CW00458785

1 MONTH OF
FREE
READING

at

www.ForgottenBooks.com

By purchasing this book you are eligible for one month membership to ForgottenBooks.com, giving you unlimited access to our entire collection of over 1,000,000 titles via our web site and mobile apps.

To claim your free month visit:
www.forgottenbooks.com/free1228274

ISBN 978-0-332-71209-3
PIBN 11228274

This book is a reproduction of an important historical work. Forgotten Books uses
state-of-the-art technology to digitally reconstruct the work, preserving the original format
whilst repairing imperfections present in the aged copy. In rare cases, an imperfection in
the original, such as a blemish or missing page, may be replicated in our edition. We do,
however, repair the vast majority of imperfections successfully; any imperfections that
remain are intentionally left to preserve the state of such historical works.

TREASURY DEPARTMENT

PUBLIC HEALTH
REPORTS

ISSUED WEEKLY
BY THE
UNITED STATES PUBLIC HEALTH SERVICE

CONTAINING INFORMATION OF THE CURRENT
PREVALENCE OF DISEASE, THE OCCURRENCE
OF EPIDEMICS, AND RELATED SUBJECTS

VOLUME 33—PART 1
NUMBERS 1-26

JANUARY–JUNE, 1918

WASHINGTON
GOVERNMENT PRINTING OFFICE
1919

PUBLIC HEALTH REPORTS

| VOL. 33 | JANUARY 4, 1918 | No. 1 |

THE CONTROL OF VENEREAL DISEASES.

For the purpose of organizing a nation-wide control of the venereal diseases the following telegram, letter, and memorandum were sent on January 2, 1918, to the health officers of all the States:

Telegram.

Control venereal infections in connection prosecution of the war constitutes most important sanitary problem now confronting public-health authorities of United States. Plan of control mailed you to-day. Request your cooperation forceful enforcement same. Venereal infections should be made reportable and quarantinable means of diagnosis and cure should be provided. Campaign wisely conducted publicity should be launched. Please inform me your action in premises.

BLUE,
Surgeon General, United States Public Health Service.

Letter.

SIR: My telegram of this date as follows is hereby confirmed:

Control venereal infections in connection prosecution of the war constitutes most important sanitary problem now confronting public health authorities of United States. Plan of control mailed you to-day. Request your cooperation, forceful enforcement same. Venereal infections should be made reportable and quarantinable; means of diagnosis and cure should be provided. Campaign wisely conducted publicity should be launched. Please inform me your action in premises.

It is evident that the prevention of venereal infections in the military population is largely dependent on the degree with which these infections are prevented in the civil community. This imposes upon the civil health authorities the duty of forcefully attacking the venereal problem upon the basis of the control of communicable disease.

There is forwarded you herewith an outline upon which it is proposed to make this attack. Manifestly, no plan which can be set forth at the present time can be complete in all its details nor can a plan be devised which in all its phases fits the requirements of each State exactly. Therefore, in the plan which I am sending you only the basic necessities have been stressed. Your cooperation in putting this plan in force is requested.

1 (1)

48333

The Public Health Service in cooperation with the Red Cross and the Medical Department of the Army is establishing venereal clinics in cities in immediate contiguity to the Army cantonments. There is even greater need for the beginning of an active antivenereal campaign in those cities which are outside of the military zones but into which soldiers go in search of recreation. Most important of all, perhaps, is the thorough education of the general public to the end that this disease group will be considered in the same light as are the other communicable infections. This will permit the free and frank discussion of this important question without offense to modesty.

I shall be pleased to have your views and suggestions as to the prosecution of further work along these lines. Whatever is to be done must be initiated promptly if we are to prevent the next increment of the draft from having the high venereal rate of the last.

Respectfully,

RUPERT BLUE,
Surgeon General.

Memorandum.

MEMORANDUM RELATIVE TO THE CONTROL OF THE VENEREAL DISEASES.

1. **Epidemiology.**
    (a) Peculiar to the human species.
    (b) Chronic diseases.
    (c) Spread by contact—not necessarily sex contact--chronic carriers.
    (d) Very prevalent in all classes of society.
    (e) Most prevalent in classes of low inhibition.
2. **Control.**
    (a) Depends upon the control of infected persons.
    (b) Control of infected persons depends upon knowledge of their whereabouts. This may be determined by:
        (1) Morbidity reports by serial number (in the case of private practitioners), name to be disclosed when infectious persons cease treatment. Case then followed up by health department which enforces quarantine act.
        (2) Morbidity reports from venereal clinic and hospital.
        (3) Legal enactment necessary to secure morbidity reports
        (4) Enact and enforce ordinance requiring pharmacists to keep record (open at all times to health department) of sales of drugs for the prevention and treatment of gonorrhea and syphilis.
    (c) Object of this control is to prevent contact between infected and non-infected persons.
    (d) May be obtained by:
        (1) Quarantine of infected persons.
        (2) Cure of infected persons.
        (3) Education of general public to avoid direct and indirect contact with persons infected or presumably infected.
3. **Quarantine of infected persons.**
    (a) Those who desire cure and can afford treatment.
        (1) These are instructed by their physicians and theoretically are thus quarantined.

3. Quarantine of infected persons—Continued.
 (*b*) Those who desire cure and can not afford treatment.
  (1) Means should be provided for the free treatment of this group.
   (*a*) Accurate diagnosis.
   (*b*) Dispensary relief.
   (*c*) Hospital relief.
 (*c*) Those who are careless or willful in the distribution of these infections through promiscuity.
  (1) These for the most part are the ignorant or the criminal classes. Careful physical examination of all persons entering jails or other public institutions, those found infected to be isolated either in a special hospital or under a probation officer who enforces dispensary relief.

4. Cure of infected persons.
 (*a*) Establishment of venereal clinics by health authorities.
  (1) Federal, in zones in close contiguity to cantonments.
  (2) State, in situations where local authorities refuse or fail to establish clinic.
  (3) City, particularly those cities in which commercialized or clandestine prostitution flourishes for the patronage of soldiers but are beyond the authority of the Secretary of War.
  (4) Country, in thickly settled rural communities.
 (*b*) By the creation of new or the utilization of existing hospital facilities.
  (1) For the treatment of those who volunteer for treatment.
  (2) For the obligatory treatment of persons under control of the courts.
 (*c*) By legal enactment.
  (1) Declaring the venereal infections to be quarantinable.
  (2) By substituting confinement to hospital for confinement to jail in the case of those convicted by courts and having venereal infections.
  (3) By substituting remanding to a probation officer for the imposition of fines.
  (4) To carry out 2 and 3 it is necessary that all persons arrested be examined by the city physician or other authorized person.
  (5) By arrest of acknowledged and clandestine prostitutes by policewomen.

5. Public education.
 (*a*) Relieve problem of all moral and social issues and place campaign solely on basis of control of communicable disease.
 (*b*) Propaganda of wisely conducted publicity.
  (1) Through public meetings addressed by forceful speakers.
  (2) Through public prints.
  (3) By placarding public toilets, placards to emphasize danger of venereal diseases and to recommend prompt treatment either by competent physician or at the free venereal clinic.
  (4) By follow-up work by social workers.
  (5) By the education of infected persons.
   (*a*) By physicians in private practice.
   (*b*) By venereal clinic and hospital.

EXTRA-CANTONMENT ZONE HEALTH REGULATIONS.

The following ordinances and regulations have been adopted in pursuance of the plan of cooperation by States and municipalities with the United States Public Health Service for the protection of military camps and the inhabitants of extra-cantonment zones:

CAMP GREENE EXTRA-CANTONMENT ZONE.

Communicable Diseases—Notification of Cases—Venereal Diseases. (Ord. of Charlotte, N. C., Oct. 22, 1917.)

1. That all physicians, osteopaths, or any other persons allowed by law to practice the art of healing the sick in the city of Charlotte, shall, within 24 hours after being called or making a diagnosis, report in writing, upon forms supplied by the health department, giving the name, except as hereinafter provided, color, age, sex, and address of all cases of typhoid fever, paratyphoid fever, continued fever of doubtful cause of more than eight days' duration, diphtheria, membranous croup, scarlet fever, measles, mumps, chicken pox, smallpox, whooping cough, infantile paralysis, epidemic cerebrospinal meningitis, tuberculosis (giving part affected), ophthalmia neonatorum, yellow fever, typhus fever, cholera, plague, leprosy, food poisoning, septic sore throat, hookworm, filariasis, dysentery (amebic, bacillary), German measles, anthrax, dengue, rabies (in man or in animal), trachoma, trichinosis, gonococcus infection, syphilis, and chancroid.

2. That in cases of gonococcus infection, syphilis, and chancroid the physician making the diagnosis or treating such patient shall keep in his office or place of business a separate record, giving the name, color, age, sex, and address and the character of disease, and such cases shall be numbered or such record kept in the numerical order of their diagnosis or treatment, and shall, within 24 hours after being diagnosed, be reported to the health department, giving the number of such case in lieu of the name of the patient.

The record kept by any physician of any of the diseases herein mentioned shall not be open to inspection by the public, but shall at all times be open to inspection by the health officer or assistant health officer of the city.

3. If any person should be afflicted with any of the above-named diseases and is not under the care of a physician, then the head of the household where such diseased person is, or the guardian of such diseased person, shall immediately report such case to the health department.

4. The proprietor or manager of any hotel, lodging house, or boarding house who shall have knowledge of or reason to believe that there is a case of any of the above-named diseases within such hotel, lodging house, or boarding house shall immediately report such fact to the health department.

5. When a physician, attendant, parent, or guardian suspects that a person under his care has any of the above-named diseases he shall immediately report the case as such and the health officer shall thereupon take such measures as are necessary to protect the public, but before declaring a quarantine he shall consult the family physician, if there be one, in charge of such case.

6. The recovery or death of all cases of the above-mentioned diseases shall be reported on forms supplied by the health department for that purpose.

7. A separate report card shall be used for reporting each case of the above-mentioned diseases.

8. Any person concealing or attempting to conceal the existence of a case of any one of the above-named diseases or violating any of the provisions of this ordinance shall upon conviction be fined not less than five dollars ($5.00) nor more than fifty dollars ($50.00).

9. This ordinance being made for the preservation of public health shall be published once in the newspapers of the city of Charlotte and shall take effect October 22, 1917.

10. That all ordinances or parts of ordinances in conflict with this ordinance are hereby repealed.

CAMP LEE EXTRA-CANTONMENT ZONE.

Foodstuffs, Sale of—Permit Required. Milk—Production and Sale. (Ord. of Richmond, Va., Nov. 15, 1917.)

1. That section 17 of chapter 25, Richmond City Code, 1910, be and the same is hereby amended and reordained so as to read as follows:

17. No person shall, within or without the city of Richmond, keep or maintain a stable, or stables, or a dairy farm for the purpose of producing milk to be sold or exposed to sale within the limits of the city of Richmond; nor shall any person within the said limits keep or operate a hotel, boarding house, café, restaurant, lunch counter, ice cream parlor or manufactory, soda fountain, or place where soda water or soft drinks are sold or manufactured; or a room, stall, store, or other place where any soda water, soft drinks, or victuals are sold, nor shall any person within the limits of the police jurisdiction of the city of Richmond, outside of the public markets of the said city, keep a room, stall, store, or other place where any milk, meat, butter, fish, fruit, or vegetable intended for human food are sold or exposed to sale without first obtaining a permit to do so from the chief health officer of the city of Richmond. Application for said permit shall be made in writing, upon a form to be prescribed by said health officer, in which application it shall be stipulated that the inspector or other health officer of the city of Richmond may from time to time inspect such places and premises and the milk produced, or victuals, food and food supplies exposed to sale thereat, and also that such applicant will conform to the requirements of this chapter, and such reasonable rules and regulations as may be established by the administrative board for the government of such place or places. Every person to whom such permit is granted, before he shall be entitled to carry on business for which he desires such permit, shall pay to the auditor of the city of Richmond a fee of $2 to cover the expenses incident to the inspection of milk, victuals, food and food supplies in the mode prescribed by this ordinance. Before granting such permit it shall be the duty of the said health officer to make, or cause to be made, an examination of the place and premises which are intended to be used in conducting any such business, or in the maintenance of said dairy farm or stable, and of such place, stall, or store where it is proposed to sell milk, meat, butter, fish, fruit, vegetables, or other food supplies, and thereafter, from time to time, inspect the same, and if found in an insanitary condition, such permit may be refused, or if granted, may at any time be revoked or suspended, without notice, by the chief health officer, if, in his judgment, such dairy, dairy farm or place is found to be in an insanitary condition.

2. This ordinance shall be in force from its passage.

CAMP SHERIDAN EXTRA-CANTONMENT ZONE.

Human Excreta—Disposal of.   (Ord. of Montgomery, Ala.)

1. That on and after November 10, 1917, every residence and building in which human beings reside, are employed, or congregate, shall be required to have a sanitary method for the disposal of human excreta, namely: Sanitary water-closet or a sanitary privy.

2. That on and after January 15, 1918, it shall be unlawful for any person, firm, or corporation to own, maintain, or operate in Montgomery, a privy or dry closet, for the reception of human excreta, unless said closet is built, rebuilt, or constructed as hereinafter provided.

3. It shall be unlawful for any person, firm, or corporation in Montgomery to throw out, deposit, or bury within the city limits any excreta from human bodies, solid or liquid, or to dispose of such excreta in any manner other than into a properly sewered water closet or a properly constructed sanitary privy.

4. All buildings or other places in said city where human beings live, are employed, or congregate, shall be provided with a properly sewered water closet or a properly constructed sanitary privy for the catchment or receiving of human discharges, which will properly dispose of and safeguard such matter.

5. *Sanitary privy.*—The term "sanitary privy" as used in this ordinance shall be construed to mean a privy which is built, rebuilt, or constructed so as to contain a privy box, which box shall conform to the following specifications:

(A) The privy boxes shall be of either the single or the double type; the double type to be installed in any privy used by more than four persons.

(B) The privy boxes shall be constructed of durable lumber, and shall be fly-tight.

(C) The single-type privy box shall be 22 inches long, 17 inches high, and 18 inches wide, all inside measurements; and shall be provided with one seat hole, about 9 inches long, the front of which shall be about 4 inches from the front of the box.

(D) The double-type privy box shall be 40 inches long, have two seat holes, and otherwise similar to the single-type box.

(E) All privy boxes shall have eight 1-inch holes in the front of the box, two inches from the floor, and shall have an opening at the upper part of the back wall 4 inches square, all of these openings to be covered with galvanized iron screen wire, at least fourteen mesh to the inch.

(F) Under each seat-hole shall be placed a galvanized-iron receptacle, with straight sides, 14-15 inches high, and 15 inches in diameter, made of 24-gauge galvanized iron. These receptacles shall be so placed as to catch all human excreta deposited in the box, being held in place by strip of wood tacked to the floor.

(G) The top of the privy box shall be hinged with metal hinges, so as to allow for the removal of the receptacles, and so as to fit flat on the top of the box at all other times.

(H) Each seat hole shall be provided with a cover or lid hinged with two hinges so as to fall into place when not being used, and which shall at all other times be kept so as to prevent the access of flies to the human excreta.

(I) A flue not less than 5 inches square shall extend from the opening in the back of the privy box to 24 inches above the lowest point of the roof of the privy. The top of this flue shall be covered so as to prevent rain from entering the privy box, but allowing the free egress of air for ventilating purposes.

6. The contents of all privy receptacles shall be removed by the city scavenger. Such removal and cleaning shall be done under the supervision of the city health officer and for such services the following charges shall be made: For cleaning each privy at private homes, one dollar and fifty cents ($1.50) per quarter in advance from each family using such privy, provided that for all privies containing more than one receptacle, a charge of twenty-five cents ($0.25) shall be made for each additional receptacle, payable quarterly in advance. The fees or charges set out in this section shall be paid at the beginning of each quarter by the occupant of said premises, or by each family using such privy, to the city clerk.

7. All sanitary privies in said city shall be kept in a cleanly condition at all times and so used that all excreta deposited therein will fall into the receptacle provided. Such receptacles shall be used only for the purpose of a toilet and no wash water, garbage, nor any refuse matter other than human excreta shall be deposited therein.

8. No privy receptacle shall be permitted to become filled to overflowing. If scavenging of privy receptacle becomes necessary oftener than hereinbefore provided

it shall be the duty of the occupant of the property to notify the sanitary department, and such privy shall be scavenged and an additional charge of ten cents shall be made for each receptacle.

9. All privies existing or maintained in said city after the date on which this ordinance takes effect which do not conform to the requirements of this ordinance or to the regulations of the city health officer issued under this ordinance shall be and are hereby declared a nuisance, dangerous to the public health, and the city of Montgomery shall proceed to abate such nuisance in accordance with law and in accordance with the ordinance of said city.

10. The city shall have the further right to make or cause to be made such alterations or constructions to such privies as are nuisances as will render them sanitary, and the entire cost of such work shall be charged against the person creating or maintaining the nuisance. All such alterations or constructions are to be prescribed and approved by the city health officer.

11. The health officer of the city of Montgomery, or a duly appointed inspector, shall personally inspect all privies in Montgomery as such,inspection shall be deemed necessary by such health officer or inspector. The city health officer, or a duly appointed inspector, is hereby empowered to enter all premises in the discharge of this duty.

12. It shall be unlawful for any person, firm, or corporation to fail or refuse to comply with the provisions of this ordinance.

13. That any person or persons, firm or corporation, or the agent of any person or persons, firm or corporation who neglects, fails, or refuses to comply with any of the provisions of this ordinance shall be deemed guilty of a misdemeanor, and when convicted shall be fined in the sum of not less than five dollars ($5.00) or more than one hundred dollars ($100.00), and each time such person or persons, firm or corporation, or the agent of any person or persons, firm or corporation neglects or refuses to comply with any of the provisions of this ordinance shall be deemed a separate offence and punished as herein provided.

14. Any ordinances or parts of ordinances in conflict herewith are hereby repealed.

15. For the preservation of the public peace, health, and safety, an emergency is hereby declared to exist, for the reason that the existing of insanitary privies in the incorporate limits of the city of Montgomery are dangerous for the public health of the inhabitants thereof, and for that reason this ordinance shall be in full force and effect from and after its passage, approval, and posting, as required by law.

NEW YORK STATE.

The following amendments to the Sanitary Code of the State of New York were adopted by the State Public Health Council at a meeting held in New York City October 30, 1917:

Health Zones Around Camps—Establishment. Permits Required for Sale of Foodstuffs.

Chapter VII of the Sanitary Code of the State of New York is hereby amended by adding thereto four new regulations, to be known as regulations 10, 11, 12, and 13, to read as follows:

REGULATION 10. *Declaration of cantonment zones.*—The State commissioner of health may from time to time declare such territory as he deems necessary in the neighborhood of a military or naval camp or cantonment a health zone, and he may from time to time change the limits of or abolish such zone.

REGULATION 11. *Permits required to sell food and beverages in all health zones.*— Whenever the State commissioner of health has declared any territory to be a health zone, as provided for in regulation 10 of this chapter, thereafter and so long as such declaration remains in effect no person shall establish or maintain any place for the sale of food or drink intended for human consumption unless such person shall first have secured from the health officer in whose jurisdiction the place is situated a written permit so to do. Such permit shall not be issued unless after an inspection the health officer has satisfied himself that the place is maintained under sanitary conditions. Such permit, unless revoked, shall be granted for one year from the date of its issuance, and shall be conspicuously displayed in the place for which it was issued. Such permits are not transferable.

REGULATION 12. *Monthly inspection by health officers.*—All places for which such permits are issued shall be inspected at least once in each month by the health officer.

REGULATION 13. *Revocation of permit.*—Any permit so issued may be revoked for cause either by the local health officer or the State commissioner of health, after giving the person holding the permit an opportunity for a hearing.

CAMP PIKE EXTRA-CANTONMENT ZONE.

Regulations governing sanitary conditions in barber shops in the civil zone around Camp Pike, near Little Rock, Ark., are enforced by the United States Public Health Service. Soldiers are not permitted by the Army authorities to patronize barber shops in which the certificate of the United States Public Health Service is not displayed. The regulations are as follows:

1. No person will be allowed to perform the work of a barber for men in uniform unless he has a certificate from the United States Public Health Service that he is free from communicable disease or venereal disease in a communicable stage.

2. All barber shops, together with all furniture, shall be kept in a clean and sanitary condition.

3. Mugs, shaving brushes, razors, scissors, clipping machines, pincers, needles, and other metal instruments shall be cleaned and sterilized either by steam, boiling water, or in alcohol of at least 60 per cent strength after each separate use.

4. Combs and brushes should be thoroughly sterilized after each separate use.

5. A separate clean towel shall be used for each person.

6. Alum or other material used to stop the flow of blood shall be applied only on a towel or other clean cloth.

7. The use of powder puffs and sponges is prohibited.

8. Every barber shop shall be kept well ventilated and provided with hot and cold water.

9. Headrests of chairs shall be covered with a towel that has been washed since having been used before, or by a clean, new paper.

10. Every barber shall cleanse his hands immediately and thoroughly before serving each customer.

11. No person shall use a barber shop as a dormitory, nor shall any part of the shop be so used.

12. No barber shall undertake to treat any disease of the skin or any lesions of the skin whatsoever, such as pimples, boils, warts, moles, and the like.

This notice must be displayed in all shops. All patrons are requested to notify the United States Public Health Service, Little Rock, Ark., of any infraction of these rules.

PREVALENCE OF DISEASE.

No health department, State or local, can effectively prevent or control disease without knowledge of when, where, and under what conditions cases are occurring.

UNITED STATES.

EXTRA CANTONMENT ZONES—CASES REPORTED WEEK ENDED JAN. 1.

Camp Beauregard, La.—City of Alexandria, meningitis 3, measles 97, German measles 6, mumps 5, pneumonia 2; for the city of Pineville, smallpox 6, measles 23, mumps 1; city of Boyce, measles 6; village of Ball, pneumonia 1; village of Wilda, measles 1; rural district at edge of Camp Beauregard, typhoid fever 1; village of Dry Prong, epidemic meningitis 4.

Camp Bowie, Tex.—Fort Worth, measles 8, diphtheria 1, German measles 4, influenza 1, mumps 1, broncho-pneumonia 2, smallpox 1.

Camp Dodge, Iowa.—Des Moines, smallpox 11, scarlet fever 4, malaria 1; Valley Junction, smallpox 1, scarlet fever 1; south Fort Des Moines, scarlet fever 2; Grimes, scarlet fever 1.

Camp Funston, Kans.—Measles 1, Ogden; measles 38, scarlet fever 2, mumps 1, smallpox 1, Manhattan; measles 18, chicken pox 3, Junction City; measles 1, Riley; measles 1, Randolph.

Camp Gordon, Ga.—Atlanta, diphtheria 1, gonococcus infection 12, measles 8, pulmonary tuberculosis 1, syphilis 3, cerebrospinal meningitis 2, scarlet fever 7. German measles 2, mumps 3; College Park, infantile paralysis 1.

Camp Greene, N. C.—Measles 36, chickenpox 2, tuberculosis 2, smallpox 1, whooping cough 3, mumps 1, chancroids 3; all in Charlotte Township.

Camp Hancock, Ga.—Measles, Augusta 8. Blythe 4; German measles. Augusta 3; typhoid fever, Augusta 1.

Fort Leavenworth, Kans.—German measles, city 3, county 1; lobar pneumonia, city 4, county 1; diphtheria, city 6; chicken pox, city 4; measles, city 1.

Camp Lee, Va.—German measles, Petersburg 10; chicken pox, Petersburg 5; diphtheria, Petersburg 1; pneumonia, Petersburg 3; tuberculosis, Petersburg 1; scarlet fever, Petersburg 1; mumps, Hopewell 1; measles, Petersburg 1.

Camp Lewis, Wash.—German measles, Dupont 4.

Camp Logan, Tex.—Diphtheria 1, chickenpox 1, German measles 24, measles 27; mumps 4, tuberculosis 8, trachoma 1, scarlet fever 1; all Houston.

Camp McClellan, Ala.—Anniston, smallpox 8, mumps 6, measles 4, chicken pox 18, pneumonia 3, German measles 1, tuberculosis 1; Precinct Thirteen, smallpox 3; Precinct Four, smallpox none; Oxford, chicken pox 1; Precinct Three, smallpox 1, pneumonia 1.

Fort Oglethorpe, Ga.—Chattanooga, German measles 9, mumps 2, scarlet fever 3, meningitis 2, diphtheria 1, pneumonia 3, typhoid fever 1; St. Elmo, tuberculosis 1, scarlet fever 1, diphtheria 1; Ridgedale, pneumonia 1, Eastlake, pneumonia 1; North Chattanooga, German measles 1; Rossville, Ga., mumps 2; Flintstone, Ga., meningitis 1; Lytle, Ga., smallpox 1.

Camp Pike, Ark. -Little Rock, measles 31, chicken pox 1, smallpox 15, tuberculosis 3, pneumonia 5, German measles 9, diphtheria 2, mumps 1, malaria 3, syphilis 2, gonorrhea 9, erysipelas 1, chancroid 1; North Little Rock, measles 3, smallpox 2, pneumonia 1, German measles 6, malaria 1, syphilis 1, gonorrhea 3; Scotts, measles 2, malaria 2, German measles 1; Kerr, dysentery 1, smallpox 1; Wrightsville, pneumonia 1; Sweethome, malaria 1.

Camp Sevier, S. C. Two measles, 1 diphtheria, Chick Springs, rural.

Camp Shelby, Miss. Hattiesburg, chicken pox 1, diphtheria 1, malaria 3, measles 3, German measles 5, pneumonia 2; Gulfport, diphtheria 1, typhoid fever 1; Biloxi, diphtheria 1; Petal, measles 8; Clyde, smallpox 2; Perry County, meningitis 1.

Camp Sheridan, Ala. —City of Montgomery, measles 17, German measles 15, mumps 2, smallpox 2, lobar pneumonia 1; Capitol Heights, measles 3, chicken pox 1, lober pneumonia 1; Cloverdale, German measles 2.

Camp Sherman, Ohio.—Cerebrospinal meningitis, Frankfort, 1; diphtheria, Chillicothe, 1; measles, Chillicothe, 5; pneumonia, lobar, Liberty Township, 1; scarlet fever, Chillicothe, 1.

Tidewater Health District, Va. —Newport News, measles 7, typhoid fever 2, whooping cough 2, cerebrospinal meningitis 1, mumps 1; Hampton, scarlet fever 2, whooping cough 3, chicken pox 1.

Camp Zachary Taylor, Ky.—Jefferson County, tuberculosis lungs 2, tubercular meningitis 1; Louisville, chicken pox 2, diphtheria 5, measles 9, scarlet fever 3, cerebrospinal meningitis 1, tuberculosis pulmonary 10.

Camp Wadsworth, S. C.--German measles, Spartanburg city 13, county 1; measles, city 3, Pauline 2; chicken pox, city 2; whooping cough, city 3; scarlet fever, city 1; pneumonia, Pauline 1, Moore 1; diphtheria, Glenn Springs 1; ptomain poisoning, Pauline 1.

Camp Wheeler, Ga. --Macon, measles 38, scarlet fever 1, mumps 2, typhoid fever 2, diphtheria 2, chicken pox 2, smallpox 2, meningitis 1, tuberculosis 1.

CAMP MACARTHUR, TEX.—EXTRA-CANTONMENT ZONE.

During the period from November 1 to December 20, 1917, 22 cases of German measles were notified in Waco and McLennan County, Tex., with the estimated number of 200 cases in the city of Waco during the period named.

CURRENT STATE SUMMARIES.

Alabama.

From Collaborating Epidemiologist Perry, telegram dated December 31, 1917:

One poliomyelitis at Lisman.

California.

From the State Board of Health of California, telegram dated January 2, 1918:

Four cases epidemic cerebrospinal meningitis last week, 2 Los Angeles County, 2 San Diego County; 1 case poliomyelitis Los Angeles County; 6 cases smallpox, Alameda County 1, Los Angeles City 1, Nevada city 2, Redlands 1, San Francisco 1; diphtheria, slightly more prevalent than preceding week, especially prevalent in large cities.

Reported by mail for the preceding week (ending Dec. 22):

Cerebrospinal meningitis	3	Mumps	38
Chicken pox	92	Pneumonia	96
Diphtheria	66	Scarlet fever	73
Dysentery	1	Smallpox	3
Erysipelas	6	Syphilis	21
German measles	63	Tetanus	1
Gonococcus infection	34	Trachoma	2
Hookworm	10	Tuberculosis	142
Malaria	2	Typhoid fever	21
Measles	265	Whooping cough	41

Connecticut.

From Collaborating Epidemiologist Black, telegram dated January 2, 1918:

Undue prevalence diphtheria New London.

Indiana.

From the State Board of Health of Indiana, telegram dated December 31, 1917:

Scarlet fever: Benham, Ripley County, Denver, Miami County; schools closed Pike Township, Huntington County. Diphtheria: Two deaths Gary. Four cases measles Huntington. Whooping cough epidemic Cornell school, Elkhart County. Epidemic smallpox: Columbus, New Haven, Allen County, 10 cases pesthouse Bloomington. Epidemic mumps Wabash Township, Parke County. One case poliomyelitis Vevay. Two cases epidemic meningitis Huntington.

Kansas.

From Collaborating Epidemiologist Crumbine, telegram dated December 31, 1917:

Epidemic meningitis: Ellsworth, 1; Aurora, 1; Wichita, 1.

Louisiana.

From Collaborating Epidemiologist Dowling, telegram dated December 31, 1917:

Four cases, 3 deaths, cerebrospinal meningitis Dry Prong, Grant; Caddo, 1 case.

Massachusetts.

From Collaborating Epidemiologist Kelley, telegram dated December 31, 1917:

Unusual prevalence diphtheria: Amesbury, 4 additional. Measles: Braintree, total December, 54; Blandford, 17 additional; Everett, 20; Medfield, total December, 19; Camp Devens, 44 additional. Typhoid fever: North Brookfield, 3 additional. Smallpox: Beverly, 1 additional, Lowell, 1; Worcester, 1.

Minnesota.

From Collaborating Epidemiologist Bracken, telegram dated December 31, 1917:

Smallpox: Anoka County, Columbus Township, 1; Carlton County, Moose Lake village, 1; Carver County, Benton township, 1; Norwood village, 2; Waconia village, 3;

12

Hennepin County, Brooklyn village, 2; Houston County, Brownsville township, 1; Marshall County, Alverado village, 1; Pine County, Banning village, 1; Pine Lake township, 1; Winona County, Pleasant Hill township, 2. One case of poliomyelitis and 3 cases of cerebrospinal meningitis reported since December 17.

Nebraska.

From the State Department of Health of Nebraska, telegram dated December 31, 1917:

Smallpox at Axtel, Lexington, North Platte, Atkinson, Rushville, and Eustis. Measles at Union and Peru. Scarlet fever at McCook, Fremont, Culbertson, Cairo, and Venango. Chicken pox at Peru. Whooping cough at Lincoln. Typhoid fever at Upland.

South Carolina.

From Collaborating Epidemiologist Hayne, telegram dated December 31, 1917:

Two cases meningitis reported from Greer and Darlington, S. C. Measles and diphtheria prevalent in all parts of the State.

Vermont.

From Collaborating Epidemiologist Dalton, telegram dated December 31, 1917:

Five cases smallpox at Barton, Orleans County. No other outbreak or unusual prevalence.

Virginia.

From Collaborating Epidemiologist Traynham, telegram dated December 31, 1917:

Smallpox reported from near Mannboro, Amelia County, and Coeburn, Wise County.

Washington.

From Collaborating Epidemiologist Tuttle, telegram dated January 2, 1918:

Six cases scarlet fever Toledo, Lewis County. No outbreaks Seattle.

CEREBROSPINAL MENINGITIS.

State Reports for November, 1917.

Place.	New cases reported.	Place.	New cases reported.
Connecticut:		Iowa:	
Fairfield County—		Johnson County	1
Bridgeport	2	Polk County	3
Shelton	1		
Hartford County—		Total	4
Hartford	1		
New Haven County		Kansas:	
New Haven	1	Bourbon County	
New London County—		Uniontown (R. D.)	1
Groton (town)	1	Butler County—	
		Douglas	1
Total	6	Dickinson County	
		Abilene	1

CEREBROSPINAL MENINGITIS—Continued.

State Reports for November, 1917—Continued.

Place.	New cases reported.	Place.	New cases reported.
Kansas—Continued.		Mississippi:	
Leavenworth County—		Attala County	2
Leavenworth	1	Carroll County	1
Marion County—		Hinds County	3
Roxbury (R. D.)	1	Sunflower County	1
Osborne County—			
Osborne (R. D.)	1	Total	7
Riley County—			
Manhattan	5	New Jersey:	
Rooks County—		Essex County	5
Stockton (R. D.)	1	Union County	1
Scott County—			
Scott City	1	Total	6
Sedgwick County—			
Wichita	1		
Wyandotte County—			
Kansas City	1		
Total	15		

City Reports for Week Ended Dec. 15, 1917.

Place.	Cases.	Deaths.	Place.	Cases.	Deaths.
Atlanta, Ga	1	2	Lowell, Mass	1	
Baltimore, Md	3	1	Milwaukee, Wis	2	1
Boston, Mass	1	1	Minneapolis, Minn	1	
Chicago, Ill	9	1	Nashua, N. H		1
Cleveland, Ohio	1		New York, N. Y	3	3
Columbus, Ohio	1		Omaha, Nebr	1	
Dayton, Ohio	3	1	Philadelphia, Pa	2	1
Detroit, Mich	3		Pittsburgh, Pa	1	1
Dubuque, Iowa		1	St. Louis, Mo	3	2
Elizabeth, N. J	1		San Francisco, Cal	2	
Evansville, Ind		1	Washington, D. C		1
Hartford, Conn	1	1	Worcester, Mass		1
Los Angeles, Cal	1				

DIPHTHERIA.

See Diphtheria, measles, scarlet fever, and tuberculosis, page 22

ERYSIPELAS.

City Reports for Week Ended Dec. 15, '

Place.	Cases.	Deaths.	Place.	Cases.	Deaths.
Ann Arbor, Mich	1		New York, N. Y		4
Baltimore, Md		2	Norfolk, Va		1
Boston, Mass	1	1	Philadelphia, Pa	7	1
Bridgeport, Conn	2		Pittsburgh, Pa	9	
Brockton, Mass	1		Pontiac, Mich	6	1
Buffalo, N. Y	4	1	Portland, Oreg	2	
Chicago, Ill	19		Reading, Pa	2	
Cincinnati, Ohio	1	2	Roanoke, Va	1	1
Cleveland, Ohio	6		Rochester, N. Y	1	
Columbus, Ohio		1	Rutland, Vt	1	
Detroit, Mich	3		St. Joseph, Mo	1	
Erie, Pa	1		St. Louis, Mo	4	2
Grand Rapids, Mich	1		St. Paul, Minn	2	
Hartford, Conn	1		Salt Lake City, Utah		1
Jersey City, N. J	1		Schenectady, N. Y	2	
Malden, Mass		1	San Francisco, Cal	2	1
Milwaukee, Wis	1		Seattle, Wash	1	
Newark, N. J	1	2	Toledo, Ohio		1
New Bedford, Mass		1	Wheeling, W. Va	1	
New Castle, Pa	1				

MALARIA.

State Reports for November, 1917.

Place.	New cases reported.	Place.	New cases reported.
Kansas:		Mississippi—Continued.	
Greenwood County –		Madison County..............	35
Severy...................	1	Marion County...............	171
		Marshall County.............	44
Mississippi:		Monroe County..............	70
Adams County................	60	Montgomery County.........	22
Alcorn County...............	36	Neshoba County.............	60
Amite County................	73	Newton County..............	31
Attala County...............	66	Noxubee County.............	24
Benton County...............	13	Oktibbeha County............	106
Bolivar County..............	604	Panola County...............	175
Calhoun County..............	39	Pearl River County..........	34
Carroll County..............	88	Perry County................	213
Choctaw County..............	94	Pike County.................	95
Claiborne County............	99	Pontotoc County.............	76
Clarke County...............	29	Prentiss County.............	25
Clay County.................	18	Quitman County..............	137
Coahoma County..............	301	Rankin County...............	85
Copiah County...............	114	Scott County................	23
Covington County............	132	Sharkey County..............	23
De Soto County..............	54	Simpson County..............	92
Franklin County.............	175	Smith County................	21
George County...............	24	Stone County................	29
Greene County...............	20	Sunflower County............	279
Grenada County..............	60	Tallahatchie County.........	131
Hancock County..............	132	Tate County.................	147
Harrison County.............	111	Tippah County...............	40
Hinds County................	252	Tishomingo County...........	50
Holmes County...............	804	Tunica County...............	218
Issaquena County............	50	Union County................	76
Itawamba County.............	71	Warren County...............	198
Jackson County..............	98	Washington County...........	324
Jasper County...............	60	Wayne County................	73
Jefferson County............	97	Webster County..............	50
Jefferson Davis County......	22	Wilkinson County............	8
Jones County................	158	Winston County..............	149
Kemper County...............	29	Yalobusha County............	71
Lafayette County............	45	Yazoo County................	140
Lamar County................	96		
Lauderdale County...........	44	Total...................	8,382
Lawrence County.............	85		
Leake County................	78	New Jersey	
Lee County..................	112	Essex County................	4
Leflore County..............	243	Hudson County...............	1
Lincoln County..............	63		
Lowndes County..............	26	Total...................	5

City Reports for Week Ended December 15, 1917.

During the week ended December 15, 1917, 1 death from malaria was reported in Memphis, Tenn., and 1 case was reported in Richmond, Va.

MEASLES.

See Diphtheria, measles, scarlet fever, and tuberculosis, page 22.

PELLAGRA.

State Reports for November, 1917.

Place.	New cases reported.	Place.	New cases reported.
Kansas:		Mississippi:	
Cherokee County—		Adams County................	3
Galena...................	2	Alcorn County...............	5
Cowley County—		Amite County................	2
Winfield.................	3	Benton County...............	1
Shawnee County—		Bolivar County..............	33
Topeka...................	1	Calhoun County..............	1
		Carroll County..............	5
Total...................	6	Choctaw County..............	1
		Claiborne County............	1

PELLAGRA—Continued.

State Reports for November, 1917—Continued.

Place.	New cases reported.	Place.	New cases reported.
Mississippi—Continued.		**Mississippi—Continued.**	
Clarke County	1	Montgomery County	2
Clay County	4	Neshoba County	7
Coahoma County	23	Newton County	4
Copiah County	8	Oktibbeha County	6
Covington County	2	Panola County	6
De Soto County	3	Pearl River County	1
Franklin County	1	Perry County	2
George County	2	Pike County	10
Hancock County	1	Pontotoc County	4
Harrison County	7	Prentiss County	4
Hinds County	16	Quitman County	4
Holmes County	4	Rankin County	4
Itawamba County	5	Scott County	1
Jackson County	3	Sharkey County	2
Jasper County	1	Simpson County	5
Jefferson County	2	Sunflower County	13
Jefferson Davis County	2	Tallahatchie County	2
Jones County	14	Tate County	4
Kemper County	4	Tippah County	3
Lafayette County	1	Tishomingo County	5
Lamar County	2	Tunica County	7
Lauderdale County	1	Union County	2
Lawrence County	3	Warren County	6
Leake County	9	Washington County	10
Lee County	7	Wayne County	2
Leflore County	7	Webster County	2
Lincoln County	9	Wilkinson County	2
Lowndes County	9	Winston County	1
Madison County	3	Yalobusha County	2
Marion County	8	Yazoo County	15
Marshall County	4		
Monroe County	5	Total	363

City Reports for Week Ended Dec. 15, 1917.

Place.	Cases.	Deaths.	Place	Cases.	Deaths.
Atlanta, Ga.		1	Memphis, Tenn	2	1
Birmingham, Ala.	4		New Orleans, La.		1
Charleston, S. C.		2	Richmond, Va.		1
Fort Worth, Tex.		1	Savannah, Ga.		1
Malden, Mass.		1	Washington, D. C.	1	

PNEUMONIA.

City Reports for Week Ended Dec. 15, 1917.

Place.	Cases.	Deaths.	Place.	Cases.	Deaths.
Allentown, Pa.	2		Lancaster, Pa.	1	
Baltimore, Md.	6	17	Lincoln, Nebr.	3	1
Berkeley, Cal.	1		Lorain, Ohio	1	
Binghamton, N. Y.	4		Los Angeles, Cal.	15	11
Boston, Mass.	30	11	Lynn, Mass.	7	7
Brockton, Mass.	2	1	McKeesport, Pa.	1	
Buffalo, N. Y.	2	6	Newark, N. J.	58	12
Cambridge, Mass.	4	6	New Bedford, Mass.	3	1
Canton, Ohio	2		Philadelphia, Pa.	108	63
Chelsea, Mass.	4	1	Pittsburgh, Pa.	37	38
Chicago, Ill.	150	67	Pittsfield, Mass.	5	2
Cincinnati, Ohio	1	4	Pontiac, Mich.	2	
Cleveland, Ohio	30	24	Quincy, Mass.	1	
Clinton, Mass.	1		Reading, Pa.	2	4
Dayton, Ohio	5	5	Rochester, N. Y.	16	3
Detroit, Mich.	9	32	Rutland, Vt	1	1
Everett, Mass.	2	1	Sacramento, Cal.	3	1
Fall River, Mass.	1	2	Sandusky, Ohio	1	
Flint, Mich.	1		San Francisco, Cal.	12	5
Grand Rapids, Mich.	1	1	Schenectady, N. Y.	3	2
Harrisburg, Pa.	1	4	Somerville, Mass.	3	1
Haverhill, Mass.	2	1	Springfield, Mass.	5	4
Jackson, Mich.	2		Stockton, Cal.	8	4
Kalamazoo, Mich.	3		Worcester, Mass.	1	5
Kansas City, Mo.	9	17			

16

POLIOMYELITIS (INFANTILE PARALYSIS).

State Reports for November, 1917.

Place	New cases reported.	Place.	New cases reported.
Colorado:		Maine:	
Boulder County	1	Androscoggin County—	
Pueblo County—		Poland (town)	1
Pueblo	2	Piscataquis County—	
		Foxcroft (town)	1
Total	3		
		Total	2
Connecticut:			
Litchfield County —		Mississippi:	
Plymouth	1	Choctaw County	2
		Harrison County	1
Iowa:		Lowndes County	1
Dickinson County	1	Pike County	1
Ida County	1	Rankin County	1
		Union County	1
Total	2		
		Total	7
Kansas:			
Coffey County—		Montana:	
Burlington (R. D.)	1	Hill County	1
Geary County —			
Junction City	1	New Jersey:	
Jewell County—		Essex County	2
Burr Oak (R. D.)	1	Mercer County	1
Johnson County —			
Ochltree (R. D.)	1	Total	3
Osborne County —			
Osborne (R. D.)	1	North Dakota:	
Saline County—		Williams County	1
Gypsum (R. D.)	1		
Washington County		South Dakota:	
Barnes (R. D.)	1	Miner County	1
Wilson County—		Minnehaha County	1
Fredonia	1	Perkins County	1
		Turner County	1
Total	8		
		Total	4

City Reports for Week Ended Dec. 15, 1917.

During the week ended Dec. 15, 1917, 3 cases of poliomyelitis were reported in Chicago, Ill.; 1 case was reported in Kansas City, Mo.; 1 death was reported in Newark, N. J.; 1 death in New York, N. Y.; 1 case in Portland, Oreg.: and 1 case in Seattle, Wash.

SCARLET FEVER.

See Diphtheria, measles, scarlet fever, and tuberculosis, page 22.

SMALLPOX.

Kansas Report for November, 1917.

Place.	New cases reported.	Deaths.	Number vaccinated within 7 years preceding attack.	Number last vaccinated more than 7 years preceding attack.	Number never successfully vaccinated.	Vaccination history not obtained or uncertain.
Kansas:						
Allen County	5				5	
Barton County—						
Great Bend (7 R. D.)	10				10	
Bourbon County	1				1	
Brown County	1				1	
Chase County	1				1	
Chautauqua County	1				1	
Cherokee County	13				13	
Clay County	2				2	
Cloud County	11				11	
Coffey County—						
Harris (R. D.)	19				19	
Comanche County	1				1	
Crawford County	1				1	
Douglas County—						
Lawrence	1				1	
Overbrook (R. D.)	13				13	
Pomona (R. D.)	1				1	
Franklin County	9				9	
Jackson County	1				1	
Jefferson County—						
Perry (13 R. D.)	14				14	
Williamstown (R. D.)	6				6	
Jewell County	15				15	
Johnson County—						
DeSoto (R. D.)	1				1	
Lenexa	1				1	
Merriam	12				12	
Olathe	1			1		
Ocheltree	3				3	
Stanley	2				2	
Kiowa County	1				1	
Labette County	3				3	
Leavenworth County	12			2	10	
Linn County	12				12	
Lyon County	2				2	
Montgomery County	1				1	
Nemaha County	1				1	
Osage County—						
Barclay	5				5	
Burlingame (11 R. D.)	17				17	
Lyndon (R. D.)	2				2	
Overbrook (5 R. D.)	16				16	
Quenemo (2 R. D.)	7			1	6	
Osborne County	2				2	
Reno County	6				6	
Republic County	1				1	
Rice County	1				1	
Rush County	1				1	
Sedgwick County	2				2	
Shawnee County	7				7	
Sumner County	1				1	
Wabaunsee County	2				2	
Washington County	1				1	
Woodson County—	1				1	
Wyandotte County—						
Kansas City (1 R. D)	134				134	
Total	384			4	380	

SMALLPOX—Continued.

Miscellaneous State Reports.

Place.	Cases.	Deaths.	Place.	Cases.	Deaths.
Colorado (Nov. 1-30):			**Maine—Continued.**		
Alamosa County..........	2	....	Hancock County—		
Arapahoe County.........	1	....	Eden (town).........	1	....
Boulder County..........	1	....	Kenebec County—		
Chaffee County..........	1	....	Gardiner.............	121	....
Delta County............	1	....	Augusta.............	2	....
Denver County—			Hallowell............	1	....
Denver..............	47	....	Randolph (town).....	20	....
Garfield County..........	1	....	West Gardiner (town)	3	....
Larimer County..........	1	....	Farmingdale (town)..	3	....
Logan County—			Pittston (town)......	2	....
Sterling.............	8	....	Oakland (town)......	1	....
Mesa County............	37	....	China (town)........	3	....
Morgan County..........	1	....	Lincoln County—		
Oterno County...........	2	....	Whitefield (town)....	1	....
Pueblo County—			Penobscot County—		
Pueblo..............	1	....	Bangor..............	1	....
Sedgwick County.........	11	....	Indian (township)...	1	....
Weld County............	2	....	Millinocket (town)...	1	....
			Enfield (town)......	2	....
Total....	117		Piscataquis County—		
			Beaver Cove........	1	....
Connecticut (Nov. 1-30):			Sagadahoc County—		
New Haven County—			Richmond (town)....	1	....
Wallingford	1		Somerset County—		
			Fairfield (town)......	1	....
Iowa (Nov. 1-30).			Jackman (plantation)	4	....
Adair County............	1	....	Waldo County—		
Appanoose County......	34	....	Knox (town)......	2	....
Audubon County.........	5	....	Washington County—		
Boone County............	2	....	Columbia Falls (town)	5	....
Bremer County...........	1	....	Jonesboro (town)....	1	....
Buchanan County........	3	....			
Cass County.............	11	....	Total.	227	
Cerro Gordo County......	5	....			
Chickasaw County........	11	....	**Mississippi (Nov. 1-30):**		
Clay County.............	7	....	Alcorn County...........	2	....
Crawford County.........	1	....	Attala County...........	1	....
Decatur County..........	12	....	Bolivar County..........	6	....
Dubuque County.........	3	....	Calhoun County.........	1	....
Floyd County............	27	....	Carroll County..........	1	....
Grundy County..........	1	....	Clarke County..........	1	....
Hamilton County........	1	....	Clay County............	16	....
Johnson County.........	1	....	De Soto County.........	1	....
Kossuth County.........	12	....	Grenada County.........	1	....
Lee County..............	3	....	Hinds County...........	2	....
Linn County.............	1	....	Holmes County..........	4	....
Louisa County...........	1	....	Jasper County..........	13	....
Marion County..........	8	....	Jones County...........	3	....
Mills County............	4	....	Lee County.............	3	....
Monroe County..........	1	....	Leflore County..........	1	....
Montgomery County......	3	....	Lincoln County..........	1	....
Palo Alto County........	2	....	Madison County.........	1	....
Plymouth County........	3	....	Sunflower County.......	1	....
Polk County.............	56	....	Tallahatchie County.....	5	....
Pott County.............	21	....	Washington County.....	10	....
Scott County............	1	....	Wayne County..........	1	....
Shelby County...........	2	....	Winston County.........	1	....
Sioux County............	3	....	Yazoo County...........	6	....
Wapello County.........	2	....			
Webster County..........	2	....	Total	82	
Total.................	251		**Montana, Nov. 1-30:**		
			Beaverhead County......	5	....
Maine (Nov. 1-30):			Cascade County.........	2	....
Androscoggin County—			Choteau County.........	3	....
Webster (town)......	1	....	Flathead County........	5	....
Aroostook County—			Kalispell	34	....
Limestone (town)....	2	....	Gallatin County........	1	....
Chapman (town).....	1	....	Bozeman............	4	....
Presque Isle (town)..	9	....	Jefferson County........	3	....
Fort Fairfield (town).	27	....	Musselshell County......	2	....
St. Francis (planta-			Park County............	1	....
tion).............	1	....	Livingston	13	....
Mars Hill (town).....	1	....	Ravalli County..........	21	....
Caribou (town)......	5	....	Silver Bow County......	27	....
Houlton (town)......	1	....	Butte................	85	....
Cumberland County—					
Portland.............	1	....			

SMALLPOX—Continued.

Miscellaneous State Reports—Continued.

Place.	Cases.	Deaths.	Place.	Cases.	Deaths.
Montana—Continued.			South Dakota (Nov. 1–30):		
Teton County............	1	....	Clark County............	6	....
Valley County............	3	....	Clay County............	39	....
Yellowstone County—			Davison County..........	5	....
Billings..............	2	....	Hamlin County..........	2	....
			Kingsbury County.......	29	....
Total...............	210	....	Lake County.............	13	....
			Miner County............	1	....
North Dakota (Nov. 1–30):			Minnehaha County.......	37	....
Benson County..........	2	....	Roberts County..........	1	....
Bottineau County........	1	....	Ziebach County..........	2	....
Burleigh County.........	2	....			
Cavlier County..........	1	....	Total................	135	....
Golden Valley County....	1	....			
Grant County............	1	....	Wyoming (Nov. 1–30):		
Griggs County...........	1	....	Laramie County.........	7	....
McKenzie County........	1	....			
McLean County..........	2	....			
Nelson County...........	3	....			
Pembina County.........	4	....			
Ramsey County..........	3	....			
Stutsman County........	4	....			
Williams County.........	10	....			
Total..................	36	....			

City Reports for Week Ended Dec. 15, 1917.

Place.	Cases.	Deaths.	Place.	Cases.	Deaths.
Akron, Ohio................	17	....	Knoxville, Tenn..........	3	....
Alton, Ill.................	6	1	La Crosse, Wis...........	7	....
Ann Arbor, Mich...........	1	....	Leavenworth, Kans........	1	....
Baltimore, Md.............	9	....	Lincoln, Nebr............	8	....
Boston, Mass..............	1	....	Lorain, Ohio.............	2	....
Bridgeport, Conn..........	1	....	Malden, Mass.............	1	....
Butler, Pa................	1	....	Memphis, Tenn...........	5	....
Butte, Mont...............	25	....	Milwaukee, Wis..........	4	....
Canton, Ohio..............	2	....	Minneapolis, Minn........	22	....
Chicago, Ill...............	8	....	New Orleans, La..........	1	....
Cincinnati, Ohio..........	6	....	New York, N. Y..........	2	....
Cleveland, Ohio...........	21	....	Oklahoma City, Okla......	4	....
Coffeyville, Kans.........	1	....	Omaha, Nebr.............	25	....
Columbus, Ohio...........	4	....	Pontiac, Mich............	6	....
Covington, Ky............	2	....	Portland, Oreg...........	1	....
Cumberland, Md...........	11	....	Quincy, Ill..............	3	....
Dayton, Ohio.............	3	....	Saginaw, Mich............	2	....
Denver, Colo..............	10	....	St. Louis, Mo............	14	....
Detroit, Mich.............	61	....	St. Paul, Minn...........	22	....
Evansville, Ind...........	3	....	Salt Lake City, Utah.....	4	....
Flint, Mich...............	14	1	Sioux City, Iowa.........	2	....
Fort Wayne, Ind..........	17	....	Springfield, Ill..........	2	....
Fort Worth, Tex..........	27	....	Springfield, Ohio.........	6	....
Grand Rapids, Mich.......	23	....	Syracuse, N. Y...........	1	....
Kansas City, Kans........	36	....	Washington, D. C.........	4	....
Kansas City, Mo..........	117	....			

TETANUS.

State Reports for November, 1917.

During the month of November, 1917, 1 case of tetanus was reported in the State of Colorado; 5 cases were reported in Kansas; and 2 cases were reported in South Dakota.

20

City Reports for Week Ended Dec. 15, 1917.

During the week ended Dec. 15, 1917, 1 fatal case of tetanus was reported in Los Angeles, Cal.; 1 case was reported in New York, N. Y.; and 1 death was reported in Wheeling, W. Va.

TUBERCULOSIS.

See Diphtheria, measles, scarlet fever, and tuberculosis, page 22.

TYPHOID FEVER.

Kansas—Eldorado.

On December 31, 1917, the epidemic of typhoid fever at Eldorado, Kans., was reported as subsiding. During the month of November, 1917, 137 cases of the disease were notified, and 23 cases were notified in December.

State Reports for November, 1917.

Place.	New cases reported.	Place.	New cases reported.
Colorado		**Connecticut—Continued.**	
Archuleta County	1	New London County—Continued.	
Boulder County	1	New London	1
Chaffee County	3	Norwich (town)	2
Denver County		Tolland County -	
Denver	5	Rockville	2
Huerfano County	8	Windham County—	
Jefferson County	1	Willamantic	1
La Plata County	2		
Larimer County	1	Total	57
Morgan County	2		
Otero County	1	**Kansas**	
Prowers County	3	Allen County	5
Pueblo County -		Anderson County	2
Pueblo	4	Atchison County	1
San Miguel County	1	Barton County	5
Weld County	1	Bourbon County	4
		Brown County	1
Total	34	Butler County—	
Connecticut:		Augusta (1 R. D.)	8
Fairfield County—		Douglas (R. D.)	1
Bridgeport		Eldorado (12 R. D.)	136
Greenwich (town)	2	Leon (R. D.)	1
Stamford	1	Roslin	2
Stratford	1	Chase County	2
Hartford County—		Chautauqua County	1
Avon	1	Cherokee County	8
East Hartford	1	Cloud County	1
Enfield	1	Coffey County	5
Glastonbury	1	Cowley County	6
Hartford	15	Crawford County	9
New Britain	4	Dickinson County	3
Simsbury	1	Doniphan County	5
South Windsor	1	Douglas County	3
West Hartford	1	Elk County	4
Wind or Locks	1	Ford County	3
Litchfield County -		Franklin County	11
Torrington	1	Greenwood County	6
Middlesex County —		Harvey County	9
Haddam	1	Jefferson County	1
Middletown	2	Jewell County	1
New Haven County—		Johnson County	1
Derby		Kingman County	3
New Haven	1	Kiowa County	2
Waterbury	3	Labette County	2
New London County—	9	Leavenworth County	9
Colchester	1	Linn County	3
Montville	1	Lyon County	2

TYPHOID FEVER—Continued.

State Reports for November, 1917—Continued.

Place.	New cases reported.	Place.	New cases reported.
Kansas—Continued.		**Mississippi—Continued.**	
Marion County	2	Monroe County	5
Meade County	1	Montgomery County	5
Miami County	1	Newton County	1
Montgomery County	13	Oktibbeha County	4
Morris County	2	Panola County	9
Neosho County	4	Pearl River County	6
Osage County	1	Perry County	1
Osborne County	2	Pike County	7
Reno County	5	Pontotoc County	8
Republic County	1	Prentiss County	5
Riley County	1	Quitman County	5
Rooks County	1	Rankin County	6
Russell County	4	Scott County	8
Saline County	4	Sharkey County	2
Sedgwick County—		Simpson County	2
Wichita (2 R. D.)	25	Smith County	3
Seward County	1	Sunflower County	10
Shawnee County	6	Tallahatchie County	6
Sherman County	2	Tate County	3
Sumner County	4	Tippah County	9
Wabaunsee County	1	Tishomingo County	2
Washington County	2	Tunica County	5
Wilson County	8	Union County	1
Woodson County	1	Warren County	1
Wyandotte County	6	Washington County	8
		Webster County	5
Total	365	Wilkinson County	14
		Winston County	5
Maine:		Yalobusha County	1
Aroostook County—		Yazoo County	3
Fort Fairfield (town)	1		
Cumberland County—		Total	364
Portland	2		
Lincoln County—		**Montana:**	
South Bristol (town)	1	Cascade County	1
Piscataquis County—		Great Falls	5
Dover (town)	4	Chouteau County	2
Foxcroft (town)	1	Custer County	1
Waldo County—		Fergus County	3
Waldo (town)	1	Flathead County	3
		Gallatin County	2
Total	10	Lewis and Clark County	1
		Missoula County	2
Mississippi:		Musselshell County	1
Adams County	4	Park County	1
Alcorn County	7	Rosebud County	6
Amite County	1	Sheridan County	4
Attala County	7	Teton County	1
Bolivar County	26	Yellowstone County	2
Calhoun County	4	Billings	2
Carroll County	4		
Choctaw County	10	Total	37
Claiborne County	2		
Clarke County	3	**Nevada:**	
Coahoma County	3	Esmeralda County	1
Copiah County	10	Humboldt County	1
De Soto County	4	Lyon County	3
Franklin County	2	Nye County	2
Greene County	4	Washoe County	5
Harrison County	12		
Hinds County	1	Total	12
Holmes County	3		
Itawamba County	2	**New Jersey:**	
Jackson County	9	Atlantic County	2
Jasper County	3	Bergen County	4
Jefferson County	5	Burlington County	13
Jefferson Davis County	20	Camden County	6
Jones County	1	Cape May County	1
Lafayette County	8	Cumberland County	2
Lamar County	2	Essex County	13
Lauderdale County	9	Gloucester County	1
Leake County	4	Hudson County	3
Lee County	15	Hunterdon County	2
Leflore County	3	Mercer County	6
Lincoln County	1	Middlesex County	2
Madison County	5	Monmouth County	4
Marion County	9	Morris County	2
Marshall County		Ocean County	1

TYPHOID FEVER—Continued.

State Reports for November, 1917—Continued.

Place.	New cases reported.	Place.	New cases reported.
New Jersey—Continued.		**North Dakota—Continued.**	
Passaic County........................	2	Stutsman County.......................	6
Somerset County......................	5	Ward County...........................	2
Union County.........................	19		
Total............................	88	Total...............................	23
		South Dakota:	
North Dakota:		Clark County..........................	1
Barnes County........................	1	Davison County.......................	1
Bottineau County.....................	3	Hutchinson County....................	6
Bowman County.......................	1	Minnehaha County....................	1
Burleigh County......................	3	Roberts County........................	1
Cass County...........................	3	Yankton County.......................	1
Foster County.........................	1		
Mercer County........................	1	Total...............................	11
Morton County........................	1	**Wyoming:**	
Nelson County.........................	1	Goshen County........................	5

City Reports for Week Ended Dec. 15, 1917.

Place.	Cases.	Deaths.	Place.	Cases.	Deaths.
Albany, N. Y...........	5	....	New Orleans, La.............	2	1
Allentown, Pa...........	2	....	New York, N. Y.............	12	6
Ann Arbor, Mich........	4	....	Niagara Falls, N. Y.........	1	....
Baltimore, Md..........	3	....	North Adams, Mass..........	1	....
Birmingham, Ala.......	2	....	Pawtucket, R. I.............	1	....
Boston, Mass...........	2	....	Philadelphia, Pa.............	4	3
Chicago, Ill............	2	1	Pittsburgh, Pa..............	2	1
Cleveland, Ohio.........	2	....	Pontiac, Mich...............	1	....
Columbus, Ohio.........	....	1	Portland, Oreg..............	1	....
Cumberland, Md.........	1	1	Quincy, Ill.................	1	1
Dayton, Ohio...........	1	....	Reading, Pa................	1	....
Denver, Colo...........	1	....	Richmond, Va..............	1	1
Detroit, Mich...........	2	5	Saginaw, Mich..............	1	....
East Orange, N. J......	1	....	St. Louis, Mo..............	2	....
Elizabeth, N. J.........	2	....	San Diego, Cal..............	2	....
El Paso, Tex...........	1	1	Savannah, Ga...............	1	....
Fall River, Mass.......	5	....	Schenectady, N. Y.........	2	....
Fort Worth, Tex.......	1	....	South Bend, Ind............	1	....
Harrisburg, Pa.........	1	....	Springfield, Ohio...........	2	1
Hartford, Conn.........	1	....	Stockton, Cal...............	2	....
Kansas City, Kans......	1	....	Syracuse, N. Y.............	1	....
Los Angeles, Cal.......	5	....	Terre Haute, Ind...........		1
Lowell, Mass...........	....	1	Troy, N. Y................	3	....
Memphis, Tenn.........	1	....	Washington, D. C...........	1	....
Milwaukee, Wis........	2	....	Wheeling, W. Va...........	1	....
Minneapolis, Minn......	2	....	Wilkes-Barre, Pa...........		1
New Castle, Pa.........	1	....	Worcester, Mass............	2	....
New Haven, Conn.......	2	....			

DIPHTHERIA, MEASLES, SCARLET FEVER, AND TUBERCULOSIS.

State Reports for November, 1917.

State.	Cases reported.			State.	Cases reported.		
	Diphtheria.	Measles.	Scarlet fever.		Diphtheria.	Measles.	Scarlet fever.
Colorado............	49	18	87	Montana............	20	22	262
Connecticut........	338	414	217	Nevada.............	4	8	10
Iowa...............	72		156	New Jersey........	674	769	369
Kansas.............	231	429	343	North Dakota......	78	8	20
Maine.............	82	359	11	South Dakota......	32	109	62
Mississippi........	155	5,792	89	Wyoming..........	49	21	57

DIPHTHERIA, MEASLES, SCARLET FEVER, AND TUBERCULOSIS—
Continued.

City Reports for Week Ended Dec. 15, 1917.

City.	Population as of July 1, 1916 (estimated by U. S. Census Bureau).	Total deaths from all causes.	Diphtheria.		Measles.		Scarlet fever.		Tuberculosis.	
			Cases.	Deaths.	Cases.	Deaths.	Cases.	Deaths.	Cases.	Deaths.
Over 500,000 inhabitants:										
Baltimore, Md.............	589,621	......	13	1	30	......	16	......	28	25
Boston, Mass.............	736,476	229	124	4	81	8	34	......	46	22
Chicago, Ill.............	2,497,722	619	249	36	43	......	101	1	547	56
Cleveland, Ohio.........	674,073	185	44	6	8	......	6	......	15	25
Detroit, Mich..........	571,784	188	71	4	27	3	44	1	41	15
Los Angeles, Cal.......	503,812	137	16	1	7	......	8	......	42	23
New York, N. Y........	5,602,841	1,459	242	29	557	10	104	4	290	180
Philadelphia, Pa.......	1,709,518	587	91	16	65	......	58	......	72	40
Pittsburgh, Pa.........	579,090	222	24	2	40	......	6	......	14	11
St. Louis, Mo..........	757,309	210	99	6	34	......	23	1	44	18
From 300,000 to 500,000 inhabitants:										
Buffalo, N. Y...........	468,558	126	23	2	8	......	10	......	28	13
Cincinnati, Ohio........	410,476	147	21	......	7	......	6	......	18	20
Jersey City, N. J.......	306,345	86	15	......	50	1	8	......	12	1
Milwaukee, Wis........	436,535	96	7	......	72	......	32	1	25	7
Minneapolis, Minn.....	363,154	......	22	......	6	......	10	......		
Newark, N. J..........	408,894	134	18	2	53	1	22	.	33	13
New Orleans, La.......	371,747	......	11	1	38	......	4	......	41	29
San Francisco, Cal.....	463,516	135	17	1	22	......	14	......	68	19
Seattle, Wash.........	348,639	......	3	......	51	......	7	......		5
Washington, D. C......	363,980	139	15	5	84	......	38	......	13	6
From 200,000 to 300,000 inhabitants:										
Columbus, Ohio.........	214,878	61	4	......	1	......	18	......	9	5
Denver, Colo...........	260,800	64	17	3	2	......	7	......		15
Kansas City, Mo........	297,847	100	16	3	14	......	11	......		12
Portland, Oreg.........	295,463	52	4	......	6	......	7	......	6	4
Providence, R. I........	254,960	72	15	3	1	2	5	......	4	9
Rochester, N. Y........	256,417	84	11	1	27	......	12	......	10	7
St. Paul, Minn.........	247,232	60	17	2	3	......	9	......	7	7
From 100,000 to 200,000 inhabitants:										
Albany, N. Y...........	104,190	......	2	......	6	......	1	......	17	......
Atlanta, Ga............	190,558	......	3	1	15	......	7	......	7	5
Birmingham, Ala.......	181,762	66	3	......	102	......	21	......	5	7
Bridgeport, Conn.......	121,579	33	6	......	9	......	1	......	3	4
Cambridge, Mass.......	112,981	36	12	1	11	......	5	......	4	6
Camden, N. J..........	106,233	......	8	......	30	......	6	......	2	......
Dayton, Ohio..........	127,224	44	11	1	3	......	3	......	3	3
Fall River, Mass.......	128,366	28	3	1	1	......	4	......	11	3
Fort Worth, Tex.......	104,562	......	3	......	56	......	2	......		2
Grand Rapids, Mich....	128,791	40	7	2	2	......	4	......	2	2
Hartford, Conn........	110,900	46	9	......	2	......	5	1	7	2
Lowell, Mass..........	113,245	32	12	......	3	......	1	......	7	2
Lynn, Mass...........	102,425	27	4	......		......	4	......	1	1
Memphis, Tenn........	148,995	53	7	1	51	1	4	......	9	7
New Bedford, Mass....	118,158	32	4	1	19	......	2	......	10	3
New Haven, Conn......	149,685	......	3	......	7	......	2	......	5	5
Omaha, Nebr..........	165,470	62	1	......	37	......	6	......		2
Reading, Pa...........	109,381	36	2	1	1	......	3	......	1	......
Richmond, Va.........	156,687	59	8	......	2	......	4	......	6	6
Salt Lake City, Utah...	117,399	27	1	......	87	......	7	......		2
Springfield, Mass......	105,942	45	13	1	3	......	10	......	1	3
Syracuse, N. Y........	155,624	35	15	2	21	......	12	......	4	4
Tacoma, Wash.........	112,770	......	4	......	5	......		......		
Toledo, Ohio..........	191,554	76	13	1	13	......	2	......	2	6
Trenton, N. J.........	111,593	45	14	1	1	......	1	......	3	3
Worcester, Mass.......	163,314	50	4	1	3	......	8	......	7	4
From 50,000 to 100,000 inhabitants:										
Akron, Ohio...........	85,625	......	7	......	1	......		......	1	.
Allentown, Pa.........	63,505	16	11	......	4	......	3	......	1	......
Atlantic City, N. J.....	57,660	......		......	1	......		......	1	......
Bayonne, N. J.........	69,893	......	3	......		......		......	1	......
Berkeley, Cal.........	57,653	14	1	1	3	......	6	1	2	......
Binghamton, N. Y.....	53,973	22	9	1	6	......	5	1	1	1
Brockton, Mass.......	67,449	13	5	......	2	......		......		1
Canton, Ohio.........	60,852	17	1	......		......		......	2	2
Charleston, S. C.......	60,734	31	3	......		......		......		2
Covington, Ky.........	57,144	28	1	2	......	......	1	......	1	4

DIPHTHERIA, MEASLES, SCARLET FEVER, AND TUBERCULOSIS—
Continued.

City Reports for Week Ended Dec. 15, 1917—Continued.

City.	Population as of July 1, 1916 (estimated by U. S. Census Bureau).	Total deaths from all causes.	Diphtheria.		Measles.		Scarlet fever.		Tuberculosis.	
			Cases.	Deaths.	Cases.	Deaths.	Cases.	Deaths.	Cases.	Deaths.
From 50,000 to 100,000 inhabitants—Continued.										
Elizabeth, N. J.	86,690	24	4	1	5	.....	6	1	4	3
El Paso, Tex.	63,705	34	1				1			12
Erie, Pa.	75,195				1		4		4	21
Evansville, Ind.	76,078	28	3	1			2		1	1
Flint, Mich.	54,772	16	3				9			1
Ft. Wayne, Ind.	76,183	16	6				2			
Harrisburg, Pa.	72,015	21	4		2		2		3	1
Hoboken, N. J.	77,214	22	4		12		1		3	2
Johnstown, Pa.	68,529	17	1		2		9			
Kansas City, Kans.	99,437		3	1	4		7		1	
Lancaster, Pa.	50,853				1					
Malden, Mass.	51,155	21	6		5		2		1	3
Manchester, N. H.	78,283	22	3		3				11	3
Mobile, Ala.	58,221	13			10					
New Britain, Conn.	53,794	17	2		1		4		4	2
Norfolk, Va.	89,612		6		16		4			2
Oklahoma City, Okla.	92,943	16	3		4		3			2
Passaic, N. J.	71,744	13	8		1				3	1
Pawtucket, R. I.	59,411	34	4	1	2		1			3
Portland, Me.	63,887	12			195					1
Rockford, Ill.	55,185	14			3					1
Sacramento, Cal.	69,895	32					4		3	5
Saginaw, Mich.	55,642	15					7			2
St. Joseph, Mo.	85,236	24	11	1	3		2			1
San Diego, Cal.	53,330	24	5		22		5		5	3
Savannah, Ga.	68,805	30			10				1	
Schenectady, N. Y.	99,319	26	6		2		1		13	5
Sioux City, Iowa.	57,078	1	2				11			
Somerville, Mass.	87,039	25	8		19		10		5	2
South Bend, Ind.	68,946	8	1				2			1
Springfield, Ill.	61,120	20	1				1			2
Springfield, Ohio.	51,550	23	1						3	1
Terre Haute, Ind.	66,083	16	5		1					1
Troy, N. Y.	77,916		1		1		5		4	3
Wilkes Barre, Pa.	76,776	29	7		6		2		2	
Wilmington, Del.	94,265	31	6		1		2			2
York, Pa.	51,630		1				2		1	
From 25,000 to 50,000 inhabitants:										
Alameda, Cal.	27,732	5	3		6				1	
Auburn, N. Y.	37,385	9	1		2					
Austin, Tex.	34,814	14	2							1
Brookline, Mass.	32,730	10	1		2		2			1
Butler, Pa.	27,632	8	2		4		2			
Butte, Mont.	43,425	6	4		4		10		13	
Chelsea, Mass.	46,192	12	9		14				1	
Chicopee, Mass.	29,319	9	2		3				1	1
Cumberland, Md.	26,074	8	3	1			1			
Danville, Ill.	32,261	9	1							
Davenport, Iowa.	48,811		2				4			1
Dubuque, Iowa.	39,873									
East Chicago, Ind.	28,743	15	2		3	1	1		1	1
East Orange, N. J.	42,458	12	3		53		1		1	
Elgin, Ill.	28,203	7								
Everett, Mass.	39,233	9	1		15	1	6		2	
Everett, Wash.	35,486	5			1					
Galveston, Tex.	41,863	3			3					2
Green Bay, Wis.	29,353	10								
Haverhill, Mass.	48,477	10	1	1					2	1
Jackson, Mich.	35,363	10	1		2		19	1		1
Kalamazoo, Mich.	48,886	10	5		11				8	1
Kenosha, Wis.	31,576	10								1
Kingston, N. Y.	26,771	8								
Knoxville, Tenn.	38,676				3				2	
La Crosse, Wis.	31,677	9	1							
Lexington, Ky.	41,097	20	1		20		1			1
Lima, Ohio.	35,384	9	6				1	1		
Lincoln, Nebr.	46,515	10	2		3		4			
Lorain, Ohio.	36,964		4							
Lynchburg, Va.	32,940	9								4
Madison, Wis.	30,699						4		2	1

DIPHTHERIA, MEASLES, SCARLET FEVER, AND TUBERCULOSIS—
Continued.

City Reports for Week Ended Dec. 15, 1917—Continued.

City.	Population as of July 1, 1916 (estimated by U. S. Census Bureau).	Total deaths from all causes.	Diphtheria.		Measles.		Scarlet fever.		Tuberculosis.	
			Cases.	Deaths.	Cases.	Deaths.	Cases.	Deaths.	Cases.	Deaths.
From 25,000 to 50,000 inhabitants—Continued.										
McKeesport, Pa.	47,521	15	2		4					1
Medford, Mass.	26,234	7					1			1
Montclair, N. J.	26,318	6	1		3	1			1	
Nashua, N. H.	27,327	11				1		1	1	
New Castle, Pa.	41,133		1				2			
Newport, R. I.	30,108	7	4	2	10					
Newton, Mass.	43,715	9	6		3				1	1
Niagara Falls, N. Y.	37,353	11	2		2		6			1
Norristown, Pa.	31,401	7	1		2				6	1
Ogden, Utah	31,404	15	1				3			
Orange, N. J.	33,080	12	3		5		3		1	2
Pasadena, Cal.	46,480	12							3	3
Pittsfield, Mass.	38,629	3	2	1			8		2	
Portsmouth, Va.	39,651	15	1		1		1			2
Quincy, Ill.	35,798	10	1		4				2	2
Quincy, Mass.	38,136	7	2						1	1
Racine, Wis.	46,486	9			1				1	
Roanoke, Va.	43,284	16	1						1	
Rock Island, Ill.	26,936	10	1							
San Jose, Cal.	38,902				3		2			
Steubenville, Ohio	27,445	10								
Stockton, Cal.	35,358		1		4				2	1
Superior, Wis.	40,226	4			2		4			1
Taunton, Mass.	36,283	16					3			1
Waltham, Mass.	30,570		3		1					2
Watertown, N. Y.	29,894				1				1	
West Hoboken, N. J.	43,139	5	2	1	2				1	
Wheeling, W. Va.	43,377	21	2	1	1		1		2	1
Williamsport, Pa.	33,809		6	1						
Wilmington, N. C.	26,892	6			2					
Winston-Salem, N. C.	31,155	17	1		22		2		1	2
Zanesville, Ohio	30,863	8								
From 10,000 to 25,000 inhabitants:										
Alton, Ill.	22,874	9	2	1	3		1		1	
Ann Arbor, Mich.	15,010	10	3		1					
Braddock, Pa.	21,685		1		4					
Cairo, Ill.	15,794	7			1					2
Clinton, Mass.	1 13,075	2			1					
Coffeyville, Kans.	17,548		1		4					
Concord, N. H.	22,669	10			2					
Galesburg, Ill.	24,276	3								
Harrison, N. J.	16,930				6					
Kearny, N. J.	23,539	8			10		3			1
Kokomo, Ind.	20,930	6					1			
Leavenworth, Kans.	1 19,363	7	3							
Long Branch, N. J.	15,395	2								
Marinette, Wis.	1 14,610	2					1			
Melrose, Mass.	17,445	5	3				1			1
Morristown, N. J.	13,284	3			1					
Nanticoke, Pa.	23,126	5	3							
Newburyport, Mass.	15,243	6							2	
New London, Conn.	20,985	12	18				1			
North Adams, Mass.	1 22,019	8	1							
Northampton, Mass.	19,926	6			3		1			1
Plainfield, N. J.	23,805	3	3						1	
Pontiac, Mich.	17,524	14	6				1		1	
Portsmouth, N. H.	11,666		1				6			
Rocky Mount, N. C.	12,067	7								
Rutland, Vt.	14,831	8					1			
Sandusky, Ohio	20,193	2			1					
Saratoga Springs, N. Y.	13,821	4							1	
Steelton, Pa.	15,548	4	2						3	1
Washington, Pa.	21,618				2		1			
Woburn, Mass.	15,969	6								

1 Population Apr. 15, 1910; no estimate made.

FOREIGN.

CUBA.

Communicable Diseases—Habana.

Communicable diseases have been notified at Habana as follows:

Diseases.	Dec. 1 10, 1917.		Remaining under treatment Dec. 10, 1917.	Diseases.	Dec. 1-10, 1917.		Remaining under treatment Dec. 10, 1917.
	New cases.	Deaths.			New cases.	Deaths.	
Diphtheria............	9	....	6	Scarlet fever..........	4	....	6
Leprosy..............	....	....	10	Smallpox.............	1	....	2
Malaria..............	32	....	¹65	Typhoid fever.........	30	6	²85
Measles..............	9	....	9	Varicella.............	2	....	2
Paratyphoid fever.....	....	....	3				

¹ From the interior, 37 cases.   ² From the interior, 54 cases.

CHOLERA, PLAGUE, SMALLPOX, AND TYPHUS FEVER.

Reports Received During Week Ended Jan. 4, 1918.[1]

CHOLERA.

Place.	Date.	Cases.	Deaths.	Remarks.
India:				
Calcutta.................	Sept. 16 Oct 6....	....	42	
Java:				
West Java................				Oct. 19 25 1917: Cases, 9, deaths, ?.
Batavia	Oct 19 25	8	2	
Persia:				
Mazanderan Province –				
Astrabad..............	July 31...	....	....	Present
Barfrush..............	July 1-27............	34	23	
Chahmirzad...........	....	....	....	25 cases reported July 31, 1917.
Chahrastagh..........	June 15-July 25...	10	8	
Kharek..............	May 28-June 11 ...	21	13	
Sari.................	July 3 29............	273	144	
Yekchambe-Bazar.....	June 3.............	6	....	
Siam:				
Bangkok.................	Sept 16 22...	1	1	

PLAGUE.

Place.	Date.	Cases.	Deaths.	Remarks.
Egypt...				Jan. 1-Nov. 15, 1917: Cases, 728; deaths, 398.
Port Said	July 23-29..........	1	2	
India:				Sept. 16-29, 1917: Cases, 18,653, deaths 13,810.
Calcutta...............	Sept. 16-29..........	....	2	
Siam:				
Bangkok.	Sept. 16-22...	1	1	
Straits Settlements:				
Singapore....	Oct 28-Nov. 3....	1	3	

[1] From medical officers of the Public Health Service, American consuls, and other sources. For reports received from June 30, 1917, to Dec 28, 1917, see Public Health Reports for Dec. 28 1917. The tables of epidemic diseases are terminated semiannually and new tables begun.

(26)

CHOLERA, PLAGUE, SMALLPOX, AND TYPHUS FEVER—Continued.

Reports Received During Week Ended Jan. 4, 1918—Continued.

SMALLPOX.

Place.	Date.	Cases.	Deaths.	Remarks.
Australia:				
New South Wales............				Oct. 12-25, 1917: Cases, 5.
Abermain................	Oct. 25.............	2	....	
Warren.................	Oct. 12-13.........	3	....	
Brazil:				
Pernambuco.................	Nov. 1-15...........	1	....	
Rio de Janeiro.............	Sept. 30-Oct. 27...	313	88	
Canada:				
Ontario—				
Hamilton..............	Dec. 16-22..........	1	....	
Sarnia.................	Dec. 9-15...........	1	....	
China:				
Amoy......................	Oct. 22-Nov. 4....	....	....	Present.
Mukden....................	Nov. 11-24.........	....	....	Do.
Tientsin..................	Nov. 11-17.........	2	....	
Egypt:				
Cairo......................	July 23-29.........	2	1	
France:				
Lyon.......................	Nov. 18-25.........	....	1	In hospital. From Givors.
Great Britain:				
Birmingham.................	Nov. 11-17.........	19	....	
Italy:				
Turin......................	Oct 29-Nov. 4....	33	6	
Java:				
Mid-Java...................	Oct. 10-16.........	8	....	
West Java..................				Oct. 19-25, 1917: Cases, 8; deaths.
Mexico:				1.
Mazatlan...................	Dec. 5-11..........	....	1	
Mexico City................	Nov. 11-17.........	9	....	
Newfoundland:				
St. Johns..................	Dec. 8-14..........	1	....	
Portuguese East Africa:				
Lourenço Marques..........	Aug. 1-Sept. 30....	....	4	
Russia:				
Moscow.....................	Aug. 26-Oct. 6....	22	2	

TYPHUS FEVER.

Place.	Date.	Cases.	Deaths.	Remarks.
Australia:				
South Australia..........				Nov. 11-17, 1917 Cases, 1.
Canada:				
Ontario—				
Kingston................	Dec. 2-8...........	3	....	
Egypt:				
Alexandria.................	Nov. 8-14..........	10	2	
Cairo......................	July 23-29.........	23	8	
Java:				
Mid-Java...................	Oct. 10-16.........	12	....	
West Java..................				Oct. 19-25, 1917: Cases, 9; deaths,
Batavia................	Oct. 18-25.........	5	1	2.
Mexico:				
Aguascalientes.............	Dec. 15............	....	2	
Mexico City................	Nov. 11-17.........	94	....	
Russia:				
Archangel..................	Sept. 1-14.........	7	2	
Moscow.....................	Aug. 26-Oct. 6....	49	2	

×

PUBLIC HEALTH REPORTS

| VOL. 33 | JANUARY 11, 1918 | No. 2 |

INDUSTRIAL EFFICIENCY.

THE BEARINGS OF PHYSIOLOGICAL SCIENCE THEREON: A REVIEW OF RECENT WORK.

By FREDERIC S. LEE, Ph. D., Consulting Physiologist to the United States Public Health Service; Professor of Physiology in Columbia University; Executive Secretary of the Committee on Industrial Fatigue.

One of the most striking features of the present war is the unprecedented use that is being made of science. In all directions one sees the laboratories called upon to direct their past discoveries and their present powers toward the devising of ways in which best to achieve the ends of the warring nations, and the men of the laboratories called upon for experimentation, for counsel, and for the guidance of the various units of the vast forces employed. This is so not only at the front where the multitudinous death-dealing and death-defying devices daily and nightly proclaim the supremacy of science, but back in the hospitals where the dying are saved from death, in the camps where the living are made fit for fighting, in the factories where the instruments of war are being rapidly produced, and even in the homes of the people where training in scientific living is being attempted on a gigantic scale. It seems impossible that this wide recognition of the utilitarian value of science and this eagerness to utilize its achievements shall altogether cease when the horrors have ended and the possibility of peaceful living returns. With the new ways of thinking and of living that are now being learned, mankind will probably continue to demand, and the laboratories will certainly continue to discover, even more efficient ways, and it seems inevitable that science will continue to maintain its proud place among the leading factors of human progress.

Industry has never been backward in accepting and utilizing scientific discoveries. Once they have been shown to be of real value in increasing the output, decreasing the cost, or improving the quality of the product, they are quickly adopted and made a part of industrial processes. Industry does not merely wait for outside contributions, but maintains its own laboratories, often upon a large scale and manned by able men, and thus scientific research has become one of its prominent features. The phenomenal industrial advances of recent decades have been due chiefly to the achievements of two

S

sciences—mechanical engineering, which has invented and developed automatic machinery, and chemistry, which has discovered new chemical substances and new chemical processes.

But all this great progress in improving industrial work on its physical side has not yet succeeded in eliminating the human being. Men and women are as necessary as ever to the performance of industrial work, however much their occupations may have been changed, and one of the great problems with which industry still has to deal is that of discovering how this human element must be utilized in order to secure its greatest efficiency and obtain from it its greatest value to the employer. Industrial medicine and sanitation have been making marked headway; efficiency engineering, or scientific management, has devised methods that under proper direction have proved valuable; and no one can dispute the fact that these agencies have contributed a considerable share in making the human factor in industrialism more effective. But none has solved the problem, and in recent years it has become gradually clearer that much light can here be derived from physiological science and that a new application of physiological principles—an industrial physiology, if one desires a specific title—has been gradually appearing.

From the standpoint of industrial physiology the industrial worker is looked upon as bringing to the general physical equipment of the factory his own bodily machine, the most intricate of all the machines used in the plant. This machine must be understood, it must be constantly watched, it must be used intelligently, and it must not be abused. Like other industrial machines it can be worked at different speeds, but unlike other industrial machines it can not be worked for an indefinite period, because it is subject to the limitation of fatigue. Fatigue delays work, diminishes output, spoils goods, causes accidents and sickness, keeps workers at home, and in all these ways is an obstacle to efficiency. How fatigue can be kept down to its lowest reasonable limit, how the working power of the individual can be maintained from day to day and from week to week and be made to yield a maximum output without detriment to itself and to others—in other words, how the human machine can be used so as to obtain from it the most profit—constitutes one of the great industrial problems of the day.

Much light had already been thrown upon the solution of this problem before the war began to make its unprecedented demands on industrialism, but progress has been much more rapid since the fateful month of August of three years ago. Various individual efforts to investigate industrialism from the physiological standpoint have now by common consent centered in Great Britain in the Health of Munition Workers Committee and in America in the Committee on Industrial Fatigue of the Advisory Commission of the Council of National

Defense, associated with the Public Health Service. These two bodies have been actively engaged in studying war industries, and the results of this study, not yet ended, are already beginning to have an important, and will, it is hoped, continue to have a lasting, influence on the industrial work of the world.

The American committee has been making a study of the hourly output of individual workers throughout the working shift. Their observations, which have been carried out under the immediate direction of Mr. P. Sargant Florence, who was formerly connected with the British investigations, when combined with previous results obtained by him and others, show that the course of output follows certain definite lines, which differ in different kinds of occupation and constitute more or less distinct types. These may be represented by typical curves. The study is not yet completed, and the curves so far obtained can not be regarded as necessarily final, nor do they necessarily comprise all possible types. They are therefore presented here as tentative and suggestive.

When in a familiar experiment of the physiological laboratory a single muscle of an animal is stimulated for a considerable period by a regular series of slight electric shocks and is made to contract with each stimulus, and with each contraction

Muscle

Attent.

Muscul.

Monot.

Night

1st. spell　　2nd. spell

Observed curves of output.

to lift a given load, the work performed in the successive contractions from the beginning to the end may be regarded as a curve which, while differing in details, is perfectly typical of all muscles (see figure). The greatest amount of work is not performed at the beginning of the working period, but the curve at first rises gradually to a maximum, indicating for a time a progressive improvement in working power. This rise is still usually called by the original name given to it, the "treppe," or "staircase." Following the maximum, there is a gradual slow decline in the curve, indicating fatigue, which may continue until the muscle is completely exhausted and totally unable to lift the load. The treppe and the fatigue are typical normal phenomena. This curve of the work of a single muscle may well be kept in mind in considering the curves of output of the industrial worker in a working spell. It should be understood, however, that in the human being the physiological conditions are infinitely more complicated than in a single muscle, for there are added the many other organs of the body whose functions may possibly modify muscular work, and especially the nervous system, with all its possibilities of wilfully changing an output curve that might otherwise represent genuine capacity. In the output curve of the human being a rise may signify, not an involuntary treppe, but a voluntary spurt; and a fall may signify, not real fatigue, but a voluntary restriction of effort. It is not always easy, and it may often prove impossible, to distinguish between the involuntary and the voluntary phenomena.

A curve of output that closely resembles the muscle curve has been found in work that requires close attention and exact muscle coordination. There is at first a gradual rise, continuing through the first hour or two, then a fall gradually increasing throughout the remainder of the working spell. After the luncheon hour the general form of the curve is repeated, but with slight changes in detail. The rise in each spell is often called the "practice effect," although it is analogous to the treppe of the muscle curve; the fall, if the work is not voluntarily restricted, is usually interpreted as indicating fatigue. The greater height of the curve just after, as compared with its height just before, the luncheon hour represents the restorative effect of rest and food; and the lower point of the curve at the end of the second, when compared with that at the end of the first spell, signifies the cumulative fatigue of the day.

In occupations that are distinguished especially by their muscular character, the output curve, although more observations are here needed, seems to show progressive fatigue, but the practice effect may be wanting, and a rise followed by a fall, appears in the latter half of the spell. This late rise indicates a temporary inhibition of fatigue, perhaps a second wind; it is less, and fatigue is more, marked in the second spell.

Where work is monotonous and where it is frequently broken by natural pauses, a curve may be obtained which for both working spells is nearly a straight and horizontal line, showing a slight practice effect but no fatigue.

The American committee has found instances of another type of output, in which the figures of the total daily production by the individual from day to day, and even from week to week, show a striking uniformity, and the inference seems to be justified that the workers are not working to their full capacity but, either voluntarily or involuntarily, have fixed upon a certain quantitative output as appropriate to a day's work. No generalized form of curve for such a method of working can yet be presented, but individual curves show usually an early fall with often a marked spurt before the close of the spell. To what degree fatigue enters into the work here is difficult to decide without further study. The frequently pronounced spurt following a decrease in production, is evidently due to the recognition by the worker that unless he bestirs himself his stint will not be finished by closing-time. The fact that a pronounced spurt is possible indicates that capacity had not before been reached. If work is actually stopped for a portion of the spell for any unusual reason, such as the breakdown of the machinery, there is a rush to accomplish the conventional amount before the end, and this often succeeds. This direct limitation, or, as Florence calls it, "stereotyping" of output, might be expected where wages are paid by the day, but it is found even where piece rates prevail and the worker is free to earn more by doing more. Its cause is probably complex and many elements may enter into it—the unthinking recognition that a certain amount is enough for a day's work; the fear, often justified, that if more is accomplished piece rates will be cut; the disinclination of many rapid workers to surpass their fellows; unwillingness or inability of the foreman to drive until individual capacity is reached; the realization by the foreman that if individual capacity is reached his department will soon exhaust all its available stock; and, last but not least, in many cases just plain human laziness. Overdriving has long been recognized as one of the evils of industrial work, but less attention has been given to underdriving. It seems reasonable that individual capacity should be among the first factors to be considered in determining the standard of output. The prevalence and causes of a maintenance of output on a stereotyped level far below the limit of individual capacity would well repay careful study.

Which, if any, of the various curves of output that have been presented represents the ideal that should always be striven for can not now be stated. Here experiment is needed. Where a genuine fatigue fall in the curve is pronounced, the cessation of work is obviously indicated. This may take the form, as circumstances may indicate, of either an intermediate recess period or the shortening of the hours spent at the factory.

This brings us to one of the most obvious problems of industrial physiology: viz. that of the duration of daily and weekly labor. At the beginning of the war, along with other evidences of the feverish haste which characterized the nation's activities, the duration of labor in the munition factories of Great Briatain was greatly increased. Besides lengthening the regular daily schedule, overtime and Sunday labor were frequently resorted to. In America, following the lead of the Council of National Defense, hours that had already been established by custom or law have in general been maintained, and unusually prolonged labor has been avoided in most factories. The result of the long British hours is what might have been predicted, the production of excessive fatigue; in America excessive fatigue seems so far to be less pronounced.

It is widely believed, and especially by employers of labor, that longer hours mean necessarily a greater output. If industrial physiology does nothing else but show the fallacy of this notion, it will have justified itself. A man can of course accomplish more in two hours than in one hour, but it does not follow that he can accomplish more in 15 hours than in 12, or more in 12 than in 10, or even more in 10 than in 8 hours.   Here the American Committee has discovered a strikingly suggestive fact in the night work of one of our large munition factories, the duration of the night shift being 12 hours. After 5 a. m. the curve of output shows a rapid decline, and during the last 40 minutes there is very little or absolutely no production. The elimination of the last two hours would be greatly to the advantage of the men and would probably result in no diminution but an actual increase in the total product turned out. Under the British Committee, Vernon has accumulated most striking statistical evidence of the beneficial results of a reduction of the hours of labor. Two instances will suffice to illustrate the point: With a group of 80 to 100 women turning aluminum fuse bodies the reduction of the weekly hours of actual work from 66.2 to 45.6, a saving of more than 20 hours, increased the gross production by 9 per cent. When the actual weekly working hours of 56 men engaged in the very heavy labor of sizing fuse bodies were reduced from 58.2 to 51.2, the gross output was increased by 21 per cent.

It is impossible in the time here allowed to go further into detail in the bearings of physiological science on industrial efficiency. Industrial physiology tells us, in the interest of a large output, not only to keep the hours of labor down to what experience has shown to be a reasonable limit, but to choose this limit in accordance with the fatiguing effects of the different specific occupations. It tells us to introduce recess periods into long spells, to omit Sunday labor, and to impose overtime on already fatigued workers only in rare emergencies and when compensation can be given by free hours later. It tells us not to keep the same workers continually on the night shift, but to alternate night with day work. It tells us that each worker and each task possesses a specific standard of strength, and it indicates in what task each worker will probably prove most efficient. It tells us that each worker has a rhythm that is best adapted to his own neuromuscular mechanism and that it is advantageous to place in a squad of workers doing a specific task only those possessing similar rhythms, eliminating the faster and the slower individuals, and then to adjust the speed of operation to the common rate. Such instances as these few reveal the scope of industrial physiology and show how it is indicating some of the ways in which the most intricate of all industrial machines, the body of the worker, must be used in order to bring out its greatest usefulness

Our Government is now rapidly making contracts for war goods
of all kinds. Our factories, heretofore engaged largely on foreign
orders, are now turning eagerly to the work required to maintain and
equip our own forces. Now is the appropriate time to place this
work upon a scientific basis and in accord with the principles of industrial physiology. I am sure that if such facts as I have been able
only briefly here to present could be understood in all their significance by our producers of war supplies, the end of this latest and most
terrible world struggle would be hastened.

MALARIA IN SOUTH CAROLINA.

PREVALENCE AND GEOGRAPHIC DISTRIBUTION, 1915 AND 1916.

The study of the prevalence and geographic distribution of malaria
in the State of South Carolina was begun in 1913. Previous reports

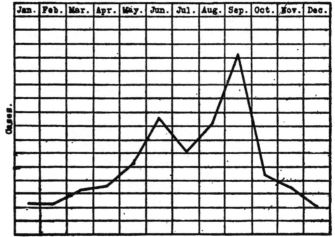

Relative prevalence of malaria in South Carolina, by months, as indicated by the number of
cases reported.

on this subject were published in the Public Health Reports of
March 13, 1914, and May 28, 1915, and issued as reprints Nos. 172
and 277.

The physicians were circularized every three months during the
calendar year 1915, and during the first, second, and fourth quarters
of the year 1916, reply postal cards being used for the purpose.

Of the cards sent to the physicians, a little more than 12.5 per
cent were returned. The number of cards sent out, the number of
schedules returned, and the number of counties represented at each
circularization are shown in Table 1.

It is to be borne in mind that the number of cases reported by the physicians does not show the cases that actually occurred, for an average of less than 13 per cent of the physicians returned the schedules. While there must have been many more cases of malaria in the State, the reports of the physicians on which this study is based are sufficient to show whether malaria was present or absent in the several counties, and reasonably accurately the relative intensity of the infection in the counties.

The cases reported throughout the State by months are shown in Table 2. The relative numbers of cases reported by months are shown in the chart.

Relative prevalence of malaria in South Carolina by counties in proportion to the population, as indicated by the number of cases reported.

The numbers of cases reported from the several counties of the State are given by race and year in Table 3.

The map above shows the relative prevalence of the disease in the several counties of the State, the heavier shaded counties being those in which the infection was heaviest, the unshaded counties those in which the infection was lightest, as indicated by the numbers of cases reported. The relative intensity of infection was determined by ascertaining the number of cases reported in each county during the period January 1, 1915, to June 30, 1916, and October 1, 1916, to December 31, 1916, inclusive, per 1,000 population. The population used was that of the 1910 census, it being impracticable to use current estimates for the purpose.

TABLE 1.—*Results of circularization of practicing physicians.*

Period.	Inquiry cards sent to physicians.	Replies received.	Percentage of replies.	Counties represented in replies.	Counties not heard from.	Cases of malaria reported.
1915.						
January to March	3,826	611	15.97	43	1	763
April to June	1,275	131	10.27	36	8	1,732
July to September	1,275	166	13.02	35	9	2,743
October to December	1,275	137	10.75	35	9	1,004
1916.						
January to March	1,275	125	9.80	35	9	457
April to June	1,275	143	11.22	34	10	988
October to December	1,275	131	10.27	35	9	947

TABLE 2.—*Cases of malaria reported by months.*

Year.	Jan.	Feb.	Mar.	Apr.	May.	June.	July.	Aug.	Sept.	Oct.	Nov.	Dec.
1915	221	217	325	361	512	859	607	816	1,320	441	356	207
1916	102	121	234	197	290	501	......	......	......	420	333	194

TABLE 3.—*Cases reported by counties, by years, and by color.*

County.	Calendar year 1915.			Jan. 1 to June 30 and Oct. 1 to Dec. 31, 1916.		
	White.	Colored.	Combined.	White.	Colored.	Combined.
Abbeville	80	72	152	....	2	2
Aiken	34	60	94	15	7	22
Anderson	14	7	21	14	9	23
Bamberg	6	6	12	....	....	...
Barnwell	122	133	255	8	12	20
Beaufort	46	45	91	3	10	13
Berkeley	55	77	132	....	....	..
Calhoun	63	92	155	25	50	75
Charleston	21	47	68	63	73	136
Cherokee	13	16	29	1	....	1
Chester	145	138	283	62	77	139
Chesterfield	21	15	36	19	7	26
Clarendon	26	14	40	29	41	70
Colleton	16	10	26	....	....	..
Darlington	62	73	135	33	69	102
Dillon	14	20	34	....	....	..
Dorchester	25	30	55	80	23	103
Edgefield	12	42	54	8	15	23
Fairfield	164	206	370	54	75	129
Florence	21	57	78	8	43	51
Georgetown	59	106	165	34	61	95
Greenville	31	29	60	1	....	1
Greenwood	16	20	36	8	5	13
Hampton	2	4	6	42	66	108
Horry	6	1	7	16	17	33
Kershaw	88	50	138	19	15	34
Lancaster	53	77	130	1	....	1
Laurens	61	32	93	12	6	18
Lee	8	12	20	18	11	29
Lexington	118	61	179	63	18	81
Marion	189	251	440	27	30	57
Marlboro	26	33	59	20	23	43
Newberry	524	591	1,115	12	14	26
Oconee	2	....	2	2	....	2
Orangeburg	393	399	792	283	192	475
Pickens	4	....	4	....	....	..
Richland	204	225	429	61	116	177
Saluda	3	4	7	6	12	18
Spartanburg	63	14	77	88	19	107
Sumter	5	8	13	....	36	36
Union	51	7	58	2	2	4
Williamsburg	40	79	119	6	6	12
York	124	49	173	55	32	87
Total	3,030	3,212	6,242	1,198	1,194	2,392

Five cases of hemoglobinuric fever were reported from Orangeburg County during the fourth quarter of 1916.

PREVALENCE OF DISEASE.

No health department, State or local, can effectively prevent or control disease without knowledge of when, where, and under what conditions cases are occurring.

UNITED STATES.

EXTRA-CANTONMENT ZONES—CASES REPORTED WEEK ENDED JAN. 8.

Camp Beauregard, La.—City of Alexandria: Meningitis 5, pneumonia 2, measles 41, diphtheria 3, gonorrhea 1, German measles 2. Pineville: Meningitis 2, measles 11 City of Boyce: Measles 13. Village of Tioga: Meningitis 1, measles 2. Rural districts of Rapides Parish: Measles 12, broncho-pneumonia 1, lobar pneumonia 1, mumps 1 The village of Moreauville, 30 miles from Alexandria, reports 6 cases meningitis, all of cases in one family; onset first case December 29, second case January 3; other 4 cases all had onset within four days of the onset second case.

Camp Bowie, Tex. Fort Worth: Measles 2, mumps 1, smallpox 2, pneumonia 2

Camp Dodge, Iowa.—Des Moines: Smallpox 31, scarlet fever 8, diphtheria 3, tuberculosis 1, measles 4. Polk City Measles 1 Urbandale Scarlet fever 1 Bloomfield Township. Diphtheria 1.

Camp Funston, Kans Measles 5, smallpox 1, Riley; measles 1, Randolph; measles 95, pneumonia 2, diphtheria 2—1 death, chicken pox 1, scarlet fever 1, meningitis 1 whooping cough 1, Manhattan; chicken pox 1, measles 1, Keats; scarlet fever 1, measles 4, chicken pox 1, Ogden; meningitis carriers, delayed reports 11. Chicken pox 2, scarlet fever 2, measles 17, smallpox 1, diphtheria 1, Junction City

Camp Gordon, Ga.—Atlanta. Chicken pox 2, diphtheria 11, German measles 2, gonococcus infection 24, measles 17, cerebrospinal meningitis 1, scarlet fever 3, smallpox 1, syphilis 10, typhoid fever 1. Decatur: German measles 3, mumps 2. Stone Mountain Measles 1.

Camp Greene, N. C.—Chancroids 3, syphilis 11, measles 22, German measles 6, syphilis and gonorrhea 1, whooping cough 10, gonorrhea 4, scarlet fever 1, typhoid fever 1, Charlotte Township.

Camp Hancock, Ga—Measles: Augusta 29, Gracewood 3, Hepzibah 5, Blythe 2, Davidson Crossing 1; chicken pox, Augusta 4; cerebrospinal meningitis, Augusta 1, German measles, Augusta 1; typhoid fever, Augusta 1; scarlet fever, Augusta 1.

Camp Jackson, S. C.—(Week ended Jan. 5.) Columbia: Roseola 10, measles 9, chicken pox 1, smallpox 1, typhoid 1, diphtheria 1.

Fort Leavenworth, Kans Measles: City 8, county 2. Whooping cough: City 4, county 2. Tuberculosis: City 2. Lobar pneumonia: City 3, county 3. Chicken pox. City 5, county 2. German measles City 5 Smallpox: City 1, county 4.

Camp Lewis, Wash German measles Dupont 10 cases, Spanway 2 cases, Park Lodge 2 cases.

Camp Logan, Tex.—Chicken pox. 6 Houston. Diphtheria: 2 Houston. German measles: 20 Houston. 1 Houston Heights. Gonorrhea: 1 Houston. Measles 27 Houston. Mumps: 1 Houston. Malaria: 1 Houston. Pneumonia: 5 Houston. Syphilis: 1 Houston. Tuberculosis: 5 Houston. Whooping cough: 1 Houston.

Camp MacArthur, Tex.—Waco: Chicken pox 4, German measles 7, gonococcus 1, malaria 1. measles 5, mumps 1, lobar pneumonia 1, scarlet fever 2, smallpox 1, syphilis 2, tuberculosis 1, typhoid 2, whooping cough 1. County: None.

Camp McClellan, Ala.—Anniston: Smallpox 6, diphtheria 3, chicken pox 20, measles 19. Oxford: Smallpox 2. Jacksonville: Chicken pox 1.

Fort Oglethorpe, Ga.—Chattanooga Scarlet fever 2, German measles 9, measles 24, mumps 3, paratyphoid 2, chicken pox 3, meningitis 1, tuberculosis 2, pneumonia 4, syphilis 1. Eastlake: Measles 4, meningitis 1, typhoid fever 1, pneumonia 1, German measles 2. Fort Cheatham: Pneumonia 1. St. Elmo: German measles 1. Rossville, Ga.: Measles 2, pneumonia 1. Lytle, Ga.: Smallpox 1.

Camp Pike, Ark.—Little Rock: Measles 39, chicken pox 7, smallpox 26, scarlet fever 4, tuberculosis —, lobar pneumonia 4, German measles 15, mumps 1, malaria 1, syphilis 9, gonorrhea 20, chancroid 5, meningitis 3. North Little Rock: Measles 5, smallpox 10, pneumonia 2. German measles 9, malaria 1, syphilis 1, meningitis 2, typhoid 1, whooping cough 1. Scotts Gonorrhea 1. Pinnacle: Measles 1. Roland: Measles 2, diphtheria 1, smallpox 1. Wynne: Measles 1. Sweethome: Pneumonia 1. Levy: Smallpox 1.

Camp Sevier, S. C.—Mills Mill 1 measles.

Camp Shelby, Miss.—Hattiesburg: Chicken pox 2, gonorrhea 4, hookworm 2, malaria 3, measles 3, German measles 5, mumps 2, pneumonia 1, smallpox 4. Saucier, Harrison County: Diphtheria 1. Biloxi, Harrison County: Diphtheria 1. McLaurin, Forrest County: Smallpox 1. Columbia, Marion County: Smallpox 1. Gulfport, Harrison County: Meningitis 1. Long Beach, Harrison County: Meningitis 1. Laurel, Jones County: Tuberculosis, pulmonary, 1. Mosells, Jones County: Tuberculosis, pulmonary, 3.

Camp Sheridan, Ala.—Montgomery: German measles 22, measles 23, smallpox 12, cerebrospinal meningitis suspect 1, diphtheria 1, chicken pox 3, scarlet fever 1, tuberculosis 1. Rural district in 5-mile zone: Measles 1, smallpox 3, chicken pox 1. Capitol Heights: German measles 1, measles 1. Cloverdale: Measles 1.

Camp Sherman, Ohio.—Chicken pox: Springfield Township 7, Kingston 1. German measles: Chillicothe 9. Gonorrhea: Chillicothe 1. Measles: Chillicothe 16. Scarlet fever: Chillicothe 1, Paint Township 1, Liberty Township 1. Smallpox: Jefferson Township 1. Whooping cough: Springfield Township 6.

Camp Zachary Taylor, Ky.—Jefferson County: Gonococcus infection 1, measles 1, rabies in animal 1, scarlet fever 1, pulmonary tuberculosis 1. Louisville: Chicken pox 3, diphtheria 6, cerebrospinal meningitis 1, German measles 9, measles 17, scarlet fever 7, tuberculosis, pulmonary, 7, smallpox 1, typhoid fever 2, whooping cough 7.

Tidewater health district, Va.—Newport News: Measles 20, chicken pox 5, lobar pneumonia 1, German measles 2, cerebrospinal meningitis 1. Hampton: Whooping cough 3, lobar pneumonia 2, diphtheria 1, measles 1. Phoebus: Chickenpox 1, whooping cough 5.

Camp Wadsworth, S. C.—Spartanburg city: German measles 22, diphtheria 1, measles 3, chicken pox 4, tuberculosis 3, whooping cough 4, scarlet fever 1, cerebrospinal meningitis 2. Pauline: Typhoid fever 1, pneumonia 1. East Spartanburg: Scarlet fever 1 Whitney: Scarlet fever 1.

CURRENT STATE SUMMARIES.

Alabama.

From Collaborating Epidemiologist Perry, telegram dated January 8, 1918:

One fatal case cerebrospinal meningitis at Silas, Choctaw County.

California.

From the State Board of Health of California, telegram dated January 8, 1918:

Nearly all reportable diseases show increase last week. Eight epidemic cerebrospinal meningitis—2 San Francisco, 2 Los Angeles, and 1 each San Jose, Orange County, Lindsay, and Ontario; 6 smallpox—2 each Los Angeles city and Imperial County, 1 each Shasta County and Grass Valley. Outbreaks of measles in San Diego city, Hanford, and Visalia. Extensive outbreak chickenpox in Stockton

Reported by mail for the preceding week (ending Dec. 29):

Cerebrospinal meningitis	4	Pneumonia	98
Chicken pox	67	Poliomyelitis	1
Diphtheria	71	Ophthalmia neonatorum	1
Erysipelas	10	Scarlet fever	57
German measles	57	Smallpox	6
Gonococcus infection	28	Syphilis	120
Malaria	2	Trachoma	1
Measles	175	Tuberculosis	155
Mumps	22	Typhoid fever	19
Pellagra	1	Whooping cough	19

Indiana.

From the State Board of Health of Indiana, telegram dated January 7, 1918:

Scarlet fever: Epidemic Winchester, school closed; Nevada, and Jackson Township, Steuben County; Pike Township, Jay County. Diphtheria deaths: One Nashville, Brown County, 1 Rushville, 1 Berne, Adams County. Smallpox: Epidemic Paragon, Morgan County, and Geneva, Adams County. Epidemic measles school children Frankfort.

Kansas.

From Collaborating Epidemiologist Crumbine, telegram dated January 7, 1918:

Epidemic meningitis: Manhattan 1, Lincoln 1, Topeka 1, Richland 1, Wichita 1. Meningococcus carriers: Junction City 11. Smallpox: Kansas City, Kans., 45.

Massachusetts.

From Collaborating Epidemiologist Kelley, telegram dated January 7, 1918:

Unusual prevalence: Diphtheria, Amesbury 3, additional; measles, Braintree 49, additional; typhoid, North Brookfield 2, additional.

Minnesota.

From Collaborating Epidemiologist Bracken, telegram dated January 7, 1918:

Smallpox: Cook County, Rosebush Township 1; Millelacs County, Borgholm Township 1; Mower County, Windom Township 3; Pope County, Lowry village 1; Stearns County, Ashley Township 1; Wright County, Frankfort Township 1. Two cases of poliomyelitis and 2 cases of cerebrospinal meningitis reported since December 31.

Washington.

From Collaborating Epidemiologist Tuttle, telegram dated January 7, 1918:

Five cases typhoid Waitsburg, Walla Walla County. No outbreaks.

CEREBROSPINAL MENINGITIS.

State Reports for November, 1917.

Place.	New cases reported.	Place.	New cases reported.
Alabama:		Alabama—Continued.	
Calhoun County	2	Montgomery County	2
Etowah County	1	Total	6
Jefferson County	1	District of Columbia	2

City Reports for Week Ended Dec. 22, 1917.

Place.	Cases.	Deaths.	Place.	Cases.	Deaths.
Augusta, Ga.	1	1	Los Angeles, Cal.	1	1
Baltimore, Md.	1	2	Louisville, Ky.		1
Berlin, N. H.		1	Lowell, Mass.		1
Boston, Mass.	2		Milwaukee, Wis.	2	1
Buffalo, N. Y.	2		Minneapolis, Minn.	1	
Chicago, Ill.	4	4	Newark, N. J.		1
Cincinnati, Ohio.	1		New York, N. Y.	3	5
Cleveland, Ohio.	1		Omaha, Nebr.		1
Columbus, S. C.	2		Orange, N. J.	1	
Dayton, Ohio.		1	Petersburg, Va.		1
Denver, Colo.		1	Philadelphia, Pa.	1	1
Des Moines, Iowa.		1	Pittsburgh, Pa.	2	
Detroit, Mich.	1	1	Providence, R. I.	1	1
Dubuque, Iowa.		1	St. Louis, Mo.	2	
East Orange, N. J.	1		San Francisco, Cal.		1
Kansas City, Mo.	4		Waltham, Mass.	1	1

DIPHTHERIA.

See Diphtheria, measles, scarlet fever, and tuberculosis, page 46.

ERYSIPELAS.

City Reports for Week Ended Dec. 22, 1917.

Place.	Cases.	Deaths.	Place.	Cases.	Deaths.
Baltimore, Md.	1	2	New York, N. Y.		3
Buffalo, N. Y.	1		Oakland, Cal.	1	
Chicago, Ill.	13	2	Philadelphia, Pa.		1
Cincinnati, Ohio.	2		Pittsburgh, Pa.	4	
Cleveland, Ohio.	3		Portland, Oreg.	1	
Denver, Colo.	6		Racine, Wis.		1
Detroit, Mich.		1	Rochester, N. Y.	2	
Duluth, Minn.	2		Rutland, Vt.	1	
Erie, Pa.	1		Sacramento, Cal.	1	
Grand Rapids, Mich.	1		Saginaw, Mich.	1	
Kalamazoo, Mich.	2		St. Joseph	1	
Los Angeles, Cal.	2		St. Louis, Mo.	8	3
Louisville, Ky.	1	1	Schenectady, N. Y.	1	
Milwaukee, Wis.	4	1	Springfield, Ill.	2	
Montclair, N. J.	1		Toledo, Ohio.		1
Newark, N. J.	8		Washington, Pa.	1	

LEPROSY.

City Report for Week Ended Dec. 22, 1917.

During the week ended December 22, 1917, one case of leprosy was reported in Cambridge, Mass.

MALARIA.

Alabama Report for November, 1917.

Place.	New cases reported.	Place.	New cases reported.
Alabama:		Alabama—Continued.	
Barbour County	1	Houston County	15
Blount County	6	Jefferson County	22
Bullock County	5	Madison County	4
Butler County	2	Mobile County	5
Calhoun County	3	Montgomery County	14
Clarke County	1	Pickens County	1
Cleburne County	4	Pike County	1
Coffee County	1	Shelby County	5
Dallas County	5	Talladega County	2
Elmore County	1	Washington County	1
Franklin County	3	Wilcox County	1
Geneva County	1		
Greene County	3	Total	107

City Reports for Week Ended Dec. 22, 1917.

Place.	Cases.	Deaths.	Places.	Cases.	Deaths.
Alexandria, La	2		Memphis, Tenn		1
Birmingham, Ala	1		Newark, N. J	1	
Little Rock, Ark	1		New Orleans, La	1	1

MEASLES.

See Diphtheria, measles, scarlet fever, and tuberculosis page 46.

PELLAGRA.

State Reports for November, 1917.

Place.	New cases reported.	Place	New cases reported.
Alabama:		Alabama—Continued.	
Autauga County	1	Limestone County	1
Calhoun County	1	Macon County	1
Chambers County	2	Madison County	1
Clarke County	3	Monroe County	1
Coffee County	1	Montgomery County	3
Covington County	1	Morgan County	3
Dallas County	1	Perry County	3
DeKalb County	3	Pike County	2
Escambia County	1	St. Clair County	2
Etowah County	3	Sumter County	1
Fayette County	1	Tallapoosa County	1
Hale County	2	Tuscaloosa County	10
Houston County	1	Washington County	1
Jackson County	1	Winston County	2
Jefferson County	25		
Lamar County	1	Total	82
Lauderdale County	1		
Lawrence County	1	District of Columbia	4

PELLAGRA—Continued.

City Reports for Week Ended Dec. 22, 1917.

Place.	Cases.	Deaths.	Place.	Cases.	Deaths.
Atlanta, Ga.		1	Lynchburg, Va.		1
Augusta, Ga.		1	Memphis, Tenn.	1	1
Birmingham, Ala.	1	1	Mobile, Ala.	1	2
Charleston, S. C.		1	Montgomery, Ala.		1
Greenville, S. C.	1	1	Savannah, Ga.		1

PNEUMONIA.

City Reports for Week Ended Dec. 22, 1917.

Place.	Cases.	Deaths.	Place.	Cases.	Deaths.
Alton, Ill.	1	1	Lincoln, Nebr.	3	2
Baltimore, Md.	14	24	Lorain, Ohio.	1	
Binghamton, N. Y.	4	1	Los Angeles, Cal.	29	15
Boston, Mass.	33	16	Manchester, N. H.	3	3
Braddeck, Pa.	2		Morristown, N. J.	1	
Brockton, Mass.	2	1	Newark, N. J.	58	10
Brookline, Mass.	2	2	New Bedford, Mass.	4	3
Buffalo, N. Y.	6	10	Newburyport, Mass.	1	1
Cambridge, Mass.	1		New Castle, Pa.	2	
Chattanooga, Tenn.	7	1	Newport, Ky.	1	1
Chelsea, Mass.	4	4	Newport, R. I.	1	
Chicago, Ill.	122	84	Newton, Mass.	6	2
Chillicothe, Ohio.	1		Petersburg, Va.	10	2
Cleveland, Ohio.	53	39	Philadelphia, Pa.	128	79
Dayton, Ohio.	12	12	Pittsburgh, Pa.	53	47
Detroit, Mich.	16	33	Pontiac, Mich.	2	1
Erie, Pa.	4		Quincy, Mass.	1	2
Fall River, Mass.	4		Reading, Pa.	3	1
Fitchburg, Mass.	5	1	Rochester, N. Y.	17	7
Flint, Mich.	2	3	Sacramento, Cal.	8	6
Grand Rapids, Mich.	2		Saginaw, Mich.	1	
Harrison, N. J.	1		St. Joseph, Mo.	2	2
Hattiesburg, Miss.	2		San Diego, Cal.	4	
Haverhill, Mass.	7	1	San Francisco, Cal.	11	14
Jackson, Mich.	1	3	Schenectady, N. Y.	1	1
Kalamazoo, Mich.	3	4	Somerville, Mass.	1	1
Kansas City, Mo.	6	20	Springfield, Mass.	2	2
Lancaster, Pa.	2		Toledo, Ohio.	1	2
Leavenworth, Kans.	1	1	Wichita, Kans.	5	2
Lexington, Ky.	2	2	Worcester, Mass.	9	1

POLIOMYELITIS (INFANTILE PARALYSIS).

Alabama Report for November, 1917.

During the month of November, 1917, cases of poliomyelitis were notified in Alabama as follows: One each in Dekalb and Jackson Counties.

City Reports for Week Ended Dec. 22, 1917.

Place.	Cases.	Deaths.	Place.	Cases.	Deaths.
Brockton, Mass.	1		Milwaukee, Wis.	1	
Chicago, Ill.	1		Pittsburgh, Pa.	1	1
Harrisburg, Pa.	5				

SCARLET FEVER.

See Diphtheria, measles, scarlet fever, and tuberculosis, page 46.

SMALLPOX.

Miscellaneous State Reports.

Place	New cases reported.	Place.	New cases reported.
Alabama (Nov. 1-30):		Alabama (Nov. 1-30)—Continued.	
Bibb County	1	Pickens County	6
Calhoun County	14	Shelby County	5
Elmore County	1	Talladega County	4
Etowah County	3		
Jefferson County	1	Total	44
Lamar County	8		
Madison County	1	District of Columbia (Nov. 1-30)	3

City Reports for Week Ended Dec. 22, 1917.

Place.	Cases.	Deaths.	Place.	Cases.	Deaths.
	5		Kenosha, Wis	1	
Mich.	2		Knoxville, Tenn	1	
	1		La Crosse, Wis	13	
	1		Leavenworth, Kans	1	
	1		Lincoln, Nebr	4	
	1		Little Rock, Ark	19	
	1		Los Angeles, Cal	2	
	17		Louisville, Ky	1	
	6		Memphis, Tenn	3	
	6		Milwaukee, Wis	6	
	1		Minneapolis, Minn	21	
	9		Montgomery, Ala	6	
	27		New Orleans, La	4	
	1		Niagara Falls, N. Y	2	
	3		North Little Rock, Ark	2	
	1		Oklahoma City, Okla	6	
	7		Omaha, Nebr	63	
	20		Pittsburgh, Pa	4	
	5		Portland, Oreg	3	
	2		Rockford, Ill	1	
	1		St. Joseph, Mo	5	
	7		St. Louis, Mo	13	
	14		Salt Lake City, Utah	8	
Ft. Wayne, Ind	11		San Francisco, Cal	1	
Ft. Worth, Tex	5		Sioux City, Iowa	7	
Grand Rapids, Mich	11		Springfield, Mass	1	
Harrisburg, Pa	2		Superior, Wis	1	
...polis, Ind	11		Wheeling, W. Va	2	
City, Kans	40		Wichita, Kans	2	
City, Mo	147				

TETANUS.

City Reports for Week Ended Dec. 22, 1917.

Place.	Cases.	Deaths.	Place.	Cases.	Deaths.
Baltimore, Md	1	1	Norristown, Pa	1	1
Chicago, Ill	1	1	Philadelphia, Pa	1	1
Lawrence, Mass	1	1	Syracuse, N. Y	1	1

TUBERCULOSIS.

See Diphtheria, measles, scarlet fever, and tuberculosis, page 46.

TYPHOID FEVER.

State Reports for November, 1917.

Place.	New cases reported.	Place.	New cases reported.
Alabama:		Alabama—Continued.	
Baldwin County	1	Lamar County	2
Barbour County	1	Lauderdale County	2
Bibb County	3	Lee County	1
Blount County	1	Limestone County	1
Bullock County	2	Lowndes County	1
Butler County	1	Madison County	30
Calhoun County	13	Marion County	1
Chambers County	2	Marshall County	2
Choctaw County	2	Mobile County	7
Clarke County	1	Monroe County	1
Coffee County	3	Montgomery County	14
Colbert County	1	Morgan County	2
Coosa County	5	Pike County	3
Covington County	2	Shelby County	1
Cullman County	1	Sumter County	2
Dallas County	3	Talladega County	2
DeKalb County	1	Tallapoosa County	2
Elmore County	10	Tuscaloosa County	7
Etowah County	2	Walker County	11
Fayette County	2	Winston County	3
Greene County	1		
Hale County	2	Total	235
Houston County	1		
Jackson County	1	District of Columbia	32
Jefferson County	77		

City Reports for Week Ended Dec. 22, 1917.

Place.	Cases.	Deaths.	Place.	Cases.	Deaths.
Alton, Ill	1		New Bedford, Mass	3	
Atlanta, Ga		1	New Castle, Pa	2	
Atlantic City, N. J	1		New Orleans, La	8	2
Baltimore, Md	5	2	New York, N. Y	10	2
Birmingham, Ala	3		Omaha, Nebr		1
Boston, Mass	3	1	Philadelphia, Pa	2	1
Buffalo, N. Y	2	1	Pittsburgh, Pa	3	
Chicago, Ill	4		Portland, Oreg		1
Cincinnati, Ohio	1	2	Providence, R. I	1	1
Cleveland, Ohio	1		Rochester, N. Y	2	
Davenport, Iowa	1		Rockford, Ill	1	
Denver, Colo		1	Sacramento, Cal		1
Detroit, Mich	2	2	Saginaw, Mich	1	
Duluth, Minn	1		St. Louis, Mo	1	2
Fall River, Mass	1		Salt Lake City, Utah	1	
Flint, Mich		1	Sandusky, Ohio	2	
Fort Worth, Tex		1	San Francisco, Cal	5	
Green Bay, Wis	2		Savannah, Ga		1
Indianapolis, Ind	2		Schenectady, N. Y	1	
Kokomo, Ind	2	1	Somerville, Mass	1	
Lawrence, Mass	4		South Bend, Ind		1
Lincoln, Nebr	1		Springfield, Ill	1	
Los Angeles, Cal	1	1	Springfield, Mass	1	
Louisville, Ky	2		Trenton, N. J	1	
Memphis, Tenn	1		Troy, N. Y	3	1
Milwaukee, Wis	1		Waltham, Mass	1	
Minneapolis, Minn	9		Washington, Pa	1	
Morristown, N. J	1		Wheeling, W. Va	2	
Nashville, Tenn	2		Wilmington, Del	2	1
Newark, N. J	4	1	Worcester, Mass	4	

TYPHUS FEVER.

City Report for Week Ended Dec. 22, 1917.

During the week ended December 22, 1917, one case of typhus fever was reported in New York City.

DIPHTHERIA, MEASLES, SCARLET FEVER, AND TUBERCULOSIS.

State Reports for November, 1917.

During the month of November, 1917, 107 cases of diphtheria, 407 cases of measles, and 139 cases of scarlet fever were notified in the State of Alabama; and 263 cases of diphtheria, 208 cases of measles, and 70 cases of scarlet fever were notified in the District of Columbia.

City Reports for Week Ended Dec. 22, 1917.

City.	Population as of July 1, 1916 estimated by U. S. Census Bureau).	Total deaths from all causes.	Diphtheria.		Measles.		Scarlet fever.		Tuberculosis	
			Cases.	Deaths.	Cases.	Deaths.	Cases.	Deaths.	Cases.	Deaths
Over 500,000 inhabitants:										
Baltimore, Md.............	589,621	254	26	1	22	1	15		18	27
Boston, Mass.............	756,476	235	118	5	85	2	47		32	23
Chicago, Ill.............	2,497,722	780	223	14	46	1	190	1	273	87
Cleveland, Ohio..........	674,073	190	50		11		8	1	55	22
Detroit, Mich............	571,784	216	62	8	16	2	34	1	21	11
Los Angeles, Cal.........	508,812	175	14		13		12		49	40
New York, N. Y..........	5,685,811	1,612	240	26	782	11	158	2	270	151
Philadelphia, Pa.........	1,709,518	629	55	8	55		55	1	104	65
Pittsburgh, Pa...........	579,090	216	29	1	113	1	9	1	29	13
St. Louis, Mo............	757,309	249	102	3	14		22		26	20
From 300,000 to 500,000 inhabitants:										
Buffalo, N. Y............	468,558	147	18	2	17		8		22	25
Cincinnati, Ohio.........	410,476	147	23	2	8		14	1	22	20
Jersey City, N. J........	348,345		9		6		14		11	
Milwaukee, Wis..........	450,515	80	10	2	33		49	1	14	4
Minneapolis, Minn.......	363,351		15		5		11			
Newark, N. J.............	408,894	134	21	2	111		10		31	17
New Orleans, La.........	371,747		22		24		1		25	29
San Francisco, Cal.......	463,516	135	24	1	35		9		28	10
From 200,000 to 300,000 inhabitants:										
Columbus, Ohio..........	214,878	70	2		4		19		9	4
Denver, Colo.............	260,800	63	6		13		11			10
Indianapolis, Ind........	271,708		37		11		40		11	
Kansas City, Mo.........	297,847		5		18		11		2	5
Louisville, Ky...........	238,910	108	10		8		11		8	9
Portland, Oreg...........	265,463	50	2		6		9		10	8
Providence, R. I.........	254,960	62	13		23		9			5
Rochester, N. Y..........	256,417	80	5	1	17		11	1	6	6
From 100,000 to 200,000 inhabitants:										
Atlanta, Ga..............	190,358		2		8		2		2	13
Birmingham, Ala.........	181,762	73			124	2	14		10	7
Bridgeport, Conn.........	121,579	38	9	1	3		1		5	5
Cambridge, Mass.........	112,841	82	6		16		4		1	10
Camden, N. J............	106,233		12		40		1		6	
Dayton, Ohio............	127,224	52	4	1	7		4		8	2
Des Moines, Iowa........	101,588	1	4		1		6			
Fall River, Mass.........	128,366	87	3	2	1		3		4	4
Fort Worth, Tex.........	104,562	52	1		34	1	4			5
Grand Rapids, Mich......	128,291	30	7	3	2		4		4	
Lawrence, Mass..........	100,560	34	3						10	3
Lowell, Mass.............	113,245	34	17	1	5		2		6	1
Lynn, Mass..............	102,425	22		1						3
Memphis, Tenn...........	148,995	54	5		93		3	1	4	3
Nashville, Tenn..........	117,067	43	4	1	6		2		1	3
New Bedford, Mass.......	118,158	40	1		11		3		17	5
New Haven, Conn........	149,685		4		2		3		2	4
Oakland, Cal.............	198,604	49	1		3		4		6	5
Omaha, Nebr.............	165,470	51	5		18		4			8
Reading, Pa.............	109,381	20	4				3		2	1
Salt Lake City, Utah.....	117,399	34			79		9			
Springfield, Mass........	105,942	37	2	1	10		10	1	5	6
Syracuse, N. Y..........	155,624	57	11	3	30	2	7		3	3
Toledo, Ohio............	191,554	53	11		4		1			7
Trenton, N. J............	111,593	45	16	2	4		2		9	3
Worcester, Mass..........	163,314	46	6		8		2		7	5

DIPHTHERIA, MEASLES, SCARLET FEVER, AND TUBERCULOSIS—
Continued.

City Reports for Week Ended Dec. 22, 1917   Continued.

City.	Population as of July 1, 1916 (estimated by U.S. Census Bureau).	Total deaths from all causes.	Diphtheria.		Measles.		Scarlet fever.		Tuberculosis.	
			Cases.	Deaths.	Cases.	Deaths.	Cases.	Deaths.	Cases.	Deaths.
From 50,000 to 100,000 inhabitants:										
Altoona, Pa.	58,659									
Atlantic City, N. J.	57,660		1		1				2	
Augusta, Ga.	50,245	11			4		2			
Bayonne, N. J.	69,893		1		2		2		2	
Berkeley, Cal.	57,653	7	1		5		5		1	
Binghamton, N. Y.	53,973	21	4		6		1		1	
Brockton, Mass.	67,449	13	3		2		4		1	
Canton, Ohio.	60,852	15	3				4		3	1
Charleston, S. C.	60,734	37	1		1					4
Chattanooga, Tenn.	60,075				13		8		2	2
Covington, Ky.	57,144	19	3				1		2	2
Duluth, Minn.	94,496	25	1		4		10	1		1
El Paso, Tex.	63,705	32	3		1					15
Erie, Pa.	75,195		6		1		1		3	32
Evansville, Ind.	76,078	19	3		1		2			2
Flint, Mich.	54,772	12	1				11			
Fort Wayne, Ind.	76,183	15	3				1			
Harrisburg, Pa.	72,015	24	1	3	1		5		2	
Hoboken, N. J.	77,214	23	2		29	1	1			1
Johnstown, Pa.	68,529	27	4	1	1		5		1	
Kansas City, Kan.	99,487		2		5		11		3	
Lancaster, Pa.	50,853				1		2			
Little Rock, Ark.	57,343	25	1		57		3		1	9
Malden, Mass.	51,155	17	1	1	4				2	1
Manchester, N. H.	78,981	23	1		4		1		1	
Mobile, Ala.	58,221	25	1		5					3
Norfolk, Va.	89,612		1	2	12		2		1	4
Oklahoma City, Okla.	92,943	22	1		3		1			2
Passaic, N. J.	71,744	17	6		1				3	
Pawtucket, R. I.	59,411	23			1		2			1
Rockford, Ill.	55,185	20								4
Sacramento, Cal.	66,895	35	2	1			7		4	2
Saginaw, Mich.	55,642	17	1				1			2
St. Joseph, Mo.	85,236	20	9	1	1				1	
San Diego, Cal.	53,330	25	3		24		3		15	5
Savannah, Ga.	68,805	39			8		2		1	4
Schenectady, N. Y.	99,519	22	6		4		3		3	1
Sioux City, Iowa.	57,078						9			
Somerville, Mass.	87,039	21	5	1	29	1	5		3	6
South Bend, Ind.	68,946	18			1		6			2
Springfield, Ill.	61,120	10	1							1
Terre Haute, Ind.	66,083	24	3						1	
Troy, N. Y.	77,916						2		2	2
Wichita, Kans.	70,722		2				4			
Wilkes-Barre, Pa.	76,776	20	6	1	3		2		3	1
Wilmington, Del.	94,265	33	3	1	1		5		1	4
York, Pa.	61,656		1				2		1	
From 25,000 to 50,000 inhabitants:										
Alameda, Cal.	27,732		5		1		1			
Austin, Tex.	34,814	15			2					2
Brookline, Mass.	32,730	14			3		5			
Butler, Pa.	27,632	9	3		8		2			
Butte, Mont.	43,425		2		2		15			
Charlotte, N. C.	39,823		1		8		1		2	
Chelsea, Mass.	46,192	12	4		6				5	
Chicopee, Mass.	29,319	9			9		1		2	1
Columbia, S. C.	34,611				17				1	
Cumberland, Md.	26,074	6	5	1					2	2
Danville, Ill.	32,261	15	1		2				2	1
Davenport, Iowa.	48,811		2		2		4			
Dubuque, Iowa.	39,573		1		3		1			1
East Chicago, Ind.	28,743	8	1		4		1			
East Orange, N. J.	42,458	8			28		1			
Elgin, Ill.	28,203	4			1					
Everett, Mass.	39,253	15	5	1	6		3		1	1
Fitchburg, Mass.	41,781	8	1						2	1
Galveston, Tex.	41,863	1			1		1		1	
Green Bay, Wis.	29,353	7	1		1					
Haverhill, Mass.	48,477	14	6		2		4		7	1

DIPHTHERIA, MEASLES, SCARLET FEVER, AND TUBERCULOSIS—
Continued.

City Reports for Week Ended Dec. 22, 1917—Continued.

City.	Population as of July 1, 1916 (estimated by U. S. Census Bureau).	Total deaths from all causes.	Diphtheria.		Measles.		Scarlet fever.		Tuberculosis.	
			Cases.	Deaths.	Cases.	Deaths.	Cases.	Deaths.	Cases.	Deaths.
From 25,000 to 50,000 inhabitants—Continued.										
Jackson, Mich	35,363	23	..		1		12	1	1	2
Kalamazoo, Mich	48,886	21	2		27	1			1	1
Kenosha, Wis	31,576	4	13				16		1	
Knoxville, Tenn	38,676		1		1		4			
La Crosse, Wis	31,677	6	3				1		1	
Lexington, Ky	41,017	20			22					2
Lima, Ohio	35,384	11	3				1			3
Lincoln, Nebr	46,515	14	2	1	12		7		2	
Lorain, Ohio	36,964		1				1			
Lynchburg, Va	32,940	11							1	2
Medford, Mass	26,234	8			3		3			1
Montclair, N. J.	26,318	4			7		1		1	
Montgomery, Ala	43,295	14			21		5			2
Newburgh, N. Y.	29,001	12			64				3	3
New Castle, Pa	41,133						2		1	
Newport, Ky	31,027	10							3	3
Newport, R. I.	30,104	7	2				2			
Newton, Mass	43,715	18	5	2	4					1
Niagara Falls, N. Y.	37,353	14	1		1		2		4	1
Norristown, Pa	31,401		1		2		1	1		1
Ogden, Utah	31,404	3	2				7			
Orange, N. J.	33,040	8	6		2					1
Pasadena, Cal	46,150	11							2	1
Perth Amboy, N. J.	41,185		3		21				2	
Petersburg, Va	25,542	21			5		1			1
Pittsfield, Mass	38,629						4	2	1	
Portsmouth, Va	39,651	19					4			2
Quincy, Mass	38,130		3		1				1	
Racine, Wis	46,486	14		2						
Roanoke, Va	43,284	11	4		3					2
Rock Island, Ill	28,926	8								
San Jose, Cal	38,902		1		7				1	
Steubenville, Ohio	27,441	12								
Superior, Wis	46,226	6			1		3			1
Taunton, Mass	36,283	16					1			1
Waltham, Mass	30,570	13	3		2				1	1
Watertown, N. Y.	29,894								3	
West Hoboken, N. J.	43,139	13	3		2		1		1	2
Wheeling, W. Va.	43,377	17	1						1	
Wilmington, N. C.	29,802	13			7					
Winston-Salem, N. C.	31,155	19			26		1		9	2
Zanesville, Ohio	30,863	16								2
From 10,000 to 25,000 inhabitants:										
Alexandria, La.	15,333	8			46					
Alton, Ill	22,874	5	2	1	1		1			
Ann Arbor, Mich	15,010	5	3		1		1			
Braddock, Pa.	21,485	4			2					
Cairo, Ill	15,794	7								1
Chillicothe, Ohio	15,470		1		19		8			
Clinton, Mass	13,075	4								
Coffeyville, Kans.	17,543				7				3	1
Concord, N. H	22,609	10								1
Galesburg, Ill	24,276	9	3		8					
Greenville, S. C.	18,181	5	1		10					
Harrison, N. J.	16,910		1		2					
Hattiesburg, Miss	16,482				9					
Kearny, N. J.	23,539	6			42					
Kokomo, Ind.	20,930	9								
Leavenworth, Kans	19,363	13	3							
Marinette, Wis.	14,610	6								2
Melrose, Mass.	17,445	6	2				1		1	
Morristown, N. J.	13,284	7							1	
Muscatine, Iowa	17,600	1								
Nanticoke, Pa.	23,126		4		1				1	
New Albany, Ind.	23,629	6			1		2			
Newburyport, Mass.	15,243	3								

¹ Population Apr. 15, 1910; no estimate made.

DIPHTHERIA, MEASLES, SCARLET FEVER, AND TUBERCULOSIS—
Continued.

City Reports for Week Ended Dec. 22, 1917—Continued.

City.	Population as of July 1, 1916 (estimated by U. S. Census Bureau).	Total deaths from all causes.	Diphtheria.		Measles.		Scarlet fever.		Tuberculosis.	
			Cases.	Deaths.	Cases.	Deaths.	Cases.	Deaths.	Cases.	Deaths.
From 10,000 to 25,000 inhabitants—Continued.										
New London, Conn	20,985	7	1						2	
North Adams, Mass	[1] 22,019	7	1							1
Northampton, Mass	19,926	9	1		1		3		4	2
North Little Rock, Ark	14,907				3				1	
Plainfield, N. J	23,805	8						1		
Pontiac, Mich	17,524	12	15	2	2		5		2	
Portsmouth, N. H	11,666						4			
Rocky Mount, N. C	12,067	3			1					
Rutland, Vt	14,831	3								
Sandusky, Ohio	20,193	11					1		1	1
Saratoga Springs, N. Y	13,821	5								
Spartanburg, S. C	21,365				2		1			1
Wilkinsburg, Pa	23,228	10			3				1	
Woburn, Mass	15,969	5								

[1] Population Apr. 15, 1910; no estimate made.

FOREIGN.

BRITISH GOLD COAST.

Plague—Axim.

Plague was reported present, January 8, 1918, at Axim, British Gold Coast, West Africa.

MALTA.

Cerebrospinal Meningitis—1916.

The report of the medical officer of the department of health of the Maltese Islands for the year 1916-17 states that cerebrospinal meningitis was not recognized in Malta previous to the year 1916. The first reported outbreak occurred in March of that year. To the end of the year under report, March 31, 1917, 11 cases with 3 fatalities were notified. The cases occurred in persons living in unfavorable sanitary conditions. Some of the cases occurred in groups. In others no connection with known cases was ascertained.

Plague, Year 1917—Plague in Rats—Previous Outbreak, 1813-14.

Eight cases of plague were notified in the island of Malta from March 2 to April 2, 1917. Of these cases, 7 were bubonic in form; 1 case was septicemic. Five of the 8 cases notified occurred at Calcara among a group of laborers from the neighboring island of Gozo, living in two tenements; the remaining cases occurred in contacts with this group. Plague was ascertained to be present in rats.

The last previously reported outbreak of plague in Malta occurred in 1813-14, with a total of 4,668 fatal cases. The epidemic of 1813-14 developed in the city of Valetta.

CHOLERA, PLAGUE, SMALLPOX, AND TYPHUS FEVER.

Reports Received During Week Ended Jan. 11, 1918.[1]

CHOLERA.

Place.	Date.	Cases.	Deaths.	Remarks.
India: Bombay	Oct 28-Nov. 3	2	1	
Java: West Java				Oct. 26-Nov. 1, 1917: Cases, 5;
Batavia	Oct. 26 Nov. 1	5	3	deaths, 3.

[1] From medical officers of the Public Health Service, American consuls, and other sources.

CHOLERA, PLAGUE, SMALLPOX, AND TYPHUS FEVER—Continued.

Reports Received During Week Ended Jan. 11, 1918—Continued

PLAGUE.

Place.	Date.	Cases.	Deaths.	Remarks.
Ceylon:				
Colombo	Oct. 14–27	4	3	
India				Oct. 21–27, 1917: Cases, 13,571;
Bombay	Oct. 28–Nov. 3	18	17	deaths, 9,390.
Karachi	Oct. 21–Nov. 10	6	5	
Madras Presidency	Oct. 31–Nov. 6	1,555	1,209	
Rangoon	Oct. 21–27	9	10	

SMALLPOX.

Place.	Date.	Cases.	Deaths.	Remarks.
Algeria.				
Algiers	Nov. 1–30	1		
Australia:				
New South Wales				Nov. 20, 1917: Cases, 1.
Abermain	Nov. 20	1		
Canada:				
Quebec—				
Montreal	Dec. 16–22	1		
China:				
Patren	Nov. 18–24	1		
Shanghai	Nov. 19–25	2	12	Cases, foreign; deaths among native population.
Egypt:				
Alexandria	Nov. 12–18	1		
France:				
Lyon	Dec. 3–9	4		
India:				
Madras	Oct. 31–Nov. 6	4	1	
Italy.				
Turin	Nov. 12–25	44	10	
Java.				
Mid-Java	Oct. 17–23	7		
West Java				Oct. 26–Nov. 1, 1917: Cases, 14; deaths, 7.
Newfoundland:				
St. Johns	Dec. 15–21	2		
Philippine Islands:				
Manila	Oct. 28–Nov. 10	3		Varioloid.
Portugal:				
Lisbon	Nov. 4–10	1		–
Russia:				
Petrograd	Aug. 31–Oct. 27	50	8	
Spain:				
Seville	Oct. 1–30		9	

TYPHUS FEVER.

Place.	Date.	Cases.	Deaths.	Remarks.
Algeria:				
Algiers	Nov. 1–30	2		
Canada:				
Quebec—				
Montreal	Dec. 16–22	2	1	
Egypt:				
Alexandria	Nov. 12–25	23	5	
Greece:				
Saloniki	Nov. 11–24		19	
Japan:				
Nagasaki	Nov. 26–Dec. 2	1		
Java:				
Mid-Java				Oct. 17–23, 1917: Cases, 6; deaths, 1.
Samarang	Oct. 17–23	3		
West Java				Oct. 26–Nov. 1, 1917: Cases, 12; deaths, 2.
Batavia	Oct. 26–Nov. 1	8	2	
Mexico:				
Mexico City	Nov. 19–Dec. 15	243		
Russia:				
Petrograd	Aug. 31–Oct. 27	22		
Sweden:				
Goteborg	Nov. 18–24	1		
Tunisia:				
Tunis	Nov. 30–Dec. 6		1	

CHOLERA, PLAGUE, SMALLPOX, AND TYPHUS FEVER Continued.

Reports Received from Dec. 29, 1917, to Jan. 4, 1918.[1]

CHOLERA.

Place.	Date.	Cases.	Deaths.	Remarks.
India:				
Calcutta	Sept. 16 Oct. 6		42	
Java:				
West Java				Oct. 19-25, 1917: Cases, 9; deaths,
Batavia	Oct. 19-25	8	2	2.
Persia:				
Mazanderan Province—				
Astrabad	July 31			Present.
Barfrush	July 1-27	31	23	
Chahmirzad				25 cases reported July 31, 1917.
Chahrastagh	June 15-July 25	10	8	
Kharek	May 28-June 11	21	13	
Sari	July 3-29	273	144	
Yekchambe-Bazar	June 3	6		
Siam:				
Bangkok	Sept. 16-22	1	1	

PLAGUE.

Place.	Date.	Cases.	Deaths.	Remarks.
British Gold Coast:				
Axim	Jan 8			Present.
Egypt:				Jan. 1–Nov. 15, 1917: Cases, 728;
Port Said	July 23-29	1	2	deaths, 398.
India:				Sept. 16-29, 1917: Cases, 18,653,
Calcutta	Sept. 16-29		2	deaths, 13,810.
Siam:				
Bangkok	Sept. 16-22	1	1	
Straits Settlements:				
Singapore	Oct. 28-Nov. 3	1	3	

SMALLPOX.

Place.	Date.	Cases.	Deaths.	Remarks.
Australia:				
New South Wales				Oct. 12-25, 1917: Cases, 5.
Abermain	Oct. 25	2		
Warren	Oct. 12-13	3		
Brazil:				
Pernambuco	Nov. 1-15	1		
Rio de Janeiro	Sept. 30-Oct. 27	313	88	
Canada:				
Ontario—				
Hamilton	Dec. 16-22	1		
Sarnia	Dec. 9-15	1		
China:				
Amoy	Oct. 22-Nov. 4			Present.
Mukden	Nov. 11-24			Do.
Tientsin	Nov. 11-17	2		
Egypt:				
Cairo	July 23-29	2	1	
France:				
Lyon	Nov. 18-25		1	In hospital. From Givors.
Great Britain:				
Birmingham	Nov. 11-17	19		
Italy:				
Turin	Oct. 29-Nov. 4	33	6	
Java:				
Mid-Java	Oct. 10-16	8		
West Java				Oct. 19-25, 1917: Cases, 8; deaths,
				1.
Mexico:				
Mazatlan	Dec. 5-11		1	
Mexico City	Nov. 11-17	9		
Newfoundland:				
St. Johns	Dec. 8-14	10		
Portuguese East Africa:				
Lourenco Marques	Aug. 1-Sept. 30		4	
Russia:				
Moscow	Aug. 26-Oct. 6	22	2	

[1] From medical officers of the Public Health Service, American consuls, and other sources. For reports received from June 30, 1917, to Dec. 28, 1917, see Public Health Reports for Dec. 28, 1917. The tables of epidemic diseases are terminated semiannually and new tables begun.

CHOLERA, PLAGUE, SMALLPOX. AND TYPHUS FEVER—Continued.

Reports Received from Dec. 29, 1917, to Jan. 4, 1918.

TYPHUS FEVER.

Place.	Date.	Cases.	Deaths.	Remarks
Australia:				
South Australia...........	....	....	....	Nov. 11–17, 1917: Cases, 1.
Canada.				
Ontario—				
Kingston...............	Dec. 2–8...........	3	....	
Egypt:				
Alexandria.................	Nov. 8–14.........	10	2	
Cairo....................	July 23–29.........	23	8	
Java:				
Mid-Java....................	Oct. 10–16.........	12	....	
West Java...............	....	....	....	Oct. 19–25, 1917: Cases, 9; deaths,
Batavia...............	Oct. 18–25.........	5	1	2.
Mexico:				
Aguascalientes.............	Dec. 15...........	....	2	
Mexico City................	Nov. 11–17.........	94	....	
Russia				
Archangel..................	Sept. 1–14.........	7	2	
Moscow	Aug. 26–Oct. 6....	49	2	

x

PUBLIC HEALTH REPORTS

| VOL. 33 | JANUARY 18, 1918 | No. 3 |

VENEREAL DISEASE LEGISLATION.

A COMPILATION OF LAWS AND REGULATIONS SHOWING THE TREND OF MODERN LEGISLATION FOR THE CONTROL OF VENEREAL DISEASES.

The following laws, ordinances, and regulations have been assembled for the purpose of presenting, in convenient form for reference, the important features of recent legislation relating to the control of venereal diseases.

No attempt has been made to secure all of the legislation on this subject, the object being to present representative laws showing measures which have been adopted by States and cities in the United States.

CALIFORNIA.

Notification—Control—Examination of Suspects—Powers and Duties of Local Health Officers—Isolation. (Reg. Bd. of H., Oct. 6, 1917.)

RULE 1. *Notification.*—Any person in attendance on a case of syphilis or gonococcus infection, or a case suspected of being one of syphilis or gonococcus infection, shall report the case immediately, by office number only, to the local health officer, who shall in turn report at least weekly on the prescribed form to the secretary of the State board of health all cases so reported to him.

NOTE 1.—In reporting by office number, an identifying number or initial shall be used which refers definitely to the physician's record of the case.

NOTE 2.—All cases of ophthalmia neonatorum, whether the infecting agent is the gonococcus or not, must be reported to the local health officer within 24 hours after the knowledge of the same, as required by chapter 724, statutes of 1915. Copies of this statute may be obtained by application to the State Board of Health, Sacramento, or the Bureau of Venereal Diseases, 525 Market Street, San Francisco. All physicians, midwives, and other persons lawfully engaged in the practice of obstetrics may obtain, without cost, the prophylactic for ophthalmia neonatorum (silver nitrate solution in wax ampoules), together with directions for its use, by applying to the Bureau of Communicable Diseases, Berkeley.

NOTE 3.—Any person in attendance on a case of syphilis or gonococcus infection who fails to report the case promptly to the local health officer is guilty of a misdemeanor, punishable by a fine of not less than $25 nor more than $500, or by imprisonment for a term of not more than 90 days, or by both such fine and imprisonment. (See public health act, sections 13 (rule 2), 16, and 21.)

NOTE 4.—Physicians attending cases of syphilis and gonococcus infection are expected to furnish to the health officer at the times of reporting the case any available useful data regarding the sources of infection, in order to assist in the control of these diseases.

RULE 2. *Diagnosis.*—The local health officer may require the submission of specimens from cases of syphilis or gonococcus infection, or cases suspected of being cases of syphilis or gonococcus infection, for the purpose of examination at a State or municipal laboratory. It shall be the duty of every physician attending a case of syphilis or gonococcus infection, or a case suspected of being one of syphilis or gonococcus infection, to secure specimens for examination when required to do so by the local health officer.

NOTE 1.—Examinations of blood for syphilis by the Wassermann test, and microscopic examinations of smears of pus for gonococcus are made without charge by the bureau of communicable diseases at Berkeley if the specimens are properly taken and mailed in the containers furnished by the bureau of communicable diseases. It is expected that the larger cities will provide adequate laboratory facilities. (See directions for sending material to the laboratory.)

5   (55)

RULE 3. *Instructions to the patient.*—It shall be the duty of the physician in attendance on a person having syphilis or gonococcus infection, or suspected of having syphilis or gonococcus infection, to instruct him in precautionary measures for preventing the spread of the disease, the seriousness of the disease, and the necessity for prolonged treatment, and the physician shall, in addition, furnish approved literature on these subjects.

NOTE 1.—Approved literature for distribution to patients may be secured from the bureau of venereal diseases of the State Board of Health, 525 Market Street, San Francisco.

NOTE 2.—The following instructions are required as a minimum by rule 2:

(a) To patients having syphilis:

1. Syphilis or pox is a contagious disease. It can usually be cured, but it requires two or more years of treatment.

2. You must not marry until a reputable physician has pronounced you cured.

3. Avoid all sexual relations.

4. Always sleep alone.

5. Do not kiss anyone.

6. Never permit anyone to use anything which has been in your mouth, such as toothpicks, toothbrushes, pipes, cigars, pencils, spoons, forks, cups, etc., or anything else that you have contaminated.

7. If you have to see a dentist, tell him about your disease before he examines your teeth.

8. Avoid patent medicines, so-called "medical institutes," and advertising "specialists."

9. Consult a reputable physician, or, in case of financial inability, the city or county physician, or a reputable dispensary such as is found in connection with most large public hospitals, and follow directions absolutely.

(b) To patients having gonorrhea:

1. Gonorrhea, "clap," or gleet, is a serious contagious disease. If properly treated it can usually be cured.

2. You must not marry until a reputable physician has pronounced you cured.

3. Avoid all sexual relations.

4. Always sleep alone, and be sure that no one uses your toilet articles, particularly your towels and wash cloths.

5. Always wash your hands thoroughly after handling the diseased parts. The discharge, if carried to your eyes, may cause blindness.

6. Avoid patent medicines, so-called "medical institutes," and advertising "specialists."

7. Consult a reputable physician, or, if financially unable to do so, the city or county physician, or a reputable dispensary such as is found in connection with most large public hospitals, and follow directions absolutely.

NOTE 3.—If any person has knowledge that a person infected with syphilis or gonococcus infection is failing to observe adequate precautions to prevent spreading infection, he shall report the facts at once to the local health officer.

RULE 4. *Health officers designated inspectors.*—All city, county, and other local health officers are, for the purpose of the control and suppression of venereal diseases, hereby designated and appointed inspectors, without salary, of the State Board of Health of California, under the provisions of section 2979 of the Political Code.

NOTE 1.—The following paragraph is quoted from section 2979 of the Political Code:

"It (the State board of health) shall have general power of inspection, examination, quarantine, and disinfection of persons, places, and things, within the State, and for the purpose of conducting the same may appoint inspectors, who, under the direction of the board, shall be vested with like powers: *Provided,* That this act shall in nowise conflict with the national quarantine laws."

RULE 5. *Investigation and control of cases.*—All city, county, and other local health officers are hereby directed to use every available means to ascertain the existence of, and immediately to investigate, all reported or suspected cases of syphilis in the infectious stages and gonococcus infection within their several territorial jurisdictions, and to ascertain the sources of such infections.

In such investigations said health officers are hereby vested with full powers of inspection, examination, isolation, and disinfection of all persons, places, and things, and as such inspectors said local health officers are hereby directed:

(a) To make examinations of persons reasonably suspected of having syphilis in the infectious stages or gonococcus infection. (Owing to the prevalence of such diseases among prostitutes, all such persons may be considered within the above class.)

(*b*) To isolate such persons whenever, in the opinion of said local health officer, the State board of health or its secretary, isolation is necessary to protect the public health. In establishing isolation the health officer shall define the limits of the area, in which the person reasonably suspected or known to have syphilis or gonococcus infections and his immediate attendant, are to be isolated, and no persons, other than the attending physicians, shall enter or leave the area of isolation without the permission of the health officer.

(*c*) In making examinations and inspections of women for the purpose of ascertaining the existence of syphilis or gonococcus infection, to appoint women physicians for said purposes where the services of a woman physician are requested or demanded by the person examined.

(*d*) In cases of quarantine or isolation, not to terminate said quarantine or isolation until the cases have become noninfectious or until permission has been given by the State board of health or its secretary.

Cases of gonococcus infection are to be regarded as infectious until at least two successive smears taken not less than 48 hours apart fail to show gonococci.

Cases of syphilis shall be regarded as infectious until all lesions of the skin or mucous membranes are completely healed.

(*e*) Inasmuch as prostitution is the most prolific source of syphilis and gonococcus infection, all health officers are directed to use every proper means of repressing the same, and not to issue certificates of freedom from venereal diseases, as such certificates may be used for purposes of solicitation.

(*f*) To keep all records pertaining to said inspections and examinations in files not open to public inspection, and to make every reasonable effort to keep secret the identity of those affected by venereal-disease control measures as far as may be consistent with the protection of the public health.

Rule 6. *Report of unusual prevalence.*—When the local health officer, through investigation, becomes aware of unusual prevalence of syphilis or gonococcus infection, or of unusual local conditions favoring the spread of these diseases, he shall report the facts at once to the bureau of venereal diseases, 525 Market Street, San Francisco.

Dispensaries, Conduct and Operation. (Reg. Bd. of H., Oct. 6, 1917.)

DISPENSARIES TREATING SYPHILIS.

1. *Special department.*—Syphilis shall be treated in a special department or the department of dermatology.

2. *Number of sessions.*—The dispensaries shall be open at least three times a week, day or evening.

3 *Staff.*—The staff shall be adequate in number and training.

4. *Equipment.*—Enough well-arranged rooms, laboratory facilities, and equipment, with instruments and apparatus, shall be provided.

5. *Beds.*—Every dispensary shall have at its disposal beds for isolation or treatment.

6. *Records.*—Adequate records of all cases shall be kept.

7. *Social service required.*—A social-service department shall be maintained and adequate measures adopted to secure a regular attendance of patients.

8. *Information to patients.*—Clinicians shall devote the amount of time necessary for intelligently informing new patients of the seriousness of their disease, the necessity for prolonged treatment, and the precautions necessary to prevent the spread of infection to others, and the clinics shall, in addition, furnish approved literature on these subjects. (This literature can be secured from the bureau of venereal diseases.)

9. *Microscopic examinations.*—Microscopic examinations of suspected initial lesions shall be made.

10. *Wassermann tests.*—Wassermann tests shall be performed in the dispensary laboratory or other approved laboratory.

11. *Administration of salvarsan or equivalents.*—Salvarsan or accepted equivalents shall be administered to all cases where there are no contraindications. (Salvarsan or approved substitutes may be obtained without cost from the bureau of venereal diseases, 525 Market Street, San Francisco, for the treatment of infectious cases of syphilis in approved dispensaries.)

12. *Procedure covering the discharge of patients.*—Suitable tests and observations shall be made of all patients for a period of not less than two years after the conclusion of adequate treatment. (See pamphlet "Modern Treatment of Syphilis," obtainable from the bureau of venereal diseases.)

13. *Transfer of patients.*—If it becomes necessary for any reason to discharge a patient still uncured, the patient shall be referred to an approved dispensary or a reputable physician.

14. *Annual report.*—An annual report of work done in the dispensary shall be made. It is suggested that this include the number of new and old patients and number of visits made, the number of patients continued under observation and treatment from one year into the next, the number of doses of salvarsan or equivalent administered (with a separate list of free doses), and the number of patients discharged as cured.

DISPENSARIES TREATING GONORRHEA.

1. *Number of sessions.*—Dispensaries shall be open at least three times a week, day or evening.

2. *Staff.*—The staff shall be adequate in number and training.

3. *Equipment.*—Enough well-arranged rooms, laboratory facilities and equipment, with instruments and apparatus, shall be provided.

4. *Beds.*—Every dispensary shall have at its disposal beds for isolation or treatment.

5. *Records.*—Adequate records of all cases shall be kept.

6. *Social service required.*—A social service department shall be maintained and adequate measures adopted to secure a regular attendance of patients.

7. *Information to patients.*—Clinicians shall devote the amount of time necessary for intelligently informing new patients of the seriousness of their disease, the necessity of treatment until cured, and the precautions necessary to prevent the spread of infection to others, and the clinic shall, in addition, furnish approved literature on these subjects. (This literature can be secured from the bureau of venereal diseases.)

8. *Microscopic examination.*—Systematic microscopic examination of discharges shall be made in departments treating patients affected with gonorrhœa.

9. *Facilities for asepsis and antisepsis.*—All departments treating patients affected with gonorrhea shall be equipped with adequate facilities for asepsis and antisepsis.

10. *Urethroscopic and cystoscopic examination.*—Facilities for urethroscopic and cystoscopic examination shall be provided and regularly employed by the attending clinicians.

11. *Procedure governing discharge of patients.*—Patients shall be discharged as cured only after repeated negative clinical and microscopic examinations.

12. *Transfer of patients.*—If it becomes necessary for any reason to discharge a patient still uncured, the patient shall be referred to an approved clinic or reputable physician.

13. *Annual report.*—An annual report of work done in the dispensary shall be made. It is suggested that this include the number of new and old patients, the number of visits made, the number of patients continued under observation and treatment from one year into the next, and the number of patients discharged as cured.

HOSPITALS TREATING SYPHILIS AND GONORRHEA.

1. *No discrimination against venereal diseases.*—Patients having venereal diseases must be accepted under the same conditions as other patients.

2. *General standard of hospital.*—The hospital shall be properly equipped and well conducted.

3. Staff and equipment.—There shall be adequate staff and equipment for the diagnosis, treatment, and keeping of records in cases of syphilis or gonococcus infection in general accord with the standards indicated for approved dispensaries.

4. Follow-up.—Social service and follow-up work shall be carried on as indicated for approved dispensaries, either by the hospital or by an approved dispensary to which patients are transferred.

School Attendance of Infected Persons.   (Act Mar. 23, 1907, as Amended.)

SEC. 17. *Infected persons not to attend school.*—No instructor, teacher, pupil, or child affected with any contagious, infectious, or communicable disease which is or might be the subject of quarantine, or has been declared reportable, or who resides in any house, building, structure, tent, or other place where such disease exists or has recently existed, shall be permitted, by any superintendent, principal, or teacher of any college, seminary, public, or private school, to attend such college, seminary, or school, except by the written permission of the local health officer.

CONNECTICUT.

Fornication or Lascivious Carriage or Behavior—Penalty.   (Ch. 6, Act Mar. 1, 1917.)

Section 1315 of the general statutes is amended to read as follows:

Every person who shall be guilty of fornication or lascivious carriage or behavior shall be fined not more than $100, or imprisoned not more than six months, or both.

Venereal Diseases in Institutions—Investigation by a Commission.   (Ch. 150, Act Apr. 17, 1917.)

SECTION 1. The governor is authorized to appoint a commission, consisting of not more than five persons, at least three of whom shall be physicians, to investigate the laws, conditions, and customs of this State pertaining to the method of diagnosis, treatment, and management of persons afflicted with venereal diseases who are confined, committed, or detained in State and county institutions, or institutions receiving State aid, and to make such other investigations as the governor shall direct.

SEC. 2. Said commission shall report its findings and recommendations to the next session of the general assembly, and shall serve without pay except that its necessary expenses, not to exceed $500, shall be paid out of the State treasury upon the order of the comptroller.

FLORIDA.

Distribution of Literature.   (Reg. Bd. of H., June 10, 1913.)

Rule 67 of the regulations of the State board of health, adopted February 27 and 28, 1912 (Public Health Reports, Dec. 6, 1912, p. 2041), was amended so as to include "venereal diseases" in the list of diseases the nature and danger of which are to be explained in literature to be distributed by local health officers and representatives of the State board of health.

ILLINOIS.

Notification—Placarding—Quarantine—Investigation—Control.   (Reg. Bd. of H., Nov. 1, 1917.)

1. *Reports.*—Every physician, nurse, attendant, hospital superintendent, druggist or other person having knowledge of a known or suspected case of venereal disease (syphilis in the infectious stages, gonococcus infection, or chancroid) must immediately report the same to the local health authorities, the report to be in accordance with the following form and setting forth at least the information therein provided for:

(Form of report.)

REPORT OF VENEREAL DISEASE.

(To be treated as confidential so far as is consistent with public safety and the Rules for the Control of Venereal Diseases.)

(1) ...., ...191..
              (City.)   (Date.)

The undersigned hereby reports a

(2) Case of...........................; (3) Laboratory findings.........;
      (Name of disease.)   (Pos. Neg. None.)

(4) Name of patient...;
      (Case or key number may be given instead of correct name under certain circumstances. See rule 1, Rules for Control of Venereal Diseases in Illinois.)

(5) Sex................; (6) Color................; (7) Age...............years;

(8) Single. married widowed. divorced...................................;

(9) Address of patient..;
      Street and house number may be omitted under certain circumstances, but name of city, town, or village must be given in accordance with rule 1.)

(10) Is living at home. in boarding house hotel, hospital, or elsewhere?.........
....
                 (Specify which.)

(11) Occupation ....

(12) Employer....................; (13) Address...............;
      (Name and address of employer may be omitted under certain circumstances, in accordance with rule 1.)

(14) Does patient handle milk. milk products, or foodstuffs?....................;

(15) Has patient discontinued employment?.............................;

(16) Probable source of infection.....................................;
      (Where a prostitute is the probable source of infection, give name and address in full.)

(17) Probable date of infection......................................;

(18) Other known cases contracted from same source....................;
             (State number of cases.)

(19) Is patient regularly under treatment with you?......................;

Signed...........................M. D.
           (Attendant.)

Address.................................
       (Of attendant.)

The requirements as to information asked for in the foregoing form may be modified only under the following circumstances and then only as hereinafter set forth:

Whenever in the opinion of the local health authorities public welfare does not require that certain information hereinafter specified in this paragraph be given in the report and the health of others is not likely to be endangered by the suppression of such information. and when (a) the patient is not a prostitute but is of good repute in the community. (b) the patient is regularly under the care of a reputable physician, (c) the physician gives the patient full and proper instructions in the rules for the control of venereal diseases and in the precautions which must be taken to prevent the spread of the infection, placing in the hands of the patient copies of the Rules for the Control of Venereal Diseases in Illinois and of the booklet of advice and information on venereal diseases published by the State department of public health. (d) the patient gives undoubted assurance of the faithful observance of all such rules and necessary precautions. and (e) the physician assumes responsibility for the faithful observance of the rules and all necessary precautions by his patient. then the correct name. explicit address of the patient, and the name and address of employer may be omitted from the report: *Provided, however*. That in the event of the infected or supposedly infected person being attached to the military or naval service of the State or Federal Government. then the correct name of the patient may be omitted from the report to the local health authority only on condition that the attendant or person having knowledge of the case shall have previously advised the medical officer of the military or naval establishment to which the patient belongs, of the correct name of the patient and the nature or supposed nature of his disease.

Whenever the patient's correct name and explicit address are omitted from the report in accordance with the conditions stated in the foregoing paragraph, the physician's case number or a "key number" by which the person reporting the case can definitely identify the same, shall be given in the report in lieu of the correct name, and the health jurisdiction (city, village, or township, as the case may be) may be indicated by name of such community, without reference to street or house number.

Whenever the name and address of the employer is omitted from the report, and the patient is employed in a food handling establishment or in any capacity wherein there is danger of imparting the infection to others, the patient shall discontinue such employment during the period the disease is infectious, and the physician assuming responsibility for the case shall see that this requirement is observed. All other items asked for in the report shall be fully and correctly supplied.

All local health authorities upon being advised of a case of venereal disease, must immediately report the same to the State department of public health on the form prescribed for that purpose. Whenever a reported case involve: a person attached to the military or naval services of the State or Federal Government, the local health authority receiving such report shall immediately advise the medical officer, of the military or naval organization to which the patient belongs, giving the name of patient, nature of disease and other data as said medical officer may desire.

Local health authorities upon being advised of a case of venereal disease in any person who is unable to pay for the necessary medicines and medical attention, shall report the case to the overseer of the poor in order that medicines and medical attention may be supplied at the expense of the county.

Reports of venereal diseases made in accordance with these rules shall be treated by local health authorities and by the State department of public health as confidential information, so far, at least, as this is consistent with public safety and the requirements of these rules.

2. *Placarding.*—Whenever a case or suspected case of venereal disease is found on premises used for immoral purposes, or upon premises where the case can not be properly isolated or controlled, and when the infected person will not consent to removal to a hospital or sanatorium where he or she can be properly isolated and controlled during the period of infectiousness, the premises on which he or she continues to reside shall be placarded in the following manner: A red card not less than 11 by 14 inches, bearing the inscription, "Venereal Disease Here, Keep Out," printed in black with bold face type not less than 3½ inches in height, shall be affixed in a conspicuous place at each outside entrance of the building, house or flat, as the case may be.

Defacement or concealment of such placards or their removal by any other than the local health authorities or the duly authorized representatives of the State department of public health is strictly prohibited.

3. *Isolation and control of patient.*—All cases of venereal diseases shall be subject to such control as will assure public safety. All persons having venereal disease are strictly prohibited from exposing others to the infection. Visitors are prohibited from entering premises placarded for venereal diseases and each infected or supposedly infected person residing on premises so placarded is prohibited from leaving such premises excepting with permission of the local health authority or the State department of health.

Responsibility for the proper control of a case in which the correct name and the explicit address is not reported to the local health authorities, under the provisions of rule 1, shall rest upon the attending physician, who shall exercise extraordinary diligence to see that the infected person shall not expose others to the infection. When the attendant has reason to believe that the infected person is not taking the precautions necessary to prevent the spread of the disease, the attendant shall immediately place the correct name and address of the infected person in the hands of the local health authorities in order that proper control may be enforced by the local health authorities.

62

The control of fully reported cases shall rest with the local health authorities in cooperation with the attending physician.

The period of control in all cases shall continue throughout the period of infectiousness of the disease. (Cases of gonococcus infection are to be regarded as infectious until at least two successive smears taken not less than 48 hours apart fail to show gonococci. Cases of syphilis shall be regarded as infectious until all lesions of the skin or mucous membranes are fully healed. Cases of chancroid shall be regarded as infectious until all lesions are fully healed.)

Whenever possible cases of venereal diseases should be removed to a hospital for treatment.

Any person having a venereal disease shall not be removed from, and is prohibited from moving out of, one health jurisdiction into another without first securing permission to do so from the local health authorities of the place from which removal is to be made, or from a duly authorized agent of the State department of public health, and such permission may be granted only under the following conditions: (1) The object of the proposed removal shall be deemed by the issuing health officer as urgent and legitimate, and not for the purpose of relieving one community of an undesirable burden at the expense of another: (2) removal can and will be made without endangering the health of others, either in transit or at destination: (3) patient agrees to place self under care of reputable physician (to be named in removal permit) on arrival at destination and attending physician assumes responsibility for fulfilment of this agreement: (4) removal shall not begin until 24 hours after notice of removal has been forwarded by first-class mail to the health officer at proposed destination of the venereally infected person, which notice shall be of the following form, made out and signed by the health authority granting permission for removal.

CASE OF VENEREAL DISEASE—REMOVAL PERMIT.

(To be forwarded by the issuing health officer by first-class mail at least 24 hours prior to hour set for beginning travel by patient.)

.........................., ..., 191..
      (City.)   (Date.)

To the local health officer

At.....................
   (Destination of patient.)

Under authority of and in compliance with the Rules for the Control of Venereal Diseases in Illinois, permission has been granted for the removal of the following described case of venereal disease:

From............................ To...............................

Beginning travel...Hour...........{A. M.
                           (Date)   {P. M.

Name of patient...
   ("Key number" may be given in place of name, when patient agrees to place self under care
   of reputable physician on arrival at destination, provided that attending physician will
   assume responsibility for fulfilment of such an agreement. See rule 1 and rule 3 of Rules
   for the Control of Venereal Diseases in Illinois.)

Sex................; Color....................; Age...............yrs.
Occupation...
Character of disease...
Will be under care of..
                           (Full name of physician at destination)
Address of physician...
                           (At destination)
Address of patient...
                           (At destination.)
   (Address of patient may be omitted only when "key number" is given in place of name, in
   accordance with rules 1 and 3 of the Rules for the Control of Venereal Diseases in Illinois.)
Purpose of visit:..
             (Signed) ...., Health Officer.
             Address..

Health officer at destination of the patient so removed shall require the recipient physician to file a report of the case and the form prescribed in rule 1 of these rules.

4. *Prohibited occupations.*—The preparation, manufacture, or handling of milk, milk products, or other foodstuffs by any person afflicted with an infectious venereal disease is strictly prohibited, and persons so afflicted shall not be employed in any milk-products or food-manufacturing or food-handling establishments.

Persons afflicted with infectious venereal diseases shall not be engaged in the care or nursing of children or of the sick, nor shall they engage in any occupation the nature of which is such that their infection may be borne to others.

5. *Investigations.*—It shall be the duty of all local health authorities to use all reasonable means to ascertain the existence of infectious venereal diseases within their respective jurisdictions, to investigate all cases that are not under the care of reputable physicians, and those of which no reports have been filed with them, and to ascertain so far as possible the sources of infection and all exposures to the same. They shall use all lawful means to make or cause to be made examinations of all such persons who may be reasonably suspected of having syphilis in the infectious stages, chancroid, or gonococcus infection. (The prevalence of such diseases among prostitutes warrants the inclusion of these within the suspected class.) In making an examination of a woman for the purpose of determining the existence of venereal disease, a woman physician should be appointed for such purpose when so requested by the person examined.

6. *Definitions.*—The term "venereal diseases" as used in these rules shall be construed to mean (a) syphilis in the infectious stages, (b) chancroid, and (c) active gonococcus infection.

The term "prostitute" used in these rules shall be construed to mean a person known to be practicing sexual intercourse promiscuously.

Notification—Furnishing of Circular of Information and Copy of Ordinance—Control. (Ord. of Chicago, June 29, 1917.)

Venereal diseases dangerous to public health.—Syphilis, gonorrhea, and chancroid, hereinafter designated venereal diseases, are hereby recognized and declared to be contagious, infectious, communicable, and dangerous to the public health.

Venereal diseases to be reported.—It shall be the duty of every licensed physician, of every superintendent or manager of a hospital or dispensary, and of every person who gives treatment for a venereal disease to mail to the department of health of the city of Chicago a card supplied by this department stating the age, sex, color, marital condition and occupation of such diseased person, the nature and previous duration of such disease and the probable origin; such card to be mailed within three days after the first examination of such diseased person: *Provided*, That, except as hereinafter required, the name and address of such diseased person shall not be reported to the department of health.

Persons afflicted with venereal diseases to be given a circular of information.—It shall be the duty of every licensed physician and of every other person who treats a person afflicted with venereal disease to give to such person at the first examination a circular of information and advice concerning venereal diseases, furnished by the department of health, and in addition to give to such diseased person a copy of this ordinance and to report to the health department that such diseased person has received the two documents herein specified.

Change of physician to be reported to physician first consulted.—When a person applies to a physician or other person for treatment of a venereal disease, it shall be the duty of the physician or person consulted to inquire of and ascertain from the person seeking treatment whether such person has theretofore consulted with or been treated by any other physicians or persons, and if so to ascertain the name and address of the physician or person last theretofore consulted. It shall be the duty of the applicant for treatment to furnish this information and a refusal to do so, or falsely stating the name and address of such physician or person consulted shall be deemed a violation of this ordinance. It shall be the duty of the physician or person consulted where the applicant has heretofore received treatment to immediately notify by mail the physician or person last theretofore treating such applicant of the change of adviser; such notification to be made upon a form furnished for that purpose by the department of health. Should the physician or person previously consulted fail to receive such notice within 10 days after the last appearance of such venereally diseased person, it shall be the duty of such physician to report to the health department the name and address of such venereally diseased person.

Protection of others from infection by venereally diseased persons.—Upon receipt of a report of a case of venereal disease it shall be the duty of the commissioner of health to institute such measures for the protection of other persons from infection by such venereally diseased person as said commissioner of health is already empowered to use to prevent the spread of other contagious, infectious, or communicable diseases.

Reports to be confidential.—All information and reports concerning persons infected with venereal diseases shall be confidential and shall be inaccessible to the public, except in so far as publicity may attend the performance of the duty imposed upon the commissioner of health in the preceding sections.

Parents responsible for the compliance of minors with the requirements of regulations.— The parents of minors acquiring venereal diseases and living with said parents shall be legally responsible for the compliance of such minors with the requirements of the ordinance relating to venereal diseases.

IOWA.

Notification—Transmission by Intercourse. (Act Mar. 29, 1913.)

SECTION 1. *Contagious diseases defined.*—That syphilis and gonorrhea are hereby declared contagious and infectious and shall be reported as contagious diseases to the local board of health.

SEC. 2. *Physicians' duty to report—Record—Name not disclosed.*—From and after the 1st day of January, A. D. 1914, it shall be the duty of every physician and surgeon practicing within the State of Iowa to report to the local board of health, within 24 hours, every case of syphilis or gonorrhea coming to his knowledge, and shall make and preserve a record of every such case so reported, numbering each case consecutively. He shall require the person to state whether or not he has been previously reported to a local board of health in this State, and if so, when, where, by whom, and under what number. The report shall state the sex of the person and the age as nearly as practicable, together with the character of the disease and the probable source of infection, and whether previously reported or not, and if so, when, where, by whom, and under what number, but shall not disclose the name of the infected person.

SEC. 3. *Failure to report—Penalty.*—Any physician or surgeon who shall be called upon to treat professionally anyone afflicted with syphilis or gonorrhea who shall fail to report the same to the local board of health within 24 hours shall be guilty of a misdemeanor, and upon conviction thereof shall be punished by a fine not exceeding $100 or imprisonment in the county jail not more than 30 days. And in addition thereto the State board of health may revoke his license or certificate to practice medicine, surgery, and obstetrics in the State of Iowa.

SEC. 4. *Transmission—Penalty.*—Any person afflicted with either of these diseases who shall knowingly transmit or assume the risk of transmitting the same by intercourse to another person shall be guilty of a misdemeanor, and upon conviction thereof be fined in the sum of not to exceed $500 or imprisoned in the county jail not to exceed one year, or both such fine and imprisonment. And in addition thereto shall be liable to the party injured in damages to be recovered in any court of competent jurisdiction.

KANSAS.

Notification—Furnishing of Circular of Instructions.   (Reg. Bd. of H., June 13, 1917.)

PART 1. RULE 2. (*a*) In addition to the diseases named in rule 1, the following are hereby declared to be infectious, contagious, or communicable in their nature and are declared to be notifiable diseases:

GROUP II. Gonorrhea, syphilis. (*b*) Hereafter, each and every physician or other practitioner of the healing art practicing in the State of Kansas, or any other person who treats or examines any person suffering from or afflicted with gonorrhea or syphilis in any of their stages or manifestations shall report by number, as hereinafter required, in writing to the State board of health the existence of such diseases.

(*c*) All such reports shall be made in writing within 48 hours after diagnosis on blank forms supplied by the State board of health, and shall give the number of the case, which number shall correspond with the serial number of the State board of health circular of instructions given to the patient; the type and stage of such disease; the color; the sex; the marital state; and the occupation of the person affected with the disease; and a statement as to whether or not the nature of the occupation or place of employment of the person afflicted with such disease makes him or her a menace to the health of any other person or persons: *Provided, however,* That nothing in this paragraph shall be construed to require the reporting of the name or address of persons afflicted with a venereal disease, as aforesaid.

(*d*) It shall be the duty of each and every physician or other practitioner of the healing art practicing in the State of Kansas, or any other person who visits, attends, advises professionally, prescribes for or renders medical or surgical assistance to, or is consulted for medical advice by any person having gonorrhea or syphilis as aforesaid, to at once give to such person a serially numbered circular of instructions furnished by the State board of health, entitled "Instructions for Preventing the Transmission of Gonorrhea or Syphilis," and to report such fact in writing to the State board of health in the report required to be made of such cases.

Serving Affected Persons in Public Bathrooms and Barber Shops.   (Reg. Bd. of H., June 13, 1917.)

PART 2. RULE 34. *Gonorrhea or syphilis; public bath.*—No person who is suffering from gonorrhea or syphilis shall be served in a public bathroom in this State; and no person suffering from syphilis shall be served in any barber shop, such prohibition to continue until 12 months has elapsed from date of infection.

Quarantine—Examination of Suspects—Suppression of Prostitution.   (Reg. Bd. of H., Nov. 2, 1917.)

RULE 1. The deputy State health officers designated for the extra-cantonment zones [1] are hereby authorized to use every available means to ascertain the existence of and immediately to investigate all suspected cases of syphilis in the infectious stages and gonococcus infections within their cantonment zone and to ascertain the source of such infection.

RULE 2. In such investigation said deputy health officers, or their duly authorized representatives, are hereby vested with full powers of inspection, examination, isolation, and disinfection of all persons, places, and things, and as such inspectors said deputy State health officers, or their duly authorized representatives, are hereby authorized:

---

[1] The zone surrounding Camp Funston (and Fort Riley) includes the counties of Riley and Geary, Kans. The zone around Fort Leavenworth consists of the county of Leavenworth, Kans.

(a) To make examination of all persons reasonably suspected of having syphilis in the infectious stages or gonococcus infection. Owing to the prevalence of such diseases among prostitutes all such persons may be considered within the above class.

(b) To isolate such persons whenever, in the opinion of said deputy State health officer, the State board of health, or its secretary, isolation is necessary to protect the public health.

In establishing isolation the health officer shall define the place and the limits of the area in which the person reasonably suspected or known to have syphilis or gonococcus infection and his (or her) attendant are to be isolated, and no persons, other than the attending physician, shall enter or leave the area of isolation without the permission of the health officer.

(c) In cases of quarantine or isolation not to terminate said quarantine or isolation until the cases have become noninfectious or until permission has been given by the deputy State health officer.

Cases of gonococcus infection are to be regarded as infectious until at least two successive smears taken not less than 48 hours apart fail to show gonococci.

Cases of syphilis are to be regarded as infectious until all lesions of skin or mucous membranes are completely healed.

(d) Inasmuch as prostitution is the most prolific source of syphilis and gonococcus infection said deputy State health officers, or their duly authorized representatives, are authorized to use every proper means to aid in suppressing the same and not to issue certificates of freedom from venereal diseases, as such certificates may be used for purposes of solicitation.

(e) Keep all records pertaining to said inspections and examinations in files not open to public inspection, and to make every reasonable effort to keep secret the identity of those affected by venereal disease control measures inasmuch as may be consistent with the protection of the public health.

KENTUCKY.

Prostitution—Disorderly Houses. (Ord. of Louisville, Oct. 6, 1917.)

1. Any person or persons who shall own, keep, or maintain, or who shall be an inmate of, or in any way connected with, a disorderly house, or house of ill fame; and any owner, proprietor, keeper, or manager of any hotel, ordinary, or house of private entertainment, boarding house, lodging house, or other like place, who shall knowingly allow prostitution or illicit sexual intercourse to be carried on therein, and any person who shall engage in prostitution in any such place, or in any other place, in the city of Louisville, Ky., shall be fined not less than $10 nor more than $50 for each offense. Every day that any person or persons shall maintain or be an inmate of, or in any way connected with, such disorderly house or houses of ill fame, shall be and constitute a separate offense.

Prostitution—Use of Vehicles. (Ord. of Louisville, Oct. 6, 1917.)

1. That any owner or chauffeur of any taxicab, jitney bus, or other vehicle who shall knowingly use the same or allow it to be used as a means of aiding or promoting prostitution or illicit sexual intercourse, or aid in any way in bringing persons together for the purpose of prostitution, or illicit sexual intercourse, shall be fined not less than $10 nor more than $50 for each offense.

LOUISIANA.

Swimming Pools—Use by Infected Persons. (Amendment to Sanitary Code, Bd. of H., Feb. 26, 1913.)

Art. 590 (f). No intoxicated person or one afflicted with scabies, favus, syphilis, gonorrhea, tuberculosis, eye trouble, or any other infectious or contagious disease, shall use or be permitted to use any swimming pool or tank.

MAINE.

Venereal Diseases in Institutions—Notification—Laboratory Tests—Treatment—Isolation—Distribution of Information. (Ch. 301, Act Apr. 7, 1917.)

SECTION 1. *R. S., c. 19, relating to public health and prevention of contagious diseases, amended.*—Chapter 19 of the revised statutes is hereby amended by adding at the end of said chapter the following sections, namely:

SEC. 125. *Venereal diseases; cases found in charitable or correctional institutions to be reported.*—It shall be the duty of every superintendent, manager, or physician in charge of any State, county, or municipal charitable or correctional institution immediately to report to the State board of health every case of venereal disease among the inmates of said institution of which he has knowledge. It shall be the duty of every superintendent, manager, or physician in charge of any State-aided, county-aided, or municipally-aided charitable institution to make a similar report to the State board of health in relation to inmates of such institution, the cost of whose care and treatment is being paid in whole or in part by the State, or by any county or municipality in the State. Said report shall be made in the form which may be required by the rules and regulations of the said State board: *Provided,* That such rules and regulations shall not require said reports to be made in a form which will disclose to the State board of health or to any other person, except the said superintendent, manager, or physician, the identity of the inmate. Said superintendents, managers, and physicians shall comply with such rules and regulations as are made by the said State board to prevent the spread of venereal disease.

SEC. 126. *Reports to be treated as confidential.*—The reports to the State board of health prescribed by the preceding section shall be confidential and shall not be accessible to the public nor shall such records and reports be deemed public records.

SEC. 127. *Examination and treatment of gonorrhea and syphilis.*—The State board of health shall provide, at the State laboratory of hygiene or elsewhere, facilities for the free bacteriological examination of discharges for the diagnosis of gonorrheal infections, and shall also provide at cost vaccine or antitoxin for the treatment of such infections. And said board shall make at the expense of the State the Wassermann test for the diagnosis of syphilis; and shall furnish the treatment known as Salvarsan or other accredited specific treatment at cost.

SEC. 128. *State board of health to include information concerning venereal diseases, in bulletins.*—The State board of health shall include in bulletins and circulars distributed by it information concerning the diseases covered by the preceding sections: *Provided,* That nothing shall be contained in such bulletins or circulars which will disclose the identity of the persons suffering from such venereal disease nor the identity of any State-aided, county-aided, or municipally-aided charitable institution in which such persons are treated or cared for.

SEC. 129. *Persons discovered afflicted, in institutions, to be treated; may be isolated; may be continued in custody; expenses after expiration of sentence.*—Any inmate of any State, county, or municipal charitable or correctional institution, or any dependent child supported or partially supported by public funds, afflicted or suspected of being afflicted with venereal disease, shall forthwith be placed under medical treatment, and if, in the opinion of the attending physician, it is necessary, shall be isolated until danger of contagion is passed. Such case shall be immediately reported to the State board of health in accordance with the latter's rules and regulations: *Provided,* That such rules and regulations shall not require information disclosing the identity of any dependent or delinquent child, and the rules and regulations of the State board of health for the examination, testing, and treatment of cases of venereal disease shall be faithfully observed. If the sentence or term of commitment of an inmate to any such State, county, or municipal charitable or correctional institution expires before such disease is cured, or if, in the opinion of the attending physician of the institution, or of such physician as the authorities thereof may consult, his discharge would be dangerous to the public health, he shall be continued under such medical treatment, care, and custody until in the opinion of such physician his discharge will not endanger the public health. The expenses of his support and treatment shall be paid by the place in which he has a pauper settlement, or by the State if he has no pauper settlement, after notice of the expiration of his sentence and of his condition to the overseers of the poor of the city or town or plantation where he was residing at the time of his commitment to the institution.

Sec. 130. *Penalty for neglect of duty.*—Any official or person who shall wilfully fail, neglect, or refuse to perform any of the duties imposed upon him by the provisions of this act shall be fined not more than $500 or be imprisoned for not more than six months.

Sec. 131. *Appropriation.*—For the purpose of enabling the State board of health to carry out the provisions of this act there is hereby appropriated for the year 1917 the sum of $4,000, and for the year 1918 the sum of $4,000.

MINNESOTA.

Making of Regulations by State Board of Health.   (Ch. 345, Act Apr. 17, 1917.)

Section 1. Section 4640, General Statutes, 1913, is hereby amended so as to read as follows:

4640. The board [State board of health] may adopt, alter, and enforce reasonable regulations of permanent application throughout the whole or any portion of the State, or for specified periods in parts thereof, for the preservation of the public health. Upon the approval of the attorney general, and the due publication thereof, such regulations shall have the force of law, except in so far as they may conflict with a statute or with the charter or ordinances of a city of the first class upon the same subject. In and by the same the board may control, by requiring the taking out of licenses or permits, or by other appropriate means, any of the following matters:

*   *   *   *   *   *   *

7. The treatment, in hospitals and elsewhere, of persons suffering from communicable diseases, including all manner of venereal diseases and infection, the disinfection and quarantine of persons and places in case of such disease, and the reporting of sicknesses and deaths therefrom:

*   *   *

NEW JERSEY.

Notification—Seller of Drugs to Report Cases—Duties of State Department of Health—Laboratory Tests.   (Ch. 232, Act Mar. 29, 1917.)

1 Every physician, superintendent, or other person having control or supervision over any State, county, or municipal hospital, sanatorium, or other public or private institution in which any person suffering from or infected with a venereal disease, such as chancroid, gonorrhea, syphilis, or any of the varieties or stages of such diseases is received for care or treatment or in which any person who is received into any such State, county, or municipal hospital, sanatorium or other public or private institution suffering from any other disease, but is found to be also infected with any venereal disease such as chancroid, gonorrhea, syphilis or any of the varieties or stages of such diseases, shall immediately after such case of sickness or disease has been received into said institution report such case of sickness or disease to the department of health of this State. Such report shall state the name, address, color, sex, and nationality of the person, and the age, as nearly as practicable, together with the character of the

disease and the probable source of infection and whether previously reported or not, and if so, when, where, and by whom; and every physician, superintendent, or other person having control or charge over any State, county, or municipal hospital, sanatorium, or other public or private institution in which any case of venereal disease set out in this section is received for cure or treatment, who shall fail to perform the above-mentioned duty at the time and in the manner named, shall be liable to a penalty of $50 for each such failure.

2. Every physician, nurse, or other person treating or attempting to treat by prescription, formula, patented or proprietary medicine or compound, or otherwise, and every physician, nurse, or other person selling or giving away any prescription, formula, patented or proprietary medicine or compound, which either by itse'f or in connection or conjunction with any other treatment, medicine, or compound is claimed to be useful, or to cure, relieve or to arrest in any way or manner any venereal disease such as chancroid, gonorrhea, syphi'is, or any of the varieties or stages thereof, shall report immediately to the department of hea'th of this State the name, sex, address, color, and nationa'ity of the said person so infected with such disease, and the age as nearly as practicable, together with the character of the disease and the probable source of infection and whether previously reported or not, and if so, when, where and by whom; and every physician, nurse, or other person treating or attempting to treat in any manner any of the venerea' diseases or varieties or stages thereof, and every physician, nurse, or other person selling or giving away any prescription, formu'a, patented or proprietary medicine or compound for the uses and purposes mentioned in this section who shall fail to perform the above-mentioned duty at the time and in the manner named, shall be liable to a pena'ty of $50 for each such failure.

3. The department of hea th of this State shall make and enforce such rules and regulations for the quarantining and treatment of venereal diseases such as chancroid, gonorrhea, syphilis, or any of the varieties or stages of such diseases reported to it as may be deemed necessary for the protection of the pub'ic. Said department of hea th shall not disclose the names or addresses of such persons reported or treated to any person other than a prosecuting officer or in court in prosecutions under this or any other State law.

4. The department of hea'th of this State shall provide facilities for the free bacteriological examination of discharges for the diagnosis of gonorrheal infections, and also shall provide, at cost, vaccines or antitoxins for the treatment of such infections. And the said department shall make, at the expense of the State, the Wasserman or other approved tests or examine smears for the diagnosis of syphilis: and shall furnish the treatment known as "Sa'varsan" or other accredited specific treatment at cost. But such diagnosis and treatment shall not be furnished until the data required for the registration of the case has been furnished by the physician, nurse, or institution treating the patient.

5. For the expenses of carrying into effect the purposes of this act, the sum of $2,000 is hereby appropriated annually, when included in any annual or supplemental appropriation bill.

Marriage or Sexual Intercourse by Infected Persons. (Ch. 23, Act Mar. 14, 1917.)

1. Any person who, knowing himself or herself to be infected with a venereal disease, such as chancroid, gonorrhea, syphilis, or any of the varieties or stages of such diseases, marries, shall be guilty of a misdemeanor.

2. Any person who, while infected with a venereal disease, such as chancroid, gonorrhea, syphilis, or any of the varieties or stages of such diseases, has sexual intercourse, shall be guilty of a misdemeanor.

NEW YORK.

Commitment of Dangerous or Careless Patients. (Ch. 559, Act May 17, 1913.)

Sec. 15. Such chapter [chap. 45, Consolidated Laws] is hereby amended by inserting therein a new section, to be section 326a, to read as follows:

Sec. 326a. *Control of dangerous and careless patients.*—Whenever a complaint shall be made by a physician to a health officer that any person is afflicted with any infectious, contagious, or communicable disease or is a carrier of typhoid fever, tuberculosis, diphtheria, or other infectious disease and is unable or unwilling to conduct himself and to live in such a manner as not to expose members of his family or household or other persons with whom he may be associated to danger of infection, the health officer shall forthwith investigate the circumstances alleged. If he shall find that any such person is a menace to others, he shall lodge a complaint against such person with a magistrate, and on such complaint the said person shall be brought before such magistrate. The magistrate after due notice and a hearing, if satisfied that the complaint of the health officer is well founded and that the person is a source of danger to others, may commit him to a county hospital for tuberculosis or to any other hospital or institution established for the care of persons suffering from any such disease or maintaining a room, ward, or wards for such person. Such person shall be deemed to be committed until discharged in the manner authorized in this section. In making such commitment the magistrate shall make such order for payment for the care and maintenance of such person as he may deem proper.

The chief medical officer of the hospital or other institution to which any such person has been committed, upon signing and placing among the permanent records of such hospital or institution a statement to the effect that such person has obeyed the rules and regulations of such hospital or institution for a period of not less than 60 days, and that in his judgment such person may be discharged without danger to the health or life of others, or for any other reason stated in full which he may deem adequate and sufficient, may discharge the person so committed. He shall report each such discharge, together with a full statement of the reasons therefor, at once to the health officer of the city, village, or town from which the patient came and at the next meeting of the board of managers or other controlling authority of such hospital or institution. Every person committed under the provisions of this section shall observe all the rules and regulations of such hospital or institution. Any patient so committed who neglects or refuses to obey the rules or regulations of the institution may by direction of the chief medical officer of the institution be placed apart from the other patients and restrained from leaving the institution. Any such patient who willfully violates the rules and regulations of the institution or repeatedly conducts himself in a disorderly manner may be taken before a magistrate by the order of the chief medical officer of the institution. The chief medical officer may enter a complaint against such person for disorderly conduct, and the magistrate, after a hearing and upon due evidence of such disorderly conduct, may commit such person for a period not to exceed six months to any institution to which persons convicted of disorderly conduct or vagrancy or of being tramps may be committed, and such institution shall keep such person separate and apart from the other inmates: *Provided,* That nothing in this section shall be construed to prohibit any person committed to any institution under its provisions from appealing to any court having jurisdiction for a review of the evidence on which commitment was made.

Advertisements Relating to Venereal Diseases and Other Sexual Ailments. (Ch. 487, Act May 15, 1917.)

Section 1. The penal law is hereby amended by adding thereto, after section 1142, a new section to be section 1142-a, to read as follows:

Sec. 1142-a. *Advertisements relating to certain diseases prohibited* —Whoever publishes, delivers or distributes or causes to be published, delivered or distributed in any manner whatsoever an advertisement concerning a venereal disease, lost manhood, lost vitality, impotency, sexual weakness, seminal emissions, varicocele, self-abuse, or excessive sexual indulgence and calling attention to a medicine, article, or preparation that may be used therefor or to a person or persons from whom or an office or place at which information, treatment, or advice relating to such disease, infirmity, habit, or condition may be obtained, is guilty of a misdemeanor, and upon conviction thereof shall be punished by imprisonment for not more than six months, or by a fine of not less than $50 nor more than $500, or by both such fine and imprisonment. This section, however, shall not apply to didactic or scientific treatises which do not advertise or call attention to any person or persons from whom or any office or place at which information, treatment, or advice may be obtained, nor shall it apply to advertisements or notices issued by an incorporated hospital, or a licensed dispensary, or by a municipal board or department of health, or by the department of health of the State of New York.

Marriage—Statements Regarding Freedom from Venereal Diseases.   (Ch. 503, Act May 16, 1917.)

A New York law makes it the duty of the town or city clerk before issuing a marriage license to secure a statement from each of the parties to the marriage in the following words

"I have not to my knowledge been infected with any venereal disease, or if I have been so infected within five years I have had a laboratory test within that period which shows that I am now free from infection from any such disease."

Furnishing of Circulars of Information to Affected Persons.   (Reg. Public Health Council, Mar. 20, 1917.)

Chapter 2 of the Sanitary Code is hereby further amended by adding thereto a new regulation to be known as regulation 29-a and to read as follows:

Reg. 29-a. *Chancroid, gonorrhea, and syphilis.*—Chancroid, gonorrhea, and syphilis are hereby declared to be infectious and communicable diseases highly dangerous to the public health

It shall be the duty of every physician when first attending a person affected with chancroid, gonorrhea, or syphilis to furnish said person with a circular of information issued or approved by the State commissioner of health and to instruct such person as to the precautions to be taken in order to prevent the communication of the disease to others.

Notification—Distribution of Literature to Affected Persons.   (Reg. Dept. of H. of New York City, June 28, 1917.)

Resolved, That section 88 of the Sanitary Code be, and is hereby, amended to read as follows:

Sec. 88. *Duty of superintendents of hospitals and dispensaries and of physicians to report cases of venereal disease.*—It shall be the duty of the manager, superintendent, or person in charge of any correctional institution and of every public or private hospital, dispensary, clinic, asylum, or charitable institution in the city of New York to report promptly to the department of health the name or initials, together with the sex, age, marital state, and address of every occupant or inmate thereof or person treated therein affected with syphilis or gonorrhea; and it shall also be the duty of every physician in the said city to promptly make a similar report to the department of health relative to any person found by such physician to be affected with syphilis or gonorrhea. All reports made in accordance with the provisions of this section, and all records of clinical or laboratory examinations indicating the presence

6

of syphilis or gonorrhea, shall be regarded as confidential and shall not be open to inspection by the public or by any person other than the official custodian of such reports or records in the department of health, the commissioner of health, and such other persons as may be authorized by law to inspect such reports or records, nor shall the custodian of any such report or record, the said commissioner of health, or any such other persons divulge any part of any such report or record so as to disclose the identity of the person to whom it relates.

It shall be the duty of every physician to furnish and deliver to every person found by such physician to be affected with syphilis or gonorrhea a circular of instruction and advice, issued or approved by the department of health of the city of New York, and to instruct such person as to the precautions to be taken in order to prevent the communication of the disease to others. No persons affected with syphilis or gonorrhea shall, by a negligent act, cause, contribute to, or promote the spread of such diseases.

Dispensaries, Conduct and Maintenance. (Regs. Dept. of H. of New York City, June 28 and July 31, 1917.)

SEC. 223. *Dispensaries: communicable disease: regulations.*—No public dispensary where communicable diseases are treated or diagnosed shall be conducted or maintained otherwise than in accordance with the regulations of the board of health. (As adopted by the board of health, June 28, 1917.)

REGULATIONS GOVERNING THE CONDUCT AND MAINTENANCE OF DISPENSARIES WHEREIN HUMAN BEINGS AFFECTED WITH SYPHILIS OR GONORRHEA ARE TREATED OR CARED FOR, AND RELATING TO SECTION 223 OF THE SANITARY CODE.

A.

SYPHILIS.

REGULATION 1. *Treatment of syphilis: special department.*—The treatment of syphilis, whatever its manifestations, shall be conducted in a special departmen t maintained for such purpose or in the department for dermatology connected with the dispensary or hospital. *Provided, however,* When the nature of the part affected, such as the eye, throat, viscera, etc., necessitates treatment in some other department of the dispensary, treatment may be given jointly by the two departments.

REG. 2. *Microscopical examination required.*—Every department for the treatment of syphilis shall make microscopical examinations of all suspected lesions.

REG. 3. *Wassermann tests.*—Laboratory facilities for making Wassermann tests should be provided in every dispensary. If such laboratory facilities are not so provided, provision shall be made for the prompt delivery of specimens to the department of health or other approved laboratories where such tests are made.

REG. 4. *Number of patients to be treated.*—The number of patients to be treated at a dispensary shall be regulated by the number of physicians in attendance and the equipment and facilities provided in the dispensary. The maximum number of patients treated by a physician shall not exceed 10 per hour.

REG. 5. *Salvarsan or its analogues to be administered.*—In view of the fact that the obligation to render a person affected with an infectious disease innocuous at the earliest possible moment rests on the institution to which the patient has applied for treatment, salvarsan or its analogues, in sufficient quantities and at proper intervals, shall be administered, with the addition of mercury or other accepted means of treatment, to all cases of syphilis.

REG. 6. *Records.*—A complete and adequate record shall be kept of every case of syphilis treated at a dispensary. Such records shall not be open to inspection by the public or to any person other than the representatives of the department of health of the city of New York, and such persons as may be authorized by law to inspect such records.

REG. 7. *Follow-up system.*—A follow-up system, approved by the department of health, to secure regular attendance by patients shall be established and maintained.

REG. 8. *Procedure governing the discharge of patients.*—A standard procedure governing the discharge of patients shall be followed. Such standard shall embrace suitable tests and subsequent persistent observations.

REG. 9. *Dispensaries to be open at least three days a week.*—Dispensaries shall be open at least three days a week.

B.

GONORRHEA.

REGULATION 1. *Microscopical examination required.*—Systematic microscopical examinations of all discharges shall be made in every department of a dispensary wherein persons affected with gonorrhea are treated or cared for.

REG. 2. *Facilities to be provided.*—Every department of a dispensary wherein persons affected with gonorrhea are treated or cared for shall be provided with and employ proper facilities for asepsis and antisepsis.

REG. 3. *Urethroscopic and cystoscopic work to be performed.*—Every dispensary shall be provided with facilities for urethroscopic and cystoscopic work, and such facilities shall be regularly employed by the physicians in attendance.

REG. 4. *Complement fixation test to be performed.*—Every such dispensary should be provided with facilities for making a complement fixation test for gonorrhea. If such facilities be not provided at the dispensary, proper provision shall be made for the prompt delivery of specimens to the department of health or other approved laboratories where such tests are made.

REG. 5. *Number of patients to be treated.*—The number of patients to be treated at a dispensary shall be regulated by the number of physicians in attendance and the equipment and facilities provided in the dispensary. The maximum number of patients treated by a physician shall not exceed 10 per hour.

REG. 6. *Records.*—A complete and adequate record shall be kept of every case of gonorrhea treated at the dispensary. Such records shall not be open to inspection by the public or any person other than the representatives of the department of health of the city of New York, and such persons as may be authorized by law to inspect such records.

REG. 7. *Procedure governing the discharge of patient.*—A standard procedure governing the discharge of patients shall be followed. Such standard shall embrace suitable tests and subsequent persistent observations.

REG. 8. *Dispensaries to be open at least three days a week.*—Dispensaries shall be open at least three days a week.

Foodstuffs—Employees—Physical Examination. (Reg. Dept. of H. of New York City, Apr. 25, 1916.)

SEC. 146. *Employment of persons affected with infectious or venereal disease prohibited.*—No person who is affected with any infectious disease, or with any venereal disease in a communicable form shall work or be permitted to work in any place where food or drink is prepared, cooked, mixed, baked, exposed, bottled, packed, handled, stored, manufactured, offered for sale, or sold. Whenever required by a medical inspector or other duly authorized physician of the department of health, or by an order of the sanitary superintendent, the director of the bureau of food and drugs, or the director of the bureau of preventable diseases of the said department, any person employed in any such place shall submit to a physical examination by a physician in the employ of the said department. Such persons, however, may, in their discretion, be examined by their own private physicians, provided such examinations are performed in accordance with the regulations of the board of health. No person who refuses to submit to such examination shall work or be permitted to work in any such place.

REGULATION 1. *Result of physical examinations to be reported on official blanks.*— The result of physical examinations performed by physicians in accordance with the provisions of section 146 of the Sanitary Code shall be reported to the department of health upon official blanks furnished for such purpose. Such blanks shall be signed by the physician making the examinations and shall contain the following information:

Name..
Age...Male—Female. Single, Married, Widowed.
Address...Borough.........................Nativity...............
Where employed..How long.......................
State special mark of identification..
Color of eyes..Color of hair............................
Skin..Mouth...
Height.................ft.........in. Weight...............lbs.

Has any laboratory test been submitted?
{ Wasserman?...
   Widal?..
   Sputum?...
   Gonorrhea smear?..

Is lues present?...Under treatment (if sick)...............
Lungs..
Has applicant ever had typhoid fever or been exposed to it?..
     I hereby certify that the above-named person is not affected with any infectious disease or any venereal disease in communicable form.
Dated..   Signed..

REG. 2. *Certificates to be issued by the department of health.*—When such official blank, properly filled out and signed, shall have been filed with the department of health, and the approval thereof given by the bureau of preventable diseases, a certificate, properly numbered and specifying the date of issue thereof, shall be issued by the department of health to the person so examined. Such certificate shall specify the date of such physical examination and shall state that the person to whom it is issued was free from any infectious disease and any venereal disease in communicable form on the date of such examination. Such certificate shall not be transferred and shall not be used by any other person than the one to whom it has been issued.

REG. 3. *Conditions under which certificates are issued.*—Certificates issued under and by virtue of the provisions of regulation 2 hereof shall not be construed to authorize the employment of persons to whom they shall have been issued where such persons thereafter contract, or are infected with, or have been or are exposed to, any infectious disease requiring isolation or exclusion from their employment by any regulation, law, or ordinance; nor shall such certificates be construed as nullifying or limiting the power of the department of health to require a reexamination of such persons in its discretion.

NORTH CAROLINA.

Notification—Control. (Ord. of Charlotte, Oct. 22, 1917.)

1. That all physicians, osteopaths, or any other persons allowed by law to practice the art of healing the sick in the city of Charlotte, shall, within 24 hours after being called or making a diagnosis, report in writing, upon forms supplied by the health department, giving the name, except as hereinafter provided, color, age, sex, and address of all cases of * * * gonococcus infection, syphilis, and chancroid.

2. That in cases of gonococcus infection, syphilis, and chancroid the physician making the diagnosis or treating such patient shall keep in his office or place of business a separate record, giving the name, color, age, sex, and address and the character of disease, and such cases shall be numbered or such record kept in the numerical order of their diagnosis or treatment and shall, within 24 hours after being diagnosed, be reported to the health department, giving the number of such case in lieu of the name of the patient.

The record kept by any physician of any of the diseases herein mentioned shall not be open to inspection by the public, but shall at all times be open to inspection by the health officer or assistant health officer of the city.

3. If any person should be afflicted with any of the above-named diseases and is not under the care of a physician, then the head of the household where such diseased person is, or the guardian of such diseased person, shall immediately report such case to the health department.

4. The proprietor or manager of any hotel, lodging house, or boarding house who shall have knowledge of or reason to believe that there is a case of any of the above-named diseases within such hotel, lodging house, or boarding house shall immediately report such fact to the health department.

5. When a physician, attendant, parent, or guardian suspects that a person under his care has any of the above-named diseases he shall immediately report the case as such and the health officer shall thereupon take such measures as are necessary to protect the public, but before declaring a quarantine he shall consult the family physician, if there be one, in charge of such case.

6. The recovery or death of all cases of the above-mentioned diseases shall be reported on forms supplied by the health department for that purpose.

7. A separate report card shall be used for reporting each case of the above-mentioned diseases.

8. Any person concealing or attempting to conceal the existence of a case of any one of the above-named diseases or violating any of the provisions of this ordinance shall upon conviction be fined not less than $5 nor more than $50.

OHIO.

Places of Prostitution Declared Nuisances—Abatement by Injunction. (Act Mar. 30, 1917.)

SECTION 1. For the purpose of this act the terms place, person, nuisance are defined as follows: Place shall include any building, erection, or place or any separate part or portion thereof or the ground itself; person shall include any individual, corporation, association, partnership, trustee, lessee, agent, or assignee; nuisance shall mean any place as above defined in or upon which lewdness, assignation, or prostitution is conducted, permitted, continued, or exists, and the personal property and contents used in conducting and maintaining any such place for any such purpose.

SEC. 2. Any person who shall use, occupy, establish, or conduct a nuisance as defined in section 1, or aid or abet therein, and the owner, agent, or lessee of any interest in any such nuisance together with the persons employed in or in control of any such nuisance by any such owner, agent, or lessee shall be guilty of maintaining a nuisance and shall be enjoined as hereinafter provided.

SEC. 3. Whenever a nuisance exists the attorney general of the State, the prosecuting attorney of the county, or any person who is a citizen of the county may bring an action in equity in the name of the State of Ohio, upon the relation of such attorney general, prosecuting attorney, or person, to abate such nuisance and to perpetually enjoin the person or persons maintaining the same from further maintenance thereof. If such action is instituted by a person other than the prosecuting attorney, or attorney general, the complainant shall execute a bond to the person against whom complaint is made, with good and sufficient surety to be approved by the court or clerk thereof, in the sum of not less than $500, to secure to the party enjoined the damages he may sustain if such action is wrongfully brought, not prosecuted to final judgment, or is dismissed, or is not maintained, or if it be finally decided that the injunction ought not to have been granted. The party thereby aggrieved by the issuance of such injunction shall have recourse against said bond for all damages suffered, including damage to his property, person, or character and including reasonable attorney's fees incurred by him in making defense to said action.

SEC. 4. Such action shall be brought in the common pleas court of the county in which the property is located. At the commencement of the action a verified petition alleging the facts constituting the nuisance shall be filed in the office of the clerk of the court. After the filing of the petition, application for a temporary injunction may be made to the court or a judge thereof who shall grant a hearing thereon within 10 days thereafter. Where such application for a temporary injunction has been made, the court or judge thereof may, on application of the complainant. issue an ex parte restraining order restraining the defendant and all other persons from removing or in any manner interfering with the personal property and contents of the place where such nuisance is alleged to exist until the decision of the court or judge granting or refusing such temporary injunction and until the further order of the court thereon. The restraining order may be served by handing to and leaving a copy of said order with any person in charge of such place or residing therein. or by posting a copy thereof in a conspicuous place at or upon one or more of the principal doors or entrances to such place. or by both such delivery and posting. The officer serving such restraining order shall forthwith make and return into court an inventory of the personal property and contents situated in and used in conducting or maintaining such nuisance. Any violation of such restraining order shall be a contempt of court and where such order is so posted mutilation or removal thereof, while the same remains in force, shall be a contempt of court, provided such posted order contains thereon or therein a notice to that effect. A copy of the complaint together with a notice of the time and place of the hearing of the application for a temporary injunction shall be served upon the defendant at least five days before such hearing. If the hearing be then continued at the instance of any defendant the temporary writ as prayed shall be granted as a matter of course. If upon hearing the allegations of the petition be sustained to the satisfaction of the court or judge the court or judge shall issue a temporary injunction without additional bond restraining the defendant and any other person or persons from continuing the nuisance.

If at the time of granting a temporary injunction, it shall further appear that the person owning, in control, or in charge of the nuisance so enjoined had received five days' notice of the hearing and unless such person shall show to the satisfaction of the court or judge that the nuisance complained of has been abated, or that such person proceeded forthwith to enforce his rights under the provisions of section 12 of this act, the court or judge shall forthwith issue an order closing the place against its use for any purpose of lewdness, assignation, or prostitution until final decision shall be rendered on the application for a permanent injunction. Such order shall also continue in effect for such further period the restraining order above provided if already issued, or, if not so issued, shall include such an order restraining for such period the removal or interference with the personal property and contents located thereat or therein as hereinbefore provided, and such restraining order shall be served and the inventory of such property shall be made and filed as hereinbefore provided: *Provided, however,* That the owner or owners of any real or personal property so closed or restrained or to be closed or restrained may appear at any time between the filing of the petition and the hearing on the application for a permanent injunction and upon payment of all costs incurred and upon the filing of a bond by the owner of the real property with sureties to be approved by the clerk in the full value of the property to be ascertained by the court, or, in vacation, by the judge, conditioned that such owner or owners will immediately abate the nuisance and prevent the same from being established or kept until the decision of the court or judge shall have been rendered on the application for a permanent injunction, then and in that case, the court, or judge in vacation, if satisfied of the good faith of the owner of the real property and of innocence on the part of any owner of the personal property of any knowledge of the use of such personal property as a nuisance and that, with reasonable care and diligence, such owner could not have known thereof, shall deliver such real or personal property or both to the respective owners thereof, and discharge or refrain from issuing at the time of the hearing on the application for the temporary injunction, as the case may be, any order or orders closing such real property or restraining the removal or interference with such personal property. The release of any real or personal property under the provisions of this section shall not release it from any judgment, lien, penalty, or liability to which it may be subjected by law.

Sec. 5. The action when brought shall be noticed for trial at the first term of the court and shall have precedence over all other cases except crimes, election contests, or injunctions. In such action evidence of the general reputation of the place or an admission or finding of guilt of any person under the criminal laws against prostitution, lewdness, or assignation at any such place shall be admissible for the purpose of proving the existence of said nuisance and shall be prima facie evidence of such nuisance and of knowledge of and of acquiescence and participation therein on the part of the person or persons charged with maintaining said nuisance as herein defined. If the complaint is filed by a person who is a citizen of the county it shall not be dismissed except upon a sworn statement by the complainant and his or its attorney, setting forth the reasons why the action should be dismissed and the dismissal approved by the prosecuting attorney in writing or in open court. If the court or judge is of the opinion that the action ought not to be dismissed, he may direct the prosecuting attorney to prosecute said action to judgment at the expense of the county, and if the action is continued more than one term of court, any person who is a citizen of the county, or has an office therein, or the attorney general or the prosecuting attorney, may be substituted for the complainant and prosecute said action to judgment. If the action is brought by a person who is a citizen of the county and the court finds that there were no reasonable grounds or cause for said action, the costs may be taxed to such person. If the existence of the nuisance be established upon the trial, a judgment shall be entered which shall perpetually enjoin the defendants and any other person or persons from further maintaining the nuisance at the place complained of and the defendants from maintaining such nuisance elsewhere.

Sec. 6. If the existence of the nuisance be admitted or established in an action as provided in this act, or in a criminal proceeding, an order of abatement shall be entered as a part of the judgment in the case, which order shall direct the removal from the place of all personal property and contents used in conducting the nuisance, and not already released under authority of the court as provided in section 4, and shall direct the sale of such thereof as belong to the defendants notified or appearing, in the manner provided for the sale of chattels under execution. Such order shall also require the renewal for one year of any bond furnished by the owner of the real property as provided in section 4, or, if not so furnished, shall continue for one year any closing order issued at the time of granting the temporary injunction, or, if no such closing order was then issued, shall include an order directing the effectual closing of the place against its use for any purpose, and so keeping it closed for a period of one year unless sooner released: *Provided, however,* That the owner of any place so closed and not released under bond as hereinbefore provided may now appear and obtain such release in the manner and upon fulfilling the requirements as hereinbefore provided. The release of the property under the provisions of this section shall not release it from any judgment, lien, penalty, or liability to which it may be subject by law. Owners of unsold personal property and contents so seized must appear and claim same within 10 days after such order of abatement is made and prove innocence, to the satisfaction of the court, of any knowledge of said use thereof and that with reasonable care and diligence they could not have known thereof. Every defendant in the action shall be presumed to have had knowledge of the general reputation of the place. If such innocence be so established, such unsold personal property and contents shall be delivered to the owner, otherwise it shall be sold as hereinbefore provided. For removing and selling the personal property and contents, the officer shall be entitled to charge and receive the same fees as he would for levying upon and selling like property on execution; and for closing the place and keeping it closed, a reasonable sum shall be allowed by the court.

Sec. 7. In case the existence of such nuisance is established in a criminal proceeding it shall be the duty of the prosecuting attorney to proceed promptly under this act to enforce the provisions and penalties thereof, and the finding of the defendant guilty in such criminal proceedings, unless reversed or set aside, shall be conclusive as against such defendant as to the existence of the nuisance. All moneys collected under this act shall be paid to the county treasurer. The proceeds of the sale of the personal property, as provided in the preceding section, shall be applied in payment of the costs of the action and abatement, including the complainant's costs or so much of such proceeds as may be necessary, except as hereinafter provided.

Sec. 8. In case of the violation of any injunction or closing order granted under provisions of this act, or of a restraining order or the commission of any contempt of court in proceedings under this act, the court, or in vacation, a judge thereof, may summarily try and punish the offender. The trial may be had upon affidavits or either party may demand the production and oral examination of the witnesses. A party found guilty of contempt under the provisions of this act shall be punished by a fine of not more than $1,000 or by imprisonment in the county jail not more than six months, or by both such fine and imprisonment.

Sec. 9. Whenever a permanent injunction issues against any person or persons for maintaining a nuisance as herein defined. there shall be imposed upon said nuisance and against the person or persons maintaining the same a tax of $300: *Provided, however*, That such tax may not be imposed upon the personal property or against the owner or owners thereof who have proven innocence as hereinbefore provided. or upon the real property or against the owner or owners thereof who shall show to the satisfaction of the court or judge thereof, at the time of the granting of the permanent injunction, that he or they have in good faith permanently abated the nuisance complained of. The imposition of said tax shall be made by the court as a part of the proceeding and the clerk of said court shall make and certify a return of the imposition of said tax thereon to the county auditor, who shall enter the same as a tax upon the property and against the persons upon which or whom the lien was imposed as and when other taxes are entered. and the same shall be and remain a perpetual lien upon all property. both personal and real, used for the purpose of maintaining said nuisance except as herein excepted until fully paid: *Provided*, That any such lien imposed while the tax books are in the hands of the auditor shall be immediately entered therein. The payment of said tax shall not relieve the persons or property from any other taxes provided by law. The provisions of the laws relating to the collection of taxes in this State. the delinquency thereof. and sale of property for taxes shall govern in the collection of the tax herein prescribed in so far as the same are applicable, and the said tax collected shall be applied in payment of any deficiency in the costs of the action and abatement on behalf of the State to the extent of such deficiency after the application thereto of the proceeds of the sale of personal property as hereinbefore provided. and the remainder of said tax, together with the unexpended portion of the proceeds of the sale of personal property. shall be distributed in the same manner as fines collected for the keeping of houses of illfame.

Sec. 10. When such nuisance has been found to exist under any proceeding as in this act provided. and the owner or agent of such place whereon the same has been found to exist was not a party to such proceeding. nor appeared therein, the said tax of $300 shall. nevertheless. be imposed against the persons served or appearing and against the property as in this act set forth. But before such tax shall be enforced against such property, the owner or agent thereof shall have appeared therein or shall be served with summons therein. and the provisions of existing laws regarding the service of process shall apply to service in proceedings under this act. The person in whose name the real estate affected by the action stands on the books of the county auditor for purposes of taxation shall be presumed to be the owner thereof, and in case of unknown persons having or claiming any ownership, right, title, or interest in property affected by the action, such may be made parties to the action by designating them in the petition as "all other persons unknown claiming any ownership, right, title, or interest in the property affected by the action" and service thereon may be had by publication in the manner prescribed by law. Any person having or claiming such ownership, right, title, or interest, and any owner or agent in behalf of himself and such owner may make defense thereto and have trial of his rights in the premises by the court: and if said cause has already proceeded to trial or to findings and judgment, the court shall by order fix the time and place of such further trial and shall modify, add to, or confirm such findings and judgment as the case may require. Other parties to said action shall not be affected thereby.

Sec. 11. Should any provision or item of this act be held unconstitutional, such fact shall not be held to invalidate the other provisions and items thereof.

Sec. 12. If a tenant or occupant of a building or tenement under a lawful title uses such place for the purposes of lewdness, assignation, or prostitution, such use shall annul and make void the lease or other title under which he holds at the option of the owner and, without any act of the owner, shall cause the right of possession to revert and vest in him, and he may without process of law make immediate entry upon the premises.

Marriage—Venereal Diseases—Physicians Allowed to Disclose Facts to Interested Persons—Advertising by Physicians—Revocation of License. (Act Apr. 26, 1915.)

Section 1. That section 1275 * * * of the General Code be amended * * * [to read] as follows:

"Sec. 1275. The State medical board may refuse to grant a certificate to a person guilty of * * * grossly unprofessional or dishonest conduct * * *. The words 'grossly unprofessional or dishonest conduct' as used in this section are hereby declared to mean:

 * * * * * * *

"Second. The willful betrayal of a professional secret. But a physician, knowing that one of the parties to a contemplated marriage has a venereal disease, and so informing the other party to such contemplated marriage, or the parent, brother, or guardian of such other party, shall not be held to answer for betrayal of a professional secret, nor shall such physician be liable in damages for truthfully giving such information to such other party, or the parent, brother, or guardian of such other party.

"Third. All advertising of medical practice in which extravagantly worded statements intended, or having a tendency, to deceive and defraud the public are made, or where specific mention is made in such advertisements of tuberculosis, consumption, cancer, Bright's disease, kidney disease, diabetes, or of venerea diseases or diseases of the genito-urinary organs.

 * * * * * * *

"Upon notice and hearing, the board, by a vote of not less than five members, may revoke or suspend a certificate for like cause or causes."

OREGON.

Marriage—Certificate of Health Required. (Chap. 187, Act Feb. 26, 1913.)

Section 1. That before any county clerk in this State shall issue a marriage license the applicant therefor shall file with the clerk from whom such license is sought a certificate from a physician duly authorized to practice medicine within the State, made under oath, within 10 days from the date of filing the same, showing that the male person thus seeking to enter the marriage relation is free from contagious or infectious venereal disease.

SEC. 2. Any physician who shall knowingly and willfully make any false statement in any certificate issued, as herein provided, shall be punished by the revocation of his license to practice his profession within the State.

SEC. 3. All fees and charges for any physician making the necessary examination of and issuing the necessary certificate to any one party, as herein provided, shall not exceed the sum of $2.50.

SEC. 4. The county physicians of the several counties shall, upon request, make the necessary examination and issue such certificate, if the same can properly be issued, without charge to the applicant, if indigent.

PENNSYLVANIA.

Notification—Quarantine.   (Res. Bd. of H. of Philadelphia, Effective Jan. 1, 1918.)

SECTION 1. *Resolved*, That on and after January 1, 1918, every physician in the city of Philadelphia shall forthwith report, in writing, to the bureau of health, on forms furnished by said bureau, the sex, color, age, marital state, and occupation of every person under his care for gonorrhea, chancroid or syphilis. All reports made in accordance with section 1 of this resolution, and all clinical and laboratory records showing the presence of gonorrhea, chancroid, or syphilis shall be confidential and not open to public inspection or be inspected by any person other than the official custodian of such reports in the bureau of health, the director of the department of public health and charities, and such other persons as may be authorized by law to inspect such reports or records; nor shall the custodian of any such report or record, the said director, or any other person, divulge any part of any such report or record, so as to disclose the identity of the person to whom it relates.

SEC. 2. *And it is further resolved*, That when a physician in Philadelphia shall report, in writing, to the bureau of health that a person afflicted with gonorrhea, chancroid, or syphilis whom he has treated or examined after January 1, 1918, can not be properly and sufficiently attended at home, then the bureau of health shall take charge of such reported person and shall quarantine or remove to a hospital the afflicted person, who shall be quarantined until duly discharged by a permit, in writing from the bureau of health. All reports and records made under section 2 of this resolution may be disclosed by the director of the department of public health and charities at his discretion.

SOUTH CAROLINA.

Wassermann Blood Test, Free.   (Act 551, Apr. 6, 1916.)

SECTION 1. *Test to be free.*—That the State board of health is required to make all Wassermann blood tests without charge as in case of other blood tests now provided for by law.

VERMONT.

Notification—Laboratory Tests and Treatment.   (Act 218, Feb. 3, 1913.)

SECTION 1. Commencing on the date of the passage of this act the superintendent or other officer in charge of public institutions such as hospitals, dispensaries, clinics, homes, asylums, charitable and correctional institutions, shall report promptly to the State board of health the name, sex, age, nationality, race, marital state, and address of every charitable patient under observation suffering from venereal diseases in any form, stating the name, character, stage, and duration of the infection, and, if obtainable, the date and source of contracting the same.

SEC. 2. Physicians shall furnish similar information concerning private patients under their care, except that the name and address of the patient shall not be reported.

Sec. 3. All information and reports in connection with persons suffering from such disease shall be regarded as absolutely confidential, and shall not be accessible by the public nor shall such records be deemed public records.

Sec. 4. The State board of health shall provide, at the expense of the State, facilities for the free bacteriological examination of discharges for the diagnosis of gonorrheal infections, and shall also provide, at cost, vaccines or antitoxins for the treatment of such infections. And said board shall make, at the expense of the State, the Wassermann test or examine smears for the diagnosis of syphilis; and shall furnish the treatment known as "Salvarsan" or other accredited specific treatment at cost. But such diagnosis and treatment shall not be furnished until the data required for the registration of the case has been furnished by the physician or institution treating the patient.

Sec. 5. The State board of health shall include in bulletins or circulars distributed by it information concerning the diseases covered by this act.

Notification—Seller of Drugs to Report—Marriage or Sexual Intercourse by Infected Persons—Making of Regulations—Educational Campaign. (Act No. 198, Mar. 23, 1915, as Amended by Act No. 238, Mar. 14, 1917.)

Section 1. A person who, having been told by a physician that he or she was infected with gonorrhea or syphilis, marries, without assurance and certification from a legally qualified practitioner of medicine and surgery that he or she is free from gonorrhea or syphilis shall be fined not more than $500 or imprisoned not more than two years.

Sec. 2. A person who, while infected with gonorrhea or syphilis, has sexual intercourse shall be fined not more than $500 or imprisoned in the house of correction for not more than one year.

Sec. 3. A physician, or any other person who knows or has reason to believe that a person whom he treats or prescribes for or to whom he sells medicine other than on a physician's prescription, has gonorrhea or syphilis, shall immediately report the name, nationality, race, marital state, address, age, and sex of such person to the secretary of the State board of health, for which report he shall receive the sum of 25 cents to be paid by the State board of health. A person who fails to make such report shall be fined not more than $200.

Sec. 4. The State board of health shall make and enforce such rules and regulations for the quarantining and treatment of cases of gonorrhea and syphilis reported to it as may be deemed necessary for the protection of the public. Said board shall not disclose the names or addresses of persons reported or treated to any person other than a prosecuting officer or in court on prosecutions under this act.

Sec. 5. Said board shall semiannually in the months of January and July pay such persons all sums due on account of such reports; and such expenditures shall be allowed in said board's accounts.

Sec. 6. The sum of $1,000 is annually appropriated for carrying out the provisions of this act.

Sec. 7. Section 2 of No. 218 of the acts of 1912 is hereby repealed.

Sec. 8. Authority is given said board under this act to conduct an educational campaign of methods of prevention and treatment and care of persons suffering from gonorrhea and syphilis, and sums so expended shall be paid from the appropriation herein named.

WASHINGTON.

Laundries—Infected Persons. (Ord. C 1848 of Spokane, Jan. 4, 1915.)

Sec. 41. It shall be unlawful for any person, firm or corporation conducting, operating, managing, or carrying on a public washhouse or laundry, to permit any person suffering from any communicable disease or venereal disease to work, lodge, sleep, or remain within or upon the premises used for the purpose of such public washhouse or laundry.

WISCONSIN.

Notification—Literature—Care of Indigent Persons—Laboratory Tests. (Ch. 235, Act May 17, 1917.)

Section 1. There is added to the statutes a new section to read:

Sec. 1417m. 1. Any person afflicted with gonorrhea or syphilis in its infective or communicable stage is hereby declared to be a menace to the public health. Any physician licensed to practice medicine in this State who is called upon to attend or treat any person infected with gonorrhea or syphilis in its communicable state, shall report to the State board of health in writing, at such time and in such manner as the State board of health may direct, the age and sex of such person and the name of the disease with which such person is afflicted. Such report shall be made on blanks furnished by the said board.

2. Every physician treating venereally infected individuals shall fully inform such persons of the danger of transmitting the disease to others and he shall advise against marriage while the person has such disease in a communicable form.

3. Whenever any person afflicted with gonorrhea or syphilis ceases taking treatment before he or she has reached the stage of the disease where it is no longer communicable or whenever any individual has been informed by a licensed physician that such individual is afflicted with gonorrhea or syphilis in the communicable stages and the person so afflicted refuses to take treatment, the physician shall forthwith notify the State board of health, giving the age, sex, and conjugal condition of the person afflicted and the nature of the disease. The State board of health shall, without delay, take such steps as shall be necessary to have said person committed to a county or State institution for treatment until such individual has reached the stage of the disease where it is no longer communicable and the person so committed shall not be released from treatment until this stage of the disease is reached unless other provisions satisfactory to the State board of health are made for suitable treatment.

4. Each county shall make such provisions as may be required by the State board of health to furnish the necessary care and treatment to all indigent individuals residing in the county who are afflicted with gonorrhea or syphilis, or to any such person who may be committed to any county institution for failure to comply with this law, until such afflicted persons have passed the infectious or communicable stage of the disease.

5. The State board of health shall prepare for free distribution upon request among the citizens of the State printed information and instructions concerning the dangers from venereal diseases, their prevention and the necessity for treatment.

6. The State laboratory of hygiene located at Madison, and all branch and co-operative laboratories located in any part of the State shall make microscopical examinations for the diagnosis of gonorrhea for any licensed physician in the State, without charge. The Psychiatric Institute at Mendota shall make the necessary examinations of blood or secretions for the diagnosis of syphilis for any licensed physician in the State, without charge.

7. Any person who shall violate any of the provisions of this section shall upon conviction be punished by a fine of not more than $100 or by imprisonment in the county jail for not more than three months, or by both such fine and imprisonment.

Marriage—Certificates of Health from Male Applicants—Laboratory Tests. (Ch. 525, Act Aug. 10, 1915, as Amended by Ch. 212, Act May 11, 1917.)

Sec. 2339m. 1. All male persons making application for license to marry shall at any time within 15 days prior to such application, be examined as to the existence or nonexistence in such person of any venereal disease, and it shall be unlawful for the county clerk of any county to issue a license to marry to any person who fails to present and file with such county clerk a certificate setting forth that such person is free from venereal diseases so nearly as can be determined by a thorough examination and by the application of the recognized clinical and laboratory tests of scientific search when in the discretion of the examining physician such clinical and laboratory tests are necessary. When a microscopical examination for gonoccocci is required, such examination shall upon the request of any physician in the S-ate be made by th S-ate laboratory of hygiene free of charge. The Wassermann test for syphilis when required shall upon application be made by the Psychiatric Institute at Mendota free of charge. Such certificate shall be made by a physician, licensed to practice in this S-ate or in the State in which such male person resides, shall be filed with the application for license to marry, and shall read as follows, to wit:

I, ... (name of physician), being a physician legally licensed to practice in the State of ...., my credentials being filed in the office of ...., in the city of ...., county of ...., State of ...., do certify that I have this .... day of ...., 19...., made a thorough examination of .... (name of person), and believe him to be free from all venereal diseases.

.... (S gnature of physician.)

2. Such examiners shall be physicians duly licensed to practice in this S+ate, or in the S-ate in which such male person resides. The fee for such examination, to be paid by the applicant for examination before the certificate shall be granted, shall not exceed $2. The county or asylum physician of any county shall upon request make the necessary examination and issue such certificate, if the same can be properly issued, without charge to the applicant if said applicant be indigent.

3. Any county clerk who shall unlawfully issue a license to marry to any person who fails to present and file the certificate provided by subsection 1 of this section, or any party or parties having knowledge of any matter relating or pertaining to the examination of any applicant for license to marry. who shall disclose the same. or any portion thereof. except as may be required by law. shall upon proof thereof be punished by a fine of not more than $100 or by imprisonment not more than six months.

4. Any physician who shall knowingly and willfully make any false statement in the certificate provided or in subsection 1 of this section shall be punished by a fine of not more than $100 or by imprisonment not more than six months.

Marriage—Certificates of Health. (Ch. 483, Act June 23, 1917.)

SECTION 1. There is added to the statutes a new section to read:

Sec. 2339n. 1. No person who has ever been afflicted with gonorrhea or syphilis shall be granted a marriage license in this State until such person shall furnish to the county clerk issuing the license a certificate from the director of the State laboratory of hygiene. or from the State board of health branch laboratory, or from one of the State cooperative laboratories controlled by the State board of health, setting forth the fact that the necessary microscopical examination has been made and that the individual named in the certificate is not in the infective or communicable state of gonorrhea. or a certificate from the director of the Psychiatric Institute at Mendota setting forth the fact that the necessary blood test for the Wasserman reaction has been made and that the person named in the certificate is not in the infective or communicable stage of syphilis. In all cases where the individual has been afflicted with both gonorrhea and syphilis both such certificates shall be furnished before such license is granted.

2. Such a certificate or certificates shall be furnished to any citizen of this State by the director of any of the laboratories mentioned, without charge.

3. The necessary smears for gonorrhea examinations and the blood for determining the presence of syphilis shall be collected and forwarded to the laboratory by physicians designated by the State board of health or the State health officer. for which a fee not to exceed $2 may be charged.

4. Any person who shall obtain any such license contrary to the provisions of this section, shall, upon conviction thereof, be punished by a fine of not less than $100 or by imprisonment in the county jail for not less than three months, or by both such fine and imprisonment.

Wassermann Test, Free.   (Ch. 307, Act June 23, 1915.)

Section 1. There is added to the statutes a new section to read:

Sec. 561jn. The board of control is hereby authorized to make necessary arrangements with the laboratory of the Psychiatric Institute of Mendota for the giving of the Wasserman test to any person confined in any State or county institution, and of making such test for any practicing physician of this State who makes application therefor in behalf of any resident of this State, free of charge.   *   *   *

UNITED STATES.

Prostitution Near Military Camps—Powers and Duties of Secretary of War.   (Act of Congress, May 18, 1917.)

Sec. 13. That the Secretary of War is hereby authorized, empowered, and directed during the present war to do everything by him deemed necessary to suppress and prevent the keeping or setting up of houses of ill fame, brothels, or bawdy houses within such distance as he may deem needful of any military camp, station, fort, post, cantonment, training, or mobilization place, and any person, corporation, partnership, or association receiving or permitting to be received for immoral purposes any person into any place, structure, or building used for the purpose of lewdness, assignation, or prostitution within such distance of said places as may be designated, or shall permit any such person to remain for immoral purposes in any such place, structure, or building as aforesaid, or who shall violate any order, rule, or regulation issued to carry out the object and purpose of this section shall, unless otherwise punishable under the Articles of War, be deemed guilty of a misdemeanor and be punished by a fine of not more than $1,000, or imprisonment for not more than 12 months, or both.

Houses of Prostitution Near Military Camps.   (Order of the President, 1917.)

2. Under authority of section 13 of the same act [act of Congress, approved May 18, 1917] the keeping or setting up of houses of ill fame, brothels, or bawdy houses within 5 miles of any military camp, station, fort, post, cantonment, training, or mobilization place being used for military purposes by the United States is prohibited.

PREVALENCE OF DISEASE.

No health department, State or local, can effectively prevent or control disease without knowledge of when, where, and under what conditions cases are occurring.

UNITED STATES.

EXTRA-CANTONMENT ZONES—CASES REPORTED WEEK ENDED JAN. 15.

Camp Beauregard, La.—For city of Alexandria: Meningitis 15, typhoid 1, measles 25, German measles 9, chickenpox 2, pneumonia 2. For city of Pineville: Measles 5, mumps 1. For city of Boyce: Measles 8. Village of Holwells: Measles 2. Boyce and Hollwells not in 5-mile zone, but make morbidity report. Total cases meningitis, Alexandria, to date 23; of these, 8 have occurred in one family whose census was 9. Four deaths have occurred in this family. Municipal hospital opened yesterday. Situation well in hand.

Camp Bowie, Tex.—Fort Worth: Mumps 1, measles 2, whooping cough 1, pneumonia 3, meningitis 3. Polytechnic: Measles 2.

Camp Dodge, Iowa.—Des Moines: Scarlet fever 9, diphtheria 2, smallpox 38, tuberculosis 2, measles 3, German measles 1. Grimes: Whooping cough 1, measles 1, chickenpox 1. Polk City: Scarlet fever 1, tuberculosis 1. Granger: Chickenpox 1, measles 72, smallpox 2, German measles 1, scarlet fever 3, diphtheria 3. Fort Des Moines: Scarlet fever 1. Bloonfield township: Smallpox 10.

Camp Gordon, Ga.—In Atlanta: Chickenpox 3, diphtheria 9, German measles 7, gonococcus infection 1, malaria 1, measles 6, epidemic cerebrospinal meningitis 4, mumps 4, lobar pneumonia 2, scarlet fever 1, smallpox 3, syphilis 2, tuberculosis 5, typhoid fever 3, whooping cough 2. In Stone Mountain: Measles 5, chickenpox 5. In Riverside: Epidemic cerebrospinal meningitis 1.

Camp Greene, N. C.—Whooping cough 8, chickenpox 6, smallpox 1, measles 52, German measles 2, gonorrhea 4, scarlet fever 1, gonorrhea and chancroid 1, gonorrhea and syphilis 1, diphtheria 1, cerebrospinal meningitis 3, syphilis 4, trachoma 1.

Camp Hancock, Ga.—Measles: Augusta 29, Davidson Crossing 1, Deans Bridge Road 1, Blythe 8, Gracewood 1, Hephzibah 2, and German measles: Augusta 8, and pulmonary tuberculosis: Augusta 3, and whooping cough: Augusta 1, and hookworm: Augusta 1, and chickenpox: Augusta 1.

Fort Leavenworth, Kans.—Measles; city 2, German measles; city 8, county 2, chickenpox; city 2, typhoid fever; city 2, paratyphoid; city 1, scarlet fever; city 1, county 1, diphtheria; city 1, tuberculosis; city 1, lobar pneumonia; county 1.

Camp Lee, Va.—Chickenpox, Petersburg 4; German measles, Petersburg 26; mumps, Petersburg 3; pneumonia. Petersburg 5; tuberculosis, Petersburg 3; whooping cough, Petersburg 3; chancroid, Petersburg 1; typhoid fever, Petersburg 1; measles, Petersburg 3; scarlet fever, Petersburg 4; malaria, Petersburg 1; German measles, Ettricks 1; scarlet fever, Hopewell 1; mumps, Chesterfield County 1; epidemic meningitis, Petersburg 1.

(85)

Camp Lewis, Wash.—German measles: Lake View 3 cases, DuPont 5, near Roy 1, Park Lodge 1, Spanway 1.

Camp Logan, Tex.—Anthrax, Houston 1. Chickenpox: Houston 6, Westfield 1. Diphtheria: Houston 2. German measles: Houston 7, Westfield 1. Gonorrhea: Houston Heights 1. Measles: Houston 16 Malaria: Goose Creek 1. Pneumonia: Houston 8. Typhoid fever: Houston 1. Tuberculosis: Houston 1. Cerebrospinal meningitis: Goose Creek 3.

Camp MacArthur, Tex.—Waco: Chickenpox 2, German measles 2, gonococcus 5, malaria 1, measles 3, tubercular meningitis 1, lobar pneumonia 5, scarlet fever 3, tuberculosis 1.

Camp McClellan, Ala.—Anniston: Smallpox 4, chickenpox 23, measles 16, cerebrospinal meningitis 3. Jacksonville: Smallpox 1. Oxford: Smallpox 4. District Four: Smallpox 7. District Fifteen: Smallpox 1.

Fort Oglethorpe, Ga.—Chattanooga: Mumps 5, measles 3, German measles 9, pneumonia 3, syphilis 3, whooping cough 4, tuberculosis 1, diphtheria 1, scarlet fever 1. North Chattanooga: Measles 1, diphtheria 2. St. Elmo: German measles 1, meningitis 1. Missionridge: Meningitis 1. Redbank: Meningitis 1, measles 2. Rossville, Ga.: Meningitis 1, measles 2.

Camp Pike, Ark.—Little Rock: Measles 31, chickenpox 2, smallpox 17, scarlet fever 1, tuberculosis 1, pneumonia 3, German measles 3, mumps 3, malaria 3, syphilis 13, gonorrhea 33, chancroid 7, meningitis 3. North Little Rock: Chickenpox 1, smallpox 6, pneumonia 1, gonorrhea 1, meningitis 2, whooping cough 2. Scotts: Measles 2, tuberculosis 1, meningitis 1, pneumonia 1. Sweethome: Measles 1, pneumonia 1. Alexander: Smallpox 1.

Camp Sevier, S. C.—Suburban Greenville: Epidemic cerebrospinal meningitis 1. Chick Springs, rural: Measles 2. Poe Mill: Measles 1. Judson Mill: Measles 2.

Camp Shelby, Miss.—Forest County, Hattiesburg: Measles 16, German measles 5, mumps 3, pneumonia 1, tuberculosis, pulmonary, 1. Carnes: Measles 8. Macedonia: Measles 1. Covington County, Mount Olive: Tuberculosis, pulmonary, 1. Sanford: Tuberculosis, pulmonary, 1. Hancock County, Bay St. Louis: Diphtheria 1.

Camp Sheridan, Ala.—Montgomery: Chickenpox 1, measles 22, mumps 2, pneumonia 1, German measles 12, scarlet fever 3, diphtheria 1, smallpox 8, tuberculosis 1. Cloverdale: Measles 1. Chisholm Measles 3. Rural district and 5-mile zone: Measles 1, smallpox 3.

Camp Sherman, Ohio.—Cerebrospinal meningitis: Chillicothe 1. Erysipelas: Chillicothe 1. German measles: Chillicothe 13 Measles: Chillicothe 13 Frankfort 1. Mumps: Chillicothe 1. Lobar pneumonia: Chillicothe 3. Scarlet fever: Chillicothe 1. East Scioto township 1, Uniontown township 1. Typhoid fever: Chillicothe 2.

Camp Zachary Taylor, Ky.—Jefferson County: Diphtheria 1, measles 1, scarlet fever 2. Louisville: Chickenpox 3, diphtheria 13, German measles 5, measles 29, mumps 2, scarlet fever 17, smallpox 1, trachoma 1, tuberculosis, pulmonary, 12, typhoid fever 2, whooping cough 1.

Tidewater Health District, Va.—Newport News: Measles 18, mumps 1, cerebrospinal meningitis 2, typhoid 1. Hampton: Measles 2, chickenpox 2, whooping cough 4.

Camp Wadsworth, S. C.—Spartanburg city: Chickenpox 9, measles 1, German measles 11, whooping cough 4, pneumonia 2, cerebrospinal meningitis 3. White Stone: Typhoid fever 1. Glenn Springs: German measles 1. Spartanburg County: German measles 3, pneumonia 1, chickenpox 2, diphtheria 1.

Camp Wheeler, Ga.—In Macon: Measles 22, diphtheria 1, mumps 12, scarlet fever 2, chickenpox 3, meningitis 1, pneumonia 1. In Bibb County: Meningitis 2. In East Macon: Measles 5, meningitis 2

CURRENT STATE SUMMARIES.
California.

From the California State Board of Health, telegram dated
January 15, 1918:

Prevalence of all communicable diseases except scarlet fever and whooping cough
decreased last week. Whooping cough especially prevalent in coast towns, while
scarlet fever is widely distributed. Three cases cerebrospinal meningitis; 2 San
Jose, 1 Los Angeles city. Three cases smallpox; 1 Maricopa, 2 Los Angeles city.
Marked reduction in typhoid, 8 cases reported last week.

Indiana.

From the Indiana State Board of Health, telegram dated January 15, 1918:

Scarlet fever: Epidemic Warsaw, Huntington, West Hartsville, Bartholomew
County, Churubusco, Allen County. Diphtheria: Death Fairmount. Measles:
Epidemic Reelhorn, Wabash County, Columbus. Smallpox: Epidemic Decatur.
Martinsville, Anderson, Clark Township, Johnson County. Whooping cough: One
death Portland, Decatur, Aurora. Rabies: Epidemic dogs Grand View, Spencer
County.

Kansas.

From Collaborating Epidemiologist Crumbine, telegram dated
January 14, 1918:

Meningitis: Arkansas City 1, Kansas City 1, Ellsworth 1, Manhattan 1, McLouth 3.
Winchester 1. Meningococcus carriers: Manhattan 3. Smallpox: Kansas City 101.
Girard 26, Neosho Falls 15, Osage County 22.

Massachusetts.

From Collaborating Epidemiologist Kelley, telegram dated January 14, 1918:

Unusual prevalence. Measles: Braintree 38, additional, Medfield, total January
40, Needham, total January 43. Typhoid fever: North Brookfield 3, additional.
Smallpox: Boston 1.

Minnesota.

From Collaborating Epidemiologist Bracken, telegram dated
January 14, 1918:

Smallpox: Clay County, Viding Township; Filmore County, Bluefield Township;
Freeborn County, Moscow Township; Sherburne County, Elk River Township;
Sibley County, Kelso Township; Todd County, Gordon Township; each 1 case;
Ramsey County, White Bear village, 2; Traverse County, Dumont village, 1; Croke
Township, 8. Poliomyelitis, cerebrospinal meningitis, 1 case each reported since
January 7.

Nebraska.

From the State Department of Health of Nebraska, telegram
dated January 15, 1918:

Smallpox at Superior, Scotts Bluff, Avoca, Manley, Weeping Water, and Genoa.
Scarlet fever at Walthill and Weeping Water. Diphtheria at Cedar Bluffs and Weeping Water.

7

88

South Carolina.

From Collaborating Epidemiologist Hayne, telegram dated January 14, 1918:

Seven new cases meningitis reported in civil population during past week; measles less prevalent; pneumonia on increase.

Virginia.

From Collaborating Epidemiologist Traynham, telegram dated January 14, 1918:

Four cases cerebrospinal meningitis Chesterfield County, 3 Bedford, 1 Portsmouth. One case smallpox King William County.

Washington.

From Collaborating Epidemiologist Tuttle, telegram dated January 14, 1918:

One case poliomyelitis San Juan County. No outbreaks of disease.

CEREBROSPINAL MENINGITIS.

City Reports for Week Ended Dec. 29, 1917.

Place.	Cases.	Deaths.	Place.	Cases.	Deaths.
Atlanta, Ga.	3		Jersey City, N. J.	2	
Baltimore, Md.	2		Los Angeles, Cal.	1	1
Birmingham, Ala.		1	Louisville, Ky.	1	
Boston, Mass.	2	2	New Britain, Conn.	1	1
Buffalo, N. Y.	3		Newport News, Va.	1	
Cambridge, Mass.	1		New York, N. Y.	3	4
Chicago, Ill.	6	3	Omaha, Nebr.	1	
Cleveland, Ohio	1	1	Philadelphia, Pa.	4	3
Columbus, Ohio	1		Providence, R. I.	1	1
Dubuque, Iowa		1	Quincy, Ill.	1	
Duluth, Minn.	1		Rockford, Ill.		1
East Orange, N. J.	1		St. Louis, Mo.		2
Fort Worth, Tex.	1	1	South Bend, Ind.	1	
Houston, Tex.		1	Troy, N. Y.	2	
Hattiesburg, Miss.	1		Washington, D. C.	2	2
Indianapolis, Ind.	1		Wichita, Kans.	1	1

DIPHTHERIA.

See Diphtheria, measles, scarlet fever, and tuberculosis, page 91.

ERYSIPELAS.

City Reports for Week Ended Dec. 29, 1917.

Place.	Cases.	Deaths.	Place.	Cases.	Deaths.
Baltimore, Md.	1	1	Los Angeles, Cal.	4	
Berkeley, Cal.	1		McKeesport, Pa.	1	
Buffalo, N. Y.	1		Malden, Mass.	1	
Camden, N. J.	1		Milwaukee, Wis.	2	
Chicago, Ill.	22	2	New York, N. Y.		11
Cleveland, Ohio	2		Philadelphia, Pa.	1	2
Denver, Colo.	3		Pittsburgh, Pa.	7	1
Detroit, Mich.		2	Plainfield, N. J.	1	
Duluth, Minn.	6		Pontiac, Mich.	2	
Evansville, Ind.		1	Portsmouth, N. H.	2	
Grand Rapids, Mich.	2		Reading, Pa.	1	
Harrisburg, Pa.	1		Rochester, N. Y.	1	
Jackson, Mich.	1		Rutland, Vt.	1	1
Johnstown, Pa.	2		St. Louis, Mo.	9	
Kansas City, Kans.	1		Salt Lake City, Utah		2
Lorain, Ohio	1		Springfield, Ill.	1	

MALARIA.

City Reports for Week Ended Dec. 29, 1917.

Place.	Cases.	Deaths.	Place.	Cases.	Deaths.
Birmingham, Ala...........		1	Louisville, Ky.............	1	....
Charleston, S. C...........		2	Memphis, Tenn............	....	1
Hattiesburg, Miss...........	3	....	North Little Rock, Ark......	1	....
Little Rock, Ark............	2	....	Stockton, Cal..............	1	....

MEASLES.

See Diphtheria, measles, scarlet fever, and tuberculosis. page 91.

PELLAGRA.

City Reports for Week Ended Dec. 29, 1917.

Place.	Cases.	Deaths.	Place.	Cases.	Deaths.
Birmingham, Ala...........		4	Little Rock, Ark...........	....	1
Charleston, S. C...........		1	Nashville, Tenn...........	....	3
Chicago, Ill...............		1	New Orleans, La...........	1	1
Fort Worth, Tex...........		1	New York, N. Y...........	....	1

PNEUMONIA.

City Reports for Week Ended Dec. 29, 1917.

Place.	Cases.	Deaths.	Place.	Cases.	Deaths.
Baltimore, Md..............	21	26	Manchester, N. H...........	1	1
Berkeley, Cal..............	1	....	Medford, Mass............	3	1
Boston, Mass..............	27	29	Melrose, Mass............	2	....
Braddock, Pa.............	1	....	Montgomery, Ala..........	2	3
Brookline, Mass...........	1	1	Nashville, Tenn...........	6	7
Cambridge, Mass..........	4	....	New Bedford, Mass........	6	2
Chattanooga, Tenn.........	3	2	New Castle, Pa...........	1	....
Chelsea, Mass.............	9	1	Newport, Ky..............	2	....
Chicago, Ill...............	344	73	Newton, Mass............	3	2
Cincinnati, Ohio...........	1	8	North Little Rock, Ark......	1	1
Cleveland, Ohio...........	34	36	Pascagoula, Miss..........	1	....
Columbia, S. C............	2	....	Philadelphia, Pa..........	106	71
Detroit, Mich.............	10	25	Pittsburgh, Pa............	59	56
Duluth, Minn.............	2	2	Pittsfield, Mass...........	1	3
Everett, Mass.............	3	2	Pontiac, Mich............	2	....
Fall River, Mass..........	9	2	Reading, Pa..............	3	5
Grand Haven, Mich........	2	1	Rochester, N. Y...........	6	....
Grand Rapids, Mich........	4	1	Sacramento, Cal..........	8	2
Hattiesburg, Miss..........	1	....	St. Joseph, Mo...........	7	2
Haverhill, Mass...........	6	1	San Diego, Cal...........	1	2
Jackson, Mich............	3	3	Sandusky, Ohio..........	2	1
Kalamazoo, Mich..........	3	2	Somerville, Mass.........	3	2
Kansas City, Kans.........	9	9	South Bethlehem, Pa......	2	....
Lancaster, Pa.............	2	....	Springfield, Mass.........	1	1
Lawrence, Mass...........	1	1	Stockton, Cal............	4	2
Leavenworth, Kans.........	1	....	Waltham, Mass...........	2	....
Little Rock, Ark..........	2	2	Wichita, Kans...........	11	3
Lorain, Ohio.............	2	....	Worcester, Mass..........	5	3
Los Angeles, Cal..........	12	10	York, Pa................	1	....

POLIOMYELITIS (INFANTILE PARALYSIS).

City Reports for Week Ended Dec. 29, 1917.

During the week ended December 29 one case of poliomyelitis was reported at each of the following-named places: Boston, Mass.; Canton, Ohio; Chicago, Ill.; Danville, Ill.; and Schenectady, N. Y. Two deaths were reported at Canton, Ohio, and one death at Chicago, Ill.

SCARLET FEVER.

See Diphtheria, measles, scarlet fever, and tuberculosis, page 91.

SMALLPOX.

City Reports for Week Ended Dec. 29, 1917.

Place.	Cases.	Deaths.	Place.	Cases.	Deaths.
Akron, Ohio	18		Little Rock, Ark	25	
Alton, Ill	5		Lorain, Ohio	1	
Ann Arbor, Mich	1		Los Angeles, Cal	1	
Anniston, Ala	4		Memphis, Tenn	8	
Braddock, Pa	1		Milwaukee, Wis	5	
Buffalo, N. Y	2		Minneapolis, Minn	13	
Butte, Mont	27		Montgomery, Ala	2	
Charlotte, N. C	1		New Orleans, La	1	
Chicago, Ill	7		North Little Rock, Ark	2	
Chillicothe, Ohio	1		Oklahoma City, Okla	5	
Cincinnati, Ohio	5		Omaha, Nebr	22	
Cleveland, Ohio	33		Pittsburgh, Pa	4	
Coffeyville, Kans	1		Portland, Oreg	1	
Columbus, Ohio	4		Rock Island, Ill	2	
Davenport, Iowa	1		St. Joseph, Mo	3	
Denver, Colo	9		St. Louis, Mo	11	
Des Moines, Iowa	14		Salt Lake City, Utah	7	
Detroit, Mich	61		Savannah, Ga	1	
Dubuque, Iowa	1		Sioux City, Iowa	13	
Fort Worth, Tex	6		Springfield, Ohio	1	
Grand Rapids, Mich	13		Superior, Wis	1	
Indianapolis, Ind	54		Tacoma, Wash	1	
Jackson, Mich	1		Toledo, Ohio	8	
Kansas City, Kans	86		Washington, D. C	1	
La Crosse, Wis	8		Wheeling, W. Va	1	
Lincoln, Nebr	1		Worcester, Mass	1	

TETANUS.

City Reports for the Week Ended Dec. 29, 1917.

During the week ended December 29, 1917, one case of tetanus was reported at Birmingham, Ala., one in New York, N. Y., and two cases in St. Louis, Mo. One death each was reported at Chicago, Ill., and Mobile, Ala.

TUBERCULOSIS.

See Diphtheria, measles, scarlet fever, and tuberculosis, page 91.

TYPHOID FEVER.

City Reports for Week Ended Dec. 29, 1917.

Place.	Cases.	Deaths.	Place.	Cases.	Deaths.
Alameda, Cal	1		Nashville, Tenn		1
Alton, Ill	1	1	New Bedford, Mass	2	
Anniston, Ala	3		New London, Conn	1	
Atlanta, Ga		1	New Orleans, La	4	
Augusta, Ga	1		New York, N. Y	13	1
Baltimore, Md	3		Oakland, Cal	1	
Birmingham, Ala	4	1	Orange, N. J	1	
Boston, Mass	1		Philadelphia, Pa	3	
Buffalo, N. Y	2	1	Portland, Oreg	1	
Chattanooga, Tenn		1	Portsmouth, N. H	1	
Chicago, Ill	5		Providence, R. I	1	
Cleveland, Ohio	1	2	Richmond, Va	1	
Denver, Colo	2		Sacramento, Cal	1	
Detroit, Mich	9	1	Salt Lake City, Utah	2	1
Everett, Mass	1		St. Louis, Mo	5	1
Hartford, Conn	2		Savannah, Ga	1	
Kalamazoo, Mich	1		Springfield, Ohio		1
Kansas City, Kans	2		Syracuse, N. Y	1	1
Lawrence, Mass	2		Toledo, Ohio	1	
Lorain, Ohio	1		Troy, N. Y	2	
Los Angeles, Cal	6		Washington, D. C	1	
Lynn, Mass	1		Wheeling, W. Va	3	1
Memphis, Tenn	2	1	Wilmington, Del	1	1
Minneapolis, Minn	5		Worcester, Mass	2	

DIPHTHERIA, MEASLES, SCARLET FEVER, AND TUBERCULOSIS.

City Reports for Week Ended Dec. 29, 1917.

City.	Population as of July 1, 1916 (estimated by U. S. Census Bureau).	Total deaths from all causes.	Diphtheria.		Measles.		Scarlet fever.		Tuberculosis.	
			Cases.	Deaths.	Cases.	Deaths.	Cases.	Deaths.	Cases.	Deaths.
Over 500,000 inhabitants:										
Baltimore, Md.	589,621	229	13	1	42	....	11	....	24	18
Boston, Mass.	756,476	257	108	11	78	2	34	2	43	27
Chicago, Ill.	2,497,722	625	192	21	55	1	74	....	344	56
Cleveland, Ohio	674,073	....	37	4	11	1	6	1	34	26
Detroit, Mich.	571,784	211	74	7	22	5	45	....	44	17
Los Angeles, Cal.	503,812	....	18	1	23	....	8	....	35	18
New York, N. Y.	5,602,841	1,516	236	30	782	8	141	1	257	186
Philadelphia, Pa.	1,709,518	598	69	13	75	....	49	1	67	60
Pittsburgh, Pa.	579,090	255	16	4	82	....	8	....	18	8
St. Louis, Mo.	757,309	211	70	3	17	....	30	1	36	21
From 300,000 to 500,000 inhabitants:										
Buffalo, N. Y.	468,558	150	12	4	6	....	3	1	28	21
Cincinnati, Ohio	410,476	123	11	3	11	....	4	....	12	19
Jersey City, N. J.	306,345	....	10	1	27	....	4	....	5	....
Milwaukee, Wis.	436,535	84	8	....	51	....	35	1	11	8
Minneapolis, Minn.	363,454	....	16	8	8	....	....	....	....	....
New Orleans, La.	371,747	153	12	....	29	....	2	....	42	25
San Francisco, Cal.	463,516	161	22	....	14	....	8	....	24	21
Seattle, Wash.	348,639	46	2	....	61	....	7	....	8	5
Washington, D. C.	363,980	147	16	....	70	3	22	....	7	13
From 200,000 to 300,000 inhabitants:										
Columbus, Ohio	214,878	67	4	....	3	....	24	....	9	5
Denver, Colo.	260,800	64	4	1	8	....	20	....	....	10
Indianapolis, Ind.	271,708	....	23	....	12	....	40	....	6	....
Kansas City, Mo.	297,847	85	9	1	12	....	13	2	....	10
Louisville, Ky.	238,910	75	4	....	19	....	5	....	11	2
Portland, Oreg.	295,463	43	....	....	6	....	5	....	4	....
Providence, R. I.	254,960	80	11	....	4	....	6	....	2	8
Rochester, N. Y.	256,417	62	8	1	15	....	8	....	7	4
From 100,000 to 200,000 inhabitants:										
Atlanta, Ga.	190,558	....	1	....	4	....	4	....	2	9
Birmingham, Ga.	181,762	70	4	....	100	....	18	....	9	5
Bridgeport, Conn.	121,579	26	6	....	4	....	1	....	2	3
Cambridge, Mass.	112,981	31	8	1	12	1	4	....	4	2
Camden, N. J.	106,233	....	5	....	76	....	1	....	1	....
Des Moines, Iowa	101,598	....	1	....	....	....	3	....	....	....
Fall River, Mass.	128,366	36	3	1	....	....	1	....	5	1
Fort Worth, Tex.	104,562	28	....	1	4	1	....	....	....	2
Grand Rapids, Mich.	128,291	39	4	1	4	....	3	....	3	1
Hartford, Conn.	110,900	47	9	2	3	....	7	....	6	4
Houston, Tex.	112,307	29	2	....	36	....	1	....	....	3
Lawrence, Mass.	100,580	21	4	....	2	....	1	....	3	1
Lowell, Mass.	113,245	36	4	....	9	....	1	....	5	3
Lynn, Mass.	102,425	27	8	....	1	....	6	....	4	4
Memphis, Tenn.	148,995	54	9	1	56	....	....	....	5	5
Nashville, Tenn.	117,057	48	1	....	6	....	2	....	3	1
New Bedford, Mass.	118,158	40	3	....	15	....	2	....	12	2
New Haven, Conn.	149,685	....	4	....	6	....	4	....	3	1
Oakland, Cal.	196,604	46	2	....	6	....	5	....	5	5
Omaha, Nebr.	165,470	44	10	1	8	....	3	....	....	1
Reading, Pa.	109,381	45	8	2	1	....	1	....	....	1
Richmond, Va.	156,687	55	9	1	8	....	1	....	2	3
Salt Lake City, Utah	117,399	....	4	....	73	....	10	....	....	....
Springfield, Mass.	105,942	34	9	1	15	....	6	2	1	....
Syracuse, N. Y.	155,024	41	9	....	45	3	10	1	1	....
Tacoma, Wash.	112,770	....	1	....	3	....	10	....	....	....
Toledo, Ohio	191,554	53	7	2	5	....	3	....	....	7
Trenton, N. J.	111,593	40	9	3	1	....	....	....	4	1
Worcester, Mass.	163,314	52	4	1	9	....	6	1	9	5
From 50,000 to 100,000 inhabitants:										
Akron, Ohio	85,625	....	6	....	....	....	3	....	....	....
Atlantic City, N. J.	57,660	....	....	....	....	....	....	....	1	....
Augusta, Ga.	50,245	18	....	....	8	....	....	....	....	....
Bayonne, N. J.	69,893	....	4	....	1	....	....	....	3	....
Berkeley, Cal.	57,653	....	....	....	1	....	5	....	3	3
Binghamton, N. Y.	53,973	18	5	....	1	....	2	....	1	1
Brockton, Mass.	67,449	13	1	....	1	....	1	....	3	....
Canton, Ohio	60,852	18	1	....	....	....	....	....	....	....

DIPHTHERIA, MEASLES, SCARLET FEVER, AND TUBERCULOSIS—
Continued.

City Reports for Week Ended Dec. 29, 1917—Continued.

City.	Population as of July 1, 1916 (estimated by U. S. Census Bureau).	Total deaths from all causes.	Diphtheria.		Measles.		Scarlet fever.		Tuberculosis.	
			Cases.	Deaths.	Cases.	Deaths.	Cases.	Deaths.	Cases.	Deaths.
From 50,000 to 100,000 inhabitants—Continued.										
Charleston, S. C.........	60,734	33	3	......	......	......	......	......	......	1
Chattanooga, Tenn.......	60,075	5	1	......	8	......	3	......	......	2
Covington, Ky............	57,144	15	......	......	......	......	2	......	......	......
Duluth, Minn............	94,405	15	......	......	5	......	2	......	2	3
Erie, Pa.................	75,193		6	......	......	......	7	......	......	3
Evansville, Ind..........	76,078	29	4	......	......	......	1	......	4	45
Fort Wayne, Ind.........	76,183	20	5	......	......	......	2	......	2	3
Harrisburg, Pa...........	72,015	34	6	1	......	......	1	......	......	2
Hoboken, N. J...........	77,214	16	1	......	16	......	8	......	1	2
Johnstown, Pa...........	68,529	22	8	......	2	......	7	......	......	2
Lancaster, Pa............	50,873		......	......	2	......	1	......	......	......
Little Rock, Ark.........	57,343	11	2	......	48	......	3	......	......	1
Malden, Mass............	51,155	18	3	1	2	......	1	......	......	2
Manchester, N. H........	78,283	24	3	1	10	......	......	......	1	1
Mobile, Ala.............	58,221	16	......	......	5	......	......	......	......	3
New Britain, Conn.......	53,794	3	......	......	......	......	3	......	2	1
Norfolk, Va.............	88,612		......	......	......	......	......	......	......	2
Oklahoma City, Okla......	92,943	11	2	1	3	......	1	......	......	1
Passaic, N. J...........	71,744	16	2	......	5	......	......	......	2	1
Pawtucket, R. I.........	59,411	24	5	......	......	......	3	......	......	3
Portland, Me............	63,467	22	5	......	57	......	3	......	......	2
Rockford, Ill...........	55,185	9	......	......	3	......	1	......	......	1
Sacramento, Cal.........	66,895	23	......	......	2	......	8	......	2	3
Saginaw, Mich...........	57,611	9	3	......	......	......	5	......	1	......
St. Joseph, Mo..........	85,395	27	15	2	3	......	3	......	3	......
San Diego, Cal..........	53,330	29	3	1	55	......	......	......	18	4
Savannah, Ga............	64,845		......	......	1	......	......	......	......	3
Schenectady, N. Y.......	99,719	26	......	......	2	......	2	......	8	5
Sioux City, Iowa........	57,078		......	......	......	......	12	......	......	......
Somerville, Mass........	87,089	18	5	......	20	......	9	......	5	1
South Bend, Ind.........	68,946	21	1	......	......	......	......	......	......	......
Springfield, Ill........	61,120	18	3	......	......	......	......	......	......	......
Springfield, Ohio.......	51,550	26	......	......	......	......	1	......	2	1
Terre Haute, Ind........	66,083	23	5	1	2	......	3	......	2	2
Troy, N. Y..............	77,716		2	......	......	......	5	......	4	1
Wichita, Kans...........	70,722		1	......	......	......	5	......	......	......
Wilkes-Barre, Pa........	79,776	24	7	1	12	......	1	......	3	1
Wilmington, Del.........	94,245	28	2	1	......	......	......	......	......	4
York, Pa................	51,656		2	......	......	......	1	......	......	......
From 25,000 to 50,000 inhabitants:										
Alameda, Cal............	27,732	9	5	1	2	......	2	......	......	......
Auburn, N. Y............	37,345	14	1	......	1	......	......	......	1	......
Brookline, Mass.........	32,730	14	1	......	16	......	3	......	......	1
Butler, Pa..............	27,632	13	1	......	20	......	3	......	......	......
Butte, Mont.............	43,425	1	2	......	2	......	13	......	......	1
Charlotte, N. C.........	39,823		......	......	29	......	......	......	1	......
Chelsea, Mass...........	46,192		4	......	18	......	1	......	5	2
Chicopee, Mass..........	29,319	6	......	......	10	......	2	......	1	1
Columbia, S. C..........	34,611	12	5	......	15	......	......	......	1	1
Cumberland, Md..........	26,074	8	2	1	......	......	......	......	......	1
Danville, Ill...........	32,261	8	......	......	......	......	......	......	......	......
Davenport, Iowa.........	48,811		......	......	......	......	3	......	......	......
Dubuque, Iowa...........	39,573		1	......	3	......	......	......	......	2
East Chicago, Ind.......	28,743	16	2	......	2	......	......	......	......	......
East Orange, N. J.......	42,458	13	3	1	35	......	......	......	......	......
Elgin, Ill..............	28,203	0	......	......	1	......	......	......	......	......
Everett, Mass...........	39,233	11	5	......	14	......	2	......	3	......
Everett, Wash...........	35,486	6	......	......	1	......	3	......	......	1
Galveston, Tex..........	41,863	10	1	......	8	......	......	......	......	1
Green Bay, Wis..........	29,353	5	2	......	9	......	......	......	1	......
Haverhill, Mass.........	48,477	8	2	......	7	......	......	......	3	......
Jackson, Mich...........	35,363	20	1	......	2	......	5	......	1	3
Kalamazoo, Mich.........	48,886	15	3	......	21	......	5	......	1	1
Kenosha, Wis............	31,576	4	5	......	......	......	6	......	......	......
Knoxville, Tenn.........	38,676		......	......	1	......	12	......	......	......
La Crosse, Wis..........	31,677	4	......	......	......	......	......	......	......	......
Lexington, Ky...........	41,097	20	2	......	15	......	1	......	......	2
Lima, Ohio..............	35,384	15	3	1	......	......	2	......	......	2

DIPHTHERIA, MEASLES, SCARLET FEVER, AND TUBERCULOSIS—
Continued.

City Reports for Week Ended Dec. 29, 1917—Continued.

City.	Population as of July 1, 1916 (estimated by U.S. Census Bureau).	Total deaths from all causes.	Diphtheria.		Measles.		Scarlet fever.		Tuberculosis.	
			Cases.	Deaths.	Cases.	Deaths.	Cases.	Deaths.	Cases.	Deaths.
From 25,000 to 50,000 inhabitants—Continued.										
Lincoln, Nebr	46,515	14	4		8		2			
Lorain, Ohio	36,064	11		1			1			
Lynchburg, Va	32,940	11					1			2
McKeesport, Pa	47,521		3		9					2
Medford, Mass	26,234	6	2		7		1			
Montclair, N.J	26,318	7			3					
Montgomery, Ala	43,285	10			16				1	
Newburg, N.Y	29,603	7	4		76		1		2	1
New Castle, Pa	41,133		1		1					
Newport, Ky	31,927	7							1	1
Newton, Mass	43,715	8	5		3					
Niagara Falls, N.Y	37,383	9	4		1	1	1		1	
Norristown, Pa	31,401	13	1		1		1			
Orange, N.J	33,060	9					1	1		
Pasadena, Cal	46,450	12							3	1
Perth Amboy, N.J	41,185		2		17		2		6	
Petersburg, Va	25,582	12	1				1		1	
Pittsfield, Mass	38,629	5			2		6		3	2
Portsmouth, Va	39,651	18	2		4				3	
Quincy, Ill	36,798	7	1	1	1					
Quincy, Mass	3,136	13	3		2				6	
Racine, Wis	46,456	11					6			1
Roanoke, Va	43,284	12			1					
Rock Island, Ill	25,026	10								
San Jose, Cal	38,902				1					
Steubenville, Ohio	27,445	9								
Stockton, Cal	35,358				2				3	2
Superior, Wis	46,226	2			1		1			
Taunton, Mass	36,283	12	1				3		1	
Waltham, Mass	30,570	4					1			
Watertown, N.Y	29,894	1			2					1
West Hoboken, N.J	43,139	7	2	1	1					
Wheeling, W. Va	43,377	21	2		1		1			1
Williamsport, Pa	33,800		3							
Winston-Salem, N.C	31,155	16	2		18		2		2	1
Zanesville, Ohio	30,463	9								
From 10,000 to 25,000 inhabitants:										
Alton, Ill	22,874	7	1		3		1			
Ann Arbor, Mich	15,010	9	4							
Anniston, Ala	14,112								1	
Braddock, Pa	21,685		2		1					
Cairo, Ill	15,794	7								1
Hattiesburg, Miss	16,452	3	1		20					
Kokomo, Ind	26,930	2	1				1		1	1
Leavenworth, Kans	¹19,363	8	6				1			1
Long Branch, N.J	15,395	4								
Melrose, Mass	17,445	6	2		1					
Morristown, N.J	13,244	6			2					
Muscatine, Iowa	17,500								1	
New Albany, Ind	22,629	4								
New London, Conn	20,985		4				2			2
Newport News, Va	26,569	9			11				1	
Plainfield, N.J	23,805	5			3					
Pontiac, Mich	17,594	6	2	1			6		1	
Saratoga Springs, N.Y	13,421	4					1		1	1
South Bethlehem, Pa	24,204		1		1		2			
Woburn, Mass	15,909	7								

¹ Population April 15, 1910; no estimate made.

FOREIGN.

CHINA.

Examination of Rats—Hongkong.

During the five weeks ended December 1, 1917, 10,793 rats were examined at Hongkong. No plague infection was found. The last plague-infected rat at Hongkong was reported found during the week ended September 22, 1917.

CUBA.

Communicable Diseases—Habana.

Communicable diseases have been notified at Habana as follows:

Disease.	Dec. 11-20, 1917.		Remaining under treatment Dec. 20, 1917.	Disease.	Dec. 11-20, 1917.		Remaining under treatment Dec. 20, 1917.
	New cases.	Deaths.			New cases.	Deaths.	
Diphtheria	7	1	9	Scarlet fever			4
Leprosy	1		11	Smallpox			2
Malaria	28	1	[1] 48	Typhoid fever	22	4	[2] 84
Measles	8		10	Varicella	4		3
Paratyphoid fever			2				

[1] From the interior, 34; foreign, 1.   [2] From the interior, 36.

JAMAICA.

Quarantine Regulations.

Under date of November 27, 1917, the quarantine board of Jamaica directed quarantine measures to be enforced at Jamaican ports as follows:

Metallic rat guards, properly adjusted and maintained, to be placed on the mooring lines leading from all vessels to wharves or other vessels; all gangways, cargo chutes, or other means of rat access, to be raised or removed between sunset and sunrise and all vessels or lighters lying alongside to be removed during the same period; night loading to be done under supervision.

Vessels which have had communication with Venezuela, Ecuador, Chile, or Peru not to be admitted to pratique until after fumigation.

Vessels arriving from the Argentine Republic, Brazil, Uruguay, Paraguay, Cape Verde Islands, Malta, Canary Islands, Hongkong, and the Azores except San Miguel, or any other country infected with plague may take first-class passengers and be admitted to pra-

tique at Jamaican ports provided they are six days out, have all well
on board, and produce a certificate of having been anchored not less
than a quarter of a mile from shore at any port of the countries
named and that cargo was not taken on board. Disinfection of
clothing and effects may be required. Vessels will then be allowed
to receive mail and passengers at Port Royal, Jamaica, during day-
light hours and to land first-class passengers and baggage at the
quarantine station.

Regulations against yellow fever.—Vessels arriving from Mexico
must be 18 days out from that country to obtain pratique at a port
in Jamaica.

Regulations against smallpox.—Passengers in transit through Panama who have not been on the Isthmus for 14 days, and passengers
from Mexico and Guatemala, desiring to land in Jamaica, must be
14 days out, show marks of recent vaccination or submit to vaccination on board, or else complete remainder of 14-day period at the
quarantine station.

VIRGIN ISLANDS.

Dengue—St. Thomas.

An outbreak of dengue occurred at St. Thomas, Virgin Islands, in
November, 1917, with an estimated number of 125 cases reported
to December 27, 1917. The disease occurred mainly among newly
arrived residents, and was generally mild in type.

CHOLERA, PLAGUE, SMALLPOX, AND TYPHUS FEVER.

Reports Received During Week Ended Jan. 18, 1918.[1]

CHOLERA.

Place.	Date.	Cases.	Deaths.	Remarks.
China:				
Antung	Nov. 26–Dec. 2....	3	1	
Java:				
West Java				Nov. 2–8,1917: Cases, 5; deaths, 2.
Batavia	Nov. 2–8..........	5	2	
Philippine Islands:				
Provinces				Nov. 18–24, 1917: Cases, 262; deaths, 167.
Antique	Nov. 18–24......	32	23	
Bohol	do......	10	9	
Iloilo	do......	57	38	
Leyte	do......	4	3	
Mindanao	do......	77	47	
Occidental Negros	do......	47	30	
Oriental Negros	do......	35	17	
Provinces				Nov. 25–Dec. 1, 1917: Cases, 251; deaths, 166.
Antique	Nov. 25–Dec. 1...	16	9	
Bohol	do......	36	19	
Capis	do......	1	1	
Iloilo	do......	67	40	
Leyte	do......	3	2	
Mindanao	do......	38	30	
Occidental Negros	do......	71	47	
Oriental Negros	do......	18	17	
Romblon	do......	1	1	

[1] From medical officers of the Public Health Service, American consuls, and other sources.

CHOLERA, PLAGUE, SMALLPOX, AND TYPHUS FEVER—Continued.

Reports Received During Week Ended Jan. 18, 1918—Continued.

PLAGUE.

Place.	Date.	Cases.	Deaths.	Remarks.
Indo-China:				
Saigon....................	Oct. 31-Nov. 18...	8	4	

SMALLPOX.

Place.	Date.	Cases.	Deaths.	Remarks.
Australia:				
New South Wales........				Sept. 28-Oct. 11, 1917: Cases, 1.
Cessnock..............	Sept. 28-Oct. 11...	3		Newcastle district.
Brazil:				
Sao Paulo.................	Oct. 21-Nov. 4....		2	
Canada:				
New Brunswick—				
Kent County.........	Dec. 4..........			Outbreak. On main line Canadian Ry., 23 miles north of Moncton.
Ontario—				
Sarnia...............	Dec. 23-Jan. 5....	3		
Windsor...........	Dec. 30-Jan. 5....	1		
Quebec—				
Montreal.............	Dec. 21-Jan. 5 ...	4		
China:				
Antung...............	Dec. 3-9....	1	1	
Chungking...........	Nov. 11-17......			Present.
Shanghai.............	Nov. 25-Dec. 2....	7	6	
Cuba:				
Habana.................	Jan. 8....	2		Nov. 8, 1917-Jan. 8, 1918: Cases, 4.
Egypt:				
Cairo.................	July 30-Aug. 5....	3		
Indo-China:				
Saigon...............	Oct. 21-Nov. 18...	41	12	
Java:				
Mid-Java..............	Oct. 21-30....	10		
West Java.............				Nov. 2-8, 1917: Cases, 10.
Batavia.............	Nov. 2-8..........	1		
Mexico:				
Piedra Negras...........	Jan. 11..........	200		
Newfoundland:				
St. Johns...........	Dec. 22-28........	2		
Spain:				
Coruna..........	Dec. 2-15........		4	
Venezuela:				
Maracaibo..............	Dec. 2-8..........		1	

TYPHUS FEVER.

Place.	Date.	Cases.	Deaths.	Remarks.
China:				
Antung..........	Dec. 3-9..........	5	1	
Egypt:				
Cairo..................	July 30-Sept. 23..	77	37	
Port Said.................	...do....	3	3	
Japan:				
Nagasaki..............	Dec. 3-9..........	3		
Java:				
East Java	Oct. 15-21........	5	2	
Mid-Java...............				Oct. 24-30, 1917: Cases, 10: deaths, 2.
Samarang...............	Oct. 24-30........	1	1	
West Java...............				Nov. 2-8, 1917: Cases, 12: deaths, 1.
Batavia.	Nov. 2-8..........	9	1	

CHOLERA, PLAGUE, SMALLPOX, AND TYPHUS FEVER—Continued.

Reports Received from Dec. 29, 1917, to Jan. 11, 1918. [1]

CHOLERA.

Place.	Date.	Cases.	Deaths.	Remarks.
India:				
Bombay	Oct. 28–Nov. 3....	2	1	
Calcutta	Sept. 16–Oct. 6....	....	42	
Java:				
West Java	....	....	....	Oct. 19–Nov. 1, 1917: Cases, 14;
Batavia	Oct. 19–Nov. 1....	8	2	deaths, 5.
Persia:				
Mazanderan Province—				
Astrabad	July 31	....	....	Present.
Barfrush	July 1–27	34	23	
Chahmirzad	....	....	....	26 cases reported July 31, 1917.
Chahrastagh	June 15–July 25...	10	8	
Kharek	May 28–June 11...	21	13	
Sari	July 3–29	273	144	
Yekchambe-Bazar	June 3	6	....	
Siam:				
Bangkok	Sept. 16–22	1	1	

PLAGUE.

Place.	Date.	Cases.	Deaths.	Remarks.
British Gold Coast:				
Axim	Jan. 8	....	....	Present.
Ceylon:				
Colombo	Oct. 14–27	4	3	Jan. 1–Nov. 15, 1917: Cases, 728;
Egypt:				deaths, 398.
Port Said	July 23–29	1	2	Sept. 16–29, 1917: Cases, 18,653;
India:				deaths, 13,810. Oct. 1–7,
Bombay	Oct. 28–Nov. 3....	18	17	1917: Cases, 13,571; deaths,
Calcutta	Sept. 16–"9	....	2	9,390.
Karachi	Oct. 1–Nov. 10...	6	5	
Madras Presidency	Oct. 31–Nov. 6...	1,555	1,200	
Rangoon	Oct. 21–27	9	10	
Siam:				
Bangkok	Sept. 16–22	1	1	
Straits Settlements:				
Singapore	Oct. 28–Nov. 3....	1	3	

SMALLPOX.

Place.	Date.	Cases.	Deaths.	Remarks.
Algeria:				
Algiers	Nov. 1–30	1	....	
Australia:				
New South Wales	....	....	....	Oct. 12–Nov. 20, 1917: Cases, 6.
Abermain	Oct. 25–Nov. 20...	3	....	
Warren	Oct. 12–13	3	....	
Brazil:				
Pernambuco	Nov. 1–15	1	....	
Rio de Janeiro	Sept. 30–Oct. 27...	313	88	
Canada:				
Ontario—				
Hamilton	Dec. 16–22	1	....	
Sarnia	Dec. 9–15	1	....	
Quebec—				
Montreal	Dec. 16–22	1	....	
China:				
Amoy	Oct. 22–Nov. 4....	....	....	Present.
Dairen	Nov. 18–24	1	....	
Mukden	Nov. 11–24	....	....	Do.
Shanghai	Nov. 18–25	2	12	Cases, foreign; deaths among
Tientsin	Nov. 11–17	2	....	natives.
Egypt:				
Alexandria	Nov. 12–18	1	....	
Cairo	July 23–29	2	1	
France:				
Lyon	Nov. 18–Dec. 9....	4	1	In hospital. From Givors.
Great Britain:				
Birmingham	Nov. 11–17	19	....	
India:				
Madras	Oct. 31–Nov. 6....	4	1	

[1] From medical officers of the Public Health Service, American consuls, and other sources. For reports received from June 30, 1917, to Dec. 28, 1917, see Public Health Reports for Dec. 28, 1917. The tables of epidemic diseases are terminated semiannually and new tables begun.

CHOLERA, PLAGUE, SMALLPOX, AND TYPHUS FEVER—Continued.

Reports Received from Dec. 29, 1917, to Jan. 11, 1918—Continued.

SMALLPOX—Continued.

Place.	Date.	Cases.	Death.	Remarks.
Italy:				
Turin...................	Oct. 29-Nov. 25...	77	16	
Java:				
Mid-Java.............	Oct. 10-23.........	15	....	
West Java...............	....	....	....	Oct. 19-Nov. 1, 1917: Cases, 62; deaths, 8.
Mexico:				
Mazatlan..............	Dec. 5-11.........	....	1	
Mexico City..............	Nov. 11-17........	9	....	
Newfoundland:				
St. Johns..............	Dec. 8-21.........	12	....	
Philippine Islands:				
Manila..................	Oct. 28-Nov. 16...	3	....	
Portugal:				
Lisbon...............	Nov. 4-10........	1	....	
Portuguese East Africa:				
Lourenço Marques.........	Aug. 1-Sept. 30...	....	4	
Russia:				
Moscow....	Aug. 26-Oct. 6....	22	2	
Petrograd..............	Aug. 31-Oct. 27...	59	3	
Spain:				
Sevilla.....................	Oct. 1-30.........	....	9	

TYPHUS FEVER.

Place.	Date.	Cases.	Death.	Remarks.
Algeria:				
Algiers.....................	Nov. 1-30.........	2	....	
Australia:				
South Australia............	....	....	....	Nov. 11-17, 1917: Cases, 1.
Canada:				
Ontario—				
Kingston..............	Dec. 2-8.........	3	....	
Quebec—				
Montreal..............	Dec. 16-22.........	2	1	
Egypt:				
Alexandria..............	Nov. 8-25.........	33	7	
Cairo.......................	July 23-29.........	23	8	
Greece:				
Saloniki.................	Nov. 11-24........	....	19	
Japan:				
Nagasaki..............	Nov. 26-Dec. 2...	1	....	
Java:				
Mid-Java..............		....	....	Oct. 10-16, 1917: Cases, 12.
Samarang.............	Oct. 17-23.........	3	....	
West Java..............		....	....	Oct. 19-Nov. 1, 1917: Cases, 21; deaths, 4.
Batavia..............	Oct. 18-Nov. 1....	13	3	
Mexico:				
Aguascalientes..............	Dec. 15.........	....	2	
Mexico City..............	Nov. 11-Dec. 15...	337	....	
Russia:				
Archangel..............	Sept. 1-14.........	7	2	
Moscow....................	Aug. 26-Oct. 6....	49	2	
Petrograd..............	Aug. 31-Oct. 27...	22	....	
Sweden:				
Goteborg.................	Nov. 18-24........	1	....	
Tunisia:				
Tunis.....................	Nov. 30-Dec. 6....	....	1	

×

PUBLIC HEALTH REPORTS

| VOL. 33 | JANUARY 25, 1918 | No. 4 |

NEGATIVE EXAMINATIONS OF TYPHOID CARRIERS.

A TYPHOID CARRIER DISCHARGED DURING CONVALESCENCE AFTER THREE NEGATIVE FECAL EXAMINATIONS—TYPHOID HISTORY IN FAMILY.

By CHARLES KRUMWIEDE, Jr., and MORRIS L. OGAN, Department of Health, New York City.

The requirement that the feces and urine should, prior to discharge of the patient, be found negative on bacteriological examination has undoubted value. Such negative examinations, however, are not conclusive evidence that the excretion of bacilli has ceased, or that if it has ceased excretion may not be resumed. The excretion during convalescence may be very irregular and a negative result may be due to the fact that the number of typhoid bacilli present is so small that they can not be isolated by our present methods. . Furthermore, actual absence from the feces would not exclude the presence of developing biliary lesions which will later discharge bacilli into the intestinal tract. Although these facts are generally known, it is seldom that we encounter such a striking illustration of their importance as the one here reported.

On April 28, 1914, we were notified of the death of Mrs. Las. An autopsy was obtained and the post-mortem findings verified the clinical diagnosis of typhoid fever. The typhoid fever was complicated by the abortion of a six months' fetus. Investigation revealed an interesting family typhoid history, showing the importance of contact infection. It also revealed the presence in the family of a chronic carrier.

Four related families were found involved. Of a total of 37 persons, 12 had developed typhoid fever. Three of the families, C., G., and Lib., are related—the mothers are sisters. Mrs. Las. is the daughter of Mrs. C. The cases of typhoid fever in the order of their onset are as follows:

C. family:
    Mike; onset September 3, 1913; age 17 years.
    Mrs.; onset October 3, 1913; age 54 years.
    Julia; onset October 3, 1913, or possibly before; age 15 years.
    George; onset October 13, 1913; probable typhoid; age 25 years.

8 (99)

G. family:

    Angelina; onset October 8, 1913; age 2 years.
    Rocco; onset October 11, 1913; age 6 years.

Lib. family: Julia; onset October 14, 1913; age 15 years.

Las. family:

    Rocco; onset March 11, 1914; age 10 years.
    Daniel; onset March 20, 1914; age 12 years.
    Louis; onset March 20, 1914; age 8 years.
    Theresa; onset March 20, 1914; age 4 years.
    Mrs.; onset April 1, 1914; died; age 30 years.

The probable sequence [1] of infection is as follows. Mrs. C. and Julia C. were probably infected nursing Mike, who did not enter the hospital till late in the course of the disease, being sent to the hospital because of the development of a peri-renal abscess. As Mike did not enter the hospital till October 11, he was probably the source of infection for George as well, rather than the more recently ill mother and sister.

The members of the G. and Lib. family visited the C. family during the illness of Mike and may have easily been infected from this source, especially considering the cramped quarters the family occupied.

With the developing of pregnancy of Mrs. Las., the mother, Mrs. C., was called upon for help in the household work, and came in more frequent contact with the members of the Las family. Although Mrs. C. was discharged from the hospital only after three negative examinations of her feces, she was found to be a carrier when examined in May, 1914, and is still excreting typhoid bacilli at the present time, although remittently. A remission of nearly six months has occurred while under our observation.

Discharge negative examinations are a safeguard only in so far as they prevent the return of convalescents to their homes while still excreting typhoid bacilli in appreciable numbers. The history of the above carrier indicates the value of a prolonged period of observation of those convalescents who are engaged in occupations where they handle foodstuffs. According to the present department procedure, such persons are now kept under observation and reexamined over a period of six months.

MALARIA IN ARKANSAS.

PREVALENCE AND GEOGRAPHIC DISTRIBUTION—1915 AND 1916.

The study of the prevalence and geographic distribution of malarial fevers in the State of Arkansas, through the circularization of the practicing physicians, was begun in 1913. Previous reports on this subject were published in the Public Health Reports of January 2, 1914, and May 28, 1915, and issued as reprints Nos. 160 and 277.

---

[1] Based on statements of family.

During 1915 and 1916 the physicians were circularized every three months, reply postal cards being used for the purpose.

Of the cards sent to the physicians about 14 per cent were returned. The number of cards sent out, the number of schedules returned, and the number of counties represented at each circularization are shown in Table 1.

It is to be borne in mind that the number of cases reported by the physicians does not show the number of cases that actually occurred, for an average of only a little more than 14 per cent of the physicians

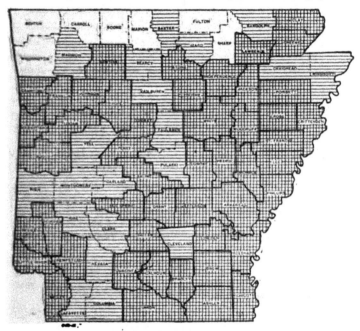

Relative prevalence of malaria in Arkansas, by counties in proportion to the population, as indicated by the number of cases reported.

returned the schedules. While there must have been many more cases of malaria in the State, the reports of the physicians on which this study is based are sufficient to show whether malaria was present or absent in the several counties, and reasonably accurately the relative intensity of the infection in the counties.

The cases reported throughout the State by months are shown in Table 2. The relative numbers of cases reported by months are shown in the chart.

The number of cases reported from the several counties of the State are given by race and year in Table 3.

The map on page 101 shows the relative prevalence of the disease in the several counties of the State, the heavier shaded counties being those in which the infection was heaviest, the unshaded counties those in which the infection was lightest, as indicated by the numbers of cases reported. The relative intensity of infection was determined

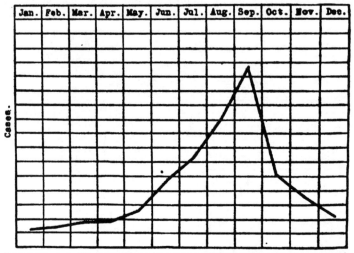

| Jan. | Feb. | Mar. | Apr. | May. | Jun. | Jul. | Aug. | Sep. | Oct. | Nov. | Dec. |

Cases.

Relative prevalence of malaria in Arkansas, by months, as indicated by the number of cases reported.

by ascertaining the number of cases reported in each county during the two years—1915 and 1916—per 1,000 population. The population used was that of the 1910 census, it being impracticable to use current estimates for the purpose.

Table 4 shows that hemoglobinuric fever was reported in 17 counties.

TABLE 1.—*Results of circularization of practicing physicians.*

Period.	Inquiry cards sent to physicians.	Replies received.	Percentage of replies.	Counties represented in replies.	Counties not heard from.	Cases of malaria reported.
1915.						
January to March	6,900	1,248	18.09	74	1	2,359
April to June	2,300	326	14.17	73	2	4,319
July to September	2,300	348	15.13	73	2	18,960
October to December	2,300	282	12.17	70	5	6,394
1916.						
January to March	2,300	284	12.35	70	5	2,167
April to June	2,300	254	11.04	69	6	4,844
July to September	2,300	267	11.61	69	6	9,095
October to December	2,300	237	10.30	70	5	4,409

TABLE 2.—*Cases of malaria reported by months.*

Year.	Jan.	Feb.	Mar.	Apr.	May.	June.	July.	Aug.	Sept.	Oct.	Nov.	Dec.
1915	586	831	942	942	1,177	2,200	3,753	5,900	9,297	3,090	1,990	1,254
1916	634	641	892	927	1,400	2,517	2,582	3,119	3,394	2,003	1,464	942

TABLE 3.—*Cases reported by counties, by years, and by color.*

County.	Calendar year 1915.			Calendar year 1916.		
	White.	Colored.	Combined.	White.	Colored.	Combined.
Arkansas	263	59	322	286	112	398
Ashley	378	230	608	65	113	178
Baxter	100	2	102	54		54
Benton	48		48	228		228
Boone	100		100	10		10
Bradley	435	129	564	471	152	623
Calhoun	105	60	165	56	29	85
Carroll	37		37			
Chicot	158	381	539	19	192	211
Clark	89	43	132	64	41	105
Clay	894		894	501		501
Cleburne	326		326	189		189
Cleveland	172	21	193	25	20	45
Columbia	61	28	89	34	11	45
Conway	940	103	1,043	116	14	130
Craighead	195	10	205	141	4	145
Crawford	1,018	198	1,216	523	94	617
Crittenden	70	238	308	70	469	539
Cross	187	20	207	169	24	193
Dallas	133	73	206	128	75	203
Desha	97	59	156	136	176	312
Drew	234	146	380	149	203	352
Faulkner	294	19	313	153	71	224
Franklin	287	3	290	244	7	251
Fulton	30		30			
Garland	235	6	241	212	8	220
Grant	407	82	489	232	146	378
Greene	355		355	248		248
Hempstead	629	473	1,102	214	55	269
Hot Spring	131	80	211	122	45	167
Howard	195	71	266	173	175	348
Independence	311	6	317	271	23	294
Izard	98	1	99	169	2	171
Jackson	252	189	441	258	203	461
Jefferson	223	223	446	213	697	910
Johnson	851	5	856	179		179
Lafayette	108	99	207	45	57	102
Lawrence	543	20	563	336	84	420
Lee	194	719	913	65	153	218
Lincoln	323	182	505	125	579	704
Little River	642	667	1,309	76	76	152
Logan	470	8	478	279	15	294
Lonoke	301	120	421	261	61	322
Madison	165	5	170	57		57
Marion	14	1	15	18		18
Miller	283	27	310	398	89	487
Mississippi	226	134	360	98	88	186
Monroe	1,099	1,773	2,872	255	258	513
Montgomery	137	8	145	123	28	151
Nevada	35	12	47	146	51	197
Newton	290		290	38		38
Ouachita	428	392	820	222	145	367
Perry	1,096	216	1,312	285	59	344
Phillips	376	378	754	217	286	503
Pike	165	16	181	108	5	113
Poinsett	708	234	942	35	1	36
Polk	108	10	118	28		28
Pope	523	52	575	116	5	121
Prairie	84	130	214	100	14	114
Pulaski	222	167	389	413	249	662
Randolph	122	1	123	165	73	238
St. Francis	130	182	312	403	175	578
Saline	275	90	365	567	92	659
Scott	555		555	174		174
Searcy	60		60	113	101	214
Sebastian	629	112	741	502	151	653

TABLE 3.—*Cases reported by counties, by years, and by color*—Continued.

County.	Calendar year 1915.			Calendar year 1916.		
	White.	Colored.	Combined.	White.	Colored.	Combined.
Sevier..................	694	99	793	436	53	489
Sharp..................	52	....	52	10	....	10
Stone..................	74	....	74	280	28	308
Union..................	246	128	374	429	227	656
Van Buren..............	176	....	176	113	....	113
Washington.............	216	....	216	116	6	122
White..................	232	38	270	267	40	307
Woodruff...............	107	153	260	308	58	366
Yell...................	279	106	. 385	183	15	198
Total..................	22,726	9,237	31,962	14,082	6,483	20,545

TABLE 4.—*Hemoglobinuric fever reported, 1916.*

County.	Cases reported.			
	First quarter.	Second quarter.	Third quarter.	Fourth quarter.
Arkansas..........			1	
Columbia..........			2	2
Conway...........				1
Crawford..........			7	
Faulkner..........	1			1
Johnson...........				
Lawrence..........	1			2
Lee..............				
Lonoke...........	4		1	
Mississippi.......	1			
Ouachita..........		1		
Perry.............			3	
Phillips..........	2		1	
Pope.............			2	
Pulaski...........			1	
Sevier............			2	
Woodruff..........			2	5

PREVALENCE OF DISEASE.

No health department, State or local, can effectively prevent or control disease without knowledge of when, where, and under what conditions cases are occurring.

UNITED STATES.

EXTRA-CANTONMENT ZONES—CASES REPORTED WEEK ENDED JAN. 22.

Camp Beauregard, La.—City of Alexandria: Pneumonia 3, measles 9, mumps 1, meningitis 2, German measles 3. For city of Pineville: Meningitis 1, pneumonia 1, measles 2, chicken pox 1. For Boyce: Measles 12, pneumonia 2, malaria 1. Village of Ball: Pneumonia 1. For rest of rural district: Measles 3, pneumonia 1.

Camp Bowie, Tex.—Fort Worth: Diphtheria 1, smallpox 13, measles 2, tuberculosis 2.

Camp Dodge, Iowa.—Des Moines: Smallpox 51, diphtheria 2, scarlet fever 11, German measles 1, measles 2, syphilis 9, gonorrhea 8, syphilis and gonorrhea 4. Polk City: Chicken pox 2, measles 1. Grimes: Pneumonia 1. Bloomfield township: Smallpox 6, scarlet fever 1.

Camp Funston, Kans.—Army City: Measles 2. Leonardville: Chicken pox 1. Green: Measles 1. Ogden: Typhoid 1, measles 1, chicken pox 2. Cleburne: Measles 1. Riley: Measles 7, smallpox 3. Milford: Measles 1. Manhattan: Measles 81, scarlet fever 6, chicken pox 1, pneumonia 2, diphtheria 1, meningitis carriers 3, whooping cough 3. Junction City: Measles 7, scarlet fever 1.

Camp Gordon, Ga.—Atlanta: Diphtheria 13, German measles 12, gonococcus infection 1, measles 4, epidemic cerebrospinal meningitis 2, tuberculous meningitis 1, mumps 3, lobar pneumonia 5, scarlet fever 2, smallpox 2, syphilis 1. East Point, Fulton County: Smallpox 1. Clarkston, Dekalb County: Measles 4. Armour Station, Fulton County: Epidemic cerebrospinal meningitis 1. Marietta Road, Fulton County: Diphtheria 1. Bolton, Fulton County: Diphtheria 1. Ashford Park, Dekalb County: Diphtheria 1. Stone Mountain, Dekalb County: Measles 1, chicken pox 1.

Camp Greene, N. C.—Chicken pox 5, chancroids 1, cerebrospinal meningitis 4, gonorrhea 1, measles 35, German measles 8, mumps 4, syphilis 3, whooping cough 5, trachoma 1, smallpox 1; all in Charlotte township.

Camp Hancock, Ga.—Measles: Augusta 22, County Home 4, Hephzibah 10, Blythe 6. German measles: Augusta 40. Chicken pox: Augusta 3. Cerebrospinal meningitis: Augusta 2, one of which was fatal. Scarlet fever: Augusta 1. Mumps: Augusta 1. Lobar pneumonia: Blythe 1.

Camp Jackson, S. C.—Columbia, week ending 19th: Roseola 9, diphtheria 2, measles 10, varicella 1, pneumonia 1, cerebrospinal meningitis 1. January 21: Columbia, Meningitis 1; extra-urban Columbia, Rose Hill 1. January 22: Extra-urban Liberty Hill: Meningitis 2.

106

Fort Leavenworth, Kans.—German measles: City 10, county 2. Measles: City 5, county 1. Diphtheria: City 2, county 2. Lobar pneumonia: City 3, county 1. Smallpox: City 1, county 6. Chicken pox: City 6. Cerebrospinal meningitis: County 1. Scarlet fever: City 5. Gonococcus infection: City 1.

Camp Lee, Va.—Petersburg: Typhoid 1, German measles 7, measles 7, pneumonia 4, acute food poisoning 1, tuberculosis 4, gonorrhea 3. Ettrick: Whooping cough 5, German measles 1, tonsilitis 1. Hopewell: Measles 4. City Point: Measles 1. Chesterfield County: Chicken pox 2, tuberculosis 1, syphilis 1. Dinwiddie County: Tuberculosis 2, malaria 1.

Camp Logan, Tex.—Houston: Chicken pox 3, German measles 15, measles 26, mumps 4, cerebrospinal meningitis 1, pneumonia 6. Houston Heights: German measles 1. Pasadena: Pneumonia 2. Park Place: Pneumonia 1.

Camp MacArthur, Tex.—Waco: Chicken pox 2, German measles 7, gonococcus 1, measles 1, epidemic meningitis 2, lobar pneumonia 1.

Camp McClellan, Ala.—Anniston: Measles 12, mumps 1, chicken pox 17, German measles 8, tuberculosis 1, typhoid fever 1, pneumonia 1, smallpox 2, poliomyelitis 1. District Fifteen: Pneumonia 1.

Fort Oglethorpe, Ga.—Chattanooga: Tuberculosis 6, syphilis 2, mumps 5, gonorrhea 2, German measles 18, pneumonia 3, scarlet fever 1, whooping cough 1. Alton Park: Tuberculosis 1, scarlet fever 4, measles 1. St. Elmo: German measles 2. Fast Lake: Pneumonia 2, mumps 1, measles 1. East Chattanooga: Measles 1. North Chattanooga: Measles 2. Rossville: Pneumonia 1, mumps 2.

Camp Pike, Ark.—Cases reported week ending January 22: Little Rock: Measles 15, chicken pox 1, smallpox 33, scarlet fever 1, tuberculosis 1, pneumonia 5, mumps 1, malaria 3, syphilis 4, gonorrhea 12, chancroid 2, meningitis 3. North Little Rock: Smallpox 5, tuberculosis 1, German measles 5, syphilis 1, chancroid 1, meningitis 1, whooping cough 1. Sweet Home: Smallpox 1. Toltec: Scarlet fever 1, pellagra 1. Scotts: German measles 1, syphilis 1, gonorrhea 6.

Camp Sevier, S. C.—Judson Mill: Four measles. Monaghan Mill: One measles. Poe Mill: One epidemic cerebrospinal meningitis.

Camp Shelby, Miss.—Week ending January 19, 1918. Forest County: Hatti sburg: chicken pox 4, malaria 5, measles 5, German measles 3, mumps 7, pneumonia 2, smallpox 4, syphilis 1. Carnes: measles 8. Macedonia: measles 3, pneumonia 1. McLaurin: diphtheria 3, smallpox 2. Stone County: Wiggins: smallpox 10. Lamar County: Richburg: measles 1. Harrison County: Gulfport: anterior poliomyelitis 1. Lamar County: Lumberton: smallpox 1.

Camp Sheridan, Ala.—Montgomery: Measles 33, German measles 32, smallpox 3, meningitis 1, scarlet fever 1, mumps 3. Capitol Heights: Measles 1. Cloverdale: Scarlet fever 1, measles 3. Rural district in 5-mile zone: Measles, smallpox 1.

Camp Sherman, Ohio.—Chicken pox: Chillicothe 1. Diphtheria: Chillicothe 1. German measles: Chillicothe 20, East Scioto Township 1. Measles: Chillicothe 8. Scarlet fever: Chillicothe 4. Syphilis: Chillicothe 2. Tuberculosis: Chillicothe 1.

Camp Zachary Taylor, Ky.—Jefferson County: Chicken pox 2, German measles 3, measles 2. Louisville: Diphtheria 7, German measles 7, measles 35, scarlet fever 5, meningitis (tubercular) 1, cerebrospinal, 2, tuberculosis 5, typhoid fever 1, whooping cough 2.

Camp Wadsworth, S. C.—Spartanburg city: Measles 1, German measles 19, whooping cough 3, chicken pox 4, diphtheria 1, cerebrospinal meningitis 2, scarlet fever 2, smallpox 1. Glenn Spring: German measles 1.

Camp Wheeler, Ga.—In Macon: Measles 15, meningitis 3, diphtheria 2, tuberculosis 3, pneumonia 4, mumps 16, chicken pox 2, scarlet fever 5. In East Macon: Measles 1.

CURRENT STATE SUMMARIES.

Alabama.

From Collaborating Epidemiologist Perry, telegram dated January 21, 1918:

Smallpox: Five cases Limestone County, 1 Monroe, 1 Shelby, 1 Sumter, 3 Walker, 1 Wilcox.

Arkansas.

From Collaborating Epidemiologist Garrison, telegram dated January 21, 1918:

For week ended 19th, have to report smallpox: Three cases Lonoke County, several Lawrence County, 75 Trumann, 1 Calico Rock, 2 Clarksville, 3 Dermott, 1 Holly Grove, 5 Phillips County, 1 Hope. One case meningitis Dermott, 1 diphtheria Camden.

California.

From the California State Board of Health, telegram dated January 22, 1918:

Sharp increase last week in chicken pox, diphtheria, and measles. Smallpox more prevalent: 9 cases reported, 2 of which just arrived from Illinois and Kansas. One case anthrax in man, Napa County. Three cases epidemic cerebrospinal menigitis, 1 Los Angeles County, 1 Los Angeles City, and 1 San Francisco. One case leprosy, Oakland. One suspected leprosy, Contra Costa County. Measles especially prevalent San Diego and Palo Alto.

Reported by mail for preceding week (ended Jan. 12):

Anthrax	1	Pneumonia	88
Cerebrospinal meningitis	4	Ophthalmia neonatorum	1
Chicken pox	134	Scarlet fever	117
Diphtheria	52	Smallpox	4
Dysentery	2	Syphilis	41
Erysipelas	13	Trachoma	1
German measles	103	Tuberculosis	93
Gonococcus infection	45	Typhoid fever	9
Malaria	8	Paratyphoid	1
Measles	309	Whooping cough	115
Mumps	74		

Connecticut.

From Collaborating Epidemiologist Black, telegram dated January 21, 1918:

One cerebrospinal meningitis navy yard, New London. One smallpox, Winsted.

Indiana.

From the State Board of Health of Indiana, telegram dated January 21, 1918:

Scarlet fever: Epidemic Vevay, Crandall, Harrison County, Banquo, Grant County, Bartholomew County, 50 cases Kosciusko County; 1 death Sullivan; Winslow, Pike County. Diphtheria: Epidemic Owensville, Gibson County, and Sheridan; 1 death

Veedersburg, Jasper. Measles: Epidemic Wayne, Shelbyville, Huntington, Martinsville. Whooping cough: Vallonia, Jackson County. Smallpox: Epidemic New Haven, Allen County, Knightsville, Clay County, South Milford, Lagrange.

Kansas.

From Collaborating Epidemiologist Crumbine, telegram dated January 22, 1918:

Week ending January 19. Poliomyelitis: Harper County 1. Meningitis: Great Bend 1, Frederick 1, Manhattan 3. Meningitis carriers: Manhattan 1. Smallpox: Kansas City 59. Diphtheria: Pleasanton 25.

Louisiana.

From Collaborating Epidemiologist Dowling, telegram dated January 21, 1918:

Meningitis (excluding Rapides): Vermilion 2, 14th; DeSoto 1, 14th; Vermilion 1, 16th; DeSoto 1, 16th; LaFourche 1, 16th; Orleans 2, 18th; St. James 1, 21st. Poliomyelitis: January 16, 1.

Massachusetts.

From Collaborating Epidemiologist Kelley, telegram dated January 21, 1918:

Unusual prevalence: Diphtheria: Waltham, January 10. Measles; Blandford, total January 18, Braintree 31 additional; Marlboro total January 100. Medfield 20 additional.

Minnesota.

From Collaborating Epidemiologist Bracken, telegram dated January 21, 1918:

Smallpox: Clay County, Elmwood Township; Filmore County, Forestville Township; Kittson County, Deerwood Township, St. Joseph Township; Roseau County, Greenbush Township; Scott County, New Margaret village; each 1 case. Four cerebrospinal meningitis, two poliomyelitis cases reported since January 14.

Mississippi.

From Collaborating Epidemiologist Leathers, telegram dated January 21, 1918:

Negro dead 20th epidemic cerebrospinal meningitis Jackson; otherwise negative.

Ohio.

From Collaborating Epidemiologist Freeman, telegram dated January 21, 1918:

No unusual prevalence. Smallpox situation improving.

South Carolina.

From Collaborating Epidemiologist Hayne, telegram dated January 21, 1918:

Five new cases meningitis in State during week, pneumonia epidemic, measles lessening.

Virginia.

From Collaborating Epidemiologist Traynham, telegram dated January 21, 1918:

Five cases smallpox Wise County, two Russell County. Two cases cerebrospinal meningitis Alexandria County, one case Norfolk.

CEREBROSPINAL MENINGITIS.

*n ∵.   **State Reports for November and December, 1917.**

Place.	New cases reported.	Place.	New cases reported.
District of Columbia (Dec. 1-31):		Massachusetts—Continued.	
District of Columbia...............	8	Suffolk County—	
		Boston..............................	2
Louisiana (Dec. 1-31):		Winthrop (town).................	1
Caddo Parish.......................	1		
De oto Parish......................	1	Total.............................	15
Rapides Parish.....................	18	Pennsylvania (Dec. 1-31):	
		Allegheny County................	7
Total..............................	20	Beaver County....................	1
		Blair County.....................	1
Maryland (Dec. 1-31):		Cambria County...................	2
Baltimore City....................	7	Chester County...................	1
Baltimore County—		Clearfield County................	1
Arlington.........................	1	Dauphin County...................	1
Dell lot..........................	1	Delaware County..................	2
Sparrows Point....................	1	Fayette County...................	2
		Lehigh County....................	1
Total..............................	10	Philadelphia County..............	11
		Tioga County.....................	1
Massachusetts (Dec. 1-31):		Venango County...................	1
Essex County—			
Beverly...........................	1	Total.............................	32
Lawrence..........................	1	Virginia (Nov. 1-30):	
Franklin County—		Augusta County...................	1
Greenfield (town).................	1	Caroline County..................	1
Middlesex County—		Essex County.....................	1
Cambridge.........................	1	Grayson County...................	2
Camp Devens.......................	1	Norfolk—	
Lowell............................	2	Portsmouth........................	1
Malden............................	1	Patrick County...................	1
Tewksbury State Infirmary.........	1	Prince George County.............	5
Waltham...........................	1	Roanoke—	
Norfolk County—		Salem.............................	1
Canton (town)....................	1	Rockbridge County................	1
Plymouth County—		Washington County................	1
Brockton..........................	1		
		Total.............................	25

1915 1913   **City Reports for Week Ended Jan. 5, 1918.**

Place.	Cases.	Deaths.	Place	Cases.	Deaths.
Albany, N. Y......................	1	......	Memphis, Tenn....................	......	1
Alexandria, La...................	7	2	Montgomery, Ala.................	1	1
Baltimore, Md....................		1	Newark, N. J....................	2	1
Boston, Mass.....................	1	1	New Bedford, Mass...............	1	1
Bridgeport, Conn.................	1		New Britain, Conn...............	1	
Buffalo, N. Y....................	1	1	Newport News, Va................	1	......
Chicago, Ill.....................	6	4	New York, N. Y..................	4	2
Cleveland, Ohio..................	2	1	North Little Rock, Ark..........	2	......
Dayton, Ohio.....................	1		Philadelphia, Pa................	1	2
Fall River, Mass.................		1	Pittsburgh, Pa..................		1
Fort Worth, Tex..................	1	1	Providence, R. L................	3	1
Hartford, Conn...................	1		Rockford, Ill...................		3
Kansas City, Mo..................	6		St. Louis, Mo...................	1	......
Lawrence, Mass...................		1	San Jose, Cal...................	1	......
Little Rock, Ark.................	2	......	San Antonio, Tex................	1	
Los Angeles, Cal.................	2	2	Toledo, Ohio....................	2	
Lowell, Mass.....................	1	......	Wichita, Kans...................	1	
Macon, Ga........................	3	3	Worcester, Mass.................	1	

DIPHTHERIA.

See Diphtheria, measles, scarlet fever, and tuberculosis, page 117.

ERYSIPELAS.

City Reports for Week Ended Jan. 5, 1918.

Place.	Cases.	Deaths.	Place.	Cases.	Deaths.
Baltimore, Md	3		Nashville, Tenn	2	
Birmingham, Ala		1	Newark, N. J	6	1
Butte, Mont		1	New York, N. Y		5
Buffalo, N. Y	3		Norristown, Pa		1
Chicago, Ill	20	5	Omaha, Nebr	2	
Cleveland, Ohio	6		Pawtucket, R. I	1	1
Denver, Colo	3		Philadelphia, Pa	1	1
Dubuque, Iowa	1		Pittsburgh, Pa	9	
Duluth, Minn	1		Pontiac, Mich	2	
Erie, Pa	1		Portland, Oreg	3	
Hartford, Conn	2		Rochester, N. Y	1	
Jackson, Fla		1	St. Louis, Mo	7	
Kansas City, Mo	1	2	Salt Lake City, Utah		1
Lancaster, Pa	1		San Francisco, Cal	4	
Lawrence, Mass		1	Schenectady, N. Y		1
Los Angeles, Cal	2		Troy, N. Y	1	
Memphis, Tenn	3		Wheeling, W. Va		2
Muscatine, Iowa	1		Wilkinsburg, Pa	1	
Milwaukee, Wis	1		Wilmington, Del		1

MALARIA.

State Reports for November and December, 1917.

Place.	New cases reported.	Place.	New cases reported
Louisiana (Dec. 1-31):		Virginia (Nov. 1-30): Continued.	
Acadia Parish	10	Gloucester County	2
Concordia Parish	8	Greensville County	5
De Soto Parish	1	Emporia	6
Iberia Parish	2	North Emporia	8
Jackson Parish	2	Halifax County	6
Madison Parish	1	South Boston	2
Ouachita Parish	1	Hanover County	21
St. Martin Parish	4	Henrico County	9
St. Mary Parish	1	Henry County—	
St. Tammany Parish	45	Martinsville	
Tensas Parish	19	Isle of Wight County	22
Vermilion Parish	3	James City County—	
West Feliciana Parish	1	Williamsburg	3
		King and Queen County	4
Total	98	Lancaster County	8
		Lee County	2
Maryland (Dec. 1-31):		Lunenburg County	2
Anne Arundel County—		Victoria	6
Camp Meade	1	Mathews County	1
		Mecklenburg County	1
Massachusetts (Dec. 1-31):		Middlesex County	8
Essex County—		Nansemond County	8
Marblehead (town)	1	Suffolk	13
Suffolk County—		Nelson County	1
Boston	1	New Kent County	5
		Norfolk County	1
Total	2	Northampton County	29
		Northumberland County	7
Virginia (Nov. 1-30):		Nottoway County	2
Accomac County	4	Crewe	7
Chincoteague	8	Pittsylvania County	1
Greenbackville	4	Powhatan County	7
Albemarle County	2	Princess Anne County	26
Alleghany County—		Prince Edward County	1
Clifton Forge	1	Farmville	2
Amelia County	1	Prince George County	11
Amherst County	1	City Point	1
Appomattox County	1	Richmond County	2
Augusta County—		Rockbridge County	1
Staunton	1	Rockingham County—	
Bedford County	1	Dayton	1
Brunswick County	11	Smyth County	1
Buckingham County	2	Southampton County	5
Campbell County	3	Stafford County	4
Caroline County	5	Surrey County	4
Dinwiddie County	7	Sussex County	15
Elizabeth City County—		Warwick County	1
Phoebus	1		
Essex County	3	Total	322
Franklin County	1		

MALARIA—Continued.

City Reports for Week Ended Jan. 5, 1918.

During the week ended January 5, 1918, three cases of malaria were reported at Birmingham, Ala., one case at North Little Rock, Ark., one case at Rocky Mount, N. C., and one case at San Francisco, Cal.

MEASLES.

See Diphtheria, measles, scarlet fever, and tuberculosis, page 117.

PELLAGRA.

State Reports for November and December, 1917.

Place.	New cases reported.	Place.	New cases reported.
Louisiana (Dec. 1-31):		Virginia (Nov. 1-30):	
Beauregard Parish..................	1	Augusta..................	1
Concordia Parish..................	1	Charles City..................	5
Tensas Parish..................	4	Chesterfield County—	
St. Tammany Parish..................	1	Winterpock..................	1
		Henrico County—	
Total..................	7	Richmond..................	1
		King and Queen County..................	1
Massachusetts (Dec. 1-31):		Pittsylvania County—	
Bristol County—		Danville..................	1
Fall River..................	1	Princess Anne County..................	6
Essex County—		Prince George County..................	2
Middleton (town)..................	1	Stafford County..................	1
Middlesex County—		Washington County..................	2
Malden..................	1		
		Total..................	21
Total..................	3		

City Reports for Week Ended Jan. 5, 1918.

Place.	Cases.	Deaths.	Place.	Cases.	Deaths.
Atlanta, Ga...		1	Macon, Ga...		3
Birmingham, Ala...	2	2	Memphis, Tenn...	1	1
Charleston, S. C...		3	New Orleans, La...	1	2
Chicago, Ill...		1	San Antonio, Tex...		6
Galveston, Tex...		1	San Diego, Cal...	1	1

POLIOMYELITIS (INFANTILE PARALYSIS).

State Reports for November and December, 1917.

Place.	New cases reported.	Place.	New cases reported.
Louisiana (Dec. 1-31):		Virginia (Nov. 1-30):	
Iberville Parish..................	1	Accomac County—	
West Feliciana Parish..................	1	Chincoteague..................	4
		Henrico County—	
Total..................	2	Richmond..................	1
Massachusetts (Dec. 1-31):		Louisa County..................	1
Bristol County—		Rockbridge County..................	1
Fall River..................	1	Rockingham County..................	1
Hampden County—			
Springfield..................	1	Total..................	8
Plymouth County—			
Brockton..................	2	West Virginia (Dec. 1-31):	
		Berkeley County..................	1
Total..................	4	Hancock County..................	2
Pennsylvania (Dec. 1-31):		Kanawha County..................	2
Allegheny County..................	2	Roane County..................	1
Blair County..................	1		
Butler County..................	1	Total..................	6
Lancaster County..................	2		
Philadelphia County..................	3		
Total..................	9		

POLIOMYELITIS (INFANTILE PARALYSIS)—Continued.

City Reports for Week Ended Jan. 5, 1918.

During the week ended January 5, 1918, two cases of poliomyelitis were reported at Chicago, Ill., one case at Cincinnati, Ohio, and one case at Taunton, Mass. One death from this disease was reported at Little Rock, Ark.

PNEUMONIA.

City Reports for Week Ended Jan. 5, 1918.

Place.	Cases.	Deaths.	Place.	Cases.	Deaths.
Alameda, Cal.	1	1	Lowell, Mass.	2	2
Auburn, N. Y.	1	1	Lynn, Mass.	2	2
Baltimore, Md.	26	23	Macon, Ga.	3	1
Bethlehem, Pa.	1		Manchester, N. H.	2	2
Boston, Mass.	56	61	Medford, Mass.	1	3
Braddock, Pa.	1		Melrose, Mass.	1	
Brockton, Mass.	3		Montgomery, Ala.	1	1
Cambridge, Mass.	3	5	Nashville, Tenn.	1	9
Canton, Ohio.	2	1	Newark, N. J.	46	14
Chattanooga, Tenn.	4	4	New Bedford, Mass.	7	2
Chelsea, Mass.	1	1	Newport, Ky.	4	1
Chicago, Ill.	169	89	Newton, Mass.	3	2
Cleveland, Ohio.	45	55	North Little Rock, Ark.	1	2
Clinton, Mass.	1		Pawtucket, R. I.	4	4
Dayton, Ohio.	4	10	Petersburg, Va.	1	
Detroit, Mich.	8	41	Philadelphia, Pa.	125	75
Duluth, Minn.	1		Pittsburgh, Pa.	10	73
Fall River, Mass.	5	3	Rochester, N. Y.	11	4
Fitchburg, Mass.	1		St. Joseph, Mo.	2	3
Grand Rapids, Mich.	5	1	San Diego, Cal.	1	3
Hagerstown, Md.	2		Sandusky, Ohio.	1	
Hattiesburg, Miss.	2		San Francisco, Cal.	19	14
Haverhill, Mass.	1		Savannah, Ga.		2
Jackson, Mich.	2	2	Schenectady, N. Y.	2	2
Kalamazoo, Mich.	4	3	Somerville, Mass.	4	2
Kansas City, Kans.	1		Springfield, Mass.	4	4
Kansas City, Mo.	9	19	Taunton, Mass.	3	1
Lancaster, Pa.	1		Toledo, Ohio.	3	3
Lawrence, Mass.	5	1	Waco, Tex.	1	
Leavenworth, Kans.	4		Waltham, Mass.	2	1
Lexington, Ky.	5	3	Wichita, Kans.	7	
Lincoln, Nebr.	8	2	Wilkinsburg, Pa.	3	3
Little Rock, Ark.	1	2	Worcester, Mass.	10	2
Los Angeles, Cal.	19	10			

SCARLET FEVER.

See Diphtheria, measles, scarlet fever, and tuberculosis, page 117.

SMALLPOX.

Texas—El Paso.

During the week ended January 21, 1918, 9 new cases of smallpox, with 2 deaths, occurred at El Paso, Tex., making a total of 44 cases. with 7 deaths, reported since December 12, 1917.

SMALLPOX—Continued.

State Reports for December, 1917.

Place	New cases reported.	Deaths.	Vaccination history of cases.			
			Number vaccinated within 7 years preceding attack.	Number last vaccinated more than 7 years preceding attack.	Number never successfully vaccinated.	Vaccination history not obtained or uncertain.
District of Columbia............	5				5	
Maryland:						
Baltimore City............	10				10	
Allegany County—						
Lonaconing............	1				1	
Cumberland............	15				15	
Westernport............	4				4	
Garrett County—						
Avilton....	9				9	
Avilton, R. D....	4				4	
Frostburg, R. D....	1				1	
Lonaconing, R. D....	1				1	
Grantsville....	7				7	
Total............	52				52	
Massachusetts:						
Essex County—						
Beverly............	2				2	
Hampden County—						
Springfield............	1				1	
Middlesex County—						
Lowell............	1			1		
Malden............	1				1	
Norfolk County—						
Brookline (town)........	1				1	
Suffolk County—						
Boston............	3			2	1	
Worcester County—						
Worcester............	1			1		
Total............	10			4	6	

Miscellaneous State Reports.

Place.	Cases.	Place.	Cases.
Louisiana (Dec. 1-31):		**Virginia (Nov. 1-30):**	
Caddo Parish............	6	Franklin............	5
Calcasieu Parish........	1	Louisa............	1
East Baton Rouge Parish............	2	Roanoke County—	
Iberia Parish............	22	Roanoke............	1
Jackson Parish............	2	Scott County............	1
Jefferson Parish............	3		
Jefferson Davis Parish............	19	Total............	8
Natchitoches Parish........	5		
Orleans Parish............	12	**West Virginia (Dec. 1-31):**	
Rapides Parish............	1	Fayette County............	5
St. Tammany Parish............	24	Harrison County............	3
		Shinston............	12
Total............	97	Kanawha County............	32
		Charleston............	14
Pennsylvania (Dec. 1-31):		Logan County............	11
Allegheny County............	14	Mason County............	1
Armstrong County............	1	Mingo County............	6
Butler County............	1	Ohio County—	
Cambria County............	2	Wheeling............	3
Centre County............	6	Roane County............	2
Clearfield County............	14	Wayne County............	1
Dauphin County............	4	Wood County............	3
Erie County............	5	Parkersburg............	3
Indiana County............	3		
Lehigh County............	1	Total............	96
McKean County............	1		
Mercer County............	3		
Somerset County............	15		
Total............	70		

SMALLPOX—Continued.

City Reports for Week Ended Jan. 5, 1918.

Place.	Cases.	Deaths.	Place.	Cases.	Deaths.
Akron, Ohio	36		Los Angeles, Cal	2	
Alton, Ill	9		Lowell, Mass	1	
Anniston, Ala	10		Memphis, Tenn	... 5	
Birmingham, Ala	1		Milwaukee, Wis	5	
Buffalo, N. Y	4		Minneapolis, Minn	26	
Butte, Mont	8		Montgomery, Ala	5	
Canton, Ohio	10		Nashville, Tenn	2	
Chicago, Ill	13		New Orleans, La	7	
Cincinnati, Ohio	6		New York, N. Y	1	
Cleveland, Ohio	22		North Little Rock, Ark	6	
Columbia, S. C	2		Oklahoma City, Okla	10	
Columbus, Ohio	11		Omaha, Nebr	28	
Dayton, Ohio	6		Pittsburgh, Pa	3	
Denver, Colo	11		Pontiac, Mich	1	
Detroit, Mich	77		Quincy, Ill	2	
Dubuque, Iowa	1		Roanoke, Va	2	
Erie, Pa	2		Saginaw, Mich	1	
Fort Wayne, Ind	14		St. Joseph, Mo	13	
Galesburg, Ill	1		St. Louis, Mo	18	
Grand Rapids, Mich	19		Salt Lake City, Utah	9	
Hattiesburg, Miss	2		San Antonio, Tex	1	1
Indianapolis, Ind	45		Sandusky, Ohio	1	
Jackson, Mich	1		Seattle, Wash	5	
Kansas City, Kans	48		Sioux City, Iowa	4	
Kansas City, Mo	104		Springfield, Ohio	1	
La Crosse, Wis	9		Toledo, Ohio	10	
Lima, Ohio	1		Wichita, Kans	1	
Lincoln, Nebr	3		Wheeling, W. Va	1	
Little Rock, Ark	20				

TETANUS.

City Report for Week Ended Jan. 5, 1918.

During the week ended January 5, 1918, one death from tetanus was reported at St. Louis, Mo.

TUBERCULOSIS.

See Diphtheria, measles, scarlet fever, and tuberculosis, page 117.

TYPHOID FEVER.

State Reports for November and December, 1917.

Place.	New cases reported.	Place.	New cases reported.
District of Columbia (Dec. 1-31):		Louisiana—Continued.	
District of Columbia	13	St. Landry Parish	4
		Tangipahoa Parish	1
Louisiana (Dec. 1-31):		Terrebonne Parish	1
Acadia Parish	2	Union Parish	1
Allen Parish	2	Vermilion Parish	1
Avoyelles Parish	1	West Feliciana Parish	1
Caddo Parish	1		
Calcasieu Parish	9	Total	66
Concordia Parish	2		
De Soto Parish	3	Maryland (Dec. 1-31):	
Evangeline Parish	1	Baltimore City	17
Iberia Parish	5	Allegany County—	
Iberville Parish	2	Cumberland	3
Jefferson Davis Parish	1	Allegany Hospital	1
Orleans Parish	21	Anne Arundel County—	
Plaquemines Parish	1	Davidsonville	2
Rapides Parish	2	Baltimore County—	
St. Charles Parish	1	St. Agnes Hospital	1
St. James Parish	2	Roslyn	1
St. John Parish	1	Fort Howard	1

TYPHOID FEVER—Continued.

State Reports for November and December, 1917—Continued.

Place.	New cases reported.	Place.	New cases reported.
Maryland—Continued.		Massachusetts—Continued.	
Caroline County—		Middlesex County—Continued.	
Denton	2	Waltham	1
Cecil County—		Watertown (town)	1
Chesapeake City (R. D.)	1	Winchester (town)	1
Rising Sun (R. D.)	1	Norfolk County—	
Elkton	1	Quincy	1
Charles County—		Weymouth (town)	1
McChonie (R. D.)	2	Suffolk County—	
Dorchester County—		Boston	5
Reids Grove	2	Worcester County—	
East New Market	1	Athol (town)	1
Wingate	1	North Brookfield (town)	13
Cambridge	2	Worcester	10
Thompsontown	1		
Eastern Shore State Hospital	2	Total	99
Frederick County—			
Frederick	2	Pennsylvania (Dec. 1-31):	
Howard County—		Adams County	6
Ellicott City	1	Allegheny County	17
Kent County—		Armstrong County	7
East Neck Island	1	Beaver County	7
Montgomery County—		Bedford County	2
Forest Glen	1	Berks County	4
Barnesville	1	Blair County	5
Clarksburg	1	Bradford County	3
Prince Georges County—		Bucks County	3
Benning (R. D.)	1	Butler County	3
Oxen Hill	1	Cambria County	1
Sharpersville (R. D.)	1	Chester County	10
Queen Annes County—		Clarion County	1
Queen Anne (R. D.)	1	Clearfield County	1
Somerset County—		Columbia County	6
Crisfield	1	Crawford County	1
Westover (R. D.)	1	Cumberland County	5
Talbot County—		Dauphin County	3
St. Michaels	1	Delaware County	6
Washington County—		Erie County	4
Hagerstown	10	Fayette County	1
Williamsport (R. D.)	1	Franklin County	1
Smithsburg	3	Greene County	1
Boonsboro	1	Jefferson County	3
Wicomico County—		Juniata County	1
Salisbury	1	Lancaster County	5
Peninsula General Hospital	1	Lawrence County	3
Worcester County—		Lebanon County	4
Girdletree	1	Lehigh County	7
		Luzerne County	4
Total	74	Lycoming County	2
		Mercer County	4
Massachusetts (Dec. 1-31):		Mifflin County	3
Barnstable County—		Montgomery County	4
Orleans (town)	1	Montour County	1
Berkshire County—		Northampton County	3
Adams (town)	3	Northumberland County	3
Lee (town)	1	Perry County	1
North Adams	1	Philadelphia County	14
Bristol County—		Potter County	2
Fall River	25	Schuylkill County	1
New Bedford	7	Somerset County	3
Swansea (town)	1	Tioga County	2
Essex County—		Venango County	1
Gloucester	1	Washington County	3
Haverhill	1	Wayne County	1
Lawrence	4	Westmoreland County	5
Lynn	2	York County	6
Peabody (town)	1		
Franklin County—		Total	184
Orange (town)	1		
Montague (town)	1	Virginia (Nov. 1-30):	
Warwick (town)	2	Accomac County	6
Hampden County—		Tangier	1
Springfield	5	Albemarle County	1
Middlesex County—		Alexandria County	1
Everett	1	Alleghany County	2
Newton	1	Covington	2
Somerville	3	Amelia County	4

TYPHOID FEVER—Continued.

State Reports for November and December, 1917—Continued.

Place.	Total cases reported.	Place.	Total cases reported.
Virginia—Continued.		Virginia—Continued.	
App. matt x County	1	Prince Edward County	5
Augusta County	5	Prince George County	3
Bath County	1	Pulaski County	1
Bedford County	1	Pulaski	1
Bland County	1	Roanoke County	1
Botetourt County	2	Rockbridge County	1
Buchanan County	9	Rockingham County	1
Buckingham County	3	Elkton	4
Campbell County—		Harrisonburg	1
Lynchburg	1	Russell County	7
Caroline County	3	Shenandoah County	4
Carroll County	3	Woodstock	1
Culpeper County	2	Smyth County	3
Culpeper	1	Southampton County	2
Dickinson County	3	Stafford County	1
Cantwood	1	Surry County—	
Dinwiddie County—		Dendron	1
Petersburg	5	Sussex County	3
Essex County	1	Wakefield	1
Fairfax County	5	Tazewell County	11
Fauquier County—		Graham	9
Warren n.	1	Pocahontas	3
Floyd County	5	Washington County	4
Franklin County	1	Abingdon	2
Grayson County	3	Damascus	6
Greene County	2	Westmoreland County	1
Hanover County	1	Wise County	3
Henrico County	7	Wise	1
Richmond	13	Wythe County—	
Henry County	1	Rural Retreat	1
Isle of Wight County	1		
King and Queen County	1	Total	227
Lancaster County	1		
Lee County	10	West Virginia (Dec. 1-31):	
Loudoun County	2	Berkeley County	1
Louisa County	1	Fayette County	3
Mathews County	2	Braxton County	2
Mecklenburg County	2	Greenbrier County	1
Middlesex County	2	Hancock County	1
Urbanna	1	Jackson County	2
Montgomery County	8	Kanawha County	5
Nelson County	3	McDowell County	1
Norfolk County	2	Marshall County	1
Portsmouth—		Mingo County	2
	1	Monroe County	2
Northampton County—		Ohio County—	
Cape Charles	1	Wheeling	19
Northumberland County	3	Summers County	1
Nottoway County—		Tucker County	4
Blackstone	1		
Patrick County	2	Total	45
Pittsylvania County	2		
Princess Anne County	2		

City Reports for Week Ended Jan. 5, 1918.

Place.	Cases.	Deaths.	Place.	Cases.	Deaths.
Akron, Ohio	1		Danville, Ill	1	
Albany, N. Y	4		Davenport, Iowa	2	
Augusta, Ga	1		Dayton, Ohio	1	
Austin, Tex		1	Detroit, Mich	9	
Baltimore, Md	3	2	Fall River, Mass	1	
Beaver Falls, Pa	1		Fort Wayne, Ind	1	1
Birmingham, Ala	1		Fort Worth, Tex	1	
Boston, Mass	1	1	Grand Rapids, Mich	1	
Buffalo, N. Y	1		Haverhill, Mass	1	
Camden, N. J	1		Indianapolis, Ind	1	
Charleston, S. C	2		Kalamazoo, Mich	1	
Chattanooga, Tenn	1		Kansas City, Kans	1	
Chicago, Ill	4		Kansas City, Mo	1	
Cleveland, Ohio	1		Lawrence, Mass		1
Columbia, S. C	1		Lincoln, Nebr		1

TYPHOID FEVER—Continued.

City Reports for Week Ended Jan. 5, 1918—Continued.

Place.	Cases.	Deaths.	Place.	Cases.	Deaths.
Lowell, Mass	1		Roanoke, Va	1	
Memphis, Tenn		1	Rochester, N. Y	1	
Milwaukee, Wis	4		Saginaw, Mich	1	
Mobile, Ala	1		St. Louis, Mo	2	
Morristown, N. J	1		Salt Lake City, Utah	1	1
Newark, N. J	7		San Antonio, Tex	1	1
New Bedford, Mass	2		San Francisco, Cal	4	
New Orleans, La	5	2	Savannah, Ga	1	
Newport News, Va		1	Schenectady, N. Y		1
New York, N. Y	7	3	Seattle, Wash	3	1
North Little Rock, Ark	1		Springfield, Mass	1	
Omaha, Nebr	1		Springfield, Ohio	1	
Petersburg, Va	1		Troy, N. Y	2	
Philadelphia, Pa	3	1	Waco, Tex	3	
Pittsfield, Mass	1		Washington, D. C	1	1
Portsmouth, N. H	1		Wheeling, W. Va		1
Racine, Wis		1	Winston-Salem, N. C	1	
Richmond, Va	1		Zanesville, Ohio	1	

TYPHUS FEVER.

City Reports for Week Ended Jan. 5, 1918.

During the week ended January 5, 1918, two deaths from typhus fever were reported at Baltimore, Md., and one case at San Antonio, Tex.

DIPHTHERIA, MEASLES, SCARLET FEVER, AND TUBERCULOSIS.

State Reports for November and December, 1917.

State.	Cases reported.			State.	Cases reported.		
	Diph-theria.	Mea-sles.	Scarlet fever.		Diph-theria.	Mea-sles.	Scarlet fever.
District of Columbia (December).	88	268	121	Pennsylvania (December).	1,551	1,620	999
Louisiana (December)	72	626	21	Virginia (November)	380	646	126
Maryland (December)	191	463	143	West Virginia (December).	73	21	59
Massachusetts (December).	1,156	1,920	671				

City Reports for Week Ended Jan. 5, 1918.

City.	Popula-tion as of July 1, 1916 (estimated by U. S. Census Bureau).	Total deaths from all causes.	Diphtheria.		Measles.		Scarlet fever.		Tuber-culosis.	
			Cases.	Deaths.	Cases.	Deaths.	Cases.	Deaths.	Cases.	Deaths.
Over 500,000 inhabitants:										
Baltimore, Md	589,621	244	13	1	45	2	13	1	26	28
Boston, Mass	756,476	298	104	15	117	4	23	1	39	21
Chicago, Ill	2,497,722	706	201	23	38	2	75	2	390	82
Cleveland, Ohio	674,073	240	18	1	13		4	1	28	29
Detroit, Mich	571,784	230	72	4	10	5	44	4	18	16
Los Angeles, Cal	503,812	128	14	1	23		10		41	19
New York, N. Y	5,602,841	1,681	163	29	705	14	95	2	170	165
Philadelphia, Pa	1,709,518	671	55	16	35		37	2	81	70
Pittsburgh, Pa	579,090	251	12	3	123		9		18	12
St. Louis, Mo	757,309	220	96	1	46		30		42	17

DIPHTHERIA, MEASLES, SCARLET FEVER, AND TUBERCULOSIS—
Continued.

City Reports for Week Ended Jan. 5, 1918—Continued.

City.	Population as of July 1, 1916 (estimated by U. S. Census Bureau).	Total deaths from all causes.	Diphtheria.		Measles.		Scarlet fever.		Tuberculosis.	
			Cases.	Deaths.	Cases.	Deaths.	Cases.	Deaths.	Cases.	Deaths.
From 300,000 to 500,000 inhabitants:										
Buffalo, N. Y.............	468,558	142	20	3	14	......	11	......	20	13
Cincinnati, Ohio..........	410,476	154	19	1	2	......	11	......	24	22
Jersey City, N. J........	306,345		14	......	16	......	4	......	25	......
Milwaukee, Wis..........	436,535	96	10	......	57	......	37	1	22	9
Minneapolis, Minn.........	363,454		21	......	19	......	11	......		
Newark, N. J.............	408,894	143	12	3	132	3	14	......	20	19
New Orleans, La..........	371,447	174	18	......	33	......	4	......	26	20
San Francisco, Cal.......	463,516	130	18	......	26	......	19	1	34	9
Seattle, Wash...........	348,639	54	7	......	71	......	7	......	9	7
Washington, D. C.........	363,680	151	14	2	70	2	26	1	15	17
From 200,000 to 300,000 inhabitants:										
Columbus, Ohio..........	214,878	84	2	......	5	......	29	......	7	6
Denver, Colo............	263,800	68	6	1	25	......	17	......		11
Indianapolis, Ind.........	271,708		33	......	21	......	30	......	3	......
Kansas City, Mo.........	297,847	115	6	2	53	......	10	......	3	13
Portland, Oreg..........	265,463	39		......	11	......	5	......	2	1
Providence, R. I.........	254,960	79	17	1	9	......	5	1	1	7
Rochester, N. Y.........	256,417	50	14	1	16	......	12	......	6	3
From 100,000 to 200,000 inhabitants:										
Albany, N. Y...........	104,199		1	......	6	......	2	......	12	......
Atlanta, Ga...........	190,558		9	2	17	......	3	......		7
Birmingham, Ala........	181,762	79	2	......	144	2	2	......	1	8
Bridgeport, Conn.......	121,579	32	10	......	2	......	2	......	1	3
Cambridge, Mass........	112,981	34	6	......	26	1	1	......	3	......
Camden, N. J..........	106,253		7	......	55	......	2	......	2	......
Dayton, Ohio..........	127,224	54	7	......	2	......	4	1	......	......
Fall River, Mass.......	128,466		6	1	6	......	1	......	9	1
Fort Worth, Tex.......	104,562	37	5	1	6	......	1	......	......	1
Grand Rapids, Mich.....	128,291	40	3	......	8	......	4	......	6	1
Hartford, Conn........	110,900	63	4	1	6	......	6	......	2	4
Houston, Tex..........	112,307	43	2	1	27	......		......	4	6
Lawrence, Mass........	100,500	30	4	......	1	......		......	4	2
Lowell, Mass..........	113,245	44		......	1	......		......	4	1
Lynn, Mass...........	102,425	22	1	......	4	......	3	......	3	1
Memphis, Tenn........	148,995	55	5	1		......	2	......	7	6
Nashville, Tenn.......	117,057	44	8	1	......	......	6	......	3	5
New Bedford, Mass.....	118,158	46	4	......	22	......	4	......	5	5
New Haven, Conn......	149,685		2	......	1	......	2	......	4	5
Oakland, Cal..........	188,604	49	1	......	1	......	6	......	6	3
Omaha, Nebr..........	115,470	41	3	......	28	......	6	......		7
Reading, Pa..........	109,381	42	8	......	1	......		......	1	9
Richmond, Va.........	156,687	75	15	2	9	......	6	......	4	6
Salt Lake City, Utah...	117,399	35		......	43	......	13	1		1
San Antonio, Tex.......	121,831		1	......	7	......		......		16
Springfield, Mass......	105,942	34	15	......	12	......	3	......	3	2
Syracuse, N. Y........	155,724		15	2	39	......	13	......	2	2
Tacoma, Wash.........	112,770		1	......		......	4	......		
Toledo, Ohio..........	191,554	55	3	......	10	......	10	......	2	5
Trenton, N. J.........	111,544	41	7	......	4	......	2	......	2	5
Worcester, Mass.......	163,314	64	1	......	15	......	4	......	4	2
From 50,000 to 100,000 inhabitants:										
Akron, Ohio...........	85,825	......	5	......	4	......	6	......		......
Allentown, Pa.........	63,505	19	6	......	3	......	2	......	2	......
Atlantic City, N. J.....	57,660			......	2	......		......	8	......
Augusta, Ga..........	50,245	12		......	19	......	1	......		......
Bayonne, N. J.........	69,863		2	......	1	......		......	1	......
Berkeley, Cal.........	57,053	15	1	......	2	......	3	......		......
Brockton, Mass.......	67,449	18		......	2	......	5	......	3	3
Canton, Ohio.........	60,852	18	2	......		......	9	......		......
Charleston, S. C.......	60,734	37	2	......	2	......		......		2
Chattanooga, Tenn.....	60,075	5		......	34	......	1	......	2	1
Covington, Ky........	57,114	19	1	......		......		......	2	1
Duluth, Minn.........	94,495	13	2	1	15	......	12	......	4	1
El Paso, Tex.........	63,705	20		......		......		......		5
Erie, Pa.............	75,195		7	......		......	4	......	2	39
Fort Wayne, Ind......	76,183	22	9	......		......		......		......
Harrisburg, Pa.......	72,015	33	2	......	3	......	5	......	3	2
Hoboken, N. J........	77,214	25	3	1	27	1	1	......		5

DIPHTHERIA, MEASLES, SCARLET FEVER, AND TUBERCULOSIS—
Continued.

City Reports for Week Ended Jan. 5, 1918—Continued.

City.	Population as of July 1, 1916 (estimated by U. S. Census Bureau).	Total deaths from all causes.	Diphtheria.		Measles.		Scarlet fever.		Tuberculosis.	
			Cases.	Deaths.	Cases.	Deaths.	Cases.	Deaths.	Cases.	Deaths.
From 50,000 to 100,000 inhabitants—Continued.										
Johnstown, Pa	68,529	24	9	1	1		6		1	
Kansas City, Kans	99,437		1		4		6		1	
Lancaster, Pa	50,853		2				2		1	
Little Rock, Ark	57,343	12			35		2		2	1
Malden, Mass	51,155		10		10		3		1	1
Manchester, N. H	78,283	25	1		7		4		3	3
Mobile, Ala	58,221	24	1		4				1	1
New Britain, Conn	53,794	9	2		1				10	
Norfolk, Va	89,612				10		4			2
Oklahoma City, Okla	92,943	16	2				2			
Passaic, N. J	71,744	17	5				1			
Pawtucket, R. I	59,411	29	3	2			3	1		
Portland, Me	63,867	24	1	1	100		1			1
Rockford, Ill	55,185	22			2		3			3
Sacramento, Cal	66,895	32			3		4		6	2
Saginaw, Mich	55,642	15	1				3		2	2
St. Joseph, Mo	85,236	14	8		1		4		2	1
San Diego, Cal	53,330	21	5		63		3			
Savannah, Ga	68,805	40			11		1		1	5
Schenectady, N. Y	99,519	28	2				3			2
Sioux City, Iowa	57,078		1				10			
Somerville, Mass	87,039	21	5		61		5		4	2
South Bend, Ind	68,946	20	1	1			1		3	1
Springfield, Ill	61,120	20	6	2	3					
Springfield, Ohio	51,550	15			1		1		3	
Terre Haute, Ind	66,063	25			2		1		1	2
Troy, N. Y	77,916				1		7		3	3
Wichita, Kans	70,722				27		7			
Wilkes-Barre, Pa	76,776	16	5		7		5	1		
Wilmington, Del	94,265	37	5		3					4
From 25,000 to 50,000 inhabitants:										
Alameda, Cal	27,732	4	6						1	1
Auburn, N. Y	37,385	11	2							1
Austin, Tex	34,814	19	1		8					
Brookline, Mass	32,730	9	2		2		3			
Butler, Pa	27,632	11	2		6					1
Butte, Mont	43,425	15	3		3		22			
Charlotte, N. C	39,823				18		2		1	
Chelsea, Mass	46,192	27			9				1	3
Chicopee, Mass	29,319	10			7	1			1	3
Columbia, S. C	34,611		1		9					
Cumberland, Md	26,074	10								
Danville, Ill	32,261	7			1					
Davenport, Iowa	48,811		1				7			
Dubuque, Iowa	39,873		1	2	1					
East Orange, N. J	42,458	9			26				2	
Elgin, Ill	28,203	5	1		5					
Everett, Mass	39,233	9	8		10		1		4	
Fitchburg, Mass	41,781	7	3	1	2				6	
Galveston, Tex	41,863	17	1		6		1			1
Green Bay, Wis	29,353	10	2		3		3			
Hagerstown, Md	25,679		2		3		1			
Haverhill, Mass	48,477	6	1		12		2		3	2
Jackson, Mich	35,363	19					10		1	3
Kalamazoo, Mich	48,686	23	8		26				1	1
Kenosha, Wis	31,576	4	11	1	1		5	1		
Knoxville, Tenn	38,676		1	1	3		3		2	2
La Crosse, Wis	31,677	12	3						1	
Lexington, Ky	41,097	18	1		26				28	11
Lima, Ohio	35,384	17	1				1			1
Lincoln, Nebr	46,515	12	6	1	5		11			
Lorain, Ohio	36,964	1	4	1	1		1			
Lynchburg, Va	32,940	12			4					
Macon, Ga	45,757	7	2		32		1			
Medford, Mass	26,234	12	2	1	6					2
Montclair, N. J	26,318	5			6		2		1	
Montgomery, Ala	43,285	7			22					
Nashua, N. H	27,327	9		2		1				
Newburgh, N. Y	29,603	9	1		46				1	
New Castle, Pa	41,133						3		6	
Newport, Ky	31,927	2	1							

DIPHTHERIA, MEASLES, SCARLET FEVER, AND TUBERCULOSIS—Continued.

City Reports for Week Ended Jan. 5, 1918—Continued.

City.	Population as of July 1, 1916 estimated by U. S. Census Bureau).	Total deaths from all causes.	Diphtheria.		Measles.		Scarlet fever.		Tuberculosis.	
			Cases.	Deaths.	Cases.	Deaths.	Cases.	Deaths.	Cases.	Deaths.
From 25,000 to 50,000 inhabitants—Continued.										
Newton, Mass.	43,715	16	3		6				1	
Niagara Falls, N. Y.	37,353	5	2				1		1	
Norristown Pa.	31,401	16			2				1	1
Ogden, Utah	31,404	5					5			
Orange, N. J.	33,080	12	1		4					
Pasadena, Cal.	46,450	6							1	2
Perth Amboy, N. J.	41,185				20		2		1	
Petersburg, Va.	25,582	10			5				1	1
Pittsfield, Mass.	38,629	5	1		8		3		1	3
Portsmouth, Va.	39,651	14	1		1					
Quincy, Ill.	36,798	6			13		2			
Quincy, Mass.	38,136	10	1		1		1		2	
Racine, Wis.	46,486	18			1		1			
Roanoke, Va.	43,284	10	2		2				1	
Rock Island, Ill.	28,938	14			3					
San Jose, Cal.	38,902				7				1	
Steubenville, Ohio	27,445	12								
Superior, Wis.	46,226	6	1		3		2			
Taunton, Mass.	36,283	8	1		1				1	
Waco, Tex.	33,385	2			6		2		1	
Waltham, Mass.	30,570	9			1					
Watertown, N. Y.	29,894	1	1		1					
West Hoboken, N. J.	43,139	9			1					
Wheeling, W. Va.	43,377	18					1		2	
Winston-Salem, N. C.	31,155				20		3			
Zanesville, Ohio	30,863	9			1				1	
From 10,000 to 25,000 inhabitants:										
Alexandria, La.	18,333	12			62					
Alton, Ill.	22,874	10	3	2	8		1			
Ann Arbor, Mich.	15,010	6		1					1	
Anniston, Ala.	14,112		3		10					
Beaver Falls, Pa.	13,532		2		1		2			
Berlin, N. ?	13,599	2								
Bethlehem, Pa.	11,142		2						2	
Braddock, Pa.	21,685		3							
Chillicothe, Ohio	15,470		1		7		2			
Clinton, Mass.	[1]13,075	6							1	1
Coffeyville, Kans.	17,548				21					
Concord, N. H.	22,609	6	2		1		3			
Galesburg, Ill.	24,276	7								
Hattiesburg, Miss.	16,482	10			7					
Kearney, N. J.	23,539	7			29				3	
Kokomo, Ind.	20,930	6								
Leavenworth, Kans.	[1]19,363	3			4				2	
Long Branch, N. J.	15,395	2	2		1					
Marinette, Wis.	[1]14,610	1								
Melrose, Mass.	17,445	5			1		2			
Morristown, N. J.	13,284	2								
Nanticoke, Pa.	23,126	4	1		1		1		1	
New Albany, Ind.	23,020	2			1		1		2	1
Newburyport, Mass.	15,243	6	1	1	1					
New London, Conn.	20,985	3	1				1			
Newport News, Va.	20,562	19	3		13					
North Adams, Mass.	[1]22,019	8	3						1	
Northampton, Mass.	19,929	9					4		3	1
North Little Rock, Ark.	14,907	2			5					
Plainfield, N. J.	23,805	12	1	1	1				1	1
Pontiac, Mich.	17,524	8	2		5		2		1	1
Portsmouth, N. H.	11,666		1	1	2		3			
Rocky Mount, N. C.	12,067	7							2	1
Rutland, Vt.	14,831	2								
Sandusky, Ohio	20,193	9					2			
Saratoga Springs, N. Y.	13,821	6			1		2		1	
Spartanburg, S. C.	21,365	9	1		5				1	
Steelton, Pa.	15,548	2							1	
Washington, Pa.	21,618				8				1	
Williamsport, Pa.	23,228	14	1		6				1	
Woburn, Mass.	15,969	4								

[1] Population Apr. 15, 1910; no estimate made.

FOREIGN.

Examination of Rats—Shanghai.

During the six weeks ended December 1, 1917, 1,617 rats were examined at Shanghai. No plague infection was found. The last plague-infected rat at Shanghai was reported found May 6, 1916.

GREAT BRITAIN.

Examination of Rats—Liverpool.

During the five weeks ended December 15, 1917, 1,843 rats were examined at Liverpool. No plague infection was found.

INDO-CHINA.

Cholera—Plague—Smallpox—Leprosy—September, 1917.

During the month of September, 1917, 74 cases of cholera, 34 cases of plague, and 193 cases of smallpox were notified in Indo-China. For the month of August, 1917, the reported prevalence was as follows: Cholera, 328 cases; plague, 50 cases; smallpox, 234 cases. The distribution of these diseases during the month of September, 1917, was as follows:

Cholera.—Province of Anam, 13 cases; Cambodia, 19 cases; Cochin-China, 32 cases; Kwang-Chow-Wan, 10 cases; total, 74 cases. The total for the corresponding month of the previous year was 107 cases.

Plague.—Province of Anam, 12 cases; Cambodia, 12 cases; Cochin-China, 10 cases; total, 34 cases. The total for September, 1916, was 26.

Smallpox.—Province of Anam, 61 cases; Cambodia, 7 cases; Cochin-China, 124 cases; Tonkin, 1 case; total, 193 cases. The total for September, 1916, was 25.

Leprosy.—During the month of September, 1917, 20 cases of leprosy were notified in Indo-China, of which 12 cases were notified in the city of Hanoi, Tonkin, and 8 in two localities in Cochin-China.

CHOLERA, PLAGUE, SMALLPOX, AND TYPHUS FEVER.

Reports Received During Week Ended Jan. 25, 1918.[1]

CHOLERA.

Place.	Date.	Cases.	Deaths.	Remarks.
India:				
Calcutta....................	Oct. 14–27............	....	26	
Indo-China:				
Provinces................			....	Sept. 1-30, 1917: Cases, 74; deaths,
Anam................	Sept. 1–30..........	13	10	37.
Cambodia..............	....do..............	19	12	
Cochin-China..........	....do..............	. 32	13	
Kwang-Chow-Wan.....	....do..............	10	2	

PLAGUE.

India...................			....	Sept. 30-Nov. 10, 1917: Cases,
Mandalay..................	Oct. 14–20............	....	20	80,105; deaths, 58,838.
Indo-China:				
Provinces................			....	Sept. 1-30, 1917: Cases, 34; deaths,
Anam................	Sept. 1–30..........	12	11	30.
Cambodia..............	....do..............	12	11	
Cochin-China..........	....do..............	10	8	

SMALLPOX.

Place.	Date.	Cases.	Deaths.	Remarks.
Australia:				
New South Wales.........			....	Dec. 5, 1917: 1 case.
Kurri Kurri.............	Dec. 5...........	1	....	
Brazil:				
Rio de Janeiro............	Oct. 28–Dec. 1.....	206	63	
Canada:				
Montreal..................	Jan. 6–12..........	1	....	
China:				
Harbin...................	May 14–June 30...	20	....	Chinese Eastern Ry.
Do...................	July 1 Oct. 15....	4	....	Do.
Manchuria Station........	May 14–June 30...	6	....	Do.
Do...................	July 1 Oct. 15....	3	....	Do.
Shanghai.................	Nov. 25-Dec. 16....	21	45	
Tientsin.................	Nov. 25-Dec. 8....	5	....	
France:				
Lyon.....................	Dec. 10-16........	2	2	
Indo-China:				
Provinces.................			....	Sept. 1–30, 1917: Cases 121;
Anam................	Sept. 1–30..........	61	12	deaths, 56.
Cambodia..............	....do..............	.	.	
Cochin-China..........	....do..............	124	44	
Tonkin..............	....do..............	1		
Italy:				
Castellamare....	Dec. 10..........	2	....	Among refugees.
Florence.................	Dec. 1–15........	17	4	
Naples................	To Dec. 10.	2	....	Do.
Newfoundland:				
St. Johns....	Dec. 29 Jan. 11....	25	....	
Philippine Islands:				
Manila..................	Dec. 2 8..........	2	....	

TYPHUS FEVER.

Brazil:				
Rio de Janeiro............	Oct. 28 Dec. 1.....	7	....	
Chosen (Formosa):				
Seoul.....................	Nov. 1 30.........	1	....	
Great Britain:				
Manchester................	Dec. 2 8..... .	1	....	
Japan:				
Nagasaki..................	Dec. 10 16..... ...	1	5	
Russia:				
Siberia—				
Vladivostok............	Oct. 29 Nov. 4....	12	1	

[1] From medical officers of the Public Health Service, American consuls, and other sources.

CHOLERA, PLAGUE, SMALLPOX, AND TYPHUS FEVER—Continued.

Reports Received from Dec. 29, 1917, to Jan. 18, 1918.[1]

CHOLERA.

Place.	Date.	Cases.	Deaths.	Remarks.
China:				
Antung	Nov. 26–Dec. 2....	3	1	
India:				
Bombay	Oct. 28–Nov. 3. ...	2	1	
Calcutta	Sept. 16–Oct. 6....	......	42	
Java:				
West Java		......	......	Oct. 19–Nov. 8, 1917: Cases, 19
Batavia	Oct. 19–Nov. 8....	13	4	deaths, 7.
Persia:				
Mazanderan Province—				
Astrabad	July 31	......	......	Present.
Barfrush	July 1–27	84	23	
Chahmirzad	......	......	......	26 cases reported July 31, 1917.
Chahrustagh	June 15–July 25..	10	8	
Kharek	May 28–June 11...	21	13	
Sari	July 3–29	273	144	
Yelchambe-Bazar	June 3	6	......	
Philippine Islands:				
Provinces		......	......	Nov. 18–24, 1917: Cases, 262;
Antique	Nov. 18–24	32	23	deaths, 167.
Bohol	do	10	9	
Iloilo	do	57	38	
Leyte	do	4	3	
Mindanao	do	77	47	
Occidental Negros	do	47	30	
Oriental Negros	do	35	17	
Provinces		......	......	Nov. 25–Dec. 1, 1917: Cases, 251;
Antique	Nov. 25–Dec. 1	18	9	deaths, 166.
Bohol	do	36	19	
Capiz	do	1	1	
Iloilo	do	67	40	
Leyte	do	3	2	
Mindanao	do	38	30	
Occidental Negros	do	71	47	
Oriental Negros	do	18	17	
Romblon	do	1	1	
Siam:				
Bangkok	Sept. 16–22	1	1	

PLAGUE.

Place.	Date.	Cases.	Deaths.	Remarks.
British Gold Coast:				
Axim	Jan. 8	......	......	Present.
Ceylon:				
Colombo	Oct. 14–27	4	3	
Egypt:				Jan. 1–Nov. 15, 1917: Cases, 728;
Port Said	July 31–22	1	2	deaths, 398.
India:				Sept. 16–29, 1917: Cases, 18,653;
Bombay	Oct. 28–Nov. 3...	18	17	deaths, 17,810. Oct. 21–27,
Calcutta	Sept. 16–29	......	2	1917: Cases, 13,571; deaths,
Karachi	Oct. 21–Nov. 10...	8	5	9,390.
Madras Presidency	Oct. 31–Nov. 6....	1,555	1,200	
Rangoon	Oct. 21–27	9	10	
Indo-China:				
Saigon	Oct. 31–Nov. 18...	8	4	
Siam:				
Bangkok	Sept. 16–22	1	1	
Straits Settlements:				
Singapore	Oct. 28–Nov. 3....	1	2	

[1] From medical officers of the Public Health Service, American consuls, and other sources. For reports received from June 30, 1917, to Dec. 28, 1917, see Public Health Reports for Dec. 28, 1917. The tables of epidemic diseases are terminated semiannually and new tables begun.

CHOLERA, PLAGUE, SMALLPOX, AND TYPHUS FEVER—Continued.

Reports Received from Dec. 29, 1917, to Jan. 18, 1918—Continued.

SMALLPOX.

Place.	Date.	Cases.	Deaths.	Remarks.
Algeria:				
Algiers.....................	Nov. 1-30.........	1	....	
Australia:				
New South Wales..........	....	....	....	Sept. 28-Nov. 20, 1917: Cases, 9.
Abermain..............	Oct. 25-Nov. 20...	3	....	
Cessnock..............	Sept. 28-Oct. 11...	3	....	Newcastle district.
Warren................	Oct. 12-13...	3	....	
Brazil:				
Pernambuco.............	Nov. 1-15.........	1	....	
Rio de Janeiro...........	Sept. 30-Oct. 27...	313	88	
Sao Paulo...............	Oct. 29-Nov. 4....	....	2	
Canada:				
New Brunswick—				
Kent County.........	Dec. 4.............	....	....	Outbreak. On main line Canadian Ry., 25 miles north of Moncton.
Ontario—				
Hamilton..............	Dec. 16-22...	1	....	
Sarnia................	Dec. 9-15...	1	....	
Windsor..............	Dec. 30-Jan. 5.....	1	....	
Quebec—				
Montreal..............	Dec. 16-Jan. 5.....	5	....	
China:				
Amoy.....................	Oct. 27-Nov. 4...	....	....	Present.
Antung...................	Dec. 3-9...	1	1	
Chungking...............	Nov. 11-17...	....	....	Do.
Dairen...................	Nov. 18-24...	1	....	
Mukden..................	Nov. 11-24...	....	....	Do.
Shanghai.................	Nov. 18-Dec. 2...	9	17	Cases, foreign; deaths among natives.
Tientsin.................	Nov. 11-17...	2	....	
Cuba:				
Habana..................	Jan. 7.............	1	....	Nov. 8, 1917; 1 case from Coruna, Dec. 5, 1917; 1 case.
Marianao................	Jan. 8.............	1	....	6 miles distant from Habana.
Egypt:				
Alexandria...............	Nov. 12-18......	1	....	
Cairo....................	July 23-Aug. 5.....	5	1	
France:				
Lyon....................	Nov. 18-Dec. 9.....	4	1	In hospital. From Givors.
Great Britain:				
Birmingham..............	Nov. 11-17...	19	....	
India:				
Madras..................	Oct. 31-Nov. 6....	4	1	
Indo-China:				
Saigon...................	Oct. 29-Nov. 18...	41	12	
Italy:				
Turin...................	Oct. 29-Nov. 25...	77	116	
Java:				
Mid-Java................	Oct. 10-30...	25	....	
West Java...............	....	....	....	Oct. 19-Nov. 8, 1917: Cases, 59; deaths, 8.
Batavia............	Nov. 2-8.........	1	....	
Mexico:				
Mazatlan................	Dec. 5-11.........	....	1	
Mexico City.............	Nov. 11-17.........	9	....	
Piedras Negras..........	Jan. 11.........	200	....	
Newfoundland:				
St. Johns...............	Dec. 8-28.........	14	....	
Philippine Islands:				
Manila..................	Oct. 28-Nov. 10...	3	....	
Portugal:				
Lisbon..................	Nov. 4-10.........	1	....	
Portuguese East Africa:				
Lourenço Marques.........	Aug. 1-Sept. 30...	....	4	
Russia:				
Moscow..................	Aug. 26-Oct. 6....	22	2	
Petrograd...............	Aug. 31-Oct. 27...	59	3	
Spain:				
Coruna.................	Dec. 2-15.........	....	4	
Seville.................	Oct. 1-30.........	....	9	
Venezuela:				
Maracaibo...............	Dec. 2-8.........	....	1	

CHOLERA, PLAGUE, SMALLPOX, AND TYPHUS FEVER—Continued.

Reports Received from Dec. 29, 1917, to Jan. 18, 1918—Continued.

TYPHUS FEVER.

Place.	Date.	Cases.	Deaths.	Remarks.
Algeria:				
Algiers	Nov. 1–30	2		
Austria:				
South Australia				Nov. 11–17, 1917: Cases, 1.
Canada:				
Ontario—				
Kingston	Dec. 2–8	3		
Quebec—				
Montreal	Dec. 16–22	2	1	
China:				
Antung	Dec. 3–9	5	1	
Egypt:				
Alexandria	Nov. 8–25	110	44	
Cairo	July 23–Sept. 23	23	8	
Port Said	July 30–Sept. 23	3	3	
Greece:				
Saloniki	Nov. 11–24		19	
Japan:				
Nagasaki	Nov. 26–Dec. 9	4		
Java:				
East Java				Oct. 15–21, 1917: Cases, 5; deaths, 2.
Mid-Java				Oct. 10–30, 1917:Cases,22;deaths,2.
Samarang	Oct. 17–30	4	1	
West Java				Oct. 19–Nov. 8, 1917: Cases, 33; deaths, 5.
Batavia	Oct. 19–Nov. 8	22	4	
Mexico:				
Aguascalientes	Dec. 15		2	
Mexico City	Nov. 11–Dec. 15	337		
Russia:				
Archangel	Sept. 1–14	7	2	
Moscow	Aug. 26–Oct. 6	49	2	
Petrograd	Aug. 31–Oct. 27	22		
Sweden:				
Goteborg	Nov. 18–24	1		
Tunisia:				
Tunis	Nov. 30–Dec. 6		1	

X

PUBLIC HEALTH REPORTS

VOL. 33.	FEBRUARY 1, 1918	No. 5

MORBIDITY STATISTICS OF WAR INDUSTRIES NEEDED.[1]

By B. S. WARREN, Surgeon, and EDGAR SYDENSTRICKER, Public Health Statistician, United States Public Health Service.

It is hardly necessary, before a group of those who understand so intimately the difficulties which beset the epidemiologist, to amplify upon the need for more accurate, uniform, and complete statistics of morbidity. This need has long been realized. It has been well said, and with the emphasis of frequent reiteration, that "no health department, State or local, can effectively prevent or control disease without knowledge of when, where, and under what conditions cases are occurring." Morbidity statistics, as an index of a population's health, are regarded without question as one of the most needed instruments and one of the most desired goals of preventive medicine.

Yet it must be confessed that we have been proceeding rather leisurely in availing ourselves of this instrument—so leisurely, in fact, that we are seriously handicapped at a time when maximum efficiency is required by national necessity of all individuals and all agencies of production and of service. There is at present no field of service in which the demand for maximum efficiency is more urgent or in which maximum efficiency is more vital than that of industrial labor, especially labor in the so-called "war industries." Such statistics of the causes of lost time by workers as we now have, indicate that while the usual major "industrial" causes of unemployment, such as slack demand for labor, have practically ceased to be operative, the time lost because of physical disability remains fairly constant.[2] In other words, to borrow the phraseology of Mr. W. H. Beveridge, we have pretty nearly reached what in normal times is the "irreducible minimum of unemployment."[3] So far as this so-called "irreducible minimum" is due to preventable sickness,

---

[1] Read before the Section on Vital Statistics of the American Public Health Association, Washington, D. C., October 18, 1917.

[2] See the statistics of unemployment among members of representative Massachusetts unions published in the Massachusetts Reports on the Statistics of Labor, and of idleness in labor unions in New York published monthly by the New York State Industrial Commission.

[3] Unemployment: A Problem of Industry, p. 72.

the responsibility for its further reduction rests upon those whose
duty it is to see that the workers' physical efficiency is at its highest
point. The obligation goes even further. While industry to-day
needs every ounce of labor force that it can get, yet in the struggle
upon which the nation has engaged itself, the length and strain of
which can not be foreseen, it is a shortsighted policy to gauge labor
efficiency in terms of the output of over-exertion. The men and
women upon whose work depends the steady productiveness of mechanical power are irreplaceable factors. To make them more efficient,
and to conserve them, it is not enough that the existing standards of
labor be maintained; it may be found advisable, just as it has been
found in Great Britain, to revise and even to raise and make more
rigid our standards. The point in this which is of vital concern to us
is that whatever may be necessary to be done should be accomplished with as great a degree of scientific accuracy and of properly
directed effort as is possible. Efficiency in the prevention of disease
among industrial workers was never more clearly indispensable than
now.

It is difficult to see how this can be accomplished without a de-
pendable current index of the health of the workers, such as a properly administered system of morbidity statistics will afford. It is
not sufficient for us to assume that certain manifestly desirable
measures, such as vigilance against specific poisons and against
excessive fatigue in occupations already recognized as hazardous
in these respects, and the wholesale sanitation of places of work and
of industrial communities, are all that are required for conserving
the health of wage-earners and their families. These measures may
be adequate, but we do not know. Certainly the inquiries of the
British Health of Munitions Workers Committee do not suggest
such a conclusion.[1] On the contrary, the problem appears to be
more complex because of the effect of certain factors already operating but not yet accurately evaluated, and because of the possible
effects of other factors which may be called into existence by new
conditions.

Some of these factors may be mentioned. For example, one of
the immediate factors which may have a relation to the health
of wage earners is the readjustment occurring in the labor supply.
New industries have been brought into existence by the war and there
has been a greatly increased activity on the part of the basic indus-

---

[1] The reader is referred to the convenient reprints of the memoranda and reports of the British Health
of Munitions Workers Committee which have been issued, in compliance with a resolution of the American Council of National Defense, by the United States Bureau of Labor Statistics as Bulletins 221, 222, 223,
and 230, and which have been, from time to time, abstracted in the Monthly Review of the Bureau of
Labor Statistics. See especially the memoranda relating to diet (in Bulletin 222), and employment of
women and children (in Bulletin 223), and the reports on causes and conditions of lost time, incentives to
work with special reference to wages, etc. (in Bulletin 230).

tries. In the face of an unprecedented demand for labor have come the withdrawal of a large number of younger male workers for the Army and Navy and for their supporting services, the entrance of more women and of older men into industry, and a tendency toward a greater employment of physically and mentally deficient persons. As the result of these readjustments, we may naturally expect some significant changes in the status of the workers' health. A second possible factor is the incentive to unusual effort on the part of workers because of higher wages, or the pressure of increased living costs, or the desire on the part of employers to obtain maximum production. The possible effects of work without necessary rest, especially on female workers, have been made a subject of study by the British munitions authorities which indicates significant conclusions. A third factor is the possible tendency toward relaxing hygienic standards in factories under what are termed "emergency conditions." The tendency is, of course, a natural one, but it is nevertheless fraught with great danger. A fourth factor, of by no means small importance, is the effect upon the health of the wage earner and his family of the lack of proper diet. There are already unmistakable evidences, for example, that the difficulties of proper distribution and the increased cost of foodstuffs are having serious effects upon the health of textile workers in certain parts of the South.

These are only a few of the factors which should be detected and evaluated. Their influence upon the health of workers is impossible of satisfactory indication or measurement unless there is a systematic recording of sickness in such a way as to permit of analysis with respect to sex, age, occupation, and various other conditions of physical status and environment of the persons concerned. The continued emphasis which Sir George Newman, the chairman of the British Health of Munitions Workers Committee, and his associates, have placed upon the adequate recording of sickness as fundamentally necessary to intelligent steps for the prevention of lessened efficiency in war industries,[1] has for us the significant implication that we should not fail to benefit by British experience without further delay. In many other lines of service the progress which ordinarily would have been reached with a tolerable degree of satisfaction in years has,

---

[1] "Every case of lost time or absence (on the part of the worker) calls for inquiry. It should be properly recorded. A study of such records is certain to disclose the existence of adverse influences or circumstances to-day unsuspected, which may denote the beginning of sickness. * * * Medical certificates should be required, correctly recorded and carefully examined. Week by week the management should scrutinize their chart of sickness returns and study their rise and fall. Only thus can they keep themselves advised of this vital matter." Memorandum No. 10 (on "Sickness and Injury") of the British Health of Munitions Workers Committee, reprinted in United States Bureau of Labor Statistics Bulletin 222: Hours, Fatigue, and Health in British Munition Factories (pp. 61-71). See also the report on "Causes and Conditions of Lost Time" by T. Loveday, reprinted in United States Bureau of Labor Statistics Bulletin 230 (pp. 42-95), especially the chapter on "Sickness" and the significance of sickness statistics (pp. 48-71).

under the spur of necessity and in a remarkable spirit of cooperation, been attained in months. The suggestion appears pertinent, therefore, that we should no longer look upon statistics of morbidity as a goal to be attained at some indefinite time in the future, but should regard it as an instrument which is immediately necessary to the task in hand.

The inadequacy of the morbidity statistics now available hardly needs to be emphasized except for the purpose of suggesting specific defects to be remedied and available agencies for the recording of sickness. What statistics we now have are fragmentary, not uniform, unrelated to conditions except in a few very general respects, and extremely scanty. The regularly collected statistics of morbidity by our Federal, State, and local health agencies consist of weekly and monthly reports of merely the number of cases of certain diseases (principally the communicable diseases) occurring among the general population. They are not available for analysis for a specific population such as the wage earners in a given industry, and they can not be correlated with age or sex or occupation. The only other morbidity records available are those of cases of disabling sickness and nonindustrial accidents among wage earners who belong to union, establishment, and other varieties of sickness insurance funds, and among the employees of a few manufacturing and transportation companies which attempt to record all cases of sickness. These records lack uniformity in many respects. The funds have different regulations governing the kinds of sickness reported and the actual proportion of reportable cases. In very few instances can they be classified according to sex, and hardly any instance has been found in which the ages of both the exposed population and the disabled individuals have been recorded. The records apply only to insured wage earners who are often a distinctly selected group, excluding those who are physically defective from chronic diseases and other causes, the temporary or casual laborers, and the large mass of those who are unable to pay the cost of insurance. Even in those establishments where the medical service is of an efficient type and where the records are kept in a businesslike and accurate manner, sex, age, and occupation are not recorded in such a way as to be expressed in relation to exposure. While several community sickness surveys have already afforded extremely valuable statistics, and this method, as well as the enumeration of serious sicknesses on census days, will yield even more important data, their usefulness is limited because they do not afford a continuous and therefore a current index to the status of a population's health.

Is it feasible to secure adequate and continuous morbidity statistics for war industries?

Let us briefly review, first, what the minimum requirements for useful statistics of morbidity should be. Tentatively the following are suggested:[1]

1. Exposure, in years or in months, of the workers who should be classifiable according to sex, age, and occupation.

2. Cases of sickness (at least those causing disability), including (a) sex, age, and occupation of persons affected, and (b) cause of sickness with time of onset, length of disability, and nature of termination.

For certain establishments where the records may be made more complete, and in special studies of the causes of sickness, various other data relating to the length of time in given occupations, the economic status, the sanitary conditions, and the like, of the exposed population and of the persons affected, are possible of collection. The foregoing, however, refers to minimum requirements for a maximum volume of data.

Second, the practicability of securing current morbidity statistics which will measure up to these requirements. It is believed that their collection is practicable within certain bounds for the following reasons:

1. A large number of industrial and transporting establishments are already in the habit of recording disabling cases of sickness, and a considerable number of the larger establishments employ industrial physicians and provide medical service. The tendency is unmistakably toward an extension of sick-benefit funds and of medical supervision and service.

2. There is a very evident willingness on the part of many employers, as well as on the part of many organizations of labor and associations for sick benefits, to cooperate in every way possible with the public health agencies. This willingness was clearly manifested before the outbreak of the war and has been undoubtedly greatly increased since the war began.

3. There already exists, therefore, a basis for an important beginning in the recording of morbidity It is believed practicable to utilize the facilities that already are available, provided, (a) that the recording of exposure and incidence be extended to all the em-

[1] In this connection reference may be made to the resolution passed by the Annual Conference of State and Territorial Health Officers with the United States Public Health Service in Washington, April 30-May 1, 1917. This resolution set forth "as minimum standard morbidity tables for publication in annual reports of State and Territorial health authorities tables giving the distribution of cases of the notifiable diseases, as follows:

"1. Chronologically by months; 2. By sex; 3. By 5-year age groups up to 25 years, and by 10-year age groups after 25 years; 4. By termination (recovery or death); 5. Geographically by counties and municipalities." (U. S. Public Health Service Public Health Reports, May 11, 1917; 32.690.)

See also "Vital Statistics: 1917 Progress Report of the Committee on Relation of 1920 Census to Vital, Statistics to the Section in Vital Statistics, American Public Health Association," by William H. Guilfoy M. D., chairman, and Edwin W. Kopf, corresponding secretary, of the committee, New York Medical Journal, Oct. 6, 1917 (CVI:633-636).

ployees of each plant, (b) that uniformity be established in the form of the medical certificate and in the records of age, sex, and occupation of the persons exposed and affected, (c) that regularity of reporting be effected, and (d) that there be a responsible central supervising, assembling, and publishing agency for the statistics recorded. There can be little doubt that with such a beginning as the cooperation of even a few large establishments would make possible, the systematic collection and analysis of morbidity statistics for not only the "war industries," but for other industries would rapidly develop.

This conclusion has been reached after a survey of the existing disability records of over 400 establishment sick-benefit funds and a more detailed inquiry into and conference with a number of establishments having such funds, or medical supervision of employees, or both, and maintaining regular records of disabling sickness for part or all of their employees. It is fully realized that considerable modifications of the suggested minimum requirements may be found advisable when further consideration is given and as experience is gained after the work is begun. The foregoing is believed to be a practical suggestion for inaugurating a method of morbidity statistics for industries which will be of great service with the least possible delay, and which will afford a foundation for later development.

Whether or not this or some other suggestion is the more feasible is, however, of less importance than the fact that morbidity records of such a kind as to afford a current index of the health of industrial labor are not merely desirable but necessary in the present emergency. They are necessary because they are an instrument without which public health administration can not meet efficiently do its important part in helping to maintain our industrial forces at their full strength. It does not seem that we can afford to continue to be handicapped in this respect.

PREVALENCE OF DISEASE.

No health department, State or local, can effectively prevent or control disease without knowledge of when, where, and under what conditions cases are occurring.

UNITED STATES.

EXTRA-CANTONMENT ZONES—CASES REPORTED WEEK ENDED JAN. 29.

Camp Bowie, Tex.—Fort Worth: Measles 19, broncho pneumonia 4, lobar pneumonia 25, smallpox 12, chicken pox 3, meningitis 2, gonorrhea 38, syphilis 18, pulmonary tuberculosis 2. Polytechnic: German measles 1. Mansfield: Pneumonia 1.

Camp Dodge, Iowa.—Des Moines: Smallpox 34, scarlet fever 6, measles 3, spinal meningitis 2, gonorrhea 1, typhoid fever 4, tuberculosis 1. Bloomfield township: Smallpox 4. Grimes: Pneumonia 1. Granger: Measles 2.

Camp Funston, Kans.—Leonardsville: Chicken pox 1, smallpox 2. Cleburne, measles 7, smallpox 1. St. George: measles 1. Pottawattamie County: smallpox 1. Junction City: Chicken pox 4, scarlet fever 3, measles 19, smallpox 2, whooping cough 1, mumps 1. Riley: Measles 13. Manhattan: measles 138, pneumonia 4, chicken pox 4, scarlet fever 4, meningitis carriers 4, mumps 5. Ogden: Diphtheria 1, measles 4, pneumonia 1.

Camp Gordon, Ga.—Atlanta: Gonococcus infection 1, scarlet fever 4, epidemic cerebrospinal meningitis 8, typhoid fever 2, German measles 5, measles 15, diphtheria 5, whooping cough 2, pneumonia 2, syphilis 1, tuberculosis 1. Decatur, DeKalb County: Measles 2, diphtheria 2. Chamblee, DeKalb County: Diphtheria 1. College Park, Fulton County: Scarlet fever 1, smallpox 1.

Camp Greene, N. C.—Chicken pox 6, measles 44, mumps 4, syphilis 10, syphilis and gonorrhea 1, German measles 4, gonorrhea 7, gonorrhea and syphilis 2, whooping cough 4, scarlet fever 2, cerebrospinal meningitis 4, gonorrhea and bubo 1, chancroids and gonorrhea 1; all in Charlotte township.

Camp Hancock, Ga.—Measles: Augusta 20, North Augusta 1, Blythe 1, Bartons Chapel 3; and German measles: Augusta 25, North Augusta 14; and lobar pneumonia: Augusta 3, Hephzibah 3, Bartons Chapel 1; and pulmonary tuberculosis: Augusta 3; and cerebrospinal meningitis: Augusta 1; and chicken pox: Augusta 1; and typhiod fever: Hephzibah 1.

Camp Jackson, S. C.—Columbia (week ending 26th): Cerebrospinal meningitis 4, mumps 2, pneumonia 1, whooping cough 3, scarlatina 1.

Fort Leavenworth, Kans.—German measles: City 37. Measles: City 7, county 5. Typhoid: City 1. Smallpox: City 3, county 1. Chicken pox: City 1, county 1. Lobar pneumonia: City 2, county 5. Diphtheria: City 1, county 1.

Camp Lewis, Wash.—German measles: Lake View 2, Spanway 7, Roy, 3 Steilacoom 1, Gravelly Lake 1, Country Club 1. Chicken pox: Spanway 3. Tuberculosis: Lake View 1.

134

Camp Logan, Tex.—Houston: Chicken pox 4, diphtheria 1, German measles 4, gonorrhea 3, measles 21, mumps 3, pneumonia 7, smallpox 2, scarlet fever 1, typhoid fever 1, tuberculosis 4. Houston Heights: Measles 1. Harrisburg: Pneumonia 1. Pasadena: Pneumonia 1.

Camp MacArthur, Tex.—Waco: Chicken pox 1, German measles 20, gonococcus 3, measles 5, meningitis, epidemic, 1, mumps 1, pneumonia 3, rabies in animals 1, smallpox 1, syphilis 1, tuberculosis 1.

Camp McClellan, Ala.—Anniston: Smallpox 3, measles 4, pneumonia 4, tuberculosis 2, chicken pox 10, German measles 5, mumps 2. Beat 2: Smallpox 2, pneumonia 1, chicken pox 1, measles 2, German measles 2. Beat 3: Smallpox 1. Beat 4: Smallpox 4. Beat 13: Smallpox 1, chicken pox 1. Beat 23: German measles 3.

Fort Oglethorpe, Ga.—Chattanooga: Scarlet fever 4, tuberculosis 4, pneumonia 4, syphilis 8, German measles 44, measles 14, mumps 8, gonorrhea 13, diphtheria 1, smallpox 3, meningitis 3, chicken pox 17. East Chattanooga: Mumps 1, chicken pox 1 North Chattanooga: Chicken pox 3, German measles 1, pneumonia 1. East Lake German measles 1, whooping cough 1, tuberculosis 1. St. Elmo: German measles 1. Lake View, Ga.: Mumps 1. Rossville, Ga.: German measles 1, mumps 1, tuberculosis 1, pneumonia 1.

Camp Pike, Ark.—Little Rock: Measles 20, chicken pox 3, smallpox 36, pneumonia 6, German measles 5, mumps 2, malaria 1, syphilis 15, gonorrhea 20, erysipelas 1, chancroid 2, meningitis 2, whooping cough 2, typhoid 1. North Little Rock: Measles 2, smallpox 6, tuberculosis 3, diphtheria 1, mumps 1, gonorrhea 1, chancroid 1. Scotts Measles 1, German measles 1, syphilis 1, pneumonia 3, septic sore throat 1. Sweet Home: Pneumonia 1, erysipelas 1, smallpox 1. Kerr: Whooping cough 2. Toltec Tuberculosis 1. Levy: Pneumonia 1, meningitis 1. McAlmont: Pneumonia 1.

Camp Sevier, S. C.—Chick Springs, rural: Two measles. Greenville, City View One epidemic cerebrospinal meningitis. Greenville: Six measles.

Camp Shelby, Miss.—Forrest County: Hattiesburg: Chicken pox 1, diphtheria 2, gonorrhea 1, malaria 2, measles 8, meningitis 1, mumps 2, pneumonia 3, smallpox 7, syphilis 1, typhoid 1. Carnes: Measles 7. Covington County: Seminary: Diphtheria 1. Collins: Smallpox 1. Green County: McLain: Smallpox 1. Harrison County: Lyman: Smallpox 1. Saucier: Diphtheria 1. Lamar County: Sumrall: Meningitis 1. Clyde: Smallpox 2.

Camp Sheridan, Ala.—Montgomery: Measles 25, German measles 10, tonsilitis 2, chicken pox 3, tuberculosis 1, pneumonia 3, smallpox 3, diphtheria 2, meningitis suspect 1. Capitol Heights: Chicken pox 2. Chisholm: Measles 1. Cloverdale Chicken pox 1, German measles 1. Rural district in 5-mile zone: Measles 1.

Camp Sherman, Ohio.—Diphtheria: Chillicothe 1. German measles: Chillicothe 39. Measles: Chillicothe 6, Liberty Township 1. Lobar pneumonia: Chillicothe 1. Scarlet fever: Chillicothe 7.

Camp Zachary Taylor, Ky.—Jefferson County: Chicken pox 1, German measles 1, typhoid fever 1. Louisville: Diphtheria 8, chicken pox 7, German measles 17, measles 39, mumps 1, pneumonia 3, meningitis, cerebrospinal 2, tubercular 1, smallpox 5, scarlet fever 4, tuberculosis, pulmonary, 26, typhoid fever 3, whooping cough 3.

Tidewater Health District, Va.—Newport News: Measles 17, pneumonia 3, tuberculosis 1, chicken pox 1. Hampton: Measles 5, tuberculosis 1. Phoebus: Pneumonia 1.

Camp Wadsworth, S. C.—Spartanburg city: Measles 2, German measles 17, whooping cough 4, chicken pox 5, smallpox 1, pneumonia 3, cerebrospinal meningitis 2, mumps 1, syphilis 2. Spartanburg County: Pneumonia 1, mumps 1, cerebrospinal meningitis 1

CURRENT STATE SUMMARIES.

Alabama.

From Collaborating Epidemiologist Perry, telegram dated January 28, 1918:

Two cases cerebrospinal meningitis, Mobile.

Arkansas.

From Collaborating Epidemiologist Garrison, telegram dated January 29, 1918:

Smallpox: Three cases Morrilton, 3 Clarksville, 6 Spadra, 1 Earle, 3 Monticello, 1 Bigelow, 3 Sebastian County, 28 Little Rock, 3 North Little Rock, 2 Sweethome, 6 Texarkana. One meningitis Little Rock. One tuberculosis Little Rock, 1 North Little Rock, 1 Toltec, 2 Sebastian County. Ten measles Little Rock, 2 North Little Rock, 2 Scotts, 1 Texarkana, 12 Thornton. Two malaria Little Rock. Thirty-two chicken pox, 1 diptheria, and 21 whooping cough, Sebastian County.

California.

From the State Board of Health of California, telegram dated January 29, 1918:

Epidemic diseases showed continued increases last week. Measles, chicken pox, and scarlet fever, especially. Smallpox: One each in Sacramento, Los Angeles, Fresno, Glendale, and Tulare County; 2 in San Francisco. Five cases epidemic cerebrospinal meningitis: One each in Oakland, Los Angeles County, and Orange County; 2 in San Diego County. Diphtheria increased in San Francisco and surrounding territory.

Reported by mail for preceding week (ended Jan. 19):

Anthrax	1	Pneumonia	67
Cerebrospinal meningitis	2	Poliomyelitis	1
Chicken pox	216	Ophthalmia neonatorum	1
Diphtheria	64	Scarlet fever	87
Erysipelas	8	Smallpox	12
German measles	176	Syphilis	37
Gonococcus infection	36	Trachoma	1
Leprosy	2	Tuberculosis	138
Malaria	7	Typhoid fever	13
Measles	376	Whooping cough	72
Mumps	68		

Indiana.

From the State Board of Health of Indiana, telegram dated January 28, 1918:

Scarlet fever: Epidemic Portland, Hanover, Laporte County, Hickville, DeKalb County; 4 cases Muncie, 3 cases Anderson. Diphtheria: Epidemic Evansville, Bloomfield; 1 death each Attica, Goshen, Martinsville. Measles: Epidemic Pleasant Lake, Greensburg. Smallpox: Sullivan County, Albion, Linton, Bloomfield, French Lick. Whooping cough: Epidemic Marion; 1 death each Boonville, Petersburg, Jonesboro.

Kansas.

From Collaborating Epidemiologist Crumbine, telegram dated January 28, 1918:

Meningitis: Salina 1, Coffeyville 2, Concordia 1, Marysville 1, Mina 2. Meningitis carriers: Manhattan 3. Smallpox: Kansas City 52; week ending January 26.

Louisiana.

From Collaborating Epidemiologist Dowling, telegram dated January 28, 1918:

Meningitis (excluding Rapides): DeSoto 1, 19th; Caddo 1, 21st; Vermilion 1, 24th; Ascension 1, 26th; Grant 1, DeSoto 1, 27th; Orleans 1, 28th.

Massachusetts.

From Collaborating Epidemiologist Kelley, telegram dated January 28, 1918:

Unusual prevalence January, to date. Diphtheria: Ashby 6, Dedham 11. Measles. Beverly 54, Hopkinton 14, Needham 60, Winchester 29. Additional for week. Measles: Marlboro 107. Scarlet fever: Shelburne 5. Whooping cough: Falmouth 22. Smallpox: Boston 1, Natick 1.

Minnesota.

From Collaborating Epidemiologist Bracken, telegram dated January 28, 1918:

Smallpox: Douglas County, Ida township 5, Isanti County, Springvale township 1, Kittson County, Hallock township 2, Rice County, Northfield city 6, Travers County, Parnell township 1, unusual prevalence; Brainard city, Crow Wing County, Mora village, Kanabeck County. Scarlet fever: Lichfield village, Meeker County. Two reports cerebrospinal meningitis since January 21.

Mississippi.

From Collaborating Epidemiologist Leathers, telegram dated January 29, 1918:

Two deaths cerebrospinal meningitis Leake County, 1 case each Holmes, Grenada, Simpson.

New Jersey.

From Collaborating Epidemiologist Bowen, telegram dated January 28, 1918:

Investigating unusual number of cases intestinal disturbance, possibly dysentery, which occurred two weeks ending January 26 in Montclair, Glen Ridge, Bloomfield, Bayonne, and possibly in some other towns using the same water supply. Extensive outbreak of same character in Elizabeth, different water supply.

South Carolina.

From Collaborating Epidemiologist Hayne, telegram dated January 28, 1918:

Thirteen new cases meningitis. Believe epidemic developing.

Vermont.

From Collaborating Epidemiologist Dalton, telegram dated January 28, 1918:

One case epidemic meningitis, Burlington. No unusual prevalence.

Virginia.

From Collaborating Epidemiologist Traynham, telegram dated January 28, 1918:

One case smallpox Wise County. One case cerebrospinal meningitis Bedford County, one case Halifax County.

Washington.

From Collaborating Epidemiologist Tuttle, telegram dated January, 28, 1918:

German measles prevalent throughout State. No unusual outbreaks of disease.

RECIPROCAL NOTIFICATION.

Minnesota.

Cases of communicable diseases referred during December, 1917, to other State health departments by department of health of the State of Minnesota.

Disease and locality of notification.	Referred to health authority of—	Why referred.
Smallpox:		
India Township, Roseau County.	Hannah, Cavalier County, N. Dak.	Exposed to smallpox at Hannah, N. Dak.
Tuberculosis:		
Mayo Clinic, Rochester, Olmsted County.	Lake Village, Chicot County, Ark.; Rock Island, Rock Island County, Ill.; Crawfordsville, Montgomery County, Ind.; Terre Haute, Vigo County, Ind.; Washington, Washington County, Iowa.; Dennison, Crawford County, Iowa; Ironwood, Gogebic County, Mich.; Glendive, Dawson County, Mont.; Poplar, Sheridan County, Mont.; Olive, Auster County, Mont.; Rulo, Richardson County, Nebr.; McClusky, Sheridan County, N. Dak.; Hankinson, Richland County, N. Dak.; Brisbane, Morton County, N. Dak.; Lead City, Lawrence County, S. Dak.; Milton Junction, Rock County, Wis.; Milwaukee, Milwaukee County, Wis.; Shullsburg, Lafayette County, Wis.; Cheyenne, Laramie County, Wyo.; Lethbridge, Alberta, Canada; Winnipeg, Manitoba, Canada; Sault Ste. Marie, Ontario, Canada; Drummer, Saskatchewan, Canada; Hazelmere, Saskatchewan, Canada; Milnor, Sergent County, N. Dak.	8 advanced cases, 12 moderately advanced, 9 apparently arrested, 1 incipient, and 1 (stage of disease not given) cases left Mayo Clinic for homes.
Thomas Hospital, Minneapolis, Hennepin County.		Open case left Thomas Hospital for home in North Dakota.
Typhoid fever:		
Breckenridge, Wilkin County.	Hankinson, Richland County, N. Dak.	Visiting at Hankinson, N. Dak., 3 weeks previous to first symptoms.
Brainerd, Crow Wing County.	Park River, Walsh County, N. Dak.	Worked as farm laborer near Park River, N. Dak., 3 weeks before first symptoms.
Abbott Hospital, Minneapolis, Hennepin County.	Hankinson, Richland County, N. Dak.	Staying at home in North Dakota 3 weeks previous to first symptoms.
Glenwood, Pope County.	Near Mauer, Saskatchewan, Canada.	Nursed typhoid case in Saskatchewan previous to her own illness.

ANTHRAX.

Massachusetts—Middlesex County.

During the month of December, 1917, 4 cases of anthrax were notified in Middlesex County, Mass. Three of the cases occurred at Woburn and 1 at Stoneham; all in persons who had been employed in or about tanneries, although 1, a carpenter, had only repaired a door in a tannery.

CEREBROSPINAL MENINGITIS.

Virginia—Norfolk.

On January 26, 1918, 5 cases of cerebrospinal meningitis were notified in Norfolk, Va., making a total of 14 cases reported among civilians up to the date of the report.

State Reports for December, 1917.

Place.	New cases reported.	Place.	New cases reported.
Kansas:		New Jersey:	
Allen County	1	Burlington County	1
Cherokee County—		Essex County	9
Galena	1	Hudson County	3
Cloud County—		Passaic County	3
Aurora	1	Somerset County	1
Ellsworth County—		Union County	2
Ellsworth	1		
Geary County—		Total	19
Junction City	2	Ohio:	
Lincoln County—		Adams County	1
Lincoln	1	Athens County	1
Sedgwick County—		Cuyahoga County	5
Wichita	1	Franklin County	4
Shawnee County—		Hamilton County	2
Auburn	1	Lucas County	3
Richland	1	Mahoning County	1
Topeka	1	Medina County	1
Wyandotte County—		Montgomery County	4
Kansas City	2	Ross County	8
Total	13	Total	30
Maine:		Rhode Island:	
Cumberland County—		Providence	3
Portland	1		
		South Carolina:	
Minnesota:		Darlington County	2
Hennepin County—		Greenville County	3
Minneapolis	1	Hampton County	1
Itasca County -		Richland County	2
Nashwauk	1		
Mower County—		Total	8
Austin	1		
Ramsey County—		South Dakota:	
St. Paul	1	Miner County	2
St. Louis County—			
Biwabik	1		
Duluth	1		
Total	6		

CEREBROSPINAL MENINGITIS Continued.

City Reports for Week Ended Jan. 12, 1918.

Place.	Cases.	Deaths.	Place.	Cases.	Deaths.
Albany, N. Y.	1	....	Los Angeles, Cal.	1	1
Alexandria, La.	11	4	Louisville, Ky.	1	1
Anniston, Ala.	1	....	Macon, Ga.	6	....
Augusta, Ga.	1	....	Milwaukee, Wis.	1	1
Boston, Mass.	1	1	Montgomery, Ala.	....	1
Buffalo, N. Y.	2	....	Newark, N. J.	3	2
Charleston, S. C.	1	....	New Orleans, La.	2	1
Charlotte, N. C.	2	....	Newport News, Va.	2	....
Chattanooga, Tenn.	3	1	New York, N. Y.	4	2
Chicago, Ill.	8	5	Norfolk, Va.	1	1
Chillicothe, Ohio.	1	....	Oklahoma City, Okla.	1	1
Cincinnati, Ohio.	1	1	Omaha, Nebr.	1	1
Cleveland, Ohio.	1	....	Philadelphia, Pa.	3	3
Columbus, Ohio.	1	....	Pittsburgh, Pa.	....	1
Dayton, Ohio.	1	1	Richmond, Va.	....	1
Duluth, Minn.	1	....	St. Louis, Mo.	2	....
Fitchburg, Mass.	1	....	San Jose, Cal.	1	....
Flint, Mich.	1	....	Spartanburg, S. C.	4	....
Hartford, Conn.	2	....	Superior, Wis.	1	....
Kansas City, Kans.	1	....	Troy, N. Y.	1	....
Kansas City, Mo.	5	2	Washington, D. C.	3	1
Kokomo, Ind.	1	1	Worcester, Mass.	1	....
Little Rock, Ark.	3	1			

DIPHTHERIA.

See Diphtheria, measles, scarlet fever, and tuberculosis, page 153.

ERYSIPELAS.

City Reports for Week Ended Jan. 12, 1918.

Place.	Cases.	Deaths.	Place.	Cases.	Deaths.
Ann Arbor, Mich.	1	....	McKeesport, Pa.	1	....
Atlanta, Ga.	....	1	Milwaukee, Wis.	3	....
Atlantic City, N. J.	1	....	Newark, N. J.	3	....
Baltimore, Md.	4	....	New Castle, Pa.	1	....
Boston, Mass.	....	2	New Orleans, La.	....	2
Buffalo, N. Y.	4	....	Norristown, Pa.	2	....
Chicago, Ill.	15	....	Oakland, Cal.	1	....
Chillicothe, Ohio.	1	....	Pasadena, Cal.	1	....
Cincinnati, Ohio.	2	....	Philadelphia, Pa.	7	1
Cleveland, Ohio.	4	1	Pittsburgh, Pa.	11	1
Denver, Colo.	8	1	Pontiac, Mich.	1	....
Detroit, Mich.	2	1	Portland, Oreg.	2	....
El Paso, Tex.	....	1	Providence, R. I.	....	1
Erie, Pa.	1	....	St. Joseph, Mo.	4	....
Everett, Mass.	1	....	St. Louis, Mo.	3	....
Flint, Mich.	1	....	St. Paul, Minn.	3	....
Grand Rapids, Mich.	1	....	Salt Lake City, Utah.	....	1
Harrisburg, Pa.	1	....	San Diego, Cal.	1	....
Kansas City, Mo.	2	....	San Francisco, Cal.	1	....
Little Rock, Ark.	....	1	Somerville, Mass.	....	1
Los Angeles, Cal.	6	1			

MALARIA.

State Reports for December, 1917.

Place.	New cases reported.	Place.	New cases reported.
Kansas:		South Carolina:	
Anderson County—		Chester County......................	1
Garnett........................	1	Dorchester County..................	12
Crawford county—		Marion County......................	1
Pittsburg (R. D.)...............	2		
Osage County—		Total........................	14
Osage City......................	1		
Total........................	4		
New Jersey:			
Essex County......................	2		
Sussex County......................	1		
Total........................	3		

City Reports for Week Ended January 12, 1918.

During the week ended January 12, 1918, one case of malaria was reported at Newark, N. J., one case at San Francisco, Cal., and two cases at Waco, Tex.

MEASLES.

See Diphtheria, measles, scarlet fever, and tuberculosis, page 152.

PELLAGRA.

State Reports for December, 1917.

Place.	New cases reported.	Place.	New cases reported.
Kansas:		South Carolina—Continued.	
Shawnee County—		Chester County.....	1
Topeka.........................	1	Greenville County.................	1
South Carolina:		Laurens County...................	1
Anderson County..................	1	Spartanburg County...............	8
Cherokee County..................	1	Total..........	13

City Reports for Week Ended Jan. 12, 1918.

Place	Cases.	Deaths.	Place.	Cases.	Deaths.
Atlanta, Ga......................	....	2	Nashville, Tenn..............	1	....
Birmingham, Ala..............	2	2	New Orleans, La.............	2	2
Charleston, S. C..............	....	1	Portsmouth, Va..............	....	1
Houston, Tex..................	....	1	Spartanburg, S. C...........	....	1
Mobile, Ala...................	....	1	Washington, D. C............	6	....

PNEUMONIA.

City Reports for Week Ended Jan. 12, 1918.

Place.	Cases.	Deaths.	Place.	Cases.	Deaths.
Akron, Ohio	1		Los Angeles, Cal	19	12
Alexandria, La	4	1	Louisville, Ky	1	17
Anniston, Ala	1		Lowell, Mass	2	3
Atlantic City, N. J	1	2	Lynn, Mass	6	4
Baltimore, Md	43	31	Macon, Ga	1	10
Boston, Mass	66	26	McKeesport, Pa	2	1
Braddock, Pa	1		Medford, Mass	1	1
Brockton, Mass	3	2	Montgomery, Ala	1	1
Butler, Pa	1		Newark, N. J	75	11
Cambridge, Mass	2	1	New Bedford, Mass	3	3
Chattanooga, Tenn	2		New Castle, Pa	3	
Chelsea, Mass	3	1	Newport, Ky	2	2
Chicago, Ill	218	91	Newport News, Va	3	3
Cleveland, Ohio	57	40	Newton, Mass	1	1
Cumberland, Md	2	2	Norristown, Pa	2	1
Dayton, Ohio	5	12	Philadelphia, Pa	235	95
Duluth, Minn	1	1	Pittsburgh, Pa	74	64
Erie, Pa	2		Providence, R. I	1	4
Everett, Mass	1	1	Reading, Pa	2	4
Fall River, Mass	9		Rochester, N. Y	3	3
Fitchburg, Mass	2	4	St. Joseph, Mo	4	2
Flint, Mich	2	3	San Antonio, Tex	2	10
Grand Haven, Mich	1		San Diego, Cal	6	2
Grand Rapids, Mich	5	2	Sandusky, Ohio	1	
Hagerstown, Md	2		San Francisco, Cal	16	13
Harrisburg, Miss	1		Schenectady, N. Y	2	3
Haverhill, Mass	2		Somerville, Mass	1	1
Jackson, Mich	4	1	Spartanburg, S. C	1	
Kalamazoo, Mich	1		Springfield, Mass	5	4
Kansas City, Kans	6		Stockton, Cal	1	
Kansas City, Mo	35	22	Toledo, Ohio	1	3
Lancaster, Pa	3		Waco, Tex	3	
Lawrence, Mass	2	4	Washington, Pa	1	
Leavenworth, Kans	4		Wichita, Kans	8	1
Lexington, Ky	1	5	Wilkinsburg, Pa	2	2
Lincoln, Nebr	7	1	Wilmington, N. C	2	4
Little Rock, Ark	4	1	Worcester, Mass	11	9

POLIOMYELITIS (INFANTILE PARALYSIS).

State Reports for November and December, 1917.

Place.	New cases reported.	Place.	New cases reported.
Minnesota (Dec. 1–31, 1917):		Ohio—Continued.	
Brown County—		Hamilton County	1
Springfield	1	Mahoning County	2
Meeker County—		Stark County	
Onamia Township	1		
Olmsted County—		Total	7
Rochester	1		
		Oregon (Nov. 1–30, 1917):	
Total	3	Clackamas County	1
		Multnomah County—	1
New Jersey (Dec. 1–31, 1917):		Portland	
Morris County	1		
		Total	2
North Dakota (Dec. 1–31, 1917):			
Walsh County	1	South Carolina (Dec. 1–31, 1917):	1
		Darlington County	1
Ohio (Dec. 1–31, 1917):		Lee County	
Clermont County	2		
Delaware County	1	Total	2

City Reports for Week Ended Jan. 12, 1918.

Place.	Cases.	Deaths.	Place.	Cases.	Deaths.
Atlanta, Ga	3		Detroit, Mich		1
Boston, Mass		1	Lowell, Mass	2	1
Chicago, Ill	1	1	New York, N. Y	1	

SCARLET FEVER.

See Diphtheria, measles, scarlet fever, and tuberculosis, page 152.

SMALLPOX.

Missouri—Kansas City.

During the period of 6 days, January 24–29, 1918, 207 cases of smallpox were notified at Kansas City, Mo.

Texas—Eagle Pass—Virulent Smallpox.

During the week ended January 28, 1918, 7 new cases of smallpox were notified at Eagle Pass, Tex., making a total of 51 cases reported since October 1, 1917. During the week from January 21 to 28, 1918, 4 deaths from smallpox were reported, making a total of 11 deaths reported at Eagle Pass since October 1, 1917.

Texas—El Paso—Correction.

The report in relation to smallpox at El Paso, Tex., as published in the Public Health Reports of January 25, 1918, on page 112, was an error. The report was for Eagle Pass instead of El Paso.

State Reports for December, 1917.

Place	New cases reported.	Deaths.	Vaccination history of cases.			
			Number vaccinated within 7 years preceding attack.	Number last vaccinated more than 7 years preceding attack.	Number never successfully vaccinated.	Vaccination history not obtained or uncertain
Kansas:						
Allen County -						
Bronson..........	1					*
Humboldt..........	2				2	
Iola..........	3				3	
Atchison County -						
Atchison..........	1				1	
Barber County—						
Hardtner..........	1			1		
Lake City..........	1				1	
Barton County—						
Hoisington..........	2			1	1	
Bourbon County --						
Fort Scott..........	1				1	
Fulton (R. D.)..........	1				1	
Brown County—						
Horton..........	1				1	
Powhattan (R. D.)..........	1				1	
Butler County—						
Augusta..........	1				1	
El Dorado (R. D.)..........	5				5	
Chase County—						
Cottonwood Falls..........	1			1		
Chautauqua County—						
Grenola (R. D.)..........	9				9	
Hewins (R. D.)..........	1				1	
Cherokee County—						
Baxter Springs..........	3				3	
Chetopa (R. D.)..........	1				1	
Columbus (R. D.)..........	5				5	
Crestline (R. D.)..........	1				1	
Galena (R. D.)..........	19				19	
Mineral..........	3				3	
Scammon..........	8				8	

SMALLPOX—Continued.

State Reports for December, 1917—Continued.

Place.	New cases reported.	Deaths.	Vaccination history of cases.			
			Number vaccinated within 7 years preceding attack.	Number last vaccinated more than 7 years preceding attack.	Number never successfully vaccinated.	Vaccination history not obtained or uncertain.
Kansas—Continued						
Cheyenne County—						
Bird City.............	2				2	
Cloud County—						
Glasco (R. D.)...........	3			1	2	
Coffey County—						
Burlington...........	1				1	
Waverly (R. D.).........	1				1	
Westphalia (R. D.)......	1				1	
Cowley County—						
Arkansas City...........	1		1			
Crawford County—						
Arma...................	1				1	
Girard.................	1					1
Dickinson County—						
Herington.............	1				1	
Doniphan County—						
Wathena (R. D.)........	1			1		
Douglas County—						
Lawrence..............	5				5	
Franklin County—						
Ottawa................	3				3	
Pomona...............	1				1	
Jackson County—						
Hoyt (1 R. D.)........	1				1	
Jefferson County—						
Oskaloosa (R. D.).........	4				4	
Perry.................	1				1	
Jewell County—						
Burr Oak.............	2				2	
Cawker City (5 R. D.)....	5				5	
Jewell (6 R. D.)........	7				7	
Lovewell (15 R. D.)......	15				15	
Mankato..............	2				2	
Randall (R. D.).........	1				1	
Johnson County—						
Gardner (R. D.).........	1				1	
Merriam (R. D.)........	1				1	
Overland Park (R. D.)...	1				1	
Rosedale (R. D.)........	1				1	
Kiowa County—						
Coldwater (R. D.)........	5				5	
Haviland County...........	1				1	
Labette County—						
Chetopa (R. D.).........	1				1	
Parsons...............	1		1			
Leavenworth County—						
Lansing..............	1				1	
Leavenworth (R. D.).....	8				8	
Linn County—						
Blue Mound (R. D.)......	6				6	
Boicourt.............	1				1	
La Cygne.............	1				1	
Mound City...........	11			1	10	
Pleasanton...........	1				1	
Logan County—						
Oakley (R. D.)...........	1				1	
Lyon County—						
Admire (R. D.).........	1				1	
Emporia..............	2				2	
Reading (R. D.)........	3				3	
Marion County—						
Hillsboro (R. D.)........	5				5	
Marshall County—						
Frankfort.............	2				2	
Irving (R. D.)...........	1			1		
Lillis.................	3				3	
Miami County—						
Drexel, Mo. (R. D.)......	2				2	
Osawatomie (R. D.).......	1				1	

SMALLPOX—Continued.

State Reports for December, 1917—Continued.

Place.	New cases reported.	Deaths.	Vaccination history of cases.			
			Number vaccinated within 7 years preceding attack.	Number last vaccinated more than 7 years preceding attack.	Number never successfully vaccinated.	Vaccination history not obtained or uncertain
Kansas—Continued.						
Mitchell County—						
Glen Elder.	2			1	1	....
Montgomery County—						
Caney.	1				1	....
Coffeyville.	4				4	....
Independence.	2				2	....
Morris County—						
Council Grove.	2				2	2.........
Neosho County—						
Chanute.	1				1	....
Norton County—						
Almena (R. D.).	1				1	....
Osage County—						
Barclay (R. D.).	27				27	....
Burlingame.	9				9	....
Carbondale.	1				1	....
Lyndon (R. D.).	1				1	....
Overbrook.	3				3	....
Quenemo.	1				1	....
Richland (R. D.).	1				1	....
Scranton (1 R. D.).	15				15	....
Osborne County—						
Alton.	1				1	....
Covert (R. D.).	1				1	....
Ottawa County—						
Delphos.	1				1	....
Minneapolis.	1				1	....
Phillips County—						
Phillipsburg.	1				1	....
Republic County—						
Belleville.	1				1	....
Narka (R. D.).	3				3	....
Republic.	3				3	....
Rice County—						
Sterling.	1				1	....
Riley County—						
Ogden.	1				1	....
Manhattan.	1				1	....
Sedgwick County—						
Wichita (R. D.).	5				5	....
Seward County—						
Plains (R. D.).	5				5	....
Shawnee County—						
Topeka.	4				4	....
Stevens County—						
Hugoton.	6				6	....
Sumner County—						
Caldwell.	1				1	....
Mulvane.	1				1	....
Wellington (R. D.).	5				5	....
Trego County—						
Collyer.	4				4	....
Wabaunsee County—						
Harveyville (R. D.).	2				2	....
Washington County—						
Cuba (R. D.).	3				3	....
Wilson County—						
Altoona.	3				3	....
Fredonia.	3				3	....
North Altoona.	9				9	....
Woodson County—						
Neosho Falls.	1				1	....
Yates Center (R. D.).	3				3	....
Wyandotte County—						
Kansas City.	178				178	....
Rosedale.	3			1	2	....
Total	519		2	8	507	2

SMALLPOX—Continued.

State Reports for December, 1917—Continued.

Place.	New cases reported.	Deaths.	Vaccination history of cases.			
			Number vaccinated within 7 years preceding attack.	Number last vaccinated more than 7 years preceding attack.	Number never successfully vaccinated.	Vaccination history not obtained or uncertain.
Michigan (Dec. 1–31, 1917):						
Alcona County..................	5	....	....	....	5	....
Allegan County..............	2	....	....	....	2	....
Alpena County..............	25	....	....	1	23	1
Arenac County..............	6	....	....	....	6	....
Barry County..............	1	....	....	....	1	....
Bay County..............	20	....	....	....	18	2
Branch County..............	1	....	....	....	1	....
Calhoun County..............	7	....	....	....	7	....
Cass County..............	4	....	....	....	4	....
Cheboygan County..............	1	....	....	....	1	....
Chippewa County..............	1	....	....	....	1	....
Clinton County..............	2	....	....	....	2	....
Eaton County..............	5	....	....	1	4	....
Genesee County..............	64	....	....	....	46	18
Gladwin County..............	2	....	....	....	2	....
Grand Traverse County......	2	....	....	....	2	....
Houghton County..............	1	....	....	....	1	....
Huron County..............	14	....	....	1	12	1
Ingham County..............	6	....	....	1	5	....
Iosco County..............	17	....	....	....	16	1
Isabella County..............	5	....	....	....	5	....
Jackson County..............	2	....	....	....	2	....
Kalkaska County..............	1	....	....	....	1	....
Kent County..............	92	....	....	2	90	....
Lapeer County..............	18	....	....	....	9	9
Lake County..............	1	....	....	....	....	1
Lenawee County..............	5	....	....	....	5	....
Livingston County..............	1	....	....	....	....	1
Macomb County..............	9	....	....	....	8	1
Mason County..............	25	....	....	....	25	....
Mecosta County..............	2	....	....	....	1	1
Menominee County..............	5	....	....	....	5	....
Missaukee County..............	12	....	....	....	12	....
Monroe County..............	1	....	....	....	1	....
Montcalm County..............	4	....	....	....	3	1
Muskegon County..............	16	1	....	....	15	1
Newaygo County..............	11	....	....	1	10	....
Oakland County..............	8	....	....	....	8	....
Oceana County..............	4	....	....	....	4	....
Ogemaw County..............	1	....	....	....	....	1
Osceola County..............	11	....	....	....	10	1
Oscoda County..............	3	....	....	....	3	....
Ottawa County..............	5	....	....	....	5	....
Presque Isle County..............	4	....	....	....	4	....
Saginaw County..............	2	....	....	....	1	1
St. Clair County..............	18	....	....	....	17	1
Sanilac County..............	3	....	....	1	2	....
Schoolcraft County..............	6	....	....	....	6	....
Shiawassee County..............	2	....	....	....	2	....
Tuscola County..............	11	....	....	....	11	....
Van Buren County..............	1	....	....	....	1	....
Washtenaw County..............	13	....	....	....	13	....
Wayne County..............	196	....	....	....	195	1
Wexford County..............	4	....	....	1	....	3
Total....................	688	1	....	9	633	46
Minnesota (Dec. 1–31, 1917):						
Aitkin County—						
Aitkin....	5	....	....	....	5	....
Anoka County—						
Columbus Township.....	1	....	....	....	1	....
Blue Earth County—						
Mankato..............	2	....	....	....	2	....
Carlton County—						
Moose Lake..............	1	....	....	....	1	....
Carver County—						
Norwood..................	2	....	....	....	2	....
Waconia..............	3	....	....	....	3	....
Benton Township.........	1	....	....	....	1	....

SMALLPOX—Continued.

State Reports for December, 1917—Continued.

Place.	New cases reported.	Deaths.	Vaccination history of cases.			
			Number vaccinated within 7 years preceding attack.	Number last vaccinated more than 7 years preceding attack.	Number never successfully vaccinated.	Vaccination history not obtained or uncertain.
Minnesota (Dec. 1-31, 1917)—Cont.						
Clay County—						
Moorhead	1				1	....
Viding Township	1				1	....
Cook County—						
Rosebush Township	1				1	
Crow Wing County—						
Brainerd	18		1	3	14	
Crosby	4		3	1	2	
Ironton	2				2	
Deerwood Township	1				1	
Douglas County—						
Alexandria	3			1	2	
Osakis	5			1	4	
Fillmore County—						
Bloomfield Township	1				1	
Hennepin County—						
Brooklyn Center	2				2	
Minneapolis	90			10	80	....
Orono Township	9				9	
Houston County—						
Brownsville Township	1				1	....
Kittson County—						
Hallock	11				11	....
Kennedy	2				2	......
Granville Township	1				1	
Lyon County—						
Marshall	7				7	....
Rock Lake Township	1				1	....
Marshall County—						
Alvarado	1			1		......
Warren	1				1	
Meeker County—						
Harvey Township	1				1	....
Mille Lacs County—						
Borgholm Township	1			1		....
Morrison County—						
Little Falls	1				1	....
Mower County—						
Austin	2				2	....
Pleasant Valley Township	1				1	....
Udolpho Township	1			1		....
Windom Township	3				3	....
Murray County—						
Slayton	7				7	....
Holly Township	1				1	....
Nicollet County—						
St. Peter	1				1	....
Olmsted County—						
Dover Township	5				5	......
Ottertail County—						
Hobart Township	13				13	....
Pine County—						
Banning	1				1	....
Pine Lake Township	1				1	....
Polk County—						
Farley Township	14			1	12	1
Fisher Township	2				2	....
Sandsville Township	3				3	....
Pope County—						
Lowry	1				1	
Ramsey County—						
St. Paul	65				65	....
White Bear	1				1	....
Renville County—						
Cairo Township	4				4	....
Rice County—						
Faribault	1				1	....
Rock County—						
Luverne	1				1	....
Kanaranzi Township	1				1	....

SMALLPOX—Continued.

State Reports for December, 1917—Continued.

Place.	New cases reported.	Deaths.	Vaccination history of cases.			
			Number vaccinated within 7 years preceding attack.	Number last vaccinated more than 7 years preceding attack.	Number never successfully vaccinated.	Vaccination history not obtained or uncertain.
Minnesota (Dec. 1-31, 1917)—Con.						
Roseau County—						
Roseau......	1				1	......
Jadis Township	2				2	......
St. Louis County—						
Duluth	3				3	......
Hibbing	1				1	......
Virginia	1				1	......
Sherburne County—						
Elk River Township	1				1	......
Sibley County—						
Kelso Township	1				1	......
Stearns County—						
Sauk Center	4				4	......
Ashley Township	2				2	......
Todd County—						
Gordon Township	1					1
Hartford Township	2				2	......
West Union Township	2				2	......
Traverse County—						
Croke Township	5			1	4	......
Watonwan County—						
Butterfield	5				5	......
Winona County—						
Pleasant Hill Township..	2				2	......
Wright County—						
Frankfort Township	1				1	......
Total	**344**	......	**4**	**21**	**317**	**2**
Ohio (Dec. 1-31, 1917):						
Allen County	1				1	......
Athens County	15				15	......
Auglaize County	6				2	4
Belmont County	1				1	......
Butler County	38				37	1
Clark County	7				7	......
Clermont County	1					1
Clinton County	1				1	......
Columbiana County	2			1	1	......
Coshocton County	1					1
Crawford County	1				1	......
Cuyahoga County	135				59	76
Darke County	28				13	15
Defiance County	3				1	2
Delaware County	1				1	......
Erie County	5				5	......
Fairfield County	9			1	4	4
Fayette County	42				5	37
Franklin County	25				23	2
Fulton County	3				1	2
Greene County	42				33	9
Guernsey County	1				1	......
Hamilton County	35			1	31	3
Hancock County	14			1	13	......
Henry County	36			1	21	14
Highland County	3				3	......
Hocking County	4				4	......
Holmes County	3				2	1
Jackson County	9				7	2
Knox County	1				1	......
Lake County	1					1
Lawrence County	10				3	7
Licking County	10			1	7	2
Logan County	4				3	1
Lorain County	8				8	......
Lucas County	20				3	17
Mahoning County	5				1	4
Medina County	44			1	43	......
Mercer County	5				5	......
Miami County	10				3	7

SMALLPOX—Continued.

State Reports for December, 1917—Continued.

Place.	New cases reported.	Deaths.	Vaccination history of cases.			
			Number vaccinated within 7 years preceding attack.	Number last vaccinated more than 7 years preceding attack.	Number never successfully vaccinated.	Vaccination history not obtained or uncertain.
Ohio (Dec. 1-31, 1917)—Continued.						
Montgomery County	22				18	4
Paulding County	4				2	2
Morrow County	1					1
Perry County	2				1	1
Pickaway County	29				12	17
Pike County	16				2	1
Portage County	46				35	11
Preble County	3				2	1
Putnam County	3				2	1
Ross County	6				6	
Scioto County	29			1	18	10
Shelby County	95			3	74	18
Stark County	31				14	17
Summit County	114				45	69
Trumbull County	16				9	
Tuscarawas County	7					1
Van Wert	1					1
Vinton County	1					
Warren County	14				14	
Washington County	1					
Wayne County	43				20	2
Williams County	1				1	
Total	**1,069**			**11**	**645**	**412**

Miscellaneous State Reports.

Place.	Cases.	Deaths.	Place.	Cases.	Deaths.
Maine (Dec. 1-31):			**Maine (Dec. 1-31)—Contd.**		
Aroostook County—			Washington County—		
Letter A (unorganized)	1		Machias (town)	1	
Chapman (town)	1		Columbia Falls (town)	3	
Mars Hill (town)	2		Eastport	60	
Perham (town)	2		Jonesport (town)	1	
Fort Fairfield (town)	27		Perry (town)	3	
St. Francis	15				
Caribou (town)	24		Total	199	
Portage (town)	1				
Davidson (unorganized)	1		**North Dakota (Dec. 1-31):**		
Van Buren (town)	1		Bottineau County	7	
Weston (town)	1		Cavalier County	29	
Range 13, No. 7 (unorganized)	2		Griggs County	1	
Kennebec County—			McKenzie County	3	
Augusta	4		McLean County	1	
Randolph (town)	9		Morton County	4	
China (town)	1		Pembina County	8	
Oakland (town)	3		Ramsey County	3	
Gardiner	4		Rolette County	10	
Oxford County—			Towner County	17	
Norway (town)	5		Walsh County	2	
Penobscot County—			Ward County	1	
Passadumkeag (town)	2		Williams County	13	
Sagadahoc County—					
Richmond (town)	1		Total	99	
Somerset County—			**Oregon (Nov. 1-30):**		
Jackman	20		Umatilla County	1	
Hartland (town)	1		Portland	2	
Fairfield (town)	1				
Waldo County—			Total	3	
Knox (town)	6		**South Carolina (Dec. 1-31):**		
			Richland County	1	

SMALLPOX—Continued.

Miscellaneous State Reports—Continued.

Place.	Cases.	Deaths.	Place.	Cases.	Deaths.
South Dakota (Dec. 1-31):			South Dakota (Dec. 1-31)—		
Brown County	18		Continued.		
Charles Mix County	1		Union County	1	
Davison County	1		Walworth County	1	
Edmunds County	7				
Faulk County	4		Total	162	
Grant County	1		Vermont (Dec. 1-31):		
Gregory County	3		Orleans County	8	
Hughes County	1		Washington County	1	
Lake County	30				
Lawrence County	1		Total	9	
McCook County	17		Wyoming (Dec. 1-31):		
Miner County	4		Laramie County	4	
Minnehaha County	59		Sheridan County	1	
Roberts County	7		Campbell County	1	
Sanborn County	1				
Spink County	2		Total	6	
Tripp County	3				

City Reports for Week Ended Jan. 12, 1918.

Place.	Cases.	Deaths.	Place.	Cases.	Deaths.
Akron, Ohio	47		La Crosse, Wis	8	
Alton, Ill	6		Leavenworth, Kans	1	
Ann Arbor, Mich	1		Lincoln, Nebr	1	
Anniston, Ala	3		Little Rock, Ark	9	
Atlanta, Ga	3		Lorain, Ohio	2	
Baltimore, Md	2		Los Angeles, Cal	2	
Boston, Mass	1		Louisville Ky	1	
Birmingham, Ala	3		Milwaukee, Wis	5	
Buffalo, N. Y	5		Minneapolis, Minn	19	
Butte, Mont	7		Montgomery, Ala	17	
Canton, Ohio	10		New Orleans, La	4	
Charlotte, N. C	1		Niagara Falls, N. Y	1	
Chicago, Ill	8	1	Oklahoma City, Okla	8	
Cincinnati, Ohio	10		Omaha, Nebr	34	
Cleveland, Ohio	27		Pontiac, Mich	1	
Coffeyville, Kans	3		Portland, Oreg	6	
Columbus, Ohio	13		Portsmouth, Va	1	
Cumberland, Md	1		Quincy, Ill	4	
Danville, Ill	1		Racine, Wis	1	
Davenport, Iowa	1		Saginaw, Mich	3	
Dayton, Ohio	6		St. Joseph, Mo	11	
Denver, Colo	7		St. Louis, Mo	29	
Des Moines, Iowa	35		St. Paul, Minn	10	
Detroit, Mich	73		Salt Lake City, Utah	13	
Dubuque, Iowa	2		San Antonio, Tex	1	
Duluth, Minn	1		Seattle, Wash	6	
Erie, Pa	2		Sioux City, Iowa	11	
Evansville, Ind	4		Springfield, Ohio	3	
Flint, Mich	11		Steelton, Pa	1	
Fort Wayne, Ind	37		Superior, Wis	2	
Fort Worth, Tex	3		Terre Haute, Ind	1	
Grand Rapids, Mich	35		Toledo, Ohio	6	
Indianapolis, Ind	62		Waco, Tex	1	
Kansas City, Kans	48		Wichita, Kans	5	
Kansas City, Mo	162				

TETANUS.

City Reports for Week Ended Jan. 12, 1918.

During the week ending January 12, 1918, one case of tetanus was reported at Philadelphia, Pa., and one death from this disease was reported at each of the following named places: New Orleans, La., Philadelphia, Pa., and Pittsburgh, Pa.

TUBERCULOSIS.

See Diphtheria, measles, scarlet fever, and tuberculosis, page 152.

TYPHOID FEVER.

State Reports for November and December, 1917.

Place.	New cases reported.	Place.	New case reported.
Kansas (Dec. 1-31):		**Kansas (Dec. 1-31)—Continued.**	
Allen County—		Morris County—	
Iola	1	Delavan (R. D.)	1
Anderson County--		Wilsey	1
Garnett	1	Morton County—	
Barton County--		Elkhart	4
Great Bend	3	Norton County—	
Bourbon County--		Norton (R. D.)	1
Fort Scott	1	Pawnee County—	
Butler County--		Belpre (R. D.)	1
Augusta (R. D.)	3	Reno County—	
El Dorado	20	Hutchinson	1
Towanda	1	Republic County—	
Whitewater	1	Belleville	1
Chautauqua County—		Riley County—	
Sedan	1	Manhattan	1
Cherokee County—		Rooks County--	
Baxter Springs	1	Woodston	4
Columbus	2	Rush County—	
Galena	2	Bison (R. D.)	1
Opolis	1	Sedgwick County—	
Picher (R. D.)	1	Wichita	1
Clay County—		Seward County—	
Idana (R. D.)	1	Liberal	1
Cowley County—		Shawnee County—	
Winfield	1	Topeka	1
Crawford County—		Washington County—	
Pittsburg	3	Barnes (R. D.)	4
Douglas County—		Wilson County—	
Lawrence	1	Altoona	2
Overbrook (R. D.)	2	Buffalo	1
Edwards County—		Fredonia	1
Haviland (R. D.)	1	Woodson County—	
Elk County		Yates Center	1
Longton	3	Wyandotte County—	
Finney County—		Kansas City	2
Garden City	1	Turner	1
Gove County			
Gove (R. D)	1	Total	121
Harper County--			
Anthony	3	**Maine (Dec 1-31):**	
Pratt City	1	Cumberland County--	
Harvey County--		Portland	6
Newton	1	Westbrook	1
Haskell County—		Hancock County—	
Santa Fe (R D.)	1	Eden (town)	1
Jackson County—		Somerset County—	
Circleville (R. D)	1	Madison (town)	1
Mayetta	1	Washington County—	
Jefferson County		Eastport	4
Valley Falls	1		
Johnson County—		Total	13
Olathe	1		
Kearny County—		**Michigan (Dec. 1 31):**	
Lakin	2	Alpena County	3
Labette County—		Bay County	4
Mound Valley	1	Benzie County	1
Parsons	3	Berrien County	1
Leavenworth County		Branch County	1
Leavenworth	1	Calhoun County	2
Linn County		Charlevoix County	1
Blue Mound (R. D.)	1	Chippewa County	1
Mound City (2 R. D.)	2	Crawford County	3
Marion County		Emmet County	1
Lehigh	1	Genesee County	5
Peabody (R. D.)	1	Gladwin County	1
Marshall County—		Gratiot County	1
Herkimer	1	Huron County	2
McPherson County--		Ingham County	2
McPherson	1	Ionia County	1
Montgomery County--		Kalamazoo County	1
Caney	1	Keweenaw County	1
Coffeyville	2	Lapeer County	1
Independence (1 R D)	2	Macomb County	1

TYPHOID FEVER—Continued.

State Reports for November and December, 1917—Continued.

Place.	New cases reported.	Place.	New cases reported.
Michigan (Dec. 1-31)—Continued.		**New Jersey (Dec. 1-31)—Continued.**	
Marquette County	2	Sussex County	1
Monroe County	2	Union County	12
Ceana County	1		
Ottawa County	1	Total	51
Saginaw County	2		
St. Clair County	1	**North Dakota (Dec. 1-31, 1917):**	
Tuscola County	1	Adams County	4
Washtenaw County	3	Burleigh County	1
Wayne County	4	Cass County	1
		Grant County	3
Total	53	McLean County	1
		Morton County	3
Minnesota (Dec. 1-31):		Mountrail County	1
Anoka County—		Stark County	1
Anoka	1	Stutsman County	2
Bigstone County—			
Graceville	1	Total	17
Blue Earth County—			
Mankato	1	**Ohio (Dec. 1-31):**	
Carlton County—		Allen County	1
Moose Lake	1	Athens County	7
Crow Wing County—		Belmont County	1
Crosby	3	Butler County	2
Freeborn County—		Clark County	7
Albert Lea	1	Clermont County	1
Goodhue County—		Columbiana County	5
Belvidere Township	1	Coshocton County	1
Hennepin County—		Cuyahoga County	6
Minneapolis	19	Darke County	4
Kanabec County—		Delaware County	1
Knife Lake Township	1	Erie County	3
Kittson County—		Franklin County	1
St. Vincent	1	Hamilton County	2
Lake County—		Harrison County	6
Two Harbors	1	Holmes County	1
Lincoln County—		Huron County	2
Hendricks	2	Lawrence County	9
Mille Lacs County—		Licking County	4
East Side Township	2	Logan County	1
Murray County—		Lorain County	1
Murray Township	1	Lucas County	4
Nicollet County—		Montgomery County	3
North Mankato	1	Muskingum County	1
Olmstead County—		Paulding County	2
Rochester	1	Portage County	2
Ottertail County—		Ross County	2
Fergus Falls	1	Scioto County	4
Pipestone County—		Summit County	3
Burke Township	1	Trumbull County	2
Red Lake County—		Warren County	4
Red Lake Falls	1	Wood County	1
Redwood County—			
Vail Township	2	Total	93
Rice County—			
Wheeling Township	1	**Oregon (Nov. 1-30):**	
St. Louis County—		Clatsop County	3
Duluth	2	Douglas County	1
Virginia	2	Harney County	1
Winona County—		Hood River County	7
Homer Township	1	Jackson County	2
		Klamath County	3
Total	49	Lane County	1
		Linn County	2
New Jersey (Dec. 1-31, 1917):		Malheur County	11
Atlantic County	2	Marion County	1
Burlington County	5	Polk County	3
Camden County	1	Union County	1
Cumberland County	1	Wallowa County	1
Essex County	12	Washington County	2
Hudson County	1	Wheeler County	2
Mercer County	2	City of Portland	19
Middlesex County	2		
Monmouth County	6	Total	60
Morris County	2		
Ocean County	1	**Rhode Island (Dec. 1-31):**	
Passaic County	2	Cranston	1
Salem County	1	Hope Valley (town)	1

TYPHOID FEVER—Continued.

State Reports for November and December, 1917—Continued.

Place.	New cases reported.	Place.	New cases reported.
Rhode Island (Dec. 1-31—Continued.		South Dakota (Dec. 1-31)—Continued.	
Pawtucket........................	1	Lake County....................	1
Providence........................	3	Minnehaha County..............	1
Total.............................	6	Total............................	4
South Carolina (Dec. 1-31):		Vermont (Dec. 1-31):	
Greenville County.................	1	Addison County.................	2
Spartanburg County...............	2	Bennington County..............	2
		Franklin County................	1
Total.............................	3	Windsor County.................	1
South Dakota (Dec. 1-31):		Total............................	6
Clark County.....................	1	Wyoming (Dec. 1-31):	
Davison County...................	1	Campbell County................	1

City Reports for Week Ended Jan. 12, 1918.

Place.	Cases.	Deaths.	Place.	Cases.	Deaths.
Albany, N. Y...................	3	....	Manchester, N. H............	1	....
Atlanta, Ga....................	1	....	Milwaukee, Wis..............	1	....
Baltimore, Md.................	3	....	New Bedford, Mass...........	2	2
Birmingham, Ala..............	4	....	New Castle, Pa..............	1	....
Boston, Mass..................	....	1	New Haven, Conn............	1	....
Braddock, Pa..................	1	....	Newport News, Va...........	1	....
Buffalo, N. Y.................	1	....	New York, N. Y.............	12	1
Camden, N. J.................	1	....	Niagara Falls, N. Y.........	2	....
Chicago, Ill...................	4	....	Oakland, Cal................	3	....
Chillicothe, Ohio.............	1	....	Philadelphia, Pa............	4	....
Cincinnati, Ohio..............	2	....	Pittsburgh, Pa..............	9	1
Cleveland, Ohio...............	4	1	Pittsfield, Mass.............	2	....
Coffeyville, Kans.............	1	....	Portland, Oreg..............	1	....
Columbus, Ohio...............	1	....	Providence, R. I............	1	....
Cumberland, Md...............	1	....	Quincy, Ill.................	....	1
Danville, Ill..................	1	1	Reading, Pa.................	1	....
Detroit, Mich.................	19	4	Saginaw, Mich..............	2	1
Elgin, Ill.....................	1	....	St. Louis, Mo...............	3	1
El Paso, Tex..................	....	1	Savannah, Ga...............	3	....
Evansville, Ind...............	1	1	Schenectady, N. Y..........	1	1
Fall River, Mass..............	2	....	South Bend, Ind............	1	....
Flint, Mich...................	4	....	Springfield, Mass...........	1	....
Grand Rapids, Mich...........	1	....	Springfield, Ohio...........	11	....
Hartford, Conn...............	1	....	Syracuse, N. Y.............	1	....
Hoboken, N. J................	1	....	Toledo, Ohio................	1	....
Houston, Tex.................	1	....	Troy, N. Y.................	7	2
Lancaster, Pa.................	1	....	Washington County, Md.....	1	....
Lawrence, Mass...............	1	1	Washington, D. C...........	5	1
Leavenworth, Kans...........	2	....	Wheeling, W. Va............	9	....
Los Angeles, Cal..............	1	....	Wilmington, Del............	1	....
Louisville, Ky................	1	....	Worcester, Mass............	1	....
Lowell, Mass..................	1	....			

DIPHTHERIA, MEASLES, SCARLET FEVER, AND TUBERCULOSIS.

State Reports for November and December, 1917.

State.	Cases reported.		
	Diphtheria.	Measles.	Scarlet fever.
Kansas (December)...	145	699	416
Maine (December)...	37	907	39
Michigan (December)..	710	516	788
Minnesota (December)...	271	183	364
New Jersey (December)..	538	1,762	356
North Dakota (December)......................................	94	18	71
Ohio (December)..	752	456	782
Oregon (November)...	21	20	57
Rhode Island (December)......................................	104	40	52
South Carolina (December)....................................	140	585	11
South Dakota (December)......................................	23	35	51
Vermont (December)..	13	20	43
Wyoming (December)...	37	48	73

DIPHTHERIA, MEASLES, SCARLET FEVER, AND TUBERCULOSIS—
Continued.

City Reports for Week Ended Jan. 12, 1918.

City.	Population as of July 1, 1916 (estimated by U. S. Census Bureau).	Total deaths from all causes.	Diphtheria.		Measles.		Scarlet fever.		Tuberculosis.	
			Cases.	Deaths.	Cases.	Deaths.	Cases.	Deaths.	Cases.	Deaths.
Over 500,000 inhabitants:										
Baltimore, Md.	589,621	....	15	1	76	..	10	....	16	..
Boston, Mass.	756,476	314	85	9	124	2	39	2	40	..
Chicago, Ill.	2,497,722	727	173	31	58	1	87	6	503	72
Cleveland, Ohio.	674,673	192	59	3	25	..	11	....	29	22
Detroit, Mich.	571,784	221	61	7	15	2	39	....	40	15
Los Angeles, Cal.	503,812	124	8	..	32	..	9	....	28	14
New York, N. Y.	5,602,841	1,907	238	31	1,102	24	140	10	268	170
Philadelphia, Pa.	1,709,518	715	41	7	55	..	62	1	98	87
Pittsburgh, Pa.	579,090	284	17	1	198	1	43	....	20	19
St. Louis, Mo.	757,309	244	61	7	30	1	28	....	34	..
From 300,000 to 500,000 inhabitants:										
Buffalo, N. Y.	468,558	151	21	..	17	..	16	2	21	..
Cincinnati, Ohio.	410,476	192	15	3	10	..	7	....	37	16
Jersey City, N. J.	306,345	....	14	..	51	..	29	....	14	..
Milwaukee, Wis.	436,535	97	12	1	60	1	41	1	18	5
Minneapolis, Minn.	363,454	....	19	..	19	..	11	....		
Newark, N. J.	408,894	....	13	2	98	..	21	....	28	15
New Orleans, La.	371,747	179	24	4	55	..	2	....	30	20
San Francisco, Cal.	464,516	138	18	1	39	1	18	1	27	12
Seattle, Wash.	349,639	....	7	..	104	..	6	....	12	3
Washington, D. C.	353,949	148	21	1	94	..	35	....	39	12
From 200,000 to 300,000 inhabitants:										
Columbus, Ohio.	224,878	70	3	..	13	..	15	....	7	5
Denver, Colo.	260,800	71	11	..	43	..	30	....		16
Indianapolis, Ind.	271,708	....	35	..	45	..	45	....	11	..
Kansas City, Mo.	297,847	124	11	1	72	3	29	....	4	5
Louisville, Ky.	238,910	101	8	1	24	..	8	1	15	7
Portland, Oreg.	285,463	57	2	..	16	..	10	....	8	3
Providence, R. I.	254,960	88	8	1	8	..	3	1	26	7
Rochester, N. Y.	256,417	75	2	1	3	1	2	....	1	5
St. Paul, Minn.	267,312	52	19	..	11	..	14	1	4	10
From 100,000 to 200,000 inhabitants:										
Albany, N. Y.	104,199	....	1	..	3	..	1	....	5	..
Atlanta, Ga.	190,558	....	10	..	13	..	1	....		13
Birmingham, Ala.	181,762	66	..	..	125	3	5	....	4	3
Bridgeport, Conn.	121,579	49	9	1	10	1	8	....	3	4
Cambridge, Mass.	112,981	43	14	2	20	1	..	....	4	4
Camden, N. J.	106,423	....	7	..	54	..	..	....	3	..
Dayton, Ohio.	127,234	52	4	..	13	..	9	....	5	..
Des Moines, Iowa.	101,598	....	3	1	1	..	5	....		
Fall River, Mass.	124,356	42	3	2	2	..	3	....	10	4
Fort Worth, Tex.	104,562	35	4	1	5	..	1	....		5
Grand Rapids, Mich.	128,291	36	5	..	9	..	6	....	5	..
Hartford, Conn.	110,900	50	3	..	8	..	7	....	2	4
Houston, Tex.	112,307	32	2	..	16	1	..	....	1	4
Lawrence, Mass.	100,560	34	1	..	1	..	..	....	3	..
Lowell, Mass.	113,245	34	2	1	9	..	1	....	5	2
Lynn, Mass.	102,425	34	2	..	9	..	3	....	5	3
Nashville, Tenn.	112,657	35	..	..	27	1	4	....	5	5
New Bedford, Mass.	118,158	43	..	..	25	1	1	....	12	4
New Haven, Conn.	149,685	....	2	1	7	1	3	....	12	6
Oakland, Cal.	198,604	45	..	..	8	..	10	....	8	..
Omaha, Nebr.	165,470	39	4	2	34	..	5	....		4
Reading, Pa.	109,381	32	4	..	3	..	1	....	9	1
Richmond, Va.	156,687	36	5	..	17	..	6	....	2	4
Salt Lake City, Utah.	117,399	23	1	..	103	..	11	....		
San Antonio, Tex.	123,851	....	..	..	12	..	2	6	7	11
Springfield, Mass.	105,942	42	6	1	20	..	6	....	3	2
Syracuse, N. Y.	155,624	44	9	..	63	1	56	....	2	5
Toledo, Ohio.	191,554	74	6	2	..	..	41	1	18	7
Trenton, N. J.	111,560	48	7	1	5	..	4	....	7	7
Worcester, Mass.	161,314	36	6	..	8	..	2	....	5	4
From 50,000 to 100,000 inhabitants:										
Akron, Ohio.	82,025	....	6	..	5	..	5	....	7	3
Atlantic City, N. J.	52,669	....	..	..	5	..	..	....	3	2
Augusta, Ga.	70,245	11	..	..	26	..	..	....	3	..
Bayonne, N. J.	69,903	....	..	..	1	..	5	....	4	..

DIPHTHERIA, MEASLES, SCARLET FEVER, AND TUBERCULOSIS—
Continued.

City Reports for Week Ended Jan. 12, 1918—Continued.

City.	Population as of July 1, 1916 (estimated by U. S. Census Bureau).	Total deaths from all causes.	Diphtheria.		Measles.		Scarlet fever.		Tuberculosis.	
			Cases.	Deaths.	Cases.	Deaths.	Cases.	Deaths.	Cases.	Deaths.
From 50,000 to 100,000 inhabitants—Continued.										
Berkeley, Cal	57,653	8			1					2
Brockton, Mass	67,449	18			6		1		1	1
Charleston, S. C	60,734	38	1							7
Chattanooga, Tenn	60,075	6	1		15				1	5
Covington, Ky	57,144	19	1		1		2		2	2
Duluth, Minn	94,495	14	4		29		8	1	2	1
East St. Louis, Ill	74,708									
Elizabeth, N. J	86,690	22	1		37		8			2
El Paso, Tex	63,705	38	1		15					10
Erie, Pa	73,195		5				1		2	32
Evansville, Ind	76,078	29	3		3		4			
Flint, Mich	54,772	14	5		3		10			1
Fort Wayne, Ind	76,183	19	4		1					
Harrisburg, Pa	72,015	37	6	2	4		9		3	1
Hoboken, N. J	77,214	16	2		15				3	3
Johnstown, Pa	68,529	22	1				12		1	1
Kansas City, Kans	99,437		9	2	13		13			
Lancaster, Pa	50,853				3		3			
Little Rock, Ark	57,343	10			47		5		1	2
Malden, Mass	51,155	14			7		4		1	
Manchester, N. H	78,283	23	2	1	23	1	5		3	1
Mobile, Ala	58,221	31			11					2
New Britain, Conn	53,794	12								1
Norfolk, Va	80,612		2	1	4		3			1
Oklahoma City, Okla	92,943	17	1		10		2			1
Passaic, N. J	71,744	26	5		2				2	2
Pawtucket, R. I	59,411	19	3							2
Portland, Me	63,867	18	3		261					1
Rockford, Ill	55,185	14			9		3		3	1
Saginaw, Mich	55,642	17	1		1		2			
St. Joseph, Mo	85,236	31	8		36		1			1
San Diego, Cal	53,330	32	1		71		3		6	6
Savannah, Ga	68,805	38	2		15				2	4
Schenectady, N. Y	99,519	26	5		10		2			3
Sioux City, Iowa	57,078						9			
Somerville, Mass	87,039	28	4		27	1			3	1
South Bend, Ind	68,946	19	1		9		5		2	1
Springfield, Ill	61,120	14	1		2					
Springfield, Ohio	51,550	24			1		1		3	3
Terre Haute, Ind	66,083	18	3		5		1		1	
Troy, N. Y	77,916		2		1				3	1
Wichita, Kans	70,722								2	
Wilkes-Barre, Pa	76,776	25	6	1	23		7		3	
Wilmington, Del	94,265	38	2	2			1		5	
From 25,000 to 50,000 inhabitants:										
Alameda, Cal	27,732	6	1		1		1		1	
Austin, Tex	34,814	17								1
Brookline, Mass	32,790	5			24		1		1	
Butler, Pa	27,632	6	3		19		1		3	
Butte, Mont	43,425	17	3	1	4		6	3		
Charlotte, N. C	39,823		1		61		1			
Chelsea, Mass	46,192	6	2		12		1		5	
Chicopee, Mass	29,319	6	3		4				3	
Columbia, S. C	34,611		2		10				1	
Cumberland, Md	26,074	10	1						1	
Danville, Ill	32,261	13			1					
Davenport, Iowa	48,811		1				5			
Dubuque, Iowa	39,873				3		1			2
East Orange, N. J	42,458	10			25		4			
Elgin, Ill	28,203	6	1		2		1		1	
Everett, Mass	39,233	8	6		5		2		1	3
Fitchburg, Mass	41,781	12	2		4		2		4	
Galveston, Tex	41,863	13	1		4		1			
Green Bay, Wis	29,353	19			12		5			
Hagerstown, Md	25,679		1		1		1		3	1
Haverhill, Mass	48,477	15	1	1	5		4		3	1
Jackson, Mich	33,363	17	1		2		36		1	1
Kalamazoo, Mich	48,886	17	5		25		1		4	1
Kenosha, Wis	31,576	2	7	1			7		1	1
Kingston, N. Y	26,771	15								2

DIPHTHERIA, MEASLES, SCARLET FEVER, AND TUBERCULOSIS - Continued.

City Reports for Week ended Jan. 12, 1918--Continued.

City.	Population as of July 1, 1916 (estimated by U. S. Census Bureau).	Total deaths from all causes.	Diphtheria.		Measles.		Scarlet fever.		Tuberculosis.	
			Cases.	Deaths.	Cases.	Deaths.	Cases.	Deaths.	Cases.	Deaths.
From 25,000 to 50,000 inhabitants--Continued.										
Knoxville, Tenn.	38,676		1		10		5			
La Crosse, Wis.	31,677	9	1				1		1	2
Lexington, Ky.	41,097	27			27		2			4
Lincoln, Nebr.	46,515	17	3		1		6			1
Lorain, Ohio	36,964		3				3		1	
Lynchburg, Va.	32,940	14			1					
Macon, Ga.	45,757	27	1		33		2			
Madison, Wis.	30,699				2		3			
McKeesport, Pa.	47,521				14					2
Medford, Mass.	26,234	6			3		1		1	
Montgomery, Ala.	45,385	12	1		32		2		2	1
Nashua, N. H.	27,227	12								1
Newburgh, N. Y.	29,603	13	1		37		1		1	
New Castle, Pa.	41,133				3		5		3	
Newport, Ky.	31,927	14							3	
Newport, R. I.	30,106	4	6	2	4		5			
Newton, Mass.	43,715	16	3	2	2		1		2	1
Niagara Falls, N. Y.	37,253	13			2		1			4
Norristown, Pa.	31,401	14	1				2			1
Ogden, Utah	31,404	3					2			
Orange, N. J.	33,080	12	1		8					
Pasadena, Cal.	46,450	17	1		1		3		4	3
Perth Amboy, N. J.	41,185	8	3		23				2	
Pittsfield, Mass.	38,629	2			4		2	2	1	
Portsmouth, Va.	39,651	12			1					1
Quincy, Ill.	36,798	13			4					
Quincy, Mass.	38,136	12								1
Racine, Wis.	46,486	9	1		1		2			
Roanoke, Va.	43,284	18	2		1		1		1	4
Rock Island, Ill.	28,926	8	2		1		2			
San Jose, Cal.	38,902				6		2			
Steubenville, Ohio	27,445	7								
Stockton, Cal.	35,358	62			12					
Superior, Wis.	46,225	12	1		3		0		2	2
Taunton, Mass.	36,283	24					1		2	1
Waco, Tex.	33,385				3		1		2	
Waltham, Mass.	30,570	9	3		3		3			1
Watertown, N. Y.	29,894	1			3					1
West Hoboken, N. J.	43,139	4	1		1		1		3	
Wheeling, W. Va.	43,377	14							1	1
Williamsport, Pa.	33,809	9			2		3			1
Wilmington, N. C.	29,892	20			15					2
Winston-Salem, N. C.	31,155	18			40				1	2
Zanesville, Ohio	30,863	9								2
From 10,000 to 25,000 inhabitants:										
Alexandria, La.	15,333	8	3	1	30					
Alton, Ill.	22,874	5			5		2			
Ann Arbor, Mich.	15,010	15			6		2			
Anniston, Ala.	14,112				4					
Beaver Falls, Pa.	13,532						1			
Braddock, Pa.	21,685				1					
Cairo, Ill.	15,794	12	1		1					1
Chillicothe, Ohio	15,470	2			20		1			
Coffeyville, Kans.	17,548		5		21		1		1	2
Concord, N. H.	22,669	13			3					
Galesburg, Ill.	24,276	9								
Greenville, S. C.	18,181	3	2		10				1	
Hattiesburg, Miss.	16,482	3			21					
Kearny, N. J.	23,539		1	1	45		2			
Kokomo, Ind.	20,930	5								
La Fayette, Ind.	21,286		1							
Leavenworth, Kans.	[1]19,363	1	1		8		1			
Long Branch, N. J.	15,395	6								1
Marinette, Wis.	[1]14,610	4	1							
Melrose, Mass.	17,445	9	3	2			1			
Morristown, N. J.	13,284	8							1	
Nanticoke, Pa.	23,126	7			1				2	
New Albany, Ind.	23,629	6								3
Newburyport, Mass.	15,243	6	1						1	

[1] Population Apr. 15, 1910; no estimate made.

DIPHTHERIA, MEASLES, SCARLET FEVER, AND TUBERCULOSIS—Continued.

City Reports for Week ended Jan. 12, 1918—Continued.

City	Population as of July 1, 1916 (estimated by U. S. Census Bureau).	Total deaths from all causes.	Diphtheria.		Measles.		Scarlet fever.		Tuberculosis.	
			Cases.	Deaths.	Cases.	Deaths.	Cases.	Deaths.	Cases.	Deaths.
From 10,000 to 25,000 inhabitants—Continued.										
New London, Conn	20,985	7	5	......	12	......	......	......	1	1
Newport News, Va	20,562	12	......	......	12	......	......	......	2	2
North Adams, Mass	¹ 22,019	4	......	......	......	......	......	......	......	1
Northampton, Mass	19,926	6	1	......	......	......	2	......	1	......
Plainfield, N. J	23,805	7	5	......	4	......	......	......	2	2
Pontiac, Mich	17,524	8	2	......	......	......	5	......	1	1
Portsmouth, N. H	11,666	......	1	......	......	......	3	......	......	......
Rocky Mount, N. C	12,067	4	......	......	2	......	......	......	......	2
Rutland, Vt	14,831	7	......	......	1	......	1	......	......	2
Sandusky, Ohio	20,193	3	2	......	1	......	......	......	......	......
Saratoga Springs, N. Y	13,821	7	......	......	1	......	1	......	1	......
South Bethlehem, Pa	24,204	......	......	......	......	......	......	......	......	......
Spartanburg, S. C	21,365	8	......	......	2	......	1	......	1	......
Steelton, Pa	15,548	2	......	......	......	......	1	......	......	......
Washington, Pa	21,618	......	......	......	10	......	......	......	......	......
Wilkinsburg, Pa	23,228	10	1	......	12	......	......	......	......	......
Woburn, Mass	15,960	5	......	......	......	......	......	......	......	......

¹ Population Apr. 15, 1910, no estimate made

FOREIGN.

CUBA.

Communicable Diseases—Habana.[1]

Communicable diseases have been notified at Habana as follows:

| Disease. | Dec. 21–31, 1917. | | Remaining under treatment Dec. 31, 1917. | Disease. | Dec. 21–31, 1917. | | Remaining under treatment Dec. 31, 1917. |
	New cases.	Deaths.			New cases.	Deaths.	
Diphtheria	5	....	4	Scarlet fever	1	....	5
Leprosy	....	....	11	Smallpox	....	....	1
Malaria	24	....	[1]51	Typhoid fever	17	6	[2]73
Measles	4	....	5	Varicella	7	....	6

[1] From the interior, 35. [2] From the interior, 32.

CHOLERA, PLAGUE, SMALLPOX, AND TYPHUS FEVER.

Reports Received During Week Ended Feb. 1, 1918.[2]

CHOLERA.

Place.	Date.	Cases.	Deaths.	Remarks.
India:				
Bombay	Oct. 21–27	9	5	
Java:				
East Java	Oct. 28–Nov. 3	1	1	
West Java				Nov. 9–29, 1917: Cases, 19; deaths,
Batavia	Nov. 9–29	15	4	28.
Philippine Islands:				
Provinces		....	....	Dec. 2–8, 1917: Cases, 188 deaths,
Bohol	Dec. 2–8	30	18	138.
Capiz	....do....	2	1	
Iloilo	....do....	43	20	
Leyte	....do....	3	4	
Mindanao	....do....	69	41	
Occidental Negros	....do....	20	14	
Oriental Negros	....do....	21	10	

PLAGUE.

Place.	Date.	Cases.	Deaths.	Remarks.
Brazil:				
Bahia	Nov. 4–Dec. 15	4	4	
India:				
Bombay	Oct. 21–27	25	23	
Java:				
East Java	Oct. 27–Nov. 10	28	7	
Straits Settlements:				
Singapore	Nov. 11–24	2	2	

[1] Correction.—In table of communicable diseases occurring at Habana during the period Nov. 11–20, 1917, published in the Public Health Reports of Dec. 21, 1917, p. 2181, footnotes 2 and 3 should be transposed. The case of smallpox originated at Coruna, Spain, and of the 20 cases of typhoid fever, 6 were from the interior.
[2] From medical officers of the Public Health Service, American consuls, and other sources.

CHOLERA, PLAGUE, SMALLPOX, AND TYPHUS FEVER –Continued.

Reports Received During Week Ended Feb. 1, 1918—Continued.

SMALLPOX.

Place.	Date.	Cases.	Deaths.	Remarks.
Australia:				
New South Wales..........				July 12–Nov. 20, 1917: Cases, 34.
Abermain.............	Oct. 25–Nov. 20...	3		
Cessnock.............	July 12–Oct. 11...	7		
Eumangla.............	Aug. 15........	1		
Mungindi.............	Aug. 13........	1		
Warren...............	July 12–Oct. 25...	22		
Brazil:				
Bahia	Nov. 10–Dec. 8....	3		
Canada:				
British Columbia—				
Winnipeg..............	Dec. 30–Jan. 5.....	1		
Ontario—				
Hamilton.............	Jan. 13–19........	2		
Sarnia...............	Jan. 6–12........	14		
China:				
Antung..............	Dec. 10–16........	5	1	
Chungking...........	Nov. 25–Dec. 1....			Present.
Hunglahotze Station.......	Oct. 28–Nov. 4....	1		On Chinese Eastern Ry.
India:				
Bombay.....................	Oct. 21–27.........	2	1	
Italy:				
Milan......................	October–	2		
Turin.....................	Nov. 26–Dec. 9....	46	4	
Java:				
East Java.............	Oct. 27–Nov. 10...	19		
Mid-Java.............	Oct. 31–Nov. 21...	30		
West Java............	Nov. 9–29.........	103	15	
Philippine Islands:				
Manila...	Dec. 2–8........	2		
Spain:				
Seville......................	Nov. 1–30........		17	
Straits Settlements:				
Singapore...................	Nov. 4–24.........	11	2	
Tunisia:				
Tunis......................	Dec. 14–20........		1	

TYPHUS FEVER.

Place	Date	Cases	Deaths	Remarks
China:				
Antung	Dec. 10–16.........	6		
Great Britain:				
Glasgow...................	Dec. 21.............	1		
Greece:				
Saloniki...................	Nov. 25–Dec. 8....		17	
Java:				
East Java..............	Oct. 28–Nov. 15...	12	1	
Mid Java..................				Oct. 31–Nov. 13, 1917: Cases, 20.
Samarang..........	Nov. 7–13.........	5		
West Java				Nov. 9–29, 1917: Cases, 3.
Batavia	Nov. 9–15.........	10	3	
Union of South Africa:				
Cape of Good Hope State..	Sept. 10–Nov. 4...	3,342	668	

Reports Received from Dec. 29, 1917, to Jan. 25, 1918.

CHOLERA.

Place.	Date.	Cases.	Deaths.	Remarks.
China:				
Antung.....................	Nov. 26–Dec. 2....	3	1	
India:				
Bombay....................	Oct. 28–Nov. 3....	2	1	
Calcutta...................	Sept. 16–Oct. 27...		68	
Indo-China:				
Provinces....................				Sept 1–30, 1917: Cases, 74; deaths, 37.
Anam.................	Sept. 1–30..........	13	10	
Cambodia	...do...........	19	12	
Cochin China.........	...do...........	32	13	
Kwang Chow-Wan ... ...do...........		10	2	

CHOLERA, PLAGUE, SMALLPOX, AND TYPHUS FEVER—Continued.

Reports Received from Dec. 29, 1917, to Jan. 25, 1918—Continued.

CHOLERA—Continued.

Place.	Date.	Cases.	Deaths.	Remarks.
Java:				
West Java...............				Oct. 19–Nov. 8, 1917: Cases, 19;
Botavia................	Oct. 19–Nov. 8....	13	4	deaths, 7.
Persia:				
Mazanderan Province—				
Astrabad...............	July 31..............			Present.
Barfrush...............	July 1–27............	34	23	
Chahmirzad............				25 cases reported July 31, 1917.
Chahrastagh...........	June 15–July 25...	10	8	
Kharek................	May 28–June 11...	21	13	
Sari...................	July 3–29............	273	144	
Yekchambe-Bazar....	June 3...............	6		
Philippine Islands:				
Provinces...............				Nov. 18–24, 1917: Cases, 262;
Antique...............	Nov. 18–24........	32	23	deaths, 167.
Bohol.................	....do.............	10	9	
Iloilo.................	....do.............	57	38	
Leyte.................	....do.............	4	3	
Mindanao.............	....do.............	77	17	
Occidental Negros.....	....do.............	47	30	
Oriental Negros.......	....do.............	35	17	
Provinces...............				Nov. 25–Dec. 1, 1917: Cases, 251;
Antique...............	Nov. 25–Dec. 1...	16	9	deaths, 166.
Bohol.................	....do.............	36	19	
Capiz.................	....do.............	1	1	
Iloilo.................	....do.............	67	10	
Leyte.................	....do.............	3	2	
Mindanao.............	....do.............	38	30	
Occidental Negros.....	....do.............	71	47	
Oriental Negros.......	....do.............	18	17	
Romblon..............	....do.............	1	1	
Siam:				
Bangkok...............	Sept. 16–22.......	1	1	

PLAGUE.

British Gold Coast:				
Axim.................	Jan. 8..............			Present.
Ceylon:				
Colombo..............	Oct. 14–27..........	4	3	
Egypt...				Jan. 1–Nov. 15, 1917: Cases, 728;
Port Said.............	July 23–29..........	1	2	deaths, 398.
India...				Sept. 16–Nov. 10, 1917: Cases,
Bombay..............	Oct. 28–Nov. 3....	18	17	98,758; deaths, 72,648.
Calcutta..............	Sept. 16–29........		2	
Karachi...............	Oct. 21–Nov. 10...	6	5	
Madras Presidency....	Oct. 31–Nov. 6....	1,555	1,309	
Mandalay.............	Oct. 14–20.........		20	
Rangoon..............	Oct. 21–27.........	9	10	
Indo-China:				
Provinces...............				Sept. 1–30, 1917: Cases, 34; deaths,
Anam.................	Sept. 1–30.........	12	11	30.
Cambodia.............	....do.............	12	11	
Cochin-China.........	....do.............	10	8	
Saigon................	Oct. 31–Nov. 18...	8	4	
Siam:				
Bangkok..............	Sept. 16–22........	1	1	
Straits Settlements:				
Singapore.............	Oct. 28–Nov. 3....	1	3	

SMALLPOX.

Algeria:				
Algiers................	Nov. 1–30.........	1		
Australia:				
New South Wales...........				Sept. 28–Dec. 5, 1917: Cases, 11.
Abermain.............	Oct. 25–Nov. 20...	3		
Cessnock.............	Sept. 28–Oct. 11...	3		Newcastle district.
Kurri Kurri...........	Dec. 5.............	1		
Warren...............	Oct. 12–13.........	3		

CHOLERA, PLAGUE, SMALLPOX, AND TYPHUS FEVER—Continued.

Reports Received from Dec. 29, 1917, to Jan. 25, 1918—Continued.

SMALLPOX—Continued.

Place.	Date.	Cases.	Deaths.	Remarks.
Brazil:				
Pernambuco...............	Nov. 1-15....	1	....	
Rio de Janeiro...............	Sept. 30-Dec. 1....	519	151	
Sao Paulo...............	Oct. 29-Nov. 4....	....	2	
Canada:				
New Brunswick—				
Kent County...........	Dec. 4...............	....	....	Outbreak. On main line Canadian Ry., 25 miles north of Moncton.
Ontario—				
Hamilton...............	Dec. 16-22....	1	....	
Sarnia...............	Dec. 9-15....	1	....	
Windsor...............	Dec. 30-Jan. 5....	1	....	
Quebec—				
Montreal...............	Dec. 16-Jan. 5....	5	....	
Do...............	Jan. 6-12....	1	....	
China:				
Amoy...............	Oct. 22-Nov. 4....	....	....	Present.
Antung...............	Dec. 3-9....	1	1	
Chungking...............	Nov. 11-17....	....	....	Do.
Dairen...............	Nov. 18-24....	1	....	
Harbin...............	May 14-June 30...	20	....	Chinese Eastern Ry.
Do...............	July 1-Oct. 15....	4	....	Do.
Manchuria Station.........	May 14-June 30...	6	....	Do.
Do...............	July 1-Oct. 15....	3	....	Do.
Mukden...............	Nov. 11-24....	....	....	Present.
Shanghai...............	Nov. 18-Dec. 16...	30	62	Cases, foreign; deaths among natives.
Tientsin...............	Nov. 11-Dec. 8....	7	....	
Cuba:				
Habana...............	Jan. 7...............	1	....	Nov. 8, 1917: 1 case from Coruna. Dec. 5, 1917: 1 case.
Marianao...............	Jan. 8...............	1	....	6 miles distant from Habana.
Egypt:				
Alexandria...............	Nov. 12-18....	1	....	
Cairo...............	July 23-Aug. 5....	5	1	
France:				
Lyon...............	Nov. 18-Dec. 16...	6	3	
Great Britain:				
Birmingham...............	Nov. 11-17....	19	....	
India:				
Madras...............	Oct. 31-Nov. 6....	4	1	
Indo-China:				
Provinces...............		....	....	Sept. 1-30, 1917: Cases 198; deaths, 70.
Anam...............	Sept. 1-30....	61	12	
Cambodia...............	....do....	7	....	
Cochin-China...............	....do....	124	44	
Tonkin...............	....do....	1	....	
Saigon...............	Oct. 29-Nov. 18...	41	12	
Italy:				
Turin...............	Oct. 20-Nov. 26...	77	116	
Castellamare...............	Dec. 10....	2	....	Among refugees.
Florence...............	Dec. 1-15....	17	4	
Naples...............	To Dec. 10....	2	....	Do.
Java:				
Mid-Java...............	Oct. 10-30....	25	....	
West Java...............		....	....	Oct. 19-Nov. 5, 1917: Cases, 29 deaths, 8.
Batavia...............	Nov. 2-8....	1	....	
Mexico:				
Mazatlan...............	Dec. 5-11....	....	1	
Mexico City...............	Nov. 11-17....	9	....	
Piedras Negras...............	Jan. 11....	200	....	
Newfoundland:				
St. Johns...............	Dec. 8-Jan. 4....	25	....	
Do...............	Jan. 5-11....	14	....	
Philippine Islands:				
Manila...............	Oct. 28-Dec. 8....	5	....	
Portugal:				
Lisbon...............	Nov. 4-10....	1	....	
Portuguese East Africa:				
Lourenço Marques.........	Aug. 1-Sept. 30...	....	4	
Russia:				
Moscow...............	Aug. 26-Oct. 6....	22	2	
Petrograd...............	Aug. 31-Oct. 27...	59	3	
Spain:				
Coruna...............	Dec. 2-15....	....	4	
Seville...............	Oct. 1-30....	....	9	
Venezuela:				
Maracaibo...............	Dec. 2-8....	....	1	

CHOLERA, PLAGUE, SMALLPOX, AND TYPHUS FEVER—Continued.

Reports Received from Dec. 29, 1917, to Jan. 25, 1918—Continued.

TYPHUS FEVER.

Place.	Date.	Cases.	Deaths.	Remarks.
Algeria:				
Algiers...............	Nov. 1–30.........	2	....	
Australia:				
South Australia...........	....	....	....	Nov. 11–17, 1917: Cases, 1.
Brazil:				
Rio de Janeiro.............	Oct. 28–Dec. 1....	7	....	
Canada:				
Ontario—				
Kingston...........	Dec. 2–8........	3	....	
Quebec—				
Montreal...............	Dec. 16–22....	2	1	
China:				
Antung................	Dec. 3–9.....	5	1	
Chosen (Formosa):				
Seoul...............	Nov. 1–30.......	1	....	
Egypt:				
Alexandria.................	Nov. 8–25.........	110	44	
Cairo....................	July 23–Sept. 23...	23	8	
Port Said................	July 30–Sept. 23...	3	3	
Great Britain:				
Manchester.................	Dec. 2–8.......	1	....	
Greece:				
Salonika.............	Nov. 11–24.......	....	19	
Japan:				
Nagasaki..............	Nov. 26–Dec. 16...	5	1	Oct. 15–21, 1917: Cases, 5; deaths, 2.
Java:				
East Java.............	....	....	....	Oct. 10–30, 1917: Cases, 22; deaths, 2.
Mid-Java:				
Samarang..............	Oct. 17–30....	4	1	Oct. 19–Nov. 8, 1917: Cases, 33; deaths, 5.
West Java...............	....	....	....	
Batavia.................	Oct. 19–Nov. 8....	22	4	
Mexico:				
Aguascalientes.............	Dec. 15....	....	2	
Mexico City.................	Nov. 11–Dec. 15...	337	....	
Russia:				
Archangel..................	Sept. 1–14.........	7	2	
Moscow..................	Aug. 26–Oct. 6....	49	2	
Petrograd................	Aug. 31–Oct. 27...	22	....	
Vladivostok...............	Oct. 29–Nov. 4....	12	1	
Sweden:				
Goteborg..................	Nov. 18–24.......	1	....	
Tunisia:				
Tunis......................	Nov. 30–Dec. 6....	....	1	

×

PUBLIC HEALTH REPORTS

VOL. 33   FEBRUARY 8, 1918   No. 6

THE QUALITY OF ANTIPNEUMOCOCCIC AND ANTIMENINGOCOCCIC SERUMS.

In order that those who use antipneumococcic and antimeningococcic serums shall be assured that such of these serums as are sold in interstate traffic are suitable for therapeutic purposes, each lot of these products made by the various manufacturers is tested at the Hygienic Laboratory of the United States Public Health Service prior to being placed on the market.

The quality of antipneumococcic serum is judged by its protective value against Type I pneumococci, using mice for test purposes.

Antimeningococcic serum is tested by agglutination and complement fixation tests, such as prove satisfactory by either test being passed.

EFFECT OF FREEZING ON THE ORGANISMS OF TYPHOID FEVER AND DIPHTHERIA.[1]

By JOSEPH BOLTEN, Passed Assistant Surgeon, United States Public Health Service

The occurrence during the summer of 1917 of an outbreak of diphtheria [2] and one of typhoid fever,[3] which seemed properly attributable to the ingestion of infected ice cream, constituted the reason for determining, under experimental conditions, how long the typhoid bacillus and the diphtheria bacterium would survive freezing, and whether freezing had any influence on the pathogenicity of the latter organism.

Results with B. typhosus.

To determine the length of time typhoid organisms would live in cream that had been frozen solid, the following experiment was undertaken on October 4, 1917.

---

[1] From the Hygienic Laboratory.
[2] McCoy, Bolten, and Bernstein, Public Health Reports, vol. 32, No. 43, Oct 26, 1917, pp. 1787-1804
[3] Personal communication from Surgeon L. L. Lumsden.

Four metal containers were sterilized and partly filled with 50 cubic centimeters of pasteurized cream. These were then inoculated with 5 cubic centimeters of a 24-hour broth culture of *B. typhosus* (Rawling's), and immediately placed in a brine tank, where they were frozen within a short period. They were permitted to remain in this condition for 24 hours, when they were removed and partly melted by placing in a 37° C. water bath for 15 to 20 minutes. A loopful of material from each container was streaked over an Endo plate. The containers were then replaced in the brine tank and the Endo plates incubated at 37° C. for 24 hours. The next day the procedure was repeated. From the Endo plates, inoculated during the preceding day, typical typhoid colonies were fished into two nutrient broth tubes and on one Russell slant tube. These were incubated at 37° C. for 24 hours. The next day, macroscopic agglutination tests were performed. One drop of a high titer anti-typhoid serum, 1:2,000, was placed in one broth tube, while the second broth tube was used as a control. The tubes were incubated at 37° C. for half an hour. At the end of this period all the tubes to which serum had been added showed a heavy flocculent precipitate. The Russell slant tube showed a red butt, with no gas and unchanged slant.

This experiment was done daily from October 4 to November 1. After this date it was performed every second day, to November 28. During the first few days there was very little change in the number of colonies per plate, but after 10 days to two weeks there were about half the number, as compared with the original plates. At the end of the month, the number of colonies developed were very few, probably less than one-twentieth of the number of colonies that developed on the first few days.

From November 28 to December 17 the containers were left undisturbed in the brine tank On December 17 the experiment was resumed. The typhoid organisms in two containers were apparently dead, as no growth appeared on the Endo plates. The other two containers still gave a growth, one colony per loop from one and six colonies from the other. The colonies at this time were not the typical grayish translucent ones of typhoid. Instead they all presented a slightly reddish center. Subcultures in broth, however, were agglutinated satisfactorily and the appearance on the Russell medium plant was characteristic of the typhoid bacillus.

If we may assume that *B. typhosus*, under natural conditions, would resist freezing in cream as long as did this laboratory culture, there is no doubt that ice cream would be a very effective agent for distributing infection.

Results with Bact. diphtheriæ.

In order to ascertain whether freezing would have any effect on viability and on the production of diphthéria toxin, 8 pure cultures of *Bact. diphtheriæ*, obtained from the epidemic referred to, were studied. These cultures were obtained from clinical cases of diphtheria and were isolated in pure cultures by plating on agar and fishing of colonies to Loeffler slants. The cultures were subjected to the following treatment:

(1) On September 26 two small Loeffler slant tubes were inoculated from each culture. These cultures were grown at 37° C. for 24 hours, after which they were each washed off with 10 cubic centimeters of 0.85 per cent salt solution and the suspension was placed in sterilized metal containers. These containers were then placed in a large wire basket and suspended in a brine tank, where in a short time they were frozen solid. They were allowed to remain in this tank in a frozen condition for 24 hours, when they were placed in a 37° C. water bath for 20 minutes, in order partly to melt the frozen solid. At the end of this period the tops were flamed and a loopful of material was inoculated on a Loeffler blood serum slant. The tubes were then incubated at 37° C. and the contents of the containers frozen again. The following day the process was repeated and the cultures of the inoculated tubes of the preceding day were examined. In all cases diphtheria bacilli were obtained. The freezing was continued for six days, and diphtheria organisms were recovered each day.

(2) On October 9 the experiment was repeated, with a slight variation. In this experiment, instead of using salt solution, 40 cubic centimeters of pasteurized cream were used. One 24-hour slant culture was washed in 5 cubic centimeters of salt solution and the 40 cubic centimeters of cream were inoculated. The cultures were frozen for four days, and then 2 per cent neutral peptone was inoculated with the frozen and the original (unfrozen) cultures.

The peptone-broth cultures were incubated at 37° C. for five days. On the fifth day 1 cubic centimeter of each of the broth cultures was injected subcutaneously into guinea pigs. Eight pigs were used for the frozen cultures and eight for the original unfrozen ones. All the pigs died within a period of three days, but without any significant difference in period of survival between those given frozen and those given the original cultures.

(3) On October 30 the experiment was again repeated. The amount of pasteurized cream used this time was 50 cubic centimeters: otherwise the details were the same as in the second experiment. The cultures were frozen for four days and then 2 per cent neutral peptone broth was inoculated with the frozen and original (unfrozen) cultures. The broth cultures were grown for four days at 37° C. and

were then used for the toxicity experiment. In the previous experiment we deemed the amount of culture used too large. In this experiment we used three dilutions, 0.5 cubic centimeter, 0.05 cubic centimeter, and 0.005 cubic centimeter, of each, frozen and unfrozen, culture. The injections were made subcutaneously.

The results of the test failed to show any difference between the toxin production of the frozen and of the unfrozen cultures.

An additional experiment of the same nature, in which the well-known diphtheria culture, Park No. 8, was frozen in the same manner for four days and then tested for toxin production, with a control of unfrozen, failed to show any difference between the two.

PREVALENCE OF DISEASE.

No health department, State or local, can effectively prevent or control disease without knowledge of when, where, and under what conditions cases are occurring.

UNITED STATES.

EXTRA-CANTONMENT ZONES—CASES REPORTED WEEK ENDED FEB. 5.

Camp Beauregard, La.—Alexandria: Meningitis 1, typhoid 1, mumps 2, measles 8, smallpox 2, pneumonia 1. Pineville: Pneumonia 1, measles 3, meningitis 1, chicken pox 1. Boyce: Measles 14. Hot Wells: Measles 1. Rural district: Measles 4, meningitis 1, located near village of Ball.

Camp Bowie, Tex.—Fort Worth: Chicken pox 1, diphtheria 2, measles 2, pneumonia 2, scarlet fever 1, syphilis 1, gonorrhea 2, smallpox 4, German measles 1.

Camp Dodge, Iowa.—Des Moines: Smallpox 36, diphtheria 3, scarlet fever 10, measles 1, German measles 1, tuberculosis 1. Ankeny: Smallpox 1. Grimes: Smallpox 1. Polk City: Scarlet fever 1, chicken pox 1.

Camp Funston, Kans.—Manhattan: Measles 89, scarlet fever 2, mumps 3, smallpox 4. Cleburne: Measles 2. Irving: Measles 1. Riley: Measles 7, smallpox 1, pneumonia 1. Junction City: Scarlet fever 2, measles 16, chicken pox 1, smallpox 1. Ogden: Diphtheria 1, measles 8, smallpox 1, chicken pox 1. Milford: Measles 3 Keats: Measles 6.

Camp Gordon, Ga.—Atlanta: Diphtheria 10, German measles 11, gonococcus infection 1, malaria 2, measles 14, epidemic cerebrospinal meningitis 5, mumps 12, scarlet fever 1, septic sore throat 1, smallpox 2, syphilis 2, tuberculosis 2. Buckhead, Fulton County: Scarlet fever 1. Carey Park, Fulton County: Tuberculosis 1. College Park, Fulton County: Epidemic cerebrospinal meningitis 1. Decatur, Dekalb County: Septic sore throat 1.

Camp Greene, N. C.—Chicken pox 1, German measles 7, gonorrhea and syphilis 1. gonorrhea 14, measles 30, mumps 2, cerebrospinal meningitis 1. syphilis 11, tuberculosis 1, whooping cough 6; all in Charlotte township.

Camp Hancock, Ga.—Measles: Augusta 24, Hophzibah 4, Blytho 7, County Home 1; and German measles: Augusta 50, North Augusta 18, Belvedere 5, Waynesboro road 1; and lobar pneumonia: Augusta 1, Blytho 1; and chicken pox: Augusta 1; and mumps: Blytho 1; and typhoid fever: Hophzibah 1; and pulmonary tuberculosis North Augusta 1.

Fort Leavenworth, Kans.—German measles: City 15. Measles: City 3, county 6. Smallpox: City 3. Lobar pneumonia: County 1. Chicken pox: City 3.

Camp Lee, Va.—Petersburg: German measles 7, pneumonia 2, measles 2, cerebrospinal meningitis 1, mumps 1, septic sore throat 1. Ettricks: Whooping cough 4. chicken pox 2, measles 3. Hopewell: Measles 3, cerebrospinal meningitis 1. Dinwiddie County: Measles 1, German measles 1. Chesterfield County: Measles 1, diphtheria 1, pneumonia, lobar. 2.

Camp Lewis, Wash.--German measles: Spanaway 7, Steilacoom 6, Du Pont 2, Hillhurst 5, Parklodge 2, Lakeview 1, Clover Creek 1.

Camp Logan, Tex.--Houston: Chicken pox 3, diphtheria 4, mumps 7, measles 22, pneumonia 10, gonorrhea 4, German measles 11, malaria 1, typhoid fever 1, tuberculosis 3.

Camp McClellan, Ala.--Anniston: Smallpox 5, chicken pox 5, measles 5, German measles 2, pneumonia 1. Oxford: German measles 1. Districts Three and Thirteen: Smallpox, 1 each. District Fifteen: Smallpox 1, chicken pox 1. District Seventeen: Cerebrospinal meningitis 2.

Fort Oglethorpe, Ga.--Chattanooga: German measles 5, tuberculosis 3, measles 3, gonorrhea 20, syphilis 6, chicken pox 2, mumps 1, pneumonia 3, meningitis 1, scarlet fever 3, smallpox 1. East Chattanooga: Smallpox 1. North Chattanooga: Mumps 2. Eastlake: Mumps 3. Rossville, Ga.: Measles 6, scarlet fever 3.

Camp Pike, Ark.--Little Rock: Measles 25, chicken pox 4, smallpox 37, scarlet fever 1, tuberculosis 4, pneumonia 15, German measles 1, diphtheria 1, mumps 3, syphilis 10, gonorrhea 13, chancroid 1, meningitis 1, trachoma 3. North Little Rock: Measles 1, smallpox 2, tuberculosis 1, German measles 3, mumps 2, gonorrhea 4, chancroid 3. Scotts: German measles 2, gonorrhea 5, syphilis 4, pellagra 1, measles 2.

Camp Sevier, S. C.--Poe Mill: Two epidemic cerebrospinal meningitis. Greenville Township, rural: One scarlet fever.

Camp Shelby, Miss.--Forrest County: Hattiesburg, chicken pox 4, malaria 2, measles 9, meningitis 2, mumps 6, pneumonia 4, smallpox 9, tuberculosis 1, whooping cough 1; Harvey, measles 1. Jefferson Davis County: White Sand, meningitis 1. Harrison County: Lyman, smallpox 1. Pearl River County: Lumberton, tuberculosis 1.

Camp Sheridan, Ala.--Montgomery: Measles 40, lobar pneumonia 3, smallpox 23, meningitis carrier 1, tuberculosis 4, German measles 20, mumps 1, scarlet fever 1, chicken pox 7. Capitol Heights: Smallpox 1. Chisholm: Smallpox 1.

Camp Sherman, Ohio.--Cerebrospinal meningitis: Chillicothe 1. Diphtheria: Chillicothe 2. Chicken pox: Green Township 1. German measles: Chillicothe 27. Measles: Chillicothe 1, Liberty Township 4. Mumps: Chillicothe 2. Lobar pneumonia: Green Township 1.

Camp Zachary Taylor, Ky.--Jefferson County: Measles 2, meningitis, cerebrospinal, 1, scarlet fever 1, trachoma 1. Louisville: Chicken pox 1, diphtheria 8, German measles 3, measles 31, pneumonia 1, scarlet fever 3, smallpox 9, tuberculosis, pulmonary, 11.

Tidewater Health District, Va.--Newport News: Measles 9, tuberculosis 1, scarlet fever 1, mumps 1, meningitis 3, whooping cough 3. Hampton: Measles 20, typhoid 2, pneumonia 3, tuberculosis 1. Phoebus: Measles 4, scarlet fever 1.

Camp Wadsworth, S. C.--Spartanburg city: German measles 9, whooping cough 13, pneumonia 5, measles 2, smallpox 1, tuberculosis 2. Drayton: Measles 3, pneumonia 1. County: Whooping cough 1.

Camp Wheeler, Ga.--In Macon: Measles 6, German measles 2, mumps 31, scarlet fever 2, diphtheria 5, meningitis 2, pneumonia 2. In East Macon: Scarlet fever 1, German measles 2. In Bibb County: Scarlet fever 1, meningitis 1.

CURRENT STATE SUMMARIES.

Alabama.

From Collaborating Epidemiologist Perry, telegram dated February 5, 1918:

Measles epidemic Smallpox. Butler 5, Chambers 3, Cherokee 1, Cullman 2, Shelby 4. Tallapoosa 88. Alker 1.

California.

From the State Board of Health of California, telegram dated February 5, 1918:

Two cases anthrax in man, Kern County. Three cases epidemic cerebrospinal meningitis; 1 Shasta County, 2 San Francisco. Two cases leprosy; 1 Monterey County, 1 San Francisco. Seven cases smallpox; 3 Nevada County, 1 Holtville, 2 Fresno, 1 Venice. Measles much more prevalent, especially in southern California. Diphtheria, mumps, scarlet fever, and whooping cough much prevalent in San Francisco Bay region. Nine of 14 typhoid cases reported are in southern California.

Reported by mail for preceding week (ended Jan. 26):

Cerebrospinal meningitis	6	Pneumonia	64
Chicken pox	139	Poliomyelitis	1
Diphtheria	69	Scarlet fever	103
Erysipelas	7	Smallpox	8
German measles	194	Syphilis	25
Gonococcus infection	22	Tuberculosis	116
Malaria	3	Typhoid fever	10
Measles	491	Whooping cough	124
Mumps	86		

Connecticut.

From Collaborating Epidemiologist Black, telegram dated February 4, 1918:

Cerebrospinal meningitis: Bridgeport 3. Greenwich 1, Cromwell 1. Smallpox: Winsted 1, Torrington 1.

Indiana.

From the State Board of Health of Indiana, telegram dated February 1, 1918:

Scarlet fever: One death Portland. Diphtheria: Epidemic Walesboro, Bartholomew County. Measles: Epidemic Anderson. German measles: Epidemic Columbus. New Castle, Seymour, Greencastle, Indianapolis, Linton. Smallpox: Epidemic Dayton, Tippecanoe County. Whooping cough: Epidemic Steuben County. Gastroenteritis or winter cholera: Epidemic Indianapolis, Anderson.

Kansas.

From Collaborating Epidemiologist Crumbine, telegram dated February 4, 1918:

Week ending February 2. Meningitis in cities: Brookville 1, Buffalo 1, Cherokee 1, De Soto 1, Ellsworth 1, Enterprise 1, Harper 1, Labette 1, Topeka 1. Meningitis carriers: Manhattan 1. Poliomyelitis: Harper County 1. Smallpox: Unusually prevalent, in counties—Cherokee 27, Crawford 49, Marion 18, Woodson 21; in cities—Coffeyville 15, Emporia 7, Kansas City 28. German measles (rubella) prevalent in every section of State.

Louisiana.

From Collaborating Epidemiologist Dowling. telegram dated February 4, 1918:

Meningitis (excluding Rapides): Bienville 1, Grant 1, Jefferson Davis 1, St. James 2, Tensas 1, Union 1, Vermilion 2, Winn 1, Orleans 2.

Massachusetts.

From Collaborating Epidemiologist Kelley, telegram dated February 5, 1918:

Unusual prevalence for week. Measles: Beverly 15, Marlboro 144, Natick 16, Winchester 14. Scarlet fever: Holden 10. Whooping cough: Canton 14.

Minnesota.

From Collaborating Epidemiologist Bracken, telegram dated February 4, 1918:

Smallpox: Mower County, Lyle village 4; Todd County, Little Sauk Township, 2; Kanabec County, Grass Lake Township; Polk County, Climax village; Roseau County, Lind Township, 1 each. One poliomyelitis, 2 cerebrospinal meningitis. Reports since January 28.

Nebraska.

From the State Board of Health of Nebraska, telegram dated February 4, 1918:

Scarlet fever at Columbus, North Bend, and Hickman. Smallpox at Davenport, Scottsbluff, Humboldt, Omaha, and Lincoln. German measles at Lincoln, McCook, and Fremont.

South Carolina.

From Collaborating Epidemiologist Hayne. telegram dated February 4, 1918:

Epidemic meningitis, 16 new cases for week ending February 3.

Virginia.

From Collaborating Epidemiologist Traynham, telegram dated February 4, 1918:

Thirteen cases cerebrospinal meningitis, Norfolk. One case smallpox, 1 case cerebrospinal meningitis, Dinwiddie County. One case infantile paralysis, Henrico County. One case varioloid, Augusta County.

Washington.

From Collaborating Epidemiologist Tuttle, telegram dated February 5, 1918:

No unusual outbreaks communicable diseases. Five cases typhoid, Kennwick, Benton County.

RECIPROCAL NOTIFICATION.

California.

Cases of communicable diseases referred during December, 1917, to other State health departments by the department of health of the State of California.

Disease and locality of notification.	Referred to health authority of—	Why referred.
Diphtheria:		
Los Angeles	El Paso, Tex.	Patient contracted disease in El Paso or en route to Los Angeles.
Gonococcus infection:		
El Centro	Mexicali, Mexico	Patient became infected while in Mexicali.
Hookworm:		
Solano County	Arkansas, 1 case. Georgia, 3 cases. Missouri, 1 case. Oklahoma, 3 cases. Tennessee, 1 case. Texas, 2 cases.	Patients resided in States named at the time they became infected.
Measles:		
Marin County	Fort Logan, Colo., 6 cases.	Patients were ill upon arrival from Colorado.
Smallpox:		
Kern County	Parker, Ariz.	History of contact with active case in Arizona.
Los Angeles	Arizona.	Infected while traveling in Arizona.
Redlands	Burlingame, Kans.	Patient contracted disease while on visit in Burlingame where smallpox was prevalent.
Maricopa	Oklahoma.	Patient was ill upon arrival from Oklahoma.
Typhoid fever:		
Sacramento	Eugene, Oregon.	Patient lived at Eugene until five days previous to attack.
El Monte	Montana, 2 cases.	Patients were ill upon arrival from Montana.
Venereal diseases:		
San Francisco	Winslow, Ariz., 1 case. Little Rock, Ark., 1 case. Denver, Colo., 4 cases. Chicago, Ill., 10 cases. Houghton, Mich., 1 case. Buhl, Minn., 1 case. Duluth, Minn., 2 cases. Everett, Minn., 1 case. Hibbing, Minn., 1 case. Keewatin, Minn., 1 case. Two Harbors, Minn., 1 case. Gilead, Nebr., 1 case. Reno, Nev., 1 case. McAlester, Okla., 1 case. Portland, Oreg., 1 case. Manila, P. I., 1 case. Fort McKinley, P. I., 1 case.	Patients resided at places named when they received their infections.

CEREBROSPINAL MENINGITIS.

Kansas—McLouth.

During the week ended February 2, 1918, one case of cerebrospinal meningitis was notified at McLouth, Kans., making a total of 7 cases reported during the present outbreak.

CEREBROSPINAL MENINGITIS—Continued.

State Reports for December, 1917.

Place.	New cases reported.	Place.	New cases reported.
California:		Mississippi:	
Fresno County—		Forrest County	2
Fowler	1	Harrison County	2
Los Angeles County	2	Hinds County	1
La Verne	1	Lowndes County	1
Los Angeles	5	Perry County	1
Orange County	1	Walthall County	1
San Diego County	3		
San Diego	3	Total	8
San Francisco (city)	2		
Solano County	1	Wisconsin:	
Sonoma County	1	Milwaukee County	4
		Rock County	1
Total	20		
		Total	5
Iowa:			
Guthrie County	1		
Jasper County	1		
Polk County	3		
Wapello County	1		
Wayne County	1		
Total	7		

City Reports for Week Ended Jan. 19, 1918.

Place.	Cases.	Deaths.	Place.	Cases.	Deaths.
Akron, Ohio	1		Indianapolis, Ind	1	
Alexandria, La	7	2	Jersey City, N. J	1	1
Anniston, Ala	2		Little Rock, Ark	3	
Atlanta, Ga	9	2	Los Angeles, Cal	1	1
Baltimore, Md	4	2	Louisville, Ky	3	2
Boston, Mass		1	Lowell, Mass	1	1
Bridgeport, Conn		1	Macon, Ga	6	4
Buffalo, N. Y	4	2	Milwaukee, Wis	2	2
Charleston, S. C	1		Minneapolis, Minn	2	
Charlotte, N. C	3		Newark, N. J	4	
Chattanooga, Tenn		1	Newport News, Va	1	1
Chicago, Ill	5	4	New York, N. Y	6	3
Chillicothe, Ohio		1	Omaha, Nebr	1	
Cincinnati, Ohio	1		Philadelphia, Pa	7	1
Columbia, S. C	1		Portsmouth, Va		1
Columbus, Ohio	1		St. Louis, Mo	1	3
Dayton, Ohio	1		San Antonio, Tex	1	
Detroit, Mich	1	2	San Francisco, Cal		1
El Paso, Tex		1	Spartanburg, S. C	3	1
Green Bay, Wis	1	1	Waco, Tex	1	
Houston, Tex	1		Washington, D. C	7	1

DIPHTHERIA.

See Diphtheria, measles, scarlet fever, and tuberculosis, page 181.

ERYSIPELAS.

City Reports for Week Ended Jan. 19, 1918.

Place.	Cases.	Deaths.	Place.	Cases.	Deaths.
Baltimore, Md	1	1	Los Angeles, Cal	2	....
Boston, Mass	....	2	Milwaukee, Wis	3	....
Braddock, Pa	1	....	Montclair, N. J	1	....
Buffalo, N. Y	1	1	Newark, N. J	10	2
Camden, N. J	1	....	New Castle, Pa	1	....
Canton, Ohio	1	....	New York, N. Y	....	4
Chicago, Ill	16	2	Omaha, Nebr	1	....
Columbus, Ohio	....	2	Philadelphia, Pa	9	1
Cleveland, Ohio	6	....	Pittsburgh, Pa	10	1
Dayton, Ohio	....	1	Pontiac, Mich	1	....
Denver, Colo	3	1	Portland, Me	....	1
Detroit, Mich	3	2	Richmond, Va	....	1
Easton, Pa	1	....	Reading, Pa	2	....
Evansville, Ind	....	1	Rochester, N. Y	3	2
Galesburg, Ill	....	1	St. Joseph, Mo	2	....
Grand Rapids, Mich	2	....	St. Louis, Mo	12	1
Harrisburg, Pa	1	....	San Diego, Cal	1	....
Jackson, Mich	3	....	Steubenville, Ohio	2	....

LEPROSY.

Mississippi—Long Beach.

During the month of December, 1917, a case of leprosy, of tuber-cular type, was reported at Long Beach, Miss., in the person of Mrs. G. J. S., aged 57 years, native of Louisiana, has lived at Long Beach 23 years, previously lived at Independence and at New Orleans, La. The patient spent 5 weeks with her mother, previous to her death from similar trouble 11 years ago.

MALARIA.

State Reports for December, 1917.

Place.	New cases reported.	Place.	New cases reported.
California:		Mississippi—Continued.	
Butte County	1	Copiah County	34
Fresno County	1	Covington County	93
Glenn County—		De Soto County	26
Orland	3	Forrest County	7
Merced County	2	Franklin County	32
Los Banos	1	George County	15
San Joaquin County	1	Greene County	9
Stockton	1	Grenada County	18
Solano County—		Hancock County	50
Vacaville	1	Harrison County	57
Yolo County	1	Hinds County	133
		Holmes County	269
Total	12	Issaquena County	51
		Itawamba County	34
Mississippi:		Jackson County	47
Adams County	50	Jasper County	60
Alcorn County	11	Jefferson County	52
Amite County	33	Jefferson Davis County	2
Benton County	2	Jones County	59
Bolivar County	385	Kemper County	10
Calhoun County	31	Lafayette County	35
Carroll County	68	Lamar County	27
Chickasaw County	5	Lauderdale County	20
Choctaw County	64	Lawrence County	46
Claiborne County	56	Leake County	44
Clarke County	27	Lee County	57
Clay County	7	Leflore County	158
Coahoma County	263	Lincoln County	21

MALARIA—Continued.
State Reports for December, 1917—Continued.

Place.	New cases reported.	Place.	New cases reported.
Mississippi—Continued.		Mississippi—Continued.	
Lowndes County	11	Simpson County	25
Madison County	16	Smith County	21
Marion County	69	Stone County	16
Marshall County	42	Sunflower County	150
Monroe County	21	Tallahatchie County	41
Montgomery County	10	Tate County	69
Neshoba County	28	Tishomingo County	21
Newton County	20	Tunica County	122
Noxubee County	10	Union County	13
Oktibbeha County	64	Walthall County	5
Panola County	95	Warren County	124
Pearl River County	25	Washington County	121
Perry County	79	Wayne County	26
Pike County	55	Webster County	22
Pontotoc County	41	Wilkinson County	4
Prentiss County	25	Winston County	72
Quitman County	117	Yalobusha County	57
Rankin County	32	Yazoo County	181
Scott County	32		
Sharkey County	63	Total	4,436

City Reports for Week Ended Jan. 19, 1918.

Place.	Cases.	Deaths.	Place.	Cases.	Deaths.
Alexandria, La.		1	Little Rock, Ark.	2	
Birmingham, Ala.	1		Memphis, Tenn.		1
Hattiesburg, Miss.	5		Savannah, Ga.	1	

MEASLES.
See Diphtheria, measles, scarlet fever, and tuberculosis, page 181.

PELLAGRA.
State Reports for December, 1917.

Place.	New cases reported.	Place.	New cases reported.
California:		Mississippi—Continued.	
San Joaquin County—		Lowndes County	6
Lodi	1	Madison County	4
		Marion County	5
Mississippi:		Marshall County	12
Adams County	1	Monroe County	2
Alcorn County	1	Montgomery County	2
Amite County	1	Neshoba County	3
Benton County	1	Newton County	1
Bolivar County	27	Noxubee County	6
Calhoun County	1	Oktibbeha County	3
Carroll County	2	Panola County	2
Chickasaw County	15	Perry County	2
Choctaw County	1	Pontotoc County	5
Clay County	6	Prentiss County	1
Coahoma County	14	Quitman County	1
Copiah County	14	Rankin County	4
Covington County	1	Sharkey County	1
De Soto County	1	Simpson County	2
George County	1	Smith County	1
Hinds County	26	Sunflower County	4
Holmes County	4	Tallahatchie County	8
Itawamba County	6	Tate County	5
Jackson County	1	Tishomingo County	4
Jasper County	1	Tunica County	6
Jefferson County	1	Union County	2
Jefferson Davis County	2	Walthall County	2
Jones County	10	Washington County	7
Kemper County	2	Webster County	3
Lamar County	1	Yalobusha County	1
Lauderdale County	4	Yazoo County	8
Lee County	5		
Leflore County	1	Total	264

PELLAGRA—Continued.

City Reports for Week Ended Jan. 19, 1918.

Place.	Cases.	Deaths.	Place.	Cases.	Deaths.
Atlanta, Ga.		2	Memphis, Tenn.	2	
Birmingham, Ala.	2	2	Mobile, Ala.	2	2
Charleston, S. C.		2	New York, N. Y.		1
Little Rock, Ark.		2	Savannah, Ga.		1
Lynchburg, Va.		1	Wilmington, N. C.		2
Macon, Ga.		3			

PLAGUE.

California—Contra Costa County—Plague-Infected Squirrels Found.

On February 1, 1918, was reported the finding of 2 plague-infected squirrels on the property of the East Bay Water Co., Contra Costa County, Cal.

PNEUMONIA.

City Reports for Week Ended Jan. 19, 1918.

Place.	Cases.	Deaths.	Place.	Cases.	Deaths.
Alexandria, La.	1	1	Little Rock, Ark.	5	2
Ann Arbor, Mich.	2	1	Long Beach, Cal.	1	1
Anniston, Ala.	2		Los Angeles, Cal.	23	11
Baltimore, Md.	92	22	Lowell, Mass.	1	3
Berkeley, Cal.	1		Lynn, Mass.	8	
Boston, Mass.	44	33	Macon, Ga.	5	8
Braddock, Pa.	1		Manchester, N. H.	2	2
Brockton, Mass.	2		Nashville, Tenn.	1	7
Cambridge, Mass.	3	6	New Albany, Ind.	1	1
Chattanooga, Tenn.	4	7	Newark, N. J.	61	14
Chelsea, Mass.	7	3	New Bedford, Mass.	6	3
Chicago, Ill.	185	84	New Castle, Pa.	2	
Chillicothe, Ohio.	2	1	Newport, Ky.	5	5
Cleveland, Ohio.	43	46	Newport News, Va.	3	3
Clinton, Mass.	1		Newton, Mass.	6	1
Columbia, S. C.	1		Pasadena, Cal.	6	1
Cumberland, Md.	2	1	Philadelphia, Pa.	187	101
Dayton, Ohio.	2	10	Pittsburgh, Pa.	42	61
Detroit, Mich.	12	62	Pontiac, Mich.	2	
Duluth, Minn.	1	1	Providence, R. I.	1	11
Easton, Pa.	2		Quincy, Mass.	2	
Evansville, Ind.	2	2	Reading, Pa.	1	2
Everett, Mass.	3		Rochester, N. Y.	12	3
Fall River, Mass.	4	2	Sacramento, Cal.	4	3
Fitchburg, Mass.	1		St. Joseph, Mo.	2	2
Flint, Mich.	2	1	San Diego, Cal.	1	
Grand Rapids, Mich.	6	3	Schenectady, N. Y.	2	
Harrisburg, Pa.	5	7	Somerville, Mass.	5	3
Hattiesburg, Miss.	1		Springfield, Mass.	8	
Houston, Tex.	1	16	Springfield, Ohio.	1	3
Jackson, Mich.	2	2	Toledo, Ohio.	2	3
Johnstown, Pa.	8	2	Waco, Tex.	3	
Lancaster, Pa.	4		Waltham, Mass.	1	
Lawrence, Mass.	4	1	Wichita, Kans.	6	1
Leavenworth, Kans.	2	1	Worcester, Mass.	10	8
Lincoln, Nebr.	2	7			

POLIOMYELITIS (INFANTILE PARALYSIS).

State Reports for December, 1917.

Place.	New cases reported.	Place.	New cases reported.
California:		Mississippi:	
Butte County	1	Newton County	2
Los Angeles County	1	Rankin County	1
Tropico	1	Smith County	2
San Francisco	1	Sunflower County	1
San Joaquin County	2		
Butter County—		Total	6
Yuba City	1		
		Wisconsin:	
Total	7	Milwaukee County	2
		Oneida County	1
Iowa:		Rock County	1
Keokuk County	1		
Washington County	1	Total	4
Total	2		

City Reports for Week Ended Jan. 19, 1918.

Place.	Cases.	Deaths.	Place.	Cases.	Deaths.
Chicago, Ill	1	1	Newark, N. J	1	
Detroit, Mich		1	New York, N. Y	1	
Duluth, Minn	1	1	Pittsburgh, Pa	1	

RABIES IN ANIMALS.

City Report for Week Ended Jan. 19, 1918.

During the week ended January 19, 1918, one case of rabies in animals was reported in Columbus, Ohio.

SCARLET FEVER.

See Diphtheria, measles, scarlet fever, and tuberculosis, page 181.

SMALLPOX.

Hawaii—Honolulu Quarantine.

On February 2, 1918, a case of smallpox was removed at the Honolulu quarantine station from the steamship *Vondel*, arrived January 31, 1918, from Yokohama.

Texas—Eagle Pass—Virulent Smallpox.

During the week ended February 4, 1918, 7 new cases of smallpox with 1 death, were notified at Eagle Pass, Tex., making a total of 58 cases, with 12 deaths, reported since October 1, 1917.

West Virginia.

On February 1, 1918, outbreaks of smallpox were reported in the coal fields of Logan, Raleigh, and Marion Counties, and also at Moundsville, Huntington, and Point Pleasant.

SMALLPOX—Continued.

California Report for December, 1917.

Place.	New cases reported.	Deaths.	Vaccination history of cases.			
			Number vaccinated within 7 years preceding attack.	Number last vaccinated more than 7 years preceding attack.	Number never successfully vaccinated.	Vaccination history not obtained or uncertain.
California:						
Alameda County............	1	....	....	....	1	....
Oakland.................	1	....	....	....	1	....
Kern County.............	1	....	....	....	1	....
Maricopa................	1	....	....	....	1	....
Los Angeles County—						
Los Angeles............	4	....	....	....	4	....
Nevada County—						
Nevada City............	2	....	....	....	2	....
Sacramento County—						
Sacramento.............	1	....	....	....	1	....
San Bernardino County—						
Redlands..............	1	....	....	....	....	1
San Francisco (city).......	2	....	....	....	2	....
Solano County.............	1	....	....	....	....	1
Total..................	15	....	....	....	13	2

Miscellaneous State Reports.

Place.	Cases.	Deaths.	Place.	Cases.	Deaths.
Colorado (Dec. 1–31):			Iowa (Dec. 1–31)—Continued.		
Arapahoe County..........	3	....	Lyon County..........	1	....
Boulder County..........	1	....	Madison County.........	11	....
Chaffee County—			Marion County.........	7	....
Salida.............	3	....	Mills County.........	4	....
Delta County............	2	....	O'Brien County.........	9	....
Denver County—			Page County.........	1	....
Denver...............	41	....	Palo Alto County.........	1	....
Eagle County............	3	....	Pocahontas County.........	2	....
Fremont County..........	1	....	Polk County.........	80	....
La Plata County..........	1	....	Pottawattamie County....	49	....
Mesa County.............	12	....	Ringgold County.........	1	....
Morgan County...........	1	....	Scott County.........	1	....
Sedgwick County.........	1	....	Shelby County.........	1	....
Logan County............	4	....	Sioux County.........	34	....
			Taylor County.........	1	....
Total.................	73	....	Wapello County.........	6	....
			Wayne County.........	8	....
Iowa (Dec. 1–31):			Woodbury County.......	2	....
Adair County.............	1	....	Wright County.........	4	....
Appanoose County.........	29	....			
Audubon County..........	1	....	Total.........	443	....
Boone County............	2	....			
Bremer County...........	1	....	Mississippi (Dec. 1–31):		
Butler County............	3	....	Alcorn County.........	26	....
Cass County.............	5	....	Benton County.........	1	....
Cerro Gordo County......	2	....	Bolivar County.........	4	....
Cherokee County.........	2	....	Calhoun County.........	5	....
Chickasaw County........	13	....	Carroll County.........	14	....
Clay County.............	1	....	Chickasaw County........	33	....
Clayton County..........	1	....	Clarke County.........	1	....
Crawford County.........	18	....	Clay County.........	10	....
Decatur County..........	109	....	De Soto County.........	7	....
Des Moines.............	4	....	Grenada County.........	12	....
Dubuque County..........	4	....	Hinds County.........	8	....
Fayette County..........	1	....	Holmes County.........	13	....
Floyd County............	3	....	Jasper County.........	13	....
Hardin County...........	1	....	Jones County.........	13	....
Harrison County.........	1	....	Lauderdale County.......	4	....
Henry County............	1	....	Lee County.........	2	....
Iowa County.............	3	....	Leflore County.........	4	....
Johnson County..........	3	....	Lowndes County.........	3	....
Kossuth County..........	4	....	Madison County.........	3	....
Linn County.............	3	....	Marion County.........	1	....

SMALLPOX—Continued.

Miscellaneous State Reports—Continued.

Place.	Cases.	Deaths.	Place.	Cases.	Deaths.
Mississippi (Dec. 1–31)—Con.			Wisconsin (Dec. 1–31)—Con.		
Marshall County..........	8	....	Chippewa County........	2	....
Newton County..........	9	....	Crawford County.........	10	....
Oktibbeha County..........	6	....	Dane County............	1	....
Panola County..........	16	....	Douglas County..........	2	....
Pearl River County.....	3	....	Dunn County............	4	....
Pontotoc County..........	1	....	Eau Claire County.......	2	....
Quitman County..........	3	....	Fond du Lac County.....	1	....
Rankin County..........	5	....	Jackson County..........	4	....
Scott County............	4	....	Juneau County..........	2	....
Sharkey County..........	3	....	Kenosha County.........	1	....
Stone County............	1	....	Kewaunee County........	2	....
Sunflower County.......	4	....	La Crosse County........	35	....
Tallahatchie County.....	19	....	Lincoln County..........	18	....
Tunica County..........	6	....	Manitowoc County.......	1	....
Union County............	2	....	Milwaukee County.......	19	....
Walthall County..........	2	....	Monroe County..........	1	....
Warren County..........	3	....	Oconto County..........	1	....
Washington County.....	1	....	Outagamie County.......	8	....
Yalobusha County.......	2	....	Pepin County...........	2	....
Yazoo County..........	22	....	Polk County............	2	....
			Racine County..........	6	....
Total...............	296	....	Rock County............	21	....
			Sauk County............	84	....
Wisconsin (Dec. 1–31):			Sheboygan County.......	1	....
Ashland County..........	1	....	Walworth County.......	1	....
Barron County..........	5	....			
Buffalo County..........	10	....	Total..................	255	....
Calumet County..........	2	....			

City Reports for Week Ended Jan. 19, 1918.

Place.	Cases.	Deaths.	Place.	Cases.	Deaths.
Akron, Ohio..............	28	....	Kokomo, Ind...........	1	....
Alton, Ill...............	13	....	La Crosse, Wis.........	15	....
Ann Arbor, Mich.........	2	....	La Fayette, Ind........	1	....
Anniston, Ala.............	1	....	Leavenworth, Kans.....	1	....
Atlanta, Ga...............	2	....	Lincoln, Nebr..........	4	....
Baltimore, Md.............	1	....	Little Rock, Ark.......	33	....
Butte, Mont..............	11	....	Lorain, Ohio...........	9	....
Canton, Ohio.............	3	....	Louisville, Ky.........	2	....
Charlotte, N. C..........	1	....	Memphis, Tenn.........	6	....
Chicago, Ill.............	13	....	Milwaukee, Wis........	10	....
Cincinnati, Ohio.........	14	....	Minneapolis, Minn.....	15	....
Cleveland, Ohio.........	37	....	Montgomery, Ala.......	5	....
Coffeyville, Kans.........	2	....	Nashville, Tenn........	1	....
Columbus, Ohio.........	8	....	New Orleans, La.......	14	....
Covington, Ky...........	2	....	Niagara Falls, N. Y....	1	....
Cumberland, Md..........	1	....	Oklahoma City, Okla....	6	....
Danville, Ill............	3	....	Omaha, Nebr...........	32	....
Dayton, Ohio...........	10	....	Pittsburgh, Pa.........	5	....
Denver, Colo...........	6	....	Pontiac, Mich..........	6	....
Des Moines, Iowa.........	53	....	Portland, Oreg.........	3	....
Detroit, Mich............	89	....	Quincy, Ill............	7	....
Dubuque, Iowa..........	1	....	Rock Island, Ill.......	1	....
El Paso, Tex............	1	1	Sacramento, Cal........	2	....
Erie, Pa................	2	....	St. Joseph, Mo........	17	....
Everett, Wash...........	3	....	St. Louis, Mo.........	16	....
Flint, Mich.............	20	....	Salt Lake City, Utah...	21	....
Fort Wayne, Ind.........	21	....	San Francisco, Cal.....	4	....
Fort Worth, Tex.........	16	....	Sioux City, Iowa.......	16	....
Grand Haven, Mich.......	1	....	Steelton, Pa...........	2	....
Grand Rapids, Mich......	26	....	Superior, Wis..........	1	....
Hattiesburg, Miss........	2	....	Syracuse, N. Y.........	1	....
Indianapolis, Ind........	67	....	Terre Haute, Ind.......	6	....
Jackson, Mich...........	2	....	Toledo, Ohio...........	4	....
Kalamazoo, Mich..........	1	....	Wheeling, W. Va.......	3	....
Kansas City, Kans........	58	....	Wichita, Kans.........	15	....
Knoxville, Tenn...........	1	....			

TETANUS.

City Reports for Week Ended Jan. 19, 1918.

Place.	Cases.	Deaths.	Place.	Cases.	Deaths.
Charleston, S. C.		1	Terre Haute, Ind		1
Detroit, Mich.		1	Worcester, Mass	1	
St. Louis, Mo.		1			

TUBERCULOSIS.

See Diphtheria, measles, scarlet fever, and tuberculosis, page 181.

TYPHOID FEVER.

State Reports for December, 1917.

Place.	New cases reported.	Place.	New cases reported.
California:		Colorado:	
Alameda County	2	Chaffee County	1
Alameda	1	Denver County—	
Berkeley	1	Denver	2
Oakland	3	Jefferson County	1
Piedmont	2	Huerfano County	1
Contra Costa County—		La Plata County	1
Richmond	1	Montrose County	1
Fresno County—		Otero County	1
Fowler	3	Prowers County	1
Fresno	3	Pueblo County—	
Imperial County	1	Pueblo	3
El Centro	1	Weld County—	
Kern County	3	Greeley	2
Los Angeles County	8		
Alhambra	1	Total	14
Burbank	1		
El Monte	2	Mississippi:	
La Verne	1	Adams County	4
Los Angeles	13	Amite County	4
Santa Monica	1	Benton County	1
Sawtelle	1	Bolivar County	3
Whittier	1	Calhoun County	1
Mariposa County	1	Carroll County	2
Mendocino County	3	Chickasaw County	4
Merced County	1	Choctaw County	6
Monterey County—		Claiborne County	1
Monterey	2	Coahoma County	2
Orange County	3	Copiah County	2
Fullerton	1	Covington County	2
Placer County—		De Soto County	2
Auburn	1	Franklin County	1
Plumas County	1	Grenada County	4
Riverside County—		Hancock County	1
Riverside	2	Harrison County	3
Blythe	7	Hinds County	7
Sacramento County—		Holmes County	1
Sacramento	2	Jasper County	9
San Bernardino County—		Jones County	10
Colton	1	Kemper County	1
San Diego County—		Lafayette County	5
San Diego	2	Lamar County	2
San Francisco (city)	18	Lauderdale County	1
San Joaquin County—		Lawrence County	1
Stockton	3	Leake County	2
San Mateo County—		Lee County	3
San Mateo	1	Leflore County	5
Santa Clara County	1	Lincoln County	4
Stanislaus County	1	Madison County	2
Modesto	1	Marion County	2
Sutter County	3	Marshall County	3
Tehama County—		Montgomery County	6
Corning	1	Newton County	2
Yolo County—		Noxubee County	1
Woodland	1	Oktibbeha County	4
	—	Panola County	5
Total	107	Pearl River County	4
		Perry County	4

TYPHOID FEVER— Continued.

State Reports for December, 1917- Continued.

Place.	New cases reported.	Place.	New cases reported
Mississippi—Continued.		Nevada:	
Pike County	2	Nye County	1
Pontotoc County	4	Washoe County	1
Prentiss County	1		
Quitman County	2	Total	1
Scott County	4		
Smith County	4	Wisconsin:	
Sunflower County	5	Bayfield County	1
Tallahatchie County	10	Chippewa County	1
Tate County	6	Eau Claire County	1
Tishomingo County	2	Jackson County	1
Tunica County	2	Jefferson County	1
Warren County	1	Juneau County	1
Washington County	6	Manitowoc County	1
Wayne County	3	Milwaukee County	1
Webster County	4	Polk County	1
Wilkinson County	3	Shawano County	1
Winston County	6	Sheboygan County	3
Yalobusha County	1	Wood County	1
Total	19?	Total	??

City Reports for Week Ended Jan. 19, 1918.

Place.	Cases.	Deaths.	Place.	Cases.	Death.
Akron, Ohio	1		Minneapolis, Minn	3	
Albany, N. Y	1		Nashville, Tenn	1	1
Alexandria, La	1		Newark, N. J	2	1
Anniston, Ala	1		New Britain, Conn	1	
Atlanta, Ga	1	1	New Castle, Pa	2	
Austin, Tex		1	New Haven, Conn	1	
Baltimore, Md	3		New Orleans, La	2	
Boston, Mass	1		Newport News, Va	3	1
Brockton, Mass	1		New York, N. Y	5	1
Buffalo, N. Y		1	Niagara Falls, N. Y	2	
Canton, Ohio		1	Oakland, Cal	1	
Chicago, Ill	4	1	Ogden, Utah	1	
Chillicothe, Ohio	1		Philadelphia, Pa	8	1
Cincinnati, Ohio	1	1	Pontiac, Mich	1	
Cleveland, Ohio	2	1	Portland, Oreg	2	
Coffeyville, Kans	4		Providence, R. I	2	
Des Moines, Iowa	3		Racine, Wis		1
Detroit, Mich	5	2	Roanoke, Va	1	
East Orange, N. J		1	Rockland, Me	1	
El Paso, Tex		3	Saginaw, Mich	1	
	1		St. Louis, Mo	2	1
	1		Savannah, Ga	1	
Grand Rapids, Mich	2	1	Schenectady, N. Y	2	
Green Bay, Wis		1	Springfield, Ohio	2	
Indianapolis, Ind	1		Stockton, Cal	1	
Kansas City, Kans	1		Toledo, Ohio	2	
Los Angeles, Cal	5	1	Troy, N. Y	2	
	2		Washington, D. C	3	
		2	Watertown, N. Y	1	
	2		Wheeling, W. Va	1	
			Zanesville, Ohio	1	

DIPHTHERIA, MEASLES, SCARLET FEVER, AND TUBERCULOSIS.

State Reports for December, 1917.

State.	Cases reported.			State.	Cases reported.		
	Diph-theria.	Measles.	Scarlet fever.		Diph-theria.	Measles.	Scarlet fever.
California..........	268	850	319	Mississippi.........	103	9,390	54
Colorado..........	84	129	124	Nevada............	2	47	19
Iowa..............	87	....	230	Wisconsin.........	244	417	461

City Reports for Week Ended Jan. 19, 1918.

City.	Popula-tion as of July 1, 1916 (estimated by U. S. Census Bureau).	Total deaths from all causes.	Diphtheria.		Measles.		Scarlet fever.		Tuber-culosis.	
			Cases.	Deaths.	Cases.	Deaths.	Cases.	Deaths.	Cases.	Deaths.
Over 500,000 inhabitants:										
Baltimore, Md.............	589,621	269	28	4	92	.....	14	.....	24	36
Boston, Mass.............	756,476	306	69	4	108	4	42	.....	28	31
Chicago, Ill.............	2,497,722	728	152	26	65	1	82	5	516	63
Cleveland, Ohio...........	674,073	218	44	3	17	.....	5	.....	39	23
Detroit, Mich.............	571,784	235	72	4	34	.....	51	.....	30	16
Los Angeles, Cal.........	503,812	158	14	1	61	.....	8	.....	52	17
New York, N. Y.........	5,602,841	1,812	262	20	968	20	136	8	493	191
Philadelphia, Pa.........	1,709,518	740	57	8	71	4	53	2	124	64
Pittsburgh, Pa...........	579,090	241	17	3	165	.....	9	.....	29	16
St. Louis, Mo............	757,309	254	61	3	40	.....	33	.....	37	13
From 300,000 to 500,000 inhabitants:										
Buffalo, N. Y............	468,558	162	16	1	27	.....	30	.....	30	18
Cincinnati, Ohio.........	410,476	159	9	.....	5	.....	10	.....	23	27
Jersey City, N. J.........	306,345	....	15	.....	41	.....	7	.....	11	.....
Milwaukee, Wis..........	436,535	....	10	4	74	.....	58	1	19	1
Minneapolis, Minn........	363,454	....	19	.....	16	.....	14	.....	.....	.....
Newark, N. J............	408,894	137	17	1	121	.....	24	.....	26	15
New Orleans, La.........	371,747	....	9	1	122	.....	1	.....	30	33
San Francisco, Cal.......	463,516	132	14	.....	26	.....	12	.....	29	10
Washington, D. C.........	363,980	165	16	1	118	1	40	1	20	14
From 200,000 to 300,000 inhabitants:										
Columbus, Ohio..........	214,878	82	3	.....	11	1	17	.....	9	7
Denver, Colo............	260,800	58	11	1	49	.....	24	1	.....	9
Indianapolis, Ind........	271,708	....	36	.....	36	.....	35	.....	6	.....
Louisville, Ky...........	238,910	113	10	1	34	.....	5	.....	5	5
Portland, Oreg..........	295,463	44	1	.....	22	.....	6	1	7	5
Providence, R. I.........	254,960	64	15	.....	7	.....	4	.....	.....	5
Rochester, N. Y.........	256,417	90	11	2	15	1	15	.....	16	5
From 100,000 to 200,000 inhabitants:										
Albany, N. Y............	104,199	....	1	.....	5	.....	.....	.....	14	.....
Atlanta, Ga.............	190,558	....	10	1	12	3	1	1	.....	10
Birmingham, Ala.........	181,762	104	.....	.....	95	1	3	1	15	14
Bridgeport, Conn........	121,579	46	9	.....	6	.....	1	.....	6	10
Cambridge, Mass.........	112,981	52	3	.....	4	.....	24	.....	3	4
Camden, N. J...........	106,233	....	4	.....	54	.....	2	.....	.....	.....
Dayton, Ohio...........	127,224	50	6	2	4	.....	4	.....	4	5
Des Moines, Iowa........	101,598	....	2	.....	.....	.....	9	.....	.....	.....
Fall River, Mass........	128,366	47	5	2	1	.....	4	.....	7	2
Fort Worth, Tex.........	104,582	37	.....	.....	5	.....	.....	.....	.....	5
Grand Rapids, Mich......	128,291	39	6	2	13	.....	10	.....	6	3
Houston, Tex...........	112,307	55	.....	.....	19	1	.....	.....	.....	1
Lawrence, Mass.........	100,560	27	5	.....	3	.....	1	.....	5	3
Lowell, Mass...........	113,245	37	.....	.....	7	.....	.....	.....	4	4
Lynn, Mass.............	102,425	16	5	.....	3	.....	1	.....	3	.....
Memphis, Tenn..........	148,995	52	5	.....	8	.....	3	1	10	12
Nashville, Tenn.........	117,057	46	3	.....	41	.....	3	.....	1	2
New Bedford, Mass.......	118,158	42	2	.....	25	.....	.....	.....	11	4
New Haven, Conn........	149,685	....	4	.....	5	.....	.....	.....	9	6
Oakland, Cal...........	196,604	50	5	.....	7	.....	7	.....	8	3
Omaha, Nebr...........	165,470	40	7	1	73	.....	8	.....	.....	5
Reading, Pa............	109,381	24	4	1	2	.....	4	.....	.....	.....

DIPHTHERIA, MEASLES, SCARLET FEVER, AND TUBERCULOSIS
Continued.

City Reports for Week Ended Jan. 19, 1918—Continued.

City.	Population as of July 1, 1916 (estimated by U. S. Census Bureau).	Total deaths from all causes.	Diphtheria.		Measles.		Scarlet fever.		Tuberculosis	
			Cases.	Deaths.	Cases.	Deaths.	Cases.	Deaths.	Cases.	Deaths.
From 100,000 to 200,000 inhabitants—Continued.										
Richmond, Va.	156,687	67	3		35		1		6	9
Salt Lake City, Utah	117,399	27	7		45		21			2
San Antonio, Tex.	123,831	114	1		3				1	16
Springfield, Mass.	103,942	29	11		17		5		4	2
Syracuse, N. Y.	155,624	43	12	2	33	1	22		2	3
Tacoma, Wash.	112,770		1		3		5			
Toledo, Ohio	191,554	68	4	1	7		8		14	7
Trenton, N. J.	111,593	54	11		6		3		4	2
Worcester, Mass.	163,314	64	5		9		6			3
From 50,000 to 100,000 inhabitants:										
Akron, Ohio	83,625		3		3		5			
Atlantic City, N. J.	57,660				3				3	1
Bayonne, N. J.	69,873		2		3		3		1	
Berkeley, Cal.	57,658	11	1		1		6			
Brockton, Mass.	67,449	10	1		3		3		2	
	60,852	31	5	1			2			2
	60,734	28	3	1						
Chattanooga, Tenn.	60,075	10			18		2		4	2
Covington, Ky.	57,144	26	1		1		1			1
Duluth, Minn.	94,495	20	1		26		5		2	2
	63,705	36	1		4					11
Erie, Pa.	75,195	15	7		2		1		3	1
Evansville, Ind.	76,078	23	2		2				13	
Flint, Mich.	84,772	13	5		2		8			
Fort Wayne, Ind.	76,183	20	3				4			
Harrisburg, Pa.	72,015	35	4		3		1		4	1
Hoboken, N. J.	77,214	23	3	1	16	1	1		2	
Jacksonville, Fla.	76,101				32		2		4	
Johnstown, Pa.	68,529	20					11		2	1
Kansas City, Kans.	99,437		1		20		17		1	
Lancaster, Pa.	50,833		1				2			
Little Rock, Ark.	57,343	14			15					
Malden, Mass.	51,155	12	1	1	6		1		3	
Manchester, N. H.	78,283	28			7		3		9	
Mobile, Ala.	58,221	36	1		34	1				2
New Britain, Conn.	53,794	22	1		4		1			1
Oklahoma City, Okla.	92,943	20			15		1			3
Passaic, N. J.	71,744	22	2						4	2
Portland, Me.	63,807	17	1		91		1			
Rockford, Ill.	55,185	16			10		1			
Sacramento, Cal.	66,495	20	2		3		5		1	3
Saginaw, Mich.	55,642	23		1			3			
St. Joseph, Mo.	85,236	30	7	1	33		2		3	2
San Diego, Cal.	53,330	24	5		112		4		2	5
Savannah, Ga.	68,805	32	1		29		1		2	
Schenectady, N. Y.	90,519	17	2		3		2		12	2
Sioux City, Iowa	57,078						13			
Somerville, Mass.	87,039	19	3		42	1	1		4	1
South Bend, Ind.	68,946	22	2	1	4		2		1	3
Springfield, Ill.	61,120	22			6				1	2
Springfield, Ohio	51,550	26	1		3		2			4
Terre Haute, Ind.	66,083	26	1		4				2	4
Troy, N. Y.	77,916		1				1		3	2
Wichita, Kans.	70,722		4		66		6		2	1
Wilkes-Barre, Pa.	76,776	30	7	1	7		2		4	3
Wilmington, Del.	94,265	30	1		3		3		2	1
From 25,000 to 50,000 inhabitants:										
Alameda, Cal.	27,732	6	1				1			
Austin, Tex.	34,814	23	2		9					
Brookline, Mass.	32,730	12			9		2		1	
Butler, Pa.	27,632	9	2	1	12		1			
Butte, Mont.	43,425	1	3	1	6					
Charlotte, N. C.	39,823				33					
Chelsea, Mass.	46,192	30	7		9		2		3	1
Chicopee, Mass.	29,319	4	1		14		3		3	1
Columbia, S. C.	34,611		2		10					
Cumberland, Md.	26,074	6			1					
Danville, Ill.	32,261	16	3		1				1	1
Davenport, Iowa	48,811		2				11			

DIPHTHERIA, MEASLES, SCARLET FEVER, AND TUBERCULOSIS—
Continued.

City Reports for Week Ended Jan. 19, 1918—Continued.

City.	Population as of July 1, 1916 (estimated by U.S. Census Bureau).	Total deaths from all causes.	Diphtheria		Measles		Scarlet fever.		Tuberculosis.	
			Cases.	Deaths.	Cases.	Deaths.	Cases.	Deaths.	Cases.	Deaths.
From 25,000 to 50,000 inhabitants—Continued.										
Dubuque, Iowa	39,873	7			7					
Easton, Pa	30,530	7	4		16					
East Orange, N.J.	42,458	10			10		2			
Elgin, Ill	28,203	16	1		4		1			2
Everett, Mass	39,233	9	5		2		1		1	
Everett, Wash	35,486				1				1	
Fitchburg, Mass	41,781	11	1		6		3		2	3
Galveston, Tex	41,863	26	1		10		3	1	2	2
Green Bay, Wis	29,353	14				8				
Jackson, Mich	35,363	24	8	3	3		50	2	4	2
Kalamazoo, Mich	45,886	23	2		16		2		3	3
Kenosha, Wis	31,576	6	5	2	2		6		2	
Kingston, N.Y.	26,771	8								1
Knoxville, Tenn	38,676				6		3			
La Crosse, Wis	31,677	9					1			
Lincoln, Nebr	46,515	18	2	1			8		1	
Long Beach, Cal	27,587	17			11		2		1	2
Lorain, Ohio	36,964						5		1	
Lynchburg, Va	32,940	20								3
Macon, Ga	45,757	38	2	1	14		5		3	1
Madison, Wis	30,699				5		1			
Medford, Mass	26,234	3	3		2		5		1	1
Montclair, N.J.	26,318				25				3	
Montgomery, Ala	43,285	26	1		31		3			1
Nashua, N.H.	27,327	12								1
Newburgh, N.Y.	28,603	13			22				2	3
New Castle, Pa	41,133		2		3		4			
Newport, Ky	31,927	12							1	1
Newport, R.I.	30,108	2					1			
Newton, Mass	43,715	5	7		13		6			
Niagara Falls, N.Y.	37,353	9			1					1
Norristown, Pa	31,401	10							3	
Ogden, Utah	31,404	7			11					
Orange, N.J.	33,080	14	1		3				2	2
Pasadena, Cal	46,450	16			2				2	3
Perth Amboy, N.J.	41,185	18	4		29		1		2	
Pittsfield, Mass	38,629	1	1		9		4		4	
Portsmouth, Va	39,651	11	1		2		4			1
Quincy, Ill	36,796	9			6					
Quincy, Mass	38,136	9	2		7		1		3	1
Racine, Wis	46,486	13								1
Roanoke, Va	43,284	14	2	1	3		3		1	2
Rock Island, Ill	28,926				3		3			
San Jose, Cal	38,902				3					
Steubenville, Ohio	27,445	8			4					
Stockton, Cal	35,358				26				3	
Superior, Wis	46,226	12			8		3			1
Taunton, Mass	36,283	9			1		1		2	
Waco, Tex	33,385	11			1		2			
Waltham, Mass	30,570	11	7						2	1
Wheeling, W.Va	43,377	20								1
Williamsport, Pa	33,809	8	6		2		1			1
Wilmington, N.C.	29,892	15			14					1
Winston-Salem, N.C.	31,155	22			39		1		4	
Zanesville, Ohio	30,863	7			2				1	
From 10,000 to 25,000 inhabitants:										
Alexandria, La	15,333	11			16					1
Alton, Ill	22,874	13	3	1	5					2
Ann Arbor, Mich	15,010	15	1		12					1
Anniston, Ala	14,112				11				1	
Berlin, N.H.	13,599	3					1			
Braddock, Pa	21,685			2		1		2		
Cairo, Ill	15,794	11	1		3					1
Chillicothe, Ohio	15,470	2	1		2				1	
Clinton, Mass	¹13,075				1					
Coffeyville, Kans	17,548				9					
Concord, N.H.	22,669	12					3			

¹ Population Apr. 15, 1910; no estimate made.

DIPHTHERIA, MEASLES, SCARLET FEVER, AND TUBERCULOSIS
Continued.

City Reports for Week Ended Jan. 19, 1918—Continued.

City.	Population as of July 1, 1916 (estimated by U. S. Census Bureau).	Total deaths from all causes.	Diphtheria.		Measles.		Scarlet fever.		Tuberculosis.	
			Cases.	Deaths.	Cases.	Deaths.	Cases.	Deaths.	Cases.	Deaths.
From 10,000 to 25,000 inhabitants—continued.										
Galesburg, Ill	24,276	12								2
Hattiesburg, Miss	16,482	6			8					
Kearny, N. J	23,539	8			25				2	1
Kokomo, Ind	20,930	7			1				2	1
La Fayette, Ind	21,286	9								
Leavenworth, Kans	19,363	2			5		4	5	1	
Long Branch, N. J	13,395	3					1		1	
Marinette, Wis	14,610	4								
Melrose, Mass	17,445	6	1		1					
Morristown, N. J	13,284	1	2						1	
Nanticoke, Pa	23,126	3	1				1			
New Albany, Ind	23,629	8			2				1	1
Newburyport, Mass	15,243	5							1	
New London, Conn	20,985	9	2						1	
Newport News, Va	20,562	14			1				2	2
North Adams, Mass	22,019	4			1					
Northampton, Mass	19,926	11								
Plainfield, N. J	23,805	6	1		4				1	
Pontiac, Mich	17,524	17	2		4		1		1	
Portsmouth, N. H	11,666		1		1		3			
Rocky Mount, N. C	12,067	6	1		1				2	1
Rutland, Vt	14,831	3					1			1
Saratoga Springs, N. Y	13,821	4							1	
South Bethlehem, Pa	24,204		1							
Spartanburg, S. C	21,365	13	1							
Steelton, Pa	15,548	3	1		2		1		6	
Washington, Pa	21,618				4					
Wilkinsburg, Pa	23,228	12			7		2			
Woburn, Mass	15,969	2								

¹ Population Apr. 15, 1910; no estimate made.

FOREIGN.

CUBA.

Communicable Diseases—Habana.

Communicable diseases have been notified at Habana as follows:

Disease.	Jan. 1-10, 1918.		Cases remaining under treatment Jan. 10, 1918.	Disease.	Jan. 1-10, 1918.		Cases remaining under treatment Jan. 10, 1918.
	New cases.	Deaths.			New cases.	Deaths.	
Cerebrospinal meningitis	1	....	[1] 1	Measles	7	....	11
Diphtheria	11	2	1	Scarlet fever	....	....	4
Leprosy	....	....	11	Smallpox	....	1	2
Malaria	19	....	[2] 37	Typhoid fever	6	5	[3] 66
				Varicella	21	....	19

[1] From the United States.
[2] From the interior, 21; imported from Mexico, 1.
[3] From the interior, 29.

SENEGAL.

Plague—St. Louis.

Plague was reported present at St. Louis, Senegal, February 2, 1918.

The presence of plague in the interior of Senegal was reported September 30, 1917.

CHOLERA, PLAGUE, SMALLPOX, AND TYPHUS FEVER.

Reports Received During Week Ended Feb. 8, 1918.[1]

CHOLERA.

Place.	Date.	Cases.	Deaths.	Remarks.
India:				
Bombay	Nov. 4-24	6	6	
Calcutta	Nov. 18-24	....	8	
Rangoon	Nov. 4-17	2	2	
Indo-China:				
Saigon	Nov. 22-28	1	....	
Philippine Islands:				
Provinces		....	....	Dec. 9-15, 1917: Cases, 130; deaths, 95.
Bobol	Dec. 9-15	35	26	
Capiz	do	4	3	
Iloilo	do	10	6	
Leyte	do	2	2	
Mindanao	do	36	21	
Occidental Negros	do	31	28	
Oriental Negros	do	12	12	
Provinces		....	....	Dec. 16-22, 1917: Cases, 161; deaths, 97.
Bobol	Dec. 16-22	36	25	
Capiz	do	5	5	
Leyte	do	1	1	
Mindanao	do	103	50	
Occidental Negros	do	8	7	
Oriental Negros	do	8	3	
Turkey in Asia:				
Bagdad	Nov. 1-15	....	40	

[1] From medical officers of the Public Health Service, American consuls, and other sources.

CHOLERA, PLAGUE, SMALLPOX, AND TYPHUS FEVER—Continued.

Reports Received During Week Ended Feb. 8, 1918—Continued.

PLAGUE.

Place.	Date.	Cases.	Deaths.	Remarks.
Ceylon:				
Colombo.................	Oct. 28–Nov. 17...	4	5	
India:				Nov. 11–24, 1917: Cases, 48,577;
Bombay................	Nov. 4–24..........	50	39	deaths, 36,615.
Henzada...............	Oct. 21–27..........	....	1	
Madras Presidency........	Nov. 11–17..........	1,739	1,351	
Mandalay..............	Nov. 3–17..........	....	69	
Rangoon...............	Oct. 28–Nov. 17...	27	25	
Senegal:				
St. Louis................	Feb. 2............	....	....	Present.
Siam:				
Bangkok...............	Oct. 28–Nov. 24...	10	6	

SMALLPOX.

Place.	Date.	Cases.	Deaths.	Remarks.
Canada:				
New Brunswick –				
Moncton:......	Jan. 20–26.........	1	....	
Restigouche County....	Jan. 19..........	60	....	
Ontario—				
Sarnia...............	Jan. 20–26.........	2	....	
China:				
Amoy....................	Nov. 5–25........	....	....	Present.
Antung..................	Dec. 17–23........	7	....	
Chungking..............	Nov. 18–24........	....	....	Do.
Shanghai................	Dec. 17–23........	11	29	Cases, foreign; deaths, Chinese.
Tientsin................	Dec. 9–22........	6	....	
India:				
Bombay.................	Nov. 4–24.........	10	3	
Madras.................	Nov. 11–17........	2	1	
Rangoon...............	Oct. 28 Nov. 17...	3	1	
Indo-China:				
Saigon..................	Nov. 22 28........	21	4	
Mexico:				
Mexico City.............	Dec. 16–29........	7	....	
Do..................	Dec. 30–Jan. 12....	8	....	
Newfoundland:				
St. Johns...............	Jan. 12–18........	4	....	
Trepassey...............	Jan. 4............	....	....	Outbreak with 11 cases reported.
Portugal:				
Lisbon..................	Dec. 9–15.........	1	....	
Russia:				
Petrograd...............	Sept. 23–Nov. 18 ..	17	....	
Siam:				
Bangkok................	Nov. 25–Dec. 1....	1	1	
Turkey in Asia:				
Bagdad................	....	....	....	Present in November, 1917.

TYPHUS FEVER.

Place.	Date.	Cases.	Deaths.	Remarks.
Egypt:				
Alexandria................	Dec. 10–16.........	11	3	
Mexico:				
Mexico City..............	Dec. 16–29........	154	....	
Do....................	Dec. 30–Jan. 12...	139	....	
Russia:				
Petrograd...............	Sept. 23–Nov. 18..	70	....	
Switzerland:				
Zurich..................	Nov. 9–15.........	2	....	

CHOLERA, PLAGUE, SMALLPOX, AND TYPHUS FEVER—Continued.

Reports Received from Dec. 29, 1917, to Feb. 1, 1918.

CHOLERA.

Place.	Date.	Cases.	Deaths.	Remarks.
China:				
Antung....................	Nov. 26-Dec. 2....	3	1	
India:				
Bombay...................	Oct. 28-Nov. 3....	11	6	..
Calcutta.................	Sept. 16-Oct. 27...	....	68	
Indo-China:				
Provinces..............	....	....	....	Sept. 1-30, 1917: Cases, 74; deaths,
Anam....................	Sept. 1-30......	13	10	37.
Cambodia...............	....do...........	19	12	
Cochin-China...........	....do...........	32	13	
Kwang-Chow-Wan........	....do...........	10	2	
Java:				
East Java..............	Oct. 28-Nov. 3....	1	1	
West Java..............	....	......	......	Oct. 19-Nov. 29, 1917: Cases, 68;
Batavia................	Oct. 19-Nov. 29...	38	8	deaths, 35.
Persia:				
Mazanderan Province—				
Astrabad..............	July 31...........	......	......	Present.
Barfrush..............	July 1-27.........	34	23	
Chahmirzad...........	....	......	......	25 cases reported July 31, 1917.
Chahrastagh..........	June 15-July 25...	10	8	
Kharek...............	May 28-June 11....	21	13	
Sari.................	July 3-29.........	273	144	
Yekchambe-Bazar.....	June 3............	6	....	
Philippine Islands:				
Provinces..............	....	......	......	Nov. 18-Dec. 8, 1917: Cases, 701;
Antique..............	Nov. 18-Dec. 1....	48	32	deaths, 471.
Bohol................	Nov. 18-Dec. 8....	76	36	
Capiz................	Nov. 25-Dec. 8....	3	2	
Iloilo...............	....do............	167	128	
Leyte................	....do............	10	9	
Mindanao.............	....do............	184	113	
Occidental Negros....	....do............	148	91	
Oriental Negros......	....do............	74	44	
Romblon..............	Nov. 25-Dec. 1....	1	1	
Siam:				
Bangkok................	Sept 16-22........	1	1	

PLAGUE.

Place.	Date.	Cases.	Deaths.	Remarks.
Brazil:				
Bahia..................	Nov. 4-Dec. 15....	4	4	
British Gold Coast:				
Axim...................	Jan. 8............	....	....	Present.
Ceylon:				
Colombo................	Oct. 14-27........	4	3	
Egypt:				Jan. 1-Nov. 15, 1917: Cases, 728;
Port Said..............	July 23-29........	1	2	deaths, 398.
India....................	....	....	....	Sept. 16-Nov. 10, 1917: Cases,
Bombay.................	Oct. 28-Nov. 3....	43	40	98,758; deaths, 72,648.
Calcutta...............	Sept. 16-29.......	......	2	
Karachi................	Oct. 21-Nov. 10...	6	5	
Madras Presidency......	Oct. 31-Nov. 6....	1,555	1,208	
Mandalay...............	Oct. 14-20........	......	20	
Rangoon................	Oct. 21-27........	9	10	
Indo-China:				Sept. 1-30, 1917: Cases, 34; deaths,
Provinces..............	....	......	......	30.
Anam..................	Sept. 1-30........	12	11	
Cambodia..............	....do............	12	11	
Cochin-China..........	....do............	10	8	
Saigon.................	Oct. 31-Nov. 18...	3	4	
Java:				
East Java..............	Oct. 27-Nov. 10...	28	27	
Siam:				
Bangkok................	Sept. 16-22.......	1	1	
Straits Settlements:				
Singapore..............	Oct. 28-Nov. 24...	3	3	

CHOLERA, PLAGUE, SMALLPOX, AND TYPHUS FEVER—Continued.

Reports Received from Dec. 29, 1917, to Feb. 1, 1918—Continued.

SMALLPOX.

Place.	Date.	Cases.	Deaths.	Remarks.
Algeria:				
Algiers...................	Nov. 1–30.........	1	....	
Australia:				
New South Wales..........				July 12–Nov. 20, 1917: Cases, 34.
Abermain..............	Oct. 25–Nov. 20...	3	....	
Cessnock...............	July 12–Oct. 11...	7	....	Newcastle district.
Eumangla..............	Aug. 15............	1	....	
Kurri Kurri...........	Dec. 5.............	1	....	
Mungindi.............	Aug. 13............	1	....	
Warren...............	July 12–Oct. 25...	22	....	
Brazil:				
Bahia.................	Nov. 10–Dec. 8....	3	....	
Pernambuco...........	Nov. 1–15..........	1	....	
Rio de Janeiro........	Sept. 30–Dec. 1....	519	151	
Sao Paulo............	Oct. 29–Nov. 4.....	....	2	
Canada:				
British Columbia—				
Winnipeg...........	Dec. 30–Jan. 5.....	1	....	
New Brunswick—				
Kent County.......	Dec. 4.............	....	....	Outbreak. On main line Canadian Ry., 25 miles north of Moncton.
Ontario—				
Hamilton..............	Dec. 16–22.........	1	....	
Do................	Jan. 13–19.........	2	....	
Sarnia................	Dec. 9–15..........	1	....	
Do................	Jan. 6–12..........	14	....	
Windsor.............	Dec. 30–Jan. 5.....	1	....	
Quebec—				
Montreal..............	Dec. 16–Jan. 5.....	5	....	
Do................	Jan. 6–12..........	1	....	
China:				
Amoy.................	Oct. 22–Nov. 4.....	....	....	Present.
Antung...............	Dec. 3–16.........	6	2	
Chungking............	Nov. 11–Dec. 1....	....	....	Do.
Dairen...............	Nov. 18–24........	1	....	
Harbin...............	May 14–June 30....	20	....	Chinese Eastern Ry.
Do................	July 1–Oct. 15....	4	....	Do.
Hungtahotse Station......	Oct. 28–Nov. 4....	1	....	Do.
Manchuria Station........	May 14–June 30....	6	....	Do.
Do................	July 1–Oct. 15....	3	....	Do.
Mukden..............	Nov. 11–24........	....	....	Present.
Shanghai.............	Nov. 18–Dec. 16...	30	62	Cases, foreign; deaths among natives.
Tientsin.............	Nov. 11–Dec. 8....	7	....	
Cuba:				
Habana...............	Jan. 7..............	1	....	Nov. 8, 1917: 1 case from Coruña. Dec. 5, 1917: 1 case.
Marianao.............	Jan. 8..............	1	....	6 miles distant from Habana.
Egypt:				
Alexandria............	Nov. 12–18.........	1	....	
Cairo.................	July 23–Aug. 5.....	5	1	
France:				
Lyon.................	Nov. 18–Dec. 16....	6	3	
Great Britain:				
Birmingham...........	Nov. 11–17.........	19	....	
India:				
Bombay...............	Oct. 21–27.........	2	1	
Madras...............	Oct. 31–Nov. 6....	4	1	
Indo-China:				
Provinces.............				Sept. 1–30, 1917: Cases, 198; deaths, 44.
Anam...............	Sept. 1–30........	61	12	
Cambodia...........	....do...........	7	....	
Cochin-China........	....do...........	124	44	
Tonkin.............	....do...........	1	....	
Saigon..............	Oct. 29–Nov. 18...	41	12	
Italy:				
Milan.................	October............	3	....	
Turin................	Oct. 29–Dec. 9....	123	120	
Castellamare..........	Dec. 10............	3	....	Among refugees.
Florence.............	Dec. 1–15.........	17	4	
Naples...............	To Dec. 10........	3	....	Do.
Java:				
East Java.............	Oct. 27–Nov. 10...	19	....	
Mid-Java.............	Oct. 10–Nov. 21...	55	....	
West Java............				Oct. 19–Nov. 29, 1917: Cases, 162, deaths, 23.
Batavia.............	Nov. 2–8..........	1	....	
Mexico:				
Mazatlan.............	Dec. 5–11..........	....	1	
Mexico City...........	Nov. 11–17.........	9	....	
Piedras Negras........	Jan. 11............	200	....	

CHOLERA, PLAGUE, SMALLPOX, AND TYPHUS FEVER—Continued.

Reports Received from Dec. 29, 1917, to Feb. 1, 1918—Continued.

SMALLPOX—Continued.

Place.	Date.	Cases.	Deaths.	Remarks.
Newfoundland:				
St. Johns................	Dec. 8–Jan. 4......	25	....	
Do............	Jan. 5–11..........	14	....	
Philippine Islands:				
Manila.....................	Oct. 28–Dec. 8.....	5	....	
Portugal:				
Lisbon..................	Nov. 4–10..........	1	....	
Portuguese East Africa:				
Lourenço Marques.........	Aug. 1–Sept. 30....	....	4	
Russia:				
Moscow...................	Aug. 26–Oct. 6....	22	2	
Petrograd................	Aug. 31–Oct. 27....	59	3	
Spain:				
Coruna...................	Dec. 2–15..........	....	4	
Seville..................	Oct. 1–Nov. 30....	....	26	
Tunisia:				
Tunis....................	Dec. 11–20.........	....	1	
Venezuela:				
Maracaibo.................	Dec. 2–8...........	....	1	

TYPHUS FEVER.

Place.	Date.	Cases.	Deaths.	Remarks.
Algeria:				
Algiers.................	Nov. 1–30..........	2	....	
Australia:				
South Australia.........	....	....	....	Nov. 11–17, 1917: Cases, 1.
Brazil:				
Rio de Janeiro..........	Oct. 28–Dec. 1.....	7	....	
Canada:				
Ontario—				
Kingston..............	Dec. 2–8...........	3	....	
Quebec—				
Montreal..............	Dec. 16–22.........	2	1	
China:				
Antung.................	Dec. 3–16..........	11	1	
Chosen (Formosa):				
Seoul..................	Nov. 1–30..........	1	....	
Egypt:				
Alexandria.............	Nov. 8–25..........	110	44	
Cairo..................	July 23–Sept. 23...	23	8	
Port Said..............	July 30–Sept. 23...	3	3	
Great Britain:				
Glasgow................	Dec. 21............	1	....	
Manchester.............	Dec. 2–8...........	1	....	
Greece:				
Saloniki...............	Nov. 11–Dec. 8.....	....	36	
Japan:				
Nagasaki...............	Nov. 26–Dec. 16...	5	5	
Java:				
East Java..............	....	....	....	Oct. 15–Nov. 15, 1917: Cases, 17; deaths, 3.
Mid Java...............	....	....	....	Oct. 10–Nov. 13, 1917: Cases, 42; deaths, 2.
Samarang..............	Oct. 17–Nov. 13...	9	1	
West Java..............	....	....	....	Oct. 19–Nov. 29, 1917: Cases, 30; deaths, 5.
Batavia..............	Oct. 19–Nov 15...	41	7	
Mexico:				
Aguascalientes.........	Dec. 15............	....	2	
Mexico City............	Nov. 11–Dec. 15...	337	....	
Russia:				
Archangel..............	Sept. 1–11.........	7	2	
Moscow.................	Aug. 26–Oct. 6....	49	2	
Petrograd..............	Aug. 31–Oct. 27...	22	....	
Vladivostok............	Oct. 29–Nov 4....	12	1	
Sweden:				
Goteborg...............	Nov. 18–24.........	1	....	
Tunisia:				
Tunis..................	Nov. 30–Dec. 6....	....	1	
Union of South Africa:				
Cape of Good Hope State...	Sept. 10–Nov. 4...	3,312	608	

X

EXTRA-CANTONMENT ZONE HEALTH REGULATIONS.

The following ordinances and regulations have been adopted in pursuance of the plan of cooperation of the United States Public Health Service, the Medical Corps of the United States Army, and State and local health authorities for the protection of the health of the troops in camps and of the inhabitants of extra-cantonment zones:

CAMP DODGE EXTRA-CANTONMENT ZONE.

Venereal Diseases—Control of. (Rules of Board of Health of Des Moines, Iowa, Jan. 11, 1918.)

Whereas by section 2575-A-6-A, supplement to the code, 1913, syphilis and gonorrhea are declared contagious and infectious; and

Whereas in recent months there has been an alarming increase in the number of persons in the city of Des Moines afflicted with these diseases; and

Whereas in order to protect the health of the thousands of our soldier boys now in training at said camp and the thousands that are yet to come, and to maintain at the highest point the efficiency and strength of these soldiers, and to prevent the spread of this plague in our own community and throughout the State, it is necessary to restrain and treat all persons so afflicted; and

Whereas by section 2571a of the 1913 supplement to the code, it is made the duty of the local board of health, through the mayor, to make such provisions as are best calculated to protect the public from contagious and infectious diseases and to remove persons afflicted with such diseases to a separate house, a house of detention, or hospital; and

Whereas there are a number of persons in the city afflicted with such diseases, with every prospect of the number increasing very rapidly unless immediate steps are taken to prevent such increase; and

Whereas the Government of the United States, through its Public Health Service, and the State of Iowa, through the governor, and the American Red Cross, have indicated a willingness to cooperate with the city in the control of venereal diseases and in bearing the expense necessary for efficient control thereof; and

Whereas the State board of health on the 3d day of January, 1918, adopted a resolution directing and ordering all local boards of health to immediately make all necessary provisions for the protection of the inhabitants of the city against danger from venereal diseases: Now, therefore,

The local board of health of the city of Des Moines, in special session, do hereby find and declare: That the rapid increase of the number of persons in the city of Des Moines afflicted with the diseases mentioned in the preamble hereof is not only alarming, but has reached the point of actual public danger, and to meet the emergency thus existing this board promulgates the following rules:

(1) Every physician, nurse, attendant, hospital superintendent, druggist, member of the police department, police magistrate, or other person having knowledge of a

known or suspected case of syphilis or gonorrhea, must immediately report the same to the mayor; such report to be in writing and to contain the necessary information from which the person afflicted with either of said diseases may be located and from which the necessity of restraining such person may be determined.

(2) It shall be the duty of the chief of police to cause all persons arrested for being found in a disorderly house, all prostitutes, and all other persons held under arrest who are suspected of having syphilis or gonorrhea in the infectious stages to be examined before released or discharged, and if any of such persons are found to be afflicted with either of said diseases to report the same promptly as required in rule 1.

(3) It shall be the duty of the mayor upon receiving notice of the existence of a case of venereal disease such as hereinabove defined to immediately issue his order to the chief of police directing that officer to cause the person afflicted with such disease to be removed to a separate house, house of detention, or hospital, and there to be restrained until the city's health physician, under proper written order, authorizes the release and discharge of said person: *Provided, however,* Whenever a reported case involves a person attached to the military or naval services of the Federal Government, the mayor, upon receiving such report, shall immediately order said person turned over to the medical officer of the military or naval organization, to be by said organization restrained until such time as such health officer authorizes his or her release or discharge.

(4) It shall be the duty of the chief of police to cause to be immediately certified to the city health department a copy of every such order so issued by the mayor, together with a brief statement of such action as has been taken thereunder by the police department, and upon receipt of such certified copy and statement, it shall be the duty of the Secretary of the health department to file the same in his office and to thereafter enter upon the record of the office a brief record of such further action taken thereunder by the department.

(5) In case any person or persons liable for the support of such person so restrained shall be financially unable to secure the proper care, provisions, or medical attendance, it shall be the duty of the mayor, through the health physician, to procure for such diseased person proper care, provisions, supplies, and medical attendance while so restrained. All bills for supplies furnished and services rendered by order of the mayor hereunder shall be authorized by the health physician and allowed and paid for only on the basis of the local market price for such provisions, services, and supplies. Such authority by the health physician shall be by written order designating the person or persons employed to furnish such services or supplies, such order to be issued before said services or supplies are actually furnished, a copy of which said order shall be attached to the bill when the same is presented for audit and payment.

(6) It shall be the duty of the health physician in all cases where persons have been restrained under the order of the mayor, as provided in these rules, to permit the person so restrained to employ at his or her own expense the physician or nurse of his or her choice, and to allow such restrained person to provide such supplies and care while so restrained, as he or she shall so require. All bills and expenses incurred in carrying out the provisions of these rules shall be filed with the secretary of the local board of health, and it shall be the duty of this board at its next regular meeting, or at a special meeting called for the purpose, to examine and audit such bills and, if found correct, approve and certify the same to the proper authorities for payment.

(7) It shall be unlawful for any person to move, cause to be moved, or assist in moving any person restrained under the order of the mayor as herein provided from one place to another within the city without first having the written permit or order of the health physician.

(8) It shall be the duty of all the local health authorities, the health physician, and the members of the police department to cooperate in every way with the United

States Public Health Service in its plan for the organization and maintenance of clinics for the control of venereal diseases and in selecting the best measures for such control, and all military police and health officers of the United States Government assigned to, and on duty in the city of Des Moines, are hereby required to observe the provisions of these rules applicable to the police department of the city and are hereby clothed with the same power to enforce the same.

(9) It shall be the duty of the secretary of the local board of health to certify these rules and regulations to the secretary of the State board of health and to cause publication thereof in the newspapers of the city and upon request furnish a copy of said rules to any resident physician or citizen.

(10) Every person who shall fail to comply with the provisions of these rules, or who shall violate any of the provisions thereof, shall be guilty of a misdemeanor and upon conviction be fined in the sum of not to exceed $100 or be imprisoned in the county jail not to exceed 30 days.

Duties of City Health Officer—Employees—Public Health Service Officer as Sanitary Adviser. (Resolution of City Council of Des Moines, Iowa, Aug. 24, 1917.)

Whereas in view of the unusual conditions existing in connection with the United States Army cantonment in this vicinity, and in view of the vital importance to both soldiers and civilians of maintaining in the city of Des Moines high-grade sanitary conditions, and in accordance with the recommendations of Surg. E. K. Sprague, United States Public Health Service, in charge of the extra-cantonment sanitary district, Camp Dodge, dated August 12, 1917; therefore be it

Resolved by the city council of the city of Des Moines, That City Health Officer H. L. Saylor be and is hereby relieved of all the official duties except those pertaining strictly to his office as city health officer in the prevention of communicable diseases; and be it further

Resolved, That City Health Officer H. L. Saylor be and is hereby authorized and empowered to employ the following assistants for the administration of public health in the city of Des Moines:

Clerical: One clerk, salary per annum, $1,200; 1 full-time stenographer, $900.

Sanitary inspectors: Three inspectors, each at $1,200; 12 inspectors, each at $1,080.

Milk inspectors: Two inspectors, each at $1,500.

Visiting nurses: Two nurses, each at $900.

Meat inspector: One meat inspector (trained in veterinary service), $1,800.

The above for the administration of public health and for the prevention of communicable diseases in the city of Des Moines, Iowa; and be it further

Resolved, That the representative of the United States Public Health Service, Surg. E. K. Sprague, be requested to act without pay as sanitary adviser to the city health officer, H. L. Saylor, in the administration of public health in the city of Des Moines, Iowa, and the said representative of the United States Public Health Service be and is hereby authorized and empowered to enforce in his official capacity any or all public health ordinances prescribed by the mayor and city council of Des Moines, Iowa.

CAMP LEE EXTRA-CANTONMENT ZONE.

Druggists to Report Sales of Certain Remedies. (Regulation of Richmond (Va.) Health Department, Jan. 16, 1918.)

All druggists and other retail dealers in drugs and remedies advertised to relieve persons suffering from contagious and infectious diseases shall require a receipt of the purchasers of such remedies, giving name and address and the name and address of the individual for whom the remedy is bought.

The dealer shall report monthly to the health department, on blanks furnished by the department, the names of the purchasers registered.

A list of the diseases of which a record is desired shall be furnished the druggist or dealer, and the name of the remedies coming within the scope of this regulation shall also, as far as they can be learned, be designated from time to time.

Foodstuffs—Protection of. Poultry Stalls. (Regulation of Richmond (Va.) Health Department, Jan. 16, 1918.)

1. All persons renting space in the city markets who wish to handle live poultry must occupy stalls especially designated for that purpose, apart from fresh meat stalls, butter dealers, etc., and such stalls must be approved by the city health department.

Lessees of said stalls, if they so desire, may, in addition to live poultry, also sell dressed poultry, eggs, and game, but nothing else.

2. All dealers handling butter, cheese, preserves, pickles, delicatessen, salads, etc., which are served without further cooking, must at all times keep such food products carefully protected from contamination by dust, flies, and the hands of passers-by.

Communicable Diseases—List of Notifiable Diseases. (Regulation of Richmond (Va.) Health Department, Jan. 16, 1918.)

The following diseases are named as reportable, and the penalty for failure by a physician to report any one of them within 24 hours after diagnosis is a fine of $10 for each 24 hours such disease remains unreported

Amebic dysentery.	Ophthalmia neonatorum.
Bubonic plague.	Pellagra.
Cancer.	Pneumonia (lobar).
Cerebrospinal meningitis.	Puerperal sepsis.
Chancroid.	Rabies.
Chicken pox.	Scabies.
Cholera.	Scarlet fever.
Diphtheria (throat, nose, and skin).	Smallpox.
Erysipelas.	Syphilis
Gonorrhea.	Tetanus.
Hookworm disease.	Tuberculosis (lungs, throat, bone, and
Infantile diarrhea.	skin).
Infantile paralysis.	Trachoma
Impetigo contagiosa.	Typhoid fever.
Leprosy	Typhus fever.
Malaria.	Whooping cough.
Measles.	Yellow fever.
Mumps.	

Physicians are expected to report the following diseases as soon as their presence is suspected

Diphtheria of the throat and nose.	Scarlet fever.
Cerebrospinal meningitis.	Smallpox.
Infantile paralysis.	Tuberculosis of lungs.
Measles.	Typhoid fever.

FORT OGLETHORPE EXTRA-CANTONMENT ZONE.

The following regulations have been issued jointly by the medical officer in charge of the work of the United States Public Health Service in the extra-cantonment zone around Fort Oglethorpe, Ga., and the commanding officer of the United States troops at Fort Oglethorpe:

Regulations for Barber Shops, Billiard Halls, and Manicuring Parlors.

[To be enforced by the United States Public Health Service and the United States Army in extra-cantonment zone.]

Owners, proprietors, and managers of barber shops, manicuring parlors, billiard halls, and similar places, who comply with the following regulations will be issued a card indicating that the establishment is approved by the United States Public Health Service, and that the United States Army gives soldiers permission to patronize the establishment. Places not complying will be denied such card and the card if already granted may be removed in case of later noncompliance. Places having no cards will receive no patronage from the men in uniform.

(Regulations marked with two asterisks apply to barber shops, manicuring parlors, billiard halls, and similar places. Those with a single asterisk apply to barber shops and manicuring parlors only. Those with no designation apply only to barber shops.)

**1. All owners, proprietors, or managers of barber shops, manicuring parlors, billiard halls, and similar places shall keep up-to-date, accurate, and complete lists of all persons employed in said barber shops, manicuring parlors, billiard halls, and similar places, indicating sex, color, and duties of each employee, and shall furnish copy of same to medical officer in charge, United States Public Health Service, which copy must be kept constantly revised to date by said owner, proprietor, or manager, and in constant agreement with all changes of personnel of employees.

*2. No owner, proprietor, or manager of a barber shop or manicuring parlor shall act, or shall knowingly permit any person to act, as a barber or manicurist, who is suffering from any communicable, especially skin or venereal, disease; and, if he so acts, shall immediately submit, and shall immediately require each person already employed, and each new employee before his employment, to submit to medical examination by the medical officer in charge, United States Public Health Service. This examination is to be made at the expense of the United States Government and without charge to the person examined. In case said barber, employee, or applicant shall be found free from said communicable diseases, he shall be permitted to continue in or enter employment in barber shop or manicuring parlor.

**3. All barber shops and manicuring parlors shall be equipped with running hot and cold water and with all such appliances, furnishings, and materials as may be necessary to enable persons employed in and about said barber shop or manicuring parlor to comply with the requirements of this regulation, and the owners, proprietors, or managers of all barber shops, manicuring parlors, billiard halls, and similar places shall keep their shops, furniture, tools, appliances, and equipment therein used in a sanitary condition at all times.

*4. All combs, hair brushes, dusters, and other articles must be washed at frequent intervals, at least once a day, and shall be kept clean at all times. All mugs, shaving brushes, razors, scissors, pinchers, needles, clippers, and other instruments must be sterilized either by the use of an approved steam sterilizer, immersion in boiling water or in compound solution of cresol of 5 per cent strength after each separate use.

5. The blade of a razor which has been stropped during the operation of shaving a customer shall be immersed in compound cresol solution of not less than 5 per cent strength, and then wiped, before being again applied to the face of a customer.

*6. No barber or manicurist shall use for service of any customer any towel or wash cloth that has not been boiled or laundered since last used.

7. All barbers must wear while serving customers washable white coats.

*8. Every barber or manicurist shall clean his hands thoroughly immediately before serving each customer.

*9. No barber or manicurist shall, to stop the flow of blood, use alum or other material unless the same is applied as a powder and with a clean towel.

10. No barber shall permit any person to use the headrest of any barber chair under his control unless the headrest is covered by clean new paper or by a fresh, clean towel.

11. No person affected with any disease of the skin or scalp shall be shaved or have his hair cut in any barber shop.

**12. No barber shop, manicuring parlor, billiard hall, or similar place shall be used as a sleeping room or dormitory. Floors must be kept free from hair at all times and must be swept and mopped daily, and all furniture and equipment must be kept free from hairs and dust.

*13. No barber or manicurist or other person in charge of a barber shop or manicuring parlor shall undertake to treat any disease of the skin.

**14. Adequate cuspidors must be furnished in every barber shop, manicuring parlor, billiard hall, or similar place; said cuspidors shall be cleaned daily, shall be kept in a clean and sanitary condition, and shall be provided at all times with a disinfectant solution consisting of 5 per cent phenol or its equivalent.

**15. All newspapers, magazines, and other reading material furnished to the public or left in the barber shop, manicuring parlor, billiard hall, or similar place shall be destroyed or removed at the end of each day.

16. No barber shall be allowed to remove the cut hairs from the face or neck of a customer by the process of blowing (i. e., blowing through the lips); mechanical bellows or sanitary brush may be used.

17. The use of rubber collar protectors is hereby prohibited.

**18. The owner, proprietor or manager of every barber shop, manicuring parlor, billiard hall, or similar place shall keep a copy of these regulations, to be furnished by the officer in charge, posted at all times in a conspicuous place in his place of business.

Hotel, Restaurant and Eating House Regulations.

To be enforced by the United States Public Health Service and the United States Army in Extra-Cantonment Zone.

Owners, proprietors, and managers of eating houses who comply with the following regulations will be issued a card indicating that the establishment is approved by the United States Public Health Service, and that the United States Army gives soldiers permission to patronize the place. Places not complying will be denied such card and the card if already granted may be removed in case of later non-compliance. Places having no card will receive no patronage from the men in uniform.

1. The various requirements of this regulation apply to hotels, restaurants, lunch counters, cafés, cafeterias, soda fountains, ice-cream parlors, soft-drink stands, and all other places, hereinafter called eating houses, where food is prepared for sale, sold, distributed, or displayed for sale. Food, as herein used, includes all articles used for food, drink, confectionery, or condiment, and all articles used in the preparation thereof.

2. All owners, proprietors, or managers of eating houses shall keep up-to-date, accurate, and complete lists of all persons employed in said eating houses, indicating

sex and color, and duties performed by each employee, and shall furnish copy of same to medical officer in charge, United States Public Health Service, which copy must be kept constantly revised up-to-date by said owner, proprietor, or manager, and in constant agreement with all changes of personnel of employees.

3. No owner, proprietor, or manager shall require or permit any person to work, nor shall any person work, in any eating house who is affected with any venereal disease, smallpox, diphtheria, scarlet fever, yellow fever, tuberculosis, trachoma, typhoid fever, dysentery, measles, mumps, German measles, whooping cough, chickenpox, or any other infectious or contagious disease.

4. Every employee, and every person desiring to work in such eating house, before entering such employment, shall secure examination by a physician designated by the medical officer in charge, United States Public Health Service, provided that medical examination shall not be required of employees in hotels and other eating places who are not in any way connected with food production, preparation, service, or sale. This examination is to be made at the expense of the United States Government and without charge to the person examined. In case said employee or applicant shall be found free from all the communicable diseases listed above, he shall be permitted to continue or enter said employment.

5. Every eating house shall be properly lighted, drained, plumbed, and ventilated, and conducted with strict regard to the influence of such conditions upon the health of the employees or other persons therein employed.

6. The floors, side walls, ceiling, furniture, receptacles, implements, and machinery of every eating house shall at all times be kept in a clean, healthful, and sanitary condition.

7. All food in the process of preparation, distribution, or display must be securely protected from flies, dust, dirt, and in so far as may be necessary by all reasonable means from all other foreign or injurious contamination.

8. All garbage, refuse, dirt, and waste products subject to decomposition or fermentation must be removed daily.

9. The clothing of all employees, clerks, and other persons therein employed must be kept clean.

10. The doors, windows, and other openings of every eating place, during such time as flies make, in the opinion of the medical officer in charge, such precaution necessary, shall be fitted with self-closing screen doors and wire window screens of not less than 14 mesh to the inch, which shall be close fitting and in good condition.

11. Every eating house shall have convenient and adequate toilet or toilet rooms separate and apart from the room or rooms where food is prepared, served, or displayed. The floors in such toilet rooms shall be of good, nonabsorbent material, and shall be kept clean and in a sanitary condition. Said toilet or toilets shall be furnished with separate ventilating flues and shall be well lighted. They shall at all times be fly-tight and every reasonable precaution must be observed to prevent the access of animals which might spread excreta or other body discharges about the premises.

12. Lavatories and wash rooms shall be adjacent to or in toilet rooms and shall be supplied with running water, soap, and individual towels, and shall be maintained in a sanitary condition. All employees and others who handle food or the ingredients of its preparation shall, before beginning work or after visiting toilet or toilets, wash their hands and arms thoroughly.

13. Cuspidors for the use of employees and other persons shall be provided whenever necessary and each cuspidor shall be thoroughly emptied and washed daily with disinfectant solution, consisting of 5 per cent phenol or its equivalent, and shall be provided at all times with at least 5 ounces of such solution.

14. No person or persons shall be allowed to live or sleep or store articles used for this purpose in the kitchen, dining room, or any other room of an eating place where food is prepared, served, stored, or displayed.

15. No owner, proprietor, or manager of an eating house shall provide or expose any toweling or similar article, except individual paper towels, for use of the public generally in any place under his control, or allow any towel or similar article to be so provided, exposed, or used there unless such towel has been laundered after each separate use.

16. All dishes, glasses, silver, and other implements used by customers shall be thoroughly washed in boiling water with soap, rinsed in clean water at the boiling temperature, and either dried with a clean towel or allowed to dry in such a place that they are protected from dirt and contamination.

17. All eating houses must be provided with running water in the kitchen with the exception of those situated in areas absolutely unprovided with main-line water supplies.

18. All straws used at soda fountains and soft drink stands shall be kept in suitable containers to keep same in a sanitary, cleanly, and safe condition, with the ends protected from dust.

19. All bottled goods must be sold and served in the original containers and straws must be inserted in the bottle for the customer's use. The contents of the bottle must not be poured into a glass.

20. All eating houses must have:

(a) A milk supply, where milk is served, which is approved by inspectors of the United States Public Health Service.

(b) Water supply free from contamination and the purity of which must be approved by the United States Public Health Service.

(c) A sanitary method of sewage disposal approved by the United States Public Health Service.

21. Eating houses outside the corporate limits of Chattanooga must comply with all provisions of the foregoing regulations which are possible and practicable in such districts as have not a public water supply.

22. The owner, proprietor, or manager of every eating house shall keep a copy of these regulations, to be furnished by the officer in charge, posted in a conspicuous place in his place of business.

PREVALENCE OF DISEASE.

No health department, State or local, can effectively prevent or control disease without knowledge of when, where, and under what conditions cases are occurring.

UNITED STATES.

EXTRA-CANTONMENT ZONES—CASES REPORTED WEEK ENDED FEB. 12

CAMP BEAUREGARD ZONE, LA

Cerebrospinal meningitis:
Rural district............................... 2
Malaria:
Pineville..................................... 1
Measles:
Alexandria................................. 5
Pineville................................... 1
Boyce....................................... 12
Melford..................................... 1
Rural district............................. 2
Mumps:
Alexandria................................. 2
Pneumonia:
Boyce....................................... 1
Pneumonia, broncho:
Pineville................................... 1
Scarlet fever:
Alexandria................................. 1
Smallpox:
Alexandria................................. 1
Pineville................................... 1
Typhoid fever:
Pineville................................... 1
Whooping cough:
Pineville................................... 7

CAMP BOWIE ZONE, TEX

Diphtheria:
Fort Worth................................. 2
Gonorrhea:
Fort Worth................................. 5
Measles:
Fort Worth................................. 4
Polytechnic................................ 2
Meningitis:
Fort Worth................................. 1
Mansfield.................................. 1
Mumps:
Fort Worth................................. 5
Pneumonia:
Fort Worth................................. 6
Mansfield.................................. 3
Saginaw.................................... 1
Scarlet fever:
Fort Worth................................. 1

CAMP BOWIE ZONE—continued

Smallpox:
Fort Worth................................. 12
Syphilis:
Fort Worth................................. 2
Tuberculosis, pulmonary:
Fort Worth................................. 2
Typhoid fever:
Fort Worth................................. 4

CAMP DODGE ZONE, IOWA.

Chicken pox:
Des Moines................................. 1
German measles:
Des Moines................................. 1
Measles:
Des Moines................................. 2
Gonorrhea:
Des Moines................................. 2
Scarlet fever:
Des Moines................................. 13
Johnson Station............................ 21
Grimes..................................... 1
Smallpox:
Des Moines................................. 28
Syphilis:
Des Moines................................. 10
Syphilis and gonorrhea:
Des Moines................................. 3

CAMP FUNSTON ZONE, KANS.

Diphtheria:
Manhattan.................................. 4
Measles:
Keats...................................... 1
Randolph................................... 7
Manhattan.................................. 88
Junction City.............................. 9
Cleburne................................... 1
Leonardville............................... 1
Mumps:
Army City.................................. 4
Ogden...................................... 1
Manhattan.................................. 8
Pneumonia:
Manhattan.................................. 4

EXTRA-CANTONMENT ZONES—CASES REPORTED WEEK ENDED FEB. 12—Continued.

CAMP FUNSTON ZONE, KANS.—continued.

Scarlet fever:
   Manhattan 5
Smallpox:
   Chapman 1
   Ogden 2
   Manhattan 11
   Junction City 2
   Cleburne 1
   Leonardville 4

CAMP GORDON ZONE, GA.

Diphtheria:
   East Point, Fulton County 1
German measles:
   Atlanta 13
Gonorrhea:
   Atlanta 5
Measles:
   Atlanta 14
Meningitis, cerebrospinal:
   Atlanta 8
   East Point, Fulton County 1
Mumps:
   Atlanta 11
   Buckhead, Fulton County 1
Pneumonia:
   Atlanta 1
Scarlet fever:
   Atlanta 4
   East Point, Fulton County 3
Septic sore throat:
   Atlanta 1
Smallpox:
   Atlanta 1
Syphilis:
   Atlanta 1
Tuberculosis:
   Atlanta 3
Whooping cough:
   Atlanta 1

CAMP GREENE ZONE, N. C.

Chicken pox:
   Charlotte Township 1
Diphtheria:
   Charlotte Township 1
German measles:
   Charlotte Township 11
Gonorrhea:
   Charlotte Township 3
Gonorrhea and chancroids:
   Charlotte Township 1
Gonorrhea and syphilis:
   Charlotte Township 2
Measles:
   Charlotte Township 27
Meningitis, cerebrospinal:
   Charlotte Township 1
   Paw Creek Township 1
Mumps:
   Charlotte Township 3

CAMP GREENE ZONE, N. C.—continued

Smallpox:
   Charlotte Township 1
   Paw Creek Township 4
Syphilis:
   Charlotte Township 5
Syphilis and chancroids:
   Charlotte Township 1
Tuberculosis:
   Charlotte Township 2

CAMP HANCOCK ZONE, GA.

Chicken pox:
   North Augusta 1
German measles:
   Augusta 12
   Martinez 1
   North Augusta 13
Measles:
   Augusta 20
   Hephzibah 1
Meningitis, cerebrospinal:
   Hagler's Brickyard 1
Mumps:
   Augusta 1
Pneumonia, lobar:
   Augusta 1
Smallpox:
   Augusta 1
Tuberculosis, pulmonary:
   Augusta 5
Whooping cough:
   Augusta 1

FORT LEAVENWORTH ZONE, KANS.

Chicken pox:
   Leavenworth 5
Diphtheria:
   Leavenworth 2
German measles:
   Leavenworth 40
Measles:
   Leavenworth 1
   Leavenworth County 1
Meningitis:
   Leavenworth 1
Mumps:
   Leavenworth 1
Pneumonia, lobar:
   Leavenworth 2
   Leavenworth County 1
Scarlet fever:
   Leavenworth 2
Smallpox:
   Leavenworth 5
   Leavenworth County 5

CAMP LEE ZONE, VA.

Chicken pox:
   Hopewell 3
   Dinwiddie County 1

EXTRA-CANTONMENT ZONES—CASES REPORTED WEEK ENDED FEB. 12—Continued.

CAMP LEE ZONE, VA.—continued.

German measles:
Ettricks... 11
Petersburg... 5
Hopewell... 4
Gonorrhea:
Prince George County............................... 3
Petersburg.. 2
Measles:
Petersburg.. 2
Hopewell.. 45
Meningitis, cerebrospinal:
Petersburg.. 1
Mumps:
Petersburg..
Hopewell..
Ettricks.. 3
Dinwiddie County.................................... 28
Pneumonia:
Petersburg.. 1
Ettricks.. 1
Septic sore throat:
Petersburg.. 1
Ettricks.. 1
Prince George County................................ 1
Tuberculosis:
Petersburg.. 2
City Point.. 1
Whooping cough:
Ettricks.. 1

CAMP LEWIS ZONE, WASH.

German measles:
Du Pont 6
American Lake....................................... 4
Steilacoom 4
Steilacoom Lake..................................... 2
Clover Creek.. 8
Spanaway.. 2
Parkland.. 1
Lacamas... 2
Tacoma.. 1

CAMP LOGAN ZONE, TEX.

Houston:
Chicken pox... 1
Diphtheria.. 3
Gonorrhea... 1
German measles...................................... 6
Measles... 28
Mumps... 6
Pneumonia... 9
Smallpox.. 2
Tuberculosis.. 4
Typhoid fever....................................... 1
Whooping cough...................................... 1

CAMP MACARTHUR ZONE, TEX.

Diphtheria:
Waco.. 1
German measles:
Waco.. 6
Precinct Four....................................... 13

CAMP MACARTHUR ZONE, TEX.—continued.

Gonorrhea:
Waco.. 1
Malaria:
Waco.. 1
Measles:
Waco.. 16
Precinct Four....................................... 4
Meningitis, cerebrospinal:
Waco.. 3
Mumps:
Waco.. 6
Pneumonia, lobar:
Waco.. 1
Smallpox:
Waco.. 1
Whooping cough:
Waco.. 2

CAMP McCLELLAN ZONE, ALA.

Chicken pox:
Anniston.. 24
Blue Mountain....................................... 1
Diphtheria:
Anniston.. 1
German measles:
District Three...................................... 6
Measles:
Anniston.. 4
Hobson City... 3
Jacksonville.. 1
Meningitis, cerebrospinal:
Anniston.. 2
Oxford.. 1
Meningitis, tubercular:
Anniston.. 1
Pneumonia:
Anniston.. 1
Blue Mountain....................................... 2
District Three...................................... 1
Pellagra:
Anniston.. 1
Smallpox:
Anniston.. 14
District Four....................................... 1
Oxford.. 4
Tuberculosis:
Anniston.. 1

FORT OGLETHORPE ZONE, GA.

Cerebrospinal meningitis:
Chattanooga, Tenn................................... 5
Eastlake, Tenn 1
North Chattanooga, Tenn............................. 1
Chicken pox:
Chattanooga, Tenn................................... 2
Rossville, Ga....................................... 4
Diphtheria:
Chattanooga, Tenn................................... 2
German measles:
Chattanooga, Tenn................................... 3
Eastlake, Tenn 1
Rossville, Ga....................................... 1

EXTRA-CANTONMENT ZONES—CASES REPORTED WEEK ENDED FEB. 12—Continued.

FORT OGLETHORPE ZONE, GA.—continued.

Gonorrhea:
Chattanooga, Tenn.. 8
Measles:
Chattanooga, Tenn.......................... 4
East Chattanooga, Tenn................... 1
Eastlake, Tenn............................. 1
St. Elmo, Tenn............................. 1
Mumps:
Chattanooga, Tenn........................ 15
East Chattanooga, Tenn................... 1
Rossville, Ga............................. 1
Pneumonia:
Chattanooga, Tenn.. 4
East Chattanooga, Tenn 1
Scarlet fever:
Chattanooga, Tenn........................ 2
Rossville, Ga............................. 1
St. Elmo, Tenn............................ 1
Smallpox:
Chattanooga, Tenn.... 1
Tuberculosis:
Chattanooga, Tenn........................ 2
Whooping cough:
Rossville, Ga.. 1

CAMP PIKE ZONE, ARK.

Cerebro-spinal meningitis:
Little Rock............ 2
Chancroid:
Little Rock............................... 5
Sweet Home................................ 1
Chicken pox:
Little Rock 4
Diphtheria:
North Little Rock 1
Dysentery:
Little Rock...... 1
German measles:
Little Rock............................... 1
Scotts.................................... 1
Gonorrhea:
Little Rock............................... 6
Malaria:
Scotts.. 1
Measles:
Little Rock............................... 22
North Little Rock......................... 7
Sweet Home................................ 1
Mumps:
Little Rock............................... 4
North Little Rock......................... 1
Pellagra:
Scotts.................................... 1
Pneumonia:
Levy 1
Little Rock............................... 5
North Little Rock......................... 1
Scarlet fever:
Little Rock....... 1
Septic sore throat:
Scotts 1

CAMP PIKE ZONE, ARK.—continued.

Smallpox:
Keo....................................... 1
North Little Rock.........................
Syphilis:
Little Rock............................... 10
Scotts.................................... 1
Tuberculosis:
Little Rock............................... 9
North Little Rock......................... 2

CAMP SEVIER ZONE, S. C.

Measles:
Butler Township.......................... 1
City View................................. 1

CAMP SHELBY ZONE, MISS.

Cerebrospinal meningitis:
Agnes..................................... 2
Hattiesburg 1
Chicken pox:
Hattiesburg............................... 1
Diphtheria:
Biloxi.................................... 2
Brooklyn.................................. 2
German measles:
Hattiesburg............................... 1
Gonorrhea:
Hattiesburg............................... 1
Malaria:
Hattiesburg............................... 12
Measles:
Hattiesburg...............................
Mumps:
Hattiesburg............................... 14
Wiggins 1
Pneumonia:
Hattiesburg............................... 4
Smallpox:
Hattiesburg............................... 20

CAMP SHERIDAN ZONE, ALA.

Cerebrospinal meningitis:
Montgomery................................
Chicken pox:
Montgomery................................ 11
Diphtheria:
Montgomery................................ 2
German measles:
Montgomery................................ 7
Measles:
Montgomery................................ 31
Rural zone................................ 1
Mumps:
Montgomery................................ 1
Pneumonia:
Montgomery................................ 2
Smallpox:
Montgomery................................ 11
Rural zone................................ 1
Tuberculosis:
Montgomery................................ 3
Typhoid fever:
Montgomery................................ 1

EXTRA-CANTONMENT ZONES—CASES REPORTED WEEK ENDED FEB. 12—Continued.

CAMP SHERMAN ZONE, OHIO.

Diphtheria:
  Chillicothe................................ 1
German measles:
  Chillicothe................................ 21
Gonorrhea:
  Chillicothe................................ 1
Measles:
  Chillicothe................................ 6
  Kingston................................... 2
  Liberty Township.......................... 3
Pneumonia, lobar:
  Chillicothe................................ 1
Scarlet fever:
  Chillicothe................................ 4
  Union Township............................ 1
Tuberculosis:
  Huntington Township....................... 1

CAMP ZACHARY TAYLOR ZONE, KY.

Cerebrospinal meningitis:
  Louisville................................ 3
Chicken pox:
  Louisville................................ 2
Diphtheria:
  Louisville................................ 3
Measles:
  Jefferson County.......................... 2
  Louisville................................ 34
Pneumonia:
  Louisville................................ 1
Scarlet fever:
  Louisville................................ 2
Smallpox:
  Jefferson County.......................... 2
  Louisville................................ 2
Trachoma:
  Jefferson County.......................... 6
Tuberculosis, pulmonary:
  Louisville................................ 4
Typhoid fever:
  Louisville................................ 1
Whooping cough:
  Jefferson County.......................... 6
  Louisville................................ 1

TIDEWATER HEALTH DISTRICT VA.

Diphtheria:
  Hampton................................... 1
German measles:
  Hampton................................... 15
  Newport News.............................. 2
  Phoebus................................... 4
Measles:
  Hampton................................... 6
  Newport News.............................. 7
  Phoebus................................... 1
Pneumonia:
  Newport News.............................. 1
  Phoebus................................... 1
Scarlet fever:
  Phoebus................................... 1
Tuberculosis, pulmonary:
  Newport News.............................. 1

TIDEWATER HEALTH DISTRICT, VA.—Con.

Whooping cough:
  Phoebus................................... 4

CAMP TRAVIS ZONE, TEX.

San Antonio:
  Cerebrospinal meningitis.................. 2
  Chicken pox............................... 2
  Erysipelas................................ 2
  Gonorrhea................................. 2
  Measles................................... 8
  Mumps..................................... 2
  Pneumonia................................. 12
  Smallpox.................................. 1
  Syphilis.................................. 2
  Tuberculosis.............................. 3
  Typhoid fever............................. 2

CAMP WADSWORTH ZONE, S. C.

Chicken pox:
  Spartanburg............................... 9
Diphtheria:
  Pauline................................... 1
German measles:
  Spartanburg............................... 21
Measles:
  Pauline................................... 2
  Saxon Mills............................... 2
  Spartanburg............................... 5
Mumps:
  Spartanburg............................... 9
Pneumonia:
  Glenn Springs............................. 3
  Saxon Mills............................... 2
  Spartanburg............................... 4
Smallpox:
  Spartanburg............................... 9
Tuberculosis:
  Spartanburg............................... 1
Whooping cough:
  Spartanburg............................... 9

CAMP WHEELER ZONE, GA.

Cerebrospinal meningitis:
  Bibb County............................... 1
  Macon..................................... 7
Chicken pox:
  Macon..................................... 1
German measles:
  Macon..................................... 1
Malaria:
  Macon..................................... 1
Measles:
  Macon..................................... 19
Mumps:
  East Macon................................ 2
  Macon..................................... 13
Pneumonia:
  Macon..................................... 1
Scarlet fever:
  Bibb County............................... 1
Smallpox:
  Macon..................................... 1

CURRENT STATE SUMMARIES.

Alabama.

From Collaborating Epidemiologist Perry, telegram dated February 11, 1918:

Measles: Epidemic many counties. Smallpox: Three cases Blount, 1 Cullman, 50 Jefferson, 20 Lowndes, 5 Wilcox. Cerebrospinal meningitis: Two Marshall County.

California.

From the State Board of Health of California, telegram dated February 13, 1918:

Measles and German measles epidemic in nearly every city of California, 1,300 cases last week. Four cases epidemic cerebrospinal meningitis in Los Angeles County and 1 in Riverside. Seven cases smallpox, 2 each Fresno County and San Francisco. 1 each Los Angeles, Madera, and Stockton.

Connecticut.

From Collaborating Epidemiologist Black, telegram dated February 11, 1918:

One leprosy West Haven, Italian alien. One typhoid carrier Myrtle (town), food handler, resident New York. One trachoma Hartford, French soldier.

Indiana.

From the State Board of Health of Indiana, telegram dated February 11, 1918:

Scarlet fever: Winamac (school closed), Laconia, Oak Ridge, Pleasant View. Harrison County. Diphtheria: Epidemic Maxwell, 3 deaths Walesboro. Small-pox: Epidemic Argos, Marshall County; West Lebanon; Mechanicsburg. Measles Epidemic Charlestown, Clark County. German measles: Epidemic Indianapolis. Medaryville, Shelbyville, Waterloo, Corydon. Whooping cough: Epidemic Beech Grove. Winter cholera: Epidemic Peru.

Kansas.

From Collaborating Epidemiologist Crumbine, telegram dated February 11, 1918:

Notified for week ended February 9. Meningitis: McLouth 1, Leavenworth 1. Niotaze 1, Langley 1, Coffeyville 1, Topeka 1, Columbus 1, Kansas City 2. Unusual prevalence. Smallpox: Emporia 32, Kansas City 58, Butler County 15. Crawford County 23, Cherokee County 39.

Louisiana.

From Collaborating Epidemiologist Dowling, telegram dated February 11, 1918:

Meningitis (excluding Rapides): Bienville 1, Caddo 1, De Soto 1, Franklin 1. Lincoln 1, Orleans 3.

CURRENT STATE SUMMARIES—Continued.

Massachusetts.

From Collaborating Epidemiologist Kelley, telegram dated February 11, 1918:

Unusual prevalence. German measles: Ayer 14, Framingham 22. Measles: Beverly 24, Marlboro 144, Winchester 28.

Minnesota.

From Collaborating Epidemiologist Bracken, telegram dated February 11, 1918:

Smallpox: Polk County, Fertile Village, 1; St. Louis County, Leiding Township, 1. Unusual prevalence scarlatina: Becker County, Lake Eunice Township; Meeker County, Litchville Village. One poliomyelitis, 3 cerebrospinal meningitis. Reports since February 4.

Nebraska.

From the State Board of Health of Nebraska, telegram dated February 12, 1918:

Smallpox: Fairfield, Chappell. Scarlet fever: Newcastle. German measles: Fremont, Peru, Lincoln, Columbus, Martel.

South Carolina.

From Collaborating Epidemiologist Hayne, telegram dated February 11, 1918:

Epidemic meningitis, 24 cases for week ending February 11. Smallpox epidemic in State.

Virginia.

From Collaborating Epidemiologist Traynham, telegram dated February 11, 1918:

One case cerebrospinal meningitis Henrico County, 2 Dinwiddie, 1 Spottsylvania, 1 Mecklenburg, 1 Hanover. One case smallpox Gloucester County, 1 Halifax, 1 Wise, 2 Hanover, 5 Washington, 2 Lee.

Washington.

From Collaborating Epidemiologist Tuttle, telegram dated February 11, 1918:

Twenty-four cases diphtheria and 12 scarlet fever in North Yakima, Yakima County. One cerebrospinal meningitis Spokane County. Three cerebrospinal meningitis in Seattle. No outbreak, but typhoid prevalent in Wenatchee, Chelan County.

CEREBROSPINAL MENINGITIS.

State Reports for December, 1917.

Place.	New cases reported.	Place.	New cases reported.
Alabama:		Connecticut:	
Calhoun County	10	Hartford County—	
Chilton County	1	East Windsor	1
Jefferson County	2	Hartford	3
Lauderdale County	1		
Madison County	1	Total	4
Total	15		

City Reports for Week Ended Jan. 26, 1918.

Place.	Cases.	Deaths.	Place.	Cases.	Deaths.
Akron, Ohio	1		La Fayette, Ind	1	
Atlanta, Ga	8	7	Louisville, Ky	2	4
Auburn, N. Y	1		Macon, Ga	3	2
Augusta, Ga	3	1	Manchester, N. H	1	
Baltimore, Md	3	1	Milwaukee, Wis	2	
Bayonne, N. J	1		Mobile, Ala	1	1
Birmingham, Ala	1	1	Newark, N. J	1	1
Boston, Mass	1		New Orleans, La	1	
Bridgeport, Conn	1		Newport News, Va	1	
Buffalo, N. Y	1	1	New York, N. Y	5	2
Charlotte, N. C	4		Norfolk, Va	1	1
Chattanooga, Tenn	3		Passaic, N. J	1	
Chicago, Ill	8	6	Philadelphia, Pa	2	3
Cincinnati, Ohio	1	1	Portsmouth, Va	1	1
Cleveland, Ohio	4	1	Providence, R. I	1	
Coffeyville, Kans	2		St. Louis, Mo	1	
Columbia, S. C	4		Schenectady, N. Y	1	
Columbus, Ohio	1		South Bend, Ind	1	
Danville, Ill	1	1	Spartanburg, S. C	1	
Detroit, Mich	3		Troy, N. Y	1	1
Greenville, S. C	1		Waco, Tex	2	
Hammond, Ind	1	1	Washington, D. C	26	
Hattiesburg, Miss	1		Worcester, Mass	1	
Kansas City, Mo		1			

DIPHTHERIA.

See Diphtheria, measles, scarlet fever, and tuberculosis, page 212.

ERYSIPELAS.

City Reports for Week Ended Jan. 26, 1918.

Place.	Cases.	Deaths.	Place.	Cases.	Deaths.
Atlanta, Ga	2		Milwaukee, Wis	1	
Baltimore, Md	3	1	Montclair, N. J	1	
Birmingham, Ala		2	Montgomery, Ala	3	
Bridgeport, Conn	3		Newark, N. J	6	
Buffalo, N. Y	8		New York, N. Y		7
Chicago, Ill	20		Niagara Falls, N. Y	2	
Cincinnati, Ohio	1		Norristown, Pa	1	1
Cleveland, Ohio	4		Oakland, Cal	1	
Denver, Colo	4		Omaha, Nebr	2	
Detroit, Mich	3	1	Philadelphia, Pa	5	
Easton, Pa	1		Pittsburgh, Pa	7	2
Erie, Pa	2		Pontiac, Mich	1	
Galesburg, Ill	1		Portland, Oreg	1	
Harrisburg, Pa	1		Richmond, Va		1
Hartford, Conn	2		St. Joseph, Mo	1	
Johnstown, Pa	2		St. Louis, Mo	9	
Lancaster, Pa	1		San Francisco, Cal	1	
Lawrence, Mass		1	Toledo, Ohio	3	1
Los Angeles, Cal	2		Troy, N. Y	1	2
Louisville, Ky	1	1	Wichita, Kans	1	
Macon, Ga	1				

LEPROSY.

New Jersey—Jersey City.

On January 30, 1918, a case of leprosy was notified in Jersey City, N. J., in the person of E. S. M., female, aged 52 years, resided at 475 Tonelle Avenue, native of Germany, came to the United States in 1882, lived in Brooklyn, N. Y., near Atlantic Docks, until 1912. The patient died from inhalation of illuminating gas January 31, 1918.

MALARIA.

Alabama Report for December, 1917.

Place.	New cases reported.	Place.	New cases reported.
Alabama:		Alabama—Continued.	
Blount County	10	Limestone County	2
Bullock County	1	Lowndes County	1
Calhoun County	3	Madison County	1
Colbert County	1	Marengo County	1
Dallas County	1	Tuscaloosa County	1
Elmore County	1		
Houston County	20	Total	50
Jefferson County	7		

City Reports for Week Ended January 26, 1918.

During the week ended January 26, 1918, one case of malaria was reported at Baltimore, Md., and one case was reported at Birmingham, Ala.

MEASLES.

See Diphtheria, measles, scarlet fever, and tuberculosis, page 212.

PELLAGRA.

Alabama Report for December, 1917.

Place.	New cases reported.	Place.	New cases reported.
Alabama:		Alabama—Continued.	
Barbour County	1	Lamar County	1
Bibb County	2	Macon County	1
Blount County	1	Madison County	2
Colbert County	1	Mobile County	11
Covington County	1	Montgomery County	4
Dekalb County	1	Pickens County	2
Elmore County	1	Shelby County	1
Etowah County	3	Sumter County	1
Franklin County	1	Talladega County	2
Greene County	1	Tuscaloosa County	5
Houston County	2	Wilcox County	1
Jackson County	1		
Jefferson County	10	Total	57

16

PELLAGRA—Continued.

City Reports for Week Ended Jan. 26, 1918.

Place.	Cases.	Deaths.	Place.	Cases.	Deaths.
Atlanta, Ga............		2	Montgomery, Ala........		2
Augusta, Ga............		1	New York, N. Y.........		1
Birmingham, Ala........		2	Richmond, Va..........		1
Charleston, S. C........		2	Rocky Mount, N. C......	1	
Macon, Ga.............		2	Rutland, Vt...........	1	1
Memphis, Tenn..........	2	1	Savannah, Ga..........		1
Mobile, Ala............		2			

PLAGUE.

Hawaii—Kukaiau--Plague-infected Rats Found.

On February 2, 1918, 2 plague-infected rats were found at Kukaiau,
Hawaii.

PNEUMONIA.

City Reports for Week Ended Jan. 26, 1918.

Place.	Cases.	Deaths.	Place.	Cases.	Deaths.
Akron, Ohio............	1		La Fayette, Ind........	1	
Alameda, Cal..........	1	1	Leavenworth, Kans......	3	
Alexandria, La.........	3	1	Long Beach, Cal........	7	1
Anniston, Ala..........	1		Los Angeles, Cal.......	19	8
Atlanta, Ga............	2	14	Louisville, Ky.........	3	11
Auburn, N. Y...........	2	2	Lowell, Mass...........	2	4
Augusta, Ga...........	3		Lynn, Mass............	1	2
Baltimore, Md..........	81	26	Macon, Ga.............	1	5
Battle Creek, Mich......	1		Manchester, N. H.......	3	3
Berkeley, Cal..........	1		Melrose, Mass..........	1	2
Boston, Mass..........	56	32	Montgomery, Ala........	3	4
Braddock, Pa..........	3		Morristown, N. J.......	1	1
Bridgeport, Conn.......	2		Muncie, Ind...........	5	5
Brockton, Mass........	3		Newark, N. J..........	10	17
Cambridge, Mass.......	13	3	New Bedford, Mass......	4	3
Canton, Ohio..........	3	1	Newburgh, N. Y........	1	2
Chattanooga, Tenn.....	3	5	New Castle, Pa........	1	
Chelsea, Mass.........	9	2	Newport, Ky...........	3	
Chicago, Ill...........	137	72	Newport News, Va......	2	1
Chillicothe, Ohio......	1		Newton, Mass..........	3	5
Cleveland, Ohio.......	26	29	Pasadena, Cal.........	2	2
Columbia, S. C........	1		Pawtucket, R. I.......	1	1
Cumberland, Md........	5		Philadelphia, Pa......	239	123
Dayton, Ohio..........	1	5	Pittsburgh, Pa........	51	39
Detroit, Mich.........	11	46	Pontiac, Mich.........	6	4
Duluth, Minn..........	1	4	Reading, Pa...........	1	2
Everett, Mass.........	3	1	Rochester, N. Y.......	6	5
Fall River, Mass......	9	4	Sacramento, Cal.......	2	1
Fitchburg, Mass.......	2		Saginaw, Mich.........	1	
Flint, Mich...........	3	1	St. Joseph, Mo........	1	4
Grand Rapids, Mich....	10	4	San Antonio, Tex......	16	16
Hagerstown, Md........	1		San Diego, Cal........	1	3
Hattiesburg, Miss.....	1		Sandusky, Ohio........	1	
Haverhill, Mass.......	5	4	San Francisco, Cal....	14	10
Holyoke, Mass.........	1	2	Schenectady, N. Y.....	4	2
Houston, Tex..........	1	14	Somerville, Mass......	3	2
Jackson, Mich.........	4		Spartanburg, S. C.....	1	
Jacksonville, Fla.....	11	10	Springfield, Mass.....	11	6
Johnstown, Pa........	10	1	Stockton, Cal.........	2	
Kalamazoo, Mich.......	3		Waco, Tex............	3	
Kansas City, Kans.....	1		Worcester, Mass.......	8	3
Kansas City, Mo.......	20	23			

POLIOMYELITIS (INFANTILE PARALYSIS).

Alabama Report for December, 1917.

During the month of December, 1917, one case of poliomyelitis was reported in the State of Alabama, Jefferson County.

City Reports for Week Ended Jan. 26, 1918.

Place.	Cases.	Deaths.	Place.	Cases.	Deaths.
Anniston, Ala	1	....	Oakland, Cal	....	1
Chicago, Ill	1	1	Tacoma, Wash	1	....
New York, N. Y	1	....			

RABIES IN MAN.

City Report for Week Ended Jan. 26, 1918.

During the week ended January 26, 1918, one case of rabies in man was reported at Waco, Tex.

RABIES IN ANIMALS.

City Reports for Week Ended Jan. 26, 1918.

During the week ended January 26, 1918, one case of rabies in animals was reported at Columbus, Ohio, one case at Taunton, Mass., and one case at Waco, Tex.

SCARLET FEVER.

See Diphtheria, measles, scarlet fever, and tuberculosis, page 212.

SMALLPOX.

Texas—Eagle Pass—Virulent Smallpox.

During the week ended February 11, 1918, 10 new cases of small-pox, with 6 deaths, were notified at Eagle Pass, Tex., making a total of 68 cases of the disease, with 18 deaths, since October 1, 1917. Of the 68 cases reported since October 1, 38 have occurred since January 1, 1918.

SMALLPOX—Continued.

Miscellaneous State Reports.

Place.	Cases.	Deaths.	Place.	Cases.	Deaths.
Alabama (Dec. 1–31):			Alabama (Dec. 1–31)—Contd.		
Blount County	12		Montgomery County	17	
Calhoun County	54		Pickens County	2	
Chilton County	2		Sumter County	3	
Coffee County	4		Talladega County	40	1
Crenshaw County	1		Tallapoosa County	1	
Etowah County	6		Tuscaloosa County	1	
Geneva County	3				
Jackson County	1		Total	168	1
Jefferson County	3				
Lamar County	14		Connecticut (Dec. 1–31):		
Lee County	1		Fairfield County—		
Madison County	1		Bridgeport	1	
Marshall County	2				

City Reports for Week Ended Jan. 26, 1918.

Place.	Cases.	Deaths.	Place.	Cases.	Deaths.
Akron, Ohio	39		Jacksonville, Fla	4	
Alexandria, La	6		Kalamazoo, Mich	1	
Alton, Ill	7		Kansas City, Kans	47	
Ann Arbor, Mich	1		Kansas City, Mo	221	
Anniston, Ala	7		Knoxville, Tenn	1	
Baltimore, Md	1		La Crosse, Wis	10	
Battle Creek, Mich	2		Lima, Ohio	5	
Birmingham, Ala	4		Little Rock, Ark	12	
Boston, Mass	1		Lorain, Ohio	6	
Buffalo, N. Y	7		Los Angeles, Cal	1	
Butte, Mont	6		Louisville, Ky	3	
Canton, Ohio	2		Madison, Wis	2	
Chattanooga, Tenn	3		Memphis, Tenn	18	
Chicago, Ill	23	1	Milwaukee, Wis	12	
Cincinnati, Ohio	8		Minneapolis, Minn	20	
Cleveland, Ohio	35		Mobile, Ala	1	
Coffeyville, Kans	1		Montgomery, Ala	4	
Columbus, Ohio	21		Muncie, Ind	6	
Covington, Ky	1		New Orleans, La	7	
Cumberland, Md	3		Oklahoma City, Okla	11	
Danville, Ill	1		Omaha, Nebr	9	
Davenport, Iowa	2		Pittsburgh, Pa	3	
Dayton, Ohio	4		Pontiac, Mich	3	
Denver, Colo	7		Portland, Oreg	2	
Detroit, Mich	78	2	Quincy, Ill	15	
Dubuque, Iowa	3		Sacramento, Cal	1	
Duluth, Minn	2		Saginaw, Mich	1	
El Paso, Tex	1		St. Joseph, Mo	11	
Evansville, Ind	2		St. Louis, Mo	27	
Flint, Mich	24		Seattle, Wash	8	
Fort Wayne, Ind	12		Sioux City, Iowa	9	
Fort Worth, Tex	9		Spartanburg, S. C	1	
Galesburg, Ill	1		Springfield, Ill	1	
Grand Rapids, Mich	15		Terre Haute, Ind	2	
Hammond, Ind	2		Toledo, Ohio	12	
Harrisburg, Pa	5		Waco, Tex	1	
Hattiesburg, Miss	9		Wheeling, W. Va	1	
Houston, Tex	2		Wichita, Kans	2	
Indianapolis, Ind	62		Winston-Salem, N. C	1	
Jackson, Mich	9				

TETANUS.

City Reports for Week Ended Jan. 26, 1918.

Place.	Cases.	Deaths.	Place	Cases	Deaths
Baltimore, Md		2	Charleston, W. Va		1
Charleston, S. C		1	Savannah, Ga		1

TUBERCULOSIS.

See Diphtheria, measles, scarlet fever, and tuberculosis, page 212.

TYPHOID FEVER.

State Reports for December, 1917.

Place.	New cases reported.	Place.	New cases reported.
Alabama:		Alabama—Continued.	
Autauga County	1	Shelby County	1
Bibb County	1	Sumter County	1
Bullock County	1	Talladega County	1
Butler County	3	Tallapoosa County	2
Calhoun County	3		
Chambers County	2	Total	90
Cherokee County	4		
Choctaw County	1	Connecticut:	
Clay County	1	Fairfield County—	
Coffee County	1	Bridgeport	2
Coosa County	1	Danbury	1
Covington County	1	Norwalk	1
Crenshaw County	1	Stamford	2
Cullman County	1	Stratford	1
Dale County	1	Hartford County—	
Dekalb County	2	Hartford	5
Elmore County	1	Windsor Locks	1
Escambia County	2	Middlesex County—	
Fayette County	1	Middletown	1
Hale County	2	New Haven County—	
Houston County	1	Milford	1
Jackson County	4	New Haven	4
Jefferson County	28	Waterbury	14
Lawrence County	1	New London County—	
Lee County	1	New London	1
Limestone County	1	Preston	2
Madison County	8	Tolland County -	
Marion County	1	Ellington	1
Marshall County	1	Windham County—	
Mobile County	2	Ashford	1
Montgomery County	4	Willimantic	1
Pike County	1		
Randolph County	1	Total	39

City Reports for Week Ended Jan. 26, 1918.

Place.	Cases.	Deaths.	Place.	Cases.	Deaths.
Atlanta, Ga	1		Louisville, Ky	1	
Auburn, N. Y	1		Lynn, Mass	2	
Baltimore, Md		1	Malden, Mass	1	
Buffalo, N. Y	2		McKeesport, Pa		1
Camden, N. J	1		Milwaukee, Wis	2	1
Charleston, W. Va	1		Minneapolis, Minn	3	
Chicago, Ill	6	1	Moline, Ill	4	1
Chicopee, Mass	1		Muncie, Ind	1	
Cleveland, Ohio	1		Newark, N. J	2	
Columbus, Ohio	1		New York, N. Y	8	1
Danville, Ill	1		Oakland, Cal	1	
Denver, Colo	1		Ogden, Utah	1	
Detroit, Mich	1	2	Oklahoma City, Okla		1
El Paso, Tex		1	Philadelphia, Pa	4	1
Evansville, Ind	1		Pittsburgh, Pa	1	1
Fall River, Mass	2		Providence, R. I		1
Flint, Mich	1		Reading, Pa	1	
Fort Worth, Tex	1		Richmond, Va	1	
Galveston, Tex	2		Roanoke, Va	1	
Grand Rapids, Mich	2	1	St. Louis, Mo	1	
Green Bay, Wis	1		San Antonio, Tex	2	
Harrisburg, Pa		1	San Diego, Cal	1	
Hattiesburg, Miss	1		San Francisco, Cal	2	1
Haverhill, Mass	2		Savannah, Ga		1
Houston, Tex	1		Seattle, Wash	1	
Indianapolis, Ind		1	Springfield, Ill	1	
Jacksonville, Fla	1		Springfield, Ohio	2	
Johnstown, Pa	1		Toledo, Ohio	1	
Kalamazoo, Mich	2		Washington, D C	1	
Kansas City, Mo		1	Wheeling, W. Va		1
Los Angeles, Cal	1		Winston-Salem, N. C	1	

DIPHTHERIA, MEASLES, SCARLET FEVER, AND TUBERCULOSIS.

State Reports for December, 1917.

During the month of December, 1917, 58 cases of diphtheria, 1,027 cases of measles, and 120 cases of scarlet fever were reported in the State of Alabama, and in the State of Connecticut 284 cases of diphtheria, 699 cases of measles, and 175 cases of scarlet fever were reported.

City Reports for Week Ended Jan. 26, 1918.

City.	Population as of July 1, 1916 (estimated by U. S. Census Bureau).	Total deaths from all causes.	Diphtheria.		Measles.		Scarlet fever.		Tuberculosis.	
			Cases.	Deaths.	Cases.	Deaths.	Cases.	Deaths.	Cases.	Deaths.
Over 500,000 inhabitants:										
Baltimore, Md............	589,621	....	14	2	94	1	8	....	48	20
Boston, Mass............	756,476	282	115	6	93	3	27	5	92	32
Chicago, Ill............	2,497,722	677	136	15	43	2	58	4	362	69
Cleveland, Ohio.........	674,073	207	20	3	16	....	4	1	27	23
Detroit, Mich...........	571,784	222	59	5	26	1	45	2	53	13
Los Angeles, Cal........	503,812	....	15	....	45	....	19	....	35	18
New York, N. Y.........	5,602,841	1,734	222	21	883	15	128	6	330	203
Philadelphia, Pa........	1,709,518	768	47	18	92	14	54	2	92	62
Pittsburgh, Pa..........	579,090	225	17	5	3	....	14	....	23	13
St. Louis, Mo...........	757,309	251	56	2	35	....	47	....	45	28
From 300,000 to 500,000 inhabitants:										
Buffalo, N. Y...........	468,558	149	8	2	29	....	8	....	33	23
Cincinnati, Ohio........	410,476	150	10	....	14	....	6	....	18	19
Jersey City, N. J.......	306,345	....	17	....	47	....	9	....	37	....
Milwaukee, Wis.........	436,535	90	11	1	73	....	45	3	13	3
Minneapolis, Minn......	363,454	....	19	3	16	....	10	....	....	9
Newark, N. J...........	408,894	148	27	2	100	1	16	....	36	12
New Orleans, La........	371,747	....	10	....	135	....	1	....	39	19
San Francisco, Cal......	463,516	160	22	3	28	1	16	....	25	22
Seattle, Wash..........	348,639	....	10	1	126	....	3	....	5	7
Washington, D. C.......	363,090	153	5	....	185	....	53	....	18	15
From 200,000 to 300,000 inhabitants:										
Columbus, Ohio.........	214,878	67	1	....	31	1	23	....	9	5
Denver, Colo...........	260,800	68	10	....	130	....	26	....	....	10
Indianapolis, Ind.......	271,708	98	26	2	57	....	32	....	14	9
Kansas City, Mo........	297,847	107	14	....	143	5	45	1	2	7
Louisville, Ky..........	238,910	106	3	1	36	1	7	....	18	12
Portland, Oreg.........	295,463	32	3	....	11	....	4	....	5	5
Providence, R. I........	254,960	78	10	3	5	....	10	1	1	10
Rochester, N. Y........	256,417	77	8	2	27	2	15	....	18	7
From 100,000 to 200,000 inhabitants:										
Atlanta, Ga............	190,558	....	11	....	10	....	2	....	....	5
Birmingham, Ala........	181,762	71	2	....	120	1	1	....	9	3
Bridgeport, Conn........	121,579	39	10	1	10	....	9	....	9	5
Cambridge, Mass........	112,981	39	8	....	18	....	2	....	3	7
Camden, N. J...........	106,234	....	9	....	20	....	1	....	4	....
Dayton, Ohio...........	127,224	50	4	2	17	....	5	....	2	2
Fall River, Mass........	128,396	52	5	3	2	....	5	....	3	2
Fort Worth, Tex........	104,562	53	4	....	5	....	....	....	....	2
Grand Rapids, Mich.....	128,291	36	4	....	5	....	5	....	6	1
Hartford, Conn.........	110,900	40	4	....	8	....	6	....	2	2
Houston, Tex...........	112,307	53	1	....	24	....	....	....	....	8
Lawrence, Mass.........	100,560	31	3	....	2	....	1	....	7	3
Lowell, Mass...........	113,245	36	2	....	3	....	....	....	1	....
Lynn, Mass............	102,425	30	2	....	4	....	2	....	4	2
Memphis, Tenn.........	148,995	64	3	....	40	....	....	....	10	11
New Bedford, Mass......	118,158	43	2	....	19	....	3	....	14	....
New Haven, Conn.......	149,685	46	1	....	7	....	....	....	8	2
Oakland, Cal...........	198,604	39	5	....	15	....	1	....	7	2
Omaha, Nebr...........	165,470	47	115	1	69	....	5	....	3	6
Reading, Pa............	109,381	41	6	....	3	....	3	....	5	3
Richmond, Va..........	156,687	54	7	....	38	....	3	....	6	8
San Antonio, Tex.......	124,831	96	2	1	8	....	1	....	15	13
Scranton, Pa...........	146,811	44	11	3	1	....	1	....	5	2
Springfield, Mass.......	105,942	72	15	1	21	....	12	1	1	5

DIPHTHERIA, MEASLES, SCARLET FEVER, AND TUBERCULOSIS—Continued.

City Reports for Week Ended Jan. 26, 1918—Continued.

City.	Population as of July 1, 1916 (estimated by U. S. Census Bureau).	Total deaths from all causes.	Diphtheria.		Measles.		Scarlet fever.		Tuberculosis.	
			Cases.	Deaths.	Cases.	Deaths.	Cases.	Deaths.	Cases.	Deaths.
From 100,000 to 200,000 inhabitants—Continued.										
Syracuse, N. Y.	155,624	49	8	2	52	2	26	......	5	3
Tacoma, Wash	112,770	......	1	......	1	......	4	......	......	......
Toledo, Ohio	191,554	83	3	1	7	......	4	......	......	11
Trenton, N. J.	111,593	47	5	1	3	......	......	......	7	2
Worcester, Mass	163,314	45	7	......	8	......	6	......	8	3
From 50,000 to 100,000 inhabitants:										
Akron, Ohio	85,625	......	11	......	5	......	4	......	13	......
Atlantic City, N. J.	57,660	......	......	......	2	......	......	......	1	1
Augusta, Ga	50,245	13	......	......	22	......	1	......	6	......
Bayonne, N. J.	69,893	......	3	......	6	......	2	......	2	......
Berkeley, Cal	57,653	......	......	......	3	......	2	......	1	......
Binghamton, N. Y.	53,973	16	2	......	13	......	4	......	4	1
Brockton, Mass	67,449	10	3	......	5	......	9	......	4	......
Canton, Ohio	60,852	17	3	......	2	......	1	......	......	2
Charleston, S. C.	60,734	36	1	......	......	......	2	......	......	......
Chattanooga, Tenn	60,075	5	1	......	56	......	3	......	5	......
Covington, Ky	57,144	33	......	......	......	......	1	1	......	4
Duluth, Minn	94,495	19	4	......	27	......	1	......	4	3
Elizabeth, N. J.	86,690	24	3	......	52	2	11	......	4	1
El Paso, Tex	63,705	......	......	......	14	......	......	......	......	11
Erie, Pa	75,195	29	3	......	......	......	4	......	10	2
Evansville, Ind	76,078	22	2	1	......	......	2	......	1	2
Flint, Mich	54,772	14	5	......	8	......	13	......	......	14
Fort Wayne, Ind	76,183	14	3	......	1	......	3	......	......	......
Harrisburg, Pa	72,015	39	7	......	4	......	......	......	5	2
Hoboken, N. J.	77,214	26	2	......	9	......	......	......	5	......
Holyoke, Mass	65,286	21	1	......	12	......	2	......	......	1
Jacksonville, Fla	76,101	42	......	......	70	......	1	......	5	1
Johnstown, Pa	68,529	29	2	1	2	......	10	......	2	1
Kansas City, Kans	99,437	......	2	......	31	......	11	......	......	......
Lancaster, Pa	50,853	......	1	......	1	......	2	......	4	......
Little Rock, Ark	57,343	14	......	......	......	......	......	......	......	1
Malden, Mass	51,155	13	7	......	3	......	......	1	2	1
Manchester, N. H.	78,283	34	1	......	10	......	1	......	9	1
Mobile, Ala	58,221	36	......	......	13	2	......	......	......	3
New Britain, Conn	53,794	19	4	......	3	......	1	......	......	1
Norfolk, Va	89,612	......	......	......	15	......	3	......	......	5
Oklahoma City, Okla	92,943	21	1	......	8	......	......	......	......	1
Passaic, N. J.	71,744	24	1	......	1	......	......	......	2	3
Pawtucket, R. I.	59,411	12	......	......	......	......	2	......	2	2
Portland, Me	63,867	15	......	......	71	......	......	......	......	2
Rockford, Ill	55,185	12	2	......	3	......	......	......	2	......
Sacramento, Cal	66,895	27	1	......	15	......	6	......	......	7
Saginaw, Mich	55,612	9	1	......	......	......	2	......	......	......
St. Joseph, Mo	85,236	21	2	1	47	......	7	......	5	1
San Diego, Cal	53,320	26	1	......	132	......	3	......	1	1
Savannah, Ga	68,805	35	1	......	20	......	1	......	2	2
Schenectady, N. Y.	99,519	29	3	1	13	......	1	......	2	3
Sioux City, Iowa	57,078	......	......	......	......	......	19	......	......	......
Somerville, Mass	87,639	26	2	......	23	......	5	......	4	3
South Bend, Ind	68,946	15	1	......	9	......	3	......	1	......
Springfield, Ill	61,120	13	2	......	2	......	......	......	......	1
Springfield, Ohio	51,550	23	......	......	7	......	......	......	5	3
Terre Haute, Ind	66,083	16	1	......	15	......	1	......	......	......
Troy, N. Y.	77,916	12	9	2	2	......	3	......	7	4
Wichita, Kans	70,722	......	1	......	136	......	6	......	3	......
Wilmington, Del	94,265	39	1	......	5	......	3	......	......	2
From 25,000 to 50,000 inhabitants:										
Alameda, Cal	27,732	8	2	......	4	......	1	......	2	......
Auburn, N. Y.	37,385	11	1	......	4	......	......	......	1	1
Battle Creek, Mich	29,480	......	4	......	12	1	4	......	......	......
Brookline, Mass	32,730	9	......	......	9	......	6	......	1	1
Butler, Pa	27,632	7	3	......	22	......	......	......	......	......
Butte, Mont	43,425	......	3	......	3	......	14	......	......	......
Cedar Rapids, Iowa	37,308	......	1	......	......	......	4	......	......	......
Charleston, W. Va	29,941	17	......	......	......	......	3	......	......	3
Charlotte, N. C.	39,823	......	......	......	48	......	1	......	......	......
Chelsea, Mass	46,192	12	4	......	19	......	1	......	4	1

DIPHTHERIA, MEASLES, SCARLET FEVER, AND TUBERCULOSIS—
Continued.

City Reports for Week Ended Jan. 26, 1918—Continued.

City.	Population as of July 1, 1916 (estimated by U. S. Census Bureau).	Total deaths from all causes.	Diphtheria. Cases.	Diphtheria. Deaths.	Measles. Cases.	Measles. Deaths.	Scarlet fever. Cases.	Scarlet fever. Deaths.	Tuberculosis. Cases.	Tuberculosis. Deaths.
From 25,000 to 50,000 inhabitants —Continued.										
Chicopee, Mass	29,319	7			7				1	
Columbia, S. C	34,611				9		1			
Cumberland, Md	26,074	4	2		1				3	2
Danville, Ill	32,261	19			1				3	2
Davenport, Iowa	48,811		3		4		8			
Dubuque, Iowa	39,873				12					1
Easton, Pa	30,530	12	1		7					
East Orange, N. J	42,458	18	1		15		2		1	2
Elgin, Ill	28,203	7			2					
Everett, Mass	39,233	4	6		8		2		2	
Everett, Wash	35,486	3			1					
Fitchburg, Mass	41,781	14	8	1	9				1	1
Galveston, Tex	41,863	10	3		7		4			
Green Bay, Wis	29,353	6			11		3			
Hagerstown, Md	25,679		1		3					
Hammond, Ind	26,171		1		2		1			
Haverhill, Mass	48,477	20	3		7				7	
Jackson, Mich	35,363	15	5		4		38	2		1
Kalamazoo, Mich	48,886	12	7		19		1		3	1
Kenosha, Wis	31,576	7	3		3		8		1	2
Kingston, N. Y	26,771	6								1
Knoxville, Tenn	38,676		1		14		2		1	1
La Crosse, Wis	31,677	13	3							
Lima, Ohio	35,384	11	1		4		2			
Long Beach, Cal	27,587	12			11				2	
Lorain, Ohio	36,964				1		1			
Lynchburg, Va	32,940	12								
Macon, Ga	45,757	29			18	1			1	1
Madison, Wis	30,699		1		9		3			
McKeesport, Pa	47,521	14	1		8					1
Medford, Mass	26,234	6	5		5		1			2
Moline, Ill	27,451	1	2		1		3			
Montclair, N. J	26,318	6			24				2	
Montgomery, Ala	43,285	26	2	1	34					2
Mount Vernon, N. Y	37,009	12	7		31					1
Muncie, Ind	25,424		1		4		6		3	2
Nashua, N. H	27,327	11								
Newburgh, N. Y	29,603	9			20					1
New Castle, Pa	41,133				6		4			
Newport, Ky	31,927	13							5	5
Newport, R. I	30,108	7	2				1			
Newton, Mass	43,715	19	5		5		1			1
Niagara Falls, N. Y	37,353	13	1						4	
Norristown, Pa	34,401	10			1					
Ogden, Utah	31,404	4			6		2		1	1
Orange, N. J	33,090	13	2		10		2		1	2
Pasadena, Cal	46,450	12			7		2		2	3
Perth Amboy, N. J	41,185	14	1		16		1		2	2
Pittsfield, Mass	38,629	10	2				2		4	2
Portsmouth, Va	39,651	8			2		2			
Quincy, Ill	36,798	12	5	1	1					2
Quincy, Mass	38,136	9	1	2	10		2		1	
Roanoke, Va	43,244	13	2		7		1		4	2
Rock Island, Ill	28,926	12	1		1					
San Jose, Cal	38,902				15		2		1	
Steubenville, Ohio	27,445	13			1		1			
Stockton, Cal	35,358		1		41		1		2	1
Superior, Wis	46,226	9			10		5			2
Taunton, Mass	36,283	11							1	
Waco, Tex	33,385		3						1	
Waltham, Mass	30,570	8	2		3		1		1	
Watertown, N. Y	29,894	1			7					1
West Hoboken, N. J	43,130	7	1		1		3		2	1
Wheeling, W. Va	43,377	15			1				2	
Wilmington, N. C	29,892	16			39					3
Winston-Salem, N. C	31,155	24	1		17		4		3	3
Zanesville, Ohio	30,863						5			

DIPHTHERIA, MEASLES, SCARLET FEVER, AND TUBERCULOSIS—
Continued.

City Reports for Week Ended Jan. 26, 1918—Continued.

City.	Population as of July 1, 1916 (estimated by U. S. Census Bureau).	Total deaths from all causes.	Diphtheria.		Measles.		Scarlet fever.		Tuberculosis.	
			Cases.	Deaths.	Cases.	Deaths.	Cases.	Deaths.	Cases.	Deaths.
From 10,000 to 25,000 inhabitants:										
Alexandria, La	15,333	6			13					1
Alton, Ill	22,874	7	2		19		3		1	1
Ann Arbor, Mich	15,010	6	2		7		4		1	
Anniston, Ala	14,112				6				1	
Berlin, N. H	13,599	6								
Braddock, Pa	21,685	..			3					
Cairo, Ill	15,794	8								1
Chillicothe, Ohio	15,470		1		12		4			
Coffeyville, Kans	17,548				25		4			
Concord, N. H	22,669	13			2		3		1	
Galesburg, Ill	24,276	9	1							
Greenville, S. C	18,181	9	1		5					
Harrison, N. J	16,950									
Hattiesburg, Miss	16,482	10	1		6		1		1	
Kearney, N. J	23,539	9	2		31		1		3	
Kokomo, Ind	20,930	8			3		2			
La Fayette, Ind	21,286	7			1		5			
Leavenworth, Kans	[1] 19,363	3	2		4				1	
Long Branch, N. J	15,395	5			2					
Marinette, Wis	[1] 14,610	1					1			
Melrose, Mass	17,445	8	3		2				2	1
Morristown, N. J	13,284	7							1	1
Nanticoke, Pa	22,126	3			2		2			
Newburyport, Mass	15,243	..								
New London, Conn	20,985	9	2							
Newport News, Va	[1] 30,562	13							1	1
North Adams, Mass	[1] 22,019	7								
Northampton, Mass	19,926	7	1		2		4			4
Plainfield, N. J	22,805	8	1		1		1		1	
Pontiac, Mich	17,524	9	1		4		5		3	2
Portsmouth, N. H	11,666		1		1		4			
Rocky Mount, N. C	12,067	13			4				4	1
Rutland, Vt	14,831	2								
Sandusky, Ohio	20,193	3			1		1			
Saratoga Springs, N. Y	13,821	9								
South Bethlehem, Pa	24,204		1						5	
Spartanburg, S. C	21,365	23			2		2			
Steelton, Pa	15,548	6					1			
Washington, Pa	21,618				8					
Wilkinsburg, Pa	23,228	10			16		1		1	
Woburn, Mass	15,969	5								

[1] Population Apr. 15, 1910; no estimate made.

FOREIGN.

CUBA.

Communicable Diseases—Habana.

Communicable diseases have been notified at Habana as follows:

Disease	Jan. 11–20, 1918.		Cases remaining under treatment Jan. 20, 1918.
	New cases.	Deaths.	
Cerebrospinal meningitis			[1]1
Diphtheria	7		4
Leprosy			11
Malaria	25		[3]39
Measles	7		14
Paratyphoid fever	1		1
Poliomyelitis			1
Scarlet fever			4
Smallpox			2
Typhoid fever	16	5	[2]74
Varicella	30		39

[1] From the United States.   [2] From the interior, 14.   [3] From the interior, 26.

INDIA.

Malaria—Bombay Presidency.

During the three-year period, 1914–1916, there were admitted to hospital in the Bombay Presidency 1,352,372 cases of malaria as compared with 1,171,600 cases admitted during the previous three-year period, 1911–1913. This increase was mainly due to a very severe incidence of malarial fever in the province of Sind, owing to excessive rains and an abnormal inundation of the Indus in the year 1916, and is not an indication that the efforts made by the Government to combat the disease in the specially malarious tracts have in any way been relaxed. A large number of cases were treated in the worst infected districts of Sind and quinine was made widely available.

(216)

CHOLERA, PLAGUE, SMALLPOX, AND TYPHUS FEVER.

Reports Received During Week Ended Feb. 15, 1918.[1]

CHOLERA.

Place.	Date.	Cases.	Deaths.	Remarks.
Java: West Java............ Batavia............	Nov. 30–Dec. 13...	13	7	Nov. 30–Dec. 13, 1917: Cases, 28; deaths, 14.

PLAGUE.

Place.	Date.	Cases.	Deaths.	Remarks.
Ceylon: Colombo..............	Nov. 18–Dec. 1....	6	5	
Java: East Java............ Surabaya............	Nov. 11–25........	2	2	Nov. 11–25, 1917: Cases, 47; deaths, 46.

SMALLPOX.

Place.	Date.	Cases.	Deaths.	Remarks.
Australia: New South Wales........ Kurri Kurri............	Dec. 7–20........	2		Dec. 7–20, 1917: Cases, 2.
Canada: British Columbia— Vancouver............ Victoria............	Jan. 13–19.... Jan. 7–20....	1 2		
New Brunswick— Kent County........ Moncton............ Northumberland County. Victoria County........ York County...........	Jan. 22......... Jan. 27–Feb. 2..... Jan. 22......... ....do............ ....do............	40 1 41 10 8		In 7 localities. In 5 localities. In Limestone and at a lumber camp.
Ontario— Sarnia..................	Jan. 27–Feb. 2.....	4		
China: Chungking............. Dairen................. Shanghai	Dec. 2–15......... Dec. 16–22........ Dec. 31–Jan. 6....	 2 4	 1 17	Present.
Java: West Java..............				Nov. 30–Dec. 6, 1917: Cases, 30; deaths, 7.
Portugal: Lisbon.................	Dec. 16–22........	5		
Portuguese East Africa: Lourenço Marquez........	Oct. 1–31.........		1	
Spain: Madrid.................				Jan. 1–Dec. 31, 1917: Deaths, 77.

TYPHUS FEVER.

Place.	Date.	Cases.	Deaths.	Remarks.
China: Antung................ Do................	Dec. 24–30........ Dec. 31–Jan. 6.....	2	 1	
Egypt: Alexandria............. Cairo.................	Dec. 22–28........ Oct. 15–21.........	13 5	5 1	
Japan: Nagasaki..............	Dec. 24–30........	2		
Java: Mid-Java............. Samarang............. West Java............. Batavia............	 Nov. 22–Dec. 5.... Nov. 30–Dec. 13...	7 6 15	 1 5	Nov. 22–Dec. 5, 1917: Cases, 7; deaths, 1. Nov. 30–Dec. 13, 1917: Cases, 19; deaths, 5.
Mexico: Aguascalientes......... Durango State— Guanacevi............	Jan. 21–27......... Feb. 11.........		3	Epidemic.
Russia: Petrograd.............	Feb. 2...........			Present.
Turkey: Janina..................	Jan. 27.........			Epidemic.

[1] From medical officers of the Public Health Service, American consuls, and other sources.

CHOLERA, PLAGUE, SMALLPOX, AND TYPHUS FEVER— Continued.

Reports Received from Dec. 29, 1917, to Feb. 8, 1918.

CHOLERA

Place.	Date.	Cases.	Deaths.	Remarks.
China:				
Antung.....................	Nov. 20–Dec. 2....	3	1	
India:				
Bombay.....................	Oct. 28–Nov. 24...	17	12	
Calcutta....................	Sept. 16–Nov. 24...		76	
Rangoon....................	Nov. 4–17...	2	2	
Indo-China:				
Provinces..................				Sept. 1–30, 1917: Cases, 74; deaths,
Anam...................	Sept. 1–30...........	13	10	37.
Cambodia..............	....do...............	19	12	
Cochin-China..........	....do...............	32	13	
Kwang-Chow-Wan......	....do...............	10	2	
Saigon....................	Nov. 22–28...........	1	....	
Java:				
East Java................	Oct. 28–Nov. 3....	1	1	
West Java................				Oct. 19–Nov. 29, 1917: Cases, 66;
Batavia.................	Oct. 19–Nov. 29...	38	8	deaths, 35.
Persia:				
Mazanderan Province—				
Astrabad..............	July 31.............			Present.
Barfrush..............	July 1–27...........	34	23	
Chahmirzad..........				25 cases reported July 31 1917.
Chahrastagh..........	June 15–July 25....	10	8	
Kharek...............	May 24–June 11....	21	13	
Sari..................	July 3–29...........	273	144	
Yekchambe-Bazar.....	June 3.............	6	....	
Philippine Islands:				
Provinces................				Nov. 18–Dec. 22, 1917: Cases, 993;
Antique................	Nov. 18–Dec. 1....	48	32	deaths, 657.
Bohol..................	Nov. 18–Dec. 22...	147	83	
Capiz..................	Nov. 25 Dec. 22...	12	10	
Iloilo..................	Nov. 25 Dec. 15...	179	134	
Leyte..................	Nov. 25–Dec. 22...	13	12	
Mindanao..............	....do...............	323	189	
Occidental Negros......	....do...............	188	123	
Oriental Negros........	....do...............	94	59	
Romblon...............	Nov. 25–Dec. 1....	1	1	
Siam:				
Bangkok..............	Sept. 16 22........	1	1	
Turkey in Asia:				
Bagdad...................	Nov. 1–15..........		40	

PLAGUE.

Place.	Date.	Cases.	Deaths.	Remarks.
Brazil:				
Bahia	Nov. 4–Dec. 15....	4	4	
British Gold Coast:				
Axim.................	Jan. 8.............			Present.
Ceylon:				
Colombo.................	Oct. 14–Nov. 17...	8	8	
Egypt...................				Jan. 1 Nov. 15, 1917: Cases, 728,
Port Said...............	July 23 29..........	1	2	deaths, 398.
India.....................				Sept. 16–Nov. 24, 1917: Cases,
Bombay.................	Oct. 28 Nov. 24...	93	79	131,804, deaths, 174,734.
Calcutta...............	Sept 16 29.........		2	
Henzada................	Oct. 21–27..........		1	
Karachi.................	Oct. 21 Nov. 10....	6	5	
Madras Presidency........	Oct. 31–Nov. 17...	3,294	2,560	
Mandalay...............	Oct. 14–Nov. 17...		89	
Rangoon................	Oct. 21 Nov. 17...	36	16	
Indo-China:				
Provinces...............				Sept. 1 30 1917: Cases, 31; deaths,
Anam..................	Sept. 1 30..........	12	11	30.
Cambodia..............	....do...............	12	11	
Cochin-China..........	....do...............	10	8	
Saigon	Oct. 31–Nov. 18...	8	4	
Java:				
East Java................	Oct. 27 Nov. 10...	28	27	
Senegal:				
St. Louis................	Feb. 2..........			Present.
Siam:				
Bangkok...	Sept. 16 Nov. 24..	11	7	
Straits Settlements:				
Singapore...............	Oct. 28–Nov. 24...	3	5	

CHOLERA, PLAGUE, SMALLPOX, AND TYPHUS FEVER—Continued.

Reports Received from Dec. 29, 1917, to Feb. 8, 1918—Continued.

SMALLPOX.

Place.	Date.	Cases.	Deaths.	Remarks.
Algeria:				
Algiers	Nov. 1-30	1		
Australia:				
New South Wales				July 12-Nov. 20, 1917: Cases, 34.
Abermain	Oct. 25-Nov. 20	3		
Cessnock	July 12-Oct. 11	7		Newcastle district.
Eumangla	Aug. 15	1		
Kurri Kurri	Dec. 5	1		
Mungindi	Aug. 13	1		
Warren	July 12-Oct. 25	22		
Brazil:				
Bahia	Nov. 10-Dec. 8	3		
Pernambuco	Nov. 1-15	1		
Rio de Janeiro	Sept. 30-Dec. 1	519	151	
Sao Paulo	Oct. 29-Nov. 4		2	
Canada:				
British Columbia—				
Winnipeg	Dec. 30-Jan. 5	1		
New Brunswick—				
Kent County	Dec. 4			Outbreak. On main line Canadian Ry., 25 miles north of Moncton.
Moncton	Jan. 20-26	1		
Restigouche County	Jan. 18	60		
Ontario—				
Hamilton	Dec. 16-22	1		
Do	Jan. 13-19	2		
Sarnia	Dec. 9-15	1		
Do	Jan. 6-26	16		
Windsor	Dec. 30-Jan. 5	1		
Quebec—				
Montreal	Dec. 16-Jan. 5	5		
Do	Jan. 6-12	1		
China:				
Amoy	Oct. 22-Nov. 25			Present.
Antung	Dec. 3-23	13	2	
Chungking	Nov. 11-Dec. 1			Do.
Dairen	Nov. 18-24			
Harbin	May 14-June 30	20		Chinese Eastern Ry.
Do	July 1-Oct. 15	4		Do.
Hungtahotze Station	Oct. 28-Nov. 4	1		Do.
Manchuria Station	May 14-June 30	6		Do.
Do	July 1-Oct. 15	3		Present.
Mukden	Nov. 11-24			
Shanghai	Nov. 18-Dec. 23	41	91	Cases, foreign; deaths among natives.
Tientsin	Nov. 11-Dec. 22	13		
Cuba:				
Habana	Jan. 7	1		Nov. 8, 1917; 1 case from Coruna. Dec. 5, 1917; 1 case.
Marianao	Jan. 8	1		6 miles distant from Habana.
Egypt:				
Alexandria	Nov. 12-18	1		
Cairo	July 23-Aug. 5	5	1	
France:				
Lyon	Nov. 18-Dec. 16	6	3	
Great Britain:				
Birmingham	Nov. 11-17	19		
India:				
Bombay	Oct. 21-Nov. 24	12	4	
Madras	Oct. 31-Nov. 17	6	2	
Rangoon	Oct. 28-Nov. 17	3	1	
Indo-China:				
Provinces				Sept. 1-30, 1917; Cases, 193; deaths, 56.
Anam	Sept. 1-30	61	12	
Cambodia	do	7		
Cochin-China	do	124	44	
Tonkin	do	1		
Saigon	Oct. 29-Nov. 28	62	16	
Italy:				
Milan				October, 1917; Cases, 2.
Turin	Oct. 29-Dec. 9	123	120	
Castellamare	Dec. 10	2		Among refugees.
Florence	Dec. 1-15	17	4	
Naples	To Dec. 10	2		Do.
Java:				
East Java	Oct. 27-Nov. 10	19		
Mid-Java	Oct. 10-Nov. 21	55		
West Java				Oct. 19-Nov. 29, 1917; Cases, 162; deaths, 23.
Batavia	Nov. 2-8	1		

CHOLERA, PLAGUE, SMALLPOX, AND TYPHUS FEVER—Continued.

Reports Received from Dec. 29, 1917, to Feb. 8, 1918—Continued.

SMALLPOX—Continued.

Place.	Date.	Cases.	Deaths.	Remarks.
Mexico:				
Mazatlan....................	Dec. 5–11....	....	1	
Mexico City.................	Nov. 11–Dec. 29...	16	....	
Do.....................	Dec. 30–Jan. 12....	8	....	
Piedras Negras..............	Jan. 11............	200	....	
Newfoundland:				
St. Johns..................	Dec. 8–Jan. 4.....	29	....	
Do.....................	Jan. 5–18..........	14	....	
Trepassey..................	Jan. 4............	....	....	Outbreak with 11 cases reported.
Philippine Islands:				
Manila....................	Oct. 28–Dec. 8...	5	....	
Portugal:				
Lisbon....................	Nov. 4–Dec. 15....	2	....	
Portuguese East Africa:				
Lourenço Marques.........	Aug. 1–Sept. 30....	....	4	
Russia:				
Moscow....................	Aug. 26–Oct. 6...	22	2	
Petrograd.................	Aug. 31–Nov. 18...	76	3	
Siam:				
Bangkok...................	Nov. 25–Dec. 1....	1	1	
Spain:				
Coruna....................	Dec. 2–13....	....	4	
Seville...................	Oct. 1–Nov. 30...	....	26	
Tunisia:				
Tunis.....................	Dec. 14–20........	....	1	
Turkey in Asia:				
Bagdad....................	....	....	....	Present in November, 1917.
Venezuela:				
Maracaibo.................	Dec. 2–8........	....	1	

TYPHUS FEVER.

Place.	Date.	Cases.	Deaths.	Remarks.
Algeria:				
Algiers....................	Nov. 1–30........	2	....	
Australia:				
South Australia............	....	....	....	Nov. 11–17, 1917: Cases, 1.
Brazil:				
Rio de Janeiro.............	Oct. 28–Dec. 1.....	7	....	
Canada:				
Ontario—				
Kingston..............	Dec. 2–8......	3	....	
Quebec—				
Montreal..............	Dec. 16–22.........	2	1	
China:				
Antung................	Dec. 3–16..	11	1	
Chosen (Formosa):				
Seoul.....	Nov. 1–30.........	1	..	
Egypt:				
Alexandria..................	Nov. 8–Dec. 16....	121	47	
Cairo.....................	July 23–Sept. 23...	23	8	
Port Said.................	July 30–Sept. 23...	3	3	
Great Britain:				
Glasgow...................	Dec. 21...........	1	....	
Manchester................	Dec. 2–8..........	1	....	
Greece:				
Saloniki..................	Nov. 11–Dec. 8....	....	36	
Japan:				
Nagasaki..................	Nov. 26–Dec. 16...	5	5	
Java:				
East Java	....	....	....	Oct. 15–Nov. 15, 1917. Cases, 17; deaths, 3.
Mid-Java..................	....	....	....	Oct. 10–Nov. 13, 1917: Cases, 42; deaths, 2.
Samarang...............	Oct. 17–Nov. 13...	9	1	
West Java..................	....	....	....	Oct. 19–Nov. 29, 1917. Cases, 36; deaths, 5.
Batavia...............	Oct. 19–Nov. 15..	41	7	
Mexico:				
Aguascalientes..............	Dec. 15...........	....	2	
Mexico City.................	Nov. 11–Dec. 29...	476	....	
Do.....................	Dec. 30–Jan. 12...	139	....	

CHOLERA PLAGUE, SMALLPOX, AND TYPHUS FEVER—Continued.

Reports Received from Dec. 29, 1917, to Feb. 8, 1918—Continued.

TYPHUS FEVER—Continued.

Place.	Date.	Cases.	Deaths.	Remarks.
Russia:				
Archangel	Sept. 1-14	7	2	
Moscow	Aug. 26-Oct. 6	49	2	
Petrograd	Aug. 31-Nov. 18	32		
Vladivostok	Oct. 29-Nov. 4	12	1	
Sweden:				
Goteborg	Nov. 18-24	1		
Switzerland:				
Zurich	Nov. 9-15	2		
Tunisia:				
Tunis	Nov. 30-Dec. 6		1	
Union of South Africa:				
Cape of Good Hope State	Sept. 10-Nov. 4	3,342	668	

x

PUBLIC HEALTH REPORTS

VOL. 33	FEBRUARY 22, 1918	No. 8

A STATE-WIDE PLAN FOR THE PREVENTION OF VENEREAL DISEASE.

By ALLAN J. McLAUGHLIN, Surgeon, United States Public Health Service, Commissioner of Health of Massachusetts.

In order to secure the greatest number of effectives in the selective draft, the prevalence of venereal disease in the civil population must be reduced. It is not necessary to discuss the reasons for a vigorous campaign for the control of venereal disease at this time. The reasons are too obvious and well recognized. The tremendous social and economic losses resulting from these diseases in times of peace are multiplied by the extraordinary conditions arising out of the world war. Furthermore, the winning of the war demands that these diseases be controlled in the entire civil population to insure the protection of the industrial army as well as that of the soldiers and sailors. To accomplish this it is not sufficient to inaugurate the campaign in the camps and a limited zone about the camps, but the control measures should include the larger cities and all parts of every State in the Union.

The successful campaign against these diseases necessitates a complex program.

1. Moral, social, and economic phases in which the health officer can assist but which are best directed by other agencies.

2. That portion of the suppressive program which is directly under the control and within the powers and duties of the health officer.

There is no part of this program in which the health officer is not interested. He has an obligation to devote his best efforts to securing results, but special activity is desired at this time in that portion of the program directly under his control.

In putting any comprehensive plan into effect it is wise to do those things which may be done at once without special law or ordinance. Time is required to secure legislative authority, and this time should be employed in establishing certain fundamentals upon which the entire campaign is based.

17 (223)

MEASURES WHICH REQUIRE MONEY BUT NO ADDITIONAL LEGISLATION.

(1) Establishment of free diagnostic facilities.

(2) Establishment of free treatment facilities.

If free diagnostic and treatment facilities are available thousands of carriers can be treated and made noninfective without compulsion of any kind. The first step necessary is to secure sufficient money to enable the State to furnish free diagnostic facilities and to secure the establishment of a chain of venereal dispensaries. This includes the manufacture or purchase of arsphenamine for free distribution. As a war measure it is possible in practically all States to secure money for a venereal disease campaign as a part of a nation-wide patriotic effort to increase the efficiency of the fighting forces.

Diagnostic Facilities.

There should be a State Wassermann laboratory, and in large cities branch laboratories may be utilized. A central Wassermann laboratory secures, by the greatly increased number of specimens examined, a much lower cost per test and much greater accuracy. The diagnostic facilities should include the simple laboratory equipment to be mentioned later in connection with the venereal dispensaries.

Venereal Dispensaries.

A chain of venereal dispensaries should be established, placed in such a manner as to furnish treatment facilities for the entire State. Sufficient money must be secured to enable the State to assist in the maintenance of those dispensaries, by furnishing free arsphenamine, and about $1,000 for each clinic for clerical or other expenses. On this basis it should be possible to establish these dispensaries preferably in connection with existing institutions, in order to "camouflage" the venereal clinic itself. These dispensaries should serve as centers to safeguard the distribution of arsphenamine, and State arsphenamine should be issued only through such dispensaries.

Massachusetts recently adopted minimum standards for clinics for venereal disease control. These standards were prepared by the writer and are presented here in detail as an illustration of the dispensary method in the program for such control.

MINIMUM REQUIREMENTS FOR ADMISSION OF VENEREAL DISEASE CLINICS OR DISPENSARIES TO LIST OF CLINICS SERVING AS DISTRIBUTORS OF ARSPHENAMINE FOR STATE DEPARTMENT OF HEALTH. (STATE APPROVED VENEREAL DISEASE CLINICS.)

1. *Maintenance.*—It shall be maintained directly by Government or municipality or receive written indorsement of municipal health authorities and the mayor.

2. *Serve as distributing center for "arsphenamine."*—It shall be a center for the distribution of State department of health "arsphenamine" (under such conditions as are outlined in memorandum on distribution of arsphenamine).

3. *Management.*—(a) If combined clinic for gonorrhea and syphilis, executive management of the clinic shall be vested in the "medical chief of the clinic" who

shall be designated as the agent of the State department of health for the distribution of arsphenamine.

(b) If separate departments treating gonorrhea and syphilis are maintained, under the executive management of an institution, some medical executive officer of the institution must be designated as agent of the State department of health for the distribution of arsphenamine.

4. *Clinic hours.*—Clinics must be open at least three times a week and must provide at least one evening clinic period per week.

5. *Chief of clinic.*—The chief of the clinic shall be a qualified physician familiar with all modern laboratory and clinical diagnostic methods, experienced in the treatment of venereal diseases, and possessing the professional confidence of the medical profession of his vicinity. He shall agree in writing to carry out the duties required of him as agent of the State department of health for distribution of arsphenamine, and he shall be otherwise acceptable to the State department of health.

6. *Staff.*—The staff other than the "chief of the clinic," shall be adequate in number and training to furnish medical, surgical, nursing, laboratory, follow-up, and clerical service commensurate with the attendance of each clinic.

7. *Laboratory service.*—Dispensary laboratory service shall comprise at least facilities for microscopic examination for the organisms of syphilis and gonorrhea and for usual microscopic and chemical examination of urine. Wassermann tests shall be made at an approved Wassermann laboratory.

8. *Equipment.*—The location, rooms, instruments, apparatus, etc., shall be satisfactory to the State department of health.

9. *Records.*—Adequate records shall be kept of all cases applying for diagnosis or treatment as well as laboratory and follow-up records of the use or distribution of arsphenamine.

10. *Hospital affiliations.*—Each State-approved venereal-disease clinic shall have at its disposal, in the same or a near-by institution, beds for isolation or treatment of cases needing the same.

11. *Educational or preventive measures.*—The clinical staff shall devote sufficient time to adequately inform all patients as to the seriousness of venereal infection and the measures necessary to prevent infection of others, and shall supplement verbal instruction by furnishing approved literature.

12. *Financing of clinics.*—Approved venereal clinics may be either free clinics or "pay clinics," but if pay clinics they shall not refuse or discriminate against any patients referred or offering themselves who are unable to pay a fee. No charge shall be made for arsphenamine.

These dispensaries should be established only in large cities, located strategically, in order to serve a wide area. The question of whether they shall be "free" or "pay" clinics should be decided locally. The self-sustained or partly self-sustaining pay clinic with a low fee and free treatment given to those unable to pay is preferable.

The following instructions for the guidance of district health officers were issued in regard to distribution of State arsphenamine:

ON THE SUPPLYING, DISTRIBUTION, AND UTILIZATION OF ARSPHENAMINE AND METHODS OF ACCOUNTING FOR SAME.

1. Emphasize (a) That the supply of arsphenamine is primarily to render cases of syphilis noninfectious.

(b) That the State is furnishing the equivalent of many thousand dollars assistance in supplying arsphenamine.

2. The "approved clinics" shall serve as centers of distribution of arsphenamine for the "area" assigned by the State department of health to the clinic.

Exception.—Arsphenamine for State institutions shall be furnished directly, when a supply is available, from the control office of the State department of health.

3. The "chief of the clinic" shall be the agent of the State department of health for the distribution of arsphenamine.

4. Ledger accounts shall be kept with each "clinic" and the "chief of the clinic". shall be charged with each dose, identified by serial number furnished to his clinic.

5. So far as the supply of arsphenamine is available, the "chief of the clinic" shall utilize arsphenamine in the following order of priority:

(a) For patients attendant upon the clinic in infective stage.

(b) For patients in infective stage in "approved" hospitals, asylums, or institutions other than in State institutions, located within the clinic area.

(c) For patients in infective stage under care of practitioners within the clinic area.

(d) For patients in noninfective stages, whether "clinic" patients, institutional patients, or patients under the care of private practitioners, in whatever order or sequence may appear best in the discretion of the "chief of the clinic."

6. All arsphenamine utilized, whether within or without the clinic, shall be identified by serial number, and reports of use made thereupon on a form furnished for that purpose.

7. The question of need for arsphenamine shall be determined as far as possible by confirmatory Wassermann test. In noninfective stage, Wassermann positive tests are to be obtained before the arsphenamine is used.

8. Hospitals and other institutions within each clinic "area" shall become "approved" institutions for utilization of arsphenamine after satisfying the "chief of the clinic" as to professional qualifications and familiarity with the special technique for the administration of arsphenamine of the medical staff of such institutions assigned to administer the same, determined by consultation with the "chief of the clinic," and agreeing to furnish reports of treatment for syphilis.

9. Private practitioners must satisfy the "chief of the clinic" as to their practical experience and familiarity with the technique of its administration before receiving arsphenamine for administration in private practice.

10. No fee for arsphenamine shall be charged under any circumstances. The "chief of the clinic" may, at his discretion, at any time discontinue the privilege of receiving arsphenamine itself, for failure to submit reports of treatment or Wassermann tests, or otherwise abusing the privilege of receiving arsphenamine.

11. Monthly the "chief of the clinic" shall forward to the State department of health a report on the doses of arsphenamine given at the clinic and furnished to institutions and physicians within the "clinic area."

The following instructions were given to Massachusetts district health officers to aid them in securing the establishment of approved clinics:

ON METHODS OF ESTABLISHING "APPROVED CLINICS."

1. No general method can be laid down. The district health officer is expected to exhibit initiative and energy in stimulating the early establishment of such clinics in the cities selected. He must study local conditions and make such concessions or modifications of the procedure outlined in these memoranda as in his judgment are necessary in individual instances, as long as he can be assured that the spirit of the minimum requirements is complied with.

2. The following groups should be interested and their support enlisted:

(1) Local board of health.

(2) Local medical profession.

(3) City officials, especially the mayor.

(4) Local committee on public safety.

(5) Large manufacturers.

(6) All organizations interested in public health.

(7) Religious bodies.

(8) Chambers of commerce, boards of trade, etc. (officially).

(9) Hospital management and boards.

(10) Local district nursing organizations.

(11) All individuals and organizations whose homes have been furnished by the Council of National Defense.

(12) Local druggists' organizations.

(13) The press (at least sufficient to insure that no antagonistic publicity is started through misunderstanding).

(14) Educators.

(15) Labor organizations (reasons same as the press).

This part of the program also calls for energetic measures on the part of the district health officer.

3. In case an energetic local campaign of education seems necessary as a preliminary to successfully launching an "approved clinic," the district health officer should not hesitate to inaugurate such a campaign. Remember, you can get for the asking direct telegraphic indorsement from the War Department and the Council of National Defense, and can readily obtain by preliminary arrangement forceful speakers from the War Department, the Massachusetts Association for the Study of Venereal Diseases, and from other bodies as women's section, Council of National Defense, Massachusetts Commission on Insane, Massachusetts Mental Hygiene Society, and other organizations.

4. If difficulty occurs in obtaining a man qualified to serve as "chief of clinic,[2] performing both executive and clinical duties, or as chief clinician under a "chief of clinic," performing only executive duties, the Boston Dispensary will furnish facilities for intensive training for physicians wishing to qualify in specialty.

5. In general urge establishment of clinics as a national duty and as a war measure; insist that they be started on a high ethical plane, not as a traditional "clap clinic"; feature their function as educational and preventive centers; strive to affiliate with hospitals where possible to better "camouflage" cause of attendance.

6. If moral issue is raised in opposition to scheme, emphasize the well-established fact, determined by the finding of British authorities, that the innocent sufferers from venereal infection form an actual majority.

7. If objection is raised from medical sources on the ground of loss of revenue, emphasize that the qualified medical profession, both of ethical and "advertising" character, is estimated at the outside to treat only 30 to 50 per cent of the total venereal infection—the remainder fall into the untreated, self-treated, and drug-store treated classes.

8 If objection is raised to the scheme locally—

(a) From the standpoint of general scepticism of the urgency of the problem and the need for action, quote such facts as the statistics of the Council of National Defense as to the comparative frequency of venereal infection in freshly drafted men and regulars.

(b) On the ground of expense involved in view of the extraordinary war-time public expenses, quote such conclusions as that of the British Royal Commission on Venereal Diseases, arrived at after a most exhaustive study in a country war-burdened to a degree this country can not yet comprehend, which says:

"That the conditions now existing and those which must follow on the conclusion of the war imperatively require that action should be taken without delay. We realize the claims of economy at the present moment, but we believe that all necessary expenditure will be recouped by the results which can be obtained.

"No short-sighted parsimony should be permitted to stand in the way of all the means that science can suggest and that organization can supply for guarding present and future generations upon whom the restoration of national prosperity must depend."

Further instructions were given to district health officers on the following points:

(1) Minimum equipment for dispensaries.

(2) Cost of equipment and maintenance.

(3) Supervision.[1]

Certain instructions given to district health officers in regard to policy may be helpful:

ON CERTAIN POLICIES TO BE EMPHASIZED AND THOROUGHLY EXPLAINED.

To a considerable degree these have been touched upon in various memoranda, but it is desired here to call to the attention of the district health officer the need for a reasonably uniform departmental policy to be followed by them in establishing clinics. It is intended that the district health officer will only modify these policies if he is certain that such modifications are necessary or desirable to insure the success of a given clinic.

1. Emphasize preventive functions of clinics, and in doing so point out that clinics can be made powerful preventive agencies in two distinct ways:

(a) By the direct benefit of lessening foci of infection, and

(b) By the correlation of repressive, correctional, and educational methods with the routine activities of the clinic.

2. Explain clearly the relationship of the "clinic" to the "clinic area." Under this head particular attention should be paid to explaining the purposes of the clinic and the methods of arsphenamine distribution, to local boards of health, management of institutions and medical profession located outside of the municipality but within the "area."

3. Relationship of clinics to hospitals. Whether the clinic is maintained as an integral part of a general hospital or not, the district health officer should devote special attention to the problem of obtaining bed facilities for patients coming under the care of the clinic who need temporary hospital care.

Another feature that will require careful explanation from the beginning will be to make the hospital and other institutional managements understand that they are not entitled to arsphenamine ad libitum by virtue of being hospitals, that they are under the same relationship to the "chief of clinic" as private practitioners and must satisfy him as to the ability to handle the product safely, and are to use it primarily for infectious cases and are to receive it for administration to other cases only in event of the supply being more than sufficient for all infective cases within the "area."

4. Relationship of clinics to medical profession. The success of the "clinics" will depend more upon the sympathetic cordial support of the medical profession of the city and "area" than upon any other factor outside the immediate management of the clinic. It is, therefore, highly essential that the support of the medical profession be obtained. This means practically an educational campaign among physicians. Each district health officer should inaugurate this at once, and push it at every opportunity.

After the clinic is inaugurated, practitioners should be urged to utilize it and should be made to feel that it is their clinic. They should be told frankly from the outset that the full success of the clinic may mean a certain loss of revenue to them, but it should also be emphasized what a small percentage of venereal cases are now being

---

[1] Details of these instructions are omitted, but if desired may be secured by addressing the State commissioner of health, Statehouse, Boston, Mass.

handled by the qualified practitioners of medicine, and they should be urged to support the clinic as a measure designed, first of all, to reach the untreated or maltreated venereal case.

Every practitioner in the "area" should have clearly explained by the district health officer, after the clinic is once begun, the relationship of the clinic management to the distribution of arsphenamine, and that special facilities for diagnosis, consultation, and treatment are open to him.

A system whereby the practitioner can refer patients, whom he does not wish to turn over permanently to the clinic for treatment, for limited or special treatment, administration of arsphenamine for example, and have them referred back to him at the end of such special treatment, should be worked out jointly by the district health officer, representative of the local medical society, and each "chief of clinic."

Practitioners should be encouraged to seek consultation either at the clinic or in the office of the practitioners respecting any case of suspected venereal disease under their care.

Every practitioner within the "area" should clearly understand that he can obtain laboratory assistance for any case of his, gratuitously, through the clinic. Each clinic should be an active Wassermann station and should make it easy for physicians to utilize the services of State or other "approved" Wassermann laboratory.

Attendance of physicians other than the regular staff at the clinic should be encouraged after the clinics are well established, but care will always have to be exercised, especially in small cities and at pay clinics, to see that attendance of physicians other than the regular staff does not tend to decrease the attendance of the clinic.

One great advantage of having several consultation rooms and an entrance to consultation rooms other than directly through the patients' waiting room is that thereby it is possible for any physician to attend and see patients he has referred to the clinic without seeing other patients. It is very desirable that as far as circumstances will permit the patients' privacy should be respected.

5. *Minimum assistance.*—In making efforts to get clinics launched, sacrifice any nonessentials, but make up your own mind as to the minimum staff necessary to insure proper handling of patients at any given clinic and then insist that the minimum staff be provided.

The following would seem to be a minimum staff for the smallest area:

One "chief of clinic," } one or both covering laboratory service.
One medical assistant, }
One qualified nurse, who is nurse, follow-up worker, and clerk.
Janitory service.

6. The relationship of the chief of clinic to the district health officer must be a particularly close and harmonious one to realize the full possibilities of the clinic scheme. He should have a free hand and not be hampered as to details. On the other hand, he should be given clearly to understand from the beginning that when he wishes to bring anything up to the State department of health, he does not need to go any further than the district health officer to obtain all the assistance, advice, and direction that the department can give.

Conversely, the district health officer should at all times bring promptly to the attention of the "chief of clinic" any and every suggestion, whether critical or commendatory, that comes to his attention. The district health officer should make it one of the prime objects of his work not only to continually keep the purposes and possibilities of the clinics before the medical profession of the "area," but also should call the same clearly to the attention of officials and others whose work is of such a character that they could utilize the services of the venereal clinics. Included in this group should be police authorities, almoners and overseers of the poor, prison physicians and chaplains, Y. M. C. A. officials, officials of the draft law, officials of rescue societies, and the like.

Personnel of dispensary.—The personality and qualifications of the chief of clinic are the most important factors in the success of the entire venereal clinic scheme. The ideal arrangement is to have him combine general executive function—i. e., management of personnel, supervision of finances, duties as distributor of arsphenamine, etc.—with the functions of the clinical specialist. In most cases this arrangement will be possible and is in all ways to be desired and urged from the standpoint of avoiding friction, divided responsibility, delays, and questions of divided authority over clinical staff and clerical staff.

In all instances the chief of clinic must enjoy the confidence of the medical profession of his vicinity. The solution of the all-important question of obtaining hearty cooperation and support from the medical profession of the city and "area" will depend upon him and the district health officer more than upon all other interested persons combined.

As official referee and distributor of arsphenamine, he must be a man of discretion, judicial temperament, and without prejudices or favorites, and not capable of being intimidated by any influences. Often he must refuse arsphenamine, and it is all essential that he make each refusal as far as possible so unmistakably based on sound grounds of best public policy that the refused party will see the reasonableness of his stand.

If he is also the chief clinician, he must be thoroughly grounded in the technique of best modern methods of diagnosis and treatment. Above all he must be a man who is interested in the preventive and educational possibilities of his clinic, and in hearty sympathy with the State department of health's policy of developing the clinics to the point where the chief clinician will actually and efficiently lessen the total incidence of venereal disease in his area. If this object is not constantly kept in mind and every effort put forth to make its accomplishment a reality, all work is in vain.

Furthermore, he must be a man who can appreciate the vital importance of keeping records and of enforcing business like methods of administration in all matters pertaining to the routine work of the clinic.

Medical and surgical staff.—The number of persons on the medical and surgical staff will vary with the size of the clinic, but the all-important point is that at least one, either the "chief of clinic" himself or, if he does not perform clinical duties, the chief clinical assistant (or assistants, if the distinct departments for gonorrhea and syphilis are maintained), shall possess special experience with venereal diseases, and a thorough knowledge of modern methods of diagnosis and treatment sufficient to give him without question an authoritative position in such matters.

Physicians of the vicinity should be encouraged to make application as temporary assistants with or without pay for the purpose of familiarizing themselves with modern methods of diagnosis and treatment; but the regular medical and surgical staff should in all instances receive compensation sufficient to represent a fair monetary return, judged by local standards, for the time devoted to the clinic, and to effect potential loss of emergency revenue from private practice due to attendance at fixed hours at the clinic.

The duties of the medical and surgical staff should include educational work with patients, making of necessary clinical records and reports, taking and transmitting material for laboratory examination and demonstrating the best methods of diagnosis and systematic treatment to physicians.

Consultations.—Consultation work by the "chief of clinic" or his clinical assistants with practitioners of the "area" should be encouraged, but clearly defined policies should be laid down for each area and generally understood and agreed to by the local profession as to the circumstances under which consultation outside of the clinic should be gratuitous or "pay" consultations. It is advisable to have a fee scale definitely fixed in advance.

Nursing staff.—The nursing staff of the clinic may often be satisfactorily filled by one female nurse reporting only at certain hours for female clinics. The nurse may be utilized for the taking of female histories to advantage. The advisability of obtaining a male nurse or "orderly" as assistant will depend on local conditions.

Laboratory staff.—The laboratory staff will depend largely upon the size of the clinic. Outside of the largest clinics, a separate laboratory staff probably will not be needed. The clinical staff in the smaller clinics should do ordinary direct microscopic and urinalysis laboratory work. Wassermanns, in most instances, will be done outside the clinic in the State or other approved Wassermann laboratories.

"Follow-up staff."—The development of a scientific yet "human" follow-up system is perhaps the most characteristic feature of the "modern" venereal dispensary, and marks it off most sharply from the policies, procedure, and results of the traditional "clap clinic."

The principal functions will be:

(a) Supervision of the prostitute patient, including enlistment of the sympathies and support of social betterment agencies for the deserving case.

(b) Establishment of good "team work" with the police and reformatory agencies for the purpose of the suppression of the incorrigible type, or at least their temporary isolation for at least a period sufficient to insure their treatment to the point where they cease to be spreaders of infection.

(c) Looking up validity of reports from patients as to sources of infection.

(d) Enlisting cooperation of employers of labor to encourage utilization of the services of the clinic.

(e) Checking up mentality of prostitute patients and enlisting the assistance of proper authorities in cases of those deserving special handling as mental deficients.

(f) Keeping track of "parole" patients of both sexes.

(g) Looking up patients still in need of treatment who fail to report at the clinic.

In some clinics the services of a full-time specially trained "follow-up" worker will be needed. In others, various part-time adjustments will be necessary.

Clerical staff.—One full-time clerical assistant will be needed in most clinics to keep up records properly, and to be available to receive requests and requisitions for arsphenamine, laboratory containers, to make appointments for the "chief of clinic," answer the telephone, etc. It is advisable to arrange if possible that State department of health money be directly utilized to provide for clerical service.

Clerical service need not be full eight hours per day nor every day in the week, but should have definite hours, well known to local medical profession, so that arsphenamine can be furnished according to the direction of the "chief of clinic" at reasonably convenient and frequent periods.

A possible combination of functions, that might prove very satisfactory in smaller clinics would be the full-time employment of one graduate nurse with social service or public health nursing experience, and have her attend female clinics, act as clerk of clinic, keeping regular office hours for that purpose, and devote the remainder of her time to follow-up work.

Control of Prostitutes for Treatment.

Prostitutes are recognized as the most prolific source of venereal disease. It is possible to do much in the suppression of prostitution by enforcement of existing laws and ordinances. It may be possible in some cities and States to secure more drastic laws for control of and elimination of this source of infection. It is certain that in many cities by enforcement of existing laws and especially by an arrangement securing the cooperation of health officers, police authorities, and city magistrates, control of thousands of prostitutes for purpose of treatment and their elimination as carriers can be effected. Preliminary to this arrangement a proper venereal dispensary and a sufficient number of beds for hospitalization must be made available. It is certain that in many States the carrier material in the person of prostitutes available for treatment under existing laws far exceeds the facilities for treatment. This lack is especially marked in hospital facilities.

Educational.

Lectures should be given by male lecturers before men's and boys' clubs and organizations, industrial groups and labor unions, fraternal and professional groups; and by female lecturers before women's clubs, groups, and organizations, employing lantern slides, moving pictures, and other devices or exhibits.

Placards should be placed in public lavatories, barber shops, railroad stations, and other places where men congregate, and pamphlets should be distributed, especially to the groups mentioned in the preceding paragraph.

MEASURES WHICH REQUIRE LEGISLATION.

In addition to the measures which probably do not require legislative authority beyond the granting of appropriations, there are certain necessary measures for which legislation should be secured.

(1) Reporting of venereal diseases.
(2) Elimination of quacks and charlatans.
(3) Prevention of treatment by drug clerks.
(4) Examination and treatment of prisoners.

None of these measures are here discussed in detail.

Reporting of Venereal Diseases.

In Massachusetts no additional legislation was necessary, the State department of health having general authority to add to the list of reportable diseases.

The following letter was sent to all physicians:

GENTLEMEN: Inclosed herewith are advance copies of the regulations adding gonorrhea and syphilis to the list of reportable diseases. This department has studied the question of reporting gonorrhea and syphilis for the last two years and sought all information possible on the subject. The method adopted by these regulations is in substance that known as the "West Australian" method of handling venereal diseases - so called because first adopted by the State of West Australia.

Because of their peculiar character any scheme for the reporting of gonorrhea and syphilis encounters difficulties which are not shared by other communicable diseases. Requiring reporting by name would be inoperative to a great degree. The alternative course is reporting by number, initials, etc. Up to a certain point the "West Australian" method has this anonymous feature, but with the proviso that when an actively infected patient fails to continue treatment, it becomes the duty of the physician to report the name and address of the patient.

When the name is reported the State department of health will report it to the local board of health having jurisdiction. Therefore it is incumbent upon the local boards of health to adopt such amendments to their rules and regulations as may seem advisable to them for the control of such cases.

It is easy to criticise features of this system, but it seems to be working better in many parts of the world than any other scheme that has yet been brought forward for the reporting of venereal diseases.

The State department of health will be glad to send on requisition to the board of health of any city or town at weekly or monthly intervals the statistical information obtained through the original anonymous reports from that city or town. This department relies confidently on the hearty cooperation of all the local boards of health in making a success of this most important war measure.

The following forms are self-explanatory and illustrate the method of reporting:

SPECIAL REGULATIONS GOVERNING THE REPORTING OF VENEREAL DISEASES PROMULGATED BY THE MASSACHUSETTS STATE DEPARTMENT OF HEALTH.

WAR MEASURE.

COMMONWEALTH OF MASSACHUSETTS STATE DEPARTMENT OF HEALTH.

GONORRHEA AND SYPHILIS ADDED TO LIST OF REPORTABLE DISEASES.

Effective February 1, 1918. Reports to be made in conformity with special regulations direct to State department of health.

Special regulations governing the reporting of these diseases are given herewith. Note carefully that all reports of gonorrhea and syphilis are to be made direct to the State department of health, statehouse, Boston, and not to local boards of health, as is the case of all other diseases dangerous to the public health.

The State department of health, at a meeting held December 12, 1917, voted, that the list of diseases declared dangerous to the public health be further amended by adding gonorrhea and syphilis, so that the said list now reads as follows:

Actinomycosis.
Anterior poliomyelitis.
Anthrax.
Asiatic cholera.
Chicken pox.
Diphtheria.
Dog bite (requiring antirabic treatment).
Dysentery:
  (a) Amebic.
  (b) Bacillary.
Epidemic cerebrospinal meningitis.

German measles.
Glanders.
Hookworm disease.
Infectious diseases of the eye:
  (a) Ophthalmia neo.
  (b) Sup. conjunctivitis.
  (c) Trachoma.
Leprosy.
Malaria.
Measles.
Mumps.
Pellagra.
Plague.

Pneumonia (lobar only).
Rabies.
Scarlet fever.
Septic sore throat.
Smallpox.
Tetanus.
Trichinosis.
Tuberculosis (all forms).
Typhoid fever.
Typhus fever.
Whooping cough.
Yellow fever.

Reportable to local boards of health in accordance with the provisions of sections 49 and 50, chapter 75, revised laws,

AND GONORRHEA, SYPHILIS,

reportable to State department of health direct, under authority of chapter 670, Laws of 1913, in accordance with the special regulations herewith promulgated.

REGULATIONS GOVERNING THE REPORTING OF GONORRHEA AND SYPHILIS.

1. Gonorrhea and syphilis are declared diseases dangerous to the public health, and shall be reported in the manner provided by these regulations promulgated under the authority of chapter 670, Laws of 1913.

2. Gonorrhea and syphilis are to be reported (in the manner provided by these regulations) on and after February 1, 1918.

3. At the time of the first visit or consultation the physician shall furnish to each person examined or treated by him a numbered circular of information and advice concerning the disease in question, furnished by the State department of health for that purpose.

4. The physician shall at the same time fill out the numbered report blank attached to the circular of advice, and forthwith mail the same to the State department of health. On this blank he shall report the following facts:

Name of the disease..............................	Marital condition and occupation of the patient....
Age..	Previous duration of disease and degree of infectiousness..
Sex..	
Color..	

THE REPORT SHALL NOT CONTAIN NAME OR ADDRESS OF PATIENT.

5. Whenever a person suffering from gonorrhea or syphilis in an infective stage applies to a physician for advice or treatment, the physician shall ascertain from the person in question whether or not such person has previously consulted with or been treated by another physician within the Commonwealth and has received a numbered circular of advice. If not, the physician shall give and explain to the patient a numbered circular of advice and shall report the case to the State department of health, as provided in the previous regulation.

If the patient has consulted with or been treated by another physician within the Commonwealth and has received the numbered circular of advice, the physician last consulted shall not report the case to the State department of health, but shall ask the patient to give him the name and address of the physician last previously treating said patient.

6. In case the person seeking treatment for gonorrhea or syphilis gives the name and address of the physician last previously consulted, the physician then being consulted shall notify immediately by mail the physician last previously consulted of the patient's change of medical adviser.

7. Whenever any person suffering from gonorrhea or syphilis in an infective stage shall fail to return to the physician treating such person for a period of six weeks later than the time last appointed by the physician for such consultation or treatment, and the physician also fails to receive a notification of change of medical advisers as provided in the previous section, the physician shall then notify the State department of health, giving name, address of patient, name of the disease and serial number, date of report and name of physician originally reporting the case by said serial number, if known.

8. Upon receipt of a report giving name and address of a person suffering from gonorrhea or syphilis in an infective stage, as provided in the previous section, the State department of health will report name and address of the person as a person suffering from a disease dangerous to the public health and presumably not under proper medical advice and care sufficient to protect others from infection to the board of health of the city or town of patient's residence or last known address. The State department of health shall not divulge the name of the physician making said report.

NOTIFICATION BLANK FROM PHYSICIAN TO ANOTHER PHYSICIAN WHO FORMERLY TREATED THE PATIENT.

....Mass.,

....191 ..

Dr..

   Street address (if known)...............................

....Mass.

DEAR DOCTOR: In accordance with section 6, Regulations Governing Reporting of Venereal Diseases, I herewith notify you that..,

                        (Name of patient.)

of .... having serial number.................................,

      (Address.)

circular of instructions for prevention of ...., formerly treated by you, has now placed himself under my care and treatment.

   Respectfully, yours,

....M. D.,

....

         (Address.)

NOTIFICATION BLANK FROM PHYSICIAN REPORTING NAME OF PATIENT WHO FAILED TO CONTINUE TREATMENT.

....Mass.,

....191...

STATE DEPARTMENT OF HEALTH,
   DIVISION OF COMMUNICABLE DISEASES,
     State House, Boston, Mass.

  GENTLEMEN: This is to notify you that ....,

                    (Name of patient.)

of .... originally reported by

      (Address of patient.)

.... as serial number ....191..,

    (Name of physician.)   (Give, if known.)

who has been under my care for treatment for.................In the infective stage

              (Specify gonorrhea or syphilis.)

has not reported to me for six weeks following date of his last appointment with me, nor have I received any notification from another physician that he has placed himself under his professional care. I am therefore reporting his name and last known address in accordance with section 7 of the Special Regulations of the State Department of Health Governing the Reporting of Gonorrhea and Syphilis.

   Sincerely, yours,

....M. D.,

.... Street,

....Mass.

CIRCULAR OF INSTRUCTIONS WHICH PHYSICIAN MUST FURNISH TO EACH PATIENT
WITH VENEREAL DISEASE.

COMMONWEALTH OF MASSACHUSETTS.

A FEW FACTS ABOUT SYPHILIS.

ISSUED BY THE MASSACHUSETTS STATE DEPARTMENT OF HEALTH, STATEHOUSE, BOSTON.

Keep—Read carefully and often—Remember your number.

1. Syphilis, also known as "pox," "blood disease," etc., is a serious contagious disease, slowly acting, which may affect all parts of the body.

2. Syphilis is caused by a minute germ, which can only be seen with a powerful microscope, which circulates through the blood and attacks every organ in the body if unchecked by proper treatment.

3. Syphilis is usually but not always transmitted by sexual intercourse.

4. Syphilis always begins by the germs entering the body through a break or abrasion of the skin or of the lining of the mouth or sexual organs. This abrasion may be so small that it can not be seen.

5. Syphilis always begins with the local sore which develops at the spot where the germs penetrate. The germ grows slowly at first and from two to eight weeks may elapse before the sore appears. This initial sore, pimple, or ulcer is usually painless and is called a "hard chancre" or the first stage.

6. Syphilis gradually develops after the chancre has apparently been cured. Skin rashes, sores in mouth, swelling of glands, fever, deep pains in bones, sore throat, falling out of hair, are some of the most frequent symptoms of this stage. Any one or more of these symptoms may occur. This is known as the second stage.

7. Syphilis, when untreated, may appear to be cured spontaneously after the second stage, but it is not. It remains in the blood and the deep parts of the body. The germs will lie quiet sometimes for years and then suddenly produce the terrible effects known as the third stage. They will slowly destroy the brain, nerves, bones, blood vessels, etc. Locomotor ataxia, paralysis, paresis, or softening of the brain, and some forms of apoplexy, are a few of the later effects of untreated syphilis. They may come on as late as 20 years after the original "chancre," but are all part of the same disease and caused by the same germs.

8. Syphilis, when uncured, may also be transmitted to unborn children through either father or mother. It is one of the greatest causes of miscarriages, children being born dead, and of weak, sickly children. When born alive, these babies often spread the disease, as their syphilis is very contagious.

9. Syphilis is extremely contagious in the first and second stages.

10. Syphilis is most easily cured in the first or "chancre" stage, is readily curable in the second stage, and may be greatly improved in the third stage.

11. Syphilis in all stages requires long thorough treatment by special remedies to insure a cure. Certain laboratory tests, especially the one known as the "Wassermann test," are of great assistance in determining when the disease is cured.

12. Syphilis can be accidentally transmitted during the first and second stages and from babies with congenital syphilis in a great variety of ways, by kissing, by articles accidentally contaminated with secretions from the sores, as towels, pipes, drinking glasses, eating utensils, etc.

13. Syphilis affects most public and clandestine or secret prostitutes. It can be best prevented by avoiding all chance of infection.

14. Syphilis can be cured, but not in a week or a month at any stage. A person with syphilis must be sure he is getting competent treatment and then stick to it a long time, until the "blood tests" and his physician say he is cured.

PERSONAL ADVICE TO PATIENT.

1. Do not forget your disease may be communicated to others by contact other than sexual intercourse.

2. It may be transmitted by any of the secretions of the body, but more especially by blood or blood serum coming from raw mucous surfaces, such as cracked or sore lips, mucous patches in the mouth and throat, discharges from syphilitic ulcers and sores.

3. Never permit the slightest opportunity for other persons to come in contact with any of these secretions.

4. To avoid this, follow these rules:

(a) Until the acutely infectious stage is passed and permission is given by the physician, you should have individual drinking cups and eating utensils. These should be sterilized by boiling after each use. Never use public drinking cups.

(b) Tooth-brushes and containers of pastes, powders, or mouth washes used in caring for the teeth should be kept in separate containers or compartments where no opportunity for contact with others is possible. Brush teeth night and morning (or better, after each meal) and keep mouth clean.

If you have bad teeth have them attended to by a dentist. Be fair to him and his next patient by telling him you have syphilis, so he may take precautions and not infect others.

(c) Use no razor or other articles used in shaving except your own, and permit no other person to use your shaving outfit. Shaving in a public barber shop is prohibited for one year after beginning of infection.

(d) Basins, lavatories, and bathtubs used should be washed out thoroughly with soap and hot water after each use by you. Separate basins are to be used wherever possible. The use of public bathtubs is prohibited.

(e) You should use individual towels.

(f) Handkerchiefs and clothing, especially underclothing, which may be soiled by secretions, should be laundered separately, or if impracticable, they must be immersed in boiling water or an approved antiseptic solution, as advised by the physician, before being added to other laundry.

(g) All dressings of sores or ulcers must be burned or otherwise destroyed. Never leave them where they are accessible to flies.

(h) Never kiss others or permit them to kiss you.

(i) Sleep alone and practice continence. Your physician will tell you good habits improve your physical tone and hasten recovery.

(j) Follow your physician's advice, and do not cease treatment until by every known laboratory method he has satisfied himself of your recovery, and assures you there is no longer danger of your transmitting the disease.

(k) Do not be led astray by promises of hasty or permanent cure by falsely advertised remedies. Cheap cures make miserable lives and expensive funerals. You gain nothing but bitter experience by deceiving yourself, and you risk the injury of those nearest and dearest to you. Play fair with yourself and with others.

5. Consult your doctor at least once a month for two years.

IMPORTANT—READ CAREFULLY—FOLLOW INSTRUCTIONS IF YOU WISH YOUR NAME KEPT SECRET.

You are given this circular of instructions with this serial number by your doctor because the law requires him to do so and to report your case to the State department of health by this number without revealing your name.

If you change doctors for any reason and wish to keep your name concealed you must see to it that the doctor you last consult notifies the doctor previously having charge of your case within six weeks.

If you fail to come for treatment at the time ordered by your doctor within the period in which your disease is infective and your doctor does not receive notice within six weeks from another doctor stating that you have placed yourself under his professional care, the doctor giving you this circular is obliged by law to report your name and address to the health authorities as a person suffering from a disease dangerous to the public health and presumably not under proper medical advice and care sufficient to protect others from infection. You will then be liable to quarantine or such other procedure as the board of health may determine. If you want your name kept secret follow these instructions carefully. Your doctor will tell you when your case is no longer infective.

No.............

BLANK FOR FIRST REPORT OF CASE BY SERIAL NUMBER ONLY.

No. ...   WAR MEASURE.   Report of a case of syphilis

COMMONWEALTH OF MASSACHUSETTS, STATE DEPARTMENT OF HEALTH.

(Date).............................191 .   (City or Town)..............................., Mass.

Patient's age...............................; sex..............................; color.............................

Marital state—Married. Single. Widowed. Divorced.*

Occupation (give specific character of occupation)..

Is occupation or sanitary surroundings at place of employment such that patient will be a menace to the health of others?.. If so, what measures of precaution have you advised?

....

....

Has your diagnosis been confirmed by laboratory tests?................. If so, which?...................

Date of onset of disease...................................191 .

Signature of reporting physician...............................M.D.

Address of reporting physician......................................

......................................Mass.

* Strike out words that do not apply, or draw circle about word indicated.

INSTRUCTIONS TO PHYSICIAN.

Tear off this slip. Fill out and mail to State Department of Health, State House, Boston, using enclosed addressed envelope. Instructions are to be given and explained to patient. The name of patient is not required. If patient can not read English and can read Armenian, Greek, Finnish, French, Italian, Lithuanian, Polish, Portuguese, Swedish or Yiddish, give patient serial numbered circular in English and request the State department of health to send to you by return mail one or more copies of unnumbered translations of circular, specifying languages and number of copies of each desired. (See back of slip for ordering.)

Elimination of Quacks.

If State laws are insufficient, proper legislation should be secured to prevent the treatment of persons suffering from venereal disease by quacks. There is sufficient law in many States to effect this, and the laws should be vigorously enforced just as soon as the treatment facilities are made available by the establishment of venereal clinics.

Prevention of Treatment by Drug Clerks.

In preparing a comprehensive program for the prevention of venereal diseases in Massachusetts it was deemed necessary to ask the legislature to pass an act prohibiting druggists from dispensing any medicines for venereal diseases except upon the prescription of a physician. Since syphilis and gonorrhea have been declared diseases dangerous to the public health and made reportable, a druggist has no more right to treat them than he has to treat smallpox, diphtheria, or scarlet fever.

The fearful results of bad treatment, especially in gonorrhea, are attributable quite as much to the treatment of cases by drug clerks over the counter as to the activity of quacks and charlatans, and it is essential that the practice of treatment of venereal diseases by drug clerks be stopped at the earliest possible moment.

Examination and Treatment of Prisoners.

One other legislative measure should be passed, viz, requirement of medical examination and treatment of prisoners. Whatever excuse we may have for not securing the treatment and elimination of the carrier in the general population, we have not the slightest excuse for discharging from our jails and reformatories thousands of prisoners with venereal disease untreated and in many instances not even diagnosed or recorded.

PREVALENCE OF DISEASE.

No health department, State or local, can effectively prevent or control disease without knowledge of when, where, and under what conditions cases are occurring.

UNITED STATES.

EXTRA-CANTONMENT ZONES—CASES REPORTED WEEK ENDED FEB. 19.

CAMP BEAUREGARD ZONE, LA.

Cerebrospinal meningitis:
Pineville.................................. 2
Diphtheria:
Alexandria................................ 2
Measles:
Alexandria................................ 5
Boyse.................................... 1
Rural district............................ 1
Mumps:
Alexandria................................ 3
Sharp.................................... 1
Smallpox:
Alexandria................................ 2
Rural district............................ 1
Typhoid fever:
Alexandria................................ 1

CAMP BOWIE ZONE, TEX.

Fort Worth:
Cerebrospinal meningitis.............. 3
Diphtheria............................ 2
Food poisoning........................ 1
Measles............................... 4
Mumps................................. 6
Pneumonia............................. 10
Scarlet fever......................... 1
Smallpox.............................. 14
Tuberculosis, pulmonary............... 3
Typhoid fever......................... 1

CAMP DODGE ZONE, IOWA

Chancroid:
Des Moines............................ 2
Diphtheria:
Des Moines............................ 8
Gonorrhea:
Des Moines............................ 11
Gonorrhea and chancroid:
Des Moines............................ 1
German measles:
Grimes................................ 1

CAMP DODGE ZONE, IOWA—continued.

Measles:
Des Moines................................ 60
Grimes.................................... 8
Pneumonia:
Grimes.................................... 4
Scarlet fever:
Des Moines................................ 10
Grimes.................................... 7
Bloomfield Township....................... 1
Smallpox:
Des Moines................................ 26
Grimes.................................... 7
Syphilis:
Des Moines................................ 3
Typhoid fever:
Des Moines................................ 1

CAMP FUNSTON ZONE, KANS.

Cerebrospinal meningitis:
Manhattan................................. 2
Army City................................. 1
Chicken pox:
Manhattan................................. 2
Junction City............................. 5
Erysipelas:
Junction City............................. 4
Measles:
Manhattan................................. 64
Junction City............................. 22
Alta Vista................................ 6
Randolph.................................. 2
Cleborne.................................. 2
Mumps:
Manhattan................................. 15
Pneumonia:
Manhattan................................. 1
Junction City............................. 1
Scarlet fever:
Manhattan................................. 3
Junction City............................. 1
Smallpox:
Manhattan................................. 8
Junction City............................. 9

CAMP GORDON ZONE, GA.

Cerebrospinal meningitis:
Atlanta.. 6
Chicken pox:
Atlanta.. 4
Diphtheria:
Atlanta.. 7
Hapeville.. 1
German measles:
Atlanta.. 9
Gonorrhea:
Atlanta.. 15
Malaria:
Atlanta.. 1
Measles:
Atlanta.. 7
Dunwoody.. 1
East Lake.. 1
Mumps:
Atlanta.. 30
Paratyphoid fever:
Atlanta.. 1
Pneumonia:
Atlanta.. 2
Dunwoody.. 1
Scarlet fever:
Atlanta.. 5
Septic sore throat:
Atlanta.. 2
Smallpox:
Atlanta.. 1
College Park....................................... 2
Syphilis:
Atlanta.. 10
Tuberculosis:
Atlanta.. 13
Typhoid fever:
Dunwoody.. 1
Whooping cough:
Atlanta.. 7
Chamblee.. 4

CAMP GREENE ZONE, N. C.

Charlotte Township:
Cerebrospinal meningitis.................... 1
Chicken pox................................... 3
Diphtheria.................................... 1
German measles................................ 5
Gonorrhea..................................... 2
Gonorrhea and syphilis........................ 1
Measles....................................... 21
Mumps... 3
Syphilis...................................... 12
Trachoma...................................... 4
Tuberculosis.................................. 2

CAMP HANCOCK ZONE, GA.

Cerebrospinal meningitis:
Augusta... 5
Chicken pox:
Augusta... 2
German measles:
Augusta... 19
Martinez.. 1
North Augusta..................................... 13

CAMP HANCOCK ZONE, GA.—continued.

Measles:
Augusta... 22
Martinez.. 1
Gracewood... 1
Blair... 1
North Augusta..................................... 1
Mumps:
Augusta... 1
Typhoid fever:
Hamburg... 1
Whooping cough:
Augusta... 1

FORT LEAVENWORTH ZONE, KANS.

Chicken pox:
Leavenworth........................... 9
Diphtheria:
Leavenworth........................... 1
German measles:
Leavenworth........................... 11
Measles:
Leavenworth........................... 2
Leavenworth County.................... 2
Pneumonia, lobar:
Leavenworth........................... 5
Leavenworth County.................... 1
Smallpox:
Leavenworth........................... 3
Leavenworth County.................... 2
Whooping cough:
Leavenworth County.................... 1

CAMP LOGAN ZONE, TEX.

Houston:
Chicken pox........................... 2
German measles........................ 11
Gonorrhea............................. 1
Measles............................... 24
Mumps................................. 4
Pneumonia............................. 16
Smallpox.............................. 6
Tuberculosis.......................... 6
Typhoid fever......................... 2
Harrisburg:
Chicken pox........................... 1

CAMP LEWIS ZONE, WASH.

German measles:
Gravelly Lake......................... 2
Roy................................... 7
Country Club.......................... 1
Lakeview.............................. 1
Spanaway.............................. 6
Parkland.............................. 8
Du Pont............................... 2
Hillhurst............................. 2

CAMP MACARTHUR ZONE, TEX.

Waco:
Cerebrospinal meningitis.............. 2
Chicken pox........................... 3
German measles........................ 9
Gonorrhea............................. 2
Measles............................... 13
Mumps................................. 10

CAMP MACARTHUR ZONE, TEX.—continued.

Waco—Continued.

Pneumonia, lobar	5
Scarlet fever	1
Smallpox	1
Whooping cough	2

CAMP M'CLELLAN ZONE, ALA.

Chicken pox:

Anniston	20
Blue Mountain	1
Precinct Three	1

German measles:

Anniston	1

Measles:

Anniston	6
Blue Mountain	6
Hobson City	2
Precinct Three	1

Pellagra:

Anniston	1

Pneumonia:

Anniston	1

Smallpox:

Anniston	10
Blue Mountain	1
Oxford	2
Precinct Two	1
Precinct Four	1
Precinct Thirteen	1

FORT OGLETHORPE ZONE, GA.

Cerebrospinal meningitis:

Chattanooga	2

Chicken pox:

Chattanooga	2
East Lake	1

Diphtheria:

Chattanooga	1

German measles:

Chattanooga	2
East Lake	1

Gonorrhea:

Chattanooga	8
North Chattanooga	1

Measles:

Chattanooga	1
East Lake	1

Mumps:

Chattanooga	9
East Lake	4

Pneumonia:

Chattanooga	1
East Lake	1

Scarlet fever:

St. Elmo	1

Smallpox:

Chattanooga	5

Syphilis:

Chattanooga	1

Tuberculosis:

Chattanooga	1

Whooping cough:

East Lake	1

CAMP PIKE ZONE, ARK.

Cerebrospinal meningitis:

Little Rock	3

Chancroid:

Little Rock	2
North Little Rock	1

Chicken pox:

Little Rock	2
North Little Rock	1

Diphtheria:

Little Rock	1

Erysipelas:

Little Rock	9

German measles:

Little Rock	4
Scotts	1

Gonorrhea:

Little Rock	30
North Little Rock	1
Scotts	1

Malaria:

Little Rock	8
North Little Rock	2

Measles:

Little Rock	19
North Little Rock	5

Mumps:

Little Rock	13
North Little Rock	1

Pellagra:

Little Rock	4

Pneumonia:

Little Rock	3
North Little Rock	1

Scarlet fever:

Little Rock	1
North Little Rock	1

Septic sore throat:

Scotts	2

Smallpox:

Little Rock	30
McAlmont	1
North Little Rock	2
Sweet Home	1

Syphilis:

Little Rock	20
Scotts	3

Tuberculosis:

Little Rock	3
North Little Rock	2
Scotts	2

Whooping cough:

Little Rock	4

CAMP SEVIER ZONE, S. C.

Measles

American Spinning Co. mill	1
Butler Township, rural	1

CAMP SHELBY ZONE, MISS.

Chicken pox:

Hattiesburg	8

Diphtheria:

Gulfport	2

Gonorrhea:

Hattiesburg	11

CAMP SHELBY ZONE, MISS —continued.

Malaria:
Hattiesburg............................. 1
Measles:
Hattiesburg............................. 2
Mumps:
Hattiesburg............................. 17
Pneumonia:
Hattiesburg............................. 1
Smallpox:
Hattiesburg............................. 11
Lumberton............................. 4
Lyman............................. 1
McHenry............................. 9
Purvis............................. 1
Syphilis:
Hattiesburg............................. 5

CAMP SHERIDAN ZONE, ALA.

Cerebrospinal meningitis:
Montgomery............................. 1
Chicken pox:
Montgomery............................. 4
Measles:
Montgomery............................. 22
Rural zone............................. 1
Pneumonia, lobar:
Montgomery............................. 3
Smallpox:
Montgomery............................. 8
Rural zone............................. 2
Tuberculosis:
Montgomery............................. 2

CAMP SHERMAN ZONE, OHIO.

Cerebrospinal meningitis:
Chillicothe............................. 1
Diphtheria:
Liberty Township............................. 1
German measles:
Chillicothe............................. 7
Measles:
Chillicothe............................. 6
Liberty Township............................. 1
Scarlet fever:
Chillicothe............................. 3

CAMP ZACHARY TAYLOR ZONE, KY.

Cerebrospinal meningitis:
Louisville............................. 3
Chicken pox:
Louisville............................. 6
Diphtheria:
Louisville............................. 13
German measles:
Jefferson County............................. 8
Measles:
Louisville............................. 53
Mumps:
Jefferson County............................. 2
Louisville............................. 5
Pneumonia:
Jefferson County............................. 2
Louisville............................. 3

CAMP ZACHARY TAYLOR ZONE, KY.—continued.

Rabies in animals:
Louisville............................. 1
Scarlet fever:
Louisville............................. 5
Smallpox:
Louisville............................. 1
Trachoma:
Jefferson County............................. 14
Tuberculosis, pulmonary:
Jefferson County............................. 3
Louisville............................. 11
Typhoid fever:
Louisville............................. 1
Whooping cough:
Louisville............................. 3

TIDEWATER HEALTH DISTRICT, VA.

Cerebrospinal meningitis:
Newport News............................. 2
German measles:
Hampton............................. 3
Newport News............................. 2
Phoebus............................. 2
Measles:
Hampton............................. 4
Newport News............................. 6
Phoebus............................. 1
Pneumonia:
Hampton............................. 2
Scarlet fever:
Fortress Monroe............................. 2
Hampton............................. 1
Phoebus............................. 1
Tuberculosis:
Newport News............................. 3
Typhoid fever:
Phoebus............................. 1
Whooping cough:
Newport News............................. 2

CAMP TRAVIS ZONE, TEX.

San Antonio:
Cerebrospinal meningitis.................... 1
Chancroid............................. 2
Dysentery............................. 1
Erysipelas............................. 1
Gonorrhea............................. 2
Measles............................. 5
Mumps............................. 2
Pneumonia............................. 9
Typhoid fever............................. 1

CAMP WADSWORTH ZONE, S. C.

Cerebrospinal meningitis:
Saxon Mills............................. 1
Chicken pox:
Spartanburg............................. 2
German measles:
Saxon Mills............................. 2
Spartanburg............................. 8
Measles:
Spartanburg............................. 10
Mumps:
Spartanburg............................. 11

CAMP WADSWORTH ZONE, S. C.—continued.		CAMP WHEELER ZONE, GA.—continued.	
Tuberculosis:		Measles:	
Greer..........................	1	East Macon..........................	6
Whooping cough:		Macon..........................	10
Spartanburg..........................	7	Mumps:	
		East Macon..........................	1
CAMP WHEELER ZONE, GA.		Macon..........................	24
Cerebrospinal meningitis:		Pneumonia:	
East Macon..........................		East Macon..........................	1
Macon..........................	4	Macon..........................	1
Chicken pox:		Scarlet fever:	
Macon..........................	1	East Macon..........................	1
Diphtheria:		Tuberculosis:	
Macon..........................	1	Macon..........................	1
German measles:			
Macon..........................	1		

CURRENT STATE SUMMARIES.

Alabama.

From Collaborating Epidemiologist Perry, telegram dated February 20, 1918:

Smallpox: Chambers County 6 cases, Cullman 4, Elmore about 40, Jefferson 40 to 50, Monroe 6. Cerebrospinal meningitis: Escambia 2 cases.

California.

From the State Board of Health of California, telegram dated February 19, 1918:

Smallpox prevalence increased, 21 cases last week: sources of infection chiefly in Mexico and Nevada. Measles still widely epidemic in San Diego and other parts of southern California. Seven cases epidemic cerebrospinal meningitis, all of which are in northern California, with one exception. Diphtheria more prevalent, especially in San Francisco and Los Angeles cities.

Reported by mail for preceding week (ended Feb. 9):

Cerebrospinal meningitis..........................	4
Chicken pox..........................	192
Diphtheria..........................	50
Dysentery..........................	1
Erysipelas..........................	15
German measles..........................	273
Gonococcus infection..........................	39
Measles..........................	1,065
Mumps..........................	138
Pneumonia..........................	58
Ophthalmia neonatorum..........................	2
Scarlet fever..........................	79
Smallpox..........................	7
Syphilis..........................	58
Trachoma..........................	1
Tuberculosis..........................	160
Typhoid fever..........................	12
Whooping cough..........................	75

Georgia.

From the State Board of Health of Georgia, telegram dated February 19, 1918:

Smallpox and measles epidemic; meningitis not epidemic, but scattered over State.

Indiana.

From the State board of health of Indiana, telegram dated February 18, 1918:

Scarlet fever: Epidemic Bloomington, Randolph County. Diphtheria: Bargersville, 1 death each Gary, Middleton, Milford, 2 deaths Elkhart. Measles: Rockport, Centerton, Greensburg, Fayette, Culver, Troy, and Danville. Smallpox: One death Indianapolis, 500 cases Bicknell, epidemic Warren, Newland, Grand View, Rockport. Whooping cough: Two deaths Hartford City, 1 death Shoals. Rabies: Epidemic in dogs Boone Township, Harrison County. Trichinosis: Eight cases 1 death Huntington.

Kansas.

From Collaborating Epidemiologist Crumbine, telegram dated February 18, 1918:

Meningitis: Reported in cities, Chanute 1, Council Grove 1, Dearing 2, Eldorado 1, Emmett 2, Greensburg 1, Hiawatha 1, Manhattan 1, Mankato 1, St. Paul 1, Topeka 1, Wichita 1. Smallpox: Kansas City 54.

Louisiana.

From Collaborating Epidemiologist Dowling, telegram dated February 18, 1918:

Meningitis (excluding Rapides): Allen 1, Caddo 1, De Soto 1, Lafayette 1, Orleans 5, Ouachita 1, Washington 1.

Massachusetts.

From Collaborating Epidemiologist Kelley, telegram dated February 18, 1918:

Unusual prevalence. Measles: Ashland 17, Beverly 22, Marlboro 119, Winchester 15, Hopkinton 42, Quincy 93, Wellesley 34. Scarlet fever: Holden 8. Smallpox: Marlboro 1.

Minnesota.

From Collaborating Epidemiologist Bracken, telegram dated February 18, 1918:

Smallpox: Aitkin County, Williams Township, Beltrami County, Sipple Township, Fillmore County, Norway Township, Grant County, Land Township, Pine County, Hinckley village, 1 each. Four cerebrospinal meningitis reports since February 11.

Mississippi.

From Collaborating Epidemiologist Leathers, telegram dated February 18, 1918:

Three cases epidemic cerebrospinal meningitis reported Coahoma County.

Nebraska.

From the State Board of Health of Nebraska, telegram dated February 18, 1918:

Smallpox: Dundy County, Trenton, Wausa, Valentine, Wayne, Sidney, Scotts Bluff County, Omaha, Lincoln. Scarlet fever: Thayer County, Pleasant Dale, Utica.

Ohio.

From Collaborating Epidemiologist Freeman, telegram dated February 18, 1918:

Salem, scarlet fever, 39 cases. Wakeman Township, Huron County, scarlet fever, 6 cases.

South Carolina.

From Collaborating Epidemiologist Hayne, telegram dated February 18, 1918:

Epidemic meningitis: Twenty-nine cases, 14 foci, in State week ended 17th.

Virginia.

From Collaborating Epidemiologist Traynham, telegram dated February 18, 1918:

Five cases smallpox Pittsylvania County, 1 Gloucester, 5 Washington, 4 Middlesex. One case cerebrospinal meningitis Sussex County, 2 Newport News.

Washington.

From Collaborating Epidemiologist Tuttle, telegram dated February 18, 1918:

Seventeen new cases diphtheria North Yakima. Cases mild and situation not alarming. No other outbreaks.

RECIPROCAL NOTIFICATION.

Massachusetts.

Cases of communicable diseases referred during January, 1918, to other State health departments by department of health of the State of Massachusetts.

Disease and locality of notification.	Referred to health authority of—	Why referred.
Smallpox: Natick........	State board of health, Columbus, Ohio.	Patient came from Elyria, Ohio, Jan. 9. Onset of disease Jan. 12.
Tuberculosis: Westfield.....	State department of health, Harrisburg, Pa.	Patient came to Westfield 3 weeks previous from Pennsylvania, where he had been a dispensary patient at Mount Alton State Sanatorium for 2 years.
Camp Devens.	State department of health, Hartford, Conn.	Discharged. Home addresses were: Bridgeport, 5; Waterbury, 4; Hartford, 1; Branford, 1; New Haven, 1; New London, 1; Guilford, 1; Milford, 1.
	State department of health, Albany, N. Y.	Discharged. Home addresses were: Brooklyn, 1; Plattsburg, 1; Hoosick Falls, 2; Herkimer, 1; Albany, 1.
	State board of health, Providence, R. I.	Discharged. Home addresses were: Providence, 2; Thornton, 1; Newport, 1; Centerdale, 1; Bradford, 1.
	State department of health, Augusta, Me.	Discharged. Home address was Ellsworth, Me.
	State board of health, Columbus, Ohio.	Discharged. Home addresses were: Columbus, 2.
	State board of health, Sacramento, Cal.	Discharged. Home address was Fort McDowd, Cal.
	State board of health, Trenton, N. J...	Discharged. Home address was Fort Hancock, N. J.
	State department of health, Springfield, Ill.	Discharged. Home address was Chicago, Ill.
	State board of health, Jefferson City, Mo.	Discharged. Home address was Jefferson Barracks, Mo.
	State board of health, Austin, Tex....	Discharged. Home address was Waco, Tex.
	State board of health, Richmond, Va..	Discharged. Home address was Portsmouth, Va.
	State department of health, Charleston, W. Va.	Discharged. Home address was Parkersburg, W. Va.
	State board of health, Burlington, Vt..	Discharged. Home addresses were: Fort Ethan Allen, 1; Shoreham, 1; Poernal Center, 1; Newport, 1; South Royalton, 1.

CEREBROSPINAL MENINGITIS.

State Reports for December, 1917, and January, 1918.

Place.	New cases reported.	Place.	New cases reported.
Kansas (Jan. 1-31):		Massachusetts—Continued.	
Barton County—		Hampden County—	
Great Bend	1	Chicopee	1
Cloud County—		Ludlow Town	1
Concordia	1	Middlesex County—	
Cowley County—		Camp Devens	1
Arkansas City	1	Lawrence	1
Crawford County—		Lowell	1
Cherokee	1	Marlboro	1
Dickinson County—		Medford	2
Enterprise	1	Norfolk County—	
Ellsworth County—		Wellesley Town	1
Frederick (R. D.)	1	Suffolk County—	
Jefferson County—		Boston	3
McLouth	2	Revere	1
Johnson County—		Worcester County—	
De Soto (R. D.)	1	Fitchburg	1
Marshall County—		Worcester	4
Marysville	1		
Mina (R. D.)	2	Total	21
Montgomery County—			
Coffeyville	2	Virginia (Dec. 1-31):	
Riley County—		Augusta County—	
Manhattan	1	Waynesboro	1
Sedgwick County—		Bedford County	1
Wichita	1	Charlotte County	1
Wilson County—		Essex County	1
Buffalo	1	Halifax County	1
Wyandotte County—		Lee County	2
Kansas City	1	Pittsylvania County	2
		Prince George County	10
Total	18	Hopewell	1
		Pulaski County	2
Maryland (Jan. 1-31):		Roanoke County—	
Baltimore City	13	Salem	1
Anne Arundel County	4	Spottsylvania County—	
Montgomery County—		Fredericksburg	1
Woodside	1	Washington County	1
Total	18	Total	25
Massachusetts (Jan. 1-31):		West Virginia (Jan. 1-31):	
Berkshire County—		Mingo County—	
Pittsfield	1	Williamson	1
Bristol County—		Summers County—	
New Bedford	1	Hinton	1
Essex County—			
Swampscott Town	1	Total	2

City Reports for Week Ended Feb. 2, 1918.

Place.	Cases.	Deaths.	Place.	Cases.	Deaths.
Atlanta, Ga	6	1	Medford, Mass	2	
Baltimore, Md	5	2	Milwaukee, Wis	1	1
Birmingham, Ala	1		Minneapolis, Minn		1
Boston, Mass		2	Montgomery, Ala		1
Bridgeport, Conn		1	Nashville, Tenn	1	2
Buffalo, N. Y	1		Newark, N. J	1	
Charlotte, N. C	5		New Haven, Conn	2	
Chattanooga, Tenn	1		New Orleans, La	2	1
Chicago, Ill	3		Newport News, Va	1	1
Chillicothe, Ohio	1		New York, N. Y	7	4
Cincinnati, Ohio	1		Norfolk, Va	5	5
Cleveland, Ohio	2		Passaic, N. J	1	1
Columbia, S. C	5		Philadelphia, Pa	11	4
Detroit, Mich	1		Pittsburgh, Pa	1	
Durham, N. C	1		Pittsfield, Mass	1	
Elizabeth, N. J	2		Providence, R. I		1
Evansville, Ind	1	1	San Antonio, Tex	1	
Harrisburg, Pa	1		Sandusky, Ohio	1	
Hartford, Conn	4		San Francisco, Cal	2	1
Indianapolis, Ind		1	Savannah, Ga	1	
Jacksonville, Fla	4	3	Schenectady, N. Y	1	
La Fayette, Ind		1	Seattle, Wash	3	3
Lansing, Mich			Spartanburg, S. C	1	1
Little Rock, Ark	2		Washington, D. C	1	1
Macon, Ga	1	2			

DIPHTHERIA.

See Diphtheria, measles, scarlet fever, and tuberculosis, page 257.

ERYSIPELAS.

City Reports for Week Ended Feb. 2, 1918.

Place.	Cases.	Deaths.	Place.	Cases.	Deaths.
Atlanta, Ga		3	McKeesport, Pa	1	
Baltimore, Md	3		Memphis, Tenn	2	
Bridgeport, Conn		1	Milwaukee, Wis	1	
Charlotte, N. C		1	Nashville, Tenn	1	
Chicago, Ill	20	2	Newark, N. J	7	
Cincinnati, Ohio	1		New York, N. Y		10
Cleveland, Ohio	5	1	Niagara Falls, N. Y	3	
Columbus, Ohio		2	Omaha, Nebr	1	
Detroit, Mich	2		Philadelphia, Pa	7	3
Duluth, Minn	3		Pittsburgh, Pa	7	1
Easton, Pa	1		Pontiac, Mich	2	
Everett, Mass	1		Portland, Oreg	1	
Galesburg, Ill		2	Quincy, Mass	1	
Hammond, Ind		1	Rochester, N. Y	5	
Jackson, Mich	3		Sacramento, Cal	2	
Kalamazoo, Mich		2	St Louis, Mo	5	
Lansing, Mich	1		Salt Lake City, Utah		1
Lexington, Ky		1	San Diego, Cal		1
Long Beach, Cal	1	1	San Francisco, Cal	9	1
Los Angeles, Cal	4		Trenton, N. J		1
Louisville, Ky	1	1	Williamsport, Pa	1	1

LEPROSY.

City Reports for Week Ended Feb. 2, 1918.

Place.	Cases.	Deaths.	Place.	Cases.	Deaths.
Galveston, Tex	3		New Orleans, La	1	
Jersey City, N. J	1	1	San Francisco, Cal	1	

MALARIA.

State Reports for December, 1917, and January, 1918.

Place	New cases reported.	Place.	New cases reported.
Maryland (Jan 1-31):		Virginia (Dec. 1-31) Continued.	
Baltimore City	1	Isle of Wight County	8
Charles County—		Smithfield	1
Pomfret (R D)	2	James City County	2
		King and Queen County	1
Total	3	Lancaster County	1
		Lee County	1
Virginia (Dec. 1-31):		Lunenberg County	1
Accomac County	8	Mecklenburg County	4
Greenbackville	5	Middlesex County	2
Appomattox County	1	Nansemond County—	
Brunswick County	2	Suffolk	20
Buckingham County	1	Northampton County	12
Caroline County	2	Nottoway County	1
Charlotte County—		Crewe	1
Charlotte Courthouse	1	Pittsylvania County	1
Chesterfield County	1	Powhatan County	9
Cumberland County	1	Princess Anne County	11
Essex County	1	Prince Edward County	4
Fluvanna County	1	Prince George County	2
Gloucester County	1	Hopewell	4
Goochland County	1	Rockingham County—	
Greensville County	5	Dayton	1
Emporia	4	Southampton County	2
North Emporia	4	Stafford County	2
Halifax County	8	Surry County	2
Houston	2	Sussex County	13
South Boston	2	Warren County	1
Hanover County	7		
Henrico County	8	Total	183

MALARIA—Continued.

City Reports for Week Ended Feb. 2, 1918.

During the week ended February 2, 1918, one case of malaria was
reported in New Orleans, La., and one death was reported in New
York, N. Y.

MEASLES.

See Diphtheria, measles, scarlet fever, and tuberculosis, page 257.

PELLAGRA.

State Reports for December, 1917, and January, 1918.

Place.	New cases reported.	Place.	New cases reported.
Virginia (Dec. 1-31):		Virginia (Dec. 1-31)—Continued.	
Augusta County	1	Henry County	1
Chesterfield County—		Lee County	1
Winterpock	1	New Kent County	1
Elizabeth City County	1	Prince Edward County	1
Fluvanna County	1		
Greensville County—		Total	11
North Emporia	1		
Halifax County—		West Virginia (Jan. 1-31):	
South Boston	1	Lewis County—	
Hanover County	1	Weston State Hospital	3

City Reports for Week Ended Feb. 2, 1918.

Place.	Cases.	Deaths.	Place.	Cases.	Deaths.
Atlanta, Ga.		1	Memphis, Tenn	1	3
Birmingham, Ala	2	1	Portland, Mo		1
Charleston, S. C.		3	Rocky Mount, N. C.		1
Charlotte, N. C.		1	Wilmington, N. C.		1
Columbus, Ga.	1				

PNEUMONIA.

City Reports for Week Ended Feb. 2, 1918.

Place.	Cases.	Deaths.	Place.	Cases.	Deaths.
Alexandria, La.	3	2	Evansville, Ind	1	1
Altoona, Pa.	4		Everett, Mass	4	
Anniston, Ala	3		Fall River, Mass	13	2
Baltimore, Md	121	59	Flint, Mich	3	2
Battle Creek, Mich	2		Fort Worth, Tex	10	10
Berkeley, Cal	2		Grand Rapids, Mich	4	1
Boston, Mass	47	23	Harrisburg, Pa	1	3
Braddock, Pa	6		Hattiesburg, Miss	5	
Bridgeport, Conn	1	3	Holyoke, Mass	3	
Brockton, Mass	3	1	Houston, Tex	8	10
Cambridge, Mass	11	3	Jacksonville, Fla	2	9
Chattanooga, Tenn	4	2	Johnstown, Pa	1	6
Chelsea, Mass	8	3	Kalamazoo, Mich	1	
Chicago, Ill	136	71	Kansas City, Kans	1	
Cincinnati, Ohio	1	13	Kokomo, Ind	1	
Cleveland, Ohio	32	36	Lancaster, Pa	1	
Clinton, Mass	1	1	Lansing, Mich	3	
Coffeyville, Kans	2		Lawrence, Mass	1	
Cumberland, Md	1		Lexington, Ky	1	4
Detroit, Mich	13	28	Lincoln, Nebr	1	
Duluth, Minn	2		Little Rock, Ark	4	3
Durham, N. C.	3		Long Beach, Cal	3	1
Easton, Pa	1	1	Los Angeles, Cal	20	11

PNEUMONIA—Continued.

City Reports for Week Ended Feb. 2, 1918—Continued.

Place.	Cases.	Deaths.	Place.	Cases.	Deaths.
Louisville, Ky	2	16	Quincy, Mass	4	2
Lowell, Mass	3	2	Rochester, N. Y	11	3
Lynn, Mass	4	1	Sacramento, Cal	1	3
Macon, Ga	2	4	St. Joseph, Mo	10	2
Manchester, N. H	2	2	Salem, Mass	1	
Melrose, Mass	1	1	San Antonio, Tex	15	15
Montgomery, Ala	2	6	San Diego, Cal	2	9
Morristown, N. J	2	1	San Francisco, Cal	18	19
Muncie, Ind	5	5	Somerville, Mass	1	
New Albany, Ind	1	1	Spartanburg, S. C	5	
Newark, N. J	65	14	Springfield, Mass	8	3
Newport, Ky	8	8	Springfield, Ohio	2	2
Newport News, Va	2	2	Toledo, Ohio	1	3
Newton, Mass	2	1	Waco, Tex	4	
Norwalk, Conn	1	2	Waltham, Mass	2	
Philadelphia, Pa	181	97	Washington, Pa	1	
Pittsburgh, Pa	46	56	Wichita, Kans	4	1
Pittsfield, Mass	1		Worcester, Mass	2	2
Pontiac, Mich	2	3			

POLIOMYELITIS (INFANTILE PARALYSIS).

State Reports for December, 1917, and January, 1918.

Place.	New cases reported.	Place.	New cases reported.
Kansas (Jan. 1-31):		Oregon (Dec. 1-31):	
Harper County—		Multnomah County—	
Anthony	1	Portland	1
		Tillamook County	1
Total	1		
		Total	2
Massachusetts (Jan. 1-31):			
Bristol County—		West Virginia (Jan. 1-31):	
Taunton	1	Fayette County	1
Middlesex County—		Morgan County	1
Lowell	4		
		Total	2
Total	5		

City Reports for Week Ended Feb. 2, 1918.

Place.	Cases.	Deaths.	Place.	Cases.	Deaths.
Chicago, Ill	1		New Haven, Conn	1	
Columbus, Ohio	1		New York, N. Y	1	
Lansing, Mich	1		Oklahoma City, Okla	1	1
Milwaukee, Wis	2		Troy, N. Y	1	

RABIES IN ANIMALS.

City Report for Week Ended Feb. 2, 1918.

During the week ended February 2, 1918, one case of rabies in animals was reported in Newark, N. J.

SCARLET FEVER.

See Diphtheria, measles, scarlet fever, and tuberculosis, page 257.

SMALLPOX.

Missouri—Kansas City.

Reports of the notification of new cases of smallpox at Kansas City, Mo., have been received as follows: February 10, 23 cases; February 13 and 14, 39 cases; February 16 to 19, 81 cases.   No reports were received for February 11, 12, and 15.

Texas—Eagle Pass.

During the week ended February 18, 1918, 15 new cases of smallpox were notified at Eagle Pass, Tex., making a total of 53 cases reported since January 1, 1918.

State Reports for January, 1918.

Place.	New cases reported.	Deaths.	Vaccination history of cases.			
			Number vaccinated within 7 years preceding attack.	Number last vaccinated more than 7 years preceding attack.	Number never successfully vaccinated.	Vaccination history not obtained or uncertain.
Kansas:						
Allen County—						
Geneva..............	1	......	....	....	1	....
Humboldt............	7	......	....	....	7	....
Iola................	2	......	....	....	2	....
Anderson County—						
Bush City (R. D.).....	1	......	....	....	1	....
Lone Elm............	1	......	....	....	1	....
Scipio..............	1	......	....	....	1	....
Westphalia..........	1	......	....	....	1	....
Atchison County—						
Atchison............	3	......	....	2	1	....
Parnell.............	1	......	....	....	1	....
Barber County—						
Hardtner............	3	......	....	....	3	....
Bourbon County—						
Fort Scott (R. D.).....	7	......	....	1	6	....
Fulton..............	5	......	....	1	4	....
Brown County—						
Hiawatha............	1	......	....	....	1	....
Horton..............	4	......	....	....	4	....
Butler County—						
Augusta.............	3	......	....	....	3	....
Douglas.............	2	......	....	1	1	....
El Dorado (R. D.).....	12	......	....	....	12	....
Rose Hill...........	2	......	....	....	2	....
Chase County—						
Strong City.........	1	......	....	....	1	....
Chautauqua County—						
Cedar Vale..........	2	......	....	....	2	....
Grenola (R. D.)......	2	......	....	....	2	....
Sedan...............	1	......	....	....	1	....
Cherokee County—						
Baxter Springs (R. D.).	11	......	....	....	11	....
Columbus............	2	......	....	....	2	....
Galena (R. D.).......	31	......	....	2	29	....
Scammon.............	2	......	....	....	2	....
Treece..............	1	......	....	....	1	....
Weir................	1	......	....	....	1	....
Cheyenne County—						
Bird City...........	2	......	....	1	1	....
Clay County—						
Broughton (R. D.)....	1	......	....	1	....	....
Clay Center (R. D.)...	2	......	....	....	2	....
Morganville (R. D.)...	1	......	....	....	1	....
Cloud County—						
Clyde...............	1	......	....	....	1	....
Glasco (R. D.).......	3	......	....	1	2	....
Miltonvale (R. D.)....	2	......	....	....	2	....

SMALLPOX—Continued.

State Reports for January, 1918—Continued.

Place.	New cases reported.	Deaths.	Number vaccinated within 7 years preceding attack.	Number last vaccinated more than 7 years preceding attack.	Number never successfully vaccinated.	Vaccination history not obtained or uncertain.
Kansas—Continued.						
Coffey County—						
Burlington (R. D.)	2				2	
Le Roy	1				1	
Cowley County—						
Arkansas City	29			2	26	
Burden	1				1	
Winfield (R. D.)	3				3	
Crawford County—						
Arma	8				8	
Chicopee	1				1	
Girard (R. D.)	51			2	44	5
Mulberry County	6				6	
Pittsburg (R. D.)	35			1	34	
Ringo	8				8	
Dickinson County—						
Abilene	1				1	
Herington	1				1	
Hope (R. D.)	1				1	
Solomon	2				2	
Doniphan County—						
Elwood	2				2	
Wathena (R. D.)	8				8	
Douglas County—						
Baldwin (R. D.)	3				3	
Lawrence (R. D.)	7			1	6	
Lecompton (R. D.)	1				1	
Edwards County—						
Kinsley (R. D.)	1				1	
Ellis County—						
Ellis	1				1	
Finney County—						
Garden City (R. D.)	1				1	
Ford County—						
Dodge City	1				1	
Franklin County—						
Ottawa	20				20	
Geary County—						
Junction City	4				4	
Gove County—						
Quinter	1				1	
Gray County—						
Cimarron (R. D.)	1				1	
Ingalls (R. D.)	1				1	
Greenwood County—						
Madison (R. D.)	2				2	
Piedmont	1				1	
Harper County—						
Anthony (R. D.)	1			1		
Jackson County—						
Delia (R. D.)	1				1	
Hoyt (R. D.)	3				3	
Soldier (R. D.)	6				6	
Jewell County—						
Formoso (R. D.)	2				2	
Lovewell	1				1	
Mankato (R. D.)	3				3	
Randall (R. D.)	2				2	
Webber (R. D.)	2				2	
Johnson County—						
Gardner (R. D.)	4				4	
Holliday	1				1	
Merriam	5				5	
Overland Park	2				2	
Spring Hill (R. D.)	1			1		
Kingman County—						
Kingman	4			1	3	
Kiowa County—						
Haviland (R. D.)	4				4	

SMALLPOX—Continued.

State Reports for January, 1918—Continued.

Place.	New cases reported.	Deaths.	Vaccination history of cases.			
			Number vaccinated within 7 years preceding attack.	Number last vaccinated more than 7 years preceding attack.	Number never successfully vaccinated.	Vaccination history not obtained or uncertain.
Kansas—Continued.						
Labette County—						
Chetopa (R. D.)........	3	....	....	....	3	....
Mound Valley (R. D.).	2	....	....	....	2	....
Oswego................	9	....	....	....	9	....
Parsons...............	7	....	....	2	5	....
Leavenworth County—						
Leavenworth (R. D.)...	9	....	1	....	8	....
Richardson...........	8	....	....	....	8	....
Linn County—						
La Cygne (R. D.)......	3	....	....	....	3	....
Mound City (R. D.)....	2	....	....	....	2	....
Pleasanton...........	1	....	....	1	....	....
Lyon County—						
Emporia..............	8	....	....	....	8	....
Marion County—						
Hillsboro (R. D.)......	3	....	....	....	3	....
Lehigh (R. D.)........	20	....	....	....	19	1
Marion...............	1	....	....	....	1	....
Peabody (R. D.).......	2	....	....	....	2	....
Marshall County—						
Frankfort............	1	....	....	....	1	....
Irving...............	5	....	....	1	4	....
McPherson County—						
McPherson...........	1	....	....	....	1	....
Miami County—						
Hillsdale (R. D.)......	3	....	....	....	3	....
Osawatomie (R. D.)....	2	....	....	....	2	....
Paola................	2	....	....	....	2	....
Mitchell County—						
Beloit...............	3	....	....	....	3	....
Cawker City.........	2	....	....	....	2	....
Glen Elder (R. D.)....	4	....	....	....	4	....
Tipton (R. D.)........	3	....	....	....	3	....
Montgomery County—						
Caney................	6	....	....	....	6	....
Coffeyville..........	20	....	....	....	18	2
Independence (R. D.)..	10	....	....	....	9	1
Morris County—						
Council Grove........	1	....	....	....	1	....
Dwight...............	1	....	....	1	....	....
Nemaha County—						
Burns (R. D.).........	2	....	....	....	2	....
Soldier (R. D.	1	....	....	....	1	....
Neosho County—						
Chanute (R. D.).......	16	....	....	....	16	....
Thayer (R. D.)........	1	....	....	....	1	....
Osage County—						
Burlingame..........	1	....	....	....	1	....
Malvern (R. D.).......	2	....	....	1	1	....
Osage City...........	2	....	....	....	2	....
Overbrook (R. D.).....	3	....	....	....	3	....
Quenemo (R. D.)......	2	....	....	....	2	....
Richland (R. D.)......	2	....	....	....	2	....
Vassar...............	1	....	....	....	1	....
Osborne County—						
Covert (R. D.)........	1	....	....	....	1	....
Downs (R. D.)........	1	....	....	....	1	....
Osborne..............	8	....	....	....	8	....
Ottawa County—						
Delphos (R. D.).......	3	....	....	....	3	....
Miltonvale (R. D.).....	6	....	....	....	6	....
Niles................	2	....	....	....	2	....
Pawnee County—						
Larned (R. D.)........	1	....	....	....	1	....
Phillips County						
Phillipsburg (R. D.)..	5	....	....	....	5	....
Pottawatomie County—						
Manhattan (R. D.).....	1	....	....	....	1	....
Onaga................	1	....	....	....	1	....
Rawlins County—						
Atwood (R. D.)........	2	....	....	....	2	....
McDonald............	3	....	....	....	3	....

SMALLPOX -Continued.

State Reports for January, 1918 - Continued.

Place.	New cases reported.	Deaths.	Vaccination history of cases.			
			Number vaccinated within 7 years preceding attack.	Number last vaccinated more than 7 years preceding attack.	Number never successfully vaccinated.	Vaccination history not obtained or uncertain.
Kansas—Continued.						
Reno County—						
Hutchinson............	2				2	
Republic County—						
Courtland (R. D.)......	2				2	
Hollis.............	1				1	
Munden (R. D.)........	3				3	
Republic..........	1				1	
Talmo (R. D.)..........	1			1		
Rice County—						
Sterling............	1				1	
Riley County—						
Cleburne.............	2				2	
Keats..........	1				1	
Leonardville (R. D.)....	3				3	
Ogden............	1				1	
Riley.............	2				2	
Rooks County—						
Webster (R. D.).......	6				6	
Russell County—						
Bunker Hill............	2				2	
Saline County—						
Falun............	1				1	
Salina (R. D.)........	2				2	
Sedgwick County –						
Garden Plain..........	3				3	
Wichita (R. D.).......	33				33	
Seward County ·						
Liberal.............	1			1		
Plains (R. D.)........	13				13	
Shawnee County—						
Richland (R. D.)......	7			1	6	
Tecumseh (R. D.)......	1				1	
Topeka............	23			1	22	
Sheridan County ·						
Hoxie (R. D.)........	4				4	
Smith County—						
Smith Center (R. D.)...	6				6	
Stafford County ·						
St. John (R. D.).	1				1	
Sumner County ·						
Belle Plaine............	1				1	
Geuda Springs.........	1				1	
Mulvane............	1				1	
Wellington..........	6				6	
Trego County –						
Utica (R. D.)........	1				1	
Washington County ·						
Haddam (R. D.).......	1				1	
Wilson County—						
Benedict	1				1	
Neodesha............	1				1	
New Albany..........	5				5	
North Altoona..........	4				4	
Woodson County—						
Neosho Falls (R. D.)....	30				30	
Vernon (R. D.)........	9				9	
Wyandotte County—						
Bonner Springs........	1				1	
Kansas City............	228				228	
Rosedale.............	2				2	
Total.................	994		1	29	954	10
Maryland:						
Baltimore City............	7			1	6	
Allegany County—						
Cumberland............	6				6	
Lonaconing (R. D.).....	1				1	
Midland..............	1				1	
Baltimore County—						
Sparrows Point........	1				1	
Total................	16			1	15	

SMALLPOX—Continued.

State Reports for January, 1918—Continued.

Place.	New cases reported.	Deaths.	Vaccination history of cases.			
			Number vaccinated within 7 years preceding attack.	Number last vaccinated more than 7 years preceding attack.	Number never successfully vaccinated.	Vaccination history not obtained or uncertain.
Massachusetts:						
Middlesex County—						
Natick (town).........	1	....	....	....	1	....
Suffolk County—						
Boston...............	2	....	....	....	2	....
Total...............	3	....	....	....	3	....
West Virginia:						
Brooke County.............	1	....	....	....	1	....
Cabell County.............	1	....	....	....	1	....
Huntington............	28	....	....	....	28	....
Fayette County............	4	....	....	....	4	....
Sun................	35	....	....	....	35	....
Gilmer County.............	1	....	....	....	1	....
Greenbrier County.........	3	....	....	....	3	....
Hancock County............	2	....	....	....	2	....
Kanawha County............	20	....	....	....	20	....
Lewis County.............	5	....	....	....	5	....
Logan County.............	48	....	....	1	47	....
McDowell County..........	10	....	....	....	10	....
Marshall County..........	20	....	1	....	19	....
Marion County............	22	....	....	....	22	....
Mason County.............	1	....	....	....	1	....
Mercer County............	4	....	....	....	4	....
Monongalia County........	5	....	....	....	5	....
Morgan County............	1	....	....	....	1	....
Ohio County..............	47	....	....	....	47	....
Raleigh County...........	18	....	....	....	18	....
Roane County.............	22	....	....	....	22	....
Taylor County............	2	....	....	....	2	....
Tucker County............	1	....	....	....	1	....
Wetzel County............	1	....	....	....	1	....
Wood County..............	19	....	....	....	19	....
Total...............	321	....	1	1	319	....

Miscellaneous State Reports.

Place.	Cases.	Deaths.	Place.	Cases.	Deaths.
Oregon (Dec. 1–31):			Virginia (Dec. 1–31):		
Multnomah County—			Lee County.............	1	....
Portland..............	7	....	Prince Edward County...	3	....
			Roanoke County—		
Virginia (Dec. 1–31):			Roanoke.............	1	....
Alleghany County—			Scott County.............	12	....
Clifton Forge..........	11	....	Gate City............	1	....
Amelia County..........	4	....	Tazewell County..........	11	....
Botetourt County—			Richlands...........	1	....
Buchanan.............	1	....	Wise County	1	....
Charlotte County.........	1	....	Big Stone Gap........	3	....
Chesterfield County.......	4	....			
Essex County.............	3	....	Total...................	59	....
Gloucester County........	1	....			

SMALLPOX—Continued.

City Reports for Week Ended Feb. 2, 1918.

Place.	Cases.	Deaths.	Place.	Cases.	Deaths.
Akron, Ohio	33		Lincoln, Nebr	5	
Alexandria, La	2		Little Rock, Ark	52	
Alton, Ill	2		Lorain, Ohio	2	
Ann Arbor, Mich	2		Los Angeles, Cal	9	
Anniston, Ala	7		Madison, Wis	3	
Baltimore, Md	1		Memphis, Tenn	20	
Battle Creek, Mich	2		Milwaukee, Wis	4	
Berlin, N. H.	4		Minneapolis, Minn	31	
Birmingham, Ala	4		Mobile, Ala	2	
Buffalo, N. Y.	2		Montgomery, Ala	18	
Butte, Mont	8		Muskegon, Mich	11	
Cairo, Ill	2		Muskogee, Okla	19	
Canton, Ohio	3		Nashville, Tenn	5	
Chicago, Ill	21		New Orleans, La	9	
Cincinnati, Ohio	6		Oak Park, Ill	1	
Cleveland, Ohio	48		Oklahoma City, Okla	12	
Coffeyville, Kans	15		Omaha, Nebr	28	
Columbus, Ga	3		Orange, N. J.	1	
Columbus, Ohio	12		Philadelphia, Pa	2	
Cumberland, Md	1		Pittsburgh, Pa	2	
Davenport, Iowa	1		Pontiac, Mich	5	
Dayton, Ohio	3		Portland, Oreg	1	
Des Moines, Iowa	32		Portsmouth, Va	1	
	53		Quincy, Ill	11	
	14		Rock Island, Ill	1	
	6		Sacramento, Cal	1	
	8		Saginaw, Mich	1	
	3		St. Joseph, Mo	7	
	21		St. Louis, Mo	11	
	27		Salt Lake City, Utah	20	
	27		Seattle, Wash	5	
	2		Sioux City, Iowa	20	
	6		South Bend, Ind	1	
	72		Springfield, Ill	4	
	2		Springfield, Ohio	3	
	3		Steelton, Pa	2	
	2		Superior, Wis	1	
	1		Tacoma, Wash	2	
Kansas City, Kans	33		Terre Haute, Ind	5	
Knoxville, Tenn	1		Toledo, Ohio	10	
La Crosse, Wis	5		Washington, D. C.	6	
Lansing, Mich	3		Wichita, Kans	4	
Leavenworth, Kans	3		Zanesville, Ohio	1	
Lima, Ohio	7				

TETANUS.

City Reports for Week Ended Feb. 2, 1918.

Place.	Cases.	Deaths.	Place.	Cases.	Deaths
Birmingham, Ala	1	1	Los Angeles, Cal	1	
Charleston, S. C.		1	Newark, N. J.	1	1
Lexington, Ky		1	San Diego, Cal		1

TUBERCULOSIS.

See Diphtheria, measles, scarlet fever, and tuberculosis, page 257.

TYPHOID FEVER.

State Reports for December, 1917, and January, 1918.

Place.	New cases reported.	Place.	New cases reported.
Kansas (Jan. 1-31):		**Maryland (Jan. 1-31)—Continued.**	
Atchison County—		Washington County—	
Atchison	1	Trego (R. D.)	1
Potter	1	Smithsburg (R. D.)	1
Bourbon County—		Yarrowsburg (R. D.)	1
Fort Scott	1	Wicomico County—	
Butler County—		Salisbury	,
Augusta	2	Worcester County—	
El Dorado (R. D.)	2	Snow Hill	1
Towanda	1		
Cherokee County—		Total	38
Baxter Springs (R. D.)	1		
Galena	2	**Massachusetts (Jan. 1-31):**	
Hallowell (R. D.)	1	Berkshire County—	
Cowley County—		Adams (Town)	1
Winfield (R. D.)	4	Pittsfield	2
Franklin County—		Bristol County—	
Ottawa	1	Fall River	6
Leavenworth County—		Mansfield (Town)	1
Leavenworth	3	New Bedford	4
Lincoln County—		Dukes County—	
Barnard (R. D.)	1	Oak Bluffs (Town)	,
Linn County—		Essex County—	
Mound City (R. D.)	1	Andover (Town)	1
Montgomery County—		Gloucester	2
Coffeyville	5	Haverhill	3
Independence	1	Ipswich (Town)	2
Pawnee County—		Lawrence	3
Larned (R. D)	1	Lynn	3
Reno County—		Methuen	1
Hutchinson	1	Hampden County—	
Riley County—		Chicopee	,
Manhattan	2	Springfield	,
Sherman County—		Hampshire County—	
Goodland	1	Northampton	,
Sumner County—		Middlesex County—	
Wellington	1	Ayer (Town)	1
Wyandotte County—		Concord (Town)	1
Kansas City	1	Everett	2
		Lowell	2
Total	35	Malden	1
		Woburn	1
Maryland (Jan. 1-31):		Norfolk County—	
Baltimore City	11	Quincy	,
Allegany County—		Plymouth County—	
Cumberland	2	Brockton	,
Anne Arundel County—		Hanover (Town)	,
Friendship	1	Suffolk County—	
Davidsonville	1	Boston	,
Baltimore County—		Worcester County—	
Lansdowne	1	Leominster	1
Highlandtown	1	North Brookfield (Town)	5
Caroline County—		Worcester	2
Denton	1		
Dorchester County—		Total	57
Crocheron	1		
Cambridge	1	**Oregon (Dec. 1-31):**	
Bishops Head	1	Klamath County	1
Frederick County—		Linn County	7
Ellerton (R. D.)	1	Multnomah County—	
Frederick	1	Portland	,
Montgomery County—		Union County	1
Dickerson	1		
Prince Georges County—		Total	13
Berwyn (R. D.)	1		
Scotchtown	1	**Virginia (Dec. 1-31):**	
Mitchellville	1	Accomac County	1
Queen Annes County—		Alexandria County	1
Bridgetown (R. D.)	1	Clarendon	1
Love Point	1	Alleghany County—	
Talbot County—		Clifton Forge	2
Tilghman	1	Covington	1

TYPHOID FEVER—Continued.

State Reports for December, 1917, and January, 1918—Continued.

Place.	New cases reported.	Place.	New cases reported.
Virginia (Dec. 1-31)—Continued.		Virginia (Dec. 1-31)—Continued.	
Appomattox County	4	Rockingham County—	
Augusta County	1	Harrisonburg	1
Staunton	4	Russell County	1
Waynesboro	1	Scott County	4
Bedford County	2	Gate City	1
Botetourt County	1	Shenandoah County	1
Buchanan County	6	New Market	1
Buckingham County	1	Smyth County	1
Campbell County	1	Southampton County	1
Caroline County	2	Spottsylvania County—	
Carroll County	3	Fredericksburg	1
Charlotte County	1	Sussex County	2
Clarke County	1	Tazewell County	4
Culpeper County	6	Graham	3
Culpeper	5	Pocahontas	1
Dickenson County	2	Tazewell	1
Dinwiddie County	2	Wise County—	
Fairfax County	1	Wise	1
Fauquier County	1	Wythe County	1
Frederick County—			
Winchester	2	Total	108
Gloucester County	1		
Grayson County—		West Virginia (Jan. 1-31):	
Galax	2	Barbour County	1
Greene County	2	Fayette County	4
Henry County	1	Greenbrier County	2
Isle of Wight County	1	Kanawha County	6
James City County—		Lewis County	1
Williamsburg	1	Lincoln County	3
Lee County	6	McDowell County	4
Loudoun County	1	Marion County	1
Lunenburg County		Mercer County	1
Middlesex County—		Monongalia County	6
Urbanna	1	Morgan County	11
Nansemond County	1	Pendleton County	6
Northumberland County	3	Raleigh County	1
Orange County	1	Ritchie County	1
Page County—		Summers County	4
Shenandoah	1	Tucker County	1
Patrick County	1	Webster County	1
Prince Edward County	3	Wetzel County	1
Roanoke County—		Wirt County	1
Roanoke	1	Wood County	1
Salem	1		
Rockbridge County—		Total	59
Buena Vista	1		

City Reports for Week Ended Feb. 2, 1918.

Place.	Cases.	Deaths.	Place.	Cases.	Deaths.
Atlanta, Ga	1		Newburgh, N. Y	4	
Baltimore, Md	3	1	New Orleans, La	3	1
Beaver Falls, Pa	2		Newport News, Va	1	
Birmingham, Ala	2	1	New York, N. Y	10	
Boston, Mass	2		Northampton, Mass	1	
Buffalo, N. Y		1	Philadelphia, Pa	4	2
Camden, N. J	1		Pittsburgh, Pa	3	2
Cleveland, Ohio	1		Plainfield, N. J	1	
Cumberland, Md	1		Pontiac, Mich	1	
Detroit, Mich	4	1	Quincy, Mass	1	
Duluth, Minn	2		Reading, Pa	1	
Elmira, N. Y	1		Roanoke, Va		1
Fall River, Mass	1		Rochester, N. Y		
Fort Worth, Tex	1		Saginaw, Mich	1	
Galveston, Tex	1		St. Louis, Mo	1	
Grand Rapids, Mich	3		San Diego, Cal	1	
Indianapolis, Ind	1		San Francisco, Cal	1	
Lansing, Mich	2		Savannah, Ga	1	
Lexington, Ky	1		Springfield, Ohio	2	1
Long Beach, Cal	1		Syracuse, N. Y	2	
Los Angeles, Cal	7		Toledo, Ohio	2	1
Louisville, Ky	1		Trenton, N. J	2	1
Milwaukee, Wis	2		Troy, N. Y	1	
Minneapolis, Minn	15		Washington, D. C	2	1
Mobile, Ala		1	Watertown, N. Y	1	
Moline, Ill	4	2	Wheeling, W. Va	2	1
Mount Vernon, N. Y	1		Wilkinsburg, Pa	1	
Newark, N. J	1		Zanesville, Ohio	2	

DIPHTHERIA, MEASLES, SCARLET FEVER, AND TUBERCULOSIS.

State Reports for December, 1917, and January, 1918.

State.	Cases reported.			State.	Cases reported.		
	Diphtheria.	Measles.	Scarlet fever.		Diphtheria.	Measles.	Scarlet fever.
Kansas (Jan. 1–31).	214	2,170	548	Oregon (Dec. 1–31).	14	41	39
Maryland (Jan. 1–31)	164	990	174	Virginia (Dec. 1–31)	195	1,086	101
Massachusetts (Jan. 1–31)	951	2,950	609	West Virginia (Jan. 1–31)	84	115	48

City Reports for Week Ended Feb. 2, 1918.

City.	Population as of July 1, 1916 (estimated by U. S. Census Bureau).	Total deaths from all causes.	Diphtheria.		Measles.		Scarlet fever.		Tuberculosis.	
			Cases.	Deaths.	Cases.	Deaths.	Cases.	Deaths.	Cases.	Deaths.
Over 300,000 inhabitants:										
Baltimore, Md.	589,621	288	18	2	111	1	17	....	34	20
Boston, Mass.	756,476	262	98	10	115	2	52	....	80	30
Chicago, Ill.	2,497,722	637	126	14	43	....	60	....	351	58
Cleveland, Ohio	674,073	171	43	3	16	....	0	....	32	21
Detroit, Mich.	571,784	201	68	9	28	....	50	3	24	15
Los Angeles, Cal.	503,812	....	17	....	143	....	12	....	39	24
New York, N. Y.	5,602,841	1,740	227	27	717	25	123	....	357	234
Philadelphia, Pa.	1,709,518	756	57	11	124	1	53	1	81	84
Pittsburgh, Pa.	579,090	223	12	2	173	2	4	....	36	10
St. Louis, Mo.	757,309	228	55	3	52	2	28	....	34	20
From 200,000 to 500,000 inhabitants:										
Buffalo, N. Y.	468,558	127	12	2	23	....	17	1	26	14
Cincinnati, Ohio	410,476	....	12	1	39	....	7	....	25	20
Jersey City, N. J.	396,345	91	22	1	48	....	16	....	6	10
Milwaukee, Wis.	436,535	....	12	....	80	....	34	3	16	5
Minneapolis, Minn.	363,454	....	11	3	22	....	18	1	....	3
Newark, N. J.	403,894	141	32	2	120	....	22	....	33	13
New Orleans, La.	371,747	208	11	....	128	1	....	....	34	30
San Francisco, Cal.	483,516	154	20	1	67	....	17	....	23	12
Seattle, Wash.	348,639	....	2	....	223	....	6	....	8	1
Washington, D. C.	363,980	166	9	....	196	....	95	1	22	15
From 200,000 to 300,000 inhabitants:										
Columbus, Ohio	214,878	64	4	....	12	....	10	....	9	5
Indianapolis, Ind.	271,708	90	34	1	80	....	45	1	9	10
Louisville, Ky.	238,910	90	10	....	60	1	4	....	19	12
Portland, Oreg.	295,463	41	....	....	24	....	5	....	7	4
Providence, R. I.	254,990	92	13	1	13	....	2	....	9	14
Rochester, N. Y.	256,417	71	4	1	13	....	6	1	16	5
From 100,000 to 200,000 inhabitants:										
Albany, N. Y.	104,199	....	4	....	9	....	1	....	9	....
Atlanta, Ga.	190,558	79	5	1	9	....	2	....	5	7
Birmingham, Ala.	181,762	78	5	2	89	4	1	....	5	4
Bridgeport, Conn.	121,579	38	7	1	3	1	2	....	3	3
Cambridge, Mass.	112,981	49	8	1	26	1	3	....	2	10
Camden, N. J.	106,233	....	8	....	48	....	1	....	2	....
Dayton, Ohio	127,224	47	....	....	8	....	5	....	8	2
Des Moines, Iowa	101,598	....	2	....	5	....	3	....	....	....
Fall River, Mass.	128,366	40	4	1	3	....	3	....	6	5
Fort Worth, Tex.	104,562	35	4	....	1	....	2	....	2	2
Grand Rapids, Mich.	128,291	44	3	1	7	....	3	....	4	2
Hartford, Conn.	110,900	61	3	....	1	....	7	....	5	7
Houston, Tex.	112,307	50	2	1	22	....	....	....	4	5
Lawrence, Mass.	100,560	34	3	1	17	....	....	....	5	3
Lowell, Mass.	113,245	20	7	1	....	....	3	....	4	2
Lynn, Mass.	102,425	38	2	....	11	....	12	....	5	1
Memphis, Tenn.	148,995	63	....	....	32	1	1	....	18	4
Nashville, Tenn.	117,057	55	....	....	66	....	2	....	6	7
New Bedford, Mass.	118,158	42	2	....	25	....	....	....	11	4
New Haven, Conn.	149,685	50	2	1	4	....	3	....	9	3
Oakland, Cal.	198,604	38	4	....	....	....	4	....	5	5

DIPHTHERIA, MEASLES, SCARLET FEVER, AND TUBERCULOSIS—Continued.

City Reports for Week Ended Feb. 2, 1918—Continued.

City.	Population as of July 1, 1916 (estimated by U. S. Census Bureau).	Total deaths from all causes.	Diphtheria.		Measles.		Scarlet fever.		Tuberculosis.	
			Cases.	Deaths.	Cases.	Deaths.	Cases.	Deaths.	Cases.	Deaths.
From 100,000 to 200,000 inhabitants—Continued.										
Omaha, Nebr.	165,470	38			68		10		1	5
Reading, Pa.	109,381	44	3	1	2		2			6
Richmond, Va.	156,687	50	5		54		7		4	7
Salt Lake City, Utah	117,399	27	6		85		12			1
San Antonio, Tex.	123,831	120	1		4				15	15
Scranton, Pa.	146,811	49	7		1		6		15	2
Springfield, Mass.	105,942	40	5	1	39		11		5	1
Syracuse, N. Y.	155,624	41	6	1	80	2	37		6	4
Tacoma, Wash.	112,770		10		3		9			
Toledo, Ohio	191,554	61	5	1	9		7	1		2
Trenton, N. J.	111,593	63	7	1	7		1		7	2
Worcester, Mass.	163,314	53	4	2	8		7		2	4
From 50,000 to 100,000 inhabitants:										
Akron, Ohio	85,625		6		14		4		2	
Altoona, Pa.	58,659		3		1				1	
Atlantic City, N. J.	57,660	6			6		1			
Bayonne, N. J.	69,893		2		2				3	
Berkeley, Cal.	57,653		3		8		4		2	1
Binghamton, N. Y.	53,973	18	1		0		8	1	10	1
Brockton, Mass.	67,449	9	2		3		6		1	1
Canton, Ohio	60,852	12	5	1			4			
Charleston, S. C.	60,734	38	1		1	2				2
Chattanooga, Tenn.	60,075	5			8	1	3		3	2
Covington, Ky.	57,144	26	1	1						2
Duluth, Minn.	94,495	18	12	1	23		3		5	1
Elizabeth, N. J.	86,690	32	4		77		9		4	1
El Paso, Tex.	63,705				5					8
Evansville, Ind.	76,078				2		1		3	3
Flint, Mich.	54,772	23	4				10		3	1
Fort Wayne, Ind.	76,183	21	3	1			1			
Harrisburg, Pa.	72,015	24	2		5		4		6	1
Hoboken, N. J.	77,214	27	1		9		5		5	7
Holyoke, Mass.	65,286		6		12		2		2	3
Jacksonville, Fla.	76,101		3	1	59				7	1
Johnstown, Pa.	68,529	30	2				9		1	1
Kansas City, Kans.	99,437		4		19		10			
Lancaster, Pa.	50,853				2		5		1	1
Little Rock, Ark.	57,343	9	1		28		1			1
Malden, Mass.	51,155	8	3		5		3		1	1
Manchester, N. H.	78,283	27			16		2		4	1
Mobile, Ala.	58,221	28			5					
New Britain, Conn.	53,794	18	3		3		1			1
Norfolk, Va.	89,612		2		25		5			2
Oklahoma City, Okla.	92,943	19			16					2
Passaic, N. J.	71,744	21	1		1		2		1	1
Portland, Me.	63,867	14	1		36		1			1
Rockford, Ill.	55,185	14	1	1	4		4			
Sacramento, Cal.	66,895	26	1		5		4		3	2
Saginaw, Mich.	55,642	21	1							
St. Joseph, Mo.	85,236	27	10		52		4		1	3
San Diego, Cal.	53,330	59	3		139		5		1	11
Savannah, Ga.	68,805	21	2		11		1		2	2
Schenectady, N. Y.	99,519	20	3		10		1		3	
Sioux City, Iowa	57,078						13			
Somerville, Mass.	87,039	24	8	2	21		6		2	2
South Bend, Ind.	68,946	20	1		3		1			1
Springfield, Ill.	61,120	19	4	2	2		1			1
Springfield, Ohio	54,550	26	2		1		1		1	1
Terre Haute, Ind.	66,083	26	4	1			1			2
Troy, N. Y.	77,916	36	1		6		5		2	2
Wichita, Kans.	70,722	23			106		5		1	1
Wilkes-Barre, Pa.	76,776	14	6		13		6			
Wilmington, Del.	94,265	33	2		9		2			2
From 25,000 to 50,000 inhabitants:										
Almeda, Cal.	27,732	4	3		7				2	
Austin, Tex.	34,814	22	1							3
Battle Creek, Mich.	29,480		8	1	11		2			
Brookline, Mass.	32,730	18			7		2		3	1
Butler, Pa.	27,632	10	1		19		1			

DIPHTHERIA, MEASLES, SCARLET FEVER, AND TUBERCULOSIS—Continued.

City Reports for Week Ended Feb. 2, 1918—Continued.

City.	Population as of July 1, 1916 (estimated by U. S. Census Bureau).	Total deaths from all causes.	Diphtheria.		Measles.		Scarlet fever.		Tuberculosis.	
			Cases.	Deaths.	Cases.	Deaths.	Cases.	Deaths.	Cases.	Deaths.
From 25,000 to 50,000 inhabitants—Continued.										
Butte, Mont.	43,425		4		3		7			
Cedar Rapids, Iowa	37,308						4			
Charlotte, N. C.	39,823				31		1		1	1
Chelsea, Mass.	46,192	14		1	5				2	1
Chicopee, Mass.	29,319	9	1		1				2	3
Columbia, S. C.	34,611	14			9					
Columbus, Ga.	25,950	8			1					
Cranston, R. I.	25,987	10	2				1			2
Cumberland, Md.	26,074	8			2		2		1	1
Danville, Ill.	32,261	7			1		2		2	
Davenport, Iowa	48,811						5			
Dubuque, Iowa	39,873		1		20					2
Durham, N. C.	25,061	3	2		4					
Easton, Pa.	30,530	15	4		9		1		1	
East Orange, N. J.	42,458	13	3		18		5		1	2
Elgin, Ill.	28,203	6			6				1	
Elmira, N. Y.	38,120		1	1	9		5		2	1
Evanston, Ill.	28,591	3								
Everett, Mass.	39,233	7	4		8		1		3	
Everett, Wash.	35,484	6			1		2		1	
Fitchburg, Mass.	41,781	9			8				3	
Fort Smith, Ark.	28,638				8					1
Galveston, Tex.	41,863	12	2		1				1	2
Green Bay, Wis.	29,353	6			1					1
Hammond, Ind.	26,171	24			2		2		2	
Jackson, Mich.	35,863	18	6	1	2		25	3	1	2
Jackson, Miss.	29,737	11	3		1					
Jamestown, N. Y.	36,540	7	2						1	1
Kalamazoo, Mich.	48,886	21	2	1	3		2		1	1
Kenosha, Wis.	31,576	5			1		6		1	
Kingston, N. Y.	26,771	13								
Knoxville, Tenn.	38,676		1	1	23		7		1	
La Crosse, Wis.	31,677	12	3							
Lansing, Mich.	40,498		5		22		10		3	
Lexington, Ky.	41,097	20			37		1		26	1
Lima, Ohio	38,384	13			2		3			2
Lincoln, Nebr.	46,515	15	3				6			
Long Beach, Cal.	27,587	14	2		20		2		1	
Lorain, Ohio	36,964		1				1		1	
Lynchburg, Va.	32,910	10								
Macon, Ga.	45,757	25	4		7		5			2
Madison, Wis.	30,699	7	1		21		1			
McKeesport, Pa.	47,521	19			7		1			
Medford, Mass.	26,234	4	3		6		1		2	
Moline, Ill.	27,451			1	3		2			1
Montclair, N. J.	26,318	5			71				1	1
Montgomery, Ala.	53,295	22		1	26		1		1	2
Mount Vernon, N. Y.	37,009	8	3	1	13		1			
Muskegon, Mich.	26,100	14								
Muskogee, Okla.	44,218		2		16		8			
Nashua, N. H.	27,327	14								
Newburgh, N. Y.	29,683	13	1		10		1			1
New Castle, Pa.	41,133				10		1			
Newport, Ky.	31,927	17								
Newport, R. I.	30,108	6								1
Newton, Mass.	43,715	2	2		14				4	
Niagara Falls, N. Y.	37,353	16			3		3		4	2
Norristown, Pa.	31,401	7	1		6					
Norwalk, Conn.	28,499									
Oak Park, Ill.	26,654	6	2		3		1			
Orange, N. J.	33,089	10	1		5				1	
Pasadena, Cal.	46,450	8			21		2			3
Perth Amboy, N. J.	41,185	7	1	1	9		1		2	3
Pittsfield, Mass.	38,029	14			3				2	1
Portsmouth, Va.	39,651	21			8		3			2
Quincy, Ill.	36,798	12	7		7		2		2	2
Quincy, Mass.	38,136	12	1		6		1		2	
Racine, Wis.	46,485	11			2		4			4
Roanoke, Va.	43,284	16	1		5		2		6	

DIPHTHERIA, MEASLES, SCARLET FEVER, AND TUBERCULOSIS—
Continued.

City Reports for Week Ended Feb. 2, 1918—Continued.

City.	Population as of July 1, 1916 (estimated by U. S. Census Bureau).	Total deaths from all causes.	Diphtheria.		Measles.		Scarlet fever.		Tuberculosis.	
			Cases.	Deaths.	Cases.	Deaths.	Cases.	Deaths.	Cases.	Deaths.
From 25,000 to 50,000 inhabitants—Continued.										
Rock Island, Ill.	28,926	11	1		2					
Salem, Mass.	48,562	12			19		1		4	
San Jose, Cal.	38,902		1		7		3		2	
Steubenville, Ohio	27,445	10								
Stockton, Cal.	35,358	9			24				1	
Superior, Wis.	46,226	3			11		4			
Taunton, Mass.	36,283	9			1				4	2
Waco, Tex.	33,385				4				1	
Waltham, Mass.	30,570	15	1		5				1	1
Watertown, N. Y.	29,894	2			3				1	1
West Hoboken, N. J.	43,139	8	1		1		3			
Wheeling, W. Va.	43,377	14	1		2		1		2	
Williamsport, Pa.	33,809	14	3	2			2			1
Wilmington, N. C.	29,892	15			2					2
Winston-Salem, N. C.	31,155	32			37				1	1
Woonsocket, R. I.	44,360		2		10					
Zanesville, Ohio	30,863								2	
From 10,000 to 25,000 inhabitants:										
Alexandria, La.	17,846	9			4					
Ann Arbor, Mich.	15,010	7			6		2			1
Anniston, Ala.	14,112				5					
Berlin, N. H.	13,599	2								
Braddock, Pa.	21,685	5								1
Cairo, Ill.	15,794	10			1					
Chillicothe, Ohio	15,470	11	2	1	1		7	1		
Clinton, Mass.	[1]13,075	5					2		2	
Coffeyville, Kans.	17,548				10		2		1	
Concord, N. H.	22,669	16			2					
Galesburg, Ill.	24,276	4								
Greenville, S. C.	18,181	4			3					
Harrison, N. J.	16,950		1		1				2	
Hattiesburg, Miss.	16,482				8				1	
Kearny, N. J.	23,539	8			29		1		1	
Kokomo, Ind.	20,930	10			3		1			1
La Fayette, Ind.	21,286	11			3		1			3
Leavenworth, Kans.	[1]19,363				3		3			
Long Branch, N. J.	15,395	3								
Melrose, Mass.	17,445				2		4			
Morristown, N. J.	13,284	3			1					
Nanticoke, Pa.	23,126	6					1			
New Albany, Ind.	23,629	8	1		2				· 1	
Newburyport, Mass.	15,243	3			2					2
New London, Conn.	20,985	6							1	1
Newport News, Va.	20,562	16					1			
North Adams, Mass.	[1]22,019	5								
Northampton, Mass.	19,926	7			2				1	
Plainfield, N. J.	23,805	12			3		1		1	
Pontiac, Mich.	17,524	11	1		5		1		1	3
Portsmouth, N. H.	11,666						4			
Rocky Mount, N. C.	12,067	11			1		2			2
Rutland, Vt.	14,831	5					1			
Sandusky, Ohio	20,193	9					1			
Saratoga Springs, N. Y.	13,821	5								
Spartanburg, S. C.	21,365	10			1	1			1	1
Steelton, Pa.	15,548	2	1				2		1	
Washington, Pa.	21,618				22				1	
Wilkinsburg, Pa.	23,228	8			11					
Woburn, Mass.	15,969	10								5

[1] Population Apr. 15, 1910; no estimate made.

FOREIGN.

JAMAICA.

Hookworm Infection.

During the month of November, 1917, out of 548 creoles and coolies examined in the 19 public general hospitals of the island of Jamaica, 416 were found to be infected with hookworm.

According to the report of the superintendent medical officer of Jamaica for the year ended March 31, 1917, 2,209 creoles and coolies were examined during the year under report in the public general hospitals of the island of Jamaica. Of these, 1,177 were found to be infected with hookworm. The returns from the Government pathologist who examined 3,247 stools sent from hospitals show that 2,460 stools were infected with hookworm.

During the year, 5,910 cases of hookworm were treated at the various hospitals in Jamaica.

VENEZUELA.

Relapsing Fever—Caracas.

According to information dated January 15, 1918, the first case of relapsing fever recognized in Venezuela was verified at Caracas during the month of January, 1918.

CHOLERA, PLAGUE, SMALLPOX, TYPHUS FEVER, AND YELLOW FEVER.

Reports Received During Week Ended Feb. 22, 1918.[1]

CHOLERA.

Place.	Date.	Cases.	Deaths.	Remarks.
India:				
Madras....................	Nov. 25-Dec. 1....	1	1	
Rangoon...................	.....do.............	1	1	
Java:				
West Java...............				Dec. 14-20, 1917: Cases, 7; deaths, 8.
Batavia................	Dec. 14-20.........	4	6	
Philippine Islands:				
Provinces...............				Dec. 23-29, 1917: Cases, 61; deaths, 36.
Bohol....................	Dec. 23-29.........	22	14	
Capiz...................	.....do.............	15	11	
Cebu....................	.....do.............	3		
Iloilo..................	.....do.............	2	1	
Mindanao...............	.....do.............	14	7	
Oriental Negros........	.....do.............	5	3	

[1] From medical officers of the Public Health Service, American consuls, and other sources.

CHOLERA, PLAGUE, SMALLPOX, TYPHUS FEVER, AND YELLOW FEVER—Continued.

Reports Received During Week Ended Feb. 22, 1918- Continued.

PLAGUE.

Place.	Date.	Cases.	Deaths.	Remarks.
India.................				Nov. 25–Dec. 1, 1917: Cases, 19 807; deaths, 15,406.
Bombay..................	Nov. 25–Dec. 1....	10	6	
Karachi..................	do.	5	4	
Rangoon..................	Nov. 18 Dec. 1....	16	12	
Java				
West Java..............				Nov. 25 Dec. 9, 1917 Cases, 45 deaths, 43.
Straits Settlements:				
Singapore.	Dec. 16–22........	1	1	

SMALLPOX.

Place.	Date.	Cases.	Deaths.	Remarks.
Algeria:				
Algiers.............	Dec. 1 31........	2	1	
Brazil:				
Rio de Janeiro...... .	Dec. 2 22..	145	33	
Canada:				
British Columbia -				
Victoria.	Jan. 27 Feb. 2....	2	....	
New Brunswick--				
Moncton..............	Feb. 3 9..........	1	....	
China:				
Antung...	Jan. 7-13......	2	....	
Harbin..............	Nov. 12-Dec. 2...	3	....	
Manchuria Station........	Nov. 18-Dec. 2....	2	....	
Shanghai............	Dec. 21 27........	6	18	Cases, foreign, deaths, native
Do.............	Dec. 28 Jan. 2....	5	11	Do.
France:				
Lyon................	Dec. 24-30... ..|	2	....	
Do............	Jan. 7-20........	5	....	
India:				
Bombay.............	Nov. 25-Dec. 1...|	4	....	
Karachi.............	Nov. 18-24.......	....	1	Nov. 11-17, 1917: 10 cases with deaths; imported on S. S. Menesa from Basreh.
Madras.......	Nov. 25 Dec. 8....	3	1	
Rangoon..	Nov. 18-24.......	1	....	
Japan:				
Taiwan--				
Taihoku	Dec. 15 21... ...	1	....	
Java:				
East Java...	Nov. 25-Dec. 9....	6	....	
Mid-Java....				Dec 6 12,1917 Cases, 8, death ,1
Samarang. ....|	Dec. 6-12..........	1	1	
West Java .. .		....	....	Dec. 14-20, 1917: Cases 25 deaths, 3.
Mexico:				
Mexico City..	Jan 13-26 ..	14	....	
Vera Cruz..	Jan 20-25.	...	3	
Newfoundland:				
St. Johns......	Jan 19 Feb. 1....|	5	...	
Straits Settlements:				
Singapore....	Nov. 25-Dec. 1....	1	1	

TYPHUS FEVER.

Place.	Date.	Cases.	Deaths.	Remarks.
Algeria:				
Algiers.	Dec. 1 31.... ...|	...	1	
Argentina:				
Rosario..	Dec. 1-31.... ....|	......	1	
Egypt:				
Alexandria................	Dec. 3-31..........	24	7	
Cairo.	Sept. 24-Nov. 25..	26	19	
Port Said.............	Nov 5 11..	2	2	
Great Britain:				
Glasgow..................	Jan 20 26	1	......	
Greece:				
Salonaki	Dec 9 29.	...|	36	
Japan				
Nagasaki	Jan 7 13..........	1	... .	

CHOLERA, PLAGUE, SMALLPOX, TYPHUS FEVER, AND YELLOW FEVER—Continued.

Reports Received During Week Ended Feb. 22, 1918—Continued.

TYPHUS FEVER—Continued.

Place.	Date.	Cases.	Deaths.	Remarks.
Java:				
East Java	Nov. 27–Dec. 9....	7	....	
Mid-Java	Dec. 6–12.	5	....	
West Java				Dec. 14–20, 1917: Cases, 18; deaths, 5.
Batavia	Dec. 14–20.	17	5	
Mexico:				
Aguascalientes	Jan. 28–Feb. 3	....	1	
Mexico City	Jan. 13–26.	144	....	
Union of South Africa:				
Cape of Good Hope State...	Nov. 5–11.	98	33	Sept. 16–Nov. 11, 1917: Cases, 3,469; deaths, 701.

YELLOW FEVER.

Place.	Date.	Cases.	Deaths.	Remarks.
Honduras:				
Tegucigalpa	Dec. 16–22.	....	1	

Reports Received from Dec. 29, 1917, to Feb. 15, 1918.

CHOLERA.

Place.	Date.	Cases.	Deaths.	Remarks.
China:				
Antung	Nov. 26–Dec. 2....	3	1	
India:				
Bombay	Oct. 28–Nov. 24...	17	12	
Calcutta	Sept. 16–Nov. 24.	....	76	
Rangoon	Nov. 4–17.	2	2	
Indo-China:				
Provinces				Sept. 1–30, 1917: Cases, 74; deaths, 37.
Anam	Sept. 1–30.	13	10	
Cambodia	....do	19	12	
Cochin-China	....do	32	13	
Saigon	Nov. 22–28.	1	....	
Kwang-Chow-Wan	Sept. 1–30.	10	2	
Java:				
East Java	Oct. 28–Nov. 3....	1	1	
West Java				Oct. 19–Dec. 13, 1917: Cases, 93; deaths, 49.
Batavia	Oct. 19–Dec. 13.	51	15	
Persia:				
Mazanderan Province—				
Astrabad	July 31.	....	....	Present.
Barfrush	July 1–27.	34	23	
Chahmirzad				25 cases reported July 31, 1917.
Chahrastagh	June 15–July 25..	10	8	
Kharek	May 28–June 11...	21	12	
Sari	July 3–29.	273	144	
Yekchambe-Bazar	June 3.	6	....	
Philippine Islands:				
Provinces				Nov. 18–Dec. 22, 1917: Cases, 992; deaths, 657.
Antique	Nov. 18–Dec. 1...	48	32	
Bobol	Nov. 18–Dec. 22..	147	83	
Capis	Nov. 25–Dec. 22...	12	10	
Iloilo	Nov. 25–Dec. 15...	179	134	
Leyte	Nov. 25–Dec. 22...	13	12	
Mindanao	....do	323	189	
Occidental Negros	....do	188	123	
Oriental Negros	....do	94	59	
Romblon	Nov. 25–Dec. 1...	1	1	
Siam:				
Bangkok	Sept. 16–22.	1	1	
Turkey in Asia:				
Bagdad	Nov. 1–15.	....	40	

CHOLERA, PLAGUE, SMALLPOX, TYPHUS FEVER, AND YELLOW FEVER—Continued.

Reports Received from Dec. 29, 1917, to Feb. 15, 1918—Continued.

PLAGUE.

Place.	Date.	Cases.	Deaths.	Remarks.
Brazil:				
Bahia....................	Nov. 4–Dec. 15 ...	4	4	
British Gold Coast:				
Axim....................	Jan. 8.................			Present
Ceylon:				
Colombo..................	Oct. 14–Dec. 1.....	14	13	
Egypt.....................				Jan. 1–Nov. 15, 1917: Cases, 72; deaths, 398.
Port Said...............	July 23–29..........	1	2	
India......................				Sept. 16–Nov. 24, 1917: Cases, 131,804; deaths, 174,734.
Bombay.................	Oct. 28–Nov. 24..	93	79	
Calcutta................	Sept. 16–20........		2	
Henzada................	Oct. 21–27...........		1	
Karachi.................	Oct. 21–Nov. 10...	6	5	
Madras Presidency........	Oct. 31–Nov. 17...	3,294	2,360	
Mandalay..............	Oct. 14–Nov. 17...		80	
Rangoon................	Oct. 21–Nov. 17...	36	16	
Indo-China:				
Provinces..............				Sept. 1–30, 1917: Cases, 31, deaths, 30.
Anam...............	Sept. 1–30..........	12	11	
Cambodia...........	....do...............	12	11	
Cochin-China.......	....do...............	10	8	
Saigon.............	Oct. 31 Nov. 18...	8	4	
Java:				
East Java...............				Oct. 27–Nov. 25, 1917: Cases 75, deaths, 73.
Surabaya.............	Nov. 11–25.........	2	2	
Senegal:				
St. Louis................	Feb. 2...............			Present.
Siam:				
Bangkok................	Sept. 16–Nov. 24..	11	7	
Straits Settlements:				
Singapore..............	Oct. 28 Nov. 24...	3	5	

SMALLPOX.

Place.	Date.	Cases.	Deaths.	Remarks.
Algeria:				
Algiers.................	Nov. 1–30...........	1		
Australia:				
New South Wales........				July 12–Dec. 20, 1917: Cases 94.
Abermain............	Oct. 25 Nov. 20...	3		
Cessnock............	July 12 Oct. 11....	7		Newcastle district
Eumangla	Aug. 15.............	1		
Kurri Kurri..........	Dec. 5 20...........	2		
Mungindi............	Aug. 13.............	1		
Warren..............	July 12–Oct. 25....	22		
Brazil				
Bahia...............	Nov. 10 Dec. 8....	3		
Pernambuco...........	Nov. 1 15...........	1		
Rio de Janeiro.........	Sept. 30– Dec. 1...	519	151	
Sao Paulo	Oct. 29 Nov. 4....		2	
Canada:				
British Columbia				
Vancouver.......	Jan. 13–19........	1		
Victoria...........	Jan. 7 20..........	2		
Winnipeg.........	Dec. 30 Jan. 5....	1		
New Brunswick				
Kent County....	Dec. 1............			Outbreak. On main line Canadian Ry., 25 miles north of Moncton
Do............	Jan. 22...........	40		In 7 localities
Northumberland County	..do............	41		In 5 localities.
Restigouche County...	Jan. 18...........	60		
Victoria County.....	Jan. 22...........	10		At Limestone and a lumber camp
Westmoreland County				
Moncton.........	Jan. 20 Feb. 2....	3		
York County	Jan. 22............	8		
Ontario				
Hamilton	Dec. 16 22........	1		
Do	Jan. 13 19 .	2		
Sarnia...........	Dec. 9 15......	1		
Do	Jan. 6 Feb. 2.....	20		
Windsor	Dec. 1 Jan. 5.....	1		
Quebec				
Montreal.........	Dec. 10 Jan. 5....	5		
Do	Jan. 6 12.....	1		

CHOLERA, PLAGUE, SMALLPOX, TYPHUS FEVER, AND YELLOW FEVER—Continued.

Reports Received from Dec. 29, 1917, to Feb. 15, 1918—Continued.

SMALLPOX—Continued.

Place.	Date.	Cases.	Deaths.	Remarks.
China:				
Amoy	Oct. 22–Nov. 25			Present.
Antung	Dec. 3–23	13	2	
Chungking	Nov. 11–Dec. 15			Do.
Dairen	Nov. 18–Dec. 22	3	1	
Harbin	May 14–June 30	20		Chinese Eastern Ry.
Dio	July 1–Oct. 15	4		Do.
Hungtahotze Station	Oct. 28–Nov. 4	1		Do.
Manchuria Station	May 14–June 30	6		Do.
Do	July 1–Oct. 15	3		Do.
Mukden	Nov. 11–24			Present.
Shanghai	Nov. 18–Dec. 23	41	91	Cases, foreign; deaths among natives.
Do	Dec. 31–Jan. 6	4	17	Do.
Tientsin	Nov. 11–Dec. 22	13		
Cuba:				
Habana	Jan. 7	1		Nov. 8, 1917: 1 case fromCoruna, Dec. 5. 1917; 1 case.
Marianao	Jan. 8	1		6 miles distant from Habana.
Egypt:				
Alexandria	Nov. 12–18	1		
Cairo	July 23–Aug. 5	5	1	
France:				
Lyon	Nov. 18–Dec. 16	6	3	
Great Britain:				
Birmingham	Nov. 11–17	19		
India:				
Bombay	Oct. 21–Nov. 24	12	4	
Madras	Oct. 31–Nov. 17	6	2	
Rangoon	Oct. 28–Nov. 17	3	1	
Indo-China:				
Provinces				Sept. 1–30, 1917: Cases, 193; deaths, 56.
Anam	Sept. 1–30	61	12	
Cambodia	do	7		
Cochin-China	do	124	44	
Saigon	Oct. 20–Nov. 28	62	8	
Tonkin	Sept. 1–30	1		
Italy:				
Milan				October, 1917: Cases, 2.
Turin	Oct. 29–Dec. 9	123	120	
Castellamare	Dec. 10	2		Among refugees.
Florence	Dec. 1–15	17	4	
Naples	To Dec. 10	2		Do.
Java:				
East Java	Oct. 27–Nov. 10	19		
Mid-Java	Oct. 10–Nov. 21	55		
West Java				Oct. 19–Dec. 6, 1917: Cases, 192; deaths, 30.
Batavia	Nov. 2–8	1		
Mexico:				
Mazatlan	Dec. 5–11		1	
Mexico City	Nov. 11–Dec. 29	16		
Do	Dec. 30–Jan. 12	8		
Piedras Negras	Jan. 11	200		
Newfoundland:				
St. Johns	Dec. 8–Jan. 4	29		
Do	Jan. 5–18	14		
Trepassey	Jan. 4			Outbreak with 11 cases reported.
Philippine Islands:				
Manila	Oct. 28–Dec. 8	5		
Portugal:				
Lisbon	Nov. 4–Dec. 15	2		
Portuguese East Africa:				
Lourenço Marques	Aug. 1–Oct. 31		5	
Russia:				
Moscow	Aug. 26–Oct. 6	22	2	
Petrograd	Aug. 31–Nov. 18	76	3	
Siam:				
Bangkok	Nov. 25–Dec. 1	1	1	
Spain:				
Coruna	Dec. 2–15		4	
Madrid				Jan. 1–Dec. 31, 1917: Deaths, 77.
Seville	Oct. 1–Nov. 30		26	
Tunisia:				
Tunis	Dec. 14–20		1	
Turkey in Asia:				
Bagdad				Present in November, 1917.
Venezuela:				
Maracaibo	Dec. 2–8		1	

CHOLERA, PLAGUE, SMALLPOX, TYPHUS FEVER, AND YELLOW FEVER—Continued.

Reports Received from Dec. 29, 1917, to Feb. 15, 1918—Continued.

TYPHUS FEVER.

Place.	Date.	Cases.	Deaths.	Remarks.
Algeria:				
Algiers..................	Nov. 1-30......	2	....	
Australia:				
South Australia...........	....	....	....	Nov. 11-17, 1917: Cases 1.
Brazil:				
Rio de Janeiro.............	Oct. 28-Dec. 1.....	7	....	
Canada:				
Ontario—				
Kingston..............	Dec. 2-8.....	3	....	
Quebec—				
Montreal..............	Dec. 16-22....	2	1	
China:				
Antung..................	Dec. 3-30........	13	1	
Do..............	Dec. 31-Jan. 6..........	....	1	
Chosen (Formosa):				
Seoul......................	Nov. 1-30........	1	....	
Egypt:				
Alexandria...............	Nov. 8-Dec. 28....	134	52	
Cairo....................	July 23-Oct. 21....	28	9	
Port Said.................	July 30-Sept. 23...	3	3	
Great Britain:				
Glasgow...............	Dec. 21........	1	....	
Manchester...............	Dec. 2-8........	1	....	
Greece:				
Saloniki..................	Nov. 11-Dec. 8.....	....	36	
Japan:				
Nagasaki..................	Nov. 26-Dec. 16...	5	5	
Java:				
East Java..............				Oct. 15-Nov. 15, 1917: Cases, 17. deaths, 3.
Mid-Java..............				Oct. 10-Dec. 5, 1917: Cases, 49. deaths, 2.
Samarang...............	Oct. 17-Dec. 5.....	15	2	
West Java..............				Oct. 19-Dec. 13, 1917: Cases, 55 deaths, 10.
Batavia...............	Oct. 19-Dec. 13....	56	12	
Mexico:				
Aguascalientes.............	Dec. 15........	....	2	
Do..............	Jan. 21-27........	....	3	
Durango, State—				
Guanacevi..........	Feb. 11..........	....	....	Epidemic.
Mexico City..............	Nov. 11-Dec. 29...	476	....	
Do..............	Dec. 30-Jan. 12....	139	....	
Russia:				
Archangel..............	Sept. 1-14........	7	2	
Moscow................	Aug. 26-Oct. 6....	49	2	
Petrograd..............	Aug. 31-Nov. 18...	32	....	
Do..............	Feb. 2............	....	....	Present.
Vladivostok..............	Oct. 29-Nov. 4....	12	1	
Sweden:				
Goteborg..............	Nov. 18-24........	1	....	
Switzerland:				
Zurich..................	Nov. 9-15........	2	....	
Tunisia:				
Tunis..................	Nov. 30-Dec. 6....	....	1	
Turkey:				
Albania—				
Janina...	Jan. 27..........	....	....	Epidemic.
Union of South Africa:				
Cape of Good Hope State...	Sept. 10-Nov. 4...	3,312	668	

×

PUBLIC HEALTH REPORTS

| VOL. 33. | MARCH 1, 1918 | No. 9 |

THE APPLICATION OF OZONE TO THE PURIFICATION OF SWIMMING POOLS.[1]

By WALLACE A. MANNHEIMER, Ph. D., Secretary American Association for Promoting Hygiene and Public Baths.

.. Recirculation and disinfection of swimming pool water may now be accepted as standard and mutually interdependent procedures in the sanitary control of plunge baths. Experimental data[2] collected during the past several years have demonstrated beyond doubt the necessity of resorting to refiltration to aid in swimming pool purification unless fresh, warm, well-filtered water is constantly supplied to the pool. In the latter process the waste of water, and of coal for heating it, coupled with the difficulty of removing all suspended matter by an initial filtration are sufficient reasons for adopting refiltration of the pool water as a standard procedure. A clear water is essential not mainly because of esthetic reasons but for the reduction of the hazard of drowning. No method in actual practice measures up to refiltration.

Concerning the methods of disinfection, the writer has already set forth[3] the data and conclusions from a comparative study of all the chemicals hitherto applied to pool water purification. Ultraviolet light in actual operation was not considered a sufficiently powerful germicide. Copper sulphate was expensive in application and unreliable unless large quantities were employed, at which time the water became disagreeable to swim in. Furthermore, the transparency of the water was impaired and the tile lining of the pool stained, entailing additional labor in cleaning the pool.

Chlorine compounds, calcium hypochlorite, sodium hypochlorite, and gaseous chlorine, while effective to a marked degree as disinfectants, required, for satisfactory use in swimming pools, a type of technical control usually not available. A study of the practical application of these chemicals to swimming pool purification has demonstrated in the large majority of pools that either the quantity added was

[1] From the Research Laboratory of the Department of Health of New York City.
[2] Am. Phy. Ed. Rev., 1912, 17, p. 669; Jour. Inf. Dis., 1914, 15, p. 159; U. S. Pub. Health Rep., Sept. 17, 1915 (reprint No. 299); Jour. Inf. Dis., 1917, 20, p. 1; Jour. Am. Soc. Promote Hyg. & Pub. Baths, 1918, vol. 1, p. 19.
[3] Jour. Inf. Dis., 1917, vol. 20, No. 1, p. 1.

insufficient to effect proper bacterial reduction or that the water had a disagreeable odor and taste due to the pressure of an excess of the reagents.   It is difficult to strike a nice balance between odor and taste on the one hand and bacterial purity on the other in the case of chemicals usable only in minimum quantities.

In consequence of the disadvantages attending the use of the common chemicals for water purification when applied in swimming pools the writer decided to attempt the application of ozone for this purpose.

The application of ozone to water purification presents no novelty. Vosmaer [1] in his comprehensive treatise gives no less than one hundred and fifty-one references to literature on this subject.   According to Spaulding [2] there are forty-nine large ozone plants abroad, having a daily water delivery capacity of over 84,000,000 gallons. The plant in Petrograd alone, delivers 24,000,000 gallons a day and the plant at Paris over 12,000,000 gallons a day.   Rosenau [3] in a summary of this question states: "Ozone is one of the most satisfactory methods of purifying water from a sanitary standpoint.   As a germicide it is the most effective of all methods used, except boiling. A well-ozonized water is practically sterile and the organic matter is partially oxidized.   It is true that a few resisting spores are not killed, but these are harmless when taken by the mouth."

The writer first applied ozone to the purification of a miniature pool.   He concluded from his experiments [4] that ozone efficiently purifies water if proper contact of ozone and water be effected; that the application of ozone to pool water is automatic in its control and reliable in disinfecting pools.   Furthermore, it can be added without objectionable result in any excess, since it is not very soluble in water.   It oxidizes most of the organic matter in the water and is inexpensive in application.

As a result of these preliminary tests, the writer, in an effort to determine the applicability on a large scale, secured the installation of a large ozone plant at the Twenty-third Street Bath, New York. The following data have been gathered from tests on that installation.

Details of Installation.

The writer soon found out in his preliminary experimental work on ozone [4] that the engineering details connected with the application of ozone on a large scale are of paramount importance.   The most important feature in the application of ozone to water is the securing of a thorough mix of ozonized air and water.   No doubt the action of

[1] Vosmaer "Ozone" D. Van Nostrand Co., 1916.
[2] Spaulding: "Report on Application of Ozone to Water Purification," N. Y. State Dept. of Health, 1915.
[3] Preventive Medicine & Hygiene, D. Appleton, 1913, p. 794.
[4] "Ozone Disinfection of Swimming Pools," Journal of the American Assn. for Promoting Hygiene & Public Baths, 1918, Vol. 1, No. 1, p. 19.

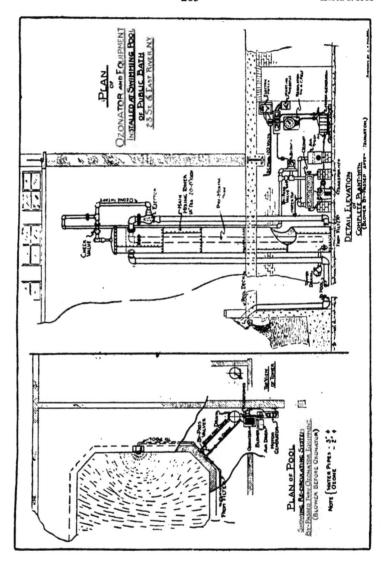

PLAN of OZONATOR and EQUIPMENT INSTALLED at SWIMMING POOL of PUBLIC BATH 23 St. & East River N.Y.

DETAIL ELEVATION of COMPLETE PLANT with (BLOWER BY-PASSED AFTER OZONATION)

PLAN of POOL SHOWING RECIRCULATING SYSTEM AIR PASSED THRU OZONATION EQUIPMENT (BLOWER BEFORE OZONATOR)

NOTE { WATER PIPES - 3"ø
       { OZONE - 2"ø

ozone on bacteria and organic matter is exceedingly rapid, as was evidenced by the preliminary work, but if the time of exposure of the water to the ozonized air is short, three parts per million of ozone (which is at least three times the necessary quantity) are required to obtain satisfactory results. A mechanical mixer was designed to insure intimate contact of the gas with water, but this was abandoned for the simpler and surer method recommended by Vosmaer, namely, the use of a tall tower.

It was finally determined to install a 20-foot tower in the Twenty-third Street Bath and to pass the water of the swimming pool into the bottom of this tower after filtration. If this tower is constructed so that the top is on a level with the surface of the pool, there is practically no additional cost in the operation of the recirculation system.[1]

Two systems of introducing the ozone into the water were installed at the same time so as to ascertain their relative merits. One was the use of a common ejector (see diagram) and the other the use of a small centrifugal air blower. The ozonized air is introduced into the pipe leading down through the center of the tower, where both water and ozone are liberated. The ozone, of course, bubbles through the water quite rapidly, the water (in its slower upward passage) being thus brought continuously into contact with fresh ozone. The ozonized water is then drawn off from the top of the tower and returned to the shallow end of the pool.

It was found when the circulating pump was stopped that water backed down into the ozonator. The air in the pipe which carries both air and water into the bottom of the mixing tower rises and carries the water with it. By a special arrangement[2] of pipes and valves, the water and ozone from this pipe are returned to the mixing tower (see diagram).

Bacterial Data.

The bacterial counts in this pool were so low after continuous operation of the ozone machine, that it was deemed advisable to add a large number of B. coli to the water in order to observe the efficiency of ozone on heavily polluted water. Accordingly a mass culture of B. coli was emulsified in salt solution and thrown into the pool. In order to secure thorough mixing of the bacteria with the pool water and to keep the pollution high, the circulating pump was shut down between 10 a. m. and 2 p. m., a long-handled brush was used to stir the water, and this, together with the agitation produced by the bathers, resulted in a uniform mix. The pool was then operated as usual and 2 hours later the tests were made.

[1] The writer is indebted to Mr. S. Palmer for many practical suggestions and for the accompanying drawings which set forth the details of installation.

[2] I am indebted to Mr. Willard A. Kitts, Jr., for the ingenious solution of this problem.

ONE PART OF OZONE PER MILLION OF WATER.

(NOTE.—All bacterial counts are averages of three or more determinations.)

Using ejector:

    Bacterial count in the artificially infected pool, 3,700 per cubic centimeter.
    After filtration and before ozonation, 1,850 per cubic centimeter.
    After ozonation, no growth in 1 cubic centimeter.
    After ozonation, no growth in 3 cubic centimeters.

In addition to plating one cubic centimeter of the water delivered from the ozone tower, three cubic centimeter samples were plated as well. In the majority of cases no growths were obtained.

Using blower:

    Pool water in the artificially infected pool, 3,500 per cubic centimeter.
    After filtration and before ozonation, 1,540 per cubic centimeter.
    After ozonation, no growth in 1 cubic centimeter.
    After ozonation, no growth in 3 cubic centimeters.

The results, using the blower, are identical with the foregoing. We conclude therefore that when one part per million of ozone is used, either with an ejector or with a centrifugal blower (which delivers more air) the pool water artificially contaminated with *B. coli* is sterilized.

USING 0.5 PART OZONE PER MILLION OF WATER.

The foregoing results were so striking that it was determined to cut down the amount of ozone supplied to the pool to ascertain the safety factor allowed when supplying one part of ozone per million of water. For this purpose the output of the ozonator was reduced to one-half by removing three of the six tubes.

Using ejector:

    Count from pool (artificially infected), 2,700 per cubic centimeter.
    After filtration and before ozonation, 1,580 per cubic centimeter.
    After ozonation, 1½ colonies per cubic centimeter.
    After ozonation, 1 to 3 colonies in 3 cubic centimeter samples.

When using half part of ozone per million of water and introducing the ozone by means of the ejector, the contaminated pool water was delivered in a relatively pure condition. A pool operated in this way, using half the quantity designed, while not delivering entirely sterile water, would be sufficiently pure for all practical purposes.

Using blower:

    Count from pool (artificially infected), 3,020 per cubic centimeter.
    After filtration and before ozonation, 1,150 per cubic centimeter.
    After ozonation, 130 per cubic centimeter.

When the blower was used a larger number of bacteria escaped destruction. This was due, in the writer's opinion, to the larger quantity of air introduced into the ozonator, resulting in a dilution of the ozone, and to the more rapid escape of the gas from the water.

A noticeable odor of ozone is observed when the blower is used, indicating that the ozone escapes without a sufficient opportunity of mixing with the water. The conclusion is reached, therefore, that the use of a turbine blower is inferior to that of an ejector, and that a great dilution of ozone in air is a disadvantage.

Cost Data.[1]

The installation cost in normal times would probably be at the rate of about 3 cents a gallon of capacity of the swimming pool. This cost will naturally vary from time to time with the cost of labor and materials. The electrical current consumption when using alternating current is 2 kilowatts per day, which amounts to from 10 to 14 cents if the cost of current varies between 5 and 7 cents per kilowatt. To this should be added 1 cent a day for the maximum cost of replacing the calcium chloride in the air dryer. The total daily cost of operation with alternating current for 60,000 gallons of water is between 11 and 15 cents. If direct current is supplied, a motor generator must be used, increasing the cost by from 10 to 15 cents a day (2 kilowatts). These figures are based upon local prices of electrical current. In plants where electrical current is generated on the premises, the cost, already very low, will be brought down still more.

The plant when once installed and adjusted is automatic and requires practically no care. The water is bleached, gradually assuming a transparent blue color, enhancing the appearance of the pool and decreasing the hazard from drowning. There is no occasion for renewal of the water, which can be retained for an indefinite period in a pure state.

The cost of water in New York City is at the rate of $1 per 1,000 cubic feet; thus, to fill the pool costs $8 for water alone. To heat the water during the cold season from the temperature in the main to that of the pool requires an average expenditure of 3 tons of coal, costing about $18. The cost of labor for cleaning the pool is about $4.[2] The total cost is about $30. By using the ozone system the saving in the course of a short time will make up for the cost of the installation, while maintaining a clean and safe pool.

The above operating and installation costs are estimated on the basis of one part of ozone per million parts of water, which under the average conditions that obtain in swimming pools allows 100 per cent safety factor in water sterilization.

---

[1] The writer is indebted to Mr. G. S. Eble, engineer in charge of baths of the borough of Manhattan, for many of the figures on cost.

[2] In municipal pools, while there would probably be no reduction of the pay roll on account of other duties to which the attendants could be assigned, nevertheless a labor saving of at least $4 is effected. Three attendants are occupied for about two and one-half hours in scrubbing out the pool.

Summary and Conclusion.

1. Refiltration combined with disinfection of swimming-pool water is a standard procedure in the sanitary control of swimming pools.

2. The methods of disinfection hitherto employed are objectionable on one score or another. Ultraviolet light in actual practice has proved ineffective; copper sulphate in low dilutions is unreliable and in high concentration is not only costly, but produces a water disagreeable to swim in; chlorine compounds, while effective as disinfectants, require a technical control usually not available in swimming pools, and when used in excess produce objectionable taste and odors in the water.

3. Ozone when properly applied to the water of a swimming pool effectively purifies the water. When one part of ozone per million parts of water is used, the result is sterile water. When half part ozone per million parts of water is used, a bacterial reduction of 99.8 per cent results, except when too great an excess of air is introduced with the ozone.

4. A study of the cost of operation of the ozonator has shown that a current consumption of 2 kilowatts per day with alternating current and of 4 kilowatts per day with direct current, plus 1 cent a day for calcium chloride, represents the total operating cost for a 60,000-gallon pool. This amounts to 11 to 15 cents a day for alternating current (at 5 to 7 cents per kilowatt) and to 21 to 29 cents a day with direct current. The cost of refilling the pool is at least $30. The use of the ozonator decreases the number of times the pool must be emptied to such an extent that the cost of the installation is soon paid for.

5. The application of ozone to the purification of swimming pools is automatic in control, reliable in action, and inexpensive in application. Accordingly, we recommend the consideration of this chemical as a standard procedure in the sanitary control of swimming pools.

The writer desires to acknowledge his appreciation of the assistance which both Mr. Todd, of the New York City bureau of public buildings and offices, and Mr. W. A. Kitts, jr., have rendered in making the above experiments possible.

PREVALENCE OF DISEASE.

No health department, State or local, can effectively prevent or control disease without knowledge of when, where, and under what conditions cases are occurring.

UNITED STATES.

EXTRA-CANTONMENT ZONES—CASES REPORTED WEEK ENDED FEB. 26.

CAMP BEAUREGARD ZONE, LA.

Cerebrospinal meningitis:
- Pineville 1

German measles:
- Alexandria 2

Measles:
- Alexandria 3
- Pineville 2
- Boyce 3

Mumps:
- Alexandria 5

Smallpox:
- Alexandria 1
- Pineville 1

Tuberculosis:
- Sharp Village 1

CAMP BOWIE ZONE, TEX.

Fort Worth:
- Chicken pox 2
- Diphtheria 1
- Measles 1
- Mumps 2
- Smallpox 10
- Tuberculosis, pulmonary 5

CAMP DEVENS ZONE, MASS.

Chicken pox:
- Littleton 7

Erysipelas:
- Lancaster 1

German measles:
- Ayer 12
- Littleton 2

Measles:
- Ayer 2
- Lancaster 2
- Westford 1

Mumps:
- Lancaster 6

CAMP DODGE ZONE, IOWA.

Cerebrospinal meningitis:
- Des Moines 1

Chicken pox:
- Des Moines 1

CAMP DODGE ZONE, IOWA—continued.

Diphtheria:
- Des Moines 6

Erysipelas:
- Woodward 1

German measles:
- Des Moines 7

Gonorrhea:
- Des Moines 9

Gonorrhea and chancroid:
- Des Moines 1

Measles:
- Des Moines 4
- Grimes 12

Mumps:
- Granger 7

Pneumonia:
- Des Moines 4

Scarlet fever:
- Des Moines 13
- Grimes 1

Smallpox:
- Des Moines 20
- Granger 1
- Madrid 1

Syphilis:
- Des Moines 5

CAMP FUNSTON ZONE, KANS.

Cerebrospinal meningitis:
- Manhattan 4

Chicken pox:
- Junction City 3
- Manhattan 1

Measles:
- Manhattan 28
- Junction City 7
- Milford 1
- Alta Vista 5
- Leonardville 5

Mumps:
- Manhattan 6
- Junction City 5
- Randolph 1

Pneumonia:
- Manhattan 2
- Riley 2

(274)

CAMP FUNSTON ZONE, KANS.—continued.

Scarlet fever:
Manhattan............................... 2
Junction City........................... 1
Smallpox:
Manhattan............................... 17
Ogden................................... 1
Randolph................................ 1
Whooping cough:
Manhattan............................... 2

CAMP GORDON ZONE, GA.

Atlanta:
Cerebrospinal meningitis................ 7
Chicken pox............................. 2
Diphtheria.............................. 6
German measles.......................... 5
Gonorrhea............................... 5
Measles................................. 9
Mumps................................... 21
Pneumonia............................... 3
Septic sore throat...................... 2
Scarlet fever........................... 5
Smallpox................................ 7
Syphilis................................ 9
Tuberculosis............................ 8
Whooping cough.......................... 3
Scottdale:
Smallpox................................ 1

CAMP GREENE ZONE, N. C.

Charlotte Township:
Chicken pox............................. 1
German measles.......................... 8
Gonorrhea............................... 9
Measles................................. 21
Mumps................................... 4
Scarlet fever........................... 1
Syphilis................................ 13
Syphilis and gonorrhea.................. 1
Tuberculosis............................ 2
Whooping cough.......................... 7

CAMP HANCOCK ZONE, GA.

Cerebrospinal meningitis:
Augusta................................. 6
New Savannah Road....................... 1
German measles:
Augusta................................. 23
North Augusta........................... 2
Measles:
Augusta................................. 26
Hephzibah............................... 2
Tuberculosis, pulmonary:
Augusta................................. 5

CAMP JACKSON ZONE, S. C.

Columbia:
Cerebrospinal meningitis................ 2
Diphtheria.............................. 2
Measles................................. 10
Mumps................................... 8
Roseola................................. 3

CAMP JOSEPH E. JOHNSTON ZONE, FLA.

Jacksonville:
Chicken pox............................. 1
Diphtheria.............................. 1
Cerebrospinal meningitis................ 5

CAMP JOSEPH E. JOHNSTON ZONE, FLA.—continued.

Jacksonville—Continued.
Measles................................. 32
Mumps................................... 5
Pellagra................................ 1
Tuberculosis............................ 5
Typhoid fever........................... 6
Whooping cough.......................... 4

FORT LEAVENWORTH ZONE, KANS.

Chicken pox:
Leavenworth............................. 16
Erysipelas:
Leavenworth............................. 1
German measles:
Leavenworth............................. 3
Leavenworth County...................... 3
Gonorrhea:
Leavenworth............................. 5
Measles:
Leavenworth............................. 1
Leavenworth County...................... 3
Mumps:
Leavenworth............................. 1
Pneumonia, lobar:
Leavenworth............................. 1
Leavenworth County...................... 3
Smallpox:
Leavenworth............................. 6
Leavenworth County...................... 5
Typhoid fever:
Leavenworth County...................... 1

CAMP LEWIS ZONE, WASH.

German measles:
Steilacoom.............................. 3
Clover Creek............................ 1
Spanaway................................ 3
Lakeview................................ 4
Parkland................................ 2
Gravelly Lake........................... 2
Mumps:
Lake City............................... 1
Scarlet fever:
Steilacoom.............................. 2
Tuberculosis:
Steilacoom Lake......................... 1
Lakeview................................ 2
Whooping cough:
Gravelly Lake........................... 1

CAMP LOGAN ZONE, TEX.

Houston:
Chicken pox............................. 4
German measles.......................... 3
Measles................................. 15
Mumps................................... 5
Pneumonia............................... 3
Scarlet fever........................... 1
Smallpox................................ 12
Tuberculosis............................ 4
Magnolia Park:
Chicken pox............................. 1

CAMP MACARTHUR ZONE, TEX.

Waco:
Chicken pox............................. 9
German measles.......................... 9
Gonorrhea............................... 2

CAMP MACARTHUR ZONE, TEX. continued

Waco—Continued.
- Measles.. 20
- Mumps.. 12
- Pneumonia, lobar........................... 3
- Smallpox...................................... 4
- Tuberculosis................................. 1

Precinct Two:
- Typhoid fever................................ 1

CAMP M'CLELLAN ZONE, ALA.

Cerebrospinal meningitis:
- Precinct Seventeen......................... 1

Chicken pox:
- Anniston..................................... 32

Measles:
- Anniston..................................... 1

Mumps:
- Anniston..................................... 1

Pneumonia:
- Anniston..................................... 3

Smallpox:
- Anniston..................................... 3
- Blue Mountain.............................. 1
- Oxford.. 1

Whooping cough:
- Anniston..................................... 1

NORFOLK COUNTY NAVAL DISTRICT, VA

Cerebrospinal meningitis:
- Portsmouth.................................. 1
- South Norfolk............................... 2

Measles:
- Portsmouth.................................. 12
- Norfolk County............................. 5

Mumps:
- Portsmouth.................................. 1

Pneumonia:
- Portsmouth.................................. 1
- Norfolk County............................. 4

Scarlet fever:
- Portsmouth.................................. 1
- Norfolk County............................. 1

Tuberculosis:
- Norfolk County............................. 4

Whooping cough:
- Portsmouth.................................. 1

FORT OGLETHORPE ZONE, GA

Cerebrospinal meningitis:
- Chattanooga................................. 2
- Ridgedale.................................... 1

Chicken pox:
- Chattanooga................................. 1
- North Chattanooga......................... 1

Diphtheria:
- Chattanooga................................. 2

German measles:
- Chattanooga................................. 2
- North Chattanooga......................... 1
- East Lake.................................... 1
- Rossville..................................... 1

Measles:
- Chattanooga................................. 2
- North Chattanooga......................... 1

FORT OGLETHORPE ZONE, GA.—continued

Measles—Continued.
- East Lake.................................... 1
- Rossville..................................... 2

Mumps:
- Chattanooga................................. 6
- North Chattanooga......................... 1
- East Lake.................................... 7

Pneumonia:
- Chattanooga................................. 4
- East Lake.................................... 4
- Rossville..................................... 4

Scarlet fever:
- Chattanooga................................. 1

Smallpox:
- Chattanooga................................. 7

Syphilis:
- Chattanooga................................. 4

Tuberculosis:
- St. Elmo..................................... 4
- Chattanooga................................. 4

CAMP SEVIER ZONE, S. C.

Cerebrospinal meningitis:
- Judson Mills................................. 4

Measles:
- Chickspring Township, rural.............. 4
- Union Bleachery............................ 4

Mumps:
- Chickspring Township, rural.............. 4

CAMP SHELBY ZONE, MISS.

Hattiesburg:
- Chicken pox.................................
- German measles............................ 4
- Malaria....................................... 4
- Measles...................................... 2
- Mumps.. 5
- Scarlet fever................................ 1
- Smallpox..................................... 5

CAMP SHERIDAN ZONE, ALA.

Montgomery:
- Cerebrospinal meningitis.................. 3
- Cerebrospinal meningitis carriers....... 2
- German measles............................ 2
- Measles...................................... 19
- Mumps.. 4
- Scarlet fever................................ 1
- Smallpox..................................... 9
- Typhoid fever............................... 1

Rural zone:
- Measles...................................... 4
- Whooping cough............................ 4

CAMP SHERMAN ZONE, OHIO

Diphtheria:
- Chillicothe................................... 4

German measles:
- Chillicothe................................... 7

Measles:
- Chillicothe................................... 1
- Liberty Township.......................... 5

Scarlet fever:
- Scioto Township............................ 4

Tuberculosis, pulmonary:
- Chillicothe................................... 4

CAMP ZACHARY TAYLOR ZONE, KY.

Cerebrospinal meningitis:
- Jefferson County............................ 1
- Louisville................................. 3

Diphtheria:
- Jefferson County............................ 1
- Louisville................................. 7

German measles:
- Jefferson County............................ 2

Measles:
- Jefferson County............................ 2
- Louisville................................. 42

Scarlet fever:
- Louisville................................. 4

Smallpox:
- Louisville................................. 3

Trachoma:
- Jefferson County............................ 4

Tuberculosis, pulmonary:
- Louisville................................. 27

Typhoid fever:
- Louisville................................. 1

Whooping cough:
- Louisville................................. 2

TIDEWATER HEALTH DISTRICT, VA.

Cerebrospinal meningitis:
- Newport News............................. 2
- Hampton................................. 1

Chicken pox:
- Newport News............................. 1

German measles:
- Hampton................................. 8
- Phoebus................................. 2

Measles:
- Newport News............................. 2
- Hampton................................. 7
- Phoebus................................. 1

Pneumonia:
- Hampton................................. 1
- Phoebus................................. 1

Tuberculosis:
- Newport News............................. 1
- Hampton................................. 1

Typhoid fever:
- Hampton................................. 1

Whooping cough:
- Newport News............................. 10

CAMP TRAVIS ZONE, TEX.

San Antonio:
- Measles.................................. 4
- Mumps.................................. 3
- Scarlet fever............................. 1
- Tuberculosis............................. 1

CAMP WADSWORTH ZONE, S. C.

Cerebrospinal meningitis:
- Drayton Mills............................ 2

CAMP WADSWORTH ZONE, S. C.—continued.

Chicken pox:
- Spartanburg............................. 1
- Glenn Springs............................ 1

Diphtheria:
- Spartanburg............................. 1

German measles:
- Spartanburg............................. 7
- Pauline................................. 2
- Cross Anchor............................ 1

Measles:
- Spartanburg............................. 20
- Pauline................................. 2
- Glenn Springs............................ 1
- Saxon Mills............................. 4
- Fair Forest............................. 1

Mumps:
- Spartanburg............................. 3

Pneumonia:
- Spartanburg............................. 3
- Pauline................................. 1
- Saxon Mills............................. 1

Tonsillitis, ulcerative:
- Glenn Springs............................ 1

Tuberculosis:
- Spartanburg............................. 1
- Glenn Springs............................ 1

Whooping cough:
- Spartanburg............................. 1

CAMP WHEELER ZONE, GA.

Cerebrospinal meningitis:
- Macon................................. 3

Chicken pox:
- Macon................................. 3

Diphtheria:
- Macon................................. 1

German measles:
- Macon................................. 2

Gonorrhea:
- Macon................................. 2

Malaria:
- Macon................................. 1

Measles:
- Macon................................. 3
- East Macon.............................. 1

Mumps:
- Macon................................. 35
- East Macon.............................. 17

Scarlet fever:
- Macon................................. 1
- East Macon.............................. 1

Smallpox:
- East Macon.............................. 10

Syphilis:
- Macon................................. 1

Tuberculosis:
- Macon................................. 1

Whooping cough
- Macon................................. 8

278

CURRENT STATE SUMMARIES.

Alabama.

From Collaborating Epidemiologist Perry, by telegraph, for week ended February 23, 1918:

Measles and smallpox abating.

California.

From the California State Board of Health, by telegraph, for week ended February 23, 1918:

Measles continues to increase in prevalence, especially in southern California; 1,400 cases in California. Fifteen cases smallpox; Fresno County 5, Imperial County 4, Los Angeles 3, San Francisco 2, Kern County 1. Six cases cerebrospinal meningitis: San Francisco 2, Oakland 2, Los Angeles 1, Orange County 1. Mumps shows great increase, particularly in San Francisco and Los Angeles.

Reported by mail for preceding week (ended Feb. 16):

Cerebrospinal meningitis	8	Pneumonia	54
Chicken pox	230	Poliomyelitis	1
Diphtheria	81	Scarlet fever	102
Erysipelas	19	Smallpox	22
German measles	303	Syphilis	31
Gonococcus infection	63	Trachoma	3
Malaria	1	Tuberculosis	107
Measles	968	Typhoid fever	11
Mumps	55	Whooping cough	67
Pellagra	1		

Connecticut.

From Collaborating Epidemiologist Black, by telegraph, for week ended February 23, 1918:

No unusual prevalence. Two cerebrospinal meningitis Stanford, 1 poliomyelitis Bristol.

Indiana.

From the State Board of Health of Indiana, by telegraph, for week ended February 23, 1918:

Scarlet fever, schools closed: Livonia, Washington County; Olive Branch, Randolph County; Longfellow School, Davies County; North Manchester College, Wabash County. Diphtheria, epidemic: Franklin, Parker, Randolph County. Measles, epidemic: Decatur, New Lisbon, Henry County, Letts, Fayette County, Rochester, New Augusta, Fort Wayne. German measles, epidemic: Gosport, Aurora, Milroy. Smallpox, epidemic: Columbus, Cartersburg, Plainville, Frankfort, Ashboro, Pike County. Whooping cough, epidemic: Lockville, Elkhart County. Epidemic gastro-enteritis: Greencastle. Rabies, epidemic, dogs: Columbus, Connorsville, Vigo County.

Kansas.

From Collaborating Epidemiologist Crumbine, by telegraph, for week ended February 23, 1918:

Meningitis, in cities: Augusta 2, Beloit 1, Kansas City 1, Leon 1, Luray 1, Manhattan 1, Seneca 1. Meningitis carriers: Topeka 1. Smallpox, in cities: Coffeyville

12, Kansas City 43, Leavenworth 7, Topeka 11, Wichita 24; in counties: Butler 10, Cherokee 14, Crawford 15.

Louisiana.

From Collaborating Epidemiologist Dowling, by telegraph, for week ended February 23, 1918:

Meningitis: Bienville 1, Caddo 1, Madison 1, Orleans 3, Vermilion 1, Winn 1.

Minnesota.

From Collaborating Epidemiologist Bracken, by telegraph, for week ended February 23, 1918:

Smallpox (new foci): Aitkin County, Solana Township 1; Mower County, Leroy Township 1; Hennepin County, Dayton village 1, Rogers village 3; Fillmore County, Arendahl Township 2; Rock County, Luverne Township 2; Yellow Medicine County, Friendship Township 2. Two cerebrospinal meningitis.

Nebraska.

From the State Board of Health of Nebraska, by telegraph, for week ended February 23, 1918:

Smallpox: Omaha, Lincoln, Holdrege, Valentine, Spencer, Wausau, Ord, Grant, Elsie. Scarlet fever: Deshler, Normal. Meningitis: Grand Island, and Nemaha County.

New Jersey.

From Collaborating Epidemiologist Bowen, by telegraph, for week ended February 23, 1918:

Measles unusually prevalent Bridgeton, Bloomfield, Montclair.

Ohio.

From Collaborating Epidemiologist Freeman, by telegraph, for week ended February 23, 1918:

Salem, scarlet fever 22 cases. Piqua, scarlet fever 14 cases. Bairdstown, diphtheria 4 cases. Wellsville, typhoid fever 8 cases. For entire State, meningitis 14 cases, including Dayton 4, Cincinnati 3.

South Carolina.

From Collaborating Epidemiologist Hayne, by telegraph, for week ended February 25, 1918:

Epidemic meningitis, 25 cases week ending 25th.

Virginia.

From Collaborating Epidemiologist Traynham, by telegraph, for week ended February 23, 1918:

Two cases smallpox Alleghany County, one Middlesex. One case cerebrospinal meningitis Buchanan County, 1 Roanoke, 1 Newport News.

RECIPROCAL NOTIFICATION.

Minnesota.

Cases of communicable diseases referred during January, 1918, to other State health departments by department of health of the State of Minnesota.

Disease and locality of notification.	Referred to health authority of—	Why referred.
Diphtheria:		
Minneapolis Health Department, Hennepin County.	State Hospital, Iowa City, Johnson County, Iowa.	Came to Minneapolis from Iowa. Jan. 21. First symptoms Jan. 19
Scarlet fever:		
Minneapolis Health Department, Hennepin County.	Camp Dodge, Iowa. (Officer on 5-day leave, quarantined—unable to return.)	Came home to Minneapolis Dec. 23 from Camp Dodge. First symptoms Dec. 31.
	Sioux Falls, Minnehaha County, S. Dak.	Came from South Dakota Jan 14, quarantined in Minneapolis Jan. 19. Child who accompanied father was desquamating when he came to Minneapolis.
Smallpox:		
Minneapolis Health Department, Hennepin County	Rothschild, Marathon County, Wis. Lyle, Mower County, Minn.........	Wife exposed to husband who contracted smallpox at Lyle, Minn., left Minneapolis to visit at Rothschild, Wis.
	Chicago, Cook County, Ill.......... Dubuque, Dubuque County, Iowa. New York City, New York County, N. Y. Pittsburgh, Allegheny County, Pa..	Case quarantined at Minneapolis exposed individuals from several localities at Chicago and Dubuque
Tuberculosis:		
Mayo Clinic, Rochester, Olmsted County.	Denver, Denver County, Colo...... Paris, Edgar County, Ill.......... Springfield, Sangamon County, Ill.. Moline, Rock Island County, Ill..... Hinsdale, Dupage County, Ill....... Colleta, Whiteside County, Ill...... Eagle, Ada County, Idaho.......... Brazil, Clay County, Ind.......... Bancroft, Kossuth County, Iowa.... Mason City, Cerro Gordo County, Iowa. Clarksville, Butler County, Iowa.... Wapello, Louisa County, Iowa...... Knoxville, Marion County, Iowa.... Wakefield, Clay County, Kans...... South Range, Houghton County, Mich. Gilman City, Harrison County, Mo. Edmonds, Stutsman County, N. Dak. Erie Cass County, N. Dak. Rock Lake, Towner County, N. Dak. Fargo, Cass County, N. Dak........ Akron, Summit County, Ohio...... Armour, Douglas County, S. Dak... Dallas, Dallas County, Texas....... Kendall, Monroe County, Wis....... Marinette, Marinette County, Wis.. Weyerhauser, Rush County, Wis... Moose Jaw, Saskatchewan, Canada.. Prince Albert, Saskatchewan, Canada. Saquith, Saskatchewan, Canada..... Blaine Lake, Saskatchewan, Canada. Danzil, Saskatchewan, Canada	11 advanced, 10 moderately advanced, 3 incipient, 4 apparently cured, 3 (stage of disease not given) cases left Mayo Clinic for homes
Thomas Hospital, Minneapolis, Hennepin County.	Badger, Webster County, Iowa.....	Open case left Thomas Hospital for home
Bemidji, Beltrami County.	Emo, Ontario, Canada..............	Sputum sent in by Minnesota physician showed tubercle bacilli present.

ANTHRAX.

Massachusetts—Winchester.

During the month of January, 1918, a case of anthrax was reported in the person of J. T. F., aged 47 years, a tanner, living at No. 36 Middlesex Street, Winchester, Mass.

CEREBROSPINAL MENINGITIS.

Kentucky—Berea.

During the period from January 17 to February 14, 1918, 16 cases of cerebrospinal meningitis occurred among students attending Berea College.

Virginia—Norfolk.

During the period from February 17 to 21, 1918, 5 cases of cerebrospinal meningitis were notified in Norfolk, Va.

State Reports for January, 1918.

Place.	New cases reported.	Place.	New cases reported.
Louisiana:		**Ohio:**	
Ascension Parish	1	Ashtabula County	2
Avoyelles Parish	6	Butler County	1
Caddo Parish	2	Columbiana County	1
DeSoto Parish	5	Cuyahoga County	6
Grant Parish	8	Franklin County	3
Iberia Parish	1	Hamilton County	3
Iberville Parish	1	Hancock County	1
Jefferson Davis Parish	1	Jefferson County	2
Lafourche Parish	1	Lucas County	1
Lincoln Parish	1	Mahoning County	3
Orleans Parish	4	Medina County	1
Rapides Parish	110	Montgomery County	3
Red River Parish	1	Noble County	1
St. James Parish	2	Ross County	6
St. Landry Parish	1	Scioto County	1
Tensas Parish	1	Seneca County	1
Union Parish	1	Summit County	4
Vermilion Parish	6		
Winn Parish	1	Total	40
Total	154	**Rhode Island:**	
		Bristol (Town)	1
Minnesota:		Providence	4
Cottonwood County—			
Rose Hill Township	1	Total	5
Carlton County—			
Barnum	1	**Vermont:**	
Hennepin County—		Chittenden County—	
Minneapolis	3	Burlington	1
St. Louis County—			
Virginia	1	**Wisconsin:**	
		Brown County	1
Total	6	Douglas County	1
		Milwaukee County	6
New Jersey:		Outagamie County	1
Bergen County	2	Sheboygan County	1
Burlington County	1	Trempealeau County	1
Essex County	11	Waupaca County	1
Hudson County	3	Wood County	2
Mercer County	1		
Passaic County	2	Total	14
Union County	3		
Total	23		

       282

CEREBROSPINAL MENINGITIS—Continued.

City Reports for Week Ended Feb. 9, 1918.

Place.	Cases.	Deaths.	Place.	Cases.	Deaths.
Akron, Ohio..............	1	....	Little Rock, Ark..............	1	....
Alexandria, La..............	1	1	Louisville, Ky..............	2	2
Atlanta, Ga..............	11	3	Macon, Ga..............	8	....
Baltimore, Md..............	4	2	Medford, Mass..............	1	....
Birmingham, Ala..............	1	1	Milwaukee, Wis..............	3	2
Boston, Mass..............	2	....	Minneapolis, Minn..............		1
Bridgeport, Conn..............	1	....	Nashville, Tenn..............	3	2
Charleston, S. C..............	2	1	Newark, N. J..............	1	1
Charlotte, N. C..............	1	....	New Britain, Conn..............		1
Chattanooga, Tenn..............	8	1	New Castle, Pa..............	1	....
Chicago, Ill..............	9	2	New Haven, Conn..............	1	....
Chillicothe, Ohio..............		1	New Orleans, La..............	3	2
Cincinnati, Ohio..............	1	1	Newport, Ky..............	2	2
Coffeyville, Kans..............	1	....	New York, N. Y..............	22	2
Columbia, S. C..............	4	....	Norfolk, Va..............	3	3
Columbus, Ohio..............	4	....	Petersburg, Va..............	1	....
Covington, Ky..............	1	1	Philadelphia, Pa..............	7	3
Dayton, Ohio..............		2	Pittsburgh, Pa..............	1	1
Fall River, Mass..............	2	1	Rochester, N. Y..............		1
Flint, Mich..............	1	1	St. Louis, Mo..............	2	....
Galveston, Tex..............	2	....	San Antonio, Tex..............	3	5
Grand Rapids, Mich..............	1	1	Schenectady, N. Y..............	1	1
Hattiesburg, Miss..............	3	....	Seattle, Wash..............	1	1
Houston, Tex..............		1	Springfield, Mass..............		1
Jamestown, N. Y..............	1	....	Troy, N. Y..............	2	....
Johnstown, Pa..............	1	....	Waco, Tex..............	2	....
Kansas City, Kans..............	1	....	Washington, D. C..............	8	2
Kansas City, Mo..............	4	3	Wilmington, Del..............	1	1
Leavenworth, Kans..............	1	....	Worcester, Mass..............	1	1
Lima, Ohio..............	1	....	Yonkers, N. Y..............	1	....

DIPHTHERIA.

See Diphtheria, measles, scarlet fever, and tuberculosis, page 295.

ERYSIPELAS.

City Reports for Week Ended Feb. 9, 1918.

Place.	Cases.	Deaths.	Place.	Cases.	Deaths.
Allentown, Pa..............	1	....	Memphis, Tenn..............	2	1
Berkeley, Cal..............	2	....	Newark, N. J..............	7	1
Boston, Mass..............		4	New Castle, Pa..............	1	....
Bridgeport, Conn..............	1	....	New York, N. Y..............		7
Buffalo, N. Y..............	3	....	Oakland, Cal..............	1	....
Chicago, Ill..............	18	2	Philadelphia, Pa..............	3	1
Cincinnati, Ohio..............	1	1	Pittsburgh, Pa..............	7	1
Cleveland, Ohio..............	10	2	Pontiac, Mich..............	3	....
Denver, Colo..............	6	1	Providence, R. I..............		1
Detroit, Mich..............	2	1	Rochester, N. Y..............	6	....
Duluth, Minn..............	1	....	St. Joseph, Mo..............	1	....
Erie, Pa..............	4	1	St. Louis, Mo..............	6	1
Harrisburg, Pa..............	1	....	Salt Lake City, Utah..............		1
Hartford, Conn..............	2	....	San Antonio, Tex..............	1	2
Kalamazoo, Mich..............	2	....	San Diego, Cal..............	1	....
Kansas City, Mo..............	2	3	San Francisco, Cal..............	4	....
Lancaster, Pa..............	2	....	Springfield, Ill..............	1	1
Los Angeles, Cal..............	6	....	Trenton, N. J..............	1	....
Louisville, Ky..............	4	2	Wilmington, Del..............		1

LEPROSY.

City Report for Week Ended Feb. 9, 1918.

During the week ended February 9, 1918, one case of leprosy was reported in Portland, Oreg.

MALARIA.

State Reports for January, 1918.

Place.	New cases reported.	Place.	New cases reported.
Louisiana:		Louisiana—Continued.	
Acadia Parish	2	Vermilion Parish	1
Assumption Parish	1	West Feliciana	3
Caddo Parish	1		
East Baton Rouge Parish	1	Total	17
East Feliciana Parish	2		
Morehouse Parish	1	New Jersey:	
Rapides Parish	1	Burlington County	1
St. John Parish	1	Essex County	1
St. Martin Parish	1	Sussex County	4
St. Mary Parish	2		
		Total	6

City Reports for Week Ended Feb. 9, 1918.

Place.	Cases.	Deaths.	Place.	Cases.	Deaths.
Birmingham, Ala	3		Newark, N. J	1	
Hagerstown, Md	1		New Orleans, La	1	
Hattiesburg, Miss	4		Savannah, Ga		1
Macon, Ga	1		Waco, Tex	2	

MEASLES.

See Diphtheria, measles, scarlet fever, and tuberculosis, page 295.

PELLAGRA.

State Reports for January, 1918.

Place.	New cases reported.	Place.	New cases reported.
Louisiana:		Vermont:	
Caldwell Parish	1	Rutland County	1
Morehouse Parish	1		
Orleans Parish	3		
Total	5		

City Reports for Week Ended Feb. 9, 1918.

Place.	Cases.	Deaths.	Place.	Cases.	Deaths.
Anniston, Ala	1		Macon, Ga		1
Atlanta, Ga		1	Nashville, Tenn	1	1
Charleston, S. C		1	New York, N. Y		1
Fort Smith, Ark		2	Portsmouth, Va		1
Houston, Tex		1	San Antonio, Tex		1

21

PNEUMONIA.

City Reports for Week Ended Feb. 9, 1918.

Place.	Cases.	Deaths.	Place.	Cases.	Deaths.
Allentown, Pa................	1	....	Los Angeles, Cal............	16	7
Altoona, Pa................	3	....	Louisville, Ky............	1	22
Anniston, Ala............	1	....	Lowell, Mass............	2	5
Atlanta, Ga............	1	11	Lynn, Mass............	3	2
Baltimore, Md....	40	26	Manchester, N. H........	5	5
Boston, Mass.........	61	....	Melrose, Mass............	1	....
Braddock, Pa........	4	....	Montgomery, Ala............	1	5
Bridgeport, Conn....	1	16	Newark, N. J............	64	19
Butler, Pa........	1	....	New Bedford, Mass........	4	8
Cambridge, Mass....	9	5	New Britain, Conn........	3	1
Chattanooga, Tenn........	4	2	Newburyport, Mass........	1	1
Chelsea, Mass........	9	3	New Castle, Pa........	1	......
Chicago, Ill........	196	81	Newport, Ky........	9	9
Chillicothe, Ohio....	1	1	Norristown, Pa........	1	1
Cleveland, Ohio....	27	30	North Adams, Mass........	2	2
Cumberland, Md....	1	1	Norwalk, Conn........	7	5
Detroit, Mich........	7	58	Oakland, Cal........	2	2
Duluth, Minn........	5	5	Pasadena, Cal........	1	......
Easton, Pa........	1	1	Petersburg, Va........	4	2
Elmira, N. Y........	2	......	Philadelphia, Pa........	171	105
Erie, Pa........	6	5	Pittsburgh, Pa........	67	82
Fall River, Mass........	7	1	Pontiac, Mich........	3	1
Fitchburg, Mass........	4	2	Providence, R. I........	5	6
Flint, Mich........	6	5	Reading, Pa........	5	4
Fort Worth, Tex........	20	20	Roanoke, Va........	2	2
Grand Rapids, Mich........	14	3	Rochester, N. Y........	8	5
Hagerstown, Md........	2	......	Sacramento, Cal........	2	......
Harrisburg, Pa........	1	3	St. Joseph, Mo........	6	4
Hattiesburg, Miss........	4	......	Salem, Mass........	1	......
Haverhill, Mass........	2	1	San Antonio, Tex........	2	62
Holyoke, Mass........	2	2	Sandusky, Ohio........	2	......
Houston, Tex........	9	10	San Francisco, Cal........	14	15
Jackson, Miss........	5	......	Schenectady, N. Y........	2	......
Jacksonville, Fla........	2	9	Somerville, Mass........	5	......
Johnstown, Pa........	5	6	South Bend, Ind........	2	2
Kalamazoo, Mich........	3	2	Springfield, Mass........	11	6
Kansas City, Kans........	2	......	Springfield, Ohio........	1	1
Kansas City, Mo........	19	24	Stockton, Cal........	10	7
Leavenworth, Kans........	2	1	Trenton, N. J........	4	......
Lexington, Ky........	3	9	Waco, Tex........	1	......
Lincoln, Nebr........	2	2	Wichita, Kans........	5	1
Little Rock, Ark........	4	5	Worcester, Mass........	7	5
Lorain, Ohio........	3	1			

POLIOMYELITIS (INFANTILE PARALYSIS).

State Reports for January, 1918.

Place.	New cases reported.	Place.	New cases reported
Louisiana:		**Ohio:**	
Jefferson Davis Parish..............	1	Ashland County.....................	1
		Franklin County.....................	1
Minnesota:		Hamilton County.....................	1
Olmsted County—		Logan County.....................	1
Kalmar Township..............	1	Warren County.....................	1
Renville County—			
Boon Lake Township...........	1	Total.....................	5
Total.......................	2	**Wisconsin:**	
		Milwaukee County.....................	2
New Jersey:		Vernon County.....................	1
Essex County..................	1	Waupaca County.....................	1
		Total.....................	4

POLIOMYELITIS (INFANTILE PARALYSIS)—Continued.

City Reports for Week Ended Feb. 9, 1918.

Place.	Cases.	Deaths.	Place.	Cases.	Deaths.
Boston, Mass		1	Pittsburgh, Pa	1	
East Orange, N. J	1		Providence, R. I	1	
Haverhill, Mass	1		Rochester, N. Y		1
New York, N. Y	3				

RABIES IN ANIMALS.

City Reports for Week Ended Feb. 9, 1918.

Place.	Cases.	Place.	Cases.
Detroit, Mich	3	New Orleans, La	1
Memphis, Tenn	2	Winston-Salem, N. C	1

SCARLET FEVER.

See Diphtheria, measles, scarlet fever, and tuberculosis, page 295.

SMALLPOX.

Alabama—Mobile.

On February 23, 1918, smallpox was reported present at Mobile, Ala., where about 20 cases of the disease had occurred.

Missouri—Kansas City.

During the period from February 21 to 26, 1918, 116 cases of small-pox were notified at Kansas City, Mo.

Texas—Eagle Pass—Virulent Smallpox.

During the period of 7 days ended February 25, 1918, 20 new cases of smallpox, with 5 deaths, were notified at Eagle Pass, Tex., making a total of 103 cases, with 23 deaths, reported since October 1, 1917. A total of 73 cases has been reported since January 1, 1918.

State Reports for January, 1918.

Place.	New cases reported.	Deaths.	Number vaccinated within 7 years preceding attack.	Number last vaccinated more than 7 years preceding attack.	Number never successfully vaccinated.	Vaccination history not obtained or uncertain.
Michigan:						
Alcona County—						
Alcona Township	1		1			
Black River Township	8				8	
Caledonia Township	9				9	
Harrisville	2					2
Alger County—						
Mathias Township	5				5	

SMALLPOX—Continued.

State Reports for January, 1918—Continued.

Place.	New cases reported.	Deaths.	Vaccination history of cases.			
			Number vaccinated within 7 years preceding attack.	Number last vaccinated more than 7 years preceding attack.	Number never successfully vaccinated.	Vaccination history not obtained or uncertain.
Michigan—Continued.						
Allegan County—						
Otsego...............	1				1	....
Wayland.............	2					....
Alpena County—						
Green Township......	14				14	....
Maple Ridge Township..	1				1	....
Sanborn Township.....	15				15	....
Alpena...............	15				15	....
Barry County—						
Hastings.............	14				14	....
Bay County—						
Fraser Township.......	2				2	....
Pinconning...........	1				1	....
Bay City.............	1				1	....
Berrien County—						
Benton Harbor.......	3				3	....
Calhoun County—						
Washington Heights....	1				1	....
Battle Creek.........	6		1		3	2
Charlevoix County—						
East Jordan.........	1				1	....
Cheboygan County—						
Koehler Township......	9				9	....
Waverly Township.....	9				9	....
Walker Township.....	1				1	....
Chippewa County—						
Sault Ste. Marie........	1					1
Clinton County—						
Ovid...............	1				1	....
Crawford County—						
Grayling.............	1		1			....
Delta County—						
Nahma Township......	1				1	....
Eaton County—						
Benton Township......	4				4	......
Genesee County—						
Burton Township......	1				1	....
Forest Township.......	1					1
Vienna Township......	2				2	....
Flint.................	66				56	10
Grand Traverse County—						
Whitewater Township..	10				10	....
Hillsdale County—						
Hillsdale Township.....	1				1	....
Hillsdale.............	4				4	....
Huron County—						
Dwight Township.....	2				2	....
Fairhaven Township....	6				6	....
Lake Township........	1					1
Lincoln Township.....	1					1
Port Austin Township..	3				3	....
Rubicon Township.....	1				1	....
Sebewaing Township....	1				1	....
Pigeon...............	1				1	....
Harbor Beach........	3				3	....
Ingham County—						
White Rock Township..	2			2		....
Lansing.............	4				3	1
Ionia County—						
North Plains Township.	1				1	......
Iosco County—						
Sherman Township....	1				1	....
Whittmore Township...	1				1	....
Isabella County—						
Vernon Township......	1				1	....
Jackson County—						
Jackson.............	11				11	....
Kalamazoo County—						
Schoolcraft Township...	2		1			•

SMALLPOX—Continued.

State Reports for January, 1918—Continued.

Place.	New cases reported.	Deaths.	Vaccination history of cases.			
			Number vaccinated within 7 years preceding attack.	Number last vaccinated more than 7 years preceding attack.	Number never successfully vaccinated.	Vaccination history not obtained or uncertain.
Michigan—Continued.						
Kalkaska County—						
Rapid River Township.	4				4	
Springfield Township...	1				1	
Kent County—						
Caledonia Township....	1				1	
Gratton Township.....	1				1	
Walker Township......	10				10	
Grand Rapids..........	110			7	103	
Lake County—						
Cherry Valley Township	5				5	
Pinvia Township......	1				1	
Luther.............	7				7	
Lapeer County—						
Attica Township.	3				1	2
Goodland Township....	1			1		
Imlay Township.......	3				3	
Metamva Township....	1				1	
Almont.......	1			1		
Imlay City.......	1				1	
Lenawee County—						
Macon Township.......	2					2
Livingston County—						
Brighton......	1				1	
Macomb County—						
Clinton Township.....	1				1	
Harrisville Township...	2			1	1	
Lake Township.......	1		1			
Sterling Township.....	1				1	
Armada.......	5				5	
Mount Clemens........	2				2	
Manistee County—						
Dickson Township.....	1				1	
Marquette County—						
Marquette.....	7				7	
Mason County—						
Summit Township......	1				1	
Ludington.....	2				2	
Mecosta County—						
Green Township.......	2				2	
Big Rapids....	2				2	
Missaukee County—						
Aetna Township.......	1				1	
Bloomfield Township...	1				1	
Caldwell Township.....	2				2	
Monroe County—						
Raisenville Township...	1				1	
Monroe.......	1		1			
Montcalm County—						
Maple Valley Township.	3				3	
Greenville....	1				1	
Muskegon County—						
Muskegon Township....	6				6	
Muskegon Heights.....	21				21	
Muskegon.....	28			1	25	2
Newaygo County—						
Sherman Township....	9				7	2
Sheridan Township....	2				2	
Newaygo.............	1				1	
Fremont.............	9			1	8	
Oakland County—						
Royal Oak Township...	1				1	
Waterford Township...	1				1	
Rochester..............	1				1	
Pontiac..............	15				15	
Oceana County—						
Crystal Township.....	2				2	
Elbridge Township.....	1				1	
Ogemaw County—						
Richland Township.....	1				1	

SMALLPOX—Continued.

State Reports for January, 1918—Continued.

Place.	New cases reported.	Deaths.	Number vaccinated within 7 years preceding attack.	Number last vaccinated more than 7 years preceding attack.	Number never successfully vaccinated.	Vaccination history not obtained or uncertain.
Michigan—Continued.						
Osceola County—						
Hartwick Township....	3	....	....	....	3	....
Sherman Township....	4	....	....	....	4	....
Otsego County—						
Dover Township........	1	....	....	....	....	1
Vanderbilt..............	1	....	....	....	1	....
Ottawa County—						
Holland Township......	1	....	....	....	....	1
Talmadge Township....	1	....	....	....	1	....
Wright Township.......	1	....	....	....	1	....
Presque Isle County—						
Belknap Township....	2	....	....	....	2	....
Saginaw County—						
Tittabawassee Township	1	....	....	....	1	....
St. Clair County—						
Brockway Township....	1	....	....	....	1	....
Berlin Township.......	1	....	....	....	1	....
China Township.......	5	....	....	....	5	....
Clyde Township......	4	....	....	....	4	....
Columbus Township....	1	....	1	....	....	....
Grant Township......	1	....	1	....	....	....
Kimball Township....	2	....	....	....	....	2
Port Huron Township..	8	....	....	....	8	....
St. Clair Township.....	2	....	....	....	2	....
Marine City...........	2	....	1	1	....	....
Port Huron...........	17	....	....	....	17	....
St. Clair	7	....	....	....	7	....
Sanilac County—						
Bridgehampton Township..............	2	....	....	....	2	....
Delaware Township....	1	....	....	....	1	....
Hartwick Township....	2	....	....	....	2	....
Speaker Township.....	6	....	....	....	6	....
Wheatland Township...	11	....	....	....	11	....
Brown City...........	1	....	....	....	1	....
Shiawassee County—						
Durand	1	....	....	....	1	....
Tuscola County—						
Fairgrove Township....	3	....	....	....	2	1
Vassar Township.......	1	....	....	....	1	....
Fairgrove.............	2	....	....	....	2	....
Reese	1	....	....	....	1	....
Vassar...............	1	....	....	....	1	....
Van Buren County—						
Breedsville Township...	1	....	....	....	1	....
Washtenaw County—						
Saline Township......	1	....	....	1	....	....
Ypsilanti Township.....	1	....	1	....	....	....
Ann Arbor...........	5	....	....	....	5	....
Wayne County—						
Greenfield Township....	2	....	....	....	....	2
Romulus Township....	3	....	....	....	3	....
Springwells Township...	5	....	....	....	5	....
Hamtramck...........	5	....	....	....	5	....
Highland Park........	28	....	....	1	19	8
Northville............	1	....	....	....	....	1
Oakwood.............	1	....	....	....	1	....
Redford.............	16	....	....	....	16	....
St. Clair Heights.......	18	....	....	....	18	....
Detroit..............	338	....	....	....	....	338
Wyandotte...........	1	....	....	....	1	....
Wexford County—						
Harrietta..............	1	....	....	....	1	....
Total..............	1,069	....	11	16	652	390

SMALLPOX- Continued.

State Reports for January, 1918—Continued.

Place.	New cases reported.	Deaths.	Number vaccinated within 7 years preceding attack.	Number last vaccinated more than 7 years preceding attack.	Number never successfully vaccinated.	Vaccination history not obtained or uncertain.
Minnesota:						
Cass County—						
Pine River Township...	1					
Clay County—						
Elmwood Township....	2				2	
Cottonwood County—						
Windom.	1				1	
Crow Wing County—						
Brainerd.	16			1	15	
Dakota County—						
Lakeville Township....	1				1	
Douglas County—						
Alexandria.	3				3	
Osakis.	4				4	
Ida Township.	5				5	
Le Grande Township...	2				2	
Fillmore County—						
Beaver Township......	1				1	
Bloomfield Township...	2				1	1
Forrestville Township...	1					1
Freeborn County—						
Moscow Township.....	4				4	
Hennepin County—						
Minneapolis...........	90			11	79	
St. Louis Park........	2			1	1	
Maple Grove Township..	1				1	
Minnetonka Township..	1				1	
Isanti County—						
Springvale Township...	1				1	
Kanabec County—						
Grass Lake Township...	1				1	
Kittson County—						
Hallock.............	1				1	
Karlstad.	1				1	
Deerwood Township....	1				1	
Hallock Township.....	2				2	
Norway Township.....	1				1	
Pelan Township......	1				1	
St. Joseph Township...	1				1	
Springbrook Township..	1				1	
Lyon County—						
Marshall............	1				1	
Morrison County—						
Little Falls...........	2				2	
Murray County—						
Slayton.............	1				1	
Olmsted County—						
Rochester............	2				2	
Ottertail County—						
Aurdal Township......	6				6	
Pipestone County—						
Jasper...............	1			1		
Polk County—						
Fisher...............	1			1		
Ramsey County—						
White Bear...........	1				1	
Rice County—						
Faribault............	1				1	
Northfield..........	6			3	3	
Roseau County—						
Greenbush...........	1				1	
Roseau.............	4				1	3
Jadis Township........	1				1	
Lind Township.........	1				1	
St. Louis County—						
Duluth..............	3			1	2	
Scott County—						
New Market........	8				8	
Stearns County—						
Sauk Center............	5				5	
Crow Lake Township...	1				1	

SMALLPOX—Continued.

State Reports for January, 1918—Continued.

Place.	New cases reported.	Deaths.	Vaccination history of cases.			
			Number vaccinated within 7 years preceding attack.	Number last vaccinated more than 7 years preceding attack.	Number never successfully vaccinated.	Vaccination history not obtained or uncertain.
Minnesota—Continued.						
Todd County—						
Little Sauk Township...	2				2	
West Union Township..	1				1	
Traverse County—						
Dumont..................	1				1	
Croke Township........	3				3	
Parnell Township.......	1				1	
Washington County—						
Oakdale Township.....	1				1	
Winona County—						
Utica...................	4				4	
Winona.................	3				3	
Yellow Medicine County—						
Hazel Run Township...	1				1	
Total..................	211			19	186	6
Ohio:						
Adams County............	82				63	19
Allen County.............	28				25	3
Athens County...........	18				17	1
Auglaize County..........	13				2	11
Belmont County..........	6				6	
Brown County............	19				19	
Butler County............	40			1	33	6
Champaign County.......	1					1
Clark County.............	6				6	
Clinton County...........	2				2	
Columbiana County.......	10			2	7	1
Coshocton County........	2				1	1
Crawford County.........	1				1	
Cuyahoga County........	145				103	42
Darke County............	7				3	4
Defiance County.........	4				1	3
Delaware County........	1					1
Erie County..............	2				2	
Fairfield County.........	7			2	5	
Franklin County..........	72			2	70	
Fulton County...........	10				6	4
Gallia County............	2				2	
Greene County...........	116			1	103	12
Guernsey County........	36				22	14
Hamilton County........	45		1	1	42	1
Hancock County.........	32			1	16	15
Harrison County.........	10			1	8	1
Henry County............	202		1	10	68	123
Highland County.........	11				10	1
Hocking County..........	11				11	
Holmes County..........	29			1	16	12
Huron County...........	2				2	
Jackson County..........	47					47
Lawrence County........	7				7	
Licking County..........	9			1	3	5
Logan County............	13				12	1
Lorain County...........	42			2	38	2
Lucas County............	59			3	42	14
Mahoning County........	15			1	12	2
Medina County..........	8				8	
Mercer County..........	34				18	16
Miami County...........	18			4	14	
Montgomery County.....	32				30	2
Morrow County..........	4				1	3
Muskingum County.......	5				4	1
Ottawa County..........	2					2
Paulding County	16					16
Perry County	6				1	5
Pickaway County........	61			3	36	22
Pike County.............	1				1	
Portage County.........	18				12	6
Preble County...........	9				6	3

SMALLPOX—Continued.

State Reports for January, 1918—Continued.

Place.	New cases reported.	Deaths.	Vaccination history of cases.			
			Number vaccinated within 7 years preceding attack.	Number last vaccinated more than 7 years preceding attack.	Number never successfully vaccinated.	Vaccination history not obtained or uncertain.
Ohio—Continued.						
Putnam County	1				1	
Richland County	1					1
Ross County	4					4
Sandusky County	1				1	
Scioto County	109			1	106	2
Seneca County	2				2	
Shelby County	64			1	18	45
Stout County	35			1	13	21
Summit County	243			3	55	185
Trumbull County	12			1	10	1
Tuscarawas County	27				6	21
Union County	2					2
Van Wert County	2					2
Vinton County	2			1		1
Warren County	16				11	5
Washington County	1					1
Wayne County	43				6	37
Williams County	4				3	1
Wood County	9					9
Wyandot County	1				1	
Total	1,957		3	43	1,148	763
Wisconsin:						
Ashland County	17			8	14	
Berron County	2				2	
Buffalo County	26		2	10	7	7
Calumet County	1				1	
Clark County	1				1	
Columbia County	4					4
Crawford County	25		17		8	
Dane County	13		17			1
Dodge County	1				1	
Douglas County	4				3	1
Dunn County	21		1	1	18	1
Eau Claire County	9				9	
Fond du Lac County	7				3	
Grant County	4			4	3	1
Green County	4				4	
Jackson County	1				1	
Jefferson County	2			1	1	
Kenosha County	1					
La Crosse County	48				48	
La Fayette County	1				1	
Lincoln County	27		13	9	5	
Manitowoc County	7		2		5	
Marathon County	4		1	2		1
Marquette County	1					1
Milwaukee County	43			4	3	36
Monroe County	6			1		1
Pepin County	22			4	9	13
Racine County	4		4			
Richland County	30				30	
Rock County	72	2		1	68	3
Sauk County	22				22	
Sawyer County	1					1
Trempealeau County	7				6	
Vernon County	8			2	5	
Waukesha County	3				3	
Winnebago County	5			1	4	
Total	459	2	73	33	283	70

SMALLPOX—Continued.

Miscellaneous State Reports.

Place.	Cases.	Deaths.	Place	Cases.	Deaths
Louisiana (Jan. 1–31):			Nebraska (Jan. 1–31)—Contd.		
Ascension Parish........	1		Keith County............	3	
Caddo Parish...........	10		Knox County............	1	
Calcasieu Parish........	3		Lancaster County........	21	
East Carroll Parish......	5		Lincoln County..........	5	
Iberville Parish.........	1		Madison County.........	36	
Lincoln Parish..........	4		Merrick County..........	1	
Morehouse Parish.......	32		Morrill County..........	5	
Orleans Parish..........	32		Nance County...........	5	
Rapides Parish..........	7		Nemaha County.........	1	
Ouachita Parish........	1		Nuckolls County........	17	
St. Mary Parish........	5		Otoe County............	4	
Tangipahoa Parish......	1		Phelps County..........	7	
Terrebonne Parish......	1		Pierce County...........	33	
			Platte County..........	12	
Total...............	72		Polk County............	6	
			Redwillow County......	1	
Nebraska (Jan. 1–31):			Richardson County......	6	
Antelope County........	4		Saline County...........	2	
Boone County..........	2		Saunders County........	4	
Buffalo County.........	1		Sheridan County........	2	
Burt County...........	3		Stanton County.........	1	
Butler County..........	14		Thayer County..........	3	
Cass County...........	13		Thurston County........	2	
Cherry County.........	6		Valley County..........	4	
Cheyenne County.......	6		Scotts Bluff County.....	4	
Clay County...........	5		Webster County.........	2	
Colfax County.........	5		Wheeler County........	23	
Custer County.........	1				
Dakota County.........	1		Total...............	449	
Dawson County........	3				
Deuel County..........	11		New Jersey (Jan. 1–31):		
Dixon County..........	10		Essex County...........	1	
Dodge County.........	6				
Douglas County........	130		Vermont (Jan. 1–31):		
Frontier County........	4		Bennington County......	1	
Furnas County.........	3		Caledonia County.......	1	
Hitchcock County......	1		Orleans County.........	3	
Holt County...........	2				
Johnson County........	3		Total...............	5	
Kearney County........	1				

City Reports for Week Ended Feb. 9, 1918.

Place.	Cases.	Deaths.	Place.	Cases.	Deaths
Akron, Ohio...................	18		Duluth, Minn...............	2	
Alexandria, La...............	1		Erie, Pa...................	5	
Alton, Ill...................	15		Evansville, Ind............	3	
Ann Arbor, Mich............	1		Flint, Mich...............	11	
Anniston, Ala..............	9		Fort Smith, Ark...........	2	
Atlanta, Ga................	1		Fort Wayne, Ind..........	9	
Austin, Tex................	1		Fort Worth, Tex..........	29	
Battle Creek, Mich.........	1		Galesburg, Ill............	1	
Berlin, N. H...............	4		Grand Rapids, Mich.......	10	
Birmingham, Ala...........	25		Hammond, Ind...........	3	
Butte, Mont...............	16		Harrisburg, Pa...........	1	
Charlotte, N. C............	3		Hattiesburg, Miss.........	19	
Chattanooga, Tenn.........	2		Houston, Tex............	2	
Chicago, Ill...............	44	1	Indianapolis, Ind.........	16	
Cincinnati, Ohio...........	7		Jackson, Mich............	3	
Cleveland, Ohio............	37		Jackson, Miss............	1	
Coffeyville, Kans..........	9		Jacksonville, Fla..........	2	
Colorado Springs, Colo......	2		Jamestown, N. Y..........	1	
Columbus, Ohio............	10		Johnstown, Pa............	1	
Council Bluffs, Iowa........	17	1	Kansas City, Kans.........	58	
Covington, Ky.............	4		Kansas City, Mo..........	219	
Dallas, Tex................	8		Knoxville, Tenn..........	8	
Danville, Ill...............	1		Kokomo, Ind............	7	
Davenport, Iowa...........	2		La Crosse, Wis...........	15	
Dayton, Ohio..............	4		Leavenworth, Kans........	1	
Denver, Colo..............	24		Lima, Ohio..............	16	
Des Moines, Iowa..........	25		Lincoln, Nebr............	8	
Detroit, Mich.............	53		Little Rock, Ark..........	36	
Dubuque, Iowa............	3		Lorain, Ohio	4	

SMALLPOX—Continued.

City Reports for Week Ended Feb. 9, 1918—Continued.

Place.	Cases.	Deaths.	Place.	Cases.	Deaths.
Los Angeles, Cal..............	1	....	Racine, Wis..............	2	....
Louisville, Ky..............	2	....	Roanoke, Va..............	1	....
Madison, Wis..............	1	....	Saginaw, Mich..............	1	....
Memphis, Tenn..............	25	....	St. Joseph, Mo..............	19	....
Milwaukee, Wis..............	3	....	St. Louis, Mo..............	17	....
Minneapolis, Minn..............	26	....	Salt Lake City, Utah..............	24	....
Mobile, Ala..............	1	....	San Antonio, Tex..............	1	....
Montgomery, Ala..............	13	....	Sandusky, Ohio..............	1	....
Muncie, Ind..............	5	....	San Francisco, Cal..............	2	....
Muskegon, Mich..............	6	....	Seattle, Wash..............	7	....
Muskogee, Okla..............	5	....	Sioux City, Iowa..............	12	....
Nashville, Tenn..............	1	....	South Bend, Ind..............	4	....
New Orleans, La..............	9	....	Springfield, Ill..............	5	....
Newport, Ky..............	1	....	Superior, Wis..............	1	....
New York, N. Y..............	1	....	Terre Haute, Ind..............	3	....
Oklahoma City, Okla..............	17	1	Toledo, Ohio..............	15	....
Omaha, Nebr..............	41	....	Waco, Tex..............	1	....
Pontiac, Mich..............	6	....	Wheeling, W. Va..............	1	....
Portland, Oreg..............	1	....	Wichita, Kans..............	15	....
Quincy, Ill..............	13	....			

TETANUS.

City Reports for Week Ended Feb. 9, 1918.

Place.	Cases.	Deaths.	Place.	Cases.	Deaths.
Chicago, Ill..............	....	1	New York, N. Y..............	1	1
El Paso, Tex..............	1	1	Portsmouth, Va..............	....	1
Lincoln, Nebr..............	1	....	St. Louis, Mo..............	1	....
Memphis, Tenn..............	....	1	San Diego, Cal..............	....	1
New Orleans, La..............	....	1			

TUBERCULOSIS.

See Diphtheria, measles, scarlet fever, and tuberculosis, page 295.

TYPHOID FEVER.

State Reports for January, 1918.

Place.	New cases reported.	Place.	New cases reported.
Louisiana:		Michigan—Continued.	
Caddo Parish..............	1	Gratiot County—	
Concordia Parish..............	1	Breckenridge..............	1
Franklin Parish..............	1	Ingham County—	
Iberville Parish..............	3	Lansing..............	1
Lafourche Parish..............	1	Ionia County—	
Orleans Parish..............	9	Lake Odessa..............	1
St. Mary Parish..............	1	Isabella County—	
Vermilion Parish..............	2	Mount Pleasant..............	1
West Carroll Parish..............	1	Kalamazoo County—	
		Kalamazoo..............	1
Total..............	29	Kent County—	
		Lowell..............	3
Michigan:		Grand Rapids..............	8
Alpene County—		Lapeer County—	
Alpena..............	1	Arcadia Township..............	1
Antrim County—		Leelanau County—	
Banks Township..............	1	Elmwood Township..............	1
Bay County—		Marquette County—	
Bay City..............	2	Marquette..............	3
Genesee County—		Mecosta County—	
Flint..............	2	Big Rapids..............	2

TYPHOID FEVER—Continued.

State Reports for January, 1918—Continued.

Place.	New cases reported.	Place.	New cases reported.
Michigan - Continued.		**New Jersey—Continued.**	
Menominee County—		Burlington County.................	1
Menominee....................	1	Camden County....................	6
Misaukee County—		Cape May County.................	2
Richland Township............	1	Essex County.....................	10
Monroe County—		Gloucester County................	4
Bedford Township............	3	Hudson County....................	1
Oakland County—		Hunterdon County................	1
Pontiac......................	1	Mercer County....................	4
Saginaw County—		Monmouth County................	3
Saginaw......................	4	Morris County....................	2
Van Buren County—		Passaic County...................	2
Port Huron..................	1	Somerset County..................	3
Washtenaw County—		Sussex County....................	1
Ann Arbor...................	1	Warren County...................	1
Wayne County—			
Ford........................	3	Total...............	50
Total......................	44	**Ohio:**	
		Ashtabula County.................	4
Minnesota:		Athens County....................	4
Anoka County—		Belmont County...................	4
Anoka.......................	1	Champaign County................	1
Beltrami County—		Clark County.....................	10
Baudette....................	1	Columbiana County...............	6
Chisago County—		Cuyahoga County.................	11
Center City..................	1	Franklin County..................	3
Rush City...................	1	Fulton County....................	9
Hennepin County—		Guernsey County.................	1
Excelsior....................	1	Hamilton County.................	3
Minneapolis..................	16	Henry County....................	1
Le Sueur County—		Logan County....................	2
Kasota Township.............	2	Lucas County....................	6
Marshall County—		Mahoning County................	3
Oslo........................	1	Monroe County...................	1
Nicollet County—		Muskingum County...............	4
St. Peter....................	1	Paulding County..................	2
Olmsted County—		Portage County...................	6
Rochester...................	1	Ross County......................	2
Otter Tail County—		Scioto County....................	2
Fergus Falls.................	1	Summit County...................	6
Ramsey County—		Trumbull County.................	3
St. Paul....................	2	Warren County...................	1
White Bear..................	1	Washington County...............	2
Red Lake County—		Williams County..................	1
Red Lake Falls..............	1	Wood County.....................	3
River Township..............	1		
Redwood County—		Total................	107
Wabasso.....................	1		
Rice County—		**Rhode Island:**	
Faribault....................	1	Providence.......................	3
Wells Township..............	1	Tiverton (town)...................	1
St. Louis County—			
Aurora......................	2	Total...............	4
Duluth......................	3		
Virginia....................	1	**Vermont:**	
Morse Township.............	1	Addison County..................	5
Stearns County—		Bennington County...............	1
St. Cloud...................	1	Orange County...................	1
Wabasha County—			
Maseppa Township..........	1	Total.......	7
Washington County—			
Stillwater...................	1	**Wisconsin:**	
		Brown County....................	2
Total..................	44	Eau Claire County................	1
		Forest County....................	1
Nebraska:		Manitowoc County................	1
Antelope County..................	1	Marathon County.................	7
Cedar County....................	1	Milwaukee County................	11
Douglas County..................	1	Price County.....................	1
Lancaster County................	1	Racine County....................	1
		Sheboygan County................	4
Total..................	4	Waupaca County..................	1
		Winnebago County................	1
New Jersey:		Wood County....................	1
Atlantic County..................	1		
Bergen County...................	2	Total........	32

TYPHOID FEVER—Continued.

City Reports for Week Ended Feb. 9, 1918.

Place.	Cases.	Deaths.	Place.	Cases.	Deaths.
Albany, N. Y	3	....	Minneapolis, Minn....	6	....
Ann Arbor, Mich.........	1	....	Moline, Ill...........	1	1
Atlantic City, N. J....	1	....	Nashville, Tenn.....	1	....
Baltimore, Md.........	2	....	New Bedford, Mass....	2	1
Boston, Mass...........	2	1	New Orleans, La......	....	2
Buffalo, N. Y...........	1	....	New York, N. Y......	30	4
Chicago, Ill...........	4	....	Petersburg, Va.......	....	1
Dayton, Ohio...........	1	1	Philadelphia, Pa.....	8	3
Detroit, Mich...........	2	....	Pittsburgh, Pa.......	4	1
East Chicago, Ind.....	1	1	Rochester, N. Y......	1	....
Elmira, N. Y...........	....	1	Sacramento, Cal......	1	1
Fall River, Mass.......	1	....	St. Louis, Mo.........	4	....
Fitchburg, Mass.......	2	....	Salt Lake City, Utah.	1	....
Galesburg, Ill.........	1	2	San Antonio, Tex.....	1	2
Hammond, Ind.........	3	....	San Francisco, Cal...	1	1
Houston, Tex...........	1	....	Seattle, Wash........	1	....
Jersey City, N. J......	1	....	Stockton, Cal........	2	....
Kansas City, Mo.......	3	....	Syracuse, N. Y......	1	1
Lancaster, Pa.........	1	....	Toledo, Ohio.........	1	1
Lawrence, Mass.......	2	....	Trenton, N. J.......	2	1
Lexington, Ky.........	1	1	Washington, D. C....	2	1
Los Angeles, Cal......	2	....	Wilkinsburg, Pa.....	2	1
Louisville, Ky.........	1	1	Wilmington, Del.....	1	....
Milwaukee, Wis........	4	2	Winston-Salem, N. C.	....	1

DIPHTHERIA, MEASLES, SCARLET FEVER, AND TUBERCULOSIS.

State Reports for January, 1918.

State.	Cases reported.			State.	Cases reported.		
	Diphtheria.	Measles.	Scarlet fever.		Diphtheria.	Measles.	Scarlet fever.
Louisiana...........	84	989	31	Ohio...............	556	997	861
Michigan...........	587	672	1,048	Rhode Island.......	87	55	45
Minnesota..........	311	456	325	Vermont...........	17	29	44
Nebraska...........	55	286	171	Wisconsin..........	241	1,122	715
New Jersey.........	420	2,423	407				

City Reports for Week Ended Feb. 9, 1918.

City.	Population as of July 1, 1916. (Estimated by U. S. Census Bureau.)	Total deaths from all causes.	Diphtheria.		Measles.		Scarlet fever.		Tuberculosis.	
			Cases.	Deaths.	Cases.	Deaths.	Cases.	Deaths.	Cases.	Deaths.
Over 500,000 inhabitants:										
Baltimore, Md..........	589,621	285	18	2	129	1	7	......	51	26
Boston, Mass..........	756,476	312	92	6	125	1	56	2	53	25
Chicago, Ill..........	2,497,722	692	103	18	51	1	47	......	409	77
Cleveland, Ohio........	674,073	215	60	7	12	1	5	......	35	23
Detroit, Mich..........	571,784	287	60	7	25	2	33	1	39	21
Los Angeles, Cal......	503,812	170	14	......	177	1	17	......	44	26
New York, N. Y.......	5,602,841	......	1,047	22	4,264	26	579	5	1,538	208
Philadelphia, Pa.......	1,709,518	729	57	12	148	2	25	1	107	93
Pittsburgh, Pa.........	579,090	232	10	1	171	3	3	......	25	9
St. Louis, Mo..........	757,309	247	47	2	63	......	24	......	34	16
From 300,000 to 500,000 inhabitants:										
Buffalo, N. Y..........	468,558	186	7	4	22	1	11	1	35	21
Cincinnati, Ohio.......	419,476	157	10	1	16	2	8	......	24	22
Jersey City, N. J......	306,345	......	12	......	46	......	12	......	6	......
Milwaukee, Wis........	436,535	98	7	1	105	......	40	......	17	3

DIPHTHERIA, MEASLES, SCARLET FEVER, AND TUBERCULOSIS—Continued.

City Reports for Week Ended February 9, 1918—Continued.

City.	Population as of July 1, 1916 (estimated by U. S. Census Bureau).	Total deaths from all causes.	Diphtheria.		Measles.		Scarlet fever.		Tuberculosis.	
			Cases.	Deaths.	Cases.	Deaths.	Cases.	Deaths.	Cases.	Deaths.
From 300,000 to 500,000 inhabitants:—Continued.										
Minneapolis, Minn	363,454	131	17		29		22	1	22	12
Newark, N. J.	408,894	131	36	2	128		10		40	15
New Orleans, La.	371,747	183	6		113				44	21
San Francisco, Cal.	463,516	134	15	1	51		16		33	10
Seattle, Wash.	348,639		5		212		8		12	2
Washington, D. C.	363,980	167	9	1	281	3	41		16	13
From 200,000 to 300,000 inhabitants:										
Columbus, Ohio	214,878	62			27		28		11	6
Denver, Colo.	260,800	77	2		182		26			12
Indianapolis, Ind.	271,708	95	20		46	1	48		12	3
Kansas City, Mo.	297,847	110	9	3	190	3	61			11
Louisville, Ky.	238,910	121	4		34		3		4	10
Portland, Oreg.	295,463	55	7		30		12			5
Providence, R. I.	254,960	86	11	4	17	1	5		1	7
Rochester, N. Y.	256,417	79	11		29	1	22	1	21	6
From 100,000 to 200,000 inhabitants:										
Albany, N. Y.	104,199		7		11				1	
Atlanta, Ga.	190,558	78	8		10		3			4
Birmingham, Ala.	181,762	88	1		122	4	6		9	1
Bridgeport, Conn.	121,579	65	8	1	5	1	4	1	4	3
Cambridge, Mass.	112,981	49	8		28	3	2		5	3
Camden, N. J.	106,233		5		30				8	
Dallas, Tex.	124,527	49	2	2	94	1			4	6
Dayton, Ohio	127,224	52			19		9	1	6	2
Des Moines, Iowa	101,598						12			
Fall River, Mass.	128,366	35	8	1	9		6		9	3
Fort Worth, Tex.	104,562	50	2		4	1	1		2	2
Grand Rapids, Mich.	128,291	41	9	2	10		1		5	
Hartford, Conn.	110,900	55	5		2		5		8	3
Houston, Tex.	112,307	47	4		11				3	5
Lawrence, Mass.	100,560	35	3		19				6	6
Lowell, Mass.	113,245	45	3		1		3		5	4
Lynn, Mass.	102,425	39	2		2		5		3	4
Memphis, Tenn.	148,995	70	2		14	2	2		12	10
Nashville, Tenn.	117,057	48			13		1		1	9
New Bedford, Mass.	118,158	45	4		13		2		8	7
New Haven, Conn.	149,685	55	3		3		4		4	3
Oakland, Cal.	198,604	36	1		26		4		6	4
Omaha, Nebr.	165,470	38	7		54		7			4
Reading, Pa.	109,381	26	1		1		1		3	1
Richmond, Va.	156,687	61	3		64	1	7		9	9
Salt Lake City, Utah	117,399	35	1		52		13			1
San Antonio, Tex.	123,531	121	2		12	1	1			14
Scranton, Pa.	146,811	51	3				3		1	4
Springfield, Mass.	105,942	40	7	1	34		4		2	5
Syracuse, N. Y.	155,624	50	17	3	95	5	23		3	1
Tacoma, Wash.	112,770		2		2		8			
Toledo, Ohio	191,554	66	2		22	1	10			2
Trenton, N. J.	111,593	36	6	1	12		1		5	2
Worcester, Mass.	163,314	57	3	1	7	1	6		6	2
From 50,000 to 100,000 inhabitants:										
Akron, Ohio	85,625		9		11		15		12	
Allentown, Pa.	63,505	22	5	1	43				1	
Altoona, Pa.	58,659		2		1		1		1	
Atlantic City, N. J.	57,660	10			5				2	1
Bayonne, N. J.	69,983		1		14		2		3	
Berkeley, Cal.	57,653	10	1		2		1			
Binghamton, N. Y.	53,973	25	1		25		7		11	1
Canton, Ohio	60,852	20			1				1	
Charleston, S. C.	60,734	32		1						2
Chattanooga, Tenn.	60,075		2		10		3		3	2
Covington, Ky.	57,144	34	2		1		2		3	2
Duluth, Minn.	94,495	20			53				5	2
El Paso, Tex.	63,705	47			19		1			12
Erie, Pa.	75,195	47	7	1	3		32		11	2
Evansville, Ind.	76,078	26	2		10		3		6	2
Flint, Mich.	51,772	20	1	1	1		5	1	7	2

DIPHTHERIA, MEASLES, SCARLET FEVER, AND TUBERCULOSIS—
Continued.

City Reports for Week Ended Feb. 9, 1918—Continued.

City.	Population as of July 1, 1916 (estimated by U. S. Census Bureau).	Total deaths from all causes.	Diphtheria.		Measles.		Scarlet fever.		Tuberculosis.	
			Cases.	Deaths.	Cases.	Deaths.	Cases.	Deaths.	Cases.	Deaths.
From 50,000 to 100,000 inhabitants—Continued.										
Fort Wayne, Ind.	76,183	25	3	....	....	....	3	....	1	2
Harrisburg, Pa.	72,015	28	7	1	5	....	2	....	2	1
Hoboken, N. J.	77,214	19	....	....	....	1	....	....	....	2
Holyoke, Mass.	65,286	....	1	....	8	1	....	....	....	2
Johnstown, Pa.	68,529	28	2	....	....	....	2	....	1	2
Kansas City, Kans.	99,437	....	1	....	40	1	11	....	1	1
Lancaster, Pa.	50,853	....	1	....	10	....	6	....	1	1
Little Rock, Ark.	57,342	21	1	....	16	....	1	....	....	3
Malden, Mass.	51,155	12	1	....	10	1	....	....	....	1
Manchester, N. H.	78,283	....	4	....	8	....	8	....	7	3
Mobile, Ala.	58,221	22	....	....	6	....	....	....	....	3
New Britain, Conn.	53,794	15	1	....	4	....	1	....	....	....
Norfolk, Va.	89,612	....	3	....	27	....	2	....	....	9
Oklahoma City, Okla.	92,943	18	1	....	15	....	1	....	....	....
Passaic, N. J.	71,744	20	2	....	1	....	1	....	....	3
Pawtucket, R. I.	59,411	13	....	....	2	....	2	....	1	....
Portland, Me.	63,867	19	1	1	32	....	....	....	....	3
Rockford, Ill.	55,185	13	1	....	9	....	....	....	....	....
Sacramento, Cal.	66,895	25	....	....	28	....	1	....	....	1
Saginaw, Mich.	55,642	28	1	....	1	....	2	....	2	....
St. Joseph, Mo.	85,236	32	2	1	60	....	2	....	1	3
San Diego, Cal.	53,330	....	2	....	200	....	5	....	14	....
Savannah, Ga.	68,805	38	3	1	24	....	....	....	2	3
Schenectady, N. Y.	99,519	18	....	....	5	....	1	....	6	3
Sioux City, Iowa.	57,078	....	1	....	....	....	20	....	....	....
Somerville, Mass.	87,039	27	2	1	42	....	3	....	3	....
South Bend, Ind.	68,946	16	1	....	6	....	1	....	....	2
Springfield, Ill.	61,120	24	1	....	7	....	....	....	....	....
Springfield, Ohio.	51,550	15	....	....	5	....	1	....	6	1
Terre Haute, Ind.	66,083	14	3	....	22	....	1	....	2	1
Troy, N. Y.	77,916	35	1	....	1	....	2	....	....	2
Wichita, Kans.	70,722	....	1	....	134	....	3	....	....	....
Wilkes-Barre, Pa.	76,776	18	2	....	23	....	5	....	4	....
Wilmington, Del.	94,265	44	....	....	5	....	....	....	....	5
Yonkers, N. Y.	99,838	115	4	....	4	....	7	....	....	....
From 25,000 to 50,000 inhabitants:										
Alameda, Cal.	27,732	4	2	....	6	....	1	....	6	2
Auburn, N. Y.	37,385	9	2	....	5	....	2	....	....	....
Austin, Tex.	34,814	19	2	....	....	....	....	....	....	3
Battle Creek, Mich.	29,480	....	6	....	16	....	2	....	....	....
Brookline, Mass.	32,730	12	5	....	15	....	1	....	1	....
Butler, Pa.	27,632	13	2	....	9	....	....	....	....	1
Butte, Mont.	43,425	....	1	....	5	....	8	....	....	....
Charlotte, N. C.	39,823	....	1	....	18	....	....	....	2	....
Chelsea, Mass.	46,192	17	....	....	7	....	2	....	1	2
Chicopee, Mass.	29,319	3	....	....	1	....	....	....	2	1
Colorado Springs, Colo.	32,971	6	....	....	18	....	1	....	5	2
Columbia, S. C.	34,611	....	1	....	2	....	....	....	3	....
Council Bluffs, Iowa.	31,484	....	....	....	3	....	2	....	....	....
Cranston, R. I.	25,987	....	....	....	....	....	1	....	1	2
Cumberland, Md.	26,074	4	1	....	....	....	....	....	....	....
Danville, Ill.	32,261	11	2	....	1	....	....	....	....	....
Davenport, Iowa.	43,811	....	....	....	....	....	10	1	....	....
Dubuque, Iowa.	39,873	....	....	....	8	....	....	....	....	3
Durham, N. C.	25,061	11	3	....	6	....	....	....	....	3
East Chicago, Ind.	28,743	16	....	....	....	....	....	....	....	3
Easton, Pa.	30,530	19	....	....	13	....	....	....	1	2
East Orange, N. J.	42,458	9	1	....	9	....	....	....	1	....
Elgin, Ill.	28,203	9	....	....	3	....	....	....	....	....
Elmira, N. Y.	38,120	7	2	....	20	....	2	....	2	2
Everett, Mass.	39,233	10	3	....	2	....	....	....	2	1
Everett, Wash.	35,486	7	....	....	....	....	....	....	1	....
Fitchburg, Mass.	41,781	9	1	....	9	....	....	....	1	1
Fort Smith, Ark.	28,638	....	1	....	5	....	....	....	....	....
Galveston, Tex.	41,863	13	1	....	....	....	1	....	....	1
Green Bay, Wis.	29,353	14	....	....	....	....	....	....	....	....
Hagerstown, Md.	25,679	....	....	....	5	....	3	....	....	....
Hammond, Ind.	26,171	10	1	1	....	....	2	....	....	....
Haverhill, Mass.	48,477	14	....	....	39	1	1	....	6	....
Jackson, Mich.	38,363	14	1	....	7	....	31	1	1	....

DIPHTHERIA, MEASLES, SCARLET FEVER, AND TUBERCULOSIS - Continued.

City Reports for Week Ended Feb. 9, 1918—Continued.

City.	Population as of July 1, 1916 (estimated by U.S. Census Bureau).	Total deaths from all causes.	Diphtheria.		Measles.		Scarlet fever.		Tuberculosis.	
			Cases.	Deaths.	Cases.	Deaths.	Cases.	Deaths.	Cases.	Deaths.
From 25,000 to 50,000 inhabitants—Continued.										
Jackson, Miss............	29,737				10				1	
Jamestown, N.Y..........	36,580	14	4						2	1
Kalamazoo, Mich.........	48,898	17	4	1	7		1		3	
Kenosha, Wis............	31,576		4				9			
Kingston, N.Y...........	26,771	10								
Knoxville, Tenn.........	38,678				13					
La Crosse, Wis..........	31,677	12	2				2			
Lexington, Ky...........	41,097	28			26		2			1
Lima, Ohio..............	35,384	12			2					1
Lincoln, Nebr...........	46,515	20	1		2		5			
Long Beach, Cal.........	27,587	16	1		31		4			1
Lorain, Ohio............	36,964	1					2		2	
Lynchburg, Va...........	32,940	15			2		1			
Macon, Ga...............	45,757	46	1		22		4			1
Madison, Wis............	30,699	11	2		10		2			2
McKeesport, Pa..........	47,521		3		24					
Medford, Mass...........	26,234	9	1		7				1	1
Moline, Ill.............	27,451	12	2		2		1		1	1
Montclair, N.J..........	26,318	3			101		3			
Montgomery, Ala.........	43,285	13	1		43				1	2
Mount Vernon, N.Y.......	37,009	9	4		61		2		7	
Muncie, Ind.............	25,424		2		7				2	
Muskegon, Mich..........	26,100	14								
Muskogee, Okla..........	44,218		2		20		3			
Newburgh, N.Y...........	29,603	7			12		2		1	2
New Castle, Pa..........	41,133		1				2			
Newport, Ky.............	31,927	15	1		2					
Newport, R.I............	30,108	3	1				1			
Newton, Mass............	43,715	6	2		23				2	
Niagara Falls, N.Y......	37,353	15	2		1		5		2	1
Norristown, Pa..........	31,401	9					1			
Oak Park, Ill...........	26,654	14			5		1			
Ogden, Utah.............	41,401		1		19		3			
Orange, N.J.............	31,040	9			20					
Pasadena, Cal...........	45,150	12			29		2			1
Perth Amboy, N.J........	41,185	13	2	1	4				1	1
Petersburg, Va..........	25,582	22			4	1			1	
Pittsfield, Mass........	38,729	20			4				1	
Portsmouth, Va..........	39,651	11			10		2			
Quincy, Ill.............	36,794	17	2		4					
Quincy, Mass............	38,136	15	3		16		1		1	1
Racine, Wis.............	46,446	20	1		15		1		6	2
Roanoke, Va.............	43,284	16	1		8				7	
Rock Island, Ill........	28,926	12			4		2			
Salem, Mass.............	44,562	17	1		16					1
San Jose, Cal...........	38,902				6					
Steubenville, Ohio......	27,445	11	1		2					
Stockton, Cal...........	35,358	10			23		1		9	5
Superior, Wis...........	46,226	9			11		1		2	2
Taunton, Mass...........	36,283	9	1		11		1		2	1
Waco, Tex...............	33,385		3		6					
Waltham, Mass...........	30,570	10			6		1		2	
Watertown, N.Y..........	29,694				33				1	1
West Hoboken, N.J.......	43,139	3	1		2					2
Wheeling, W.Va..........	43,377	17							1	1
Wilmington, N.C.........	29,892	21								2
Winston-Salem, N.C......	31,155	22			40				8	
Zanesville, Ohio........	30,863	11								
From 10,000 to 25,000 inhabitants.										
Alexandria, La..........	17,846	6			2		1			
Alton, Ill..............	22,874	11			18					3
Ann Arbor, Mich.........	15,010	5	2		14		2			
Anniston, Ala...........	14,112		1		1				1	
Berlin, N.H.............	13,599	3	1							
Braddock, Pa............	21,685	11			2				1	1
Cairo, Ill..............	15,794	7							1	1
Chillicothe, Ohio.......	15,470	7			5		4			1
Clinton, Mass	¹13,075	2								1

¹ Population Apr. 15, 1910; no estimate made.

DIPHTHERIA, MEASLES, SCARLET FEVER, AND TUBERCULOSIS—
Continued.

City Reports for Week Ended Feb. 9, 1918—Continued.

City.	Population as of July 1, 1916 (estimated by U. S. Census Bureau).	Total deaths from all causes.	Diphtheria.		Measles.		Scarlet fever.		Tuberculosis.	
			Cases.	Deaths.	Cases.	Deaths.	Cases.	Deaths.	Cases.	Deaths.
From 10,000 to 25,000 inhabitants—Continued.										
Coffeyville, Kans...........	17,548	......	1	......	13	......	1	......	2	......
Concord, N. H............	22,669	8	2	......	......	......	1	......	......	1
Galesburg, Ill............	24,276	7	......	......	......	......	1	......	......	......
Greenville, S. C..........	18,181	4	......	......	2	......	......	......	......	......
Harrison, N. J............	16,950	......	......	......	......	......	......	......	......	......
Hattiesburg, Miss.........	16,482	10	......	......	2	......	......	......	1	......
Kearny, N. J..............	23,539	9	......	......	25	......	3	......	1	......
Kokomo, Ind..............	20,930	7	2	......	......	......	......	......	......	......
Leavenworth, Kans........	1 19,363	6	1	......	5	......	2	1	......	......
Marinette, Wis...........	1 14,610	4	......	......	......	......	1	......	......	......
Melrose, Mass............	17,445	1	1	......	1	......	2	......	......	......
Muscatine, Iowa..........	17,500	......	......	......	......	......	1	......	......	......
Nanticoke, Pa............	23,126	10	1	......	......	......	1	......	......	......
New Albany, Ind..........	22,629	6	......	......	4	......	......	......	......	1
Newburyport, Mass........	15,243	6	......	......	4	......	......	......	2	......
New London, Conn........	20,965	4	......	......	2	......	1	......	2	......
North Adams, Mass........	1 22,019	11	......	......	......	......	......	......	......	......
Northampton, Mass........	19,926	12	1	......	......	......	......	......	2	2
Plainfield, N. J...........	23,905	9	......	......	......	......	......	......	2	......
Pontiac, Mich............	17,524	16	......	......	5	......	2	......	2	1
Portsmouth, N. H.........	11,566	......	......	......	......	......	2	......	......	......
Rocky Mount, N. C........	12,067	3	1	......	2	......	......	......	......	1
Sandusky, Ohio...........	20,193	4	......	......	......	......	......	......	2	......
Saratoga Springs, N. Y....	13,821	4	......	......	5	......	1	......	1	......
Spartanburg, S. C.........	21,365	15	......	......	3	......	2	......	1	2
Steelton, Pa..............	15,548	......	......	......	......	......	1	......	......	......
Washington, Pa...........	21,618	......	......	......	26	......	......	......	2	......
Wilkinsburg, Pa..........	23,228	8	1	......	11	......	1	......	2	......
Woburn, Mass............	16,969	6	......	......	......	......	......	......	......	......

1 Population Apr. 15, 1910; no estimate made.

22

FOREIGN.

CUBA.

Communicable Diseases—Habana.

Communicable diseases have been notified at Habana as follows:

Diseases.	Jan. 21–31, 1918.		Cases remaining under treatment Jan. 31, 1918.	Diseases.	Jan. 21–31, 1918.		Cases remaining under treatment Jan. 31, 1918.
	New cases.	Deaths.			New cases.	Deaths.	
Cerebrospinal meningitis.......	....	....	1	Paratyphoid fever...	....	....	1
Diphtheria.........	12	1	5	Scarlet fever.......	1	....	3
Leprosy............	....	....	11	Smallpox...........	....	....	2
Malaria............	20	....	¹ 21	Typhoid fever......	16	1	¹ 89
Measles............	10	....	21	Varicella...........	61	....	76

¹ About one-half from the interior.

INDIA.

Cholera—Plague—Smallpox—Madras Presidency—Year, 1916.

During the year 1916, 875,013 deaths were notified in the Presidency of Madras. Of these, 16,735 were due to cholera, 11,498 to plague, and 21,903 to smallpox.

The number of deaths from cholera showed a progressive decrease from the number reported in 1914, viz, 68,449, and that for 1915, viz, 30,098. One district remained free from the disease and in one only 11 deaths from cholera were notified. Thirty deaths from cholera were notified in Madras city.

The number of deaths from plague rose from 3,889 in 1915 to 11,498 in 1916. The disease was especially prevalent in the districts of Coimbatore, Salem, and Bellary. The chief remedial measure was evacuation of infected villages.

Smallpox was present in 1916 in all districts of the Madras Presidency, but with a lower mortality than in 1915, the number of deaths being 21,903 as against 24,038. Fifteen municipalities remained free from the disease. A large proportion of the deaths occurred among children under 11 years of age.

The population of the Madras Presidency on which vital statistics were returned was 40,005,735.

Malaria—1916.

Malaria investigations were not generally carried out owing to war conditions. Itinerant dispensaries were operated in certain districts, and antimalarial measures were generally undertaken by the local bodies concerned, including quinine administration to all persons in the infected areas.

PORTUGAL.

Typhus Fever—Lisbon—Oporto.

On February 21, 1918, typhus fever was reported present at Lisbon, Portugal, with a few cases, and at Oporto in epidemic form.

CHOLERA, PLAGUE, SMALLPOX, TYPHUS FEVER, AND YELLOW FEVER.

Reports Received During Week Ended Mar. 1, 1918.[1]

CHOLERA.

Place.	Date.	Cases.	Deaths.	Remarks.
Philippine Islands:				
Provinces—				Dec. 30, 1917–Jan. 5, 1918: Cases 134; deaths, 98.
Bohol	Dec. 30–Jan. 5	16	15	
Capiz	do	6	7	
Cebu	do	21	11	
Iloilo	do	14	10	
Mindanao	do	74	52	
Oriental Negros	do	3	3	
Provinces—				Jan. 6–12, 1918: Cases, 91; deaths, 72.
Bohol	Jan. 6–12	23	21	
Capiz	do	12	11	
Cebu	do	3	1	
Iloilo	do	12	8	
Mindanao	do	40	30	
Oriental Negros	do	1	1	

PLAGUE.

Place.	Date.	Cases.	Deaths.	Remarks.
Ecuador—				Sept. 1–Nov. 30, 1917: Cases, 68; deaths, 24.
Guayaquil	Sept. 1–30	3	1	
Do	Oct. 1–31	20	8	
Do	Nov. 1–30	45	15	

SMALLPOX.

Place.	Date.	Cases.	Deaths.	Remarks.
Canada:				
Nova Scotia—				
Sydney	Feb. 3–9	1		
Prince Edward Island—				
Charlottetown	Feb. 7–13	1		
Ecuador				Sept. 1–Nov. 30, 1917: Cases, 26; deaths, 2.
Guayaquil	Sept. 1–30	8		
Do	Oct. 1–31	14	1	
Do	Nov. 1–30	4	1	
Egypt:				
Cairo	Nov. 12–18	1		
Italy:				
Leghorn	Jan. 7–13	7		
Mexico:				
Aguascalientes	Feb. 4–10		1	
Mazatlan	Jan. 29–Feb. 5	2		
Vera Cruz	Jan. 27–Feb. 9	4		

[1] From medical officers of the Public Health Service, American consuls, and other sources.

CHOLERA, PLAGUE, SMALLPOX, TYPHUS FEVER, AND YELLOW FEVER—Continued.

Reports Received During Week Ended Mar. 1, 1918—Continued.

SMALLPOX—Continued.

Place.	Date.	Cases.	Deaths.	Remarks.
Porto Rico:				
San Juan	Jan. 28–Feb. 3	1		Varioloid.
Portugal:				
Lisbon	Dec. 23–29	1		
Do	Dec. 30–Jan. 19	2		
Portuguese East Africa:				
Lourenço Marques	Nov. 1–30		4	

TYPHUS FEVER.

Mexico:				
Aguascalientes	Feb. 4–10		10	
Portugal:				
Lisbon	Feb. 21			Present.
Oporto	do			Epidemic.
Switzerland:				
Basel	Jan. 6–12		1	
Zurich	Jan. 13–19	2		

YELLOW FEVER.

Ecuador				Sept 1–Nov. 30, 1917: Cases, &
Guayaquil	Sept. 1–30	1	1	deaths, 3.
Do	Oct. 1–31	1		
Do	Nov. 1–30	2	2	
Yaguachi	do	1		
Honduras:				
Tegucigalpa	Jan. 7–19		1	

Reports Received from Dec. 29, 1917, to Feb. 22, 1918.

CHOLERA.

Place.	Date.	Cases.	Deaths.	Remarks.
China:				
Antung	Nov. 26–Dec. 2	3	1	
India:				
Bombay	Oct. 28–Nov. 24	17	12	
Calcutta	Sept. 16–Nov. 24		76	
Madras	Nov. 25–Dec. 1	1	1	
Rangoon	Nov. 4–Dec. 1	3	3	
Indo-China				
Provinces				Sept. 1–30, 1917 Cases, 74, deaths,
Anam	Sept. 1–30	13	10	37.
Cambodia	do	19	12	
Cochin-China	do	32	13	
Saigon	Nov. 22–29	1		
Kwang-Chow-Wan	Sept. 1–30	10	2	
Java:				
East Java	Oct. 28–Nov. 3	1	1	
West Java				Oct. 19–Dec. 20, 1917: Cases, 100;
Batavia	Oct. 19–Dec. 20	55	21	deaths, 57.
Persia:				
Mazanderan Province--				
Astrabad	July 31			Present.
Barfrush	July 1–27	34	23	
Chahmirzad				25 cases reported July 31, 1917.
Chahradagh	June 15–July 27	10	8	
Kharek	May 28–June 11	21	13	
Sari	July 3–29	273	144	
Yekchambe-Bazar	June 3	6		

CHOLERA, PLAGUE, SMALLPOX, TYPHUS FEVER, AND YELLOW FEVER—Continued.

Reports Received from Dec. 29, 1917, to Feb. 22, 1918—Continued.

CHOLERA—Continued.

Place.	Date.	Cases.	Deaths.	Remarks.
Philippine Islands:				
Provinces				Nov. 18–Dec. 29, 1917: Cases,
Antique	Nov. 18–Dec. 1	45	32	1,053; deaths, 693.
Bohol	Nov. 18–Dec. 29	169	111	
Capis	Nov. 25–Dec. 29	27	21	
Cebu	Dec. 23–29	3		
Iloilo	Nov. 25–Dec. 29	179	135	
Leyte	Nov. 25–Dec. 22	13	12	
Mindanao	Nov. 25–Dec. 29	337	195	
Occidental Negros	Nov. 25–Dec. 22	177	123	
Oriental Negros	Nov. 25–Dec. 29	99	62	
Romblon	Nov. 25–Dec. 1	1	1	
Siam:				
Bangkok	Sept. 16–22	1	1	
Turkey in Asia:				
Bagdad	Nov. 1–15		40	

PLAGUE.

Place.	Date.	Cases.	Deaths.	Remarks.
Brazil:				
Bahia	Nov. 4–Dec. 15	4	4	
British Gold Coast:				
Axim	Jan. 8			Present.
Ceylon:				
Colombo	Oct. 14–Dec. 1	14	13	
Egypt				Jan. 1–Nov. 15, 1917: Cases, 728;
Port Said	July 23–29	1	2	deaths, 308.
India				Sept. 16–Dec. 1, 1917: Cases,
Bombay	Oct. 28–Dec. 1	103	85	151,751; deaths, 113,434.
Calcutta	Sept. 16–29		2	
Henzada	Oct. 21–27		1	
Karachi	Oct. 21–Dec. 1	11	9	
Madras Presidency	Oct. 31–Nov. 17	3,294	2,560	
Mandalay	Oct. 14–Nov. 17		89	
Rangoon	Oct. 21–Dec. 1	32	38	
Indo-China:				
Provinces				Sept. 1–30, 1917: Cases, 34; deaths,
Anam	Sept. 1–30	12	11	30.
Cambodia	do	12	11	
Cochin-China	do	10	8	
Saigon	Oct. 31–Nov. 18	8	4	
Java:				
East Java				Oct. 27–Nov. 25, 1917: Cases, 75;
Surabaya	Nov. 11–25	2	2	deaths, 73.
West Java				Nov. 25–Dec. 9, 1917: Cases, 45; deaths, 45.
Senegal:				
St. Louis	Feb. 2			Present.
Siam:				
Bangkok	Sept. 16–Nov. 24	11	7	
Straits Settlements:				
Singapore	Oct. 28–Dec. 22	4	6	

SMALLPOX.

Place.	Date.	Cases.	Deaths.	Remarks.
Algeria:				
Algiers	Nov. 1–Dec. 31	3	1	
Australia:				
New South Wales				July 12–Dec. 20, 1917: Cases, 36.
Abermain	Oct. 25–Nov. 20	3		Newcastle district.
Cessnock	July 12–Oct. 11	7		
Eumangia	Aug. 15	1		
Kurri Kurri	Dec. 5–20	2		
Mungindi	Aug. 13	1		
Warren	July 12–Oct. 25	22		
Brazil:				
Bahia	Nov. 10–Dec. 8	3		
Pernambuco	Nov. 1–15	1		
Rio de Janeiro	Sept. 30–Dec. 22	664	134	
Sao Paulo	Oct. 29–Nov. 4			

CHOLERA, PLAGUE, SMALLPOX, TYPHUS FEVER, AND YELLOW FEVER—Continued.

Reports Received from Dec. 29, 1917, to Feb. 22, 1918—Continued.

SMALLPOX—Continued.

Place.	Date.	Cases.	Deaths.	Remarks.
Canada:				
British Columbia—				
Vancouver	Jan. 13–19	3		
Victoria	Jan. 7–Feb. 2	2		
Winnipeg	Dec. 30–Jan. 5	1		
New Brunswick—				
Kent County	Dec. 4			Outbreak. On main line Canadian Ry., 25 miles north of Moncton.
Do	Jan. 22	40		In 7 localities.
Northumberland County.	do	41		In 5 localities.
Restigouche County	Jan. 18	60		
Victoria County	Jan 22	10		At Limestone and a lumber camp.
Westmoreland County.				
Moncton	Jan. 20–Feb. 9.	4		
York County	Jan. 22	8		
Ontario—				
Hamilton	Dec. 16–22	1		
Do	Jan. 13–19	2		
Sarnia	Dec. 9–15	1		
Do	Jan. 6–Feb. 2	20		
Windsor	Dec. 30–Jan. 5	1		
Quebec—				
Montreal	Dec. 16–Jan. 5	5		
Do	Jan. 6–12	1		
China:				
Amoy	Oct. 27–Nov. 25			Present.
Antung	Dec. 3–23	13	2	
Do	Jan. 7–13	2		
Chungking	Nov. 11–Dec. 15			Do.
Dairen	Nov. 18–Dec. 22	3	1	
Harbin	May 14–June 30	20		Chinese Eastern Ry.
Do	July 1–Dec. 2	7		Do.
Hungtahotse Station	Oct. 28–Nov. 4	1		Do.
Manchuria Station	May 14–June 30	6		Do.
Do	July 1–Dec. 2	5		Do.
Mukden	Nov. 11–24			Present.
Shanghai	Nov. 18–Dec. 23	41	91	Cases, foreign; deaths among natives
Do	Dec. 31–Jan. 6	9	28	Do.
Tientsin	Nov. 11–Dec. 22	13		
Cuba:				
Habana	Jan. 7	1		Nov. 8, 1917: 1 case from Coruna, Dec. 5, 1917: 1 case.
Marianao	Jan. 8	1		6 miles distant from Habana.
Egypt:				
Alexandria	Nov. 12–18	1		
Cairo	July 23–Aug. 5	5	1	
France:				
Lyon	Nov. 18–Dec. 16	6	3	
Do	Jan. 7–20	5		
Great Britain:				
Birmingham	Nov. 11–17	10		
India:				
Bombay	Oct. 21–Dec. 1	16	4	
Karachi	Nov. 18–24		1	Nov. 11–17, 1917: 10 cases with 4 deaths; imported on s. s. Meness from Basreh.
Madras	Oct. 31–Dec. 8	9	3	
Rangoon	Oct. 28–Nov. 24	4	1	
Indo-China:				
Provinces				Sept. 1–30, 1917: Cases, 193; deaths, 56.
Anam	Sept. 1–30	61	12	
Cambodia	do	7		
Cochin-China	do	124	44	
Saigon	Oct. 20–Nov. 28	62	8	
Tonkin	Sept. 1–30	1		
Italy:				
Milan				October, 1917: Cases, 2.
Turin	Oct. 29–Dec. 9	123	120	
Castellamare	Dec. 10	2		Among refugees.
Florence	Dec. 1–15	17	4	
Naples	To Dec. 10	2		Do.
Japan:				
Taiwan—				
Taihoku	Dec. 15–21	1		

CHOLERA, PLAGUE, SMALLPOX, TYPHUS FEVER, AND YELLOW FEVER—Continued.

Reports Received from Dec. 29, 1917, to Feb. 22, 1918—Continued.

SMALLPOX—Continued.

Place.	Date.	Cases.	Deaths.	Remarks.
Java:				
East Java..................	Oct. 27–Dec. 9.....	25	....	Oct. 10–Dec. 12, 1917: Cases, 63; deaths, 1.
Mid-Java..................				
Samarang..............	Dec. 6–12...........	1	1	
West Java................				Oct. 19–Dec. 20, 1917: Cases, 217; deaths, 33.
Batavia..............	Nov. 2–8...........	1	....	
Mexico:				
Mazatlan..............	Dec. 5–11...........	....	1	
Mexico City..............	Nov. 11–Dec. 29...	16	....	
Do...............	Dec. 30–Jan. 26....	22	....	
Piedras Negras..............	Jan. 11.............	200	....	
Vera Cruz..............	Jan. 20–26.........	....	3	
Newfoundland:				
St. Johns..................	Dec. 8–Jan. 4......	29	....	
Do..................	Jan. 5–Feb. 1......	19	....	
Trepassey..............	Jan. 4.............	....	....	Outbreak with 11 cases reported.
Philippine Islands:				
Manila..................	Oct. 28–Dec. 8....	5	....	
Portugal:				
Lisbon..................	Nov. 4–Dec. 15....	2	....	
Portuguese East Africa:				
Lourenço Marques........	Aug. 1–Oct. 31....	....	5	
Russia:				
Moscow..................	Aug. 26–Oct. 6....	22	2	
Petrograd..................	Aug. 31–Nov. 18...	76	3	
Siam:				
Bangkok..................	Nov. 25–Dec. 1....	1	1	
Spain:				
Coruna..................	Dec. 2–15...........	....	4	
Madrid..................				Jan. 1–Dec. 31, 1917: Deaths, 77.
Seville..................	Oct. 1–Nov. 30...	....	26	
Straits Settlements:				
Singapore..............	Nov. 25–Dec. 1....	1	1	
Tunisia:				
Tunis..................	Dec. 14–20.........	....	1	
Turkey in Asia:				
Bagdad..................	....	....	....	Present in November, 1917.
Venezuela:				
Maracaibo..............	Dec. 2–8............	....	1	

TYPHUS FEVER.

Place.	Date.	Cases.	Deaths.	Remarks.
Algeria:				
Algiers..................	Nov. 1–Dec. 31....	2	1	
Argentina:				
Rosario..................	Dec. 1–31...........	....	1	
Australia:				
South Australia..........	....	....	....	Nov. 11–17, 1917: Cases, 1.
Brazil:				
Rio de Janeiro..............	Oct. 28–Dec. 1.....	7	....	
Canada:				
Ontario—				
Kingston..............	Dec. 2–8...........	3	....	
Quebec—				
Montreal..............	Dec. 16–22.........	2	1	
China:				
Antung..................	Dec. 3–30...........	13	1	
Do...............	Dec. 31–Jan. 6......	....	1	
Chosen (Formosa):				
Seoul..................	Nov. 1–30.........	1	....	
Egypt:				
Alexandria..............	Nov. 8–Dec. 28....	57	15	
Cairo..................	July 23–Nov. 25...	126	64	
Port Said..............	July 30–Nov. 11...	5	5	
Great Britain:				
Glasgow..................	Dec. 21.............	1	....	
Do..................	Jan. 20–26.........	1	....	
Manchester..............	Dec. 2–8...........	1	....	
Greece:				
Saloniki..................	Nov. 11–Dec. 29...	....	72	
Japan:				
Nagasaki..................	Nov. 26–Dec. 16...	5	5	
Do..................	Jan. 7–13...........	1	....	

CHOLERA, PLAGUE, SMALLPOX, TYPHUS FEVER, AND YELLOW FEVER—Continued.

Reports Received from Dec. 29, 1917, to Feb. 22, 1918—Continued.

TYPHUS FEVER—Continued.

Place.	Date.	Cases.	Deaths.	Remarks.
Java:				
East Java.............	....	....	....	Oct. 15-Dec. 9, 1917: Cases, 34; deaths, 3.
Mid-Java.............				Oct. 10-Dec. 12, 1917: Cases, 54; deaths, 2.
Samarang.............	Oct. 17-Dec. 5.....	15	2	
West Java.............	....	....	....	Oct. 19-Dec. 20, 1917: Cases, 73; deaths, 15.
Batavia.............	Oct. 19-Dec. 20....	73	17	
Mexico:				
Aguascalientes...........	Dec. 15...........	....	2	
Do.............	Jan. 21-Feb. 3.....	....	4	
Durango, State—				
Guanacevi...........	Feb. 11...........	....	....	Epidemic.
Mexico City.............	Nov. 11-Dec. 29....	476	....	
Do.............	Dec. 30-Jan. 26....	183	....	
Russia:				
Archangel.............	Sept. 1-14........	7	2	
Moscow.............	Aug. 26-Oct. 6....	49	2	
Petrograd.............	Aug. 31-Nov. 18...	32	....	
Do.............	Feb. 2...........	....	....	Present.
Vladivostok.............	Oct. 29-Nov. 4....	12	1	
Sweden:				
Goteborg.............	Nov. 18-24........	1	....	
Switzerland:				
Zurich.............	Nov. 9-15.........	2	....	
Tunisia:				
Tunis.............	Nov. 30-Dec. 6....	....	1	
Turkey:				
Albania—				
Janina.............	Jan. 27...........	....	....	Epidemic.
Union of South Africa:				
Cape of Good Hope State...	Sept. 10-Nov. 11...	3,409	701	

YELLOW FEVER.

Place.	Date.	Cases.	Deaths.	Remarks.
Honduras:				
Tegucigalpa.............	Dec. 16-22........	....	1	

✗

PUBLIC HEALTH REPORTS

VOL. 33	MARCH 8, 1918	No. 10

SCHOOL INSPECTION IN EXTRA-CANTONMENT ZONES.

Medical inspection of school children is one of the activities undertaken by the United States Public Health Service to prevent the carrying of communicable diseases to the troops. Such inspection has already been commenced in practically all of the zones surrounding the Army cantonments.

An officer of the Service is detailed to give his full time to the work and has an office and the assistance of school nurses or other help. The expenses, as a rule, are met jointly by the Red Cross, the local health authorities, and the Public Health Service. Regular inspection of the work is carried on by a Service expert familiar with the best standards of school hygiene.

In but few of the places where this work has been commenced had school inspection been previously practiced and in none had the full-time services of a physician been devoted to it. Now, with a skilled officer giving his full time to the work in each locality, much is expected to be accomplished. In communities where school inspection has been adequately carried out, the result has been a remarkable reduction in the incidence of contagious diseases in the general population. The same result is expected in the areas around the cantonments.

The plan is for the Service officer and nurse, through cooperation with the teachers, to keep a close watch on each school for the early detection of contagious diseases. The parents are then notified, the quarantine rules are enforced, vaccination is practiced where it fits the case, and all possible is done to prevent the disease from reaching the cantonment. The protection of the troops is the great aim; but at the same time the other benefits to be derived from school inspection are not overlooked. Thus, while all of the children in the areas around the cantonments are examined frequently for communicable disease, they are also to be examined at least once a year for physical defects. These defects tend to lower individual resistance and increase the susceptibility of a child to contagious diseases. They also retard intellectual development and prepare the way for degenerative diseases in later life. When the defects are found the parents are informed and urged to have them corrected. The great number debarred from the Army and Navy

23   (307)

recently because of physical disability indicates that many such defects, which could have been corrected in childhood had they been known, remained uncorrected, with a resulting loss in national efficiency at this crucial moment.

In the examinations every effort is made to consider the parents' wishes in regard to inspection of their children. Where a doctor's certificate is presented, the child may be excused from the physical examination.

The nurses not only assist in making the examinations, but go to the homes, follow up cases of communicable disease, tell the parents how to prevent the spread of the infection, look up children reported as absent to see if they are sick, and give advice in regard to personal hygiene. Clinics are established wherever possible, in order to give the necessary operative treatment to needy children. Where such clinics are not feasible, an effort is made to arrange with local physicians for the treatment of such cases.

An attempt is also made to determine cases of defective or retarded children, so that they may be given special instruction fitted to make them useful citizens. Encouragement is also given to the teaching of personal hygiene in the schools. Furthermore, the sanitary conditions of the schools themselves are looked into, and the school authorities are given advice as to improvements in toilet arrangements, heating, ventilation, humidity, illumination, size of desks, playgrounds, etc. These features, and in fact all of the work, are conducted with a view to interesting nearby localities in school inspection. It is recognized that to effect any great improvement in the sanitary conditions of the country it is necessary to educate the school children in regard to the principles underlying public health.

EXTRA-CANTONMENT ZONE SANITATION.

NEWPORT NEWS, VA., AND VICINITY.[1]

By S. B. Grubbs, Surgeon, United States Public Health Service.

The United States Public Health Service has, as a part of its war duties, taken charge of the sanitation of many of the extra-cantonment zones. In addition to the common difficulties of lack of authority, intense business activity, and limited funds, each has presented its own special problems.

That district of Virginia between the York and James Rivers is of especial importance, as there will be gathered for both training and embarkation the pick of all branches of the Army. Langley Field and Morrison Aviation Field, as well as Fort Monroe with the Artillery School, are in this district. Two large embarkation camps—

---

[1] Feb. 1, 1918.

Camp Stuart and Camp Hill—will contain a military population already trained whose health is of vital importance to the country. In addition, the Newport News Shipbuilding & Drydock Co. employs over 10,000 workmen engaged largely in Government work. The two counties, which cover about 100 square miles, normally have a population of about 55,000. This is now about 100,000 in addition to troops. Newport News, for example, has increased 50 per cent in six months. The local health administration was entirely inadequate for the strain of the intensive military activity, which was to crowd the district first with workmen and then with troops, but the authorities willingly delegated their powers to Service officers and cooperated with them.

Existing health organizations.—Newport News has a board of health elected·by the city council. The president of the board of health is the health officer and must be a physician. He is paid on a part-time basis. There are also a chief sanitary inspector, a food and dairy inspector, a sanitary inspector, and a clerk. Elizabeth City County has a board of health, with a part-time health officer and part-time inspector. Warwick County has a board of health and a part-time health officer. All of these organizations were willing to cooperate with the Service. It was also evident that arrangements might be made for these three health departments to operate together, and there was an opportunity to establish a district organization that might outlast the necessities of the war. The matter was taken up with the press, representative organizations, and prominent citizens, and after necessary publicity a called meeting was held, which indorsed the plan of combining the health activities of the two counties under a full-time district health officer whose salary and expenses were to be paid by Newport News and the two counties, in proportion to the population of each. The meeting also approved the appointment of an advisory health committee of twelve. Those appointed on this committee are public-spirited and active citizens, and among its members are the three health officers of Newport News, Elizabeth City County, and Warwick County. This committee, as the name signifies, has no legal authority, but the advice and moral support of such citizens is of inestimable value.

After being approved by the advisory health committee each local government was asked to indorse the program and to make special health appropriations. In each case this was done without a dissenting vote. The appropriations voted were as follows.

Newport News:

Full-time health officer	$1,666.60
Malaria control	800.00
Contagious-disease hospital	500.00
Incidentals	100.00

Elizabeth City County:

Full-time health officer	1,125.81
Malaria control	300.00
Filth-borne diseases	200.00
Contagious-disease hospital	225.00
Incidentals	100.00

Warwick County:

Full-time health officer	166.70
Malaria control	200.00
Filth-borne diseases	200.00
Contagious-disease hospital	50.00
Incidentals	50.00

As there were no legal provisions for either a district health officer or a service officer to act in local health matters, authority was delegated by appointing both of these officials as special inspectors of the State board of health and as deputy health officers of each of the three communities comprising the district. In order to better identify the district organization the advisory committee has adopted the name of the "Tidewater Health Organization."

Red Cross sanitary unit.—As soon as plans of organization were completed a request was made to the newly created division of sanitary service of the American Red Cross for the creation of a sanitary unit. This request embodied in it a report of local conditions and a proposed plan of operation. The result was the creation of sanitary unit No. 9 with an allotment of $21,000. Mr. Caleb D. West, of Newport News, was chosen business manager.

Red Cross funds, being immediately available, have been of the greatest value. These funds have made it possible to undertake measures against malaria-bearing mosquitoes involving an expenditure of several thousand dollars, which money could not reasonably be expected from either local property owners or the Federal Government, and have supplied promptly public health nurses, sanitary inspectors and other personnel and allowed work to be extended into the country by furnishing automobiles, for which Government money is not available.

Plan of operations.—In order to concentrate on essentials it was decided to limit the district work to the control of communicable diseases and malaria, to proper disposal of excreta, to safeguarding the supply of milk and water, and to the inspection of schools. Later, the sanitary control of establishments selling food and drink was undertaken in connection with the Army. The matters of garbage disposal, abatement of nuisances, the inspection of stores, and the like were left entirely with the local health authorities, although assistance has been given at times.

Communicable diseases.—The first essential for the control of communicable disease being their prompt recognition and reporting, all the physicians in the district have been asked verbally,.by letter, and through their societies, to report to the district health office all cases that are in fact or suspected to be communicable. Not only is this emphasized as a public duty, but in return assistance in diagnosis is given when asked for and our diagnostic laboratory helps the physicians in every way possible. Reports of disease are received either by mail or telephone and the epidemiology of each case is immediately studied. Contacts are examined and proper measures to isolate carriers of disease and those already in the incubation stage are taken. Contagious diseases among troops and laborers on camp sites are cared for by the Army, but there is the closest cooperation between military and civil health authorities and the various camps report each day details of all cases. This is necessary for effective work, as many of those employed in camp construction live in the towns and the systematic entertainment of troops by organizations and families makes the association between the soldier and civilian peculiarly intimate.

If requested, the medical officer visits each case with the visiting physician to confirm the diagnosis, or independently to get epidemiological data, deal with contacts, and to establish room isolation. The public-health nurse of the Red Cross sanitary unit accompanies the physician or visits the case as soon as possible. Room isolation, rather than house quarantine, is always established and maintained by the nurse, who continues her visits every day, if necessary, and demonstrates aseptic nursing. Where necessary, "kits" consisting of galvanized iron washtubs, pails, disinfectant, and the like, are loaned in order that the essential equipment may be quickly available.

The control of the ordinary contagious diseases has heretofore been largely in the hands of the practicing physician. On his report the case was placarded and at his request the placard was removed. This increased the work of the conscientious physician but put no check upon any one either as to reporting or subsequent care. It is believed that the present system has removed a great responsibility from the practitioner, especially where the opportunities for spread of communicable diseases by contact infection are greatly increased by the crowded living conditions. It is believed the work has justified itself in meningitis and diphtheria, as in both these diseases several foci of infection have been discovered and cleaned up.

Contagious-disease hospital.—There are three excellent private hospitals in Newport News and one in Hampton. They have no outpatient departments and will not receive any communicable diseases except typhoid fever. Anticipating that crowded living conditions would increase the incidence of infection, it was considered advisable to provide some place where, at least in emergencies, contagious cases could be given hospital care.

As a part of the plan of community organization, amounts aggregating $775 were asked from Newport·News and the two counties. With this a farmhouse about 2 miles from Newport News, on one of the roads leading to Hampton, was rented for the duration of the war. This has been repaired and equipped. The equipment was furnished largely by private subscription. Owing to the urgent need for hospitalization of venereal disease carriers, the contagious-disease hospital has been used almost entirely for that purpose.

Laboratory.—It was immediately recognized that a fully equipped public-health laboratory would be of the greatest value, as there was no such laboratory in this district and none available nearer than that of the State department of health at Richmond. As a result of some rapid work a complete laboratory equipment was received within two weeks and was installed as rapidly as rooms and workmen were available. While the cities of this district are furnished good water, there are many wells that required laboratory examination. The most important work of the laboratory, however, is for the diagnosis of communicable diseases, especially diphtheria, cerebrospinal meningitis, and venereal diseases. In the five months it has been operated the "Tidewater Laboratory" has handled all of this work for the civil population and has done a large amount of work of all kinds for the various Army camps, whose laboratories are not yet ready. It was possible to limit the spread of diphtheria in the fall of 1917 to a few cases in spite of congested living conditions, as a large number of swabs could be handled and prompt reports obtained. Special cultural work for epidemic meningitis was the most important work in December, 1917, and January, 1918, as all the contacts of the cases among civilians have been cultured and several carriers isolated.

It is expected that the new city farm to be established by the city of Newport News will make provision not only for contagious venereal but also for other communicable diseases.

Malaria.—No statistics are available of the prevalence of malaria, but this entire peninsula is considered malarious. The general opinion of physicians is that this disease causes a large part of the disability and a number of deaths. Asst. Surg. Gen. H. R. Carter, Asst. Epidemiologist Griffitts and party made a complete Anopheles survey of all parts of this district ordinarily frequented by soldiers. Practically all the territory surrounding the camps was found breeding Anopheles profusely, especially on two sides of Camp Stuart, one place having the distinction of being the most profuse breeder of Anopheles Asst. Surg. Gen. Carter had in his long experience ever seen. However, there is no serious engineering problem, as the country is practically level, but careful preliminary surveys are necessary. These are under way and will be completed by March

1, 1918, when it is planned to begin extensive ditching and draining operations. During the late summer a certain amount of oiling was done as a temporary measure. In this work the military forces are cooperating, and the draining work done or planned within the camps is based on the work to be done outside. During the severe cold weather, when field work had to be discontinued, a census of those living near the camps was made in order to locate the persons who had active malaria during the past year and as many as possible were induced to take quinine, which was furnished free of charge.

Typhoid fever.—The rate of prevalence of typhoid fever is high. Since the principal cities of the peninsula are supplied with excellent water by the Newport News Light & Water Co., it is probable that public water supplies are not a factor in the causation of this disease. The milk supply is not properly protected against contamination. The methods of disposal of human excreta are generally faulty. In view of the condition of the milk supply and of the faulty systems of excreta disposal and of the especially high incidence of the disease in the summer and fall seasons, it appears that the chief factors of typhoid infection in the peninsula are flies, milk, and private water supplies, all of which operate to convey the infection from its invariable source, "insanitary deposits of human excreta."

Tuberculosis.—This disease has been reported very imperfectly in the past and is undoubtedly quite prevalent. Reporting is now being stimulated and cases are discovered by our public health nurses and those of the Visiting Nurses Association. All of the patients are encouraged to take suitable precautions and are furnished sputum cups and other supplies when needed.

Excreta disposal.—A survey has been made which has discovered about 900 privies in Newport News and over 600 in Hampton and Phoebus. All are of the insanitary type and poorly scavenged. An ordinance was recommended and passed by the Newport News City Council requiring the installation of sanitary-can privies and providing for a city scavenging system and a disposal plant connected with the city sewer. For this purpose $5,000 was appropriated and construction work has begun. A similar ordinance has been submitted to the cities of Hampton and Phoebus, where, on account of near-by oyster beds, the installation of a sludge tank and chlorination plant according to plans furnished by the Hygienic Laboratory has been recommended. Outside of the cities attention has thus far been paid especially to schoolhouses and to districts where typhoid fever prevailed. A large number of privies have been built by our rural sanitation force. The best type of privy for the rural districts is not yet settled, as unusual difficulties have been encountered, especially from the high level of the ground water.

When concrete has been used it has been necessary to buy both sand and gravel, which adds materially to the cost.

Water.—The cities of Newport News, Hampton, and Phoebus, much of the thickly settled rural community, and all of the military camps are supplied by the Newport News Light & Water Co. The source is an impounded surface stream, subject to a long period of storage followed by coagulation with alum, sedimentation, and filtration, and finally disinfection by hypochlorite of lime. A survey of the watershed and repeated bacteriological examinations confirm the opinion that the quality of the water is good. Laboratory examination of this water, at first made every day, is now made once a week and results are reported to the water company and the military authorities.

There are, however, many wells in use both in the cities and the country. These are all shallow, as the ground water is within 4 to 6 feet of the surface. The water from driven wells is of a fair sanitary quality, but open wells are universally bad. A systematic examination of these wells has been made and where local conditions and laboratory findings were bad the wells have been closed. In certain cases signs stating that the water is not fit for drinking purposes have been posted and the use of the water for washing purposes is allowed.

Milk.—The milk supply of the district is inadequate in quantity and not properly guarded, as was shown by the occurrence of two milk-borne epidemics of typhoid fever in 1914 and 1916. On the other hand, a survey made by representatives of the Department of Agriculture at our request shows a fair degree of cleanliness and good quality of milk. The supply of Newport News is from tuberculin tested cows and 62 per cent of the dairies scored 70 per cent or over. Only one-third of the herds supplying the eastern part of the district were tuberculin tested and but 40 per cent scored 70 per cent. It was recognized that not only should milk be safeguarded to prevent the transmission of disease but the supply should be increased, as in spite of high prices—20 cents per quart—there is a milk shortage that is constantly growing on account of the rapidly increasing population.

It was recommended that a privately owned but publicly controlled pasteurizing plant be built in Newport News and that pasteurization be made compulsory. As this would eliminate retail delivery of milk by the producers, the project was not opposed by the local dairymen and additional milk has been promised from farms at a distance.

Many residents and the Chamber of Commerce of Newport News indorsed the plan, but the company has not yet been organized, although the necessary capital has been assured. It is believed that when the great business rush caused by the building of the cantonments passes, the project will go through. Until then the milk supply will be inadequate, the prices high, and the risk of milk-borne disease ever present. The dairy inspection maintained by the city health department is fairly effective along the lines of cleanliness, but such inspection can not prevent milk-borne diseases, as it does not oversee the health of those handling milk or milk products. It has been estimated by the Public Health Service expert who studied the situation, that the saving made possible by the elimination of multiple deliveries in the same territory, and the saving on bad debts and bottle losses, would more than pay for the cost of pasteurization.

School inspection.—Newport News, through its school board, has this year for the first time employed a full-time school physician, who is assisted by a white and a colored nurse. The work was begun some years ago and has gradually developed as the advantage has become evident. In order to extend this work to the communities outside and to control communicable diseases in the schools, a preliminary survey was made by Surg. Taliaferro Clark and regular work was begun under an acting assistant surgeon. A school nurse has since been employed and it is hoped to cover every school in the district during the school year. The work consists of (1) physical examination of children with special reference to defects that are referred through the parents to a physician or dentist for correction; (2) examination of children that appear sick in order to find contagious cases; (3) visits at their houses of those absent for three consecutive days on account of sickness or without known reason; (4) general control of communicable diseases in the schools; (5) sanitation of school environment; (6) establishment of school republics.

Venereal Diseases.—While these diseases constitute one of the most serious public health problems, their control has seldom been attempted and such efforts have usually met with slight success or with absolute failure. The public health aspects of these diseases are so closely allied to those of morality and law enforcement that the health officer has hesitated until recently to engage in this field.

With the necessity for military efficiency the subject can be no longer ignored and the lines of action are being drawn. These are: (1) Recreative amusements and education of the soldier both within and without the camps; (2) the enforcement of laws against public and clandestine prostitutes both in brothels and on the streets; (3) the treatment of persons in the infective stages of these diseases, with the isolation of patients that can not be otherwise controlled.

Under the first heading may be mentioned the effective work in this same done by the Army and the Young Men's Christian Association within the camps and the numerous activities outside that have been coordinated by the Commission on Training Camp Activities; under the second heading are the municipal and military police, supported by the police court, and assisted by a representative of the Commission on Training Camp Activities, together with an Army Sanitary Corps officer experienced in social hygiene. It was evident that in this locality prostitution was extensive and increasing with the influx of soldiers and well-paid workmen. A military order prohibiting soldiers entering a certain district of the city of Newport News gave the matter such prominence that indifference to this health menace was no longer to be tolerated. It must be said, however, that many prominent citizens did not wait for military action. Several meetings had been held and organizations interested in the vice question were at work. No definite action had been taken in public health lines, but during more than two months the extra-cantonment sanitation office has been formulating plans in which the Public Health Service, the Army, and the Red Cross were to cooperate. These plans call for an increased police force, two policewomen, and one or more probation officers. The city of Newport News was asked to establish a jail farm on which there would be a contagious-disease hospital. It was planned also to establish a clinic that would pay especial attention to venereal diseases.

Women convicted of prostitution were by order of the court to be examined and if found to be carriers of a venereal disease were to be sent to the hospital, there to be held in quarantine and treated. When no longer in an infective stage the case was to be returned to the court, which would, in its discretion, release the person under bond to continue treatment and stop the practice of prostitution. It is a function of the probation officer to see that such women continue treatment either under a regular physician or at the clinic above mentioned. The probation officers and policewomen will also deal with the clandestine prostitute and the nonprofessional persons who on account of promiscuous relations are spreading the disease. These may be induced to receive treatment and change their practices in order to avoid the publicity of arrest.

Reports of venereal disease are being received from practicing physicians, from druggists, and from the Army medical officers. In them the name of the patient is not disclosed, but the physician asks the source of the infection and gives this information in the report. It is recognized that great care must be exercised when these reports indicate as infecting agents other persons than known prostitutes, but when evidence accumulates it should be possible by social service methods to cure the infection and possibly effect a moral reform.

At present writing the above program is in force, but the time is too short to report results or draw conclusions. The Tidewater Hospital for Contagious Diseases has been filled, and the clinic has occupied rooms in the Public Health Service building and patients are beginning to come in. The amount of good accomplished will depend largely upon the energy and skill of those in immediate charge. All expenses for this movement are being paid by the bureau of sanitary service, American Red Cross, except that the hospital building is furnished by the Tidewater Health Organization, and a medical officer of the Public Health Service has been detailed for the work. It is intended that as soon as the proposed city farm is in operation, hospital patients will be taken there. Already a special committee has recommended a bond issue of $25,000 for the purchase and equipment of such a farm. The entire plan is still in the formative stage, but the progress already made is gratifying.

Education and publicity.—It was necessary, especially at the beginning, to arouse public interest in the prevention of disease. While the intelligent minority saw at once that war activities and increasing congestion would create new difficulties, as is usual the general attitude toward preventable sickness and death was that of the fatalist. With war activities working at high pressure there have been unusual claims upon the time and energy of the citizen, but moral and financial support for an extensive health program has never been lacking. It is believed that this cooperation has been made possible by the publicity carried on through the press, especially during the first three months of the work. News items regarding public-health work have appeared nearly every day, and a series of editorials were written by Mr. W. S. Copeland, strongly indorsing various health movements, such as the district organization, good milk supply, and venereal-disease control. For six weeks a series of articles, prepared in this office and averaging about a half column, appeared on the editorial page of both morning and evening papers. This column was entitled "Here's to your health," and the articles were written in popular style, the publications of the Public Health Service and local departments of health being freely used. Over a hundred addresses have been delivered by members of the force, no invitation to speak having been refused. In this way a direct appeal has been made to business organizations, societies, committees, schools, and the general public, and a certain amount of public-health instruction has been disseminated. The marked interest and sympathy shown have doubtless been due in a large measure to the efforts in health education and publicity.

Office work has always been reduced as much as possible, but it is interesting to note that during the past six months administrative branches have grown from desk room in the old city health office to the entire second and third floors of the Barrett Building, in all, 14 rooms, 4 of which are used by the laboratory and 2 by the dispensary.

Present force and organization.—On January 1 there were on duty in this district the following:

United States Public Health Service.—Two commissioned officers, two acting assistant surgeons, two bacteriologists, one scientific assistant, two sanitary inspectors, and two stenographers.

Division of sanitary service, American Red Cross.—Two sanitary inspectors, four Public-Health nurses, one hospital matron, and one clerk.

The full-time district health officer works as a part of the regular force.

Assistance of the greatest value has been given by outside agencies. The Virginia State department of health furnished both personnel and advice during the period of organization. The Dairy Division of the United States Department of Agriculture made a survey and the Virginia State department of health has sent its inspectors at our request.

Sanitary, milk, and malarial surveys, which were necessary for the intelligent prosecution of the work, were made by properly qualified experts of the Public Health Service.

The Hygienic Laboratory has furnished temporarily two bacteriologists for special work in water analysis and cerebrospinal meningitis.

The proximity of Washington, facilitating advice or visits from the Service experts, has been of the greatest help.

Conclusion.—Intensive extra-cantonment sanitation has been made possible on account of the war, which has justified the expenditure of more money than the local communities could be expected to contribute. Among the troops this work should cause a decided decrease in physical disability that would otherwise result from communicable diseases, especially malaria and venereal infections. Upon the civil population it should act as a protection against infectious diseases brought in by troops which are gathered, especially at a military port of embarkation, from all parts of the country. Especially important among these infections may be mentioned measles, diphtheria, and cerebrospinal meningitis.

In addition, a great deal may be done to curtail the increase among the civil population of certain diseases, such as typhoid fever and tuberculosis, that thrive on congestion and poor sanitation.

One indirect result of our efforts will be the advancement of health education. Those people who have experienced the comfort and satisfaction derived from good sanitation and the feeling of security afforded by a well-equipped health department, that deals promptly and vigorously with all communicable diseases, will not be satisfied with the old fatalistic attitude that has been common in this country.

PREVALENCE OF DISEASE.

No health department, State or local, can effectively prevent or control disease without knowledge of when, where, and under what conditions cases are occurring.

UNITED STATES.

EXTRA-CANTONMENT ZONES—CASES REPORTED WEEK ENDED MAR. 5.

CAMP BEAUREGARD ZONE, LA.

Cerebrospinal meningitis:
Alexandria	1

Measles:
Alexandria	3
Boyce	3

Mumps:
Alexandria	4

Smallpox:
Alexandria	2
Pineville	1

Typhoid fever:
Pineville	1

CAMP BOWIE ZONE, TEX.

Fort Worth:
Cerebrospinal meningitis	3
Chancroid	2
Chicken pox	3
Gonorrhea	2
Mumps	12
Pneumonia, lobar	1
Scarlet fever	1
Smallpox	4
Syphilis	7
Tuberculosis, pulmonary	2

CAMP DEVENS ZONE, MASS.

Chicken pox:
Ayer	1
Littleton	8

German measles:
Ayer	2
Littleton	2

Measles:
Lancaster	2
Ayer	1
Shirley	1

Mumps:
Lancaster	6

CAMP DODGE ZONE, IOWA.

Chicken pox:
Des Moines	1

Diphtheria:
Des Moines	1

CAMP DODGE ZONE, IOWA—continued.

German measles:
Grimes	1
Urbandale	15

Measles:
Des Moines	6
Grimes	12

Scarlet fever:
Des Moines	6

Smallpox:
Des Moines	26
Carney	1

Syphilis:
Des Moines	6

Syphilis and chancroid:
Des Moines	1

Syphilis and urethritis:
Des Moines	1

Typhoid fever:
Des Moines	1

CAMP GORDON ZONE, GA.

Atlanta:
Cerebrospinal meningitis	1
Chicken pox	3
Diphtheria	6
German measles	12
Gonorrhea	5
Measles	5
Mumps	16
Pneumonia	4
Scarlet fever	2
Smallpox	4
Syphilis	5
Tuberculosis	17
Typhoid fever	1
Whooping cough	5

CAMP GREENE ZONE, N. C.

Charlotte Township:
Cerebrospinal meningitis	2
Chancroid and gonorrhea	1
Diphtheria	1
German measles	4
Gonorrhea	2
Gonorrhea and syphilis	3
Malaria	2

CAMP GREENE ZONE, N. C.—continued.

Charlotte Township—Continued.
Measles.................................. 15
Scarlet fever............................. 1
Smallpox................................. 1
Syphilis.................................. 9
Trachoma................................. 1
Tuberculosis............................. 4
Typhoid fever............................ 1
Whooping cough.......................... 4

CAMP HANCOCK ZONE, GA.

Cerebrospinal meningitis:
Augusta.............................. 4
Chicken pox:
Augusta.............................. 2
German measles:
Augusta.............................. 14
Wrightsboro Road..................... 3
Measles:
Augusta.............................. 9
Wrightsboro Road..................... 3
Scarlet fever:
Augusta.............................. 2
Smallpox:
Augusta.............................. 1
Tuberculosis, pulmonary:
Augusta.............................. 1

CAMP JACKSON ZONE, S. C.

Columbia:
Cerebrospinal meningitis............. 1
Measles.............................. 1
Mumps................................ 4
Roseola.............................. 1
Tuberculosis......................... 1

CAMP JOSEPH E. JOHNSTON ZONE, FLA.

Jacksonville:
Cerebrospinal meningitis............. 1
Chicken pox.......................... 4
Erysipelas........................... 1
Measles.............................. 29
Mumps................................ 2
Pneumonia............................ 1
Trachoma............................. 2
Tuberculosis......................... 6
Typhoid fever........................ 3

FORT LEAVENWORTH ZONE, KANS.

Leavenworth:
Chicken pox.......................... 14
Diphtheria........................... 1
German measles....................... 10
Measles.............................. 4
Scarlet fever........................ 1
Smallpox............................. 1
Leavenworth County:
Smallpox............................. 1

CAMP LEE ZONE, VA.

Cerebrospinal meningitis:
Petersburg........................... 1
Hopewell............................. 1
Chicken pox:
Petersburg........................... 1

CAMP LEE ZONE, VA.—continued.

Diphtheria:
Petersburg........................... 4
German measles:
Petersburg........................... 1
Ettricks............................. 8
Prince George County................. 6
Gonorrhea:
Petersburg........................... 2
Dinwiddie County..................... 1
Measles:
Petersburg........................... 1
Hopewell............................. 26
Ettricks............................. 1
Prince George County................. 7
Chesterfield County.................. 3
City Point........................... 1
Mumps:
Petersburg........................... 1
Hopewell............................. 12
Prince George County................. 8
Pneumonia:
Petersburg........................... 4
Septic sore throat:
Petersburg........................... 5
Ettricks............................. 4
Chesterfield County.................. 1
Dinwiddie County..................... 1
Tuberculosis:
Petersburg........................... 2
Ettricks............................. 1
Whooping cough:
Hopewell............................. 1
Ettricks............................. 2
Prince George County................. 8

CAMP LEWIS ZONE, WASH.

Chicken pox:
Spanaway............................. 1
German measles:
Spanaway............................. 7
Roy.................................. 9
Steilacoom Lake...................... 1
Parkland............................. 1
Scarlet fever:
Steilacoom........................... 2

CAMP LOGAN ZONE, TEX.

Houston:
Cerebrospinal meningitis............. 3
Chicken pox.......................... 9
Diphtheria........................... 1
Measles.............................. 47
Mumps................................ 20
Pneumonia............................ 4
Smallpox............................. 6
Tuberculosis......................... 5
Typhoid fever........................ 1

CAMP MACARTHUR ZONE, TEX.

Waco:
Cerebrospinal meningitis............. 1
Chicken pox.......................... 7
Diphtheria........................... 1
German measles....................... 1
Measles.............................. 6
Mumps................................ 10

CAMP MACARTHUR ZONE, TEX.—continued.

Waco—Continued.
Pneumonia. lobar 4
Smallpox 1
Tuberculosis 1
Whooping cough 8
Precinct 4:
Smallpox 1

CAMP M'CLELLAN ZONE, ALA.

Chicken pox:
Anniston 10
German measles:
Anniston 4
Precinct 2 1
Measles:
Anniston 17
Precinct 3 2
Mumps:
Anniston 2
Pneumonia:
Anniston 9
Precinct 2 1
Smallpox:
Anniston 27
Bobson 1
Oxford 3
Piedmont 2
Blue Mountain 1
Precinct 1 1
Precinct 13 4
Precinct 20 1

NORFOLK COUNTY NAVAL DISTRICT, VA.

Cerebrospinal meningitis:
Titustown 1
Dysentery, amebic:
Portsmouth 1
Gonorrhea:
Portsmouth 7
Malaria:
Portsmouth 2
Measles:
Portsmouth 16
Norfolk County 9
Mumps:
Portsmouth 8
Pneumonia:
Norfolk County 1
Scarlet fever:
Portsmouth 1
Port Norfolk 1
Smallpox:
Port Norfolk 1
Titustown 1
Syphilis:
Portsmouth 5
Tuberculosis:
Portsmouth 1
Great Bridge 1
Benefit 1

FORT OGLETHORPE ZONE, GA.

Cerebrospinal meningitis:
Chattanooga 1
North Chattanooga 1

FORT OGLETHORPE ZONE, GA.—continued.

Chicken pox:
Chattanooga 3
Dysentery:
East Lake 4
German measles:
Chattanooga 1
East Chattanooga 1
East Lake 1
Rossville 1
Gonorrhea:
Chattanooga 0
Measles:
Chattanooga 2
North Chattanooga 2
Mumps:
Chattanooga 68
North Chattanooga 4
East Chattanooga 3
East Lake 2
Pneumonia:
Chattanooga 2
North Chattanooga 1
Scarlet fever:
St. Elmo 4
Smallpox:
Chattanooga 7
Syphilis:
Chattanooga 4
Tuberculosis:
Chattanooga 3
East Lake 2
Whooping cough:
Chattanooga 10
North Chattanooga 1
East Lake 1

CAMP SEVIER ZONE, S. C.

Greenville Township.
Cerebrospinal meningitis 2
Mumps 6

CAMP SHELBY ZONE, MISS.

Chicken pox:
Hattiesburg 5
Bon Homme 1
Diphtheria:
Hattiesburg 4
Gonorrhea:
Hattiesburg 4
Malaria:
Hattiesburg 1
Eastabutchie 1
Measles:
Hattiesburg 9
Mumps:
Hattiesburg 6
Pneumonia:
Hattiesburg 9
Smallpox:
Hattiesburg 3
Collins 3
Syphilis:
Hattiesburg 4
Tuberculosis, pulmonary:
Hattiesburg 1
Eastabutchie 1

CAMP SHERMAN ZONE, OHIO.

Diphtheria:
  Chillicothe................................. 1
German measles:
  Chillicothe................................. 6
Gonorrhea:
  Chillicothe................................. 2
Measles:
  Kingston................................... 1
  Liberty Township........................... 18
Pneumonia, lobar:
  Frankfort.................................. 1
Scarlet fever:
  Chillicothe................................. 6

CAMP ZACHARY TAYLOR ZONE, KY.

Cerebrospinal meningitis:
  Jefferson County........................... 1
Chicken pox:
  Louisville.................................. 4
Diphtheria:
  Jefferson County........................... 2
  Louisville.................................. 2
German measles:
  Jefferson County........................... 1
Measles:
  Jefferson County........................... 4
  Louisville.................................. 24
Scarlet fever:
  Louisville.................................. 6
Smallpox:
  Louisville.................................. 1
Trachoma:
  Jefferson County........................... 17
Tuberculosis:
  Jefferson County........................... 1
Tuberculous pulmonary
  Louisville................................. 11
Tuberculosis peritoneum.
  Louisville................................. 1
Typhoid fever
  Louisville................................. 1

TIDEWATER HEALTH DISTRICT, VA.

Cerebrospinal meningitis:
  Newport News.............................. 4
  Hampton................................... 1
German measles:
  Newport News.............................. 8
  Hampton................................... 5
  Phoebus................................... 6
La grippe:
  Newport News.............................. 1
Measles:
  Phoebus................................... 1
Mumps:
  Newport News.............................. 4
  Hampton................................... 3
  Phoebus................................... 1
Pneumonia:
  Newport News.............................. 1
  Hampton................................... 2
Whooping cough:
  Phoebus................................... 1

CAMP TRAVIS ZONE, TEX.

San Antonio:
  Cerebrospinal meningitis................... 1
  Gonorrhea.................................. .
  Measles.................................... 4
  Mumps..................................... 2
  Roseola.................................... 1
  Pneumonia................................. 2
  Syphilis................................... 1
  Tuberculosis............................... 2
  Typhoid fever.............................. 2

CAMP WADSWORTH ZONE, S. C.

Cerebrospinal meningitis:
  Fairforest................................. 1
Chicken pox:
  Spartanburg................................ 2
  White Stone................................ 1
Diphtheria:
  Spartanburg................................ 4
German measles:
  Spartanburg................................ .
Measles:
  Spartanburg................................ 9
  Pauline.................................... 9
Mumps:
  Spartanburg................................ 4
  Hayne..................................... 1
Smallpox:
  Spartanburg................................ .
Tuberculosis:
  Spartanburg................................ .
Whooping cough:
  Spartanburg................................ 11
  Saxon Mills................................ 3

CAMP WHEELER ZONE, GA.

Cerebrospinal meningitis:
  Bibb County................................ .
Chicken pox:
  Macon...................................... .
German measles:
  East Macon................................. .
Malaria:
  East Macon................................. .
Measles:
  Macon...................................... 8
  East Macon................................. 1
Mumps:
  Macon...................................... 28
  East Macon................................. 4
Scarlet fever:
  Macon...................................... 2
  East Macon................................. 1
Tuberculosis:
  Macon...................................... .
Whooping cough
  Macon...................................... .

DISEASE CONDITIONS AMONG TROOPS IN THE UNITED STATES.

The following data are taken from telegraphic reports received in the office of the Surgeon General, United States Army, for the week ended February 22, 1918:

Annual admission rate per 1,000 (disease only):

All troops	1,506.7
National Guard camps	1,192.5
National Army camps	1,835.9
Regular Army	1,360.1

Nonaffective rate per 1,000 on day of report:

All troops	50.8
National Guard camps	44.8

Nonaffective rate per 1,000 on day of report—Continued.

National Army camps	58.6
Regular Army	45.3

Venereal diseases—annual admission rate per 1,000:

National Guard camps	51.1
National Army camps	62.9
Regular Army	81.3

New cases of special diseases reported during the week ended Feb. 22, 1918.

Camps.	Pneumonia.	Dysentery.	Malaria.	Venereal.	Paratyphoid.	Typhoid.	Measles.	Meningitis.	Scarlet fever.	Deaths.	Noneffective per 1,000 on day of report.
Wadsworth	3			34				1		1	27.0
Hancock	8			14			19	2	8	0	27.0
McClellan	9			12		1	16	1	3	1	32.5
Sevier	9		1	20			7	2	3	8	69.9
Wheeler	17	1	4	43			1			4	52.2
Logan	11		4	59			48		1	2	35.3
Cody	46			14			2	2	4	13	37.7
Doniphan	2		1	15				1		5	45.5
Bowie	22		1	63			1	3	1	3	70.9
Sheridan				6			4			2	23.5
Shelby	3			26			4	2	1	3	56.3
Beauregard	6			17			1			8	61.2
Kearney	9			5			2		9	1	49.8
Devens	5			15			10	1	3	3	38.5
Upton	8			20			4		2	1	24.6
Dix	2			34			26		6	2	43.6
Meade	2			26			9	2	6	4	31.4
Lee	15			50			14	3		9	63.6
Jackson	10		1	31			6	0	2	6	80.2
Gordon	12			24			2	1	0	6	34.1
Sherman	4			34			61		16	2	52.9
Taylor	19			13			5		1	7	71.4
Custer	3			15			16		5	6	44.7
Grant	4			43			23	1	17	5	38.3
Pike	19		4	87			7		9	7	97.1
Dodge	9			27			19		18	9	68.7
Funston	4			7			1	2	7	2	104.6
Travis	46			22			4	2	1	7	98.0
Lewis	21			47			40	2	26	2	60.9
Regulars	132	4	5	585	1	2	519	25	129	66	45.3
National Guard in Departments	1			22			58			0	
National Army in Departments	12		1	148			31		32	2	

Annual rate per 1,000 for special diseases.

[Week ending Feb. 22, 1918.]

Disease.	All troops in United States.	Regulars in United States.	National Guard, all camps.	National Army, all camps.	Expeditionary Forces.[1]
Pneumonia	21.2	18.3	22.6	23.2	18.5
Dysentery	0.2	0.5	0.1	0.0	0.2
Malaria	0.8	0.7	1.2	0.6	0.2
Venereal	70.7	81.3	51.1	62.9	51.7
Paratyphoid	0.04	0.1	0.0	0.0	0.2
Typhoid	0.1	0.3	0.1	0.0	0.0
Measles	42.9	72.1	16	31.4	26.4
Meningitis	2.8	3.5	2.2	2.9	4.2
Scarlet fever	13.8	17.9	4.7	15.1	11.1

[1] Week ending Feb. 14, 1918.

CURRENT STATE SUMMARIES.

Alabama.

From Collaborating Epidemiologist Perry, **by telegraph, for week** ended March 2, 1918:

Smallpox: Augusta 3, Bibb 4, Butler 9, Chambers 8, Cullman 9, Jefferson 129, Montgomery 1, Pickens 13. Cerebrospinal meningitis: Jefferson 3.

California.

From the State Board of Health of California, **by telegraph, for** week ended March 2, 1918:

Smallpox and measles continue to increase in prevalence, 1,300 cases measles for week. Twenty-five cases smallpox widely distributed. One case poliomyelitis Kern County. One case leprosy Oakland. Three cases cerebrospinal meningitis; 2 Alameda County, 1 San Francisco.

Reported by mail for preceding week (ended Feb. 23):

Cerebrospinal meningitis	7	Pneumonia	63
Chicken pox	246	Ophthalmia neonatorum	1
Diphtheria	49	Scarlet fever	85
Dysentery	1	Smallpox	15
Erysipelas	17	Syphilis	35
German measles	372	Tetanus	1
Gonococcus infection	50	Trachoma	2
Malaria	7	Tuberculosis	132
Measles	1,192	Typhoid fever	13
Mumps	306	Whooping cough	96
Pellagra	2		

Connecticut.

From Collaborating Epidemiologist Black, **by telegraph, for week** ended March 2, 1918:

Smallpox: Bloomfield 3, Hartford 4, Norwich 1. Cerebrospinal meningitis: Bridgeport 2, New Haven 1.

Indiana.

From the State Board of Health of Indiana, **by telegraph, for week** ended March 2, 1918:

Scarlet fever: Schools closed Green Township, Jay County, 1 death Huntington, 2 deaths each Wabash and Morocco. Smallpox: Epidemic Gary, Hammond, Crown Point, Lowell, Anderson, Richmond. Diphtheria: One death each Gary and Greensburg. Measles: Epidemic Cayuga, Akron, Greencastle. Infantile paralysis: One case Bloomington. 2 cases Columbus. Rabies: Epidemic, dogs, Perry County.

Kansas.

From Collaborating Epidemiologist Crumbine, **by telegraph, for** week ended March 2, 1918:

Meningitis: In cities, Augusta 1, Cherokee 1, Corbin 1, Junction City 1, Kanopolis 1, Kansas City 3, Madison 2, Paola 1, Pittsburg 1 Wichita 1. Smallpox: In cities Kansas City 30, Topeka 10. Winfield 27.

Louisiana.

From Collaborating Epidemiologist Dowling, by telegraph, for week ended March 2, 1918:

Meningitis, excluding Rapides: Caddo 1, De Soto 1, Jackson 1, Lincoln 4, Orleans 2, Vermilion 1.

Massachusetts.

From Collaborating Epidemiologist Kelley, by telegraph, for week ended March 2, 1918:

Unusual prevalence. German measles: Framingham 37, Newton 63, Salem 35, Ashland 40, Beverly 26, Marlboro 55, Quincy 57, Wellesley 30, Winchester 19. Smallpox: Boston 1, Marlboro 3. Typhus: Chelsea 1.

Minnesota.

From Collaborating Epidemiologist Bracken, by telegraph, for week ended March 2, 1918:

Smallpox (new foci): Fillmore County, Sumner Township; Marshall County, Moylan Township; Polk County, Garfield Township. 1 each; Mower County, Lansing Township; St. Louis County, Proctor village; Wadena County, Meadow Township, 2 each. One poliomyelitis and 4 cerebrospinal meningitis reported since February 25.

Nebraska.

From the State Board of Health of Nebraska, by telegraph, for week ended March 2, 1918

Smallpox: Holdrege, Despler, Wassa, Bruning, Gordon, Valentine, Omaha, Lincoln. German measles: Fillmore County, Lincoln, Peru. Measles: Omaha.

Ohio.

From Collaborating Epidemiologist Freeman, by telegraph, for week ended March 2, 1917:

Zanesville, typhoid fever 8 cases. Cuyahoga Falls, typhoid fever 5 cases. Meningitis, entire State 5 cases. Poliomyelitis, Warren 1 case.

South Carolina.

From Collaborating Epidemiologist Hayne, by telegraph, for week ended March 2, 1918:

Twenty cases meningitis. Five additional suspected cases.

Vermont.

From Collaborating Epidemiologist Dalton, by telegraph, for week ended March 2, 1918:

Smallpox: Island Pond, 4 cases. No other outbreak or unusual prevalence.

Virginia.

From Collaborating Epidemiologist Traynham, by telegraph, for week ended March 2, 1918:

Four cases smallpox Wise County, 1 case Northampton, 1 Louisa. Two cases cerebrospinal meningitis Henrico County, 1 Hanover, 1 Roanoke, 1 Prince George.

Washington.

From Collaborating Epidemiologist Tuttle, by telegraph, for week ended March 2, 1918:

Scarlet fever: Tacoma 21 cases, Steilacoom 4, Ellensburg 4. Measles: Vancouver 27. Diphtheria: Leavenworth 4. German measles: Prevalent.

CEREBROSPINAL MENINGITIS.

Arkansas—Morrillton.

On February 27, 1918, the presence of cerebrospinal meningitis was reported at Morrillton, Ark., where 8 cases had recently occurred.

State Reports for January, 1918.

Place.	New cases reported.	Place.	New cases reported.
Arkansas:		Mississippi—Continued.	
Chicot County	5	Jasper County	2
Conway County	1	Jefferson County	1
Phillips County	1	Lamar County	1
Pulaski County	10	Panola County	1
		Perry County	1
Total	26	Quitman County	1
		Rankin County	2
Colorado:		Washington County	1
Alamosa County	1		
Mineral County	2	Total	15
Total	3	Pennsylvania:	
		Allegheny County	2
Connecticut:		Armstrong County	1
Fairfield County—		Cambria County	2
Bridgeport	3	Lackawanna County	3
Greenwich	1	Lawrence County	1
Hartford County—		Luzerne County	2
Bristol	2	Philadelphia County	12
Hartford	4	Schuylkill County	1
New Britain	1	Somerset County	1
Windsor Locks	1		
New Haven County—		Total	27
Guilford	1		
New Haven	3	South Carolina:	
Orange	1	Anderson County	1
Waterbury	1	Calhoun County	1
Middlesex County—		Charleston County	1
Cromwell	1	Chester County	2
New London County—		Deerfield County	1
Groton	2	Florence County	2
		Greenville County	6
Total	21	Hampton County	1
		Horry County	1
District of Columbia	37	Kershaw County	1
		Lexington County	3
Iowa:		Newberry County	1
Cass County	1	Oconee County	1
Linn County	1	Orangeburg County	3
Polk County	4	Pickens County	2
Van Buren County	2	Richland County	4
		Robeson County	1
Total	8	Spartanburg County	6
		Union County	1
Mississippi:			
Adams County	1	Total	105
Forrest County	1		
Grenada County	1	South Dakota:	
Hinds County	1	Brown County	1

City Reports for Week Ended Feb. 16, 1918.

Place.	Cases.	Deaths.	Place.	Cases.	Deaths.
Akron, Ohio	1	....	Louisville, Ky	1	2
Alexandria, La	....	1	Lowell, Mass	1	1
Anniston, Ala	2	....	Macon, Ga	7	1
Atlanta, Ga	5	5	Manchester, N. H	1	....
Augusta, Ga	5	....	Milwaukee, Wis	3	2
Baltimore, Md	3	1	Montgomery, Ala	2	3
Birmingham, Ala	....	1	Nashville, Tenn	1	1
Charleston, S. C	4	1	Newark, N. J	1	....
Charlotte, N. C	2	....	New Orleans, La	5	1
Chattanooga, Tenn	1	2	New York, N. Y	7	7
Chelsea, Mass	1	2	Norfolk, Va	1	....
Chicago, Ill	5	2	Omaha, Nebr	1	....
Chillicothe, Ohio	1	1	Philadelphia, Pa	12	5
Cincinnati, Ohio	2	....	Pittsburgh, Pa	3	1
Cleveland, Ohio	2	2	Providence, R. I	2	1
Columbia, S. C	2	....	Racine, Wis	....	1
Dayton, Ohio	2	....	Richmond, Va	1	....
Durham, N. C	....	1	Saginaw, Mich	1	....
Elizabeth, N. J	....	1	St. Louis, Mo	3	1
Ft. Wayne, Ind	1	....	San Antonio, Tex	2	7
Galveston, Tex	1	....	San Francisco, Cal	1	....
Hagerstown, Md	1	....	Savannah, Ga	1	....
Jacksonville, Fla	9	1	Schenectady, N. Y	1	....
Kearny, N. J	2	....	Waco, Tex	3	....
Lexington, Ky	....	1	Washington, D. C	7	2
Little Rock, Ark	1	....	Worcester, Mass	1	....

DIPHTHERIA.

See Diphtheria, measles, scarlet fever, and tuberculosis, page 335.

ERYSIPELAS.

City Reports for Week Ended Feb. 16, 1918.

Place.	Cases.	Deaths.	Place.	Cases.	Deaths.
Alameda, Cal	2	....	New Orleans, La	....	1
Ann Arbor, Mich	1	....	New York, N. Y	....	8
Atlanta, Ga	1	....	Oakland, Cal	1	....
Baltimore, Md	2	2	Ogden, Utah	1	....
Beaver Falls, Pa	1	1	Oklahoma City, Okla	1	1
Bridgeport, Conn	....	1	Omaha, Nebr	1	....
Brockton, Mass	1	....	Philadelphia, Pa	5	1
Buffalo, N. Y	9	....	Pittsburgh, Pa	6	2
Chicago, Ill	11	1	Providence, R. I	....	1
Cleveland, Ohio	6	....	Quincy, Ill	....	1
Denver, Colo	2	1	Rochester, N. Y	3	....
Detroit, Mich	5	2	Rock Island, Ill	1	....
Harrisburg, Pa	1	....	St. Joseph, Mo	1	....
Jackson, Miss	1	....	St. Louis, Mo	16	2
Jamestown, N. Y	1	....	Salt Lake City, Utah	....	1
Johnstown, Pa	1	....	San Antonio, Tex	1	2
Los Angeles, Cal	7	....	San Diego, Cal	2	....
Louisville, Ky	3	....	San Francisco, Cal	3	1
Memphis, Tenn	3	3	Schenectady, N. Y	1	....
Milwaukee, Wis	1	....	Toledo, Ohio	....	1
Newark, N. J	8	....	Troy, N. Y	1	....
New Castle, Pa	1	....			

LEPROSY.

City Reports for Week Ended Feb. 16, 1918.

During the week ended February 16, 1918, one case of leprosy was reported at New Orleans, La.

MALARIA.

State Reports for January, 1918.

Place.	New cases reported.	Place.	New cases reported.
Arkansas:		**Mississippi—Continued.**	
Ashley County	27	Lafayette County	14
Calhoun County	6	Lamar County	19
Craighead County	12	Lauderdale County	21
Greene County	4	Lawrence County	46
Jefferson County	3	Leake County	4
Ouachita County	1	Lee County	43
Perry County	4	Leflore County	64
Phillips County	2	Lincoln County	14
Pulaski County	9	Madison County	22
Scott County	1	Marion County	60
Sebastian County	8	Marshall County	22
Sevier County	60	Monroe County	30
St. Francis County	21	Montgomery County	3
White County	6	Neshoba County	60
		Newton County	9
Total	164	Noxubee County	9
		Oktibbeha County	50
Mississippi:		Panola County	40
Adams County	27	Pearl River County	3
Alcorn County	5	Perry County	14
Amite County	38	Pike County	54
Attala County	30	Pontotoc County	14
Benton County	3	Prentiss County	15
Bolivar County	380	Quitman County	110
Calhoun County	12	Rankin County	14
Carroll County	50	Scott County	5
Chickasaw County	6	Sharkey County	45
Choctaw County	23	Simpson County	20
Claiborne County	40	Smith County	35
Clarke County	21	Tallahatchie County	94
Coahoma County	199	Tate County	38
Copiah County	43	Tippah County	30
Covington County	37	Tunica County	78
De Soto County	9	Stone County	18
Forrest County	7	Sunflower County	166
Franklin County	50	Union County	11
George County	5	Walthall County	4
Greene County	12	Warren County	123
Grenada County	12	Washington County	101
Hancock County	32	Wayne County	11
Harrison County	43	Webster County	12
Hinds County	103	Wilkinson County	9
Holmes County	261	Winston County	70
Issaquena County	30	Yalobusha County	34
Itawamba County	10	Yazoo County	225
Jackson County	23		
Jasper County	43	Total	3,652
Jefferson County	57		
Jefferson Davis County	9	**South Carolina:**	
Jones County	36	Marion County	2
Kemper County	13		

City Reports for Week Ended Feb. 16, 1918.

Place.	Cases.	Deaths.	Place.	Cases.	Deaths.
Hattiesburg, Miss	9		Little Rock, Ark	3	
Houston, Tex		1	Macon, Ga	1	
Jackson, Miss	4				

MEASLES.

See Diphtheria, measles, scarlet fever, and tuberculosis, page 335.

PELLAGRA.

State Reports for January, 1918.

Place.	New cases reported.	Place.	New cases reported.
Arkansas:		**Mississippi—Continued.**	
Faulkner County	1	Lee County	5
Pulaski County	1	Leflore County	4
Sebastian County	5	Lincoln County	9
		Lowndes County	6
Total	7	Madison County	2
		Marion County	7
Connecticut:		Marshall County	6
Fairfield County—		Monroe County	7
Bridgeport	1	Neshoba County	24
New London County—		Newton County	1
Old Lyme	1	Noxubee County	4
		Oktibbeha County	1
Total	2	Panola County	2
		Pearl River County	1
Mississippi:		Perry County	3
Adams County	1	Pike County	2
Alcorn County	1	Pontotoc County	5
Attala County	1	Quitman County	3
Bolivar County	10	Rankin County	3
Carroll County	2	Sharkey County	2
Chickasaw County	8	Simpson County	1
Claiborne County	2	Stone County	1
Clay County	2	Sunflower County	6
Coahoma County	13	Tallahatchie County	13
Copiah County	3	Tippah County	1
Covington County	4	Tishomingo County	8
De Soto County	1	Tunica County	4
Franklin County	1	Union County	1
George County	1	Warren County	1
Greene County	1	Washington County	8
Harrison County	1	Wayne County	2
Hinds County	6	Webster County	2
Holmes County	3	Wilkinson County	1
Jackson County	2	Winston County	3
Jefferson County	1		
Jefferson Davis County	3	Total	226
Jones County	4		
Kemper County	2	**South Carolina:**	
Lamar County	2	Spartanburg County	3
Leake County	2		

City Reports for Week Ended Feb. 16, 1918.

Place.	Cases.	Deaths.	Place.	Cases.	Deaths.
Anniston, Ala	1		Little Rock, Ark	1	
Augusta, Ga		1	Los Angeles, Cal	1	
Birmingham, Ala	1	3	Memphis, Tenn	2	
Charleston, S. C		1	San Antonio, Tex		1
Houston, Tex		1	Spartansburg, S. C		1

PNEUMONIA.

City Reports for Week Ended Feb. 16, 1918.

Place.	Cases.	Deaths.	Place.	Cases.	Deaths.
Akron, Ohio	2		Cleveland, Ohio	23	22
Altoona, Pa	3		Detroit, Mich	29	47
Atlanta, Ga	10	16	Duluth, Minn	2	1
Baltimore, Md	65	48	Durham, N. C	4	1
Braddock, Pa	1		Elmira, N. Y	1	1
Bridgeport, Conn	3	12	Fall River, Mass	4	2
Brockton, Mass	5	4	Fort Worth, Tex	11	11
Cambridge, Mass	10	6	Grand Rapids, Mich	5	1
Chattanooga, Tenn	1	3	Hagerstown, Md	1	
Chelsea, Mass	10	5	Harrisburg, Pa	1	2
Chicago, Ill	196	83	Haverhill, Mass	2	3
Chicopee, Mass	2	1	Houston, Tex	2	6

PNEUMONIA—Continued.

City Reports for Week Ended Feb. 16, 1918—Continued.

Place.	Cases.	Deaths.	Place.	Cases.	Deaths.
Jackson, Mich..............	3	....	Newton, Mass.............	2	1
Jackson, Miss..............	8	....	North Adams, Mass........	3	1
Jacksonville, Fla...........	4	....	Northampton, Mass........	1	....
Kalamazoo, Mich...........	1	1	Oakland, Cal.............	8	10
Lancaster, Pa..............	1	....	Philadelphia, Pa..........	127	93
Lawrence, Mass............	7	4	Pittsburgh, Pa............	47	34
Leavenworth, Kan..........	5	2	Pontiac, Mich.............	1	....
Lexington, Ky.............	2	5	Providence, R. I...........	1	6
Lincoln, Nebr.............	2	....	Roanoke, Va.............	2	3
Long Beach, Cal...........	3	....	Rochester, N. Y...........	17	3
Los Angeles, Cal..........	19	12	Sacramento, Cal..........	1	3
Louisville, Ky............	8	13	St. Joseph, Mo...........	3	4
Lowell, Mass..............	1	4	Salem, Mass..............	3	3
Macon, Ga................	3	8	San Antonio, Tex..........	2	43
Malden, Mass.............	3	1	San Francisco, Cal........	20	13
Manchester, N. H..........	4	4	Schenectady, N. Y........	7	1
Melrose, Mass.............	2	....	Somerville, Mass..........	5	3
Montgomery, Ala..........	1	....	Springfield, Mass.........	3	....
Muskegon, Mich...........	1	....	Steubenville, Ohio........	1	....
Newark, N. J..............	49	14	Stockton, Cal.............	1	1
New Bedford, Mass.........	3	2	Waco, Tex...............	4	....
New Castle, Pa............	2	c	Wichita, Kans............	11	1
Newport, Ky..............	5	5	Worcester, Mass..........	5	10

POLIOMYELITIS (INFANTILE PARALYSIS).

State Reports for January, 1918.

Place.	New cases reported.	Place.	New cases reported.
Colorado:		Mississippi:	
Otero County.....................	1	Calhoun County.................	1
		Choctaw County................	1
Connecticut:		Harrison County................	1
Windham County—			
Woodstock......................	1	Total.....................	3
Iowa:		Pennsylvania:	
Dallas County....................	1	Allegheny County...............	1
Humboldt County.................	1	Cambria County................	2
Total.....................	2	Total.....................	3

City Reports for Week Ended Feb. 16, 1918.

Place.	Cases.	Deaths.	Place.	Cases.	Deaths.
Denver, Colo...............	....	1	Pittsburgh, Pa............	1	1
Milwaukee, Wis............	4	....	San Francisco, Cal.........	1	....
New York, N. Y............	1	1			

RABIES IN ANIMALS.

New York—Rochester.

On February 26, 1918, the prevalence of rabies among dogs was reported in Rochester, N. Y., where several cases of the disease had occurred since February 1, 1918.

City Reports for Week Ended Feb. 16, 1918.

During the week ended February 16, 1918, one case of rabies in animals was reported at Louisville, Ky., and one case at Memphis, Tenn.

SMALLPOX.

Alabama—Mobile.

During the week ended March 2, 1918, 10 new cases of smallpox were notified at Mobile, Ala., making a total of 36 cases recently reported.

Missouri—Kansas City.

During the 4 days from February 27 to March 2, 1918, 71 cases of smallpox were notified at Kansas City, Mo., and during the 2 days of March 4 and 5, 52 cases were notified.

Texas—Eagle Pass—Virulent Smallpox.

During the week ended March 4, 1918, 11 new cases of smallpox, with 1 death, were notified at Eagle Pass, Tex., making a total of 134 cases, with 29 deaths, reported since October 1, 1917. Since January 1, 1918, 101 cases have been reported.

Miscellaneous State Reports for January, 1918.

Place.	Cases.	Deaths.	Place.	Cases.	Deaths.
Arkansas:			**Colorado—Continued.**		
Ashley County	1		Mesa County	8	
Calhoun County	2		Morgan County	2	
Chicot County	10		Otero County	1	
Clay County	15		Phillips County	4	
Conway County	16		Pueblo County	2	
Craighead County	20		Weld County	2	
Crittenden County	1				
Dallas County	6		Total	175	
Drew County	3				
Faulkner County	12		**Connecticut:**		
Grant County	65		Litchfield County—		
Greene County	10		Colebrook	1	
Hempstead County	1		Winchester	2	
Howard County	6				
Izard County	47		Total	3	
Jefferson County	6				
Johnson County	12		District of Columbia	7	
Little River County	1				
Miller County	8		**Iowa:**		
Mississippi County	6		Adair County	2	
Monroe County	8		Appanoose County	10	
Ouachita County	3		Audubon County	2	
Perry County	3		Benton County	4	
Phillips County	29		Boone County	2	
Poinsett County	75		Bremer County	4	
Prairie County	1		Butler County	1	
Pulaski County	156		Calhoun County	4	
Scott County	2		Cass County	7	
Searcy County	17		Cerro Gordo County	1	
Sebastian County	17		Cherokee County	1	
Sevier County	5		Chickasaw County	12	
St. Francis County	4		Clay County	1	
Union County	7		Crawford County	8	
White County	25		Dallas County	3	
			Decatur County	3	
Total	600		Des Moines County	11	
			Dubuque County	13	
Colorado:			Emmet County	1	
Arapahoe County	2		Franklin County	11	
Chaffee County	11		Fremont County	2	
Denver County	58		Greene County	1	
Eagle County	4		Grundy County	1	
El Paso County	41		Hardin County	2	
Fremont County	1		Harrison County	1	
Garfield County	1		Henry County	1	
Jefferson County	33		Humboldt County	7	
Lincoln County	5		Iowa County	1	

SMALLPOX—Continued.

Miscellaneous State Reports for January, 1918—Continued.

Place.	Cases.	Deaths.	Place.	Cases.	Deaths.
Iowa—Continued.			**Mississippi:**		
Jackson County	2		Alcorn County	27	
Jasper County	1		Attala County	4	
Jefferson County	1		Benton County	4	
Johnson County	1		Bolivar County	5	
Jones County	1		Calhoun County	11	
Keokuk County	6		Carroll County	15	
Linn County	2		Chickasaw County	31	
Louisa County	2		Clarke County	25	
Lucas County	10		Clay County	32	
Lyon County	6		Coahoma County	11	
Madison County	13		Copiah County	4	
Marion County	3		Forrest County	10	
Marshall County	3		Franklin County	1	
Mills County	9		Greene County	5	
Monroe County	5		Grenada County	6	
Montgomery County	1		Harrison County	3	
O'Brien County	4		Hinds County	47	
Page County	13		Holmes County	3	
Palo Alto County	21		Itawamba County	3	
Polk County	192	2	Jasper County	45	
Pottowattamie County	83		Jones County	37	
Ringgold County	18		Kemper County	5	
Scott County	7		Lafayette County	4	
Shelby County	2		Lamar County	4	
Sioux County	30		Lee County	5	
Story County	10		Leflore County	17	
Union County	1		Lincoln County	2	
Wapello County	40		Lowndes County	7	
Wayne County	7		Madison County	9	
Webster County	11		Marshall County	3	
Winneshiek County	1		Noxubee County	4	
Woodbury County	11		Oktibbeha County	8	
Wright County	12		Panola County	67	
			Pearl River County	3	
Total	650	2	Pike County	3	
Maine:			Pontotoc County	5	
Aroostook County—			Quitman County	5	
Portage (town)	1		Rankin County	3	
Frenchville (town)	1		Scott County	11	
Mapleton (town)	1		Sharkey County	2	
Fort Fairfield (town)	7		Smith County	1	
Perham (town)	1		Stone County	9	
Wallagrass (planta-			Sunflower County	2	
tation)	1		Tallahatchie County	8	
Davidson	3		Tate County	11	
Bancroft (town)	1		Tippah County	5	
Van Buren (town)	2		Tunica County	4	
Caribou (town)	7		Union County	9	
Franklin County—			Warren County	6	
Chain-of-Ponds	3		Washington County	6	
Eustis (town)	4		Webster County	20	
Hancock County—			Winston County	1	
Bucksport (town)	1		Yalobusha County	3	
Eden (town)	1		Yazoo County	51	
Kennebec County—					
Oakland (town)	9		Total	631	
Augusta	3				
Penobscot County—			**North Dakota:**		
Brewer	8		Bottineau County	11	
Patten (town)	2		Cass County	3	
Lincoln (town)	1		Eddy County	1	
Sagadahoc County—			Griggs County	4	
Bowdoinham (town)	1		Morton County	1	
Somerset County—			Nelson County	1	
Mercer (town)	1		Pembina County	12	
Rockwood	1		Pierce County	1	
Long Pond (planta-			Ramsey County	4	
tion)	1		Sargent County	3	
Norridgewock (town)	2		Towner County	4	
Jackman (plantation)	13		Ward County	8	
Washington County—			Williams County	9	
Lubec (town)	5				
Baileyville (town)	1		Total	63	
Millbridge (town)	6				
Jonesport (town)	1		**Pennsylvania:**		
Eastport	3		Allegheny County	26	
			Beaver County	3	
Total	92		Center County	2	
			Clearfield County	6	

SMALLPOX—Continued.

Miscellaneous State Reports for January, 1918—Continued.

Place.	Cases.	Deaths.	Place.	Cases.	Deaths.
Pennsylvania—Continued.			South Dakota—Continued.		
Dauphin County.........	20		Clark county..........	6	
Erie County....	11		Codington county.......	6	
Franklin County....	1		Davison county.......	7	
Indiana County....	5		Day county....	2	
Mercer County....	4		Edmunds county....	1	
Northumberland County.	4		Haakon County....	4	
Potter County....	2		Hamlin County....	5	
Somerset County....	1		Hughes County....	5	
Westmoreland County....	1		Jerauld County....	1	
			Lake County....	12	
Total..............	86		McCook County....	1	
			Miner County....	5	
South Carolina:			Minnehaha County......	17	
Richland County........	2		Roberts County....	2	
Spartanburg County.....	2		Spink county....	3	
			Tripp County....	1	
Total...............	4		Union County....	5	
			Walworth county........	2	
South Dakota:			Yankton County.........	1	
Bon Homme County....	1		Ziebach County....	1	
Brown county....	7				
Charles Mix County.....	3		Total.................	108	

City Reports for Week Ended Feb. 16, 1918.

Place.	Cases.	Deaths.	Place.	Cases.	Deaths.
Akron, Ohio....	13		Kalamazoo, Mich....	1	
Alexandria, La....	1		Kansas City, Kans....	54	
Alton, Ill....	6		Knoxville, Tenn....	5	
Ann Arbor, Mich....	1		La Crosse, Wis....	9	
Anniston, Ala....	16		Leavenworth, Kans....	5	
Atlanta, Ga....	2		Lima, Ohio....	6	
Austin, Tex....	2	1	Lincoln, Nebr....	3	
Baltimore, Md....	2		Little Rock, Ark....	29	
Battle Creek, Mich....	2		Lorain, Ohio....	2	
Berlin, N. H....	4		Los Angeles, Cal....	3	
Birmingham, Ala....	46	2	Louisville, Ky....	2	
Butte, Mont....	6		Madison, Wis....	5	
Cairo, Ill....	1		Memphis, Tenn....	22	
Canton, Ohio....	6		Milwaukee, Wis....	7	
Charlotte, N. C....	1		Minneapolis, Minn....	15	
Chattanooga, Tenn....	5		Mobile, Ala....	6	
Chicago, Ill....	16		Moline, Ill....	1	
Cincinnati, Ohio....	17	1	Montgomery, Ala....	11	
Cleveland, Ohio....	45		Muncie, Ind....	5	
Coffeyville, Kans....	9		Muskegon, Mich....	8	
Columbus, Ohio....	11	1	Muskogee, Okla....	7	
Council Bluffs, Iowa....	23		New Orleans, La....	13	
Covington, Ky....	2		Newport, Ky....	1	
Cumberland, Md....	3		New York, N. Y....	1	
Davenport, Iowa....	1		Oakland, Cal....	1	
Dayton, Ohio....	11		Ogden, Utah....	1	
Des Moines, Iowa....	26		Oklahoma City, Okla....	20	
Detroit, Mich....	40		Omaha, Nebr....	33	
Dubuque, Iowa....	2		Pittsburgh, Pa....	1	
Duluth, Minn....	1		Pontiac, Mich....	3	
Elmira, N. Y....	1		Portland, Oreg....	5	
El Paso, Tex....	1		Quincy, Ill....	4	
Erie, Pa....	1		Roanoke, Va....	2	
Evanston, Ill....	1		Rockford, Ill....	1	
Evansville, Ind....	8		Saginaw, Mich....	1	
Everett, Wash....	4		St. Joseph, Mo....	10	
Flint, Mich....	16		St. Louis, Mo....	24	
Fort Wayne, Ind....	10		Salt Lake City, Utah....	30	
Fort Worth, Tex....	27		San Antonio, Tex....	1	
Galesburg, Ill....	1		San Francisco, Cal....	3	
Grand Rapids, Mich....	14		Scranton, Pa....	1	
Harrisburg, Pa....	2		Seattle, Wash....	1	
Hattiesburg, Miss....	17		Sioux City, Iowa....	16	
Houston, Tex....	7	1	Springfield, Ill....	2	
Indianapolis, Ind....	50	1	Springfield, Ohio....	1	
Jackson, Mich....	1		Toledo, Ohio....	5	
Jackson, Miss....	3		Waco, Tex....	1	
Jacksonville, Fla....	1		Wichita, Kans....	3	
Jersey City, N. J....	1				

TETANUS.

City Reports for Week Ended February 16, 1918.

During the week ended February 16, 1918, two deaths from tetanus were reported at Chicago, Ill., two cases at Newark, N. J., and one case at Philadelphia, Pa.

TYPHOID FEVER.

State Reports for January, 1918.

Place.	New cases reported.	Place.	New cases reported.
Arkansas:		**Mississippi—Continued.**	
Clay County	1	Jasper County	5
Newton County	1	Jefferson Davis County	2
Pulaski County	2	Kemper County	1
Sebastian County	4	Leake County	2
		Lee County	2
Total	8	LeBore County	3
		Lincoln County	5
Colorado:		Lowndes County	15
Archuleta County	1	Marion County	1
Denver County	1	Marshall County	1
Larimer County	1	Oktibbeha County	1
Lincoln County	1	Pearl River	2
Rio Blanco County	1	Pike County	5
		Pontotoc County	3
Total	5	Prentiss County	1
		Scott County	1
Connecticut:		Sunflower County	2
Fairfield County—		Tallahatchie County	8
New Canaan	1	Tate County	1
Hartford County—		Tippah County	2
Hartford	1	Tishomingo County	21
New Britain	2	Tunica County	1
Southington	1	Union County	2
Middlesex County—		Warren County	2
Middletown	7	Washington County	10
New Haven County—		Wayne County	1
New Haven	2	Webster County	3
Wallingford	1	Wilkinson County	3
Windham County—		Winston County	2
Plainfield	2	Yalobusha County	1
Windham	1	Yazoo County	1
Total	18	Total	148
District of Columbia	10	**Nevada:**	
		Lander County	1
Maine:		Washoe County	1
Cumberland County—			
Portland	1	Total	2
Knox County—			
Hope (town)	1	**North Dakota:**	
Rockland	1	Barnes County	1
Sagadahoc County—		Bowman County	2
Bath	1	Grant County	4
Waldo County—		Hettinger County	1
Knox (town)	1	Morton County	5
Washington County—		Stutsman County	2
Eastport	6		
		Total	15
Total	11		
		Pennsylvania:	
Mississippi:		Allegheny County	25
Adams County	2	Armstrong County	14
Amite County	6	Beaver County	2
Attala County	3	Bedford County	1
Benton County	2	Berks County	3
Bolivar County	3	Blair County	4
Carroll County	2	Bradford County	5
Choctaw County	1	Butler County	3
Clarke County	3	Cambria County	2
Coahoma County	2	Chester County	2
Copiah County	3	Crawford County	1
DeSoto County	1	Dauphin County	6
Hinds County	4	Delaware County	1
Holmes County	3	Erie County	2

TYPHOID FEVER—Continued.

State Reports for January, 1918—Continued.

Place.	New cases reported.	Place.	New cases reported.
Pennsylvania—Continued.		Pennsylvania—Continued.	
Fayette County	2	Washington County	4
Huntingdon County	2	Westmoreland County	2
Lancaster County	1	York County	7
Lawrence County	5		
Lebanon County	2	Total	146
Lehigh County	4		
Mercer County	10	South Carolina:	
Mifflin County	1	Chester County	2
Montgomery County	5	Richland County	1
Montour County	1	Spartanburg County	2
Northampton County	2		
Northumberland County	1	Total	5
Perry County	1		
Philadelphia County	18	South Dakota:	
Schuylkill County	2	Codington County	1
Sullivan County	1	Spink County	1
Susquehanna County	2		
Union County	1	Total	2
Warren County	1		

City Reports for Week Ended Feb. 16, 1918.

Place.	Cases.	Deaths.	Place.	Cases.	Deaths.
Alameda, Cal		1	Montgomery, Ala	1	
Albany, N. Y	4		Newark, N. J	1	
Alexandria, La	1		Newburgh, N. Y	1	1
Altoona, Pa	1		New Castle, Pa	1	
Baltimore, Md	2	1	New Haven, Conn		1
Brockton, Mass	1		New York, N. Y	5	1
Buffalo, N. Y		1	Norfolk, Va		1
Canton, Ohio			Philadelphia, Pa	3	1
Chicago, Ill	5		Pittsburgh, Pa	5	2
Cleveland, Ohio	2	1	Portland, Oreg	2	
Columbus, Ohio		1	Richmond, Va	1	
Detroit, Mich		1	Roanoke, Va	1	
Elizabeth, N. J	1		Salt Lake City, Utah	1	
Fall River, Mass	3		San Antonio, Tex	3	1
Fort Worth, Tex	1		San Diego, Cal		1
Galesbury, Ill		1	San Francisco, Cal	1	
Houston, Tex	2		Savannah, Ga		1
Indianapolis, Ind	2		Springfield, Ohio	6	1
Jacksonville, Fla	2		Stockton, Cal	1	1
Jamestown, N. Y	1		Syracuse, N. Y	1	
Kalamazoo, Mich	1		Trenton, N. J	1	
Lawrence, Mass	1		Troy, N. Y		1
Los Angeles, Cal	1		Washington, D. C	1	1
Louisville, Ky	1		Wheeling, W. Va	3	
Lynn, Mass	1		Wichita, Kans	1	
Minneapolis, Minn	6		Williamsburg, Pa	3	
Moline, Ill	5		Wilmington, Del	1	

DIPHTHERIA, MEASLES, SCARLET FEVER, AND TUBERCULOSIS.

State Reports for January, 1918.

State.	Cases reported.			State.	Cases reported.		
	Diphtheria.	Measles.	Scarlet fever.		Diphtheria.	Measles.	Scarlet fever.
Arkansas	15	1,064	72	Mississippi	72	15,348	216
Colorado	68	491	173	Nevada	2	20	56
Connecticut	322	705	178	North Dakota	39	30	129
Dist. of Columbia	57	576	268	Pennsylvania	1,003	3,050	151
Iowa	58		422	South Carolina	59	219	10
Maine	19	727	27	South Dakota	15	112	108

DIPHTHERIA, MEASLES, SCARLET FEVER, AND TUBERCULOSIS—Continued.

City Reports for Week Ended Feb. 16, 1918.

City.	Population as of July 1, 1916 (estimated by U. S. Census Bureau).	Total deaths from all causes.	Diphtheria.		Measles.		Scarlet fever.		Tuberculosis.	
			Cases.	Deaths.	Cases.	Deaths.	Cases.	Deaths.	Cases.	Deaths.
Over 500,000 inhabitants:										
Baltimore, Md	589,621	317	11	1	116	3	8	....	28	32
Chicago, Ill	2,497,722	738	102	19	52	2	63	1	129	82
Cleveland, Ohio	674,073	189	61	6	19	....	6	....	31	21
Detroit, Mich	571,784	229	69	8	24	3	33	....	38	25
Los Angeles, Cal	503,812	131	27	1	221	....	16	....	37	19
New York, N. Y	5,602,841	1,740	189	30	1,061	21	129	5	241	190
Philadelphia, Pa	1,709,518	702	47	2	172	5	44	....	80	78
Pittsburgh, Pa	579,090	213	14	3	181	2	12	....	27	9
St. Louis, Mo	757,309	280	51	5	87	....	36	....	41	28
From 300,000 to 500,000 inhabitants:										
Buffalo, N. Y	468,558	139	12	4	42	2	13	....	28	15
Cincinnati, Ohio	410,476	170	13	1	20	1	12	....	16	20
Jersey City, N. J	306,345	....	22	....	70	....	15	....	19	....
Milwaukee, Wis	436,535	97	5	2	136	....	60	2	16	3
Minneapolis, Minn	363,454	....	11	2	31	....	31	1	....	14
Newark, N. J	408,894	....	21	2	156	3	6	2	44	23
New Orleans, La	371,747	158	18	1	102	2	1	....	31	77
San Francisco, Cal	463,516	167	12	....	69	....	14	....	29	19
Seattle, Wash	348,639	....	6	....	219	....	8	....	19	4
Washington, D. C	363,960	155	4	2	244	4	40	....	19	13
From 200,000 to 300,000 inhabitants:										
Columbus, Ohio	214,878	70	....	....	19	....	24	....	7	6
Denver, Colo	260,800	82	1	....	190	....	34	....	....	13
Indianapolis, Ind	271,708	77	16	3	83	....	32	1	17	10
Louisville, Ky	238,910	101	11	....	46	....	4	....	12	11
Portland, Oreg	295,463	61	1	....	61	....	5	....	5	2
Providence, R. I	254,960	96	12	....	18	3	8	....	20	14
Rochester, N. Y	256,417	78	21	1	51	1	16	....	16	8
From 100,000 to 200,000 inhabitants:										
Albany, N. Y	104,199	....	2	....	19	....	1	....	13	....
Atlanta, Ga	190,558	74	6	....	30	....	5	1	11	5
Birmingham, Ala	181,762	88	....	....	49	4	1	....	8	5
Bridgeport, Conn	121,579	56	6	1	5	....	1	....	7	5
Cambridge, Mass	112,981	41	4	....	83	....	....	....	2	4
Camden, N. J	106,733	....	5	....	34	....	5	....	7	....
Dayton, Ohio	127,224	39	3	....	26	....	8	....	5	3
Des Moines, Iowa	101,598	....	5	2	4	....	7	....	....	....
Fall River, Mass	128,366	46	3	....	4	1	16	....	9	4
Fort Worth, Tex	104,562	39	4	....	2	....	2	....	1	1
Grand Rapids, Mich	128,291	28	9	....	16	....	3	....	3	....
Hartford, Conn	110,900	....	4	....	5	1	4	....	4	2
Houston, Tex	112,307	35	1	....	26	....	....	....	4	2
Lawrence, Mass	100,560	36	4	....	17	....	1	....	5	2
Lowell, Mass	113,245	51	1	....	4	....	2	1	3	4
Lynn, Mass	102,425	29	2	....	16	....	8	....	2	....
Memphis, Tenn	148,995	73	6	....	29	....	4	....	20	15
Nashville, Tenn	117,057	48	1	....	10	....	2	....	4	7
New Bedford, Mass	118,158	41	2	....	29	....	2	....	13	8
New Haven, Conn	149,685	r	r	....	8	1	2	....	8	5
Oakland, Cal	198,604	44	2	....	32	....	5	....	6	4
Omaha, Nebr	165,470	28	3	....	57	....	17	....	1	4
Reading, Pa	109,381	38	2	1	4	....	1	....	1	2
Richmond, Va	156,687	74	1	....	42	....	5	....	8	6
Salt Lake City, Utah	117,399	29	6	....	56	1	12	1	....	6
San Antonio, Tex	123,831	74	3	2	14	1	3	....	....	17
Scranton, Pa	146,811	52	6	....	5	....	7	....	....	3
Springfield, Mass	105,942	39	6	....	64	....	5	....	6	2
Syracuse, N. Y	155,621	63	6	....	85	10	21	1	3	2
Tacoma, Wash	112,770	....	1	....	3	....	8	....	....	....
Toledo, Ohio	191,554	80	6	....	15	....	10	1	37	6
Trenton, N. J	111,383	51	2	1	14	....	4	....	4	6
Worcester, Mass	163,314	66	2	1	12	....	11	....	7	6
From 50,000 to 100,000 inhabitants:										
Akron, Ohio	85,625	....	3	....	24	....	6	....	5	....
Altoona, Pa	58,651	....	3	....	....	....	....	....	2	....
Atlantic City, N. J	57,699	....	....	....	2	....	....	....	....	....
Augusta, Ga	50,245	20	....	....	29	....	....	....	....	....

DIPHTHERIA, MEASLES, SCARLET FEVER, AND TUBERCULOSIS—Continued.

City Reports for Week Ended Feb. 16, 1918—Continued.

City.	Population as of July 1, 1916 (estimated by U. S. Census Bureau).	Total deaths from all causes.	Diphtheria.		Measles.		Scarlet fever.		Tuberculosis.	
			Cases.	Deaths.	Cases.	Deaths.	Cases.	Deaths.	Cases.	Deaths.
From 50,000 to 100,000 inhabitants—Continued.										
Bayonne, N. J.	69,893				32		4		2	
Berkeley, Cal.	57,653	9	1		5		4		2	
Binghamton, N. Y.	53,973	19	2		20		5		2	1
Brockton, Mass.	67,449	20			9		4		4	2
Canton, Ohio.	60,852	13	4				4			2
Charleston, S. C.	60,734	24					1			
Chattanooga, Tenn.	60,075	8	1		1				1	3
Covington, Ky.	57,144	27	1		1				2	4
Duluth, Minn.	94,495	10	4		39		3		2	2
Elizabeth, N. J.	89,190		5	1	65	1	4		7	
El Paso, Tex.	63,705	31	1		19		1			10
Erie, Pa.	75,185	36	8		2		2		1	3
Evansville, Ind.	76,078	35	6	1	3				1	3
Flint, Mich.	64,772	9	4		2		11	1	5	
Fort Wayne, Ind.	76,183	21	4	1			4		1	1
Harrisburg, Pa.	72,015	13	2		7		6		6	2
Hoboken, N. J.	77,214	29	2		11	1			7	4
Jacksonville, Fla.	76,101				55				2	
Johnstown, Pa.	68,629	24	2				15		3	1
Kansas City, Kans.	99,437		2		31		7			
Lancaster, Pa.	50,853		1		10		5			
Little Rock, Ark.	57,343				19					
Malden, Mass.	51,155	13	1		4		2		1	1
Manchester, N. H.	78,-83	29	1		6		1		5	1
Mobile, Ala.	55,221	25	1		1				1	1
New Britain, Conn.	53,794	20	3		5		4		1	1
Norfolk, Va.	8,612		1		15		3		1	7
Oklahoma City, Okla.	92,943	12	1	1	13					
Passaic, N. J.	71,744	21	3				4		1	2
Portland, Me.	6?,867	24	2		26	1	4			1
Rockford, Ill.	5?,185	17			9		8		2	1
Sacramento, Cal.	66,895	30	1		37		5		5	6
Saginaw, Mich.	55,642	22		1	1		3			
St. Joseph, Mo.	85,236	36	2		78		1		1	5
San Diego, Cal.	55,330	14			113		6		4	5
Savannah, Ga.	68,805		1		10				4	
Schenectady, N. Y.	99,519	22	4	1	7		6		12	3
Sioux City, Iowa.	57,078	1	1	1			19			
Somerville, Mass.	87,039	22	2		25		4		1	1
South Bend, Ind.	68,946	15			9				1	
Springfield, Ill.	61,120	18	3		3					2
Springfield, Ohio.	51,550	21	1		2		4		2	5
Terre Haute, Ind.	66,083	23	2		0				1	2
Troy, N. Y.	77,916	35			2		5		2	2
Wichita, Kans.	70,722		2		132		5			
Wilkes-Barre, Pa.	76,776	21	2		22		3		3	
Wilmington, Del.	94,265	44			10		1			1
From 25,000 to 50,000 inhabitants:										
Alameda, Cal.	27,732	5	1		10		1		2	
Austin, Tex.	34,814		1	1						1
Battle Creek, Mich.	29,480		7	1	30		2		1	2
Bellingham, Wash.	32,185	7							2	2
Brookline, Mass.	32,730	7	3	1	10		1		2	
Butler, Pa.	27,632	11			26		1			
Butte, Mont.	43,425		2		3		6			
Cedar Rapids, Iowa.	37,308						3			
Charlotte, N. C.	39,823				31		1			
Chelsea, Mass.	46,192	20			18				6	1
Chicopee, Mass.	29,319	10			1				2	1
Clinton, Iowa.	27,386		1				6			
Columbia, S. C.	34,611	19	2		10				2	
Council Bluffs, Iowa.	31,484				1		1			
Cranston, R. I.	24,187		1				1			2
Cumberland, Md.	26,074	6	1		2		5		1	1
Danville, Ill.	32,261	6	1		37		2		1	
Davenport, Iowa.	48,811				3		7			
Dubuque, Iowa.	39,873				3		1			
Durham, N. C.	25,061	4	1		10					
Easton, Pa.	30,530	9	2	1	7				1	3

DIPHTHERIA, MEASLES, SCARLET FEVER, AND TUBERCULOSIS—
Continued.

City Reports for Week Ended Feb. 16, 1918—Continued.

City.	Population as of July 1, 1916 (estimated by U. S. Census Bureau).	Total deaths from all causes.	Diphtheria.		Measles.		Scarlet fever.		Tuberculosis.	
			Cases.	Deaths.	Cases.	Deaths.	Cases.	Deaths.	Cases.	Deaths.
From 25,000 to 50,000 inhabitants—Continued.										
East Orange, N. J.	42,458	8	1	....	14	....	2	....	3	....
Elgin, Ill.	28,203	8	....	....	2	....	1	....	2	....
Elmira, N. Y.	38,120	2	1	....	26	....	3	....	2	1
Evanston, Ill.	28,591	6	1	....	22	....	1	....	....	....
Everett, Mass.	39,233	8	5	....	6	....	....	....	2	1
Everett, Wash.	35,486	6	....	....	1	....	....	....	....	1
Fitchburg, Mass.	41,781	13	....	....	....	....	....	....	....	1
Galveston, Tex.	41,863	15	....	....	2	....	....	....	....	....
Green Bay, Wis.	29,353	12	....	....	....	....	....	....	....	1
Hagerstown, Md.	25,679	....	2	....	3	....	2	....	....	....
Haverhill, Mass.	48,477	15	1	....	15	1	4	....	2	2
Jackson, Mich.	35,363	18	....	....	5	....	29	2	1	....
Jackson, Miss.	29,737	18	....	....	3	....	....	....	....	....
Jamestown, N. Y.	36,580	12	2	....	7	....	....	....	4	....
Kalamazoo, Mich.	48,886	20	1	....	12	....	1	....	2	1
Kenosha, Wis.	31,576	6	8	....	1	....	6	....	....	....
Knoxville, Tenn.	38,676	....	1	....	21	....	1	....	2	1
La Crosse, Wis.	31,677	11	9	2	....	....	....	....	....	1
Lexington, Ky.	41,097	32	....	....	33	....	1	....	....	4
Lima, Ohio.	35,784	11	....	....	10	....	1	....	....	....
Lincoln, Nebr.	46,515	12	1	....	1	....	3	....	1	....
Long Beach, Cal.	27,587	12	....	....	30	....	....	....	1	1
Lorain, Ohio.	36,964	....	3	....	....	....	....	....	....	....
Lynchburg, Va.	32,940	11	....	....	....	....	....	....	....	....
Macon, Ga.	45,757	21	1	....	8	....	....	....	1	....
Madison, Wis.	30,609	7	....	....	12	....	3	....	....	....
Medford, Mass.	26,234	25	1	....	6	....	3	....	2	1
Moline, Ill.	27,451	9	....	....	2	....	2	....	....	....
Montclair, N. J.	26,318	6	....	....	110	....	1	....	1	1
Montgomery, Ala.	43,285	28	1	....	22	....	....	....	2	4
Mount Vernon, N. Y.	37,009	....	3	....	16	....	....	....	....	1
Muncie, Ind.	27,424	....	2	....	4	....	....	....	1	....
Muskegon, Mich.	26,100	13	....	....	1	....	....	....	....	....
Muskogee, Okla.	44,218	....	....	....	29	....	....	....	....	....
Nashua, N. H.	27,327	6	....	....	....	....	....	....	....	....
Newburgh, N. Y.	29,603	13	....	....	1	....	1	....	....	1
New Castle, Pa.	41,133	....	1	....	14	....	2	....	....	....
Newport, Ky.	31,927	10	1	1	....	....	....	....	1	1
Newport, R. I.	30,108	6	1	1	....	....	1	....	....	....
Newton, Mass.	43,715	6	2	....	27	....	....	....	....	....
Niagara Falls, N. Y.	37,533	14	....	....	3	....	1	....	1	1
Norristown, Pa.	31,401	14	....	....	8	....	1	....	....	1
Norwalk, Conn.	26,839	....	1	....	....	....	....	....	....	....
Ogden, Utah.	31,464	7	....	....	18	....	1	....	....	....
Orange, N. J.	33,060	8	....	....	1	....	....	....	2	....
Pasadena, Cal.	45,400	13	....	....	58	....	1	....	4	4
Perth Amboy, N. J.	41,185	13	....	....	5	....	....	....	....	3
Petersburg, Va.	25,582	....	....	....	4	....	....	....	6	2
Pittsfield, Mass.	38,629	9	1	....	2	....	....	....	3	1
Portsmouth, Va.	39,651	17	1	....	11	....	1	....	....	1
Quincy, Ill.	36,708	11	2	....	11	1	....	....	....	1
Quincy, Mass.	38,136	17	1	....	76	....	4	....	2	3
Racine, Wis.	45,486	9	1	....	18	....	2	....	3	2
Roanoke, Va.	43,284	12	2	....	8	....	....	....	3	1
Rock Island, Ill.	28,936	....	1	....	20	....	9	....	....	....
Salem, Mass.	48,562	19	....	....	26	....	1	....	2	4
San Jose, Cal.	38,902	....	3	....	21	....	....	....	1	....
Steubenville, Ohio.	27,445	11	....	....	2	....	1	....	....	....
Stockton, Cal.	35,358	13	....	....	44	1	....	....	5	3
Superior, Wis.	46,226	5	....	....	20	....	3	....	....	....
Taunton, Mass.	36,283	5	1	....	....	....	1	....	4	3
Waco, Tex.	33,385	....	....	....	20	....	....	....	....	1
Waltham, Mass.	30,570	10	3	....	2	....	....	....	....	1
Watertown, N. Y.	29,884	1	....	....	17	....	....	....	....	....
West Hoboken, N. J.	43,139	7	....	....	....	....	....	....	....	....
Wheeling, W. Va.	43,377	12	1	....	7	....	....	....	1	3
Williamsport, Pa.	33,809	10	5	....	....	....	....	....	....	....
Wilmington, N. C.	29,892	18	....	....	1	....	....	....	....	....
Winston-Salem, N. C.	31,155	19	....	....	30	....	....	....	4	1
Woonsocket, R. I.	44,360	....	....	....	20	....	....	....	....	....
Zanesville, Ohio.	30,863	9	....	....	....	....	....	....	1	1

DIPHTHERIA, MEASLES, SCARLET FEVER, AND TUBERCULOSIS—Continued.

City Reports for Week Ended Feb. 16, 1918—Continued.

City.	Population as of July 1, 1916 (estimated by U. S. Census Bureau).	Total deaths from all causes.	Diphtheria. Cases.	Diphtheria. Deaths.	Measles. Cases.	Measles. Deaths.	Scarlet fever. Cases.	Scarlet fever. Deaths.	Tuberculosis. Cases.	Tuberculosis. Deaths.
From 10,000 to 25,000 inhabitants:										
Alexandria, La...............	15,333	8	2		7					
Alton, Ill..................	22,874	9	2		17		2			
Ann Arbor, Mich...........	15,010	5	2		21		1		2	
Anniston, Ala..............	14,112				16					
Braddock, Pa..............	21,685	13	1							
Cairo, Ill.................	15,794	12			10					3
Chillicothe, Ohio..........	15,470	7	1	1	5		3			1
Clinton, Mass.............	13,075	4			4				1	1
Coffeyville, Kans..........	17,548				18				1	
Concord, N. H.............	22,669	11			1		1		2	1
Galesburg, Ill.............	24,276	14	1		1					
Greenville, S. C...........	18,181	3			7					
Harrison, N. J.............	16,950		1							
Hattiesburg, Miss..........	16,482	4			2					
Kearny, N. J...............	23,539	9			26		3			
Kokomo, Ind...............	20,930	9			6					2
La Fayette, Ind...........	21,286	1			3		3			
Leavenworth, Kans........	19,363	10	4		2					2
Long Branch, N. J.........	15,395	9								
Marinette, Wis............	14,610	4					1			1
Melrose, Mass.............	17,445	9	2		1			1		
Morristown, N. J..........	13,284	7					1			
Muscatine, Iowa...........	17,500				6		3			
Nanticoke, Pa.............	23,126	9					3			
New Albany, Ind..........	23,629	8			2					3
Newburyport, Mass........	15,243	5			1		1			
North Adams, Mass........	22,019	11							1	
Northampton, Mass........	19,926	12					4			2
Plainfield, N. J...........	23,805	10			2					
Pontiac, Mich.............	17,524	12	3		5		6			
Rocky Mount, N. C........	12,067	4	1		1				1	
Rutland, Vt...............	14,831	11								1
Sandusky, Ohio............	20,193	7					2			
Saratoga Springs, N. Y....	13,821	4			2					
Spartanburg, S. C.........	21,365	22			7					3
Steelton, Pa..............	15,548				1		2			
Washington, Pa...........	21,618				24				1	
Wilkinsburg, Pa...........	23,228	6			13		1		1	
Woburn, Mass.............	15,969	4								1

¹ Population Apr. 15, 1910; no estimate made.

25

FOREIGN.

CHINA.

Cerebrospinal Meningitis—Hongkong.

An outbreak of cerebrospinal meningitis, with 113 cases, of which 58 were fatal, occurring during the period from February 9 to 23, 1918, has been reported at Hongkong.

CUBA.

Communicable Diseases—Habana.

Communicable diseases have been notified at Habana as follows:

Disease.	Feb. 1-10, 1918.		Cases remaining under treatment Feb. 10, 1918.	Disease.	Feb. 1-10, 1918.		Cases remaining under treatment Feb. 10, 1918.
	New cases.	Deaths.			New cases.	Deaths.	
Cerebrospinal meningitis			1	Paratyphoid fever			¹1
Diphtheria	5	1	4	Scarlet fever			3
Leprosy			11	Smallpox			3
Malaria	7		17	Typhoid fever	13	3	²62
Measles	9		17	Varicella	20		7

¹ Imported from the United States.　² From the interior, 16

GUATEMALA.

Typhus Fever—Guatemala City.

Typhus fever was reported present at Guatemala City, Guatemala, March 3, 1918.

INDO-CHINA.

Cholera—Plague—Smallpox—Leprosy—October, 1917.

During the month of October, 1917, 39 cases of cholera, 36 cases of plague, and 152 cases of smallpox were notified in Indo-China, as compared with 74 cases of cholera, 34 cases of plague, and 193 cases of smallpox notified during the month of September, 1917. The distribution of these diseases, by Provinces, during the month of October, 1917, was as follows:

Cholera.—Anam, 6 cases; Cambodia, 22; Cochin-China, 11; total, 39. The total for the corresponding month of 1916 was 103 cases.

Plague.—Anam, 13 cases; Cambodia, 18; Cochin-China, 5; total, 36 cases. The total for the corresponding month of 1916 was 27 cases.

Smallpox.—Anam, 42 cases; Cambodia, 3; Cochin-China, 98; Laos, 1 case; Tonkin, 8 cases; total, 152 cases. The total for the corresponding month of 1916 was 71 cases.

Leprosy.—Ten cases of leprosy were reported in Indo-China during the month of October, 1917.

PERU.

Plague—Dec. 1, 1917–Jan. 15, 1918.

During the period from December 1, 1917, to January 15, 1918, 106 cases of plague were notified in Peru. The cases were distributed according to Departments as follows: Ancachs, 2 cases occurring at Casma; Lambayeque, 22 cases occurring at Chiclayo, Ferrenafe, Jayanca, and Lambayeque; Libertad, 72 cases occurring at five localities and in the country district of Trujillo; Lima, 9 cases occurring in the city and surrounding country; and Piura, 1 case at Catacaos.

CHOLERA, PLAGUE, SMALLPOX, TYPHUS FEVER, AND YELLOW FEVER.

Reports Received During Week Ended Mar. 8, 1918.[1]

CHOLERA.

Place.	Date.	Cases.	Deaths.	Remarks.
India:				
Calcutta	Dec. 2–8		5	
Indo-China—				
Provinces				Oct. 1–31, 1917: Cases, 39; deaths,
Anam	Oct. 1–31	6	3	20.
Cambodia	...do...	29	13	
Cochin-China	...do...	11	4	
Saigon	Nov. 26–Dec. 9	3	3	
Persia:				
Mazandaran Province				July 30–Sept. 3, 1917: Cases, 384;
Achraf	July 30–Aug. 16	90	88	deaths, 276.
Barfrush	...do...	5	2	
Charoud	Aug. 26–Sept. 3	4	2	
Damghan	Aug. 26			Present.
Meched	Aug. 18–Sept. 2	174	82	
Ousoun Dare	Aug. 8			Do.
Sebzevar	Aug. 24			Do.
Sari	July 30–Aug. 16	97	97	
Semnan	Aug. 31–Sept. 2	14	5	
Philippine Islands:				
Provinces				Jan. 13–19, 1918: Cases, 222 deaths
				122.
Bohol	Jan. 13–19	18	16	
Capiz	...do...	23	17	
Cebu	...do...	12	5	
Iloilo	...do...	16	9	
Mindanao	...do...	100	53	
Occidental Negros	...do...	45	15	
Oriental Negros	...do...	8	7	

[1] From medical officers of the Public Health Service, American consuls, and other sources.

CHOLERA, PLAGUE, SMALLPOX, TYPHUS FEVER, AND YELLOW FEVER—Continued.

Reports Received During Week Ended Mar. 8, 1918—Continued.

PLAGUE.

Place.	Date.	Cases.	Deaths.	Remarks.
Brazil:				
Bahia	Dec. 30–Jan. 12	3	2	
Rio de Janeiro	Dec. 23–29	1		
Do	Jan. 6–12	1	1	
Indo-China:				
Provinces				Oct. 1–31, 1917: Cases, 36; deaths, 34.
Anam	Oct. 1–31	13	13	
Cambodia	do	18	18	
Cochin-China	do	5	3	
Saigon	Dec. 3–23	9	2	
Peru:				Dec. 1, 1917–Jan. 15, 1918: Cases, 108.
Ancachs Department—				
Casma	Dec. 1–Jan. 15	2		
Lambayeque Department	do	22		At Chiclayo, Ferrenafe, Jayanca, Lambayeque.
Libertad Department	do	72		At Guadalupe, Mansiche, Pacasmayo, Salaverry San Jose San Pedro, and country district of Trujillo
Lima Department	do	9		City and country
Piura Department—				
Catacaos	do	1		
Siam:				
Bangkok	Dec. 9–29	2	2	

SMALLPOX.

Place.	Date.	Cases.	Deaths.	Remarks.
Australia:				
New South Wales				Jan. 4–17, 1918: Cases, 1.
Warren	Jan. 4–17	1		
Brazil:				
Rio de Janeiro	Dec. 23–29	39	6	
Do	Dec. 30–Jan. 19	120	33	
Canada:				
British Columbia—				
Vancouver	Feb. 10–16	1		
New Brunswick—				
Moncton	Feb. 10–23	4		
Ontario—				
Sarnia	do	5		
Toronto	Feb. 10–16	1		
China:				
Amoy	Dec. 3–30			Present.
Antung	Jan. 13–27	2	2	Do.
Chungking	Dec. 16–29			
Dairen	Dec. 30–Jan. 12	2		
Hongkong	Dec. 23–29	1		
Shanghai	Jan. 7–20	11	40	Cases, foreign; deaths, native
Tientsin	Dec. 30–Jan. 19	5		
Egypt:				
Alexandria	Jan. 8–14	3		
Indo-China:				
Provinces				Oct. 1–31, 1917: Cases, 152; deaths, 43.
Anam	Oct. 1–31	43	3	
Cambodia	do	3	5	
Cochin-China	do	96	32	
Saigon	Nov. 26–Dec. 30	58	13	
Laos	Oct. 1–31	1		
Tonkin	do	4	4	
Italy:				
Leghorn	Jan. 14–27	10	5	
Messina	Jan. 13–19	1		
Milan				Nov. 1–30, 1917: Cases, 15.
Japan:				
Nagasaki	Jan. 14–27	3	1	
Taihoku	Jan. 8–14	1		
Yokohama	Jan. 17–23	2		
Mexico:				
Mazatlan	Feb. 6–12	2		
Mexico City	Jan. 27–Feb. 2	8		
Newfoundland:				
St. Johns	Feb. 2–15	6		
Philippine Islands:				
Manila	Jan. 13–19	3		
Spain:				
Seville	Dec. 1–30		40	

CHOLERA, PLAGUE, SMALLPOX, TYPHUS FEVER, AND YELLOW FEVER—Continued.

Reports Received During Week Ended Mar. 8, 1918—Continued.

TYPHUS FEVER.

Place.	Date.	Cases.	Deaths.	Remarks.
China:				
Antung...................	Jan. 13-27.........	2	1	
Egypt:				
Alexandria................	Oct. 22-28.........	13	7	
Do...................	Jan. 8-14.........	20	7	
Cairo....................	Dec. 3-16..........	11	6	
Guatemala:				
Guatemala City...........	Mar. 3.............	....	.....	Present.
Japan:				
Nagasaki................	Jan. 21-27.........	2	....	
Mexico:				
Mexico City................	Jan. 27-Feb. 2.....	54	....	

Reports Received from Dec. 29, 1917, to Mar. 1, 1918.

CHOLERA.

Place.	Date.	Cases.	Deaths.	Remarks.
China:				
Antung...................	Nov. 26-Dec. 2....	3	1	
India:				
Bombay..................	Oct. 28-Nov. 24...	17	12	
Calcutta.................	Sept. 16-Nov. 24..	....	76	
Madras..................	Nov. 25-Dec. 1....	1	1	
Rangoon.................	Nov. 4-Dec. 1.....	3	3	
Indo-China:				
Provinces................	....	....	....	Sept. 1-30, 1917: Cases, 74; deaths, 37.
Anam..............	Sept. 1-30.........	13	10	
Cambodia..........	....do...........	19	12	
Cochin-China......	....do...........	32	13	
Saigon...........	Nov. 22-28.......	1	....	
Kwang-Chow-Wan....	Sept. 1-30.........	10	2	
Java:				
East Java.................	Oct. 28-Nov. 3....	1	1	
West Java................	....	....	....	Oct. 19-Dec. 20, 1917: Cases, 100; deaths, 57.
Batavia...........	Oct. 19-Dec. 20...	55	21	
Persia:				
Mazanderan Province—				
Astrabad..............	July 31.............	....	....	Present.
Barfrush.............	July 1-27...........	34	23	
Chahmirzad..........	....	....	....	25 cases reported July 31, 1917.
Chahrastagh..........	June 15-July 25...	10	8	
Kharek..............	May 28-June 11...	21	13	
Sari................	July 3-29...........	273	144	
Yekchambe-Bazar....	June 3.............	6	....	
Philippine Islands:				
Provinces................	....	....	....	Nov. 18-Dec. 29, 1917: Cases, 1,053; deaths, 693. Dec. 30, 1917-Jan. 12, 1918: Cases, 225; deaths, 70.
Antique..............	Nov. 18-Dec. 1...	48	32	
Bohol...............	Nov. 18-Dec. 29...	169	111	
Do...............	Dec. 30-Jan. 12...	39	36	
Capiz...............	Nov. 25-Dec. 29...	27	21	
Do...............	Dec. 30-Jan. 12...	18	18	
Cebu................	Dec. 23-29.........	3	....	
Do...............	Dec. 30-Jan. 12...	24	12	
Iloilo...............	Nov. 25-Dec. 29...	179	135	
Do...............	Dec. 30-Jan. 12...	26	18	
Leyte...............	Nov. 26-Dec. 22...	13	12	
Mindanao............	Nov. 25-Dec. 29...	337	196	
Do...............	Dec. 30-Jan. 12...	114	82	
Occidental Negros.....	Nov. 25-Dec. 29...	177	123	
Oriental Negros.......	Nov. 25-Dec. 29...	99	62	
Do...............	Dec. 30-Jan. 12...	4	4	
Romblon.............	Nov. 25-Dec. 1....	1	1	
Siam:				
Bangkok...............	Sept. 16-22........	1	1	
Turkey in Asia:				
Bagdad................	Nov. 1-15..........	....	40	

CHOLERA, PLAGUE, SMALLPOX, TYPHUS FEVER, AND YELLOW FEVER—Continued.

Reports Received from Dec. 29, 1917, to Mar. 1, 1918—Continued.

PLAGUE.

Place.	Date.	Cases.	Deaths.	Remarks
Brazil:				
Bahia	Nov. 4-Dec. 15	4	4	
British Gold Coast:				
Axim	Jan. 8			Present.
Ceylon:				
Colombo	Oct. 14-Dec. 1	14	13	
Ecuador				Sept. 1-Nov. 30, 1917: Cases, 68; deaths, 26.
Guayaquil	Sept. 1-30	3	1	
Do	Oct. 1-31	20	8	
Do	Nov. 1-30	45	16	
Egypt.				Jan. 1-Nov. 15, 1917: Cases, 722; deaths, 398.
Port Said	July 23-29	1	2	
India.				Sept. 16-Dec. 1, 1917: Cases, 153,751; deaths, 113,694.
Bombay	Oct. 28-Dec. 1	103	85	
Calcutta	Sept. 16-29		2	
Henzada	Oct. 21-27		1	
Karachi	Oct. 21-Dec. 1	11	9	
Madras Presidency	Oct 31-Nov. 17	3,291	2,560	
Mandalay	Oct. 14-Nov. 17		80	
Rangoon	Oct. 21-Dec. 1	32	38	
Indo-China:				
Provinces				Sept. 1-30, 1917: Cases, 34; deaths, 30.
Anam	Sept. 1-30	12	11	
Cambodia	do	12	11	
Cochin-China	do	10	8	
Saigon	Oct. 31-Nov. 18	8	4	
Java:				
East Java				Oct. 27-Nov. 25, 1917: Cases, 78; deaths, 73.
Surabaya	Nov. 11-25	2	2	
West Java				Nov. 25-Dec. 9, 1917: Cases, 45; deaths, 45.
Senegal:				
St. Louis	Feb. 2			Present.
Siam:				
Bangkok	Sept. 16-Nov. 24	11	7	
Straits Settlements:				
Singapore	Oct. 28-Dec. 22	4	6	

SMALLPOX.

Place.	Date.	Cases.	Deaths.	Remarks
Algeria:				
Algiers	Nov. 1-Dec. 31	3	1	
Australia:				July 12-Dec. 28, 1917: Cases, 35.
New South Wales				
Abermain	Oct. 25-Nov. 29	3		Newcastle district.
Cessnock	July 12-Oct. 11	7		
Eumaugla	Aug. 15	1		
Kurri Kurri	Dec. 5-20	2		
Mungindi	Aug. 13	1		
Warren	July 12-Oct. 25	22		
Brazil:				
Bahia	Nov. 10-Dec. 8	2		
Pernambuco	Nov. 1-15	1		
Rio de Janeiro	Sept. 30-Dec. 22	684	126	
Sao Paulo	Oct. 29-Nov. 4		2	
Canada:				
British Columbia—				
Vancouver	Jan. 13-19	3		
Victoria	Jan. 7-Feb. 2	3		
Winnipeg	Dec. 30-Jan. 5	1		
New Brunswick—				
Kent County	Dec. 4			Outbreak. On main line Canadian Ry., 25 miles north of Moncton.
Do	Jan. 22	48		In 7 localities.
Northumberland County.	do	42		In 5 localities.
Restigouche County	Jan. 18	60		
Victoria County	Jan. 22	19		At Limestone and a lumber camp.
Westmoreland County, Moncton	Jan. 20-Feb. 9	4		
York County	Jan. 22	8		
Nova Scotia:				
Sydney	Feb. 3-9	1		

CHOLERA, PLAGUE, SMALLPOX, TYPHUS FEVER, AND YELLOW FEVER—Continued.

Reports Received from Dec. 29, 1917, to Mar. 1, 1918—Continued.

SMALLPOX—Continued.

Place.	Date.	Cases.	Deaths.	Remarks.
Canada—Continued.				
Ontario—				
Hamilton..............	Dec. 16-22........	1	....	
Do...............	Jan. 13-19........	2	....	
Sarnia................	Dec. 9-15.........	1	....	
Do...............	Jan. 6-Feb. 2.....	20	....	
Windsor.............	Dec. 30-Jan. 5....	1	....	
Prince Edward Island—				
Charlottetown........	Feb. 7-13.........	1	....	
Quebec—				
Montreal.............	Dec. 16-Jan. 5....	5	....	
Do...............	Jan. 6-12.........	1	....	
China:				
Amoy................	Oct. 22-Nov. 25..			Present.
Antung..............	Dec. 3-23.........	13	2	
Do...............	Jan. 7-13.........	2	....	
Chungking...........	Nov. 11-Dec. 15...			Do.
Dairen...............	Nov. 18-Dec. 22...	3	1	
Harbin...............	May 14-June 30...	20	....	Chinese Eastern Ry.
Do...............	July 1-Dec. 2.....	7	....	Do.
Hungchotze Stati n..	Oct. 28-Nov. 4....	1	....	Do.
Manchuria Stati n...	May 14-June 30...	6	....	Do.
Do...............	July 1-Dec. 2.....	3	....	Do.
Mukden..............	Nov. 11-24........			Present.
Shanghai............	Nov. 18-Dec. 23...	41	91	Cases, foreign; deaths among natives.
Do...............	Dec. 31-Jan. 6....	9	28	Do.
Tientsin.............	Nov. 11-Dec. 22...	13	....	
Cuba:				
Habana..............	Jan. 7............	1	....	Nov. 8, 1917: 1 case from Coruna, Dec. 5, 1917: 1 case.
Marianao............	Jan. 8............	1	....	6 miles distant from Habana.
Ecuador:				
Guayaquil...........	Sept. 1-30........	8	....	Sept. 1-Nov. 30, 1917: Cases, 26, deaths, 2.
Do...............	Oct. 1-31.........	14	1	
Do...............	Nov. 1-30.........	4	1	
Egypt:				
Alexandria..........	Nov. 12-18........	1	....	
Cairo...............	July 23-Nov. 12...	6	1	
France:				
Lyon................	Nov. 18-Dec. 16...	6	3	
Do...............	Jan. 7-20.........	5	....	
India:				
Bombay.............	Oct. 21-Dec. 1....	18	4	
Karachi.............	Nov. 18-24........		1	Nov. 11-17, 1917: 10 cases with 4 deaths; imported on s. s. Monesa from Basreh.
Madras..............	Oct. 31-Dec. 8....	9	3	
Rangoon............	Oct. 28-Nov. 24...	4	1	
Indo-China:				
Provinces...........				Sept. 1-30, 1917: Cases, 193 deaths, 56.
Anam.............	Sept. 1-30........	61	12	
Cambodia..........	...do............	7	....	
Cochin-China......	...do............	124	44	
Saigon.........	Oct. 20-Nov. 28...	62	8	
Tonkin...........	Sept. 1-30........	1	....	
Italy:				
Leghorn............	Jan. 7-13.........	7	....	
Milan...............				October, 1917: Cases, 2.
Turin...............	Oct. 29-Dec. 9....	223	129	
Castellamare........	Dec. 10...........	2	....	Among refugees.
Florence............	Dec. 1-15.........	17	4	
Naples..............	To Dec. 10........	2	....	Do.
Japan:				
Taiwan—				
Taihoku...........	Dec. 15-21........	1	....	
Java:				
East Java...........	Oct. 7-Dec. 9.....	25	....	
Mid-Java...........	Oct. 10-Nov. 21...	55	....	Oct. 10-Dec. 12, 1917: Cases, 69; deaths, 1.
Samarang........	Dec. 6-12.........	1	1	
West Java...........				Oct. 19-Dec. 20, 1917: Cases, 217; deaths, 33.
Batavia...........	Nov. 2-8..........	1	....	
Mexico:				
Aguascalientes......	Feb. 4-10.........		2	
Mazatlan...........	Dec. 5-11.........		1	
Do...............	Jan. 29-Feb. 5....	2	....	
Mexico City.........	Nov. 11-Dec. 29...	16	....	
Do...............	Dec. 30-Jan. 26...	22	....	
Piedras Negras......	Jan. 11...........	200	....	
Vera Cruz...........	Jan. 20-Feb. 9....	4	3	

CHOLERA, PLAGUE, SMALLPOX, TYPHUS FEVER, AND YELLOW FEVER—Continued.

Reports Received from Dec. 29, 1917, to March 1, 1918—Continued.

SMALLPOX—Continued.

Place.	Date.	Cases.	Deaths.	Remarks.
Newfoundland:				
St. Johns	Dec. 8–Jan. 4	29		
Do	Jan. 5–Feb. 1	19		
Trepassey	Jan. 4			Outbreak with 11 cases reported.
Philippine Islands:				
Manila	Oct. 28–Dec. 8	5		
Porto Rico:				
San Juan	Jan. 28–Feb. 3	1		Varioloid.
Portugal:				
Lisbon	Nov. 4–Dec. 15	2		
Do	Dec. 30–Jan. 19	2		
Portuguese East Africa:				
Lourenço Marques	Aug. 1–Nov. 30		9	
Russia:				
Moscow	Aug. 26–Oct. 6	22	2	
Petrograd	Aug. 31–Nov. 18	76	3	
Siam:				
Bangkok	Nov. 25–Dec. 1	1	1	
Spain:				
Coruna	Dec. 9–15		4	
Madrid				Jan. 1–Dec. 31, 1917: Deaths, 77.
Seville	Oct. 1–Nov. 30		26	
Straits Settlements:				
Singapore	Nov. 25–Dec. 1	1	1	
Tunisia:				
Tunis	Dec. 14–20		1	
Turkey in Asia:				
Bagdad				Present in November, 1917.
Venezuela:				
Maracaibo	Dec. 2–8		1	

TYPHUS FEVER.

Place.	Date.	Cases.	Deaths.	Remarks.
Algeria:				
Algiers	Nov. 1–Dec. 31	2	1	
Argentina:				
Rosario	Dec. 1–31		1	
Australia:				
South Australia				Nov. 11–17, 1917: Cases, 1.
Brazil:				
Rio de Janeiro	Oct. 28–Dec. 1	7		
Canada:				
Ontario—				
Kingston	Dec. 2–8	3		
Quebec—				
Montreal	Dec. 16–22	2	1	
China:				
Antung	Dec. 3–30	13	1	
Do	Dec. 31–Jan. 6		1	
Chosen (Formosa):				
Seoul	Nov. 1–30	1		
Egypt:				
Alexandria	Nov. 8–Dec. 28	57	15	
Cairo	July 23–Nov. 25	126	64	
Port Said	July 30–Nov. 11	5	5	
Great Britain:				
Glasgow	Dec. 21	1		
Do	Jan. 20–26	1		
Manchester	Dec. 2–8	1		
Greece:				
Saloniki	Nov. 11–Dec. 29		72	
Japan:				
Nagasaki	Nov. 26–Dec. 16	5	5	
Do	Jan. 7–13	1		
Java:				
East Java				Oct. 15–Dec. 9, 1917: Cases, 24; deaths, 3.
Mid-Java				Oct. 10–Dec. 12, 1917: Cases, 44; deaths, 2.
Samarang	Oct. 17–Dec. 5	15	2	
West Java				Oct. 19–Dec. 20, 1917: Cases, 72; deaths, 15.
Batavia	Oct. 19–Dec. 20	73	17	

CHOLERA, PLAGUE, SMALLPOX, TYPHUS FEVER, AND YELLOW FEVER—Continued.

Reports Received from Dec. 29, 1917, to March 1, 1918—Continued.

TYPHUS FEVER—Continued.

Place.	Date.	Cases.	Deaths.	Remarks.
Mexico:				
Aguascalientes.............	Dec. 15............	....	2	
Do..............	Jan. 21–Feb. 10....	....	14	
Durango, State—				
Guanacevi.............	Feb. 11............	....	....	Epidemic.
Mexico City................	Nov. 11–Dec. 29...	476	....	
Do..............	Dec. 30–Jan. 26....	183	....	
Portugal:				
Lisbon.................	Feb. 21............	....	....	Present.
Oporto..................	.....do.............	....	....	Epidemic.
Russia:				
Archangel.................	Sept. 1–14.........	7	2	
Moscow....................	Aug. 26–Oct. 6....	49	2	
Petrograd.................	Aug. 31–Nov. 18...	32	....	
Do..............	Feb. 2.............	....	....	Present.
Vladivostok................	Oct. 29–Nov. 4.....	12	1	
Sweden:				
Goteborg..................	Nov. 18–24........	1	....	
Switzerland:				
Basel.....................	Jan. 6–12..........	....	1	
Zurich....................	Nov. 9–15.........	2	....	
Do......................	Jan. 13–19.........	2	....	
Tunisia:				
Tunis.....................	Nov. 30–Dec. 6....	....	1	
Turkey:				
Albania—				
Janina....................	Jan. 27............	....	....	Epidemic.
Union of South Africa:				
Cape of Good Hope State...	Sept. 10–Nov. 11...	3,469	701	

YELLOW FEVER

Place.	Date.	Cases.	Deaths.	Remarks.
Ecuador......................		....	....	Sept. 1–Nov. 30, 1917: Cases, 5; deaths, 3.
Guayaquil..................	Sept. 1 30.........	1	1	
Do......................	Oct. 1 31..........	1	....	
Do......................	Nov. 1–30..........	2	2	
Yaguachi..................	.....do.............	1	....	
Honduras:				
Tegucigalpa................	Dec. 16–22.........	....	1	
Do......................	Jan. 6–19..........	....	1	

X

PUBLIC HEALTH REPORTS

| VOL. 33 | MARCH 15, 1918 | No. 11 |

METHODS FOR FIELD STUDY OF INDUSTRIAL FATIGUE.[1]

By P. Sargant Florence, Member of Committee on Industrial Fatigue, Advisory Commission of the Council of National Defense; Supervising Field Investigator (Scientific Assistant), United States Public Health Service.

Field investigation into industrial fatigue means investigation carried out in the factory itself, where fatigue is produced by ordinary work, as contrasted with experiments carried on in the laboratory, where fatigue is produced artificially and "ad hoc." These field investigations fall into two classes, investigations which measure ordinary natural fatigue by means of artificial "tests," such as the tests of reaction time or tests of sense acuity, carried out notably by Prof. Stanley Kent under the British Home Office and described in his two interim reports of 1915 and 1916, and investigations which measure fatigue by the ordinary events of industrial life, such as output (quantity and quality), accidents, power consumption, sickness, labor turnover. The most usual measure to take is that of quantity of output, wherever this does not depend exclusively on the speed of the machine. The data of the investigator are here either found ready for him in factory records kept for purposes of checking wages or measuring efficiency, or the investigator may observe and record the industrial processes himself. The output measure has been used recently by the British Health of Munition Workers Committee. Dr. Vernon, in Memoranda 12 and 18, has compared the output of the same individual workers in the same factory under different hourly schedules, i. e., he has compared the output per hour in a 70-hour working week against the output per hour in a 60-hour week. This was also the method pursued by Dr. Abbé in his famous experiment at the Zeiss Optical Works in reducing hours from 9 to 8 per day. Again in their interim report the British Health of Munition Workers Committee compared the output per hour on night work against the output per hour of the same workers when on the day shift, and they also compared the output per hour under different incentives.

---

[1] Read before the Section on Industrial Hygiene of the American Public Health Association, Washington, D. C., Oct. 19, 1917.

Now, all these investigations have compared the output of a given number of individuals before with the output after a change. Yet changes in hours are very distasteful to most factory owners. They require thought and involve many incidental rearrangements. The field for the "before and after" comparison is therefore strictly limited, and what I wish to put before you to-day is a method of testing fatigue which shall not depend immediately on any change in factory schedules.

This test may be called that of the "hourly output curve." Curiously enough, it was first used on a large scale by the United States Government in the report on Women and Child Wage Earners[1] (1910–1912). In volume 11 a table is given stating the output from stamping presses for every hour of the day. Twenty-three machines were observed from 1 to 7 days each and the output for each hour, (8 to 9, 9 to 10, etc.) added up in a total, 10 working hours being compared. Similarly in the Federal report on the Conditions of Employment in the Iron and Steel Industry[2] (1911) the number of blows from two Bessemer converters is given for 8 months for every hour of two 12-hour shifts.

Fatigue consists in a diminution of activity that is itself caused by activity. As activity proceeds activity falls, and the theory is that a comparison of the output of consecutive hours will show exactly to what extent the unrelaxed tension of activity will result in fatigue toward the end of a spell and toward the end of the working day, and exactly how far rest pauses, meal intervals, and a night's sleep will allow human capacity to gain recovery.

But it was peculiarly unfortunate that the two operations chosen by the Federal Government were of a nature not yielding definite evidence of fatigue. Work on a stamping press is extremely monotonous, and only subjectively, not objectively, tiring, while in the operation of the Bessemer converter, numerous pauses allowing for recuperation occur in the work. Between every blow the men have to wait for the completion of the material process. The result in both cases was a straight line of output throughout the day instead of a falling curve.

In collecting material for the British Association Committee on Fatigue from the Economic Standpoint (1915) I obtained several output curves which differed radically from those collected by the Federal Government. The operations I chose consisted mainly in soldering by hand or in labeling biscuit tins, work requiring a certain degree of attentiveness and coordination and capable of being carried on without any pauses whatever. Comparing the different hours of the spell, a curve was obtained not very unlike the fatigue curve yielded by the contractions of a continuously stimulated muscle.

The Federal Government was discouraged by the lack of any signs of fatigue in the curves they collected, and this discouragement seems

---

[1] 61st Cong., 2d Sess., Doc. 645.   [2] 62d Cong., 1st Sess., Doc. 110, Vol. IV.

to have spread to investigations elsewhere. Nevertheless, there seem to me to be some very good reasons why the hourly output tests should be developed and extended.

First of all, the record of output is usually easy to secure every hour. Foremen often keep it for their own benefit in estimating at any given time how the day's work is progressing. Often also there are automatic registers attached to machines to record each unit of output as on a cyclometer, and the total attained each hour may be read off at a glance.

Secondly, the output curve can be accompanied by curves in other very significant events of factory life. I refer to accidents and to the consumption of power. Just as output can be plotted from hour to hour, so can the number of accidents occuring in any factory and the amount of electrical power consumed. And with these latter tests the evidence of fatigue can not be isolated except by hourly curves. It gives no indication of fatigue to compare the rate of accidents for the whole factory during long periods under different schedules, since the rate of accidents depends so largely on the type of machine used and the experience of the workers, and these factors vary enormously at different periods. Further, in the investigations into output made hitherto, the same workers were selected for comparison before and after the change in hours, but it is impossible to do this in the case of accidents, since such selected workers may never have any accidents at all. Accidents must always be studied over the factory as a whole. Similarly with power consumption, it is very seldom that a factory keeps any records of the power consumed on certain machines or by certain special workers. The record has to be made for the factory as a whole, and with power records as with accidents it is always hard to keep all the disturbing factors constant where different and often far-distant periods are compared.

The accident curve for different hours of the working day, it is true, has often been rejected as an index of fatigue, owing to the curve showing a peak one hour from the end, rather than at the end of the spell. Why there should be a drop in the last hour it is difficult to explain. My own theory is that the anticipation of a break in his work and of food and rest makes the worker more alert and he becomes more alive to the dangers in his surroundings. But whatever the theory, an analysis of the circumstances of accidents will show a surprisingly high percentage of occurrences which the injured man could have avoided either by a quick reaction to danger or by more attention or better coordination. Accidents due purely to mechanical causes are usually not more than 5 or 10 per cent of the whole number. In my opinion, therefore, a rise in accidents must form an admirable measure of fatigue, particularly of a psychological fatigue affecting attention and alertness rather than rapidity of motion.

There is, however, one element in the accident curve that leads to confusion. It is obvious that the more frequently a man's hands pass certain danger points in a given period of time, the more liable are accidents to occur; thus the accident curve depends partly on the worker's speed of production and will tend to rise as output is increased. To this extent, a rise in accidents will measure a rise in working capacity and not a fall. It is necessary, therefore. to eliminate this factor in the accident curve and to correct the figures to some standard output. But accidents, as we have said before, can be measured only over the whole factory and to obtain a measure of output for the whole factory also with all its varying operations and productive and nonproductive duties, is practically impossible. In this dilemma the curve of power consumption comes to our aid. Wherever, as is usually the case, the machinery and the workman jointly combine in setting the pace, it is a curve corresponding roughly to the output and yet it is obtained for the whole factory If therefore the number of accidents per hour be divided by the amount of power consumed each hour, we shall get the curve representing the worker's loss of capacity in attention and alertness quite irrespective of the amount of work he is doing. It is this composite curve together with the curve of output described above that may yield one of the most nearly perfect measures of fatigue in the factory.

A third advantage of the hourly curve is the subtle distinction it brings out between the fatiguing effect of different types of work and possibly of different types of conditions also. Dr. Lee was able to demonstrate that monotonous work, work requiring attention, and work involving muscular strain, might yield several different shapes of curves. Unless the change of hours in a factory is very frequent the "before-and-after" comparison does not yield more than one or two combinations. It is the great number of readings composing the curve, usually 10 a day, that renders possible a more subtle analysis.

I can not close honestly without admitting one disadvantage to the hourly curve method. In their practical application the results of the curve do not point so directly to any one policy as the "before-and-after" type of investigation. The curve is obtained under one factory schedule. It is not in itself a comparison of two different schedules one of which can be declared superior to the other. If an output or power consumption curve should fall or an accident curve rise steeply, conditions are obviously wrong, but what condition may lead to better results is not directly indicated by the figures.

However, if a sufficient number of observations is made, the curves obtained permit comparisons between different factories and different conditions in the same factory that would be impossible to secure by the direct before-and-after method. In using the curves, no comparison of absolute figures is contemplated. Absolute figures of output are determined not merely by human capacity but by the efficiency of machines, the quality of material, the discipline exercised by the foreman and the general coordination of the factory staff. If compared directly, the hourly output of one factory against the hourly output of another factory, even on exactly the same process, might demonstrate nothing more than superior machines and superior foremen and superior materials in the one, as against the other. It would not show necessarily any superior schedule of hours. The curve method involves only a comparison of figures determined under the same conditions. The figures are yielded hour to hour in the same factory or section of the factory. Between the hours there can be no changes in factory organization or equipment. If the output curve in one factory drops heavily as work increases in length, while in another factory on the same operation the output curve continues steadily, then we may conclude that the latter factory has so arranged its hours and conditions of work that the workers do not suffer from undue fatigue at the end of their day.

I include a consideration of factory conditions advisedly, because the occurrence of fatigue, though running parallel with the length and intensity of activity, may yet be retarded or expedited in its course by different degrees of heat, damp, noise, dust, smell, comfort of posture, and so on, and as soon as accurate instruments are devised for grading each condition, its peculiar effect on the curves may be investigated just as scientifically as the effect of long hours, and the investigation will be just as important.

PREVALENCE OF DISEASE.

No health department, State or local, can effectively prevent or control disease without knowledge of when, where, and under what conditions cases are occurring.

UNITED STATES.

EXTRA-CANTONMENT ZONES—CASES REPORTED WEEK ENDED MARCH 12.

CAMP BEAUREGARD ZONE, LA.

Alexandria:
Smallpox.................................... 2
Tuberculosis............................... 1

CAMP BOWIE ZONE, TEX.

Fort Worth:
Cerebrospinal meningitis.................. 2
Diphtheria................................. 1
Gonorrhea.................................. 5
Malaria.................................... 2
Measles.................................... 4
Pneumonia, lobar........................... 4
Smallpox................................... 11
Syphilis................................... 2
Tuberculosis, pulmonary.................... 1

CAMP DEVENS ZONE, MASS.

German measles:
Ayer....................................... 1
Lancaster.................................. 5
Lunenburg.................................. 2
Westford................................... 1
Measles:
Westford................................... 4
Mumps:
Lancaster.................................. 7
Pneumonia, lobar:
Westford................................... 1

CAMP DODGE ZONE, IOWA

Diphtheria:
Des Moines................................. 9
German measles:
Des Moines................................. 2
Grimes..................................... 1
Gonorrhea:
Des Moines................................. 3
Measles:
Des Moines................................. 6
Grimes..................................... 5
Pneumonia:
Grimes..................................... 2
Scarlet fever:
Des Moines................................. 13
Grimes..................................... 1
Bloomfield Township........................ 1

CAMP DODGE ZONE, IOWA—continued.

Smallpox:
Des Moines................................. 12
Syphilis:
Des Moines.................................

CAMP FUNSTON ZONE, KANS.

Chicken pox:
Manhattan..................................
Diphtheria:
Manhattan.................................. 1
Measles:
Junction City.............................. 5
Ogden...................................... 1
Cleburne................................... 3
Army City.................................. 1
Riley...................................... 3
Manhattan.................................. 6
Mumps:
Junction City.............................. 9
Ogden...................................... 1
Cleburne................................... 1
Manhattan.................................. 9
Pneumonia:
Junction City..............................
Scarlet fever:
Junction City.............................. 3
Manhattan.................................. 3
Smallpox:
Manhattan..................................
Riley......................................
Whooping cough:
Junction City..............................

CAMP GORDON ZONE, GA.

Atlanta:
Cerebrospinal meningitis................... 4
Chicken pox................................ 2
Diphtheria................................. 2
Dysentery, amebic.......................... 2
German measles............................. 2
Gonorrhea.................................. 24
Hookworm infection......................... 4
Malaria.................................... 1
Measles.................................... 16
Mumps...................................... 3
Pneumonia.................................. 4
Scarlet fever.............................. 4
Septic sore throat.........................

CAMP GORDON ZONE, GA.—continued.

Atlanta—Continued.
Smallpox.................................... 7
Syphilis.................................... 10
Typhoid fever............................. 1
. Tuberculosis............................. 4
Whooping cough.......................... 2
Scottdale:
Typhoid fever............................. 1
Smallpox.................................. 1
Kirkwood:
Smallpox.................................. 1

CAMP GREENE ZONE, N. C.

Charlotte Township:
Chancroid................................. 1
Chicken pox.............................. 2
German measles........................... 6
Gonorrhea................................. 10
Malaria.................................... 4
Measles.................................... 7
Mumps..................................... 5
Syphilis................................... 9
Tuberculosis.............................. 8
Typhoid fever............................. 1
Whooping cough.......................... 7

CAMP JACKSON ZONE, S. C.

Columbia:
Cerebrospinal meningitis................. 1
Measles.................................... 4
Mumps..................................... 6
Pneumonia................................. 1
Scarlet fever.............................. 1
Tuberculosis.............................. 2
Typhoid fever............................. 1
Whooping cough.......................... 5

CAMP JOSEPH E. JOHNSTON ZONE, FLA.

Jacksonville:
Chicken pox.............................. 3
Erysipelas................................ 2
Measles.................................... 4
Mumps..................................... 6
Scarlet fever.............................. 1
Trachoma.................................. 3
Tuberculosis.............................. 4
Typhoid fever............................. 3
Whooping cough.......................... 1
East Port:
Mumps..................................... 1

FORT LEAVENWORTH ZONE, KANS.

Chicken pox:
Leavenworth.............................. 4
German measles:
Leavenworth.............................. 7
Leavenworth County...................... 3
Measles:
Leavenworth.............................. 7
Leavenworth County...................... 1
Mumps:
Leavenworth County...................... 1
Pneumonia, lobar:
Leavenworth.............................. 1
Leavenworth County...................... 2

FORT LEAVENWORTH ZONE, KANS.—continued.

Scarlet fever:
Leavenworth.............................. 2
Smallpox:
Leavenworth.............................. 5
Leavenworth County...................... 3
Tuberculosis:
Leavenworth.............................. 1

CAMP LEE ZONE, VA.

Cerebrospinal meningitis:
Prince George County.................... 1
Chicken pox:
Prince George County.................... 1
Chancroid:
Petersburg................................ 1
German measles:
Prince George County.................... 4
Dinwiddie County......................... 1
Ettricks................................... 2
Gonorrhea:
Petersburg................................ 1
Malaria:
Dinwiddie County......................... 1
Measles:
Petersburg................................ 2
Hopewell.................................. 31
Ettricks................................... 1
Mumps:
Hopewell.................................. 15
Chesterfield County...................... 1
Ettricks................................... 1
City Point................................. 1
Pellagra:
Petersburg................................ 1
Pneumonia:
Petersburg................................ 3
Scarlet fever:
Prince George County.................... 1
Septic sore throat:
Petersburg................................ 2
Chesterfield County...................... 2
Dinwiddie County......................... 1
Ettricks................................... 1
Tuberculosis:
Petersburg................................ 2

CAMP LOGAN ZONE, TEX.

Houston:
Chicken pox.............................. 9
Measles.................................... 45
Mumps..................................... 6
Pneumonia................................. 3
Scarlet fever.............................. 2
Smallpox.................................. 3
Syphilis................................... 1
Trachoma.................................. 1
Typhoid fever............................. 2
Magnolia Park:
Smallpox.................................. 1

CAMP LEWIS ZONE, WASH.

Chicken pox:
Lakeview.................................. 1
German measles:
Steilacoom Lake.......................... 3
American Lake............................ 2

CAMP LEWIS ZONE, WASH.—continued.

German measles—Continued.
Gravelly Lake	1
Spanaway	6
Lake City	3
Steilacoom	4
Custer	1
Roy	7

Measles:
American Lake	1

Pneumonia, lobar:
Murray	1

Whooping cough:
Steilacoom Lake	3
Lakeview	1

CAMP MACARTHUR ZONE, TEX.

Waco:
German measles	5
Gonorrhea	3
Measles	22
Mumps	26
Pneumonia, lobar	6
Smallpox	3
Tuberculosis	2
Whooping cough	1

Precinct One:
Cerebrospinal meningitis	1

Precinct Four:
Mumps	1

CAMP M'CLELLAN ZONE, ALA.

Cerebrospinal meningitis:
Precinct Thirteen	1

Chicken pox:
Anniston	14

Diphtheria:
Anniston	1

German measles:
Anniston	3

Measles:
Anniston	5
Precinct Two	17

Mumps:
Anniston	2

Pneumonia:
Anniston	1

Smallpox:
Anniston	26
Precinct Nine	1
Precinct Fifteen	1
Precinct Twenty-three	1

Tuberculosis:
Anniston	1

Whooping cough:
Anniston	1

NORFOLK COUNTY NAVAL DISTRICT, VA.

Cerebrospinal meningitis:
South Norfolk	1
Norfolk County	1

Chicken pox:
Portsmouth	2

Diphtheria:
Portsmouth	1
Port Norfolk	1

Dysentery:
Portsmouth	1
South Norfolk	1

NORFOLK COUNTY NAVAL DISTRICT, VA.—continued.

Measles:
Portsmouth	12

Mumps:
South Norfolk	3

Pellagra:
South Norfolk	1

Pneumonia:
South Norfolk	1

Rabies:
Portsmouth	1

Scarlet fever:
Portsmouth	2

Smallpox:
Port Norfolk	3
Pinners Point	4

Tuberculosis:
South Norfolk	1
St. Brides	1

FORT OGLETHORPE ZONE, GA.

Cerebrospinal meningitis:
Chattanooga	2
St. Elmo	1

Chicken pox:
Chattanooga	4

Gonorrhea:
Chattanooga	2

Measles:
Chattanooga	4
East Lake	2
Rossville	8

Mumps:
Chattanooga	22
North Chattanooga	1
East Lake	1
Rossville	2

Pneumonia:
Chattanooga	2
Rossville	2

Scarlet fever:
East Lake	1

Smallpox:
Chattanooga	2

Syphilis:
Chattanooga	3
Lakeview	1

Tuberculosis:
St. Elmo	2
Alton Park	1

Typhoid fever:
Chattanooga	1

Whooping cough:
Chattanooga	2
Rossville	1

CAMP PIKE ZONE, ARK.

Cerebrospinal meningitis:
Little Rock	1
North Little Rock	2

Chancroid:
Little Rock	1
Scotts	1

Chicken pox:
Little Rock	2

Diphtheria:
Little Rock	1
North Little Rock	1

CAMP PIKE ZONE, ARK.—continued.

German measles:
Little Rock 1
Gonorrhea:
Little Rock 10
North Little Rock 2
Hookworm:
Marche 1
Malaria:
Little Rock 8
North Little Rock 1
Measles:
Little Rock 10
North Little Rock 1
Mumps:
Little Rock 22
North Little Rock 4
Scotts 1
Pellagra:
Scotts 2
Pneumonia:
Little Rock 16
North Little Rock 5
Scarlet fever:
North Little Rock 1
Smallpox:
Little Rock 32
Camp Pike 1
Browns Camp 1
Syphilis:
Little Rock 6
North Little Rock 1
Scotts 6
Trachoma:
North Little Rock 1
Tuberculosis:
Little Rock 8
North Little Rock 1
Scotts 1
Sweet Home 1
Typhoid fever:
Little Rock 1
Tuckerman 1
Whooping cough:
Little Rock 1
Toltec 6

CAMP SEVIER ZONE, S. C.

Greenville Township:
Cerebrospinal meningitis 2
Measles 1
Scarlet fever 1
Typhoid fever 1
Chick Springs Township:
Measles 1

CAMP SHERIDAN ZONE, ALA.

Chicken pox:
Montgomery 8
Capitol Heights 1
German measles:
Montgomery 2
Measles:
Montgomery 13
Rural district 2
Scarlet fever:
Montgomery 1

CAMP SHERIDAN ZONE, ALA.—continued.

Smallpox:
Montgomery 6
Rural district 2

CAMP SHERMAN ZONE, OHIO.

Cerebrospinal meningitis:
Chillicothe 4
Chicken pox:
Chillicothe 4
Measles:
Chillicothe 1
Liberty Township 1
Hallsville 2
Mumps:
Liberty Township 4
Pneumonia, lobar:
Chillicothe 4
Syphilis:
Chillicothe 4
Scarlet fever:
Chillicothe 5
Liberty Township 1
Trachoma:
Union Township 9

CAMP ZACHARY TAYLOR ZONE, KY.

Jefferson County:
Measles 2
Trachoma 5
Louisville:
Cerebrospinal meningitis 2
Chicken pox 3
Diphtheria 4
Measles 15
Mumps 1
Pneumonia, lobar 1
Scarlet fever 1
Smallpox 3
Trachoma 2
Tuberculosis, pulmonary 6
Typhoid fever 1

TIDEWATER HEALTH DISTRICT, VA.

Chicken pox:
Newport News 2
Cerebrospinal meningitis:
Newport News 1
German measles:
Newport News 2
Hampton 18
Phoebus 6
Measles:
Newport News 4
Hampton 8
Phoebus 6
Mumps:
Newport News 3

CAMP TRAVIS ZONE, TEX.

San Antonio:
Gonorrhea 1
Measles 1
Mumps 2
Roseola 2
Syphilis 1
Trachoma 2

CAMP TRAVIS ZONE, TEX -continued.

San Antonio—Continued.
Tuberculosis................................. 3
Typhoid fever............................... 1

CAMP WADSWORTH ZONE, S C.

Cerebrospinal meningitis:
Arkwright Mills........................... 1
Chicken pox:
Spartanburg............................... 1
Diphtheria:
Pauline.................................... 1
White Stone............................... 1
German measles:
Saxon Mills............................... 1
Glenn Springs............................. 2
Measles:
Spartanburg............................... 8
Pauline................................... 3
Mumps:
Spartanburg............................... 4
Pneumonia:
Pauline................................... 2
Smallpox:
Inman..................................... 2

CAMP WADSWORTH ZONE, S C.-continued

Tuberculosis:
Spartanburg............................... 1
Whooping cough:
Spartanburg............................... 13
Fair Forest............................... 2
Hayne..................................... 1
Pauline................................... 4

CAMP WHEELER ZONE, GA

East Macon:
Mumps..................................... 4
Macon:
Cerebrospinal meningitis.................. 1
Chicken pox............................... 3
Gonorrhea................................. 2
Measles................................... 6
Mumps..................................... 22
Pellagra.................................. 1
Pneumonia................................. 1
Scarlet fever............................. 2
Tuberculosis.............................. 2
Typhoid fever,............................ 2

DISEASE CONDITIONS AMONG TROOPS IN THE UNITED STATES.

The following data are taken from telegraphic reports received in the office of the Surgeon General, United States Army, for the week ended March 1, 1918:

Annual admission rate per 1,000 (disease only):
All troops...... .... 1,372.2
National Guard camps.................. 1,101.7
National Army camps.................. 1,557.1
Regular Army........................... 1,334.6
Noneffective rate per 1,000 on day of report:
All troops... .... 47.8
National Guard camps................. 42.2

Noneffective rate per 1,000 on day of report Con.
National Army camps.............. 54.5
Regular Army..................... 42.9
Annual death rate per 1,000:
All troops...................... 6.4
National Guard camps............ 6.4
National Army camps............. 5.9
Regular Army.................... 7.9

New cases of special disease reported during the week ended Mar. 1, 1918.

Camps.	Pneumonia.	Dysentery.	Malaria.	Venereal.	Measles.	Meningitis.	Scarlet fever.	Deaths.	Annual admission rate per 1,000 (disease only).	Noneffective per 1,000 on day of report.
Wadsworth...........	7			15	4	1		2	591.6	22.6
Hancock.............	6			23	10	6	3	2	432.2	28.9
McClellan...........	5			18	10		2	1	745.5	28.7
Sevier...............			2	22	2		1	3	1,670.1	70.0
Wheeler.............	9	1	3	45	2			6	1,360.6	48.6
Logan...............	8			70	32		2	2	1,127.2	34.6
Cody................	30			7		1		2	634.8	37.5
Doniphan............	11		1	8			3	8	1,772.2	47.6
Bowie...............	17			74	3	2	1	3	2,058.2	64.0
Sheridan............	2			10	3	1	3		443.1	51.5
Shelby..............	2		1	20				2	1,232.0	54.2
Beauregard..........	56		2	16		2		7	1,318.1	55.4
Kearney.............				6	1		4	4	1,181.3	47.1
Devens..............	9			68	6		3	5	1,077.5	28.4
Upton...............	7			21				4	575.4	23.6
Dix.................	1			64	11		9	1	1,560.9	44.7
Meade...............	9			19	15	6		1	508.6	30.9
Lee.................	14			49	10	2		4	474.3	56.0
Jackson.............	5			29	7		4	4	794.0	71.4
Gordon..............	1			118	1			3	1,333.7	34.9
Sherman.............	10			31	35		27	3	994.7	61.3
Taylor..............	11			48	13	1	2	5	1,812.0	60.6
Custer..............	5			6	9		6	2	1,171.4	48.9

New cases of special disease reported during the week ended Mar. 1, 1918—Continued.

Camps.	Pneumonia.	Dysentery.	Malaria.	Venereal.	Measles.	Meningitis.	Scarlet fever.	Deaths.	Annual admission rate per 1,000 (disease only).	Noneffective per 1,000 on day of report.
Grant	7	1	......	10	12	......	9	3	919.3	31.3
Pike	15	1	......	138	17	2	9	3	3,056.9	96.6
Dodge	8	......	......	111	54	1	11	2	1,577.3	54.4
Funston	7	......	......	55	......	3	2	3	2,081.7	97.3
Travis	23	1	......	68	26	......	......	8	3,081.8	72.3
Lewis	3	......	......	31	52	2	37	......	1,401.0	65.8
Northeastern Department	......	......	......	13	1	......	......	......	884.8	31.9
Eastern Department	11	......	2	16	10	1	2	1	684.5	27.0
Southeastern Department	4	1	......	29	13	1	6	5	1,456.7	46.7
Southern Department	22	1	......	85	84	3	4	11	1,111.8	43.2
Central Department	4	......	......	31	10	2	9	1	1,499.6	47.8
Western Department	12	......	......	39	42	......	8	7	986.5	31.5
Aviation, Signal Corps	41	......	3	125	146	3	29	19	1,680.8	44.9
Camp Greene	11	......	......	17	13	1	......	......	980.0	39.8
Camp Fremont	4	......	1	26	3	......	......	1	1,304.7	45.5
El Paso	......	......	......	5	3	......	......	......	847.1	4.6
Fort Slocum	1	......	......	12	4	......	1	2	1,762.2	39.2
Columbus Barracks	2	......	......	13	......	......	2	......	1,970.5	60.5
Fort Thomas	......	......	......	6	......	1	......	4	1,634.3	77.6
Jefferson Barracks	4	......	......	7	14	......	6	......	2,025.2	127.1
Fort Logan	5	......	......	2	7	......	3	......	2,249.3	74.9
Fort McDowell	......	......	......	2	6	......	1	......	1,696.6	52.0
Disciplinary Barracks, Fort Leavenworth	......	......	......	1	......	......	......	......	1,388.4	30.5
Disciplinary Barracks, Alcatraz	......	......	......	......	......	......	......	......	656.1	15.7
Aberdeen Proving Ground	......	......	......	......	1	......	......	......	2,451.0	54.0
Allentown, Artillery Concentration Camp	7	......	......	1	2	......	......	......	1,516.6	33.2
Camp Humphreys	......	......	......	11	......	......	......	......	1,858.5	18.9
J. E. Johnston	1	......	......	25	17	......	1	......	913.3	32.0
Camp Meigs	2	......	......	11	7	......	1	......	2,648.6	35.3
Camp Merritt	17	......	......	20	5	......	37	4	1,526.4	62.2
Camp Stuart	19	......	......	9	8	1	1	5	1,754.1	53.7
West Point, N. Y	......	......	......	......	19	......	......	......	1,052.0	20.2
National Guard Departments	1	......	......	16	24	......	4	2	......	......
National Army Departments	15	......	1	136	46	......	25	2	......	......
Total	464	6	16	2,282	820	37	284	157	1,372.2	47.8

Annual rate per 1,000 for special diseases.

	All troops in United States.[1]	Regulars in United States.[1]	National Guard, all camps.[1]	National Army, all camps.[1]	Expeditionary Forces.[2]
Pneumonia	19.7	22.0	20.6	16.8	21.3
Dysentery	.2	.2	.1	.3	.4
Malaria	.5	.8	1.3	......	.4
Venereal	97.1	121.5	53.4	.6	55.3
Typhoid	.2	.6	......	.1	......
Measles	34.7	54.7	10.2	31.1	26.9
Meningitis	1.5	1.7	1.9	1.3	6.0
Scarlet fever	12.0	14.6	2.9	14.5	10.5

[1] Week ended Mar. 1, 1918.   [2] Week ended Feb. 21, 1918.

CURRENT STATE SUMMARIES.

Alabama.

From Collaborating Epidemiologist Perry, by telegraph, for week ended March 9, 1918:

Smallpox, by counties: Butler 9, Jefferson 107. Mobile 25. Epidemic meningitis, by counties: Jefferson 12, Tuscaloosa 2.

Arkansas.

From Collaborating Epidemiologist Garrison, by telegraph, for week ended March 9, 1918:

Smallpox: Crossett 1 case, Pine Bluff 4, Fort Smith 10, Black Rock 1, Booneville 1, Texarkana 1, Forest City 7; by counties, Drew 9, Greene 12, Izard 7, Craighead 1, Perry 6, Clark 2, Cross 4. Measles: Crossett 5, Rogers 6, Datto 1, Gurdon 7, Fouke 21, Texarkana 4, Banks 2, Forest City 2, Dermott 5, Huttig 1, Conway 1; by counties, Drew 40, Izard 4, Perry 4, Clark 52. Chicken pox: Gurdon 1, Camden 4; by counties, Drew 16, Perry 2. Tuberculosis: Rogers 3, Gurdon 2, Lonsdale 1, Conway 1, Higden 1; by counties, Greene 1, Clark 6. Meningitis: Augusta 1, Perry County 1. Diphtheria: Gurdon 1. Scarlet fever: Gurdon 2, Izard County 1. Whooping cough: Gurdon 1, Fouke 3, Lonsdale 2, Higden 3; by counties, Greene 8, Perry 10. Report exclusive of Pulaski and Lonoke Counties.

California.

From the State Board of Health of California, by telegraph, for week ended March 9, 1918:

Increases in prevalence of all communicable diseases, especially diphtheria, measles, and smallpox. Of 34 cases smallpox, 16 are in San Francisco. Four epidemic cerebrospinal meningitis, 1 each in Stockton, Riverside County, San Bernardino, and Los Angeles. Two poliomyelitis, 1 San Jose and 1 Tulare County.

Reported by mail for preceding week (ended March 2):

Cerebrospinal meningitis	3	Mumps	182
Chicken pox	185	Pneumonia	65
Diphtheria	51	Poliomyelitis	1
Dysentery	1	Ophthalmia neonatorum	2
Erysipelas	9	Scarlet fever	74
German measles	295	Smallpox	25
Gonococcus infection	51	Syphilis	40
Hookworm	1	Trachoma	2
Leprosy	1	Tuberculosis	170
Malaria	2	Typhoid fever	12
Measles	1,298	Whooping cough	85

Connecticut.

From Collaborating Epidemiologist Black, by telegraph, for week ended March 9, 1918:

Smallpox: Hartford 5, Montville 1. Meningitis: Hartford 1, New Milford 1, Wallingford 1, Ansonia 1.

Indiana.

From the State Board of Health of Indiana, by telegraph, for week ended March 9, 1918:

Scarlet fever: Epidemic Lucerne, Warren, Wolf Lake. Measles: Epidemic Rensselaer, Crown Point, Fountain City, Jonesville, Scottsburg, Elizabethtown. Smallpox: Epidemic Odon, South Bend. Diphtheria: Epidemic Wawaka; 1 death Decatur. Whooping cough: Epidemic Zionsville. Infantile paralysis: One case Howe.

Kansas.

From Collaborating Epidemiologist Crumbine, by telegraph, for week ended March 9, 1918:

Meningitis: Augusta 1 (total since February 6 for Butler County 9 cases), Corbin 1, De Soto 1, Eldorado 1, Hollister 1, Little River 1, Towanda 2. Smallpox: In cities, Topeka 16, Wichita 15; in counties, Atchison 24, Crawford 10.

Louisiana.

From Collaborating Epidemiologist Dowling, by telegraph, for week ended March 9, 1918:

Meningitis, excluding Rapides Parish: By parishes, Avoyelles 1, Caddo 1, Catahoula 1, Morehouse 1, Orleans 3, Saint Landry 2.

Massachusetts.

From Collaborating Epidemiologist Kelley, by telegraph, for week ended March 9, 1918:

Unusual prevalence. German measles: Danvers 31, Framingham 36, Newton 50. Measles: Beverly 104, Dartmouth 21, Quincy 70. Smallpox: Lowell 1, Marlboro 1, Milton 1.

Minnesota.

From Collaborating Epidemiologist Bracken, by telegraph, for week ended March 9, 1918:

Smallpox, new foci: Clearwater County, Clearbrook village; Douglas County, Carlos village; Kittson County, Poppleton Township, Lancaster village; Murray County, Lake Wilson village; Ottertail County, Aurdal Township; Pennington County, Reinner Township; Scott County, Shakopee city; each 1 case; Millelacs County, Milaca village, 2; Mower County, Adams Township, 1; Lodi Township, 2. One cerebrospinal meningitis reported since March 4.

Nebraska.

From the State Board of Health of Nebraska, by telegraph, for week ended March 9, 1918:

Smallpox: Winnebago, Plattsmouth, Scotts Bluff, southern part of Cherry County. Poliomyelitis: Howells. Scarlet fever: Winnebago.

Ohio.

From Collaborating Epidemiologist Freeman, by telegraph, for week ended March 9, 1918:

Zanesville, typhoid fever 8 cases; Middleport, typhoid fever 5 cases.

South Carolina.

From Collaborating Epidemiologist Hayne, by telegraph, for week ended March 9, 1918:

Eight cases meningitis; 1 suspected case; week ended March 10.

Vermont.

From Collaborating Epidemiologist Dalton, by telegraph, for week ended March 9, 1918:

Smallpox: Barre 1, Rutland 3. No other outbreak or unusual prevalence.

Virginia.

From Collaborating Epidemiologist Traynham, by telegraph, for week ended March 9, 1918:

Six cases cerebrospinal meningitis Newport News, 3 Gloucester County. 1 Buchanan County, 1 Petersburg. One case smallpox Louisa County.

Washington.

From Collaborating Epidemiologist Tuttle, by telegraph, for week ended March 9, 1918:

Unusual prevalence communicable diseases in State: Thirty-seven cases scarlet fever Tacoma; German measles epidemic Seattle, Tacoma, and generally over the State.

CEREBROSPINAL MENINGITIS.

California Report for January, 1918.

Place.	New cases reported.	Place.	New cases reported.
California:		California—Continued.	
Alameda County		San Bernardino County	
Oakland	1	Ontario	1
Los Angeles County	2	Santa Clara County	
Los Angeles	4	San Jose	2
Orange County	2	Shasta County	1
Napa County	1	Solano County	
Riverside County	1	Mare Island	4
San Diego County -		Tulare County	
Naval Training Station	2	Lindsay	1
San Francisco County -			
Presidio	1	Total	5
San Francisco	4		

City Reports for Week Ended Feb. 23, 1918.

Place.	Cases.	Deaths.	Place.	Cases.	Deaths.
Alexandria, La		1	Fall River, Mass	1	
Anniston, Ala	1		Flint, Mich	2	
Atlanta, Ga	6	2	Greenville, S. C	2	4
Augusta, Ga	2	2	Hammond, Ind	2	1
Austin, Tex		1	Indianapolis, Ind		
Baltimore, Md	6	1	Kansas City, Kans	1	
Birmingham, Ala	3	1	Little Rock, Ark	1	
Boston, Mass	5	2	Los Angeles, Cal	1	4
Cambridge, Mass	1		Louisville, Ky	13	4
Charleston, S. C	3	1	Lowell, Mass	1	
Chattanooga, Tenn	2	2	Macon, Ga	3	1
Chelsea, Mass	1		Memphis, Tenn	1	
Chicago, Ill	7	2	Milwaukee, Wis	1	
Cincinnati, Ohio	1		Minneapolis, Minn	1	
Columbia, S. C	2		Montgomery, Ala	3	
Columbus, Ohio	1	1	Nashville, Tenn		
Council Bluffs, Iowa	2	2	New Albany, Ind	2	1
Davenport, Iowa	1		Newark, N. J	5	1
Dayton, Ohio	4	5	New Haven, Conn	1	
Detroit, Mich	2		New Orleans, La	3	1
Elizabeth, N. J	1		New York, N. Y	19	11
Evansville, Ind	2	1	Norfolk, Va	3	2

City Reports for Week Ended Feb. 23, 1918—Continued.

Place.	Cases.	Deaths.	Place.	Cases.	Deaths.
Oakland, Cal	2	....	Salt Lake City, Utah	1	....
Passaic, N. J	....	1	Sandusky, Ohio	....	1
Philadelphia, Pa	6	5	San Francisco, Cal	2	....
Pittsburgh, Pa	....	1	Schenectady, N. Y	1	....
Providence, R. I	7	....	Washington, D. C	12	....
Roanoke, Va	1	....	Wilkesbarre, Pa	1	....
Saginaw, Mich	....	1	Worcester, Mass	....	1
St. Louis, Mo	2	1			

DIPHTHERIA.

See Diphtheria, measles, scarlet fever, and tuberculosis, page 368.

ERYSIPELAS.

City Reports for Week Ended Feb. 23, 1918.

Place.	Cases.	Deaths.	Place.	Cases.	Deaths.
Alameda, Cal	1	....	New Britain, Conn	1	....
Altoona, Pa	2	1	Newburgh, N. Y	....	1
Atlanta, Ga	2	1	Newton, Mass	....	1
Baltimore, Md	2	....	New York, N. Y	....	3
Bridgeport, Conn	1	....	Omaha, Nebr	....	....
Chicago, Ill	13	....	Philadelphia, Pa	3	3
Cleveland, Ohio	4	....	Pittsburgh, Pa	9	....
Cumberland, Md	1	....	Pontiac, Mich	1	....
Dayton, Ohio	1	....	Portland, Oreg	2	....
Denver, Colo	1	1	Portsmouth, Va	....	2
Detroit, Mich	4	....	Providence, R. I	....	1
Easton, Pa	1	....	Rochester, N. Y	....	1
Erie, Pa	2	....	St. Joseph, Mo	2	....
Fall River, Mass	....	1	St. Louis, Mo	4	1
Jackson, Mich	3	....	St. Paul, Minn	1	....
Johnstown, Pa	1	1	Salt Lake City, Utah	....	1
Leavenworth, Kans	1	....	San Diego, Cal	....	....
Little Rock, Ark	2	....	San Francisco, Cal	1	....
Los Angeles, Cal	8	....	Schenectady, N. Y	1	....
Louisville, Ky	2	....	Seattle, Wash	1	....
Memphis, Tenn	2	1	Toledo, Ohio	....	1
Milwaukee, Wis	2	....	Trenton, N. J	....	1
Montclair, N. J	1	....	Wichita, Kans	1	....
Newark, N. J	4	....	Williamsport, Pa	1	....

LEPROSY.

City Reports for Week Ended Feb. 23, 1918.

During the week ended February 23, 1918, one case of leprosy was reported at New Orleans, La., and one death from this disease was reported at Syracuse, N. Y.

MALARIA.

California Report for January, 1918.

Place.	New cases reported.	Place.	New cases reported.
California:		California—Continued.	
Butte County	5	San Francisco County—	
Chico	8	San Francisco	1
Glenn County—		U. S. N. Training Station	1
Orland	1	San Joaquin County	1
Kern County—		Yolo County—	
Bakersfield	1	Woodland	1
Placer County—			
Rocklin	2	Total	21

MALARIA—Continued.

City Reports for Week Ended Feb. 23, 1918.

Place.	Cases.	Deaths.	Place.	Cases.	Deaths.
Atlanta, Ga..........	1	....	Little Rock, Ark..........	5	....
Kokomo, Ind..........	....	1	Macon, Ga..........	1	....

MEASLES.

See Diphtheria, measles, scarlet fever, and tuberculosis, page 368.

PELLAGRA.

California Report for January, 1918.

During the month of January, 1918, 2 cases of pellagra were notified in the State of California. 1 case each in San Diego and San Francisco Counties.

City Reports for Week Ended Feb. 23, 1918.

Place.	Cases.	Deaths.	Place.	Cases.	Deaths.
Birmingham, Ala..........	....	3	Mobile, Ala..........	....	2
Charleston, S. C..........	....	1	Montgomery, Ala..........	....	1
Houston, Tex..........	....	1	Petersburg, Va..........	1	......
Lexington, Ky..........	....	3	Portsmouth, Va..........	....	1
Lynchburg, Va..........	....	1	Spartanburg, S. C..........	2	....
Macon, Ga..........	....	1			

PNEUMONIA.

City Reports for Week Ended Feb. 23, 1918.

Place.	Cases.	Deaths.	Place.	Cases.	Deaths.
Alameda, Cal	1	1	Lawrence, Mass..........	4	1
Anniston, Ala.	6	....	Lincoln, Nebr.	3	1
Atlanta, Ga.	2	3	Little Rock, Ark..........	12	....
Atlantic City, N. J.	1	1	Long Beach, Cal..	2	1
Auburn, N. Y.	2		Lorain, Ohio.	1	
Baltimore, Md.	88	23	Los Angeles, Cal..	21	9
Boston, Mass.	72	48	Louisville, Ky..	3	13
Bridgeport, Conn.	2	12	Lynn, Mass.	6	2
Brockton, Mass.	2	....	Manchester, N. H.	2	2
Cambridge, Mass.	26	8	McKeesport, Pa.	2	
Charleston, W. Va.	1	1	Melrose, Mass..	3	
Chattanooga, Tenn.	2	....	Nashville, Tenn.		3
Chelsea, Mass.	13	7	Newark, N. J.	51	9
Chicago, Ill.	168	88	New Bedford, Mass..........	2	1
Chicopee, Mass.	2	....	Newport, Ky.	4	4
Cleveland, Ohio.	34	24	North Little Rock, Ark......	4	2
Covington, Ky.	3	....	Norwalk, Conn.	1	1
Cranston, R. I.	2	2	Oak Park, Ill..........	1	
Cumberland, Md.	4	....	Pasadena, Cal..	5	4
Dayton, Ohio.	1	3	Philadelphia, Pa..	185	90
Detroit, Mich.	15	42	Pittsburgh, Pa..	32	31
Duluth, Minn.	1	1	Pontiac, Mich..	3	1
Everett, Mass.	3	1	Quincy, Mass..........	2	2
Fall River, Mass.	2	1	Reading, Pa..	2	....
Fitchburg, Mass.	2	1	Rochester, N. Y..........	16	2
Flint, Mich.	1	1	Rutland, Vt..	1	
Grand Rapids, Mich.	2	1	Sacramento, Cal.	1	2
Hammond, Ind.	2	3	St. Joseph, Mo..........	2	
Harrisburg, Pa.	1	4	San Francisco, Cal..........	13	11
Hattiesburg, Miss.	1	....	Schenectady, N. Y..........	4	2
Haverhill, Mass.	7	1	Somerville, Mass..........	6	1
Houston, Tex.	5	3	Spartanburg, S. C..	1	
Jackson, Mich.	3	1	Springfield, Mass..........	14	4
Jackson, Miss.	8	....	Stockton, Cal..........	4	....
Johnstown, Pa.	4	6	Taunton, Mass..........	3	2
Kalamazoo, Mich.	4	1	Wichita, Kans..........	2	2
Kansas City, Kans.	3	....	Woburn, Mass..........	22	9
Lancaster, Pa.	3	....	Yonkers, N. Y..........	3	3

POLIOMYELITIS (INFANTILE PARALYSIS).

California Report for January, 1918.

Place.	New cases reported.	Place.	New cases reported.
California:		California—Continued.	
Alameda County—		Sonoma County.....................	2
Oakland.......................	1	Tulare County—	
Los Angeles County—		Visalia..........................	1
Whittier......................	1	Yuba County.....................	1
Plumas County.....................	2		
Sacramento County—		Total...........................	9
Sacramento...................	1		

City Reports for Week Ended Feb. 23, 1918.

Place.	Cases.	Deaths.	Place.	Cases.	Deaths.
Milwaukee, Wis..............	6	....	Quincy, Ill.....	1	....
New York, N. Y.............	1	1	Rochester, N. Y.............	1	1
Philadelphia, Pa.............	1	1	Somerville, Mass..............	1	....

RABIES IN MAN.

City Reports for Week Ended Feb. 23, 1918.

During the week ended February 23, 1918, two deaths from rabies were reported at Erie, Pa.

SCARLET FEVER.

See Diphtheria, measles, scarlet fever, and tuberculosis, page 368.

SMALLPOX.

Missouri—Kansas City.

During the period from March 6 to 12, 1918, 108 cases of smallpox were notified at Kansas City, Mo.

Texas—Eagle Pass—Virulent Smallpox.

During the week ended March 11, 1918, 10 new cases of smallpox, with 1 death, were notified at Eagle Pass, Tex., making a total of 108 cases of the disease, with 18 deaths, reported since January 1, 1918.

Texas—Lamar County.

On March 11, 1918, the presence of smallpox was reported in Lamar County, Tex., where about 250 cases of the disease, with 1 death, had occurred since December 1, 1917.

27

SMALLPOX—Continued.

California Report for January, 1918.

Place	New cases reported.	Deaths.	Vaccination history of cases			
			Number vaccinated within 7 years preceding attack.	Number last vaccinated more than 7 years preceding attack.	Number never successfully vaccinated.	Vaccination history not obtained or uncertain.
California:						
Fresno County—						
Fresno..............	3	....	....	1	2	....
Imperial County..........	1	....	....	....	1	....
El Centro..............	1	....	....	....	1	....
Holtville..............	2	....	....	....	2	....
Kern County—						
Bakersfield............	1	....	....	....	1	....
Maricopa..............	2	....	....	....	....	2
Los Angeles County—						
Glendale.............	1	....	....	1	....	....
Los Angeles..........	5	....	....	....	5	....
Venice..............	1	....	....	....	1	....
Nevada County..........	3	....	....	....	3	....
Grass Valley..........	1	....	....	....	1	....
Nevada City..........	3	....	....	....	3	....
Orange County..........	1	....	....	....	1	....
Santa Ana........ ...	1	....	....	....	1	....
Riverside County—						
Riverside..........	1	....	....	....	1	....
Sacramento County — ·						
Sacramento..........	3	....	....	....	3	....
San Bernardino County—						
San Bernardino........	1	....	....	....	1	....
Needles......	1	....	....	....	1	....
Redlands..........	2	....	....	....	2	....
San Francisco County--						
San Francisco..........	6	....	....	....	6	....
Shasta County..........	1	....	....	....	....	....
Ventura County..........	1	....	....	....	.	....
Total................	42	....	....	2	37	3

Miscellaneous State Reports.

During the month of December, 1917, 18 cases of smallpox were reported in the State of Idaho, and during January, 1918, 5 cases were reported in the same State.

City Reports for Week Ended Feb. 23, 1918.

Place.	Cases.	Deaths.	Place.	Cases	Deaths
Akron, Ohio.............	20	....	Covington, Ky..	2	....
Alexandria, La.............	1	....	Davenport, Iowa......	3	....
Alton, Ill.............	6	....	Dayton, Ohio..........	11	....
Anniston, Ala.............	5	....	Denver, Colo...	47	....
Atlanta, Ga.............	1	....	Des Moines, Iowa ..	24	....
Austin, Tex.............	2	1	Detroit, Mich	54	1
Berlin, N. H.............	9	....	Dubuque, Iowa......	7	....
Birmingham, Ala.............	72	....	Durham, N. C..........	1	....
Butte, Mont.............	6	....	Erie, Pa ..	6	....
Canton, Ohio.............	5	....	Evansville, Ind..	5	....
Cedar Rapids, Iowa..........	1	....	Flint, Mich.........	8	....
Charleston, W. Va.............	2	....	Fort Smith, Ark.	5	....
Chattanooga, Tenn...... ...	6	....	Fort Wayne, Ind ..	17	....
Chicago, Ill.............	6	....	Galesburg, Ill. . .	1	....
Cincinnati, Ohio.............	15	....	Grand Rapids, Mich ...	11	....
Cleveland, Ohio.............	88	....	Hammond, Ind.	4	....
Coffeyville, Kans.............	11	....	Harrisburg, Pa ..	1	....
Colorado Springs.............	1	....	Hattiesburg, Miss........	3	....
Columbus, Ga.............	3	....	Houston, Tex......	9	....
Columbus, Ohio.............	7	....	Indianapolis, Ind	79	....
Council Bluffs, Iowa.............	20	....	Johnstown, Pa......	1	....

SMALLPOX—Continued.

City Reports for Week Ended Feb. 23, 1918—Continued.

Place.	Cases.	Deaths.	Place.	Cases.	Deaths.
Kansas City, Kans..........	45	....	New Orleans, La............	16	....
Knoxville, Tenn.............	6	....	New York, N. Y.............	1	....
Kokomo, Ind................	1	....	North Little Rock, Ark......	2	....
La Crosse, Wis..............	10	....	Ogden, Utah...............	2	....
Leavenworth, Kans..........	7	....	Oklahoma City, Okla........	33	....
Lexington, Ky..............	1	....	Omaha, Nebr...............	42	....
Lincoln, Nebr..............	5	....	Pontiac, Mich..............	12	....
Little Rock, Ark...........	35	....	Portland, Oreg.............	2	....
Lorain, Ohio...............	2	....	Quincy, Ill................	12	....
Los Angeles, Cal...........	4	....	St. Joseph, Mo.............	19	....
Louisville, Ky.............	1	....	St. Louis, Mo..............	27	....
Lowell, Mass...............	1	....	St. Paul, Minn.............	4	....
Macon, Ga..................	10	....	Salt Lake City, Utah........	27	....
Madison, Wis...............	2	....	San Francisco, Cal..........	2	....
Milwaukee, Wis.............	2	....	Sioux City, Iowa...........	16	....
Minneapolis, Minn..........	35	....	South Bend, Ind............	1	....
Mobile, Ala................	17	....	Steelton, Pa...............	1	....
Montgomery, Ala............	7	....	Terre Haute, Ind...........	3	....
Muncie, Ind................	10	....	Toledo, Ohio...............	19	....
Muskogee, Okla.............	4	....	Wheeling, W. Va............	1	....
Nashville, Tenn............	3	....	Wichita, Kans..............	24	....

TETANUS.

City Reports for Week Ended Feb. 23, 1918.

Place.	Cases.	Deaths.	Place.	Cases.	Deaths.
Harrisburg, Pa..............	1	1	New York, N. Y.............	....	1
Mobile, Ala.................	....	2	Philadelphia, Pa............	1	2

TUBERCULOSIS.

See Diphtheria, measles, scarlet fever, and tuberculosis, page 368.

TYPHOID FEVER.

State Reports for December, 1917, and January, 1918.

Place.	New cases reported.	Place.	New cases reported.
California (Jan. 1-31, 1918):		California (Jan. 1-31, 1918)—Continued.	
Alameda County—		San Bernardino County—	
Emeryville.....................	1	Needles.....................	1
Oakland......................	6	San Bernardino..............	1
Hayward.....................	1	San Diego County—	
Colusa County—		San Diego...................	3
Colusa.......................	1	San Francisco County—	
Fresno County.................	4	San Francisco...............	7
Clovis.......................	1	San Joaquin County..........	3
Fresno.......................	1	Stockton....................	3
Humboldt County..............	1	San Mateo County...........	2
Lassen County—		Santa Barbara County—	
Susanville...................	2	Santa Maria.................	1
Los Angeles County—		Santa Clara County..........	3
Alhambra....................	1	Siskiyou County.............	1
Long Beach..................	3	Dunsmuir...................	3
Los Angeles.................	11	Sutter County...............	1
Monterey County—		Stanislaus County—	
Monterey....................	2	Modesto.....................	1
Orange County—		Tehama County..............	1
Brea........................	1	Corning.....................	2
Placer County.................	1		
Riverside County..............	3	Total....................	81
Sacramento County............	3	Idaho (Dec. 1-31, 1917).............	10
Sacramento..................	1		
San Benito County—			
Hollister....................	1		

TYPHOID FEVER—Continued.

City Reports for Week Ended Feb. 23, 1918.

Place.	Cases.	Deaths.	Place.	Cases.	Deaths.
Altoona, Pa	2	....	New Haven, Conn.....	1	....
Baltimore, Md	3	....	New Orleans, La.....	1	....
Birmingham, Ala	1	....	New York, N. Y.....	7	....
Boston, Mass	2	....	Norfolk, Va.....	....	2
Braddock, Pa	1	....	Norristown, Pa.....	1	....
Brockton, Mass	2	....	Oakland, Cal.....	1	1
Chicago, Ill	3	....	Omaha, Nebr.....	2	....
Cincinnati, Ohio	....	1	Philadelphia, Pa.....	7	1
Columbus, Ohio	....	1	Pittsburgh, Pa.....	2	1
Detroit, Mich	1	1	Quincy, Ill.....	....	1
East Chicago, Ind	1	....	Reading, Pa.....	1	....
Erie, Pa	....	1	Richmond, Va.....	1	....
Everett, Mass	1	....	St. Louis, Mo.....	2	1
Fitchburg, Mass	2	....	San Francisco, Cal.....	3	....
Flint, Mich	2	....	Seattle, Wash.....	1	....
Hammond, Ind	7	1	Springfield, Ohio.....	2	1
Harrisburg, Pa	1	....	Stockton, Cal.....	2	....
Indianapolis, Ind	2	....	Tacoma, Wash.....	1	....
Kansas City, Kans	1	....	Trenton, N. J.....	1	....
Kokomo, Ind	1	....	Wheeling, W. Va.....	....	1
Little Rock, Ark	1	....	Wichita, Kans.....	1	....
Long Branch, N. J	1	....	Wilkinsburg, Pa.....	2	....
Los Angeles, Cal	4	....	Wilmington, N. C.....	....	....
Minneapolis, Minn	10	2	Winston-Salem, N. C.....	1	1
Moline, Ill	2	....	York, Pa.....	1	....
New Bedford, Mass	1	....	Zanesville, Ohio.....	8	1
New Britain, Conn	1	....			

TYPHUS FEVER.

Massachusetts—Chelsea.

On February 27, 1918, a case of typhus fever was reported in Chelsea, Mass., in the person of L. T., male, aged 47 years, a storekeeper, who had lived at 137 Walnut Street for a period of 2 years, had not visited any other place during the last month previous to the attack. The symptoms and history of the case were typical, but the source of infection could not be determined. Careful investigation failed to show any vermin on persons in the family or in the residence.

DIPHTHERIA, MEASLES, SCARLET FEVER, AND TUBERCULOSIS.

State Reports for November, 1917, and January, 1918.

State.	Cases reported.		
	Diph-theria.	Measles.	Scarlet fever.
California, Jan. 1-31, 1918	340	2,561	129
Idaho, Nov. 1-30, 1917	....	....	16
Idaho, Jan. 1-31, 1918	21	5	9

DIPHTHERIA, MEASLES, SCARLET FEVER, AND TUBERCULOSIS—
Continued.

City Reports for Week Ended Feb. 23, 1918.

City.	Population as of July 1, 1916. (Estimated by U. S. Census Bureau.)	Total deaths from all causes.	Diphtheria.		Measles.		Scarlet fever.		Tuberculosis.	
			Cases.	Deaths.	Cases.	Deaths.	Cases.	Deaths.	Cases.	Deaths.
Over 500,000 inhabitants:										
Baltimore, Md	589,621	266	16	1	152	.....	13	.....	65	32
Boston, Mass	756,476	298	66	11	143	2	27	1	59	33
Chicago, Ill	2,497,722	661	144	18	55	1	62	1	319	69
Cleveland, Ohio	674,073	166	54	1	14	.....	10	.....	23	21
Detroit, Mich	571,784	239	53	8	22	6	43	1	43	23
Los Angeles, Cal	503,812	162	16	1	302	.....	17	.....	42	25
New York, N. Y	5,602,841	1,579	227	16	1,125	26	116	2	251	172
Philadelphia, Pa	1,709,518	655	42	4	245	1	44	2	108	67
Pittsburgh, Pa	579,090	191	22	.....	90	1	3	.....	28	9
St. Louis	757,309	220	61	3	147	1	33	1	65	20
From 300,000 to 500,000 inhabitants:										
Cincinnati, Ohio	410,476	145	13	4	18	.....	1	.....	19	19
Jersey City, N. J	306,345	.....	13	.....	76	.....	13	.....	11	.....
Milwaukee, Wis	436,535	95	5	.....	168	.....	34	.....	23	2
Minneapolis, Minn	363,454	.....	7	1	37	.....	24	1	.....	6
Newark, N. J	408,894	.....	18	1	209	3	13	.....	55	21
New Orleans, La	371,747	.....	26	.....	81	1	2	.....	36	25
San Francisco, Cal	463,516	.....	10	1	80	.....	10	.....	27	22
Seattle, Wash	348,639	.....	8	.....	71	.....	9	.....	4	6
Washington, D. C	363,980	149	14	.....	271	4	23	.....	31	16
From 200,000 to 300,000 inhabitants:										
Columbus, Ohio	214,878	76	.....	.....	40	.....	26	.....	8	6
Denver, Colo	260,800	77	1	.....	280	.....	28	.....	4	13
Indianapolis, Ind	271,708	77	16	.....	103	.....	35	.....	19	12
Louisville, Ky	238,910	99	6	2	33	.....	2	.....	7	7
Portland, Oreg	295,463	52	.....	.....	86	.....	3	.....	7	4
Providence, R. I	251,960	77	7	1	5	.....	5	1	.....	6
Rochester, N. Y	256,417	77	13	1	59	.....	19	.....	13	4
St. Paul, Minn	247,232	53	17	1	35	.....	29	1	15	6
From 100,000 to 200,000 inhabitants:										
Albany, N. Y	104,199	.....	2	.....	21	.....	2	.....	5	.....
Atlanta, Ga	190,558	67	6	.....	6	.....	4	.....	6	9
Birmingham, Ala	181,762	68	3	.....	61	.....	2	.....	6	1
Bridgeport, Conn	121,579	32	11	.....	6	.....	3	.....	7	3
Cambridge, Mass	112,981	58	6	.....	63	1	1	.....	8	7
Camden, N. J	106,233	.....	3	.....	29	.....	3	.....	1	.....
Dayton, Ohio	127,224	55	2	.....	32	.....	12	.....	9	2
Des Moines, Iowa	101,598	.....	3	.....	2	.....	12	.....	.....	.....
Fall River, Mass	128,366	32	3	.....	3	.....	14	.....	5	5
Grand Rapids, Mich	128,291	36	2	1	11	.....	2	.....	2	2
Hartford, Conn	110,900	50	10	.....	3	.....	6	.....	3	7
Houston, Tex	112,307	47	.....	.....	13	.....	.....	.....	3	7
Lawrence, Mass	100,560	37	2	1	17	.....	.....	.....	5	7
Lowell, Mass	113,215	39	5	1	4	.....	.....	.....	.....	5
Lynn, Mass	102,425	20	2	.....	9	1	2	.....	2	1
Memphis, Tenn	148,995	62	11	1	25	2	2	.....	10	6
Nashville, Tenn	117,057	46	1	.....	11	.....	.....	.....	6	8
New Bedford, Mass	118,158	37	3	.....	22	.....	1	.....	6	1
New Haven, Conn	149,685	46	2	1	1	.....	3	.....	5	4
Oakland, Cal	198,604	54	2	.....	31	.....	2	.....	5	5
Omaha, Nebr	165,470	35	7	.....	67	.....	15	.....	.....	7
Reading, Pa	109,381	23	3	.....	4	.....	4	.....	12	1
Richmond, Va	156,687	67	5	1	41	.....	5	.....	3	6
Salt Lake City, Utah	117,399	32	2	.....	19	.....	15	.....	.....	111
Scranton, Pa	146,811	56	5	.....	3	.....	4	.....	1	3
Springfield, Mass	105,942	43	7	1	39	.....	4	.....	16	3
Syracuse, N. Y	155,624	51	6	1	85	5	20	.....	5	2
Tacoma, Wash	112,770	.....	.....	.....	1	.....	18	.....	.....	.....
Toledo, Ohio	191,554	60	3	1	9	.....	5	.....	.....	5
Trenton, N. J	111,593	47	2	1	13	.....	1	.....	6	5
Worcester, Mass	163,314	51	1	.....	4	.....	2	.....	12	2
From 50,000 to 100,000 inhabitants:										
Akron, Ohio	85,025	.....	10	.....	11	.....	5	.....	4	.....
Altoona, Pa	58,659	.....	5	3	.....	.....	.....	.....	1	.....
Atlantic City, N. J	57,660	.....	.....	.....	4	.....	.....	.....	3	.....
Augusta, Ga	50,245	.....	.....	.....	15	.....	.....	.....	3	1
Bayonne, N. J	69,893	.....	2	.....	85	.....	5	.....	2	.....
Berkeley, Cal	57,633	11	.....	.....	6	.....	3	.....	1	.....

DIPHTHERIA, MEASLES, SCARLET FEVER, AND TUBERCULOSIS—
Continued.

City Reports for Week Ended Feb. 23, 1918—Continued.

City.	Population as of July 1, 1916 (Estimated by U. S. Census Bureau.)	Total deaths from all causes.	Diphtheria.		Measles.		Scarlet fever.		Tuberculosis.	
			Cases.	Deaths.	Cases.	Deaths.	Cases.	Deaths.	Cases.	Deaths.
From 50,000 to 100,000 inhabitants—Continued.										
Binghamton, N. Y........	53,973	10	1	......	14		8		1	1
Brockton, Mass..........	67,449	18	1	......	10	1	7	......	3	2
Canton, Ohio............	60,852	19	1	......	2		1			2
Charleston, S. C.........	60,734	25	5	......				......		
Chattanooga, Tenn.......	60,075	6	1	......	6		1		1	4
Covington, Ky...........	57,144	25	2	......	2				3	2
Duluth, Minn............	94,495	13	2	......	23		3		4	3
Elizabeth, N. J..........	86,090	21	5	......	69		3	......	1	3
El Paso, Tex.............	63,705	40		......	14					
Erie, Pa.................	75,195	31	6	1	3	......	5	......	4	4
Evansville, Ind..........	76,078	30	3	......	12		4	......	2	6
Flint, Mich.............	54,772	17	2	......	4		6	1	4	3
Fort Wayne, Ind.........	76,183	22	4	......			1	......	1	2
Harrisburg, Pa..........	72,015	26	2	......	13		5		4	
Hoboken, N. J...........	77,214	19	1	1	11		2		4	1
Holyoke, Mass...........	65,286	15	1	......	9		2		1	
Johnstown, Pa...........	68,520	34	2	......	9		1		2	
Kansas City, Kans.......	99,437	......	1	......	29		5	1	1	......
Lancaster, Pa...........	50,854		1	......	9		6			
Little Rock, Ark........	57,314	14	2	......	30		3		4	1
Manchester, N. H.......	78,283	19	5	......	13		5			
Mobile, Ala.............	58,221	21	2	......						1
New Britain, Conn......	73,794	21	2	1	14	1	2			1
Norfolk, Va.............	80,612		5	......	14		2			1
Oklahoma City, Okla.....	92,943	21		......	16					
Passaic, N. J...........	71,744	20	2	1	4		1	......	3	1
Pawtucket, R. I.........	59,111	20		......	4					1
Portland, Me...........	65,867	24		......	9		1			
Rockford, Ill...........	55,185	13	1	......	19		4		1	
Sacramento, Cal........	66,895	23		......	39		1	1	1	1
Saginaw, Mich..........	55,642	17	2	......			3		1	......
St. Joseph, Mo.........	85,236	32	4	......	37		1			
San Diego, Cal.........	53,390	11		......	20	1	2		1	
Schenectady, N. Y......	99,519	28	3	......	13				2	3
Sioux City, Iowa	57,078			......			23			
Somerville, Mass	87,689	21	4	1	20		5		6	1
South Bend, Ind........	68,915	22	4	1	9				1	
Springfield, Ill........	61,120	13	1	......	32					
Springfield, Ohio......	51,550	18		......	9					
Terre Haute, Ind.......	66,083	21	5	1	4					
Troy, N. Y.............	77,916	22	2	......	4		2	......		5
Wichita, Kans..........	70,722			......	159				3	1
Wilkes-Barre, Pa.......	76,776	17	5	......	59		3		3	
Wilmington, Del.......	91,215	43		......	11		1			1
Yonkers, N. Y.........	99,838		1	......	6		5			
York, Pa..............	51,656	......	2	......	10		2		6	
From 25,000 to 50,000 inhabitants:										
Alameda, Cal..........	27,732	11		......	7		1		1	......
Auburn, N. Y.........	37,385	13		......	7		1			3
Austin, Tex...........	34,814	31		......						
Brookline, Mass.......	32,730	9	1	1	9		5		1	
Butler, Pa............	27,632	10	3	1	50					
Butte, Mont..........	43,425	17	2	......						
Cedar Rapids, Iowa....	37,308			......			4			
Charleston, W. Va.....	29,911	15	1	......	6					
Charlotte, N. C.......	39,523		1	......	18				4	4
Chelsea, Mass.........	46,192	20	2	......	28	2	2		1	......
Chicopee, Mass........	29,319	4	1	......	3					
Clinton, Iowa.........	27,386			......			28			
Colorado Springs, Colo..	32,971	14	2	1	23		1		4	7
Columbia, S. C........	34,611	25	2	......	10					2
Columbus, Ga.........	25,950	6		......						1
Council Bluffs, Iowa....	31,484			......	5		2			1
Cranston, R. I........	25,997	8	1	......	1		1		1	1
Cumberland, Md.......	28,074	6	1	......	2		11		1	1
Danville, Ill.........	32,201	10	1	......	53		1		1	......
Davenport, Iowa......	48,811		1	1	4		16			1
Dubuque, Iowa........	39,873			......	8					1
Durham, N. C.........	25,061	5		......	7					

DIPHTHERIA, MEASLES, SCARLET FEVER, AND TUBERCULOSIS—Continued.

City Reports for Week Ended Feb. 23, 1918—Continued.

City.	Population as of July 1, 1916. (Estimated by U.S. Census Bureau.)	Total deaths from all causes.	Diphtheria.		Measles.		Scarlet fever.		Tuberculosis.	
			Cases.	Deaths.	Cases.	Deaths.	Cases.	Deaths.	Cases.	Deaths.
From 25,000 to 50,000 inhabitants—Continued.										
East Chicago, Ind.	28,743	11	1		11					1
Easton, Pa.	30,530	23								
East Orange, N.J.	42,458	8	1		20		2		1	1
Elgin, Ill.	28,203	9			3					
Elmira, N.Y.	38,120	4		1	43		1	1	3	1
Evanston, Ill.	28,591	7			20					
Everett, Mass.	39,233	9	6		10		2		6	
Fitchburg, Mass.	41,781	11			12		1		3	
Fort Smith, Ark.	28,638				1					
Galveston, Tex.	41,863	16			1				4	
Green Bay, Wis.	29,353	6			8		2			
Hammond, Ind.	26,171	21	1		2		3		1	
Haverhill, Mass.	48,477	9			18		3	1	4	
Jackson, Mich.	35,363	18	9		6		15	2	1	1
Kalamazoo, Mich.	48,886	11	2	1	5		1		4	1
Kenosha, Wis.	31,576	3	8		4		3	1		
Kingston, N.Y.	26,771	7								
Knoxville, Tenn.	38,076		1		65				1	1
La Crosse, Wis.	31,677	6	3				2		1	
Lexington, Ky.	41,097	16			24		3			3
Lincoln, Nebr.	46,515	10			7		5		1	1
Long Beach, Cal.	27,587	15			64		4			
Lorain, Ohio	36,964		2				1			
Lynchburg, Va.	32,940	14	1		7				4	
Macon, Ga.	45,757	23	1		12		3		1	2
Madison, Wis.	30,699	8	1		25		3		1	1
McKeesport, Pa.	47,521	14	2		14		1			2
Medford, Mass.	26,234	8	1		5		2		1	1
Moline, Ill.	27,451	9	1		8		2			
Montclair, N.J.	26,318	3			116		2		1	
Montgomery, Ala.	43,285	11			19		1			3
Muncie, Ind.	25,424	8	1		6				1	1
Muskogee, Okla.	44,218		1		14					
Nashua, N.H.	27,327	12	1							
Newburgh, N.Y.	29,603	7	2		8				2	1
New Castle, Pa.	41,133				20					
Newport, Ky.	31,927	11							1	1
Newport, R.I.	30,108	8	2		1		1			
Newton, Mass.	43,715	16	2	1	37		1		1	2
Niagara Falls, N.Y.	37,353	10			1		1		1	
Norristown, Pa.	31,401	7			1		1			2
Norwalk, Conn.	26,899								1	2
Oak Park, Ill.	26,654	10	1		18		3		1	1
Ogden, Utah	31,404	4			24					
Orange, N.J.	33,080	13			14				3	2
Pasadena, Cal.	46,450	17			74				3	1
Perth Amboy, N.J.	41,185	15			1				2	2
Petersburg, Va.	25,582		1		9		1		4	
Pittsfield, Mass.	38,629	7			5		3		1	3
Portsmouth, Va.	39,651	17			11		1			2
Quincy, Ill.	36,798	11			8		1			
Quincy, Mass.	38,136	17	2		49		3		1	2
Racine, Wis.	46,488	14	1		21		2		2	
Roanoke, Va.	43,284	13			18					3
Rock Island, Ill.	28,926		5	1	21		4			
San Jose, Cal.	38,002		1		31		2		4	
Steubenville, Ohio	27,415	15			1					
Stockton, Cal.	35,358	14			41		1			
Superior, Wis.	46,226	12			17		1			
Taunton, Mass.	36,283	11			1				10	4
Waltham, Mass.	30,570	7			3		1			1
Watertown, N.Y.	29,894	3	1		16					3
West Hoboken, N.J.	43,139	8			1					
Wheeling, W. Va.	43,377	13			2					3
Williamsport, Pa.	33,800	8	4		1		1			3
Wilmington, N.C.	29,892	19			3					3
Winston-Salem, N.C.	31,155	26			35				7	
Zanesville, Ohio	30,863	8							7	2

DIPHTHERIA, MEASLES, SCARLET FEVER, AND TUBERCULOSIS—Continued.

City Reports for Week Ended Feb. 23, 1918—Continued.

City.	Population as of July 1, 1916. (Estimated by U. S. Census Bureau.)	Total deaths from all causes.	Diphtheria.		Measles.		Scarlet fever.		Tuberculosis.	
			Cases.	Deaths.	Cases.	Deaths.	Cases.	Deaths.	Cases.	Deaths.
From 10,000 to 25,000 inhabitants:										
Alexandria, La.	15,333	6			4					1
Alton, Ill.	22,871	11	2		10					1
Ann Arbor, Mich.	15,010	7	3		14		1		2	
Anniston, Ala.	14,112				3					
Beaver Falls, Pa.	13,532				1					
Berlin, N. H.	13,599	2	1							
Braddock, Pa.	21,685	5			5					
Cairo, Ill.	15,794	12								4
Chillicothe, Ohio	15,470	3			2					
Clinton, Mass.	13,075	5			2		2			1
Coffeyville, Kans.	17,548				22					
Concord, N. H.	22,609	10	2	2	2		1			
Galesburg, Ill.	21,276	8			5		1			
Greenville, S. C.	18,181	7			5				1	
Hattiesburg, Miss.	16,482				3		1			
Kearney, N. J.	25,789	11			11		1		1	1
Kokomo, Ind.	20,930	11			3		1		1	
La Fayette, Ind.	21,286	6			2		2			
Leavenworth, Kans.	19,363	4								
Long Branch, N. J.	13,395	2								
Marinette, Wis.	14,610	4					1			1
Melrose, Mass.	17,445	4			2					
Muscatine, Iowa	17,500				3		1			
Nanticoke, Pa.	23,126	9	1				5			
New Albany, Ind.	23,629	12			1					
Newburyport, Mass.	15,213	7			2					1
North Adams, Mass.	22,019	12							1	
Northampton, Mass.	19,936	13					3		1	1
North Little Rock, Ark.	14,907	2			4		1		2	
Plainfield, N. J.	23,905	11					1		1	
Pontiac, Mich.	17,524	15	2		1		4		2	2
Portsmouth, N. H.	11,466	1	1		7		4	1		
Rocky Mount, N. C.	12,067	4	1		2				2	
Rutland, Vt.	14,831	9								
Sandusky, Ohio	20,193	6								
Saratoga Springs, N. Y.	13,821	3								
Spartanburg, S. C.	21,395	9			7	3			1	
Steelton, Pa.	15,518	2	1		1		5			
Washington, Pa.	21,618				101		1			
Wilkinsburg, Pa.	23,228	14			6					
Woburn, Mass.	15,169	6								

[1] Population Apr 15, 1910; no estimate made.

FOREIGN.

CHOLERA, PLAGUE, SMALLPOX, TYPHUS FEVER, AND YELLOW FEVER.

Reports Received During Week Ended Mar. 15, 1918.[1]

PLAGUE.

Place.	Date.	Cases.	Deaths.	Remarks.
Indo-China:				
Cochin-China—				
Saigon..................	Dec. 31–Jan. 6.....	2	....	
Straits Settlements:				
Singapore....................	Dec. 23–29...	1	1	

SMALLPOX.

Place.	Date.	Cases.	Deaths.	Remarks.
Algeria:				
Algiers......................	Jan. 1–31...........	2	....	
Brazil:				
Rio de Janeiro..............	Jan. 19–26.........	38	9	
Canada:				
Nova Scotia—				
Sydney...................	Feb. 17–23 .	2	....	
Ontario—				
Sarnia.................	Feb. 21–Mar. 2....	3	....	
China:				
Chungking..................	Dec. 30–Jan. 12....	....	....	Present.
Dairen.....................	Jan. 20–26........	2	....	
Shanghai.................	Jan. 21–27........	5	7	
Tientsin..................	Jan. 20–26........	4	....	
Indo-China:				
Cochin-China—				
Saigon..................	Dec. 31–Jan. 6.....	17	10	
Italy:				
Turin.....................	Jan. 14–Feb. 3.....	53	6	
Mexico:				
Aguascalientes.............	Feb. 11–17........	....	1	
Mazatlan...................	Feb. 13–19........	....	1	
Vera Cruz..................	Feb. 10–16........	2	....	
Newfoundland:				
St. Johns.................	Feb. 16–22........	4	....	
Porto Rico:				
San Juan....................	Feb. 11–17........	1	....	
Russia:				
Archangel..................	Sept. 1–Oct. 31....	7	....	
Straits Settlements:				
Singapore...................	Dec. 23–29........	2	....	
Do.................	Dec. 30–Jan. 5.....	1	....	

TYPHUS FEVER.

Place.	Date.	Cases.	Deaths.	Remarks.
Great Britain:				
Belfast......................	Feb. 10–16.........	4	1	
Greece:				
Saloniki.....................	Dec. 30–Jan. 19....	....	11	
Japan:				
Nagasaki....................	Jan. 28–Feb. 3.....	2	....	
Union of South Africa:				
Cape of Good Hope State...	Nov. 19–25........	37	7	Sept. 10–Nov. 25, 1917: Cases, 3,724 (European, 31; native, 3,093); deaths. 761 (European, 5; native, 756).

[1] From medical officers of the Public Health Service, American consuls, and other sources.

CHOLERA, PLAGUE, SMALLPOX, TYPHUS FEVER, AND YELLOW FEVER—Continued.

Reports Received from Dec. 29, 1917, to Mar. 8, 1918.

CHOLERA.

Place.	Date.	Cases.	Deaths.	Remarks.
China:				
Antung................	Nov. 26–Dec. 2....	3	1	
India:				
Bombay...............	Oct. 28–Nov. 24...	17	12	
Calcutta..............	Sept. 16–Dec. 8....	....	81	
Madras................	Nov. 25–Dec. 1....	1	1	
Rangoon..............	Nov. 4–Dec. 1.....	3	3	
Indo-China:				
Provinces............		....	....	Sept. 1–Oct. 31, 1917: Cases, 113; deaths, 57.
Anam.............	Sept. 1–Oct. 31...	17	13	
Cambodia........	....do...........	41	25	
Cochin-China....	....do...........	43	17	
Saigon...........	Nov. 22–Dec. 9...	4	3	
Kwang-Chow-Wan.....	Sept. 1–30.........	10	2	
Java:				
East Java.............	Oct. 28–Nov. 3....	1	1	
West Java............		....	....	Oct. 19–Dec. 20, 1917: Cases, 102; deaths, 57.
Batavia..........	Oct. 19–Dec. 20...	55	21	
Persia:				
Mazanderan Province.....		....	....	July 30–Sept. 3, 1917: Cases, 381, deaths, 276.
Achraf...........	July 30–Aug. 16...	90	88	
Astrabad.........	July 31...........	....	....	Present.
Barfrush.........	July 1–Aug. 16....	39	25	
Chahmirzad.......		....	....	25 cases reported July 31, 1917.
Chahrastagh......	June 15–July 25...	10	8	
Charoud.........	Aug. 26–Sept. 3...	4	2	
Damghan.........	Aug. 26..........	....	....	Present.
Kharek..........	May 28–June 11...	21	13	
Meched..........	Aug. 18–Sept. 2...	174	82	
Ouzoun Dare......	Aug. 8...........	....	....	Do.
Sabzevar.........	Aug. 24..........	....	....	Do.
Sari.............	July 3–29.........	273	144	
Semnan..........	Aug. 31–Sept. 2...	14	5	
Yekchambe-Bazar....	June 3...........	6	....	
Philippine Islands:				
Provinces............		....	....	Nov. 18–Dec. 29, 1917: Cases, 1,053; deaths, 693. Dec. 30, 1917–Jan. 19, 1918: Cases, 447, deaths, 192.
Antique..........	Nov. 18–Dec. 1...	48	32	
Bohol...........	Nov. 18–Dec. 29...	169	111	
Do...........	Dec. 30–Jan. 19...	57	52	
Capiz...........	Nov. 25–Dec. 29...	27	21	
Do...........	Dec. 30–Jan. 19...	41	35	
Cebu............	Dec. 23–29........	3	....	
Do...........	Dec. 30–Jan. 19...	36	17	
Iloilo...........	Nov. 25–Dec. 29...	179	135	
Do...........	Dec. 30–Jan. 19...	42	27	
Leyte...........	Nov. 25–Dec. 22...	13	12	
Mindanao........	Nov. 25–Dec. 29...	337	196	
Do...........	Dec. 30–Jan. 19...	224	135	
Occidental Negros.....	Nov. 25–Dec. 22...	177	123	
Do...........	Jan. 13–19........	45	15	
Oriental Negros......	Nov. 25–Dec. 29...	99	62	
Do...........	Dec. 30–Jan. 19...	12	11	
Romblon.........	Nov. 25–Dec. 1...	1	1	
Siam:				
Bangkok..............	Sept. 16–22.......	1	1	
Turkey in Asia:				
Bagdad...............	Nov. 1–15.........	....	40	

PLAGUE.

Place.	Date.	Cases.	Deaths.	Remarks.
Brazil:				
Bahia.................	Nov. 4–Dec. 13....	4	4	
Do..............	Dec. 30–Jan. 12...	3	2	
Rio de Janeiro........	Dec. 23–29........	1	....	
Do..............	Jan. 6–12.........	1	1	
British Gold Coast:				
Axim.................	Jan. 8............	....	....	Present.
Ceylon:				
Colombo..............	Oct. 14–Dec. 1....	14	13	
Ecuador...............		....	....	Sept. 1–Nov. 30, 1917: Cases, 68; deaths, 24.
Guayaquil............	Sept. 1–30........	3	1	
Do..............	Oct. 1–31.........	20	8	
Do..............	Nov. 1–30.........	45	15	

CHOLERA, PLAGUE, SMALLPOX, TYPHUS FEVER, AND YELLOW FEVER—Continued.

Reports Received from Dec. 29, 1917, to Mar. 8, 1918—Continued.

PLAGUE—Continued.

Place.	Date.	Cases.	Deaths.	Remarks.
Egypt..............				Jan. 1–Nov. 15, 1917: Cases, 728;
Port Said	July 23–29.........	1	2	deaths, 398.
India..............				Sept. 16–Dec. 1, 1917: Cases,
Bombay...........	Oct. 28–Dec. 1....	103	85	151,751; deaths, 113,434.
Calcutta...........	Sept. 16–29		2	
Henzada...........	Oct. 21–27......		1	
Karachi............	Oct. 21–Dec. 1....	11	9	
Madras Presidency........	Oct. 31–Nov. 17..	3,294	2,560	
Mandalay.........	Oct. 14–Nov. 17...		89	
Rangoon...........	Oct. 21–Dec. 1.....	32	38	
Indo-China:				
Provinces...........				Sept. 1–Oct. 31, 1917: Cases, 70;
Anam...........	Sept. 1–Oct. 31....	25	24	deaths, 64.
Cambodia............	....do...........	30	19	
Cochin-China.........	....do..........	15	11	
Saigon............	Oct. 31–Dec. 23....	17	6	
Java:				
East Java..				Oct. 27–Nov. 25, 1917: Cases, 75;
Surabaya............	Nov. 11–25.......	2	2	deaths, 73.
West Java..........				Nov. 25–Dec. 9, 1917: Cases, 45;
				deaths, 45.
Peru...				Dec. 1, 1917–Jan. 15, 1918: Cases,
Ancache Department –				106.
Casma.............	Dec. 1–Jan. 15.....	2	....	
Lambayeque Department..	....do...........	22	....	At Chiclayo, Ferrenafe, Jayanca,
				Lambayeque.
Libertad Department......	....do...........	72	....	At Guadalupe, Mansiche, Pacas-
				mayo, Salaverry, San Jose, San
				Pedro, and country district of
				Trujillo
Lima Department.........	....do...........	9	....	City and country.
Piura Department—				
Catacaos............	....do...........	1	....	
Senegal:				
St. Louis...	Feb. 2..........			Present.
Siam:				
Bangkok..	Sept 16–Dec. 23...	13	9	
Straits Settlements:				
Singapore.................	Oct. 28–Dec. 22....	4	6	

SMALLPOX.

Place.	Date.	Cases.	Deaths.	Remarks.
Algeria:				
Algiers	Nov. 1 Dec. 31....	3	1	
Australia:				July 12–Dec. 20, 1917: Cases, 36.
New South Wales............				Jan. 1–17, 1918: Cases, 1.
Abermain............	Oct. 25–Nov. 29...	3	....	Newcastle district.
Cessnock............	July 12–Oct. 11...	7	....	
Eumongla	Aug. 15...........	1	....	
Kurri Kurri............	Dec. 5–20........	2	....	
Mungindi............	Aug. 13...........	1	....	
Warren............	July 12–Oct. 25...	22	....	
Do............	Jan. 1–17.........	1	....	
Brazil.				
Bahia...	Nov. 10–Dec. 8....	3	....	
Pernambuco..............	Nov. 1–15......	1	....	
Rio de Janeiro..............	Sept. 30 Dec. 29...	703	190	
Do..............	Dec. 30 Jan. 19....	120	33	
Sao Paulo.............	Oct. 29 Nov. 4....		2	
Canada:				
British Columbia –				
Vancouver............	Jan. 13 Feb. 16....	4	....	
Victoria............	Jan. 7–Feb. 2......	2	....	
Winnipeg............	Dec. 30 Jan. 5.....	1	....	
New Brunswick—				
Kent County..........	Dec. 4..............		....	Outbreak. On main line Cana-
				dian Ry., 25 miles north of
				Moncton.
Do..............:	Jan. 22............	40	....	In 7 localities.
Northumberland	....do............	41	....	In 5 localities.
County.				
Restigouche County. ..	Jan. 18............	60	....	
Victoria County........	Jan. 22............	10	....	At Limestone and a lumber
Westmoreland County,	Jan. 20–Feb 23....	8	....	camp.
Moncton.				
York County..........	Jan. 22............	8	....	

CHOLERA, PLAGUE, SMALLPOX, TYPHUS FEVER, AND YELLOW FEVER—Continued.

Reports Received from Dec. 29, 1917, to Mar. 8, 1918—Continued.

SMALLPOX—Continued.

Place.	Date.	Cases.	Deaths.	Remarks.
Canada—Continued.				
Nova Scotia—				
Sydney	Feb. 3-9	1		
Ontario—				
Hamilton	Dec. 16-22	1		
Do	Jan. 13-19	2		
Sarnia	Dec. 9-15	1		
Do	Jan. 6-Feb. 23	25		
Toronto	Feb. 10-16	1		
Windsor	Dec. 30-Jan. 5	1		
Prince Edward Island—				
Charlottetown	Feb. 7-13	1		
Quebec—				
Montreal	Dec. 16-Jan. 5	5		
Do	Jan. 6-12	1		
China:				
Amoy	Oct. 29-Dec. 30			Present.
Antung	Dec. 3-23	13	2	
Do	Jan. 7-27	4	2	
Chungking	Nov. 11-Dec. 29			Do.
Dairen	Nov. 18-Dec. 22	3	1	
Do	Dec. 30-Jan. 12	2		
Harbin	May 14-June 30	20		Chinese Eastern Ry.
Do	July 1-Dec. 2	7		Do.
Hongkong	Dec. 23-29	1		
Hungtahotze Station	Oct. 28-Nov. 4	1		Do.
Manchuria Station	May 14-June 30	6		Do.
Do	July 1-Dec. 2	3		Do.
Mukden	Nov. 11-24			Present.
Shanghai	Nov. 18-Dec. 23	41	91	Cases, foreign; deaths among natives.
Do	Dec. 31-Jan. 20	20	68	Do.
Tientsin	Nov. 11-Dec. 22	13		
Do	Dec. 30-Jan. 19	5		
Cuba:				
Habana	Jan. 7	1		Nov. 8, 1917, 1 case from Coruna. Dec. 5, 1917, 1 case.
Marianao	Jan. 8	1		6 miles distant from Habana.
Ecuador:				Sept. 1-Nov. 30, 1917: Cases, 26, deaths, 2.
Guayaquil	Sept. 1-30	8		
Do	Oct. 1-31	14	1	
Do	Nov. 1-30	4	1	
Egypt:				
Alexandria	Nov. 12-18	1		
Do	Jan. 8-14	3		
Cairo	July 23-Nov. 12-18	6	1	
France:				
Lyon	Nov. 18-Dec 16	6	3	
Do	Jan. 7-20	5		
India:				
Bombay	Oct. 21-Dec. 1	16	4	
Karachi	Nov. 18-24		1	Nov. 11-17, 1907: 10 cases with 4 deaths; imported on a Manesa from Basreh.
Madras	Oct. 31-Dec. 8	9	3	
Rangoon	Oct. 28-Nov. 24	4	1	
Indo-China:				
Provinces				Sept. 1-Oct. 31, 1917: Cases, 345; deaths, 99.
Anam	Sept. 1-Oct. 31	103	15	
Cambodia	do	10	3	
Cochin-China	do	222	76	
Saigon	Oct. 20-Dec. 30	120	26	
Laos	Oct. 1-31	1		
Tonkin	Sept. 1-Oct. 31	9	4	
Italy:				
Castellamare	Dec. 10	2		Among refugees.
Florence	Dec. 1-15	17	4	
Leghorn	Jan. 7-27	17	5	
Messina	Jan. 3-19	1		
Milan				Oct. 1-Nov. 20, 1917: Cases, 17.
Naples	To Dec. 10	2		Among refugees.
Turin	Oct. 29-Dec. 9	123	120	
Japan:				
Nagasaki	Jan. 14-27	3	1	Island of Taiwan (Formosa).
Taihoku	Dec. 1-31	1		Do.
Do	Jan. 8-14	1		
Yokohama	Jan. 17-24	2		

CHOLERA, PLAGUE, SMALLPOX, TYPHUS FEVER, AND YELLOW FEVER—Continued.

Reports Received from Dec. 29, 1917, to Mar. 8, 1918—Continued.

SMALLPOX—Continued.

Place.	Date.	Cases.	Deaths.	Remarks.
Java:				
East Java..................	Oct. 7-Dec. 9.....	25	....	
Mid-Java..................	Oct. 10-Nov. 21...	55	....	Oct. 10-Dec. 12, 1917: Cases, 63;
Samarang...............	Dec. 6-12..........	1	1	death, 1.
West Java................	....	....	....	Oct. 19-Dec. 20, 1917: Cases, 217;
Batavia...............	Nov. 2-8..........	1	....	deaths, 33.
Mexico:				
Aguascalientes...........	Feb. 4-10..........	....	1	
Mazatlan................	Dec. 5-11..........	....	1	
Do....	Jan. 29-Feb. 12....	4	....	
Mexico City..............	Nov. 11-Dec. 29...	16	....	
Do.................	Dec. 30-Feb. 2....	30	....	
Piedras Negras...........	Jan. 11............	200	....	
Vera Cruz................	Jan. 20-Feb. 9....	4	3	
Newfoundland:				
St. Johns................	Dec. 8-Jan. 4.....	29	....	
Do.................	Jan. 5-Feb. 15.....	25	....	
Trepassey..............	Jan. 4............	....	....	Outbreak with 11 cases reported.
Philippine Islands:				
Manila	Oct. 28-Dec. 8....	5	....	
Do.................	Jan. 13-19.........	3	....	
Porto Rico:				
San Juan..............	Jan. 28-Feb. 3.....	1	....	Varioloid.
Portugal:				
Lisbon.................	Nov. 4-Dec. 15....	2	....	
Do.................	Dec. 30-Jan. 19...	2	....	
Portuguese East African:				
Lourenço Marques........	Aug. 1-Nov. 30...	....	9	
Russia:				
Moscow................	Aug. 26-Oct. 6...	22	2	
Petrograd..............	Aug. 31-Nov. 18...	76	3	
Siam:				
Bangkok...............	Nov. 25-Dec. 1....	1	1	
Spain:				
Coruna................	Dec. 2-15.........	....	4	
Madrid................	....	....	....	Jan. 1-Dec. 31, 1917: Deaths, 77.
Seville................	Oct. 1-Dec. 30....	....	66	
Straits Settlements:				
Singapore..............	Nov. 25-Dec. 1....	1	1	
Tunisia:				
Tunis	Dec. 14-20........	....	1	
Turkey in Asia:				
Bagdad..............	....	....	....	Present in November, 1917.
Venezuela:				
Maracaibo.............	Dec. 2-8..........	....	1	

TYPHUS FEVER.

Place.	Date.	Cases.	Deaths.	Remarks.
Algeria:				
Algiers.................	Nov. 1-Dec. 31....	2	1	
Argentina:				
Rosario................	Dec. 1-31.........	....	1	
Australia:				
South Australia	....	....	....	Nov. 11-17, 1917: Cases, 1.
Brazil:				
Rio de Janeiro...........	Oct. 28-Dec. 1.....	7	....	
Canada:				
Ontario—				
Kingston..............	Dec. 2-8..........	3	....	
Quebec—				
Montreal..............	Dec. 16-22........	2	1	
China:				
Antung................	Dec. 3-30.........	13	1	
Do.................	Dec. 31-Jan. 27....	2	2	
Chosen (Formosa):				
Seoul.................	Nov. 1-30........	1	....	
Egypt:				
Alexandria.............	Nov. 8-Dec. 28....	57	13	
Do.................	Jan. 8-14.........	20	7	
Cairo.................	July 23-Dec. 16...	137	70	
Port Said.............	July 30-Nov. 11...	5	5	
Great Britain:				
Glasgow...............	Dec. 21...........	1	....	
Do.................	Jan. 20-26........	1	....	
Manchester.............	Dec. 2-8..........	1	....	

CHOLERA, PLAGUE, SMALLPOX, TYPHUS FEVER, AND YELLOW FEVER—Continued.

Reports Received from Dec. 29, 1917, to Mar. 8, 1918—Continued.

TYPHUS FEVER—Continued.

Place.	Date.	Cases.	Deaths.	Remarks.
Greece:				
Saloniki...................	Nov. 11–Dec. 29...	....	72	
Japan:				
Nagasaki..................	Nov. 26–Dec. 16....	5	5	
Do...................	Jan. 7–27...........	3	....	
Java:				
East Java................				Oct. 15–Dec. 9, 1917: Cases, 24; deaths, 3.
Mid-Java:				Oct. 10–Dec. 12, 1917: Cases, 54, deaths, 2.
Samarang..............	Oct. 17–Dec. 5.....	15	2	
West Java................				Oct. 19–Dec. 20, 1917: Cases, 73, deaths, 15.
Batavia................	Oct. 19–Dec. 20....	73	17	
Mexico:				
Aguascalientes............	Dec. 15............		2	
Do...................	Jan. 21–Feb. 10....		14	
Durango, State—				
Guanacevi............	Feb. 11............			Epidemic.
Mexico City..............	Nov. 11–Dec. 29...	476	....	
Do...................	Dec. 30–Feb. 2....	257	....	
Portugal:				
Lisbon...................	Feb. 21............			Present.
Oporto..................	...do.............			Epidemic.
Russia:				
Archangel................	Sept. 1–14.........	7	2	
Moscow..................	Aug. 26–Oct. 6....	49	2	
Petrograd................	Aug. 31–Nov. 18...	32	....	
Do...................	Feb. 2............			Present.
Vladivostok..............	Oct. 29–Nov. 4....	12	1	
Sweden:				
Goteborg.................	Nov. 18–24........	1	....	
Switzerland:				
Basel....................	Jan. 6–12..........		1	
Zurich..................	Nov. 9–15.........	2	....	
Do...................	Jan. 13–19.........	2	....	
Tunisia:				
Tunis...................	Nov. 30–Dec. 6....		1	
Turkey:				
Albania—				
Janina...............	Jan. 27...........		....	Epidemic.
Union of South Africa:				
Cape of Good Hope State...	Sept. 10–Nov. 11...	3,469	701	

YELLOW FEVER.

Place.	Date.	Cases.	Deaths.	Remarks.
Ecuador...........				Sept. 1–Nov. 30, 1917: Cases, 5; deaths, 3.
Guayaquil.................	Sept. 1–30.........	1	1	
Do...................	Oct. 1–31..........	1	....	
Do...................	Nov. 1–30..........	2	2	
Yaguachi.................	...do.............	1	....	
Honduras:				
Tegucigalpa...............	Dec. 16–22.........	....	1	
Do...................	Jan. 6–19..........	....	1	

PUBLIC HEALTH REPORTS

| VOL. 33 | MARCH 22, 1918 | No. 12 |

HEALTH HAZARDS FROM THE USE OF THE AIR HAMMER IN CUTTING INDIANA LIMESTONE.

By J. P. LEAKE, Passed Assistant Surgeon, United States Public Health Service.

1. The Industry.

Indiana limestone from the vicinity of Bedford, Ind., is at present the most important building stone in America. Beside its architectural qualities, its value is due largely to the ease with which it can be quarried and worked in large quantities. It is of fine texture, of the class called oölitic because of the small egg-like fossils of which it is composed, of even consistency, and comparatively soft to the tool.

The center of the industry is Bedford, a city of 10,000 population, the county seat of Lawrence County; Bloomington, a city of about the same size, the county seat of Monroe County, adjoining Lawrence County on the north, is next in importance as a stone center; Ellettsville and Stinesville, north of Bloomington, are smaller centers. Bedford has railroad shops and other small factories, but it is essentially a town of one industry—stone—while Bloomington is the seat of the State university and enjoys more varied activities.

There are 39 stone companies in the district. Though some of these engage in both branches of the work, a sharp line is drawn between the production of rough or machine-tooled stone and the production of dressed or cut stone. It is only the latter with which this investigation is concerned.

The greater part of the quarrying for Bedford is near Oolitic, a town of about a thousand inhabitants, 4 miles northwest of Bedford. For all but the preliminary squaring off of the blocks (the process called scabbling) the stone is brought to the mills in Bedford. These mills are very large buildings, some operating as many as seven 10 or 15 ton electric cranes and containing tracks for the loading and unloading of freight cars. On account of their size and height, and the wide doors, they are difficult to heat; moreover, they contain no intrinsic source of heat, such as the furnaces of a steel mill.

In general, the blocks of stone from the quarries are first sawed into large slabs by reciprocating gang saws. These are strips of steel without teeth, the abrasion being furnished by a mixture of sand and

water, which i-
large circular
This is also a w
over the circula
dressing follow
planers, circular
stone. In the
bed beneath th
coarse powder, p
were formerly cu

The stonecutt
main craneways
gation, the air h
except in the ca
mallet in the old
or carving more
capitals (Fig. 3),
"cleaning up."
shaped to the forn
hammer or wooden
this part of the w
the finishing or "c
appear to be used
division between "re
plain stonecutting a

There are normall
in Bloomington, and
On account of inactiv
were found employed
In general, however,
permanent; the stonec
owning excellent home
8 per day and 4 on Sa
time of the investigatio
not hired directly by the
who employ other carver

In the stone industry,
on granites and the harde
duced in Bedford about :
became universal in this d
pression is maintained by
pounds per square inch, and
ible pressure hose connects
is turned on for each hamme
about 3 feet from the hamm

... parts of the air hammer. The cylinder piston.
... three-quarter inch hammer are shown to the
... rule, and those of the 1-inch hammer to the
... foot rule. The hose is coupled to the head, the
... inserted in the other end of the cylinder. In the
... inch hammer the exhaust is in the head. In
... in the cylinder near the head.

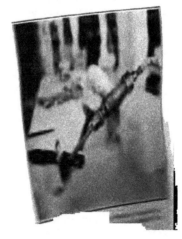

matic hammers were seen. The three parts of each of the two sizes of a hammer frequently used are shown in figure 4. The reciprocating strokes are produced by the piston alternately opening and closing inlet and exhaust openings at various points on the interior of the cylinder (piston valve) and thus responding to the force of the air pressure.

The tool is not attached to the hammer, but must be held in the point of the hammer by the hand. The tools are about 10 inches long, including a butt of about 1½ inches which fits into the hammer. The diameter is variable, frequently about half an inch, giving a weight of about 9 ounces.

The dimensions of the two hammers are approximately as follows:

	Three-quarter inch.	1 inch.
Length	6.7 inches	8 inches.
Weight (without tool)	1¼ pounds.	3¼ pounds.
diameter	1.2 inches.	1.6 inches.
diameter	½ inch.	1 inch.
length (cylinder)	2.6 inches.	2.8 inches.
of stroke	0.9 inch.	1.07 inches.
of piston	½ inch.	1 inch.
of piston proper	1.7 inches.	1.75 inches.
of piston rod (for impact against tool)	0.9 inch.	1.5 inches.
of piston (with rod)	3 ounces.	6 ounces.

means of the tuning-fork mechanism shown in figure 5 and matically in figure 6, the rate of vibration of various tools measured.[1] The apparatus consisted simply of a copper platen by an adjustable clamp to the tool whose vibration was to ured. The platen was smoked after being fixed to the tool, ng it over a bit of ignited camphor. While the tool was d on a piece of stone, a tuning fork with tracing point was drawn rapidly across the platen. If the tool were not the resulting curve would show merely the smooth vibra- tuning fork. If the tool vibrated at the same time, the urve would show a certain number of the smooth tuning ns and also the sharp strokes of the tool, giving peaks hape, height, and number from those caused by the The ratio of the number of the former peaks to the latter in a given distance on the tracing gives the of the tool when that of the fork is known.

of the same size and type, and with the and to give rather widely varying ntly on the pressure exerted by on the lubrication and amount found that with a range of be gaug accurately

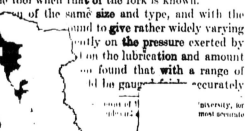

of 1
mos

niversity, for
most accurate

Fig 4 —The three parts of the air hammer. The cylinder, piston, and head of the three-quarter inch hammer are shown to the left of the foot rule, and those of the 1-inch hammer to the right of the foot rule. The hose is coupled to the head, the tool being inserted in the other end of the cylinder. In the three-quarter inch hammer the exhaust is in the head; in the 1-inch it is in the cylinder near the head.

Fig 5 —Platen for measuring vibration frequency attached to the tool in an air hammer. One tuning fork is in position for recording. This is more clearly shown in figure 6.

matic hammers were seen. The three parts of each of the two sizes of a hammer frequently used are shown in figure 4. The reciprocating strokes are produced by the piston alternately opening and closing inlet and exhaust openings at various points on the interior of the cylinder (piston valve) and thus responding to the force of the air pressure.

The tool is not attached to the hammer, but must be held in the point of the hammer by the hand. The tools are about 10 inches long, including a butt of about $1\frac{1}{2}$ inches which fits into the hammer. The diameter is variable, frequently about half an inch, giving a weight of about 9 ounces.

The dimensions of the two hammers are approximately as follows:

	Three-quarter inch.	1 inch.
Total length	6.7 inches	8 inches.
Total weight (without tool)	$1\frac{1}{2}$ pounds	$3\frac{1}{2}$ pounds.
Outside diameter	1.2 inches	1.6 inches.
Inside diameter	$\frac{3}{4}$ inch	1 inch.
Inside length (cylinder)	2.6 inches	2.8 inches.
Length of stroke	0.9 inch	1.07 inches.
Diameter of piston	$\frac{3}{4}$ inch	1 inch.
Length of piston proper	1.7 inches	1.73 inches.
Length of piston rod (for impact against tool)	0.9 inch	1.5 inches.
Weight of piston (with rod)	3 ounces	6 ounces.

By means of the tuning-fork mechanism shown in figure 5 and diagrammatically in figure 6, the rate of vibration of various tools was measured.[1] The apparatus consisted simply of a copper platen attached by an adjustable clamp to the tool whose vibration was to be measured. The platen was smoked after being fixed to the tool, by moving it over a bit of ignited camphor. While the tool was being used on a piece of stone, a tuning fork with tracing point attached, was drawn rapidly across the platen. If the tool were not vibrating, the resulting curve would show merely the smooth vibrations of the tuning fork. If the tool vibrated at the same time, the compound curve would show a certain number of the smooth tuning fork vibrations and also the sharp strokes of the tool, giving peaks different in shape, height, and number from those caused by the tuning fork. The ratio of the number of the former peaks to the number of the latter in a given distance on the tracing gives the rate of vibration of the tool when that of the fork is known.

Various hammers, even of the same size and type, and with the same registered air pressure, were found to give rather widely varying rates of vibration, dependent apparently on the pressure exerted by the stonecutter against the stone and on the lubrication and amount of wear of the hammer. It was soon found that with a range of tuning forks the rate of vibration could be gauged fairly accurately

[1] The writer is indebted to Prof. A. L. Foley of the Department of Physics, Indiana University, for suggesting and perfecting the details of this apparatus. It is simple and appeared to be the most accurate of several which were considered.

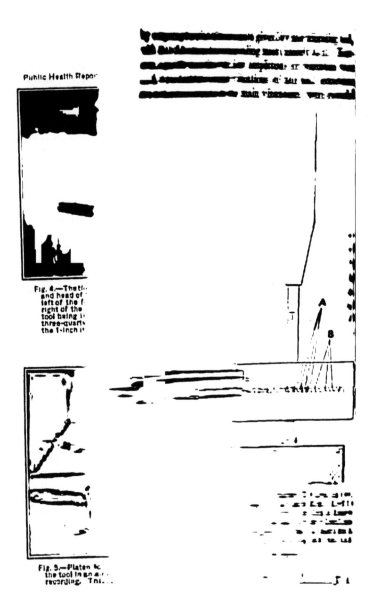

Fig. 4.—The th...
and head of...
left of the f...
right of the...
tool being i...
three-quart...
the f-inch i...

Fig. 5.—Platen &...
the tool in an a...
recording. Thi...

much more rapid than the figures usually given, and still does not take account of the more rapid accessory vibrations.

The method of using the air hammer may be seen in figures 2 and 3. The hammer itself is held by a right-handed person in the right hand, between the thumb and forefingers in much the same way as a pencil or pen is held. Some of the stonecutters regulate the power of the stroke by holding the thumb or forefinger over the exhaust. This may create a callus or a small area of insensibility at times, but does not appear to be productive of any serious results. The tool is held in the left hand, the most powerful part of the grasp and that controlling the direction of the cutting edge being exerted by the ulnar part of the hand. The direction of the hammer and tool is diagonal to the surface of the stone, and the rotation of the chisel about its own axis as well as the depth of the cut must be controlled very accurately. Since the tool is slender and rotates freely in the hammer, this necessitates a very firm and constant grip with the left hand. These points are important, as will be shown later. Some of the air hammers, presumably those which were considerably worn, were observed to discharge air along the piston rod and tool, against the fingers of the hand which held the tool. This was not observed to cause serious discomfort, but may have interfered with the power of the stroke.

The work is fairly continuous. Frequent changes of position and interruptions to blow away dust, make measurements, and change tools occur, but the hammer is in the hand and operating for the greater part of the time. Competition in speed, in part stimulated by the foremen or subcontractors, in part natural to the stonecutters, is probably keener than in smaller shops under the old conditions of stonecutting; in Bedford, stonecutting has been transformed to a factory occupation.

Heat was furnished in one of three ways: First, by hot air conduits opening in the vicinity of the stonecutters, as shown in Figure 2; second, by steam pipes around the side of the building; third, by coke-burning salamanders. Of these the latter appeared to be the most efficient, and the mills were so open that danger from carbon monoxide poisoning was minimal. However, since cold appears to be a factor in the production of discomfort from the use of the tool, it would be advisable to install radiators or other devices for heating the tools and the hands on cold mornings, in closer proximity to the cutters than the hot-air conduits and the steam pipes. The temperature in the mills is much less severe than in the open sheds where stonecutting has customarily been done. In one mill when the outside temperature was 16° F. at 7.30 a. m., the temperature where the stonecutting took place was observed to be 38° F. at the same time. In another mill the inside temperature was 40° F. when the outside temperature was 22° F.; in a third the inside temperature was 40° F. when the outside temperature was 26° F. In two metal plants where pneumatic tools were being used the temperatures were 45° F. and 62° F. when the outside temperatures were 19° F. and 21° F., respectively.

As regards lighting, conditions were satisfactory. The stonecutting is usually done at one side of the mill and therefore near windows.

2. Other Uses of Vibrating Pneumatic Tools.

The use of pneumatic tools was also observed and tried in drilling holes in limestone, in cutting granite and other hard stone, in riveting metal plates, in calking boilers, in chipping castings, in cutting metal preparatory to calking, and in cutting grooves on sheet metal.

In the mills and at the quarries, reciprocating pneumatic drills, called "plug drills," are used for drilling holes in the blocks of stone for hoisting and for breaking. These drills are much larger than the air hammers used in stonecutting, especially in length of stroke, and the rate of vibration is much slower. The hammer has a pistol or shovel grip, and the tool, or drill proper, is guided by the left hand only at the first application to the stone; when the hole has been started, both hands grasp the hammer. Moreover, the drill is of larger diameter than the tool in stonecutting, and the grasp does not need to be as rigid or to direct the point as accurately as in the latter work.

In granite and monument cutting, the air hammer and tools are like those used in the Indiana limestone belt. Part of the granite cutting, however, is a pulverization of the stone, with the hammer and tool held perpendicular to the surface. It is apparent that when the work is of this character the grip on the tool is not of necessity as firm as when diagonal cutting is done. The main vibratory rates and the accessory vibrations were found to be similar to those in the limestone mills. The tendency toward vasomotor spasticity in the left hand (to be described later) was observed in the granite cutters, but not as uniformly nor to as marked a degree as in the limestone cutters.

In hot riveting outdoors and in hot and cold riveting in shops and mills the largest hand air hammers are used, those with pistons $1\frac{1}{16}$-inches diameter and a 9-inch stroke being a common size. These give about 20 vibrations per second. Here both hands are on the hammer, which usually has a pistol grip; the cap or "set" which hits the rivet is attached to the hammer by a spring clutch and does not need to be held. Riveting by sledge hammer was also observed; a rivet is headed as quickly by this method as by the use of the pneumatic hammer, but the strain on the men is much more severe. No cases of vasomotor spasticity were discovered among pneumatic rivet men.

In calking metal seams, a smaller hammer is used th 'n in riveting, and the calking tool is held in the hand, but a firm, rigid grasp is not necessary, as the action of the hammer is perpendicular to the surface and the tool guides itself to a large extent.

The chipping preparatory to this calking, on the contrary, is inclined work. A triangular ribbon of steel is cut from the upper plate in order to make a bevel for calking. Grooving a sheet of metal is a somewhat similar process. Not so much attention, however, is directed in these cases to make the finished job smooth in appearance as in stonecutting, and the grasp on the tool is consequently not so rigid or continuous. The vibration rate is about 50 per second.

Chipping rough projections from castings is like the processes just described, but frequently larger hammers are used. Some of the tools used for this purpose have a hexagonal butt which fits into a six-sided opening in the end of the hammer snugly enough to prevent turning, but allowing free up and down motion. With the pistol grip, which is almost universal in pneumatic hammers for metal work, this enables the operator to guide the tool well with the hammer hand, and to relax the grasp on the tool to some extent. None of the metal workers who used air hammers admitted the blanching of the hands which was found so frequently in limestone cutters.

In a search in Pittsburgh through hospital records, interrogation of physicians with large practices among the metal workers, and an examination of several gangs of men chipping shell cases and steel wheels, the only case of pathological blanching of the hands which was found was in a man who had acquired it while cutting granite. This man did not complain of the hand condition but quit stone-cutting for more sedentary metal work because of a subdeltoid bursitis with sudden onset 16 years after he began to use the air hammer. The chippers, who had been working with the air hammer for 3 to 12 years, had no complaint; it was noted, however, that these were men of stocky build and that they diminished the amplitude of the vibration by bracing their bodies against the hammers. The hammer used had a piston diameter of $1\frac{1}{8}$ inches and a 3-inch stroke. At 100 pounds pressure about 32 strokes per second or 1,800 per minute were delivered. The very fine secondary vibrations, or "overtones" were much more rapid than in the stone tools, being 20 to 40 times as frequent as the main strokes; but it is probable that these secondary vibrations in either case, on account of their very low amplitude and force, are practically negligible. In chipping the tool does not need to be guided with great accuracy and some of the more skillful chippers do not hold the tool at all except in starting and finishing.

It is thus seen that in these other uses of the pneumatic hammer (except granite cutting, which is somewhat similar to limestone cutting) the rate of vibration is slower and the grasp on the tool less constrained and constant than in the occupation under consideration. We should therefore expect that if the vibration itself had any deleterious effect, this would be at a maximum in the case of the stonecutters.

3. The Pulmonary Hazard.

Though this investigation was primarily directed to ascertain the possible effects of the air hammer in producing nervous disorders, it was deemed worth while to secure some data on the pulmonary hazard, since dust is commonly supposed to be the one great danger in the stonecutting trade. The infiltration of the lung with dust particles is known as pneumokoniosis, in the case of stone dust, as chalicosis: the result is a fibroid phthisis giving rise to dyspnœa, less often to cough and expectoration, at times fatal in itself, but more commonly found at necropsy when the direct cause of death has been tuberculosis. We may therefore consider the dust as predisposing to pulmonary infection with tubercle bacilli—less often with pneumococci or other organisms—and we may expect to find chalicosis expressed in the death records as pulmonary tuberculosis.

All prior statistics based on this assumption class stonecutting as a somewhat hazardous occupation. In this country the census of 1900 [1] recorded 33 per cent of the deaths among marble and stonecutters as due to pulmonary tuberculosis, while for all occupations (males) the percentage was only 14.5. In 1909 [2] 28.6 per cent of marble and stonecutters, 14.8 per cent of all occupied males, and 21 per cent of all occupied females who died, died of pulmonary tuberculosis. Hoffman [3] has reported the experience of the Prudential Life Insurance Co., 1907–1910: 47.8 per cent of the deaths among stone workers 25 to 44 years of age and 32.3 per cent of those 45 to 64 years of age were due to tuberculosis; among all occupied males the percentages for the two age groups were 38.5 and 14.1, respectively.

Through the courtesy of the officers of the Journeymen Stone Cutters' Association of North America, part of the death records of this organization were summarized. Of 343 deaths among stonecutters with assigned cause, 56 per cent were credited to pulmonary tuberculosis, stonecutter's consumption, and fibroid phthisis. On every count, then, stonecutters have suffered severely from chronic pulmonary disease, presumably caused by the stone dust.

[1] Twelfth Census of the United States. Vital Statistics, Part 1, Table 8, p. 151. Washington: United States Census Office, 1902.

[2] Mortality Statistics, 1909. Tenth Annual Report. Table VIII, pp. 402, 3ss. Washington: Government Printing Office 1912.

[3] Hoffman, F. E. Exhibits of the Prudential Insurance Co. of America. International Congress on Hygiene and Demography. Pp. 29, 24. Washington, 1912.

I am indebted to Dr. Harvey Voyles, registrar of Bedford, for access to the original mortality records of that city, which are in good shape for the past 10 years, except for some uncertainty (as is common in death records) as to stillbirths; on this latter account only persons over 1 year of age were considered. To secure a basis for comparison, the United States Mortality Records were similarly summarized for 1910–1915, the middle six years of the past decade, since the records for 1916 and 1917 are not available. For the registration area, 11.3 per cent of all deaths in this age-group (11.9 per cent in males, 10.5 per cent in females) were due to tuberculosis of the lungs, for Indiana 11.5 per cent. For Lawrence County, Ind., 12.6 per cent of deaths at all ages were due to pulmonary tuberculosis; for the registration area 9.4 per cent at all ages, and for Indiana either as a whole or disregarding cities of over 10,000 population in 1910, 9.9 per cent. The population of Bedford was 8,716 at the last census. The tuberculosis proportional rate in Lawrence County is thus seen to be above normal. But beside Bedford and the limestone mills, Lawrence County contains the town of Mitchell, near which are large cement factories. Many cement works are notoriously dusty, and both locally and generally have a reputation for high consumptive rates. The death rate per thousand from pulmonary tuberculosis in the registration area for the six-year period was 1.31, in Indiana 1.29, in rural Indiana including all of Lawrence County 1.24, in Lawrence County 1.60.

Among stonecutters in Bedford 15 per cent of the deaths during the 10 years were due to pulmonary tuberculosis. Among all the workers in the stone mills, including the planer men, 12 per cent of the deaths were assigned to this cause. No disproportionately high number of deaths was assigned to other respiratory or heart disease, under which titles might be found fatalities really due to chalicosis. Among all other males of the same age group (23 to 72 years) the proportional rate was 13 per cent; among all females 21 per cent; among all persons over 1 year of age the proportional rate (from tuberculosis of the lungs) was 13.3 per cent, corresponding to 11.3 per cent for the registration area.

Objections might be justly raised to absolute conclusions from these statistics alone in that for some items there were only a small number of deaths—only two deaths from phthisis were recorded for Belfast stonecutters during the 10 years; also that the age groups were very broad and that proportionate percentages instead of actual death rates were compared. In regard to the small size of the items, it is to be noted that the classes are not subject to the allowances made for samples, but that they represent the total number of deaths. The age distribution was not strikingly dissimilar in the different classes. The possibility of consumptive stonecutters having left the trade or sought other climates is to be considered, but the higher percentage of tuberculosis in Bedford among females than among males would argue against the assumption; for if the affected stonecutters had left the trade, while still remaining in Bedford, we should expect a disproportionately high rate among the males of that age-group as compared with the sex which is not subject to the hazard.

It accordingly appears that while Bedford has a proportional death percentage from phthisis slightly above normal, it has been no higher for stoneworkers than for other classes of the population, including females.

This agrees with what could be learned from a canvass of the physicians of Bedford and from the stonecutters themselves. The only case of consumption in stonecutters about which information could be obtained in this way was in a man who developed the disease nursing his wife through a fatal tuberculosis. No X-ray chest plates were made, but in examining the men no symptom or sign which could be attributed to pneumokoniosis was found.

The mills were not as dusty as several granite monument shops which were visited, but the difference was not striking, except for the fact that in the monument shops the dust was in the air, while in the limestone mills the dust was almost entirely on surfaces. There are at least four conceivable explanations for the comparative immunity of the Bedford stonecutters: (1) The particles may be larger and heavier than in the cutting of other stones; as one looked down the stonecutting aisles of these mills the visible cloud of dust from each tool stopped far below the face of the worker. In general the exhaust from the pneumatic tool blows what dust is formed away from the breathing zone. In limestone cutting the action of the tool is chipping at an acute angle with the surface of the stone; as explained before, in granite cutting the action is frequently perpendicular to the surface and possibly more pulverizing. (2) The blocks of stone as they reach the cutter in the mills, though not visibly wet, retain some of the moisture from the sawing processes. This reduces the dustiness of the cutting. (3) It is possible that the particles from the oolitic limestone are rounder and smoother than those from other stones; an accurate microscopical comparison was not made. (4) By some theories, calcium salts have a beneficial action in tuberculosis, aiding in walling off chance lesions from further activity. In general, the cutting of limestone has been held to be less perilous than the cutting of sandstone or granite. In any case, stonecutters appear to suffer less in Bedford than elsewhere from the dust hazard.

Associated with the dust hazard is the hazard from flying chips, largely an ocular one. Only a small proportion of the men were observed to wear protecting goggles. But on account of the inclination of the hammer the direction of the chipping is away from the worker's eyes. The physicians and oculists in Bedford state that while eye injuries occur in the stone mills, the most numerous and severe are not among the workmen who handle the stone, but among the metal workers, machinists and tool sharpeners; stone particles rarely cause more than temporary injury.

4. The Nervous Hazard.

At the outset of the investigation it was observed that the stone-cutters on cold mornings were likely to have the fingers and ulnar side of the left hand white, cold, and numb. The investigation was primarily directed toward ascertaining the seriousness of this condition and whether other nervous troubles might be attributable to the use of the air hammer. The general findings and conclusions in this regard are given in Prof. Edsall's report. The writer is deeply indebted to Dr. Edsall for advice and collaboration, and for making by far the greater part of the more thorough examinations.

Many have considered the action of pneumatic tools to be unduly fatiguing or to subject the nervous system to some mysterious injury, but no data have been available sufficient for drawing conclusions in the matter. Southard and Solomon[1] have reported a case of pain and numbness in the hand of a granite cutter, in whom they found a slight anesthesia demonstrable only by Martin's electrical sensory test. This cutter had used a pneumatic tool for 15 years; the Wassermann reaction was positive. In this investigation it was felt that changes in sensation perceptible to the examiner only by use of a faradic current and not by any of the ordinary tests or by functional ability, in the first place must be very slight, and in the second place, especially in the question of occupational neurosis, might be rather dubious.

The following form was used to record the histories obtained at the time of examination:

Name...................... Residence.................. Age..................
Years with air hammer.... Years with mallet.... Type hammer used....Stone....
Character of work (roughing, finishing, carving)........... Where...............
Finger complaint........... Location.......... When first noticed...........
(Underline condition observed at examination.)
Other complaints:
    Sleep....... Pain....... Numbness....... Cold......... Breath........
Exhaust control...................... Along tool...............................
Opinion as to best form of hammer and character of work.......................
Date examined........... Hour.................. Location..................
Temperature outside.............. Temperature where examined.................

---

[1] Southard, E. E. and Solomon, H. C.: Occupation Neurosis, p. 288 in Kober & Hanson's Diseases of Occupation and Vocational Hygiene. Philadelphia: 1916.

Beside the 19 men examined by Dr. Edsall, three other cases were examined in detail because they were commonly reported to be among the most severe sufferers from the use of the air hammer. Two were said to have stopped stonecutting on this account, and had left the Bedford district. In none of the three was there evidence of any organic change of consequence which could be attributed to the hammer. On the right forefinger of one man there was an area of diminished temperature sense; this was the finger used in controlling the exhaust. Callouses interfered with pain and touch sensitiveness over part of the hands, and when the parts were cold all sensibility was obtunded, but not more in any of the three cases than was the case with the hands of the examiner.

Of those who had changed their employment supposedly on account of objections to the air hammer, one stated that he quit because he had a disagreement with the foreman about another matter, a second had sought easier and steadier work, but found that two years of indoor occupation made him more nervous than cutting stone with the air hammer. A third had been badly frightened by hearing a severe prognosis made as to the possible effects of the hammer; he was habitually nervous and apprehensive in using the pneumatic tool, but stated voluntarily that he would like to go back if it were improved so as to relieve the strain.

When the stone mills were visited soon after work started in the morning the greater part of the cutters and carvers showed a blanching of the ulnar part of the hand which held the tool, with numbness and lowered temperature. They stated that this occurred commonly, but not uniformly in any one subject, in winter and on cold, damp, spring mornings. It also occurred frequently when the hands were subjected to cold in any way. It could be brought out in many of the men weeks or months after they had stopped work by plunging the hands for a few moments into snow or cold water. The hands of the examiner, used as a control, would under those circumstances show the normal hyperemic reaction, as did also the right hands of the stonecutters usually. On the left hand, typically, the little finger and hyperthenar eminence, the ring finger, and the tip of the middle finger became white and nearly bloodless. This might involve other fingers and the palm of the hand. If the person were left-handed, the right hand would show the phenomenon.

Designating the digits as 1, 2, 3, 4, 5, in order from the thumb to the little finger, the following table indicates the distribution of this vasomotor hypertonicity as to the fingers affected:

TABLE 1.—*Distribution of blanching, by fingers.*

Case.	Tool hand.	Hammer hand.	Case.	Tool hand.	Hammer hand.
1	5	....	22	3,4,5	....
2	5	....	23	3,4,5	....
3	5	....	24	3,4,5	2
4	5	....	25	3,4,5	2
5	4,5	....	26	3,4,5	3
6	4,5	....	27	¹2,3,4	....
7	4,5	....	28	3,4,5	2,3
8	4,5	....	29	2,3,4,5	....
9	4,5	2,3,4	30	2,3,4,5	....
10	3,4,5	....	31	2,3,4,5	....
11	3,4,5	....	32	2,3,4,5	....
12	3,4,5	....	33	2,3,4,5	....
13	3,4,5	....	34	2,3,4,5	....
14	3,4,5	....	35	2,3,4,5	....
15	3,4,5	....	36	2,3,4,5	....
16	3,4,5	....	37	2,3,4,5	2
17	3,4,5	....	38	2,3,4,5	2
18	3,4,5	....	39	1,2,3,4,5	....
19	3,4,5	....	40	1,2,3,4,5	....
20	3,4,5	....	41	1,2,3,4,5	....
21	3,4,5	....	42	1,2,3,4,5	1,3

¹ Little finger held under tool.

The greater number of the cutters showed the condition on the cold winter mornings during which the investigation was in progress: In one mill 5 out 6, in other mills 6 out of 7, 2 out of 4, 4 out of 7, 8 out of 11, and 5 out of 7. Usually, decided discomfort was experienced when the blood returned to the hand, but the work was not seriously interfered with. The apprentices, who did not use the air hammer, had colder left hands than right, but no clear history was obtained of the typical reaction in its marked form in men who used the mallet exclusively. A former boiler builder, now one of the sales force for a boiler factory, who never used a penumatic tool and had not heard of the above condition, described the same phenomenon as occurring in his left hand, following the use of hand tools in the boiler shop.

It is noteworthy that many of the older stonecutters state that they formerly had trouble of this sort, but do not have it at present. It is their belief that the younger workmen grip the tool too tightly. This spastic anemia, however, was sluggish in onset, taking months or more than a year for full development, and lasting equally long after the cause was removed; it occurred only in cold weather, and not continuously then. In spite of thorough search for the worst cases in and out of Bedford, no suggestion of any more severe changes than those described was obtained. There seemed no tendency for the anemia to go on to frostbite or necrosis. The use of gloves did not prevent the blanching.

Other nervous symptoms encountered bore more or less relation to the hand phenomenon. Sleep was disturbed in some cases by the hands and arms becoming numb very readily. Pains, particularly confined to the left side and extremities, were occasionally described, but did not appear to be more severe than would be encountered among groups of workmen of the same age and habits who did not use pneumatic tools. Those unaccustomed to the air hammer unquestionably suffered more severely from these functional nervous symptoms. A few minutes' early morning use of the hammer in cutting stone (longer than a momentary trial) gave the writer an unpleasant, cramped, slightly painful sensation in the 5th digit and ulnar side of the left hand, during the entire evening, with observable redness and swelling. The phenomenon was noticed before the use of the hammer was recalled. Recovery was complete over night. The factors concerned were evidently similar to the ordinary local fatigue and strain such as are commonly experienced from an unaccustomed employment. This is in agreement with the frequent statement of the stonecutters that their chief difficulty as regards nervousness and sleeplessness was when they began to use the tool, but that as they became used to cutting stone with the air hammer, these symptoms wore off. The development of the white fingers, however, is said to be more gradual, coming on in the winter after the pneumatic tool had been in use for some months.

It appears, then, that the continued use of the air hammer in cutting limestone leads to a disorder shown by a blanching of parts of the left hand, with cold and numbness; that this is not a serious disease, but in some cases decidedly disagreeable, and that measures should be instituted to prevent it. Of the three assigned causes, cold would appear to be merely the exciting cause. It would nevertheless be advisable to provide radiators or other means of heating the hands and tools of the stonecutters, giving a source of heat nearer to the working places than the present pipes and hot air conduits. Of the two other factors, the strain caused by the cramped position of the hand in grasping the narrow tool, and the vibration, the former would appear to be dominant but the vibration can not be eliminated as a cause since the phenomenon apparently does not occur in metal workers who use hammers with much lower vibratory rates, but who nevertheless guide the tool in somewhat the same way as do the stonecutters. The sensation imparted to the hand by the slower vibration is very different from that felt in the use of the air hammer in the stone works.

It has been suggested that changes along one or more of the four lines indicated below might be effective, but the problem is essentially a mechanical one, the object being to make the grasp of the left hand more comfortable and less straining, and also if possible to relieve some of the vibration received by that hand. Until an effective method is in use, it is advised that there be periods of rest from the use of the hammer and narrow tool, to enable the muscles of the left hand to relax and change their position.

1. A tool of larger diameter would permit a more hygienic grasp. It is possible that due to the softness of the stone and the necessary accurateness of the work, the impact of a light tool is preferable to that of a heavy one, but it would appear that if pressed against the stone, it is the construction of the hammer and the air pressure which determine the impact rather than the weight of the tool. A heavy tool, moreover, would reduce the vibratory effect felt by the left hand.

2. The shank of the tool might be provided with a tight fitting cover of asbestos or other similar material. This would need to be very rigid in order to permit proper guiding of the tool.

3. Instead of a tight handle, as above, a handle permitting reciprocal but no rotary motion could be used.

4. The end of the hammer might be prolonged over the tool so that the left hand in guiding grasps this instead of the tool. The tool should then have a square or triangular shank or be provided with grooves to prevent any rotary motion, and should also have a spring catch such as the rivet set in a pneumatic riveter.

5. Conclusions.

1. The pulmonary hazard is much less in stonecutting in the Bedford plants than in stonecutting in general. This is unquestionably the great hazard in the trade and its relative absence in this center makes the occupation of a stonecutter here more healthful than elsewhere. The workmen are not exposed to severe weather, the workrooms are large and well ventilated. In some of the mills the sanitary conveniences and guards against the spread of intestinal infection are satisfactory, but in others improvements should be made.

2. There exists in the hands of stonecutters who use pneumatic hammers a hypertonicity of the blood vessels which shows itself as an exaggerated reaction to low temperatures.

This is not serious as to life or function, but is uncomfortable at times, and should be remedied. It is believed that this can be done without eliminating the tool, and suggestions are made to that end.

SUPPOSED PHYSICAL EFFECTS OF THE PNEUMATIC HAMMER ON WORKERS IN INDIANA LIMESTONE.

By DAVID L. EDSALL, M. D., Consultant in Industrial Hygiene, United States Public Health Service.

The following report is based upon a visit to Bedford, Ind., made by the writer for the purpose of consulting with Dr. Leake in regard to the effect of the pneumatic hammer on the health of stonecutters. In very considerable part the statements concern points which Dr. Leake had elicited. The mills were inspected in company with Dr. Leake, and the men were observed while at work, talked to, and examined. A visit was also made to Bloomington, Ind., for the purpose of examining additional stonecutters.

We requested Mr. Griggs, president of the Journeymen Stone-cutters' Association of North America, the local officers of the stone-cutters' association, and many of the men in both Bedford and Bloomington to bring to us those who complained most, or we got their addresses and went to their homes. None of the men that we examined were sent to us through the employers, and none were examined in the presence of the employers or their representatives. In Bedford we reached them chiefly in their homes. This had the advantage of making them and their households feel quite free to talk in regard to their condition. In Bloomington, Mr. Walters, the secretary of the local branch of the stonecutters' association, brought the men to us. In both places the men seemed extremely frank and open in what they said. They are, as a class, superior men in personality, education, and manner of living. It rapidly became apparent that because the symptoms that I shall describe occur frequently, and fear had been aroused in various ways that they might grow worse, the anxiety of the men was due more to this fear of further and more serious results than to anything known to have occurred. In fact, several of those with the most pronounced manifestations said that if that was all, they thought it of comparatively slight consequence. Their fears of bad results had apparently been largely aroused within two years by their interpretation of the opinions of some physicians who had seen some affected men, but who, so far as we could learn, had not actually studied the cases or the men's work carefully, but had somewhat naturally based their advice upon the men's own apprehensions.

The symptoms seemed, from the statements of these men, as well as from statements of men who use the air hammer in other trades, to be confined almost exclusively, if not entirely, to stoneworkers, and among the stoneworkers they occur almost entirely in those who work with soft stone, such as the Indiana limestone. The reason for this becomes apparently clear when one observes accurately the manner in which these latter workmen use the air hammer, and especially the manner in which they use the stonecutting or stonecarving tools, and compares this with the details of the work of others who use the air hammer. At the same time, this offers a clear reason for the location of the symptoms and to a considerable extent at least for their character, and it furthermore suggests some very apparent expedients that may be expected to reduce the discomfort, and that if properly developed through experimentation would probably entirely or almost entirely do away with the effects which now, while apparently never serious, are easily demonstrated, uncomfortable, and justify a demand for a definite effort to overcome them.

The matter will be most evident if I first describe the symptoms and then the character of the work. As to the symptoms: We examined very carefully 19 men, and in going through the mills and upon other occasions we examined casually and talked with as many more. Dr. Leake, before and after my visit, saw many others. Nearly all of these men stated that they had then or had previously had, in very slight degree, up to a decided degree, the condition that we were there to study. This consists of temporary blanching and numbness of the fingers when the hands are chilled. It occurs almost entirely when the weather is cold or at least quite cool and when the workers are exposed to the cold—not when they are in well-heated buildings. One or two however believed that they sometimes felt it in summer, and several said that it annoyed them when "in swimming" in summer. It occurs chiefly when they start work in the morning before they get "warmed up" and lasts from a few minutes up to one and a half or two hours. A few men said it tended to recur during the day when at work. It also tends to occur when they walk or drive in cold weather, and when the hands are plunged into cold water or snow it can be brought out in a few moments. Indeed, any exposure to cold causes it to recur. In appearance and in sensation they say it is precisely like over-chilling the fingers in winter so that they "go dead," the first stage of frost bite of the fingers. As in the condition just mentioned, there may be some tingling or actual pain when it comes on and there is usually tingling when the blanching passes off, at which time it is succeeded by a flush and congestion for a little time, and at this time there may be a good deal of discomfort or actual pain which is such as most people have experienced with chilled fingers, and may extend up the arms. Occasionally this is described as severe, but usually they say "annoying" is a sufficiently descriptive term. The numbness usually does not interfere appreciably with the use of their hands. Occasionally they state that it makes them clumsy, slower and less accurate in their work while it lasts. Its distribution is striking and important in relation to its causation. In the great majority of the cases it is

29

noticed first in the ends of the ring and little fingers of the left hand; later it is felt predominantly--in many cases solely—in the fingers of the left hand. In most instances, when definitely developed, it is felt chiefly, and is often even later confined to, an area on the ulnar side, extending back to include the two distal phalanges of the little finger or the whole finger, and running diagonally across to the index finger, where it involves only the last phalanx or a little more. It gradually increases in some cases until it involves the whole of all the fingers of the left hand, occasionally going back along the ulnar side to the wrist or over the whole hand to the wrist. The right hand is less frequently affected than the left, and then usually less markedly. When it occurs at all in the right hand, it is noticed chiefly in the thumb and index and middle fingers. In a very few cases it appears to involve the whole of both hands. The only instance of that extent that I actually saw was, however, in a man with whom questioning brought out the fact that it had not appeared, as is usual, toward the tips of the fingers and slowly increased in area, but had come suddenly over the whole area when he had "frozen" his hands during a long drive in cold weather and had subsequently, upon exposure to cold, been always of that same extent, slowly diminishing in intensity. In this case, therefore, while work with the air hammer brought out the symptoms after they had once appeared, it did not seem to have excited them in the beginning.

The distribution of the symptoms seems to be explained by the manner in which these men hold the tool in the left hand and the hammer in the right, and in the right hand a factor of importance seems to be the practice of some of the men of controlling the exhaust from the hammer by pressing the thumb, index, or sometimes the middle finger over the exhaust hole, a practice which the more skillful men say is unnecessary and undesirable.

Sometimes after prolonged work the men have flexor contraction of the fingers of the left hand for a few moments as they cease work— evidently because of the prolonged constrained grip on the tool. This is significant chiefly in suggesting the origin of their trouble.

The men sometimes complain of lameness in the arms, shoulders, or chest. Two said they slept badly and twitched and turned in their sleep after working hard with the hammer. These two, however, were in poor general condition. Various other symptoms of vague character and significance were elicited in some of the men. I may, however, for brevity's sake state here that neither questioning the men nor careful physical examination showed evidence that the symptoms mentioned or any others outside those in the hands were of any particular significance. They were rather such symptoms as some members of any group of men will always show when doing work, of whatever kind, that is at times hard work and often carried out in constrained positions. In making this last statement I exclude any consideration of the effects of dust upon the lungs. I was not asked to study that and did not do so. I would say, however, that I was not impressed with any noteworthy need of studying the dust hazard, which in working with this particular stone seems surprisingly mild.

Some excitement had been caused by the fact that one stonecutter had died insane. This case the men themselves now dismiss, however, as having been due to general paresis. One man we saw had had an ordinary acute facial paralysis. Quite naturally, in the apprehension that had been aroused, such occurrences and various vague rumors and suggestions had led to fears of "paralysis," Raynaud's disease, and a variety of other grave results. We could find absolutely nothing to justify such fears, even in the stories we were told. It is entirely conceivable that a neurotic subject might grow decidedly neurasthenic from dwelling on the disagreeable sensation that these small pneumatic hammers produce. Some of the men said that the sensation was exceedingly disagreeable to them at first, but all except the nervously over-sensitive soon get so accustomed to it that they pay no attention to it. It is in this respect like many other accompaniments of industry, as for instance the noise in many forms of work.

The symptoms in the hands, then, seem to constitute all the recognizable effects of the stonecutting and carving with the air hammer and in describing the results of physical examination and in considering the cause and nature of the condition and the possible remedies, I should be understood as referring solely to these hand symptoms.

Physical examination: When the men were at work in the mills in the early part of the day, many of them showed in mild form and extent the blanching described above. The fingernails and the affected fingers were sometimes cyanosed instead of blanched. When seen in houses or in our rooms just after they had come in from the cold the same conditions existed. It was severe cold weather during my stay there. After a short period in the warmth the affected area became flushed and then after a further period looked, and the men said felt, normal. As I said, except for occasional other symptoms that seemed to have no distinctive relation to the work, nothing else was observed and the men almost all stated that this was the whole trouble. One man showed fibrillation of the muscles of the left hand, but it was so slight as to be scarcely observable and such as is occasionally seen without definite cause and since no one else showed it, it was probably of no significance. None showed tremor except one who admitted the rather generous use of alcohol, and in him it was of the usual alcoholic character. When cold and blanched the finger movements were somewhat clumsy. When warm the motor power was normal. There was no muscle atrophy observable. The hand grip was normal, as were the wrist and elbow reflexes, in all instances. Sensation was tested to touch, to pain and to heat and cold. When blanched, the sensation to pain and to heat and cold was of course often moderately blunted over the affected area but became normal in the warmth. In two instances there was apparently very slight persistent reduction of sensation in the last phalanges of the third and fourth fingers of the left hand. Three men showed much reduced pain sense in entirely irregular and changing areas over the hands and forearms, but one of these was mildly alcoholized at the time and the other two were of distinctly neurotic character, and since the sensory disturbance was quite as marked over the forehead, face and neck on both sides, it appeared to be unrelated to the vasomotor disturbance in the hands and of no significance in relation to the actual effects of the air hammer except that a study of the hands and arms alone might easily have led to the decision that there were organic nerve changes.

It is to be noted also that most of these men, owing to the grit from the stone and the use of the tool and hammer, develop a very remarkable degree of callous on the palmar surface, and naturally this is found particularly in the areas especially likely to be involved by the phenomenon under study. The thickening of the skin frequently extends up the sides of the fingers, so as to leave soft skin on only the back surface of the fingers, approximately three-fourths the finger surface being often somewhat calloused and also much of the palm and the outer ulnar surface. Naturally, over calloused skin the sensation, especially to pain, is somewhat lessened, but this was of course equally the case in those men who had symptoms and those who had none. It is important only in showing that one might easily think, mistakenly, that there were persistent changes in sensation even when the hands were warm and normal-looking.

In the 19 examined the stereognostic sense was normal. It was examined especially because Mr. Griggs stated that the men sometimes could not distinguish coins by their feeling. In the 19 men I examined carefully the heart and blood pressure were normal in all but one, who showed a moderately high pressure. He told me, however, that he had had syphilis. In all the 19 the blood vessels felt normal, and in all, pulsation of normal characters could be felt in both radial and ulnar arteries.

Aside from the callous there was no observable persistent change in the skin. It was interesting that there was, even in the men who had had symptoms for years, none of the redness and desquamation that one sees after mild frostbite, and they had no persistent itching or burning.

The condition seems, then, to be purely a local vasomotor irritability and there seems to be no evidence of any nervous or other organic changes, except possibly, in one or two cases, extremely slight and very localized sensory peripheral nerve changes. These were, however, doubtful; they seemed insignificant at most, and may occasionally be noticed in any workingmen who bring to bear as much and as prolonged local pressure as these men do. In view of the fact that the men who get symptoms usually do so within six months to two years of the time when they begin the use of the air hammer and that a large proportion of the men we examined, as well as very many others, have used the air hammer for many years, and nevertheless no worse results could be discovered, it is wholly reasonable to conclude that this comprises the sum of the results and no organic changes or more disturbing functional changes are likely to occur.[1]

We were unable to see or to learn of any cases in which the condition described actually interfered with the men's occupation as stoneworkers, though we were told of two or three cases in which they gave up this work, either because of the discomfort it caused in cold weather or because of apprehension that it might grow worse. There does seem some possibility of its being a distinct disadvantage if the man wishes to go into certain other forms of work that cause exposure to cold. One man told me he had originally been a car builder, and after using the air hammer in stonework he tried to go back to his old trade because he had had difficulties with the foreman in the stone mill, but had to give it up because he could not hold a cold chisel firmly with his numb fingers in cold weather.

We were told of several young stonecutters who had been drafted into the National Army and who were said to be having a very uncomfortable time in the cold weather, especially in carrying a rifle. Gloves do not suffice to prevent the effect of very cold weather.

However, skilled stonecutters usually stick to their trade and, as stated, I found none whose stonework was either prevented or seriously interfered with. One man of those seen had given up working on limestone and was using the hammer with comfort in working on granite, perhaps because both tool and hammer are used differently on granite. Five men stated that they had earlier had the trouble decidedly, but that it had gradually lessened until it had almost entirely disappeared. They attribute this to having learned to use the tool with greater skill and especially with an easier and less cramped

---

[1] It is of some interest to note that one, and I think also a second, man said that when seen a few days before by Dr. Leake he had tried to bring out the phenomenon by plunging his hands into snow, but was surprised to find it would not appear, though usually marked. He said that he remembered afterward that he "had had a couple of drinks of whisky just before." This is of interest and some importance in that it indicates both the mild character of the disturbance and its apparently purely vasomotor origin, since it was entirely overcome by the mild vasodilator action of the moderate amount of alcohol.

grip. Other experienced workmen told me the older and more skill-ful men have less bother than the younger and less skilled and attributed this to the same cause and to the fact that the young men use the mallet little in "roughing out," while the older have more familiarity with the mallet and use it a good deal. Mr. Griggs stated also that it is more common in the young men than in the older. He believed this due to the more common use recently of the larger hammer, but the older men state that they use the larger hammers as much as do the younger.

In considering the cause, the precise character of the work must be appreciated. It is easy to see, when one tries personally some of the various uses of the pneumatic hammer, why peculiar results may occur with soft-stone workers. In the first place they use hammers of very rapid action. We were unable to get a reliable and definite statement as to the number of blows delivered by these and other air hammers. Dr. Leake is endeavoring to determine the number accurately. It is said to be, with the smaller of these ham-mers, approximately 3,000 to 3,500 a minute, with the larger, 2,000 to 3,000. Whatever the exact figures, the blows are so frequent that they can not be appreciated individually by the ear, but make a continuous note, whereas the hammers used in riveting and most other metal work act much more slowly and the individual blows can be heard. The vibrations are therefore much finer and more frequent in the hammers used by the stonecutters. The difference one appreciates at once when holding the hammers at work.

Probably much more important in explaining the special occur-rence of these symptoms in the soft-stone workers is the manner in which they hold the hammer, and more especially the fact that they work with a tool held by the left hand in a peculiar manner. The riveter simply grasps his larger hammer with both hands in a manner convenient to reach the rivet with it. There is no loose tool to be held. The granite worker holds the hammer perpendicularly grasped in his right hand, and while he does use a tool in the left hand it does not need to be gripped firmly or guided forcibly except in doing lettering or other fine work. These workers in limestone, however, hold the hammer in the right hand as one uses a pen, whatever force is exerted upon it being exercised by the thumb, fore, and middle fingers; the tool, like the hammer, is held obliquely, but of course in the left hand, is gripped firmly, held closely against the stone, and guided, by a pressure exerted especially by the last two fingers and running along a line which is practically that which I described as de-limiting the extent, toward the hand, of the vasomotor phenomenon as usually seen in the left hand. The use of the left hand in calking and chipping seems superficially to be much the same, but when one tries it, it is at once apparent that in these operations the tool needs relatively little guiding or pressure, and for this reason and because the tool is larger (the shank of the stonecutting tool is only half an inch or often less), the grip of the left hand is very much less forceful and constrained than the soft-stone workers.

It will, I think, be apparent that the symptoms in the latter correspond in area closely to those areas of the fingers that are forcefully used and extend from there peripherally. It is to be remembered that these men use their hands continually for most of their working days in this manner, unless they get frequent change by using the mallet. But most of them nowadays use the mallet little. It is interesting that some of the men state that they had the same symptoms when working in earlier years with the mallet, but apparently this was unusual and the symptoms then ordinarily were, they said, slight.

There are three chief factors that evidently may play a part in producing the symptoms: Cold, constriction, and vibration. Cold is evidently the chief factor that temporarily excites the symptoms, as few of the men have any trouble except in the cold. But in the many other trades in which the hands are equally exposed to cold this phenomenon appears to be unusual. In fact, the stonecutters were, in earlier years, when they used the mallet, more exposed to cold than now. I am inclined to believe that cold elicits the symptoms rather than produces them, but it nevertheless gives the men discomfort. The factors more peculiar to this trade are the constriction of the grip exercised and the vibration. The vibration occurs almost equally, if not equally, in other work in which the air hammer is used, with relatively little or no such effect; also, if the vibration were the chief cause, the affection would be expected to occur more diffusely over the hands (since the whole hand feels the vibration), and in more irregular distribution, and particularly it would be expected to spread radially from the source of vibration, instead of being, as it is, observed peripherally only, in most cases, and usually first in the finger tips. It seems probable that the most important factor and hence the one to be especially obviated is the continuous constriction. Much the same phenomenon may be temporarily brought out easily in most persons in cold weather by a similarly strained continued grip. It can not, however, be either denied or affirmed with the evidence at hand that the vibration is a factor of importance.

It is obvious that certain simple things may be done to attempt to eliminate the trouble. First of all, the shank of the tool, where it is held, could be made larger, so that the grip need not be so strained. In doing this it would be well to use some substance that would conduct cold or heat poorly, instead of, as at present, intensifying the effect of cold by holding the cold metal. Asbestos suggests itself, and its practicability could be tried. Some of the men have tried rubber hose drawn over the tool, but said it tended to work upward on the tool and choke the action of the hammer. One man, however, said that he soaked the hose in oil, drew it on his tools, and allowed the softened rubber to adhere to the tool in drying and thereby was able to use it successfully. He said that he had earlier had "dead fingers" but is no longer troubled by them. Asbestos, if practical, would have evident advantages. Some such handle would perhaps serve also to some extent as a shock absorber and thus reduce the possible effects of the vibration. It is possible, too, that practicable methods of keeping the tools warm in cold weather could be easily devised and would reduce the discomfort. It is also to be noted that the practice of controlling the exhaust with the thumb or fingers of the right hand should be discontinued. In the same connection it is to be observed that in some hammers, due either to their construction or to wear, the exhaust leaks out downward along the tool—which it should not do—giving a slight constant blast of cold air on the left hand. This should be obviated. Heating the compressed air has, I believe, been tried, but meets with difficulties, and I do not believe it would be of much value if successfully done.

Reducing the time spent at any disadvantageous work and shifting to other forms of work is in many kinds of industrial disorders sufficient largely to overcome the trouble. In this instance there is an obvious way of accomplishing this—by requiring the men to use the mallet in suitable parts of the work, especially in "roughing out." The operators say they have always preferred that this should be done, especially because compressed air is expensive, but that the men will not do it. The men admit they use the hammer in such work when they do not need to, partly because they get more done, but they say that unless they do the foremen look unfavorably upon them and are likely to drop them because they do not work so fast. Evident adjustments and understandings are needed on both sides here. Both the men and the operators and their foremen should recognize that the frequent shift to the mallet may go far to obviate the trouble. While the tool is held in much the same way when employing the mallet, there is a slight, almost automatic, relaxation of the grip on both the tool and the mallet handle after each blow, and this alternating relaxation and contraction is just the desirable offset to the constant constriction exercised when using the air hammer.

Mr. Griggs stated that he believed the 1-inch hammer should be done away with in this work and only the ⅞-inch hammer used. The men differ very much on this point. Many think the smaller hammer gives them more discomfort. Certainly the immediate sensation one gets in using it is more disagreeable than with the larger hammer, owing to the more frequent and finer vibrations. I do not believe that with the evidence at hand it is possible to say whether limiting them to the smaller hammer would help directly, but it would perhaps lead the men to use the air hammer less in "roughing out," and if that were the case it would probably indirectly do good.

Besides these obvious measures, there is little doubt that having in mind the above-mentioned factors that are probably active in producing the trouble, an ingenious person of mechanical training and familar with the practical needs in the work could by some study and experiment devise changes in the tools or the hammer, or other changes, that would improve upon the above suggestions; and if the latter were not of the character needed, he could devise means that would be successful. While the disorder is not, under present conditions, such as to justify any fear of more serious results, it is uncomfortable and possibly of some economic disadvantage to the men, and it is due to them that such studies as the above be made by the manufacturers of the hammer, or more especially by the soft-stone operators, since of those who use the pneumatic hammer it is their interests that are particularly involved.

PHYSICAL FATIGUE AS A FACTOR IN INCREASING SUSCEPTIBILITY TO COMMUNICABLE DISEASE.

Fatigue in its relation to health has been the subject of many investigations. With the beginning of the present world war and the immediate need for soldiers, sailors, and munitions, the question became one of great importance. The effects of fatigue in the making of soldiers, sailors, and munitions should be very carefully watched with a view to maintaining the output of training camps and munition factories at its highest level during the war. No necessary sacrifice of men should be questioned at this time, but when methods employed for speeding up this output are liable to "invite disaster," such methods should be carefully revised.

In the investigations made into the prevalence of communicable diseases by the Division of Sanitation, Bureau of Medicine and Surgery, Navy Department, the conclusion was reached that fatigue was a factor in their spread, and that "the attempt to make a sailor too rapidly is to invite disaster."

In view of these findings and their apparent relation to the civil population, and especially the industrial army, the reports are published here in full:

Notes on Preventive Medicine for Medical Officers, United States Navy.

Bulletin No. 12, Division of Sanitation.

DEPARTMENT OF THE NAVY,
BUREAU OF MEDICINE AND SURGERY,
Washington, D. C., February 15, 1918.

Epidemiological study of cerebrospinal fever under conditions obtaining in the Navy indicates that the incidence of carriers and the incidence of the disease must be considered separately. Where carriers are found it does not necessarily follow that cases of cerebrospinal fever will occur.

The dissemination of meningococci resulting in multiplication of carriers is due to causes which have been pointed out many times—overcrowding, close contact, bad ventilation, the prevalence of catarrhal infections with coughing and sneezing, mess gear or similar articles contaminated with fresh moist discharges from the nose and throat, etc.

Without the meningococcus cerebrospinal fever could not occur. On the other hand, it is now well known that although many persons in a camp may harbor the meningococcus in the nasopharynx, relatively few of the men exposed contract the disease, although many of them become meningococcus carriers. All meningococci may not be and probably are not virulent. Individuals vary in susceptibility, and indeed susceptibility seems to vary from time to time in the same individual. Other infections, age, exposure, fatigue, mental depression, digestive disturbances, lack of food, and unsuitable clothing, individually or collectively, undoubtedly play an important rôle.

Recent epidemiological study at the naval training stations at Great Lakes, Hampton Roads, and Norfolk, Va., has resulted in the accumulation of some interesting data relative to the factors which are concerned in causing an outbreak of this disease.

In the first place the normal 21-day period of detention was broken. This period of detention is the most important single factor in preventing the introduction of communicable disease and its spread on the station. This detention is necessary not only to detect carriers of such organisms as the diphtheria bacillus and the meningococcus, and to detect such diseases as measles and scarlet fever in their incubative stages, but also in order that sufficient time may be devoted to the preparation of recruits for the rigorous course of training to come. The recruit upon entering a naval training station, particularly in the wintertime, must adapt himself to a complete change in habits and environment. He must become accustomed to naval discipline, learn to take care of himself, become accustomed to a radical change in apparel, and to a change in diet; learn to sleep in a hammock in barracks, make new acquaintances, and possibly overcome a certain amount of homesickness.

Experience at the larger stations shows that these changes must be brought about gradually, because all these things have a decided influence in tending to lower resistance to infectious diseases. While the recruit is in detention it is necessary that he be immunized against smallpox, typhoid, and paratyphoid infections. It would be folly not to recognize that so potent an influence for good did not also have a certain degree of resistance-lowering influence, a further and important reason for avoiding strenuous training activities during the detention period. All in all, these views may be summarized in the statement that "the attempt to make a sailor too rapidly is to invite disaster."

The carrier problem is of the greatest importance, and, as already stated, overcrowding either in barracks, at moving-picture entertainments, or in other places of assembly, such as the Y. M. C. A. building, is an important factor in the dissemination of pathogenic organisms through the method of the droplet infection.

The great technical difficulties in the laboratory procedures for the detection of meningococcus and pneumococcus carriers, as well as the recognized intermissions of the carrier state, render it practically impossible to prevent the introduction of carriers into the training camp proper. Much of the success in eliminating carriers from the training station will depend upon the percentage of carriers in the civil population and the season of the year. The multiplication of carriers in the training camp proper will be restricted by limiting the number of men quartered in any one compartment, providing a proper amount of floor area for each man, and by the elimination of unnecessary points of contact.

There has been a striking parallelism in the incidence of cerebro-spinal fever and lobar pneumonia at the naval training stations. It has also been noted that epidemics of bronchitis and coryza have preceded outbreaks of both of these diseases. Certain factors concerned in the development of either lobar pneumonia or cerebro-spinal fever must be considered in contradistinction to the factors involved in the spread of the organisms. Experience seems to show that one of the most important of these is the fatigue factor. It is a well-recognized axiom that the prevalence of communicable disease is at a minimum among thoroughly seasoned and disciplined forces. In connection with the recent outbreak of communicable diseases at Great Lakes it may be observed that incoming detention was broken, and then for several thousand recruits the excellent but intensive system of training in vogue at that station was begun too early and too precipitately.   About the same time two severe blizzards occurred and it was necessary to employ several thousand apprentice seamen to clear the roads and walks of snow, 3 to 6 feet deep.   There was thus involved an unusual amount of hard work combined with exposure, which brought about a degree of fatigue and lowering of resistance to infection in many instances.   Shortly thereafter there was a wide prevalence of bronchitis and coryza, followed by an outbreak of various communicable diseases of the respiratory type, including lobar pneumonia and cerebrospinal fever.   The same sequence of events without the extra amount of work necessitated by the heavy fall of snow was noted at the Norfolk Training Station, where by reason of unprecedented weather the exposure was even greater because of poorer housing facilities and lack of heat and ventilation.

At Great Lakes the regiments which suffered most from the incidence of disease were three which were recruited in December and transferred to the training camp proper after only a few days in detention.   The men of two of these regiments were subjected to the same kind of hard manual labor as that performed by older regiments.   By the time that the last of these new regiments was recruited it was already recognized that new recruits could not be subjected to the same amount of exposure and work as the more seasoned men, and this regiment suffered less than the other two new regiments.   During this period only a few cases of cerebrospinal fever occurred in the older regiments on the station.

In respect to the length of time which those who became ill with the disease had been on the station it may be said that no cases developed until the third week and that the outbreak reached its height between the sixth and seventh weeks, after which it rapidly declined.

The lack of an outgoing detention camp, equal in capacity to that used for incoming detention, contributed to the introduction of disease into other stations.   Without a full period of outgoing detention the transference of infection from one station to another is almost certain to occur.

In conclusion it will do no harm to repeat that from the standpoint of preventive medicine "the attempt to make a sailor too rapidly is to invite disaster."

Bulletin No. 13, Division of Sanitation.

DEPARTMENT OF THE NAVY,
BUREAU OF MEDICINE AND SURGERY,
Washington, D. C., February 22, 1918.

Physical fatigue, from the standpoint of preventive medicine, must be given careful consideration as one of the important etiological factors tending to lower blood and tissue resistance to infectious diseases, with special reference to cerebrospinal fever, lobar pneumonia, and other coccus infections.

Epidemiological investigations indicate that body fatigue plays an important rôle, potentially, in an outbreak of communicable disease in a closely housed military organization when the source of infection is present. In fact, in the training of recruits it may be the most prominent factor in determining the number of individuals who will become ill following exposure, if immediate steps are not taken, after early detection of disease and prompt isolation of patients, to interdict physical exertion and to place those not already ill under the best possible circumstances favorable to physical well-being. Mental depression or nerve fatigue, which is not to be differentiated altogether, either from the secretory state of the thyroid and other ductless glands or from muscle fatigue, deserves consideration as a subject unto itself, and is not to be touched upon here except in so far as nerve fatigue is associated with muscle fatigue.

In a previous number attention was directed to some of the untoward results which follow unwise attempts to hasten the early training of naval recruits. Competitive athletics have for years played a very prominent part in the national life, and it is perhaps natural for college experience and college methods of training to influence, more or less, those engaged in the training of recruits, especially now when it is necessary to expand the Navy quickly.

It must be borne in mind, however, that in the training for competitive athletics ordinarily everything in the system of training is subordinated to the object of winning the big final event of the year, and usually, too, the system is calculated to eliminate all but the most fit and to develop, with scant regard to the danger of causing some permanent physical damage, the few remaining to the desired point where a temporary and not to be maintained state of physical power is reached. Such methods obviously are not to be considered in fitting men for arduous manual occupations. They are not used even in training teams for professional baseball, a seasonal occupation which begins each year with easy work for previously trained athletes. Somewhere between the natural hardening of the laborer and the systematic training for the baseball season lies the happy medium which should guide in the training of recruits. It may be taken for granted that the training should begin gently, particularly as a large majority of the recruits are young and physically immature.

There are certain principles which may be laid down as the result of practical experience in training men physically, and in preparing them for athletic contests. Where men are trained in groups, physical strain should be regulated so that the weaker members will not suffer. The speed of the whole group should be governed to protect the weaker physiques. If it is considered necessary to train the older and stronger recruits expeditiously, the younger and less developed should be placed in a separate group and a more moderate application of training methods should be made, thus gradually bringing them up to the point of maximum efficiency. If the potentially strong are developed at the expense of the less fit, an unnecessarily large number of the latter must be lost to the service through medical survey for physical disability of one kind or another. Of course, it is recognized that military training is calculated quite properly, to eliminate men who are constitutionally unfit, mentally or physically, but for economic reasons undue prodigality with the excellent recruit material now available for training will serve no good purpose.

Some college trainers have developed winning teams by a system under which the weaker physiques are quickly eliminated, leaving only the most fit to be coached into final form. These trainers have had an abundance of material to work with, of course, and they have had no consideration for the harm done to those eliminated during the period of training. There have been other very successful trainers, who, forced, perhaps, by a comparative scarcity of material, have preferred to give careful consideration to men less perfect in physique; to conserve vitality always, and to develop gradually those of weaker physique. These men in the end generally obtain even better results than those who use the more forceful method. The conservation method was consistently carried out for years by a famous varsity crew coach. Quite frequently he would take under his observation a freshman who to the average trainer would have offered little promise of developing into varsity material. By a system of carefully graduated exercises and constant supervision he would bring such an individual to a state where after three years he would make the first crew in a boat which was accustomed to win the big event year after year. It is needless to say that many of his athletes would not only have failed to make the crew under forced training but some of them would doubtless have suffered irreparable physical damage.

In many instances the accumulation of fatigue substances incident to excessive metabolism taking place during the course of a single long race, where fatigue has occurred before reaching the goal, has made it necessary to put an athlete to bed for several days in order to enable him to recuperate sufficiently to enter another event a week or 10 days later. Had such students been brought into contact with sources of infection, it is not to be doubted that they would have contracted in severe form communicable diseases to which they were at other times comparatively immune. It is a common experience to observe a lessened immunity to staphylococcus infection among athletes undergoing hard training, especially as they approach the point of becoming overtrained or "stale."

Applied physical exercises in ordinary drills, continued day after day, even in comparatively small dosage, without proper periods of rest, will have the same effect as a short period of physical strain carried to the limit of endurance. Many men in training for athletic contests never reach the point of making the first team. They drop out finally because of damage done to their hearts and nervous systems. Too close an analogy should not be drawn between systems of training for athletic events and the daily drills and setting-up exercises incident to the training of naval recruits, but, after all, the effect on the individual is very similar and the same bad results occur if the training is forced. The cumulative effects of fatigue, caused by smaller doses of physical exercise improperly prolonged, and without suitable rest periods, produce in the end the same kind of physical damage. In fact, the development of the individual may be retarded or actually prevented.

It may be laid down as a general principle that for men under training no drill or physical exercise should cause such a degree of fatigue that reaction fails to follow quickly after a brief rest. To quote Medical Inspector J. A. Murphy, United States Navy:

> Strenuous effort should be approached slowly, as the exercises are not used to test the limit of power. Prolonged effort is to be avoided in order that a condition of stimulation will occur rather than exhaustion. Exercise should produce the simple symptoms of physical activity, such as a general sense of warmth and well-being, animation, sparkling eyes, cheerfulness, and mental exhilaration, instead of the opposite effect of overactivity, such as a vague sensation of discomfort about the heart, with constricting girdle sense, obscuration of vision, confused ideas, blunted sensation, and air hunger.

Drills should stop at the point where the men will look forward to subsequent drills with pleasure rather than to regard them as laborious tasks. Certainly after a short rest and a shower all men should emerge clear of eye and physically alert.

The old saying, "haste makes waste," can be substantiated by scientific investigation. Training methods which take into consideration different degrees of physical development and endurance will result not only in reduced admission rates for disease but will develop from the men who begin the course of training the maximum number capable of maintaining a high standard of physical fitness. In connection with speeding-up methods, investigations in munition factories have shown that the output in a working day of eight hours—two four-hour periods—was materially increased by taking 10 minutes for rest out of each four-hour period. It was also shown that the night shift which was required to work nine hours—divided into a four and a five hour period—gave results in the four-hour period which did not differ materially from those given in the first day period, but during the five-hour period very little output was secured in the last hour. By eliminating an hour from this period the total output for the night shift was actually increased.

PREVALENCE OF DISEASE.

No health department, State or local, can effectively prevent or control disease without knowledge of when, where, and under what conditions cases are occurring.

UNITED STATES.

EXTRA-CANTONMENT ZONES—CASES REPORTED WEEK ENDED MARCH 19.

CAMP BEAUREGARD ZONE, LA.

	Cases.
Measles:	
Alexandria	3
Boyce	1
Mumps:	
Alexandria	3
Pneumonia:	
Boyce	1
Pneumonia, lobar:	
Alexandria	1
Smallpox:	
Pineville	1

CAMP BOWIE ZONE, TEX.

Fort Worth:	
Chicken pox	1
Gonorrhea	3
Pneumonia, lobar	1
Smallpox	2
Syphilis	3
Typhoid fever	2

CAMP DEVENS ZONE, MASS.

Chicken pox:	
Shirley	1
German measles:	
Ayer	1
Lancaster	13
Lunenburg	3
Measles:	
Ayer	13
Shirley	1
Mumps:	
Lancaster	3
Pneumonia, lobar:	
Lancaster	1
Shirley	1

CAMP DODGE ZONE, IOWA.

Des Moines:	
Cerebrospinal meningitis	2
Chancroid	2
Diphtheria	1
Gonorrhea	1

CAMP DODGE ZONE, IOWA—continued.

	Cases.
Des Moines—Continued.	
Scarlet fever	2
Smallpox	25
Syphilis	5
Grimes:	
Measles	3

CAMP EBERTS ZONE, ARK.

Cerebrospinal meningitis:	
Kerr	1
Erysipelas:	
England (R. D. 2)	1
German measles:	
Lonoke	1
Lonoke (R. D. 1)	1
Cabot	1
Ward	4
Malaria:	
England	2
Cabot	2
Ward	1
Measles:	
Lonoke	1
Lonoke (R. D. 1)	3
Lonoke (R. D. 4)	11
England	4
England (R. D. 3)	1
Coy	3
Mumps:	
Lonoke (R. D. 1)	1
England	3
Austin	2
Coy	1
Ward	5
Pneumonia:	
Lonoke (R. D. 1)	5
Lonoke (R. D. 4)	1
England	2
England (R. D. 2)	2
Austin	1
Kerr	2

(410)

CAMP EBERTS ZONE, ARK.—continued.

Smallpox:	Cases.
Lonoke	1
Lonoke (R. D. 1)	3
England	1
Austin (R. D. 1)	1
Coy	2
Kerr	1
Pettus	1
Syphilis:
Lonoke	1
Tuberculosis:
England	1
Austin (R. D. 1)	2
Typhoid fever:
Cabot	1
Whooping cough:
Lonoke (R. D. 1)	2
England	2

CAMP FUNSTON ZONE, KANS.

Chicken pox: |
---|---
Junction City | 1
Measles: |
Junction City | 5
Cleburne | 2
Leonardville | 3
Manhattan | 21
Mumps: |
Junction City | 3
Manhattan | 12
Milford | 1
Pneumonia: |
Manhattan | 2
Scarlet fever: |
Junction City | 2
Manhattan | 6
Smallpox: |
Manhattan | 1
Stockdale | 2
Whooping cough: |
Junction City | 1

CAMP GORDON ZONE, GA.

Atlanta: |
---|---
Chicken pox | 8
Diphtheria | 1
German measles | 8
Gonorrhea | 2
Measles | 10
Mumps | 30
Pneumonia | 17
Scarlet fever | 2
Septic sore throat | 2
Smallpox | 1
Syphilis | 4
Tuberculosis | 11
Whooping cough | 2
Chamblee: |
Mumps | 1

CAMP GREENE ZONE, N. C.

Charlotte Township: |
---|---
Chancroid | 2
Chicken pox | 1
Diphtheria | 3
Gonorrhea | 5

CAMP GREENE ZONE, N. C.—continued.

Charlotte Township—Continued.	Cases.
Gonorrhea and chancroid	2
Gonorrhea and syphilis	3
Measles	3
Mumps	2
Ophthalmia neonatorum	1
Syphilis	4
Tuberculosis	5
Typhoid fever	3
Whooping cough	5

GULFPORT HEALTH DISTRICT, MISS.

Cerebrospinal meningitis: |
---|---
Gulfport | 1
Chicken pox: |
Lyman | 6
Diphtheria: |
Biloxi | 1
Malaria: |
Gulfport | 1
Measles: |
Gulfport | 3
Whooping cough: |
Lyman | 1

CAMP HANCOCK ZONE, GA.

Chicken pox: |
---|---
Augusta | 1
German measles: |
Augusta | 11
North Augusta | 2
Measles: |
Augusta | 20
Wrightsboro Road | 1
Pneumonia, lobar: |
Augusta | 1
Scarlet fever: |
North Augusta | 1
Syphilis: |
Augusta | 1
Tuberculosis, pulmonary: |
Augusta | 3

CAMP JACKSON ZONE, S. C.

Columbia: |
---|---
Cerebrospinal meningitis | 1
Diphtheria | 1
Measles | 7
Mumps | 9
Pneumonia | 1
Scarlet fever | 1
Tuberculosis | 1
Typhoid fever | 3
Whooping cough | 1

CAMP JOSEPH E. JOHNSTON ZONE, FLA.

Chicken pox: |
---|---
Jacksonville | 3
German measles: |
Murray Hill | 1
Gonorrhea: |
Jacksonville | 1
Measles: |
Jacksonville | 18
East Port | 1
Mumps: |
Jacksonville | 3

CAMP JOSEPH E. JOHNSTON ZONE, FLA.—contd.

	Cases.
Pneumonia:	
Jacksonville	3
Smallpox:	
Jacksonville	1
Trachoma:	
Jacksonville	5
Tuberculosis:	
Jacksonville	5
Typhoid fever:	
Jacksonville	5
Fishers Corner	1
Whooping cough:	
Jacksonville	1

FORT LEAVENWORTH ZONE, KANS.

Chicken pox:	
Leavenworth	3
Diphtheria:	
Leavenworth	1
Erysipelas:	
Leavenworth County	1
Gonorrhea:	
Leavenworth	6
Measles:	
Leavenworth	7
Pneumonia:	
Leavenworth	1
Leavenworth County	1
Scarlet fever:	
Leavenworth County	1
Smallpox:	
Leavenworth	3
Leavenworth County	2
Typhoid fever:	
Leavenworth County	1

CAMP LEE ZONE, VA.

Chicken pox:	
Ettricks	1
Prince George County	2
German measles:	
Ettricks	14
Chesterfield County	1
Prince George County	3
Measles:	
Ettricks	3
Hopewell	21
Petersburg	3
Meningitis, tubercular:	
Prince George County	1
Mumps:	
Ettricks	6
Hopewell	11
Prince George County	4
Septic sore throat:	
Dinwiddie County	1
Ettricks	3
Petersburg	11
Tuberculosis:	
Petersburg	1
Typhoid fever:	
Petersburg	2
Whooping cough:	
Ettricks	1

CAMP LEWIS ZONE, WASH.

	Cases.
Chicken pox:	
Spanaway	2
German measles:	
Loveland	2
Parkland	4
Spanaway	9
Measles:	
Dupont	2
Whooping cough:	
Steilacoom Lake	6
Gravelly Lake	1

CAMP LOGAN ZONE, TEX.

Houston:	
Chicken pox	3
Gonorrhea	51
Measles	31
Mumps	8
Pneumonia	2
Smallpox	2
Syphilis	40

CAMP MACARTHUR ZONE, TEX.

Waco:	
Chicken pox	4
German measles	1
Gonorrhea	1
Measles	10
Mumps	62
Pneumonia, lobar	4
Smallpox	2
Whooping cough	1

CAMP M'CLELLAN ZONE, ALA.

Cerebrospinal meningitis:	
Anniston	*
Chicken pox:	
Anniston	5
Diphtheria:	
Anniston	2
German measles:	
Precinct Two	4
Measles:	
Anniston	3
Precinct Two	14
Meningitis, tubercular:	
Anniston	*
Mumps:	
Anniston	4
Precinct Two	3
Pneumonia:	
Precinct Two	*
Scarlet fever:	
Anniston	*
Smallpox:	
Anniston	14
Blue Mountain	1
Precinct Two	2
Precinct Twenty	1
Typhoid fever:	
Anniston	*
Whooping cough:	
Anniston	*

NORFOLK COUNTY NAVAL DISTRICT, VA

Cerebrospinal meningitis:	Cases.
Brighton	1
Ocean View	1
Portsmouth	3
South Norfolk	1
Diphtheria:	
Portsmouth	1
Influenza:	
Churchland	1
Malaria:	
Prentis Park	1
Measles:	
Portsmouth	7
Rodmans Heights	1
South Norfolk	1
Meningitis, tubercular:	
Titustown	1
Mumps:	
Portsmouth	7
Pellagra:	
Titustown	1
Pneumonia:	
Portsmouth	1
South Norfolk	1
Scarlet fever:	
Portsmouth	1
Smallpox:	
Pinners Point	1
Syphilis:	
Portsmouth	1
Tuberculosis:	
Hickory	1
Portsmouth	4

FORT OGLETHORPE ZONE, GA.

Chicken pox:	
Chattanooga	1
German measles:	
Chattanooga	1
Gonorrhea:	
Chattanooga	9
East Chattanooga	1
Measles:	
Chattanooga	3
East Chattanooga	1
Rossville	8
Mumps:	
Chattanooga	46
East Chattanooga	4
East Lake	1
Fort Cheatham	2
Rossville	2
Pneumonia:	
East Chattanooga	1
Smallpox:	
Chattanooga	1
Syphilis:	
Chattanooga	3
Tuberculosis:	
St. Elmo	1
Whooping cough:	
Chattanooga	10
East Lake	1
Rossville	1

CAMP PIKE ZONE, ARK.

Cerebrospinal meningitis:	Cases.
Little Rock	1
North Little Rock	2
Chancroid:	
Little Rock	0
Chicken pox:	
Little Rock	5
North Little Rock	2
Diphtheria:	
Little Rock	2
German measles:	
Little Rock	0
Gonorrhea:	
Little Rock	12
North Little Rock	1
Scotts	3
Malaria:	
Little Rock	3
North Little Rock	3
Measles:	
Little Rock	0
Mumps:	
Little Rock	20
North Little Rock	8
Pellagra:	
Kerr	1
England	2
Pneumonia:	
Little Rock	4
Scarlet fever:	
Little Rock	4
North Little Rock	2
Smallpox:	
Little Rock	17
North Little Rock	1
Scotts	1
Levy	4
Syphilis:	
Little Rock	3
North Little Rock	2
Scotts	4
Trachoma:	
Little Rock	1
Tuberculosis:	
Little Rock	5
North Little Rock	2
Kerr	1
Typhoid fever:	
Little Rock	2

CAMP SEVIER ZONE, S. C.

Measles:	
Chick Springs Township	8
Greenville Township	1
Mumps:	
Greenville Township	4

CAMP SHELBY ZONE, MISS.

Chicken pox:	
Hattiesburg	8
Gonorrhea:	
Hattiesburg	11
Malaria:	
Hattiesburg	4
Measles:	
Hattiesburg	8

CAMP SHELBY ZONE, MISS.—continued.

	Cases.
Mumps:	
Hattiesburg	10
Smallpox:	
Hattiesburg	3
Lucedale	1
Pinola	1
Purvis	1
Syphilis:	
Hattiesburg	7
Tuberculosis:	
Hattiesburg	2

CAMP SHERIDAN ZONE, ALA.

Chicken pox:	
Montgomery	2
Diphtheria:	
Montgomery	1
Measles:	
Montgomery	9
Chisholm	1
Rural district	1
Mumps:	
Montgomery	5
Septic sore throat:	
Montgomery	1
Smallpox:	
Montgomery	5
Rural district	2

CAMP SHERMAN ZONE, OHIO.

Chicken pox:	
Scioto Township	2
Diphtheria:	
Chillicothe	4
Measles:	
Chilicothe	3
Liberty Township	3
Pneumonia:	
Liberty Township	1
Scarlet fever:	
Chillicothe	5

CAMP ZACHARY TAYLOR ZONE, KY.

Cerebrospinal meningitis:	
Louisville	1
Chicken pox:	
Louisville	3
Diphtheria:	
Jefferson County	3
Louisville	2
German measles:	
Jefferson County	1
Measles:	
Jefferson County	1
Louisville	24
Mumps:	
Louisville	4
Scarlet fever:	
Louisville	1
Smallpox:	
Louisville	3
Trachoma:	
Jefferson County	1
Louisville	1

CAMP ZACHARY TAYLOR ZONE, KY.—continued.

	Cases.
Tuberculosis, pulmonary:	
Louisville	19
Whooping cough:	
Louisville	2

TIDEWATER HEALTH DISTRICT, VA.

Cerebrospinal meningitis:	
Newport News	4
Diphtheria:	
Newport News	1
German measles:	
Newport News	4
Phoebus	4
Measles:	
Newport News	18
Hampton	1
Phoebus	12
Mumps:	
Newport News	3
Pneumonia:	
Newport News	3
Hampton	1
Phoebus	1
Scarlet fever:	
Newport News	1
Tuberculosis:	
Newport News	4
Phoebus	1

CAMP TRAVIS ZONE, TEX.

San Antonio:	
Chicken pox	1
Gonorrhea	1
Malaria	1
Mumps	1
Pneumonia	2
Syphilis	2
Tuberculosis	5

CAMP WADSWORTH ZONE, S. C.

Diphtheria:	
Spartanburg	1
German measles:	
Spartanburg	3
Pauline	1
Measles:	
Spartanburg	13
Pauline	3
Mumps:	
Spartanburg	6
Pauline	1
Pneumonia:	
Pauline	1
Smallpox:	
Spartanburg	2
Tuberculosis:	
Spartanburg	3
Typhoid fever:	
Pauline	1
Whooping cough:	
Spartanburg	16
Moores	2
Pauline	1

CAMP WHEELER ZONE, GA.	Cases.	CAMP WHEELER ZONE, GA.—continued.	Cases.
Chicken pox:		Pneumonia:	
Macon	1	Macon	2
Gonorrhea:		Scarlet fever:	
Macon	1	Macon	.
East Macon	1	Smallpox:	
Itch:		Macon	1
Macon	1	East Macon	2
Measles:		Tuberculosis:	
Macon	1	Macon	.
Mumps:		Typhoid fever:	
Macon	27	Macon	1
East Macon	2	East Macon	1

DISEASE CONDITIONS AMONG TROOPS IN THE UNITED STATES.

The following data are taken from telegraphic reports received in the office of the Surgeon General, United States Army, for the week ended March 8, 1918:

Annual admission rate per 1,000 (disease only):
- All troops... 1,412.8
- National Guard camps... 1,103.6
- National Army camps... 1,731.2
- Regular Army... 1,221.8

Noneffective rate per 1,000 on day of report:
- All troops... 47.5
- National Guard camps... 42.1

Noneffective rate per 1,000 on day of report—Con.
- National Army camps... 54.2
- Regular Army... 42

Annual death rate per 1,000 (disease only):
- All troops... 6.6
- National Guard camps... 6.2
- National Army camps... 6
- Regular Army... 7.5

New cases of special diseases reported during the week ended Mar. 8, 1918.

Camps.	Pneumonia.	Dysentery.	Malaria.	Venereal.	Measles.	Meningitis.	Scarlet fever.	Deaths.	Annual admission rate per 1,000 (disease only).	Noneffective per 1,000 on day of report.
Wadsworth	10			17	4			1	537.1	23.7
Hancock	4		1	15	9		2	3	437.7	25.1
McClellan				23	10		2	3	728	30.3
Sevier	14		1	23	1	3	2	2	1,736.1	70.5
Wheeler	13	1	3	35		1		4	1,280.2	42.2
Logan	4		2	146	22	2	1	3	1,586	44
Cody	11			2	1			6	578.5	35.2
Doniphan	5			18			3	5	1,702.3	46.9
Bowie	15		1	52		2		6	1,717.4	58
Sheridan	2			7	1		2		544.7	34.2
Shelby	4	1		24	1	1		5	1,286.1	32.9
Beauregard	3		2	18	1	3		3	1,299.4	54.5
Kearney	2			2	2		7	1	1,160.6	46.7
Devens	12			63	10			4	1,377.1	39.4
Upton	21			40	1		3	6	1,140.8	28.7
Dix	5			82	5	1	10	1	2,365.4	51.4
Meade	8			23	19	1	13	3	860.7	33.8
Lee	15		1	116	9	1		4	1,523.5	56.7
Jackson	6			302	6			3	2,005	59.3
Gordon	6			178	8	2		2	1,626.2	37.6
Sherman	12			47	90	1	29	4	1,745	61.5
Taylor	13			41	23			4	1,725.7	68.2
Custer				14	6	2	4	3	990.9	45.7
Grant	11			28	20		5	2	1,029.3	30.1
Pike	24		1	127	19		9	4	3,084.1	84.1
Dodge	19			121	52		7	4	1,744.1	48.1
Funston	10	1		45		3	4	5	2,017.2	82.8
Travis	29	1	3	52	23	1	2	2	2,975.7	68.9
Lewis	9			17	44		35	6	1,502.2	78.6
Northeastern Department				14	7			1	1,177.6	30.3
Eastern Department	11			29	18	1	1	3	843.6	26.0
Southeastern Department	9		4	25	17	2	1	6	1,015.2	48.7
Southern Department	16			71	55	2	14	10	1,066.6	39.9
Central Department	6			22	21		7	4	1,487.9	43.2
Western Department	9			30	39		5	9	1,136.2	32.4

*New cases of special diseases reported during the week ended Mar. 8, 1918—*Continued

Camps.	Pneumonia.	Dysentery.	Malaria.	Venereal.	Measles.	Meningitis.	Scarlet fever.	Deaths.	Annual admission rate per 1,000 (disease only).	Noneffective per 1,000 on day of report.
Aviation, S. C.	21			91	133	3	12	17	1,381.2	45.4
Camp Greene	8		1	36	15	4	6	2	464.7	33.5
Camp Fremont	6		1	39	15				1,099.1	43.3
El Paso				5	12		1		1,012.3	6.5
Fort Slocum	2			11	8				1,810	39.1
Columbus Barracks	1			16	1		3		1,876.5	51.3
Fort Thomas				1					1,108.8	53
Jefferson Barracks	1			10	5		13	5	2,272.3	117.2
Fort Logan	1			1	22		5	1	2,496.6	70.8
Fort McDowell				5	5		1		1,132.1	53.7
Disciplinary Barracks, Fort Leavenworth									1,692.4	35.2
Disciplinary Barracks, Alcatraz									852.5	13.1
Aberdeen, P. G.					1		1	1	1,368.4	29.2
A. A. Humphreys				9					1,275.5	12.2
J. E. Johnston				27	4	1	1	1	940.1	33.5
Edgewood						1			1,642.1	140.3
Camp Merritt	16			65	16	1	26	5	1,944.8	74.2
Camp Stuart	9			11	6		1	4	1,694.7	54.2
West Point, N. Y.	1			1	7				1,053.8	17.4
General Hospital No. 1								1		
National Guard departments	4			12	33		1	2		
National Army departments	25	4	1	181	50		14	3		
Total	435	8	22	2,390	877	39	256	171	1,412.8	47.5

¹ All troops.

Annual rate per 1,000 for special diseases.

Diseases.	All troops in United States.¹	Regulars in United States.¹	National Guard, all camps.¹	National Army, all camps¹	Expeditionary forces.²
Pneumonia	18.2	15.1	13.5	22.8	26
Dysentery	.3		.3	.2	.2
Malaria	.9	.7	1.3	.5	
Venereal	100.2	67.2	59.1	146.3	44.2
Typhoid					.4
Measles	36.7	52.7	8	37.8	13.7
Meningitis	1.6	1.9	1.8	1.3	3
Scarlet fever	10.7	13.1	2.9	13.6	13.6

¹ Week ended Mar. 8, 1918.   ² Week ended Feb. 28, 1918.

CURRENT STATE SUMMARIES.

Alabama.

From Collaborating Epidemiologist Perry, by telegraph, for week ended March 16, 1918:

Smallpox: By counties, Autauga 1, Butler 13, Cullman 15, Jefferson 104, Marengo 4, Sumter 1, Tuscaloosa 2, Winston 1. Meningitis: By counties, Jefferson 6, Talladega 1, Tuscaloosa 1.

California.

From the State Board of Health of California, by telegraph, for week ended March 16, 1918:

Sixteen hundred cases measles in California, making total of 12,500 since January 1. Twenty cases smallpox, more prevalent than at any time since 1914. Five cases cerebrospinal meningitis. Other reportable diseases stationary.

Connecticut.

From Collaborating Epidemiologist Black, by telegraph, for week ended March 16, 1918:

Trachoma: New Britain 1. Meningitis: Fairfield 1, Greenwich 1. Smallpox: East Windsor 1.

Illinois.

From the State Department of Health of Illinois, by telegraph, for week ended March 16, 1918:

Smallpox, very mild type: Prevalent southern portion of State, Herrin, Odin, Virden, Chester, Harrisburg, Peoria, Chicago. Diphtheria: Much less than usual prevalence. Scarlet fever: Much less than usual, but showing tendency to increase some points. Measles increasing. Meningitis: Total 9 cases; Chicago 3, Springfield 2, one each Lake Forest, Virden, Gillespie, near Quincy. Poliomyelitis: Total 6 cases; Chicago 3, Taylorville 1, Christian County 1, Henry County 1.

Indiana.

From the State Board of Health of Indiana, by telegraph, for week ended March 16, 1918:

Scarlet fever: Epidemic Morocco, 1 death each Jamestown and South Bend. Measles: Epidemic Shiloh, Americus, Rensselaer, Princeton, Remington, Kokomo. Smallpox: Epidemic Ingalls. Diphtheria: One death each Wabash and Acton. Infantile paralysis: One case Gosport, 1 death Bringhurst. Epidemic meningitis: 1 case Madison, 2 cases Indianapolis. Rabies: Epidemic dogs, Troy; 1 case each Terre Haute, Cannelton, Corydon, Hazleton, Montezuma, Mount Vernon. Botulinis poisoning: Four deaths Decatur. Typhoid: Three cases Whiting and Nuntington.

Kansas.

From Collaborating Epidemiologist Crumbine, by telegraph, for week ended March 16, 1918:

Poliomyelitis: Elwood 1, Hutchinson 1. Meningitis: Chereokee 1, Corona 1, Eldorado 1, Hoisington 1, Horton 1, Kansas City 6, Osawatomic 1, Otego 1, Parsons 3, Towanda 1, Topeka 1. Smallpox, more than 10 cases: In counties, Allen 21, Butler 14, Cowley 11, Crawford 12, Miami 20, Sedgwick—not including Wichita—17; in cities, Kansas City 80, Wichita 19.

Louisiana.

From Collaborating Epidemiologist Dowling, by telegraph, for week ended March 16, 1918:

Meningitis, excluding Rapides Parish: By parishes, Caddo 1, Calcasieu 1, East Carroll 1, Morehouse 1, Orleans 1, Ouachita 1.

Massachusetts.

From Collaborating Epidemiologist Kelley, by telegraph, for week ended March 16, 1918:

Unusual prevalence. German measles: Danvers 20, Framingham 29, Newton 55. Measles: Ashland 36, Ayer 17, Beverly 50, Hudson 15, Quincy 88. Smallpox: Marlboro 1.

Minnesota.

From Collaborating Epidemiologist Bracken, by telegraph, for week ended March 16, 1918:

Smallpox, new foci: Anoka County, Columbia Heights village 2, Cass County, Backus village 1, Chisago County, Rush City village 2, Houston County, Wilmington Township 8. One cerebrospinal meningitis, 1 poliomyelitis, reported since March 11.

Nebraska.

From the State Board of Health of Nebraska, by telegraph, for week ended March 16, 1918:

Smallpox: Roseland, Kearney, Plattsmouth, Cherry County, Brock, Steinauer. Scarlet fever: Bigspring.

Ohio.

From Collaborating Epidemiologist Freeman, by telegraph, for week ended March 16, 1918:

Typhoid fever: Niles, 10 cases. Poliomyelitis: Norwood, 1 case. Meningitis: Entire State 4 cases.

South Carolina.

From Collaborating Epidemiologist Hayne, by telegraph, for week ended March 16, 1918:

Eighteen cases meningitis; 4 additional suspected cases.

Vermont.

From Collaborating Epidemiologist Dalton, by telegraph, for week ended March 16, 1918:

Smallpox: Rochester 1, Barton 2, Fairfax 1. No other outbreak or unusual prevalence.

Virginia.

From Collaborating Epidemiologist Traynham, by telegraph, for week ended March 16, 1918:

Five cases smallpox Prince William County, 1 Craig, 6 Alleghany. One case cerebrospinal meningitis Newport News, 1 Caroline County. One case poliomyelitis Norfolk County, 1 Lynchburg City.

Washington.

From Collaborating Epidemiologist Tuttle, by telegraph, for week ended March 16, 1918:

German measles still prevalent throughout State. Scarlet fever epidemic Tacoma remains unabated; 55 cases reported.

CEREBROSPINAL MENINGITIS.

Kentucky—Glasgow and Tracy.

During the period from March 3 to 15, 1918, 4 cases of cerebrospinal meningitis, with 3 deaths, were notified at Glasgow, Ky., and 1 case was notified at Tracy, 20 miles from Glasgow.

CEREBROSPINAL MENINGITIS—Continued.

City Reports for Week Ended Mar. 2, 1918.

Place.	Cases.	Deaths.	Place.	Cases.	Deaths.
Anniston, Ala	1	....	Milwaukee, Wis	1	....
Atlanta, Ga	3	1	Montgomery, Ala	2	....
Augusta, Ga	6	1	New Albany, Ind	1	1
Baltimore, Md	7	....	Newark, N. J	4	....
Birmingham, Ala	1	....	New Haven, Conn	1	1
Boston, Mass	8	3	New Orleans, La	2	1
Bridgeport, Conn	1	1	Newport, Ky	1	1
Buffalo, N. Y	1	....	New York, N. Y	5	9
Cambridge, Mass	1	....	Niagara Falls, N. Y	1	1
Charleston, S. C	2	2	Norfolk, Va	1	....
Charleston, W. Va	1	....	Passaic, N. J	1	1
Charlotte, N. C	2	....	Petersburg, Va	1	....
Chattanooga, Tenn	1	1	Philadelphia, Pa	6	3
Chicago, Ill	6	1	Pittsburgh, Pa	4	....
Cincinnati, Ohio	1	1	Pittsfield, Mass	2	1
Cleveland, Ohio	2	....	Pontiac, Mich	1	....
Colorado Springs, Colo	1	....	Portsmouth, Va	1	....
Columbia, S. C	1	....	Providence, R. I	2	1
Davenport, Iowa	1	....	Richmond, Va	1	....
Dayton, Ohio	....	3	Roanoke, Va	....	1
Detroit, Mich	4	....	Rock Island, Ill	1	....
Durham, N. C	1	1	St. Louis, Mo	1	....
Evansville, Ind	....	1	San Francisco, Cal	1	....
Greenville, S. C	1	....	Savannah, Ga	3	....
Hartford, Conn	1	....	Spartanburg, S. C	....	1
Houston, Tex	3	2	Springfield, Ohio	1	....
Indianapolis, Ind	1	1	Troy, N. Y	1	....
Kansas City, Kans	2	1	Waco, Tex	1	....
Little Rock, Ark	5	2	Washington, D. C	6	2
Louisville, Ky	1	1	Wichita, Kans	1	....
Lowell, Mass	2	....	Wilkes-Barre, Pa	....	1
Macon, Ga	2	1	Worcester, Mass	1	....
Memphis, Tenn	3	2	York, Pa	1	1

DIPHTHERIA.

See Diphtheria, measles, scarlet fever, and tuberculosis, page 423.

ERYSIPELAS.

City Reports for Week Ended Mar. 2, 1918.

Place.	Cases.	Deaths.	Place.	Cases.	Deaths.
Allentown, Pa	2	....	Memphis, Tenn	....	2
Boston, Mass	....	2	Milwaukee, Wis	2	....
Bridgeport, Conn	1	....	Montclair, N. J	1	....
Brockton, Mass	2	....	Newark, N. J	7	....
Buffalo, N. Y	3	....	New York, N. Y	....	7
Chicago, Ill	17	3	Norristown, Pa	1	....
Cleveland, Ohio	14	....	Omaha, Nebr	1	2
Cumberland, Md	1	....	Philadelphia, Pa	7	1
Dayton, Ohio	1	....	Pittsburgh, Pa	6	....
Denver, Colo	4	....	Pontiac, Mich	2	....
Detroit, Mich	2	1	Portland, Me	1	....
Duluth, Minn	1	....	Providence, R. I	....	1
Erie, Pa	1	....	Reading, Pa	1	....
Evansville, Ind	....	1	Rochester, N. Y	1	....
Harrisburg, Pa	1	....	Sacramento, Cal	1	....
Jackson, Mich	1	....	St. Louis, Mo	6	3
Johnstown, Pa	1	....	San Francisco, Cal	1	....
Lancaster, Pa	1	....	Springfield, Ill	1	....
Lawrence, Mass	....	1	Toledo, Ohio	....	1
Lincoln, Nebr	1	....	Troy, N. Y	1	....
Little Rock, Ark	2	....	Wheeling, W. Va	1	....
Long Beach, Cal	1	....	Wichita, Kans	3	....
Los Angeles, Cal	4	1	Winston-Salem, N. C	2	....
Louisville, Ky	4	1			

LEPROSY.

Massachusetts—Cambridge—Correction.

The report of a case of leprosy at Cambridge, Mass., during the week ended December 22, 1917, published in the Public Health Reports of January 11, 1918, page 42, was an error, information to that effect having been received from the city health officer of Cambridge.

City Reports for Week Ended Mar. 2, 1918.

During the week ended March 2, 1918, one case of leprosy was reported at Galveston, Tex., and one case at Oakland, Cal.

MALARIA.

City Reports for Week Ended Mar. 2, 1918.

Place.	Cases.	Deaths.	Place.	Cases.	Deaths.
Birmingham, Ala	1	....	Macon, Ga	1	....
Charlotte, N. C	2	....	Savannah, Ga	....	1
Hattiesburg, Miss	5	....	Stockton, Cal	1	....
Little Rock, Ark	1	....	Wilmington, N. C	2	....

MEASLES.

See Diphtheria, measles, scarlet fever, and tuberculosis, page 423.

PELLAGRA.

City Reports for Week Ended Mar. 2, 1918.

Place.	Cases.	Deaths.	Place.	Cases.	Deaths.
Charleston, S. C	....	2	Petersburg, Va	....	1
Houston, Tex	....	1	Providence, R. I	....	1
Lexington, Ky	....	1	Richmond, Va	....	2
Memphis, Tenn	1	....	Savannah, Ga	....	1
Mobile, Ala	....	1	Wilmington, N. C	....	1
New Orleans, La	3	2	Winston-Salem, N. C	1	....

PNEUMONIA.

City Reports for Week Ended Mar. 2, 1918.

Place.	Cases.	Deaths.	Place.	Cases.	Deaths.
Alameda, Cal	1	1	Haverhill, Mass	4	1
Allentown, Pa	6	....	Holyoke, Mass	1	1
Anniston, Ala	8	....	Houston, Tex	4	9
Auburn, N. Y	2	1	Jackson, Mich	2	2
Baltimore, Md	74	36	Jamestown, N. Y	1	2
Berkeley, Cal	2	2	Kalamazoo, Mich	3	3
Boston, Mass	64	46	Kansas City, Kans	3	....
Braddock, Pa	1	....	Lancaster, Pa	1	....
Bridgeport, Conn	1	11	Lawrence, Mass	4	2
Brockton, Mass	9	1	Leavenworth, Kans	1	....
Cambridge, Mass	4	1	Lincoln, Nebr	4	1
Chattanooga, Tenn	2	1	Little Rock, Ark	17	....
Chelsea, Mass	1	2	Long Beach, Cal	1	1
Chicago, Ill	300	104	Los Angeles, Cal	19	7
Cleveland, Ohio	19	23	Lowell, Mass	3	6
Cranston, R. I	1	....	Lynn, Mass	5	....
Cumberland, Md	1	1	Malden, Mass	1	....
Dayton, Ohio	1	6	Manchester, N. H	2	2
Detroit, Mich	13	29	McKeesport, Pa	3	....
Fall River, Mass	6	1	Melrose, Mass	3	....
Flint, Mich	9	....	Newark, N. J	59	13
Galesburg, Ill	2	....	New Bedford, Mass	3	2
Grand Rapids, Mich	4	2	New Britain, Conn	4	12
Harrisburg, Pa	2	8	Newburyport, Mass	2	....
Hattiesburg, Miss	2	....	Newport, Ky	1	1

PNEUMONIA—Continued.

City Reports for Week Ended Mar. 2, 1918—Continued.

Place.	Cases.	Deaths.	Place.	Cases.	Deaths.
Newton, Mass	1	3	Salem, Mass	7	4
Norristown, Pa	1	....	San Diego, Cal	9	....
Norwalk, Conn	1	....	San Francisco, Cal	13	17
Oakland, Cal	1	7	Schenectady, N. Y	4	2
Oak Park, Ill	1	1	Somerville, Mass	9	2
Orange, N. J	1	2	Spartanburg, S. C	4	....
Pasadena, Cal	3	3	Springfield, Mass	15	6
Philadelphia, Pa	150	82	Steubenville, Ohio	1	....
Pittsburgh, Pa	31	38	Stockton, Cal	3	....
Pittsfield, Mass	3	....	Taunton, Mass	1	3
Pontiac, Mich	4	2	Toledo, Ohio	2	2
Poughkeepsie, N. Y	1	....	Waco, Tex	3	....
Quincy, Mass	4	2	Washington, Pa	1	....
Reading, Pa	1	....	Wichita, Kans	7	1
Rochester, N. Y	24	5	Worcester, Mass	7	5
Rutland, Vt	1	....	York, Pa	1	....
Sacramento, Cal	4	2			

POLIOMYELITIS (INFANTILE PARALYSIS).

City Reports for Week Ended Mar. 2, 1918.

Place.	Cases.	Deaths.	Place.	Cases.	Deaths.
Chicago, Ill	2	....	Milwaukee, Wis	3	....
Columbus, Ohio	1	....	New York, N. Y	1	....
Everett, Mass	1	....	Pittsburgh, Pa	2	....
Hoboken, N. J	1	....			

RABIES IN ANIMALS.

City Reports for Week Ended Mar. 2, 1918.

During the week ended March 2, 1918, one case of rabies in animals was reported at Detroit, Mich., and two cases were reported at Troy, N. Y.

RABIES IN MAN.

City Report for Week Ended Mar. 2, 1918.

During the week ended March 2, 1918, one death from rabies was reported at Pittsburgh, Pa.

SCARLET FEVER.

See Diphtheria, measles, scarlet fever, and tuberculosis, page 423.

SMALLPOX.

Illinois—Pekin.

On March 16, 1918, smallpox was reported prevalent in Pekin, Ill.

SMALLPOX—Continued.

Missouri—Kansas City.

During the period from March 11 to 18, 1918, 102 cases of smallpox were notified in Kansas City, Mo.

Texas—Eagle Pass—Virulent Smallpox.

During the period from March 12 to 18, 1918, 7 new cases of smallpox were notified at Eagle Pass, Tex., making a total of 115 cases of the disease reported at that place since January 1, 1918. Eighteen deaths from smallpox have been reported in Eagle Pass during the period from January 1 to March 18, 1918.

City Reports for Week Ended Mar. 2, 1918.

Place.	Cases.	Deaths.	Place.	Cases.	Deaths.
Akron, Ohio	38		Lexington, Ky	1	
Alexandria, La	3		Lima, Ohio	18	
Alton, Ill	7		Lincoln, Nebr	5	
Anniston, Ala	24		Little Rock, Ark	24	
Atlanta, Ga	3		Lorain, Ohio	2	
Augusta, Ga	1		Los Angeles, Cal	2	
Baltimore, Md	4		Louisville, Ky	4	
Birmingham, Ala	120		Madison, Wis	6	
Boston, Mass	1		Memphis, Tenn	28	
Butte, Mont	7		Milwaukee, Wis	7	
Cairo, Ill	1		Minneapolis, Minn	30	
Canton, Ohio	3		Mobile, Ala	10	
Charleston, W. Va	2		Montgomery, Ala	10	
Charlotte, N. C	1		Morristown, N. J	2	
Chattanooga, Tenn	10		Muskegon, Mich	2	
Chicago, Ill	11		Muskogee, Okla	2	
Cincinnati, Ohio	14		Nashville, Tenn	4	
Cleveland, Ohio	42		New Orleans, La	17	
Coffeyville, Kans	6		New York N. Y	2	
Columbus, Ga	7		Norfolk, Va	1	
Columbus, Ohio	15		Oakland, Cal	1	
Council Bluffs, Iowa	28		Oklahoma City, Okla	18	
Covington, Ky	4		Omaha, Nebr	40	
Cumberland, Md	1		Pittsburgh, Pa	3	
Danville, Ill	1		Pontiac, Mich	5	
Davenport, Iowa	2		Portland, Oreg	4	
Dayton, Ohio	11		Quincy, Ill	11	
Denver, Colo	21	1	Racine, Wis	1	
Des Moines, Iowa	23		Roanoke, Va	1	
Detroit, Mich	45		Sacramento, Cal	1	
Dubuque, Iowa	1		St. Louis, Mo	22	
Erie, Pa	5		San Diego, Cal	1	
Evanston, Ill	13		Sandusky, Ohio	4	
Everett, Wash	4		San Francisco, Cal	4	
Flint, Mich	7	1	Schenectady, N. Y	1	
Fort Smith, Ark	4		Seattle, Wash	4	
Fort Wayne, Ind	10		Sioux City, Iowa	15	
Grand Rapids, Mich	8		South Bend, Ind	1	
Green Bay, Wis	1		Spartanburg, S. C	4	
Hartford, Conn	2		Springfield, Ill	1	
Harrisburg, Pa	1		Superior, Wis	1	
Houston, Tex	7	1	Tacoma, Wash	2	
Indianapolis, Ind	81		Terre Haute, Ind	2	
Johnstown, Pa	1		Toledo, Ohio	6	1
Kansas City, Kans	29		Topeka, Kans	10	
Knoxville, Tenn	7	1	Waco, Tex	6	
Kokomo, Ind	2		Washington, D. C	2	
La Crosse, Wis	8		Wichita, Kans	15	
Leavenworth, Kans	2		Winston-Salem, N. C	2	

TETANUS.

City Reports for Week Ended Mar. 2, 1918.

During the week ended March 2, 1918, one death from tetanus was reported at each of the following-named cities: Los Angeles, Cal., New Orleans, La., New York, N. Y., and Trenton, N. J.

TUBERCULOSIS.

See Diphtheria, measles, scarlet fever, and tuberculosis, below.

TYPHOID FEVER.

City Reports for Week Ended Mar. 2, 1918.

Place.	Cases.	Deaths.	Place.	Cases.	Deaths.
Allentown, Pa	1	....	La Crosse, Wis	1	....
Altoona, Pa	2	....	Lancaster, Pa	1	....
Atlanta, Ga	1	1	Lawrence, Mass	2	....
Baltimore, Md	....	1	Los Angeles, Cal	2	1
Birmingham, Ala	1	1	Louisville, Ky	2	....
Boston, Mass	1	1	Minneapolis, Minn	5	1
Buffalo, N. Y	2	....	Moline, Ill	1	....
Charlotte, N. C	1	....	Nashville, Tenn	3	....
Chicago, Ill	3	2	New Castle, Pa	1	....
Cincinnati, Ohio	2	1	New Orleans, La	1	....
Cleveland, Ohio	3	1	New York, N. Y	14	4
Colorado Springs, Colo	1	....	North Adams, Mass	1	....
Columbus, Ohio	....	1	Oakland, Cal	1	....
Detroit, Mich	4	1	Orange, N. J	1	....
Duluth, Minn	1	....	Philadelphia, Pa	8	2
Easton, Pa	....	1	Pittsburgh, Pa	5	2
Elizabeth, N. J	2	....	Providence, R. I	1	2
Evansville, Ind	....	....	Racine, Wis	....	1
Everett, Mass	....	1	Reading, Pa	....	1
Fall River, Mass	3	....	Roanoke, Va	1	....
Fitchburg, Mass	....	....	Rochester, N. Y	1	....
Flint, Mich	9	1	Rockford, Ill	1	....
Galesburg, Ill	1	....	St. Louis, Mo	4	1
Grand Rapids, Mich	1	....	San Francisco, Cal	2	1
Green Bay, Wis	....	1	Saratoga Springs, N. Y	1	....
Hammond, Ind	2	2	Topeka, Kans	1	....
Harrisburg, Pa	....	1	Troy, N. Y	1	1
Hartford, Conn	1	....	Wilkinsburg, Pa	3	....
Haverhill, Mass	1	....	Wilmington, N. C	1	1
Houston, Tex	1	....	Winston-Salem, N. C	1	....
Indianapolis, Ind	1	....	Zanesville, Ohio	8	....
Kokomo, Ind	....	1			

DIPHTHERIA, MEASLES, SCARLET FEVER, AND TUBERCULOSIS.

City Reports for Week Ended Mar. 2, 1918.

City.	Population as of July 1, 1916 (estimated by U. S. Census Bureau).	Total deaths from all causes.	Diphtheria.		Measles.		Scarlet fever.		Tuberculosis.	
			Cases.	Deaths.	Cases.	Deaths.	Cases.	Deaths.	Cases.	Deaths.
Over 500,000 inhabitants:										
Baltimore, Md	589,621	....	13	......	107	1	15	......	22	29
Boston, Mass	756,476	345	96	5	190	2	36	1	80	37
Chicago, Ill	2,497,722	754	117	11	74	......	50	1	279	74
Cleveland, Ohio	674,073	210	92	5	29	......	10	......	23	43
Detroit, Mich	571,784	251	50	10	33	10	42	2	38	32
Los Angeles, Cal	503,812	163	14	3	309	......	8	......	57	28
New York, N. Y	5,602,841	1,787	213	33	1,303	27	161	8	298	193
Philadelphia, Pa	1,709,518	673	75	12	309	2	49	3	129	82
Pittsburgh, Pa	579,090	222	17	4	177	2	8	......	33	21
St. Louis, Mo	757,309	264	47	3	95	......	27	1	67	26

DIPHTHERIA, MEASLES, SCARLET FEVER, AND TUBERCULOSIS—Con.

City Reports for Week Ended Mar. 2, 1918—Continued.

City.	Population as of July 1, 1916 (estimated by U. S. Census Bureau).	Total deaths from all causes.	Diphtheria.		Measles.		Scarlet fever.		Tuberculosis.	
			Cases.	Deaths.	Cases.	Deaths.	Cases.	Deaths.	Cases.	Deaths.
From 300,000 to 500,000 inhabitants:										
Buffalo, N. Y.	468,558	156	13	2	67	1	11	....	36	14
Cincinnati, Ohio	410,476	154	9	....	28	1	5	....	28	17
Jersey City, N. J.	306,345	95	13	....	54	....	11	1	38	8
Milwaukee, Wis.	436,535	124	4	....	260	2	44	....	17	10
Minneapolis, Minn.	363,454		11	4	37		43	....		6
Newark, N. J.	408,894	159	31	2	262	2	8	....	71	27
New Orleans, La.	371,747	144	27	1	54	....			24	23
San Francisco, Cal.	463,516	173	19	1	40	....	13	....	45	21
Seattle, Wash.	348,639		2	....	69	....	3	....	7	4
Washington, D. C.	363,980	143	10	2	349	1	41	....	26	12
From 200,000 to 300,000 inhabitants:										
Columbus, Ohio	214,878	65	5	1	32	....	39	....	8	6
Denver, Colo.	260,800	72	6	....	237	....	29			12
Indianapolis, Ind.	271,708	102	32	3	107	....	25	....	25	12
Louisville, Ky.	238,910	117	5	....	38	1	6	....	29	10
Portland, Oreg.	295,463	53	3	1	158	....	6	....	14	1
Providence, R. I.	254,960	86	14	....	12	....	11	1		9
Rochester, N. Y.	256,417	81	7	1	69	....	17	....	27	5
From 100,000 to 200,000 inhabitants:										
Atlanta, Ga.	190,558	74	5	1	4	....	2	....	2	7
Birmingham, Ala	181,762	58	1	....	73	....	1	....	9	5
Bridgeport, Conn	121,579	45	7	2	3	....			1	5
Cambridge, Mass	112,981		5	....	53	2	1	....	8	14
Camden, N. J.	106,233		4	....	34	....	6	....	4	
Dayton, Ohio	127,224	41	2	....	45	....	10	....	9	1
Des Moines, Iowa	101,598		1	....	4	....	6			
Fall River, Mass.	128,366	39	9	....	8	....	7	....	13	6
Grand Rapids, Mich	128,291		2	1	11	....	5	....	4	1
Hartford, Conn	110,900	64	1	....	2	....	4	1	4	2
Houston, Tex	112,307	45			31	....	2	....	3	2
Lawrence, Mass	100,570	35	2	....	5	....	2	....	5	4
Lowell, Mass	113,245	42	2	....	1	....			14	2
Lynn, Mass	102,425	22	2	....	15	....	6	1	4	2
Memphis, Tenn	148,995	77	7	....	12	....	3	1	18	4
Nashville, Tenn	117,657	49	1	1	8	....	1	....	4	5
New Bedford, Mass	118,158	51	2	....	27	....			16	8
New Haven, Conn	149,685	65	2	....	48	....	3	....	4	2
Oakland, Cal.	198,604	41	1	....	48	....	6	....	17	3
Omaha, Nebr	165,470	43	6	1	45	....	17	....		6
Reading, Pa.	109,381	44	3	1	11	....	4	....	1	5
Richmond, Va.	156,687	76	3	....	61	1	7	....	6	8
Scranton, Pa.	146,811	70	1	....	1	....	1	....		2
Springfield, Mass.	105,942	60	2	2	64	....	6	....	10	6
Syracuse, N. Y.	155,624	50	6	....	85	1	12	....	6	5
Tacoma, Wash	112,770		2	....	7	....	22	....		
Toledo, Ohio	191,554	57	1	....	15	....	8	....		6
Trenton, N. J.	111,593	70	1	....	10	....	4	....	9	4
Worcester, Mass	163,314	53	1	....	3	....	3	....	11	6
From 50,000 to 100,000 inhabitants:										
Akron, Ohio	85,625		14	....	14	....	17	....	3	
Allentown, Pa.	63,505	20	3	1	9	....	1	....	4	
Altoona, Pa.	58,659		4	....	21	....	1	....		
Atlantic City, N. J.	57,660				13	....			5	1
Augusta, Ga.	50,245	19	....	....	31	....	2	....	1	1
Bayonne, N. J.	69,893		2	....	97	....			2	
Berkeley, Cal.	57,653	17			16	....	1	....	1	
Binghamton, N. Y.	53,973	30	3	....	16	....	2	....		1
Brockton, Mass.	67,449	19	2	....	6	....	2	....	3	2
Canton, Ohio	60,852	12	1	....	3	....	4	....		
Charleston, S. C.	60,734	33	2	....	1	....			1	4
Chattanooga, Tenn	60,075	3	1	....	3	....			3	1
Covington, Ky.	57,141	24	1	....	6	....	2	....	2	2
Duluth, Minn.	94,495	22	6	....	37	....			3	2
Elizabeth, N. J.	86,600	35	4	....	81	1	72	....	4	3
El Paso, Tex.	63,705	40	3	....	16	....	3	....		9
Erie, Pa.	73,195	24	8	1	4	....	4	....	7	1
Evansville, Ind.	76,078	23	3	....	22	....	1	....	15	1
Flint, Mich.	54,772	21	1	....	7	....	9	1	2	
Fort Wayne, Ind.	76,183	24	6	....			5	....	2	....

DIPHTHERIA, MEASLES, SCARLET FEVER, AND TUBERCULOSIS—Con.

City Reports for Week Ended Mar. 2, 1918—Continued.

City.	Population as of July 1, 1916 (estimated by U. S. Census Bureau).	Total deaths from all causes.	Diphtheria.		Measles.		Scarlet fever.		Tuberculosis.	
			Cases.	Deaths.	Cases.	Deaths.	Cases.	Deaths.	Cases.	Deaths.
From 50,000 to 100,000 inhabitants—Continued.										
Harrisburg, Pa	72,015	37	1		11		3		1	
Hoboken, N. J	77,214	20			4	1	2		6	3
Holyoke, Mass	65,286		1		2		1		3	1
Johnstown, Pa	68,529	20	2				11			
Kansas City, Kans	99,437		4		28		3			
Lancaster, Pa	50,853		2		23		11		1	
Little Rock, Ark	57,343	7			8		2		3	1
Malden, Mass	51,155	10	1		5		4		3	1
Manchester, N. H	78,283	18	1		28		1		4	1
Mobile, Ala	58,221	28	1		1					2
New Britain, Conn	53,794	16	2		12				10	
Norfolk, Va	89,612		3	1	11		1			6
Oklahoma City, Okla	92,943	17	2		15					2
Passaic, N. J	71,744	24	5	1	1			2	1	
Portland, Me	63,867	17	4		27					2
Rockford, Ill	55,185	10	1	1	19		5		2	
Sacramento, Cal	66,896	19	1		94		2		7	2
Saginaw, Mich	55,642	21	3				4			1
San Diego, Cal	53,330	10	1		218	2	8		4	7
Savannah, Ga	68,805	27			7		1		2	6
Schenectady, N. Y	99,519	19	4		9				4	1
Sioux City, Iowa	57,078	1					24			
Somerville, Mass	87,089	30	2		26		1		6	3
South Bend, Ind	68,946	13	2		12		3		1	1
Springfield, Ill	61,120	18	1		20					3
Springfield, Ohio	51,550		1		3					3
Terre Haute, Ind	66,083	24	5		1				1	2
Troy, N. Y	77,916	36	1		4		6	1	6	5
Wichita, Kans	70,722		1		102		1		1	
Wilkes-Barre, Pa	76,776	15	2		56		5		7	1
Wilmington, Del	94,265	43	3		12		1			3
Yonkers, N. Y	99,838		7		9		4		7	2
York, Pa	51,656	1	2		14		2		2	
From 25,000 to 50,000 inhabitants:										
Alameda, Cal	27,732	5	3		7		1		1	1
Auburn, N. Y	37,385	14			15					
Battle Creek, Mich	29,480		6		14		3			
Brookline, Mass	32,730	7			12		1			2
Butler, Pa	27,632	9	3	1	26					
Butte, Mont	43,425		1		1		7			
Cedar Rapids, Iowa	37,908						5			
Charleston, W. Va	29,941	9	1		3		1			5
Charlotte, N. C	39,823		1		16		2		4	
Chelsea, Mass	46,192	14	1		9		1		1	2
Chicopee, Mass	29,319	7	2						1	
Clinton, Iowa	27,386	1					31	1		
Colorado Springs, Colo	32,971	7			20				4	2
Columbia, S. C	34,611	12			5				1	
Columbus, Ga	25,950	4								
Council Bluffs, Iowa	31,484				1		3			
Cranston, R. I	25,987	4	1		1					
Cumberland, Md	26,074	9			2		10			1
Danville, Ill	32,261	17			87		1		3	2
Davenport, Iowa	48,811		1		4		8			
Decatur, Ill	39,631	11			2					3
Dubuque, Iowa	39,873				3					1
Durham, N. C	25,061	10			31					
East Chicago, Ind	28,743	9	1							
Easton, Pa	30,530	19	3		13					2
East Orange, N. J	42,458	8	1		23		6		1	
Elgin, Ill	28,203	6	1				3		1	
Elmira, N. Y	38,120	6	2	1	58				3	2
Evanston, Ill	28,591	5			10		1			
Everett, Mass	39,233	10	5		9		2		5	
Everett, Wash	35,486	4		1						1
Fitchburg, Mass	41,781	11								2
Fort Smith, Ark	28,638				3		1			
Galveston, Tex	41,863	1			1				1	
Green Bay, Wis	29,353	14			9		8		1	
Hammond, Ind	26,171	18								2
Haverhill, Mass	48,477	9	3	1	26		5		6	1

DIPHTHERIA, MEASLES, SCARLET FEVER, AND TUBERCULOSIS—Con.

City Reports for Week Ended Mar. 2, 1918—Continued.

City.	Population as of July 1, 1916 (estimated by U. S. Census Bureau).	Total deaths from all causes.	Diphtheria.		Measles.		Scarlet fever.		Tuberculosis.	
			Cases.	Deaths.	Cases.	Deaths.	Cases.	Deaths.	Cases.	Deaths.
From 25,000 to 50,000 inhabitants—Continued.										
Jackson, Miss	35,363	16	1		4		24		2	1
Jamestown, N. Y	36,580	12							2	3
Kalamazoo, Mich	48,886	35	2		7				1	2
Kingston, N. Y	26,771	7								2
Knoxville, Tenn	38,676				7		7		2	2
La Crosse, Wis	31,677	13	2				2			2
Lexington, Ky	41,097	30			20					6
Lima, Ohio	35,384	12	1		5		2			1
Lincoln, Nebr	46,515	11	1		6		6		1	2
Long Beach, Cal	27,587	8			35		1		2	1
Lorain, Ohio	36,964						1		1	
Lynchburg, Va	32,940	10			6		3		5	1
Macon, Ga	45,757	10			11		3		5	1
Madison, Wis	30,699	7			8		1		1	
McKeesport, Pa	47,521		1		20					
Medford, Mass	26,234	9	4	1	10		3			
Moline, Ill	27,451	20			16		4	1		
Montclair, N. J	26,318	5			76		1			1
Montgomery, Ala	43,285	16			15				2	
Mount Vernon, N. Y	37,009	8	3	1	11					
Muskegon, Mich	26,100	9			1					
Muskogee, Okla	44,218				7					
Nashua, N. H	27,327	8	3		1					2
Newburgh, N. Y	29,603	11	1		7				3	1
New Castle, Pa	41,133				20					
Newport, Ky	31,927	12					1		2	2
Newport, R. I	30,108	7	2	1			1		1	
Newton, Mass	43,715	21			33		3		2	
Niagara Falls, N. Y	37,353	23			3		2		1	2
Norristown, Pa	31,401	11			3		2		1	
Norwalk, Conn	26,899								1	
Oak Park, Ill	26,654	14	4	1	16		2	1		
Orange, N. J	33,080	13	1		31		1		5	1
Pasadena, Cal	46,450	14			83				2	3
Perth Amboy, N. J	41,185	9			4				8	2
Petersburg, Va	25,582		3		6				2	
Pittsfield, Mass	38,629	13	1		6		3		1	1
Portsmouth, Va	39,651	15			8		3			1
Poughkeepsie, N. Y	30,390				22		1		10	
Quincy, Ill	36,798	10	1		8	1	2		1	1
Quincy, Mass	38,136		2		70		1			
Racine, Wis	46,486	14			40		5			1
Roanoke, Va	43,284	19	1		33	1				1
Rock Island, Ill	28,926		3		16		3			
Salem, Mass	48,562				34				2	.
San Jose, Cal	38,902				17				1	
Steubenville, Ohio	27,445	12			4		2		2	
Stockton, Cal	35,358	11			78					
Superior, Wis	46,226	14			11					
Taunton, Mass	36,281	20					1		4	1
Topeka, Kans	18,726				3		15			
Waco, Tex	33,385		1		13		1		1	
Waltham, Mass	30,570	9			1	1	1		1	2
Watertown, N. Y	29,894	2			16				1	
West Hoboken, N. J	43,139	5							2	1
Wheeling, W. Va	43,377	15	2		4				4	
Williamsport, Pa	33,809	7	2						7	
Wilmington, N. C	29,892	7			10					1
Winston-Salem, N. C	31,155	19			28		1		16	8
Zanesville, Ohio	30,863	9							1	
From 10,000 to 25,000 inhabitants:										
Alexandria, La	15,333	4			2					
Alton, Ill	22,874	13		1	5		2			2
Ann Arbor, Mich	15,010	11	2		31		3			
Anniston, Ala	14,112				10					
Braddock, Pa	21,685	9	2		1				2	
Cairo, Ill	15,794	2	2							
Chillicothe, Ohio	15,470	6	2		1		1		1	
Clinton, Mass	13,070	6	2							1

[1] Population Apr. 15, 1910; no estimate made.

DIPHTHERIA, MEASLES, SCARLET FEVER, AND TUBERCULOSIS—Con.

City Reports for Week Ended Mar. 2, 1918—Continued.

City.	Population as of July 1, 1916 (estimated by U. S. Census Bureau).	Total deaths from all causes.	Diphtheria.		Measles.		Scarlet fever.		Tuberculosis.	
			Cases.	Deaths.	Cases.	Deaths.	Cases.	Deaths.	Cases.	Deaths.
From 10,000 to 25,000 inhabitants—Continued.										
Coffeyville, Kans	17,540				13		1			
Concord, N. H	22,669	13								
Dover, N. H	13,272	4								
Galesburg, Ill	24,276	5	1	1	6					
Greenville, S. C	18,181	10			3					
Hattiesburg, Miss	16,482	9			2				1	
Kearny, N. J	23,539	7			26		2		1	
Kokomo, Ind	20,930	8			5		1		1	
La Fayette, Ind	21,286	3			2					
Leavenworth, Kans	1 19,363	4			2		1			
Long Branch, N. J	15,395	1			1					
Marinette, Wis	1 14,610	2	2							1
Melrose, Mass	17,445	7	1		1					1
Morristown, N. J	13,284	9		1	1					
Muscatine, Iowa	17,500				11					
Nanticoke, Pa	23,126	7			1		2			
New Albany, Ind	23,629	8	1		1		1			
Newburyport, Mass	15,243	6			1				1	1
North Adams, Mass	1 22,019	11							1	1
Northampton, Mass	19,926	10					1		3	1
Pontiac, Mich	17,524	9	4		2		3		2	
Portsmouth, N. H	11,666						5			
Rocky Mount, N. C	12,067	3			3				1	
Rutland, Vt	14,831								1	
Sandusky, Ohio	20,193	8								
Saratoga Springs, N. Y	13,821	2			1				2	
Spartanburg, S. C	21,365	16	1		34	1			7	1
Washington, Pa	21,618				108		1			
Wilkinsburg, Pa	23,228	13			12		1			

1 Population Apr. 15, 1910; no estimate made.

31

FOREIGN.

CHINA.

Further Relative to Cerebrospinal Meningitis—Hongkong.[1]

During the two weeks ended March 16, 1918, 215 cases of cerebrospinal menginitis were notified at Hongkong.

CUBA.

Communicable Diseases—Habana.

Communicable diseases have been notified at Habana as follows:

Disease.	Feb. 11-20, 1918.		Cases remaining under treatment Feb. 20, 1918.	Disease.	Feb. 11-20, 1918.		Cases remaining under treatment Feb. 20, 1918.
	New cases.	Deaths.			New cases.	Deaths.	
Diphtheria...........	6	1	2	Scarlet fever........	1	....	2
Leprosy.............	....	....	11	Smallpox..........	....	....	2
Malaria.............	34	....	[1] 34	Typhoid fever........	21	4	[1] 74
Measles.............	40	....	44	Varicella...........	47	....	85

[1] From the interior, 33.   [1] From the interior, 32.

CHOLERA, PLAGUE, SMALLPOX, TYPHUS FEVER, AND YELLOW FEVER.

Reports Received During Week Ended Mar. 22, 1918.[1]

CHOLERA.

Place.	Date.	Cases.	Deaths.	Remarks.
Philippine Islands:				
Provinces....................				Jan. 20-26, 1918: Cases, 116;
Bohol....................	Jan. 20-26.........	34	29	deaths, 81.
Capiz....................	...do.............	23	16	
Cebu....................	...do.............	15	6	
Iloilo....................	...do.............	25	15	
Mindanao....................	...do.............	19	15	
Occidental Negros........	...do.............		3	
Provinces....................				Jan. 27-Feb. 2, 1918: Cases, 103;
Bohol....................	Jan. 27-Feb. 2.....	60	44	deaths, 84.
Capiz....................	...do.............	22	19	
Cebu....................	...do.............	9	9	
Iloilo....................	...do.............	8	6	
Occidental Negros........	...do.............	4	6	

PLAGUE.

Place.	Date.	Cases.	Deaths.	Remarks.
India........................	....	....	....	Dec. 2-8, 1917: Cases, 19,441; deaths, 15,436. Dec. 23-29, 1917: Cases, 18,753, deaths, 15,162.
Indo-China:				
Cochin-China -				
Saigon.................	Jan. 7-27.........	22	7	

[1] Public Health Reports, Mar. 8, 1918, p. 340.
[1] From medical officers of the Public Health Service, American consuls, and other sources.

CHOLERA, PLAGUE, SMALLPOX, TYPHUS FEVER, AND YELLOW FEVER—Continued.

Reports Received During Week Ended Mar. 22, 1918—Continued.

SMALLPOX.

Place.	Date.	Cases.	Deaths.	Remarks.
Canada:				
New Brunswick—				
St. John	Mar. 3–9	2		
Nova Scotia—				
Halifax	Feb. 24–Mar. 2	1		
Sydney	do	1		
Ontario—				
Ottawa	Mar. 4–10	1		
Quebec—				
Montreal	Feb. 24–Mar. 9	6		
China:				
Chungking	Jan. 13–19			Present.
Dairen	Jan. 27–Feb. 16	11	4	
Nanking	Feb. 3–9			Epidemic.
Shanghai	Jan. 25–Feb. 10	8	17	
Swatow	Jan. 18			Unusually prevalent.
Tientsin	Jan. 27–Feb. 9	5		
France:				
Marseille	Jan. 1–31		2	
Paris	Jan. 27–Feb. 2	1		
Great Britain:				
Cardiff	Feb. 3–9	4		
Honduras:				
Santa Barbara Department.	Jan. 1–7			Present in interior.
Indo-China:				
Cochin-China—				
Saigon	Jan. 7–27	111	36	
Italy:				
Genoa	Dec. 2–31	11	3	
Do	Jan. 2–31	30	2	
Leghorn	Jan. 28–Feb. 3	7		
Japan:				
Taihoku	Jan. 15–Feb. 11	4	2	
Tokyo	Feb. 11–18	8		City and suburbs.
Yokohama	Jan. 28–Feb. 3	2		
Mexico:				
Mexico City	Feb. 3–16	15		
Vera Cruz	Feb. 24–Mar. 2	1		
Newfoundland:				
St. Johns	Feb. 23–Mar. 1	4		
Philippine Islands:				
Manila	Jan. 20–Feb. 2	5		
Siam:				
Bangkok	Jan. 6–12	1		

TYPHUS FEVER.

Place.	Date.	Cases.	Deaths.	Remarks.
France:				
Marseille	Dec. 1–31		1	
Great Britain:				
Glasgow	Feb. 3–9	2		
Japan:				
Nagasaki	Feb. 11–17	1		
Mexico:				
Mexico City	Feb. 3–16	115		
Portugal:				
Oporto				Dec. 24, 1917–Mar. 9, 1918: About 250 cases reported.
Sweden:				
Goteborg	Dec. 9–15	1		
Switzerland:				
Basel	Jan. 13–19	1		

CHOLERA, PLAGUE, SMALLPOX, TYPHUS FEVER, AND YELLOW FEVER—Continued.

Reports Received from Dec. 29, 1917, to Mar. 15, 1918.

CHOLERA.

Place.	Date.	Cases.	Deaths.	Remarks.
China:				
Antung	Nov. 26–Dec. 2	3	1	
India:				
Bombay	Oct. 28–Nov. 24	17	12	
Calcutta	Sept. 16–Dec. 8		81	
Madras	Nov. 25–Dec. 1	1	1	
Rangoon	Nov. 4–Dec. 1	3	3	
Indo-China:				
Provinces				Sept. 1–Oct. 31, 1917: Cases, 113; deaths, 57.
Anam	Sept. 1–Oct. 31	17	13	
Cambodia	...do...	41	25	
Cochin-China	...do...	43	17	
Saigon	Nov. 22–Dec. 9	4	3	
Kwang-Chow-Wan	Sept. 1–30	10	2	
Java:				
East Java	Oct. 28–Nov. 3	1	1	
West Java				Oct. 19–Dec. 20, 1917: Cases, 100; deaths, 57.
Batavia	Oct. 19–Dec. 20	55	21	
Persia:				
Mazanderan Province				July 30–Sept. 3, 1917: Cases, 384; deaths, 276.
Achraf	July 30–Aug. 16	90	88	
Astrabad	July 31			Present.
Barfrush	July 1–Aug. 16	39	25	
Chahmirzad				25 cases reported July 31, 1917.
Chahrastagh	June 15–July 25	10	8	
Charoud	Aug. 26–Sept. 3	4	2	
Damghan	Aug. 28			Present.
Kharek	May 28–June 11	21	13	
Meched	Aug. 18–Sept. 2	174	82	
Ouzoun Dare	Aug. 8			Do.
Sabzevar	Aug. 24			Do.
Sari	July 3–29	273	144	
Semnan	Aug. 31–Sept. 2	14	5	
Yekchambe-Bazar	June 3	6		
Philippine Islands.				
Provinces				Nov. 18–Dec. 29, 1917: Cases, 1,053; deaths, 603. Dec. 30, 1917–Jan. 19, 1918: Cases, 447; deaths, 192.
Antique	Nov. 18–Dec. 1	48	32	
Bohol	Nov. 18–Dec. 29	169	111	
Do	Dec. 30–Jan. 19	57	52	
Capiz	Nov. 25–Dec. 29	27	21	
Do	Dec. 30–Jan. 19	41	35	
Cebu	Dec. 23–29	3		
Do	Dec. 30–Jan. 19	36	17	
Iloilo	Nov. 25–Dec. 29	179	135	
Do	Dec. 30–Jan. 19	42	27	
Leyte	Nov. 25–Dec. 22	13	12	
Mindanao	Nov. 25–Dec. 29	337	196	
Do	Dec. 30–Jan. 19	224	135	
Occidental Negros	Nov. 25–Dec. 22	177	123	
Do	Jan. 13–19	45	15	
Oriental Negros	Nov. 25–Dec. 29	99	62	
Do	Dec. 30–Jan. 19	12	11	
Romblon	Nov. 25–Dec. 1	1	1	
Siam:				
Bangkok	Sept. 16–22	1	1	
Turkey in Asia:				
Bagdad	Nov. 1–15		40	

PLAGUE.

Place.	Date.	Cases.	Deaths.	Remarks.
Brazil:				
Bahia	Nov. 4–Dec. 15	4	4	
Do	Dec. 30–Jan. 12	3	2	
Rio de Janeiro	Dec. 23–29	1		
Do	Jan. 6–12	1	1	
British Gold Coast:				
Axim	Jan. 8			Present.
Ceylon:				
Colombo	Oct. 14–Dec. 1	14	13	
Ecuador				Sept. 1–Nov. 30, 1917: Cases, 66; deaths, 24.
Guayaquil	Sept. 1–30	3	1	
Do	Oct. 1–31	20	8	
Do	Nov. 1–30	43	15	
Egypt				Jan. 1–Nov. 15, 1917: Cases, 728; deaths, 398.
Port Said	July 23–29	1	2	

CHOLERA, PLAGUE, SMALLPOX, TYPHUS FEVER, AND YELLOW FEVER—Continued.

Reports Received from Dec. 29, 1917, to Mar. 15, 1918—Continued.

PLAGUE—Continued.

Place.	Date.	Cases.	Deaths.	Remarks.
India....................				Sept. 16–Dec. 1, 1917: Cases, 151,751; deaths, 113,434.
Bombay...................	Oct. 28–Dec. 1.....	103	85	
Calcutta..................	Sept. 16–29........		2	
Henzada..................	Oct. 21–27.........		1	
Karachi..................	Oct. 21–Dec. 1.....	11	9	
Madras Presidency........	Oct. 31–Nov. 17....	3,294	2,560	
Mandalay.................	Oct. 14–Nov. 17....		89	
Rangoon..................	Oct. 21–Dec. 1.....	32	38	
Indo-China:				
Provinces................				Sept. 1–Oct. 31, 1917: Cases, 70; deaths, 64.
Anam................	Sept. 1–Oct. 31....	25	24	
Cambodia............	...do...........	30	19	
Cochin-China........	...do...........	15	11	
Saigon..............	Oct. 31–Dec. 23....	17	6	
Do.............	Dec. 31–Jan. 6.....	2		
Java:				
East Java...............				Oct. 27–Nov. 25, 1917: Cases, 75; deaths, 73.
Surabaya............	Nov. 11–25.........	2	2	
West Java..............				Nov. 25–Dec. 9, 1917: Cases, 45; deaths, 45.
Peru......................				Dec. 1, 1917–Jan. 15, 1918: Cases, 106.
Ancachs Department—				
Casma..............	Dec. 1–Jan. 15....	2		
Lambayeque Department..	...do...........	22		At Chiclayo, Ferrenafe, Jayanca, Lambayeque.
Libertad Department......	...do...........	72		At Guadalupe, Mansiche, Pacasmayo, Salaverry, San Jose, San Pedro, and country district of Trujillo.
Lima Department.........	...do...........	9		City and country.
Piura Department—				
Catacaos............	...do...........	1		
Senegal:				
St. Louis..............	Feb. 2............			Present.
Siam:				
Bangkok...............	Sept. 16–Dec. 23...	13	9	
Straits Settlements:				
Singapore................	Oct. 28–Dec. 29....	5	7	

SMALLPOX.

Place.	Date.	Cases.	Deaths.	Remarks.
Algeria:				
Algiers................	Nov. 1–Dec. 31....	3	1	
Do................	Jan. 1–31.........	2		
Australia:				
New South Wales........				July 12–Dec. 20, 1917: Cases, 36. Jan. 4–17, 1918: Cases, 1. Newcastle district.
Abermain...........	Oct. 25–Nov. 29...	3		
Cessnock...........	July 12–Oct. 11...	7		
Eumangla...........	Aug. 15...........	1		
Kurri Kurri.........	Dec. 5–20.........	2		
Mungindi...........	Aug. 13...........	1		
Warren.............	July 12–Oct. 25...	22		
Do.............	Jan. 1–17.........	1		
Brazil:				
Bahia...............	Nov. 10–Dec. 8....	3		
Pernambuco.........	Nov. 1–15.........	1		
Rio de Janeiro......	Sept. 30–Dec. 29...	703	190	
Do.............	Dec. 30–Jan. 26...	158	42	
Sao Paulo..........	Oct. 29–Nov. 4....		2	
Canada:				
British Columbia—				
Vancouver..........	Jan. 13–Feb. 16...	4		
Victoria...........	Jan. 7–Feb. 2.....	2		
Winnipeg...........	Dec. 30–Jan. 5.....	1		
New Brunswick—				
Kent County........	Dec. 4............			Outbreak. On main line Canadian Ry., 25 miles north of Moncton.
Do..............	Jan. 22...........	40		In 7 localities.
Northumberland County.	...do...........	41		In 5 localities.
Restigouche County...	Jan. 18...........	60		
Victoria County.......	Jan. 22...........	10		At Limestone and a lumber camp.
Westmoreland County, Moncton.	Jan. 20–Feb. 23...	8		
York County..........	Jan. 22...........	8		

CHOLERA, PLAGUE, SMALLPOX, TYPHUS FEVER, AND YELLOW FEVER—Continued.

Reports Received from Dec. 29, 1917, to Mar. 15, 1918—Continued.

SMALLPOX—Continued.

Place	Date.	Cases.	Deaths.	Remarks.
Canada—Continued.				
Nova Scotia—				
Sydney................	Feb. 3-23........	3	....	
Ontario—				
Hamilton...........	Dec. 16-22....	1	....	
Do.................	Jan. 13-19........	2	....	
Sarnia.............	Dec. 9-15........	1	....	
Do.................	Jan. 6-Mar. 2....	28	....	
Toronto............	Feb. 10-16....	1	....	
Windsor............	Dec. 30-Jan. 5....	1	....	
Prince Edward Island—				
Charlottetown........	Feb. 7-13....	1	....	
Quebec—				
Montreal.............	Dec. 16-Jan. 5....	5	....	
Do.................	Jan. 6-12....	1	....	
China:				
Amoy................	Oct. 22-Dec. 30....	....	....	Present.
Antung..............	Dec. 3-23....	13	2	
Do.................	Jan. 7-27....	4	2	
Chungking...........	Nov. 11-Dec. 29....	....	....	Do.
Do.................	Dec. 30-Jan. 12....	....	....	Do.
Dairen..............	Nov. 18-Dec. 22....	3	1	
Do.................	Dec. 30-Jan. 26....	4	....	
Harbin..............	May 14-June 30....	20	....	Chinese Eastern Ry.
Do.................	July 1-Dec. 2....	7	....	Do.
Hongkong............	Dec. 23-29....	1	....	
Hungtahotze Station...	Oct. 28-Nov. 4....	1	....	Do.
Manchuria Station.....	May 14-June 30...	6	....	Do.
Do.................	July 1-Dec. 2....	3	....	Do.
Mukden.............	Nov. 11-24....	....	....	Present.
Shanghai............	Nov. 18-Dec. 23....	41	91	Cases, foreign; deaths among natives.
Do.................	Dec. 31-Jan. 27....	25	75	Do.
Tientsin............	Nov. 11-Dec. 22....	13	....	
Do.................	Dec. 30-Jan. 26....	9	....	
Cuba:				
Habana.............	Jan. 7........	1	....	Nov. 8, 1917: 1 case from Coruna; Dec. 5, 1917, 1 case.
Marianao...........	Jan. 8.........	1	....	6 miles distant from Habana.
Ecuador	....	....	....	Sept. 1-Nov. 30, 1917: Cases, 26; deaths, 2.
Guayaquil..........	Sept. 1-30......	8	....	
Do.................	Oct. 1-31........	14	1	
Do.................	Nov. 1-30.......	4	1	
Egypt:				
Alexandria.........	Nov. 12-18...	1	....	
Do.................	Jan. 8-14....	3	....	
Cairo..............	July 23-Nov. 12-18	6	1	
France:				
Lyon...............	Nov. 18-Dec. 16...	6	3	
Do.................	Jan. 7-20....	5	....	
India:				
Bombay.............	Oct. 21-Dec. 1....	16	4	
Karachi............	Nov. 18-24....	....	1	Nov. 11-17, 1917: 10 cases with 4 deaths; imported on s. s. Meness from Basreh.
Madras.............	Oct. 31-Dec. 8....	9	3	
Rangoon............	Oct. 28-Nov. 24...	4	1	
Indo-China:				
Provinces...........	....	....	....	Sept. 1-Oct. 31, 1917: Cases, 345; deaths, 98.
Anam..............	Sept. 1-Oct. 31....	103	15	
Cambodia..........	....do......	10	3	
Cochin-China.......	....do......	222	76	
Saigon.............	Oct. 20-Dec. 30...	120	26	
Do.................	Dec. 31-Jan. 6...	17	10	
Laos..............	Oct. 1-31......	1	....	
Tonkin............	Sept. 1-Oct. 31....	9	4	
Italy:				
Castellamare	Dec. 10 ..	2	......	Among refugees.
Florence	Dec. 1-15....	17	4	
Leghorn	Jan. 7-27....	17	5	
Messina	Jan. 3-19....	1	....	
Milan.............	....	....	....	Oct. 1-Nov. 30, 1917. Cases, 17.
Naples.............	To Dec. 10......	2	....	Among refugees.
Turin..............	Oct. 20-Dec. 29....	123	120	
Do.................	Jan. 21-Feb. 3....	24	3	
Japan:				
Nagasaki...........	Jan. 14-27....	3	1	
Taihoku............	Dec. 15-21....	1	....	Island of Taiwan (Formosa).
Do.................	Jan. 8-11....	1	....	Do.
Yokohama..........	Jan. 17-23....	2	....	

CHOLERA, PLAGUE, SMALLPOX, TYPHUS FEVER, AND YELLOW FEVER—Continued.

Reports Received from Dec. 29, 1917, to Mar. 15, 1918—Continued.

SMALLPOX—Continued.

Place.	Date.	Cases.	Deaths.	Remarks.
Java:				
East Java...................	Oct. 7–Dec. 9.....	25	....	
Mid-Java...................	Oct. 10–Nov. 21...	55	....	Oct. 10–Dec. 12, 1917: Cases, 63;
Samarang...............	Dec. 6–12.........	1	1	death, 1.
West Java...................	....	....	....	Oct. 19–Dec. 20, 1917: Cases, 217;
Batavia.................	Nov. 2–8.........	1	....	deaths, 33.
Mexico:				
Aguascalientes.............	Feb. 4–17.........	....	2	
Mazatlan..................	Dec. 5–11.........	....	1	
Do.....	Jan. 29–Feb. 19...	4	1	
Mexico City................	Nov. 11–Dec. 20...	16	....	
Do.................	Dec. 30–Feb. 2....	30	....	
Piedras Negras.............	Jan. 11..........	200	....	
Vera Cruz................	Jan. 20–Feb. 16....	6	3	
Newfoundland:				
St. Johns...................	Dec. 8–Jan. 4.....	20	....	
Do...................	Jan. 5–Feb. 22....	29	....	
Trepassey...............	Jan. 4............	....	....	Outbreak with 11 cases reported.
Philippine Islands:				
Manila..................	Oct. 28–Dec. 8.....	5	....	
Do.................	Jan. 13–19........	3	....	
Porto Rico:				
San Juan...............	Jan. 28–Feb. 17...	2	....	
Portugal:				
Lisbon...................	Nov. 4–Dec. 15....	2	....	
Do...................	Dec. 30–Jan. 19...	2	....	
Portuguese East Africa:				
Lourenço Marques........	Aug. 1–Nov. 30....	....	9	
Russia:				
Archangel...............	Sept. 1–Oct. 31...	7	....	
Moscow..................	Aug. 26–Oct. 6...	22	2	
Petrograd...............	Aug. 31–Nov. 18...	76	3	
Siam:				
Bangkok.................	Nov. 25–Dec. 1....	1	1	
Spain:				
Coruna..................	Dec. 2–15.........	....	4	
Madrid..................	....	....	....	Jan. 1–Dec. 31, 1917: Deaths, 77.
Seville..................	Oct. 1–Dec. 30....	....	66	
Straits Settlements:				
Singapore................	Nov. 25–Dec. 1....	1	1	
Do.................	Dec. 30–Jan. 5....	1	....	
Tunisia:				
Tunis..................	Dec. 14–20........	....	1	
Turkey in Asia:				
Bagdad..................	....	....	....	Present in November, 1917.
Venezuela:				
Maracaibo.................	Dec. 2–8..........	....	1	

TYPHUS FEVER.

Place.	Date.	Cases.	Deaths.	Remarks.
Algeria:				
Algiers.....................	Nov. 1–Dec. 31.....	2	1	
Argentina:				
Rosario....................	Dec. 1–31..........	....	1	
Australia:				
South Australia...........	....	....	....	Nov. 11–17, 1917: Cases, 1.
Brazil:				
Rio de Janeiro.............	Oct. 28–Dec. 1.....	7	....	
Canada:				
Ontario—				
Kingston..............	Dec. 2–8............	3	....	
Quebec—				
Montreal..............	Dec. 16–22..........	2	1	
China:				
Antung..................	Dec. 3–30..........	13	1	
Do.................	Dec. 31–Jan. 27....	2	2	
Chosen (Formosa):				
Seoul.................	Nov. 1–30..........	1	....	
Egypt:				
Alexandria.............	Nov. 8–Dec. 28.....	57	15	
Do.................	Jan. 8–14..........	20	7	
Cairo..................	July 23–Dec. 16....	137	70	
Port Said..................	July 30–Nov. 11...	5	5	

CHOLERA, PLAGUE, SMALLPOX, TYPHUS FEVER, AND YELLOW FEVER—Continued.

Reports Received from Dec. 29, 1917, to Mar. 15, 1918—Continued.

TYPHUS FEVER—Continued.

Place.	Date.	Cases.	Deaths.	Remarks.
Great Britain:				
Belfast...................	Feb. 10–16.........	4	1	
Glasgow...............	Dec. 21..........	1	....	
Do...................	Jan. 20–26.........	1	....	
Manchester...............	Dec. 2–8.........	1	....	
Greece:				
Saloniki................	Nov. 11–Dec. 29...	....	72	
Do...................	Dec. 30–Jan. 19...	....	11	
Japan:				
Nagasaki................	Nov. 26–Dec. 16...	5	5	
Do...................	Jan. 7–Feb. 3.....	5	....	
Java:				
East Java.................		....	....	Oct. 15–Dec. 9, 1917: Cases, 24; deaths, 3.
Mid-Java.................				Oct. 10–Dec. 12, 1917: Cases, 54;
Samarang...............	Oct. 17–Dec. 5....	15	2	deaths, 2.
West Java.................				Oct. 19–Dec. 20, 1917: Cases, 73;
Batavia................	Oct. 19–Dec. 20...	73	17	deaths, 15.
Mexico:				
Aguascalientes...........	Dec. 15..........	....	2	
Do...................	Jan. 21–Feb. 10....	....	14	
Durango, State—				
Guanaceví.............	Feb. 11..........	....	....	Epidemic.
Mexico City................	Nov. 11–Dec. 29...	476	....	
Do...................	Dec. 30–Feb. 2....	237	....	
Portugal:				
Lisbon...................	Feb. 21..........	....	....	Present.
Oporto.................	......do.......	....	....	Epidemic.
Russia:				
Archangel...............	Sept. 1–14......	7	2	
Moscow................	Aug. 26–Oct. 6...	49	2	
Petrograd...............	Aug. 31–Nov. 18...	32	....	
Do...................	Feb. 2...........	....	....	Present.
Vladivostok................	Oct. 29–Nov. 4....	12	1	
Sweden:				
Goteborg...............	Nov. 18–24.......	1	....	
Switzerland:				
Basel..............	Jan. 6–12.........	....	1	
Zurich...................	Nov. 9–15........	2	....	
Do...................	Jan. 13–19........	2	....	
Tunisia:				
Tunis...................	Nov. 30–Dec. 6....	....	1	
Turkey:				
Albania -				
Janina................	Jan. 27..........	....	....	Epidemic.
Union of South Africa:				
Cape of Good Hope State...	....	....	....	Sept. 10–Nov. 25, 1917: Cases, 3,724 (European, 31; native, 3,693); deaths, 761 (European, 5; native, 756).

YELLOW FEVER.

Place.	Date.	Cases.	Deaths.	Remarks.
Ecuador...................	....	....	....	Sept. 1–Nov. 30, 1917: Cases, 5; deaths, 3.
Guayaquil.................	Sept. 1–30.......	1	1	
Do...................	Oct. 1–31........	1	....	
Do...................	Nov. 1–30........	2	2	
Yaguachi...................	......do..........	1	....	
Honduras:				
Tegucigalpa............	Dec. 16–22......	....	1	
Do...................	Jan. 6–19........	....	1	

×

Suggestions for State Board of Health Regulations for the Prevention of Venereal Diseases.

Approved by—
     Surgeon General of the Army.
     Surgeon General of the Navy.
     Surgeon General of the Public Health Service.

Venereal diseases declared dangerous to the public health.—Syphilis, gonorrhea, and chancroid, hereinafter designated venereal diseases, are hereby declared to be contagious, infectious, communicable, and dangerous to the public health.

Rule 1. Venereal diseases to be reported.—Any physician or other person who makes a diagnosis in, or treats, a case of syphilis, gonorrhea, or chancroid, and every superintendent or manager of a hospital, dispensary, or charitable or penal institution, in which there is a case of venereal disease, shall report such case immediately in writing to the local health officer, stating the name and address or the office number, age, sex, color, and occupation, of the diseased person, and the date of onset of the disease, and the probable source of the infection, provided, that the name and address of the diseased person need not be stated except as hereinafter specifically required. The report shall be inclosed in a sealed envelope and sent to the local health officer, who shall report weekly [1] on the prescribed form to the State board of health, all cases reported to him.

Rule 2. Patients to be given information.—It shall be the duty of every physician and of every other person who examines or treats a person having syphilis, gonorrhea, or chancroid, to instruct him in measures for preventing the spread of such disease, and inform him of the necessity for treatment until cured, and to hand him a copy of the circular of information obtainable for this purpose from the State board of health.

Rule 3. Investigation of cases.—All city, county, and other local health officers shall use every available means to ascertain the existence of, and to investigate, all cases of syphilis, gonorrhea, and

---

[1] Substitute period required for other communicable diseases.

chancroid within their several territorial jurisdictions, and to ascertain the sources of such infections. Local health officers are hereby empowered and directed to make such examinations of persons reasonably suspected of having syphilis, gonorrhea, or chancroid, as may be necessary for carrying out these regulations. Owing to the prevalence of such diseases among prostitutes and persons associated with them, all such persons are to be considered within the above class.

Rule 4. Protection of others from infection by venereally diseased persons.—Upon receipt of a report of a case of venereal disease it shall be the duty of the local health officer to institute measures for the protection of other persons from infection by such venereally diseased person.

(a) Local health officers are authorized and directed to quarantine persons who have, or are reasonably suspected of having syphilis, gonorrhea, or chancroid whenever, in the opinion of said local health officer, or the State board of health, or its secretary, quarantine is necessary for the protection of the public health. In establishing quarantine the health officer shall designate and define the limits of the area in which the person known to have, or reasonably suspected of having, syphilis, gonorrhea, or chancroid and his immediate attendant are to be quarantined and no persons other than the attending physicians shall enter or leave the area of quarantine without the permission of the local health officer.

No one but the local health officer shall terminate said quarantine, and this shall not be done until the diseased person has become noninfectious, as determined by the local health officer or his authorized deputy through the clinical examination and all necessary laboratory tests, or until permission has been given him so to do by the State board of health or its secretary.

(b) The local health officer shall inform all persons who are about to be released from quarantine for venereal disease, in case they are not cured, what further treatment should be taken to complete their cure. Any person not cured before release from quarantine shall be required to sign the following statement after the blank spaces have been filled to the satisfaction of the health officer:

I, ..., residing at ...., hereby acknowledge the fact that I am at this time infected with ...., and agree to place myself under the medical care of ...., ... within .... hours,
<small>Name of physician or clinic.   Address</small>
and that I will remain under treatment of said physician or clinic until released by the health officer of ...., or until my case is transferred with the approval of said health officer to another regularly licensed physician or an approved clinic

I hereby agree to report to the health officer within four days after beginning treatment as above agreed, and will bring with me a statement from the above physician or clinic of the medical treatment applied in my case, and thereafter will report as often as may be demanded of me by the health officer.

I agree, further, that I will take all precautions recommended by the health officer to prevent the spread of the above disease to other persons, and that I will not perform any act which would expose other persons to the above disease.

I agree, until finally released by the health officer, to notify him of any change of address and to obtain his consent before moving my abode outside his jurisdiction

....
Signature.

....
Date.

All persons signing the above agreement shall observe its provisions, and any failure so to do shall be a violation of these regulations. All such agreements shall be filed with the health officer and kept inaccessible to the public as provided in rule 10.

Rule 5. Conditions under which the name of a patient is required to be reported.—(a) When a person applies to a physician or other person for the diagnosis or treatment of syphilis, gonorrhea, or chancroid, it shall be the duty of the physician or person so consulted to inquire of and ascertain from the person seeking such diagnosis or treatment whether such person has theretofore consulted with or has been treated by any other physician or person and, if so, to ascertain the name and address of the physician or person last consulted. It shall be the duty of the applicant for diagnosis or treatment to furnish this information, and a refusal to do so or a falsification of the name and address of such physician or person consulted by such applicant shall be deemed a violation of these regulations. It shall be the duty of the physician or other person whom the applicant consults to notify the physician or other person last consulted of the change of advisers. Should the physician or person previously consulted fail to receive such notice within 10 days after the last date upon which the patient was instructed by him to appear, it shall be the duty of such physician or person to report to the local health officer the name and address of such venereally diseased person.

(b) If an attending physician or other person knows or has good reason to suspect that a person having syphilis, gonorrhea, or chancroid is so conducting himself or herself as to expose other persons to infection, or is about so to conduct himself or herself, he shall notify the local health officer of the name and address of the diseased person and the essential facts in the case.

Rule 6. Druggists forbidden to prescribe for venereal diseases.—No druggist or other person not a physician licensed under the laws of the State shall prescribe or recommend to any person any drugs, medicines, or other substances to be used for the cure or alleviation of gonorrhea, syphilis, or chancroid, or shall compound any drugs or medicines for said purpose from any written formula or order not written for the person for whom the drugs or medicines are compounded and not signed by a physician licensed under the laws of the State.

438

Rule 7. Spread of venereal disease unlawful.—It shall be a violation of these regulations for any infected person knowingly to expose another person to infection with any of the said venereal diseases or for any person to perform an act which exposes another person to infection with venereal disease.

Rule 8. Prostitution to be repressed.—Prostitution is hereby declared to be a prolific source of syphilis, gonorrhea, and chancroid, and the repression of prostitution is declared to be a public-health measure. All local and State health officers are therefore directed to cooperate with the proper officials whose duty it is to enforce laws directed against prostitution and otherwise to use every proper means for the repression of prostitution.

Rule 9. Giving certificates of freedom from venereal diseases prohibited.—Physicians, health officers, and all other persons are prohibited from issuing certificates of freedom from venereal disease, provided this rule shall not prevent the issuance of necessary statements of freedom from infectious diseases written in such form or given under such safeguards that their use in solicitation for sexual intercourse would be impossible.

Rule 10. Records to be secret.—All information and reports concerning persons infected with venereal diseases shall be inaccessible to the public except in so far as publicity may attend the performance of the duties imposed by these regulations and by the laws of the State.

Notes and Suggestions.

Note 1.—A rule providing penalties for violation of these regulations should be added if penalties are not specified by statute. It is thought preferable that the statute should prescribe a penalty for violation of regulations of the State board of health. In any case the State law should be examined to make sure that it either prescribes penalties or gives the State board of health power to do so. The statutes should also give the State board of health the powers suggested by the following wording: "The State board of health shall have power to make such regulations concerning venereal diseases, including the reporting thereof and quarantine of infected persons, as it may from time to time deem advisable."

Note 2.—It is recommended that provision for intensive treatment in suitable hospitals while patients are under quarantine shall be made by the municipalities, counties, or the State at public expense, and that adequate hospitals and clinic facilities of high standards shall be made available to voluntary and compulsory patients.

Note 3.—For the enforcement of these regulations it is recommended that States establish bureaus or divisions of venereal diseases under the State boards of health and appropriate the necessary funds.

Note 4.—The issuance of arsphenamine or equivalents to health officers, institutions, and physicians at State expense under suitable restrictions is a valuable measure for preventing syphilis, as these substances render cases of syphilis noninfectious in the shortest possible time.

Note 5. Provision should be made for the examination of prisoners for venereal diseases and their treatment. If they are still infectious when their prison terms have expired, they should be quarantined and treated until they can be released with safety to the public health.

Note 6.—Laboratory tests for syphilis and gonorrhea should be made for physicians by the laboratories of the State board of health and the health departments of large cities.

Note 7.—Due provision should be made for follow-up work and social service in connection with the prevention of venereal diseases.

Note 8.—Institutions are needed for the segregation of persons who are, or are almost certain to become, venereal-disease carriers and who can not be adequately controlled in any other way. Sufficient provision for the segregation of the feeble-minded is most important.

Note 9.—It is recommended that the "floating" or "passing on" of persons having venereal disease from one community to another be prevented.

Note 10.—It is suggested that the bureau of venereal diseases carry on a campaign of public education in venereal-disease prevention, and in the conditions responsible for the dissemination of venereal diseases.

PREVALENCE OF DISEASE.

No health department, State or local, can effectively prevent or control disease without knowledge of when, where, and under what conditions cases are occurring.

UNITED STATES.

EXTRA-CANTONMENT ZONES—CASES REPORTED WEEK ENDED MAR. 26.

CAMP BEAUREGARD ZONE, LA.

Mumps:
Alexandria 3
Smallpox:
Alexandria 1
Tioga 3
Tuberculosis:
Boyce 1

CAMP BOWIE ZONE, TEX.

Fort Worth:
Chicken pox 2
Diphtheria 11
Gonorrhea 8
Malaria 1
Measles 1
Pneumonia, lobar 4
Scarlet fever 3
Syphilis 2

CAMP DEVENS ZONE, MASS

Chicken pox:
Littleton 6
German measles:
Ayer 1
Graniteville 1
Lancaster 2
Measles
Ayer 7
Graniteville 4
Lancaster 1
Shirley 2
Mumps:
Littleton 4

CAMP DODGE ZONE, IOWA.

Cerebrospinal meningitis
Ankeny 1
Chicken pox
Des Moines 1
Diphtheria
Des Moines 3
German measles
Polk City 1

CAMP DODGE ZONE, IOWA—continued.

Measles:
Ankeny 1
Des Moines 23
Scarlet fever:
Des Moines 14
Smallpox:
Des Moines 20
Syphilis
Des Moines 6

CAMP EBERTS ZONE, ARK

Cerebrospinal meningitis
England 1
Kerr 1
Erysipelas
Lonoke, route 1 1
England, route 2 1
German measles
England 6
Gonorrhea
England 7
Hookworm
England 1
Malaria.
Lonoke, route 1 2
England 10
England, route 2 1
Carlisle 4
Cabot 3
Cabot, route 2 1
Austin 1
Measles
Lonoke 3
Lonoke, route 4 5
England 7
Keo 1
Mumps
Carlisle 1
Lonoke 4
England 5

(448)

CAMP EBERTS ZONE, ARK.—continued.

Pellagra:
England...................................... 1
England, route 1............................ 1
Cabot, route 2.............................. 1
Pneumonia:
Lonoke, route 2............................ 2
England.................................... 8
Keo....................................... 1
Pettus.................................... 1
Scarlet fever:
Lonoke.................................... 1
Smallpox:
England................................... 2
Syphilis:
England................................... 2
Tuberculosis:
England................................... 1
Cabot..................................... 1
Carlisle.................................. 1
Typhoid fever:
England................................... 1
Whooping cough: .
Lonoke.................................... 6
England................................... 1

CAMP FUNSTON ZONE, KANS.

Chicken pox:
Stockdale................................. 2
Diphtheria:
Junction City............................. 1
Measles:
Junction City............................. 3
Stockdale................................. 3
Manhattan................................. 4
Alta Vista................................ 1
Mumps:
Junction City............................. 1
Army City................................. 1
Manhattan................................. 6
Scarlet fever:
Manhattan................................. 4
Smallpox:
Green..................................... 1
Junction City............................. 1
Stockdale................................. 1

CAMP GORDON ZONE, GA.

Chicken pox:
Atlanta................................... 1
Diphtheria:
Atlanta................................... 7
German measles:
Atlanta................................... 2
Gonorrhea:
Atlanta................................... 3
Malaria:
Atlanta................................... 2
Measles:
Atlanta................................... 14
Mumps:
Atlanta................................... 24
Decatur................................... 1
Scottdale................................. 1
Pneumonia:
Atlanta................................... 1
Scarlet fever:
Atlanta................................... 2

CAMP GORDON ZONE, GA.—continued.

Septic sore throat:
Atlanta................................... 3
Smallpox:
Atlanta................................... 6
East Point................................ 1
Lithonia.................................. 1
Scottdale................................. 1
Syphilis:
Atlanta................................... 1
Tuberculosis:
Atlanta................................... 8
Decatur................................... 1
Whooping cough:
Atlanta................................... 1
Chamblee.................................. 1
Clarkston................................. 1

CAMP GREENE ZONE, N. C.

Charlotte Township:
Chancroid................................. 3
German measles............................ 2
Gonorrhea................................. 15
Measles................................... 7
Mumps..................................... 3
Scarlet fever............................. 1
Smallpox.................................. 3
Syphilis.................................. 18
Tuberculosis.............................. 3
Whooping cough............................ 4

GULFPORT HEALTH DISTRICT, MISS.

Measles:
Biloxi.................................... 1
Gulfport.................................. 1
Pass Christian............................ 1
Pneumonia:
Gulfport.................................. 2

CAMP HANCOCK ZONE, GA.

Augusta:
Cerebrospinal meningitis.................. 2
Diphtheria................................ 1
German measles............................ 3
Measles................................... 14
Tuberculosis.............................. 2
Typhoid fever............................. 1
North Augusta:
German measles............................ 1

CAMP JACKSON ZONE, S. C.

Columbia:
Cerebrospinal meningitis.................. 1
Diphtheria................................ 3
Measles................................... 4
Mumps..................................... 4
Pneumonia................................. 1
Roseola................................... 1
Tuberculosis.............................. 1
Typhoid fever............................. 1

FORT LEAVENWORTH ZONE, KANS.

Leavenworth:
Cerebrospinal meningitis.................. 2
Chicken pox............................... 6
German measles............................ 1
Gonorrhea................................. 1
Measles................................... 11
Mumps..................................... 2

FORT LEAVENWORTH ZONE, KANS.—continued.

Leavenworth—Continued.
Pneumonia, lobar........................ 3
Smallpox.... 4
Syphilis................................ 1
Leavenworth County:
Chicken pox............................ 1
Measles................................ 1
Pneumonia, lobar...................... 1
Smallpox............................... 1

CAMP LEE ZONE, VA.

Cerebrospinal meningitis:
Petersburg............................. 1
Chicken pox:
Prince George County................ 2
Diphtheria:
Petersburg............................. 1
German measles:
Ettricks............................... 5
Petersburg............................. 1
Gonorrhea:
Petersburg............................. 2
Malaria:
Petersburg............................. 1
Measles:
Dinwiddie County...................... 1
Ettricks............................... 1
Hopewell.............................. 21
Petersburg............................ 10
Mumps:
City Point............................. 1
Ettricks.............................. 12
Hopewell.............................. 11
Petersburg 1
Prince George County................ 1
Pneumonia:
Ettricks............................... 2
Petersburg............................. 2
West Hopewell......................... 2
Septic sore throat:
Ettricks............................... 3
Petersburg............................. 2
Tuberculosis:
Petersburg............................. 3
Whooping cough:
Ettricks.............................. 10

CAMP LEWIS ZONE, WASH.

German measles:
Lakeview............................... 1
Roy................................... 5
Spanaway............................... 3
Steilacoom............................ 13
Pneumonia, lobar:
Lakeview............................... 1
Scarlet fever:
Lakeview............................... 3
Whooping cough:
Steilacoom Lake....................... 1

CAMP LOGAN ZONE, TEX.

Cerebrospinal meningitis:
Houston 1
Chancroids:
Houston 4
Chicken pox:
Moonshine Hill 1

CAMP LOGAN ZONE, TEX.—continued.

Diphtheria:
Houston............................... 4
German measles:
Houston............................... 9
Gonorrhea:
Goose Creek............................ 1
Houston.............................. 13
Moonshine Hill........................ 1
Malaria:
Moonshine Hill 1
Measles:
Goose Creek........................... 4
Houston.............................. 47
Moonshine Hill........................ 1
Laport................................ 9
Mumps:
Goose Creek............................ 2
Houston................................ 1
Moonshine Hill........................ 2
Pneumonia:
Houston 1
Pneumonia, lobar:
Moonshine Hill........................ 4
Smallpox:
Houston 1
Syphilis:
Houston.............................. 22
Westfield.............................. 1
Typhoid fever:
Goose Creek........................... 1
Laport................................ 1
Tuberculosis:
Houston 15
Westfield 4
Whooping cough:
Moonshine Hill........................ 1

CAMP MACARTHUR ZONE, TEX.

Waco:
Chicken pox 2
German measles........................ 3
Gonorrhea.............................. 1
Measles............................... 16
Mumps................................ 76
Scarlet fever 3
Tuberculosis 2
Typhoid fever.......................... 1
Whooping cough 9

CAMP M CLELLAN ZONE, ALA.

Chicken pox:
Anniston 8
Blue Mountain 1
Measles:
Anniston 2
Blue Mountain 2
Precinct One 1
Precinct Two 2
Mumps:
Anniston 6
Pneumonia:
Precinct Three 1
Smallpox:
Anniston 16
Precinct Two.......................... 1
Tuberculosis:
Anniston.............................. 8

NORFOLK COUNTY NAVAL DISTRICT, VA.

Cerebrospinal meningitis:
Portsmouth.................................. 1
Diphtheria:
Portsmouth.................................. 1
Measles:
Expo.. 1
Portsmouth.................................. 19
Pneumonia:
Port Norfolk................................ 1
Pinners Point............................... 1
South Norfolk............................... 1
Scarlet fever:
Pinners Point............................... 1
Portsmouth.................................. 4
Tuberculosis:
Portsmouth.................................. 1

FORT OGLETHORPE ZONE, GA.

Cerebrospinal meningitis:
Chattanooga................................. 1
Chicken pox:
Rossville, Ga............................... 2
Diphtheria:
Chattanooga................................. 1
German measles:
Dewberry Town, Ga........................... 1
Gonorrhea:
Lytle, Ga................................... 1
Measles:
Chattanooga................................. 1
East Chattanooga............................ 7
East Lake................................... 1
Mumps:
Chattanooga................................. 17
East Chattanooga............................ 4
East Lake................................... 2
Pneumonia:
East Lake................................... 4
Smallpox:
Chattanooga................................. 1
Scarlet fever:
Chickamauga Park, Ga........................ 1
Syphilis:
Chattanooga................................. 1
Tuberculosis:
Chattanooga................................. 1
Typhoid fever:
Alton Park.................................. 1
Chattanooga................................. 1
East Lake................................... 1
Whooping cough:
Chattanooga................................. 12
East Lake................................... 2

CAMP PIKE ZONE, ARK.

Cerebrospinal meningitis:
North Little Rock........................... 1
Sweet Home.................................. 1
Chancroid:
Little Rock................................. 3
Scotts...................................... 3
Chicken pox:
Little Rock................................. 1
Diphtheria:
Little Rock................................. 1
Scotts...................................... 1

CAMP PIKE ZONE, ARK.—continued.

German measles:
Little Rock................................. 1
Gonorrhea:
Little Rock................................. 23
North Little Rock........................... 6
Scotts...................................... 4
Malaria:
Little Rock................................. 51
North Little Rock........................... 3
Measles:
Little Rock................................. 0
Mumps:
Little Rock................................. 11
North Little Rock........................... 4
Pellagra:
Kerr.. 1
Scotts...................................... 1
Pneumonia:
Little Rock................................. 14
North Little Rock........................... 2
Toltec...................................... 1
Scarlet fever:
Little Rock................................. 5
North Little Rock........................... 1
Septic sore throat:
Scotts...................................... 1
Smallpox:
Jacksonville................................ 1
Little Rock................................. 14
North Little Rock........................... 1
Syphilis:
Little Rock................................. 9
North Little Rock........................... 1
Scotts...................................... 3
Trachoma:
Little Rock................................. 1
Tuberculosis:
Galloway.................................... 1
Kerr.. 1
Little Rock................................. 1
Scotts...................................... 1
Whooping cough:
Little Rock................................. 1

CAMP SEVIER ZONE, S. C.

Cerebrospinal meningitis:
Greenville Township......................... 1
Measles:
Chicksprings Township....................... 10
Greenville Township......................... 1
Pneumonia:
Chicksprings Township....................... 1
Smallpox:
Greenville Township......................... 1

CAMP SHELBY ZONE, MISS.

Hattiesburg:
Chicken pox................................. 2
Malaria..................................... 2
Measles..................................... 1
Mumps....................................... 5
Pneumonia................................... 1
Smallpox.................................... 2
Tuberculosis................................ 3
Whooping cough.............................. 2
Richburg, Lamar County:
Smallpox.................................... 4

CAMP SHERIDAN ZONE, ALA.

Chisholm:
Measles............................... 2

Montgomery:
Chicken pox........................... 1
Measles............................... 9
Mumps................................ 8
Scarlet fever......................... 1
Smallpox.............................. 4

CAMP SHERMAN ZONE, OHIO.

Chicken pox:
Scioto Township....................... 1
Diphtheria:
Chillicothe........................... 5
Scioto Township....................... 1
Measles:
Chillicothe........................... 14
Liberty Township...................... 6
Meningitis, tuberculous:
Liberty Township...................... 1
Scarlet fever:
Chillicothe........................... 5
Smallpox:
Chillicothe........................... 1
Trachoma:
Concord Township...................... 1

CAMP ZACHARY TAYLOR ZONE, KY.

Jefferson County:
Diphtheria............................ 1
German measles........................ 1
Measles............................... 1
Trachoma.............................. 12
Tuberculosis.......................... 1
Louisville:
Cerebrospinal meningitis.............. 2
Chicken pox........................... 4
Diphtheria............................ 8
Measles............................... 11
Rabies................................ 1
Scarlet fever......................... 2
Smallpox.............................. 5
Tuberculosis.......................... 10
Whooping cough........................ 3

TIDEWATER HEALTH DISTRICT, VA.

Chicken pox:
Newport News.......................... 2
Phoebus............................... 1
German measles:
Newport News.......................... 1
Phoebus............................... 1

TIDEWATER HEALTH DISTRICT VA.—continued.

Measles:
Hampton............................... 1
Newport News.......................... 15
Phoebus............................... 15
Mumps:
Hampton............................... 3
Pneumonia:
Phoebus............................... 4
Scarlet fever:
Hampton............................... 3
Smallpox:
Newport News.......................... 4
Tuberculosis:
Hampton............................... 1
Newport News.......................... 2

CAMP TRAVIS ZONE, TEX.

San Antonio:
Cerebrospinal meningitis.............. 1
Chicken pox........................... 1
Gonorrhea............................. 20
Malaria............................... 6
Measles............................... 7
Mumps................................. 15
Pneumonia............................. 7
Septic sore throat.................... 2
Syphilis.............................. 2
Tuberculosis.......................... 14
Typhoid fever......................... 1
Whooping cough........................ 1

CAMP WHEELER ZONE, GA.

Chicken pox:
Macon................................. 9
Diphtheria:
Macon................................. 4
German measles:
Macon................................. 3
Mumps:
East Macon............................ 5
Macon................................. 20
Pneumonia:
Macon................................. 3
Scarlet fever:
Bibb County........................... 2
Smallpox:
Macon................................. 4
Tuberculosis:
East Macon............................ 1
Macon................................. 2

DISEASE CONDITIONS AMONG TROOPS IN THE UNITED STATES.

The following data are taken from telegraphic reports received in the office of the Surgeon General, United States Army, for the week ended March 15, 1918:

Annual admission rate per 1,000 (disease only):

All troops	1,566.0
National Guard camps	975.1
National Army camps	2,075.0
Regular Army	1,279.1

Noneffective rate per 1,000 on day of report:

All troops	50.6
National Guard camps	40.2

Noneffective rate per 1,000 on day of report—Continued.

National Army camps	58.8
Regular Army	44.2

Annual death rate per 1,000 (disease only):

All troops	7.5
National Guard camps	4.2
National Army camps	9.1
Regular Army	7.9

New cases of special diseases reported during the week ended Mar. 15, 1918.

Camp.	Pneu-monia.	Dys-en-tery.	Ma-laria.	Venereal.	Measles.	Men-in-gitis.	Scar-let fever.	Deaths.	Annual admission rate per 1,000 (disease only).	Non-effective per 1,000 on day of report.
Wadsworth	9			21	9	1	2	2	590.0	22.7
Hancock	6			26	12		1	3	390.6	23.6
McClellan	4			19	17	1			814.2	30.3
Sevier	5			35				1	1,201.9	68.2
Wheeler	12	1	1	43				6	1,107.1	41.6
Logan	9		1	40	12	1			1,093.9	39.2
Cody	12			5		2		3	511.7	33.0
Doniphan	6			10	1		1	4	1,521.3	43.1
Bowie	14			34	2	2		2	1,616.7	59.2
Sheridan	1			62	1		1		573.8	25.5
Shelby				21				5	1,217.5	49.8
Beauregard	10		1	31	1	2		1	1,213.8	49.3
Kearney	3			2	1		7	1	1,172.7	49.7
Devens	17			33	9		6	3	1,381.2	41.3
Upton	27			63	5		1	15	1,855.3	35.6
Dix	11	2		27	13		6	2	3,075.0	53.5
Meade	30			21	2	2	24	5	929.8	36.0
Lee	11			124	5			6	1,686.3	60.8
Jackson	22	1		169	5	3	1	3	1,790.5	56.3
Gordon	7			133	10	1		4	1,533.6	42.8
Sherman	15			51	19		24	8	2,231.1	64.1
Taylor	20			17	30	2	2	5	1,968.5	70.4
Custer				12	1		3	1	1,040.0	48.7
Grant	19			19	13	2	28	1	878.2	31.5
Pike	11		11	148	20		12	7	3,320.7	79.6
Dodge	16			51	61		16	7	2,432.3	66.4
Funston	18		1	13	6	2	1	5	4,058.5	117.3
Travis	24		5	33	53			6	3,167.0	68.4
Lewis	7			35	41	1	25	3	1,875.5	83.5
Northeastern Department	3			32				1	1,075.7	34.1
Eastern Department	6			26	16	3		4	1,542.0	36.6
Southeastern Department	3			73	9	1	7	5	958.4	43.6
Central Department	13		1	29	19		17	4	1,693.3	45.0
Southern Department	9		1	102	22		11	7	1,040.7	40.2
Western Department	9			33	50	1	27	7	996.0	26.8
Aviation, Signal Corps	21	1	2	91	134	4	26	21	1,522.8	48.2
Camp Greene	9	1	2	42	22	1	6		696.5	23.5
Camp Fremont	1			28	9		2		1,072.9	45.9
El Paso				8	5		3		1,434.3	8.0
Columbus Barracks	2			23	2		3	1	2,079.3	55.5
Jefferson Barracks	5			96	6		4	1	2,006.0	121.5
Fort Logan	1			2	8		2		2,520.0	86.0
Fort McDowell				6	7		1	1	1,396.0	45.0
Fort Slocum	9			11	1			1	2,305.8	47.9
Fort Thomas	2			3				1	995.4	57.4
Disciplinary Barracks, Alcatraz									652.0	15.0
Disciplinary Barracks, Fort Leavenworth				3	1				1,486.0	34.0
A. A. Humphreys				5	1				1,111.0	11.1
J. E. Johnston			1	12	2	1			733.6	31.4

*New cases of special diseases reported during the week ended Mar. 15, 1918—*Continued.

Camp	Pneu-monia.	Dys-en-tery.	Ma-laria.	Venereal.	Measles.	Men-in-gitis.	Scar-let fever.	Deaths.	Annual admission rate per 1.000 (disease only).	Non-effective per 1,000 on day of report.
Camp Merritt..........	17	....	....	79	9	....	26	4	2,304.6	84.4
Camp Stuart..........	28	....	....	19	7	4	1	9	1,681.3	46.4
West Point, N. Y......				16				1	1,509.8	20.3
Edgewood.............				1				1	2,036.1	26.1
General hospitals......	3	....	....	28	7		1	3		
National Guard depart-ments..............	2	....	....	22	16	....	....			
National Army depart-ments..............	7	....	4	62	67	....	15	4		
Total............	496	6	31	2,136	795	37	312	184	[1] 1,566.0	[1] 30.6

[1] All troops.

Annual rate per 1,000 for special diseases.

	All troops in United States.[1]	Regulars in United States.[1]	National Guard, all camps.[1]	National Army, all camps.[1]	Expedi-tionary forces.[2]
Pneumonia...............................	21.0	16.9	14.1	29.5	36.5
Dysentery...............................	.2	.2	.1	.3	1.0
Malaria.................................	1.3	.8	.4	1.9	.4
Venereal................................	90.6	90.4	54.6	109.8	48.5
Measles.................................	33.7	43.6	8.7	33.9	16.2
Meningitis..............................	1.6	1.8	1.4	1.5	6.6
Scarlet fever...........................	13.2	16.3	1.9	17.2	21.2

[1] Week ended Mar. 15, 1918.   [2] Week ended Mar. 7, 1918.

CURRENT STATE SUMMARIES.

Alabama.

From Collaborating Epidemiologist Perry, by telegraph, for week ended March 23, 1918:

Smallpox: Greatly decreased. Meningitis: Colbert 3, Jefferson 3.

Arkansas.

From Collaborating Epidemiologist Garrison, by telegraph, for week ended March 23, 1918:

Smallpox: Scranton 2, Gurdon 1, Pine Bluff 5. Hot Springs 4, Dewitt 1, Croley 8, . Paris 2, Logan County 6, Phillips 2, Johnson 1, Drew 12, Perry 2, Jefferson 4, Sebastian 1, Franklin 2.   Malaria: Gurdon 8, Ouachita County 22, Drew 5, Perry 4, Jefferson 3, Sebastian 2.   Pellagra: Ouachita County 1, Perry 1, Gurdon 1.   Tuberculosis: Gurdon 1, Kingsland 1, Ouachita 6, Drew 1, Perry 2, Jefferson 2.   Typhoid: Gurdon 1, Sebastian 1, Ouachita 2.   Scarlet fever: Gurdon 2, Sebastian County 9.   Measles: Paris 12, Corley 7, Gurdon 7, Texarkana 1, Hot Springs 2, Sebastian 184, Perry 6, Drew 18, Johnson 4.   Whooping cough: Sebastian County 59, Perry 3, Ouachita 1, Gurdon 1.   Diphtheria: Jefferson 1, Kingsland 1.

California.

From the State Board of Health of California, by telegraph, for week ended March 23, 1918:

State-wide epidemic measles and German measles continues unabated. Diphtheria shows sharp increase, 79 cases, 32 of which are in Los Angeles; 26 cases smallpox, most of which are in San Francisco and Fresno County; 2 cases of leprosy, 1 San Francisco, 1 Los Angeles; 4 cases epidemic cerebrospinal meningitis, 2 in Contra Costa County, 1 San Francisco, 1 Stockton.

Reported by mail for preceding week (ended March 16):

Cerebrospinal meningitis	6	Pneumonia	66
Chicken pox	175	Ophthalmia neonatorum	3
Diphtheria	57	Scarlet fever	82
Dysentery	1	Smallpox	22
Erysipelas	10	Syphilis	95
German measles	332	Tetanus	1
Gonococcus infection	104	Trachoma	2
Malaria	3	Tuberculosis	142
Measles	1,461	Typhoid fever	11
Mumps	224	Whooping cough	110
Pellagra	1		

Connecticut.

From Collaborating Epidemiologist Black, by telegraph, for week ended March 23, 1918:

Smallpox: Hartford 3, New Britain 1. Meningitis: Hartford 1.

Illinois.

From the State Board of Health of Illinois, by telegraph, for week ended March 23, 1918:

Smallpox: New cases 160, prevalent Galesburg. Alton, Quincy, Granite City, Herrin, Odin. Chenoa, Peoria, Freeburg, Virden, Millstadt, Chicago, and rural sections southern State counties. Scarlet fever: One hundred and thirteen, of which 61 in Chicago. Dipththeria: One hundred and eighty-three, of which Chicago 138, Streator 10, Galesburg 5. Meningitis: Sixteen, of which Chicago 10, and 1 each Quincy, Springfield, East St. Louis, Westville, Winnebago County, and St. Charles Township (Kane County). Poliomyelitis: Four, of which 1 each Chicago, Wheaton, Lovington; Mackinaw. Measles: Increasing.

Indiana.

From the State Board of Health of Indiana, by telegraph, for week ended March 23, 1918:

Measles: Epidemic—Hardinsburg, Dublin, Athens, Rockport. Diphtheria: Epidemic—Fort Wayne, Wawaka; one death each, Evansville, Goshen. Smallpox: Epidemic—Fowlerton, Irondale, Muncie, Odon. Epidemic rabies, dogs, Bordon, Clark County, Evansville.

Kansas.

From Collaborating Epidemiologist Crumbine, by telegraph, for week ended March 23, 1918:

Meningitis: In cities—Coldwater 1, Colbin 4. Hoisington 1, Leavenworth 2. Towanda 1, Whiting 1, Wichita 1. Smallpox (10 or more cases): In cities—Hutchinson 10, Wichita 12; in counties—Allen 14, Cherokee 12. Lyon 10.

Louisiana.

From Collaborating Epidemiologist Dowling, by telegraph, for week ended March 23, 1918:

Meningitis: By parishes, Bienville 1, Caddo 1, Orleans 1, Richland 1. Poliomyelitis: Evangeline Parish 1.

Massachusetts.

From Collaborating Epidemiologist Kelley, by telegraph, for week ended March 23, 1918:

Unusual prevalence. Diphtheria: Wakefield 19. German measles: Danvers 12, Framingham 28, Newton 40. Measles: Beverly 93, Norwood 32, Quincy 65. Smallpox: Hardwick 1.

Minnesota.

From Collaborating Epidemiologist Bracken, by telegraph, for week ended March 23, 1918:

Smallpox, new foci: Blue Earth County, Beauford Township; Chippewa County, Crate Township; Fillmore County, Peterson village; Jackson County, La Rosse Township; Kittson County, Richardsville Township; Norman County, Bear Park Township; Rice County, Dennison village; each 1 case; Brown County, Leavenworth Township, 2; Pipestone County, Pipestone village, 4. Unusual prevalence scarlet fever Stearns County, St. Cloud City. Two cases cerebrospinal meningitis reported since March 18.

Nebraska.

From the State Board of Health of Nebraska, by telegraph, for week ended March 23, 1918:

Smallpox: Inman, Holdredge, Steinauer, Kearney, Bartlett, College View, Omaha, Lincoln, Johnson County, Otoe County. Scarlet fever: College View.

South Carolina.

From Collaborating Epidemiologist Hayne, by telegraph, for week ended March 23, 1918:

Six cases meningitis State at large.

Vermont.

From Collaborating Epidemiologist Dalton, by telegraph, for week ended March 23, 1918:

Smallpox: Barre 2. Epidemic meningitis: Colchester 1. No other outbreak or unusual prevalence.

Virginia.

From Collaborating Epidemiologist Traynham, by telegraph, for week ended March 23, 1918:

One case smallpox Northampton County. One case poliomyelitis James City County. Four cases cerebrospinal meningitis Norfolk County, 1 case Warwick County, 1 Fauquier County, 2 Bedford County.

Washington.

From Collaborating Epidemiologist Tuttle, by telegraph, for week ended March 23, 1918:

Seattle: Scarlet fever 21 cases. Tacoma: Slight decrease in scarlet fever, 43 cases reported during week. One case cerebrospinal meningitis Tacoma.

RECIPROCAL NOTIFICATION.

Massachusetts.

Cases of communicable diseases referred during February, 1918, to other State health departments by department of health of the State of Massachusetts.

Disease and local-ity of notification.	Referred to health authority of—	Why referred.
Scarlet fever: Mercersburg, Pa.	Massachusetts State Department of Health notified by Pennsylvania State Department of Health.	Scarlet fever outbreak in Mercersburg Academy, Mercersburg, Pa., and students left before they could be quarantined, for their homes in Massachusetts, as follows: Quincy, Dracut, Boston, Newton, Somerville, Worcester.
Burlington, Vt.	Massachusetts State Department of Health notified by Vermont State Board of Health.	Patient exposed to scarlet fever in Lawrence, Mass., Feb. 2, and later developed the disease.
Smallpox: Marlboro......	State department of health, Augusta, Me.	Patient came from Gardiner, Me., Jan. 24, and the disease was unrecognized. Later a case developed in a man who lived in the same house with the unrecognized case.
Tuberculosis: Camp Devens, Ayer.	State department of health, Hartford, Conn.	Rejected by Camp Devens, Ayer, Mass., on account of chronic pulmonary tuberculosis, to the following addresses: Waterbury, 2 cases; Bridgeport, 7 cases; Manchester, 1 case; Milford, 1 case; Hartford, 3 cases; Ansonia, 1 case; Norwich, 1 case; Meriden, 1 case; New Haven, 1 case.
Do........	State department of health, Augusta, Me.	Rejected by Camp Devens, Ayer, Mass., to the following addresses: Portland, 1 case; Lewiston, 1 case; Ellsworth, 1 case.
Worcester.....	.....do...............................	Rejected by local exemption board; intended address: Dennysville.
Camp Devens, Ayer.	State board of health, Lansing, Mich..	Rejected by Camp Devens; intended address: Detroit.
Do........	State board of health, Concord, N. H..	Rejected by Camp Devens, Ayer, Mass., to the following addresses: Manchester, 1 case; Hanover, 1 case.
Do........	State department of health, Trenton, N. J.	Rejected by Camp Devens, Ayer, Mass., intended address: East Orange.
Worcester.....	.....do...............................	Rejected by local exemption board; intended address: Trudeau Sanitarium, Trudeau.
Camp Devens, Ayer.	State department of health, Albany, N. Y.	Rejected by Camp Devens, Ayer, Mass.; intended addresses: Glen Falls, 2 cases, Johnstown, 1 case; New York City, 1 case;
Boston........	State department of health, Columbus, Ohio.	Patient reported with pulmonary tuberculosis. Home address: Dayton, Ohio.
Camp Devens, Ayer.	State department of health, Harrisburg, Pa.	Rejected by Camp Devens, Ayer, Mass.; intended address: Pittsburgh.
Do........	State board of health, Providence, R. I.	Rejected by Camp Devens, Ayer, Mass.; intended addresses: Providence, 1 case; Pawtucket, 1 case.
Taunton......	.....do...............................	Rejected by local exemption board; intended address: Providence.
Boston........	.....do...............................	Rejected by local exemption board; intended address: Providence.
Camp Devens, Ayer.	State board of health, Burlington, Vt..	Rejected by Camp Devens, Ayer, Mass.; intended addresses: Middlebury, 2 cases; Bennington, 2 cases.
Typhoid fever: Warwick......	State board of health, Concord, N. H..	Patient came from Hillsboro, N. H., where he was employed as a mill hand.
Williamstown.	State department of health, Albany, N. Y.	Patient reported as typhoid fever by Williamstown, Feb. 4. Taken to Troy, N. Y., Jan. 31.

Minnesota.

Cases of communicable diseases referred during February. 1918. to other State health departments by the department of health of the State of Minnesota.

Disease and locality of notification.	Referred to health authority of -	Why referred.
Epidemic cerebrospinal meningitis:		
Minneapolis City Hospital, Hennepin County.	Phillips Lumber Camp, Phillips, Rice County, Wis.	Laborer at camp when taken sick. Meningococci found in spinal fluid.
Smallpox:		
Aurdal Township, Ottertail County.	Waverly, Bremer County, Iowa.....	Visited at Waverly, Iowa, where smallpox was prevalent. Developed smallpox after return home, and infected rest of family (6 members).
Minneapolis Health Department, Hennepin County.	Miles City, Custer County, Mont....	Worked as news agent running into Miles City, Mont., for a week after first symptoms.
	New York City, New York County, N. Y.	Stopped at New York hotel while in infective stage.
	Fargo, Cass County, N. Dak.........	Traveling film agent stopped at home of relative in Fargo while in infective stage.

ANTHRAX.

Massachusetts.

During the months of January and February, 1918, 5 cases of anthrax were notified in Massachusetts. Three of the cases occurred in persons handling raw wool and 2 cases were in handlers of hides.

CEREBROSPINAL MENINGITIS.

State Reports for January and February, 1918.

Place.	New cases reported.	Place.	New cases reported.
Alabama (Jan. 1 31):		Louisiana (Feb 1-28)—Continued.	
Calhoun County.....................	9	Washington Parish................	1
Jefferson County.....................	1	Winn Parish.	1
Lee County	1		
Marshall County.....................	1	Total.......................	31
Mobile County.....................	1		
Montgomery County.................	4	Maryland (Feb. 1-28):	
Morgan County.....................	1	Baltimore........	23
Talladega County...................	1	Baltimore County—	
Tuscaloosa County...................	3	Mount Pleasant...............	1
		Highlandtown................	2
Total............	22		
		Total.................	26
Connecticut (Feb. 1 28):		Massachusetts (Feb. 1-28):	
Fairfield County		Berkshire County-	
Bridgeport.....................	2	Pittsfield...............	1
Stamford.....................	1	Bristol County—	
New Haven County—		Fall River.................	2
Ansonia....	1	New Bedford.................	1
New Haven.....................	4	Hampden County—	
Orange.....................	1	Springfield.................	1
Wallingford.....................	1	Hampshire County—	
		Easthampton (town)	1
Total.....................	10	Middlesex County—	
		Cambridge................	1
District of Columbia (Feb. 1 28).........	32	Lowell....................	4
		Medford.................	1
Louisiana (Feb. 1 28):		Wayland (town).............	1
Allen Parish......	1	Norfolk County—	
Bienville Parish...................	4	Holbrook (town).............	1
Caddo Parish...................	4	Plymouth County –	
De Soto Parish	3	Hanson (town).............	1
Franklin Parish...................	1	Suffolk County —	
Jackson Parish...................	1	Boston....................	12
Lafayette Parish...................	1	Chelsea...................	2
Madison Parish	1	Worcester County —	
Orleans Parish.	13	Leominster..................	1
Ouachita Parish.	1	Worcester	4
Rapides Parish	1		
Vermilion Parish	2	Total	37

CEREBROSPINAL MENINGITIS—Continued.

State Reports for January and February, 1918—Continued.

Place.	New cases reported.	Place.	New cases reported.
Minnesota (Feb. 1-28):		Virginia (Jan. 1-31)—Continued.	
Hennepin County—		Halifax County.....................	2
Minneapolis.....................	5	Henry County.....................	1
St. Louis County—		King William County................	2
Virginia.........................	1	Lee County........................	2
Stearns County—		Mecklenburg County................	1
St. Joseph.......................	1	Norfolk County....................	5
		Norfolk........................	12
Total......................	7	Patrick County....................	1
		Pittsylvania County................	1
Ohio (Feb. 1-28):		Prince George County..............	1
Allen County....................	1	Princess Anne County..............	9
Butler County...................	1	Pulaski County....................	1
Clark County....................	1	Rockingham County................	2
Crawford County.................	1	Scott County......................	3
Cuyahoga County.................	5	Warwick County—	
Franklin County.................	4	Newport News................	3
Erie County.....................	1		
Greene County...................	4	Total..................	53
Hamilton County.................	1		
Hancock County..................	1	Washington (Jan. 1-31):	
Jefferson County.................	1	Pierce County.....................	1
Mahoning County.................	2	Spokane County—	
Montgomery County...............	8	Spokane......................	1
Pickaway County.................	1		
Ross County.....................	6	Total......................	2
Stark County....................	4		
Summit County...................	3	Wisconsin (Feb. 1-28):	
Trumbull County.................	1	Door County......................	1
Van Wert County.................	1	Forest County.....................	1
		Green Lake County................	1
Total......................	47	Iowa County......................	1
		Milwaukee County.................	8
Virginia (Jan. 1-31):		Rock County......................	1
Alexandria County...............	2	Waukesha County..................	1
Chesterfield County..............	3		
Fauquier County.................	1	Total......................	14
Floyd County—			
Floyd.........................	1		

City Reports for Week Ended Mar. 9, 1918.

Place.	Cases.	Deaths.	Place.	Cases.	Deaths.
Alexandria, La.................	1	1	Lowell, Mass..................	1	....
Anniston, Ala..................	1	....	Macon, Ga....................	1	....
Atlanta, Ga....................	2	4	Madison, Wis.................		1
Augusta, Ga...................	6	1	McKeesport, Pa...............	1	....
Austin, Tex...................	1	1	Memphis, Tenn................	1	....
Baltimore, Md.................	2	2	Milwaukee, Wis...............	1	....
Bayonne, N. J.................	1	....	Minneapolis, Minn............	1	1
Birmingham, Ala..............	5	1	Montgomery, Ala.............	2	1
Boston, Mass.................	3	4	Nanticoke, Pa.................	1	....
Buffalo, N. Y.................	....	1	Nashville, Tenn...............	1	....
Cambridge, Mass..............	1	....	Newark, N. J..................	3	2
Charleston, S. C..............		1	New Orleans, La..............	3	3
Charleston, W. Va.............		1	New York, N. Y...............	13	9
Chattanooga, Tenn............	4	....	Niagara Falls, N. Y............		1
Chicago, Ill..................	10	6	Norfolk, Va...................	2	1
Cincinnati, Ohio..............	1	1	North Little Rock, Ark........	1	....
Cleveland, Ohio...............	3	2	Omaha, Nebr..................	2	....
Columbia, S. C...............	1	....	Passaic, N. J..................	1	....
Columbus, Ohio...............	1	....	Petersburg, Va................		1
Dallas, Tex...................	....	2	Philadelphia, Pa..............	5	10
Detroit, Mich.................	3	....	Providence, R. I..............	2	2
East Orange, N. J.............	1	....	St. Louis, Mo.................	5	....
Fall River, Mass..............	1	....	Salem, Mass..................	1	....
Hattiesburg, Miss.............	1	....	Springfield, Ill...............	2	....
Indianapolis, Ind.............	2	....	Springfield, Ohio.............		1
Jacksonville, Fla..............		1	Stockton, Cal.................	1	....
Kansas City, Kans............	4	1	Tacoma, Wash................	1	....
La Fayette, Ind...............	2	....	Toledo, Ohio.................	1	1
Lexington, Ky................	1	....	Troy, N. Y...................	1	1
Little Rock, Ark..............	1	2	Washington, D. C.............	3	....
Los Angeles, Cal..............	1	....	Wichita, Kans................	1	....

33

DIPHTHERIA.

See Diphtheria, measles, scarlet fever, and tuberculosis, page 468.

ERYSIPELAS.

City Reports for Week Ended Mar. 9, 1918.

Place.	Cases.	Deaths.	Place.	Cases.	Deaths.
Akron, Ohio	1		Minneapolis, Minn		1
Baltimore, Md	1	1	Newark, N. J	10	
Buffalo, N. Y	3		New York, N. Y		7
Charleston, S. C		1	Oklahoma City, Okla	3	1
Chicago, Ill	17	4	Omaha, Nebr	1	
Cleveland, Ohio	8		Petersburg, Va	1	
Cumberland, Md	1		Philadelphia, Pa	5	
Detroit, Mich	3	2	Pittsburgh, Pa	8	1
Duluth, Minn	1		Quincy, Ill		1
Fall River, Mass		1	Reading, Pa	1	1
Flint, Mich	1		Richmond, Va	1	
Fort Smith, Ark		1	Rochester, N. Y	2	
Fort Wayne, Ind	1		St. Louis, Mo	6	2
Green Bay, Wis		1	St. Paul, Minn	3	
Hartford, Conn	4		Salt Lake City, Utah		1
Jackson, Mich	1		San Diego, Cal	1	
Jacksonville, Fla	2		San Francisco, Cal	3	1
Lancaster, Pa	1		Toledo, Ohio		1
Lincoln, Nebr	1		Troy, N. Y	1	
Los Angeles, Cal	3		Wichita, Kans	1	
Louisville, Ky		1	Williamsport, Pa	1	
Milwaukee, Wis	3		Yonkers, N. Y		1

LEPROSY.

Connecticut—West Haven.

During the month of February, 1918, a case of leprosy was notified at West Haven, Conn., in the person of G. C., Italian, aged 21 years, male, who had lived at West Haven for a period of 6 months, had previously lived in New Haven and Bristol, Conn., and has been in the United States for 4 years and 8 months. The patient has been isolated at New Haven.

City Reports for Week Ended Mar. 9, 1918.

There were reported during the week ended March 9, 1918, one case of leprosy at New Orleans, La., and one death at New York, N. Y.

MALARIA.

State Reports for January and February, 1918.

Place.	New cases reported.	Place.	New cases reported.
Alabama (Feb. 1-28):		Alabama (Feb. 1-28)—Continued.	
Barbour County	1	Madison County	1
Butler County	1	Perry County	1
Cherokee County	1	Pickens County	1
Dallas County	1	Sumter County	1
Houston County	20	Talladega County	1
Jefferson County	5	Tuscaloosa County	1
Lamar County	1		
Limestone County	2	Total	36

MALARIA—Continued.

State Reports for January and February, 1918—Continued.

Place.	New cases reported.	Place.	New cases reported.
Louisiana (Feb. 1-28):		**Virginia—Continued.**	
Acadia Parish	1	Chesterfield County	1
Avoyelles Parish	1	Winterpock	3
Concordia Parish	2	Cumberland County	2
De Soto Parish	1	Fluvanna County	1
East Feliciana Parish	2	Franklin County	40
Ouachita Parish	2	Gloucester County	4
Rapides Parish	1	Greensville County	5
St. John Parish	1	Emporia	5
St. Landry Parish	5	North Emporia	5
Tensas Parish	2	Halifax County	9
Vermilion Parish	2	South Boston	2
West Feliciana Parish	2	Henrico County	4
		Isle of Wight County	6
Total	22	James City County	2
		King and Queen County	4
		King George County	2
Maryland (Feb. 1-28):		King William County	4
Anne Arundel County—		Lunenburg County	2
Camp Meade	1	Mecklenburg County	1
Washington County—		Middlesex County	1
Hagerstown	1	Nansemond County	1
		Suffolk	2
Total	2	Northampton County	10
		Northumberland County	8
		Pittsylvania County	2
Massachusetts (Feb. 1-28):		Powhatan County	4
Middlesex County—		Prince Edward County	1
Cambridge	1	Prince George County	3
		Hopewell	1
		Rockingham County—	
Virginia (Jan. 1-31):		Dayton	2
Accomac County	15	Stafford County	4
Albemarle County	1	Surry County	2
Augusta County—		Sussex County	22
Staunton	1	Washington County	1
Buckingham County	3	Westmoreland County	2
Campbell County	1		
Caroline County	2	Total	193
Charles City County	2		

City Reports for Week Ended Mar. 9, 1918.

Place.	Cases.	Deaths.	Place.	Cases.	Deaths.
Birmingham, Ala	1	1	Jackson, Miss	3	
Charlotte, N. C	4		Little Rock, Ark	3	
Detroit, Mich	1		New Orleans, La	1	
Hattiesburg, Miss	2		North Little Rock, Ark	1	1

MEASLES.

See Diphtheria, measles, scarlet fever, and tuberculosis, page 468.

PELLAGRA.

State Reports for January and February, 1918.

Place.	New cases reported.	Place.	New cases reported.
Alabama (Jan. 1-31):		**Alabama—Continued.**	
Barbour County	1	Marion County	1
Butler County	1	Mobile County	11
Calhoun County	2	Montgomery County	3
Cherokee County	1	Pickens County	1
Etowah County	3	Talladega County	1
Hale County	1	Tallapoosa County	1
Houston County	1	Tuscaloosa County	9
Jackson County	1		
Jefferson County	14	Total	57
Madison County	5		

PELLAGRA—Continued.

State Reports for January and February, 1918—Continued.

Place.	New cases reported.	Place.	New cases reported.
Louisiana (Feb. 1-28):		Virginia—Continued.	
Cadde Parish	1	Augusta County	1
East Baton Rouge Parish	1	Staunton	1
Lafourche Parish	1	Elisabeth City County	1
Orleans Parish	3	Hampton	1
Red River Parish	1	Grayson County	1
Vernon Parish	2	Henry County	1
		Pittsylvania County	1
Total	9	Rockbridge County	1
Virginia (Jan. 1-31):		Total	9
Amherst County	1		

City Reports for Week Ended Mar. 9, 1918.

Place.	Cases.	Deaths.	Place.	Cases.	Deaths.
Atlanta, Ga		2	Macon, Ga	1	
Birmingham, Ala	1		Memphis, Tenn		1
Charleston, S. C			Minneapolis, Minn		4
Charlotte, N. C		3	Nashville, Tenn	1	
Chicago, Ill		1	New York, N. Y		1
Dallas, Tex		1	Petersburg, Va	1	
Jackson, Miss	2		Wilmington, N. C		1
Lexington, Ky		1	Winston-Salem, N. C	2	1
Little Rock, Ark		2			

PNEUMONIA.

City Reports for Week Ended Mar. 9, 1918.

Place.	Cases.	Deaths.	Place.	Cases.	Deaths.
Akron, Ohio	1		Los Angeles, Cal	19	9
Allentown, Pa	7		Lowell, Mass	2	5
Altoona, Pa	6		Lynn, Mass	10	7
Anniston, Ala	3		Manchester, N. H	4	4
Atlanta, Ga	6	3	McKeesport, Pa	1	
Baltimore, Md	66	27	Medford, Mass	1	
Boston, Mass	39	38	Morristown, N. J	2	
Bridgeport, Conn	2	11	Newark, N. J	61	11
Brockton, Mass	5	1	New Bedford, Mass	3	4
Brookline, Mass	1	1	Newburyport, Mass	1	1
Cambridge, Mass	1	1	New Castle, Pa	1	
Charleston, W. Va	1	1	Newport, Ky	4	
Chattanooga, Tenn	2	3	Newton, Mass	6	2
Chelsea, Mass	3	1	North Little Rock, Ark	1	1
Chicago, Ill	287	145	Oakland, Cal	1	11
Chillicothe, Ohio	1		Petersburg, Va	4	3
Cleveland, Ohio	36	13	Philadelphia, Pa	142	76
Cranston, R. I	1	1	Pittsburgh, Pa	26	31
Cumberland, Md	2		Pittsfield, Mass	2	3
Detroit, Mich	10	40	Providence, R. I	1	10
Duluth, Minn	8	3	Reading, Pa	1	3
Elmira, N. Y	3	3	Rochester, N. Y	23	6
Erie, Pa	8	2	Sacramento, Cal	3	
Everett, Mass	3	1	Salem, Mass	1	
Fall River, Mass	7	1	San Diego, Cal	14	1
Flint, Mich	4	4	Sandusky, Ohio	2	2
Grand Rapids, Mich	5	1	San Francisco, Cal	29	17
Harrisburg, Pa	2	4	Schenectady, N. Y	3	1
Harrison, N. J	2		Somerville, Mass	9	4
Hattiesburg, Miss	4	1	Springfield, Mass	5	4
Holyoke, Mass	2	1	Springfield, Ohio	2	2
Jamestown, N. Y	1	1	Stockton, Cal	7	
Kalamazoo, Mich	3		Waco, Tex	6	
Lawrence, Mass	3	2	Waltham, Mass	4	
Lexington, Ky	1	5	Wichita, Kans	13	
Lincoln, Nebr	2		Worcester, Mass	6	6
Little Rock, Ark	11	2	York, Pa	3	
Lorain, Ohio	1				

POLIOMYELITIS (INFANTILE PARALYSIS).

State Reports for January and February, 1918.

Place.	New cases reported.	Place.	New cases reported.
Alabama (Jan. 1-31):		Ohio (Feb. 1-28):	
Calhoun County....................	1	Franklin County.................	1
Jefferson County..................	1	Licking County..................	1
		Stark County....................	1
Total......................	2	Trumbull County.................	1
		Washington County...............	1
Connecticut (Feb. 1-28):			
Hartford County—		Total......................	5
Bristol......................	1		
New Haven County—		Virginia (Jan. 1-31):	
New Haven...................	1	Wise County....................	1
Total......................	2	Washington (Jan. 1-31):	
		King County....................	1
Massachusetts (Feb. 1-28):		Kittitas County—	
Essex County—		Ellensburg..................	1
Haverhill...................	1	Pierce County—	
Middlesex County—		Tacoma.....................	1
Dracut (town)...............	1		
Somerville..................	1	Total......................	3
Total......................	3	West Virginia (Feb. 1-28):	
		Harrison County................	1
Minnesota (Feb. 1-28):			
Olmstead County—		Wisconsin (Feb. 1-28):	
Rochester...................	1	Milwaukee County...............	13
Washington County—		Waupaca County.................	1
Stillwater..................	1		
		Total......................	14
Total......................	2		

City Reports for Week Ended Mar. 9, 1918.

Place.	Cases.	Deaths.	Place.	Cases.	Deaths.
Baltimore, Md.................	2	2	Milwaukee, Wis...............	6	1
Chicago, Ill...................	3	1	St. Louis, Mo................	1	....
Cleveland, Ohio...............	1	....	San Jose, Cal................	1	....
Columbus, Ohio...............	....	1			

RABIES IN ANIMALS.

City Reports for Week Ended Mar. 9, 1918.

During the week ended March 9, 1918, there were reported one case of rabies in animals at Detroit, Mich., one at St. Paul, Minn., and two at Toledo, Ohio.

RABIES IN MAN.

Texas—Galveston.

On March 20, 1918, a case of rabies in a colored boy, C. J., 9 years of age, was reported at Galveston, Tex. The patient was bitten by a dog February 28 and died March 19, 1918.

SCARLET FEVER.

See Diphtheria, measles, scarlet fever, and tuberculosis, page 468.

SMALLPOX.

Indiana—Newcastle.

During the period from March 15 to 21, 1918, 3 cases of smallpox were notified at Newcastle, Ind.

Missouri—Kansas City.

During the period from March 18 to 25, 1918, 87 cases of smallpox were notified at St. Louis, Mo.

State Reports for February, 1918.

Place	New cases reported.	Deaths.	Vaccination history of cases.			
			Number vaccinated within 7 years preceding attack.	Number last vaccinated more than 7 years preceding attack.	Number never successfully vaccinated.	Vaccination history not obtained or uncertain.
District of Columbia..............	2				2	
Maryland:						
Baltimore.............	5				5	
Allegany County—						
Cumberland............	4				4	
Baltimore County—						
Orangeville............	1				1	
Highlandtown..........	2				2	
Total...................	12				12	
Massachusetts:						
Middlesex County—						
Lowell.................	1				1	
Marlborough...........	1				1	
Total...................	2				2	
Michigan:						
Alcona County—						
Black River Township....	1				1	
Alger County—						
Au Train Township......	1				1	
Alpena County—						
Ossineki Township.....	1				1	
Wellington Township.....	4				4	
Alpena..............	7				7	
Antrim County—						
Banks Township.........	3				3	
Central Lake........	7				7	
Arenac County—						
Mason Township.....	5				5	
Bay County—						
Pinconning Township.....	5				5	
Bay City............	1					1
Barry County—						
Barry Township..	2				2	
Rutland Township.......	2				2	
Middleville...........	1					1
Hastings.................	23				23	
Niles..............	13				13	
Branch County—						
Mattison Township......	1				1	
Coldwater..—.....	1				1	
Colburn County—						
Bedford Township......	1					1
Claredon Township......	1					1
Marshall Township......	1					1
Albion............	1				1	
Battle Creek........	5				5	
Marshall............	1				1	
Cass County—						
Cassopolis............	1					1
Dowagiac..............	3				2	1

SMALLPOX—Continued.

State Reports for February, 1918—Continued.

Place.	New cases reported.	Deaths.	Vaccination history of cases.			
			Number vaccinated within 7 years preceding attack.	Number last vaccinated more than 7 years preceding attack.	Number never successfully vaccinated.	Vaccination history not obtained or uncertain.
Michigan—Continued.						
Charlevoix County—						
East Jordan............	6				6	
Chippewa County—						
Sault Ste. Marie.........	1			1		
Clare County—						
Freeman Township......	1					1
Clinton County—						
Duplain Township.......	1					1
Eaton County—						
Benton Township........	2				2	
Oneida Township.........	1				1	
Genesee County—						
Flint Township...........	1					1
Richland Township.......	1				1	
Vienna Township........	6				6	
Clio.....................	5				5	
Flint....................	30				30	
Gratiot County—						
Wheeler Township......	1				1	
Hillsdale County—						
Adams Township........	3				3	
Allen Township..........	1				1	
Cambria Township......	3				3	
Hillsdale Township......	3				3	
Ransom Township.......	1				1	
Scipo Township.........	4				4	
Hillsdale...............	35				35	
Huron County—						
Dwight Township.......	4				4	
Fair Haven Township....	3				3	
Huron Township........	1					1
Port Austin Township....	1				1	
Harbor Beach..........	1				1	
Ingham County—						
Lansing Township........	6				6	
Locke Township.........	4				4	
Williamston Township....	1				1	
Webberville............	1				1	
Williamston.............	3				3	
East Lansing............	2				2	
Lansing................	4				4	
Ionia County—						
North Plains Township...	1				1	
Belding................	1				1	
Iosco County—						
Oscoda Township........	15				15	
Sherman Township......	3				3	
Au Sable...............	1				1	
Isabella County—						
Chippewa Township......	7				6	1
Mount Pleasant........	1				1	
Jackson County—						
Henrietta Township......	1				1	
Jackson................	3				3	
Kalamazoo County—						
Kalamazoo Township.....	2				2	
Bangor.................	1				1	
Kalkaska County—						
Clear Water Township....	1			1		
Rapid River Township....	5				5	
Kent County—						
Gratton Township........	2				2	
Sparta Township........	2			1	1	
Vergennes Township.....	1				1	
Walker Township........	3				3	
Grand Rapids...........	35				35	
Lake County—						
Chase Township.........	6				6	
Cherry Valley Township..	2				2	
Pinvia Township........	3				2	1

SMALLPOX—Continued.

State Reports for February, 1918—Continued.

Place.	New cases reported.	Deaths.	Number vaccinated within 7 years preceding attack.	Number last vaccinated more than 7 years preceding attack.	Number never successfully vaccinated.	Vaccination history not obtained or uncertain.
Michigan—Continued.						
Lapeer County—						
Oregon Township	1				1	
Almont	1				1	
Leelanau County—						
Leelanau Township	1				1	
Lenawee County—						
Adrian Township	9				9	
Macon Township	1				1	
Tecumseh Township	1				1	
Tecumseh	2			1	1	
Livingston County—						
Iosco Township	3				3	
Mackinac County—						
Newton Township	1				1	
Macomb County—						
Sterling Township	2				2	
Mount Clemens	4				4	
Marquette County—						
Marquette	7				7	
Mason County—						
Hamlin Township	1			1		
Riverton Township	4				4	
Victory Township	2				2	
Ludington	2				2	
Mecosta County—						
Big Rapids	3				3	
Missaukee County—						
Aetna Township	2				2	
Bloomfield Township	1				1	
Caldwell Township	5				5	
Norwich Township	4				4	
Monroe County—						
Bedford Township	1				1	
Monroe Township	2				1	1
Monroe	5				5	
Montcalm County—						
Howard City	1				1	
Greenville	1				1	
Muskegon County—						
Norton Township	1				4	
Ravenna Township	1				1	
Muskegon Township	3				3	
Muskegon Heights	6				6	
Muskegon	16				16	
Newaygo County—						
Big Prairie Township	6				6	
Croton Township	2				1	1
Dayton Township	3				3	
Sheridan Township	7				6	1
Fremont	7			1	6	
Oakland County—						
Avon Township	2				2	
Bloomfield Township	4				4	
Rose Township	1					1
Waterford Township	2				2	
Rochester	5				5	
Pontiac	31			2	29	
Oceana County—						
Crystal Township	19				19	
Elbridge Township	1				1	
Grant Township	1				1	
Ogemaw County—						
Richland Township	4				2	-
Otsego County—						
Vanderbilt	1				1	
Ottawa County—						
Crockery Township	3				3	
Holland Township	1				1	
Wright Township	1				1	

SMALLPOX—Continued.

State Reports for February, 1918—Continued.

Place.	New cases reported.	Deaths.	Vaccination history of cases.			
			Number vaccinated within 7 years preceding attack.	Number last vaccinated more than 7 years preceding attack.	Number never successfully vaccinated.	Vaccination history not obtained or uncertain.
Michigan—Continued.						
Presque Isle County—						
Belknap Township.......	2				2	
Saginaw County—						
Birch Run Township....	1				1	
Saginaw...............	9				9	
St. Clair County—						
Clyde Township........	11				11	
Cotterville Township....	2				2	
Emmett Township......	1				1	
Kenockee Township....	2				2	
Kimball Township......	1				1	
St. Clair Township......	2				2	
Port Huron............	8				8	
St. Joseph County—						
Fabius Township.......	8				8	
Mendon Township......	1				1	
Sanilac County—						
Bridgehampton Township	2				2	
Elmer Township........	1				1	
Carsonville...........	3				3	
Peck...............	1				1	
Schoolcraft County—						
Hiawatha Township....	1				1	
Shiawassee County—						
Vernon Township.......	1				1	
Tuscola County—						
Almer Township........	1					1
Tuscola Township.......	1					1
Vassar Township.......	10				10	
Akron...............	3				3	
Kingston..............	4				4	
Vassar................	2				2	
Washtenaw County—						
Augusta Township.......	4				4	
Freedom Township......	1				1	
Saline Township.......	4				4	
Chelsea..............	1				1	
Ann Arbor.............	3				3	
Wayne County—						
Brownstown Township..	1					1
Grosse Isle Township....	1					1
Monguagon Township....	1					1
Romulus Township......	1					1
Ford...............	1				1	
Hamtramck............	3				3	
Highland Park.........	9				9	
Redford.............	1				1	
St. Clair Heights........	15				15	
Detroit..............	210				209	
Wyandotte............	1				1	
Wexford County—						
Clam Lake Township.....	4				4	
Henderson Township....	3				3	
South Branch Township..	5				4	1
Cadillac..............	15				15	
Total..................	**885**			**8**	**852**	**25**
Minnesota:						
Aitkin County—						
Solana Township........	1				1	
Williams Township.....	1				1	
Beltrami County—						
Zippel Township........	1				1	
Cass County—						
Pine River............	2				1	1
Maple Township........	1				1	
Clay County—						
Moorhead............	1				1	
Crow Wing County—						
Brainerd..............	10			1	9	
Pequot...............	5				4	1

SMALLPOX—Continued.

State Reports for February, 1918—Continued.

Place.	New cases reported.	Deaths.	Number vaccinated within 7 years preceding attack.	Number last vaccinated more than 7 years preceding attack.	Number never successfully vaccinated.	Vaccination history not obtained or uncertain.
Minnesota—Continued.						
Dakota County—						
South St. Paul	1				1	
Dodge County—						
Canister Township	1				1	
Douglas County—						
Alexandria	1				1	
Osakis	1					1
Fillmore County—						
Rushford	1				1	
Arendahl Township	3			2	1	
Bloomfield Township	1				1	
Norway Township	2				2	
Sumner Township	1				1	
Freeborn County—						
London Township	1				1	
Moscow Township	9				9	
Goodhue County—						
Red Wing	5				5	
Grant County						
Land Township	1				1	
Hennepin County						
Dayton	1				1	
Minneapolis	105		1	7	97	
Osseo	2				2	
Rogers	3				3	
Corcoran Township	3				3	
Maple Grove Township	5				5	
Houston County—						
Black Hammer Township	2				2	
Jackson County—						
Jackson	1				1	
Kanabec County—						
Grass Lake Township	4		1		3	
Kittson County—						
Hallock	1				1	
Lac qui Parle County—						
Baxter Township	1				1	
Marshall County—						
Moylan Township	1				1	
Martin County—						
Fairmont	1				1	
Meeker County—						
Litchfield	6		2	1	3	
Mower County—						
Austin	1				1	
Lyle	9				9	
Lansing Township	2				2	
Leroy Township	1				1	
Murray County—						
Cameron Township	1				1	
Nicollet County—						
St. Peter	1				1	
Olmsted County						
Rochester	5				5	
Pennington County						
Thief River Falls	2				2	
Pine County						
Hinckley	1					
Polk County						
Climax	1					
Fertile	1					1
Garfield Township	1			1		
Ramsey County						
St. Paul	25				25	
Renville County						
Buffalo Lake	1					
Rice County						
Faribault	1					
Northfield	1				1	
Rock County—						
Luverne Township	2				2	

SMALLPOX—Continued.

State Reports for February, 1918—Continued.

Place.	New cases reported.	Deaths.	Vaccination history of cases.			
			Number vaccinated within 7 years preceding attack.	Number last vaccinated more than 7 years preceding attack.	Number never successfully vaccinated.	Vaccination history not obtained or uncertain.
Minnesota—Continued						
Roseau County—						
Roseau	3				3	
St. Louis County—						
Duluth	4				4	
Proctor	2				2	
Virginia	2			1	1	
Sibley County—						
Gibbon	1				1	
Stearns County—						
St. Cloud	1				1	
Sauk Center	13				13	
Todd County—						
Gordon Township	4				4	
Wadena County—						
Meadow Township	2				2	
Washington County—						
Stillwater	2				2	
Watonwan County—						
Madelia	2				2	
Winona County—						
St. Charles	1				1	
Utica	5				5	
Yellow Medicine County—						
Friendship Township	2				2	
Total	295		4	14	273	4
Ohio:						
Adams County	15				8	
Allen County	44			3	41	
Athens County	7				5	2
Auglaize County	1				1	
Brown County	5					5
Butler County	52				51	1
Carroll County	1					
Champaign County	1					1
Clark County	4				2	2
Clinton County	2				2	
Columbiana County	13			1	10	2
Coshocton County	8				3	5
Crawford County	9				7	2
Cuyahoga County	222				74	148
Darke County	5				5	
Defiance County	2				1	
Erie County	6		1		4	1
Fairfield County	14			2	5	7
Fayette County	10				5	5
Franklin County	54			1	48	5
Fulton County	6				2	4
Gallia County	7				5	1
Greene County	49			1	48	
Guernsey County	9				3	6
Hamilton County	60				54	6
Hancock County	18			3	9	6
Henry County	61				51	10
Highland County	8			1	7	
Hocking County	23					23
Holmes County	18			1	10	7
Jackson County	8					8
Jefferson County	4				1	3
Knox County	6					6
Lawrence County	20				7	13
Licking County	7				5	2
Logan County	3				2	1
Lorain County	15				14	1
Lucas County	57		1	1	22	3
Madison County	1				1	
Mahoning County	2				1	1
Medina County	2				2	
Meigs County	2				1	1
Mercer County	12				10	2

SMALLPOX—Continued.

State Reports for February, 1918—Continued.

Place.	New cases reported.	Deaths.	Vaccination history of cases.			
			Number vaccinated within 7 years preceding attack.	Number last vaccinated more than 7 years preceding attack.	Number never successfully vaccinated.	Vaccination history not obtained or uncertain.
Ohio—Continued.						
Miami County	13			1	7	5
Montgomery County	41				34	7
Morgan County	8					8
Muskingum County	2				1	1
Ottawa County	1				1	
Paulding County	1					1
Perry County	25				1	24
Pickaway County	5					5
Pike County	2					2
Portage County	2				2	
Treble County	6				6	
Putnam County	5				4	1
Madison County	7				5	1
Sandusky County	3			1	1	2
Scioto County	65			1	56	8
Seneca County	6				6	
Shelby County	11			1	7	3
Stark County	28				6	22
Summit County	127				35	92
Trumbull County	5				3	2
Tuscarawas County	23				13	10
Union County	1				1	
Van Wert County	4					4
Vinton County	21				7	13
Warren County	24			1	23	
Wayne County	19				7	12
Williams County	8				6	2
Wood County	5					5
Total	1,341		2	22	730	538
Wisconsin:						
Ashland County	3		1	1	1	
Bayfield County	7			1	6	
Brown County	7					1
Buffalo County	7				6	
Chippewa	7			1	5	2
Clark County	2				2	
Crawford County	9				8	
Dane County	16		1		8	
Dodge County	16		16			
Douglas County	1				1	
Dunn County	2				2	
Forest County	5		5			
Grant County	10		1	1	8	2
Green County	2					2
Juneau County	5				5	
La Crosse County	5					5
Lafayette County	43		1		42	
Langlade County	3				1	2
Lincoln County	2		2			
Manitowoc County	9		6		3	
Marathon County	4				4	
Milwaukee County	9		5	3		1
Monroe County	20				1	19
Oconto County	3			1	1	1
Pepin County	2		2			
Pierce County	3					3
Price	2				2	
Racine County	1				1	
Richland County	4		4			
Rock County	1				1	
St. Croix County	105	6	32	4	55	14
Sauk County	10				7	3
Sheboygan County	16			2	14	
Vernon County	1				1	
Winnebago County	1					1
Wood County	12			3	9	
	1				1	
Total	334	6	76	17	187	54

SMALLPOX—Continued.

Miscellaneous State Reports.

Place.	Cases.	Deaths.	Place.	Cases.	Deaths.
Alabama (Jan. 1–31):			**Vermont (Feb. 1–28):**		
Baldwin County	1		Essex County	5	
Bullock County	22		Rutland County	1	
Butler County	7		Washington County—		
Calhoun County	40		Barre	1	
Chambers County	14				
Chilton County	2		Total	7	
Cleburne County	5				
Covington County	2		**Virginia (Jan. 1–31):**		
Elmore County	40		Alleghany County	2	
Etowah County	28		Clifton Forge	2	
Greene County	1		Lowmoor	1	
Jefferson County	47		Botetourt County	2	
Lee County	12		Floyd County	1	
Limestone County	10		Halifax County	2	
Lowndes County	1		King William County	6	
Macon County	1		Montgomery County	4	
Madison County	3		Norfolk County—		
Mobile County	4		Norfolk	1	
Monroe County	6		Pittsylvania County	13	
Montgomery County	47		Prince George County	1	
Pickens County	14		Roanoke County—		
Pike County	2		Roanoke	1	
Randolph County	11		Rockbridge County	1	
Sumter County	2		Russell County	19	
Talladega County	73		Lebanon	1	
Tallapoosa County	101		Scott County	62	
Tuscaloosa County	2		Gate City	2	
Washington County	2		Tazewell County	1	
Wilcox County	2		Pocahontas	1	
			Washington County	1	
Total	497		Wise County	15	
			Norton	1	
Connecticut (Feb. 1–28):					
Litchfield County—			Total	146	
Torrington	1				
New London County—			**Washington (Jan. 1–31):**		
Norwich	1		Adams County	1	
			Chelan County—		
Total	2		Wenatchee	1	
			Ferry County	2	
Louisiana (Feb. 1–28):			King County	3	
Acadia Parish	1		Lewis County—		
Avoyelles Parish	7		Centralia	3	
Bienville Parish	1		Pend Oreille County—		
Bossier Parish	2		Ione	1	
Caddo Parish	18		Newport	1	
Concordia Parish	2		Skamania County	2	
De Soto Parish	2		Snohomish County	1	
East Carroll Parish	1		Everett	13	
Evangeline Parish	2		Spokane County—		
Grant Parish	2		Spokane	36	
Iberia Parish	1		Walla Walla County	2	
Jefferson Davis Parish	1		Yakima County	2	
Lincoln Parish	8				
Madison Parish	1		Total	68	
Morehouse Parish	5				
Natchitoches Parish	2		**West Virginia (Feb. 1–28):**		
Orleans Parish	60		Barbour County	1	
Ouachita Parish	7		Berkeley County	2	
Rapides Parish	10		Cabell County	2	
Richland Parish	1		Clay County	11	
St. Landry Parish	5		Fayette County	4	
Tangipahoa Parish	1		Gilmer County	11	
Tensas Parish	2		Hancock County	1	
Terrebonne Parish	3		Jackson County	1	
Union Parish	1		Kanawha County	25	
Vermilion Parish	10		Lewis County	2	
Washington Parish	1		Lincoln County	17	
Winn Parish	2		Logan County	17	
			Marshall County	15	
Total	157		Marion County	24	
			Mercer County	1	
Oregon (Jan. 1–31):			Morgan County	4	
Portland	12		Ohio County	2	
Clatsop County	1		Raleigh County	2	
Douglas County	1		Wayne County	2	
Wasco County	3		Wirt County	3	
			Wood County	5	
Total	17				
			Total	152	

SMALLPOX--Continued.

City Reports for Week Ended Mar. 9, 1918.

Place.	Cases.	Deaths.	Place	Cases	Deaths.
Akron, Ohio	28		Kokomo, Ind	2	
Alexandria, La	1		La Crosse, Wis	5	
Alton, Ill	11		Leavenworth, Kans	5	
Anniston, Ala	37		Lexington, Ky	1	
Atlanta, Ga	7		Lima, Ohio	6	
Austin, Tex	1		Lincoln, Nebr	3	
Baltimore, Md	1		Little Rock, Ark	23	
Birmingham, Ala	50		Lorain, Ohio	1	
Buffalo, N. Y	9		Los Angeles, Cal	4	
Butte, Mont	7		Madison, Wis	10	
Canton, Ohio	1		Memphis, Tenn	18	
Cedar Rapids, Iowa	2		Milwaukee, Wis	5	
Chattanooga, Tenn	4		Minneapolis, Minn	13	
Chicago, Ill	9	1	Mobile, Ala	2	
Cincinnati, Ohio	21		Montgomery, Ala	10	
Cleveland, Ohio	65		Muncie, Ind	6	
Coffeyville, Kans	4		Muskegon, Mich	5	
Columbus, Ohio	13		Muskogee, Okla	6	
Council Bluffs, Iowa	37		New Orleans, La	12	
Covington, Ky	3		Newport, Ky	1	
Dallas, Tex	16		Norfolk, Va	2	
Danville, Ill	1		North Little Rock, Ark	5	
Davenport, Iowa	1		Ogden, Utah	1	
Detroit, Mich	33	1	Oklahoma City, Okla	33	
Dubuque, Iowa	2		Omaha, Nebr	30	
El Paso, Tex	2		Portland, Oreg	3	
Erie, Pa	3		Quincy, Ill	3	
Evanston, Ill	1		Roanoke, Va	5	
Evansville, Ind	1		Sacramento, Cal	1	
Everett, Wash	3		St. Joseph, Mo	34	
Flint, Mich	9		St. Louis, Mo	14	
Fort Smith, Ark	10		St. Paul, Minn	4	
Fort Wayne, Ind	11		Salt Lake City, Utah	17	
Galveston, Tex	1		San Diego, Cal	1	
Grand Rapids, Mich	1		San Francisco, Cal	16	
Hammond, Ind	1		Seattle, Wash	5	
Hartford, Conn	4		Sioux City, Iowa	14	
Hattiesburg, Miss	3		South Bend, Ind	2	
Houston, Tex	3		Spartanburg, S. C	1	
Indianapolis, Ind	50		Springfield, Ill	3	
Jackson, Mich	1		Tacoma, Wash	3	
Jackson, Miss	5		Terre Haute, Ind	3	
Johnstown, Pa	2		Toledo, Ohio	12	
Kalamazoo, Mich	8		Waco, Tex	1	
Kansas City, Kans	31		Wheeling, W. Va	1	
Knoxville, Tenn	3		Wichita, Kans	16	

TETANUS.

City Reports for Week Ended Mar. 9, 1918.

During the week ended March 9, there were reported 4 deaths from tetanus; 1 each at Moline, Ill., and Newburgh, N. Y., and 2 at New Orleans, La. One case was reported at St. Louis, Mo.

TUBERCULOSIS.

See Diphtheria, measles, scarlet fever, and tuberculosis, page 468.

TYPHOID FEVER.

State Reports for January and February, 1918.

Place.	New cases reported.	Place.	New cases reported.
Alabama (Jan. 1–31):		**Maryland—Continued.**	
Calhoun County	1	Cecil County—	
Cleburne County	1	Elkton	1
Coosa County	2	Chesapeake City	1
Covington County	3	Frederick County—	
Cullman County	1	Knoxville	1
Escambia County	1	Frederick Hospital	1
Etowah County	1	Kent County—	
Geneva County	1	Swan Point	1
Hale County	1	Montgomery County—	
Henry County	1	Poolesville	1
Jefferson County	15	Prince Georges County—	
Lamar County	1	Capitol Heights	1
Madison County	4	Washington County—	
Mobile County	1	Hagerstown	3
Monroe County	1	Millstone	1
Perry County	2	Worcester County—	
Randolph County	1	Snow Hill	1
St. Clair County	1		
Sumter County	1	Total	29
Talladega County	1		
Tallapoosa County	1	**Massachusetts (Feb. 1–28):**	
Tuscaloosa County	2	Barnstable County—	
		Provincetown (town)	2
Total	44	Berkshire County—	
		North Adams	1
Connecticut (Feb. 1–28):		Williamstown (town)	1
Fairfield County—		Bristol County—	
Danbury	1	Fall River	6
Stratford	1	New Bedford	3
Hartford County—		Essex County—	
New Britain	1	Lawrence	5
Windsor Locks	1	Lynn	1
Middlesex County—		Marblehead (town)	1
Middletown	1	Salem	1
New Haven County—		Franklin County –	
New Haven	1	Warwick (town)	1
Wallingford	1	Hampden County—	
New London County—		Westfield (town)	1
New London	1	Middlesex County—	
Stonington	1	Everett	1
		Norfolk County—	
Total	9	Dedham (town)	1
		Plymouth County—	
District of Columbia (Feb. 1–28)	6	Brockton	3
		Plymouth (town)	1
Louisiana (Feb. 1–28):		West Bridgewater (town)	2
Avoyelles Parish	1	Suffolk County—	
Caddo Parish	1	Boston	8
Concordia Parish	2	Worcester County—	
Iberville Parish	3	Fitchburg	2
Orleans Parish	3	Westminster (town)	2
Ouachita Parish	5		
Rapides Parish	1	Total	43
St. James Parish	3		
St. Landry Parish	2	**Michigan (Feb. 1–28):**	
St. Mary Parish	1	Bay County—	
Tangipahoa Parish	1	Bay City	1
Vermilion Parish	1	Benzie County—	
		Frankfort	2
Total	24	Berrien County—	
		Chickaming Township	1
Maryland (Feb. 1–28):		Benton Harbor	1
Baltimore	6	Niles	2
Allegany County—		Chippewa County—	
Cumberland	1	Sault Ste. Marie	1
Eckhart	1	Clinton County—	
Western Maryland Hospital	1	St. Johns	1
Anne Arundel County—		Eaton County—	
Annapolis	1	Grand Ledge	1
Jewell	1	Genesee County—	
Jewell (R. F. D.)	1	Flint	8
Baltimore County—		Gratiot County—	
Canton	1	Wheeler Township	2
Highlandtown	2	St. Louis	3
Hamilton	1	Huron County –	
Calvert County—		Meade Township	1
Poplars	1		

TYPHOID FEVER—Continued.

State Reports for January and February, 1918—Continued.

Place.	New cases reported.	Place.	New cases reported.
Michigan—Continued.		**Ohio—Continued.**	
Jackson County—		Defiance County	2
Rives Township	1	Erie County	1
Tompkins Township	1	Fairfield County	1
Kalamazoo County—		Guernsey County	1
Kalamazoo	1	Hamilton County	2
Kent County—		Henry County	1
Lowell	3	Highland County	1
Grand Rapids	2	Hocking County	3
Macomb County—		Holmes County	5
Mount Clemens	1	Lawrence County	15
Midland County—		Lucas County	1
Midland Township	1	Mahoning County	5
Midland City	5	Meigs County	3
Montcalm County—		Montgomery County	2
Howard	1	Muskingum County	17
Ogemaw County—		Portage County	2
Churchill Township	1	Scioto County	1
Saginaw County—		Seneca County	1
Saginaw	1	Stark County	2
St. Clair County—		Summit County	7
Cotterville Township	1	Trumbull County	10
Wayne County—		Wood County	1
Ford	1		
Wyandotte	3	Total	106
Total	47	**Oregon (Jan. 1-31):**	
		Linn County	10
Minnesota (Feb. 1-28):		Portland	5
Becker County—			
Carsonville Township	1	Total	15
Beltrami County—		**Vermont (Feb. 1-28):**	
Blackduck	1	Caledonia County	1
Bigstone County—		Orleans County	1
Ortonville	1	Rutland County	4
Blue Earth County—			
Mankato	1	Total	6
Crow Wing County—		**Virginia (Jan. 1-31):**	
Brainerd	1	Alleghany County	
Hennepin County—		Clifton Forge	1
Minneapolis	31	Amelia County	2
Koochiching County—		Amherst County	1
International Falls	1	Appomattox County	1
Lac qui Parle County—		Augusta County	1
Riverside Township	1	Botetourt County	3
Olmsted County		Buchanan County	2
Rochester	1	Culpeper County	2
Eyota Township	1	Culpeper	5
Otter Tail County		Dickenson County	2
Fergus Falls	3	Fairfax County	1
Dane Prairie Township	1	Grayson County	2
Pennington County—		Halifax County	1
St. Hilaire	1	Henrico County	1
Ramsey County—		Loudoun County	1
St. Paul	5	Mecklenburg County	1
Rice County—		Norfolk County	
Faribault	2	Norfolk	5
St. Louis County—		Northampton County	1
Biwabik	2	Cape Charles	1
Duluth	1	Northumberland County	1
Eveleth	1	Nottoway County	1
Steele County—		Crewe	1
Owatonna	1	Prince Edward County	1
Wadena County—		Roanoke County—	
Wadena	1	Roanoke	2
Wright County—		Scott County	1
Stockholm Township	1	Gate City	4
		Smyth County	1
Total	59	Sussex County	1
Ohio (Feb. 1-28):		Tazewell County	2
Allen County	2	Warwick County—	
Ashtabula County	1	Newport News	3
Athens County	1	Washington County	1
Belmont County	4	Westmoreland County	1
Butler County	2	Wise County	1
Clark County	8	Norton	1
Columbiana County	23		
Cuyahoga County	5	Total	56

TYPHOID FEVER—Continued.

State Reports for January and February, 1918—Continued.

Place.	New cases reported.	Place.	New cases reported.
Washington (Jan. 1–31):		West Virginia—Continued.	
Benton County............	1	Marion County............	11
Cheland County...........	1	Mercer County............	3
Wenatchee..............	5	Monongalia County.........	2
Grays Harbor County—		Ohio County..............	3
Elma..................	1	Ritchie County...........	1
King County..............	1	Roane County............	1
Kirkland..............	1	Wirt County.............	1
Skagit County............	2		
Mount Vernon..........	6	Total..............	32
Walla Walla County........	3		
Waitsburg.............	1	Wisconsin (Feb. 1–28):	
Whatcom County—		Douglas County...........	5
Bellingham............	1	Eau Claire County........	3
Whitman County—		Green Lake County........	1
Pullman...............	2	La Crosse County.........	1
Yakima County...........	2	Marathon County.........	1
North Yakima..........	1	Milwaukee County........	10
		Outagamie County........	1
Total..............	28	Portage County..........	1
		Racine County...........	1
West Virginia (Feb. 1–28):		Sheboygan County........	4
Barbour County...........	2	Trempealeau County.......	2
Braxton County...........	2	Wood County............	1
Grant County............	4		
Jackson County...........	1	Total..............	31
Kanawha County..........	1		

City Reports for Week Ended Mar. 9, 1918.

Place.	Cases.	Deaths.	Place.	Cases.	Deaths.
Altoona, Pa...............	2	....	Little Rock, Ark.........	2	....
Atlanta, Ga..............	1	....	Los Angeles, Cal........	6	....
Baltimore, Md...........	3	1	Macon, Ga.............	2	....
Beaver Falls, Pa........	2	....	Memphis, Tenn.........	2	....
Birmingham, Ala........	3	....	Milwaukee, Wis........	7	....
Boston, Mass...........	1	....	Minneapolis, Minn......	1	....
Brockton, Mass.........	1	....	Moline, Ill.............	2	....
Buffalo, N. Y...........	2	....	Newark, N. J..........	2	....
Charleston, N. C........	1	....	New Orleans, La........	4	....
Charlotte, N. C.........	1	....	New York, N. Y........	7	4
Chattanooga, Tenn......	1	....	Norfolk, Va...........	1	....
Chicago, Ill............	3	1	Oakland, Cal..........	1	....
Cleveland, Ohio........	1	....	Omaha, Nebr..........	2	2
Clinton, Mass..........	3	....	Philadelphia, Pa.......	9	2
Coffeyville, Kans......	1	....	Pittsburgh, Pa.........	1	1
Columbia, S. C........	1	....	Portland, Me..........	1	....
Columbus, Ohio........	1	....	Quincy, Ill...........	1	....
Detroit, Mich..........	6	1	Rochester, N. Y........	....	1
Dubuque, Iowa.........	11	1	St. Louis, Mo..........	1	....
Elizabeth, N. J........	2	....	St. Paul, Minn........	....	2
Everett, Mass.........	1	....	Sandusky, Ohio........	1	1
Fall River, Mass.......	....	1	San Francisco, Cal......	1	....
Flint, Mich...........	6	....	Scranton, Pa..........	1	....
Galveston, Tex........	1	....	Seattle, Wash.........	2	....
Grand Rapids, Mich....	1	....	South Bend, Ind.......	1	1
Hammond, Ind........	2	....	Toledo, Ohio..........	2	....
Houston, Tex..........	2	....	Troy, N. Y...........	2	1
Indianapolis, Ind......	2	....	Watertown, N. Y.......	1	....
Jackson, Miss.........	1	....	Wilkinsburg, Pa.......	6	....
Jacksonville, Fla......	5	1	Worcester, Mass.......	1	....
Jersey City, N. J......	1	....	York, Pa.............	2	....
Kokomo, Ind..........	1	....	Zanesville, Ohio.......	3	....
Lawrence, Mass........	1	....			

TYPHUS FEVER.

City Report for Week Ended Mar. 9, 1918.

There were reported during the week ended March 9, 1918, one case and one death from typhus fever at Boston, Mass.

DIPHTHERIA, MEASLES, SCARLET FEVER, AND TUBERCULOSIS.

State Reports for January and February, 1918.

State.	Cases reported.			State.	Cases reported.		
	Diph-theria.	Measles.	Scarlet fever.		Diph-theria.	Measles.	Scarlet fever.
Alabama (Jan.)........	52	2,237	45	Ohio (Feb.)............	562	1,629	994
Connecticut (Feb.)....	173	601	190	Oregon (Jan.)...........	6	112	53
Dist. of Columbia(Feb.)	37	1,084	165	Vermont (Feb.).........	11	33	39
Louisiana (Feb.).......	84	822	8	Virginia (Jan.)........	121	2,565	102
Maryland (Feb.).......	123	1,243	217	Washington (Jan.)......	50	731	53
Massachusetts (Feb.)...	677	3,471	539	West Virginia (Feb.)...	28	163	52
Michigan (Feb.).....	485	549	828	Wisconsin (Feb.).....	156	2,296	645
Minnesota (Feb.)......	214	549	547				

City Reports for Week Ended Mar. 9, 1918.

DIPHTHERIA, MEASLES, SCARLET FEVER, AND TUBERCULOSIS—Contd.

City Reports for Week Ended Mar. 9, 1918—Continued.

City.	Population as of July 1, 1916 (estimated by U. S. Census Bureau).	Total deaths from all causes.	Diphtheria.		Measles.		Scarlet fever.		Tuberculosis.	
			Cases.	Deaths.	Cases.	Deaths.	Cases.	Deaths.	Cases.	Deaths.
From 100,000 to 200,000 inhabitants—Continued.										
Grand Rapids, Mich	128,291	24	3		6		5		7	2
Hartford, Conn	110,900	45	9		10		4		8	1
Houston, Tex	112,307	40	1		37				3	4
Lawrence, Mass	100,560	46	3		10				8	4
Lowell, Mass	113,245	41	1		4		2		8	3
Lynn, Mass	102,425	36	2	1	18		1		8	3
Memphis, Tenn	148,995	51	6		13		4		18	9
Nashville, Tenn	117,057	44	2		11		3		4	1
New Bedford, Mass	118,158	33	1		25		2		17	5
New Haven, Conn	149,685	36	3		4				8	6
Oakland, Cal	198,604	61	2		46		2	1	3	3
Omaha, Nebr	165,470	44	1		38		19	1		4
Reading, Pa	109,381	35	4		16		4			2
Richmond, Va	156,687	67	4		38		19		13	12
Salt Lake City, Utah	117,399		6	2	27		14			2
Scranton, Pa	146,811	53	11		1		5		5	2
Springfield, Mass	105,942	33	2	1	28		9		5	
Syracuse, N. Y	155,624	43	6		127		13		7	7
Tacoma, Wash	112,770		1		3		42			
Toledo, Ohio	191,554	66	2		10		5	2	21	6
Trenton, N. J	111,593	40	4		11		2		8	5
Worcester, Mass	163,314	60	6		7				7	4
From 50,000 to 100,000 inhabitants:										
Akron, Ohio	85,623		9		18		10		4	
Allentown, Pa	63,505	18	2		11		1		2	
Altoona, Pa	58,659		4		7		1		1	
Atlantic City, N. J	57,660				14				7	1
Bayonne, N. J	69,893				95		1		1	
Berkeley, Cal	57,653	10	1		11		10		1	1
Binghamton, N. Y	53,973	19	2		11		2		3	2
Brockton, Mass	67,449	11			10		4		1	
Canton, Ohio	60,852	16	2		3		2			2
Charleston, S. C	60,734	28	2		5	1			2	5
Chattanooga, Tenn	60,075	7			3					4
Covington, Ky	57,144	19		1			1		2	6
Duluth, Minn	94,495	18	1		18		1		4	1
Elizabeth, N. J	86,690	30	5		90	3	5		3	6
El Paso, Tex	63,705	43	3		14					10
Erie, Pa	75,195	22			4		3		9	2
Evansville, Ind	76,078	27	3		11		4		3	2
Flint, Mich	54,772	14	2	2	3		7		3	
Fort Wayne, Ind	76,183	24	5					1	1	1
Harrisburg, Pa	72,015	22	3		14		7		13	1
Holyoke, Mass	65,286		1		4		4		2	2
Jacksonville, Fla	76,101	31			6	1	1		3	1
Johnstown, Pa	68,529	20	7	1	8		10			2
Kansas City, Kans	99,437		4		21		5		2	
Lancaster, Pa	50,853				45		5		1	
Little Rock, Ark	57,343	15	1		12		1		3	2
Malden, Mass	51,155	18	3		2		4		5	1
Manchester, N. H	78,283	30	2		66		5		8	2
Mobile, Ala	58,221	12	1		2				1	2
New Britain, Conn	53,794	13	1		8		4			
Norfolk, Va	99,612				18		2			4
Oklahoma City, Okla	92,943	18	2		11		2			
Passaic, N. J	71,744	21	3		1				4	2
Pawtucket, R. I	59,411	22	1		9		2			3
Portland, Me	63,867	27	3	1	21	1				3
Rockford, Ill	55,185	25	2	1	10		1			
Sacramento, Cal	66,895	15			93		1		6	3
Saginaw, Mich	55,642	16			20		4		8	1
St. Joseph, Mo	85,236	29	7		20					
San Diego, Cal	53,330	6	2	1	228	1	2		9	2
Schenectady, N. Y	99,519	23	1		18		2		7	2
Sioux City, Iowa	57,078						19			
Somerville, Mass	87,039	35	7	1	26		2		6	2
South Bend, Ind	68,946	19	1		10		1		5	2
Springfield, Ill	61,120	16	2		25					4
Springfield, Ohio	51,550	23			4				1	4
Terre Haute, Ind	66,083	28	1						1	3

DIPHTHERIA, MEASLES, SCARLET FEVER, AND TUBERCULOSIS—Contd.

City Reports for Week Ended Mar. 9, 1918—Continued.

City.	Popula- tion as of July 1, 1916 (estimated by U. S. Census Bureau).	Total deaths from all causes.	Diphtheria.		Measles.		Scarlet fever.		Tuber- culosis.	
			Cases.	Deaths.	Cases.	Deaths.	Cases.	Deaths.	Cases.	Deaths.
From 50,000 to 100,000 inhabit- ants—Continued.										
Troy, N. Y.............	77,916	45	3	......	6	......	4	......	6	2
Wichita, Kans........	70,722		.....	......	71	......	3	......	1	
Wilkes-Barre, Pa......	78,770	22	2	......	55	......	3	......	2	
Wilmington, Del.......	94,285	41	3	......	21	......	3	.....	.....	4
Yonkers, N. Y........	99,635		7	......	10	......	7	3	.....	2
York, Pa..............	51,636		1	......	3	......	..	..	3	
From 25,000 to 50,000 inhabitants:										
Alameda, Cal.........	37,713		3	......	21	......	...	...	...	...
Auburn, N. Y.........	37,385	6	3	......	26	......	2	......	...	...
Austin, Tex..........	34,814	15	3	......	2	......	.....	......	...	3
Battle Creek, Mich....	29,680	1	3	......	36	......	7	1	...	...
Brookline, Mass......	32,730	11	2	......	11	......	3	1	.....	1
Butler, Pa............	27,632	8	2	3	44	1	1	......	3	1
Butte, Mont..........	43,435	28	2	......	4	......	3	......	2	...
Cedar Rapids, Iowa...	37,308		...	......	...	......	2	1	...	...
Charleston, W. Va....	29,941	5	...	......	5	......	2	......	...	...
Charlotte, N. C.......	39,823	15	...	......	...	......	.....	......	7	...
Chelsea, Mass........	49,192	14	...	......	17	......	.....	......	6	...
Chicopee, Mass.......	29,319	4	1	......	...	......	.....	......	2	...
Clinton, Iowa........	27,344		...	......	26	......	22	......	...	...
Columbia, S. C.......	34,611	21	...	......	6	......	1	......	2	...
Council Bluffs, Iowa..	31,494		...	......	...	......	6	......	...	...
Cranston, R. I.......	25,947	6	2	......	...	......	2	......	...	...
Cumberland, Md......	26,074	7	2	......	3	......	12	......	1	...
Danville, Ill.........	32,251	12	1	......	103	......	.....	......	7	2
Davenport, Iowa.....	48,811		...	......	5	......	14	......	...	...
Decatur, Ill..........	39,631	10	...	......	6	......	3	......	...	4
Dubuque, Iowa.......	30,673		...	......	4	......	.....	......	...	...
Durham, N. C........	25,061	3	...	......	6	......	.....	......	...	...
Easton, Pa...........	30,530	16	...	......	29	......	1	......	3	1
East Orange, N. J....	43,456	13	2	......	22	......	3	......	3	1
Elgin, Ill............	29,303	2	...	......	6	......	.....	......	3	...
Elmira, N. Y.........	38,130	4	1	......	57	......	2	......	6	1
Evanston, Ill.........	29,501	5	...	......	...	......	1	......	...	...
Everett, Mass........	39,713	13	...	......	20	......	1	......	4	1
Everett, Wash........	33,446	2	...	......	...	......	1	......	4	1
Fort Smith, Ark......	26,615	12	...	......	3	......	.....	......	...	...
Galveston, Tex.......	41,863	18	...	......	...	......	.....	......	1	2
Green Bay, Wis.......	29,353	15	...	......	...	......	.....	......	...	1
Hammond, Ind........	26,171	10	2	1	2	......	2	......	1	......
Jackson, Mich........	33,383	26	1	......	12	......	18	......	4	......
Jackson, Miss........	29,737	15	...	......	11	......	.....	......	4	......
Jamestown, N. Y.....	36,740	14	...	......	...	......	1	......	3	......
Kalamazoo, Mich.....	49,666	11	4	......	3	......	1	......	3	......
Kenosha, Wis.........	31,576	11	3	......	1	......	14	......	...	......
Kingston, N. Y.......	28,771	13	3	......	1	......	.....	......	...	......
Knoxville, Tenn......	38,676		2	......	11	......	.....	......	1	......
La Crosse, Wis.......	31,677	12	3	......	...	......	.....	......	1	......
Lexington, Ky.......	41,097	20	...	......	29	......	2	......	22	3
Lima, Ohio...........	35,384	16	1	......	17	......	.....	......	...	3
Lincoln, Nebr........	49,515	13	...	......	...	......	.....	......	1	4 1
Long Beach, Cal......	37,867	14	...	......	26	......	5	......	1	1
Lorain, Ohio.........	36,964		2	......	...	......	.....	......	...	......
Lynchburg, Va.......	32,640		8	......	26	......	.....	......	3	2
Macon, Ga...........	43,757	27	...	......	3	......	2	......	3	1
Madison, Wis........	30,699	14	1	......	27	......	2	......	...	1
McKeesport, Pa......	47,631		...	......	15	......	.....	......	...	...
Medford, Mass.......	26,234	10	...	......	6	......	.....	......	3	1
Moline, Ill...........	27,431	11	...	......	23	......	1	......	...	1
Montclair, N. J.......	28,319	6	...	......	196	......	1	......	3	...
Montgomery, Ala.....	43,295	10	2	......	17	......	1	......	.....	...
Muncie, Ind.........	29,424	6	1	......	2	......	1	......	3	2
Muskegon, Mich......	34,100	11	...	......	2	......	.....	......	...	...
Muskogee, Okla......	44,218		...	......	12	......	.....	......	...	...
Nashua, N. H........	27,327	10	2	......	5	......	1	......	...	2
Newburgh, N. Y......	29,602	5	...	......	7	......	.....	......	...	...
New Castle, Pa.......	41,123		...	......	9	......	.....	......	4	......
Newport, Ky.........	31,927	17	1	......	...	......	.....	......	1	......
Newport, R. I........	30,196		1	1	...	......	1	......	...	......
Newton, Mass........	43,715	11	1	......	...	......	.....	......	1	1
Niagara Falls, N. Y...	37,332	13	1	......	41	......	1	......	1	1
Norristown, Pa.......	31,602	4	...	......	1	......	.....	......	...	......

DIPHTHERIA, MEASLES, SCARLET FEVER, AND TUBERCULOSIS—Contd.

City Reports for Week Ended Mar. 9, 1918—Continued.

City.	Population as of July 1, 1917 (estimated by U. S. Census Bureau).	Total deaths from all causes.	Diphtheria.		Measles.		Scarlet fever.		Tuberculosis.	
			Cases.	Deaths.	Cases.	Deaths.	Cases.	Deaths.	Cases.	Deaths.
From 25,000 to 50,000 inhabitants—Continued										
Oak Park, Ill.	26,654	9	2		26		3			
Ogden, Utah	31,404	12			26		1			
Orange, N. J.	33,080	21	1		36		3		2	4
Pasadena, Cal.	46,450	8			76		1		2	1
Perth Amboy, N. J.	41,185	15			10				14	
Petersburg, Va.	25,582				6				2	1
Pittsfield, Mass.	38,629	19	1		2		3		2	3
Portsmouth, Va.	39,651	13	1		15		6			1
Quincy, Ill.	36,798	12	1		5					2
Quincy, Mass.	38,136	10	2		82		4		2	
Racine, Wis.	46,486	15								1
Roanoke, Va.	43,284	20	1		24	1	1		2	2
Salem, Mass.	48,562	11	1		23					
San Jose, Cal.	38,902				27		3			
Steubenville, Ohio.	27,445	8							2	
Stockton, Cal.	35,358	9	2		93				2	
Superior, Wis.	46,226	9	9				3			1
Taunton, Mass.	36,283	14	1		1		6		6	1
Waco, Tex.	33,385				21				2	
Waltham, Mass.	30,570	10	1		4		1		1	1
Watertown, N. Y.	29,894	4			22					2
West Hoboken, N. J.	43,139	5	1		7		1		2	1
Wheeling, W. Va.	43,377	17			19		1		2	3
Williamsport, Pa.	33,809	17	2				1			2
Wilmington, N. C.	29,892	11			5					
Winston-Salem, N. C.	31,155	16			23		1		4	1
Zanesville, Ohio.	30,863	9								
From 10,000 to 25,000 inhabitants:										
Alexandria, La.	15,333	8			2				1	
Alton, Ill.	22,874	19	1		5					5
Ann Arbor, Mich.	15,010	9	4		25		3		1	
Anniston, Ala.	14,112		1		3				1	
Beaver Falls, Pa.	13,532				2					
Berlin, N. H.	13,599	2								
Braddock, Pa.	21,685	11	1		4				2	
Cairo, Ill.	15,794	5								1
Chillicothe, Ohio.	15,470	5			1		10			
Clinton, Mass.	1 13,075	2			3					1
Coffeyville, Kans.	17,548				9					
Concord, N. H.	22,669	16			1					
Dover, N. H.	13,272	4								
Galesburg, Ill.	24,276	10			23					
Harrison, N. J.	16,950		1							
Hattiesburg, Miss.	16,482		1		2					
Kearney, N. J.	23,539	8			21					
Kokomo, Ind.	20,930	1	1		14		1		2	1
La Fayette, Ind.	21,2-6	11			2		2		1	
Leavenworth, Kans.	1 19,362	5	1		6		1			
Long Branch, N. J.	15,395	5			1					
Marinette, Wis.	1 14,610	3								
Melrose, Mass.	17,445	7			3					1
Morristown, N. J.	13,284	9			2					
Muscatine, Iowa.	17,500				10					
Nanticoke, Pa.	23,126	8			5				1	
Newburyport, Mass.	15,243	3			2				1	
North Adams, Mass.	1 22,019	4							2	1
Northampton, Mass.	19,926	4			6		2		3	1
North Little Rock, Ark.	14,907	2			2				1	1
Plainfield, N. J.	23,805	6	1				2			
Portsmouth, N. H.	11,666				7		7			
Rocky Mount, N. C.	12,067	5			1					1
Rutland, Vt.	14,831	3								
Sandusky, Ohio.	20,193	6								
Saratoga Springs, N. Y.	13,821	4			1		1		2	1
Spartanburg, S. C.	21,365	10	2		7				1	1
Steelton, Pa.	15,548	12					1		3	
Washington, Pa.	21,618				164		1		2	
Wilkinsburg, Pa.	23,228	6			14		1		2	1
Woburn, Mass.	15,969	8								

1 Population Apr. 15, 1910; no estimate made.

FOREIGN.

CHINA.

Examination of Rats—Shanghai.

During the three weeks ended December 29, 1917, 808 rats were examined at Shanghai, and during the five weeks ended February 2, 1918, 1,220 rats were examined. No plague infection was found. The last plague-infected rat at Shanghai was reported found May 6, 1916.

CUBA.

Communicable Diseases—Habana.

Communicable diseases have been notified at Habana as follows:

Disease.	Feb. 21-28, 1918.		Cases remaining under treatment Feb. 28, 1918.	Disease.	Feb. 21-28, 1918.		Cases remaining under treatment Feb. 28, 1918.
	New cases.	Deaths.			New cases.	Deaths.	
Diphtheria..	2	....	4	Paratyphoid fever..	3	....	3
Leprosy..	....	....	11	Scarlet fever....	1	....	3
Malaria............	11	....	¹ 32	Typhoid fever.....	10	....	² 65
Measles............	15	1	46	Varicella.	24	....	88

¹ From the interior, 27.   ² From the interior, 29.

CHOLERA, PLAGUE, SMALLPOX, TYPHUS FEVER, AND YELLOW FEVER.

Reports Received During Week Ended Mar. 29, 1918.[1]

CHOLERA.

Place.	Date.	Cases.	Deaths.	Remarks.
India:				
Bombay...................	Dec. 30-Jan. 5	74	67	
Calcutta.................	Dec. 9-15..	....	11	
Madras...................	Jan. 6-12.........	2	3	
Rangoon.................	Dec. 30-Jan. 5....	1	1	Nov. 1-30, 1917: Cases, 2, deaths, 2.
Java:				
West Java...............	....	....	....	Dec. 23-29, 1917: Cases, 16, deaths, 4.
Batavia	Dec. 23-29.........	10	1	
Philippine Islands:				
Provinces..	....	....	....	Feb. 3-9, 1918: Cases, 248, deaths, 186.
Antique.............	Feb. 3-9...........	4	4	
Bohol...............	...do........	62	56	
Capiz	...do........	35	31	
Cebu...................	...do........	9	4	
Iloilo.................	...do........	7	5	
Leyte..	...do........	9	8	
Mindanao	...do........	108	70	
Occidental Negros ...	...do........	11	6	
Oriental Negros..	...do........	3	2	

[1] From medical officers of the Public Health Service, American consuls, and other sources.

CHOLERA, PLAGUE, SMALLPOX, TYPHUS FEVER, AND YELLOW FEVER—Continued.

Reports Received During Week Ended Mar. 29, 1918—Continued.

PLAGUE.

Place.	Date.	Cases.	Deaths.	Remarks.
Ceylon:				
Colombo...............	Dec. 9-29..........	6	6	
Do................	Dec. 30-Jan. 12....	6	5	
Ecuador:				
Guayaquil............	....	....	....	Reported outbreak occurring about Jan. 17, 1918.
Egypt:				
Alexandria..............	Jan. 14-28........	1	2	
India......	....	....	....	Dec. 30, 1917-Jan. 5, 1918: Cases, 28,304; deaths, 22,677.
Bassein..................	Dec. 9-29....	....	8	
Do..................	Dec. 30-Jan. 5....	....	2	
Bombay.................	....do..........	19	11	
Karachi................	Dec. 23-29....	6	5	
Madras Presidency..........	Jan. 6-12..........	1,503	1,177	
Mandalay................	Dec. 9-29....	....	259	
Do................	Dec. 30-Jan. 5.	....	167	
Myingyan.................	Dec. 9-29....	....	80	
Do................	Dec. 30-Jan. 5....	....	37	
Rangoon.................	Dec. 24-29....	11	11	
Do................	Dec. 30-Jan. 5....	15	14	Nov. 1-30, 1917: Cases, 37, deaths, 34.
Toungoo................	Dec. 9-29....	....	5	
Do................	Dec. 30-Jan. 5....	....	3	
Java:				
East Java................	Dec. 9-22..........	56	56	

SMALLPOX.

Place.	Date.	Cases.	Deaths.	Remarks.
Canada:				
British Columbia—				
Vancouver............	Mar. 3-9..........	1	....	
Ontario—				
Sarnia................	Mar. 3-16..........	1	....	
China:				
Amoy.................	Dec. 31-Feb. 3....	....	....	Present.
Antung...............	Feb. 11-17........	1	....	
Changsha..............	Jan. 28-Feb. 3....	....	1	
Chefoo...............	Jan. 27-Feb. 9....	....	....	Present.
Dairen...............	Feb. 3-9....	4	1	
Nanking................	Feb. 10-16....	....	....	Epidemic.
Tsingtau..............	Feb. 4-10..........	1	....	
Egypt:				
Alexandria................	Jan. 29-Feb. 4.....	1	1	
France:				
Lyon..................	Jan. 21-Feb. 17....	6	2	
India:				
Bombay...............	Dec. 31-Jan. 5.....	26	5	
Karachi................	Dec. 23-29.........	1	1	
Madras................	Jan. 6-12..........	15	7	Nov. 1-30, 1917: Cases, 3; deaths 1.
Rangoon..............	Dec. 30-Jan. 5.....	1	....	
Italy:				
Leghorn..................	Feb. 12-18........	5	1	
Taormina..............	Jan. 20-Feb. 9....	6	....	
Java:				
East Java.............	Dec. 9-23..........	17	....	
Mid-Java..............	Dec. 12-23..........	17	....	
West Java.............	Dec. 23-29..........	71	8	
Mexico:				
Ciudad Juarez..............	Mar. 3-9..........	1	1	
Mazatlan..................	Feb. 27-Mar. 5....	....	2	
Mexico City................	Feb. 24-Mar. 2....	7	....	
Newfoundland:				
St. Johns.............	Mar. 2-8..........	1	....	
Philippine Islands:				
Manila................	Feb. 3-9..........	4	....	Varioloid.
Porto Rico:				
San Juan..............	Feb. 25-Mar. 3....	21	....	
Union of South Africa:				
Cape of Good Hope State...	Oct. 1-Dec. 31.....	28	....	

CHOLERA, PLAGUE, SMALLPOX, TYPHUS FEVER, AND YELLOW FEVER—Continued.

Reports Received During Week Ended Mar. 29, 1918—Continued.

TYPHUS FEVER.

Place.	Date.	Cases.	Deaths.	Remarks.
Egypt:				
Alexandria	Jan. 14–Feb. 4	64	15	
Great Britain:				
Glasgow	Feb. 17–23	1		
Japan:				
Nagasaki	Feb. 4–10	2	2	
Mexico:				
Mexico City	Feb. 24–Mar. 2	39		
Tunisia:				
Tunis	Feb. 9–15	2		

Reports Received from Dec. 29, 1917, to Mar. 22, 1918.

CHOLERA.

Place.	Date.	Cases.	Deaths.	Remarks.
China				
Antung	Nov. 26–Dec. 2	3	1	
India				
Bombay	Oct. 28–Nov. 24	17	12	
Calcutta	Sept. 16–Dec. 8		81	
Madras	Nov. 25–Dec. 1	1	1	
Rangoon	Nov. 4–Dec. 1	3	3	
Indo-China				
Provinces				Sept. 1–Oct. 31, 1917: Cases, 113;
Anam	Sept. 1 Oct. 31	17	13	deaths 57.
Cambodia	do	41	25	
Cochin-China	do	43	17	
Saigon	Nov. 22–Dec. 9	4	3	
Kwang-Chow-Wan	Sept. 1 30	10	2	
Java				
East Java	Oct. 28 Nov 3	1	1	
West Java				Oct. 19 Dec 29, 1917: Cases, 100;
Batavia	Oct 19 Dec 29	55	21	deaths, 57.
Persia				
Mazanderan Province				July 30 Sept 3, 1917: Cases, 384;
Achraf	July 30 Aug. 16	90	88	deaths, 275
Astrabad	July 31			Present
Barfrush	July 1–Aug. 16	39	25	
Chahmirzad				25 cases reported July 31, 1917.
Chahrastagh	June 15–July 25	10	8	
Charud	Aug 26 Sept 3	4	2	
Damghan	Aug 26			Present.
Khatek	May 28 June 11	21	13	
Meched	Aug. 18 Sept. 2	174	82	
Ouzoun Dare	Aug. 8			Do.
Sabzevar	Aug. 24			Do.
Sari	July 3 29	273	144	
Semnan	Aug 31 Sept. 2	11	5	
Yekchamhe-Bazar	June 3	6		
Philippine Islands				Nov. 18–Dec. 29, 1917: Cases,
Provinces				1,053, deaths, 693. Dec. 30,
Antique	Nov 18 Dec 1	48	32	1917–Feb. 2, 1918: Cases, 666;
Bohol	Nov 18 Dec 29	109	111	deaths, 360.
Do	Dec. 30–Feb. 2	151	125	
Capiz	Nov. 25 Dec 29	27	21	
Do	Dec. 30–Feb. 2	86	70	
Cebu	Dec 23 29	3		
Do	Dec. 23–Feb. 2	60	32	
Iloilo	Nov. 25–Dec 29	179	135	
Do	Dec 30 Feb. 2	75	48	
Leyte	Nov. 25–Dec. 22	13	12	
Mindanao	Nov. 25–Dec. 29	337	196	
Do	Dec. 30 Jan. 26	263	150	
Occidental Negros	Nov 25 Dec 22	177	123	
Do	Jan 13 26	49	31	
Oriental Negros	Nov . Dec 29	99	62	
Do	Dec 30 Jan 19	12	11	
Romblon	Nov. 25 Dec. 1	1	1	
Siam				
Bangkok	Sept 16 22	1	1	
Turkey in Asia				
Bagdad	Nov 1 15		40	

CHOLERA, PLAGUE, SMALLPOX, TYPHUS FEVER, AND YELLOW FEVER—Continued.

Reports Received from Dec. 29, 1917, to Mar. 22, 1918—Continued.

PLAGUE.

Place.	Date.	Cases.	Deaths.	Remarks.
Brazil:				
Bahia	Nov. 4–Dec. 15....	4	4	
Do	Dec. 30–Jan. 12....	3	2	
Rio de Janeiro	Dec. 23–29....	1		
Do	Jan. 6–12....	1	1	
British Gold Coast:				
Axim	Jan. 8....			Present.
Ceylon:				
Colombo	Oct. 14–Dec. 1....	14	13	
Ecuador				Sept. 1–Nov. 30, 1917: Cases, 68; deaths, 24.
Guayaquil	Sept. 1–30....	3	1	
Do	Oct. 1–31....	20	8	
Do	Nov. 1–30....	45	15	
Egypt				Jan. 1–Nov. 15, 1917: Cases, 728; deaths, 396.
Port Said	July 23–29....	1	2	
India				Sept. 16–Dec. 8, 1917: Cases, 171,192; deaths, 128,870. Dec. 23–29, 1917: Cases, 18,753; deaths, 15,162.
Bombay	Oct. 28–Dec. 1....	103	85	
Calcutta	Sept. 16–29....		2	
Henzada	Oct. 21–27....		1	
Karachi	Oct. 21–Dec. 1....	11	9	
Madras Presidency	Oct. 31–Nov. 17....	3,294	2,560	
Mandalay	Oct. 14–Nov. 17....		89	
Rangoon	Oct. 21–Dec. 1....	32	38	
Indo-China:				
Provinces				Sept. 1–Oct. 31, 1917: Cases, 70; deaths, 64.
Anam	Sept. 1–Oct. 31....	25	24	
Cambodia	....do....	30	19	
Cochin-China	....do....	15	11	
Saigon	Oct. 31–Dec. 23....	17	6	
Do	Dec. 31–Jan. 27....	24	7	
Java:				
East Java				Oct. 27–Nov. 25, 1917: Cases, 75; deaths, 73.
Surabaya	Nov. 11–25....	2	2	
West Java				Nov. 25–Dec. 9, 1917: Cases, 45; deaths, 45.
Peru				Dec. 1, 1917–Jan. 15, 1918: Cases, 106.
Ancachs Department—				
Casma	Dec. 1–Jan. 15....	2		
Lambayeque Department	....do....	22		At Chiclayo, Ferrenafe, Jayanca, Lambayeque.
Libertad Department	....do....	72		At Guadalupe, Mansiche, Pacasmayo, Salaverry, San Jose, San Pedro, and country district of Trujillo.
Lima Department	....do....	9		City and country.
Piura Department—				
Catacaos	....do....	1		
Senegal:				
St. Louis	Feb. 2....			Present.
Siam:				
Bangkok	Sept. 16–Dec. 23....	13	9	
Straits Settlements:				
Singapore	Oct. 28–Dec. 29....	5	7	

SMALLPOX.

Place.	Date.	Cases.	Deaths.	Remarks.
Algeria:				
Algiers	Nov. 1–Dec. 31....	3	1	
Do	Jan. 1–31....	2		
Australia:				
New South Wales				July 12–Dec. 20, 1917: Cases, 36, Jan. 4–17, 1918: Case, 1. Newcastle district.
Abermain	Oct. 25–Nov. 29....	3		
Cessnock	July 12–Oct. 11....	7		
Eumangla	Aug. 15....	1		
Kurri Kurri	Dec. 5–20....	2		
Mungindi	Aug. 13....	1		
Warren	July 12–Oct. 25....	22		
Do	Jan. 1–17....	1		
Brazil:				
Bahia	Nov. 10–Dec. 8....	3		
Pernambuco	Nov. 1–15....	1		
Rio de Janeiro	Sept. 30–Dec. 29....	703	190	
Do	Dec. 30–Jan. 26....	158	42	
Sao Paulo	Oct. 29–Nov. 4....		2	

CHOLERA, PLAGUE, SMALLPOX, TYPHUS FEVER, AND YELLOW FEVER—Continued.

Reports Received from Dec. 29, 1917, to Mar. 22, 1918—Continued.

SMALLPOX—Continued.

Place.	Date.	Cases.	Deaths.	Remarks.
Canada:				
British Columbia—				
Vancouver	Jan. 13–Feb. 16	4		
Victoria	Jan. 7–Feb. 2	2		
Winnipeg	Dec. 30–Jan. 5	1		
New Brunswick—				
Kent County	Dec. 4			Outbreak. On main line Canadian Ry., 25 miles north of Moncton.
Do	Jan. 22	40		In 7 localities.
Northumberland County.	....do	41		In 5 localities.
Restigouche County	Jan. 18	60		
St. John County—				
St. John	Mar. 3–9	2		
Victoria County	Jan. 22	10		At Limestone and a lumber camp.
Westmoreland County—				
Moncton	Jan. 20–Feb. 23	8		
York County	Jan. 22	8		
Nova Scotia—				
Halifax	Feb. 24–Mar. 2	1		
Sydney	Feb. 3–Mar. 2	4		
Ontario—				
Hamilton	Dec. 16–22	1		
Do	Jan. 13–19	2		
Ottawa	Mar. 4–10	1		
Sarnia	Dec. 9–15	1		
Do	Jan. 6–Mar. 2	28		
Toronto	Feb. 10–16	1		
Windsor	Dec. 30–Jan. 5	1		
Prince Edward Island—				
Charlottetown	Feb. 7–13	1		
Quebec—				
Montreal	Dec. 16–Jan. 5	5		
Do	Jan. 6–Mar. 9	7		
China:				
Amoy	Oct. 22–Dec. 30			Present.
Antung	Dec. 3–23	13	2	
Do	Jan. 7–27	4	2	
Chungking	Nov. 11–Dec. 29			Do.
Do	Dec. 30–Jan. 19			Do.
Dairen	Nov. 18–Dec. 22	3	1	
Do	Dec. 30–Feb. 16	15		
Harbin	May 14–June 30	20		Chinese Eastern Ry.
Do	July 1–Dec. 2	7		Do.
Hongkong	Dec. 23–29	1		
Hungtahotze Station	Oct. 28–Nov. 4	1		Do.
Manchuria Station	May 14–June 30	6		Do.
Do	July 1–Dec. 2	3		Do.
Mukden	Nov. 11–24			Present.
Nanking	Feb. 3–9			Epidemic.
Shanghai	Nov. 18–Dec. 23	41	91	Cases, foreign; deaths among natives.
Do	Dec. 31–Feb. 10	33	92	Do.
Swatow	Jan. 18			Unusually prevalent.
Tientsin	Nov. 11–Dec. 22	13		
Do	Dec. 30–Feb. 9	14		
Cuba:				
Habana	Jan. 7	1		Nov. 8, 1917: 1 case from Coruna; Dec. 5, 1917, 1 case.
Marianao	Jan. 8	1		6 miles distant from Habana.
Ecuador:				Sept. 1–Nov. 30, 1917: Cases, 26; deaths, 2.
Guayaquil	Sept. 1–30	8		
Do	Oct. 1–31	14	1	
Do	Nov. 1–30	4	1	
Egypt:				
Alexandria	Nov. 12–18	1		
Do	Jan. 8–14	3		
Cairo	July 23–Nov. 18	6	1	
France:				
Lyon	Nov. 18–Dec. 16	8	3	
Do	Jan. 7–20	8		
Marseille	Jan. 1–31		2	
Paris	Jan. 27–Feb. 2	1		

CHOLERA, PLAGUE, SMALLPOX, TYPHUS FEVER, AND YELLOW FEVER—Continued.

Reports Received from Dec. 29, 1917, to Mar. 22, 1918—Continued.

SMALLPOX—Continued.

Place.	Date.	Cases.	Deaths.	Remarks.
Great Britain:				
Cardiff...................	Feb. 3–9..........	4	....	
Honduras:				
Santa Barbara Department.	Jan. 1–7...........	......	....	Present in interior.
India:				
Bombay.................	Oct. 21–Dec. 1.....	16	4	
Karachi.................	Nov. 18–24.....	......	1	Nov. 11–17, 1917: 10 cases with 4
Madras.................	Oct. 31–Dec. 8.....	9	3	deaths; imported on s. s. Me-
Rangoon................	Oct. 28–Nov. 24...	4	1	nesa from Basreh.
Indo-China:				
Provinces.............				Sept. 1–Oct. 31, 1917: Cases, 345;
Anam.................	Sept. 1–Oct. 31....	103	15	deaths, 98.
Cambodia.............	....do............	10	3	
Cochin-China.........	....do............	222	76	
Saigon.............	Oct. 20–Dec. 30....	120	26	
Do...............	Dec. 31–Jan. 27....	128	46	
Laos...............	Oct. 1–31.........	1	....	
Tonkin.............	Sept. 1–Oct. 31....	9	4	
Italy:				
Castellamare...........	Dec. 10...........	2	....	Among refugees.
Florence...............	Dec. 1–15.........	17	4	
Genoa.................	Dec. 2–31.........	11	3	
Do..................	Jan. 2–31.........	30	2	
Leghorn...............	Jan. 7–Feb. 3.....	24	5	
Messina...............	Jan. 3–19.........	1	....	
Milan.................		......	....	Oct. 1–Nov. 30, 1917: Cases, 17.
Naples................	To Dec. 10.......	2	....	Among refugees.
Turin.................	Oct. 29–Dec. 29...	123	120	
Do..................	Jan. 21–Feb. 3....	24	3	
Japan:				
Nagasaki...............	Jan. 14–27........	3	1	
Taihoku...............	Dec. 15–21........	1	....	Island of Taiwan (Formosa).
Do..................	Jan. 8–Feb. 11....	5	2	Do.
Tokyo.................	Feb. 11–18........	8	....	City and suburbs.
Yokohama..............	Jan. 17–Feb. 3....	4	....	
Java:				
East Java..............	Oct. 7–Dec. 9.....	25	....	
Mid-Java...............		......	....	Oct. 10–Dec. 12, 1917: Cases, 63;
Samarang............	Dec. 6–12.........	1	1	death, 1.
West Java..............		......	....	Oct. 19–Dec. 20, 1917: Cases, 217;
Batavia.............	Nov. 2–8..........	1	....	deaths, 33.
Mexico:				
Aguascalientes.........	Feb. 4–17.........	......	2	
Mazatlan..............	Dec. 5–11.........	......	1	
Do..................	Jan. 29–Feb. 19....	4	1	
Mexico City............	Nov. 11–Dec. 29...	16	....	
Do..................	Dec. 30–Feb. 16...	45	....	
Piedras Negras.........	Jan. 11..........	200	....	
Vera Cruz..............	Jan. 20–Mar. 2....	7	3	
Newfoundland:				
St. Johns..............	Dec. 8–Jan. 4.....	29	....	
Do..................	Jan. 5–Mar. 1.....	33	....	
Trepassey..............	Jan. 4............	......	....	Outbreak with 11 cases reported.
Philippine Islands:				
Manila................	Oct. 28–Dec. 8.....	5	....	
Do..................	Jan. 13–Feb. 2.....	8	....	
Porto Rico:				
San Juan..............	Jan. 28–Feb. 17....	2	....	
Portugal:				
Lisbon................	Nov. 4–Dec. 15....	2	....	
Do..................	Dec. 30–Jan. 19...	2	....	
Portuguese East Africa:				
Lourenço Marques........	Aug. 1–Nov. 30....	......	9	
Russia:				
Archangel.............	Sept. 1–Oct. 31....	7	....	
Moscow...............	Aug. 26–Oct. 6....	22	2	
Petrograd.............	Aug. 31–Nov. 18...	76	3	
Siam:				
Bangkok...............	Nov. 25–Dec. 1....	1	1	
Do..................	Jan. 6–12.........	1	....	
Spain:				
Coruna................	Dec. 2–15.........	......	4	
Madrid................		......	....	Jan. 1–Dec 31, 1917: Deaths, 77.
Seville................	Oct. 1–Dec. 30....	......	66	
Straits Settlements:				
Singapore......	Nov. 25–Dec. 1....	1	1	
Do..........	Dec. 30–Jan. 5....	1	....	

CHOLERA, PLAGUE, SMALLPOX, TYPHUS FEVER, AND YELLOW FEVER—Continued.

Reports Received from Dec. 29, 1917, to Mar. 22, 1918—Continued.

SMALLPOX—Continued.

Place.	Date.	Cases.	Deaths.	Remarks.
Tunisia:				
Tunis	Dec. 14-20		1	
Turkey in Asia:				
Bagdad				Present in November, 1917.
Venezuela:				
Maracaibo	Dec. 2-8		1	

TYPHUS FEVER.

Place.	Date.	Cases.	Deaths.	Remarks.
Algeria:				
Algiers	Nov. 1-Dec. 31	2	1	
Argentina:				
Rosario	Dec 1-31		1	
Australia:				
South Australia				Nov. 11-17, 1917. Cases, 1.
Brazil:				
Rio de Janeiro	Oct. 28-Dec. 1	7		
Canada:				
Ontario—				
Kingston	Dec. 2-8	3		
Quebec—				
Montreal	Dec. 16-22	2	1	
China:				
Antung	Dec 3-30	13	1	
Do	Dec 31-Jan. 27	2	2	
Chosen (Formosa):				
Seoul	Nov. 1-20	1		
Egypt:				
Alexandria	Nov. 8-Dec. 28	57	15	
Do	Jan. 8-14	20	7	
Cairo	July 23-Dec. 16	147	70	
Port Said	July 30-Nov. 11	5	5	
France.				
Marseille	Dec 1-31		1	
Great Britain:				
Belfast	Feb. 10-16	4	1	
Glasgow	Dec. 21	1		
Do	Jan. 20-Feb. 9	3		
Manchester	Dec 2-8	1		
Greece:				
Saloniki	Nov. 11-Dec 29		72	
Do	Dec. 30-Jan. 19		11	
Japan				
Nagasaki	Nov. 26-Dec. 16	5	5	
Do	Jan. 7-Feb. 17	6		
Java				
East Java				Oct. 15-Dec. 9, 1917: Cases, 24, deaths, 3.
Mid Java				Oct. 10-Dec. 12, 1917: Cases, 54, deaths, 2.
Samarang	Oct. 17-Dec. 5	15	2	
West Java				Oct. 19-Dec. 20, 1917: Cases, 73, deaths, 15.
Batavia	Oct. 19-Dec. 20	73	17	
Mexico				
Aguascalientes	Dec. 15		2	
Do	Jan. 21-Feb. 10		14	
Durango, State				
Guanacevi	Feb. 11			Epidemic.
Mexico City	Nov. 11-Dec. 29	476		
Do	Dec. 30-Feb. 16	452		
Portugal.				
Lisbon	Feb. 21			Present.
Oporto	do			Epidemic. Dec. 24, 1917-Mar. 9, 1918: About 250 cases reported.
Russia:				
Archangel	Sept 1-14	7	2	
Moscow	Aug. 26-Oct. 6	49	2	
Petrograd	Aug. 31-Nov. 18	52		
Do	Feb. 2			Present.
Vladivostok	Oct. 29-Nov. 4	12	1	
Sweden				
Goteborg	Nov. 18-Dec. 15	2		

CHOLERA, PLAGUE, SMALLPOX, TYPHUS FEVER, AND YELLOW FEVER—Continued.

Reports Received from Dec. 29, 1917, to Mar. 22, 1918.

TYPHUS FEVER—Continued.

Place.	Date.	Cases.	Deaths.	Remarks.
Switzerland:				
Basel....................	Jan. 6-19.........	1	1	
Zurich..................	Nov. 9-15.........	2	....	
Do..................	Jan. 13-19........	2	....	
Tunisia:				
Tunis..................	Nov. 30-Dec. 6....	....	1	
Turkey:				
Albania—				
Janina...............	Jan. 27...........	....	....	Epidemic.
Union of South Africa:				
Cape of Good Hope State...	....	....	....	Sept. 10-Nov. 25, 1917: Cases, 3,724 (European, 31; native, 3,693); deaths, 761 (European, 5; native, 756).

YELLOW FEVER.

Place.	Date.	Cases.	Deaths.	Remarks.
Ecuador.......................	....	....	....	Sept. 1-Nov. 30, 1917: Cases, 5; deaths, 3.
Guayaquil................	Sept. 1-30.........	1	1	
Do.................	Oct. 1-31..........	1	....	
Do.................	Nov. 1-30.........	2	2	
Yaguachi................	.....do..........	1	....	
Honduras:				
Tegucigalpa...............	Dec. 16-22........	....	1	
Do....................	Jan. 6-19.........	....	1	

×

i

PUBLIC HEALTH REPORTS

| VOL. 33 | APRIL 5, 1918 | No. 14 |

PELLAGRA.

ITS NATURE AND PREVENTION.

By JOSEPH GOLDBERGER, Surgeon, United States Public Health Service.

In the following paper an attempt is made to answer, as simply as possible, the more important questions which the general public frequently asks in regard to pellagra.

Symptoms.

Although the fully developed disease makes a picture which, when once seen, can hardly ever be wrongly diagnosed even by one who is not a physician, the recognition of the disease is by no means simple, because the fully developed or classical types of cases form only a small proportion of the total.

The following sketch of the symptoms is presented, therefore, not with the idea that it will enable the untrained to recognize the disease, but rather to call attention to those symptoms or combinations of symptoms which should be looked upon as suspicious and as calling for the simple and effective measures of prevention to be outlined.

In a fairly well developed though not advanced case the disease shows itself by a variety of symptoms, of which weakness, nervousness, indigestion, and an eruption form the most distinctive combination.

Eruption.—The eruption is the most characteristic telltale of the disease and the main reliance in its recognition. When the eruption first shows itself it may look very much like a sunburn, the deceptive resemblance to which may, in some cases, be heightened by the subsequent peeling with or without the formation of blisters. In many cases the inflamed-looking skin first turns to a somewhat dirty brown, frequently parchmentlike, then quickly becomes rough and scaly, or cracks and peels. In many instances, however, the beginning redness is not noticed or does not occur, the first and perhaps the only thing observed being the dirty-looking scaly patch of skin very much

35 (481)

like and frequently thought to be no more than a simple weathering or chapping.

Among the most distinctive peculiarities of the eruption is its preference for certain parts of the body surface. The backs of the hands in adults and the backs of the feet in children are its favorite sites. Other parts not infrequently attacked are the sides or front of the neck or both, the face, elbows, and knees. From these or other points, for it may attack any part of the body, it may spread to a varying degree. Another marked peculiarity of the eruption is its tendency to appear at about the same time, and to cover similar areas, both as to extent and peculiarities of outline, on both sides of the body. Thus it may be stated as the rule that if the back of one hand or of one foot, one elbow, one knee, one side of the neck, one cheek, or the lid of one eye is affected, then the corresponding part on the other side of the body is affected, and affected to almost exactly the same extent. This rule, however, is not without many exceptions. It must not be assumed, because the back of one hand or of one foot or of one side of the neck alone seems to be involved, or is involved to so slight an extent as to be almost nothing in comparison with the involvement of the other side, that the possibility of the disease being pellagra may be thrown out of court without further ado.

Suspicious symptoms.—Although the main reliance in the recognition of the disease, the eruption of pellagra not infrequently is very tardy in making its appearance. While, until it appears, it is ordinarily impossible to determine the presence or absence of the disease with certainty, a shrewd suspicion may, nevertheless, be formed from a careful consideration of the other symptoms. This applies only to a limited extent to children, in most of whom the manifestations of the disease, other than the eruption, are slight and frequently difficult or impossible to make out. It has happened more than once in the experience of the writer that the liveliest of a group of children was found with a well-developed eruption. Notwithstanding this, however, careful questioning of the mother, if she be observant, not infrequently develops the fact that the child seems to her less active than common; in some cases it is evidently listless and fretful and the mother may also recognize that it has fallen off in weight. In older individuals a complaint of loss of strength with indigestion or nervousness or both coming on or made worse in the spring or summer and improving in the fall and winter are very frequently met with. The patient will complain of being "worked out," of having "blind staggers" (dizziness, vertigo), of discomfort or pain in the pit of the stomach, frequently of headache, sometimes of wakefulness, frequently also of sluggishness of the bowels, requiring the habitual use of medicine to move them. Although, as has already been said, these symptoms alone or even with the addition of such symptoms as a burning or scalded feeling of the mouth, reddened tongue, burning of the hands or feet and loose bowels are not enough to distinguish pellagra from other conditions, they are ample to justify a suspicion of the disease, especially if such individual is known to be finicky or a nibbler about food, or has been living on a diet made up largely of biscuits, corn bread, grits, gravy, and sirup, with little or no milk or lean meat; in other words, on a diet mainly of cereals, starches, and fat, with but little, if any, of the animal flesh (protein) foods.

The suspicion of pellagra may with confidence be dismissed in one who is known to be, and to have been, a habitual milk drinker and meat eater. It is well to be warned, however, that it is very easy to be misled about what and how much the individual actually eats.

Insanity.—In a small proportion of cases, fortunately much smaller than is commonly believed, the mind is affected to a degree requiring asylum care. Many of these cases get well under treament. Recovery of the mind is not to be expected, however, where the pellagra occurs in a person whose insanity is due to some other (incurable) cause.

Importance and Distribution.

Under proper treatment and with careful nursing only a small percentage of cases die; nevertheless, the actual number of deaths is deplorably large. Indeed, in nearly all the Southern States pellagra is one of the foremost causes of death. Thus, in 1916, it ranked fourth in Mississippi, third in Alabama, and second in South Carolina. In that year, probably an average one so far as pellagra is concerned, this disease was charged with having caused 677 deaths in Alabama, 840 in Mississippi, 467 in North Carolina, 627 in South Carolina, 607 in Tennessee, and 452 in Texas, or an aggregate of some 3,700 deaths for these six States alone. As the fatality rate, counting all types of cases, was probably not in excess of 5 per cent, it can readily be seen that not only is this disease among the most important as a cause of death, but it probably ranks with the first in importance as a cause of sickness and lowered physical efficiency of the people in the area affected. In the six States named there probably occurred some 70,000 definite cases of pellagra. As it is quite safe to assume that there were in the remaining 7 of the 13 States south of the Potomac and Ohio Rivers—the section most seriously affected—at least half as many more, there probably occurred in this region in 1916 upward of 100,000 cases. The incomplete figures at hand indicate a considerable increase of the disease in 1917. It seems safe to assume that this increase averaged about 25 per cent, so that it may

be estimated that in 1917, in the part of the country mentioned, fully
125,000 people were attacked.

In other parts of the country the disease is very much less common.
The explanation for this has not been fully worked out. It depends
in part, at least, on a difference in dietary habit. The people of the
South are known to eat much less of the animal foods, such as milk
and lean meat, than do the people in other sections. This, in its
turn, is due in part to the fact that, by comparison, much less of the
animal foods is raised in the South, and, therefore, in many localities they are hard to get or are too expensive for poor people to buy.

Relation to Living Cost.

It is the poor man who is the chief sufferer from this disease. This
explains why hard times, especially when accompanied by rising
food prices, are likely to be followed by an increase in the disease.
This is well illustrated by the great increase that took place in 1915
following the hard times brought on by the outbreak of the war in
Europe in the summer of 1914, and by the great decrease in 1916 following the improvement in conditions that developed during 1915.
Unfortunately, the upward trend of living cost in the fall and winter
of 1916 brought about an increase of pellagra in 1917 in many localities, an increase which was forecast months in advance by the
United States Public Health Service.

Cause.

Pellagra not "catching."—The apparently rapid spread of the disease following the discovery of its presence in this country about 10
years ago caused great alarm and with certain other circumstances
gave rise to the opinion that pellagra was a communicable disease.
Fortunately, the investigations of the Public Health Service now
permit one to answer the oft-repeated question, "Is pellagra catching?" in the negative.

Experimental tests and careful observations show that pellagra is
not a communicable disease. No germ that can properly be considered its cause has ever been found. Attempts to give persons
pellagra by inoculations of blood or saliva and other body discharges
from severe cases of pellagra have failed completely. On the other
hand, when 11 convicts were fed on an unbalanced diet composed
mainly of biscuit, corn bread, grits, rice, gravy, and sirup, with only
a few vegetables and no milk, meat, or fruit, at least six developed the
disease. In an asylum where many of the inmates developed pellagra
year after year it was observed that the doctors, nurses, and helpers
who lived with them never developed the disease. The only discover-
able reason for the exemption of the nurses and helpers was a better

diet. The nurses and helpers had a liberal allowance of lean meat and some milk, while the inmates had very little or none. When this observation was tested by giving the inmates a better diet—that is, by giving them more meat, milk, fruit, and vegetables—it was found that the inmates stopped having pellagra. This test was also carried out at three orphanages where there had been many cases in the children every spring for several years, and always with the same result. After the diet was improved, although no other change was made, pellagra disappeared. Attempts to prevent pellagra by supposedly other means have succeeded only when, whether intentionally so or not, some change in diet took place at the same time.

Caused by unbalanced diet.—These facts, together with others not mentioned here, show that pellagra is caused by eating a faulty or unbalanced diet, and that people who consume a mixed, well-balanced, and varied diet, such, for example, as that furnished to our soldiers and sailors, do not have the disease. In other words, if all persons provided themselves and ate a well-selected and properly varied diet there would be no pellagra. It is very important to realize that having good food on the family table is of itself not enough to keep one from having pellagra. There may be plenty of milk or eggs or meat, but if you don't eat them, or if you just pick at them and prefer to live, as the convicts in the experiment lived, mainly on cereals, starchy foods, and sweets, the milk and eggs will do you no good, and if you persist long enough pellagra may result.

Balanced Ration Prevents Pellagra.

A properly selected or well-balanced diet is one that includes in sufficient quantities and in proper form all the elements needed by the body for its healthy growth and normal activities. In order that a proper balance may be assured, the diet should include, besides the cereals, starches, sweets, and fats, a sufficient quantity of milk or some lean meat and an abundance of green vegetables and fruit and preferably some of all of these classes of foods. How such a diet operates to prevent pellagra or, indeed, just how an unbalanced or faulty diet acts so that the symptoms of pellagra are developed is still obscure and the subject of study by many scientists. The vitally important practical thing, however, is that the right kind of a diet will keep people from having the disease and will cure those who have it if the cases are not too far advanced.

Milk is the most important single food in balancing a diet and preventing or curing pellagra, and when lean meat, green vegetables, and fruits are for any reason not included in the diet or only infrequently or in very small quantities, it is most important that at least three glassfuls (1½ pints), and preferably more, of milk (sweet or

buttermilk) be taken daily. This single addition to the customary
daily diet will in practically all instances protect the individual from
an attack of pellagra. Milk for the family in these quantities is,
however, frequently hard to procure. For this and other reasons it is
wiser under such circumstances to use certain other classes of foods
as substitutes or, preferably, as additions to the available milk supply.

Lean meat (fowl, fish, pork, beef, etc.) helps in an important degree
to give proper balance to a diet, especially the diet of those who take
but little milk. Under these circumstances an allowance of half a
pound at least three or four times a week should be made. Part of
the meat may be replaced by eggs or cheese. It will be wiser, however, not to make any reduction in the meat allowance recommended,
but rather to add eggs and cheese to the diet.

It is often declared that Americans eat too much meat. No doubt
there are many who do. It is important to recognize, however, that
there are even more who do not eat enough.

In seasons when lean meats are difficult to procure or are exces-
sively expensive, the use of the dried soya bean as a substitute for
flesh food is to be highly recommended. It is but little known and
relatively little used as human food in this country, though an extensively used staple in the Orient. From a nutritive standpoint, it is
probably the most valuable of the dried beans and peas. Recent
studies have shown it to be decidedly superior to the dried navy bean,
lima bean, and the pea. The soya bean may be eaten boiled or baked
and, in the form of soy-bean meal, may be included to great advantage in the biscuit or the corn bread to the extent of one-fifth to one-
fourth of the flour or the corn meal.

Generous helpings of green vegetables (cabbage, collards, turnip
greens, spinach, string beans, or snap beans), or fruits (apples,
peaches, prunes, apricots), and preferably of both, should be included
in the daily diet, especially when milk is not used or used only in
small amounts. This is particularly important during the late winter and spring, the season when people have the fewest number and
the least variety of things to eat.

As an illustration of the practical application of the above recommendations for a health-preserving, pellagra-preventing diet, the following outline of a bill of fare is presented:

Pellagra-Preventing Bill of Fare.

BREAKFAST.

Sweet milk, daily.
Boiled oatmeal with butter or with milk every other day.
Boiled hominy grits or mush with a meat gravy or with milk every other day.
Light bread or biscuit (one-fourth soy-bean meal), with butter, daily.

A meat dish (beefstew, hash, or pot roast, ham or shoulder of pork, boiled or roast fowl, broiled or fried fish, or creamed salmon or codfish cakes, etc.), at least every other day.

Macaroni with cheese, once a week.

Dried beans (boiled cowpeas with or without a little meat, baked or boiled soya beans with or without a little meat), two or three times a week.

Potatoes (Irish or sweet), four or five times a week.

Rice, two or three times a week, on days with the meat stew or the beans.

Green vegetables (cabbage, collards, turnip greens, spinach, snap beans or okra), three or four times a week.

Corn bread (one-fifth soy-bean meal), daily.

Buttermilk, daily.

Light bread or biscuit (one-fourth soy-bean meal), daily. .

Butter, daily.

Milk (sweet or buttermilk), daily.

Stewed fruit (apples, peaches, prunes, apricots), three or four times a week, on days when there is no green vegetable for dinner.

Peanut butter, once or twice a week.

Sirup, once or twice a week.

It will be recognized that this bill of fare is primarily for older children and adults. The intelligent housewife will, of course, make such modifications as the age of her children, the tastes of her family, and her particular circumstances suggest or make necessary. Various additions may be made to give greater variety and attractiveness to the meals. The quantities of some of the foods may be reduced and replaced, in part or in whole, by other similar foods, but so far as possible no reduction should be made in the quantities of milk and lean meats. In the case of young children eggs make a very desirable addition and the relative quantity of milk allowed them may advantageously be increased.

Treatment.

While the above recommendations have in view primarily pellagra prevention, the same diet serves satisfactorily also in the treatment and cure of the average case. For severe cases a more liberal allowance of milk should be made and eggs added. In some instances, in fact, only liquids can be taken. In these, milk, fresh-meat juice, meat broth, bean, pea, or potato puree, and pot liquor should form the diet until more substantial food (milk toast, soft boiled or coddled eggs) can be added. The food should be given at regular intervals just as is done with medicine. Indeed, for the cure of pellagra the only medicine we have is the diet. The only use that medicines serve in pellagra is the alleviation of painful symptoms and in the treatment of complicating conditions. The sooner this is realized the sooner will the quacks, both within and without the profession, be put out of business. The money that is now being wasted on useless and quack medicines is well-nigh sufficient to procure for the poor, deluded sufferers the food from the lack of which they are suffering.

A change of climate is of itself not an essential in the treatment and cure of pellagra. A change from city, village, or "camp" to a farm in the country has not infrequently been found to be beneficial. The benefit derived is to be attributed, however, not to the change of air, as is commonly thought, but rather to the fact that in the country the diet is improved by an abundance of milk, eggs, etc. Practically all the benefits of a "change of climate" may be had at home at the cost of two quarts of milk and half a dozen eggs or half a pound of stew beef a day. .

The patient should be warned that a proper diet is not to be considered as a temporary thing which can be dispensed with after recovery from the attack. To avoid a recurrence of the disease and permanently to maintain health and vigor a properly selected diet is essential and must be maintained at all times. It is worth while emphasizing that if all people provided themselves and, at all times, ate a well-balanced diet, pellagra would disappear from the face of the earth. The gain to the country from the consequent reduction of sickness, invalidism, and death, and the increased physical vigor and happiness of the people can not be overestimated.

EFFECT OF THE AIR HAMMER ON THE HANDS OF STONE-CUTTERS.

In the Public Health Reports of March 22, 1918, appeared reports of investigations made by officers of this service in regard to health hazards from the use of the air hammer in cutting Indiana limestone.

A similar investigation has recently been made by Dr. Alice Hamilton for the Bureau of Labor Statistics of the United States Department of Labor. Her report will appear in the April, 1918, issue of the monthly review of that bureau. Through the courtesy of Dr. Royal Meeker, Commissioner of Labor Statistics, there is given below the summary of the report made by Dr. Alice Hamilton:

Summary.

Among users of the air hammer for cutting stone there appears very commonly a disturbance in the circulation of the hands, which consists in spasmodic contraction of the blood vessels of certain fingers, making them blanched, shrunken, and numb.

These attacks come on under the influence of cold, and are most marked, not while the man is at work with the hammer, but usually early in the morning or after work. The fingers affected are in right-handed men the little, ring, middle, and more rarely, the index of the left hand, and the tips of the fingers of the right hand, with sometimes the whole of the index finger and sometimes the thumb. In left-handed men this condition in the two hands is reversed.

The fingers affected are numb and clumsy while the vascular spasm persists. As it passes over there may be decided discomfort and even pain, but the hands soon become normal in appearance and as a usual thing the men do not complain of discomfort between the attacks. There are no serious secondary effects following these attacks.

The condition is undoubtedly caused by the use of the air hammer; it is most marked in those branches of stonework where the air hammer is most continuously used and it is absent only in the one branch where the air hammer is used little or not at all. Stonecutters who do not use the air hammer do not have this condition of the fingers.

Apparently, once the spastic anemia has been set up it is very slow in disappearing. Men who have given up the use of the air hammer for many years still may have their fingers turn white and numb in cold weather.

According to the opinion of the majority of stonecutters, the condition does not impair the skill in the fingers for ordinary interior stonecutting and carving, but may make it impossible for a man to do outside cutting in cold weather or to take up a skilled trade which exposes the hands to cold.

The trouble seems to be caused by three factors—long continued muscular contraction of the fingers in holding the tool, the vibrations of the tool, and cold. It is increased by too continuous use of the air hammer, by grasping the tool too tightly, by using a worn, loose air hammer, and by cold in the working place. If these features can be eliminated the trouble can probably be decidedly lessened.

PREVALENCE OF MALARIA IN CERTAIN STATES DURING JANUARY, 1918.

The study of the prevalence and geographic distribution of malaria by the circularization of physicians has been carried on by the United States Public Health Service for several years. In cooperation with the State health authorities, the Public Health Service mails each month to the physicians in certain States cards on which each physician is asked to report the number of new cases of malaria occurring in his practice during the month. The reports show also the types of infection and whether or not the diagnoses were confirmed by the use of the microscope.

Reports for the month of January, 1918, have been received from physicians in Georgia, New Jersey, Ohio, the eastern part of Texas, and Virginia. The following table shows the results of the circularization in these States:

Summary of postal-card reports of malaria for the month of January, 1918.

	Georgia.	New Jersey.	Ohio.	Texas (eastern half).	Virginia.
Cards mailed	3,421	3,012	7,912	3,450	2,420
Cards returned unclaimed	60	83	100	109	27
Replies received	164	980	1,262	620	810
Percentage of replies received	4.88	32.43	16.15	18.55	33.84
Counties represented in replies	103	21	51	104	100
Counties from which no replies were received	47		37	9	
Towns or cities represented in replies	242	218	316	277	440
Cases of malaria reported	120	79	11	572	219
Types of infection:					
Tertian	53	57	7	239	103
Quartan	12	5		111	22
Estivo-autumnal	18	6	2	82	41
Cases reported confirmed microscopically:					
Tertian	7	11	2	56	18
Quartan	2			9	6
Estivo-autumnal	4	4	1	24	11
Cases of hemoglobinuric fever reported				7	

PREVALENCE OF DISEASE.

No health department, State or local, can effectively prevent or control disease without knowledge of when, where, and under what conditions cases are occurring.

UNITED STATES.

EXTRA-CANTONMENT ZONES—CASES REPORTED WEEK ENDED APR. 2.

CAMP BEAUREGARD ZONE, LA.

	Cases.
Cerebrospinal meningitis:	
Rapides Parish, rural	1
Measles:	
Alexandria	1
Mumps:	
Alexandria	6
Pellagra:	
Alexandria	1
Pneumonia:	
Alexandria	2
Boyce	1
Pineville	1
Smallpox:	
Pineville	1
Typhoid fever:	
Pineville	1

CAMP BOWIE ZONE, TEX.

Fort Worth:	
Cerebrospinal meningitis	1
Diphtheria	1
Gonorrhea	2
Mumps	4
Pneumonia, lobar	1
Scarlet fever	2
Smallpox	4
Syphilis	3
Typhoid fever	1

CAMP DEVENS ZONE, MASS

Chicken pox:	
Lancaster	1
Littleton	1
Lunenburg	1
German measles:	
Ayer	1
Littleton	2
Lunenburg	12
Measles:	
Ayer	7

CAMP DEVENS ZONE, MASS.—continued.

	Cases.
Mumps:	
Lancaster	8
Pneumonia, lobar:	
Ayer	0

CAMP DODGE ZONE, IOWA.

Bloomfield Township:	
Chicken pox	4
Des Moines:	
Chancroid	1
Gonorrhea	5
Measles	5
Scarlet fever	8
Smallpox	21
Syphilis	18
Tuberculosis	1
Whooping cough	5
Fort Des Moines:	
Chicken pox	1
Smallpox	1

CAMP FUNSTON ZONE, KANS.

Cerebrospinal meningitis:	
Manhattan	4
Chicken pox:	
Junction City	1
Stockdale	2
Diphtheria:	
Manhattan	4
Erysipelas:	
Manhattan	4
Measles:	
Junction City	7
Manhattan	19
Mumps:	
Junction City	1
Manhattan	9
Pneumonia:	
Manhattan	

CAMP FUNSTON ZONE, KANS.—continued.

Scarlet fever: Cases.
    Junction City............................. 1
    Manhattan................................ 7
    Pottawatomie County..................... 2
    Riley.................................... 1
Smallpox:
    Manhattan................................ 3
Whooping cough:
    Junction City............................ 4
    Manhattan................................ 1

CAMP GORDON ZONE, GA.

Cerebrospinal meningitis:
    Atlanta.................................. 2
Chicken pox:
    Atlanta.................................. 5
Diphtheria:
    Atlanta.................................. 1
German measles:
    Atlanta.................................. 4
Gonorrhea:
    Atlanta.................................. 6
Measles:
    Atlanta.................................. 19
Mumps:
    Atlanta.................................. 41
    Decatur.................................. 1
Pneumonia:
    Atlanta.................................. 3
    Dunwoody................................. 1
Scarlet fever:
    Atlanta.................................. 4
Smallpox:
    Atlanta.................................. 1
Syphilis:
    Atlanta.................................. 9
Tuberculosis:
    Atlanta.................................. 3
    Chamblee................................. 1
Typhoid fever:
    Atlanta.................................. 9

CAMP GREENE ZONE, N. C.

Charlotte Township:
    Cerebrospinal meningitis................. 2
    Chancroid................................ 3
    Chicken pox.............................. 1
    Diphtheria............................... 1
    Gonorrhea................................ 10
    Measles.................................. 6
    Mumps.................................... 7
    Rabies in animals........................ 1
    Smallpox................................. 4
    Syphilis................................. 6
    Tuberculosis............................. 2
    Typhoid fever............................ 1

GULFPORT HEALTH DISTRICT, MISS.

Gulfport:
    Chicken pox.............................. 1
    Gonorrhea................................ 1
    Malaria.................................. 4
    Measles.................................. 7
    Mumps.................................... 3
    Pellagra................................. 2
    Tuberculosis............................. 1

CAMP HANCOCK ZONE, GA.

Cerebrospinal meningitis: Cases.
    Augusta.................................. 1
Chicken pox:
    Augusta.................................. 1
German measles:
    Augusta.................................. 7
    North Augusta............................ 1
Measles:
    Augusta.................................. 21
Mumps:
    Augusta.................................. 2
Scarlet fever:
    Augusta.................................. 2
    North Augusta............................ 1
Tuberculosis:
    Augusta.................................. 2
Typhoid fever:
    Augusta.................................. 1
Whooping cough:
    Augusta.................................. 2

CAMP JACKSON ZONE, S. C.

Columbia:
    Measles.................................. 5
    Mumps.................................... 8
    Roseola.................................. 1
    Tuberculosis............................. 1

CAMP JOSEPH E. JOHNSTON ZONE, FLA.

Cerebrospinal meningitis:
    Jacksonville............................. 1
Chicken pox:
    Jacksonville............................. 10
Diphtheria:
    Jacksonville............................. 1
Dysentery:
    Jacksonville............................. 2
    Seaboard Air Line shops.................. 13
Gonorrhea:
    Jacksonville............................. 4
Malaria:
    Jacksonville............................. 1
Measles:
    Jacksonville............................. 9
    Fishers' Corner.......................... 1
Mumps:
    Jacksonville............................. 5
    Seaboard Air Line shops.................. 1
    Eastport................................. 2
Pneumonia:
    Seaboard Air Line shops.................. 1
Smallpox:
    Jacksonville............................. 2
Syphilis:
    Jacksonville............................. 2
    Murray Hill.............................. 1
Trachoma:
    Jacksonville............................. 2
Tuberculosis:
    Jacksonville............................. 9
Typhoid fever:
    Jacksonville............................. 1
Whooping cough:
    Jacksonville............................. 1

FORT LEAVENWORTH ZONE, KANS.

	Cases.
Leavenworth:	
Chicken pox	2
Diphtheria	3
German measles	2
Gonorrhea	1
Measles	11
Scarlet fever	3
Smallpox	1
Leavenworth County:	
Chicken pox	1
Measles	3
Pneumonia, lobar	1
Scarlet fever	1

CAMP LEWIS ZONE, WASH.

German measles:	
Roy	7
Lake City	3
Spanaway	6
Parkland	6
Stellacoom Lake	1
Mumps:	
Dupont	1
Whooping cough:	
Parkland	3
Stellacoom Lake	1

CAMP LOGAN ZONE, TEX.

Cerebrospinal meningitis:	
Houston	1
Chancroid:	
Houston	2
Goose Creek	1
Chicken pox:	
Houston	4
Diphtheria:	
Houston	3
German measles:	
Houston	3
Gonorrhea:	
Houston	30
Tomball	1
Humble	1
Goose Creek	1
Magnolia Park	1
Westfield	1
Malaria:	
Moonshine Hill	1
Measles:	
Houston	26
Goose Creek	1
Mumps:	
Houston	6
Goose Creek	1
Pneumonia:	
Houston	13
Magnolia Park	2
Moonshine Hill	1
Scarlet fever:	
Houston	1
Syphilis:	
Houston	27
Humble	1

CAMP LOGAN ZONE, TEX.—continued.

	Cases.
Trachoma:	
Houston	1
Tuberculosis:	
Houston	6
Whooping cough:	
Houston	4

CAMP MACARTHUR ZONE, TEX.

Waco:	
Chicken pox	8
Measles	15
Mumps	50
Pneumonia, lobar	3
Scarlet fever	2
Smallpox	2
Typhoid fever	4
Whooping cough	6

CAMP M'CLELLAN ZONE, ALA.

Chicken pox:	
Anniston	6
Oxford	1
Diphtheria:	
Anniston	4
Measles:	
Precinct 2	6
Mumps:	
Anniston	3
Pneumonia:	
Anniston	4
Scarlet fever:	
Anniston	1
Smallpox:	
Anniston	7
Oxford	2
Jacksonville	1
Precinct 4	1
Tuberculosis:	
Anniston	4

NORFOLK COUNTY NAVAL DISTRICT, VA.

Diphtheria:	
Portsmouth	1
Port Norfolk	1
Measles:	
Portsmouth	7
Ocean View	1
Mumps:	
Portsmouth	4
Pneumonia:	
Portsmouth	4
Port Norfolk	1
Gilmerton	3
Scarlet fever:	
West Norfolk	1
Willoughby	1
Tetanus:	
Portsmouth	4
Tuberculosis:	
Portsmouth	9
Whooping cough:	
Oakwood	3
Ocean View	1

CAMP PIKE ZONE, ARK.

	Cases.
Chancroid:	
Little Rock	1
Chicken pox:	
Little Rock	4
Diphtheria:	
Little Rock	1
German measles:	
Little Rock	1
Gonorrhea:	
Scotts	3
Little Rock	17
North Little Rock	2
Malaria:	
Little Rock	2
North Little Rock	3
Levy	1
Measles:	
Kerr	1
Little Rock	5
North Little Rock	1
Mumps:	
Little Rock	20
North Little Rock	1
Pellagra:	
Keo	1
Scotts	1
Pneumonia:	
Little Rock	4
North Little Rock	6
Galloway	1
Scarlet fever:	
Little Rock	4
Smallpox:	
Little Rock	15
North Little Rock	3
Syphilis:	
Scotts	7
Little Rock	7
Trachoma:	
Little Rock	1
Tuberculosis:	
Little Rock	2
North Little Rock	3
Scotts	1
Kerr	1
Keo	2
Typhoid fever:	
Little Rock	1
Whooping cough:	
Little Rock	4
North Little Rock	1

CAMP SEVIER ZONE, S. C.

Cerebrospinal meningitis:	
Butler Township	1
Measles:	
Chicksprings Township	1
Mumps:	
Chicksprings Township	1
Pneumonia:	
Chicksprings Township	1
Whooping cough:	
Greenville Township	1

CAMP SHELBY ZONE, MISS.

	Cases.
Hattiesburg:	
Malaria	1
Mumps	18
Pellagra	1
Pneumonia, lobar	3
Scarlet fever	1
Tuberculosis	1
Whooping cough	10
Richton, Perry County:	
Chicken pox	2
Smallpox	3

CAMP SHERIDAN ZONE, ALA.

Montgomery:	
Chancroid	1
Chicken pox	1
Diphtheria	1
Gonorrhea	8
Measles	7
Mumps	4
Pneumonia	1
Ringworm	2
Smallpox	2
Syphilis	2
Whooping cough	3
Rural district in 5-mile zone:	
Measles	3
Smallpox	1

CAMP SHERMAN ZONE, OHIO.

Diphtheria:	
Chillicothe	2
Measles:	
Chillicothe	4
Jefferson Township	6
Mumps:	
Chillicothe	4
Liberty Township	1
Pneumonia, lobar:	
Clarksburg	1
Scarlet fever:	
Chillicothe	8
South Salem	2
Union Township	3
Smallpox:	
Chillicothe	3
Franklin Township	1
Tuberculosis:	
Chillicothe	1

CAMP ZACHARY TAYLOR ZONE, KY.

Jefferson County:	
Diphtheria	3
Measles	3
Pneumonia, lobar	2
Rabies in animals	1
Trachoma	1
Tuberculosis, pulmonary	5
Louisville:	
Cerebrospinal meningitis	2
Chicken pox	1
Diphtheria	4
Measles	17
Mumps	1

CAMP ZACHARY TAYLOR ZONE, KY.—continued.

Louisville—Continued.	Cases.
Pneumonia	3
Scarlet fever	5
Smallpox	3
Trachoma	1
Tuberculosis, pulmonary	21
Typhoid fever	1

TIDEWATER HEALTH DISTRICT, VA.

Cerebrospinal meningitis:
Newport News	3
Hampton	2

Chicken pox:
Newport News	3

Diphtheria:
Newport News	1

German measles:
Newport News	3

Measles:
Newport News	7
Hampton	5
Phoebus	7

Mumps:
Newport News	4
Phoebus	2

Smallpox:
Newport News	1

Typhoid fever:
Hampton	1

CAMP TRAVIS ZONE, TEX.

San Antonio:
Cerebrospinal meningitis	1
Chancroid	1
Diphtheria	1
Gonorrhea	22
Measles	4
Mumps	5
Pneumonia	6

CAMP TRAVIS ZONE, TEX.—continued.

San Antonio—Continued.	Cases.
Syphilis	3
Tuberculosis	9
Whooping cough	2

CAMP WADSWORTH ZONE, S. C.

Chicken pox:
Spartanburg	2

German measles:
Spartanburg Junction	1
Pauline	2

Measles:
Spartanburg	5
Saxon Mills	1
Glenn Springs	2

Mumps:
Spartanburg	4
Glenn Springs	1

Pneumonia:
Spartanburg	1

Scarlet fever:
Spartanburg	1

Smallpox:
Spartanburg	1

Whooping cough:
Spartanburg	14
Drayton Mills	8

CAMP WHEELER ZONE, GA.

Macon:
Chicken pox	1
Measles	3
Mumps	9
Pneumonia	2
Scarlet fever	1
Smallpox	2
Tuberculosis	1

East Macon:
Mumps	5

DISEASE CONDITIONS AMONG TROOPS IN THE UNITED STATES.

The following data are taken from telegraphic reports received in the office of the Surgeon General, United States Army, for the week ended March 22, 1918:

Annual admission rate per 1,000 (disease only):
All troops	1,464.2
National Guard camps	893.6
National Army camps	1,870.0
Regular Army	1,390.2

Noneffective rate per 1,000 on day of report:
All troops	48.7
National Guard camps	37.8

Noneffective rate per 1,000 on day of report—Continued:
National Army camps	57.6
Regular Army	43.0

Annual death rate per 1,000 (disease only):
All troops	8.9
National Guard camps	2.8
National Army camps	13.1
Regular Army	9.3

New cases of special diseases reported during the week ended Mar. 22, 1918.

Camp.	Pneumonia.	Dysentery.	Malaria.	Venereal.	Measles.	Meningitis.	Scarlet fever.	Deaths.	Annual admission rate per 1,000 (disease only).	Noneffective per 1,000 on day of report.
Wadsworth	9			12	1		6	2	381.5	21.7
Hancock	7			15	6	1	2	2	355.8	24.1
McClellan	5		2	15	5		1	0	732.5	26.2
Sevier	3		1	18				1	1,056.5	45.5
Wheeler	4		6	28				1	964.6	37.6
Logan	7			54	4			0	1,036.7	39.2
Cody	9			7	1			2	483.6	32.6
Doniphan				16	1	2	1	1	1,484.2	44.3
Bowie	21			26				4	1,529.2	57.0
Sheridan	1			21			2	0	433.9	24.6
Shelby	4			13	2	1		1	935.3	46.4
Beauregard	5		20	17	1			3	1,234.7	53.9
Kearney	1			10	5		11	3	1,374.6	47.2
Devens	11			12	8		1	2	1,292.6	48.4
Upton	35			48	7	3	1	12	1,118.2	30.#
Dix	20	1	1	19	5	1	5	4	1,851.3	44.0
Meade	29			7	6		5	8	911.8	34.0
Lee	11			238			5	10	1,877.6	63.3
Jackson	15		2	24	3	10		5	1,547.0	53.2
Gordon	7		2	32	12			0	1,488.6	44.3
Sherman	23			41	13		20	13	1,888.1	58.9
Taylor	12			52	122	1		9	2,228.0	71.5
Custer	1			15	2		7	5	1,454.2	41.3
Grant	9			17	14	1	10	4	753.1	28.2
Pike	19	2	3	185	18		6	10	2,911.6	75.8
Dodge	33			37	110		22	11	3,077.6	78.5
Funston	28			17	6	4	1	14	3,004.9	86.8
Travis	26			50	53			7	2,761.6	71.9
Lewis	8			27	40		28	3	1,600.7	83.4
Northeastern Department				16	5			0	1,128.3	33.1
Eastern Department	14			40	15		1	6	1,625.2	30.4
Southeastern Department	21		1	41	11	2	2	4	890.1	40.9
Central Department	17			29	38		14	9	1,507.3	43.4
Southern Department	10			94	23		8	5	1,176.8	43.3
Western Department	2		1	24	7	2	11	1	844.8	26.8
Aviation, S. C.	49			128	119	7	48	32	1,636.0	48.9
Camp Greene	3			48	27	1	6	2	800.5	27.8
Camp Fremont				42	12		1	0	1,423.1	53.3
El Paso				7	4		1	0	1,177.1	7.9
Columbus Barracks	1			31	1		2	0	2,046.8	50.7
Jefferson Barracks	12			67	20		3	4	2,957.0	99.3
Fort Logan	4			2	2		2	0	2,714.1	93.1
Fort McDowell	1		2	13	11			0	2,602.9	55.2
Fort Slocum	17			11	1			4	2,548.9	51.8
Fort Thomas	1			6				0	1,260.6	58.5
D. B. Alcatraz								0	648.0	6.2
D. B. Fort Leavenworth								0	9,089.6	133.0
A. A. Humphreys	1			4				0	962.9	11.2
J. E. Johnston			1	15		1		1	829.2	33.5
Camp Merritt	16		2	49	5		6	11	1,254.9	63.9
Camp Stuart	12			29	6		1	7	1,783.3	47.4
West Point, N. Y.					2			0	2,614.5	19.8
Edgewood	1			4				0	2,865.8	30.4
General hospitals	1		1	42	1		1	2		
National Guard departments			1	10	17		1	1		
National Army departments	16		1	58	53	1	29	5		
Total	563	3	47	1,883	825	38	266	231	¹1,464.2	¹48.7

¹ All troops.

Annual rate per 1,000 for special diseases.

Disease.	All troops in United States.[1]	Regulars in United States.[1]	National Guard, all camps.[1]	National Army, all camps.[1]	Expeditionary Forces.[2]
Pneumonia	23.5	22.4	11.9	33.3	36.2
Dysentery	.1	.0	.0	.3	.7
Malaria	1.9	.8	4.5	.9	.0
Venereal	78.5	85.9	39.4	95.3	46.2
Paratyphoid	.04	.0	.0	.1	.0
Typhoid	.1	.0	.0	.3	.2
Measles	34.4	37.9	4.0	48.6	16.5
Meningitis	1.6	1.6	.6	2.3	2.5
Scarlet fever	11.1	13.0	3.6	12.3	30.9

[1] Week ended Mar. 22, 1918.   [2] Week ended Mar. 14, 1918.

CURRENT STATE SUMMARIES.

Alabama.

From Collaborating Epidemiologist Perry, by telegraph, for week ended March 30, 1918:

Jefferson County: Smallpox 52, meningitis 5. No other unusual prevalence.

Arkansas.

From Collaborating Epidemiologist Garrison, by telegraph, for week ended March 30, 1918:

Smallpox: Helena 2, Forest City 4, Dumas 1, Pine Bluff 5, Monroe County 4, Sebastian 1, Woodruff 1, Ashley 17, Jefferson 3, Izard 7. Malaria: Cabot 2, Wilmot 4, Rison 1, Osceola 1, Sebastian 5, Johnson 2, Ashley 5, Drew 13, Jefferson 3, Izard 2, Phillips 1. Measles: Wilmot 2, Helena 1, Forest City 3, Sebastian 78, Johnson 4, Ashley 19, Drew 9, Pine Bluff 3, Phillips 1, Izard 4. Chicken pox: Prairie Grove 2, Sebastian 34, Johnson 4, Phillips 2. Diphtheria: Pine Bluff 1, Sebastian 1. Typhoid: Jefferson 1, Sebastian 2. Scarlet fever: Sebastian 5. Meningitis: Woodruff 1. Tuberculosis: Wilmot 2, Helena 1, Sebastian 1, Ashley 2, Jefferson 1.

California.

From the State Board of Health of California, by telegraph, for week ended March 30, 1918:

Eleven cases epidemic cerebrospinal meningitis; 3 San Francisco, 3 San Diego, 2 Los Angeles city, 1 Los Angeles County, 1 Monrovia, 1 San Diego County. Fourteen cases smallpox, 7 of which were in Los Angeles County. One case leprosy at Visalia. Measles still epidemic throughout California.

Reported by mail for preceding week (ended Mar. 23):

Cerebrospinal meningitis	5	Mumps	170
Chicken pox	149	Pneumonia	61
Diphtheria	82	Scarlet fever	61
Erysipelas	16	Smallpox	29
German measles	396	Syphilis	53
Gonococcus infection	36	Trachoma	2
Leprosy	2	Tuberculosis	141
Malaria	7	Typhoid fever	18
Measles	1,234	Whooping cough	122

Illinois.

From the State Board of Health of Illinois, by telegraph, for week ended March 30, 1918:

Smallpox: One hundred and fifty-eight new cases; prevalent in Quincy, Edgar, and Elbridge Township (Edgar County), Springfield, East St. Louis, Duquoin, Alton, Belleville, Sullivan, White City, and Chicago. Diphtheria: One hundred and eighty-five cases, of which 144 in Chicago. Scarlet fever: One hundred and thirty-six of which 68 cases in Chicago, other cases widely distributed. Epidemic meningitis: Fourteen cases; Chicago, 12, Thompsonville 1, and 1 in Mount Pleasant Township (Warren County). Poliomyelitis: Oak Park 1, Springfield 1. Measles and German measles increasing.

Indiana.

From the State Board of Health of Indiana, by telegraph, for week ended March 30, 1918:

Scarlet fever: Epidemic Chamberlain school, Elkhart County, Brook. Measles: Epidemic Martinsville and Morgan County. Smallpox: Epidemic Waverly, Reynolds. Rabies: Epidemic (dogs) Evansville, Orange County.

Kansas.

From Collaborating Epidemiologist Crumbine, by telegraph, for week ended March 30, 1918:

Meningitis: Coffeyville 1, Corbin 1, Kansas City 4, Lakin 1 (suspect), Manhattan 1, Sabetha 1, Wichita 2. Smallpox, over 10 cases: In counties--Butler 34, Crawford 21, Elk 25, Miami 11; in cities—Kansas City 66, Salina 22, Wichita 37. Scarlet fever, over 10 cases. In counties Clay 15, Stafford 15.

Louisiana.

From Collaborating Epidemiologist Dowling, by telegraph, for week ended March 30, 1918:

Meningitis, excluding Rapides Parish: Ascension Parish 1, Caddo 1, De Soto 1, Calcasieu 1, Pointe Coupee 1.

Massachusetts.

From Collaborating Epidemiologist Kelley, by telegraph, for week ended March 30, 1918:

Unusual prevalence. German measles: Framingham 31, Newton 24. Measles: Beverly 55, Quincy 25. Smallpox: At Tewkesbury State Infirmary.

Minnesota.

From Collaborating Epidemiologist Bracken, by telegraph, for week ended March 30, 1918:

Smallpox, new foci: Aitkin County, Pliny Township 1; Hennepin County, Hassan Township 13; Roseau County, Mickinock Township 2; Grimstad Township 1; Stearns County, Sartell village 5; Wadena County, Aldrich Township 1. Five cerebrospinal meningitis reported since March 25.

South Carolina.

From Collaborating Epidemiologist Hayne, by telegraph, for week ended March 30, 1918:

Five cases meningitis, 1 suspected case.

Vermont.

From Collaborating Epidemiologist Dalton, by telegraph, for week ended March 30, 1918:

Mumps prevalent in Burlington. One case epidemic meningitis Castleton.

Virginia.

From Collaborating Epidemiologist Traynham, by telegraph, for week ended March 30, 1918:

Ten cases smallpox Bedford County, 1 Loudon, 5 Newport News. One case poliomyelitis Rockingham, 1 Shenandoah. One case cerebrospinal meningitis Petersburg, 3 cases Newport News.

Washington.

From Collaborating Epidemiologist Tuttle, by telegraph, for week ended March 30, 1918:

Unusual prevalence contagious diseases. La Center, Clarke County, 1 case epidemic cerebrospinal meningitis. Tacoma, 48 cases scarlet fever.

CEREBROSPINAL MENINGITIS.

State Reports for February, 1918.

Place.	New cases reported.	Place.	New cases reported.
Colorado:		Kansas:	
Sedgwick County	1	Chautauqua County—	
		Niotaze	1
Iowa:		Cherokee County—	
Boone County	1	Columbus	1
Dallas County	1	Crawford County—	
Polk County	4	Cherokee	1
Pottawattamie County	2	Pittsburg	1
Scott County	1	Ellsworth County—	
Van Buren County	1	Ellsworth	1
Wapello County	1	Kanopolis	1
Washington County	1	Geary County—	
		Junction City	2
Total	12	Greenwood County—	
		Madison	2
Kansas:		Harper County—	
Brown County—		Harper	1
Hiawatha	1	Jefferson County—	
Butler County—		McLouth	2
Augusta	2	Jewell County—	
El Dorado	3	Burr Oak	1
Leon	1	Ionia	1

CEREBROSPINAL MENINGITIS—Continued.

State Reports for February, 1918—Continued.

Place.	New cases reported.	Place.	New cases reported.
Kansas—Continued.		**New Jersey—Continued.**	
Kiowa County—		Passaic County	2
Greensburg	1	Union County	2
Leavenworth County—			
Leavenworth	1	Total	25
McPherson County—			
McPherson	1	**Pennsylvania:**	
Miami County -		Allegheny County	15
Paola	1	Berks County	1
Montgomery County—		Cambria County	2
Coffeyville	1	Clearfield County	1
Dearing	2	Delaware County	5
Morris County -		Lackawanna County	1
Council Grove	1	Lawrence County	1
Nemaha County—		Lebanon County	2
Seneca	1	Luzerne County	4
Neosho County—		Northampton County	1
St. Paul	1	Philadelphia County	3
Pottawatomie County—		Potter County	1
Emmett	2	Somerset County	1
Rice County -		Tioga County	1
Little River	2	Union County	1
Riley County -		Washington County	2
Manhattan	5		
Saline County		Total	42
Brookville	1		
Sedgwick County—		**Rhode Island:**	
Wichita	2	North Providence	1
Shawnee County—		Providence	6
Topeka	1		
Wyandotte County --		Total	7
Kansas City	6		
		South Carolina:	
Total	51	Abbeville County	1
		Aiken County	1
Mississippi.		Anderson County	4
Bolivar County	5	Calhoun County	2
Calhoun County	1	Charleston County	12
Carroll County	1	Cherokee County	3
Coahoma County	13	Chesterfield County	2
Copiah County	2	Dillon County	2
Forrest County	4	Edgefield County	1
Harrison County	3	Florence County	2
Hinds County	1	Greenville County	16
Madison County	1	Greenwood County	1
Panola County	2	Lancaster County	1
Perry County	1	Laurens County	5
Quitman County	1	Lexington County	1
Tallahatchie County	1	Marion County	6
Tippah County	3	Marlboro County	4
Tishomingo County		Newberry County	4
		Orangeburg County	2
Total	40	Pickens County	1
		Richland County	25
Nebraska:		Spartanburg County	7
Cuming County	1	Union County	3
Nuckolls County	2		
Pawnee County	1	Total	107
Total	4	**South Dakota**	
		Codington County	2
New Jersey		Sully County	1
Bergen County	4	Turner County	1
Burlington County	2	Walworth County	1
Essex County	11		
Hudson County	2	Total	5
Mercer County	2		

CEREBROSPINAL MENINGITIS—Continued.

City Reports for Week Ended Mar. 16, 1918.

Place.	Cases.	Deaths.	Place.	Cases.	Deaths.
Albany, N. Y................	3	....	Manchester, N. H...........	1	....
Anniston, Ala..............	1	....	Memphis, Tenn.............	....	1
Atlanta, Ga................	1	3	Milwaukee, Wis............	3	1
Baltimore, Md..............	5	3	Minneapolis, Minn.........	....	1
Birmingham, Ala...........	4	2	Muncie, Ind...............	1	....
Boston, Mass..............	4	2	Nashville, Tenn...........	1	1
Brockton, Mass............	1	....	New Orleans, La...........	1	1
Charleston, S. C...........	3	....	New York, N. Y............	16	12
Chattanooga, Tenn.........	1	1	North Little Rock, Ark.....	4	4
Chelsea, Mass.............	1	....	Oakland, Cal..............	2	1
Chicago, Ill...............	4	2	Omaha, Nebr..............	....	1
Chillicothe, Ohio..........	1	....	Petersburg, Va...........	1	....
Cincinnati, Ohio...........	2	2	Philadelphia, Pa..........	8	3
Cleveland, Ohio...........	3	....	Pittsburgh, Pa...........	....	1
Columbia, S. C............	1	....	Saginaw, Mich...........	....	1
Des Moines, Iowa..........	1	1	St. Joseph, Mo...........	1	1
Detroit, Mich.............	7	....	St. Louis, Mo...........	4	2
Fall River, Mass..........	....	1	San Francisco, Cal........	1	....
Greenville, S. C...........	1	....	Schenectady, N. Y.........	1	....
Indianapolis, Ind.........	3	1	Scranton, Pa.............	1	....
Jersey City, N. J..........	1	1	Somerville, Mass.........	....	1
Kansas City, Kans.........	2	1	Springfield, Ill..........	1	....
Kansas City, Mo...........	9	2	Tacoma, Wash............	1	....
Little Rock, Ark..........	1	....	Washington, D. C.........	3	2
Los Angeles, Cal..........	1	....	Wichita, Kans...........	1	1
Louisville, Ky............	4	1	Wilkes-Barre, Pa.........	1	1
Lowell, Mass.............	3	1	Wilmington, Del..........	1	1
Macon, Ga................	....	1	Worcester, Mass.........	1	....

DIPHTHERIA.

See Diphtheria, measles, scarlet fever, and tuberculosis, page 515.

ERYSIPELAS.

City Reports for Week Ended Mar. 16, 1918.

Place.	Cases.	Deaths.	Place.	Cases.	Deaths.
Ann Arbor, Mich...........	2	....	New York, N. Y...........	....	5
Atlanta, Ga..............	1	2	Northampton, Mass........	....	1
Baltimore, Md............	2	....	Omaha, Nebr.............	2	....
Bayonne, N. J............	1	....	Philadelphia, Pa.........	13	....
Berkeley, Cal............	1	....	Pittsburgh, Pa...........	7	....
Boston, Mass.............	....	1	Pontiac, Mich............	1	....
Chicago, Ill.............	20	2	Portland, Me.............	....	....
Cincinnati, Ohio.........	2	....	Portland, Oreg...........	2	....
Cleveland, Ohio..........	6	....	Providence, R. I.........	....	1
Cumberland, Md...........	1	....	Racine, Wis..............	1	....
Denver, Colo.............	6	....	Reading, Pa..............	2	....
Detroit, Mich............	2	1	Richmond, Va............	4	1
Duluth, Minn............	....	1	Rochester, N. Y..........	2	....
Fall River, Mass.........	....	1	Sacramento, Cal.........	....	1
Hartford, Conn...........	2	....	St. Louis, Mo............	12	1
Houston, Tex............	....	1	St. Paul, Minn...........	2	1
Jacksonville, Fla.........	1	....	San Francisco, Cal.......	4	1
Kansas City, Mo..........	2	....	Scranton, Pa............	1	....
Lincoln, Nebr............	....	1	Somerville, Mass.........	....	....
Los Angeles, Cal.........	4	1	Wheeling, W. Va..........	1	1
Louisville, Ky...........	5	1	Wilkinsburg, Pa..........	1	....
Malden, Mass............	....	1	Winston-Salem, N. C......	1	....
Memphis, Tenn...........	1	....	Yonkers, N. Y...........	1	1
Milwaukee, Wis...........	3	....	York, Pa................	2	....
Newark, N. J.............	2	....			

INFLUENZA.

Kansas—Haskell.

On March 30, 1918, the occurrence of 18 cases of influenza of severe type, from which 3 deaths resulted, was reported at Haskell, Kans.

LEPROSY.

City Report for Week Ended Mar. 16, 1918.

There was reported during the week ended March 16, 1918, one case of leprosy at New Orleans, La.

MALARIA.

State Reports for February, 1918.

Place.	New cases reported.	Place.	New cases reported.
Colorado:		Mississippi—Continued.	
Larimer County...................	1	Neshoba County..................	50
		Newton County..................	20
Mississippi:		Noxubee County.................	10
Adams County..................	19	Oktibbeha County...............	44
Alcorn County..................	12	Panola County..................	60
Amite County..................	57	Pearl River....................	24
Attala County..................	70	Perry County...................	89
Benton County.................	5	Pike County....................	76
Bolivar County.................	407	Pontotoc County................	66
Calhoun County................	19	Prentiss County................	25
Carroll County.................	153	Quitman County................	154
Chickasaw County..............	12	Rankin County.................	28
Choctaw County...............	14	Scott County...................	13
Claiborne County..............	39	Sharkey County................	56
Clarke County.................	27	Simpson County................	40
Clay County..................	12	Smith County..................	23
Coahoma County...............	274	Stone County..................	14
Copiah County.................	38	Sunflower.....................	130
Covington County..............	104	Tallahatchie County............	64
De Soto County................	43	Tate County...................	78
Forrest County................	21	Tippah County.................	30
Franklin County...............	33	Tishomingo County.............	45
George County................	13	Tunica County.................	122
Green County.................	11	Union County..................	21
Grenada County...............	9	Walthall County................	3
Hancock County...............	19	Warren County.................	127
Harrison County...............	59	Washington County.............	134
Hinds County.................	78	Wayne County.................	14
Holmes County................	118	Webster County................	8
Issaquena County..............	45	Wilkinson County..............	10
Itawamba County..............	22	Winston County................	86
Jackson County...............	38	Yalobusha County..............	47
Jasper County.................	68	Yazoo County.................	344
Jefferson County...............	40		
Jefferson Davis County..........	25	Total....................	4,659
Jones County.................	36		
Kemper County...............	19	New Jersey:	
Lafayette County..............	17	Burlington County..............	1
Lamar County.................	43	Essex County..................	1
Lauderdale County.............	11		
Lawrence County..............	48	Total....................	2
Leake County.................	21		
Lee County...................	87	South Carolina:	
Leflore County................	248	Beaufort County................	8
Lincoln County................	29	Chester County................	12
Lowndes County...............	30	Dorchester County.............	10
Madison County...............	16	Laurens County................	1
Marion County................	99	Marlboro County...............	1
Marshall County...............	24	Williamsburg County...........	3
Monroe County...............	30		
Montgomery County............	23	Total....................	35

MALARIA—Continued.

City Reports for Week Ended Mar. 16, 1918.

Place.	Cases.	Deaths.	Place.	Cases.	Deaths.
Atlanta, Ga	1	....	New York, N. Y	....	1
Dallas, Tex	....	1	North Little Rock, Ark	2	....
Hattiesburg, Miss	1	....	Richmond, Va	1	....
Jackson, Miss	4	....	Stockton, Cal	1	....
Jersey City, N. J	1	....	Wilmington, N. C	1	....
Little Rock, Ark	3	....			

MEASLES.

See Diphtheria, measles, scarlet fever, and tuberculosis, page 515.

PELLAGRA.

State Reports for February, 1918.

Place.	New cases reported.	Place.	New cases reported.
Mississippi:		Mississippi—Continued.	
Adams County	8	Marshall County	7
Alcorn County	2	Monroe County	3
Amite County	1	Montgomery County	2
Bolivar County	36	Neshoba County	7
Calhoun County	2	Oktibbeha County	4
Carroll County	2	Panola County	7
Chickasaw County	8	Pearl River County	1
Choctaw County	2	Perry County	7
Claiborne County	1	Pike County	8
Clay County	5	Pontotoc County	5
Coahoma County	25	Quitman County	11
Copiah County	5	Rankin County	1
Covington County	5	Sharkey County	1
De Soto County	7	Smith County	3
Forrest County	2	Sunflower County	4
Franklin County	2	Tallahatchie County	9
George County	4	Tate County	1
Green County	3	Tippah County	2
Hancock County	1	Tunica County	7
Harrison County	1	Union County	2
Hinds County	20	Walthall County	1
Holmes County	4	Warren County	3
Issaquena County	1	Wayne County	2
Ittawamba County	6	Webster County	1
Jasper County	1	Wilkinson County	1
Jefferson County	1	Winston County	2
Jefferson Davis County	4	Yazoo County	12
Jones County	6		
Kemper County	2	Total	321
Lamar County	1		
Lauderdale County	6	South Carolina:	
Lawrence County	1	Laurens County	2
Lee County	9	Marion County	1
Leflore County	7	Spartanburg County	3
Lincoln County	6	Williamsburg County	1
Lowndes County	6		
Marion County	4	Total	7

City Reports for Week Ended Mar. 16, 1918.

Place.	Cases.	Deaths.	Place.	Cases.	Deaths.
Atlanta, Ga	....	2	Michigan City, Ind	1	1
Baltimore, Md	....	1	Nashville, Tenn	....	1
Birmingham, Ala	5	1	New Orleans, La	....	2
Charlotte, N. C	....	1	San Diego, Cal	1	....
Dallas, Tex	....	1	Spartanburg, S. C	1	....
Fort Worth, Tex	1	....	Washington, D. C	1	....
Jacksonville, Fla	1	....	Winston-Salem, N. C	2	....
Lexington, Ky	....	1	Worcester, Mass	1	....
Memphis, Tenn	1	....			

PNEUMONIA.

City Reports for Week Ended Mar. 16, 1918.

Place.	Cases.	Deaths.	Place.	Cases.	Deaths.
Akron, Ohio	6		Louisville, Ky	1	8
Alameda, Cal	3	3	Lowell, Mass	4	6
Ann Arbor, Mich	1		Lynn, Mass	11	3
Atlanta, Ga	2	4	Macon, Ga	3	3
Baltimore, Md	95	28	Malden, Mass	5	1
Battle Creek, Mich	1		Manchester, N. H	3	3
Boston, Mass	38	29	McKeesport, Pa	5	
Braddock, Pa	1		Muskegon, Mich	2	1
Bridgeport, Conn	4	18	Newark, N. J	71	22
Brockton, Mass	4	3	New Bedford, Mass	4	1
Cambridge, Mass	10	3	Newburgh, N. Y	1	1
Chelsea, Mass	9	3	Newburyport, Mass	2	
Chicago, Ill	427	143	Newport, Ky	2	2
Chicopee, Mass	2		Newton, Mass	5	4
Cleveland, Ohio	26	22	Northampton, Mass	2	1
Clinton, Mass	2		North Little Rock, Ark	1	1
Columbia, S. C	1		Oakland, Cal	5	13
Detroit, Mich	11	50	Oak Park, Ill	2	2
Easton, Pa	2		Parkersburg, W. Va	2	1
Everett, Mass	4	2	Pasadena, Cal	2	
Fall River, Mass	5	3	Philadelphia, Pa	180	116
Fort Worth, Tex	6	6	Pittsburgh, Pa	37	31
Grand Rapids, Mich	13	1	Pontiac, Mich	4	1
Harrisburg, Pa	2	6	Quincy, Mass	1	3
Harrison, N. J	1		Reading, Pa	1	
Haverhill, Mass	4	1	Richmond, Va	1	8
Houston, Tex	3	5	Rochester, N. Y	16	8
Jackson, Mich	1		St. Joseph, Mo	2	3
Jackson, Miss	1		Salem, Mass	1	
Jacksonville, Fla	2	1	San Diego, Cal		2
Johnstown, Pa	4	3	San Francisco, Cal	12	13
Kalamazoo, Mich	3	1	Schenectady, N. Y	8	2
Kansas City, Kans	3		Somerville, Mass	6	1
Kansas City, Mo	9	15	Springfield, Mass	13	4
Lancaster, Pa	1		Springfield, Ohio	2	1
Lawrence, Mass	4	4	Stockton, Cal	3	
Leavenworth, Kans	2		Waco, Tex	4	1
Lincoln, Nebr	1	1	Wichita, Kans	2	1
Little Rock, Ark	11	1	Wilkinsburg, Pa	1	1
Long Beach, Cal	2	1	Worcester, Mass	4	4
Los Angeles, Cal	7	4	Yonkers, N. Y	3	2

POLIOMYELITIS (INFANTILE PARALYSIS).

State Reports for February, 1918.

Place.	New cases reported.	Place.	New cases reported.
Colorado:		**Pennsylvania:**	
Delta County	1	Allegheny County	4
		Armstrong County	1
Iowa:		Mercer County	1
Clayton County	1	Northampton County	1
Dickinson County	1		
		Total	7
Total	2		
		Rhode Island:	
Mississippi:		Providence	1
Marion County	1		
Tishomingo County	1	**South Dakota:**	
		Roberts County	1
Total	2		
New Jersey:			
Essex County	3		
Hudson County	1		
Total	4		

POLIOMYELITIS (INFANTILE PARALYSIS)—Continued.

City Reports for Week Ended Mar. 16, 1918.

Place.	Cases.	Deaths.	Place.	Cases.	Deaths.
Boston, Mass.	1	....	Lynchburg, Va.	1	....
Chicago, Ill.	2	1	Milwaukee, Wis.	6	....
Columbus, Ohio	2	1	Pawtucket, R. I.	....	4

RABIES IN ANIMALS.

City Reports for Week Ended Mar. 16, 1918.

Place.	Cases.	Place.	Cases.
Charleston, S. C.	1	Kokomo, Ind.	3
Detroit, Mich.	1	Newark, N. J.	1
Jacksonville, Fla.	1	St. Paul, Minn.	1
Kansas City, Mo.	1		

SCARLET FEVER.

See Diphtheria, measles, scarlet fever, and tuberculosis, page 515.

SMALLPOX.

New Jersey—Atlantic City.

During the period from February 13 to March 28, 1918, 17 cases of smallpox of mild type were notified at Atlantic City, N. J.

Kansas Report for February, 1918.

Place.	New cases reported.	Deaths.	Vaccination history of cases.			
			Number vaccinated within 7 years preceding attack.	Number last vaccinated more than 7 years preceding attack.	Number never successfully vaccinated.	Vaccination history not obtained or uncertain.
Kansas:						
Allen County—						
Humboldt	3				3	....
Iola	11				9	2
Anderson County—						
Colony	7				7	....
Kincaid	1			1	....	....
Westphalia	2				2	....
Atchison County—						
Atchison	2			2	....	....
Huron	1				1	....
Muscotah	1				1	....
Potter	1				1	....
Barton County—						
Great Bend	9			1	7	1
Heizer	1				1	....
Hoisington	1				1	....
Pawnee Rock	8				8	....
Bourbon County—						
Bronson	3				3	....
Fort Scott	6				6	....
Fulton	7				7	....
Hammond	1				1	....
Mapleton	2				2	....
Brown County—						
Hiawatha	18				18	....
Horton	6				5	1

SMALLPOX—Continued.

Kansas Report for February, 1918—Continued.

Place.	New cases reported.	Deaths.	Number vaccinated within 7 years preceding attack.	Number last vaccinated more than 7 years preceding attack.	Number never successfully vaccinated.	Vaccination history not obtained or uncertain.
Kansas—Continued.						
Butler County—						
Augusta............	7	....	....	....	7	....
Benton............	1	....	....	1	....	....
Douglass...........	3	....	1	....	2	....
Eldorado...........	26	....	....	....	26	....
Rose Hill...........	1	....	....	....	1	....
Chase County—						
Cottonwood Falls.....	2	....	....	1	1	....
Chautauqua County—						
Chautauqua..........	1	....	....	1	....	....
Cherokee County—						
Baxter Springs.........	10	....	....	....	10	....
Columbus...........	3	....	....	....	3	....
Crestline...........	1	....	....	....	1	....
Galena.............	25	....	....	1	23	1
Mineral............	5	....	....	....	5	....
Scammon...........	5	....	....	....	5	....
Skidmore...........	3	....	....	....	3	....
Treece.............	22	....	....	....	22	....
Turk..............	2	....	....	....	2	....
Weir..............	1	....	....	....	1	....
Clark County—						
Minneola...........	1	....	....	....	1	....
Clay County—						
Clay Center..........	2	....	....	....	2	....
Wakefield...........	1	....	....	....	1	....
Cloud County—						
Clyde.............	5	....	....	....	5	....
Courtland...........	1	....	....	....	1	....
Hollis.............	2	....	....	....	2	....
Coffey County—						
Burlington...........	2	....	....	....	2	....
Hartford...........	1	....	....	....	1	....
Le Roy............	5	....	....	....	5	....
Cowley County—						
Arkansas City..........	39	....	....	1	37	1
Cambridge...........	7	....	....	....	7	....
Grand Summit.........	3	....	....	....	3	....
Cowley County—						
Geuda Springs.........	1	....	....	....	1	....
Maple City..........	1	....	....	....	1	....
Rock.............	1	....	....	....	1	....
Winfield............	8	....	....	....	8	....
Crawford County—						
Arcadia............	1	....	....	....	1	....
Arma.............	18	....	....	....	17	1
Cherokee...........	1	....	....	....	1	....
Frontenac...........	10	....	....	....	10	....
Girard.............	31	....	1	1	29	....
Pittsburg...........	46	....	....	....	46	....
Radley.............	2	....	....	....	2	....
Ringo.............	1	....	....	1	....	....
Walnut............	1	....	....	....	1	....
Decatur County—						
Danbury, Nebr., R. D.....	1	....	....	....	1	....
Oberlin............	1	....	....	....	1	....
Dickinson County—						
Abilene............	3	....	....	....	3	....
Chapman...........	1	....	....	....	1	....
Herington...........	1	....	....	....	1	....
Doniphan County—						
Troy..............	1	....	....	....	1	....
Wathena...........	1	....	....	....	1	....
White Cloud..........	1	....	....	....	1	....
Douglas County—						
Baldwin............	2	....	....	....	2	....
Eudora............	7	....	....	....	7	....
Lawrence...........	14	....	....	....	13	1
Ellis County—						
Ellis..............	11	....	....	....	11	....
Hays..............	1	....	....	....	1	....

SMALLPOX—Continued.

Kansas Report for February, 1918—Continued.

Place.	New cases reported.	Deaths.	Number vaccinated within 7 years preceding attack.	Number last vaccinated more than 7 years preceding attack.	Number never successfully vaccinated.	Vaccination history not obtained or uncertain.
Kansas—Continued.						
Ellsworth County—						
Langley	1			1		
Marquette	3				3	
Finney County—						
Garden City	2				2	
Ford County—						
Fort Dodge	1				1	
Franklin County—						
Ottawa	12				12	
Geary County—						
Junction City	13		2	1	10	
Milford	1				1	
Gove County—						
Quinter	4				4	
Graham County—						
Hill City	13				13	
Palco	3				3	
Penokee	7				7	
Gray County—						
Cimarron	6				6	
Greenwood County—						
Climax	1				1	
Eureka	1				1	
Piedmont	4				4	
Harper County—						
Anthony	2				2	
Harvey County—						
Newton	3				3	
Jackson County—						
Holton	1		1			
Soldier	3				3	
Jefferson County—						
Grantville	3				3	
McLouth	12				12	
Perry	5				5	
Williamstown	2				2	
Jewell County—						
Burr Oak	4				4	
Formoso	4				4	
Mankato	2				2	
Johnson County—						
DeSoto	3				3	
Lenexa	1				1	
Merriam	3				3	
Olathe	1				1	
Overland Park	1				1	
Springhill	2				2	
Stanley	1				1	
Stillwell	1				1	
Washita	1				1	
Kingman County—						
Rago	1				1	
Kiowa County—						
Greensburg	4				4	
Haviland	9				9	
Labette County—						
Bartlett	1				1	
Chetopa	5				5	
Edna	2				2	
Oswego	1				1	
Parsons	10			3	7	
Lane County—						
Healy	1				1	
Leavenworth County—						
Bain City	2				2	
Easton	1				1	
Lansing	3				3	
Leavenworth	20			3	17	
Linwood	4				4	
Richardson	1				1	
Lincoln County—						
Barnard	4				4	
Lincoln	1				1	

SMALLPOX—Continued.

Kansas Report for February, 1918—Continued.

Place.	New cases reported.	Deaths.	Number vaccinated within 7 years preceding attack.	Number last vaccinated more than 7 years preceding attack.	Number never successfully vaccinated.	Vaccination history not obtained or uncertain.
Kansas —Continued.						
Linn County—						
Blue Mound	1				1	
Boiscourt	1				1	
Centerville	1			1		
Fontana	1				1	
Fulton	1				1	
Lane	1				1	
Logan County—						
Ben Allen	1				1	
Lyon County—						
Americus	4				4	
Emporia	33				43	10
Madison	2				2	
Plymouth	1				1	
Marion County—						
Durham	1				1	
Hillsboro	6			2	4	
LeHigh	23				23	
Marion	2			1	1	
Peabody	4				4	
Marshall County—						
Blue Rapids	1				1	
Irving	1				1	
Lees Summitt	1				1	
Marysville	2			1	1	
Waterville	1				1	
Miami County—						
Fontana	1				1	
Hillsdale	1				1	
Osawatomie	16			1	15	
Mitchell County—						
Glen Elder	2				2	
Tipton	1				1	
Montgomery County—						
Bolton	3				3	
Caney	9				9	
Cherryvale	1				1	
Coffeyville	37				37	
Dearing	1				1	
Independence	20			1	19	
Morris County—						
Council Grove	5			1	4	
White City	2				2	
Nemaha County—						
Corning	1				1	
Neosho County—						
Chanute	1				1	
Norton County—						
Almena	3				3	
Osage County—						
Burlingame	4				4	
Carbon Dale	4				4	
Lyndon	6				6	
Olivet	2			1	1	
Osage City	9			1	8	
Overbrook	2				2	
Scranton	4				4	
Osborne County—						
Osborne	1				1	
Ottawa County—						
Delphos	1				1	
Minneapolis	4				1	
Niles	5				5	
Tescott	2				2	
Pawnee County—						
Burdett	1			1		
Larned	13				13	
Rozel	1				1	
Rush Center	9				9	
Phillips County						
Gretna	2					
Long Island	3				3	
Prairie View	12				12	

SMALLPOX—Continued.

Kansas Report for February, 1918—Continued.

Place.	New cases reported.	Deaths.	Vaccination history of cases.			
			Number vaccinated within 7 years preceding attack.	Number last vaccinated more than 7 years preceding attack.	Number never successfully vaccinated.	Vaccination history not obtained or uncertain.
Kansas—Continued.						
Pottawatomie County—						
Belvue	2				2	
Wamego	1				1	
Pratt County—						
Pratt	1				1	
Reno County—						
Hutchinson	10				10	
Turon	1				1	
Republic County—						
Belleville	1				1	
Courtland	1				1	
Hollis	2				2	
Munden	3				3	
Republic	2				2	
Talmo	1				1	
Riley County—						
Cleburne	1				1	
Leonardville	4			2	2	
Manhattan	43				43	
Ogden	4				4	
Randolph	1				1	
Riley	1				1	
Winkler	1				1	
Rush County—						
Otis	1				1	
Saline County—						
Gypsum	2				2	
New Cambria	5				5	
Salina	15				15	
Sedgwick County—						
Garden Plain	3				3	
Kechi	3				3	
Sedgwick	2				2	
Valley Center	2				2	
Wichita	67				67	
Seward County—						
Liberal	4			1	3	
Shawnee County—						
Oakland	1				1	
Richland	1				1	
Topeka	37			5	32	
Smith County—						
Bellaire	3				3	
Smith Center	3				3	
Stafford County—						
St. John	7				7	
Stevens County—						
Hugoton	1				1	
Sumner County—						
Argonia	2				2	
Conway Springs	6				6	
Oxford	1				1	
South Haven	3			1	2	
Wellington	10				10	
Thomas County—						
Rexford	1				1	
Trego County—						
Collyer	4				4	
Washington County—						
Haddam	4				4	
Wilson County—						
New Albany	8				8	
Woodson County—						
Buffalo	1				1	
Gridley	2				2	
Neosho Falls	2				2	
Yates Center	8				7	1
Wyandotte County—						
Kansas City	187				187	
Total	1,419		8	39	1,353	19

SMALLPOX—Continued.

Miscellaneous State Reports.

Place.	Cases.	Deaths.	Place.	Cases.	Deaths.
Colorado (Feb. 1-28):			**Iowa—Continued.**		
Alamosa County	2		Woodbury County	1	
Boulder County	1		Wright County	15	
Delta County	14				
Denver County	95		Total	561	
Eagle County	1				
El Paso County	21		**Maine (Feb. 1-28):**		
Jefferson County	9		Aroostook County—		
Larimer County	8		Portage (town)	1	
Mesa County	1		Dyer Brook (town)	5	
Montezuma County	1		Van Buren (town)	8	
Otero County	1		Mapleton (town)	3	
Phillips County	1		Frenchville (town)	28	
Pueblo County	6		St. Francis	4	
Sedgwick County	10		Smyrna (town)	1	
Weld County	5		Oakfield (town)	4	
			Fort Fairfield (town)	1	
Total	176		Cumberland County—		
			Brunswick (town)	6	
Iowa (Feb. 1-28):			Hancock County—		
Adair County	2		Bucksport (town)	2	
Appanoose County	1		Kennebec County—		
Audubon County	9		Rome (town)	2	
Benton County	3		Augusta	3	
Boone County	10		Oxford County—		
Bremer County	2		Buckfield (town)	2	
Buchanan County	2		Albany (town)	5	
Butler County	9		Gilead (town)	3	
Calhoun County	1		Penobscot County—		
Cass County	3		Bangor	1	
Cerro Gordo County	4		Orono (town)	2	
Cherokee County	2		Piscataquis County—		
Crawford County	4		Greenville (town)	5	
Dallas County	8		Somerset County—		
Decatur County	2		Mercer (town)	2	
Des Moines County	4		Washington County—		
Dickinson County	16		Milbridge (town)	5	
Emmet County	1		Centerville (town)	3	
Fayette County	1		Eastport	7	
Fremont County	2				
Greene County	6		Total	103	
Grundy County	5				
Hancock County	13		**Mississippi (Feb. 1-28):**		
Hardin County	8		Adams County	2	
Henry County	1		Alcorn County	15	
Jasper County	2		Amite County	2	
Jefferson County	3		Benton County	1	
Johnson County	5		Bolivar County	31	
Kossuth County	9		Calhoun County	10	
Linn County	4		Carroll County	4	
Lucas County	11		Chickasaw County	27	
Madison County	10		Choctaw County	1	
Mahaska County	1		Clarke County	25	
Marion County	3		Clay County	17	
Mills County	11		Coahoma County	10	
Mitchell County	16		Covington County	5	
Monona County	3		De Soto County	2	
Monroe County	4		Forrest County	19	
Montgomery County	1		Greene County	1	
O'Brien County	4		Harrison County	1	
Page County	5		Hinds County	42	
Palo Alto County	10		Holmes County	5	
Plymouth County	4		Itawamba County	1	
Polk County	127		Jasper County	72	
Pottawattamie County	98		Jefferson Davis County	1	
Poweshiek County	2		Jones County	47	
Ringgold County	6		Kemper County	1	
Sac County	1		Lafayette County	2	
Scott County	9		Lamar County	14	
Shelby County	1		Lauderdale County	1	
Sioux County	14		Leake County	1	
Story County	5		Lee County	11	
Tama County	1		Leflore County	87	
Wapello County	23		Lincoln County	1	
Warren County	2		Lowndes County	4	
Washington County	5		Madison County	19	
Wayne County	12		Marshall County	2	
Webster County	10		Monroe County	2	
Winnebago County	4		Montgomery County	2	

SMALLPOX—Continued.

Miscellaneous State Reports—Continued.

Place.	Cases.	Deaths.	Place.	Cases.	Deaths.
Mississippi—Continued.			**Pennsylvania (Feb. 1-28):**		
Neshoba County	4		Allegheny County	11	
Newton County	13		Beaver County	5	
Oktibbeha County	17		Bucks County	1	
Panola County	33		Cambria County	14	
Pearl River County	3		Center County	2	
Pike County	2		Clearfield County	7	
Pontotoc County	24		Dauphin County	5	
Prentiss County	8		Erie County	18	
Quitman County	8		Fayette County	7	
Rankin County	12		Franklin County	4	
Scott County	7		Indiana County	8	
Sharkey County	8		Lackawanna County	1	
Smith County	1		McKean County	8	
Sunflower County	12		Mercer County	4	
Tallahatchie County	18		Mifflin County	1	
Tate County	12		Northumberland County	1	
Tippah County	2		Philadelphia County	3	
Tunica County	6		Potter County	1	
Union County	4		Somerset County	7	
Warren County	5		Washington County	1	
Washington County	9		Westmoreland County	1	
Wayne County	5				
Webster County	12		**Total**	111	
Winston County	2				
Yalobusha County	4		**South Carolina (Feb. 1-28):**		
Yazoo County	31		Chester County	4	
			Lexington County	3	
Total	690		Spartanburg County	4	
			York County	5	
New Jersey (Feb. 1-28):					
Hudson County	1		**Total**	16	
Morris County	1				
			South Dakota (Feb. 1-28):		
Total	2		Davison County	5	
			Day County	1	
North Dakota (Feb. 1-28):			Grant County	3	
Bottineau County	11		Gregory County	1	
Cass County	4		Hand County	4	
Cavalier County	3		Kingsbury County	8	
Grand Forks County	1		Minnehaha County	6	
McKenzie County	2		Roberts County	9	
Pembina County	10		Turner County	5	
Ramsey County	1		Walworth County	12	
Renville County	1		Yankton County	6	
Rolette County	10		Lake County	7	
Ward County	2				
Williams County	2		**Total**	67	
Total	47		**Wyoming (Feb. 1-28):**		
			Sweetwater County	4	
Oregon (Feb. 1-28):			Washakie County	2	
Marion County	1		Laramie County	3	
Wasco County	1		Carbon County	1	
Portland	13				
			Total	10	
Total	15				

City Reports for Week Ended Mar. 16, 1918.

Place.	Cases.	Deaths.	Place.	Cases.	Deaths.
Akron, Ohio	22		Chicago, Ill	11	
Alton, Ill	9		Cincinnati, Ohio	17	
Anniston, Ala	18		Cleveland, Ohio	44	
Atlanta, Ga	3		Clinton, Iowa	1	
Baltimore, Md	3		Coffeyville, Kans	3	
Birmingham, Ala	83		Columbus, Ohio	19	
Buffalo, N. Y	6		Council Bluffs, Iowa	18	
Canton, Ohio	3		Dallas, Tex	12	
Cedar Rapids, Iowa	2		Davenport, Iowa	2	
Charleston, W. Va	2		Denver, Colo	26	
Charlotte, N. C	1		Des Moines, Iowa	24	
Chattanooga, Tenn	1		Detroit, Mich	37	

SMALLPOX—Continued.

City Reports for Week Ended Mar. 16, 1918—Continued.

Place.	Cases.	Deaths.	Place.	Cases.	Deaths.
Dubuque, Iowa	5		Muskegon, Mich	8	
Duluth, Minn	1		Muskogee, Okla	17	
Evansville, Ind	2		Nashville, Tenn	2	
Fort Smith, Ark	6		New Albany, Ind	1	
Fort Wayne, Ind	19		New Orleans, La	17	
Fort Worth, Tex	32		Norfolk, Va	2	
Fresno, Cal	2		Oak Park, Ill	1	
Galesburg, Ill	1		Ogden, Utah	2	
Galveston, Tex	1		Oklahoma City, Okla	36	
Grand Rapids, Mich	8		Omaha, Nebr	43	
Hammond, Ind	2		Parkersburg, W. Va	1	
Hattiesburg, Miss	2		Philadelphia, Pa	1	
Houston, Tex	2		Pittsburgh, Pa	2	
Indianapolis, Ind	48		Pontiac, Mich	2	
Jackson, Mich	2		Portland, Oreg	1	
Jacksonville, Fla	1		Quincy, Ill	8	
Jamestown, N. Y	2		Roanoke, Va	6	
Kalamazoo, Mich	1		Rock Island, Ill	1	
Kansas City, Kans	36		St. Joseph, Mo	17	
Kansas City, Mo	100	1	St. Louis, Mo	20	
Knoxville, Tenn	8		St. Paul, Minn	4	
Kokomo, Ind	3		Salt Lake City, Utah	17	
La Crosse, Wis	6		San Diego, Cal	1	
Leavenworth, Kans	2		Sandusky, Ohio	7	
Lima, Ohio	12		San Francisco, Cal	9	
Lincoln, Nebr	12		Seattle, Wash	2	
Little Rock, Ark	24		Sioux City, Iowa	19	
Lorain, Ohio	1		South Bend, Ind	4	
Louisville, Ky	4		Springfield, Ill	5	
Lowell, Mass	1		Springfield, Ohio	2	
Macon, Ga	2		Steelton, Pa	1	
Madison, Wis	1		Steubenville, Ohio	1	
Memphis, Tenn	22		Superior, Wis	2	
Michigan City, Ind	2		Tacoma, Wash	2	
Milwaukee, Wis	12		Terre Haute, Ind	3	
Minneapolis, Minn	18		Toledo, Ohio	5	
Mobile, Ala	8		Waco, Tex	4	
Montgomery, Ala	8		Wichita, Kans	29	
Morristown, N. J	1		Winston-Salem, N. C	5	
Muncie, Ind	7		York, Pa	1	

TETANUS.

City Reports for Week Ended Mar. 16, 1918.

Place.	Cases.	Deaths.	Place.	Cases.	Deaths.
Baltimore, Md		1	Philadelphia, Pa		1
Cincinnati, Ohio		1	St. Louis, Mo		1
Elizabeth, N. J	1		San Diego, Cal	1	1
New Orleans, La		4	Schenectady, N. Y		1
New York, N. Y		1			

TUBERCULOSIS.

See Diphtheria, measles, scarlet fever, and tuberculosis, page 515.

TYPHOID FEVER.

State Reports for February, 1918.

Place.	New cases reported.	Place.	New cases reported.
Colorado:		**Mississippi—Continued.**	
Denver	1	Lincoln County	1
Jefferson County	1	Lowndes County	6
San Miguel County	1	Madison County	1
Weld County	1	Marion County	2
		Marshall County	5
Total	4	Montgomery County	6
		Pearl River County	2
Kansas:		Pike County	4
Allen County—		Pontotoc County	5
La Harpe	3	Prentiss County	1
Moran	3	Scott County	1
Brown County—		Simpson County	1
Morrill	1	Smith County	3
Butler County—		Sunflower County	3
El Dorado	3	Tallahatchie County	3
Cherokee County—		Tippah County	1
Galena	1	Tishomingo County	2
Clark County—		Union County	2
Ashland	1	Warren County	14
Franklin County—		Washington County	2
Ottawa	2	Webster County	2
Geary County—		Wilkinson County	4
Junction City	1	Yalobusha County	2
Leavenworth County—		Yazoo County	8
Lansing	2		
Mitchell County—		Total	141
Scottsville	2		
Montgomery County—		**Nebraska:**	
Cherryvale	1	Douglas County	2
Independence	2	Richardson County	1
Pawnee County—			
Larned	1	Total	3
Republic County—			
Belleville	1	**New Jersey—**	
Sedgwick County—		Atlantic County	1
Wichita	1	Bergen County	1
Shawnee County—		Burlington County	6
Topeka	1	Camden County	1
Sumner County—		Cape May County	1
Wellington	1	Cumberland County	1
Wyandotte County—		Essex County	3
Kansas City	3	Gloucester County	3
		Hudson County	2
Total	30	Mercer County	3
		Monmouth County	5
Maine:		Morris County	1
Knox County—		Ocean County	1
Camden	1	Passaic County	1
Washington County—		Union County	2
Eastport	4		
		Total	32
Total	5		
		North Dakota:	
Mississippi:		Barnes County	2
Adams County	2	Nelson County	1
Alcorn County	3	Walsh County	1
Amite County	5	Wells County	1
Benton County	3	Williams County	1
Bolivar County	2		
Calhoun County	1	Total	6
Chickasaw County	2		
Choctaw County	5	**Oregon:**	
Clarke County	3	Clackamas County	1
Copiah County	3	Hood River County	1
De Soto County	1	Portland	2
Grenada County	6		
Hancock County	1	Total	4
Harrison County	1		
Hinds County	1	**Pennsylvania:**	
Holmes County	1	Allegheny County	98
Ittawamba County	6	Armstrong County	47
Jackson County	3	Beaver County	7
Jasper County	2	Bedford County	1
Jefferson Davis County	3	Berks County	8
Jones County	1	Blair County	7
Leake County	1	Bradford County	5
Leflore County	4	Bucks County	10

TYPHOID FEVER—Continued.

State Reports for February, 1918—Continued.

Place.	New cases reported.	Place.	New cases reported.
Pennsylvania—Continued.		**Pennsylvania—Continued.**	
Butler County	3	Union County	1
Carbon County	1	Warren County	1
Chester County	3	Washington County	1
Clarion County	1	Westmoreland County	6
Crawford County	3	York County	13
Cumberland County	2		
Delaware County	1	Total	301
Erie County	1		
Fayette County	2	**Rhode Island:**	
Franklin County	1	Hope Valley (town)	1
Huntingdon County	1	Providence	7
Jefferson County	1		
Lackawanna County	1	Total	8
Lancaster County	6		
Lawrence County	5	**South Carolina:**	
Lebanon County	2	Aiken County	1
Lehigh County	3	Greenville County	1
Luzerne County	1	Laurens County	3
Lycoming County	1	Lexington County	1
McKean County	1	Orangeburg County	1
Mercer County	15	Richland County	1
Montgomery County	10		
Montour County	1	Total	8
Northampton County	5		
Northumberland County	2	**South Dakota:**	
Perry County	3	Miner County	1
Philadelphia County	16		
Somerset County	1	**Wyoming:**	
Sullivan County	1	Washakie County	1
Susquehanna County	2		

City Reports for Week Ended Mar. 16, 1918.

Place.	Cases.	Deaths.	Place.	Cases.	Deaths.
Albany, N. Y	1		Milwaukee, Wis	6	2
Altoona, Pa	3		Minneapolis, Minn	12	1
Anniston, Ala	1		Moline, Ill	3	1
Baltimore, Md	6	1	Morgantown, W. Va	2	
Battle Creek, Mich	1		New Bedford, Mass		
Birmingham, Ala	2		New Haven, Conn	1	
Boston, Mass	1		New Orleans, La	4	
Brockton, Mass			Newport, Ky	1	
Buffalo, N. Y	3	1	Newton, Mass	1	
Canton, Ohio	1		New York, N. Y	7	2
Charlotte, N. C	2		Oakland, Cal	1	
Chicago, Ill	6	1	Omaha, Nebr		1
Columbia, S. C	3		Parkersburg, W. Va	2	
Columbus, Ohio	1		Passaic, N. J	1	
Dallas, Tex	1		Philadelphia, Pa	3	1
Danville, Ill	1	1	Pittsburgh, Pa	6	4
Denver, Colo	1		Pontiac, Mich	1	
Detroit, Mich	1		Portland, Me	1	
Dubuque, Iowa	19		Quincy, Ill	1	
Duluth, Minn	1		Reading, Pa	2	
Elmira, N. Y	2		Richmond, Va	1	
Evansville, Ind	1		Rock Island, Ill	1	
Galveston, Tex		1	Saginaw, Mich	2	
Grand Rapids, Mich	2		St. Louis, Mo	6	1
Hammond, Ind	7	1	St. Paul, Minn		1
Hoboken, N. J	1		Salt Lake City, Utah	4	
Holyoke, Mass	1		San Diego, Cal	1	
Jackson, Miss	1		San Francisco, Cal	2	2
Jacksonville, Fla	3	2	Scranton, Pa		1
Jersey City, N. J	1	2	South Bend, Ind	1	
Kansas City, Mo	1		Stockton, Cal	2	
Lima, Ohio		1	Syracuse, N. Y	2	
Little Rock, Ark	1		Toledo, Ohio	4	
Lorain, Ohio	1		Washington, D. C	3	1
Los Angeles, Cal	1		Wheeling, W. Va		1
Louisville, Ky	1		Wilkes-Barre, Pa	1	
Macon, Ga	1		Wilmington, N. C	2	1
Manchester, N. H	1	1	Yonkers, N. Y	1	1
Memphis, Tenn	1		Zanesville, Ohio	7	

DIPHTHERIA, MEASLES, SCARLET FEVER, AND TUBERCULOSIS.

State Reports for February, 1918.

State.	Cases reported.			State.	Cases reported.		
	Diph-theria.	Measles.	Scarlet fever.		Diph-theria.	Measles.	Scarlet fever.
Colorado	36	482	244	North Dakota	29	57	177
Iowa	78	....	447	Oregon	13	392	31
Kansas	88	2,391	464	Pennsylvania	1,049	4,432	• 972
Maine	15	217	22	Rhode Island	64	87	48
Mississippi	54	10,985	24	South Carolina	45	276	6
Nebraska	34	293	217	South Dakota	6	337	81
New Jersey	361	3,695	337	Wyoming	19	110	44

City Reports for Week Ended Mar. 16, 1918.

City.	Population as of July 1, 1916 (estimated by U. S. Census Bureau).	Total deaths from all causes.	Diphtheria.		Measles.		Scarlet fever.		Tuberculosis.	
			Cases.	Deaths.	Cases.	Deaths.	Cases.	Deaths.	Cases.	Deaths.
Over 500,000 inhabitants:										
Baltimore, Md	589,621	286	5	.....	408	8	2	.....	50	42
Boston, Mass	756,476	289	68	2	255	3	24	2	59	20
Chicago, Ill	2,497,722	760	110	15	70	1	36	1	494	79
Cleveland, Ohio	674,073	199	60	3	22	.....	5	1	30	23
Detroit, Mich	571,784	244	35	4	19	5	35	.....	32	27
Los Angeles, Cal	503,812	153	16	1	314	1	4	.....	27	23
New York, N. Y	5,602,841	1,939	249	26	1,475	37	153	2	323	208
Philadelphia, Pa	1,709,518	729	52	8	534	1	53	2	124	95
Pittsburgh, Pa	579,090	196	20	.....	239	5	12	.....	26	14
St. Louis, Mo	757,309	265	66	1	99	1	32	.....	49	21
From 300,000 to 500,000 inhabitants:										
Buffalo, N. Y	468,558	134	10	.....	119	.....			33	16
Cincinnati, Ohio	410,476	163	17	1	27	1	7	1	32	22
Jersey City, N. J	306,345	120	10	3	67	3	9	.....	13	14
Milwaukee, Wis	436,535		1	1	315	2	35	3	15	8
Minneapolis, Minn	363,454		17	1	18	.....	21	.....	34	9
Newark, N. J	408,894	155	20	3	321	3	20	.....	37	21
New Orleans, La	371,747		16	.....	29	.....			36	24
San Francisco, Cal	463,516	157	9	.....	69	1	21	.....	43	12
Seattle, Wash	348,639		3	.....	64	2		1	9	5
Washington, D. C	363,980	182	11	.....	464	1	43	2	21	25
From 200,000 to 300,000 inhabitants:										
Columbus, Ohio	214,878	75	1	.....	28	.....	23	.....	8	.....
Denver, Colo	260,800	72	7	.....	197	.....	39	.....	.....	17
Indianapolis, Ind	271,708	79	18	1	121	.....	36	.....	11	9
Kansas City, Mo	297,847	99	15	2	81	.....	20	.....	2	15
Louisville, Ky	238,910	111	9	1	61	.....	5	.....	31	11
Portland, Oreg	295,463	79	.....	.....	239	.....	4	.....	8	8
Providence, R. I	254,960	80	11	.....	37	.....	5	1	.....	7
Rochester, N. Y	256,417	75	11	.....	91	.....	18	.....	19	6
St. Paul, Minn	247,232	59	18	.....	19	.....	35	2	17	5
From 100,000 to 200,000 inhabitants:										
Albany, N. Y	104,199	.....	3	.....	17	.....	1	.....	9	.....
Atlanta, Ga	190,558	60	1	.....	8	.....	4	.....	13	3
Birmingham, Ala	181,762	77	.....	.....	48	.....			17	18
Bridgeport, Conn	121,579	62	9	1	2	.....	2	.....	4	8
Cambridge, Mass	112,981	31	8	.....	56	.....	6	.....	5	3
Camden, N. J	106,233	.....	2	.....	28	.....	2	.....	4	.....
Dallas, Tex	124,527	9	.....	.....	3	.....	1	.....	2	6
Des Moines, Iowa	101,598	.....	1	.....	.....	.....	2	.....	.....	.....
Fall River, Mass	128,366	44	6	.....	6	.....	4	.....	9	7
Fort Worth, Tex	104,562	25	1	1	6	1	.....	.....	.....	.....
Grand Rapids, Mich	128,291	34	11	.....	10	.....	9	.....	2	.....
Hartford, Conn	110,900	46	2	1	12	.....	3	.....	4	3
Houston, Tex	112,307	55	.....	.....	46	.....	2	.....	.....	7
Lawrence, Mass	100,560	29	1	.....	1	.....	.....	.....	3	3
Lowell, Mass	113,245	37	4	2	3	.....	2	.....	2	2
Lynn, Mass	102,425	19	1	.....	31	.....	4	.....	6	2

DIPHTHERIA, MEASLES, SCARLET FEVER, AND TUBERCULOSIS—Continued.

City Reports for Week Ended Mar. 16, 1918—Continued.

City.	Population as of July 1, 1916 (estimated by U.S Census Bureau).	Total deaths from all causes.	Diphtheria.		Measles.		Scarlet fever.		Tuberculosis.	
			Cases.	Deaths.	Cases.	Deaths.	Cases.	Deaths.	Cases.	Deaths.
From 100,000 to 200,000 inhabitants—Continued.										
Memphis, Tenn	148,995	54	3		20		6		8	5
Nashville, Tenn	117,057	51			14		3		4	3
New Bedford, Mass	118,158	31			10		2		19	2
New Haven, Conn	149,685	63	2		5				7	2
Oakland, Cal	198,604	66			39		9		9	7
Omaha, Nebr	165,470	32	3		23		13		1	3
Reading, Pa	109,381	36	4		37		6		1	2
Richmond, Va	156,687	61	2		90		7		9	4
Salt Lake City, Utah	117,399	41	8		12		10			3
Scranton, Pa	146,811	48	4	1	2		5		5	5
Springfield, Mass	105,942	33	7	1	36	1	4		1	2
Syracuse, N. Y	155,624	53	15		86		17		3	2
Tacoma, Wash	112,770		3		4		43			
Toledo, Ohio	191,554	73	7		19		12	1	2	11
Trenton, N. J	111,593	56	4		11				6	2
Worcester, Mass	163,314	55	3		5				4	7
From 50,000 to 100,000 inhabitants:										
Akron, Ohio	85,625		10		14		7		8	
Altoona, Pa	58,659		1		9				1	
Atlantic City, N. J	57,660				31				3	
Bayonne, N. J	69,893		1		94		4		6	
Berkeley, Cal	57,653	13			10		4		5	1
Binghamton, N. Y	53,073	27	1		10		5		6	
Brockton, Mass	67,449	27	1		8		7		3	
Canton, Ohio	60,852	15			2		1			1
Charleston, S. C	60,734	29	3	1	5		1			5
Chattanooga, Tenn	60,075	4			5					1
Covington, Ky	57,144	24	1		8				2	5
Duluth, Minn	94,495	13	2		23		6		2	1
Elizabeth, N. J	86,090	26	5		46	1	3		7	3
El Paso, Tex	63,705	40		1	11		3			9
Erie, Pa	75,195	38	5		2		7		6	3
Evansville, Ind	76,078	29	2	1	25		1		9	3
Fort Wayne, Ind	76,183	34	5		3					
Harrisburg, Pa	72,015	26	1	1	20		4			3
Hoboken, N. J	77,214	32	2		7				5	3
Holyoke, Mass	65,286	13	1		16		2		3	2
Jacksonville, Fla	76,101	31			16				7	4
Johnstown, Pa	68,529	28	5		6		11		4	1
Kansas City, Kans	99,437	16	1		12		4		2	
Lancaster, Pa	50,853		1		26		9		8	
Little Rock, Ark	57,343	13	2		7		2		5	2
Malden, Mass	51,155	14	4		11		1		1	
Manchester, N. H	78,283	21	3		8		3		4	2
Mobile, Ala	58,221	15	1		3					3
New Britain, Conn	53,794	15	3		10		4			1
Norfolk, Va	89,612				34		5			6
Oklahoma City, Okla	92,943	29			6		2			3
Passaic, N. J	71,744	21	1		2		1		6	2
Pawtucket, R. I	59,411	20	1		9		3			
Portland, Me	63,467	22			11					1
Rockford, Ill	55,183	19			25		4		5	
Sacramento, Cal	66,893	25			95		3		3	5
Saginaw, Mich	55,642	9	1		1		1		9	
St. Joseph, Mo	85,236	38	5		10		1		4	4
San Diego, Cal	53,630	5	4		125		8		19	3
Schenectady, N. Y	99,519	36	4	1	13				4	
Sioux City, Iowa	57,078						21			
Somerville, Mass	87,039	32	6		25		2		3	1
South Bend, Ind	68,946	13			18		4		1	
Springfield, Ill	61,120	17			45		2			1
Springfield, Ohio	51,550	20			5				2	3
Terre Haute, Ind	66,083	21			1					7
Troy, N. Y	77,916	13	1		7		4		2	1
Wichita, Kans	70,722				64		4	1	2	1
Wilkes Barre, Pa	76,776	25	9		55		3		3	
Wilmington, Del	114,260	30	3	1	25		2			4
Yonkers, N. Y	99,838		6		18		2		4	
York, Pa	51,65	17	2		10				2	1

DIPHTHERIA, MEASLES, SCARLET FEVER, AND TUBERCULOSIS—
Continued.

City Reports for Week Ended Mar. 16, 1918—Continued.

City.	Population as of July 1, 1916 (estimated by U. S. Census Bureau).	Total deaths from all causes.	Diphtheria.		Measles.		Scarlet fever.		Tuberculosis.	
			Cases.	Deaths.	Cases.	Deaths.	Cases.	Deaths.	Cases.	Deaths.
From 25,000 to 50,000 inhabitants:										
Alameda, Cal.	27,732	9	2	1	15				3	
Auburn, N. Y.	37,385	19			31					1
Austin, Tex.	34,814	15								
Battle Creek, Mich.	29,480		4		22		5		2	
Bellingham, Wash.	32,985				6					
Brookline, Mass.	32,730	7	4		17		2			1
Butler, Pa.	27,632	3	4		15		1			
Butte, Mont.	43,425	17	1		7		14	2		
Cedar Rapids, Iowa	37,308						6			
Charleston, W. Va.	29,941	7			6		2			
Charlotte, N. C.	39,823	15	1		1	1			4	
Chelsea, Mass.	46,192	21			23		2		2	3
Chicopee, Mass.	29,319	8	2		1					1
Clinton, Iowa	27,386		1		60		1			
Colorado Springs, Colo.	32,971	11							3	4
Columbia, S. C.	34,611	26	2		7		1		1	
Council Bluffs, Iowa	31,484		1	1	1		1			1
Cranston, R. I.	25,987	9			4		1			
Cumberland, Md.	26,074	12			12		5		1	
Danville, Ill.	32,261	13	1		89					
Davenport, Iowa	48,811		2		6		5			
Decatur, Ill.	39,631	10			4				8	
Dubuque, Iowa	39,873		3		6					
Durham, N. C.	25,061	9			8				2	
Easton, Pa.	30,530	14	2		15				1	
East Orange, N. J.	42,458	8	1		33		7		1	
Elgin, Ill.	28,203	7			2				1	2
Elmira, N. Y.	38,120	3			62				4	
Evanston, Ill.	28,591	3			10		2			
Everett, Mass.	39,233	13	2	1	8		4		1	1
Fort Smith, Ark.	28,638	8	1		5	2			1	
Fresno, Cal.	34,958	6			12					
Galveston, Tex.	41,863	19	1		2					3
Green Bay, Wis.	29,353	7			11		1			2
Hammond, Ind.	26,171	18	4		1		2			2
Haverhill, Mass.	48,477	13	3	1	34				1	1
Jackson, Mich.	35,363	13			17		16	1	1	2
Jackson, Miss.	29,737	13							1	
Jamestown, N. Y.	36,580	12	2						1	2
Kalamazoo, Mich.	48,896	17	1		10		2			
Kenosha, Wis.	31,576	3	7		4		2			
Kingston, N. Y.	26,771	4								1
Knoxville, Tenn.	38,676				15					
La Crosse, Wis.	31,677	10	3							
Lexington, Ky.	41,097	28	1		21					5
Lima, Ohio.	35,384	15	2							1
Lincoln, Nebr.	46,515	18	1		1		3			
Long Beach, Cal.	27,587	13	2		33					
Lynchburg, Va.	32,940	16	1		4		1		1	3
Macon, Ga.	45,757	24			3		1		4	3
Madison, Wis.	30,699	14	2	1	23		4			1
McKeesport, Pa.	47,521				21					
Medford, Mass.	26,234	5	1		5		5		3	
Moline, Ill.	27,451	12	2	1	36		2	1		1
Montgomery, Ala.	43,285		1		5					
Mount Vernon, N. Y.	37,009	9	1		12	1			2	
Muncie, Ind.	25,424	8			1		1			2
Muskegon, Mich.	26,100	14			2		1		1	
Muskogee, Okla.	44,218		1		16					
Newburgh, N. Y.	29,003	12			2		1		4	3
New Castle, Pa.	41,133		1		4		1			
Newport, Ky.	31,927	9							1	1
Newport, R. I.	30,108	5	2							1
Newton, Mass.	43,715	16	1		29				1	
Niagara Falls, N. Y.	37,383	16			2		2		4	3
Norristown, Pa.	31,401	9			1					1
Norwalk, Conn.	26,899									1
Oak Park, Ill.	26,654	7	2		15		3			
Ogden, Utah	31,404	13	1		25				2	2
Orange, N. J.	33,080	18			57		2		2	2
Oshkosh, Wis.	36,065	4					1		2	
Pasadena, Cal.	46,450	9			280				2	2
Perth Amboy, N. J.	41,185	14			15				9	1

DIPHTHERIA, MEASLES, SCARLET FEVER, AND TUBERCULOSIS—Continued.

City Reports for Week Ended Mar. 16, 1918—Continued.

City.	Population as of July 1, 1916 (estimated by U. S. Census Bureau).	Total deaths from all causes.	Diphtheria.		Measles.		Scarlet fever.		Tuberculosis.	
			Cases.	Deaths.	Cases.	Deaths.	Cases.	Deaths.	Cases.	Deaths.
From 25,000 to 50,000 inhabitants—Continued.										
Petersburg, Va.............	25,582	......	2	1	8	......	......	......	......	2
Pittsfield, Mass...........	38,629	16	2	1	4	......	1	......	4	1
Poughkeepsie, N. Y.......	30,390	......	2	1	72	......	......	......	3	1
Quincy, Ill................	36,798	7	2	......	2	......	......	......	......	......
Quincy, Mass.............	38,136	12	1	......	87	......	2	......	3	2
Racine, Wis...............	46,486	10	......	......	23	......	4	......	1	......
Roanoke, Va..............	43,284	13	......	......	21	......	......	......	1	2
Rock Island, Ill...........	28,926	14	......	......	34	......	3	......	1	......
Salem, Mass..............	48,562	13	......	......	24	......	1	......	3	......
San Jose, Cal.............	38,902	......	......	......	27	......	......	......	1	1
Sheboygan, Wis...........	28,550	8	......	......	1	......	......	......	......	......
Steubenville, Ohio.........	27,445	6	1	......	1	......	......	......	......	......
Stockton, Cal.............	35,358	12	7	......	61	......	......	......	1	......
Superior, Wis.............	46,226	12	1	......	1	......	......	......	......	......
Taunton, Mass............	36,283	13	......	......	......	......	2	......	4	......
Waco, Tex................	33,345	15	......	......	14	......	......	......	......	......
Waltham, Mass...........	30,570	8	......	......	......	......	1	......	2	......
Watertown, N. Y..........	29,894	......	......	......	32	......	......	......	4	1
West Hoboken, N. J.......	43,139	6	3	......	5	......	......	......	1	1
Wheeling, W. Va..........	43,377	10	......	......	10	......	......	......	......	......
Wilmington, N. C.........	29,892	13	......	......	35	......	......	......	1	1
Winston-Salem, N. C......	31,155	12	1	......	48	......	......	......	5	1
Woonsocket, R. I..........	44,380	......	2	1	......	......	1	......	......	......
Zanesville, Ohio...........	30,863	11	......	......	......	......	......	......	......	2
From 10,000 to 25,000 inhabitants:										
Alton, Ill.................	22,874	11	......	......	1	......	......	......	......	1
Ann Arbor, Mich..........	15,010	12	1	......	24	......	1	......	......	......
Anniston, Ala.............	14,112	......	2	......	24	......	1	......	......	......
Beaver Falls, Pa..........	13,532	......	......	......	1	......	1	......	......	......
Berlin, N. H..............	13,509	3	......	......	......	......	......	......	......	......
Braddock, Pa.............	21,685	14	......	......	......	......	1	......	......	......
Cairo, Ill.................	15,794	6	1	......	......	......	......	......	......	......
Chillicothe, Ohio..........	15,470	5	1	......	2	......	3	......	......	......
Clinton, Mass.............	13,075	1	......	......	4	......	......	......	1	......
Coffeyville, Kans.........	17,548	......	1	......	2	......	......	......	1	......
Concord, N. H............	22,669	9	1	......	2	......	......	......	......	......
Galesburg, Ill.............	24,276	9	......	......	16	......	......	......	......	1
Greenville, S. C...........	18,181	5	......	......	2	......	......	......	......	......
Harrison, N. J............	16,950	......	3	......	2	......	......	......	......	......
Hattiesburg, Miss.........	16,482	9	......	......	1	......	......	......	2	......
Janesville, Wis...........	14,399	......	......	......	2	......	4	......	......	1
Kearney, N. J.............	23,539	8	......	......	29	......	2	......	1	......
Kokomo, Ind..............	20,930	5	......	......	18	......	......	......	......	1
La Fayette, Ind...........	21,245	10	......	......	......	......	......	......	1	......
Leavenworth, Kans........	19,363	5	1	......	7	......	1	......	1	......
Marinette, Wis............	14,610	2	......	......	......	......	3	......	......	......
Melrose, Mass............	17,445	3	1	......	1	......	2	......	1	......
Michigan City, Ind........	21,512	12	......	......	1	......	1	......	1	1
Morgantown, W. Va.......	13,709	8	......	......	......	......	......	......	1	......
Morristown, N. J..........	13,284	7	......	......	......	......	......	......	2	1
Moundsville, W. Va.......	11,153	3	......	......	......	......	......	......	......	......
Muscatine, Iowa...........	17,500	......	......	......	5	......	......	......	......	......
Nanticoke, Pa.............	23,126	9	......	......	1	......	3	......	1	......
New Albany, Ind..........	23,629	10	1	......	......	......	......	......	2	3
Newburyport, Mass........	15,243	6	......	......	1	......	......	......	......	1
North Adams, Mass.......	22,019	9	......	......	......	......	......	......	......	......
Northampton, Mass........	19,926	5	......	......	1	......	1	......	1	......
North Little Rock, Ark....	14,907	5	......	......	......	......	2	......	2	......
Parkersburg, W. Va.......	20,612	8	......	......	9	......	......	......	......	......
Plainfield, N. J...........	23,805	6	1	1	5	......	3	......	5	......
Pontiac, Mich.............	17,524	10	5	......	2	......	3	......	......	......
Portsmouth, N. H.........	11,666	......	......	......	5	......	6	......	......	......
Rocky Mount, N. C........	12,067	1	......	......	......	......	......	......	......	1
Rutland, Vt...............	14,831	11	......	......	......	......	......	......	......	......
Sandusky, Ohio...........	20,193	8	......	......	......	......	......	......	1	1
Saratoga Springs, N. Y....	13,821	6	......	......	2	......	1	......	1	1
Spartanburg, S. C.........	21,365	5	1	......	5	......	......	......	3	1
Steelton, Pa...............	15,548	2	......	......	1	......	......	......	1	......
Washington, Pa...........	21,618	......	......	......	139	......	......	......	1	......
Wilkinsburg, Pa...........	23,728	10	1	1	13	......	......	......	......	......
Woburn, Mass............	15,949	4	......	......	......	......	......	......	......	2

1 Population Apr. 15, 1910; no estimate made.

FOREIGN.

CUBA.

Communicable Diseases—Habana.

Communicable diseases have been notified at Habana as follows:

Disease.	Mar. 1-10, 1918.		Cases remaining under treatment Mar. 10, 1918.
	New cases.	Deaths.	
Diphtheria	4	....	4
Leprosy	1	....	12
Malaria	12	·1	[1] 38
Measles	11	....	45
Paratyphoid fever	....	....	3
Scarlet fever	....	....	2
Typhoid fever	20	2	[2] 72
Varicella	14	....	68

[1] From the interior, 33.   [2] From the interior, 28.

INDO-CHINA.

Cholera—Plague—Smallpox—Leprosy—November, 1917.

During the month of November, 1917, 39 cases of cholera, 19 of plague, and 201 of smallpox were notified in Indo-China, as compared with 39 cases of cholera, 36 of plague, and 152 of smallpox notified during the month of October, 1917. The distribution of the cases according to Provinces was as follows:

Cholera.—Anam, 1 case; Cambodia, 31 cases; Cochin-China, 7 cases; total, 39 cases. The total for the corresponding month of the year 1916 was 151. The largest number of cases notified in November, 1917, occurred in the Province of Cambodia, 31, of which 12 were due to an outbreak of the disease occurring in the prison at Pnompenh.

Plague.—Anam, 3 cases; Cambodia, 9; Cochin-China, 7; total, 19. The total for the corresponding month of the year 1916 was 24.

Smallpox.—Anam, 60 cases; Cambodia, 6; Cochin-China, 131; Laos, 1 case; Tonkin, 3 cases; total, 201 cases. The total for the corresponding month of the year 1916 was 128.

Leprosy.—There were notified during the month of November, 1917, 11 cases of leprosy, of which 10 cases occurred at Hanoi, capital of the Province of Tonkin.

(519)

CHOLERA, PLAGUE, SMALLPOX, TYPHUS FEVER, AND YELLOW FEVER.

Reports Received During Week Ended Apr. 5, 1918.[1]

CHOLERA.

Place.	Date.	Cases.	Deaths.	Remarks.
India:				
Bombay	Dec. 3–15	2	2	
Calcutta	Dec. 30–Jan. 12		14	
Madras	Dec. 16–22	1	1	
Do	Dec. 30–Jan. 5	1		
Rangoon	Dec. 9–22	2	2	
Indo-China:				
Provinces				Nov. 1–30, 1917: Cases, 39; deaths, 32.
Anam	Nov. 1–30	1		
Cambodia	do	31	27	
Cochin-China	do	7	5	
Java:				
West Java				Dec. 30, 1917–Jan. 10, 1918
Batavia	Dec. 21–27	4	2	Cases, 22; deaths, 9.
Do	Dec. 28–Jan. 10	15	1	

PLAGUE.

Place.	Date.	Cases.	Deaths.	Remarks.
India				Dec. 9–22, 1917: Cases, 38,689; deaths, 30,711.
Bassein	Jan. 6–12		1	
Bombay	Dec. 2–29	44	38	
Calcutta	Dec. 30–Jan. 12		3	
Karachi	Dec. 2–22	10	6	
Madras	Dec. 30–Jan. 5	1		
Madras Presidency	Dec. 15–29	2,332	1,748	
Do	Dec. 30–Jan. 5	1,281	947	
Mandalay	Jan. 6–12		69	
Rangoon	Dec. 9–22	19	18	
Indo-China:				
Provinces				Nov. 1–30, 1917: Cases, 19; deaths, 14.
Anam	Nov. 1–30	3	1	
Cambodia	do	9	9	
Cochin-China	do	7	4	
Saigon	Jan. 28–Feb. 3	12	2	
Java:				
East Java	Dec. 9–23	56	56	

SMALLPOX.

Place.	Date.	Cases.	Deaths.	Remarks.
Canada:				
New Brunswick—				
Moncton	Mar. 17–23	1		
St. John	Mar. 17–23	1		
Nova Scotia—				
Sydney	Mar. 9–23	4		
Ontario—				
Ottawa	Mar. 18–24	4		
Sarnia	Mar. 17–23	1		
China:				
Chungking	Jan. 20–Feb. 2			Present.
Dairen	Feb. 17–23	6		
Hongkong	Jan. 26–Feb. 9	6	1	
Egypt:				
Alexandria	Feb. 12–28	2		
France:				
Paris	Feb. 17–23	1		
Greece:				
Saloniki	Jan. 27–Feb. 9		7	
India:				
Bombay	Dec. 2–29	34	8	
Karachi	Dec. 2–22	3		
Madras	Dec. 9–29	9	5	
Do	Dec. 30–Jan. 5	6	3	
Rangoon	Dec. 9–22	2		
Indo-China:				
Provinces				Nov. 1–30, 1917: Cases, 201; deaths, 48.
Anam	Nov. 1–30	60	10	
Cambodia	do	6	5	
Cochin-China	do	131	32	
Saigon	Jan. 28–Feb. 3	60	17	
Laos	do	1	1	
Tonkin	do	3		

[1] From medical officers of the Public Health Service, American consuls, and other sources.

CHOLERA, PLAGUE, SMALLPOX, TYPHUS FEVER, AND YELLOW FEVER—Continued.

Reports Received During Week Ended Apr. 5, 1918—Continued.

SMALLPOX—Continued.

Place.	Date.	Cases.	Deaths.	Remarks.
Italy:				
Leghorn	Feb. 19-24	1	1	
Java:				
East Java	Dec. 9-29	17		
Mid-Java	Dec. 13-26	17		
West Java	Dec. 21-27	61	3	
Do	Dec. 28-Jan. 10	24	3	
Newfoundland:				
St. John	Mar. 9-15	1		
Portugal:				
Lisbon	Feb. 10-22	2		
Portuguese East Africa:				
Lourenço Marquez	Dec. 1-31		7	
Union of South Africa:				
East Liverpool	Jan. 20-26	1		Varioloid.

TYPHUS FEVER.

Place.	Date.	Cases.	Deaths.	Remarks.
Egypt:				
Alexandria	Feb. 5-25	130	32	
Great Britain:				
Belfast	Feb. 17-Mar. 2	11	1	
Java:				Dec. 9-23, 1917: Cases, 11; deaths, 1.
East Java				
Surabaya	Dec. 17-23	6	1	Dec. 13-30, 1917: Cases, 9. Dec. 27, 1917-Jan. 2, 1918: Cases, 4.
Mid-Java				
Samarang	Dec. 13-26	1		
Do	Dec. 27-Jan. 2	1		
West Java				Dec. 21-27, 1917: Cases, 5; deaths, 1. Dec. 28, 1917-Jan. 10, 1918: Cases, 20; deaths, 10.
Batavia	Dec. 21-27	2	1	
Do	Dec. 28-Jan. 10	9		
Norway:				
Bergen	Feb. 1-16	3		

Reports Received from Dec. 29, 1917, to Mar. 29, 1918.

CHOLERA.

Place.	Date.	Cases.	Deaths.	Remarks.
China:				
Antung	Nov. 26-Dec. 2	3	1	
India:				
Bombay	Oct. 28-Nov. 24	17	12	
Do	Dec. 30-Jan. 5	74	67	
Calcutta	Sept. 16-Dec. 15		92	
Madras	Nov. 25-Dec. 1	1	1	
Do	Jan. 6-12	2	3	
Rangoon	Nov. 4-Dec. 1	3	3	
Do	Dec. 30-Jan. 5	1	1	Nov. 1-30, 1917: Cases, 2; deaths, 2.
Indo-China:				
Provinces				Sept. 1-Oct. 31, 1917: Cases, 118; deaths, 57.
Anam	Sept. 1-Oct. 31	17	13	
Cambodia	do	41	25	
Cochin-China	do	43	17	
Saigon	Nov. 22-Dec. 9	4	3	
Kwang-Chew-Wan	Sept. 1-30	10	2	
Java:				
East Java	Oct. 28-Nov. 3	1	1	
West Java				Oct. 19-Dec. 29, 1917: Cases, 116; deaths, 61.
Batavia	Oct. 19-Dec. 29	65	22	

CHOLERA, PLAGUE, SMALLPOX, TYPHUS FEVER, AND YELLOW FEVER—Continued.

Reports Received from Dec. 29, 1917, to Mar. 29, 1918—Continued.

CHOLERA—Continued.

Place.	Date.	Cases.	Deaths.	Remarks.
Persia:				
Mazanderan Province......				July 30–Sept. 3, 1917: Cases, 384;
Achraf...............	July 30–Aug. 16...	90	88	deaths, 276.
Astrabad............	July 31...........			Present.
Barfrush............	July 1–Aug. 16....	39	25	
Chahmirzad.........				25 cases reported July 31, 1917.
Chahrastagh........	June 15–July 25..	10	8	
Charoud............	Aug. 26–Sept. 3..	4	2	
Damghan...........	Aug. 26..........			Present.
Kharek.............	May 28–June 11...	21	13	
Meched............	Aug. 18–Sept. 2...	174	82	
Ouzoun Dare........	Aug. 8...........			Do.
Sabzevar...........	Aug. 24..........			Do.
Sari...............	July 3–29........	273	144	
Semman............	Aug. 31–Sept. 2...	14	5	
Yekchambe-Bazar.....	June 3...........	6		
Philippine Islands:				
Provinces..........				Nov. 18–Dec. 29, 1917: Cases,
Antique............	Nov. 18–Dec. 1...	48	32	1,053; deaths, 693. Dec. 30,
Do.............	Feb. 3–9.........	4	4	1917–Feb. 9, 1918: Cases, 914;
Bohol.............	Nov. 18–Dec. 29..	169	111	deaths, 546.
Do.............	Dec. 30–Feb. 9...	213	181	
Capiz.............	Nov. 25–Dec. 29..	27	21	
Do.............	Dec. 30–Feb. 9...	121	101	
Cebu..............	Dec. 23–29.......	3		
Do.............	Dec. 30–Feb. 9...	69	36	
Iloilo.............	Nov. 25–Dec. 29..	179	135	
Do.............	Dec. 30–Feb. 9...	82	53	
Leyte.............	Nov. 25–Dec. 22..	13	12	
Do.............	Feb. 3–9.........	9	8	
Mindanao..........	Nov. 25–Dec. 29..	337	196	
Do.............	Dec. 30–Feb. 9...	351	220	
Occidental Negros..	Nov. 25–Dec. 22..	177	123	
Do.............	Jan. 13–Feb. 9...	60	40	
Oriental Negros.....	Nov. 25–Dec. 29..	99	62	
Do.............	Dec. 30–Feb. 9...	15	13	
Romblon...........	Nov. 25–Dec. 1...	1	1	
Siam:				
Bangkok...........	Sept. 16–22......	1	1	
Turkey in Asia:				
Bagdad............	Nov. 1–15........		40	

PLAGUE.

Place.	Date.	Cases.	Deaths.	Remarks.
Brazil:				
Bahia..............	Nov. 4–Dec. 15....	4	4	
Do.............	Dec. 30–Jan. 12...	3	2	
Rio de Janeiro......	Dec. 23–29........	1		
Do.............	Jan. 6–12.........	1	1	
British Gold Coast:				
Axim..............	Jan. 8............			Present.
Ceylon:				
Colombo...........	Oct. 14–Dec. 1....	14	12	
Do.............	Dec. 30–Jan. 12...	6	5	
Ecuador............				Sept. 1–Nov. 30, 1917: Cases, 68;
Guayaquil..........	Sept. 1–30........	3	1	deaths, 24. Reported outbreak
Do.............	Oct. 1–31.........	20	8	occurring about Jan. 17, 1918.
Do.............	Nov. 1–30.........	45	15	
Egypt..............				Jan. 1–Nov. 15, 1917: Cases, 728;
Alexandria........	Jan. 14–28........	1	2	deaths, 398.
Port Said.........	July 23–29........	1	2	
India.............				Sept. 16–Dec. 8, 1917: Cases,
Bassein...........	Dec. 9–29........		8	171,192; deaths, 128,870. Dec.
Do.............	Dec. 30–Jan. 5...		2	23–29, 1917: Cases, 18,753;
Bombay...........	Oct. 28–Dec. 1...	103	85	deaths, 15,162. Dec. 30, 1917–
Do.............	Dec. 30–Jan. 5...	19	11	Jan. 5, 1918: Cases, 26,304;
Calcutta..........	Sept. 16–29.......		2	deaths, 22,677.
Henzada..........	Oct. 21–27........		1	
Karachi...........	Oct. 21–Dec. 29..	17	14	
Madras Presidency..	Oct. 31–Nov. 17..	3,294	2,560	
Do.............	Jan. 6–12.........	1,503	1,177	
Mandalay.........	Oct. 14–Nov. 17..		89	
Do.............	Dec. 30–Jan. 5...		167	
Myingyan.........	Dec. 30–Jan. 5...		37	

CHOLERA, PLAGUE, SMALLPOX, TYPHUS FEVER, AND YELLOW FEVER—Continued.

Reports Received from Dec. 29, 1917, to Mar. 29, 1918—Continued.

PLAGUE—Continued.

Place.	Date.	Cases.	Deaths.	Remarks.
India—Continued.				
Rangoon	Oct. 21–Dec. 1	32	38	
Do	Dec. 30–Jan. 5	15	14	Nov. 1–30, 1917: Cases, 27; deaths, 34.
Toungoo	Dec. 9–29		5	
Do	Dec. 30–Jan. 5		3	
Indo-China:				
Provinces				Sept. 1–Oct. 31, 1917: Cases, 70; deaths, 54.
Anam	Sept. 1–Oct. 31	25	24	
Cambodia	....do	30	19	
Cochin-China	....do	15	11	
Saigon	Oct. 31–Dec. 23	17	6	
Do	Dec. 31–Jan. 27	24	7	
Java:				
East Java				Oct. 27–Dec. 22, 1917: Cases, 131; deaths, 129.
Surabaya	Nov. 11–25	2	2	
West Java				Nov. 25–Dec. 9, 1917: Cases, 45 deaths, 45.
Peru				Dec. 1, 1917–Jan. 15, 1918: Cases, 106.
Ancachs Department—				
Casma	Dec. 1–Jan. 15	2		At Chiclayo, Ferrenafe, Jayanca, Lambayeque.
Lambayeque Department	....do	22		
Libertad Department	....do	72		At Guadalupe, Mansiche, Pacasmayo, Salaverry, San Jose, San Pedro, and country district of Trujillo.
Lima Department	....do	9		City and country.
Piura Department—				
Catacaos	....do	1		
Senegal:				
St. Louis	Feb. 2			Present.
Siam:				
Bangkok	Sept. 16–Dec. 23	13	9	
Straits Settlements:				
Singapore	Oct. 28–Dec. 29	5	7	

SMALLPOX.

Place.	Date.	Cases.	Deaths.	Remarks.
Algeria:				
Algiers	Nov. 1–Dec. 31	8	1	
Do	Jan. 1–31	2		
Australia:				
New South Wales				July 12–Dec. 20, 1917: Cases, 36. Jan. 4–17, 1918: Case, 1. Newcastle district.
Abermain	Oct. 25–Nov. 29	3		
Cessnock	July 12–Oct. 11	7		
Eumangla	Aug. 15	1		
Kurri Kurri	Dec. 5–20	2		
Mungindi	Aug. 13	1		
Warren	July 12–Oct. 25	22		
Do	Jan. 1–17	1		
Brazil:				
Bahia	Nov. 10–Dec. 8	3		
Pernambuco	Nov. 1–15	1		
Rio de Janeiro	Sept. 30–Dec. 29	703	190	
Do	Dec. 30–Jan. 26	158	42	
Sao Paulo	Oct. 29–Nov. 4		2	
Canada:				
British Columbia—				
Vancouver	Jan. 13–Mar 9	5		
Victoria	Jan. 7–Feb. 2	2		
Winnipeg	Dec. 30–Jan. 5	1		
New Brunswick—				
Kent County	Dec. 4			Outbreak. On main line Canadian Ry., 25 miles north of Moncton.
Do	Jan. 22	40		In 7 localities.
Northumberland County.	....do	41		In 5 localities.
Restigouche County	Jan. 18	60		
St. John County—				
St. John	Mar. 3–9	2		
Victoria County	Jan. 22	10		At Limestone and a lumber camp.
Westmoreland County—				
Moncton	Jan. 20–Feb. 23	8		
York County	Jan. 22	8		

CHOLERA, PLAGUE, SMALLPOX, TYPHUS FEVER, AND YELLOW FEVER—Continued.

Reports Received from Dec. 29, 1917, to Mar. 29, 1918—Continued.

SMALLPOX—Continued.

Place.	Date.	Cases.	Deaths.	Remarks.
Canada—Continued.				
Nova Scotia—				
Halifax	Feb. 24–Mar. 2	1		
Sydney	Feb. 3–Mar. 2	4		
Ontario—				
Hamilton	Dec. 16–22	1		
Do	Jan. 13–19	2		
Ottawa	Mar. 4–10	1		
Sarnia	Dec. 9–15	1		
Do	Jan. 6–Mar. 16	29		
Toronto	Feb. 10–16	1		
Windsor	Dec. 30–Jan. 5	1		
Prince Edward Island—				
Charlottetown	Feb. 7–13	1		
Quebec—				
Montreal	Dec 16–Jan 5	5		
Do	Jan. 6–Mar. 9	7		
China:				
Amoy	Oct. 22–Dec. 30			Present.
Do	Dec. 31–Feb. 3			Do.
Antung	Dec 2–23	13	2	
Do	Jan. 7–Feb. 17	5	2	
Changsha	Jan. 28–Feb. 3		1	
Chefoo	Jan. 27–Feb 9			Do.
Chungking	Nov. 11–Dec 29			Do.
Do	Dec. 30–Jan. 19			Do.
Dairen	Nov 18–Dec 22	3	1	
Do	Dec. 30–Feb. 16	19	1	
Harbin	May 14–June 30	20		Chinese Eastern Ry.
Do	July 1–Dec. 2	7		Do.
Hongkong	Dec. 23 29	1		
Hungchutze Station	Oct 28–Nov. 4	1		Do.
Manchuria station	May 14–June 30	6		Do.
Do	July 1–Dec. 2	3		Do.
Mukden	Nov. 11–24			Present.
Nanking	Feb. 3–16			Epidemic.
Shanghai	Nov. 18–Dec. 23	41	91	Cases, foreign; deaths among natives.
Do	Dec. 31–Feb. 10	33	92	Do.
Swatow	Jan. 18			Unusually prevalent.
Tientsin	Nov. 11–Dec. 22	13		
Do	Dec. 30–Feb. 9	14		
Tsingtau	Feb. 4–10	1		
Cuba:				
Habana	Jan. 7	1		Nov. 8, 1917: 1 case from Coruna; Dec. 5, 1917, 1 case.
Marianao	Jan. 9	1		6 miles distant from Habana.
Ecuador:				Sept. 1–Nov. 30, 1917: Cases, 26; deaths, 2.
Guayaquil	Sept. 1–30	8		
Do	Oct. 1 31	14	1	
Do	Nov. 1 30	4	1	
Egypt:				
Alexandria	Nov. 12 18	2	1	
Do	Jan. 8 Feb. 4	3		
Cairo	July 28 Nov. 18	6	1	
France:				
Lyon	Nov. 18 Dec. 16	6	3	
Do	Jan. 7 Feb. 17	11	2	
Marseille	Jan. 1 31		2	
Paris	Jan. 27 Feb. 2	1		
Great Britain:				
Cardiff	Feb. 3–9	4		
Honduras:				
Santa Barbara Department	Jan. 1–7			Present in interior.
India				
Bombay	Oct 21 Dec. 1	16	4	
Do	Dec. 31 Jan. 5	26	5	
Karachi	Nov. 18 Dec. 29	1	2	Nov. 11–17, 1917: 10 cases with 4 deaths; imported on s. s. Menesa from Basreh.
Madras	Oct. 31 Dec. 8	9	3	
Do	Jan. 6 12	15	7	
Rangoon	Oct. 28 Nov. 24	4	1	
Do	Dec. 30 Jan. 5	1		Nov. 1–30, 1917: Cases, 3; deaths, 1.

CHOLERA, PLAGUE, SMALLPOX, TYPHUS FEVER, AND YELLOW FEVER—Continued.

Reports Received from Dec. 29, 1917 to Mar. 29, 1918—Continued.

SMALLPOX—Continued.

Place.	Date.	Cases.	Deaths.	Remarks.
Indo-China:				
Provinces...................				Sept. 1–Oct. 31, 1917: Cases, 343;
Anam..................	Sept. 1–Oct. 31....	103	15	deaths, 98. ....
Cambodia..............	.....do............	10	3	
Cochin-China..........	.....do............	222	76	
Saigon................	Oct. 20–Dec. 30....	120	26	
Do................	Dec. 31–Jan. 27....	128	45	
Laos..................	Oct. 1–31..........	1	....	
Tonkin................	Sept. 1–Oct. 31....	9	4	
Italy:				
Castellamare..............	Dec. 10............	2	....	Among refugees.
Florence..................	Dec. 1–15..........	17	4	
Genoa....................	Dec. 2–31..........	11	3	
Do....................	Jan. 2–31..........	30	2	
Leghorn..................	Jan. 7–Feb. 18.....	29	6	
Messina..................	Jan. 3–19..........	1	....	
Milan....................				Oct. 1–Nov. 30, 1917: Cases, 17.
Naples...................	To Dec. 10.........	2	....	Among refugees.
Taormina................	Jan. 20–Feb. 9.....	6	....	
Turin....................	Oct. 29–Dec. 29....	123	120	
Do....................	Jan. 21–Feb. 3.....	24	3	
Japan:				
Nagasaki.................	Jan. 14–27.........	3	1	
Taihoku.................	Dec. 15–21.........	1	....	Island of Taiwan (Formosa).
Do..................	Jan. 9–Feb. 11.....	5	2	Do.
Tokyo...................	Feb. 11–18.........	8	....	City and suburbs.
Yokohama...............	Jan. 17–Feb. 3.....	4	....	
Java:				
East Java................	Oct. 7–Dec. 23.....	42	....	
Mid-Java................				Oct. 10–Dec. 23, 1917: Cases, 80;
Samarang............	Dec. 6–12..........	1	1	death, 1.
West Java................				Oct. 19–Dec. 29, 1917: Cases, 288;
Batavia..............	Nov. 2–8...........	1	....	deaths, 41.
Mexico:				
Aguascalientes...........	Feb. 4–17..........	....	2	
Ciudad Juarez............	Mar. 3–9...........	1	1	
Mazatlan................	Dec. 5–11..........	....	1	
Do................	Jan. 29–Mar. 5.....	4	3	
Mexico City..............	Nov. 11–Dec. 29....	16	....	
Do..............	Dec. 30–Mar. 2.....	52	....	
Piedras Negras...........	Jan. 11............	100	....	
Vera Cruz................	Jan. 20–Mar. 2.....	7	3	
Newfoundland:				
St. Johns................	Dec. 8–Jan. 4......	29	....	
Do................	Jan. 5–Mar. 8......	34	....	
Trepassey...............	Jan. 4.............	....	....	Outbreak with 11 cases reported.
Philippine Islands:				
Manila..................	Oct. 28–Dec. 8.....	5	....	
Do..................	Jan. 13–Feb. 9.....	12	....	
Porto Rico:				
San Juan................	Jan. 28–Mar. 3.....	23	....	
Portugal:				
Lisbon..................	Nov. 4–Dec. 15.....	2	....	
Do..................	Dec. 30–Jan. 19....	2	....	
Portuguese East Africa:				
Lourenço Marques.........	Aug. 1–Nov. 30.....	....	5	
Russia:				
Archangel................	Sept. 1–Oct. 31....	7	....	
Moscow..................	Aug. 26–Oct. 6.....	22	2	
Petrograd................	Aug. 31–Nov. 18...	76	3	
Siam:				
Bangkok.................	Nov. 25–Dec. 1.....	1	1	
Do.................	Jan. 6–12..........	1	....	
Spain:				
Coruna...................	Dec. 2–15..........	....	4	
Madrid..................				Jan. 1–Dec. 31, 1917: Deaths, 77.
Seville..................	Oct. 1–Dec. 30.....	....	66	
Straits Settlements:				
Singapore................	Nov. 25–Dec. 1.....	1	1	
Do................	Dec. 30–Jan. 5.....	1	....	
Tunisia:				
Tunis...................	Dec. 24–2	1	....	
Turkey in Asia:				
Bagdad.................				Present in November, 1917.
Union of South Africa:				
Cape of Good Hope State...	Oct. 1–Dec. 31.....	28	....	
Venezuela:				
Maracaibo...............	Dec. 2–8...........	....	1	

CHOLERA, PLAGUE, SMALLPOX, TYPHUS FEVER, AND YELLOW FEVER—Continued.

Reports Received from Dec. 29, 1917, to Mar. 29, 1918—Continued.

TYPHUS FEVER.

Place.	Date.	Cases.	Deaths.	Remarks.
Algeria:				
Algiers	Nov. 1–Dec. 31	2	1	
Argentina:				
Rosario	Dec. 1–31		1	
Australia:				
South Australia				Nov. 11–17, 1917: Cases, 1.
Brazil:				
Rio de Janeiro	Oct. 28–Dec. 1	7		
Canada:				
Ontario—				
Kingston	Dec. 2–8	3		
Quebec—				
Montreal	Dec. 16–22	2	1	
China:				
Antung	Dec. 3–30	13	1	
Do	Dec. 31–Jan. 27	2	2	
Chosen (Formosa):				
Seoul	Nov. 1–20	1		
Egypt:				
Alexandria	Nov. 8–Dec. 28	57	15	
Do	Jan. 8–Feb. 4	84	22	
Cairo	July 23–Dec. 16	137	70	
Port Said	July 30 Nov. 11	5	5	
France:				
Marseille	Dec. 1–31		1	
Great Britain:				
Belfast	Feb. 10–16	4	1	
Glasgow	Dec. 21	1		
Do	Jan. 20–Feb. 23	4		
Manchester	Dec. 2–8	1		
Greece:				
Saloniki	Nov. 11–Dec. 29		72	
Do	Dec. 30–Jan. 19		11	
Japan:				
Nagasaki	Nov. 26–Dec. 16	5	5	
Do	Jan. 7–Feb. 17	8	2	
Java:				
East Java				Oct. 15–Dec. 9, 1917: Cases, 34; deaths, 3.
Mid-Java				Oct. 10–Dec. 12, 1917: Cases, 54;
Samarang	Oct. 17 Dec. 5	15	2	deaths, 2.
West Java				Oct. 19–Dec. 20, 1917: Cases, 73;
Batavia	Oct. 19 Dec 20	57	14	deaths, 17.
Mexico:				
Aguascalientes	Dec. 15		2	
Do	Jan. 21–Feb. 10		14	
Durango State -				
Guanacevi	Feb. 11			Epidemic.
Mexico City	Nov. 11 Dec. 29	476		
Do	Dec. 30–Mar. 2	491		
Portugal:				
Lisbon	Feb. 21			Present.
Oporto	do			Epidemic. Dec. 24, 1917–Mar. 9, 1918: About 250 cases reported.
Russia:				
Archangel	Sept. 1 14	7	2	
Moscow	Aug. 26–Oct. 6	49	2	
Petrograd	Aug. 31–Nov. 18	32		
Do	Feb 2			Present.
Vladivostok	Oct. 29 Nov. 4	12	1	
Sweden:				
Goteborg	Nov. 18 Dec. 15	2		
Switzerland:				
Basel	Jan. 6 19	1	1	
Zurich	Nov. 9–15	2		
Do	Jan 13–19	2		
Tunisia:				
Tunis	Nov. 30 Dec. 6		1	
Do	Feb. 9–15	2		
Turkey:				
Albania -				
Janina	Jan 27			Epidemic.
Union of South Africa:				
Cape of Good Hope State				Sept. 10 Nov. 25, 1917: Cases, 3,724 (European, 31; native, 3,693); deaths, 761 (European, 5; native, 756).

CHOLERA, PLAGUE, SMALLPOX, TYPHUS FEVER, AND YELLOW FEVER—Continued.

Reports Received from Dec. 29, 1917, to Mar. 29, 1918—Continued.

YELLOW FEVER.

Place.	Date.	Cases.	Deaths.	Remarks.
Ecuador				Sept. 1–Nov. 30, 1917: Cases, 5; deaths, 3.
Guayaquil	Sept. 1–30	1	1	
Do	Oct. 1–31	1		
Do	Nov. 1–30	2	2	
Yaguachi	do	1		
Honduras:				
Tegucigalpa	Dec. 16–22		1	
Do	Jan. 6–19		1	

×

PUBLIC HEALTH REPORTS

| VOL. 33 | APRIL 12, 1918 | No. 15 |

A NEW DISINFECTANT TESTING MACHINE.

By A. M. STIMSON, Surgeon, and M. H. NEILL, Passed Assistant Surgeon, United States Public Health Service.

In performing laboratory tests to determine the bactericidal power of disinfectants; some of the organisms, living or dead, upon which the disinfecting solutions have been allowed to act, are transferred at stated intervals from the disinfectant solutions to test tubes containing nutrient broth. The bacteria are thus placed in favorable conditions for multiplication, if they have not been killed by the disinfectant solution. As growth will appear in those tubes into which live organisms have been introduced, the results of the tests may be observed and from these observations an opinion formed as to the efficiency of the disinfectant under the conditions of the test. In testing a disinfectant a number of dilutions are used, thus necessitating a number of transfers for each time interval.

It is obvious that in performing these transfers by hand only one transfer can be made at a time; thus the conditions throughout the experiment may constantly be subjected to certain variations in those important factors of time and temperature upon which the uniformity of the tests depends. Moreover, as these transfers must be made in sequence, a single error in technique, disturbing the sequence of manipulation, may ruin the entire experiment. The precise inoculation of a considerable number of tubes at intervals of 15 seconds, as is sometimes required, and in a certain sequence, using different suspensions of bacteria, is a tedious task even if correctly done by an expert in the work. The serial inoculation may well be dispensed with if a method equally satisfactory, as regards the accuracy of the results, can be devised.

In performing disinfectant tests, the use of a machine has a certain obvious advantage over a technique depending wholly upon manual dexterity, in so far as the precision of a mechanical device is substituted for the variations in accuracy of the hand movements of one or more laboratory workers. In addition to this general advantage the machine to be described has certain other definite advantages when contrasted with the hand technique. By the use of the machine, all the transfers due to be made at any particular

time interval are made at the same time and in the same way, thus
securing identical conditions for each dilution of the disinfectant or
disinfectants used. Furthermore, the machine makes 15 transfers
at once, thus doing away with the strain of inoculating a large number of tubes singly in a certain sequence.

It has been recognized that in using a machine greater difficulty
as regards the exclusion of air contamination is likely to be encountered; however, this machine has been so designed as to overcome
that disadvantage.

Actual comparison of the two methods has shown that the use of
the machine greatly simplifies the practice of disinfectant testing.

Construction of the Machine.[1]

A table (T), 31 inches high, 36 inches wide, and 30 inches from
front to back, supports the following essential parts of the apparatus:
A water bath (B), a large test tube rack (R3), a traveling carriage
(Ca), and a flaming device (F.).

The water bath (B) is countersunk, so that half of its depth is
below the level of the table top. The external dimensions of the bath
are 30¼ by 10 by 10 inches; the internal dimensions are 26¼ by 5¼ by
7½ inches. The space between the outer wooden casing of the bath
and its galvanized iron lining (Li), is occupied with sawdust (Sd), for
insulation. Two galvanized-iron racks hang in the bath supported
at the ends. The first (R1), consists of an angled piece of galvanized
iron 26 inches long. To the vertical portion of the rack are riveted
15 brass clips into which fit 15 disinfectant tubes (Td), their bottoms
resting on the horizontal portion of the rack. The clips are so arranged that the centers of the tubes are exactly 1¾ inches from each
other. Clear glass test tubes, 3 inches by ⅝ inch, are used. They are
plugged with cotton and sterilized by dry heat. The second rack
consists of three sheets of galvanized iron 26 inches long by 2½ inches
wide, the upper two being perforated with a row of 15 holes 1 inch in
diameter. Into these fits a row of tubes for the test bacteria (Te),
exactly similar to those used in rack No. 1. The tubes in rack
No. 2 are so placed that their centers are 1¾ inches apart and that
they are exactly in line with the corresponding tubes in rack No. 1.
The water level (W. L.) in the bath is maintained about an inch
below the top of the lining of the bath.

The test tube rack (R3) consists of 3 sheets of galvanized iron,
26¼ by 10½ inches, joined together by uprights at the ends. The top
of the rack is 3¾ inches above the table top and is perforated for test
tubes, as is the second sheet, which is secured 3 inches below the top.

[1] The letters refer to similar designations on the illustrations. They are repeated with a complete list
of the parts to which they refer at the close of the article.

The bottom sheet rests upon the table top and supports the test tubes. The holes for the test tubes are ⅝ inch in diameter. They are arranged in six rows of 15 each. In these holes are placed test tubes (B. T.), 6 inches by ½ inch, containing about 7 c.c. of sterile

DISINFECTANT TESTING MACHINE

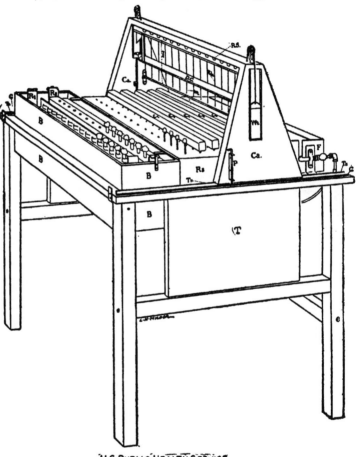

U.S. PUBLIC HEALTH SERVICE

Fig. 1.

broth. The rack is so adjusted on the table by means of guides as to bring the test tubes into alignment with the tubes in rack No. 2. The centers of the tubes in the rows are 1¾ inches apart, and the rows are this same distance from each other. When the usual cotton plugs are removed from the tubes, each row is covered by a galvanized-iron cover (C), previously sterilized by dry heat. The covers are 24 inches long, 1½ inches wide, and 2 inches high, and are open only on

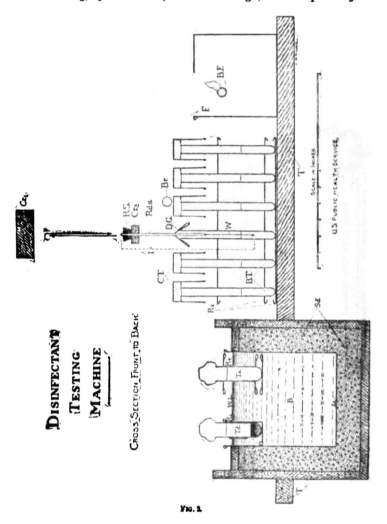

Fig. 2.

their inferior aspect, so as to fit over the rows of tubes. Two small projections serve to secure a layer of cotton (Ct) at the top of the cover inside, thus making them dustproof when applied to the mouths of the test tubes.

The traveling carriage (Ca) consists of two triangular-shaped wooden uprights 16 inches high. These are placed 31 inches apart and are connected with a crosspiece (CR). Small wheels are set into the bottoms of the uprights which rest upon two tracks (Tr), running from the front to the back of the table. Thus the carriage may be moved forward and backward on the table. Pins (P) on the uprights engage in holes in guides (G), running parallel to the tracks and external to them. These holes are so placed that the carriage may be accurately brought to a standstill, so that the center of the crosspiece will be exactly above the various rows of tubes described above. The inoculator (I) is hung from the crosspiece at its ends by pulleys and is so counterbalanced by weights (Wt) that after use the device will always return to its position under the crosspiece (Cr1). The inoculator consists of a crosspiece (Cr2), to the ends of which are attached vertical guides carrying small wheels (2 at each end). The wheels run upon metal tracks on the inner surfaces of the uprights of the carriage, making it possible to raise and lower the inoculator in a plane at right angles with the table top but parallel with the rows of tubes in the racks. This crosspiece is perforated with 15 holes into which fit No. 3 rubber stoppers (RS). The stoppers have one perforation in the center into which No. 8 gauge aluminum rods (Rds) 5½ inches in length are fitted. The lower ends of the rods are flattened and here are attached pieces of No. 23 gauge nichrome wire (Wi). The wires continue downward in line with the rods for 3 inches and terminate in 4 coils, used for transferring the culture after exposure to the disinfectant. They are made of nichrome wire, No. 23 B. & S. gauge.

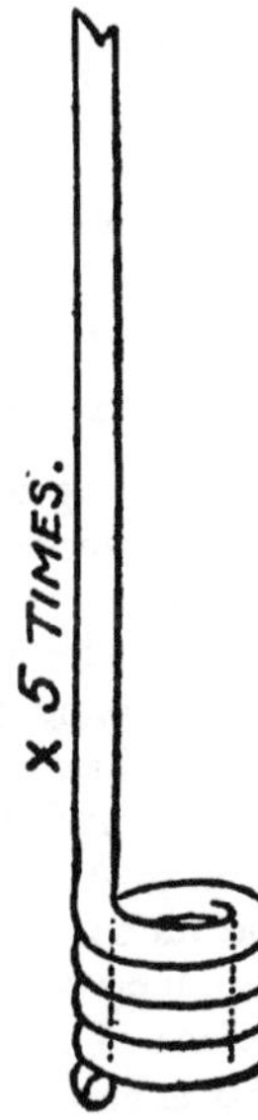

Fig. 3.—Coil for inoculator.

A close cylindrical spiral is made by winding the wire as tightly as possible about a piece of steel or other hard wire having a diameter of 0.072 inch (No. 13 B. & S. gauge). Wind about five full turns, bend the remainder of the wire sharply at a right angle to the wound portion, and parallel to the axis of the cylinder. Remove from the core and cut off the lower end, to leave exactly four complete turns. When completed the successive turns of the spiral must touch one another continuously. The coils are 7¼ inches below the crosspiece of the inoculator.

The centers of the holes in the crosspiece are 1¾ inches apart, and the machine has been so constructed that as the traveling carriage is moved back and forth the centers of the corresponding tubes in the racks will be directly below them. As the wire coils are directly below the centers of the holes in the crosspiece, they are directly above the centers of the mouths of the test tubes. Two and one-half inches below the crosspiece, and extending entirely across the inoculator, is the dust guard (D. G.). This is attached to the guides of the inoculator and is perforated to allow the aluminum rods to pass through it. It is made of galvanized iron, and in cross section has the shape of an inverted V. An expansion device consisting of a brass cylinder fitting snugly into a metal sleeve serves to connect the dust guard with the guide of the inoculator on the right. It has been so placed as to fit snugly over the mouths of the broth test tubes in rack 3 when the inoculator is lowered. The carriage is strengthened by a brace (Br), which is an iron rod extending across the carriage, and is attached to the side pieces 6½ inches from their bottoms and 2 inches back of the center line. The flaming device (F) consists of a Bunsen burner to which is attached a horizontal brass tube closed at the distal end. The tube is slotted every 1¾ inches, and when the apparatus is lighted the wires of the inoculator can be lowered into the flames (B, F) from these slots and sterilized.

The Performance of Disinfectants—Tests, Using the Machine.

Following is a description of a method for substituting the machine above described for hand manipulations in the testing of disinfectants. It is not our purpose at this time to discuss the technique of disinfectant tests in general, nor to describe them in particular.

In making the tests, the machine should be in a room free from dust and air currents. Before beginning work, the crosspieces of the carriage and inoculator and the internal surfaces of the uprights of the carriage are wiped clean and free from dust. The water bath is filled, and its contents are brought to the desired temperature just before beginning work. The operator now thoroughly flames the interior surface of the dust guard and the rods and wires projecting below. This is conveniently done with an ordinary Bunsen burner attached to a long rubber hose. The flaming device may be conveniently lighted at this time.

The broth tubes are now placed in rack No. 3. Just before putting each tube in its place the stopper is ignited and the mouth of the tube is quickly flamed and the stopper extinguished. When all the broth tubes are in place the stoppers are quickly removed from the row nearest the operator, and this row is covered with its sterile galvanized-iron cover as quickly as possible. The stoppers are removed from the remainder of the tubes and the covers placed on the remaining rows in like manner.

Next, the operator places the tubes containing disinfectant dilutions and the test cultures in racks No. 1 and No. 2, respectively. The cotton stoppers are now removed from the tubes in these racks and the dilutions of disinfectants in the tubes in rack No. 1 are simultaneously poured upon the test cultures in the corresponding tubes in rack No. 2. This is done by taking rack No. 1 away from the operator through an arc of 90 degrees.

At the instant of pouring, the time is taken and the experiment begins. The tubes in rack No. 2, now containing various dilutions of disinfectants and organisms, are covered by a semicylindrical galvanized-iron cover, previously flamed, and are gently agitated to mix the contents.

The carriage is now placed in such a position that the coils of the inoculator are over the mouths of the test tubes in rack 2, and after the proper time has elapsed the tubes are uncovered and the inoculator is lowered, immersing the wire coils in the contents of the tubes. The inoculator is raised and the tubes are covered. The operator now removes the cover from the row of broth tubes nearest him and rests it on the crosspiece of the carriage. The carriage is then pushed into such a position that the coils are over this row, the inoculator is lowered, and the coils, bearing organisms from the disinfectant-bacteria suspension, are immersed in the first row of broth tubes. The inoculator is raised, the carriage pushed back to a position over the flaming device, and the cover replaced on the first row of tubes. The inoculator is lowered, bringing the wires and coils into the Bunsen flames, which sterilize them. The operator now raises the inoculator and brings the carriage back to a position over the tubes containing disinfectant and bacteria. When the proper interval has elapsed after the first transfer, the operations described above are repeated, inoculating the 2nd row of broth tubes, and so on until the 3d, 4th, 5th, and 6th rows of tubes have been inoculated, the proper time intervals being carefully observed. The experiment is now completed and rack 2, with tubes and covers in place, is removed from the machine and placed in the incubator.

It has been found advisable to agitate gently the tubes in rack No. 2 just before each transfer is made, and to continuously and withdraw the wire coils several times from the tubes, repeating this period in the broth tubes each time a transfer is made.

Comparison of Various and Head Tests

The following table shows . . . .

In this comparison the hand test is not taken as a standard of accuracy, as it is quite likely that the machine test represents the more reliable results. It will be noted throughout both tests that the values for the phenol control correspond very closely with the usual values obtained.

The presence or absence of growth in the broth tubes is indicated by plus or minus signs.

TABLE I a.

Disinfectant A.

HYGIENIC LABORATORY PHENOL COEFFICIENT USING MACHINE.

Temperature of experiment, 20° C.
Culture used, *B. typhosus*, 24-hour infusion broth, filtered.
Proportion of culture and disinfectant, 0.1 cc. + 5 cc.

Sample.	Dilu-tion.	Time culture exposed to action of disinfectant for minutes.						Phenol coefficient.
		2½	5	7½	10	12½	15	
Phenol	1-80	−	−	−	−	−	−	
	1-90	−	−	−	−	−	−	
	1-100	+	−	−	−	−	−	
	1-110	+	+	−	−	−	−	$\frac{175}{90}+\frac{350}{110}$
	1-120	+	+	+	+	+	+	
Disinfectant A	1-150	−	−	−	−	−	−	$\frac{}{2}=$
	1-175	−	−	−	−	−	−	
	1-200	+	−	−	−	−	−	
	1-225	+	−	−	−	−	−	$\frac{1.94+3.18}{2}=$
	1-250	+	−	−	−	−	−	
	1-275	+	+	−	−	−	−	
	1-300	+	+	−	−	−	−	2.56 coeffi-cient.
	1-325	+	+	+	−	−	−	
	1-350	+	+	+	+	−	−	
	1-375	+	+	+	+	+	+	

TABLE I b.

Disinfectant A.

HYGIENIC LABORATORY PHENOL COEFFICIENT USING HAND TECHNIQUE.

Temperature of experiment, 20° C.
Culture used, *B. typhosus*, 24-hour meat infusion broth, filtered.
Proportion of culture and disinfectant, 0.1 cc. + 5 cc.

Sample.	Dilu-tion.	Time culture exposed to action of disinfectant for minutes.						Phenol coefficient.
		2½	5	7½	10	12½	15	
Phenol	1-80	−	−	−	−	−	−	
	1-90	−	−	−	−	−	−	
	1-100	+	+	−	−	−	−	
	1-110	+	+	+	−	−	−	$\frac{200}{90}+\frac{350}{110}$
	1-120	+	+	+	+	+	+	
Disinfectant A	1-150	−	−	−	−	−	−	$\frac{}{2}=$
	1-175	−	−	−	−	−	−	
	1-200	−	−	−	−	−	−	
	1-225	+	−	−	−	−	−	$\frac{2.22+3.18}{2}=$
	1-250	+	+	−	−	−	−	
	1-275	+	+	+	−	−	−	
	1-300	+	+	+	+	−	−	2.7 coeffi-cient.
	1-325	+	+	+	+	+	−	
	1-350	+	+	+	+	+	−	
	1-375	+	+	+	+	+	+	

TABLE II a.

Disinfectant B.

HYGIENIC LABORATORY PHENOL COEFFICIENT USING MACHINE.

Temperature of experiment, 20° C.
Culture used, *B. typhosus*, 24-hour meat infusion broth.
Proportion of culture and disinfectant, 0.1 cc. + 5 cc.

Sample.	Dilution.	Time culture exposed to action of disinfectant for minutes.						Phenol coefficient.
		2½	5	7½	10	12½	15	
Phenol............................	1-60	—	—	—	—	—	—	
	1-90	—	—	—	—	—	—	
	1-100	+	+	—	—	—	—	
	1-110	+	+	+	+	—	—	$\frac{\frac{225}{90}+\frac{300}{110}}{2}=$
	1-120	+	+	+	+	—	+	
Disinfectant B......................	1-150	—	—	—	—	—	—	
	1-175	—	—	—	—	—	—	
	1-200	—	—	—	—	—	—	
	1-225	—	—	—	—	—	—	$\frac{2.5+2.73}{2}=2.61$
	1-250	—	—	—	—	—	—	
	1-275	+	—	—	—	—	—	coefficient.
	1-300	+	+	—	—	—	—	
	1-325	+	+	+	+	—	—	
	1-350	+	+	+	+	+	+	
	1-375	+	+	+	+	+	+	

TABLE II b.

Disinfectant B.

HYGIENIC LABORATORY PHENOL COEFFICIENT USING HAND TECHNIQUE.

Temperature of experiment, 20° C.
Culture used, *B. typhosus* 24-hour meat infusion broth.
Proportion of culture and disinfectant, 0.1 cc. + 5 cc.

Sample.	Dilution.	Time culture exposed to action of disinfectant for minutes.						Phenol coefficient.
		2½	5	7½	10	12½	15	
Phenol............................	1-80	—	—	—	—	—	—	
	1-90	+	—	—	—	—	—	
	1-100	+	—	+	—	—	—	
	1-110	+	+	+	+	—	—	$\frac{\frac{225}{80}+\frac{300}{110}}{2}=$
	1-120	+	+	+	+	+	+	
Disinfectant B......................	1-150	—	—	—	—	—	—	
	1-175	—	—	—	—	—	—	
	1-200	—	—	—	—	—	—	
	1-225	—	—	—	—	—	—	$\frac{2.81+2.73}{2}=2.77$
	1-250	+	—	—	—	—	—	
	1-275	+	+	+	+	—	—	coefficient.
	1-300	+	+	+	+	+	—	
	1-325	+	+	+	+	+	+	
	1-350	+	+	+	+	+	+	
	1-375	+	+	+	+	+	+	

TABLE III a.

Disinfectant C.

HYGIENIC LABORATORY PHENOL COEFFICIENT USING MACHINE.

Temperature of experiment, 20° C.
Culture used, B. typhosus, 24-hour meat infusion broth.
Proportion of culture and disinfectant, 0.1 cc.+5 cc.

Samples.	Dilu- tion.	Time culture exposed to action of disinfectant for minutes.						Phenol coefficient.
		2½	5	7½	10	12½	15	
Phenol................................	1- 80	–	–	–	–	–	–	
	1- 90	–	–	–	–	–	–	
	1-100	–	–	–	–	–	–	
	1-110	+	+	+	–	–	–	
	1-120	+	+	+	+	–	+	$\frac{275}{90} + \frac{350}{110}$
Disinfectant C........................	1-150	–	–	–	–	–	–	$\overline{2}$
	1-175	–	–	–	–	–	–	
	1-200	–	–	–	–	–	–	
	1-225	–	–	–	–	–	–	$\frac{3.06 + 3.18}{2}$
	1-250	–	–	–	–	–	–	
	1-275	–	–	–	–	–	–	
	1-300	+	–	–	–	–	–	3.11 coefficient.
	1-325	+	–	+	–	–	–	
	1-350	+	+	+	–	+	–	
	1-375	+	+	+	+	+	+	

TABLE III b.

Disinfectant C.

HYGIENIC LABORATORY PHENOL COEFFICIENT USING HAND TECHNIQUE.

Temperature of experiment, 20° C.
Culture used B. typhosus, 24-hour meat infusion broth.
Preparation of culture and disinfectant, 0.1 cc.+5 cc.

Samples.	Dilu- tion.	Time culture exposed to action of disinfectant for minutes.						Phenol coefficient.
		2½	5	7½	10	12½	15	
Phenol................................	1- 80	–	–	–	–	–	–	
	1- 90	+	–	–	–	–	–	
	1-100	+	–	+	–	–	–	
	1-110	+	+	+	+	–	–	
	1-120	+	+	+	+	+	+	$\frac{250}{80} + \frac{350}{110}$
Disinfectant C........................	1-150	–	–	–	–	–	–	$\overline{2}$
	1-175	–	–	–	–	–	–	
	1-200	–	–	–	–	–	–	
	1-225	–	–	–	–	–	–	$\frac{3.12 + 3.18}{2}$
	1-250	–	–	–	–	–	–	
	1-275	+	–	–	–	–	–	
	1-300	+	–	–	–	–	–	3.15 coefficient.
	1-325	+	+	+	+	–	–	
	1-350	+	+	+	+	–	–	
	1-375	+	+	+	+	+	+	

List of Parts of the Machine.

B.   =Water bath.
B. F.   =Bunsen flame.
Br.   =Brace.
B. T.   =Broth tubes.
C.   =Covers for broth tubes.
Ca.   =Carriage.
Cr. 1. =Cross piece of carriage.
Cr. 2. =Cross piece of inoculator.
Ct.   =Cotton.
D. G.   =Dust guard.
F.   =Flaming device.
G.   =Guides.
I.   =Inoculator.
Li.   =Lining of water bath.

P.   =Pins.
R. 1.   =Rack for disinfectant tubes.
R. 2.   =Rack for tubes for test organisms.
R. 3.   =Broth tube rack.
R. S.   =Rubber stoppers.
Rds.   =Rods.
T.   =Table.
Td.   =Disinfectant tubes.
Te.   =Tubes for test organisms.
Tr.   =Tracks.
Sd.   =Sawdust.
Wi.   =Wires.
W. L.   =Water level.
Wt.   =Weight.

ARSPHENAMINE (SALVARSAN) AND NEO-ARSPHENAMINE (NEO-SALVARSAN).

LICENSES ORDERED AND RULES AND STANDARDS PRESCRIBED FOR THEIR MANUFACTURE.

Upon the recommendation of the Public Health Service the rules and standards copied below were adopted by the Federal Trade Commission on March 4, 1918, for the control of establishments licensed for the manufacture and sale of arsphenamine and neo-arsphenamine.

So far licenses for the manufacture of these products have been issued to the following establishments:

Dermatological Research Laboratories, 1818 Lombard Street, Philadelphia, Pa.

Takamine Laboratory (Inc.), 120 Broadway, New York City.

Farbwerke-Hoechst Co., 122 Hudson Street, New York City.

Diarsenol Co. (Inc.), 475 Ellicott Square, Buffalo, N. Y.

RULES AND STANDARDS PRESCRIBED BY THE UNITED STATES PUBLIC HEALTH SERVICE FOR THE CONTROL OF LICENSEES FOR THE MANUFACTURE AND SALE OF ARSPHE-NAMINE.

(1) Except as provided in paragraph (3) hereof, only the abbreviated chemical term Arsphenamine immediately followed by the descriptive chemical name shall be used on packages to designate the preparation.

(2) Arsphenamine shall be offered for sale only in colorless glass ampules containing an atmosphere of an inert gas.

(3) Each package shall be plainly marked so as to show the license number, the lot number, the name of the preparation, the actual amount of arsphenamine in the container, and the name and address of the manufacturer, in the following manner:

License No. ――――. Lot No. ――――.

This package contains ―――― grams of Arsphenamine (hydrochloride of 3-diamino-4-dihydroxy-1-arsenobenzene), prepared under regulations issued by the Federal Trade Commission, and conforms with tests approved by the United States Public Health Service. Made by ――――

No names of diseases or symptoms shall appear on any label or package.

The licensee shall use the name Arsphenamine, immediately followed by the extended scientific name of the article. The word Arsphenamine, when used upon labels attached to packages and cartons, shall be printed in 10-point Roman capitals. On ampules, 8-point Roman capitals may be used.

The licensee may, if he desires, use upon labels and packages his particular brand or trade name, provided that whenever any such brand or trade name is used it shall invariably be accompanied without intervening printed matter, with the name Arsphenamine and the extended scientific name of the article, as provided in the preceding paragraph.

(4) Before placing on the market, each lot shall be tested by the manufacturer as regards toxicity and arsenic content, and shall comply with the requirements of paragraphs (5) and (6) following. Detailed and permanent records of these tests shall be kept by the manufacturer and copies furnished to the commission immediately upon the completion of the tests.

(5) The total arsenic content of the air-dried drug shall not be below 29.5 nor above 31.57 per cent.

(6) The maximum tolerated dose for healthy albino rats shall not be below 60 milligrams per kilo body weight when a 2 per cent slightly alkaline solution of the drug in freshly glass-distilled water is injected intravenously at the rate of not more than 0.5 cubic centimeter per minute.

For each toxicity test à series of animals of not less than four shall be used, and at least 75 per cent of the animals injected with the maximum tolerated dose should survive 48 hours from the time of injection.

The rats shall not be anesthetized for the injection and shall weigh between 100 and 150 grams. Pregnant animals shall not be used.

(7) In addition to tests by the manufacturer, tests shall be made from time to time . by the United States Public Health Service. For this purpose samples of each lot shall be forwarded by the manufacturer to the Hygienic Laboratory of the United States Public Health Service. The number of samples supplied shall be not less than 10 ampules from any lot, and from lots of over 1,000 ampules, 1 per cent shall be furnished. Each ampule forwarded shall contain at least 0.6 gram of Arsphenamine.

Officers of said service or of the Federal Trade Commission, when duly detailed, may enter establishments for the purpose of securing samples and conducting inspections.

(8) When lots have passed satisfactorily the prescribed tests, they may be offered for sale, but the right is reserved to require the withdrawal from the market of any lot designated by the Federal Trade Commission.

(9) Manufacturers shall retain 2 per cent of the ampules from each lot for a period of three months from the time the preparation is put in ampules; but the number retained need not exceed 10 ampules from each lot.

RULES AND STANDARDS PRESCRIBED BY THE UNITED STATES PUBLIC HEALTH SERVICE FOR THE CONTROL OF LICENSEES FOR THE MANUFACTURE AND SALE OF NEO-ARSPHENAMINE.

(1) Except as provided in paragraph (3) hereof, only the abbreviated chemical term Neo-Arsphenamine, immediately followed by the descriptive designation, shall be used on packages to designate the preparation.

(2) Neo-Arsphenamine shall be offered for sale only in colorless glass ampules containing an atmosphere of an inert gas.

(3) Each package shall be plainly marked so as to show the license number, the lot number, the name of the preparation, the actual amount of Neo-Arsphenamine in the container, and the name and address of the manufacturer in the following manner:

License No. ———. Lot No. ———.

This package contains ——— grams of Neo-Arsphenamine (a compound prepared from Arsphenamine by means of formaldehyd-sulphoxylate), prepared under regulations issued by the Federal Trade Commission, and conforms with tests approved by the United States Public Health Service. Made by ———.

No name of diseases or symptoms shall appear on any label or package.

The licensee shall use the name Neo-Arsphenamine, immediately followed by the descriptive designation of the article. The word Neo-Arsphenamine, when used upon labels attached to packages and cartons, shall be printed in 10-point roman capitals. On ampules 8-point roman capitals may be used.

The licensee may, if he desires, use upon labels and packages his particular brand or trade name, provided that whenever any such brand or trade name is used it shall invariably be accompanied, without intervening printed matter, with the name Neo-Arsphenamine and the descriptive designation of the article, as provided in the preceding paragraph.

(4) Before placing on the market, each lot shall be tested by the manufacturer as regards toxicity and arsenic content, and shall comply with the requirements of paragraphs (5) and (6), following. Detailed and permanent records of these tests shall be kept by the manufacturer and copies furnished to the commission immediately · upon the completion of the tests.

(5) The total arsenic content of the air-dried drug shall not be below 18 per cent nor above 20 per cent.

(6) The maximum tolerated dose for healthy albino rats shall not be below 90 milligrams per kilo body weight when a 2 per cent aqueous solution of the drug in freshly glass-distilled water is injected intravenously at the rate of not more than 0.5 cubic centimeter per minute.

For each toxicity test a series of animals of not less than four shall be used, and at least 75 per cent of the animals injected with the maximum tolerated dose should survive seven days from the time of injection.

The rats shall not be anesthetized for the injection and shall weigh between 100 and 150 grams. Pregnant animals shall not be used.

(7) In addition to tests by the manufacturer, tests shall be made from time to time by the United States Public Health Service. For this purpose samples of each lot shall be forwarded by the manufacturer to the hygienic laboratory of the United States Public Health Service. The number of samples supplied shall not be less than 10 ampules from any lot, and from lots of over 1,000 ampules 1 per cent shall be furnished. Each ampule forwarded shall contain at least 0.9 gram of Neo-Arsphenamine

Officers of said service or of the Federal Trade Commission, when duly detailed, may enter establishments for the purpose of securing samples and conducting inspections.

(8) When lots have passed satisfactorily the prescribed tests, they may be offered for sale; but the right is reserved to require the withdrawal from the market of any lot designated by the Federal Trade Commission.

(9) Manufacturers shall retain 2 per cent of the ampules from each lot for a period of three months from the time the preparation is put in ampules, but the number retained need not exceed 10 ampules from any lot.

PREVALENCE OF DISEASE.

No health department, State or local, can effectively prevent or control disease without knowledge of when, where, and under what conditions cases are occurring.

UNITED STATES.

EXTRA-CANTONMENT ZONES—CASES REPORTED WEEK ENDED APR. 9.

CAMP BEAUREGARD ZONE, LA.

Alexandria:	Cases.
Chicken pox	2
Diphtheria	1
Malaria	1
Mumps	28
Pellagra	2
Pneumonia	2
Smallpox	4
Typhoid fever	1
Whooping cough	2

Boyce:	
Pneumonia	2

Pineville:	
Mumps	3
Smallpox	2

CAMP BOWIE ZONE, TEX.

Fort Worth:	
Cerebrospinal meningitis	1
Chicken pox	3
Gonorrhea	1
Measles	1
Scarlet fever	2
Smallpox	3
Syphilis	1

CAMP DEVENS ZONE, MASS.

Chicken pox:	
Lancaster	4
Lunenburg	4

German measles:	
Lancaster	1
Lunenburg	14

Measles:	
Ayer	7
Lancaster	1
Shirley	2

Mumps:	
Lancaster	3

CAMP DODGE ZONE, IOWA.

Des Moines:	
Gonorrhea	10
Measles	3
Scarlet fever	21
Smallpox	9
Syphilis	15
Whooping cough	1

CAMP DODGE ZONE, IOWA—continued.

Ankeny:	Cases.
Diphtheria	1
Gonorrhea	1
Scarlet fever	1

CAMP FUNSTON ZONE, KANS.

Chicken pox:	
Manhattan	4

Diphtheria:	
Randolph	1

Measles:	
Army City	1
Manhattan	11

Mumps:	
Junction City	2
Manhattan	8

Pneumonia:	
Manhattan	2

Scarlatina:	
Riley	1

Scarlet fever:	
Manhattan	3

Whooping cough:	
Junction City	8

CAMP GORDON ZONE, GA.

Cerebrospinal meningitis:	
Atlanta	4

Chicken pox:	
Atlanta	9

Diphtheria:	
Atlanta	4

German measles:	
Atlanta	6

Gonorrhea:	
Atlanta	9

Malaria:	
Atlanta	4

Measles:	
Atlanta	14

Mumps:	
Atlanta	21
Clarkston	1
Decatur	3
Engleside	5
Scottdale	1

CAMP GORDON ZONE, GA.—continued.

	Cases.
Pneumonia:	
Atlanta	3
Decatur	3
Scottdale	1
Scarlet fever:	
Atlanta	3
Syphilis:	
Atlanta	3
Tuberculosis:	
Atlanta	8
Typhoid fever:	
Atlanta	3
Whooping cough:	
Scottdale	1
Stone Mountain	1

CAMP GREENE ZONE, N. C.

Charlotte Township:	
Diphtheria carrier	1
German measles	3
Gonorrhea	10
Measles	6
Mumps	1
Syphilis	10
Trachoma	3
Whooping cough	5

GULFPORT HEALTH DISTRICT, MISS.

Gulfport Health District:	
Cerebrospinal meningitis	1
Conjunctivitis	1
Dysentery	5
Malaria	9
Measles	7
Mumps	2
Pneumonia	1
Syphilis	1
Tuberculosis, pulmonary	1

CAMP HANCOCK ZONE, GA.

Augusta:	
Cerebrospinal meningitis	1
Chicken pox	1
German measles	1
Measles	22
Mumps	2
Pneumonia, lobar	1
Whooping cough	1

CAMP JACKSON ZONE, S. C.

Columbia:	
Cerebrospinal meningitis	2
Diphtheria	1
Measles	2
Mumps	1

CAMP JOSEPH E. JOHNSTON ZONE, FLA.

Diarrhea:	
Fishers Corner	1
Dysentery:	
Highway	2
Jacksonville	7
South Jacksonville	1
Youkon	1
Gonorrhea:	
Fishers Corner	1
Hookworm:	
Highway	2

CAMP JOSEPH E. JOHNSTON ZONE, FLA.—continued.

	Cases.
Malaria:	
Eastport	1
Jacksonville	1
Mandarin	1
Measles:	
Jacksonville	14
South Jacksonville	2
Mumps:	
Jacksonville	9
Smallpox:	
Jacksonville	2
Syphilis:	
Jacksonville	9
Trachoma:	
Jacksonville	4
Tuberculosis:	
Jacksonville	9
Whooping cough:	
Jacksonville	25

FORT LEAVENWORTH ZONE, KANS.

Leavenworth:	
Chicken pox	1
Diphtheria	5
German measles	1
Measles	14
Mumps	1
Pneumonia, lobar	2
Smallpox	2
Tuberculosis	1
Leavenworth County:	
Measles	7
Scarlet fever	1
Smallpox	3

CAMP LEE ZONE, VA.

Chicken pox:	
Hopewell	1
Prince George County	6
Diphtheria:	
Hopewell	1
Petersburg	2
German measles:	
Ettricks	2
Petersburg	1
Malaria:	
Hopewell	4
Measles:	
City Point	1
Ettricks	3
Hopewell	11
Petersburg	6
Mumps:	
Ettricks	6
Hopewell	4
Pneumonia:	
Ettricks	4
Septic sore throat:	
Chesterfield County	1
Ettricks	3
Petersburg	5
Tuberculosis:	
Petersburg	9
Typhoid fever:	
Petersburg	4
Whooping cough:	
Ettricks	4

CAMP LEWIS ZONE, WASH.

	Cases.
German measles:	
Dupont	2
Lakeview	1
Oak Knoll	3
Parkland	2
Spanaway	1
Steilacoom Lake	2
Mumps:	
Dupont	1
Scarlet fever:	
Dupont	1
Parkland	1
Tuberculosis:	
Clover Creek	1
Greendale	1
Tenino	1
Whooping cough:	
Parkland	4

CAMP LOGAN ZONE, TEX.

Houston:	
Cerebrospinal meningitis	1
German measles	1
Gonorrhea	124
Measles	17
Mumps	7
Pneumonia	3
Syphilis	31
Tuberculosis	1
Whooping cough	1
Humble:	
Gonorrhea	1
Syphilis	6
Magnolia Park:	
Measles	1

CAMP MACARTHUR ZONE, TEX.

Waco:	
Chicken pox	10
Measles	13
Meningitis, tubercular	1
Mumps	41
Pneumonia, lobar	4
Poliomyelitis	1
Smallpox	3
Tuberculosis	1
Typhoid fever	1
Whooping cough	1

CAMP MCCLELLAN ZONE, ALA.

Chicken pox:	
Anniston	2
Measles:	
Anniston	1
Precinct 23	3
Mumps:	
Anniston	3
Pneumonia:	
Anniston	2
Smallpox:	
Anniston	9
Oxford	1
Precinct 15	1
Precinct 22	1
Tuberculosis:	
Anniston	2

FORT OGLETHORPE ZONE, GA.

	Cases.
Cerebrospinal meningitis:	
Chattanooga	1
Chicken pox:	
Chattanooga	2
Gonorrhea:	
Chattanooga	2
Rossville	1
Measles:	
East Lake	1
Mumps:	
Chattanooga	13
East Chattanooga	7
East Lake	1
Scarlet fever:	
North Chattanooga	1
Smallpox:	
Chattanooga	3
Tuberculosis:	
Chattanooga	1
Typhoid fever:	
Chattanooga	2
Whooping cough:	
Chattanooga	20

CAMP PIKE ZONE, ARK.

Little Rock:	
Chancroid	2
Chicken pox	2
Diphtheria	2
Gonorrhea	13
Malaria	5
Measles	4
Mumps	10
Pneumonia	16
Scarlet fever	3
Smallpox	6
Syphilis	12
Tetanus	1
Trachoma	1
Tuberculosis	3
Typhoid fever	1
North Little Rock:	
German measles	1
Mumps	3
Pneumonia	2
Smallpox	2
Tuberculosis	1
Scotts:	
Diphtheria	1
Mumps	1
Syphilis	1

CAMP SEVIER ZONE, S. C.

Cerebrospinal meningitis:	
Greenville Township	1
Pneumonia, broncho:	
Chick Springs Township	1

CAMP SHELBY ZONE, MISS.

Hattiesburg:	
Chicken pox	2
Hookworm	2
Malaria	7
Measles	1
Mumps	21

CAMP SHELBY ZONE, MISS.—continued.

Hattiesburg—Continued.	Cases.
Pneumonia, lobar	5
Smallpox	5
Tuberculosis, pulmonary	6
Typhoid fever	1
Whooping cough	6

CAMP SHERIDAN ZONE, ALA.

Montgomery: |
---|---
Chancroid | 2
Chicken pox | 2
Gonorrhea | 4
Malaria | 63
Measles | 6
Mumps | 8
Ringworm | 20
Smallpox | 3
Syphilis | 3
Rural district in 5-mile zone: |
Smallpox | 1

CAMP SHERMAN ZONE, OHIO.

Chancroid: |
---|---
Chillicothe | 1
Gonorrhea: |
Chillicothe | 2
Measles: |
Chillicothe | 19
Green Township | 1
Jefferson Township | 10
Liberty Township | 4
Mumps: |
Chillicothe | 2
Scioto Township | 1
Scarlet fever: |
Chillicothe | 4
Smallpox: |
Chillicothe | 1
Typhoid fever: |
Chillicothe | 1

CAMP ZACHARY TAYLOR ZONE, KY.

Jefferson County: |
---|---
Cerebrospinal meningitis | 1
Rabies in animals | 1
Tuberculosis, pulmonary | 2
Typhoid fever | 1
Louisville: |
Cerebrospinal meningitis | 3
Chicken pox | 3
Diphtheria | 12
Measles | 18
Pneumonia, lobar | 3
Rabies in animals | 1
Scarlet fever | 5
Smallpox | 8
Trachoma | 2
Tuberculosis, pulmonary | 26
Typhoid fever | 1
Whooping cough | 3

TIDEWATER HEALTH DISTRICT, VA.

Chicken pox:	Cases.
Newport News	1
Phoebus	1
German measles:
Phoebus	3
Measles:
Hampton	2
Newport News	12
Phoebus	7
Mumps:
Newport News	9
Pneumonia:
Phoebus	1
Scarlet fever:
Hampton	1
Newport News	6
Phoebus	1
Smallpox:
Newport News	2
Tuberculosis:
Newport News	3
Whooping cough:
Newport News	1

CAMP TRAVIS ZONE, TEX.

San Antonio: |
---|---
Dysentery | 2
Erysipelas | 1
Gonorrhea | 26
Measles | 9
Mumps | 3
Pneumonia | 4
Syphilis | 6
Tuberculosis | 9

CAMP WADSWORTH ZONE, S. C.

Glenn Springs: |
---|---
Chicken pox | 3
Gonorrhea | 2
Pauline: |
Chicken pox | 1
German measles | 1
Spartanburg: |
Diphtheria | 2
German measles | 1
Measles | 4
Mumps | 3
Ophthalmia neonatorum | 1
Pneumonia | 1
Smallpox | 3
Tuberculosis | 4
Whooping cough | 4

CAMP WHEELER ZONE, GA.[1]

East Macon: |
---|---
Mumps | 9
Macon: |
Chicken pox | 6
German measles | 1
Mumps | 11
Scarlet fever | 1
Smallpox | 1

[1] For week ended Apr. 6, 1918.

DISEASE CONDITIONS AMONG TROOPS IN THE UNITED STATES.

The following data are taken from telegraphic reports received in the office of the Surgeon General, United States Army, for the week ended March 29, 1918:

Annual admission rate per 1,000 (disease only):

All troops............................ 1,522.0
National Guard camps.............. 1,103.5
National Army camps................ 1,814.7
Regular Army...................... 1,513.8

Noneffective rate per 1,000 on day of report:

All troops........................... 49.4

Noneffective rate per 1,000—Continued.

National Guard camps............... 39.1
National Army camps............... 58.7
Regular Army...................... 44.4

Annual death rate per 1,000 (disease only):

All troops......................... 9.8
National Guard camps............... 3.6
National Army camps............... 14.0
Regular Army...................... 10.1

New cases of special diseases reported during the week ended Mar. 29, 1918.

Camps.	Pneumonia.	Dysentery.	Malaria.	Venereal.	Measles.	Meningitis.	Scarlet fever.	Deaths.	Annual admission rate per 1,000 (disease only).	Noneffective per 1,000 on day of report.
Wadsworth..................	2	......	......	14	8	1	4	1	628.4	22.3
Hancock....................	......	......	......	24	5	......	1	4	413.2	26.2
McClellan..................	5	......	1	17	......	1	......	1	838.4	29.6
Sevier.....................	6	......	1	15	2	......	......	1	1,044.9	37.5
Wheeler....................	4	......	4	36	......	......	......	4	773.7	36.3
Logan......................	8	......	......	45	4	1	......	4	1,080.0	34.2
Cody.......................	5	......	......	10	......	......	......	5	673.7	30.8
Doniphan...................	11	......	......	46	......	......	1	3	1,981.3	44.5
Bowie......................	23	......	1	35	......	......	......	2	2,634.6	67.0
Sheridan...................	2	......	......	14	......	......	......	1	438.4	24.2
Shelby.....................	......	......	......	25	1	......	1	2	1,117.2	50.9
Beauregard.................	13	......	8	21	......	1	......	1	1,472.5	53.8
Kearney....................	......	......	......	34	......	......	3	......	1,337.2	53.7
Devens.....................	16	......	......	16	10	2	3	4	1,360.4	46.9
Upton......................	16	......	......	60	13	......	1	9	811.2	28.4
Dix........................	4	......	......	9	7	1	1	4	969.2	35.7
Meade......................	19	......	......	5	11	......	6	6	578.6	32.5
Lee........................	2	......	......	180	15	1	......	6	1,295.5	60.5
Jackson....................	17	......	......	31	22	6	......	6	1,730.4	56.4
Gordon.....................	9	......	......	19	16	3	1	2	1,433.6	45.3
Sherman....................	16	......	......	53	2	......	20	6	1,328.5	53.2
Taylor.....................	30	......	......	10	107	1	2	2	2,028.0	78.9
Custer.....................	5	......	......	24	4	......	8	5	1,712.3	45.1
Grant......................	11	......	......	4	6	......	5	5	704.6	26.2
Pike.......................	42	......	1	58	17	2	7	20	3,531.4	87.0
Dodge......................	44	......	......	25	83	2	12	15	2,741.1	52.8
Funston....................	24	1	......	10	11	2	3	18	1,679.2	82.2
Travis.....................	25	2	8	39	38	3	......	6	4,799.2	90.1
Lewis......................	9	......	......	40	13	......	17	4	3,087.6	94.7
Northeastern Department.....	6	......	......	20	2	......	1	......	1,673.5	44.6
Eastern Department	3	......	1	23	15	1	......	5	1,170.3	30.0
Southeastern Department.....	11	......	2	34	30	5	4	3	1,199.1	50.2
Central Department.........	31	......	......	33	17	......	25	9	2,219.2	50.4
Southern Department........	13	2	......	67	15	2	11	8	1,242.4	43.1
Western Department.........	9	......	......	48	9	1	7	2	1,747.8	37.9
Aviation, S. C.............	62	2	......	165	105	......	56	30	1,462.5	41.4
Camp Greene...............	11	......	......	38	22	1	5	4	1,004.8	39.0
Camp Fremont..............	4	......	1	28	7	......	......	......	1,739.9	73.3
El Paso....................	......	......	......	11	3	......	1	......	932.8	7.4
Columbus Barracks.........	1	......	......	15	4	......	4	1	2,054.2	65.6
Jefferson Barracks.........	21	......	......	59	16	......	5	2	3,128.1	112.5
Fort Logan.................	5	......	......	3	7	......	2	2	2,562.9	78.5
Fort McDowell.............	5	......	......	2	11	......	3	2	2,329.8	51.9
Fort Slocum...............	3	......	......	13	3	......	......	4	2,085.7	45.1
Disciplinary Barracks, Alcatraz.	......	......	......	......	......	......	......	......	1,561.6	27.0
Disciplinary Barracks, Fort Leavenworth............	15	......	......	......	......	......	......	2	3,864.5	56.6
A. A. Humphreys............	1	......	......	4	......	......	......	......	654.8	3.7
J. E. Johnston.............	1	......	......	24	4	......	1	1	1,152.3	39.7
Camp Merritt...............	43	......	2	45	8	......	12	9	1,303.4	57.
Camp Stuart................	40	......	......	29	6	1	3	5	2,170.4	57
West Point, N. Y...........	......	......	......	......	......	......	......	1	1,484.6	

New cases of special diseases reported during the week ended Mar. 29, 1918—Continued.

Camps.	Pneumonia.	Dysentery.	Malaria.	Venereal.	Measles.	Meningitis.	Scarlet fever.	Deaths.	Annual admission rate per 1,000 (disease only).	Noneffective per 1,000 on day of report.
Edgewood-Aberdeen	2			4	1				2,313.9	25.8
Provisional depot for corps and Army troops	2			24	12	2	3		1,431.7	34.4
Camp Holabird				1					6,246.2	3.0
Camp Raritan						1				
General hospitals	1		1	31	2	1		2		
National Guard in departments	2			8	2			3		
National Army in departments	24			91	41		29	7		
Fort Thomas	4			6	2				1,573.3	64.4
Total	692	7	31	1,745	741	48	269	249	1,522.0	49.4

[1] All troops.

Annual rate per 1,000 for special diseases.

Disease.	All troops in United States.[1]	Regulars in United States.[1]	National Guard, all camps.[1]	National Army, all camps.[1]	Expeditionary forces.[2]
Pneumonia	31.7	43.4	13	34.9	46.4
Dysentery	.3	.5		.3	.5
Malaria	1.3	.7	2.5	1.1	.2
Venereal	74.3	87.2	55.4	70.4	39
Paratyphoid					.2
Measles	31.5	37.7	3.3	45.3	8.9
Meningitis	2.1	2.5	.6	2.8	1.5
Scarlet fever	11.4	17.9	1.8	19.4	22.6

[1] Week ended Mar. 29, 1918.   [2] Week ended Mar. 21, 1918.

CURRENT STATE SUMMARIES.

Arkansas.

From Collaborating Epidemiologist Garrison, by telegraph, for week ended April 6, 1918:

Smallpox: Union County 5, Mississippi 2, Faulkner 1, Drew 3, Jefferson 2, Fort Smith 3, Logan 4, Washington 34, Monroe 2. Measles: Drew 3, Sebastian 28, Fort Smith 1, Lee 1, Logan 15, Desha 7. Chicken pox: Sebastian 36, Fort Smith 2, Logan 20, Chicot 1. Malaria: Lafayette 1, Traskwood 2, Jefferson 1, Sebastian 1, Logan 1, Ouachita 1, Chicot 2. Tuberculosis: Drew 3, Jefferson 1, Logan 4, Ouachita 2. Scarlet fever: Sebastian 6. Diphtheria: Jefferson 1, Lee 1.

Connecticut.

From Collaborating Epidemiologist Black, by telegraph, for week ended April 6, 1918:

Infantile paralysis: Hartford 1. Meningitis: New London 1, Windsor Locks 1.

Illinois.

From Collaborating Epidemiologist Drake, by telegraph, for week ended April 6, 1918:

Smallpox: One hundred and thirty-three, of which Chicago 9, Quincy 14, Bryant 5, Virden 6, White City 7, Alton 15, Peoria 15, Belleville 5, Harlem Township 7, Millcreek 8. Scarlet fever: One hundred and seven, of which Chicago 60. Meningitis: Chicago 10, Washington 1. Poliomyelitis: Chicago 3, Springfield 1. Diphtheria: One hundred and twenty-eight, of which Chicago 94.

Indiana.

From the State Board of Health of Indiana, by telegraph, for week ended April 6, 1918:

Measles: Epidemic North Manchester, South Bend. Diphtheria: One death each Brownsburg, Anderson, Greensburg, Phlox; epidemic Salem, Napoleon. Smallpox: Epidemic Davies County, Lawrenceburg. Whooping cough: Epidemic Banta; one death Windfall. Gastroenteritis: Shop workers, munition plant Kokomo, Michigan City, South Bend.

Kansas.

From Collaborating Epidemiologist Crumbine, by telegraph, for week ended April 6, 1918:

Smallpox (10 or more cases): By counties—Allen 14, Bourbon 10, Cherokee 30, Crawford 15, Graham 28, Jackson 14, Kingman 15, Labette 13; by cities—Kansas City 16, Topeka 14, Wichita 13. Meningitis: By cities—Eldorado 1, De Soto 1, Edna 1, Chanute 1, Norton 1, Kansas City 2. Scarlet fever (over 10 cases): Topeka 26.

Louisiana.

From Collaborating Epidemiologist Dowling, by telegraph, for week ended April 6, 1918:

Meningitis, excluding Rapides Parish: Calcasieu Parish, Gerstnerfield 1, Orleans Parish 1. Poliomyelitis 1.

Massachusetts.

From Collaborating Epidemiologist Hitchcock, by telegraph, for week ended April 6, 1918:

Unusual prevalence. German measles: Attleboro 14, Brookline 41, Lunenburg 25, Manchester 20, Nahant 8, Newton 33. Measles: Beverly 34, Brookline 45, Chelsea 48, Newbury 10, Norwood 18, Quincy 58, Woburn 14.

Minnesota.

From Collaborating Epidemiologist Bracken, by telegraph, for week ended April 6, 1918:

Smallpox (new foci): Carver County, Cologne village 3; Clay County, Oakport Township 1; Douglas County, Drandon Township 1; Filmore County, Spring Valley Township 2, Forestville Township 1; Kittson County, Humboldt village 4, Hill Township 2, St. Vincent Township 24; Pine County, Rock Creek Township 4; Traverse County, Monson Township 1; Wright County, Cokato Township 18. Five cerebrospinal meningitis, 1 poliomyelitis reported since April 1.

Nebraska.

From the State Board of Health of Nebraska, by telegraph, for week ended April 6, 1918:

Smallpox: Harvard, Allen, Miller, Red Cloud, Omaha, Pawnee City, Burchard, Steinauer, Mayberry, Tamora, Clay County. Scarlet fever: Clay Center. Cerebrospinal meningitis: Nebraska City.

New Jersey.

From Collaborating Epidemiologist Bowen, by telegraph, for week ended April 6, 1918:

Measles: Unusually prevalent in Newark, East Orange, Paterson.

South Carolina.

From Collaborating Epidemiologist Hayne, by telegraph, for week ended April 8, 1918:

Meningitis: Greenville 2, Charleston 3, Hartsville 1, Darlington 1, Richland 1, Columbia 1.

Vermont.

From Collaborating Epidemiologist Dalton, by telegraph, for week ended April 6, 1918:

Smallpox: Guild Hall 1, Canaan 1. No other outbreak or unusual prevalence.

Virginia.

From Collaborating Epidemiologist Traynham, by telegraph, for week ended April 6, 1918:

Smallpox: By counties—Franklin 5, Alleghany 3, Alexandria 2, Botetourt 2, York 1, city of Newport News 3. Cerebrospinal meningitis: Newport News 1, Culpeper County 3.

Washington.

From Collaborating Epidemiologist Tuttle, by telegraph, for week ended April 6, 1918:   .

Investigating outbreak of possible meningitis in Douglas County. Scarlet fever in Tacoma seems to be subsiding.

ANTHRAX.

Louisiana.

During the month of March, 1918, 2 cases of anthrax were notified in Louisiana, 1 case from Caddo Parish and 1 from Vermilion Parish. The source of infection was not positively determined in either case.

CEREBROSPINAL MENINGITIS.

State Reports for February, 1918.

Place.	New cases reported.	Place.	New cases reported.
Alabama:		California—Continued.	
Calhoun County	9	Orange County	1
Colbert County	2	Merced County	1
Houston County	1	Riverside County—	
Jefferson County	20	Riverside	1
Lamar County	1	San Diego County—	
Limestone County	1	Naval Training Camp	2
Madison County	1	Camp Kearney	1
Marshall County	1	San Francisco County—	
Montgomery County	3	San Francisco	4
Morgan County	3	Solano County	1
Tuscaloosa County	10	Mare Island	3
		Stanislaus County—	
Total	52	Modesto	1
California:		Total	24
Alameda County	2		
Oakland	2	Nevada:	
Contra Costa County—		Nye County	1
Martinez	1		
Los Angeles County	3		
Los Angeles	1		

City Reports for Week Ended Mar. 23, 1918.

Place.	Cases.	Deaths.	Place.	Cases.	Deaths.
Augusta, Ga	1		Muncie, Ind		1
Baltimore, Md	7	2	Nashville, Tenn	2	
Birmingham, Ala	3	2	Newark, N. J	4	1
Boston, Mass	6	6	Newburyport, Mass	1	
Buffalo, N. Y		1	New Haven, Conn	1	
Charlotte, N. C		1	New Orleans, La	1	1
Chattanooga, Tenn	1		New York, N. Y	7	11
Chicago, Ill	7	6	North Little Rock, Ark	1	
Cleveland, Ohio	1		Omaha, Nebr	1	
Columbia, S. C	1		Orange, N. J	1	
Dallas, Tex	1		Petersburg, Va		1
Dayton, Ohio	2		Philadelphia, Pa	4	8
Detroit, Mich	1		Pittsburgh, Pa	2	1
Elizabeth, N. J	2		Portsmouth, Va	1	
Evansville, Ind	1		Poughkeepsie, N. Y	1	
Fall River, Mass	1	1	Providence, R. I	3	2
Flint, Mich	1	1	Quincy, Mass	1	1
Fort Wayne, Ind	1	1	Richmond, Va		1
Grand Haven, Mich	1		St. Louis, Mo	2	2
Hartford, Conn	1		St. Paul, Minn	1	
Haverhill, Mass	1	1	Salt Lake City, Utah	1	1
Houston, Tex	1		San Francisco, Cal	1	
Jersey City, N. J		2	Savannah, Ga	2	1
Kansas City, Kans	2		Scranton, Pa	1	2
Lawrence, Mass	2		Seattle, Wash	1	
Leavenworth, Kans	2	1	Somerville, Mass	1	
Louisville, Ky		1	Springfield, Ill	1	
Lowell, Mass		1	Stockton, Cal	1	
Macon, Ga		1	Troy, N. Y	1	
Manchester, N. H	2	1	Washington, D. C	3	
Milwaukee, Wis	8	5	Wichita, Kans	1	
Minneapolis, Minn	1	1	Wilkes-Barre, Pa	1	
Montgomery, Ala	7		Worcester, Mass	1	

DIPHTHERIA.

See Diphtheria, measles, scarlet fever, and tuberculosis, page 558.

552

ERYSIPELAS.

City Reports for Week Ended Mar. 23, 1918.

Place.	Cases.	Deaths.	Place.	Cases.	Deaths.
Bridgeport, Conn..............	2	....	Oakland, Cal...........	1	....
Buffalo, N. Y................	5	1	Oklahoma City, Okla........	3	....
Chicago, Ill................	25	1	Passaic, N. J...........	2	1
Cincinnati, Ohio.............	3	1	Peoria, Ill............	....	1
Cleveland, Ohio.............	8	1	Petersburg, Va.........	....	....
Dayton, Ohio..............	1	....	Philadelphia, Pa........	1	1
Detroit, Mich..............	5	1	Pittsburgh, Pa.........	9	2
Dubuque, Iowa.............	1	....	Pontiac, Mich..........	1	....
Fargo, N. Dak.............	1	....	Portland, Oreg.........	3	....
Flint, Mich...............	1	....	Providence, R. I........	1	1
Grand Forks, N. Dak........	1	....	Racine, Wis............	1	....
Hartford, Conn............	1	....	Richmond, Va...........	2	....
Jacksonville, Fla............	1	....	Rochester, N. Y........	1	....
Lexington, Ky.............	....	1	Sacramento, Cal........	1	....
Los Angeles, Cal............	5	1	St. Louis, Mo..........	9	1
Louisville, Ky.............	4	....	St. Paul, Minn.........	1	....
Milwaukee, Wis............	6	....	San Francisco, Cal......	5	....
Morristown, N. J...........	1	....	Springfield, Ill.........	1	....
Nashville, Tenn...........	1	....	Steubenville, Ohio.......	1	....
Newark, N. J..............	6	....	Superior, Wis..........	1	1
New Orleans, La...........	....	1	Wilkinsburg, Pa.........	1	....
New York, N. Y............	....	7	Yonkers, N. Y..........	1	1

LEPROSY.

California—Los Angeles.

On April 9, 1918, a case of leprosy was notified at Los Angeles, Cal., in the person of W. G., living at 500 East Ninth Street.

City Reports for Week Ended Mar. 23, 1918.

During the week ended March 23, 1918, there were three cases of leprosy reported; one at Los Angeles, Cal., one at New Orleans, La., and one at San Francisco, Cal. There was also one death from this disease reported at New Orleans.

MALARIA.

State Reports for February, 1918.

Place.	New cases reported.	Place.	New cases reported.
Alabama:		California:	
Bullock County.....................	1	Glenn County...................	3
Butler County.....................	1	Los Angeles County.............	4
Chambers County..................	1	Merced County.................	1
Houston County...................	1	San Francisco County—	
Jefferson County..................	4	U. S. N. Training Station......	1
Lee County.......................	1	San Joaquin County.............	1
Limestone County.................	2	Stockton.....................	1
Madison County..................	1		
Shelby County....................	2	Total......................	11
Talladega County.................	1		
Tuscaloosa County................	3		
Total.......................	18		

MALARIA—Continued.

City Reports for Week Ended Mar. 23, 1918.

Place.	Cases.	Deaths.	Place.	Cases.	Deaths.
Atlanta, Ga.	2	....	Little Rock, Ark.	1	....
Berkeley, Cal.	2	....	Newark, N. J.	1	....
Birmingham, Ala.	1	....	North Little Rock, Ark.	4	....
Evansville, Ind.	....	1	Pittsfield, Mass.	1	....
Hattiesburg, Miss.	1	....			

MEASLES.

See Diphtheria, measles, scarlet fever, and tuberculosis, page 558.

PELLAGRA.

State Reports for February, 1918.

Place.	New cases reported.	Place.	New cases reported.
Alabama:		Alabama—Continued.	
Bibb County	1	Shelby County	1
Calhoun County	2	Tuscaloosa County	7
Elmore County	1	Winston County	1
Etowah County	2		
Hale County	1	Total	56
Henry County	1		
Jackson County	3	California:	
Jefferson County	13	Los Angeles County—	
Lamar County	1	Los Angeles	4
Macon County	1	San Diego County—	
Madison County	8	San Diego	2
Mobile County	6		
Montgomery County	6	Total	3
Pickens County	1		

City Reports for Week Ended Mar. 23, 1918.

Place.	Cases.	Deaths.	Place.	Cases.	Deaths.
Atlanta, Ga.	....	1	Memphis, Tenn.	....	1
Austin, Tex.	....	1	New Orleans, La.	1	....
Birmingham, Ala.	2	....	Norfolk, Va.	....	1
Boston, Mass.	1	1	Philadelphia, Pa.	....	1
Charleston, S. C.	....	1	Somerville, Mass.	1	....
Dallas, Tex.	1	1	Wilmington, N. C.	....	1
Fort Worth, Tex.	1	1	Worcester, Mass.	1	....
Lexington, Ky.	....	1			

PNEUMONIA.

City Reports for Week Ended Mar. 23, 1918.

Place.	Cases.	Deaths.	Place.	Cases.	Deaths.
Akron, Ohio	1	....	Boston, Mass.	40	30
Alameda, Cal.	1	1	Braddock, Pa.	4	....
Altoona, Pa.	9	....	Bridgeport, Conn.	17	23
Anderson, Ind.	1	1	Brockton, Mass.	2	1
Anniston, Ala.	1	....	Brookline, Mass.	1	1
Atlanta, Ga.	7	5	Bainbridge, Mass.	7	2
Baltimore, Md.	112	37	Charlestown, W. Va.	1	1
Barre, Vt.	1	....	Chelsea, Mass.	12	8
Battle Creek, Mich.	2	....	Chicago, Ill.	444	162
Berkeley, Cal.	1	1	Chicopee, Mass.	2	1

PNEUMONIA—Continued.

City Reports for Week Ended Mar. 23, 1918—Continued.

Place.	Cases.	Deaths.	Place.	Cases.	Deaths.
Cleveland, Ohio	55	24	Moundsville, W. Va	5	2
Clinton, Mass	3	2	Newark, N. J	190	42
Columbia, S. C	1		New Bedford, Mass	4	4
Dallas, Tex	3	7	New Britain, Conn	3	1
Dayton, Ohio	2	8	Newburyport, Mass	1	
Detroit, Mich	26	41	Newcastle, Pa	1	
Fall River, Mass	1	1	Newport, Ky	2	2
Flint, Mich	6	3	Newton, Mass	4	1
Fort Worth, Tex	7	7	Northampton, Mass	1	
Grand Rapids, Mich	14	2	North Little Rock, Ark	1	1
Hagerstown, Md	2		Oakland, Cal	7	15
Harrisburg, Pa	2	7	Parkersburg, W. Va	2	1
Hattiesburg, Miss	1		Philadelphia, Pa	150	121
Haverhill, Mass	6	1	Pittsburg, Pa	37	30
Holyoke, Mass	1		Pittsfield, Mass	1	8
Jackson, Mich	1		Pontiac, Mich	3	2
Jacksonville, Fla	2	6	Richmond, Va	3	6
Jersey City, N. J		25	Rochester, N. Y	21	2
Kalamazoo, Mich		1	Rutland, Vt	2	2
Kansas City, Kans	25		St. Joseph, Mo	1	3
Lancaster, Pa	2		San Diego, Cal	23	15
Lawrence, Mass	3	3	Schenectady, N. Y	4	1
Leavenworth, Kans	2	3	Sheboygan, Wis	1	1
Lexington, Ky	3	7	Somerville, Mass	4	1
Lincoln, Nebr	4	1	Springfield, Mass	17	7
Little Rock, Ark	17	2	Springfield, Ohio	1	3
Long Beach, Cal	3	1	Steubenville, Ohio	1	
Lorain, Ohio	1		Stockton, Cal	4	
Los Angeles, Cal	2	6	Waco, Tex	2	
Lowell, Mass	2	5	Waltham, Mass	1	1
Lynn, Mass	6	5	Wichita, Kans	5	1
Manchester, N. H	2	2	Worcester, Mass	23	5
Michigan City, Ind	1	1	Yonkers, N. Y	13	3
Morgantown, W. Va	7		York, Pa	2	
Morristown, N. J	1				

POLIOMYELITIS (INFANTILE PARALYSIS).

California Report for February, 1918.

During the month of February, 1918, 1 case of poliomyelitis was reported at Delano, Kern County, Cal.

City Reports for Week Ended Mar. 23, 1918.

Place.	Cases.	Deaths.	Place.	Cases.	Deaths.
Cambridge, Mass	1		Newark, N. J	2	
Chicago, Ill	1		New York, N. Y	2	1
Cleveland, Ohio	1	1	Pittsburgh, Pa	3	1
Fall River, Mass	1		Racine, Wis	1	1
Lowell, Mass	2		Toledo, Ohio	1	
Milwaukee, Wis	17	10			

RABIES IN MAN.

City Reports for Week Ended Mar. 23, 1918.

There were 2 deaths from rabies reported during the week ended March 23, 1918; 1 at Galveston, Tex., and 1 at Louisville, Ky.

RABIES IN ANIMALS.

City Report for Week Ended Mar. 23, 1918.

During the week ended March 23, 1918, there was 1 case of rabies in animals reported at Detroit, Mich.

SCARLET FEVER.

See Diphtheria, measles, scarlet fever, and tuberculosis, page 558.

SMALLPOX.

Kansas—Fort Scott.

During the period from April 1 to 6, 1918, 2 cases of smallpox were notified at Fort Scott, Kans., making a total of 24 cases reported at that place since the beginning of the outbreak, December 10, 1917.

California Report for February, 1918.

Place.	New cases reported.	Deaths.	Vaccination history of cases.			
			Number vaccinated within 7 years preceding attack.	Number last vaccinated more than 7 years preceding attack.	Number never successfully vaccinated.	Vaccination history not obtained or uncertain.
California:						
Alameda County..............	1				1	
Oakland...................	2		1		1	
Fresno County................	4				4	
Fresno....................	3				3	
Selma.....................	1				1	
Imperial County..............	4				4	
Calexico..................	2				2	
Kern County.................	2			1	1	
Lake County.................	1				1	
Madera County...............	1				1	
Marin County—						
Sausalito.................	1				1	
Orange County...............	3				1	2
Santa Ana.................	5				5	
Los Angeles County...........	3				3	
Los Angeles..............	9				7	2
Riverside County.............	3				3	
Sacramento County—						
Sacramento...............	1				1	
San Bernardino County.......	2				2	
San Diego County—						
San Diego................	2				1	
San Francisco County—						
San Francisco.............	12				12	
San Joaquin County..........	1			1		
Stockton.................	1				1	
San Mateo County............	1				1	
Shasta County—						
Redding..................	1				1	
Siskiyou County—						
Dunsmuir.................	3				3	
Tehama County...............	5			1	1	3
Total......................	74		1	3	61	9

SMALLPOX—Continued.

Miscellaneous State Reports.

Place.	Cases.	Deaths.	Place.	Cases.	Deaths.
Alabama (Feb. 1-28):			**Alabama (Feb. 1-28)—Con.**		
Autauga County	3		Limestone County	2	
Baldwin County	11		Macon County	2	
Barbour County	1		Madison County	1	
Bibb County	5		Mobile County	51	
Butler County	14		Monroe County	2	
Calhoun County	50		Montgomery County	54	
Chambers County	14		Morgan County	3	
Cherokee County	6		Pickens County	16	
Chilton County	3		Pike County	6	
Cleburne County	6		Shelby County	6	1
Coffee County	1		St. Clair County	12	
Colbert County	1		Sumter County	1	
Coosa County	6		Talladega County	90	
Covington County	4		Tuscaloosa County	5	
Cullman County	8		Washington County	3	
Dale County	25				
DeKalb County	2		Total	925	4
Etowah County	10				
Fayette County	1		**Nevada (Feb. 1-28):**		
Greene County	1		Elko County	8	
Jefferson County	472	3	Nye County	3	
Lamar County	6		Washoe County	1	
Lauderdale County	4				
Lee County	5		Total	12	

City Reports for Week Ended Mar. 23, 1918.

Place.	Cases.	Deaths.	Place.	Cases.	Deaths.
Akron, Ohio	26		Jacksonville, Fla	1	
Alton, Ill	17		Janesville, Wis	5	
Anderson, Ind	8		Kalamazoo, Mich	2	
Ann Arbor, Mich	1		Kansas City, Mo	41	
Anniston, Ala	17		Knoxville, Tenn	5	
Atlanta, Ga	8		Kokomo, Ind	1	
Baltimore, Md	3		La Crosse, Wis	8	
Barre, Vt	2		La Fayette, Ind	1	
Battle Creek, Mich	5		Leavenworth, Kans	3	
Birmingham, Ala	64		Lima, Ohio	7	
Butte, Mont	2		Lincoln, Nebr	7	
Canton, Ohio	6		Little Rock, Ark	11	
Cedar Rapids, Iowa	4		Lorain, Ohio	2	
Charlotte, N. C	1		Los Angeles, Cal	1	
Chicago, Ill	12		Louisville, Ky	8	
Cincinnati, Ohio	16		Macon, Ga	1	
Cleveland, Ohio	47		Madison, Wis	1	
Clinton, Iowa	2		Memphis, Tenn	22	
Coffeyville, Kans	3		Michigan City, Ind	14	
Colorado Springs, Colo	1		Milwaukee, Wis	12	
Columbus, Ohio	10		Minneapolis, Minn	20	
Council Bluffs, Iowa	20		Mishawaka, Ind	1	
Dallas, Tex	35		Missoula, Mont	1	
Davenport, Iowa	2		Mobile, Ala	8	
Dayton, Ohio	6		Moline, Ill	2	
Des Moines, Iowa	22		Montgomery, Ala	5	
Detroit, Mich	30		Muncie, Ind	8	
Dubuque, Iowa	6		Muskegon, Mich	6	
East Chicago, Ind	1		Muskogee, Okla	1	
El Paso, Tex	1		Nashville, Tenn	5	
Elwood, Ind	3		New Britain, Conn	1	
Erie, Pa	1		New Castle, Ind	2	
Evansville, Ind	3		New Orleans, La	9	
Flint, Mich	6		New York, N. Y	1	
Fort Wayne, Ind	11		Norfolk, Va	1	
Fort Worth, Tex	16		North Little Rock, Ark	1	
Fresno, Cal	4		Oakland, Cal	1	
Galesburg, Ill	26		Oklahoma City, Okla	29	
Grand Forks, N. Dak	8		Omaha, Nebr	53	
Grand Rapids, Mich	3		Oshkosh, Wis	2	
Harrisburg, Pa	1		Parkersburg, W. Va	1	
Hartford, Conn	2		Peoria, Ill	6	
Hattiesburg, Miss	1		Pittsburgh, Pa	6	
Indianapolis, Ind	64		Pontiac, Mich	7	

SMALLPOX—Continued.

City Reports for Week Ended Mar. 23, 1918—Continued.

Place.	Cases.	Deaths.	Place.	Cases.	Deaths.
Pueblo, Colo	2	....	San Francisco, Cal	9	....
Quincy, Ill	6	....	Seattle, Wash	4	....
Racine, Wis	1	....	Shelbyville, Ind	1	....
Richmond, Ind	2	....	South Bend, Ind	4	....
Richmond, Va	1	....	Spartanburg, S. C	5	....
Roanoke, Va	4	....	Superior, Wis	7	....
Rock Island, Ill	1	....	Terre Haute, Ind	5	....
Rutland, Vt	2	....	Toledo, Ohio	12	....
St. Joseph, Mo	10	....	Topeka, Kans	5	....
St. Louis, Mo	15	....	Washington, D. C	1	....
St. Paul, Minn	2	....	Wichita, Kans	12	....
Salt Lake City, Utah	27	....	Winston-Salem, N. C	4	....
Sandusky, Ohio	5	....	York, Pa	2	....

TETANUS.

City Reports for Week Ended Mar. 23, 1918.

There were reported during the week ended March 23, 1918, three deaths from tetanus; one each at Cincinnati, Ohio, Mobile, Ala., and New Orleans, La.

TUBERCULOSIS.

See Diphtheria, measles, scarlet fever, and tuberculosis, page 558.

TYPHOID FEVER.

State Reports for February, 1918.

Place.	New cases reported.	Place.	New cases reported.
Alabama:		California—Continued.	
Colbert County	1	Merced County	1
Conecuh County	1	Monterey County	1
Cullman County	3	Orange County—	
Etowah County	1	Fullerton	1
Fayette County	1	Riverside County—	
Franklin County	1	Riverside	4
Houston County	1	Sacramento County—	
Jefferson County	32	Sacramento	4
Lamar County	1	San Francisco County—	
Limestone County	2	San Francisco	4
Madison County	1	San Diego County—	
Mobile County	3	San Diego	2
Montgomery County	2	San Mateo County	2
Pike County	1	Santa Barbara County	1
Washington County	1	Santa Clara County	3
		San Joaquin County—	
Total	52	Stockton	7
		Siskiyou County—	
California:		Etna	1
Alameda County—			
Oakland	2	Total	53
Colusa County	1		
Fresno County	3	Nevada:	
Fresno	2	Washoe County	1
Imperial County	2	White Pine County	1
Brawley	1		
Calexico	4	Total	2
Los Angeles County	1		
Los Angeles	9		

TYPHOID FEVER—Continued.

City Reports for Week Ended Mar. 23, 1918.

Place.	Cases.	Deaths.	Place.	Cases.	Deaths.
Altoona, Pa.	1		Lowell, Mass.	1	
Anderson, Ind.	1		Macon, Ga.	1	
Atlanta, Ga.	1		Manchester, N. H.	2	1
Atlantic City, N. J.	2		McKeesport, Pa.	2	
Austin, Tex.		1	Milwaukee, Wis.		1
Baltimore, Md.	5	1	Minneapolis, Minn.	6	1
Birmingham, Ala.	1		Moline, Ill.	1	1
Boston, Mass.	1	1	Morgantown, W. Va.	1	
Brookline, Mass.	1		New Bedford, Mass.	3	1
Buffalo, N. Y.	1	2	Newburgh, N. Y.	10	
Charleston, S. C.	1		New Orleans, La.	2	1
Charleston, W. Va.	1		Newton, Mass.	1	
Chattanooga, Tenn.	1		New York, N. Y.	4	3
Chicago, Ill.	8	2	Norristown, Pa.	1	
Cincinnati, Ohio.	2	1	Oakland, Cal.	1	
Cleveland, Ohio.	2		Philadelphia, Pa.	2	1
Columbia, S. C.	1		Pittsburgh, Pa.	6	1
Covington, Ky.	1		Pontiac, Mich.	1	
Cumberland, Md.	1		Portland, Me.	1	
Denver, Colo.	1		Portland, Oreg.	1	
Detroit, Mich.	4	2	Pueblo, Colo.	1	1
Dubuque, Iowa.	5		Quincy, Ill.	2	
Duluth, Minn.	1		Rock Island, Ill.	1	
East Chicago, Ind.	5		Saginaw, Mich.	2	
East Orange, N. J.	1		Salt Lake City, Utah.	1	
Elizabeth, N. J.	1		Sandusky, Ohio.	1	
Elwood, Ind.	1		San Francisco, Cal.		1
Green Bay, Wis.		1	Schenectady, N. Y.	1	
Hammond, Ind.	2		Somerville, Mass.	1	
Haverhill, Mass.	1		Superior, Wis.		1
Hoboken, N. J.	1		Syracuse, N. Y.	3	
Holyoke, Mass.	1		Taunton, Mass.	1	
Indianapolis, Ind.	1		Toledo, Ohio.		1
Kansas City, Kans.	3		Washington, D. C.	1	
Kenosha, Wis.	1		Washington, Pa.	2	
La Crosse, Wis.	1	1	Wheeling, W. Va.	2	1
Lorain, Ohio.	1		Wilmington, Del.	1	
Los Angeles, Cal.	3		Winston-Salem, N. C.	1	
Louisville, Ky.		1			

DIPHTHERIA, MEASLES, SCARLET FEVER, AND TUBERCULOSIS.

State Reports for February, 1918.

For the month of February, 1918, there were reported in Alabama 35 cases of diphtheria, 1,345 cases of measles, and 28 cases of scarlet fever; in California, 262 cases of diphtheria, 5,299 cases of measles, and 407 cases of scarlet fever; in Nevada, 8 cases of measles and 24 cases of scarlet fever.

City Reports for Week Ended Mar. 23, 1918.

City.	Population as of July 1, 1916. (Estimated by U. S. Census Bureau.)	Total deaths from all causes	Diphtheria		Measles.		Scarlet fever.		Tuberculosis.	
			Cases.	Deaths.	Cases.	Deaths.	Cases.	Deaths.	Cases.	Deaths.
Over 500,000 inhabitants:										
Baltimore, Md.	589,621	311	9		420	2	11	1	33	43
Boston, Mass.	756,476	89	3		192	2	35	1	79	32
Chicago, Ill.	2,497,722	883	116	17	61		51	1	393	102
Cleveland, Ohio.	674,073	210	18		19	1	8		33	31
Detroit, Mich.	571,744	241	60	10	37	1	53		49	30
Los Angeles, Cal.	503,812	135	32		195		10		31	24
New York, N. Y.	5,602,841	2,246	267	31	1,562	41	153	3	230	300
Philadelphia, Pa.	1,709,518	796	58	9	525		50	1	118	105
Pittsburgh, Pa.	579,090	228	21	3	139	3	12		43	16
St. Louis, Mo.	757,309	252	33	1	119		30	1	48	21

DIPHTHERIA, MEASLES, SCARLET FEVER, AND TUBERCULOSIS—Continued.

City Reports for Week Ended Mar. 23, 1918—Continued.

City.	Population as of July 1, 1916. (Estimated by U. S. Census Bureau.)	Total deaths from all causes.	Diphtheria.		Measles.		Scarlet fever.		Tuberculosis.	
			Cases.	Deaths.	Cases.	Deaths.	Cases.	Deaths.	Cases.	Deaths.
From 300,000 to 500,000 inhabitants:										
Buffalo, N. Y.	468,558	144	11	3	84	....	6	....	27	17
Cincinnati, Ohio	410,476	160	10	2	25	1	7	....	24	26
Jersey City, N. J.	306,345	137	15	1	61	2	46	....	9	12
Milwaukee, Wis.	436,535	127	5	1	281	2	45	1	22	7
Minneapolis, Minn	363,454	....	14	1	28	1	16	1	....	....
Newark, N. J.	408,894	....	23	....	369	8	96	1	39	20
New Orleans, La.	371,747	199	12	....	7	....	1	....	48	23
San Francisco, Cal	463,516	175	16	....	124	2	14	....	30	13
Seattle, Wash.	348,639	....	....	....	62	3	....	....	11	5
Washington, D. C.	363,080	211	9	....	510	2	41	1	17	22
From 200,000 to 300,000 inhabitants:										
Columbus, Ohio	214,878	74	....	....	31	....	18	....	9	8
Denver, Colo.	260,800	79	6	....	211	....	40	....	....	19
Indianapolis, Ind.	271,708	90	20	....	65	....	31	1	14	10
Louisville, Ky.	238,910	98	7	....	13	....	1	....	16	17
Portland, Oreg.	295,463	58	3	....	281	....	7	....	....	5
Providence, R. I.	254,960	87	10	1	51	....	9	....	....	8
Rochester, N. Y.	255,417	77	6	....	59	1	16	1	11	7
St. Paul, Minn	247,232	64	35	1	26	....	41	2	18	7
From 100,000 to 200,000 inhabitants:										
Atlanta, Ga.	190,558	51	5	....	17	....	2	....	8	7
Birmingham, Ala.	181,762	56	4	....	33	1	1	....	7	8
Bridgeport, Conn.	121,579	77	11	1	9	1	3	....	7	5
Cambridge, Mass.	112,981	29	8	....	57	1	6	....	4	5
Camden, N. J.	106,233	....	2	....	24	....	5	....	4	....
Dallas, Tex.	124,527	11	2	....	40	1	1	....	3	1
Dayton, Ohio	127,224	....	3	....	43	....	5	....	....	5
Des Moines, Iowa	101,598	....	9	1	10	....	12	1	....	....
Fall River, Mass.	128,366	54	3	4	3	....	2	....	11	6
Fort Worth, Tex.	104,562	30	4	1	....	....	9	....	....	....
Grand Rapids, Mich.	128,291	45	5	2	14	....	10	....	6	5
Hartford, Conn.	110,900	52	3	....	5	....	8	....	9	2
Houston, Tex.	112,307	41	2	....	34	....	....	....	9	4
Lawrence, Mass.	100,560	32	1	....	16	1	....	....	6	3
Lowell, Mass.	113,245	40	6	1	8	....	3	....	7	1
Lynn, Mass.	102,425	33	5	1	21	....	7	....	4	2
Memphis, Tenn	148,995	74	12	....	23	....	7	....	29	13
Nashville, Tenn.	117,057	57	....	....	9	....	1	....	3	8
New Bedford, Mass.	118,158	48	2	....	10	....	2	....	12	4
New Haven, Conn.	140,685	56	3	....	1	....	....	....	15	5
Oakland, Cal.	198,604	56	....	....	45	....	6	....	11	6
Omaha, Nebr.	165,470	48	3	1	20	....	9	....	....	5
Reading, Pa.	109,381	29	9	5	50	....	10	....	....	1
Richmond, Va.	156,687	55	6	1	42	....	11	....	8	7
Salt Lake City, Utah	117,399	38	5	....	27	....	18	1	....	3
Scranton, Pa.	146,811	45	3	....	3	....	7	....	....	5
Springfield, Mass.	105,942	39	5	1	25	1	8	....	4	4
Syracuse, N. Y.	155,624	46	8	....	200	3	12	....	8	6
Tacoma, Wash.	112,770	....	1	....	8	....	31	....	....	....
Toledo, Ohio	191,554	77	....	....	18	....	11	....	52	10
Trenton, N. J.	111,592	51	....	....	8	....	1	....	12	7
Worcester, Mass.	163,314	....	5	2	13	....	4	....	7	4
From 50,000 to 100,000 inhabitants:										
Akron, Ohio	85,625	....	9	....	18	....	8	....	3	....
Altoona, Pa.	58,659	....	6	....	8	....	....	....	1	....
Atlantic City, N. J.	57,660	....	....	....	18	....	....	•	5	1
Augusta, Ga.	50,245	28	....	....	16	....	....	....	....	3
Bayonne, N. J.	69,893	....	2	....	140	....	2	....	1	....
Berkeley, Cal.	57,653	12	....	....	4	....	3	....	....	....
Binghamton, N. Y.	53,973	22	1	1	9	....	6	....	2	2
Brockton, Mass.	67,449	14	1	....	13	....	5	....	1	....
Canton, Ohio	60,452	13	1	....	2	....	3	....	2	1
Charleston, S. C.	60,734	31	1	1	4	1	....	....	....	3
Chattanooga, Tenn.	60,075	7	....	....	1	....	....	....	1	3
Covington, Ky.	57,144	30	1	....	10	....	1	....	2	7
Duluth, Minn.	94,495	24	6	1	12	....	1	....	5	4
Elizabeth, N. J.	86,690	41	4	....	47	....	7	....	11	5

DIPHTHERIA, MEASLES, SCARLET FEVER, AND TUBERCULOSIS—Continued.

City Reports for Week Ended Mar. 23, 1918—Continued.

City.	Population as of July 1, 1916. (Estimated by U. S. Census Bureau.)	Total deaths from all causes.	Diphtheria.		Measles.		Scarlet fever.		Tuberculosis.	
			Cases.	Deaths.	Cases.	Deaths.	Cases.	Deaths.	Cases.	Deaths.
From 50,000 to 100,000 inhabitants—Continued:										
El Paso, Tex.	63,705	34	1	....	19	....	....	....	....	8
Erie, Pa	75,195	33	4	1	16	....	7	....	10	5
Evansville, Ind.	76,078	35	5	....	11	....	2	....	8	3
Flint, Mich.	54,772	26	7	....	1	....	3	....	2	....
Fort Wayne, Ind.	76,183	24	8	....	....	....	2	....	....	1
Harrisburg, Pa.	72,015	38	2	....	27	....	5	....	10	5
Hoboken, N. J.	77,214	27	4	2	8	....	....	....	10	4
Holyoke, Mass.	65,286	21	....	....	3	....	3	....	1	1
Jacksonville, Fla.	76,101	29	1	1	13	....	....	....	8	2
Johnstown, Pa.	68,529	25	7	....	1	....	10	....	3	1
Kansas City, Kans.	99,437	....	1	....	2	....	4	1	7	....
Lancaster, Pa.	50,853	....	....	....	40	....	3	....	....	....
Little Rock, Ark.	57,343	17	....	....	7	....	4	....	....	1
Malden, Mass.	51,155	13	5	2	9	....	4	....	4	2
Manchester, N. H.	78,263	27	1	....	41	....	3	....	12	2
Mobile, Ala.	58,221	20	....	....	1	....	....	....	....	2
New Britain, Conn.	53,794	16	2	....	27	....	8	....	....	1
Norfolk, Va.	89,612	....	1	....	11	....	2	....	....	1
Oklahoma City, Okla.	92,943	18	1	....	....	....	1	....	....	5
Passaic, N. J.	71,744	26	4	....	4	....	....	....	4	3
Pawtucket, R. I.	59,411	....	....	....	3	2	....	....	....	2
Peoria, Ill.	71,458	24	1	....	10	....	1	....	....	3
Portland, Me.	63,867	17	1	....	7	....	2	....	....	....
Pueblo, Colo.	54,462	12	1	....	9	....	1	....	....	....
Rockford, Ill.	55,185	20	....	....	34	....	....	....	3	2
Sacramento, Cal.	66,895	21	....	....	50	....	3	....	1	4
Saginaw, Mich.	55,642	25	....	....	7	....	2	....	....	3
St. Joseph, Mo.	85,236	31	5	1	7	....	....	....	3	1
San Diego, Cal.	53,330	21	3	....	101	1	4	....	5	1
Savannah, Ga.	68,505	24	....	....	5	....	1	....	3	3
Schenectady, N. Y.	99,519	21	1	....	17	....	3	....	8	1
Somerville, Mass.	87,039	24	8	....	31	....	5	....	3	4
South Bend, Ind.	68,946	14	1	....	28	....	3	....	4	....
Springfield, Ill.	61,120	17	1	....	65	....	....	....	....	2
Springfield, Ohio	51,550	....	1	....	3	....	....	....	4	2
Terre Haute, Ind.	66,083	16	5	....	2	....	1	....	....	4
Troy, N. Y.	77,916	24	1	....	6	....	10	....	8	3
Wichita, Kans.	70,722	....	....	....	42	1	3	....	4	....
Wilkes-Barre, Pa.	76,776	31	....	....	28	....	7	....	1	....
Wilmington, Del.	94,265	58	8	....	58	....	2	....	....	7
Yonkers, N. Y.	99,838	....	1	1	15	....	1	....	....	2
York, Pa.	51,656	32	....	....	17	....	1	....	1	....
From 25,000 to 50,000 inhabitants:										
Alameda, Cal.	27,732	9	3	....	12	....	2	....	1	1
Austin, Tex.	34,814	18	....	....	....	....	....	....	....	5
Battle Creek, Mich.	29,480	....	7	2	65	....	3	....	....	....
Bellingham, Wash.	32,985	7	....	....	1	....	....	....	....	....
Brookline, Mass.	32,730	9	....	....	48	....	1	....	3	....
Burlington, Iowa	25,030	6	....	....	....	....	1	....	....	....
Butler, Pa.	27,632	11	5	1	35	....	....	....	....	1
Butte, Mont.	43,425	29	2	....	5	....	13	....	....	....
Cedar Rapids, Iowa	37,308	....	....	....	....	....	7	....	....	....
Charleston, W. Va.	29,941	7	1	....	14	....	....	....	....	....
Charlotte, N. C.	39,523	23	3	....	8	....	....	....	5	....
Chelsea, Mass.	46,192	24	2	....	42	....	1	....	2	....
Chicopee, Mass.	29,319	6	3	....	1	....	1	....	3	2
Clinton, Iowa	27,386	....	....	....	42	....	2	....	....	....
Colorado Springs, Colo.	32,971	17	3	....	38	....	....	....	3	5
Columbia, S. C.	34,611	....	3	....	4	....	....	....	1	....
Council Bluffs, Iowa	31,484	....	....	....	....	....	5	....	....	....
Cranston, R. I.	25,967	6	....	....	4	....	3	....	....	....
Cumberland, Md.	26,074	10	....	....	2	....	11	....	3	1
Danville, Ill.	32,261	10	....	....	123	....	....	....	1	1
Davenport, Iowa	48,811	....	....	....	4	....	12	....	....	2
Dubuque, Iowa	39,873	....	....	....	3	....	....	....	....	1
Durham, N. C.	25,061	5	....	....	7	....	....	....	....	1
East Chicago, Ind.	28,743	12	....	....	....	....	....	....	....	....
Easton, Pa.	30,530	18	1	....	17	....	....	....	1	....
East Orange, N. J.	42,458	12	....	....	43	....	....	....	....	....

DIPHTHERIA, MEASLES, SCARLET FEVER, AND TUBERCULOSIS—Continued.

City Reports for Week Ended Mar. 23, 1918—Continued.

City.	Population as of July 1, 1916. (Estimated by U. S. Census Bureau.)	Total deaths from all causes.	Diphtheria.		Measles.		Scarlet fever.		Tuberculosis.	
			Cases.	Deaths.	Cases.	Deaths.	Cases.	Deaths.	Cases.	Deaths.
From 25,000 to 50,000 inhabitants—Continued										
Elgin, Ill	28,203	12			8		2			
Elmira, N. Y	38,190		1		52		1		6	
Evanston, Ill	28,591	6					1			
Everett, Mass	39,233				18		1		5	
Everett, Wash	35,486	2	4				4		5	
Fitchburg, Mass	41,781	14								
Fresno, Cal	34,958	5			17					
Galveston, Tex	41,863	18								2
Green Bay, Wis	29,353	9								1
Hagerstown, Md	25,679				1		1			
Hammond, Ind	26,171	12	1		1					
Haverhill, Mass	48,477	16	5		21		5	1	3	
Jackson, Mich	35,363	13	4		10		23		1	1
Jamestown, N. Y	38,580	17	2						1	
Kalamazoo, Mich	48,886	30	2		3					
Kenosha, Wis	31,576	8	7		5		4		3	4
Knoxville, Tenn	38,676				6					
La Crosse, Wis	31,677	3							2	1
Lexington, Ky	41,097	20	1		12				1	2
Lima, Ohio	35,384	15	3		10					
Lincoln, Nebr	46,515	17	4				8	1	1	
Long Beach, Cal	27,587	12	1		26				1	
Lorain, Ohio	36,964						1			
Lynchburg, Va	32,940	11	2		15				3	1
Macon, Ga	45,757	20			5		1		2	3
Madison, Wis	30,609	16		1				1		
McKeesport, Pa	47,521		1		19					
Medford, Mass	26,234	8	4		6		3			
Moline, Ill	27,451	11			25				1	
Montclair, N. J	26,318	4			78					
Montgomery, Ala	43,285	21			11		1			
Mount Vernon, N. Y	37,009	11	2		5		1		1	
Muncie, Ind	25,424	8			4		1		1	1
Muskegon, Mich	26,100	11			1					
Muskogee, Okla	44,218				10					1
Nashua, N. H	27,327		3				5			
Newburgh, N. Y	29,603	11	1		6				3	3
New Castle, Pa	41,133				10		1			
Newport, Ky	31,927	9							2	2
Newport, R. I	30,108	3	1				3			
Newton, Mass	43,715	7	1		23	2	1		1	2
Niagara Falls, N. Y	37,353	7	1		3		5		1	1
Norristown, Pa	31,401	12	2		1					2
Norwalk, Conn	26,899		1		6				1	1
Oak Park, Ill	26,654	12	4		34			1	1	
Orange, N. J	33,090	9			56		1		2	1
Oshkosh, Wis	36,065	7							4	2
Pasadena, Cal	46,450	18			248				1	3
Perth Amboy, N. J	41,185	15	1		25		1		3	
Petersburg, Va	25,582		1		9				1	1
Pittsfield, Mass	38,629	19		1	1		5			2
Portsmouth, Va	39,851	17	2		15		2			1
Poughkeepsie, N. Y	30,390		1	1	58		1		1	
Quincy, Ill	36,796	11	1		6		3		1	
Quincy, Mass	38,136	18	5		73		6			3
Racine, Wis	46,496	11			33		9			2
Roanoke, Va	43,284	16			55				2	3
Rock Island, Ill	28,926	12			45		2		1	
Salem, Mass	48,562	23	3		30				3	2
San Jose, Cal	38,002				28					
Sheboygan, Wis	28,559	7			4				1	1
Steubenville, Ohio	27,445	22			3					
Stockton, Cal	35,358		5		58				3	
Superior, Wis	46,226	11					4			1
Taunton, Mass	36,283	16							3	2
Topeka, Kans	43,726				63		20			
Waco, Tex	33,385	18			11		3			
Waltham, Mass	30,570	14								2

DIPHTHERIA, MEASLES, SCARLET FEVER, AND TUBERCULOSIS—
Continued.

City Reports for Week Ended Mar. 23, 1918—Continued.

City.	Population as of July 1, 1916. (Estimated by U. S. Census Bureau.)	Total deaths from all causes.	Diphtheria.		Measles.		Scarlet fever.		Tuberculosis.	
			Cases.	Deaths.	Cases.	Deaths.	Cases.	Deaths.	Cases.	Deaths.
From 25,000 to 50,000 inhabitants—Continued.										
Watertown, N. Y	29,894	3	2		98					
West Hoboken, N. J	43,139	3			9		1			
Wheeling, W. Va	43,377	13	1		15				2	2
Williamsport, Pa	33,400	11	1							
Wilmington, N. C	29,492	12			11					
Winston-Salem, N. C	31,155	16			24				3	1
Woonsocket, R. I	44,360		3	1			1			
Zanesville, Ohio	30,863	12								2
From 10,000 to 25,000 inhabitants:										
Alton, Ill	22,874	19	1	1			2		1	5
Anderson, Ind	23,906	8	2		3		2		1	
Ann Arbor. Mich	15,010	13	5		43				1	
Anniston. Ala	14,112				22				3	
Barre, Vt	12,189	2	1							
Bedford, Ind	10,349	1								
Berlin, N. H	13,599	3								1
Braddock, Pa	21,985	8			1				1	
Cairo, Ill	15,794	7			1					
Chillicothe, Ohio	15,470	3	5		5		3			
Clinton, Mass	13,075	6			8		1			
Coffeyville, Kans	17,548				5					
Dover. N. H	13,272	6								
Elkhart, Ind	21,858								1	
Elwood, Ind	11,028	4			3					
Fargo. N. Dak	17,389	2	2		8				1	
Galesburg, Ill	24,276	7	2		26					
Grand Forks, N. Dak	15,837				1		3			
Greenville, S. C	18,181	1							3	
Hackensack, N. J	16,943		1		1		1			
Hattiesburg, Miss	16,482	3			1				1	
Janesville, Wis	14,439		1				3			
Kearny, N. J	23,539	9			27				3	
Kokomo, Ind	20,930	7			7		1			1
La Fayette, Ind	21,286	8					1			1
Leavenworth, Kans	19,353	21		1	12		2			1
Marinette, Wis	14,610	1					2			
Martinsburg, W. Va	12,666				1					
Melrose, Mass	17,445	6	1		4					
Michigan City, Ind	21,512	9							2	2
Mishawaka, Ind	16,385	7							1	
Missoula, Mont	18,214	4								
Morgantown, W. Va	13,709	6							2	
Morristown, N. J	13,284	4								
Moundsville, W. Va	11,153	5			1				2	2
Nanticoke Pa	23,126	14	1		3		6			
New Albany Ind	23,629	10	1						1	1
Newburyport. Mass	15,243	4							1	
Newcastle, Ind	13,241	3								
New London. Conn	20,985	9			1	1	1		1	1
North Adams. Mass	22,019	8								1
North Little Rock, Ark	14,907	1					1			
Northampton, Mass	19,926	7					1		2	2
Parkersburg, W. Va	20,612	5			1		1		1	
Plainfield. N. J	23,405	8			11		1		1	1
Pontiac, Mich	17,534	13	7		6		7		3	
Portsmouth N. H	11,668				6		7			
Richmond, Ind	24,697	8							4	
Rocky Mount, N. C	12,067	3			2				4	
Rutland Vt	14,831	7								
Sandusky, Ohio	20,193	6							1	
Saratoga Springs, N. Y	13,821	7			1				1	1
Shelbyville, Ind	10,965	3								
Spartanburg. S. C	21,365	15			5		1		2	3
Steelton, Pa	15,548	1								
Washington, Pa	21,618				115					
Wilkinsburg, Pa	23,228	17	1		28				1	2
Woburn, Mass	15,969	2								

FOREIGN.

CHOLERA, PLAGUE, SMALLPOX, TYPHUS FEVER, AND YELLOW FEVER.

Reports Received During Week Ended Apr. 12, 1918.[1]

CHOLERA.

Place.	Date.	Cases.	Deaths.	Remarks.
India:				
Bombay	Jan. 6-26	126	103	
Karachi	Dec. 30-Jan. 26	25	6	
Madras	Jan. 20-26	10	4	

PLAGUE.

Place.	Date.	Cases.	Deaths.	Remarks.
Ceylon:				
Colombo	Jan. 13-19	1	....	Jan. 6-26, 1918: Cases, 95,630; deaths, 76,273.
India		....	....	
Bassein	Jan. 5-19	......	11	
Bombay	Jan. 5-26	62	48	
Henzada	Jan. 5-19	......	5	
Karachi	Dec. 30-Jan. 26	16	14	
Madras Presidency	Jan. 20-26	1,526	1,162	
Myingyan	Jan. 5-12	......	73	
Prome	....do...	......	1	
Rangoon	Jan. 6-26	64	60	
Toungoo	Jan. 13-19	....	1	

SMALLPOX.

Place.	Date.	Cases.	Deaths.	Remarks.
Brazil:				
Rio de Janeiro	Feb. 3-Mar. 9	73	41	
Canada:				
New Brunswick—				
Moncton	Mar. 25-30	2	....	
Nova Scotia—				
Halifax	Mar. 17-23	2	....	
Sydney	Mar. 25-30	5	....	
Ontario—				
Ottawa	Mar. 25-31	1	....	
Sarnia	Mar. 24-30	2	....	
Quebec—				
Montreal	....do	3	....	
China:				
Amoy	Feb. 4-10	....	....	Present.
Shanghai	Feb. 11-Mar. 3	3	10	Cases, foreign; deaths, native.
Tientsin	Feb. 18-23	3	....	
India:				
Bombay	Jan. 6-26	132	39	
Madras	Jan. 20-26	27	5	
Rangoon	Jan. 6-26	6	2	
Italy:				
Milan	Dec. 1-31	15	....	
Mexico:				
Ciudad Juares	Mar. 18-23	1	....	
Mexico City	Mar. 3-9	9	....	
Porto Rico:				
San Juan	Mar. 11-17	9	....	Varioloid.
Spain:				
Coruna	Jan. 20-Feb. 23	....	5	
Madrid	Dec. 1-31	....	12	
Seville	Jan. 1-31	....	20	

[1] From medical officers of the Public Health Service, American consuls, and other sources.

CHOLERA, PLAGUE, SMALLPOX, TYPHUS FEVER, AND YELLOW FEVER—Continued.

Reports Received During Week Ended Apr. 12, 1918—Continued.

TYPHUS FEVER.

Place.	Date.	Cases.	Deaths.	Remarks.
Great Britain:				
Belfast.........................	Mar. 3–9............	1	1	
Glasgow......................	...do............	5	....	
Greece:				
Arta.........................	Feb. 19............	2	....	
Janina......................	Feb. 14............	110	....	
Mexico:				
Mexico City...............	Mar. 3–9............	37	....	
Union of South Africa:				
Cape of Good Hope State....	....	......	....	Sept. 10, 1917–Jan. 13, 1918: Cases, 4,158; deaths, 854.
Natal.........................	....	......	....	To Jan. 13, 1918: Cases, 37; deaths, 10.

Reports Received from Dec. 29, 1917, to Apr. 5, 1918.

CHOLERA.

Place.	Date.	Cases.	Deaths.	Remarks.
China:				
Antung......................	Nov. 26–Dec. 2....	3	1	
India:				
Bombay....................	Oct. 28–Dec. 15....	19	14	
Do...................	Dec. 30–Jan. 5....	74	67	
Calcutta...................	Sept. 16–Dec. 15..	....	92	
Do...................	Dec. 30–Jan. 12..	....	14	
Madras....................	Nov. 25 Dec. 22	2	2	
Do...................	Dec. 30–Jan. 12....	3	3	
Rangoon..................	Nov. 4–Dec. 22....	5	5	
Do...................	Dec. 30–Jan. 5. ...	1	1	
Indo-China:				
Provinces..................	....	......	......	Sept. 1 Nov. 30, 1917: Cases, 152; deaths, 89
Anam.....................	Sept. 1–Nov. 30...	18	13	
Cambodia...............	.....do.......	72	52	
Cochin-China...........	.....do.......	50	22	
Saigon...............	Nov. 22 Dec. 9....	4	3	
Kwang-Chou-Wan.....	Sept. 1 30... ...	10	2	
Java:				
East Java	Oct. 28 Nov. 3....	1	1	
West Java.................	....	......	......	Oct. 19 Dec. 27, 1917: Cases, 107; deaths, 56 Dec. 28, 1917 Jan. 10, 1918: Cases, 22; deaths, 9.
Batavia	Oct. 19 Dec. 27....	49	23	
Persia:				
Mazanderan Province .....'	....	......	......	July 30 Sept. 3, 1917: Cases, 384; deaths, 276.
Achraf...................	July 30–Aug. 16....	90	88	
Astrabad................	July 31.	......	......	Present.
Barfrush................	July 1–Aug. 16....	39	25	
Chahmirzad............	....	......	......	25 cases reported July 31, 1917.
Chahrastagh............	June 15–July 25....	10	8	
Charoud................	Aug 26–Sept 3...	4	2	
Damghan................	Aug 26	......	......	Present.
Kharek	May 28 June 11...	21	13	
Meched................	Aug 18–Sept.2....	174	82	
Ouroun Dare...........	Aug 8....	......	......	Do.
Sabzevar...............	Aug 24	......	......	Do.
Sari.....................	July 3 29	273	144	
Semman..................	Aug 31 Sept.2....	14	5	
Yekchambe-Bazar.....	June 3........	6	......	
Philippine Islands:				
Provinces	....	......	......	Nov. 18–Dec. 29, 1917: Cases, 1,063; deaths, 865. Dec. 30, 1917–Feb. 9, 1918: Cases, 914; deaths, 546.
Antique..................	Nov. 18–Dec. 1....	48	32	
Do..................	Feb. 3–9........	4	4	
Bohol....................	Nov. 18–Dec 29....	169	111	
Do..................	Dec 30–Feb 9.....	213	181	
Capiz....................	Nov 25–Dec 29....	27	21	
Do..................	Dec 30–Feb.9.....	121	101	
Cebu....................	Dec 23–29....	3	....	
Do..................	Dec 30–Feb 9	69	36	
Iloilo....................	Nov 25–Dec 29....	179	135	
Do..................	Dec 30–Feb.9.....	82	53	
Leyte....................	Nov. 25–Dec 22....	13	12	
Do..................	Feb 3 9........	9	8	

CHOLERA, PLAGUE, SMALLPOX, TYPHUS FEVER, AND YELLOW FEVER—Continued.

Reports Received from Dec. 29, 1917, to Apr. 5, 1918—Continued.

CHOLERA—Continued.

Place.	Date.	Cases.	Deaths.	Remarks.
Philippine Islands—Continued.				
Provinces—Continued.				
Mindanao	Nov. 25–Dec. 29	337	196	
Do	Dec. 30–Feb. 9	351	220	
Occidental Negros	Nov. 25–Dec. 22	177	123	
Do	Jan. 13–Feb. 9	60	40	
Oriental Negros	Nov. 25–Dec. 29	99	62	
Do	Dec. 30–Feb. 9	15	13	
Romblon	Nov. 25–Dec. 1	1	1	
Siam:				
Bangkok	Sept. 16–22	1	1	
Turkey in Asia:				
Bagdad	Nov. 1–15		40	

PLAGUE.

Place.	Date.	Cases.	Deaths.	Remarks.
Brazil:				
Bahia	Nov. 4–Dec. 15	4	4	
Do	Dec. 30–Jan. 12	3	2	
Rio de Janeiro	Dec. 23–29	1		
Do	Jan. 6–12	1	1	
British Gold Coast:				
Axim	Jan. 8			Present.
Ceylon:				
Colombo	Oct. 14–Dec. 1	14	13	
Do	Dec. 30–Jan. 12	6	5	
Ecuador				Sept. 1–Nov. 30, 1917: Cases, 68; deaths, 24. Reported outbreak occurring about Jan. 17, 1918.
Guayaquil	Sept. 1–30	3	1	
Do	Oct. 1–31	20	8	
Do	Nov. 1–30	45	15	
Egypt				Jan. 1–Nov. 15, 1917: Cases, 728; deaths, 398.
Alexandria	Jan. 14–28	1	2	
Port Said	July 23–29	1	2	
India				Sept. 16–Dec. 22, 1917: Cases, 228,834; deaths, 174,743. Dec. 30, 1917–Jan. 5, 1918: Cases, 28,304; deaths, 22,677.
Bassein	Dec. 9–29		8	
Do	Dec. 30–Jan. 12		3	
Bombay	Oct. 28–Dec. 29	147	123	
Do	Dec. 30–Jan. 5	19	11	
Calcutta	Sept. 16–29		2	
Do	Dec. 30–Jan. 12		3	
Henzada	Oct. 21–27		1	
Karachi	Oct. 21–Dec. 29	27	20	
Do	Dec. 30–Jan. 5	1		
Madras Presidency	Oct. 31–Nov. 17	3,294	2,560	
Do	Jan. 6–12	2,784	2,124	
Mandalay	Oct. 14–Nov. 17		89	
Do	Dec. 30–Jan. 12		236	
Myingyan	Dec. 30–Jan. 5		37	
Rangoon	Oct. 21–Dec. 22		56	
Do	Dec. 30–Jan. 5	15	14	Nov. 1–30, 1917: Cases, 37; deaths, 34.
Toungoo	Dec. 9–29		5	
Do	Dec. 30–Jan. 5		3	
Indo-China:				
Provinces:				Sept. 1–Nov. 30, 1917: Cases, 89; deaths, 68.
Anam	Sept. 1–Nov. 30	28	25	
Cambodia	do	39	28	
Cochin-China	do	22	15	
Saigon	Oct. 31–Dec. 23	17	6	
Do	Dec. 31–Feb. 3	36	9	
Java:				
East Java				Oct. 27–Dec. 23, 1917: Cases, 189; deaths, 186.
Surabaya	Nov. 4–25	3	3	
West Java				Nov. 25–Dec. 9, 1917: Cases, 45; deaths, 45.
Peru				Dec. 1, 1917–Jan. 15, 1918: Cases, 106.
Ancachs Department—				
Casma	Dec. 1–Jan. 15	2		
Lambayeque Department	do	22		At Chiclayo, Ferrenafe, Jayanca, Lambayeque.
Libertad Department	do	72		At Guadalupe, Mansiche, Pacasmayo, Salaverry, San Jose, San Pedro, and country district of Trujillo.
Lima Department	do	9		City and country.
Piura Department—				
Catacaos	do	1		

CHOLERA, PLAGUE, SMALLPOX, TYPHUS FEVER, AND YELLOW FEVER—Continued.

Reports Received from Dec. 29, 1917, to Apr. 5, 1918—Continued.

PLAGUE—Continued.

Place.	Date.	Cases.	Deaths.	Remarks.
Senegal:				
St. Louis..................	Feb. 2..............	....	....	Present.
Siam:				
Bangkok..................	Sept. 16–Dec. 23....	13	9	
Straits Settlements:				
Singapore..................	Oct. 28–Dec. 29....	5	7	

SMALLPOX.

Place.	Date.	Cases.	Deaths.	Remarks.
Algeria:				
Algiers....................	Nov. 1–Dec. 31....	3	1	
Do.	Jan. 1–31..........	2	....	
Australia:				
New South Wales.........				July 12–Dec. 20, 1917: Cases, 36.
Abermain.................	Oct. 25–Nov. 29..	3	....	Jan. 4–17, 1918: Cases, 1.
Cessnock................	July 12–Oct. 11...	7	....	Newcastle district.
Eumangla...............	Aug. 15............	1	....	
Kurri Kurri............	Dec. 5–20..........	2	....	
Mungindi..............	Aug. 13............	1	....	
Warren.................	July 12–Oct. 25....	22	....	
Do.	Jan. 1–17..........	1	....	
Brazil:				
Bahia....................	Nov. 10–Dec. 8....	3	....	
Pernambuco..............	Nov. 1–15.........	1	....	
Rio de Janeiro............	Sept. 30–Dec. 29...	703	190	
Do.	Dec. 30–Jan. 26....	158	42	
Sao Paulo................	Oct. 29–Nov. 4....	....	2	
Canada:				
British Columbia—				
Vancouver...........	Jan. 13–Mar. 9....	5	....	
Victoria...............	Jan. 7–Feb. 2.....	2	....	
Winnipeg.............	Dec. 30–Jan. 5.....	1	....	
New Brunswick—				
Kent County...........	Dec. 4..............			Outbreak. On main line Canadian Ry., 25 miles north of Moncton.
Do.	Jan. 22............	40		In 7 localities.
Northumberland County	....do...........	41		In 5 localities.
Restigouche County....	Jan. 18............	60		
St. John County—				
St. John	Mar. 3–9...........	2		
Victoria County.	Jan. 22...........	10		At Limestone and a lumber camp.
Westmoreland County—				
Moncton..........	Jan. 20–Mar. 23....	9		
St. John............	Mar. 17–23.....	1		
York County..........	Jan. 22...........	8		
Nova Scotia—				
Halifax...............	Feb. 24–Mar. 2....	1		
Sydney...............	Feb. 3–Mar. 23 ...	8		
Ontario—				
Hamilton...........	Dec. 16–22........	1		
Do.	Jan. 13–19........	2		
Ottawa.	Mar. 4–24.........	5		
Sarnia..............	Dec. 9–15.........	1		
Do.	Jan. 6–Mar. 23 ...	30		
Toronto...........	Feb. 10–16........	1		
Windsor	Dec. 30–Jan. 5.....	1		
Prince Edward Island—				
Charlottetown........	Feb. 7–13.........	1		
Quebec—				
Montreal..............	Dec. 16–Jan. 5....	5		
Do.	Jan. 6–Mar. 9.....	7	....	
China:				
Amoy...............,	Oct. 22–Dec. 30...			Present.
Do.	Dec. 31–Feb. 3....			Do.
Antung.................	Dec. 2–23.........	13	2	
Do.	Jan. 7–Feb. 17....	5	2	
Changsha.............	Jan. 28–Feb. 3....	....	1	
Chefoo	Jan. 27–Feb. 9....			Do.
Chungking.............	Nov. 11–Dec. 29...	....	....	Do.
Do.	Dec. 30–Feb. 2....			Do.
Dairen	Nov. 18–Dec. 22...	3	1	
Do.	Dec. 30–Feb. 23....	25	1	

CHOLERA, PLAGUE, SMALLPOX, TYPHUS FEVER, AND YELLOW FEVER—Continued.

Reports Received from Dec. 29, 1917, to Apr. 5, 1918—Continued.

SMALLPOX—Continued.

Place.	Date.	Cases.	Deaths.	Remarks.
China—Continued.				
Harbin	May 14–June 30	20		Chinese Eastern Ry.
Do	July 1–Dec. 2	7		Do.
Hongkong	Dec. 23–29	1		
Do	Jan. 26–Feb. 9	6	1	
Hungtahotze Station	Oct. 28–Nov. 4	1		Do.
Manchuria Station	May 14–June 30	1		Do.
Do	July 1–Dec. 2	3		Do.
Mukden	Nov. 11–24			Present.
Nanking	Feb. 3–16			Epidemic.
Shanghai	Nov. 18–Dec. 23	41	91	Cases, foreign; deaths among natives.
Do	Dec. 31–Feb. 10	33	92	Do.
Swatow	Jan. 18			Unusually prevalent.
Tientsin	Nov. 11–Dec. 22	13		
Do	Dec. 30–Feb. 9	14		
Tsingtau	Feb. 4–10	1		
Cuba:				
Habana	Jan. 7	1		Nov. 8, 1917; 1 case from Coruna; Dec. 5, 1917, 1 case.
Marianao	Jan. 8	1		6 miles distant from Habana.
Ecuador				Sept. 1–Nov. 30, 1917; Cases, 26; deaths, 2.
Guaysquil	Sept. 1–30	8		
Do	Oct. 1–31	14	1	
Do	Nov. 1–30	4	1	
Egypt:				
Alexandria	Nov. 12–18	2	1	
Do	Jan. 8–Feb. 28	5		
Cairo	July 23–Nov. 18	6	1	
France:				
Lyon	Nov. 18–Dec. 16	6	3	
Do	Jan. 7–Feb. 17	11	2	
Marseille	Jan. 1–31		2	
Paris	Jan. 27–Feb. 23	2		
Great Britain:				
Cardiff	Feb. 3–9	4		
Greece:				
Saloniki	Jan. 27–Feb. 9		7	
Honduras:				
Santa Barbara Department	Jan. 1–7			Present in interior.
India:				
Bombay	Oct. 21–Dec. 29	50	12	
Do	Dec. 31–Jan. 5	26	5	
Karachi	Nov. 18–Dec. 29	4	2	Nov. 11–17, 1917: 10 cases with 4 deaths; imported on s. s. Menesa from Basreh.
Madras	Oct. 31–Dec. 29	18	8	
Do	Dec. 30–Jan. 12	21	10	
Rangoon	Oct. 28–Dec. 22	6	1	
Do	Dec. 30–Jan. 5	1		
Indo-China:				
Provinces				Sept. 1–Nov. 30, 1917: Cases, 546; deaths, 146.
Anam	Sept. 1–Nov. 30	163	25	
Cambodia	do	16	8	
Cochin-China	do	353	109	
Saigon	Oct. 20–Dec. 30	120	26	
Do	Dec. 31–Feb. 3	188	63	
Laos	Oct. 1–31	1		
Do	Jan. 20–Feb. 3	1	1	
Tonkin	Sept. 1–Oct. 31	9	4	
Do	Jan. 26–Feb. 3	3		
Italy:				
Castellamare	Dec. 10	2		Among refugees.
Florence	Dec. 1–15	17	4	
Genoa	Dec. 2–31	11	3	
Do	Jan. 2–31	30	2	
Leghorn	Jan. 7–Feb. 24	30	6	
Messina	Jan. 3–19	1		
Milan				Oct. 1–Nov. 30, 1917: Cases, 17.
Naples	To Dec. 10	2		Among refugees.
Taormina	Jan. 20–Feb. 9	6		
Turin	Oct. 29–Dec. 29	123	120	
Do	Jan. 21–Feb. 3	24	3	
Japan:				
Nagasaki	Jan. 14–27	3	1	
Taihoku	Dec. 15–21	1		Island of Taiwan (Formosa).
Do	Jan. 8–Feb. 11	5	2	Do.
Tokyo	Feb. 11–18	8		City and suburbs.
Yokohama	Jan. 17–Feb. 3	4		

CHOLERA, PLAGUE, SMALLPOX, TYPHUS FEVER, AND YELLOW FEVER—Continued.

Reports Received from Dec. 29, 1917, to Apr. 5, 1918—Continued.

SMALLPOX—Continued.

Place.	Date.	Cases.	Deaths.	Remarks.
Java:				
East Java....................	Oct. 7–Dec. 23.....	50	....	
Mid-Java.....................				Oct. 10–Dec. 26, 1917: Cases, 86;
Samarang...............	Nov. 6–Dec. 12....	4	1	death, 1.
West Java....................				Oct. 19–Dec. 27, 1917: Cases, 231;
Batavia.................	Nov. 2–8....	1	....	deaths, 36. Dec. 28, 1917–Jan. 10, 1918: Cases, 47; deaths, 4.
Mexico:				
Aguascalientes.............	Feb. 4–17.........	....	2	
Ciudad Juares.............	Mar. 3–9...........	1	1	
Mazatlan....................	Dec. 5–11..........	....	1	
Do..................	Jan. 29–Mar. 5...	4	3	
Mexico City...............	Nov. 11–Dec. 29...	16	....	
Do..................	Dec. 30–Mar. 2....	52	....	
Piedras Negras.............	Jan. 11...........	200	....	
Vera Cruz.................	Jan. 20–Mar. 2....	7	3	
Newfoundland:				
St. Johns..................	Dec. 8–Jan. 4.....	29	....	
Do..................	Jan. 5–Mar. 15.....	35	....	
Trepassey.................	Jan. 4...........	....	....	Outbreak with 11 cases reported.
Philippine Islands:				
Manila....................	Oct. 28–Dec. 8....	5	........r.	
Do..................	Jan. 13–Feb. 9.....	12	....	
Porto Rico:				
San Juan.................	Jan. 28–Mar. 3.....	28	....	
Portugal.				
Lisbon....................	Nov 4–Dec. 15....	2	....	
Do.................	Dec. 30–Feb. 22...	4	....	
Portuguese East Africa:				
Lourenço Marques........	Aug. 1–Dec. 31....	....	16	
Russia:				
Archangel................	Sept. 1–Oct. 31...	7	....	
Moscow...................	Aug. 26–Oct. 6.....	22	2	
Petrograd................	Aug. 31–Nov. 18...	76	3	
Siam:				
Bangkok..................	Nov. 25–Dec. 1....	1	1	
Do..................	Jan. 6–12.........	1	....	
Spain:				
Coruna...................	Dec. 2–15.........	....	4	
Madrid...................				Jan. 1–Dec. 31, 1917: Deaths, 77.
Seville...................	Oct. 1–Dec. 30....	....	66	
Straits Settlements:				
Singapore................	Nov. 25–Dec. 1....	1	1	
Do.................	Dec. 30–Jan. 5.....	1	....	
Tunisia:				
Tunis....................	Dec. 14–20........	1	....	
Turkey in Asia:				
Bagdad...................				Present in November, 1917.
Union of South Africa:				
Cape of Good Hope State...	Oct. 1–Dec. 31....	28	....	
East Liverpool............	Jan. 20–26........	1	....	Varioloid.
Venezuela:				
Maracaibo.................	Dec. 2–8..........	....	1	

TYPHUS FEVER.

Place.	Date.	Cases.	Deaths.	Remarks.
Algeria:				
Algiers...	Nov. 1–Dec. 31...	2	1	
Argentina:				
Rosario....	Dec. 1–31..	....	1	
Australia:				
South Australia	....	....	....	Nov. 11–17, 1917. one case.
Brazil:				
Rio de Janeiro	Oct. 28–Dec. 1.....	7	....	
Canada:				
Ontario				
Kingston..............	Dec. 2–8...........	3	....	
Quebec-				
Montreal..............	Dec. 16–22.......	2	1	
China:				
Antung....................	Dec. 3–30.........	13	1	
Do....................	Dec. 31–Jan. 27....	2	2	
Chosen (Formosa):				
Seoul.....................	Nov. 1–20.........	1	....	

CHOLERA, PLAGUE, SMALLPOX, TYPHUS FEVER, AND YELLOW FEVER—Continued.

Reports Received from Dec. 29, 1917, to Apr. 5, 1918—Continued.

TYPHUS FEVER—Continued.

Place.	Date.	Cases.	Deaths.	Remarks.
Egypt:				
Alexandria	Nov. 8–Dec. 28	57	15	
Do	Jan. 8–Feb. 25	223	54	
Cairo	July 23–Dec. 16	137	70	
Port Said	July 30–Nov. 11	5	5	
France:				
Marseille	Dec. 1–31		1	
Great Britain:				
Belfast	Feb. 10–Mar. 2	15	2	
Glasgow	Dec. 21	1		
Do	Jan. 20–Feb. 23	4		
Manchester	Dec. 2–8	1		
Greece:				
Saloniki	Nov. 11–Dec. 29		72	
Do	Dec. 30–Jan. 19		11	
Japan:				
Nagasaki	Nov. 26–Dec. 16	5	5	
Do	Jan. 7–Feb. 17	8	2	
Java:				
East Java				Oct. 15–Dec. 23, 1917: Cases, 35; deaths, 6.
Surabaya	Dec. 17–23	6	1	
Mid-Java:				Oct. 10–Dec. 26, 1917: Cases, 63; deaths, 2.
Samarang	Oct. 9–Dec. 26	20	2	
Do	Dec. 27–Jan. 2	1		
West Java				Oct. 19–Dec. 27, 1917: Cases, 94; deaths, 17.
Batavia	Oct. 19–Dec. 27	59	15	
Mexico:				
Aguascalientes	Dec. 15		2	
Do	Jan. 21–Feb. 10		14	
Durango State—				
Guanacevi	Feb. 11			Epidemic.
Mexico City	Nov. 11–Dec. 29	476		
Do	Dec. 30–Mar. 2	491		
Norway:				
Bergen	Feb. 1–16	3		
Portugal:				
Lisbon	Feb. 21			Present.
Oporto	do			Epidemic. Dec. 24, 1917–Mar. 9, 1918. About 250 cases reported.
Russia:				
Archangel	Sept. 1–14	7	2	
Moscow	Aug. 26–Oct. 6	49	2	
Petrograd	Aug. 31–Nov. 18	32		
Do	Feb. 2			Present.
Vladivostok	Oct. 29–Nov. 4	12	1	
Sweden:				
Goteborg	Nov. 18–Dec. 15	2		
Switzerland:				
Basel	Jan. 6–19	1	1	
Zurich	Nov. 9–15	2		
Do	Jan. 13–19	2		
Tunisia:				
Tunis	Nov. 30–Dec. 6		1	
Do	Feb. 9–15	2		
Turkey:				
Albania				
Janina	Jan. 27			Epidemic.
Union of South Africa:				
Cape of Good Hope State				Sept. 10–Nov. 25, 1917: Cases, 3,724 (European, 31; native, 3,693); deaths, 761 (European, 5; native, 756).

YELLOW FEVER.

Place.	Date.	Cases.	Deaths.	Remarks.
Ecuador				Sept. 1–Nov. 30, 1917: Cases, 5; deaths, 3.
Guayaquil	Sept.-1-30	1	1	
Do	Oct. 1–31	1		
Do	Nov. 1–30	2	2	
Yaguachi	do	1		
Honduras:				
Tegucigalpa	Dec. 16–22		1	
Do	Jan. 6–19		1	

X

BREEDING OF ANOPHELES QUADRIMACULATUS IN DEEP WATER AND AT A DISTANCE FROM SHORE.

By H. R. CARTER, Assistant Surgeon General, United Statse Public Health Service.

It is generally stated that Anopheles do not breed in deep water or at a distance from shore. This is usually true because (1) such water does not furnish food for the larvæ: (2) they are drowned by wave action; and (3) they are eaten by fish.

In the course of malaria surveys made by the United States Public Health Service near the United States Marine Barracks, Quantico, Va., in September, 1917, the contrary was found to be true.

Examination up to July 29 had shown no production of Anopheles in either Quantico or Chappawampsic Creek and no production of *A. quadrimaculatus* anywhere except in pools near the mouth of Creek No. 1. Since this was scanty and had not been found up to July 16, it was feared that this species would appear in Quantico and Chappawampsic Creeks as the season advanced. Being large, these creeks would warm up more slowly and hence breed later than small pools, and this species is not an early breeder.

On September 3 an examination was made of a number of houses at Quantico and *A. quadrimaculatus* were found in them in such number and distribution as to indicate an important source to the northeast of the village. In addition 442 mosquitoes were taken in an isolated group of tents one-third mile distant from the lower part of the Chappawampsic. No other water not under control was within a mile.

Examination of Quantico and Chappawampsic Creeks was made by boat by Mr. Messer of the Virginia State Board of Health and myself. In both creeks there were large masses, acres in extent, of "floatage" over the wild celery (*Vallisneria spiralis*).

This plant was growing in water from 2½ feet to over 6 feet deep and extended in places from one-quarter to possibly one-half mile from shore. Its long blades floated just level with the surface of the water rising and falling with the tide and pointing down the current. The "floatage" was formed mainly of the broken pieces of these blades—they are quite fragile—and an enormous amount of pollen of the same plant; it was then in flower. In a

41   (571)

few places the "floatage" was bound together by a growth of algæ, but mainly adherent without it. In these creeks there was the heaviest breeding of *Anophelas quadrimaculatus* I have ever seen over a large area. The patches of "floatage" were measurable in acres and fractions of an acre rather than in square yards. In Quantico Creek they were at both sides of the channel, but none within 300 feet, say, of the shore. In Chappawampsic Creek they were mainly near the mouth and on the side next to the camp. Here they were within half a mile, maybe less, of the tents in which we found the Anopheles and were most probably their source. Quantico Creek is about a mile wide where this "floatage" was found. Chappawampsic is about 1¾ or 2 miles wide at its mouth. We estimated the average number of larvæ per dip at 8, but one dipper took 52. They were of all sizes, and pupæ were also present. In addition to the breeding in this "floatage" there was breeding in some of the lotus beds, where the leaves of this plant fell into the water and adhered together as they decayed. Where the leaf stood up above the water there was no breeding. The same conditions, breeding in floatáge in deep water, had been noted on Broad River, S. C., and other places in our work on Impounded Waters, but none so spectacular as this.

In all of these cases the matting of the "floatage" prevented the breaking of the waves, which passed through it in long smooth swells, and furnished a perfect protection against fish. It must also have provided a good food supply.

The problem of the control of this breeding is a very difficult one.

EFFECT OF ANOPHELES PUNCTIPENNIS ON THE NATURAL CONVEYANCE OF MALARIAL FEVER.

By H. R. CARTER, Assistant Surgeon General, United States Public Health Service.

There is no question that *A. punctipennis* is capable of conveying malarial fever. King first (1915) showed that mosquitoes of this species were readily infectible and that the malaria parasite underwent complete sporogenous development in them. Mitzmain later (1916) produced malarial fever in men by the bites of infected mosquitoes of this species. To what extent they convey malaria *in nature*, however, is not determined.

It has been shown (Public Health Bulletin No. 79) that this mosquito is rarely found in residences—houses occupied by men—in the day time. Where both species are breeding to the same extent *A. quadrimaculatus* is found in such houses in far greater numbers than *A. punctipennis*. If this is because *A. punctipennis* do not enter the residence to feed, it would imply that they are less efficient as vectors of malaria than *A. quadrimaculatus*. It may be, however, that they enter residences at night, feed and leave before morning. Such evidence as we have is against this, but it is not enough to be convincing. It was purposed to determine this point last summer, but owing to the war this study could not be carried out. Indeed, observations to determine the general problem "To what extent is *A. punctipennis* a vector in nature" had been planned from several sides, biological and epidemiological, but were necessarily abandoned when the extra-cantonment work was taken up. The following epidemiological observations, however, bearing on this subject, were made:

A malaria survey was made in August 1917 of Camp Meade, Md., and its environment—about 18 square miles. Eight residences gave a history of malarial fever in 1916 and 1917 at four places. Examination of 74 places breeding Anopheles showed 5 of them producing *A. quadrimaculatus* or *A. crucians*. The remaining places were breeding only *A. punctipennis*. Punctipennis were also found in three of the other places with the other species.

Note that malaria was reported in houses near all the places producing *Anopheles quadrimaculatus* or *crucians* except one.[1] Of some 300 houses where the malaria history was taken, the great majority of which were near places producing punctipennis, only one reported malaria. The country was, as seen from the number of houses, very thickly settled, mainly by whites, and in the part most thickly settled the breeding of Anopheles (punctipennis) was as general as I have ever seen. I don't mean as profuse, although it was free and in places profuse.

It is obvious that the diagnosis of malaria based on the statements of patients can not be accepted without reserve, but at four of these houses (all near breeding places of *A. quadrimaculatus* or *A. crucians*) the history of repeated chills and fevers, given by intelligent people, was very clear, and Derivaux states that he found a number of such cases (in 1915) near the other place breeding quadrimaculatus. The statement of those claiming freedom from malaria can, I think, generally be accepted, as it involved freedom from any kind of sickness. The census of the houses was made by the State board of health, but special inquiries, at five of the houses, were made by myself.

In this locality, then, the production of *A. punctipennis* in large number and adjacent to many white people was not associated with malarial fever, while that of *A. quadrimaculatus* and *A. crucians* was.

This may be correlated with our observations at Greenville, S. C., in 1914 and 1915. In June, August, and September a stream run-

---

[1] There was a house near this place, but it probably was not visited or there was no one at home when it was visited.

ning through the heart of this town was absolutely swarming with
A. punctipennis larvæ and the imagos were abundant in culverts,
spring inclosures, etc. Yet Greenville was practically free from
malaria. There was some malaria, but it was scarcely a sanitary
problem. The same was true of Rock Hill, S. C.: a large production
of *A. punctipennis* and only a very moderate amount of malaria.
The same appears to be true of the country around Atlanta. Grimm,
of the Public Health Service, states that in a large number of blood
specimens examined at Spartanburg, S. C., during two and one-
half years, he failed to find the malaria parasites except in cases
that had recently come from malaria sections. Yet Le Prince reports
A. punctipennis breeding freely in this section last fall, and I think
this was true in 1914 also.

During the investigation of impounded waters some country
neighborhoods were found with a large number of punctipennis and
only a moderate amount of malaria, contrasted with communities in
which quadrimaculatus was prevalent and malaria decidedly common.
For instance, a survey of the Valley of Broad River, S. C., from
Dawkins to Blair, was made by Griffitts in 1916. Punctipennis was
breeding freely in all of this section, which, however, was not considered as malarious (measured by the standard of this section)
except at the Buckhead Settlement. Here it was prevalent, notoriously so, and here *A quadrimaculatus* was breeding freely in some
large ponds. More imagoes of this species were taken in the first
house examined at Buckhead than in the 12 days' work in the
punctipennis district. Several somewhat similar instances could be
given from these investigations. Observations consistent with the
above have been made at other places.

I have never found malaria prevalent where only punctipennis
was breeding, but Brumfield of Virginia has reported quite an outbreak of malaria where this was the only species. There was also a
sharp epidemic at Greenville, S. C., in 1912, although whether punctipennis was the only form then present is not known.

The above report of conditions about Camp Meade is made so that
other men may be encouraged to record observations of similar (or
contrasting) conditions, i. e., the relation of the prevalence of *A. punctipennis* to the presence or absence of malarial fevers. The definite
determination of the efficiency of this species as a vector *in nature*
compared with *A. quadrimaculatus* and *A. crucians*, is of very great
importance to the sanitarian. If it is not a vector of serious sanitary
importance for which there is certainly some evidence—we will
avoid undertaking the very large amount of work required for the
control of its production. Its breeding habits are quite different
from those of *A. quadrimaculatus* (and to a lesser degree from those
of *A. crucians*) both in character of place and in season, and special

April 19, 1918

measures are required for the control of this species not needed for the others. Over the whole United States the cost of these and other measures for controlling punctipennis would run into many millions each year, which should not be expended if the malaria averted by them—for punctipennis unquestionably does convey some malaria—causes less loss than would the expense of averting it. To spend a dollar in sanitation and get less than one hundred cents' benefit is not only bad business, but bad sanitation.

To what extent each of the three species of Anopheles most common east of the Rocky Mountains, *A. quadrimaculatus*, *A. crucians*, and *A. punctipennis*, is a factor in the *natural* conveyance of malaria is possibly the most important of our field problems.

PREVALENCE OF DISEASE.

No health department, State or local, can effectively prevent or control disease without knowledge of when, where, and under what conditions cases are occurring

UNITED STATES.

EXTRA-CANTONMENT ZONES—CASES REPORTED WEEK ENDED APR. 16.

CAMP BEAUREGARD ZONE, LA.

	Cases.
Alexandria:	
Chicken pox	1
Malaria	1
Measles	2
Mumps	12
Pellagra	1
Smallpox	5
Whooping cough	1
Pineville:	
Erysipelas	1
Smallpox	1

CAMP BOWIE ZONE, TEX.

Fort Worth:	
Chicken pox	1
Smallpox	4
Syphilis	1

CAMP DEVENS ZONE, MASS.

Chicken pox:	
Lancaster	3
German measles:	
Lunenburg	1
Pepperell	2
Measles:	
Ayer	3
Graniteville	18

CAMP DODGE ZONE, IOWA.

Chicken pox:	
Bloomfield Township	1
Fort Des Moines	1
Diphtheria	
Bloomfield Township	3
Des Moines	5
Gonorrhea	
Des Moines	6
Measles	
Des Moines	5
Scarlatina	
Bloomfield Township	1

CAMP DODGE ZONE, IOWA—continued.

	Cases.
Scarlet fever:	
Bloomfield Township	2
Des Moines	26
Smallpox:	
Bloomfield Township	3
Des Moines	13
Fort Des Moines	1
Syphilis:	
Des Moines	4
Typhoid fever:	
Des Moines	4
Whooping cough:	
Des Moines	4

CAMP FUNSTON ZONE, KANS.

Measles:	
Manhattan	5
Milford	10
Riley	6
Mumps:	
Junction City	2
Manhattan	5
Pneumonia:	
Manhattan	4
Scarlet fever:	
Junction City	4
Manhattan	1
Riley	5
Smallpox:	
Manhattan	1
Milford	2
Whooping cough:	
Manhattan	4

CAMP GORDON ZONE, GA.

Atlanta:	
Cerebrospinal meningitis	1
Chicken pox	7
Diphtheria	1
German measles	2
Gonorrhea	3
Measles	12

(576)

CAMP GORDON ZONE, GA.—continued.

Atlanta—Continued.   Cases.

Mumps	18
Pneumonia	5
Scarlet fever	4
Smallpox	1
Syphilis	3
Tuberculosis	4
Typhoid fever	1
Whooping cough	1

Chamblee:

Measles	2

Decatur:

Measles	1

East Point:

Smallpox	5

CAMP GREENE ZONE, N. C.

Charlotte Township:

Chancroid	2
Chicken pox	2
Gonorrhea	12
Measles	16
Mumps	3
Scarlet fever	1
Syphilis	13
Tuberculosis	3
Whooping cough	8

GULFPORT HEALTH DISTRICT, MISS.

Gulfport Health District:

Cerebrospinal meningitis	1
Diphtheria	1
Dysentery	1
Malaria	4
Measles	4
Varioloid	1
Whooping cough	2

CAMP HANCOCK ZONE, GA.

Augusta:

German measles	3
Malaria	5
Measles	27
Pneumonia, lobar	1

Gracewood:

Measles	1

CAMP JACKSON ZONE, S. C.

Columbia:

Measles	5
Mumps	3
Whooping cough	6

CAMP JOSEPH E. JOHNSTON ZONE, FLA.

Chicken pox:

Jacksonville	2

Dysentery:

Jacksonville	5
Seaboard Air Line Shops	1
South Jacksonville	1
Fisher's Corner	1
Panama Park	2

Gonorrhea:

Jacksonville	27
Panama Park	1

CAMP JOSEPH E. JOHNSTON ZONE, FLA.—continued.

Hookworm: Cases.

Seaboard Air Line Shops	2

Malaria:

Jacksonville	2
Mandarin	1

Measles:

Jacksonville	11
South Jacksonville	1
Seaboard Air Line Shops	2
Mandarin	1
Fisher's Corner	1

Mumps:

Jacksonville	4

Pellagra:

Jacksonville	1

Pneumonia:

Jacksonville	4

Syphilis:

Jacksonville	36

Trachoma:

Jacksonville	2

Tuberculosis:

Jacksonville	6

Typhoid fever:

Jacksonville	4

Whooping cough:

Jacksonville	18
Ortega	1

FORT LEAVENWORTH ZONE, KANS.

Leavenworth:

Chicken pox	2
Diphtheria	2
German measles	1
Measles	27
Smallpox	6
Whooping cough	2

Leavenworth County:

Diphtheria	2
Measles	4
Pneumonia, lobar	1
Smallpox	5

CAMP LEE ZONE, VA.

Cerebrospinal meningitis:

Hopewell	1

Chancroid:

Petersburg	1

Chicken pox:

Ettricks	1
Prince George County	3

Gonorrhea:

Petersburg	1

Measles:

Hopewell	1

Mumps:

Ettricks	8
Hopewell	2
Petersburg	3

Pneumonia:

Ettricks	2

Septic sore throat:

Ettricks	2
Petersburg	4

CAMP LEE ZONE, VA.—continued.

Tuberculosis:	Cases.
Petersburg	3
Whooping cough:	
Ettricks	1
Petersburg	1
Prince George County	1

CAMP LEWIS ZONE, WASH.

German measles:	
Lake City	5
Parkland	4
Spanaway	1
Mumps:	
Du Pont	3
Nisqually	2
Scarlet fever:	
Du Pont	1
Parkland	1
Whooping cough:	
Parkland	3

CAMP LOGAN ZONE, TEX.

Chancroid:	
Houston	1
Chicken pox:	
Houston	1
Diphtheria:	
Houston	2
Gonorrhea:	
Houston	10
Louetta	1
Tomball	1
Malaria:	
Houston	1
Measles:	
Houston	24
Spring	24
Mumps:	
Houston	4
Pneumonia:	
Houston	1
Syphilis:	
Beaumont	1
Goose Creek	1
Houston	20
Tuberculosis:	
Houston	8
Whooping cough:	
Houston	3

CAMP M'ARTHUR ZONE, TEX.

Waco:	
Chicken pox	7
German measles	1
Measles	11
Mumps	26
Pneumonia, lobar	5
Scarlet fever	2
Tuberculosis	1
Whooping cough	3
Precinct 4:	
Smallpox	1

CAMP M'CLELLAN ZONE, ALA

Chicken pox:	
Anniston	3
Measles:	
Anniston	1
Mumps:	
Anniston	3

CAMP M'CLELLAN ZONE, ALA.—continued.

Pneumonia:	Cases.
Anniston	1
Smallpox:	
Anniston	6
Oxford	1
Precinct 15	1
Precinct 22	1

NORFOLK COUNTY NAVAL DISTRICT, VA.

Cerebrospinal meningitis:	
Fairmount Park	1
South Norfolk	1
Diphtheria:	
Norfolk County	1
Malaria:	
Gilmerton	1
Measles:	
Norfolk	8
Portsmouth	11
Mumps:	
Ocean View	3
Willoughby	1
Pneumonia:	
Gilmerton	2
Portsmouth	3
Scarlet fever:	
Norfolk	1
Norfolk County	1
Portsmouth	1
Smallpox:	
Portsmouth	1
Tuberculosis:	
Portsmouth	4
Whooping cough:	
Portsmouth	7

FORT OGLETHORPE ZONE, GA.

Cerebrospinal meningitis:	
Chattanooga	9
Chicken pox:	
Chattanooga	1
Measles:	
Chattanooga	1
East Lake	1
Mumps:	
Chattanooga	13
East Lake	1
Rossville	1
Pneumonia:	
Chattanooga	1
Rossville	1
Scarlet fever:	
Chattanooga	1
Smallpox:	
Chattanooga	5
Tuberculosis:	
Chattanooga	2
Hixson	1
Whooping cough:	
Chattanooga	4

CAMP SEVIER ZONE, S. C.

Cerebrospinal meningitis:	
Greenville, suburban	1
Measles:	
Greenville, suburban	3
Union Bleachery	8
Typhoid fever:	
American Spinning Co	1

CAMP SHELBY ZONE, MISS.

Hattiesburg:	Cases.
German measles	1
Malaria	7
Measles	2
Mumps	21
Pneumonia, lobar	2
Scarlet fever	1
Smallpox	2
Tuberculosis, pulmonary	1
Venereal	9
Whooping cough	6

CAMP SHERIDAN ZONE, ALA.

Montgomery:

Chancroid	2
Diphtheria	1
Gonorrhea	7
Hookworm	1
Measles	5
Mumps	11
Ringworm	12
Smallpox	4
Syphilis	7

Rural district in 5-mile zone:

Measles	1
Mumps	1

CAMP SHERMAN ZONE, OHIO.

Gonorrhea:

Chillicothe	1

Measles:

Chillicothe	17
Green Township	4
Jefferson Township	1
Liberty Township	2
Scioto Township	2

Mumps:

Liberty Township	2

Scarlet fever:

Chillicothe	6
Huntington Township	1

Typhoid fever:

Chillicothe	1

CAMP ZACHARY TAYLOR ZONE, KY.

Jefferson County:

Diphtheria	1
Measles	2
Typhoid fever	1

Louisville:

Cerebrospinal meningitis	1
Chancroid	6
Chicken pox	2
Diphtheria	7
Gonorrhea	26
Measles	9
Mumps	1
Pneumonia	2
Scarlet fever	1
Smallpox	4
Syphilis	25
Tuberculosis, pulmonary	12
Typhoid fever	2
Whooping cough	2

TIDEWATER HEALTH DISTRICT, VA.

Cerebrospinal meningitis:	Cases.
Newport News	3

Chicken pox:

Newport News	2

German measles:

Hampton	6

Measles:

Newport News	24
Phoebus	2

Mumps:

Hampton	3
Newport News	11
Phoebus	1

Pneumonia:

Phoebus	1

Scarlet fever:

Hampton	1
Newport News	2
Phoebus	3

Smallpox:

Newport News	9

Typhoid fever:

Hampton	1
Newport News	1

CAMP TRAVIS ZONE, TEX.

San Antonio:

Chancroid	1
Dysentery	1
Gonorrhea	18
Influenza	2
Malaria	1
Measles	4
Mumps	4
Pneumonia	4
Syphilis	4
Tuberculosis	6

CAMP WADSWORTH ZONE, S. C.

Cerebrospinal meningitis:

Spartanburg	1

Diphtheria:

Spartanburg	1

German measles:

Spartanburg	1
Spartanburg County	3

Gonorrhea:

Pauline	1

Measles:

Saxon Mills	3
Spartanburg	1

Mumps:

Spartanburg	9

Tuberculosis:

Whitestone	1

Whooping cough:

Pauline	2
Saxon Mills	1
Spartanburg	2

CAMP WHEELER ZONE, GA.

East Macon:

Cerebrospinal meningitis	1
Mumps	2

CAMP WHEELER ZONE, GA.—continued.

Macon:

Chancroid	1
Gonorrhea	8
Measles	1
Mumps	10
Pneumonia	2
Scarlet fever	2

CAMP WHEELER ZONE, GA.—continued.

Macon—Continued.

Smallpox	1
Syphilis	3
Tuberculosis	4
Typhoid fever	4

South Macon:

Cerebrospinal meningitis	4

DISEASE CONDITIONS AMONG TROOPS IN THE UNITED STATES.

The following data are taken from telegraphic reports received in the office of the Surgeon General, United States Army, for the week ended April 5, 1918:

Annual admission rate per 1,000 (disease only):

All troops	1,685.1
National Guard camps	1,478.3
National Army camps	1,943.7
Regular Army	1,518.5

Noneffective rate per 1,000 on day of report:

All troops	47.8
National Guard camps	41.4

Noneffective rate per 1,000 on day of report—Continued.

National Army camps	54.3
Regular Army	43.5

Annual death rate per 1,000 (disease only):

All troops	11.6
National Guard camps	5.9
National Army camps	14.1
Regular Army	13.6

New cases of special disease reported during the week ended Apr. 5, 1918.

Camps.	Pneumonia.	Dysentery.	Malaria.	Venereal.	Measles.	Meningitis.	Scarlet fever.	Deaths.	Annual admission rate per 1,000 (disease only).	Noneffective per 1,000 on day of report.
Wadsworth	5			14	5		2	4	1,313.9	28.9
Hancock	7		1	8	3	1	1	4	472.1	26.4
McClellan	4		2	15	1			1	904.2	30.3
Sevier	7			23	5	1		3	1,639.3	37.7
Wheeler	6		7	32				2	1,150.2	38.7
Logan	9		2	40	6			2	1,674.3	44.1
Coly	14			4	1			10	1,208.3	32.3
Doniphan	17			12				6	2,007.6	43.1
Bowie	32			70				5	4,174.6	78.2
Sheridan	3			57	8		1	1	811.9	24.4
Shelby	5		2	12			1	1	1,132.3	50.8
Beauregard	2		16	38	1	1		3	1,361.6	53.1
Kearney			1	1			7		1,185.5	45.9
Devens	28			65	6	1	2	6	1,628.5	43.0
Upton	16			74	8		15	9	919.5	37.7
Dix	6			50	10		7		1,264.8	38.3
Meade	4			7	13		4	2	547.7	30.2
Lee	12			495	9	1		1	1,911.6	54.8
Jackson	20		4	357	32	4		8	1,714.4	52.0
Gordon	8		1	142	14	1	1	2	1,630.3	41.6
Sherman	10			81	5		21	7	1,632.7	53.5
Taylor	30			43	87			13	2,062.7	69.7
Custer	11			116	5		14	16	2,293.1	38.0
Grant	1			11	11	6		5	802.4	26.0
Pike	29			79	14	1	8	17	2,851.8	74.4
Doge	34			99	24	1	15	26	3,093.7	106.5
Funston	19		1	109	16	2	6	10	1,702.5	76.2
Travis	35	1	5	41	44	1	1	6	3,772.9	72.7
Lewis	15			167	19		23	1	4,100.6	87.0
Northeastern Department	2			22			1	3	2,200.0	44.4
Eastern Department	9		2	20	14		1	2	1,108.2	33.0
Southeastern Department	3		1	21	27		2	6	1,561.7	45.8
Central Department	29	1		79	17		15	13	1,907.4	47.7
Southern Department	28		1	80	13	3		8	1,588.6	59.3
Western Department	5			25	14		44	4	1,194.6	30.4
Aviation, S. C.	15	1	5	104	70	8	42	27	1,658.4	41.3
Camp Greene	0	1	3	39	22	1	2	4	715.3	24.1
Camp Lewis	2		2	32	18			2	1,361.8	57.4
El Paso	1			11	5				989.2	7.2
Columbia Barracks	7			7	1		1	4	1,853.3	61.3
Jefferson Barracks	14			35	10		8	8	2,304.7	110.2
Fort Logan	9			2			7	7	1,937.4	75.2

New cases of special disease reported during the week ended Apr. 5, 1918—Continued.

Camps.	Pneumonia.	Dysentery.	Malaria.	Venereal.	Measles.	Meningitis.	Scarlet fever.	Deaths.	Annual admission rate per 1,000 (disease only).	Noneffective per 1,000 on day of report.
Fort McDowell.............	.....	.....	.....	2	7	.....	.....	2	1,709.4	50.9
Fort Slocum...............	5	.....	.....	11	2	.....	.....	.....	1,113.6	41.6
Disciplinary Barracks, Fort Leavenworth.............	.....	.....	.....	1	.....	.....	.....	4	1,440.1	40.3
A. A. Humphreys.........	1	.....	.....	2	.....	.....	.....	.....	577.8	7.4
J. E. Johnston...........	4	.....	.....	49	8	1	.....	2	1,440.4	41.4
Camp Merritt.............	20	1	4	90	4	.....	5	10	1,636.4	56.0
Camp Stuart.............	31	.....	.....	68	12	2	1	11	1,411.8	55.5
West Point, N. Y........	.....	.....	.....	2	1	.....	.....	.....	1,000.6	14.2
Edgewood-Aberdeen.......	1	.....	.....	.....	8	.....	4	.....	1,481.3	34.9
Provision depot for corps and Army troops........	7	.....	.....	7	49	.....	1	2	2,235.3	46.5
Camp Holabird...........	.....	.....	.....	1	.....	.....	.....	.....	.....	.....
Camp Raritan.............	.....	.....	.....	.....	2	.....	.....	.....	1,054.7	21.2
Fort Thomas.............	4	.....	.....	4	2	.....	.....	1	3,234.6	79.5
National Guard in departments.............	3	.....	.....	15	11	.....	.....	1	.....	.....
National Army in departments.............	13	.....	2	160	50	1	40	5	.....	.....
Total...............	643	5	62	3,113	714	37	269	296	1,685.1	¹ 47.8

¹ All troops.

Annual rate per 1,000 for special diseases.

Disease.	All troops in United States.¹	Regulars in United States.¹	National Guard, all camps.¹	National Army, all camps.¹	Expeditionary Forces.²
Pneumonia..........................	26.6	29.1	18.4	31.1	40.4
Dysentery..........................	0.3	0.5	0.0	0.1	0.5
Malaria...........................	2.7	2.2	5.1	1.2	0.0
Venereal..........................	128.9	83.3	54.0	215.0	48.7
Paratyphoid fever..................	0.0	0.0	0.0	0.0	0.0
Typhoid fever......................	0.04	0.0	0.0	0.0	0.0
Measles...........................	29.5	37.7	5.0	35.2	9.2
Meningitis.........................	1.5	1.8	0.5	2.0	1.7
Scarlet fever......................	11.1	10.0	1.8	13.0	15.2

¹ Week ended Apr. 5, 1918.   ² Week ended Mar. 28, 1918.

CURRENT STATE SUMMARIES.

Connecticut.

From Collaborating Epidemiologist Black, by telegraph, for week ended April 13, 1918:

Cerebrospinal meningitis: Bridgeport 1, Waterbury 2.

Illinois.

From Collaborating Epidemiologist Drake, by telegraph, for week ended April 13, 1918:

Smallpox: One hundred and three; of which Chicago 4, Honeypoint Township, Macoupin County 5, Alton 22, Peoria 13, Quincy 16, Belleville 5, East St. Louis 8. Scarlet fever: One hundred and six; of which Chicago 49. Meningitis: Chicago 12, Wheaton 1, Winfield Township, Dupage County 1, West Warren Township, Williamson County 1, Virden 4, Minook Township, Woodford County 2. Poliomyelitis: Chicago 6, Beardstown 1.

Indiana.

From the State Board of Health of Indiana, by telegraph, for week ended April 13, 1918:

Smallpox: Epidemic Crown Point, Rushville. Measles: Epidemic Wawaka. Scarlet fever: Epidemic Newcastle. Epidemic meningitis: Two cases Charleston, Clark County. La Grippe: Epidemic Fort Wayne, Anderson, Muncie.

Kansas.

From Collaborating Epidemiologist Crumbine, by telegraph, for week ended April 13, 1918:

Meningitis: McLouth 1. Smallpox (10 or more cases): By counties—Brown 15, Butler 15, Decatur 10, Reno 27, Seward 11, Woodson 10; by cities—Kansas City 20, Wichita 18, Ottawa 12, Pottawatomie 10. Scarlet fever (over 10 cases): Riley County 11, Topeka city 20. Scarlatina prevalent over entire State.

Louisiana.

From Collaborating Epidemiologist Dowling, by telegraph, for week ended April 13, 1918:

Meningitis (excluding Rapides Parish): De Soto Parish 1.

Massachusetts.

From Collaborating Epidemiologist Hitchcock, by telegraph, for week ended April 13, 1918:

Unusual prevalence. Diphtheria: Malden, 17. German measles: Brookline, 45; Chelmsford, 8; Mansfield, 23; Manchester, 10; Rockland, 12. Measles: Brookline, 34; Chelsea, 38; Haverhill, 50; Waltham, 58. Scarlet fever: Colerain, 7.

Minnesota.

From Collaborating Epidemiologist Bracken, by telegraph, for week ended April 13, 1918:

Smallpox (new foci): Lyon County, Stanley Township, 1; Mower County, Austin Township, 1; Norman County, Strand Township, 3; Renville County, Bandon Township, 3

Nebraska.

From the State Board of Health of Nebraska, by telegraph, for week ended April 13, 1918:

Poliomyelitis: One case, Tilden. Typhoid fever: One case, Davenport. Smallpox: Red Cloud, Emerson, Henderson, Broken Bow, Scottsbluff, Atkinson, Upland, Humphrey, Omaha, Lincoln, Tecumseh, Antioch, Holland, Brewster, Murdock, Tamora, Culbertson, Wayne Scarlet fever: Pakmer, Omaha, Emerson, License. Measles. Scottsbluff, Omaha, Bee, Leigh. Diphtheria: Shelby, Geneva. German measles: Lyons Septic sore throat: Lyons

New Jersey.

From Collaborating Epidemiologist Bowen, by telegraph, for week ended April 13, 1918:

Unusual prevalence. Measles. East Orange, Bayonne, Paterson. Whooping cough: Paterson.

South Carolina.

From Collaborating Epidemiologist Hayne, by telegraph, for week ended April 15, 1918:

Epidemic meningitis: Six cases week ended 15th.

Virginia.

From Collaborating Epidemiologist Traynham, by telegraph, for week ended April 13, 1918:

Smallpox: By counties—Pulaski 12, Lee 1, Smyth 1, Caroline 2, Russell several, Spottsylvania several, Middlesex 1, Wise 1, Pittsylvania 1, Carroll 16, Suffolk 1, Newport News city 6. Cerebrospinal meningitis: By counties—Lunenburg 1, Prince William 1, Sussex 2, Roanoke 1, Prince George 1, Norfolk 1; Newport News city 4, Richmond city 1. Poliomyelitis: By counties—Accomac 1, Mecklenburg 1.

Washington.

From Collaborating Epidemiologist Tuttle, by telegraph, for week ended April 13, 1918:

Unusual prevalence. Scarlet fever: Prevalent Kent, King County. Smallpox: Thirteen cases in quarantine at Arlington, Snohomish County. Scarlet fever: Twenty-nine cases in Tacoma.

CEREBROSPINAL MENINGITIS.

State Reports for February and March, 1918.

Place.	New cases reported.	Place.	New cases reported.
Maryland (Mar. 1-31):		North Carolina (Feb. 1-28):	
Baltimore	27	Cherokee County	3
Anne Arundel County	1	Cumberland County	1
Shipley	1	Currituck County	1
Baltimore County—		Durham County	1
St. Helena	1	Franklin County	1
Hamilton	1	Gaston County	5
Catonsville	1	Guilford County	2
Highlandtown	1	Halifax County	1
Montgomery County—		Haywood County	1
Bethesda	2	Henderson County	1
		Johnston County	1
Total	35	Martin County	1
		Mecklenburg County	2
New York (Mar. 1-31):		Montgomery County	1
Albany County	9	Pasquotank County	1
Cattaraugus County	1	Pitt County	1
Cortland County	1	Randolph County	1
Dutchess County	1	Richmond County	1
Erie County	6	Yadkin County	1
Niagara County	1		
Oneida County	1	Total	27
Rensselaer County	6		
Schenectady County	1	Vermont (Mar. 1-31):	
Westchester County	2	Chittenden County	1
		Rutland County	1
Total	29		
		Total	2

CEREBROSPINAL MENINGITIS—Continued.

City Reports for Week Ended Mar. 30, 1918.

Place.	Cases.	Deaths.	Place.	Cases.	Deaths.
Amarillo, Tex	2		Malden, Mass		
Ann Arbor, Mich	1		Manitowoc, Wis	1	
Atlanta, Ga	2	1	Marion, Ind	1	
Atlantic City, N. J	1		McKeesport, Pa	2	
Augusta, Ga	1	2	Memphis, Tenn	2	1
Baltimore, Md	9	5	Milwaukee, Wis	1	2
Beaumont, Tex		1	Nashville, Tenn	1	
Birmingham, Ala	3		Newark, N. J	4	1
Boston, Mass	4	1	New London, Conn	1	1
Buffalo, N. Y	3	1	New York, N. Y	19	11
Charleston, S. C	2	1	Petersburg, Va	1	1
Charleston, W. Va	1		Philadelphia, Pa	7	4
Charlotte, N. C	1		Pittsburgh, Pa	2	
Chelsea, Mass	1	1	Poughkeepsie, N. Y	1	
Chicago, Ill	5	4	Providence, R. I	1	1
Cincinnati, Ohio		2	Richmond, Va	2	1
Cleveland, Ohio	3		St. Louis, Mo	2	
Coffeyville, Kans	4		San Diego, Cal	2	3
Detroit, Mich			San Francisco, Cal	2	2
Elizabeth, N. J	2		Savannah, Ga	3	1
Evansville, Ind	1		Shelbyville, Ind	1	2
Indianapolis, Ind	2	2	Springfield, Ohio	1	1
Kansas City, Kans	2		Tacoma, Wash	1	
La Crosse, Wis	1	1	Wichita, Kans	2	
Lexington, Ky			Wilkes-Barre, Pa	2	1
Los Angeles, Cal	2	1	Winston-Salem, N. C	2	2
Louisville, Ky	4		Worcester, Mass	2	
Lowell, Mass	1		York, Pa	1	1

DIPHTHERIA.

See Diphtheria, measles, scarlet fever, and tuberculosis, page 591.

ERYSIPELAS.

City Reports for Week Ended Mar. 30, 1918.

Place.	Cases.	Deaths.	Place.	Cases.	Deaths.
Akron, Ohio	1		Marshall, Tex	1	
Baltimore, Md	4	1	Milwaukee, Wis	2	
Billings, Mont	2		Minneapolis, Minn		2
Bridgeport, Conn	2		Mobile, Ala		1
Brockton, Mass	1		Newark, N. J	2	
Buffalo, N. Y	4		New Castle, Pa	1	
Butler, Pa	1		Newton, Mass		1
Charlotte, N. C		1	New York, N. Y		12
Chicago, Ill	18	2	Oklahoma City, Okla	2	
Colorado Springs, Colo		1	Omaha, Nebr	1	
Concord, N. H			Peoria, Ill	1	
Denver, Colo	6		Pawtucket, R. I		1
Detroit, Mich	6		Philadelphia, Pa	7	
Duluth, Minn	2		Pittsburgh, Pa	8	1
Flint, Mich	2		Pittsfield, Mass	2	1
Fort Worth, Tex	1	1	Portland, Oreg	4	
Harrisburg, Pa	2		Quincy, Mass		1
Hartford, Conn	1		Reading, Pa	2	
Jackson, Mich	1	1	Rochester, N. Y	9	
Lancaster, Pa	1		Sacramento, Cal	1	
Leavenworth, Kans		1	St. Joseph, Mo	1	
Lexington, Ky		1	St. Louis, Mo	10	3
Lincoln, Nebr			San Francisco, Cal	9	1
Los Angeles, Cal	6		Seattle, Wash	2	
Louisville, Ky	5		Wheeling, W. Va	1	
Malden, Mass		1	Wichita, Kans	2	
Manitowoc, Wis	1				

MALARIA.

Maryland Report for March, 1918.

During the month of March, 1918, cases of malaria were reported in Maryland as follows: Caroline County, Hillsboro, 1; Worcester County, Girdletree, 1.

MALARIA—Continued.

City Reports for Week Ended Mar. 30, 1918.

Place.	Cases.	Deaths.	Place.	Cases.	Deaths.
Birmingham, Ala	2		Newark, N. J	1	
Hattiesburg, Miss	1		Newcastle, Ind.	1	
Little Rock, Ark	5		New Orleans, La	1	
Marshall, Tex	1		New York, N. Y		1

MEASLES.

Alaska—Ketchikan.

During the period from April 1 to 6, 1918, 16 cases of measles were notified at Ketchikan, Alaska.

See also Diphtheria, measles, scarlet fever, and tuberculosis, page 591.

PELLAGRA.

City Reports for Week Ended Mar. 30, 1918.

Place.	Cases.	Deaths.	Place.	Cases.	Deaths.
Abilene, Tex	1		Little Rock, Ark		2
Atlanta, Ga		2	Marshall, Tex	1	
Birmingham, Ala	2	4	Milwaukee, Wis		1
Cambridge, Mass	1		Mobile, Ala	1	
Charleston, S. C		1	Petersburg, Va	1	
Dallas, Tex	2		Spartanburg, S. C	3	
Hattiesburg, Miss	1		Wilmington, N. C		1

PNEUMONIA.

City Reports for Week Ended Mar. 30, 1918.

Place.	Cases.	Deaths.	Place.	Cases.	Deaths.
Alameda, Cal	1		Harrison, N. J	4	
Altoona, Pa	5		Hattiesburg, Miss	1	
Amarillo, Tex	1		Haverhill, Mass	7	2
Ann Arbor, Mich	1		Holyoke, Mass	10	4
Anniston, Ala	1		Houston, Tex	5	4
Atlanta, Ga	2	11	Jamestown, N. Y	3	
Auburn, N. Y	6	2	Kalamazoo, Mich	2	1
Baltimore, Md	96	31	Kansas City, Kans	15	
Battle Creek, Mich	1		Lancaster, Pa	1	
Boston, Mass	27	31	Lawrence, Mass	3	4
Braddock, Pa	7		Leavenworth, Kans	2	
Bridgeport, Conn	6	29	Lexington, Ky	2	8
Brockton, Mass	4		Lincoln, R. I	1	
Brookline, Mass	2		Little Rock, Ark	9	1
Cambridge, Mass	3	1	Long Beach, Cal	1	
Charleston, W. Va	3	3	Los Angeles, Cal	25	10
Chelsea, Mass	4	3	Louisville, Ky	2	13
Chicago, Ill	400	158	Lynn, Mass	10	5
Chicopee, Mass	3	4	Macon, Ga	5	3
Cleveland, Ohio	60	42	Manitowoc, Wis	1	1
Clinton, Mass	2	3	Marshall, Tex	1	
Dayton, Ohio	5	5	McKeesport, Pa	1	
Detroit, Mich	19	49	Melrose, Mass	2	1
Elmira, N. Y	4	1	Morgantown, W. Va	1	
Elwood, Ind	1	1	Muskegon, Mich	2	2
Everett, Mass	2		Nashville, Tenn	1	8
Fall River, Mass	2	1	Newark, N. J	175	49
Flint, Mich	10	13	New Bedford, Mass	4	2
Fort Worth, Tex	11	11	New Britain, Conn	4	3
Fresno, Cal	1		New Castle, Ind	1	1
Grand Forks, N. Dak	1		New Castle, Pa	1	
Grand Rapids, Mich	6	1	Newport, Ky	4	4
Hammond, Ind	2	2	Newton, Mass	2	1

PNEUMONIA—Continued.

City Reports for Week Ended Mar. 30, 1918.

Place.	Cases.	Deaths.	Place.	Cases.	Deaths.
Northampton, Mass............	1	....	Saginaw, Mich................	1	1
Norwalk, Conn...............	3	2	St. Joseph, Mo................	3	5
Oakland, Cal.................	5	....	Salem, Mass..................	1	....
Oak Park, Ill................	1	2	Sandusky, Ohio...............	1	....
Oklahoma City, Okla..........	1	1	San Francisco, Cal............	16	16
Parkersburg, W. Va...........	4	2	Schenectady, N. Y.............	7	4
Philadelphia, Pa.............	150	96	Somerville, Mass..............	5	4
Pittsburgh, Pa...............	49	66	Springfield, Mass.............	18	7
Pittsfield, Mass.............	2	....	Steelton, Pa.................	3	3
Pontiac, Mich...............	10	1	Taunton, Mass................	2	1
Providence, R. I.............	1	12	Toledo, Ohio.................	2	4
Quincy, Mass................	1	3	Topeka, Kans.................	1	5
Reno, Nev...................	1	....	Washington, Pa...............	1	....
Richmond, Va................	3	7	Wichita, Kans................	8	2
Rochester, N. Y..............	33	9	Worcester, Mass..............	17	6
Rutland, Vt.................	1	1	Yonkers, N. Y................	12	3
Sacramento, Cal.............	3	1	York, Pa....................	2	....

POLIOMYELITIS (INFANTILE PARALYSIS).

State Reports for March, 1918.

During the month of March, 1918, 1 case of poliomyelitis was reported at Baltimore, Md., 1 case in St. Lawrence County, N. Y., and 1 case in Henderson County, N. C.

City Reports for Week Ended Mar. 30, 1918.

Place.	Cases.	Deaths.	Place.	Cases.	Deaths.
Abilene, Tex.................	1	....	Oak Park, Ill................	1	....
Hartford, Conn..............	1	....	Racine, Wis.................	1	....
Newark, N. J................	4	1	Richmond, Va................	1	....
New York, N. Y..............	5	3	Springfield, Ill..............	....	1

RABIES IN ANIMALS.

City Reports for Week Ended Mar. 30, 1918.

During the week ended March 30, 1918, there was one case of rabies in animals reported at each of the following places: Akron, Ohio; Charlotte, N. C.; and Evansville, Ind.

RABIES IN MAN.

City Report for Week Ended Mar. 30, 1918.

During the week ended March 30, 1918, there were reported at Ogden, Utah, 1 case and 1 death from rabies in man.

SCARLET FEVER.

See Diphtheria, measles, scarlet fever, and tuberculosis, page 591.

SMALLPOX.

Oklahoma—Lawton.

On April 10, 1918, 15 cases of smallpox were reported in quarantine at Lawton, Okla.

SMALLPOX—Continued.

State Reports for March, 1918.

Place.	New cases reported.	Deaths.	Vaccination history of cases.			
			Number vaccinated within 7 years preceding attack.	Number last vaccinated more than 7 years preceding attack.	Number never successfully vaccinated.	Vaccination history not obtained or uncertain.
Maryland:						
Baltimore.................	10			1	9	
Allegany County—						
Cumberland.............	1				1	
Anne Arundel County—						
Brooklyn, R. F. D.......	2			1	1	
Baltimore County—						
Highlandtown...........	1				1	
Dorchester County—						
Cambridge...............	1				1	
Harford County..............	2				2	
Total....................	17			2	15	
New York:						
Chautauqua County—						
Dunkirk...................	1			1		
Chemung County—						
Elmira...................	1					4
Erie County—						
Buffalo..................	10					10
East Hamburg...........	1				1	
Genesee County—						
Batavia.................	3				3	
Herkimer County—						
Ilion.....................	1				1	
Mohawk.................	2		1		1	
Frankfort...............	1			1		
Oneida County—						
Rome....................	4				4	
Utica....................	7			3	4	
Clayville................	1				1	
St. Lawrence County—						
Brasher.................	1				1	
Schenectady County—						
Schenectady.............	1					
Seneca County—						
Covert..................	3			1	2	
Interlaken..............	3			1	2	
Lodi....................	1					1
Wyoming County—						
Warsaw.................	1				1	
Total....................	42		1	7	21	13

Miscellaneous State Reports.

Place.	New cases reported.	Place.	New cases reported.
North Carolina (Feb. 1-28):		North Carolina (Feb. 1-28)—Continued.	
Alamance County..................	1	Swain County........................	2
Anson County....................	1	Iredell County......................	3
Buncombe County.................	4	Surry County........................	1
Cabarrus County.................	3	Jackson County......................	35
Catawba County.................	2	Johnston County.....................	1
Chatham County.................	1	Stanly County.......................	19
Cherokee County.................	1	Lee County..........................	4
Cleveland County.................	1	Lincoln County......................	1
Cumberland County...............	1	Scotland County	1
Durham County	1	Martin County.......................	1
Edgecombe County	10	Mc owell County....................	2
Forsyth County..................	2	Mecklenburg County.................	2
Gaston County...................	3	Pitt County.........................	2
Graham County..................	4	Richmond County....................	1
Harnett County..................	8	Robeson County.....................	11
Henderson County................	2	Rockingham County.................	6

SMALLPOX—Continued.

Miscellaneous State Reports—Continued.

Place.	New cases reported.	Place.	New cases reported.
North Carolina (Feb. 1-28)—Continued.		Vermont (Mar. 1-31):	
Rowan County	5	Essex County	1
Rutherford County	21	Orleans County	2
Wake County	2	Rutland County	2
Wayne County	1	Washington County	2
Yancey County	2	Windsor County	1
Total	168	Total	8

City Reports for Week Ended Mar. 30, 1918.

Place.	Cases.	Deaths.	Place.	Cases.	Deaths.
Abilene, Tex	8		Keokuk, Iowa	1	
Akron, Ohio	65		Knoxville, Tenn	2	
Alton, Ill	34		La Crosse, Wis	4	
Amarillo, Tex	20		Lansing, Mich	6	
Anderson, Ind	8		Leavenworth, Kans	3	
Anniston, Ala	17		Lima, Ohio	44	
Atlanta, Ga	7		Lincoln, Nebr	12	
Atlantic City, N. J	2		Little Rock, Ark	13	
Baltimore, Md	2		Lorain, Ohio	1	
Bedford, Ind	4		Los Angeles, Cal	6	
Bellingham, Wash	1		Louisville, Ky	4	
Billings, Mont	1		Macon, Ga	3	
Birmingham, Ala	40		Madison, Wis	3	
Bloomington, Ind	8		Marion, Ind	1	
Burlington, Iowa	2		Marshall, Tex	3	
Butte, Mont	4		Memphis, Tenn	22	
Canton, Ohio	4		Michigan City, Ind	10	
Cedar Rapids, Iowa	6		Milwaukee, Wis	10	
Charleston, W. Va	2		Minneapolis, Minn	8	
Charlotte, N C	6		Mishawaka, Ind	1	
Chattanooga, Tenn	3		Missoula, Mont	1	
Chicago, Ill	15		Moline, Ill	1	
Chillicothe, Ohio	4		Montgomery, Ala	2	
Cincinnati, Ohio	12		Morgantown, W. Va	1	
Cleveland, Ohio	29		Muncie, Ind	3	
Coffeyville, Kans	7		Muskogee, Okla	9	
Colorado Springs, Colo	2		Nashville, Tenn	4	
Columbus, Ohio	9		Newark, N. J	1	
Council Bluffs, Iowa	12		Newcastle, Ind	1	
Cumberland, Md	1		New Orleans, La	12	
Dallas, Tex	15		New York, N. Y	6	
Danville, Ill	2		Oakland, Cal	1	
Davenport, Iowa	1		Ogden, Utah	1	
Dayton, Ohio	7		Oklahoma City, Okla	31	
Decatur, Ill	1		Omaha, Nebr	49	
Denver, Colo	26		Peoria, Ill	8	
Des Moines, Iowa	20		Philadelphia, Pa	8	
Detroit, Mich	23		Pontiac, Mich	3	
Dubuque, Iowa	2		Portland, Oreg	1	
Duluth, Minn	4		Quincy, Ill	15	
El Paso, Tex	2		Richmond, Ind	1	
Elwood, Ind	1		Roanoke, Va	3	
Evansville, Ind	2		St. Joseph, Mo	29	
Fargo, N Dak	2		St Louis, Mo	15	
Flint, Mich	9		Salt Lake City, Utah	18	
Fort Wayne, Ind	12		San Francisco, Cal	1	
Fort Worth, Tex	32		Seattle, Wash	3	
Galesburg, Ill	2		Shelbyville, Ind	2	
Grand Forks, N Dak	2		Sioux City, Iowa	10	
Grand Rapids, Mich	6		South Bend, Ind	2	
Greeley, Colo	2		Spartanburg, S. C	2	
Hammond, Ind	1		Spokane, Wash	12	
Harrisburg, Pa	3		Springfield, Ill	4	
Hattiesburg, Miss	1		Springfield, Ohio	1	
Independence, Kans	5		Terre Haute, Ind	12	
Indianapolis, Ind	49		Toledo, Ohio	6	
Kalamazoo, Mich	2		Topeka, Kans	10	
Kansas City, Kans	23		Wichita, Kans	36	
Kenosha, Wis	4		Winston-Salem, N. C	1	

TETANUS.

City Reports for Week Ended Mar. 30, 1918.

Place.	Cases.	Deaths.	Place.	Cases.	Deaths.
Baltimore, Md.		1	McKeesport, Pa.	1	
Charleston, S. C.		1	Minneapolis, Minn.		1
Corpus Christi, Tex.	1	1	New York, N. Y.	1	1
Fall River, Mass.	1	1	Portsmouth, Va.		1
Lexington, Ky.		1	Wilmington, N. C.		1

TUBERCULOSIS.

See Diphtheria, measles, scarlet fever, and tuberculosis, page 591.

TYPHOID FEVER.

State Reports for February and March, 1918.

Place.	New cases reported.	Place.	New cases reported.
Maryland (Mar. 1-31):		New York (Mar. 1-31)—Continued.	
Baltimore	22	Clinton County—	
Allegany County—		Plattsburg	4
National	1	Columbia County—	
Cresaptown	1	Kinderhook (town)	1
Westernport	1	Germantown (town)	1
Cumberland	1	Dutchess County—	
Franklin	1	Poughkeepsie (town)	2
Lonaconing	1	Erie County—	
Western Maryland Hospital	2	Buffalo	7
Anne Arundel County—		Tonawanda	1
Annapolis	1	Elma (town)	3
Baltimore County—		Angola	1
Highlandtown	14	Essex County—	
Sparrows Point	2	Ticonderoga (town)	2
Catonsville	1	Franklin County—	
Reisterstown	1	Westville (town)	1
Guilford	2	Malone (town)	2
Gardenville	1	Fort Covington (town)	1
St. Agnes Hospital	1	Genesee County—	
Caroline County—		Batavia	5
Ridgely	2	Greene County—	
Dorchester County—		Catskill	1
Reids Grove	1	Greenville (town)	1
Frederick County—		Jefferson County—	
Brunswick	2	Watertown	1
Libertytown	1	Alexandria Bay	2
Garrett County—		Brownville (town)	2
Kempton	1	Wilna (town)	3
Oakland	1	Henderson (town)	1
Grantsville	2	Cape Vincent	1
Howard County—		Madison County—	
Elkridge	1	Georgetown (town)	4
Prince Georges County—		Montgomery County—	
Riverdale	1	Amsterdam	4
Somerset County—		Niagara County—	
Pocomoke City	1	North Tonawanda	3
Washington County—		Lockport	4
Brownsville	1	Niagara Falls	1
Hagerstown	2	Oneida County—	
Wicomico County—		Augusta (town)	4
Salisbury	2	Onondaga County—	
		Syracuse	6
Total	71	Clay (town)	2
		Minoa	1
New York (Mar. 1-31):		Ontario County—	
Albany County—		Geneva	1
Albany	8	Orange County—	
Watervliet	1	Newburgh	10
Ravena	1	Montgomery (town)	3
Coeymans (town)	2	Hamptonburg (town)	1
Green Island	1	Oswego County—	
Cattaraugus County—		Hannibal (town)	4
Franklinville	1	Otsego County—	
Cattaraugus	1	Oneonta	4
Chemung County—		Rensselaer County—	
Elmira	2	Troy	7
Southport (town)	7		

TYPHOID FEVER—Continued.

State Reports for February and March, 1918—Continued.

Place.	New cases reported.	Place.	New cases reported.
New York Mar. 1–31—Continued.		New York Mar. 1–31—Continued.	
St. Lawrence County—		Westchester County—	
Massena	1	Yonkers	4
De Kalb (town)	1	Yates County—	
Saratoga County—		Jerusalem (town)	1
Mechanicsville	4	Rushville	1
Schenectady County—		Starkey (town)	1
Schenectady	2		
Schoharie County—		Total	138
Cobleskill	1		
Seneca County—		North Carolina (Feb. 1–28):	
Seneca Falls	3	Avery County	4
Steuben County—		Columbus County	1
Corning	1	Davidson County	1
Suffolk County—		Durham County	3
Huntington (town)	2	Lenoir County	1
Sullivan County—		Lincoln County	1
Callicoon (town)	1	Martin County	1
Thompson (town)	1	Montgomery County	1
Fallsburg (town)	1	Robeson County	1
Tioga County—		Rutherford County	1
Candor	1	Sampson County	1
		Swain County	1
Ulster County—		Vance County	1
Kingston	2	Wake County	2
Marlborough (town)	4	Washington County	1
Shawangunk (town)	2	Wilson County	1
Warren County –			
Glens Falls	1	Total	21
Hague (town)	1		

City Reports for Week Ended Mar. 30, 1918.

Place.	Cases.	Deaths.	Place.	Cases.	Deaths.
Amarillo, Tex	1	1	Milwaukee, Wis	8	1
Atlanta, Ga	2		Minneapolis, Minn	20	4
Augusta, Ga	1	1	Moline, Ill	2	
Austin, Tex		1	Nashville, Tenn	1	
Baltimore, Md	7		Newark, N. J	6	
Birmingham, Ala	2	2	New Bedford, Mass	2	
Boston, Mass	1		New Britain, Conn	1	
Buffalo, N. Y	1	1	Newburgh, N. Y	1	
Charleston, W. Va	1		New Orleans, La	3	1
Chicago, Ill	1	1	New York, N. Y	7	3
Cincinnati, Ohio	1		Parkersburg, W. Va	1	
Corpus Christi, Tex	1	1	Philadelphia, Pa	6	
Covington, Ky	1		Pittsburgh, Pa	2	
Davenport, Iowa	1		Pontiac, Mich		1
Detroit, Mich	2	2	Reading, Pa		1
Dubuque, Iowa	1		Rockford, Ill	2	
Elizabeth, N. J	1		Rutland, Vt	1	
Elmira, N. Y	2		Saginaw, Mich	2	
Fall River, Mass	1		St. Louis, Mo	1	
Flint, Mich		1	Salt Lake City, Utah	1	
Grand Rapids, Mich	6		San Francisco, Cal	5	
Hammond, Ind	2	1	Steubenville, Ohio	1	
Hoboken, N. J	1	1	Syracuse, N Y	1	1
Indianapolis, Ind	1		Toledo, Ohio	2	
Jackson, Mich	1		Trenton, N. J	1	1
Johnstown, Pa			Troy, N. Y	1	
Little Rock, Ark	1		Washington, Pa	1	
Long Branch, N. J	2		Wheeling, W. Va	1	
Los Angeles, Cal	2		Wilkinsburg, Pa	3	
Louisville, Ky	1	1	Wilmington, N. C	1	
Lowell, Mass	1		Wilmington, Del		3
Manchester, N. H	1		Zanesville, Ohio	2	
McKeesport, Pa	1				

DIPHTHERIA, MEASLES, SCARLET FEVER, AND TUBERCULOSIS.

State Reports for February and March, 1918.

During the month of March, 1918, there were reported in Maryland, 91 cases of diphtheria, 2,625 cases of measles, and 209 cases of scarlet fever; in New York, 469 cases of diphtheria, 7,061 cases of measles, and 768 cases of scarlet fever; in Vermont, 13 cases of diphtheria, 36 cases of measles, and 16 cases of scarlet fever. During the month of February there were reported in North Carolina 13 cases of diphtheria, 36 cases of measles, and 16 cases of scarlet fever.

City Reports for Week Ended Mar. 30, 1918.

City.	Population as of July 1, 1916 (estimated by U. S. Census Bureau).	Total deaths from all causes.	Diphtheria.		Measles.		Scarlet fever.		Tuberculosis.	
			Cases.	Deaths.	Cases.	Deaths.	Cases.	Deaths.	Cases.	Deaths.
Over 500,000 inhabitants:										
Baltimore, Md............	589,621	....	5	3	487	1	8	.....	59	40
Boston, Mass.............	756,476	....	100	1	227	8	27	1	68	24
Chicago, Ill.............	2,497,722	844	110	5	59	......	50	.....	396	90
Cleveland, Ohio..........	674,073	216	12	1	25	1	7	......	27	26
Detroit, Mich............	571,784	236	51	1	53	4	34	2	46	33
Los Angeles, Cal.........	503,812	140	12	3	186	......	17	......	46	17
New York, N. Y..........	5,602,841	2,381	255	39	1,601	44	128	5	309	270
Philadelphia, Pa.........	1,709,518	658	62	9	687	3	49	......	123	91
Pittsburgh, Pa...........	579,090	253	16	1	199	2	12	1	......	29
St. Louis, Mo............	757,309	261	39	6	115	1	19	......	49	24
From 300,000 to 500,000 inhabitants:										
Buffalo, N. Y............	468,558	180	11	3	104	2	14	1	42	.....
Cincinnati, Ohio.........	410,476	156	14	1	39	4	6	......	33	21
Jersey City, N. J........	306,345	139	13	2	53	1	10	1	39	17
Milwaukee, Wis..........	436,535	110	4	1	395	4	30	1	7	12
Minneapolis, Minn.......	363,454	....	21	2	23	......	14	......	......	10
Newark, N. J............	408,894	201	22	2	396	7	17	1	54	17
New Orleans, La.........	371,747	141	8	......	2	......	......	......	34	27
San Francisco, Cal.......	463,516	187	17	......	161	......	16	......	33	28
Seattle, Wash...........	348,639	....	3	......	67	......	8	......	14	......
From 200,000 to 300,000 inhabitants:										
Columbus, Ohio..........	214,878	72	......	......	18	......	30	......	10	8
Denver, Colo............	260,800	97	8	......	149	......	34	......	......	17
Indianapolis, Ind........	271,708	....	25	1	60	......	25	1	17	14
Louisville, Ky...........	238,910	96	5	1	24	......	5	......	21	6
Portland, Oreg..........	295,463	61	1	......	341	1	3	......	4	4
Providence, R. I.........	254,960	140	4	2	70	1	6	1	......	13
Rochester, N. Y.........	256,417	76	11	......	78	......	19	......	15	7
From 100,000 to 200,000 inhabitants:										
Atlanta, Ga.............	190,558	62	6	......	11	......	6	......	7	6
Birmingham, Ala........	181,762	52	1	......	30	1	5	......	13	4
Bridgeport, Conn........	121,579	73	9	1	15	......	2	......	10	5
Cambridge, Mass........	112,981	27	19	......	44	......	......	......	5	2
Camden, N. J...........	106,233	....	6	......	21	......	8	......	10	......
Dallas, Tex.............	124,527	8	......	......	26	......	2	......	5	4
Dayton, Ohio...........	127,224	....	1	......	14	......	1	......	2	2
Des Moines, Iowa........	101,598	....	1	......	2	......	7	......	......	......
Fall River, Mass........	128,366	44	7	......	2	......	4	......	9	4
Fort Worth, Tex........	104,562	53	1	1	2	......	1	......	3	3
Grand Rapids, Mich......	123,291	36	7	1	13	......	9	......	4	3
Hartford, Conn..........	110,900	75	10	......	4	......	5	......	2	2
Houston, Tex...........	112,307	40	2	......	16	......	......	......	4	3
Lawrence, Mass.........	100,560	38	1	1	16	......	......	......	7	4
Lowell, Mass...........	113,245	40	7	1	5	......	1	......	4	2
Lynn, Mass.............	102,425	27	1	......	28	......	4	......	4	2
Memphis, Tenn..........	148,995	56	4	2	20	......	9	......	15	9
Nashville, Tenn.........	117,057	52	1	......	15	......	......	......	9	6
New Bedford, Mass......	118,158	40	......	......	11	......	2	......	10	6
New Haven, Conn........	149,685	56	8	2	2	......	2	......	14	9
Oakland, Cal............	198,604	57	1	......	43	......	3	......	5	2

DIPHTHERIA, MEASLES, SCARLET FEVER, AND TUBERCULOSIS—
Continued.

City Reports for Week Ended Mar. 30, 1918—Continued.

City.	Population as of July 1, 1916 (estimated by U. S. Census Bureau).	Total deaths from all causes.	Diphtheria.		Measles.		Scarlet fever.		Tuberculosis.	
			Cases.	Deaths.	Cases.	Deaths.	Cases.	Deaths.	Cases.	Deaths.
From 100,000 to 200,000 inhabitants—Continued.										
Omaha, Nebr	165,470	34	5	1	8	......	21	1	......	2
Reading, Pa	109,381	22	5	1	44	......	5	......	1	1
Richmond, Va	156,687	58	8	1	79	1	3	......	11	10
Salt Lake City, Utah	117,399	37	10	......	8	......	7	......	......	2
Scranton, Pa	146,811	51	4	......	5	......	4	......	7	4
Spokane, Wash	150,323	......	......	......	4	......	6	......	......	
Springfield, Mass	105,942	44	2	......	37	......	6	......	7	4
Syracuse, N. Y	155,624	61	7	1	136	6	6	......	4	3
Tacoma, Wash	112,770	......	3	......	2	......	48	......		
Toledo, Ohio	191,554	62	3	1	13	......	10	......	15	11
Trenton, N. J	114,563	37	3	1	7	......	......	......	7	1
Worcester, Mass	163,514	65	4	......	2	......	3	1	8	5
From 80,000 to 100,000 inhabitants:										
Akron, Ohio	83,625	......	18	......	17	......	14	......	14	......
Altoona, Pa	58,659	......	4	......	15	......	......	......		
Atlantic City, N. J	57,680	......	1	......	30	......	......	......	2	1
Augusta, Ga	59,245	18	1	......	22	......	2	......	......	4
Bayonne, N. J	90,593	......	7	......	114	......	1	......	3	......
Berkeley, Cal	57,673	6	1	......	12	......	3	......	1	......
Binghamton, N. Y	53,973	25	2	......	9	......	11	......	2	......
Brockton, Mass	67,149	12	......	......	11	......	5	......	3	2
Canton, Ohio	60,852	13	1	......	4	......	5	......		3
Charleston, S. C	60,734	30	7	1	8	1	......	......	1	4
Chattanooga, Tenn	60,075	6	1	......	5	......	......	......	1	4
Covington, Ky	57,114	24	......	......	4	......	2	......	2	3
Duluth, Minn	94,195	14	5	......	6	1	4	......	6	1
Elizabeth, N. J	86,090	31	10	......	37	1	10	......	1	4
El Paso, Tex	63,705	30	1	1	12	1	1	......		6
Erie, Pa	75,195	34	1	......	6	......	4	......	11	5
Evansville, Ind	76,078	24	2	......	6	......	1	......	3	3
Flint, Mich	54,772	10	2	......	6	......	4	......	4	4
Fort Wayne, Ind	76,183	27	2	......	......	......	4	......	2	2
Harrisburg, Pa	72,015	20	1	......	15	......	......	......	3	1
Hoboken, N. J	77,114	32	4	1	7	......	......	......	7	2
Holyoke, Mass	65,286	34	1	......	1	......	......	......	3	4
Johnstown, Pa	88,529	19	4	1	......	......	10	......	......	1
Kansas City, Kans	99,447	......	......	......	16	......	4	......	2	......
Lancaster, Pa	50,853	......	......	......	31	......	3	......		
Little Rock, Ark	57,343	6	1	......	7	......	4	......	3	2
Malden, Mass	51,155	21	3	......	15	......	3	1	2	2
Manchester, N. H	78,283	28	2	......	19	......	2	......	2	2
Mobile, Ala	58,221	18	......	......	1	......	......	......		
New Britain, Conn	53,794	18	5	......	23	......	7	......	9	1
	89,612	......	1	......	27	......	4	......		2
Oklahoma City, Okla	92,943	16	......	......	......	......	1	......	2	3
Passaic, N. J	71,744	19	2	1	2	......	......	......	3	......
Pawtucket, R. I	59,411	29	2	......	3	1	......	......	......	2
	71,458	19	......	......	9	......	1	......	......	3
	63,867	15	2	......	3	......	......	......	......	1
	55,185	20	1	......	13	......	5	......	4	1
	66,895	20	......	......	45	......	4	......	2	1
	55,612	15	1	......	4	......	2	......	1	1
		44	7	......	......	3	......	......	......	1
	54,490	25	4	......	58	......	5	......	8	1
	68,805	39	2	1	7	......	......	......	1	7
Y	99,519	31	6	......	15	......	......	......	4	3
	57,078	1	2	......	......	......	22	......		
	87,689	24	3	......	28	......	5	......	5	2
	68,946	23	1	......	30	......	1	......	1	2
	61,120	21	1	......	59	......	2	......	......	2
	51,550	11	......	......	2	......	......	......	......	2
	66,083	18	1	1	......	......	......	1	3	1
	77,916	31	3	......	......	......	......	......	6	4
	70,722	......	......	......	48	2	5	......	3	2
	76,776	28	3	......	37	......	3	......	4	......
	44,67	37	3	......	44	1	......	......	......	4
	99,518	......	4	......	15	......	......	......	......	4
	51,556	......	......	......	11	......	......	1	......	2

DIPHTHERIA, MEASLES, SCARLET FEVER, AND TUBERCULOSIS—Continued.

City Reports for Week Ended Mar. 30, 1918—Continued.

City.	Population as of July 1, 1916 (estimated by U.S. Census Bureau).	Total deaths from all causes.	Diphtheria.		Measles.		Scarlet fever.		Tuberculosis.	
			Cases.	Deaths.	Cases.	Deaths.	Cases.	Deaths.	Cases.	Deaths.
From 25,000 to 50,000 inhabitants:										
Alameda, Cal	27,732	7			20				3	1
Auburn, N. Y	37,385	11			14					1
Austin, Tex	34,814	18								3
Battle Creek, Mich	29,480		4		56		3			2
Beaumont, Tex	27,711	8								
Bellingham, Wash	32,985				1					
Brookline, Mass	32,730	13	1		32		9		2	
Burlington, Iowa	25,030	11					2			
Butler, Pa	27,632	10			25					
Butte, Mont	43,425	51	2		1		7	3		
Cedar Rapids, Iowa	37,308						5			
Central Falls, R. I	25,636				2					
Charleston, W. Va	29,941	16			4		1		2	2
Charlotte, N. C	39,823	16			3				1	2
Chelsea, Mass	46,192	16	4		39	1	5		2	
Chicopee, Mass	29,319	14	3	2			1		2	
Clinton, Iowa	27,386				15					
Colorado Springs, Colo	32,971	19			35				3	9
Columbia, S. C	34,611				5				1	
Council Bluffs, Iowa	31,484				1		3			
Cranston, R. I	25,987	10			2		1		1	1
Cumberland, Md	26,074	7			12		6		1	
Danville, Ill	32,261	12			78	1			1	1
Davenport, Iowa	48,811		2				12			
Decatur, Ill	39,631	7			40					4
Dubuque, Iowa	39,873		1				2			2
Durham, N. C	25,061	6			1					
Easton, Pa	30,530	19			15				2	
East Orange, N. J	42,458	7	1		32		2		3	1
Elgin, Ill	28,203	5			4					
Elmira, N. Y	38,120	4	1		42					3
Evanston, Ill	28,591	4			11					
Everett, Mass	39,233	8	2		17		2		4	
Everett, Wash	35,486	7			2		1			
Fresno, Cal	34,958	6			13				1	
Galveston, Tex	41,863	20	1		2		1			1
Green Bay, Wis	29,353	7			5		2			1
Hammond, Ind	26,171	15	1		2		2		1	1
Haverhill, Mass	48,477	14			50		5		1	1
Jackson, Mich	35,363	18			17		30		3	2
Jamestown, N. Y	36,580	14	2				1		5	
Kalamazoo, Mich	48,886	28					1			1
Kenosha, Wis	31,576	10	7		2		4		1	1
Kingston, N. Y	26,771	9								1
Knoxville, Tenn	38,676	4			19				4	4
La Crosse, Wis	31,677	8	1							
Lansing, Mich	40,498		2		29		2			
Lexington, Ky	41,097	32	1		19					5
Lima, Ohio	35,384	15	2		1					
Lincoln, Nebr	46,515	19	1		2		6			1
Long Beach, Cal	27,587	9	3		28				1	
Lorain, Ohio	36,964	1	3	1			1			
Lynchburg, Va	32,940	12	2		12				1	
Macon, Ga	45,757	26	1		3		2		2	
Madison, Wis	30,699	10			32		13			1
McKeesport, Pa	47,521				6					
Medford, Mass	26,234	6	2		9		3		2	
Moline, Ill	27,451	10	1		18		1			1
Montclair, N. J	26,318	2	1		39				2	
Montgomery, Ala	43,585	16			16					
Muncie, Ind	25,424	7			3		1		1	1
Muskegon, Mich	26,100	15			1				1	
Muskogee, Okla	44,218				5					
Nashua, N. H	27,327	8								1
Newburgh, N. Y	29,603	11	1		2					1
New Castle, Pa	41,133		1		9					
Newport, Ky	31,927	13					1		3	3
Newport, R. I	30,108	11			1	1	4			1
Newton, Mass	43,715	13	1	1	17		2		1	1

DIPHTHERIA, MEASLES, SCARLET FEVER, AND TUBERCULOSIS—Continued.

City Reports for Week Ended Mar. 30, 1918—Continued.

City.	Population as of July 1, 1916 (estimated by U. S. Census Bureau).	Total deaths from all causes.	Diphtheria.		Measles.		Scarlet fever.		Tuberculosis.	
			Cases.	Deaths.	Cases.	Deaths.	Cases.	Deaths.	Cases.	Deaths.
From 25,000 to 50,000 inhabitants—Continued.										
Norristown, Pa	31,401	9		1	1					
Norwalk, Conn	26,899				1					2
Oak Park, Ill	26,654	13	1		9					
Ogden, Utah	31,404	11			18					
Orange, N. J	33,080	19			30				1	3
Oshkosh, Wis	36,065	9	3	2					2	1
Perth Amboy, N. J	41,185	11	1		14		1	1	2	
Petersburg, Va	25,582				4				4	
Pittsfield, Mass	38,629	19	1		1		4		2	5
Portsmouth, Va	28,741	27			13					7
Poughkeepsie, N. Y	30,390	15		1	69		1		3	1
Quincy, Ill	36,798	9			8					7
Quincy, Mass	38,136	9	1		65				1	
Racine, Wis	46,486	14			37		3			1
Roanoke, Va	43,284	21			20					3
Rock Island, Ill	28,928	10	1		32				4	
Salem, Mass	48,562	18	2		30				4	1
San Jose, Cal	38,002				32				2	
Sheboygan, Wis	28,559	13	2				1		5	6
Steubenville, Ohio	27,445	19	1				1			
Superior, Wis	46,226	5	1				4			
Taunton, Mass	39,283	8			1		1		3	2
Topeka, Kans	48,726	18	1		2		10		1	
Walla Walla, Wash	25,136		3		2					
Waltham, Mass	30,570	13	4	1	5				1	
Warwick, R. I	29,909				2					
Watertown, N. Y	29,894	6			138	3			2	
West Hoboken, N. J	43,139	15	2		4				1	2
Wheeling, W. Va	43,377	17			10		2		4	1
Williamsport, Pa	33,809	11	2						1	1
Wilmington, N. C	29,892	5			30				3	
Winston-Salem, N. C	31,155	29			27				4	
Woonsocket, R. I	44,360		2				1			
Zanesville, Ohio	30,863	17					1		1	2
From 10,000 to 25,000 inhabitants:										
Abilene, Tex	14,238	1					4		2	
Alton, Ill	22,874	10	1		3		1			3
Amarillo, Tex	19,124	15			7		4	1	4	4
Ann Arbor, Mich	15,010	9	4		27		1		2	
Anniston, Ala	14,112		1		7				1	
Appleton, Wis	17,834				2		2			
Barre, Vt	12,109	2	1							1
Bedford, Ind	10,349	2								
Berlin, N. H	13,599	5								1
Billings, Mont	14,422						1			
Bloomington, Ind	11,383	3					3			
Braddock, Pa	21,685	11	1		1		1		3	
Cairo, Ill	15,794	9			1					2
Chillicothe, Ohio	15,470	5	5		12		9		1	2
Clinton, Mass	¹13,075	14			3				1	2
Coffeyville, Kans	17,548				4					
Concord, N. H	22,669	11			1					
Corpus Christi, Tex	10,432	4	2							
Dover, N. H	13,272	3	1		1		1			
East Providence, R. I	18,113		1		1		1			
Elwood, Ind	¹11,028	6			7		1			
Fargo, N. Dak	17,389	5	2		4				2	
Galesburg, Ill	24,276	5			20					1
Grand Forks, N. Dak	15,837	9					1		1	
Greeley, Colo	11,420	4					6			
Greensboro, N. C	19,577								3	
Greenville, S. C	18,181	6			1					
Harrison, N. J	16,930		1		1		2			
Hattiesburg, Miss	16,462	6							2	
Independence, Kans	14,500				9				1	
Janesville, Wis	14,339				4		4			
Kearny, N. J	23,530	8			22					
Keokuk, Iowa	¹14,008				5		11			
Kokomo, Ind	20,930	8	2		7					2
La Fayette, Ind	21,386	10	1				3			

¹ Population Apr. 15, 1910, no estimate made.

DIPHTHERIA, MEASLES, SCARLET FEVER, AND TUBERCULOSIS—
Continued.

City Reports for Week Ended Mar. 30, 1918—Continued.

City.	Population as of July 1, 1916 (estimated by U. S. Census Bureau).	Total deaths from all causes.	Diphtheria.		Measles.		Scarlet fever.		Tuberculosis.	
			Cases.	Deaths.	Cases.	Deaths.	Cases.	Deaths.	Cases.	Deaths.
From 10,000 to 25,000 inhabitants—Continued.										
Leavenworth, Kans........	[1] 19,363	9	3	......	11	1	......	......	......	......
Lincoln, R. I.............	10,383	3	......	......	......	1	......	......	......	......
Long Branch, N. J........	15,395	6	......	......	......	......	......	......	......	......
Manitowoc, Wis...........	13,805	6	2	......	15	......	......	......	1	1
Marinette, Wis...........	[1] 14,610	2	......	......	......	......	......	......	......	......
Marion, Ind..............	19,834	1	......	......	......	......	......	......	......	......
Marshall, Tex............	13,172	6	1	......	......	......	......	......	2	......
Melrose, Mass............	17,445	8	......	......	1	......	......	......	1	1
Michigan City, Ind.......	21,512	11	......	......	......	......	1	......	......	3
Mishawaka, Ind..........	16,285	5	......	......	4	......	......	......	1	......
Missoula, Mont...........	18,214	8	......	......	......	......	1	1	......	......
Morgantown, W. Va.......	13,709	3	......	......	......	......	......	......	......	......
Morristown, N. J.........	13,284	5	......	......	......	......	......	......	......	1
Moundsville, W. Va.......	11,153	3	......	......	......	......	......	......	......	......
Muscatine, Iowa..........	17,500	......	......	......	5	......	......	......	......	......
Nanticoke, Pa............	23,126	9	......	......	2	......	......	......	3	......
New Albany, Ind.........	23,629	6	......	......	......	......	......	......	......	2
Newburyport, Mass........	15,243	5	1	......	1	......	......	......	......	......
New Castle, Ind..........	13,241	4	1	......	......	......	......	......	......	......
New London, Conn........	20,985	......	......	......	1	......	2	......	......	1
North Adams, Mass........	[1] 22,019	8	......	......	4	......	......	......	2	1
Northampton, Mass........	19,926	12	1	......	4	......	......	......	1	3
North Yakima, Wash......	20,951	......	......	......	22	......	......	......	......	......
Parkersburg, W. Va.......	20,612	7	......	......	6	......	......	......	1	......
Plainfield, N. J..........	23,805	8	1	......	6	......	......	......	......	2
Pontiac, Mich............	17,524	7	6	......	1	......	3	......	......	1
Portsmouth, N. H.........	11,666	......	......	......	8	......	1	......	......	......
Reno, Nev...............	14,869	5	......	......	1	......	1	......	......	......
Richmond, Ind...........	24,697	6	......	......	......	......	1	......	2	......
Rocky Mount, N. C........	12,067	6	......	......	1	......	......	......	2	1
Rutland, Vt..............	14,831	10	......	......	......	......	......	......	......	......
Sandusky, Ohio...........	20,193	2	......	......	......	......	......	......	......	......
Saratoga Springs, N. Y....	13,821	4	......	......	1	......	2	......	1	......
Shelbyville, Ind..........	10,965	4	......	......	......	......	1	......	......	......
Spartansburg, S. C........	21,365	8	2	......	2	......	2	......	1	......
Steelton, Pa.............	15,548	6	......	......	......	......	......	......	2	1
Vancouver, Wash.........	13,180	......	......	......	18	......	......	......	......	......
Washington, Pa..........	21,618	......	1	......	70	......	......	......	......	......
West Orange, N. J........	13,550	4	1	......	15	......	1	......	......	1
Wilkinsburg, Pa..........	23,228	9	......	......	17	......	......	......	......	......

[1] Population Apr. 15, 1910, no estimate made.

FOREIGN.

CHINA.

Cerebrospinal Meningitis—Shanghai.

Cerebrospinal meningitis was reported present at Shanghai, March 14, 1918.

Examination of Rats—Hongkong.

Examination of rats at Hongkong has been reported as follows: Three weeks ended December 29, 1917, 8,320 rats; period from December 30, 1917, to February 9, 1918, 11,486 rats. No plague infection was found. The last plague-infected rat at Hongkong was reported found during the week ended September 22, 1917.

Examination of Rats—Shanghai.

During the period from February 3 to March 9, 1918, 1,331 rats were examined at Shanghai. No plague infection was found. The last plague-infected rat at Shanghai was reported found May 6, 1916.

Plague—Nanking.

Plague was reported present in pneumonic form at Nanking, China, April 12, 1918.

Plague—North China.

During the month of January, 1918, plague was reported present, in pneumonic form, in north China. In February, 1918, the disease was reported prevalent in the vicinity of Kalgan, an important trade center in Chili Province, and in Shansi Province.

CUBA.

Communicable Diseases—Habana.

Communicable diseases have been notified at Habana as follows:

Disease.	Mar. 11-20, 1918.		Cases remaining under treatment Mar 20, 1918.	Disease.	Mar. 11-20, 1918.		Cases remaining under treatment Mar. 20, 1918.
	New cases.	Deaths.			New cases.	Deaths.	
Diphtheria	8		9	Paratyphoid fever			2
Leprosy			12	Scarlet fever	9		[2]7
Malaria	13		[1]40	Typhoid fever	11	6	[1]41
Measles	6	1	49	Varicella	22		68

[1] From the interior, 33.　　[2] From the interior, 7.　　[3] From the interior, 20.

GREAT BRITAIN.

Examination of Rats—Liverpool.

During the period from December 30, 1917, to March 9, 1918, 1,525 rats were examined at Liverpool. No plague infection was found.

CHOLERA, PLAGUE, SMALLPOX, TYPHUS FEVER, AND YELLOW FEVER.

Reports Received During Week Ended Apr. 19, 1918.[1]

CHOLERA.

Place.	Date.	Cases.	Deaths.	Remarks.
India:				
Calcutta	Dec. 16-29		29	
Do	Jan. 13-26		10	
Madras	Jan. 27-Feb. 2	16	7	
Indo-China:				
Cochin-China—				
Saigon	Feb. 4-17	4		
Java:				
West Java				Dec. 28, 1917–Jan. 31, 1918: Cases, 27; deaths, 7.
Batavia	Dec. 28–Jan. 31	24	1	
Philippine Islands:				
Provinces				Feb. 10-16, 1918: Cases, 104; deaths, 79.
Bohol	Feb. 10-16	23	23	
Capiz	do	31	22	
Cebu	do	3		
Iloilo	do	13	9	
Leyte	do	15	14	
Occidental Negros	do	17	10	
Oriental Negros	do	2	1	
Provinces				Feb. 17-23, 1918: Cases, 102; deaths, 80.
Bohol	Feb. 17-23	53	37	
Capiz	do	34	28	
Cebu	do	4	4	
Iloilo	do	1		
Leyte	do	4	4	
Occidental Negros	do	6	7	
Provinces				Feb. 24-Mar. 2, 1918: Cases, 138; deaths, 93.
Bohol	Feb. 24-Mar. 2	50	33	
Capiz	do	16	17	
Cebu	do	3	2	
Iloilo	do	1	1	
Leyte	do	10	7	
Misamis	do	33	21	
Occidental Negros	do	5		
Surigao	do	8	5	
Zamboanga	do	12	7	

PLAGUE.

Place.	Date.	Cases.	Deaths.	Remarks.
China:				
North China				Present in January, 1918; pneumonic form.
Chili Province—				
Kalgan				Vicinity. Present in February, 1918.
Shansi Province				Present in February, 1918; 116 cases estimated.
India:				
Madras Presidency	Jan. 27-Feb. 2	1,006	774	
Indo-China:				
Cochin-China—				
Saigon	Feb. 4-17	17	9	
Java:				
East Java				Dec. 25-31, 1917: Cases, 32; deaths, 31. Jan. 1-14, 1918: Cases, 22; deaths, 21.
Do				
Surabaya	Dec. 25-31	3	3	
Do	Jan. 7-14	10	10	
Siam:				
Bangkok	Jan. 13-Feb. 9	15	11	
Straits Settlements:				
Singapore	Jan. 6-Feb. 16	29	28	

[1] From medical officers of the Public Health Service, American consuls, and other sources.

CHOLERA, PLAGUE, SMALLPOX, TYPHUS FEVER, AND YELLOW FEVER—Continued.

Reports Received During Week Ended Apr. 19, 1918—Continued.

SMALLPOX.

Place.	Date.	Cases.	Deaths.	Remarks.
Canada:				
New Brunswick—				
Moncton	Mar. 31–Apr. 6	5	....	
St. John	Mar. 24–30	2	....	
Nova Scotia—				
Halifax	....do	2	....	
Sydney	Mar. 31–Apr. 6	2	....	
Ontario—				
Arnprior	....do		1	
Toronto	....do	1	....	
China:				
Antung	Mar. 4–10	1	....	
Dairen	Feb. 24–Mar. 2	14	1	
Nanking	Feb. 17–23			Epidemic.
Shanghai	Mar. 4–10	....	4	
Tientsin	Feb. 24–Mar. 9	8	....	
Tsingtau	Feb. 17–23	2	....	
India:				
Madras	Jan. 27–Feb. 2	32	13	
Indo-China:				
Cochin-China—				
Saigon	Feb. 4–17	102	37	
Italy:				
Leghorn	Mar. 4–10	2	1	
Turin	Feb. 4–Mar. 3	32	....	
Japan:				
Nagasaki	Mar. 4–10	3	1	
Taihoku	Feb. 12–Mar. 11	20	3	
Tokyo	Feb. 28–Mar. 6	18	....	City and suburbs.
Java:				
East Java	....	....	....	Dec. 25–31, 1917: Cases, 7. Jan. 1–14, 1918: Cases, 3.
Do	....	....	....	
Surabaya	Dec. 25–31	1	....	
Mid-Java	Dec. 28–Jan. 23	23	....	
West Java	Dec. 28 Jan. 31	116	17	
Newfoundland:				
St. Johns	Mar. 16 29	26	....	
Philippine Islands:				
Manila	Feb. 10–Mar. 2	3	2	Varioloid, 33.
Portugal:				
Lisbon	Mar. 10–16	2	....	
Siam:				
Bangkok	Jan. 13 19		1	

TYPHUS FEVER.

Place.	Date.	Cases.	Deaths.	Remarks.
Chosen (Korea):				
Seoul	Feb. 1–28	3	2	
Great Britain:				
Belfast	Mar. 10–16	1	....	
Greece:				
Saloniki	Feb. 10–Mar. 2	....	11	
Japan:				
Nagasaki	Feb. 18–Mar. 10	5	3	
Java:				
East Java	....	....	....	Dec. 25–31, 1917: Cases, 4: death, 1. Jan. 1–14, 1918: Cases, 11: deaths, 2.
Do	....	....	....	
Surabaya	Dec. 25–31	3	....	
Do	Jan. 1–14	10	1	
Mid-Java				Dec. 28, 1917–Jan. 23, 1918: Cases, 11.
Samarang	Jan. 3–15	9	....	
West Java				Dec. 28, 1917–Jan. 31, 1918: Cases, 53: death, 1.
Batavia	Dec. 28–Jan. 31	27	1	
Mexico:				
Aguascalientes	Mar. 24–30		1	
Portugal:				
Lisbon	Mar. 3 16	8	....	
Spain:				
Corcubion	Apr. 11	....	....	Present. Province of Coruña, west coast.
Tunisia:				
Tunis	Feb. 23–Mar. 8	4	1	
Union of South Africa:				
Cape of Good Hope State	Sept. 10–Dec. 30	4,035	830	European, cases 31: deaths, European, 5.
Natal	To Dec. 30	31	10	

CHOLERA, PLAGUE, SMALLPOX, TYPHUS FEVER, AND YELLOW FEVER—Continued.

Reports Received from Dec. 29, 1917, to Apr. 12, 1918.

CHOLERA.

Place.	Date.	Cases.	Deaths.	Remarks.
China:				
Antung...................	Nov. 26–Dec. 2....	3	1	
India:				
Bombay.................	Oct. 28–Dec. 15....	19	14	
Do..................	Dec. 30–Jan. 26....	200	170	
Calcutta................	Sept. 16–Dec. 15...	....	92	
Do..................	Dec. 30–Jan. 12....	....	14	
Karachi................	Dec. 30–Jan. 26....	25	6	
Madras.................	Nov. 25–Dec. 22....	3	2	
Do..................	Dec. 30–Jan. 26....	13	7	
Rangoon................	Nov. 4–Dec. 22....	5	5	
Do..................	Dec. 30–Jan. 5....	1	1	
Indo-China:				
Provinces..............		....	....	Sept. 1–Nov. 30, 1917: Cases, 152; deaths, 80.
Anam..............	Sept. 1–Nov. 30...	18	13	
Cambodia..........	....do............	72	52	
Cochin-China........	....do............	50	22	
Saigon............	Nov. 22–Dec. 9...	4	3	
Kwang-Chow-Wan.....	Sept. 1–30........	10	2	
Java:				
East Java..............	Oct. 28–Nov. 3....	1	1	
West Java..............		....	....	Oct. 19–Dec. 27, 1917: Cases, 102; deaths, 56. Dec. 28, 1917–Jan. 10, 1918: Cases, 22; deaths, 9.
Batavia............	Oct. 19–Dec. 27...	49	23	
Persia:				
Mazanderan Province......		....	....	July 30–Sept. 3, 1917: Cases, 384; deaths, 276.
Achraf.............	July 30–Aug. 16...	90	88	
Astrabad............	July 31...........	....	....	Present.
Barfrush............	July 1–Aug. 16....	39	25	
Chahmirzad..........		....	....	25 cases reported July 31, 1917.
Chahrastagh........	June 15–July 25...	10	8	
Charoud............	Aug. 26–Sept. 3...	4	2	
Damghan............	Aug. 26...........	....	....	Present.
Kharek.............	May 28–June 11...	21	13	
Meched.............	Aug. 18–Sept. 2...	174	82	
Ouzoun Dare.........	Aug. 8............	....	....	Do.
Sabzevar............	Aug. 24...........	....	....	Do.
Sari................	July 3–29.........	273	144	
Semnan.............	Aug. 31–Sept. 2...	14	5	
Yekchambe-Bazar.....	June 3............	6	....	
Philippine Islands:				
Provinces..............		....	....	Nov. 18–Dec. 29, 1917: Cases, 1,053; deaths, 693. Dec. 30, 1917–Feb. 9, 1918: Cases, 914; deaths, 546.
Antique............	Nov. 18–Dec. 1....	48	32	
Do..............	Feb. 3–9..........	4	4	
Bohol..............	Nov. 18–Dec. 29...	160	111	
Do..............	Dec. 30–Feb. 9....	213	181	
Capiz..............	Nov. 25–Dec. 29...	27	21	
Do..............	Dec. 30–Feb. 9....	121	101	
Cebu...............	Dec. 23–29........	3	....	
Do..............	Dec. 30–Feb. 9....	60	36	
Iloilo..............	Nov. 25–Dec. 29...	179	135	
Do..............	Dec. 30–Feb. 9....	82	53	
Leyte..............	Nov. 25–Dec. 22...	13	12	
Do..............	Feb. 3–9..........	9	8	
Mindanao...........	Nov. 25–Dec. 29...	337	196	
Do..............	Dec. 30–Feb. 9....	351	220	
Occidental Negros......	Nov. 25–Dec. 29...	177	123	
Do..............	Jan. 13–Feb. 9....	60	40	
Oriental Negros........	Nov. 25–Dec. 29...	99	62	
Do..............	Dec. 30–Feb. 9....	15	13	
Romblon............	Nov. 25–Dec. 1....	1	1	
Siam:				
Bangkok............	Sept. 16–22.......	1	1	
Turkey in Asia:				
Bagdad.............	Nov. 1–15.........	....	40	

PLAGUE.

Brazil:				
Bahia..............	Nov. 4–Dec. 15....	4	4	
Do..............	Dec. 30–Jan. 12....	3	2	.
Rio de Janeiro............	Dec. 23–29.........	1	....	
Do..............	Jan 6–12..........	1	1	
British Gold Coast:				
Axim...............	Jan. 8............	....	....	Present.

CHOLERA, PLAGUE, SMALLPOX, TYPHUS FEVER, AND YELLOW FEVER—Continued.

Reports Received from Dec. 29, 1917, to Apr. 12, 1918—Continued.

PLAGUE—Continued.

Place.	Date.	Cases.	Deaths.	Remarks.
Ceylon:				
Colombo.................	Oct. 14–Dec. 1.....	14	13	
Do..................	Dec. 30–Jan. 19....	7	5	
Ecuador...................				Sept. 1–Nov. 30, 1917: Cases, 68; deaths, 24. Reported outbreak occuring about Jan. 17, 1918.
Guayaquil..............	Sept. 1–30..........	3	1	
Do..................	Oct. 1–31...........	20	8	
Do..................	Nov. 1–30..........	45	15	
Egypt...................				Jan. 1–Nov. 15, 1917: Cases, 736; deaths, 398.
Alexandria..............	Jan. 14–28..........	1	2	
Port Said..............	July 23–29..........	1	2	
India....................				Sept. 16–Dec. 29, 1917: Cases, 228,834; deaths, 174,743. Dec. 30, 1917–Jan. 26, 1918: Cases, 125,934; deaths, 98,950.
Bassein................	Dec. 9–29..........		8	
Do..................	Dec. 30–Jan. 19....		14	
Bombay................	Oct. 28–Dec. 29....	147	123	
Do..................	Dec. 30–Jan. 26....	81	59	
Calcutta...............	Sept. 16 29........		2	
Do..................	Dec. 30–Jan. 12....		3	
Henzada...............	Oct. 21–27.........		1	
Do..................	Jan. 5–19..........		5	
Karachi................	Oct. 21–Dec. 29....	27	20	
Do..................	Dec. 30–Jan. 26....	16	14	
Madras Presidency......	Oct. 31–Nov. 17...	3,294	2,560	
Do..................	Jan. 6–26..........	4,310	3,286	
Mandalay..............	Oct. 14–Nov. 17...		89	
Do..................	Dec. 30–Jan. 12....		236	
Myingyan..............	....do.............		110	
Prome.................	Jan. 5–12..........		1	
Rangoon...............	Oct. 21–Dec. 22....		56	
Do..................	Dec. 30 Jan. 26....	79	74	
Toungoo...............	Dec. 9–29..........		5	
Do..................	Dec. 30–Jan. 19...		4	
Indo-China:				
Provinces..............				Sept. 1–Nov. 30, 1917: Cases, 89; deaths, 68.
Anam...............	Sept. 1–Nov. 30...	28	25	
Cambodia............	....do.............	39	28	
Cochin-China........	....do.............	22	15	
Saigon..............	Oct. 31–Dec. 23...	17	6	
Do..............	Dec. 31–Feb. 3....	36	9	
Java:				
East Java..............				Oct. 27–Dec. 23, 1917: Cases, 199; deaths, 198.
Surabaya...........	Nov. 4–25..........	3	3	
West Java..............				Nov. 25–Dec. 9, 1917: Cases, 45; deaths, 45.
Peru....................				Dec. 1, 1917–Jan. 15, 1918: Cases, 106.
Ancachs Department -				
Casma.............	Dec. 1–Jan. 15.....	2		
Lambayeque Department..	...do..........	22		At Chiclayo, Ferronafe, Jayanca, Lambayeque.
Libertad Department....	...do..........	72		At Guadalupe, Mansiche, Pacasmayo, Salaverry, San Jose, San Pedro, and country district of Trujillo.
Lima Department........	.do...........	9		City and country.
Piura Department -				
Catacaos..............	do...........	1		
Senegal:				
St. Louis..............	Feb. 2.........			Present.
Siam:				
Bangkok............	Sept. 16–Dec. 23.	13	9	
Straits Settlements:				
Singapore...........	Oct. 28–Dec. 29....	5	7	

SMALLPOX.

Place.	Date.	Cases.	Deaths.	Remarks.
Algeria:				
Algiers..................	Nov. 1 Dec. 31.....	3	1	
Do..................	Jan. 1 31..........	2		
Australia:				
New South Wales.				July 12–Dec. 20, 1917: Cases, 36. Jan. 4–17, 1918: Case, 1. Newcastle district.
Abermain............	Oct. 25 Nov. 29...	3		
Cessnock............	July 12 Oct. 11...	7		
Eumangla............	Aug. 15...........	1		
Kurri Kurri..........	Dec. 5 30..........	1		
Mungindi............	Aug. 15...........	1		
Warren..............	July 12–Oct. 25....	22		
Do.................	Jan. 1 17..........	1		

CHOLERA, PLAGUE, SMALLPOX, TYPHUS FEVER, AND YELLOW FEVER—Continued.

Reports Received from Dec. 29, 1917, to Apr. 12, 1918—Continued.

SMALLPOX—Continued.

Place.	Date.	Cases.	Deaths.	Remarks.
Brazil:				
Bahia	Nov. 10–Dec. 8....	3	....	
Pernambuco	Nov. 1–15........	1	....	
Rio de Janeiro	Sept. 30–Dec. 29 ...	703	190	
Do	Dec. 30–Mar. 9....	231	83	
Sao Paulo	Oct. 29–Nov. 4....		2	
Canada:				
British Columbia—				
Vancouver	Jan. 13–Mar. 9.....	5	....	
Victoria	Jan. 7–Feb. 2......	2	....	
Winnipeg	Dec. 30–Jan. 5.....	1	....	
New Brunswick—				
Kent County	Dec. 4..............	....	....	Outbreak. On main line Canadian Ry., 25 miles north of Moncton.
Do	Jan. 22.............	40	....	In 7 localities.
Northumberland County.	....do.............	41	....	In 5 localities.
Restigouche County....	Jan. 18.............	60	....	
St. John County—				
St. John	Mar. 3–23..........	3	....	
Victoria County	Jan. 22.............	10	....	At Limestone and a lumber camp.
Westmoreland County—				
Moncton	Jan. 20–Mar. 30....	11	....	
York County	Jan. 22.............	8	....	
Nova Scotia—				
Halifax	Feb. 24–Mar. 23....	1	....	
Sydney	Feb. 3–Mar. 30.....	13	....	
Ontario—				
Hamilton	Dec. 16–22.........	1	....	
Do	Jan. 13–19.........	2	....	
Ottawa	Mar. 4–24..........	5	....	
Sarnia	Dec. 9–15..........	1	....	
Do	Jan. 6–Mar. 30.....	32	....	
Toronto	Feb. 10–16.........	1	....	
Windsor	Dec. 30–Jan. 5.....	1	....	
Prince Edward Island—				
Charlottetown	Feb. 7–13...........	1	....	
Quebec—				
Montreal	Dec. 16–Jan. 5.....	5	....	
Do	Jan. 6–Mar. 30.....	10	....	
China:				
Amoy	Oct. 22–Dec. 30....	....	....	Present.
Do	Dec. 31–Feb. 10....	....	....	Do.
Antung	Dec. 2–23..........	13	2	
Do	Jan. 7–Feb. 17.....	5	2	
Changsha	Jan. 28–Feb. 3.....	....	1	
Chefoo	Jan. 27–Feb. 9.....	....	....	Do.
Chungking	Nov. 11–Dec. 29...	....	....	Do.
Do	Dec. 30–Feb. 2.....	....	....	Do.
Dairen	Nov. 18–Dec. 22...	3	1	
Do	Dec. 30–Feb. 23...	25	1	
Harbin	May 14–June 30....	20	....	Chinese Eastern Ry.
Do	July 1–Dec. 2......	7	....	Do.
Hongkong	Dec. 23–29.........	1	....	
Do	Jan. 26–Feb. 9.....	6	1	
Hungtahoize Station	Oct. 28–Nov. 4....	1	....	Do.
Manchuria Station	May 14–June 30....	6	....	Do.
Do	July 1–Dec. 2......	3	....	Do.
Mukden	Nov. 11–24.........	....	....	Present.
Nanking	Feb. 3–16..........	....	....	Epidemic.
Shanghai	Nov. 18–Dec. 23...	41	91	Cases, foreign; deaths among natives.
Do	Dec. 31–Mar. 3....	36	102	Do.
Swatow	Jan. 18.............	....	....	Unusually prevalent.
Tientsin	Nov. 11–Dec. 22...	13	....	
Do	Dec. 30–Feb. 23...	17	....	
Tsingtau	Feb. 4–10..........	1	....	
Cuba:				
Habana	Jan. 7..............	1	....	Nov. 8, 1917: 1 case from Coruna; Dec. 5, 1917, 1 case.
Marianao	Jan. 8..............	1	....	6 miles distant from Habana.

CHOLERA, PLAGUE, SMALLPOX, TYPHUS FEVER, AND YELLOW FEVER—Continued.

Reports Received from Dec. 29, 1917, to Apr. 12, 1918—Continued.

SMALLPOX—Continued.

Place.	Date.	Cases.	Deaths.	Remarks.
Ecuador.				Sept. 1–Nov. 30, 1917: Cases, 26; deaths, 2.
Guayaquil.	Sept. 1–30.	8		
Do.	Oct. 1–31.	14	1	
Do.	Nov. 1–30.	4	1	
Egypt:				
Alexandria.	Nov. 12–18.	2	1	
Do.	Jan. 8–Feb. 28.	5		
Cairo.	July 23–Nov. 18.	6	1	
France:				
Lyon.	Nov. 18–Dec. 16.	6	3	
Do.	Jan. 7–Feb. 17.	11	2	
Marseille.	Jan. 1–31.		2	
Paris.	Jan. 27–Feb. 23.	2		
Great Britain:				
Cardiff.	Feb. 3–9.	4		
Greece:				
Saloniki.	Jan. 27–Feb. 9.		7	
Honduras:				
Santa Barbara Department.	Jan. 1–7.			Present in interior.
India:				
Bombay.	Oct. 21–Dec. 29.	50	12	
Do.	Dec. 31–Jan. 26.	26	5	
Karachi.	Nov. 18–Dec. 29.	4	2	Nov. 11–16, 1917: 10 cases with 4 deaths; imported on s. s. Mcnesa from Basreh.
Madras.	Oct. 31–Dec. 29.	18	8	
Do.	Dec. 30–Jan. 26.	48	15	
Rangoon.	Oct. 28–Dec. 22.	6	1	
Do.	Dec. 30–Jan. 26.	7	2	
Indo-China:				
Provinces.				Sept. 1–Nov. 30, 1917: Cases, 546; deaths, 146.
Anam.	Sept. 1–Nov. 30.	163	25	
Cambodia.	do.	16	8	
Cochin-China.	do.	353	108	
Saigon.	Oct. 20–Dec. 30.	120	26	
Do.	Dec. 31–Feb. 3.	188	63	
Laos.	Oct. 1–31.	1		
Do.	Jan. 26–Feb. 3.	1	1	
Tonkin.	Sept. 1–Oct. 31.	9	4	
Do.	Jan. 26–Feb. 3.	3		
Italy:				
Castellamare.	Dec. 10.	2		Among refugees.
Florence.	Dec. 1–15.	17	4	
Genoa.	Dec. 2–31.	11	3	
Do.	Jan. 2–31.	30	2	
Leghorn.	Jan 7–Feb. 24.	30	6	
Messina.	Jan. 3–19.	1		
Milan.	To Dec. 10.			Oct. 1–Dec. 31, 1917: Cases, 33.
Naples.		2		Among refugees.
Taormina.	Jan. 20–Feb. 9.	6		
Turin.	Oct. 29–Dec. 29.	123	120	
Do.	Jan. 21–Feb. 3.	24	3	
Japan:				
Nagasaki.	Jan. 14–27.	3	1	
Taihoku.	Dec. 15–21.	1		Island of Twaiwan (Formosa).
Do.	Jan. 8–Feb. 11.	5	2	Do.
Tokyo.	Feb. 11–18.	8		City and suburbs.
Yokohama.	Jan. 17–Feb. 3.	4		
Java:				
East Java.	Oct. 7–Dec. 23.	50		
Mid-Java.				Oct. 10–Dec. 26, 1917: Cases, 88; death, 1.
Samarang.	Nov. 6–Dec. 12.	4	1	
West Java.				Oct. 19–Dec. 27, 1917: Cases, 221. deaths, 36. Dec. 28, 1917–Jan. 10, 1918: Cases, 47; deaths, 6.
Batavia.	Nov. 2–8.	1		
Mexico				
Aguascalientes.	Feb. 4–17.		2	
Ciudad Juarez.	Mar. 3–23.	2	1	
Mazatlan.	Dec. 5–11.		1	
Do.	Jan. 29–Mar. 5.	4	3	
Mexico City.	Nov. 11–Dec. 29.	16		
Do.	Dec. 30–Mar. 9.	61		
Piedras Negras.	Jan. 11.	200		
Vera Cruz.	Jan. 20–Mar. 2.	7	3	
Newfoundland:				
St. Johns.	Dec. 8–Jan. 4.	29		
Do.	Jan. 5–Mar. 15.	35		
Trepassey.	Jan. 4.			Outbreak with 11 cases reported.

CHOLERA, PLAGUE, SMALLPOX, TYPHUS FEVER, AND YELLOW FEVER—Continued.

Reports Received from Dec. 29, 1917, to Apr. 12, 1918—Continued.

SMALLPOX—Continued.

Place.	Date.	Cases.	Deaths.	Remarks.
Philippine Islands:				
Manila	Oct. 28–Dec. 8.....	5	....	
Do	Jan. 13–Feb. 9.....	12	....	
Porto Rico:				
San Juan	Jan. 28–Mar. 17....	32	....	Varioloid.
Portugal:				
Lisbon	Nov. 4–Dec. 15....	2	....	
Do	Dec. 30–Feb. 22...	4	....	
Portuguese East Africa:				
Lourenço Marques	Aug. 1–Dec. 31....	....	16	
Russia:				
Archangel	Sept. 1–Oct. 31....	7	....	
Moscow	Aug. 26–Oct. 6....	22	2	
Petrograd	Aug. 31–Nov. 18...	76	3	
Siam:				
Bangkok	Nov. 25–Dec. 1....	1	1	
Do	Jan. 6–12	1	....	
Spain:				
Coruna	Dec. 2–15	....	4	
Do	Jan 20–Feb. 23....	....	5	
Madrid		....	....	Jan. 1–Dec. 31, 1917: Deaths, 77.
Seville	Oct. 1–Dec. 30....	....	66	
Do	Jan. 1–31	....	20	
Straits Settlements:				
Singapore	Nov. 25–Dec. 1....	1	1	
Do	Dec. 30–Jan. 5....	1	....	
Tunisia:				
Tunis	Dec. 14–20	1	....	
Turkey in Asia:				
Bagdad		....	....	Present in November, 1917.
Union of South Africa:				
Cape of Good Hope State	Oct. 1–Dec. 31.....	28	....	
East Liverpool	Jan. 20–26	1	....	Varioloid.
Venezuela:				
Maracaibo	Dec. 2–8	....	1	

TYPHUS FEVER.

Place.	Date.	Cases.	Deaths.	Remarks.
Algeria:				
Algiers	Nov. 1–Dec. 31....	2	1	
Argentina:				
Rosario	Dec. 1–31	....	1	
Australia:				
South Australia		....	....	Nov. 11–17, 1917: Cases, 1.
Brazil:				
Rio de Janeiro	Oct. 28–Dec. 1.....	7	....	
Canada:				
Ontario—				
Kingston	Dec. 2–8	3	....	
Quebec—				
Montreal	Dec. 16–22	2	1	
China:				
Antung	Dec. 3–30	13	1	
Do	Dec. 31–Jan. 27....	2	2	
Chosen (Formosa):				
Seoul	Nov. 1–20	1	....	
Egypt:				
Alexandria	Nov. 8–Dec. 28....	57	15	
Do	Jan. 8–Feb. 25....	223	54	
Cairo	July 23–Dec. 16...	137	70	
Port Said	July 30–Nov. 11...	5	5	
France:				
Marseille	Dec. 1–31	....	1	
Great Britain:				
Belfast	Feb. 10–Mar. 9....	16	3	
Glasgow	Dec. 21	1	....	
Do	Jan. 20–Mar. 9....	9	....	
Manchester	Dec. 2–8	1	....	
Greece:				
Arta	Feb. 19	2	....	
Janina	Feb. 14	110	....	Jan. 27, epidemic.
Saloniki	Nov. 11–Dec. 29...	....	72	
Do	Dec. 30–Jan. 19....	....	11	

43

CHOLERA, PLAGUE, SMALLPOX, TYPHUS FEVER, AND YELLOW FEVER—Continued.

Reports Received from Dec. 29, 1917, to Apr. 12, 1918—Continued.

TYPHUS FEVER—Continued.

Place.	Date.	Cases.	Deaths.	Remarks.
Japan:				
Nagasaki	Nov. 26–Dec. 16....	5	5	
Do.	Jan. 7–Feb. 17.....	8	2	
Java:				
East Java.				Oct. 15–Dec. 23, 1917: Cases, 26;
Surabaya.	Dec. 17–23.......	6	1	deaths, 6.
Mid-Java.				Oct. 10–Dec. 26, 1917: Cases, 63;
Samarang.	Oct. 9–Dec. 26.....	20	2	deaths, 2.
Do.	Dec. 27–Jan. 2....	9		
West Java.				Oct. 19–Dec. 27, 1917: Cases, 94;
Batavia.	Oct. 19–Dec. 27....	59	15	deaths, 17.
Mexico:				
Aguascalientes.	Dec. 15.........		2	
Do.	Jan. 21–Feb. 10....		14	
Durango State—				
Guanacevi.	Feb. 11..........			Epidemic.
Mexico City.	Nov. 11–Dec. 29 ..	476		
Do.	Dec. 30–Mar. 9....	528		
Norway:				
Bergen.	Feb. 1–16........	3		
Portugal:				
Lisbon.	Feb. 21..........			Present.
Oporto.	...do...........			Epidemic. Dec. 24, 1917–Mar. 9, 1918: About 260 cases reported.
Russia:				
Archangel.	Sept. 1–14........	7	2	
Moscow.	Aug. 26–Oct. 6...	49	2	
Petrograd.	Aug. 31–Nov. 18...	32		
Do.	Feb. 2..........			Present.
Vladivostok.	Oct. 29–Nov. 4....	12	1	
Sweden:				
Goteborg.	Nov. 18–Dec. 15...	2		
Switzerland:				
Basel.	Jan. 6–19........	1	1	
Zurich.	Nov. 9–15........	2		
Do.	Jan. 13–19.......	2		
Tunisia:				
Tunis.	Nov. 30–Dec. 6....		1	
Do.	Feb. 9–15........	2		
Union of South Africa:				
Cape of Good Hope State.				Sept. 10–Nov. 26, 1917: Cases, 3,724 (European, 31; native, 3,693); deaths, 761 (European, 5; native, 756). Total to Jan. 13, 1918: Cases, 4,158 (European, 32; native, 4,126); deaths, 854 (European, 5; native, 849).
Natal.				Dec., 1917–Jan. 13, 1918: Cases, 37; deaths, 10. (No Europeans.)

YELLOW FEVER.

Ecuador.				Sept. 1–Nov. 30, 1917: Cases, 5; deaths, 3.
Guayaquil.	Sept. 1–30........	1	1	
Do.	Oct. 1–31........	1		
Do.	Nov. 1–30........	2	2	
Yaguachi.	...do...........	1		
Honduras:				
Tegucigalpa.	Dec. 16–22.......		1	
Do.	Jan. 6–19........		1	

X

PUBLIC HEALTH REPORTS

| VOL. 33 | APRIL 26, 1918 | No. 17 |

THE PRESENT STATUS OF OUR KNOWLEDGE OF FATIGUE PRODUCTS.[1]

By ERNEST L. SCOTT, Associate in Physiology, Columbia University; Member of Committee on Industrial Fatigue, Advisory Commission of the Council of National Defense; Physiological Chemist (Scientific Assistant) to the United States Public Health Service.

In 1865 Johannes Ranke (1), then lecturer in the Physiological Institute at Munich, published a book of nearly 500 pages in which he gave the results which he had obtained from his studies on the physiology of muscle. In many ways this book has never been superseded. Among other things he here developed the idea of fatigue substances. At that time Ranke brought out the fact that fatigue is due, at least to a great extent, to something which arises within the organ rather than to the absence of anything used up by the process of muscular contraction. That is, fatigue is to be explained on the basis of a full ash pit rather than an empty coal bin. His principal evidence consisted of the fact that when a fatigued muscle was irrigated with an indifferent fluid, as salt solution, it resumed its power of contraction. Now, it was argued, since the irrigating fluid could not have supplied anything necessary to the muscle, it must have removed something detrimental to it. The substances supposed to have been removed are the fatigue substances.

Obviously, the next point is their isolation and identification. Their identification has been attempted both by chemical comparison of fatigued material with resting material and by the injection into the nonfatigued preparation of substances which are suspected of being fatigue substances. Though the results so far at hand are somewhat disappointing, we have some definite data upon which to base our conclusions.

One of Ranke's experiments consisted in treating a muscle with lactic acid, and by this treatment he obtained fatigue phenomena. Lactic acid was therefore placed in the list of fatigue substances, and has been maintained there. So far as lactic acid is concerned we have progressed considerably beyond the point where Ranke left us.

[1] Read before the Section on Industrial Hygiene of the American Public Health Association, Washington, D. C., Oct. 19, 1917.

43

About 10 years ago Fletcher and Hopkins (2) published a very important paper on the origin of lactic acid in muscle. Though there are some rather discouraging difficulties in the analytical technic which have never been satisfactorily removed, the work reported by these authors leaves no doubt that there is an accumulation of lactic acid or of its salts in excised muscle during fatigue. They further show that the accumulation of lactic acid results from an insufficient supply of oxygen, and that an abundant supply of oxygen prevents the accumulation of the lactic acid or causes its removal in case it has already accumulated. Fletcher and Hopkins have summarized their work in a recent Croonian Lecture (3). At about the time of the appearance of the first paper by Fletcher and Hopkins two articles appeared by Lee (4, 5), in which he gives a very convincing series of tracings obtained from muscles which had been irrigated with solutions containing lactic acid or its salts. These tracings show not only that the onset of fatigue is hastened and that its results are intensified by the presence of lactic acid, but that the familiar phenomenon of treppe, which up to that time had been without satisfactory explanation, was caused by the same substance. Thus treppe, or the augmentation of the contractions which occurs in the early stages of a series, is due to the same material which later causes exhaustion. In a sense it may be considered as the first indication of fatigue. Lee calls attention to the apparent conflict between this fact and the general biological law that metabolic products are harmful to the protoplasm in which they are formed. This conflict is apparent rather than real, for we are in all probability dealing with at least two phenomena, the rate of activity of one of which may be reduced while that of the other may at the same time be augmented. One of these phenomena is the production of lactic acid; another is the effect of this acid, or possibly more accurately of its hydrogen ion, upon the contractile mechanism. The law, in all probability, is, in part, a special application of the more general chemical law of mass action, and if sufficiently accurate methods were at hand it could probably be demonstrated that the rate of formation of the acid is progressively decreased during activity. This is, however, quite apart from the effect of the acid upon the muscle fibers. The activity of these may be augmented or depressed according to the concentration of the acid.

Some years after the articles by Lee appeared, Burridge (6) published the results of a similar set of experiments. While the experiments of Burridge differed somewhat in detail from those of Lee the essential principles involved were the same and the results of the two experimenters agreed. In addition to lactic acid both authors perfused muscle with salts of lactic acid; notably with the lactates of sodium, potassium, and ammonium. Lee found that the salts produced effects similar to those produced by the acid, though perhaps in a somewhat less marked degree, and concluded that both the positive and negative ions were functional in producing fatigue. Burridge worked with the advantage of the beautiful work of Mines (7) before him. A comparison of his results with those of Mines led him to believe that the effects were wholly those of the positive ions. This phase of the problem is distinctly in need of more work.

Since the hydrogen ion seems to be of much importance, one would expect other metabolic products which increase the concentration of this ion to be effective producers of fatigue. In line with this idea, Lee gives records, obtained after treatment of the muscles with carbon dioxide or with potassium dihydrogen phosphate, which show results very similar to those obtained after treatment with lactic acid.

The question of the effect of the negative ion of acids other than lactic arises at this time. Other organic acids may be eliminated in a group from further discussion by the simple statement that normally they are present in very small amounts, if present at all, and that not enough is known concerning them to warrant any discussion at this time. Lee (19) does, however, find that when muscles are perfused with β oxy-butyric acid and its salts, results are obtained which are similar to those given by lactic acid. A study of the effect of the acids derived from glucose and of the fatty acids in their relation to fatigue would be highly interesting and might throw some valuable light on the course of events in intermediate metabolism.

Among the inorganic acids it may be said that no chlorine ion is formed during fatigue because all the chlorine of the body is, so far as we know, present only in the ionic form. There is, however, some modification in the chlorine metabolism. Thus Tissiè (8) found in a 24-hour bicycle race by a professional cyclist that the urinary chlorine output was slightly below normal on the day of work and markedly so on the following day. Harper and Holliday (9) also noted the same reduction in chloride output. This is, however, closely bound up with the chlorine excreted in the perspiration, as shown by Viale (10), who measured the chlorine output per square centimeter of skin area as taken on the foreheads of marching soldiers. He found that the perspiration averaged 0.85 per cent chlorine, but that while the rate of water excretion diminished with the progress of the march that of chlorine increased. So far as I know, there are no figures showing whether or not there is a change of the chlorine relationships in any organ of the body during fatigue. I do not think we are warranted at present in believing that hydrochloric acid or any of its salts stands in any causal relation to fatigue.

Of the other inorganic acids the increased concentration of carbon dioxide is best substantiated. That the concentration of this acid is of great importance is made evident by the very abundant literature on the subject. However, I am not clear as to what extent this substance is effective apart from its rôle as a modifier of hydrogen ion concentration.

Tissié on his bicyclist and Garratt on himself, as a bicyclist, both observed an increase in the output of phosphates and sulphates in the urine after work. Their experiments were conducted under more or less severe conditions, but I think I am warranted in saying that a man doing ordinary work to which he is daily accustomed secretes somewhat more sulphate at night than he does in the morning. The sulphur, it seems to me, is derived from broken-down protein and may be related to the fact noted by Lee, Scott, and Colvin (11) that muscles capable of doing more severe work contain more protein sulphur. The phosphorous output is thought by most observers to represent a disintegration of the nucleins. Dunlop (16) and co-authors find that the increased phosphorous excretion takes place only in untrained men, though one would hardly expect Tissié's professional bicyclist to be an untrained man. Here, again, very little is known as to whether phosphoric and sulphuric acids have any effect except that of their hydrogen ion or that resulting from the sweeping of alkalies and alkaline earths from the body.

Many organic extractives have been named as fatigue substances, but the claims for very few, if indeed any, bear careful analysis. One of the earliest of these to be proposed was creatin. This was one of the original list proposed by Ranke, though later he failed to confirm his earlier experiments, and consequently it does not appear in his later lists. Folin's colorometric method for creatinine gave a great impulse to the study of creatin and creatinine and has resulted in a very extensive bibliography on this subject. Among these papers there are several having to do with creatinine or creatin after fatigue. These papers, however, taken as a whole, only add to the confusion, for while Scaffidi (12) and some others report no change in the amount of either creatin or creatinine, Gregor (13) reports a decreased urinary output, while Oddi and Tarulli (14) and others report increases in the amount present in either the muscle or urine after fatigue. Work in our own laboratory indicates clearly that the amount of creatin or of creatinine in muscle is independent of the work done, and this whether the muscle is worked in situ or whether it is excised.

The evidence in regard to uric acid is also more or less conflicting. Judging from what has been said as to the increased output of phosphoric acid and the supposed origin of this acid from the nucleins, one would expect some additional evidence of nuclein metabolism. An increased output of uric acid would be the most probable change.

Tissiè found in the urine of his cyclist on the day of the race about double the amount of uric acid that Folin (15) gives as the average of his 30 normal urines, while on the following day there was a still greater rise. Garratt, again using himself as subject, finds that a slight increase is usual after work, but that in one case, when out of training, the increase was more marked. Dunlop (16) and coauthors think there is no rise when the subject is in training, but otherwise there is an increased excretion of uric acid. They interpret the rise to mean a destruction of protein outside the muscles and suggest that it may be due to a mobilization of the protein of the more inactive portions of the body somewhat akin to the mobilization which takes place during starvation. In their interpretation Garratt agrees with them. Bearing on purine metabolism, attention should be called to the work in which Scaffidi (17) showed that there was no accumulation of uric acid in excised muscles which had been exhausted by fatigue, though there was a loss of fixed purine base. This hardly bears out Dunlop's contention, but on the other hand indicates that the source of the uric acid is the working muscle itself and that perhaps the trained muscle differs from the untrained in its power of breaking up the uric acid, or in the path taken in the disintegration of the purine.

Of course there are numerous other disintegration products which might be expected to arise, as by-products of the working muscle, but evidence that such exist or that they have any bearing on fatigue is even poorer than is that for creatin and uric acid. There is even some question as to whether any protein is destroyed during muscular activity. However, in spite of the fact that according to Luciani (18) Succi excreted no more nitrogen on the twelfth day of his fast when he took exercise than on the eleventh, which he spent in bed, and in spite of the fact that Benedict and Cathcart's (20) experiments indicate no change of urinary nitrogen during work, I feel warranted in believing that there is a definite, though perhaps limited, increased nitrogen output resulting from increased muscular work. Tissiè, again working on the urine of his bicycle rider, reports a normal nitrogen excretion on the day of the race, while on the following day there was an increase of 85 per cent. Garratt agrees with Tissiè in finding no increase during the actual work period, and finds a distinct rise beginning at once after the cessation of work and reaching a maximum some 12 hours later. The excretion did not return to normal for some 30 hours after the work had ceased. This rise followed a different curve from that which followed the taking of food and in addition it occurred during the abstinence from food. Again, Frentzel (21) gives similar results following work done by fasting dogs.

The destruction of protein suggests the possibility that certain of the protein disintegration products may have some bearing upon fatigue. Lee (19) has performed perfusion experiments with indol, skatol, methyl mercaptan, and phenol. In every case he obtained results similar to those obtained with lactic acid or carbon dioxide. These effects were noted in some cases with very small concentrations. There is a general idea extant that the fatigued organism works to less advantage in many ways than does the nonfatigued organism. Normally, the toxic property of such substances as those named is reduced or destroyed by the union of the toxic body with an acid, as sulphuric or gluceronic acid. We are now conducting a series of experiments in the Public Health Service by means of which we hope to show not only whether the output of these bodies is increased during the work day, but also whether the organism can as effectually de-toxify them after as it can before a period of work.

If the destruction of protein is granted, one might expect specific protein toxins which could truthfully be called fatigue toxins, which would be comparable to the bacterial toxins. Such Weichardt (22) claimed to have found and named "kinitoxin." This he originally prepared from the muscle of fatigued animals and when it was injected into the blood streams of normal animals it was reported to produce the phenomena of fatigue. Weichardt himself soon abandoned his original line of research and became interested in some bizarre experiments which apparently led to nothing of present interest. Other workers have found it difficult or impossible to repeat his work, and finally Korff-Peterson (23) and Lee and Aronovitch (24) conclude definitely that no such bodies result in the course of normal fatigue.

To summarize, we may conclude that—

1. Substances carrying hydrogen ions, as lactic, β oxy-butyric acids, potassium, dihydrogen phosphate and carbon dioxide, stand as causal agents of fatigue.

2. Certain products of protein disintegration, as indol, skatol and phenol may produce fatigue symptoms and may be active agents in producing normal fatigue.

3. There is some evidence that the negative ion of lactic and β oxy-butyric acids and that certain positive ions, especially that of potassium, are capable of producing certain fatigue phenomena.

4. There is no evidence that the negative ions of carbonic, phosphoric or sulphuric acids are fatigue substances.

5. There is no evidence at present for the existence of specific fatigue substances as proposed by Weichardt.

6. There is very little probability that creatin or creatinine have any relation to fatigue or to muscle work in general.

7. There are no doubt numerous bodies, as purine bases, uric acid, etc., which may be increased by work, but which have no causal bearing on fatigue.

Literature Referred to.

(1) Ranke, Tetanus, book, Leipzig, 1865.

(2) Fletcher and Hopkins, Lactic Acid in Amphibian Muscle, Journal of Physiology, 1904, XXX, 414.

(3) Croonian Lecture: The respiratory Process in Muscle and the Nature of Muscular Motion, Proceed. Roy. Soc., B. 1917, LXXXIX, 444.

(4) Lee, The Cause of Treppe, Am. Journ. Physiol., 1907, XVIII, 267.

(5) The Normal Action of Fatigue Substances on Muscle, Am. Journ. Physiol., 1907, XX, 170.

(6) Butridge, An Inquiry into some Chemical Factors of Fatigue, Journ. Physiol., 1910, XLI, 285.

(7) Mines, On the Spontaneous Movements of Amphibian Skeletal Muscle in Saline Solutions. Journ. Physiol., 1908, XXXVII, 408.

(8) Tissiè, Observations Physiologiques concernant un Record Vélocipédique., Arch. de Physiol., 1894, VI, 822.

(9) Harper and Holliday, A Contribution to the Chemistry of Fatigue. Journ. Am. Chem. Soci., 1903, XXV, 33.

(10) Viale, The Excretion of Sodium Chloride in the Perspiration During Fatigue. Atti accad. Lincei., 1913, XXII, 180.

(11) Lee, Scott and Colvin, Some of the Chemical Characters of Certain Mammalian Muscles. Am. Journ. Physiol., 1916, XL, 474.

(12) Scaffidi, Sur la présence de créatinine dans les muscles et sur le mode de comporter de la créatine durant la fatigue. Arch. Ital. Biol., 1914, LXI, 168.

(13) Gregor, Beiträge zur Physiolog. des Kreatinins. Ztsch. Physiol. Chem., 190 0, XXI, 98.

(14) Oddi and Tarulli, Bul. del' Accad. Med. di Roma, 1893, XIX, 57.

(15) Folin, Approximately complete analyses of thirty normal urines, Am. Journ. Physiol., 1905, XIII, 45.

(16) Dunlop and others, Muscular Exercises and Metabolism, Journ. Physiol., 1897, XXII, 68.

(17) Scaffidi, Ueber das Verhalten der Purinebasen der Muskeln während Arbeit, Biochem. Ztsch., 1911, XXX, 473.

(18) Luciani, Das Hungern, p. 123, book, 1900.

(19) Lee, The Causes of Fatigue in Certain Pathological States, Brit. Med. Journ., 1906, II, 1806.

(20) Benedict and Cathcart, Muscular Work. Carnegie Pub., 1913, p. 98.

(21) Frentzel, Ein Beitrag zur Frage nach der Quelle der Muskelkraft, Pfluger's Archive, 1897, LXVIII, 212.

(22) Weichardt, Ueber Ermüdungsstoffe, book, 1912.

(23) Korff-Peterson, Untersuchungen über Kenotoxin. Ztsch. Hyg., 1914, LXXVIII, 37.

(24) Lee and Aronovitch, Does a Fatigue Toxin Exist? Proc. Soc. Exp. Biol. and Med., 1917, XIV, 153.

Additional literature will be found in the article on fatigue by Ioteyko in Richet's Dictionaire de Physiologie, Vol. 6, 1904.

PREVALENCE OF DISEASE.

No health department, State or local, can effectively prevent or control disease without knowledge of when, where, and under what conditions cases are occurring.

UNITED STATES.

EXTRA-CANTONMENT ZONES—CASES REPORTED WEEK ENDED APR. 23.

CAMP BEAUREGARD ZONE, LA.

Alexandria:	Cases.
Cerebrospinal meningitis	1
Diphtheria	2
Gonorrhea	3
Mumps	11
Pneumonia	2
Whooping cough	6
Pineville:	
Mumps	2
Typhoid fever	1

CAMP BOWIE ZONE, TEX.

Fort Worth:	
Herpes genitalis	1
Pneumonia	1
Scabies	1
Syphilis	2
Typhoid fever	2

CAMP DEVENS ZONE, MASS.

Chicken pox:	
Lunenburg	1
German measle:	
Ayer	1
Lunenburg	2
Measles:	
Ayer	1

CAMP DODGE ZONE, IOWA.

Des Moines:	
Chancroid	1
Diphtheria	7
Gonorrhea	19
Measles	3
Scarlet fever	26
Smallpox	23
Syphilis	17
Oralalet	
Typhoid fever	1

CAMP DONIPHAN ZONE, OKLA.

Faxon:	Cases.
Smallpox	15
Lawton:	
Diphtheria	1
German measles	1
Gonorrhea	2
Smallpox	16

CAMP EBERTS ZONE, ARK.

Cerebrospinal meningitis:	
Scotts, route 2	.
Dysentery:	
England	1
Carlisle	1
Erysipelas:	
Ward	.
Gonorrhea:	
Austin	2
Scotts	3
Scotts, route 1	8
Malaria:	
England	6
England, route 1	1
England, route 2	1
England, route 3	1
Lonoke	1
Austin, route 2	1
Plum Bayou	3
Scotts, route 2	1
Measles:	
England	4
England, route 1	1
England, route 2	5
Lonoke, route 3	6
Eberts Field	1
Mumps:	
England	2
England, route 1	1
Lonoke	2

CAMP EBERTS ZONE, ARK.—continued.

Mumps—Continued.	Cases.
Eberts Field	1
Cabot	1
Ward	1
Ophthalmia neonatorum:	
England	1
Pellagra:	
England	2
Pneumonia:	
Cabot	1
Septic sore throat:	
England, route 2	1
Smallpox:	
England	1
England, route 2	4
England, route 3	1
Lonoke	1
Plum Bayou	1
Syphilis:	
Scotts	3
Scotts, route 1	4
Tonsilitis:	
Cabot	1
Tuberculosis:	
England, route 1	1
England, route 3	2
Lonoke	1
Carlisle	1
Pettus	1
Kerr, route 1	1
Scotts, route 1	4
Whooping cough:	
England, route 4	1
Plum Bayou	1

CAMP FUNSTON ZONE, KANS.

Chicken pox:	
Manhattan	2
Measles:	
Cleburne	2
Manhattan	5
Stockdale	1
Mumps:	
Junction City	4
Manhattan	8
Scarlet fever:	
Manhattan	1
Whooping cough:	
Junction City	3

CAMP GORDON ZONE, GA.

Cerebrospinal meningitis:	
Atlanta	4
Diphtheria:	
Atlanta	1
Doraville	1
Malaria:	
Atlanta	2
Measles:	
Atlanta	7
Decatur	3
Mumps:	
Atlanta	11
Chamblee	1
Decatur	3
Ingleside	2

CAMP GORDON ZONE, GA.—continued.

Pneumonia:	Cases.
Atlanta	5
Kirkwood	1
Scottdale	1
Stone Mountain	1
Scarlet fever:	
Atlanta	3
East Point	1
Septic sore throat:	
Atlanta	2
Smallpox:	
Atlanta	3
Clarkston	1
Tuberculosis:	
Atlanta	3
Scottdale	2
Typhoid fever:	
Atlanta	2
Decatur	1

CAMP GREENE ZONE, N. C.

Charlotte Township:	
German measles	2
Gonorrhea	19
Malaria	2
Measles	10
Mumps	1
Scarlet fever	3
Smallpox	1
Syphilis	18
Tuberculosis	6
Typhoid fever	1

GULFPORT HEALTH DISTRICT, MISS.

Gulfport Health District:	
Chicken pox	1
Gonorrhea	1
Malaria	1
Measles	4
Mumps	2
Whooping cough	1

CAMP HANCOCK ZONE, GA.

Augusta:	
Chicken pox	1
German measles	1
Measles	16
Pneumonia, lober	1
Tuberculosis, pulmonary	3
Whooping cough	5

CAMP JACKSON ZONE, S C.

Columbia:	
Measles	3
Mumps	17
Pellagra	1
Whooping cough	6

CAMP JOSEPH E. JOHNSTON ZONE, FLA.

Chicken pox:	
Jacksonville	∎
Diphtheria:	
Jacksonville	▲
Dysentery:	
Jacksonville	15

CAMP JOSEPH E. JOHNSTON ZONE. FLA.—continued.

Gonorrhea:	Cases.
Jacksonville	2
Mandarin	1

Malaria:

Eastport	4
Jacksonville	1
Mandarin	1
Moncrief	1

Measles:

| Fishers Corner | 1 |
| Jacksonville | 8 |

Mumps:

| Jacksonville | 14 |

Pellagra:

| Jacksonville | 1 |

Pneumonia:

| Eastport | 1 |
| Jacksonville | 6 |

Syphilis:

| Dinsmore | 1 |
| Jacksonville | 2 |

Trachoma:

| Jacksonville | 1 |

Tuberculosis:

| Jacksonville | 7 |
| South Jacksonville | 1 |

Whooping cough:

| Jacksonville | 20 |
| Ortega | 2 |

FORT LEAVENWORTH ZONE, KANS.

Leavenworth:

Measles	33
Pneumonia, lobar	2
Scarlet fever	1
Smallpox	1
Typhoid fever	1

Leavenworth County:

Measles	16
Scarlet fever	3
Whooping cough	4

CAMP LEE ZONE, VA.

Chicken pox:

| Chesterfield County | 2 |
| Prince George County | 1 |

German measles:

Ettricks	4
Petersburg	3
Prince George County	3

Gonorrhea:

Hopewell	1
Petersburg	1
Prince George County	1

Malaria:

| Ettricks | 1 |
| Petersburg | 1 |

Measles:

Ettricks	1
Hopewell	5
Petersburg	1
Prince George County	2

Mumps:

Ettricks	2
Hopewell	5
Petersburg	4
Prince George County	1

CAMP LEE ZONE, VA.—continued.

Pneumonia:	Cases.
Ettricks	1
Petersburg	1

Septic sore throat:

Chesterfield County	1
Dinwiddie County	2
Petersburg	5
Prince George County	2

Tuberculosis:

| Ettricks | 4 |

Whooping cough:

Ettricks	1
Hopewell	3
Chesterfield County	1

CAMP LEWIS ZONE, WASH.

Chicken pox:

| Parkland | 4 |

German measles:

Greendale	1
Oak Knoll	1
Parkland	3
Spanaway	6

Mumps:

Du Pont	2
Flett Station	1
Roy	1
Spanaway	2

Tuberculosis, pulmonary:

| Du Pont | 4 |

Whooping cough:

| American Lake | 4 |
| Parkland | 3 |

CAMP LOGAN ZONE, TEX.

Chancroid:

| Houston | 1 |

Diphtheria:

| Houston | 1 |

Dysentery:

| Moonshine Hill | 4 |

German measles:

| Houston | 1 |

Gonorrhea:

Houston	25
Humble	1
Hufsmith	1
Westfield	1
Cottage Grove	1

Malaria:

| Houston | 4 |

Measles:

Houston	4
Louetta	5
Spring	1

Mumps:

| Houston | 9 |

Pneumonia:

| Houston | 9 |

Syphilis:

Houston	29
Humble	1
Brooksmith	1
Brookshire	1
Goose Creek	1

Tuberculosis:

| Houston | 1 |
| Louetta | 1 |

Typhoid fever:	Cases.
Houston	3
Whooping cough:	
Houston	4

CAMP MACARTHUR ZONE, TEX.

Waco:
Gonorrhea	1
Measles	6
Mumps	25
Pneumonia, lobar	1
Smallpox	6
Tuberculosis	1

CAMP M'CLELLAN ZONE, ALA.

Chicken pox:	
Anniston	1
Diphtheria:	
Oxford	1
Measles:	
Anniston	1
Mumps:	
Anniston	1
Scarlet fever:	
Anniston	1
Smallpox:	
Anniston	8
Oxford	1
Precinct Four	1

CAMP PIKE ZONE, ARK.

Cerebrospinal meningitis:	
Little Rock	1
Chancroid:	
Little Rock	1
North Little Rock	2
Chicken pox:	
Little Rock	2
Erysipelas:	
Little Rock	3
German measles:	
North Little Rock	1
Gonorrhea:	
Little Rock	18
North Little Rock	1
Scotts	7
Malaria:	
Little Rock	12
Measles:	
Little Rock	2
Mumps:	
Little Rock	6
North Little Rock	3
Pneumonia:	
Little Rock	3
North Little Rock	2
Scarlet fever:	
Little Rock	4
Smallpox:	
Little Rock	9
North Little Rock	4
Syphilis:	
Little Rock	3
Scotts	7

Tuberculosis:	Cases.
Little Rock	10
Altheimer	1
Typhoid fever:	
Little Rock	4
Whooping cough:	
Little Rock	4

NORFOLK COUNTY NAVAL DISTRICT, VA.

Diphtheria:	
South Norfolk	4
Gonorrhea:	
South Norfolk	4
Malaria:	
Ocean View	9
Measles:	
Portsmouth	7
Ocean View	2
South Norfolk	1
Mumps:	
Ocean View	3
South Norfolk	2
Pneumonia:	
Portsmouth	2
Pinners Point	1
Norfolk County	2
South Norfolk	2
Scarlet fever:	
Portsmouth	3
Tuberculosis:	
Oakwood	1
Portsmouth	1
Willoughby	1
Varicella:	
Ocean View	4

FORT OGLETHORPE ZONE, GA.

Chicken pox:	
Chattanooga	2
German measles:	
Missionridge	4
Gonorrhea:	
Chattanooga	51
Measles:	
East Lake	4
Mumps:	
Chattanooga	1
East Chattanooga	1
Pneumonia:	
Chattanooga	2
Alton Park	1
Scarlet fever:	
Chattanooga	3
Smallpox:	
Chattanooga	4
Syphilis:	
Chattanooga	17
Churchville	1
Tuberculosis:	
Chattanooga	2
Whooping cough:	
Chattanooga	9

CAMP SEVIER ZONE, S. C.

Cerebrospinal meningitis: Cases.
- Butler Township 1
- Greenville, suburban 1

Measles:
- Judson Mills 2
- Union Bleachery 9

Mumps:
- Union Bleachery 2

Pneumonia:
- Chick Springs Township 1

Typhoid fever:
- American Spinning Co. 1

CAMP SHELBY ZONE, MISS.

Hattiesburg:
- German measles 1
- Malaria 30
- Mumps 14
- Pneumonia, lobar 1
- Tuberculosis 1
- Venereal 8
- Whooping cough 10

CAMP SHERIDAN ZONE, ALA.

Montgomery:
- German measles 1
- Measles 9
- Mumps 7
- Ringworm 6
- Smallpox 1
- Tuberculosis 1

CAMP SHERMAN ZONE, OHIO.

Gonorrhea:
- Chillicothe 1

Measles:
- Chillicothe 7
- Green Township 1

Mumps:
- Chillicothe 3
- Liberty Township 1

Pneumonia, lobar:
- Chillicothe 1

Scarlet fever:
- Chillicothe 5
- Union Township 1
- Scioto Township 1

Tuberculosis, pulmonary:
- Chillicothe 1

Typhoid fever:
- Chillicothe 1

Whooping cough:
- Chillicothe 1

CAMP ZACHARY TAYLOR ZONE, KY.

Jefferson County:
- Measles 1
- Pneumonia, lobar 1
- Tuberculosis, pulmonary 1
- Typhoid fever 1
- Whooping cough 3

CAMP ZACHARY TAYLOR ZONE, KY.—continued.

Louisville: Cases.
- Cerebrospinal meningitis 1
- Chicken pox 2
- Diphtheria 2
- Malaria 1
- Measles 14
- Pneumonia, lobar 8
- Scarlet fever 2
- Smallpox 5
- Rabies in animals 1
- Tuberculosis, pulmonary 12
- Typhoid fever 2
- Whooping cough 5

U. S. Government clinic:
- Chancroid 5
- Gonorrhea 22
- Syphilis 39

TIDEWATER HEALTH DISTRICT, VA.

Hampton:
- Measles 3
- Mumps 1
- Tuberculosis 2
- Typhoid fever 1

Newport News:
- Cerebrospinal meningitis 2
- Chicken pox 3
- German measles 4
- Measles 16
- Mumps 18
- Scarlet fever 3
- Smallpox 2
- Whooping cough 1

Phœbus.
- Scarlet fever 3

CAMP TRAVIS ZONE, TEX.

San Antonio:
- Chancroid 2
- Gonorrhea 35
- Influenza 3
- Measles 11
- Mumps 9
- Otitis media 1
- Pellagra 1
- Pneumonia 5
- Syphilis 7
- Tuberculosis 30
- Typhoid fever 6

CAMP WHEELER ZONE, GA.

Macon:
- Cerebrospinal meningitis 1
- Chicken pox 4
- Gonorrhea 6
- Mumps 8
- Scarlet fever 6
- Smallpox 2
- Syphilis 1
- Typhoid fever 1

DISEASE CONDITIONS AMONG TROOPS IN THE UNITED STATES.

The following data are taken from telegraphic reports received in the office of the Surgeon General, United States Army, for the week ended April 12, 1918:

Annual admission rate per 1,000 (disease only):	
All troops	1,627.1
National Guard camps	1,232.2
National Army camps	1,959.4
Regular Army	1,502.5
Noneffective rate per 1,000 on day of report:	
All troops	48
National Guard camps	37.8

Noneffective rate per 1,000 on day of report—Continued.	
National Army camps	55.7
Regular Army	44.8
Annual death rate per 1,000 (disease only):	
All troops	11.3
National Guard camps	3.4
National Army camps	17.9
Regular Army	10.3

New cases of special diseases reported during the week ended Apr. 12, 1918.

Camp.	Pneumonia.	Dysentery.	Malaria.	Venereal.	Measles.	Meningitis.	Scarlet fever.	Deaths.	Annual admission rate per 1,000 (disease only).	Noneffective per 1,000 on day of report.
Wadsworth	4			16	3		1	0	846.1	24.6
Hancock	4			32	10		2	1	602.0	26.8
McClellan	5			21	1	2		0	1,263.8	35.6
Sevier	16			20	9	2	1	5	1,021.4	30.0
Wheeler	3	1	2	23		2		3	1,355.1	55.3
Logan	12		2	32	14		6	0	1,653.0	35.0
Cody	26			11				8	610.7	27.3
Doniphan								0	1,065.0	14.9
Bowie	35			54				3	2,260.1	54.0
Sheridan	6			20		1	2	1	1,204.4	36.1
Shelby			1	13				0	1,470.9	52.5
Beauregard	9		13	40		1		0	1,454.7	56.0
Kearney	38		1	2			11	1	1,131.8	45.0
Devens	38			50	5		7	10	1,623.6	47.0
Upton	20			50	17	1	5	6	827.8	32.0
Dix	5	1		163	11	1	10	2	1,733.8	41.2
Meade	25			15	5	1	1	7	497.2	31.4
Lee	15			179	14	1		6	1,751.2	60.2
Jackson	29			14	24	2		5	1,533.5	55.5
Gordon	26		1	129	38	1	6	3	2,282.7	46.3
Sherman	25	1		184	9		16	19	2,207.0	55.7
Taylor	28			26	57		3	15	3,272.9	95.4
Custer	72		1	77	6		12	15	1,403.0	36.2
Grant	7			13	10	1	7	8	842.2	27.4
Pike	22		3	55	23	2	6	10	2,715.4	71.1
Dodge	90			57	29		23	34	2,693.5	120.6
Funston	31			85	19		4	11	1,837.0	83.9
Travis	21	2	1	41	28	1		7	4,839.4	70.4
Lewis	27			87	1		17	7	1,882.1	56.3
Northeastern Department	6			20	9		1	5	1,863.0	45.9
Eastern Department	10		1	62	10			5	1,329.8	33.0
Southeastern Department	9		3	34	13		1	7	1,323.8	49.1
Central Department	23	1	1	30	17	2	23	8	1,451.6	44.3
Southern Department	21	2	2	56	16		9	6	1,934.9	55.3
Western Department	8		1	28	10		7	3	1,187.4	27.0
Aviation, S. C.	34		2	88	86	1	48	27	1,490.0	40.4
Camp Greene	9			32	9	2	3	3	1,330.3	45.8
Camp Fremont	3			13	19	2		1	2,457.8	78.8
El Paso	1			11	1		1	0	1,476.3	6.7
Columbus Barracks	3			10	2			3	1,471.4	56.6
Jefferson Barracks	5			62	3		10	3	4,247.4	125.1
Fort Logan	7			1	2		6	6	2,065.9	86.2
Fort McDowell			1	5	1	1	5	0	1,914.1	64.4
Fort Slocum				10	1			1	1,743.0	50.0
Fort Thomas	4			2	6			0	1,431.2	67.3
D. B. Alcatraz								0		
D. B. Fort Leavenworth	2			1				2	1,167.0	38.4
A. A. Humphreys					1			0		
J. E. Johnston	2	1	1	44	7	1	1	0	1,472.4	37.3
Camp Merritt	20			112	4	2	14	7	1,412.0	50.6
Camp Stuart	19			144	8	2	1	11	1,545.7	64.8

New cases of special diseases reported during the week ended Apr. 12, 1918—Continued.

Camp.	Pneumonia.	Dysentery.	Malaria.	Venereal.	Measles.	Meningitis.	Scarlet fever.	Deaths.	Annual admission rate per 1,000 (disease only).	Noneffective per 1,000 on day of report.
West Point, N. Y.				2	7			0	451.9	12.4
Edgewood-Aberdeen	1			2	7		1	0	1,396.8	40.1
Provisional depot for corps and Army troops	11		1	23	20			1	1,868.7	44.5
Camp Holabird				1				0		
Camp Raritan				1	2			0	672.4	20.5
National Guard departments	2			17	9		1	1		
National Army departments	35		3	167	81	1	22	9		
Total	838	9	41	2,485	677	35	294	296	1,627.1	48.0

[1] All troops.

Annual rate per 1,000 for special diseases.

Disease.	All troops in United States.[1]	Regulars in United States[1]	National Guard, all camps.[1]	National Army, all camps.[1]	Expeditionary forces[2]
Pneumonia	31.6	23	19.9	52.9	35.4
Dysentery	0.4	0.5	0.16	0.4	1.0
Malaria	1.7	1.6	3.1	0.7	0.0
Venereal	102.8	95.5	46.7	134.8	49.2
Paratyphoid fever	0.0	0.0	0.0	0.0	0.1
Typhoid fever	0.04	0.1	0.0	0.0	0.3
Measles	28	31.9	6	32.6	10.3
Meningitis	1.4	1.6	1.3	1.4	3.3
Scarlet fever	12.1	16.4	3.6	13	14.7

[1] Week ended Apr. 12, 1918.   [2] Week ended Apr. 4, 1918.

CURRENT STATE SUMMARIES.

Alabama.

From Collaborating Epidemiologist Perry, by telegraph, for week ended April 20, 1918:

Jefferson County, smallpox 43, meningitis 1.

California.

From the State Board of Health of California, by telegraph, for week ended April 20, 1918:

Prevalence of reportable diseases in California reduced, except diphtheria and smallpox. Diphtheria: More prevalent in southern California than in other parts of State. Measles greatly reduced but still prevalent in southern California. Mumps, German measles, and whooping cough prevalent in San Francisco. Smallpox epidemic in Brawley, Imperial County. Eight cases of epidemic cerebrospinal meningitis. 4 in San Joaquin County, 2 Napa County, 1 each San Francisco and Los Angeles.

Reported by mail for preceding week (ended April 13):

CURRENT STATE SUMMARIES—Continued.

Cerebrospinal meningitis	9	Pneumonia	67
Chicken pox	153	Poliomyelitis	2
Diphtheria	67	Ophthalmia neonatorum	1
Erysipelas	13	Scarlet fever	70
German measles	271	Smallpox	14
Gonococcus infection	59	Syphilis	41
Leprosy	1	Tetanus	1
Malaria	11	Trachoma	2
Measles	923	Tuberculosis	87
Mumps	298	Typhoid fever	14
Pellagra	2	Whooping cough	160

Connecticut.

From Collaborating Epidemiologist Black, by telegraph, for week ended April 20, 1918:

Smallpox: Hartford, 6 cases. Cerebrospinal meningitis: Hartford, 1, New Haven 1, Naugatuck 1, Wallingford 1, Ledyard 1. Scarlet fever: Norwalk 16 cases, institutional.

Georgia.

From Collaborating Epidemiologist Abercrombie, by telegraph, for week ended April 20, 1918:

Cerebrospinal meningitis: Dalton 6 cases, 2 deaths. Dysentery: Dallas 8 cases, 2 deaths, Surrency 3 new cases, 2 deaths. Smallpox: General throughout State.

Illinois.

From Collaborating Epidemiologist Drake, by telegraph, for week ended April 20, 1918:

Smallpox: One hundred and sixty-six; of which in Chicago 10, Quincy 17, Riverside Township (Adams County) 10, Bryant 5, Farmington 6, Alton 28, Peoria 21, Belleville 5, Millcreek 13. Diphtheria: One hundred and seventy-six; of which in Chicago 113, Quincy 4, Altamont 4, Edwardsville 4. Scarlet fever: One hundred and sixty-nine; of which in Chicago 55, De Kalb 5, East Galesburg 4, Virdin 4, Keithsburg 42, Moline 6. Poliomyelitis: Chicago 5, De Kalb 1, Waukegan 1. Meningitis: Chicago 9, Springfield 1, Rockford 1.

Indiana.

From the State Board of Health of Indiana, by telegraph, for week ended April 20, 1918:

Scarlet fever: One death each Winamac, Decatur, Fremont, Bloomington. Whooping cough: One death each Kokomo, Peru. Measles: Epidemic Warsaw, Huntington, Grant City. Diphtheria: One death each Anderson, Greensburg. Rabies: Epidemic Pike County. Grippe: Epidemic Warsaw, Newcastle, Huntington, Bluffton, Muncie, Gary.

Kansas.

From Collaborating Epidemiologist Crumbine, by telegraph, for week ended April 20, 1918:

Smallpox (10 or more cases): By counties—Butler 17, Cowley 14, Ness, 11; by cities—Coffeyville 12, Fort Scott 20, Hutchinson 16, Iola 11, Kansas City 15,

CURRENT STATE SUMMARIES—Continued.

Kansas—Continued.

Salina 17, Wichita 20. Scarlet fever (10 or more cases): By counties—Clay 16, Kiowa 14; by cities—Dodge City 10, Hutchinson 11, Topeka 20. Meningitis: In cities—Eldorado 1, Frankfort 1, Lebo 1, Manhattan 1, Plains 1, Reece 1, Topeka 1, Wichita 1. Poliomyelitis: Newton 1.

Louisiana.

From Collaborating Epidemiologist Dowling, by telegraph, for week ended April 20, 1918:

Meningitis, excluding Rapides Parish: Orleans Parish 3.

Massachusetts.

From Collaborating Epidemiologist Hitchcock, by telegraph, for week ended April 20, 1918:

Unusual prevalence. German measles: Lynn 46. Measles: Brookline 35, Chelsea 37, Chelmsford 12, Haverhill 58, Newberry 6, Shirley 21, Westford 15. Smallpox: State Infirmary 1.

Minnesota.

From Collaborating Epidemiologist Bracken, by telegraph, for week ended April 20, 1918:

Smallpox (new loci): Hubbard County, Nevis village; Kittson County, section 14, township 162, range 45; Lyon County, Clifton Township; Mahnomen County, Wauon village, Roseau County, Malung Township; Wabasha County, Greenfield Township; one case each. Two cerebrospinal meningitis reported since March 8.

Nebraska.

From the State Board of Health of Nebraska, by telegraph, for week ended April 20, 1918:

Rabies Cass County. Smallpox: Lincoln, Omaha, Johnson County, Broken Bow, Wakefield. Scarlet fever: Ashland, Culbertson. Cerebrospinal meningitis: Crete 1 case.

South Carolina.

From Collaborating Epidemiologist Hayne, by telegraph, for week ended April 22, 1918:

Four cases epidemic meningitis.

Vermont.

From Collaborating Epidemiologist Dalton, by telegraph, for week ended April 20, 1918:

Smallpox: Rochester 1. No other outbreak or unusual prevalence.

Virginia.

From Collaborating Epidemiologist Traynham, by telegraph, for week ended April 20, 1918.

Five cases smallpox Newport News, 1 Tazewell County, 18 Pulaski, 1 Washington. Two cases cerebrospinal meningitis Newport News, 1 Norfolk, 1 Bedford County, 1 Prince George.

CURRENT STATE SUMMARIES—Continued.

Washington.

From Collaborating Epidemiologist Tuttle, by telegraph, for week ended April 20, 1918:

Two cases epidemic cerebrospinal meningitis Camas, Clarke County, onset of cases March 10 and 12. One case in Seattle. Forty scarlet fever in Tacoma. Fourteen cases smallpox Arlington, Snohomish County.

RECIPROCAL NOTIFICATION.

Massachusetts.

Cases of communicable diseases referred during March, 1918, to other State health departments by department of health of the State of Massachusetts.

Disease and locality of notification.	Referred to health authority of—	Why referred.
Diphtheria; Milton, N. Y..	State department of health, Albany, N. Y., notified Massachusetts department of health.	Two possible diphtheria carriers left Milton, N. Y., for Holyoke.
Lobar pneumonia: Pittsfield......	State department of health, Albany, N. Y.	Case reported by the Pittsfield board of health. Residence of patient, Braynard, N. Y.
Tuberculosis: Camp Devens.	State department of health, Des Moines, Iowa.	Discharged from Camp Devens and returned to his home in Iowa.
	State department of health, Hartford, Conn.	4 cases. Discharged from Camp Devens and returned to their homes in Connecticut.
	State department of health, Augusta, Me.	Discharged from Camp Devens and returned to his home in Maine.
	State board of health, Concord, N. H..	Discharged from Camp Devens and returned to his home in New Hampshire.
	State department of health, Albany, N. Y.	10 cases. Discharged from Camp Devens and returned to their homes in New York.
	State board of health, Burlington, Vt..	Discharged from Camp Devens and returned to his home in Vermont.
Smallpox: Boston........	State board of health, Concord, N. H...	Patient came from Groveton, N. H., to Boston February 27. Onset of disease February 17.
Milton........	State department of health, Hartford, Conn.	Patient was a traveling salesman and had been in Hartford, Waterbury, and Litchfield, Conn., until February 20. Onset of disease February 23 or 24.

CEREBROSPINAL MENINGITIS.

State Reports for February and March, 1918.

Place.	New cases reported.	Place.	New cases reported.
California (Mar.):		California—Continued.	
Alameda County	4	San Joaquin County—	
Oakland......................	2	Stockton......................	3
Contra Costa County..................	1		
Martines....................	1	Total........................	32
Los Angeles County..................	2		
Los Angeles...................	4	District of Columbia (Mar.).............	11
Monrovia.....................	1		
Riverside County..................	1	Louisiana (Mar.):	
Perris......................	2	Avoyelles Parish...................	1
San Bernardino County..............	1	Ascension Parish...................	1
San Bernardino...............	1	Bienville Parish..................	1
San Diego County—		Caddo Parish....................	4
San Diego...................	3	Calcasieu Parish.................	2
Fort Rosecrans	1	Catahoula Parish.................	1
San Francisco......................	5	De Soto Parish	1

44

CEREBROSPINAL MENINGITIS—Continued.

State Reports for February and March, 1918—Continued.

Place.	New cases reported.	Place.	New cases reported.
Louisiana—Continued.		**Rhode Island (Mar.):**	
East Carroll Parish	1	Providence County—	
Lincoln Parish	4	North Smithfield	1
Morehouse Parish	2	Providence	6
Orleans Parish	5	Woonsocket	1
Ouchita Parish	1		
Pointe Coupee Parish	1	Total	8
Rapides Parish	12		
Richland Parish	1	**Virginia (Feb.):**	
St. Landry Parish	2	Buchanan County	2
		Caroline County	1
Total	40	Henrico County—	
		Richmond	2
Massachusetts (Mar.):		Henry County	1
Bristol County—		Lee County	2
Fall River	2	Loudoun County	1
Essex County—		Louisa County	1
Danvers (Town)	1	Montgomery County	1
Gloucester	1	Nelson County	2
Haverhill	1	Norfolk County—	
Lawrence	2	Portsmouth	1
Newburyport	1	Prince George County—	2
Salem	3	Camp Lee	7
Franklin County—		Hopewell	2
Greenfield (Town)	1	Scott County	1
Middlesex County—		Spottsylvania County	1
Camp Devens, Ayer	1	Sussex County	2
Billerica (Town)	1	Warren County—	
Cambridge	2	Front Royal	1
Lowell	5	Warwick County—	
Malden	1	Newport News	7
Somerville	1	Washington County	1
Norfolk County—			
Quincy	1	Total	38
Plymouth County—			
Brockton	1	**West Virginia (Mar.):**	
Suffolk County—		Gilmer County	1
Boston	18	Boone County	1
Chelsea	3	Roane County	1
Worcester County—		Summers County	1
Winchendon (Town)	1		
Worcester	4	Total	4
Total	51		

City Reports for Week Ended Apr. 6, 1918.

Place.	Cases.	Deaths.	Place.	Cases.	Deaths.
Albany, N. Y	1		Louisville, Ky	2	
Atlanta, Ga	1	2	Lowell, Mass	1	1
Atlantic City, N. J	1	1	Marion, Ind		2
Augusta, Ga	1		Memphis, Tenn	5	5
Baltimore, Md	11	3	Milwaukee, Wis	4	2
Birmingham, Ala	1		Nashville, Tenn	2	1
Boston, Mass	4	2	Newark, N. J	3	1
Buffalo, N. Y		1	New Haven, Conn	1	
Cambridge, Mass	1		New Orleans, La	1	1
Chanute, Kans	1		New York, N. Y	18	7
Charleston, S. C	1	1	Norfolk, Va	1	1
Charlotte, N. C	1		Oklahoma City, Okla	1	
Chattanooga, Tenn	1		Omaha, Nebr	1	1
Chelsea, Mass	2		Peoria, Ill		1
Chicago, Ill	9	4	Petersburg, Va		
Cincinnati, Ohio	2	1	Philadelphia, Pa	11	2
Cleveland, Ohio	4	3	Pittsburgh, Pa	5	2
Columbia, S. C	2		Providence, R. I	3	3
Columbus, Ohio		1	Racine, Wis		1
Detroit, Mich	1	1	Richmond, Va	1	
East Orange, N. J	1		Roanoke, Va	1	1
Erie, Pa	1	1	St. Joseph, Mo	1	
Greenville, S. C	1		St. Louis, Mo	2	1
Hackensack, N. J		1	San Francisco, Cal	1	
Hartford, Conn		1	Savannah, Ga	2	1
Houston, Tex	1		Scranton, Pa	1	
Indianapolis, Ind	1		Toledo, Ohio		1
Johnstown, Pa	1		Troy, N. Y	1	
Kansas City, Kans	2	1	Wilmington, N. C	2	2
Lawrence, M	1		Wilkes-Barre, Pa	2	
Lexington, K	1		Winston-Salem, N. C	3	2
Los Angeles, Cal	1	1	Worcester, Mass		1

DIPHTHERIA.

See Diphtheria, measles, scarlet fever, and tuberculosis, page 631.

ERYSIPELAS.

City Reports for Week Ended Apr. 6, 1918.

Place.	Cases.	Deaths	Place.	Cases.	Deaths.
Akron, Ohio...............	2	....	Newark, N. J....	6	1
Anderson, Ind....	1	....	New York, N. Y....	....	11
Ann Arbor, Mich............	1	....	Oklahoma City, Okla........	1	1
Baltimore, Md....	1	....	Parkersburg, W. Va....	1	....
Birmingham, Ala...........	....	1	Passaic, N. J...	1	....
Buffalo, N. Y....	2	....	Peoria, Ill....	....	1
Chicago, Ill...	14	1	Philadelphia, Pa....	7	....
Cleveland, Ohio...	7	....	Pittsburgh, Pa....	6	1
Colorado Springs, Colo......	1	....	Pontiac, Mich....	1	....
Columbus, Ohio...	....	1	Portland, Oreg....	3	....
Corsicana, Tex....	1	....	Reading, Pa....	1	....
Denver, Colo....	5	....	Redlands, Cal....	1	....
Detroit, Mich....	4	2	St. Joseph, Mo....	2	....
Easton, Pa....	1	....	St. Louis, Mo....	11	1
El Paso, Tex....	....	1	St. Paul, Minn....	3	1
Fargo, N. Dak....	1	....	San Francisco, Cal....	3	....
Jackson, Mich....	1	....	Somerville, Mass....	....	1
Johnstown, Pa....	1	....	Stockton, Cal....	1	....
Lancaster, Pa....	1	....	Superior, Wis....	1	....
Lincoln, Nebr....	1	....	Syracuse, N. Y....	....	1
Los Angeles, Cal....	5	....	Trinidad, Ohio....	1	....
Louisville, Ky....	3	....	Troy, N. Y....	1	....
Marshall, Tex....	1	....	Wichita, Kans....	1	....
Milwaukee, Wis....	....	1	Zanesville, Ohio....	....	1
Nashville, Tenn....	4	....			

MALARIA.

State Reports for February and March, 1918.

Place.	New cases reported.	Place.	New cases reported.
California (Mar.):		Louisiana—Continued.	
Alameda County—		St. John Parish....	2
Berkeley....	2	St. Martin Parish....	10
Fresno County....	2	St. Mary Parish....	1
Glenn County—		St. Tammany Parish....	30
Orland....	1	Union Parish....	2
Kern County....	1	Vermilion Parish....	9
Merced County....	1	Washington Parish....	1
San Joaquin County....	4	W. Feliciana Parish....	2
Stockton....	1		
Tracy....	2	Total....	104
Tehama County....	2		
Tulare County....	1	Massachusetts (Mar.):	
San Francisco County—		Essex County—	
Presidio....	1	Lynn....	1
Yolo County....	3	Middlesex County—	
		Newton....	1
Total....	21		
		Total....	2
Louisiana (Mar.):			
Acadia Parish....	2	Virginia (Feb.):	
Allen Parish....	1	Accomac County....	1
Ascension Parish....	1	Chincoteague....	7
Bienville Parish....	1	Greenbackville....	5
Concordia Parish....	3	Albemarle County....	2
De Soto Parish....	1	Augusta County—	
E. Baton Rouge Parish....	3	Staunton....	2
E. Feliciana Parish....	5	Botetourt County....	2
La Salle Parish....	2	Buckingham County....	2
Madison Parish....	1	Caroline County....	9
Natchitoches Parish....	6	Charles City County....	3
Pointe Coupee Parish....	2	Chesterfield County—	
Rapides Parish....	17	Winterpock....	3
St. Charles Parish....	2	Culpeper County....	1
St. Helena Parish....	1	Cumberland County....	3

MALARIA—Continued.

State Reports for February and March, 1918—Continued.

Place	New cases reported.	Place.	New cases reported.
Virginia—Continued.		Virginia—Continued.	
Dinwiddie County	3	Nottoway County	1
Elizabeth City County	2	Blackstone	2
Essex County	3	Burkeville	2
Gloucester County	4	Crewe	1
Greensville County	13	Page County	1
Halifax County	24	Pittsylvania County	5
Hanover County	7	Powhatan County	5
Henrico County	9	Prince Edward County—	
Isle of Wright County	3	Farmville	1
James City County	5	Prince George County	2
Williamsburg	3	Camp Lee	1
King William County	1	Hopewell	6
Lancaster County	2	Princess Anne County	14
Londoun County	5	Prince William County	2
Louisa County	2	Southampton County	10
Lunenburg County	4	Stafford County	3
Victoria	2	Surry County	5
Mecklenburg County	4	Sussex County	7
Nansemond County	1	Wise County	1
Suffolk	9	York County	1
Nelson County	2		
Northampton County	8	Total	263
Northumberland County	6		

City Reports for Week Ended Apr. 6, 1918.

Place.	Cases.	Deaths.	Place.	Cases.	Deaths.
Alexandria, La	1		Little Rock, Ark	5	
Birmingham, Ala	2	1	Montgomery, Ala	63	
Corsicana, Tex	6		Petersburg, Va	1	1
Hattiesburg, Miss	5		Richmond, Va	1	

MEASLES.

See Diphtheria, measles, scarlet fever, and tuberculosis, page 631.

PELLAGRA.

State Reports for February and March, 1918.

Place.	New cases reported.	Place.	New cases reported.
California (Mar.):		Massachusetts (Mar.)—Continued.	
San Diego County—		Middlesex County—	
San Diego	1	Cambridge	1
Oceanside	1		
		Total	2
Total	2		
		Virginia (Feb):	
Louisiana (Mar):		Accomac County—	
Caddo Parish	3	Tangier	1
De Soto Parish	2	Amherst County	1
Natchitoches Parish	1	Chesterfield County	1
Orleans Parish	1	Floyd County	1
Rapides Parish	4	Henry County	1
St. Mary Parish	1	James City County	1
		Orange County	3
Total	12	Pittsylvania County—	
		Danville	2
Massachusetts (Mar):		Rockbridge County	1
Hampshire County –		Rockingham County	1
Northampton	1		
		Total	13

PELLAGRA—Continued.

City Reports for Week Ended Apr. 6, 1918.

Place.	Cases.	Deaths.	Place.	Cases.	Deaths.
Alexandria, La	2		Mobile, Ala		1
Birmingham, Ala	2	1	Plainfield, N. J		4
Hartford, Conn	1		Richmond, Va	1	1
Houston, Tex	2	2	Savannah, Ga		1
Lexington, Ky		1	Worcester, Mass		1
Little Rock, Ark		1			

PNEUMONIA.

City Reports for Week Ended Apr. 6, 1918.

Place.	Cases.	Deaths.	Place.	Cases.	Deaths.
Alexandria, La	1		Lowell, Mass	5	2
Altoona, Pa	1		Lynn, Mass	5	5
Anderson, Ind	1		Manchester, N. H	1	1
Ann Arbor, Mich	1		McKeesport, Pa	3	
Anniston, Ala	2		Medford, Mass	1	
Atlanta, Ga	4	16	Melrose, Mass	2	3
Baltimore, Md	42	30	Michigan City, Ind	2	2
Battle Creek, Mich	5	2	Montgomery, Ala	1	
Berkeley, Cal	1		Montpelier, Vt	1	1
Billings, Mont	1		Morgantown, W. Va	1	
Boston, Mass	24	42	Nashville, Tenn	2	7
Braddock, Pa	3		Newark, N. J	134	42
Bridgeport, Conn	6	16	New Bedford, Mass	6	1
Brockton, Mass	6	2	New Britain, Conn	9	2
Buffalo, N. Y	12	23	Newburgh, N. Y	1	6
Burlington, Vt	1	1	Newburyport, Mass	1	
Butler, Pa	3		Newport, Ky	3	3
Cambridge, Mass	7	2	Newton, Mass	4	1
Canton, Ohio	6	7	North Adams, Mass	1	1
Charleston, W. Va	1	4	North Little Rock, Ark	4	2
Chelsea, Mass	12	5	Oak Park, Ill	6	
Chicago, Ill	486	218	Oshkosh, Wis	4	3
Chicopee, Mass	1		Parkersburg, W. Va	1	1
Cincinnati, Ohio	1	27	Petersburg, Va	1	1
Cleveland, Ohio	53	44	Philadelphia, Pa	165	102
Clinton, Mass	3	1	Pittsburgh, Pa	82	84
Corsicana, Tex	10	3	Pittsfield, Mass	3	
Cumberland, Md	3	1	Pontiac, Mich	5	2
Detroit, Mich	25	58	Providence, R. I	1	12
Duluth, Minn	2	4	Reading, Pa	4	4
Elmira, N. Y	4	3	Richmond, Va	2	
Everett, Mass	1	1	Rochester, N. Y	41	15
Fall River, Mass	4	1	Rutland, Vt	1	1
Grand Rapids, Mich	14	1	Sacramento, Cal	3	1
Hammond, Ind	4	8	St. Paul, Minn	1	10
Harrison, N. J	2		Salem, Mass	2	
Hattiesburg, Miss	5		San Diego, Cal	5	5
Haverhill, Mass	7	5	San Francisco, Cal	20	16
Holyoke, Mass	12	3	Schenectady, N. Y	12	5
Houston, Tex	4	2	Somerville, Mass	7	1
Jackson, Mich	5	1	Spartanburg, S. C	1	
Jacksonville, Fla	1	3	Springfield, Mass	28	13
Kalamazoo, Mich	2		Springfield, Ohio	2	2
Kansas City, Kans	6		Steubenville, Ohio	1	
Lawrence, Mass	5	5	Stockton, Cal	4	
Leavenworth, Kans	1	1	Topeka, Kans	3	
Lexington, Ky	2	2	Waco, Tex	5	1
Lincoln, Nebr	1		Waltham, Mass	1	
Little Rock, Ark	15	1	Wichita, Kans	10	3
Lorain, Ohio	1		Wilkinsburg, Pa	3	3
Los Angeles, Cal	13	7	Worcester, Mass	42	11
Louisville, Ky	4	16	York, Pa	1	

POLIOMYELITIS (INFANTILE PARALYSIS).

State Reports for February and March, 1918.

Place.	New cases reported.	Place.	New cases reported.
California (Mar.):		Massachusetts (Mar.):	
Sonoma County	1	Bristol County—	
Santa Clara County—		Fall River	1
San Jose	1	Middlesex County—	
Tulare County	1	Cambridge	1
Ventura County	1	Everett	1
		Lowell	2
Total	4	Suffolk County—	
		Boston	1
Louisiana (Mar.):			
Catahoula Parish	1	Total	6
Evangeline Parish	1		
		Virginia (Feb.):	
Total	2	Albemarle County	4

City Reports for Week Ended Apr. 6, 1918.

Place.	Cases.	Deaths.	Place.	Cases.	Deaths.
Baltimore, Md		1	Milwaukee, Wis	6	4
Boston, Mass		1	New York, N. Y	3	1
Chicago, Ill	1	1	Racine, Wis		1
Grand Rapids, Mich	1		Springfield, Ill	1	
Lowell, Mass		1	Waco, Tex	1	

RABIES IN ANIMALS.

City Reports for Week Ended Apr. 6, 1918.

During the week ended April 6, 1918, one case of rabies in animals was reported at Charlotte, N. C., and one case at Corsicana, Tex.

SCARLET FEVER.

See Diphtheria, measles, scarlet fever, and tuberculosis, page, 631.

SMALLPOX.

State Reports for March, 1918.

Place.	New cases reported.	Deaths.	Vaccination history of cases.			
			Number vaccinated within 7 years preceeding attack.	Number last vaccinated more than 7 years preceeding attack.	Number never successfully vaccinated.	Vaccination history not obtained or uncertain.
California:						
Alameda County	3				2	1
Oakland	2			1	1	
Butte County	1				1	
Colusa County	1		1			
Fresno County	12				7	5
Fresno	7					7
Kern County	3				3	
Los Angeles County	6			1	5	
Glendale	1			1		
Los Angeles	11				6	5
Vernon	1					1
Madera County	1				1	

SMALLPOX—Continued.

State Reports for March, 1918—Continued.

Place.	New cases reported.	Deaths.	Vaccination history of cases.			
			Number vaccinated within 7 years preceding attack.	Number last vaccinated more than 7 years preceding attack.	Number never successfully vaccinated.	Vaccination history not obtained or uncertain.
California—Continued.						
Nevada County—						
Grass Valley	1				1	
Orange County	3				3	
Placer County	1				1	
Riverside County	2					2
Blythe	1				1	
Sacramento	1				1	
San Diego County	2				1	1
Camp Kearney	2					2
San Diego	1					1
San Francisco	35			3	32	
San Mateo County—						
Camp Fremont	1					1
Siskiyou County—						
Dunsmuir	1				1	
Stanislaus County	1					1
Tehama County	1				1	
Tulare County	4					4
Visalia	1					1
Total	107		1	6	68	32
District of Columbia	1				1	
Massachusetts:						
Middlesex County—						
Marlboro	5				5	
Lowell	1				1	
Tewksbury State Infirmary	1				1	
Norfolk County—						
Milton (town)	1				1	
Suffolk County—						
Boston	1				1	
Worcester County—						
Hardwick (town)	1			1		
Total	10			1	9	

Miscellaneous State Reports.

Place.	Cases.	Deaths.	Place.	Cases.	Deaths.
Louisiana (Mar.):			Louisiana (Mar.)—Continued.		
Avoyelles Parish	4		Union Parish	1	
Bienville Parish	1		Vermilion Parish	5	
Caddo Parish	23		Vernon Parish	1	
Calcasieu Parish	1				
Caldwell Parish	7		Total	153	
Claiborne Parish	3				
Evangeline Parish	1		Virginia (Feb.):		
Iberia Parish	7		Alleghany County	3	
Iberville Parish	2		Augusta County—		
Jefferson Parish	1		Basic City	6	
Lafourche Parish	1		Caroline County	1	
Lincoln Parish	3		Franklin County	20	
Morehouse Parish	8		Gloucester County	9	
Natchitoches Parish	2		Grayson County	2	
Orleans Parish	51		Halifax County	6	
Rapides Parish	4		Montgomery County	4	
Red River Parish	4		Northampton County—		
St. Landry Parish	1		Cape Charles	1	
St. Martin Parish	10		Orange County	9	
St. Tammany Parish	11		Pittsylvania County	29	
Terrebonne Parish	1		Princess Anne County	10	

SMALLPOX—Continued.

Miscellaneous State Reports—Continued.

Place.	Cases.	Deaths.	Place.	Cases.	Deaths.
Virginia (Feb.)—Continued.			West Virginia—Continued.		
Prince William County...			Lincoln County.........	7	....
Roanoke County—			McDowell County........	6	....
Roanoke.............	6	....	Marshall County........	2	....
Russell County...........	12	....	Marion County.........	8	....
Scott County............	8	....	Mercer County.........	10	....
Tazewell County—			Mingo County..........	2	....
Pocahontas...........	2	....	Monongalia County.....	4	....
Wise County.............	30	....	Monroe County.........	7	....
Big Stone Gap........	6	....	Morgan County.........	1	....
Norton..............	5	....	Nicholas County........	2	....
			Ohio County...........	2	....
Total................	172	....	Pocahontas County......	1	....
			Raleigh County.........	2	....
West Virginia (Mar.):			Roane County..........	3	....
Berkeley County.........	1	....	Summers County........	1	....
Braxton County.........	1	....	Tucker County.........	1	....
Cabell County...........	2	....	Taylor County.........	14	....
Clay County.............	38	....	Wayne County..........	1	....
Fayette County..........	14	....	Wirt County...........	2	....
Gilmer County...........	8	....	Wood County...........	7	....
Hancock County.........	11	....	Wyoming County........	4	....
Harrison County........	1	....			
Jackson County.........	14	....	Total................	186	....
Kanawha County........	7	....			

City Reports for Week Ended Apr. 6, 1918.

Place.	Cases.	Deaths.	Place.	Cases.	Deaths.
Abilene, Tex.............	16	....	Greeley, Colo...........	1	....
Akron, Ohio.............	29	....	Hammond, Ind..........	3	....
Alexandria, La..........	2	....	Harrisburg, Pa.........	3	....
Alton, Ill...............	24	....	Houston, Tex...........	1	....
Anderson, Ind..........	4	....	Independence, Kans.....	4	....
Anniston, Ala...........	5	....	Indianapolis, Ind......	38	....
Atlanta, Ga.............	3	....	Jacksonville, Fla.......	2	....
Baltimore, Md..........	1	....	Janesville, Wis.........	2	....
Battle Creek, Mich......	3	....	Johnstown, Pa.........	1	....
Berlin, N. H............	5	....	Kalamazoo, Mich.......	13	....
Billings, Mont..........	1	1	Kansas City, Kans......	16	....
Birmingham, Ala........	32	....	Knoxville, Tenn........	2	....
Bloomington, Ind.......	1	....	La Crosse, Wis.........	7	....
Burlington, Iowa.......	2	....	Leavenworth, Kans.....	2	....
Butte, Mont............	1	....	Lima, Ohio.............	10	....
Canton, Ohio...........	1	....	Lincoln, Nebr..........	9	....
Chanute, Kans..........	5	....	Little Rock, Ark.......	10	....
Charleston, W. Va......	2	....	Lorain, Ohio...........	1	....
Chattanooga, Tenn......	5	....	Los Angeles, Cal.......	4	....
Chicago, Ill............	9	....	Louisville, Ky.........	7	....
Cincinnati, Ohio........	5	....	Macon, Ga.............	1	....
Cleveland, Ohio.........	26	1	Madison, Wis..........	2	....
Coffeyville, Kans.......	4	....	Marion, Ind...........	6	....
Columbus, Ohio........	2	....	Marshall, Tex..........	2	....
Council Bluffs, Iowa....	11	....	Mason City, Iowa......	2	....
Covington, Ky..........	1	....	Memphis, Tenn.........	19	....
Cumberland, Md........	9	....	Michigan City, Ind.....	3	....
Danville, Ill...........	1	....	Milwaukee, Wis........	4	....
Davenport, Iowa........	2	....	Minneapolis, Minn......	11	....
Dayton, Ohio...........	3	....	Mobile, Ala...........	3	....
Decatur, Ill............	1	....	Moline, Ill............	1	....
Denver, Colo............	41	....	Montgomery, Ala.......	5	....
Des Moines, Iowa.......	12	....	Morgantown, W. Va.....	2	....
Detroit, Mich...........	32	1	Muncie, Ind...........	7	....
Dubuque, Iowa.........	1	....	Muskogee, Okla........	11	....
Eau Claire, Wis........	4	....	Nashville, Tenn........	6	....
El Paso, Tex............	....	2	New Orleans, La.......	6	....
Erie, Pa................	1	....	New York, N. Y........	2	....
Evansville, Ind........	2	....	Niagara Falls, N. Y....	2	....
Fort Scott, Kans.......	2	....	Norfolk, Va...........	1	....
Fort Wayne, Ind.......	13	1	North Little Rock, Ark..	5	....
Fresno, Cal............	3	....	Ogden, Utah...........	2	....
Galesburg, Ill..........	3	....	Oklahoma City, Okla....	7	....
Grand Forks, N. Dak....	2	....	Omaha, Nebr...........	27	....
Grand Rapids, Mich.....	5	....	Parkersburg, W. Va.....	2	....

SMALLPOX—Continued.

City Reports for Week Ended Apr. 6, 1918—Continued.

Place.	Cases.	Deaths.	Place.	Cases.	Deaths.
Peoria, Ill.	9	....	Spartanburg, S. C.	1	....
Portsmouth, Va.	1	....	Spokane, Wash.	11	....
Quincy, Ill.	10	....	Springfield, Ill.	1	....
Racine, Wis.	1	....	Springfield, Mo.	5	....
Richmond Ind.	3	....	Springfield, Ohio.	1	....
Roanoke, Va.	3	....	Steubenville, Ohio.	1	....
St. Joseph, Mo.	23	....	Superior, Wis.	3	....
St. Louis, Mo.	26	....	Terre Haute, Ind.	4	....
St. Paul, Minn.	12	....	Toledo, Ohio.	3	....
Salina, Kans.	10	....	Topeka, Kans.	14	....
Salt Lake City, Utah.	18	....	Waco, Tex.	4	....
Sandusky, Ohio.	1	....	Washington, D. C.	2	....
San Francisco, Cal.	1	....	Wichita, Kans.	13	....
Seattle, Wash.	12	....	Woonsocket, R. I.	1	....
Shelbyville, Ind.	2	....	York, Pa.	1	....
Sioux City, Iowa.	8	....			

TETANUS.

City Reports for Week Ended Apr. 6, 1918.

Place.	Cases.	Deaths.	Place.	Cases.	Deaths.
Birmingham, Ala.	2	....	New York, N. Y.	1	2
Buffalo, N. Y.	....	1	St. Louis, Mo.	1	....
Morristown, N. J.	....	1			

TUBERCULOSIS.

See Diphtheria, measles, scarlet fever, and tuberculosis, page 631.

TYPHOID FEVER.

State Reports for February and March, 1918.

Place.	New cases reported.	Place.	New cases reported.
California (Mar.):		California (Mar.)—Con.	
Alameda County.	1	San Joaquin County—	
Oakland.	2	Stockton.	1
Colusa County—		Santa Barbara County—	
Colusa.	2	Santa Barbara.	1
Glenn County.	1	Santa Clara County.	1
Contra Costa County.	1	Santa Clara.	1
Richmond.	1	Shasta County—	
Pinole.	1	Redding.	1
Kern County—		Siskiyou County—	
Bakersfield.	1	Dunsmuir.	1
Los Angeles County.	1	Yreka.	2
Alhambra.	1	Sonoma County.	3
Los Angeles.	12	Solano County.	1
Marin County.	3	Rio Vista.	2
Monterey County.	1	Riverside County—	
Sacramento County—		Blythe.	7
Represa.	1		
San Benito County.	3	Total.	62
San Diego County—			
San Diego.	1	District of Columbia.	5
San Francisco.	8		

TYPHOID FEVER—Continued.

State Reports for February and March, 1918.

Place.	New cases reported.	Place.	New cases reported.
Louisiana (Mar.):		**Rhode Island (Mar.):**	
Acadia Parish	1	Kent County—	
Allen Parish	1	West Warwick (town)	1
Avoyelles Parish	2	Washington County—	
Caddo Parish	2	Charlestown (town)	1
Evangeline Parish	1		
Iberville Parish	1	Total	2
Jefferson Davis Parish	1		
Lafayette Parish	1	**Virginia (Feb.):**	
Orleans Parish	14	Accomac County	1
Rapides Parish	3	Alleghany County—	
St. Martin Parish	3	Clifton Forge	2
St. Mary Parish	1	Covington	1
Tensas Parish	1	Amherst County	1
Terrebonne Parish	7	Appomattox County	1
Vermilion Parish	1	Botetourt County	2
West Feliciana Parish	1	Buchanan County	1
		Culpeper County	3
Total	41	Elizabeth City County—	
		Phoebus	1
		Franklin County	1
Massachusetts (Mar.):		Frederick County	1
Bristol County—		Henrico County—	
Fall River	2	Richmond	2
New Bedford	3	Highland County	1
Taunton	1	Loudoun County	1
Essex County—		Montgomery County—	1
Haverhill	2	Christiansburg	1
Lawrence	1	Nansemond County—	
Methuen	2	Suffolk	2
Franklin County—		Nelson County	1
New Salem (town)	1	Nottoway County—	
Orange (town)	1	Crewe	1
Hampshire County—		Pittsylvania County	2
Holyoke	2	Pulaski County	3
Middlesex County—		Roanoke County—	
Everett	1	Roanoke	2
Framingham (town)	1	Russell County	5
Lowell	2	Scott County	2
Newton	2	Southampton County	1
North Reading (town)	1	Spotsylvania County	1
Reading (town)	1	Tazewell County	1
Somerville	1	Pocahontas	1
Stoneham (town)	1	Washington County	4
Nantucket County—		Westmoreland County	4
Nantucket (town)	2	Wise County	4
Norfolk County—			
Brookline (town)	1	Total	57
Norwood (town)	1		
Walpole (town)	1	**West Virginia (Mar.):**	
Plymouth County—		Boone County	10
Bridgewater (town)	2	Braxton County	1
Brockton	2	Fayette County	1
Suffolk County—		Jackson County	2
Boston	3	Kanawha County	4
Worcester County—		Marion County	2
Clinton (town)	1	Monongalia County	6
Leominster	1	Morgan County	1
Winchendon (town)	1	Ohio County	3
Worcester	1	Roane County	1
		Wood County	2
Total	41		
		Total	33

TYPHOID FEVER—Continued.

City Reports for Week Ended Apr. 6, 1918.

Place.	Cases.	Deaths.	Place.	Cases.	Deaths.
Albany, N. Y.	1		Minneapolis, Minn.	11	7
Alton, Ill.	1		Moline, Ill.	4	
Atlanta, Ga.	2		Morgantown, W. Va.	1	
Baltimore, Md.	8	1	Nashville, Tenn.	4	
Birmingham, Ala.	1	1	Newark, N. J.	2	
Boston, Mass.	1		New Britain, Conn.	3	
Buffalo, N. Y.	1		Newburgh, N. Y.	3	
Chanute, Kans.	3		New Castle, Pa.	2	
Charleston, W. Va.	4		New Orleans, La.	1	1
Charlotte, N. C.	1		New York, N. Y.	21	
Chattanooga, Tenn.	2		Norfolk, Va.	3	
Chicago, Ill.	2		Oakland, Cal.	1	
Cleveland, Ohio.	1	1	Philadelphia, Pa.	5	2
Covington, Ky.	1		Pittsburgh, Pa.	1	3
Danville, Ill.	1		Portland, Oreg.	2	
Decatur, Ill.	1		Reno, Nev.	1	
Denver, Colo.	1		Richmond, Va.	2	
Detroit, Mich.	3		Rochester, N. Y.	1	
Duluth, Minn.	1		Sacramento, Cal.	1	
East Chicago, Ind.	2	1	Saginaw, Mich.	1	
Erie, Pa.	1	1	St. Louis, Mo.	4	1
Evansville, Ind.	2	1	St. Paul, Minn.	1	
Fall River, Mass.	1		San Francisco, Cal.	1	
Fort Wayne, Ind.	1		Savannah, Ga.	1	
Fresno, Cal.	1		Seattle, Wash.	1	
Grand Rapids, Mich.	2	3	Steubenville, Ohio.	1	
Hammond, Ind.	4	1	Syracuse, N. Y.	1	
Hartford, Conn.	1		Toledo, Ohio.	2	
Hoquiam, Wash.	1		Trenton, N. J.	1	
Independence, Kans.	1		Waco, Tex.	5	
Indianapolis, Ind.	3	1	Waltham, Mass.	1	
Jackson, Mich.	1		Washington, Pa.	1	
Johnstown, Pa.	1		Washington, D. C.	1	
Kansas City, Kans.	1		Watertown, N. Y.	2	
Knoxville, Tenn.	1		Wheeling, W. Va.	3	
La Fayette, Ind.	1	1	Wilkes-Barre, Pa.	1	
Lawrence, Mass.	1		Wilmington, Del.		1
Long Beach, Cal.	1		Winston-Salem, N. C.	3	
Los Angeles, Cal.	2		Woonsocket, R. I.	2	
Louisville, Ky.		1	Zanesville, Ohio.	1	1
Milwaukee, Wis.	6	2			

DIPHTHERIA, MEASLES, SCARLET FEVER, AND TUBERCULOSIS.

State Reports for February and March, 1918.

State.	Cases reported.			State.	Cases reported.		
	Diphtheria.	Measles.	Scarlet fever.		Diphtheria.	Measles.	Scarlet fever.
California (March)..	295	5,273	379	Rhode Island (March).	79	271	62
District of Columbia (March).	49	2,090	161	Virginia (February)	111	3,808	114
Louisiana (March).	51	644	13	West Virginia (March).	19	340	25
Massachusetts (March).	747	4,018	537				

DIPHTHERIA, MEASLES, SCARLET FEVER, AND TUBERCULOSIS—Continued.

City Reports for Week Ended Apr. 6, 1918.

City.	Population as of July 1, 1916 (estimated by U.S. Census Bureau).	Total deaths from all causes.	Diphtheria.		Measles.		Scarlet fever.		Tuberculosis.	
			Cases.	Deaths.	Cases.	Deaths.	Cases.	Deaths.	Cases.	Deaths.
Over 500,000 inhabitants:										
Baltimore, Md.	569,621	322	17		456	4	10		63	62
Boston, Mass.	756,476	283	61	8	262	5	26		57	28
Chicago, Ill.	2,497,722	879	89	16	67	2	55	2	345	86
Cleveland, Ohio	674,073	211	15	1	25	1	6		31	31
Detroit, Mich.	571,784	258	46	2	56	3	37	1	48	32
Los Angeles, Cal.	503,812	131	25		232	1	7		49	11
New York, N.Y.	5,602,841	2,160	280	41	1,388	36	153	6	366	232
Philadelphia, Pa.	1,709,518	697	48	15	679	2	39	3	179	92
Pittsburgh, Pa.	579,090	276	17	2	344	2	15	1	41	22
St. Louis, Mo.	757,309	229	38	6	116		34		53	18
From 300,000 to 500,000 inhabitants:										
Buffalo, N.Y.	468,558	176	7	1	101	1	16		35	22
Cincinnati, Ohio	410,476	199	12		27		7		29	33
Jersey City, N.J.	306,345		8	1	43	1	12		16	9
Milwaukee, Wis.	436,535	103	4	1	313	1	25		42	5
Minneapolis, Minn.	363,454		20	2	35		22			8
Newark, N.J.	408,894	180	27	4	471	8	16		54	22
New Orleans, La.	371,747	144	9		10	1	1		37	36
San Francisco, Cal.	463,516	140	2		81		9		31	13
Seattle, Wash.	348,639		3		46		10			
Washington, D.C.	363,980	150	7		558	4	39	3	24	12
From 200,000 to 300,000 inhabitants:										
Columbus, Ohio	214,878	79	1		21		20		7	5
Denver, Colo.	260,800	109	13	3	95		43	1	4	21
Indianapolis, Ind.	271,708		20	2	45		37	1	15	13
Louisville, Ky.	238,910	104	9		15		5		21	17
Portland, Oreg.	295,463	54			291		4	1	5	2
Providence, R.I.	254,960	110	12	3	150		7		2	10
Rochester, N.Y.	256,417	82	10	1	58		24		23	6
St. Paul, Minn.	247,232	83	18		15		31	4	15	5
From 100,000 to 200,000 inhabitants:										
Albany, N.Y.	104,199				16				3	
Atlanta, Ga.	190,558	61	1		12		3		21	7
Birmingham, Ala.	181,762		1		18	1			6	5
Bridgeport, Conn.	121,579	45	10		7		2		8	4
Cambridge, Mass.	112,981	32	19		44	1	2		3	4
Camden, N.J.	106,233		5		16		5		6	
Dallas, Tex.	124,527		2		28					6
Dayton, Ohio	127,224		3		10		2			3
Des Moines, Iowa	101,598				2		19			
Fall River, Mass.	128,366	35	1		3		5		11	3
Grand Rapids, Mich.	128,291	39	3	1	7		5		1	1
Hartford, Conn.	110,900	60	6	1	7		2		9	4
Houston, Tex.	112,307	52			15				4	4
Lawrence, Mass.	100,560	32	3	2	29				2	4
Lowell, Mass.	113,245	46	2	1	7		4		6	7
Lynn, Mass.	102,425	22	4		19		5		11	2
Memphis, Tenn.	148,995	46	4		9		2		32	8
Nashville, Tenn.	117,057	49	1		13		2		4	2
New Bedford, Mass.	118,158	46			11				20	9
New Haven, Conn.	149,685		1		3				6	7
Oakland, Cal.	198,604	50			37		1		8	7
Omaha, Nebr.	165,470	51	4		17		16			5
Reading, Pa.	109,381	44	5		40		2		6	4
Richmond, Va.	156,687	52	4		64	1	4		9	4
Salt Lake City, Utah	117,399	39			20	1	7			1
Scranton, Pa.	146,811	41	6	1	8		3			3
Spokane, Wash.	150,323						1			
Springfield, Mass.	105,942	44	4		39		4		6	3
Syracuse, N.Y.	155,624	77	3	1	146	2	11		5	3
Tacoma, Wash.	112,770				1		6			
Toledo, Ohio	191,554	78	2		31		4		10	13
Trenton, N.J.	111,593	80	3		4		1		7	9
Worcester, Mass.	163,314	55	4	1	7	1	5		6	

DIPHTHERIA, MEASLES, SCARLET FEVER, AND TUBERCULOSIS—Continued.

City Reports for Week Ended Apr. 6, 1918—Continued.

City.	Population as of July 1, 1916 (estimated by U.S. Census Bureau).	Total deaths from all causes.	Diphtheria.		Measles.		Scarlet fever.		Tuberculosis.	
			Cases.	Deaths.	Cases.	Deaths.	Cases.	Deaths.	Cases.	Deaths.
From 50,000 to 100,000 inhabitants:										
Akron, Ohio	85,625		6		18		8		5	
Altoona, Pa.	58,659		1		9		2			
Atlantic City, N.J.	57,660				26				1	
Augusta, Ga.	50,245	12			14		2			2
Bayonne, N.J.	69,893		2		115		1		1	
Berkeley, Cal.	57,653	13			1				3	
Binghamton, N.Y.	53,973	24	2		9		10		1	3
Brockton, Mass.	67,449	17	1		16		11		3	3
Canton, Ohio	60,852	25			3		1			
Charleston, S.C.	60,734	23	3	1	3					3
Chattanooga, Tenn.	60,075	6							1	3
Covington, Ky.	57,144	33	1		7		1			8
Duluth, Minn.	94,495	20	2		3		1		6	5
Elizabeth, N.J.	95,090	34	4	1	44	4	8	1	3	5
El Paso, Tex.	63,705	36	1		16		1			12
Erie, Pa.	75,195	26		1	23		2		4	3
Evansville, Ind.	76,078	27			12		3		2	3
Fort Wayne, Ind.	76,183	35	6	1	16		3		2	2
Harrisburg, Pa.	72,015	34	2		29		6		1	1
Hoboken, N.J.	77,214	23	1		6		1		6	2
Holyoke, Mass.	65,286	23	1		5		1		3	2
Jacksonville, Fla.	76,101	32			17				2	1
Johnstown, Pa.	68,529	28	3				11			
Kansas City, Kans.	99,437		2		16		3		3	
Lancaster, Pa.	50,853				19		5		3	
Little Rock, Ark.	57,343	6	3		4		6			
Malden, Mass.	51,155	19	4	2	17		6		1	3
Manchester, N.H.	78,283	16	4		32				7	5
Mobile, Ala.	58,221	17				1			1	5
New Britain, Conn.	53,794	18	4		27		2		9	6
Norfolk, Va.	89,612		1		39		6		1	6
Oklahoma City, Okla.	92,943	28			18		2		7	2
Passaic, N.J.	71,744	21	3		8		1		4	1
Pawtucket, R.I.	59,411	26			3	1	1			2
Peoria, Ill.	71,458	21	1		5		1			1
Portland, Me.	63,867	21		1	4		1			
Rockford, Ill.	55,185	14			13					2
Sacramento, Cal.	66,895	31			74		3		5	4
Saginaw, Mich.	55,642	24	1						9	1
St. Joseph, Mo.	85,236	36	2	2	6	1			2	
San Diego, Cal.	53,330	28	2	1	40		3		5	4
Savannah, Ga.	68,805	25	1		5				2	4
Schenectady, N.Y.	99,519	20	3		3		1		6	
Sioux City, Iowa	57,078						13	1		
Somerville, Mass.	87,039	30	8	4	55		3		4	1
South Bend, Ind.	68,946	19			6					3
Springfield, Ill.	61,120	16	1		97	1	1			3
Springfield, Ohio	51,550	21			3		1		2	3
Terre Haute, Ind.	66,083	27	3		2				2	2
Troy, N.Y.	77,916	39	1	1	1		4	1	2	5
Wichita, Kans.	70,722		1		38		4		5	1
Wilkes-Barre, Pa.	76,776	20	6		27		3		1	1
Wilmington, Del.	94,265	46	1	1	38		1			1
York, Pa.	51,656				8		2		3	
From 25,000 to 50,000 inhabitants:										
Alameda, Cal.	27,732	5	3		38		2		1	1
Austin, Tex.	34,814	10	3				3			
Battle Creek, Mich.	29,480		1		73		1			
Beaumont, Tex.	27,711	12								
Bellingham, Wash.	32,985				1					
Brookline, Mass.	32,730	3	1		31		2		1	
Burlington, Iowa	25,030	7								
Butler, Pa.	27,632	14	7		20		1			
Butte, Mont.	43,425	57	1		1		1			
Central Falls, R.I.	25,636		1		2					
Charleston, W.Va.	29,941	13	1		14	1				1
Charlotte, N.C.	39,823	14	1		4					3
Chelsea, Mass.	46,192	21	7		43		1		4	1

DIPHTHERIA, MEASLES, SCARLET FEVER, AND TUBERCULOSIS—Continued.

City Reports for Week Ended Apr. 6, 1918—Continued.

City.	Population as of July 1, 1916 (estimated by U. S. Census Bureau).	Total deaths from all causes.	Diphtheria.		Measles.		Scarlet fever.		Tuberculosis.	
			Cases.	Deaths.	Cases.	Deaths.	Cases.	Deaths.	Cases.	Deaths.
From 25,000 to 50,000 inhabitants—Continued.										
Chicopee, Mass	29,319	12	4		3		2		2	5
Clinton, Iowa	27,386				3		1			
Colorado Springs, Colo	32,971	14	2		22				3	1
Columbia, S. C	34,611		1		2					
Council Bluffs, Iowa	31,484	18			2		1			
Cumberland, Md	26,074	5			13		8		3	
Danville, Ill	32,261	5	1		57				3	1
Davenport, Iowa	48,811				2		6			
Decatur, Ill	39,631	11			17				2	1
Dubuque, Iowa	39,873		1	2						
Durham, N. C	25,061	6			2					2
East Chicago, Ind	28,743	14			6					2
Easton, Pa	30,530	10	1		29					
East Orange, N. J	42,458	9	2		60		2	1	3	
Elgin, Ill	28,203	6			1					
Elmira, N. Y	38,120	8	1		30				14	4
Evanston, Ill	28,591	4							1	
Everett, Mass	39,233	11		2	8				4	2
Fitchburg, Mass	41,781	18	1		7		1		1	4
Fresno, Cal	34,958	5	1		22					
Galveston, Tex	41,863	8			4				1	1
Green Bay, Wis	29,353	9			3		1			
Hammond, Ind	28,171	21	1				1			1
Haverhill, Mass	48,477				45				4	
Jackson, Mich	35,363	16	1		10		35		4	1
Joliet, Ill	38,010				4		1		2	
Kalamazoo, Mich	48,886	22			12				1	1
Kenosha, Wis	31,576	8	3		2		4		1	
Knoxville, Tenn	38,676		1		10				5	5
La Crosse, Wis	31,677	7	2						1	1
Lexington, Ky	41,097	31			20				18	5
Lima, Ohio	35,384	15			2					
Lincoln, Nebr	46,515	7	1		1		4			
Long Beach, Cal	27,587	7	1		20					
Lorain, Ohio	36,964		1						1	
Lynchburg, Va	32,940	9			6				1	1
Macon, Ga	45,757	8			1		1			1
Madison, Wis	30,699	10			1		2			1
McKeesport, Pa	47,521		1		11		1			
Medford, Mass	26,234	6	5		7		3		1	2
Moline, Ill	27,451	11	5	1	16		1			1
Montclair, N. J	26,318	4			36				1	
Montgomery, Ala	43,285	11	1		4				1	
Mount Vernon, N. Y	37,009	10	4		6		1		1	
Muncie, Ind	25,424	8			2		2		1	1
Muskogee, Okla	44,218		1		1					
Nashua, N. H	27,327	6	1							
Newburgh, N. Y	29,603	19			3					1
New Castle, Pa	41,133		1		6				3	
Newport, Ky	31,927	11								
Newport, R. I	30,108	6	2				3			
Newton, Mass	43,715	16			18				5	1
Niagara Falls, N. Y	37,353	20	4	1	1		5		2	1
Norristown, Pa	31,401	6			1					1
Oak Park, Ill	26,654	6	7		21				2	3
Ogden, Utah	31,401	17			45		3			
Orange, N. J	33,080	14	1		34				1	1
Oshkosh, Wis	36,065	5			4		1		3	
Pasadena, Cal	46,450	7			234		1			
Perth Amboy, N. J	41,185	20		1						
Petersburg, Va	25,582		1		8				3	1
Pittsfield, Mass	38,629	11					7		4	2
Portsmouth, Va	39,651	14	1		10		3			1
Poughkeepsie, N. Y	30,390	13			114		1		4	2
Quincy, Ill	36,798	13	4		14					1
Quincy, Mass	38,136	11			63				3	
Racine, Wis	46,486	15			57		1		4	3
Roanoke, Va	43,284	24			40				4	2
Rock Island, Ill	28,926	11	1		19		3		1	

DIPHTHERIA, MEASLES, SCARLET FEVER, AND TUBERCULOSIS—
Continued.

City Reports for Week Ended Apr. 6, 1918—Continued.

City.	Population as of July 1, 1916 (estimated by U. S. Census Bureau).	Total deaths from all causes.	Diphtheria.		Measles.		Scarlet fever.		Tuberculosis.	
			Cases.	Deaths.	Cases.	Deaths.	Cases.	Deaths.	Cases.	Deaths.
From 25,000 to 50,000 inhabitants—Continued.										
Salem, Mass	48,562	19	1	......	20	1	1	......	4	3
San Jose, Cal	38,902	......	......	......	15	......	......	......	......	......
Sheboygan, Wis	28,559	9	2	......	......	......	1	......	2	3
Springfield, Mo	40,341	10	......	......	1	......	2	1	......	2
Steubenville, Ohio	27,445	16	......	......	......	......	2	......	2	......
Stockton, Cal	35,358	14	3	......	56	......	......	......	1	......
Superior, Wis	46,226	6	......	......	......	......	3	......	......	......
Taunton, Mass	36,283	14	1	......	......	......	......	......	5	2
Topeka, Kans	48,726	......	1	......	2	......	24	......	1	......
Waco, Tex	33,385	8	......	......	6	......	1	......	......	......
Walla Walla, Wash	25,136	......	......	......	......	......	1	......	......	......
Waltham, Mass	30,570	10	1	......	15	......	......	......	1	......
Watertown, N. Y	29,894	......	......	......	62	......	......	......	......	1
West Hoboken, N. J	43,139	13	......	......	8	......	2	......	2	......
Wheeling, W. Va	43,377	20	......	......	6	......	......	......	1	......
Williamsport, Pa	33,809	9	2	......	......	......	3	......	......	......
Wilmington, N. C	29,892	8	......	......	32	......	......	......	......	......
Winston-Salem, N. C	31,155	25	......	......	11	......	1	......	4	......
Zanesville, Ohio	30,863	16	......	......	......	......	......	......	1	1
From 10,000 to 25,000 inhabitants:										
Abilene, Tex	14,238	4	......	......	2	......	2	......	......	......
Alexandria, La	15,333	5	1	......	1	......	......	......	......	1
Alton, Ill	22,874	11	1	......	......	......	......	......	......	......
Anderson, Ind	23,996	7	......	......	6	......	1	......	1	......
Ann Arbor, Mich	15,010	13	1	......	36	......	3	......	......	......
Anniston, Ala	14,112	......	......	......	......	......	1	......	2	......
Appleton, Wis	17,834	......	......	......	......	......	3	1	......	......
Asbury Park, N. J	14,007	2	......	......	......	......	......	......	......	1
Barre, Vt	12,160	4	......	......	......	......	......	......	......	......
Beaver Falls, Pa	13,532	......	......	......	......	......	2	......	......	......
Bedford, Ind	10,349	2	......	......	......	......	......	......	......	1
Beloit, Wis	18,072	......	......	......	12	......	2	......	......	1
Berlin, N. H	13,599	3	......	......	......	......	......	......	......	......
Billings, Mont	14,422	......	......	......	3	......	3	......	......	......
Bloomington, Ind	11,383	6	......	......	......	......	......	1	......	......
Braddock, Pa	21,685	5	......	......	1	......	3	......	......	......
Burlington, Vt	21,617	6	1	......	......	......	......	......	......	......
Cairo, Ill	15,794	14	......	......	1	......	......	......	......	2
Chanute, Kans	12,455	......	......	......	4	......	......	......	1	......
Chillicothe, Ohio	15,470	3	......	......	17	......	3	......	......	......
Clinton, Mass	¹13,075	3	......	......	11	......	1	......	2	......
Coffeyville, Kans	17,548	......	1	......	3	......	......	......	......	......
Concord, N. H	22,669	13	......	......	1	......	......	......	......	......
Corpus Christi, Tex	10,432	1	1	......	......	......	......	......	1	......
Corsicana, Tex	10,022	5	1	......	15	......	......	......	4	1
Crawfordsville, Ind	11,164	2	6	......	......	......	......	......	......	......
Dover, N. H	13,272	6	......	......	......	......	......	......	......	......
East Providence, R. I	18,113	......	......	......	1	......	......	......	......	......
Eau Claire, Wis	18,807	......	......	......	36	......	......	......	......	......
Elwood, Ind	¹11,028	......	......	......	1	......	......	......	......	......
Fargo, N. Dak	17,389	3	1	......	2	......	......	......	......	......
Fort Scott, Kans	10,550	12	......	......	4	......	......	......	......	......
Galesburg, Ill	24,276	10	......	......	12	......	......	......	......	1
Grand Forks, N. Dak	15,837	14	......	......	......	......	......	1	......	......
Greeley, Colo	11,420	5	......	......	......	......	5	......	......	......
Greensboro, N. C	19,577	2	......	......	......	......	......	......	2	......
Greenville, S. C	18,181	6	......	......	......	......	......	......	......	......
Hackensack, N. J	16,945	7	1	......	10	......	2	......	......	......
Harrison, N. J	16,950	......	2	......	2	......	......	......	......	......
Hattiesburg, Miss	16,482	......	......	......	......	......	1	......	6	......
Independence, Kans	14,506	3	......	......	1	......	......	......	......	1
Janesville, Wis	14,399	4	......	......	......	......	4	......	......	......
Kearny, N. J	23,599	10	......	......	24	......	1	......	......	......
Kokomo, Ind	20,930	5	3	......	......	......	......	......	......	2
La Fayette, Ind	21,296	8	1	......	1	......	......	......	1	......
Leavenworth, Kans	¹19,363	6	3	......	15	......	3	......	1	......
Lincoln, R. I	19,383	2	......	......	......	......	......	......	......	1

¹ Population Apr. 15, 1910; no estimate made.

DIPHTHERIA, MEASLES, SCARLET FEVER, AND TUBERCULOSIS—
Continued.

City Reports for Week Ended Apr. 6, 1918—Continued.

City.	Population as of July 1, 1914 (estimated by U. S. Census Bureau).	Total deaths from all causes.	Diphtheria.		Measles.		Scarlet fever.		Tuberculosis.	
			Cases.	Deaths.	Cases.	Deaths.	Cases.	Deaths.	Cases.	Deaths.
From 10,000 to 25,000 inhabitants—Continued.										
Logansport, Ind.	21,046	9			1				1	
Long Branch, N. J.	15,398	1								
Manitowoc, Wis.	13,805	2								
Marinette, Wis.	¹14,610	1	1				1			
Marion, Ind.	19,834	3			3					
Marshall, Tex.	13,712	5	1						1	
Martinsburg, W. Va.	12,666		2							
Mason City, Iowa	14,457	1	1		2					
Melrose, Mass.	17,445	9			2		1		1	
Michigan City, Ind.	21,512	8	1		3		4	1		
Mishawaka, Ind.	16,385		1		3					
Missoula, Mont.	18,214	8					1			1
Morgantown, W. Va.	13,709	6								
Morristown, N. J.	13,284	7					1			
Moundsville, W. Va.	11,153	1								
Nanticoke Pa.	23,126	10	1							
New Albany, Ind.	23,629	10								3
Newburyport, Mass.	15,243	5			2				1	
New Castle, Ind.	13,241	3					3			
New London, Conn.	20,985	13	1		1		3		1	
North Adams, Mass.	¹22,019	9							4	
Northampton, Mass.	19,926	10							1	
North Little Rock, Ark.	14,907				1				1	1
North Yakima, Wash.	20,951				4		2		3	
Parkersburg, W. Va.	20,612	9			2		1			
Plainfield, N. J.	23,805	12			9				1	1
Pontiac, Mich.	17,524	8	1		5				1	1
Portsmouth, N. H.	11,666		1		5	1	4			
Raleigh, N. C.	20,127	8			8				1	1
Redlands, Cal.	14,000	3			31					
Reno, Nev.	14,869	5	·1							
Richmond, Ind.	24,697	9			1				3	
Rocky Mount, N. C.	12,067	7			1				1	2
Rutland, Vt.	14,831	5							1	1
Sandusky, Ohio	20,193	10								1
Saratoga Springs, N.Y.	13,821	3			1					
Shelbyville, Ind.	10,965	4								
Spartanburg, S. C.	21,365	10			4				1	
Steelton, Pa.	15,548	3			2					
Trinidad, Colo.	13,875				3					
Vancouver, Wash.	13,180				30		1			
Wausau, Wis.	19,239	3			28		2	1		
Washington, Pa.	21,618				44					
West Orange, N. J.	13,550	3	1		26					2
Wilkinsburg, Pa.	23,228	13	1		25		2			1
Woburn, Mass.	15,969	7								

¹ Population Apr. 15, 1910; no estimate made.

FOREIGN.

CHINA.

Plague—Anhwei Province.

An outbreak of pneumonic plague was reported February 27, 1918, in Anhwei Province, China, with 9 fatal cases notified at Fengyang-hsien, and 1 fatal case at Pengpu.

GUATEMALA.

Yellow Fever—Retalhuleu.

Yellow fever was reported present in Guatemala, April 22, at Retalhuleu, a town situated on the Guatemala Central Railroad and about 25 miles from the port of Champerico.

MEXICO.

Yellow Fever—Merida.

A fatal case of yellow fever was notified at Merida, State of Yucatan, Mexico, April 18, 1918.

PORTUGAL.

Further Relative to Typhus Fever—Oporto.[1]

Typhus fever has been reported at Oporto, Portugal, as follows: Month of December, 1917, 23 cases; period January 1 to March 8, 1918, 1,811 cases.

CHOLERA, PLAGUE, SMALLPOX, TYPHUS FEVER, AND YELLOW FEVER.

Reports Received During Week Ended Apr. 26, 1918.[2]

CHOLERA.

Place.	Date.	Cases.	Deaths.	Remarks.
India:				
Calcutta	Oct. 7–Nov. 10		43	
Madras	Jan. 13–19	6	3	
Philippine Islands:				
Provinces				Mar. 10–16, 1918: Cases, 75;
Bohol	Mar. 10–16	39	32	deaths, 57.
Capiz	do	3	1	
Davao	do	10	8	
Leyte	do	6	3	
Misamis	do	17	13	

[1] Public Health Reports, Mar. 1, 1918, p. 301.
[2] From medical officers of the Public Health Service, American consuls, and other sources.

CHOLERA, PLAGUE, SMALLPOX, TYPHUS FEVER, AND YELLOW FEVER—Continued.

Reports Received During Week Ended Apr. 26, 1918—Continued.

PLAGUE.

Place.	Date.	Cases.	Deaths.	Remarks.
Brazil:				
Bahia	Feb. 17–23	1	1	
China:				
Anhwei Province—				
Fengyanghsien	Feb. 27		9	Pneumonic.
Pengpu	do		1	Do.
Ecuador:				
Babahoyo	Feb. 1–15	1		
Duran	do	1	1	
Guayaquil	do	44	18	
Do	Mar. 1–15	20	7	
India:				
Madras Presidency	Jan. 13–19	1,746	1,368	Oct. 21–27, 1917: Cases, 1,158; deaths, 902. Nov. 18–24, 1917: Cases, 1,304; deaths, 1,057.
Indo-China:				
Cochin China—				
Saigon	Feb. 18–21	19	13	
Java:				
East Java				Oct. 8–Dec. 31, 1917: Cases, 196; deaths, 193.
Kediri	Oct. 8–Dec. 31	1	1	
Madioen	do	49	49	
Samarang	do	110	109	
Surabaya	do	25	23	
Surakarta	do	11	11	

SMALLPOX.

Place.	Date.	Cases.	Deaths.	Remarks.
Algeria:				
Algiers	Feb. 1–28	11	1	
Canada:				
British Columbia—				
Winnipeg	Mar. 24–30	1		
Nova Scotia—				
Halifax	Mar. 31–Apr. 6	2		
Quebec—				
Montreal	Mar. 31–Apr. 6	2		
China:				
Chungking	Feb. 3–16			Present.
Dairen	Mar. 10–16	8	1	
Hankow	Feb. 25–Mar. 3	1		
Nanking	Feb. 24–Mar. 16			Epidemic.
Tientsin	Feb. 10–16	2		
Ecuador:				
Guayaquil	Feb. 1–15	3	3	
France:				
Paris	Feb. 25–Mar. 2	3	1	
Great Britain:				
Hull	Mar. 17–23	1		
Greece:				
Saloniki	Mar. 3–16		2	
India:				
Madras	Jan. 13–19	16	4	Nov. 19–24, 1917: Cases, 2.
Indo-China:				
Cochin-China—				
Saigon	Feb. 18–24	114	46	
Mexico:				
Mazatlan	Mar. 27–Apr. 2		1	
Mexico City	Mar. 10–30	29		
Philippine Islands:				
Manila	Mar. 10–16	5	2	Varioloid, 23.
Porto Rico:				
San Juan	Mar. 25–31	1		Varioloid.
Spain:				
Valencia	Jan. 27–Feb. 2	1		

CHOLERA, PLAGUE, SMALLPOX, TYPHUS FEVER, AND YELLOW FEVER—Continued.

Reports Received During Week Ended Apr. 26, 1918—Continued.

TYPHUS FEVER.

Place.	Date.	Cases.	Deaths.	Remarks.
Egypt:				
Alexandria	Feb. 26–Mar. 11...	186	44	
Great Britain:				
Belfast	Mar. 17–30	4		
Dublin	Mar. 24–30	3		
Glasgow	Mar. 17–23	3	1	
Greece:				
Saloniki	Mar. 3–16		5	
Italy:				
San Remo	Mar. 10–16	2		
Mexico:				
Aguascalientes	Apr. 1–7		1	
Mexico City	Mar. 10–30	99		
Portugal:				
Oporto	Dec. 1–31	23	4	
Do	Jan. 1–Mar. 8	1,811	161	
Tunisia:				
Tunis	Mar. 9–15	29	4	Of these, 26 in outbreak in prison.
Union of South Africa:				
Cape of Good Hope State...	Sept. 10–Jan. 27...	4,248	866	European cases, 32; deaths, 5.

YELLOW FEVER.

Place.	Date.	Cases.	Deaths.	Remarks.
Ecuador:				
Babahoyo	Feb. 1–15	1	1	....
Guayaquil	...do	1		
Do	Mar. 1–15	1	1	
Milagro	Feb. 1–15	1	1	
Guatemala:				
Retalhuleu	Apr. 22			Present. About 25 miles from Champerico, Pacific port.
Mexico:				
Yucatan, State—				
Merida	Apr. 18	1	1	

Reports Received from Dec. 29, 1917, to Apr. 19, 1918.

CHOLERA.

Place.	Date.	Cases.	Deaths.	Remarks.
China:				
Antung	Nov. 26–Dec. 2....	3	1	
India:				
Bombay	Oct. 28–Dec. 15....	19	14	
Do	Dec. 30–Jan. 26....	200	170	
Calcutta	Sept. 16–Dec. 15..		92	
Do	Dec. 30–Jan. 26....		24	
Karachi	...do	25	6	
Madras	Nov. 25–Dec. 22..	2	2	
Do	Dec. 30–Feb. 2....	29	14	
Rangoon	Nov. 4–Dec. 22....	5	5	
Do	Dec. 30–Jan. 5.....	1	1	
Indo-China:				
Provinces				Sept. 1–Nov. 30, 1917: Cases, 152; deaths, 89.
Anam	Sept. 1–Nov. 30...	18	13	
Cambodia	...do	72	52	
Cochin-China	...do	50	22	
Saigon	Nov. 22–Dec. 9....	4	3	
Do	Feb. 4–17	4		
Kwang-Chow-Wan	Sept. 1–30	10	2	
Java:				
East Java	Oct. 28–Nov. 3....	1	1	
West Java				Oct. 19–Dec. 27, 1917: Cases, 108; deaths, 56. Dec. 28, 1917–Jan. 31, 1918: Cases, 27; deaths, 7.
Batavia	Oct. 19–Dec. 27....	49	23	
Do	Dec. 28–Jan. 31....	24	1	

CHOLERA, PLAGUE, SMALLPOX, TYPHUS FEVER, AND YELLOW FEVER—Continued.

Reports Received from Dec. 29, 1917, to Apr. 19, 1918—Continued.

CHOLERA—Continued.

Place.	Date.	Cases.	Deaths.	Remarks.
Persia:				
Mazanderan Province......				July 30–Sept. 3, 1917: Cases, 384; deaths, 276.
Achraf................	July 30–Aug. 16...	90	88	
Astrabad.............	July 31............			Present.
Borfrush.............	July 1–Aug. 16....	39	25	
Chahmirzad..........				25 cases reported July 31, 1917.
Chahrastagh.........	June 15–July 25...	10	8	
Charoud.............	Aug. 26–Sept. 3...	4	2	
Damghan.............	Aug. 26............			Present.
Kharek..............	May 28–June 11...	21	13	
Meched.............	Aug. 18–Sept. 2...	174	82	
Ouzoun Dare........	Aug. 8.............			Do.
Sabzevar............	Aug. 24............			Do.
Sari................	July 3–29..........	273	144	
Semman.............	Aug. 31–Sept. 2...	14	5	
Yekchambe-Bazar....	June 3.............	6		
Philippine Islands:				
Provinces...........				Nov. 18–Dec. 29, 1917: Cases, 1,053; deaths, 663. Dec. 30, 1917–Mar. 2, 1918: Cases, 1,258; deaths, 796.
Antique.............	Nov. 18–Dec. 1...	48	32	
Do................	Feb. 3–9...........	4	4	
Bohol...............	Nov. 18–Dec. 29...	169	111	
Do................	Dec. 30–Mar. 2....	339	274	
Capiz...............	Nov. 25–Dec. 29...	27	21	
Do................	Dec. 30–Mar. 2....	202	168	
Cebu...............	Dec. 23–29.........	3		
Do................	Dec. 30–Mar. 2....	79	42	
Iloilo..............	Nov. 25–Dec. 29...	179	135	
Do................	Dec. 30–Mar. 2....	97	63	
Leyte..............	Nov. 25–Dec. 22...	13	12	
Do................	Feb. 3–Mar. 2.....	38	33	
Mindanao...........	Nov. 25–Dec. 29...	337	196	
Do................	Dec. 30–Feb. 9....	351	220	
Misamis............	Feb. 24–Mar. 2....	33	21	
Occidental Negros...	Nov. 25–Dec. 22...	177	123	
Do................	Jan. 13–Mar. 2....	88	57	
Oriental Negros.....	Nov. 25–Dec. 29...	99	62	
Do................	Dec. 30–Feb. 16...	17	14	
Romblon............	Nov. 25–Dec. 1....	1	1	
Surigao............	Feb. 24–Mar. 2....	8	5	
Zamboanga..........	.....do...........	12	7	
Siam:				
Bangkok............	Sept. 16–22........	1	1	
Turkey in Asia:				
Bagdad.............	Nov. 1–15.........		40	

PLAGUE.

Place.	Date.	Cases.	Deaths.	Remarks.
Brazil:				
Bahia.............	Nov. 4–Dec. 15....	4	4	.... ..
Do...............	Dec. 30–Jan. 12....	3	2	
Rio de Janeiro............	Dec. 23–29.........	1		....
Do...............	Jan. 6–12..........	1	1	
British Gold Coast:				... ..
Axim............	Jan. 8.............			Present.
Ceylon:				
Colombo...........	Oct. 14–Dec. 1.....	14	13	. ...
Do...............	Dec. 30–Jan. 19....	7	5	
China:				
North China.......				Present in January, 1918; pneumonic form.
Chili Province—				
Kalgan.........				Vicinity. Present in February, 1918.
Shansi Province......				Present in February, 1918; 116 cases estimated.
Ecuador..............				Sept. 1–Nov. 30, 1917: Cases, 68; deaths, 24. Reported outbreak occuring about Jan. 17, 1918.
Guayaquil...........	Sept. 1–30........	3	1	
Do...............	Oct. 1–31.........	20	8	
Do...............	Nov. 1–30.........	45	15	
Egypt...............				Jan. 1–Nov. 15, 1917: Cases, 735; deaths, 806.
Alexandria..........	Jan 14 28.........	1	2	
Port Said...........	July 23 29........	1	2	

CHOLERA, PLAGUE, SMALLPOX, TYPHUS FEVER, AND YELLOW FEVER—Continued.

Reports Received from Dec. 29, 1917, to Apr. 19, 1918—Continued.

PLAGUE—Continued.

Place.	Date.	Cases.	Deaths.	Remarks.
India...				Sept. 16-Dec. 29, 1917: Cases, 228,834; deaths, 174,743. Dec. 30, 1917-Jan. 26, 1918: Cases, 123,934; deaths, 98,950.
Bassein...	Dec. 9-29...		8	
Do...	Dec. 30-Jan. 19...		14	
Bombay...	Oct. 28-Dec. 29...	147	123	
Do...	Dec. 30-Jan. 26...	81	59	
Calcutta...	Sept. 16-29...		2	
Do...	Dec. 30-Jan. 12...		3	
Henzada...	Oct. 21-27...		1	
Do...	Jan. 5-19...		5	
Karachi...	Oct. 21-Dec. 29...	27	20	
Do...	Dec. 30-Jan. 26...	16	14	
Madras Presidency...	Oct. 31-Nov. 17...	3,294	2,560	
Do...	Jan. 6-Feb. 2...	5,318	4,060	
Mandalay...	Oct. 14-Nov. 17...		89	
Do...	Dec. 30-Jan. 12...		236	
Myingyan...	....do...		110	
Prome...	Jan. 5-12...		1	
Rangoon...	Oct. 21-Dec. 22...		56	
Do...	Dec. 30-Jan. 26...	79	74	
Toungoo...	Dec. 9-29...		5	
Do...	Dec. 30-Jan. 19...		4	
Indo-China:				Sept. 1-Nov. 30, 1917: Cases, 89; deaths, 68.
Provinces...				
Anam...	Sept. 1-Nov. 30...	28	25	
Cambodia...	...do...	39	28	
Cochin-China...	...do...	22	15	
Saigon...	Oct. 31-Dec. 23...	17	6	
Do...	Dec. 31-Feb. 17...	55	18	
Java:				Oct. 27-Dec. 31, 1917: Cases, 221; deaths, 217.
East Java...				Jan. 1-14, 1918: Cases, 22; deaths, 21.
Do...				
Surabaya...	Nov. 4-Dec. 31...	6	6	
Do...	Jan. 7-14...	10	10	
West Java...				Nov. 25-Dec. 9, 1917: Cases, 45; deaths, 45. Dec. 1, 1917-Jan. 15, 1918: Cases, 106.
Peru:				
Ancachs Department—				
Casma...	Dec. 1-Jan. 15...	2		
Lambayeque Department...	...do...	22		At Chiclayo, Ferrenafe, Jayanca, Lambayeque.
Libertad Department...	...do...	72		At Guadalupe, Mansiche, Pacasmayo, Salaverry, San Jose, San Pedro, and country district of Trujillo.
Lima Department...	...do...	9		City and country.
Piura Department—				
Catacaos...	...do...	1		
Senegal:				
St. Louis...	Feb. 2...			Present.
Siam:				
Bangkok...	Sept. 16-Dec. 23...	13	9	
Do...	Jan. 13-Feb. 9...	15	11	
Straits Settlements:				
Singapore...	Oct. 28-Dec 29...	5	7	
Do...	Jan. 6-Feb. 16...	29	28	

SMALLPOX.

Place.	Date.	Cases.	Deaths.	Remarks.
Algeria:				
Algiers...	Nov. 1-Dec. 31...	3	1	
Do...	Jan. 1-31...	2		
Australia:				
New South Wales...				July 12-Dec. 20, 1917: Cases, 36. Jan. 4-17, 1918: Case, 1. Newcastle district.
Abermain...	Oct. 25-Nov. 29...	3		
Cessnock...	July 12-Oct. 11...	7		
Eumangla...	Aug. 15...	1		
Kurri Kurri...	Dec. 5-20...	2		
Mungindi...	Aug. 13...	1		
Warren...	July 12-Oct. 25...	22		
Do...	Jan. 1-17...	1		

CHOLERA, PLAGUE, SMALLPOX, TYPHUS FEVER, AND YELLOW FEVER—Continued.

Reports Received from Dec. 29, 1917, to Apr. 19, 1918—Continued.

SMALLPOX—Continued.

Place.	Date.	Cases.	Deaths.	Remarks.
Brazil:				
Bahia	Nov. 10–Dec. 8....	3		
Pernambuco	Nov. 1–15....	1		
Rio de Janeiro	Sept. 30–Dec. 29...	703	190	
Do	Dec. 30–Mar. 9...	281	83	
Sao Paulo	Oct. 29–Nov. 4....		2	
Canada:				
British Columbia—				
Vancouver	Jan. 13–Mar. 9....	5		
Victoria	Jan. 7–Feb. 2....	2		
Winnipeg	Dec. 30–Jan. 5....	1		
New Brunswick—				
Kent County	Dec. 4.			Outbreak. On main line Canadian Ry., 25 miles north of Moncton.
Do	Jan. 22	40		In 7 localities.
Northumberland County.	.....do	41		In 5 localities.
Restigouche County	Jan. 18	60		
St. John County—				
St. John	Mar. 3–Apr. 6....	5		
Victoria County	Jan. 22	10		At Limestone and a lumber camp.
Westmoreland County—				
Moncton	Jan. 20–Apr. 6....	16		
York County	Jan. 22	8		
Nova Scotia—				
Halifax	Feb. 24–Mar. 30...	3		
Sydney	Feb. 3–Apr. 6....	15		
Ontario—				
Arnprior	Mar. 31–Apr. 6....		1	
Hamilton	Dec. 16–22....	1		
Do	Jan. 13–19....	2		
Ottawa	Mar. 4–24....	5		
Sarnia	Dec. 9–15....	1		
Do	Jan 6–Mar. 30....	32		
Toronto	Feb. 10–Apr. 6....	2		
Windsor	Dec. 30–Jan. 5....	1		
Prince Edward Island—				
Charlottetown	Feb. 7–13....	1		
Quebec—				
Montreal	Dec. 16–Jan. 5....	5		
Do	Jan. 6–Mar. 30....	10		
China:				
Amoy	Oct. 22–Dec. 30....			Present.
Do	Dec. 31–Feb. 10....			Do.
Antung	Dec. 2–23....	13	2	
Do	Jan. 7–Feb. 17....	6	2	
Changsha	Jan. 28–Mar. 10....		1	
Chefoo	Jan. 27–Feb. 9....			Do.
Chungking	Nov. 11–Dec. 29....			Do.
Do	Dec. 30–Feb. 2....			Do.
Dairen	Nov. 18–Dec. 22....	3	1	
Do	Dec. 30–Mar. 2....	89	2	
Harbin	May 14–June 30...	20		Chinese Eastern Ry.
Do	July 1–Dec. 2....	7		Do.
Hongkong	Dec. 23–29....	1		
Do	Jan. 26–Feb. 9....	6	1	
Hungtahotze Station	Oct. 28–Nov. 4....	1		Do.
Manchuria Station	May 14–June 30...	6		Do.
Do	July 1–Dec. 2....	3		Do.
Mukden	Nov. 11–24....			Present.
Nanking	Feb. 3–23....			Epidemic.
Shanghai	Nov. 18–Dec. 23...	41	91	Cases, foreign; deaths among natives.
Do	Dec. 31–Mar. 10...	36	106	Do.
Swatow	Jan. 18.			Unusually prevalent.
Tientsin	Nov. 11–Dec. 22...	13		
Do	Dec. 30–Mar. 9....	25		
Tsingtau	Feb. 4–23....	3		
Cuba:				
Habana	Jan. 7	1		Nov. 8, 1917: 1 case from Coruna; Dec. 5, 1917, 1 case.
Marianao	Jan. 8	1		6 miles distant from Habana.

CHOLERA, PLAGUE, SMALLPOX, TYPHUS FEVER, AND YELLOW FEVER—Continued.

Reports Received from Dec. 29, 1917, to Apr. 19, 1918—Continued.

SMALLPOX—Continued.

Place.	Date.	Cases.	Deaths.	Remarks.
Ecuador:				Sept. 1–Nov. 30, 1917: Cases, 26;
Guayaquil	Sept. 1–30	8		deaths, 2.
Do	Oct. 1–31	14	1	
Do	Nov. 1–30	4	1	
Egypt:				
Alexandria	Nov. 12–18	2	1	
Do	Jan. 8–Feb. 28	5		
Cairo	July 23–Nov. 18	6	1	
France:				
Lyon	Nov. 18–Dec. 16	6	3	
Do	Jan. 7–Feb. 17	11	2	
Marseille	Jan. 1–31		2	
Paris	Jan. 27–Feb. 23	2		
Great Britain:				
Cardiff	Feb. 3–9	4		
Greece:				
Saloniki	Jan. 27–Feb. 9		7	
Honduras:				
Santa Barbara Department	Jan. 1–7			Present in interior.
India:				
Bombay	Oct. 21–Dec. 29	50	12	
Do	Dec. 31–Jan. 26	26	5	
Karachi	Nov. 18–Dec. 29	4	2	Nov. 11–16, 1917: 10 cases with 4
Madras	Oct. 31–Dec. 29	18	8	deaths; imported on s. s. Mc-
Do	Dec. 30–Feb. 2	80	28	nessa from Basreh.
Rangoon	Oct. 28–Dec. 22	6	1	
Do	Dec. 30–Jan. 26	7	2	
Indo-China:				
Provinces				Sept. 1–Nov. 30, 1917: Cases, 546;
Anam	Sept. 1–Nov. 30	163	25	deaths, 146.
Cambodia	do	16	8	
Cochin-China	do	353	108	
Saigon	Oct. 20–Dec. 30	120	26	
Do	Dec. 31–Feb. 17	290	100	· · ·
Laos	Oct. 1–31	1		
Do	Jan. 26–Feb. 3	1	1	
Tonkin	Sept. 1–Oct. 31	9	4	
Do	Jan. 26–Feb. 3	3		
Italy:				
Castellamare	Dec. 10	2		Among refugees.
Florence	Dec. 1–15	17	4	
Genoa	Dec. 2–31	11	3	
Do	Jan. 2–31	30	2	
Leghorn	Jan. 7–Mar. 10	32	7	
Messina	Jan. 3–19	1		
Milan				Oct. 1–Dec. 31, 1917: Cases, 32.
Naples	To Dec. 10	2		Among refugees.
Taormina	Jan. 20–Feb. 9	6		
Turin	Oct. 29–Dec. 29	123	120	· · ·
Do	Jan. 21–Mar. 3	56	3	
Japan:				
Nagasaki	Jan. 14–Mar. 10	6	2	
Taihoku	Dec. 15–21	1		Island of Taiwan (Formosa).
Do	Jan. 8–Mar. 11	25	5	Do.
Tokyo	Feb. 11–Mar. 6	26		City and suburbs.
Yokohama	Jan. 17–Feb. 3	4		
Java:				
East Java	Oct. 7–Dec. 23	50		Dec. 25–31, 1917: Cases, 7. Jan.
Surabaya	Dec. 25–31	1		1–14, 1918: Cases, 3.
Mid-Java:				Oct. 10–Nov. 26, 1917: Cases, 86;
Samarang	Nov. 6–Dec. 12	4	1	death, 1. Dec. 28, 1917–Jan. 28,
				1918: Cases, 23.
West Java:				Oct. 19–Dec. 27, 1917: Cases, 231;
Batavia	Nov. 2–8	1		deaths, 36. Dec. 28, 1917–Jan.
				31, 1918: Cases, 116; deaths, 17.
Mexico:				
Aguascalientes	Feb. 4–17		2	
Ciudad Juarez	Mar. 3–23	2	1	
Mazatlan	Dec. 5–11		1	
Do	Jan. 29–Mar. 5	4	3	
Mexico City	Nov. 11–Dec. 29	16		
Do	Dec. 30–Mar. 9	61		
Piedras Negras	Jan. 11	200		
Vera Cruz	Jan. 20–Mar. 2	7	3	

CHOLERA, PLAGUE, SMALLPOX, TYPHUS FEVER, AND YELLOW FEVER—Continued.

Reports Received from Dec. 29, 1917, to Apr. 19, 1918—Continued.

SMALLPOX—Continued.

Place.	Date.	Cases.	Deaths.	Remarks.
Newfoundland:				
St. Johns...................	Dec. 8–Jan. 4......	29	....	
Do......................	Jan. 5–Mar. 29.....	61	....	
Trepassey.................	Jan. 4............	....	....	Outbreak with 11 cases reported.
Philippine Islands:				
Manila...................	Oct 28–Dec. 8......	5	....	
Do......................	Jan. 13–Mar. 2.....	15	2	Varioloid, 33.
Porto Rico:				
San Juan.................	Jan. 28–Mar. 17....	32	....	Varioloid.
Portugal:				
Lisbon...................	Nov. 4–Dec. 15....	2	....	
Do......................	Dec. 30–Mar. 16...	6	....	
Portuguese East Africa:				
Lourenço Marques.........	Aug. 1–Dec. 31....	....	16	
Russia:				
Archangel.................	Sept. 1–Oct. 31....	7	....	
Moscow...................	Aug. 26–Oct. 6.....	22	2	
Petrograd.................	Aug. 31–Nov. 18...	76	3	
Siam:				
Bangkok..................	Nov. 25–Dec. 1....	1	1	
Do......................	Jan. 6–19.........	1	1	
Spain:				
Coruna...................	Dec. 2–15.........	....	4	
Do......................	Jan. 20–Feb. 23....	....	5	
Madrid...................		....	....	Jan. 1–Dec. 31, 1917: Deaths, 77
Seville...................	Oct. 1–Dec. 30.....	....	66	
Do......................	Jan. 1–31.........	....	20	
Straits Settlements:				
Singapore................	Nov. 25–Dec. 1....	1	1	
Do......................	Dec. 30–Jan. 5....	1	....	
Tunisia:				
Tunis....................	Dec. 14–20........	1	....	
Turkey in Asia:				
Bagdad...................		....	....	Present in November, 1917.
Union of South Africa:				
Cape of Good Hope State...	Oct. 1–Dec. 31.....	28	....	
East Liverpool............	Jan. 20–26........	1	....	Varioloid.
Venezuela:				
Maracaibo................	Dec. 2–8..........	....	1	

TYPHUS FEVER.

Place.	Date.	Cases.	Deaths.	Remarks.
Algeria:				
Algiers...................	Nov. 1–Dec. 31....	2	1	
Argentina:				
Rosario..................	Dec. 1–31.........	....	1	
Australia:				
South Australia...........		....	....	Nov. 11–17, 1917: Cases, 1.
Brazil:				
Rio de Janeiro............	Oct. 28–Dec. 1.....	7	....	
Canada:				
Ontario—				
Kingston...............	Dec. 2–8..........	3	....	
Quebec—				
Montreal...............	Dec. 16–22........	2	1	
China:				
Antung..................	Dec. 3–30.........	13	1	
Do......................	Dec. 31–Jan. 27....	2	2	
Chosen (Formosa):				
Seoul....................	Nov. 1–20.........	1	....	
Do......................	Feb. 1–28.........	3	2	
Egypt:				
Alexandria................	Nov. 8–Dec. 28....	57	15	
Do......................	Jan. 8–Feb. 25....	223	54	
Cairo	July 23–Dec. 16....	137	70	
Port Said................	July 30–Nov. 11...	5	5	
France:				
Marseille.................	Dec. 1–31.........	....	1	
Great Britain:				
Belfast	Feb. 10–Mar. 16...	17	3	
Glasgow.................	Dec. 21...........	1	....	
Do	Jan. 20–Mar. 9.....	9	....	
Manchester...............	Dec. 2–8..........	1	....	

CHOLERA, PLAGUE, SMALLPOX, TYPHUS FEVER, AND YELLOW FEVER—Continued.

Reports Received from Dec. 29, 1917, to Apr. 19, 1918—Continued

TYPHUS FEVER—Continued.

Place.	Date.	Cases.	Deaths.	Remarks.
Greece:				
Arta........................	Feb. 10............	2	....	
Janina......................	Feb. 14............	110	....	Jan. 27, epidemic.
Saloniki....................	Nov. 11–Dec. 29...	....	72	
Do.......................	Dec. 30–Mar. 2....	....	22	
Japan:				
Nagasaki....................	Nov. 26–Dec. 16...	5	5	
Do.......................	Jan. 7–Mar. 10.....	13	5	
Java:				
East Java...................	....	....	....	Oct. 15–Dec. 31, 1917: Cases, 39;
Surabaya.................	Dec. 17–31.........	9	1	deaths, 7. Jan. 1–14, 1918:
Do....................	Jan. 1–14.........	10	1	Cases, 11; deaths, 2.
Mid-Java....................				Oct. 10 Dec. 26, 1917: Cases, 63;
Samarang.................	Oct. 9–Dec. 26....	20	2	deaths, 2. Dec. 28, 1917–Jan.
Do....................	Dec. 27–Jan. 15...	18		23, 1918: Cases, 11.
West Java...................				Oct. 19–Dec .27, 1917: Cases, 94;
Batavia..................	Oct. 19–Dec. 27...	59	15	deaths, 17. Dec. 28, 1917–Jan
Do....................	Dec. 28–Jan. 31...	27	1	31, 1918: Cases, 53; death, 1.
Mexico:				
Aguascalientes.............	Dec. 15............	....	2	
Do.......................	Jan. 21–Mar. 30....	....	14	
Durango State—				
Guanacevi...............	Feb. 11............	....	....	Epidemic.
Mexico City................	Nov. 11–Dec. 29...	476	....	
Do.......................	Dec. 30–Mar. 9....	528	....	
Norway:				
Bergen......................	Feb. 1–16..........	3	....	
Portugal:				
Lisbon......................	Mar. 3–16..........	8	....	Feb. 21: Present.
Oporto......................	Feb. 21............	....	....	Epidemic. Dec. 24, 1917–Mar. 9,
				1918: About 250 cases reported.
Russia:				
Archangel...................	Sept. 1–14.........	7	2	
Moscow.....................	Aug. 26–Oct. 6....	49	2	
Petrograd...................	Aug. 31–Nov. 18...	32	....	
Do.......................	Feb. 2.............	....	....	Present.
Vladivostok.................	Oct. 29–Nov. 4....	12	1	
Spain:				
Corcubion...................	Apr. 11............	....	....	Present. Province of Coruna,
				west coast.
Sweden:				
Goteborg....................	Nov. 18–Dec. 15...	2	....	
Switzerland:				
Basel.......................	Jan. 6–19..........	1	1	
Zurich......................	Nov. 9–15..........	2	....	
Do.......................	Jan. 13–19.........	2	....	
Tunisia:				
Tunis.......................	Nov. 30–Dec. 6.....	....	1	
Do.......................	Feb. 9–Mar. 8.....	6	1	
Union of South Africa:				
Cape of Good Hope State...	Sept. 10–Dec. 30...	4,035	830	Sept. 10–Nov. 25, 1917: Cases, 3,724 (European, 31; native, 3,693); deaths, 761 (European, 5; native, 756). Total to Jan. 13, 1918: Cases, 4,158 (European, 32; native, 4,126); deaths, 854 (European, 5; native, 849).
Natal.......................	....	....	....	From date of outbreak in December, 1917, to Jan. 27, 1918: Cases, 34; deaths, 10.

YELLOW FEVER.

Ecuador........................	....	....	....	Sept. 1–Nov. 30, 1917: Cases, 5;
Guayaquil....................	Sept. 1–30.........	1	1	deaths, 3.
Do.......................	Oct. 1–31..........	1	....	
Do.......................	Nov. 1–30..........	2	2	
Yaguachi....................	...do..............	1	....	
Honduras:				
Tegucigalpa.................	Dec. 16–22.........	....	1	
Do.......................	Jan. 6–19..........	....	1	

×

PUBLIC HEALTH REPORTS

VOL. 33	MAY 3, 1918	No. 18

The Dietary Deficiency of Cereal Foods with Reference to Their Content in "Antineuritic Vitamine."

By CARL VOEGTLIN, G. C. LAKE, and C. N. MYERS, Division of Pharmacology, Hygienic Laboratory, United States Public Health Service, Washington, D. C.

Introduction.—Recent experimental work has called attention to the importance of certain so-called accessory foods or vitamines in their relation to proper nutrition. The work of Stepp, Hopkins, Funk, Osborne and Mendel, McCollum and Davis, and others, has demonstrated that a diet is not complete and does not permit of adequate nutrition unless it contains sufficient amounts of two accessory substances. One of these substances is essential in the prevention and cure of beriberi in man or polyneuritis of fowls, and has been termed the "antineuritic vitamine" or the water soluble B. The other substance occurs in certain foods rich in fat (butter, etc.), and has been designated as fat soluble A by McCollum and his coworkers.

This paper deals with the occurrence of the antineuritic vitamine in foods derived from wheat or corn. Researches of a similar nature have been made by other investigators, and the fact has been thoroughly established that all natural cereals contain an abundance of antineuritic vitamine, an amount considerably in excess of that needed when these cereals form the exclusive diet of animals.

Valuable as these investigations are in regard to the feeding of animals and the purely scientific aspects of nutrition, the previous investigators have not sufficiently taken into consideration the fact that cereals in the form of the entire grain are only rarely consumed by man. The bulk of the cereal component of the diet of our people is represented by wheat or corn bread. Wheat and corn bread are largely prepared from flour or corn meal which represents only part of the wheat or corn kernel. The commonly used "patent" flour, for instance, contains only about 70 per cent of the wheat from which it is milled. The question, therefore, arises as to whether or not bread made from "white" flour or "highly milled" corn meal includes all the essential food elements contained in the intact grain.

The present paper reports a continuation of work done by others with respect to the antineuritic vitamine of corn and wheat products used in nutrition. In a succeeding paper certain other dietary attributes of these foods will be considered in their relation to growth.

Previous work.—Experimental and clinical work on the etiology of beriberi has demonstrated the fact that polished rice may give rise to beriberi in man and to polyneuritis in fowls when used to the more or less complete exclusion of other foods. It has, furthermore, been shown that substitution of unpolished rice for polished rice prevents the occurrence of beriberi and polyneuritis. Moreover, it has been found that the rice polishings contained the antineuritic vitamine, the substance which is responsible for the prevention and cure of beriberi. Thus unquestionable proof was furnished that the "highly milled" (polished or white) rice has been deprived of an essential dietary element resident in the peripheral layers of the intact grain.

Because of these results with rice, the attention of investigators interested in this field was soon attracted to wheat bread. Thus Holst (1907), in experimental studies relating to ship beriberi and scurvy, carried out on pigeons a few experiments with rye and wheat bread, baked with yeast or baking powder. The pigeons on wheat bread developed symptoms and nerve degeneration characteristic of polyneuritis. The addition of yeast to the wheat flour seemed to delay the onset of the symptoms, but did not prevent a gradual loss of body weight (30 per cent). The pigeons fed on rye bread or whole wheat bread, however, lived for four months without showing any abnormalities. Holst does not mention the kind of wheat flour used in his experiments beyond stating that it was "the flour ordinarily used by Norwegian sailors in tropical waters."

Simpson and Edie (1911) describe a few additional experiments on the feeding of "whole wheat" bread and "white" bread to pigeons. On the "whole wheat" bread the birds continued active and well, and two pigeons paired and successfully hatched the two eggs. The pigeons fed "white" bread died after an average of 29 days with an average loss of weight of 26 per cent. Typical paralytic symptoms were observed in these animals and marked degenerative changes were found in their peripheral nerves. Several of these birds were treated when extremely weak with either yeast or beans. Great improvement in the condition of the birds followed this treatment.

The reports of Little (1912 and 1914) concerning his five years' experience with epidemics of beriberi in Newfoundland are very important, as they show that in this locality beriberi was due to a diet limited to "white" bread made from highly milled flour, molasses, a small quantity of fish, and tea. This author furthermore presents evidence to the effect that the substitution of "whole wheat" bread for the "white" bread was followed by a disappearance of the disease, in spite of the fact that the other dietary and hygienic conditions were apparently left unchanged.

At Little's suggestion, Ohler (1914) carried out a number of experiments with chickens, in order to furnish experimental proof for the contention that a more or less exclusive diet of "white" bread was the chief cause of the occurrence of beriberi in Newfoundland. Fourteen chickens fed on "white" bread, made from "highly milled" flour with or without the addition of yeast, died within 28 to 40 days. Before death the birds exhibited symptoms of polyneuritis, and histological examination of the peripheral nerves revealed considerable degeneration. Five fowls fed on "whole-wheat" bread and two on whole wheat lived in perfect health for 75 days, when the experiment was discontinued.

Similar experiments were carried out by Wellmann and Bass (1913) and by Voegtlin, Sullivan, and Myers (1916).

Nature of the present experiments.—Pigeons and chickens were used in these experiments for the reason that they are better adapted for feeding experiments with cereals than other animals. Only full-grown birds were used. The symptoms resulting from a deficiency of the diet in antineuritic vitamine are easily recognized in fowls, and curative experiments yield striking results. The observations made on birds were confirmed in experiments on dogs, hogs, and a large number of white mice (these results will be published elsewhere). As a rule, the birds were given as much of the various corn and wheat foods as they cared to eat. In a few experiments, by mistake they did not receive sufficient food, a fact which caused them to lose in body weight (experiments Nos. 18, 20, and 25). The appearance of polyneuritic symptoms was regarded as indicating that the particular food in question was deficient in antineuritic vitamine. The polyneuritic symptoms were always preceded by a gradual loss in body weight. The peripheral nerves of a large number of the birds were examined histologically at the end of the period of observation, and always confirmed the conclusions drawn from clinical observations. Birds exhibiting polyneuritic symptoms during life always showed marked myelin degeneration of their peripheral nerves.

The corn and wheat products were obtained in the open market and came from various modern roller mills, old-fashioned buhr mills and various bakeries.

As a rule, the total phosphorus pentoxide content of the dried products was determined, as it had been shown by other investigators that the phosphorus and vitamine contents of rice of various degrees of milling run roughly parallel.

In order definitely to prove that the symptoms observed in the animals kept on deficient foods were due to a deficient supply of antineuritic vitamine, some of the pigeons were treated after the onset of the disease with various vitamine preparations (Funk's vitamine fraction) obtained from brewer's yeast, ox liver, or rice polishings. Further evidence was obtained from protective experiments in which there was added to the deficient food a small quantity of a vitamine preparation. This material was prepared according to the method described by Seidell (1914). The so-called activated Lloyd's reagent consists of fuller's earth (Lloyd's reagent), which has been treated with autolyzed yeast filtrate. It contains an average of 2.3 per cent of total nitrogen, which is derived from the basic substances of autolyzed yeast filtrate.

As it was confirmed in the course of the investigation that white bread was deficient in antineuritic vitamine, a few experiments were made to determine the effect of adding an extract of "whole-wheat" bread to the diet of "white" bread. This extract was prepared as follows: Two hundred and eighty grams of "whole-wheat" bread were extracted twice at room temperature with one liter of 50 per cent alcohol containing 25 cubic centimeters of concentrated hydrochloric acid. The filtered extract was concentrated in vacuo to a small volume, so that 1 cubic centimeter of the extract corresponded to 1 gram of fresh "whole-wheat" bread. The extract was free from fat and contained 11.5 per cent of solids.

The animals were kept in wire cages, tap water being supplied daily and grit from time to time.

The bread was fed in the form in which it was received from the dealer. Water was added to the flour, which was made into cakes. The cakes were dried at 45° C. and broken up into pieces of suitable size.

Throughout this paper the words "highly milled" are meant to indicate that the product was milled in a manner to eliminate most of the superficial layers and the germ of the grain. "White" bread is the ordinary wheat bread made from "highly milled" flour. "Patent" flour is the word applied by the milling industry to a flour which is of very fine texture and almost white in appearance. It contains practically no bran or germ. By "old-fashioned" Graham flour is meant a wheat flour which is obtained by grinding wheat in buhrstone mills with the omission of bolting. "Whole-wheat" flour is a designation of a flour which contains the whole-wheat berry, with the exception of part of the bran. "First-clear" flour resembles "patent" flour but contains a small amount of the peripheral portions of the grain. Similar designations have been used for the corn foods. The following tables and charts will illustrate the main results obtained in this investigation.

EXPERIMENT 1.—*"Old-fashioned" Graham flour milled in the presence of one of authors (V) in an old-fashioned buhr mill in Spartanburg, S. C.*

[Appearance: Typical Graham flour, containing considerable bran and germ. P_2O_5 content: 0.866 per cent.]

(Beginning with the twenty-fifth day of the experiment, a similar Graham flour was substituted for the above product.)

No. of pigeon.	First appearance of polyneuritis.	Period of observation.	Change in body weight in per cent of original weight.	Notes.
		Days.		
308	No symptoms......................	118	+ 2	Sciatic normal.
309	.....do.........................	118	+ 9	Do.
312	.....do.........................	123	+21	Sciatic not examined.
313	.....do.........................	96	+12	Do.
311	.....do.........................	113	+13	Do.

Remarks.—On the 25th day of the experiment the food was changed to another old-fashioned Graham flour ($P_2O_5=0.82$ per cent), obtained from another buhrstone mill in Spartanburg, S. C. This mill had been in operation for at least 50 years. Slight changes were made in its power plant, substituting turbines for the "water wheels." The process of milling, however, was still the same as at the time of the opening of the mill.

Both of these flours contained sufficient antineuritic vitamine to prevent polyneuritic symptoms and loss of body weight. Their P_2O_5 content is almost as high as that of whole wheat.

EXPERIMENT 2.—*"Whole wheat flour" milled in St. Louis, Mo.*

[Appearance: Grayish white. P_2O_5 content: 0.61 per cent.]

No. of pigeon.	First appearance of polyneuritis.	Period of observation.	Change in body weight in per cent of original weight.	Notes.
		Days.		
332	No symptoms......................	90	+21	Sciatic normal.
333	.....do.........................	90	−28	Do.
336	.....do.........................	91	−33	Do.
337	.....do.........................	103	−22	Do.
335	.....do.........................	96	−36	Do.

Remarks.—Pigeon 337 died apparently from accidental causes, as the necropsy revealed a piece of copper wire, which had perforated the craw and prevented the animal from eating. The other pigeons appeared in perfect health until a few days previous to end of period of observation. No definite paralytic symptoms were observed in any of these birds and the histological examination of the sciatic nerves also yielded negative results.

This flour contained sufficient antineuritic vitamine to prevent polyneuritic symptoms and fatty degeneration of the peripheral nerves. Its P_2O_5 content is somewhat lower than that of whole wheat.

EXPERIMENT 3.—*Wheat flour obtained from old-fashioned buhr mill, Roebuck, S. C.*

[Appearance: White, with yellowish tinge; contains particles of bran. P_2O_5 content: 0.265 per cent.]

No. of pigeon.	First appearance of polyneuritis.	Period of observation.	Change in body weight in per cent of original weight.	Notes.
315	No definite symptoms..........	Died after 109 days......	−36	No treatment.
317	Twenty-second day.............	Died after 27 days......	−15	Do.
318	No definite symptoms..........	Killed after 158 days....	−28	Do.
319	No symptoms...................	......do................	+ 4	Do.

Remarks.—Sciatic nerves of pigeons 315 and 319 did not reveal any degenerative changes and were to all appearances normal. Sciatic nerve of pigeon 318 revealed a slight degeneration.

This flour represents a fairly "highly milled" product. It was bolted through a fine silk cloth, which eliminated a considerable part of the germ and bran. In physical appearance this flour is not as refined as "patent" flour. It obviously contains more antineuritic vitamine than "patent" flour but not as much as "whole-wheat" flour. The P_2O_5 content is also low.

EXPERIMENT 3a.—*Wheat flour obtained from old-fashioned buhr mill, Spartanburg, S. C.*

Appearance: White with yellowish tinge; contains small particles of bran. P_2O_5 content: 0.27 per cent.]

No. of pigeon.	First appearance of polyneuritis.	Period of observation.	Change in body weight in per cent of original weight.	Notes.
338	Remained well.................	Killed after 118 days.....	−13	Not treated.
339	No symptoms...................	Died after 102 days......	−12	Do.
340	Remained well.................	Killed after 118 days.....	− 6	Do.
341	...do........................	...do..................	− 5	Do.
343	Thirtieth day, doubtful........	Died after 38 days.......	−34	Do.

Remarks.—Sciatic nerve of pigeon 339 showed slight degeneration. There were never noticed any definite symptoms of polyneuritis in this bird. Sciatic nerve of pigeons 338 and 340 did not exhibit any degeneration; that of pigeon 341 revealed slight degeneration, although the bird seemed to be in perfect health when it was killed.

EXPERIMENT 4.—*"Patent wheat flour" obtained from a Maryland roller mill.*

[Appearance. Pure white; no bran can be detected. P_2O_5 content: 0.25 per cent.]

No. of pigeon.	First appearance of polyneuritis.	Period of observation.	Change in body weight in per cent of original weight.	Notes.
326	Twenty-second day.............	Died after 43 days......	−22	Relieved symptoms on thirtieth day by an extract of rice polishings.
327	Fifteenth day.................	Died after 67 days......	−44	Relieved symptoms on thirtieth and fifty-seventh days by yeast vitamine.
328	......do	Died after 26 days......	−21	Not treated.
329	Tenth day....................	Died after 16 days......	−31	Do.
330	...do......................	Died after 12 days......	− 7	Do.
331	Twenty-second day............	Died after 46 days......	−20	Relieved symptoms on twenty-eighth day by an extract of rice polishings.

Remarks.—Pigeon 326 received, on thirtieth day of experiment, 0.5 cubic centimeter of Funk's vitamine fraction from an extract of rice polishings. Bird was greatly improved as a result of this treatment, but gradually developed a relapse several days later. Pigeon 327 received, on thirtieth and fifty-seventh days of experiment, 0.5 cubic centimeter autolyzed yeast vitamine, prepared by means of Lloyd's reagent (dose equivalent to 40 cubic centimeters autolyzed yeast filtrate).

The pigeons of this series all developed polyneuritis within three weeks. The flour was "highly milled" and had a low phosphorus content. The administration of an active preparation of antineuritic vitamine promptly relieved the symptoms.

EXPERIMENT 5.—*"Patent" wheat flour obtained from a roller mill in Virginia.*

[Appearance: Pure white; no particles of bran or germ. P_2O_5 content: 0.20 per cent.]

No. of pigeon.	First appearance of polyneuritis.	Period of observation.	Change in body weight in per cent of original weight.	Notes.
344	Fifteenth day...................	Died after 29 days.......	−37	Not treated.
345	Twenty-second day..............	Died after 30 days.......	−34	Do.
346	Tenth day.....................	Died after 26 days.......	−43	Do.
347	Fifteenth day..................	Died after 39 days.......	−37	Do.
348	Tenth day.....................	Died after 36 days.......	−14	Temporary improvement after administration of "vitamine."
349	Fifteenth day..................	Died after 19 days.......	−28	Not treated.

Remarks.—All of the pigeons of this lot developed typical polyneuritis between the tenth and twenty-second days after feeding was begun, and died with marked loss in body weight. Pigeon 348 was given one dose of 0.3 cubic centimeter of a fluid antineuritic preparation, obtained from autolyzed brewers' yeast, which caused a temporary improvement in the symptoms.

EXPERIMENT 6.—*"Patent flour" milled in a Michigan roller mill.*

[Appearance: Pure white; contains no bran. P_2O_5 content: 0.206 per cent.]

No. of pigeon.	First appearance of polyneuritis.	Period of observation.	Change in body weight in per cent of original weight.	Notes.
320	Tenth day.....................	Died after 38 days.......	−27	Not treated.
321	Fifteenth day..................	.....do...................	−13	Do.
322	Eighteenth day................	Died after 34 days.......	−43	Symptoms relieved on the eighteenth day by a preparation made from rice polishings.
323	Fifteenth day..................	Died after 18 days......	−38	Not treated.
324	.....do.....................	Died after 40 days......	−30	Do.
325	.....do.....................	Died after 83 days.......	−43	Symptoms relieved on twentieth and thirty-third days by a preparation made from yeast.

Remarks.—Pigeon 322 received 0.5 cubic centimeter of a dilute extract of rice polishings (vitamine fraction), which caused complete disappearance of severe symptoms of paralysis. Pigeon 325 was given, on the twentieth day, 0.5 cubic centimeter of an extract of brewers' yeast (vitamine fraction); severe paralytic symptoms disappeared within 24 hours. On the thirty-third day another attack of polyneuritis was completely relieved by a dose of 1 cubic centimeter autolyzed yeast vitamine, prepared by means of Lloyd's reagent (dose equivalent to 40 cubic centimeters autolyzed yeast filtrate). The pigeon remained free from any symptoms after this treatment for about 25 days.

EXPERIMENT 7.—*"Straight patent flour" milled from winter wheat at a roller mill in South Carolina.*

[Appearance. White; contains a few particles of bran.　P₂O₅ content: 0.216 per cent.]

No. of pigeon.	First appearance of polyneuritis.	Period of observation.	Change in body weight in per cent of original weight.	Notes.
351	Twentieth day..................	Died after 36 days.......	−27	Not treated.
352	....do..................	Died after 38 days......	−39	Do.
353	Twenty-sixth day..............	Killed after 118 days.....	¹−34	Relieved symptoms on twenty-sixth day by a preparation made from ox liver. on thirty-fourth day with yeast preparation. Diet changed on Fortieth day.
354	Twentieth day	Died after 32 days.......	−28	Relieved symptoms on twenty-sixth day by a preparation made from ox liver.
350	Twenty-sixth day..............	Died after 57 days.......	−48	Not treated.

¹ Fortieth Day.

Remarks.—Diet of pigeon 353 was changed, on fortieth day of experiment, to a wheat flour obtained from an old-fashioned buhrmill in South Carolina. This change caused the pigeon to regain some of the lost weight (original weight 249 grams, weight at period of dietary change 165 grams; weight at end of experiment, 43 days later, 188 grams). Pigeon was killed after 118 days, being free from symptoms of polyneuritis. Sciatic nerve did not reveal any degenerated fibers.

This experiment, in conjunction with those preceding, shows that a "highly milled" flour with low phosphorus content leads to polyneuritis within about three weeks. The symptoms are due to a deficiency of this food in antineuritic vitamine, as demonstrated by the curative effect of a small quantity of an antineuritic extract from yeast or ox liver.

EXPERIMENT 8　*"Patent wheat flour" obtained from a Minnesota roller mill through the open market.*

[Appearance: Pure white; no bran can be detected.　P₂O₅ content: 0.25 per cent.]

No. of pigeon.	First appearance of polyneuritis.	Period of observation.	Change in body weight in per cent of original weight.	Notes.
		Days.		
1	Twentieth day..................	25	−39	Died of polyneuritis, sciatic degenerated.
2	Eighteenth day..................	37	−40	Do.
3	Thirty-first day..................	38	−33	Severe paralysis relieved with antineuritic material.
4	Twenty-second day..............	28	−35	Do.
5	Twelfth day	17	−22	Died of polyneuritis; sciatic degenerated.
6	Twenty-eighth day..............	36	−24	Do.

Remarks.—On this flour the birds developed polyneuritis in about the same time as on highly milled rice. Marked degeneration of the sciatic was found on histological examination. The P_2O_5 content of the flour was low (less than one-third that of "whole wheat").

EXPERIMENT 9.—"*White-wheat bread*" *obtained from a bakery in Washington, D. C.*

[Appearance: Good; no bran. P_2O_5 content: 0.26 per cent.]

No. of pigeon.	First appearance of polyneuritis.	Period of observation.	Change in body weight in per cent of original weight.	Notes.
		Days.		
37	Forty-second day.................	45	−36	Polyneuritis cured by extract of "whole-wheat bread."
38	Forty-fifth day....................	80	−42	Not treated; died of polyneuritis; sciatic degenerated.
39	Fifty-fourth day..................	64	−23	Severe polyneuritis cured by extract of "whole-wheat bread."
40	Eighteenth day...................	40	−38	Do.
41	Thirty-first day..................	35	−41	Not treated; died of polyneuritis; sciatic degenerated.
42	Seventeenth day.................	40	−39	Do.

Remarks.—The bread used in this experiment was made from a mixture of "patent" and "first clear" flour, yeast, sodium chloride, compound lard, molasses, and evaporated milk. The exact formulas could not be obtained. This bread had a low phosphorus content and led to polyneuritic symptoms in the pigeons of this series in about three to five weeks. It is seen that the incubation period is somewhat longer (three to five weeks) than in birds kept on "patent" flour (2 to 3 weeks). This incubation period is also longer than that observed when polished rice forms the exclusive diet of pigeons. Three of the pigeons were given an extract of the "whole-wheat" bread used in experiment 15. Chart 3 illustrates the gradual loss in body weight on a diet of white bread and the slow recovery after treatment with the extract of "whole-wheat" bread was begun. The addition of yeast and evaporated milk to the flour, in the process of bread making, did not seem to furnish sufficient antineuritic vitamine to prevent polyneuritis.

EXPERIMENT 10.—*White-wheat bread, ordinary baker's bread, purchased on the open market in Washington, D. C., and Spartanburg, S. C.*

[Appearance: White, contained no bran. P_2O_5 content: 0.26 and 0.19 per cent.]

No. of pigeon.	First appearance of polyneuritis.	Died after—	Change in body weight in per cent of original weight.
		Days.	
116	Thirty-second day..........................	32	Not determined.
120	Twentieth day.............................	21	Do.
300	Twenty-fifth day...........................	42	−15.
304	Twenty-first day...........................	29	−29.
305	Twenty-fourth day.........................	43	−4.
307	Twenty-fifth day...........................	46	−18.
401	Fourteenth day............................	15	Not determined.
402	Fortieth day...............................	40	Do.

Remarks.—From these experiments it would seem that the incubation period of polyneuritis is somewhat prolonged (about 14 days) as a result of the addition of yeast and evaporated milk to the highly milled flour in the process of bread making. Both yeast and milk are known to contain antineuritic vitamine.

Experiment 11.—*High grade "patent" wheat flour + Lloyd's reagent (inactive).* **This** *flour was obtained from a Minnesota roller mill and 1 per cent of Lloyd's reagent incorporated with it.*

[Appearance: White; no coarse particles. P₂O₅ content: 0.25 per cent.]

No. of pigeon.	First appearance of polyneuritis.	Period of observation.	Change in body weight in per cent of original weight.	Notes.
		Days.		
13	Thirty-first day..................	38	−43	Experiment discontinued after 38 days.
14	Thirty-eighth day................	38	−27	Do.
15	Twenty-fifth day.................	38	−40	Died of polyneuritis; sciatic nerve degenerated.
16	Thirty-first day..................	38	−38	Experiment discontinued after 38 days.
17	.....do...........................	38	−32	Do.
18	.....do...........................	54	−48	On fifty-fourth day pigeon was dying; killed with chloroform; sciatic degenerated.

Remarks.—This experiment shows that "patent" flour, with the addition of Lloyd's reagent (fuller's earth) which has not been activated by autolyzed yeast, does not prevent the appearance of polyneuritis in pigeons. These results are in marked contrast with experiments illustrated by chart 5.

May 3, 1918.

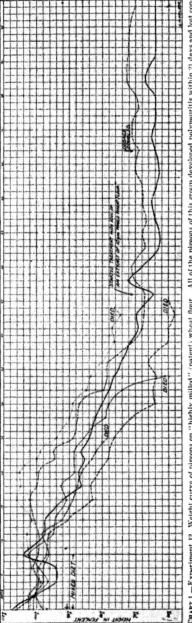

CHART 1.—Experiment 12. Weight curve of pigeons on "highly milled" (patent) wheat flour. All of the pigeons of this group developed polyneuritis within 21 days and lost considerable body weight. Four of the birds died after having been on this diet 17, 26, 36, and 37 days, respectively. The two remaining birds received an extract of "whole wheat" flour and were cured of their paralytic symptoms, but did not recover their lost body weight during the next 40 days.

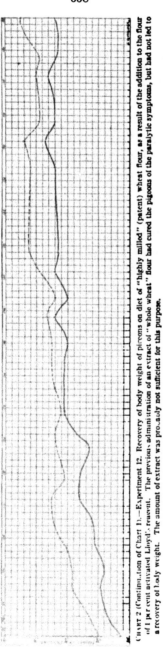

CHART 2 (Continuation of Chart 1).—Experiment 12. Recovery of body weight of pigeons on diet of "highly milled" (patent) wheat flour, as a result of the addition to the flour of 1 per cent activated Lloyd's reagent. The previous administration of an extract of "whole wheat" flour had cured the pigeons of the paralytic symptoms, but had not led to a recovery of body weight. The amount of extract was probably not sufficient for this purpose.

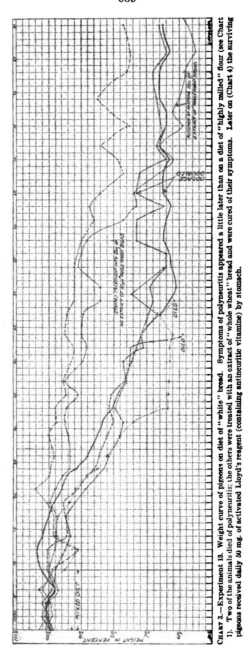

CHART 3.—Experiment 13. Weight curve of pigeons on diet of "white" bread. Symptoms of polyneuritis appeared a little later than on a diet of "highly milled" flour (see Chart 1). Two of the animals died of polyneuritis; the others were treated with an extract of "whole wheat" bread and were cured of their symptoms. Later on (Chart 4) the surviving pigeons received daily 50 mg. of activated Lloyd's reagent (containing antineuritic vitamine) by stomach.

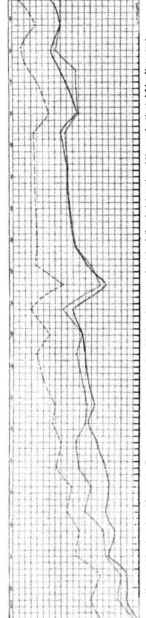

CHART 1 (Continuation of Chart 3).—Recovery of pigeons on diet of "white bread" as a result of the daily administration of 50 mg. of activated Lloyd's reagent.

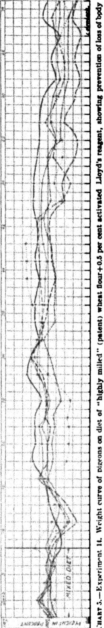

CHART 3.—Experiment 14. Weight curve of pigeons on diet of "highly milled" (patent) wheat flour + 0.5 per cent activated Lloyd's reagent, showing prevention of loss of body weight in pigeons on this mixture. In another experiment, the same amount of *inactive* Lloyd's reagent was added to the patent flour. The pigeons developed polyneuritis within three weeks and lost about 30 per cent of body weight, thus showing that fullers' earth per se can not prevent polyneuritis.

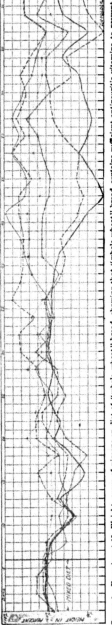

CHART 6.—Experiment 15. Weight curve of pigeons on diet of "whole wheat" bread, showing that "whole wheat" bread contains sufficient antineuritic vitamine to prevent a loss in body weight of pigeons fed exclusively on this diet. The birds of this series did not develop any symptoms of polyneuritis.

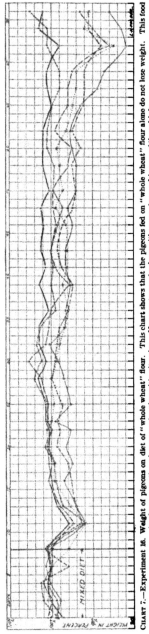

CHART 7.—Experiment 16. Weight of pigeons on diet of "whole wheat" flour. This chart shows that the pigeons fed on "whole wheat" flour alone do not lose weight. This food is adequate as the sole source of antineuritic vitamine. No symptoms of polyneuritis were observed in any of these birds.

EXPERIMENT 17.—*Whole corn.*

[P₂O₅ content: 0.76 per cent.]

No of chicken.	First appearance of polyneuritis.	Period of observation.	Change in body weight in per cent of original weight.
		Days.	
6	No symptoms...	222	− 14
10	......do..	428	− 5
11	......do..	188	− 7

Remarks.—The animals of this group were healthy, full-grown chickens. They were kept in individual small cages throughout the period of observation. The lack of cage space may account for the trivial loss in body weight, as it is very difficult to keep fowls in perfect condition in such narrow confinement for so long a time.

EXPERIMENT 18.—*"Old process water-ground corn meal"* obtained from an old-fashioned buhr mill in Georgia.

[Appearance: Contains large particles of bran and germ. P₂O₅ content: 0.659 per cent.]

No. of pigeon.	First appearance of polyneuritis.	Period of observation.	Change in body weight in per cent of original weight.	Notes.
		Days.		
66	No symptoms.....................	150	−30	Not treated.
67	......do...........................	73	−36	Do.

Remarks—Pigeons 66 and 67 remained perfectly well, but lost considerable weight. This loss of weight was due to the underfeeding of these birds. They received only 10 grams corn meal daily, instead of 15 to 20 grams. In spite of the loss of weight, these animals did not exhibit the slightest signs of polyneuritis during the long period of observation.

EXPERIMENT 19.—*Corn grits (hominy)* obtained from an old-fashioned buhrstone mill in South Carolina.

[Appearance: Practically all the bran and germ mixed with the finer endosperm. P₂O₅ content: 0.658 per cent.]

No. of pigeon.	First appearance of polyneuritis.	Period of observation.	Change in body weight in per cent of original weight.	Notes.
		Days.		
98	No symptoms	152	−11	Not treated.
99	No symptoms, escaped...........	98	(¹)	Do.
96	No symptoms...................	77	+9	Do.

¹ Not determined.

E⁻ ⸱.MENT 19a.—*Same as used in experiment 19, except that the larger particles of bran were removed by passing through a coarsely meshed sieve.*

[P₂O₅ content: 0.59 per cent.]

No. of pigeon.	First appearance of polyneuritis.	Period of observa- tion.	Change in body weight in per cent of original weight.	Notes.
		Days.		
102	No symptoms.....................	152	− 8	Not treated.
103	.....do.............................	152	− 6	Do.
100	.....do.............................	152	−10	Do.

EXPERIMENT 20.—*Corn meal used at Milledgeville State Hospital, Milledgeville, Ga.*

[Appearance: Contains considerable bran and germ. P₂O₅ content: 0.677 per cent.]

No. of pigeon.	First appearance of polyneuritis.	Period of observa- tion.	Change in body weight in per cent of original weight.	Notes.
		Days.		
72	No symptoms.....................	52	−38	Not treated.
73	.....do.............................	84	−15	Do.

Remarks.--Both pigeons were underfed, receiving only 10 grams of cornmeal daily. This fact accounts for the loss of body weight.

Pigeon 73 also received old process corn meal, obtained from the United States Penitentiary, Atlanta, Ga. (0.77 per cent P₂O₅). This bird remained well and apparently in perfect health for a period of 84 days when the experiment was discontinued. No symptoms of polyneuritis were exhibited.

EXPERIMENT 21.—*Corn grits obtained from State institutions in Alabama and Georgia.*

[Appearance: Highly milled. P₂O₅ content: 0.169 and 0.201 per cent.]

No. of pigeon.	First appearance of polyneu- ritis.	Period of observation.	Change in body weight in per cent of original weight.	Notes.
61	Twenty-second day..............	41 days.................	[1] −22	Beginning with twenty-second day, daily dose 0.2 c. c yeast extract.
62	Twentieth day...................	45 days.................	([2])	Beginning with twen- tieth day, daily dose 0.2 c. c. yeast extract.
64	Eighteenth day.................	Died after 34 days.......	−48	Not treated.
411	.....do...........................	Died after 31 days.......	−33	Do.

[1] Twenty-second day of experiment.   [2] Not determined.

Remarks.—Pigeons 61 and 62 received grits which was used in the State hospital in Alabama (P₂O₅ content=0.169 per cent). Pigeon 64 received grits used in a hospital for the insane in Georgia (P₂O₅ content=0.201 per cent). All of these products contained very little bran and germ and were products of roller mills. Pigeons 61 and 62 responded very well to the treatment with yeast extract (disappearance of polyneuritic symptoms) and were in excellent condition at the end of the period of observation.

47

EXPERIMENT 22.—"*Highly milled*" *corn grits obtained from a roller mill in North Carolina.*

[Appearance: Contains a trace of bran and germ.　P_2O_5 content: 0.21 per cent.]

No. of pigeon.	First appearance of polyneuritis.	Period of observation.	Change in body weight in per cent of original weight.	Notes.
91	Thirty-first day.........	Died after 72 days.......	Not determined...	Symptoms relieved on sixty-fourth day by yeast extract.
92	Twenty-third day.......	Died after 92 days.......	.....do............	Improved on sixty-seventh day by alcoholic extract of yeast.
93	Thirty-first day.........	Died after 91 days.......	.....do............	Improved on seventy-third day by yeast extract.
94	Forty-seventh day......	Died after 95 days.......	.....do............	Marked improvement on sixty-fifth day by 0.2 gm. alcoholic yeast extract.
97	Thirty-first day.........	Died after 64 days.......	.....do............	Not treated.

EXPERIMENT 23.—*Highly milled corn grits and wheat bran. The grits were obtained from a roller mill in North Carolina and the bran from an old-process (stone) mill in South Carolina. The grits were the same as used in Experiment 22.*

[P_2O_5 content of corn grits: 0.21 per cent.　P_2O_5 content of wheat bran: 2.48 per cent.]

No. of pigeon.	First appearance of polyneuritis.	Period of observation.	Change in body weight in per cent of original weight.	Diet.
87	No symptoms..................	149 days.................	0	35 gm. corn grits + 10 gm. wheat bran.
85	.....do...........	.....do...........	+ 3	
86	.....do...........	.....do...........	− 9	
88	Sixty-seventh day..............	Died after 68 days.......	(1)	40 gm. corn grits + 5 gm. wheat bran.
89	One hundred and forty-ninth day	226 days................	+ 8	
90	One hundred and fiftieth day...	Died after 158 days......	−31	

1 Not determined.

Remarks.—Pigeons 85, 86, and 87 remained in perfect condition throughout the period of observation. Pigeons 88, 89, and 90 developed polyneuritic symptoms after a considerable length of time and two of the birds died of the disease. Pigeon 89, however, recovered from the paralytic attack, regained its lost body weight and appeared perfectly well at the end of the period of observation (226 days).

EXPERIMENT 24.—*Highly milled corn grits with addition of corn bran. The grits were the same as used in experiment 22, and the bran was obtained from old-process corn meal by passing the latter through a wide-meshed sieve.*

[P_2O_5 content of corn grits: 0.21 per cent.　P_2O_5 content of corn bran: 0.787 per cent.]

No. of pigeon.	First appearance of polyneuritis.	Period of observation.	Change in body weight in per cent of original weight.	Notes.
81	Seventy-third day......	Died after 113 days......	Not determined...	Symptoms relieved on seventy-third day by 10 c. c. of dilute yeast extract.
101	.....do..................	Died after 115 days......	.....do............	Do.

Remarks.—Both pigeons of this lot received a mixture of 15 grams of corn grits and 5 grams of corn bran. The addition of corn bran caused a very considerable delay in the onset of polyneuritis (about 40 days). This furthermore seems to indicate that corn bran is probably not as rich in antineuritic substance as either wheat bran or possibly corn germ. On examination of the corn bran it was noticed that very little of the so-called aleuron layer adhered to the cellulose layer of the bran.

Both pigeons recovered temporarily from their paralytic symptoms as a result of a single dose of an antineuritic yeast preparation. The birds again recovered their lost appetite and remained free from symptoms for 38 days (pigeon 81) and 41 days (pigeon 101), respectively.

In order to discover whether a larger addition of corn bran would offer complete protection from polyneuritis, pigeon 74 was fed on a mixture of 10 grams highly milled corn grits (0.20 per cent P_2O_5) and 10 grams corn bran (0.78 per cent P_2O_5). The corn grits used were the same as fed to pigeon 411 (experiment 21) and had caused symptoms of polyneuritis on the eighteenth day after feeding was begun. Pigeon 74 remained well on this diet for two months, when the experiment was discontinued.

EXPERIMENT 25.—*Corn germ obtained from a roller mill in Indiana.*

[P_2O_5 content: 2.81 per cent.]

No. of pigeon.	First appearance of polyneuritis.	Period of observation.	Change in body weight in per cent of original weight.	Notes.
70	No symptoms..................................	Days. 85	−17	Not treated.
71	.....do..	92	−20	Do.

Remarks.—These pigeons were underfed (see p. 649), receiving only 10 grams of food daily. They never exhibited the slightest symptoms of polyneuritis and were lively throughout the period of observation.

Conclusions.—(1) The results obtained in this investigation clearly show that for pigeons an exclusive diet of whole wheat or corn furnishes an adequate supply of antineuritic vitamine.

(2) The antineuritic vitamine seems to reside in the peripheral layers and the germ of these seeds, whereas the endosperm is relatively poor in this substance.

(3) If wheat and corn foods containing only a small percentage of the peripheral layers and germ of the seed are fed to pigeons and chickens exclusive of other food, polyneuritic symptoms appear on an average of three weeks after the beginning of the feeding period. The appearance of polyneuritis is preceded by a gradual loss in body weight. The birds can be relieved of their paralysis in a striking way by the oral or subcutaneous administration of a highly concentrated preparation of antineuritic vitamine derived from "whole-wheat" bread, yeast, ox liver, rice polishings, or beans.

(4) The addition of yeast (in amounts used by bakers) in the preparation of bread from highly milled flour does not prevent the appearance of polyneuritis in birds fed on this food, but prolongs slightly the period of incubation.

(5) The addition to "highly milled" flour, or bread made from "highly milled" flour, of a small amount of antineuritic vitamine preparation will correct this particular dietary deficiency, and will prevent the appearance of polyneuritis and the loss of body weight.

(6) The total phosphorus content of corn and wheat foods is a fairly satisfactory i: ' ' the amount of antineuritic vitamine contained in these foods. way, it can be said that a high total phosphorus content is an indication that the particular corn or wheat product is relatively rich in antineuritic vitamine.

References.

HOLST, 1907, J. Hyg., vol. 7, p. 629.
LITTLE, 1912, J. Am. M. Ass., vol. 58, p. 2029.
———— 1914, ibid., vol. 63, p. 1287.
OHLER, 1914, J. Med. Research, vol. 31, p. 239.
SIMPSON and EDIE, 1911-12, Ann. Trop. Med. & Parasit., vol. 5, p. 321.
SEIDELL, 1914, Public Health Reports, February 18, p. 364.
VOEGTLIN, SULLIVAN, and MYERS, 1916, Public Health Reports. August 14, p. 935.
WELLMANN and BASS, 1913, Am. J. Trop. Dis. & Prev. Med.

PREVALENCE OF DISEASE.

o health department, State or loca~~~ ~~~~ View... ~~ or control disease without
knowledge of when, where, and una~~~ ~~~ ~~~~~~~~~ cases are occurring.

UNITED STATES.

TRA-CANTONMENT ZONES—CASES REPORTED WEEK ENDED APR. 30.

CAMP BEAUREGARD ZONE, LA.

dria:	Cases.
Cerebrospinal meningitis	1
Diphtheria	1
Malaria	6
Mumps	22
Smallpox	5
Tuberculosis	1
Whooping cough	4

ural district:

Measles	2

CAMP BOWIE ZONE, TEX.

ort Worth:

Chicken pox	3
Gonorrhea	5
Measles	1
Mumps	12
Smallpox	15
Typhoid fever	2

CAMP DEVENS ZONE, MASS.

cken pox:

Lancaster	1

erman measles:

Ayer	1

easles:

Ayer	4
Lancaster	2

CAMP DODGE ZONE, IOWA.

s Moines:

Diphtheria	4
Gonorrhea	11
Measles	1
Scarlet fever	23
Smallpox	19
Syphilis	6
Typhoid fever	1
Whooping cough	2

CAMP DONIPHAN ZONE, OKLA.

llpox:

Faxon	4
Lawton	4

CAMP EBERTS ZONE, ARK.

Cerebrospinal meningitis:	Cases.
Keo	1
Chancroid:	
England	1
Gonorrhea:	
Lonoke	2
England	3
Keo	1
Cabot, route 1	1
Hookworm:	
England, route 1	1
Malaria:	
Lonoke, route 4	1
England	17
England, route 1	1
England, route 2	1
England, route 3	1
Keo	2
Measles:	
Lonoke	1
Lonoke, route 3	1
England	1
England, route 2	4
Cabot	3
Carlisle	2
Mumps:	
England	9
Pellagra:	
Lonoke, route 3	2
Pneumonia:	
Austin	2
Carlisle	2
Smallpox:	
Lonoke	1
England	6
Keo	1
Syphilis:	
Lonoke, route 1	1
England	1
Tuberculosis:	
England	3
Jacksonville, route 1	1
Whooping cough:	
England	3

CAMP FUNSTON ZONE, KANS.

Chicken pox:	Cases.
Manhattan	2

Erysipelas:
| |
--- | ---
Manhattan | 1

Measles:
| |
--- | ---
Junction City |
Manhattan | 3
Riley | 4

Mumps:
| |
--- | ---
Junction City | 9
Manhattan | 8

Pneumonia:
| |
--- | ---
Manhattan | 3

Scarlet fever:
| |
--- | ---
Manhattan | 4
Riley | 1

Whooping cough:
| |
--- | ---
Manhattan | 1

CAMP GORDON ZONE, GA.

Atlanta:
| |
--- | ---
Chicken pox | 4
Diphtheria | 2
Gonorrhea | 5
Measles | 5
Mumps | 10
Pneumonia | 2
Scarlet fever | 1
Septic sore throat | 1
Smallpox | 4
Syphilis | 6
Tuberculosis | 13
Whooping cough | 2

Decatur:
| |
--- | ---
Mumps | 4

CAMP GREENE ZONE, N. C.

Charlotte Township:
| |
--- | ---
Diphtheria | 2
Gonorrhea | 14
Measles | 9
Mumps | 3
Scarlet fever | 1
Syphilis | 8
Trachoma | 6
Tuberculosis | 2
Whooping cough | 6

GULFPORT HEALTH DISTRICT, MISS.

Gulfport Health District:
| |
--- | ---
Chicken pox | 4
Gonorrhea | 2
Malaria | 7
Measles | 8
Mumps | 3

CAMP JOSEPH E. JOHNSTON ZONE, FLA.

Chicken pox:
| |
--- | ---
Jacksonville | 3
Seaboard Air Line | 1

Dysentery:
| |
--- | ---
Jacksonville | 3

Gonorrhea:
| |
--- | ---
Highway | 1
Jacksonville | 8

Malaria:
| |
--- | ---
Eastport | 3
Jacksonville | 1

CAMP JOSEPH E. JOHNSTON ZONE, FLA.—contd.

Measles:	Cases.
Jacksonville	7
South Jacksonville	1

Mumps:
| |
--- | ---
Jacksonville | 5

Pellagra:
| |
--- | ---
Jacksonville | 1

Pneumonia:
| |
--- | ---
Jacksonville | 2

Syphilis:
| |
--- | ---
Jacksonville | 3

Trachoma:
| |
--- | ---
Jacksonville | 1

Tuberculosis:
| |
--- | ---
Jacksonville | 7
Panama | 1

Typhoid fever:
| |
--- | ---
Jacksonville | 4

Whooping cough:
| |
--- | ---
Jacksonville | 21
Ortega | 2
South Jacksonville | 1

FORT LEAVENWORTH ZONE, KANS.

Leavenworth:
| |
--- | ---
Chicken pox | 4
Diphtheria | 1
Measles | 15
Mumps | 1
Scarlet fever | 2
Smallpox | 1

Leavenworth County:
| |
--- | ---
Erysipelas | 1
Measles | 10
Smallpox | 1
Typhoid fever | 1

CAMP LEE ZONE, VA.

German measles:
| |
--- | ---
Ettricks | 4
Dinwiddie County | 1
Prince George County | 4

Gonorrhea:
| |
--- | ---
Dinwiddie County | 1

Measles:
| |
--- | ---
Ettricks | 2
Hopewell | 3
Petersburg | 7
Prince George County | 1

Mumps:
| |
--- | ---
Ettricks | 6
Hopewell | 1
Chesterfield County | 3
Prince George County | 2

Scarlet fever:
| |
--- | ---
Hopewell | 2
Petersburg | 2

Septic sore throat:
| |
--- | ---
Ettricks | 2
Prince George County | 2

Tuberculosis:
| |
--- | ---
Petersburg | 1

Whooping cough:
| |
--- | ---
Ettricks | 2
Hopewell | 4
Prince George County | 9

CAMP LEWIS ZONE, WASH.

German measles: | Cases.
Gravelly Lake............................ 1
Lake City................................ 3
Loveland................................. 6
Shawaney................................. 1

Measles:
Du Pont.................................. 4

Mumps:
Du Pont.................................. 4

Whooping cough:
Du Pont.................................. 3

CAMP LOGAN ZONE, TEX.

Chancroid:
Brookline................................ 1
Goose Creek.............................. 1
Houston.................................. 1

Diphtheria:
Houston.................................. 1

Gonorrhea:
Houston.................................. 24
Hufsmith................................. 1

Measles:
Houston.................................. 14
Moonshine Hill........................... 2

Malaria:
Houston.................................. 1
Moonshine Hill........................... 8

Mumps:
Houston.................................. 5

Pneumonia:
Houston.................................. 4

Scarlet fever:
Houston.................................. 1

Smallpox:
Houston.................................. 1

Syphilis:
Goose Creek.............................. 1
Houston.................................. 12

Tuberculosis:
Houston.................................. 2

Whooping cough:
Houston.................................. 4

CAMP MACARTHUR ZONE, TEX.

Waco:
Chicken pox.............................. 1
German measles........................... 1
Measles.................................. 2
Mumps.................................... 25
Pneumonia, lobar......................... 1
Scarlet fever............................ 1
Tuberculosis............................. 1
Typhoid fever............................ 1
Whooping cough........................... 6

CAMP M'CLELLAN ZONE, ALA.

Anniston:
Chicken pox.............................. 2
Measles.................................. 1
Mumps.................................... 4
Pneumonia................................ 1
Smallpox................................. 8
Typhoid fever............................ 1
Whooping cough........................... 2

Blue Mountain:
Smallpox................................. 2

Precinct 15:
Smallpox................................. 1

NORFOLK COUNTY NAVAL DISTRICT, VA.

Gonorrhea: | Cases.
Berkley.................................. 1

Malaria:
Gilmerton................................ 1
South Norfolk............................ 2

Measles:
Norfolk.................................. 14
Ocean View............................... 3
Lenox.................................... 3
Berkley.................................. 1
South Norfolk............................ 5
Portsmouth............................... 13

Mumps:
Gilmerton................................ 2
South Norfolk............................ 2
Portsmouth............................... 1
Norfolk.................................. 2

Pellagra:
Gilmerton................................ 1

Pneumonia:
South Norfolk............................ 1

Scarlet fever:
Norfolk.................................. 3
Willoughby............................... 1
Portsmouth............................... 1
Norfolk County........................... 1

Smallpox:
Norfolk.................................. 1

Tuberculosis:
Portsmouth............................... 3
West Norfolk............................. 1
Brighton................................. 1

Varicella:
Pinners Point............................ 1
Port Norfolk............................. 1

FORT OGLETHORPE ZONE, GA.

Chattanooga:
Cerebrospinal meningitis................. 2
Chicken pox.............................. 1
Diphtheria............................... 2
Gonorrhea................................ 26
Measles.................................. 1
Mumps.................................... 5
Pneumonia................................ 2
Scarlet fever............................ 1
Smallpox................................. 4
Syphilis................................. 7
Whooping cough........................... 3

East Chattanooga:
Mumps.................................... 3

East Lake:
Scarlet fever............................ 2

CAMP PIKE ZONE, ARK.

Cerebrospinal meningitis:
Little Rock.............................. 1

Chancroid:
Little Rock.............................. 3
North Little Rock........................ 3

Chicken pox:
Little Rock.............................. 6

Diphtheria:
Little Rock.............................. 3

Gonorrhea:
Little Rock.............................. 10
North Little Rock........................ 3
Scotts...................................

CAMP PIKE ZONE, ARK.—continued.

Malaria:	Cases.
Little Rock	3
Measles:	
Little Rock	2
Mumps:	
Little Rock	2
North Little Rock	2
Scotts	1
Pneumonia:	
Little Rock	5
Scarlet fever:	
Little Rock	4
North Little Rock	1
Septic sore throat:	
Scotts	1
Smallpox:	
Little Rock	10
North Little Rock	1
Syphilis:	
Little Rock	5
North Little Rock	3
Tuberculosis:	
Little Rock	1
Scotts	1
Kerr	1
Typhoid fever:	
Little Rock	1
Whooping cough:	
Little Rock	3

CAMP SHELBY ZONE, MISS.

Hattiesburg:	
Hookworm	5
Malaria	8
Measles	1
Mumps	11
Pneumonia	7
Tuberculosis	5
Typhoid fever	2
Venereal	6
Whooping cough	6

CAMP SHERIDAN ZONE, ALA.

Montgomery:	
Chancroid	4
Gonorrhea	29
Malaria	2
Measles	5
Mumps	5
Pneumonia, lobar	2
Ringworm	27
Syphilis	2
Tuberculosis	15
Rural district in 5-mile zone.	
Chicken pox	2
Measles	1
Mumps	1
Smallpox	1

CAMP SHERMAN ZONE, OHIO.

Gonorrhea:	
Chillicothe	2

CAMP SHERMAN ZONE, OHIO—continued.

Measles:	Cases.
Chillicothe	6
Liberty Township	6
Scioto Township	1
Mumps:	
Liberty Township	2
Scarlet fever:	
Chillicothe	7
Smallpox:	
Chillicothe	2
Tuberculosis, pulmonary:	
Chillicothe	1
Springfield Township	1

CAMP ZACHARY TAYLOR ZONE, KY.

Jefferson County:	
Diphtheria	1
Measles	3
Trachoma	2
Tuberculosis, pulmonary	4
Tuberculosis, granular	1
Whooping cough	1
Louisville:	
Cerebrospinal meningitis	2
Chicken pox	2
Diphtheria	13
Malaria	1
Measles	7
Mumps	3
Pneumonia, lobar	6
Rabies in animals	3
Scarlet fever	1
Septic sore throat	1
Smallpox	1
Syphilis	2
Tuberculosis, pulmonary	30
Typhoid fever	2
Whooping cough	5
United States Government clinic:	
Chancroid	6
Gonorrhea	22
Syphilis	27

TIDEWATER HEALTH DISTRICT, VA.

Hampton:	
Diphtheria	1
Tuberculosis	1
Typhoid fever	2
Newport News:	
Cerebrospinal meningitis	1
Chicken pox	2
German measles	1
Measles	12
Mumps	9
Pneumonia	1
Scarlatina	1
Scarlet fever	1
Tuberculosis	1
Typhoid fever	2
Whooping cough	1
Phoebus:	
Tuberculosis	1

CAMP WADSWORTH ZONE, S. C.

Spartanburg:	Cases.
Chicken pox	1
Diphtheria	1
Gonorrhea	2
Measles	8
Mumps	5
Syphilis	2
Whooping cough	2
Pauline:	
German measles	1
Measles	2

CAMP WHEELER ZONE, GA.

East Macon:	Cases.
Gonorrhea	1
Measles	1
Mumps	1
Macon:	
Diphtheria	1
Gonorrhea	1
Malaria	1
Mumps	1
Scarlet fever	2
Tuberculosis	1
Typhoid fever	2

DISEASE CONDITIONS AMONG TROOPS IN THE UNITED STATES.

The following data are taken from telegraphic reports received in the office of the Surgeon General, United States Army, for the week ended April 19, 1918:

Annual admission rate per 1,000 (disease only):
- All troops... 1,745.5
- National Guard camps... 2,053.0
- National Army camps... 1,742.0
- Regular Army... 1,515.8

Noneffective rate per 1,000 on day of report:
- All troops... 49.1
- National Guard camps... 46.8

Noneffective rate per 1,000 on day of report—Continued.
- National Army camps... 54.2
- Regular Army... 43.6

Annual death rate per 1,000 (disease only):
- All troops... 12.9
- National Guard camps... 6.5
- National Army camps... 17.3
- Regular Army... 12.4

New cases of special diseases reported during week ended Apr. 19, 1918.

Camps.	Pneumonia.	Dysentery.	Malaria.	Venereal.	Measles.	Meningitis.	Scarlet fever.	Deaths.	Annual admission rate per 1,000 (disease only).	Noneffective per 1,000 on day of report.
Wadsworth	2			99	1			7	529.0	22.9
Hancock	2			32		1	1	1	653.5	25.2
McClellan	4			5	1				2,783.5	43.6
Sevier	16			25	21	1	9	4	732.8	27.0
Wheeler	24		3	12				8	4,818.5	85.1
Logan	14		2	73	11		9	2	3,393.4	51.7
Cody	19			2				5	450.6	26.2
Doniphan	23			7				4	2,648.2	68.4
Bowie	22		2	67				7	1,554.3	50.5
Sheridan	5			17	3		1	1	2,698.5	45.4
Shelby	8			17	3			6	4,536.7	87.4
Beauregard	15		18	27		1		2	2,083.3	65.4
Kearney	1		1	1			6	2	1,178.0	42.3
Devens	37			27	3			7	881.4	42.5
Upton	13			48	19		7	11	953.1	43.0
Dix	11			73	14	1	8	4	1,169.2	35.9
Meade	17			69	6		1	6	1,282.7	43.1
Lee	11	1	2	212	5		1	3	1,730.4	59.7
Jackson	14	1	6	15	17			3	1,950.0	67.4
Gordon	32			44	22	1	4	9	2,554.0	51.6
Sherman	29			58	1	1	20	16	1,580.0	46.7
Taylor	37			21	48	2		11	4,640.5	82.4
Custer	28			37	4		8	6	937.7	32.0
Grant	7			15	5		3	20	772.8	28.3
Pike	28			90	31	2	3	9	2,807.0	71.6
Dodge	75			63	19	3	44	29	1,896.6	107.0
Funston	41			20	15	2		9	1,163.8	66.4
Travis	27			37	18			13	3,394.9	62.0
Lewis	23		1	75	5		13	4	1,241.0	48.5
Northeastern Department				9	4	1	1	7	1,167.3	35.3
Eastern Department	9	1		14	15		1	6	978.5	33.0
Southeastern Department	11		4	37	13		1	4	1,609.2	58.5
Central Department	6			37	33	3	20	3	1,221.5	40.4
Southern Department	6		1	89	21	13		14	2,161.4	53.2
Western Department	8			53	15	1	2	2	1,367.1	29.2

Massachusetts.

From Collaborating Epidemiologist Hitchcock, by telegraph, for week ended April 27, 1918:

Unusual prevalence. German measles: Gardner 22, Mansfield 56. Measles: Chelsea 42, Brookline 45, Chelmsford 60, Quincy 24, Shirley 11, Westford 10. Scarlet fever: Holliston 97, Brewster 5, Adams 8. (April 14: Smallpox; Chelsea 1.)

Minnesota.

From Collaborating Epidemiologist Bracken, by telegraph, for week ended April 27, 1918:

Smallpox (new focus): Beltrami County, Kelliher Township 1. Three cerebrospinal meningitis reported since April 22.

New Jersey.

From Collaborating Epidemiologist Bowen, by telegraph, for week ended April 27, 1918:

Unusual prevalence measles Hackensack, Haddonfield, Bridgeton, Montclair, Orange, Pitman, Newton.

Ohio.

From Collaborating Epidemiologist Freeman, by telegraph, for week ended April 27, 1918:

Meningitis: Seven cases scattered throughout State. Poliomyelitis: Two cases. Smallpox decreasing.

South Carolina.

From Collaborating Epidemiologist Hayne, by telegraph, for week ended April 29, 1918:

Four cases epidemic meningitis.

Virginia.

From Collaborating Epidemiologist Traynham, by telegraph, for week ended April 27, 1918:

One case smallpox Henrico County, 1 Smyth, 2 Amherst, 8 Spottsylvania. One case cerebrospinal meningitis Newport News, 1 Salem. One case poliomyelitis Amelia County.

Washington.

From Collaborating Epidemiologist Tuttle, by telegraph, for week ended April 27, 1918:

Communicable disease situation unchanged.

RECIPROCAL NOTIFICATION.

Minnesota.

Cases of communicable diseases referred during March, 1918, to other State health departments by Department of Health of the State of Minnesota.

Disease and locality of notification.	Referred to health authority of—	Why referred.
Scarlet fever: Minneapolis health department, Hennepin County.	Grand Rapids, Kent County, Mich. (2 cases).	Man and wife exposed to scarlet fever in Michigan developed disease in Minnesota. Husband died.
Smallpox: Minneapolis health department, Hennepin County.	Cresco, Howard County, Iowa; Owatonna, Steele County, Minn.; Excelsior, Hennepin County, Minn.	Quarantined at Minneapolis; traveled in Iowa and two Minnesota towns while in infectious stage.
	Cedar Rapids, Linn County, Iowa....	Salesman quarantined in Minneapolis traveled in Iowa while in infectious stage.
	Fargo, Cass County, N. Dak.........	Quarantined in Minneapolis; developed first symptoms before leaving North Dakota.
	Toronto, Deuel County, S. Dak.......	Exposed to smallpox Mar. 14 in Minnesota through consulting chiropractor, who developed first symptoms Mar. 8.
	Superior, Douglas County, Wis........	Salesman, quarantined in Minneapolis. Traveled in Wisconsin while in infectious stage.
Tuberculosis: Mayo Clinic, Rochester, Olmsted County.	Rochelle, Ogle County, Ill. Oak Park, Cook County, Ill. Rock Falls, Whiteside County, Ill. Chicago, Cook County, Ill. Freeport, Stephenson County, Ill. Ligonier, Nobles County, Ind. Sioux City, Woodbury County, Iowa. Schaller, Sac County, Iowa. Buxton, Monroe County, Iowa. Rake, Winnebago County, Iowa. Hanlontown, Worth County, Iowa. Glen Elder, Mitchell County, Kans. Stambaugh, Iron County, Mich. Gladstone, Delta County, Mich. Iron River, Iron County, Mich. Maryville, route No. 3, Nodaway County, Mo. Conception, Nodaway County, Mo. Livingston, Park County, Mont. Birney, Rosebud County, Mont. Outlook, Sheridan County, Mont. Geyser, Cascade County, Mont. Surrey, Ward County, N. Dak. Devils Lake, Ramsey County, N. Dak. Lawton, Ramsey County, N. Dak. Carrington, Foster County, N. Dak. Edmore, Ramsey County, N. Dak. (4 cases)	4 incipient, 1 apparently arrested, 2 apparently cured, 4 (stage of disease not given) 5 advanced, and 14 moderately advanced cases left Mayo Clinic for homes.
	Mohall, Renville County, N. Dak. Ashland, Saunders County, Nebr. Shawnee, Pottawatomie County, Okla. Gettysburg, Adams County, Pa. Brandon, Minnehaha County, S. Dak. Roslyn, Day County, S. Dak. (2 cases). Orleans, Faulk County, S. Dak. McLaughlin, Corson County, S. Dak. Sioux Falls, Minnehaha County, S. Dak. Merrill, Lincoln County, Wis. Hamburg, Marathon County, Wis. Cecil, Shawano County, Wis. Neillsville, Clark County, Wis. Pine River, Waushara County, Wis. Neepawa, Manitoba, Canada. Winnipeg, Manitoba, Canada. Lanigan, Saskatchawan, Canada. Darmody, Saskatchawan, Canada.	1 (stage of disease not given), 7 advanced, 7 moderately advanced, 3 apparently arrested cases left Mayo Clinic for homes.
Pokegama Sanatorium, Pine County.	Bismarck, Burleigh County, N. Dak. Stevens Point, Portage County, Wis.	2 incipient cases left Pokegama Sanatorium for homes.
Thomas Hospital, Minneapolis, Hennepin County.	Seattle, King County, Wash. Bruce, Brookings County, S. Dak.....	Open case left sanatorium for home. Deceased case removed from Thomas Hospital to home.

CEREBROSPINAL MENINGITIS.

State Reports for March, 1918.

Place.	New cases reported.	Place.	New cases reported.
Connecticut:		Kansas—Continued.	
Fairfield County—		...n County—	
Bridgeport	1	Horton	1
Fairfield	1	Butler County—	
Greenwich	1	Augusta	2
Hartford County—		Eldorado	2
Hartford	2	Towanda	3
New Haven County—		Cherokee County—	
Ansonia	1	Curona	1
Naugatuck	1	Comanche County—	
Wallingford	1	Coldwater	1
Waterbury	1	Cowley County—	
New Haven	1	Arkansas City	1
New London County—		Crawford County—	
New London	1	Cherokee	1
Litchfield County—		Greenwood County--	
New Milford	1	Madison	1
		Jackson County—	
Total	12	Whiting	1
		Johnson County—	
Illinois:		De Soto	1
Adams County—		Kearny County—	
Quincy	1	Lakin	1
Bond County—		Labette County—	
Greenville	1	Edna	1
Cook County—		Parsons	3
Chicago	29	Leavenworth County -	
Dekalb County—		Leavenworth	3
Sandwich	1	Miami County —	
Dewitt County—		Osawatomie	1
Rutledge Township	1	Montgomery County—	
Franklin County—		Coffeyville	2
Thompsonville	1	Nemaha County—	
Henry County—		Sabetha	1
Alpha	1	Neosho County—	
Oxford Township	1	Chanute	1
Kane County—		Riley County-	
St. Charles Township	1	Manhattan	1
Lake County—		Sedgwick County—	
Lake Forest	1	Wichita	2
Waukegan	1	Sumner County--	
Macoupin County—		Corbin	1
Gillespie	1	Wyandotte County —	
Virden	2	Kansas City	12
Madison County—			
Venice	1	Total	54
McLean County—			
Saybrook	1	Minnesota:	
Pike County—		Blue Earth County	
Pleasantvale Township	1	Mankato	1
Saline County-		Freeborn County-	
Galatia	1	Albert Lea	1
Sangamon County--		Albert Lea Township	1
Springfield	3	Hennepin County -	
St. Clair County—		Minneapolis	1
East St. Louis	1	Ottertail County	
Vermilion County—		Deer Creek	1
Georgetown Township	1	Pope County	
Westville	1	Glenwood	1
Warren County—		Ramsey County -	
Roseville Township	1	St. Paul	1
Point Pleasant Township	1	St. Louis County	
Will County—		Eveleth	1
Wilmington	1		
Winnebago County -		Total	9
Rockford	3		
Camp Grant	1	Mississippi	
		Bolivar County	8
Total	59	Carroll County	1
Iowa:		Coahoma County	3
Polk County	5	Harrison County	1
Scott County	4	Jones County	1
		Pearl River County	1
Total	9	Tallahatchie County	1
		Tate County	1
Kansas:		Warren County	1
Barton County -		Washington County	7
Holsington	2		
Bourbon County -		Total	25
Hollister	1		
Redfield	1		

CEREBROSPINAL MENINGITIS—Continued.

State Reports for March, 1918—Continued.

Place.	New cases reported.	Place.	New cases reported.
Nebraska:		**Pennsylvania—Continued.**	
Dodge County	1	Fayette County	1
Douglas County	3	Lackawanna County	2
Hall County	2	Luzerne County	9
Merrick County	1	Montgomery County	1
		Northampton County	1
Total	7	Philadelphia County	20
		Schuylkill County	1
New Jersey:		Washington County	1
Atlantic County	1	Westmoreland County	4
Bergen County	1	York County	1
Burlington County	5		
Camden County	3	Total	79
Cape May County	1		
Essex County	15	**South Carolina:**	
Hudson County	5	Aiken County	2
Mercer County	2	Barnwell County	1
Passaic County	4	Charleston County	12
Union County	4	Chester County	1
		Darlington County	3
Total	41	Fairfield County	1
		Florence County	1
North Carolina:		Greenville County	26
Avery County	1	Horry County	2
Bladen County	1	Laurens County	1
Cabarrus County	1	Lee County	1
Catawba County	1	Newberry County	4
Cherokee County	1	Orangeburg County	1
Cleveland County	1	Richland County	12
Cumberland County	1	Saluda County	1
Currituck County	1	Spartanburg County	6
Forsyth County	2	Sumter County	1
Gaston County	2	York County	6
Graham County	2		
Hyde County	2	Total	82
Martin County	1		
Montgomery County	1	**South Dakota:**	
Pasquotank County	1	Codington County	2
Pitt County	2	Lake County	1
Total	21	Total	3
Pennsylvania:		**Wisconsin:**	
Allegheny County	19	Calumet County	1
Armstrong County	1	Dane County	2
Cambria County	2	La Crosse County	1
Cameron County	1	Manitowoc County	1
Chester County	1	Milwaukee County	14
Clarion County	5	Rock County	1
Clearfield County	1	Sheboygan County	4
Dauphin County	1	Waupaca County	1
Delaware County	2		
Elk County	5	Total	25

City Reports for Week Ended Apr. 13, 1918.

Place.	Cases.	Deaths.	Place.	Cases.	Deaths.
Akron, Ohio	2	....	Fall River, Mass	2	....
Atlanta, Ga	1	2	Flint, Mich		1
Baltimore, Md	4	4	Indianapolis, Ind	2	....
Birmingham, Ala	1	....	Jacksonville, Fla		1
Boston, Mass	7	3	Jamestown, N. Y	1	....
Bridgeport, Conn	1	1	Jersey City, N. J	1	5
Buffalo, N. Y	1		Little Rock, Ark	1	....
Chattanooga, Tenn	6	4	Los Angeles, Cal	2	....
Chicago, Ill	8	2	Louisville, Ky	2	2
Cincinnati, Ohio	1	1	Macon, Ga	1	1
Cleveland, Ohio	2	1	Memphis, Tenn	1	....
Covington, Ky	1		Milwaukee, Wis	4	4
Dayton, Ohio		4	Nashville, Tenn	1	....
Detroit, Mich	6	1	Newark, N. J	5	....
Duluth, Minn	1	....	Newcastle, Ind	1	1
Evansville, Ind		1	New York, N. Y	22	5

CEREBROSPINAL MENINGITIS—Continued.

City Reports for Week Ended Apr. 13, 1918—Continued.

Place.	Cases.	Deaths.	Place.	Cases.	Deaths.
Niagara Falls, N. Y	1		Salt Lake City, Utah		1
Norfolk, Va	2	2	San Diego, Cal	1	
North Little Rock, Ark	1		San Francisco, Cal	4	2
Passaic, N. J	1	1	Scranton, Pa	1	
Philadelphia, Pa	6	3	Seattle, Wash	1	
Pittsburgh, Pa	6		Syracuse, N. Y	1	
Pittsfield, Mass	1		Tacoma, Wash	1	
Portsmouth, Va	1		Troy, N. Y	1	
Poughkeepsie, N. Y		1	Washington, D. C	1	1
Providence, R. I	2		Wilkes-Barre, Pa	3	
Rockford, Ill	1		Winston-Salem, N. C	1	
St. Louis, Mo	4		Worcester, Mass	5	3

DIPHTHERIA.

See Diphtheria, measles, scarlet fever, and tuberculosis, page 702.

ERYSIPELAS.

City Reports for Week Ended Apr. 13, 1918.

Place.	Cases.	Deaths.	Place.	Cases.	Deaths.
Baltimore, Md	3	1	Malden, Mass		1
Beloit, Wis	2		Marshall, Tex	1	
Boston, Mass		1	Medford, Mass		1
Bridgeport, Conn	1		Milwaukee, Wis	1	
Brockton, Mass	2		Newark, N. J	9	
Buffalo, N. Y	4	2	New York, N. Y		1
Chicago, Ill	18	2	Omaha, Nebr	4	1
Cincinnati, Ohio	1	1	Passaic, N. J	1	
Cleveland, Ohio	6		Philadelphia, Pa	9	
Denver, Colo	7		Pittsburgh, Pa	12	2
Detroit, Mich	1	1	Portland, Oreg	3	
Easton, Pa	1		Providence, R. I		1
Erie, Pa	2	2	Provo, Utah	1	
Jackson, Mich	2		St. Louis, Mo	16	
Johnstown, Pa		1	St. Paul, Minn	3	
Joplin, Mo	1	6	San Francisco, Cal	4	
Kansas City, Kans	2		Seattle, Wash	2	
Los Angeles, Cal	1		Wichita, Kans	1	
Louisville, Ky	3		York, Pa	1	

LEPROSY.

City Reports for Week Ended Apr. 13, 1918.

During the week ended April 13, 1918, two cases of leprosy were reported; one case at Los Angeles, Cal., and one case at Riverside, Cal.

MALARIA.
State Reports for March, 1918.

Place.	New cases reported.	Place.	New cases reported.
Illinois:		**Mississippi—Continued.**	
Bureau County—		Jasper County..............	104
Mineral.....................	1	Jefferson County..........	101
Coles County—		Jefferson Davis County...........	26
Seven Hickory Township......	1	Jones County..............	62
Crawford County—		Kemper County............	35
Robinson....................	4	Lafayette County..........	36
Franklin County—		Lamar County.............	55
Macedonia...................	6	Lauderdale County........	35
Grundy County—		Lawrence County..........	64
Saratoga Township...........	3	Leake County.............	87
Jackson County—		Lee County...............	110
Elkville..................	15	Leflore County...........	13 1
Jasper County—		Lincoln County...........	38
Newton..................	3	Lowndes County...........	20
Knox County—		Madison County...........	11
Walnut Grove Township.......	4	Marion County............	108
Livingston County—		Marshall County..........	47
Long Point.................	1	Monroe County............	37
Pike County—		Montgomery County........	41
Kinderhook.................	3	Neshoba County...........	59
Pope County—		Newton County............	22
Golconda....................	6	Noxubee County...........	12
Pulaski County—		Oktibbeha County.........	41
Ullin......................	2	Panola County............	100
Putnam County—		Pearl River County.......	75
Hennepin...................	1	Perry County.............	81
Randolph County—		Pike County..............	67
Coulterville...............	2	Pontotoc County..........	71
Red Bud.................	1	Prentiss County..........	30
Sangamon County—		Quitman County...........	140
Talkington Township..........	1	Rankin County............	53
Union County—		Scott County.............	46
Jonesboro..................	2	Sharkey County...........	49
Williamson County—		Simpson County...........	71
Cambria....................	4	Smith County.............	36
		Stone County.............	24
Total....................	60	Sunflower County.........	234
		Tallahatchie County......	173
Kansas:		Tate County..............	138
Chautauqua County:		Tippah County............	41
Sedan................	1	Tishomingo County........	32
		Tunica County............	145
Mississippi:		Union County.............	45
Adams County...............	18	Walthall County..........	14
Alcorn County..............	28	Warren County............	211
Amite County...............	74	Washington County........	170
Attala County..............	64	Wayne County.............	25
Benton County..............	11	Webster County...........	26
Bolivar County.............	332	Wilkinson County.........	9
Calhoun County.............	30	Winston County...........	63
Carroll County.............	44	Yalobusha County.........	29
Chickasaw County...........	31	Yazoo County.............	262
Choctaw County.............	51		
Claiborne County...........	51	Total.................	6,084
Clarke County..............	31		
Clay County................	34	**New Jersey:**	
Coahoma County.............	391	Bergen County............	1
Copiah County..............	56	Burlington County........	3
Covington County...........	83	Essex County.............	3
De Soto County.............	27	Hudson County............	1
Forrest County.............	22		
Franklin County............	45	Total.................	8
George County..............	13		
Greene County..............	25	**Pennsylvania:**	
Grenada County.............	24	Huntingdon County................	1
Hancock County.............	31		
Harrison County............	73	**South Carolina:**	
Hinds County...............	166	Barnwell County..................	1
Holmes County..............	203	Marion County............	2
Issaquena County...........	37		
Itawamba County............	25	Total........................	3
Jackson County.............	39		

MALARIA—Continued.

City Reports for Week Ended Apr. 13, 1918.

Place.	Cases.	Deaths.	Place.	Cases.	Deaths.
Alexandria, La.	1	....	Jacksonville, Fla.	1	....
Atlanta, Ga.	1	....	Joplin, Mo.	4	....
Augusta, Ga.	5	....	Little Rock, Ark.	4	....
Birmingham, Ala.	2	1	Newton, Mass.	1	....
Charleston, S. C.	..	1	Palestine, Tex.	4	....
Fort Smith, Ark.	1	....	Rahway, N. J.	1	....
Hattiesburg, Miss.	6	....			

MEASLES.

See Diphtheria, measles, scarlet fever, and tuberculosis, page 702.

PELLAGRA.

State Reports for March, 1918.

Place.	New cases reported.	Place.	New cases reported.
Connecticut:		Mississippi—Continued.	
Hartford County—		Lee County	21
Hartford	1	Leflore County	7
		Lincoln County	12
Illinois:		Lowndes County	9
Sangamon County—		Madison County	1
Talkington Township	1	Marion County	9
Jacksonville State Hospital	1	Marshall County	12
		Montgomery County	5
Total	2	Neshoba County	10
		Newton County	1
Kansas:		Noxubee County	3
Reno County—		Oktibbeha County	2
Hutchinson	1	Panola County	6
		Pearl River County	3
Mississippi:		Perry County	6
Adams County	2	Pike County	6
Alcorn County	4	Pontotoc County	7
Amite County	2	Prentiss County	2
Benton County	1	Quitman County	8
Bolivar County	48	Rankin County	5
Calhoun County	4	Scott County	6
Carroll County	2	Simpson County	2
Chickasaw County	15	Stone County	7
Claiborne County	1	Sunflower County	12
Clarke County	3	Tallahatchie County	27
Clay County	7	Tate County	13
Coahoma County	43	Tippah County	3
Copiah County	17	Tishomingo County	5
Covington County	7	Tunica County	14
De Soto County	8	Union County	7
Forrest County	5	Walthall County	4
George County	5	Warren County	2
Grenada County	1	Washington County	23
Hinds County	39	Wayne County	2
Holmes County	2	Webster County	4
Issaquena County	1	Wilkinson County	1
Itawamba County	6	Winston County	3
Jackson County	1	Yalobusha County	2
Jefferson County	1	Yazoo County	30
Jefferson Davis County	5		
Jones County	4	Total	556
Kemper County	3		
Lafayette County	3	South Carolina:	
Lamar County	1	Greenville County	1
Lauderdale County	3	Spartanburg County	5
Lawrence County	4		
Leake County	3	Total	6

PELLAGRA—Continued.

City Reports for Week Ended Apr. 13, 1918.

Place.	Cases.	Deaths.	Place.	Cases.	Deaths.
Alexandria, La	1	....	Mobile, Ala	1	1
Atlanta, Ga	....	1	Montgomery, Ala	....	2
Birmingham, Ala	....	2	Nashville, Tenn	....	....
Charleston, S. C	....	1	New Orleans, La	2	....
Dallas, Tex	....	2	Northampton, Mass	1	....
Fort Worth, Tex	1	1	Palestine, Tex	1	....
Jacksonville, Fla	1	....	Passaic, N. J	....	7
Los Angeles, Cal	1	1	Savannah, Ga	....	1
Marshall, Tex	3	....	Schenectady, N. Y	....	1
Memphis, Tenn	2	....	Winston-Salem, N. C	1	....

PNEUMONIA.

City Reports for Week Ended Apr. 13, 1918.

Place.	Cases.	Deaths.	Place.	Cases.	Deaths.
Alexandria, La	1	....	Little Rock, Ark	13	....
Ann Arbor, Mich	2	1	Lorain, Ohio	2	....
Anniston, Ala	2	....	Los Angeles, Cal	10	10
Atlanta, Ga	5	24	Lowell, Mass	9	6
Baltimore, Md	76	36	Lynn, Mass	9	2
Barre, Vt	1	1	Macon, Ga	2	5
Battle Creek, Mich	1	....	Manchester, N. H	4	4
Berkeley, Cal	2	2	Marshall, Tex	3	....
Binghamton, N. Y	8	....	McKeesport, Pa	3	8
Boston, Mass	25	30	Michigan City, Ind	5	5
Braddock, Pa	14	....	Montgomery, Ala	4	....
Bridgeport, Conn	6	19	Newark, N. J	122	21
Brockton, Mass	4	3	New Bedford, Mass	7	3
Buffalo, N. Y	12	31	Newburyport, Mass	2	1
Cambridge, Mass	10	6	New Castle, Pa	7	....
Chattanooga, Tenn	1	3	Newport, Ky	1	1
Chelsea, Mass	15	1	Newton, Mass	2	....
Chicago, Ill	569	193	North Little Rock, Ark	1	1
Chicopee, Mass	1	1	Oshkosh, Wis	2	1
Cleveland, Ohio	53	60	Palestine, Tex	2	....
Clinton, Mass	1	1	Pasadena, Cal	1	....
Coffeyville, Kans	1	....	Philadelphia, Pa	165	91
Dayton, Ohio	2	2	Pittsburgh, Pa	151	132
Detroit, Mich	69	98	Pittsfield, Mass	4	3
Duluth, Minn	19	13	Pontiac, Mich	9	3
Elmira, N. Y	8	3	Providence, R. I	1	22
Erie, Pa	17	10	Provo, Utah	2	....
Fall River, Mass	14	2	Quincy, Mass	2	....
Fargo, N. Dak	1	1	Reading, Pa	7	8
Fitchburg, Mass	5	2	Redlands, Cal	1	....
Flint, Mich	3	5	Rochester, N. Y	29	17
Fort Worth, Tex	9	9	Sacramento, Cal	2	2
Grand Rapids, Mich	6	1	St. Paul, Minn	2	16
Hammond, Ind	2	5	Salem, Mass	3	2
Harrisburg, Pa	2	4	Sandusky, Ohio	2	1
Harrison, N. J	1	....	San Francisco, Cal	26	17
Hattiesburg, Miss	1	....	San Jose, Cal	1	....
Haverhill, Mass	7	....	Saratoga Springs, N. Y	1	1
Holyoke, Mass	7	....	Schenectady, N. Y	13	6
Jackson, Mich	5	5	Somerville, Mass	4	1
Jacksonville, Fla	5	1	Springfield, Mass	13	6
Jamestown, N. Y	1	2	Springfield, Ohio	3	5
Janesville, Wis	2	2	Steelton, Pa	1	....
Johnstown, Pa	5	8	Steubenville, Ohio	2	....
Joplin, Mo	2	....	Toledo, Ohio	3	19
Kalamazoo, Mich	7	1	Waco, Tex	4	....
Kansas City, Kans	13	....	Waltham, Mass	1	....
Lancaster, Pa	1	....	Wichita, Kans	4	1
Lawrence, Mass	6	3	Worcester, Mass	32	16
Lincoln, Nebr	7	1	York, Pa	4	....

POLIOMYELITIS (INFANTILE PARALYSIS).

State Reports for March, 1918.

Place.	New cases reported.	Place.	New cases reported.
Connecticut:		Michigan—Continued.	
Hartford County—		Wayne County—	
Hartford..................	1	Highland Park................	1
		Wexford County—	
Illinois:		Cadillac...................	1
Christian County—			
Assumption Township.........	1	Total....................	5
Taylorville....................	1		
Cook County—		Minnesota:	
Chicago.....................	8	Olmsted County—	
Cicero......................	1	Rochester.................	1
Oak Park....................	1		
Du Page County—		Mississippi:	
Wheaton.................	1	Adams County.............	1
Henry County—		Bolivar County............	1
Lynn Township..............	1	Rankin County.............	1
Moultrie County—		Tate County...............	2
Lovington...............	1		
Sangamon County—		Total....................	5
Springfield...............	1		
Talkington Township..........	1	Nebraska:	
Tazewell County—		Colfax County.............	1
Mackinaw.	1	York County..............	1
Williamson County—			
Herrin.................	1	Total....................	2
Total......................	19	New Jersey:	
		Essex County..............	5
Iowa:			
Crawford County.................	1	North Carolina:	
Dickinson County................	1	Chowan County............	1
Hamilton County................	1	Franklin County............	1
Mills County...................	1		
		Total....................	2
Total.....................	4		
		North Dakota:	
Kansas:		Walsh County..............	1
Brown County—			
Hamlin......................	1	Pennsylvania:	
Harper County—		Allegheny County..........	4
Anthony...................	1	Berks County	1
Harvey County—		Fayette County............	1
Newton....................	1	Lancaster County..........	2
Reno County—		Mercer County.............	2
Hutchinson................	1	Union County	1
Total......................	4	Total....................	11
Michigan:		Wisconsin:	
Lenawee County—		Bayfield County............	1
Clayton	1	Milwaukee County..........	46
Kent County—		Racine County.............	2
Grand Rapids...............	1	Rock County...............	1
Van Buren County —			
Keeler Township..............	1	Total....................	50

City Reports for Week Ended Apr. 13, 1918.

Place.	Cases.	Deaths.	Place.	Cases.	Deaths.
Chicago, Ill.	3	2	Milwaukee, Wis..............	7	2
Columbus, Ohio................	5	3	New Castle, Pa...............	1	....
Jersey City, N. J..............		1	New York, N. Y..............	4	1
Los Angeles, Cal..............	1	....	Pittsburgh, Pa...............	1	....
Lowell, Mass.................	1	1	St. Joseph, Mo...............	1	....
Medford, Mass.................	1	....	San Francisco, Cal...........	1	1

RABIES IN ANIMALS.

City Reports for Week Ended Apr. 13, 1918.

During the week ended April 13, 1918, one case of rabies in animals was reported at Atlantic City, N. J., one case at Louisville, Ky., one case at Reno, Nev., and one case at Winston-Salem, N. C.

ROCKY MOUNTAIN SPOTTED FEVER.

Montana—Missoula County.

On April 29, 1918, one case of Rocky Mountain spotted fever was reported from O'Brien Creek, Missoula County, Mont.

SCARLET FEVER.

See Diphtheria, measles, scarlet fever, and tuberculosis, page 702.

SMALLPOX.

State Reports for March, 1918.

Place.	New cases reported.	Deaths.	Vaccination history of cases.			
			Number vaccinated within 7 years preceding attack.	Number last vaccinated more than 7 years preceding attack.	Number never successfully vaccinated.	Vaccination history not obtained or uncertain.
Kansas:						
Allen County—						
Carlyle	5				5	
Concreto	1				1	
Gas	2				2	
Humboldt	2				2	
Iola	47		1	1	45	
Moran	2				2	
Anderson County—						
Colony	2				2	
Atchison County—						
Atchison	6			2	4	
Huron	16				16	
Lancaster	2				2	
Muscotah	5				5	
Nortonville	1				1	
Barber County—						
Kiowa	1				1	
Barton County—						
Ellinwood	1				1	
Great Bend	6			1	5	
Heizer	1				1	
Pawnee Rock	2				2	
Bourbon County—						
Fort Scott	10			1	9	
Fulton	2				2	
Garland	15				15	
Hammond	5				5	
Uniontown	1				1	
Brown County—						
Everest	4				4	
Hiawatha	14			1	13	
Horton	1				1	
Morrill	4				4	
Netawaka	1				1	
Butler County—						
Atlanta	1				1	
Augusta	6				6	
Douglass	6				6	
Eldorado	59				51	8
Oil Hill	1				1	
Whitewater	1				1	

SMALLPOX—Continued.

State Reports for March, 1918—Continued.

Place.	New cases reported.	Deaths.	Number vaccinated within 7 years preceding attack.	Number last vaccinated more than 7 years preceding attack.	Number never successfully vaccinated.	Vaccination history not obtained or uncertain.
Kansas—Continued.						
Chautauqua County—						
Longton.................	1				1	
Sedan.................	3				3	
Cherokee County—						
Baxter Springs.......	2				2	
Columbus.............	2				2	
Galena...............	25				25	
Melrose..............	1				1	
Scammon.............	17				17	
Weir.................	6				6	
West Mineral........	7				7	
Cheyenne County—						
St. Francis..........	3				3	
Jaqua...............	1				1	
Clark County—						
Minneola............	8				8	
Clay County—						
Clay Center.........	2				2	
Cloud County—						
Aurora..............	3				3	
Clyde...............	1				1	
Concordia...........	1				1	
Coffey County—						
Burlington..........	8				8	
Halls Summit........	1				1	
Leroy...............	2				2	
Waverly.............	1				1	
Comanche County—						
Protection..........	9				9	
Cowley County—						
Arkansas City.......	18				18	
Atlanta.............	4				4	
Cambridge...........	2				2	
Udall...............	2				2	
Winfield............	4			1	3	
Crawford County—						
Arma................	4				4	
Breezy Hill.........	1				1	
Cherokee............	2				2	
Englevale...........	5				5	
Farlington..........	2				2	
Franklin............	1				1	
Frontenac...........	9				9	
Girard..............	13				13	
McCune..............	3			1	2	
Mulberry............	2				2	
Pittsburg...........	25				20	5
Radley..............	7				7	
Decatur County—						
Jennings............	1				1	
Oberlin.............	2				2	
Dickinson County—						
Barrett.............	1				1	
Elmo................	1				1	
Herington...........	9				9	
Hope................	2				2	
Navarre.............	1				1	
Doniphan County—						
Huron...............	1				1	
Severance...........	5				5	
Troy................	6				6	
Wathena.............	1				1	
White Cloud.........	1				1	
Douglas County—						
Eudora..............	1				1	
Lawrence............	3				3	
Edwards County—						
Kinsley.............	1				1	
Kinsley.............	3			1	2	
Elk County—						
Grenola.............	1				1	
Howard..............	30			1	29	

SMALLPOX—Continued.

State Reports for March, 1918—Continued.

Place.	New cases reported.	Deaths.	Vaccination history of cases.			
			Number vaccinated within 7 years preceding attack.	Number last vaccinated more than 7 years preceding attack.	Number never successfully vaccinated.	Vaccination history not obtained or uncertain.
Kansas—Continued.						
Ellsworth County—						
Kanopolis.............	1	....	....	....	1	....
Wilson...................	1	....	....	....	1	....
Finney County—						
Holcomb.............	1	....	....	....	1	....
Ford County—						
Dodge City...........	2	....	....	....	2	....
Franklin County—						
Ottawa................	12	....	....	....	12	....
Gove County—						
Utica.................	4	....	....	....	4	....
Graham County—						
Edmond...............	1	....	....	....	1	....
Hill City.............	85	....	....	....	85	....
Lenora...............	5	....	....	....	5	....
Morland..............	7	....	....	....	7	....
Palco................	1	....	....	....	1	....
Studley..............	1	....	....	....	1	....
Gray County—						
Cimarron.............	7	....	....	....	7	....
Ensign...............	1	....	....	....	1	....
Greenwood County—						
Climax...............	1	....	....	....	1	....
Eureka...............	11	....	....	....	11	....
Reece................	1	....	....	....	1	....
Toronto..............	2	....	....	....	2	....
Harper County—						
Anthony..............	2	....	....	....	2	....
Danville.............	3	....	....	....	3	....
Harper...............	6	....	....	....	6	....
Harvey County—						
Newton...............	11	....	....	....	11	....
Valley Center........	1	....	....	....	1	....
Walton...............	1	....	....	....	1	....
Jackson County—						
Holton...............	2	....	....	....	2	....
Hoyt.................	4	....	....	....	4	....
Straight Creek........	12	....	....	....	12	....
Jefferson County—						
Boyle................	1	....	....	....	1	....
Dunavant.............	2	....	....	....	2	....
McLouth..............	3	....	....	....	3	....
Oskaloosa............	1	....	....	....	1	....
Perry................	1	....	....	....	1	....
Valley Falls.........	1	....	....	....	1	....
Williamstown.........	1	....	....	....	1	....
Jewell County—						
Reubens..............	3	....	....	....	3	....
Webber...............	5	....	....	....	5	....
Johnson County—						
Lenexa...............	1	....	....	....	1	....
Merriam..............	1	....	....	....	1	....
Overland Park........	1	....	....	....	1	....
South Park...........	1	....	....	....	1	....
Zarah................	1	....	....	....	1	....
Kingman County—						
Cheney...............	4	....	....	....	4	....
Nashville............	1	....	....	....	1	....
Pretty Prairie.......	10	....	....	....	10	....
Kiowa County—						
Haviland.............	2	....	....	....	2	....
Labette County—						
Altamont.............	1	....	....	....	1	....
Bartlett.............	1	....	....	....	1	....
Chetopa..............	6	....	....	....	6	....
Edna.................	13	....	....	....	13	....
Parsons..............	16	....	....	1	15	....
Oswego...............	1	....	....	....	1	....
Lane County—						
Healy................	2	....	....	....	2	....

SMALLPOX—Continued.

State Reports for March, 1918—Continued.

Place.	New cases reported.	Deaths.	Vaccination history of cases.			
			Number vaccinated within 7 years preceding attack.	Number last vaccinated more than 7 years preceding attack.	Number never successfully vaccinated.	Vaccination history not obtained or uncertain.
Kansas—Continued.						
Leavenworth County—						
Bain City	3				3	
Easton	5				5	
Leavenworth	13			1	12	
Tonganoxie	1				1	
Lincoln County—						
Beverly	1				1	
Milo	1				1	
Linn County—						
Parker	8			1	7	
Lyon County—						
Admire	1				1	
Dunlap	1				1	
Emporia	15				14	1
Marion County—						
Durham	1				1	
Hillsboro	17				17	
Lehigh	6				6	
Marion	1				1	
Peabody	5				5	
Tampa	12				12	
Marshall County—						
Blue Rapids	4				4	
Irving	2				2	
Lellis	1				1	
Vermilion	7				7	
McPherson County—						
Galva	1				1	
Marquette	2				2	
Miami County—						
Beagle	1				1	
Hillsdale	1				1	
Osawatomie	25				24	1
Paola	8				8	
Wellsville	7				7	
Mitchell County—						
Beloit	1				1	
Blue Hill	1				1	
Cawker City	6				6	
Montgomery County—						
Caney	4				4	
Cherryvale	11				11	
Coffeyville	28			3	25	
Dearing	1				1	
Independence	8				7	1
Morris County—						
Dunlap	1				1	
Council Grove	1				1	
White City	3				2	1
Nemaha County—						
Corning	3				3	
Neosho County—						
Chanute	6				6	
Earlton	1				1	
Erie	1				1	
St. Paul	1				1	
Osage County—						
Lyndon	3				3	
Olivet	3				3	
Osage City	3				2	1
Overbrook	4				4	
Scranton	6				6	
Osborne County—						
Portis	1				1	
Wooton	1				1	
Pawnee County—						
Larned	4				4	
Phillips County—						
Longford	1				1	
Woodruff	1			1		

SMALLPOX—Continued.

State Reports for March, 1918—Continued.

Place.	New cases reported.	Deaths.	Number vaccinated within 7 years preceding attack.	Number last vaccinated more than 7 years preceding attack.	Number never successfully vaccinated.	Vaccination history not obtained or uncertain.
Kansas—Continued.						
Pottawatomie County—						
Belvue	2				2	
Blaine	1				1	
Garrison	1				1	
Louisville	2				2	
Wamego	1				1	
Pratt County—						
Pratt	1				1	
Reno County—						
Abbyville	1				1	
Haven	4				4	
Hutchinson	25				25	
Turon	4				4	
Whiteside	1				1	
Republic County—						
Belleville	3			1	1	
Cuba	1				1	
Rydal	4				4	
Rice County—						
Little River	2				2	
Lyons	2				1	1
Raymond	1				1	
Wherry	1				1	
Riley County—						
Green	1				1	
Keats	1				1	
Manhattan	7			3	4	
Stockdale	11				11	
Rooks County—						
Plainville	1				1	
Woodston	2					2
Russell County—						
Bunker Hill	1			1		
Lucas	2				2	
Luray	2				2	
Saline County—						
Assaria	1				1	
Gypsum	4			1	3	
New Cambria	2				2	
Salina	38				38	
Scott County—						
Scott City	3		1		2	
Sedgwick County—						
Furley	13				13	
Goddard	1				1	
Koobi	6				6	
Valley Center	4				4	
Whitewater	1				1	
Wichita	102				102	
Seward County—						
Liberal	10				10	
Shawnee County—						
Topeka	43				43	
Sheridan County—						
Studley	3				3	
Smith County—						
Lebanon	7				7	
Smith Center	2				2	
Stevens County—						
Hugoton	3				3	
Rolla	1				1	
Sumner County—						
Ashton	5				5	
Belle Plaine	1				1	
Caldwell	1				1	
Oxford	2				2	
South Haven	1				1	
Wellington	2				2	
Trego County—						
Collyer	2				2	
Ogallah	1				1	

SMALLPOX—Continued.

State Reports for March, 1918—Continued.

Place.	New cases reported.	Deaths.	Vaccination history of cases.			
			Number vaccinated within 7 years preceding attack.	Number last vaccinated more than 7 years preceding attack.	Number never successfully vaccinated.	Vaccination history not obtained or uncertain.
Kansas—Continued.						
Wabaunsee County—						
Alta Vista...........	1				1	
Belvue...............	5				5	
Paxico..............	2				2	
Washington County—						
Washington.......	1			1		
Wilson County—						
Altoona.............	3				3	
Fredonia...........	2				2	
Neodesha...........	8				8	
Roper..............	1				1	
Woodson County—						
Rose...............	1				1	
Yates Center......	7				7	
Wyandotte County—						
Bethel.............	3				3	
Bonner Springs.....	2				2	
Edwardsville.......	1				1	
Muncie.............	4			2	2	
Kansas City........	153				153	
Rosedale...........	35			1	34	
Total...............	1,604		2	27	1,553	22
Michigan:						
Alcona County—						
Curtis Township....	1				1	
Harrisville Township..	1				1	
Alpena County—						
Ossiniki Township.....	1				1	
Antrim County—						
Banks Township........	1				1	
Arenac County—						
Mason Township...	1				1	
Standish Township....	1				1	
Barry County—						
Johnston Township...	1				1	
Rutland Township..	5				5	
Pinconning Township...	6				6	
Pinconning............	1				1	
Berrien County—						
Sodas Township.......	1				1	
Niles.................	3				3	
Branch County—						
Coldwater.........	2				2	
Calhoun County—						
Albion.............	34				74	
Battle Creek.........	8				8	
Marshall.............	1				1	
Cass County—						
Valinia Township.......	1					1
Dowagiac...........	3				3	
Charlevoix County—						
Charlevoix.........	1				1	
Chippewa County—						
Sault Ste. Marie..........	5		1	2	3	
Clinton County—						
Duplain Township.......	2				2	
Dickinson County—						
Norway...............	6			2	1	
Eaton County—						
Benton Township.......	5				5	
Oneida Township.......	1				1	
Emmet County—						
Pleasant View Township..	1					1
Genesee County—						
Montrose Township	9				9	
Richfield Township.	2				2	
Thetford Township	2				2	
Vienna Township.	2				2	
Cho	10				10	
Flint..	53				53	

SMALLPOX—Continued.

State Reports for March, 1918—Continued.

Place.	New cases reported.	Deaths.	Vaccination history of cases.			
			Number vaccinated within 7 years preceding attack.	Number last vaccinated more than 7 years preceding attack.	Number never successfully vaccinated.	Vaccination history not obtained or uncertain.
Michigan—Continued.						
Grand Traverse County—						
Mayfield Township	1				1	
Paradise Township	4				4	
Traverse City	2				2	
Hillsdale County—						
Hillsdale Township	1				1	
Ransom Township	4				4	
Reading Township	1		1			
Hillsdale	4				4	
Huron County—						
Lincoln Township	3				3	
Wright Township	1				1	
Port Hope	1				1	
Bad Axe	1				1	
Ingham County—						
Aurelius Township	1				1	
Delhi Township	1				1	
Lansing Township	2				2	
Leroy Township	1				1	
Locke Township	6				6	
Meridian Township	1				1	
Webberville	7				7	
Williamston	2				2	
Lansing	25				25	
Ionia County—						
Lake Odessa	1				1	
Ionia	3				3	
Iosco County—						
Oscoda Township	5				5	
Sherman Township	10				10	
Wilber Township	1				1	
Jackson County—						
Columbia Township	1				1	
Liberty Township	1				1	
Jackson	3			1	2	
Kalamazoo County—						
Schoolcraft	1				1	
Kalamazoo	20				20	
Kent County—						
Plainfield Township	1				1	
Sparta	1				1	
Grand Rapids	21		7		14	
Lake County—						
Chase Township	2				2	
Lenawee County—						
Adrian Township	4				4	
Dover Township	1				1	
Mackinac County—						
Newton Township	2				2	
Macomb County—						
Clinton Township	1				1	
Mount Clemens	2				2	
Manistee County—						
Norman Township	1			1		
Manistee	1				1	
Mason County—						
Ludington	2				2	
Mecosta County—						
Colfax Township	6				6	
Big Rapids	8				8	
Missaukee County—						
Norwich Township	1				1	
Richland Township	1				1	
McBain	1				1	
Monroe County—						
Welan Township	1			1		
Monroe	16				16	
Montcalm County—						
Fairplains Township	1					
Pierson Township	2					
Howard City	5					
Sheridan	1					

SMALLPOX—Continued.

State Reports for March, 1918—Continued.

Place.	New cases reported.	Deaths.	Vaccination history of cases.			
			Number vaccinated within 7 years preceding attack.	Number last vaccinated more than 7 years preceding attack.	Number never successfully vaccinated.	Vaccination history not obtained or uncertain.
Michigan.— Continued.						
Montmorency County—						
Avery Township..........	1				1	
Muskegon County—						
Muskegon Township......	9				9	
Norton Township........	2				2	
Montague...............	1				1	
Muskegon...............	6				6	
Muskegon Heights.......	8				8	
Newago County—						
Monroe Township........	2				2	
Sherman Township.......	3			2	1	
Wilcox Township........	4				4	
Oakland County—						
Highland Township......	1				1	
Royal Oak Township.....	1				1	
Rochester..............	5				5	
Pontiac................	11				11	
Oceana County—						
Crystal Township	2				2	
Shelby Township........	1				1	
Ogemaw County—						
Mills Township.........	1				1	
Osceola County—						
Middle Branch Town ł.łp.	1				1	
Rose Lake Township.....	4				2	2
Leroy..................	3				2	1
Oscoda County—						
Mentor Township........	2				2	
Otsego County —						
Gaylord	1				1	
Ottawa County —						
Bendon Township...	1				1	
Holland Township.......	1				1	
Wright Township........	1				1	
Presque Isle County —						
Posen Township.........	3				7	
Onaway................	1				1	
St. Clair County—						
Clyde Township.........	2				2	
St. Joseph County —						
Mendon	9				9	
Three Rivers...........	2				2	
Sanilac County—						
Bridgehampton Township.	3				3	
Delaware Township.	1				1	
Lamotte Township	4				1	
Lexington Township	1		1			
Marlette Township	3				3	
Sanilac Township	1				1	
Washington Township....	4				4	
Watertown Township	1				1	
Wheatland Township	2				2	
Lexington	1				1	
Schoolcraft County —						
Manistique	1				1	
Shiawassee County —						
Antrim Township	1					
Durand	1			1		
Tuscola County—						
Akron Township	7				7	
Almer Township	11				11	
Columbia Township	4				1	
Kingston Township	5				5	
Akron	6				6	
Van Buren County						
Paw Paw	1					
Washtenaw County						
Lodi Township	2				2	
Ann Arbor	1				1	

SMALLPOX—Continued.

State Reports for March, 1918—Continued.

Place.	New cases reported.	Deaths.	Number vaccinated within 7 years preceding attack.	Number last vaccinated more than 7 years preceding attack.	Number never successfully vaccinated.	Vaccination history not obtained or uncertain.
Michigan—Continued.						
Wayne County—						
Brownston Township.....	1				1	
Nankin Township........	1		1			
Redford Township........	1				1	
Dearborn.................	4				4	
Ecorse...................	1				1	
Ford.....................	1				1	
Highland Park...........	12				12	
Northville...............	1				1	
St. Clair Heights.........	12				12	
Detroit..................	133				133	
Wyandotte..............	2				2	
Wexford County—						
Cherry Grove Township...	1				1	
Henderson Township.....	3				3	
Liberty Township........	1				1	
Cadillac.................	12				12	
Total...................	683	....	12	9	662	6
Minnesota:						
Aitkin County—						
Pliny Township..........	1				1	
Anoka County—						
Columbia Heights........	2				2	
Beltrami County—						
Bemidji..................	7			1	6	
Blue Earth County—						
Mankato.................	1				1	
Beauford Township.......	1			1		
Brown County—						
Leavenworth Township...	2				2	
Cass County—						
Backus..................	1				1	
Chippewa County—						
Crate Township..........	1				1	
Chisago County—						
Rush City...............	2			1	1	
Clay County—						
Moorhead................	2			1	1	
Cromwell Township.......	1				1	
Clearwater County—						
Leon Township..........	2				2	
Crow Wing County—						
Brainerd.................	22				22	
Dakota County—						
Farmington..............	3			1	2	
Douglas County—						
Alexandria..............	1				1	
Carlos...................	1				1	
Osakis...................	5				5	
Faribault County—						
Elmore..................	1				1	
Fillmore County—						
Peterson................	1				1	
Arendahl Township......	1				1	
Freeborn County—						
Hayward Township......	1				1	
Moscow Township.......	2				2	
Goodhue County—						
Red Wing...............	5		2		2	
Hennepin County—						
Minneapolis.........	72			13	59	
Wayzata............	1				1	
Bloomington Township...	1				1	
Corcoran Township.....	1				1	
Dayton Township........	2				2	
Hassan Township.......	13				13	
Maple Grove Township...	1				1	
Houston County—						
Wilmington Township....	16				16	

SMALLPOX—Continued.

State Reports for March, 1918—Continued.

Place.	New cases reported.	Deaths.	Number vaccinated within 7 years preceding attack.	Number last vaccinated more than 7 years preceding attack.	Number never successfully vaccinated.	Vaccination history not obtained or uncertain.
Minnesota—Continued						
Itasca County—						
Bovey....	1					
Jackson County—						
Heron Lake.	1				1	
La Crosse Township	1				1	....
Kittson County—						
Hallock	4				4	
Lancaster	2		1		1	
Hill Township	2				2	
Poppleton Township	2				2	
Richardville Township	1			1		
St. Vincent Township	24				24	
Koochiching County—						
International Falls	1				1	
Lyon County						
Marshall	4			2	2	
Marshall County—						
Augsburg Township	1				1	
Meeker County—						
Litchfield	17		2	6	9	
Forest City Township	1				1	
Mille Lacs County						
Milaca	7				7	
Mower County—						
Austin	1				1	
Adams Township	4				4	
Lodi Township	2				2	
Murray County—						
Lake Wilson	2				2	
Norman County—						
Bear Park Township	1				1	
Olmsted County—						
Rochester	8			1	7	
Ottertail County—						
Aurdal Township	1				1	
Pennington County—						
Reiner Township	1				1	
Pine County—						
Hinckley	1			1		....
Pipestone County—						
Jasper	4				4	
Pipestone	13			2	2	9
Polk County—						
Fertile	1				1	
Ramsey County—						
St. Paul	11				11	....
Rice County—						
Dennison	1				1	
Rock County—						
Rose Dell Township	2				2	
Roseau County						
Jadis Township	2				2	
Grimstad Township	1				1	
Mickmock Township	2				2	
St. Louis County—						
Duluth	5				5	....
Proctor	8				8	....
Virginia	1				1	....
Scott County—						
Shakopee	2			1		
Stearns County—						
St. Cloud	1				1	....
Sartell	5				5	.. ..
Todd County—						
Osakis	2				2	....
West Union Township	1				1	....
Wadena County—						
Aldrich Township	1				1	....
Meadow Township	6			1	5	....
Washington County—						
Stillwater	1				1	....

SMALLPOX—Continued.

State Reports for March, 1918—Continued.

Place.	New cases reported.	Deaths.	Vaccination history of cases.			
			Number vaccinated within 7 years preceding attack.	Number last vaccinated more than 7 years preceding attack.	Number never successfully vaccinated.	Vaccination history not obtained or uncertain.
Minnesota—Continued.						
Watonwan County—						
St. James	2				2	
St. James Township	2				2	
Wright County—						
Cokato Township	18					18
Total	355		5	33	288	29
New Jersey:						
Atlantic County	19			2	17	
Essex County	1					1
Morris County	3					3
Passaic County	1					1
Total	24			2	17	5
Wisconsin:						
Ashland County	4			2		2
Bayfield County	3					3
Buffalo County	8				8	
Burnett County	9		3		6	
Chippewa County	44		1	2	23	18
Crawford County	12			1	10	1
Dane County	16		15			1
Douglas County	10		1	1	6	2
Fond du Lac County	1					1
Grant County	24		1	5	18	
Green County	1				1	
Jackson County	4				4	
Jefferson County	12		4	1	5	2
Kenosha County	6				2	4
La Crosse County	26			1	25	
Langlade County	4			4		
Lincoln County	9		7		2	
Manitowoc County	1				1	
Marathon County	1				1	
Milwaukee County	39					39
Monroe County	28		1	2	5	20
Oconto County	2				1	1
Racine County	2		2			
Rock County	21			1	17	3
St. Croix County	5				3	2
Sheboygan County	5				4	1
Trempealeau County	1		1			
Washburn County	1					1
Washington County	2				2	
Waukesha County	1		1			
Waupaca County	1					1
Winnebago County	5				5	
Wood County	5				5	
Total	313		37	20	154	102

Miscellaneous State Reports for March, 1918.

Connecticut:
  Hartford County—
    Bloomfield ....
    East Windsor ....
    Hartford ....
    New Britain ....
  New London County –
    Montville ....

    Total ....

Illinois:
  Adams County –
    Fall Creek Township ....
    Loraine ....
    Quincy ....
  Brown County –
    Elkhorn Township .. ..
  Bureau County—
    Arispie Township ....
    Mineral ....
    Mineral Township ....

SMALLPOX—Continued.

Miscellaneous State Reports for March, 1918—Continued.

Place.	Cases.	Deaths.	Place.	Cases.	Deaths.
Illinois—Continued.			**Illinois—Continued.**		
Calhoun County.........			Jackson County—		
Batchtown............	1	....	Bradley Township....	4	....
Cass County—	2	....	Campbell Hill........	3	....
Beardstown...........			Degognia Township..	1	....
Champaign County—	4	....	De Soto.............	1	....
Champaign...........			De Soto Township....	3	....
Urbana..............	1	....	Elk Township........	5	....
Christian County—	1	....	Murphysboro........	1	....
Taylorville..........	2	....	Jefferson County—		
Morrisonville........	3	....	Elk Prairie Township.	2	....
Ricks Township......	4	....	Mount Vernon.......	1	....
Clinton County—			Jersey County—		
Lake Township......	1	....	Jerseyville..........	12	....
Wade Township......	1	....	Ruyle Township.....	4	....
Coles County—			Jo Daviess County—		
East Oakland Town-			Galena..............	2	....
ship............	1	....	Johnson County—		
Cook County—			Vienna.............	1	....
Chicago.............	50	....	Knox County—		
Cicero..............	1	....	Galesburg..........	18	....
Evanston............	1	....	La Salle County—		
La Grange..........	1	....	Richland Township..	1	....
La Grange Park.....	1	....	Lawrence County—		
Lemont.............	2	....	Dennison Township..	2	....
Oak Park...........	1	....	Lawrenceville.......	3	....
Cumberland County—			Logan County—		
Sumpter Township...	1	....	Lincoln.............	1	....
Toledo..............	1	....	Macon County—		
Union Township.....	1	....	Decatur............	4	....
Douglas County—			Friends Creek Town-		
Sargent Township....	1	....	ship............	1	....
Edgar County—			Macoupin County—		
Edgar Township.....	7	....	Barr Township......	1	....
Elbridge Township...	6	....	Bunker Hill Town-		
Hume...............	1	....	ship............	1	....
Kansas.............	2	....	Carlinville.........	2	....
Paris...............	1	....	Gillespie...........	1	....
Effingham County—			Hilyard Township....	2	....
Effingham...........	2	....	Honey Point Town-		
Fayette County—			ship............	1	....
Ramsey Township...	2	....	Medora............	12	....
Sefton Township.....	1	....	Mount Olive Town-		
Seminary Township..	5	....	ship............	38	....
St. Elmo...........	1	....	Pease Township.....	2	....
St. Peter...........	1	....	Scottville..........	1	....
Wilberton Township.	7	....	Shipman............	3	....
Vandalia Township...	1	....	South Otter Town-		
Franklin County—			ship............	1	....
Benton.............	8	....	Palmyra............	7	....
Buckner............	1	....	South Palmyra Town-		
Cave Township......	8	....	ship............	4	....
Christopher.........	1	....	Staunton...........	6	....
Good Hope Township.	9	....	Virden.............	20	....
Six Mile Township...	7	....	White City.........	29	....
Sesser..............	1	....	Madison County—		
West City..........	4	....	Alton..............	75	....
Ziegler.............	4	....	Collinsville.........	19	....
Fulton County—			East Alton.........	1	....
Canton.............	1	....	Fosterburg Township	1	....
Farmington.........	5	....	Granite City	27	....
Greene County—			Godfrey Township....	2	....
Bluffdale Township..	1	....	Madison............	4	....
Carrollton..........	4	....	Venice.............	13	....
Patterson Township..	1	....	Wood River........	2	....
Rockybridge Town-			Marion County—		
ship............	1	....	Odin...............	20	....
Hamilton County—			Odin Township......	3	....
Flannigan Township.	4	....	Salem Township.....	2	....
Knights Prairie			Mason County—		
Township........	1	....	Easton.............	1	....
Hancock County—			Massac County—		
Basco..............	2	....	Metropolis..........	1	....
Hardin County.........	2	....	McDonough County—		
Henderson County—			Bushnell...........	4	....
Stronghurst.	2	....	Emmet Township....	5	....
Henry County—			Good Hope..........	3	....
Annawan...........	8	....	McLean County—		
Kewanee	2	....	Bloomington........	1	....
Loraine Township...	1	....	Chenoa	1	....
Iroquois County—			Le Roy	1	....
Watseka............	1	....	Money Creek Town-		
			ship............	1	....

SMALLPOX—Continued.

Miscellaneous State Reports for March, 1918—Continued.

Place.	Cases.	Deaths.	Place.	Cases.	Deaths.
Illinois—Continued.			Illinois—Continued.		
Montgomery County—			Tazewell County—		
Coffeen	6		Cincinnati Township	1	
East York Township	2		East Peoria	3	
Morgan County—			Pekin	1	
Jacksonville	5		South Pekin	1	
Moultrie County—			Union County—		
Sullivan	6		Dongola	4	
Peoria County—			Vermilion County—		
Averyville	2		Danville	3	
Brimfield	1		Wabash County—		
Brimfield Township	1		Mount Carmel	1	
Chillicothe Township	1		Warren County—		
Kickapoo Township	1		Monmouth	1	
Limestone Township	1		Washington County—		
Peoria	31		Nashville	1	
Peoria Heights	1		Wayne County—		
Perry County—			Indian Prairie Township	1	
Duquoin	14		White County—		
Piatt County—			Enfield	1	
Cisco	1		Whitesides County—		
Willow Branch Township	3		Fulton	3	
Pike County—			Williamson County—		
Atlas Township	1		Blairsville Township	6	
Flint Township	1		Bush	3	
Neuberg Township	1		Cambria	5	
Pleasant Hill	1		Carterville	5	
Pleasant Hill Township	1		Carterville Township	10	
Pulaski County—			Creal Springs	2	
Mound City	3		East Marion Township	3	
Randolph County—			Eight Mile Township	2	
Percy	11		Energy	5	
Red Bud	3		Herrin	22	
Rockwood	2		Hurst	2	
Rockwood Precinct	9		Marion	1	
Richland County—			Stonefort Township	1	
Olney Township	1		Winnebago County—		
Rock Island County—			Rockford	4	
Moline	3		Rockton	3	
Rock Island	2		Woodford County—		
Saline County—			Greene Township	1	
East Eldorado Township	2		Palestine Township	2	
Eldorado	9		Seco	1	
Galatia Township	5		Southern Illinois Penitentiary	3	
Gaskins City	4				
Harrisburg	6		Total	999	
Harrisburg Township	3				
Independence Township	2		Iowa:		
Sangamon County—			Adair County	3	
Chatham Township	1		Adams County	10	
Springfield	8		Appanoose County	4	
Williamsville	1		Audubon County	4	
Shelby County—			Benton County	1	
Herrick Township	8		Blackhawk County	4	
Shelbyville	2		Boone County	5	
St. Clair County—			Bremer County	5	
Belleville	15		Buena Vista County	1	
Centerville Township	1		Butler County	5	
Dupo	1		Cass County	5	
East St. Louis	12		Cedar County	2	
Englemann Township	1		Cerro Gordo County	17	
Freeburg	12		Cherokee County	2	
Marissa	4		Clay County	1	
Mascoutah	3		Clayton County	7	
Millstadt	8		Crawford County	1	
New Baden	3		Dallas County	3	
Smithton	1		Davis County	2	
St. Clair Township	2		Decatur County	2	
Swansea	1		Des Moines County	7	
Stark County—			Dickinson County	4	
Toulon	1		Dubuque County	16	
Stephenson County—			Emmet County	2	
Dakota	1		Fremont County	7	
Freeport	6		Grundy County	1	
			Guthrie County	1	
			Hancock County	5	

SMALLPOX—Continued.

Miscellaneous State Reports for March, 1918—Continued.

Place.	Cases.	Deaths.	Place.	Cases.	Deaths.
Illinois—Continued.			Illinois—Continued.		
Calhoun County—			Jackson County—		
Batchtown	1		Bradley Township	4	
Cass County—	2		Campbell Hill	3	
Board:town	4		Degognia Township	1	
Champaign County—			De Soto	1	
Champaign	1		De Soto Township	3	
Urbana	1		Elk Township	5	
Christian County—			Murphysboro	1	
Taylorville	2		Jefferson County—		
Morrisonville	3		Elk Prairie Township	2	
Ricks Township	4		Mount Vernon	1	
Clinton County—			Jersey County—		
Lake Township	1		Jerseyville	12	
Wade Township	1		Ruyle Township	4	
Co'es County—			Jo Daviess County—		
East Oakland Township	1		Galena	2	
Cook County—			Johnson County—		
Chicago	50		Vienna	1	
Cicero	1		Knox County—		
Evanston	1		Galesburg	15	
La Grange	1		La Salle County—		
La Grange Park	1		Richland Township	1	
Lemont	2		Lawrence County—		
Oak Park	1		Dennison Township	2	
Cumberland County—			Lawrenceville	3	
Sumpter Township	1		Logan County—		
Toledo	1		Lincoln	1	
Union Township	1		Macon County—		
Douglas County—			Decatur	4	
Sargent Township	1		Friends Creek Township	1	
Edgar County –			Macoupin County—		
Edgar Township	7		Barr Township	1	
Elbridge Township	6		Bunker Hill Township	1	
Hume	1		Carlinville	2	
Kansas	2		Gillespie	1	
Paris	1		Hilyard Township	2	
Effingham County –			Honey Point Township	1	
Effingham	2		Medora	12	
Fayette County –			Mount Olive Township	38	
Ramsey Township	2		Pease Township	2	
Sefton Township	1		Scottville	1	
Seminary Township	5		Shipman	3	
St Elmo	1		South Otter Township	1	
St. Peter	1		Palmyra	7	
Wilberton Township	7		South Palmyra Township	4	
Vandalia Township	1		Staunton	6	
Franklin County—			Virden	20	
Benton	8		White City	29	
Buckner	1		Madison County—		
Cavo Township	8		Alton	75	
Christopher	1		Collinsville	19	
Good Hope Township	9		East Alton	1	
Six Mile Township	7		Fosterbury Township	1	
Sesser	1		Granite City	27	
West City	4		Godfrey Township	2	
Ziegler	4		Madison	4	
Fulton County—			Venice	13	
Canton	1		Wood River	2	
Farmington	5		Marion County—		
Greene County—			Odin	20	
Bluffdale Township	1		Odin Township	3	
Carrollton	4		Salem Township	2	
Patterson Township	1		Mason County—		
Rockybridge Township	1		Easton	1	
Hamilton County—			Massac County—		
Flannigan Township	4		Metropolis	1	
Knights Prairie Township	1		McDonough County—		
Hancock County—			Bushnell	4	
Basco	2		Emmet Township	5	
Hardin County	2		Good Hope	3	
Henderson County—			McLean County—		
Stronghurst	2		Bloomington	1	
Henry County—			Chenoa	1	
Annawan	8		Le Roy	1	
Kewanee	2		Money Creek Township	1	
Loraine Township	1				
Iroquois County –					
Watseka	1				

Place.					
Illinois—Continued.					
Montgomery County—					
Coffeen					
East York Township					
Morgan County—					
Jacksonville					
Moultrie County—					
Sullivan					
Peoria County—					
Averyville					
Brimfield					
Brimfield Township					
Chillicothe Township					
Kickapoo Township					
Limestone Township					
Peoria					
Peoria Heights					
Perry County—					
Duquoin					
Piatt County—					
Cisco					
Willow Branch Township					
Pike County—					
Atlas Township					
Flint Township					
Newburg Township					
Pleasant Hill					
Pleasant Hill Township					
Pulaski County—					
Mound City					
Randolph County—					
Percy					
Red Bud					
Rockwood					
Rockwood Precinct					
Richland County—					
Olney Township					
Rock Island County—					
Moline					
Rock Island					
Saline County—					
Eldorado Township						1
Eldorado					
...th Township						2
...kee City						6
...bury						1
...ford Township						15
...dence Township						5
						21
...quois County—						13
Onarga Township					
...ngfield					
...ville						50

SMALLPOX—Continued.

Miscellaneous State Reports for March, 1918—Continued.

Place.	Cases.	Deaths.	Place.	Cases.	Deaths.
Iowa—Continued.			**Mississippi—Continued.**		
Hardin County	1		Quitman County	5	
Harrison County	12		Rankin County	7	
Henry County	2		Scott County	5	
Howard County	5		Sharkey County	1	
Humboldt County	4		Stone County	7	
Jasper County	8		Sunflower County	33	
Johnson County	7		Tallahatchie County	44	
Kossuth County	5		Tate County	31	
Linn County	14		Tippah County	2	
Lyon County	1		Tishomingo County	1	
Madison County	11		Tunica County	1	
Marion County	2		Union County	6	
Mills County	6		Warren County	11	
Mitchell County	14		Washington County	7	
O'Brien County	1		Webster County	4	
Palo Alto County	2		Yalobusha County	4	
Pocahontas County	1		Yazoo County	9	
Polk County	120				
Pottawattamie County	95	1	Total	622	
Poweshiek County	3				
Ringgold County	3		**Nebraska:**		
Scott County	5		Adams County	14	
Sioux County	3		Antelope County	4	
Taylor County	3		Arthur County	6	
Van Buren County	36		Boone County	2	
Wapello County	40		Box Butte County	6	
Warren County	1		Boyd County	1	
Washington County	2		Buffalo County	6	
Wayne County	5		Burt County	5	
Webster County	7		Butler County	2	
Winnebago County	6		Cass County	3	
Winneshiek County	2		Cherry County	45	
Woodbury County	2		Cheyenne County	53	
			Custer County	19	
Total	556	1	Dixon County	5	
			Douglas County	161	
Mississippi:			Fillmore County	31	
Adams County	4		Franklin County	2	
Alcorn County	3		Furnas County	11	
Amite County	16		Grant County	6	
Attala County	10		Greeley County	2	
Benton County	1		Hall County	6	
Bolivar County	21		Hitchcock County	6	
Calhoun County	4		Holt County	12	
Carroll County	12		Johnson County	3	
Chickasaw County	16		Lancaster County	54	
Clarke County	10		Madison County	50	
Clay County	6		Nance County	23	
Coahoma County	15		Nemaha County	1	
Copiah County	2		Otoe County	45	
Covington County	3		Pawnee County	12	
Forrest County	6		Phelps County	2	
George County	2		Platte County	1	
Greene County	1		Polk County	4	
Grenada County	2		Red Willow County	1	
Harrison County	2		Richardson County	24	
Hinds County	36		Saunders County	4	
Holmes County	13		Scotts Bluff County	1	
Issaquena County	2		Seward County	10	
Itawamba County	6		Sheridan County	10	
Jasper County	73		Sherman County	1	
Jones County	11		Sioux County	9	
Lafayette County	4		Thayer County	13	
Lauderdale County	11		Thurston County	14	
Lee County	16		Valley County	1	
Leflore County	30		Washington County	15	
Lincoln County	2		Wayne County	34	
Lowndes County	10		Webster County	5	
Madison County	15		Wheeler County	4	
Marshall County	1		York County	1	
Monroe County	1				
Montgomery County	6		Total	734	
Oktibbeha County	10				
Panola County	23		**North Carolina:**		
Pearl River County	5		Alleghany County	4	
Perry County	9		Ashe County	1	
Pike County	1		Avery County	12	
Pontotoc County	13		Buncombe County	4	
Prentiss County	6		Cabarrus County	2	

SMALLPOX—Continued.

Miscellaneous State Reports for March, 1918—Continued.

Place.	Cases.	Deaths.	Place.	Cases.	Deaths.
North Carolina—Continued.			**Pennsylvania—Continued.**		
Catawba County	1		Indiana County	2	
Clay County	1		Lackawanna County	1	
Columbus County	2		Mercer County	3	
Cumberland County	2		McKean County	1	
Currituck County	1		Mifflin County	1	
Edgecombe County	19		Philadelphia County	7	
Forsyth County	4		Potter County	2	
Gaston County	9		Somerset County	1	
Haywood County	6		Tioga County	7	
Jackson County	10		Westmoreland County	2	
Johnston County	1		York County	7	
Lee County	4				
McDowell County	4		Total	89	
Perqimans County	4				
Randolph County	4		**South Carolina:**		
Rowan County	10		Greenville County	2	
Stanly County	24		Spartanburg County	10	
Surry County	5				
Swain County	2		Total	12	
Union County	1				
Wayne County	1		**South Dakota:**		
Wilkes County	1		Bon Homme County	1	
			Brown County	21	
Total	137		Clay County	26	
			Codington County	8	
North Dakota:			Davison County	2	
Bottineau County	4		Deuel County	7	
Burleigh County	1		Edmunds County	1	
Cass County	4		Hand County	15	
Foster County	8		Hanson County	2	
Grand Forks County	15		Hughes County	2	
Griggs County	1		Hyde County	5	
La Moure County	6		Jones County	1	
McKenzie County	3		Kingsbury County	2	
Mountrail County	5		Lake County	1	
Nelson County	2		Lawrence County	1	
Pembina County	1		McCook County	12	
Ramsey County	2		Minnehaha County	2	
Renville County	2		Roberts County	4	
Richland County	3		Union County	6	
Sargent County	5		Walworth County	3	
Ward County	6		Yankton County	2	
Williams County	4				
			Total	124	
Total	72				
			Wyoming:		
Pennsylvania:			Laramie County	2	
Allegheny County	14		Johnson County	6	
Armstrong County	2		Hot Springs County	1	
Cambria County	10		Niobrara County	1	
Clearfield County	2		Albany County	1	
Dauphin County	18		Washakie County	5	
Elk County	1		Natrona County	21	
Erie County	5		Carbon County	13	
Fayette County	1				
Greene County	2		Total	50	

City Reports for Week Ended Apr. 13, 1918.

Place.	Cases.	Deaths.	Place.	Cases.	Deaths.
Akron, Ohio	17		Chanute, Kans	1	
Alton, Ill	21		Chattanooga, Tenn	5	
Ann Arbor, Mich	1		Chicago, Ill	4	
Anniston, Ala	11		Chillicothe, Ohio	1	
Appleton, Wis	1		Cincinnati, Ohio	14	
Atlanta, Ga	6		Cleveland, Ohio	22	
Baltimore, Md	5		Coffeyville, Kans	5	
Beloit, Wis	2		Colorado Springs, Colo	1	
Birmingham, Ala	25		Columbus, Ohio	1	
Butte, Mont	1		Council Bluffs, Iowa	13	
Canton, Ohio	3		Covington, Ky	1	
Cape Girardeau, Mo	3		Dallas, Tex	3	
Centralia, Ill	1		Davenport, Iowa	1	

SMALLPOX—Continued.

City Reports for Week Ended Apr. 13, 1918—Continued.

Place.	Cases.	Deaths.	Place.	Cases.	Deaths.
Dayton, Ohio	1		Mason City, Iowa	1	
Denver, Colo	30		Memphis, Tenn	14	
Des Moines, Iowa	9		Milwaukee, Wis	10	
Detroit, Mich	17		Minneapolis, Minn	20	
Dubuque, Iowa	4		Mobile, Ala	5	
Elmira, N. Y	2		Montgomery, Ala	3	
El Paso, Tex	3		Muncie, Ind	5	
Everett, Wash	1		Muskogee, Okla	11	
Fargo, N. Dak	1		Nashville, Tenn	8	
Flint, Mich	1		New Albany, Ind	1	
Fort Scott, Kans	19		New Castle, Ind	2	
Fort Smith, Ark	4		New Orleans, La	5	
Fort Wayne, Ind	1		North Little Rock, Ark	2	
Fort Worth, Tex	17			1	
Fresno, Cal	1		Okla	23	
Galesburg, Ill	1			30	
Grand Forks, N. Dak	2		Va	5	
Grand Rapids, Mich	3			1	
Greeley, Colo	3		O	1	
Hammond, Ind	1		P	1	
Hattiesburg, Miss	3		Portland, Oreg	1	
Houston, Tex	2		Provo, Utah	3	
Indianapolis, Ind	40		Quincy, Ill	22	
Iola, Kans	10		Richmond, Ind	1	
Janesville, Wis	3		Roanoke, Va	1	
Joplin, Mo	3		Saginaw, Mich	3	
Kalamazoo, Mich	4		St. Joseph, Mo	8	
Kansas City, Kans	21		St. Louis, Mo	9	
Kenosha, Wis	5		St. Paul, Minn	9	
Knoxville, Tenn	1		Salina, Kans	5	
Kokomo, Ind	1		Salt Lake City, Utah	14	
La Crosse, Wis	1		San Francisco, Cal	4	
Lawrence, Kans	3		Seattle, Wash	6	
Leavenworth, Kans	3		Sioux City, Iowa	9	
Lexington, Ky	2		South Bend, Ind	1	
Lincoln, Nebr	15		Spokane, Wash	6	
Little Rock, Ark	7		Springfield, Ill	1	
Logansport, Ind	2		Stoelton, Pa	1	
Lorain, Ohio	3		Steubenville, Ohio	2	
Los Angeles, Cal	3		Terre Haute, Ind	7	
Louisville, Ky	4		Toledo, Ohio	1	
Macon, Ga	1		Topeka, Kans	3	
Madison, Wis	3		Winston-Salem, N. C	4	
Marion, Ind	2		York, Pa	2	
			Zanesville, Ohio	2	

TETANUS.

City Reports for Week Ended Apr. 13, 1918.

Place.	Cases.	Deaths.	Place.	Cases.	Deaths.
Los Angeles, Cal	1		Providence, R. I		1
Macon, Ga		1	Saginaw, Mich	1	
Newark, N. J	1				

TUBERCULOSIS.

See Diphtheria, measles, scarlet fever, and tuberculosis, page 702.

TYPHOID FEVER.

State Reports for March, 1918.

Place.	New cases reported.	Place.	New cases reported.
Connecticut:		**Illinois—Continued.**	
Fairfield County—		Saline County—	
Norwalk	1	Eldorado	1
Hartford County—		Schuyler County—	
Bristol	1	Rushville Township	1
Hartford	1	Stephenson County—	
New Britain	1	Dakota	2
Windsor Locks	1	St. Clair County—	
New Haven County—		East St. Louis	1
Ansonia	1	Vermilion County—	
New Haven	1	Danville	1
Wallingford	1	Warren County—	
Waterbury	1	Monmouth Township	1
New London County—		Wayne County—	
Jewett City	1	Sims	1
Tolland County—		Will County—	
Stafford Springs	1	Joliet Township	3
		Williamson County—	
Total	11	Cambria	1
		Winnebago County—	
Illinois:		Rockford	3
Adams County—			
Quincy	4	Total	91
Clinton County—			
Carlyle Township	1	**Kansas:**	
Cook County—		Allen County—	
Chicago	21	Iola	1
Glencoe	1	Anderson County—	
Mount Prospect	1	Garnett	1
Cumberland County—		Atchison County—	
Sumpter Township	1	Atchison	1
Douglas County—		Huron	1
Tuscola Township	1	Muscotah	1
Edgar County—		Bourbon County—	
Paris	1	Redfield	1
Franklin County—		Butler County—	
Macedonia	5	El Dorado	2
Fulton County—		Cherokee County—	
Lewistown	1	Treece	1
Henry County—		Cloud County—	
Kewanee	1	Glasco	1
Iroquois County—		Coffey County—	
Woodland	2	Lebo	1
Jo Daviess County—		Dickinson County—	
Galena	1	Elmo	1
Kane County—		Greenwood County—	
Batavia	1	Eureka	1
Kankakee County—		Toronto	2
Kankakee	1	Kingman County—	
Lake County—		Nashville	1
Lake Forest	2	Leavenworth County—	
North Chicago	1	Lansing	2
Waukegan	3	Lincoln County—	
La Salle County—		Vesper	1
Freedom Township	1	Lyon County—	
Peru	1	Allen	1
Livingston County—		Miami County—	
Pontiac	2	Paola	1
Macon County—		Montgomery County—	
Decatur	1	Coffeyville	1
Madison County—		Independence	1
Granite City	1	Morton County—	
Monroe County—		Elkhart	1
Du Long Township	1	Neosho County—	
Montgomery County—		Chanute	2
Harvel	1	St. Paul	1
Marshall County—		Reno County—	
Wenona	1	Hutchinson	1
McHenry County—		Republic County—	
Crystal Lake	1	Belleville	2
Pike County—		Rice County—	
Pleasant Hill	2	Sterling	1
Randolph County—		Riley County—	
Sparta	3	Ogden	2
Rock Island—		Saline County—	
East Moline	3	Salina	1
Moline	8	Smith County—	
Rock Island	1	Smith Center	1

TYPHOID FEVER—Continued.

State Reports for March, 1918—Continued.

Place.	New cases reported.	Place.	New cases reported.
Kansas—Continued.		**Minnesota—Continued.**	
Wallace County—		Pennington County—	
Wallace............................	1	St. Hilaire...................	1
Wilson County—		Thief River Falls..............	1
North Altoona.................	12	Ramsey County—	
Woodson County—		St. Paul.....................	1
Yates Center..................	2	Red Lake County—	
Wyandotte County—		Red Lake Falls...............	1
Kansas City...................	5	River Township..............	3
		Redwood County—	
Total........................	56	Wabasso...................	2
Michigan:		Roseau County—	
Alpena County—		Roseau.....................	1
Alpena..........................	1	St. Louis County—	
Bay County—		Duluth.....................	3
Bay City........................	5	Ely........................	1
Calhoun County—		Eveleth....................	1
Battle Creek....................	1	Iron Junction..............	1
Delta County—		Wright County—	
Escanaba........................	13	Cokato....................	1
Genessee County—			
Flint...........................	6	Total........................	81
Ingham County—		**Mississippi:**	
Lansing.........................	2	Adams County...............	6
Isabella County—		Amite County...............	1
Mount Pleasant.................	1	Attala County...............	2
Kent County—		Benton County...............	4
Lowell..........................	2	Bolivar County...............	3
Grand Rapids....................	10	Calhoun County...............	1
Lenawee County—		Carroll County...............	6
Adrian Township...............	1	Claiborne County.............	1
Cambridge Township............	1	Clarke County...............	4
Marquette County—		Coahoma County...............	2
Marquette......................	1	Copiah County...............	4
Negaunee.......................	2	Covington County.............	1
Midland County—		De Soto County...............	1
Midland.........................	1	Forrest County...............	8
Montcalm County—		Franklin County...............	3
Howard City....................	2	Hancock County...............	1
Oakland County—		Hinds County...............	2
Royal Oak......................	5	Jackson County...............	2
Pontiac.........................	2	Jasper County...............	2
Ontonagon County—		Jefferson County.............	1
Ontonagon......................	1	Jones County...............	4
Saginaw County—		Lafayette County.............	8
Saginaw.........................	5	Lauderdale County.............	2
St. Clair County—		Lawrence County.............	3
Ira Township...................	1	Leflore County...............	2
Van Buren County—		Madison County...............	3
Paw Paw........................	1	Marion County...............	1
Wayne County—		Marshall County.............	1
Ford............................	2	Oktibbeha County.............	3
Wyandotte.......................	3	Panola County...............	3
		Pearl River County...........	3
Total........................	69	Pike County...............	2
Minnesota:		Pontotoc County.............	2
Beltrami County—		Prentiss County.............	1
Baudette.......................	1	Rankin County...............	2
Bigstone County—		Scott County...............	1
Graceville......................	1	Sharkey County.............	2
Carlton County—		Simpson County.............	2
Barnum.........................	1	Smith County...............	7
Cloquet.........................	1	Stone County...............	1
Carver County—		Sunflower County.............	9
Watertown Township............	3	Tate County...............	2
Goodhue County—		Tippah County...............	2
Red Wing.......................	1	Tishomingo County...........	3
Hennepin County—		Union County...............	1
Minneapolis....................	50	Warren County...............	2
Wayzata........................	1	Washington County...........	3
Lyon County—		Wayne County...............	1
Cottonwood.....................	1	Webster County.............	2
Morrison County		Wilkinson County.............	3
Piers...........................	1	Winston County.............	3
Mower County—		Yazoo County...............	15
Austin..........................	2		
Ottertail County—		Total........................	155
Fergus Falls....................	2		

TYPHOID FEVER--Continued.

State Reports for March, 1918—Continued.

Place.	New cases reported.	Place.	New cases reported.
Nebraska:		**Pennsylvania—Continued.**	
Douglas County	2	Columbia County	3
Richardson County	1	Cumberland County	2
		Dauphin County	1
Total	3	Delaware County	10
		Fayette County	7
Nevada:		Franklin County	1
Clark County	3	Huntingdon County	2
Lander County	1	Jefferson County	2
White Pine County	3	Juniata County	5
		Lackawanna County	6
Total	7	Lancaster County	7
		Lawrence County	4
New Jersey:		Lebanon County	2
Atlantic County	2	Lehigh County	11
Bergen County	3	Luzerne County	3
Burlington County	5	Lycoming County	1
Cumberland County	1	Mercer County	14
Essex County	11	Montgomery County	6
Gloucester County	3	Montour County	2
Hudson County	7	Northampton County	3
Mercer County	1	Northumberland County	1
Monmouth County	5	Philadelphia County	20
Morris County	1	Schuylkill County	7
Ocean County	1	Somerset County	4
Passaic County	1	Tioga County	1
Salem County	1	Union County	1
Union County	3	Venango County	1
		Washington County	10
Total	45	Westmoreland County	12
		Wyoming County	1
North Carolina:		York County	15
Alamance County	1		
Anson County	3	Total	329
Craven County	1		
Cumberland County	1	**South Carolina:**	
Davidson County	1	Charleston County	2
Edgecombe County	1	Greenville County	1
Gaston County	2	Laurens County	1
Jackson County	1	Richland County	2
Johnston County	1	Spartanburg County	4
Lenoir County	1		
Martin County	2	Total	10
Montgomery County	1		
Pitt County	3	**South Dakota:**	
Rockingham County	2	Brown County	1
Rowan County	3	Corson County	1
Swain County	1	Davison County	1
Warren County	1	Grant County	1
		Minnehaha County	2
Total	26	Walworth County	7
North Dakota:		Total	13
Dunn County	2		
Golden Valley County	1	**Wisconsin:**	
Morton County	1	Barron County	2
Pierce County	1	Bayfield County	2
Renville County	1	Dane County	1
Williams County	2	Douglas County	14
		Kenosha County	1
Total	8	La Crosse County	1
		Lafayette County	3
Pennsylvania:		Milwaukee County	21
Adams County	2	Outagamie County	1
Allegheny County	76	Pepin County	1
Armstrong County	36	Rock County	1
Beaver County	3	Sheboygan County	2
Bedford County	4	Trempealeau County	5
Berks County	4	Washington County	1
Blair County	12		
Bradford County	1	Total	56
Bucks County	5		
Butler County	3	**Wyoming:**	
Cambria County	1	Uinta County	1
Chester County	14	Washakie County	1
Clarion County	1		
Clearfield County	1	Total	2

TYPHOID FEVER—Continued.

City Reports for Week Ended Apr. 13, 1918.

Place.	Cases.	Deaths.	Place.	Cases.	Deaths.
Alexandria, La	1	....	Macon, Ga	1	....
Alton. Ill	1	....	McKeesport, Pa	....	1
Atlanta, Ga	2	....	Milwaukee, Wis	3	2
Baltimore, Md	....	1	Minneapolis, Minn	6	....
Bedford, Ind	1	....	Mobile, Ala	2	....
Beloit, Wis	1	....	Moline, Ill	1	....
Berkeley, Cal	1	....	Morgantown, W. Va	2	....
Birmingham, Ala	3	....	Nashville, Tenn	2	....
Boston, Mass	3	....	Newark, N. J	1	....
Buffalo, N. Y	2	1	New Britain, Conn	1	1
Burlington, Vt	1	1	New Haven, Conn	2	....
Cambridge, Mass	1	....	New Orleans, La	4	....
Charlotte, N. C	....	1	Newton, Mass	1	....
Chicago, Ill	4	....	New York, N. Y	7	2
Chillicothe, Ohio	2	....	North Yakima, Wash	1	....
Cincinnati, Ohio	1	....	Oakland. Cal	2	....
Cleveland, Ohio	3	1	Ogden, Utah	1	....
Covington, Ky	2	1	Oshkosh, Wis	1	....
Davenport, Iowa	1	....	Parkersburg, W. Va	1	....
Dayton, Ohio	....	1	Philadelphia, Pa	5	....
Denver, Colo	1	....	Pittsburgh, Pa	4	2
Detroit, Mich	6	1	Portland, Oreg	3	....
Easton, Pa	1	....	Providence, R. I	3	1
Elmira, N. Y	1	....	Reading, Pa	1	....
Fall River, Mass	2	....	Richmond, Va	....	1
Fitchburg, Mass	1	....	Saginaw, Mich	1	....
Flint, Mich	1	....	Salt Lake City, Utah	1	....
Fort Wayne, Ind	1	1	Sandusky, Ohio	1	....
Fort Worth, Tex	1	....	Schenectady, N. Y	1	....
Grand Rapids, Mich	....	1	Scranton, Pa	....	1
Hattiesburg, Miss	....	....	Sheboygan, Wis	1	....
Hoboken, N. J	2	....	Springfield, Ill	....	1
Jacksonville, Fla	1	....	Troy, N. Y	....	1
Jersey City, N J	1	....	Washington, D. C	1	1
Knoxville, Tenn	1	1	Watertown, N. Y	1	....
Lawrence, Mass	2	....	Winston-Salem, N. C	1	....
Little Rock, Ark	2	....	Woonsocket, R. I	1	....
Los Angeles, Cal	1	....	Zanesville, Ohio	1	....
Louisville, Ky	1	....			

DIPHTHERIA, MEASLES, SCARLET FEVER, AND TUBERCULOSIS.

State Reports for March, 1918.

State.	Cases reported.			State.	Cases reported.		
	Diph-theria.	Measles.	Scarlet fever.		Diph-theria.	Measles.	Scarlet fever.
Connecticut	203	773	178	New Jersey	402	5,541	400
Illinois	796	4,096	682	North Carolina	50	1,707	15
Iowa	73	....	385	North Dakota	49	287	134
Kansas	128	1,504	576	Pennsylvania	1,046	8,146	1,119
Michigan	479	969	715	South Carolina	68	197	9
Minnesota	339	513	809	South Dakota	27	375	156
Mississippi	335	7,742	26	Wisconsin	138	4,034	669
Nebraska	21	214	143	Wyoming	19	227	90
Nevada	3	76	6				

DIPHTHERIA, MEASLES, SCARLET FEVER, AND TUBERCULOSIS—Contd.

City Reports for Week Ended Apr. 13, 1918.

City.	Population as of July 1, 1916 (estimated by U. S. Census Bureau).	Total deaths from all causes.	Diphtheria.		Measles.		Scarlet fever.		Tuberculosis.	
			Cases.	Deaths.	Cases.	Deaths.	Cases.	Deaths.	Cases.	Deaths.
Over 500,000 inhabitants:										
Baltimore, Md	589,021	283	14	3	443	4	3	......	27	31
Boston, Mass	756,476		70	7	321	6	24	......	63	36
Chicago, Ill	2,497,722	904	114	21	68	3	45	3	340	85
Cleveland, Ohio	674,073	277	12	1	43	2	5	......	59	27
Detroit, Mich	571,784	329	43	3	53	1	38	......	46	26
Los Angeles, Cal	503,812	118	22	1	160	......	6	......	20	17
New York, N. Y	5,602,841	1,910	320	34	1,471	37	118	6	533	248
Philadelphia, Pa	1,709,518	602	69	4	625	2	41	1	222	88
Pittsburgh, Pa	579,090	309	11	1	240	2	9	......	35	8
St. Louis, Mo	757,309	251	52	1	99	......	31	1	45	26
From 300,000 to 500,000 inhabitants:										
Buffalo, N. Y	468,558	171	12	2	96	......	15	......	48	21
Cincinnati, Ohio	410,476	177	10	1	23	......	2	......	18	26
Jersey City, N. J	306,345		27	......	52	......	16	1	12	10
Milwaukee, Wis	436,535	135	12	......	410	3	25	......	48	11
Minneapolis, Minn	363,454		26	......	36	......	25	......		
Newark, N. J	408,894	159	29	3	413	8	17	2	54	21
New Orleans, La	371,747		5	......	4	......		......	40	26
San Francisco, Cal	463,516	177	23	2	71	......	11	1	27	27
Seattle, Wash	348,639		5	......	32	......	17	......		
Washington, D. C	363,980	161	7	......	476	3	35	......	35	13
From 200,000 to 300,000 inhabitants:										
Columbus, Ohio	214,878	92	......	......	35	......	22	......	8	9
Denver, Colo	260,800	101	11	......	33	......	28	......		16
Indianapolis, Ind	271,708	123	18	2	40	......	43	2	17	15
Louisville, Ky	238,910	97	11	1	11	1	3	......	8	7
Portland, Oreg	295,463	79	1	......	502	......	5	......	11	7
Providence, R. I	254,960	125	10	1	170	1	8	2	2	8
Rochester, N. Y	256,417	90	8	1	57	......	16	......	9	6
St. Paul, Minn	247,232	82	18	3	17	......	33	3	15	7
From 100,000 to 200,000 inhabitants:										
Atlanta, Ga	190,558	89	1	......	13	......	3	......	2	10
Birmingham, Ala	181,762	44	2	......	28	......	1	......	7	5
Bridgeport, Conn	121,579	49	9	1	9	......	1	......	6	3
Cambridge, Mass	112,981	52	30	......	56	1	......	......	6	7
Camden, N. J	106,233		4	......	21	......	4	......	9	......
Dallas, Tex	124,527		......	......	18	......	1	......	2	3
Dayton, Ohio	127,224		1	......	6	......	3	......	4	2
Des Moines, Iowa	101,598		5	......		......	22	1	......	......
Fall River, Mass	128,356	47	2	......	4	......		......	9	8
Fort Worth, Tex	104,562	29		......	9	......	3	......		
Grand Rapids, Mich	128,291	56	2	......	9	......	11	......	11	1
Hartford, Conn	110,900	61	10	......	5	......	5	......	10	1
Houston, Tex	112,307	45	3	......	5	......		......		2
Lawrence, Mass	100,560	30	3	......	9	......		......	15	5
Lowell, Mass	113,245	56		......	10	......	1	......	9	5
Lynn, Mass	102,425	34	3	......	17	......	7	......	2	5
Memphis, Tenn	148,995	57	7	......	6	1	5	......	13	10
Nashville, Tenn	117,057	66		......	18	1	2	......	6	5
New Bedford, Mass	118,158	43	3	1	4	......	4	1	6	5
New Haven, Conn	149,685	74	4	......	9	......		......	6	5
Oakland, Cal	198,604	51	2	......	12	1	3	......	5	5
Omaha, Nebr	165,470	51	4	......	15	......	19	......		2
Reading, Pa	109,381	42	1	......	66	......	6	......	2	1
Richmond, Va	156,687	57	3	......	83	......		......		2
Salt Lake City, Utah	117,399	44	3	......	23	......	16	......		
Scranton, Pa	146,811	73	9	2	11	......	4	......	9	4
Spokane, Wash	150,323		1	......		......	3	......		
Springfield, Mass	105,942	44	8	......	28	1	5	......	3	4
Syracuse, N. Y	155,624	90	7	1	77	3	6	......	6	4
Tacoma, Wash	112,770		1	......	8	......	29	......		
Toledo, Ohio	191,554	106	2	......	14	......	15	......	16	10
Trenton, N. J	111,593	50	6	......	9	......		......	6	3
Worcester, Mass	163,314	74	8	1	7	......	4	......	9	3
From 50,000 to 100,000 inhabitants:										
Akron, Ohio	85,625		2	......	8	......	7	......	6	......
Atlantic City, N. J	57,660		1	1	26	......	1	......	3	......
Augusta, Ga	50,245	19	......	......	33	......		......	1	......

DIPHTHERIA, MEASLES, SCARLET FEVER, AND TUBERCULOSIS—Contd.

City Reports for Week Ended Apr. 13, 1918—Continued.

City.	Population as of July 1, 1916 (estimated by U. S. Census Bureau).	Total deaths from all causes.	Diphtheria.		Measles.		Scarlet fever.		Tuberculosis.	
			Cases.	Deaths.	Cases.	Deaths.	Cases.	Deaths.	Cases.	Deaths.
From 50,000 to 100,000 inhabitants—Continued.										
	69,893	....	5		31				4	
	57,653	14			11		1		2	1
	53,973	15	2		17		4		6	
	67,449	25			4		5		5	2
	60,852	23			2	1	2			2
	60,734	37	10	1	5				3	2
	60,075	9			1		1		3	2
	57,144	21			6				1	3
	94,495	30	3				1		6	2
	63,705	63			9		2			19
	75,195	46	1		33		3		9	6
	76,078	31	1		5		1		3	1
	54,772	18	2		6		4		8	1
	76,183	38	2	1	25		2		2	2
	72,015	36	1				2		4	4
	77,214	25	2		2				6	3
	65,296	24	2		2		2		6	3
	76,101	22			7	1			5	3
	68,529	38	2				10	1	1	1
Kansas City, Kans	99,137		1		15		1		7	
Lancaster, Pa	50,853				28					
Little Rock, Ark	57,343				8		2		6	
Ma'den, Mass	51,155	13	17		21		2			
Manchester, N. H	78,283	31	3	1	9				5	3
Mobile, Ala	58,221	25								1
New Britain, Conn	53,794	24	5		24		5			1
Norfolk, Va	80,612				22		2			2
Oklahoma City, Okla	92,943	23			8		2		2	2
Passaic, N. J	71,744	20	5		4				2	1
Portland, Me	63,847	35	4	1	1		2			2
Rockford, Ill	55,185	29			9		1		5	1
Sacramento, Cal	66,895		2	1	25		4			3
Saginaw, Mich	55,642	15	1		8		2			1
St. Joseph, Mo	85,236	40	2		4		1		3	3
San Diego, Cal	53,330	32		1	49		6	1		6
Savannah, Ga	68,905	39					3		1	6
Schenectady, N. Y	99,519	31	1		24				3	2
Sioux City, Iowa	57,078		2				10			
Somerville, Mass	87,039	18	4	1	36		3		3	1
South Bend, Ind	68,946	17	1		5				3	2
Springfield, Ill	61,120	11	2		48		1			1
Springfield, Ohio	51,550	26			3				5	2
Terre Haute, Ind	66,083	14	1		2				1	4
Troy, N. Y	77,916	32	3	1	2		5		7	5
Wichita, Kans	70,722				48		3			
Wilkes-Barre, Pa	76,776	34	3	1	34		2	1	1	2
Wilmington, Del	94,285	53	3	1	46	2	2			3
York, Pa	51,656		1		14		1		1	
From 25,000 to 50,000 inhabitants:										
Alameda, Cal	27,782	5	1	1	22		1		1	
Auburn, N. Y	37,345	14			8		1			1
Battle Creek, Mich	29,480		2		109		1			
Beaumont, Tex	27,711	8								
Bellingham, Wash	32,945		1							
Bloomington, Ill	27,258	4	1				1			
Brookline, Mass	32,730	2	3		35		1			
Burlington, Iowa	25,030	6								1
Butler, Pa	27,032	5	8		19					
Butte, Mont	43,125						5			
Charlotte, N. C	39,823	16		1	8					
Chelsea, Mass	46,192	9	2		38		4		1	
Chicopee, Mass	29,319	7		1					4	
Clinton, Iowa	27,389				5		1			
Colorado Springs, Colo	32,971	10	2		8				5	3
Columbia, S. C	34,611				5					
Council Bluffs, Iowa	31,484	12			7		3	1		
Cumberland, Md	28,074	4	1		19		8	1	2	1
Danville, Ill	32,204	11			30					
Davenport, Iowa	48,811		1		2		2			
Dubuque, Iowa	39,873				1					

DIPHTHERIA, MEASLES, SCARLET FEVER, AND TUBERCULOSIS—Contd.

City Reports for Week Ended Apr. 13, 1918—Continued.

City.	Population as of July 1, 1916 (estimated by U. S. Census Bureau).	Total deaths from all causes.	Diphtheria.		Measles.		Scarlet fever.		Tuberculosis.	
			Cases.	Deaths.	Cases.	Deaths.	Cases.	Deaths.	Cases.	Deaths.
From 25,000 to 50,000 inhabitants—Continued.										
Durham, N. C.	25,061	8			7				1	1
Easton, Pa.	30,530	20			15				1	1
East Orange, N. J.	42,456	12	4		58		2	1	2	2
Elgin, Ill.	28,203	14	1		1		1			
Elmira, N. Y.	38,120	5	1		18			1		1
Evanston, Ill.	28,591	5								
Everett, Mass.	39,235	11	1		11		3		2	
Everett, Wash.	35,486						1			
Fitchburg, Mass.	41,781	13			13		3		6	1
Fort Smith, Ark.	28,638	5			3					
Fresno, Cal.	34,958	11			10	1	1			
Galveston, Tex.	41,863	10	1		5					1
Green Bay, Wis.	29,353	13	2		2		1		1	
Hammond, Ind.	26,171	16								1
Haverhill, Mass.	48,477	11	2		48				1	1
Jackson, Mich.	35,363	19		1	13		17	1	1	1
Jamestown, N. Y.	36,580	14	2						4	2
Joplin, Mo.	33,216				2		1		2	
Kalamazoo, Mich	48,896	30					1	1	6	1
Kenosha, Wis.	31,576	13	10		1		11		1	
Knoxville, Tenn.	38,676				9				4	4
La Cross, Wis.	31,677	6					1			
Lexington, Ky.	41,097	22			15					2
Lincoln, Nebr.	46,515	17			1		1			1
Long Beach, Cal	27,587	8			23		1		1	
Lorain, Ohio	36,964		1		2					
Lynchburg, Va.	32,940	10			6				1	1
Macon, Ga.	45,757	25			1				1	1
Madison, Wis.	30,699	13	1				8			
McKeesport, Pa.	47,521	15	1		12					
Medford, Mass.	26,234	9			6		9			1
Moline, Ill.	27,451	16	2	1	9		4			
Montclair, N. J.	26,318	4			26				3	
Montgomery, Ala.	43,285	23	1		11					1
Mount Vernon, N. Y.	37,009		1		10					2
Muncie, Ind.	25,424	11			1		2		2	1
Muskogee, Okla.	44,218				9					
Nashua, N. H.	27,327	11								1
Newburgh, N. Y.	29,603	15								5
New Castle, Pa.	41,133				10		2			
Newport, Ky.	31,927	12	1						3	3
Newport, R. I.	30,108	4					3			
Newton, Mass.	43,715	10	1		16		1		3	2
Niagara Falls, N. Y.	37,353	19	1		2		3		5	1
Norristown, Pa.	31,401	7	1		2				7	1
Oak Park, Ill.	26,654	11	4		12		1			
Ogden, Utah	31,404	6	1		31		1			
Orange, N. J.	33,080	12	1		30		1			1
Oshkosh, Wis.	36,065	13			3		2		2	
Pasadena, Cal.	46,450	14			240				2	
Perth Amboy, N. J.	41,185	23			6					2
Petersburg, Va.	25,582	1			2				2	
Pittsfield, Mass.	38,620	12	2		2		6		2	
Portsmouth, Va.	39,651	13			10		1			2
Poughkeepsie, N. Y.	30,390	12			72		2		3	1
Quincy, Ill.	36,798	11	3	1	4		1			2
Quincy, Mass.	38,136	9	1		36		1			3
Racine, Wis.	46,486	8			50		3		4	4
Roanoke, Va.	43,234	18			42					
Rock Island, Ill.	28,926	12	4		18		3		3	
Salem, Mass.	48,562	14			25				3	2
San Jose, Cal.	38,902				6		1			
Sheboygan, Wis.	28,559	3			2					
Springfield, Mo.	40,341	6	1	1			2			
Steubenville, Ohio	27,445	13	1							
Superior, Wis.	46,226	16			1		3			
Taunton, Mass.	36,283	9					2		8	
Topeka, Kans.	48,726	13	1		7		20			
Waco, Tex.	33,385	18			12		1		2	
Walla Walla, Wash.	25,136		1							
Waltham, Mass.	30,570	8	4		55				2	2

DIPHTHERIA, MEASLES, SCARLET FEVER, AND TUBERCULOSIS—Contd.

City Reports for Week Ended Apr. 13, 1918—Continued.

City.	Population as of July 1, 1916 (estimated by U. S. Census Bureau).	Total deaths from all causes.	Diphtheria.		Measles.		Scarlet fever.		Tuberculosis.	
			Cases.	Deaths.	Cases.	Deaths.	Cases.	Deaths.	Cases.	Deaths.
From 25,000 to 50,000 inhabitants—Continued.										
Warwick, R. I.	29,969				3					
Watertown, N. Y.	29,894	1			118					
West Hoboken, N. J.	43,139	6			10		9			
Wheeling, W. Va.	43,377	33			9					
Wilmington, N. C.	29,892	11			17				1	4
Winston-Salem, N. C.	31,155	22			3				12	5
Zanesville, Ohio.	30,863	12					1		1	2
From 10,000 to 25,000 inhabitants:										
Aberdeen, S. Dak.	15,218	2								
Alexandria, La.	15,333	7			2					
Alton, Ill.	22,874	15	2							
Ann Arbor, Mich.	15,010	13			49		1			
Anniston, Ala.	14,112				3					
Appleton, Wis.	17,834				1				1	
Asbury Park, N. J.	14,007	3								
Bakersfield, Cal.	16,874	10			5		1		2	1
Barre, Vt.	12,169	4							1	1
Beaver Falls, Pa.	13,332				2					
Bedford, Ind.	10,349	2								
Beloit, Wis.	18,072	2			14				1	
Braddock, Pa.	21,685	5	1		1					
Burlington, Vt.	21,617	14	1					1		
Cairo, Ill.	15,794	9								
Cape Girardeau, Mo.	10,775	7	1							3
Centralia, Ill.	11,538						3			
Chanute, Kans.	12,455	2	4	1	2		2		3	
Chillicothe, Ohio.	15,470	1			2		1			
Clinton, Mass.	13,075	4			16		5			
Coffeyville, Kans.	17,548	5			1		1			
Concord, N. H.	22,669	1	1		1		6			
Corpus Christi, Tex.	10,432	12								
Dover, N. H.	13,272	3								
Dunkirk, N. Y.	20,743	2			3					
East Providence, R. I.	18,113	7	1		4		1		1	1
Eau Claire, Wis.	18,807				18		2			
Elwood, Ind.	11,028				7					
Eureka, Cal.	14,684	2					1			
Fargo, N. Dak.	17,389	3	1	1	5					
Fort Scott, Kans.	10,550	2			6				1	
Galesburg, Ill.	24,276	7	4		30					
Grand Forks, N. Dak.	15,837	1								
Greeley, Colo.	11,420	11	3				1	4	2	
Greensboro, N. C.	19,577				1					
Greenville S. C.	18,181	10			1				2	
Hackensack, N. J.	16,145	9	1		15					
Harrison, N. J.	16,950		2		1				3	
Hattiesburg, Miss.	16,482	15			1				1	
Iola, Kans.	11,068		1						1	
Janesville Wis.	14,789	4			4		3			
Kokomo, Ind.	20,430	11			4				2	2
La Fayette, Ind.	21,286	9					2		1	
Lawrence Kans.	13,324		1						2	1
Leavenworth, Kans.	19,363	9	4		24				1	
Logansport, Ind.	21,046	3			2					
Long Branch, N. J.	15,395	8								1
Manitowoc, Wis.	13,805	5								
Marinette, Wis.	14,610	10					1			
Marion Ind.	19,834	1	2		1					
Marshall, Tex.	13,712	4	1						1	
Mason City, Iowa.	14,457	3					2			
Melrose Mass.	17,445	7								
Michigan City, Ind.	21,512	13	1						1	
Mishawaka, Ind.	16,885	4	1		11				1	
Missoula, Mont.	18,214	6								2
Morgantown, W. Va.	13,709	4								
Morristown, N. J.	13,284	7			2					
Moundsville W. Va.	11,173	8								2
Nanticoke Pa.	23,126	9	1		1		3			
New Albany, Ind.	23,629	10							1	
Newburyport, Mass.	15,243	6			7					1
New Castle, Ind.	13,241	4	1				4			

¹ Population Apr. 15, 1910; no estimate made.

DIPHTHERIA, MEASLES, SCARLET FEVER, AND TUBERCULOSIS—Contd.

City Reports for Week Ended Apr. 13, 1918—Continued.

City.	Population as of July 1, 1916 (estimated by U. S. Census Bureau).	Total deaths from all causes.	Diphtheria.		Measles.		Scarlet fever.		Tuberculosis.	
			Cases.	Deaths.	Cases.	Deaths.	Cases.	Deaths.	Cases.	Deaths.
From 10,000 to 25,000 inhabitants—Continued.										
New London, Conn	20,985	13	1	......	3	......	1	......	1	......
North Adams, Mass	[1] 22,019	7	......	......	1	......	......	......	1	......
Northampton, Mass	19,926	12	1	......	3	......	......	......	1	2
North Little Rock, Ark	14,907	2	......	......	4	......	......	......	1	1
North Yakima, Wash	20,951	......	1	......	26	......	......	......	......	......
Palestine, Tex	11,854	5	......	......	6	......	......	......	1	......
Parkersburg, W. Va	20,612	5	......	......	2	......	......	......	......	......
Plainfield, N. J	23,805	18	2	......	7	......	3	......	......	......
Pomona, Cal	13,150	6	......	......	10	......	......	......	......	......
Pontiac, Mich	17,524	17	6	......	4	......	4	......	......	1
Portsmouth, N. H	11,666	......	......	......	6	......	5	......	......	......
Provo, Utah	10,645	4	1	......	......	......	......	......	......	1
Rahway, N. J	10,219	......	......	......	1	......	......	......	1	......
Raleigh, N. C	20,127	12	......	......	11	2	......	......	......	1
Redlands, Cal	14,600	3	......	......	12	......	......	......	......	1
Reno, Nev	14,860	6	2	......	......	......	1	......	......	1
Richmond, Ind	24,697	9	3	......	......	......	......	......	......	2
Riverside, Cal	19,763	8	......	......	......	......	......	......	......	......
Rocky Mount, N. C	12,067	5	1	......	2	......	......	......	......	......
Salina, Kans	12,098	......	......	......	7	......	1	......	......	......
Sandusky, Ohio	20,193	8	1	......	......	......	1	......	......	......
Santa Ana, Cal	10,627	2	......	......	24	......	......	......	......	......
Saratoga Springs, N. Y	13,821	6	......	......	1	......	3	......	......	......
Shelbyville, Ind	10,965	• 6	......	......	......	......	......	......	......	2
Spartanburg, S. C	21,365	15	2	......	2	......	......	......	3	2
Steelton, Pa	15,548	3	3	......	......	......	1	......	2	......
Vallejo, Cal	13,461	5	......	......	9	......	......	......	......	......
Vancouver, Wash	13,180	......	......	......	15	......	......	......	......	......
Washington, Pa	21,618	......	......	......	27	......	......	......	3	......
Wausau, Wis	19,239	3	......	......	1	......	5	......	......	1
West Orange, N. J	13,560	7	......	......	20	......	......	......	......	......
West Warwick, R. I	15,782	4	1	......	......	......	......	......	......	2
Wilkinsburg, Pa	23,228	7	1	......	16	......	......	......	......	......
Woburn, Mass	15,969	5	......	......	......	......	......	......	......	......

[1] Population Apr. 15, 1910; no estimate made.

FOREIGN.

Epidemic Smallpox—Algiers.

Smallpox in epidemic form was reported, April 23, 1918, at Algiers, with 200 cases present. The occurrence was reported both among Europeans and natives.

CHINA.

Cerebrospinal Meningitis—Amoy.

Cerebrospinal meningitis was reported present at Amoy, China, March 12, 1918. The cases occurred in the native city.

Cerebrospinal Meningitis—Hankow.

Cerebrospinal meningitis was reported prevalent among children in the native city of Hankow, China, March 22, 1918.

Further Relative to Plague—Shansi Province.[1]

The outbreak of pneumonic plague previously reported as occurring in Shansi Province, China, in February, 1918, was first observed in the vicinity of Wuyuan and Saratsi during the latter part of December, 1917. Reports under date of February 18, 1918, show an extensive prevalence of the disease in the Province, with an estimated occurrence from January 14 to 18 of 1,000 fatal cases in the vicinity of Paotongchen.

CUBA.

Deratization of Vessels from New Orleans—Habana.

According to Cuban quarantine circular dated April 15, 1918, vessels arriving at Habana from New Orleans will be required to be deratized only once in three months, provided such vessels, while at New Orleans, have remained not less than 8 feet from the wharf with their cables protected with rat guards.

---

[1] Public Health Reports, Apr. 19, 1918, p 596.

CHOLERA, PLAGUE, SMALLPOX, TYPHUS FEVER, AND YELLOW FEVER.

Reports Received During Week Ended May 3, 1918.[1]

CHOLERA.

Place.	Date.	Cases.	Deaths.	Remarks.
India:				
Madras....................	Feb. 3-9..........	2	2	
Rangoon..................	Jan. 27-Feb. 2....	1	....	
Indo-China:				
Cochin-China—				
Saigon.................	Feb. 25-Mar. 11...	3	3	
Philippine Islands:				Mar. 3-9, 1918: Cases, 91; deaths,
Provinces..............		....	....	70.
Bohol...............	Mar. 3-9...........	43	30	
Capiz...............	....do.............	5	5	
Cebu...............	....do.............	4	3	
Leyte...............	....do.............	6	2	
Misamis............	....do.............	22	17	
Occidental Negros....	....do.............	8	6	
Zamboanga..........	....do.............	3	7	

PLAGUE.

Place.	Date.	Cases.	Deaths.	Remarks.
British East Africa:				
Mombasa................	Oct. 1-Dec. 31.....	31	18	
China:				
Nanking.................	Mar. 18	....	....	Present.
India:				
Bassein.................	Jan. 20-Feb. 2....	....	23	
Henzada..............	....do.............	....	20	
Madras.................	Feb. 3-9...........	2	1	
Madras Presidency........	....do.............	1,587	1,171	
Mandalay..............	Jan. 11-Feb. 2....	....	391	
Myingyan..............	....do.............	....	125	
Rangoon...............	Jan. 27-Feb. 9....	109	102	
Toungoo	Jan. 20-Feb. 2....	....	8	
Indo-China:				
Cochin-China—				
Saigon.................	Feb. 25-Mar. 17...	24	16	
Siam:				
Bangkok..................	Feb. 10-Mar. 2....	9	5	

SMALLPOX.

Place.	Date.	Cases.	Deaths.	Remarks.
Algeria:				
Algiers.................	Apr. 23............	200	....	Apr. 1-23, 1918: Deaths, 30.
British East Africa:				
Mombasa..:......11........	Oct. 1-Dec. 31.....	9	5	
Canada:				
British Columbia—				
Winnipeg..............	Apr. 7-13..........	2	....	
China:				
Tsingtau...................	Mar. 10-23.........	5	....	
France:				
Paris......................	Mar. 3-9...........	3	1	
India:				
Madras.................	Feb. 3-9...........	6	6	
Rangoon.................	Jan. 27-Feb. 9.....	28	4	
Indo-China:				
Cochin-China—				
Saigon.................	Feb. 25-Mar. 17...	283	94	
Italy:				
Genoa......................	Mar. 1-15..........	11	3	
Japan:				
Nagasaki.................	Mar. 18-31.........	3	1	
Newfoundland:				
St. Johns.................	Mar. 30-Apr. 12...	15	....	
Philippine Islands:				
Manila...................	Mar. 3-9...........	1	....	Varioloid, 13.
Porto Rico:				
San Juan..................	Apr. 1-7...........	....	....	Varioloid, 31
Siam:				
Bangkok..................	Feb. 10-Mar. 2....	14	5	

[1] From medical officers of the Public Health Service, American consuls, and other sources.

CHOLERA, PLAGUE, SMALLPOX, TYPHUS FEVER, AND YELLOW FEVER—
Continued.

Reports Received During Week Ended May 3, 1918—Continued.

TYPHUS FEVER.

Place.	Date.	Cases.	Deaths.	Remarks.
Austria-Hungary:				
Hungary....................	....	....	....	Present in December, 1917.
Germany......................	....	....	....	Jan. 1–30, 1918: Cases, 66.
Japan:				
Nagasaki....................	Mar. 18–31.........	1	1	
Lithuania......................	....	....	....	Dec. 30, 1917–Jan. 5, 1918: Cases, 195.
Newfoundland:				
St. Johns..................	Mar. 30–Apr. 5....	1	1	
Poland..........................	....	....	....	Dec. 23, 1917–Jan. 12, 1918: Cases 3,026; deaths, 315.

Reports Received from Dec. 29, 1917, to Apr. 26, 1918.

CHOLERA.

Place.	Date.	Cases.	Deaths.	Remarks.
China:				
Antung....................	Nov. 26–Dec. 2....	3	1	
India:				
Bombay....................	Oct. 28–Dec. 15..	19	14	
Do.......................	Dec. 30–Jan. 26....	200	170	
Calcutta..................	Sept. 16–. ec. 15..	....	135	
Do.......................	Dec. 30–Jan. 26....	....	24	
Karachi...................	.....do...........	25	6	
Madras....................	Nov. 25–Dec. 22..	2	2	
Do.......................	Dec. 30–Feb. 2....	35	17	
Rangoon..................	Nov. 4–Dec. 22...	5	5	
Do.......................	Dec. 30–Jan. 5....	1	1	
Indo-China:				
Provinces..................				Sept. 1–Nov. 30, 1917: Cases, 132. deaths, 89.
Anam....................	Sept. 1–Nov. 30...	18	13	
Cambodia................	.....do...........	72	52	
Cochin-China............	.....do...........	50	22	
Saigon..................	Nov. 22–Dec. 9...	4	3	
Do.....................	Feb. 4–17.........	4	....	
Kwang-Chow-Wan.....	Sept. 1–30.........	10	2	
Java:				
East Java.................	Oct. 28–Nov. 3....	1	1	
West Java................				Oct. 19–Dec. 27, 1917: Cases, 102; deaths, 56. Dec. 28, 1917–Jan. 31, 1918: Cases, 27; deaths, 7.
Batavia................	Oct. 19–Dec. 27...	49	23	
Do....................	Dec. 28–Jan. 31...	24	1	
Persia:				
Mazanderan Province.......				July 30–Sept. 3, 1917: Cases, 384, deaths, 276.
Achraf....................	July 30–Aug. 16..	90	88	
Astrabad................	July 31...........	....	....	Present.
Barfrush................	July 1–Aug. 16...	39	25	
Chahmirzad.............				25 cases reported July 31, 1917.
Chahrastagh...........	June 15 July 25...	10	8	
Charoud...............	Aug. 26–Sept. 3...	4	2	
Damghan...............	Aug. 26..........	....	....	Present.
Kharek.................	May 28–June 11...	21	13	
Meched................	Aug. 18–Sept. 2....	174	82	
Ouzoun Pare...........	Aug. 8............	....	....	Do.
Sabzevar...............	Aug. 24...........	....	....	Do.
Sari...................	July 3–29..........	273	144	
Semman................	Aug. 31–Sept. 2....	14	5	
Yekchambe Bazar.....	June 3............	6	....	
Philippine Islands:				
Provinces.................				Nov. 18–Dec. 29, 1917: Cases, 1,053, deaths, 693. Dec. 30, 1917–Mar. 2, 1918: Cases, 1,256; deaths, 798.
Antique..................	Nov. 18–Dec. 1...	48	32	
Do.....................	Feb. 3 9	4	4	
Bohol..................	Nov. 18–Dec. 29...	160	111	
Do.....................	Dec. 30–Mar. 2....	339	274	
Capiz..................	Nov. 25–Dec. 29...	27	21	
Do.....................	Dec. 30–Mar. 2....	202	168	
Cebu..................	Dec. 23 29	3	....	
Do..................	Dec. 30 Mar. 2....	79	42	
Iloilo..................	Nov. 25–Dec. 29...	179	135	
Do..................	Dec. 30 Mar. 2....	97	63	
Leyte..................	Nov. 25–Dec. 22...	13	12	
Do..................	Feb. 3 Mar. 2....	38	33	

CHOLERA, PLAGUE, SMALLPOX, TYPHUS FEVER, AND YELLOW FEVER—
Continued.
Reports Received from Dec. 29, 1917, to Apr. 26, 1918—Continued.
CHOLERA—Continued.

Place.	Date.	Cases.	Deaths.	Remarks.
Philippine Islands—Contd.				
Provinces—Contd.				
Mindanao	Nov. 25–Dec. 29	337	196	
Do	Dec. 30–Feb. 9	351	220	
Misamis	Feb. 24–Mar. 2	33	21	
Occidental Negros	Nov. 25–Dec. 22	177	123	
Do	Jan. 13–Mar. 2	88	57	
Oriental Negros	Nov. 25–Dec. 29	99	62	
Do	Dec. 30–Feb. 16	17	14	
Romblon	Nov. 25–Dec. 1	1	1	
Surigao	Feb. 24–Mar. 2	8	5	
Zamboanga	do	12	7	
Siam:				
Bangkok	Sept. 16–22	1	1	
Turkey in Asia:				
Bagdad	Nov. 1–15		40	

PLAGUE.

Place.	Date.	Cases.	Deaths.	Remarks.
Brazil:				
Bahia	Nov. 4–Dec. 15	4	4	
Do	Dec. 30–Feb. 23	4	3	
Rio de Janeiro	Dec. 23–29	1		
Do	Jan. 6–12	1	1	
British Gold Coast:				
Axim	Jan. 8			Present.
Ceylon:				
Colombo	Oct. 14–Dec. 1	14	13	
Do	Dec. 30–Jan. 19	7	5	
China				Present in North China in January, 1918: pneumonic form.
Anhwei Province—				
Fengyanghsien	Feb. 27		9	Pneumonic.
Pengpu	do		1	Do.
Chili Province—				
Kalgan				Vicinity. Present in February, 1918.
Shansi Province				Present in February, 1918, 116 cases estimated.
Ecuador				
Babahoyo	Feb. 1–15	1		
Duran	do	1	1	
Guayaquil	Sept. 1–Nov. 30	64	24	Reported outbreak occurring about Jan. 17, 1918.
Do	Feb. 1–15	44	18	
Do	Mar. 1–15	20	7	
Egypt				Jan. 1–Nov. 15, 1917: Cases, 728; deaths, 399.
Alexandria	Jan. 14–28	1	2	
Port Said	July 23–29	1	2	
India				Sept. 16–Dec. 29, 1917: Cases, 22,634; deaths, 17,430. Dec. 30, 1917–Jan. 26, 1918: Cases, 125,564; deaths, 94,364.
Bassein	Dec. 9–29		6	
Do	Dec. 30–Jan. 19		14	
Bombay	Oct. 28–Dec. 29	147	123	
Do	Dec. 30–Jan. 26	81	55	
Calcutta	Sept. 16–29		3	
Do	Dec. 30–Jan. 12		3	
Henzada	Oct. 21–27		1	
Do	Jan. 6–19			
Karachi	Oct. 21–Dec. 29	27	20	
Do	Dec. 30–Jan. 26	14	14	
Madras Presidency	Oct. 21–Nov. 24	5,796	4,107	
Do	Jan. 6–Feb. 2	7,462	5,424	
Mandalay	Oct. 14–Nov. 17		46	
Do	Dec. 30–Jan. 12		109	
Myingyan	do			
Prome	Jan. 6–12		3	
Rangoon	Jan. 5–Jan. 22		5	
Do	Jan. 30–Jan. 26	79	74	
Toungoo	Jan. 6–26			
Do	Jan. 30–Jan. 19		4	
Indo-China				Aug. 1–Nov. 30, 1917: Cases, 603; deaths, 341.
Provinces				
Annam	Aug. 1–Nov. 30	20	17	
Cambodia	do	39	29	
Cochin-China	do	22	17	
Saigon	Jan. 6–Jan. 12	17	4	
Do	Jan. 30–Feb. 26	74	5	

CHOLERA, PLAGUE, SMALLPOX, TYPHUS FEVER, AND YELLOW FEVER—
Continued.

Reports Received from Dec. 29, 1917, to Apr. 26, 1918—Continued.

PLAGUE—Continued.

Place.	Date.	Cases.	Deaths.	Remarks.
Java:				
East Java................	....	....	....	Oct. 8-Dec. 31, 1917: Cases, 196; deaths, 193.
Do............	....	....	....	Jan. 1-14, 1918: Cases, 22; deaths, 21.
Residences—				
Kediri............	Oct. 8-Dec. 31.....	1	1	
Madioen............	....do............	49	49	
Samarang............	....do............	110	109	
Surabaya............	....do............	25	23	
Surakarta............	....do............	11	11	
West Java............				Nov. 25-Dec. 9, 1917: Cases, 46; deaths, 45.
Do............				Dec. 1, 1917-Jan. 15, 1918: Cases, 106.
Peru:				
Ancachs Department—				
Casma...............	Dec. 1-Jan. 15.....	2	....	
Lambayeque Department..	....do...........	23	....	At Chiclayo, Ferronafe, Jayanca, Lambayeque.
Libertad Department......	....do............	72	....	At Guadalupe, Mansiche, Pacasmayo, Salaverry, San Jose, San Pedro, and country district of Trujillo.
Lima Department............	....do............	9	....	City and country.
Piura Department—				
Catacaos................	....do............	1	....	
Senegal:				
St. Louis................	Feb. 2............	....	....	Present.
Siam:				
Bangkok............	Sept. 16-Dec. 23...	13	9	
Do................	Jan. 13-Feb. 9....	15	11	
Straits Settlements:				
Singapore............	Oct. 28-Dec. 29...	5	7	
Do................	Jan. 6-Feb. 16....	29	28	

SMALLPOX.

Place.	Date.	Cases.	Deaths.	Remarks.
Algeria:				
Algiers............	Nov. 1-Dec. 31...	3	2	
Do............	Jan. 1-Feb. 28...	13	....	
Australia:				
New South Wales............				July 12-Dec. 20, 1917: Cases, 36. Jan. 4-17, 1918: Cases, 1.
Abermain............	Oct. 25-Nov. 29...	3	....	Newcastle district.
Cessnock............	July 12-Oct. 11...	7	....	
Eumangla............	Aug. 15............	1	....	
Kurri Kurri............	Dec. 5-20............	2	....	
Mungindi............	Aug. 13............	1	....	
Warren............	July 12-Oct. 25...	22	....	
Do............	Jan. 1-17............	1	....	
Brazil:				
Bahia............	Nov. 10-Dec. 8...	3	....	
Pernambuco............	Nov. 1-15............	1	....	
Rio de Janeiro............	Sept. 30-Dec. 29...	703	190	
Do............	Dec. 30-Mar. 9...	231	83	
Sao Paulo............	Oct. 29-Nov. 4...	....	2	
Canada:				
British Columbia—				
Vancouver............	Jan. 13-Mar. 9...	5	....	
Victoria............	Jan. 7-Feb. 2.....	2	....	
Winnipeg............	Dec. 30-Mar. 30...	2	....	
New Brunswick—				
Kent County............	Dec. 4............	....	....	Outbreak. On main line Canadian Ry., 25 miles north of Moncton.
Do............	Jan. 22............	40	....	In 7 localities.
Northumberland County.	....do............	41	....	In 5 localities.
Restigouche County....	Jan. 18............	60	....	
St. John County—				
St. John............	Mar. 3 Apr. 6....	5	....	
Victoria County.......	Jan. 22............	10	....	At Limestone and a lumber camp.
Westmoreland County				
Moncton............	Jan. 20 Apr. 6...	16	....	
York County............	Jan. 22............	8	....	

CHOLERA, PLAGUE, SMALLPOX, TYPHUS FEVER, AND YELLOW FEVER—
Continued.

Reports Received from Dec. 29, 1917, to Apr. 26, 1918—Continued.

SMALLPOX—Continued.

Place.	Date.	Cases.	Deaths.	Remarks.
Canada—Continued.				
Nova Scotia—				
Halifax	Feb. 24–Apr. 6	6		
Sydney	Feb. 3–Apr. 6	15		
Ontario—				
Arnprior	Mar. 31–Apr. 6		1	
Do	Dec. 16–22	1		
Hamilton	Jan. 13–19	2		
Ottawa	Mar. 4–24	5		
Sarnia	Dec. 9–15	1		
Do	Jan. 6–Mar. 30	32		
Toronto	Feb. 10–Apr. 6	2		
Windsor	Dec. 30–Jan. 5	1		
Prince Edward Island—				
Charlottetown	Feb. 7–13	1		
Quebec—				
Montreal	Dec. 16–Jan. 5	5		
Do	Jan. 6–Apr. 6	12		
China:				
Amoy	Oct. 22–Dec. 30			Present.
Do	Dec. 31–Feb. 10			Do.
Antung	Dec. 2–23	13	2	
Do	Jan. 7–Feb. 17	6	2	
Changsha	Jan. 28–Mar. 10		1	
Chefoo	Jan. 27–Feb. 9			Do.
Chungking	Nov. 11–Dec. 29			Do.
Do	Dec. 30–Feb. 16			Do.
Dairen	Nov. 18–Dec. 22	3	1	
Do	Dec. 30–Mar. 16	39	2	
Hankow	Feb. 25–Mar. 3	1		
Harbin	May 14–June 30	20		Chinese Eastern Ry.
Do	July 1–Dec. 2	7		Do.
Hongkong	Dec. 23–29	1		
Do	Jan. 26–Feb. 9	6	1	
Hungtahotze Station	Oct. 28–Nov. 4	1		Do.
Manchuria Station	May 14–June 30	6		Do.
Do	July 1–Dec. 2	3		Do.
Mukden	Nov. 11–24			Present.
Nanking	Feb. 3–Mar. 16			Epidemic.
Shanghai	Nov. 18–Dec. 23	41	91	Cases, foreign; deaths among natives.
Do	Dec. 31–Mar. 10	36	106	Do.
Swatow	Jan. 18			Unusually prevalent.
Tientsin	Nov. 11–Dec. 22	13		
Do	Dec. 30–Mar. 9	27		
Tsingtau	Feb. 4–23	3		
Cuba:				
Habana	Jan. 7	1		Nov. 8, 1917: 1 case from Coruna; Dec. 5, 1917, 1 case.
Marianao	Jan. 8	1		6 miles distant from Habana.
Ecuador:				
Guayaquil	Sept. 1–Nov. 30	26	2	
Do	Feb. 1–15	3	3	
Egypt:				
Alexandria	Nov. 12–18	2	1	
Do	Jan. 8–Feb. 28	5		
Cairo	July 23–Nov. 18	6	1	
France:				
Lyon	Nov. 18–Dec. 16	6	3	
Do	Jan. 7–Feb. 17	11	2	
Marseille	Jan. 1–31		2	
Paris	Jan. 27–Mar. 2	5	1	
Great Britain:				
Cardiff	Feb. 3–9	4		
Hull	Mar. 17–23	1		
Greece:				
Saloniki	Jan. 27–Mar. 16		9	
Honduras:				
Santa Barbara Department	Jan. 1–7			Present in interior.
India:				
Bombay	Oct. 21–Dec. 29	50	12	
Do	Dec. 31–Jan. 26	26	5	
Karachi	Nov. 18–Dec. 29	4	2	Nov. 11–16, 1917: 10 cases with 4 deaths; imported on s. s. Menesa from Basreh.
Madras	Oct. 31–Dec. 29	20	8	
Do	Dec. 30–Feb. 2	96	32	
Rangoon	Oct. 28–Dec. 22	6	1	
Do	Dec. 30–Jan. 26	7	2	

CHOLERA, PLAGUE, SMALLPOX, TYPHUS FEVER, AND YELLOW FEVER—
Continued.

Reports Received from Dec. 29, 1917, to Apr. 26, 1918—Continued.

SMALLPOX—Continued.

Place.	Date.	Cases.	Deaths.	Remarks.
Indo-China:				
Provinces...............				Sept. 1 Nov. 30, 1917: Cases, 346;
Anam...............	Sept. 1-Nov. 30....	163	25	deaths, 146.
Cambodia...........	do............	16	8	
Cochin-China.......	do............	353	108	
Saigon.............	Oct. 20-Dec. 30.	120	26	
Do............	Dec. 31 Feb. 24.	404	146	
Laos...............	Oct. 1-31......	1	....	
Do............	Jan. 26-Feb. 3.	1	1	
Tonkin.............	Sept. 1-Oct. 31.	9	4	
Do............	Jan. 26-Feb. 3.	3	....	
Italy:				
Castellamare.............	Dec. 10....	2	....	Among refugees.
Florence..............	Dec. 1-15....	17	4	
Genoa...............	Dec. 2 31....	11	3	
Do...............	Jan. 2-31....	30	2	
Leghorn.............	Jan. 7-Mar. 10.	32	7	
Messina.............	Jan. 3-19....	1	....	
Milan...............				Oct. 1-Dec. 31, 1917: Cases, 22.
Naples...............	To Dec. 10...	2	....	Among refugees.
Taormina.............	Jan. 20-Feb. 9.	6	....	
Turin...............	Oct. 29-Dec. 29.	128	129	
Do...............	Jan. 21 Mar. 3.	34	3	
Japan:				
Nagasaki.............	Jan. 14-Mar. 10.	6	2	
Taihoku.............	Dec. 15-31....	1	....	Island of Taiwan (Formosa).
Do............	Jan. 5-Mar. 11.	28	5	Do.
Tokyo...............	Feb. 11-Mar. 6.	28	....	City and suburbs.
Yokohama...........	Jan. 17-Feb. 3.	4	....	
Java:				
East Java.............	Oct. 7-Dec. 23.	89	....	Dec. 25-31, 1917: Cases, 7. Jan.
Surabaya.........	Dec. 25 31....	1	....	1-14, 1918: Cases, 3.
Mid-Java.............				Oct. 10-Dec. 26, 1917: Cases, 86.
Samarang.........	Nov. 6-Dec. 12.	4	1	death, 1. Dec. 28, 1917-Jan. 23,
				1918: Cases, 28.
West Java.............				Oct. 10-Dec. 27, 1917: Cases, 231;
Batavia...........	Nov. 3-8....	1	....	deaths, 26. Dec. 28, 1917-Jan.
				31, 1918: Cases, 110; deaths, 17.
Mexico:				
Aguascalientes.......	Feb. 4-17....	....	3	
Ciudad Juarez.......	Mar. 3-23....	2	1	
Mazatlan.............	Dec. 5 11....	....	1	
Do...............	Jan. 20-Apr. 2.	4	4	
Mexico City..........	Nov. 11-Dec. 29.	16	....	
Do...............	Dec. 30-Mar. 30.	90	....	
Piedras Negras.......	Jan. 11....	208	....	
Vera Cruz...........	Jan. 20-Mar. 2.	7	3	
Newfoundland:				
St. Johns.............	Dec. 8-Jan. 4.	29	....	
Do...............	Jan. 5 Mar. 29.	61	....	
Trepassey.............	Jan. 4....	....	....	Outbreak with 11 cases reported.
Philippine Islands:				
Manila...............	Oct. 29-Dec. 8.	8	....	
Do...............	Jan. 13 Mar. 16.	28	4	Varioloid, 56.
Porto Rico:				
San Juan.............	Jan. 28-Mar. 31.	33	....	Varioloid.
Portugal:				
Lisbon...............	Nov. 4-Dec. 15.	2	....	
Do...............	Dec. 30 Mar. 16.	6	....	
Portuguese East Africa:				
Lourenço Marques.......	Aug. 1-Dec. 31.	....	16	
Russia:				
Archangel.............	Sept. 1 Oct. 31.	7	....	
Moscow...............	Aug. 26 Oct. 6.	22	2	
Petrograd.............	Aug. 31-Nov. 18.	76	3	
Siam:				
Bangkok.............	Nov. 25 Dec. 1.	1	1	
Do...............	Jan. 6-19....	1	1	
Spain:				
Coruna...............	Dec. 2-15....	....	4	
Do...............	Jan. 20 Feb. 23.	....	5	
Madrid...............				Jan. 1-Dec. 31, 1917: Deaths, 77.
Seville...............	Oct. 1 Dec. 30.	....	65	
Do...............	Jan. 1-31....	....	30	
Valencia.............	Jan. 27 Feb. 2.	1	....	
Straits Settlements:				
Singapore.............	Nov. 25 Dec. 1.	1	1	
Do...............	Dec. 30-Jan. 5.	3	....	

CHOLERA, PLAGUE, SMALLPOX, TYPHUS FEVER, AND YELLOW FEVER—
Continued.

Reports Received from Dec. 29, 1917, to Apr. 26, 1918—Continued.

SMALLPOX—Continued.

Place.	Date.	Cases.	Deaths.	Remarks.
Tunisia:				
Tunis......................	Dec. 14–20.......	1	....	
Turkey in Asia:				
Bagdad.....................	....	....	....	Present in November, 1917.
Union of South Africa:				
Cape of Good Hope State...	Oct. 1–Dec. 31.....	29	....	
East Liverpool............	Jan. 20–26.........	1	....	Varioloid.
Venezuela:				
Maracaibo.................	Dec. 2–8...........	....	1	

TYPHUS FEVER.

Place.	Date.	Cases.	Deaths.	Remarks.
Algeria:				
Algiers....................	Nov. 1–Dec. 31....	2	1	
Argentina:				
Rosario...................	Dec. 1–31..........	.....	1	
Australia:				
South Australia..........	....	.....	.....	Nov. 11–17, 1917: Cases, 1.
Brazil:				
Rio de Janeiro............	Oct. 28–Dec. 1....	7	.....	
Canada:				
Ontario—				
Kingston.............	Dec. 2–8..........	3	....	
Quebec—				
Montreal.............	Dec. 16–22........	2	1	
China:				
Antung....................	Dec. 3–30.........	13	1	
Do....................	Dec. 31–Jan. 27...	2	2	
Chosen (Korea):				
Seoul.....................	Nov. 1–20.........	1	....	
Do....................	Feb. 1–28.........	3	2	
Egypt:				
Alexandria................	Nov. 8–Dec. 28....	57	15	
Do....................	Jan. 8–Mar. 11....	409	98	
Cairo.....................	July 23–Dec. 16...	137	70	
Port Said.................	July 30–Nov. 11...	5	5	
France:				
Marseille.................	Dec. 1–31.........	.....	1	
Great Britain:				
Belfast...................	Feb. 18–Mar. 30...	21	3	
Dublin....................	Mar. 24–30........	3	....	
Glasgow...................	Dec. 21...........	1	....	
Do....................	Jan. 20–Mar. 23...	12	....	
Manchester................	Dec. 2–8..........	1	....	
Greece:				
Arta......................	Feb. 19...........	2	....	
Janina....................	Feb. 14...........	110	....	Jan. 27, epidemic.
Saloniki..................	Nov. 11–Dec. 29...	.....	72	
Do....................	Dec. 30–Mar. 16...	.....	27	
Italy:				
San Remo..................	Mar. 10–16........	2	....	
Japan:				
Nagasaki..................	Nov. 26–Dec. 16...	5	5	
Do....................	Jan. 7–Mar. 10....	13	5	
Java:				
East Java.................				Oct. 15–Dec. 31, 1917: Cases, 39;
Surabaya..............	Dec. 17–31........	9	1	deaths, 7. Jan. 1–14, 1918:
Do....................	Jan. 1–14.........	10	1	Cases, 11; deaths, 2.
Mid-Java..................				Oct. 10–Dec. 26, 1917: Cases, 63;
Samarang..............	Oct. 9–Dec. 26....	20	2	deaths, 2. Dec. 28, 1917–Jan.
Do....................	Dec. 27–Jan. 15...	18	.....	23, 1918: Cases, 11.
West Java.................				Oct. 19–Dec. 27, 1917: Cases, 94;
Batavia...............	Oct. 19–Dec. 27...	59	15	deaths, 17. Dec. 28, 1917–Jan.
Do....................	Dec. 28–Jan. 31...	27	1	31, 1918; Cases, 53; deaths, 1.
Mexico:				
Aguascalientes............	Dec. 15...........	.....	3	
Do....................	Jan. 21–Apr. 7....	.....	14	
Durango State—				
Guanacevi............	Feb. 11...........	.....	.....	Epidemic.
Mexico City...............	Nov. 11–Dec. 29...	476	....	
Do....................	Dec. 30–Mar. 30...	627	....	
Norway:				
Bergen....................	Feb. 1–16.........	3	....	

CHOLERA, PLAGUE, SMALLPOX, TYPHUS FEVER, AND YELLOW FEVER—
Continued.

Reports Received from Dec. 29, 1917, to Apr. 26, 1918—Continued.

TYPHUS FEVER—Continued.

Place.	Date.	Cases.	Deaths.	Remarks.
Portugal:				
Lisbon........................	Mar. 3-16...........	8	....	Feb. 21: Present.
Oporto.......................	Dec. 1-31...........	23	4	
Do.........................	Jan. 1-Mar. 8......	1,811	161	
Russia:				
Archangel...................	Sept. 1-14.........	7	2	
Moscow......................	Aug. 26-Oct. 6.....	49	2	
Petrograd...................	Aug. 31-Nov. 18...	32	....	
Do.........................	Feb. 2.............	....	....	Present.
Vladivostok.................	Oct. 29-Nov. 4.....	12	1	
Spain:				
Corcubion....................	Apr. 11............	....	....	Present. Province of Coruna, west coast.
Sweden:				
Goteborg....................	Nov. 18-Dec. 15...	2	....	
Switzerland:				
Basel.......................	Jan. 6-19..........	1	1	
Zurich......................	Nov. 9-15..........	2	....	
Do.........................	Jan. 13-19.........	2	....	
Tunisia:				
Tunis.......................	Nov. 30-Dec. 6.....	....	1	
Do.........................	Feb. 9-Mar. 15.....	35	5	Of these, 26 in outbreak in prison.
Union of South Africa:				
Cape of Good Hope State...	Sept. 10-Dec. 30...	4,035	830	Sept. 10-Nov. 25, 1917: Cases, 3,734 (European, 31); deaths, 761 (European, 5). Total to Jan. 27, 1918: Cases, 4,248 (European, 32); deaths, 869 (European, 5).
Natal.......................	....	....	....	From date of outbreak in December, 1917, to Jan. 27, 1918: Cases, 34; deaths, 10.

YELLOW FEVER.

Place.	Date.	Cases.	Deaths.	Remarks.
Ecuador:				
Babahoyo...................	Feb. 1-15..........	1	1	
Guayaquil..................	Sept. 1-Nov. 30...	5	3	
Do.........................	Feb. 1-15..........	1	....	
Do.........................	Mar. 1-15..........	1	1	
Milagro....................	Feb. 1-15..........	1	1	
Yaguachi...................	Nov. 1-30..........	1	....	
Guatemala:				
Retalhuleu.................	Apr. 22............	....	....	Present. About 25 miles from Champerico, Pacific port.
Honduras:				
Tegucigalpa................	Dec. 16-22.........	....	1	
Do.........................	Jan. 6-19..........	....	1	

×

PUBLIC HEALTH REPORTS

| VOL. 33 | MAY 10, 1918 | No. 19 |

THE PROBLEM OF ACUTE INFECTIOUS JAUNDICE IN THE UNITED STATES.

By M. H. NEILL, Passed Assistant Surgeon, United States Public Health Service.

Acute infectious jaundice is an acute infectious disease characterized by malaise, prostration, and gastrointestinal symptoms at onset, by fever of varying degree and by jaundice of varying intensity and duration. In severe cases bleeding from mucous surfaces and albuminuria are common. In moderately severe cases the rather high fever, marked prostration, and absence of local signs tend to exclude local disease of the biliary tract and present the clinical picture of an acute infection. Light cases of this affection, however, seem to be clinically indistinguishable from ordinary catarrhal jaundice and therefore are seldom diagnosed correctly in the absence of an outbreak of the disease, which naturally directs attention to the probably infectious character of the malady.

In presenting this brief paper the writer desires to:

1. Emphasize the aspects of the disease which are of special interest to sanitarians in the United States.

2. Briefly outline the epidemiological problems of the disease.

3. Indicate the procedures for their study by laboratory methods.

Prevalence of the Disease Among Troops in Europe.

It is well known that outbreaks of jaundice have occurred at different times among the French, British, Italian, German, and Russian troops. The geographical range of prevalence has been from Belgium to Gallipoli. In most of the outbreaks the mortality has been low, but in some of the commands the attack rate has been high. At this time the weight of evidence indicates that the disease in the great majority of instances, if not in all, has been due to the *"Spirochæta icterohæmorrhagiæ"* of Inada (1916) and his coworkers. This organism was first demonstrated as the cause of a severe form of the disease prevalent in Japan.

Prevalence of the Spirochæta Icterohæmorrhagiæ Among Wild Rats in the United States.

Noguchi (1917) found that rats captured about New York City were infested with a spirochæta identical in appearance with that causing acute spirochætal jaundice in man. This worker, by means of cross immunity tests, presented further evidence that the parasites causing the human disease in Europe and Japan and those found in New York rats were the same. Jobling (1917) found that of more than a hundred rats captured in Nashville, Tenn., at least ten per cent carried similar spirochætes in their kidneys. The writer has found a similar prevalence of the *Spirochæta icterohæmorrhagiæ* in wild rats captured in Washington, D. C. As far as can be made out the organisms found by different workers in the United States correspond very closely in appearance and pathogenicity for guinea pigs with those infecting human beings in the trenches in Europe and in the mines of Japan. The evidence then seems to indicate pretty conclusively that the *Spirochæta icterohæmorrhagiæ*, the cause of acute spirochætal jaundice in man, is rather widely disseminated among wild rats living under such different conditions of environment as obtain in New York, Washington, and Nashville. Reports of the degree of prevalence of these parasites in the rats throughout the country are awaited with considerable interest.

Reported Occurrence of Epidemic Jaundice in the United States.

A search of the literature reveals a number of outbreaks of jaundice occurring from time to time in this country. Even though few and far between, on account of the prevalence of the causative agent in wild rats and the fact that outbreaks of jaundice tend to occur among troops, these reports deserve at least a passing consideration.

An account of an outbreak of jaundice among troops in the War of 1812 has come down to us. Acute infectious jaundice has been stated to have been highly prevalent during the Civil War and various numerical estimates of its prevalence appear in the literature. The following quotation is taken from the Medical and Surgical History of the War of the Rebellion prepared under direction of the Surgeon General, United States Army: "Jaundice occurred frequently in the progress of the malarial or other fevers as the result of morbid changes affecting the liver or blood. The yellow coloration in these cases was mostly an incident or symptom of the well-defined primary disease. There were, however, a large number of hepatic or hæmatic disorders in which the alteration of color represented so prominent a symptom that the disease was recorded under the heading of jaundice. Not less than 71,691 cases of this kind were reported among white troops (Union Army). Generally the cases were sporadic, but sometimes a series occurred in a command constituting a local epidemic."

While in the report just quoted the association of jaundice with disease of the liver and malaria is recognized, the records contain several accounts of clear-cut outbreaks of jaundice and fever corresponding pretty closely to the descriptions of the trench jaundice observed in the present war. It seems, then, that while outbreaks of acute infectious jaundice, very likely due to spirochætes, occurred during the Civil War, a numerical estimate of the prevalence of the disease should not be attempted.

A search of the literature reveals a number of reports of outbreaks of jaundice among the civil population in the United States. In the majority of these reports no special prevalence of other febrile diseases is mentioned in connection with the cases reported. In many of the cases the observers were impressed with the fact that they were dealing with a condition they had never seen before, basing their diagnosis on the description of the disease as it occurs in Europe.

In all the American reports most of the patients experienced nausea or vomiting, some abdominal-distress or pain, headache, and fever of varying degree, followed in a few days by jaundice of varying intensity. In fact from many of the descriptions there is little to suggest a specific infectious disease, aside from the fact that a number of cases as described above would appear at about the same time in a community which was both previously and subsequently free from the disease. Several reports indicate a high mortality among pregnant women. In some outbreaks children seem to have been chiefly attacked, in others adults, and in still others adults and children were equally affected. In some outbreaks males were principally affected, while in others both sexes were affected about equally. In several outbreaks the symptomatology in the fatal cases was strikingly similar, suggestive of rapid necrosis of the liver cells as occurs in acute yellow atrophy of the liver. There is no information as to the occupation of those ill with the disease, nor is it possible to gain any comprehensive idea of the sanitary situation as regards water and food supply, sewage disposal, and the like, under which the disease has occurred in the United States. No adequate study of the pathology of the disease in man in this country has come to the writer's attention. Barker and Sladen found that the blood serum of their cases agglutinated a strain of *B. paratyphosus*.

There is some evidence to suggest that direct contact may have occasionally played a part in transmitting the disease, as in Hanover, N. H. (Gile, 1908), where a number of college students were engaged in surveying roads in the vicinity, camping out at night. From time to time one would become ill with jaundice and fever and return to college. Then cases began to appear in the college itself where the disease had formerly been unknown. Again at Ann Arbor, Mich.

(Cummings, 1915), 12 of the 19 cases had been in contact with a sick college mate previous to contracting the disease. In this outbreak the food supply was apparently not a factor, as nearly all those attacked ate at separate boarding houses.

Outbreaks of Infectious Jaundice in the United States (Civil Population).

Place.	Approximate population.	Year.	Months.	Cases.	Deaths.	Reported by—
Rocky Mount, N. C.	?	1849-50	Nov., Dec., Jan.	About 40...	Not stated.	Pittman, N. Orleans Med. J., v. 6, p. 694.
Halifax Court House, Va.	?	1857-58	Fall and winter.	Not stated.	Apparently none.	Faulkner, Md. & Va. Med. J., v. 15, p. 355.
Savannah, Ga....	30,000	1880	Jan., Feb....	80..........	None......	Nunn, Atlanta Med. & Surg J., v. 24, p. 6.
Birmingham, Ala.	3,000	1881-82	Sept.-Jan....	"Many"...	"Few"....	Sears, Trans M'd. Assoc. State of Alabama.
Plainfield, Mich..	100	1886-87	Dec., Jan....	22..........	None.......	Green, Phys. & Surg , v 9, p.190.
Geneva, N. Y....	7,000	1888	Spring......	200.........	None mentioned.	Sweet, Med. Regist., v. 3, p. 317.
Troy, Me........	?	1887	.....do...	Not stated.	.....do.....	Dodge, Rept. State Bd. Health, Maine, v. 4, p 266.
Sparta, Wis......	3,000	1898	Aug., Sept., Oct.	"Few"....	"Few"....	Beebe, Trans. Med. Soc., Wis., v. 32, p. 183.
Calumet, Mich., and vicinity.	30,000	1897-98	June-Jan....	675.........	None......	Pomeroy, Trans. Mich. State Med. Soc., v. 22, p 347.
Hanover, N. H...	4,000	1899	Not stated..	About 25...	.....do.....	Gile, Trans. N. Hampshire Med. Soc., 1909, p. 181.
Stirling, Kans....	2,200	1905	Sept., Oct., Nov.	30..........	2...........	Ross, J. Kansas Med. Soc , 1906, p. 407.
Montevallo, Ala..	....	1906	Nov., Dec...	Not stated.	None.......	Wilkinson, Ala. Med. J., v. 19, No. 6.
Talladega, Ala....	5,500	1907	Summer and fall.	About 200..	2...........	Dixon, Ala Med. J., v. 20, p. 320.
Baltimore, Md...	558,500	1908	Nov., Dec...	6 cases, of 700 inmates of jail.	None......	Barker & Sladen, Bull. Johns Hopkins Hosp., v. 20, p. 316.
Andover, Me.....	750	1908-09	Oct.-Feb....	135..........	.....do.....	Leslie, Bost. Med. & Surg. J., v. 161, p. 672
Austin, Minn....	6,960	1910	Sept.-Dec...	About 200..	.....do.....	Collins, J. Minnesota State Med. Asso., v 31, p. 303.
New York City...	4,900,000	1912-13	Oct.-Jan....	25 studied at author's clinic	1...........	Herrman, Trans. Amer. Ped. Soc , v. 25, p 85.
Hetland, S. Dak..	223	1913	June.-Sept..	Not stated.	Not stated.	Grove, St. Paul Med. J., v. 16, p. 109.
Ann Arbor, Mich.	15,000	1915	Spring......	25..........	None.......	Cummings, J. Mich. State Med. Soc., v. 14, p. 293.

From the table it is evident that, while in certain of the outbreaks a fairly large proportion of the community has been attacked, the case-fatality rate has always been low. As regards seasonal prevalence, it would seem that the fewest cases occurred in the warmer months of the year. Detailed analysis of the reports shows very few cases occurring in the summer as compared with the fall and winter. This is in accordance with a part of the observation of Japanese and European workers, that the disease does not occur in the hottest or coldest weather.

Before closing the discussion as to the prevalence of epidemics of jaundice in the United States it seems fair, in the absence of more definite knowledge, to ask whether such a disease as a separate entity has existed or whether all the outbreaks were not manifestations of some other disease such as typhoid fever or malaria. With regard to malaria it may be said that, while estivo-autumnal malaria undoubtedly caused outbreaks of jaundice in the Civil War, it is contrary to our present knowledge of the distribution of this disease to ascribe such outbreaks as occurred in Maine, New Hampshire, Minnesota, and Wisconsin to this cause. To infer that these cases were due to some vagary of *B. typhosus* would contradict a great mass of clinical experience, which shows that jaundice is a very rare symptom of typhoid fever. The same may be said with regard to paratyphoid infection. In general the seasonal prevalence of acute infectious jaundice seems to be at its lowest just when so-called filth-borne diseases are most prevalent.

Whatever may be the weight attached to such facts as have been stated above they indicate that epidemics of jaundice closely simulating those now known to be caused by the *Spirochæta icterohæmorrhagiæ* have occasionally appeared in this country, and that they were possibly due to this parasite. This latter statement is strengethened by the finding by A. M. Stimson (personal communication) of spirochætes in sections of the kidney of a man who died in New Orleans of a disease characterized by jaundice and fever. These sections prepared by Levaditi's method show spirochætes morphologically similar to the causative agent of acute spirochætal jaundice.

The Problem of the Rat as a Carrier of the Spirochæta Icterohæmorrhagiæ.

The following quotation from Noguchi is well adapted as a starting point in this discussion: "The finding of the causative organism of infectious jaundice among wild rats in America and the identification of this strain with those found in Asia and Europe seem to be particularly important in revealing a latent danger to which we have been constantly exposed but from which we escape as long as sanitary conditions are not disturbed by untoward events."

Long before the present war acute infectious jaundice was recognized to occur especially among troops, among sewer workers, agricultural laborers working in wet soil, and in mine workers. People who handle food as butlers and cooks, in Japan at least, are also said to be attacked with especial frequency. With the universal adoption of trench warfare in the present conflict acute infectious jaundice took a more or less prominent place in the category of trench diseases. Stokes (1917) observed a definite increase in the number of cases among troops during wet spells of weather, followed by a diminution in cases when the weather became dry. It was also noted that a regiment which had a number of cases in the line—i. e., wet trenches—was not infected while in rest billets, but again produced cases when it returned to the trenches. In Japan, Inada

(1916) and his coworkers found that cases of acute infectious jaundice occurred in the wet shafts of the mine, but not in the dry shafts nor on the surface. Some evidence has been presented to show that the hot and cold months of the year are unfavorable to the spread of the disease. Several laboratory workers have been directly infected by the blood of guinea pigs suffering from the disease, at least once with fatal outcome.

The credit of first finding the *Spirochæta icterohæmorrhagiæ* in rodents belongs to the Japanese investigators, who first demonstrated these parasites in the kidneys of field mice. Further investigations in the coal-mining regions of Japan showed that 40 per cent of the wild rats harbored organisms resembling these parasites. Many cases of infectious jaundice in human beings, due to spirochætes, occur in this region. With regard to the spirochætes found in the rats, it was observed that they live in the kidney without injury to the animal, and are excreted in the urine. By means of tests with immune sera, evidence was obtained which indicated that the spirochætes which came from the rats were quite similar to, if not identical with, those derived from human sources. The various strains of these spirochætes all produced the same striking pathological picture in experimentally infected guinea pigs. Guinea pigs were infected by allowing rats to bite them, and it was demonstrated also that the organisms would pass through the unbroken skin of these animals.

English and French workers soon demonstrated the presence of the *Spirochæta icterohæmorrhagiæ* in rats taken from the trenches in which the disease had appeared among troops. Thus Stokes (1917) found 6 out of 15 rats to be infected. On the other hand, Courmont and Durand (1917) examined 50 rats taken in a region where acute infectious jaundice was unknown. The rats appeared perfectly healthy', but four of them were proved by guinea-pig inoculation to harbor the *Spirochæta icterohæmorrhagiæ*. These figures approximate the rate of incidence later obtained for wild rats in the United States. Rat infestation has been demonstrated in other portions of France.

With regard to the relation between rat infestation and human infection with *Spirochæta icterohæmorrhagiæ*, two possibilities present themselves. First, it is possible that no transfer from rats to man takes place, or only exceptionally as in case of a bite. It may be that some cause is at work in the trenches and mines which tends to infect man and rats with the *Spirochæta icterohæmorrhagiæ* entirely independently of each other. On the other hand, it seems more probable that the spirochætes may be interchanged indiscriminately among men and rats living in such environments as obtain in the trenches, by means of their urine. There is evidence to show that infection can take place either through the skin or by the mouth.

There is no adequate evidence that any insect plays a part in the transmission of the disease in nature, although the experimental evidence in this regard is by no means complete. The epidemiology of the disease seems to point rather definitely to a moist soil, at an equable temperature, as a means of keeping alive the virus.

While the problem of the rat in relation to acute infectious jaundice has not been completely worked out, the following statement of the mode of transfer forms a reasonable hypothesis. About 10 per cent of all wild rats wherever located probably carry the *Spirochæta icterohæmorrhagiæ* in their kidneys and excrete them in their urine. If this organism finds a favorable environment in the soil, a sufficient number may live long enough to infect a human being who gets them in the mouth or on the skin. Under these conditions a larger number of rats also take up the spirochætes.

Much more work needs to be done to place the whole matter on a sound scientific basis and to do this it is essential to (1) recognize cases of the disease in man, (2) determine the general prevalence of the *Spirochæta icterohæmorrhagiæ* in wild rats, living in various environments.

Detection of the Spirochæta Icterohæmorrhagiæ by Laboratory Methods.

A. *In Man.*

·The following methods have been successfully employed in detecting infection with the *Spirochæta icterohæmorrhagiæ* in human beings:

1. Examination of blood films. These have been stained for spirochætes by one of the Romanowski stains or one of the silver impregnation methods.

2. Examination of the blood by dark field illumination.

3. Injection of the blood into the peritoneal cavity of a guinea pig.

In these three methods, the earlier in the course of the disease the blood is obtained the better the chances of success. In the first two methods search must be made with the microscope for the spirochætes and as they are not very numerous in the blood of human cases, and somewhat difficult to stain these methods are not highly satisfactory. On the other hand, in early cases guinea-pig inoculation with blood is a valuable procedure and should always be done, unless the patient is first seen late in the disease. If the *Spirochæta icterohæmorrhagiæ* are present in the inoculated blood the guinea pig will usually sicken and die in about ten days. Post-mortem examination will show a well marked combination of jaundice and hemorrhage such as, so far as known, is not produced by any other infection.

In a light-skinned guinea pig a distinct yellowish tinge, especially noticeable in the ears and about the genitals, is usually observed. On dividing the skin of the abdomen in a case of this disease, the operator is at once struck with the widespread hemorrhages which lie beneath the skin and between the connective tissue planes.

They range from minute petechiæ up to massive effusions of blood perhaps a centimeter in diameter. The hemorrhages are especially well marked about the axillary and inguinal lymph-nodes and as the skin is reflected hemorrhagic areas will be seen between the fascia covering the skeletal muscles. The skin is usually quite yellow and the abdominal muscles frequently show a yellowish tinge. On opening the body cavity the liver appears distinctly enlarged and of a brownish yellow color. The spleen is not enlarged. The intestines are stained yellow and hemorrhages into the intestinal walls are of frequent occurrence. Post-peritoneal hemorrhages are frequent and abundant, especially about the kidney and adrenal. This organ is frequently the seat of marked effusions of blood. In the thorax the lungs especially attract attention, being the seat of the most characteristic gross change observed in the guinea pig. These consist of numerous sharply defined hemorrhagic foci. The description, by the Japanese, of the lungs as resembling the mottled wings of a butterfly is a very apt one. Histologically the liver and kidneys show the most characteristic changes. The liver shows an exudation of polymorphonuclear leucocytes about the bile ducts, and widespread degenerative changes of the parenchyma. Many of the cells contain an abnormal amount of pigment, while others show pronounced vacuolization and dispersion. The kidneys show an acute exudative nephritis with hemorrhages throughout the cortex.

The tissues of the guinea pig contain many spirochætes, which may be best demonstrated by staining portions of the liver by the older method of Levaditi, making sections and examining by the microscope. Dark field examination of the liver pulp will also usually reveal them.

4. Microscopic examination of the urine for spirochætes.

The urine is centrifugalized and the sediment examined by the dark field method, or films are made and stained by India ink, Romanowsky stain or a silver impregnation method. It will be recalled that the urine contains spirochætes in a variety of conditions, and one must be entirely familiar with the morphology of the *Spirochæta icterohæmorrhagiæ* to hazard a diagnosis by a microscopic examination of the urine.

The microscopic examination of the urine has a special field in expert hands to determine whether a convalescent is excreting the spirochætes in his urine and is therefore a carrier.

5. Injection of urinary sediment into the peritoneal cavity of a guinea pig.

This method has frequently been followed by positive results and should be regularly practiced. As in the injection of blood it has the decided advantage that positive results are well marked, causing the definite pathological changes in the guinea pig, above referred to.

6. Examination of tissues obtained at necropsy by the older method of Levaditi.

By this method the spirochætes may frequently be demonstrated in the viscera, especially in the kidneys.

In general, it may be stated that for the diagnosis of the disease in the living patient by laboratory procedures, guinea pig inoculation appears to be most reliable, and the method of choice; next in practical importance is the microscopical examination of blood and urine for spirochætes; and finally, attempts to cultivate the organism directly from the human subject, which appears to be a matter of considerable difficulty.

B. *In Rodents.*

Here, as in the detection of the disease in man, guinea-pig inoculation is the method of choice and reliability. The rats should preferably be taken alive, killed, and the kidneys removed at once, with precautions not to contaminate them. The kidneys should then be emulsified and the emulsion injected into the peritoneal cavity of a guinea pig, if possible using a guinea pig for each rat. The guinea pigs should then be observed for at least two weeks. If the *Spirochæta icterohæmorrhagiæ* are present the pig will become ill, show some rather variable pyrexia, become slightly jaundiced, collapse, and die in about 10 days, and at post-mortem examination will show the marked picture of jaundice and hemorrhage referred to above. Spirochætes may be demonstrated in the tissues, as previously indicated.

Bibliography.

The following available articles dealing with the *Spirochæta icterohæmorrhagiæ* will be found to contain the essentials of our present knowledge of this organism and the effects it produces in man and animals.

Chambers, Graham.
> 1917: An outbreak of infectious jaundice occurring among the soldiers of the British forces.
> J. Roy. Army Med. Corps, v. 29, p. 108.

Costa, S., and Troisier, J.
> 1916: Sur la Spirochétose ictéro-hémorragique.
> Compt. rend. Soc. d. Biol., Paris, v. 79, p. 1038.

Courmont, Jules, and Durand, Paul.
> 1917: Le rat d'égout "Reservoir de virus pour la Spirochétose ictéro-hémorrhagique."
> Bull. et mém. Soc. méd. hôp., Paris, 1917, 3d ser., 33d year, p. 115.

Dawson, Bertrand, and Hume, W. E.
> 1917: Jaundice of infective origin.
> Quart. J. Med., v. 10, p. 90.

Dawson, Bertrand, Hume, W. E., and Bedson, S. P.
> 1917: Infective jaundice.
> Brit. M. J., 1917, Sept. 15, p. 345.

Garnier, Marcel, and Reilly, J.
    1917: L'ictèro infectieux à spirochètes.
        Bull. et mém. Soc. méd. hôp. Paris, Dec. 22, 1916.
Ido, Yutaka, Hoki, Rokuro, Ito, Hiroshi, and Wani, H.
    1916: The prophylaxis of Weil's disease (spirochætosis icterohæmorrhagica).
        J. Exper. Med., v. 24, p. 471.
    1917: The rat as a carrier of *Spirochæta icterohæmorrhagiæ*, the causative agent of
        Weil's disease (spirochætosis icterohæmorrhagica).
        J. Exper. Med., v. 26, p. 341.
Inada, Ryokichi.
    1917: The clinical aspects of spirochætosis icterohæmorrhagica or Weil's disease.
        J. Exper. Med., v. 26, p. 355.
Inada, Ryokichi, Ido, Yutaka, Hoki, Rokuro, Ito, Hiroshi, and Wani, Hidetsune.
    1918: Intravenous serotherapy of Weil's disease (spirochætosis icterohæmorrhagica).
        J. Exper. Med., v. 27, p. 283.
Inada, Ryokichi, Ido, Yutaka, Hoki, Rokuro, Kaneko, Renjiro, and Ito Hiroshi.
    1916: The etiology, mode of infection, and specific therapy of Weil's disease
        (spirochætosis icterohæmorrhagica).
        J. Exper. Med., v. 23, p. 377.
Ito, Tetsuta, and Matsuyaki, Haruichiro.
    1916: The pure cultivation of *Spirochæta icterohæmorrhagiæ* (Inada).
        J. Exper. Med., v. 23, p. 557.
Jobling, James W., and Eggstein, A. A.
    1917: The wild rats of the Southern States as carriers of *Spirochæta ictero-
        hæmorrhagiæ*.
        J. Am. Med. Assoc., v. 69, p. 1787.
Kaneko, Renjiro, and Okuda, Kikuyo.
    1917: The distribution in the human body of *Spirochæta icterohæmorrhagiæ*.
        J. Exper. Med., v. 26, p. 325.
    1918: Distribution of *Spirochæta icterohæmorrhagiæ* in the organs after serum
        treatment.
        J. Exper. Med., v. 27, p. 305.
Martin, August, and Pettit, Louis.
    1917: La Spirochétose ictero-hémorragique en France.
        Presse med., 1916, no. 69.
    1917: Présence de *Spirochæta icterohæmorrhagiæ* chez le surmulot de la zone des
        armées.
        Compt. rend. Soc. de Biol., Paris, v. 80, p. 10.
    1917: Présence de *Spirochæta icterohæmorrhagiæ* chez les surmulot de l'intériéur.
        Compt. rend. Soc. de Biol., Paris, v. 80, p. 574.
Martin, August, Pettit, Louis, and Voudremer, Albert.
    1917: Culture du *Spirochæta icterohæmorrhagiæ*.
        Compt. rend. Soc. oe Biol., Paris, v. 80, p. 197.
Noguchi, Hideyo.
    1917: *Spirochæta icterohæmorrhagiæ* in American wild rats and its relation to
        Japanese and European strains.
        J. Exper. Med., v. 25, p. 755.
Stokes, A., Ryle, J. A., and Tytler, W. H.
    1917: Weil's disease (Spirochætosis icterohæmorrhagica) in the British Army
        in Flanders.
        Lancet, v. 192, p. 142.
Wilmaers, L., and Renaux, E.
    1917: Quarante-sept cas de spirochétose, ictéro-hémorrhagique, étude clinique
        et notes laboratoire.
        Arch. méd. Belges, v. 70, p. 115, 207.

PREVALENCE OF DISEASE.

No health department, State or local, can effectively prevent or control disease without knowledge of when, where, and under what conditions cases are occurring.

UNITED STATES.

EXTRA-CANTONMENT ZONES—CASES REPORTED WEEK ENDED MAY 7.

CAMP BEAUREGARD ZONE, LA.

	Cases.
Chicken pox:	
Alexandria	1
Gonorrhea:	
Alexandria	1
Malaria:	
Alexandria	2
Measles:	
Alexandria	2
Pineville	1
Mumps:	
Alexandria	28
Pineville	3
Pneumonia:	
Alexandria	5
Pineville	1
Poliomyelitis:	
Ward No. 2	6
Smallpox:	
Alexandria	1
Tuberculosis:	
Alexandria	1
Pineville	1
Whooping cough:	
Alexandria	4

CAMP BOWIE ZONE, TEX.

Fort Worth:	
Chicken pox	6
Diphtheria	1
Gonorrhea	2
Malaria	1
Measles	1
Mumps	31
Pneumonia	2
Scarlet fever	10
Smallpox	22
Sore eyes	1
Tonsilitis	3
Typhoid fever	3
Whooping cough	2

CAMP DEVENS ZONE, MASS.

German measles.	
Lancaster	1
Mumps:	
Ayer	1
Lancaster	1

CAMP DODGE ZONE, IOWA.

	Cases.
Chancroid:	
Des Moines	1
Diphtheria:	
Des Moines	.
Gonorrhea:	
Des Moines	5
Scarlet fever:	
Ankeny	1
Des Moines	17
Grimes	1
Smallpox:	
Des Moines	14
Syphilis:	
Des Moines	0

CAMP EBERTS ZONE, ARK.

Arthritis, acute:	
England	1
Gonorrhea:	
Cabot	1
Carlisle	1
England	1
Lonoke	3
Malaria:	
Carlisle	4
England	9
Lonoke	1
Measles:	
Carlisle	2
England	8
Lonoke	1
Lonoke, route 4	2
Mumps:	
Carlisle	1
England	5
Keo	1
Pellagra:	
England	0
Pneumonia:	
England	1
Kerr	1
Lonoke	1
Smallpox:	
England	7
Lonoke, route 2	1
Syphilis:	
England	2

CAMP EBERTS ZONE, ARK.—continued.

	Cases.
Tuberculosis:	
England	3
Typhoid fever:	
Carlisle	2
England	1
Whooping cough:	
England	2

CAMP GORDON ZONE, GA.

Atlanta:	
Chicken pox	5
Diphtheria	2
German measles	1
Gonorrhea	16
Measles	3
Mumps	17
Pneumonia	2
Scarlet fever	2
Syphilis	11
Smallpox	1
Tuberculosis	13
Typhoid fever	1
Whooping cough	1
Decatur:	
Typhoid fever	1
Stone Mountain:	
Whooping cough	6

CAMP GREENE ZONE, N. C.

Charlotte Township:	
Diphtheria	1
Gonorrhea	22
Measles	6
Mumps	11
Scarlet fever	3
Syphilis	11
Trachoma	1
Tuberculosis	6
Whooping cough	10

GULFPORT HEALTH DISTRICT, MISS.

Gulfport Health District:	
Gonorrhea	5
Malaria	11
Measles	4
Mumps	3
Syphilis	1
Tuberculosis, pulmonary	2

CAMP HANCOCK ZONE, GA.

Augusta:	
Cerebrospinal meningitis	1
Chancroid	4
Chicken pox	6
German measles	1
Gonorrhea	9
Measles	12
Syphilis	12

CAMP JOSEPH E. JOHNSTON ZONE, FLA.

Atlantic Beach:	
Measles	1
Eastport:	
Malaria	1

CAMP JOSEPH E. JOHNSTON ZONE, FLA.—contd.

	Cases.
Jacksonville:	
Chicken pox	4
Enteritis	4
Gonorrhea	1
Measles	2
Mumps	9
Pneumonia	2
Smallpox	2
Syphilis	2
Tuberculosis	5
Typhoid fever	4
Whooping cough	22
Mandarin:	
Malaria	4

FORT LEAVENWORTH ZONE, KANS.

Leavenworth:	
German measles	1
Measles	5
Smallpox	4
Tuberculosis	4
Leavenworth County:	
Diphtheria	1
Measles	9
Pneumonia, lobar	1
Scarlet fever	3
Smallpox	1
Typhoid fever	2

CAMP LEE ZONE, VA.

Chancroid:	
Petersburg	1
Chicken pox:	
Prince George County	9
German measles:	
Ettricks	4
Prince George County	4
Gonorrhea:	
Petersburg	9
Measles:	
Ettricks	1
Hopewell	1
Petersburg	2
Mumps:	
Ettricks	9
Hopewell	3
Petersburg	1
Prince George County	2
Pneumonia:	
Petersburg	4
Scarlet fever:	
Hopewell	1
Petersburg	1
Septic sore throat:	
Ettricks	4
Syphilis:	
Petersburg	4
Tuberculosis:	
Petersburg	4
Whooping cough:	
Ettricks	3
Hopewell	1

CAMP LEWIS ZONE, WASH.

German measles: Cases.

Greendale 2
Loveland 6
Spanaway 1

Measles:

Du Pont 2

Mumps:

Du Pont 3
Parkland 1

Scarlet fever:

Parkland 1

Syphilis:

Lakeview 1

Tuberculosis, pulmonary:

American Lake 1
Lakeview 1
Parkland 1

Whooping cough:

American Lake 8
Parkland 1

CAMP LOGAN ZONE, TEX.

Chancroid:

Houston 2

Diphtheria:

Houston 2

Dysentery:

Moonshine Hill 1

Gonorrhea:

Houston 20

Malaria:

Eureka 1
Moonshine Hill 5

Measles:

Cypress 1
Houston 10
Moonshine Hill 3

Mumps:

Moonshine Hill 1

Smallpox:

Hufsmith 1

Syphilis:

Goose Creek 1
Houston 23
Humble 1

Trachoma:

Houston 1

Tuberculosis:

Houston 3

CAMP MACARTHUR ZONE, TEX.

Waco:

Chicken pox 3
Malaria 1
Mumps 27
Scarlet fever 1
Smallpox 2
Tuberculosis 4

CAMP M'CLELLAN ZONE, ALA.

Anniston:

Chicken pox 3
Diphtheria 1
Measles 1
Mumps 14
Pellagra 1

CAMP M'CLELLAN ZONE, ALA.—continued.

Anniston—Continued.   Cases.

Pneumonia 2
Smallpox 4
Tuberculosis 1
Whooping cough 1

Blue Mountain:

Smallpox 1

Precinct 20:

Mumps 1

NORFOLK COUNTY NAVAL DISTRICT, VA.

Chicken pox:

Lafayette Park Reservation 1

Diphtheria:

Norfolk 1

Malaria:

Ocean View 2

Measles:

Norfolk 13
Portsmouth 12
Larchmont 1
South Norfolk 3

Mumps:

Ocean View 3
Willoughby 1
Norfolk 5
Portsmouth 1

Ophthalmia neonatorum:

Portsmouth 1

Pneumonia:

Norfolk 2

Scarlet fever:

Portsmouth 2
Norfolk 1
Norfolk County 1

Smallpox:

Norfolk 2

Syphilis:

Norfolk 1

Typhoid fever:

Norfolk 1

Tuberculosis:

Portsmouth 2
Ocean View 1

FORT OGLETHORPE ZONE, GA.

Cerebrospinal meningitis:

Chattanooga 1

Diphtheria:

Chattanooga 1

Gonorrhea:

Chattanooga 17

Mumps:

Chattanooga 3
Rossville 7

Paratyphoid fever:

Chattanooga 1

Pneumonia:

East Lake 1
Rossville 1

Scarlet fever:

Chattanooga 3
St. Elmo 1

FORT OGLETHORPE ZONE, GA.—continued.

Smallpox: Cases.
- Chattanooga 5
- North Chattanooga 1

Syphilis:
- Chattanooga 15

Tuberculosis:
- Chickamauga 1

Typhoid fever:
- Alton Park 1
- Chattanooga 1

Whooping cough:
- Chattanooga 3

CAMP PIKE ZONE, ARK.

Little Rock:
- Cerebrospinal meningitis 3
- Chancroid 1
- German measles 1
- Gonorrhea 13
- Malaria 8
- Measles 1
- Mumps 4
- Pellagra 2
- Pneumonia 12
- Scarlet fever 2
- Smallpox 11
- Syphilis 12
- Tuberculosis 20
- Typhoid fever 1

North Little Rock:
- Gonorrhea 1
- Malaria 4
- Mumps 2
- Pellagra 1
- Smallpox 3
- Syphilis 1

Scott:
- Gonorrhea 2

CAMP SEVIER ZONE, S. C.

Measles:
- Judson Mills 1
- Union Bleachery 1

Mumps:
- Union Bleachery 3

Smallpox:
- Poe Mill 1

CAMP SHELBY ZONE, MISS.

Hattiesburg:
- Chicken pox 1
- Malaria 2
- Measles 1
- Mumps 55
- Pellagra 3
- Septic sore throat 1
- Venereal 10
- Whooping cough 8

CAMP SHERIDAN ZONE, ALA.

Montgomery:
- Chancroid 4
- Chicken pox 1
- Gonorrhea 16
- Malaria 76
- Measles 5

CAMP SHERIDAN ZONE, ALA.—continued.

Montgomery—Continued.   Cases.
- Mumps 6
- Ophthalmia neonatorum 1
- Ringworm 34
- Smallpox 2
- Tuberculosis 2

CAMP SHERMAN ZONE, OHIO.

Diphtheria:
- Chillicothe 2

Measles:
- Chillicothe 5
- Liberty Township 1
- Springfield Township 2

Scarlet fever:
- Chillicothe 1
- Springfield Township 1

Smallpox:
- Chillicothe 3

Tuberculosis, pulmonary:
- Chillicothe 4

CAMP ZACHARY TAYLOR ZONE, KY.

Jefferson County:
- Cerebrospinal meningitis 1
- Measles 2
- Smallpox 3

Louisville:
- Chicken pox 4
- Diphtheria 6
- Measles 8
- Mumps 1
- Rabies in animals 1
- Scarlet fever 2
- Smallpox 2
- Tuberculosis, pulmonary 2

U. S. Government clinic:
- Chancroid 2
- Gonorrhea 29
- Syphilis 12

TIDEWATER HEALTH DISTRICT, VA.

Chancroid:
- Newport News 9

Chicken pox:
- Hampton 1
- Newport News 4

Gonorrhea:
- Newport News 7

Measles:
- Hampton 1
- Newport News 12

Mumps:
- Hampton 4
- Newport News 18
- Phoebus 1

Scarlet fever:
- Newport News 2

Smallpox:
- Newport News 2

Syphilis:
- Newport News 9

Trachoma:
- Hampton 4

TIDEWATER HEALTH DISTRICT, VA.—continued.

Tuberculosis:	Cases.
Hampton	1
Typhoid fever:	
Hampton	1
Phoebus	1
Whooping cough:	
Hampton	1
Newport News	2

CAMP TRAVIS ZONE, TEX.

San Antonio:

Diphtheria	1
Dysentery	2
Enteritis, gastro	1
Erysipelas	1
Gonorrhea	50
Malaria	1
Measles	8
Mumps	6
Pneumonia	2
Syphilis	7
Tuberculosis	23
Typhoid fever	9

CAMP WADSWORTH ZONE, S. C.

Measles:	
Moores	1
Spartanburg	3

CAMP WADSWORTH ZONE, S. C.—continued.

Mumps:	Cases.
Spartanburg	10
Pellagra:	
Glenn Springs	1
Moores	1
Pauline	2
Pneumonia: lobar:	
Cedar Springs	1
Saxon Mills	1
Spartanburg	1
Smallpox:	
Spartanburg	2
Tuberculosis:	
Saxon Mills	1
Whooping cough:	
Spartanburg	9

CAMP WHEELER ZONE, GA.

Bibb County:	
Malaria	1
Macon:	
Malaria	1
Measles	1
Mumps	1
Scarlet fever	4
Smallpox	2
Tuberculosis	2
Typhoid fever	1

DISEASE CONDITIONS AMONG TROOPS IN THE UNITED STATES.

The following data are taken from telegraphic reports received in the office of the Surgeon General, United States Army, for the week ended April 26, 1918:

Annual admission rate per 1,000 (disease):

All troops	1,279.4
National Guard camps	1,313.8
National Army camps	1,304.2
Regular army	1,257.2

Noneffective rate per 1,000 on day of report:

All troops	42.9
National Guard camps	37.6

Noneffective rate per 1,000 —Continued.

National Army camps	50.5
Regular Army	40

Annual death rate per 1,000 (disease only):

All troops	10.4
National Guard camps	8.3
National Army camps	13
Regular Army	9.8

New cases of special diseases reported during the week ended Apr. 26, 1918.

	Pneumonia.	Dysentery.	Malaria.	Venereal.		Measles.	Meningitis.	Scarlet fever.	Deaths.	Annual admission rate per 1,000 (disease only).	Noneffective per 1,000 on day of report.
				Total.	New infections.						
Wadsworth	4			17	12	4	1	2	1	332	17.2
Hancock	4			15	15	2		1		478	26.6
McClellan	17		1	15	15		1		5	1,065	29.4
Sevier	8		6	43	24	6		3	3	538	25
Wheeler	62		2	9	3				13	1,634	44.4
Logan	20			61	49	10	1	11	4	2,855	40.4
Cody	5			5	1		1		5	377	22.1
Doniphan	6			8					8	1,783	64.9
Bowie	11		1	65	64				3	1,016	54.6
Sheridan	10			13	10				3	902	28.7

New cases of special diseases reported during the week ended Apr. 26, 1918—Continued.

	Pneumonia.	Dysentery.	Malaria.	Venereal.		Measles.	Meningitis.	Scarlet fever.	Deaths.	Annual admission rate per 1,000 (disease only).	Noneffective per 1,000 on day of report.
				Total.	New infections,						
Shelby	11	1		17	7	3			4	2,546	51.3
Beauregard	23		13	29	5	1	1		2	2,138	70.2
Kearny	4		1	6	6			5		1,612	46.4
Devens	49			47	5	8		6	8	867	45.9
Upton	15			34	12	14	1	1	3	716	36.4
Dix	8			53	17	12		6	3	953	32.7
Meade	9			18	9	8		2	1	779	30.4
Lee	2		1	223	16	3	1		6	1,311	61.8
Jackson	9			21	4	17	1		1	1,422	61.9
Gordon	11		2	17	17	25	2	1	21	1,560	57.1
Sherman	21			25	7	6		20	8	1,119	46.8
Taylor	17					33		2	15	1,788	73.9
Custer	12			31	2	6	1	7	3	743	31.8
Grant	9			26	1	20		4	2	853	29.3
Pike	21	2		60	12	16	5	5	11	1,703	62.9
Dodge	41			39		22	1	18	19	1,555	99.5
Funston	16			30	12	7		3	5	961	59.3
Travis	11		3	31	3	22			7	3,578	59.4
Lewis	1		1	92	13	4		13		1,055	43.1
Northeastern Department	1			8	6	4			2	936.8	32.9
Eastern Department	5			26	8	16	2		3	967.3	32.4
Southeastern Department	2		8	28	21	13	1		5	1,189.1	51
Central Department	14			32	14	18		18	2	1,120.9	39.7
Southern Department	30		1	85	51	11	1	4	12	1,570.9	47.3
Western Department	7			23	15	8			3	1,064.9	25.8
Aviation Section, Signal Corps	31	1	4	132		43	2	32	23	1,344.1	34.4
Camp Greene	10			11		5			2	615.9	21.8
Camp Fremont	3		1	12	4	15		1	1	908.5	43.5
El Paso	1			11	11	1		1		1,079.7	4.9
Columbus Barracks	2			18	1				2	1,465.6	60.2
Jefferson Barracks	3			27	1	4		7	1	3,557.3	130.5
Fort Logan	8					2		4	5	4,036.5	114.2
Fort McDowell				4	2					1,325.8	47.4
Fort Slocum			1	2		1			1	612.7	37.5
Fort Thomas	1			2		7				1,248.3	55.5
Disciplinary Barracks, Alcatraz										1,155.5	25.4
Disciplinary Barracks, Fort Leavenworth	3			2					1	1,310.7	35.3
A. A. Humphreys	1									761.8	44.6
J. E. Johnston	1			35	25	6	1	1		1,337.5	39.7
Hoboken	21		1	158	20	8		4	11	1,383	51.6
Newport News	9		2	54	17	32			7	1,257.4	63.3
West Point, N. Y	1									387.1	8.1
Edgewood	1			1						658.5	19.2
Prov. Depot for Corps and Army troops	7			19	1	5		1	6	1,199.5	41.7
Camp Holabird				1						4,666.7	51.3
Camp Raritan				2		1				1,150.4	21
Springfield Armory										839.7	37.6
National Guard Departments	2			9	2	4					
National Army Departments	15		3	76	32	56		9	7		
Total	616	4	52	1,828	572	509	24	192	258	[1]1,279.4	[1]42.9

[1] All troops.

Annual rate per 1,000 for special diseases.

Disease.	All troops in United States.[1]	Regulars in United States.[1]	National Guard, all camps.[1]	National Army, all camps.[1]	Expedition-ary Forces.[2]
Pneumonia	26.6	21.1	32.6	29.1	21.3
Dysentery	0.17	0.13	0.17	0.2	0.0
Malaria	2.2	2.3	4.2	0.8	0.7
Venereal	78.9	90.5	53.3	86.2	52.8
Paratyphoid	0.13	0.13	0.0	0.0	0.0
Typhoid	0.04	0.0	0.0	0.1	0.1
Measles	21.9	26.1	4.5	25.7	5.2
Meningitis	1.0	0.9	0.88	1.4	3.4
Scarlet fever	8.3	9.5	3.87	10.1	6.7

[1] Week ended Apr. 26, 1918.　　　　[2] Week ended Apr. 19, 1918.

CURRENT STATE SUMMARIES.

Alabama.

From Collaborating Epidemiologist Perry, by telegraph, for week ended May 4, 1918:

Smallpox: By counties—Cullman 1, Jackson 39, Jefferson 43, Tuscaloosa 1, Wilcox 4. No other unusual prevalence.

California.

From the State Board of Health of California, by telegraph, for week ended May 4, 1918:

Twenty-three cases smallpox; 7 in Stockton, 4 in Tehama, 4 in San Francisco, remainder scattered over State. Six cases epidemic cerebrospinal meningitis; 1 in Berkeley, 2 in San Francisco, 2 in Los Angeles, 1 in San Joaquin County. One case poliomyelitis in Santa Monica. Prevalence of measles and other diseases that have been epidemic throughout the State now greatly reduced. Twenty-three cases of hookworm reported from mines in Amador County.

Reported by mail for preceding week (ended April 27):

Cerebrospinal meningitis	6	Poliomyelitis	1
Chicken pox	121	Scarlet fever	63
Diphtheria	61	Smallpox	17
Erysipelas	12	Syphilis	39
German measles	262	Tetanus	2
Gonococcus infection	49	Trachoma	2
Hookworm	13	Tuberculosis	124
Malaria	5	Typhoid fever	16
Measles	829	Whooping cough	173
Pneumonia	45	Mumps	176

Connecticut.

From Collaborating Epidemiologist Black, by telegraph, for week ended May 4, 1918:

Smallpox: Hartford 3, Cheshire 1. Cerebrospinal meningitis: Hartford 1, Waterbury 1.

Illinois.

From Collaborating Epidemiologist Drake, by telegraph, for week ended May 4, 1918:

Smallpox: One hundred and fifteen, of which in Quincy 9, Chandlerville 6, Elk Township (Jackson County) 6, Decatur 5, Alton 7, Woodriver Township (Madison County) 7, Peoria 20, East St. Louis 8, Millcreek 8, Chicago 5. Diphtheria: One hundred and thirty-two, of which in Chicago 97. Scarlet fever: Ninety-three, of which Oak Park 6, East Alton 7, Moline 5, Chicago 40. Poliomyelitis: Three, of which Chicago 2, Joliet 1. Meningitis: Nineteen, of which one each in Macon Township (Effingham County), Geneva, Nilwood, Petersburg Precinct (Menard County), Springfield 2, Chicago 13.

Indiana.

From the State Board of Health of Indiana, by telegraph, for week ended May 4, 1918:

Diphtheria: One death each—Tipton, Michigan City, Vevay. Smallpox: Epidemic—Logansport, Anderson. Measles: Epidemic—Prairie Creek, Benton County, Henry County. Whooping cough: One death each—Middleton, Hearsey, Henry County.

Kansas.

From Collaborating Epidemiologist Crumbine, by telegraph, for week ended May 4, 1918:

Meningitis: In cities—Junction City 1, Pittsburgh 1, Wichita 1. Poliomyelitis. Wathena 1. Smallpox (10 or more cases): In counties—Allen 14, Butler 13, Cherokee 14, Crawford 19, Graham 13, Montgomery 10, Osborne 30; in cities—Wichita 17. Scarlet fever (over 10 cases): Neosho County, including Chanute, 34.

Louisiana.

From Collaborating Epidemiologist Dowling, by telegraph, for week ended May 4, 1918:

Meningitis 3, smallpox 27, typhoid fever 15, measles 18, pneumonia 16.

Massachusetts.

From Collaborating Epidemiologist Hitchcock, by telegraph, for week ended May 4, 1918:

Unusual prevalence. Diphtheria: Templeton 6. German measles: Gardner 16, Mansfield 20. Measles: Brookline 36, Lawrence 125, Quincy 37, Westford 15, Woburn 14. Scarlet fever: Billerica 5. Smallpox: Lynn 1.

Minnesota.

From Collaborating Epidemiologist Bracken, by telegraph, for week ended May 4, 1918:

Smallpox (new foci): Chippewa County, Leenthrop Township, 1; Freeborn County, Riceland Township, 2; Goodhue County, Kenyon village, 78; Cherry Grove Township, 19; Meeker County, Dassel village, 1; Renville County, Camp Township, 4; Fairfax village, 2; Rice County, Richland Township, 9. One poliomyelitis, nine cerebrospinal meningitis, reported since April 29.

Nebraska.

From the State board of health of Nebraska, by telegraph, for week ended May 4, 1918:

Smallpox: Scotts Bluff County, Stella, Upland, and still existing at Omaha, Lincoln, and Syracuse. Scarlet fever: Scotts Bluff County.

South Carolina.

From Collaborating Epidemiologist Hayne, by telegraph, for week ended May 6, 1918:

Two cases epidemic meningitis.

Virginia.

From the State Board of Health of Virginia, by telegraph, for week ended May 4, 1918:

Two cases smallpox Northampton County, several King William, one Charlotte, several Wise, two Pittsylvania, one Loudoun. One case cerebrospinal meningitis Buckingham County, one Montgomery, one Nansemond. One case poliomyelitis Accomac, one Pittsylvania.

Washington.

From Collaborating Epidemiologist Tuttle, by telegraph, for week ended May 4, 1918:

German measles still widely prevalent, but epidemic decreasing. Scarlet fever situation much improved in Tacoma. Seattle, 30 cases scarlet fever. Yakima County, 35 cases whooping cough.

CEREBROSPINAL MENINGITIS.

State Reports for March, 1918.

Place.	New cases reported.	Place.	New cases reported.
Alabama:		Ohio—Continued.	
Bibb County	1	Lucas County	2
Calhoun County	4	Mahoning County	2
Colbert County	4	Medina County	1
Etowah County	1	Montgomery County	4
Houston County	1	Muskingum County	1
Jefferson County	22	Pike County	3
Montgomery County	2	Ross County	1
Morgan County	1	Scioto County	3
Tuscaloosa County	3	Shelby County	1
		Summit County	6
Total	39	Trumbull County	1
Ohio:		Total	57
Ashland County	1		
Ashtabula County	2	Washington:	
Belmont County	2	Clark County—	
Butler County	1	Camas	2
Clark County	2	Pierce County—	
Clinton County	2	Tacoma	3
Columbiana County	1	Whatcom County—	
Cuyahoga County	11	Sumas	1
Franklin County	1	King County—	
Guernsey County	1	Seattle	1
Hamilton County	6		
Henry County	1	Total	7
Jackson County	1		

CEREBROSPINAL MENINGITIS—Continued.

City Reports for Week Ended Apr. 20, 1918.

Place.	Cases.	Deaths.	Place.	Cases.	Deaths.
Atlanta, Ga	3	1	Newark, N. J	14	3
Baltimore, Md	7	4	New Haven, Conn	1	
Bayonne, N. J	1		New Orleans, La	3	2
Birmingham, Ala	1	1	New York, N. Y	28	7
Boston, Mass	7	2	Niagara Falls, N. Y	1	1
Buffalo, N. Y	1		Norfolk, Va	2	1
Cambridge, Mass	1		Oakland, Cal		1
Centralia, Ill	1		Philadelphia, Pa	2	1
Chicago, Ill	9	2	Pittsburgh, Pa	2	1
Cincinnati, Ohio	4	1	Pittsfield, Mass	1	
Cleveland, Ohio	2	1	Providence, R. I	1	
Davenport, Iowa	1		Richmond, Va		1
Dayton, Ohio		1	St. Joseph, Mo	1	
Detroit, Mich	2		St. Louis, Mo	2	3
Fort Wayne, Ind	1		San Francisco, Cal	1	2
Hartford, Conn		1	Schenectady, N. Y	1	
Holyoke, Mass	1	1	Scranton, Pa	1	
Indianapolis, Ind	1	1	Seattle, Wash	1	1
Lawrence, Mass	1	2	Shenandoah, Pa	2	
Lexington, Ky	1	1	Spartanburg, S. C	1	
Lincoln, Nebr	1		Springfield, Ill	1	
Los Angeles, Cal	1	2	Topeka, Kans	1	
Louisville, Ky	2	2	Warren, Ohio	1	1
Macon, Ga	2		Washington, D. C	4	1
Manchester, N. H	1	1	Wichita, Kans	1	
Manitowoc, Wis	1		Wilkes-Barre, Pa		1
Milwaukee, Wis	6	4	Winston-Salem, N. C	2	
Nashville, Tenn	2	1	Worcester, Mass	3	2

DIPHTHERIA.

See Diphtheria, measles, scarlet fever, and tuberculosis, page 744.

ERYSIPELAS.

City Reports for Week Ended Apr. 20, 1918.

Place.	Cases.	Deaths	Place.	Cases.	Deaths.
Alameda, Cal	1		Milwaukee, Wis	3	
Austin, Tex		2	Newark, N. J	7	
Baltimore, Md	4		New Castle, Pa	1	
Berkeley, Cal	1		New York, N. Y		4
Bridgeport, Conn	1		Oklahoma City, Okla		1
Buffalo, N. Y	7	1	Palestine, Tex	1	
Cambridge, Mass		1	Philadelphia, Pa		2
Charlotte, N. C		1	Pittsburgh, Pa	7	1
Chicago, Ill	13	2	Pontiac, Mich	1	
Cincinnati, Ohio	2		Portland, Oreg	2	
Cleveland, Ohio	5		Quincy, Ill		1
Denver, Colo	1		Reading, Pa	1	
Detroit, Mich	5	1	Richmond, Ind		1
Duluth, Minn	1		Rochester, N. Y	1	
El Paso, Tex		1	St. Joseph, Mo	1	
Erie, Pa	1		St. Louis, Mo	16	2
Kansas City, Kans	1		San Francisco, Cal	2	1
Los Angeles, Cal	6		Steubenville, Ohio	2	
Louisville, Ky	3	4	Tacoma, Wash	2	
Manchester, N. H	1	1	Utica, N. Y		1
Manitowoc, Wis	1		Yonkers, N. Y	1	
Memphis, Tenn		1			

LEPROSY.

City Report for Week Ended Apr. 20, 1918.

During the week ended April 20, 1918, one case of leprosy was reported at San Francisco, Cal.

MALARIA.

State Reports for March, 1918.

Place.	New cases reported.	Place.	New cases reported.
Alabama:		Alabama—Continued.	
Butler County	2	Mobile County	1
Calhoun County	3	Shelby County	1
Colbert County	2	Tuscaloosa County	8
Elmore County	1		
Escambia County	1	Total	38
Etowah County	1		
Greene County	2	Ohio:	
Houston County	1	Gallia County	4
Jefferson County	6	Harrison County	2
Madison County	5		
Marshall County	4	Total	6

City Reports for Week Ended Apr. 20, 1918.

Place.	Cases.	Deaths.	Place.	Cases.	Deaths.
Austin, Tex		1	Louisville, Ky	1	1
Bakersfield, Cal	1		Marshall, Tex	1	
Birmingham, Ala	1		Memphis, Tenn	3	2
Hattiesburg, Miss	14		Palestine, Tex	14	
Little Rock, Ark	3		Richmond, Va	2	
Cape Girardeau, Mo	4		Tuscaloosa, Ala	1	

MEASLES.

See Diphtheria, measles, scarlet fever, and tuberculosis, page 744.

PELLAGRA.

State Reports for March, 1918.

Place.	New cases reported.	Place.	New cases reported.
Alabama:		Alabama—Continued.	
Bibb County	1	Pickens County	1
Calhoun County	2	Shelby County	1
Chambers County	1	St. Clair County	3
Colbert County	1	Sumter County	1
Dallas County	3	Tuscaloosa County	13
Escambia County	1	Walker County	2
Etowah County	1	Wilcox County	1
Henry County	2		
Jackson County	3	Total	67
Jefferson County	12		
Lamar County	1	Ohio:	
Limestone County	1	Lawrence County	1
Madison County	14	Paulding County	1
Marion County	1		
Montgomery County	1	Total	2

City Reports for Week Ended Apr. 20, 1918.

Place.	Cases.	Deaths.	Place.	Cases.	Deaths.
Augusta, Ga		1	Little Rock, Ark		1
Austin, Tex		1	Marshall, Tex	1	
Beaumont, Tex		1	Memphis, Tenn		2
Birmingham, Ala	1	2	Mobile, Ala		1
Charleston, S. C		3	Montgomery, Ala		1
Charlotte, N. C		1	Nashville, Tenn	1	
Chelsea, Mass		1	New Orleans, La	1	
Columbia, S. C	1		Palestine, Tex	2	
Dallas, Tex		2	Providence, R. I	1	
Greenville, S. C		1	Roanoke, Va		
Houston, Tex	1		Rocky Mount, N. C		1
Lincoln, Nebr	1		Winston-Salem, N. C	1	

PLAGUE.

Hawaii—Laupahoehoe.

On May 5, 1918, one death from plague was reported at Laupa-hoehoe, Hawaii.

PNEUMONIA.

City Reports for Week Ended Apr. 20, 1918.

Place.	Cases.	Deaths.	Place.	Cases.	Deaths.
Amsterdam, N. Y	5	1	Long Beach, Cal	1	
Atlanta, Ga	2	30	Los Angeles, Cal	11	6
Auburn, N. Y	4	1	Louisville, Ky	5	20
Baltimore, Md	57	21	Lowell, Mass	6	4
Barre, Vt	1	1	Lynn, Mass	8	5
Battle Creek, Mich	1	1	Manchester, N. H	3	3
Berkeley, Cal	1		Manitowoc, Wis	2	2
Boston, Mass	25	40	Mansfield, Ohio	2	1
Braddock, Pa	3		Marshall, Tex	1	
Brockton, Mass	8	2	McKeesport, Pa	8	10
Buffalo, N. Y	7	37	Melrose, Mass	1	1
Burlington, Vt	1		Michigan City, Ind	2	2
Butler, Pa	1		Morgantown, W. Va	1	
Cambridge, Mass	12	5	Morristown, N. J	1	1
Centralia, Ill	2		Newark, N. J	66	21
Chattanooga, Tenn	2	1	New Bedford, Mass	9	3
Chelsea, Mass	2	3	Newburyport, Mass	5	4
Chicago, Ill	432	185	New Castle, Ind	3	
Chillicothe, Ohio	1		New Castle, Pa	2	
Cleveland, Ohio	74	59	Newport, Ky	3	
Clinton, Mass	1		Newton, Mass	3	3
Collesville, Kans	1		Northampton, Mass	1	1
Cumberland, Md	1		Oak Park, Ill	1	3
Dallas, Tex	1	9	Palestine, Tex	4	2
Dayton, Ohio	8	9	Philadelphia, Pa	129	66
Detroit, Mich	54	114	Pittsburgh, Pa	119	142
Duluth, Minn	2	9	Pittsfield, Mass	1	2
Erie, Pa	4	7	Pontiac, Mich	2	1
Fall River, Mass	6	1	Quincy, Mass	4	1
Findlay, Ohio	1		Reading, Pa	7	4
Flint, Mich	9	2	Rochester, N. Y	16	12
Fort Worth, Tex	11	11	Sacramento, Cal	2	2
Fresno, Cal	1		Saginaw, Mich	2	1
Grand Rapids, Mich	29	4	Salem, Mass	1	1
Hammond, Ind	2	3	San Francisco, Cal	24	26
	1	4	Schenectady, N. Y	10	3
	1		Somerville, Mass	8	3
	15	1	Springfield, Mass	17	3
	2	1	Steelton, Pa	1	1
	1	5	Steubenville, Ohio	1	
	6	3	Stockton, Cal	9	4
Johnstown, Pa	1	12	Waco, Tex	1	
Kalamazoo, Mich	4	3	Waltham, Mass	1	3
Kansas City, Kans	6		Warren, Ohio	3	3
Keokuk, Iowa	4		Wichita, Kans	3	
Kokomo, Ind	1		Wilkinsburg, Pa	4	5
Lancaster, Pa	3		Worcester, Mass	26	9
	4	2	Yonkers, N. Y	1	2
Leavenworth, Kans	2	1	York, Pa	1	
Lincoln, Nebr	1	1	Youngstown, Ohio	4	15
Little Rock, Ark	4				

POLIOMYELITIS (INFANTILE PARALYSIS).

State Reports for March, 1918.

Place.	New cases reported.	Place.	New cases reported.
Alabama		Ohio—Continued	
Lawson County	1	Lucas County	1
Ohio		Mercer County	1
Cuyahoga County		Wyandot County	1
Franklin County	2		
Hamilton County	1	Total	8

POLIOMYELITIS (INFANTILE PARALYSIS)—Continued.

City Reports for Week Ended Apr. 20, 1918.

Place.	Cases.	Deaths.	Place.	Cases.	Deaths.
Cambridge, Mass.	2	1	New York, N. Y.	1	
Chicago, Ill.	4	1	Orange, N. J.		3
Milwaukee, Wis.	6	1	Warren, Ohio.	1	

RABIES IN ANIMALS.

City Reports for Week Ended Apr. 20, 1918.

During the week ended April 20, 1918, two cases of rabies in animals were reported at Detroit, Mich., and one case at Louisville, Ky.

SCARLET FEVER.

See Diphtheria, measles, scarlet fever, and tuberculosis, page 744.

SMALLPOX.

Kentucky—Laurel County.

On April 29, 1918, smallpox was reported in Laurel County, Ky., from 40 to 60 cases of the disease having occurred in two or three localities in the county.

State Reports for March, 1918.

Place.	New cases reported.	Deaths.	Vaccination history of cases.			
			Number vaccinated within 7 years preceding attack.	Number last vaccinated more than 7 years preceding attack.	Number never successfully vaccinated.	Vaccination history not obtained or uncertain.
Ohio:						
Adams County	9				3	6
Allen County	79			1	78	
Ashland County	6				1	5
Ashtabula County	5				4	1
Athens County	6			1	2	3
Auglaize County	6				3	3
Brown County	2				1	1
Butler County	78			1	77	
Clark County	4				4	
Clermont County	1				1	
Clinton County	2				2	
Columbiana County	19				16	3
Coshocton County	13				4	9
Crawford County	6				4	2
Cuyahoga County	216				59	157
Darke County	8			1	5	2
Delaware County	1				1	
Erie County	15			1	14	
Fairfield County	23			1	18	4
Fayette County	2				1	1
Franklin County	64				60	4
Fulton County	21				21	
Gallia County	20				16	4
Greene County	14				11	3
Guernsey County	29				7	22
Hamilton County	88			2	79	7
Hancock County	33				16	14
Henry County	26			1	20	5

SMALLPOX—Continued.

State Reports for March, 1918—Continued.

Place.	New cases reported.	Deaths.	Vaccination history of cases.			
			Number vaccinated within 7 years preceding attack.	Number last vaccinated more than 7 years preceding attack.	Number never successfully vaccinated.	Vaccination history not obtained or uncertain.
Ohio—Continued.						
Hocking County	12				9	3
Huron County	11				2	9
Jackson County	3				1	2
Jefferson County	3				1	2
Knox County	9				1	8
Lake County	3				3	
Lawrence County	12				8	4
Licking County	20				3	17
Logan County	11				5	6
Lorain County	22			1	8	13
Lucas County	43		1		2	40
Mahoning County	28				6	22
Medina County	1				1	
Meigs County	30					30
Mercer County	11				7	4
Miami County	7			3	4	
Montgomery County	35				34	1
Morgan County	1				1	
Muskingum County	23				6	17
Ottawa County	1				1	
Paulding County	4				2	2
Perry County	23				1	22
Pickaway County	3			1	2	
Portage County	41				2	39
Preble County	1				1	
Putnam County	4				4	
Richland County	1				1	
Ross County	6				6	
Sandusky County	4				4	
Scioto County	53			1	43	9
Seneca County	6				6	
Shelby County	8			1	5	2
Stark County	27		1	1	6	19
Summit County	217			2	71	144
Trumbull County	17				15	2
Warren County	24			3	11	7
Van Wert County	5				4	1
Vinton County	14				4	10
Warren County	15				15	
Washington County	2				1	1
Wayne County	20					20
Williams County	1				1	
Wood County	25				18	7
Wyandot County	9				7	2
Total	1,618		2	22	737	864

Miscellaneous State Reports for March, 1918.

Place.	Cases.	Deaths.	Place.	Cases.	Deaths.
Alabama:			Alabama—Continued.		
Baldwin County	1		Escambia County	1	
Barbour County	2	1	Etowah County	24	
Bibb County	29		Jackson County	1	
Butler County	20		Jefferson County	340	1
Calhoun County	168	1	Lamar County	2	
Chambers County	1	1	Limestone County	3	
Cherokee County	3		Madison County	1	
Chilton County	5		Mobile County	41	
Choctaw County	3		Montgomery County	35	
Cleburne County	4		Morgan County	28	
Coffee County	1		Pike County	3	
Colbert County	8	1	Randolph County	1	
Cullman County	2		Shelby County	2	
Elmore County	7		St. Clair County	8	

SMALLPOX—Continued.

Miscellaneous State Reports for March, 1918—Continued.

Place.	Cases.	Deaths.	Place.	Cases.	Deaths.
Alabama—Continued.			**Washington—Continued.**		
Sumter County.........	3	....	Ferry County—		
Tallapoosa County.......	8	....	Republic..........	9	....
Tuscaloosa County......	4	....	King County..........	3	....
Walker County..........	3	....	Seattle..........	15	....
Washington County.....	12	....	Kittitas County..........	6	....
Wilcox County..........	2	....	Okanogan County........	2	....
Winston County..........	1	....	Pierce County—		
			Steilacoom..........	1	....
Total..................	721	5	Tacoma..........	5	....
			Skagit County..........	1	....
Oregon:			Snohomish County......	4	....
Baker County..........	4	....	Arlington..........	29	....
Clackamas County.......	2	....	Everett..........	4	....
Clatsop County..........	1	....	Marysville..........	1	....
Jackson County..........	1	....	Spokane County..........	10	....
Marion County..........	8	....	Cheney..........	9	....
Umatilla County..........	1	....	Hillyard..........	10	....
Wallowa County..........	3	....	Spokane..........	76	....
Wasco County..........	1	....	Stevens County..........	2	....
Portland..............	11	....	Walla Walla County.......	3	....
			Whatcom County—		
Total..................	32	....	Bellingham..........	3	....
			Whitman County..........	6	....
Washington:			Lacrosse..........	1	....
Douglas County—					
Mansfield.............	1	....	Total..............	172	....

City Reports for Week Ended Apr. 20, 1918.

Place.	Cases.	Deaths.	Place.	Cases.	Deaths.
Akron, Ohio.................	24	....	Fremont, Ohio..........	1	....
Alton, Ill..................	16	....	Fresno, Cal..........	1	....
Atlanta, Ga..............	4	....	Galesburg, Ill..........	1	....
Bakersfield, Cal..........	1	....	Grand Forks, N. Dak......	2	....
Baltimore, Md..........	3	....	Grand Rapids, Mich........	3	....
Beaumont, Tex..........	1	....	Greeley, Colo..........	3	....
Bellingham, Wash..........	1	....	Hamilton, Ohio..........	10	....
Birmingham, Ala..........	27	....	Harrisburg, Pa..........	3	....
Braddock, Pa..........	1	....	Hartford, Conn..........	6	....
Buffalo, N. Y..........	1	....	Independence, Mo..........	8	....
Burlington, Iowa..........	3	....	Indianapolis, Ind..........	50	....
Canton, Ohio..........	1	....	Iola, Kans..........	3	....
Cedar Rapids, Iowa..........	4	....	Jamestown, N. Y..........	2	....
Chanute, Kans..........	1	....	Janesville, Wis..........	1	....
Charleston, W. Va..........	1	....	Kalamazoo, Mich..........	9	....
Chattanooga, Tenn..........	3	....	Kansas City, Kans..........	13	....
Chicago, Ill..........	11	....	Knoxville, Tenn..........	7	....
Cincinnati, Ohio..........	19	....	La Crosse, Wis..........	3	....
Cleveland, Ohio..........	34	....	La Fayette, Ind..........	1	....
Coffeyville, Kans..........	12	....	Lancaster, Ohio..........	4	....
Colorado Springs, Colo......	1	....	Leavenworth, Kans..........	4	....
Columbus, Ohio..........	4	....	Lima, Ohio..........	15	....
Council Bluffs, Iowa........	19	....	Lincoln, Nebr..........	5	....
Crawfordsville, Ind..........	1	....	Little Rock, Ark..........	9	....
Danville, Ill..........	4	....	Logansport, Ind..........	1	....
Davenport, Iowa..........	1	....	Lorain, Ohio..........	2	....
Dayton, Ohio..........	1	....	Los Angeles, Cal..........	1	....
Denver, Colo..........	25	....	Louisville, Ky..........	4	....
Des Moines, Iowa..........	23	....	Madison, Wis..........	2	....
Detroit, Mich..........	18	1	Marion, Ind..........	1	....
Dubuque, Iowa..........	2	....	Massillon, Ohio..........	3	....
Durham, N. C..........	1	....	Memphis, Tenn..........	6	....
Elmira, N. Y..........	1	....	Michigan City, Ind..........	1	....
El Paso, Tex..........	2	....	Middletown, Ohio..........	1	....
Elyria, Ohio..........	1	....	Milwaukee, Wis..........	3	....
Erie, Pa..........	1	....	Minneapolis, Minn..........	17	....
Fargo, N. Dak..........	1	....	Mobile, Ala..........	2	....
Flint, Mich..........	3	....	Montgomery, Ala..........	1	....
Fort Scott, Kans..........	6	....	Morgantown, W Va..........	1	....
Fort Smith, Ark..........	3	....	Muncie, Ind..........	3	....
Fort Wayne, Ind..........	2	....	Muskogee, Okla..........	8	....
Fort Worth, Tex..........	20	....	Nashville, Tenn..........	1	....

DIPHTHERIA, MEASLES, SCARLET FEVER, AND TUBERCULOSIS.

State Reports for March, 1918.

Place.	Cases reported.			Place.	Cases reported.		
	Diph-theria.	Measles.	Scarlet fever.		Diph-theria.	Measles.	Scarlet fever.
Alabama	37	1,178	30	Oregon	10	1,579	43
Ohio	574	2,202	940	Washington	44	867	326

City Reports for Week Ended Apr. 20, 1918.

City.	Popula-tion as of July 1, 1916 (estimated by U. S. Census Bureau).	Total deaths from all causes.	Diphtheria.		Measles.		Scarlet fever.		Tuber-culosis.	
			Cases.	Deaths.	Cases.	Deaths.	Cases.	Deaths.	Cases.	Deaths.
Over 500,000 inhabitants:										
Baltimore, Md	589,621	281	4	2	623	4	11		70	45
Boston, Mass	756,476	286	71	6	326	4	37		69	35
Chicago, Ill	2,497,722	862	107	15	83		37		493	111
Cleveland, Ohio	674,073	267	23	3	52		8		43	32
Detroit, Mich	571,784	333	56	7	80	4	44	1	44	33
Los Angeles, Cal	503,812	155	20		157		6	1	41	34
New York, N. Y	5,602,841	1,735	285	46	1,467	43	130	5	290	221
Philadelphia, Pa	1,709,518	628	58	6	770	6	30		102	72
Pittsburgh, Pa	579,090		12		434		15		33	
St. Louis, Mo	757,309	239	43	4	116	2	34		43	14
From 300,000 to 500,000 inhabitants:										
Buffalo, N. Y	468,558	177	13	2	99		17		34	20
Cincinnati, Ohio	410,476		18	1	32	1	2		30	22
Jersey City, N. J	306,345	98	13	1	62	1	27		15	11
Milwaukee, Wis	436,535	178	8	2	321	3	30	2	45	8
Minneapolis, Minn	363,454		18	3	25		23	3	18	15
Newark, N. J	408,894		25	1	556	8	23		37	22
New Orleans, La	371,747	172	8	1	2		1		42	17
San Francisco, Cal	463,516	190	16		56		7		25	30
Seattle, Wash	348,639		6		91		19		10	
Washington, D. C	363,980	181	8		553	2	30	2	28	17
From 200,000 to 300,000 inhabitants:										
Columbus, Ohio	214,878	76			44		35		7	8
Denver, Colo	260,800	98	6		86		31	1		14
Indianapolis, Ind	271,708		12	1	11		51	3	11	
Louisville, Ky	238,910	109	2		16		2		21	12
Portland, Oreg	295,463	64	2		223	4	8		12	7
Providence, R. I	254,960	102	11	1	174	1	8		2	10
Rochester, N. Y	256,417	77	6		60		13	2	17	3
From 100,000 to 200,000 inhabitants:										
Atlanta, Ga	190,558	97	3	1	4		2		7	6
Birmingham, Ala	181,762	98	1		9	1			9	9
Bridgeport, Conn	121,579	39	7		6		2		11	5
Cambridge, Mass	112,981	29	9		75		4		6	4
Camden, N. J	106,243		2		28		4		15	
Dallas, Tex	124,527	16	1		22	1				4
Dayton, Ohio	127,224	43	2		6		4		7	2
Des Moines, Iowa	101,598		10				24			
Fall River, Mass	128,365	46	3		2				9	6
Fort Worth, Tex	104,562	34	1		1		1		2	2
Grand Rapids, Mich	128,291	45	1		11		9		6	
Hartford, Conn	119,700	60	4	1	7		3		7	5
Houston, Tex	112,307	40	1		20				2	5
Lawrence, Mass	100,763	31	3		36	2	1		6	4
Lowell, Mass	113,245	43	1		17				4	4
Lynn, Mass	102,425	28	2		52		3		2	1
Memphis, Tenn	148,995	64	8		4		5		21	6
Nashville, Tenn	115,057	87			26	2	2		3	4
New Bedford, Mass	118,158		2		6				13	6
New Haven, Conn	149,685		2		3				11	3
Oakland, Cal	198,604	45	4	1	13		3		7	3

DIPHTHERIA, MEASLES, SCARLET FEVER, AND TUBERCULOSIS—Contd.

City Reports for Week Ended Apr. 20, 1918—Continued.

City.	Population as of July 1, 1916 (estimated by U. S. Census Bureau).	Total deaths from all causes.	Diphtheria.		Measles.		Scarlet fever.		Tuberculosis.	
			Cases.	Deaths.	Cases.	Deaths.	Cases.	Deaths.	Cases.	Deaths.
From 100,000 to 200,000 inhabitants—Continued.										
Omaha, Nebr.	165,470	45	13	2	11	....	23	1	....	....
Reading, Pa.	109,381	....	2	....	77	....	5	....	....	....
Richmond, Va.	156,687	68	2	....	92	....	3	....	9	6
Salt Lake City, Utah	117,399	32	7	....	14	....	4	....	1	....
Scranton, Pa.	146,811	....	4	....	8	....	1	....	2	....
Spokane, Wash.	150,323	....	....	....	....	....	2	....	....	....
Springfield, Mass.	105,942	39	5	2	32	....	5	....	2	6
Syracuse, N. Y.	155,624	62	5	....	126	1	6	....	12	6
Tacoma, Wash.	112,770	....	5	....	9	....	40	....	....	....
Toledo, Ohio	191,554	77	5	....	23	....	11	....	23	11
Trenton, N. J.	111,593	46	4	1	8	....	....	....	8	2
Worcester, Mass.	163,314	75	2	1	4	....	4	....	8	4
Youngstown, Ohio	108,385	....	....	....	24	....	....	....	4	4
From 50,000 to 100,000 inhabitants:										
Akron, Ohio	85,625	....	9	....	10	....	18	....	10	....
Allentown, Pa.	63,505	....	1	....	22	....	1	....	4	....
Altoona, Pa.	58,659	....	6	....	12	....	3	....	....	....
Atlantic City, N. J.	57,660	....	....	....	46	....	....	....	3	1
Augusta, Ga.	50,245	21	....	....	13	....	....	....	3	3
Bayonne, N. J.	69,893	....	....	....	27	....	1	....	3	....
Berkeley, Cal.	57,653	10	1	....	9	....	2	....	....	2
Binghamton, N. Y.	53,973	18	6	....	16	....	5	....	2	1
Brockton, Mass.	67,449	19	3	1	14	....	4	....	3	2
Canton, Ohio	60,852	13	1	....	4	....	1	....	....	1
Charleston, S. C.	60,734	35	1	....	1	....	....	....	....	4
Chattanooga, Tenn.	60,075	3	....	....	....	....	3	....	2	1
Covington, Ky.	57,144	26	1	....	10	....	....	....	2	4
Duluth, Minn.	94,495	31	2	....	5	....	....	....	5	1
Elizabeth, N. J.	86,690	11	6	....	111	....	3	....	7	1
El Paso, Tex.	63,705	57	1	....	16	2	4	....	....	15
Erie, Pa.	75,195	....	1	....	41	....	3	....	15	....
Evansville, Ind.	76,078	38	....	....	9	....	....	....	2	7
Flint, Mich.	54,772	23	2	....	6	....	10	....	3	2
Fort Wayne, Ind.	76,183	44	7	....	22	....	1	....	3	3
Harrisburg, Pa.	72,015	....	3	....	8	....	4	....	....	....
Hoboken, N. J.	77,214	23	7	....	5	....	....	....	5	4
Holyoke, Mass.	65,286	15	1	1	4	....	....	....	2	....
Johnstown, Pa.	68,529	....	2	....	5	....	5	....	....	....
Kansas City, Kans.	99,437	....	2	....	43	....	5	....	7	....
Lancaster, Pa.	50,853	....	....	....	35	....	5	....	2	....
Little Rock, Ark.	57,343	12	....	....	2	....	3	....	8	1
Malden, Mass.	51,155	8	....	....	21	....	1	....	....	....
Manchester, N. H.	78,283	22	2	....	16	....	2	....	4	2
Mobile, Ala.	58,221	23	....	....	....	....	....	....	....	4
New Britain, Conn.	53,794	12	2	....	20	....	5	....	....	3
Norfolk, Va.	89,612	....	....	....	13	....	4	....	....	6
Oklahoma City, Okla.	92,943	22	....	....	....	....	2	....	....	5
Passaic, N. J.	71,744	14	4	....	21	....	....	....	1	1
Pawtucket, R. I.	50,411	24	....	....	24	....	1	....	....	3
Peoria, Ill.	71,458	29	....	....	7	....	....	....	....	1
Portland, Me.	63,867	21	....	....	3	....	1	....	....	....
Rockford, Ill.	55,185	25	....	1	13	....	1	....	....	3
Sacramento, Cal.	66,895	32	1	1	31	....	3	....	....	3
Saginaw, Mich.	55,642	21	1	....	3	....	1	....	....	2
St. Joseph, Mo.	85,236	23	6	1	3	....	1	....	1	1
San Diego, Cal.	53,330	22	5	....	35	1	2	....	....	....
Schenectady, N. Y.	99,519	31	4	....	13	....	1	....	3	3
Sioux City, Iowa	57,078	1	....	....	....	....	11	....	....	1
Somerville, Mass.	87,039	27	3	....	58	....	4	....	3	3
South Bend, Ind.	68,946	13	1	....	5	....	....	....	2	1
Springfield, Ill.	61,120	28	1	....	80	....	....	....	....	3
Springfield, Ohio	51,550	27	....	....	3	....	....	....	4	2
Terre Haute, Ind.	66,083	48	5	1	3	....	4	....	....	3
Troy, N. Y.	77,916	35	1	....	3	....	2	....	4	3
Utica, N. Y.	85,692	24	1	....	52	....	1	....	6	....
Wichita, Kans.	70,722	....	....	....	38	....	1	....	3	1
Wilkes-Barre, Pa.	76,776	....	7	....	66	....	4	....	1	....
Wilmington, Del.	94,265	40	....	....	36	....	3	....	....	2
Yonkers, N. Y.	99,838	22	....	....	32	2	5	....	....	3
York, Pa.	51,656	....	3	....	9	....	2	....	4	....

DIPHTHERIA, MEASLES, SCARLET FEVER, AND TUBERCULOSIS—Contd.

City Reports for Week Ended Apr. 20, 1918—Continued.

City.	Population as of July 1, 1916 (estimated by U. S. Census Bureau).	Total deaths from all causes.	Diphtheria.		Measles.		Scarlet fever.		Tuberculosis.	
			Cases.	Deaths.	Cases.	Deaths.	Cases.	Deaths.	Cases.	Deaths.
From 25,000 to 50,000 inhabitants:										
Alameda, Cal..............	27,732	10			37		1		5	
Amsterdam, N. Y..........	37,103	2	1		5				1	1
Auburn, N. Y.............	37,385	10			3				2	1
Austin, Tex..............	34,814	22	1			1	1			3
Battle Creek, Mich.......	29,480		2		78		5		1	
Beaumont, Tex............	27,711	19	1			1				3
Bellingham, Wash.........	32,985				1		1			
Brookline, Mass..........	32,730	7	1		35		1		1	1
Burlington, Iowa.........	25,030	8					2			
Butler, Pa...............	27,632		2		11		4		1	
Butte, Mont.............	43,425	51	1		2		6	2	3	
Cedar Rapids, Iowa.......	37,308						7			
Central Falls, R. I......	25,636		1							
Charleston, W. Va........	29,941	17			3	1	1		1	3
Charlotte, N. C..........	39,823	16			13				7	1
Chelsea, Mass............	46,192	12	2		37	2	1		2	1
Chester, Pa..............	41,396		1		6				2	
Chicopee, Mass...........	29,310	10	3	1	1				5	1
Clinton, Iowa............	27,386				6		2			
Cohoes, N. Y.............	25,211	5					1		1	
Colorado Springs, Colo...	32,971	15	2		7				5	6
Columbia, S. C...........	34,611				3					
Council Bluffs, Iowa.....	31,484	12			2		4			
Cranston, R. I...........	25,757	11			1					1
Cumberland, Md...........	26,074	5			11		9		3	
Danville, Ill............	32,261	19	1		17				4	4
Davenport, Iowa..........	48,811						2			
Durham, N. C.............	25,061	9			11					1
Easton, Pa...............	30,530		4		16				3	
East Orange, N. J........	42,458	5			77		3		1	1
Elgin, Ill...............	28,203	8			1		1			
Elmira, N. Y.............	38,120	7	1		28				4	
Evanston, Ill............	28,591	8								
Everett, Mass............	39,233	7	1		11		1		1	
Everett, Wash............	35,495				5					
Fort Smith, Ark..........	28,638				1				1	
Fresno, Cal..............	34,958	11			9					
Galveston, Tex...........	41,863	11	1						1	3
Green Bay, Wis...........	29,353	12	1		40		2			2
Hamilton, Ohio...........	40,496	12			3		1			
Hammond, Ind.............	26,171	9	1		2					
Haverhill, Mass..........	48,477	15	2		19	1	1		1	1
Hazleton, Pa.............	28,491		2		22					
Jackson, Mich............	35,363	12	4		8		24			1
Jamestown, N. Y..........	36,580	18	1		25				2	2
Kalamazoo, Mich..........	48,886	19			4				4	2
Kenosha, Wis.............	31,576	16	6	2	1		2	1	1	1
Knoxville, Tenn..........	38,676		1		12				2	3
La Crosse, Wis...........	31,677	9	1							
Lexington, Ky............	41,097	20			12				1	2
Lima, Ohio...............	35,384	14	1				1			
Lincoln, Nebr............	46,515	8	3				7			
Long Beach, Cal..........	27,587	10			9		2			
Lorain, Ohio.............	36,964				1		1			
Lynchburg, Va............	32,940	8			8				4	1
Macon, Ga................	45,757	16					7			1
Madison, Wis.............	30,699	13			2		2			1
McKeesport, Pa...........	47,521				14					
Medford, Mass............	26,231	5	2		8		1			1
Moline, Ill..............	27,451	18	2		26		5	1		
Montclair, N. J..........	28,318	4			22				3	2
Montgomery, Ala..........	43,285	30			8					1
Muncie, Ind..............	25,424	8	1		2		1		1	2
Muskogee, Okla...........	44,218		1							
Natchez, N. H............	27,327	6					1			
Newark, Ohio.............	29,665				8					
Newburgh, N. Y...........	29,607	11			3				4	
New Castle, Pa...........	41,533				5					
Newport, Ky..............	31,927	12							2	2
Newport, R. I............	30,198	5	1							
Newton, Mass.............	43,715	12			5		1		3	1
Niagara Falls, N. Y......	37,553	13	1		1		2		1	
Norristown, Pa...........	31,191				1				2	
Norwalk, Conn............	33,880					1	19	2	11	3

DIPHTHERIA, MEASLES, SCARLET FEVER, AND TUBERCULOSIS—Contd.

City Reports for Week Ended Apr. 20, 1918—Continued.

City.	Population as of July 1, 1916 (estimated by U. S. Census Bureau).	Total deaths from all causes.	Diphtheria Cases.	Deaths.	Measles Cases.	Deaths.	Scarlet fever Cases.	Deaths.	Tuberculosis Cases.	Deaths.
From 25,000 to 50,000 inhabitants—Continued.										
Oak Park, Ill.	26,654	12	1		24		1			
Ogden, Utah	31,404				31				1	1
Orange, N. J.	33,080	13			38				2	..
Oshkosh, Wis	36,065	5					3		1	
Pasadena, Cal	46,450	11	1		59		1		4	3
Pittsfield, Mass	38,629	19			1		1		3	
Portsmouth, Va	39,651	17			12		3			1
Poughkeepsie, N. Y.	30,390	12	1		130		1		3	2
Quincy, Ill.	36,798	21	4	1	15					
Quincy, Mass	38,136	21	5	1	56	1	1		4	1
Racine, Wis	46,496	17			27		1	1	2	2
Roanoke, Va	43,284	21	1		51				1	
Rock Island, Ill	28,926	10	5		17		1			
Salem, Mass	48,562				17				3	
San Jose, Cal	38,902				22					
Sheboygan, Wis	28,559	16	1		2	1	2	2		2
Shenandoah, Pa	29,201		2						4	
Springfield, Mo	40,341	18			1		2			6
Steubenville, Ohio	27,445	25			1				2	
Stockton, Cal	35,358	16	1		8				1	1
Superior, Wis	46,226	24					3			
Taunton, Mass	36,283	22			11			1		2
Topeka, Kans	48,726						20			
Waco, Tex.	33,385	16			10		1			
Walla Walla, Wash	25,136				1					
Waltham, Mass	30,570	12			25				1	1
Waterloo, Iowa	35,559	4			1		3		1	
Watertown, N. Y.	29,894	1			74				1	
West Hoboken, N. J.	43,139	8			9		2			
Wheeling, W. Va	43,377	20	1		7		4		3	2
Williamsport, Pa	33,809		2				2			
Winston-Salem, N. C.	31,155	24			5				5	4
Zanesville, Ohio	30,863	7								
From 10,000 to 25,000 inhabitants:										
Alton, Ill.	22,874	11					1			1
Ann Arbor, Mich	15,010	8			21					2
Anniston, Ala.	14,112		1		2					
Appleton, Wis	17,834	3			4					1
Asbury Park, N. J.	14,007	6	2		2		1			
Ashtabula, Ohio	21,498	7			2					
Bakersfield, Cal	16,874	5			6		1		1	2
Barre, Vt.	12,169	4					2			1
Bedford, Ind.	10,349	4								3
Beloit, Wis	18,072	9		1	10		1		1	
Bethlehem, Pa	14,142				21		2		3	
Bloomington, Ind.	11,383	2					1			
Braddock, Pa	21,686		1	1						
Burlington, Vt.	21,617	8	1							
Cairo, Ill.	15,794	10			1					
Cape Girardeau, Mo.	10,775						3		1	
Carlisle, Pa.	10,726		1							
Centralia, Ill.	11,538						1			
Chanute, Kans.	12,455				6					
Cheyenne, Wyo.	¹11,320		2				2		1	
Chillicothe, Ohio	15,470	3			8		4		1	
Clinton, Mass	13,075	3			9					
Coatesville, Pa	14,455				8		1			
Coffeyville, Kans.	17,548		1		2		9			
Concord, N. H.	22,669	9	1		5				1	
Connellsville, Pa	15,455				12					
Corpus Christi, Tex.	10,432	6								2
Crawfordsville, Ind	11,164	1	6	1						
Dover, N. H.	13,272	4			1		1			
Du Bois, Pa	14,665		1		3					
Dunmore, Pa	20,776		1				1			
Elyria, Ohio	18,618	10							1	
Fairmont, W. Va.	15,506				1					
Fargo, N. Dak	17,389	5	2	1	4					
Farrell, Pa.	¹10,190				3					
Findlay, Ohio	¹14,858	7	1		36				3	

¹ Population Apr. 15, 1910, no estimate made.

DIPHTHERIA, MEASLES, SCARLET FEVER AND TUBERCULOSIS—Contd.

City Reports for Week Ended Apr. 20, 1918—Continued.

City.	Population as of July 1, 1916 (estimated by U. S. Census Bureau).	Total deaths from all causes.	Diphtheria.		Measles.		Scarlet fever.		Tuberculosis.	
			Cases.	Deaths.	Cases.	Deaths.	Cases.	Deaths.	Cases.	Deaths.
From 10,000 to 25,000 inhabitants—Continued.										
Fort Scott, Kans	10,550	4			2					
Fremont, Ohio	10,882				7					
Galesburg, Ill	24,276	9	1		17		1			
Gardner, Mass	17,140	2	1		2				1	1
Greeley, Colo	11,420						6			
Greensboro, N. C	19,577	5	1		4					
Greensburg, Pa	15,483				1					
Greenville, S. C	18,181	9			1		1			1
Hackensack, N. J	16,945	6	1		6					1
Harrison, N. J	16,950				6		3		3	1
Hattiesburg, Miss	16,482	8			2				2	1
Homestead, Pa	22,466				6		1		1	
Independence, Kans	14,506	5							1	1
Independence, Mo	11,672	7	2				4			
Iola, Kans	11,068				1					
Janesville, Wis	14,339	5			1		1			
Kearny, N. J	23,539	9	1		29		1			
Keokuk, Iowa	¹11,008				11		6		1	1
Kokomo, Ind	20,930	11			2				2	
Lafayette, Ind	21,286	10	1							1
Lancaster, Oh o	15,670				4		7		2	2
Lawrence, Kans	13,321		1							
Leavenworth, Kans	¹19,363	9			31		1			
Lincoln, R. I	10,383				6					
Logansport, Ind	21,046	8			6				2	1
Long Branch, N. J	15,395	2			1		4		1	1
Mahanoy City, Pa	17,463		1		3					
Manitowoc, Wis	13,805	7			1		5			
Mansfield, Ohio	22,734	7			33				1	2
Marinette, Wis	14,610	4			1		2	1		
Marion, Ind	19,834	2			2					
Marshall, Tex	13,712	1								
Mason City, Iowa	14,457	5								1
Massillon, Ohio	15,310	3	1		3		1		1	1
Meadville, Pa	13,802				3					
Melrose, Mass	17,445	4			1				1	
Michigan City, Ind	21,512	3	5							
Middletown, Ohio	15,623	6			1					
Mishawaka, Ind	16,385	2	2		22					
Missoula, Mont	18,214	4					2			
Monessen, Pa	21,630		4		10					1
Morgantown, W. Va	13,709	2			1		1		3	
Morristown, N. J	13,281	7	1		1					
Moundsville, W. Va	11,153	3							2	2
Mount Carmel, Pa	20,268								3	
Muscatine, Ia	17,500				2					
Nanticoke, Pa	23,126		1						1	
New Albany, Ind	23,629	10	1						1	1
Newburyport, Mass	15,243	14			8					
New Castle, Ind	13,241	4					3		1	
New London, Conn	20,985	12					1		2	
North Adams, Mass	¹22,019	8							1	1
Northampton, Mass	19,926	7								1
North Braddock, Pa	15,148						1		1	
North Little Rock, Ark	14,907	1	1						1	
North Yakima, Wash	20,951		1		14				1	
Oil City, Pa	19,297				2				1	
Palestine, Tex	11,854	10			14					1
Parkersburg, W. Va	20,612	7			5				1	
Phoenixville, Pa	11,714								1	
Preston, Pa	18,599				3					
Plainfield, N. J	23,895	12	2		6		1			1
Pontiac, Mich	17,524	6	1		1		3		4	2
Portsmouth, N. H	11,666				3		3			
Pottsville, Pa	22,872		3		4					
Provo, Utah	10,645	3								
Rahway, N. J	10,219				2					
Raleigh, N. C	20,127	9			11					
Redlands, Cal	14,000				2					

¹ Population Apr. 15, 1910, no estimate made.

DIPHTHERIA, MEASLES, SCARLET FEVER, AND TUBERCULOSIS—Contd.

City Reports for Week Ended Apr. 20, 1918—Continued.

City.	Population as of July 1, 1916 (estimated by U. S. Census Bureau).	Total deaths from all causes.	Diphtheria.		Measles.		Scarlet fever.		Tuberculosis.	
			Cases.	Deaths.	Cases.	Deaths.	Cases.	Deaths.	Cases.	Deaths.
From 10,000 to 25,000 inhabitants—Continued.										
Reno, Nev	14,869	10								
Richmond, Ind	24,697	9	3	2					1	1
Rocky Mount, N. C	12,067	3			1				1	
Rutland, Vt	14,831	4								
Salina, Kans	12,098				12		7			
Sandusky, Ohio	20,193	5			1				1	1
Santa Ana, Cal	10,627	3			18					
Santa Cruz, Cal	14,594	4			2					
Saratoga Springs, N. Y	13,821	10			11					
Shamokin, Pa	21,119						1			
Sharon, Pa	18,616				10					
Shelbyville, Ind	10,965	1								
Spartanburg, S. C	21,365	11	4		3					2
Steelton, Pa	15,548		1				1		4	
Sunbury, Pa	16,260		1		1					
Tiffin, Ohio	12,867	4			5					1
Tuscaloosa, Ala	10,488	6			3					
Uniontown, Pa	20,780				1					
Vallejo, Cal	13,461	8			12					2
Vancouver, Wash	13,180				57		1			
Warren, Ohio	13,059	4	2		3				3	
Warren, Pa	14,737								1	
Washington, Pa	21,618				18		2			
Wausau, Wis	19,239	3					1			
West Orange, N. J	13,550	3			30				1	
West Warwick, R. I	15,782	7								
Wilkinsburg, Pa	23,228		1		16					
Woburn, Mass	15,969	6								

FOREIGN.

CUBA.

Communicable Diseases—Habana.

Communicable diseases have been notified at Habana as follows:

Disease.	Mar. 21–31, 1918.		Remaining under treatment Mar. 31, 1918.	Disease.	Mar. 21–31, 1918.		Remaining under treatment Mar. 31, 1918.
	New cases.	Deaths.			New cases.	Deaths.	
Diphtheria............	2	1	6	Paratyphoid fever......			2
Leprosy.................	....	....	12	Scarlet fever...........			[1]7
Malaria................	5	1	[1]37	Typhoid fever..........	21	3	[2]50
Measles................	5	....	49	Varicella...............	6	....	15

[1] From the interior, 30.   [2] From the interior, 7.   [3] From the interior, 25.

DOMINICAN REPUBLIC.

Dengue.

Dengue was reported present in the Dominican Republic during the week ended March 30, 1918, as follows: La Vega, 3 cases; Puerto Plata, 2 cases; San Francisco de Macoris, 1 case.

CHOLERA, PLAGUE, SMALLPOX, TYPHUS FEVER, AND YELLOW FEVER.

Reports Received During Week Ended May 10, 1918.[1]

CHOLERA.

Place.	Date.	Cases.	Deaths.	Remarks.
India:				
Bombay..................	Jan. 27–Feb. 16....	16	20	
Calcutta..................	Jan. 27–Feb. 2.....	......	5	
Madras...................	Feb. 10–23........	5	3	
Indo China:				
Cochin-China—				
Saigon...............	Mar. 4–10.........	1	....	
Philippine Islands:				
Provinces................	....	....	....	Mar. 17–23, 1918: Cases, 180; deaths, 125.
Bohol...................	Mar. 17–23........	71	55	
Capiz....................	...do.	9	8	
Cebu.....................	...do.	12	7	
Misamis..................	...do.	34	16	
Occidental Negros.....	...do.............	34	20	
Surigao..................	...do.............	6	4	
Zamboanga.............	...do.............	20	15	

[1] From medical officers of the Public Health Service, American consuls, and other sources.

CHOLERA, PLAGUE, SMALLPOX, TYPHUS FEVER, AND YELLOW FEVER—
Continued.

Reports Received During Week Ended May 10, 1918—Continued.

PLAGUE.

Place.	Date.	Cases.	Deaths.	Remarks.
Ceylon:				
Colombo..................	Jan. 20–Feb. 16....	13	12	
China:				
Nanking..................	Mar. 17–23........	....	15	
Ecuador:				
Duran....................	Mar. 16–30........	1	....	
Guayaquil...............	....do............	17	7	
Hawaii:				
Laupahoehoe.............	May 5.............	1	1	
India....................	....	....	....	Jan. 27–Feb. 16, 1918. Cases;
				116,066; deaths, 93,199.
Bassein..................	Feb. 3–16.........	....	37	
Bombay..................	Jan. 27–Feb. 16....	71	53	
Calcutta.................	Jan. 27–Feb. 2.....	....	1	
Henzada.................	Feb. 3–16.........	....	32	
Karachi.................	Jan. 27–Feb. 23....	20	14	
Madras..................	Feb. 10–16........	1	1	
Madras Presidency........	....do............	1,832	1,510	
Myingyan...............	Feb. 3–10.........	....	51	
Pegu....................	Feb. 10–16........	....	1	
Rangoon.................	....do............	78	75	
Toungoo.................	Feb. 3–16.........	....	21	
Indo-China:				
Cochin-China—				
Saigon...............	Mar. 4–10........	17	13	

SMALLPOX.

Place.	Date.	Cases.	Deaths.	Remarks.
Canada:				
New Brunswick—				
Moncton..............	Apr. 14–20........	3	....	
St. John..............	Apr. 21–27........	4	....	
Nova Scotia—				
Halifax..............	Apr. 14–20........	3	....	
China:				
Changsha...............	Mar. 2–8..........	6	....	
Dairen.................	Mar. 17–30........	23	3	
Hongkong..............	Feb. 24–Mar. 9....	4	2	
Nanking...............	Mar. 17–23........	....	....	Present.
Tientsin...............	Mar. 10–16........	10	....	
Ecuador:				
Guayaquil.............	Mar. 16–31........	1	....	
Great Britain:				
Hull....................	Mar. 24–30........	2	....	
India:				
Bombay.................	Jan. 27–Feb. 2.....	320	129	
Calcutta................	....do............	....	3	
Karachi................	Jan. 27–Feb. 23....	24	12	
Madras.................	Feb. 10–23........	20	10	
Rangoon................	Feb. 10–16........	7	1	
Indo-China:				
Cochin-China—				
Saigon...............	Mar. 4–10........	108	33	
Italy:				
Genoa..................	Mar. 25–31........	2	1	
Mexico:				
Guadalajara............	Mar. 1–31.........	21	4	
Philippine Islands:				
Manila.................	Mar. 17–23........	15	1	Varioloid, 21.
Portugal:				
Lisbon.................	Mar. 17–30........	11	....	
Spain:				
Madrid.................	Feb. 1–28.........	....	3	
Malaga................	Oct. 1–31.........	....	19	
Tunisia:				
Tunis..................	Mar. 16–22........	1	....	

CHOLERA, PLAGUE, SMALLPOX, TYPHUS FEVER, AND YELLOW FEVER—
Continued.

Reports Received During Week Ended May 10, 1918—Continued.

TYPHUS FEVER.

Place.	Date..	Cases.	Deaths.	Remarks.
Great Britain:				
Glasgow	Mar. 31–Apr. 13	3		
Mexico:				
Aguascalientes	Apr. 15–21		1	
Guadalajara	Mar. 1–31	6	3	
Portugal:				
Lisbon	Mar. 17–30	10		
Tunisia:				
Tunis	Mar. 23–29	2	3	Mar. 11, 1918: Epidemic in regions of Tala and Tozer.

YELLOW FEVER.

Place.	Date.	Cases.	Deaths.	Remarks.
Ecuador:				
Guayaquil	Mar. 16–31	11	6	

Reports Received from Dec. 29, 1917, to May 3, 1918.

CHOLERA.

Place.	Date.	Cases.	Deaths.	Remarks.
China:				
Antung	Nov. 26–Dec. 2	3	1	
India:				
Bombay	Oct. 28–Dec. 15	19	14	
Do	Dec. 30–Jan. 26	200	170	
Calcutta	Sept. 16–Dec. 15		135	
Do	Dec. 30–Jan. 26		24	
Karachi	do	25	6	
Madras	Nov. 25–Dec. 22	2	2	
Do	Dec. 30–Feb. 9	37	19	
Rangoon	Nov. 4–Dec. 22	5	5	
Do	Dec. 30–Feb. 2	2	1	
Indo-China:				
Provinces		18	13	Sept. 1–Nov. 30, 1917: Cases, 152; deaths, 89.
Anam	Sept. 1–Nov. 30	18	13	
Cambodia	do	72	52	
Cochin-China	do	50	22	
Saigon	Nov. 22–Dec. 9	4	3	
Do	Feb. 4–Mar. 11	7	3	
Kwang-chow-Wan	Sept. 1–30	10	2	
Java:				
East Java	Oct. 28–Nov. 3	1	1	
West Java				Oct. 19–Dec. 27, 1917: Cases, 102; deaths, 56. Dec 28, 1917–Jan. 31, 1918: Cases, 27; deaths, 7.
Batavia	Oct. 19–Dec. 27	49	23	
Do	Dec. 28–Jan. 31	24	1	
Persia:				
Mazanderan Province				July 30–Sept. 3, 1917: Cases, 384, deaths, 276.
Achraf	July 30–Aug. 16	90	85	
Astrabad	July 31			Present.
Barfrush	July 1–Aug. 16	39	25	
Chahmurrad				25 cases reported July 31, 1917.
Chahra Ingh	June 15–July 25	10	8	
Charood	Aug. 26–Sept. 3	4	2	
Damavan	Aug. 26			Present.
Kiarek	May 28–June 11	21	13	
Meerel	Aug. 18–Sept. 2	174	82	
Ouzem Dare	Aug. 8			Do.
Shoxar	Aug. 24			Do.
Sari	July 29	273	144	
Semnan	Aug. 31–Sept. 2	14	5	
Yeke-ut-ia Bazar	June 3	6		
Philippine Islands:				
Provinces				Nov. 18–Dec. 29, 1917: Cases, 1,053, deaths, 693. Dec. 30, 1917–Mar. 16, 1918: Cases, 1,424; deaths, 925.
Antique	Nov. 18–Dec. 1	48	32	
Do	Feb. 19	4	4	
Bohol	Nov. 18–Dec. 29	169	111	
Do	Dec. 30–Mar. 16	421	336	
Capiz	Nov. 25–Feb. 29	27	21	
Do	Dec. 30–Mar. 2	210	174	
Cebu	Dec. 2–29	3		
Do	Dec. 30–Mar. 9	83	45	

CHOLERA, PLAGUE, SMALLPOX, TYPHUS FEVER, AND YELLOW FEVER—
Continued.

Reports Received from Dec. 29, 1917, to May 3, 1918—Continued.

CHOLERA—Continued.

Place.	Date.	Cases.	Deaths.	Remarks.
Philippine Islands—Contd.				
Provinces—Continued.				
Davao	Mar. 10–16	10	8	
Iloilo	Nov. 25–Dec. 29	179	135	
Do	Dec. 30–Mar. 2	97	63	
Leyte	Nov. 25–Dec. 22	13	12	
Do	Feb. 3–Mar. 16	50	38	
Mindanao	Nov. 25–Dec. 29	337	196	
Do	Dec. 30–Feb. 9	351	220	
Misamis	Feb. 24–Mar. 16	72	51	
Occidental Negros	Nov. 25–Dec. 22	177	123	
Do	Jan. 13–Mar. 9	96	63	
Oriental Negros	Nov. 25–Dec. 29	99	82	
Do	Dec. 30–Feb. 16	17	14	
Romblon	Nov. 25–Dec. 1	1	1	
Surigao	Feb. 24–Mar. 2	8	5	
Zamboanga	Feb. 24–Mar. 9	15	14	
Siam:				
Bangkok	Sept. 16–22	1	1	
Turkey in Asia:				
Bagdad	Nov. 1–15		40	

PLAGUE.

Place.	Date.	Cases.	Deaths.	Remarks.
Brazil:				
Bahia	Nov. 4–Dec. 15	4	4	
Do	Dec. 30–Feb. 23	4	3	
Rio de Janeiro	Dec. 23–29	1		
Do	Jan. 6–12	1	1	
British East Africa:				
Mombasa	Oct. 1–Dec. 31	31	18	
British Gold Coast:				
Axim	Jan. 8			Present.
Ceylon:				
Colombo	Oct. 14–Dec. 1	14	13	
Do	Dec. 30–Jan. 19	7	5	
China				Present in North China in January, 1918; pneumonic form.
Anhwei Province—				
Fengyanghsien	Feb. 27		9	Pneumonic.
Pengpu	do		1	Do.
Chili Province—				
Kalgan				Vicinity. Present in February, 1918.
Kiangsu Province—				
Nanking	Mar. 18			Present.
Shansi Province				Present in February, 1918; 116 cases estimated.
Ecuador:				
Babahoyo	Feb. 1–15	1		
Duran	do	1	1	
Guayaquil	Sept. 1–Nov. 30	68	24	Reported outbreak occurring about Jan. 17, 1918.
Do	Feb. 1–15	44	18	
Do	Mar. 1–15	20	7	
Egypt				Jan. 1–Nov. 15, 1917: Cases, 728; deaths, 398.
Alexandria	Jan. 14–28	1	2	
Port Said	July 23–29	1	2	
India				Sept. 16–Dec. 29, 1917: Cases, 228,834; deaths, 174,743. Dec. 30, 1917–Jan. 26, 1918: Cases, 123,934; deaths, 98,950.
Bassein	Dec. 9–29		8	
Do	Dec. 30–Feb. 2		37	
Bombay	Oct. 28–Dec. 29	147	123	
Do	Dec. 30–Jan. 26	81	59	
Calcutta	Sept. 16–29		2	
Do	Dec. 30–Jan. 12		3	
Henzada	Oct. 21–27		1	
Do	Jan. 5–Feb. 2		25	
Karachi	Oct. 21–Dec. 29	27	20	
Do	Dec. 30–Jan. 26	16	14	
Madras	Feb. 3–9	2	1	
Madras Presidency	Oct. 31–Nov. 24	5,786	4,519	
Do	Jan. 6–Feb. 9	8,599	6,599	
Mandalay	Oct. 14–Nov. 17		89	
Do	Dec. 30–Feb. 2		627	
Myingyan	do		235	
Promo	Jan. 5–12		1	
Rangoon	Oct. 21–Dec. 22		56	
Do	Dec. 30–Feb. 9	188	176	
Toungoo	Dec. 9–29		5	
Do	Dec. 30–Jan. 19		4	

CHOLERA, PLAGUE, SMALLPOX, TYPHUS FEVER, AND YELLOW FEVER—
Continued.

Reports Received from Dec. 29, 1917, to May 3, 1918—Continued.

PLAGUE—Continued.

Place.	Date.	Cases.	Deaths.	Remarks.
Indo-China:				
Provinces....................				Sept. 1-Nov. 30, 1917: Cases, 99; deaths, 68.
Anam..................	Sept. 1-Nov. 30...	28	25	
Cambodia.............	do.....	30	26	
Cochin-China..........	do.....	22	15	
Saigon...............	Oct. 31-Dec. 23....	17	6	
Do.............	Dec. 31-Mar. 17....	98	47	
Java:				
East Java.......................				Oct. 8-Dec. 31, 1917: Cases, 196; deaths, 193.
Do......................				Jan. 1-14, 1918: Cases, 22; deaths, 21.
Residences—				
Kediri.............	Oct. 8-Dec. 31.....	1	1	
Madioen............	do.....	49	49	
Samarang...........	do.....	110	109	
Surabaya...........	do.....	25	23	
Surakarta..........	do.....	11	11	
West Java..................				Nov. 26-Dec. 9, 1917: Cases, 45; deaths, 45. Dec. 1, 1917-Jan. 15, 1918: Cases, 108.
Peru:				
Ancachs Department—				
Casma.............	Dec. 1-Jan. 15....	2		
Lambayeque Department..	do....	22		At Chiclayo, Ferrenafe, Jayanca, Lambayeque.
Libertad Department.......	do....	72		At Guadalupe, Mansiche, Pacasmayo, Salaverry, San Jose, San Pedro, and country district of Trujillo.
Lima Department..........	do....	9		City and country.
Piura Department—				
Catacaos..............	do....	1		
Senegal.				
St. Louis..................	Feb. 2..			Present.
Siam:				
Bangkok..................	Sept. 16-Dec. 23...	13	9	
Do..................	Jan. 13-Mar. 2....	34	16	
Straits Settlements:				
Singapore..................	Oct. 28-Dec. 29....	5	7	
Do..................	Jan. 6-Feb. 16.....	29	28	

SMALLPOX.

Place.	Date.	Cases.	Deaths.	Remarks.
Algeria:				
Algiers....................	Nov. 1-Dec. 31....	3	2	
Do....................	Jan 1-Apr. 23.....	213		
Australia:				
New South Wales..........				July 12-Dec. 20, 1917: cases, 18; Jan. 4-17, 1918; case, 1.
Abermain..............	Oct. 25-Nov. 29....	3		Newcastle district.
Cessnock	July 12-Oct. 11...	7		
Eumangla.............	Aug. 15....	1		
Kurri Kurri...........	Dec. 5-20....	2		
Mungindi.............	Aug. 13.....	1		
Warren...............	July 12-Oct. 25....	22		
Do...............	Jan. 1-17.....	1		
Brazil:				
Bahia.................	Nov. 10-Dec. 8....	3		
Pernambuco...........	Nov. 1-15...	1		
Rio de Janeiro..........	Sept. 30-Dec. 29...	703	190	
Do..........	Dec. 30-Mar. 9.....	231	83	
Sao Paulo.	Oct. 29-Nov. 4.....		2	
British East Africa:				
Mombasa..............	Oct. 1-Dec. 31.....	9	5	
Canada:				
British Columbia—				
Vancouver...........	Jan. 13-Mar. 9.....	5		
Victoria.............	Jan. 7-Feb. 2.....	2		
Winnipeg	Dec. 30-Apr. 13...	4		
New Brunswick—				
Kent County...........	Dec. 4.....			Outbreak. On main line Canadian Ry., 25 miles north of Moncton.
Do	Jan 22.............	40		In 7 localities.
Northumberland County..	do.............	41		In 5 localities.
Restigouche County....	Jan. 18.............	60		

CHOLERA, PLAGUE, SMALLPOX, TYPHUS FEVER, AND YELLOW FEVER—
Continued.

Reports Received from Dec. 29, 1917, to May 3, 1918—Continued.

SMALLPOX—Continued.

Place.	Date.	Cases.	Deaths.	Remarks.
Canada—Continued.				
New Brunswick—Contd.				
St. John County—				
St. John.............	Mar. 3-Apr. 6.....	5	....	
Victoria County.......	Jan. 22.............	10	....	At Limestone and a lumber camp.
Westmoreland County—				
Moncton...........	Jan. 29-Apr. 6.....	16	....	
York County............	Jan. 22.............	8	....	
Nova Scotia—				
Halifax..............	Feb. 24-Apr. 6.....	6	....	
Sydney...............	Feb. 3-Apr. 6.....	15	....	
Ontario—				
Arnprior............	Mar. 31-Apr. 6.....	....	1	
Hamilton.............	Dec. 16-22.........	1	....	
Do.............	Jan. 13-19.........	2	....	
Ottawa..............	Mar. 4-24.........	5	....	
Sarnia...............	Dec. 9-15.........	1	....	
Do.............	Jan. 6-Mar. 30.....	32	....	
Toronto..............	Feb. 10-Apr. 6.....	2	....	
Windsor..............	Dec. 30-Jan. 5.....	1	....	
Prince Edward Island—				
Charlottetown........	Feb. 7-13........	1	....	
Quebec—				
Montreal..............	Dec. 16-Jan. 5.....	5	....	
Do..............	Jan. 6-Apr. 6.....	12	....	
China:				
Amoy.................	Oct. 22-Dec. 30...	....	....	Present.
Do.............	Dec. 31-Feb. 10...	....	....	Do.
Antung.............	Dec. 2-23.........	13	2	
Do.............	Jan. 7-Feb. 17...	6	2	
Changsha..............	Jan. 28-Mar. 10...	....	1	
Chefoo....	Jan. 27-Feb. 9...	....	....	Do.
Chungking..............	Nov. 11-Dec. 29...	....	....	Do.
Do.............	Dec. 30-Feb. 16...	....	....	Do.
Dairen..............	Nov. 18-Dec. 22...	3	1	
Do.............	Dec. 30-Mar. 16...	39	2	
Hankow..............	Feb. 25-Mar. 3...	1	....	
Harbin..............	May 14-June 30...	20	....	Chinese Eastern Ry.
Do.............	July 1-Dec. 2.....	7	....	Do.
Hongkong..............	Dec. 23-29.........	1	....	
Do.............	Jan. 26-Feb. 9....	6	1	
Hungtahotse Station.....	Oct. 28-Nov. 4....	1	....	Do.
Manchuria Station.........	May 14-June 30...	6	....	Do.
Do.............	July 1-Dec. 2.....	3	....	Do.
Mukden..............	Nov. 11-24...	....	....	Present.
Nanking..............	Feb. 3-Mar. 16...	....	....	Epidemic.
Shanghai..............	Nov. 18-Dec. 23...	41	91	Cases, foreign; deaths among natives.
Do.............	Dec. 31-Mar. 10...	36	106	
Swatow..............	Jan. 18.............	....	....	Unusually prevalent.
Tientsin..............	Nov. 11-Dec. 22...	13	....	
Do.............	Dec. 30-Mar. 9....	27	....	
Tsingtau..............	Feb. 4-Mar. 23...	8	....	
Cuba:				
Habana..............	Jan. 7.............	1	....	Nov. 8, 1917: 1 case from Coruna; Dec. 5, 1917, 1 case.
Mariano..............	Jan. 8.............	1	....	6 miles distant from Habana.
Ecuador:				
Guayaquil..............	Sept. 1-Nov. 30...	26	2	
Do.............	Feb. 1-15.........	3	3	
Egypt:				
Alexandria..............	Nov. 12-18.......	2	1	
Do.............	Jan. 8-Feb. 28....	5	....	
Cairo..............	July 23-Nov. 18...	6	1	
France:				
Lyon..............	Nov. 18-Dec. 16...	6	3	
Do.............	Jan. 7-Feb. 17.....	11	2	
Marseille..............	Jan. 1-31.........	....	2	
Paris..............	Jan. 27-Mar. 9....	8	2	
Great Britain:				
Cardiff..............	Feb. 3-9.........	4	....	
Hull..............	Mar. 17-23.........	1	....	
Greece:				
Saloniki..............	Jan. 27-Mar. 10....	....	9	
Honduras:				
Santa Barbara Department	Jan. 1-7..........	....	....	Present in interior.

CHOLERA, PLAGUE, SMALLPOX, TYPHUS FEVER, AND YELLOW FEVER—
Continued.

Reports Received from Dec. 29, 1917, to May 3, 1918—Continued.

SMALLPOX—Continued.

Place.	Date.	Cases.	Deaths.	Remarks.
India:				
Bombay	Oct. 21–Dec. 29...	50	12	
Do.	Dec. 31–Jan. 26...	26	5	
Karachi	Nov. 18–Dec. 29...	4	2	Nov. 11–16, 1917: 10 cases with 4
Madras	Oct. 31–Dec. 29...	20	8	deaths; imported on s. s. Me-
Do.	Dec. 30–Feb. 9...	102	38	nesa from Basreh.
Rangoon	Oct. 28–Dec. 22...	6	1	
Do.	Dec. 30–Feb. 9...	35	6	
Indo-China:				
Provinces				Sept. 1–Nov. 30, 1917: Cases, 542;
Anam	Sept. 1–Nov. 30...	161	25	deaths, 146.
Cambodia	...do....	16	8	
Cochin-China	...do....	353	108	
Saigon	Oct. 20–Dec. 30...	120	26	
Do.	Dec. 31–Mar. 17...	687	240	
Laos	Oct. 1–31...	1		
Do.	Jan. 26–Feb. 3...	1	1	
Tonkin	Sept. 1–Oct. 31...	9	4	
Do.	Jan. 26–Feb. 3...	3		
Italy:				
Castellamare	Dec. 10...	2		Among refugees.
Florence	Dec. 1–15...	17	4	
Genoa	Dec. 2–31...	11	3	
Do.	Jan. 2–Mar. 15...	41	5	
Leghorn	Jan. 7–Mar. 10...	32	7	
Messina	Jan. 3–19...	1		
Milan				Oct. 1–Dec. 31, 1917: Cases, 32.
Naples	Dec. 10...	2		Among refugees.
Taormina	Jan. 20–Feb. 9...	6		
Turin	Oct. 29–Dec. 29...	121	120	
Do.	Jan. 21–Mar. 3...	56	3	
Japan:				
Nagasaki	Jan. 14–Mar. 31...	9	3	
Taihoku	Dec. 15–21...	1		Island of Taiwan (Formosa).
Do.	Jan. 8–Mar. 11...	25	5	Do.
Tokyo	Feb. 11–Mar. 6...	26		City and suburbs.
Yokohama	Jan. 17–Feb. 3...	4		
Java:				
East Java	Oct. 7–Dec. 23...	50		Dec. 25–31, 1917: Cases, 7. Jan.
Surabaya	Dec. 25–31...	1		1–14, 1918: Cases, 3.
Mid-Java				Oct. 10–Dec. 26, 1917: Cases, 89;
Samarang	Nov. 6–Dec. 12...	4	1	death, 1. Dec. 28, 1917–Jan. 27
				1918: Cases, 23.
West Java				Oct. 19–Dec. 27, 1917: Cases, 221;
Batavia	Nov. 2–8...	1		deaths, 36. Dec. 28, 1917–Jan.
				31, 1918. Cases, 116; deaths, 17.
Mexico:				
Aguascalientes	Feb. 4–17...		2	
Ciudad Juarez	Mar. 3–23...	2	1	
Mazatlan	Dec. 5–11...		1	
Do.	Jan. 29–Apr. 2...	4	4	
Mexico City	Nov. 11–Dec. 29...	16		
Do.	Dec 30–Mar. 30...	90		
Piedras Negras	Jan. 11...	200		
Vera Cruz	Jan. 20–Mar. 2...	7	3	
Newfoundland:				
St. Johns	Dec. 8–Jan. 4...	29		
Do.	Jan. 5–Apr. 12...	76		
Trepassey	Jan. 4...			Outbreak with 11 cases reported.
Philippine Islands:				
Manila	Oct 28–Dec. 8...	5		
Do.	Feb. 3–Mar. 16...	12	3	Varioloid, 78.
Porto Rico:				
San Juan	Jan. 28–Apr. 7...	37		Of these, 36 varioloid.
Portugal:				
Lisbon	Nov. 4–Dec. 15...	2		
Do.	Dec. 30–Mar. 16...	6		
Portuguese East Africa:				
Lourenço Marques	Aug. 1–Dec. 31...		16	
Russia:				
Archangel	Sept. 1–Oct. 31...	7		
Moscow	Aug. 26–Oct. 6...	22	2	
Petrograd	Aug. 31–Nov. 18...	76	3	
Siam:				
Bangkok	Nov. 25–Dec. 1...	1	1	
Do.	Jan. 6–Mar. 2...	15	6	

CHOLERA, PLAGUE, SMALLPOX, TYPHUS FEVER, AND YELLOW FEVER—
Continued.

Reports Received from Dec. 29, 1917, to May 3, 1918—Continued.

SMALLPOX—Continued.

Place.	Date.	Cases.	Deaths.	Remarks.
Spain:				
Coruna	Dec. 2-15		4	
Do	Jan. 20-Feb. 23		5	
Madrid				Jan. 1-Dec. 31, 1917: Deaths, 77.
Seville	Oct. 1-Dec. 30		66	
Do	Jan. 1-31		20	
Valencia	Jan. 27-Feb. 2	1		
Straits Settlements:				
Singapore	Nov. 25-Dec. 1	1	1	
Do	Dec. 30-Jan. 5	1		
Tunisia:				
Tunis	Dec. 14-20	1		
Turkey in Asia:				
Bagdad				Present in November, 1917.
Union of South Africa:				
Cape of Good Hope State	Oct. 1-Dec. 31	28		
East Liverpool	Jan. 20-26	1		Varioloid.
Venezuela:				
Maracaibo	Dec. 2-8		1	

TYPHUS FEVER.

Place.	Date.	Cases.	Deaths.	Remarks.
Algeria:				
Algiers	Nov. 1-Dec. 31	2	1	
Argentina:				
Rosario	Dec. 1-31		1	
Australia:				
South Australia				Nov. 11-17, 1917: Cases, 1.
Austria-Hungary:				
Hungary				Present in December, 1917.
Brazil:				
Rio de Janeiro	Oct. 28-Dec. 1	7		
Canada:				
Ontario—				
Kingston	Dec. 2-8	3		
Quebec—				
Montreal	Dec. 16-22	2	1	
China:				
Antung	Dec. 3-30	13	1	
Do	Dec. 31-Jan. 27	2	2	
Chosen (Korea):				
Seoul	Nov. 1-20	1		
Do	Feb. 1-28	3	2	
Egypt:				
Alexandria	Nov. 8-Dec. 28	57	15	
Do	Jan. 8-Mar. 11	409	98	
Cairo	July 23-Dec. 16	137	70	
Port Said	July 30-Nov. 11	5	5	
France:				
Marseille	Dec. 1-31		1	
Germany				Jan. 1-30, 1918: Cases, 66.
Great Britain:				
Belfast	Feb. 10-Mar. 30	21	3	
Dublin	Mar. 24-30	3		
Glasgow	Dec. 21	1		
Do	Jan. 20-Mar. 23	12		
Manchester	Dec. 2-8	1		
Greece:				
Arta	Feb. 19	2		
Janina	Feb. 14	110		Jan. 27, epidemic.
Saloniki	Nov. 11-Dec. 29		72	
Do	Dec. 30-Mar. 16		27	
Italy:				
San Remo	Mar. 10-16	2		
Japan:				
Nagasaki	Nov. 26-Dec. 16	5	5	
Do	Jan. 7-Mar. 31	14	6	
Java:				
East Java				Oct. 15-Dec. 31, 1917: Cases, 39; deaths, 7. Jan. 1-14, 1918:
Surabaya	Dec. 17-31	9	1	Cases, 11; deaths, 2.
Do	Jan. 1-14	10	1	
Mid-Java				Oct. 10-Dec. 26, 1917: Cases, 63;
Samarang	Oct. 9-Dec. 26	20	2	deaths, 2. Dec. 26, 1917-Jan.
Do	Dec. 27-Jan. 15	18		23, 1918: Cases, 11.

CHOLERA, PLAGUE, SMALLPOX, TYPHUS FEVER, AND YELLOW FEVER—
Continued.

Reports Received from Dec. 29, 1917, to May 3, 1918—Continued.

TYPHUS FEVER—Continued.

Place.	Date.	Cases.	Deaths.	Remarks.
Java—Continued.				
West Java.....				Oct. 19–Dec. 27, 1917: Cases, 94;
Batavia..............	Oct. 19–Dec. 27....	59	15	deaths, 17. Dec. 28, 1917–Jan.
Do..............	Dec. 28–Jan. 31....	27	1	31, 1918; Cases, 53; deaths, 1.
Lithuania...........				Dec. 30, 1917–Jan. 5, 1918: Cases, 195.
Mexico:				
Aguascalientes.............	Dec. 15.....		3	
Do..............	Jan. 21–Apr. 7....		14	
Durango State—				
Guanacevi.............	Feb. 11.....			Epidemic.
Mexico City..............	Nov. 11–Dec. 29...	476	....	
Do..............	Dec. 30–Mar. 30...	627	....	
Newfoundland:				
St. John's.............	Mar. 30–Apr. 5....	1	1	
Norway:				
Bergen..............	Feb. 1–16....	3		
Poland............				Dec. 23, 1917–Jan. 12, 1918: Cases, 3,026; deaths, 315.
Portugal:				
Lisbon............	Mar. 3–16.....	8		Feb. 21: Present.
Oporto............	Dec. 1–31.....	23	4	
Do..............	Jan. 1–Mar. 8......	1,811	161	
Russia:				
Archangel..............	Sept. 1–14.....	7	2	
Moscow............	Aug. 26–Oct. 6....	49	2	
Petrograd............	Aug. 31–Nov. 18...	32	....	
Do..............	Feb. 2.....			Present.
Vladivostok..............	Oct. 29–Nov. 4....	12	1	
Spain:				
Corcubion............	Apr. 11.....			Present. Province of Coruna, west coast.
Sweden:				
Goteborg............	Nov. 18–Dec. 15...	2	....	
Switzerland:				
Basel............	Jan. 6–19....	1	1	
Zurich..............	Nov. 9–15.....	2	....	
Do..............	Jan. 13–19.....	2	....	
Tunisia:				
Tunis............	Nov. 30–Dec. 6.....		1	
Do..............	Feb. 9–Mar. 15....	35	5	Of these, 26 in outbreak in prison.
Union of South Africa:				
Cape of Good Hope State...	Sept. 10–Dec. 30...	4,035	830	Sept. 10–Nov. 25, 1917: Cases, 3,724 (European, 31); deaths, 761 (European, 5). Total to Jan. 27, 1918: Cases, 4,248 (European, 32), deaths, 866 (European, 5).
Natal............				From date of outbreak in December, 1917, to Jan. 27, 1918: Cases, 34; deaths, 10.

YELLOW FEVER.

Place.	Date.	Cases.	Deaths.	Remarks.
Ecuador:				
Babahoyo..................	Feb. 1–15..........	1	1	
Guayaquil..............	Sept. 1–Nov. 30...	5	3	
Do..............	Feb. 1–15....	1	....	
Do..............	Mar. 1–15....	1	1	
Milagro..................	Feb. 1–15....	1	1	
Yaguachi.............	Nov. 1–30....	1	....	
Guatemala:				
Retalhuleu..................	Apr. 22.........			Present. About 25 miles from Champerico, Pacific port.
Honduras:				
Tegucigalpa..................	Dec. 16–22..........		1	
Do..................	Jan. 6–19..........		1	

×

PUBLIC HEALTH REPORTS

| VOL. 33 | MAY 17, 1918 | No. 20 |

ANNUAL CONFERENCE OF HEALTH OFFICERS.

The Sixteenth Annual Conference of State and Territorial Health Authorities with the United States Public Health Service will be held in Washington, D. C., June 3 and 4, 1918.

Provisional Program.

Opening remarks by the Surgeon General.
Roll call of delegates.
Appointment of committees.

REPORTS OF STANDING COMMITTEES.

Matters related to war—Dr. H. M. Biggs.
Morbidity Returns—Dr. A. J. Chesley.
Sanitation of Public Conveyances—Dr. Oscar Dowling.
Rural Sanitation—Dr. W. S. Rankin.
Trachoma—Dr. A. W. Freeman.
Increasing Efficiency of Confe. ences—Dr. W. C. Woodward.

NEW BUSINESS.

1. Sanitation of extra-cantonment areas, especially as related to the work of State and local health authorities.
2. The venereal diseases: Their control, with reference to the relation of the United States Public Health Service to States and cities in handling this problem.
3. Better control of communicable diseases and disease carriers, especially in the case of cerebrospinal meningitis and typhoid fever.
4. Use of records of drafted men for public health purposes.
5. Relation to public health of industrial hygiene and sanitation, especially in war industries.
6. Care of health of tuberculous soldiers and relation to the public health, especially after their return to civil life.
7. Trachoma and its bearing on the public health of the military forces.
8. Hookworm disease: The importance of its prevalence and control among the military forces.

9. Effects on the public health of the forthcoming shortage in the medical profession.

10. Better morbidity reports: How to secure them.

(a) Fees to physicians.

(b) Appointments of collaborating epidemiologists in every State and assistant collaborating epidemiologists in every county.

(c) Issuance of weekly bulletins containing detailed summaries of reports from 100 representative cities.

(d) Creation of registration area.

11. Railroad water supplies.

12. Pellagra.

On the completion of the regular program members may bring before the conference other subjects to be taken up in so far as time permits.

SOME OBSERVATIONS ON THE PERSONALITY OF FEEBLE-MINDED CHILDREN IN THE GENERAL POPULATION.

By WALTER L. TREADWAY, Passed Assistant Surgeon, United States Public Health Service.

In studies of school children with reference to mental development the investigations made by the Public Health Service emphasize the necessity of making careful studies of those children who grade below the normal limits as to intelligence. Children in this group show greater differences in make-up or personality than children in the normal group. It is not sufficient to grade the children in any school by formal psychological tests.

In making studies of the mental development of any group of children the formal psychological tests may be relied upon to grade the intelligence. But those children who grade below certain normal limits or who by their conduct show unusual traits of character should be studied more carefully by one having psychiatric training.

Investigations conducted by the Public Health Service have afforded the opportunity to grade, by the Binet-Simon scale, the intelligence of a large number of rural American school children, white and colored, and of some immigrant children. The results showed a considerable variation in the degree of intelligence among mentally normal children.[1]

When such children were compared, there were also found differences in make-up or personality. When children who graded below the limits of normal intelligence were compared, a somewhat greater difference in intelligence was observed, and some of these children possessed constitutional traits approaching those of the psychopathic make-up. The recognition of these personalities may serve as a

---

[1] "Rural school sanitation, including physical and mental status of school children in Porter County, Ind;" By Taliaferro Clark, O. L. Collins and W. L. Treadway; Public Health Bulletin No. 77. "Mental status of rural school children, report of preliminary sanitary survey made in New Castle County, Del., with a description of the tests employed;" By E. H. Mullan; Reprint No. 377 from Public Health Reports. Reports of other investigations of this character by officers of the Service have not yet been published.

means to differentiate the mentally defective child from one who is merely retarded and prove of practical value in determining the care and treatment necessary.

Binet and Simon,[1] in discussing the psychology of the feeble-minded child, claim that he does not resemble a normal child whose mental development is simply retarded. In the case of the former, the retardation has not been uniform, showing as an end result a greater development of intelligence in some respects than in others. Binet and Simon, therefore, conclude that the mental equipment of the feeble-minded lacks equilibrium or proper balance. They also state that feeble-minded children who are assumed to resemble, by reason of retarded intellect, much younger normal children, show defects of reasoning, understanding and imagination which do not appear in the latter. These authors are of the opinion that the mental powers of the feeble-minded child show individual peculiarities of a pathological kind.

Howe claimed that mental defectives resemble the insane in that they both show intellectual or moral degradation, or a combination of the two. Hoffbauer thought this was true in the case of the higher grade mental defectives, because he considered that their powers of judgment were clouded with evil and because they had passionate attacks of anger. It appears that a number of classifications have been devised which confound insanity and mental deficiency. This confusion is partly explained by the fact that certain peculiarities of make-up or affective reactions of the feeble-minded resemble certain types of insanity, and partly by the fact that some insane cases, because of affective reactions which put them out of harmony with their environment, show a more or less low grade of intelligence when the Binet-Simon scale or other psychological test for the grading of intelligence is applied. This confusion arises because these tests fail to characterize or measure the affective reactions.

However, it is very probable that it will be impossible to devise a series of tests which will measure the affective reactions, because: First, the situations which call forth these reactions are very complex; and, second, by reason of the very nature of their complexity, they can not be exactly reproduced experimentally. Even if this were possible, the results would perhaps lack the real flavor of the reactions as observed in their natural state.

In the absence of tests to measure the affective reactions some substitute is necessary. The usual questionnaires to record mental traits, no doubt of value for the purpose intended, afford little aid, and the same is true of attempts to apply the teachings of formal psychology to the understanding of traits which make for good or bad adaptative capabilities. It is necessary, therefore, to turn to

---

[1] Binet and Simon. "Mentally defective children," authorized translation by W. B. Drummon. Published by Edw. Arnold. 1914.

psychiatry for a guide to the understanding of collective reactions as observed, either habitually or episodically. By means of the psychiatric approach the differences of personality as recognized in the feeble-minded children may be better understood.

To illustrate the plan for psychiatric study and the tentative classification of feeble-minded children, five types are discussed below and a few case histories obtained in the course of surveys of the Public Health Service are presented. These types of personality or make-up are recognized in the field of psychiatry as making for poor capabilities for adaptability to environment.

Types Showing "Shut-In" Tendencies.

Hoch [1] called attention to a group of individuals to whom he applied the term "shut-in" personality. These persons do not have a natural tendency to be "open" or to get into contact with their environment. They are reticent and seclusive, and are often sensitive, stubborn, and hard to influence. They show little interest in what is going on and often do not participate in the pleasures, cares, and pursuits of those about them. They do not, as a rule, let others know of their conflicts, do not unburden their minds, are shy, and have a tendency to live in a world of fancies. Beneath their ordinary daily activities there is usually a variety of internal dissensions quite incompatible with that feeling of satisfaction which goes with good bodily and mental health. There is no longer any question that the traits of character shown by this so-called "shut-in" personality serve in the genesis of dementia præcox, a malignant mental disorder arising during early adolescence.

Anyone who has come in intimate contact with cases of dementia præcox must have been impressed with the wide variation in the intellectual endowment of persons suffering from this disorder. Observations made upon a large group of American school children, however, show no cases possessing the "shut-in" type of personality who grade as exceptionally intelligent by the Binet-Simon scale. Many of these cases grade as normal, some under average, and others exceptionally below the average.

The last type may be illustrated by a boy 13 years and 5 months of age. He never played like other boys, was quiet, and cared little for companionship, but was fond of little children and much liked by boys of 10 and 11 years of age. At times when boys came to his house he went into the house to sleep. He always enjoyed being petted by his mother and seemed not to care whether any one else liked him. He slept with his mother until 12½ years old and has since had a cot near by. Children at school and in his own family

[1] Constitutional Factors in the Dementia Præcox Group   By August Hoch; Review Neurol. & Psychiat., August, 1910

teased him and called him "mother's pet." It is evident that this boy possessed "shut-in" tendencies in his make-up.

Although he showed a certain habitual reaction which interferred with his social adaptation, he also manifested certain defects in the intellectual fields. He could not be trusted to do more than the simplest tasks, because he forgot them. For instance, he was never trusted by his mother to carry out more than one command. His mother had failed after repeated attempts to teach him to tell the hour by the clock. He began school at 6 years of age and made very slow progress, being classed at the time of this study with the second and third grade pupils. He was recognized by his teacher as exceptionally backward and by his fellow-pupils as subnormal. Although his intellectual attainments have been of a very low order, he has occasionally done some work, but could accomplish very little, being unable to endure continued application. He graded by the Binet-Simon scale 7.8 years.

The classification of mental age characterizes, in a measure, his intelligence but leaves much to be desired in characterizing his difference from a case with simple retarded intellect. According to certain standards or customs this boy would be classed as either a high-grade imbecile or a low-grade moron, but he also shows certain fundamental differences in make-up from a case of retardation. These differences may be characterized as "shut-in tendencies," a term descriptive of his habitual affective reactions or personality. It is at present impossible to determine whether this individual may or may not develop a psychosis in later life. Future observation of such types will furnish data for improvement in their control and a better understanding of atypical clinical cases in mental medicine.

Cases Showing the Manic Depressive Reaction.

Another type of individual, because of collective affective reactions, occurring more or less habitually, is liable to show poor adaptative capabilities. His traits have been sufficiently observed to show that they serve in the genesis of mental disorders characterized by mood disturbances.

Because of variability of mood, this type has been called "manic depressive," "manic make-up," "hypomanic make-up," "cyclothemic make-up," or, to be more descriptive, "obtrusive make-up." The type shows emotional variability and fluctuations in capacity and efficiency sufficiently marked to attract attention. The fact must not be lost sight of that these traits, when faintly developed, may be useful qualities and indeed appear to belong to normal experience, but that when exaggerated they interfere with efficiency and frequently serve in the genesis of a frank attack of manic depressive insanity.

It is a well-known fact that the manic depressive reaction occurs during the course of various organic mental disorders and that in the functional mental disorders the reaction occurs in individuals who have shown the hypomanic or "obtrusive make-up."

The following illustrates this reaction in an imbecile boy 12 years of age, whose mental enfeeblement was complicated by an organic mental defect and convulsive seizures. He was considered normal until 2 years old. At that time he had frequent spasms, followed by a permanent right-sided paralysis. He did not learn to talk until 5 years of age. At 10 he had convulsive seizures for two weeks, as many as 12 a day. Since then the convulsions have recurred at varying intervals. At home he was untidy, was regarded as simple, and thought it a great joke when his mother died. He could do but the simplest tasks, as pumping water or carrying wood. He was never allowed to handle animals, because of his cruelty, nor to handle tools for fear of his injuring himself. At school, which he began at 7 and attended for three years, he learned nothing. When observed he showed a marked press of activity. For example, in attempting to chop wood, he swung the ax violently toward any part of the woodpile without concerted direction of his efforts, and ran about the yard without apparent purpose. Associated with this motor activity was a continuous stream of words, little of which could be understood, because of a speech defect. His grandmother, with whom he lived, stated that at times he was easily irritated, at others he was playful, and that he became more excitable when strangers were about.

This type of individual as he grows older becomes a source of danger and nuisance in the community, because of an obtrusive and sometimes violent manner. These cases are often committed to hospitals for the insane, where their maniclike reactions render them a charge upon the State for various periods of time.

The type which occurs or seems to occur without the admixture of organic features is shown by the following case:

A young woman, 20 years of age, has since 1904 made her home with foster parents. She developed very rapidly, and is now a strong, excitable, stubborn, and defiant young woman. She loses her temper easily, but is never violent. She has often shown a press of activity, rushing about vigorously and noisily at her work, even, it is said, splitting her clothing in these attacks of energy. She chases after men and boys; watches from the window for carriages or automobiles and goes to the door to call out as they pass. At times she neglects her work at home, and seeks every opportunity to be away by working for her neighbors. She spends all her spare money on perfume and powder, and shows a tendency to bedeck herself with trifles. She is jovial and pleasant in her manner. She is evidently of a hypomanic or obtrusive make-up, or one in whom the transition to a manic attack of insanity seems plausible.

She attended school until 15 years of age, and is said by her guardians to have learned rapidly. Upon examination, however, her grasp of general and school knowledge is found to be very meager. She grades according to the Binet scale 8 years. By customary standards she would be classed as a low-grade moron, but this does not give any idea of the clinical picture beyond the characterization of her intelligence in terms of mental age.

The family is of interest in respect to make-up and social adjustment. The father's brother had some mental disorder and was an inmate of the local county almshouse. A half brother died of spasms; another, with obtrusive make-up and grading 2 years by intelligence scale, is an inmate of the local county almshouse. A half sister deserted her husband, and eloped with two men; another half sister has a feeble intellect, with seclusive or shut-in tendencies.

Cases Allied to Those Showing the Manic-Depressive Reaction.

There are types of individuals who resemble in make-up those showing the manic-depressive reaction.

The following cases of brothers, one 22 and one 16 years of age, are of interest as regards their make-up. Both are arrogant, boastful, rather talkative and dictatorial in manner. Neither possesses that jovial, care-free manner that the pure manic-depressive personality shows, but instead there is an attitude of superiority unaccompanied by the usual mood of elation. They both make a good deal of their opportunity to impress, display unusual vanity, and tend to be somewhat pompous in their attitude. Their robust physical development tends to add to their ability to impress certain groups of individuals.

The older left school at 15 years, having reached the second or third grade. The younger left school at 14 years, never progressing beyond the primary grade. Neither, in the opinion of their teachers could learn. Both had speech defects in early childhood. According to the Binet-Simon scale the older graded 7 and the younger 6 years of age.

In addition to the intellectual enfeeblement, certain constitutional traits of character or "make-up" are in the foreground. It would be impractical to venture on opinion as to the eventual adaptation of these persons to their environment. The writer has seen, in ward practice, individuals of this type who ran an acute course of hallucinosis precipitated by alcohol. In individuals of this type who develop a hallucinosis the manic features are usually prominent. These individuals, who have a personality resembling or allied to the manic-depressive reaction, have considerable difficulties in adapting themselves to conventional standards. They frequently undertake tasks for which they are illy suited, and when they do not complete them with credit, are apt to develop paranoic ideas. In other words, being unable to recognize their own shortcoming, they tend to develop ideas that will place the blame on some one else.

Cases Showing Egoistic and Epileptic Temperaments.

The next type of personality observed to interfere with proper adaptation to environment has been called the "epileptic temperament." In this character, two qualities dominate, one an egotism which will not permit the individual to recognize the rights of others; the other an inclination to piety. Clark[1] calls attention to these habitually occurring affective reactions in essential epilepsy. There are also other affective reactions that occur episodically, namely, convulsions and attacks of irritability. Because of his egotism the epileptic has considerable difficulty in adjusting himself to discipline. He requires an unusual share of attention and perceives slights when none are intended. He is suspicious and given to misinterpretations which fit his own egotistical make-up.

The characteristics described above are not wholly confined to the epileptic, and for this reason the term "egoistic temperament" has been suggested to include those cases in which egotism alone stands as the dominant constitutional trait which interferes with good adaptative capabilities.

A case illustrating the "egoistic make-up" in a feeble-minded individual follows.

A boy, 11 years 2 months of age, graded according to the Binet-Simon scale 7.6 years. At home he is stubborn, is easily angered and has no control over his temper. When angry he will bite his arms. Most of the time it is difficult for him to get along with any one. For the most part, he is selfish and arrogant and shows no affection or regard for those with whom he comes in intimate contact. His foster parents regarded him as an unusual child because he did not allow any one to pet him. He is destructive and seems to have no appreciation of the consequence of his acts. He will build fires anywhere and has thrown fire into fodder pens, and about the barns at his home.

He began school at 6 years of age and has made very slow progress. He is classed as a second grade pupil, but his teacher stated that he could not do the work of public schools and is so low mentally that he gives him special work as an ungraded pupil. His fellow pupils recognize his defect. They tease him some, but he is cruel and fights on the least provocation. He has no chums, would rather be alone and seldom if ever plays with children except at school.

It is impossible to determine what this boy is liable to develop in later years. Most epileptics, even before the convulsive seizures

---

[1] "Clinical Studies in Epilepsy." Utica State Hospital Press 1917, by L. Pierce Clark.

have developed, show this egoistic temperament, whereas others never have convulsions.

There is another group of individuals whose constitutional traits seem to be intimately related to the egoistic make-up. These children are prone to be cruel, have no regard for the rights of others, are arrogant, insulting, and seem to have little conception of the consequences of their acts. They are liars and thieves, and are prone to commit sexual offenses. They are adept pupils in sexual irregularities and often early acquire homosexual practices. They are usually disobedient toward their parents; but to others in authority they are servile, unduly kind and readily promise anything, only to break the promise when such authority is removed. These traits closely resemble those of the epileptic.

The following case illustrates the reaction of the epileptic temperament:

A young man, 19 years of age, graded according to the Binet-Simon scale 7.6 years. When a child he had convulsive attacks which have tended, in later years, to grow worse. The attacks are associated with violence, when he refuses to sit at table with his family, threatens to kill, swears and runs about a good deal. Between these attacks he is arrogant and wilful, interests himself in religious subjects and tries to convert those in the neighborhood.

This person is evidently a so-called epileptic, but, in addition to his spells, he shows well-defined constitutional traits.

It is observed in the last two cases, as in the preceding ones, that the characterization of the intellect in terms of mental age, leaves much to be desired.

Cases Showing a Fatuous Temperament.

Another type of reaction or temperament occurs in persons possessing an exceptionally retarded intellect. For the want of a better term the word "fatuous make-up" is applied to them. The type shows more or less self-complacency and comprises the silly and stupid cases.

The peculiar affectation that these individuals show leads to the assumption that they might develop reactions resembling the psychoneurotic. Anyone who has come in intimate contact with the psychoneuroses must have been impressed with the childlike behavior of their emotional adjustments.

The following case of defective development illustrates the type:

A girl, 16 years of age, graded by the Binet-Simon scale 8.8 years. She did not learn to talk until more than 5 years of age. Until 13 years of age she occasionally wet her clothing while at school. She showed little self-control and grinned inordinately more than could be expected of a girl of her age. She is agreeable, obedient, kind and easily controlled. Her foster mother stated that she had little temper, as she harbored no resentment toward persons who attempted to take advantage of her. She is not especially sociable, but likes to be with children from 10 to 12 years of age. She has always had an antipathy for boys and will never go to parties because she is afraid that during some game boys might kiss, or even touch, her. She wants to remain a girl and wishes never to marry nor bear children.

Her teacher and school children regard her as being mentally defective. She began school at 6 years of age and has been exceedingly slow in her school work.

This type of affective adjustment is not uncommon in the mentally defective group.

Conclusions.

1. In addition to certain formal psychological tests the children who grade below certain normal limits, or who show certain unusual traits of character, should be studied by psychiatric methods.

2. Certain constitutional traits occur with sufficient frequency in the mental defectives to warrant their being recognized as types for future study. The following tentative classification is suggested: (a) those with shut-in tendencies; (b) those with manic-depressive-like reactions; (c) those allied to the manic-depressive group; (d) those who show the egoistic and epileptic temperament; and (e) those who show a fatuous temperament.

3. Constitutional traits must be taken into account when making a diagnosis of mental deficiency, or feeble-mindedness, as it is more often termed. Future studies in the field may show that they are of practical value in differentiating the mentally defective child from one merely retarded.

4. A knowledge of psychiatry is an important requisite in the diagnosis of feeble-mindedness. This becomes of more importance when it is realized that a close relationship exists between psychic disorders usually regarded as insanity and the higher types of mental deficiency or feeble-mindedness.

5. The recognition of these constitutional traits will permit a better understanding of impure or atypical cases in mental medicine and, furthermore, offer a means of recognizing antisocial traits in the mental defective before society has paid the penalty of their inherent antisocial tendencies.

6. The understanding of these traits permits, early in the career of the feeble-minded, the inauguration of prophylaxis which may serve to prevent much sorrow and disgrace to their immediate families; first, by segregating certain types in institutions early in life, regardless of the financial status of the family, and second, by replacing through early training vicious tendencies which the feeble-minded child easily adopts and which are not readily overcome when once developed.

Poster on Malaria Issued by Public Health Service Available for Distribution to Health Officers.

Health officers and sanitarians may secure, without charge, copies of the poster reproduced below, in numbers suitable to their needs, by applying to the Surgeon General, United States Public Health Service.

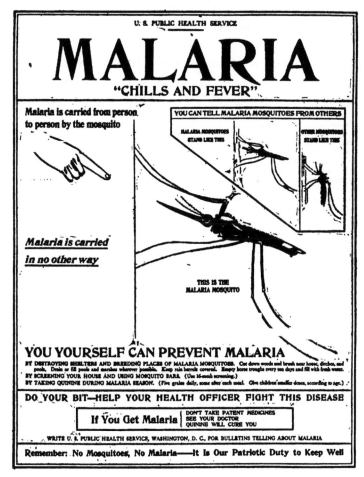

The poster is printed in two colors, on paper 20 by 16 inches in size. Copies have been sent to post offices and railroad stations in the Southern States.

PREVALENCE OF DISEASE.

No health department, State or local, can effectively prevent or control disease without knowledge of when, where, and under what conditions cases are occurring.

UNITED STATES.

EXTRA-CANTONMENT ZONES—CASES REPORTED WEEK ENDED MAY 14.

CAMP BEAUREGARD ZONE, LA.

Alexandria:	Cases.
Chicken pox	3
Gonorrhea	2
Malaria	3
Measles	1
Mumps	15
Pneumonia	2
Smallpox	2
Typhoid fever	1
Whooping cough	7
Pineville:	
Cerebrospinal meningitis	1
Mumps	3

CAMP BOWIE ZONE, TEX.

Fort Worth:	
Chicken pox	15
Gonorrhea	3
Malaria	1
Measles	1
Mumps	46
Pneumonia	2
Scarlet fever	9
Smallpox	28
Syphilis	8
Tonsilitis	5
Tuberculosis	4
Typhoid fever	2
Whooping cough	5

CAMP DEVENS ZONE, MASS

Chicken pox:	
Ayer	2
German measles:	
Lancaster	1
Measles:	
Ayer	1
Forge Village	16
Graniteville	1
Westford	1
Tuberculosis, pulmonary:	
Lancaster	1

CAMP DODGE ZONE, IOWA.

Cerebrospinal meningitis:	Cases.
Des Moines	1
Diphtheria:	
Bloomfield Township	1
Des Moines	4
Fort Des Moines	1
Scarlet fever:	
Des Moines	21
Grimes	1
Smallpox:	
Des Moines	12
Fort Des Moines	1
Syphilis:	
Des Moines	1
Urethritis, specific:	
Des Moines	1

CAMP DONIPHAN ZONE, OKLA.

Gonorrhea:	
Lawton	5
Mumps:	
Fletcher	1
Pneumonia, lobar:	
Lawton	1
Smallpox:	
Fletcher	1
Lawton	1
Tinney	1
Tuberculosis, pulmonary:	
Fletcher	1
Whooping cough:	
Fletcher	5

CAMP EBERTS ZONE, ARK.

Chancroid:	
England	1
Chicken pox:	
Cabot	2
German measles:	
Ward	2
Gonorrhea:	
England	5
Lonoke	1
Scott	1

CAMP EBERTS ZONE, ARK.—continued.

Malaria:	Cases.
England	6
Cabot	1
Keo	1
Ward	2

Measles:
Lonoke, route 1	4
Cabot	13
Keo	3
Ward	1
Ward, route 1	2
Austin, route 1	2

Mumps:
Lonoke, route 1	1
England	1
Eberts Field	1
Keo	3

Pellagra:
Ward	1

Pneumonia:
Lonoke, route 1	1
England	1
Scott, route 1	1
Kerr	2

Smallpox:
Eberts Field	1

Syphilis:
England	3

Tuberculosis:
England	2
Keo	1
Scott, route 1	2
Kerr, route 1	1

Whooping cough:
Keo	4

CAMP FUNSTON ZONE, KANS.

Chicken pox:
Manhattan	4

Diphtheria:
Junction City	1

Measles:
Junction City	2
Manhattan	3
Riley	2

Mumps:
Junction City	3
Manhattan	8
Randolph	1

Pneumonia:
Manhattan	3
Ogden	2

Scarlet fever:
Junction City	1
Manhattan	2

Smallpox:
Junction City	1
Manhattan	1

Whooping cough:
Junction City	2

CAMP GORDON ZONE, GA.

Chicken pox:
Atlanta	4
Decatur	1

CAMP GORDON ZONE, GA.—continued.

Diphtheria:	Cases
Atlanta	1

German measles:
Atlanta	a

Gonorrhea:
Atlanta	7

Malaria:
Atlanta	2

Measles:
Atlanta	22
Stone Mountain	1

Mumps:
Atlanta	13
Decatur	2
Norcross	3

Pneumonia:
Atlanta	4

Scarlet fever:
Atlanta	3
Decatur	1
Hapeville	1

Smallpox:
Atlanta	9

Syphilis:
Atlanta	9

Tuberculosis:
Atlanta	5
Norcross	1
Chamblee	1

Typhoid fever:
Tucker	1

Whooping cough:
Atlanta	4

CAMP GREENE ZONE, N. C.

Charlotte Township:
Chancroid	3
Chicken pox	1
German measles	2
Gonorrhea	26
Measles	6
Mumps	5
Scarlet fever	1
Syphilis	15
Tuberculosis	2
Whooping cough	12

Paw Creek Township:
Syphilis	4

GULFPORT HEALTH DISTRICT, MISS.

Gulfport Health District:
Malaria	4
Measles	2
Mumps	1

CAMP HANCOCK ZONE, GA.

Augusta:
Chicken pox	2
Gonorrhea	3
Measles	7
Syphilis	5
Tuberculosis, pulmonary	1
Whooping cough	2

Richmond County:
Syphilis	4

CAMP JOSEPH E. JOHNSTON ZONE, FLA.

	Cases.
Chicken pox:	
Jacksonville	3
Dysentery:	
Jacksonville	4
Panama	3
Murray Hill	2
Fishers Corner	1
Lackawanna	1
Ortega	2
Gonorrhea:	
Jacksonville	2
Measles:	
Jacksonville	7
Fishers Corner	1
Lackawanna	4
Mumps:	
Jacksonville	3
Panama	5
Pellagra:	
Fishers Corner	1
Pneumonia:	
Jacksonville	5
Panama	1
Scabies:	
Fishers Corner	2
Syphilis:	
Jacksonville	1
Tuberculosis:	
Jacksonville	5
Panama	1
Murray Hill	2
Lackawanna	2
Typhoid fever:	
Jacksonville	2
Fishers Corner	1
Lackawanna	1
Grand Crossing	2
Whooping cough:	
Jacksonville	11
Lackawanna	4

FORT LEAVENWORTH ZONE, KANS.

Leavenworth	
Diphtheria	1
Measles	3
Smallpox	1
Leavenworth County:	
Diphtheria	1
Measles	1
Pneumonia, lobar	3
Scarlet fever	1
Whooping cough	3

CAMP LEE ZONE, VA.

Chancroid:	
Petersburg	1
Diphtheria:	
Petersburg	1
German measles.	
Prince George County	12
Gonorrhea	
Petersburg	9
Malaria:	
Chesterfield County	1
Petersburg	1

CAMP LEE ZONE, VA — continued.

	Cases.
Measles:	
Ettricks	1
Hopewell	4
Prince George County	6
Mumps:	
Dinwiddie County	8
Ettricks	3
Hopewell	2
Petersburg	2
Prince George County	7
Septic sore throat:	
Ettricks	2
Petersburg	7
Scarlet fever:	
Prince George County	1
Syphilis:	
Petersburg	6
Tuberculosis:	
Petersburg	3

CAMP LOGAN ZONE, TEX.

Houston:	
Chancroid	1
Diphtheria	1
Gonorrhea	49
Measles	13
Malaria	1
Mumps	1
Pneumonia	1
Scarlet fever	1
Smallpox	1
Syphilis	12
Tuberculosis	1
Typhoid fever	3

CAMP M'ARTHUR ZONE, TEX.

Waco:	
Chicken pox	2
Mumps	14
Pneumonia, lobar	2
Rabies in animals	2
Smallpox	5
Tuberculosis	4

CAMP M'CLELLAN ZONE, ALA.

Anniston:	
Chicken pox	1
German measles	1
Malaria	1
Measles	1
Mumps	2
Smallpox	3
Whooping cough	1
Precinct 15:	
Smallpox	6
Precinct 17:	
Smallpox	1

NORFOLK COUNTY NAVAL DISTRICT, VA.

Chicken pox:	
Norfolk County	1
Lafayette Residence Park	1
Malaria	
Ocean View	2
Norfolk County	1
Deep Creek	3

NORFOLK COUNTY NAVAL DISTRICT, VA.—contd.

Measles:	Cases.
Norfolk County	2
Portsmouth	8
Norfolk	8
South Norfolk	1
Mumps:	
Norfolk	8
Ocean View	1
Gilmerton	2
South Norfolk	1
Pneumonia:	
Gilmerton	1
Norfolk	1
Scarlet fever:	
Norfolk	10
Tuberculosis:	
Ocean View	1
Typhoid fever:	
Norfolk	1
Whooping cough:	
Norfolk	1
Ocean View	2

FORT OGLETHORPE ZONE, GA.

Cerebrospinal meningitis:	
East Lake	1
North Chattanooga	1
Chicken pox:	
Chattanooga	1
East Lake	1
Gonorrhea:	
Chattanooga	113
Measles:	
Chattanooga	1
Mumps:	
Chattanooga	3
East Chattanooga	2
Scarlet fever:	
Chattanooga	2
St. Elmo	1
Syphilis:	
Chattanooga	55
Tuberculosis:	
Hornsville	1
Typhoid fever:	
Chattanooga	1

CAMP PIKE ZONE, ARK.

Little Rock:	
Cerebrospinal meningitis	1
Chancroid	1
Chicken pox	3
Diphtheria	1
Gonorrhea	8
Malaria	6
Measles	6
Mumps	4
Pneumonia	6
Smallpox	5
Syphilis	9
Trachoma	1
Tuberculosis	10
Whooping cough	2

CAMP PIKE ZONE, ARK.—continued.

North Little Rock:	Cases.
Cerebrospinal meningitis	1
Chicken pox	1
Gonorrhea	2
Malaria	2
Mumps	4
Orchitis	2
Pneumonia	1
Syphilis	1
Scotts:	
Gonorrhea	3
Pellagra	1
Syphilis	3
Tuberculosis	3

CAMP SEVIER ZONE, S. C.

Mumps:	
Chick Springs Township	1
Smallpox:	
Duncan Mills	1
Tuberculosis:	
Chick Springs Township	1

CAMP SHELBY ZONE, MISS.

Hattiesburg:	
Chicken pox	4
Malaria	5
Mumps	14
Tuberculosis	1
Typhoid fever	1
Venereal	3
Whooping cough	4

CAMP SHERIDAN ZONE, ALA.

Montgomery:	
Cerebrospinal meningitis	1
Chicken pox	2
Gonorrhea	14
Malaria	5
Measles	5
Mumps	1
Ophthalmia neonatorum	1
Ringworm	12
Scarlet fever	2
Smallpox	3
Syphilis	1
Tuberculosis	1
Typhoid fever	2
Whooping cough	2
Montgomery County:	
Cerebrospinal meningitis	1
Measles	1

CAMP SHERMAN ZONE, OHIO.

Cerebrospinal meningitis:	
Chillicothe	1
Diphtheria:	
Chillicothe	1
Gonorrhea:	
Chillicothe	3
Green Township	1
Measles:	
Chillicothe	1
Liberty Township	2

CAMP SHERMAN ZONE, OHIO—continued.

	Cases.
Scarlet fever:	
Chillicothe	3
Smallpox:	
Chillicothe	1
Tuberculosis, pulmonary:	
Springfield Township	1
Whooping cough:	
Chillicothe	5

CAMP ZACHARY TAYLOR ZONE, KY.

Jefferson County:	
Diphtheria	1
Tuberculosis, pulmonary	1
Typhoid fever	2
Louisville:	
Chicken pox	1
Diphtheria	6
Measles	11
Mumps	1
Pneumonia, lobar	6
Smallpox	4
Tuberculosis, pulmonary	14
Typhoid fever	3
Whooping cough	2
U. S. Government Clinic:	
Chancroid	2
Gonorrhea	28
Syphilis	25

TIDEWATER HEALTH DISTRICT, VA.

Cerebrospinal meningitis:	
Hampton	1
Chancroid:	
Newport News	2
Chicken pox:	
Newport News	2
German measles:	
Hampton	1
Gonorrhea:	
Newport News	6
Measles:	
Newport News	4
Phoebus	1
Mumps:	
Hampton	4
Newport News	7
Pneumonia:	
Phoebus	2
Scarlet fever:	
Newport News	1
Smallpox:	
Denbigh	1
Newport News	1

TIDEWATER HEALTH DISTRICT, VA.—continued.

	Cases.
Tuberculosis:	
Newport News	3
Phoebus	1
Whooping cough:	
Phoebus	2

CAMP TRAVIS ZONE, TEX.

San Antonio:	
Bronchitis	1
Chancroid	2
Dysentery	6
Enterocolitis	1
Gonorrhea	34
Malaria	5
Measles	9
Mumps	7
Pneumonia	2
Syphilis	9
Tetanus	1
Tuberculosis	7
Typhoid fever	5

CAMP WADSWORTH ZONE, S. C.

Pauline:	
German measles	1
Measles	1
Pneumonia	1
Whooping cough	1
Spartanburg:	
Chicken pox	4
Diphtheria	1
Measles	2
Mumps	12
Pellagra	1
Smallpox	1
Tuberculosis	1
Whooping cough	10

CAMP WHEELER ZONE, GA.

East Macon:	
Gonorrhea	1
Measles	1
Scarlet fever	1
Typhoid fever	1
Macon:	
Cerebrospinal meningitis	1
Chicken pox	2
Gonorrhea	22
Malaria	3
Mumps	3
Smallpox	5
Syphilis	7
Tuberculosis	3
Whooping cough	1

DISEASE CONDITIONS AMONG TROOPS IN THE UNITED STATES.

The following data are taken from telegraphic reports received in the office of the Surgeon General, United States Army, for the week ended May 3, 1918:

Annual admission rate per 1,000 (disease only):

All troops 1,109.7
National Guard camps 994
National Army camps 1,222.4
Regular Army 1,054.1

Noneffective rate per 1,000 on day of report:

All troops 39.1
National Guard camps 35.6

Noneffective rate per 1,000 on day of report—Continued.

National Army camps 43.8
Regular Army 37.4

Annual death rate per 1,000 (disease only):

All troops 6.3
National Guard camps 3.6
National Army camps 6.3
Regular Army 8.19

New cases of special diseases reported during the week ended May 3, 1918.

Camp.	Pneumonia.	Dysentery.	Malaria.	Venereal.		Measles.	Meningitis.	Scarlet fever.	Deaths.	Annual admission rate per 1,000 (disease only).	Noneffective per 1,000 on day of report.
				Total.	New infections.						
Wadsworth..................	6			9	7	2	1		4	223.6	12.9
Hancock...................	1			553	16	1			1	514.4	34.5
McClellan..................	4		1	106	12	2			2	818.8	28.1
Wheeler...................	15		22	24	1				4	953.7	39
Sevier....................	8		5	120	53	20	2	3	1	770.6	29.4
Logan.....................	8		2	193	117	18	1	5	1	1,976.2	41.3
Cody......................	6			2	1				1	367.8	22
Doniphan..................	2			16						1,901.9	57.3
Bowie.....................	7		3	47	43	1			2	1,125.7	41.2
Sheridan..................	6			19	15			1	3	420.2	25.2
Shelby....................	3	2		7		2				845.6	42.4
Beauregard................	21		21	44	4	3			2	1,634.7	63.2
Kearny....................	9			5		1			1	1,706.3	38.3
Devens....................	19			21	4	5		4	3	704.4	38.5
Upton.....................	16			324	16	10		4	3	1,172.1	39.2
Dix.......................	5			88	17	16		3	1	873.2	31.2
Meade.....................	4			9	2	6			2	683.5	26.5
Lee.......................	5		1	106	8	16	1		4	879.4	44.8
Jackson...................	13	1	7	231	7	17	3	1	3	1,355.9	46
Gordon....................	3		1	110	7	44	4	1	8	1,390.3	47.1
Sherman...................	10		1	103	4	25		9	6	1,159.6	40.3
Taylor....................	7			137	15	36	2	1	1	1,393.9	61.9
Custer....................	10			138	6	8		10	5	847.6	32.1
Grant.....................	8			10		23	1	5	3	635.6	27.5
Pike......................	5	2		66	8	32	5	1	4	1,848.6	62.6
Dodge.....................	27			83		24	2	8	12	1,871.9	84.9
Funston...................	31			115	14	6	2	3	9	1,432.3	52.8
Travis....................	6	1	4	67	3	7		1	2	2,097.7	40.5
Lewis.....................	5		1	475	11	15	1	12	2	1,617.6	43
Northeastern Department...				10	3	5		5		991.8	32.2
Eastern Department........	8			24	7	13		1	7	762.1	27.8
Southeastern Department...	2		4	38	24	14		1	2	812.7	44.8
Central Department........	2			25	11	5		3	4	1,285.1	46.6
Southern Department.......	21	2	2	75	39	0		17	12	1,110.8	44.8
Western Department........	2			30	15	4		1	3	895.7	27.4
Aviation S. C.............	22	3	4	97		28	3	15	18	1,126.7	34.2
Camp Greene...............		2		39		1			1	523.7	22.8
Camp Fremont..............	2		2	17	3	9		1	1	757.7	42.1
El Paso...................				11	11	2		1		628.6	3.1
Columbus Barracks.........	1			26	3	2			1	1,077.6	39.1
Jefferson Barracks........	14			30	2	5		4	3	2,303.7	100.7
Fort Logan................	7					1		3	6	2,242.7	103.0
Fort McDowell.............			1	17	1	1				1,598.8	46.8
Fort Slocum...............				14		1			2	1,265.0	45.1
Fort Thomas...............	1		1	3		2				1,165.9	45.4
D. B. Alcatraz............				1						3,199.9	
D. B. Fort Leavenworth....				2			1		1	1,034.8	35.7
A. A. Humphreys...........	4			4		5				434.6	7.0
J. E. Johnston............	3			24	18	11	1	1		1,359.9	38.8
Hoboken, N. J.............	24		1	147		31		12	8	907.1	35.6
Camp Stuart...............	16			193	8	12	2	1	7	2,006.7	63.3
West Point, N. Y..........										612.9	32.2
Edgewood-Aberdeen.........						1				784.5	25.1
Provisional depot for corps and Army troops.........	6			12		1			2	945.8	40.2
Camp Holabird.............				1						661.3	46.2
Camp Raritan..............				2						742.8	23.6
Springfield Armory........											
National Guard Departments.	1			9	7	5		2	1		
National Army Departments.	11	1	2	69	24	68	4	7	7		
Total..................	417	14	67	3,561	567	574	36	147	176	1,109.7	39.1

Annual rate per 1,000 for special diseases.

Disease.	All troops in United States.[1]	Regulars in United States.[1]	National Guard, all camps.[1]	National Army, all camps.[1]	Expeditionary Forces.[2]
Pneumonia	16.6	17.3	17.2	16.7	28.4
Dysentery	0.5	0.9	0.3	0.38	0.1
Malaria	2.6	2.0	6.1	1.4	1.3
Venereal	145.8	108.2	115.9	200.3	40.5
Paratyphoid	0.0	0.0	0.0	0.0	0.0
Typhoid	0.04	0.0	0.17	0.0	0.0
Measles	22.9	20.6	9.0	27.9	6.2
Meningitis	1.4	0.9	0.7	2.0	2.3
Scarlet fever	5.8	8.4	1.6	6.0	9.7

[1] Week ended May 3, 1918.   [2] Week ended Apr. 26, 1918.

CURRENT STATE SUMMARIES.

Alabama.

From Collaborating Epidemiologist Perry, by telegraph, for week ended May 11, 1918:

One infantile paralysis Autauga County, 1 meningitis Wilcox County.

Connecticut.

From Collaborating Epidemiologist Black, by telegraph, for week ended May 11, 1918:

Smallpox: Hartford 1. Cerebrospinal meningitis: Greenwich 1. Poliomyelitis: Voluntown 1.

Illinois.

From Collaborating Epidemiologist Drake, by telegraph, for week ended May 11, 1918:

Diphtheria: One hundred and twenty-two, of which in Chicago 86, Peoria 7, Oak Park 6. Scarlet fever: Ninety-seven, of which in Chicago, 41, Prophetstown 9, Rockford 5, Roscoe Township (Winnebago County) 6. Smallpox: One hundred and forty-eight, of which in Quincy 17, Pulaski 8, Belleville 7, Millcreek 14, Danville 6, Cropsey Township (McLean County) 6, Lincoln State School and Colony 6. Meningitis: Fifteen, of which in Chicago 10, 1 each Girard, Tamaroa, Standard, Moline, Moweaqua. Poliomyelitis: Springfield 1, Frankfort Township (Will County) 1, Chicago 2.

Indiana.

From the State board of health of Indiana, by telegraph, for week ended May 11, 1918:

Smallpox: Epidemic Idaville. Scarlet fever: Epidemic Ligonier, Portland. Measles: Epidemic Sheridan, Marengo, Celestine, Hayden. Whooping cough: Epidemic Newcastle, Boone County, Dearborn County. Diphtheria: Epidemic Hamburg. Braytown, Milroy. Rabies: Epidemic Corydon.

Kansas.

From Collaborating Epidemiologist Crumbine, by telegraph, for week ended May 11, 1918:

Smallpox (10 or more cases): By counties—Franklin 15, Reno 19, Wyandotte 14; by cities—Coffeyville 10, Kansas City 13, Topeka 17, Wichita 38. Scarlet fever (over 10 cases): In cities—Topeka 15. Meningitis: In cities—Independence 1, Kansas City 1, Wichita 1.

Louisiana.

From Collaborating Epidemiologist Dowling, by telegraph, for week ended May 11, 1918:

Meningitis 2, dengue 69, typhoid fever 37, smallpox 8, diphtheria 9.

Massachusetts.

From Collaborating Epidemiologist Hitchcock, by telegraph, for week ended May 11, 1918:

Unusual prevalence. Diphtheria: Templeton 6. Measles: Chelmsford 21, Lawrence 139, Malden 70, Natick 27, Quincy 36, Salem 71, Westford 20. Smallpox: Boston 2.

Minnesota.

From Collaborating Epidemiologist Bracken, by telegraph, for week ended May 11, 1918:

Smallpox (new foci): Chisago County, Amador Township, 1; Crow Wing County, Garrison Township, 1; Goodhue County, Halden Township, 4; Lac qui Parle County Madison city, 1; Lincoln County, Diamond Lake Township, 1; Martin County, Truman Township, 2. One poliomyelitis, 6 cerebrospinal meningitis reported since May 6.

Virginia.

From the State Board of Health of Virginia, by telegraph, for week ended May 11, 1918:

Twelve cases smallpox Culpeper County, 2 Bedford, 3 Warwick, 1 Norfolk. One case cerebrospinal meningitis, Spotsylvania County, 1 Hanover.

Washington.

From Collaborating Epidemiologist Tuttle, by telegraph, for week ended May 11, 1918:

Unusual prevalence. Poliomyelitis: One case Wenatchee. Cerebrospinal meningitis: One case each Seattle, Tacoma, Waterville. Scarlet fever: Tacoma 50 cases, Seattle 17. Smallpox: Spokane 11 cases.

CEREBROSPINAL MENINGITIS.

City Reports for Week Ended Apr. 27, 1918.

Place.	Cases.	Deaths.	Place.	Cases.	Deaths.
Akron, Ohio	1	....	Cleveland, Ohio	1	....
Atlanta, Ga	1	....	Columbus, Ohio	1	....
Baltimore, Md	11	2	Dayton, Ohio	....	2
Berkeley, Cal	1	....	Detroit, Mich	....	1
Birmingham, Ala	2	....	Evansville, Ind	1	1
Boston, Mass	5	2	Fall River, Mass	....	1
Buffalo, N. Y	1	1	Fitchburg, Mass	1	....
Cambridge, Mass	5	1	Galesburg, Ill	....	1
Centralia, Ill	1	....	Greenville, S. C	1	1
Chattanooga, Tenn	2	....	Indianapolis, Ind	3	2
Chicago, Ill	10	3	Jersey City, N. J	....	1
Cincinnati, Ohio	2	1	Lincoln, Nebr	1	1

CEREBROSPINAL MENINGITIS—Continued.

City Reports for Week Ended Apr. 27, 1918—Continued.

Place.	Cases.	Deaths.	Place.	Cases.	Deaths.
Little Rock, Ark...........	2	....	Roanoke, Va............	2	....
Louisville, Ky............	2	3	Rockford, Ill............	....	2
Lowell, Mass.	2	....	St. Joseph, Mo..........	1	....
Marion, Ind............	....	1	St. Louis, Mo........	4	1
Memphis, Tenn...........	....	1	San Francisco, Cal......	4	3
Milwaukee, Wis..........	1	1	Saratoga Springs, N. Y......	1	1
Newark, N. J.	4	2	Savannah, Ga..	1	....
New Bedford, Mass....	1	....	Schenectady, N. Y.......	1	....
New Orleans, La........	1	....	Springfield, Ill.........	1	....
Newport, R. I........	2	1	Springfield, Mo.........	1	1
New York, N. Y........	20	11	Superior, Wis...........	1	2
Oklahoma City, Okla.......	1	1	Tacoma, Wash.........	1	....
Philadelphia, Pa........	3	2	Troy, N. Y........	1	....
Pittsburgh, Pa...........	1	....	Washington, D. C.......	1	1
Port Chester, N. Y......	....	1	West Warwick, R. I......	....	1
Providence, R. I........	....	2	Wilkes-Barre, Pa........	1	....
Racine, Wis.............	2	....	Winston-Salem, N. C......	2	1
Richmond, Va............	1	1	Worcester, Mass....	2	1

DIPHTHERIA.

See Diphtheria, measles, scarlet fever, and tuberculosis, page 783.

ERYSIPELAS.

City Reports for Week Ended Apr. 27, 1918.

Place.	Cases.	Deaths.	Place.	Cases.	Deaths.
Akron, Ohio..............	2	....	Milwaukee, Wis........	3	....
Baltimore, Md............	1	....	Minneapolis, Minn.......	....	1
Barre, Vt.............	1	....	Morristown, N. J........	1	....
Birmingham, Ala.........	....	1	Newark, N. J........	4	1
Buffalo, N. Y............	4	1	New Britain, Conn......	1	....
Chicago, Ill.............	11	....	New York, N. Y........	....	4
Cincinnati, Ohio.........	1	....	Oakland, Cal........	....	1
Cleveland, Ohio..........	6	2	Philadelphia, Pa........	14	1
Colorado Springs, Colo......	....	1	Plainfield, N. J........	....	1
Columbus, Ohio.........	....	1	Portland, Oreg........	1	....
Denver, Colo...........	4	2	Richmond, Va........	2	....
Detroit, Mich............	6	1	Sacramento, Cal........	1	....
Duluth, Minn............	2	....	Saginaw, Mich........	2	....
Fargo, N. Dak............	1	....	St. Joseph, Mo.........	1	....
Fort Worth, Tex.........	1	1	St. Louis, Mo........	12	2
Hagerstown, N. Y........	1	....	San Francisco, Cal......	2	....
Jackson, Mich...........	4	1	Somerville, Mass........	....	1
Kansas City, Kans........	3	....	Syracuse, N. Y........	....	1
Los Angeles, Cal.........	4	1	Toledo, Ohio........	1	1
Louisville, Ky...........	2	2	Utica, N. Y........	....	1
Memphis, Tenn...........	1	....	Wichita, Kans........	1	....

LEPROSY.

City Reports for Week Ended Apr. 27, 1918.

There was reported during the week ended April 27, 1918, at Louisville, Ky., one case of leprosy. One death from the same disease was reported at Philadelphia, Pa.

MALARIA.

City Reports for Week Ended Apr. 27, 1918.

Place.	Cases.	Deaths.	Place.	Cases.	Deaths.
Atlanta, Ga..............	1	....	Louisville, Ky..............	1	....
Birmingham, Ala............	4	....	Marshall, Tex..............	3	....
Centralia, Ill..............	3	....	Memphis, Tenn..........	1	....
Fort Smith, Ark.............	2	....	Montgomery, Ala..........	2	....
Hattiesburg, Miss..........	17	....	Oklahoma City, Okla........	....	1
Jacksonville, Fla..........	....	1	Palestine, Tex..............	35	....
Little Rock, Ark............	12	....	Tuscaloosa, Ala..............	2	....

MEASLES.

New York—Fulton.

Telegraphic report from the city health officer of Fulton, N. Y., stated that during the period from May 10 to 14, 1918, 14 cases of measles were notified in Fulton.

See also Diphtheria, measles, scarlet fever, and tuberculosis, page 783.

PELLAGRA.

City Reports for Week Ended Apr. 27, 1918.

Place.	Cases.	Deaths.	Place.	Cases.	Deaths.
Atlanta, Ga............:	....	2	Lynchburg, Va..............	....	1
Birmingham, Ala..........	1	5	Memphis, Tenn.............	4	1
Charleston, S. C...........	....	2	Nashville, Tenn.............	3	1
Coffeyville, Kans..........	1	....	New Orleans, La.............	3	3
Dallas, Tex................	....	1	Palestine, Tex..............	1	....
Durham, N. C..............	....	1	Providence, R. I.............	1	....
Greenville, S. C...........	....	2	Raleigh, N. C..............	1	1
Houston, Tex..............	1	....	Rocky Mount, N. C.........	1	....
Jacksonville, Fla..........	1	2	Spartanburg, S. C...........	2	....
Lexington, Ky.............	....	1	Wilmington, N. C..........	....	1
Little Rock, Ark..........	....	1	Winston-Salem, N. C........	1	....

PNEUMONIA.

City Reports for Week Ended Apr. 27, 1918.

Place.	Cases.	Deaths.	Place.	Cases.	Deaths.
Akron, Ohio..............	1	....	Cleveland, Ohio.............	56	50
Amsterdam, N. Y..........	6	....	Coffeyville, Kans...........	1	....
Ann Arbor, Mich..........	1	....	Cranston, R. I.............	1	1
Anniston, Ala.............	1	....	Cumberland, Md...........	2	....
Atlanta, Ga..............	3	18	Danville, Ill..............	5	5
Baltimore, Md............	43	12	Dayton, Ohio..............	6	8
Battle Creek, Mich........	1	....	Detroit, Mich..............	37	76
Berkeley, Cal.............	1	3	Duluth, Minn..............	7	9
Boston, Mass..............	23	43	Fall River, Mass............	11	2
Bridgeport, Conn...........	4	8	Fitchburg, Mass............	1	....
Brockton, Mass............	3	3	Flint, Mich................	5	3
Buffalo, N. Y.............	1	18	Fort Worth, Tex............	8	8
Cambridge, Mass..........	6	4	Grand Rapids, Mich........	16	5
Cambridge, Ohio..........	1	....	Hagerstown, Md...........	4	....
Centralia, Ill.............	10	2	Hammond, Ind.............	3	6
Chattanooga, Tenn........	1	5	Hattiesburg, Miss..........	9	....
Chelsea, Mass.............	10	2	Haverhill, Mass............	11	4
Chicago, Ill..............	337	136	Holyoke, Mass..............	3	1
Chicopee, Mass............	1	....	Houston, Tex..............	1	6

PNEUMONIA—Continued.

City Reports for Week Ended Apr. 27, 1918—Continued.

Place.	Cases.	Deaths.	Place.	Cases.	Deaths.
Independence, Mo............	2	1	Oakland, Cal...................	1	6
Jackson, Mich................	4	4	Oak Park, Ill.................	2	....
Jacksonville, Fla............	1	2	Oshkosh, Wis.................	4	4
Jamestown, N. Y.............	11	2	Palestine, Tex...............	8	2
Kalamazoo, Mich.............	10	4	Parkersburg, W. Va.........	3	2
Kansas City, Kans..........	3	....	Philadelphia, Pa.............	120	53
Lawrence, Mass..............	10	2	Pittsfield, Mass.............	9	1
Lexington, Ky...............	1	2	Pontiac, Mich...............	3	....
Little Rock, Ark............	2	1	Provo, Utah.................	1	....
Long Beach, Cal.............	1	2	Quincy, Mass................	5	1
Lorain, Ohio................	1	....	Redlands, Cal...............	1	....
Los Angeles, Cal............	9	5	Richmond, Va...............	1	4
Louisville, Ky..............	7	22	Rochester, N. Y.............	8	12
Lowell, Mass................	1	7	Salem, Mass.................	1	....
Lynn, Mass..................	9	2	Sandusky, Ohio.............	3	....
Manchester, N. H...........	4	4	San Francisco, Cal..........	16	19
Montgomery, Ala............	1	3	Schenectady, N. Y..........	8	4
Newark, N. J................	54	9	Somerville, Mass............	7	5
New Bedford, Mass..........	9	5	Springfield, Mass...........	5	3
Newburyport, Mass..........	2	1	Springfield, Ohio...........	2	....
New Castle, Ind.............	4	1	Toledo, Ohio................	3	9
New Castle, Pa.............	1	....	Waco, Tex..................	2	....
Newport, Ky................	3	3	Watertown, N. Y............	1	1
Newton, Mass...............	2	1	Westfield, Mass.............	2	1
North Adams, Mass..........	5	1	Wichita, Kans..............	1	....
Northampton, Mass..........	3	2	Worcester, Mass............	24	7
North Little Rock, Ark.....	2	1	Yonkers, N. Y..............	2	5
North Tonawanda, N. Y.....	2	....	Youngstown, Ohio...........	2	8

POLIOMYELITIS (INFANTILE PARALYSIS).

City Reports for Week Ended Apr. 27, 1918.

Place.	Cases.	Deaths.	Place.	Cases.	Deaths.
Battle Creek, Mich...........	1	1	Omaha, Nebr................	....	1
Detroit, Mich...............	1	1	Pittsburgh, Pa..............	1	....
Kenosha, Wis...............	1	....	Racine, Wis................	1	....
Milwaukee, Wis.............	3	....	Springfield, Mass...........	1	1
New York, N. Y.............	1	....	Troy, N. Y.................	....	6

RABIES IN ANIMALS.

City Report for Week Ended Apr. 27, 1918,

There was reported at Detroit, Mich., during the week ended April 27, 1918, one case of rabies in animals.

SCARLET FEVER.

See Diphtheria, measles, scarlet fever, and tuberculosis, page 783.

SMALLPOX.

Maryland—Cumberland—Correction.

The publication of 9 cases of smallpox at Cumberland, Md., in the Public Health Reports of April 26, 1918, page 628, was an error. No cases of smallpox were reported in Cumberland during the week ended April 6, 1918.

SMALLPOX—Continued.

Colorado Report for March, 1918.

Place.	New cases reported.	Deaths.	Vaccination history of cases.			
			Number vaccinated within 7 years preceding attack.	Number last vaccinated more than 7 years preceding attack.	Number never successfully vaccinated.	Vaccination history not obtained or uncertain.
Colorado:						
Alamosa County	5					5
Arapahoe County	1					1
Bent County	1				1	
Boulder County	1				1	
Chaffee County	1		1			
Crowley County	2				2	
Delta County	2				2	
Denver	117		15		100	2
El Paso County	8		2		3	3
Huerfano County	1				1	
Kit Carson County	19		1		18	
Larimer County	14		1		4	9
Mesa County	26		2		3	21
Morgan County	1				1	
Otero County	1				1	
Phillips County	6				5	1
Pueblo	10				6	4
Rio Blanco County	1				1	
Rio Grande County	2				2	
Weld County	21		1		11	9
Yuma County	10				8	2
Total	250		23		170	57

City Reports for Week Ended Apr. 27, 1918.

Place.	Cases.	Deaths.	Place.	Cases.	Deaths.
Abilene, Tex	25		Evansville, Ind	3	
Akron, Ohio	17		Everett, Wash	2	
Alton, Ill	6		Fargo, N. Dak	1	
Anniston, Ala	8		Fort Scott, Kans	7	
Ashtabula, Ohio	5		Fort Smith, Ark	3	
Atlanta, Ga	6		Fort Wayne, Ind	5	
Bellingham, Wash	2		Fremont, Ohio	4	
Billings, Mont	1		Fresno, Cal	1	
Birmingham, Ala	14		Galesburg, Ill	2	
Bloomington, Ind	5		Grand Rapids, Mich	1	
Buffalo, N. Y	3		Greeley, Colo	1	
Butte, Mont	2		Greensburg, Pa	1	
Cape Girardeau, Mo	9		Hamilton, Ohio	10	
Cedar Rapids, Iowa	3		Houston, Tex	3	
Chanute, Kans	3		Independence, Kans	4	
Charleston, W. Va	3		Independence, Mo	9	
Chattanooga, Tenn	2		Indianapolis, Ind	23	
Chelsea, Mass	1		Iola, Kans	11	
Cheyenne, Wyo	1		Jamestown, N. Y	1	
Chicago, Ill	8		Janesville, Wis	1	
Chillicothe, Ohio	2		Johnstown, Pa	2	
Cincinnati, Ohio	14		Kalamazoo, Mich	5	
Cleveland, Ohio	30		Kansas City, Kans	14	
Coffeyville, Kans	3		Kenosha, Wis	2	
Columbus, Ohio	3		Knoxville, Tenn	1	
Council Bluffs, Iowa	8		Kokomo, Ind	1	
Dallas, Tex	5		La Crosse, Wis	4	
Davenport, Iowa	5		Lancaster, Ohio	1	
Dayton, Ohio	4		Lawrence, Kans	1	
Denver, Colo	30		Leavenworth, Kans	1	
Des Moines, Iowa	18		Lima, Ohio	3	
Detroit, Mich	55		Lincoln, Nebr	8	
Dubuque, Iowa	2		Little Rock, Ark	5	
Elgin, Ill	1		Lorain, Ohio	1	
Elmira, N. Y	1		Los Angeles, Cal	2	
El Paso, Tex	1		Louisville, Ky	1	
Elyria, Ohio	1		Lynchburg, Va	3	

SMALLPOX—Continued.

City Reports for Week Ended Apr. 27, 1918—Continued.

Place.	Cases.	Deaths.	Place.	Cases.	Deaths.
Madison, Wis	1		Quincy, Ill	6	
Marion, Ind	1		Richmond, Ind	1	
Mason City, Iowa	4		Roanoke, Va	3	
Memphis, Tenn	9		St. Joseph, Mo	13	
Milwaukee, Wis	3		St. Louis, Mo	13	
Minneapolis, Minn	14		Salt Lake City, Utah	4	
Mobile, Ala	8		San Francisco, Cal	5	
Montgomery, Ala	2		Seattle, Wash	9	
Muncie, Ind	3		Shelbyville, Ind	3	
Muskogee, Okla	5		Sioux City, Iowa	12	
Nashville, Tenn	6		South Bend, Ind	2	
New Albany, Ind	1		Spartanburg, S. C	1	
Newark, Ohio	1		Spokane, Wash	6	
New Orleans, La	5		Springfield, Ill	2	
New York, N. Y	1		Springfield, Mo	2	
Niagara Falls, N. Y	1		Springfield, Ohio	1	
Norfolk, Va	1		Steelton, Pa	2	
North Little Rock, Ark	2		Tacoma, Wash	1	
Norwood, Ohio	1		Terre Haute, Ind	3	
Ogden, Utah	1		Toledo, Ohio	14	
Oklahoma City, Okla	25		Topeka, Kans	8	
Omaha, Nebr	27		Tuscaloosa, Ala	3	
Oshkosh, Wis	2		Waco, Tex	6	
Parkersburg, W. Va	8		Waterloo, Iowa	7	
Peoria, Ill	9		Wichita, Kans	18	
Philadelphia, Pa	2		Winston-Salem, N. C	2	
Portland, Oreg	1				

TETANUS.

City Reports for Week Ended Apr. 27, 1918.

During the week ended April 27, 1918, one death from tetanus was reported at Savannah, Ga., and one at Wilmington, N. C.

TUBERCULOSIS.

See Diphtheria, measles, scarlet fever, and tuberculosis, page 783.

TYPHOID FEVER.

Colorado Report for March, 1918.

Place.	New cases reported.	Place.	New cases reported.
Colorado:		Colorado—Continued.	
Denver	3	Weld County	2
Larimer County	1		
Mesa County	2	Total	11
Pueblo County	3		

City Reports for Week Ended Apr. 27, 1918.

Place.	Cases.	Deaths.	Place.	Cases.	Deaths.
Altoona, Pa	1		Charleston, W. Va	2	1
Baltimore, Md	8	2	Chicago, Ill	4	1
Bethlehem, Pa	1		Chillicothe, Ohio	1	
Birmingham, Ala	1	1	Cincinnati, Ohio	1	
Boston, Mass	3		Cleveland, Ohio		2
Buffalo, N. Y	2		Detroit, Mich	6	3
Burlington, Vt	1		Dubuque, Iowa		1
Charleston, S. C	2		Duluth, Minn	3	

TYPHOID FEVER—Continued.

City Reports for Week Ended Apr. 27, 1918—Continued.

Place.	Cases.	Deaths.	Place.	Cases.	Deaths.
Elmira, N. Y.	1		New Castle, Pa.	2	
Erie, Pa.	2		New Haven, Conn.	1	
Evansville, Ind.	1		New Orleans, La.	3	2
Fairmont, W. Va.	1		New York, N. Y.	13	1
Flint, Mich.	1	1	Orange, N. J.	1	
Fort Smith, Ark.	1		Palestine, Tex.	1	
Fremont, Ohio	1		Pawtucket, R. I.	1	
Grand Rapids, Mich.	2		Philadelphia, Pa.	3	
Greeley, Colo.	3		Pittsburgh, Pa.	4	
Hammond, Ind.	2	1	Portland, Oreg.	2	
Hattiesburg, Miss.	1		Portsmouth, N. H.		1
Hoboken, N. J.	1		Providence, R. I.	1	
Houston, Tex.	1		Quincy, Ill.	1	
Indianapolis, Ind.	1		Richmond, Va.	3	
Jacksonville, Fla.	6		St. Louis, Mo.	5	2
Jersey City, N. J.		2	Sandusky, Ohio.	1	
Lawrence, Mass.		1	San Francisco, Cal.	7	1
Lorain, Ohio.	2		Scranton, Pa.	2	
Los Angeles, Cal.	1	1	Shamokin, Pa.	1	
Louisville, Ky.	1		Somerville, Mass.	2	
Madison, Wis.	2		Syracuse, N. Y.	1	
Manchester, N. H.	1		Toledo, Ohio.	1	
Milwaukee, Wis.	1	1	Waco, Tex.	1	1
Minneapolis, Minn.	4	1	Washington, D. C.	1	
Mobile, Ala.	1		Washington, Pa.	1	
Moline, Ill.	1		West Chester, Pa.	1	
Morgantown, W. Va.	1		Wheeling, W. Va.	4	1
Morristown, N. J.	1		Wilmington, Del.	1	
Nashville, Tenn.	3	1	Worcester, Mass.	1	
New Albany, Ind.	1		Youngstown, Ohio.	1	1
Newark, N. J.		1	Zanesville, Ohio.	2	1

TYPHUS FEVER.

Massachusetts—Chelsea.

On May 14, 1918, 1 case of typhus fever was notified at Chelsea, Mass.

DIPHTHERIA, MEASLES, SCARLET FEVER, AND TUBERCULOSIS.

Colorado Report for March, 1918.

There were reported during the month of March, 1918, from Colorado, 48 cases of diphtheria, 498 cases of measles, and 285 cases of scarlet fever.

City Reports for Week Ended Apr. 27, 1918.

City.	Population as of July 1, 1916 (estimated by U. S. Census Bureau).	Total deaths from all causes.	Diphtheria.		Measles.		Scarlet fever.		Tuberculosis.	
			Cases.	Deaths.	Cases.	Deaths.	Cases.	Deaths.	Cases.	Deaths.
Over 500,000 inhabitants:										
Baltimore, Md.	589,621	216	8	1	668	4	9		52	33
Boston, Mass.	756,476	273	71	3	383	7	24		58	36
Chicago, Ill.	2,497,722	800	121	11	113	3	41		339	120
Cleveland, Ohio.	674,073	263	23		48		14	2	35	33
Detroit, Mich.	571,784	288	53	5	78	4	55	4	65	25
Los Angeles, Cal.	503,812		18	2	143		6		38	31
New York, N. Y.	5,602,841	1,601	227	34	1,125	33	128	6	310	206
Philadelphia, Pa.	1,709,518	610	53	12	899	12	39		154	88
Pittsburgh, Pa.	579,090		14		266		12		23	
St. Louis, Mo.	757,309	288	44	3	84	1	24	1	59	21

DIPHTHERIA, MEASLES, SCARLET FEVER, AND TUBERCULOSIS—Contd.

City Reports for Week Ended Apr. 27, 1918—Continued.

City.	Population as of July 1, 1916 (estimated by U. S. Census Bureau).	Total deaths from all causes.	Diphtheria.		Measles.		Scarlet fever.		Tuberculosis.	
			Cases.	Deaths.	Cases.	Deaths.	Cases.	Deaths.	Cases.	Deaths.
From 300,000 to 500,000 inhabitants:										
Buffalo, N. Y............	468,558	168	14	4	152	1	20	......	28	12
Cincinnati, Ohio..........	410,476	137	17	......	36	......	2	......	13	23
Jersey City, N. J..........	306,345	87	......	......	......	3	......	......	......	10
Milwaukee. Wis..........	436,535	158	4	......	419	2	37	2	25	11
Minneapolis, Minn........	363,454	......	19	......	28	3	19	1	26	12
Newark, N. J............	408,894	131	26	4	383	11	18	......	43	20
New Orleans, La..........	371,747	174	6	......	6	......	......	......	28	33
San Francisco, Cal........	463,516	144	18	......	61	1	18	......	29	17
Seattle, Wash...........	348,639	......	2	......	61	......	37	......	......	......
Washington, D. C.........	363,980	152	24	......	412	4	31	......	29	17
From 200,000 to 300,000 inhabitants:										
Columbus, Ohio..........	214,878	71	2	......	31	......	28	......	10	7
Denver, Colo.............	260,800	104	6	1	65	......	15	......	......	21
Indianapolis, Ind.........	271,708	140	22	2	18	1	47	1	9	22
Louisville, Ky...........	238,910	127	7	1	8	......	......	......	25	15
Portland, Oreg...........	295,463	55	1	......	196	......	5	......	10	6
Providence, R. I..........	254,960	80	12	2	137	3	12	......	......	20
Rochester, N. Y..........	256,417	72	6	1	60	......	19	......	19	7
From 100,000 to 200,000 inhabitants										
Atlanta, Ga.............	190,558	71	2	......	9	......	2	......	10	9
Birmingham, Ala.........	181,762	106	......	......	2	2	3	......	13	8
Bridgeport, Conn.........	121,578	42	8	......	8	......	3	1	6	2
Cambridge, Mass.........	112,981	35	10	......	73	1	1	......	5	4
Camden, N. J............	106,233	......	3	......	19	......	5	......	12	......
Dallas, Tex..............	124,527	16	2	......	13	1	......	......	4	3
Dayton, Ohio............	127,224	52	2	......	2	......	1	......	4	5
Des Moines, Iowa........	101,598	......	4	......	......	......	21	......	......	......
Fall River, Mass.........	128,366	46	3	......	11	......	3	......	10	9
Fort Worth, Tex.........	104,562	36	2	......	2	......	4	......	5	3
Grand Rapids, Mich.......	128,291	59	6	1	12	......	4	......	2	3
Hartford, Conn..........	110,900	32	15	......	3	......	1	......	7	1
Houston, Tex............	112,307	45	......	......	7	......	......	......	......	3
Lawrence, Mass..........	100,560	41	6	2	57	......	1	......	6	5
Lowell, Mass............	113,245	48	1	......	10	......	1	......	6	7
Lynn, Mass..............	102,425	28	5	1	26	......	2	......	5	2
Memphis, Tenn..........	118,995	51	6	......	7	......	......	......	22	5
Nashville, Tenn..........	117,057	80	1	1	27	......	2	......	4	11
New Bedford, Mass.......	118,158	57	1	......	10	......	1	......	8	8
New Haven, Conn........	149,685	37	3	......	9	......	1	......	9	7
Oakland, Cal............	198,604	47	1	......	21	......	2	......	6	4
Omaha, Nebr............	165,470	39	14	2	18	......	13	......	1	4
Reading, Pa.............	109,341	......	......	......	75	......	3	......	7	......
Richmond, Va...........	156,687	50	3	......	85	1	2	......	4	4
Salt Lake City, Utah......	117,399	32	4	......	31	......	10	1	......	1
Scranton, Pa............	146,811	......	5	......	9	......	2	......	......	......
Spokane, Wash..........	150,323	......	3	......	......	......	3	......	......	......
Springfield, Mass.........	105,942	18	5	2	52	......	7	1	6	3
Syracuse, N. Y..........	155,624	64	8	......	122	3	12	......	15	4
Tacoma, Wash...........	112,770	......	1	......	7	......	24	......	......	......
Toledo, Ohio............	191,554	80	1	......	12	......	6	1	3	14
Trenton, N. J............	111,593	46	7	2	8	......	1	......	3	2
Worcester, Mass.........	163,314	60	4	......	12	......	2	......	9	7
Youngstown, Ohio........	108,385	43	......	......	25	......	3	......	......	3
From 50,000 to 100,000 inhabitants										
Akron, Ohio.............	85,625	......	15	......	17	......	21	......	6	......
Allentown, Pa...........	63,505	......	4	......	33	......	3	......	......	......
Altoona, Pa.............	58,659	......	3	......	21	......	......	......	......	......
Atlantic City, N. J........	57,049	......	......	......	24	......	......	......	......	1
Augusta, Ga.............	50,215	21	......	......	9	......	2	......	1	......
Bayonne, N. J...........	69,804	......	5	......	31	......	4	......	3	......
Berkeley, Cal...........	57,653	11	......	......	10	......	......	......	......	......
Binghamton, N. Y........	53,973	25	5	......	23	......	......	......	2	1
Brockton, Mass..........	67,449	17	1	......	43	......	4	1	3	1
Canton, Ohio............	69,552	23	......	......	1	......	2	......	1	3
Charleston, S. C.........	60,734	39	3	......	......	......	......	......	......	6
Chattanooga, Tenn.......	60,075	7	1	......	......	......	2	......	......	2
Covington, Ky...........	57,144	20	1	......	6	......	......	......	3	7

DIPHTHERIA, MEASLES, SCARLET FEVER, AND TUBERCULOSIS—Contd.

City Reports for Week Ended Apr. 27, 1918—Continued.

City.	Population as of July 1, 1916 (estimated by U. S. Census Bureau).	Total deaths from all causes.	Diphtheria.		Measles.		Scarlet fever.		Tuberculosis.	
			Cases.	Deaths.	Cases.	Deaths.	Cases.	Deaths.	Cases.	Deaths.
From 50,000 to 100,000 inhabitants—Continued.										
Duluth, Minn	94,495	28	2	....	4	....	....	....	4	1
El Paso, Tex	63,705	41	1	....	13	....	4	1	4	7
Erie, Pa	75,195	....	6	....	54	....	1	....	7	....
Evansville, Ind	76,078	32	....	....	11	....	1	....	3	3
Flint, Mich	54,772	17	2	....	7	....	6	1	7	....
Fort Wayne, Ind	76,183	36	3	....	....	....	....	....	5	4
Harrisburg, Pa	72,015	....	3	....	12	....	....	....	....	....
Hoboken, N. J	77,214	23	3	1	1	....	5	....	7	5
Holyoke, Mass	65,286	13	3	....	5	....	1	....	1	....
Jacksonville, Fla	76,101	33	....	....	6	....	....	....	8	2
Johnstown, Pa	68,529	....	6	....	....	....	14	....	1	....
Kansas City, Kans	99,437	....	....	....	34	....	5	....	5	....
Lancaster, Pa	50,853	....	....	....	21	....	1	....	....	....
Little Rock, Ark	57,343	7	....	....	2	....	1	....	2	2
Manchester, N. H	78,283	27	1	1	11	1	....	....	8	3
Mobile, Ala	58,221	17	....	....	....	....	....	....	....	1
New Britain, Conn	53,794	21	1	1	9	....	2	....	....	2
Norfolk, Va	89,612	....	....	....	25	....	2	....	....	6
Oklahoma City, Okla	92,943	20	1	....	10	1	....	....	....	5
Passaic, N. J	71,744	28	2	....	21	....	2	....	....	3
Pawtucket, R. I	59,411	23	1	....	32	3	1	....	....	1
Peoria, Ill	71,458	26	1	....	7	....	2	....	....	2
Portland, Me	63,867	20	2	....	3	....	....	....	....	2
Rockford, Ill	55,185	18	....	....	17	....	....	....	....	2
Sacramento, Cal	66,895	20	2	....	12	....	5	....	3	4
Saginaw, Mich	55,642	....	....	....	1	....	....	....	....	1
St. Joseph, Mo	85,236	41	2	1	....	....	....	....	....	2
San Diego, Cal	53,330	18	....	....	23	....	3	....	....	2
Savannah, Ga	68,805	30	....	....	....	....	1	....	2	2
Schenectady, N. Y	99,519	21	1	....	24	....	1	....	5	....
Sioux City, Iowa	57,078	....	1	....	....	....	3	....	....	....
Somerville, Mass	87,039	27	6	....	98	....	4	....	10	1
South Bend, Ind	68,946	17	1	....	5	....	....	....	3	3
Springfield, Ill	61,120	21	1	....	35	....	....	....	....	3
Springfield, Ohio	51,550	32	....	....	1	1	1	....	7	5
Terre Haute, Ind	66,083	25	4	....	2	....	1	....	1	1
Troy, N. Y	77,916	36	....	....	2	....	5	1	6	4
Utica, N. Y	85,692	40	2	....	63	3	2	....	4	1
Wichita, Kans	70,722	....	....	....	39	....	1	....	6	....
Wilkes-Barre, Pa	76,776	....	4	....	37	....	4	....	11	....
Wilmington, Del	94,265	45	....	....	62	....	....	....	....	3
Yonkers, N. Y	99,838	22	2	....	42	....	3	....	....	3
York, Pa	51,656	....	4	....	20	....	4	....	3	....
From 25,000 to 50,000 inhabitants:										
Alameda, Cal	27,732	8	5	1	17	....	1	....	....	....
Amsterdam, N. Y	37,103	....	6	1	2	....	1	....	6	1
Austin, Tex	34,814	20	1	....	....	....	1	....	....	3
Battle Creek, Mich	29,480	....	3	....	104	....	....	....	1	1
Beaumont, Tex	27,711	18	....	....	....	....	....	....	....	2
Bellingham, Wash	32,985	5	....	....	....	....	....	....	....	....
Boise, Idaho	33,846	9	....	....	1	....	1	....	....	....
Brookline, Mass	32,730	9	2	....	45	....	....	....	5	....
Burlington, Iowa	25,030	10	....	....	....	....	4	....	....	....
Butler, Pa	27,632	....	....	....	18	....	....	....	....	....
Butte, Mont	43,425	....	....	....	....	....	3	....	....	....
Cedar Rapids, Iowa	37,308	....	1	....	....	....	5	....	....	....
Charleston, W. Va	29,941	13	1	....	9	....	1	....	....	5
Charlotte, N. C	39,823	21	2	....	7	....	2	....	1	1
Chelsea, Mass	46,192	20	2	....	42	....	3	....	5	....
Chester, Pa	41,396	....	....	....	6	....	....	....	2	....
Chicopee, Mass	29,319	9	1	....	4	....	....	....	2	1
Clinton, Iowa	27,386	....	....	....	21	....	....	....	....	....
Cohoes, N. Y	25,211	12	1	1	4	....	....	....	....	1
Colorado Springs, Colo	32,971	8	3	....	13	....	1	....	5	2
Council Bluffs, Iowa	31,484	14	2	1	5	....	13	1	....	....
Cranston, R. I	25,987	6	....	....	4	....	1	....	....	....
Cumberland, Md	26,074	6	....	....	23	....	15	....	3	1
Danville, Ill	32,261	14	....	....	20	....	....	....	1	1
Davenport, Iowa	48,811	....	....	....	....	....	4	....	2	....
Dubuque, Iowa	39,573	....	2	....	....	....	1	....	....	3

DIPHTHERIA, MEASLES, SCARLET FEVER, AND TUBERCULOSIS—Contd.

City Reports for Week Ended Apr. 27, 1918—Continued.

City.	Population as of July 1, 1916 (estimated by U. S. Census Bureau).	Total deaths from all causes.	Diphtheria.		Measles.		Scarlet fever.		Tuberculosis.	
			Cases.	Deaths.	Cases.	Deaths.	Cases.	Deaths.	Cases.	Deaths.
From 25,000 to 50,000 inhabitants—Continued.										
Durham, N. C.	25,061	8			17					
East Chicago, Ind	28,743	21			2				1	
Easton, Pa.	30,530				14					
East Orange, N. J.	42,458	5	2		47		2		3	
Elgin, Ill.	28,203	6								
Elmira, N. Y.	38,120	4			14		1			1
Evanston, Ill.	28,591	9			12		1			
Everett, Mass.	33,233	7	1		5		4		1	2
Everett, Wash.	35,480				1		1			
Fitchburg, Mass.	41,781	14			11		1		3	1
Fort Smith, Ark.	28,638	7			4		2		1	
Fresno, Cal.	31,958	6			6					
Galveston, Tex.	41,863	16	1		11		2			2
Green Bay, Wis.	29,353	9			4					1
Hagerstown, Md.	25,679				2					
Hammond, Ind.	26,171	16	3	1			2		1	1
Haverhill, Mass.	48,477	27	4		27		5		6	1
Hazleton, Pa.	28,491		3		27		1			
Jackson, Mich.	35,396	21	3		6		22	2	4	1
Jamestown, N. Y.	36,780	7	1		26		1		1	
Kalamazoo, Mich.	48,858				1				5	2
Kenosha, Wis.	31,576	15	13	1			8		4	2
Knoxville, Tenn	38,076				8				3	3
La Crosse, Wis.	31,677	10							1	1
Lexington, Ky.	41,097	25	1		13					4
Lima, Ohio	35,384	11	3				2			
Lincoln, Nebr.	46,515	14	3	1			2			
Long Beach, Cal.	27,587	19			20		1	1	4	1
Lorain, Ohio	36,946						1			
Lynchburg, Va.	32,940	12	1		3				2	2
Madison, Wis.	30,699	21			60		10			1
McKeesport, Pa.	47,521				13				1	
Medford, Mass.	26,234	5	2		12		1		1	
Moline, Ill.	27,451	16	2		14		2	1		
Montclair, N. J.	26,318	6			31	1	1		1	1
Montgomery, Ala.	43,285	17			10				15	
Muncie, Ind.	25,424	7					3		1	2
Muskogee, Okla	44,210		1		1					2
Nashua, N. H.	27,327	18								2
Newark, Ohio	29,635	14			2		2			1
Newburgh, N. Y.	29,603	7	1		1					
New Castle, Pa.	41,133		1		9					
Newport, Ky.	31,927	9							2	2
Newport, R. I.	30,108	8								1
Newton, Mass.	43,715	13	1		18				1	1
Niagara Falls, N. Y.	37,353	16			2		8			2
Norristown, Pa.	31,101				7					
Norwalk, Conn	26,899			4			8		1	2
Oak Park, Ill.	26,651	10	1		13		1			
Ogden, Utah	31,404	8			43		1			
Orange, N. J.	33,089	11			25		2		2	
Oshkosh, Wis.	36,067	13			4		4		1	
Pasadena, Cal	40,651	14			130				5	1
Perth Amboy, N. J.	41,185	11	1		1				3	
Petersburg, Va.	25,582	9			5				1	
Pittsfield, Mass.	38,609	18			2		2		8	3
Poughkeepsie, N. Y.	30,340	13			80		1		3	
Quincy, Ill.	36,798	12	1		16				1	
Quincy, Mass.	38,135	13			33		2		1	
Racine, Wis.	46,486	25			33		4			1
Roanoke, Va	43,184	13	1		32				1	1
Rock Island, Ill.	28,929	8	2		29		6			1
Salem, Mass.	48,552	12	2		39				2	1
San Jose, Cal	38,902				17				1	
Sheboygan, Wis.	28,551	14	1				1	1	1	1
Shenandoah, Pa.	29,401		1						2	
Sedalia, Mo.	4,411	10	1							1
Steubenville, Ohio	27,145	19			1				1	
Superior, Wis.	40,266	17	1		1		10			2

DIPHTHERIA, MEASLES, SCARLET FEVER, AND TUBERCULOSIS—Contd.

City Reports for Week Ended Apr. 27, 1918—Continued.

City.	Population as of July 1, 1916 (estimated by U. S. Census Bureau).	Total deaths from all causes.	Diphtheria.		Measles.		Scarlet fever.		Tuberculosis.	
			Cases.	Deaths.	Cases.	Deaths.	Cases.	Deaths.	Cases.	Deaths.
From 25,000 to 50,000 inhabitants—Continued.										
Taunton, Mass.	36,283	12			1		3		3	
Topeka, Kans.	48,726		1	1	6		16	1		
Waco, Tex.	33,385	25			6		1		1	
Waltham, Mass.	30,570	7	2		54					3
Waterloo, Iowa.	35,559	19			1		5			
Watertown, N. Y.	29,894	3	1	1	132	1				
West Hoboken, N. J.	43,139	1			6		1			
Wheeling, W. Va.	43,377	23	1		5		1		3	1
Wilmington, N. C.	29,892	13			13				1	
Winston-Salem, N. C.	31,155	13			5				1	1
Woonsocket, R. I.	44,360		1							
Zanesville, Ohio.	30,863	10								1
From 10,000 to 25,000 inhabitants:										
Abilene, Tex.	14,238				5		5			
Alton, Ill.	28,874	11								1
Ann Arbor, Mich.	15,010	9	1		31		1		1	1
Anniston, Ala.	14,118				2		1			
Appleton, Wis.	17,834	8					1			
Asbury Park, N. J.	14,007	3			6		1			
Ashtabula, Ohio.	21,498	7			1		5		3	1
Bakersfield, Cal.	16,874	7	1		2				3	2
Barre, Vt.	12,109	1	1							
Beloit, Wis.	18,072	8	4		25		3			
Bethlehem, Pa.	14,142				32		1			
Bellaire, Ohio.	14,348	5	1	1	1					
Billings, Mont.	14,422		1				1			
Bloomington, Ind.	11,383	7					1			1
Braddock, Pa.	21,685		1		9					
Bradford, Pa.	[1]14,544				9					
Burlington, Vt.	21,617	11	1							
Cairo, Ill.	15,794	13				1				4
Cambridge, Ohio.	13,483				2					
Carbondale, Pa.	19,248				1		1			
Carlisle, Pa.	10,726		1		5					
Carnegie, Pa.	11,692				1					
Centralia, Ill.	11,538	2	1		1				2	
Chambersburg, Pa.	12,380						1			
Chanute, Kans.	12,455									
Cheyenne, Wyo.	[1]11,320		1		4		2			
Chillicothe, Ohio.	15,470	6			4		5		1	
Clinton, Mass.	[1]13,075	3			3				3	
Coatesville, Pa.	14,455				1		2		3	
Coffeyville, Kans.	17,548				1		2		2	1
Concord, N. H.	22,669	15			2					
Connellsville, Pa.	15,455			3	7					
Corpus Christi, Tex.	10,432	6								
Dover, N. H.	13,272	4			1		2			
Du Bois, Pa.	14,665		1		3					
Dunkirk, N. Y.	20,743	5								
Dunmore, Pa.	20,776		3							
East Providence, R. I.	18,113				2		2			
Eau Claire, Wis.	18,807				23					
Elwood, Ind.	[1]11,028		1		14					
Elyria, Ohio.	18,618	6							1	1
Eureka, Cal.	14,684	3					2			
Fargo, N. Dak.	17,389	5			4					1
Farrell, Pa.	[1]10,190				3					
Fort Scott, Kans.	10,550	4	1							
Fostoria, Ohio.	10,770	3								
Fremont, Ohio.	10,882				1		2			
Galesburg, Ill.	24,276	11	1		10					
Gardner, Mass.	17,140		2		22		1			
Greeley, Colo.	11,420	8					3			1
Greensboro, N. C.	19,377			1	8					
Greensburg, Pa.	15,483				1		1			
Greenville, S. C.	18,181	16			1					1

[1] Population Apr. 15, 1910; no estimate made.

DIPHTHERIA, MEASLES, SCARLET FEVER, AND TUBERCULOSIS—Contd.

City Reports for Week Ended Apr. 27, 1918—Continued.

City.	Population as of July 1, 1916 (estimated by U. S. Census Bureau).	Total deaths from all causes.	Diphtheria.		Measles.		Scarlet fever.		Tuberculosis.	
			Cases.	Deaths.	Cases.	Deaths.	Cases.	Deaths.	Cases.	Deaths.
From 10,000 to 25,000 inhabitants—Continued.										
Hackensack, N. J.	16,945	5			19					
Harrison, N. J.	16,950		2				1			
Hattiesburg, Miss	16,482				1					
Homestead, Pa	22,466		1		6				4	
Independence, Kans	14,506	3			9			1		
Independence, Mo	11,672	8	3		1			1		
Iola, Kans	11,068				1					
Jacksonville, Ill	15,481	3			8					
Janesville, Wis	14,339	3			1		3			
Kokomo, Ind	20,930	11	5		4		1			
La Fayette, Ind	21,246	7								1
Lancaster, Ohio	15,670				12		3		1	1
Lawrence, Kans	13,324						1			
Leavenworth, Kans	¹ 19,363	6			16		1			1
Lebanon, Pa	20,779								2	
Lincoln, R. I.	10,383		1		3					
Mahanoy City, Pa	17,463				4					
Long Branch, N. J.	15,395	7			1		1			
Manitowoc, Wis	13,805									
Marinette, Wis	¹ 14,610	8			19		1	1		1
Marion, Ind	19,834	3			2					1
Marshall, Tex	13,712	4								
Martinsburg, W. Va	12,666						1			
Mason City, Iowa	14,457	7								
Massillon, Ohio	15,310	5	1		2		2			
Meadville, Pa	13,802				2		1			
Melrose, Mass	17,445	6			3					
Michigan City, Ind	21,512	6	1	1	1				1	1
Mishawaka, Ind	16,385	4			1					
Monessen, Pa	21,833		5							1
Morgantown, W. Va	13,709	5			1					
Morristown, N. J.	13,281	3								
Moundsville, W. Va	11,153	4	1							
Mt. Carmel, Pa	20,268		1							
Mt. Vernon, Ohio	10,628								1	
Muscatine, Iowa	17,533				1					
Nanticoke, Pa	23,126		1				2			
New Albany, Ind	23,620	6	1				2		1	
Newburyport, Mass	15,243	5			0				1	
New Castle, Ind	13,241	3								
New London, Conn	20,985	11					2		1	
North Adams, Mass	¹ 22,019	11							2	1
Northampton, Mass	19,926	11					1			1
North Braddock, Pa	15,148		2		6					
North Little Rock, Ark	14,907	1								
North Tonawanda, N. Y.	13,768	5							1	
North Yakima, Wash	20,951				19					
Norwood, Ohio	22,286	6					2			1
Oil City, Pa	19,207				2		3			
Old Forge, Pa	14,902		2		2		1			
Palestine, Tex	11,854		1		1	2	1		4	
Parkersburg, W. Va	20,612	8			2					
Plainfield, N. J.	23,845	7	1	1	13		1		2	
Plymouth, Pa	19,100						1		1	
Pomona, Cal	13,170				6				1	
Pontiac, Mich	17,524				1		2		2	
Port Chester, N. Y.	16,183	5			10		1		1	
Portsmouth, N. H.	11,666	3	1	1	3					1
Pottsville, Pa	22,372				7					
Provo, Utah	10,645	6					1			
Rahway, N. J.	10,219				3					
Raleigh, N. C.	20,127	3			12				1	
Redlands, Cal	14,000				15					
Richmond, Ind	21,667	9								
Riverside, Cal	19,341	3			1					
Rocky Mount, N. C.	12,067	2								
Rutland, Vt	14,831	9						1		
Sandusky, Ohio	20,193	4						1		

¹ Population Apr 15, 1910, no estimate made.

DIPHTHERIA, MEASLES, SCARLET FEVER, AND TUBERCULOSIS—Contd.

City Reports for Week Ended Apr. 27, 1918—Continued.

City.	Population as of July 1, 1916 (estimated by U. S. Census Bureau).	Total deaths from all causes.	Diphtheria.		Measles.		Scarlet fever.		Tuberculosis.	
			Cases.	Deaths.	Cases.	Deaths.	Cases.	Deaths.	Cases.	Deaths.
From 10,000 to 25,000 inhabitants—Continued.										
Santa Ana, Cal	10,627	2			18					
Santa Cruz, Cal	14,592	4			5					
Saratoga Springs, N. Y	13,821	7			3				1	2
Shamokin, Pa	21,129		1		1		3			
Shelbyville, Ind	10,965	3							2	
Spartanburg, S. C	21,365	7	1		4					2
Steelton, Pa	15,548				1		1		3	
Sunbury, Pa	16,360						1			
Tuscaloosa, Ala	10,488	3	1	1	5				2	
Uniontown, Pa	20,780				12					
Vallejo, Cal	13,461	3			2				1	1
Vancouver, Wash	13,180				14					
Warren, Pa	14,737		1						1	
Washington, Pa	21,618				12					
Wausau, Wis	19,239	4					1			
West Chester, Pa	13,176		1		11		2		1	
Westfield, Mass	18,391	10			13		1		1	1
West Orange, N. J	13,550	2			60				2	
West Warwick, R. I	15,782	4								
Wilkinsburg, Pa	21,228		2		9		1			
Winthrop, Mass	12,692		2		10					
Woburn, Mass	15,969	9								

FOREIGN.

BRAZIL.

Yellow Fever—Bahia.

A case of yellow fever was notified at Bahia, Brazil, during the week ended March 16, 1918.

CHINA.

Further Relative to Cerebrospinal Meningitis—Hankow.[1]

On April 8, 1918, cerebrospinal meningitis was reported still prevalent at Hankow, China, with frequent occurrence among adults.

CUBA.

Communicable Diseases—Habana.

Communicable diseases have been notified at Habana as follows:

Disease.	Apr. 1-10, 1918.		Remaining under treatment Apr. 10, 1918.	Disease.	Apr. 1-10, 1918.		Remaining under treatment Apr. 10, 1918
	New cases.	Deaths.			New cases.	Deaths.	
Diphtheria	1		5	Paratyphoid fever	4		3
Leprosy			12	Scarlet fever	1		[2] 5
Malaria	11		[1] 33	Typhoid fever	22	3	[3] 47
Measles	6		8	Varicella	32		28

[1] From the interior, 25. [2] From the interior, 4. [3] From the interior, 22.

RUSSIA.

Cholera—Tashkentnine—Tzaritsin.

Cholera was reported present at Tashkentnine and Tzaritsin, Russia, May 13, 1918.

VENEZUELA.

Mortality, 1917.

During the period from January 1 to June 30, 1917, 30,167 deaths were notified in Venezuela, the highest mortality being reported in January with 6,736 deaths and the lowest in April with 4,375 deaths. Of the total number of deaths reported, 4,927 were due to malarial fever, 1,382 occurring in January and 575 in June, 1917. Typhoid fever caused 941 deaths and infantile tetanus 1,085 deaths.

---

[1] Public Health Reports, May 3, 1918, p. 708.

During the six months ended December 31, 1917, 27,647 deaths were notified in Venezuela. Of these, 4,258 were due to malarial fever, 814 to typhoid fever, and 442 to tetanus. (Population of Venezuela, 2,713,700.)

———

CHOLERA, PLAGUE, SMALLPOX, TYPHUS FEVER, AND YELLOW FEVER.

Reports Received During the Week Ended May 17, 1918.[1]

CHOLERA.

Place.	Date.	Cases.	Deaths.	Remarks.
India:				
Calcutta..............	Feb. 3–23..........	....	24	
Philippine Islands:				
Provinces..............	....	....	....	Mar. 24–30, 1918: Cases, 54; deaths, 35.
Bohol..............	Mar. 24–30..........	29	22	
Cebu..............	.....do..........	5	2	
Occidental Negros......	.....do..........	14	10	
Oriental Negros......	.....do..........	6	1	
Russia:				
Tashkentnine..............	May 13..........	....	....	Present.
Tsaritsin	.....do..........	....	....	Do.

PLAGUE.

Place.	Date.	Cases.	Deaths.	Remarks.
Egypt:				
Cairo..............	Dec. 17–23........	2	....	
Port Said..............	July 2–Dec. 23.....	13	7	
Sues..............	July 2–Oct. 20.....	62	38	
Siam:				
Bangkok..............	Mar. 3–16..........	13	11	
Straits Settlements:				
Singapore..............	Feb. 17–Mar. 9.....	35	29	

SMALLPOX.

Place.	Date.	Cases.	Deaths.	Remarks.
Brazil:				
Rio de Janeiro..............	Mar. 10–23..........	20	1	
Canada:				
New Brunswick—				
Moncton..............	Apr. 21–27......	1	....	
St. John..............	Apr. 28–May 4.....	1	....	
Nova Scotia—				
Cape Sable Island......	May 3..........	....	....	Present at Clarks Harbor.
Halifax..............	Apr. 21–27.........	4	....	
Sydney..............	.....do..........	1	....	
Quebec—				
Quebec..............	.....do..........	2	....	
China:				
Amoy..............	Feb. 18–Mar. 10....	....	....	Present and in vicinity.
Antung..............	Mar. 24–Apr. 6.....	7	1	
Chungking..............	Feb. 17–Mar. 9.....	....	....	Present.
Dairen..............	Mar. 31–Apr. 6.....	2	....	
Hongkong..............	Feb. 24–Mar. 16.....	6	3	
Mukden..............	Feb. 10–Mar. 30....	....	....	Do.
Nanking..............	Mar. 24–30..........	....	....	Do.
Shanghai..............	Mar. 11–Apr. 1.....	2	13	Cases foreign; deaths, native.
Tientsin..............	Mar. 17–Apr. 6.....	9	....	
Tsingtau..............	Mar. 25–31..........	2	2	
Egypt:				
Alexandria..............	Mar. 19–25..........	5	....	
France:				
Paris..............	Mar. 24–30........	1	1	
Rouen..............	Mar. 31–Apr. 6....	26	4	
India:				
Calcutta..............	Feb. 3–23..........	....	10	
Italy:				
Leghorn..............	Apr. 1–7..........	1	....	

[1] From medical officers of the Public Health Service, American consuls, and other sources.

CHOLERA, PLAGUE, SMALLPOX, TYPHUS FEVER, AND YELLOW FEVER—
Continued.

Reports Received from Dec. 29, 1917, to May 10, 1918—Continued.

PLAGUE—Continued.

Place.	Date.	Cases.	Deaths.	Remarks.
China				Present in North China in January, 1918; pneumonic form.
Anhwei Province—				
Fengyanghsien	Feb. 27		9	Pneumonic.
Pengpu	....do		1	Do.
Chili Province—				
Kalgan				Vicinity. Present in February, 1918.
Kiangsu Province—				
Nanking	Mar. 17-23		15	
Shansi Province				Present in February, 1918; 116 cases estimated.
Ecuador:				
Bababoyo	Feb. 1-15	1	1	
Duran	Feb. 16-Mar. 30	2	1	
Guayaquil	Sept. 1-Nov. 30	68	24	Reported outbreak occurring about Jan. 17, 1918.
Do	Feb. 1-15	44	18	
Do	Mar. 1-30	37	14	
Egypt:				Jan. 1-Nov. 15, 1917: Cases 726; deaths, 398.
Alexandria	Jan. 14-28	1	2	
Port Said	July 23-29	1	2	
Hawaii:				
Laupahoehoe	May 5	1	1	
India				Sept. 16-Dec. 29, 1917: Cases, 228,834; deaths, 174,743. Dec. 30, 1917-Feb. 16, 1918: Cases, 240,000; deaths, 192,149.
Bassein	Dec. 9-29		8	
Do	Dec. 30-Feb. 16		74	
Bombay	Oct. 28-Dec. 29	147	123	
Do	Dec. 30-Feb. 16	152	112	
Calcutta	Sept. 16-29		2	
Do	Dec. 30-Feb. 2		4	
Henzada	Oct. 21-27		1	
Do	Jan. 5-Feb. 16		57	
Karachi	Oct. 21-Dec. 29	27	20	
Do	Dec. 30-Feb. 23	36	28	
Madras	Feb. 3-16	3	2	
Madras Presidency	Oct. 31-Nov. 24	5,786	4,519	
Do	Jan. 6-Feb. 16	10,431	8,100	
Mandalay	Oct. 14-Nov. 17		89	
Do	Dec. 30-Feb. 2		627	
Myingyan	Dec. 30-Feb. 10		286	
Pegu	Feb. 10-16		1	
Prome	Jan. 5-12		1	
Rangoon	Oct. 21-Dec. 22		36	
Do	Dec. 30-Feb. 16	266	251	
Toungoo	Dec. 9-29		5	
Do	Dec. 30-Feb. 16		25	
Indo-China:				Sept. 1-Nov. 30, 1917: Cases, 89; deaths, 68.
Provinces				
Anam	Sept. 1-Nov. 30	28	25	
Cambodia	....do	39	26	
Cochin-China	....do	22	15	
Saigon	Oct. 31-Dec. 23	17	6	
Do	Dec. 31-Mar. 17	115	60	
Java:				Oct. 8-Dec. 31, 1917 Cases, 196; deaths, 193.
East Java				
Do				Jan. 1-14, 1918: Cases, 22; deaths, 21.
Residencies				
Kediri	Oct. 8-Dec. 31	1	1	
Madiwen	....do	49	49	
Samarang	....do	110	109	
Surabaya	....do	25	23	
Surakarta	....do	11	11	
West Java				Nov. 25-Dec. 9, 1917: Cases, 45; deaths, 45. Dec. 1, 1917-Jan. 15, 1918: Cases, 106.
Peru:				
Ancachs Department—				
Casma	Dec. 1-Jan. 15	2		
Lambayeque Department	....do	22		At Chiclayo, Ferrenafe, Jayanca, Lambayeque.
Libertad Department	....do	72		At Guadalupe, Mansiche, Pacasmayo, Salaverry, San Jose, San Pedro, and country district of Trujillo.
Lima Department	....do	9		City and country.
Piura Department—				
Catacaos	....do	1		

CHOLERA, PLAGUE, SMALLPOX, TYPHUS FEVER, AND YELLOW FEVER—
Continued.

Reports Received from Dec. 29, 1917, to May 10, 1918—Continued.

PLAGUE—Continued.

Place.	Date.	Cases.	Deaths.	Remarks.
Senegal:				
St. Louis...............	Feb. 2............			Present.
Siam:				
Bangkok..................	Sept. 16–Dec. 23...	13	9	
Do...............	Jan. 13–Mar. 2.....	24	16	
Straits Settlements:				
Singapore.................	Oct. 28–Dec. 29....	5	7	
Do........................	Jan. 6–Feb. 16.....	29	28	

SMALLPOX.

Place.	Date.	Cases.	Deaths.	Remarks.
Algeria:				
Algiers.................	Nov. 1–Dec. 31....	3	2	
Do................	Jan. 1–Apr. 23....	213		
Australia:				
New South Wales.........				July 12–Dec. 20, 1917: cases, 36;
Abermain...........	Oct. 25–Nov. 29...	3		Jan 4–17, 1918; case, 1.
Cessnock...........	July 12–Oct. 11...	7		Newcastle district.
Eumangla...........	Aug. 15..........	1		
Kurri Kurri.........	Dec. 5–20.........	2		
Mungindi...........	Aug. 13..........	1		
Warren.............	July 12–Oct. 25...	22		
Do...............	Jan. 1–17.........	1		
Brazil:				
Bahia...................	Nov. 10–Dec. 8....	3		
Pernambuco.............	Nov. 1–15.........	1		
Rio de Janeiro..........	Sept. 30–Dec. 29..	703	190	
Do................	Dec. 30–Mar. 9....	231	83	
Sao Paulo..............	Oct. 29–Nov. 4....		2	
British East Africa:				
Mombasa...............	Oct. 1–Dec. 31....	9	5	
Canada:				
British Columbia—				
Vancouver............	Jan. 13–Mar. 9....	5		
Victoria............	Jan. 7–Feb. 2.....	2		
Winnipeg—...........	Dec. 30–Apr. 13...	4		
New Brunswick—				
Kent County..........	Dec. 4............			Outbreak. On main line Canadian Ry., 25 miles north of Moncton.
Do................	Jan. 22...........	40		In 7 localities.
Northumberland County.	.....do...........	41		In 5 localities.
Restigouche County....	Jan. 18...........	60		
St. John County—				
St. John............	Mar. 3–Apr. 27...	9		
Victoria County......	Jan. 22...........	10		At Limestone and a lumber camp.
Westmoreland County—				
Moncton............	Jan. 29–Apr. 20...	19		
York County.........	Jan. 22...........	8		
Nova Scotia—				
Halifax..............	Feb. 24–Apr. 20...	6		
Sydney..............	Feb. 3–Apr. 6.....	18		
Ontario—				
Arnprior.............	Mar. 31–Apr. 6...		1	
Hamilton............	Dec. 16–22........	1		
Do................	Jan. 13–19........	2		
Ottawa..............	Mar. 4–24.........	5		
Sarnia..............	Dec. 9–15.........	1		
Do...............	Jan. 6–Mar. 30...	32		
Toronto.............	Feb. 10–Apr. 6...	2		
Windsor.............	Dec. 30–Jan. 5....	1		
Prince Edward Island—				
Charlottetown.......	Feb. 7–13.........	1		
Quebec—				
Montreal............	Dec. 16–Jan. 5....	5		
Do................	Jan. 6–Apr. 6.....	12		
China:				
Amoy..................	Oct. 22–Dec. 30...			Present.
Do................	Dec. 31–Feb. 10...			Do.
Antung...............	Dec. 2–23.........	13	2	
Do................	Jan. 7–Feb. 17....	6	2	
Changsha.............	Jan. 28–Mar. 10...	6	1	
Chefoo...............	Jan. 27–Feb. 9....			Do.

PUBLIC HEALTH REPORTS

| VOL. 33 | MAY 24, 1918 | No. 21 |

PROGRESS IN VENEREAL DISEASE CONTROL.

By J. G. WILSON, Passed Assistant Surgeon, United States Public Health Service.

Public Health Reports of March 29, 1918, contained the suggestions for State board of health regulations approved by the Surgeons General of the Army, Navy, and Public Health Service as most feasible for the control of venereal diseases.

Although several States had already previously adopted regulations along the lines indicated in these "suggestions," the response to the printed appeal has resulted in very large additions to the list. The work has also been stimulated by an offer of the Surgeon General of the Public Health Service to give practical aid to State health departments in the establishment of divisions of venereal disease. On April 25 the following telegram was sent to State health officers:

"As a result of conference with the Surgeon General of the Army, the Public Health Service will appoint a man in your State to assume charge of venereal disease control under your direction, you to be consulted as to appointment. Salary to be paid by State and Federal Government jointly according to special needs, but appointee to wear uniform of Public Health Service officer. Wire if such cooperation desired and letter will follow." [1]

This telegram resulted in a large number of acceptances of the offer and many inquiries for further details. Letters have been written to all the State health officials and Public Health Service officers detailed to venereal disease control duty in order to further explain the plan and perfect arrangements for its execution. The details of the plan were briefly set forth in the following memorandum:

"Explanation of Organization of Work.

"There should be a division or bureau of venereal disease created in the State health department and the work should be undertaken along the general lines indicated in bureau letter to the State health

---

[1] Kansas and North Carolina were omitted because the Surgeon General of the Army had already detailed officers to those States for this purpose.

officer. This bureau should have its activities grouped under the
following four headings:

"1. Notification of cases of venereal disease to the health authorities.

"2. Repressive measures, looking toward isolation and treatment
in detention hospitals of infected persons who are unable or unwilling
to take measures to prevent their becoming a menace to others;
also measures for the suppression of prostitution.

"3. Educational measures, including measures for informing the
general public as well as infected individuals in regard to the nature
and manner of spread of venereal diseases and the steps that shou'd
be taken to combat them.

"4. Extension of facilities for early diagnosis and treatment.
State to be systematically divided and organized for this purpose
with representatives of the division of venereal disease in charge of
the work in each area.

"The time is opportune for immediate active cooperation between
the Public Health Service and State departments of health in carrying out all the measures mentioned under the four preceding heads.
It is believed, however, that the whole program can be most advantageously carried out if special stress is laid upon the last feature,
because with the organization of each State into districts and the
establishment of venereal clinics in strategic areas, the machinery
necessary for the entire plan will automatically be set in motion.
Although the operation of this machinery will at first undoubtedly
be imperfect, the following twofold results should be immediately
accomplished.

"First. Establishment of centers for carrying out workable regulations on reporting and the institution of repressive and educational
measures appropriate to particular communities.

"Second. Immediate reduction in venereal-disease foci with a
marked decrease in the prevalence of such diseases in both the
civilian and military population.

"The first aim, therefore, of the State bureau and division of
venereal diseases should be to establish a chain of venereal-disease
clinics. The operation of these clinics should be standardized
according to methods to be presented and agreed upon at the State
health officers' conference in June, but in the meantime it is not
advisable to await the perfection of all the details before starting
the work.

"An emergency exists and the clinics should be opened without
delay. One small clinic in a populous community is worth more
than a ton of literature distributed broadcast over the entire country."

The V. D. campaign, as waged by the United States Public Health
Service, by the "Section on combating V. D." of the Surgeon

General's Office, United States Army, and by the "Law Enforcement Division, of the Commission on Training Camp Activities," together with numbers of State and private and semiofficial organizations, has already developed in the following definite results:

1. *It is becoming rapidly recognized that health departments must also assume their share in the fight against venereal diseases which has heretofore been chiefly waged by educational and police organizations.*

Acting upon this principle, notification laws or regulations requiring reporting of these diseases to health authorities have been passed as follows: [1]

States in which venereal disease is reported by name:

Colorado.	Maryland.	Ohio.
Indiana.	New Jersey.	Vermont.

States in which venereal disease is reported by serial number:

Alabama.	Iowa.	Rhode Island.
Arizona.	Kansas.	South Dakota.
Arkansas.	Louisiana.	Tennessee.
California.	Massachusetts.	Texas.
Connecticut.	Michigan.	Utah.
Florida.	Minnesota.	Virginia.
Georgia.	New Mexico.	Washington.
Hawaii.	New York.	Wisconsin.
Illinois.	Oregon.	

States in which venereal disease is reportable by name when the patient fails to observe proper precautions:

Alabama.	Iowa.	New Mexico.
Arizona.	Kansas.	New York.
Arkansas.	Massachusetts.	Texas.
California.	Michigan.	Virginia.
Georgia.	Minnesota.	Washington.
Illinois.	Mississippi.	

2. *It is becoming rapidly recognized that the principles governing the control of venereal disease are essentially the same as those of any other communicable disease.*

This principle is admitted in fact when persons suffering from such diseases are subject to quarantine. Following is a list of States in which persons who are a menace to the public health on account of venereal infections may be isolated until such danger is past:

Alabama.	Iowa.	New York.
Arizona.	Kansas.	Ohio.
Arkansas.	Maryland.	Oregon.
California.	Minnesota.	South Dakota.
Colorado.	Mississippi.	Texas.
Illinois.	New Jersey.	Washington.
Indiana.	New Mexico.	Wisconsin.

---

[1] States making venereal disease notifiable are rapidly increasing. The list as given will undoubtedly be incomplete by the time this article is in press.

Acting upon the recognition of the foregoing principles, the machinery for control of venereal disease is being rapidly put in operation.

This machinery for actual control so far consists chiefly in the establishment of venereal disease bureaus and venereal disease clinics for diagnosis and early treatment.

. States which have bureaus or divisions especially devoted to the control of venereal diseases:

Arkansas.	Illinois.	Minnesota.
California.	Indiana.	Ohio.
Colorado.	Louisiana.	Pennsylvania.
Georgia.	Michigan.	Virginia.

States where arrangements have been made to place an officer of the United States Public Health Service in charge of venereal disease bureau:

Alabama.	Louisiana.	Ohio.
Colorado.	Maryland.	Rhode Island.
Georgia.	Massachusetts.	South Carolina.
Indiana.	Minnesota.	Virginia.
Iowa	Missouri.	Mississippi.
Kentucky.	New Hampshire.	

Both these lists are being rapidly increased. North Carolina and Kansas have medical officers of the Army as directors of their venereal disease control activities.

States which have already established venereal disease clinics as part of the machinery for control:

Alabama.	Indiana.	Minnesota.
California.	Massachusetts.	Ohio.
Connecticut.	Michigan.	Pennsylvania.

Location of venereal disease clinics operated jointly by the United States Public Health Service and American Red Cross for the protection of the civilian and military population in extra-cantonment zones:

Alexandria, La.	Des Moines, Iowa.	Macon, Ga.
Anniston, Ala.	El Paso, Tex.	Montgomery, Ala.
Atlanta, Ga.	Fort Worth, Tex.	Newport News, Va.
Augusta, Ga.	Greenville, S. C.	Petersburg, Va.
Chattanooga, Tenn.	Hattiesburg, Miss.	Portsmouth, Va.
Charlotte, N. C.	Houston, Tex.	San Antonio, Tex.
Chalicothe, Ohio.	Jacksonville, Fla.	Spartanburg, S. C.
Columbia, S. C.	Louisville, Ky.	

To insure the success of the Federal Government program for the suppression of venereal disease, it is essential that that program should have the support of every practicing physician in every State. The best thought in the medical profession of to-day concedes that every doctor should consider himself a health officer without pay.

PREVALENCE OF MALARIA IN CERTAIN STATES.

The table given below shows the results of the circularization of physicians for the purpose of ascertaining the prevalence and type of malaria during the months of January and February, 1918. A similar summary for the month of January, 1918, for Georgia, New Jersey, Ohio, Virginia, and the eastern half of Texas was published in the Public Health Reports April 5, 1918, pages 489–490.

Summary of postal-card reports of malaria.

	Ohio, Feb., 1918.	Oklahoma.		Texas (eastern half), Feb., 1918	Virginia, Feb., 1918.
		Jan., 1918.	Feb., 1918.		
Cards mailed to physicians	7,912	2,634	2,634	3,450	2,420
Cards returned unclaimed	82	18	13	65	18
Replies received	1,113	301	195	515	759
Percentage of replies received	14.21	11.50	7.43	15.21	31.59
Counties represented in replies	44	73	67	96	98
Counties not heard from	44	4	10	16	2
Towns or cities represented in replies	307	188	140	256	422
Cases of malaria reported	11	278	217	419	154
Types of infection:					
Tertian	8	195	92	177	65
Quartan	3	23	39	29	20
Estivo-autumnal		33	41	38	19
Cases reported confirmed microscopically:					
Tertian	3	38	12	38	10
Quartan		3	1	3	4
Estivo-autumnal		6	7	16	7
Cases reported confirmed, type not stated		10	34	34	
Cases of hemoglobinuric fever reported				[1] 1	[2] 1

[1] Chambers County.   [2] Southampton County.

PREVALENCE OF DISEASE.

No health department, State or local, can effectively prevent or control disease without knowledge of when, where, and under what conditions cases are occurring.

UNITED STATES.

EXTRA-CANTONMENT ZONES—CASES REPORTED WEEK ENDED MAY 21.

CAMP BEAUREGARD ZONE, LA.

	Cases.
Chicken pox:	
Alexandria	7
Dysentery:	
Rural district	1
Gonorrhea:	
Alexandria	1
Malaria:	
Alexandria	7
Pineville	1
Tioga	1
Measles:	
Alexandria	1
Mumps:	
Alexandria	19
Pellagra:	
Alexandria	1
Pneumonia:	
Pineville	1
Smallpox:	
Alexandria	3
Tuberculosis:	
Alexandria	4
Typhoid fever:	
Alexandria	2
Pineville	2
Whooping cough:	
Alexandria	2

CAMP BOWIE ZONE, TEX.

Fort Worth:	
Cerebrospinal meningitis	1
Chicken pox	3
Diphtheria	1
Gonorrhea	18
Malaria	2
Measles	6
Mumps	9
Pneumonia	1
Scabies	1
Scarlet fever	5
Smallpox	17
Syphilis	9
Tonsillitis	1
Tuberculosis	2
Typhoid fever	3

CAMP DEVENS ZONE, MASS.

	Cases.
Chicken pox:	
Lancaster	1
Lunenburg	2
Diphtheria:	
Townsend	1
German measles:	
Lunenburg	1
Measles:	
Forge Village	1
Graniteville	2
Lunenburg	1
Westford	7
Mumps:	
Ayer	1
Lancaster	2
Tuberculosis, pulmonary:	
Ayer	1
Lunenburg	1
Whooping cough	
Townsend	1

CAMP DODGE ZONE, IOWA.

Diphtheria:	
Des Moines	2
Gonorrhea:	
Des Moines	8
Measles:	
Des Moines	1
Scarlet fever:	
Des Moines	17
Grimes	1
Polk City	1
Smallpox:	
Des Moines	12
Enterprise	2
Syphilis:	
Des Moines	6

CAMP DONIPHAN ZONE, OKLA.

Measles:	
Apache	1
Smallpox:	
Cache	1

CAMP EBERTS ZONE, ARK.

	Cases.
Erysipelas:	
Austin	1
Gonorrhea:	
England	2
Kerr	2
Lonoke	2
Malaria:	
Carlisle	1
Cabot	2
England	2
Keo, route 1	3
Ward	2
Measles:	
Austin, route 1	2
Ward	2
Mumps:	
Eberts Field	2
England	1
Keo	1
Pellagra:	
Scotts	1
Pneumonia:	
Kerr	1
Kerr, route 1	1
Scarlet fever:	
Austin, route 1	1
Septic sore throat:	
Ward	1
Smallpox:	
England route 2	2
Lonoke	1
Syphilis:	
England	2
Lonoke	1
Tetanus:	
England	1
Tuberculosis:	
England	1
Scotts	1

CAMP FUNSTON ZONE, KANS.

Army City:	
Tuberculosis	1
Junction City:	
Cerebrospinal meningitis	2
Measles	4
Mumps	9
Smallpox	2
Manhattan:	
Chicken pox	3
Measles	3
Mumps	7
Pneumonia	1
Smallpox	2
Whooping cough	3

CAMP GORDON ZONE, GA.

Chicken pox:	
Atlanta	10
Diphtheria:	
Atlanta	5
Dysentery, bacillary:	
Atlanta	2
German measles:	
Atlanta	2

CAMP GORDON ZONE, GA.—continued.

	Cases.
Gonorrhea:	
Atlanta	9
Measles:	
Atlanta	8
Mumps:	
Atlanta	24
Doraville	1
Scottdale	1
Pneumonia:	
Atlanta	2
Decatur	1
Scarlet fever:	
Atlanta	1
Hapeville	1
Septic sore throat:	
Atlanta	1
Smallpox:	
Atlanta	5
East Point	1
Syphilis:	
Atlanta	2
Stone Mountain	1
Tuberculosis:	
Atlanta	2
Typhoid fever:	
Atlanta	1
Whooping cough:	
Atlanta	4
Scottdale	4

CAMP GREENE ZONE, N. C.

Charlotte Township:	
Chancroid	3
Chicken pox	3
Diphtheria	3
Gonorrhea	15
Measles	2
Mumps	9
Scarlet fever	1
Syphilis	18
Tuberculosis	1
Typhoid fever	1
Whooping cough	16

GULFPORT HEALTH DISTRICT, MISS.

Gulfort Health District:	
Chicken pox	2
Malaria	7
Measles	4
Typhoid fever	2

CAMP HANCOCK ZONE, GA.

Augusta:	
Chicken pox	2
Measles	5
Typhoid fever	1

CAMP JOSEPH E. JOHNSTON ZONE, FLA.

Chicken pox:	
Jacksonville	9
Dysentery:	
Jacksonville	7
Gonorrhea:	
Jacksonville	1

CAMP JOSEPH E. JOHNSTON ZONE, FLA.—contd.

	Cases.
Hookworm:	
Grand Crossing	3
Malaria:	
Eastport	1
South Jacksonville	1
Measles:	
Fisher's Corner	3
Jacksonville	12
Panama	1
Mumps:	
Jacksonville	8
Pellagra:	
Jacksonville	3
South Jacksonville	1
Pneumonia:	
Jacksonville	1
Moncrief	1
Panama	1
Syphilis:	
Jacksonville	1
Tuberculosis:	
Eastport	1
Jacksonville	6
Typhoid fever:	
Fisher's Corner	2
Grand Crossing	1
Jacksonville	6
Lackawanna	1
Whooping cough:	
Eastport	1
Fisher's Corner	4
Jacksonville	22
Lackawanna	10
Murray Hill	1
Panama	1
Youkon	1

FORT LEAVENWORTH ZONE, KANS.

Leavenworth:	
Measles	3
Pneumonia, lobar	1
Scarlet fever	4
Smallpox	3
Tuberculosis	1
Typhoid fever	1
Whooping cough	1
Leavenworth County:	
Pneumonia, lobar	1
Smallpox	1
Whooping cough	1

CAMP LEE ZONE, VA.

Cerebrospinal meningitis:	
Petersburg	2
Diphtheria:	
Hopewell	1
German measles:	
Prince George County	11
Gonorrhea:	
Petersburg	15
Measles:	
Chesterfield County	1
Mumps:	
Chesterfield County	1
Hopewell	2
Prince George County	5

CAMP LEE ZONE, VA—continued.

	Cases.
Pneumonia:	
Prince George County	1
Scarlet fever:	
Hopewell	2
Petersburg	1
Septic sore throat:	
Petersburg	1
Smallpox:	
Hopewell	4
Syphilis:	
Petersburg	2
Tonsilitis:	
Chesterfield County	1
Tuberculosis:	
Petersburg	1
Typhoid fever:	
Petersburg	1
Whooping cough:	
Petersburg	1

CAMP LEWIS ZONE, WASH.

Cerebrospinal meningitis:	
Parkland	1
Mumps:	
Custer	1
Dupont	1
Locamas	1
Scarlet fever:	
Park Lodge	1
Steilacoom Lake	1
Tuberculosis, pulmonary:	
Roy	1

CAMP LOGAN ZONE, TEX.

Goose Creek:	
Syphilis	2
Houston:	
Chancroid	4
Gonorrhea	23
Malaria	1
Measles	3
Mumps	1
Pneumonia	1
Syphilis	21
Smallpox	1
Tuberculosis	3
Round Top:	
Gonorrhea	4

CAMP MACARTHUR ZONE, TEX.

Waco:	
Chicken pox	2
Dysentery, bacillary	1
Gonorrhea	2
Measles	4
Mumps	31
Pneumonia, lobar	1
Scarlet fever	1
Smallpox	1
Syphilis	3
Tuberculosis	2
Typhoid fever	1

CAMP M'CLELLAN ZONE, ALA.

Anniston:	
Chicken pox	1
Erysipelas	1

CAMP M'CLELLAN ZONE, ALA.—continued.

Anniston—Continued. Cases.

Malaria.. 1
Measles... 1
Tuberculosis..................................... 4

Precinct 20:
Chicken pox.................................... 3

NORFOLK COUNTY NAVAL DISTRICT, VA.

Cerebrospinal meningitis:
Labor Camp.................................. 1
Norfolk... 1
Quartermaster Terminal.................. 2
Conjunctivitis:
Norfolk County.............................. 1
Portsmouth................................... 1
Diphtheria:
Ocean View.................................. 1
Measles:
South Norfolk................................ 5
Norfolk... 16
Portsmouth................................... 3
Deep Creek................................... 1
Ocean View.................................. 1
Norfolk County.............................. 1
Mumps:
Norfolk... 5
Ocean View.................................. 2
Pneumonia:
Ocean View.................................. 1
Scarlet fever:
Norfolk County.............................. 1
Ocean View.................................. 1
Norfolk... 1
Smallpox:
Quartermaster Terminal.................. 1
Tuberculosis:
Ocean View.................................. 1
Portsmouth................................... 2
Norfolk County.............................. 1
Logan Park................................... 1
Varicella:
Norfolk County.............................. 1

FORT OGLETHORPE ZONE, GA.

Chicken pox:
Alton Park.................................... 1
Chattanooga................................. 1
Gonorrhea:
Chattanooga................................. 6
Measles:
Chattanooga................................. 1
East Lake..................................... 1
Mumps:
Chattanooga................................. 1
East Chattanooga.......................... 2
North Chattanooga........................ 1
St. Elmo...................................... 1
Scarlet fever:
Chattanooga................................. 1
St. Elmo...................................... 1
Smallpox:
Chattanooga................................. 1
Syphilis:
Chattanooga................................. 16

FORT OGLETHORPE ZONE, GA.—continued.

Tuberculosis: Cases.
St. Elmo...................................... 1
Whooping cough:
Chattanooga................................. 1

CAMP PIKE ZONE, ARK.

Little Rock:
Chicken pox.................................. 2
Gonorrhea.................................... 6
Malaria.. 8
Measles....................................... 5
Mumps.. 5
Pleurisy....................................... 1
Pneumonia................................... 5
Scarlet fever................................. 4
Smallpox...................................... 2
Syphilis.. 8
Tuberculosis................................. 3
Whooping cough............................ 2
North Little Rock:
Chicken pox.................................. 2
Gonorrhea.................................... 4
Mumps.. 4
Tuberculosis................................. 1
Syphilis.. 1
Protho:
Gonorrhea.................................... 1
Scotts:
Gonorrhea.................................... 2
(Not located:)
Malaria.. 1

CAMP SEVIER ZONE, S. C.

Chicken pox:
Greenville Township....................... 2
Dysentery:
Butler Township............................ 1
Mumps:
Chick Springs Township.................. 6
Pneumonia:
Greenville Township....................... 1

CAMP SHELBY ZONE, MISS.

Hattiesburg:
Chicken pox.................................. 2
Hookworm.................................... 2
Malaria.. 6
Mumps.. 10
Tuberculosis, pulmonary.................. 1
Venereal....................................... 6
Whooping cough............................ 10

CAMP SHERIDAN ZONE, ALA

Montgomery:
Chancroid..................................... 6
Chicken pox.................................. 5
Gonorrhea.................................... 28
Measles....................................... 3
Mumps.. 8
Ringworm..................................... 19
Smallpox...................................... 4
Syphilis.. 6
Tuberculosis................................. 2

CAMP SHERIDAN ZONE, ALA.—continued.

Montgomery County: Cases.
  Malaria...................................... 1
  Measles..................................... 2

CAMP SHERMAN ZONE, OHIO.

Diphtheria:
  Chillicothe................................. 1
Measles:
  Chillicothe................................. 1
  Liberty Township........................... 3
Mumps:
  Chillicothe................................. 3
Rabies in animals:
  Chillicothe................................. 1
Scarlet fever:
  Chillicothe................................. 4
  Scioto Township............................ 1

TIDEWATER HEALTH DISTRICT, VA.

Hampton:
  Mumps..................................... 4
  Whooping cough............................ 2
Newport News:
  Chancroid.................................. 1
  Chicken pox................................ 2
  Gonorrhea................................. 10
  Measles.................................... 4
  Mumps..................................... 3
  Syphilis................................... 2
Phoebus:
  Whooping cough............................ 4

CAMP TRAVIS ZONE, TEX.

San Antonio:
  Chancroid.................................. 2
  Colitis.................................... 1
  Diphtheria................................. 2
  Dysentery.................................. 1
  Gonorrhea................................. 28
  Mumps..................................... 2
  Otitis media............................... 1
  Pneumonia................................. 1

CAMP TRAVIS ZONE, TEX.—continued.

San Antonio—Continued.   Cases.
  Syphilis.................................... 7
  Tuberculosis................................ 4
  Typhoid fever.............................. 6

CAMP WADSWORTH ZONE, S. C.

Chicken pox:
  Spartanburg................................ 1
German measles:
  Moore...................................... 1
  Pauline.................................... 2
Measles:
  Pauline.................................... 1
  Spartanburg................................ 8
Mumps:
  Drayton Mills.............................. 1
  Spartanburg................................ 2
  White Stone................................ 1
Smallpox:
  Pauline.................................... 1
Syphilis:
  Spartanburg................................ 1
Tuberculosis:
  Cedar Springs.............................. 1
  Spartanburg................................ 2
Whooping cough:
  Drayton Mills.............................. 5
  Spartanburg................................ 6

CAMP WHEELER ZONE, GA.

East Macon:
  Hookworm.................................. 1
  Typhoid fever.............................. 1
Macon:
  Chicken pox................................ 1
  Gonorrhea.................................. 9
  Malaria.................................... 4
  Measles.................................... 2
  Mumps..................................... 4
  Pellagra................................... 1
  Smallpox................................... 4
  Syphilis................................... 5
  Tuberculosis............................... 2
  Whooping cough............................ 1

DISEASE CONDITIONS AMONG TROOPS IN THE UNITED STATES.

The following data are taken from telegraphic reports received in the office of the Surgeon General, United States Army, for the week ended May 10, 1918:

Annual admission rate per 1,000 (disease only):
  All troops............................... 1,335 5
  National Guard camps................. 917 3
  National Army camps................. 1,459 5
  Regular Army......................... 1,148 2
Noneffective rate per 1,000 on day of report:
  All troops 40 8
  National Guard camps................. 37.7

Noneffective rate per 1,000 on day of report—Continued.
  National Army camps................. 46.7
  Regular Army......................... 37
Annual death rate 1,000 (disease only):
  All troops................................ 5.3
  National Guard camps................. 2.8
  National Army camps................. 6
  Regular Army......................... 5.9

New cases of special diseases reported during the week ended May 10, 1918.

Camps.	Pneumonia.	Dysentery.	Malaria.	Venereal.		Measles.	Meningitis.	Scarlet fever.	Deaths.	Annual admission rate per 1,000 (disease only).	Noneffective per 1,000 on day of report.
				Total.	New infections.						
Wadsworth	1			37		1				1,083.3	48.8
Hancock				22		1				515.2	35.8
McClellan	2		3	29	19		1		2	582.4	29.2
Sevier	1		2	28	16		2		4	293.3	29.9
Wheeler	2	2	2	22	3				4	987.6	43.7
Logan	8	2		31	20	8	1	6	1	2,105.7	68.7
Cody	9			3						449.3	23.6
Bowie	3		1	41	41	1			12	1,254.1	38.6
Sheridan				21	14					462.4	28
Shelby	1	6	1	13		1			2	864.5	41
Beauregard	9		13	25	3				2	1,935.3	60.7
Kearny	3		1	5		3	1	1	2	1,162.9	35.5
Devens	15			686	3	18	1	2	1	868.3	42.8
Upton	9			231	16	5		6	4	1,308.4	41.7
Dix	1			175	3	25		39	1	1,309.2	31.6
Meade	10			124	4	6	2	3	4	1,070.7	30.9
Lee	4		1	202	10	26	2		1	977.5	38.7
Jackson	23		2	236	5	20	1		1	2,771.2	66.7
Gordon	56		2	85	85	88	5	2	7	2,207.8	56.4
Sherman	9			153	6	12		10	3	1,252.3	39.7
Taylor	17			42	2	19		2	3	2,115.1	69.7
Custer	38			364	3	9		9	8	1,621.2	31.8
Grant	8			45		12		2	3	764.9	29.1
Pike	25		4	61	9	22	2		2	2,340.2	66.3
Dodge	46			97		36		6	17	1,885.3	79.5
Funston	55			38	12	13	3	4	9	1,305.1	49.4
Travis	16		4	164		5			2	3,041.5	55.1
Lewis	9		1	252	4	9	1	16	3	1,466.5	37.3
Northeastern Department				9		2		4		837	30.3
Eastern Department	3			31	10	3		1	5	988.6	29.6
Southeastern Department	1		4	56	10	6	1		4	1,058.8	31.7
Central Department	8			12	9	8		9	1	1,188.3	44
Southern Department	10		1	96	31	7		16	14	1,220.2	41.4
Western Department	2	2	3	18	11	10		5	1	854.4	24.4
Aviation, Signal Corps	23	5	5	132		26	2	20	15	1,158.1	32.5
Camp Greene	1		1	19	19	4				570.4	18.8
Camp Fremont		1	1	12	5	14				866.1	36.7
El Paso				6	6			1		794.7	4.6
Columbus Barracks				11						796.5	23.2
Jefferson Barracks	7			44	4	3		4	3	1,933	60.5
Fort Logan	2			3	2	4		2	1	1,387.9	78.9
Fort McDowell			1	41						2,157.1	58.5
Fort Slocum	1			33		1			2	1,495	38.4
Fort Thomas				8		8			1	1,256.7	29.5
Disciplinary Barracks, Alcatraz										330.1	6.3
Disciplinary Barracks, Fort Leavenworth				2						1,438.3	45.9
A. A. Humphreys	8			25		7				563.5	9.2
J. E. Johnston	10		2	42	25	13	3	6	1	1,355.5	37.3
Hoboken, N. J	16		1	245	17	13	3	10	8	1,070.4	49.9
Camp Stuart	13	1	3	107	16	17	3	1	5	1,605.8	55.8
West Point, N. Y										609.1	6.2
Edgewood-Aberdeen								1	1	487.7	17.3
Prov. Depot for Corps and Army Troops	3		1	45	4	4		1		1,404.2	47.1
Camp Holabird				2						448.7	3.2
Camp Raritan										493.7	26.3
Springfield Armory	1					1				1,599.9	35.9
National Guard departments				14	7	3	1				
National Army departments	10		1	316	53	34	1	11	5		
MacArthur						1			1	810.1	50.2
Doniphan	5			19		2	1	5	1	3,888.1	97.6
Total	504	19	60	4,580	487	531	37	205	167	1,335.5	40.8

Annual rate per 1,000 for special diseases.

Disease.	All troops in United States.[1]	Regulars in United States.[1]	National Guard, all camps.[1]	National Army, all camps.[1]	Expeditionary forces.[2]
Pneumonia	20.0	13.8	8.3	31.2	23.5
Dysentery	.7	1.1	2.1	0.0	.7
Malaria	2.4	2.6	4.9	1.3	1.2
Venereal	182.5	12 3.3	59.1	270.9	35.1
Paratyphoid	.2	.6			
Typhoid	.1	.3			.2
Measles	21.1	18.6	3.2	29.8	8.5
Meningitis	1.4	1.57	1.0	1.5	2.4
Scarlet fever	8.1	10.4	1.5	9.2	8.3

[1] Week ended May 10, 1918.   [2] Week ended May 2, 1918.

CURRENT STATE SUMMARIES.

California.

From the State Board of Health of California, by telegraph, for the week ended May 18, 1918:

Three cases cerebrospinal meningitis; 1 Lindsay, 1 San Francisco, 1 Los Angeles. Three cases poliomyelitis; 1 San Francisco, 1 Los Angeles, 1 Riverside County. Thirty cases smallpox; 11 reported from Tehama County, also prevalent in Imperial and Tulare Counties. Measles still prevalent in Los Angeles city and San Francisco; about 500 cases throughout California.

Reported by mail for preceding week (ended May 11):

Cerebrospinal meningitis	4	Pellagra	2
Chicken pox	129	Pneumonia	53
Diphtheria	53	Poliomyelitis	1
Dysentery	2	Scarlet fever	71
Erysipelas	13	Smallpox	54
German meas'es	110	Syphilis	50
Gonococcus infection	79	Tetanus	1
Malaria	14	Trachoma	2
Measles	598	Tuberculosis	166
Mumps	129	Typhoid fever	27
Paratyphoid	1	Whooping cough	138

Connecticut.

From Collaborating Epidemiologist Black, by telegraph, for week ended May 18, 1918:

Meningitis. Hartford 1, New Britain 1, New Haven 1, Bridgeport 1. Smallpox: Colebrook 1.

Illinois.

From Collaborating Epidemiologist Drake, by telegraph, for week ended May 18, 1918:

Diphtheria: 128, of which in Chicago 111. Scarlet fever: 96, of which in Chicago 57. Smallpox: 126, of which in Quincy 9, Canton 5, Onarga 16, Alton 6, Peoria 7, Evansville 6, Belleville 6. Meningitis 13, of which in Chicago 12, Spring Lake Township (Tazewell County) 1. Poliomyelitis: Chicago 2.

Indiana.

From the State Board of Health of Indiana, by telegraph, for week ended May 18, 1918:

Smallpox: Epidemic Orleans. Scarlet fever: Epidemic Portland. Measles: One death Cannelton. Whooping cough: Epidemic Rushville, 2 deaths Carthage, 1 death each Colfax, Rushville. Rabies: Epidemic dogs Pike County.

Kansas.

From Collaborating Epidemiologist Crumbine, by telegraph, for week ended May 18, 1918:

Small pox (10 or more cases): In counties—Butler 17, Linn 15, Pawnee 10, Reno 10, Sedgwick 11; in cities—Coffeyville 14, Topeka 12. Scarlet fever (10 or more cases): In cities—Hutchinson 11, Topeka 14, Kansas City 10. Meningitis: Caney 1.

Louisiana.

From Collaborating Epidemiologist Dowling, by telegraph, for week ended May 18, 1918:

Meningitis 1, smallpox 29, typhoid 29, malaria 31.

Massachusetts.

From Collaborating Epidemiologist Hitchcock, by telegraph, for week ended May 18, 1918:

Unusual prevalence. Measles: Foxboro 22, Hingham 22, Hopedale 16, Lawrence 177, Malden 77, Stoneham 49, Upton 19, Waltham 53, Westford 22.

Minnesota.

From Collaborating Epidemiologist Bracken, by telegraph, for week ended May 18, 1918:

Smallpox, new foci: Carver County, Watertown Township, 6; Rice County, Walcott Township, 1. Seven cerebrospinal meningitis, 1 poliomyelitis, reported since May 13.

Nebraska.

From State Board of Health of Nebraska, by telegraph, for week ended May 18, 1918:

Typhoid fever: Winside. Smallpox: Marion, Albion, Verdon.

New Jersey.

From Collaborating Epidemiologist Bowen, by telegraph, for week ended May 18, 1918:

Unusual prevalence. German measles: Dover (Morris County), Westfield. Whooping cough: Paterson. Measles: Lakewood, Passaic, Paterson, Elizabeth, Ramsey, Northampton Township, Palmyra Township, East Orange, Orange, Westfield.

CEREBROSPINAL MENINGITIS—Continued.

City Reports for Week Ended May 4, 1918.

Place.	Cases.	Deaths.	Place.	Cases.	Deaths.
Atlanta, Ga.		2	Milwaukee, Wis.	3	2
Baltimore, Md.	7	4	Moline, Ill.	1	
Birmingham, Ala.	2	2	Newark, N. J.	2	3
..... Mass.	5	4	New York, N. Y.	7	10
..... Ill.	1		North Braddock, Pa.	1	
Chattanooga, Tenn.	1		Omaha, Nebr.	1	1
Chicago, Ill.	13	3	Philadelphia, Pa.	10	4
Cincinnati, Ohio.	2	2	Pittsfield, Mass.	1	
Cleveland, Ohio.	4		Portland, Oreg.	1	1
Columbia, S. C.	2		Providence, R. I.	3	1
Council Bluffs, Iowa.	1		St. Louis, Mo.	8	2
Dallas, Tex.	1	1	San Francisco, Cal.	2	
Detroit, Mich.	3	4	Savannah, Ga.	1	1
Dubuque, Iowa.		1	Scranton, Pa.	1	
Fall River, Mass.		1	Sioux City, Iowa.	1	1
Fitchburg, Mass.	1		Springfield, Ill.	1	
Greenville, S. C.	1		Troy, N. Y.		
Hartford, Conn.			Washington, D. C.	4	1
Indianapolis, Ind.	1	1	Wheeling, W. Va.	1	
Kansas City, Kans.	1		Wichita, Kans.	1	
Los Angeles, Cal.	2		Worcester, Mass.	1	
Lowell, Mass.	1		York, Pa.	2	

DENGUE.

Louisiana.

During the period from May 4 to 19, 1918, 119 cases of dengue of very mild type were notified in Louisiana.

DIPHTHERIA.

See Diphtheria, measles, scarlet fever, and tuberculosis, page 825.

ERYSIPELAS.

City Reports for Week Ended May 4, 1918.

Place.	Cases.	Deaths.	Place.	Cases.	Deaths.
Baltimore, Md.	2	1	Milwaukee, Wis.	3	
Bayonne, N. J.	1		Morgantown, W. Va.	1	
Beloit, Wis.		1	Mount... N. J.	1	
Berkeley, Cal.	1		Newark, N. J.	10	
Boston, Mass.	1	5	New York, N. Y.		7
Brockton, Mass.	1		Omaha, Nebr.	2	1
Buffalo, N. Y.	4		Philadelphia, Pa.	7	3
Chicago, Ill.	29	2	Portland, Oreg.	2	
Cleveland, Ohio.	6	1	Providence, R. I.		2
Denver, Colo.		1	Richmond, Va.	1	1
Detroit, Mich.	5	1	Rochester, N. Y.	1	
Duluth, Minn.	1		Rock Island, Ill.	1	
Grand Rapids, Mich.	1		Saginaw, Mich.	1	
Hagerstown, Md.	1		St. Joseph, Mo.	1	
Kansas City, Kans.	1		St. Louis, Mo.	8	2
Los Angeles, Cal.	1	1	Steubenville, Ohio.	1	
Louisville, Ky.	1		Superior, Wis.		1
Marinette, Wis.	1		Wheeling, W. Va.	1	
Memphis, Tenn.	2	1			

MALARIA.

State Reports for April, 1918.

Place.	New cases reported.	Place.	New cases reported.
Louisiana:		Louisiana—Continued.	
Ascension Parish	2	St. Tammany Parish	8
Avoyelles Parish	3	Vermilion Parish	7
Bienville Parish	1	Washington Parish	2
East Feliciana Parish	6	Webster Parish	1
Iberia Parish	1	West Feliciana Parish	1
Lafayette Parish	2		
Livingston Parish	1	Total	126
Madison Parish	4		
Morehouse Parish	1	Massachusetts:	
Natchitoches Parish	2	Essex County—	
Ouachita Parish	6	Lynn	1
Rapides Parish	57	Middlesex County—	
St. Charles Parish	1	Newton	1
St. Helena Parish	3	Norfolk County—	
St. James Parish	1	Dedham (town)	2
St. John Parish	2	Suffolk County—	
St. Landry Parish	2	Boston (town)	1
St. Martin Parish	11		
St. Mary Parish	1	Total	5

City Reports for Week Ended May 4, 1918.

Place.	Cases.	Deaths.	Place.	Cases.	Deaths.
Austin, Tex		1	Macon, Ga	1	
Beaumont, Tex	1		Marshall, Tex	2	
Birmingham, Ala	3		Montgomery, Ala	75	
Cape Girardeau, Mo	14		New Orleans, La	1	
Centralia, Ill	2		Orange, N. J		1
Dallas, Tex		1	Palestine, Tex	18	
Hattiesburg, Miss	2		Savannah, Ga		1
Little Rock, Ark	4		Tuscaloosa, Ala	1	
Lynn, Mass	1				

MEASLES.

See Diphtheria, measles, scarlet fever, and tuberculosis page 825.

PELLAGRA.

State Reports for April, 1918.

Place.	New cases reported.	Place.	New cases reported.
Louisiana:		Massachusetts:	
Jackson Parish	1	Hampshire County—	
Jefferson Davis Parish	1	Northampton	1
Lincoln Parish	1	Middlesex County—	
Morehouse Parish	4	Cambridge	1
Natchitoches Parish	1		
Orleans Parish	5	Total	2
Rapides Parish	4		
St. John Parish	1	Nebraska:	
St. Martin Parish	1	Lancaster County	1
Total	19		

58

PELLAGRA—Continued.

City Reports for Week Ended May 4, 1918.

Place.	Cases.	Deaths.	Place.	Cases.	Deaths.
Atlanta, Ga		1	Mobile, Ala	2	1
Austin, Tex		1	Montgomery, Ala	1	
Birmingham, Ala	8	7	New Orleans, La	2	2
Charleston, S. C		2	Northampton, Mass		1
Columbia, S. C	1		Palestine, Tex	2	
Fort Worth, Tex	3	3	Richmond, Va	1	
Los Angeles, Cal		1	Spartanburg, S. C	1	
Marshall, Tex	1		Washington, D. C	1	1
Memphis, Tenn	3				

PNEUMONIA.

City Reports for Week Ended May 4, 1918.

Place.	Cases.	Deaths.	Place.	Cases.	Deaths.
Abilene, Tex	2		Little Rock, Ark	8	1
Alameda, Cal	1	1	Lorain, Ohio	2	
Amsterdam, N. Y	3	1	Los Angeles, Cal	13	11
Anderson, Ind	2		Louisville, Ky	8	9
Anniston, Ala	1		Lowell, Mass	2	3
Ashtabula, Ohio			Lynn, Mass	3	1
Atlanta, Ga	1	15	Manchester, N. H	3	3
Attleboro, Mass	6		Marshall, Tex	1	
Auburn, N. Y	3		Melrose, Mass	1	
Baltimore, Md	25	9	Middletown, N. Y	1	
Berkeley, Cal	1		Montgomery, Ala	1	
Beverly, Mass	3	1	Morgantown, W. Va	1	
Binghamton, N. Y	3		Muskegon, Mich	1	1
Boston, Mass	34	30	Newark, N. J	73	7
Brockton, Mass	2	1	New Bedford, Mass	3	2
Buffalo, N. Y	2	12	New Britain, Conn	1	2
Cambridge, Mass	10	2	Newburyport, Mass	2	1
Centralia, Ill	3		New Castle, Pa	2	2
Chattanooga, Tenn	1	1	Newport, Ky	3	3
Chelsea, Mass	4		Newton, Mass	2	
Chicago, Ill	237	108	Norfolk, Va	1	4
Cleveland, Ohio	31	20	North Adams, Mass	1	
Clinton, Mass	3	2	Northampton, Mass	1	1
Cumberland, Md	5	1	South Attleboro, Mass	1	
Dallas, Tex	2	4	Oakland, Cal	1	10
Dayton, Ohio	2	1	Oak Park, Ill	3	3
Detroit, Mich	16	52	Ogden, Utah	3	
Duluth, Minn	8	2	Oshkosh, Wis	4	4
Elmira, N. Y	3	7	Paris, Tex	2	2
Everett, Mass	1		Parkersburg, W. Va	3	3
Fall River, Mass	5	2	Petersburg, Va	1	1
Fargo, N. Dak	1	1	Philadelphia, Pa	112	61
Fitchburg, Mass	1		Pontiac, Mich	1	
Flint, Mich	7	3	Port Chester, N. Y	1	
Fort Worth, Tex	4	4	Richmond, Va	8	3
Framingham, Mass	3		Rochester, N. Y	9	4
Fremont, Ohio	2	2	Salem, Mass	3	1
Grand Rapids, Mich	16	3	San Diego, Cal	6	6
Hagerstown, Md	3		Sandusky, Ohio	1	2
Harrison, N. J	1		San Francisco, Cal	13	9
Haverhill, Mass	9	2	Schenectady, N. Y	5	3
Holyoke, Mass	1	2	Somerville, Mass	7	2
Independence, Mo	1	2	Springfield, Mass	6	5
Jamestown, N. Y	13	3	Toledo, Ohio	1	7
Kalamazoo, Mich	2	3	Wichita, Kans	1	
Kansas City, Kans	4		Winthrop, Mass	2	
Kokomo, Ind	2		Worcester, Mass	14	10
Lackawanna, N. Y	4		Yonkers, N. Y	6	3
Lawrence, Mass	3	2	Youngstown, Ohio	2	3

POLIOMYELITIS (INFANTILE PARALYSIS).

State Reports for April, 1918.

Place.	New cases reported.	Place.	New cases reported.
Maryland:		**Nebraska:**	
Allegany County—		Madison County......................	1
Westernport...................,....	2		
Garrett County—		**New York:**	
Cove..............................	1	Cattaraugus County—	
		Olean...........................	1
Total........................	3	Dutchess County—	
		Poughkeepsio.....................	1
Massachusetts:		Westchester County—	
Essex County—		Yonkers...........................	1
Methuen.......................	1		
Hampden County—		Total........................	3
Springfield.....................	1		
Middlesex County—		**Wisconsin:**	
Cambridge.....................	1	Kenosha County....................	1
Lowell.........................	1	Milwaukee County.................	25
Medford.......................	1	Racine County....................	1
Suffolk County—		Winnebago County.................	1
Boston.........................	1		
		Total........................	28
Total........................	6		

City Reports for Week Ended May 4, 1918.

Place.	Cases.	Deaths.	Place.	Cases.	Deaths.
Battle Creek, Mich...........	....	1	New York, N. Y..............	1	1
Chicago, Ill...................	2	....	Omaha, Nebr.................	1	....
Los Angeles, Cal..............	1	....	St. Louis, Mo................	1	1
Milwaukee, Wis..............	1	....			

RABIES IN ANIMALS.

City Reports for Week Ended May 4, 1918.

There were reported during the week ended May 4, 1918, three cases of rabies in animals at Louisville, Ky., and two cases at Winston-Salem, N. C.

ROCKY MOUNTAIN SPOTTED FEVER.

Montana.

On May 20, 1918, 2 cases of Rocky Mountain spotted fever were reported in Montana, 1 at Hamilton and 1 at Bridger.

SCARLET FEVER.

See Diphtheria, measles, scarlet fever, and tuberculosis, page 825.

SMALLPOX.

State Reports for April, 1918.

Place.	New cases reported.	Deaths.	Vaccination history of cases.			
			Number vaccinated within 7 years preceding attack.	Number last vaccinated more than 7 years preceding attack.	Number never successfully vaccinated.	Vaccination history not obtained or uncertain.
Massachusetts:						
Middlesex County—						
Tewksbury	1				1	
Suffolk County—						
Chelsea	1				1	
Total	2				2	
New York:						
Albany County—						
Coeymans	1				1	
Westerlo	8			1	7	
Chautauqua County—						
Jamestown	3				3	
Carroll (town)	1				1	
Poland (town)	1			1		
Chemung County—						
Elmira	2				2	
Horseheads (town)	3				3	
Chenango County—						
Norwich	1				1	
Greene	5		1	2	2	
Smyrna (town)	1					1
Delaware County—						
Meredith	2			1	1	
Erie County						
Buffalo	8				5	3
Depew	3				3	
Lancaster	2				2	
Jefferson County—						
Watertown	9				9	
Niagara County—						
Niagara Falls	4				4	
Oneida County—						
Utica	1				1	
Kirkland (town)	1				1	
Whitestown (town)	1					1
Otsego County						
Morris	2				2	
New York City	2			1	1	
	61		2	5	49	5

Miscellaneous State Reports for March and April, 1918.

Place.	Cases.	Deaths.	Place.	Cases.	Deaths.
Louisiana (North):			Louisiana—Continued.		
Alba Parish	2		Lincoln Parish	1	
Caldwell Parish	8		Morehouse Parish	6	
Caroll Parish	1		Ouachita Parish	20	
Claiborne Parish	4		Richland Parish	1	
Catahoula Parish	1		Rapides Parish	15	
Grant Parish	1		Red River Parish	1	
Concordia Parish	14		Tensas Parish	4	
Franklin Parish	1		West Parish	13	
East Parish	4				
DeSoto Parish	2		Total	141	
Lafourche Parish	1				

SMALLPOX—Continued.

Miscellaneous State Reports for March and April, 1918—Continued.

Place.	Cases.	Deaths.	Place.	Cases.	Deaths.
Maine (March):			**Nebraska —Continued.**		
Androscoggin County—			Clay County............	4	....
Lewiston.............	2	....	Colfax County...........	10	....
Aroostook County—			Custer County...........	58	....
St. Francis (planta-			Dawes County...........	24	....
tion)...............	1	....	Dixon County...........	21	....
Frenchville (town)...	12	....	Douglas County..........	98	....
Dyer Brook (town)...	2	....	Fillmore County.........	11	....
Glasier Lake.........	1	....	Franklin County.........	4	....
Stockholm (town)....	1	....	Furnas County...........	10	....
Madawaska (town)...	2	....	Gage County............	2	....
Fort Fairfield (town).	11	....	Grant County...........	3	....
Smyrna (town).......	1	....	Hall County.............	56	....
Cumberland County—			Hamilton County........	1	....
Brunswick (town)....	1	....	Hitchcock County........	8	....
Kennebec County—			Holt County.............	1	....
Augusta.............	13	....	Howard County..........	2	....
Rome (town)........	2	....	Jefferson County.........	1	....
Oxford County—			Johnson County..........	5	....
Bethel (town)........	1	....	Knox County............	1	....
Penobscot County—			Lancaster County........	37	....
Old town............	4	....	Madison County.........	35	....
Orono (town)........	3	....	Merrick County..........	7	....
Piscataquis County—			Otoe County.............	15	....
Foxcroft (town)......	1	....	Pawnee County..........	37	....
Greenville (town).....	33	....	Phelps County...........	1	....
Sagadahoc County—			Platt County............	1	....
Richmond (town)....	2	....	Polk County.............	6	....
Somerset County—			Richardson County.......	11	....
Madison (town)......	3	....	Scotts Bluff County......	25	....
Norridgewock (town).	1	....	Seward County..........	39	....
Caratunk (plantation)	3	....	Sheridan County.........	13	....
The Forks (planta-			Thayer County..........	2	....
tion)...............	1	....	Washington County......	2	....
West Forks (planta-			Wayne County...........	1	....
tion)...............	11	....	Webster County.........	11	....
Holeb Township......	2	....	Wheeler County.........	1	....
Washington County—			York County............	2	....
Lubec (town)........	12	....			
Columbia (town)	1	....	Total.................	613	....
Baileyville (town)...	3	....			
Trescott (town)......	2	....	**Wisconsin (April):**		
			Bayfield County..........	1	....
Total.............	132	....	Buffalo County...........	2	....
			Chippewa County.........	44	....
Maryland (April):			Columbia County.........	2	....
Allegany County—			Crawford County.........	1	....
Cumberland.........	1	....	Dane County.............	15	....
Anne Arundel County—			Douglas County..........	5	....
Brooklyn............	2	....	Eau Claire County........	4	....
Baltimore County—			Fond du Lac County......	1	....
Sparrows Point......	3	....	Grant County...........	27	....
Caroline County—			Green County............	80	....
Federalburg..........	2	....	Jackson County..........	1	....
Cecil County—			Jefferson County.........	5	....
Principio Furnace....	1	....	Juneau County..........	6	....
Charles County—			Kenosha County.........	7	....
Waldorf.............	1	....	La Crosse County........	15	....
Dorchester County—			Lincoln County..........	16	....
Cambridge...........	2	....	Manitowoc County.......	6	....
Howard County—			Marathon County........	11	....
Jessup...............	1	....	Marquette County........	8	....
Savage..............	9	....	Milwaukee County.......	22	....
Prince George County—			Monroe County..........	9	....
Laurel..............	4	....	Oconto County..........	5	....
Somerset County—			Oneida County..........	1	....
Rouds Point........	2	....	Outagamie County.......	1	....
Smiths Island.......	3	....	Price County............	2	....
Baltimore.................	10	....	Racine County..........	1	.1.......
			Rock County............	16	....
Total.................	41	....	Rusk County............	2	....
			St. Croix County........	11	....
Nebraska (April):			Sheboygan County.......	1	....
Adams County............	16	....	Trempealeau County.....	1	....
Blaine County............	2	....	Vernon County..........	11	....
Box Butte County........	4	....	Waukesha County........	2	....
Burt County.............	4	....	Waupaca County.........	6	....
Butler County............	5	....	Winnebago County.......	6	....
Cass County.............	5	....	Wood County............	12	....
Cherry County...........	16	....			
Cheyenne County........	25	....	Total.................	369	....

SMALLPOX—Continued.

City Reports for Week Ended May 4, 1918.

Place.	Cases.	Deaths.	Place.	Cases.	Deaths.
Abilene, Tex	5		Knoxville, Tenn	4	
Alton, Ill	7		La Crosse, Wis	2	
Anderson, Ind	6		Leavenworth, Kans	1	
Anniston, Ala	12		Lima, Ohio	4	
Ashtabula, Ohio	2		Little Rock, Ark	7	
Atlanta, Ga	3		Lorain, Ohio	2	
Baltimore, Md	1		Louisville, Ky	8	
Birmingham, Ala	31		Lynchburg, Va	3	
Bloomington, Ind	2		Lynn, Mass	1	
Buffalo, N. Y	2		Macon, Ga	2	
Burlington, Iowa	3		Madison, Wis	4	
Cairo, Ill	1		Marion, Ind	2	
Cape Girardeau, Mo	1		Marshalltown, Iowa	12	
Centralia, Ill	1		Mason City, Iowa	2	
Chanute, Kans	1		Memphis, Tenn	6	
Chattanooga, Tenn	3		Milwaukee, Wis	6	
Cheyenne, Wyo	2		Minneapolis, Minn	15	
Chicago, Ill	6		Missoula, Mont	1	
Chillicothe, Ohio	3		Mobile, Ala	7	
Cincinnati, Ohio	13		Montgomery, Ala	1	
Cleveland, Ohio	33		Muncie, Ind	6	
Coffeyville, Kans	9		Muscatine, Iowa	2	
Columbus, Ohio	2		Muskegon, Mich	7	
Council Bluffs, Iowa	11		New Albany, Ind	8	
Covington, Ky	1		New Orleans, La	3	
Dallas, Tex	14		New Rochelle, N. Y		1
Davenport, Iowa	1		Norfolk, Va	1	
Dayton, Ohio	4		Ogden, Utah	2	
Denver, Colo	38		Oklahoma City, Okla	22	
Des Moines, Iowa	16		Omaha, Nebr	20	
Detroit, Mich	12		Parkersburg, W. Va	3	
Dubuque, Iowa	2		Peoria, Ill	6	
Duluth, N. Y	1		Philadelphia, Pa	2	
East Liverpool, Ohio	3		Pittsburgh, Pa	1	
Eau Claire, Wis	1		Pontiac, Mich	10	
Elmira, N. Y	1		Provo, Utah	1	
Erie, Pa	4		Quincy, Ill	10	
Evansville, Ind	3		Roanoke, Va	3	
Everett, Wash	1		St. Joseph, Mo	8	
Fairmont, W. Va	1		St. Louis, Mo	7	
Fargo, N. Dak	2		Salina, Kans	3	
Farrell, Pa	1		Salt Lake City, Utah	10	
Flint, Mich	2		San Francisco, Cal	4	
Fort Scott, Kans	4		Seattle, Wash	12	
Fort Smith, Ark	2		Sioux City, Iowa	10	
Fort Wayne, Ind	2		South Bend, Ind	8	
Fort Worth, Tex	17		Spartanburg, S. C	2	
Fresno, Cal	2		Spokane, Wash	8	
Galesburg, Ill	3		Springfield, Ill	3	
Galveston, Tex	1		Springfield, Mo	8	
Grand Rapid, Mich	1		Steelton, Pa	2	
Greeley, Colo	4		Tacoma, Wash	1	
Hammond, Ind	5		Topeka, Kans	1	
Independence, Kans	2		Tuscaloosa, Ala	1	
Independence, Mo	4		Utica, N. Y	3	
Indianapolis, Ind	49		Waco, Tex	1	
Iola, Kans	3		Washington, D. C	1	
Jamestown, N. Y	5		Waterloo, Iowa	2	
Junction City, Wis	1		Wichita, Kans	17	
Kalamazoo, Mich	7		Winston-Salem, N. C	6	
Kansas City, Kans	14		York, Pa	1	

TETANUS.

City Reports for Week Ended May 4, 1918.

During the week ended May 4, 1918, there were reported one case and one death from tetanus at New York, N. Y., one death at Petersburg, Va., and one death at Richmond, Va.

TUBERCULOSIS.

See Diphtheria, measles, scarlet fever, and tuberculosis, page 825.

TYPHOID FEVER.

State Reports for March and April, 1918.

Place.	New cases reported.	Place.	New cases reported.
Louisiana (April):		**Maryland—Continued.**	
Assumption Parish	2	Washington County—	
Avoyelles Parish	2	Hagerstown	1
Caddo Parish	1	Williamsport	1
Calcasieu Parish	2	Funkstown	1
Caldwell Parish	1	Wicomico County—	
Concordia Parish	6	Parsonsburg	1
Iberia Parish	2	Worcester County—	
Lafayette Parish	3	Stockton	2
Lafourche Parish	7	Pocomoke City	1
Natchitoches Parish	1		
Orleans Parish	12	Total	64
Plaquemines Parish	1		
Rapides Parish	2	**Massachusetts (April):**	
Red River Parish	1	Barnstable County—	
St. James Parish	3	Orleans (town)	4
St. Landry Parish	9	Berkshire County—	
St. Martin Parish	4	North Adams	4
Union Parish	1	Bristol County—	
Vermilion Parish	2	Fairhaven (town)	1
West Feliciana Parish	1	Fall River	8
		Essex County—	
Total	83	Beverly	1
		Lawrence	8
Maine (March):		Methuen	1
Cumberland County—		Franklin County—	
Portland	2	Orange (town)	1
Piscataquis County—		Hampden County—	2
Foxcroft (town)	2	Longmeadow (town)	
Somerset County—		Middlesex County—	
Madison (town)	2	Cambridge	2
		Lowell	1
Total	6	Marlborough	1
		Medford	1
		Newton	1
Maryland (April):		Sherborn (town)	1
Baltimore	21	Somerville	3
Allegany County—		Stoneham (town)	2
Hazen	1	Waltham	1
Anne Arundel County—		Woburn	1
Jones	1	Norfolk County—	
Annapolis	1	Holbrook (town)	1
Bristol	1	Quincy	1
Baltimore County—		Plymouth County—	
Highlandtown	6	Wareham (town)	4
Govans	1	Suffolk County—	
Sparrows Point	1	Boston	7
Caroline County—		Chelsea	1
Marydel	1	Revere	2
Calvert County—		Worcester County—	
Olivet	1	Brookfield (town)	1
Carroll County—		Fitchburg	1
Union Bridge	2	Webster (town)	1
Mariottsville	1	Worcester	1
Gist	1		
Taneytown	2	Total	51
New Windsor	1		
Frederick County—		**Nebraska (April):**	
Frederick	1	Burt County	1
Brunswick	1	Colfax County	1
Garrett County—		Nuckolls County	2
Lonaconing	1	Thayer County	2
Bittinger	1		
Kempton	3	Total	6
Prince Georges County—			
Upper Marlboro	4	**New York (April):**	
Capitol Heights	1	Albany County—	
Somerset County—		Albany	7
Crisfield	1	Cohoes	1
Westover	1	Water.liet	3
Talbot County—		Coeymans (town)	1
Longwood	1	Ravena	1

TYPHOID FEVER—Continued.

State Reports for March and April, 1918—Continued.

Place.	New cases reported.	Place.	New cases reported.
New York—Continued.		**New York—Continued.**	
Allegany County—		Rensselaer County—	
Alma (town)	2	Troy	2
Wellsville	2	Petersburg (town)	1
Broome County—		Castleton	1
Lisle	1	St. Lawrence County—	
Cattaraugus County—		De Kalb (town)	1
Little Valley	2	Saratoga County—	
New Albion (town)	1	Mechanicville	9
Cayuga County—		Corinth	1
Auburn	1	South Glens Falls	8
Chautauqua County—		Stillwater	1
Dunkirk	1	Schenectady County—	
Chemung County—		Schenectady	1
Elmira	1	Seneca County—	
Southport (town)	7	Seneca Falls	5
Clinton County—		Steuben County—	
Plattsburg	2	Corning	3
Chazy (town)	1	Corning (town)	1
Ellenburgh (town)	1	Dansville (town)	1
Columbia County—		Painted Post	1
Stockport (town)	1	Jasper (town)	1
Dutchess County—		Hammondsport	1
Fishkill	1	Suffolk County—	
Erie County—		Southampton (town)	1
Buffalo	9	Sullivan County—	
Buffalo State Hospital	2	Callicoon (town)	1
Tonawanda	4	Rockland (town)	1
Essex County—		Thompson (town)	1
Ticonderoga (town)	3	Ulster County—	
Greene County—		Kingston	1
Catskill (town)	1	New Paltz	1
Catskill	1	Warren County—	
Jefferson County—		Glens Falls	1
Watertown	3	Wayne County—	
Cape Vincent	1	Newark	1
Hounsfield (town)	1	Sodus (town)	1
Livingston County—		Walworth (town)	1
Conesus (town)	1	Westchester County—	
Madison County—		Port Chester	1
Brookfield (town)	1	Yonkers	1
Earlville	1	Tarrytown	2
Nelson (town)	1	Wyoming County—	
Monroe County—		Wyoming	1
Rochester	4		
Niagara County—		**Total**	118
Lockport	5		
North Tonawanda	1	**Wisconsin (April).**	
Oneida County—		Bayfield County	2
Utica	2	Buffalo County	1
Onondaga County—		Chippewa County	1
Syracuse	1	Clark County	1
Orange County—		Dane County	3
Middletown	1	Douglas County	1
Newburgh	4	Monroe County	1
Newburgh (town)	3	Marathon County	1
Orleans County—		Milwaukee County	21
Ridgeway (town)	1	Oneida County	3
Oswego County—		Richland County	1
Oswego	3	Rock County	1
Scriba (town)	1	Sheboygan County	2
Otsego County—		Trempealeau County	2
Oneonta	1	Winnebago County	1
Oneonta (town)	2	**Total**	42

TYPHOID FEVER—Continued.

City Reports for Week Ended May 4, 1918.

Place.	Cases.	Deaths.	Place.	Cases.	Deaths.
Allentown, Pa	1		Minneapolis, Minn	1	
Altoona, Pa	1		Mobile, Ala	1	1
Anniston, Ala	1		Moline, Ill	1	
Atlanta, Ga	1		New Albany, Ind	2	
Baltimore, Md	5	2	Newark, N. J	1	
Birmingham, Ala	1		New Castle, Pa	1	
Buffalo, N. Y		1	New London, Conn	1	
Camden, N. J	1		New Orleans, La	3	1
Cape Girardeau, Mo	1		New York, N. Y	13	1
Carbondale, Pa	1		Norfolk, Va	1	
Charleston, S. C	1	1	North Adams, Mass	2	
Chester, Pa	1		Oswego, N. Y	1	
Chicago, Ill	1	1	Palestine, Tex	1	
Cleveland, Ohio	2	1	Parkersburg, W. Va	1	1
Cohoes, N. Y	2		Pawtucket, R. I	1	
Columbia, S. C	2		Philadelphia, Pa	7	1
Columbus, Ohio	1		Pittsburgh, Pa	1	
Dallas, Tex	2		Port Chester, N. Y	1	
Danville, Ill	1	1	Pottsville, Pa	1	
Detroit, Mich	4		Providence, R. I	1	
Dover, N. H	1		Quincy, Ill	2	
Erie, Pa	2		Redlands, Cal	1	
Fall River, Mass	3	2	Richmond, Va	1	
Grand Rapids, Mich	1		Saginaw, Mich		1
Green Bay, Wis	1		St. Louis, Mo	1	
Harrisburg, Pa	2		San Francisco, Cal	2	
Hattiesburg, Miss	1		Saratoga Springs, N. Y	1	
Haverhill, Mass	1		Schenectady, N. Y	1	
Indianapolis, Ind	1		Seattle, Wash	2	
Ithaca, N. Y	1		Spokane, Wash	1	
Jackson, Mich		1	Superior, Wis	2	1
Kansas City, Kans	1		Taunton, Mass	1	
Keokuk, Iowa	1		Toledo, Ohio	1	2
Lancaster, Pa	1		Trenton, N. J	2	
Lawrence, Mass		1	Utica, N. Y	1	
Lebanon, Pa	3		Washington, D. C	2	
Little Rock, Ark	2		Wheeling, W. Va	17	
Los Angeles, Cal	1		Wichita, Kans	1	
Louisville, Ky	3	1	Yonkers, N. Y	1	
Macon, Ga	3		Youngstown, Ohio	1	1
Milwaukee, Wis	3	2			

DIPHTHERIA, MEASLES, SCARLET FEVER, AND TUBERCULOSIS.

State Reports for March and April, 1918.

Place.	Cases reported.			Place.	Cases reported.		
	Diph-theria.	Measles.	Scarlet fever.		Diph-theria.	Measles.	Scarlet fever.
Louisiana (April)	49	213	9	Nebraska (April)	57	460	192
Maine (March)	54	206	31	New York (April)	400	8,839	770
Maryland (April)	92	3,939	164	Wisconsin (April)	130	4,066	475
Massachusetts (April)	667	5,210	626				

DIPHTHERIA, MEASLES, SCARLET FEVER, AND TUBERCULOSIS—Contd.

City Reports for Week Ended May 4, 1918.

City.	Population as of July 1, 1916 (estimated by U. S. Census Bureau).	Total deaths from all causes.	Diphtheria. Cases.	Diphtheria. Deaths.	Measles. Cases.	Measles. Deaths.	Scarlet fever. Cases.	Scarlet fever. Deaths.	Tuberculosis. Cases.	Tuberculosis. Deaths.
Over 500,000 inhabitants:										
Baltimore, Md	589,621	241	16	4	526	3	4	.....	50	33
Boston, Mass	756,476	275	59	4	326	6	33	1	80	33
Chicago, Ill	2,497,722	692	92	13	92	3	39	1	421	86
Cleveland, Ohio	674,073	221	24	4	61	1	8	1	40	34
Detroit, Mich	571,784	247	40	4	107	4	43	1	41	18
Los Angeles, Cal	503,812	159	20	.....	112	.....	10	.....	35	26
New York, N. Y	5,692,841	1,585	327	32	1,358	24	147	7	358	170
Philadelphia, Pa	1,709,518	573	54	5	868	4	31	4	176	78
Pittsburgh, Pa	579,090	.....	15	.....	330	.....	6	.....	34	.....
St. Louis, Mo	757,309	269	65	2	88	.....	25	1	51	23
From 300,000 to 500,000 inhabitants:										
Buffalo, N. Y	468,558	133	11	4	144	2	14	.....	41	15
Cincinnati, Ohio	410,476	147	16	.....	48	.....	5	.....	22	26
Jersey City, N. J	306,345	.....	14	.....	27	.....	11	.....	26	.....
Milwaukee, Wis	439,535	139	4	.....	436	8	27	2	21	8
Minneapolis, Minn	363,454	.....	23	2	47	.....	32	4	27	19
Newark, N. J	408,894	134	15	1	510	6	26	.....	35	22
New Orleans, La	371,747	165	7	.....	3	.....	1	.....	35	76
San Francisco, Cal	463,516	132	17	1	38	.....	12	.....	59	21
Seattle, Wash	348,639	.....	2	.....	75	.....	30	.....	12	.....
Washington, D. C	363,980	166	25	.....	271	2	22	.....	15	18
From 200,000 to 300,000 inhabitants:										
Columbus, Ohio	214,878	69	1	.....	28	.....	23	.....	6	1
Denver, Colo	260,800	77	5	2	44	.....	28	1	.....	14
Indianapolis, Ind	271,708	.....	17	1	15	.....	49	.....	12	17
Louisville, Ky	234,910	67	10	.....	8	.....	2	.....	16	8
Portland, Oreg	295,463	57	.....	.....	118	2	8	.....	15	6
Providence, R. I	254,960	64	19	1	193	1	10	1	.....	9
Rochester, N. Y	256,417	64	7	.....	94	1	13	.....	8	8
From 100,000 to 200,000 inhabitants:										
Atlanta, Ga	190,558	73	1	.....	3	.....	2	.....	8	6
Birmingham, Ala	181,762	81	2	.....	4	.....	3	.....	15	7
Bridgeport, Conn	121,576	60	5	1	10	.....	4	.....	5	6
Cambridge, Mass	112,921	.....	10	.....	108	.....	3	.....	3	3
Camden, N. J	106,233	.....	5	.....	32	.....	.....	.....	4	.....
Dallas, Tex	124,527	11	2	.....	20	.....	.....	.....	5	5
Dayton, Ohio	127,244	44	1	.....	11	.....	1	.....	1	5
Des Moines, Iowa	101,598	.....	5	.....	.....	.....	19	.....	.....	.....
Fall River, Mass	128,366	40	1	.....	13	.....	1	.....	8	5
Fort Worth, Tex	104,562	29	.....	.....	3	.....	3	.....	3	3
Grand Rapids, Mich	128,291	41	1	.....	12	.....	4	.....	5	2
Hartford, Conn	110,900	50	.....	.....	.....	.....	.....	1	.....	3
Houston, Tex	112,307	32	2	.....	7	.....	1	.....	5	2
Lawrence, Mass	101,760	31	7	2	124	2	1	.....	7	2
Lowell, Mass	113,245	38	2	.....	29	.....	3	.....	4	6
Lynn, Mass	102,425	22	2	.....	33	.....	3	.....	6	2
Memphis, Tenn	148,995	66	4	1	8	1	7	.....	26	14
New Bedford, Mass	118,158	39	1	.....	3	.....	1	.....	7	10
New Haven, Conn	149,685	58	3	.....	1	.....	1	.....	6	3
Oakland, Cal	198,604	52	1	.....	29	.....	6	1	10	4
Omaha, Nebr	165,470	40	17	1	76	.....	19	.....	2	4
Reading, Pa	109,381	.....	2	.....	132	.....	4	.....	.....	.....
Richmond, Va	156,687	62	.....	.....	98	.....	5	.....	1	10
Salt Lake City, Utah	117,804	35	2	2	20	.....	32	.....	1	1
Scranton, Pa	146,811	.....	6	.....	.....	.....	2	.....	4	.....
Spokane, Wash	139,823	.....	3	.....	1	.....	3	.....	2	.....
Springfield, Mass	105,942	42	2	.....	74	.....	3	.....	2	3
Syracuse, N. Y	153,624	51	6	1	42	2	9	.....	7	8
Tacoma, Wash	112,770	.....	1	.....	5	.....	1	.....	.....	.....
Toledo, Ohio	191,554	75	3	1	8	.....	7	.....	20	7
Trenton, N. J	111,703	46	1	.....	.....	.....	1	.....	3	4
Worcester, Mass	168,411	76	2	.....	14	.....	6	.....	8	6
Youngstown, Ohio	108,385	51	1	.....	9	1	3	.....	3	6
From 50,000 to 100,000 inhabitants:										
Allentown, Pa	63,705	.....	4	.....	48	.....	8	.....	.....	.....
Altoona, Pa	58,790	.....	6	.....	24	.....	3	.....	1	.....
Atlantic City, N. J	55,646	.....	.....	.....	31	.....	.....	.....	13	4
Austin, Tex	30,345	13	.....	.....	14	.....	.....	.....	.....	1
Bayonne, N. J	61,593	.....	4	.....	11	.....	3	.....	2	.....

DIPHTHERIA, MEASLES, SCARLET FEVER, AND TUBERCULOSIS—Contd.

City Reports for Week Ended May 4, 1918—Continued.

City.	Population as of July 1, 1916 (estimated by U. S. Census Bureau).	Total deaths from all causes.	Diphtheria.		Measles.		Scarlet fever.		Tuberculosis.	
			Cases.	Deaths.	Cases.	Deaths.	Cases.	Deaths.	Cases.	Deaths.
From 50,000 to 100,000 inhabitants—Continued.										
Berkeley, Cal	57,653	.....	2	......	4	......	2	......	......	1
Binghamton, N. Y	53,973	20	3	......	29	......	6	......	6	......
Brockton, Mass	67,449	12	......	......	51	......	2	......	2	1
Canton, Ohio	60,852	17	......	......	1	......	1	......	......	......
Charleston, S. C	60,734	35	1	......	6	1	......	......	......	3
Chattanooga, Tenn	60,075	8	2	......	1	......	2	......	......	7
Covington, Ky	57,144	19	3	......	......	......	1	......	2	4
Duluth, Minn	94,495	18	3	......	1	......	2	......	5	......
El Paso, Tex	63,705	44	......	......	8	......	1	......	......	7
Erie, Pa	75,195	......	1	......	123	......	1	......	4	......
Evansville, Ind	76,078	28	1	......	5	......	......	......	1	1
Flint, Mich	54,772	10	2	......	6	......	5	......	10	......
Fort Wayne, Ind	78,183	24	1	......	17	......	2	......	2	2
Harrisburg, Pa	72,015	......	1	......	14	......	2	......	......	......
Hoboken, N. J	77,214	14	5	......	5	......	......	......	4	2
Holyoke, Mass	65,286	......	3	......	2	......	......	......	4	2
Johnstown, Pa	68,520	......	1	......	2	......	5	......	3	......
Kansas City, Kans	99,437	......	......	......	43	......	7	......	7	......
Lancaster, Pa	50,853	......	......	......	25	......	3	......	......	......
Little Rock, Ark	57,343	4	1	......	1	......	3	......	17	1
Malden, Mass	51,155	10	8	......	41	......	......	......	2	1
Manchester, N. H	78,283	32	1	......	14	......	1	......	11	2
Mobile, Ala	58,221	26	......	......	6	1	......	......	1	3
New Britain, Conn	53,794	12	1	......	3	......	1	......	8	1
Norfolk, Va	89,612	......	1	......	15	......	7	......	......	6
Oklahoma City, Okla	92,943	23	1	......	......	......	3	......	1	2
Passaic, N. J	71,744	18	3	......	31	......	1	......	4	3
Pawtucket, R. I	59,411	22	2	......	12	1	5	......	......	1
Peoria, Ill	71,458	19	3	......	13	1	1	......	......	2
Portland, Me	63,867	31	2	......	4	......	......	......	......	2
Rockford, Ill	55,185	22	1	......	21	......	5	......	19	......
Sacramento, Cal	66,495	31	2	......	23	......	2	......	9	5
Saginaw, Mich	53,642	17	......	......	2	......	2	......	1	1
St. Joseph, Mo	85,236	35	4	2	......	......	2	......	......	1
San Diego, Cal	53,330	......	......	......	20	......	2	......	7	2
Savannah, Ga	68,805	31	1	......	......	......	1	......	......	2
Schenectady, N. Y	99,519	31	3	......	26	1	2	......	4	2
Sioux City, Iowa	57,078	3	......	1	......	......	7	......	......	1
Somerville, Mass	87,039	28	4	......	51	......	3	......	2	1
South Bend, Ind	68,946	22	2	1	1	......	1	......	1	......
Springfield, Ill	61,120	20	......	......	41	......	......	......	......	2
Springfield, Ohio	51,550	......	......	......	8	......	......	......	1	......
Terre Haute, Ind	66,093	31	3	1	......	......	2	......	2	4
Troy, N. Y	77,016	32	2	......	3	......	1	......	5	1
Utica, N. Y	85,692	36	......	......	63	2	4	......	11	2
Wichita, Kans	70,722	......	......	......	21	......	1	......	4	......
Wilkes-Barre, Pa	75,770	......	2	......	10	......	2	......	3	......
Wilmington, Del	94,265	......	1	1	......	......	......	......	......	......
Yonkers, N. Y	99,838	24	6	1	80	1	......	......	......	2
York, Pa	51,656	......	4	......	16	......	5	......	3	......
From 25,000 to 50,000 inhabitants:										
Alameda, Cal	27,732	9	1	......	46	......	2	......	......	1
Amsterdam, N. Y	37,103	......	3	......	4	......	......	......	2	2
Auburn, N. Y	37,385	11	1	......	14	......	1	......	......	......
Austin, Texas	34,814	29	1	......	......	......	......	......	......	8
Battle Creek, Mich	29,480	...	1	1	73	......	2	......	2	1
Beaumont, Tex	27,711	8	......	......	......	......	......	......	......	......
Boise, Idaho	33,846	2	......	......	3	......	......	1	......	......
Brookline, Mass	32,730	9	......	......	30	......	4	......	6	......
Burlington, Iowa	25,690	7	......	......	......	......	......	......	......	......
Butler, Pa	27,632	......	2	......	13	......	......	......	......	......
Charlotte, N. C	39,823	17	1	......	......	......	......	......	6	......
Chelsea, Mass	46,192	26	4	......	16	......	3	......	2	4
Chester, Pa	41,596	......	......	......	7	......	......	......	6	......
Chicopee, Mass	29,319	12	......	......	2	......	......	......	4	2
Clinton, Iowa	27,386	......	1	......	10	......	......	......	......	......
Cohoes, N. Y	25,211	6	......	1	......	......	......	......	......	......
Columbia, S. C	34,611	......	1	......	2	......	......	......	......	......
Council Bluffs, Iowa	31,484	11	2	1	4	......	6	1	......	......

DIPHTHERIA, MEASLES, SCARLET FEVER, AND TUBERCULOSIS—Contd.

City Reports for Week Ended May 4, 1918—Continued.

City.	Population as of July 1, 1916 (estimated by U. S. Census Bureau).	Total deaths from all causes.	Diphtheria.		Measles.		Scarlet fever.		Tuberculosis.	
			Cases.	Deaths.	Cases.	Deaths.	Cases.	Deaths.	Cases.	Deaths.
From 25,000 to 50,000 inhabitants—Continued.										
Cranston, R. I.	25,987	9			6					
Cumberland, Md	26,074	6	1		14		11			
Danville, Ill	32,261	18			7		1			1
Davenport, Iowa	48,811				1		2			
Dubuque, Iowa	39,873		2				1			
Durham, N. C	25,061	6	1		11					2
Easton, Pa	30,530				24					
East Orange, N. J	42,458	11	1		59		1		2	1
Elgin, Ill	28,263	8	1		1					
Elmira, N. Y	38,120		1		26		3		1	1
Evanston, Ill	28,591	5	1							
Everett, Mass	39,233	14			7		1			
Everett, Wash	35,486				1					
Fitchburg, Mass	41,781	11			33				2	1
Fort Smith, Ark	28,643	6			1					
Fresno, Cal	34,968	12			4					
Galveston, Tex	41,863	12			7	1				
Green Bay, Wis	29,353	6			6	2				
Hagerstown, Md	25,679				2					
Hammond, Ind	26,171	7	3	1	1		3		1	1
Haverhill, Mass	48,477	16	2		25	1	1		2	2
Hazelton, Pa	28,491		1		30					
Jackson, Mich	35,396	16	1		15		14			2
Jamestown, N. Y	36,580				42				4	
Kalamazoo, Mich	48,886	20			4				3	1
Kenosha, Wis	31,576	13	3		4		6			
Knoxville, Tenn	38,670				5				5	5
La Crosse, Wis	31,677	6							2	1
Lexington, Ky	41,097	19			12		1		23	1
Lima, Ohio	35,384	7								1
Long Beach, Cal	27,587	11	1		21		2		1	1
Lorain, Ohio	36,946				1					
Lynchburg, Va	32,840	13	1		8					
Macon, Ga	45,757	28	1				3			5
Madison, Wis	30,199	9	1		16		9			
McKeesport, Pa	47,521		1		14					
Medford, Mass	26,234				19					1
Moline, Ill	27,451	10	3		24		5			1
Montclair, N. J	26,418	6			9				1	
Montgomery, Ala	44,285	24			3				2	
Muncie, Ind	25,424	8	3		2					2
Muskegon, Mich	26,100	5	2							1
Muskogee, Okla	44,210				2					
Nashua, N. H	27,327	10								
Newark, Ohio	26,035	9			1		2			
Newburgh, N. Y	29,046	8								
New Castle, Pa	41,143		1		11		1		6	
Newport, Ky	31,827	6							1	1
Newport, R. I	30,108		1							
New Rochelle, N. Y	37,559	9			24		1		1	
Newton, Mass	44,715	8	1		9					
Niagara Falls, N. Y	37,553	19	1		3		3			2
Norristown, Pa	31,401				2					
Norwalk, Conn	29,859						8	2		1
Oak Park, Ill	26,651	9	5		16		6			
Ogden, Utah	31,401		1		42	1	4		1	1
Orange, N. J			10		47		1			
Oshkosh, Wis	36,075	9	1		3		2		3	2
Pasadena, Cal	46,450	8			30					4
Perth Amboy, N. J	41,185	10			2				2	
Petersburg, Va	35,582	8			2		1		4	2
Pittsfield, Mass	41,129	7			2		6		4	2
Poughkeepsie, N. Y	30,294	13			72	1	1		2	2
Quincy, Ill	36,587	16	1		11					2
Quincy, Mass	38,159		1		55				4	2
Racine, Wis	44,751	12	1		27		9			3
Roanoke, Va	44,584	13			55				1	
Rock Island, Ill	28,261	12	3		10		3		1	
Salem, Mass	45,413		2		50	2			4	
San Jose, Cal	45,912		1		10				1	

DIPHTHERIA, MEASLES, SCARLET FEVER, AND TUBERCULOSIS—Contd.

City Reports for Week Ended May 4, 1918—Continued.

City.	Population as of July 1, 1916 (estimated by U. S. Census Bureau).	Total deaths from all causes.	Diphtheria. Cases.	Diphtheria. Deaths.	Measles. Cases.	Measles. Deaths.	Scarlet fever. Cases.	Scarlet fever. Deaths.	Tuberculosis. Cases.	Tuberculosis. Deaths.
From 25,000 to 50,000 inhabitants—Continued.										
Sheboygan, Wis	28,559	12			1		1			3
Shenandoah, Pa	29,201						2		4	
Springfield, Mo	40,341	17					2			
Steubenville, Ohio	27,445	12			1					
Superior, Wis	46,266	13			1		5			2
Taunton, Mass	30,283	7					3		1	
Topeka, Kans	48,726			1	10		4			
Waco, Tex	33,385	10							4	2
Walla Walla, Wash	25,136						1			
Waltham, Mass	30,570	7			51					
Waterloo, Iowa	35,559	13	1				2			
Watertown, N. Y	29,894	3				2				
West Hoboken, N. J	43,139	7			10		1		3	
Wheeling, W. Va	43,377	15			3		2			
Williamsport, Pa	33,809		3							
Wilmington, N. C	29,892	11			4					
Winston-Salem, N. C	31,155	16	1						6	6
Zanesville, Ohio	30,803	11								1
From 10,000 to 25,000 inhabitants:										
Aberdeen, Wash	20,334				3		1			
Abilene, Tex	14,238	11	1				3			
Alton, Ill	22,871	11					1			
Anderson, Ind	23,996	7	2		4		1		1	
Ann Arbor, Mich	15,010	11			50					
Anniston, Ala	14,112		1		1				1	
Appleton, Wis	17,834	3			2					
Asbury Park, N. J	14,007	1					1			
Ashtabula, Ohio	21,498	8								1
Attleboro, Mass	19,282				1					
Bakersfield, Cal	16,874	14			3				1	2
Beacon, N. Y	11,555	2								2
Bellaire, Ohio	14,318	6	1	1			1			
Beloit, Wis	18,072	9		1	27	1	1			
Bethlehem, Pa	14,142		1		68		1		4	
Beverly, Mass	21,645				6					
Bloomington, Ind	11,383	5					4			1
Braddock, Pa	21,685		3		18		1			
Cairo, Ill	15,794	11								2
Cape Girardeau, Mo	10,775		1		1					1
Carlisle, Pa	10,726		1		1					
Carnegie, Pa	11,692				1					
Centralia, Ill	11,538		1		2					
Chanute, Kans	12,465	1			8					
Cheyenne, Wyo	11,320		1							
Chillicothe, Ohio	15,470	7			7		3	1		1
Clinton, Mass	13,075	4			2					
Coatesville, Pa	14,455		2		1		4			
Coffeyville, Kans	17,548						3			
Columbia, Pa	[1]11,454				2					
Concord, N. H	22,669	7	1		1					
Corning, N. Y	15,106	6	1		2				1	
Cortland, N. Y	13,069	3			1				1	
Dover, N. H	13,272	3			2		1			
Du Bois, Pa	14,665				9					
Dunkirk, N. Y	20,743	4								
Dunmore, Pa	20,776		3		1				2	
East Liverpool, Ohio	22,586				1		3			
East Providence, R. I	18,113									
Eau Claire, Wis	18,907				11					
Fairmont, W. Va	15,706								1	
Fargo, N. Dak	17,389	3								
Farrell, Pa	[1]10,190				2		1			
Fort Scott, Kans	10,750	4								
Framingham, Mass	13,982	2			2		4			
Fremont, Ohio	10,582	2			2					
Fulton, N. Y	11,508	4								
Galesburg, Ill	24,276	10			14					2
Gardner, Mass	17,110		1		14				1	

[1] Population Apr. 15, 1910; no estimate made.

DIPHTHERIA, MEASLES, SCARLET FEVER, AND TUBERCULOSIS—Contd.

City Reports for Week Ended May 4, 1918—Continued.

City.	Population as of July 1, 1916 (estimated by U. S. Census Bureau).	Total deaths from all causes.	Diphtheria.		Measles.		Scarlet fever.		Tuberculosis.	
			Cases.	Deaths.	Cases.	Deaths.	Cases.	Deaths.	Cases.	Deaths.
From 10,000 to 25,000 inhabitants—Continued.										
Greeley, Colo.	11,420	7					8			2
Greensboro, N. C.	19,577	1			2					
Greensburg, Pa.	15,483				1		1			
Greenville, S. C.	18,181	4					1			
Hackensack, N. J.	16,945	5	1		7					
Harrison, N. J.	16,950				12					
Hattiesburg, Miss.	16,482	7							1	1
Homestead, Pa.	22,469		1							
Hoquiam, Wash.	11,666				6		1			
Hudson, N. Y.	12,705								1	
Independence, Kans.	14,595	3	2		2		4			1
Independence, Mo.	11,673	8			6					
Ithaca, N. Y.	15,548				2		1		2	
Janesville, Wis.	14,339	5	1		1		4			1
Johnstown, N. Y.	10,646			1	4					
Kearny, N. J.	23,539	7			12					
Keokuk, Iowa.	14,008						4		1	
Kokomo, Ind.	30,930	5	1		1				1	
La Fayette, Ind.	31,296	7								
Lackawanna, N. Y.	15,987	11					1			
Lancaster, Ohio.	15,670				12		8			
Leavenworth, Kans.	19,363	7	2		15		1		1	
Lebanon, Pa.	20,779						2			
Lincoln, R. I.	10,385				2					
Little Falls, N. Y.	13,451								2	1
Long Branch, N. J.	15,395	1			13					
Mahanoy City, Pa.	17,465		3		3					
Manitowoc, Wis.	13,845	5			5		2			
Marinette, Wis.	14,610	5			9		1			
Marion, Ind.	19,844	1								
Marshall, Tex.	13,712	4								
Marshalltown, Iowa.	14,490		1		1					
Mason City, Iowa.	14,457	2					1			
Massillon, Ohio.	15,410	2			1				1	
McKees Rocks, Pa.	19,949		1		37		1		2	
Meadville, Pa.	13,802				2					
Melrose, Mass.	17,445	11			1					2
Methuen, Mass.	13,921	6			19	1				
Michigan City, Ind.	21,512	2					1		1	
Middletown, N. Y.	15,840				3					
Milford, Mass.	14,110	9								
Mishawaka, Ind.	16,85	3			3					
Missoula, Mont.	18,214	7					1			
Monessen, Pa.	21,6?0		5		7				1	
Morgantown, W. Va.	19,704	2			3				1	1
Morristown, N. J.	14,284	3			2		2			
Mount Carmel, Pa.	20,4??								2	1
Muscatine, Iowa.	17,549	1			2					1
Nanticoke, Pa.	24,126	6					1			
New Albany, Ind.	30,629	9								2
Newburyport, Mass.	15,243	4			5					
New Castle, Ind.	14,241	3								
New London, Conn.	30,985				5		10		1	
North Adams, Mass.	22,019	10	1						1	
Northampton, Mass.	19,925	10			6				2	1
North Attleboro, Mass.	11,611	2			29				2	
North Braddock, Pa.	15,148		1		3				1	
North Tonawanda, N. Y.	16,768								1	
North Yakima, Wash.	20,93?				18				2	
Norwood, Ohio.	22,28?	4					1			
Oil City, Pa.	19,247				3		1		1	
Olean, N. Y.	16,924	6								
Oswego, N. Y.	24,101				3		6		2	
Palestine, Tex.	11,854	2	1							
Parkersburg, W. Va.	20,012	7			4				1	1
Phoenixville, Pa.	11,414				2					
Pittston, Pa.	18,594		3		4					
Plainfield, N. J.	22,809	8			7		1		2	2

¹ Population Apr. 15, 1910, no estimate made.

DIPHTHERIA, MEASLES, SCARLET FEVER, AND TUBERCULOSIS—Contd.

City Reports for Week Ended May 4, 1918—Continued.

City.	Population as of July 1, 1916 (estimated by U. S. Census Bureau).	Total deaths from all causes.	Diphtheria.		Measles.		Scarlet fever.		Tuberculosis.	
			Cases.	Deaths.	Cases.	Deaths.	Cases.	Deaths.	Cases.	Deaths.
From 10,000 to 25,000 inhabitants—Continued.										
Plymouth, Pa...............	19,100				1					
Pontiac, Mich..............	17,524		2		3		7		2	2
Port Chester, N. Y..........	16,183	5			18					
Pottsville, Pa..............	22,372		1		6				1	
Provo, Utah...............	10,645	2					1			
Rahway, N. J..............	10,219				1					
Raleigh, N. C..............	20,127	7			13		1			
Redlands, Cal..............	14,000	1			6					
Richmond, Ind.............	24,697	5								
Riverside, Cal.............	19,763	8			2					2
Rocky Mount, N. C.........	12,067	7							2	
Rome, N. Y...............	23,737		1		3				3	
Rutland, Vt...............	11,831	5						●		1
Salina, Kans...............	12,098				15		3			
Sandusky, Ohio............	20,193	5			1		1			
Saratoga Springs, N. Y....	13,621	2			15		1		2	
Shamokin, Pa..............	21,139		1				1			
Sharon, Pa................	18,616		1		40		1			
Southbridge, Mass..........	14,205	3	2						2	
Spartanburg, S. C..........	21,365	9	1		5				4	
Steelton, Pa...............	15,548		1		2				4	
Tuscaloosa, Ala............	10,488	4			9		●		4	
Uniontown, Pa.............	20,780		1		1					
Vallejo, Cal...............	13,461	2			17					
Vancouver, Wash...........	13,180		1		17					
Warwick, R. I.............	13,302						1			
Washington, Pa............	21,618		3		18		2		2	..
Watertown, Mass...........	14,867	7			3		2		2	1
Wausau, Wis..............	19,239	7	1		4		5		2	
West Chester, Pa...........	13,176				5					
West Orange, N. J..........	13,550	6			37					2
West Warwick, R. I........	15,782	4			4					
White Plains, N. Y.........	22,465	4			2					
Wilkinsburg, Pa...........	23,228				11					
Winchester, Mass..........	10,603	4	1		2					
Winona, Minn.............	18,583	3								
Winthrop, Mass............	12,692				9		3			
Woburn, Mass.............	15,969	4						1		1

FOREIGN.

CORRECTION.

Typhus Fever—South Australia.

The report of a case of typhus fever which appears in the Public Health Reports of January 4, 1918, page 27, as having occurred in South Australia during the week ended November 17, 1917, was an error.

CUBA.

Communicable Diseases—Habana.

Communicable diseases have been notified at Habana as follows:

Disease.	Apr. 11-20, 1918.		Remaining under treatment Apr. 20, 1918.	Disease.	Apr. 11-20, 1918.		Remaining under treatment Apr. 20, 1918.
	New cases.	Deaths.			New cases.	Deaths.	
Diphtheria	7		9	Paratyphoid fever	2		5
Leprosy	1		13	Scarlet fever	1	1	2
Malaria	19	1	¹ 43	Typhoid fever	35		² 70
Measles	6		10	Varicella	5		15

¹ From the interior, 36.　　² From the interior, 33; 1 foreign.

INDO-CHINA.

Cholera—Plague—Smallpox—Month of December, 1917.

During the month of December, 1917, 16 cases of cholera, 82 of plague, and 154 of smallpox were notified in Indo-China, as compared with 39 cases of cholera, 19 of plague, and 201 of smallpox notified during the month of November, 1917. The cases were distributed according to provinces as follows:

Cholera.—Anam, 6 cases; Cambodia, 2 cases; Cochin-China, 8 cases. The total for the corresponding month of 1916 was 77. The epidemic of cholera which was present in the prison at Pnompenh in October and November, 1917,[1] was declared extinct in December, 1917.

Plague.—Anam, 17 cases; Cambodia, 56 cases; Cochin-China, 9 cases. The total for the corresponding month of 1916 was 15. Of the 56 cases notified in the Province of Cambodia, 54 cases occurred at Pnompenh. A recrudescence of plague at Pnompenh has been

[1] Public Health Reports, Apr 5, 1918, p 513.

observed in the months of December and January during a period of years as follows: January, 1911, 32 cases; December, 1912, 59 cases; January, 1913, 73 cases; January, 1914, 41 cases; December, 1915, 27 cases; January, 1916, 39 cases. The increase is associated with the ingress of rats into houses.

Smallpox.—Anam, 57 cases; Cambodia, 3 cases; Chochin-China, 87 cases; Laos, 6 cases; Tonkin, 1 case. The total for the corresponding month of 1916 was 236 cases. In Anam the district of Quang-Ngai presented the greatest prevalence of smallpox.

GUATEMALA.

Yellow Fever Increasing.

According to information received May 23, 1918, yellow fever continues present at Retalhuleu and is spreading along the Pacific coast of Guatemala.

MEXICO.

Measures Against Importation of Yellow Fever.

According to information dated May 7, 1918, received from Mexico City, communication with Guatemala by land and sea routes has been suspended by order of the board of health of Mexico on account of the prevalence of yellow fever in Guatemala.

CHOLERA, PLAGUE, SMALLPOX, TYPHUS FEVER, AND YELLOW FEVER.

Reports Received During Week Ended May 24, 1918.[1]

CHOLERA.

Place.	Date.	Cases.	Deaths.	Remarks.
India:				
Rangoon	Feb. 24–Mar. 2	5	2	
Madras	Mar. 3–9	2	2	
Indo-China:				
Provinces				Dec. 1–31, 1917: Cases, 16; deaths 6.
Anam	Dec. 1–31	6	2	
Cambodia	do	2	2	
Cochin-China	do	8	2	
Palestine				Dec. 28, 1917–Feb. 5, 1918: Cases, 31. Occurring at 7 localities; 2 cases in encampments.
Deir Seneid	Dec. 28–Jan 31	13		
Sukkarieh	do	13		

PLAGUE.

Place.	Date.	Cases.	Deaths.	Remarks.
China:				
Amoy	Mar. 11–31			Present in vicinity.
Nanking	Mar. 17–Apr. 5	19		
India:				
Bassein	Feb. 17–23		25	
Henzada	do		14	
Karachi	Feb. 24–Mar. 2	12	6	
Madras	Mar. 3–9	1	1	
Madras Presidency	do	651	482	

[1] From medical officers of the Public Health Service, American consuls, and other sources.

CHOLERA, PLAGUE, SMALLPOX, TYPHUS FEVER, AND YELLOW FEVER—Continued.

Reports Received During Week Ended May 24, 1918—Continued.

PLAGUE—Continued.

Place.	Date.	Cases.	Deaths.	Remarks.
India—Continued.				
Mandalay	Feb. 10-16		154	
Moulmein	Feb. 17-23		1	
Myingyan	Feb. 3-16		121	
Pegu	Feb. 17-23		1	
Rangoon	Feb. 17-Mar. 2	175	169	
Toungoo	Feb. 17-23		7	
Indo-China:				
Provinces				Dec. 1-31, 1917: Cases, 82; deaths,
Anam	Dec. 1-31	17	3	60.
Cambodia	do	56	55	
Cochin-China	do	9	2	

SMALLPOX.

Place.	Date.	Cases.	Deaths.	Remarks.
Canada:				
New Brunswick—				
St. John	May 5-11	10		
China:				
Amoy	Mar. 11-31			Present.
Chungking	Mar. 10-16			Do.
Hongkong	Mar. 17-30	7	5	
Nanking	Mar. 31-Apr. 6			Epidemic.
India:				
Karachi	Feb. 25-Mar. 2	7	6	
Madras	Mar. 3-9	21	1	
Rangoon	Feb. 25-Mar. 2	21	4	
Indo-China:				
Provinces				Dec. 1-31, 1917: Cases, 151; deaths,
Anam	Dec. 1-31	57	5	34.
Cambodia	do	43	3	
Cochin-China	do	87	25	
Laos	do	6	1	
Tonkin	do	1		
Italy:				
Genoa	Apr. 1-15	9	3	
Turin	Mar. 4-10	16	3	
Mesopotamia:				
Bagdad	Jan. 1-31		10	
Mexico:				
Vera Cruz	Apr. 22-28	1		
Newfoundland:				
St. Johns	Apr. 27-May 3	7		
Tunis:				
Tunis	Apr. 6-12	1		

TYPHUS FEVER.

Place.	Date.	Cases.	Deaths.	Remarks.
Germany				July 29-Dec. 8, 1917: Cases, 74. Of these, 9 in prison camps.
Great Britain:				
Glasgow	Apr. 14-20		1	
Poland:				Nov. 18-Dec. 8, 1917: Cases,
Lodz	Nov. 18-Dec. 8	219	25	2,368; deaths, 218. In region
Warsaw	do	1,461	141	occupied by German troops.

YELLOW FEVER.

Place.	Date.	Cases.	Deaths.	Remarks.
Guatemala:				
Retalhuleu	May 23			Present. Spreading along Pacific coast.

CHOLERA, PLAGUE, SMALLPOX, TYPHUS FEVER, AND YELLOW FEVER—Continued.

Reports Received from Dec. 29, 1917, to May 17, 1918.

CHOLERA.

Place.	Date.	Cases.	Deaths.	Remarks.
China:				
Antung....................	Nov. 26–Dec. 2....	3	1	
India:				
Bombay....................	Oct. 28–Dec. 15....	19	14	
Do....................	Dec. 30–Jan. 26....	216	190	
Calcutta..................	Sept. 16–Dec. 15....	....	135	
Do....................	Dec. 30–Feb. 23....	....	53	
Karachi..................	....do............	25	6	
Madras...................	Nov. 25–Dec. 22....	2	2	
Do....................	Dec. 30–Feb. 23....	42	22	
Rangoon..................	Nov. 4–Dec. 22....	5	5	
Do....................	Dec. 30–Feb. 2....	2	1	
Indo-China:				
Provinces.................		....	....	Sept. 1–Nov. 30, 1917: Cases, 152; deaths, 89.
Anam..................	Sept. 1–Nov. 30...	18	13	
Cambodia..............	....do............	72	52	
Cochin-China..........	....do............	50	22	
Saigon................	Nov. 22–Dec. 9....	4	3	
Do................	Feb. 4–Mar. 11....	8	3	
Kwang-Chow-Wan....	Sept. 1–30.........	10	2	
Java:				
East Java..............	Oct. 28–Nov. 3....	1	1	
West Java..............		....	....	Oct. 19–Dec. 27, 1917: Cases, 102; deaths, 56. Dec. 28, 1917–Jan. 31, 1918: Cases, 27; deaths, 7.
Batavia..............	Oct. 10–Dec. 27....	49	23	
Do................	Dec. 28–Jan. 31....	24	1	
Persia....................		....	....	July 30–Sept. 3, 1917: Cases, 384; deaths, 276.
Achraf................	July 30–Aug. 16...	90	88	
Astrabad..............	July 31............	....	....	Present.
Barfrush..............	July 1–Aug. 16....	39	25	
Chahmirzad...........		....	....	26 cases reported July 31, 1917.
Chahrastagh...........	June 15–July 25...	10	8	
Charoud..............	Aug. 26–Sept. 3....	4	2	
Damghan..............	Aug. 26............	....	....	Present.
Kharek...............	May 28–June 11...	21	13	
Meched...............	Aug. 18–Sept. 2....	174	82	
Ouzoun Dare..........	Aug. 8............	....	....	Do.
Sabzevar..............	Aug. 24............	....	....	Do.
Sari..................	July 3–29..........	273	144	
Semman...............	Aug. 31–Sept. 2....	14	5	
Yekchambe Bazar........	June 3............	6	....	
Philippine Islands:				
Provinces.................		....	....	July 1–Dec. 29, 1917: Cases, 5,964; deaths, 3,655. Dec. 30, 1917–Mar. 30, 1918: Cases, 1,664; deaths, 1,185.
Antique...............	Nov. 18–Dec. 1....	48	32	
Do................	Feb. 3–9..........	4	4	
Bohol................	Nov. 18–Dec. 29....	169	111	
Do................	Dec. 30–Mar. 30....	521	413	
Capiz................	Nov. 25–Dec. 29....	27	21	
Do................	Dec. 30–Mar. 23....	219	182	
Cebu.................	Dec. 23–29.........	3	....	
Do................	Dec. 30–Mar. 30....	100	54	
Davao................	Mar. 10–16.........	10	8	
Iloilo................	Nov. 25–Dec. 29....	179	135	
Do................	Dec. 30–Mar. 2....	97	63	
Leyte................	Nov. 25–Dec. 22....	13	12	
Do................	Feb. 3–Mar. 16....	50	38	
Mindanao.............	Nov. 25–Dec. 29....	337	196	
Do................	Dec. 30–Feb. 9....	341	220	
Misamis..............	Feb. 24–Mar. 23....	106	67	
Occidental Negros......	Nov. 25–Dec. 22....	177	123	
Do................	Jan. 13–Mar. 30....	144	83	
Oriental Negros........	Nov. 25–Dec. 29....	99	62	
Do................	Dec. 30–Mar. 30....	23	15	
Romblon..............	Nov. 25–Dec. 1....	1	1	
Surigao...............	Feb. 24–Mar. 23...	14	9	
Zamboanga............	....do............	35	29	
Russia:				
Tashkentnine..............	May 13............	....	....	Present.
Tzaritsin..................	....do............	....	....	Do.
Siam:				
Bangkok..................	Sept. 16–22........	1	1	
Turkey in Asia:				
Bagdad...................	Nov. 1–15..........	....	40	

836

CHOLERA, PLAGUE, SMALLPOX, TYPHUS FEVER, AND YELLOW FEVER—Continued.

Reports Received from Dec. 29, 1917, to May 17, 1918—Continued.

PLAGUE.

Place.	Date.	Cases.	Deaths.	Remarks.
Brazil:				
Bahia	Nov. 4-Dec. 15	4	4	
Do	Dec. 30-Feb. 23	4	3	
Rio de Janeiro	Dec. 23-29	1		
Do	Jan. 6-12	1	1	
British East Africa:				
Mombasa	Oct. 1-Dec. 31	31	18	
British Gold Coast:				
Axim	Jan. 8			Present.
Ceylon:				
Colombo	Oct. 14-Dec. 1	14	13	
Do	Dec. 30-Feb. 16	20	17	
China				Present in North China in January, 1918; pneumonic form.
Anhwei Province—				
Fengyanghsien	Feb. 27		9	Pneumonic.
Pengpu	do		1	Do.
Chili Province—				
Kalgan				Vicinity. Present in February, 1918.
Kiangsu Province—				
Nanking	Mar. 17-23		15	
Shansi Province				Present in February, 1918; 116 cases estimated.
Ecuador:				
Babahoyo	Feb. 1-15	1		
Duran	Feb. 16-Mar. 30	2	1	
Guayaquil	Sept. 1-Nov. 30	68	24	Reported outbreak occurring about Jan. 17, 1918.
Do	Feb. 1-15	44	18	
Do	Mar. 1-30	37	14	
Egypt				Jan. 1-Nov. 15, 1917: Cases, 728; deaths, 398.
Alexandria	Jan. 14-28	1	2	
Cairo	Dec. 17-23	2		
Port Said	July 2 Dec. 23	13	7	
Suez	July 2-Oct. 20	62	38	
Hawaii:				
Laupahoehoe	May 5	1	1	
India				Sept. 16-Dec. 29, 1917: Cases, 228,834; deaths, 174,743. Dec. 30, 1917-Feb. 16, 1918: Cases, 240,000; deaths, 192,149.
Bassein	Dec. 9-29		8	
Do	Dec. 30 Feb. 16		74	
Bombay	Oct. 28-Dec. 29	147	123	
Do	Dec. 30 Feb. 16	152	112	
Calcutta	Sept. 16-29		2	
Do	Dec. 30 Feb. 2		4	
Henzada	Oct. 21 27		1	
Do	Jan. 5 Feb. 16		57	
Karachi	Oct. 21 Dec. 29	27	20	
Do	Dec. 30 Feb. 23	36	28	
Madras	Feb. 3 16	3	2	
Madras Presidency	Oct. 31 Nov. 24	5,786	4,519	
Do	Jan. 6 Feb. 16	10,431	8,109	
Mandalay	Oct. 14 Nov. 17		89	
Do	Dec. 30 Feb. 2		627	
Myingyan	Dec. 30 Feb. 10		286	
Pegu	Feb. 10 16		1	
Prome	Jan. 5 12		1	
Rangoon	Oct. 21 Dec. 22		56	
Do	Dec. 30 Feb. 16	266	251	
Toungoo	Dec. 9 29		5	
Do	Dec. 30 Feb. 16		25	
Indo-China:				
Provinces				Sept. 1-Nov. 30, 1917: Cases, 99; deaths, 68.
Anam	Sept. 1 Nov. 30	26	25	
Cambodia	do	39	28	
Cochin-China	do	22	15	
Saigon	Oct. 31 Dec. 23	17	6	
Do	Dec. 31 Mar. 17	115	60	
Java:				
East Java				Oct. 8-Dec. 31, 1917: Cases, 196; deaths, 193.
Do				Jan. 1-14, 1918: Cases, 22; deaths, 21.
Residencies—				
Kediri	Oct. 8-Dec. 31	1	1	
Madison	do	49	49	
Samarang	do	110	109	
Surabaya	do	25	23	
Surakarta	do	11	11	
West Java				Nov. 25-Dec. 9, 1917: Cases, 48; deaths, 45. Dec. 1, 1917-Jan. 15, 1918: Cases, 108.

CHOLERA, PLAGUE, SMALLPOX, TYPHUS FEVER, AND YELLOW FEVER—Continued.

Reports Received from Dec. 29, 1917, to May 17, 1918—Continued.

PLAGUE—Continued.

Place.	Date.	Cases.	Deaths.	Remarks.
Peru:				
Ancachs Department—				
Casma................	Dec. 1–Jan. 15.....	2	....	
Lambayeque Department..	.....do............	22	....	At Chiclayo, Ferrenafe, Jayanca, Lambayeque.
Libertad Department.....	.....do............	72	....	At Guadalupo, Mansiche, Pacasmayo, Salaverry, San Jose, San Pedro, and country district of Trujillo.
Lima Department..........	.....do............	9	....	City and oouutry.
Piura Department—				
Catacaos................	.....do............	1	....	
Senegal:				
St. Louis..............	Feb. 2.............	....	....	Present.
Siam:				
Bangkok..................	Sept. 16–Dec. 23....	13	9	
Do..................	Jan. 13–Mar. 16....	37	27	
Straits Settlements:				
Singapore................	Oct. 28–Dec. 29....	¹5	7	
Do..................	Jan. 6–Mar. 9......	64	57	

SMALLPOX.

Place.	Date.	Cases.	Deaths.	Remarks.
Algeria:				
Algiers..................	Nov. 1–Dec. 31....	3	2	
Do..................	Jan. 1–Apr. 23.....	213	....	
Australia:				
New South Wales.........				July 12–Dec. 20, 1917: Cases, 36; Jan. 4–17, 1918; case, 1. Newcastle district.
Abermain..............	Oct. 25–Nov. 29..	3	....	
Cessnock..............	July 12–Oct. 11...	7	....	
Eumangla.............	Aug. 15...........	1	....	
Kurri Kurri...........	Dec. 5–20.........	2	....	
Mungindi.............	Aug. 13...........	1	....	
Warren..............	July 12–Oct. 25....	22	....	
Do..................	Jan. 1–17.........	1	....	
Brazil:				
Bahia..................	Nov. 10–Dec. 8....	3	....	
Pernambuco.............	Nov. 1–15.........	1	....	
Rio de Janeiro..........	Sept. 30–Dec. 29..	703	190	
Do..................	Dec. 30–Mar. 23...	251	84	
Sao Paulo...............	Oct. 29–Nov. 4....	....	2	
British East Africa:				
Mombasa..................	Oct. 1–Dec. 31....	9	5	
Canada:				
British Columbia—				
Vancouver............	Jan. 13–Mar. 9....	5	....	
Victoria.............	Jan. 7–Feb. 2.....	2	....	
Winnipeg.............	Dec. 30–Apr. 13...	4	....	
New Brunswick—				
Kent County..........	Dec. 4............	....	....	Outbreak. On main line Canadian Ry., 25 miles north of Moncton.
Do..................	Jan. 22...........	40	....	In 7 localities.
Northumberland County.	.....do............	41	....	In 5 localities.
Restigouche County....	Jan. 18...........	60	....	
St. John County—				
St. John...........	Mar. 3–May 4.....	10	....	
Victoria County........	Jan. 2...........	10	....	At Limestone and a lumber camp.
Westmoreland County—				
Moncton..........	Jan. 29–Apr. 27....	20	....	
York County...........	Jan. 22...........	8	....	
Nova Scotia—				
Cape Sable Island.....	....	....	....	Present May 8 at Clarks Harbor.
Halifax..............	Feb. 24–Apr. 27..	10	....	
Sydney..............	Feb. 3–Apr. 27....	19	....	
Ontario—				
Arnprior..............	Mar. 31–Apr. 6.....	....	1	
Hamilton..............	Dec. 16–22........	1	....	
Do..................	Jan. 13–19.........	2	....	
Ottawa..............	Mar. 4–24.........	5	....	
Sarnia................	Dec. 9–15.........	1	....	
Do..................	Jan. 6–Mar. 30....	32	....	
Toronto...............	Feb. 10–Apr. 6....	2	....	
Windsor...............	Dec. 30–Jan. 5.....	1	....	

CHOLERA, PLAGUE, SMALLPOX, TYPHUS FEVER, AND YELLOW FEVER—Continued.

Reports Received from Dec. 29, 1917, to May 17, 1918—Continued.

SMALLPOX—Continued.

Place.	Date.	Cases.	Deaths.	Remarks.
Canada—Continued.				
Prince Edward Island—				
Charlottetown..........	Feb. 7–13..........	1	....	
Quebec—				
Montreal..............	Dec. 16–Jan. 5.....	5	....	
Do..................	Jan. 6–Apr. 6......	12	....	
Quebec...............	Apr. 21–27.........	2	....	
China:				
Amoy...................	Oct. 22–Dec. 30....	....	....	Present.
Do...................	Dec. 31–Mar. 10....	....	....	Do.
Antung.................	Dec. 2–23..........	13	2	
Do...................	Jan. 7–Apr. 6......	13	3	
Changsha..............	Jan. 28–Mar. 10....	6	1	
Chefoo................	Jan. 27–Feb. 9.....	....	....	Do.
Chungking............	Nov. 11–Dec. 29....	....	....	Do.
Do..................	Dec. 30–Mar. 9.....	....	....	Do.
Dairen................	Nov. 18–Dec. 22....	3	1	
Do..................	Dec. 30–Apr. 6.....	64	5	
Hankow...............	Feb. 25–Mar. 3.....	1	....	
Harbin................	May 14–June 30....	20	....	Chinese Eastern Ry.
Do..................	July 1–Dec. 2......	7	....	Do.
Hongkong.............	Dec. 23–29.........	1	....	
Do..................	Jan. 26–Mar. 16....	12	4	
Hungtahotze Station ..	Oct. 28–Nov. 4.....	1	....	Do.
Manchuria Station	May 14–June 30....	6	....	Do.
Do..................	July 1–Dec. 2......	3	....	Do.
Mukden...............	Nov. 11–24.........	....	....	Present.
Do..................	Feb. 10–Mar. 30....	....	....	Do.
Nanking..............	Feb. 3–Mar. 30.....	....	....	Do.
Shanghai..............	Nov. 18–Dec. 23....	41	91	Cases, foreign; deaths among natives.
Do..................	Dec. 31–Apr. 1....	38	119	Do.
Swatow...............	Jan. 18............	....	....	Unusually prevalent.
Tientsin..............	Nov. 11–Dec. 22....	13	....	
Do..................	Dec. 30–Apr. 6.....	46	....	
Tsingtau.............	Feb. 4–Mar. 31....	10	2	
Cuba:				
Habana...............	Jan. 7.............	1	....	Nov. 8, 1917: 1 case from Coruna, Dec. 5, 1917, 1 case.
Marianao.............	Jan. 8.............	1	....	6 miles distant from Habana.
Ecuador:				
Guayaquil............	Sept. 1–Nov. 30 ...	26	2	
Do..................	Feb. 1–Mar. 31....	4	3	
Egypt:				
Alexandria............	Nov. 12–18........	2	1	
Do..................	Jan. 8–Mar. 25....	10	....	
Cairo.................	July 23–Nov. 18....	6	1	
France:				
Lyon..................	Nov. 18–Dec. 16....	6	3	
Do..................	Jan. 7–Feb. 17.....	11	2	
Marseille.............	Jan. 1–31..........	....	2	
Paris.................	Jan. 27–Mar 30....	9	3	
Rouen................	Mar. 31–Apr. 6....	26	4	
Great Britain:				
Cardiff...............	Feb. 3–9...........	4	....	
Hull.................	Mar. 17–30.........	3	....	
Greece:				
Saloniki..............	Jan. 27–Mar. 16....	....	9	
Honduras:				
Santa Barbara Department.	Jan. 1–7..........	....	....	Present in interior.
India:				
Bombay...............	Oct. 21 Dec. 29....	50	12	
Do..................	Dec. 31 Feb. 2....	346	134	
Calcutta..............	Jan. 27 Feb. 23....	....	13	
Karachi..............	Nov. 18 Dec. 29....	4	2	
Do..................	Jan. 27–Feb. 23....	24	12	Nov. 11–16, 1917: 10 cases with 4 deaths; imported on s. s. Menesa from Basreh.
Madras...............	Oct. 31–Dec. 29....	20	8	
Do..................	Dec. 30 Feb. 23....	122	134	
Rangoon..............	Oct. 28–Dec. 22....	6	1	
Do..................	Dec. 30 Feb. 16....	42	7	
Indo China:				
Provinces.............	....	....	....	Sept. 1–Nov. 30, 1917: Cases, 546; deaths, 146.
Anam................	Sept. 1 Nov. 30....	163	25	
Cambodia............	......do...........	16	8	
Cochin China........	......do...........	330	108	
Saigon..............	Oct. 20 Dec. 30....	120	20	
Do..................	Dec. 31–Mar. 17....	705	278	

CHOLERA, PLAGUE, SMALLPOX, TYPHUS FEVER, AND YELLOW FEVER—Continued.

Reports Received from Dec. 29, 1917, to May 17, 1918—Continued.

SMALLPOX—Continued.

Place.	Date.	Cases.	Deaths.	Remarks.
Indo-China—Continued.				
Provinces—Continued.				
Laos	Oct. 1–31	1		
Do	Jan. 26–Feb. 3	1	1	
Tonkin	Sept. 1–Oct. 31	9	4	
Do	Jan. 26–Feb. 3	3		
Italy:				
Castellamare	Dec. 10	2		Among refugees.
Florence	Dec. 1–15	17	4	
Genoa	Dec. 2–31	11	3	
Do	Jan. 2–Mar. 31	43	6	
Leghorn	Jan. 7–Apr. 7	33	7	
Messina	Jan. 3–19	1		
Milan				Oct. 1–Dec. 31, 1917: Cases, 32.
Naples	To Dec. 10	2		Among refugees.
Taormina	Jan. 20–Feb. 9	6		
Turin	Oct. 29–Dec. 29	123	120	
Do	Jan. 21–Mar. 3	56	3	
Japan:				
Nagasaki	Jan. 14–Apr. 14	10	3	
Taihoku	Dec. 15–21	1		Island of Taiwan (Formosa).
Do	Jan. 8–Apr. 8	49	8	Do.
Tokyo	Feb. 11–Apr. 14	26		City and suburbs.
Yokohama	Jan. 17–Feb. 3	63		
Java:				
East Java	Oct. 7–Dec. 23	50		Dec. 25–31, 1917: Cases, 7. Jan. 1–14, 1918: Cases, 3.
Surabaya	Dec. 25–31	1		
Mid-Java				Oct. 10–Dec. 26, 1917: Cases, 86; death, 1. Dec. 28, 1917–Jan. 23, 1918: Cases, 23.
Samarang	Nov. 6–Dec. 12	4	1	
West Java				Oct. 19–Dec. 27, 1917: Cases, 231; deaths, 36. Dec. 28, 1917–Jan. 31, 1918: Cases, 116; deaths, 17.
Batavia	Nov. 2–8	1		
Mexico:				
Aguascalientes	Feb. 4–17		2	
Ciudad Juarez	Mar. 3–23	2	1	
Guadalajara	Mar. 1–31	21	4	
Mazatlan	Dec. 5–11		1	
Do	Jan. 29–Apr. 2	4	4	
Mexico City	Nov. 11–Dec. 29	16		
Do	Dec. 30–Apr. 13	111		
Piedras Negras	Jan. 11	200		
Vera Cruz	Jan. 20–Apr. 21	15	3	
Newfoundland:				
St. Johns	Dec. 8–Jan. 4	29		45 cases in hospital.
Do	Jan. 5–Apr. 26	82		
Trepassey	Jan. 4			Outbreak with 11 cases reported.
Philippine Islands:				
Manila	Oct. 28–Dec. 8	5		Varioloid, 130.
Do	Feb. 3–Mar. 30	81	35	
Porto Rico:				
San Juan	Jan. 28–Apr. 7	37		Of these, 36 varioloid.
Portugal:				
Lisbon	Nov. 4–Dec. 15	2		
Do	Dec. 30–Mar. 30	17		
Portuguese East Africa:				
Lourenço Marquez	Aug. 1–Dec. 31		16	
Do	Jan. 1–31		6	
Russia:				
Archangel	Sept. 1–Oct. 31	7		
Moscow	Aug. 26–Oct. 6	22	2	
Petrograd	Aug. 31–Nov. 18	76	3	
Siam:				
Bangkok	Nov. 25–Dec. 1	1	1	
Do	Jun. 6–Mar. 10	26	14	
Spain:				
Coruna	Dec. 2–15		4	
Do	Jan 20–Feb. 23		5	
Madrid	Jan. 1–Feb. 28		9	Jan. 1–Dec. 31, 1917: Deaths, 77.
Malaga	Oct. 1–31		19	
Seville	Oct. 1–Dec. 30		66	
Do	Jan. 1–31		20	
Valencia	Jan. 27–Feb. 2	1		
Straits Settlements:				
Singapore	Nov. 25–Dec. 1	1	1	
Do	Dec. 30–Jan. 5	1		

CHOLERA, PLAGUE, SMALLPOX, TYPHUS FEVER, AND YELLOW FEVER—Continued.

Reports Received from Dec. 29, 1917, to May 17, 1918—Continued.

SMALLPOX—Continued.

Place.	Date.	Cases.	Deaths.	Remarks.
Tunisia:				
Tunis...................	Dec. 14-20..........	1	....	
Do...................	Mar. 16-22..........	1	....	
Turkey in Asia:				
Bagdad...............	....	....	....	Present in November, 1917.
Union of South Africa:				
Cape of Good Hope State..	Oct. 1-Dec. 31.....	28	....	
East Liverpool.........	Jan. 20-26.........	1	....	Varioloid.
Transvaal—				
Johannesburg..........	Jan. 1-31..........	4	....	
Venezuela:				
Maracaibo..............	Dec. 2-8..........	....	1	

TYPHUS FEVER.

Place.	Date.	Cases.	Deaths.	Remarks.
Algeria:				
Algiers..................	Nov. 1-Dec. 31....	2	1	
Argentina:				
Rosario.................	Dec. 1-31.........	....	1	
Austria-Hungary:				
Hungary................	....	....	....	Present in December, 1917.
Brazil:				
Rio de Janeiro............	Oct. 28-Dec. 1.....	7	....	
Canada.				
Ontario—				
Kingston.............	Dec. 2-8..........	3	....	
Quebec—				
Montreal.............	Dec. 16-22........	2	1	
China:				
Antung.................	Dec. 3-20.........	13	1	
Do...................	Dec. 31-Mar. 30...	3	2	
Chosen (Korea):				
Seoul..................	Nov. 1-20.........	1	....	
Do...................	Feb. 1-28.........	3	2	
Egypt:				
Alexandria.............	Nov. 8-Dec. 28....	57	15	
Do...................	Jan. 8-Apr. 1......	688	157	
Cairo..................	July 23 Dec. 23....	143	74	
Port Said..............	July 30-Nov. 11...	5	5	
France				
Marseille..............	Dec. 1-31.........	....	1	
Germany	....	....	....	Jan. 1-30, 1918; Cases, 66.
Great Britain:				
Belfast................	Feb. 10 Mar 30...	21	3	
Dublin................	Mar. 24 30........	3	....	
Glasgow...............	Dec. 21...........	1	....	
Do	Jan. 20-Apr. 13...	15	....	
Manchester............	Dec. 2-8..........	1	....	
Greece:				
Arta..................	Feb. 19...........	2	....	
Janina................	Feb. 14...........	110	....	Jan. 27, epidemic.
Saloniki..............	Nov. 11-Dec. 29...	....	72	
Do...................	Dec. 30-Mar. 16...	....	27	
Italy:				
San Remo..............	Mar. 10 16........	2	....	
Japan:				
Nagasaki..............	Nov. 26 Dec. 16...	5	5	
Do...................	Jan. 7 Apr 14.....	18	6	
Java:				
East Java..............	....	....	....	Oct. 15-Dec. 31, 1917; Cases, 39; deaths, 7. Jan. 1-14, 1918.
Surabaya.............	Dec 17-31.........	9	1	Cases, 11; deaths, 2.
Do.................	Jan. 1-14.........	10	1	
Mid-Java	....	....	....	Oct. 10-Dec. 26, 1917; Cases, 63; deaths, 2. Dec. 28, 1917-Jan. 23, 1918; Cases, 11.
Samarang............	Oct. 9 Dec 26.....	20	2	
Do.................	Dec. 27 Jan. 15...	9	....	
West Java	....	....	....	Oct. 19-Dec. 27, 1917; Cases, 94; deaths, 17. Dec. 28, 1917-Jan. 31, 1918; Cases, 53; deaths, 1.
Batavia	Oct 1 Dec 27.....	50	15	
Do.................	Dec 28 Jan 31....	27	1	
Lithuania	....	....	....	Dec. 30, 1917-Jan. 5, 1918; Cases, 195.
Mexico:				
Aguascalientes........	Dec 15	....	3	
Do.................	Jan. 21-Apr 28....	....	17	
Durango State—				
Goahuila..............	Feb. 11	....	....	Epidemic.

CHOLERA, PLAGUE, SMALLPOX, TYPHUS FEVER, AND YELLOW FEVER—Continued.

Reports Received from Dec. 29, 1917, to May 17, 1918—Continued.

TYPHUS FEVER—Continued.

Place.	Date.	Cases.	Deaths.	Remarks.
Mexico—Continued.				
Mexico City	Nov. 11–Dec. 29...	476	....	
Do	Dec. 30–Apr. 13...	704	....	
Newfoundland:				
St. Johns	Mar. 30–Apr. 5....	1	1	
Norway:				
Bergen	Feb. 1–16	3	....	
Poland		....	....	Dec. 23, 1917–Jan. 12, 1918: Cases, 3,026; deaths, 315.
Portugal:				
Lisbon	Mar. 3–30	18	....	Feb. 21: Present.
Oporto	Dec. 1–31	23	4	
Do	Jan. 1–Mar. 8	1,811	161	
Russia:				
Archangel	Sept. 1–14	7	2	
Moscow	Aug. 26–Oct. 6....	49	2	
Petrograd	Aug. 31–Nov. 18...	32	....	
Do	Feb. 2	....	....	Present.
Vladivostock	Oct. 29–Nov. 4....	12	1	
Spain:				
Corcubion	Apr. 11	....	....	Present. Province of Coruna, west coast.
Madrid	Jan. 1–31	....	1	
Sweden:				
Goteborg	Nov. 18–Dec. 15...	2	....	
Switzerland:				
Basel	Jan. 6–19	1	1	
Zurich	Nov. 9–15	2	....	
Do	Jan. 13–19	2	....	
Tunisia:				
Tala	Mar. 18	....	....	Epidemic.
Tozer	...do	....	1	Do.
Tunis	Nov. 30–Dec. 6....	....	....	
Do	Feb. 9–Apr. 5	37	13	Of these, 26 in outbreak in prison.
Union of South Africa:				
Cape of Good Hope State...	Sept. 10–Dec. 30...	4,035	830	Sept. 10–Nov. 25, 1917: Cases, 3,724 (European, 31); deaths, 761 (European, 5). Total to Feb. 17, 1918: Cases, 4,386 (European, 32); deaths, 887 (European, 5).
Natal		....	....	From Dec. 1, 1917–Feb. 17, 1918: Cases, 43; deaths, 11.

YELLOW FEVER.

Place.	Date.	Cases.	Deaths.	Remarks.
Brazil:				
Bahia	Mar. 10–16	1	1	
Ecuador:				
Babahoyo	Feb. 1–15	1	1	
Guayaquil	Sept. 1–Nov. 30	5	3	
Do	Feb. 1–15	1	....	
Do	Mar. 1–31	12	7	
Milagro	Feb. 1–15	1	1	
Yauguachi	Nov. 1–30	1	....	
Guatemala:				
Retalhuleu	Apr. 22	....	....	Present. About 25 miles from Champerico, Pacific port.
Honduras:				
Tegucigalpa	Dec. 16–22	....	1	
Do	Jan. 6–19	....	1	

X

VOL. 33   MAY 31, 1918   No. 22

THE GROWTH-PROMOTING PROPERTIES OF FOODS DERIVED FROM CORN AND WHEAT.

By CARL VOEGTLIN and C. N. MYERS, Division of Pharmacology, Hygienic Laboratory, United States Public Health Service.

The authors in a preceding paper have shown that the whole wheat or corn grain contains an abundance of antineuritic vitamine, whereas the "highly milled" products derived from these cereals are deficient in this respect. This conclusion was drawn from experiments on adult animals. As growing animals require the presence of all dietary constituents to a greater extent than do adults, it seemed desirable to continue the investigation along this line. Recent studies on growth have furnished the necessary information to answer the question as to what constitutes a diet complete enough to insure growth. It is now generally held that a physiologically sufficient diet must contain an adequate caloric value derived from protein of proper composition, carbohydrate, and fat. In addition it must contain a sufficient amount of antineuritic and fat-soluble vitamines and of necessary inorganic salts.

The dietary deficiencies of the whole wheat and corn kernel in the diet of growing animals have already been investigated. Thus Hart and McCollum (1914), working with young albino rats and hogs, have shown that normal growth is obtained when the wheat kernel is supplemented by the addition of inorganic salts, fat-soluble vitamine, and casein. Subnormal growth was observed with rations consisting of wheat plus casein and salts; wheat plus casein and butter fat; wheat plus salts and butter fat.

McCollum, Simmonds, and Pitz (1916) have made similar observations with corn. In this case also the grain requires an improvement in its protein moiety, its salt content, and an added supply of fat-soluble vitamine. Of these three additions the correction of the deficiency in certain inorganic salts seemed to be of the greatest importance, inasmuch as this correction in itself furnished a ration on which rats did grow fairly well for several months.

Hart, Halpin, and Steenbock (1917) report experiments with pullets weighing 2 to 3 pounds on corn and wheat rations These investigators found that corn and wheat meal do not support growth in this species of animals; fortifying the cereals with an appropriate inorganic salt mixture, protein of proper composition, and a small amount of fat-soluble vitamine (2 per cent butter fat) leads to normal growth. These authors also call attention to the possibility of intoxication as a result of excessive wheat feeding, which they attribute to the presence of some toxic substance in the wheat kernel.

The purpose of the present investigation was to answer the question as to whether the corn and wheat products used in human nutrition exhibit similar dietary deficiencies as those of the whole grains. The bulk of the corn and wheat foods of the American dietary are derived from the wheat and corn kernel by means of a process of milling (roller mills) which is known to eliminate most of the germ and superficial layers of the grain. It, therefore, seemed to us a question of practical importance to determine whether the milling process improves, or causes a decrease in, the dietary value of the milled product. Moreover, it was desirable to decide whether or not the food additions made to flour (yeast, salt, milk) in the preparation of bread improve the nutritive value of this food.

Experimental.

The experiments were carried out on squabs, young albino mice, and a few hogs. Most of the work was done with wheat, and only a few incomplete experiments were made with foods obtained from corn.

We are not aware of any previous records where squabs have been used for studies on growth. For this reason the following details are given, as they may be of interest to workers in this field. The growth period of pigeons is extremely short, as will be seen from the records. Almost maximum body weight is reached, on an adequate diet, within 40 days after the squabs are hatched. The feathers develop gradually, and by the time full growth is reached the body is completely covered. The birds begin to fly at the age of about 40 days. This is usually followed by a slight loss of body weight, which is probably due to the strenuous muscular work performed in flying. It should be pointed out that squabs can not feed themselves during the first two weeks of life. During this period the parents feed the young by regurgitating food which has been softened in their crops. The function of the crop consists in the preparation of the cereal food for gastric digestion. It is very doubtful whether active digestion takes place within the crop, and it is more likely that this organ simply softens the food by means of water in order to facilitate its disintegration by the stomach. In the absence of the crop, gastric digestion of cereals would be a rather slow process, even in the case of the bird's stomach with its powerful muscular wall and the gravel which takes the place of millstones.

In order to obtain a sufficient number of squabs for experiments on growth, about 70 to 100 healthy pigeons were kept in a well-ventilated room containing numerous cages (wire screened), the doors of which were left open. Usually the birds built their nests in these cages and after laying the eggs the parents were caught, confined to the cage, and put on the diet to be tested for its growth-promoting properties. When it happened that eggs were laid outside of the cages, the pigeons were allowed to hatch and the young squabs were then transferred, with the nest and the parent birds, to the nearest cage. We found that it was impossible to move the eggs, as the birds refused to sit after the eggs had been handled. The sitting period of pigeons is about 17 days. The male bird sits from about 9 a. m. to 5 p. m.; the female from 5 p. m. to 9 a. m.

The stock pigeons were fed for nearly two years, while this work was in progress, on an exclusive diet of corn and wheat, crushed oyster shells, and river sand. Fresh running water was supplied. On this diet the birds bred very well throughout the year, with the exception of the moulting season.

The average egg weighed about 16 grams; the contents, minus the shell, weighed about 15 grams, and the weight of the squab immediately after hatching was about 13 grams. It was found that squabs which were below the average body weight and those that had difficulty in hatching, were of low vitality. The squabs were weighed as soon after hatching as possible and every three days thereafter during the morning hours (9 a. m.). The growth curve during the first 10 days is almost a straight line, slight deviations being due to variations of crop content. The birds which died as a result of a diet of inadequate composition were necropsied and the sciatic nerves examined for the presence of myelin degeneration.

The great advantage of using squabs for growth experiments is due to the possibility of immediately starting the newborn animal on a ration which is to be investigated. It is obvious that this can not be done when mammals are used.

The experiments with albino mice were carried out on young animals weighing approximately 6 to 8 grams and obtained from a healthy stock kept in the laboratory. Recent work has sufficiently demonstrated that mice are as well suited for growth experiments as albino rats. The animals were placed in wide glass jars with a wire screened top. Sawdust was used as bedding. Under these conditions the mice could be kept in excellent health on an adequate diet for nearly a year. The animals were weighed every three or four days.[1]

The hogs used were young animals, either purchased on the open market or raised in the laboratory. They were kept in stalls with a concrete floor. The bedding was wheat straw, some of which was eaten by the animals. Tap water was supplied. The experiments on hogs are somewhat complicated, as the straw and tap water may perhaps be considered as a source of inorganic salts and fat-soluble vitamine. However, this factor remained approximately constant in each experiment.

Food used.—When the whole wheat was fed to mice it was usually crushed in an ordinary kitchen mill. The wheat flour, either alone or with other foods, was made into cakes by means of water. The wet cakes were dried at 45° C. and broken up into small pieces. The white flour used was bought under the name of "patent" flour and came from one of the largest roller mills of the West. The wheat "middlings" were obtained from a roller mill in Washington, D. C. The "whole wheat" bread used was purchased in Washington, D. C., and the bakery volunteered the following information in regard to the food materials used in the preparation of this bread: Standard loaves were made from crushed whole wheat, with the addition of canned eggs, some salt, olive oil, molasses, compound lard, wheat bran, and pressed yeast. The accurate proportions of the various constitutents could not be obtained. The "white" bread was made from "highly milled" wheat flour, with the addition of sodium chloride, compound lard, yeast, and evaporated milk. For 900 standard loaves of this bread, 588 pounds of flour, 47 pounds of evaporated milk, and 8¾ pounds of pressed yeast were used.

In the experiments where the "white" bread was supplemented by other foods, the bread was first dried at 40 to 50° C., crushed in a mill, and mixed with the other food in the desired proportions. The casein was a purified preparation made in this laboratory. The crushed oyster shells, fed to the pigeons, consisted largely of calcium carbonate, with traces of organic matter. When the rations contained chemically pure calcium carbonate in place of the oyster shells, exactly the same results were obtained so far as the growth of squabs was concerned. The grit was

---

[1] The normal growth curve of mice was taken from the article by Mitchell, J., Biol. Chem., 1916, vol. 26, p. 24.

well-washed river sand, consisting mainly of silicates. The so-called "activated" Lloyd's reagent was used as a source of antineuritic vitamine.[1]

In some experiments the "inactive" Lloyd's reagent was included in the rations. Fuller's earth, which had not been in contact with the yeast filtrate, was used in this case. The highest proportion of activated Lloyd's reagent contained in any of the rations was 3 per cent. In most cases 0.6 per cent or 1.5 per cent were used with equal success. When the activated Lloyd's reagent forms 0.6 or 1.5 per cent of the ration, the total nitrogen derived from this source represents only 15 to 37 milligrams.

It should be pointed out that squabs do not well tolerate the addition of considerable quantities of fat to the diet. In some experiments, where 5 per cent of lard was incorporated in the ration, the birds showed diarrhea and poor growth, followed by decline and death.

Summary.

It seems superfluous to enter into a detailed discussion of the results obtained in this investigation, as the accompanying charts illustrate the results in a comprehensive manner. For this reason only the main points will be referred to in this summary.

1. The "highly milled" products are, without exception, inferior in dietary value, as regards growth, to foods prepared from the whole grain. It is rather surprising that such delicate organs as the gastrointestinal tract of young mice can tolerate a diet containing a large amount of bran. This fact, however, does not necessarily mean that it is advantageous to include the bran in foods intended for human nutrition. On the contrary, the experiences with "war bread" would rather indicate that persons with delicate digestion are subject to temporary digestive disturbances as a result of a change from "white" bread to bread containing a considerable percentage of bran ("war bread"). On the other hand, from the standpoint of dietary completeness, a bread including all of the grain, with the exception of the superficial cellulose layer, is undoubtedly superior to the so-called white bread, made from "highly milled" flour, and would not possess the above-mentioned objectionable features.

2. The "white" bread used in these experiments was not adequate for maintaining normal growth, in spite of the fact that it was prepared with some evaporated milk and yeast. The most significant defect of "white" flour is the deficiency in antineuritic and fat-soluble vitamine; it is also deficient in adequate protein and inorganic salts.

3. A wheat flour, containing a considerable part of the germ and superficial layers of the grain, supports growth of mice and pigeons especially well when supplemented with inorganic salts. The same is true of "whole wheat" bread.

[1] It was prepared from autolyzed brewer's yeast by treatment with hydrochloric acid and filtration. This yeast filtrate was then treated with a special grade of fuller's earth, which removed a considerable part of the active vitamine from the yeast filtrate. The dried preparation was free of protein and gave negative tests for tryptophan, cystin, and tyrosin. No lysin could be isolated but the activated Lloyd's reagent contained a substance which in its reactions resembled histidine. The total nitrogen content of the dried reagent was about 25 per cent, and this consisted largely of adenine and other basic substances derived from yeast filtrate.

4. "Highly milled" corn grits, forming the exclusive food of young hogs, leads to failure of growth in these animals, whereas the whole corn kernel, supplemented by inorganic salts, promotes growth.

5. Newborn squabs are suitable animals for growth experiments.

6. No evidence of a toxic action of a whole wheat diet was obtained in the experiments on squabs which were fed on whole wheat meal, supplemented by a suitable salt mixture.

7. In the light of our present knowledge, it would appear that bread made from "whole wheat" flour, or old-fashioned corn meal, should be used in preference to "white" bread and "highly milled" corn foods, whenever the diet is restricted to these cereal foods to the more or less complete exclusion of other foods possessing greater dietary values.

Bibliography.

Hart, Halpin, and Steenbock. 1917. J. Biol. Chem., vol. 31, p. 415.
Hart and McCollum. 1914. J. Biol. Chem., vol. 19, p. 373.
McCollum, Simmonds, and Pitz. 1916. J. Biol. Chem., vol. 28, p. 153.
Mitchell. 1916. J. Biol. Chem., vol. 26, p. 24.

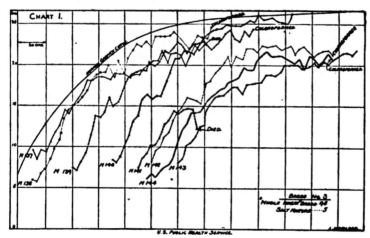

CHART 1 —Shows satisfactory growth of mice when "whole wheat" bread is supplemented with 5 per cent of salt mixture. Evidently the whole wheat bread used in this experiment was slightly deficient in inorganic salts, as seen from chart 2, where the bread was fed without the addition of the salt mixture. The composition of the salt mixture used in this investigation was as follows: NaCl, 0.50 gm.; K_2HPO_4, 1.21 gm.; $CaH_4(PO_4)_2$, H_2O, 0.256 gm.; Calcium lactate, 2.944 gm.; Ferric citrate, 0.100 gm.

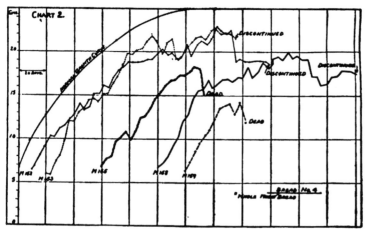

CHART 2 —Illustrates the growth of mice on "whole wheat" bread. The retardation of growth is mainly due to the deficiency of this diet in inorganic salts. (See chart 1.)

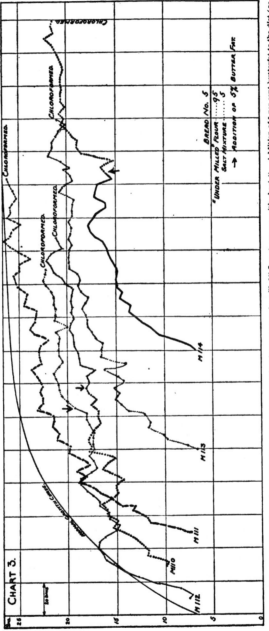

CHART 3.—Growth of mice. Shows beneficial effect of the addition of salt mixture to "undermilled" flour (compare with chart 4). Addition of 5 per cent butterfat to the diet (as indicated by arrows) increased rate of growth of mouse 114, but not of mice 110 and 112. From charts 3 and 4 it seems that this "undermilled" flour is deficient in certain inorganic salts and possibly fat soluble vitamine.

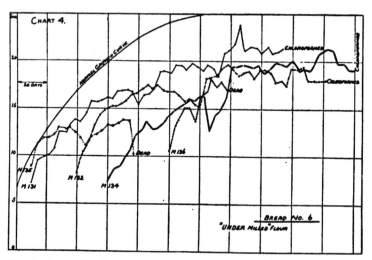

CHART 4 —Illustrates the subnormal growth of mice on a diet of "under milled" flour. This flour was obtained from a roller mill and was bought as "second clear." It contained 0 92 per cent P_2O_5 From the phosphorous content of this flour it would appear that this product is the grade of flour intermediate between a "first and second clear."

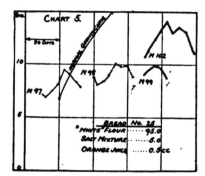

CHART 5.—Shows insignificant growth of mice when "white" flour is supplemented with a salt mixture. The orange juice was added to the drinking water with the idea of preventing scorbutic symptoms. The "white" flour was bought under the name of "patent" flour and contained 0.25 per cent of P_2O_5. The sciatic nerves of mouse 102, 98, and 97 showed marked myelin degeneration. These animals probably died of polyneuritis.

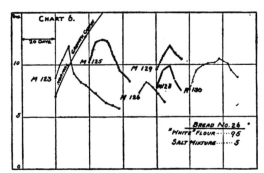

CHART 6.—Illustrates early failure of growth, followed by death of mice on a diet of "white" flour plus salt mixture. The sciatic nerves of these mice showed marked myelin degeneration. The results of this experiment are therefore identical with the one which is illustrated by chart 5.

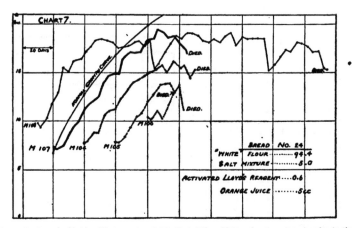

CHART 7.—Growth of mice. Illustrates beneficial effect of the addition of antineuritic vitamine in the form of activated Lloyd's reagent to a mixture of "white" flour and inorganic salts. Compare with charts 5 and 6. Bread No. 24 is not a complete diet, probably deficient in fat-soluble vitamine and certain essential amino acids.

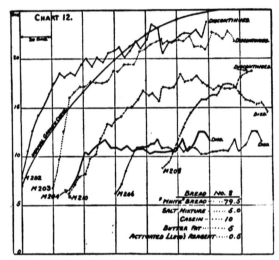

CHART 12.—Illustrates the fairly good growth of mice on bread No. 8. Completion of growth was not obtained with all the mice of this series. Mice 204 and 206 did not grow well after having reached about 12 gm. of body weight.

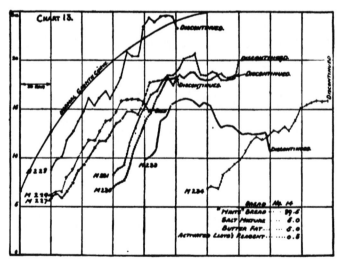

CHART 13.—Growth of mice.

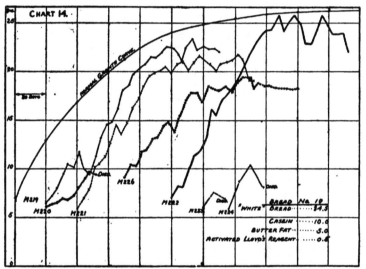

CHART 14.—Shows retardation of growth of mice on bread No. 10, deficient in inorganic salts.

55640°—18——2

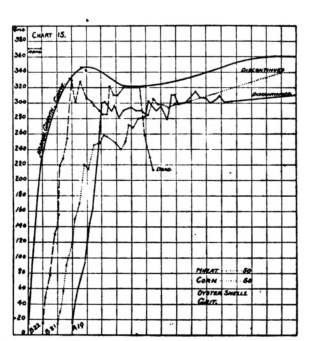

CHART 15. -Shows satisfactory growth of squabs on a diet limited to the corn and wheat kernel, supplemented by the addition of calcium carbonate (oyster shells). The oyster shells were crushed and fed to the parents ad libitum. Squab B22 reached normal body weight in 20 days, but died suddenly at the age of 75 days The cause of death is unknown. The other two squabs of this series showed normal growth and development and lived for 150 days, when the experiment was discontinued. The appearance of the birds at this time was normal in every respect.

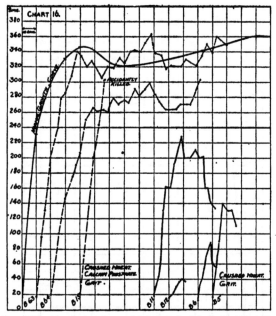

CHART 16.—Shows failure of growth of squabs on a diet of whole wheat alone. The birds evidently suffered from privation of mineral salts. The skeleton was poorly developed, calcification being very deficient. When the wheat kernel was supplemented by the addition of calcium phosphate practically normal growth was obtained. Sciatic nerve of Squab B11, B5, and B6 shows no myelin degeneration.

858

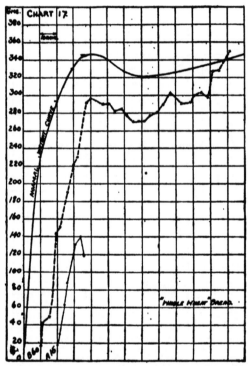

CHART 17.—Shows delayed growth and failure of growth of squabs on "whole wheat bread." This food is deficient in calcium salts. Compare with chart 18. Sciatic nerve of squab A15 did not reveal any myelin degeneration.

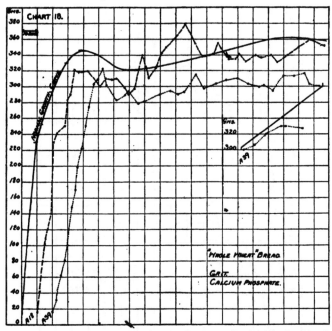

CHART 18.—Illustrates normal growth and development of squabs on a diet of "whole wheat" bread and calcium phosphate. The parents of these two squabs raised two other pairs of squabs while being fed on this diet. This proves that growth, reproduction, and maintenance of normal nutrition are possible on a simple diet as "whole wheat" bread supplemented by calcium salts.

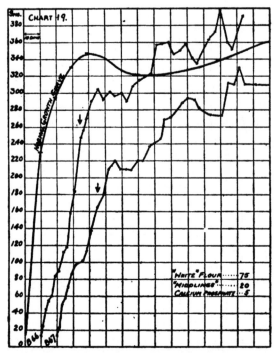

CHART 19.—Growth of squabs. Shows beneficial effect of addition of "middlings" and calcium phosphate to "highly milled" flour. The "middlings" fed with the mixture for the first 25 days of the experiment had the appearance of wheat bran and contained 1.98 per cent P_2O_5. The mixture of "white" flour and "middlings" contained 1.21 per cent P_2O_5. Compare this chart with chart 26.

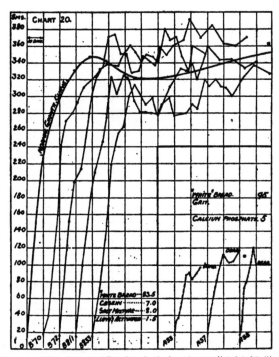

CHART 20.—Illustrates failure of growth, followed by death of squabs, on a diet of "white" bread and calcium phosphate (A33, A37, and A38). When the "white" bread is further supplemented by casein and a preparation containing antineuritic vitamine, normal growth and development results. Squabs B70 72,811, 833 reached nearly maximum normal weight at the age of about 30 days. Sciatic nerves of A33 A37, and A38 exhibit myelin degeneration.

862

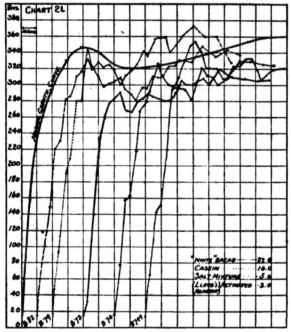

CHART 21.—Shows satisfactory growth of squabs when the "white" bread is supplemented by protein of proper composition, inorganic salts, and antineuritic vitamine. In this experiment the amount of the latter food accessory is twice as large as in the experiments illustrated by chart 20.

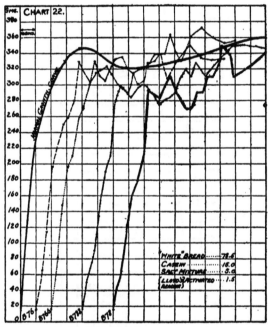

CHART 22.—Growth of squabs. The diet used in this experiment must be considered as physiologically complete. The "white" bread evidently contains sufficient fat-soluble vitamine (derived from evaporated milk) to render this ration adequate for growth.

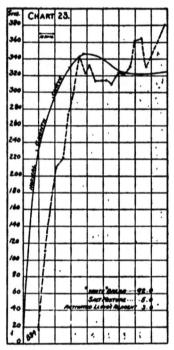

CHART 23.—Shows good growth of a squab on a diet of "white bread," which was supplemented by inorganic salts and antineuritic vitamine. Evidently the "white bread" used in this investigation was prepared with sufficient evaporated milk to correct the deficiency of the highly milled flour in fat-soluble vitamine and protein of proper composition.

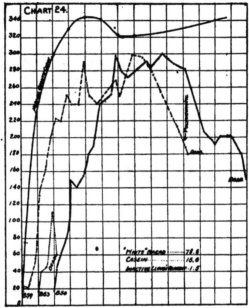

CHART 24.—Shows subnormal growth of squabs on a diet which is deficient in inorganic salts and anti-neuritic vitamine. The inactive l loyd's reagent which was added to the diet had not been treated with autolyzed yeast and therefore did not contain the antineuritic substance. Both birds developed poly-neuritic symptoms shortly before death.

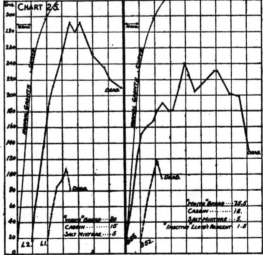

CHART 25.—Shows subnormal growth of squabs, followed by polyneuritis and death, when the "white" bread is supplemented by casein and a salt mixture (L2 and L1). The addition of "inactive" Lloyd's reagent, which has not been treated with autolyzed yeast, does not alter the result (B55 and B52).

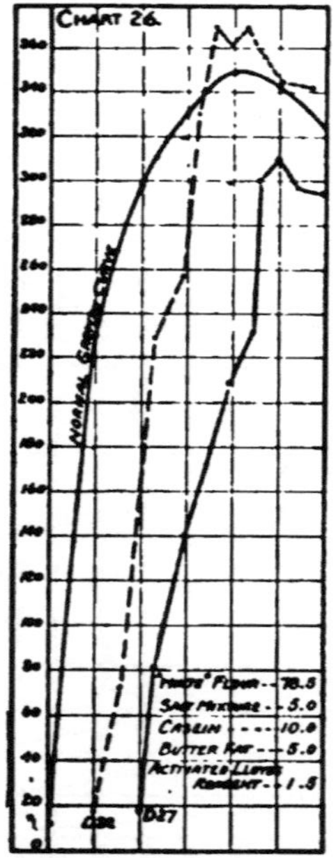

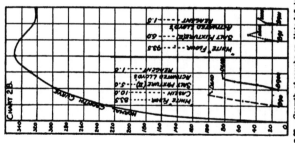

CHART 28.—Growth of squabs on diets deficient in fat soluble vitamine (B90 and B900) or fat soluble vitamine and protein of proper composition (B91 and B901).

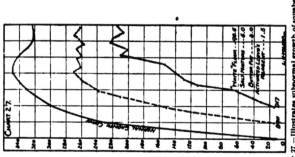

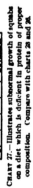

CHART 27.—Illustrates subnormal growth of squabs on a diet which is deficient in protein of proper composition. (Compare with charts 26 and 28.

CHART 26.—Shows that squabs grow normally when the "white" flour is supplemented by inorganic salts, protein of proper composition, fat soluble vitamine, and antineuritic vitamins

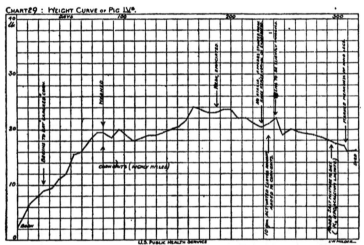

CHART 29 : WEIGHT CURVE OF PIG IV^B.

U.S. PUBLIC HEALTH SERVICE

CHART 29.—Illustrates the failure of growth of young hogs on a diet of "highly milled" corn grits. This food was obtained from a roller mill and represents the endosperm of the corn kernel. The animal was born of a hog which had been raised in the laboratory on a diet of cracked corn, wheat straw, and tap water. On the corn grits the animal did not gain more than a few pounds during nine months, in spite of the addition of a supplementary salt mixture and antineuritic vitamine. The animal finally died. The necropsy revealed the following abnormalities: Emphysema of lungs, chronic gastritis, small injected areas in small intestine, chronic passive congestion of liver, congestion of spleen, no scorbutic changes. Sciatic shows marked myelin degeneration. Another pig of the same litter showed a similar growth curve on a diet of corn grits. Here also correction of the salt content and antineuritic vitamine of the diet did not prevent death. Necropsy findings were the same as in Pig IVB.

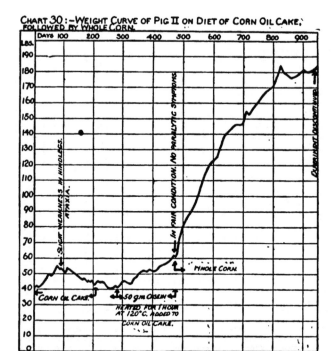

CHART 30 :—WEIGHT CURVE OF PIG II ON DIET OF CORN OIL CAKE, FOLLOWED BY WHOLE CORN.

CHART 30.—Illustrates failure of growth of a hog fed on corn oil cake. This product is obtained commercially on a large scale by pressing out the oil from the corn embryo. As soon as this diet was changed to whole corn a rapid increase in the rate of growth followed. This animal reached nearly full size and was in excellent condition at the end of the experiment. Compare this chart with chart 29, where "highly milled" corn grits was fed.

BIOLOGICAL PRODUCTS.

ESTABLISHMENTS LICENSED FOR THE PROPAGATION AND SALE OF VIRUSES, SERUMS, TOXINS, AND ANALOGOUS PRODUCTS.

The following table contains a list of the establishments holding licenses issued by the Treasury Department in accordance with the act of Congress approved July 1, 1902, entitled "An act to regulate the sale of viruses, serums, toxins, and analogous products in the District of Columbia, to regulate interstate traffic in said articles, and for other purposes."

The licenses granted to the following establishments for the products mentioned do not imply an indorsement of the claims made by the manufacturers for their respective preparations. The granting of a license means that inspections of the establishment concerned and laboratory examinations of samples of its products are made regularly to insure the observance of safe methods of manufacture, to ascertain freedom from contamination, and to determine the potency of diphtheria antitoxin, tetanus antitoxin, antidysenteric serum, antimeningococcic serum, antipneumococcic serum, and typhoid vaccine, the only products for which potency standards or tests have been established.

The enumeration of the products is as follows: Serums are placed first, the antitoxins, being the older and more important, heading the list. The other products called antigens because they are supposed to stimulate the production of antibodies are arranged generally in the order of their origin, those considered most important being placed first. The items in each class are arranged alphabetically.

The order may be resumed thus:

1. Antitoxins (alphabetically).
2. Other serums (alphabetically).
3. Vaccine virus.
4. Rabies vaccine.
5. Tuberculins—
   Old.
   T. R.
   B. E.
   B. F.
   Miscellaneous.
6. Bacterial vaccines (alphabetically by bacteria).
7. Sensitized bacterial vaccines (alphabetically by bacteria).
8. Miscellaneous products (alphabetically).

Establishments Licensed and Products for which Licenses have been Issued.

AMERICAN ESTABLISHMENTS.

Parke, Davis & Co., Detroit, Mich.—License No. 1:

Diphtheria antitoxin; tetanus antitoxin; antigonococcic serum; antimeningococcic serum; antipneumococcic serum; antistreptococcic serum; hemostatic serum (Lapenta); normal horse serum, thyroidectomized horse serum; vaccine virus; rabies vaccine (Cumming); tuberculin old; tuberculin T. R.; tuberculin B. E.; tuberculin B. F.; bacterial vaccines made from acne bacillus, acne diplococcus, colon bacillus, Friedländer bacillus, gonococcus, influenza bacillus, meningococcus, micrococcus catarrhalis, paratyphoid bacillus A, paratyphoid bacillus B, pertussis bacillus, pneumococcus, prodigiosus bacillus, pseudodiphtheria bacillus, staphylococcus albus, staphylococcus aureus, staphylococcus citreus, streptococcus, and typhoid bacillus; cholera prophylactic (Strong); diphtheria toxin-antitoxin mixture; modified bacterial derivatives prepared from colon bacillus, diphtheria bacillus, gonococcus, paratyphoid bacillus A, paratyphoid bacillus B, pneumococcus, pyocyaneus bacillus, staphylococcus albus, staphylococcus aureus, staphylococcus citreus, streptococcus and typhoid bacillus; pollen extract.

H. K. Mulford Co., Philadelphia, Pa.—License No. 2:

Diphtheria antitoxin; tetanus antitoxin; antianthrax serum; antidysenteric serum; antimelitensis serum; antimeningococcic serum; antipneumococcic serum; antistreptococcic serum; normal horse serum; vaccine virus; rabies vaccine; tuberculin old; tuberculin T. R.; tuberculin B. E.; tuberculin B. F.; tuberculin proteose-free (Lyons); bacterial vaccines prepared from acne bacillus, cholera vibrio, colon bacillus, diphtheria bacillus, dysentery bacillus, Friedländer bacillus, gonococcus, influenza bacillus, meningococcus, micrococcus catarrhalis, paratyphoid bacillus A, paratyphoid bacillus B, pertussis bacillus, plague bacillus, pneumococcus, pseudodiphtheria bacillus, pyocyaneus bacillus, staphylococcus albus, staphylococcus aureus, streptococcus, and typhoid bacillus; sensitized bacterial vaccines prepared from acne bacillus, cholera vibrio, colon bacillus, Friedländer bacillus, gonococcus, influenza bacillus, meningococcus, micrococcus catarrhalis, paratyphoid bacillus A, paratyphoid bacillus B, pertussis bacillus, pneumococcus, pseudodiphtheria bacillus, staphylococcus albus, staphylococcus aureus, streptococcus, and typhoid bacillus; pollen extract.

The Cutter Laboratory, Berkeley, Cal.—License No. 8:

Diphtheria antitoxin; tetanus antitoxin; antimeningococcic serum; antipneumococcic serum; antistreptococcic serum; normal horse serum; vaccine virus; rabies vaccine; tuberculin old; tuberculin T. R.; tuberculin B. E.; tuberculin B. F.; bacterial vaccines prepared from acne bacillus, colon bacillus, Friedländer bacillus, gonococcus, influenza bacillus, meningococcus, micrococcus catarrhalis, pertussis bacillus, pneumococcus, pseudodiphtheria bacillus, staphylococcus albus, staphylococcus aureus, streptococcus, and typhoid bacillus.

Bureau of Laboratories, Department of Health, New York City.—License No. 14:

Diphtheria antitoxin; tetanus antitoxin; antimeningococcic serum, antipneumococcic serum; normal horse serum; vaccine virus; rabies vaccine; tuberculin old, and bacterial vaccines prepared from gonococcus, paratyphoid bacillus A, paratyphoid bacillus B, pertussis bacillus, pneumococcus, staphylococcus albus, staphylococcus aureus, streptococcus, and typhoid bacillus; diphtheria toxin-antitoxin mixture.

National Vaccine and Antitoxin Institute, Washington, D. C.—License No. 16:

Diphtheria antitoxin, tetanus antitoxin; normal horse serum; rabies vaccine; bacterial vaccines prepared from acne bacillus, colon bacillus, Friedländer bacillus, gonococcus, influenza bacillus, meningococcus, micrococcus catarrhalis, micrococcus tetragenus, paratyphoid bacillus A, paratyphoid bacillus B, pertussis bacillus, pneumococcus, pseudodiphtheria bacillus, pyocyaneus bacillus, staphylococcus albus, staphylococcus aureus, staphylococcus citreus, streptococcus, and typhoid bacillus.

Lederle Antitoxin Laboratories, Pearl River, N. Y.—License No 17:

Diphtheria antitoxin, tetanus antitoxin, antidysenteric serum, antigonococcic serum, antimeningococcic serum, antipneumococcic serum, antistreptococcic serum, normal horse serum, vaccine virus, rabies vaccine, tuberculin B. F., tuberculin bacillary suspension, bacterial vaccines prepared from acne bacillus, cholera vibrio, colon bacillus, Friedländer bacillus, gonococcus, influenza bacillus, meningococcus, micrococcus catarrhalis, paratyphoid bacillus A, paratyphoid bacillus B, pertussis bacillus, plague bacillus, pneumococcus, pseudodiphtheria bacillus, pyocyaneus bacillus, staphylococcus albus, staphylococcus aureus, staphylococcus citreus, streptococcus, and typhoid bacillus, diphtheria toxin-antitoxin, pollen extract.

Bacterio-Therapeutic Laboratory, Asheville, N. C.—License No. 23:

Tuberculin o d, tuberculin B. E., watery extract of tubercle bacilli (von Ruck), modified tubercle bacillus derivative (von Ruck).

Dr. G. H. Sherman, 444 Jefferson Avenue, Detroit, Mich.—License No 30:

Bacterial vaccines prepared from acne bacillus, colon bacillus, Friedländer bacillus, gonococcus, influenza bacillus, meningococcus, micrococcus catarrhalis, nonvirulent tubercle bacillus, paratyphoid bacillus A, paratyphoid bacillus B, pertussis bacillus, pneumococcus, pseudodiphtheria bacillus, staphylococcus albus, staphylococcus aureus, staphylococcus citreus, streptococcus, and typhoid bacillus.

Hygienic Laboratory, California State Board of Health, Berke'ey, Cal.—License No. 40:
 Rabies vaccine, sensitized sedimented typhoid vaccine (Gay-Claypo'e).
The Abbott Laboratories, 4735 East Ravenswood Avenue, Chicago, Ill.—License No 43:
 Bacterial vaccines prepared from acne bacillus, colon bacillus, Fried'änder bacillus, gonococcus, micro-
  coccus catarrhalis, pertussis bacillus pneumococcus, staphylococcus albus, staphylococcus aureus,
  streptococcus, and typhoid bacillus.
Dr. W. T. McDougall, 640 Minnesota Avenue, Kansas City, Kans.—License No. 49:
 Rabies vaccine.
St. Louis Pasteur Institute, 928 North Grand Avenue, St. Louis, Mo.—License No. 50:
 Rabies vaccine (dilution method).
The Upjohn Co., Kalamazoo, Mich.—License No. 51:
 Bacterial vaccines prepared from colon bacillus, Friedländer bacillus, gonococcus, influenza bacillus,
  micrococcus catarrhalis, micrococcus tetragenus, paratyphoid bacillus A, paratyphoid bacillus B,
  pertussis bacillus, pneumococcus, pse idodiphtheria bacillus, staphylococcus albus, staphylococcus
  aureus, staphylococcus citreus, streptococcus, and typhoid bacillus.
E. R. Squibb & Sons' Research and Biological Laboratories, New Brunswick, N. J.—License No. 52:
 Diphtheria antitoxin, tetanus antitoxin, antigonococcic serum, antimeningococcic serum, antipneumococcic serum, antistreptococcic serum, normal horse serum, vaccine virus, rabies vaccine, bacterial
  vaccines prepared from acne bacillus, cho'era vibrio, colon bacillus, dysentery bacillus, Friedländer
  bacillus, gonococcus, influenza bacillus, meningococcus, micrococcus catarrhalis, ozena bacillus,
  paratyphoid bacillus A, paratyphoid bacillus B, pertussis bacillus, pneumococcus, pseudodiphtheria bacillus, pyocyaneus bacillus, staphylococcus albus, staphylococcus aureus, staphylococcus
  citreus, streptococcus, and typhoid bacillus, leucocytic extract from the horse.
Laboratory of Clinical Pathology, 1208 Wyandotte Street, Kansas City, Mo.—License No. 53:
 Rabies vaccine.
Dr. James McI. Phillips, 2057 North High Street, Columbus, Ohio.—License No. 54:
 Rabies vaccine.
Eli Lilly & Co., Indianapolis, Ind.—License No. 56:
 Diphtheria antitoxin, tetanus antitoxin, antistreptococcic serum, normal horse serum, normal sheep
  serum, vaccine virus, rabies vaccine (Harris), tuberculin old, tuberculin T. R., tuberculin B. E.,
  tuberculin B. F., bacterial vaccines prepared from acne bacillus, cholera vibrio, colon bacillus,
  diphtheria bacillus, Friedländer bacillus, gonococcus, influenza bacillus, meningococcus, micrococcus
  catarrhalis, micrococcus tetragenus, paratyphoid bacillus A, paratyphoid bacillus B, pertussis
  bacillus, plague bacillus, pneumococcus, pyocyaneus bacillus, staphylococcus albus, staphylococcus
  aureus, staphylococcus citreus, streptococcus, and typhoid bacillus.
Swan Myers Co., 219 North Senate Avenue, Indianapolis, Ind.—License No. 58:
 Bacterial vaccines prepared from acne bacillus, colon bacillus, Friedländer bacillus, gonococcus, in
  fluenza bacillus, micrococcus catarrhalis, micrococcus tetragenus, paratyphoid bacillus A, paratyphoid bacillus B, pertussis bacillus, pneumococcus, pseudodiphtheria bacillus, staphylococcus albus,
  staphylococcus aureus, streptococcus, and typhoid bacillus.
Greeley Laboratories (Inc.), 655 Huntington Avenue, Boston, Mass.—License No. 60:
 Bacterial vaccines prepared from acne bacillus, colon bacillus, gonococcus, micrococcus catarrhalis,
  pertussis bacillus, pneumococcus, pseudodiphtheria bacillus, staphylococcus albus, staphylococcus
  aureus, staphylococcus citreus, and streptococcus.
Gilliland Laboratories, Ambler, Pa.—License No. 63:
 Diphtheria antitoxin; tetanus antitoxin; normal horse serum; vaccine virus; rabies vaccine; tuber-
  culin, old; tuberculin, T. R.; tuberculin B. E.; tuberculin B. F.; bacterial vaccine prepared from
  the typhoid bacillus.
Antitoxin and Vaccine Laboratory, Massachusetts State Department of Health, Boston, Mass.—License
 No. 64:
 Diphtheria antitoxin; vaccine virus; bacterial vaccines prepared from paratyphoid bacillus A, para-
  typhoid bacillus B, and typhoid bacillus.
United States Standard Serum Co., Woodworth, Wis.—License No. 65:
 Diphtheria antitoxin.

FOREIGN ESTABLISHMENTS.

Institut Pasteur de Paris, Paris, France —License No. 11. Selling agents for the United States: Pasteur
 Laboratories of America, 399 West Eleventh Street, New York City:
 Diphtheria antitoxin tetanus antitoxin, venom antitoxin; antidysenteric serum; antimeningococcic
  serum. antiplague serum, antistreptococcic serum, bacterial vaccine prepared from plague bacillus.
Burroughs, Wellcome & Co., London, England.—License No. 18:
 Diphtheria antitoxin, tetanus antitoxin; anticolon bacillus serum; antidysenteric serum antigonococcic serum; antimeningococcic serum, antistaphylococcic serum; antistreptococcic serum; anti-
  typhoid serum; normal horse serum tuberculin, old; tuberculin, T. R. tuberculin, B. E.; tuberculin, B. F ; tuberculin (Wellcome), bacterial vaccines prepared from acne bacillus, cholera vibrio,
  colon bacillus, influenza bacillus, gonococcus, micrococcus catarrhalis, micrococcus melitensis, pneumococcus, septus bacillus, staphylococcus albus, staphylococcus aureus, staphylococcus citreus,
  streptococcus, and typhoid bacillus.

Swiss Serum and Vaccine Institute, Berne, Switzerland—License No. 21:

Diphtheria antitoxin, tetanus antitoxin; antidysenteric serum, antimeningococcic serum; antiplague serum, antipneumococcic serum, antistreptococcic serum, tuberculin, old, bacterial vaccines prepared from cholera vibrio, colon bacillus, plague bacillus, pneumococcus, staphylococcus albus, staphylococcus aureus, streptococcus, and typhoid bacillus.

Institut Bactériologique de Lyon, Lyon, France.—License No. 22:

Diphtheria antitoxin, normal goat serum.

Dr. Carl Spengler, Davos-Platz, Switzerland.—License No. 35:

Antituberculc blood (Spengler).

Laboratorio di Terapia Sperimentale (Bruschettini), Genoa, Italy.—License No. 38:

Tuberculosis serum extract (Bruschettini); tuberculosis extract (Bruschettini).

Inoculation Department, St. Mary's Hospital, London, England. —License No. 48:

Bacterial vaccines prepared from acne bacillus, gonococcus, influenza bacillus, pneumococcus, staphylococcus albus, staphylococcus aureus, staphylococcus citreus, and streptococcus; pollen extract.

PREVALENCE OF DISEASE.

No health department, State or local, can effectively prevent or control disease without knowledge of when, where, and under what conditions cases are occurring.

UNITED STATES.

EXTRA-CANTONMENT ZONES—CASES REPORTED WEEK ENDED MAY 28.

CAMP BEAUREGARD ZONE, LA.

Alexandria: Cases.
  Gonorrhea................................. 2
  Malaria................................... 3
  Measles................................... 1
  Mumps..................................... 23
  Smallpox.................................. 7
  Tuberculosis.............................. 2
  Typhoid fever............................. 1
Pineville:
  Mumps..................................... 2
Rural district:
  Malaria................................... 2

CAMP BOWIE ZONE, TEX.

Fort Worth:
  Chicken pox............................... 8
  Gonorrhea................................. 16
  Malaria................................... 1
  Measles................................... 2
  Mumps..................................... 8
  Scarlet fever............................. 1
  Smallpox.................................. 33
  Syphilis.................................. 19
  Tuberculosis.............................. 2
  Typhoid fever............................. 2
  Whooping cough............................ 1

CAMP DEVENS ZONE, MASS.

Chicken pox:
  Lunenburg................................. 2
Measles:
  Forge Village............................. 2
  Townsend.................................. 1
  Westford.................................. 4
Tuberculosis, pulmonary:
  Ayer...................................... 1
Whooping cough:
  Ayer...................................... 1

CAMP DONIPHAN ZONE, OKLA.

Cerebrospinal meningitis:
  Elgin..................................... 1
Smallpox:
  Cache..................................... 6
  Fletcher.................................. 2
  Letitia................................... 1

CAMP DONIPHAN ZONE, OKLA—continued.

Syphilis: Cases.
  Lawton.................................... 1
Typhoid fever:
  Lawton.................................... 4
Whooping cough:
  Lawton.................................... 4

CAMP EBERTS ZONE, ARK.

Chancroid:
  England................................... 4
Chicken pox:
  Carlisle.................................. 1
  Cabot..................................... 2
Diphtheria:
  Scott, route 2............................ 4
Gonorrhea:
  Carlisle.................................. 1
  Lonoke.................................... 2
  Kerr...................................... 1
  Kerr, route 1............................. 1
Malaria:
  England................................... 1
  Carlisle.................................. 2
  Lonoke.................................... 2
  Kerr...................................... 1
  Kerr, route 1............................. 1
  Cabot..................................... 2
  Cabot, route 1............................ 1
Measles:
  England, route 1.......................... 1
  Ward...................................... 1
  Cabot, route 3............................ 4
  Austin.................................... 1
  Austin, route 2........................... 4
Mumps:
  England................................... 4
  Lonoke.................................... 1
  County Farm............................... 3
  Scott, route 1............................ 2
Pellagra:
  Lonoke.................................... 4
Smallpox:
  England................................... 2
  Carlisle.................................. 1
  Kerr, route 1............................. 1
  Scott, route 1............................ 1

874

Syphilis:	Cases.
Lonoke	2
Scott	1
Tuberculosis:	
Scott, route 1	1
Whooping cough:	
England, route 2	1

CAMP FUNSTON ZONE, KANS.

Junction City:

Mumps	3
Manhattan:	
Measles	1
Mumps	4
Smallpox	2
Whooping cough	1

CAMP GORDON ZONE, GA.

Cerebrospinal meningitis:	
Decatur	1
Chicken pox:	
Atlanta	1
Diphtheria:	
Atlanta	1
Gonorrhea:	
Atlanta	8
Hookworm:	
Atlanta	1
Measles	
Atlanta	4
Decatur	3
Mumps	13
Atlanta	
Scarlet fever:	
Atlanta	1
Hapeville	1
Smallpox:	
Atlanta	9
Armour	1
Syphilis:	
Atlanta	1
Doraville	1
Tuberculosis:	
Atlanta	9
Tucker	1
Whooping cough:	
Atlanta	5

CAMP GREENE ZONE, N. C.

Charlotte Township:

Chicken pox	4
Chancroid	3
Gonorrhea	13
Measles	7
Syphilis	9
Tuberculosis	2
Whooping cough	41

GULFPORT HEALTH DISTRICT, MISS.

Gulfport Health District.

Malaria	9
Mumps	4
Typhoid fever	2

CAMP HANCOCK ZONE, GA.

Augusta: Cases.

Cerebrospinal meningitis	1
Chicken pox	5
German measles	1
Gonorrhea	1
Malaria	3
Measles	4
Tuberculosis, pulmonary	2
Typhoid fever	1
Whooping cough	1

CAMP JOSEPH E. JOHNSTON ZONE, FLA.

Chicken pox:	
Jacksonville	5
Dysentery:	
Jacksonville	5
Lackawanna	1
Malaria:	
Fishers Corner	1
Measles:	
Jacksonville	7
Fishers Corner	4
Mumps:	
Jacksonville	7
Panama	1
Pellagra:	
Jacksonville	1
Pneumonia:	
Jacksonville	2
Syphilis:	
Fishers Corner	1
Panama	1
Trachoma:	
Jacksonville	1
Tuberculosis.	
Jacksonville	3
Orange Park	1
Ortega	1
Typhoid fever:	
Jacksonville	2
Whooping cough:	
Jacksonville	21
Lackawanna	3

FORT LEAVENWORTH ZONE, KANS.

Leavenworth:	
Measles	1
Pneumonia, lobar	1
Smallpox	5
Leavenworth County:	
Measles	21
Pneumonia, lobar	2
Scarlet fever	2
Smallpox	5
Typhoid fever	1

CAMP LEE ZONE, VA.

Chancroid:	
Peter burg	4
Chicken pox	
Prince George County	4
Gonorrhea	
Petersburg	9

CAMP LEE ZONE, VA.—continued.

Malaria:	Cases.
Ettricks	2
Petersburg	4
Mumps:	
Hopewell	7
Petersburg	2
Prince George County	5
Pneumonia:	
Prince George County	1
Scarlet fever:	
Hopewell	1
Syphilis:	
Petersburg	4
Tuberculosis:	
Ettricks	1
Dinwiddie County	2
Petersburg	1

CAMP LEWIS ZONE, WASH.

German measles:	
Parkland	1
Mumps:	
Dupont	1
Lacamas	1
Parkland	1
Spanaway	3
Whooping cough:	
Parkland	1

CAMP LOGAN ZONE, TEX.

Houston:	
Chancroid	2
Diphtheria	1
Gonorrhea	31
Measles	1
Malaria	2
Mumps	1
Pneumonia	1
Syphilis	24
Tuberculosis	1
Typhoid fever	1
Goose Creek:	
Gonorrhea	1

CAMP MACARTHUR ZONE, TEX.

Waco:	
Measles	1
Mumps	8
Poliomyelitis	3
Syphilis	1
Tuberculosis	1
Typhoid fever	1
Whooping cough	3

CAMP M'CLELLAN ZONE, ALA.

Anniston:	
Diphtheria	1
Measles	7
Mumps	2

NORFOLK COUNTY NAVAL DISTRICT, VA.

Chicken pox:	
Norfolk County	2
Diphtheria:	
Ocean View	1

NORFOLK COUNTY NAVAL DISTRICT, VA.—contd.

Malaria:	Cases.
Port Norfolk	1
Ocean View	2
Measles:	
Pinners Point	1
Norfolk	1
South Norfolk	1
Portsmouth	1
Mumps:	
South Norfolk	2
Norfolk County	1
Norfolk	4
Portsmouth	2
Scarlet fever:	
Portsmouth	1
Tuberculosis:	
Norfolk County	1
Ocean View	1
Whooping cough:	
Norfolk	1

PORT OGLETHORPE ZONE, GA.

Gonorrhea:	
Chattanooga	9
Malaria:	
Greens Lake	1
Mumps:	
Chattanooga	1
East Chattanooga	1
Paratyphoid fever:	
North Chattanooga	2
Pneumonia:	
Chattanooga	1
Scarlet fever:	
Chattanooga	1
Smallpox:	
Chattanooga	11
Syphilis:	
Chattanooga	7
Chickamauga, Ga	1
Tuberculosis:	
Chattanooga	9
Whooping cough:	
Chattanooga	8

CAMP PIKE ZONE, ARK.

Cerebrospinal meningitis:	
Little Rock	1
Chancroid:	
North Little Rock	1
Chicken pox:	
Little Rock	2
Diphtheria:	
Little Rock	1
Gonorrhea:	
Little Rock	10
North Little Rock	2
Malaria:	
Little Rock	15
North Little Rock	1
Scotts	1
Nonresidents treated	1
Measles:	
Little Rock	2
Nonresidents treated	

CAMP PIKE ZONE, ARK.—continued.

Mumps: Cases.
    Little Rock............................ 3
    North Little Rock...................... 1
Pellagra:
    Galloway.............................. 1
Pneumonia:
    Little Rock............................ 1
Scarlet fever:
    Little Rock............................ 2
Smallpox:
    Little Rock............................ 10
    Little Maumelle....................... 1
Syphilis:
    Little Rock 7
    North Little Rock...................... 2
    Baucum............................... 1
Tuberculosis:
    Little Rock.... 10
    Wrightsville 1
Whooping cough.
    Little Rock............................ 1

CAMP SEVIER ZONE, S. C.

Cerebrospinal meningitis:
    Chick Springs Township................ 2
Mumps:
    Chick Springs Township................ 3
Tuberculosis, pulmonary.
    Chick Springs Township................ 1
    Greenville Township 1

CAMP SHELBY ZONE, MISS.

Hattiesburg:
    Chicken pox........................... 3
    Malaria............................... 7
    Mumps................................ 10
    Pellagra.............................. 1
    Smallpox.............................. 1
    Typhoid fever. 1
    Venereal.............................. 2
    Whooping cough....................... 8

CAMP SHERIDAN ZONE, ALA.

Montgomery:
    Chancroid 2
    Chicken pox........................... 1
    Gonorrhea............................ 22
    Malaria.............................. 37
    Measles.. 2
    Mumps............................... 2
    Syphilis.............................. 2
    Tuberculosis.......................... 2
    Typhoid fever......................... 2
    Whooping cough... 2

CAMP SHERMAN ZONE, OHIO.

Chillicothe:
    Chicken pox........................... 1
    Diphtheria............................ 1
    Gonorrhea............................ 2
    Scarlet fever.......................... 5
    Smallpox............................. 1
    Tuberculosis pulmonary 1
Liberty Township
    Measles 3
    Scarlet fever......................... 1

CAMP ZACHARY TAYLOR ZONE, KY.

Jefferson County: Cases.
    Trachoma............................. 3
    Typhoid fever......................... 2
Louisville:
    Chicken pox................ 1
    Diphtheria............................ 2
    Malaria............................... 1
    Measles............................... 5
    Mumps................................ 2
    Scarlet fever.......................... 1
    Smallpox............................. 3
    Trachoma............................. 1
    Tuberculosis, pulmonary............... 16
    Whooping cough....................... 5
New Albany, Ind.:
    Tuberculosis, pulmonary............... 1
United States Government clinic:
    Chancroid............................ 2
    Gonorrhea............................ 23
    Syphilis.............................. 34

TIDEWATER HEALTH DISTRICT, VA.

Cerebrospinal meningitis:
    Phoebus.............................. 1
Chancroid:
    Newport News......................... 4
Chicken pox:
    Hampton.............................. 4
German measles:
    Newport News......................... 4
Gonorrhea:
    Newport News......................... 14
Measles:
    Newport News......................... 7
Mumps:
    Newport News......................... 9
Scarlet fever:
    Newport News......................... 6
    Hampton.............................. 2
Smallpox:
    Newport News......................... 4
Syphilis:
    Newport News......................... 4
Tuberculosis:
    Morrison............................. 4
Whooping cough:
    Phoebus.............................. 9

CAMP WHEELER ZONE, GA.

Bibb County:
    Gonorrhea............................ 1
East Macon:
    Chicken pox........................... 1
    Syphilis.............................. 2
Macon:
    Chicken pox........................... 1
    Gonorrhea............................ 7
    Malaria 2
    Measles............................... 1
    Scarlet fever.......................... 1
    Smallpox............................. 5
    Syphilis.............................. 16
    Tuberculosis.......................... 3
    Typhoid fever......................... 2

DISEASE CONDITIONS AMONG TROOPS IN THE UNITED STATES.

The following data are taken from telegraphic reports received in the office of the Surgeon General, United States Army, for the week ended May 17, 1918:

Annual admission rate per 1,000 (disease only):

All troops	1,166.2
Divisional camps	736
Cantonments	1,227.2
Departmental and other troops	1,177.3

Noneffective rate per 1,000 on day of report:

All troops	39.5
Divisional camps	33

Noneffective rate per 1,000 on day of report—Continued.

Cantonments	44.7
Departmental and other troops	38.4

Annual death rate per 1,000 (disease only):

All troops	6.3
Divisional camps	3.1
Cantonments	9.9
Departmental and other troops	4.2

NOTE.—On account of frequent changes in organizations and personnel, it is no longer practicable to group troops separately as National Army, National Guard, and Regular Army as has been done previously in this report. The new grouping is considered more accurate.

New cases of special diseases reported during the week ended May 17, 1918.

Camp.	Pneumonia.	Dysentery.	Malaria.	Venereal.		Measles.	Meningitis.	Scarlet fever.	Deaths.	Annual admission rate per 1,000 (disease only).	Noneffective per 1,000 on day of report.
				Total.	New infections.						
Beauregard	8		19	40	4	2			5	1,084.1	53.5
Bowie	3		4	80	74					870.9	31.1
Cody	10	1		5	2				3	432.3	22.7
Doniphan	1			10					1	2,176.2	68.6
Fremont	3			46	45	28		1	1	1,209.2	38.5
Greene				6	6	3			1	540.1	23.4
Kearny	3		2	6		3		1	5	885.1	33.1
Logan	3	3	2	40	21	1	2	1		514.9	29.7
MacArthur									1	749.5	47.3
McClellan				95	21					884.5	31.5
Fevier	3		4	46	20	9	1	1	2	242.4	20.7
Shelby		4	2	12	2	1	1		2	652.4	36.9
Sheridan	1		2	20	13			4	2	398.9	20.3
Wadsworth				116		4		1		1,305.8	31.8
Wheeler	2	1		11	4		1		1	774.7	42.7
Custer	26			45	2	5	1		6	630.3	25
Devens	9			35	6	23		2	5	782.9	43.4
Dix	9		3	108	21	25		3	1	994.1	32.8
Dodge	36			133		44		3	14	1,543.3	82.6
Funston	42		1	23	11	13	1	2	3	1,016.2	44.1
Gordon	57		3	30	1	68	1		19	2,036	66.3
Grant	15			33	1	22		15	4	500.6	24.2
Jackson	31	1	1	334	3	26	1		14	1,888.4	59.7
J. F. Johnston	24		1	30	20	12			1	1,017.5	34.7
A. A. Humphreys	2			18	2	18			2	883	16.2
Lee	6		1	243	16	11			6	908.3	43.9
Lewis	17		5	74	5	10		11	2	1,023.3	34.7
Meade	14			74	17	5	4	1	2	901	33
Pike	37			63	16	21	2	2	10	2,036.7	71.4
Sherman	4			114	6	12		5	3	1,145.4	39.4
Taylor	14			69	2	13		3	5	909.4	57.4
Travis	55	2	6	74	3	4			11	2,503.2	40.2
Upton	14			218	43	3	2	6	3	1,016.1	31.3
Northeastern department	1			35	23	3				835.7	50.2
Eastern Department	1		3	31	25	9		2	4	851.3	27.7
Southeastern Department	1			75	8	6		1	3	1,100.7	32.4
Central Department	3			22	14	16		7		1,263.5	62.3
Southern Department	10		3	170	69	8		6	6	1,418.4	41.7
Western Department	3			38	17	7		6	2	1,007	18.5
Aviation, Signal Corps	21		2	103		14	3	13	11	1,228.1	34.8
Alcatraz Disciplinary Barracks										645.9	15.5
Columbus Barracks	1			8				1	1	643	21.1
Depot, Provisional Corps, and Army troops	10		1	62		3	5	2		1,715.3	35.7
Edgewood-Aberdeen						1				413.2	13.3
El Paso										268.3	13.3

New cases of special diseases reported during the week ended May 17, 1918—Continued.

| Camp. | Pneumonia. | Dysentery. | Malaria. | Venereal. | | Measles. | Meningitis. | Scarlet fever. | Deaths. | Annual admission rate per 1,000 (disease only). | Noneffective per 1,000 on day of report. |
				Total.	New infections.						
Hoboken	14	.....	2	113	9	13	3	7	3	647.1	49.4
Holabird.................						1				478.5	4.1
Jefferson Barracks.........	6	.....	.....	371	2	7	1	3	2	3,549	84.9
Leavenworth Disciplinary											
Barracks....	.....	.....	.....	.....	.....	.....	.....	.....	.....	1,160.1	40.7
Logan, Fort...........	.....	.....	.....	6	2	1		5	.....	1,608.3	77
McDowell, Fort..........	.....	.....	1	63	.....	2	.....	1	.....	2,740.5	78.4
Newport News............	10	4	3	146	3	5	1	1	4	1,245.1	53.4
Raritan.............	3	.....	.....	33	.....	.....	.....	.....	1	1,059.5	34.2
Slocum, Fort..........	3	.....	.....	33	.....	.....	.....	.....	1	1,039.5	34.2
Springfield Armory.......	.....	.....	.....	.....	.....	.....	.....	.....	.....	804.1	21.9
Thomas, Fort...........	2	.....	.....	24	.....	5	.....	.....	.....	1,622.9	77.6
Watervliet............	.....	.....	.....	2	.....	.....	.....	.....	.....	405.2	39
West Point...........	.....	.....	.....	.....	.....	.....	.....	.....	.....	449.8	8.6
National Guard departments.	.....	.....	.....	13	.....	7	1	1	.....	.....	.....
National Army departments..	8	.....	1	293	115	23	1	39	1	.....	.....
Total.................	**543**	**16**	**72**	**3,901**	**666**	**522**	**32**	**161**	**178**	**1,106.2**	**30.5**

¹ All troops.

Annual rate per 1,000 for special diseases.

Disease.	All troops in United States.¹	Departmental and other troops.¹	Divisional camps.¹	Cantonments.¹	Expeditionary forces.¹
Pneumonia.........................	21.8	12.5	6.7	26.7	21.7
Dysentery.........................	0.6	0.58	1.6	0.2	0.1
Malaria...........................	2.9	2.1	6.4	1.8	1.1
Venereal..........................	156.9	194.1	98	151.2	22.3
Paratyphoid.......................	0.0	0.0	0.0	0.0	0.0
Typhoid...........................	0.0	0.0	0.0	0.0	0.2
Measles...........................	21	14.6	0.5	30.2	9.3
Meningitis........................	1.28	1.9	0.9	1.1	2.1
Scarlet fever.....................	6.4	8	1.6	17.1	6.4

¹ Week ended May 17, 1918.   ² Week ended May 9, 1918.

CURRENT STATE SUMMARIES.

Connecticut.

From Collaborating Epidemiologist Black, by telegraph, **for week** ended May 25, 1918:

Smallpox Hartford 1, Voluntown 1, Griswold 4: contact with a Griswold case located State pier, New London. Meningitis, Bridgeport 2. Poliomyelitis, Essex 1. Septic sore throat: Farmington 50; in private school, epidemic abated.

Georgia.

From Collaborating Epidemiologist Abercrombie, by telegraph, for week ended May 25. 1918:

Dysentery, bacillary, Washington County 28 cases, 6 deaths.

Illinois.

From Collaborating Epidemiologist Drake, by telegraph, for week ended May 25, 1918:

Diphtheria: One hundred forty-one, of which in Chicago 122. Scarlet fever: Seventy-eight, of which in Chicago 51. Smallpox: One hundred twenty-three, of which in Morrisonville 9, Evansville 7, Eldorado 12, Springfield 6, Belleville 8, East St. Louis 7, Quincy 5, Onarga 5, Danville 5. Meningitis: Six, of which in Chicago 4, Chicago Heights 1, Springfield 1. Poliomyelitis: Six, of which in Woodstock 2, Chicago 4.

Indiana.

From the State Board of Health of Indiana, by telegraph, for week ended May 25, 1918:

Smallpox: Epidemic Kendallville, Seymour. Rabies (dogs): Sullivan. Mauckport, Anderson, Francesville, Evansville.

Kansas.

From Collaborating Epidemiologist Crumbine, by telegraph, for week ended May 25, 1918:

Smallpox (10 or more cases): By counties—Bourbon 11, Cherokee 24. Haskell 12, Pratt 10; by cities—Fort Scott 20, Kansas City 17, Salina 13, Wichita 51. Meningitis: By cities—Belvue 1, Bendena 1, Junction City 2.

Louisiana.

From Collaborating Epidemiologist Dowling, by telegraph, for week ended May 25, 1918:

Dengue: Iberia Parish 3. Typhoid fever 51, smallpox 60, malaria 85.

Massachusetts.

From Collaborating Epidemiologist Hitchcock, by telegraph, for week ended May 25, 1918:

Unusual prevalence. Measles: Lawrence 185, Malden 51, Norwood 26, Shirley 12, Waltham 29. Scarlet fever: Erving 6, Montague 16. Whooping cough: Avon 19, Whitman 30.

Minnesota.

From Collaborating Epidemiologist Bracken, by telegraph, for week ended May 25, 1918:

Smallpox (new foci): Faribault County, Emerald Township; Fillmore County, Preston village; Kittson County, St. Joseph Township; Millelacs County, Onamia village; Norman County, Fossum Township; each 1 case; Goodhue County, Welch Township, 7.

Nebraska.

From the State Board of Health of Nebraska, by telegraph, for week ended May 25, 1918:

Smallpox: North part Garden County, Merrick County, and Neligh. Scarlet fever: Omaha.

New Jersey.

From Collaborating Epidemiologist Bowen, by telegraph, for week ended May 25, 1918:

Unusual prevalence measles Clifton city.

South Carolina.

From Collaborating Epidemiologist Hayne, by telegraph, for week ended May 25, 1918:

Meningitis: McClellanville 1, Mount Pleasant 1.

Virginia.

From the State Board of Health of Virginia, by telegraph, for week ended May 25, 1918:

One case smallpox Montgomery County, 1 Prince George, 1 Halifax. Two cases cerebrospinal meningitis Grayson County, 1 Charlotte, 1 Petersburg.

Washington.

From Collaborating Epidemiologist Tuttle, by telegraph, for week ended May 25, 1918:

Scarlet fever: Four cases Ritzville (Adams County), 36 cases Tacoma, 20 cases Seattle. Measles: Fifty-one cases Seattle, 13 cases Tacoma, 3 cases Walla Walla. Typhoid. Elma 5 cases, Wenatchee 2 cases.

RECIPROCAL NOTIFICATION.

Minnesota.

Cases of communicable diseases referred during April, 1918, to other State health departments by department of health of the State of Minnesota.

Disease and locality of notification.	Referred to health authority of—	Why referred.
Diphtheria: Duluth Health Department, St. Louis County.	Turtle Lake, Barron County, Wis.....	Taken sick at Turtle Lake, Mar. 24, quarantined in Duluth Apr. 1.
Paratyphoid: Minneapolis Health Department, Hennepin County.	Winter, Sawyer County, Wis.........	Taken sick at Winter—came to Minneapolis, where he was admitted to City Hospital.
Smallpox: Minneapolis Health Department, Hennepin County.	Woodstock, McHenry County, Ill.....	Father, mother, and son exposed to smallpox at Minneapolis, left for home in Illinois.
Stillwater, Washington County.	Peoria, Peoria County, Ill............	Patient broke quarantine, left Minnesota for Illinois.
Minneapolis Health Department, Hennepin County.	Holdrege, Phelps County, Nebr.......	Sick on arrival in Minnesota from Nebraska.
St. Paul Bureau of Health, Ramsey County.	Lisbon, Ransom County, N. Dak.....	Traveling salesman, stopped at Lisbon while in infectious stage.
St. Louis Park, Hennepin County.	Pittsburgh, Allegheny County, Pa....	Exposed to smallpox in Minnesota; left for Pennsylvania.
Pipestone, Pipestone County...	Flandreau, Moody County, S. Dak....	Contracted smallpox after visit to South Dakota.
Tuberculosis: Mayo Clinic, Rochester, Olmsted County.	Marion County, Ind.; e, Madison County, Ind.; Bourbon, Marshall County, Ind.; Fort Wayne, Allen County, Ind.; Belmond, Wright County, Iowa; Le Mars, Plymouth County, Iowa (2 cases); New Hampton, Chickasaw County, Iowa; Mason City, Cerro Gordo County, Iowa; Hubbard, Hardin County, Iowa; Pike, R. No. 1, Grundy County, Iowa; Burlington, Des Moines County, Iowa; Nora Springs, Floyd County, Iowa; Burlington, Des Moines County, Iowa; Hubbell, Houghton County, Mich.; Hancock, Houghton County, Mich.; Sault Ste. Marie, Chippewa County, Mich.; Maryville, Nodaway County, Mo.; St. Louis, St. Louis County, Mo.; Carl Junction, Jasper County, Mo.; Great Falls, Cascade County, Mont.; Burwell, Garfield County, Nebr.; Holdrege, Phelps County, Nebr.; Enderlin, Ransom County, N. Dak.; Dresden, Cavalier County, N. Dak.; Ravenna, Portage County, Ohio; Sioux Falls, Minnehaha County, S. Dak.; Westport, Brown County, S. Dak.; Hatland, Kingsbury County, S. Dak.; Aberdeen, Grays Harbor County, Wash.; Minong, Washburn County, Wis.; Emo, Ontario, Canada; Indian Head, Saskatchewan, Canada; Luseland, Saskatchewan, Canada.	6 moderately advanced, 11 advanced, 5 incipient, 1 apparently cured, 2 apparently arrested, 3 (stage of disease not given) cases left Mayo Clinic for homes. 3 moderately advanced, 2 advanced, 1 (stage of disease not given) cases left Mayo Clinic for home.
Pokegama sanatorium, Pine County.	Havre, Hill County, Mont.; Spokane, Spokane County, Wash; Liberty, Sullivan County, N. Y.	Improved cases left Pokegama sanatorium for homes.
Thomas Hospital............	Enderlin, Ransom County, N. Dak.; Grafton, Walsh County, N. D.; Milwaukee, Milwaukee County, Wis.; Sprague, Manitoba, Canada.	2 improved cases, 2 (stage of disease not given) cases left Thomas Hospital for homes.
Ottertail County sanatorium, Ottertail County.	McClusky, Sheridan County, N. Dak..	Case left Ottertail County sanatorium for home.

CEREBROSPINAL MENINGITIS.

State Reports for April, 1918.

Place.	New cases reported	Place.	New cases reported.
District of Columbia...................	8	Pennsylvania—Continued.	
		Luzerne County.......................	19
Minnesota:		Lycoming County.....................	1
Blue Earth County—		Mercer County.......................	2
Mankato.......................	1	Philadelphia County.................	35
Fillmore County—		Schuylkill County....................	2
York Township................	1	Tioga County........................	1
Hennepin County—		Westmorland County.................	1
Dunwoody Institute...........	1	York County.........................	3
St. Louis County—			
Duluth.......................	2	Total.......................	92
Scott County—			
Belle Plaine Borough...........	1	Rhode Island:	
Stearns County—		Bristol County—	
St. Cloud.....................	1	Warren (town)..................	1
St. Augusta Township..........	1	Newport County—	
		Newport......................	4
Total.......................	8	Providence County—	
		Johnston (town)...............	1
North Carolina:		Providence...................	9
Durham County...................	2		
Forsyth County..................	9	Total.......................	13
Graham County..................	1		
Guilford County.................	1	South Carolina:	
Hyde County	2	Charleston County..............	3
Madison County.................	1	Darlington County..............	2
Mecklenburg County.............	1	Greenville County..............	12
Montgomery County.............	1	Laurens County................	2
Pasquotank County..............	1	Richland County	6
Sampson County................	1	Spartanburg County............	2
		Union County..................	1
Total.......................	20	York County...................	3
Pennsylvania:		Total.......................	31
Allegheny County................	14		
Beaver County...................	1	South Dakota:	
Berks County	1	Hyde county...................	1
Clearfield County................	1	Lake County...................	1
Dauphin County.................	1		
Delaware County................	2	Total.......................	2
Elk County	2		
Erie County.....................	1	West Virginia:	
Lackawanna County	4	Summers County................	1
Lehigh County	1		

City Reports for Week Ended May 11, 1918.

Place.	Cases.	Deaths.	Place.	Cases.	Deaths.
Atlanta, Ga.		1	Minneapolis, Minn....	1	1
Baltimore, Md.	5		Nashville, Tenn...............	2	.... ..
Boston, N. Y.		1	Newark, N. J.	1	1
Berkeley, Cal.	1		New Britain, Conn	1	1
Birmingham, Ala.	4		New Orleans, La.	1	..
Boston, Mass.	2	2	Newport, R. I...............	1	....
Buffalo, N. Y.	2		New York, N. Y.	22	7
Chicago, Ill.	10	2	Passaic, N. J.	1	...
Chattanooga, Ohio			Paterson, Pa................	5	5
Chester, Pa.	1		Pittsburgh, Pa...............	6	...
Dayton, Ohio		1	Portland, Me................		1
Detroit, Mich	1		Providence, R. I.............	3	...
Elwood, Ind.			Raleigh, N. C................	1	...
Fall River, Mass.	4		St. Louis, Mo...............	3	1
Flint, Mich.		1	San Diego, Cal..............	3	1
Galveston, Tex.			Schenectady, N. Y...........	1	...
Hackensack, N. J.		2	Scranton, Pa................	1	...
Indianapolis, Ind	1		Sioux City, Iowa............	1	
Indianapolis, Ind.	1	...	Washington, D. C............	2	1
Lexington, Ky.	1		Waltham, Pa................	1	...
Lima, Ohio		1	Wilkes Barre, Pa............	1	
Little Rock, Ark.	3		Worcester, Mass.............	1	...
Lynn, Mass.	1		Youngstown, Ohio	1	
Milwaukee, Wis............	6	6	Zanesville, Ohio............	1	

DIPHTHERIA.

See Diphtheria, measles, scarlet fever, and tuberculosis, page 894.

ERYSIPELAS.

City Reports for Week Ended May 11, 1918.

Place.	Cases.	Deaths.	Place.	Cases.	Deaths.
Akron, Ohio	1		Henderson, Ky		1
Alameda, Cal	1		Jackson, Mich	1	
Anderson, Ind	1		Kalamazoo, Mich	2	
Atlanta, Ga	1		Los Angeles, Cal	3	
Baltimore, Md	1		Louisville, Ky	1	1
Bayonne, N. J	1		Manitowoc, Wis	1	
Beacon, N. Y		2	Milwaukee, Wis	1	4
Beloit, Wis	1		Minneapolis, Minn	4	2
Berkeley, Cal	1		Mishawaka, Ind		1
Brockton, Mass	1		Moline, Ill		1
Buffalo, N. Y	2	1	Moundsville, W. Va	1	
Burlington, Vt	1	1	Newark, N. J	5	2
Cambridge, Mass		1	New York, N. Y		6
Camden, N. J	2		North Attleboro, Mass		1
Charleston, W. Va	1		Oklahoma City, Okla		1
Chicago, Ill	12		Peoria, Ill		1
Cincinnati, Ohio	2		Philadelphia, Pa	5	
Cleveland, Ohio	4		Pittsfield, Mass		1
Danville, Ill	1		Portland, Oreg	1	
Denver, Colo	1		Providence, R. I		2
Detroit, Mich	4		Rome, N. Y	1	
Duluth, Minn	3		St. Louis, Mo	10	1
Elgin, Ill	1		San Francisco, Cal	6	1
Fort Wayne, Ind		2	Schenectady, N. Y	1	
Frederick, Md	1		Troy, N. Y		1

MALARIA.

State Report for April, 1918.

Place.	New cases reported.	Place.	New cases reported.
South Carolina:		South Carolina—Continued.	
Abbeville County	4	Edgefield County	2
Beaufort County	2	Laurens County	2
Calhoun Conty	25	Marion County	8
Chester County	3		
Chesterfield County	18	Total	64

City Reports for Week Ended May 11, 1918.

Place.	Cases.	Deaths.	Place.	Cases.	Deaths.
Alexandria, La	3		Memphis, Tenn	1	
Birmingham, Ala	4		Montgomery, Ala	2	
Charleston, W. Va	1		Natick, Mass	1	
Hattiesburg, Miss	4		New Orleans, La		1
Independence, Mo	1	1	New York, N. Y		1
Joplin, Mo	3		North Little Rock, Ark	2	
Little Rock, Ark	4		Palestine, Tex	31	
Long Beach, Cal	1		Richmond, Va		2
Macon, Ga	5		Tuscaloosa, Ala	2	
Marshall, Tex	1		Waco, Tex	1	

MEASLES.

See Diphtheria, measles, scarlet fever, and tuberculosis, page 894.

PELLAGRA.

State Report for April, 1918.

Place.	New cases reported.	Place.	New cases reported.
South Carolina:		South Carolina—Continued.	
Abbeville County	3	Laurens County	4
Beaufort County	1	Richland County	2
Chester County	1	Spartanburg County	10
Chesterfield County	3		
Edgefield County	2	Total	27
Greenville County	1		

City Reports for Week Ended May 11, 1918.

Place.	Cases.	Deaths.	Place.	Cases.	Deaths.
Alexandria, La	6		Los Angeles, Cal	1	
Anniston, Ala	1		Louisville, Ky		1
Atlanta, Ga		2	Marshall, Tex	1	
Augusta, Ga		2	Memphis, Tenn	3	
Beaumont, Tex		1	Montgomery, Ala		1
Birmingham, Ala	1	1	Nashville, Tenn	3	2
Charleston, S. C		3	North Little Rock, Ark	1	
Concord, N. H		1	Palestine, Tex	2	
Corpus Christi, Tex	1		Raleigh, N. C		1
El Paso, Tex		1	Richmond, Va		1
Hattiesburg, Miss	3		Rocky Mount, N. C	1	
Houston, Tex		2	Tuscaloosa, Ala	1	1
Lincoln, Nebr		1	Winston-Salem, N. C		1

PNEUMONIA.

City Reports for Week Ended May 11, 1918.

Place.	Cases.	Deaths.	Place.	Cases.	Deaths.
Alameda, Cal	1	1	Hattiesburg, Miss	1	
Amesbury, Mass	1		Haverhill, Mass	2	
Anderson, Ind	1		Holyoke, Mass	2	1
Anniston, Ala	1		Hornell, N. Y	1	
Arlington, Mass	2		Houston, Tex	1	5
Auburn, N. Y	2	2	Hudson, N. Y	1	1
Bakersfield, Cal	1	1	Jackson, Mich	1	1
Baltimore, Md	40	10	Jamestown, N. Y	4	1
Battle Creek, Mich	1	1	Joplin, Mo	1	
Berkeley, Cal	1		Kalamazoo, Mich	3	
Beverly, Mass			Kansas City, Kans	2	
Boston, Mass	17	20	Kewanee, Ill	2	2
Bridgeport, Conn	1	3	Lawrence, Mass	4	1
Buffalo, N. Y	2	13	Little Rock, Ark	6	3
Cambridge, Mass	2	2	Los Angeles, Cal	9	5
Cadiz, Ohio	2	2	Louisville, Ky	5	9
Chelsea, Mass	6		Lynn, Mass	2	2
Chicago, Ill	184	104	Manchester, N. H	4	4
Cincinnati, Ohio	1	6	Marion, Ohio	1	1
Cleveland, Ohio	2	27	McKeesport, Pa	2	1
Clinton, Mass	1		Medford, Mass	4	
Colon, N. Y	1	1	Morristown, N. Y	2	1
Dayton, Ohio	2	7	Morgantown, W. Va	3	
Detroit, Mich	14	40	Natick, Mass	1	
Duluth, Minn	12	2	New Albany, Ind		1
Elmira, N. Y	3	3	Newark, N. J	2	12
Everett, Mass	1	1	New Bedford, Mass	6	4
Everett, Wash	2		New Castle, Ind	1	1
Fort Worth, Tex	3		Newport, Ky	2	3
Galveston, Tex	1	1	Newton, Mass	4	1
Gloucester, Mass	1		North Little Rock, Ark	2	1
Grand Rapids, Mich	2	2	Oakland, Cal	2	1
Great Falls, Mich	7	4	Oswego, N. Y	2	
Green Bay, Mass	1		Passaic, N. J	1	
Harrison, N. J	1		Philadelphia, Pa	102	54
			Pittsfield, Mass	3	2

PNEUMONIA—Continued.

City Reports for Week Ended May 11, 1918—Continued.

Place.	Cases.	Deaths.	Place.	Cases.	Deaths
Pontiac, Mich	1	1	Springfield, Mass	10	2
Quincy, Mass	5	1	Toledo, Ohio	1	2
Rochester, N. Y	4	7	Waco, Tex	1	
Sacramento, Cal	1	1	Waterloo, Iowa	1	
San Francisco, Cal	12	6	Westfield, Mass	3	4
San Diego, Cal	4	3	Wichita, Kans	7	1
Santa Cruz, Cal	1		Winthrop, Mass	1	
Schenectady, N. Y	4	2	Worcester, Mass	5	6
Sheboygan, Wis	2	2	Yonkers, N. Y	5	1
Somerville, Mass	5		Youngstown, Ohio	6	7
Spartanburg, S. C	1				

POLIOMYELITIS (INFANTILE PARALYSIS).

State Reports for April, 1918.

Place.	New cases reported.	Place.	New cases reported.
Michigan:		**Pennsylvania:**	
Kent County—		Allegheny County	2
Grand Rapids	1	Beaver County	1
Calhoun County—		Dauphin County	2
Battle Creek	1	Lawrence County	1
Bay County—		Tioga County	1
Frankenlust Township	1	Washington County	1
Total	3	Total	7
Minnesota:		**South Dakota:**	
Olmsted County—		Spink County	1
Rochester	1		
Polk County—			
Roome Township	1		
Total	2		

City Reports for Week Ended May 11, 1918.

Place.	Cases.	Deaths.	Place.	Cases.	Deaths.
Cambridge, Mass	1		New York, N. Y	1	1
Framingham, Mass	2		Palestine, Tex	1	
Milwaukee, Wis	1	1	San Francisco, Cal	1	
Minneapolis, Minn	1	1			

RABIES IN ANIMALS.

City Reports for Week Ended May 11, 1918.

Place.	Cases.	Place.	Cases.
Ann Arbor, Mich	1	Rochester, N. Y	1
Hudson, N. Y	1	Waco, Tex	2
Louisville, Ky	1		

RABIES IN MAN.

City Reports for Week Ended May 11, 1918.

During the week ended May 11, 1918, there were reported at Birmingham, Ala., one case and one death from rabies in man.

SCARLET FEVER.

See Diphtheria, measles, scarlet fever, and tuberculosis, page 894.

SMALLPOX.

State Reports for April, 1918.

Place.	New cases reported.	Deaths.	Vaccination history of cases.			
			Number vaccinated within 7 years preceding attack.	Number last vaccinated more than 7 years preceding attack.	Number never successfully vaccinated.	Vaccination history not obtained or uncertain.
Michigan:						
Alcona County—						
Curtis Township.........	6				6	
Mitchel Township.........	5				5	
Alpena County—						
Green Township.........	1				1	
Ossinike Township.......	1				1	
Antrim County—						
Banks Township.........	7			3	4	
Bay County –						
Pinconning Township.....	5			2	3	
Williams Township......	3			1	2	
Benzie County—						
Benzonia Township......	1				1	
Inland Township	2				2	
Berrien County—						
Benton Harbor...........	9				9	
Niles	3				3	
Calhoun County-						
Bedford Township.... ...	1					
Albion	21				21	
Charlevoix County--						
Boyne Valley Township..	1					
Cheboygan County—						
Aloha Township.........	1				1	
Chippewa County—						
Sault Ste Marie.........	4				4	
Dickinson County—						
Norway	2				2	
Eaton County—						
Grand Ledge.............	2				2	
Genesee County--						
Benton Township	1				1	
Flushing Township....	2				1	1
Richfield Township.....	1				1	
Vienna Township	1			1		1
Clio	1					
Mount Morris	4				4	
Flint	5				5	
Gladwin County						
Butman Township......	1				1	
Gratiot County						
Newark Township......	1				1	
Hillsdale County						
Fayette Township	2				2	
Hillsdale Township.... ..	3				3	
Scipio Township..........	1				1	
Huron County						
Dwight Township........	1				1	
Meade Township	2				2	
Ingham County						
Alaiedon Township.....	1				1	
Delhi Township	2				2	
Meridian Township	3				3	
Lansing	12				12	
Iosco County						
Sherman Township......	1				1	
Wilber Township......	5				5	
Isabella County						
Coldwater Township.....	2				2	
Jackson County						
Columbia Township.	1				1	
Kalamazoo County						
Comstock Township	3				2	1
Kalamazoo Township ...	1					1
Kalamazoo................	31			1	25	5

SMALLPOX—Continued.

State Reports for April, 1918—Continued.

Place.	New cases reported.	Deaths.	Vaccination history of cases.			
			Number vaccinated within 7 years preceding attack.	Number last vaccinated more than 7 years preceding attack.	Number never successfully vaccinated.	Vaccination history not obtained or uncertain.
Michigan—Continued.						
Kalkaska County—						
Rapid River Township...	5	....	....	....	1	4
Kent County—						
Grand Rapids Township..	1	....	....	....	1	....
Sparta Township.........	1	....	....	....	....	1
Tyrone Township........	6	....	....	....	6	....
Sparta.................	1	....	....	....	1	....
Grand Rapids...........	11	....	....	....	11	....
Lapeer County—						
Goodland Township......	1	....	....	....	1	....
Lenawee County—						
Ogden Township........	1	....	....	....	1	....
Hudson................	1	....	....	....	1	....
Livingston County—						
Geneva Township........	1	....	....	....	1	....
Macomb County—						
Memphis Township......	1	....	....	....	1	....
Mount Clemens........	2	....	....	....	2	....
Manistee County—						
Filer Township.........	7	....	....	....	7	....
Norman Township.......	1	....	....	....	1	....
Manistee.............	9	....	....	....	9	....
Marquette County—						
Marquette.............	4	....	....	....	4	....
Mecosta County—						
Fork Township.........	7	....	....	....	7	....
Menominee County—						
Menominee.............	2	....	....	....	2	....
Monroe County—						
Bedford Township......	1	....	....	....	1	....
La Salle Township......	1	....	....	....	1	....
Monroe Township......	1	....	....	....	1	....
Monroe...............	6	....	....	....	6	....
Montcalm County—						
Pierson Township.......	1	....	....	....	1	....
Montmorency County—						
Avery Township........	1	....	....	....	1	....
Muskegon County—						
Muskegon Township.....	1	....	....	....	1	....
Norton Township.......	1	....	....	....	1	....
Montague.............	1	....	....	1	1	....
Muskegon.............	2	....	....	....	2	....
Newaygo County—						
Sheridan Township......	2	....	....	....	2	....
Fremont..............	1	....	....	1	....	....
Oakland County—						
Novi Township........	1	....	....	1	....	....
Southfield Township....	1	....	....	....	1	....
Twy Township.........	1	....	....	....	....	1
Pontiac..............	19	....	....	....	19	....
Oceana County—						
Crystal Township.......	1	....	....	....	1	....
Ogemaw County—						
Hill Township..........	1	....	....	....	1	....
Osceola County—						
Sherman Township......	1	....	....	....	1	....
Sylvan Township........	1	....	....	....	1	....
Otsego County—						
Gaylord..............	1	....	....	....	1	....
Ottawa County—						
Crockery Township......	2	....	....	....	2	....
Holland..............	1	....	....	....	1	....
Presque Isle County—						
North Allis Township.....	1	....	....	....	....	1
Saginaw County—						
Saginaw..............	3	....	....	....	3	....
St. Clair County—						
Clyde Township........	2	....	....	....	2	....
Columbus Township.....	2	....	....	....	2	....
Kimball Township.......	2	....	....	....	2	....
St. Clair Township......	1	....	....	....	1	....
St. Clair..............	2	....	....	1	1	....

SMALLPOX—Continued.

State Reports for April, 1918—Continued.

Place.	New cases reported.	Deaths.	Number vaccinated within 7 years preceding attack.	Number last vaccinated more than 7 years preceding attack.	Number never successfully vaccinated.	Vaccination history not obtained or uncertain.
Michigan—Continued.						
St. Joseph County—						
Florence Township........	1				1	
Centerville...............	2				2	
Colon....................	2				2	
Mendon..................	3				3	
Three Rivers.............	3				3	
Sanilac County—						
Argyle Township..........	1			1		
Lamotte Township........	2				2	
Moore Township..........	1				1	
Sanilac Township.........	1				1	
Croswell.................	1				1	
Sandusky................	1				1	
Tuscola County—						
Almer Township	17				12	5
Juanita Township........	1				1	
Koylton Township........	1				1	
Akron...................	1				1	
Van Buren County—						
Gobleville	3				3	
Washtenaw County—						
Ann Arbor	1				1	
Wayne County—						
Highland Park...........	4				3	1
Northville	2			1		1
St. Clair Heights.........	4				4	
Detroit	91					91
Wexford County—						
Cherry Grove Township...	1				1	
Liberty Township........	2				2	
Selma Township.........	4				4	
Cadillac................	4				4	
Total..............	411			14	312	115
Minnesota:						
Beltrami County—						
Bemidji	2				2	
Kelliher Township	1				1	
Carver County—						
Chaska.................	2				2	
Cologne................	3				3	
Chisago County—						
Rush City..............	1				1	
Clay County—						
Moorhead..............	1			1		
Oak Port Township......	1				1	
Crow Wing County—						
Brainerd	5			1	4	
Douglas County—						
Holmes City Township......	1				1	
Faribault County—						
East	1				1	
Fillmore County—						
Rushford	3			1	2	
Forestville Township.....	4					1
Spring Valley Township..	4				2	2
Freeborn County—						
Riceland Township......	2			1		1
Goodhue County—						
Kenyon	71				71	
Cherry Grove Township..	19			1	18	
Hennepin County.........	1					1
Minneapolis.............	64			6	61	
Eden Prairie Township...	1				1	
Houston County—						
Spring Grove...........	2				2	
Hubbard County—						
Akeley.................	1				1	
Nevis..................	1				1	

SMALLPOX—Continued.

State Reports for April, 1918—Continued.

Place.	New cases reported.	Deaths.	Vaccination history of cases.			
			Number vaccinated within 7 years preceding attack.	Number last vaccinated more than 7 years preceding attack.	Number never successfully vaccinated.	Vaccination history not obtained or uncertain.
Minnesota—Continued.						
Isanti County—						
Maple Ridge Township....	1				1	
Jackson County—						
Heron Lake..........	1				1	
Alba Township...........	1				1	
La Crosse Township.......	4				4	
Kittson County—						
Humboldt..........	4				4	
Lancaster....	1				1	
Township 162, R. 45.....	1				1	
Lyon County—						
Clifton Township.........	1				1	
Stanley Township........	1				1	
Mahnomen County—						
Waubon.....	1				1	
Meeker County—						
Dassel.......	1				1	
Mower County—						
Austin......	4				4	
Adams Township........	1				1	
Austin Township........	1				1	
Murray County—						
Lake Wilson..........	1				1	
Norman County—						
Strand Township........	3			3		
Olmsted County—						
Rochester.....	11				11	
Pine County—						
Rock Creek Township....	4				4	
Pipestone County—						
Pipestone.....	1					▲
Polk County—						
Climax.....	1				1	
Ramsey County—						
St. Paul.....	26				26	
Renville County—						
Fairfax.....	2			1	1	
Morton....	1					1
Bandon Township.......	3				3	
Camp Township.........	4				4	
Wellington Township.....	1				1	
Rice County—						
Richland Township.......	9				9	
Roseau County—						
Malung Township........	1				1	
Mickinock Township......	1				1	
St. Louis County—						
Duluth..............	3				3	
Virginia.........	1				1	
Stearns County—						
St. Cloud.....	1				1	
Traverse County—						
Monson Township........	1				1	
Wabasha County—						
Greenfield Township......	1				1	
Washington County—						
Forest Lake........	1			1		
Wilkin County—						
Breckenridge...........	6				6	
Winona County—						
St Charles.....	1				1	
Winona.....	2				2	
Wright County—						
Cokato Township.......	1				1	
French Lake Township...	1				1	
Total.....	**304**			**16**	**281**	**7**
Rhode Island:						
Woonsocket..............	1	1			1	

SMALLPOX—Continued.

Miscellaneous State Reports for April, 1918.

Place.	Cases.	Deaths.	Place.	Cases.	Deaths.
District of Columbia.........	5	....	South Carolina:		
			Spartanburg County......	5	....
North Carolina:			Union County.............	3	....
Anson County.............	1	....			
Ashe County..............	1	....	Total.............	8	....
Avery County.............	13	....			
Bladen County............	1	....	South Dakota:		
Buncombe County........	5	....	Bon Homme County.....	1	....
Burke County............	2	....	Brown County...........	8	....
Cabarrus County.........	3	....	Charles Mix County......	10	....
Caswell County...........	1	....	Clark County............	1	....
Cherokee County.........	4	....	Codington County.......	7	....
Cumberland County......	1	....	Davison County..........	3	....
Currituck County........	1	....	Dewey County...........	2	....
Davidson County........	1	....	Gregory County.........	1	....
Durham County..........	1	....	Hutchinson County......	6	....
Edgecombe County......	3	....	Hyde County............	11	1
Forsyth County..........	9	....	Lake County............	2	....
Gaston County...........	5	....	McCook County.........	8	....
Haywood County.........	3	....	Miner County...........	4	....
Henderson County.......	4	....	Minnehaha County......	4	....
Lee County..............	3	....	Perkins County..........	1	....
Macon County...........	1	....	Spink County...........	4	....
Madison County.........	6	....	Sully County............	2	....
McDowell County........	4	....	Turner County..........	1	....
Mecklenburg County.....	2	....	Yankton County.........	5	....
Montgomery County.....	5	....			
Pitt County.............	1	....	Total.............	79	1
Robeson County.........	4	....			
Rockingham County.....	15	....	Vermont:		
Rowan County...........	2	....	Caledonia County.......	10	....
Rutherford County......	1	....	Orleans County.........	6	....
Stanly County...........	1	....	Windsor County.........	3	....
Surry County	3	....			
Swain County............	3	....	Total.............	19	....
Total.............	109	....	West Virginia:		
			Calwell County.........	5	....
Pennsylvania:			Calhoun County.........	11	....
Adams County...........	1	....	Fayette County.........	10	....
Allegheny County.......	4	....	Harrison County........	1	....
Armstrong County......	9	....	Kanawha County........	21	....
Beaver County..........	1	....	Lewis County...........	3	....
Blair County............	1	....	Lincoln County.........	29	....
Cambria County........	11	....	Logan County...........	4	....
Center County..........	1	....	McDowell County........	3	....
Clarion County.........	1	....	Marion County..........	3	....
Clearfield County.......	12	....	Mercer County..........	7	....
Crawford County.......	1	....	Mingo County...........	22	....
Dauphin County........	13	....	Monongalia County......	3	....
Delaware County.......	1	....	Nicholas County........	9	....
Erie County.............	2	....	Ohio County............	1	....
Franklin County........	5	....	Pendleton County.......	10	....
Huntingdon County.....	3	....	Putnam County.........	7	....
Lackawanna County....	1	....	Ritchie County..........	2	....
Luzerne County........	1	....	Raleigh County.........	24	....
Mercer County..........	4	....	Roane County...........	1	....
Mifflin County..........	1	....	Tyler County...........	2	....
Philadelphia County.....	7	....	Taylor County..........	5	....
Somerset County........	9	....	Webster County.........	2	....
Warren County..........	1	....	Wirt County............	1	....
Westmoreland County...	1	....	Wood County...........	16	....
York County............	10	....			
			Total.............	200	....
Total.............	101	....			

SMALLPOX—Continued.

City Reports for Week Ended May 11, 1918.

Place.	Cases.	Deaths.	Place.	Cases.	Deaths.
cron, Ohio	10	....	Kalamazoo, Mich	7	....
exandria, La	1	....	Kansas City, Kans	3	....
ton, Ill	2	....	Knoxville, Tenn	9	....
iderson, Ind	2	....	Leavenworth, Kans	1	....
iniston, Ala	8	....	Lima, Ohio	9	....
lanta, Ga	3	....	Lincoln, Nebr	11	....
igusta, Me	2	....	Little Rock, Ark	7	....
rberton, Ohio	2	....	Louisville, Ky	4	....
llings, Mont	1	....	Macon, Ga	4	....
rmingham, Ala	17	....	Madison, Wis	3	....
ston, Mass	2	....	Massillon, Ohio	1	....
ffalo, N. Y	1	....	Memphis, Tenn	3	....
tte, Mont	3	....	Menominee, Mich	2	....
iro, Ill	1	....	Middletown, Ohio	4	....
nton, Ohio	7	....	Milwaukee, Wis	5	....
iar Rapids, Iowa	2	....	Minneapolis, Minn	16	....
arleston, W. Va	2	....	Mobile, Ala	3	....
attanooga, Tenn	4	....	Montgomery, Ala	1	....
icago, Ill	1	....	Muscatine, Iowa	1	....
illicothe, Ohio	1	....	Muscogee, Okla	5	....
cinnati, Ohio	10	....	Nashville, Tenn	7	....
veland, Ohio	38	....	Newark, Ohio	1	....
nton, Iowa	1	....	New Orleans, La	1	....
leyville, Kans	10	....	New York, N. Y	1	....
umbia, S. C	1	....	Oklahoma City, Okla	30	....
numbus, Ohio	5	....	Omaha, Nebr	37	....
ncil Bluffs, Iowa	7	....	Oshkosh, Wis	1	....
nville, Ill	6	....	Owensboro, Ky	2	....
venport, Iowa	1	....	Parkersburg, W. Va	1	....
yton, Ohio	1	....	Peoria, Ill	4	....
nver, Colo	24	....	Philadelphia, Pa	1	....
s Moines, Iowa	10	....	Pittsburgh, Pa	1	....
roit, Mich	19	....	Pocatello, Idaho	1	....
buque, Iowa	10	....	Pontiac, Mich	4	....
luth, Minn	2	....	Portland, Me	1	....
st Liverpool, Ohio	4	....	Quincy, Ill	21	....
in, Ill	1	....	Rock Island, Ill	1	....
ria, Ohio	3	....	St. Joseph, Mo	8	....
insville, Ind	2	....	St. Louis, Mo	19	....
go, N. Dak	3	....	Salt Lake City, Utah	25	....
nt, Mich	3	....	Sandusky, Ohio	1	....
t Scott, Kans	1	....	San Francisco, Cal	3	....
t Smith, Ark	5	....	Shelbyville, Ind	2	....
t Worth, Tex	31	....	Sioux City, Iowa	4	....
sno, Cal	3	....	Spartanburg, S. C	2	....
veston, Tex	2	....	Spokane, Wash	11	....
y, Ind	1	....	Springfield, Mo	4	....
nd Rapids, Mich	2	....	Springfield, Ohio	1	....
eley, Colo	2	....	Steelton, Pa	2	....
nmond, Ind	4	.... :	Steubenville, Ohio	1	....
tford, Conn	1	....	Superior, Wis	1	....
tiesburg, Miss	1	....	Toledo, Ohio	14	....
ston, Tex	1	....	Waco, Tex	5	....
pendence, Kans	2	....	Warren, Ohio	3	....
apendence, Mo	4	....	Washington, D. C	2	....
ianapolis, Ind	31	....	Waterloo, Iowa	2	....
. Kans	4	....	Wichita, Kans	40	....
iestown, N. Y	1	....	Winona, Minn	2	....
lin, Mo	2	....	Youngstown, Ohio	3	....

TETANUS.

City Reports for Week Ended May 11, 1918.

Place.	Cases.	Deaths.	Place.	Cases.	Deaths.
ısta, Ga	....	1	Schenectady, N. Y	....	1
ningham, Ala	1	....	Taunton, Mass	1	1
lington, Vt	1	1	Toledo, Ohio	....	1
shall, Tex	1	....	Warren, Ohio	....	1
stine, Tex	2	....	Yonkers, N. Y	1	....

TUBERCULOSIS.

ee Diphtheria, measles, scarlet fever, and tuberculosis, page 894.

TYPHOID FEVER.

State Reports for April, 1918.

Place.	New cases reported.	Place.	New cases reported.
District of Columbia..................	6	**Michigan—Continued.**	
		Gratiot County—	
Minnesota:		North Star Township..........	1
Beltrami County—		Ingham County—	
Bemidji..................	2	Stockbridge................	1
McDougald Township..........	1	Ionia County—	
Bigstone County—		Muir......................	1
Graceville..................	1	Isabella County—	
Blue Earth County—		Denver Township..........	2
Mankato..................	1	Jackson County—	
Carlton County—		Blackman Township..........	1
Cloquet..................	1	Kent County—	
Cass County—		Grand Rapids..............	4
State Sanatorium..............	3	Lapeer County—	
Slater Township..........	1	Lapeer....................	11
Chippewa County—		Mecosta County—	
Montevideo..............	1	Big Rapids................	1
Crow Wing County—		Midland County—	
Brainerd.................	1	Wells Township..........	1
Faribault County—		Midland................	2
Clark Township..........	1	Oakland County—	
Freeborn County—		Southfield Township..........	1
Alden Township..........	1	Saginaw County—	
Goodhue County—		Saginaw	1
Red Wing.................	1	Shiawassee County -	
Zumbrota..................	3	Bennington Township..........	1
Hennepin County—			
Minneapolis..............	23	Total.............	47
Champlin Township..........	1		
Jackson County —		**North Carolina:**	
Jackson		Buncombe County..........	1
Kittson County—		Duplin County..........	2
Cannon Township	1	Durham County..........	2
Hampden Township..........	1	Forsyth County..........	7
Koochiching county		Gaston County..........	2
International Falls..........	1	Graham County..........	4
Lesueur County—		Guilford County..........	1
Waterville..........	1	Harnett County..........	1
Marshall County—		Johnston County..........	2
Oslo..........	1	Madison County..........	1
Mower County—		Martin County..........	3
Racine Township..........	1	Mecklenburg County..........	1
Norman County—		Northampton County..........	1
Halstad..........	1	Pitt County..........	1
Olmsted County—		Richmond County..........	2
Rochester..........	1	Robeson County..........	2
Ottertail County—		Stokes County..........	1
Fergus Falls..........	1	Swain County..........	1
Renville county—		Warren County..........	1
Renson..........	1	Wayne County..........	1
St. Louis County—		Wilson County..........	1
Duluth..........	2	Yancey County..........	1
Eveleth..........	1		
Hibbing..........	1	Total..........	38
Virginia..........	2		
Bovine Township..........	1	**Pennsylvania:**	
Wabasha County—		Allen County..........	5
Mazeppa..........	1	Allegheny County..........	30
		Armstrong County..........	3
Total..........	61	Beaver County..........	11
		Bedford County..........	2
Michigan:		Berks County..........	6
Alpena County—		Blair County..........	4
Long Rapids Township..........	1	Bradford County..........	5
Bay County—		Bucks County..........	12
Bay City..........	7	Butler County..........	2
Berrien County—		Cambria County..........	3
West........	1	Columbia County..........	1
Calhoun County—		Centre County..........	5
Township..........	1	Chester County..........	1
Battle Creek..........	1	Clearfield County..........	1
Dickinson County—		Clinton County..........	6
Iron Mountain..........	1	Columbia County..........	2
Eaton County—		Cumberland County..........	6
Charlotte..........	1	Dauphin County..........	8
Genesee County—		Delaware County..........	4
Flint..........	3	Erie County..........	5
Gladwin County—		Fayette County..........	5
Gladwin..........	1	Franklin County..........	6

TYPHOID FEVER—Continued.

State Reports for April, 1918—Continued.

Place.	New cases reported.	Place.	New cases reported.
nsylvania—Continued.		South Caro'ina:	
Huntingdon County	2	Calhoun County	1
Jefferson County	2	Charleston County	4
Lackawanna County	7	Chesterfie'd County	2
Lancaster County	16	Greenville County	1
Lawrence County	5	Marion County	1
Lebanon County	10	Richland County	2
Lehigh County	11		
Luzerne County	6	Total	11
Lycoming County	2		
Mercer County	5	South Dakota:	
Mifflin County	1	Miner County	4
Montgomery County	20	Perkins County	1
Montour County	1	Yankton County	2
Northampton County	4		
Northumberland County	18	Total	7
Philadelphia County	7		
Schuylkill County	11	Vermont:	
Somerset County	3	Bennington County	1
Tioga County	1		
Union County	1	West Virginia:	
Venango County	1	Braxton County	4
Warren County	1	Clay County	2
Washington County	7	Fayette County	2
Westmore'and County	5	Hardy County	2
York County	5	Kanawha County	16
		Logan County	4
Total	288	McDowell County	2
		Marion County	18
e Island:		Mercer County	2
ent County—		Mingo County	3
Warwick (town)	1	Mononga'ia County	10
West Warwick (town)	2	Monroe County	1
rovidence County—		Morgan County	1
Johnston (town)	10	Ohio County	31
Pawtucket	1	Putnam County	2
Providence	6	Randolph County	6
Woonsocket	3	Tucker County	1
ashington County—			
Westerly (town)	1	Total	107
Total	24		

City Reports for Week Ended May 11, 1918.

Place.	Cases.	Deaths.	Place.	Cases.	Deaths.
, Ohio	1		Fort Scott, Kans	1	
wn, Pa	4		Fresno, Cal		1
a, Pa	1		Grand Rapids, Mich	3	
ore, Md	2		Greeley, Colo	1	
Creek, Mich	1		Hartford, Conn	1	
gham, Ala	1	1	Hattiesburg, Miss	1	
, Mass	3	1	Houston, Tex	1	
ine, Mass	1		Indianapolis, Ind	1	
, N. Y	1	2	Ithaca, N. Y	1	
ton, Vt	1		Kewanee, Ill	1	
dge, Mass	1		Lawrence, Mass	1	
ton, S. C	2		Louisville, Ky	2	
ton, W. Va		1	Lynchburg, Va	2	
tooga, Tenn	1		Macon, Ga	1	
, Mass	1		Memphis, Tenn	1	1
, Ill	7	1	Middletown, Ohio	1	
nd, Ohio	2	2	Milwaukee, Wis	3	
ia, S. C	1		Minneapolis, Minn	3	
us, Ohio	1		Moline, Ill	1	
Christi, Tex	1		Newark, N. J		1
, Mich	5	2	New Castle, Pa	1	
, N. H	2		New Haven, Conn	1	
ie, Iowa	1		New Orleans, La	8	5
verpool, Ohio		2	Newton, Mass		1
ange, N. J	1		New York, N. Y	17	2
nt, W. Va	1		North Adams, Mass	1	
ver, Mass	3		Oakland, Cal	1	1

TYPHOID FEVER—Continued.

City Reports for Week Ended May 11, 1918—Continued.

Place.	Cases.	Deaths.	Place.	Cases.	Deaths.
Ogden, Utah	1	1	Shenandoah, Pa	1	
Omaha, Nebr		1	South Bend, Ind		1
Orange, N. J	1		Spokane, Wash	1	
Oswego, N. Y	2	1	Springfield, Ill	1	
Peoria, Ill		1	Springfield, Ohio	1	1
Philadelphia, Pa	13	2	Trenton, N. J	1	
Pittsburgh, Pa	2		Troy, N. Y		1
Portland, Oreg	1		Walla Walla, Wash	2	
Providence, R. I	1		Warren, Ohio	1	
Reno, Nev	1		Washington, D. C	1	
Richmond, Va	1		West Warwick, R. I	1	
St. Joseph, Mo	1	1	Wheeling, W. Va	5	1
St. Louis, Mo	2		Wichita, Kans	2	1
Salt Lake City, Utah	2		Wilkes-Barre, Pa	1	
San Francisco, Cal	2		Wilmington, N. C	3	
Scranton, Pa	1		Yonkers, N. Y	1	
Seattle, Wash	1		York, Pa	3	
Sheboygan, Wis	1	1	Zanesville, Ohio	1	

DIPHTHERIA, MEASLES, SCARLET FEVER, AND TUBERCULOSIS.

State Reports for April, 1918.

State.	Cases reported.			State.	Cases reported.		
	Diphtheria.	Measles.	Scarlet fever.		Diphtheria.	Measles.	Scarlet fever.
District of Columbia	55	2,007	132	Rhode Island	92	1,022	72
Michigan	377	1,285	720	South Carolina	93	240	2
Minnesota	364	409	607	South Dakota	7	301	87
North Carolina	57	1,498	29	Vermont	18	56	20
Pennsylvania	1,602	10,593	665	West Virginia	27	430	31

City Reports for Week Ended May 11, 1918.

City.	Population as of July 1, 1916, estimated by U. S. Census Bureau.	Total deaths from all causes.	Diphtheria		Measles.		Scarlet fever.		Tuberculosis.	
			Cases.	Deaths.	Cases.	Deaths.	Cases.	Deaths.	Cases.	Deaths.
Over 500,000 inhabitants:										
Baltimore, Md	589,621		15	2	463	5	14	1	26	44
Boston, M	756,47	274	14	1	385	8	40	2	100	35
Chicago, Ill	2,445,722		78	14	165	1	33		422	96
Cleveland, Ohio	6,1,	292	11	1	74	1	7		28	27
Detroit, M	571,784		19	4	15	7	36	4	40	37
Los Angeles, Cal	7,512	121	15	1	131	1	8		66	25
New York, N. Y	5,601,11	1,7	293	21	1,101	31	101	5	360	246
Philadelphia, Pa	1,200,75	649	68	12	845	12	42	1	165	69
Pittsburgh, Pa			25		319		20		65	
St. Louis, Mo	757,49	227	55	1	88		28	1	50	30
From 300,000 to 500,000 inhabitants:										
Buffalo, N. Y	468,55	158	11		166		13	1	30	23
Cincinnati, Ohio	417,07		18	1	39	1	8		20	21
Jersey City, N. J	3,305		11		36		11		21	
Milwaukee, Wis	4	116	7	1	383	4	21	1	30	10
Minneapolis, Minn			14	5	79	3	29	2	6	9
Newark, N. J	4,804	117	17	1	475		12	1	63	15
New Orleans, La	371,147	166	8	1	13	3	2		40	33
Seattle, Wash	16,755	14	19		45	1	17		36	12
			2				17		14	
Washington, D. C	363,551	10	12	1	242	4	21	1	37	15

PHTHERIA, MEASLES, SCARLET FEVER, AND TUBERCULOSIS—Continued.

City Reports for Week Ended May 11, 1918—Continued.

City.	Population as of July 1, 1916 (estimated by U. S. Census Bureau).	Total deaths from all causes.	Diphtheria.		Measles.		Scarlet fever.		Tuberculosis.	
			Cases.	Deaths.	Cases.	Deaths.	Cases.	Deaths.	Cases.	Deaths.
200,000 to 300,000 inhabitants:										
Columbus, Ohio	214,878	66	3		24		19	1	6	9
Denver, Colo	260,800	79	3		45		38			11
Indianapolis, Ind	271,708		18	2	31		38		10	12
Louisville, Ky	238,910	74	8		13		1		18	6
Portland, Oreg	295,463	66	3		140	1	5		7	6
Providence, R. I	254,960	64	15	2	157	2	11		1	10
Rochester, N. Y	256,417	80	12	2	127		15		9	5
St. Paul, Minn	247,232	78	36	2	10		24		21	7
100,000 to 200,000 inhabitants:										
Atlanta, Ga	190,558	54	1		16		2		13	5
Birmingham, Ala	181,762	71			11		2		8	5
Bridgeport, Conn	121,576	38	1		8		8		4	5
Cambridge, Mass	112,921	31	12	1	79		2		10	3
Camden, N. J	106,233		1		11		2		5	
Dayton, Ohio	127,244				3		3		4	6
Des Moines, Iowa	101,598		3				17			
Fall River, Mass	128,366	42	4	1	12		4		12	6
Fort Worth, Tex	104,562	20			1		3		1	1
Grand Rapids, Mich	128,291	38	4	2	19		11		6	1
Hartford, Conn	110,900	50	5		2		4		4	1
Houston, Tex	112,307	51	1		9		1		1	2
Lawrence, Mass	100,560	27			148	1			6	4
Lowell, Mass	113,245	33	2		23		1		5	2
Lynn, Mass	102,425	26	3		60		1		4	2
Memphis, Tenn	148,995	46	9	1	11		11		10	8
Nashville, Tenn	117,057	49			30		1		2	6
New Bedford, Mass	118,158	42	1		10		2		11	6
New Haven, Conn	149,685	56	1		7				13	5
Oakland, Cal	198,604	51	2	1	14		4		7	7
Omaha, Nebr	165,470	53	12	1	20		11			1
Reading, Pa	109,381		1		116		3		2	
Richmond, Va	156,687	73	2		54	2	4			6
Salt Lake City, Utah	117,399	30	3	1	34		17	1		
Scranton, Pa	146,811		8		17		6			
Spokane, Wash	150,323						2		1	
Springfield, Mass	105,942	33	6	1	65		7		11	2
Syracuse, N. Y	155,624	45	4		74	2	14		14	5
Tacoma, Wash	112,770		1		17		50			
Toledo, Ohio	191,554	82	1	1	11		3			12
Trenton, N. J	111,593	38	2		6				6	6
Worcester, Mass	163,314	51	3	1	8		7		14	8
Youngstown, Ohio	108,385	22			19		3		3	1
50,000 to 100,000 inhabitants:										
Akron, Ohio	85,625	20	3		9		7		10	
Allentown, Pa	63,505		5		39		3		4	
Altoona, Pa	58,659		1		10		1			
Atlantic City, N. J	57,660				17		2		2	1
Augusta, Ga	56,245	24			6		1		1	1
Bayonne, N. J	69,803		4		42		2		3	
Berkeley, Cal	57,653	6			5		3		2	1
Brockton, Mass	67,449	17	2		59		2		4	1
Canton, Ohio	60,852	16					3			1
Charleston, S. C	60,734	33			1	1				3
Chattanooga, Tenn	61,075	3					3			1
Covington, Ky	57,144	25	1		3		1		2	3
Duluth, Minn	94,495	23	3		4		8		5	3
El Paso, Tex	63,705	44	1		8				3	8
Erie, Pa	73,195		4		199		2			
Evansville, Ind	76,078	23	2		10				6	3
Flint, Mich	54,772	22	2	1	3		4			2
Fort Wayne, Ind	76,183	20	4		25				5	
Harrisburg, Pa	72,015		4		11		1			
Hoboken, N. J	77,214	8	4		5		5			
Holyoke, Mass	63,286	14	1		8				2	2
Johnstown, Pa	68,529		16		19		8		1	
Kansas City, Kans	99,437		2		30		1		4	
Lancaster, Pa	50,853				14		1			

DIPHTHERIA, MEASLES, SCARLET FEVER, AND TUBERCULOSIS—
Continued.

City Reports for Week Ended May 11, 1918—Continued.

City.	Popula-tion as of July 1, 1916 (estimated by U. S. Census Bureau).	Total deaths from all causes.	Diphtheria.		Measles.		Scarlet fever.		Tuber-culosis.	
			Cases.	Deaths.	Cases.	Deaths.	Cases.	Deaths.	Cases.	Deaths.
From 50,000 to 100,000 inhab-itants—Continued.										
Little Rock, Ark...........	57,343	10			1		1		4	1
Malden, Mass.............	51,155	10	3		78		1		3	1
Manchester, N. H.........	78,283	23	2		10				12	1
Mobile, Ala..............	58,221	20	1		7				1	5
New Britain, Conn.......	53,794	23			8					
Oklahoma City, Okla......	92,943	22				1	3	1		2
Passaic, N. J.............	71,744	19			33				3	2
Peoria, Ill...............	71,458	27	4		4		2			3
Portland, Me.............	63,867	23			4					1
Rockford, Ill.............	55,185	18			36		2			3
Sacramento, Cal..........	65,895	24			9		5		3	3
Saginaw, Mich...........	55,642	16	2		2		2			1
St. Joseph, Mo...........	85,236	32	2							
San Diego, Cal...........	53,589	24			10		2			
Schenectady, N. Y.......	99,519	21	1		38				18	3
Sioux City, Iowa..........	57,078						5			
Somerville, Mass.........	87,039	18	4		46		2		7	5
South Bend, Ind..........	68,916	25			3					
Springfield, Ill...........	61,120	25			40					2
Springfield, Ohio	51,750	20	1		4		1		1	2
Terre Haute, Ind.........	66,093	14	1		1		2		3	2
Troy, N. Y..............	77,916	39	2	1	9		2		7	2
Wichita, Kans...........	70,722				21		1		1	
Wilkes-Barre, Pa.........	76,776		6		45		1		5	
Wilmington, Del..........	94,265	32	1	1	16		4			2
Yonkers, N. Y...........	99,888	20	7	1	185		1			2
York, Pa................	51,656		4		24		3			
From 25,000 to 50,000 inhabitants.										
Alameda, Cal.............	27,732	3	3		29		1		1	
Auburn, N. Y............	37,385	8	1		19		1			1
Battle Creek, Mich.......	29,180		1		76		4	1		
Beaumont, Tex...........	27,711	10				1				2
Boise, Idaho.............	33,846				3					
Brookline, Mass..........	32,740	4	1		25		1			1
Butler, Pa..............	27,652				9				4	
Butte, Mont.............	43,425						16			
Cedar Rapids, Iowa	37,498						6			
Central Falls, R. I.	25,436		1	1						
Charleston, W. Va	29,941	12	2		12					
Charlotte, N. C..........	39,823	13			3		2		2	3
Chelsea, Mass...........	46,119	11			18		4		4	
Chester, Pa.............	41,965		3		12		3		4	
Chicopee, Mass..........	29,319	5			1				2	1
Clinton, Iowa............	27,068		1		20					
Color...., N. Y..........	25,211	4								1
Colorado Springs, Colo....	32,971	11	3	1	7		2		1	7
Columbia, S. C...........	34,611				2					
Council Bluffs, Iowa.......	31,184	7			11		3			
Cranston, R. I............	25,987	4			15					1
Cumberland, Md..........	25,974	9	1	1	32		3		2	1
Danville, Ill............	32,261	16			5					1
Davenport, Iowa.........	48,811	1			1		6	1		
Dubuque, Iowa...........	39,873		1		1					1
Durham, N. C...........	22,084	5			8					1
Easton, Pa..............	30,790				20				1	
East Orange, N. J.........	42,458	8			31		1		1	1
Elgin, Ill...............	28,245	5			1				1	1
Elmira, N. Y............	38,120	3			40		2			
Evanston, Ill............	28,501	8					1			
Everett, Mass...........	39,752	7	2		10		1		7	
Everett, Wash...........	37,484									
Fort Smith, Ark..........	28,618	6	1		2		1			
Fresno, Cal..............	31,968	14			12					
Galveston, Tex...........	41,863	15			1				1	
Green Bay, Wis..........	29,353	9			4		1			
Hammond, Ind...........	29,171	10					3		4	
Haverhill, Mass..........	48,477		2		17	1				
Hoboken, Pa............	28,491				42					
Jackson, Mich...........	35,952	8			17		13			
Jamestown, N. Y.........	36,983	11	1		28		1		4	

PHTHERIA, MEASLES, SCARLET FEVER, AND TUBERCULOSIS—Continued.

City Reports for Week Ended May 11, 1918—Continued.

City.	Population as of July 1, 1916 (estimated by U. S. Census Bureau).	Total deaths from all causes	Diphtheria.		Measles.		Scarlet fever.		Tuberculosis.	
			Cases.	Deaths.	Cases.	Deaths.	Cases.	Deaths.	Cases.	Deaths.
25,000 to 50,000 inhabitants—Continued.										
oplin, Mo	23,216				5		2		6	
alamazoo, Mich	48,886	18			3				3	
enosha, Wis	31,576	6	4		13		4		1	
noxville, Tenn	38,676		1		3				1	1
a Crosse, Wis	31,677	7	1						1	
exington, Ky	41,097	16	1		11				1	2
ima, Ohio	35,384	7								1
incoln, Nebr	46,515	10	5	1	2		4			
ong Beach, Cal	27,587	12	1		18	1			2	
orain, Ohio	36,946				3					
ynchburg, Va	32,940	9			5				2	1
acon, Ga	45,757	28			2		1		4	1
adison, Wis	30,699	8	1		27		16			
cKeesport, Pa	47,521		3		4					
edford, Mass	26,234	6	2		10		2		2	1
oline, Ill	27,451	9	1		32		1			
ontclair, N. J	26,318	2	1		13				1	
ontgomery, Ala	43,285	11			8					1
ount Vernon, N. Y	37,009	7	1		12		1		2	
uncie, Ind	25,424	6	2						1	1
uskegon, Mich	26,100	5							2	
uskogee, Okla	44,210				4					
ashua, N. H	27,327	6								
ewark, Ohio	29,635	2			6					
ewburgh, N. Y	29,603	11	1		1		1			4
ew Castle, Pa	41,133				10		1			
ewport, Ky	31,927	5							1	1
ewport, R. I	30,108	2	2		1		3			
ewton, Mass	43,715	12	7	1	11		1		1	
iagara Falls, N. Y	37,353	14			2		3		3	1
orristown, Pa	31,401				1					
orwalk, Conn	28,899						2			
ak Park, Ill	26,654	10	1		11				2	
gden, Utah	31,404	10			36				1	
range, N. J	33,080	13	1		63				10	1
shkosh, Wis	36,095	13							1	1
asadena, Cal	45,450	11	1		65		2		1	2
etersburg, Va	25,582	18							1	3
ittsfield, Mass	38,029	17			3		2		4	
oughkeepsie, N. Y	30,370	10	2		51		1		3	
uincy, Ill	36,708	11			2					1
uincy, Mass	38,136	12	2		57		5		5	
acine, Wis	46,486	14							2	1
oanoke, Va	43,284	13	1		30				1	1
ock Island, Ill	28,926		2		20		6			
alem, Mass	48,562	16			51		2		1	2
an Jose, Cal	38,902				18				1	
heboygan, Wis	28,559	1	1				2			
henandoah, Pa	29,201		1							2
pringfield, Mo	40,341	15			1		4			2
teubenville, Ohio	27,415	12			7		1		3	
uperior, Wis	46,266	19	1				6			1
aunton, Mass	36,283	17	1		2					2
aco, Tex	33,385	12					1		4	2
altham, Mass	30,570	10	1		50					
arwick, R. I	29,999						1			—
aterloo, Iowa	35,550	11			4					
atertown, N. Y	29,804		1							
est Hoboken, N. J	43,039	7			4		2		3	
heeling, W. Va	43,377	17	2		3		1	1		
illiamsport, Pa	33,709						1			
ilmington, N. C	29,592	17			10					
inston-Salem, N. C	31,155	22	1	1	2				4	5
…ville, Ohio	30,463				2					2
10,000 to 25,000 inhabitants:										
erdeen, S. Dak	15,218									1
lexandria, La	15,533	5			3				1	
lton, Ill	22,874	8			2		1		1	1
mesbury, Mass	10,157	2	2						1	
nderson, Ind	23,996	6			3		1			

DIPHTHERIA, MEASLES, SCARLET FEVER, AND TUBERCULOSIS—
Continued.

City Reports for Week Ended May 11, 1918—Continued.

City.	Population as of July 1, 1916 (estimated by U. S. Census Bureau).	Total deaths from all causes.	Diphtheria.		Measles.		Scarlet fever.		Tuberculosis.	
			Cases.	Deaths.	Cases.	Deaths.	Cases.	Deaths.	Cases.	Deaths.
From 10.000 to 25,000 inhabitants—Continued.										
Ann Arbor, Mich	15,010	11			20					
Anniston, Ala	14,112				4					
Ansonia, Conn	16,704				2		1		1	
Appleton, Wis	17,834	5			2					
Arlington, Mass	12,811	2			1				1	
Asbury Park, N. J	14,007	1			22					
Ashtabula, Ohio	21,498	7							1	
Attleboro, Mass	19,282	3							2	1
Augusta, Me	14,170				1					
Bakersfield, Cal	16,874	17			2					4
Barberton, Ohio	13,212		4				1	1		1
Barre, Vt	12,169	3	2							1
Beaver Falls, Pa	13,532				7					
Bedford, Ind	10,349	2								
Bellaire, Ohio	14,348	6					1			
Beloit, Wis	18,072	7	3		26	2				
Bethlehem, Pa	14,142		4		29		1		4	
Beverly, Mass	21,645	3			8					
Billings, Mont	14,422		1		1		3			
Bloomington, Ind	11,383	2								
Braddock, Pa	21,685				18					
Bradford, Pa	14,544				17					
Burlington, Vt	21,617	12			1		1			1
Cairo, Ill	15,794	7			1					
Cambridge, Ohio	13,183	2								
Canton, Ill	13,262	5		1	1					
Cape Girardeau, Mo	10,775		1							
Carbondale, Pa	19,242				5					
Carlisle, Pa	10,726				1					
Carnegie, Pa	11,672				6				1	
Chanute, Kans	12,455				8		2			
Chillicothe, Ohio	15,470	4	3		2		2		1	1
Clinton, Mass	13,075	7			9					
Coatesville, Pa	14,455				1				1	
Coffeyville, Kans	17,548				4		3		1	
Concord, N. H	22,669	9			4					1
Corpus Christi, Tex	10,132	4								
Cortland, N. Y	13,064	2								
Dedham, Mass	10,453				6				1	
Dover, N. H	13,372	4					1			
Dunkirk, N. Y	20,543	6	1		1					
Dunmore, Pa	20,776		1		1					
East Liverpool, Ohio	22,559	7					2			1
East Providence, R. I	18,114						1			
Eau Claire, Wis	18,507		1		16					1
Elwood, Ind	11,068	6	1		1					1
Elyria, Ohio	18,618	3	1		2					1
Fairmont, W. Va	15,599		1							
Fargo, N. Dak	17,489	9	1							
Farrell, Pa	10,190									
Findlay, Ohio	14,845				95					
Fort Scott, Kans	10,550	10			1					
Fostoria, Ohio	10,770	2			1					
Framingham, Mass	13,982				1		2		2	1
Frederick, Md	11,112	2								
Fremont, Ohio	10,582	2			5					
Fulton, N. Y	11,608	7								1
Galesburg, Ill	24,276	6							2	
Gardner, Mass	17,140	1			16				2	
Gary, Ind	16,802	8	3				2			
Glens Falls, N. Y	16,884	4			1				2	
Gloversville, Colo	11,430		1		1		5			
Greenfield, Mass	11,998	2			4				2	
Greensboro, N. C	19,577	4			1					
Greensburg, Pa	15,484						1			
Hackensack, N. J	18,995	7	1		9				3	
Haddon, N. J	16,950		1		8				2	
Hattiesburg, Miss	16,182				1				1	1

[1] Population Apr 15, 1910, no estimate made.

DIPHTHERIA, MEASLES, SCARLET FEVER, AND TUBERCULOSIS—Continued.

City Reports for Week Ended May 11, 1918—Continued.

City.	Population as of July 1, 1916 (estimated by U. S. Census Bureau).	Total deaths from all causes.	Diphtheria.		Measles.		Scarlet fever.		Tuberculosis.	
			Cases.	Deaths.	Cases.	Deaths.	Cases.	Deaths.	Cases.	Deaths.
10,000 to 25,000 inhabitants—Continued.										
enderson, Ky	12,192	7								
omestead, Pa	22,466						1			
opkinsville, Ky	10,762						3			
ornell, N. Y	14,685	2			2					
udson, N. Y	12,705	2			2	1			1	
idependence, Kans	14,506	6			2					
idependence, Mo	11,672	6	1		4				1	1
la, Kans	11,068				0					
haca, N. Y	15,848	2			3					
nesville, Wis	14,339	5					3			1
hnstown, N. Y	20,646				7					
ankakee, Ill	14,220				0					
arny, N. J	23,539	7			19		2		2	
wanee, Ill	13,561	7	1		3		3			1
okomo, Ind	20,930	6	1		0					
ckawanna, N. Y	15,987	5								
Fayette, Ind	21,286	9							1	1
ncaster, Ohio	15,670				4		8			
avenworth, Kans	19,363	7	1		5					
ncoln, R. I	10,383				5					
tle Falls, N. Y	13,451	2								
nitowoc, Wis	13,806	7	1						2	1
nsfield, Ohio	22,734				14				1	
rinette, Wis	14,610	4			12		1	1		
rion, Ind	19,834	1								
rshall, Tex	13,712	3	1						2	
ssillon, Ohio	15,310	5			3					
lrose, Mass	17,445	6	2							
aomimee, Mich	10,507	8					5			
higan City, Ind	21,512	5								
lletown, N. Y	15,810	1			1				1	
idl town, Ohio	15,625	7			2				1	
lville, N. J	13,624		1		5					
hawaka, Ind	16,385	3								
soula, Mont	18,214	5							1	1
es en, Pa	21,630		5		5		1			
antown, W. Va	13,709	4			3					
ristown, N. J	13,284				29				3	
indsville, W. Va	11,153	3								
nt Carmel, Pa	20,268		3		2					
atine, Iowa	17,500				1					
ticoke, Pa	23,126						3			
k, Mass	10,102	3			12				1	1
Albany, Ind	23,629	4							1	
buryport, Mass	15,243	10	1		4					
Castle, Ind	13,241	1					2			
London, Conn	20,985	9	1		3		5			2
h Adams, Mass	22,019	9	2				1		1	
hampton, Mass	19,926	8			4		2		1	2
h Attleboro, Mass	11,014	4	3		7					
h Braddock, Pa	15,148		1		2					
h Little Rock, Ark	14,907	2			2				1	1
h Yakima, Wash	20,951				5		3			
rood, Ohio	22,286	1								
, N. Y	16,621	5								
go, N. Y	24,101		1		2		5		1	
sboro, Ky	17,784	10	1		1	1	1			2
tine, Tex	11,854		1		1				2	
riburg, W. Va	20,612	3			1				1	1
nixville, Pa	11,714				3					
field, N. J	23,805	6			5				1	
burgh, N. Y	12,837	3							1	
outh, Mass	13,743	3								
outh, Pa	19,100		1							
ello, Idaho	12,293				1					
ic, Mich	17,524		7		3		1			3
hester, N. Y	16,183	4			10	1			1	

1 Population Apr. 15, 1910; no estimate made.

DIPHTHERIA, MEASLES, SCARLET FEVER, AND TUBERCULOSIS—Continued.

City Reports for Week Ended May 11, 1918—Continued.

City.	Population as of July 1, 1916 (estimated by U. S. Census Bureau).	Total deaths from all causes.	Diphtheria.		Measles.		Scarlet fever.		Tuberculosis.	
			Cases.	Deaths.	Cases.	Deaths.	Cases.	Deaths.	Cases.	Deaths.
From 10,000 to 20,000 inhabitants—Continued.				ɔ		ɔ				
Pottsville, Pa.	23,372				4				1	
Provo, Utah	10,645	3							1	
Rahway, N. J.	10,219								1	
Raleigh, N. C.	20,127	12			11				2	2
Redlands, Cal.	14,000	1			5				1	1
Reno, Nev.	14,889	6	1							
Richmond, Ind.	24,697	7								
Riverside, Cal.	19,703	7			2					
Rocky Mount, N. C.	12,067	7								2
Rome, N. Y.	23,737		3						1	
Rutland, Vt.	14,831	8								
Sandusky, Ohio	20,193	4	1		1					
Sanford, Me.	10,916	3								
Santa Ana, Cal.	10,627	4			15					
Santa Cruz, Cal.	14,592	5			5					1
Saratoga Springs, N. Y.	13,821	3			5				1	1
Shamokin, Pa.	21,129		4					3		1
Shelbyville, Ind.	10,905	6								
Southbridge, Mass	14,205	2			4				1	
Spartanburg, S. C.	21,305	8			5				1	1
Steelton, Pa	15,548							1	2	
Tuscaloosa, Ala	10,488	3	1		1				2	1
Uniontown, Pa	20,790				3					
Vallejo, Cal	13,461				3					
Vancouver, Wash.	13,180				22			3		
Warren, Ohio	13,059	12			3					
Warren, Pa	14,737							1		
Washington, Pa	21,618		4		20			4	2	
Watertown, Mass	14,687	3			5			2	1	
Wausau, Wis	19,239	5						3	1	1
West Chester, Pa.	13,176				4			1		
Westfield, Mass	18,391	10	1		18			1		2
West Warwick, R. I.	15,782	6								1
White Plains, N. Y.	22,405	6			4			3		
Wilkinsburg, Pa.	23,228				11			1		
Winchester, Mass.	10,443	4			1					
Winona, Minn.	¹18,583	3								2
Winthrop, Mass.	12,092		1		7			5	1	

¹ Population Apr. 15, 1910, no estimate made.

FOREIGN.

CUBA.

Communicable Diseases—Habana.

mmunicable diseases have been notified at Habana as follows:

Disease.	Apr. 21-30, 1918.		Cases remaining under treatment Apr. 30, 1918.	Disease.	Apr. 21-30, 1918.		Cases remaining under treatment Apr. 30, 1918.
	New cases.	Deaths.			New cases.	Deaths.	
ria.............	12	....	18	Paratyphoid fever......	....	....	1
....	....	....	13	Scarlet fever...........	1	....	¹2
....	8	....	¹43	Typhoid fever.........	44	2	²86
....	1	....	8	Varicella............	17	....	22

¹ From the interior, 38.
² From the interior, 1.
³ From the interior, 41. Foreign, 1: from Regla, 1.

ERA, PLAGUE, SMALLPOX, TYPHUS FEVER, AND YELLOW FEVER.

Reports Received During Week Ended May 31, 1918.[1]

CHOLERA.

Place.	Date.	Cases.	Deaths.	Remarks.
ay................	Feb. 17-23.......	3	3	
Java..............				Feb. 1-21, 1918: Cases, 1L
atavia........	Feb. 1-21..........	11	....	
Islands:				
tevs.				Mar 31-Apr. 6, 1918: Cases, 96; deaths, 85.
.h ol.................	Mar. 31-Apr. 6.....	28	23	
isamis........	.....do.............	48	31	
Oriental Negros......	.....do.............	2	5	
rigao................	.....do.............	18	26	

PLAGUE.

.y.................	Feb. 17-23..........	35	30	Feb. 17-23, 1918: Cases, 36,768; deaths, 20,709.
.:				
....	Mar. 18-31..........	25	14	
.va...........				Jan. 15-Feb. 4, 1918: Cases, 60; deaths, 60
.baya..............	Jan. 15-Feb 4.....	17	17	

om medical officers of the Public Health Service, American consuls, and other sources.

(901)

CHOLERA, PLAGUE, SMALLPOX, TYPHUS FEVER, AND YELLOW FEVER—Continued.

Reports Received During Week Ended May 31, 1918—Continued.

SMALLPOX.

Place.	Date.	Cases.	Deaths.	Remarks.
Algeria:				
Algiers	Mar. 1–31	36	6	
Canada:				
New Brunswick—				
St. John				May 13, 1918: 14 cases.
Nova Scotia—				
Halifax	Apr. 28–May 11	9		
Sydney	May 5–11	1		
Ontario—				
Sarnia	May 11–18	2		
Quebec—				
Quebec	May 5–11	1		
France:				
Paris	Mar. 31–Apr. 6		1	
India:				
Bombay	Feb. 17–23	179	72	
Indo-China:				
Saigon	Mar. 18–24	300	97	
Java:				
East Java				Jan. 15–Feb. 4, 1918: Cases, 11.
Surabaya	Jan. 29–Feb. 4	1		
Mid-Java				Jan. 30–Feb 13, 1918: Cases, 18.
West Java				Feb. 1–21, 1918; Cases, 141; deaths, 43.
Batavia	Feb. 1–7	1		
Newfoundland:				
St. Johns	May 4–14	14		
Philippine Islands:				
Manila	Mar. 31–Apr. 6	17	11	Varioloid, 41.
Spain:				
Coruna	Mar. 1–Apr. 6		14	
Madrid	Mar. 1–31		7	

TYPHUS FEVER.

Place.	Date.	Cases.	Deaths.	Remarks.
Java:				
East Java				Jan. 15–Feb. 11, 1918: Cases, 28; deaths, 5.
Surabaya	Jan. 15–Feb 11	19	3	
Mid-Java				Jan. 24–Feb. 13, 1918: Cases, 13; deaths, 2.
Samarang	Jan. 31–Feb. 6	2		
West Java				Feb. 1–21, 1918: Cases, 3.
Batavia	Feb. 1–21	20	1	
Mexico				
Aguascalientes	Apr. 29–May 5		1	
Spain:				
Madrid	Mar. 1–31		1	
Tunis:				
Tunis	Apr. 12–19	3	3	
Union of South Africa:				
Cape of Good Hope State				Sept 10, 1917–Mar 17, 1918: Cases, 4,444 (European, 34), deaths, 962 (European, 15).
Natal				Dec 1, 1917–Mar 17, 1918: Cases, 50; deaths, 11.

OLERA, PLAGUE, SMALLPOX, TYPHUS FEVER, AND YELLOW FEVER—Continued.

Reports Received from Dec. 29, 1917, to May 24, 1918—Continued.

CHOLERA.

Place.	Date.	Cases.	Deaths.	Remarks.
ntung	Nov. 26–Dec. 2....	3	1	
lombay	Oct. 28–Dec. 15....	19	14	
Do	Dec. 30–Jan. 26....	216	190	
alcutta	Sept. 16–Dec. 15...	....	135	
Do	Dec. 30–Feb. 23....	....	53	
arachl	....do........	25	6	
ladras	Nov. 25–Dec. 22...	2	2	
Do	Dec. 30–Mar. 9....	44	24	
angoon	Nov. 4–Dec. 22....	·5	5	
Do	Dec. 30–Mar. 2....	7	3	
China:				
rovinces	....	....	....	Sept. 1–Dec. 31, 1917: Cases, 168; deaths, 95.
Anam	Sept. 1–Dec. 31...	24	15	
Cambodia	....do........	74	54	
Cochin-China	....do........	58	24	
Saigon	Nov. 22–Dec. 9....	4	3	
Do	Feb. 4–Mar. 11....	8	3	
Kwang-Chow-Wan	Sept. 1–30.........	10	2	
ist Java	Oct. 28–Nov. 3....	1	1	
e:t Java	....	....	....	Oct. 19–Dec. 27, 1917: Cases, 102; deaths, 56. Dec. 28, 1917–Jan. 31, 1918: Cases, 27; deaths, 7.
Batavia	Oct. 10–Dec. 27....	49	23	
Do	Dec. 28–Jan. 31....	24	1	
ine	....	....	....	Dec. 28, 1917–Feb. 5, 1918: Cases, 31. Occurring at 7 localities; 2 cases in encampments.
ir Seneid	Dec. 28–Jan. 31....	13	....	
kkarieh	....do........	13	....	
hral	July 30–Aug. 16....	90	88	July 30–Sept. 3, 1917: Cases, 384; deaths, 276.
trabad	July 31...........	....	....	Present.
rírush	July 1–Aug. 16....	39	25	
ahmirzad	....	....	....	25 cases reported July 31, 1917.
ahrastagh	June 15–July 25...	10	8	
aroud	Aug. 26–Sept. 3....	4	2	
mghan	Aug. 26.........	....	....	Present.
arek	May 28–June 11...	21	13	
hed	Aug. 18–Sept. 2...	174	82	
oun Dare	Aug. 8.........	....	....	Do.
zevar	Aug. 24.........	....	....	Do.
i	July 3–29.........	273	144	
inan	Aug. 31–Sept. 2...	14	5	
chambe Bazar	June 3.........	6	....	
ine Islands:				
vinces	....	....	....	July 1–Dec. 29, 1917: Cases, 5,964; deaths, 3,655. Dec. 30, 1917–Mar. 30, 1918: Cases, 1,664; deaths, 1,135.
Antique	Nov. 18–Dec. 1....	48	32	
Do	Feb. 3–9.........	4	4	
Bohol	Nov. 18–Dec. 29...	169	111	
Do	Dec. 30–Mar. 30...	521	413	
Capiz	Nov. 25–Dec. 29...	27	21	
Do	Dec. 30–Mar. 23...	219	182	
ebu	Dec. 23–29.........	3	....	
Do	Dec. 30–Mar. 30...	100	54	
Davao	Mar. 10–16.........	10	8	
loilo	Nov. 25–Dec. 29...	179	135	
Do	Dec. 30–Mar. 2....	97	63	
æyte	Nov. 25–Dec. 22...	13	12	
Do	Feb. 3–Mar. 16....	50	38	
lindanao	Nov. 25–Dec. 29...	337	196	
Do	Dec. 30–Feb. 9....	341	220	
Isamis	Feb. 24–Mar. 23...	106	67	
ccidental Negros	Nov. 25–Dec. 22...	177	123	
Do	Jan. 13–Mar. 30...	144	83	
riental Negros	Nov. 25–Dec. 29...	99	62	
Do	Dec. 30–Mar. 30...	23	15	
omblon	Nov. 25–Dec. 1....	1	1	
irigno	Feb. 24–Mar. 23...	14	9	
mboanga	....do........	35	29	
antnine	May 13...........	....	....	Present.
iin	....do...........	....	....	Do.
ok	Sept. 16–22........	1	1	
Asia:				
i	Nov. 1–15........	....	40	

904

CHOLERA, PLAGUE, SMALLPOX, TYPHUS FEVER, AND YELLOW FEVER—Continued

Reports Received from Dec. 29, 1917, to May 24, 1918—Continued.

PLAGUE.

Place.	Date.	Cases.	Deaths.	Remarks.
Brazil:				
Bahia...................	Nov. 4- Dec. 15....	4	4	
Do.........	Dec. 30 Feb. 23...	4	3	
Rio de Janeiro............	Dec. 23 29.........	1	....	
Do.........	Jan. 6-12.........	1	1	
British East Africa:				
Mombassa............	Oct. 1-Dec. 31.....	31	18	
British Gold Coast:				
Axim...............	Jan. 8............			Present.
Ceylon:				
Colombo................	Oct. 14-Dec. 1.....	14	13	
Do.........	Dec. 30-Feb. 16...	20	17	
China..........				Present in North China in January, 1918, pneumonic form.
Anhwei Province—				
Fengyanghsien........	Feb. 27............		9	Pneumonic.
Pengpu.........	...do.........		1	Do.
Chili Province—				
Kalgan...........				Vicinity. Present in February, 1918.
Fukien Province—				
Amoy............	Mar. 11-31.......			Present in vicinity.
Kiangsu Province—				
Nanking...........	Mar. 17-Apr. 5...	19	15	
Shanshi Province.........				Present in February, 1918; 116 cases estimated.
Ecuador.				
Babahoyo..............	Feb. 1 15.........	1	....	
Duran...........	Feb 16 Mar. 30....	2	1	
Guayaquil...........	Sept. 1 Nov. 30....	66	24	Reported outbreak occurring about Jan. 17, 1918.
Do.........	Feb. 1 15.........	44	18	
Do.........	Mar. 1 30.........	37	14	
Egypt.				Jan. 1-Nov. 15, 1917; Cases, 725; deaths, 398.
Alexandria.......	Jan. 14 28........	1	2	
Cairo...............	Dec. 17 23........	2	....	
Port Said...........	July 2 Dec. 23....	13	7	
Suez...	July 2 Oct. 20....	62	28	
Hawaii:				
Laupahoehoe............	May 5............	1	1	
India............				July 1 Dec. 29, 1917: Cases, 260,258, deaths, 212,622. Dec. 30, 1917 Feb. 16, 1918: Cases, 240,000, deaths, 192,149.
Bassein.........	Dec. 9 29		8	
Do.........	Dec 30 Feb 23....		99	
Bombay...........	Oct 28 Dec. 29....	147	123	
Do.........	Dec. 30 Feb. 16...	152	112	
Calcutta...........	Sept. 16 29		2	
Do.........	Dec. 30 Feb. 2....		4	
Henzada...........	Oct. 21 27........		1	
Do.........	Jan. 5 Feb. 23....		71	
Karachi...........	Oct. 21 Dec 29 ...	27	20	
Do.........	Dec. 30 Mar. 2....	48	34	
Madras...........	Feb. 3 Mar. 9....	3	3	
Madras Presidency.........	Oct 31 Nov. 24...	5,786	4,519	
Do.........	Jan. 6 Mar. 9 ...	11,082	8,591	
Mandalay...........	Oct 14 Nov. 17...		69	
Do.........	Dec 30 Feb. 16...		782	
Moulmein...........	Feb. 1 23		1	
Myingyan.........	Dec. 30 Feb. 16...		607	
Pegu...........	Feb. 10-23........		2	
Prome...........	Jan. 5 12		1	
Rangoon.........	Oct. 21-Dec. 22...		86	
Do.........	Dec. 30 Mar. 2...	441	400	
Toungoo...........	Dec. 9 29........		5	
Do.........	Dec. 30 Feb. 23 ..		32	
Indo-China				
Provinces.........				Sept. 1-Dec. 31, 1917: Cases, 171; deaths, 125.
Anam............	Sept. 1-Dec. 31...	45	29	
Cambodia............	...do.........	95	83	
Cochin-China	...do.........	31	17	
Saigon.........	Oct 31 Dec. 23...	17	6	
Do.........	Dec. 31 Mar. 17...	115	60	
Java:				
East Java.........				Oct. 8-Dec. 31, 1917: Cases, 196; deaths, 188
Do.........				Jan 1-16, 1918. Cases, 23; deaths, 21.
Residencies—				
Kediri...........	Oct. 8-Dec. 31.....	1	1	
Madioen	...do.........	49	49	
Samarang.........	...do.........	110	100	
Surabaya........	...do.........	25	23	
Surakarta.........	...do.........	11	11	
West Java.........				Nov. 25-Dec. 9, 1917: Cases, 46; deaths, 46. Dec. 1, 1917-Jan. 15, 1918: Cases, 160.

OLERA, PLAGUE, SMALLPOX, TYPHUS FEVER, AND YELLOW FEVER—Continued.

Reports Received from Dec. 29, 1917, to May 24, 1918—Continued.

PLAGUE—Continued.

Place.	Data.	Cases.	Deaths.	Remarks.
ncachs Department—				
Casma..................	Dec. 1–Jan. 15.....	2	....	
ambayeque Department..	.....do............	22	....	At Chiclayo, Ferrenafe, Jayanca, Lambayeque.
bertad Department.......	.....do............	72	....	At Guadalupe, Mansiche, Pacasmayo, Salaverry, San Jose, San Pedro, and country district of Trujillo.
ma Department..........	.....do............	9	....	City and country.
ura Department—				
Catacaos...............	.....do............	1	....	
.l:				
Louis...................	Feb. 2.............		....	Present.
ngkok....................	Sept. 16–Dec. 23...	13	9	
Do....................	Jan. 13–Mar. 16...	37	27	
Settlements:				
rupore...................	Oct. 28–Dec. 29....	5	7	
Do....................	Jan. 6–Mar. 9......	64	57	

SMALLPOX.

Place.	Data.	Cases.	Deaths.	Remarks.
iers....................	Nov. 1–Dec. 31....	3	2	
Do....................	Jan. 1–Apr. 23.....	213	....	
ia:				
v South Wales..........				July 12–Dec. 20, 1917: Cases, 36; Jan. 4–17, 1918: case, 1. Newcastle district.
Abermain.............	Oct. 25–Nov. 29...	3	....	
Cessnock..............	July 12–Oct. 11...	7	....	
Eumangla.............	Aug. 15...........	1	....	
Kurri Kurri...........	Dec. 5–20..........	2	....	
Mungindi	Aug. 13...........	1	....	
Warren...............	July 12–Oct. 25...	22	....	
Do.................	Jan. 1–17.........	1	....	
.a....................	Nov. 10–Dec. 8....	3	....	
ambuco..............	Nov. 1–15.........	1	....	
de Janeiro............	Sept. 30– Dec. 29..	703	190	
Do..................	Dec. 30–Mar. 23...	251	84	
Paulo................	Oct. 29–Nov. 4....		2	
East Africa:				
basa.................	Oct. 1–Dec. 31.....	9	5	
sh Columbia—				
'ancouver.............	Jan. 13–Mar. 9....	5	....	
'ictoria..............	Jan. 7–Feb. 2......	2	....	
Vinnipeg.............	Dec. 30–Apr. 13...	4	....	
Brunswick—				
Kent County..........	Dec. 4.............		....	Outbreak. On main line Canadian Ry., 25 miles north of Moncton.
Do..............	Jan. 22............	40	....	In 7 localities.
orthumberland	.....do............	41	....	In 5 localities.
County.				
estigouche County....	Jan. 18............	60	....	
:. John County—				
St. John............	Mar. 3–May 11....	20	....	
ictoria County........	Jan. 2.............	10	....	At Limestone and a lumber camp.
'estmorelandCounty—				
Moncton..........	Jan. 29–Apr. 27...	20	....	
ork County...........	Jan. 22............	8	....	
Scotia—				
pe Sable Island.......			....	Present May 8 at Clarks Harbor
ilifax.................	Feb. 24–Apr. 27...	10	....	
dney.................	Feb. 3–Apr. 27....	19	....	
o—				
nprior...............	Mar. 31–Apr. 6....		1	
imilton	Dec. 16 22........	1	....	
Do.................	Jan. 13–19.........	2	....	
tawa................	Mar. 4–24..........	5	....	
nia..................	Dec. 9–15..........	1	....	
Do.................	Jan. 6–Mar. 30.....	32	....	
ronto................	Feb. 10–Apr. 6....	2	....	
ndsor................	Dec. 30–Jan. 5.....	1	....	

CHOLERA, PLAGUE, SMALLPOX, TYPHUS FEVER, AND YELLOW FEVER—Continued.

Reports Received from Dec. 29, 1917, to May 24, 1918—Continued.

SMALLPOX—Continued.

Place.	Date.	Cases.	Deaths.	Remarks.
Canada—Continued.				
Prince Edward Island—				
Charlottetown..........	Feb. 7-13........	1	....	
Quebec—				
Montreal.............	Dec. 16-Jan. 5....	5	....	
Do.............	Jan. 6-Apr. 6.....	12	....	
Quebec.............	Apr. 21-27.......	2	....	
China:				
Amoy...............	Oct. 22-Dec. 30....	....	....	Present.
Do...............	Dec. 31-Mar. 31...	....	....	Do.
Antung..............	Dec. 2-23.......	13	2	
Do...............	Jan. 7-Apr. 6.....	13	3	
Changsha............	Jan. 28-Mar. 10...	6	1	
Chefoo..............	Jan. 27-Feb. 9....	....	....	Do.
Chungking...........	Nov. 11-Dec. 29...	....	....	Do.
Do...............	Dec. 30-Mar. 16...	....	....	Do.
Dairen.............	Nov. 18-Dec. 22...	3	1	
Do...............	Dec. 30-Apr. 6....	64	5	
Hankow.............	Feb. 25-Mar. 3....	1	....	
Harbin..............	May 14-June 30...	20	....	Chinese Eastern Ry.
Do...............	July 1-Dec. 2.....	7	....	Do.
Hongkong...........	Dec. 23-29.......	1	....	
Do...............	Jan. 26-Mar. 30...	19	9	
Hungtahotze Station...	Oct. 28-Nov. 4....	1	....	Do.
Manchuria Station.....	May 14-June 30...	6	....	Do.
Do...............	July 1-Dec. 2.....	3	....	Do.
Mukden.............	Nov. 11-24......	....	....	Present.
Do...............	Feb. 10-Mar. 30...	....	....	Do.
Nanking............	Feb. 3-Apr. 6.....	....	....	Do.
Shanghai............	Nov. 18-Dec. 23...	41	91	Cases, foreign; deaths among natives.
Do...............	Dec. 31-Apr. 1....	38	119	Do.
Swatow.............	Jan. 18........	....	....	Unusually prevalent.
Tientsin............	Nov. 11-Dec. 22...	13	....	
Do...............	Dec. 30-Apr. 6....	46	....	
Tsingtau............	Feb. 4-Mar. 31....	10	2	
Cuba:				
Habana.............	Jan. 7.........	1	....	Nov. 8, 1917: 1 case from Coruna; Dec. 5, 1917, 1 case
Marianao...........	Jan. 8.........	1	....	6 miles distant from Habana.
Ecuador.				
Guayaquil...........	Sept. 1-Nov. 30....	26	2	
Do...............	Feb. 1-Mar. 31....	4	3	
Egypt:				
Alexandria...........	Nov. 12-18......	2	1	
Do...............	Jan. 5-Mar. 25	10	....	
Cairo...............	July 23-Nov. 18...	6	1	
France.				
Lyon	Nov. 18-Dec. 16...	6	3	
Do...............	Jan. 7-Feb. 17....	11	2	
Marseille............	Jan. 1-31.......	....	2	
Paris	Jan. 27-Mar. 30...	9	3	
Rouen.............	Mar. 31-Apr. 6....	26	4	
Great Britain:				
Cardiff.............	Feb. 3-9.......	4	....	
Hull..............	Mar. 17-30......	3	....	
Greece.				
Saloniki.	Jan. 27-Mar. 16 ...	....	9	
Honduras.				
Santa Barbara Department	Jan. 1-7........	....	....	Present in interior.
India.				
Bombay.............	Oct. 21-Dec. 29...	80	12	
Do	Dec. 31-Feb. 2....	348	134	
Calcutta	Jan. 27-Feb. 23 ...	....	12	
Karachi	Nov. 18-Dec. 29...	4	2	Nov. 11-16, 1917: 10 cases with 4 deaths; imported on s. s. Mecca from Bassreh.
Do	Jan. 27-Mar. 2....	31	17	
Madras	Oct. 31-Dec. 29...	20	5	
Do	Dec. 30-Mar. 9....	143	135	
Rangoon............	Oct. 28-Dec. 22...	8	1	
Do	Dec. 30-Mar. 2....	63	11	
Indo-China.				
Provinces		....	....	Sept. 1-Dec. 31, 1917: Cases, 659, deaths, 150.
Annam	Sept. 1-Dec. 31...	210	20	
Do	...do..........	19	11	
Cambodia	...do..........	440	133	
Saigon	Oct. 20-Dec. 30 ...	120	26	
Do	Dec. 31-Mar. 17...	795	272	
Laos	Oct. 1-Dec. 31	8	1	
Tonkin.............	Sept. 1-Dec. 31...	18	5	

CHOLERA, PLAGUE, SMALLPOX, TYPHUS FEVER, AND YELLOW FEVER—Continued.

Reports Received from Dec. 29, 1917, to May 24, 1918—Continued.

SMALLPOX—Continued.

Place.	Date.	Cases.	Deaths.	Remarks.
..ly:				
Castellamare...............	Dec. 10............	2	....	Among refugees.
Florence...............	Dec. 1–15........	17	4	
Genoa................	Dec. 2–31........	11	3	
Do..............	Jan. 2–Apr. 15....	52	9	
Leghorn...............	Jan. 7–Apr. 7....	33	7	
Messina............	Jan. 3–19........	1	....	
Milan............		....	....	Oct. 1–Dec. 31, 1917: Cases, 32.
Naples...............	To Dec. 10........	2	....	Among refugees.
Taormina.............	Jan. 20–Feb. 9....	6	....	
Turin................	Oct. 29–Dec. 29..	123	120	
Do..............	Jan. 21–Mar. 10....	72	6	
..an:				
Nagasaki...............	Jan. 14–Apr. 14....	10	3	
Taihoku................	Dec. 15–21........	1	....	Island of Taiwan (Formosa).
Do..............	Jan. 8–Apr. 8....	49	8	Do.
Tokyo..................	Feb. 11–Apr. 14....	26	....	City and suburbs.
Yokohama............	Jan. 17–Feb. 3....	63	....	
..a:				
East Java...............	Oct. 7–Dec. 23.....	50	....	Dec. 25–31, 1917: Cases, 7. Jan. 1–14, 1918: Cases, 3.
Surabaya...........	Dec. 25–31........	1	....	
Mid-Java................		....	....	Oct. 10–Dec. 26, 1917: Cases, 86; death, 1. Dec. 28, 1917–Jan. 23, 1918: Cases, 23.
Samarang.............	Nov. 6–Dec. 12....	4	1	
West Java...............		....	....	Oct. 19–Dec. 27, 1917: Cases, 231; deaths, 36. Dec. 28, 1917–Jan. 31, 1918: Cases, 116; deaths, 17.
Batavia...............	Nov. 2–8..........	1	....	
..potamia—				
Bagdad.............	Jan. 1–31........	....	10	
..co:				
Aguascalientes.............	Feb. 4–17........	....	2	
Ciudad Juarez.............	Mar. 3–23........	2	1	
Guadalajara.............	Mar. 1–31........	21	4	
Mazatlan.............	Dec. 5–11........	....	1	
Do.............	Jan. 29–Apr. 2.....	4	4	
Mexico City.............	Nov. 11–Dec. 29....	16	....	
Do.............	Dec. 30–Apr. 13....	111	....	
Piedras Negras.............	Jan. 11........	200	....	
Vera Cruz.............	Jan. 20–Apr. 28....	16	3	
..oundland:				
St. Johns...............	Dec. 8–Jan. 4......	29	....	
Do..............	Jan. 5–May 3......	89	....	45 cases in hospital.
Trepassey............	Jan. 4........	....	....	Outbreak with 11 cases reported.
..pine Islands:				
Manila...............	Oct. 28–Dec. 8.....	5	....	
Do...............	Feb. 3–30........	81	35	Varioloid, 13 .
..Rico:				
San Juan...................	Jan. 28–Apr. 7....	37	....	Of these, 30 varioloid.
..gual:				
Lisbon............	Nov. 4–Dec. 15....	2	....	
Do...............	Dec. 30–Mar. 30...	17	....	
..guese East Africa:				
Lourenço Marquez........	Aug. 1–Dec. 31.....	....	16	
Do.............	Jan. 1–31........	....	6	
..r.				
Archangel...............	Sept. 1–Oct. 31...	7	....	
Moscow..................	Aug. 26–Oct. 6....	23	2	
Petrograd..................	Aug. 31–Nov. 18...	76	3	
..:				
Bangkok...............	Nov. 25–Dec. 1....	1	1	
Do...............	Jan. 6–Mar. 16....	26	14	
..:				
Coruna.............	Dec. 2–15........	....	4	
Do.............	Jan. 20–Feb. 23...	....	5	
Madrid.............	Jan. 1–Feb. 28....	....	9	Jan. 1–Dec. 31, 1917: Deaths, 77.
Malaga.............	Oct. 1–31........	....	19	
Seville.............	Oct. 1–Dec. 30....	....	66	
Do.............	Jan. 1–31........	....	20	
Valencia.............	Jan. 27–Feb. 2.....	1	....	
..Settlements:				
Singapore.................	Nov. 25–Dec. 1....	1	1	
Do...............	Dec. 30–Jan. 5....	1	....	
..:				
Tunis.............	Dec. 14–20........	1	....	
Do...................	Mar. 16–Apr. 12...	2	....	

CHOLERA, PLAGUE, SMALLPOX, TYPHUS FEVER, AND YELLOW FEVER—Continued.

Reports Received from Dec. 29, 1917, to May 24, 1918—Continued.

SMALLPOX—Continued.

Place.	Date.	Cases.	Deaths.	Remarks.
Turkey in Asia:				
Bagdad...............	....	....	....	Present in November, 1917.
Union of South Africa:				
Cape of Good Hope State...	Oct. 1–Dec. 31.....	28	....	
East Liverpool.........	Jan. 20–26.........	1	....	Varioloid.
Transvaal—				
Johannesburg..........	Jan. 1–31..........	4	....	
Venezuela:				
Maracaibo..................	Dec. 2–8............	....	1	

TYPHUS FEVER.

Place.	Date.	Cases.	Deaths.	Remarks.
Algeria:				
Algiers.....................	Nov. 1–Dec. 31....	2	1	
Argentina:				
Rosario....................	Dec. 1–31.........	....	1	
Austria-Hungary:				
Hungary..................	....	....	....	Present in December, 1917.
Brazil:				
Rio de Janeiro..............	Oct. 28–Dec. 1.....	7	....	
Canada:				
Ontario—				
Kingston..............	Dec. 2–8...........	3	....	
Quebec—				
Montreal..............	Dec. 16–22.........	2	1	
China:				
Antung..................	Dec. 3–20..........	13	1	
Do......................	Dec 31–Mar. 30...	3	2	
Chosen (Korea):				
Seoul....................	Nov. 1–30.........	1	....	
Do......................	Feb. 1–28..........	3	2	
Egypt:				
Alexandria................	Nov. 8 Dec. 28....	57	15	
Do......................	Jan 8–Apr 1.......	688	157	
Cairo....................	July 25 Dec. 23....	143	74	
Port Said................	July 30–Nov. 11...	5	5	
France:				
Marseille.................	Dec 1–31..........	....	1	
Germany..................	....	....	....	Jan. 1–30, 1918: Cases, 66.
Great Britain:				
Belfast...................	Feb. 10–Mar 30...	21	3	
Dublin	Mar. 24 30........	3	....	
Glasgow.................	Dec. 21............	1	....	
Do......................	Jan. 20 Apr. 20...	16	....	
Manchester..............	Dec. 2–8..........	1	....	
Greece:				
Arta	Feb. 19............	2	....	
Janina..................	Feb. 14...........	110	....	Jan. 27, epidemic.
Saloniki.................	Nov. 11 Dec 29...	....	72	
Do......................	Dec. 30 Mar. 16...	....	27	
Italy:				
San Remo................	Mar. 10–16........	2	....	
Japan:				
Nagasaki................	Nov 26 Dec 16....	5	5	
Do......................	Jan. 7–Apr. 14....	16	6	
Java:				
East Java................				Oct 15–Dec 31, 1917: Cases, 39;
Surabaya........	Dec 17–31.........	9	1	deaths, 7 Jan 1–14, 1918:
Do.	Jan. 1–14.........	10	1	Cases, 11; deaths, 2
Mid-Java ...				Oct 10 Dec. 26, 1917 Cases, 62
Samarang	Oct 9 Dec. 26.....	20	2	deaths, 2. Dec 28, 1917–Jan.
Do	Dec 27–Jan. 15....	16	....	23, 1918 Cases, 11.
West Java................				Oct 19 Dec 27, 1917 Cases, 94;
Batavia	Oct 1 Dec 27......	50	15	deaths, 17. Dec 28 to17–Jan.
Do	Dec. 28 Jan. 31....	27	1	31, 1918 Cases, 33, deaths, 1
Lithuania................				Dec 30, 1917 Jan. 5, 1918. Cases, 105.
Mexico:				
Aguascalientes..........	Dec 15	....	3	
Do.	Jan 21–Apr 28.....	....	17	
Durango State –				
Gomez...........	Feb 11............	....	....	Epidemic.
Mexico City.............	Nov 11 Dec 29.....	476	....	
Do......................	Dec. 30–Apr. 13...	704	....	

CHOLERA, PLAGUE, SMALLPOX, TYPHUS FEVER, AND YELLOW FEVER—Continued.

Reports Received from Dec. 29, 1917, to May 24, 1918—Continued.

TYPHUS FEVER—Continued.

Place.	Date.	Cases.	Deaths.	Remarks.
Newfoundland:				
St. Johns..................	Mar. 30-Apr. 5....	1	1	
Norway:				
Bergen....................	Feb. 1-16..........	3	....	
Poland......................	....	....	....	Nov. 18-Dec. 8, 1917: Cases, 2,568;
Lodz...................	Nov. 18-Dec. 8....	219	25	deaths, 218. Dec. 23, 1917-
Warsaw..............	.....do..........	1,461	141	Jan. 12, 1918: Cases, 3,026; deaths, 315.
Portugal:				
Lisbon....................	Mar. 3-30..........	18	....	Feb. 21: Present.
Oporto..................	Dec. 1-31..........	23	4	
Do..................	Jan. 1-Mar. 8.....	1,811	161	
Russia:				
Archangel.................	Sept. 1-14........	7	2	
Moscow..................	Aug. 26-Oct. 6....	49	2	
Petrograd..............	Aug. 31-Nov. 18...	32	....	
Do..................	Feb. 2............	....	....	Present.
Vladivostok..............	Oct. 29-Nov. 4....	12	1	
Spain:				
Corcubion...............	Apr. 11...........	....	....	Present. Province of Coruna, west coast.
Madrid....................	Jan. 1-31..........	....	1	
Sweden:				
Goteborg..................	Nov. 18-Dec. 15...	2	....	
Switzerland:				
Basel....................	Jan. 6-19..........	1	1	
Zurich..................	Nov. 9-15.........	2	....	
Do..................	Jan 13-19.........	2	....	
Tunisia:				
Tala.....................	Mar. 18...........	....	....	Epidemic.
Tozer....................	.....do..........	....	....	Do.
Tunis....................	Nov. 30-Dec. 6....	....	1	
Do..................	Feb. 9-Apr. 5.....	37	13	Of these, 26 in outbreak in prison.
Union of South Africa:				
Cape of Good Hope State...	Sept. 10-Dec. 30...	4,035	830	Sept. 10-Nov. 25, 1917: Cases, 3,724 (European, 31); deaths, 761 (European, 5). Total to Feb. 17, 1918: Cases, 4,386 (European, 32); deaths, 887 (European, 5).
Natal..................	....	....	....	From Dec. 1, 1917-Feb. 17, 1918: Cases, 43; deaths, 11.

YELLOW FEVER.

Place.	Date.	Cases.	Deaths.	Remarks.
Brazil:				
Bahia.......................	Mar. 10-16........	1	1	
Ecuador:				
Babahoyo..................	Feb. 1-15.........	1	1	
Guayaquil.................	Sept. 1-Nov. 30...	5	3	
Do..................	Feb. 1-15.........	1	....	
Do..................	Mar. 1-31..........	12	7	
Milagro...................	Feb. 1-15.........	1	1	
Naguachi.................	Nov. 1-30.........	1	....	
Guatemala:				
Retalhuleu................	Apr. 22-May 23...	....	....	Present. About 25 miles from Champerico, Pacific port. Disease spreading along Pacific coast.
Honduras:				
Tegucigalpa.................	Dec. 16-22........	....	1	
Do.....................	Jan. 6-19..........	....	1	

PUBLIC HEALTH REPORTS

OL. 33   JUNE 7, 1918   No. 23

BULLETIN ON COLOR BLINDNESS.

The importance of differentiating between those who are dan-
erously color blind—that is, unable at all times to distinguish
etween red and green—and those who are only slightly color blind
 brought out in a recent study conducted by Surg. George L.
ollins, United States Public Health Service, and published as
ublic Health Bulletin No. 92. The following conclusions were
ached:

Conclusions.

Color blindness is best detected by testing with colored lights of
1own spectral composition.

The Edridge-Green lantern will satisfactorily divide the color
ind into the dangerously color blind and the harmlessly color
ind, after an understanding of the principles of the test is gained.

The Jennings self-recorded worsted test should not be used for
sting sailors or trainmen, but possesses certain practical features
hich render it superior to other tests where great accuracy and
assification of color defects are not essential.

Among healthy individuals in America, color blindness occurs
 about 8.6 per cent of men and 2.2 per cent of women. Dan-
rous color blindness occurs in about 3.1 per cent of men and 0.7
r cent of women.

Among refractive conditions of the eye, color blindness occurs
ast frequently in eyes apparently without demonstrable refractive
ror and most frequently in eyes showing mixed astigmatism.

HOSPHOROUS AS AN INDICATOR OF THE "VITAMINE" CONTENT OF CORN AND WHEAT PRODUCTS.

CARL VOEGTLIN and C. N. MYERS, Division of Pharmacology, Hygienic Laboratory, United States Public Health Service.

Previous work by the writers has demonstrated that the vitamines
e not evenly distributed throughout the corn and wheat kernel.
1us it was shown that the starchy part of these cereals is very defi-
ent in vitamines, whereas the other portions of the grain (bran and

germ)[1] contain a considerable amount of these substances. These results were obtained from experiments on fowls by feeding the particular cereal product in question and noting the time necessary for the appearance of polyneuritic symptoms. When the symptoms appeared after an average of two to three weeks on a given diet, the diet was considered as containing only an insignificant amount of antineuritic vitamine. In case the symptoms appeared after three to four weeks the product was regarded as being deficient, but not entire y lacking in this substance. Finally, if no symptoms appeared within 60 days or longer, the diet was considered adequate in this respect.

Information concerning the fat soluble vitamine was furnished by growth experiments on mice and squabs. In this case it was determined whether or not it was necessary to supplement a particular corn or wheat product with fat-soluble vitamine, in the form of butter fat, in order to produce growth in these animals. When the product did not lead to practically normal growth, in spite of the fact that the other dietary deficiencies of the food with the exception of the fat-soluble vitamine were corrected, the product was considered as being deficient in this substance.

These biological procedures for the approximate estimation of the vitamine content obviously have the great disadvantage of being time consuming. On the other hand, chemical methods for the direct quantitative determination of vitamines are not available. Under these circumstances the search for more convenient means, which would permit at least a rough estimate of these food accessories in cereal foods, is urgently needed.

So far as the fat-soluble vitamine is concerned, an estimation of the fat content of the cereal product might yield the necessary information, inasmuch as it has been found that the germ seems to contain most of the fat as well as the fat-soluble vitamine of the grain. The following figures very clearly show the differences in the fat content of the most important corn and wheat products:

CORN [2]	Fat in per cent.	WHEAT [3]	Fat in per cent.
Corn (whole)	3 62	Wheat (whole)	2 74
Corn grits	. 48	Flour, patent	1. 45
Corn meal	1. 41	Flour, low grade	3. 86
Germ	23. 79	Germ	15. 61
Bran	6. 71	Bran	5. 03

There seems to exist a similar relationship between the fat content and the antineuritic substance of wheat and corn foods. In practice this theoretical deduction may very well prove of value.

[1] The terms bran and germ are applied throughout this paper to mill products of a varying degree of purity. Thus the germ is not the pure embryo of the grain, but is always contaminated with some bran. The bran always contains a small amount of the starchy part of the cereal.

[2] Winton, Burnet and Bornmann, U. S. Dept. Agr. Bull. No. 216 (1915).

[3] Richardson, Cl. U. S. Dept. Agr. Bull. No. 4 (1884).

However, the present investigation was confined exclusively to the
elation between phosphorus and vitamine content, for the reason
hat previous work with rice milled to various degrees had demon-
trated the intimate relation between phosphorus and antineuritic
itamine. Thus, Fraser and Stanton (1909)[1] on the basis of a wide
xperience with beri-beri in the East went even so far as to reject as
nsafe any rice with a phosphoric oxide content of less than 0.4
er cent when this food formed the principal article of the diet.

The object of the present communication is to correlate the phos-
horus content of corn and wheat foods with their content in anti-
euritic and fat-soluble vitamine. Special emphasis is placed on the
istribution of phosphorus in the various products obtained from
odern corn and flour mills.

Experimental.

The phosphoric oxide determinations were made on samples dried at 110° C. to
nstant weight. Five to ten grams of the dried sample are ashed by the Neumann
thod. Considerable patience is required in the early stages of the process to pre-
nt excessive foaming. It has been found advantageous to allow the sample to rein in contact with concentrated sulphuric acid for about 24 hours before the ashing
h nitric acid takes place. The ashed material is neutralized with ammonia until
s alkaline to litmus. After cooling, enough water is added to bring up the volume
bout 250 cubic centimeters and the solution made just acid with nitric acid (lit-
s). One cubic centimeter of 10 per cent nitric acid and 25 cubic centimeters
monium nitrate [2] are then added. The flask containing the solution is then
nersed in a water bath, kept at 65° to 68° C. After the contents of the flasks have
ched this temperature, a sufficient amount of molybdate solution [3] acidified by
ing 5 cubic centimeters of concentrated HNO_3 (sp. gr. 1.42) with 100 cubic centi-
ers of molybdate solution, is added with constant shaking.

he flasks are then heated for 15 minutes in the water bath. The yellow ammonium
sphomolybdate precipitate is now at once filtered off through a Gooch crucible
1 asbestos filter. The filtrate is always tested for complete precipitation by adding
esh amount of ammonium nitrate and molybdate solution and reheating in the
er bath. The flask and the precipitate are well washed with a 1 per cent ammo-
n nitrate solution until neutral to litmus, and finally with a little distilled water.
precipitate is now returned to the flask with the addition of about 200 cubic centi-
ers of distilled water. To this mixture N/2 sodium hydroxide, measured from a
tte, is added until the yellow precipitate is completely dissolved. There should
to 10 cubic centimeters of alkali in excess. One cubic centimeter of neutral
nolphthalein solution is added as indicator and the solution immediately titrated
with N/2 sulphuric acid until the pink color just disappears.

o difference between the sulphuric acid and the sodium hydroxide represents
amount of N/2 sodium hydroxide used to neutralize the insoluble precipitate
)$_3PO_412MoO_3$.

ser and Stanton. 1909. Studies from the Institute of Medical Research, Federated Malay States.
iology of beri-beri.

epared as follows: 3,750 gm. of ammonium nitrate, C. P., are dissolved in 2,500 cc. of hot distilled
after cooling to room temperature this solution is diluted with distilled water to 5,000 cc. and filtered.
is molybdate solution is prepared as follows: 100 gm. of molybdic acid are dissolved in 144 cc. of
nium hydroxide (sp. gr. 0.£0) and 271 cc. of water. This solution is poured slowly and with constant
g into a mixture of 489 cc. of nitric acid (sp. gr. 1.42) and 1,149 cc. of water contained in a large por-
dish. This mixture is kept in a warm place for several days, or until a portion heat- d to 40° C.
ts no yellow sediment, and preserved in glass-stoppered bottles.

One cubic centimeter of $N/2$ NaOH is equivalent to 1.5440 milligrams P_2O_5.

In regard to the phosphoric oxide determinations, it should be pointed out that the procedure just described will yield reliable results, as shown by the striking agreement of duplicate analyses. However, the results obtained by this method can not be compared with results obtained by other methods, as different analytical procedures will yield slightly different results.

The following tables give the results of the phosphorus determinations, as well as an estimate of both the antineuritic and fat soluble vitamines of these cereal products. The data referring to the vitamine content are taken from two previous papers by the authors.

In order to illustrate the distribution of the phosphorus of the original grain in the course of roller milling, Table 4 is offered. For a better understanding of this table a brief outline [1] of the process of milling is added.

The wheat as received by the mill is first put through a cleaning machine, which is known as the "milling separator." This consists of a series of metallic sieves. The perforations of the first two sieves are just large enough for a kernel of wheat to pass through, and therefore, oats, straw, and other impurities larger than wheat are separated from the wheat. The lowest sieve of the series has perforations considerably smaller than a kernel of wheat, which permit the smaller mustard seeds and other impurities to pass through.

From the milling separator the wheat is passed through the "wheat scourer," which consists of an upright perforated cylinder, in the center of which, revolving about the shaft, are large beaters. The wheat falls down in the center, is struck by the beaters, and is thrown against the outer case, and after revolving a number of times against the casing is passed through the bottom of the cylinder. While it is falling through the cylinder, a strong air current, passing upward, carries off the dust from the scourings.

The wheat (61) [2] now passes to the first set of corrugated rolls. After passing through these rolls it (62) goes into one end of a long reel, covered with coarse bolting cloth. The middlings (63) pass through the cloth and what remains of the wheat goes to the second reduction rolls, which are similar to the first.

This process is repeated five times, and after the middlings are taken out after the fifth reduction, all that is left of the wheat is the bran (79).

Before the middlings can be reduced to flour, the fine bran and dust must be taken out of them, or, in other words, they must be purified. Before purification can be accomplished thoroughly the middlings must be divided into various grades with respect to size. This is accomplished by running the middlings into one end of a long reel which is covered with bolting cloth of various degrees of fineness. On the head of the reel is a very fine cloth through which the flour passes; the next section is covered with a coarser cloth through which the first grade of middlings passes; the cloth of the next section is still coarser, and so on up to the end of the reel. What is too coarse to go through the last section of the reel passes over the end and is called the coarsest middlings (68).

After the middlings are graded they pass on to the "middlings purifier." This is a long narrow sieve with a strong current of air passing upward through the cloth The middlings travel from one end of the sieve very gradually to the other end The air current carries off the fine dust into a dust collector, and the fine bran, being lighter than the middlings, is suspended by the air current from the cloth, while the middlings go through the cloth The bran (69) is carried by the current of air to the tail of the machine, and is thus separated from the middlings (70).

---

[1] We are indebted for this description and the samples referred to in Table 4 to the manager of one of the largest flour mills in this country.

[2] The figures given in parentheses in this and the following paragraphs correspond with those of the diagram and represent the serial numbers of the samples used for the phosphorus determinations.

This process is the same for the various grades of middlings. After the purification the middlings are reduced similarly to the whole wheat, except that instead of corrugated rolls smooth rolls are used. The coarsest grade of middlings is ground, then passed on to a reel, covered with a very fine cloth, through which the flour (74) passes and goes to the flour bin. Particles of the middlings that are too coarse to pass through the cloth go over the end of the reel to another set of rolls and are ground again. This process is repeated for all grades of middlings until all have been reduced to flour. The "clears" and lower grades of flour are made from the fine bran and dust that are taken out of the middlings during the process of purification. This is done by grinding between smooth rolls the fine bran and dust. The bran will not break up, but flattens out. The product is passed on to a reel covered with fine cloth, through which the flour passes. This flour contains very fine particles of bran which is impossible to separate from it, and therefore this flour can not be run into the highest grades of flour. It is sold as either "first clear" (75), "second clear"(76), "red dog" (77), according to the amount of bran it contains.

Conclusions.

The phosphoric anhydride determination of wheat and corn products yields fairly satisfactory information as to the content of these products in accessory foods. A low phosphoric anhydride content indicates that the product is poor in vitamines.

TABLE 1.—Corn products—Content in P_2O_5 and vitamines.

Nature of product.	Source.	Degree of milling.	P_2O_5 in per cent.	Estimated vitamine content (from feeding experiments).	
				Fat-soluble vitamine.	Antineuritic vitamine.
Corn, whole.....	Connecticut.......	Not milled......	0.77	Relatively high.	High.
.....do......	California..........	.....do........	.84	.....do......	Do.
.....do......	Indiana...........	.....do........	.73	.....do......	Do.
.....do......	Tennessee.........	.....do........	.69	.....do......	Do.
.....do......	Alabama..........	.....do........	.57	.....do......	Do.
.....do......	Georgia...........	.....do........	.61	.....do......	Do.
Corn meal......	Georgia (b u h r mill).	Undermilled; considerable bran and germ.	.77	.....do......	Do.
.....do......	South Carolina....	.....do........	.79	.....do......	Do.
.....do......	Tennessee (buhr mill).	.....do........	.67	.....do......	Do.
.....do......	Georgia (b u h r mill).	.....do........	.66	.....do......	Do.
.....do......	South Carolina (buhr mill).	.....do........	.67	.....do......	Do.
.....do......	.....do........	.....do........	.63	.....do......	Do.
Corn grits......	.....do........	.....do........	.67	.....do......	Do.
Hominy..........	.....do........	.....do........	.64	.....do......	Do.
Corn bran.......	.....do........	Undermilled; contains some germ.	.78	Doubtful (not estimated).	Fairly high. Prevents polyneuritis when added to highly milled corn grits in proportion of 10 gms. to 35 gms.
Corn germ.......	Indiana (roller mill).	Germ plus traces of bran.	2.81	High..........	High.
Corn meal......	Maryland (roller mill).	Highly milled...	.29	Low..........	Very low. Produced polyneuritis in 3 weeks.
Corn grits.......	North Carolina (roller mill).	.....do........	.13	.....do......	Do.
.....do..........	Mississippi State Hospital.	.....do........	.18	.....do......	Do.
.....do..........	Georgia..........	.....do........	.17	.....do......	Do.
.....do..........	Georgia (U. S. penitentiary).	.....do........	.20	.....do......	Do.
.....do..........	Mississippi........	.....do........	.17	.....do......	Do.
.....do..........	South Carolina....	.....do........	.18	.....do......	Do.

TABLE 2.—*P_2O_4 content of various products from same run of corn (Maryland roller mill).*

Sample No.	Nature of product.	Appearance.	P_2O_4 in per cent.
37	Corn	Whole	0.80
39	"Table meal"	Considerable bran and germ	.81
40	"Table hominy"	No bran or germ	.17
41	"Cream meal"	do	.15
43	Corn flour	White; no bran or germ	.21
42	Corn germ	Largely germ; little bran	2.57
44	Corn bran	Largely bran	.69

TABLE 3.—*Wheat products—content in P_2O_4 and vitamines.*

Sample No.	Nature of product.	Source.	Degree of milling.	P_2O_4 in per cent.	Estimated vitamine content (from feeding experiments).	
					Fat-soluble vitamine.	Antineuritic vitamine
49	Wheat (whole)			1.12	Considerable	High.
61	do			1.01	do	Do.
86	do	South Carolina		.85	do	Do.
85	"Graham" flour from wheat No. 86	South Carolina (buhr mill)	Undermilled	.86	do	Do.
92	"Graham" flour	do	do	.82	do	Do.
84	Wheat bran	do	Undermilled; white material adhering to cellulose	2.12	Probably deficient (not estimated).	Do.
97	"Whole-wheat" flour.	Missouri (roller mill)	Undermilled, contains some germ and bran.	62	Considerable	Do.
98	"Red dog" feed	Washington, D. C. (roller mill)	Undermilled	.92	do	Do.
103	"White" middling	do	do	1.65	do	Do.
101	"Brown" middling.	do	do	1.88	do	Do
88	Wheat flour from No. 86.	South Carolina (buhr mill).	Highly milled	.26	Very deficient	Deficient.
91	"Patent" flour	Virginia	do	.20	do	Very deficient.
94	do	Michigan	do	.21	do	Do.
95	do	Maryland	do	.25	do	Do
93	do	South Carolina	do	22	do	Do.

Diagram of flour milling process and distribution of phosphorus.

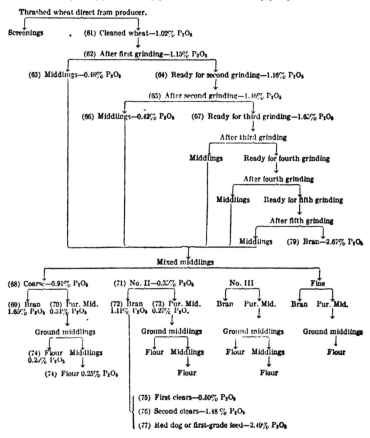

PREVALENCE OF DISEASE.

No health department, State or local, can effectively prevent or control disease without knowledge of when, where, and under what conditions cases are occurring.

UNITED STATES.

EXTRA-CANTONMENT ZONES—CASES REPORTED WEEK ENDED JUNE 4.

CAMP BEAUREGARD ZONE, LA.

Alexandria: Cases

Gonorrhea	2
Malaria	1
Measles	1
Mumps	17
Smallpox	3
Whooping cough	1

Pineville:

Cerebrospinal meningitis	1
Typhoid fever	1

CAMP BOWIE ZONE, TEX.

Fort Worth:

Chicken pox	3
Continued fever	1
Diphtheria	1
Gonorrhea	16
Scarlet fever	1
Smallpox	15
Syphilis	12
Typhoid fever	5

CAMP DEVENS ZONE, MASS.

Chicken pox:

Lunenburg	4

German measles:

Lunenburg	3

Measles:

Ayer	3
Littleton	1

Mumps:

Lancaster	3

CAMP DODGE ZONE, IOWA.

Diphtheria:

Des Moines	2

Gonorrhea:

Des Moines	10

Measles:

Polk City	1

Scarlet fever:

Des Moines	6
Grimes	2

CAMP DODGE ZONE, IOWA—continued.

Smallpox: Cases.

Des Moines	11
Fort Des Moines	1

Syphilis:

Des Moines	12

Tuberculosis:

Des Moines	3

Typhoid fever:

Des Moines	9

CAMP DONIPHAN ZONE, OKLA.

Pneumonia:

Lawton	1

Smallpox:

Elgin	1
Fletcher	2

Typhoid fever:

Lawton	4

CAMP EBERTS ZONE, ARK.

Chancroid:

England	1

Gonorrhea:

Lonoke	7
England	2
Carlisle	1

Malaria:

Lonoke, route 1	2
Lonoke, route 4	2
England	11
England, route 4	1
Keo	1
Ward	3
Eberts Field	2
Wattensaw	1

Measles:

Lonoke	2
Lonoke, route 1	1
Cabot, route 1	6
Ward	2

Mumps:

England	3
Kerr	1

(918)

CAMP EBERTS ZONE, ARK.—continued.

Pellagra:	Cases.
Keo	2
Pneumonia:	
Wattensaw	2
Septic sore throat:	
Ward	1
Smallpox:	
Scotts	1
Syphilis:	
Lonoke	1
Tonsilitis:	
Lonoke, route 1	1
Wattensaw	1
Tuberculosis:	
Ward	1
Typhoid fever:	
Lonoke, route 4	1
Ward	1

CAMP FUNSTON ZONE, KANS.

Junction City:	
Mumps	1
Whooping cough	3
Manhattan:	
Chicken pox	1
Mumps	3
Smallpox	1
Whooping cough	1

CAMP GORDON ZONE, GA.

Chicken pox:	
Atlanta	4
Diphtheria:	
Atlanta	1
Dysentery, bacillary:	
Atlanta	5
Gonorrhea:	
Atlanta	6
Malaria:	
Atlanta	3
Measles:	
Atlanta	11
Mumps:	
Atlanta	14
Scarlet fever:	
Atlanta	1
Smallpox:	
Atlanta	6
Chamblee	1
Syphilis:	
Atlanta	11
Tuberculosis:	
Atlanta	9
Typhoid fever:	
Chamblee	1
Decatur	2
Wesley Chapel	1
Whooping cough:	
Atlanta	9

CAMP GREENE ZONE, N. C.

Charlotte Township:	
Chancroid	3
German measles	1
Gonorrhea	23

CAMP GREENE ZONE, N. C.—continued.

Charlotte Township—Continued.	Cases.
Measles	4
Mumps	2
Syphilis	9
Trachoma	78
Tuberculosis	2
Typhoid fever	1
Whooping cough	20

GULFPORT HEALTH DISTRICT, MISS.

Gulfport Health District:	
Diphtheria	1
Measles	1
Mumps	1

CAMP HANCOCK ZONE, GA.

Augusta:	
Chicken pox	1
Diphtheria	1
Gonorrhea	2
Measles	4
Syphilis	21
Typhoid fever	2

CAMP JACKSON ZONE, S. C.[1]

Columbia:	
Chicken pox	7
Measles	2
Mumps	15
Tuberculosis	4
Typhoid fever	1
Whooping cough	20
New Brookland:	
Typhoid fever	1
South Shandon:	
Paratyphoid	2

CAMP JOSEPH E. JOHNSTON ZONE, FLA.

Chancroid:	
Jacksonville	9
Dysentery:	
Jacksonville	9
Gonorrhea:	
Jacksonville	41
Cummers Mill	1
Hookworm:	
Fishers Corner	1
Panama	2
Malaria:	
Jacksonville	2
Measles:	
Jacksonville	1
Mumps:	
Jacksonville	2
Panama	1
Syphilis:	
Jacksonville	35
Fishers Corner	1
Trachoma:	
Jacksonville	2
Tuberculosis:	
Jacksonville	9
Typhoid fever:	
Fishers Corner	1
Jacksonville	4
South Jacksonville	1

[1] Report for week ended June 1, 1918.

CAMP JOSEPH E. JOHNSTON ZONE, FLA.—contd.

Whooping cough:	Cases.
Fishers Corner	1
Jacksonville	30
Lackawanna	1
Ortega	2
Seaboard Air Line shops	1

FORT LEAVENWORTH ZONE, KANS.

Leavenworth:	
Diphtheria	3
Measles	1
Scarlet fever	1
Smallpox	4
Tuberculosis	3
Leavenworth County:	
Pneumonia, lobar	1

CAMP LEWIS ZONE, WASH.

Mumps:	
Parkland	1
Roy	1
Steilacoom	1
Scarlet fever:	
Roy	3
Spanaway	1
Tuberculosis:	
Clover Creek	1
Whooping cough:	
American Lake	8
Parkland	1

CAMP LOGAN ZONE, TEX.

Chicken pox:	
Houston	2
Gonorrhea:	
Houston	26
Humble	1
Pasadena	1
Mumps:	
Houston	2
Syphilis:	
Houston	13
Humble	1
Goose Creek	1
Typhoid fever:	
Houston	1
Whooping cough:	
Houston	1

CAMP MACARTHUR ZONE, TEX.

Waco:	
Gonorrhea	1
Mumps	3
Poliomyelitis	1
Tuberculosis	2
Typhoid fever	4

CAMP M'CLELLAN ZONE, ALA.

Diphtheria:	
Anniston	1
Malaria:	
Precinct 15	3
Measles:	
Anniston	1
Smallpox:	
Anniston	2
Precinct 2	1
Precinct 21	2
Typhoid fever:	
Anniston	1

NORFOLK COUNTY NAVAL DISTRICT, VA.

Cerebrospinal meningitis:	Cases.
Winona	1
Chicken pox:	
Edgewater	1
Norfolk	2
Malaria:	
Portsmouth	1
South Norfolk	1
Measles:	
Norfolk	2
Portsmouth	4
South Norfolk	1
Mumps:	
Camp Ostella	1
Norfolk	1
Norfolk County	1
Portsmouth	2
Quartermaster Terminal	4
Scarlet fever:	
Norfolk	1
Norfolk County	1
Portsmouth	1
Smallpox:	
Quartermaster Terminal	1
Tetanus:	
South Norfolk	1
Typhoid fever:	
Norfolk	1
Whooping cough:	
Portsmouth	1

FORT OGLETHORPE ZONE, GA.

Cerebrospinal meningitis:	
Missionary Ridge	1
Gonorrhea:	
Chattanooga	7
Missionary Ridge	1
Mumps:	
East Lake	1
Scarlet fever:	
Chattanooga	3
Fort Lake	1
Syphilis:	
Chattanooga	3
Missionary Ridge	1
Tuberculosis:	
Chattanooga	3
Typhoid fever:	
Chattanooga	1
East Lake	1
Whooping cough:	
Chattanooga	1

CAMP PIKE ZONE, ARK.

Cerebrospinal meningitis:	
Little Rock	1
Chicken pox:	
Little Rock	1
Diphtheria:	
Little Rock	2
Dysentery:	
North Little Rock	1
Gonorrhea:	
Little Rock	9
Scarlet fever:	3

CAMP PIKE ZONE, ARK.—continued.

Malaria:	Cases.
Little Rock	12
North Little Rock	2
Nonresidents	3

Measles:	
Little Rock	5

Mumps:	
Little Rock	2
North Little Rock	2

Pellagra:	
Little Rock	1

Pneumonia:	
Little Rock	1

Scarlet fever:	
Little Rock	2

Smallpox:	
Little Rock	2

Syphilis:	
Little Rock	10
Scotts	1

Tuberculosis:	
Little Rock	5
Keo	1

CAMP SEVIER ZONE, S. C.

Chick Springs Township:	
Cerebrospinal meningitis	2
Dysentery	1
Mumps	2
Tuberculosis, pulmonary	1

Greenville Township:	
Tuberculosis, pulmonary	1

CAMP SHELBY ZONE, MISS.

Hattiesburg:	
Chicken pox	1
Dysentery	1
Hookworm	2
Malaria	20
Meningitis, tubercular	1
Mumps	5
Tuberculosis, pulmonary	2
Typhoid fever	1
Venereal	6
Whooping cough	8

CAMP SHERIDAN ZONE, ALA.

Montgomery:	
Chancroid	4
Chicken pox	1
Gonorrhea	11
Measles	1
Syphilis	3
Tuberculosis, pulmonary	5
Typhoid fever	1

United States Government clinic:	
Gonorrhea	4
Gonorrhea, chronic	1
Syphilis	9

CAMP SHERMAN ZONE, OHIO.

Chillicothe:	
Diphtheria	2
Gonorrhea	2
Measles	2
Mumps	1
Ophthalmia neonatorum	1
Scarlet fever	3

CAMP ZACHARY TAYLOR ZONE, KY.

Jefferson County:	Cases.
Cerebrospinal meningitis	1
Gonorrhea	1
Measles	2
Trachoma	1
Typhoid fever	1

Louisville:	
Cerebrospinal meningitis	1
Chicken pox	3
Diphtheria	5
Malaria	2
Measles	1
Mumps	2
Pneumonia	1
Rabies in animal	1
Scarlet fever	1
Smallpox	2
Tuberculosis, pulmonary	5
Typhoid fever	3
Whooping cough	2

United States Government clinic:	
Chancroid	1
Gonorrhea	47
Syphilis	44

TIDEWATER HEALTH DISTRICT, VA.

Hampton:	
Mumps	2
Whooping cough	7

Newport News	
Chancroid	4
Gonorrhea	3
Measles	4
Mumps	2
Scarlatina	1
Smallpox	1
Syphilis	2
Typhoid fever	1
Whooping cough	3

Phoebus:	
Whooping cough	0

CAMP TRAVIS ZONE, TEX.

San Antonio:	
Dysentery	1
Gonorrhea	35
Measles	1
Mumps	4
Pneumonia	1
Syphilis	11
Tuberculosis	1
Typhoid fever	14

CAMP WADSWORTH ZONE, S. C.

Chicken pox:	
Spartanburg	

Diphtheria:	
Spartanburg	

Gonorrhea.	
Pauline	1
Spartanburg	11

Measles.	
Moores	
Pauline	1
Spartanburg	2

CAMP WADSWORTH ZONE, S. C.—continued.

Mumps: Cases.
   Spartanburg................................. 4
Smallpox:
   Arcadia...................................... 1
Syphilis:
   Spartanburg................................. 3
Typhoid fever:
   Arcadia...................................... 2
Whooping cough:
   Spartanburg................................. 7

CAMP WHEELER ZONE, GA.

Macon: Cases.
   Chancroid................................... 1
   Chicken pox................................ 1
   Gonorrhea.................................. 2
   Hookworm................................. 1
   Malaria..................................... 1
   Measles.................................... 2
   Mumps...................................... 2
   Scarlet fever............................... 2
   Syphilis..................................... 7
   Typhoid fever.............................. 1
   Whooping cough........................... 1

DISEASE CONDITIONS AMONG TROOPS IN THE UNITED STATES.

The following data are taken from telegraphic reports received in the office of the Surgeon General, United States Army, for the week ended May 24, 1918:

Annual admission rate per 1,000 (disease only):
   All troops............................. 1,068.1
   Divisional camps..................... 764.5
   Cantonments.......................... 1,200.9
   Departmental and other troops........ 1,109.1
Noneffective rate per 1,000 on day of report:
   All troops............................. 39.8
   Divisional camps..................... 33.4

Noneffective rate per 1,000 on day of report—Con.
   Cantonments.......................... 46.4
   Departmental and other troops........ 35.8
Annual death rate per 1,000 (disease only):
   All troops............................. 8.7
   Divisional camps..................... 1.9
   Cantonments.......................... 9.6
   Departmental and other troops........ 4.1

New cases of special diseases reported during the week ended May 24, 1918.

Camp.	Pneumonia.	Dysentery.	Malaria.	Venereal. Total.	Venereal. New infections.	Measles.	Meningitis.	Scarlet fever.	Deaths.	Annual admission rate per 1,000 (disease only).	Noneffective per 1,000 on day of report.
Beauregard..............	5	8	23	40	5	1				1,168.4	48.8
Bowie....................	4	.....	2	24	22					990.4	30.9
Cody....................	5	.....	.....	6	.....			1		531.3	23.2
Doniphan................		1	.....	12	.....					2,447.3	59.1
Fremont.................	6	.....	.....	34	19	13		3	3	1,097.2	34.6
Greene..................				4	4	8			1	516.4	20.1
Hancock................		.....	.....	51	.....		1			1,071.9	55.4
Kearny..................	2	.....	1	2	.....	2	1		3	833.0	27.4
Logan...................		.....		13	1	2				299.3	26.6
MacArthur..............										723.8	30.4
McClellan..............	1	.....	1	20	14	3				546.8	27.6
Sevier..................	10	.....		33	11	4			2	493.4	37.4
Shelby.................	1	6	3	12	4	1	1		3	1,020.9	41.2
Sheridan...............	2	.....	4	35	14			1		514.4	20.0
Wadsworth.............	1	.....		83	.....	15		1		1,153.5	34.9
Wheeler................	2	.....		21	6	.....			1	572.0	35.9
Custer..................	10	.....		117	4	1			4	673.4	24.4
Devens.................	37	.....	1	28	6	25			4	661.1	30.0
Dix.....................	3	2	1	63	4	9	1	4	2	893.7	39.2
Dodge..................	33	.....		97	.....	10	1	13	12	1,261.9	78.0
Funston................	13	.....	1	176	63	5	3	3	3	1,031.1	50.7
Gordon.................	24	.....	2	97	2	41	2		14	2,296.5	76.3
Grant..................	5	.....		14	.....	5	2	8	4	437.7	23.9
Jackson................	17	1	2	81	.....	30	2		15	3,500.9	64.6
J. E. Johnston........	5	.....	1	43	23	5			3	869.9	37.0
A. A. Humphreys......	11	.....		11	7	11	1		2	909.1	21.8
Lee....................			1	123	1	11			2	1,062.7	41.7
Lewis..................	13	.....		58	4	7		3	1	777.7	32.5
Meade.................	6	.....		10	6	4	1	1	2	982.5	31.5
Pike...................	10	.....	3	71	14	17	3		13	1,554.4	63.6
Sherman...............	2	.....		81	5	14	1	5	4	1,014.6	43.5
Taylor.................	11	.....		4	.....	14			3	911.9	58.0
Travis.................	33	1	5	50	3	20		1	11	2,345.1	40.0
Upton..................	5	.....		142	35	.....		2	2	843.8	40.7
Northeastern Department..	.....	.....	.....	11	1	3	1			602.8	27.3

New cases of special diseases reported during the week ended May 24, 1918—Continued.

Camp.	Pneumonia.	Dysentery.	Malaria.	Venereal.		Measles.	Meningitis.	Scarlet fever.	Deaths.	Annual admission rate per 1,000 (disease only).	Noneffective per 1,000 on day of report.
				Total.	New Infections.						
Eastern Department			1	22	12	4	:....		3	871.8	23.9
Southeastern Department	1			62	35	9			3	996.1	31.9
Central Department	3			24	10	8		4	3	1,226.2	62.0
Southern Department	19	3	3	156	37	70	1	11	6	1,166.6	33.7
Western Department				31	7	12		3	1	722.2	23.2
Aviation, Signal Corps	9		3	124		14	2	4	11	1,134.5	31.4
Alcatraz, Disciplinary Barracks				1						478.5	18.4
Columbus Barracks	1			8	2			1		643.0	21.1
Depot, Provisional Corps and Army Troops	1		3	4					1	1,174.9	46.6
Edgewood-Aberdeen						1				306.5	11.1
El Paso			1	2	1	1				596.5	19.1
Hoboken	7			165	11	12		3	4	979.2	55.3
Holabird				3						610.8	3.9
Jefferson Barracks	5		1	188	3	5				2,305.4	86.1
Leavenworth, Disciplinary Barracks	1							1	2	1,166.2	37.4
Logan, Fort	1			5					3	1,233.3	70.6
McDowell, Fort	2			43		1				2,437.5	86.2
Newport News	10		2	99	34	8		1	5	800.1	48.1
Raritan										480.6	27.7
Slocum, Fort	2			26		1				2,311.3	44.4
Springfield Armory										276.6	21.3
Thomas, Fort	1			17		8			1	1,383.7	38.4
Watervliet										536.0	51.5
West Point				2						801.4	11.7
National Guard Departments				15	7	2		1	1		
National Army Departments	9	1	1	481	158	20		8	4		
Total	352	21	65	3,145	595	456	24	84	161	1,063.1	39.8

Annual rate per 1,000 for special diseases.

Disease.	All troops in United States.[1]	Departmental and other troops.[1]	Divisional camps.[1]	Cantonments.[1]	Expeditionary forces.[2]
Pneumonia	14.4	8.5	6.9	23.3	12.8
Dysentery	.98	.6	2.6	.4	.3
Malaria	2.66	1.6	6.0	1.6	1.0
Venereal	129.0	176.2	09.0	123.1	37.8
Paratyphoid	.0	.0	.0	.0	.0
Typhoid	.1	.1	.0	.2	.0
Measles	18.27	21.0	8.7	21.2	12.8
Meningitis	.98	.4	.5	1.6	1.4
Scarlet fever	3.4	4.7	.7	.38	5.7

[1] Week ended May 24, 1918.   [2] Week ended May 16, 1918.

CURRENT STATE SUMMARIES.

Connecticut.

From Collaborating Epidemiologist Black, by telegraph, for week ended June 1, 1918:

Smallpox: Voluntown 1, Hartford 1. Cerebrospinal meningitis: New Milford 1, Bridgeport 1. Tetanus: East Lyme 1.

CURRENT STATE SUMMARIES—Continued.

Illinois.

From Collaborating Epidemiologist Drake, by telegraph, for week ended June 1, 1918:

Diphtheria: 133, of which in Chicago 105, Quincy 5, Alton 5. Scarlet fever: 46, of which in Chicago 22. Smallpox: 109, of which in Quincy 11, Argenta 9, Peoria 6, East Moline 7, Springfield 13, Elgin State Hospital 13. Meningitis: 8, of which in Quincy 1, Chicago 7. Poliomyelitis: 4, of which in Blue Island 1, Alton 2, Petersburg 1.

Indiana.

From the State Board of Health of Indiana, by telegraph, for week ended June 1, 1918:

Smallpox: Epidemic Clark County; cases at Columbus, Princeton, Bloomington, Anderson, Rome City. Infantile paralysis: One death Newpoint, Decatur County. Rabies: Epidemic dogs Boonville, Warrick County.

Louisiana.

From Collaborating Epidemiologist Dowling, by telegraph, for week ended June 1, 1918:

Meningitis 4, smallpox 22, typhoid 26, diphtheria 44.

Massachusetts.

From Collaborating Epidemiologist Hitchcock, by telegraph, for week ended June 1, 1918:

Unusual prevalence: Measles: Lawrence 139, Malden 51, Methuen 39, Salem 46, Waltham 61. Scarlet fever; Gill 11, Montague 9. Whooping cough; Whitman 28.

Minnesota.

From Collaborating Epidemiologist Bracken, by telegraph, for week ended June 1, 1918:

Smallpox, new foci: Cottonwood County, Rosehill Township, 1; Mahnomen County, Pembina Township, 3; Pine County, Pine City Township 1. One cerebrospinal meningitis, 2 poliomyelitis, reported since May 27.

Nebraska.

From the State Board of Health of Nebraska, by telegraph, for week ended June 1, 1918:

Smallpox. Gretna, Grand Island, Marion, Tekamah, Elkhorn. Scarlet fever; Culbertson.

New Jersey.

From Collaborating Epidemiologist Bowen, by telegraph, for week ended June 1, 1918:

Unusual prevalence. Measles: Pamsey Borough.

Ohio.

From Collaborating Epidemiologist Freeman, by telegraph, for week ended June 1, 1918:

Typhoid: Coitsville Township, Mahoning County, 21 cases. Diphtheria: Warren Township, Washington County, 7 cases.

Virginia.

From the State Board of Health of Virginia, by telegraph, for week ended June 1, 1918:

Smallpox: Stafford County 1, Culpepper 1, Newport News 7. Cerebrospinal meningitis: Charlotte County 1, Elizabeth City 1, Petersburg 1.

Washington.

From Collaborating Epidemiologist Tuttle, by telegraph, for week ended June 1, 1918:

Scarlet fever: Seattle 25, Tacoma 28, Camas 3, Hoquiam 5. Cerebrospinal meningitis: Seattle 1, Tacoma 1, Bremerton 2. Smallpox: Columbia County 9, Seattle 3. One suspected anterior poliomyelitis Cowlitz County.

CEREBROSPINAL MENINGITIS.

State Reports for February, March, and April, 1918.

Place.	New cases reported.	Place.	New cases reported.
Alabama (April):		California (April)—Continued.	
Barbour County	1	Orange County	1
Colbert County	2	Santa Ana	1
Coneugh County	1	Riverside County—	
Coosa County	1	Perris	2
Fayette County	1	San Diego County—	
Henry County	1	San Diego	1
Madison County	3	San Francisco	9
Morgan County	2	San Joaquin County	1
Tallacega County	1	Stockton	1
Wilcox County	2	San Mateo County—	
		Camp Fremont	2
Total	15		
		Total	29
Arkansas (February):			
Calhoun County	1	Illinois (April):	
Chicot County	1	Cook County—	
Conway County	18	Chicago	39
Craighead County	1	Henry County—	
Perry County	1	Kewanee	1
Phillips County	1	Jefferson County—	
Saline County	4	Mount Vernon	4
		Kane County—	
Total	27	Geneva	4
		Macoupin County—	
California (April):		Nilwood	1
Alameda County—		Virden	4
Oakland	1	Pulaski County—	
Berkeley	1	Karnak	4
Butte County	1	Sangamon County—	
Kern County	1	Thayer	4
Los Angeles County—		Woodford County—	
Los Angeles	4	Roanoke Township	1
Lassen County	2		
Napa County	1	Total	50
Napa	1		

CEREBROSPINAL MENINGITIS—Continued.

State Reports for February, March, and April, 1918—Continued.

Place.	New cases reported.	Place.	New cases reported.
Iowa (April):		**North Dakota (April):**	
Keokuk County	1	Foster County	3
Muscatine County	2	Emmons County	1
Pottawattamie County	1		
Scott County	1	Total	4
Total	5	**Ohio (April):**	
		Belmont County	1
Kansas (April):		Cuyahoga County	13
Barton County—		Erie County	1
Great Bend	1	Franklin County	1
Bourbon County—		Hamilton County	10
Fort Scott	1	Lake County	1
Butler County—		Licking County	1
Eldorado (R. D.)	1	Madison County	1
Coffey County—		Montgomery County	1
Lebo (R. D.)	1	Ottawa County	1
Crawford County—		Ross County	1
Pittsburg (R. D.)	1	Scioto County	4
Doniphan County—		Trumbull County	1
Bendena (R. D.)	1	Wood County	1
Geary County—			
Junction City	1	Total	38
Greenwood County—			
Salem Township	1	**Virginia (March):**	
Jefferson County—		Alexandria County	1
McLouth	1	Bedford County	1
Johnson County—		Buchanan County	1
De Soto	1	Caroline County	1
Marshall County—		Elizabeth City County	1
Winfield	1	Fauquier County	2
Meade County—		Goochland County	1
Plains	1	Halifax County	1
Pottawatomie County—		Henrico County—	
Emmett	2	Richmond	3
Riley County—		Lee County	2
Manhattan	1	Louisa County	1
Sedgwick County—		Nelson County	1
Wichita	3	Norfolk County—	
Shawnee County—		Norfolk	4
Topeka	1	Northampton County	1
Wyandotte County—		Page County	1
Kansas City	4	Prince George County	6
		Prince William County	3
Total	21	Rappahannock County	1
		Rockbridge County—	
Mississippi (April):		Buena Vista	4
Alcorn County	1	Spotsylvania County—	
Bolivar County	3	Fredericksburg	4
Calhoun County	1	Sussex County—	
Coahoma County	1	Wakefield	4
De Soto County	1	Warwick County—	
Harrison County	2	Newport News	10
Hinds County	1	Washington County	4
Holmes County	1	Wythe County	1
Lowndes County	1		
Tate County	1	Total	51
Warren County	2		
Washington County	2	**Washington (April):**	
Yazoo County	3	Coslin County	1
		Clarke County—	
Total	21	Camas	4
		King County—	
Nevada (April):		Seattle	4
Humboldt County	1	Pierce County—	
		Tacoma	2
New Jersey (April):		Camp Lewis	1
Atlantic County	1		
Bergen County	3	Total	8
Burlington County	3		
Essex County	29	**Wyoming (April):**	
Gloucester County	3	Natrona County	1
Hudson County	3		
Passaic County	3		
Salem County	1		
Union County	1		
Total	46		

CEREBROSPINAL MENINGITIS—Continued.

City Reports for Week Ended May 18, 1918.

Place.	Cases.	Deaths.	Place.	Cases.	Deaths.
Birmingham, Ala	2		New York. N. Y	15	11
Boston, Mass	3	2	North Little Rock, Ark	1	
Bridgeport, Conn	1		Oklahoma City, Okla	1	
Cambridge, Mass	2		Petersburg, Va	1	
Chattanooga, Tenn		1	Pittston, Pa	1	
Chicago, Ill	12		Plainfield, N. J	1	
Cleveland, Ohio	2	1	Portland, Oreg		1
Cranston, R. I	1		Providence, R. I	4	
Dayton, Ohio	1		Quincy, Mass	1	
Detroit, Mich	3		Racine, Wis		1
Fall River, Mass	1		Roanoke, Va		1
Greenville, S. C	1		St. Joseph, Mo		1
Hartford, Conn	1	1	St. Louis, Mo	1	
Indianapolis, Ind	3		Salt Lake City, Utah	1	
Little Falls, N. Y	1	1	San Diego, Cal	2	
Little Rock, Ark	2		San Francisco, Cal	1	
Louisville, Ky	1	1	Savannah, Ga	1	
Lowell, Mass	1		Somerville, Mass	1	
Lynn, Mass		1	Syracuse, N. Y	1	1
Macon, Ga		1	Tacoma, Wash	1	
Milwaukee, Wis	3	3	Taunton, Mass	1	
Montgomery, Ala	2	1	Troy, N. Y	1	
Nashville, Tenn	1	2	Washington, D. C	5	1
Newark, N. J	2	1	Watertown, Mass	1	
New Bedford, Mass	1	1	Waycross, Ga		1
New Haven, Conn	1		West Springfield, Mass	1	1
New London, Conn		1	Youngstown, Ohio		1
New Orleans, La	1	1			

DIPHTHERIA.

See Diphtheria, measles, scarlet fever, and tuberculosis, page 948.

ERYSIPELAS.

City Reports for Week Ended May 18, 1918.

Place.	Cases.	Deaths.	Place.	Cases.	Deaths.
Brockton, Mass	1		Milwaukee, Wis	4	
Buffalo, N. Y	2		Minneapolis, Minn	2	
Burlington, Vt		1	Nashville, Tenn	1	1
Chicago, Ill	17	5	Newark, N. J	11	
Cleveland, Ohio	2	2	New York, N. Y		2
Clinton, Iowa	1		Niagara Falls, N. Y	2	
Denver, Colo	2		Norfolk, Va	1	
Duluth, Minn	4		Oakland, Cal	2	
Flint, Mich	1		Omaha, Nebr	2	
Harrison, N. J	1		Palestine, Tex	1	
Henderson, Ky	1		Portland, Oreg	6	
Hornell, N. Y		5	Providence, R. I		1
Jackson, Mich	2		Racine, Wis	1	
Joplin, Mo	1	8	Richmond, Va		1
Kansas City, Kans	1		Rochester, N. Y		
Leavenworth, Kans		1	St. Joseph, Mo	2	
Lincoln, Nebr			St. Louis, Mo	1	
Long Beach, Cal	1		St. Paul, Minn	6	
Los Angeles, Cal	2		San Francisco, Cal	5	1
Louisville, Ky	5	1	Schenectady, N. Y	5	1
Macon, Ga		1	Steubenville, Ohio	1	
Manitowoc, Wis	1		Trinidad, Colo	2	
Milford, Mass	1	1	Wichita, Kans	1	

LEPROSY.

New Jersey—Phillipsburg.

In July, 1917, two cases of leprosy were discovered in Blackwells Island (N. Y.) Hospital. The patients were brothers, aged 11 and 14 years, respectively. The family were Italians. The children were returned to their father's residence at Phillipsburg, N. J. The mother of these children died in June, 1917. The death certificate gave embolism as the cause of death, but the symptoms were similar to those of the children.

MALARIA.

State Reports for February, March, and April, 1918.

Place.	New cases reported.	Place.	New cases reported.
Alabama (April):		**California (April)—Continued.**	
Bullock County	1	Placer County—	
Calhoun County	1	Lincoln	2
Coffee County	1	Rocklin	2
Colbert County	5	San Joaquin County	1
Cullman County	3	Stockton	2
Dallas County	5	Yolo County	2
Escambia County	3	Yuba County—	
Geneva County	1	Marysville	2
Houston County	32	San Diego County	2
Jefferson County	11	Camp Kearny	2
Lauderdale County	3	Tuolumne County	1
Lawrence County	1		
Limestone County	1	Total	26
Madison County	6		
Mobile County	1	**Illinois (April):**	
Morgan County	1	Hardin County—	
Pike County	1	Rosiclare	4
Shelby County	5	Kankakee County—	
Sumter County	1	Waldron	4
Tuscaloosa County	8	Lake County—	
Walker County	1	Grays Lake	4
		Perry County —	
Total	92	St. Joseph	4
		Rock Island County—	
Arkansas (February):		East Moline	1
Ashley County	8	Union County—	
Bradley County	55	Jonesboro	2
Chicot County	1	Wabash County—	
Clark County	20	Bellmont	2
Craighead County	35	Williamson County—	
Drew County	16	Cambria	3
Greene County	15		
Hot Spring County	7	Total	12
Izard County	7		
Jefferson County	6	**Mississippi (April):**	
Little River County	4	Adams County	17
Logan County	1	Alcorn County	62
Miller County	48	Amite County	80
Ouachita County	18	Attala County	84
Phillips County	4	Benton County	21
Saline County	20	Bolivar County	69
Sebastian County	3	Calhoun County	33
Sevier County	46	Carroll County	53
St. Francis County	25	Chickasaw County	21
White County	10	Choctaw County	68
		Claiborne County	30
Total	349	Clarke County	8
		Clay County	146
California (April):		Coahoma County	351
Butte County	3	Copiah County	94
Colusa County—		Covington County	175
Colusa	2	De Soto County	54
Contra Costa County —		Forrest County	66
Hercules	1	Franklin County	109
Fresno County—		George County	62
Clovis	1	Greene County	82
Kern County	3	Grenada County	29

MALARIA—Continued.

State Reports for February, March, and April, 1918—Continued.

Place.	New cases reported.	Place.	New cases reported.
Mississippi (April)—Continued.		**Virginia (March):**	
Hancock County	75	Accomac County	16
Harrison County	149	Greenbackville	3
Hinds County	262	Alleghany County	1
Holmes County	207	Amelia County	2
Issaquena County	54	Amherst County	1
Itawamba County	39	Bedford County	8
Jackson County	39	Brunswick County	3
Jasper County	93	Buchanan County	1
Jefferson County	102	Campbell County	4
Jefferson Davis County	61	Caroline County	8
Jones County	128	Charlotte County	1
Kemper County	57	Keysville	1
Lafayette County	57	Chesterfield County—	
Lamar County	92	Winterpock	3
Lauderdale County	24	Cumberland County	3
Lawrence County	124	Dinwiddie County	2
Leake County	51	Elizabeth City County	1
Lee County	114	Essex County	3
Leflore County	341	Gloucester County	2
Lincoln County	108	Greensville County	6
Lowndes County	67	North Emporia	6
Madison County	48	Halifax County	6
Marion County	184	South Boston	1
Marshall County	21	Hanover County	3
Monroe County	134	Henrico County	3
Montgomery County	59	Richmond	3
Neshoba County	21	Isle of Wight County	11
Newton County	48	Smithfield	8
Noxubee County	40	James City County	4
Oktibbeha County	96	King and Queen County	4
Panola County	114	King William County	1
Pearl River County	74	Lancaster County	3
Perry County	160	Lee County	1
Pike County	122	Louisa County	3
Pontotoc County	105	Lunenburg County	6
Prentiss County	54	Victoria	1
Quitman County	249	Mathews County	2
Rankin County	71	Mecklenburg County	1
Scott County	54	Middlesex County	8
Sharkey County	155	Nansemond County	13
Simpson County	42	Suffolk	4
Smith County	45	Northampton County	10
Stone County	47	Cape Charles	2
Sunflower County	445	Northumberland County	4
Tallahatchie County	241	Nottaway County	1
Tate County	123	Crewe	1
Tippah County	54	Pittsylvania County	7
Tishomingo County	84	Powhatan County	6
Tunica County	181	Prince George County	8
Union County	62	Hopewell	3
Warren County	217	Princess Anne County	29
Washington County	228	Prince William County	1
Wayne County	85	Rockingham County—	
Webster County	36	Bridgewater	3
Wilkinson County	30	Southampton County	3
Winston County	59	Franklin	2
Yalobusha County	59	Spotsylvania County	2
Yazoo County	279	Stafford County	3
		Surry County	12
Total	8,707	Sussex County	8
		Washington County—	
New Jersey (April):		Abingdon	1
Bergen County	1	York County	3
Burlington County	1		
Essex County	1	Total	270
Somerset County	1		
Total	4		

MALARIA—Continued.

City Reports for Week Ended May 18, 1918.

Place.	Cases.	Deaths.	Place.	Cases.	Deaths.
Alexandria, La	6	....	Memphis, Tenn	2	2
Anniston, Ala	2	....	Mobile, Ala	....	1
Berkeley, Cal	1	....	Montgomery, Ala	3	....
Birmingham, Ala	2	....	North Little Rock, Ark	2	....
Dallas, Tex	....	1	Oklahoma City, Okla	....	1
Hattiesburg, Miss	7	....	Palestine, Tex	15	....
Houston, Tex	....	1	Passaic, N. J	1	....
Joplin, Mo	4	....	San Francisco, Cal	2	....
Laurel, Miss	8	....	Savannah, Ga	....	1
Little Rock, Ark	4	....	Tuscaloosa, Ala	4	....
Macon, Ga	3	....	Waycross, Ga	....	1
Marshall, Tex	2	....	Yonkers, N. Y	....	1
McAlester, Okla	2	....			

MEASLES.

See Diphtheria, measles, scarlet fever, and tuberculosis, page 948.

PELLAGRA.

State Reports for February, March, and April, 1918.

Place.	New cases reported.	Place.	New cases reported.
Alabama (April):		**Illinois (April):**	
Autauga County	2	Southern Illinois State Penitentiary	1
Calhoun County	1		
Chilton County	1	**Kansas (April):**	
Clay County	1	Cherokee County—	
Colbert County	2	Galena (1 R. D.)	4
Cullman County	1	Montgomery County—	
Etowah County	1	Coffeyville	4
Hale County	1	Sedgwick County—	
Houston County	1	Wichita	1
Jefferson County	21		
Lauderdale County	2	Total	4
Lee County	1		
Limestone County	1	**Mississippi (April):**	
Lowndes County	2	Adams County	2
Madison County	9	Alcorn County	6
Mobile County	1	Amite County	2
Montgomery County	5	Attala County	1
Pickens County	1	Benton County	5
Russell County	1	Bolivar County	65
Shelby County	1	Calhoun County	2
Tuscaloosa County	11	Carroll County	2
Walker County	1	Chickasaw County	14
Winston County	1	Claiborne County	4
		Clarke County	6
Total	70	Clay County	9
		Coahoma County	76
Arkansas (February):		Copiah County	27
Ashley County	1	De Soto County	7
Clark County	1	Forrest County	2
Craighead County	1	Franklin County	1
Hempstead County	1	George County	6
Hot Spring County	4	Greene County	9
Saline County	2	Hancock County	2
Sebastian County	4	Harrison County	14
		Hinds County	39
Total	14	Holmes County	11
		Issaquena County	1
California (April):		Itawamba County	4
Fresno County	1	Jackson County	3
Kern County	1	Jasper County	7
Los Angeles County—		Jefferson County	8
Los Angeles	1	Jefferson Davis County	8
Orange County—		Jones County	8
Anaheim	1	Kemper County	4
San Bernardino County	1	Lafayette County	2
		Lamar County	2
Total	5	Lauderdale County	4
		Lawrence County	6

PELLAGRA—Continued.

State Reports for February, March, and April, 1918—Continued.

Place.	New cases reported.	Place.	New cases reported.
Mississippi (April)—Continued.		**Mississippi (April)—Continued.**	
Lee County	24	Yalobusha County	4
Leflore County	15	Yazoo County	25
Lincoln County	17		
Lowndes County	7	Total	780
Madison County	11		
Marion County	18	**Virginia (March):**	
Marshall County	2	Accomac County	1
Monroe County	3	Albemarle County—	
Montgomery County	2	Charlottesville	1
Neshoba County	3	Amherst County	1
Newton County	2	Augusta County	1
Noxubee County	10	Brunswick County	1
Oktibbeha County	6	Chesterfield County	1
Panola County	7	Winterpock	2
Pearl River County	1	Dinwiddie County—	
Perry County	8	Petersburg	1
Pike County	14	Fairfax County	1
Pontotoc County	5	Grayson County	1
Prentiss County	4	Greenesville County	1
Quitman County	20	Halifax County	1
Rankin County	6	Hanover County	2
Scott County	5	Henry County	3
Sharkey County	7	James City County	2
Simpson County	2	Lee County	3
Sunflower County	48	Mecklenburg County	1
Tallahatchie County	35	Northampton County	1
Tate County	13	Richmond County	1
Tippah County	2	Roanoke County—	
Tishomingo County	14	Roanoke	1
Tunica County	16	Spottsylvania County—	
Union County	9	Fredericksburg	1
Warren County	22	Wise County	1
Washington County	18	Big Stone Gap	2
Wayne County	3	York County	2
Webster County	6		
Wilkinson County	2	Total	33

City Reports for Week Ended May 18, 1918.

Place.	Cases.	Deaths.	Place.	Cases.	Deaths.
Alexandria, La	1		Memphis, Tenn	2	1
Atlanta, Ga		2	Nashville, Tenn	3	
Augusta, Ga		1	New Orleans, La	2	2
Birmingham, Ala	1		Petersburg, Va	1	
Charleston, S. C		3	Pontiac, Mich	2	
Chicago, Ill		1	Richmond, Va	1	
Houston, Tex	1	1	Spartanburg, S. C	1	1
Laurel, Miss	2		Waycross, Ga		1
Little Rock, Ark		2	Wilmington, N. C		1
Macon, Ga	1	1			

PLAGUE.

Hawaii—Lauparothoe—Plague Rat Found.

The finding of a plague-infected rat was reported May 18, 1918, at Lauparothoe, Hawaii.

PNEUMONIA.

City Reports for Week Ended May 18, 1918.

Place.	Cases.	Deaths.	Place.	Cases.	Deaths.
Alexandria, La	1	....	Manchester, N. H	1	1
Atlanta, Ga	2	11	Marquette, Mich	1	....
Binghamton, N. Y	1	....	Marshall, Tex	1	....
Boston, Mass	15	22	McAlester, Okla	2	....
Brockton, Mass	1	1	Melrose, Mass	2	....
Brookline, Mass	1	....	Michigan City, Ind	1	1
Cambridge, Mass	4	1	Middletown, Ohio	1	....
Chelsea, Mass	2	1	Milford, Mass	1	....
Chicago, Ill	185	73	Morgantown, W. Va	1	....
Cincinnati, Ohio	1	10	Mount Vernon, N. Y	1	....
Cleveland, Ohio	12	25	New Albany, Ind	1	....
Dayton, Ohio	1	2	Newark, N. J	54	15
Detroit, Mich	7	33	New Bedford, Mass	1	....
Duluth, Minn	14	3	North Adams, Mass	1	....
Elmira, N. Y	3	3	North Little Rock, Ark	2	1
Evansville, Ind	2	2	North Yakima, Wash	1	....
Fall River, Mass	2	1	Oakland, Cal	1	1
Fitchburg, Mass	1	....	Oshkosh, Wis	2	2
Flint, Mich	7	2	Oswego, N. Y	5	....
Fort Scott, Kans	2	....	Palestine, Tex	6	....
Fort Worth, Tex	2	2	Pittsfield, Mass	3	1
Fremont, Ohio	1	....	Pontiac, Mich	1	....
Grand Rapids, Mich	5	3	Port Chester, N. Y	2	1
Harrison, N. J	1	....	Quincy, Mass	1	....
Holyoke, Mass	3	....	Reno, Nev	2	3
Houston, Tex	1	2	Richmond, Va	1	3
Independence, Mo	3	2	Rochester, N. Y	12	2
Iola, Kans	3	....	Rutland, Vt	4	....
Irvington, N. J	1	2	Sacramento, Cal	1	3
Jackson, Mich	2	1	San Diego, Cal	5	5
Joplin, Mo	1	....	San Francisco, Cal	3	10
Kalamazoo, Mich	2	1	Schenectady, N. Y	5	5
Kansas City, Kans	3	....	Somerville, Mass	2	2
Kansas City, Mo	8	11	Springfield, Mass	10	1
Lackawanna, N. Y	3	1	Stockton, Cal	3	3
Laurel, Miss	1	....	Troy, N. Y	2	2
Little Rock, Ark	3	2	Waco, Tex	1	....
Los Angeles, Cal	9	6	Watertown, Mass	1	1
Louisville, Ky	2	1	Wichita, Kans	4	....
Lynn, Mass	3	2	Worcester, Mass	8	4
Madison, Wis	1	3	Youngstown, Ohio	1	1

POLIOMYELITIS (INFANTILE PARALYSIS).

State Reports for March and April, 1918.

Place.	New cases reported.	Place.	New cases reported.
Alabama (April):		Illinois (April)—Continued.	
Autauga County	1	Cook County—	
Clay County	1	Chicago	10
		Greene County—	
Total	2	Roodhouse	1
		Kankakee County—	
California (April):		Kankakee	1
Imperial County—		Lake County—	
Holtville	1	Waukegan	1
Los Angeles County—		La Salle County—	
Los Angeles	1	La Salle	1
San Francisco	1	Will County—	
Santa Clara County—		Joliet	1
Palo Alto	1		
Siskiyou County	1	Total	14
Total	6	Kansas (April):	
Colorado (April):		Doniphan County—	
Weld County	1	Wathena	1
Illinois (April):		Maine (April):	
Cass County—		Piscataquis County—	
Beardstown	1	Foxcroft (town)	1

POLIOMYELITIS (INFANTILE PARALYSIS)—Continued.

State Reports for March and April, 1918—Continued.

Place.	New cases reported.	Place.	New cases reported.
Mississippi (April):		Virginia (March):	
Itawamba County	1	Accomac County	2
Panola County	1	Bedford County	1
		Campbell County—	
Total	2	Lynchburg	1
		Caroline County	1
New Jersey (April):		Henrico County—	
Bergen County	1	Richmond	2
Hudson County	1	James City County—	
Hunterdon County	1	Williamsburg	1
		Rockingham County	5
Total	3	Bridgewater	5
		Smyth County	2
Ohio (April):			
Allen County	1	Total	20
Fairfield County	2		
Franklin County	3	Washington (April):	
Knox County	1	Chelan County	1
Scioto County	1	Douglas County	2
Trumbull County	1		
		Total	3
Total	9		

City Reports for Week Ended May 18, 1918.

Place.	Cases.	Deaths.	Place.	Cases.	Deaths.
Chicago, Ill	2	....	La Crosse, Wis	1	1
Cleveland, Ohio	1	....	Toledo, Ohio	1	1
Duluth, Minn	1	....			

RABIES IN ANIMALS.

City Reports for Week Ended May 18, 1918.

During the week ended May 18, 1918, there were reported five cases of rabies in animals at Detroit, Mich., three cases at Greeley, Colo., one case at Rochester, N. Y., and one case at Winston-Salem, N. C.

SCARLET FEVER.

See Diphtheria, measles, scarlet fever, and tuberculosis, page 948.

SMALLPOX.

State Reports for April, 1918.

Place.	New cases reported.	Deaths.	Vaccination history of cases.			
			Number vaccinated within 7 years preceding attack.	Number last vaccinated more than 7 years preceding attack.	Number never successfully vaccinated.	Vaccination history not obtained or uncertain.
California:						
Fresno County	2	....	....	....	2	....
Fresno City	6	....	....	....	6	....
Kern County	2	....	....	....	2	....
Bakersfield	1	....	....	1	....	....
Kings County—						
Hanford	1	....	....	....	1	....
Imperial County—						
Brawley	3	....	....	....	3	....
Calexico	4	....	....	....	4	....

SMALLPOX—Continued.

State Reports for April, 1918—Continued.

Place.	New cases reported.	Deaths.	Number vaccinated within 7 years preceding attack.	Number last vaccinated more than 7 years preceding attack.	Number never successfully vaccinated.	Vaccination history not obtained or uncertain.
California—Continued.						
Los Angeles County—						
Los Angeles	10			1	8	
Orange County	5				5	
Riverside County—						
Corona	2				2	
Blythe	5				5	
San Francisco	16				15	1
San Joaquin County—						
Stockton	4				4	
Siskiyou County	2				2	
Stanislaus County	3				3	
Modesto	2				2	
Tulare County—						
Tulare City	4				4	
Total	72			2	68	2
Colorado:						
Adams County	4				4	
Arapahoe County	1				1	
Boulder County	3					3
Cheyenne County	1				1	
Crowley County	1				1	
Delta County	2					2
Douglas County	5				5	
Denver	141		22		115	4
El Paso County	1					1
Garfield County	11				11	
Huerfano County	1				1	
Jefferson County	4				3	1
Kit Carson County	7				6	1
Larimer County	1				1	
Mesa County	5				1	4
Morgan County	1				1	
Otero County	1				1	
Pitkin County	1				1	
Pueblo County	6				2	4
Rio Blanco County	8				5	3
Rio Grande County	4			1	3	
Washington County	2				2	
Weld County	21			1	11	9
Yuma County	7			1	2	4
Total	239		25		178	36
Kansas:						
Allen County—						
Humboldt (R. D.)	1				1	
Iola	19			1	17	1
La Harpe (R. D.)	7				7	
Moran	2				2	
Atchison County—						
Atchison	6			3	3	
Effingham	1				1	
Huron	1				1	
Muscotah (R. D.)	1				1	
Barton County—						
Ellinwood	1				1	
Great Bend (R. D.)	2				2	
Heizer	2				2	
Pawnee Rock	1				1	
Bourbon County—						
Fort Scott (2 R. D.)	36			1	35	
Mapleton (R. D.)	3				3	
Uniontown (R. D.)	4			1	3	
Brown County—						
Hiawatha	3				3	
Horton	8			1	7	
Morrill	3				3	
Penkomi	1				1	

SMALLPOX—Continued.

State Reports for April, 1918—Continued.

Place.	New cases reported.	Deaths.	Number vaccinated within 7 years preceding attack.	Number last vaccinated more than 7 years preceding attack.	Number never successfully vaccinated.	Vaccination history not obtained or uncertain.
Kansas—Continued.						
But'er County—						
Augusta	11				11	
Douglas (R. D.)	2				2	
Eldorado (4 R. D.)	38				38	
Latham (2 R. D.)	3				3	
Oil Hill	2				2	
Towanda (R. D.)	4				4	
Whitewater (R. D.)	1				1	
Chase County—						
Florence	2				2	
Chautauqua County—						
Cedra Vale (1 R. D.)	2				2	
Sedan (2 R. D.)	3				3	
Cherokee County—						
Baxter Springs	3				3	
Columbus (6 R. D.)	8				8	
Galena	9			1	8	
Hallowell	1				1	
Scammon	5				5	
Sherwin	1				1	
Weir (1 R. D.)	7				7	
Cheyenne County—						
Jaqua	1				1	
St. Francis (2 R. D.)	6				6	
Clark County—						
Ashland (R. D.)	9			1	8	
Minneola (3 R. D.)	4				4	
Clay County—						
Clay Center	1				1	
Clifton	1				1	
Cloud County—						
Clyde (2 R. D.)	12				12	
Concordia	3				3	
Jamestown	1				1	
Coffey County—						
Burlington	2				2	
Waverly	4				4	
Comanche County—						
Coldwater (3 R. D.)	4				4	
Protection (9 R. D.)	14				14	
Wilmore	2				2	
Cowley County—						
Arkansas City	11			1	9	▲
Dale	1				1	
Udall	1				1	
Winfield (1 R. D.)	7				7	
Crawford County—						
Arcadia	1				1	
Chicopee	1				1	
Croweburg	1				1	
Farlington (R. D.)	7				7	
Franklin	1				1	
Frontenac	15				15	
Girard (7 R. D.)	11				11	
Midway	1				1	
Mulberry	2				2	
Pittsburg (6 R. D.)	10				10	
Radley	1				1	
Yale	1				1	
Decatur County—						
Cedar Bluffs (R. D.)	1				1	
Lyle	8				8	
Oberlin (5 R. D.)	12				10	2
Doniphan County—						
Elwood	4				4	
Severance (R. D.)	2				2	
Troy (R. D.)	6				6	
Douglas County—						
Lakeview	1				1	
Lawrence (1 R. D.)	5				5	
Edwards County—						
Belpre (2 R. D.)	5				5	
Fellsburg	3				3	
Kinsley	3			2	1	

SMALLPOX—Continued.
State Reports for April, 1918—Continued.

Place.	New cases reported.	Deaths.	Number vaccinated within 7 years preceding attack.	Number last vaccinated more than 7 years preceding attack.	Number never successfully vaccinated.	Vaccination history not obtained or uncertain.
Kansas—Continued.						
Ellis County—						
Ellis....................	1				1	
Hays....................	1				1	
Ellsworth County—						
Ellsworth..............	4		1		3	
Kanopolis..............	1				1	
Langley................	1				1	
Wilson.................	1				1	
Ford County—						
Dodge City............	2				2	
Sears..................	1				1	
Franklin County—						
Ottawa.................	1				1	
Princeton (11 R. D.).....	13				13	
Rantoul................	2				2	
Geary County—						
Junction City..........	1				1	
Milford................	3				3	
Graham County—						
Bogue (R. D.)..........	3				3	
Hill City (7 R. D.)......	9			1	8	
Morland (R. D.)........	15				15	
Gray County—						
Cimarron...............	1				1	
Ingalls................	1				1	
Greenwood County—						
Reece..................	1				1	
Harper County—						
Danville...............	1				1	
Freeport...............	1				1	
Harper.................	2				2	
Harvey County—						
Burrton................	1				1	
Hesston................	3				3	
Newton (5 R. D.).......	6				6	
Whitewater (R. D.).....	1				1	
Jackson County ·						
Straight Creek.........	2				2	
Jefferson County—						
Dunavant...............	1				1	
Perry (1 R. D.).........	2				2	
Williamstown (R. D.)....	2				2	
Jewell County—						
Cawker.................	1				1	
Glen Elder.............	1				1	
Ionia..................	1				1	
Mankato (R. D.)........	3				2	1
Superior, Nebr. (R. D.)...	1				1	
Johnson County—						
Olathe.................	2				2	
Kingman County—						
Mount Vernon..........	3				3	
Kiowa County						
Mullinville............	1				1	
Labette County—						
Altemont (R. D.).......	1				1	
Bartlett (R. D.)........	1				1	
Chetopa...............	3				3	
Oswego (R. D.).........	2				2	
Parsons...............	8		1		7	
Leavenworth County—						
Bonner Springs (R. D.)...	1				1	
Easton.................	3				3	
Lansing (R. D.).........	2				2	
Leavenworth (1 R. D.)...	9				9	
Tonganoxie.............	1				1	
Lincoln County—						
Lincoln................	1			1		
Shady Bend............	1				1	
Linn County—						
Centerville............	5				5	
Parker (7 R. D.)........	16			2	14	
Pleasanton (R. D.)......	1				1	
Logan County—						
Oakley.................	2				2	

SMALLPOX—Continued.

State Reports for April, 1918—Continued.

Place.	New cases reported.	Deaths.	Vaccination history of cases.			
			Number vaccinated within 7 years preceding attack.	Number last vaccinated more than 7 years preceding attack.	Number never successfully vaccinated.	Vaccination history not obtained or uncertain.
Kansas—Continued.						
Lyon County—						
Emporia	2				2	
Osage City (R. D.)	1				1	
Marion County—						
Hillsboro	1				1	
Marion (2 R. D.)	3			1	2	
Tampa (R. D.)	1				1	
Marshall County—						
Barretts	2				2	
Beattie	1				1	
Blue Rapids	14				14	
Marysville	1				1	
Frankfort	1				1	
McPherson County—						
Inman	3				3	
McPherson	1				1	
Mound Ridge	1				1	
Miami County—						
Louisburg (2 R. D.)	3				3	
Osawatomie	13			2	10	1
Paola (1 R. D.)	5				5	
Mitchell County—						
Cawker City (R. D.)	3				3	
Montgomery County—						
Caney	4				4	
Cherryvale	7			1	6	
Coffeyville	27			1	26	
Dearing	3				3	
Independence	6				6	
Nemaha County—						
Centralia (R. D.)	2				2	
Corning (R. D.)	2				2	
Oneida	4				4	
Seneca	3				3	
Sabetha	1				1	
Neosho County—						
Chanute (1 R. D.)	9				7	2
Norton County—						
Norton	1				1	
Osage County—						
Overbrook (1 R. D.)	1				1	
Quenemo	1				1	
Wakarusa (R. D.)	2				2	
Osborne County—						
Alton	4				4	
Osborne (2 R. D.)	31				31	
Tipton (R. D.)	2				2	
Ottawa County—						
Culver	1				1	
Longford	2				2	
Minneapolis (8 R. D.)	9				9	
Pawnee County—						
Larned	1				1	
Rozel (10 R. D.)	16			1	15	
Rush Center	1				1	
Phillips County—						
Logan (R. D.)	1				1	
Phillipsburg	1				1	
Pottawatomie County—						
Blaine	1				1	
Garrison (R. D.)	8				8	
Pratt County—						
Cullison (R. D.)	2				2	
Pratt	1				1	
Reno County—						
Castleton (R. D.)	1				1	
Haven	21				21	
Hutchinson (13 R. D.)	29				26	3
Whiteside (R. D.)	1				1	
Republic County—						
Belleville (1 R. D.)	4			1	3	
Courtland (5 R. D.)	12				12	
Scandia	1				1	

SMALLPOX—Continued.

State Reports for April, 1918—Continued.

Place.	New cases reported.	Deaths.	Vaccination history of cases.			
			Number vaccinated within 7 years preceding attack.	Number last vaccinated more than 7 years preceding attack.	Number never successfully vaccinated.	Vaccination history not obtained or uncertain.
Kansas—Continued.						
Rice County—						
Lyons	1				1	
Riley County—						
Manhattan (1 R. D.)	3				3	
Rooks County—						
Webster (R D.)	2				2	
Woodston	1				1	
Russell County—						
Bunker Hill (R. D.)	5				5	
Russell (R. D.)	3				3	
Saline County—						
Assaria (R. D)	1				1	
Salina (3 R D)	27				27	
Solomon (R. D.)	1				1	
Sedgwick County—						
Cheney	2				2	
Furley	2				2	
Kechi (R. D)	1				1	
Wichita (3 R. D.)	78				78	
Seward County—						
Liberal	6				6	
Shawnee County—						
Shorey	1				1	
Tecumseh	1				1	
Topeka	32				32	
Sheridan County—						
Hoxie	2				2	
Studley (R. D.)	1				1	
Smith County—						
Bellaire	1				1	
Stafford County—						
Hudson (2 R. D.)	2				2	
Macksville	7				7	
Stevens County—						
Moscow	9				9	
Sumner County—						
Belle Plaine	1				1	
Hunnewell	1				1	
Oxford	1				1	
Wellington	1				1	
Thomas County—						
Colby	1				1	
Trego County						
Collyer	1					
Wakeeney	2			1	2	
Wabaunsee County—						
Belvue (R. D)	1				1	
Maple Hill (R. D.)	1				1	
McFarland	1				1	
Washington County—						
Haddam	1				1	
Washington	1				1	
Wilson County						
Fredonia (R. D)	1				1	
Neodesha	1				1	
Woodson County—						
Vernon	5				5	
Yates Center	13				13	
Wyandotte County—						
Bonner Springs	1				1	
Kansas City	77				76	1
Rosedale	4				4	
Total	1,130		2	26	1,090	12
Ohio:						
Allen County	44				41	3
Ashland County	10					10
Ashtabula County	7				6	1
Athens County	10					10
Auglaize County	1				1	
Brown County	6					6

SMALLPOX—Continued.

State Reports for April, 1918—Continued.

Place.	New cases reported.	Deaths.	Vaccination history of cases.			
			Number vaccinated within 7 years preceding attack.	Number last vaccinated more than 7 years preceding attack.	Number never successfully vaccinated.	Vaccination history not obtained or uncertain.
Ohio—Continued.						
Butler County	85	....	2	1	46	36
Clark County	2					2
Clinton County	7					7
Columbiana County	54		4	1	29	20
Coshocton County	4				2	2
Crawford County	8				7	1
Cuyahoga County	139				1	138
Darke County	1					1
Defiance County	3				3	
Delaware County	5				5	
Erie County	3				1	2
Fairfield County	8				6	2
Payette County	3					3
Franklin County	17				14	3
Fulton County	6				1	5
Gallia County	15				14	1
Green County	9			1	8	
Guernsey County	13					13
Hamilton County	67			1	19	47
Hancock County	5				2	3
Hardin County	4					4
Henry County	25				20	5
Highland County	1					1
Hocking County	10				10	
Holmes County	17				5	11
Huron County	2		1			1
Jackson County	11			1		11
Jefferson County	14				12	2
Knox County	1					1
Lake County	1				1	
Lawrence County	8				4	4
Licking County	8				4	4
Logon County	2				1	
Lorain County	12		2		3	7
Lucas County	22		7		11	4
Mahoning County	12				2	10
Medina County	19		1	1	12	5
Meigs County	1					1
Mercer County	4			2	2	
Miami County	5				3	2
Montgomery County	21				1	20
Morgan County	5					5
Morrow County	1					1
Muskingum County	15				4	11
Ottawa County	6					6
Paulding County	4					4
Perry County	20					20
Pickaway County	14					14
Pike County	4					4
Portage County	48		1		5	42
Preble County	2					2
Putnam County	2				1	1
Richland County	6				1	5
Ross County	4				1	3
Sandusky County	7				5	2
Scioto County	58				55	3
Seneca County	2				2	....
Shelby County	6				6	
Stark County	9				2	7
Summit County	120			2	26	92
Trumbull County	9				9	....
Tuscarawas County	30			1	25	4
Van Wert County	11				1	10
Warren County	9				7	2
Wavne County	15				2	13
Williams County	2				2	
Wood County	8				4	4
Wyandot County	15				3	12
Total	1,161	....	19	11	458	676

SMALLPOX—Continued.

Miscellaneous State Reports.

Place.	Cases.	Deaths.	Place.	Cases.	Deaths.
Alabama (April):			**Illinois (April)—Continued.**		
Autauga County	6		Alexander County—		
Baldwin County	3		Cairo	1	
Barbour County	3		Bureau County—		
Bibb County	4		Mineral	4	
Butler County	3		Cass County—		
Calhoun County	51		Beardstown	2	
Cherokee County	2		Chandlerville	4	
Chilton County	5		Champaign County—		
Choctaw County	1		Champaign	4	
Clarke County	1		Sidney Township	2	
Clay County	4		St. Joseph Township	3	
Colbert County	30		Urbana	1	
Crenshaw County	3		Christian County—		
Dallas County	3		Morrisonville	2	
Escambia County	1		Pana	2	
Etowah County	3		Taylorville	2	
Hale County	1		Clinton County—		
Jackson County	12		Aviston	1	
Jefferson County	166		Breese	4	
Lauderdale County	6		Breese Township	1	
Lee County	6	1	Coles County—		
Madison County	3		Charleston	2	
Mobile County	20		Cook County—		
Monroe County	1		Chicago	31	
Montgomery County	12		Chicago Heights	1	
Morgan County	6		Cicero	3	
Pike County	5		Cumberland County—		
Randolph County	3		Toledo	1	
Shelby County	20		Edgar County—		
St. Clair County	6		Kansas	1	
Tallapoosa County	7		Paris	4	
Tuscaloosa County	7		Franklin County—		
Walker County	3		Benton Township	5	
Wilcox County	1		Christopher	2	
			Goode Township	2	
Total	408	1	Rovalton	3	
Arkansas (February):			Six Mile	2	
Arkansas County	16		West City	4	
Ashley County	18		Ziegler	4	
Bradley County	11		Fulton County—		
Clark County	2		Bryant	10	
Conway County	19		Buckhart Township	2	
Craighead County	19		Canton Township	1	
Dallas County	6		Gallatin County —		
Desha County	3		Greene	1	
Drew County	24		Ridgeway	1	
Faulkner County	4		Greene County—		
Franklin County	3		Wrights Township	6	
Garland County	3		Hamilton County—		
Greene County	12		Knights Prairie		
Hempstead County	12		Township	2	
Hot Spring County	8		Harden County—		
Izard County	7		Hicks Township	1	
Jefferson County	33		Henry County —		
Lee County	2		Alba Township	2	
Lincoln County	25		Colona Township	1	
Little River County	2		Kewanee	1	
Logan County	8		Jackson County—		
Monroe County	4		Degognia Township	2	
Ouachita County	28		Elk Township	12	
Phillips County	10		Murphysboro	2	
Poinsett County	12		Jefferson County—		
Randolph County	1		Dodds Township	5	
Saline County	30		Jersey County—		
Sebastian County	12		Jerseyville	2	
Sevier County	3		Johnson County—		
Sharp County	20		Vienna	2	
St. Francis County	13		Kane County—		
Washington County	6		Aurora	3	
White County	200		Elgin	1	
			Montgomery	1	
Total	596		Kankakee County—		
Illinois (April):			Sumner Township	2	
Adams County—			Knox County—		
Melrose Township	1		E. Galesburg	1	
Quincy	51		Henderson Township	3	
Riverside Township	14		Salem Township	1	
Ursa Township	1		Yates City	7	

SMALLPOX—Continued.

Miscellaneous State Reports—Continued.

Place.	Cases.	Deaths.
Illinois (April)—Continued.		
Livingston County—		
Belle Prairie Township	2	....
Logan County—		
Lincoln	1	....
Macon County—		
Decatur	7	....
Macon	2	....
Milan Township	2	....
Macoupin County—		
Verden	4	....
White City	7	....
Madison County—		
Alton	64	....
Collinsville	11	....
E. Alton	5	....
Nameoki Township	1	....
Wood River Township	19	....
Marion County—		
Oden	1	....
Mason County—		
Manito Township	2	....
McDonough County—		
Bushnell	4	....
McHenry County—		
Harvard	1	....
McLean County—		
Bloomington	1	....
LeRoy	1	....
West Township	1	....
Montgomery County—		
Coffeen	4	....
E. York Township	1	....
Morgan County—		
Jacksonville	9	....
Peoria County—		
Averyville	8	....
Chillicothe Township	2	....
Limestone Township	1	....
Peoria	65	....
Perry County—		
Duquoin Township	2	....
Randolph County—		
Chester	1	....
Chester precinct	1	....
Rock Island County—		
Moline	1	....
Rock Island	1	....
Saline County—		
Cottage Township	1	....
Harrisburg	4	....
Sangamon County—		
Curran Township	2	....
Shelby County—		
Cold Springs Township	1	....
Stark County—		
Goshen Township	1	....
St. Clair County—		
East Carondolet	2	....
Marissa	1	....
Stephenson County—		
Redott Township	2	....
Tazewell County—		
Cincinnati Township	1	....
Pekin	4	....
Pekin Township	2	....
Union County—		
Douglas	7	....
Vermilion County—		
Danville	5	....
Hoopeston	2	....
Wabash County—		
Mount Carmel	1	....
Warren County—		
Monmouth	1	....
Illinois (April)—Continued.		
Wayne County—		
Jasper Township	1	....
Mount Erie Township	1	....
Will County—		
Joliet	1	....
Williamson County—		
Cambria	1	....
Energy	1	....
Herrin	3	....
Winnebago County—		
Petaconica	2	....
Rockton	2	....
Woodford County—		
Montgomery Township	1	....
State Institutions—		
Jacksonville State Hospital	3	....
Lincoln State School and Colony	2	....
Soldiers and Sailors Home	1	....
Total	534	....
Iowa (April):		
Adair County	1	....
Appanoose County	2	....
Audubon County	1	....
Boone County	2	....
Bremer County	2	....
Cass County	8	....
Cerro Gordo County	9	....
Chickasaw County	2	....
Clay County	2	....
Clayton County	10	....
Crawford County	1	....
Dallas County	9	....
Davis County	4	....
Delaware County	1	....
Des Moines County	7	....
Dubuque County	2	....
Emmet County	3	....
Fayette County	2	....
Floyd County	2	....
Grundy County	4	....
Guthrie County	4	....
Hancock County	3	....
Hardin County	4	....
Harrison County	3	....
Henry County	7	....
Jasper County	7	....
Johnson County	11	....
Kossuth County	3	....
Linn County	19	....
Lucas County	1	....
Madison County	2	....
Mahaska County	7	....
Marion County	6	....
Marshall County	2	....
Mills County	2	....
Mitchell County	1	....
Monona County	4	....
Monroe County	10	....
Montgomery County	2	....
Osceola County	1	....
Palo Alto County	2	....
Plymouth County	3	....
Polk County	83	....
Pottowattamie County	61	....
Poweshiek County	6	....
Ringgold County	3	....
Scott County	5	....
Shelby County	2	....
Sioux County	6	....
Union County	1	....
Van Buren County	2	....

SMALLPOX—Continued.

Miscellaneous State Reports—Continued.

Place.	Cases.	Deaths.	Place.	Cases.	Deaths.
Iowa (April)—Continued.			**Mississippi (April)—Contd.**		
Wapello County.........	42	....	Sunflower County.......	71	....
Washington County.....	2	....	Tallahatchie County.....	28	....
Wayne County..........	1	....	Tate County.............	23	....
Webster County........	7	....	Tippah County..........	10	....
Winnebago County......	1	....	Tunica County..........	7	....
Woodbury County.......	1	....	Union County...........	4	....
Worth County..........	2	....	Warren County..........	17	....
Wright County.........	7	....	Washington County......	13	....
			Winston County.........	2	....
Total...............	410	....	Yalobusha County.......	1	....
Maine (April):			Yazoo County...........	11	....
Aroostook County—					
Fort Fairfield (town).	1	....	Total...............	662	....
Sherman (town).....	6	....			
St. John (plantation).	1	....	**Nevada (April):**		
Kennebec County—			Elko County............	1	....
Augusta.............	2	....	Humboldt County.......	1	....
Benton (town)......	7	....			
Oxford County—			Total...............	2	....
Bethel (town).......	1	....			
Rumford (town).....	1	....	**New Jersey (April):**		
Penobscot County—			Atlantic County........	8	....
Exeter (town).......	1	....			
Bangor..............	2	....	**North Dakota (April):**		
Piscataquis County—			Adams County..........	1	....
Greenville (town).....	2	....	Bottineau County.......	3	....
Somerset County—			Burleigh County........	1	....
Caratunk (plantation)	1	....	Cass County............	4	....
Madison (town)......	4	....	Hettinger County.......	1	....
			La Moure County.......	3	....
Total...............	29	....	McHenry County........	1	....
Mississippi (April):			McKenzie County.......	6	....
Adams County..........	2	....	McLean County.........	2	....
Alcorn County.........	9	....	Mountrail County.......	3	....
Attala County.........	5	....	Pembina County........	1	....
Benton County.........	10	....	Pierce County..........	2	....
Bolivar County........	3	....	Ramsey County.........	1	....
Calhoun County........	2	....	Renville County........	2	....
Carroll County........	5	....	Rolette County.........	1	....
Chickasaw County......	5	....	Stutsman County........	4	....
Clarke County.........	5	....	Towner County.........	1	....
Clay County...........	12	....	Traill County..........	2	....
Coahoma County........	10	....	Ward County...........	3	....
Copiah County.........	3	....	Wells County..........	1	....
Covington County......	13	....	Williams County........	5	....
De Soto County........	10	....			
Forrest County........	2	....	Total...............	51	....
Franklin County.......	1	....			
Greene County.........	2	....	**Virginia (March):**		
Harrison County.......	2	....	Albemarle County -		
Hinds County..........	31	....	Charlottesville.......	2	....
Holmes County.........	19	....	Alexandria County......	2	....
Issaquena County......	6	....	Alleghany County.......	4	....
Jasper County.........	11	....	Clifton Forge.......	2	....
Jefferson Davis County...	1	....	Bedford County.........	10	....
Jones County..........	17	....	Botetourt County.......	5	....
Kemper County........	3	....	Franklin County........	6	....
Lafayette County......	24	....	Gloucester County......	6	....
Lamar County.........	1	....	Grayson County........	5	....
Lauderdale County......	60	....	Halifax County.........	20	....
Lee County............	4	....	Henrico County —		
Leflore County........	78	....	Richmond..........	1	....
Lincoln County........	11	....	Lancaster County.......	1	....
Lowndes County.......	8	....	Lee County............	10	....
Montgomery County.....	5	....	Loudoun County........	1	....
Newton County........	1	....	Louisa County.........	4	....
Oktibbeha County......	7	....	Norfolk County —		
Panola County.........	46	....	Norfolk..........	4	....
Pearl River County.....	5	....	Northampton County....	1	....
Perry County..........	7	....	Cape Charles........	2	....
Pike County...........	7	....	Orange County.........	2	....
Pontotoc County.......	3	....	Pittsylvania County......	19	....
Prentiss County.......	1	....	Roanoke County -		
Quitman County........	6	....	Roanoke..........	18	....
Sharkey County........	11	....	Russell County.........	2	....
Smith County..........	5	....	Scott County...........	4	....
Stone County..........	1	1	Spotsylvania County....	10	....
			Stafford County........	12	....

SMALLPOX—Continued.

Miscellaneous State Reports—Continued.

Place.	Cases.	Deaths.	Place.	Cases.	Deaths.
Virginia (March)—Contd.			Washington (April)—Contd.		
Tazewell County	13	....	Spokane County	11	....
Pocahontas	3	....	Cheney (Tyler)	12	....
Warwick County—			Hillyard	4	....
Newport News	5	....	Spokane	75	....
Washington County	4	....	Stevens County	3	....
Wise County	29	....	Thurston County—		
East Stone Gap	1	....	Olympia	3	....
York County	1	....	Whatcom County	2	....
			Bellingham	2	....
Total	209	....	Yakima County—		
			Zillah	1	....
Washington (April):					
Benton County	1	....	Total	190	....
Chelan County	2	....			
Ferry County	2	....	Wyoming (April):		
Republic	2	....	Albany County	2	....
King County	3	....	Converse County	2	....
Seattle	31	....	Fremont County	1	....
Kittitas County—			Hot Springs County	3	....
Cle Elum	1	....	Johnson County	20	....
Klickitat County	2	....	Laramie County	3	....
Pierce County	9	....	Natrona County	17	....
Tacoma	5	....	Sheridan County	1	....
Wilkeson	3	....	Uinta County	1	....
Snohomish County	5	....			
Arlington	8	....	Total	50	....
Everett	4	....			

City Reports for Week Ended May 18, 1918.

Place.	Cases.	Deaths.	Place.	Cases.	Deaths.
Akron, Ohio	25	....	Fremont, Ohio	1	....
Alexandria, La	4	....	Fresno, Cal	2	....
Alton, Ill	5	....	Galesburg, Ill	2	....
Anniston, Ala	2	....	Grand Rapids, Mich	8	....
Atlanta, Ga	5	....	Greeley, Colo	2	....
Barberton, Ohio	1	....	Houston, Tex	1	....
Beloit, Wis	1	....	Independence, Kans	2	....
Birmingham, Ala	11	....	Independence, Mo	6	....
Buffalo, N. Y	3	....	Indianapolis, Ind	34	....
Cairo, Ill	1	....	Iola, Kans	9	....
Canton, Ohio	4	....	Joplin, Mo	3	....
Cape Girardeau, Mo	2	....	Kalamazoo, Mich	7	....
Cedar Rapids, Iowa	3	....	Kansas City, Kans	7	....
Chanute, Kans	4	....	Kansas City, Mo	30	....
Charleston, W. Va	6	....	Knoxville, Tenn	3	....
Chattanooga, Tenn	1	....	La Crosse, Wis	3	....
Chicago, Ill	2	....	Laurel, Miss	3	....
Cincinnati, Ohio	9	....	Leavenworth, Kans	3	....
Cleveland, Ohio	32	....	Lebanon, Pa	1	....
Clinton, Iowa	1	....	Lima, Ohio	2	....
Coffeyville, Kans	14	....	Lincoln, Nebr	9	....
Columbus, Ohio	3	....	Little Rock, Ark	2	....
Council Bluffs, Iowa	7	....	Lorain, Ohio	1	....
Dallas, Tex	7	....	Louisville, Ky	2	....
Danville, Ill	4	....	Ludington, Mich	1	....
Davenport, Iowa	7	....	Macon, Ga	2	....
Dayton, Ohio	4	....	Madison, Wis	1	....
Denver, Colo	35	....	Marion, Ind	1	....
Des Moines, Iowa	24	....	Marshall, Tex	1	....
Detroit, Mich	11	....	McAlester, Okla	1	....
Dubuque, Iowa	4	....	Memphis, Tenn	2	....
Dunkirk, N. Y	6	....	Middletown, Ohio	7	....
Elmira, N. Y	1	....	Minneapolis, Minn	16	....
El Paso, Tex	1	....	Missoula, Mont	1	....
Elyria, Ohio	3	....	Mobile, Ala	7	....
Evansville, Ind	4	....	Moline, Ill	1	....
Fairmont, W. Va	1	....	Montgomery, Ala	5	....
Flint, Mich	4	....	Muncie, Ind	5	....
Fort Dodge, Iowa	2	....	Muscatine, Iowa	1	....
Fort Scott, Kans	4	....	Muskegon, Mich	6	....
Fort Worth, Tex	13	....	New Orleans, La	2	....

SMALLPOX—Continued.

City Reports for Week Ended May 18, 1918—Continued.

Place.	Cases.	Deaths.	Place.	Cases.	Deaths.
Niagara Falls, N. Y	1	....	Sioux City, Iowa	5	....
North Little Rock, Ark	2	....	Spartanburg, S. C	1	....
Oklahoma City, Okla	24	....	Spokane, Wash	17	....
Omaha, Nebr	16	....	Springfield, Ill	6	....
Parkersburg, W. Va	2	....	Springfield, Mo	5	....
Peoria, Ill	6	....	Stockton, Cal	2	....
Pine Bluff, Ark	2	....	Superior, Wis	1	....
Pontiac, Mich	9	....	Toledo, Ohio	1	....
Quincy, Ill	4	....	Topeka, Kans	12	....
Richmond, Ind	1	....	Utica, N. Y	8	....
Roanoke, Va	2	....	Waco, Tex	2	....
Rockford, Ill	1	....	Walla Walla, Wash	1	....
St. Joseph, Mo	28	....	Warren, Ohio	1	....
St. Louis, Mo	26	....	Washington, D. C	2	....
Salt Lake City, Utah	5	....	Waterloo, Iowa	3	....
San Francisco, Cal	3	....	Wichita, Kans	17	....
Sault Ste. Marie, Mich	1	....	Winston-Salem, N. C	1	....
Seattle, Wash	2	....			

TETANUS.

City Reports for Week Ended May 18, 1918.

Place.	Cases.	Deaths.	Place.	Cases.	Deaths.
Cairo, Ill	1	1	Kansas City, Mo	7	1
Chicago, Ill	1	1	Marshall, Tex	1	....
Columbus, Ohio	....	1	Montgomery, Ala	....	1
Dayton, Ohio	....	1	Pine Bluff, Ark	1	....

TUBERCULOSIS.

See Diphtheria, measles, scarlet fever, and tuberculosis, page 948.

TYPHOID FEVER.

State Reports for February, March, and April, 1918.

Place.	New cases reported.	Place.	New cases reported.
Alabama (April):		Arkansas (February):	
Barbour County	1	Benton County	1
Bullock County	1	Carroll County	1
Calhoun County	1	Logan County	32
Cherokee County	2	Saline County	1
Chilton County	1		
Colbert County	1	Total	35
Covington County	1		
Cullman County	1	California (April):	
Dallas County	7	Alameda County—	
Etowah County	1	Oakland	3
Franklin County	1	Alameda	1
Jefferson County	12	Berkeley	1
Lauderdale County	2	Butte County	1
Marion County	3	Contra Costa County—	
Mobile County	7	Pittsburg	1
Monroe County	1	Richmond	4
Montgomery County	1	Imperial County	2
Morgan County	4	Calexico	2
Tuscaloosa County	1	Los Angeles County	1
Walker County	3	Glendale	1
		Long Beach	1
Total	52	Los Angeles	6
		Whittier	1

TYPHOID FEVER—Continued.

State Reports for February, March, and April, 1918—Continued.

Place.	New cases reported.	Place.	New cases reported.
California (April)—Continued.		**Illinois (April)—Continued.**	
Fresno County—		Macon County—	
Fresno City	1	Decatur	1
Madera County	2	Madison County—	
Merced County	1	Alton	1
Orange County	2	Mason County—	
Riverside County—		Easton	1
Blythe	3	McHenry County—	
Corona	1	Crystal Lake	1
Sacramento County	1	Platt County—	
Sacramento	2	Monticello	1
San Bernardino County—		Pike County—	
Ontario	1	Pleasant Hill	4
San Diego County—		Rock Island County—	
Chula Vista	1	Moline	6
National City	1	Rock Island	1
San Joaquin County	1	Sangamon County—	
Stockton	3	Pleasant Plains	1
San Francisco	8	Rochester	1
San Mateo County—		Rochester Township	1
Daly City	1	Vermilion County—	
Santa Barbara County—		Danville	4
Santa Barbara	1	Wabash County—	
Santa Cruz County—		Bellmont	1
Santa Cruz	1	Will County—	
Sonoma County—		Frankfort	1
Santa Rosa	1	Joliet Township	1
Stanislaus County	2	Williamson County—	
Newman	1	Cambria	1
Sutter County—			
Yuba City	1	Total	66
Yolo County	2		
		Kansas (April):	
Total	65	Anderson County—	
		Garnett	1
Colorado (April):		Bourbon County—	
Chaffee County	4	Hiattville	1
Denver	2	Cloud County—	
Huerfano County	1	Hollis (R. D.)	1
Las Animas County	2	Crawford County—	
Mesa County	1	Pittsburg	1
Montrose County	5	Ellis County—	
Otero County	1	Ellis	1
Pueblo	1	Greenwood County—	
Weld County	6	Eureka (1 R. D.)	5
		Hamilton	1
Total	23	Jefferson County—	
		Winchester (R. D.)	1
Illinois (April):		Johnson County—	
Adams County—		Springhill	1
Quincy	1	Kearny County—	
Cook County—		Lakin	1
Chicago	13	Kiowa County—	
Crawford County—		Greensburg	1
Oblong	2	Labette County—	
De Kalb County—		Chetopa	1
Sycamore	1	Leavenworth County—	
Fulton County—		Bonner Springs (R. D.)	2
Lewistown	1	Lansing (State Prison)	1
Henry County—		Leavenworth	1
Cambridge	1	Lincoln County—	
Geneseo Township	1	Sylvan Grove	1
Wethersford	1	Vesper	1
Iroquois County—		Lyon County—	
Woodland	3	Olpe	1
Jersey County—		Montgomery County—	
Jerseyville	2	Caney	1
Kane County—		Cherryvale	1
St. Charles	1	Independence	1
Lake County—		Morris County—	
Lake Forest	1	Council Grove	2
Waukegan	2	Delavan (R. D.)	1
La Salle County—		Nemaha County—	
La Salle	1	Corning	1
Oglesby	1	Osage County—	
Sheridan	1	Osage City (R. D.)	1
Livingston County—		Reno County—	
Dwight	8	Haven (R. D.)	1

TYPHOID FEVER—Continued.

State Reports for February, March, and April, 1918—Continued.

Place.	New cases reported.
Kansas (April)—Continued.	
Rush County—	
Loretta (R. D.)	2
Russell County—	
Russell (R. D.)	1
Sedgwick County—	
Wichita (I R. D.)	3
Shawnee County—	
Silver Lake	1
Washington County—	
Greenleaf	3
Morrowville	1
Wilson County—	
Fredonia	1
North Altoona	10
Neodesha (R D.)	1
Wyandotte County—	
Bonner Springs (R. D.)	1
Kansas City	1
Rosedale	1
Total	58
Maine (April):	
Cumberland County—	
Portland	1
Lincoln County—	
Wiscasset (town)	1
Penobscot County—	
Old Town	1
Sagadahoc County—	
Bowdoinham (town)	1
Somerset County -	
Madison (town)	1
Total	5
Mississippi (April):	
Adams County	4
Amite County	1
Attala County	1
Benton County	1
Bolivar County	17
Calhoun County	2
Carroll County	2
Choctaw County	2
Claiborne County	1
Clarke County	5
Coahoma County	1
Copiah County	5
Covington County	2
De Soto County	2
Forrest County	2
Hancock County	1
Hinds County	2
Holmes County	1
Issaquena County	1
Jackson County	3
Jasper County	3
Jones County	5
Lamar County	1
Lauderdale County	2
Lawrence County	3
Leake County	4
Leflore County	2
Lincoln County	2
Lowndes County	3
Madison County	4
Marion County	1
Neshoba County	2
Oktibbeha County	2
Panola County	5
Pike County	5
Pontotoc County	1
Rankin County	2
Scott County	1
Sharkey County	1
Stone County	1
Sunflower County	15

Place.	New cases reported.
Mississippi (April)—Continued.	
Tallahatchie County	3
Tate County	3
Tippah County	1
Tishomingo County	3
Tunica County	2
Union County	2
Warren County	7
Washington County	3
Webster County	2
Wilkinson County	1
Yazoo County	4
Total	154
Nevada (April):	
Lander County	2
Washoe County	1
Total	3
New Jersey (April):	
Atlantic County	1
Bergen County	2
Burlington County	3
Camden County	1
Cumberland County	4
Essex County	4
Hudson County	5
Mercer County	2
Middlesex County	3
Monmouth County	3
Morris County	1
Passaic County	3
Total	16
North Dakota (April):	
McHenry County	1
Walsh County	2
Williams County	1
Total	4
Ohio (April):	
Ashtabula County	2
Athens County	1
Belmont County	5
Columbiana County	9
Cuyahoga County	9
Defiance County	4
Erie County	4
Guernsey County	1
Hamilton County	2
Hardin County	2
Harrison County	1
Jefferson County	3
Lawrence County	12
Lorain County	1
Lucas County	3
Mahoning County	3
Meigs County	4
Miami County	2
Monroe County	2
Muskingum County	4
Ottawa County	3
Preble County	1
Putnam County	1
Ross County	1
Sandusky County	1
Scioto County	1
Seneca County	3
Summit County	1
Trumbull County	6
Tuscarawas County	1
Warren County	1
Wood County	3
Total	98

TYPHOID FEVER—Continued.

State Reports for February, March, and April, 1918—Continued.

Place.	New cases reported.	Place.	New cases reported.
Virginia (March):		**Virginia (March)—Continued.**	
Alleghany County	2	Washington County	2
Clifton Forge	3	Wise County	1
Amherst County	1	Norton	2
Botetourt County	4		
Buchanan County	3	Total	65
Campbell County	1		
Brookneal	1	**Washington (April):**	
Chesterfield County	1	Benton County	2
Culpeper County	1	Prosser	1
Dickenson County	2	Chelan County—	
Fairfax County	1	Wenatchee	3
Floyd County	2	Grays Harbor County	1
Fluvanna County	1	King County—	
Halifax County	1	Seattle	1
Hanover County	1	Okanogan County—	
Henrico County—		Brewster	1
Richmond	1	Pacific County—	
King William County	1	Raymond	1
Louisa County	2	Pierce County—	
Mechlenburg County	2	Tacoma	1
Middlesex County	1	Skagit County—	
Nelson County	2	Anacortes	1
Norfolk County—		Spokane County—	
Norfolk	1	Spokane	2
Northampton County	1	Thurston County—	
Orange County—		Tenino	1
Orange	1	Walla Walla County—	
Prince Edward County	1	Waitsburg	1
Princess Anne County	3	Yakima County—	3
Pulaski County	1	Yakima	2
Roanoke County—			
Salem	1	Total	21
Rockbridge County	1		
Rockingham County	1	**Wyoming:**	
Scott County	2	Goshen County	1
Shenandoah County	1	Johnson County	3
Southampton County			
Tazewell County	9	Total	4
Pocahontas	2		

City Reports for Week Ended May 18, 1918.

Place.	Cases.	Deaths.	Place.	Cases.	Deaths.
Akron, Ohio	1		Galveston, Tex	1	
Alexandria, La	3	1	Grand Rapids, Mich	1	
Ashtabula, Ohio		1	Hartford, Conn	1	
Atlanta, Ga	1		Houston, Tex	5	
Bellaire, Ohio	1		Independence, Mo	2	
Berkeley, Cal	2		Indianapolis, Ind	1	
Birmingham, Ala	2		Ithaca, N. Y	1	
Bloomington, Ind	1		Kansas City, Kans	2	
Boston, Mass	3		Lackawanna, N. Y	2	
Buffalo, N. Y	1	1	Leavenworth, Kans	1	
Chanute, Kans	2		Lima, Ohio	1	
Charleston, S. C	2		Los Angeles, Cal	3	1
Charlotte, N. C	1		Louisville, Ky	3	
Chattanooga, Tenn	1		Macon, Ga	3	
Chelsea, Mass	3		Marlboro, Mass		1
Chicago, Ill	3	1	Marshall, Tex	1	
Cincinnati, Ohio	1		Memphis, Tenn	2	
Cleveland, Ohio	2	1	Milwaukee, Wis	5	
Columbia, S. C	1		Minneapolis, Minn	1	
Danville, Ill	1		Mobile, Ala	1	
Dayton, Ohio	1		Montgomery, Ala	2	
Denver, Colo	1		Morgantown, W. Va	2	
Detroit, Mich	3		Nashville, Tenn	1	1
Dover, N. H	1		New Bedford, Mass	1	
Duluth, Minn	1		New Castle, Pa	3	
Evansville, Ind	1	1	New Orleans, La	5	3
Fall River, Mass	1		Newport, R. I		1
Fort Worth, Tex	1		New York, N. Y	17	3

TYPHOID FEVER—Continued.

City Reports for Week Ended May 18, 1918—Continued.

Ltate.	Cases.	Deaths.	State.	Cases.	Deaths.
Norfolk, Va..........	1	....	St. Louis, Mo..........	....	1
North Yakima, Wash.......	1	....	Salt Lake City, Utah........	2	1
Norwalk, Conn..........	1	1	San Francisco, Cal..........	2	....
Ogdensburg, N. Y..........	1	....	Saratoga Springs, N. Y.....	1	....
Omaha, Nebr...	....	1	Savannah, Ga..........	2	....
Oswego, N. Y..........	....	2	Syracuse, N. Y..........	....	1
Palestine, Tex..........	1	....	Troy, N. Y..........	....	1
Petersburg, Va..........	1	1	Washington, D. C..........	2	....
Pittsburgh, Pa..........	2	....	Watertown, Mass..........	1	....
Portland, Oreg..	1	....	Wausau, Wis..........	1	....
Portsmouth, N. H..........	1	1	West Warwick, R. I........	1	....
Reno, Nev......	1	....	Wheeling, W. Va..........	2	....
Richmond, Va..........	....	1	Wilkinsburg, Pa..........	1	....
Riverside, Cal..	1	....	York, Pa..........	2	....
Saginaw, Mich..........	1	....	Youngstown, Ohio..........	1	....

DIPHTHERIA, MEASLES, SCARLET FEVER, AND TUBERCULOSIS,

State Reports for February, March, and April, 1918.

State.	Disease.			State.	Disease.		
	Diph-theria.	Measles	Scarlet fever.		Diph-theria.	Measles	Scarlet fever.
Alabama (April).........	26	408	22	Mississippi (April)......	35	4,041	42
Arkansas (February)....	13	1,736	60	New Jersey (April)......	498	6,701	462
California (April).........	283	3,599	265	Nevada (April)......	2	155	16
Colorado (April).........	62	289	258	North Dakota (April)......	52	69	94
Illinois (April)...........	725	3,337	583	Ohio (April).........	358	2,294	754
Iowa (April)...........	74	....	422	Virginia (March).........	96	4,685	62
Kansas (April)...........	138	2,219	533	Washington (April).......	44	976	133
Maine (April)...........	15	65	22	Wyoming (April).......	17	179	40

City Reports for Week Ended May 18, 1918.

City.	Popula-tion as of July 1, 1916 (estimated by U. S. Census Bureau).	Total deaths from all causes.	Diphtheria.		Measles.		Scarlet fever.		Tuber-culosis.	
			Cases.	Deaths.	Cases.	Deaths.	Cases.	Deaths.	Cases.	Deaths.
Over 500,000 inhabitants:										
Baltimore, Md..........	589,621	242	75	6	306	4	31	....	77	33
Boston, Mass..........	756,476	643	108	12	160	2	53	....	335	54
Chicago, Ill..........	2,497,722	172	11	2	87	....	10	....	63	34
Cleveland, Ohio..........	674,073	196	45	5	113	10	22	....	67	26
Detroit, Mich..........	571,784	141	16	3	80	3	10	1	36	30
Los Angeles, Cal..........	503,812	1,426	264	32	1,121	30	105	6	262	173
New York, N. Y..........	5,602,841	090	7	....	256	....	11	....	19	....
Pittsburgh, Pa..........	579,090	199	57	1	76	....	22	....	56	27
St. Louis, Mo..........	757,309									
From 300,000 to 500,000 inhab-itants:										
Buffalo, N. Y..........	468,558	154	9	1	133	2	10	....	37	24
Cincinnati, Ohio..........	410,476	198	10	....	76	....	4	....	63	11
Milwaukee, Wis..........	438,535	101	7	1	342	4	17	....	20	13
Minneapolis, Minn..........	363,454	....	19	2	98	1	20	1	20	8
Newark, N. J..........	408,894	125	9	1	497	7	10	1	46	14
New Orleans, La..........	371,747	180	23	....	2	2	....	....	20	22
San Francisco, Cal..........	465,516	165	19	4	81	....	....	....	20	21
Seattle, Wash..........	348,639	....	3	....	61	....	26	....	....	....
Washington, D. C..........	363,980	108	13	2	216	2	19	....	34	19

DIPHTHERIA, MEASLES, SCARLET FEVER, AND TUBERCULOSIS—Contd.

City Reports for Week Ended May 18, 1918—Continued.

City.	Population as of July 1, 1916 (estimated by U. S. Census Bureau).	Total deaths from all causes.	Diphtheria.		Measles.		Scarlet fever.		Tuberculosis.	
			Cases.	Deaths.	Cases.	Deaths.	Cases.	Deaths.	Cases.	Deaths.
From 200,000 to 300,000 inhabitants:										
Columbus, Ohio	214,878	64	1	......	16	1	23	1	6	7
Denver, Colo	260,800	62	16	1	24	......	16	......	6	8
Indianapolis, Ind	271,708	......	17	6	28	......	21	......	6	9
Kansas City, Mo	297,874	28	8	......	36	3	8	1	1	10
Louisville, Ky	238,910	73	3	1	8	......	......	......	12	11
Portland, Oreg	295,465	60	2	......	156	1	16	......	15	6
Providence, R. I	254,960	72	9	1	191	4	12	......	......	7
Rochester, N. Y	256,417	58	12	1	116	1	10	......	29	7
From 100,000 to 200,000 inhabitants:										
Atlanta, Ga	190,558	67	2	......	8	......	2	......	11	4
Birmingham, Ala	181,762	72	......	......	8	......	4	......	5	11
Bridgeport, Conn	121,576	18	2	......	13	......	3	......	4	1
Cambridge, Mass	112,921	29	14	......	100	1	2	......	7	4
Dallas, Tex	124,527	5	......	......	7	......	2	......	1	3
Dayton, Ohio	127,244	36	2	......	5	......	2	......	7	6
Des Moines, Iowa	101,598	......	4	......	......	......	19	......	......	......
Fall River, Mass	128,366	34	3	......	5	......	1	......	15	6
Fort Worth, Tex	104,562	21	......	......	......	......	2	......	1	1
Grand Rapids, Mich	128,291	43	3	.1	11	......	8	......	6	4
Hartford, Conn	110,900	26	5	......	5	......	2	......	5	3
Houston, Tex	112,307	35	2	......	10	......	1	......	......	7
Lawrence, Mass	100,560	28	......	......	179	4	......	......	6	3
Lowell, Mass	113,245	37	1	......	21	......	......	......	7	3
Lynn, Mass	102,425	30	4	......	56	......	......	......	6	4
Memphis, Tenn	148,995	43	2	......	15	......	4	......	14	4
Nashville, Tenn	117,057	53	......	......	23	......	1	......	5	9
New Bedford, Mass	118,158	28	......	......	5	......	1	......	6	4
New Haven, Conn	149,685	......	2	......	......	......	......	......	8	2
Oakland, Cal	198,604	46	2	......	12	......	5	......	......	4
Omaha, Nebr	165,170	28	14	......	13	......	22	......	1	1
Reading, Pa	109,381	......	4	......	67	......	2	......	5	......
Richmond, Va	156,687	40	1	......	67	1	1	......	11	5
Salt Lake City, Utah	117,399	24	5	......	23	......	17	1	1	1
Scranton, Pa	146,811	......	3	......	12	......	1	......	7	......
Spokane, Wash	150,323	......	1	......	......	......	4	......	......	......
Springfield, Mass	105,942	28	1	......	47	......	7	......	4	3
Syracuse, N. Y	155,624	......	3	......	73	1	7	......	12	6
Tacoma, Wash	112,770	......	1	......	27	......	32	......	......	......
Toledo, Ohio	191,554	51	1	......	6	......	7	......	19	11
Worcester, Mass	163,314	42	3	......	5	......	10	......	12	2
Youngstown, Ohio	108,385	35	......	......	15	......	2	......	4	4
From 50,000 to 100,000 inhabitants:										
Akron, Ohio	85,625	33	7	1	4	......	8	......	5	......
Allentown, Pa	63,505	......	2	......	27	......	......	......	1	......
Altoona, Pa	58,659	......	3	......	17	......	......	......	1	......
Augusta, Ga	50,245	15	......	......	8	......	......	......	......	......
Bayonne, N. J	69,993	......	1	......	24	......	3	......	4	......
Berkeley, Cal	57,453	11	1	......	4	......	2	......	4	1
Binghamton, N. Y	53,973	10	4	1	42	......	......	......	5	1
Brockton, Mass	67,449	14	......	......	52	......	......	......	3	1
Canton, Ohio	69,852	7	......	......	......	......	2	......	......	1
Charleston, S. C	60,734	36	1	......	......	......	......	1	......	3
Chattanooga, Tenn	60,075	5	......	......	1	......	......	......	......	2
Duluth, Minn	94,495	22	......	......	4	......	3	......	4	2
El Paso, Tex	63,705	50	2	1	8	2	1	......	......	12
Erie, Pa	75,195	......	10	......	141	......	3	......	10	......
Evansville, Ind	76,078	18	......	......	5	......	......	......	......	2
Flint, Mich	54,772	13	......	......	10	......	2	......	4	1
Fort Wayne, Ind	76,183	27	4	......	20	......	......	......	1	......
Harrisburg, Pa	72,015	......	2	......	5	......	1	......	......	......
Hoboken, N. J	77,214	10	2	......	1	1	4	1	2	3
Holyoke, Mass	65,286	10	......	......	1	......	1	......	2	2
Johnstown, Pa	68,029	......	2	......	19	......	5	......	4	......
Kansas City, Kans	99,437	......	......	......	57	......	10	......	1	......
Lancaster, Pa	50,453	......	......	......	10	......	2	......	1	......
Little Rock, Ark	57,443	10	1	......	4	......	2	......	5	......
Malden, Mass	51,155	13	3	3	52	......	1	......	2	2
Manchester, N. H	78,383	22	2	......	29	......	1	......	12	2
Mobile, Ala	58,221	......	1	......	1	......	......	......	1	4

DIPHTHERIA, MEASLES, SCARLET FEVER, AND TUBERCULOSIS—Contd.

City Reports for Week Ended May 18, 1918—Continued.

City.	Population as of July 1, 1916 (estimated by U. S. Census Bureau).	Total deaths from all causes.	Diphtheria.		Measles.		Scarlet fever.		Tuberculosis.	
			Cases.	Deaths.	Cases.	Deaths.	Cases.	Deaths.	Cases.	Deaths.
From 50,000 to 100,000 inhabitants—Continued.										
Norfolk, Va...	80,612				14		2			6
Oklahoma City, Okla...	92,943	18					1			3
Passaic, N. J...	71,744	14	3		60				2	1
Peoria, Ill...	71,458	22	2		11		1			4
Portland, Me...	63,867	15			2		3			2
Rockford, Ill...	55,185	19			24				5	2
Sacramento, Cal...	66,805	35	5	1	18		4		7	5
Saginaw, Mich...	55,642	19			1					1
St. Joseph, Mo...	85,236	34								
San Diego, Cal...	53,330	23	1		8		1		6	5
Savannah, Ga...	68,805	35					1		1	3
Schenectady, N. Y...	99,519	19			28		1		5	2
Sioux City, Iowa...	57,078						4			
Somerville, Mass...	87,039	21	6		60		4		4	
South Bend, Ind...	68,946	15			1				2	2
Springfield, Ill...	61,120	15			18		1		1	
Springfield, Ohio...	51,550	8	2	1	9				2	
Terre Haute, Ind...	66,093	27	3		4		1		2	5
Troy, N. Y...	77,916	21			1		1		6	1
Utica, N. Y...	85,692	29			70		3		6	4
Wichita, Kans...	70,722		1		8		1		3	
Wilkes-Barre, Pa...	76,776		3		30		2		4	
Yonkers, N. Y...	99,838	23	4		114		1			4
York, Pa...	51,656				17		2			
From 25,000 to 50,000 inhabitants:										
Alameda, Cal...	27,732	4	1		32				1	
Auburn, N. Y...	37,385	7	2		36		1		3	
Austin, Tex...	34,814	20								5
Beaumont, Tex...	27,711	21								4
Boise, Idaho...	33,846	3			4		1		1	
Brookline, Mass...	32,730	6	1		20				1	
Butler, Pa...	27,632		3		3					
Butte, Mont...	43,425		1				1			
Cedar Rapids, Iowa...	37,308						4			
Central Falls, R. I...	25,646				2		1			
Charleston, W. Va...	29,941	7			5					
Charlotte, N. C...	39,823		3		6		2		1	
Chelsea, Mass...	46,192	17	4		13		1		4	2
Chester, Pa...	41,396				15		1		5	
Clinton, Iowa...	27,386		1		27					
Cohoes, N. Y...	25,211	5			2				2	
Colorado Springs, Colo...	32,971	11	2		5		1		4	3
Columbia, S. C...	34,611		1		4					
Council Bluffs, Iowa...	31,484	11			8		2	1	2	
Cranston, R. I...	25,987	5			5				2	1
Danville, Ill...	32,261	11							1	1
Davenport, Iowa...	48,811		1		1		5			
Dubuque, Iowa...	39,873						1			
Durham, N. C...	25,061	6			5				2	
Easton, Pa...	30,540				8					
East Orange, N. J...	42,458	8			61				4	2
Elgin, Ill...	28,233	3			1					
Elmira, N. Y...	38,120				23				4	1
Evanston, Ill...	28,591	8								
Everett, Mass...	39,243	8	5		9				3	3
Fitchburg, Mass...	41,781	6			31				2	2
Fresno, Cal...	34,059	5			6		1		1	
Galveston, Tex...	41,863	12			1					2
Green Bay, Wis...	29,353				4		1			
Hammond, Ind...	26,171	11		2			1		1	1
Hazleton, Pa...	28,491				36					
Jackson, Mich...	35,396	16	1		19		14	1	1	1
Joplin, Mo...	35,216	8			6		1		5	
Kalamazoo, Mich...	48,486	12			3				2	
Kenosha, Wis...	31,576	6	1		15					
Knoxville, Tenn...	38,676		1		3				5	5
La Crosse, Wis...	31,677	12		1					1	
Lima, Ohio...	35,244	14	1		1		4			3
Lincoln, Nebr...	46,515	12			3		3			
Long Beach, Cal...	27,587	8			16		3			
Lorain, Ohio...	34,948		2				1		1	

PHTHERIA, MEASLES, SCARLET FEVER, AND TUBERCULOSIS—Contd.

City Reports for Week Ended May 18, 1918—Continued.

City.	Population as of July 1, 1916 (estimated by U.S. Census Bureau).	Total deaths from all causes.	Diphtheria.		Measles.		Scarlet fever.		Tuberculosis.	
			Cases.	Deaths.	Cases.	Deaths.	Cases.	Deaths.	Cases.	Deaths.
n 25,000 to 50,000 inhabitants—Continued.										
Macon, Ga	45,757	18			1				2	3
Madison, Wis	30,699	12	1		16		8		4	1
McKeesport, Pa	47,521				21		2			
Moline, Ill	27,451	12			45	1	1	1		
Montclair, N. J	26,318	5	1		7				3	
Montgomery, Ala	43,285	13			1				1	
Mount Vernon, N. Y	37,009	7	1		20				2	
Muncie, Ind	25,424	5	2	1					1	1
Muskogee, Okla	44,210		1		4		1			
Nashua, N. H	27,327	6	1							
Newark, Ohio	29,635	5			2					
Newburgh, N. Y	29,603	6			2		1		1	
New Castle, Pa	41,133		1		12		1			
Newport, Ky	31,927	9					1		1	1
Newport, R. I	30,108	11	1				3	1	1	
New Rochelle, N. Y	37,759	9	1		21				1	
Niagara Falls, N. Y	37,353	14	3		3					2
Norristown, Pa	31,401				6		1		6	
Norwalk, Conn	26,899		1						5	2
Oak Park, Ill	26,654	5	1	1	17		1			
Ogden, Utah	31,404	14			23		3			
Orange, N. J	33,080	13			46		1		1	1
Oshkosh, Wis	36,065	7							1	1
Pasadena, Cal	46,450	18			30		3		3	4
Perth Amboy, N. J	41,185	8								
Petersburg, Va	25,582	8					1		2	1
Pittsfield, Mass	38,629	14			7		3		2	1
Poughkeepsie, N. Y	30,390	7			37				2	1
Quincy, Ill	36,798	9			10		1			1
Quincy, Mass	38,136	3	1		42		2		3	
Racine, Wis	46,498	14			30	1	3	1		3
Roanoke, Va	43,284	17			32				2	2
Rock Island, Ill	28,926	4	1		21		2			
Salem, Mass	48,562	7			49				3	
San Jose, Cal	38,972				12		2		1	
Sheboygan, Wis	28,559	9	1				1		1	1
Springfield, Mo	40,341	15					1			1
Steubenville, Ohio	27,445	12	2				1			
Stockton, Cal	35,358	13			2		1			
Superior, Wis	40,266	11					4			
Taunton, Mass	36,283	10	1		2				3	1
Topeka, Kans	48,726		1		12		13		1	
Waco, Tex	33,385	19			1				1	
Walla Walla, Wash	25,136				1					
Warwick, R. I	29,999						1			
Waterloo, Iowa	35,559	18			2		2			3
Watertown, N. Y	29,804	3								3
West Hoboken, N. J	43,139	5			10				3	2
Wheeling, W. Va	43,377	9			6		2	1		
Williamsport, Pa	33,809		3				1		18	
Wilmington, N. C	29,892	9			5				1	
Winston-Salem, N. C	31,155	18			3				1	5
Zanesville, Ohio	30,863	6								
n 10,000 to 25,000 inhabitants:										
Albuquerque, N. Mex	14,025	9			3					8
Alexandria, La	15,333	3							2	
Alton, Ill	22,874	7								1
Anniston, Ala	14,112								8	
Appleton, Wis	17,834	7			2		2			
Asbury Park, N. J	14,007	4			3					
Ashtabula, Ohio	21,498	3								
Attleboro, Mass	19,282	6			4					
Bakersfield, Cal	16,874	8			1					1
Barberton, Ohio	13,210			1						
Barre, Vt	12,199		2				1			
Batavia, N. Y	12,350	1			4		1			
Beatrice, Nebr	10,297	9					2			
Bedford, Ind	10,349	3								
Bellaire, Ohio	14,348	3			7					
Beloit, Wis	15,072	8	3		24	1	2			
Bethlehem, Pa	14,142		1		36				1	

DIPHTHERIA, MEASLES, SCARLET FEVER, AND TUBERCULOSIS—Contd.

City Reports for Week Ended May 18, 1918—Continued.

City.	Population as of July 1, 1916 (estimated by U. S. Census Bureau).	Total deaths from all causes.	Diphtheria.		Measles.		Scarlet fever.		Tuberculosis.	
			Cases.	Deaths.	Cases.	Deaths.	Cases.	Deaths.	Cases.	Deaths.
From 10,000 to 25,000 inhabitants—Continued.										
Beverly, Mass.		4			2					
Billings, Mont.	14,422				7					
Bloomfield, N. J.	18,966				3					
Bloomington, Ind.	11,383		1				1		3	1
Braddock, Pa.	21,985		1	1	11					
Bristol, Conn.		3					2			
Burlington, Vt.		9					1			2
Canton, Ill.	13,362	3			12					
Cape Girardeau, Mo.	10,775		1							
Carbondale, Pa.	19,242				1					
Carlisle, Pa.			1		2					
Chanute, Kans.	12,445				9					
Cheyenne, Wyo.	¹11,320						7			
Coatesville, Pa.	14,455				4					
Coffeyville, Kans.	17,518				2		5		1	
Concord, N. H.	²22,069	7	1							
Connellsville, Pa.	15,455				3		1			
Corning, N. Y.	15,406	5								
Corpus Christi, Tex.	10,432	5	1							
Cortland, N. Y.	13,069	1			2				1	
Dedham, Mass.	10,433		1							
Dover, N. H.	13,272	3			2		1			
Dunkirk, N. Y.	20,743	6							1	1
Dunmore, Pa.	20,776		1		2		2			
East Liverpool, Ohio	23,586	6					2			4
East Providence, R. I.	18,113		1		1		1			
Elwood, Ind.	¹11,028	4	1		1					
Elyria, Ohio	18,618	8	1		4					
Englewood, N. J.	12,231	2			20					
Escanaba, Mich.	15,485						1		1	
Eugene, Oreg.	13,572				7					
Eureka, Cal.	14,684	2								
Fairmount, W. Va.	15,506				1					
Fargo, N. Dak.	17,389	3	2							
Farrell, Pa.	¹10,190				2					
Findlay, Ohio	¹14,588		1		62		1		2	1
Fort Dodge, Iowa	20,618	2	2				4			
Fort Scott, Kans.	10,550	6							1	
Fostoria, Ohio	10,770	2								
Framingham, Mass.	13,982	4			5				2	1
Frederick, Md.	11,112	2			6				1	
Fremont, Ohio	10,882				5					
Fulton, N. Y.	11,498	4			22				2	
Galesburg, Ill.	24,276	10			8					
Geneva, N. Y.	13,711	5			21				3	
Glens Falls, N. Y.	16,894	5			3					
Granite City, Ill.	15,142	2	1		5					
Greeley, Colo.	11,420		3		1		3			
Greenfield, Mass.	11,998	5			1				1	
Greenville, S. C.	18,181	3								
Greenwich, Conn.	19,159				14					
Hackensack, N. J.	16,945	5			11				2	1
Hancock, Mich.	12,079				2		2		2	
Harrison, N. J.	16,520		2		16					
Hattiesburg, Miss.	16,482	2							2	1
Henderson, Ky.	12,162	7								3
Holland, Mich.	12,183				1				1	1
Hoquiam, Wash.	11,602						3			
Hornell, N. Y.	14,685				8					
Independence, Kans.	14,566	6			2					
Independence, Mo.	11,672	7	1		5		4		2	1
Iola, Kans.	11,998				1					
Irvington, N. J.	16,613	7			16				1	
Ithaca, N. Y.	15,888	5			3				1	
Janesville, Wis.	14,542	6	2	1			5			1
Johnstown, N. Y.	10,016	2			1					
Kearny, N. J.	23,559	7	1		22				3	1
Keokuk, Iowa	14,008				7		2			
Kokomo, Ind.	20,940	7			3		1			
Lackawanna, N. Y.	15,987	8			1					1

¹ Population Apr. 15, 1910, no estimate made.

DIPHTHERIA, MEASLES, SCARLET FEVER, AND TUBERCULOSIS—Contd.

City Reports for Week Ended May 18, 1918—Continued.

City.	Population as of July 1, 1916 (estimated by U. S. Census Bureau).	Total deaths from all causes.	Diphtheria.		Measles.		Scarlet fever.		Tuberculosis.	
			Cases.	Deaths.	Cases.	Deaths.	Cases.	Deaths.	Cases.	Deaths.
From 10,000 to 25,000 inhabitants—Continued.										
Lafayette, Ind	21,286	3								
Lancaster, Ohio	15,670				5		8			
Laurel, Miss	11,779	3								
Leavenworth, Kans	1 19,363	6			2		3		1	
Lebanon, Pa	20,779		2		1		7			
Little Falls, N. Y	13,451	2								
Long Branch, N. J	15,395	5			31					1
Ludington, Mich	10,367	2								
Manitowoc, Wis	13,805	4					2		2	1
Mansfield, Ohio	22,734		2		18					
Marinette, Wis	1 14,610	3			2		1			
Marion, Ind	19,834	1							1	
Marlboro, Mass	15,187	4							1	1
Marquette, Mich	12,409	9					4			
Marshall, Tex	13,712	4							2	
Massillon, Ohio	15,310				1					
Melrose, Mass	17,445	5					1		1	
Michigan City, Ind	21,512				3				3	3
Middletown, N. Y	15,810				3				1	
Middletown, Ohio	15,625	4			10					
Mishawaka, Ind	16,385	6			1				1	
Missoula, Mont	18,214	11	8							
Monessen, Pa	21,630		1		6		2		1	
Morgantown, W. Va	13,709	2			2					
Morristown, N. J	13,284	2			14					
Moundsville, W. Va	11,153	2							1	1
Mount Carmel, Pa	20,208		1						1	
Muscatine, Iowa	17,500				1					
Nanticoke, Pa	23,126								5	
Natick, Mass	10,102	3	2		29				1	1
New Albany, Ind	23,629	6			1					
New London, Conn	20,985	12	1		3		4		2	2
North Adams, Mass	1 22,019	11		1					1	2
Northampton, Mass	19,926	9			3				2	2
North Att'eboro, Mass	11,014	3	1		11		1			
North Braddock, Pa	15,148				3		1			
North Litt'e Rock, Ark	14,907	2			2				2	1
North Yakima, Wash	20,951				11					
Norwood, Ohio	22,286	3			3		1		2	
Ogdensburg, N. Y	16,718	9							2	
Oil City, Pa	19,297				4				5	
Olean, N. Y	16,624	4								1
Ossining, N. Y	13,705		1	1	31					
Oswego, N. Y	24,101	11			3				2	3
Palestine, Tex	11,845	3			2				5	3
Parkersburg, W. Va	20,612	7							1	1
Peabody, Mass	18,360	4	1		1				3	
Peekskill, N. Y	18,530	5				2				
Phoenixville, Pa	11,714				1					
Pine Bluff, Ark	17,477						1			
Piqua, Ohio	14,152	3			1		1			
Pittston, Pa	18,599		1		3					
Plainfield, N. J	23,905	5	2		13				2	1
Plattsburg, N. Y	12,837	1								
Pocatello, Idaho	12,293				1					
Pomona, Cal	13,150	6			9		1			
Pontiac, Mich	17,534	3	1		9				1	1
Port Chester, N. Y	16,183	2			15		2		1	
Portsmouth, N. H	11,666	1								
Pottstown, Pa	16,794		3							
Pottsville, Pa	22,372				2					
Rahway, N. J	10,219				3					
Raleigh, N. C	20,127	13			6				1	1
Red Lands, Cal	14,000	2			5				1	
Reno, Nev	14,389	9								
Richmond, Ind	24,697	7	2		1		1			
Riverside, Cal	19,763	3			5					2
Rocky Mount, N. C	12,067	4			1					
Rutland, Vt	14,831	6					2			
St. Cloud, Minn	11,817	7					3			
Sandusky, Ohio	20,193	6			2				1	1

1 Population Apr. 15, 1910; no estimate made.

DIPHTHERIA, MEASLES, SCARLET FEVER, AND TUBERCULOSIS—Contd.

City Reports for Week Ended May 18, 1918—Continued.

City.	Popula-tion as of July 1, 1916 (estimated by U. S. Census Bureau).	Total deaths from all causes.	Diphtheria.		Measles.		Scarlet fever.		Tuber-culosis.	
			Cases.	Deaths.	Cases.	Deaths.	Cases.	Deaths.	Cases.	Deaths.
From 10,000 to 25,000 inhabit-ants—Continued.										
Sanford, Me.	10,916	5								1
Santa Ana, Cal.	10,627	6			14		1			
Santa Barbara, Cal.	14,846	7								
Santa Cruz, Cal.	14,594	1								
Saratoga Springs, N. Y.	13,821	8			9				4	
Shamokin, Pa.	21,129		2		1					
Sharon, Pa.	18,618		1		22		1			
Sioux Falls, S. Dak.	16,499	2			1		1			
Southbridge, Mass.	14,205	3								
Spartanburg, S. C.	21,395	4	1		7				1	1
Steelton, Pa.	15,548				1				1	
Sunbury, Pa.	16,260				2		1			
Tiffin, Ohio.	12,867	10								1
Trinidad, Colo.	13,875				1		1			
Tuscaloosa, Ala.	10,488	4	1						1	
Uniontown, Pa.	20,780				3					
Vallejo, Cal.	43,161	2								
Vancouver, Wash.	13,180				5					
Wakefield, Mass.	12,733				2		1		2	
Warren, Ohio.	13,059	8	1		5					
Washington, Pa.	21,618				3					
Watertown, Mass.	14,867	4			5					
Wausau, Wis.	19,239	2					3	1		1
West Chester, Pa.	13,176				5					
Westfield, Mass.	18,391	2	2		16				1	
West Orange, N. J.	13,550	3			25					
West Springfield, Mass.	10,555	1			5				2	
West Warwick, R. I.	15,782	8	1		2				1	1
White Plains, N. Y.	22,465		1		1		2	1	2	1
Wilkinsburg, Pa.	23,228				4		2		1	
Winchester, Mass.	10,603	3			2				1	
Winona, Minn.	18,583	8								
Woburn, Mass.	15,469	6								

[1] Population Apr. 15, 1910; no estimate made.

FOREIGN.

CHOLERA, PLAGUE, SMALLPOX, TYPHUS FEVER, AND YELLOW FEVER.
Reports Received During Week Ended June 7, 1918.[1]

CHOLERA.

Place.	Date.	Cases.	Deaths.	Remarks.
India:				
Bombay	Feb. 24–Mar. 9....	3	4	
Calcutta	Mar. 3–16		102	
Madras	Mar. 10–16	3	2	
Rangoon	Mar. 3–16	4	3	
Java:				
Cheribon	May 6–29			Present.
Philippine Islands:				
Provinces				Apr. 7–13, 1918: Cases, 31; deaths,
Bohol	Apr. 7–13	18	10	15.
Davao	....do	2	2	
Surigao	....do	11	3	

PLAGUE.

Place.	Date.	Cases.	Deaths.	Remarks.
Ceylon:				
Colombo	Feb. 13–Mar. 9....	12	11	
India				Feb. 24–Mar. 9, 1918: Cases,
Bassein	Feb. 24–Mar. 16...		82	79,572; deaths, 64,170.
Bombay	Feb. 24–Mar. 9...	88	71	
Henzada	Feb. 24–Mar. 16...		46	
Karachi	Mar. 8–14	46	38	
Madras Presidency	Mar. 10–16	567	421	
Mandalay	Feb. 17–Mar. 16...		284	
Moulmein	Feb. 24–Mar. 16...		73	
Myingyan	....do		84	
Pegu	....do		3	
Rangoon	Mar. 3–16	256	239	
Toungoo	Feb. 24–Mar. 16...		37	

SMALLPOX.

Place.	Date.	Cases.	Deaths.	Remarks.
Canada:				
New Brunswick—				
St. John	May 19–25	7		
Nova Scotia—				
Halifax	May 12–18	3		
China:				
Chungking	Mar. 26–Apr. 6			Present.
Dairen	Apr. 6–13	8	1	
Tientsin	Apr. 6–20	4		
Egypt:				
Alexandria	Apr. 9–15	1		
France:				
Paris	Apr. 7–13	2	1	
Rouen	Apr. 21–27	5	2	Including varioloid.
India:				
Bombay	Feb. 24–Mar. 9....	393	175	
Calcutta	Mar. 3–16		21	
Karachi	Mar. 8–14	25	14	
Madras	Mar. 10–16	14	5	
Rangoon	Mar. 3–16	17	8	
Italy:				
Turin	Mar. 8–Apr. 7.....	24	4	
Japan:				
Nagasaki	Apr. 15–28	4	1	
Nagoya	Mar. 24–30	1		
Taihoku	Mar. 26–Apr. 22...	27	13	Island of Taiwan.
Tokyo	Apr. 15–May 4.....	14		
Philippine Islands:				
Manila	Apr. 7–20	117	48	Varioloid, 94 cases; 4 deaths.

[1] From medical officers of the Public Health Service, American consuls, and other sources.

CHOLERA, PLAGUE, SMALLPOX, TYPHUS FEVER, AND YELLOW FEVER—Continued.

Reports Received During Week Ended June 7, 1918—Continued.

TYPHUS FEVER.

Place.	Date.	Cases.	Deaths.	Remarks.
Austria-Hungary:				
Hungary...............				Nov. 26, 1917–Jan. 20, 1918: Ca---
Budapest.............	Nov. 26–Jan. 20...	2	....	16; deaths, 2.
Egypt:				
Alexandria.................	Apr. 2–22...........	562	124	
Germany..............				Dec. 23, 1917–Feb. 23, 1914: Ca-
Breslau District............	Feb. 3–23...........	4	....	112; deaths, 9.
Königsberg District........	....do...........	1		Prisoner of war.
Lorraine...................				Dec. 23, 1917–Feb. 23, 1918 C-
Metz..................	Dec. 23–Feb. 2....	17	3	77; deaths, 4. Of the-, 5-.--
Posen District............	Feb. 3–23..........	7	....	1 death, in workmen's --- at Pontingen and Werni.. :
Great Britain:				
Dublin....................	Apr. 21–27........	1	....	
Glasgow..................	Apr. 21–May 4.....	2	....	
Greece:				
Saloniki.................	Mar. 17–Apr. 6....	....	15	
Italy:				
Bagnasco...................	Mar. 18–Apr. 7....	4	....	Province of Cuneo.
Japan:				
Nagasaki..................	Apr. 15–21.........	1	2	

Reports Received from Dec. 29, 1917, to May 31, 1918.

CHOLERA.

Place.	Date.	Cases.	Deaths.	Remarks.
China:				
Antung....................	Nov. 26–Dec. 2....	3	1	
India:				
Bombay....................	Oct. 28–Dec. 15....	19	14	
Do.................	Dec. 30–Feb. 23....	216	190	
Calcutta.................	Sept. 16–Dec. 15...		135	
Do.................	Dec. 30–Feb. 23...		53	
Karachi....................	....do.........	25	6	
Madras...................	Nov. 25–Dec. 22...	2	2	
Do.................	Dec. 30–Mar. 9....	44	24	
Rangoon..................	Nov. 4 Dec. 22....	5	5	
Do.................	Dec. 30–Mar. 2....	7	3	
Indo-China:				
Provinces..................		....	....	Sept. 1–Dec. 31, 1917: Cases, 168.
Anam..................	Sept. 1–Dec. 31....	21	15	deaths, 95.
Cambodia..............	....do.........	74	54	
Cochin-China..........	....do.........	58	24	
Saigon................	Nov. 22–Dec. 9....	4	3	
Do..........	Feb. 4–Mar. 11....	8	3	
Kwang-Chow-Wan.....	Sept. 1–30.........	10	2	
Java:				
East Java..................	Oct. 28–Nov. 3....	1	1	
West Java.				Oct. 19–Dec. 27, 1917: Cases, 102;
Batavia..............	Oct. 10 Dec. 27....	49	23	deaths, 56. Dec. 28, 1917–Feb.
Do.................	Dec. 28–Feb. 21...	35	1	21, 1918 Cases, 38, deaths, 7.
Palestine..................				Dec. 28, 1917–Feb. 5, 1918: Cases,
Deir Seneid..............	Dec 28 Jan. 31....	13	....	31. Occurring at 7 localities 2
Sukkarieh.................	....do.........	13		cases in encampments.
Persia....................				July 30–Sept. 3, 1917: Cases, 334;
Achraf	July 30 Aug. 16...	90	88	deaths, 270.
Astrabad.............	July 31..........			Present.
Barfresh................	July 1–Aug. 16....	39	25	
Chahmurzad				25 cases reported July 31, 1917.
Chahra tagh.............	June 15 July 25...	10	8	
Chroud	Aug. 26 Sept. 3...	4	2	
Damghan................	Aug. 26.........			Present.
Khareh................	May 28 June 11...	21	13	
Meched...............	Aug. 18 Sept. 2...	174	82	
Ouzein Dare.............	Aug. 9.........			Do.
Sabzevar................	Aug 24.........			Do.
Sari	July 3 29.......	273	144	
Semnan..................	Aug 31 Sept. 2...	14	5	
Yekchambe Bazar.........	June 3...........	6	....	

CHOLERA, PLAGUE, SMALLPOX, TYPHUS FEVER, AND YELLOW FEVER—Continued.

Reports Received from Dec. 29, 1917, to May 31, 1918—Continued.

CHOLERA—Continued.

Place.	Date.	Cases.	Deaths.	Remarks.
Philippine Islands:				July 1–Dec. 29, 1917: Cases, 5,964; deaths, 3,655. Dec. 30, 1917–Apr. 6, 1918: Cases, 1,760, deaths, 1,270.
Provinces				
Antique	Nov. 18–Dec. 1	48	32	
Do	Feb. 3–9	4	4	
Bohol	Nov. 18–Dec. 29	169	111	
Do	Dec. 30–Apr. 6	549	436	
Capiz	Nov. 25–Dec. 29	27	21	
Do	Dec. 30–Mar. 23	219	182	
Cebu	Dec. 23–29	3		
Do	Dec. 30–Mar. 30	100	54	
Davao	Mar. 10–16	10	8	
Iloilo	Nov. 25–Dec. 29	179	135	
Do	Dec. 30–Mar. 2	97	63	
Leyte	Nov. 25–Dec. 22	13	12	
Do	Feb. 3–Mar. 16	50	38	
Mindanao	Nov. 25–Dec. 29	337	196	
Do	Dec. 30–Feb. 9	341	220	
Misamis	Feb. 24–Apr. 6	154	98	
Occidental Negros	Nov. 25–Dec. 22	177	123	
Do	Jan. 13–Apr. 6	146	88	
Oriental Negros	Nov. 25–Dec. 29	99	62	
Do	Dec. 30–Mar. 30	23	15	
Romblon	Nov. 25–Dec. 1	1	1	
Surigao	Feb. 24–Apr. 6	32	35	
Zamboanga	do	35	29	
Russia:				
Tashkentnine	May 13			Present.
Tzaritsin	do			Do.
Siam:				
Bangkok	Sept. 16–22	1	1	
Turkey in Asia:				
Bagdad	Nov. 1–15		40	

PLAGUE.

Place.	Date.	Cases.	Deaths.	Remarks.
Brazil:				
Bahia	Nov. 4–Dec. 15	4	4	
Do	Dec. 30–Feb. 23	4	3	
Rio de Janeiro	Dec. 23–29	1		
Do	Jan. 6–12	1	1	
British East Africa:				
Mombassa	Oct. 1–Dec. 31	31	18	
British Gold Coast:				
Axim	Jan. 8			Present.
Ceylon:				
Colombo	Oct. 14–Dec. 1	14	13	
Do	Dec. 30–Feb. 16	20	17	
China				Present in North China in January, 1918; pneumonic form.
Anhwei Province—				
Fengyanghsien	Feb. 27		9	Pneumonic.
Pengpu	do		1	Do.
Chili Province—				
Kalgan				Vicinity. Present in February 1918.
Fukien Province—				
Amoy	Mar. 11–31			Present in vicinity.
Kiangsu Province—				
Nanking	Mar. 17–Apr. 5	19	15	
Shanshi Province				Present in February, 1918; 116 cases estimated.
Ecuador:				
Babahoyo	Feb. 1–15	1		
Duran	Feb. 16–Mar. 30	2	1	
Guayaquil	Sept. 1–Nov. 30	66	24	Reported outbreak occurring about Jan. 17, 1918.
Do	Feb. 1–15	44	18	
Do	Mar. 1–30	37	14	
Egypt				Jan. 1–Nov. 15, 1917: Cases, 728; deaths, 396.
Alexandria	Jan. 14–28	1	2	
Cairo	Dec. 17–23	2		
Port Said	July 2–Dec. 23	13	7	
Suez	July 2–Oct. 20	62	38	
Hawaii:				
Leupahoehoe	May 5	1	1	

CHOLERA, PLAGUE, SMALLPOX, TYPHUS FEVER, AND YELLOW FEVER—Continued.

Reports Received from Dec. 29, 1917, to May 31, 1918—Continued.

PLAGUE—Continued.

Place.	Date.	Cases.	Deaths.	Remarks.
India....				July 1–Dec. 29, 1917: Cases 240,258; deaths, 212,022 — 30, 1917–Feb. 23, 1918 Cases 276,768; deaths, 221,855.
Bussein....	Dec. 9–29....		8	
Do....	Dec. 30–Feb. 23..		99	
Bombay....	Oct. 28–Dec. 29....	147	123	
Do....	Dec. 30–Feb. 23...	187	142	
Calcutta....	Sept. 16–29....		2	
Do....	Dec. 30–Feb. 2....		4	
Henzada....	Oct. 21–27....		1	
Do....	Jan. 5–Feb. 23....		71	
Karachi....	Oct. 21–Dec. 29....	27	20	
Do....	Dec. 30–Mar. 2....	48	34	
Madras....	Feb. 3–Mar. 9....	3	3	
Madras Presidency....	Oct. 31–Nov. 24..	5,746	4,519	
Do....	Jan. 6–Mar. 9....	11,082	8,591	
Mandalay....	Oct. 14–Nov. 17...		89	
Do....	Dec. 30–Feb. 16..		781	
Moulmein....	Feb. 17–23...		1	
Myingyan....	Dec. 30–Feb. 16..		407	
Pegu....	Feb. 10–23....		2	
Prome....	Jan. 5–12....		1	
Rangoon....	Oct. 21–Dec. 22..		56	
Do....	Dec. 30–Mar. 2....	441	400	
Toungoo....	Dec. 9–29....		5	
Do....	Dec. 30–Feb. 23..		32	
Indo-China:				
Provinces....				Sept 1–Dec. 31, 1917: Cases, 173 deaths, 128.
Anam....	Sept. 1–Dec. 31...	45	28	
Cambodia....	....do....	95	83	
Cochin-China....	....do....	31	17	
Saigon....	Oct 31 Dec. 23...	17	6	
Do....	Dec. 31–Mar. 31..	140	74	
Java:				
East Java....				Oct 8–Dec 31, 1917: Cases, 19 deaths, 193.
Do....				Jan 1–Feb 4, 1918: Cases, 6 deaths, 91.
Residences—				
Kediri....	Oct. 8–Dec 31...	1	1	
Madioen....	....do....	49	49	
Samarang....	....do....	110	109	
Surabaya....	....do....	23	23	
Do....	Jan. 15–Feb. 4....	17	17	
Surakarta....	Oct. 8–Dec. 31....	11	11	
West Java....				Nov. 25–Dec. 9, 1917: Cases, 47 deaths, 45 Dec 1, 1917 Jan 15, 1918: Cases, 105.
Peru:				
Ancachs Department—				
Casma....	Dec. 1–Jan. 15....	2		
Lambayeque Department.	....do....	22		At Chiclayo, Ferrenafe, Jayanca, Lambayeque.
Libertad Department....	....do....	72		At Guadalupe, Mansiche, Laredo, Salaverry, San Jose San Pedro, and country district of Trujillo.
Lima Department....	....do....	9		City and country.
Piura Department—				
Catacaos....	....do....	1		
Senegal:				
St. Louis....	Feb. 2...			Present.
Siam:				
Bangkok....	Sept 16 Dec 23...	13	9	
Do....	Jan. 13–Mar. 16...	37	27	
Straits Settlements.				
Singapore....	Oct. 28–Dec. 29...	5	7	
Do....	Jan. 6–Mar. 9....	64	57	

SMALLPOX.

Place.	Date.	Cases.	Deaths.	Remarks.
Algeria:				
Algiers....	Nov 1–Dec 31....	3	2	
Do....	Jan 1–Apr 23....	249	6	
Australia:				
New South Wales....				July 12–Dec. 20, 1917: Cases, 38 Jan. 4–17, 1918: Case, 1.
Aberdeen....	Oct 25 Nov 29...	3		
Cessnock....	July 12 Oct. 11...	7		Newcastle district.

CHOLERA, PLAGUE, SMALLPOX, TYPHUS FEVER, AND YELLOW-FEVER—Continued.

Reports Received from Dec. 29, 1917, to May 31, 1918—Continued.

SMALLPOX—Continued.

Place.	Date.	Cases.	Deaths.	Remarks.
Australia—Continued.				
New South Wales—Contd.				
Eumangla	Aug. 15	1		
Kurri Kurri	Dec. 5–20	2		
Mungindi	Aug. 13	1		
Warren	July 12–Oct. 25	22		
Do	Jan. 1–17	1		
Brazil:				
Bahia	Nov. 10–Dec. 8	3		
Pernambuco	Nov. 1–15	1		
Rio de Janeiro	Sept. 30–Dec. 29	703	190	
Do	Dec. 30–Mar. 23	251	84	
Sao Paulo	Oct. 29–Nov. 4		2	
British East Africa:				
Mombasa	Oct. 1–Dec. 31	9	5	
Canada:				
British Columbia—				
Vancouver	Jan. 13–Mar. 9	5		
Victoria	Jan. 7–Feb. 2	2		
Winnipeg	Dec. 30–Apr. 13	4		
New Brunswick—				
Kent County	Dec. 4			Outbreak. On main line Canadian Ry., 25 miles north of Moncton.
Do	Jan. 22	40		In 7 localities.
Northumberland County.	...do	41		In 5 localities.
Restigouche County	Jan. 18	60		
St. John County—				
St. John	Mar. 3–May 11	20		May 13, 1918: Cases present, 14.
Victoria County	Jan. 2	10		At Limestone and a lumber camp.
Westmoreland County—				
Moncton	Jan. 29–Apr. 27	20		
York County	Jan. 22	8		
Nova Scotia—				
Cape Sable Island				Present May 8 at Clarks Harbor.
Halifax	Feb. 24–May 11	19		
Sydney	Feb. 3–May 11	20		
Ontario—				
Arnprior	Mar. 31–Apr. 6		1	
Hamilton	Dec. 16–22	1		
Do	Jan. 13–19	2		
Ottawa	Mar. 4–24	5		
Sarnia	Dec. 9–15	1		
Do	Jan. 6–May 18	34		
Toronto	Feb. 10–Apr. 6	2		
Windsor	Dec. 30–Jan. 5	1		
Prince Edward Island—				
Charlottetown	Feb. 7–13	1		
Quebec—				
Montreal	Dec. 16–Jan. 5	5		
Do	Jan. 6–Apr. 6	12		
Quebec	Apr. 21–May 11	3		
China:				
Amoy	Oct. 22–Dec. 30			Present.
Do	Dec. 31–Mar. 31			Do.
Antung	Dec. 2–23	13	2	
Do	Jan. 7–Apr. 6	13	3	
Changsha	Jan. 28–Mar. 10	6	1	
Chefoo	Jan. 27–Feb. 9			Do.
Chungking	Nov. 11–Dec. 29			Do.
Do	Dec. 30–Mar. 16			Do.
Dairen	Nov. 18–Dec. 22	3	1	
Do	Dec. 30–Apr. 6	64	5	
Hankow	Feb. 25–Mar. 3	1		
Harbin	May 14–June 30	20		Chinese Eastern Ry.
Do	July 1–Dec. 2	7		Do.
Hongkong	Dec. 23–29	1		
Do	Jan. 26–Mar. 30	19	9	
Hungtahotze Station	Oct. 28–Nov. 4	1		Do.
Manchuria Station	May 14–June 30	6		Do.
Do	July 1–Dec. 2	3		Do.
Mukden	Nov. 11–24			Present.
Do	Feb. 10–Mar. 30			Do.
Nanking	Feb. 3–Apr. 6			Do.

CHOLERA, PLAGUE, SMALLPOX, TYPHUS FEVER, AND YELLOW FEVER—Continued.

Reports Received from Dec. 29, 1917, to May 31, 1918—Continued.

SMALLPOX—Continued.

Place.	Date.	Cases.	Deaths.	Remarks.
China—Continued.				
Shanghai	Nov. 18–Dec. 23	41	91	Cases, foreign; deaths among natives.
Do	Dec. 31–Apr. 1	38	119	Do.
Swatow	Jan. 18			Unusually prevalent.
Tientsin	Nov. 11–Dec. 22	13		
Do	Dec. 30–Apr. 6	46		
Tsingtau	Feb. 4–Mar. 31	10	2	
Cuba:				
Habana	Jan. 7	1		Nov. 8, 1917: 1 case from Coruna; Dec. 5, 1917, 1 case
Marianao	Jan. 8	1		6 miles distant from Habana.
Ecuador:				
Guayaquil	Sept. 1–Nov. 30	26	2	
Do	Feb. 1–Mar. 31	4	3	
Egypt:				
Alexandria	Nov. 12–18	2	1	
Do	Jan. 8–Mar. 25	10		
Cairo	July 23–Nov. 18	6	1	
France:				
Lyon	Nov. 18–Dec. 16	6	3	
Do	Jan. 7–Feb. 17	11	2	
Marseille	Jan. 1–31		2	
Paris	Jan. 27–Apr. 6	9	4	
Rouen	Mar. 31–Apr. 6	26	4	
Great Britain:				
Cardiff	Feb. 3–9	4		
Hull	Mar. 17–30	3		
Greece:				
Saloniki	Jan. 27–Mar. 16		9	
Honduras.				
Santa Barbara Department	Jan. 1–7			Present in interior.
India:				
Bombay	Oct. 21–Dec. 29	50	12	
Do	Dec. 31–Feb. 23	525	206	
Calcutta	Jan. 27–Feb. 23		13	
Karachi	Nov. 18–Dec. 29	4	2	
Do	Jan. 27–Mar. 2	31	17	Nov. 11–16, 1917: 10 cases with 4 deaths imported on s. s. Menesa from Basreh.
Madras	Oct. 31–Dec. 29	20	8	
Do	Dec. 30–Mar. 9	143	135	
Rangoon	Oct. 28–Dec. 22	6	1	
Do	Dec. 30–Mar. 2	63	11	
Indo-China:				
Provinces				Sept. 1–Dec. 31, 1917: Cases, 40; deaths, 180.
Anam	Sept. 1–Dec. 31	210	30	
Cambodia	do	19	11	
Cochin-China	do	440	133	
Saigon	Oct. 28–Dec. 30	120	26	
Do	Dec. 31–Mar. 24	1,095	370	
Laos	Oct. 1–Dec. 31	8	1	
Tonkin	Sept. 1–Dec. 31	18	5	
Italy:				
Castellamare	Dec. 10	2		Among refugees.
Florence	Dec. 1–15	17	4	
Genoa	Dec. 2–31	11	3	
Do	Jan. 2–Apr. 15	52	9	
Leghorn	Jan. 7–Apr. 7	33	7	
Messina	Jan. 3–19	1		
Milan				Oct. 1–Dec. 31, 1917: Cases, 32.
Naples	Dec. 10	2		Among refugees.
Taormina		6		
Turin	Dec. 29	123	120	
Do	Jan. 1–Mar. 10	72	6	
Japan:				
Nagasaki	Jan. 14–Apr. 14	10	3	
Taihoku	Dec. 15–21	1		Island of Taiwan (Formosa).
Do	Jan. 8–Apr. 8	49	8	Do.
Tokyo	Feb. 11–Apr. 14	26		City and suburbs.
Yokohama	Jan. 17–Feb. 3	63		
Java:				
East Java	Oct. 7–Dec. 23	50		Dec. 25–31, 1917: Cases, 7. Jan. 1–Feb. 4, 1918: Cases, 14.
Surabaya	Dec. 27–31	1		
Do	Jan. 29–Feb. 4	1		
Mid-Java.				Oct. 10–Dec. 26, 1917: Cases, 35; death, 1. Dec. 26, 1917–Feb. 13, 1918: Cases, 41.
Samarang	Nov. 6–Dec. 12	4	1	

CHOLERA, PLAGUE, SMALLPOX, TYPHUS FEVER, AND YELLOW FEVER—Continued.

Reports Received from Dec. 29, 1917, to May 31, 1918—Continued.

SMALLPOX—Continued.

Place.	Date.	Cases.	Deaths.	Remarks.
Java—Continued.				
West Java		1		Oct. 19–Dec. 27, 1917: Cases, 231;
Batavia	Nov. 2–8	1		deaths, 36. Dec. 28, 1917–Feb.
Do	Feb. 1–7	1		21, 1918: Cases, 257; deaths, 60.
Mesopotamia:				
Bagdad	Jan. 1–31		10	
Mexico:				
Aguascalientes	Feb. 4–17		2	
Ciudad Juarez	Mar. 3–23	2	1	
Guadalajara	Mar. 1–31	21	4	
Mazatlan	Dec. 5–11		1	
Do	Jan. 29–Apr. 2	4	4	
Mexico City	Nov. 11–Dec. 29	16		
Do	Dec. 30–Apr. 13	111		
Piedras Negras	Jan. 11	200		
Vera Cruz	Jan. 20–Apr. 28	16	3	
Newfoundland;				
St. Johns	Dec. 8–Jan. 4	29		
Do	Jan. 5–May 14	103		45 cases in hospital.
Trepassey	Jan. 4			Outbreak with 11 cases reported.
Philippine Islands:				
Manila	Oct. 28–Dec. 8	5		
Do	Feb. 3–Apr. 6	98	46	Varioloid, 130.
Porto Rico:				
San Juan	Jan. 28–Apr. 7	37		Of these, 36 varioloid.
Portugal:				
Lisbon	Nov. 4–Dec. 15	2		
Do	Dec. 30–Mar. 30	17		
Portuguese East Africa:				
Lourenço Marques	Aug. 1–Dec. 31		16	
Do	Jan. 1–31		6	
Russia:				
Archangel	Sept. 1–Oct. 31	7		
Moscow	Aug. 26–Oct. 6	22	2	
Petrograd	Aug. 31–Nov. 18	76	3	
Siam:				
Bangkok	Nov. 25–Dec. 1	1	1	
Do	Jan. 6–Mar. 16	26	14	
Spain:				
Coruna	Dec. 2–15		4	
Do	Jan. 20–Apr. 6		19	
Madrid	Jan. 1–Mar. 31		16	Jan. 1–Dec. 31, 1917: Deaths, 77.
Malaga	Oct. 1–31		19	
Seville	Oct. 1–Dec. 30		66	
Do	Jan. 1–31		20	
Valencia	Jan. 27–Feb. 2	1		
Straits Settlements:				
Singapore	Nov. 25–Dec. 1	1	1	
Do	Dec. 30–Jan. 5	1		
Tunisia:				
Tunis	Dec. 14–20	1		
Do	Mar. 16–Apr. 12	2		
Turkey in Asia:				
Bagdad				Present in November, 1917.
Union of South Africa:				
Cape of Good Hope State	Oct. 1–Dec. 31	28		
East Liverpool	Jan. 20–26	1		Varioloid.
Transvaal—				
Johannesburg	Jan. 1–31	4		
Venezuela:				
Maracaibo	Dec. 2–8			

TYPHUS FEVER.

Place.	Date.	Cases.	Deaths.	Remarks.
Algeria:				
Algiers	Nov. 1–Dec. 31	2	1	
Argentina:				
Rosario	Dec. 1–31		1	
Austria-Hungary:				
Hungary				Present in December, 1917.
Brazil:				
Rio de Janeiro	Oct. 28–Dec. 1	7		

CHOLERA, PLAGUE, SMALLPOX, TYPHUS FEVER, AND YELLOW FEVER—Continued.

Reports Received from Dec. 29, 1917, to May 31, 1917—Continued.

TYPHUS FEVER—Continued.

Place.	Date.	Cases.	Deaths.	Remarks.
Canada:				
Ontario—				
Kingston	Dec. 2-8	3		
Quebec—				
Montreal	Dec. 16-22	2	1	
China:				
Antung	Dec. 3-20	13	1	
Do	Dec. 31-Mar. 30	3	2	
Chosen (Korea):				
Seoul	Nov. 1-20	1		
Do	Feb. 1-28	3	2	
Egypt:				
Alexandria	Nov. 8-Dec. 28	57	15	
Do	Jan. 8-Apr. 1	688	157	
Cairo	July 23-Dec. 23	143	74	
Port Said	July 30-Nov. 11	5	5	
France:				
Marseille	Dec. 1-31		1	
Germany				Jan. 1-30, 1918: Cases, 66.
Great Britain:				
Belfast	Feb. 10-Mar. 30	21	3	
Dublin	Mar. 24-30	3		
Glasgow	Dec. 21	1		
Do	Jan. 20-Apr. 20	16		
Manchester	Dec. 2-8	1		
Greece:				
Arta	Feb. 19	2		
Janina	Feb. 14	110		Jan. 27, epidemic.
Saloniki	Nov. 11-Dec. 29		72	
Do	Dec. 30-Mar. 16		27	
Italy:				
San Remo	Mar. 10-16	2		
Japan:				
Nagasaki	Nov. 26-Dec. 16	5	5	
Do	Jan. 7-Apr. 14	18	6	
Java:				
East Java				Oct. 15-Dec. 31, 1917: Cases, 32;
Surabaya	Dec. 17-31	9	1	deaths, 7. Jan. 1-Feb. 11,
Do	Jan. 1-Feb. 11	29	4	1918: Cases, 36; deaths, 7
Mid-Java				Oct. 10-Dec. 26, 1917: Cases, 63
Samarang	Oct. 9-Dec. 26	20	2	deaths, 2. Dec. 28, 1917-Feb.
Do	Dec. 27-Feb. 6	20		13, 1918: Cases, 24, deaths, 2
West Java				Oct. 19 Dec. 27, 1917: Cases, 94;
Batavia	Oct. 1-Dec. 27	50	15	deaths, 17. Dec. 28, 1917-Feb.
Do	Dec. 28 Feb. 21	47	2	21, 1918: Cases, 56, deaths, 1
Lithuania				Dec. 30, 1917 Jan. 5, 1918: Cases,
Mexico:				195.
Aguascalientes	Dec. 15		3	
Do	Jan. 21-May 5		18	
Durango State—				
Gumaevi	Feb. 11			Epidemic.
Mexico City	Nov. 11 Dec. 29	476		
Do	Dec. 30-Apr. 13	704		
Newfoundland:				
St. John ns	Mar. 30-Apr. 5	1	1	
Norway:				
Bergen	Feb. 1-16	3		
Poland				Nov. 18 Dec. 8,1917: Cases, 2, 368;
Lodz	Nov. 18 Dec. 8	219	25	deaths, 218. Dec. 23, 1917-
Warsaw	do	1,461	141	Jan. 12, 1918: Cases, 3,036;
				deaths, 315.
Portugal:				
Lisbon	Mar. 3 30	18		Feb. 21: Present.
Oporto	Dec. 1 31	23	4	
Do	Jan 1-Mar. 8	1,811	161	
Russia:				
Archangel	Sept 1 14	7	2	
Moscow	Aug. 26 Oct. 6	49	2	
Petrograd	Aug 31 Nov. 18	32		
Do	Feb. 2			Present.
Vladivostok	Oct. 29 Nov. 4	12	1	
Spain:				
Corcubion	Apr. 11			Present. Province of Coruna,
				west coast.
Madrid	Jan. 1-Mar. 31		3	

CHOLERA, PLAGUE, SMALLPOX, TYPHUS FEVER, AND YELLOW FEVER—Continued.

Reports Received from Dec. 29, 1917, to May 31, 1918—Continued.

TYPHUS FEVER—Continued.

Place.	Date.	Cases.	Deaths.	Remarks.
Sweden:				
Goteborg	Nov. 18–Dec. 15...	2	....	
Switzerland:				
Basel	Jan. 6–19	1	1	
Zurich	Nov. 9–15	2	....	
Do	Jan. 13–19	2	....	
Tunisia:				
Tala	Mar. 18	....	....	Epidemic.
Tozer	...do	....	....	Do.
Tunis	Nov. 30–Dec. 6	....	1	
Do	Feb. 9–Apr. 19	4	16	Of these, 26 in outbreak in prison.
Union of South Africa:				
Cape of Good Hope State...	....	....	....	Sept. 10, 1917–Mar. 17, 1918: Cases, 4,444 (European, 34); deaths, 902 (European, 15).
Natal	....	....	....	Dec. 1, 1917–Mar. 17, 1918: Cases, 50; deaths, 11.

YELLOW FEVER.

Place.	Date.	Cases.	Deaths.	Remarks.
Brazil:				
Bahia	Mar. 10–16	1	1	
Ecuador:				
Babahoyo	Feb. 1–15	1	1	
Guayaquil	Sept. 1–Nov. 30...	5	3	
Do	Feb. 1–15	1	....	
Do	Mar. 1–31	12	7	
Milagro	Feb. 1–15	1	1	
Yaguachi	Nov. 1–30	1	....	
Guatemala:				
Retalhuleu	Apr. 22–May 23	....	....	Present. About 25 miles from Champerico, Pacific port. Disease spreading along Pacific coast.
Honduras:				
Tegucigalpa	Dec. 16–22	....	1	
Do	Jan. 6–19	....	1	

×

PUBLIC HEALTH REPORTS

| VOL. 33 | JUNE 14, 1918 | No. 24 |

RESOLUTIONS ADOPTED AT ANNUAL CONFERENCE OF HEALTH OFFICERS.

The following resolutions were adopted at the sixteenth annual conference of State and Territorial health authorities with the United States Public Health Service held in Washington, D. C., on June 3 and 4, 1918:

Rural Sanitation—Federal Aid Extension.

Whereas the advancement of rural sanitation is urgently necessary for the conservation of the health and strength of this Nation; and

Whereas the need of rural sanitation imposes an obligation alike on National, State, and local rural governments; and

Whereas the principle of Federal aid extension is admirably designed to meet obligations common to National, State, and local governments; and

Whereas the principle of Federal aid extension has already been established and is now being applied in several departments of our National Government; and

Whereas the measures carried out under the Federal aid extension laws for improving rural conditions have proved highly effective and popular to all concerned: Therefore be it

Resolved, That the sixteenth annual conference of State and Territorial health authorities with the United States Public Health Service indorses the principle of Federal aid extension as the best means for the coordination of and making effective the work of the National, State, and local rural governments for the advancement of rural sanitation; and be it further

Resolved, That this conference respectfully urge the United States Public Health Service to take such steps as to secure the necessary suitable Federal legislation; and be it further

Resolved, That the State health organizations represented in this conference pledge their active support to the United States Public Health Service in the efforts to secure the aforesaid legislation.

61566°—18——1

Safeguarding the Health of Industrial Workers.

Whereas the need for the conservation of man power makes it imperative to safeguard the health of the industrial army; and

Whereas adequate measures to this end are a major problem in public health, involving the cooperation of the Federal Government with State and local health and labor authorities; and

Whereas the Public Health Service is the civil executive branch of the Federal Government dealing with the public health: Therefore be it

Resolved, That the members of this conference of State and Territorial health officers with the Public Health Service advocate that a Federal system of supervision of the health of war industrial centers be established by cooperation of the Public Health Service with State and local health and labor authorities and that the necessary executive authorization be obtained in order effectively to bring this about.

Vaccination Against Smallpox.

Whereas the safeguarding of public health is one of the chief functions of governments; and

Whereas vaccination against smallpox is recognized as the only method of controlling and eradicating this disease: Therefore be it

Resolved, By the Sixteenth Annual Conference of State and Territorial Health Authorities with the United States Public Health Service at Washington, that the State of Arkansas, through its governor, Hon. Chas. H. Brough, be congratulated on having a compulsory vaccination law sustained and further commend the supreme court for interpreting the law on broad principles which affect the general welfare of the Commonwealth.

Control of Venereal Disease.

Whereas it is universally recognized that venereal diseases constitute the chief menace to the health of the military forces, incapacitating more men for duty than wounds received in action, and furthermore because of the universal recognition of the following facts:

1. These diseases have their chief source of origin within the civilian population from which the military forces are drawn.

2. The conservation of the health of the civilian population is primarily a function for the supervision of the State health officials acting in cooperation with the United States Public Health Service.

3. The machinery for the control of venereal diseases is seriously handicapped both on account of insufficient funds and proper law for coordinating the State health functions with those exercised by the United States Public Health Service.

4. The Chamberlain-Kahn bill, known as Senate bill 4608 and House bill 12258, appears to embody all the features essential for

the successful solution of the venereal disease problem in the civilian population as well as to render necessary aid to the Surgeons General of the Army and Navy in combating such diseases among the military forces: Therefore be it

Resolved, in view of the foregoing facts, That the Sixteenth Conference of the State and Territorial Health Officials with the United States Public Health Service places itself on record as indorsing the principle of the above-mentioned bill.

Committee on Sanitary Disposal of Human Excreta.

Resolved, That the Sixteenth Annual Conference of State and Territorial Health Authorities with the United States Public Health Service respectfully recommends the appointment by the Surgeon General of the United States Public Health Service of a committee for a study of the problem of sanitary disposal of human excreta in unsewered communities.

Resolved, further, That the said committee should be composed of members with such training and experience as will enable them to conduct practical studies of the problem from a biological, chemical, and engineering standpoint, with a definite view to the preparation of plans and specifications for standard types of closets suitable to the variety of economic, geologic, and climatic conditions of this country.

And resolved further, That the committee consider and report upon the practicability of model State legislation encouraging the extensive adoption of the standard types of closets agreed upon.

Loss of Personnel from State and Local Health Organizations.

Be it resolved, That the United States Public Health Service ascertain by questionnaire the number of public-health workers in the employ of the States that have left for Federal service and the number of workers that probably will be lost in the next few months, the results thus obtained to be submitted to the proper authorities, to the end that a statement be forthcoming as to the attitude of the Federal authorities on this question of depletion of State health organizations.

Whereas the demands of the military and naval services of the United States upon the medical profession, upon sanitary engineers, and upon graduate nurses have depleted the numbers of persons engaged in such callings and thereby seriously impaired the efficiency of many of the State and local sanitary organizations, and threaten further impairment and even disintegration of some of them; and

Whereas such harm as has already been done can be repaired and disaster averted only by the wisest possible distribution of such

future demands as may be made by the military and naval forces
upon the physicians, sanitary engineers, and nurses among the
various sources of supply from which services of these kinds are
ordinarily obtained; and

Whereas the maintenance of the efficiency of the Federal, State,
and local health agencies, to the end that the health of the people
may be conserved and promoted, is a necessary and important
element in the war program: Be it

Resolved, That a committee of five be appointed by the chairman
to confer with the committee on sanitary policy under war conditions
of the Conference of State and Provincial Boards of Health of North
America, and that this be made a special order of business at 2.30
p. m., June 5.

DEVELOPMENT OF COUNTY HEALTH WORK.[1]

By K. E. MILLER, Assistant Surgeon, United States Public Health Service.

A discussion of county health work must be somewhat specific if it
is to be intelligible, because the 3,000 counties of the United States
vary widely in size, population, altitude, climate, wealth, and pursuits. Since we are met here as health officers of North Carolina,
this discussion, although quite applicable to county health work in
general, will endeavor to adapt itself particularly to the average
county of this State. This county will be about 600 square miles in
size, will have a population of about 30,000, with a notable proportion of negroes, will be economically prosperous but not rich, and
will be distinctly rural.

In attacking the county health problem a sharp distinction between rural and municipal conditions must be drawn. In a city of
30,000 population the area covered is perhaps from 10 to 15 square
miles, whereas the area may be 600 square miles in a county of similar
population. While disease incidence in rural districts is lessened
somewhat by the comparative lack of personal contact, the administrative difficulties are multiplied enormously by the area over which
the health officer must work, the bad or impassable roads during certain months of the year, the lack of sanitary inspectors, policemen,
and nurses, and the fact that rural people are not so accustomed to
rules and regulations and are therefore harder to control. Thus,
rural health administration requires special training. While I do
not wish to discount the value of the special instruction for health
officers given by the medical schools, I do wish to say that not one of
the courses is conducted from the standpoint of rural needs and con-

---

[1] Read before the meeting of the North Carolina Health Officers' Association, Pine-
hurst, N. C., April 15, 1918.

ditions and that, therefore, the student is not fitted for rural health work. Nowhere is the man himself so important as in rural health work. In comparison, the personality of the municipal official is insignificant, since he is fortified by a routine system which keeps him more or less behind the scenes.

The first problem in county health work is that of funds. Inasmuch as the whole program hinges upon this factor, it is deserving of special consideration. Probably no county has a surplus above current expenditures. It is the universal belief of the citizen that he is paying all the taxes he can stand, an impression neither always true nor always false. As regards expenditures for health protection, there are, obviously, limits beyond which we would not be justified in going, especially in view of the fact that there is no such thing as absolute protection of health. On the other hand, there is a minimum below which organized and efficient health work in a county can not be undertaken, this minimum being about $3,000 a year, or in a county of 30,000 population, 10 cents per capita. That this is not excessive is shown by the fact that certain purely rural counties are now exceeding this amount and are proud of their investment. Indeed, if the money now spent in most counties in the old haphazard way in the absence of an adequate health machine were applied to the conduct of a business-like health department, the increase necessary to reach 10 cents per capita would be surprisingly small.

Two thousand of the three thousand dollars above mentioned should be set aside for the salary of the health officer, and the remainder for running expenses.

In order to attempt effective health work certain other minimal requirements must be provided for, as follows:

1. Equipment. (*a*) Automobile, bought and operated by county money. (*b*) Stationery and office furniture. (*c*) By all means an adequate system of preserving records. This is one of the weakest points in county health establishments generally. (*d*) Office help. Under the above budget not much can be invested in this way, but it is very essential to have some one, if only a child, always in the office to answer telephone calls and to keep the simple but necessary records.

2. A well-trained medical man who has the instinct for work and the personality and judgment suitable for accomplishing the desired ends. The idea of making health officers out of nonmedical men has gained popularity in some quarters, but in county health work there are many reasons making this even more of a mistake than elsewhere. In any case, the health officer must be a full-time man.

Starting with the foregoing minimal requirements, other facilities may be added ad infinitum. Roughly speaking, a county can get as much health protection as it is able and willing to pay for. For the average county these minimal requirements are about all that can be expected at first. The health officer should recognize the limitations of his position, and be prepared to sacrifice cheerfully the less important activities for the more important, so that his full capacities may be applied at the strategic points. One of the favorite fetishes which die so hard is, for instance, a laboratory. Unless the one-man health officer divorces himself from the idea early, he will waste precious time and good money, providing always that such good services are obtainable from the State laboratory as we now enjoy. Many recent developments in public health work, such as measures to meet the venereal problem, prenatal care, welfare work of various kinds, eugenics, and life extension work, are very attractive, but can not be actively incorporated into the early stages of rural health work.

As regards contagious diseases, the rural health officer has no choice. These constitute emergencies and he must attend to them as they arise. In connection with them he finds a duty in the performance of which he must be tireless—the training of his people in the prompt reporting of diseases. This will require time, patience, sometimes the pressure of law, and every atom of the health officer's ingenuity. The many devices which may be employed to secure more complete reporting can not be discussed here for lack of time. Suffice it to say that if the health officer secures good reporting the remainder of contagious-disease control becomes practically automatic. The practice of quarantining by registered mail is looked upon as particularly well adapted to rural needs, but it should not be employed as a routine measure.

All health establishments in their infancy will find themselves confronted with almost universally dangerous filth-disposal systems, or lack of any at all, in the home. No real progress can be made toward control of filth-borne diseases, therefore, until these insanitary practices are supplanted by sanitary measures. This may not be accomplished completely until the millennium, but much can be done. It has been found in the extensive rural sanitation work done by the United States Public Health Service during the past three years that better returns from small amounts of sanitary reform are secured than are really deserved. A very notable drop in the typhoid-fever rate has invariably followed the rural sanitation campaigns, even when the actual numbers of sanitary privies constructed bore but a small ratio to the total. It is fortunate that labors in this field are so rewarded, because the business is sordid and unattractive and health officers might persuade themselves to neglect it if the fruits were not so unmistakable. The health officer must plan to devote the major portion of his energies to this problem, especially during the summer months.

As to malaria, this is a disease of sectional prevalence, but in the average southern county there are most likely to be localities where the damage wrought by it is very extensive, the disease ranking very close to the white plague itself as a menace to human health, welfare, and life. Although malaria is one of the diseases capable of complete eradication, the best method to be used, namely, drainage, is unfortunately far too expensive to be undertaken on a comprehensive scale in many rural districts, unless the results at the same time contribute some adequate economic benefit, such as the reclaiming of waste land, or rendering more productive that already in cultivation. Consequently the cooperation of the health officer with the agricultural agencies in the extension of cultivation projects will furnish a sound basis for antimalaria work by the one-man health officer. For more immediate results the routine administration of quinine should be adopted as a policy and given persistent publicity.

It is quite within the power of a one-man health officer, also, to obtain a good general anopheline survey of his county by means of sampling collections of water wherever he may happen to be in the county. Having once determined the principal foci of infection, a limited amount of intensive antimalaria work will be found possible and of most value as a demonstration. Even the one-man health force is able to do this effectively by selecting a small unit, such as one school district, and making a house-to-house canvess of it, teaching the people what to do and how to do it and urging their faithfulness in pursuing the course prescribed.

During the fall and winter months the health officer has work which compares favorably with the foregoing in importance. This is the physical examination of school children, together with some system of follow-up work.

Two other basic problems, tuberculosis and infant welfare, are unfortunately beyond the direct reach of the one-man health officer, although it is possible and essential for him to stress these subjects in an educational way from every possible angle.

The foundation of all rural health work, of course, must be education. In the large cities methods of compulsion may be tolerated, but not so in county work. It does not come within the province of this article, however, to discuss the various aspects which educational work may assume. No method or practice which will accomplish the desired end can be disregarded.

A characteristic mistake in trying to develop county health work is to attempt to get results by an overabundance of new rules and laws, on the theory that, even if only 10 per cent of the laws are enforced, more will be accomplished with many laws than with few. This practice tends rather to disorganize than to develop health work. Good health legislation should be such that its effect should be its own recommendation. No laws should be passed except those capable of from 90 to 100 per cent enforcement with the machinery the health officer has at hand. A few reasonable laws which can be made to mean just what they say will inculcate in the people the habit of observing health laws. These will then serve as a nucleus around which other laws may be developed.

When an engineer lays out a drainage system he so executes the plans that the smallest branches bear a definite relation to the main collecting channel. In the scheme of health administration we find a close parallel, in which the county organization represents the smallest branches or indivisible units and the State and Federal organizations, respectively, the larger ones. Each has its own separate functions to perform, but can not operate successfully independently of the others. While this fact is so simple that its statement seems a mere platitude, a glaring disregard of it is sometimes seen.

When the turmoil of war subsides, we may confidently look for a great impetus to internal development in this country. Unquestionably, health matters will receive greater recognition than ever before. We may therefore conceive of the time, not far distant, when funds may be available for a cooperative health program in which county, State, and Federal Governments will all share. Such a scheme would necessarily bring about a close coordination of policy in the different units and wipe out all barriers to interdependent co-operation now existing. But whether this plan is ever realized or not, the wise health officer, in developing the work of a county, will go about his task with the idea that the health forces of our country constitute an organic whole, of which the county organization is an inseparable unit.

PREVALENCE OF MALARIA IN CERTAIN STATES.

The table given below shows the results of the circularization of physicians for the purpose of ascertaining the prevalence and types of malaria during the month of March, 1918.　Similar summaries appeared in the Public Health Reports, April 5, 1918, pages 489–490, and May 24, 1918, page 805.

Summary of postal-card reports of malaria for the month of March, 1918.

	Ohio.	Okla-homa.	Texas (eastern half).	Virginia.
Cards mailed	7,912	2,634	3,450	2,420
Cards returned unclaimed	87	20	54	16
Replies received	1,167	234	478	798
Percentage of replies received	14.91	8.95	14.07	33.19
Counties represented in replies	43	71	94	99
Counties from which no replies were received	45	6	19	1
Towns or cities represented in replies	302	167	250	441
Cases of malaria reported	25	284	426	323
Types of infection—				
Tertian	10	159	175	198
Quartan		36	24	27
Estivo-autumnal	8	36	66	18
Cases reported confirmed microscopically—				
Tertian	4	24	33	15
Quartan		1		1
Estivo-autumnal	1	1	7	2
Cases reported confirmed, types not stated		14	49	20

PREVALENCE OF DISEASE.

*No health department, State or local, can effectively prevent or control disease without
knowledge of when, where, and under what conditions cases are occurring.*

UNITED STATES.

EXTRA-CANTONMENT ZONES—CASES REPORTED WEEK ENDED JUNE 11.

CAMP BEAUREGARD ZONE, LA.

Alexandria:	Cases.
Chicken pox	2
Gonorrhea	3
Malaria	6
Mumps	16
Smallpox	1
Tuberculosis	2
Whooping cough	5
Ball:	
Typhoid fever	1
Boyce:	
Mumps	3
Whooping cough	3
Rural district:	
Malaria	1

CAMP BOWIE ZONE, TEX.

Fort Worth:	
Diphtheria	3
Gonorrhea	23
Mumps	3
Smallpox	12
Syphilis	19
Trachoma	1
Tuberculosis	2
Typhoid fever	12
Polytechnic:	
Smallpox	2

CAMP DEVENS ZONE, MASS.

Chicken pox:	
Leominster	4
Diphtheria:	
Fitchburg	1
German measle:	
Lancaster	1
Leominster	1
Pneumonia:	
Leominster	1
Whooping cough:	
Ayer	1

CAMP DIX ZONE, N. J.[1]

Measles	Cases.
New Hanover Township	2
Pemberton Township	2
Whooping cough:	
Pemberton Township	1
Plumstead Township	2

CAMP DODGE ZONE, IOWA.

Des Moines:	
Diphtheria	4
Gonorrhea	7
Scarlet fever	5
Smallpox	7
Syphilis	4
Tuberculosis	1
Typhoid fever	1

CAMP DONIPHAN ZONE, OKLA.

Chancroid:	
Lawton	1
Diphtheria:	
Cache	1
Gonorrhea:	
Lawton	2

CAMP PIKE ZONE, ARK.

Diphtheria:	
Lonoke	1
Dysentery:	
Cabot	1
Cabot, route 1	1
Cabot route 2	1
German measles:	
Hartsfield	1
Wattensaw	1
Gonorrhea:	
Lonoke	6
Lonoke, route 2	1
England	1
Scott	3
Malaria:	
Lonoke, route 4	2
England	1

Malaria—Continued.	Cases.
Carlisle	6
Carlisle, route 1	1
Carlisle, route 5	2
Cabot, route 1	1
Austin, route 1	1
Kerr, route 1	1
Measles:	
Lonoke	1
Austin, route 1	3
Mumps:	
Lonoke	22
Lonoke, route 2	1
England	2
Carlisle	1
Eberts Field	2
Keo	1
Wattensaw	1
Pellagra:	
Lonoke	1
England	1
Smallpox:	
England	2
Scotts, route 1	1
Syphilis:	
Lonoke	2
England	1
Scotts	2
Tuberculosis:	
Lonoke	1
Lonoke, route 3	1
Scotts, route 1	1
Scotts, route 2	1

CAMP FUNSTON ZONE, KANS.

Erysipelas:	
Manhattan	1
Measles:	
Junction City	2
Mumps:	
Manhattan	5
Whooping cough:	
Junction City	9
Manhattan	3

CAMP GORDON ZONE, GA.

Chicken pox:	
Atlanta	3
Conjunctivitis, acute, infectious:	
Atlanta	1
Diphtheria:	
East Point	1
Dysentery:	
Chattahoochee	2
Dysentery, bacillary:	
Atlanta	1
Clarkston	3
Simsille	1
German measles:	
Atlanta	1
Gonorrhea:	
Atlanta	8

Malaria:	Cases.
Bolton	1
Measles:	
Atlanta	7
Chamblee	1
College Park	1
Mumps:	
Atlanta	16
Scarlet fever:	
Atlanta	2
Smallpox:	
Atlanta	9
College Park	1
East Point	1
Syphilis:	
Atlanta	0
Tuberculosis:	
Atlanta	4
Typhoid fever:	
Atlanta	2
Dunwoody	1
Roswell Road	1
Whooping cough:	
Atlanta	0

CAMP GREENE ZONE, N. C.

Charlotte Township:	
Chancroid	1
German measles	2
Gonorrhea	31
Measles	8
Mumps	2
Scarlet fever	1
Syphilis	20
Trachoma	4
Typhoid fever	2
Whooping cough	21

GULFPORT HEALTH DISTRICT, MISS.

Gulfport Health District:	
Malaria	18
Mumps	4
Typhoid fever	1
Whooping cough	7

CAMP HANCOCK ZONE, GA.

Augusta:	
Chicken pox	1
German measles	1
Measles	3
Tuberculosis	3
Typhoid fever	7
Whooping cough	1
Gracewood:	
Tuberculosis, pulmonary	1
Waynesboro:	
Typhoid fever	4

CAMP JACKSON ZONE, S. C.[1]

Columbia:	
Mumps	14
Typhoid fever	4
Whooping cough	19

[1] Report for week ended June 8, 1918.

CAMP JOSEPH E. JOHNSTON ZONE, FLA.

	Cases.
Chancroid:	
Jacksonville	3
Chicken pox:	
Fisher's Corner	1
Jacksonville	15
Diphtheria:	
Jacksonville	1
Dysentery:	
Jacksonville	2
Gonorrhea:	
Jacksonville	56
Malaria:	
Jacksonville	3
Measles:	
Jacksonville	1
Panama	1
Mumps:	
Fisher's Corner	1
Jacksonville	4
Pellagra:	
Jacksonville	1
St. Nicholas	1
Pneumonia:	
Brentwood	1
Scarlet fever:	
Jacksonville	1
St. Nicholas	1
Smallpox:	
Jacksonville	2
Syphilis:	
Jacksonville	28
Trachoma:	
Lackawanna	2
Tuberculosis:	
Jacksonville	2
Seaboard Air Line	1
Typhoid fever:	
Jacksonville	2
Whooping cough:	
Fisher's Corner	1
Jacksonville	31
Lackawanna	7
Ortega	1

FORT LEAVENWORTH ZONE, KANS.

Leavenworth:	
Gonorrhea	2
Smallpox	1
Leavenworth County:	
Diphtheria	1
Scarlet fever	1
Smallpox	1
Whooping cough	2

CAMP LEE ZONE, VA.

Gonorrhea:	
Petersburg	3
Malaria:	
Petersburg	5
Mumps:	
Hopewell	2
Pneumonia:	
Fort Corp Co. N.Y.	1
Syphilis:	
Petersburg	3

CAMP LEE ZONE, VA.—continued.

	Cases.
Tuberculosis:	
Petersburg	1
Typhoid fever:	
Petersburg	4
Whooping cough:	
Hopewell	6

CAMP LEWIS ZONE, WASH.

Mumps:	
Parkland	1
Steilacoom	1
Steilacoom Lake	1
Tuberculosis, pulmonary:	
Parkland	4
Whooping cough:	
Parkland	4

CAMP LOGAN ZONE, TEX.

Chancroid:	
Houston	2
Chicken pox:	
Moonshine Hill	4
Dysentery:	
Houston	4
Gonorrhea:	
Houston	33
Goose Creek	4
Ellington Field	1
Chenango	1
Pasadena	1
La Porte	1
Malaria:	
Humble	4
Measles:	
Houston	1
Moonshine Hill	2
Mumps:	
Houston	1
Moonshine Hill	1
Syphilis:	
Houston	28
Goose Creek	1
Pasadena	1
Humble	1
Tuberculosis:	
Houston	6
Typhoid fever:	
Houston	1
Goose Creek	1

CAMP MACARTHUR ZONE, TEX.

Precinct 2:	
Malaria	4
Precinct 4:	
Whooping cough	4
Waco:	
Chicken pox	3
Measles	1
Pneumonia	1
Smallpox	2
Syphilis	1
Typhoid fever	6
Whooping cough	2

CAMP McCLELLAN ZONE, ALA.

Anniston:	Cases.
Malaria	1
Measles	2
Typhoid fever	1
Precinct 21:	
Malaria	1

FORT OGLETHORPE ZONE, GA.

Chattanooga:	
Cerebrospinal meningitis	1
Chicken pox	1
Gonorrhea	3
Scarlet fever	3
Smallpox	2
Syphilis	13
Tuberculosis	1
Typhoid fever	1
Whooping cough	7
East Chattanooga:	
Syphilis	1

CAMP SEVIER ZONE, S. C.

Chick Springs Township:	
Dysentery	1
Mumps	1
Whooping cough	4
Greenville Township:	
Dysentery	1

CAMP SHELBY ZONE, MISS.

Hattiesburg:	
Chicken pox	1
Malaria	14
Mumps	4
Scarlet fever	2
Typhoid fever	2
Venereal	10
Whooping cough	6
Seminary:	
Smallpox	6

CAMP SHERIDAN ZONE, ALA.

Montgomery:	
Gonorrhea	1
Scarlet fever	1
Syphilis	1
Tuberculosis, pulmonary	2
Typhoid fever	4
Montgomery County:	
Malaria	63
Typhoid fever	2
U. S. Government Clinic:	
Chancroid	7
Gonorrhea	28
Syphilis	7

CAMP SHERMAN ZONE, OHIO.

Diphtheria:	
Union Township	1
Chillicothe	1
Gonorrhea:	
Chillicothe	6
Measles:	
Liberty Township	1

CAMP SHERMAN ZONE, OHIO—continued.

Mumps:	Cases.
Liberty Township	1
Scarlet fever:	
Chillicothe	4

CAMP ZACHARY TAYLOR ZONE, KY.

Jefferson County:	
Measles	4
Tuberculosis, pulmonary	1
Louisville:	
Diphtheria	8
Measles	5
Mumps	1
Rabies in animal	1
Tuberculosis, pulmonary	22
Typhoid fever	3
Whooping cough	2
United States Government clinic:	
Chancroid	2
Gonorrhea	33
Syphilis	28

TIDEWATER HEALTH DISTRICT, VA.

Chancroid:	
Newport News	4
Diphtheria:	
Hampton	1
Gonorrhea:	
Newport News	6
Measles:	
Hampton	1
Newport News	2
Mumps:	
Newport News	2
Scarlet fever:	
Hampton	1
Newport News	2
Smallpox:	
Newport News	4
Syphilis:	
Newport News	2
Tuberculosis:	
Hampton	1
Newport News	1
Typhoid fever:	
Hampton	1
Newport News	2
Whooping cough:	
Hampton	4
Phoebus	19

CAMP TRAVIS ZONE, TEX.

San Antonio:	
Cerebrospinal meningitis	2
Chancroid	2
Diphtheria	1
Dysentery	2
Gonorrhea	35
Malaria	2
Mumps	3
Pneumonia	1
Scarlet fever	1
Syphilis	14
Tuberculosis	3
Typhoid fever	26

CAMP WADSWORTH ZONE, S. C.	
Gonorrhea:	Cases.
Spartanburg	8
Measles:	
Spartanburg	1
White Stone	3
Whitney	1
Pauline	1
Mumps:	
Spartanburg	3
White Stone	1
Whitney	1
Glenn Springs	1
Smallpox:	
Spartanburg	1
Tuberculosis:	
Spartanburg	2
Typhoid fever:	
Pauline	1
Saxon Mills	1

CAMP WADSWORTH ZONE, S. C.—continued.	
Whooping cough:	Cases.
Spartanburg	1
Whitney	9
CAMP WHEELER ZONE, GA.	
Bibb County:	
Diphtheria	4
East Macon:	
Typhoid fever	1
Macon:	
Chicken pox	4
Gonorrhea	9
Hookworm	2
Malaria	1
Syphilis	6
Typhoid fever	2
Whooping cough	2

DISEASE CONDITIONS AMONG TROOPS IN THE UNITED STATES.

The following data are taken from telegraphic reports received in the office of the Surgeon General, United States Army, for the week ended May 31, 1918:

Annual admission rate per 1,000 (disease only):
All troops 611.5
Divisional camps 777.8
Cantonments 1,086
Departmental and other troops 372.4

Noneffective rate per 1,000 on day of report:
All troops 38.9
Divisional camps 47.7
Cantonments 44.1
Departmental and other troops 32.7

Annual death rate per 1,000 (disease only):
All troops 4.01
Divisional camps 2.5
Cantonments 6
Departmental and other troops 2.7

New cases of special diseases reported during the week ended May 31, 1918

Camp.	Pneumonia.	Dysentery.	Malaria.	Venereal.		Measles.	Meningitis.	Scarlet fever.	Deaths.	Annual admission rate per 1,000 (disease only).	Noneffective rate per 1,000 on day of report.
				Total.	New infections.						
Beauregard		4	15	44	3		1		3	1,074.3	44.8
	1		2	62	50				2	774.8	28.8
	1			6			1			340.6	14.4
	1		3	21		1			1	324.4	17.5
	17	1		10	4	19	1	1	3	532.0	44.0
	1			43		1				571.4	23.2
	2			4		9			1	683.5	22.8
	1			24	12				1	587.6	27.3
				10	17				1	552.7	27.8
	1		6	17	9	9			1	436.3	32.6
				18		3		2		772.6	24.3
						18		5	1	913.3	27.1
			1			15				2,236.3	33.1
Wheeler		2	6	6					4	530.7	34.7
	1			8	3	6			3	535.3	21.0
			18	21	5	16	1		2	649.3	39.1

New cases of special diseases reported during the week ended May 31, 1918—Continued.

Camp.	Pneumonia.	Dysentery.	Malaria.	Venereal. Total.	New infections.	Measles.	Meningitis.	Scarlet fever.	Deaths.	Annual admission rate per 1,000 (disease only).	Noneffective per 1,000 on day of report.
Dix.............			1	79	2	11	2	2	2	814.2	32.8
Dodge.............	15			82		23	2	1	7	1,189.7	67.4
Funston............	4		1	63	10	10	3	1	7	919.0	56.2
Gordon.............	8		1	194	5	40	1		11	1,891.6	61.3
Grant.............	2			15		13		3	4	336.0	16.7
Jackson............	11	1	1	276		45	2	1	6	1,763.1	57.4
J. E. Johnston......	6		3	40		9			3	1,047.8	37.8
A. A. Humphreys..	2			21	8	4	2			622.0	15.9
Lee.............	1			804		7			1	2,090.6	91.0
Lewis.............	5			271	4	12	1	17	1	1,063.3	32.1
Meade.............	4			21	16	6			3	862.0	27.7
Pike.............	11	1	13	59	7	7	2		7	1,377.0	64.3
Sherman............	2			94		4				1,001.4	53.8
Taylor.............				76	7	32	2		3	979.7	47.7
Travis.............	15	5	11	56	1	34		1	4	1,499.0	39.5
Upton.............				261	12	1			3	836.5	34.8
Northeastern Department........				43	32				1	858.6	28.4
Eastern Department........	3		4	163	100	16		2	5	785.4	20.0
Southeastern Department...........	1		5	121	95	3			3	1,100.7	33.7
Central Department	7			114	69	15		8	1	1,384.0	44.8
Southern Department.............	7	2	8	237	31	11		2	7	1,250.6	38.9
Western Department.............	3		1	54	22	9		6	5	785.8	22.3
Aviation, Signal Corps...........	7	16	2	127	17	17		6	10	1,009.7	27.8
Alcatraz Disciplinary Barracks.....										626.6	15.0
Columbus Barracks.	1			27	1	1				875.2	23.9
Edgewood Arsenal..	1									513.1	8.9
El Paso.............										400.8	17.3
Hoboken............	6		6	105	15	17	1	12	2	532.4	32.0
Holabird............						1				218.6	1.2
Jefferson Barracks.	3			154	1	7			1	1,543.9	88.3
Leavenworth Disciplinary Barracks.........	1			2						809.7	34.2
Fort Logan........	1			19	3	1		5		3,407.5	75.6
Fort McDowell.....			2	30		1		1		1,713.7	84.6
Newport News.....	7		5	333	16	22	1	1	5	1,169.6	47.6
Raritan............						1				502.6	19.3
Fort Slocum.......				18	1	1				850.7	35.2
Springfield Armory.										1,100.5	10.6
Fort Thomas.......				12		5			1	1,663.8	55.8
Watervliet........										319.0	36.8
West Point........				1						384.7	8.0
Total........	205	35	109	4,573	597	499	23	80	127	974.5	36.8

Annual rate per 1,000 for special diseases.

Diseases.	All troops in United States.[1]	Departmental and other troops.[1]	Divisional camps.[1]	Cantonments.[1]	Expeditionary forces.[2]
Pneumonia..........	7.9	5.27	7.5	10.3	20.8
Dysentery..........	1.35	1.97	1.7	0.64	1.7
Malaria............	4.2	3.6	7.5	2.85	0.77
Venereal...........	176.4	171.5	83	232	75.4
Paratyphoid........	0.0	0.0	0.0	0.0	0.67
Typhoid...........	0.08	0.1	0.0	0.09	0.19
Measles............	19.2	14	14.7	26	9.7
Meningitis.........	0.89	0.2	0.5	1.65	1.1
Scarlet fever.......	3.08	4.7	1.5	2.58	3

[1] Week ended May 31, 1918.   [2] Week ended May 23, 1918.

CURRENT STATE SUMMARIES.

Connecticut.

From Collaborating Epidemiologist Black, by telegraph, for week ended June 8, 1918:

Meningitis: Bridgeport 1, East Hartford 1. Smallpox: Hartford 1. Leprosy Bridgeport 1. Rabies: Waterbury 1, human.

Illinois.

From Collaborating Epidemiologist Drake, by telegraph, for week ended June 8, 1918:

Diphtheria: One hundred and sixty-eight, of which in Chicago 138. Chicago Heights 6. Scarlet fever: Thirty-seven, of which in Chicago 23. Smallpox: Ninety-eight of which in Johnson Township (Clark County) 8, Peoria 7, Alton 2, Quincy 3, Steelville precinct (Randolph County) 14. Meningitis: Four, of which in Chicago 2, East St. Louis 1, Mount Carmel 1. Poliomyelitis: Springfield 1.

Kansas.

From Collaborating Epidemiologist Crumbine, by telegraph, for week ended June 8, 1918:

Smallpox (over 10 cases): By counties—Butler 18, Cherokee 34, Dickinson 15, Montgomery (including Coffeyville) 11, Sedgwick (including Wichita) 12, Shawnee (including Topeka) 14. Meningitis: Kansas City 1, Oskaloosa 1. Poliomyelitis Wellington 1.

Louisiana.

From Collaborating Epidemiologist Dowling, by telegraph, for week ended June 8, 1918:

Meningitis: State (excepting Rapides Parish) 2. Typhoid fever: State 44. Smallpox: State 25. Diphtheria: State 22.

Massachusetts.

From Collaborating Epidemiologist Hitchcock, by telegraph, for week ended June 8, 1918:

Unusual prevalence. Measles: Lawrence 121, Malden 41, Manchester 31, Salem 32, Waltham 30. Whooping cough: Whitman 14.

Minnesota.

From Collaborating Epidemiologist Bracken, by telegraph, for week ended June 8, 1918:

Smallpox, new foci: Douglas County, Hudson Township, 1; Mower County, Dexter Township, 1. Pine County, Terry Township, 1. One poliomyelitis and 1 cerebrospinal meningitis reported since June 3.

Nebraska.

From the State Board of Health of Nebraska, by telegraph, for week ended June 8, 1918:

Smallpox: Comstock, Bloomington, Monowi.   Typhoid fever: Thurston.

Virginia.

From the State Board of Health of Virginia, by telegraph, for week ended June 8, 1918:

One case smallpox King and Queen County, 3 Bedford, 1 Fauquier, 1 Norfolk, 14 Wise, 1 Newport News.   One case cerebrospinal meningitis Hanover County, 1 Norfolk, 1 James City.

Washington.

From Collaborating Epidemiologist Tuttle, by telegraph, for week ended June 8, 1918:

Scarlet fever: Seattle 26 cases, Hoquiam 3, Tacoma 37.   Poliomyelitis: Ferry County 1.   No unusual outbreaks other communicable diseases.

CEREBROSPINAL MENINGITIS.

Oregon Report for April, 1918.

During the month of April, 1918, one case of cerebrospinal meningitis was reported in Clatsop County, Oreg., and two cases were reported in Portland, Oreg.

City Reports for Week Ended May 25, 1818.

Place.	Cases.	Deaths.	Place.	Cases.	Deaths.
Augusta, Ga.	1	1	Newburyport, Mass.	1	1
Bakersfield, Cal.	1		New York, N. Y.	11	6
Baltimore, Md.	3	2	Norfolk, Va.	1	
Boston, Mass.	2	1	Petersburg, Va.	1	1
Bridgeport, Conn.	2		Philadelphia, Pa.	6	2
Cambridge, Mass.		1	Piqua, Ohio.	1	1
Canton, Ohio.	1	1	Pittsburgh, Pa.	1	
Cape Girardeau, Mo.	1		Plattsburg, N. Y.		1
Chicago, Ill.	3	1	Providence, R. I.	1	
Cincinnati, Ohio.	1		Racine, Wis.	1	
Cleveland, Ohio.	1		St. Louis, Mo.	2	1
Dayton, Ohio.	1		St. Paul, Minn.		1
Detroit, Mich.	1	2	San Diego, Cal.	1	1
Galesburg, Ill.		1	San Francisco, Cal.	3	1
Greenville, S. C.		1	Savannah, Ga.	1	
Kansas City, Mo.	1		Seattle, Wash.	1	
Little Rock, Ark.	1	1	Taunton, Mass.		1
Los Angeles, Cal.	1	1	Utica, N. Y.		1
Lynchburg, Va.	1		Washington, D. C.	3	
Milwaukee, Wis.	3		Washington, Pa.	1	
Minneapolis, Minn.		1	Winston-Salem, N. C.	2	1
Newark, N. J.		1	Worcester, Mass.	2	1

DIPHTHERIA.

See Diphtheria, measles, scarlet fever, and tuberculosis, page 986.

61566°—18——2

ERYSIPELAS.

City Reports for Week Ended May 25, 1918.

Place.	Cases.	Deaths.	Place.	Cases.	Deaths.
Anniston, Ala...............	1	....	Los Angeles, Cal............	3	....
Atlanta, Ga................	1	....	Louisville, Ky..............	2	....
Baltimore, Md..............	1	1	McAlester, Okla............	1	....
Berkeley, Cal..............	1	....	Milwaukee, Wis.............	3	....
Boston, Mass..............	....	2	Newark, N. J...............	7	....
Buffalo, N. Y..............	2	....	New York, N. Y.............	....	3
Cape Girardeau, Mo........	1	....	Niagara Falls, N. Y........	2	....
Chicago, Ill...............	11	3	Norfolk, Va................	1	....
Cleveland, Ohio............	2	....	Omaha, Nebr................	1	....
Cumberland, Md............	1	....	Philadelphia, Pa...........	3	1
Detroit, Mich..............	3	....	Portland, Oreg.............	2	....
Duluth, Minn..............	1	....	Rochester, N. Y............	2	....
East Liverpool, Ohio.......	....	1	St. Louis, Mo..............	9	....
El Paso, Tex...............	....	1	St. Paul, Minn.............	1	1
Flint, Mich................	3	....	San Francisco, Cal.........	1	....
Fort Collins, Colo.........	2	....	Schenectady, N. Y..........	....	1
Fort Wayne, Ind...........	....	1	Superior, Wis..............	....	1
Gardner, Mass.............	1	....	Tyler, Tex.................	1	....
Jackson, Mich.............	1	....	Warren, Ohio...............	1	1
Joplin, Mo................	....	5	Wheeling, W. Va............	2	....
Kansas City, Kans.........	1	....	Wichita, Kans..............	1	....
Kansas City, Mo...........	4	....			

LEPROSY.

City Report for Week Ended May 25, 1918.

During the week ended May 25, 1918, one case of leprosy was reported at New Orleans, La.

MALARIA.

City Reports for Week Ended May 25, 1918.

Place.	Cases.	Deaths.	Place.	Cases.	Deaths.
Alexandria, La.............	5	....	McAlester, Okla............	2	....
Beaumont, Tex.............	1	....	Memphis, Tenn.............	2	....
Birmingham, Ala...........	3	....	Montgomery, Ala...........	7	....
Corsicana, Tex............	6	....	Newark, N. J..............	1	....
Holland, Mich.............	1	....	New Orleans, La...........	3	1
Joplin, Mo................	2	....	North Little Rock, Ark.....	1	....
Little Rock, Ark..........	1	....	Palestine, Tex.............	30	....
Louisville, Ky............	2	....	Richmond, Va..............	2	....
Lynn, Mass................	1	....	Trenton, N. J..............	1	....
Macon, Ga................	5	....	Tuscaloosa, Ala...........	4	....
Marshall, Tex.............	1	....			

MEASLES.

See Diphtheria, measles, scarlet fever, and tuberculosis, page 986.

PELLAGRA.

City Reports for Week Ended May 25, 1918.

	Cases.	Deaths.	Place.	Cases.	Deaths.
Atlanta, Ga................	....	4	New Orleans, La...........	2	2
Birmingham, Ala...........	7	2	Norfolk, Va................	....	1
Boston, Mass..............	1	....	Palestine, Tex.............	4	....
Chelsea, Mass.............	1	....	Perry, Mich................	....	1
Corsicana, Tex............	1	....	Raleigh, N. C..............	3	....
El Paso, Tex..............	....	1	Richmond, Va..............	1	....
Hartford, Conn............	1	1	Savannah, Ga..............	....	1
Hattiesburg, Miss.........	1	....	Spartanburg, S. C..........	3	1
Lexington, Ky.............	....	1	Springfield, Mo............	1	....
Lynchburg, Va.............	2	....	Tuscaloosa, Ala...........	1	....
Macon, Ga................	....	2	Wilmington, N. C..........	....	1
Marshall, Tex.............	1	....	Winston-Salem, N. C.......	2	....
Memphis, Tenn............	2	....	Youngstown, Ohio..........	1	....
Montgomery, Ala..........	....	2			

PNEUMONIA.

City Reports for Week Ended May 25, 1918.

Place.	Cases.	Deaths.	Place.	Cases.	Deaths.
Amsterdam, N. Y	2	1	Los Angeles, Cal	8	6
Ann Arbor, Mich	1	....	Lynn, Mass	8	2
Arlington, Mass	1	....	Manitowoc, Wis	1	1
Baltimore, Md	19	8	Marquette, Mich	1	....
Battle Creek, Mich	1	....	Marshall, Tex	1	....
Beaumont, Tex	1	....	Melrose, Mass	1	....
Boston, Mass	9	15	Natick, Mass	1	....
Brockton, Mass	1	1	Newark, N. J	40	14
Buffalo, N. Y	1	11	New Bedford, Mass	1	1
Cambridge, Mass	2	1	Newburgh, N. Y	1	1
Cape Girardeau, Mo	2	....	Newburyport, Mass	1	....
Chattanooga, Tenn	1	2	Newton, Mass	1	....
Chelsea, Mass	1	....	North Adams, Mass	1	....
Chicago, Ill	111	55	North Little Rock, Ark	2	1
Cleveland, Ohio	18	10	Palestine, Tex	6	2
Council Bluffs, Iowa	1	1	Peabody, Mass	1	....
Dayton, Ohio	1	1	Philadelphia, Pa	48	34
Detroit, Mich	10	23	Pittsfield, Mass	1	1
Evansville, Ind	1	1	Port Chester, N. Y	1	1
Everett, Mass	1	1	Quincy, Mass	1	....
Fall River, Mass	3	1	Richmond, Va	1	1
Flint, Mich	4	1	Rochester, N. Y	14	2
Framingham, Mass	1	....	Rutland, Vt	2	....
Fremont, Ohio	2	....	Salem, Mass	1	1
Grand Rapids, Mich	2	....	San Francisco, Cal	6	11
Greenwich, Conn	2	....	Santa Cruz, Cal	1	1
Hancock, Mich	1	....	Sault Ste. Marie, Mich	1	....
Harrison, N. J	1	....	Schenectady, N. Y	3	3
Holland, Mich	1	....	Somerville, Mass	3	....
Houston, Tex	2	4	Springfield, Mass	3	1
Jackson, Mich	1	....	Springfield, Ohio	1	1
Kansas City, Kans	1	....	Tacoma, Wash	4	....
Kansas City, Mo	2	7	Tuscaloosa, Ala	3	....
Lackawanna, N. Y	5	....	Waco, Tex	1	....
Leavenworth, Kans	2	1	Wichita, Kans	2	....
Lincoln, Nebr	1	....	Wilmington, Del	3	3
Little Rock, Ark	4	....	Worcester, Mass	6	4
Long Beach, Cal	1	2	Youngstown, Ohio	3	2

POLIOMYELITIS (INFANTILE PARALYSIS).

City Reports for Week Ended May 25, 1918.

Place.	Cases.	Deaths.	Place.	Cases.	Deaths.
Bakersfield, Cal	1	....	Moundsville, W. Va	1	....
Birmingham, Ala	....	1	Newark, N. J	1	1
Chicago, Ill	1	....	New York, N. Y	1	....
Lowell, Mass	....	1	Palestine, Tex	1	....
Marshall, Tex	1	....	San Diego, Cal	1	....
Milwaukee, Wis	1	....	Toledo, Ohio	....	1

RABIES IN ANIMALS.

City Reports for Week Ended May 25, 1918.

Place.	Cases.	Place.	Cases.
Buffalo, N. Y	1	Pueblo, Colo	2
Chillicothe, Ohio	1	Schenectady, N. Y	2
Fort Collins, Colo	2		

SCARLET FEVER.

See Diphtheria, measles, scarlet fever, and tuberculosis, page 986.

SMALLPOX.
Oregon Report for April, 1918.

Place.	Cases.	Deaths.	Place.	Cases.	Deaths.
Oregon:			Oregon—Continued.		
Clackamas County	9	....	Multnomah County—		
Clatsop County	2	....	Portland	2	....
Columbia County	1	....	Wallowa County	1	....
Grant County	3	....	Wasco County	1	....
Jefferson County	1	....	Wheeler County	2	....
Malheur County	2	....			
			Total	24	....

City Reports for Week Ended May 25, 1918.

Place.	Cases.	Deaths.	Place.	Cases.	Deaths.
Abilene, Tex	6	....	Kalamazoo, Mich	15	....
Akron, Ohio	18	....	Kansas City, Kans	17	....
Alexandria, La	6	....	Kansas City, Mo	32	....
Alton, Ill	3	....	Knoxville, Tenn	15	....
Anniston, Ala	1	....	Laurel, Miss	2	....
Atlanta, Ga	10	....	Lawrence, Kans	4	....
Bakersfield, Cal	1	....	Leavenworth, Kans	3	....
Baltimore, Md	5	....	Lincoln, Nebr	10	....
Beatrice, Nebr	1	....	Little Falls, N. Y	1	....
Benton Harbor, Mich	1	....	Little Rock, Ark	5	....
Birmingham, Ala	19	....	Lorain, Ohio	5	....
Buffalo, N. Y	2	....	Los Angeles, Cal	1	....
Burlington, Iowa	2	....	Louisville, Ky	5	....
Butte, Mont	2	....	Macon, Ga	8	....
Canton, Ill	1	....	Madison, Wis	1	....
Canton, Ohio	2	....	Marinette, Wis	1	....
Cape Girardeau, Mo	5	....	Marion, Ind	2	....
Chanute, Kans	1	....	Marshall, Tex	1	....
Charleston, W. Va	5	....	Marshalltown, Iowa	9	....
Chattanooga, Tenn	11	....	McAlester, Okla	4	....
Cheyenne, Wyo	1	....	Memphis, Tenn	4	....
Chicago, Ill	3	....	Middletown, Ohio	4	....
Chillicothe, Ohio	1	....	Milwaukee, Wis	3	....
Cincinnati, Ohio	7	....	Minneapolis, Minn	11	....
Cleveland, Ohio	24	....	Mobile, Ala	1	....
Coffeyville, Kans	2	....	Montgomery, Ala	2	....
Colorado Springs, Colo	1	....	Muncie, Ind	3	....
Columbus, Ohio	4	....	Muskogee, Okla	6	....
Corsicana, Tex	1	....	New Orleans, La	3	....
Council Bluffs, Iowa	2	....	New York, N. Y	2	....
Covington, Ky	2	....	North Little Rock, Ark	1	....
Dallas, Tex	4	....	Ogden, Utah		....
Danville, Ill	2	....	Oklahoma City, Okla	24	....
Davenport, Iowa	6	....	Omaha, Nebr	10	....
Dayton, Ohio	1	....	Parkersburg, W. Va	2	....
Denver, Colo	30	....	Peoria, Ill	7	....
Detroit, Mich	4	....		6	....
Duluth, Minn	1	....			....
East Liverpool, Ohio	2	....		5	....
El Paso, Tex	1	....		2	....
Elyria, Ohio	1	....		1	....
Erie, Pa	1	....		5	....

TETANUS.

City Reports for Week Ended May 25, 1918.

Place.	Cases.	Deaths.	Place.	Cases.	Deaths.
Baltimore, Md.................		2	Newark, N. J.................	1	1
Cleveland, Ohio.............	1		New Orleans, La.............		1
Flint, Mich..................	1	1	New York, N. Y.............		1
Kansas City, Mo.............	9	1	Omaha, Nebr................		1
Lawrence, Mass.............		1	Savannah, Ga...............		1
Marshalltown, Iowa..........	2		Wilmington, Del.............	1	1

TUBERCULOSIS.

See Diphtheria, measles, scarlet fever, and tuberculosis, page 986.

TYPHOID FEVER.

Oregon Report for April, 1918.

Place.	New cases reported.	Place.	Now cases reported.
Oregon:		Oregon—Continued.	
Douglas County......................	1	Umatilla.................	2
Jackson County....................	1	Wallowa...................	2
Multnomah County—			
Portland......................	4	Total.....................	10

City Reports for Week Ended May 25, 1918.

Place.	Cases.	Deaths.	Place.	Cases.	Deaths.
Alexandria, La................	1		Joplin, Mo................	1	
Allentown, Pa................	1		Kansas City, Mo...........		1
Altoona, Pa..................	1		Knoxville, Tenn...........	2	
Arlington, Mass.............	1		La Crosse, Wis............	1	
Augusta, Ga.................	1		Lancaster, Pa.............	1	
Baltimore, Md...............	1	1	Lo, Angeles, Cal...........	2	1
Berkeley, Cal...............	1		Macon, Ga................	2	
Billings, Mont..............	1		Manchester, N. H.........	1	
Birmingham, Ala............	2		Marshall, Tex.............	1	
Boston, Mass...............	5	1	Massillon, Ohio...........	1	
Braddock, Pa...............	1		McAlester, Okla...........	1	1
Charleston, S. C............	2		Memphis, Tenn............	1	
Chester, Pa.................	1		Middletown, N. Y..........	1	
Chicago, Ill................	4		Milwaukee, Wis...........	1	
Chicopee, Mass.............	1		Minneapolis, Minn.........	2	1
Cincinnati, Ohio...........	1		Mobile, Ala...............	3	
Cleveland, Ohio............	1		Moline, Ill...............	6	
Coatesville, Pa.............	1		Montgomery, Ala..........	1	
Columbia, S. C.............	2		Morgantown, W. Va........	2	
Danville, Ill...............	1		Muscatine, Iowa..........	1	
Detroit, Mich..............	1	1	New Albany, Ind..........	1	1
East Liverpool, Ohio.......		2	Newark, N. J.............	3	
El Paso, Tex...............	1		New Bedford, Mass........	1	
Erie, Pa...................	1		Newburgh, N. Y...........	4	
Fall River, Mass...........	2		Newburyport, Mass........	1	
Flint, Mich................	2		New Orleans, La..........	9	1
Fort Collins, Colo..........	1		New York, N. Y...........	9	1
Fort Scott, Kans...........	1		North Braddock, Pa.......	1	
Fort Wayne, Ind...........	1		Oakland, Cal.............	4	
Fort Worth, Tex...........	3		Oklahoma City, Okla......	1	
Galveston, Tex.............	3		Omaha, Nebr.............	1	
Geneva, N. Y..............	1		Oswego, N. Y.............	1	
Grand Rapids, Mich........	1		Palestine, Tex............	3	
Green Bay, Wis............	1		Philadelphia, Pa..........	6	
Greenville, S. C...........	2		Pittsburgh, Pa............	1	
Houston, Tex..............	1		Portland, Me.............	1	
Independence, Mo..........	2		Portland, Oreg...........	1	
Indianapolis, Ind..........	3		Portsmouth, N. H.........	1	
Ithaca, N. Y...............	1		Quincy, Ill...............	1	
Jersey City, N. J...........	1		Reading, Pa..............	2	
Johnstown, Pa.............	1		Richmond, Va.............	2	

TYPHOID FEVER—Continued.

City Reports for Week Ended May 25, 1918—Continued.

Place.	Cases.	Deaths.	Place.	Cases.	Deaths
Riverside, Cal..	1	1	Terre Haute, Ind.		1
Sacramento, Cal.	3		Toledo, Ohio.	1	
Saginaw, Mich.	1		Waco, Tex.	2	
Salt Lake City, Utah.	2		Walla Walla, Wash.	3	
Savannah, Ga.	3		West Warwick, R. I.	1	
Scranton, Pa.	3		Washington, D. C.	2	
Sheboygan, Wis.	1		Wheeling, W. Va.	2	
Shenandoah, Pa.	1		Wilkinsburg, Pa.	2	
Springfield, Mo.		1	Winston-Salem, N. C.	2	
Taunton, Mass.	1				

TYPHUS FEVER.

City Report for Week Ended May 25, 1918.

Two cases of typhus fever were reported at New York, N. Y., during the week ended May 25, 1918.

DIPHTHERIA, MEASLES, SCARLET FEVER, AND TUBERCULOSIS.

Oregon Report for April, 1918.

During the month of April, 1918, there were reported in Oregon, 9 cases of diphtheria, 450 cases of measles, and 60 cases of scarlet fever.

City Reports for Week Ended May 25, 1918.

City.	Population as of July 1, 1916 (estimated by U. S. Census Bureau).	Total deaths from all causes.	Diphtheria.		Measles.		Scarlet fever.		Tuberculosis.	
			Cases.	Deaths.	Cases.	Deaths.	Cases.	Deaths.	Cases.	Deaths.
Over 500,000 inhabitants:										
Baltimore, Md.	589,621	249	15		266	5	3		36	38
Boston, Mass.	756,476	215	65	4	315	4	32		74	24
Chicago, Ill.	2,497,722	630	119	12	115	3	38	2	477	75
Cleveland, Ohio	674,073	164	9		161		7		28	27
Detroit, Mich.	571,784	215	34	6	80	3	54	2	27	35
Los Angeles, Cal.	503,812	164	16	1	90		11		21	12
New York, N. Y.	5,602,841	1,253	324	20	852	30	120	8	263	149
Philadelphia, Pa.	1,709,518	567	54	9	913	8	31	1	130	46
Pittsburgh, Pa.	579,090		10	1	215		6		27	
St. Louis, Mo.	757,309	206	79	2	75	3	18		30	20
From 300,000 to 500,000 inhabitants:										
Buffalo, N. Y.	468,558	128	8	3	230		16		28	15
Cincinnati, Ohio.	410,476	124	16		67	1	5		22	19
Jersey City, N. J.	300,615		12		26		4		14	
Milwaukee, Wis.	439,735	94	11	1	289	4	20	2	40	16
Minneapolis, Minn.	363,454		13	1	72	1	38	1	30	14
Newark, N. J.	408,894	128	14	1	305	7	14		46	17
New Orleans, La.	371,747		3		6	2			40	17
San Francisco, Cal.	463,516	132	11		61		7		34	15
Seattle, Wash.	315,654		2		51		20			
Washington, D. C.	363,980	112	23	1	140	2	19		36	12
From 200,000 to 300,000 inhabitants:										
Columbus, Ohio.	214,878	72	1		23		15		7	8
Denver, Colo.	260,800	57	14	2	19		27			11
Indianapolis, Ind.	271,708		17	1	27		18		18	9
Kansas City, Mo.	297,874	23	6	5	19		14	1	7	7
Louisville, Ky.	238,910	66	4	1	5		2		39	17
Portland, Oreg.	275,095		2		129		9		12	4
Providence, R. I.	254,960	56	7		181	5	2		1	
Rochester, N. Y.	256,417		5	1	130		15		21	7
St. Paul, Minn.	247,232	65	16	1	1		28	2	11	4

DIPHTHERIA, MEASLES, SCARLET FEVER, AND TUBERCULOSIS—Contd.

City Reports for Week Ended May 25, 1918—Continued.

City.	Population as of July 1, 1916 (estimated by U.S. Census Bureau).	Total deaths from all causes.	Diphtheria.		Measles.		Scarlet fever.		Tuberculosis.	
			Cases.	Deaths.	Cases.	Deaths.	Cases.	Deaths.	Cases.	Deaths.
From 100,000 to 200,000 inhabitants:										
Atlanta, Ga	190,558	69	3	...	2	...	1	...	3	4
Birmingham, Ala	181,762	63	...	...	15	...	1	...	10	3
Bridgeport, Conn	121,576	29	11	1	19	...	4	...	5	6
Cambridge, Mass	112,921	27	4	...	75	2	...	...	8	3
Camden, N.J	106,233	...	6	...	11	...	3	...	6	...
Dallas, Tex	124,527	6	...	...	2	...	...	...	...	3
Dayton, Ohio	127,244	38	1	...	...	...	...	...	3	5
Fall River, Mass	128,360	32	2	1	10	...	2	...	10	4
Fort Worth, Tex	104,562	28	...	...	...	...	...	...	2	2
Grand Rapids, Mich	128,291	25	2	...	25	...	11	...	4	1
Hartford, Conn	110,900	...	7	...	2	...	2	...	4	3
Houston, Tex	112,307	38	3	...	1	...	...	...	2	3
Lawrence, Mass	100,560	26	1	...	189	2	...	...	3	2
Lowell, Mass	113,245	...	...	...	17	...	1	...	5	4
Lynn, Mass	102,425	27	3	...	54	...	...	...	1	3
Memphis, Tenn	148,995	55	...	...	10	...	4	...	18	7
New Bedford, Mass	118,158	29	1	...	4	...	1	...	8	6
New Haven, Conn	149,685	...	1	...	2	1	1	...	6	3
Oakland, Cal	196,604	35	3	...	12	...	4	...	4	4
Omaha, Nebr	165,470	50	14	4	11	...	26	...	...	5
Reading, Pa	109,381	...	1	...	19	...	1	...	...	...
Richmond, Va	156,687	40	1	...	76	1	3	...	11	5
Salt Lake City, Utah	117,399	30	1	...	27	...	15	...	1	...
Scranton, Pa	146,811	...	4	...	5	...	...	...	11	...
Spokane, Wash	150,323	...	3	...	...	...	6	...	...	...
Springfield, Mass	105,942	29	3	...	40	...	3	...	5	2
Syracuse, N.Y	155,624	41	4	...	73	1	9	...	8	3
Tacoma, Wash	112,770	...	1	...	13	...	36	...	4	...
Toledo, Ohio	191,554	70	3	...	8	...	2	...	15	8
Trenton, N.J	111,593	28	79	1	6	...	...	...	6	...
Worcester, Mass	163,314	41	6	1	12	...	9	...	10	4
Youngstown, Ohio	108,385	35	2	...	13	...	...	...	3	2
From 50,000 to 100,000 inhabitants:										
Akron, Ohio	85,625	50	6	...	26	...	15	...	14	10
Allentown, Pa	63,505	...	4	...	102	...	4	...	...	...
Altoona, Pa	58,659	...	3	...	18	...	1	...	1	...
Atlantic City, N.J	57,660	6	...	...	10	...	...	...	4	2
Augusta, Ga	50,245	16	...	...	5	...	...	...	...	1
Bayonne, N.J	69,893	...	2	...	8	...	...	...	5	...
Berkeley, Cal	57,653	8	8	1	9	...	1	...	2	1
Binghamton, N.Y	53,973	17	3	...	61	...	1	...	3	6
Brockton, Mass	67,449	14	...	...	26	...	3	...	2	...
Canton, Ohio	60,852	14	...	...	...	...	...	...	...	1
Charleston, S.C	60,734	26	...	1	...	1	1	...	1	1
Chattanooga, Tenn	60,075	3	...	...	...	...	1	...	3	...
Covington, Ky	57,144	17	2	...	4	...	1	...	3	3
Duluth, Minn	94,495	25	...	...	...	...	1	...	5	...
El Paso, Tex	63,705	...	...	...	4	...	1	...	...	10
Erie, Pa	75,195	...	...	...	120	...	...	...	1	...
Evansville, Ind	76,078	13	6	1	7	...	...	...	6	3
Flint, Mich	54,772	15	2	1	7	...	6	...	...	...
Fort Wayne, Ind	76,183	17	2	1	18	...	1	...	7	2
Harrisburg, Pa	72,015	...	2	...	7	...	...	...	...	...
Hoboken, N.J	77,214	13	3	...	3	...	2	...	4	4
Holyoke, Mass	65,286	22	...	...	1	...	1	...	3	2
Johnstown, Pa	68,529	...	...	...	14	...	3	...	...	...
Kansas City, Kans	99,437	...	1	...	27	...	6	...	3	...
Lancaster, Pa	50,853	...	...	...	2	...	1	...	...	...
Little Rock, Ark	57,343	12	...	...	3	...	4	...	8	...
Malden, Mass	51,155	14	5	...	68	...	1	...	1	...
Manchester, N.H	78,283	21	...	...	3	...	1	...	1	4
Mobile, Ala	58,221	12	1	...	3	...	...	...	1	3
New Britain, Conn	53,794	16	...	...	5	...	3	...	...	1
Norfolk, Va	89,612	...	1	...	5	...	5	...	...	2
Oklahoma City, Okla	92,943	19	...	...	...	...	...	...	...	2
Passaic, N.J	71,744	...	4	...	87	...	2	...	4	2
Pawtucket, R.I	59,411	23	...	...	12	2	2	...	...	3
Peoria, Ill	71,458	33	...	...	13	1	6	...	...	3
Portland, Mo	63,867	13	1	...	6	...	...	...	...	4
Pueblo, Colo	54,462	18	...	...	17	...	2	...	...	1
Rockford, Ill	55,185	16	...	...	26	...	...	1	...	3

DIPHTHERIA, MEASLES, SCARLET FEVER, AND TUBERCULOSIS—Contd.

City Reports for Week Ended May 25, 1918—Continued.

City.	Population as of July 1, 1916 (estimated by U. S. Census Bureau).	Total deaths from all causes.	Diphtheria.		Measles.		Scarlet fever.		Tuberculosis.	
			Cases.	Deaths.	Cases.	Deaths.	Cases.	Deaths.	Cases.	Deaths.
From 50,000 to 100,000 inhabitants—Continued.										
Sacramento, Cal	66,895	27	1		16		7		4	3
Saginaw, Mich	55,642	9	1	1	3					1
St. Joseph, Mo	85,236	22	1				1			1
San Diego, Cal	53,330	23	1		11		1			3
Savannah, Ga	68,805	32			3		1		3	3
Schenectady, N. Y	99,519	24			25				8	4
Sioux City, Iowa	57,078						2			
Somerville, Mass	87,039	31	8		50	1			5	2
South Bend, Ind	68,946	13			2				2	1
Springfield, Ohio	51,550	16			5	1			1	1
Terre Haute, Ind	66,093	19			3					
Utica, N. Y	85,692	33	4		43		3		32	4
Wichita, Kans	70,722				1				4	
Wilkes-Barre, Pa	75,776		4		31		2		4	
Wilmington, Del	94,265	31	1		12	1	1		1	1
Yonkers, N. Y	99,818	21	4	2	88		2		1	3
York, Pa	51,656				11		3		3	
From 25,000 to 50,000 inhabitants:										
Alameda, Cal	27,732	6	1	1	36		3			
Amsterdam, N. Y	37,103	1			2					1
Auburn, N. Y	37,385	12			13		1		2	1
Austin, Tex	34,811	17								4
Battle Creek, Mich	29,480		3		29		3		1	
Beaumont, Tex	27,711	11								
Boise, Idaho	33,846	2			6					
Brookline, Mass	32,730	8			12		1		1	
Burlington, Iowa	25,030	7					1			
Butler, Pa	27,042			1	2					
Butte, Mont	43,125		3	1	2		7			
Cedar Rapids, Iowa	37,408		2				3			
Central Falls, R. I	25,636				1		2			
Charleston, W. Va	29,911	7			7					1
Charlotte, N. C	39,823	4		1					2	
Chelsea, Mass	46,192	9	4		20		2		9	
Chester, Pa	41,396				11				2	
Chicopee, Mass	29,519	3	1		19				3	4
Clinton, Iowa	27,389				19					
Cohoes, N. Y	25,211	5	1						2	1
Colorado Springs, Colo	32,971	11	1						12	1
Columbia, S. C	34,011								1	
Council Bluffs, Iowa	31,481	5			2		4			
Cranston, R. I	25,987	3			1					
Cumberland, Md	26,074	5			16		13		2	
Danville, Ill	32,283	12			1		2			
Davenport, Iowa	48,811									
Dubuque, Iowa	39,883		4							
Durham, N. C	25,094	10			10					4
Easton, Pa	30,530				11					
East Orange, N. J	42,408	11	1		37		1		4	1
Elgin, Ill	28,204	8								1
Elmira, N. Y	38,130				36					
Evanston, Ill	28,004	5					1			
Everett, Mass	39,103	7	1		6				7	5
Everett, Wash	34,105				1					
Fresno, Cal	34,508	10			11		1		3	
Galveston, Tex	41,863	12	1		3		1			1
Green Bay, Wis	29,753	12			1		1			
Hammond, Ind	29,171	15	3		1		3		1	2
Hoboken, Pa	28,394				39					
Jackson, Mich	35,996	20	3	1	22		5	2	4	1
Joplin, Mo	33,454				4		1		2	
Kalamazoo, Mich	48,889	15			3				6	
Kenosha, Wis	31,576	10	6	3	11		1			
Knoxville, Tenn	38,679				4				2	2
La Crosse, Wis	31,677	9								
Lexington, Ky	41,697	20			6					5
Lincoln, Nebr	46,915	9	1		2					
Long Beach, Cal	27,757	11			10		3			1
Lorain, Ohio	36,940		1						1	
Lynchburg, Va	32,940	4					1			
Macon, Ga	45,757	20			1		1		3	

DIPHTHERIA, MEASLES, SCARLET FEVER, AND TUBERCULOSIS—Contd.

City Reports for Week Ended May 25, 1918—Continued.

City.	Population as of July 1, 1916 (estimated by U. S. Census Bureau).	Total deaths from all causes.	Diphtheria.		Measles.		Scarlet fever.		Tuberculosis.	
			Cases.	Deaths.	Cases.	Deaths.	Cases.	Deaths.	Cases.	Deaths.
From 25,000 to 50,000 inhabitants—Continued.										
Madison, Wis	30,699	14			9		2			2
McKeesport, Pa	47,521		1		15					
Medford, Mass	26,234	4			20		4		2	
Moline, Ill	27,451	4			35	1	1			
Montclair, N. J	26,318	2			4		1			
Montgomery, Ala	43,285	29			6				4	2
Mount Vernon, N. Y	37,009	7			10		1		1	
Muncie, Ind	25,424	9	1							2
Nashua, N. H	27,327	6								2
Newburgh, N. Y	29,603	12	2	1					3	2
New Castle, Pa	41,133				7					
Newport, Ky	31,927	7							2	2
Newport, R. I	30,108	5	2				3			
Newton, Mass	43,715	10	2		9		1		1	
Niagara Falls, N. Y	37,353	15	2		4		1		2	
Norwalk, Conn	26,899								1	1
Oak Park, Ill	26,654	13	1		11		1			
Ogden, Utah	31,404	9			24		2		1	
Orange, N. J	33,080	8	1		59				4	
Oshkosh, Wis	36,065	12							2	2
Pasadena, Cal	46,450	13			71		10		5	
Perth Amboy, N. J	41,185	6			6					1
Petersburg, Va	25,582	12							1	3
Pittsfield, Mass	38,629		1				9		2	2
Poughkeepsie, N Y	30,390	8	1		15				2	
Quincy, Ill	36,798	11	4	1	7				1	2
Quincy, Mass	38,136	12	3		49		2		1	2
Racine, Wis	46,486	15	2		8		3		1	
Roanoke, Va	43,284	8	1		17					1
Rock Island, Ill	28,926	8	2		23		6		3	
Salem, Mass	48,562	13	1		55		1			1
San Jose, Cal	38,902				8				2	
Sheboygan, Wis	28,559	6			1		3			
Shenandoah, Pa	29,201		2						1	
Springfield, Mo	40,341	14								2
Steubenville, Ohio	27,445	11			3				1	
Superior, Wis	46,266	10	1		3		5			
Taunton, Mass	36,283	17	1		7				2	3
Topeka, Kans	48,726	20			8		9		1	1
Waco, Tex	33,385	19			4		1		3	2
Walla Walla, Wash	25,136				1		2			
Waltham, Mass	30,570	4								
Waterloo, Iowa	35,559	14					6			
Watertown, N. Y	29,891	3								3
Wheeling, W. Va	43,377	12			4					
Wilmington, N. C	29,892	11			4	1			2	
Winston-Salem, N. C	31,155	21			4		2		8	4
Zanesville, Ohio	30,863	8								3
From 10,000 to 25,000 inhabitants:										
Aberdeen, S. Dak	15,218									1
Abilene, Tex	14,238						6			
Adams, Mass	14,214	1								1
Alexandria, La	15,333	9			2				3	
Alton, Ill	22,874	7								1
Ann Arbor, Mich	15,010	9	2		12					
Anniston, Ala	14,112				8				1	
Ansonia, Conn	16,704	2							1	
Appleton, Wis	17,834	7					1			
Arlington, Mass	12,811	2	2		1				2	
Asbury Park, N. J	14,007	4			15				1	2
Attleboro, Mass	19,282	5								
Bakersfield, Cal	16,874	8								1
Batavia, N. Y	13,350	3					2		1	1
Beacon, N. Y	11,555	1								
Beatrice, Nebr	10,287	5			8		2			
Bedford, Ind	10,349	1								
Bellaire, Ohio	14,348	6			3				1	1
Beloit, Wis	18,072	5	2		20				1	
Benton Harbor, Mich	10,833				5					
Berlin, N. H	13,599	9				1				
Bethlehem, Pa	14,142		1		25				7	
Billings, Mont	14,422				12					

DIPHTHERIA, MEASLES, SCARLET FEVER, AND TUBERCULOSIS—Cont.

City Reports for Week Ended May 25, 1918—Continued.

City.	Population as of July 1, 1916 (estimated by U.S. Census Bureau).	Total deaths from all causes.	Diphtheria.		Measles.		Scarlet fever.		Tuberculosis.	
			Cases.	Deaths.	Cases.	Deaths.	Cases.	Deaths.	Cases.	Deaths.
From 10,000 to 25,000 inhabitants—Continued.										
Bloomfield, N. J.	18,466	1			1		2		6	1
Braddock, Pa.	21,685		1		10		9			
Bradford, Pa.	15,029				16		9			
Bristol, Conn.	15,927	2							2	1
Burlington, Vt.	21,617	10			1		1			1
Cairo, Ill.	15,794	4								
Canton, Ill.	13,262	2			3					1
Cape Girardeau, Mo.	10,775		1				1		3	
Carbondale, Pa.	19,212				1					
Carlisle, Pa.	10,726		3							
Carnegie, Pa.	11,692				1					
Chanute, Kans.	12,445				3		1			
Chillicothe, Ohio	15,470	3	3				5		1	1
Clinton, Mass.	13,075	4			1					
Coatesville, Pa.	14,455				8					
Coffeyville, Kans.	17,518				2		2			
Columbia, Pa.	11,451				2					
Concord, N. H.	22,669	4			3				1	
Corning, N. Y.	15,406	5	1							
Corpus Christi, Tex.	10,432	8								2
Corsicana, Tex.	10,022	4							1	1
Cortland, N. Y.	13,069	4			1					
Cumberland, R. I.	10,848		2		10				1	
Dedham, Mass.	10,433	2							1	
Dover, N. H.	13,252	2	1		4		1			
Dunkirk, N. Y.	20,743	3								
Dunmore, Pa.	20,570				2					
East Liverpool, Ohio	22,386	11					5			3
Eau Claire, Wis.	18,807				17		2			
Elwood, Ind.	11,028	3			2		1			
Elyria, Ohio	18,618	7	1							1
Englewood, N. J.	12,231	4			9					
Enid, Okla.	20,307	4							1	2
Escanaba, Mich.	15,185	9	1				3			
Eugene, Oreg.	13,572				14					
Fargo, N. Dak.	17,669	7								1
Farrell, Pa.	10,190				8					
Findlay, Ohio	14,858		1		41					
Fort Collins, Colo.	11,451	4			8		1			
Fort Scott, Kans.	10,530	1			1		1			
Framingham, Mass.	13,982	4			5		1			
Frederick, Md.	11,112	7			2					1
Fremont, Ohio	10,582								1	
Fulton, N. Y.	11,598	2			8					
Galesburg, Ill.	24,276	5			1					
Gardner, Mass.	17,110	1	6		2				1	1
Geneva, N. Y.	13,711	2			27		1			
Glens Falls, N. Y.	16,894	5	1		1					
Gloucester City, N. J.	11,109	2			7					
Granite City, Ill.	15,142	4	1		2					
Greenfield, Mass.	11,998	6			3					
Greensboro, N. C.	19,557	3			2					
Greenville, S. C.	18,181	3			1					
Greenwich, Conn.	19,170		1		6					1
Hackensack, N. J.	16,945	11	2		13				1	1
Hamtramck, Mich.	12,059	3	2				2			
Harrison, N. J.	16,952				9					
Henderson, Ky.	12,192	8								3
Hopewell, N. Y.	14,685	3	1		11					
Hudson, N. Y.	12,765									
Independence, Kans.	14,599	2			2		1		1	1
Independence, Mo.	11,872	4			4		4			
Iola, Kans.	11,098				3					
Iowa City, Iowa	11,414				4		1			
Irvington, N. J.	16,049				15				2	
Ithaca, N. Y.	15,048	5			1				2	1
Jacksonville, Ill.	15,481	10							1	
Jamestown, W...			1				1			
Johnstown, N. Y.	10,436	3	1		5					
Kearny, N. J.		6	1		20				2	
Keokuk, Iowa	14,008				5		2			

¹ Population Apr. 15, 1910; no estimate made.

DIPHTHERIA, MEASLES, SCARLET FEVER, AND TUBERCULOSIS—Contd.

City Reports for Week Ended May 25, 1918—Continued.

City.	Population as of July 1, 1916 (estimated by U. S. Census Bureau).	Total deaths from all causes.	Diphtheria.		Measles.		Scarlet fever.		Tuberculosis.	
			Cases.	Deaths.	Cases.	Deaths.	Cases.	Deaths.	Cases.	Deaths.
From 10,000 to 25,000 inhabitants— Continued.										
Kokomo, Ind	20,930	6							1	1
Lackawanna, N. Y	15,987	2			3				2	1
La Fayette, Ind	21,2.6	1								
Lancaster, Ohio	15,670				5		1		1	
Lawrence, Kans	13,324								2	
Leavenworth, Kans	[1] 19,363	12			2		1			
Lincoln, R. I	10,383				1					
Little Falls, N. Y	13,451	1							1	
Long Branch, N. J	15,395				23					
Mahanoy, Pa	17,463				4					
Manitowoc, Wis	13,805	7					1		4	1
Mansfield, Ohio	22,734				7					
Marinette, Wis	[1] 14,610	6			1					
Marion, Ind	19,834	2								2
Marlboro, Mass	15,187	1							1	
Marquette, Mich	12,409	5					2		4	2
Marshall, Tex	13,712	3								
Mason City, Iowa	14,475	6								
Massillon, Ohio	15,310	3			1					
Mattoon, Ill	12,582	5			23					
Maywood, Ill	10,529	3								
McAlester, Okla	18,504	1								
Meadville, Pa	13,802				2					
Melrose, Mass	17,445	2							2	
Middletown, N. Y	15,810				2				2	1
Middletown, Ohio	15,625	3			2					1
Milford, Mass	14,110	4			1					1
Mishawaka, Ind	16,385	1								
Missoula, Mont	18,214	3	5							1
Monessen, Pa	21,630		7				1			
Morgantown, W. Va	13,709	5			5					
Morristown, N. J	13,284	3			13					
Moundsville, W. Va	11,153	3								
Muscatine, Iowa	17,500				1					
Nanticoke, Pa	23,126				1		1			
Natick, Mass	10,102	6	2	1	20				1	
New Albany, Ind	23,639	8							1	
Newburyport, Mass	15,243	5	1		6		2		1	
New Castle, Ind	13,241	4								
New London, Conn	20,985	9			1		3			1
North Adams, Mass	[1] 22,019	7		1					1	
Northampton, Mass	19,926	7			13					1
North Attleboro, Mass	11,014	2			6		1			
North Braddock, Pa	15,148		1		2					
North Little Rock, Ark	14,907	3			1				3	2
North Tonawanda, N. Y	13,768	3					1			
Norwood, Ohio	22,286				5					
Ogdensburg, N. Y	16,718	3							1	
Oil City, Pa	19,297				3					
Olean, N. Y	16,624	4								
Ossining, N. Y	13,705	5	1	1	6					
Oswego, N. Y	24,101	3			3				1	
Palestine, Tex	11,845	4							3	1
Parkersburg. W. Va	20,612	6			1					
Peabody, Mass	18,360	3	1		20		1			
Peekskill, N Y	18,530	4								
Phoenixville, Pa	11,714				2					
Piqua, Ohio	14,152	6					2		1	1
Plainfield, N. J	23,803	4			6		1			
Plattsburg, N. Y	12,837	5								
Plymouth, Mass	13,743	1								
Pomona, Cal	13,150				10		4			
Pontiac, Mich	17,524	3			3		2			1
Port Chester, N. Y	16,183	4			3					
Pottstown, Pa	16,794		1		2		1			
Pottsville, Pa	22,372						1			
Provo, Utah	10,645	1								
Rahway, N. J	10,219	2			3					
Raleigh, N. C	20,127	11	2						6	
Redlands, Cal	14,000	1	1		10				1	

[1] Population Apr. 15, 1910; no estimate made.

DIPHTHERIA, MEASLES, SCARLET FEVER, AND TUBERCULOSIS—Contd.

City Reports for Week Ended May 25, 1918—Continued.

City.	Population as of July 1, 1916 (estimated by U. S. Census Bureau).	Total deaths from all causes.	Diphtheria.		Measles.		Scarlet fever.		Tuberculosis.	
			Cases.	Deaths.	Cases.	Deaths.	Cases.	Deaths.	Cases.	Deaths.
From 10,000 to 25,000 inhabitants—Continued.										
Richmond, Ind	24,697	6							2	
Riverside, Cal	19,763	3			6				1	1
Rocky Mount, N. C	12,067	3			1					
Rome, N. Y	23,737		1		2		1		3	
Rutland, Vt	14,831	3					1			
San Bernardino, Cal	16,945		1		1					
Sandusky, Ohio	20,193	3			2					
Sanford, Me	10,916	2								
Santa Barbara, Cal	14,846	1								
Santa Cruz, Cal	14,594	4			1					
Saratoga Springs, N. Y	13,821	4			6					
Sault Ste. Marie, Mich	13,919	2			1					
Shamokin, Pa	21,129		2		2					
Shelbyville, Ind	10,965	1								
Sioux Falls, S. Dak	16,499	3			1				1	
Southbridge, Mass	14,205	2								
Spartanburg, S. C	21,363	12	1		3				1	1
Steelton, Pa	15,548		1						2	
Sunbury, Pa	16,290						1			
Tuscaloosa, Ala	10,488	3			2					
Tyler, Tex	11,865		1							
Uniontown, Pa	20,780		1							
Vallejo, Cal	13,461	9								
Vancouver, Wash	13,180				5		1			
Warren, Ohio	13,059	14			8					
Warren, Pa	14,737				9		1			
Washington, Pa	21,618				3				2	
Watertown, Mass	14,867	4	1		2				1	1
Wausau, Wis	19,239	2								
West Chester, Pa	13,176				1					
Westfield, Mass	18,391	5			3					
West Warwick, R. I	15,782	5			2					
Wilkinsburg, Pa	23,228		2							
Winchester, Mass	10,603	1			2					
Winthrop, Mass	12,692				4		2			
Woburn, Mass	15,969	7					1			

FOREIGN.

CEREBROSPINAL MENINGITIS ON VESSEL.

An outbreak of epidemic cerebrospinal meningitis on the steamship *Anyo Maru* from Panama to Callao, Peru, was reported May 21, 1918.

CHINA.

Examination of Rats—Hongkong.

During the period from February 10 to March 30, 1918, 14,350 rats were examined at Hongkong. No plague infection was found. The last plague-infected rat at Hongkong was reported found during the week ended September 22, 1917.

Examination of Rats—Shanghai.

Rats have been examined at Shanghai as follows: Week ended March 16, 1918, 351 rats; four weeks ended April 20, 1918, 1,120 rats. No plague infection was found.

CHOLERA, PLAGUE, SMALLPOX, TYPHUS FEVER, AND YELLOW FEVER.

Reports Received During Week Ended June 14, 1918.[1]

CHOLERA.

Place.	Date.	Cases.	Deaths.	Remarks.
Indo-China:				
Saigon...................	Apr. 1-14.........	7	5	
Palestine...............				Feb. 7-24, 1918: 90 cases, at 16 localities.
Deir Seneid.............	Feb. 17-24.........	52	....	
Jaffa..................	......do...........	4	....	
Ludd..................	Mar. 22...........	1	....	
Sukkarieh.............	......do...........	11	....	
Persia:				
Bender Bouchir...........	Apr. 22...........	....	....	Present. On Persian Gulf.

PLAGUE.

Place.	Date.	Cases.	Deaths.	Remarks.
Ceylon:				
Colombo.................	Mar. 10-23.........	5	5	
China:				
Hongkong................	Apr. 14-20.........	1	1	
Indo-China:				
Saigon................	Apr. 1-14.........	33	22	
Straits Settlements:				
Penang................	Mar. 17-23.........	1	....	
Singapore................	Mar. 10-23.........	17	15	

[1] From medical officers of the Public Health Service, American consuls, and other sources.

CHOLERA, PLAGUE, SMALLPOX, TYPHUS FEVER, AND YELLOW FEVER—Continued.

Reports Received During Week Ended June 14, 1918—Continued.

SMALLPOX.

Place.	Date.	Cases.	Deaths.	Remarks.
Canada:				
British Columbia—				
Winnipeg	May 19–25	1		
New Brunswick—				
Moncton	May 12–25	2		
Nova Scotia—				
Halifax	May 19–25	3		
Sydney	May 12–25	7		
China:				
Amoy	Apr. 9–15			Present.
Antung	Apr. 21–27	1		
Dairen	Apr. 14–27	18	6	
Hongkong	Mar. 31–Apr. 13	3	1	
Tientsin	Apr. 21–27	3		
Tsingtau	Apr. 22–28	1		
France:				
Paris	Apr. 14–20		1	
Rouen	Apr. 6–20	12	4	Including varioloid.
Indo-China:				
Saigon	Apr. 1–14	312	67	
Japan:				
Kobe	Apr. 21–27	1		
Nagasaki	Apr. 29–May 5	4	1	
Nagoya	Apr. 7–13	2		
Mexico:				
Ciudad Juarez	May 26–June 1	2	1	
Guadalajara	Apr. 1–30	3	1	
Mexico City	Apr. 14–May 11	35		
Newfoundland:				
St. Johns	May 8–24	5		
Portugal:				
Lisbon	Mar. 31–May 6	21		
Russia:				
Vladivostok	Apr. 19–24	6	2	
Straits Settlements:				
Penang	Feb. 24–Mar. 2	1	1	
Singapore	Mar. 17–23	3	1	

TYPHUS FEVER.

Place.	Date.	Cases.	Deaths.	Remarks.
Austria-Hungary:				
Hungary—				Jan 21–Feb. 24, 1918: Cases, 21.
Budapest	Jan. 21–Feb. 24	14		
Brazil:				
Pernambuco	Mar. 16–31	1		
Egypt:				
Alexandria	Mar. 12–18	127	29	
Germany:				Mar. 3–23, 1918: Cases, 28, of which 11 occurred among prisoners of war, Danzig and Marienwerder districts.
Berlin	Mar. 2–23	1		
Great Britain:				
Belfast	May 5–11	1		
Lithuania				Jan 27–Mar 2, 1918. Cases, 1663. In regions occupied by German troops.
Mexico:				
Aguas dientes	May 6–12		4	
Guadalajara	Apr. 1–30	2	2	
Mexico City	Apr. 14–May 21	144		
Poland:				Feb. 10–Mar. 9, 1918: Cases, 3,377, deaths, 522.
Lodz	Feb 10–Mar. 9	292	35	
Warsaw	do	2,747	331	
Russia:				
Vladivostok	Apr. 19–25	3		
Spain:				
Madrid	Apr. 1–15	1	1	
Tunis:				
Tunis	Apr. 29–May 3	6	4	

CHOLERA, PLAGUE, SMALLPOX, TYPHUS FEVER, AND YELLOW FEVER—Continued.

Reports Received from Dec. 29, 1917, to June 7, 1918.

CHOLERA.

Place.	Date.	Cases.	Deaths.	Remarks.
China:				
Antung..................	Nov. 26- Dec. 2....	3	1	
India:				
Bombay.................	Oct. 28-Dec. 15....	19	14	
Do...................	Dec. 30-Mar. 9....	219	191	
Calcutta................	Sept. 16-Dec. 15...		135	
Do...................	Dec. 30 Mar. 16...		135	
Karachi................	Dec. 30-Feb. 23...	25	6	
Madras.................	Nov. 25-Dec. 22...	2	2	
Do...................	Dec. 30-Mar. 16...	47	26	
Rangoon................	Nov. 4-Dec. 22....	5	5	
Do...................	Dec. 30-Mar. 16...	11	6	
Indo-China:				
Provinces..............				Sept. 1-Dec. 31, 1917: Cases, 168;
Anam...........	Sept. 1-Dec. 31....	24	15	deaths, 95.
Cambodia.......	....do...........	71	51	
Cochin-China....	....do...........	58	24	
Saigon.........	Nov. 22 Dec. 9....	4	3	
Do............	Feb. 4-Mar. 11....	8	3	
Kwang-Chow-Wan....	Sept. 1-30........	10	2	
Java:				
East Java...............	Oct. 28-Nov. 3....	1	1	
West Java...............				Oct. 19-Dec. 27, 1917: Cases, 102;
Batavia.........	Oct. 10-Dec. 27...	49	23	deaths, 56. Dec 28, 1917-Feb.
Do............	Dec. 28-Feb. 21...	35	1	21, 1918: Cases, 38; deaths, 7.
Palestine..................				Dec. 28, 1917-Feb. 5, 1918: Cases,
Deir Seneid.............	Dec. 28-Jan. 31...	13		31. Occurring at 7 localities; 2
Sukkarieh..............	....do...........	13		cases in encampments.
Persia....................				July 30-Sept. 3, 1917: Cases, 384;
Achraf.................	July 30-Aug. 16...	90	88	deaths, 276.
Astrabad...............	July 31...........			Present.
Barfrush...............	July 1-Aug. 16....	39	25	
Chahmirzad.............				25 cases reported July 31, 1917.
Chahrastagh............	June 15-July 25...	10	8	
Chraud................	Aug. 26 Sept. 3...	4	2	
Damghan...............	Aug. 26...........			Present.
Kharek................	May 28-June 11....	21	13	
Meshed................	Aug. 18 Sept. 2...	174	82	
Onz au Dare...........	Aug. 8............			Do.
Sabzevar..............	Aug. 21...........			Do.
Sari..................	July 3 29.........	273	144	
Semnan................	Aug. 31 Sept. 2...	14	5	
Yekehambe Bazar........	June 3............	6		
Philippine Islands:				July 1-Dec. 29, 1917: Cases, 5,964;
Provinces..............				deaths, 3,655. Dec. 30, 1917-
Antique........	Nov. 18 Dec. 1....	48	32	Apr. 13, 1918: Cases, 1,791;
Do............	Feb. 3 9..........	4	4	deaths, 1,285.
Bohol..........	Nov. 18 Dec. 29...	169	111	
Do............	Dec. 30 Apr. 13...	567	446	
Capiz..........	Nov. 25 Dec. 29...	27	21	
Do............	Dec. 30 Mar. 23...	219	182	
Cebu...........	Dec. 23 29........	3		
Do............	Dec. 30 Mar. 30...	100	54	
Davao..........	Mar. 10 Apr. 13...	12	11	
Iloilo.........	Nov. 25 Dec. 29...	179	135	
Do............	Dec. 30 Mar. 2....	97	63	
Leyte..........	Nov 25 Dec. 22....	13	12	
Do............	Feb. 3 Mar. 16....	50	38	
Mindanao.......	Nov. 25 Dec. 29...	337	196	
Do............	Dec. 30 Feb. 9....	341	220	
Misamis........	Feb. 21 Apr. 6....	154	98	
Occidental Negros....	Nov 25 Dec. 22...	177	123	
Do............	Jan. 13 Apr. 6....	146	88	
Oriental Negros....	Nov. 25 Dec. 29...	99	62	
Do............	Dec. 30 Mar. 30...	23	15	
Romblon........	Nov. 25 Dec. 1....	1	1	
Surigao........	Feb. 24 Apr. 13...	43	38	
Zamboanga......	Feb. 24-Apr. 6....	35	29	
Russia:				
Tashkentuine...........	May 13............			Present.
Tzaritsin..............	....do...........			Do.
Siam:				
Bangkok................	Sept. 16-22........	1	1	
Turkey in Asia:				
Bagdad................	Nov. 1-15.........		40	

CHOLERA, PLAGUE, SMALLPOX, TYPHUS FEVER, AND YELLOW FEVER—Continued.

Reports Received from Dec. 29, 1917, to June 7, 1918—Continued.

PLAGUE.

Place.	Date..	Cases.	Deaths.	Remarks.
Brazil:				
Bahia	Nov. 4–Dec. 15	4	4	
Do	Dec. 30–Feb. 23	4	3	
Rio de Janeiro	Dec. 23–29	1		
Do	Jan. 6–12	1	1	
British East Africa:				
Mombasa	Oct. 1–Dec. 31	31	18	
British Gold Coast:				
Axim	Jan. 8			Present.
Ceylon:				
Colombo	Oct. 14–Dec. 1	14	13	
Do	Dec. 30–Mar. 9	32	28	
China				Present in North China in January, 1918; pneumonic form.
Anhwei Province—				
Fengyanghsien	Feb. 27		9	Pneumonic.
Pengpu	....do		1	Do.
Chili Province—				
Kalgan				Vicinity. Present in February 1918.
Fukien Province—				
Amoy	Mar. 11–31			Present in vicinity.
Kiangsu Province—				
Nanking	Mar. 17–Apr. 5	19	15	
Shanshi Province				Present in February, 1918; 118 cases estimated.
Ecuador:				
Babahoyo	Feb. 1–15	1		
Duran	Feb. 16–Mar. 30	2	1	
Guayaquil	Sept. 1–Nov. 30	68		Reported outbreak occurring about Jan. 17, 1918.
Do	Feb. 1–15	44	24	
Do	Mar. 1–30	37	11	
Egypt				Jan. 1–Nov. 15, 1917: Cases, 735; deaths, 398.
Alexandria	Jan. 14–28	1	2	
Cairo	Dec. 17–23	2		
Port Said	July 2–Dec. 23	13	7	
Suez	July 2–Oct. 20	62	38	
Hawaii:				
Laupahoehoe	May 5	1	1	
India				July 1–Dec. 29, 1917: Cases 240,258; deaths, 212,022. Dec. 30, 1917–Feb. 23, 1918: Cases, 276,768; deaths, 221,558.
Bassein	Dec. 9–29		8	
Do	Dec. 30–Mar. 16		181	
Bombay	Oct. 28–Dec. 29	147	123	
Do	Dec. 30–Mar. 9	275	213	
Calcutta	Sept. 16–29		2	
Do	Dec. 30–Feb. 2		4	
Henzada	Oct. 21–27		1	
Do	Jan. 5–Mar. 16		117	
Karachi	Oct. 21–Dec. 29	27	20	
Do	Dec. 30–Mar. 14	94	72	
Madras	Feb. 3–Mar. 9	3	3	
Madras Presidency	Oct. 31–Nov. 24	5,786	4,519	
Do	Jan. 6–Mar. 16	11,649	9,012	
Mandalay	Oct. 14–Nov. 17		89	
Do	Dec. 30–Mar. 16		1,065	
Moulmein	Feb. 17–Mar. 16		74	
Myingyan	Dec. 30–Mar. 16		440	
Pegu	Feb. 10–Mar. 16		5	
Prome	Jan. 5–12		1	
Rangoon	Oct. 21–Dec. 22		56	
Do	Dec. 30–Mar. 16	697	639	
Toungoo	Dec. 9–29		5	
Do	Dec. 30–Mar. 16		69	
Indo-China:				
Provinces				Sept. 1–Dec. 31, 1917: Cases, 171; deaths, 128.
Anam	Sept. 1–Dec. 31	45	28	
Cambodia	....do	95	83	
Cochin China	....do	31	17	
Saigon	Oct. 31–Dec. 23	17	6	
Do	Dec. 31–Mar. 31	140	71	
Java:				
East Java				Oct. 8–Dec. 31, 1917: Cases, 196; deaths, 193. Jan. 1–Feb. 4, 1918: Cases, 82; deaths, 81.
Do				
Residency—				
Kediri	Oct. 8–Dec. 31	1	1	
Madoen	....do	49	49	
Semarang	....do	110	109	
Surabaya	....do	25	23	
Do	Jan. 1–Feb. 4	17	17	
Surakarta	Oct. 8–Dec. 31	11	11	
West Java				Nov. 25–Dec. 9, 1917: Cases, 43; deaths 45. Dec. 1, 1917–Jan. 15, 1918: Cases, 106.

CHOLERA, PLAGUE, SMALLPOX, TYPHUS FEVER, AND YELLOW FEVER—Continued.

Reports Received from Dec. 29, 1917, to June 7, 1918—Continued.

PLAGUE—Continued.

Place.	Date.	Cases.	Deaths.	Remarks.
Peru:				
Ancachs Department—				
Casma...............	Dec. 1–Jan. 15....	2	....	
Lambayeque Department..	.....do............	22	....	At Chiclayo, Ferrenafe, Jayanca, Lambayeque.
Libertad Department......	.....do............	72	....	At Guadalupe. Mansiche, Pacasmayo, Salaverry, San Jose, San Pedro. and country district of Trujillo.
Lima Department........	.....do............	9	....	City and country.
Piura Department—				
Catacaos..................	.....do............	1	....	
Senegal:				
St. Louis...............	Feb. 2.............			Present.
Siam:				
Bangkok................	Sept. 16–Dec. 28...	13	9	
Do................	Jan. 13–Mar. 16....	37	27	
Straits Settlements:				
Singapore...............	Oct. 28–Dec. 29....	5	7	
Do...............	Jan. 6–Mar. 9......	64	57	

SMALLPOX.

Place.	Date.	Cases.	Deaths.	Remarks.
Algeria:				
Algiers.....................	Nov. 1–Dec. 31....	3	2	
Do.....................	Jan. 1–Apr. 28....	249	6	
Australia:				
New South Wales..........				July. 12–Dec. 20, 1917; Cases, 36; Jan. 4–17, 1918: Case, 1. Newcastle district.
Abermain...............	Oct. 25–Nov. 29...	5	....	
Cessnock...............	July 12–Oct. 11...	7	....	
Eumangla..............	Aug. 18...........	1	....	
Kurri Kurri...........	Dec. 5–20..........	2	....	
Mungindi..............	Aug. 13...........	1	....	
Warren................	July 12–Oct. 25...	22	....	
Do................	Jan. 1–17..........	1	....	
Brazil:				
Bahia....................	Nov. 10–Dec. 8....	3	....	
Pernambuco...............	Nov. 1–15.........	1	....	
Rio de Janeiro...........	Sept. 30–Dec. 29...	705	190	
Do..................	Dec. 30–Mar. 23...	251	84	
Sao Paulo...............	Oct. 29–Nov. 4....		2	
British East Africa:				
Mombasa..................	Oct. 1–Dec. 31.....	9	5	
Canada:				
British Columbia—				
Vancouver.............	Jan. 13–Mar. 9.....	5	....	
Victoria..............	Jan. 7–Feb. 2.....	2	....	
Winnipeg..............	Dec. 30–Apr. 13...	4	....	
New Brunswick—				
Kent County...........	Dec. 4.............		....	Outbreak. On main line Canadian Ry., 25 miles north of Moncton.
Do................	Jan. 22............	40	....	In 7 localities.
Northumberland County.	.....do............	41	....	In 5 localities.
Restigouche County....	Jan. 18............	60	....	
St. John County—				
St. John............	Mar. 3–May 25....	27	....	May 13, 1918: Cases present, 14.
Victoria County.......	Jan. 2.............	10	....	At Limestone and a lumber camp.
Westmoreland County—				
Moncton.............	Jan. 29–Apr. 27....	20	....	
York County..........	Jan. 22............	8	....	
Nova Scotia—				
Cape Sable Island......				Present May 8 at Clarks Harbor.
Halifax................	Feb. 24–May 18...	22	....	
Sydney................	Feb. 3–May 11....	20	....	
Ontario—				
Arnprior...............	Mar. 31–Apr. 6....		1	
Hamilton..............	Dec. 16–22.........	1	....	
Do................	Jan. 13–19.........	2	....	
Ottawa................	Mar. 4–24..........	5	....	
Sarnia................	Dec. 9–15..........	1	....	
Do................	Jan. 6–May 18.....	24	....	
Toronto...............	Feb. 10–Apr. 6....	2	....	
Windsor...............	Dec. 30–Jan. 5.....	1	....	

CHOLERA, PLAGUE, SMALLPOX, TYPHUS FEVER, AND YELLOW FEVER—Continued.

Reports Received from Dec. 29, 1917, to June 7, 1918—Continued.

SMALLPOX—Continued.

Place.	Date.	Cases.	Deaths.	Remarks.
Canada—Continued.				
Prince Edward Island—				
Charlottetown	Feb. 7–13	1		
Quebec—				
Montreal	Dec. 16–Jan. 5	5		
Do	Jan. 6–Apr. 6	12		
Quebec	Apr. 21–May 11	3		
China:				
Amoy	Oct. 22–Dec. 30			Present.
Do	Dec. 31–Mar. 31			Do.
Antung	Dec. 2–23	13	2	
Do	Jan. 7–Apr. 6	13	3	
Changsha	Jan. 28–Mar. 10	6	1	
Chefoo	Jan. 27–Feb. 9			Do.
Chungking	Nov. 11–Dec. 29			Do.
Do	Dec. 30–Apr. 6			Do.
Dairen	Nov. 18–Dec. 22	3	1	
Do	Dec. 30–Apr. 13	72	6	
Hankow	Feb. 25–Mar. 3	1		
Harbin	May 14–June 30	20		Chinese Eastern Ry.
Do	July 1–Dec. 2	7		Do.
Hongkong	Dec. 23–29	1		
Do	Jan. 26–Mar. 30	19	9	
Hungtahotze Station	Oct. 28–Nov. 4	1		Do.
Manchuria Station	May 14–June 30	6		Do.
Do	July 1–Dec. 2	3		Do.
Mukden	Nov. 11–24			Present.
Do	Feb. 10–Mar. 30			Do.
Nanking	Feb. 3–Apr. 6			Do.
Shanghai	Nov. 18–Dec. 22	41	91	Cases, foreign; deaths among natives.
Do	Dec. 31–Apr. 1	38	119	Do.
Swatow	Jan. 18			Unusually prevalent.
Tientsin	Nov. 11–Dec. 22	13		
Do	Dec. 30–Apr. 6	46		
Tsingtau	Feb. 4–Mar. 31	10	2	
Cuba:				
Habana	Jan. 7	1		Nov. 8, 1917: 1 case from Coruna; Dec. 5, 1917, 1 case.
Marianao	Jan. 8	1		6 miles distant from Habana.
Ecuador:				
Guayaquil	Sept. 1–Nov. 30	26	2	
Do	Feb. 1–Mar. 31	4	3	
Egypt:				
Alexandria	Nov. 12–18	2	1	
Do	Jan. 8–Apr. 15	11		
Cairo	July 23–Nov. 18	6	1	
France:				
Lyon	Nov. 18–Dec. 16	8	3	
Do	Jan. 7–Feb. 17	11	2	
Marseille	Jan. 1–31		2	
Paris	Jan. 27–Apr. 13	11	5	
Rouen	Mar. 31–Apr. 27	31	6	Including varioloid.
Great Britain:				
Cardiff	Feb. 3–9	4		
Hull	Mar. 17–30	3		
Greece:				
Saloniki	Jan. 27–Mar. 16		9	
Honduras:				
Santa Barbara Department	Jan. 1–7			Present in interior.
India:				
Bombay	Oct. 21–Dec. 29	50	12	
Do	Dec. 31–Mar. 9	918	381	
Calcutta	Jan. 27–Mar. 16		34	
Karachi	Nov. 18–Dec. 29	4	2	Nov. 11–16, 1917: 10 cases with 6 deaths; imported on s. s. Monea from Basrah.
Do	Jan. 27–Mar. 14	56	31	
Madras	Oct. 31–Dec. 29	20	8	
Do	Dec. 30–Mar. 16	157	140	
Rangoon	Oct. 28–Dec. 22	6	1	
Do	Dec. 30–Mar. 16	80	19	
Indo-China:				
Provinces				Sept. 1–Dec. 31, 1917: Cases, 656; deaths, 180.
Anam	Sept. 1–Dec. 31	210	30	
Cambodia	do	19	11	
Cochin-China	do	440	133	
Saigon	Oct. 20–Dec. 30	120	26	
Do	Dec. 31–Mar. 24	1,095	370	
Laos	Oct. 1–Dec. 31	8	1	
Tonkin	Sept. 1–Dec. 31	18	5	

CHOLERA, PLAGUE, SMALLPOX, TYPHUS FEVER, AND YELLOW FEVER—Continued.

Reports Received from Dec. 29, 1917, to June 7, 1918—Continued.

SMALLPOX—Continued.

Place.	Date.	Cases.	Deaths.	Remarks.
Italy:				
Castellamare	Dec. 10	2		Among refugees.
Florence	Dec. 1–15	17	4	
Genoa	Dec. 2–31	11	3	
Do	Jan. 2–Apr. 15	52	9	
Leghorn	Jan. 7–Apr. 7	23	7	
Messina	Jan. 3–19	1		
Milan				Oct. 1–Dec. 31, 1917: Cases, 32.
Naples	To Dec. 10	2		Among refugees.
Taormina	Jan. 20–Feb. 9	6		
Turin	Oct. 29–Dec. 29	123	120	
Do	Jan. 21–Apr. 7	96	10	
Japan:				
Nagasaki	Jan. 14–Apr. 28	14	4	
Nagoya	Mar. 24–30	1		
Taihoku	Dec. 15–21	1		Island of Taiwan (Formosa).
Do	Jan. 8–Apr. 22	76	21	Do.
Tokyo	Feb. 11–Apr. 22	40		City and suburbs.
Yokohama	Jan. 17–Feb. 3	63		
Java:				
East Java	Oct. 7–Dec. 23	50		Dec. 25–31, 1917: Cases, 7. Jan. 1–Feb. 4, 1918: Cases, 14.
Surabaya	Dec. 25–31	1		
Do	Jan. 29–Feb. 4	1		
Mid-Java				Oct. 10–Dec. 26, 1917: Cases, 86; death, 1. Dec. 28, 1917–Feb. 13, 1918: Cases, 41.
Samarang	Nov. 6–Dec. 12	4	1	
West Java				Oct. 19–Dec. 27, 1917: Cases, 231; deaths, 36. Dec. 28, 1917–Feb. 21, 1918: Cases, 257; deaths, 60.
Batavia	Nov. 2–8	1		
Do	Feb. 1–7	1		
Mesopotamia:				
Bagdad	Jan. 1–31		10	
Mexico:				
Aguascalientes	Feb. 4–17		2	
Ciudad Juarez	Mar. 3–23	2	1	
Guadalajara	Mar. 1–31	21	4	
Mazatlan	Dec. 5–11		1	
Do	Jan. 29–Apr. 2	4	4	
Mexico City	Nov. 11–Dec. 29	16		
Do	Dec. 30–Apr. 13	111		
Piedras Negras	Jan. 11	200		
Vera Cruz	Jan. 20–Apr. 28	16	3	
Newfoundland:				
St. Johns	Dec. 8–Jan. 4	29		
Do	Jan. 5–May 14	103		45 cases in hospital.
Trepassey	Jan. 4			Outbreak with 11 cases reported.
Philippine Islands:				
Manila	Oct. 28–Dec. 8	5		
Do	Feb. 3–Apr. 20	215	94	Varioloid, 224.
Porto Rico:				
San Juan	Jan. 28–Apr. 7	37		Of these, 36 varioloid.
Portugal:				
Lisbon	Nov. 4–Dec. 15	2		
Do	Dec. 30–Mar. 30	17		
Portuguese East Africa:				
Lourenço Marques	Aug. 1–Dec. 31		16	
Do	Jan. 1–31		6	
Russia:				
Archangel	Sept. 1–Oct. 31	7		
Moscow	Aug. 26–Oct. 6	22	2	
Petrograd	Aug. 31–Nov. 18	76	3	
Siam:				
Bangkok	Nov. 25–Dec. 1	1	1	
Do	Jan. 6–Mar. 16	26	14	
Spain:				
Coruna	Dec. 2–15		4	
Do	Jan. 20–Apr. 6		19	
Madrid	Jan. 1–Mar. 31		16	Jan. 1–Dec. 31, 1917: Deaths, 77.
Malaga	Oct. 1–31		19	
Seville	Oct. 1–Dec. 30		66	
Do	Jan. 1–31		20	
Valencia	Jan. 27–Feb. 2	1		
Straits Settlements:				
Singapore	Nov. 25–Dec. 1	1	1	
Do	Dec. 30–Jan. 5	1		
Tunisia:				
Tunis	Dec. 14–20	1		
Do	Mar. 16–Apr. 12	2		

CHOLERA, PLAGUE, SMALLPOX, TYPHUS FEVER, AND YELLOW FEVER—Continued.

Reports Received from Dec. 29, 1917, to June 7, 1918—Continued.

SMALLPOX,—Continued.

Place.	Date.	Cases.	Deaths.	Remarks.
Turkey in Asia:				
Bagdad				Present in November, 1917.
Union of South Africa:				
Cape of Good Hope State...	Oct 1–Dec. 31.....	28		
East London............	Jan. 20–26......	1		Varioloid.
Transvaal –				
Johannesburg..........	Jan. 1–31..........	4		
Venezuela:				
Maracaibo.................	Dec. 2–8...........		1	

TYPHUS FEVER.

Place.	Date.	Cases.	Deaths.	Remarks.
Algeria:				
Algiers....................	Nov. 1–Dec. 31.....	2	1	
Argentina				
Rosario.................	Dec. 1–31..........		1	
Austria-Hungary:				
Hungary..............				Nov. 26, 1917–Jan. 20, 1918. Cases,
Budapest...............	Nov. 26–Jan. 20...	2		16; deaths, 2.
Brazil:				
Rio de Janeiro............	Oct. 28–Dec. 1.....	7		
Canada:				
Ontario –				
Kingston..............	Dec. 2–8..........	3		
Quebec –				
Montreal..............	Dec. 16–22.........	2	1	
China:				
Antung................	Dec 3–20	13	1	
Do.................	Dec. 31–Mar. 30...	3	2	
Chosen (Korea):				
Seoul.................	Nov. 1–20.........	1		
Do.................	Feb. 1–28..........	3	2	
Egypt:				
Alexandria............	Nov. 8–Dec 28....	57	15	
Do...............	Jan. 8–Apr. 22.....	1,250	281	
Cairo................	July 23 Dec. 23...	143	74	
Port Said.............	July 30–Nov 11...	5	5	
France:				
Marseille..............	Dec. 1–31..........		1	
Germany...............				Dec 23, 1917–Feb. 23, 1918: Cases,
Breslau District	Feb. 3–23..........	4		112; deaths, 9.
Kottbus District........	do.........	1		Prisoner of war.
Lorraine				Dec 23, 1917–Feb 23, 1918: Cases,
Metz	Dec 23–Feb 2....	17	3	77, deaths, 4 Of these, 59 cases
Posen District.............	Feb. 3–23.........	7		1 death, in workmen's camps
				at Pontingen and Werningen.
Great Britain:				
Belfast...............	Feb. 10–Mar 30...	21	3	
Dublin...............	Mar 24–Apr. 27...	4		
Glasgow..............	Dec. 21...........	1		
Do...............	Jan. 20–May 4.....	18		
Manchester...........	Dec. 2–8..........	1		
Greece:				
Arta.................	Feb. 19...........	2		
Janina................	Feb 14...........	110		Jan. 27, epidemic.
Saloniki..............	Nov. 11–Dec 29....		72	
Do..............	Dec 30–Apr. 6....		42	
Italy				
Barnasco.............	Mar 18–Apr. 7....	4		Province of Cuneo.
San Remo.............	Mar. 10–16........	2		
Japan				
Nagasaki.............	Nov 26–Dec 16...	5	5	
Do...............	Jan. 7–Apr. 21.....	19	8	
Java				
East Java				Oct. 15–Dec. 31, 1917: Cases, 39;
Surabaya...............	Dec 17–31........	9	1	deaths, 7 Jan. 1–Feb. 11,
Do	Jan 1–Feb. 11....	29	4	1918: Cases, 34; deaths, 7.
Mid-Java				Oct. 19–Dec. 26, 1917: Cases, 62;
Samarang	Oct 9 Dec 26....	20	2	deaths, 2 Dec. 26, 1917–Feb.
Do	Dec 27 Feb 6....	20		13, 1918: Cases, 24; deaths, 2.
West Java				Oct. 19–Dec. 27, 1917: Cases, 94;
Batavia	Oct 1 Dec 27....	50	15	deaths, 17. Dec. 28, 1917–Feb.
Do..............	Dec. 28–Feb 21...	47	3	21, 1918: Cases, 56; deaths, 1.

CHOLERA, PLAGUE, SMALLPOX, TYPHUS FEVER, AND YELLOW FEVER—
Continued.

Reports Received from Dec. 29, 1917, to June 7, 1918—Continued.

TYPHUS FEVER—Continued.

Place.	Date.	Cases.	Deaths.	Remarks.
Lithuania.............				Dec. 30, 1917–Jan. 5, 1918: Cases, 195.
Mexico:				
Aguascalientes..............	Dec. 15...............		3	
Do....	Jan. 21–May 5....		18	
Durango State—				
Guanacevi.............	Feb. 11.			Epidemic.
Mexico City...............	Nov. 11–Dec. 29...	476		
Do...............	Dec. 30–Apr. 13...	704		
Newfoundland:				
St. Johns....................	Mar. 30–Apr. 5....	1	1	
Norway:				
Bergen....................	Feb. 1–16..........	3		
Poland....................				Nov. 18–Dec 8, 1917: Cases, 2,568; deaths. 218 Dec. 23, 1917–Jan. 12. 1918. Cases, 3,026; deaths, 315.
Lodz....................	Nov. 18–Dec. 8....	219	25	
Warsaw....................	....do.............	1,461	141	
Portugal:				
Lisbon.....................	Mar. 3–30..........	18		Feb. 21: Present.
Oporto...................	Dec 1–31..........	23	4	
Do...................	Jan. 1–Mar. 8......	1,811	161	
Russia:				
Archangel.................	Sept. 1–14........	7	2	
Moscow.................	Aug. 26–Oct 6....	49	2	
Petrograd................	Aug. 31–Nov. 18...	32		
Do................	Feb. 2...........			Present.
Vladivostok...............	Oct. 29–Nov. 4....	12	1	
Spain:				
Corcubion..................	Apr. 11...........			Present. Province of Coruña.
Madrid...................	Jan. 1–Mar. 31......		2	
Sweden:				
Goteborg...................	Nov. 18–Dec. 15...	2		
Switzerland:				
Basel.....................	Jan. 6–19..........	1	1	
Zurich.....................	Nov. 9–15.........	2		
Do.....................	Jan. 13–19.........	2		
Tunisia:				
Tala......................	Mar. 18...........			Epidemic.
Tozer......................	....do...........			Do.
Tunis....................	Nov. 30–Dec. 6....		1	
Do....................	Feb. 9–Apr. 19....	4	16	Of these, 26 in outbreak in prison.
Union of South Africa:				
Cape of Good Hope State...				Sept. 10, 1917–Mar. 17, 1918: Cases, 4,444 (European. 34); deaths, 902 (European, 25).
Natal.....................				Dec. 1, 1917–Mar. 17, 1918: Cases, 50; deaths, 11.

YELLOW FEVER.

Place.	Date.	Cases.	Deaths.	Remarks.
Brazil:				
Bahia....................	Mar. 10–16.........	1	1	
Ecuador:				
Babahoyo.................	Feb. 1–15..........	1	1	
Guayaquil................	Sept. 1–Nov. 30...	5	3	
Do................	Feb. 1–15..........	1		
Do................	Mar. 1–31.........	12	7	
Milagro..................	Feb. 1–15..........	1	1	
Yaguachi.................	Nov. 1–30.........	1		
Guatemala:				
Retalhuleu..............	Apr. 22–May 23....			Present. About 25 miles from Champerico, Pacific port. Disease spreading along Pacific coast.
Honduras:				
Tegucigalpa..............	Dec. 16–22.........		1	
Do..................	Jan. 6–19..........		1	

✗

PUBLIC HEALTH REPORTS

| VOL. 33 | JUNE 21, 1918 | No. 25 |

Influenza a Probable Cause of Fever of Undetermined Nature in Southern States.

Fevers of an undetermined nature were reported during April and May at various points from Norfolk to Louisiana. An examination of the records and reports of the physicians who have treated these cases leads to the belief that these fevers were mainly influenza of mild type.

It is possible, however, that all cases reported were not of the same disease, and in one locality in Louisiana dengue may have occurred.

North Carolina Enforcing Law Requiring Morbidity Reports.

A determined effort is being made by the State Board of Health of North Carolina to secure the reporting of cases of communicable disease by physicians throughout the State and the prompt transmission of the reports to the State Board of Health.

During the week ended June 8, 1918, two physicians were prosecuted and fined for failure to report cases of notifiable diseases as required by the State law. A county quarantine officer was also prosecuted for failure to perform the duties of his office. He pleaded guilty, and the case was dismissed upon his promise to comply with the law in the future.

Some Qualitative and Quantitative Tests for Arsphenamine (3, 3'-Diamino – 4, 4'-Dioxy-Arsenobenzene Dihydrochloride) and Neo-Arsphenamine (Sodium-3, 3'-Diamino-4, 4'-Dihydroxy-Arsenobenzene-Methanal-Sulphoxalate).

By C. N. MYERS, Organic Chemist, and A. O. DuMEz, Technical Assistant, Hygienic Laboratory, United States Public Health Service.

Previous to the year 1914, all of the arsphenamine (salvarsan) and neo-arsphenamine (neosalvarsan) on the market was manufactured by a single German firm under the supervision of Paul Ehrlich, one of the patentees. Naturally the products were fairly uniform in their composition and properties.

As a result of the present war in Europe, the protection afforded these products in the allied countries, through licenses or patents, has been temporarily withdrawn, and they are now being manufactured in England, France, Japan, Canada, and the United States.

Examinations made by the authors, as well as evidence presented by clinicians (Martin and others, 1916), have revealed the fact that the products of different manufacturers appearing on the market in this country are not all uniform with respect to either their chemical or their physiological properties. Even the last of the German supplies received are stated to be more toxic than the products obtained before the beginning of hostilities in Europe (Ormsby and Mitchell, 1916).

Tentative standards for these preparations (arsphenamine and neo-arsphenamine) have been adopted by the Federal Trade Commission on the recommendation of the United States Public Health Service, but these do not appear to meet all exigencies. It is for this reason and for the purpose of better defining the properties of good preparations that the following qualitative and quantitative tests have been worked out and compiled.

Arsphenamine—Physical Properties.

Appearance: Arsphenamine is a pale yellow, microcrystalline, hygroscopic powder very unstable in the air. When properly dried, it is free from lumps.

Odor: The pure product is odorless.[1]

Taste: It has a sour astringent taste.

Solubility: Arsphenamine is soluble in water, 1 to 5 parts, methyl alcohol, 1 to 3 parts, and ethyl alcohol, 1 to 12 parts (Wilcox and Webster, 1916). It is readily soluble in ethylene glycol and glycerin, but only slightly soluble in glacial acetic acid, acetone, ether and concentrated hydrochloric acid (Ehrlich and Bertheim, 1912).

The aqueous solution is greenish-yellow[2] in color and reacts strongly acid to litmus.

Moisture content: When dried to constant weight in an atmosphere of dry hydrogen at 105° C., arsphenamine should lose not more than 7.6 per cent of its weight, which corresponds to the loss of 2 molecules of water of crystallization (Gaebel, 1911).

Arsphenamine—Chemical Properties.

Behavior toward acids: Dilute mineral acids, with the exception of dilute sulphuric acid, have no noticeable effect on aqueous solu-

[1] Commercial samples frequently have the odor of ether due to the incomplete removal of this solvent which is used in the preparation and washing the product

[2] A brownish-yellow, or brown color sometimes observed in solutions prepared from commercial samples, is thought to be an indication of the presence of oxidation products or other impurities.

tions of arsphenamine [1] (distinction from *neo-arsphenamine*, which yields a precipitate with all dilute mineral acids).

The addition of dilute sulphuric acid, however, produces a yellowish-white precipitate.[2]

The addition of any of the concentrated mineral acids, with the exception of phosphoric, to an aqueous solution of arsphenamine causes the formation of a precipitate (distinction from *neo-arsphenamine*, which is precipitated by phosphoric acid).

In the case of concentrated nitric acid, the precipitate dissolves on the addition of an excess of acid yielding a red solution.

Acetic acid (36 per cent) produces no noticeable effect when added to an aqueous solution of arsphenamine (distinction from *neo-arsphenamine*, which yields an orange-yellow precipitate on heating the liquid).

Carbon dioxide immediately precipitates arsphenamine from aqueous solutions.

Behavior toward alkalies: The addition of sodium hydroxide test solution to an aqueous solution of arsphenamine produces a precipitate which dissolves in an excess of the reagent.[3]

Solutions of barium and calcium hydroxides also yield precipitates.

The alkali carbonates produce precipitates which are not soluble in an excess of the reagent.

Behavior toward oxidizing agents: The addition of chlorine or bromine water, ferric chloride, or chromic acid to an aqueous solution of arsphenamine causes the liquid to become red or brownish red in color.

Behavior toward general alkaloidal reagents: An aqueous solution of arsphenamine slowly reduces gold and platinic chloride test solutions in the cold, yielding characteristic precipitates. Reduction is hastened by heating.

Mercuric chloride test solution produces a light-yellow colored precipitate which becomes white on heating.

Mayer's reagent gives a heavy, orange-yellow precipitate.

Picric acid test solution produces a copious yellow precipitate (distinction from *neo-arsphenamine*, aqueous solutions of which become only slightly turbid on the addition of picric acid test solution).

---

[1] For carrying out the above tests, or those which follow, a 1 in 1,000 aqueous solution of the product was used, unless otherwise mentioned.

All of the test solutions employed were made according to the U. S. P. IX, unless differently stated.

[2] Precipitation also occurs on the addition of sulphates.

[3] Precipitation first begins when 1 mol of sodium hydroxide has been added for each mol of arsphenamine in solution. If the addition of sodium hydroxide is continued until precipitation is complete, a further addition of alkali will cause the precipitate to go into solution as the phenolate (Ehrlich and Bertheim, 1912).

Phosphotungstic acid test solution [1] produces a dirty gray colored precipitate, insoluble in an excess of the reagent, but which dissolves upon the addition of sodium carbonate, or ammonia water, yielding a deep blue colored solution.

Phosphomolybdic acid test solution gives a similar color reaction if the liquid is made acid with hydrochloric acid after the addition of the alkali (Gaebel, 1911b).

Behavior toward other reagents: The addition of a freshly prepared solution of ferric chloride and potassium ferricyanide to an aqueous solution of arsphenamine immediately produces a copious precipitate of Prussian blue.

Nessler's reagent is instantly reduced.

The addition of silver nitrate test solution first causes a yellow color to appear, then the formation of a gelatinous precipitate which changes to a black powder on heating. The black precipitate is soluble in dilute nitric acid.

Millon's reagent gives a copious yellow precipitate.

If a drop of copper sulphate solution (4 in 100) be added to 5 cubic centimeters of an aqueous solution of salvarsan (1 in 1,000), to which has been added 0.5 cubic centimeter of hydrogen dioxide solution and 0.5 cubic centimeter of ammonia water, an intense bluish-green color will develop. If the blue solution is poured into alcohol (90 per cent), a blue precipitate, which can be separated by centrifugation, will be obtained (Denigès and Labat, 1911).

To 2 or 3 cubic centimeters of an aqueous solution of arsphenamine (1 in 1,000) add 3 or 4 drops of dilute hydrochloric acid (an amount sufficient to cause the disappearance of most of the yellow color) cool the solution by holding the test tube in ice water and add 3 or 4 drops of a solution of sodium nitrite (5 in 1,000). This results in the formation of a diazo compound having a greenish-yellow fluorescence (distinction from *neo-arsphenamine*, which forms a brown solution).

If a small portion of the solution containing the diazo compound be added drop by drop to an alcoholic solution of α-naphthylamine hydrochloride, a beautiful violet color will develop (Gaebel, 1911b).

With an alcoholic solution of β-naphthylamine hydrochloride, a light-brown color develops (distinction from *atoxyl*, which yields a red-colored solution, Wilcox and Webster, 1916).

If some of the diazotized solution be added to a freshly prepared solution of resorcinol (1 part in 20 parts of a 10 per cent sodium hydroxide solution), a deep red color will develop (Abelin, 1911).

The direct addition of Ehrlich and Pauly's (1904) diazo reagent to an aqueous solution of arsphenamine produces a brownish-red color.

[1] The phosphotungstic acid test solution used in the above test was prepared according to the method of Folin and Denis (1912).

Tests for arsenic: A positive test for arsenic is obtained by applying the Reinsch test. ,}

The Marsh test gives positive results if the arsphenamine is first decomposed by oxidation with nitric and sulphuric acids and the resulting solution reduced by the addition of potassium metabisulphite (Wilcox and Webster, 1916).

Under the foregoing conditions, the Gutzeit's test also gives positive results.

The biological test with *Penicillium brevicaule*, carried out according to the method of Abel and Buttenberg, gives the characteristic garlic odor (Gaebel, 1911b).

Tests for impurities: An aqueous solution of arsphenamine yields no precipitate with hydrogen sulphide, even after the addition of hydrochloric acid and warming (absence of *inorganic arsenic compounds*).

If 4 cubic centimeters of sodium acetate test solution are added to 5 cubic centimeters of an aqueous solution of arsphenamine (1 in 10), the mixture heated for a few minutes and the precipitate removed by filtration, the filtrate should not yield a precipitate within 12 hours on being made alkaline with 3 cubic centimeters of ammonia water and the addition of magnesia mixture (absence of *inorganic arsenic compounds*, Moeller and Thoms, 1914).

If about 0.1 gram of arsphenamine be placed in a test tube, a small quantity of zinc dust and some dilute hydrochloric acid added,[1] and the mouth of the tube covered with a piece of filter paper moistened with a 5 per cent solution of cadmium chloride, the paper should not be stained yellow within a few minutes (absence of *sulphur compounds*).[2]

Dissolve exactly 1.0 gram of arsphenamine in 10 cubic centimeters of methyl alcohol contained in a 100 cubic centimeter volumetric flask. Dilute the solution with 75 cubic centimeters of distilled water, add 1.5 grams of precipitated calcium carbonate, and shake to precipitate the salvarsan base. Dilute with distilled water to exactly 100 cubic centimeters and filter. To exactly 50 cubic centimeters of the filtrate add 75 cubic centimeters of water, 5 cubic centimeters of N/1 hydrochloric acid volumetric solution, and titrate with N/20 iodine volumetric solution. The amount of iodine volumetric solution consumed, expressed in cubic centimeters, represents the percentage of *amino-oxy-phenyl-arsenoxide* present in the material. The

---

[1] A drop of platinic chloride test solution may be added to start the reaction.

[2] Arsinsulphide and Arsinsesquisulphide have been suggested as possible impurities in arsphenamine (Schamberg, Kolmer, and Raizies, 1917).

Most of the commercial samples of arsphenamine examined in this laboratory gave a positive test for sulphur by the method described above.

amount of the oxide present in good products varies from 0.5 to 0.8 per cent [1] (Ehrlich and Bertheim, 1912).

Neo-Arsphenamine—Physical Properties.

Appearance: Neo-arsphenamine is an orange-yellow, microcrystalline powder which changes rapidly in the air, becoming dark brown in color.

Odor: The pure preparation is odorless.[2]

Taste: It has a taste somewhat resembling that of garlic.[3]

Solubility: Neo-arsphenamine is readily soluble in water or glycerin, but only slightly soluble in methyl alcohol, ethyl alcohol, acetone, and ether.

The aqueous solution, when freshly prepared, is yellow in color and reacts neutral toward litmus. The solution rapidly becomes brown on exposure to the air.

Neo-Arsphenamine—Chemical Properties.

Behavior toward acids: Dilute as well as concentrated mineral acids yield precipitates with an aqueous solution of neo-arsphenamine. Precipitation does not occur immediately, but is first noticeable after several minutes (distinction from *arsphenamine*, which is not precipitated by dilute mineral acids or concentrated phosphoric acid, but yields a precipitate immediately with concentrated hydrochloric, sulphuric, and nitric acids).

The addition of acetic acid (36 per cent) to an aqueous solution of neo-arsphenamine yields a yellow colored precipitate when the liquid is heated (distinction from *arsphenamine*, which is not precipitated .

Behavior toward alkalies: The addition of sodium hydroxide test solution to an aqueous solution of neo-arsphenamine produces no noticeable effect (distinction from *arsphenamine*, a solution of which yields a precipitate).

Solutions of barium and calcium hydroxides yield turbid solutions or faint precipitates.

Solutions of the alkali carbonates do not produce precipitates (distinction from *arsphenamine*).

Behavior toward oxidizing agents: Similar to the reactions with *arsphenamine*.

Behavior toward general alkaloidal reagents: Similar to the reactions with *arsphenamine*, except that the precipitate with picric acid test solution develops slowly and is relatively small in amount.

---

[1] The amount of oxide found in the commercial sample examined in this laboratory varied from 0.5 to 2.8 per cent.

[2] Commercial samples sometimes have an odor of garlic, due apparently to slight decomposition.

[3] Commercial samples frequently have a saline taste, probably due to the presence of sodium chloride which is said to be used as a diluent for products high in arsenic content.

Mayer's reagent does not yield a precipitate until the solution has been made acid with dilute hydrochloric acid (distinction from a solution of *arsphenamine*, which yields a precipitate on the direct addition of the reagent).

Behavior toward other reagents: The behavior of an aqueous solution of neo-arsphenamine toward a freshly prepared solution of ferric chloride and potassium ferricyanide, silver nitrate test, and Nessler's reagent is similar to that described under *arsphenamine*.

Millon's reagent yields a copious brown-colored precipitate.

If 5 cubic centimeters of dilute hydrochloric acid be added to 10 cubic centimeters of an aqueous solution of neo-arsphenamine (1 in 100) and the mixture heated, the irritating odor of sulphur dioxide will be developed (New and Nonofficial Remedies, 1917).

If about 0.1 gram of neo-arsphenamine be placed in a test tube, a small quantity of zinc dust and some dilute hydrochloric acid added and the mouth of the tube covered with a piece of filter paper moistened with a 5 per cent solution of cadmium chloride, the paper will be stained yellow within a few minutes (distinction from *arsphenamine*).

If 5 cubic centimeters of an aqueous solution of neo-arsphenamine be boiled with 1 cubic centimeter of dilute hydrochloric acid, a violet color will develop on the addition of a few drops of Schiff's reagent [1] (distinction from *arsphenamine*, Denigès and Labat, 1913).

The diazotized solution [2] of neo-arsphenamine gives color reactions with α-naphthylamine hydrochloride and resorcinol similar to those described under *arsphenamine*. With β-naphthylamine hydrochloride, a brownish-red color develops.

Tests for arsenic: The reactions are similar to those noted under *arsphenamine*.

Tests for impurities: An aqueous solution of neo-arsphenamine [3] yields no precipitate on passing in hydrogen sulphide gas (absence of *inorganic arsenic compounds*).

If 5 cubic centimeters of acetic acid (36 per cent) be added to 5 cubic centimeters of an aqueous solution of neo-arsphenamine, the mixture heated a few minutes and the precipitate removed by filtration, the filtrate should not yield a precipitate within 12 hours on the addition of an excess of ammonia water and some magnesia mixture (absence of *inorganic arsenic compounds*).

---

[1] By boiling with hydrochloric acid, the methylene group of the neo-arsphenamine is detached and oxidized to formic aldehyde.

[2] In diazotizing the solution, add the sodium nitrite solution first, then the hydrochloric acid in order to avoid precipitation.

[3] Hydrochloric acid should not be added, as acids produce a precipitate.

Arsphenamine and Neo-Arsphenamine—Quantitative Determination of Arsenic.

The methods for the quantitative determination of arsenic in organic compounds, described in the literature, are both numerous and varied in their manner of execution. Most of them, however, are more or less complicated and are, therefore, not suitable for use in routine work where the number of samples of material to be analyzed is large. They involve, for example, such processes as fusion (methods of La Coste and Michaelis, 1880; of Pringsheim, 1904; of Little, Cahen, and Morgan, 1909; and of St. Warunis, 1912); or distillation (methods of Schneider and Fyfe, 1906; of Jannasch and Seidel, 1910; and of Bohrisch and Kürschner, 1911); and the subsequent estimation of the arsenic by gravimetric or volumetric methods.

Among the simpler and more practical procedures, which have received special mention in connection with the estimation of the arsenic in arsphenamine or neo-arsphenamine, are the methods of Gaebel (1911c) and Denigès and Labat (1911), in which an aqueous solution of the material is titrated directly with iodine or potassium permanganate volumetric solution. In this class are, likewise, the methods of Norton and Koch (1905), Lehmann (1912), and Ewins (1916). In these methods the arsenic is, first, either oxidized or reduced by digesting the material with suitable reagents and then estimated by titration in one of the usual ways.

For the purpose of determining which one of these simpler methods is the most accurate, and can be depended upon to give the best results in the hands of different operators, a few preliminary analyses were carried out. The results obtained indicated that the methods of Gaebel, Ewins, and Lehmann offered the greatest possibilities for fulfilling these conditions.[1] A large number of samples of both arsphenamine and neo-arsphenamine were, therefore, subjected to analysis by these methods. For comparison, a number of gravimetric determinations were also made. Detailed descriptions of these methods, together with the data obtained in the analyses, follow:

Gaebel's titration method: Weigh out accurately about 0.2 gram of arsphenamine and dissolve it in 100 cubic centimeters of distilled water contained in an Erlenmeyer flask. Add 1 cubic centimeter of starch test solution and titrate with N/20 iodine volumetric solution to a permanent blue color.[2] One cubic centimeter of N/20 iodine volumetric solution is equivalent to 0.001875 gram of arsenic.

---

[1] The method of Denigès and Labat was eliminated from the field of possibilities, as the end point obtained in the titration is too infrequent to yield accurate results in the hands of different analysts.

The Ewins method was given preference over that of Norton and Koch, as it is essentially an improved modification of the latter.

[2] As the greenish-yellow color of the arsphenamine solution becomes less and less pronounced and finally vanishes on the addition of iodine solution, the titration may also be carried out without the use of an indicator.

Ewins's method: Weigh out accurately 0.1 to 0.2 gram of the substance and transfer it to a long-necked Kjeldahl flask of 300 cubic centimeters capacity. Add 10 grams of potassium sulphate and 0.2 to 0.3 gram of starch (after a little experience the amount can be sufficiently accurately estimated and need not be weighed). Wash in any solid adhering to the neck of the flask with a little water. Cautiously add 20 cubic centimeters of concentrated sulphuric acid and heat the mixture on wire gauze over a Bunsen flame. As soon as the contents of the flask begin to froth, lower the flame somewhat until the frothing diminishes, which generally takes place within 10 to 15 minutes from the commencement of heating. Again turn on the flame and continue heating until the liquid becomes colorless or of a very pale yellow tint. Shake the flask once or twice during digestion, in order to wash down any material adhering to the walls. The time required for the complete oxidation of the material is usually about 4 hours.

After the liquid has cooled, transfer it quantitatively to an Erlenmeyer flask of 350 cubic centimeters capacity and make it just distinctly alkaline by the addition of sodium hydroxide solution (10 to 12N). A small piece of litmus paper added to the contents of the flask serves as the most convenient indicator. Cool the flask and its contents to about 30° to 40° C. and add concentrated sulphuric acid, drop by drop, until the solution is again distinctly acid (care should be taken that no drops of sodium hydroxide solution remain on the inside of the neck of the flask, which should be well washed down with water, or the flask may be stoppered and shaken). Now add from a burette a saturated solution of sodium hydrogen carbonate, until the solution becomes distinctly alkaline and an excess of 5 to 10 cubic centimeters of the reagent is present

To this solution, add 2 cubic centimeters of a 1 per cent solution of starch, and titrate the arsenious acid present with N/20 iodine volumetric solution. Toward the end of the reaction, the solution usually develops a reddish-violet tint, which fades on standing. The end-point, however, is reached when the solution acquires the characteristic deep blue color given by free iodine in the presence of starch. From the amount of iodine consumed, the percentage of arsenic present is easily calculated. One cubic centimeter of N/20 iodine volumetric solution is equivalent to 0.001875 gram of arsenic.

Gravimetric method: Weigh out accurately about 0.2 gram of the product and transfer it to a Kjeldahl flask of 300 cubic centimeters capacity. Add 1.5 grams of a mixture of equal parts of sodium nitrate and potassium nitrate, 200 cubic centimeters of distilled water and 5 cubic centimeters of concentrated sulphuric acid. Heat the mixture slowly under a hood to allow the escape of the nitric acid fumes. Add a small quantity of concentrated or fuming nitric acid from time to time, until oxidation is completed, which is generally indicated by the disappearance of the yellow color.[1] Continue the digestion until the volume of the liquid has been reduced to about 15 cubic centimeters,[2] cool, add 100 cubic centimeters of distilled water and again concentrate to about 15 cubic centimeters, in order to remove the last trace of nitric acid. If the product has been completely oxidized and all traces of nitric acid have been removed, the liquid will be water clear at this point. After cooling, cautiously neutralize the liquid with strong ammonia water and transfer it to a 300 cubic centimeter beaker, using a small quantity of distilled water for rinsing the flask.

To the solution, which will now contain all of the arsenic in the form of arsenate, add 10 to 20 cubic centimeters of 2N ammonium chloride solution for every 50 cubic centimeters of the liquid, then 20 cubic centimeters of magnesia mixture, drop by drop, with constant stirring. Finally add an amount of strong ammonia water, equal to one-third the volume of the liquid, and 2 cubic centimeters of alcohol. After allowing the mixture to stand for 12 hours, collect the precipitate, with the aid of a suction pump, in a Gooch crucible, which has been prepared as follows:

Cover the bottom of the crucible with a thin layer of asbestos, which has previously been washed with ammonia water (2.5 per cent), and dry in an oven at 110° C. Remove the crucible from the oven and place it in a larger porcelain crucible, fitted with an asbestos ring so that the sides and bottom of the two will not touch, put on the cover and heat slowly over an open flame until there is a light red glow on the outer crucible (Treadwell-Hall, 1905). Remove the Gooch crucible, cool in a desiccator and weigh.

After the precipitate has been collected, dry the crucible as described above, but add a crystal of ammonium nitrate before heating over the open flame. Finally cool the crucible and weigh. The weight of the precipitate multiplied by 0.48275 represents the amount of arsenic present in the sample taken for analysis.

Lehmann's method: Weigh out accurately about 0.2 gram of the substance and transfer to a 200 cubic centimeter Erlenmeyer flask.[3] Add 1 gram of finely powdered potassium permanganate and 5 cubic centimeters of dilute sulphuric acid and allow the mixture to stand for about 10 minutes. Rotate the flask frequently during this time to insure the complete mixing of the materials. Now add 10 cubic centimeters of concentrated sulphuric acid, in portions of about 2 cubic centimeters, rotating the flask after each addition.

---

[1] Sometimes the liquid may still have a pale yellow tint.
[2] Concentration should be effected in such a manner that the formation of sulphuric acid fumes in large quantities will be avoided.
[3] An Erlenmeyer flask, fitted with a glass stopper, is most suitable for this purpose.

When the reaction has ceased, add a quantity (about 5 to 7 cubic centimeters) of hydrogen dioxide solution sufficient to dissolve all of the brown precipitate. Toward the end, the hydrogen dioxide solution should be added, drop by drop, to avoid any great excess. Dilute the liquid with 25 cubic centimeters of distilled water and boil over wire gauze for about 10 minutes, or until the excess of hydrogen dioxide has been completely removed.[1]

After dilution with 50 cubic centimeters more of distilled water, cool the solution and add 2.5 grams of potassium iodide. Stopper the flask tightly and allow it to stand in a cool place for 1 hour. Finally titrate the liberated iodine with N/10 sodium thiosulphate volumetric solution without the use of starch test solution as an indicator.[2] One cubic centimeter of N/10 sodium thiosulphate solution is equivalent to 0.003748 gram of arsenic.

TABLE 1.--*Arsenic content of commercial samples of arsphenamine.*

Manufacturer.	Name of product.	Lot number.	Per cent of arsenic.			
			Direct titration with N/20 iodine V. S.	Ewins's method.	Gravimetric method.	Lehmann's method.
Dermatological Research Laboratories, Philadelphia, Pa.	Arsenobenzol	630		30.06		
Do.	do.	652		29.61		
Do.	do.	721		29.11		
Do.	do.	740	29.92	30.33	31.58	31.32
Do.	do.	750	29.24		31.16	31.34
Do.	do.	755	29.34	29.26	31.13	30.94
Do.	do.	757	28.43	29.90		
Do.	do.	767	29.53	29.20		
Do.	do.	788	29.38	29.27		
Do.	do.	791	29.19	29.26		
Do.	do.	799	29.29	29.89	31.52	31.40
Do.	do.	809	29.95	29.59	30.87	30.46
Do.	do.	826		29.20		
Do.	do.	841	29.28	29.19	31.54	31.38
Do.	do.	845	29.07	29.30		
Do.	do.	862	29.52	29.91		
Do.	do.	873	29.53	29.71	31.38	31.22
Do.	do.	875		29.74		
Do.	do.	886	29.53	30.22	31.46	31.18
Do.	do.	890	29.23		31.35	31.22
Do.	do.	900	29.42	29.70	31.07	30.94
Do.	do.	914		28.71		
Do.	do.	928	29.56	30.06	31.17	31.03
Do.	do.	952	29.62	30.33	31.07	31.03
Do.	do.	954		31.24		
Do.	do.	966		29.45		
Do.	do.	973		30.51		
Do.	do.	980				30.46 / 30.52
Do	do.	1008				30.56 / 30.63
Do.	do.	1013				30.44 / 30.73
Do.	do.	1017				31.16 / 31.00

[1] Experience has shown that it is practically impossible to remove all of the hydrogen dioxide by boiling, unless the solution be evaporated to a very small volume, when it is very liable to become colored brown, due to the further action of the hot concentrated acid. In the analyses made by the authors the last trace of hydrogen dioxide was removed by the addition of a drop or two of permanganate solution (1 per cent) and the resulting pink color removed by the addition of oxalic acid solution in very slight excess.

[2] A blank test should be carried out under exactly the same conditions and the proper corrections made. The blank tests usually consume from 0.1 to 0.3 cubic centimeter of the iodine solution.

TABLE 1.—*Arsenic content of commercial samples of arsphenamine*—Continued.

Manufacturer.	Name of product.	Lot number.	Per cent of arsenic.			
			Direct titration with N/20 iodine V. S.	Ewins's method.	Gravimetric method.	Lehmann's method.
Dermatological Research Laboratories, Philadelphia, Pa.	Arsenobenzol..........	1020	....	....	....	{ 21 22 \ 31 28
Do..........	....do..........	1048	....	....	....	30 29
Do..........	....do..........	1062	....	....	....	31 41
Do..........	....do..........	1072	....	....	....	31 15
Do..........	....do..........	1077	....	....	....	30 25
Do..........	....do..........	1095	....	....	....	
Do..........	....do..........	1103	....	....	....	30 43
Do..........	....do.... ?......	1125	....	....	....	30 23
Do..........	....do..........	1135	....	....	....	30 43
Do..........	....do..........	1142	....	....	....	31 53
Farbwerke-Hoechst Co., at H. A. Metz Laboratories (Inc.), New York.	Salvarsan..........	BDB	29 23	31.10	....	....
Do..........	....do..........	BFB	30.60	31.30	....	....
Do..........	....do..........	BJB	29.02	31.38	....	....
Do..........	....do..........	BLB	29.40	....	....	....
Do..........	....do..........	BMB	29.88	29.98	....	....
Do..........	....do..........	BUB	29.34	30.88	....	....
Do..........	....do..........	BVB	29.69	31.44	....	....
Do..........	....do..........	BXB	29.43	30 35	....	....
Do..........	....do..........	DBB	28.87	29.63	31.16	30 72
Do..........	....do..........	DFB	29.97	31.30	31.47	31 23
Do..........	....do..........	DHB	30.05	{ 30.76 \ 31.22 }	....	....
Do..........	....do..........	DHB	30.24	30.76	....	....
Do..........	....do..........	DJB	29.60	31.65	....	....
Do..........	....do..........	DLB	30.63	31.95	....	....
Do..........	....do..........	DMB	{ 29.07 \ 29.62 }	{ 30.72 \ 29.57 }	....	31 40
Do..........	....do..........	DUB	29.16	30.31	....	....
Do..........	....do..........	FBB	29.72	{ 31.00 \ 31.54 }	31 85	31.53
Do..........	....do..........	HBB	30.74	31.64	31.65	31.28
Do..........	....do..........	JBB	....	30.43	....	....
Do..........	....do..........	LBB	....	....	31.24	31 30, 32 24, 32 24, 32 43
Do..........	....do..........	MBB	....	....	....	32 44, 32 76, 32 43
Do..........	....do..........	UBB	....	....	....	31 29, 30 27
Do..........	....do..........	XBB	....	....	....	30 43
Do..........	....do..........	I75	....	....	31.15	30 63, 30 73
Do..........	....do..........	I76	....	....	31.15	31 43, 31 58
Do..........	....do..........	I77	....	....	31.80	31.64, 31 88, 30 62
Do..........	....do..........	I78	....	....	....	30 42, 30 43, 30 94
Do..........	....do..........	I79	....	....	31.56	31 38, 31 38
Do..........	....do..........	I81	....	....	....	32 18
Do..........	....do..........	I82	....	....	....	31 97
Les Établissements Poulenc Frères, Paris	Arsenobenzol "Billon"	DC32	....	29.63	....	30.74
The Parsenol Co. (Ltd.), Toronto, Canada.	Parsenol..........	B87320	28.80	29.92	....	....
Do..........	....do..........	B87521	29.06	....	....	30 14
Do..........	....do..........	1275	....	....	....	30 73
Fankoo & Co., Tokyo........	Arminol..........	68	29.95	31.26	....	31 94
Do..........	....do..........	54	29.89	31.20	....	32 38
Arsemin Co., Tokyo..........	Neo Arsemin ("Salvarsan sol.)	DE1A	....	21.04	....	....
Do..........	....do..........	DE18	....	20.73	20.47	20 50

TABLE 2.—*Arsenic content of commercial samples of neo-arsphenamine.*

Manufacturer.	Name of product.	Lot number.	Per cent of arsenic.		
			Ewins's method.	Gravimetric method.	Lehmann's method.
Farbwerke vorm. Meister Lucius & Bruning, Hoechst a. M.	Neosalvarsan	HV	18.38	19.82	20.12
Les Etablissements Poulenc Frères, Paris.	Novarsenobenzol "Billon"	B1539	17.80	20.34	19.93
Do	do	B2126	18.98	....	20.21
Do	do	B2137	18.06	19.96	19.74
Do	do	8750	18.19	20.35	19.93
Do	do	9651	18.24	20.05	20.12
Anglo-French Drug Co. (Ltd.), London.	Ampsalvs	....	18.28	....	{ 19.81 19.65.
Kokusan-Seiyakusho, Tokyo	Neotanvarsan	19	18.26		
Do	do	20	18.15	{ 18.27 18.34 }	18.40
Do	do	21	18.10	18.19	18.30
Banyu Co., Tokyo	Neochramisol	CHA	18.82	....	a 17.93
Do	do	CHA	18.47	....	18.41
Sankyo & Co , Tokyo	Neoarsaminol	N139	16.56	16.96	17.04
Do	do	N153	16.81	....	16.70
Do	do	N183			{ 17.21 17.44 17.27
Do	do	N185	16.80	16.96	16.89
Synthetic Drug Co., Toronto	Neodiarsenol	180	....	....	16.69
Do	do	181	....	....	15.50
Do	do	182	....	....	16.68
Do	do	183	....	....	17.55
Do	do	189	....	{ 15.79 16.05 }	b 15.33
Do	do	262	....	....	16.35
Do	do	264	....	....	{ 15.37 15.29
Do	do	267	....	....	{ 15.46 15.30

a The tube had been opened for a considerable length of time previous to analysis and the product was oxidized to a considerable extent.
b The sample was not uniform.

A survey of the preceding tables shows that the results obtained by the Lehmann and the gravimetric methods are nearly identical, while those obtained by direct titration with iodine volumetric solution are relatively low in all cases. With the Ewins method, the results are occasionally of the same magnitude as those obtained by the gravimetric determination, but, as a rule, they are also relatively low.

With respect to the titration method, Gaebel (1911c) states that the reaction between arsphenamine and iodine is a reversible one, viz:

$$C_{12}H_{12}O_2N_2As_2.2HCl.2H_2O + 8I + 4H_2O \rightleftharpoons 2C_6H_4O_4NAs.HCl + 8HI.$$

As a consequence a state of equilibrium is reached before all of the arsphenamine has been oxidized and the amount of iodine solution consumed is less than that required by theory. This investigator states further that the reagents (sodium bicarbonate, sodium acetate, borax, etc.) usually employed for overcoming this difficulty in iodometric titrations of arsenious compounds are of no value in this case, a condition which has also been observed by the authors. This method appears, therefore, to be of little value.

The low percentages obtained by the Ewins method are apparently the result of a loss of arsenic through volatilization. It was thought that this loss might be avoided by slowing the rate of digestion. A number of samples were, therefore, digested for some time in the cold and then slowly over a low flame. Samples from the same tubes were also digested rapidly in order to obtain data for comparison. The results obtained follow:

TABLE 3.—*Effect of rate of digestion on the results obtained by the Ewins method.*

Manufacturer.	Name of product.	Lot number.	Per cent of arsenic, Ewins's method.	
			Slow digestion.	Rapid digestion.
Dermatological Research Laboratories, Philadelphia.......	Arsenobenzol.	740	30.33	28.64
Do............	....do......	750	....	29.75
Do............	....do......	799	29.69	29.70
Do............	....do......	873	29.71	29.40
Do............	....do......	886	30.22	29.72
Do............	....do......	890	....	29.85
Do............	....do......	952	30.33	29.62

The above data indicate that the rate at which digestion is allowed to proceed is a factor which influences the final result to a very considerable extent. But they also show that the results are low even when digestion is carried out very slowly. It appears, therefore, that this method in its present form is objectionable. It is possible that greater accuracy might be attained by condensing the fumes which escape during digestion, reuniting the distillate with the contents of the Kjeldahl flask previous to neutralization, and finally titrating the mixture. Work along this line is, however, necessary before a positive statement can be made.

The method of Lehmann, with the slight modifications recommended in the footnotes, is accurate and reliable. It is simple, requires but small quantities of inexpensive reagents, and can be completed in about one and one-half hours. It, therefore, appears to be superior to any of the other methods mentioned for the routine analysis of these products.

Bibliography.

ABELIN. J.
1911. Ueber eine neue Methode, das Salvarsan nachzuweisen. Münch. med. Wchnschr., v. 58, p. 1002-1003.
AMERICAN MEDICAL ASSOCIATION (Council on Pharmacy and Chemistry).
1917. New and Nonofficial Remedies, Chicago, Am. M. Assoc.
BOHRISCH, P., and KÜRSCHNER, F.
1911. Zur quantitativen Bestimmung des Arsens organischen Substanzen, mit besonderer Berücksichtung organischer Arsenverbindungen (Salvarsan usw.). Pharm. Zentralh., v. 52, p. 1365-1369.

DENIGÈS and LABAT.
1911. Réactions et dosage de l'arsénobenzol ou 606. Répert. de Pharm., v. 23, p. 251-253.
DENIGÈS and LABAT.
1913. Réactions et dosage du néosalvarsan. Répert. de Pharm., v. 25, p. 9-10.
EHRLICH, P., and BERTHEIM, A.
1912. Ueber das salzsaure 3,3'-Diamino-4,4'-dioxyarsenobenzol und seine nächsten Verwandten. Ber. deutsch. chem. Gesellsch., v. 45, p. 756-766.
EHRLICH, P., and PAULY, H.
1904. 'Ueber die Konstitution des Histidins. Ztschr. physiol. Chem., v. 42, p. 508.
EWINS, ARTHUR J.
1916. The Estimation of Arsenic in Organic Compounds. J. Chem. Soc. (Trans.), v. 109, pt. 2. p. 1355-1358.
FOLIN, OTTO, and DENIS, W.
1912. On Phosphotungstic-Phosphomolybdic Compounds as Color Reagents. J. Biol. Chem., v. 12, p. 240.
GAEBEL, G. OTTO.
1911a. Die quantitative Zusammensetzung des Salvarsan. Apoth.-Ztg., v. 26, p. 215-216.
GAEBEL. G. OTTO.
1911b. Das Salvarsan beim gerichtlichen Arsennachweis. Arch. Pharm., v. 249, p. 49-56.
GAEBEL. G. OTTO.
1911c. Titration von Salvarsan mit Jodlösung. Arch. Pharm., v. 249, p. 241-247.
GIUSEPPE. BRESSANIN.
1911. Methode zum Nachweis und zur Bestimmung von Arsen in organischen Verbindungen. Chem. Centralbl., v. 82, p. 1965, from Boll. Chim. Farm., v. 50, p. 727-730.
JANNASCH. P., and SEIDEL, J.
1910. Ueber die quantitative Verflüchtigung des Arsens aus Lösung unter Reduktion des Arsenchlorids zu Arsenchlorür durch Hydrazinsalze. Ber. deutsch. chem. Gesellsch., v. 43, p, 1218-1223.
LA COSTE. W. and MICHAELIS. A.
1880. Ueber aromatische Arsenverbindungen. Ann. Chem., v. 201, p. 224.
LEHMANN, F.
1912. Ueber die Bestimmung des Arsens in Salvarsan und Neosalvarsan. Apoth.-Ztg., v. 27, p. 545-546.
LITTLE. HARRY F. V., CAHEN, EDWARD, and MORGAN, GILBERT T.
1909. The Estimation of Arsenic in Organic Compounds. J. Chem. Soc. (Trans.), v. 95. p. 1477-1482.
MARTIN, E. H.
1916. Alarming Symptoms Caused by Diarsenol. J. Am. M. Assoc., v. 66, p. 1155.
MOELLER, JOSEPH and THOMS, HERMANN.
1914. Real-Enzyklopädie der Gesamten Pharmazie, v. 14, p. 35.
NORTON, F. A. and KOCH, A. E.
1905. A Method for the Detection and Determination of Arsenic and Antimony in the Presence of Organic Matter. J. Am. Chem. Soc., v. 27, p. 1247-1251.

Ormsby, Oliver S. and Mitchell, James H.
　　1916. Toxicity of the Present Supply of Salvarsan and Neosalvarsan. J. Am. M. Assoc., v. 67, p. 1756.

Pringsheim, Hans H.
　　1904. The Analysis of Organic Substances with the Help of Sôdium Peroxide. Am. Chem. J., v. 31, p. 386-395.

Puckner, W. A. and Hilpert, W. S.
　　1910. The Chemical Properties of Salvarsan ("606"). J. Am. M. Assoc., v. 55, p. 2311.

Rupp, E. and Lehmann, F.
　　1911. Ueber eine vereinfachte Bestimmung des Arsens in Atoxyl und Arsacetin. Apoth.-Ztg., v. 26, p. 203-204.

Schamberg, Jay F., Kolmer, John A., and Raiziss, George W.
　　1917. Experimental and Clinical Studies of the Toxicity of Dioxydiamino-Arsenobenzol Dihydrochloride. Reprint from J. Cutaneous Dis., May-June, p. 1-52.

St. Warunis, Theodor.
　　1912. Bestimmung des Arsens in organischen Verbindungen. Chem. Ztg , v. 36, p. 1205-1206.

Schneider and Fyfe.
　　Quoted by Schmidt, 1906, Pharmazeutische Chemie. Friedr. Vieweg. & Sohn, Braunschweig, v. 1, p. 379.

Treadwell-Hall.
　　1905. Analytical Chemistry. John Wiley & Sons, New York, v. 2, p. 25.

Willcox, William H. and Webster, John.
　　1916. The Toxicology of Salvarsan, Dioxy-diamino-arsenobenzol. Brit. M. J., v. 1, p. 474.

PREVALENCE OF DISEASE.

No health department, State or local, can effectively prevent or control disease without knowledge of when, where, and under what conditions cases are occurring.

UNITED STATES.

EXTRA-CANTONMENT ZONES—CASES REPORTED WEEK ENDED JUNE 18.

CAMP BEAUREGARD ZONE, LA.

	Cases.
Gonorrhea:	
Alexandria	1
Malaria:	
Alexandria	5
Mumps:	
Alexandria	11
Pineville	1
Tuberculosis:	
Alexandria	2
Rural district	1
Typhoid fever:	
Pineville	1
Whooping cough:	
Alexandria	3

CAMP BOWIE ZONE, TEX.[1]

Fort Worth:	
Chicken pox	1
Erysipelas	1
Gonorrhea	17
Measles	3
Mumps	2
Smallpox	2
Syphilis	18
Typhoid fever	7
Whooping cough	5

CAMP DEVENS ZONE, MASS.

Measles:	
Ayer	1
Littleton	1
Whooping cough:	
Ayer	3

CAMP DODGE ZONE, IOWA.

Des Moines:	
Diphtheria	2
Gonorrhea	10
Measles	2
Scarlet fever	6
Smallpox	4
Syphilis	4

CAMP DODGE ZONE, IOWA—continued.

	Cases.
Grimes:	
Scarlet fever	2
Runnells:	
Diphtheria	1

CAMP DONIPHAN ZONE, OKLA.

Lawton:	
Gonorrhea	6
Mumps	1

CAMP EBERTS ZONE, ARK.

Chancroid:	
Allport	1
Diphtheria:	
Kerr, route 1	1
Dysentery:	
Cabot	1
Kerr, route 1	1
Erysipelas:	
England, route 1	1
Gonorrhea:	
Lonoke	3
England	2
Malaria:	
Lonoke	1
Lonoke, route 1	1
Lonoke, route 2	2
Lonoke, route 3	1
England	9
England, route 2	1
Cabot	1
Keo	2
Carlisle	7
Austin, route 1	3
Ward	4
Kerr, route 1	1
Measles:	
Lonoke, route 1	2
England	4
Keo	1
Mumps:	
Lonoke	1

[1] Report for week ended June 15, 1918.

CAMP EBERTS ZONE, ARK.—continued.

Pellagra: Cases.
    Lonoke, route 2............................. 1
    England................................... 1
Septic sore throat:
    Ward..................................... 1
Smallpox:
    England................................... 1
    Kerr, route 1.............................. 1
Syphilis:
    England................................... 1
Tuberculosis:
    Lonoke, route 1........................... 1
    Ward..................................... 1

CAMP FUNSTON ZONE, KANS.

Junction City:
    Mumps.................................... 1
    Smallpox.................................. 1
    Tuberculosis.............................. 1
Manhattan:
    Measles................................... 1
    Mumps.................................... 6
    Whooping cough.......... 1

CAMP GORDON ZONE, GA.[1]

Cerebrospinal meningitis:
    Atlanta................................... 2
Gonorrhea:
    Atlanta................................... 21
Malaria.
    Atlanta................................... 3
Measles
    Atlanta................................... 15
Meningitis, tubercular:
    Atlanta................................... 1
Mumps:
    Atlanta................................... 20
Pellagra:
    Atlanta................................... 1
Pneumonia:
    Atlanta................................... 5
Scarlet fever:
    Atlanta................................... 1
    Decatur................................... 1
Smallpox:
    Atlanta................................... 3
    College Park.............................. 1
    Decatur................................... 1
    Fairburn.................................. 1
    Orchard Knob.............................. 1
Syphilis
    Atlanta................................... 5
Tuberculosis:
    Atlanta................................... 11
Typhoid fever:
    Atlanta................................... 2
Whooping cough:
    Atlanta................................... 4
    Decatur................................... 2

CAMP GREENE ZONE, N. C

Charlotte Township.
    Gonorrhea................................. 4
    Measles................................... 2

[1] Report for June 12 to 15, 1918.

CAMP GREENE ZONE, N. C.—continued.

Charlotte Township—Continued.   Cases
    Mumps.................................... 1
    Scarlet fever.............................. 5
    Syphilis.................................. 1
    Typhoid fever............................. 1
    Whooping cough........................... 15

GULFPORT HEALTH DISTRICT, MISS.

Gulfport health district:
    Cancer.................................... 1
    Dysentery................................. 1
    Gonorrhea................................. 1
    Malaria................................... 17
    Measles................................... 1
    Mumps.................................... 7
    Pellagra.................................. 5
    Tuberculosis.............................. 1
    Whooping cough........................... 2

CAMP HANCOCK ZONE, GA.

Augusta:
    Chicken pox............................... 3
    German measles............................ 1
    Malaria................................... 2
    Measles................................... 4
    Typhoid fever............................. 2
    Whooping cough........................... 4

CAMP JACKSON ZONE, S. C.[1]

Columbia:
    Mumps.................................... 9
    Typhoid fever............................. 6
    Whooping cough........................... 20

CAMP JOSEPH E. JOHNSTON ZONE, FLA.

Cerebrospinal meningitis:
    Jacksonville.............................. 1
Chancroid:
    Jacksonville.............................. 4
Chicken pox:
    Jacksonville........................ ... 11
Dysentery:
    Fishers Corner............................ 1
    Grand Crossing........................... 1
    South Jacksonville........................ 4
Gonorrhea:
    Jacksonville.............................. 5
Hookworm:
    Grand Crossing........................... 3
    Lackawanna............................... 4
    Panama................................... 3
Malaria:
    Jacksonville.............................. 1
Measles.
    Jacksonville.............................. 2
Mumps:
    Jacksonville.............................. 2
Pellagra:
    Jacksonville.............................. 2
Syphilis:
    Jacksonville.............................. 41
Trachoma:
    Jacksonville.............................. 4
Tuberculosis:
    Jacksonville.... 5

[1] Report for week ended June 15, 1918.

CAMP JOSEPH E. JOHNSTON ZONE, FLA.—contd.

Typhoid fever: Cases.
    Jacksonville 3
    Ortega 1
    Riverview 1
Whooping cough:
    Jacksonville 20
    St. John Park 1

FORT LEAVENWORTH ZONE, KANS.

Leavenworth:
    Diphtheria 3
    Gonorrhea 5
    Pneumonia, lobar 1
    Scarlet fever 2
    Smallpox 2
    Tuberculosis 2
Leavenworth County:
    Diphtheria 2

CAMP LEE ZONE, VA.

Chancroid:
    Petersburg 2
German measles:
    Petersburg 1
Gonorrhea:
    Petersburg 3
    Hopewell 3
Mumps:
    Hopewell 1
    Prince George County 3
Syphilis:
    Petersburg 1
Typhoid fever:
    Hopewell 1
Whooping cough:
    Hopewell 1

CAMP LOGAN ZONE, TEX.

Cerebrospinal meningitis:
    Houston 1
Chancroid:
    Houston 1
    Goose Creek 1
Diphtheria:
    Houston 2
Gonorrhea:
    Houston 15
    Park Place 1
Syphilis:
    Houston 14
    Goose Creek 1
    Magnolia Park 1
Tuberculosis:
    Houston 5
Typhoid fever:
    Houston 2

CAMP M'ARTHUR ZONE, TEX.

Waco:
    Mumps 1
    Poliomyelitis 3
    Tuberculosis 3
    Typhoid fever 5
    Whooping cough 4

CAMP M'CLELLAN ZONE, ALA.

Malaria:
    Anniston 2
Measles:
    Anniston 1

CAMP M'CLELLAN ZONE, ALA.—continued.

Pellagra: Cases
    Anniston 1
Tuberculosis:
    Anniston 2
    Blue Mountain 1
Typhoid fever:
    Anniston 1
    Blue Mountain 1
    Precinct 23 1
Whooping cough:
    Anniston 4

NORFOLK COUNTY NAVAL DISTRICT, VA.

Measles:
    Portsmouth 1
    Ocean View 1
    Norfolk 1
Mumps:
    Expo 1
    Norfolk County 2
    Portsmouth 1
    Brighton 1
Scarlet fever:
    Norfolk 2
    Portsmouth 2
Typhoid fever:
    Portsmouth 2
    Pleasant Grove District 1
    Ocean View 1
Whooping cough:
    Portsmouth 4
    Ocean View 2
    Norfolk 1

FORT OGLETHORPE ZONE, GA.

Cerebrospinal meningitis:
    Chattanooga 4
Dysentery:
    Rossville 4
Gonorrhea:
    Chattanooga 11
    St. Elmo 1
    Whiteside 1
Scarlet fever:
    Chattanooga 4
Syphilis:
    Chattanooga 11
Whooping cough:
    Chattanooga 17

CAMP PIKE ZONE, ARK.

Keo:
    Malaria 4
Little Rock:
    Dysentery 3
    Gonorrhea 11
    Malaria 8
    Measles 2
    Mumps 7
    Pellagra 1
    Pneumonia 1
    Poliomyelitis 1
    Syphilis 3
    Tuberculosis 2
    Typhoid fever 2
    Whooping cough 1
North Little Rock:
    Gonorrhea 1
    Malaria 4
    Typhoid fever 2
    Whooping cough 6

CAMP PIKE ZONE, ARK.—continued.

Scotts:	Cases.
Malaria	3
Mumps	1

CAMP SEVIER ZONE, S. C.

Dysentery: |
--- | ---
Bates Township | 1
Malaria: |
Bates Township | 2
Mumps: |
Chick Springs Township | 3
Smallpox: |
Greenville Township | 1
Tuberculosis: |
Toris Mountain Township | 2
Bates Township | 1
Typhoid fever: |
Bates Township | 2
Greenville Township | 1
Whooping cough: |
Butler Township | 1

CAMP SHELBY ZONE, MISS.

Hattiesburg: |
--- | ---
Chicken pox | 1
Dysentery, amebic | 1
Hookworm | 2
Malaria | 14
Pellagra | 1
Tuberculosis | 1
Typhoid fever | 4
Whooping cough | 4
McHenry: |
Typhoid fever | 1
Sumrall: |
Typhoid fever | 1

CAMP SHERIDAN ZONE, ALA.

Montgomery |
--- | ---
Gonorrhea | 6
Mumps | 1
Syphilis | 2
Tuberculosis, pulmonary | 2
Typhoid fever | 4
Montgomery County: |
Mumps | 1
Typhoid fever | 4
Whooping cough | 3
United States Government Clinic. |
Chancroid | 7
Gonorrhea | 2s
Syphilis | 6

CAMP SHERMAN ZONE, OHIO.

Diphtheria |
--- | ---
Chillicothe | 2
Hillsville | 1
Gonorrhea: |
Chillicothe | 5
Measles |
Chillicothe | 2
Scioto Township | 1
Scarlet fever: |
Chillicothe | 2
Tuberculosis, pulmonary: |
Chillicothe | 1

CAMP ZACHARY TAYLOR ZONE, KY.

Jefferson County:	Cases.
Diphtheria	7
Tuberculosis, pulmonary	2
Typhoid fever	1
Louisville:
Chicken pox	3
Diphtheria	2
Malaria	1
Measles	2
Mumps	2
Trachoma	1
Tuberculosis, pulmonary	10
Typhoid fever	2
Whooping cough	7
New Albany, Ind.:
Smallpox	4
United States Government clinic:
Chancroid	2
Gonorrhea	25
Syphilis	24

TIDEWATER HEALTH DISTRICT, VA.

Hampton: |
--- | ---
Typhoid fever | 1
Newport News. |
Cerebrospinal meningitis | 1
Chancroid | 4
Gonorrhea | 22
Measles | 1
Mumps | 2
Scarlatina | 1
Syphilis | 9
Tuberculosis | 1
Typhoid fever | 2
Whooping cough | 1
Phoebus: |
Tuberculosis | 1
Whooping cough | 7

CAMP TRAVIS ZONE, TEX.

San Antonio |
--- | ---
Chancroid | 4
Diphtheria | 1
Gonorrhea | 20
Mumps | 1
Syphilis | 9
Tuberculosis | 1
Typhoid fever | 21

CAMP WADSWORTH ZONE, S. C.

Gonorrhea |
--- | ---
Spartanburg | 22
Measles: |
Spartanburg | 1
Dun an | 2
Mumps |
Spartanburg | 9
Whitney | 12
Syphilis |
Spartanburg | 9
Typhoid fever: |
Glendale | 1
Dun an | 1
Roebuck | 2
Whooping cough: |
White Stone | 1

CAMP WHEELER ZONE, GA.[1]

Macon: |
--- | ---
Pneumonia | 1
Typhoid fever | 2

[1] Report for week ended June 15, 1918.

DISEASE CONDITIONS AMONG TROOPS IN THE UNITED STATES.

The following data are taken from telegraphic reports received in the office of the Surgeon General, United States Army, for the week ended June 7, 1918:

Annual admission rate per 1,000 (disease only):
- All troops............................... 1,056.1
- Divisional camps...................... 1,135.3
- Cantonments........................... 975.6
- Departmental and other troops........ 1,101.1

Noneffective rate per 1,000 on day of report:
- All troops.........................,..... 37.8
- Divisional camps...................... 36.8

Noneffective rate per 1,000 on day of report—Continued.
- Cantonments........................... 42.2
- Departmental and other troops....... 33.6

Annual death rate per 1,000 (disease only):
- All troops............................... 3.16
- Divisional camps...................... 3.2
- Cantonments........................... 3.6
- Departmental and other troops....... 2.58

New cases of special diseases reported during the week ended June 7, 1918.

Camp.	Pneumonia.	Dysentery.	Malaria.	Venereal. Total.	Venereal. New infections.	Measles.	Meningitis.	Scarlet fever.	Deaths.	Annual admission rate per 1,000 (disease only).	Noneffective per 1,000 on day of report.
Beauregard.....................	4	5	22	129	4	2	2		2	927.3	47.0
Bowie.........................	4		2	52	51	2			1	764.1	25.3
Cody.........................	11			3	3			1	3	967.8	24.5
Doniphan.....................				15		3		1	2	1,579.5	44.0
Fremont......................	8		2	14	7	6		1	4	1,016.9	38.6
Hancock......................				74		1				985.8	43.5
Kearny.......................	4		1	4		4	1	1	3	370.7	20.0
Logan........................	2			44					2	3,198.0	15.0
MacArthur....................						3				1,032.0	37.2
McClellan....................	2		4	26	10	3				582.2	25.0
Sevier.......................	10		7	269	4	7				1,346.3	46.5
Shelby.......................			8	15	3	2		1		1,007.3	39.2
Sheridan.....................			1	35		6				613.6	35.0
Wadsworth....................	2		1	94		18			3	1,257.0	29.9
Wheeler......................	4			25	5				6	2,846.2	50.9
Custer.......................	4		1	68	9	11			2	509.3	20.5
Devens.......................	16		1	32	7	10	3		6	682.2	36.4
Dix..........................	3	1	1	170	2	8	1	6	2	871.3	34.3
Dodge........................	4		2	99		14		2	3	1,239.9	59.1
Funston......................	3			50	4	6	2		2	787.1	55.4
Gordon.......................	14		2	149	5	34	2		7	1,591.5	87.6
Grant........................	1			34		3	2		2	373.9	17.0
Jackson......................	9		1	114		58			1	1,412.7	57.7
J. E. Johnston...............	2			74	64	6		2		1,198.9	41.6
Lee..........................	9		5	272			6		4	626.6	57.5
Lewis........................	4		3	235	3	3	3	9	5	1,007.9	33.1
Meade........................	3			18	4	2	1		1	559.7	29.4
Pike.........................	14	4	15	72	12	44	2		5	1,684.2	60.7
Sherman......................	2		1	74		4		1		1,334.8	88.5
Taylor.......................	7			102		16				1,017.4	42.0
Travis.......................	1		6	69	6	26	1	1	2	1,366.1	39.3
Upton........................	8		1	283	34		1	1	5	740.7	27.2
Northeastern Department.....	2			27	14	3			1	735.5	28.5
Eastern Department..........	11		4	148	46	8	1	1	3	900.5	23.3
Southeastern Department.....			3	236	18	5			2	1,614.0	43.3
Central Department..........	2			78	37	5		2	1	1,591.5	42.2
Southern Department.........	8	2	1	337	90	13		9	6	1,172.5	34.4
Western Department..........	5			69	28	15		6	2	915.9	23.0
Aviation, S. C...............	16	7	4	205		14		3	14	1,055.7	30.8
Alcatraz, Disciplinary Barracks										800.0	12.3
Columbus Barracks...........				22	1				1	570.0	18.7
Edgewood Arsenal............				1	1				1	779.0	20.0
Hoboken......................	5		7	225	19	37	4		3	802.9	29.5
Jefferson Barracks...........	3			177	2	4		3	1	1,598.6	77.5
Leavenworth, Disciplinary Barracks				6		1				895.4	33.3
Logan, Fort..................				10				1	2	1,691.5	50.3
McDowell, Fort...............	2	1		45		5		1		3,824.5	101.0
Newport News................	10		4	328	12	11	2	1	3	1,462.4	61.6
Slocum, Fort.................	2			160	2				1	2,058.7	47.0
Springfield Armory...........											
Thomas, Fort.................	1		1	17		4				985.0	29.0
Watervliet...................										600.0	25.9
West Point...................				1						785.4	13.8
Total.......................	222	20	111	4,806	507	425	34	54	114	1,056.1	37.8

CEREBROSPINAL MENINGITIS.

State Reports for May, 1918.

Place.	New cases reported.	Place.	New cases reported.
District of Columbia...................	16	Massachusetts—Continued.	
Maryland:		Hampden County—	
Baltimore...........................	19	West Springfield (town)........	1
Allegany County....................	4	Middlesex County...................	
Cumberland....................	1	Cambridge.....................	
Baltimore County—		Lowell........................	
Canton......................	1	Newton........................	
Fort Howard....................	1	Somerville......................	1
Harford County—		Watertown (town)...............	1
Whiteford......................	1	Norfolk County—	
		Braintree (town)...............	
Total.......................	27	Quincy......................	
		Suffolk County—	
Massachusetts:		Boston........................	
Berkshire County—		Revere........................	1
Pittsfield....	1	Worcester County—	
Bristol County—		Blackstone (town)...............	1
Fall River.......................	3	Fitchburg.....................	
New Bedford....................	1	Northbridge (town).............	
Taunton......................	1	Worcester......................	
Essex County—			
Lynn........................	1	Total.......................	30
Newburyport..................	1		

City Reports for Week Ended June 1, 1918.

Place.	Cases.	Deaths.	Place.	Cases.	Deaths.
Aberdeen, S. Dak.............		1	Milwaukee, Wis..............	3	3
Abilene, Tex.................	1		Missoula, Mont..............		1
Baltimore, Md..............	4	2	Nashville, Tenn.............		1
Bayonne, N. J..............	1		Newark, N J...............		
Birmingham, Ala............	1	1	New Orleans, La.............	2	1
Boston, Mass...............	2	1	New York, N. Y.............	14	7
Bridgeport, Conn............	1		Petersburg, Va.............	1	
Chicago, Ill.	3	4	Philadelphia, Pa............	2	2
Cincinnati, Ohio............		1	Providence, R. I............	2	1
Cleveland, Ohio.............	1	1	Quincy, Ill.................	1	
Detroit, Mich..............		1	Riverside, Cal.............	1	1
Evansville, Ind............	1		Rochester, N. Y............		1
Everett, Wash.............		1	St Louis, Mo...............	2	3
Flint, Mich		1	Scranton, Pa...............	1	
Galesburg, Ill.............		1	Tacoma, Wash.............	1	
Independence, Kans........	2	2	Troy, N. Y................	1	
Indianapolis, Ind..........	1	2	Washington, D C...........	2	1
Iola, Kans....	1		Wheeling, W. Va...........	1	
Kansas City, Mo...........		1	Wichita, Kans.............	1	
Louisville, Ky..............		1	Winston-Salem, N.C........		1

DIPHTHERIA.

See Diphtheria, measles, scarlet fever, and tuberculosis, page 1033.

ERYSIPELAS.

City Reports for Week Ended June 1, 1918.

Place.	Cases.	Deaths.	Place.	Cases.	Deaths.
Akron, Ohio	2		Milwaukee, Wis	2	
Ann Arbor, Mich	4		Minneapolis, Minn	3	
Bakersfield, Cal	1		Mount Vernon, N. Y	1	
Baltimore, Md	1		Newark, N. J	4	
Battle Creek, Mich	1		Newburgh, N. Y		1
Berkeley, Cal	1		New York, N. Y		3
Boston, Mass		1	Norfolk, Va	1	
Bridgeport, Conn	1		Oakland, Cal	1	1
Buffalo, N. Y	2		Passaic, N. J	2	
Cambridge, Mass		1	Philadelphia, Pa	2	1
Chicago, Ill	10		Sacramento, Cal	1	
Cleveland, Ohio	1		St. Joseph, Mo	1	
Denver, Colo	1		St. Louis, Mo	4	
Detroit, Mich	1	1	St. Paul, Minn	1	1
Kalamazoo, Mich		2	San Francisco, Cal	5	1
Kansas City, Kans	1		Seattle, Wash	1	
Kansas City, Mo	2	1	Sioux City, Iowa	1	
Long Beach, Cal	1		Somerville, Mass		1
Los Angeles, Cal	1		Tacoma, Wash	1	
Louisville, Ky	1	1	Topeka, Kans	2	1
Melrose, Mass	1				

LEPROSY.

California—Rio Vista and San Francisco.

During the month of May, 1918, 2 cases of leprosy were notified in the State of California; 1 at Rio Vista, in the person of R. W., female, aged 14 years, born in Hawaiian Islands, came to the United States 7 years ago, and has lived in Rio Vista 3½ years, and in San Francisco for the same length of time; the other case at San Francisco, in the person of L. J., male, aged 20 years, native of China, came to the United States 8 years ago, has lived in San Francisco 1 month, and before that lived in Portland, Oreg.

Massachusetts—Boston—On Vessel.

On May 7, 1918, a case of leprosy in the person of W. C., native of East Indies, aged 22 years, recently arrived on the steamship *Gunene*, was reported at Boston, Mass. The patient was an alien and was deported on the same vessel on which he arrived.

MALARIA.

State Reports for May, 1918.

Place.	New cases reported.	Place.	New cases reported.
Maryland:		Massachusetts:	
Anne Arundel County.............	2	Essex County—	
Calvert County—		Lynn........................	2
Prince Frederick................	1	Suffolk County—	
Frederick County—		Boston...................	2
Walkersville...................	1		
Kent County—		Total.................	4
Rock Hall.....................	1		
Chestertown	1		
Total.......................	6		

City Reports for Week Ended June 1, 1918.

Place.	Cases.	Deaths.	Place.	Cases.	Deaths.
Albany, Ga.................	2	....	Marshall, Tex...........	2	....
Atlanta, Ga.................	1	....	Memphis, Tenn..........	5	1
Beaumont, Tex.............	1	1	Mobile, Ala.............	..	1
Birmingham, Ala...........	1	1	Montgomery, Ala........	30	....
Boston, Mass..............	2	....	Newark, N. J...........	1	....
Cape Girardeau, Mo........	4	....	New Orleans, La.........	1	1
Charleston, S. C...........	..	2	New York, N. Y.........	..	2
Corsicana, Tex............	2	....	North Little Rock, Ark....	1	....
Hattiesburg, Miss..........	14	....	Palestine, Tex...........	6	....
Jersey City, N. J...........	1	....	Petersburg, Va..........	3	....
Little Rock, Ark............	18	....	Rahway, N. J............	1	....
Louisville, Ky.............	2	....	Rocky Mount, N. C.......	1	1
Macon, Ga.................	3	1			

MEASLES.

See Diphtheria, measles, scarlet fever, and tuberculosis, page 1033.

PELLAGRA.

State Reports for May, 1918.

Place.	New cases reported.	Place.	New cases reported.
District of Columbia....................	1	Massachusetts:	
		Norfolk County –	
Maryland:		Foxboro (town)...............	1
Dorchester County—		Suffolk County –	
Woolford......................	1	Boston......................	1
Madison......................	1	Chelsea.....................	1
Total........................	2	Total........................	3

City Reports for Week Ended June 1, 1918.

Place.	Cases.	Deaths.	Place.	Cases.	Deaths.
Albany, Ga.................	1	....	Macon, Ga..............		1
Albuquerque, N. Mex.......		1	Memphis, Tenn..........		2
Atlanta, Ga................		1	Mobile, Ala.............		1
Austin, Tex...............		2	Nashville, Tenn.........	5	1
Birmingham, Ala...........	5	2	New Orleans, La.........	1	1
Charlotte, N. C............		2	New York, N. Y.........		1
Corsicana, Tex.............	1	1	Raleigh, N. C...........	1	1
Dallas, Tex................	1	2	Richmond, Va...........	1	....
Durham, N. C.............	1	2	Rocky Mount, N. C......	1	1
Fort Worth, Tex...........	1	1	Spartanburg, S. C.......	1	1
Greenville, S. C...........		1	Washington, D. C.......	1	....
Lexington, Ky.............		1	Winston-Salem, N. C......	1	1
Little Rock, Ark...........		2			

PLAGUE.

California—Contra Costa County—Plague-Infected Squirrel Found.

On June 8, 1918, a plague-infected squirrel was shot 5 miles west of Martinez, Contra Costa County, Cal.

PNEUMONIA.

City Reports for Week Ended June 1, 1918.

Place.	Cases.	Deaths.	Place.	Cases.	Deaths.
Adams, Mass.............	1	1	Long Beach, Cal............	2	....
Amarillo, Tex............	1	....	Los Angeles, Cal............	8	8
Amsterdam, N. Y..........	2	1	Louisville, Ky.............	1	8
Atlanta, Ga.............	1	3	Lowell, Mass.............	1	2
Baltimore, Md..............	15	9	Lynn, Mass.............	2	1
Battle Creek, Mich..........	1	....	Malden, Mass.............	1	1
Beverly, Mass....	1	....	Manchester, N. H.........	1	1
Binghamton, N. Y..........	1	....	Manitowoc, Wis..........	1	....
Boston, Mass..	6	11	Marshall, Tex.............	1	....
Buffalo, N. Y............	3	7	Milford, Mass.............	3	....
Cambridge, Mass............	5	2	Newark, N. J............	32	4
Chelsea, Mass...........	2	....	Newburgh, N. Y..........	1	1
Chicago, Ill.............	64	87	Newport, Ky.............	1	1
Cleveland, Ohio............	13	....	North Little Rock, Ark.......	2	1
Clinton, Mass............	2	....	North Tonawanda, N. Y....	1	....
Corsicana, Tex...........	1	1	Oakland, Cal............	1	5
Cumberland, Md............	4	....	Ogden, Utah.............	3	....
Dayton, Ohio.............	1	1	Ossining, N. Y............	2	....
Detroit, Mich.............	6	13	Oswego, N. Y............	1	....
Elmira, N. Y............	4	2	Palestine, Tex.............	1	....
Everett, Mass...........	1	1	Parkersburg, W. Va.........	1	1
Fall River, Mass............	4	....	Philadelphia, Pa............	28	29
Fort Worth, Tex...........	1	1	Pontiac, Mich.............	1	1
Grand Rapids, Mich..........	2	....	Richmond, Va.............	1	2
Greenfield, Mass..........	1	....	Riverside, Cal............	1	1
Hartford, Conn...........	1	....	Rochester, N. Y............	3	5
Haverhill, Mass...........	2	....	St. Cloud, Minn............	3	....
Holyoke, Mass............	2	....	San Francisco, Cal.........	8	9
Independence, Mo...........	1	....	Sault Ste. Marie, Mich.......	1	....
Jackson, Mich............	1	1	Schenectady, N. Y.........	2	2
Jamestown, N. Y..........	1	....	Springfield, Mass..........	5	2
Kansas City, Mo...........	2	9	Toledo, Ohio.............	1	1
Lackawanna, N. Y..........	3	....	Waltham, Mass............	1	3
Lawrence, Mass...........	2	1	Westfield, Mass............	1	....
Lincoln, Nebr.............	1	1	Worcester, Mass............	3	1

POLIOMYELITIS (INFANTILE PARALYSIS).

State Reports for May, 1918.

Place.	New cases reported.	Place.	New cases reported.
Maryland:		Massachusetts:	
Baltimore County—		Middlesex County—	
Lauraville.............	1	Cambridge................	1
Kingsville.............	1	Framingham (town)...........	2
Frederick County—		Suffolk County—	
Myersville.............	1	Boston................	1
Howard County—		Braintree (town)...............	1
Laurel.............	1	Worcester County—	
		Barre (town)....................	1
Total...............	4	Total................	6

City Reports for Week Ended June 1, 1918.

Place.	Cases.	Deaths.	Place.	Cases.	Deaths.
Alton, Ill..................	2	....	Natick, Mass..................	1	....
Indianapolis, Ind.............	1	....	Richmond, Ind.............	1	1
Milwaukee, Wis............	1	1	Springfield, Ill.............	1	....
Moundsville, W. Va..........	1	....	Waco, Tex.............	4	1

RABIES IN ANIMALS.

City Reports for Week Ended June 1, 1918.

Place.	Cases.	Place.	Cases.
Detroit, Mich............................	1	Pueblo, Colo............................	2
Louisville, Ky............................	1	Schenectady, N. Y......................	3
Memphis, Tenn...........................	1		

ROCKY MOUNTAIN SPOTTED FEVER.

California.

During the month of May, 1918, 3 cases of Rocky Mountain spotted fever were reported in California; 2 cases in Plumas County and 1 in Lassen County.

Montana.

During the month of May, 1918, 3 cases of Rocky Mountain spotted fever were reported in Montana; 2 cases in Ravalli County and 1 in Yellowstone County.

SCARLET FEVER.

See Diphtheria, measles, scarlet fever, and tuberculosis, page 1033.

SMALLPOX.

State Reports for May, 1918.

Place.	New cases reported.	Deaths.	Vaccination history of cases.			
			Number vaccinated within 7 years preceding attack.	Number last vaccinated more than 7 years preceding attack.	Number never successfully vaccinated.	Vaccination history not obtained or uncertain.
District of Columbia...............	11				11	
Maryland:						
Baltimore.......................	9				9	....
Allegany County--						
Mount Savage.............	1				1	....
Baltimore County -						
Turners Station	1				1	....
Sparrows Point	1				1	....
Carroll County						
Westminster.............	1				1	....
Howard County -						
Savage	2				2	....
Prince Georges County--						
Laurel....................	2				2	....
Somerset County -						
Tylerton..................	2				2	....
Total...................	19				19	
Massachusetts						
Essex County—						
Lynn	1				1	....
Suffolk County -						
Boston..	2				2	....
Total	3				3	....

Vermont Report for May, 1918.

During the month of May smallpox was reported in Vermont as follows: Essex County, 1; Rutland County, 3; Windham County, 1.

City Reports for Week Ended June 1, 1918.

Place.	Cases.	Deaths.	Place.	Cases.	Deaths.
Aberdeen, Wash	1		Kansas City, Mo	21	
Abilene, Tex	6		Knoxville, Tenn	2	
Akron, Ohio	3		Kokomo, Ind	3	
Alton, Ill	1		La Crosse, Wis	1	
Ann Arbor, Mich	1		Leavenworth, Kans	7	
Atlanta, Ga	8		Lebanon, Pa	2	
Baltimore, Md	2		Lexington, Ky	1	
Battle Creek, Mich	1		Lincoln, Nebr	5	
Beaumont, Tex	3		Little Rock, Ark	1	
Benton Harbor, Mich	2		Los Angeles, Cal	2	
Billings, Mont	1		Louisville, Ky	3	
Birmingham, Ala	9		Macon, Ga	2	
Bloomington, Ind	1		Madison, Wis	2	
Boise, Idaho	1		Marshall, Tex	1	
Buffalo, N. Y	5		Mason City, Iowa	8	
Burlington, Iowa	1		Memphis, Tenn	2	
Canton, Ill	1		Michigan City, Ind	2	
Chanute, Kans	3		Middletown, Ohio	5	
Charleston, W. Va	1		Milwaukee, Wis	4	1
Chicago, Ill	2		Minneapolis, Minn	17	1
Cincinnati, Ohio	10		Muscatine, Iowa	2	
Cleveland, Ohio	19		Muskegon, Mich	1	
Coffeyville, Kans	12		Muskogee, Okla	7	
Columbus, Ohio	5		Nashville, Tenn	3	
Corsicana, Tex	1		New Albany, Ind	3	
Council Bluffs, Iow	7		New Castle, Pa	3	
Dallas, Tex	1		New Orleans, La	3	
Danville, Ill	1		Oklahoma City, Okla	23	
Davenport, Iowa	2		Omaha, Nebr	24	
Denver, Colo	17			1	
Des Moines, Iowa	11		Peoria, Ill	7	
Detroit, Mich	12		Philadelphia,	1	
Dubuque, Iowa	5		Pontiac, Mich	7	
Duluth, Minn	2		Provo, Utah	2	
Elgin, Ill	1		Quincy, Ill	8	
Erie, Pa	4		Roanoke, Va	1	
Evansville, Ind	1		St. Joseph, Mo	17	
Fairmont, W. Va	1		St. Louis, Mo	26	
Flint, Mich	4			3	
Fond du Lac, Wis	1		Salt Lake City,	5	
Fort Collins, Colo	1		San Francisco, Cal	4	
Fort Scott, Kans	7		Santa Ana, Cal	6	
Fort Wayne, Ind	1		Seattle, Wash	3	
Fort Worth, Tex	24		Sioux City, Iowa	6	
Grand Rapids, Mich	2		Sioux Falls, S. Dak	1	
Granite City, Ill	4		Spartanburg, S. C	1	
Greeley, Colo	7		Spokane, Wash	6	
Greenville, S. C	1		Springfield, Ill	14	
Harrisburg, Pa	1		Springfield, Mo	3	
Hartford, Conn	1		Stockton, Pa	1	
Hattiesburg, Miss	1		Tacoma, Wash	1	
Houston, Tex	1			1	
Independence, Kans	2			3	
Independence, Mo	2			4	
Indianapolis, Ind	25			1	
Iola, Kans	15			5	
Iowa City, Iowa	4			3	
Jacksonville, Ill	2		C	3	
Kalamazoo, Mich	34			11	
Kansas City, Kans	7		N. C	4	

TETANUS.

City Reports for Week Ended June 1, 1918.

Place.	Cases.	Deaths.	Place.	Cases.	Deaths.
Cleveland, Ohio	1	1	New York, N. Y	1	1
Louisville, Ky		1	Richmond, Va		1
Mobile, Ala		1	Worcester, Mass		1

1032

TUBERCULOSIS.

See Diphtheria, measles, scarlet fever, and tuberculosis, page 1033.

TYPHOID FEVER.

Florida—Pensacola.

During the period from May 1 to June 14, 1918, 28 cases of typhoid fever, with 5 deaths, were reported at Pensacola, Fla.

State Reports for May, 1918.

Place.	New cases reported.	Place.	New cases reported.
District of Columbia	7	Massachusetts:	
		Berkshire County—	
Maryland:		Adams (town)	1
Baltimore	13	Lanesboro (town)	1
Anne Arundel County—		North Adams	3
Shady Side	1	Bristol County—	
Baltimore County—		Easton (town)	1
Woodlawn	1	Fall River	10
Sparrows Point	1	New Bedford	2
Rossville	1	Taunton	1
Roland Park	2	Westport (town)	1
Highlandtown	2	Essex County—	
Arlington	1	Haverhill	3
Calvert County—		Lawrence	1
Willows	2	Lynn	3
Wallsville	1	Saugus (town)	1
Poplars	1	Franklin County—	
Carroll County—		Orange (town)	1
New Windsor	2	Hampden County—	
Tyrone	1	Chicopee	1
Cecil County—		Springfield	3
Chesapeake City	1	Middlesex County—	
Cayetts Corner	1	Arlington (town)	1
Union Hospital	1	Cambridge	1
Charles County—		Malden	6
Indian Head	1	Stoneham (town)	1
Dorchester County—		Sudbury (town)	1
Secretary	1	Watertown (town)	1
Bishops Head	1	Woburn	1
Maryland Hospital	1	Norfolk County—	
Frederick County—		Brookline (town)	1
Brunswick	1	Sharon (town)	1
Walkersville	4	Weymouth (town)	1
Dayville	1	Plymouth County—	
Garrett County—		Brockton	1
Friendsville	1	East Bridgewater (town)	2
Howard County—		Lakeville (town)	1
Ellicott City	1	Plymouth (town)	1
Montgomery County—		Suffolk County—	
Rockville	1	Boston	12
Prince Georges County—		Chelsea	4
Aquasco	3	Revere	1
Laurel	1	Worcester County—	
Takoma Park	1	Northbridge (town)	1
Queen Annes County—			
Centerville	1	Total	70
Stevensville	1		
Washington County—		Vermont:	
Hagerstown	1	Caledonia County	1
Worcester County—		Chittenden County	2
Pocomoke City	1	Orleans County	4
Snepmxent	1	Rutland County	1
Stockton	4	Washington County	5
Total	59	Total	13

TYPHOID FEVER—Continued.

City Reports for Week Ended June 1, 1918.

Place.	Cases.	Deaths.	Place.	Cases.	Deaths.
Aberdeen, S. Dak		1	Marquette, Mich	1	
Allentown, Pa	1		Marshall, Tex	1	
Arlington, Mass	1		Martinsburg, W. Va		1
Austin, Tex	2		Memphis, Tenn	1	
Baltimore, Md	7	1	Milwaukee, Wis	1	
Beaumont, Tex		1	Minneapolis, Minn	1	
Billings, Mont	2		Mobile, Ala	2	1
Birmingham, Ala	5	1	Montgomery, Ala	2	
Boise, Idaho	1		Morgantown, W. Va	1	
Boston, Mass	1		Nashville, Tenn	3	
Braddock, Pa	1		New Castle, Pa	1	
Brockton, Mass	1	1	New Orleans, La	4	2
Buffalo, N. Y	2		New York, N. Y	14	2
Cambridge, Mass	1		Norfolk, Va	1	
Camden, N. J	1		Norristown, Pa	1	
Cape Girardeau, Mo	1	1	Oakland, Cal	1	
Chanute, Kans	1		Ogden, Utah	1	
Charleston, S. C		1	Peoria, Ill	1	1
Charleston, W. Va	2		Petersburg, Va	1	
Chelsea, Mass	1	1	Philadelphia, Pa	7	2
Chicago, Ill	1		Pittsburgh, Pa	1	
Coatesville, Pa	2		Portland, Me	1	
Columbia, S. C	1		Redlands, Cal	1	
Dallas, Tex	1		Richmond, Ind	1	
Des Moines, Iowa	5		Richmond, Va	6	
Detroit, Mich	5	1	Saginaw, Mich	1	
Duluth, Minn	1		St. Louis, Mo	3	1
Durham, N. C	1		Salt Lake City, Utah	1	
Fairmont, W. Va	2		San Diego, Cal	1	
Fall River, Mass	3		San Francisco, Cal	2	
Fremont, Ohio	1		Saratoga Springs, N. Y	1	
Galveston, Tex	2		Sault Ste. Marie, Mich	3	1
Greenville, S. C	1		Sheboygan, Wis	1	
Hammond, Ind		1	Somerville, Mass		1
Hattiesburg, Miss	1		Springfield, Mass	2	
Homestead, Pa	1		Terre Haute, Ind		1
Houston, Tex	5		Toledo, Ohio	5	1
Independence, Kans	2	1	Trenton, N. J	3	
Indianapolis, Ind	3		Uniontown, Pa	1	
Jacksonville, Ill	1		Waco, Tex	2	
Kansas City, Mo	1	1	Wheeling, W. Va	5	1
Little Falls, N. Y	1		Wichita, Kans	1	
Los Angeles, Cal	6		Wilmington, Del	2	
Louisville, Ky	1		Winston-Salem, N. C	2	
Lynchburg, Va	1	1	York, Pa	3	
Macon, Ga	4		Youngstown, Ohio	5	
Malden, Mass	1		Zanesville, Ohio		1

DIPHTHERIA, MEASLES, SCARLET FEVER, AND TUBERCULOSIS.

State Reports for May, 1918.

State.	Cases reported.			State.	Cases reported.		
	Diphtheria.	Measles.	Scarlet fever.		Diphtheria.	Measles.	Scarlet fever.
District of Columbia	72	865	91	Massachusetts	663	6,334	487
Maryland	91	3,294	144	Vermont	8	161	27

DIPHTHERIA, MEASLES, SCARLET FEVER, AND TUBERCULOSIS—Contd.

City Reports for Week Ended June 1, 1918.

City.	Population as of July 1, 1916 (estimated by U. S. Census Bureau).	Total deaths from all causes.	Diphtheria.		Measles.		Scarlet fever.		Tuberculosis.	
			Cases.	Deaths.	Cases.	Deaths.	Cases.	Deaths.	Cases.	Deaths.
Over 500,000 inhabitants:										
Baltimore, Md.	589,621		16		287	4	10		45	13
Boston, Mass.	756,476	188	47	4	263	5	23		65	2
Chicago, Ill.	2,497,722	539	98	11	100	3	18		447	74
Cleveland, Ohio	674,073	170	10		80		9		40	
Detroit, Mich.	571,784	172	39	2	77	8	22	2	57	22
Los Angeles, Cal.	503,812	123	26		72		10		39	22
New York, N.Y.	5,602,841	1,181	245	30	716	19	92	3	141	175
Philadelphia, Pa	1,709,518	458	36	4	918	6	32		80	57
Pittsburgh, Pa.	579,090		7		119		5		15	
St. Louis, Mo.	757,309	207	31		62		16		60	13
From 300,000 to 500,000 inhabitants:										
Buffalo, N.Y.	468,558	120	11		162	3	14		41	11
Cincinnati, Ohio	410,476	136	13	1	123	1	10		21	19
Jersey City, N.J.	306,345		14		31		7		19	
Milwaukee, Wis.	436,535	94	5		217	3	23	1	17	14
Minneapolis, Minn.	363,454		15	1	85		31	3	8	12
Newark, N.J.	408,894	94	18	1	328	3	11		28	17
New Orleans, La.	371,747	144	40		3	1			21	22
San Francisco, Cal.	463,516	137	6		43		11		45	13
Seattle, Wash.	348,639		3		25		25		11	
Washington, D.C.	363,980	114	9	1	80		17		23	13
From 200,000 to 300,000 inhabitants:										
Columbus, Ohio	214,878	68			12	1	15		5	8
Denver, Colo	260,800	70	19		21	1	25			10
Indianapolis, Ind.	271,708		17	4	9		24		13	
Kansas City, Mo.	297,874	80	5		10		8	1	4	12
Louisville, Ky.	248,910	80	3	1	4				13	13
Portland, Oreg.	295,463	72	3	1	90		9		12	4
Providence, R.I.	254,960	73	13	1	114	2	7	2	6	6
Rochester, N.Y.	256,417	71	9	1	73	2	8		18	4
St. Paul, Minn	247,232	54	19		7		29	1	4	4
From 100,000 to 200,000 inhabitants:										
Atlanta, Ga.	190,558	71			11		1		4	13
Birmingham, Ala	181,762	57			7		2		10	7
Bridgeport, Conn	121,576	29	4	2	13		2		16	3
Cambridge, Mass	112,981	24	10		51	4	4		4	5
Camden, N.J.	105,233		3		12		3		4	
Dallas, Tex.	124,527	8			1		4		10	6
Dayton, Ohio	127,224		2		3	1	4		4	3
Des Moines, Iowa	101,598		2				6		3	
Fall River, Mass.	128,366		3		6		1		9	3
Fort Worth, Tex.	104,562	23							4	4
Grand Rapids, Mich.	128,291	31	2		12		5		6	
Hartford, Conn.	110,900		4		15		1		4	3
Houston, Tex.	112,307	28	1				2			2
Lawrence, Mass.	100,560	37	6	1	133	8			4	5
Lowell, Mass.	113,245	36	2	1	28				7	7
Lynn, Mass.	102,425	16	3		65		2		3	4
Memphis, Tenn	148,995	55	2		6		12		23	10
Nashville, Tenn	117,057	47	1		8				5	3
New Bedford, Mass.	118,158	22							6	2
New Haven, Conn.	149,685	42			2				6	4
Oakland, Cal.	198,604	34			15		4		7	2
Omaha, Nebr.	165,470	36	20	2	10		19	1		2
Reading, Pa.	107,481				20		1			
Richmond, Va	139,687	66	1		48		2		12	6
Salt Lake City, Utah	117,849		4	1	19		17			1
Scranton, Pa.	146,811		2		3		1		5	
Spokane, Wash.	150,423		2				3			
Springfield, Mass.	105,942	27	3	1	25		1		3	
Syracuse, N.Y.	155,233	43	1		45	1	1		6	5
Tacoma, Wash.	112,770		1		10		28			
Toledo, Ohio	191,734	48	2		8	1	4			
Trenton, N.J.	111,503	25	2	1	11				4	2
Worcester, Mass	163,314	43	2		6		2		8	6
Youngstown, Ohio	168,385	35			7		1		2	3

DIPHTHERIA, MEASLES, SCARLET FEVER, AND TUBERCULOSIS—Contd.

City Reports for Week Ended June 1, 1918—Continued.

City.	Population as of July 1, 1916 (estimated by U. S. Census Bureau).	Total deaths from all causes.	Diphtheria.		Measles.		Scarlet fever.		Tuberculosis.	
			Cases.	Deaths.	Cases.	Deaths.	Cases.	Deaths.	Cases.	Deaths.
From 50,000 to 100,000 inhabitants:										
Akron, Ohio	85,625	34	3		14		2		4	
Allentown, Pa	63,505		2		102		3			
Atlantic City, N. J	57,660	7			5				6	
Bayonne, N. J	69,893		3		5		1		3	
Berkeley, Cal	57,653	6	4		11		1		2	
Binghamton, N. Y	53,973	20	3		42		3		4	1
Brockton, Mass	67,449	13	1		20		5		5	1
Canton, Ohio	60,852	15	1						2	
Charleston, S. C	60,734	41								5
Chattanooga, Tenn	60,075	3					4		1	2
Covington, Ky	57,144	16	2		10	1			3	2
Duluth, Minn	94,495	19	1						4	
Erie, Pa	75,195		1		70		1		9	
Evansville, Ind	76,078		2	1	8				5	2
Flint, Mich	54,772	9	1		1		5		1	1
Fort Wayne, Ind	76,183	26	6		48				3	1
Harrisburg, Pa	72,015				1					
Hoboken, N. J	77,214	17	6		1				5	3
Holyoke, Mass	65,286	9	1		2		1		7	2
Johnstown, Pa	68,529		2		8		1			
Kansas City, Kans	99,437		2		13		5		2	
Lancaster, Pa	50,853		2		3		1			
Little Rock, Ark	57,343	6	3		2		2		4	
Malden, Mass	51,155	9	1		42		2			
Manchester, N. H	78,283	21	1				1		7	4
Mobile, Ala	58,221	24			5				2	3
New Britain, Conn	53,794	13	2		5		1		5	2
Norfolk, Va	89,612				1		1			3
Oklahoma City, Okla	92,943	21			2		1			3
Passaic, N. J	71,744	18	3		65	1	1		2	2
Pawtucket, R. I	59,411	18	3		26	2	1			1
Peoria, Ill	71,458	36			5					1
Portland, Me	63,867	21			1					2
Rockford, Ill	55,185	12	1	1	23		1			2
Sacramento, Cal	66,895	19	1		3		3		1	2
Saginaw, Mich	55,642	16	1		1		1		1	2
St. Joseph, Mo	85,236	24	1	1	1		1		1	1
San Diego, Cal	53,330	34	1	1	3		2		4	
Schenectady, N. Y	99,519	10	2		13		3		4	
Sioux City, Iowa	57,078						3			
Somerville, Mass	87,039	16	4		22		1		8	1
Springfield, Ill	61,120	29			19					2
Springfield, Ohio	51,550	11	1		11		1		5	
Terre Haute, Ind	66,053	26	1		5		4		1	
Troy, N. Y	77,916	24	2		7		1		1	4
Utica, N. Y	85,692	24	1		38		1		5	3
Wichita, Kans	70,722				4		1		1	
Wilkes-Barre, Pa	76,776		1		13				5	
Wilmington, Del	94,265	18			10		1		3	3
Yonkers, N. Y	99,838	16	14	1	130		2			1
York, Pa	51,656						1		6	
From 25,000 to 50,000 inhabitants:										1
Alameda, Cal	27,732	4			37		1			1
Austin, Tex	34,814	26	2							3
Battle Creek, Mich	29,480		2		22		2			
Beaumont, Tex	27,711	18								4
Boise, Idaho	33,846	1			3		1			
Brookline, Mass	32,730	6			13		2			
Burlington, Iowa	25,030	1					1			
Butler, Pa	27,632		1		1					
Butte, Mont	43,425		2		1		13			
Central Falls, R. I	25,636				1					
Charleston, W. Va	22,941	8	1		2		1			2
Charlotte, N. C	39,823				4					1
Chelsea, Mass	46,192	15			16		1			
Chester, Pa	41,396				6				1	
Chicopee, Mass	29,319	10	3		9		1		1	4
Clinton, Iowa	27,386				17					
Cohoes, N. Y	25,211									2
Colorado Springs, Colo	32,971	11	8		5		3		34	4

DIPHTHERIA, MEASLES, SCARLET FEVER, AND TUBERCULOSIS—Contd.

City Reports for Week Ended June 1, 1918—Continued.

City.	Population as of July 1, 1916 (estimated by U. S. Census Bureau).	Total deaths from all causes.	Diphtheria.		Measles.		Scarlet fever.		Tuberculosis.	
			Cases.	Deaths.	Cases.	Deaths.	Cases.	Deaths.	Cases.	Deaths.
From 25,000 to 50,000 inhabitants—Continued.										
Columbia, S.C.	34,611				2				4	
Council Bluffs, Iowa	31,184	10			2		7			1
Cranston, R. I.	25,087	8			6				1	
Cumberland, Md.	26,074	6			10		1		1	1
Danville, Ill.	32,261	10								
Davenport, Iowa	48,811				4		3			
Dubuque, Iowa	39,873		3		1					
Durham, N.C.	25,061	8			3					1
Easton, Pa.	30,530		1		6					
East Orange, N.J.	42,458	2			24				3	1
Elgin, Ill.	28,203	9	1							1
Elmira, N. Y.	38,120				67					
Evanston, Ill.	28,591	4					1			
Everett, Mass.	39,233	6	3		4		2			
Everett, Wash.	35,186	10			3					
Fitchburg, Mass.	41,781	13			16	1			1	1
Galveston, Tex.	41,863	12	1							1
Green Bay, Wis.	29,353	10								2
Hammond, Ind.	26,171	7	1	1						
Haverhill, Mass.	48,477	9	2		9	1	1		4	
Hazelton, Pa.	28,491		2		21					
Jackson, Mich.	33,396	10			10		9	1	1	1
Jamestown, N.Y.	36,580				88				7	2
Kalamazoo, Mich.	48,886				1				3	1
Kenosha, Wis.	31,576	3			16					
Knoxville, Tenn.	38,676				3					
La Crosse, Wis.	31,677	6	2	1					1	
Lexington, Ky.	41,097	16			1					1
Lima, Ohio	35,384	2			3		1			
Lincoln, Nebr.	46,515	12			1					
Long Beach, Cal.	27,587	9	1		16		2			
Lorain, Ohio	36,946		1						1	
Lynchburg, Va.	32,940	9								1
Macon, Ga.	45,757	13			2				2	
Madison, Wis.	30,699	11			3					1
McKeesport, Pa.	47,521		1		7					
Medford, Mass.	26,234	8	1		23		3			2
Moline, Ill.	27,451				44		2			
Montclair, N.J.	26,318	3			1				2	
Montgomery, Ala.	43,285	12							3	
Mount Vernon, N.Y.	37,009	12			9					
Muncie, Ind.	25,424	7	2	1					1	1
Muskogee, Okla.	44,210				1					
Nashua, N. H.	27,327	9								
Newburgh, N. Y.	29,603	11	1		1					
New Castle, Pa.	41,133		2		8					
Newport, Ky.	31,927								3	2
Newport, R. I.	30,108	8	1				1			
New Rochelle, N.Y.	37,759	6	1		4					
Newton, Mass.	43,715	5	1		10				2	
Niagara Falls, N. Y.	37,353	17	1		1		1		2	
Norristown, Pa.	31,401		3		2		1			
Norwalk, Conn.	26,989							1	1	
Oak Park, Ill.	26,654	10	2		9					1
Ogden, Utah	31,104	10			18		3			
Orange, N. J.	33,080	12	1		32	1			3	2
Oshkosh, Wis.	36,065	8								
Pasadena, Cal.	46,130	13			40		3		5	
Perth Amboy, N. J.	41,185	12			2					
Petersburg, Va.	25,582	9							1	1
Poughkeepsie, N.Y.	30,490	9	1	1	14		1		1	
Quincy, Ill.	36,798	7	3		7					1
Quincy, Mass.	38,136	7			14		2		6	1
Racine, Wis.	46,186	11			21		4		12	
Roanoke, Va.	43,284	14			13		1		1	
San Jose, Cal.	38,392				8					
Sheboygan, Wis.	28,759	3								
Shenandoah, Pa.	29,401								5	
Springfield, Mo.	40,341	8								
Steubenville, Ohio	27,445	12	2		1				1	
Superior, Wis.	46,266	6			6		2			

DIPHTHERIA, MEASLES, SCARLET FEVER, AND TUBERCULOSIS—Contd.

City Reports for Week Ended June 1, 1918—Continued.

City.	Population as of July 1, 1916 (estimated by U. S. Census Bureau).	Total deaths from all causes.	Diphtheria.		Measles.		Scarlet fever.		Tuberculosis.	
			Cases.	Deaths.	Cases.	Deaths.	Cases.	Deaths.	Cases.	Deaths.
From 25,000 to 50,000 inhabitants—Continued.										
Taunton, Mass....	36,283	6					1		1	1
Topeka, Kans....	48,726		1		5		4			
Waco, Tex....	33,385	19							2	2
Walla Walla, Wash....	25,136		1				2			
Waltham, Mass....	30,570	9			60				2	
Waterloo, Iowa....	35,559	14			3		6			
Watertown, N. Y....	29,894	4				1				1
West Hoboken, N. J....	43,139	11	1		13		2		1	1
Wheeling, W. Va....	43,377	8	1		3					1
Wilmington, N. C....	29,892	15			2					1
Winston-Salem, N. C....	31,155	22			2				3	6
Zanesville, Ohio....	30,863	15								2
From 10,000 to 25,000 inhabitants:										
Aberdeen, S. Dak....	15,218	3								
Abilene, Tex....	14,238						4			
Adams, Mass....	14,214	2								1
Albany, Ga....	10,604				6					
Albuquerque, N. Mex....	14,025	7								2
Alton, Ill....	22,874	7	6							
Amarillo, Tex....	19,124	10	1							
Ann Arbor, Mich....	15,010	13	3		5					
Ansonia, Conn....	16,704	3								
Appleton, Wis....	17,834	7								
Arlington, Mass....	12,811	5			3					3
Asbury Park, N. J....	14,007	5			3					
Astoria, Oreg....	10,363	5			3					1
Attleboro, Mass....	19,282	2			1					
Bakersfield, Cal....	16,874	5			2				2	
Barre, Vt....	12,169	1								1
Beacon, N. Y....	11,555	2								
Beatrice, Nebr....	10,287	4			1					
Bedford, Ind....	10,349	3							1	1
Bellaire, Ohio....	14,348				6				3	
Belleville, N. J....	12,393		1		1					
Beloit, Wis....	18,072	5			17					8
Benton Harbor, Mich....	10,833	4			10					
Berlin, N. H....	13,599	1								
Bethlehem, Pa....	14,142		1		19					
Beverly, Mass....	21,645	3							2	
Billings, Mont....	14,422		1		9					
Bloomfield, N. J....	18,466				1					
Bloomington, Ind....	11,383	3	1		3		1		1	2
Braddock, Pa....	21,685		1		3				1	
Bristol, Conn....	15,927								1	
Burlington, Vt....	21,617	2								
Cairo, Ill....	15,794	2	1	r.						1
Cambridge, Ohio....	13,183	5			2	A.				
Canton, Ill....	13,262	5			4					
Cape Girardeau, Mo....	10,775								2	
Carbondale, Pa....	19,242								1	
Carlisle, Pa....	10,726		3							
Carnegie, Pa....	11,692				2					
Centralia, Ill....	11,538				2					
Chanute, Kans....	12,445				14		1			
Cheyenne, Wyo....	¹11,320		3				2			
Chillicothe, Ohio....	15,470		1		1		2			
Clinton, Mass....	¹13,075	6			2					
Coatesville, Pa....	14,455				4					
Coffeyville, Kans....	17,548				3		4		1	
Concord, N. H....	22,669	5								
Connellsville, Pa....	15,455						1		6	
Corpus Christi, Tex....	10,432		5							
Corsicana, Tex....	10,022		5						2	
Cortland, N. Y....	13,069	4							1	
Cumberland, R. I....	10,848			1		2		1			
Dedham, Mass....	10,433	1								1
Dover, N. H....	13,272	6								
Dunmore, Pa....	20,776				1					
East Providence, R. I....	18,113		2							
Eau Claire, Wis....	18,807				29		2		2	
Englewood, N. J....	12,231	3			13					

¹ Population April 15, 1910; no estimate made.

DIPHTHERIA, MEASLES, SCARLET FEVER, AND TUBERCULOSIS—Cont'd.

City Reports for Week Ended June 1, 1918—Continued.

City.	Population as of July 1, 1916 (estimated by U. S. Census Bureau).	Total deaths from all causes.	Diphtheria.		Measles.		Scarlet fever.		Tuberculosis.	
			Cases.	Deaths.	Cases.	Deaths.	Cases.	Deaths.	Cases.	Deaths.
From 10,000 to 25,000 inhabitants—Continued.										
Enid, Okla	20,307	2								
Fairmont, W. Va	15,506				1					
Fargo, N. Dak	17,389	3					1			
Farrell, Pa	10,190				1					
Findlay, Ohio	14,858	3			32					
Fond du Lac, Wis	21,113	8					3	1		
Fort Collins, Colo	11,451	6			1					
Fort Dodge, Iowa	20,648						1			
Fort Scott, Kans	10,550	2								
Fostoria, Ohio	10,770	4								
Frederick, Md	11,112	3			8		1			
Fremont, Ohio	10,582				2		3			
Fulton, N. Y	11,908	6			6					
Galesburg, Ill	24,276	11			4					1
Gardner, Mass	17,140		5		4				2	
Geneva, N. Y	12,711	3			8					
Granite City, Ill	15,142	6			1					
Greeley, Colo	11,420		1		2					
Greenfield, Mass	11,998	5			2		1			
Greensboro, N. C	19,577	7			1					1
Greenville, S. C	18,181	4			1					1
Greenwich, Conn	19,159				7					
Hackensack, N. J	16,945	6	1		16					
Hancock, Mich	12,979	1								
Harrison, N. J	16,960				9					
Hattiesburg, Miss	16,482								2	
Henderson, Ky	12,192	1								
Homestead, Pa	22,466				5		3			
Hornell, N. Y	14,685	1			59					
Hoquiam, Wash	11,666						5			
Hudson, N. Y	12,705								3	
Independence, Kans	14,806	6			1					1
Independence, Mo	11,672	2							1	
Iola, Kans	11,068				2				2	
Iowa City, Iowa	11,413				1					
Ishpeming, Mich	12,448		1	1	1					
Ithaca, N. Y	15,848	5							3	
Jacksonville, Ill	15,481	11								
Janesville, Wis	14,339	1					1			
Kankakee, Ill	14,230				3					
Kearny, N. J	23,539	8			6		2		2	1
Kokomo, Ind	20,930	6			1				2	
Lackawanna, N. Y	15,987	1							1	
La Fayette, Ind	21,268	10	1							
Laurel, Miss	11,779									
Leavenworth, Kans	19,363	9	1		1		1		3	
Lebanon, Pa	20,779		1				3			
Little Falls, N. Y	12,451	7					1			
Long Branch, N. J	15,395	4			34				2	
Mahanoy City, Pa	17,463		1		1					
Manchester, Conn	15,551	2			1				4	2
Manitowoc, Wis	12,805	4	1						1	1
Marinette, Wis	14,610	4			2					1
Marlboro, Mass	15,187	3								
Marquette, Mich	12,409	4					3			
Marshall, Tex	13,712	6							1	
Martinsburg, W. Va	12,666	1								
Mason City, Iowa	14,457	4					2			
Massillon, Ohio	15,310		2							
Mattoon, Ill	12,582	4			15					
McKees Rocks, Pa	19,949		1		26					
Melrose, Mass	17,145	2					1		1	
Middletown, N. Y	15,810	1			2				3	1
Middletown, Ohio	15,625	6			5		1			
Milford, Mass	14,110	4								
Mishawaka, Ind	16,385	3								
Missoula, Mont	18,211	4	5							
Monessen, Pa	21,630		1							
Morgantown, W. Va	13,709	3					6		1	
Morristown, N. J	13,284	2			4					
Moundsville, W. Va	11,153	1								

[1] Population Apr. 15, 1910; no estimate made.

DIPHTHERIA, MEASLES, SCARLET FEVER, AND TUBERCULOSIS—Contd.

City Reports for Week Ended June 1, 1918—Continued.

City.	Population as of July 1, 1916 (estimated by U. S. Census Bureau).	Total deaths from all causes.	Diphtheria.		Measles.		Scarlet fever.		Tuberculosis.	
			Cases.	Deaths.	Cases.	Deaths.	Cases.	Deaths.	Cases.	Deaths.
From 10,000 to 25,000 inhabitants—Continued.										
Mount Carmel, Pa.	20,268	1			1				2	
Nanticoke, Pa.	23,126				1					
Natick, Mass.	10,102		3	1	12				2	
New Albany, Ind.	23,629	7							2	2
Newburyport, Mass.	15,243	4			4				2	
New Castle, Ind.	13,241	2								
New London, Conn.	20,985	9	2				3			1
North Adams, Mass.	22,019	5	1						2	2
Northampton, Mass.	19,926	6	1		6				1	
North Attleboro, Mass.	11,014				3					
North Braddock, Pa.	15,148				1					
North Little Rock, Ark.	14,907	2			1				2	1
North Tonawanda, N. Y.	13,768	5								
North Yakima, Wash.	20,951				18					
Ossining, N. Y.	13,705		1		33				2	
Oswego, N. Y.	24,104				4				2	
Palestine, Tex.	11,854	2							2	1
Parkersburg, W. Va.	20,612	5							1	1
Peabody, Mass.	18,360	4			8				2	
Peekskill, N. Y.	18,530	6								
Piqua, Ohio.	14,152	3			1					
Pittston, Pa.	18,599				3					
Plainfield, N. J.	23,805	5			2		1			
Plattsburg, N. Y.	12,837	3								1
Pontiac, Mich.	17,524	9			12		8			2
Port Chester, N. Y.	16,183	2			5				1	
Portsmouth, N. H.	11,666		1							
Pottsville, Pa.	22,372		1		5					
Provo, Utah.	10,645	1								
Rahway, N. J.	10,219	5			4					
Raleigh, N. C.	20,127	17		1	2		1		1	1
Redlands, Cal.	14,000	2	1		7					
Richmond, Ind.	24,697	7								
Riverside, Cal.	19,763	10			1					
Rocky Mount, N. C.	12,067	6							1	1
Rome, N. Y.	23,737								1	
Rutland, Vt.	14,831	4			3	1				
St. Cloud, Minn.	11,817	8							1	
San Bernardino, Cal.	16,945				4					
Sandusky, Ohio.	20,193	6			2				2	
Santa Ana, Cal.	10,627	7			18		1			1
Santa Barbara, Cal.	14,846	10								2
Santa Cruz, Cal.	14,594	2			3					
Saratoga Springs, N. Y.	13,821	5			9					
Sault Ste. Marie, Mich.	13,919	2								
Sharon, Pa.	18,616				34					
Sioux Falls, S. Dak.	16,499	3								
Southbridge, Mass.	14,205	2								
Spartanburg, S. C.	21,365	7	1		3				1	1
Steelton, Pa.	15,548						1		1	
Streator, Ill.	14,304	5								
Tiffin, Ohio.	12,867	2								
Trinidad, Colo.	13,875				2					
Vallejo, Cal.	13,461	3			1					
Vancouver, Wash.	13,190				2					
Wakefield, Mass.	12,733		1		1				2	
Warren, Ohio.	13,059	12			3					
Warren, Pa.	14,737				2					
Washington, Pa.	21,618		3							
Watertown, Mass.	14,867	2	1		1				1	
Wausau, Wis.	19,239	4								
West Chester, Pa.	13,176		1		7					
Westfield, Mass.	18,391	8			3		1		1	3
West Orange, N. J.	13,550	1			20				1	
West Warwick, R. I.	15,782	4	1							
Wilkinsburg, Pa.	23,228		1		6		1			
Winchester, Mass.	10,603	1			1					
Winona, Minn.	¹18,583	3							1	
Winthrop, Mass.	12,692		3		4				1	
Woburn, Mass.	15,969	5								

¹ Population Apr. 15, 1910; no estimate made.

FOREIGN.

Plague on Vessel.

Two cases of plague were reported, May 9, 1918, on the steamship *Quilpue*, at Callao, Peru.

CUBA.

Communicable Diseases—Habana.

Communicable diseases have been notified at Habana as follows:

Disease.	May 11-20, 1918.		Remaining under treatment May 20, 1918.	Disease.	May 11-20, 1918.		Remaining under treatment May 20, 1918.
	New cases.	Deaths.			New cases.	Deaths.	
Cerebrospinal meningitis...... ..	2	....	¹ 3	Measles............	....	....	4
Diphtheria.........	4	....	16	Paratyphoid fever..	3	....	¹ 3
Leprosy............	....	....	13	Scarlet fever.......	3	....	¹ 5
Malaria............	9	....	² 26	Typhoid fever......	42	3	⁴ 11
				Varicella..........	3	....	12

¹ Foreign, 3.
² From the interior, 25.
³ From the interior, 1.
⁴ From the interior, 61; from Regla, 3; foreign, 1.

ECUADOR.

Yellow Fever—Guayaquil.

Yellow fever was reported present at Guayaquil, June 8, 1918.

GREAT BRITAIN.

Examination of Rats—Liverpool.

During the period from March 10 to May 4, 1918, 1,332 rats were examined at Liverpool, England. No plague infection was found.

PERU.

Plague—February 16–March 31, 1918.

During the period from February 16 to March 31, 1918, 113 cases of plague were notified in Peru. The cases were distributed according to departments as follows: Ancachs, 5 cases; Callao, 1 case; Junin, 1 case; Lambayeque, 16 cases; Libertad, 68 cases; Lima, 22 cases.

CHOLERA, PLAGUE; SMALLPOX, TYPHUS FEVER, AND YELLOW FEVER.

Reports Received During Week Ended June 21, 1918.[1]

CHOLERA.

Place.	Date.	Cases.	Deaths.	Remarks.
India:				
Rangoon	Mar. 17-23	2	2	
Indo-China:				
Saigon	Apr. 15-28	13	10	
Philippine Islands:				Apr. 14-20, 1918: Cases, 165;
Provinces	Apr. 14-20			deaths, 105.
Bohol	Apr. 14-20	14	14	
Capiz	do	11	8	
Cebu	do	18	14	
Misamis	do	103	55	
Surigao	do	19	14	

PLAGUE.

Place.	Date.	Cases.	Deaths.	Remarks.
India:				
Bassein	Feb. 17-23		12	
Henzada	do		12	
Karachi	Mar. 24-Apr. 6	167	118	
Moulmein	Feb. 17-23		9	
Myingyan	Feb. 10-16		16	
Pegu	Feb. 17-23		1	
Prome	do		5	
Rangoon	Mar. 17-23	70	65	
Toungoo	Feb. 17-23		11	
Indo-China:				
Saigon	Apr. 15-28	25	11	
Peru				Feb. 16-Mar. 31, 1918: Cases, 113.
Departments—				
Ancachs	Feb. 16-Mar. 31	5		
Callao	do	1		
Junin	do	1		
Lambayeque	do	16		
Libertad	do	68		
Lima	do	22		
Siam:				
Bangkok	Apr. 7-20	22	17	
On vessel:				
S. S. Quilpue	May 9	2		At Callao, Peru.

SMALLPOX.

Place.	Date.	Cases.	Deaths.	Remarks.
Arabia:				
Aden	Apr. 4-10		1	
Canada:				
Nova Scotia—				
Halifax	May 26-June 1	3		
Sydney	do	1		
Prince Edward Island—				
Charlotte Town	May 30-June 5	1		
China:				
Antung	Apr. 7-20	1	1	
Tientsin	May 5-11	1		
Colombia:				
Cartagena	May 21			Present in suburbs.
India:				
Karachi	Mar. 24-Apr. 6	53	35	
Rangoon	Mar. 17-23	10	4	
Indo-China:				
Saigon	Apr. 15-28	159	45	
Newfoundland:				
Badger	May 25-31	2		Present.
Conche	do			Do.
Englee	do			
Philippine Islands:				
Manila	Apr. 14-May 4	141	76	
Siam:				
Bangkok	Apr. 7-20	5	4	
Straits Settlements:				
Penang	Apr. 7-13	5		
Singapore	Mar. 31-Apr. 20	16	11	

[1] From medical officers of the Public Health Service, American consuls, and other sources.

CHOLERA, PLAGUE, SMALLPOX, TYPHUS FEVER, AND YELLOW FEVER—
Continued.

Reports Received During Week Ended June 21, 1918—Continued.

TYPHUS FEVER.

Place.	Date.	Cases.	Deaths.	Remarks.
China:				
Antung................	Apr. 7-13.........	1	....	
Great Britain:				
Glasgow...............	May 12 18.........	4	....	
Spain:				
Lira....................	Apr. 6............	11	3	Vicinity of Corcubion, Province of Coruna.
Tunisia:				
Tunis................	May 4-17.........	2	2	

YELLOW FEVER.

Place	Date	Cases	Deaths	Remarks
Ecuador:				
Guayaquil................	June 8...........	....	....	Present.

Reports Received from Dec. 29, 1917, to June 14, 1918.

CHOLERA.

Place.	Date.	Cases.	Deaths.	Remarks.
China:				
Antung................	Nov. 26-Dec. 2....	3	1	
India:				
Bombay..................	Oct. 28- Dec. 15....	19	14	
Do...............	Dec. 30 Mar. 9....	219	194	
Calcutta...............	Sept. 16- Dec. 15...	....	135	
Do...............	Dec. 30-Mar. 16....	....	155	
Karachi.................	Dec. 30-Feb. 23...	26	6	
Madras..................	Nov. 25-Dec. 22...	3	2	
Do.................	Dec. 30-Mar. 16...	47	26	
Rangoon.................	Nov. 4 Dec. 22...	6	5	
Do.................	Dec. 30 Mar. 16...	11	6	
Indo-China:				
Provinces................				Sept. 1 Dec. 31, 1917: Cases, 165; deaths, 93.
Anam...............	Sept. 1- Dec. 31...	21	15	
Cambodia..........	....do.......	74	54	
Cochin-China...........	....do.......	56	24	
Saigon............	Nov. 22 Dec. 9...	4	3	
Do............	Feb. 4 Apr. 14....	15	8	
Kwang-Chow-Wan...	Sept. 1-30.........	10	2	
Java:				
East Java..............	Oct. 28 Nov. 3....	1	1	
West Java..............				Oct. 19 Dec. 27, 1917: Cases, 102; deaths, 56. Dec. 28, 1917-Feb. 21, 1918: Cases, 38; deaths, 7. Dec. 28, 1917-Feb. 24, 1918: Cases, 121
Batavia..............	Oct. 10 Dec. 27...	49	23	
Do..............	Dec. 28 Feb. 21...	35	1	
Palestine..............				
Deir Seneid............	Dec. 28 Feb. 24...	65	....	
Jaffa..................	Feb. 17 24.........	4	....	
Ludd..................	Mar. 22...........	1	....	
Sukkarieh.............	Dec. 28 Mar. 22...	24	....	
Persia..................				July 30-Sept. 2, 1917: Cases, 364; deaths, 276.
Achraf.................	July 30 Aug. 16...	90	88	Present.
Astrabad...............	July 31...........	....	....	
Barfrush...............	July 1 -Aug. 16....	39	26	
Bender Bouchir.........				Present. On Persian Gulf. 25 cases reported July 31, 1917.
Chahrirzad.............				
Chahrastugh............	June 15 July 25....	10	8	
Chroud...............	Aug. 26 Sept. 3...	4	2	
Damghan...............	Aug. 26...........	....	....	Present.
Khrack................	May 28 June 11...	21	13	
Mehed.................	Aug. 18 Sept. 2...	171	82	
Ouroun Pare	Aug. 8...........	....	....	Do.
Sabzevar...............	Aug. 24...........	....	....	Do.
Sari..................	July 1 29.........	273	144	
Semnan	Aug. 31 Sept. 2...	14	5	
Yekehambe Bazar........	June 3............	6	....	

CHOLERA, PLAGUE, SMALLPOX, TYPHUS FEVER, AND YELLOW FEVER—
Continued.

Reports Received from Dec. 29, 1917, to June 14, 1918—Continued.

CHOLERA—Continued.

Place.	Date.	Cases.	Deaths.	Remarks.
Philippine Islands:				
Provinces....................	....	....	....	July 1–Dec. 29, 1917: Cases, 5,964;
Antique.................	Nov. 18–Dec. 1...	48	32	deaths, 3,655. Dec. 30, 1917–
Do..............	Feb. 3–9.........	4	4	Apr. 13, 1918: Cases, 1,791;
Bohol.................	Nov. 18–Dec. 29...	169	111	deaths, 1,285.
Do..............	Dec. 30–Apr. 13...	567	446	
Capiz.................	Nov. 25–Dec. 29...	27	21	
Do..............	Dec. 30–Mar. 23...	219	182	
Cebu.................	Dec. 23–29...	3	....	
Do..............	Dec. 30–Mar. 30...	100	54	
Davao.................	Mar. 10–Apr. 13...	12	11	
Iloilo.................	Nov. 25–Dec. 29...	179	135	
Do..............	Dec. 30–Mar. 2...	97	63	
Leyte.................	Nov. 25–Dec. 22...	13	12	
Do..............	Feb. 3–Mar. 16...	50	38	
Mindanao.............	Nov. 25–Dec. 29...	337	196	
Do..............	Dec. 30–Feb. 9...	341	220	
Misamis.............	Feb. 24–Apr. 6...	154	98	
Occidental Negros.....	Nov. 25–Dec. 22...	177	123	
Do..............	Jan. 13–Apr. 6...	146	88	
Oriental Negros........	Nov. 25–Dec. 29...	99	62	
Do..............	Dec. 30–Mar. 30...	23	15	
Romblon.............	Nov. 25–Dec. 1...	1	1	
Surigao.............	Feb. 24–Apr. 13...	43	36	
Zamboanga.............	Feb. 24–Apr. 6...	35	29	
Russia:				
Tashkentnine.............	May 13...........	....	....	Present.
Tzaritsin.................	...do..........	....	....	Do.
Siam:				
Bangkok.................	Sept. 16–22.......	1	1	
Turkey in Asia:				
Bagdad.................	Nov. 1–15.......	....	40	

PLAGUE.

Place.	Date.	Cases.	Deaths.	Remarks.
Brazil:				
Bahia.....................	Nov. 4–Dec. 15...	4	4	
Do.....................	Dec. 30–Feb. 23...	4	3	
Rio de Janeiro.............	Dec. 23–29...	1	....	
Do.....................	Jan. 6–12.........	1	1	
British East Africa:				
Mombasa.............	Oct. 1–Dec. 31...	31	18	
British Gold Coast:				
Axim.....................	Jan. 8...........	....	....	Present.
Ceylon:				
Colombo.................	Oct. 14–Dec. 1...	14	13	
Do.................:	Dec. 30–Mar. 23...	37	33	
China.....................				Present in North China in January, 1918; pneumonic form.
Anhwei Province—				
Fengyanghsien.........	Feb. 27...........	....	9	Pneumonic.
Pengpu.............	....do..........	....	1	Do.
Chili Province—				
Kalgán.............	....	....	....	Vicinity. Present in February, 1918.
Fukien Province—				
Amoy.................	Mar. 11–31...	....	....	Present in vicinity.
Hongkong.............	Apr. 14–20...	1	1	
Kiangsu Province—				
Nanking.............	Mar. 17–Apr. 5...	19	15	
Shanshi Province.............	....	....	....	Present in February, 1918; 116 cases estimated.
Ecuador:				
Babahoyo.............	Feb. 1–15.........	1	....	
Duran.....................	Feb. 16–Mar. 30...	2	1	
Guayaquil.............	Sept. 1–Nov. 30...	68	24	Reported outbreak occurring about Jan. 17, 1918.
Do.....................	Feb. 1–15.........	44	18	
Do.....................	Mar. 1–30...	37	14	
Egypt.....................				Jan. 1–Nov. 15, 1917: Cases, 728; deaths, 398.
Alexandria.............	Jan. 14–28...	1	2	
Cairo.....................	Dec. 17–23...	2	....	
Port Said.................	July 2–Dec. 23...	13	7	
Suez.....................	July 2–Oct. 20...	62	38	
Hawaii:				
Laupahoehoe.............	May 5...........	1	1	

CHOLERA, PLAGUE, SMALLPOX, TYPHUS FEVER, AND YELLOW FEVER.—
Continued.

Reports Received from Dec. 29, 1917, to June 14, 1918—Continued.

PLAGUE—Continued.

Place.	Date.	Cases.	Deaths.	Remarks.
India				July 1-Dec. 29, 1917: Cases, 280,258; deaths, 212,022. Dec. 30, 1917-Feb. 23, 1918: Cases, 276,708; deaths, 221,856.
Bassein	Dec. 9 29		8	
Do	Dec. 30-Mar. 16		181	
Bombay	Oct. 28-Dec. 29	147	123	
Do	Dec. 30-Mar. 9	275	213	
Calcutta	Sept. 16-29		2	
Do	Dec. 30-Feb. 2		4	
Henzada	Oct. 21 27		1	
Do	Jan. 5-Mar. 16		117	
Karachi	Oct. 21-Dec. 29	27	20	
Do	Dec. 30 Mar. 14	94	72	
Madras	Feb. 3-Mar. 9	3	3	
Madras Presidency	Oct. 31-Nov. 24	5,786	4,519	
Do	Jan. 6-Mar. 16	11,049	9,012	
Mandalay	Oct. 14-Nov. 17		80	
Do	Dec. 30-Mar. 16		1,065	
Moulmein	Feb. 17-Mar. 16		74	
Myingyan	Dec. 30-Mar. 16		480	
Pegu	Feb. 10-Mar. 16		5	
Prome	Jan. 5 12		1	
Rangoon	Oct. 21-Dec. 22		56	
Do	Dec. 30 Mar. 16	697	639	
Toungoo	Dec. 9 29		5	
Do	Dec. 30 Mar. 16		69	
Indo-China:				
Provinces				Sept. 1-Dec. 31, 1917: Cases, 171; deaths, 128.
Anam	Sept. 1-Dec. 31	45	28	
Cambodia	do	95	83	
Cochin-China	do	31	17	
Saigon	Oct. 31-Dec. 31	17	6	
Do	Dec. 31-Apr. 14	173	96	
Java:				
East Java				Oct. 8-Dec. 31, 1917: Cases, 198; deaths, 193. Jan. 1-Feb. 4, 1918: Cases, 82; deaths, 81.
Do				
Residences—				
Kediri	Oct. 8-Dec. 31	1	1	
Madioen	do	49	49	
Samarang	do	110	109	
Surabaya	do	23	23	
Do	Jan. 15 Feb. 4	17	17	
Surakarta	Oct. 8-Dec. 31	11	11	
West Java				Nov. 25-Dec. 9, 1917: Cases, 45; deaths, 45. Dec. 1, 1917-Jan. 15, 1918: Cases, 106.
Peru:				
Ancachs Department—				
Casma	Dec 1-Jan. 15	2		
Lambayeque Department	do	22		At Chiclayo, Ferrenafe, Jayanca, Lambayeque.
Libertad Department	do	72		At Guadalupe, Mansiche, Pacasmayo, Salaverry, San Jose, San Pedro, and country district of Trujillo.
Lima Department	do	9		City and country.
Piura Department				
Catacaos	do	1		
Senegal:				
St. Louis	Feb. 2			Present.
Siam:				
Bangkok	Sept 16-Dec 23	13	9	
Do	Jan. 13-Mar. 16	37	27	
Straits Settlements:				
Penang	Mar 17 23	1		
Singapore	Oct 28 Dec 29	5	7	
Do	Jan. 6 Mar 23	51	72	

CHOLERA, PLAGUE, SMALLPOX, TYPHUS FEVER, AND YELLOW FEVER—
Continued.

Reports Received from Dec. 29, 1917, to June 14, 1918—Continued.

SMALLPOX.

Place.	Date.	Cases.	Deaths.	Remarks.
Algeria:				
Algiers....................	Nov. 1–Dec. 31....	3	2	
Do...................	Jan. 1–Apr. 23....	249	6	
Australia:				
New South Wales.........				July 12–Dec. 20, 1917: Cases, 36; Jan. 4–17, 1918: Case, 1.
Abermain.............	Oct. 25–Nov. 29...	3		
Cessnock.............	July 12–Oct. 11....	7		Newcastle district.
Eumangla.............	Aug. 15............	1		
Kurri Kurri..........	Dec. 5–20.........	2		
Mungindi.............	Aug. 13............	1		
Warren..............	July 12–Oct. 25...	22		
Do.................	Jan. 1–17..........	1		
Brazil:				
Bahia................	Nov. 10–Dec. 8....	3		
Pernambuco..........	Nov. 1–15..........	1		
Rio de Janeiro...........	Sept. 30–Dec. 29...	703	190	
Do................	Dec. 30–Mar. 23...	251	84	
Sao Paulo...............	Oct. 29–Nov. 4.....		2	
British East Africa:				
Mombasa.................	Oct. 1–Dec. 31.....	9	5	
Canada:				
British Columbia—				
Vancouver............	Jan. 13–Mar. 9.....	5		
Victoria.............	Jan. 7–Feb. 2	2		
Manitoba—				
Winnipeg.............	Dec. 30–May 25....	5		
New Brunswick—				
Kent County..........	Dec. 4.............			Outbreak. On main line Canadian Ry., 25 miles north of Moncton.
Do.................	Jan. 22............	40		In 7 localities.
Northumberland County.	....do...........	41		In 5 localities.
Restigouche County....	Jan. 18............	60		
St. John County—				
St. John...........	Mar. 3–May 25.....	27		May 13, 1918: Cases present, 14.
Victoria County.......	Jan. 2.............	10		At Limestone and a lumber camp.
Westmoreland County—				
Moncton...........	Jan. 29–May 25....	22		
York County..........	Jan. 22............	8		
Nova Scotia—				
Cape Sable Island.....				Present May 8 at Clarks Harbor.
Halifax..............	Feb. 24–May 25....	25		
Sydney..............	Feb. 3–May 25.....	27		
Ontario—				
Arnprior.............	Mar. 31–Apr. 6.....		1	
Hamilton............	Dec. 16–22.........	1		
Do...............	Jan. 13–19.........	2		
Ottawa..............	Mar. 4–24.........	5		
Sarnia..............	Dec. 9–15.........	1		
Do...............	Jan. 6–May 18.....	34		
Toronto.............	Feb. 10–Apr. 6.....	2		
Windsor.............	Dec. 30–Jan. 5.....	1		
Prince Edward Island—				
Charlottetown........	Feb. 7–13..........	1		
Quebec—				
Montreal.............	Dec. 16–Jan. 5.....	5		
Do................	Jan. 6–Apr. 6......	12		
Quebec..............	Apr. 21–May 11....	3		
China:				
Amoy...................	Oct. 22–Dec. 30....			Present.
Do...................	Dec. 31–Apr. 15....			Do.
Antung.................	Dec. 2–23..........	14	2	
Do...................	Jan. 7–Apr. 27.....	13	3	
Changsha...............	Jan. 28–Mar. 10....	6	1	
Chefoo.................	Jan. 27–Feb. 9.....			Do.
Chungking..............	Nov. 11–Dec. 29....			Do.
Do...................	Dec. 30–Apr. 6.....			Do.
Dairen.................	Nov. 18–Dec. 22....	3	1	
Do...................	Dec. 30–Apr. 27...	90	12	
Hankow................	Feb. 25–Mar. 2.....	1		
Harbin.................	May 14–June 30...	20		Chinese Eastern Ry.
Do...................	July 1–Dec. 2......	7		Do.
Hongkong..............	Dec. 23–29.........	1		
Do...................	Jan. 26–Apr. 13....	22	10	
Hungtahotze Station.......	Oct. 28–Nov. 4.....	1		Do.

CHOLERA, PLAGUE, SMALLPOX, TYPHUS FEVER, AND YELLOW FEVER—
Continued.

Reports Received from Dec. 29, 1917, to June 14, 1918—Continued.

SMALLPOX—Continued.

Place.	Date.	Cases.	Deaths.	Remarks.
China—Continued.				
Manchuria Station.........	May 14–June 30...	6	....	Chinese Eastern Ry.
Do................	July 1–Dec. 2......	3	....	Do.
Mukden..................	Nov. 11 21.........	....	....	Present.
Do................	Feb. 10–Mar. 30...	....	....	Do.
Nanking.................	Feb. 3–Apr. 6......	....	....	Do.
Shanghai................	Nov. 18–Dec. 23...	41	91	Cases, foreign; deaths among natives.
Do................	Dec. 31–Apr. 1.....	38	119	Do.
Swatow.................	Jan. 18............	....	....	Unusually prevalent.
Tientsin...............	Nov. 11–Dec. 22...	13	....	
Do................	Dec. 30 Apr. 27...	49	....	
Tsingtau...............	Feb. 4–Apr. 28....	11	2	
Cuba:				
Habana.................	Jan. 7.............	1	....	Nov. 8, 1917: 1 case from Coruna; Dec. 5, 1917, 1 case.
Marianao...............	Jan. 8.............	1	....	6 miles distant from Habana.
Ecuador:				
Guayaquil...............	Sept. 1–Nov. 30...	26	2	
Do................	Feb. 1–Mar. 31....	4	3	
Egypt:				
Alexandria.............	Nov. 12–18........	2	1	
Do................	Jan. 8 Apr. 15.....	11	....	
Cairo..................	July 23–Nov. 18...	6	1	
France:				
Lyon..................	Nov. 18–Dec. 16...	6	3	
Do................	Jan. 7–Feb. 17....	11	2	
Marseille..............	Jan. 1 31..........	....	2	
Paris..................	Jan. 27–Apr. 20...	11	5	
Rouen.................	Mar. 31–Apr. 27...	43	10	Including varioloid.
Great Britain:				
Cardiff................	Feb. 3–9...........	4	....	
Hull..................	Mar. 17–30........	3	....	
Greece:				
Salonild...............	Jan. 27–Mar. 16...	....	9	
Honduras:				
Santa Barbara Department.	Jan. 1–7...........	....	....	Present in interior.
India:				
Bombay................	Oct. 21–Dec. 29...	50	12	
Do................	Dec. 31 Mar. 9....	918	381	
Calcutta...............	Jan. 27 Mar. 16...	....	34	
Karachi................	Nov. 18–Dec. 29...	4	2	
Do................	Jan. 27–Mar. 14...	56	31	Nov. 11–16, 1917: 10 cases with 4 deaths; imported on s. s. Mesnes from Basreh.
Madras................	Oct. 31–Dec. 29...	20	8	
Do................	Dec. 30–Mar. 16...	157	140	
Rangoon...............	Oct. 28–Dec. 22...	6	1	
Do................	Dec. 30–Mar. 22...	80	19	
Indo-China:				
Provinces..............		....	....	Sept. 1–Dec. 31, 1917: Cases, 466; deaths, 180.
Anam................	Sept. 1–Dec. 31...	210	30	
Cambodia............	....do............	19	11	
Cochin-China.........	....do............	440	133	
Saigon............	Oct. 20 Dec. 30...	120	26	
Do.............	Dec. 31–Apr. 14...	1,407	437	
Laos................	Oct. 1 Dec. 31....	8	1	
Tonkin..............	Sept. 1–Dec. 31...	18	5	
Italy:				
Castellamare...........	Dec. 10............	2	....	Among refugees.
Florence...............	Dec. 1–15.........	17	4	
Genoa	Dec. 2 31..........	11	3	
Do................	Jan. 2–Apr. 15.....	52	9	
Leghorn...............	Jan. 7–Apr. 7.....	33	7	
Messina...............	Jan. 3 19..........	1	....	
Milan.................	....	....	....	Oct. 1 Dec. 31, 1917: Cases, 22.
Naples...............	To Dec. 10........	2	....	Among refugees.
Taormina.............	Jan. 20 Feb. 9.....	6	....	
Turin	Oct. 29 Dec. 29...	123	120	
Do................	Jan. 21–Apr. 7....	96	10	
Japan:				
Kobe..................	Apr. 21–27.........	1	....	
Nagasaki..............	Jan. 14–May 5.....	18	4	
Nagoya...............	Mar. 24–Apr. 13...	3	....	
Taihoku..............	Dec. 15 21.........	1	....	Island of Taiwan (Formosa).
Do................	Jan. 8 Apr. 22	76	21	Do.
Tokyo................	Feb. 11 Apr. 22...	40	....	City and suburbs.
Yokohama.............	Jan. 17–Feb. 3.....	63	....	

CHOLERA, PLAGUE, SMALLPOX, TYPHUS FEVER, AND YELLOW FEVER—
Continued.

Reports Received from Dec. 29, 1917, to June 14, 1918—Continued.

SMALLPOX—Continued.

Place.	Date.	Cases.	Deaths.	Remarks.
Java:				
East Java...................	Oct. 7–Dec. 23....	50	....	Dec. 25–31, 1917: Cases, 7. Jan.
Surabaya..............	Dec. 25–31.........	1	....	1–Feb. 4, 1918: Cases, 14.
Do...............	Jan. 29–Feb. 4....	1	....	
Mid-Java.............			....	Oct. 10–Dec. 26, 1917: Cases, 86;
Samarang............	Nov. 6–Dec. 12...	4	1	death, 1. Dec. 28, 1917–Feb. 13, 1918: Cases, 41.
West Java.............			....	Oct. 19–Dec. 27, 1917: Cases, 231;
Batavia.............	Nov. 2–8..........	1	....	deaths, 36. Dec. 28, 1917–Feb.
Do...............	Feb. 1–7..........	1	....	21, 1918: Cases, 257; deaths, 60.
Mesopotamia:				
Bagdad.............	Jan. 1–31.........	....	10	
Mexico:				
Aguascalientes............	Feb. 4–17.........	....	2	
Ciudad Juarez.............	Mar. 3–June 1.....	4	2	
Guadalajara.............	Mar. 1–Apr. 30...	24	5	
Mazatlan.............	Dec. 5–11.........	....	1	
Do...............	Jan. 29–Apr. 2....	4	4	
Mexico City.............	Nov. 11–Dec. 29...	16	....	
Do...............	Dec. 30–May 11....	146	....	
Piedras Negras.............	Jan. 11............	200	....	
Vera Cruz.............	Jan. 20–Apr. 28...	16	3	
Newfoundland:				
St. Johns.............	Dec. 8–Jan. 4.....	20	....	
Do...............	Jan. 5–May 24....	108	....	
Trepassey.............	Jan. 4.............	....	....	Outbreak with 11 cases reported.
Philippine Islands:				
Manila.............	Oct. 28–Dec. 8....	5	....	
Do...............	Feb. 3–Apr. 20...	215	94	Varioloid, 224.
Porto Rico:				
San Juan.............	Jan. 28–Apr. 7...	37	....	Of these, 36 varioloid.
Portugal:				
Lisbon.............	Nov. 4–Dec. 15...	2	....	
Do...............	Dec. 30–May 6....	38	....	
Portuguese East Africa:				
Lourenço Marquez.........	Aug. 1–Dec. 31....	....	16	
Do...............	Jan. 1–31.........	....	6	
Russia:				
Archangel.............	Sept. 1–Oct. 31...	7	....	
Moscow.............	Aug. 26–Oct. 6....	22	2	
Petrograd.............	Aug. 31–Nov. 18...	76	3	
Vladivostok.............	Apr. 19–24....	6	2	
Siam:				
Bangkok.............	Nov. 25–Dec. 1....	1	1	
Do...............	Jan. 6–Mar. 16....	26	14	
Spain:				
Coruna.............	Dec. 2–15.........	....	4	
Do...............	Jan. 20–Apr. 6....	....	19	
Madrid.............	Jan. 1–Mar. 31...	....	16	Jan. 1–Dec. 31, 1917: Deaths, 77.
Malaga.............	Oct. 1–31.........	....	19	
Seville.............	Oct. 1–Dec. 30....	....	66	
Do...............	Jan. 1–31.........	....	20	
Valencia.............	Jan. 27–Feb. 2....	1	....	
Straits Settlements:				
Penang.............	Feb. 24–Mar. 2....	1	1	
Singapore.............	Nov. 25–Dec. 1....	1	1	
Do...............	Dec. 30–Mar. 23....	4	....	
Tunisia:				
Tunis.............	Dec. 14–20........	1	....	
Do...............	Mar. 16–Apr. 12...	2	....	
Turkey in Asia:				
Bagdad.............		....	....	Present in November, 1917.
Union of South Africa:				
Cape of Good Hope State...	Oct. 1–Dec. 31...	28	....	
East London...........	Jan. 20–26........	1	....	Varioloid.
Transvaal—				
Johannesburg.........	Jan. 1–31.........	4	....	
Venezuela:				
Maracaibo.............	Dec. 2–8..........	....	1	

CHOLERA, PLAGUE, SMALLPOX, TYPHUS FEVER, AND YELLOW FEVER—
Continued.

Reports Received from Dec. 29, 1917, to June 14, 1918—Continued.

TYPHUS FEVER.

Place.	Date.	Cases.	Deaths.	Remarks.
Algeria:				
Algiers	Nov. 1–Dec. 31	2	1	
Argentina:				
Rosario	Dec. 1–31		1	
Austria-Hungary:				
Hungary				Nov. 25, 1917–Jan. 20, 1918: Cases, 16; deaths, 2. Jan. 21–Feb. 24, 1918: Cases, 21.
Budapest	Nov. 25–Jan. 20	2		
Do	Jan. 21–Feb. 24	14		
Brazil:				
Pernambuco	Mar. 16–31	1		
Rio de Janeiro	Oct. 28–Dec. 1	7		
Canada:				
Ontario—				
Kingston	Dec. 2–8	3		
Quebec—				
Montreal	Dec. 16–22	2	1	
China:				
Antung	Dec. 3–20	13	1	
Do	Dec. 31–Mar. 30	3	2	
Chosen (Korea):				
Seoul	Nov. 1–20	1		
Do	Feb. 1–28	3	2	
Egypt:				
Alexandria	Nov. 8–Dec. 28	57	15	
Do	Jan. 8–Apr. 22	1,377	310	
Cairo	July 23–Dec. 23	143	74	
Port Said	July 30–Nov. 11	5	5	
France:				
Marseille	Dec. 1–31		1	
Germany				Dec. 23, 1917–Mar. 23, 1918: Cases, 106, deaths, 9.
Berlin	Mar. 2–23	1		
Breslau District	Feb. 3 23	4		
Konigsberg District	do	1		Prisoner of war.
Lorraine				Dec. 23, 1917–Feb 23, 1918: Cases, 77; deaths, 4. Of these, 10 cases, 1 death, in workmen's camps at Pontingen and Worningen.
Metz	Dec. 23–Feb. 2	17	3	
Posen District	Feb. 3–23	7		
Great Britain:				
Belfast	Feb. 10–Mav 11	22	3	
Dublin	Mar. 24–Apr. 27	4		
Glasgow	Dec. 21	1		
Do	Jan. 20 May 4	18		
Manchester	Dec. 2–8	1		
Greece:				
Arta	Feb. 19	2		
Janina	Feb. 14	110		Jan. 27, epidemic.
Saloniki	Nov. 11–Dec. 29		72	
Do	Dec. 30–Apr. 6		42	
Italy:				
Bagnasco	Mar. 18 Apr. 7	4		Province of Cuneo.
San Remo	Mar. 10–10	2		
Japan:				
Nagasaki	Nov. 25 Dec 16	5	5	
Do	Jan. 7 Apr. 21	19	8	
Java:				
East Java				Oct. 15–Dec. 31, 1917: Cases, 39; deaths, 7. Jan. 1–Feb. 11, 1918: Cases, 34; deaths, 7.
Surabaya	Dec. 17–31	9	1	
Do	Jan. 1 Feb 11	29	4	
Mid-Java				Oct. 10–Dec. 26, 1917: Cases, 62; deaths, 2. Dec. 28, 1917–Feb. 13, 1918: Cases, 34; deaths 2.
Samarang	Oct. 9 Dec 26	20	2	
Do	Dec. 27 Feb. 6	20		
West Java				Oct. 19–Dec. 27, 1917: Cases, 91; deaths, 17. Dec. 28, 1917–Feb. 21, 1918: Cases, 56; deaths, 1.
Batavia	Oct. 1 Dec 27	50	15	
Do	Dec. 28–Feb. 21	47	2	
Lithuania				Dec. 30, 1917–Mar. 2, 1918. Cases, 1,878.
Mexico:				
Aguascalientes	Dec 15		3	
Do	Jan. 21 May 12		22	
Durango State—				
Guanacevi	Feb. 11			Epidemic.
Guadalajara	Apr. 1 30	2	2	
Mexico City	Nov. 11–Dec 29	476		
Do	Dec. 30–May 21	848		
Newfoundland:				
St. Johns	Mar. 30–Apr. 5	1	1	

CHOLERA, PLAGUE, SMALLPOX, TYPHUS FEVER, AND YELLOW FEVER—
Continued.

Reports Received from Dec. 29, 1917, to June 14, 1918—Continued.

TYPHUS FEVER--Continued.

Place.	Date.	Cases.	Deaths.	Remarks.
Norway:				
Bergen.....................	Feb. 1-16...........	3	....	
Poland.......................				Nov. 18-Dec. 8, 1917: Cases, 2,568;
Lodz......................	Nov. 18-Dec. 8....	219	25	deaths, 218. Dec. 23, 1917-
Do......................	Feb. 10-Mar. 9....	292	35	Mar. 9, 1918: Cases, 8,403;
Warsaw....................	Nov. 18-Dec. 8....	1,461	141	deaths, 315.
Do......................	Feb. 10, Mar. 9....	2,747	331	
Portugal:				
Lisbon....................	Mar. 3-30..........	18	....	Feb. 21: Present.
Oporto...................	Dec. 1-31..........	23	4	
Do....................	Jan. 1-Mar. 8......	1,811	161	
Russia:				
Archangel.................	Sept. 1-14........	7	2	
Moscow....................	Aug. 26-Oct. 6....	40	2	
Petrograd.................	Aug. 31-Nov. 18...	32	....	
Do....................	Feb. 2............			Present.
Vladivostok...............	Oct. 29-Nov. 4....	12	1	
Do....................	Apr. 19-25........	3	....	
Spain:				
Almeria...................	Apr. 1-15..........	1	1	
Corcubion.................	Apr. 11...........			Present. Province of Coruna.
Madrid...................	Jan. 1-Mar. 31....	....	2	
Sweden:				
Goteborg.................	Nov. 18-Dec. 15...	2	....	
Switzerland:				
Basel....................	Jan. 6-19.........	1	1	
Zurich...................	Nov. 9-15..........	2	....	
Do....................	Jan. 13-19........	2		
Tunisia:				
Tala.....................	Mar. 18...........			Epidemic.
Tozer....................	...do...........			Do.
Tunis....................	Nov. 30-Dec. 6....		1	
Do....................	Feb. 9-May 3......	46	20	Of these, 26 in outbreak in prison.
Union of South Africa:				
Cape of Good Hope State..	....			Sept. 10, 1917-Mar. 17, 1918: Cases, 4,444 (European, 34); deaths, 902 (European, 15).
Natal....................	....			Dec. 1, 1917-Mar. 17, 1918: Cases, 50; deaths, 11.

YELLOW FEVER.

Place.	Date.	Cases.	Deaths.	Remarks.
Brazil:				
Bahia.....................	Mar. 10-16........	1	1	
Ecuador:				
Babahoyo.................	Feb. 1-15.........	1	1	
Guayaquil................	Sept. 1-Nov. 30...	5	3	
Do.................	Feb. 1-15.........	1	....	
Do.................	Mar. 1-31.........	12	7	
Milagro..................	Feb. 1-15.........	1	1	
Yaguachi................	Nov. 1-30.........	1	....	
Guatemala:				
Retalhuleu...............	Apr. 22-May 23....	....	....	Present. About 25 miles from Champerico, Pacific port. Disease spreading along Pacific coast.
Honduras:				
Tegucigalpa..............	Dec. 16-22........	....	1	
Do....................	Jan. 6-19.........	....	1	

×

PUBLIC HEALTH REPORTS

| VOL. 33 | JUNE 28, 1918 | No. 26 |

VACCINATION AGAINST SMALLPOX AND TYPHOID FEVER.

TREASURY DEPARTMENT,
OFFICE OF THE SECRETARY,
Washington, June 4, 1918.

To persons in charge of establishments manufacturing war materials:

From the standpoint of health conservation and labor efficiency, it is imperative that such communicable diseases as smallpox and typhoid fever be prevented in all establishments manufacturing materials for the Federal Government. This is of special importance at the present time in view of the constant movement of labor from one locality to another, which facilitates so greatly the spread of disease.

The experience of every civilized country shows that complete protection is furnished against smallpox by vaccination, and temporary immunity against typhoid by inoculation with typhoid vaccine.

In order to prevent such diseases, upon the recommendation of the Surgeon General of the United States Public Health Service, persons in charge of plants engaged in the manufacture of war materials are urged to require every person employed under them to be vaccinated against smallpox and inoculated against typhoid fever, as now done in the case of our military forces.

The medical staff should be instructed to take the necessary steps for the enforcement of these measures. The need for them has already been demonstrated by the occurrence of isolated outbreaks of smallpox in establishments engaged in the production of war materials through imported labor. These outbreaks not only cause the quarantine of the personnel, but also interfere seriously with the production of materials necessary to the conduct of the war.

The Public Health Service is ready to cooperate in enforcing these measures, and any persons calling at any of the service stations will, on request, be vaccinated against smallpox or typhoid fever free of cost.

J. H. MOYLE,
Acting Secretary.

61563°—18——1

DRIED MILK POWDER.

A REVIEW OF BRITISH EXPERIENCE.

The local Government board of Great Britain has recently issued a series of reports under the general classification "Food Reports No. 24" upon the preparation, composition, and nutritive values of dried milk powders, with special reference to their use in infant feeding. It is stated that this article is coming into rather large use in the preparation of certain foodstuffs and in the feeding of infants. In view of these facts and of certain claims which have been made as to the advantages of this product over ordinary cow's milk, especially from the point of view of freedom from bacteria of a dangerous sort, a somewhat extensive inquiry into the entire subject has been deemed advisable.

History, Manufacture, and Uses.

The first branch of this inquiry related to the use of dried milk in infant feeding and was carried out by Dr. F. J. H. Coutts with the assistance of Prof. Delépine. A brief history of dried milk and of its methods of preparation is first given. It is stated that as early as 1868 "desiccated milk" was an article of commerce. Since that time, and especially during the past 20 years, considerable advance has been made in the methods of preparation, the general purpose being to secure a dry residue by evaporation at the lowest possible temperature and in the shortest time. Most of the processes employed use one or another form of revolving heated drum, upon the surface of which a thin milk layer is spread and from which the dried product is scraped. The most recent processes inject a stream of partially condensed milk into a heated chamber in the form of a fine spray, the evaporation taking place in the air and the dry powder falling to the floor. In the factories the conditions of manufacture, as regards general cleanliness, were found to be excellent. The author, however, does not agree with the commonly expressed view of the desirability of small-scale manufacture upon the farm. He found in many such cases that the most elementary precautions as to cleanliness were being neglected. The importance of placing this industry under the supervision and control of public health officials is emphasized. About 5,000,000 pounds of milk powder were imported into England during 1915 of which one-half came from the United States, and the importance of some form of guarantee as to the conditions of manufacture of imported products is also noted.

The market product is of three main varieties, namely, full-cream, half cream, and skimmed. Certain firms, however, make other preparations, including some with additional cream. Certain preparations also contain added cane sugar.

Dried milk is used as a basis of certain proprietary infant foods. It is also employed in admixture with cocoa and sugar, with egg powder and sugar as a custard powder, and in various other combinations. Dried milk is said to be used extensively in many of the industries, . particularly in the baking and confectionery trades. Reference is also made to a so-called synthetic dried milk made entirely from vegetable materials. The use of the word milk in this connection is considered rather unfortunate. The ethics of labeling and advertisement are discussed, and the investigations showed on the whole a reasonable regard to accuracy, although in some instances advertisements were decidedly objectionable.

Physical and Chemical Characteristics.

The literature on the physical and chemical characteristics of milk powders is quoted at length. Dr. Monier-Williams reported in 1909 upon a sample of whole milk powder, dried upon a drum at $100° +$, C. Upon mixing with a small amount of water, stirring until homogeneous, and then adding cold, previously boiled, distilled water to make a 12.5 per cent solution, a product was obtained which did not have the homogeneous appearance of fresh milk. It had a slight smell of boiled milk and the fat separated quickly as a yellow layer at the surface. The curd produced by rennet was flocculent and finely divided; that produced by acetic acid was similar to that produced from normal milk. The reconstituted milk did not contain the active enzymes of fresh milk as shown by the peroxydase reaction. The fat globules viewed under the microscope were in most cases larger than those in fresh milk and there was observed a considerable amount of undissolved proteid. A considerable proportion of the lactalbumen had been converted into a form insoluble in magnesium sulphate. The milk sugar had undergone no alteration. A somewhat extensive compilation of various analyses of milk powders is given. Among the foreign substances found are cane sugar, bicarbonate of soda, various preservatives, coloring matter, starch, foreign fat, dirt, and traces of certain metals.

Bacteriology.

A similar comprehensive review of the literature of the bacteriology of dried milk is given. In view of the small amount of information available, a further investigation was made by the author and 42 samples of commercial preparations were submitted to the Lister Institute. Ten per cent solutions of the powder showed aerobic bacteria growing at $22° C.$, ranging in numbers from 100 to 757,000 per cc. and at $37° C.$, from 100 to 892,000 per cc. The results for th part, however, ranged under 10,000 per cc. in each ca presence of streptococci, enteriditis, and *B. coli* was recorded in many of the samples. There was no evidence of tuberculosis in guinea pigs inoculated from these samples.

Investigations made at the factory indicated an enormous reduction in bacteria during the process of drying and a subsequent recontamination during handling and packing. The experiment was tried of running through the drying process a specimen of milk from a tubercular cow and one heavily inoculated with a potato culture of tubercle bacilli. Subsequent inoculations of guinea pigs indicated that living tubercle bacilli may survive the process of manufacture of dried milk, but "the course of the disease produced by the bacteria was very much slower than that of the disease produced in guinea pigs inoculated with the same amount of untreated tubercular milk." No evidence of tubercular infection was obtained by feeding experiments upon four young rabbits.

Infant Feeding.

Upon the basis of a review of the experience of many authorities and of information obtained by personal visits to several large infant feedings stations, the opinion is expressed that when breast feeding is impossible dried milk is a very valuable food for infant feeding. This statement applies, however, only to milk of recent manufacture, made from a good quality of cow's milk under hygienic conditions. It is probably no better than and perhaps slightly inferior to fresh cow's milk, but under the present conditions in cities, and especially in hot weather, it is often desirable to use it in preference to the latter, and this can be safely done without fear of prejudicing the health and progress of the infant. Many infants suffering from digestive troubles show excellent progress on dried milk. Scurvy and rickets are rare in infants fed on this preparation, although the occasional use of fruit juice is desirable.

Increasingly large quantities of milk powder are being used in maternity and child welfare stations supported by public health authorities and voluntary agencies in England and Wales. A list is given of some 75 districts, including some of the principal cities of Great Britain, in which this is the case. At Leicester a dried-milk depot is open every day and consultations are held twice each week. The milk powder is supplied in packages with directions and in three grades, namely, full cream, three-quarters cream, and half cream. The very poor obtain this material at less than cost or even free, while the average purchaser pays a slight margin of profit. Similar details of the operation of some of the other large welfare stations are given.

For administrative purposes, under the "Sale of food and drugs act," milk powders are classed with condensed milk. An extensive bibliography closes the section.

Nutritive Value.

This section is a report of the investigation conducted by George Winfield, M. A., on behalf of the medical research committee. The conclusions are based in part upon observations at infant welfare centers in Leeds and Sheffield and in part on animal feeding experiments. The growth curves of children fed exclusively upon dried milk from birth closely resemble the average growth curve of breast-fed children, although at somewhat lower levels by reason of the more delicate condition of these children. The conclusion is reached "that cow's milk, during the process of desiccation, loses none of the characters which are necessary for the support of normal growth in infants." Teething and walking begin at normal ages, and there is no greater liability of rickets and scurvy. The experiments on rats led to the conclusion that dried milk as a sole food maintains an animal in good health and permits normal growth for periods which long outlast those corresponding with infancy and early childhood in the human subject.

Examination of Milk Powders.

This section of the report, prepared by Sir James Dobbie, Government chemist, presents in detail the methods of chemical examination employed and the analytical results obtained upon a large number of commercial samples of all sorts. These results are summarized in Dr. Coutts's report.

STATE AND FEDERAL COOPERATION IN COMBATING THE VENEREAL DISEASES.

By J. G. WILSON, Passed Assistant Surgeon, United States Public Health Service.

In the Public Health Reports for May 24 an article entitled, "Progress in Venereal Disease Control," showed that the States were rapidly adopting regulations which made these infections notifiable and placed them on much the same footing as other communicable diseases.

Since this article was written further progress has been made. Of the 48 States, 37 now have laws which require notification of the venereal diseases. Most of these States have adopted regulations modeled after suggestions approved by the Surgeons General of the Army, the Navy, and the Public Health Service.[1]

Following is a list of 24 States in which definite arrangements have been made to cooperate with the Federal Government by having an officer of the Public Health Service assume charge of venereal

---

[1] Suggestions for State Board of Health Regulations for the Prevention of Venereal Diseases, approved by the Surgeon General of the Army, the Surgeon General of the Navy, and the Surgeon General of the Public Health Service, Reprint No. 459 from the Public Health Reports, Mar. 29, 1918.

disease control under the joint supervision of the State health department and the United States Public Health Service:

Alabama.	Kentucky.	Montana.
Arizona.	Louisiana.	New Hampshire.
Arkansas.	Maine.	Ohio.
Colorado.	Massachusetts.	Oregon.
Florida.	Minnesota.	Rhode Island.
Georgia.	Mississippi.	South Carolina.
Indiana.	Missouri.	Virginia.
Iowa.	Maryland.	Washington.

In addition to the foregoing, arrangements are being perfected as rapidly as possible with 12 other States whose health officers have expressed a desire to cooperate in the same way.

In most of the 24 States where arrangements have been made for State and Federal cooperation the work is well under way, and in many of them very definite results have already been accomplished. In practically all of these States regulations have been passed which provide ample legal authority for dealing with the problem according to the plan approved by the Surgeons General of the Army, the Navy, and the United States Public Health Service. Consequently the work of the medical officer in charge of venereal-disease control is largely directed toward the organization of the State to carry out the program already agreed upon. The campaign for this organization naturally follows four principal channels, to wit:

(1) Educational: Acquainting the public with the nature of the diseases and the objects desired to be accomplished.

(2) Law enforcement: Securing cooperation of the physicians in reporting cases, and of the police in apprehending prostitutes, vagrants, and such other persons as can be reasonably suspected of having venereal disease in communicable stages.

(3) Propaganda to secure local funds for providing detention homes and hospital facilities for isolation and treatment of venereal-disease carriers who by their habits are a menace to the public health.

(4) Establishment of increased facilities for early diagnosis and treatment.

The following report of progress by Scientific Assistant L. W. Feezer, chief of division of venereal diseases, Minnesota, is a good example of what can be accomplished in a short time by well-directed efforts along the foregoing lines:

St. Paul, Minn., *June 11, 1918.*

Surgeon General,
    United States Public Health Service,, Washington, D. C.

Sir: The following is submitted as a summary of the activities of the Minnesota State Board of Health in connection with the control of venereal diseases during the month of May, 1918:

Reporting of Cases.

A few scattered reports of cases of gonorrhea and syphilis have been voluntarily made by physicians. The official reporting card to be used for making such reports has not yet been received from the printers, and it is not the intention to require such reports until the necessary forms can be supplied. The report card will constitute the back cover of a pamphlet of information and instructions which the physician is required to give the patient at the time he first comes for treatment.

A survey was made of the prisoners in the Minneapolis city workhouse on Sunday, May 26. The survey consisted of the examination of 187 prisoners, 42 women and 145 men, for the detection of venereal disease. The examinations were made with the assistance of a number of internes and nurses from the State University Hospital and was done under the supervision of Dr. H. G. Irvine, director of the division of venereal diseases. A Wassermann was taken in each case. Smears were made from all women and from men who showed a discharge. The results were as follows:

	Wassermann's positive.	Active gonorrhea.
Males	50	7
Females	19	14

Treatment.

The city workhouse of Minneapolis has made arrangements for treatment of venereal cases in its custody. A physician has already been employed, who will give half of his time to this work, and facilities are being provided for the treatment of a considerable number of cases at one time in the workhouse buildings. Particularly in the case of women prisoners is it necessary to have proper facilities.

The city of St. Paul, through the department of public safety, has likewise undertaken to provide the necessary equipment and personnel for treating city prisoners, especially those held for offenses involving prostitution. The city architect has prepared the plans for a treatment room in accordance with suggestions from the State Board of Health. The University Hospital has agreed to place at the disposal of the syphilis clinic 12 beds for the treatment of cases requiring hospital care.

Distribution of Arsphenamine.

In accordance with the plans for supplying free arsphenamine to competent physicians for the treatment of indigent syphilitics in the infectious stage of the disease and to dispensaries and hospitals complying with certain standards for similar use, arsphenamine has been supplied to the University Hospital Dispensary, the Minneapolis City Workhouse physician. and the St. Paul City and County Hospital, in all 170 ampules.

Educational Work.

Twenty-five thousand pamphlets have been procured and are being distributed to all applicants. Several hundred signs have been posted in public toilets and 3,000 more are in preparation.

Two courses of lectures have been held at the State university, one for juniors and seniors and one for graduate students. Five courses of 10 lectures each have been introduced into each of the 5 State normal schools. These have reached 2,000 students, all of whom will become teachers within a year. Courses of lectures by two members of the staff of the division have been arranged for the university summer school to begin in June. Circular letters have been sent to the Women's Council of National Defense in each county and to the Parents and Teachers Associations in the Twin

Cities. Five lectures have been given in the Minneapolis City Hospital to student nurses, and an educational motion-picture film has been shown to teachers in St. Paul and Minneapolis.

A series of six articles explaining the State and Federal campaign for control of venereal diseases is now in process of publication in one of the city papers, and a Duluth paper has asked for a similar series.

Members of the divisional staff have addressed the 3 county medical societies, 2 rotary clubs and approximately 25 women's clubs.

Law Enforcement.

As a result of a conference between officers of this department, municipal judges and police authorities, the municipal courts of the Twin Cities have agreed to hold persons arrested for offenses involving prostitution, without the option of bail, for medical examination, and the imposition of workhouse sentences without the option of fine has been made the routine punishment for all such cases.

Reports from military authorities of sources of infection of soldiers have been reported to police authorities, and in some cases have led to arrest and sentence. A number of persons so arrested are now under treatment.

Through the social service agencies of this division, prostitutes reported as having infected soldiers have been located and in certain instances examinations have been made and treatment instituted. The social worker and protective officer have investigated the matter of soliciting and prostitution in parks and regions adjoining the military training places and other amusement places.

Summary.

Summarized, the innovations made by the city authorities in the Twin Cities as a result of the activities of this board are as follows:

Minneapolis: Three men added to the park police force, employment of workhouse physician, provision of funds for treatment, room and equipment at workhouse. Discontinuance of fine and bail privileges in cases of arrest for offenses involving prostitution. Uniform workhouse punishment for offenses involving prostitution. Assignment of beds for dispensary treatment of syphilis at University Hospital.

St. Paul: Provision for treatment of cases held at workhouse. Provision for control and equipment for the treatment rooms at the workhouse. Medical examination of persons arrested for offenses involving prostitution. Discontinuance of fines and bail and uniform workhouse sentences in cases of arrest involving prostitution.

Respectfully,

L. W. FERRER,
Scientific Assistant.

PREVALENCE OF DISEASE.

No health department, State or local, can effectively prevent or control disease without knowledge of when, where, and under what conditions cases are occurring.

UNITED STATES.

EXTRA-CANTONMENT ZONES—CASES REPORTED WEEK ENDED JUNE 25.

CAMP BEAUREGARD ZONE, LA.

	Cases.
Leprosy:	
Alexandria	1
Malaria:	
Alexandria	8
Pineville	2
Ball	1
Tioga	1
Mumps:	
Alexandria	22
Pellagra:	
Boyce	2
Smallpox:	
Alexandria	2
Tuberculosis:	
Alexandria	1
Pineville	1
Typhoid fever:	
Alexandria	1
Boyce	1
Pineville	2
Whooping cough:	
Alexandria	12

CAMP DEVENS ZONE, MASS.

Measles:	
Littleton	1
Westford	2
Mumps:	
Lancaster	3
Whooping cough:	
Littleton	5
Shirley	3

CAMP DIX ZONE, N. J.[1]

Tuberculosis:	
Pemberton Township	1

CAMP DODGE ZONE, IOWA.

Des Moines:	
Conjunctivitis	2
Diphtheria	8
Measles	8
Mumps	6

CAMP DODGE ZONE, IOWA—continued.

	Cases
Des Moines—Continued.	
Pneumonia	6
Scarlet fever	4
Smallpox	5
Tuberculosis	1
Whooping cough	5
Grimes:	
Scarlet fever	2

CAMP EBERTS ZONE, ARK.

Chancroid:	
Cabot	1
Dysentery:	
Cabot	10
Gonorrhea:	
England	1
Malaria:	
Lonoke, route 3	1
England, route 2	3
Cabot	4
Carlisle	6
Keo	1
Measles:	
Cabot	1
Keo	2
Pellagra:	
England, route 1	1
Pettus	1
Scotts, route 3	1
Smallpox:	
Scotts, route 3	2
Tonsilitis:	
Cabot	1
Tuberculosis:	
Carlisle	2
Scotts, route 1	1
Scotts, route 2	1
Whooping cough:	
Cabot	6

CAMP FUNSTON ZONE, KANS.

Mumps:	
Junction City	1
Manhattan	2

[1] Report for week ended June 22, 1918.

CAMP FUNSTON ZONE, KANS.—continued.

Tuberculosis:	Cases.
Junction City	1
Whooping cough:	
Ogdent	4

CAMP GORDON ZONE, GA.

Atlanta:

German measles	2
Gonorrhea	11
Malaria	3
Measles	1
Mumps	11
Pneumonia	1
Smallpox	3
Scarlet fever	2
Syphilis	5
Tuberculosis	12
Typhoid fever	3
Whooping cough	10

Chamblee:

Mumps	1

Scottdale:

Dysentery	1

CAMP GREENE ZONE, N. C.

Charlotte Township:

Chancroid	3
Gonorrhea	29
Measles	3
Mumps	1
Scarlet fever	14
Syphilis	25
Tuberculosis	2
Typhoid fever	5
Whooping cough	22

GULFPORT HEALTH DISTRICT, MISS.

Gulfport health district:

Dysentery	1
Malaria	8
Measles	1
Mumps	2
Pellagra	1
Syphilis	1
Tuberculosis	3
Typhoid fever	6
Whooping cough	6

CAMP HANCOCK ZONE, GA.

Augusta:

Gonorrhea	1
Malaria	2
Measles	3
Tuberculosis	2
Typhoid fever	4
Whooping cough	7

CAMP JACKSON ZONE, S. C.

Columbia:

Chicken pox	1
Diphtheria	1
Measles	1
Mumps	5
Whooping cough	16

CAMP JOSEPH E. JOHNSTON ZONE, FLA.

Chancroid:	Cases.
Jacksonville	1
Youkon	1
Chicken pox:	
Jacksonville	1
Lackawanna	1
Fishers Corner	2
Dysentery:	
Brentwood	1
Jacksonville	2
Lackawanna	1
Gonorrhea:	
Jacksonville	6
Hookworm:	
Fishers Corner	1
Lackawanna	4
Malaria.	
Jacksonville	4
South Jacksonville	2
Mumps:	
Jacksonville	2
Lackawanna	1
Syphilis:	
Jacksonville	34
Trachoma:	
Lackawanna	1
Tuberculosis:	
Jacksonville	14
Typhoid fever:	
Fishers Corner	2
Jacksonville	4
Lackawanna	2
Whooping cough:	
Fishers Corner	2
Jacksonville	2
Panama	4
South Jacksonville	1

FORT LEAVENWORTH ZONE, KANS

Leavenworth

Diphtheria	4
German measles	1
Gonorrhea	3

Leavenworth County:

Diphtheria	1
Measles	3
Scarlet fever	21

CAMP LEE ZONE, VA.

Chancroid:

Petersburg	6

Chicken pox:

Petersburg	1

Gonorrhea:

Petersburg	42

Malaria:

Petersburg	4

Mumps:

Ettrick	5
Hopewell	3

Syphilis:

Petersburg	19

Tuberculosis:

Petersburg	4

[1] Report for week ended June 22, 1918.

CAMP LEE ZONE, VA.—continued.

Typhoid fever: Cases.
   Hopewell.................................. 1
   Petersburg................................ 1
Whooping cough:
   Ettricks.................................. 1
   Hopewell.................................. 4
   Petersburg................................ 2

CAMP LEWIS ZONE, WASH.

German measles:
   Lake City................................. 1
Mumps:
   Parkland.................................. 3
   Steilacoom................................ 2
Scarlet fever:
   Steilacoom................................ 1

CAMP LOGAN ZONE, TEX.

Houston:
   Gonorrhea................................. 13
   Pneumonia................................. 1
   Syphilis.................................. 16
   Tuberculosis.............................. 5
   Typhoid fever............................. 5
Humble:
   Syphilis.................................. 1
Magnolia Park:
   Tuberculosis.............................. 1

CAMP M'ARTHUR ZONE, TEX.

Waco:
   Chicken pox............................... 2
   Diphtheria................................ 1
   Gonorrhea................................. 2
   Malaria................................... 1
   Mumps..................................... 2
   Syphilis.................................. 1
   Tuberculosis.............................. 1
   Typhoid fever............................. 4

CAMP M'CLELLAN ZONE, ALA.

Chicken pox:
   Precinct 20............................... 2
Diphtheria:
   Anniston.................................. 1
Pellagra:
   Anniston.................................. 2
Pneumonia:
   Anniston.................................. 3
   Precinct 15............................... 1
Tuberculosis:
   Anniston.................................. 1
   Blue Mountain............................. 1
   Jacksonville.............................. 1
   Piedmont.................................. 3
Typhoid fever:
   Anniston.................................. 1
   Blue Mountain............................. 1
   Precinct 23............................... 1

NORFOLK COUNTY NAVAL DISTRICT, VA.

Chancroid:
   Lincoln Park.............................. 1
Diphtheria:
   Norfolk County............................ 1

NORFOLK COUNTY NAVAL DISTRICT, VA.—contd.

Dysentery: Cases.
   Expo...................................... 1
Gonorrhea:
   Norfolk................................... 10
   Portsmouth................................ 2
Malaria:
   Brighton.................................. 1
   Norfolk County............................ 2
Measles:
   Norfolk................................... 3
   South Norfolk............................. 1
Mumps:
   Quartermaster Terminal.................... 1
Smallpox:
   Norfolk................................... 1
Syphilis:
   Norfolk................................... 3
   Portsmouth................................ 1
Tuberculosis:
   Portsmouth................................ 2
   South Norfolk............................. 2
Typhoid fever:
   Mount Hermon.............................. 1
   Norfolk................................... 2
   Norfolk County............................ 1
   Portsmouth................................ 1
Whooping cough:
   Brighton.................................. 1
   Campostella............................... 1
   Norfolk................................... 2
   Ocean View................................ 4
   Portsmouth................................ 2

FORT OGLETHORPE ZONE, GA.

Chattanooga:
   Gonorrhea................................. 25
   Scarlet fever............................. 1
   Smallpox.................................. 1
   Syphilis.................................. 11
   Whooping cough............................ 30
North Chattanooga:
   Paratyphoid............................... 1
St. Elmo:
   Syphilis.................................. 1

CAMP PIKE ZONE, ARK.

Dysentery:
   Little Rock............................... 4
Gonorrhea:
   Little Rock............................... 5
   North Little Rock......................... 4
   Camp Pike................................. 2
   Scotts.................................... 1
Malaria:
   Little Rock............................... 10
   North Little Rock......................... 4
   Galloway.................................. 1
   Outside of county......................... 2
Scarlet fever:
   Little Rock............................... 1
Syphilis:
   Little Rock............................... 9
   Scotts.................................... 2
Typhoid fever:
   Little Rock............................... 2

CAMP SEVIER ZONE, S. C.

	Cases.
Dysentery:	
Chick Springs Township	1
Mumps:	
Chick Springs Township	1
Smallpox:	
Greenville Township	1
Tuberculosis:	
Greenville Township	1
Typhoid fever:	
Greenville Township	1
Whooping cough:	
Butler Township	1

CAMP SHELBY ZONE, MISS.

Hattiesburg:	
Malaria	10
Measles	1
Venereal	1
Typhoid fever	1
Whooping cough	3
Laurel:	
Cerebrospinal meningitis	1

CAMP SHERIDAN ZONE, ALA.

Montgomery:	
Gonorrhea	16
Malaria	4
Syphilis	10
Tuberculosis, pulmonary	2
Typhoid fever	2
Montgomery County:	
Diphtheria	1
Typhoid fever	2
United States Government Clinic:	
Chancroid	5
Gonorrhea	16
Syphilis	9

CAMP SHERMAN ZONE, OHIO.

Chillicothe:	
Diphtheria	8
Tuberculosis, pulmonary	9
Liberty Township:	
Chicken pox	1
Measles	1
United States Government Clinic:	
Gonorrhea	1
Syphilis	3

CAMP ZACHARY TAYLOR ZONE, KY.

Cerebrospinal meningitis:	
Louisville	1
Diphtheria:	
Louisville	6
Gonorrhea:	
U. S. Government clinic	43
Measles:	
Jefferson County	3
Mumps:	
Louisville	1
Syphilis:	
U. S. Government clinic	31
Trachoma:	
Louisville	1

CAMP ZACHARY TAYLOR ZONE, KY.—continued.

	Cases.
Tuberculosis, pulmonary:	
Louisville	
Clark County, Ind	
Typhoid fever:	
Louisville	4
Jefferson County	2
Jeffersonville	1
Whooping cough:	
Louisville	

TIDEWATER HEALTH DISTRICT, VA.

Hampton:	
Scarlet fever	
Newport News:	
Chancroid	
Gonorrhea	
Syphilis	3
Smallpox	1
Typhoid fever	1
Phoebus:	
Pellagra	2
Whooping cough	

CAMP TRAVIS ZONE, TEX.

San Antonio:	
Cerebrospinal meningitis	
Chancroid	2
Gonorrhea	
Malaria	1
Measles	
Mumps	2
Syphilis	4
Tuberculosis	
Typhoid fever	
Whooping cough	

CAMP WADSWORTH ZONE, S. C.

Saxon Mills:	
Tuberculosis	
Spartanburg:	
Diphtheria	1
Gonorrhea	
Measles	
Mumps	
Syphilis	
Typhoid fever	
Whooping cough	

CAMP WHEELER ZONE, GA.

Bibb County:	
Pneumonia	
Macon:	
Chicken pox	1
Gonorrhea	1
Malaria	4
Pellagra	1
Pneumonia	2
Smallpox	1
Tuberculosis	1
Typhoid fever	5
U. S. Government Clinic:	
Gonorrhea	15
Syphilis	7

DISEASE CONDITIONS AMONG TROOPS IN THE UNITED STATES.

The following data are taken from telegraphic reports received in the office of the Surgeon General, United States Army, for the week ended June 14, 1918:

Annual admission rate per 1,000 (disease only):

All troops	987. 2
Divisional camps	978
Cantonments	1, 044. 4
Departmental and other troops	930. 6

Noneffective rate per 1,000 on day of report:

All troops	38. 3
Divisional camps	35. 4
Cantonments	44. 6
Departmental and other troops	33. 2

Annual death rate per 1,000 (disease only):

All troops	3. 31
Divisional camps	2. 9
Cantonments	4. 89
Departmental and other troops	1. 86

New cases of special diseases reported during the week ended June 14, 1918.

Camp.	Pneumonia.	Dysentery.	Malaria.	Venereal. Total.	Venereal. New infections.	Measles.	Meningitis.	Scarlet fever.	Deaths.	Annual admission rate per 1,000 (disease only.)	Noneffective per 1,000 on day of report.
Beauregard			26	52	3	2			1	815. 8	43. 4
Bowie	1	4	3	54	39	2				716. 7	25. 5
Cody	27			23	3	12			4	942. 2	22. 2
Doniphan				25					3	1, 816. 3	44. 3
Fremont	15			13	1	18	1	1	3	923. 5	39. 5
Hancock	1			19					1	868. 2	41. 5
Kearny	2			2		3			1	413. 4	19. 5
Logan	3			17		3				1, 916. 2	83. 5
MacArthur	3					6			1	1, 506. 9	45. 0
McClellan	4		2	13	6	1				634. 8	39. 5
Sevier	10	1	8	56	16	21			1	876. 7	50. 6
Shelby				14	6	1				948. 8	40. 2
Sheridan	3		4	26		17			2	802. 2	37. 7
Wadsworth	2		3	573	12	13			1	1, 711. 3	27. 8
Wheeler	8			68	4		1		3	696. 8	29. 8
Custer	4		1	65	6	16			1	496. 0	20. 3
Devens	10			35	5	19			4	582. 7	36. 3
Dix	3		1	94	1	8	2		3	625. 5	36. 8
Dodge	6		1	138		29		1	7	1, 457. 9	61. 1
Funston	1			69	2	4		1	4	792. 8	53. 6
Gordon	6		2	577	5	18	2		5	2, 606. 1	65. 0
Grant	3			17	1	15		2		396. 2	16. 9
Jackson	10			259	1	76	1		5	1, 645. 5	50. 7
J. E. Johnston	6		3	20	13	15			1	985. 5	37. 8
Lee	3		1	219		20	1		2	781. 7	62. 0
Lewis	17		1	175	5	18		8	8	1, 013. 7	33. 9
Meade	2			19	8	3			4	583. 8	26. 9
Pike	12		29	53	4	26	1		5	1, 496. 3	60. 4
Sherman	1			98		2	2		2	1, 314. 8	73. 4
Taylor	4			43	1	44			3	951. 0	58. 2
Travis	3	6	8	28		11			2	1, 562. 3	49. 1
Upton	11			132	12	2	2		4	643. 1	34. 7
Northeastern Department			2	27	10	5			3	791. 6	27. 8
Eastern Department	9		2	205	70	18			2	758. 3	21. 7
Southeastern Department			5	38	23	1			1	923. 5	37. 3
Central Department	1		1	51	26	18		7	3	1, 211. 1	39. 5
Southern Department	7		10	128	46	5	2	2	4	809. 5	32. 5
Western Department	1		1	111	40	6	1	7	2	881. 3	26. 8

New cases of special diseases reported during the week ended June 14, 1918—Contd.

Camp.	Pneumonia.	Dysentery.	Malaria.	Venereal.		Measles.	Meningitis.	Scarlet fever.	Deaths.	Annual admission rate per 1,000 (disease only.)	Noneffective per 1,000 on day of report.
				Total.	New infections.						
Air Service.........	6	12	3	160	....	16	3	1	12	1,035.4	2. :
Alcatraz Disciplinary Barracks......	......	......	......	......	....	......	......	......	......	314.2	9. •
Columbus Barracks..	......	......	......	7	....	1	......	......	......	394.7	3. •
Edgewood Arsenal..	......	......	......	1	1	......	......	......	......	303.4	1 : 4
Hoboken..........	8	2	5	302	8	29	1	4	3	940.6	27 1
Jefferson Barracks..	3	......	......	91	5	4	......	2	......	1,477.5	80 5
Leavenworth Disciplinary Barracks.....	......	......	......	......	....	......	1	......	......	804.0	34.4
Logan, Fort......	3	......	......	2	....	1	......	......	......	1,504.4	78.4
McDowell, Fort....	3	......	......	16	2	......	......	......	......	2,243.5	145.6
Newport News.....	2	......	5	103	5	6	......	......	2	976.2	41 4
Slocum, Fort......	......	......	......	27	....	......	......	......	......	865.4	77. •
Springfield Armory.	......	......	......	1	....	......	......	......	......	509.4	4 4
Thomas, Fort......	......	......	1	10	....	5	......	......	......	1,134.1	61.4
Watervliet........	......	......	......	......	....	......	......	......	......	135.4	1.4
West Point........	......	......	......	1	....	......	......	......	......	32K.1	4.4
Greenleaf.........	1	......	2	35	....	22	......	......	1	1,159.4	54.9
War Prisoners Barracks No. 1.....	......	......	......	......	....	......	......	......	......	165.1	8 5
Keogh, Fort.......	......	......	......	......	....	......	......	......	......	349.0	4.7
Watertown Arsenal.	......	......	......	1	....	......	......	......	......	706.2	4.4
Total.........	230	25	127	4,312	390	563	20	36	115	957.2	34.3

[1] All troops.

Annual rate per 1,000 for special diseases.

Diseases.	All troops in United States.[1]	Departmental and other troops.[1]	Divisional camps.[1]	Cantonments[1]	Forwarding army forces[1]
Pneumonia..........................	8.57	4.32	13.5	9.87	10.5
Dysentery...........................	.93	1.37	.8	.55	3
Malaria.............................	4.73	3.34	7.9	4.34	.9
Venereal............................	160.7	129.4	163.8	188.4	24.4
Paratyphoid.........................	....	....	....	....	.04
Typhoid.............................	.04	....	.17	....	....
Measles.............................	21.0	13.6	17.0	30.5	....
Meningitis..........................	.74	.60	.3	1.04	1.7
Scarlet fever........................	1.34	2.26	.17	1.1	3.3

[1] Week ended June 14, 1918.   [2] Week ended June 7, 1918.

CURRENT STATE SUMMARIES.

California.

From the State Board of Health of California, by telegraph, for week ended June 22, 1918:

Most communicable diseases reduced in prevalence. Increase in gonococcus infection and syphilis. Typhoid fever begins its seasonal rise, 24 cases during week, well distributed over the State, except in Imperial County, where many cases reported. One case poliomyelitis in San Diego. Two cases human anthrax; 1 in Amador and 1 in Tuolumne County. Four cases epidemic cerebrospinal meningitis, 1 Los Angeles and 3 San Francisco. Twenty-two cases of smallpox; well scattered throughout the State.

Reported by mail for preceding week (ended June 15):

Cerebrospinal meningitis	1	Pneumonia	42
Chicken pox	129	Poliomyelitis	2
Diphtheria	54	Scarlet fever	51
Erysipelas	7	Smallpox	18
German measles	66	Syphilis	36
Gonococcus infection	60	Tetanus	1
Malaria	4	Trachoma	2
Measles	457	Tuberculosis	131
Mumps	132	Typhoid fever	12
Pellagra	2	Whooping cough	128

Connecticut.

From Collaborating Epidemiologist Black, by telegraph, for week ended June 22, 1918:

Typhoid fever: Stratford 2, Waterbury 3, total in State 10. Cerebrospinal meningitis: New Britain 1, Waterbury 1. Diphtheria: New London 7, total in State 36. Scarlet fever: New Britain 10, total in State 27. Smallpox: South Windsor 1.

Illinois.

From Collaborating Epidemiologist Drake, by telegraph, for week ended June 22, 1918:

Diphtheria: One hundred and forty-four, of which in Chicago 121, Chicago Heights, 5. Scarlet fever: Fifty, of which in Chicago 31. Smallpox: Thirty-five in Alton, 3 Springfield. Meningitis: Chicago 4. Poliomyelitis: Six, of which in Kewanee Township (Henry County), 1, Okawville Township (Washington County) 1, Chicago 4.

Indiana.

From the State Board of Health of Indiana, by telegraph, for week ended June 22, 1918:

Typhoid fever: South Bend 3 cases. Smallpox: Princeton 3 cases.

Louisiana.

From Collaborating Epidemiologist Dowling, by telegraph, for week ended June 22, 1918:

Infantile paralysis 1, meningitis 1, typhoid fever 65, diphtheria 69, malaria 74.

Massachusetts.

From Collaborating Epidemiologist Hitchcock, by telegraph, for week ended June 22, 1918:

Unusual prevalence. Measles: Fitchburg 64, Haverhill 24, Lawrence 55, Northampton 17, Stoughton (total in June) 25, Waltham 28.

Minnesota.

From Collaborating Epidemiologist Bracken, by telegraph, for week ended June 22, 1918:

Smallpox, new foci: Lesueur County, Tyrone Township; McLeod County, Rich Valley Township; Washington County, Dayton Township; Wilkin County, Champion Township; each 1 case. Wright County, Cokato Village, 5. One poliomyelitis report since June 17.

Nebraska.

From the State Board of Health of Nebraska, by telegraph, for week ended June 22, 1918:

Smallpox at Neligh.

New Jersey.

From Collaborating Epidemiologist Bowen, by telegraph, for week ended June 22, 1918:

Unusual prevalence. Measles: Asbury Park. Smallpox: Paulsboro.

Virginia.

From the State Board of Health of Virginia, by telegraph, for week ended June 22, 1918:

Several cases smallpox Bedford County, 1 Norfolk.

Washington.

From the State Board of Health of Washington, by telegraph, for week ended June 22, 1918:

One cerebrospinal meningitis South Bend. Thirty-one scarlet fever Tacoma, 19 Seattle. Nine cases smallpox Farmington (Whitman County), and 4 cases Chewelah (Stevens County).

RECIPROCAL NOTIFICATION.

Minnesota.

Cases of communicable diseases referred during May, 1918, to other State health departments by department of health of the State of Minnesota.

Disease and locality of notification.	Referred to health authority of—	Why referred.
Cerebrospinal meningitis: Minneapolis Health Department, Hennepin County.	Dolan 1, Spink County, S Dak........	Rural school-teacher per Dolan 1 came to Minneapolis May 4, taken sick May 7. Meningococci demonstrated.
Smallpox: Willmar, Kandiyohi County.	Omaha, Douglas County, Nebr........	Taken sick 5 days after a visit of 2 months in Nebraska.
Minneapolis Health Department, Hennepin County.	Kansas City, Jackson County, Mo...	Taken sick in Minneapolis 5 days after exposure to smallpox in Missouri.
	Crosby, Divide County, N Dak ... Fredonia, Wells County, N Dak.. Berwick, McHenry County, N Dak.. Hamlet, Wells County, N Dak.... Fargo, Cass County, N Dak........ Cloquet, Cook County, Ill .... Baxter, Itasca County, Iowa....... Wilton, Burleigh County, Pa... Mobridge, Perkins County, S Dak ... Lemmon, Perkins County, S Dak ... New Richmond, St Croix County, Wis. Rochester, Olmsted County, Minn ... La Crosse, La Crosse County, Wis...	Traveling salesman in transit on arrival in Minnesota from North Dakota, where he was 1 per in several different towns. Quarantined on arrival in Minnesota from S. Dakota, exposed 1 per on train.
Tuberculosis: Mayo Clinic, Rochester, Olmsted County.	Lewiston, Nez Perce County, Idaho... Philipsburg, Granite County, Mont... Brooklyn, Kings County, N Y...... Sawyer, Ward County, N Dak ...... Tr. in Lawrence County, S Dak..... Milwaukee, Milwaukee County, Wis.. New Lisbon, Juneau County, Wis.... Rhinelander, Oneida County, Wis.... Butternut, Ashland County, Wis...... Casper, Natrona County, Wyo........ Red Deer, Alberta, Canada...........	4 advanced, 5 moderately advanced, 1 fibroid case. 1 apparently arrested, case left Mayo Clinic for home.

Cases of communicable diseases referred during May, 1918, to other State health departments by department of health of the State of Minnesota—Continued.

Disease and locality of notification.	Referred to health authority of—	Why referred.
Tuberculosis—Continued.		
Pokegama Sanatorium, Pine County.	Hanlontown, Worth County, Iowa.... Ambrose, Divide County, N. Dak..... Fairdale, Walsh County, N. Dak...... Aberdeen, Brown County, S. Dak..... Denzil, Saskatchewan, Canada	1 removal on account of death, and 4 cases left Pokegama Sanatorium in an improved condition for homes.
Thomas Hospital, Minneapolis, Hennepin County.	Flandreau, Moody County, S. Dak.... Wautoma, Waushara County, Wis....	1 incipient and 1 moderately advanced case left Thomas Hospital for homes.
State Reformatory, St. Cloud, Stearns County.	Springfield, Bon Homme County, S. Dak.	An apparently arrested case left reformatory for home in South Dakota.
Typhoid fever:		
Abbott Hospital, Minneapolis, Hennepin County.	Eau Clair, Eau Clair County, Wis.....	Convalescent typhoid case left Minnesota for Wisconsin.
Minneapolis Health Department, Hennepin County.	Chelsea, Taylor County, Wis..........	Typhoid case brought for treatment to Minneapolis from Wisconsin.

CEREBROSPINAL MENINGITIS.

State Reports for April and May, 1918.

Place.	New cases reported.	Place.	New cases reported.
California (May):		Montana (May):	
San Francisco.....................	6	Sanders County...................	1
Alameda County—			
Berkeley.......................	1	New York (May):	
San Mateo County................	1	Albany County—	
San Joaquin County..............	1	Albany........................	2
Tulare County—		Broome County—	
Lindsay.......................	2	Binghamton...................	1
Los Angeles County—		Cattaraugus County—	
Los Angeles...................	4	Allegany......................	1
San Diego County................	1	Erie County—	
San Diego.....................	3	Buffalo.......................	3
Kern County—		Herkimer County—	
Bakersfield...................	1	Little Falls (town)...........	1
Riverside County—		Monroe County—	
Riverside.....................	1	Rochester....................	4
		Onondaga County—	
Total.....................	21	Syracuse.....................	2
Connecticut (April):		Rensselaer County—	
Fairfield County—		Troy..........................	1
Bridgeport....................	1	Rockland County—	
Hartford County—		Suffern.......................	1
Hartford......................	2	Schenectady County—	
Windsor Locks................	1	Schenectady..................	1
New Haven County—		Wayne County—	
Naugatuck....................	1	Newark.......................	1
New Haven....................	3	Westchester County—	
Wallingford...................	1	Bedford (town)...............	1
Waterbury....................	2		
New London County—		Total.....................	19
Ledyard......................	1	Rhode Island (May):	
Lyme.........................	1	Providence County...............	10
New London..................	1	Newport County.................	1
Windham County—			
Sterling......................	1	Total.....................	11
Total.....................	15	West Virginia (May):	
Louisiana (May):		Ohio County.....................	2
Allen Parish....................	1	Wisconsin (May):	
Caldwell Parish.................	1	Dane County....................	1
Evangeline Parish..............	1	Lincoln County..................	1
Grant Parish...................	1	Milwaukee County...............	18
Orleans Parish..................	4	Oneida County..................	3
Ouachita Parish................	1	Sheboygan County..............	1
Rapides Parish..................	2	Waupaca County................	1
St. Martin Parish...............	1	Winnebago County..............	1
Total.....................	12	Total.....................	26

CEREBROSPINAL MENINGITIS—Continued.

City Reports for Week Ended June 8, 1918.

Place.	Cases.	Deaths.	Place.	Cases.	Deaths.
Amsterdam, N. Y.	1		Kansas City, Kans.	1	
Astoria, Oreg.	1	1	Little Rock, Ark.	1	
Baltimore, Md.	3	5	Los Angeles, Cal.	1	1
Bethlehem, Pa.	1		Louisville, Ky.	1	2
Boston, Mass.	2	1	Lowell, Mass.		1
Bridgeport, Conn.	1		Milwaukee, Wis.	1	1
Cambridge, Mass.	2		New York, N. Y.	7	4
Cedar Rapids, Iowa.	1		Philadelphia, Pa.	3	1
Charleston, W. Va.		1	Pittsburgh, Pa.	1	
Chattanooga, Tenn.	1		Pittsfield, Mass.		1
Chicago, Ill.	2	2	Providence, R. I.		1
Cleveland, Ohio.	3	1	St. Louis, Mo.		1
Covington, Ky.			Troy, N. Y.	1	
Dayton, Ohio.		1	Washington, D. C.		
Detroit, Mich.	1	1	Washington, Pa.	1	
Duluth, Minn.		1	Worcester, Mass.	1	
Evansville, Ind.	1	1	York, Pa.	1	
Galveston, Tex.		1			

DIPHTHERIA.

See Diphtheria, measles, scarlet fever, and tuberculosis, page 1080.

ERYSIPELAS.

City Reports for Week Ended June 8, 1918.

Place.	Cases.	Deaths.	Place.	Cases.	Deaths.
Akron, Ohio.	1		Marshall, Tex.	1	
Bakersfield, Cal.	1		Minneapolis, Minn.	1	
Baltimore, Md.	1		Moline, Ill.	1	1
Belleville, N. J.	1		Newark, N. J.	3	
Buffalo, N. Y.	1		New York, N. Y.		5
Chicago, Ill.	8	2	Omaha, Nebr.	2	
Cleveland, Ohio.	1		Pasadena, Cal.	1	
Denver, Colo.	5		Philadelphia, Pa.	9	3
Detroit, Mich.	1		Portland, Oreg.	2	
Duluth, Minn.	1		Sacramento, Cal.	1	
Fond du Lac, Wis.		1	St. Louis, Mo.	1	
Jackson, Mich.	2		St. Paul, Minn.	2	
Kansas City, Mo.		2	San Diego, Cal.	2	1
Los Angeles, Cal.	1		Syracuse, N. Y.		1
Louisville, Ky.	1	1	Tacoma, Wash.	1	

LEPROSY.

City Reports for Week Ended June 8, 1918.

During the week ended June 8, 1918, one case of leprosy at each of the following places was reported: Abilene, Tex.; Boston, Mass.; Bridgeport, Conn.; New Orleans, La. There was also one death from this disease reported at New Orleans, La.

MALARIA.

State Reports for May, 1918.

Place.	New cases reported.	Place.	New cases reported.
California:		Louisiana:	
Alameda County—		Acadia Parish	11
Berke'ey	1	Allen Parish	1
Butte County	11	Assumption Parish	9
Chico	3	Avoyelles Parish	1
Calaveras County	2	Beauregard Parish	2
Colusa County	5	Ca'casieu Parish	1
Colusa	2	Caldwell Parish	2
Glenn County	6	De Soto Parish	5
Los Ange'es County—		East Fe'iciana Parish	10
Los Ange'es	1	Jefferson Davis Parish	4
Merced County—		Lafayette Parish	1
Merced	2	Morehouse Parish	1
Placer County	1	Ouachita Parish	26
Linco'n	2	Rapides Parish	111
Ro:klin	1	St. Char'es Parish	12
San Francisco County	1	St. John the Baptist Parish	12
Presidio	1	St. Martin Parish	6
San Joaquin County	1	St. Mary Parish	13
Stockton	1	St. Tammany Parish	43
So'ano County—		Tangipahoa Parish	1
Benicia	3	Tensas Parish	17
Stanislaus County—		Vormi'ion Parish	12
Oakda'e	2		
Tehama County—		Total	301
Corning	1		
Tulare County	1		
Yo'o County—			
Wood'and	1		
Yuba County	1		
Marysvil'e	1		
Total	51		

City Reports for Week Ended June 8, 1918.

Place.	Cases.	Deaths.	Place.	Cases.	Deaths.
Albany, Ga	3		Memphis, Tenn	3	1
Atlanta, Ga	2		New Orleans, La	5	
Birmingham, Ala	2		North Little Rock, Ark	2	
Camden, N. J	2		Palestine, Tex	3	
Cape Girardeau, Mo	4		Petersburg, Va	1	
Corsicana, Tex	1		Richmond, Va	1	
Dedham, Mass	1		Rocky Mount, N. C	1	
Hattiesburg, Miss	18		Sedalia, Mo	4	
Little Rock, Ark	6		Trenton, N. J	1	
Macon, Ga	1	1	Tuscaloosa, Ala	3	1
Marshall, Tex	2				

MEASLES.

See Diphtheria, measles, scarlet fever, and tuberculosis, page 1080

PELLAGRA.

State Reports for May, 1918.

Place.	New cases reported.	Place.	New cases reported.
California:		Louisiana—Continued.	
Los Angeles County	1	Morehouse Parish	10
Los Angeles	1	Orleans Parish	6
La Verne	1	Ouachita Parish	3
Total	3	Rapides Parish	1
		Richland Parish	1
Louisiana:		St. Mary Parish	1
Assumption Parish	5	St. Tammany Parish	1
Concordia Parish	1	West Carroll Parish	1
De Soto Parish	1	Total	36
East Baton Rouge Parish	2		
East Feliciana Parish	1	West Virginia:	
Iberia Parish	2	Randolph County	1

PELLAGRA—Continued.

City Reports for Week Ended June 8, 1918.

Place.	Cases.	Deaths.	Place.	Cases.	Deaths.
Albany, Ga	1	1	Nashville, Tenn	3	2
Atlanta, Ga		6	New Orleans, La	3	3
Augusta, Ga		1	Northampton, Mass	1	1
Baltimore, Md	1		Petersburg, Va		6
Birmingham, Ala	7	1	Raleigh, N. C		2
Chicago, Ill		1	Richmond, Va	3	
Corsicana, Tex	2	3	Roanoke, Va		1
Durham, N. C	2	1	Rocky Mount, N. C	1	
Houston, Tex		1	Sedalia, Mo	2	
Independence, Mo	1		Spartanburg, S. C	4	
Lexington, Ky		1	Washington, D. C	2	
Mobile, Ala	1	2	Wilmington, N. C		1

PLAGUE.

California—Plague-Infected Squirrels Found.

During the period from June 8 to 24, 1918, 5 plague-infected squirrels were found in California, in Alameda and Contra Costa Counties, making a total of 6 cases reported from two weeks of hunting.

PNEUMONIA.

City Reports for Week Ended June 8, 1918.

Place	Cases.	Deaths.	Place.	Cases.	Deaths.
Amsterdam, N. Y	4	1	Lynn, Mass	4	1
Astoria, Oreg	4	4	Manchester, N. H	1	1
Auburn, N. Y	2	1	Marquette, Mich	1	
Baltimore, Md	7	3	Millard, Mass		4
Berkeley, Cal	1	1	Newark, N J	26	6
Beverly, Mass	1		New Britain, Conn	1	
Boston, Mass	5	7	North Little Rock, Ark	1	2
Brockton, Mass	2		Oshkosh, Wis	3	
Cambridge, Mass	5		Parkersburg, W. Va	1	1
Chicago, Ill	62	29	Plainfield, Pa	45	2
Cleveland, Ohio	8	11	Rochester, N. Y	7	1
Dallas, Tex	1	2	Sacramento, Cal	2	1
Dayton, Ohio	1	2	St. Cloud, Minn	1	
Detroit, Mich	4	12	San Diego, Cal	3	3
Flint, Mich	1	1	Schenectady, N. Y	4	
Fort Worth, Tex	1	1	Sedalia, Mo	3	
Framingham, Mass	1	1	Sheboygan, Wis		
Greenwich, Conn	1		Somerville, Mass	1	
Kansas City, Kans	1		Springfield, Mass	4	
Kansas City, Mo	2	10	Utica, N. Y	1	1
Lackawanna, N. Y	1		Wilmington, Del	2	2
Little Rock, Ark	2		Worcester, Mass	3	1
Los Angeles, Cal	7	1	Youngstown, Ohio	1	
Lowell, Mass	1	2			

POLIOMYELITIS (INFANTILE PARALYSIS).

State Reports for May, 1918.

Place.	New cases reported.	Place.	New cases reported.
California:		New York:	
Los Angeles County—		Albany County—	
Los Angeles...................	1	New Scotland (town)...........	1
Santa Monica..................	1	Lewis County—	
San Francisco.................	1	Croghan (town)................	1
Madera County................	1	St. Lawrence County—	
San Diego County—		Massena......................	1
San Diego....................	1		
Riverside County..............	1	Total......................	3
Kern County—			
Bakersfield..................	1	West Virginia:	
		Marshall County....................	3
Total........................	7		
		Wisconsin:	
Michigan:		Dane County......................	1
Calhoun County—		Dodge County....................	1
Battle Creek..................	1	La Crosse County.................	1
Huron County—		Milwaukee County.................	6
Harbor Beach.................	1	Walworth County.................	1
Kalamazoo County—		Waukesha County.................	1
Vicksburg....................	1		
		Total......................	11
Total........................	3		

City Reports for Week Ended June 8, 1918.

Place.	Cases.	Deaths.	Place.	Cases.	Deaths.
Cleveland, Ohio..............	1	....	Richmond, Va.................	....	1
Evansville, Ind..............	1	1	Rochester, N. Y..............	....	1
Kansas City, Mo.............	1	....	San Diego, Cal..............	1	....
New York, N. Y.............	1	1	Springfield, Ohio............	1	1
Pittsburgh, Pa..............	1	....			

RABIES IN ANIMALS.

City Reports for Week Ended June 8, 1918.

Place.	Cases.	Place.	Cases.
Detroit, Mich............................	1	Rochester, N. Y......................	1
Louisville, Ky...........................	1	Schenectady, N. Y....................	1
Passaic, N. J............................	1		

SCARLET FEVER.

See Diphtheria, measles, scarlet fever, and tuberculosis, page 1080.

SMALLPOX.

State Reports for May, 1918.

Place.	New cases reported.	Deaths.	Vaccination history of cases.			
			Number vaccinated within 7 years preceding attack.	Number last vaccinated more than 7 years preceding attack.	Number never successfully vaccinated.	Vaccination history not obtained or uncertain.
California:						
Contra Costa County—						
Martinez	1				1	
Imperial County	9				9	
Brawley	9				9	
Fresno County	5				5	
Fresno	6				6	
Kern County	2				2	
Bakersfield	1			1		
Los Angeles County—						
Los Angeles	4				4	
Orange County	1				1	
Santa Ana	7				7	
San Bernardino County—						
Ontario	4			1	3	
Riverside County—						
Blythe	1				1	
San Francisco	14			2	12	
San Diego County—						
San Diego	1				1	
San Joaquin County	8				8	
Stockton	12				12	
Tracy	1				1	
Siskiyou County	3				3	
Sacramento County	2				2	
Stanislaus County	7				7	
Turlock	1				1	
Tehama County	50			2	57	
Tulare County	4			1	3	
Porterville	8				8	
Tulare	2				2	
Total	172			7	168	
Michigan:						
Alcona County—						
Mitchell Township	3				3	
Bay County—						
Pinconning Township	1				1	
Benzie County—						
Inland Township	5				1	
Berrien County—						
Bainbridge Township	1			1		
Branch County—						
Ovid Township	1				1	
Coldwater	6				6	
Calhoun County—						
Clarendon Township	1				1	
Homer	4				1	
Washington Heights	1					
Albion	14				14	
Battle Creek	2				2	
Charlevoix County—						
Boyne Falls	1			1		
Boyne City	2				2	
Chippewa County—						
Sault Ste. Marie	2				2	
Eaton County—						
Grand Ledge	1				1	
Genesee County—						
Burton Township	1				1	
Richfield Township	2				2	
Flint	12				8	4
Gladwin County—						
Beaverton Township	1					
Grand Traverse County—						
Traverse City	1				1	
Gratiot County—						
Alma	2				2	
Hillsdale County—						
Hillsdale Township	8			1		7
Pittsford Township	4				4	

SMALLPOX—Continued.

State Reports for May, 1918—Continued.

Place.	New cases reported.	Deaths.	Vaccination history of cases.			
			Number vaccinated within 7 years preceding attack.	Number last vaccinated more than 7 years preceding attack.	Number never successfully vaccinated.	Vaccination history not obtained or uncertain.
Michigan—Continued.						
Ingham County—						
Lansing....................	5				5	....
Ionia County—						
Lyons Township.........	3				3	....
Iosco County—						
Oscoda Township........	17				17	....
Isabella County—						
Nottawa Township......	1				1	....
Wise Township..........	5				5	....
Jackson County—						
Pulaski Township........	3			1	1	....
Tompkins Township......	1				1	....
Kalamazoo County—						
Brady Township.........	3				3	....
Comstock Township.....	6				6	....
Pavilion Township.......	1				1	....
Vicksburg...............	1			1	....	....
Kalamazoo...............	70				70	....
Kent County—						
Grand Rapids............	14				14	....
Lapeer County—						
North Branch Township..	1				1	....
Leelanau County—						
Elmwood Township.....	1				1	....
Lenawee County—						
Blissfield................	1					
Macomb County—						
New Baltimore..........	1				1	....
Mount Clemens..........	1				1	....
Manistee County—						
Bear Lake Township.....	6				6	....
Filer Township..........	8				8	....
Manistee................	5				5	....
Marquette County—						
Marquette...............	2				2	....
Mason County—						
Ludington...............	1				1	....
Mecosta County—						
Austin Township........	2				2	....
Deerfield Township......	23				23	....
Fork Township..........	2				2	....
Menominee County—						
Menominee..............	3				1	....
Missaukee County—						
Aetna Township........	2				2	....
Richland Township......	2				2	....
Monroe County—						
Berlin Township........	1				1	....
Monroe Township........	1				1	....
Monroe..................	7				7	....
Montcalm County—						
Eureka Township........	1				1	....
Muskegon County—						
Muskegon Township......	1				1	....
Muskegon Heights........	1				1	....
Muskegon...............	1				1	....
Newaygo County—						
Croton Township........	1				1	....
Dayton Township.......	2				2	....
Sheridan Township......	1			1	....	....
Oakland County—						
Royal Oak..............	1				1	....
Springfield Township.....	1				1	....
Troy Township..........	1				....	1
Pontiac.................	24				22	2
Oceana County—						
Elbridge Township......	1				1	....
Ogemaw County—						
Hill Township...........	2				2	....
Ottawa County—						
Spring Lake Township....	1				1	....
Grand Haven............	8				8	....

SMALLPOX—Continued.

State Reports for May, 1918—Continued.

Place.	New cases reported.	Deaths.	Vaccination history of cases.			
			Number vaccinated within 7 years preceding attack.	Number last vaccinated more than 7 years preceding attack.	Number never successfully vaccinated.	Vaccination history not obtained or uncertain.
Michigan—Continued.						
St. Clair County—						
Clyde Township	1				1	
Ira Township	1				1	
St. Joseph County—						
Centreville	2				2	
Three Rivers	5				5	
Sanilac County—						
Applegate	1				1	
Speaker Township	3				3	
Sandusky	1				1	
Van Buren County—						
Covert Township	2				2	
Washtenaw County -						
Ann Arbor	2				2	
Wayne County—						
Ecorse	1			1		
Grosse Pointe	2				2	
Oakland	11				10	1
Detroit	49					49
Highland Park	14		1	2	3	8
Wexford County -						
Cadilla	3				3	
Total	121		3	7	330	
New York:						
Albany County—						
Coeymans (town)	1				1	
Broome County—						
Endicott	1				1	
Cattaraugus County—						
Little Valley	1				1	
Chautauqua County—						
Dunkirk	2				1	1
Jamestown	13				12	1
Poland (town)	2				2	
Pomfret (town)	1				1	
Chemung County -						
Elmira	1					1
Erin (town)	1				1	
Erie County						
Buffalo	8				8	
Clarence (town)	1				1	
Lancaster	3				3	
West Seneca (town)	1				1	
Herkimer County—						
Little Falls	1				1	
Ilion	1					
Jefferson County -						
Watertown	2				2	
Madison County -						
Nelson (town)	2				2	
Niagara County -						
Lockport	16			1	15	
Niagara Falls	1				1	
Oneida County -						
Utica	15			1	11	3
Kirkland (town)	2				2	
Washington County—						
Cambridge (town)	7			3	4	
Westchester County—						
New Rochelle	1			1		
Wyoming County—						
Arcade	6			1	5	
Java (town)	2				2	
Total	92		2	8	78	7

SMALLPOX—Continued.

Miscellaneous State Reports for April and May, 1918.

Place.	Cases.	Deaths.	Place.	Cases.	Deaths.
Connecticut (April):			West Virginia (May):		
Hartford County—			Calhoun County..........	1	....
Cheshire............	3	....	Fayette County........	11	....
Hartford............	9	....	Hampshire County......	9	....
			Kanawha County........	25	....
Total..............	12	....	Lewis County..........	9	....
			Lincoln County........	26	....
Louisiana (May):			Marion County.........	4	....
Acadia Parish............	11	....	Mingo County..........	5	....
Allen Parish............	3	....	Roane County..........	9	....
Ascension Parish........	2	....	Taylor County.........	6	....
Assumption Parish.......	1	....	Tucker County.........	1	....
Caddo Parish...........	6	....	Webster County........	3	....
Caldwell Parish..........	1	....	Wood County...........	10	....
De Soto Parish..........	1	....	Charleston............	14	....
Iberville Parish..........	6	....	Fairmont..............	4	....
Jackson Parish..........	2	....	Parkersburg...........	8	....
Jefferson Parish.........	5	....			
Lafourche Parish........	2	....	Total..............	145	....
Orleans Parish..........	12	....	Wisconsin (May):		
Ouachita Parish.........	1	....	Brown County.........	1	....
Rapides Parish..........	12	....	Burnett County........	1	....
Red River Parish........	1	....	Chippewa County......	21	....
St. Landry Parish.......	1	....	Clark County.........	7	....
St. Martin Parish.......	4	....	Columbia County......	8	....
St. Mary Parish........	5	....	Crawford County......	2	....
Tangipahoa Parish......	22	....	Dane County..........	17	....
Winn Parish............	36	....	Douglas County.......	7	....
			Dunn County..........	1	....
Total..............	136	....	Eau Claire County.....	2	....
			Fond du Lac County....	7	....
Montana (May):			Grant County.........	8	....
Beaverhead County......	2	....	Green County.........	2	....
Broadwater County......	2	....	Iowa County..........	1	....
Cascade County.........	6	....	Jefferson County......	4	....
Great Falls..........	3	....	Juneau County........	3	....
Custer County..........	1	....	La Crosse County.....	8	....
Dawson County.........	4	....	Lafayette County.....	5	....
Deerlodge County—			Lincoln County.......	8	....
Anaconda............	8	....	Manitowoc County.....	5	....
Fergus County..........	3	....	Marinette County.....	3	....
Fallon County..........	1	....	Milwaukee County.....	20	1
Flathead County........	25	....	Monroe County........	1	....
Gallatin County—			Oconto County........	6	....
Bozeman............	1	....	Polk County..........	3	....
Hill County............	13	....	Portage County.......	6	....
Lewis and Clark County—			Richland County......	3	....
Helena..............	4	....	Rock County..........	4	....
Missoula County—			St. Croix County.....	4	....
Missoula............	2	....	Sauk County..........	1	....
Sheridan County........	2	....	Sawyer County........	1	....
Silver Bow County......	1	....	Sheboygan County.....	1	....
Butte..............	5	....	Vernon County........	12	....
Teton County..........	1	....	Waukesha County......	1	....
Yellowstone County—			Waupaca County.......	19	....
Billings............	1	....	Winnebago County.....	2	....
			Wood County..........	19	....
Total..............	85	....	Total..............	224	1

City Reports for Week Ended June 8, 1918.

Place.	Cases.	Deaths.	Place.	Cases.	Deaths.
Abilene, Tex.................	3	....	Boone, Iowa..............	4	....
Akron, Ohio.................	7	....	Buffalo, N. Y............	2	....
Alexandria, La..............	1	....	Burlington, Iowa.........	1	....
Alton, Ill..................	1	....	Butte, Mont..............	1	....
Anniston, Ala..............	2	....	Cedar Rapids, Iowa.......	1	....
Atlanta, Ga................	5	....	Chattanooga, Tenn........	2	....
Baltimore, Md..............	4	....	Chicago, Ill.............	2	....
Barberton, Ohio............	8	....	Cincinnati, Ohio.........	8	....
Beatrice, Nebr.............	1	....	Cleveland, Ohio..........	20	....
Billings, Mont.............	1	....	Coffeyville, Kans........	2	....
Birmingham, Ala............	5	....	Colorado Springs, Colo...	2	....

SMALLPOX—Continued.

City Reports for Week Ended June 8, 1918—Continued.

Place.	Cases.	Deaths.	Place.	Cases.	Deaths.
Columbus, Ohio	5		Marshalltown, Iow...a	6	
Council Bluffs, Iowa	7		Memphis, Tenn	4	
Dallas, Tex	2		Middletown, Ohio	4	
Davenport, Iowa	3		Milwaukee, Wis	1	
Dayton, Ohio	3		Minneapolis, Minn	10	
Denver, Colo	18		Mobile, Ala	1	
Des Moines, Iowa	6		Muncie, Ind	5	
Detroit, Mich	27		Muskogee, Okla	2	
Dubuque, Iowa	4		Nashville, Tenn	2	
El Paso, Tex	1		New Orleans, La	6	
Erie, Pa	2		North Little Rock, Ark	2	
Evansville, Ind	1		Ogden, Utah	2	
Fairmont, W. Va	1		Oklahoma City, Okla	19	
Flint, Mich	1		Omaha, Nebr	20	
Fond du Lac, Wis	1		Peoria, Ill	7	
Fort Wayne, Ind	1		Philadelphia, Pa	2	
Fort Worth, Tex	4		Piqua, Ohio	1	
Grand Rapids, Mich	4		Quincy, Ill	4	
Granite City, Ill	2		Richmond, Ind	1	
Greeley, Colo	2		Riverside, Cal	1	
Green Bay, Wis	2		Roanoke, Va	2	
Hartford, Conn	1		St. Joseph, Mo	10	
Houston, Tex	2		St. Louis, Mo	21	
Indianapolis, Ind	19		St. Paul, Minn	2	
Iola, Kans	6		Salt Lake City, Utah	6	
Johnstown, Pa	1		Seattle, Wash	4	
Kalamazoo, Mich	16		Sedalia, Mo	4	
Kansas City, Kans	8		Sioux City, Iowa	7	
Kansas City, Mo	24	1	Spokane, Wash	3	
Knoxville, Tenn	3		Springfield, Ill	1	
Kokomo, Ind	2		Tacoma, Wash	5	
La Crosse, Wis	1		Toledo, Ohio	3	
Laurel, Miss	1		Topeka, Kans	9	
Leavenworth, Kans	1		Trinidad, Colo	1	
Lincoln, Nebr	5		Tuscaloosa, Ala	2	
Little Rock, Ark	1		Vancouver, Wash	1	
Lorain, Ohio	1		Washington, D. C	2	
Louisville, Ky	1		Waterloo, Iowa	1	
Madison, Wis	10		Wichita, Kans	7	
Mansfield, Ohio	1		Youngstown, Ohio	4	
Marshall, Tex	1				

TETANUS.

City Reports for Week Ended June 8, 1918.

Place.	Cases.	Deaths.	Place.	Cases.	Deaths.
Boston, Mass		1	St. Louis, Mo	1	1
Colorado Springs, Colo		1	Trenton, N. J	1	
East Orange, N. J		1	Worcester, Mass	1	

TUBERCULOSIS.

See Diphtheria, measles, scarlet fever, and tuberculosis, page 1080.

TYPHOID FEVER.

State Reports for April and May, 1918.

Place.	New cases reported.	Place.	New cases reported.
California (May):		**Louisiana (May):**	
Alameda County—		Acadia Parish	2
Berkeley	4	Ascension Parish	8
Oakland	7	Assumption Parish	4
Butte County—		Avoyelles Parish	2
Chico	1	Beauregard Parish	2
Colusa County	1	Calcasieu Parish	10
Fresno County—		East Baton Rouge Parish	4
Fresno	2	Iberia Parish	11
Glenn County	1	Iberville Parish	4
Imperial County—		Jefferson Davis Parish	3
Brawley	2	Lafayette Parish	4
Calexico	1	Lafourche Parish	1
Kern County	1	Livingston Parish	5
Lassen County	3	Morehouse Parish	2
Los Angeles County	1	Orleans Parish	24
Glendale	1	Ouachita Parish	6
Los Angeles	18	Plaquemines Parish	7
Madera County	1	Pointe Coupee Parish	2
Merced County	9	Rapides Parish	5
Merced	2	Richland Parish	1
Orange County	3	St. Charles Parish	3
Mendocino County—		St. James Parish	12
Willits	1	St. Martin Parish	5
Ukiah	1	St. Mary Parish	11
Monterey County—		St. Tammany Parish	2
King City	1	Tangipahoa Parish	4
Riverside County	2	Tensas Parish	6
Blythe	10	Terrebonne Parish	4
Riverside	1	Vermilion Parish	2
San Diego County—		Winn Parish	1
National City	11		
San Diego	1	Total	157
Sacramento County	6		
San Bernardino County—		**Michigan (May):**	
Redlands	2	Allegan County—	
San Francisco	8	Cheshire Township	.
San Joaquin County	1	Barry County—	
San Mateo County	1	Hastings	.
Santa Clara County	1	Bay County—	
Mountain View	1	Bay City	3
Siskiyou County—		Berrien County—	
Dunsmuir	1	Watervliet Township	1
Sisson	1	Calhoun County—	
Placer County—		Burlington Township	2
Lincoln	1	Sheridan Township	1
Stanislaus County	1	Albion	1
Solano County	1	Battle Creek	1
Sonoma County	1	Chippewa County—	
Santa Rosa	2	Sault Ste. Marie	4
Yolo County	1	Crawford County—	
Tulare County	2	Grayling	2
Dinuba	1	Eaton County—	
		Potterville	1
Total	118	Genesee County—	
		Flint	.
Connecticut (April):		Hillsdale County—	
Fairfield County—		Wootten Township	1
Danbury	1	Ionia County—	
Norwalk	1	Portland	.
Hartford County—		Kent County—	
Glastonbury	1	Grand Rapids	.
Hartford	2	Lenawee County—	
New Britain	2	Fairfield Township	.
Rocky Hill	2	Marquette County—	
New Haven County—		Marquette	.
New Haven	3	Montmorency County—	
Waterbury	1	Hillmore Township	.
New London County—		Oakland County—	
New London	1	Farmington Township	1
Litchfield County—		Independence Township	1
New Hartford	1	Otsego County—	
Winchester	1	Gaylord	.
		Ottawa County—	
Total	16	Holland Township	.

TYPHOID FEVER—Continued.

State Reports for April and May, 1918—Continued.

Place.	New cases reported.	Place.	New cases reported.
Michigan (May)—Continued.		**New York (May)—Continued.**	
Saginaw County—		Onondaga County—	
Birch Run Township..........	1	Syracuse.............	1
Saginaw.................	2	Solvay................	1
Tuscola County—		Ontario County—	
Novesta Township..........	1	Canandaigua.........	1
Wexford County—		Geneva.............	
South Branch Township.......	1	Orange County—	
		Newburgh...........	4
Total.............	35	Highlands (town)...........	1
		Oswego County—	
Montana (May):		Oswego..............	6
Blaine County.................	2	Sandy Creek (town)........	1
Flathead County..............	1	Scriba (town)...........	1
Billings......................	2	Otsego County—	
		Pittsfield (town)...........	1
Total.............	5	Saint Lawrence County—	
		Ogdensburg...........	3
New York (May):		De Kalb (town).........	1
Albany County—		Gouverneur (town).......	1
Albany.................	7	Gouverneur...........	1
Watervliet.............	2	Norwood....	3
Coymans (town)...........	1	Saratoga County—	
Ravena............	1	Saratoga Springs........	2
Green Island...........	1	Mechanicville..........	1
Allegany County—		Schuylerville...........	
Grove (town)...........	1	Waterford............	1
Wellsville.............	8	Schoharie County—	
Broome County—		Middleburg...........	1
Binghamton...........	1	Seward (town)...........	1
Union.................	1	Seneca Falls...........	2
Cattaraugus County—		Steuben County—	
Salamanca.............	1	Corning............	9
East Otto (town)...........	1	Jasper (town)...........	1
Franklinville (town)..........	1	Suffolk County—	
Cayuga County—		Brookhaven (town).......	1
Cayuga...............	1	Huntington (town)............	1
Chautauqua County—		Sullivan County—	
Dunkirk............	1	Rockland (town)........	1
Carroll (town).............	1	Tompkins County—	
Chenango County—		Ithaca............	3
Oxford (town).............	1	Lansing (town)..........	1
Clinton County—		Ulster County—	
Plattsburg.............	4	Kingston............	1
Ellenburg (town)...........	3	Lloyd (town)...........	1
Mooers (town)...........	1	Wayne County—	
Cortland County—		Newark............	1
Marathon (town)............	1	Marion (town)...........	1
Dutchess County—			
Fishkill................	5	Total.............	175
La Grange (town).............	1		
Erie County—		**Rhode Island (May):**	
Buffalo.............	4	Providence....	1
Lackawanna............	2	Pawtucket............	1
Tonawanda.............	1	Warren (town)...........	1
Gowanda State Hospital.......	2	Westerly (town)........	1
Franklin County—		West Warwick (town)...........	6
Chateaugay (town)...........	1		
Greene County—		Total.............	6
Athens.............	1		
Catskill............	2	**West Virginia (May):**	
Hamilton County—		Berkeley County.........	1
Inlet (town)...........	1	Kanawha County..........	13
Jefferson County—		Lewis County...........	5
Watertown.............	1	Marion County...........	1
Philadelphia (town)...........	1	Mercer County..........	1
Madison County—		Monongalia County.......	2
Georgetown (town).............	1	Ohio County...........	31
Montgomery County—		Raleigh County..........	4
Amsterdam (town).............	1	Randolph County..........	2
Niagara County—		Tucker County...........	2
Lockport	9	Wood County...........	1
Niagara Falls............	1		
North Tonawanda.............	1	Total.............	65
Wheatfield (town)..........	1		
Oneida County—		**Wisconsin (May):**	
Rome.................	1	Bayfield County..........	1
Utica................	1	Brown County..........	3

TYPHOID FEVER—Continued.

State Reports for April and May, 1918—Continued.

Place.	New cases reported.	Place.	New cases reported.
Wisconsin (May)—Continued.		**Wisconsin (May)—Continued.**	
Clark County	5	Marathon County	1
Crawford County	1	Milwaukee County	13
Dane County	1	Outagamie County	11
Door County	1	Sheboygan County	3
Douglas County	2	Trempealeau County	1
Fond du Lac County	1	Wood County	2
La Crosse County	1		
Manitowoc County	1	Total	36

City Reports for Week Ended June 8, 1918.

Place.	Cases.	Deaths.	Place.	Cases.	Deaths.
Anniston, Ala	3		Louisville, Ky	5	
Atlanta, Ga	2		Lynchburg, Va	1	1
Baltimore, Md	4	1	Lynn, Mass	1	
Berkeley, Cal	1	1	Macon, Ga	4	
Billings, Mont	1		Malden, Mass		1
Birmingham, Ala	3		Manchester, Conn	1	
Boston, Mass	1		Memphis, Tenn	1	
Buffalo, N. Y	2		Middletown, N. Y	1	
Camden, N. J	1		Milwaukee, Wis	4	1
Charleston, S. C	6		Montgomery, Ala	3	1
Charleston, W. Va	8		Nashville, Tenn	3	
Charlotte, N. C	1		Newark, N. J	1	
Chattanooga, Tenn	1		Newcastle, Pa	1	
Chicago, Ill	6		New Orleans, La	3	1
Cincinnati, Ohio		1	Newton, Mass	1	
Cleveland, Ohio	1	1	New York, N. Y	28	2
Coffeyville, Kans	1		Norfolk, Va	1	
Columbia, S. C	4		North Tonawanda, N. Y	1	
Columbus, Ohio	1		Oakland, Cal	3	
Corpus Christi, Tex	1		Omaha, Nebr		1
Corsicana, Tex	1		Philadelphia, Pa	6	
Covington, Ky	1		Pittsburgh, Pa	1	
Dallas, Tex	5		Portland, Me	2	1
Danville, Ill	1		Portland, Oreg	1	1
Denver, Colo	1		Rahway, N. J	2	
Des Moines, Iowa	4		Richmond, Va	6	
Detroit, Mich	1		Riverside, Cal	1	
Duluth, Minn	1		Rochester, N. H	1	
Erie, Pa	1		Rocky Mount, N. C	2	
Fairmont, W. Va	4		Saginaw, Mich	1	
Fall River, Mass	2	1	St. Joseph, Mo	1	
Galveston, Tex	5		St. Louis, Mo	3	1
Grand Rapids, Mich	2		Salt Lake City, Utah	1	1
Greenville, S. C	1		Sandusky, Ohio	2	
Harrisburg, Pa	1		Saratoga Springs, N. Y	3	
Hartford, Conn	1	1	Sault Ste. Marie, Mich	1	
Hattiesburg, Miss	2		Sedalia, Mo	4	
Holyoke, Mass	1		Sheboygan, Wis	1	
Houston, Tex	4		Springfield, Mass	1	
Independence, Kans	2		Syracuse, N. Y	1	
Ithaca, N. Y	1	1	Taunton, Mass	1	
Jacksonville, Ill	1		Toledo, Ohio	5	2
Johnstown, Pa	1		Trenton, N. J	1	
Kansas City, Kans	1		Troy, N. Y	1	
Kansas City, Mo	2		Uniontown, Pa	1	
Kokomo, Ind	3		Walla Walla, Wash	2	
La Crosse, Wis	3		Washington, D. C	5	1
La Fayette, Ind	2		Washington, Pa	1	
Laurel, Miss	2		West Chester, Pa	1	
Lawrence, Mass		1	Wichita, Kans	1	1
Lexington, Ky		1	York, Pa	7	
Los Angeles, Cal	6		Youngstown, Ohio	1	

TYPHUS FEVER.

Georgia—Dalton.

On June 19, 1918, 2 cases of typhus fever were notified at Dalton. Ga., in the persons of J. C. L. and W. L., mother and daughter, the case in the mother being of very light type and that in the daughter more severe.

City Reports for Week Ended June 8, 1918.

During the week ended June 8, 1918, one case of typhus fever was reported at New York, N. Y., and one case and one death from this disease were reported at Palestine, Tex.

DIPHTHERIA, MEASLES, SCARLET FEVER, AND TUBERCULOSIS.

State Reports for April and May, 1918.

State.	Cases reported.			State.	Cases reported		
	Diph-theria.	Measles.	Scarlet fever.		Diph-theria.	Measles.	Scarlet fever
California (May)....	289	2,993	438	New York (May)...	402	9,774	384
Connecticut (April)	208	851	175	Rhode Island (May)	70	1,009	--
Louisiana (May)...	95	134	9	West Virginia (May)	11	134	14
Michigan (May)....	365	1,040	*530	Wisconsin (May)...	171	4,637	472
Montana (May)....	50	272	147				

City Reports for Week Ended June 8, 1918.

City.	Popula-tion as of July 1, 1916 (estimated by U. S. Census Bureau).	Total deaths from all causes.	Diphtheria.		Measles.		Scarlet fever.		Tuber-culosis.	
			Cases.	Deaths.	Cases.	Deaths.	Cases.	Deaths.	Cases.	Deaths.
Over 500,000 inhabitants:										
Baltimore, Md.............	589,621	190	11	1	159	5	6	2	35	27
Boston, Mass.............	756,476	216	45	2	280	1	10	......	77	28
Chicago, Ill.............	2,497,722	546	132	14	114	3	22	1	417	44
Cleveland, Ohio.........	674,073		17	1	63		8	......	50	77
Detroit, Mich...........	571,784	191	55	2	125	3	20	1	78	25
Los Angeles, Cal.........	543,812		32		48	1	5	......	32	11
New York, N Y...........	5,602,841	1,244	359	25	619	20	78	3	338	131
Philadelphia, Pa.........	1,709,518	531	46	8	746	8	23	......	212	46
Pittsburgh, Pa...........	579,090		11		156		6	......	34	
St Louis, Mo	757,309	166	25	1	54	3	13	......	47	16
From 300,000 to 500,000 inhabit-ants:										
Buffalo, N. Y.............	468,558	220	14	2	184	4	5	......	45	24
Cincinnati, Ohio.........	410,476	89	7	1	65	1	4	......	19	10
Jersey City, N J.........	306,345	......	18		33		5	......	12	--
Milwaukee, Wis...........	436,535	86	8		227	1	21	......	25	6
Minneapolis, Minn........	363,454		8		76	4	15	......	34	11
Newark, N J.............	408,894	105	17		290	8	6	......	45	15
New Orleans, La.........	371,747	......	15	1	2	1	......	......	33	20
Seattle, Wash.........	348,639		2		48		26	......	11	--
Washington, D C..	363,980	122	13	2	82	......	8	......	30	8
From 200,000 to 300,000 inhabit-ants:										
Columbus, Ohio...........	214,878	63	1		8	......	12	......	5	18
Denver, Colo..	261,800	88	18	3	23	......	24	......		13
Indianapolis, Ind.........	271,708	64	16	4	14	......	15	......	24	7
Kansas City, Mo.........	297,874	92	4	2	2	1	1	......	2	13
Louisville, Ky...........	248,910	60	10		1		1	......	22	11
Portland, Oreg...........	265,463	60	4	1	64	1	11	1	5	4
Providence, R I..........	254,960	68	5	1	121	2	3	......		4
Rochester, N Y...........	256,417	40	3		109	1	5	......	2	7
St Paul, Minn...........	247,232	49	18	1	7	......	10	......	19	8
From 100,000 to 200,000 inhabit-ants:										
Atlanta, Ga.............	190,558	72			10	......	2	......	9	3
Birmingham, Ala.........	181,762	56	1		10	......	1	......	4	11
Bridgeport, Conn.........	121,579	33	4		29	1		......	8	3
Cambridge, Mass.........	112,921	30	4		59		2	......	3	6
Camden, N J	106,234	......	1		4		2	......	8	
Dallas, Tex	124,527	4			6	......		......		2
Dayton, Ohio.............	127,244	41	1			......	3	......		6

DIPHTHERIA, MEASLES, SCARLET FEVER, AND TUBERCULOSIS—Contd.

City Reports for Week Ended June 8, 1918—Continued.

City.	Population as of July 1, 1916 (estimated by U. S. Census Bureau).	Total deaths from all causes.	Diphtheria.		Measles.		Scarlet fever.		Tuberculosis.	
			Cases.	Deaths.	Cases.	Deaths.	Cases.	Deaths.	Cases.	Deaths.
From 100,000 to 200,000 inhabitants—Continued.										
Des Moines, Iowa	101,598	...	4	1			5		1	...
Fall River, Mass	128,366	43	2		9	1	2		3	6
Fort Worth, Tex	104,162	28	3						4	4
Grand Rapids, Mich	128,291	20			14		13		4	2
Hartford, Conn	110,900	37	1		5				4	3
Houston, Tex	112,307	37			2				12	8
Lawrence, Mass	100,560		8		118	2	1		2	...
Lowell, Mass	113,245	31	1	1	22		1		3	2
Lynn, Mass	102,425	15	3		28				5	...
Memphis, Tenn	148,995	45	2		4		3		12	7
Nashville, Tenn	117,057	37			7				5	2
New Bedford, Mass	118,158	35			15		1		11	5
New Haven, Conn	149,085		2		5				21	2
Oakland, Cal	198,604	37			6		5		18	3
Omaha, Nebr	165,470	35	12	2	11		13		..	6
Reading, Pa	109,381		1		4					
Richmond, Va	156,687	51	2		35				8	9
Salt Lake City, Utah	117,399	26			18		7			1
Spokane, Wash	150,323		1		3		7			
Springfield, Mass	105,942	24	2		36	1		1	7	5
Syracuse, N. Y	153,024	40	2		23		1		4	2
Tacoma, Wash	113,770				14		37		1	
Toledo, Ohio	191,554	50	4		4		5		23	6
Trenton, N. J	111,503	43	2				1		8	2
Worcester, Mass	163,314	33	4		8		1		6	7
Youngstown, Ohio	108,385	50			13				1	2
From 50,000 to 100,000 inhabitants:										
Akron, Ohio	85,625	27	8	1	21		10		8	...
Allentown, Pa	63,505		2		163				3	...
Altoona, Pa	58,659		7		5		1			
Atlantic City, N. J	57,660	14			10		1		2	2
Augusta, Ga	50,245	4			4				2	3
Bayonne, N. J	66,863				5				1	
Berkeley, Cal	57,653	13	1		5				2	
Binghamton, N. Y	53,973	19	1		45				1	1
Brockton, Mass	67,449	8	1		35		7		1	1
Canton, Ohio	60,852	11			1		1			1
Charleston, S. C	60,734	19	1							
Chattanooga, Tenn	60,075	2					3			2
Covington, Ky	57,144	16			5	1				
Duluth, Minn	94,495	16			6		3		5	2
El Paso, Tex	63,705	36			3	1	2			8
Erie, Pa	75,195		1		32		3		7	...
Evansville, Ind	76,078				1		1		3	4
Flint, Mich	54,778	12	1		3		3			1
Fort Wayne, Ind	76,183	26	3		12		1			6
Harrisburg, Pa	72,015		1		3					
Hoboken, N. J	77,214	11								1
Holyoke, Mass	65,286	17							2	...
Johnstown, Pa	68,529				10				3	...
Kansas City, Kans	99,437		1		14		2		2	...
Lancaster, Pa	50,853				2					
Little Rock, Ark	57,343	9			4		1		4	...
Malden, Mass	51,155	10	5		45				2	1
Manchester, N. H	78,283	22			1				2	2
Mobile, Ala	58,221	33			1					6
New Britain, Conn	53,794	14	6	1	7		3			1
Norfolk, Va	89,612				1					2
Oklahoma City, Okla	92,943	11					4		2	1
Passaic, N. J	71,744	19			96	1	1		2	1
Pawtucket, R. I	59,411	24	5		18		2			
Peoria, Ill	71,458	22	1		3					1
Portland, Me	63,867	17			4					2
Rockford, Ill	55,185	20	1	1	12		1			4
Sacramento, Cal	66,895	17	3		9		5		7	3
Saginaw, Mich	55,642	12	2				1			3
St. Joseph, Mo	85,236	30							1	3
San Diego, Cal	53,330	30	1		8		1		17	2
Schenectady, N. Y	99,519	22			11				20	1
Sioux City, Iowa	57,078						3			...

DIPHTHERIA, MEASLES, SCARLET FEVER, AND TUBERCULOSIS—Contd.

City Reports for Week Ended June 8, 1918—Continued.

City.	Population as of July 1, 1916 (estimated by U.S. Census Bureau).	Total deaths from all causes.	Diphtheria. Cases.	Diphtheria. Deaths.	Measles. Cases.	Measles. Deaths.	Scarlet fever. Cases.	Scarlet fever. Deaths.	Tuberculosis. Cases.	Tuberculosis. Deaths.
From 50,000 to 100,000 inhabitants—Continued.										
Somerville, Mass.	87,039	17	2	1	24		1		4	1
South Bend, Ind.	68,946	14			1		1		2	
Springfield, Ill.	61,120	9			10					1
Springfield, Ohio	51,550	13			17				1	1
Terre Haute, Ind.	66,083	16	1		8		1		2	
Troy, N. Y.	77,916	18			10				6	3
Utica, N. Y.	85,692	24	5	1	41		1		10	4
Wichita, Kans.	70,722				5		1			
Wilkes-Barre, Pa.	76,776				3					
Wilmington, Del.	94,265	27	2		10	1	1		4	4
Yonkers, N. Y.	99,838	18	3	1	68				15	3
York, Pa.	51,051				12		3		1	
From 25,000 to 50,000 inhabitants:										
Alameda, Cal.	27,732	3	3		33		2		1	
Amsterdam, N. Y.	37,103		1		11					
Auburn, N. Y.	37,385	12			11		3		5	
Bellingham, Wash.	32,985						1			
Boise, Idaho	33,846	3			10					
Brookline, Mass.	32,730	9	3		12				1	2
Burlington, Iowa	25,030	5								
Butler, Pa.	27,632		4		3				1	
Butte, Mont.	43,425				2		12	2		
Cedar Rapids, Iowa	37,308		2							
Charleston, W. Va.	29,941	11			3					
Charlotte, N. C.	39,823	18			10		1		1	2
Chelsea, Mass.	46,192	7			4				1	2
Chester, Pa.	41,356		3		25		2		6	
Clinton, Iowa	27,383				10					
Cohoes, N. Y.	25,211	7								
Colorado Springs, Colo.	32,971		1				2		2	5
Council Bluffs, Iowa	31,484	5			1		3	1	1	1
Cranston, R. I.	25,987				13		1		1	1
Cumberland, Md.	26,074	5			6		1		1	1
Danville, Ill.	32,261	9								1
Davenport, Iowa	48,811				2		1			
Dubuque, Iowa	39,873		4		1		2			
Durham, N. C.	25,061	8			1					2
Easton, Pa.	30,599				4					
East Orange, N. J.	42,458	5	1		44		1		1	
Elgin, Ill.	28,203	3			2					1
Elmira, N. Y.	38,120						68		4	
Evanston, Ill.	28,591	10	1		8					
Everett, Mass.	39,233	3	3		3				3	1
Everett, Wash.	35,480				3				2	
Fitchburg, Mass.	41,781	7			15				2	1
Galveston, Tex.	41,863	15	1							
Green Bay, Wis.	29,353	5	1				1			
Hammond, Ind.	29,171	10	1	1	1					2
Haverhill, Mass.	48,477	10	2		17				3	1
Hazleton, Pa.	28,491		3		30					
Jackson, Mich.	35,396	15			28		2		4	
Jamestown, N. Y.	36,580	8			76				1	2
Kalamazoo, Mich.	48,883	15			4				2	
Kenosha, Wis.	31,576	4	1		14		1			
Knoxville, Tenn.	38,676				3		2		3	1
La Crosse, Wis.	31,677	16	1		4				1	1
Lexington, Ky.	41,097	21			4				12	1
Lincoln, Nebr.	46,515	8	1		1		4			
Long Beach, Cal.	27,587	11			8					
Lorain, Ohio	36,946				1		2		1	
Lynchburg, Va.	32,940	12			2					
Macon, Ga.	45,757	21								4
Madison, Wis.	30,699	2					1			
McKeesport, Pa.	47,521		2		9				1	
Medford, Mass.	26,234	10	4		17		1		1	1
Moline, Ill.	27,451				35					
Montclair, N. J.	26,418				3					
Montgomery, Ala.	43,285	17			1				3	
Muncie, Ind.	25,424	6	4		2					
Nashua, N. H.	27,327	10								1
Newark, Ohio	29,655	6					1		1	1

DIPHTHERIA, MEASLES, SCARLET FEVER, AND TUBERCULOSIS—Contd.

City Reports for Week Ended June 8, 1918—Continued.

City.	Population as of July 1, 1916 (estimated by U. S. Census Bureau).	Total deaths from all causes.	Diphtheria.		Measles.		Scarlet fever.		Tuberculosis.	
			Cases.	Deaths.	Cases.	Deaths.	Cases.	Deaths.	Cases.	Deaths.
From 25,000 to 50,000 inhabitants—Continued.										
Newburgh, N. Y.	29,603	9	2		3		1			
New Castle, Pa.	41,133								7	
Newport, Ky.	31,927	5							1	1
Newport, R. I.	30,108	5	2	1	1					
Newton, Mass.	43,715	10			4				1	
Niagara Falls, N. Y.	37,353	24			1					1
Norwalk, Conn.	26,499									1
Oak Park, Ill.	26,645	11	2		3			1		1
Ogden, Utah.	31,404	6			14		3			
Orange, N. J.	33,080	10			19				3	2
Oshkosh, Wis.	36,065	8								
Pasadena, Cal.	46,450	9			18		1		1	1
Perth Amboy, N. J.	41,185	9							2	1
Petersburg, Va.	25,582	11			1				2	4
Pittsfield, Mass.	38,029	10			5		1		2	
Poughkeepsie, N. Y.	30,390	10			4				2	
Quincy, Ill.	36,798	9	1		6				4	
Quincy, Mass.	38,136	4	2		18		1		2	1
Racine, Wis.	46,486	18			13	1	1			1
Roanoke, Va.	43,284	12			10					2
Rock Island, Ill.	28,926	5			11					
San Jose, Cal.	38,902	1			3		2		1	
Sheboygan, Wis.	28,550	5					1			
Shenandoah, Pa.	29,201								2	
Springfield, Mo.	40,341	3								1
Steubenville, Ohio.	27,445	9								
Superior, Wis.	46,266	8			6		5			1
Taunton, Mass.	36,283	13			1				3	2
Topeka, Kans.	48,726	11			5		3	1	1	
Waltham, Mass.	30,570	5			37				3	1
Waterloo, Iowa.	35,550	9			1		3			
Watertown, N. Y.	29,894	2								1
West Hoboken, N. J.	43,139	4			3		1		2	1
Williamsport, Pa.	33,809		1							
Wilmington, N. C.	29,892	12								2
Winston-Salem, N. C.	31,155	25								7
Zanesville, Ohio.	30,863	7								1
From 10,000 to 25,000 inhabitants:										
Abilene, Tex.	14,238						2			
Adams, Mass.	14,214	2			1		1			
Albany, Ga.	10,604	4			3				1	
Alexandria, La.	15,333	8							2	3
Alton, Ill.	22,874	16					1			
Ann Arbor, Mich.	15,010	6			13					
Anniston, Ala.	14,112		1		1					
Ansonia, Conn.	16,704	3							4	
Appleton, Wis.	17,834	4								
Arlington, Mass.	12,811	4							2	1
Asbury Park, N. J.	14,007	2			9					
Astoria, Oreg.	10,363	7								
Attleboro, Mass.	19,282		2		1					
Bakersfield, Cal.	16,874	7			1					
Barberton, Ohio.	13,210	3					1			
Beatrice, Nebr.	10,287	2		1		1				
Beaver Falls, Pa.	13,532		1		3		2			
Bedford, Ind.	10,349	2							1	1
Bellaire, Ohio.	14,348	5							1	1
Belleville, N. J.	12,393				8					
Beloit, Wis.	18,072	5	2		5					3
Benton Harbor, Mich.	10,533				4					
Bethlehem, Pa.	14,142		3		31					
Beverly, Mass.	21,645		2		1				2	
Billings, Mont.	14,422				12		1		32	
Bloomfield, N. J.	18,466		2		3					
Boone, Iowa.	11,185		1				1			
Braddock, Pa.	21,685		1		19					
Bradford, Pa.	[1]14,544				3		4			
Bristol, Conn.	15,927	2							4	
Burlington, Vt.	21,617	14								1

[1] Population Apr. 15, 1910; no estimate made.

DIPHTHERIA, MEASLES, SCARLET FEVER, AND TUBERCULOSIS—Contd.

City Reports for Week Ended June 8, 1918—Continued.

City.	Popula-tion as of July 1, 1916 (estimated by U. S. Census Bureau).	Total deaths from all causes.	Diphtheria.		Measles.		Scarlet fever.		Tuber-culosis.	
			Cases.	Deaths.	Cases.	Deaths.	Cases.	Deaths.	Cases.	Deaths.
From 10,000 to 25,000 inhabitants—Continued.										
Cairo, Ill	15,794	7								2
Canton, Ill	13,262	1			5	1				
Cape Girardeau, Mo	10,775	1							1	
Carbondale, Pa	19,242				1					
Carnegie, Pa	11,692				1					
Cheyenne, Wyo	¹11,320		1	1						1
Chillicothe, Ohio	15,470	8	2		1		4			1
Clinton, Mass	¹13,075	6			2					1
Coatesville, Pa	14,455				5					
Coffeyville, Kans	17,518								1	
Concord, N. H	22,609	5	1		3				1	
Corpus Christi, Tex	10,432	3							1	
Corsicana, Tex	10,022	6								
Cortland, N. Y	13,099	2			2					1
Cumberland, R. I	10,518	1	1		4					
Dedham, Mass	10,433	1			4					
Dover, N. H	13,272	3								1
Dunmore, Pa	20,776		1		1					
East Providence, R. I	18,113		4		2					
Eau Claire, Wis	18,807				12					
Englewood, N. J	12,281	5			11					
Escanaba, Mich	15,185	5					1			
Eugene, Oreg	13,572				6					
Fairmont, W. Va	15,566				1		1			
Fargo, N. Dak	17,389	6	3							3
Farrell, Pa	¹10,190				1					
Findlay, Ohio	¹14,858	6			3					
Fond du Lac, Wis	21,113	6			2					
Fort Scott, Kans	10,550	4								
Fostoria, Ohio	10,770	1								
Framingham, Mass	13,982	10			1		1		1	
Frederick, Md	11,112				6				1	
Fulton, N. Y	11,908	2			1		2		1	
Gardner, Mass	17,140		2		9					
Geneva, N. Y	13,711				12		1		1	
Glens Falls, N. Y	16,894	6			1					
Granite City, Ill	15,142	2			1					
Greeley, Colo	11,420						2			
Greenfield, Mass	11,798	3							1	
Greensboro, N. C	19,577	2	2							
Greenville, S. C	18,181	9								
Greenwich, Conn	19,159		2		3					
Hackensack, N. J	19,945	5	1		17					1
Harrison, N. J	16,950				5					
Hattiesburg, Miss	16,482						2			
Holland, Mich	12,180	1			2					
Hornell, N. Y	14,687	6			24					
Independence, Kans	14,235	4			1					
Independence, Mo	11,672	2					1		1	
Ithaca, N. Y	15,548	8								
Jacksonville, Ill	15,481	8			1				1	1
Janesville, Wis	14,339	3					1			1
Johnstown, N. Y	10,146	6			2					
Kankakee, Ill	14,230		1							
Kokomo, Ind	23,990	7	1						3	
Lackawanna, N. Y	15,987	2	1		4					
La Fayette, Ind	21,286	5	5							
Laurel, Miss	11,759						1			
Lawrence, Kans	14,321	2								
Leavenworth, Kans	¹19,363	9	2							
Lebanon, Pa	26,779	1							1	
Lincoln, R. I	10,188				1					
Little Falls, N. Y	13,153	4								
Long Branch, N. J	15,394				46					
Mahanoy City, Pa	17,963				5					
Manchester, Conn	15,551	1			2				1	1
Mardstown, Wis	14,905	4					1			
Mansfield, Ohio	22,744	2			7					
Marinette, Wis	¹14,610						1			

¹ Population Apr. 15, 1910, no estimate made.

DIPHTHERIA, MEASLES, SCARLET FEVER, AND TUBERCULOSIS—Contd.

City Reports for Week Ended June 8, 1918—Continued.

City.	Population as of July 1, 1916 (estimated by U. S. Census Bureau).	Total deaths from all causes.	Diphtheria.		Measles.		Scarlet fever.		Tuberculosis.	
			Cases.	Deaths.	Cases.	Deaths.	Cases.	Deaths.	Cases.	Deaths.
From 10,000 to 25,000 inhabitants—Continued.										
Marquette, Mich..	12,409	4					5			1
Marshall, Tex..	13,712	5								
Marshalltown, Iowa..	14,360		1		1					
Mason, City..	14,457	7								
Mattoon, Ill..	12,582	2			8					
Meadville, Pa..	13,802				6					
Melrose, Mass..	17,445	4	1		7				1	1
Middletown, N. Y...	15,810				2				1	
Middletown, Ohio..	15,625	2			1					
Milford, Mass..	14,110	11			4	4				1
Mishawaka, Ind..	16,385	3								
Missoula, Mont..	18,214	6	1		3					
Morgantown, W. Va..	13,709	3			3					
Morristown, N. J..	13,284	5			8		1			
Moundsville, W. Va..	11,153	2								
Mount Carmel, Pa..	20,268								1	
Muscatine, Iowa..	17,500	1								1
Nanticoke, Pa..	23,126				1					
Natick, Mass..	10,102	2	2		20					
New Albany, Ind..	23,629	4								2
Newburyport, Mass..	15,243	3			2					
New London, Conn..	20,985	8			1		4			2
North Adams, Mass..	22,019	8	1							4
Northampton, Mass..	19,926	7			14		1			1
North Attleboro, Mass..	11,014	2	1		2					
North Little Rock, Ark...	14,907	3							1	1
North Tonawanda, N. Y..	13,768	4							1	
North Yakima, Wash..	20,951				3					
Norwood, Ohio..	22,286	2	1		6					
Oil City, Pa..	19,297				5			6		
Olean, N. Y..	16,624	3								
Oneonta, N. Y..	10,962	5			1		1			
Ossining, N. Y..	13,705	6			21				1	
Oswego, N. Y..	24,101	7			4		3		2	
Palestine, Tex..	11,854	2								
Parkersburg, W. Va..	20,612	5								
Peabody, Mass..	18,360	2	1		26					
Peekskill, N. Y..	18,530	1								
Phillipsburg, N. J..	15,605	3	1						1	
Phoenixville, Pa..	11,714		1		3					
Piqua, Ohio..	14,152	3								
Plainfield, N. J..	23,805	8			1					
Plymouth, Mass..	13,743	6							1	
Plymouth, Pa..	19,100								2	
Pontiac, Mich..	17,524	9	1		8		2		2	
Port Chester, N. Y..	16,183	3	1		1					
Portsmouth, N. H..	11,666				1					
Pottstown, Pa..	16,794		2							
Rahway, N. J..	10,219	5			2					1
Raleigh, N. C..	20,127	6	1		4					
Redlands, Cal..	14,000	3								
Richmond, Ind..	24,697	2					1			
Riverside, Cal..	19,763	2			6			3		
Rocky Mount, N. C..	12,067	4								1
Rome, N. Y..	23,737		2					1		
Rutland, Vt...	14,831	2								
St. Cloud, Minn..	11,817	2								
San Angelo, Tex..	[1] 10,321	4								1
San Bernardino, Cal..	16,945	2			2					
Sandusky, Ohio..	20,193	3			3			1		
Santa Barbara, Cal..	14,846	5								
Santa Cruz, Cal..	14,594	5								
Saratoga Springs, N. Y..	13,821	6			6				1	
Sault Ste. Marie, Mich..	13,919	2			1					
Sedalia, Mo..	19,449	3	3		17			29		
Shamokin, Pa..	21,129		2		1					
Sharon, Pa..	18,616				2					
Sioux Falls, S. Dak..	16,499	4								
Southbridge, Mass..	14,205	3			3					

[1] Population Apr. 15, 1910; no estimate made.

DIPHTHERIA, MEASLES, SCARLET FEVER, AND TUBERCULOSIS—Contd.

City Reports for Week Ended June 8, 1918—Continued.

City.	Popula-tion as of July 1, 1916 (estimated by U. S. Census Bureau).	Total deaths from all causes.	Diphtheria.		Measles.		Scarlet fever.		Tuber-culosis.	
			Cases.	Deaths.	Cases.	Deaths.	Cases.	Deaths.	Cases.	Deaths.
From 10,000 to 25,000 inhabitants—Continued.										
Spartanburg, S. C.	21,365	14							1	1
Streator, Ill.	14,304	3								
Trinidad, Colo.	13,875				2					
Tuscaloosa, Ala.	10,488	6								
Vallejo, Cal.	13,461	3			2					
Vancouver, Wash.	13,180				6				1	
Warren, Ohio.	13,059	5	1		4					
Warren, Pa.	14,737				3					
Washington, Pa.	21,618		4		26		3		1	
Watertown, Mass.	14,867	4			7					1
Wausau, Wis.	19,239	2							1	
West Chester, Pa.	13,176				1					
Westfield, Mass.	18,391	9			2		1		1	
West New York, N. J.	18,773				2				2	
West Orange, N. J.	13,550	1			20					
White Plains, N. Y.	22,465	6					1			1
Wilkinsburg, Pa.	23,228		1		4		1		1	
Winchester, Mass.	10,603						1			
Winona, Minn.	1 18,583	7							1	1
Winthrop, Mass.	12,092		1		2		1		2	
Woburn, Mass.	15,969	5								

1 Population Apr. 15, 1910; no estimate made.

FOREIGN.

CUBA.

Communicable Diseases—Habana.

Communicable diseases have been notified at Habana as follows:

Disease.	May 1-10, 1918.		Remaining under treatment May 10, 1918.	Disease.	May 1-10, 1918.		Remaining under treatment May 10, 1918.
	New cases.	Deaths.			New cases.	Deaths.	
Cerebrospinal meningitis.........	1	....	¹1	Measles............	3	....	8
Diphtheria.........	7	....	17	Paratyphoid fever..	1	....	¹2
Leprosy...........	....	....	13	Scarlet fever.......	2	....	¹4
Malaria............	12	....	²32	Typhoid fever.....	54	12	³106
				Varicella...........	20	....	25

¹ From the interior, 1.   ² From the interior, 30.   ³ From the interior, 54; 2 foreign; 2 from Regla.

SPAIN.

Undetermined Disease—Valencia.

A disease of undetermined nature was reported present, May 28, 1918, at Valencia, Spain. The disease was stated to be characterized by high fever, to be of short duration, and to resemble grippe. A number of cases similar to those which were reported at Valencia have been notified in other cities in Spain.

CHOLERA, PLAGUE, SMALLPOX, TYPHUS FEVER, AND YELLOW FEVER.

Reports Received During Week Ended June 28, 1918.[1]

CHOLERA.

Place.	Date.	Cases.	Deaths.	Remarks.
India:				
Calcutta.................	Mar. 17-Apr. 6....	....	210	
Philippine Islands:				
Provinces................		....	....	Apr. 21-27, 1918: Cases, 23;
Bohol..................	Apr. 21-27........	21	13	deaths, 15.
Capiz.................	.....do..........	2	2	

PLAGUE.

India........................		....	....	Mar. 3-30, 1918: Cases, 139,832;
Calcutta....................	Mar. 17-Apr. 6....	....	12	deaths, 112,472.
Siam:				
Bangkok..................	Mar. 17-May 4.....	43	41	

[1] From medical officers of the Public Health Service, American consuls, and other sources.

(1087)

CHOLERA, PLAGUE, SMALLPOX, TYPHUS FEVER AND YELLOW FEVER—Continued.

Reports Received During Week Ended June 28, 1918—Continued.

SMALLPOX.

Place.	Date.	Cases.	Deaths.	Remarks.
Brazil:				
Rio de Janeiro..............	Mar. 24–May 4.....	46	8	
Canada:				
British Columbia—				
Victoria...............	May 26–June 8....	3	....	
Manitoba—				
Winnipeg..............	June 2–8..........	2	....	
New Brunswick—				
St. John..............	....do............	1	....	
Prince Edward Island—				
Summerside...........	June 1–7..........	1	....	
Quebec				
Montreal............	June 9–15.........	1	....	
Quebec..............	Jun: 2 8..........	2	....	
China:				
Amoy....................	Apr. 22–May 4.....	....	....	Present.
Antung..................	May 7–13...	2	....	
Changsha...............	Mar. 29 Apr. 5....	2	....	
Chungking..............	Mar. 17 May 11...	....	....	Do.
Dairen..................	Apr. 30–May 6....	14	6	
Hankow.................	Apr. 15–21........	1	....	Do.
Nanking................	Apr. 7–May 4.....	....	....	
Tientsin................	Apr. 22 May 18...	5	1	Death in European.
Tsingtau...............	Apr. 15 May 5....	4	....	
France				
Rouen..................	Apr. 28–May 11...	6	....	Including varioloid.
India:				
Calcutta...............	Mar. 17–23........	....	55	
Italy:				
Genoa..................	Apr. 17–May 15....	16	6	
Japan:				
Nagasaki...............	May 6 19..........	10	....	
Taihoku................	Apr. 23–May 13....	23	3	
Tokyo..................	May 13 19.........	2	....	
Mexico:				
Mazatlan...............	May 29–June 4....	1	....	
Mexico City............	May 12–18.........	14	....	
Newfoundland:				
St. Johns..............	June 1–7..........	3	....	
Philippine Islands:				
Manila.................	Apr. 21–27........	82	39	Varioloid, 47.
Portuguese East Africa:				
Lourenço Marques.........	Feb. 1–28.........	....	3	
Russia				
Vladivostok............	Apr. 1 30.........	51	12	
Siam				
Bangkok................	Mar. 17 May 4....	8	9	
Spain:				
Seville................	Mar. 1 31.........	....	3	
Valencia...	May 5 18..........	2	....	

TYPHUS FEVER.

Algeria:				
Algiers...................	Apr. 1–30........	....	1	
China:				
Antung..................	May 7 13.........	2	....	
Hankow.................	Apr. 22 28........	2	....	European.
Chosen (Korea):				
Seoul...................	Mar. 1 31.........	4	1	Apr. 24–30, 1918: Cases, 2.
Egypt:				
Alexandria..............	Apr. 23 May 4....	449	96	
Greece:				
Saloniki................	Apr. 7 27.........	....	6	
Japan:				
Nagasaki...............	May 6 19.........	3	....	
Mexico:				
Aguascalientes..........	June 3 9..........	....	1	
Mexico City............	May 12–18........	29	....	
Vera Cruz.	June 3–9..........	....	2	
Russia				
Vladivostok.............	Apr 1 30..........	....	4	

YELLOW FEVER.

Mexico				
Acapulco.................	June 16..........	1	....	

CHOLERA, PLAGUE, SMALLPOX, TYPHUS FEVER AND YELLOW FEVER—Continued.

Reports Received from Dec. 29, 1917, to June 28, 1918.

CHOLERA.

Place.	Date.	Cases.	Deaths.	Remarks.
China:				
Antung...................	Nov. 26–Dec. 2....	3	1	
India:				
Bombay..................	Oct. 28–Dec. 15....	19	14	
Do...................	Dec. 30–Mar. 9....	219	194	
Calcutta................	Sept. 16–Dec. 15...	....	135	
Do...................	Dec. 30–Apr. 6....	....	365	
Karachi.................	Dec. 30–Feb. 23...	25	6	
Madras..................	Nov. 25–Dec. 22...	2	2	
Do...................	Dec. 30–Mar. 16...	47	26	
Rangoon................	Nov. 4–Dec. 22....	5	5	
Do...................	Dec. 30–Mar. 23...	13	8	
Indo-China:				
Provinces...............		....	....	Sept. 1–Dec. 31, 1917: Cases, 168;
Anam.................	Sept. 1–Dec. 31....	24	15	deaths, 95.
Cambodia.............	.....do...........	74	54	
Cochin-China.........	.....do...........	58	24	
Saigon...............	Nov. 22–Dec. 9...	4	3	
Do.................	Feb. 4–Apr. 28...	28	18	
Kwang-Chow-Wan....	Sept. 1–30........	10	2	
Java:				
East Java..............	Oct. 28–Nov. 3....	1	1	
West Java..............		....	....	Oct. 19–Dec. 27, 1917: Cases, 102;
Batavia...............	Oct. 10–Dec. 27...	49	23	deaths, 56. Dec. 28, 1917–Feb.
Do.................	Dec. 28–Feb. 21...	35	1	21, 1918: Cases, 38; deaths, 7.
Palestine................				Dec. 28, 1917–Feb. 24, 1918: Cases,
Deir Seneid...........	Dec. 28–Feb. 24...	65	....	121.
Jaffa..................	Feb. 17–24........	4	....	
Ludd..................	Mar. 22...........	1	....	
Sukkarieh.............	Dec. 28–Mar. 22...	24	....	
Persia...................		....	....	July 30–Sept. 3, 1917: Cases, 384;
Achraf................	July 30–Aug. 16...	90	88	deaths, 276.
Astrabad..............	July 31...........	....	....	Present.
Barfrush..............	July 1–Aug. 16....	39	25	
Bender Bouchir........		....	....	Present. On Persian Gulf.
Chahmirzad...........		....	....	25 cases reported July 31, 1917.
Chahrastagh..........	June 15–July 25...	10	8	
Chroud...............	Aug. 26–Sept. 3...	4	2	
Damghan.............	Aug. 26...........	....	....	Present.
Kharek...............	May 28–June 11...	21	13	
Meched...............	Aug. 18–Sept. 2...	174	82	
Ouzoun Dare..........	Aug. 8............	....	....	Do.
Sabzevar.............	Aug. 24...........	....	....	Do.
Sari..................	July 3–29.........	273	144	
Semnan...............	Aug. 31–Sept. 2...	14	5	
Yekchambe Bazar......	June 3............	6	....	
Philippine Islands:				
Provinces..............		....	....	July 1–Dec. 29, 1917: Cases, 5,964;
Antique..............	Nov. 18–Dec. 1....	48	32	deaths, 3,655. Dec. 30, 1917–
Do.................	Feb. 3–9..........	4	4	Apr. 27, 1918: Cases, 1,980,
Bohol................	Nov. 18–Dec. 29...	169	111	deaths, 1,407.
Do.................	Dec. 30–Apr. 27...	602	473	
Capiz................	Nov. 25–Dec. 29...	27	21	
Do.................	Dec. 30–Apr. 27...	232	192	
Cebu.................	Dec. 23–29........	3	....	
Do.................	Dec. 30–Apr. 20...	118	68	
Davao................	Mar. 10–Apr. 13...	12	11	
Iloilo................	Nov. 25–Dec. 29...	179	135	
Do.................	Dec. 30–Mar. 2....	97	63	
Leyte................	Nov. 25–Dec. 22...	13	12	
Do.................	Feb. 3–Mar. 16....	50	38	
Mindanao............	Nov. 25–Dec. 29...	337	196	
Do.................	Dec. 30–Feb. 9....	341	220	
Misamis..............	Feb. 24–Apr. 20...	257	153	
Occidental Negros....	Nov. 25–Dec. 22...	177	123	
Do.................	Jan. 13–Apr. 6....	146	88	
Oriental Negros......	Nov. 25–Dec. 29...	99	62	
Do.................	Dec. 30–Mar. 30...	23	15	
Romblon.............	Nov. 25–Dec. 1....	1	1	
Surigao..............	Feb. 24–Apr. 20...	62	52	
Zamboanga...........	Feb. 24–Apr. 6....	35	29	
Russia:				
Tashkentnine..........	May 13............	....	....	Present.
Tzaritsin.............	.....do...........	....	....	Do.
Siam:				
Bangkok..............	Sept. 16–22........	1	1	
Turkey in Asia:				
Bagdad...............	Nov. 1–15.........	....	40	

CHOLERA, PLAGUE, SMALLPOX, TYPHUS FEVER AND YELLOW FEVER—Continued.

Reports Received from Dec. 29, 1917, to June 28, 1918—Continued.

PLAGUE.

Place.	Date.	Cases.	Deaths.	Remarks.
Brazil:				
Bahia	Nov. 4–Dec. 15....	4	4	
Do	Dec. 30–Feb. 23...	4	3	
Rio de Janeiro	Dec. 23–29..........	1		
Do	Jan. 6–12...........	1	1	
British East Africa:				
Mombasa	Oct. 1–Dec. 31.....	31	18	
British Gold Coast:				
Axim	Jan. 8...........			Present.
Ceylon:				
Colombo	Oct. 14–Dec. 1.....	14	13	
Do	Dec. 30–Mar. 23...	37	33	
China				Present in North China in January, 1918; pneumonic form.
Anhwei Province—				
Fengyanghsien	Feb. 27............		9	Pneumonic.
Pengpu	....do...........		1	Do.
Chili Province—				
Kalgan				Vicinity. Present in February, 1918.
Fukien Province—				
Amoy	Mar. 11–31........			Present in vicinity.
Hongkong	Apr. 14–20.........	1	1	
Kiangsu Province—				
Nanking	Mar. 17–Apr. 5.....	19	15	
Shanshi Province				Present in February, 1918; 116 cases estimated.
Ecuador:				
Babahoyo	Feb. 1–15..........	1		
Duran	Feb. 16–Mar. 30...	2	1	
Guayaquil	Sept. 1–Nov. 30...	68	24	Reported outbreak occurring about Jan. 17, 1918.
Do	Feb. 1–15..........	44	18	
Do	Mar. 1–30..........	37	14	
Egypt				Jan. 1–Nov. 15, 1917: Cases, 735; deaths, 398.
Alexandria	Jan. 14–28.........	1	2	
Cairo	Dec. 17–23.........	2		
Port Said	July 2–Dec. 23.....	13	7	
Suez	July 2–Oct. 20.....	62	38	
Hawaii.				
Laupahoehoe	May 5.............	1	1	
India				July 1–Dec. 29, 1917: Cases, 280,258; deaths, 212,032. Dec. 30, 1917–Feb. 23, 1918: Cases, 276,768; deaths, 221,556. Mar. 3–30, 1918: Cases, 139,532; deaths, 112,473.
Bassein	Dec. 9–29..........		8	
Do	Dec. 30–Mar. 16...		193	
Bombay	Oct. 28–Dec. 29....	147	123	
Do	Dec. 30–Mar. 9...,	275	213	
Calcutta	Sept. 16–29........		2	
Do	Dec. 30–Apr. 6.....		16	
Henzada	Oct. 21–27.........		1	
Do	Jan. 5–Mar. 16.....		129	
Karachi	Oct. 21–Dec. 29....	27	20	
Do	Dec. 30–Apr. 6.....	261	190	
Madras	Feb. 3–Mar. 9......	3	2	
Madras Presidency	Oct. 31–Nov. 24....	5,786	4,519	
Do	Jan. 6–Mar. 16.....	11,649	9,012	
Mandalay	Oct. 14–Nov. 17...		89	
Do	Dec. 30–Mar. 16...		1,065	
Moulmein	Feb. 17–Mar. 16...		83	
Myingyan	Dec. 30–Mar. 16...		496	
Pegu	Feb. 10–Mar. 16...		6	
Prome	Jan. 5–Feb. 23.....		6	
Rangoon	Oct. 21–Dec. 22....		56	
Do	Dec. 30–Mar. 23...	767	704	
Toungoo	Dec. 9–29..........		5	
Do	Dec. 30–Mar. 16...		80	
Indo-China:				
Provinces—				Sept. 1–Dec. 31, 1917: Cases, 171; deaths, 126.
Anam	Sept. 1–Dec. 31....	45	28	
Cambodia	....do............	95	83	
Cochin China	..do	31	17	
Saigon	Oct. 31–Dec. 23....	17	6	
Do	Dec. 31–Apr. 28...	198	107	
Java:				
East Java				Oct. 8–Dec. 31, 1917: Cases, 198; deaths, 193.
Do				Jan. 1–Feb. 4, 1918: Cases, 62; deaths, 51.

CHOLERA, PLAGUE, SMALLPOX, TYPHUS FEVER AND YELLOW FEVER—Continued.

Reports Received from Dec. 29, 1917, to June 28, 1918—Continued.

PLAGUE—Continued.

Place.	Date.	Cases.	Deaths.	Remarks.
Java—Continued.				
East Java—Continued.				
Residences—				
Kediri	Oct. 8–Dec. 31	1	1	
Madioen	do	49	49	
Samarang	do	110	109	
Surabaya	do	25	23	
Do	Jan. 15–Feb. 4	17	17	
Surakarta	Oct. 8–Dec. 31	11	11	
West Java				Nov. 25–Dec. 9, 1917: Cases, 45; deaths, 45. Dec. 1, 1917–Jan. 15, 1918: Cases, 106.
Peru				Dec. 1, 1917–Jan. 15, 1918: Cases, 106. Feb. 16–Mar. 31, 1918: Cases, 113.
Departments—				
Ancachs	Dec. 1–Jan. 15	2		At Casma.
Do	Feb. 16–Mar. 31	5		
Callao	do	1		
Junin	do	1		
Lambayeque	Dec. 1–Jan. 15	22		At Chiclayo, Ferrenafe, Jayanca, Lambayeque.
Do	Feb. 16–Mar. 31	16		
Libertad	Dec. 1–Jan. 15	72		At Guadelupe, Mansiche, Pacasmayo, Salaverry, San Jose, San Pedro, and country district of Trujillo.
Do	Feb. 16–Mar. 31	68		
Lima	Dec. 1–Jan. 15	9		City and country.
Do	Feb. 16–Mar. 31	22		
Piura	Dec. 1–Jan. 15	1		At Catacaos.
Senegal:				
St. Louis	Feb. 2			Present.
Siam:				
Bangkok	Sept. 16–Dec. 23	13	9	
Do	Jan. 13–May 4	80	68	
Straits Settlements:				
Penang	Mar. 17–23	1		
Singapore	Oct. 28–Dec. 29	5	7	
Do	Jan. 6–Mar. 28	81	72	
On vessel:				
S. S. Quilpue	May 9	2		At Callao, Peru.

SMALLPOX.

Place.	Date.	Cases.	Deaths.	Remarks.
Algeria:				
Algiers	Nov. 1–Dec. 31	3	2	
Do	Jan. 1–Apr. 23	249	6	
Arabia:				
Aden	Apr. 4–10		1	
Australia:				
New South Wales				July 12–Dec. 20, 1917: Cases, 36; Jan. 4–17, 1918: Case, 1.
Abermain	Oct. 25–Nov. 29	3		Newcastle district.
Cessnock	July 12–Oct. 11	7		
Eumangla	Aug. 15	1		
Kurri Kurri	Dec. 5–29	2		
Mungindi	Aug. 13	1		
Warren	July 12–Oct. 25	22		
Do	Jan. 1–17	1		
Brazil:				
Bahia	Nov. 10–Dec. 8	3		
Pernambuco	Nov. 1–15	1		
Rio de Janeiro	Sept. 30–Dec. 29	708	190	
Do	Dec. 30–May 4	297	92	
Sao Paulo	Oct. 29–Nov. 4		2	
British East Africa:				
Mombasa	Oct. 1–Dec. 31	9	5	
Canada:				
British Columbia—				
Vancouver	Jan. 13–Mar. 9	5		
Victoria	Jan. 7–June 8	5		
Manitoba—				
Winnipeg	Dec. 30–June 8	7		

CHOLERA, PLAGUE, SMALLPOX, TYPHUS FEVER AND YELLOW FEVER—Continued.

Reports Received from Dec. 29, 1917, to June 28, 1918—Continued.

SMALLPOX—Continued.

Place.	Date.	Cases.	Deaths.	Remarks.
Canada—Continued.				
New Brunswick—				
Kent County..........	Dec. 4..............			Outbreak. On main line Canadian Ry., 25 miles north of Moncton.
Do...............	Jan. 22.............	40	....	In 7 localities.
Northumberland County.	....do............	41	....	In 5 localities.
Restigouche County....	Jan. 18.............	60	....	
St. John County—				
St. John..........	Mar. 3–June 8.....	28	....	May 13, 1918: Cases present, 14.
Victoria County.......	Jan. 2.............	10	....	At Limestone and a lumber camp.
Westmoreland County—				
Moncton..........	Jan. 29–May 25....	22	....	
York County..........	Jan. 22.............	8	....	
Nova Scotia—				
Cape Sable Island......				Present May 8 at Clarks Harbor.
Halifax.............	Feb. 24–June 1....	28	....	
Sydney.............	Feb. 3–June 1.....	30	....	
Ontario—				
Arnprior...........	Mar. 31–Apr. 6....		1	
Hamilton..........	Dec. 16–22........	1	....	
Do............	Jan. 13–19........	2	....	
Ottawa............	Mar. 4–24.........	5	....	
Sarnia.............	Dec. 9–15.........	1	....	
Do............	Jan. 6–May 18.....	34	....	
Toronto............	Feb. 10–Apr. 6....	2	....	
Winsor............	Dec. 30–Jan. 5....	1	....	
Prince Edward Island—				
Charlottetown........	Feb. 7–June 5.....	2	....	
Summerside..........	June 1–7..........	1	....	
Quebec—				
Montreal............	Dec. 16–Jan. 5....	5	....	
Do............	Jan. 6–June 15....	13	....	
Quebec.............	Apr. 21–June 8....	5	....	
China:				
Amoy...............	Oct. 29–Dec. 30...			Present.
Do............	Dec. 31–May 4.....			Do.
Antung.............	Dec. 2–23.........	14	2	
Do............	Jan. 7–May 13.....	16	4	
Changsha...........	Jan. 28–Apr. 5....	8	1	
Chefoo.............	Jan. 27–Feb. 9....			Do.
Chungking..........	Nov. 11–Dec. 29...			Do.
Do.............	Dec. 30–May 11....			Do.
Dairen.............	Nov. 18–Dec. 22...	3	1	
Do............	Dec. 30–May 6.....	104	18	
Hankow............	Feb. 25–Apr. 21...	2	....	
Harbin.............	May 14–June 30....	20	....	Chinese Eastern Ry.
Do............	July 1–Dec. 2.....	7	....	Do.
Hongkong...........	Dec. 23–29.........	1	....	
Do............	Jan. 20–Apr. 13...	22	10	
Hunchshotze Station....	Oct. 28–Nov. 4....	1	....	Do.
Manchuria Station......	May 14–June 30....	6	....	Do.
Do............	July 1–Dec. 2.....	3	....	Do.
Mukden............	Nov. 11–24........			Present.
Do............	Feb. 10–Mar. 30...			Do.
Nanking............	Feb. 3–May 4......			Do.
Shanghai...........	Nov. 18–Dec. 23...	41	91	Cases, foreign; deaths among natives.
Do............	Dec. 31–Apr. 1....	38	119	Do.
Swatow............	Jan. 18...........			Unusually prevalent.
Tientsin...........	Nov. 11–Dec. 22...	13	....	
Do............	Dec. 30–May 18....	55	1	
Tsingtau...........	Feb. 4–May 5......	15	2	
Colombia:				
Cartagena............				Present in suburbs, May 27, 1918.
Cuba:				
Habana.............	Jan. 7............	1	....	Nov. 8, 1917: 1 case from Coruna; Dec. 5, 1917, 1 case.
Marianao...........	Jan. 8............	1	....	6 miles distant from Habana.
Ecuador:				
Guayaquil...........	Sept. 1–Nov. 20...	26	2	
Do............	Feb. 1–Mar. 31....	4	3	

CHOLERA, PLAGUE, SMALLPOX, TYPHUS FEVER AND YELLOW FEVER—Continued.

Reports Received from Dec. 29, 1917, to June 28, 1918—Continued.

SMALLPOX—Continued.

Place.	Date.	Cases.	Deaths.	Remarks.
Egypt:				
Alexandria	Nov. 12-18	2	1	
Do	Jan. 8-Apr. 15	11		
Cairo	July 23-Nov. 18	6	1	
France:				
Lyon	Nov. 18-Dec. 16	6	3	
Do	Jan 7-Feb. 17	11	2	
Marseille	Jan. 1-31		2	
Paris	Jan. 27-Apr. 20	11	5	
Rouen	Mar. 31-May 11	49	10	Including varioloid.
Great Britain:				
Cardiff	Feb. 3-9	4		
Hull	Mar. 17-30	3		
Greece:				
Saloniki	Jan. 27-Mar. 16		9	
Honduras:				
Santa Barbara Department	Jan. 1-7			Present in interior.
India:				
Bombay	Oct. 21-Dec. 29	50	12	
Do	Dec. 31-Mar. 9	918	381	
Calcutta	Jan. 27-Mar. 23		89	
Karachi	Nov. 18-Dec. 29	4	2	
Do	Jan. 27-Apr. 6	109	66	Nov. 11-16, 1917: 10 cases with 4
Madras	Oct. 31-Dec. 29	20	8	deaths; imported on s. s. Me-
Do	Dec. 30-Mar. 16	157	140	nesa from Basreh.
Rangoon	Oct. 28-Dec. 22	6	1	
Do	Dec. 30-Mar. 23	90	23	
Indo-China:				
Provinces				Sept. 1-Dec. 31, 1917; Cases, 690;
Anam	Sept. 1-Dec. 31	210	30	deaths, 180.
Cambodia	do	19	11	
Cochin-China	do	440	133	
Saigon	Oct. 20—Dec. 30	120	26	
Do	Dec. 31-Apr. 28	1,566	482	
Laos	Oct. 1-Dec. 31	8	1	
Tonkin	Sept. 1-Dec. 31	18	5	
Italy:				
Castellamare	Dec. 10	2		Among refugees.
Florence	Dec. 1-15	17	4	
Genoa	Dec. 2-31	11	3	
Do	Jan. 2-May 15	68	15	
Leghorn	Jan. 7-Apr. 7	33	7	
Messina	Jan. 3-19	1		
Milan				Oct. 1-Dec. 31, 1917; Cases, 32.
Naples	To Dec. 10	2		Among refugees.
Taormina	Jan. 20-Feb. 9	6		
Turin	Oct. 20-Dec. 29	121	120	
Do	Jan. 21-Apr. 7	96	10	
Japan:				
Kobe	Apr. 21-27	1		
Nagasaki	Jan. 14-May 19	28	4	
Nagoya	Mar. 24-Apr. 13	3		
Taihoku	Dec. 15-21	1		Island of Taiwan (Formosa).
Do	Jan. 8-May 13	99	24	Do.
Tokyo	Feb. 11-May 19	42		City and suburbs.
Yokohama	Jan. 17-Feb. 3	63		
Java:				
East Java	Oct. 7-Dec. 23	50		Dec. 25-31, 1917; Cases, 7. Jan.
Surabaya	Dec. 25-31	1		1-Feb. 4, 1918: Cases, 14.
Do	Jan. 29-Feb. 4	1		
Mid-Java				Oct. 10-Dec. 26, 1917; Cases, 86;
Samarang	Nov. 6-Dec. 12	4	1	death, 1. Dec. 26, 1917-Feb.
				13, 1918: Cases, 41.
West Java				Oct. 19-Dec. 27, 1917; Cases, 221;
Batavia	Nov. 2-8	1		deaths, 36. Dec. 28, 1917-Feb.
Do	Feb. 1-7	1		21, 1918: Cases, 257; deaths, 60.
Mesopotamia:				
Bagdad	Jan. 1-31		10	
Mexico:				
Aguascalientes	Feb. 4-17		2	
Ciudad Juarez	Mar. 3-June 1	4	2	
Guadalajara	Mar. 1-Apr. 30	24	5	
Mazatlan	Dec. 5-11		1	
Do	Jan. 29-June 4	5	4	
Mexico City	Nov. 11-Dec. 29	16		
Do	Dec. 30-May 18	160		
Piedras Negras	Jan. 11	200		
Vera Cruz	Jan. 20-Apr. 28	16	3	

CHOLERA, PLAGUE, SMALLPOX, TYPHUS FEVER AND YELLOW FEVER—Continued.

Reports Received from Dec. 29, 1917, to June 28, 1918—Continued.

SMALLPOX—Continued.

· Place.	Date.	Cases.	Deaths.	Remarks.
Newfoundland:				
Badger Brook.............	May 25–31........	2	....	
St. Johns..................	Dec. 8–Jan. 4......	29	....	
Do.....................	Jan. 5–June 7......	111	....	
Trepassey.................	Jan. 4.............	....	....	Outbreak with 11 cases reported.
Philippine Islands:				
Manila..................	Oct. 28–Dec. 8.....	5	......	
Do.....................	Feb. 3–Apr. 27....	291	136	Varioloid, 312.
Port Rico:				
San Juan................	Jan. 28–Apr. 7.....	37	....	Of these, 36 varioloid.
Portugal:				
Lisbon..................	Nov. 4–Dec. 15....	2	....	
Do.....................	Dec. 30–May 6.....	38	....	
Portuguese East Africa:				
Lourenço Marquez.........	Aug. 1–Dec. 31....	....	16	
Do.....................	Jan. 1–Feb. 28....	....	9	
Russia:				
Archangel...............	Sept. 1–Oct. 31....	7	....	
Moscow.................	Aug. 26–Oct. 6....	22	2	
Petrograd...............	Aug. 31–Nov. 18...	76	3	
Vladivostok.............	Apr. 1–30..........	51	12	
Siam:				
Bankok.................	Nov. 25–Dec. 1....	1	1	
Do.....................	Jan. 6–May 4......	39	27	
Spain:				
Corunna.................	Dec. 2–15.........	....	4	
Do.....................	Jan. 20–Apr. 6....	....	19	
Madrid.................	Jan. 1–Mar. 31....	....	16	Jan. 1–Dec 31, 1917: Deaths, 77.
Malaga.................	Oct. 1–31..........	....	19	
Seville.................	Oct. 1–Dec. 30....	....	66	
Do.....................	Jan. 1–Mar. 31....	....	23	
Valencia................	Jan. 27–May 18....	3	....	
Straits Settlements:				
Penang..................	Feb. 24–Apr. 13....	6	1	
Singapore...............	Nov. 25–Dec. 1....	1	1	
Do.....................	Dec. 30–Apr. 20...	20	11	
Tunisia:				
Tunis..................	Dec. 14–20........	1	....	
Do.....................	Mar. 16–Apr. 12...	2	....	
Turkey in Asia:				
Bagdad..................	.			Present in November, 1917.
Union of South Africa:				
Cape of Good Hope State...	Oct. 1–Dec. 31.....	28	....	
East London...........	Jan. 20–26........	1	....	Varioloid.
Transvaal—				
Johannesburg..........	Jan. 1–31..........	4	....	
Venezuela:				
Maracaibo................	Dec. 2–8..........	....	1	

TYPHUS FEVER.

Place	Date	Cases	Deaths	Remarks
Algeria:				
Algiers..................	Nov. 1–Dec. 31....	2	1	
Do...................	Apr. 1–30).........	....	1	
Argentina:				
Rosario.................	Dec. 1–31..........	....	1	
Austria-Hungary:				
Hungary.................	....	....	....	Nov. 26, 1917–Jan. 20, 1918: Cases, 16; deaths, 2. Jan. 21–Feb. 24, 1918: Cases, 21.
Budapest...............	Nov. 26–Jan. 20...	2	....	
Do..................	Jan. 21–Feb. 24....	14	....	
Brazil:				
Pernambuco.............	Mar. 16–31........	1	....	
Rio de Janeiro...........	Oct. 28–Dec. 1.....	7	....	
Canada:				
Ontario—				
Kingston..............	Dec. 2–8..........	3	....	
Quebec—				
Montreal..............	Dec. 16–22........	2	1	
China:				
Antung.................	Dec. 3–20........	13	1	
Do.....................	Dec. 31–May 13....	6	2	
Hankow.................	Apr. 2–22.........	2	....	European.

CHOLERA, PLAGUE, SMALLPOX, TYPHUS FEVER AND YELLOW FEVER—Continued.

Reports Received from Dec. 29, 1917, to June 28, 1918—Continued.

TYPHUS FEVER—Continued.

Place.	Date.	Cases.	Deaths.	Remarks.
Chosen (Korea):				
Seoul	Nov. 1-20	1		
Do	Feb. 1-Apr. 30	9	3	
Egypt:				
Alexandria	Nov. 8-Dec. 28	57	15	
Do	Jan. 8-May 4	1,826	406	
Cairo	July 23-Dec. 23	142	74	
Port Said	July 30-Nov. 11	5	5	
France:				
Marseille	Dec. 1-31		1	
Germany				Dec. 23, 1917-Mar. 23, 1918: Cases, 106; deaths, 9.
Berlin	Mar. 2-23	1		
Breslau District	Feb. 3-23	4		
Königsoerg District	do	1		Prisoner of war.
Lorraine				Dec. 23, 1917-Feb. 23, 1918: Cases, 77; deaths, 4. Of these 59 cases, 1 death, in workmen's camps at Pontingen and Werningen.
Metz	Dec. 23-Feb. 2	17	3	
Posen District	Feb. 3-23	7		
Great Britain:				
Belfast	Feb. 10-May 11	22	3	
Dublin	Mar. 24-Apr. 27	4		
Glasgow	Dec. 21	1		
Do	Jan. 20-May 18	22		
Manchester	Dec. 2-8	1		
Greece:				
Arta	Feb. 19	2		
Janina	Feb. 14	110		Jan. 27, epidemic.
Saloniki	Nov. 11-Dec. 29		72	
Do	Dec. 30-Apr. 27		48	
Italy:				
Bagnasco	Mar. 18-Apr. 7	4		Province of Cuneo.
San Remo	Mar. 10-16	2		
Japan:				
Nagasaki	Nov. 26-Dec. 16	5	5	
Do	Jan. 7-May 19	22	8	
Java:				
East Java				Oct. 15-Dec. 31, 1917: Cases, 39; deaths, 7. Jan. 1-Feb. 11, 1918: Cases, 34; deaths, 7.
Surabaya	Dec. 17-31	9	1	
Do	Jan. 1-Feb. 11	29	4	
Mid-Java				Oct. 10-Dec. 26, 1917: Cases, 63; deaths, 2. Dec. 28, 1917-Feb. 13, 1918: Cases, 24; deaths, 2.
Samarang	Oct. 9-Dec. 26	20	2	
Do	Dec. 27-Feb. 6	20		
West Java				Oct. 19-Dec. 27, 1917: Cases, 94; deaths, 17. Dec. 28, 1917-Feb. 21, 1918: Cases, 56; deaths, 1.
Batavia	Oct. 1-Dec. 27	50	15	
Do	Dec. 28-Feb. 21	47	2	
Lithuania				Dec. 30, 1917-Mar. 2, 1918: Cases, 1,878.
Mexico:				
Aguascalientes	Dec. 15		3	
Do	Jan. 21-June 9		23	
Durango State—				
Guanacevi	Feb. 11			Epidemic.
Guadalajara	Apr. 1-30	2	2	
Mexico City	Nov. 11-Dec. 29	476		
Do	Dec. 30-May 21	877		
Vera Cruz	June 3-9		2	
Newfoundland:				
St. Johns	Mar. 30-Apr. 5	1	1	
Norway:				
Bergen	Feb. 1-16	3		
Poland				Nov. 18-Dec. 8, 1917: Cases, 2,568; deaths, 218 Dec. 23, 1917-Mar. 9, 1918: Cases, 8,403; deaths, 315.
Lodz	Nov. 18-Dec. 8	219	25	
Do	Feb. 10-Mar. 9	292	35	
Warsaw	Nov. 18-Dec. 8	1,461	141	
Do	Feb. 10-Mar. 9	2,747	331	
Portugal:				
Lisbon	Mar. 3-30	18		Feb. 21: Present.
Oporto	Dec. 1-31	23	4	
Do	Jan. 1-Mar. 8	1,811	161	
Russia:				
Archangel	Sept. 1-14	7	2	
Moscow	Aug. 26-Oct. 6	49	2	
Petrograd	Aug. 31-Nov. 18	32		
Do	Feb. 2			Present.
Vladivostok	Oct. 29-Nov. 4	12	1	
Do	Apr. 1-30	4		

CHOLERA, PLAGUE, SMALLPOX, TYPHUS FEVER AND YELLOW FEVER—Continued.

Reports Received from Dec. 29, 1917, to June 28, 1918—Continued.

TYPHUS FEVER—Continued.

Place.	Date.	Cases.	Deaths.	Remarks.
Spain:				
Almeria	Apr. 1-15	1	1	
Corcubion	Apr. 11			Present. Province of Coruna.
Lira	Apr. 6	11	3	Vicinity of Corcubion.
Madrid	Jan. 1-Mar. 31		2	
Sweden:				
Goteborg	Nov. 18-Dec. 15	2		
Switzerland:				
Basel	Jan. 6-19	1	1	
Zurich	Nov. 9-15	2		
Do	Jan. 13-19	2		
Tunisia:				
Tala	Mar. 18			Epidemic.
Tozer	....do			Do.
Tunis	Nov. 30-Dec. 6		1	
Do	Feb. 9-May 17	48	22	Of these 26 in outbreak in prison
Union of South Africa:				
Cape of Good Hope State				Sept. 10, 1917-Mar. 17, 1918: Cases, 4,444 (European, 54); deaths, 902 (European, 15).
Natal				Dec. 1, 1917-Mar. 17, 1918: Cases, 50; deaths, 11.

YELLOW FEVER.

Place.	Date.	Cases.	Deaths.	Remarks.
Brazil:				
Bahia	Mar. 10-16	1	1	
Ecuador:				
Babahoyo	Feb 1-15	1	1	
Guayaquil	Sept. 1-Nov. 30	5	3	
Do	Feb. 1-15	1		
Do	Mar. 1-31	12	7	June 8, 1918: Present.
Milagro	Feb. 1-15	1	1	
Yaguachi	Nov. 1-30	1		
Guatemala:				
Retalhuleu	Apr. 22-May 22			Present. About 25 miles from Champerico, Pacific port. Disease spreading along Pacific coast.
Honduras:				
Tegucigalpa	Dec. 16-22		1	
Do	Jan. 6-19		1	
Mexico:				
Acapulco	June 16	1		

✖

INDEX.

A.

D.

Mc.

MacArthur, Camp—Disease cases reported. (*See* Extra-cantonment zones.)

McClellan, Camp—Disease cases reported. (*See* Extra-cantonment zones.

McLaughlin, Allan J.—Venereal disease control—State-wide plan_____ **Page.** 223

M.

O

DARE
TO
LOVE

THE TRUTH AND DARE DUET
LYLAH JAMES

DARE TO LOVE

Copyright © 2020 by Lylah James

This is a work of fiction. Names, characters, places, brands, media, and incidents are either the products of the author's imagination or are used fictitiously.

DARE
TO
LOVE

THE TRUTH AND DARE DUET
LYLAH JAMES

To my amazing readers–
Thank you for loving Maddox and Lila as much as I do.

A gripping, heart-wrenching and slow burn enemies-to-friends-to-lovers romance.

What happens when a dare goes too far?

Maddox Coulter. Reckless bad boy. Infamous playboy. He was my nemesis, then my best friend.

Maddox promised to always be there for me. I vowed I'd never leave him.

We teetered over the line of love and obsession for many years. The irresistible attraction between us became more – it burned us and we laid in the ashes of our mistakes. Our relationship was something precious and we fought, we bled… and we fell deeper into this game of love.

We were never meant to cross paths in the first place because Maddox held a secret that would be the cause of our ruination.

But maybe it was kismet…

Truth or Dare?

Truth: He loved me. I loved him. But it was never simple.
Dare: I dare you to read our story. Nothing is what it seems to be.

DARE TO LOVE is the complete TRUTH AND DARE DUET collection and a never seen before Christmas Novella.

DO YOU DARE?

TRUTH AND DARE DUET BOOK 1

PROLOGUE

Lila

His presence was a warm heat behind me as we walked into the bar. He was close; really, *really* close. I could *feel* him. I could *smell* him. He was so close, yet so far out of reach. A dangerous temptation dangling right in front of me.

I wanted to turn around and wrap my arms around him, bask in his warmth. We've hugged and cuddled plenty of times before, but since the Charity Gala, everything has been different.

He has been different.

Somehow, there was a wall between us now. I couldn't break it or walk around it. It was exhausting and scary – watching the change in him, seeing him so…cold and withdrawn from me. Sometimes, it felt like he was battling something inside his head. I waited silently for him to come to me, to speak of his worries, so I could find a way to soothe him. Like always.

Except…it started to feel as if *I* was the problem. As if he was hiding

from *me*.

A week in Paris. This was supposed to be fun and exciting. An adventure for us. Day one and it was already going to waste.

I chewed on my bottom lip as we walked further inside the dim room. It wasn't overly crowded, but everyone here looked fancy. After all, this was one of the famous hotels of Paris; wealthy and posh people came here often. "I didn't think the hotel would have its own bar. Fancy. I like it."

"It's nice," he replied. There was a roughness in his voice, except his tone was robotic. No emotions whatsoever.

What's wrong with you? What did I do?

I paused in my steps, expecting him to bump into me. He didn't. Instead, I felt his arm slide around my waist as he curled it around me. Our bodies collided together softly, and I sucked in a quiet breath. His rock-hard chest was to my back, pressing against me, and I could feel every intake of breath he took. His touch was a sweet, sweet torture.

Fuck you, for making me feel this way, for tempting me and leaving me hanging and...for making me fall in love with you...

"This way." His lips lingered near my ear as he whispered the words. He steered me toward the bar stools.

We sat side by side. From the corner of my eye, I watched him as he ordered our drinks. His voice was smooth, and it slid over my skin like silk. Soft and gentle.

Lost in my thoughts, I didn't notice the man standing next to me until his hand touched my shoulder. I swiveled to the left, my eyes catching the intruder. Yes, intruder. He was interrupting my time with *him*.

Maddox Coulter – the balm to my soul but also the stinging pain in my chest. He was sweet heaven and the bane of my existence.

"Remember me?" the man in the suit asked with a tiny grin.

Yup, I did. He was the owner of the hotel. We met him when we checked in yesterday.

"I saw you across the bar, and I knew instantly, you had to be the pretty girl I met last night." His English was perfect, but it was laced with a husky French accent. I had to admit, it was kind of sexy. Mr. Frenchman stood between our stools, separating Maddox and me. He blocked my view of Maddox and I. Did. Not. Like. That.

"Thank you for helping us yesterday," I replied sweetly, masking my irritation.

His emerald eyes glimmered, and his grin widened. Mr. Frenchman was your typical tall, dark, and handsome eye candy. And he wore an expensive suit that molded to his body quite nicely. "It was all my pleasure."

I nodded, a little lost at what else I could say. I wasn't shy or uncomfortable around men. But this one was a little too close for my liking, and since I had zero interest in him, even though he could definitely be my type, given the fact that *someone else* had all my attention, I didn't want to continue this conversation.

"Lucien Mikael." He presented me with his hand. I remembered he told us his name last night, but I didn't tell him mine.

I took his palm in mine, shaking it. "You can call me, Lila. It's nice to make your acquaintance."

Instead of shaking my hand, he turned it over and brought my hand to his lips. He kissed the back of it, his lips lingering there for a second too long. His eyes met mine over our entwined hands. "My pleasure, *ma belle.*"

Oh dear. Yup. Mr. Frenchman was flirting.

I glanced around Lucien and saw that Maddox was lounging back in his stool, his long legs stretched out in front of him, a drink in his hand, and he was staring directly at me. His face was expressionless.

Lucien turned to the bartender and said something to him in French. I didn't understand the words, but I quickly figured out what he said when he turned back to me.

"It's on me. A treat for a lovely lady."

I was already shaking my head. "Oh. You didn't have to –"

His hand tightened around mine. "Please, allow me."

"Thank you."

Lucien opened his mouth to say something else, but he was interrupted by the ringing of his phone. "Excuse me, *chérie*."

As he moved away, I caught sight of Maddox again. Our eyes met, and I stopped breathing. His gaze was dark, and his jaw was clenched so tightly that I wondered if it'd crack under the pressure. I could see the ticks in his sharp jaw as he gritted his teeth. His face – I didn't know how to describe it. Anger made his eyes appear darker, almost deadly. A shadow loomed over his face, his expression almost threatening. There was a predatory feel in his glare as he watched me closely.

He constantly pushed me away, putting more and more distance between us. Why was he so angry now? I couldn't tell. I. Couldn't. Think. Especially when he stared at me like *this*.

Maddox was maddening. He pulled and pushed; he loved and hated. I always thought I understood him better than anyone else. But right now, he confused the hell out of me.

"Lila." My eyes snapped away from Maddox, and I looked at Lucien. He was apparently done with his phone call, and his attention was back on me. Before I could pull away, he gripped my hand in his once more. "If you need anything while you are in Paris, please call me. I could take you sightseeing. I know many beautiful places."

He let go of my hand, and I turned my palm over to see his business card. Smooth trick, Mr. Frenchman. "Umm, thank you."

Lucien leaned down and quickly placed a chaste kiss on both my cheeks before pulling away. "Au revoir, *chérie*."

I didn't watch him leave. All my attention was on the man sitting beside me. He took a large gulp of his drink.

"He likes you," he said, once Lucien was out of hearing range.

"Jealous?" I shot back immediately.

A smirk crawled onto his face, and he chuckled, his wide chest rumbling with it. "He wants you, Lila."

My stomach clenched, goosebumps breaking out over my skin. My breath left me in a whoosh. His words were spoken dangerously low, although the harshness in his voice could not be mistaken.

"How would you know?" I retorted, angry and confused. He played with my feelings, turning my emotions into a little game of his. Maddox had me in knots, twisting me around like a little plaything.

He grunted, shaking his head, and then he let out a laugh. As if he was sharing an inside joke with himself. "I'm a man, like him. I know what he was thinking about when he looked at you like that."

"Maybe he wasn't thinking about sex. Maybe he's a gentleman. Unlike you." I was playing with fire, I knew that. I was testing him, testing *us*.

"*I dare you*," he whispered so softly, I almost missed it. Maddox looked down at his glass, his fingers clenched around it. Even in the dim lights, I could see the way his knuckles were starting to turn white.

He was giving me a dare *now*?

He didn't finish his sentence, and I wondered if he was contemplating his dare. Maddox's jaw flexed from obvious frustration. For a brief moment, I thought maybe he wasn't angry at *me*. Maybe, he was angry at *himself*. He was fighting *himself*. Could it be that the problem wasn't me?

He drank the rest of his drink in one gulp and then slammed his glass on the counter, before swiveling around in his stool to face me. Maddox stood up and walked a step closer to me, until my knees were touching his strong thighs. He leaned forward, caging me in between the counter and his body. Our gaze locked, and he licked his lips. He had me captivated for a moment until he mercilessly broke the spell.

"I dare you to sleep with him."

I reared back in shock. *Wh-at?* No, I must have misheard him. This couldn't be...

"What?" I whispered, my throat dry, and my tongue suddenly heavy in my mouth.

Maddox's eyes bore into mine, staring into my soul. When he spoke again, his deep accented voice danced over my skin dangerously. "I dare you to fuck him, Lila."

A trembling started in my core and then moved through my body like a storm. Not just a quiet storm. A tsunami of emotions hit me all at once, reckless in its assault. I submerged under the dark waves, suffocating, and then I was being split open, so viciously, it sent tiny cracks of my heart and fissures of my soul in all directions. I clamped my teeth together to stop myself from saying something –anything that would make it worse.

We had done too many dares to simply count on our fingers. Countless silly dares over the years, but we had never dared each other to sleep with other people. Granted, I had asked him to kiss a girl once; they made out, but it was years ago. But our dares had never crossed that line.

Sex... that was never on the table. We never explicitly talked about it, but it was almost an unspoken rule.

"What's with that look, Lila?"

My eyes closed. I refused to look at him, to look into his beautiful eyes and see nothing but pitch black darkness. He wasn't looking at me like he used to. The light in his eyes was gone.

It scared me.

It hurt me.

It was destroying the rest of what was left of me.

"Look. At. Me."

I didn't want to. I didn't want him to see the hurt in my eyes.

"Open your eyes, Lila," he said in his rich baritone voice.

I did as I was commanded. He crowded into my personal space, forcing me to inhale his scent and feel the warmth of his body. "Are you serious? Or are you already drunk?" I asked quietly. It was hard to breathe with him this close.

"I never take back a dare."

And I never lose. He knew that. We were both very competitive, and to this day, neither of us had backed down from a dare.

Maddox's hand came up, and he cupped my jaw. His fingers kissed my skin softly. He smiled, but it didn't match the look in his eyes. "What's wrong? You don't want to do it?"

"I don't play to lose." *Asshole.*

Maddox leaned closer, his face barely an inch away from mine. Our noses were almost touching. My heart fluttered when he tipped my head back. *Take back your dare. Take back your dare, Maddox. Don't make me do this.*

He curled his index finger around the lock of hair that had fallen out from my bun. His minty breath, mixed with the smell of alcohol, feathered over my lips. I wanted to beg him with my eyes. Maddox tugged on my hair slightly before tucking it behind my ear. He moved, and my eyes fluttered close once again…*waiting…* a desperate breath locked in my throat, my chest caving, and my stomach clenching.

He pressed his cheek against mine, and his lips lingered over my ear. "Don't disappoint me, *chérie.*"

My body shuddered, and I breathed out a shaky breath. He tore my heart open and left me bleeding. He pulled away and stared down at me.

Maddox was mocking me. Taunting me.

He never stopped being a jerk. He just hid it behind a sexy smile and a nonchalant expression.

I thought he had left his asshole ways behind. But no, I was wrong. So goddamn wrong about him. About *us.*

Friends. We were friends.

I thought maybe… he wanted *more.* More of me. More of us, of what we were or could be. I was so goddamn wrong.

Maddox Coulter was still an asshole behind a pretty mask.

And I was the stupid girl who fell in love with her best friend.

CHAPTER ONE

Lila

Three and a half years ago

"**M**otherfu–" My mouth snapped shut before I hissed out another painful breath as my knees threatened to buckle under me.

The coffee table stared back at me innocently, and I glared in response. *Little shit.* I gave it a kick, with my uninjured leg, just for the heck of it.

My morning was a mess already, and I fought the urge to take out my anger on the coffee table. Granted, it just bruised my knees, but in reality, the fault was mine.

My alarm didn't go off, which obviously meant I woke up late. *Very late.* First period classes had already ended, and it was halfway through second period. Then, in my struggle to get dressed hurriedly, I ended up tearing a hole in my white and pristine school blouse. Great. What a lovely morning already.

Scrambling away from the little table, I ran out of my grandparents' house and quickly locked the door behind me. I had to catch the bus in two minutes, or else I was going to be mega-late. The next bus wouldn't be here for another thirty-five minutes.

As I ran to the nearest bus stop, I quickly went over my morning list in my head. Four very important things. Phone – yes. Earphones – yes. Keys – yes. My English assignment – yes.

Everything seemed to be in order. Now, I just had to make it on time for my third period class, so I could submit my English essay on time. Or else...

I shook my head, refusing to even think of the consequences. My heart started to race and beat erratically at the mere thought of getting a zero on this assignment.

No way. It would ruin my perfect record of straight As. My grandma liked to joke and say I was paranoid and a little *too* OCD about my marks. My grandpa, with a proud little laugh, would say I was a perfectionist. They weren't exactly wrong.

My perfect GPA, plus my thousand hours of community service and volunteer work, would get me into Harvard. And it was all that mattered. Harvard was my path. It was my destination, and it was where I belonged. Maybe my grandparents were right. Maybe I was obsessed with the idea of *"perfection."* But I didn't care. If perfection would get me everything I wanted, then *Miss Perfectionist* I'd be.

The bus came on time, and I successfully climbed in without any more bad luck. My favorite seat at the back of the bus was waiting for me. It gave me the perfect view of the whole bus, and it was a window seat. Once my earphones were in, "Hands to Myself" by Selena Gomez started to blast in my ears. I leaned my forehead against the cool window and watched the world move.

This was probably my favorite part of my morning routine. I'd always been an observer, and one could learn a lot in a ten-minute bus ride.

Not long after, the bus came to a stop, and I walked out; I stopped on the pavement for the briefest moment to stare at the large and old, yet hauntingly beautiful and fancy, building in front of me.

The Berkshire Academy of Weston.

The private school for the rich and the corrupted. Kids of infamous judges, senators, government associates, and some of the highest paid lawyers and doctors in the United States.

I wasn't one of them. My father *was* a high school teacher. My mother *was* a nurse. And I was the quiet and poor girl amongst all the famous, wealthy spawns of the devils themselves. I didn't belong here. But I *chose* to be here.

48.2% of Berkshire Academy of Weston graduates end up at an Ivy League College – Yale, Princeton, Dartmouth, or Harvard.

That little fact was the reason why I chose to enroll in this school during my junior year. Now, I was a senior at Berkshire. A few more months, and I'd be out of here.

I took in a deep breath and inhaled the fresh September air. It wasn't too cold yet. The fall season had just begun, and the leaves were just starting to turn red, orange, and yellow. It was a beautiful time of year – the time where the trees end up naked, silently awaiting their rebirth once again. The end of something beautiful, while waiting for a new beginning.

"Lila!"

My thoughts came to a halt, and I turned to see Riley coming my way. She waved animatedly, and I couldn't help but smile. Riley was a sweet, wild girl, and my only friend at Berkshire.

Her pretty blonde locks bounced as she hopped over to me. "Are you late, too?"

I nodded with a sigh. She perked up cheekily. "No way! Miss Smarty Pants is late? Jesus, I need to write this down. ASAP."

The urge to roll my eyes was strong, but I refrained from doing so. "You have Advanced Calculus next, right?" I asked, switching the subject.

I usually loved to join in on the teasing, but I wasn't in the mood today. Waking up late had made me a tad grumpier. My knee was sore and ached every time I took a step – a constant reminder of how *amazing* my morning had been so far. Grumpy Lila was no fun.

Riley looked thoughtful for a second. "Yeah. I do," she responded after a long second. "You?"

"English. We have twenty minutes before our classes start."

"I actually need to see my teacher before class. Did I mention I hate math? Yeah, I probably did a hundred times. We have a test next week, and I'm pretty sure I'm going to flunk it." Riley's normal cheerfulness disappeared, and her brows tensed with a frown. She looked deeply saddened for a moment, but just as quickly, her expression changed, and she was back to happy Riley once again. "I'll see you at lunch?"

I grabbed her hand before she could leave. "If you want, I can help you this weekend with Calculus."

She smiled brightly, her whole face shining like the moon. "Really? Thank you, babe. How about we talk more about it at lunch? We can pick a time and place."

"Sounds good to me." I let her hand go, and she waved before running through the gates.

I looked down at my phone. Fifteen minutes until my next class. It was enough time for me to grab an iced latte. *Perfect.* Maybe sugar would help my mood.

The coffee shop was only a few feet away, sitting right next to the campus. It was pretty much only visited by the students of Berkshire. It wasn't lunch yet, so when I walked in, the shop was fairly quiet. I ordered myself an iced latte with extra whip cream and went to stand next to the heater. "Sugar" by Maroon 5 continued to play in my ear, and I softy hummed along to the song.

When a blast of cool air hit the back of my legs, I turned around to see a group of loud boys walking into the coffee shop. I instantly recognized a few of them from my classes. The Bennett Twins were part of the group. The boys kept the door opened, standing right at the entrance. Half of the group were wearing the required Berkshire uniform – pants, shirt, tie and blazer. The other half were in their gym clothes or football uniforms.

Jocks. *Ugh.*

Rich. Loud. Foul-mouthed. Annoying. A bit *too* wild. Everything I stayed away from, and everything I despised.

Whatever.

Ignorance was bliss. I turned back around and focused on my playlist instead, my foot tapping impatiently on the floor. The barista was taking forever, and I desperately needed my sugar. I could feel the group of boys coming closer to me, and I half-listened to them order their own drinks. In my peripheral, I could see them pushing each other around, bumping shoulders, and shaking with laughter. Their teasing rung louder than the music blasting in my ears.

"Here you go!" I lifted my head up when the voice called out in a singsong tone. Finally! My mouth watered as the young lady handed me the iced latte, and I almost drooled at the sight of extra whip cream. *Heaven.*

"Thank you." I cleared my throat and sent her a grateful smile. *God bless your soul, woman.*

I swiveled around while simultaneously putting the straw into my mouth. But I never got the chance to take the first sip of my heavenly goodness. Nope. My happiness only lasted for two seconds flat.

Before I knew what was happening, a rock-hard wall bumped into me. I heard someone swear under his breath. It happened fast, too quickly for me to catch on until it was too late. The world spun and tilted on its axis. My eyes closed as I expected the impact of me hitting the floor, but my face didn't kiss the ground. I stayed suspended in the air, my body bent backward.

Someone was holding onto my arm…really…*really* tightly. Two heartbeats later, I was back on my feet again. I finally opened my eyes, and a shaky breath expelled from my lungs.

The first thing I noticed was that his navy colored blazer was wet. My coffee… "Shit. Sorry. I am so sorry," I muttered, absolutely horrified.

Then, I inwardly groaned. First – why was I apologizing? *He* bumped into *me*. His fault. Not mine. Second – My iced latte was gone.

My heart was still beating too fast and too hard after the little scare, and it felt like it would thump right out of my chest. *Wait...*

I looked down at myself and saw that my white shirt was soaked, and my pink bra was now quite visible to everyone. Oh, that was where my iced latte went. *Amaaaazing.*

Mood level: Extra grumpy with just a touch of bitchiness.

I let my eyes travel the length of the *wall* that bumped into me. Okay, not a wall then. He was definitely human. But a rock nonetheless. I had felt those hard muscles when he knocked me over. It was like a truck hitting me, and I swore he must have given me a concussion from that whiplash.

My gaze went up and up…and up. *Jesus Christ,* he was tall. I was basically a midget next to him at five foot two inches.

My eyes stayed longer on his stomach, and for a brief moment, I wondered if he had six-pack abs. His wide chest caught my attention next. He was tall and lean, but still muscular and a bit bigger for his age. I could instantly tell he played football – his strong arms and muscular shoulders told me so, and he had a gym/sports bag thrown over his right shoulder. His school blazer molded to his upper body perfectly. Deliciously.

Sweet Mother Mary... I was supposed to be angry, right?

When my gaze finally landed on his face, my eyes decided they'd been blessed. A classic gorgeous boy. Chiseled jawline that could give you a papercut if you touched it? Check. Piercing eyes? Check. Thick eyebrows? Check. Plump lips made for kissing? Check. Intense good looks? Double check. He was a fine specimen, and I wanted to put him

24

under my microscope for a closer look.

His dirty blond hair was curly and the tight curls ended a good inch or two above his shoulders. It gave him a surfer look, a bit wild and outgoing.

Wait. Hold up.

I stumbled a step back and took a good look at his face. My lips parted, completely dumbstruck, and I choked on my saliva silently. *Are you kidding me?*

Out of everyone… out of 325 boys at Berkshire, I had to bump into HIM?

He eyed me up and down, his gaze scanning my body leisurely like I had done to him. My cheeks flamed, not because he was checking me out – no, because he had obviously caught *me* checking *him* out. Could this day get any worse?

He cocked his head to the side, his deep blue eyes flashing with mischief. His eyes caressed my bare legs and then he followed the path up. My beige school skirt came to mid-thigh, only a few inches above my knees. He seemed to take great pleasure in watching my bare skin.

Slowly, his gaze moved up. Mister-Who-Bumped-Into-Me blatantly stared at my boobs. He was so goddamn obvious. The corner of his lips tilted up, and he gave me the perfect swoon worthy smirk.

He chuckled, a deep laugh that came out roughly from within his chest. "Well, I guess that'll perk them up a little."

Huh?

His buddies snickered and chortled with laughter. Cole Bennett, one of the twins, even doubled over and wheezed like he had just heard the best joke of the century.

I followed his gaze to my chest and then I looked back at him. Wait… was he…did he…just…?

My body tensed, and I straightened my spine. "Excuse me?"

My brain had finally caught on, and I could feel the steam coming out of my ears. How dare he!

I crossed my arms over my chest, my cheeks burning hot, and I held back an irritated growl. Yes, my boobs were *petite*. The two mounds were almost non-existent compared to the other girls my age, and they basically stopped growing when I was fourteen.

But. He. Did. Not. Have. To. Rub. That. In. My. Face.

Oh wait, I forgot. He was an asshole. *The* asshole.

Maddox Coulter.

Berkshire Academy's Star Quarterback.

Reckless bad boy. Infamous playboy.

The Casanova of the senior class and its golden boy.

And yes, a Class-A jerk, with unparalleled levels of douchebaggery.

Maddox was well-known in Berkshire. His face was catalogued into everyone's brain and heart, and I wanted nothing to do with him. Except, out of 325 boys in our school, I had to bump into him today.

He was still smirking, and I let out an irritated sigh. "Are you going to apologize to me or not? You bumped into me," I seethed, shoving my empty cup between us.

His dark blue eyes narrowed on my boobs again. Apparently, Mr. Coulter had a short attention span because he chose to ignore my words and decided to focus on my tits instead. The same tits he just insulted.

I crossed my arms over my chest again and glowered at him and his buddies. His gaze finally met mine, and I hated that he had such beautiful eyes. He didn't deserve them.

Maddox shrugged, quite nonchalantly. "You were in my way. Whoops."

Is he serious?

He took a step forward, his bigger body closing in on my small frame. "I have an extra shirt in my locker. I'll give it to you, considering the one you're wearing is soaked."

His voice lowered into a raspy tone when he spoke his next words.

"But one condition. If I give you my shirt, I get to keep your bra. It's *cute*. I love the little flowers on them, baby."

I stumbled back, aghast. I knew he was immature, rude, and vulgar, but this was a whole other level of douchebaggery. *Murder is a crime, Lila. You could go to prison for a very long time.* My eyes narrowed on him. "You know what? I don't have time for this. Go take your shitty attitude and try to impress another girl with it."

Maddox blinked, his goofy smile disappearing for a nanosecond, before his eyes lit up, almost as if he loved me rebuffing him.

I swiveled around, dumped my empty coffee cup into the garbage, and decided to walk away from Maddox. Too bad he was standing in my way, refusing to budge. I inwardly rolled my eyes and pushed past him. He was standing so close that I was forced to touch him, our bodies slightly rubbing against each other as I went by. A cocky smirk was plastered on his stupidly handsome face.

Fine. He wanted to play… then I'd play.

After taking two steps forward, I did a little side twist, which allowed my bag to hit him. *Bullseye.* When I heard a hiss of pain, I knew that the corner of my bag had bumped into his crotch, and his dick probably felt the impact, too.

I turned my head and gave Maddox a look over my shoulder. He had doubled over and was cupping himself between the legs. "You were in my way. Whoops," I said lazily, repeating his earlier words.

My middle name is 'Petty Bitch.' I didn't have time for a reckless bad boy, but I also wouldn't let him play me like his other fangirls.

His ocean blue eyes locked on mine, and they darkened the slightest bit. Maddox straightened his spine and stood at his full height again. He was imposing, his presence almost owning the whole coffee shop. I sent him a sugary sweet smile before walking away.

If I didn't leave this coffee shop in one minute, I was going to be late for my English class.

The intensity of his gaze burned into my back. I could feel the heat of it, of *him*. My cheeks flamed, and my body grew warmer. I knew he was looking at my ass. I could *feel* it.

Maddox Coulter was officially on my shit list.

CHAPTER TWO

Lila

I was on time for my English class and successfully submitted my essay – all thanks to the spare shirt I had in my locker. The one I wore this morning was soaked from my spilled iced coffee by the boy who shall not be named.

As soon as the bell rang, indicating the start of class, Mrs. Levi started her lecture about Greek Mythology. She went back and forth from the textbook and writing notes on the chalkboard.

Science might be my passion, but English was my favorite subject. I loved reading, loved learning about the language - every little piece of it. My interest began with Shakespeare, although it was Edgar Allen Poe who made me fall in love with English.

"Deep into that darkness peering, long I stood there, wondering, fearing, doubting, dreaming dreams no mortal ever dared to dream before."

I may or may not have memorized most of his poems after reading them over and over again. There was just something eerily beautiful with the way he weaved his words together.

"Medusa has several myths about her life, the most common ones are of her death and her, rather, painful demise." Mrs. Levi's voice snapped me to the present as she introduced us to the history of Medusa. "This will be our focus for the next two weeks. Your next assignment will be based on this particular topic, so make sure you're doing your research at home and come to class with your questions. The essay will be fifteen percent of your final mark. We'll be discussing it in more depth the next couple of days."

She continued to talk about Medusa, and I wrote down all my notes, marking the important ones with my red pen. I liked to keep my things organized, even though to other people, it seemed a bit too OCD.

Halfway through Mrs. Levi's lecture, my hand paused, and my pen came to halt. It had been a few minutes now, and I couldn't ignore the *feeling* anymore. My skin prickled, and my back seemed to warm under someone's intense stare. I could feel the tiny hairs on my arms stand on end. It was a strange feeling, and I couldn't concentrate on Mrs. Levi anymore.

I always sat in the front row of all my classes, but usually, I was invisible to everyone.

Today though… someone was staring at me *hard.*

It was impossible not to *feel* it.

The stare burned into my back, scorching me… waiting for a reaction, until I was forced to peek over my shoulder.

Our eyes met first.

Mine – widening with surprise. *His* – with amusement.

My jaw went slack, and I stared back, hard. No way.

He was sitting in the last row at the back of the class, in the corner, next to the wall. There was a large gap between us, but I still felt him.

Maddox Coulter had both his elbows on the desk, his fingers threaded with his chin resting on them. His blue eyes danced with mischief, and when I continued to stare back, his lips crooked up in a lazy grin.

Well... shit.

I faced the front of the class again and mentally berated myself. Could this day get any worse?

How could I have missed him?

It was only the third week of school, and I never paid attention to whoever was sitting at the back. My focus had always been on Mrs. Levi and whatever she was teaching.

Knowing Maddox, he had probably skipped more than half of the classes in the past three weeks. I knew of his reputation. He rarely came to class, and when he did... he came with drama and a whole lot of assholery.

I mentally face-palmed while chewing on my lower lip, nervously. In the heat of the moment, I acted without thinking; granted, he was the douchebag in this situation, but nobody ever crossed Maddox without dealing with the repercussions.

With my best nonchalant expression, I quickly peeked over my shoulder again. He was still staring... and he caught me looking, *again*. His eyes were the deepest blue, shimmering with intensity. He lazily rubbed his thumb back and forth across his squared jaw while he cocked his head to the side, raising one lonely eyebrow almost mockingly.

Maddox watched me like he was sizing up his *prey*.

I didn't like the look he was giving me, and I didn't have any interest of being on his radar.

He might be *the* player, but I wasn't about to be played. *Try again, Coulter.*

Giving him the most exaggerated eyeroll I could muster, I sent him a frigid smile and then turned back around to face Mrs. Levi.

During the rest of the class, I tried my hardest not to pay attention to Maddox. It was the longest fifty minutes of my life as I fought hard not to fidget in my chair. He continued to stare, and I could feel it – feel him smirking and silently taunting me.

My fingers clenched and unclenched around my pen, and when the bell finally rang for lunch, I let out the deepest sigh of relief.

"Maddox, I'm going to need you to stay back for two minutes," Mrs. Levi announced, with a hard look.

"Can't, Teach. Got stuff to do."

"You either stay or you have detention for two weeks. Decide, Mr. Coulter."

There was one very important fact about Mrs. Levi, and it was why she was my favorite teacher: she took no bullshit from *anyone*. She wasn't intimated by Maddox or *who* he was.

All the students looked back and forth between Mrs. Levi and Maddox, holding their breath and *waiting*.

"Class, you may leave for lunch."

There were groans and whispers as everyone got up and started piling out of the classroom. Everyone had been waiting for drama – with Maddox in the middle of it. *Ha!*

I stood up too, following the herd. Curiosity got the best of me, and I looked back over my shoulder, one final time. Maddox was still sitting back in his chair, his arms crossed over his broad chest. His gaze followed me as I walked out of the class, and by *me*, I meant my ass.

I noticed Colton Bennett, twin number one, standing beside Maddox's chair. They muttered something to each other, and Colton's gaze found mine before he chuckled at something else Maddox said.

Maddox might be on my shit list, but… I had a feeling I was on his now, too.

Riley waved at me as I stepped into the loud cafeteria. She was already sitting at a table, and I smiled, walking to her. "Hey!" She spoke through a bite of her chicken sandwich. "I got you one, too."

"Thanks, babe." I settled opposite her and took the sandwich she offered. It was our thing. Sometimes, I would buy her lunch, and other days, she'd return the favor.

"So, what exactly do you need help with in Math?" I munched on my cold sandwich and watched Riley pout.

"Everything," she mumbled, pouting even harder. "It makes no sense to me! The only genius who can help me is you."

I raised an eyebrow at her. "Why do I have a feeling this friendship is only one-sided?"

"Bitch, yes, I'm using you for your abilities to teach me Math."

It was a lie; we both knew that. Riley and I stared at each other for a second before we chuckled.

We became friends during junior year, after Jasper – another football star of Berkshire Academy -- broke her heart. That was a tamed way of putting it. They dated for six months; he was the perfect gentleman at first. When she finally gave him her virginity, he broke up with her two days later. She later found out Jasper had been cheating on her all along, and he only dated her to win a stupid bet. He spent the rest of the year spreading stupid rumors about her. She lost her cheerleader friends and sweet Riley…? She became another outcast. I was there and watched her crumble – going from Miss Popular to a nobody.

What happens when outcast number one meets outcast number two?
Of course, they became best friends. I was the new student, and Riley was my first friend. It was a done deal.

"So… I heard whispers in the hallway," she started, eyeing me closely. "Huh?"

"About a girl who dumped coffee on Maddox Coulter this morning." Riley left the sentence hanging before taking another bite of her sandwich.

My heart thudded in my chest, so hard and so fast. Choking back a cough, I quickly sputtered, "Dumped coffee on him? Excuse me! He *bumped* into *me* and spilled my coffee down the front of *me*."

Riley sat back in her chair, taking the last bite of her lunch. "I didn't say it was you, but thanks for confirming that," she replied around a mouthful. "Your name was mentioned once, but I didn't want to believe anything until I heard it myself from you."

Sweet Lord! Rumors were already going around?

"So, he bumped into you?" Riley pushed, looking quite amused at this sudden turn of events.

"*Yes*," I hissed under my breath. "He didn't even apologize! My shirt got wet, but thank God, I had a spare in my locker."

"Why am I not surprised? Do you think Maddox is the type of guy to apologize? Think again, babe. I've known him since elementary school. Coulter doesn't apologize. *Ever*. Everyone bows down to him."

I huffed in response, and Riley shrugged. "He's the golden boy."

To the people of Berkshire Academy, he was a god amongst mortals.

To me? He was just another boy who had too much power in his hands and didn't know how to use it. Maddox was no hero to me.

If he expected me to worship the ground he walked on, like all of his fangirls, he was about to be thoroughly disappointed.

Riley leaned forward and tapped me on the nose with her index finger. "Stay out of his way, Lila. He'll mess you up so bad and leave you broken. Boys like him can't be trusted."

Her voice was thick, and I could see the emotions playing on her face. Jasper really broke her. Her scars were not visible; she hid them with a pretty smile, but I knew she still hurt inside.

"Don't worry. I have no plans to play his game."

Riley squinted at me. "I don't believe you. You're competitive by nature, Lila. If he pushes, you're going to push back twice as hard."

I bit my lower lip and gave her a sheepish look. She was right...

"How about this? I promise not to fall for him."

"One less girl in Maddox's harem," she agreed.

I rolled my eyes. "Okay, today is Thursday. How about we meet up on Saturday? I'll go over whatever you need help on with you then."

Riley nodded before her cheeks flushed. "You'll have to start at the beginning. Don't kill me."

"This is going to be a loooong Saturday." She kicked me under the table, and I hissed out a laugh.

"Bitch." Riley threw her empty plastic bottle at my head, laughing.

The rest of my day was uneventful. I stayed out of Maddox's way. There were a few whispers in the halls about me, but I ignored them, too.

I felt pretty confident that, after today, everyone would forget about the coffee shop scene, and Maddox would most definitely forget about my existence. He had plenty of girls to distract him.

Except... I had never been more wrong in my life.

The next day, my nightmare began.

35

CHAPTER THREE

Lila

The next morning, I found Maddox outside our English class. He was leaning against the wall, his long legs crossed at the ankle with his hands stuffed in his pockets. His expensive leather shoes were shiny and wrinkled free. He was missing his navy blazer, but his pristine white shirt was rolled to his elbows, exposing his strong forearms. His tie hung loosely around his neck.

He was *pretty* to look at – I had to admit, but the sight of him annoyed me.

There was a curvy blonde girl attached to his side, practically plastered against him. She whispered something into his ear, but he wasn't paying attention. Maddox looked bored, and the poor girl was trying too hard. *Run away, don't fall for his charms.* I wanted to shake some sense into her.

The moment his gaze fell on me, he slowly grinned.

My blood simmered, and I pressed my lips firmly together, refusing to acknowledge him. I tilted my chin up and marched forward. If I ignored him, he'd go away – I told myself.

Too bad it was nothing but false hope.

When I tried to walk into the classroom, Maddox pulled himself away from the girl. She protested, but it died in her throat when she noticed it was useless.

He shifted sideways and placed his arm out, blocking the door and effectively stopping me from stepping inside. "Hey, Garcia."

Maddox threw me his signature smirk in an attempt to *melt* me. I rolled my eyes. "Coulter," I said in acknowledgment. "You're in my way."

I tried to push past him, but he didn't budge; granted, he was a whole foot taller than me, but Maddox was an immovable wall. "It's quite comical that you think you can move me."

There was just *something* about Maddox that irritated me. It was like he had hit a nerve I didn't know I had. He made me feel edgy. I didn't know why I felt like that, but I was defensive around him.

"A knee between your legs will move you alright. So, either you move with no injuries, or your baby making machine will be in danger." I cocked my head to the side while holding my bag over my shoulder and waiting for him to move.

My lips crooked up in my fakest and sweetest smile.

Maddox stared me down for a second before he eventually moved, bending slightly to his waist and putting his arm out to motion inside the classroom. "Ladies first. After you."

I rolled my eyes a-fucking-gain because he was so goddamn annoying. Pushing past his hard body, I walked into class with a huff and settled in my chair. He sauntered inside like he owned the room and walked past me to his desk at the back of the classroom.

Maddox purposely brushed against my shoulder as he did so. "Whoops, my bad," he muttered gruffly. I could hear the laughter in his voice.

My fingers clenched into a fist, but I held back.

My days continued like this.

I noticed him following me around. Sometimes, he would call out my name loudly in the hallways, bringing everyone's attention to me. Other times, he would purposely bump into me in class or the cafeteria. I often caught him doing nothing but following silently behind me. He knew it annoyed me, and he did it on purpose. To. Irritate. Me.

A week ago, I was completely invisible to Maddox Coulter.

Now, I was the center of his attention.

The deal breaker was when he broke into my locker and stole my spare shirt. He even left a note: *What's the color of your bra today?*

Actually no, that wasn't the worst part.

The worst part was when he decided to reenact a scene from Romeo and Juliet in the cafeteria...

He was Romeo, standing on the table, and loudly confessing his undying love to Juliet for the whole room to hear.

Who was Juliet?

Oh me...

He was being dramatic and overly exaggerated his performance for one reason only: to embarrass me.

Everyone stared... snickered... laughed, until Riley and I were forced to leave the cafeteria; we ended up having to eat lunch under a staircase. I hated hiding, I hated the attention, and Riley... she was about to blow up.

Maddox was waiting for a reaction, he was egging me on... pushing and pushing, waiting for me to *snap*, like I did in the coffee shop. But I vowed I wouldn't play his stupid games.

He would eventually stop, I convinced myself. He'd grow bored of me soon enough, I told myself. I was wrong again.

On Thursday, a week after handling his nonsense, Maddox still hadn't given up.

"Uh-oh. He's here. Maybe we should make a run for it now." Riley went to stand up, taking her lunch tray with her.

"Sit down," I hissed. "We're not running away. We're going to eat lunch, and we're going to ignore him."

"He's coming our way," she reported, shaking her head. "Oh shit, here we go again."

My back straightened, and I prepared myself for what was coming. I nodded at Riley, letting her know it was okay. Her eyebrows pulled together with a frown before she leveled a hard glare at whoever was standing behind me.

I felt Maddox before I saw him. His presence surrounded me, and I locked my jaw, gritting my teeth together. He grabbed the chair beside me and turned it around before sitting down, straddling it. Maddox leaned forward, using the back of the chair as an armrest. His friends settled around our table, grabbing their own chairs and joining us. Riley released a long, exasperated sigh.

Without speaking to me, he reached for my tray and grabbed my apple. With great annoyance, I forced myself to look at his face. His long dirty blond hair was pulled back into a small, messy man-bun. The rest of him was immaculate. The small diamond stud in his ear glinted in the light, briefly catching my attention. Maddox locked eyes with me, before taking a bite of my red apple. "Hmm juicy."

"That's my apple."

"It was lonely. I'm giving it some attention," he said, taking another huge bite.

I dropped my fork with a loud clank. "Put. The. Apple. Down."

Maddox was unfazed. "Or what?"

"You'll regret it, Coulter."

He let out a deep chuckle, as if my threat meant *nothing* to him. "You're all bark and no bite, Sweet Cheeks."

Sweet Cheeks? Excuse me...?

"You know what you remind me of? A little chihuahua trying to fight a bigger and stronger dog when she knows she can't win. Careful or you'll end up with a nasty bite, Garcia."

I snatched my apple from his hand and leaned forward, bringing our faces closer. "Did you know that chihuahuas are known as an aggressive breed when they're moody, and when they *do* bite, they bite *hard*. Careful, or you'll end up with a nasty bite, Coulter."

I brought the apple to my mouth and took a bite before I realized what I was doing. Maddox's eyes flared before his lips quirked up. "I think we just shared our first indirect kiss."

Oh, for God's sake!

Colton snickered before stealing a brownie from Riley's tray. She hissed, and her eyes hardened with a glare. The girl before Jasper would have exploded. The new Riley? She stayed quiet.

"That was a lousy kiss. You can do better than that, man," Colton said, his six-foot-something frame shaking with mirth.

Maddox grabbed my chair and pulled me closer to him, the four legs making a loud screeching sound. The whole cafeteria was watching now. I could feel their stares burning into me.

"What do you say, Garcia? Shall we put on a show for these asswipes?" His voice lowered, holding a suggestive tone.

"Not interested. Your lips probably hold more disease than a pig's asshole." I handed him back the apple, giving him my best smile. "Consider this charity. Next time, I won't be so gracious."

The boys hollered at my response.

Maddox stared, his blue eyes pointedly holding mine. He was still grinning. I didn't know why he kept doing that – smiling like he was having the best time of his life verbally sparring with me.

I found it neither entertaining nor funny.

Pushing away from the table, I stood up and grabbed my empty tray. Riley followed suit, and we left the cafeteria.

Maddox and his buddies didn't follow.

Mrs. Levi gave me a nod of approval, and I let out a relieved sigh. "That was a fabulous explanation, Lila."

"Thank you." I started to take my seat, feeling quite pleased with myself. I had spent two hours last night writing my essay, rereading all my notes and writing out this analysis.

"I disagree." A deep baritone voice interrupted my happy moment.

Heat crept up my neck, and I flushed under the sudden scrutinizing stares coming from the rest of the class. Including *his*.

"Excuse me?" I said through gritted teeth, turning around to face Maddox. He was sitting, laid-back, in his chair.

Maddox leaned forward in his chair, crossing his arms over the desk. When he spoke, his tone was flat and disinterested. "Sometimes we're thrown into a difficult situation where we need to make a difficult choice. Sometimes, it's not the best *or* the right choice. But maybe, it's the only option we have."

"Could you elaborate on that, Maddox?" Mrs. Levi demanded.

"Throughout Greek history and mythology, Medusa has always been viewed as a villain. You made a good point that Athena is an anti-hero, but you also went ahead and painted Medusa as a villain, yet again. Medusa was once a very beautiful woman - one who was an avowed priestess of Athena. She spent her days and nights in Athena's temple. Here's what we all know… she was punished for breaking her vow of celibacy. Athena cursed her, and Medusa became the woman with serpent heads. But… was it really her fault? History said she had an affair with Poseidon. Some say he seduced her, but the article that Mrs. Levi assigned us to read revealed that it was a lie to hide the fact that, in reality, Poseidon had raped her. She was never given the chance to plead her case or to speak for herself. Poseidon said Medusa seduced him, and in a fit of anger and jealousy, Athena cursed her. Once turned into a monster, she brought terror to the temple and anyone who stepped foot inside was instantly turned into stone. Now, it's easy to categorize Athena as the antagonist. After all, *she* was the one who gave the magical mirror to the warrior, which was used to turn Medusa into stone and eventually killed her. But could it be an act of mercy?" Maddox paused, cocking his head to the side, thoughtfully. "Maybe Athena regretted turning Medusa into a monster. Maybe Athena discovered the truth about Poseidon. Maybe… killing Medusa was the only way of granting her peace. Neither Medusa nor Athena is a villain. I would say they're both anti-heroes who were thrown into a very shitty situation."

"Wow… umm that's a very interesting way of looking at it, Maddox. A very in-depth analysis, I have to say." I could hear the shock in Mrs. Levi's voice. She probably wasn't expecting that.

Me? My whole body strummed with embarrassment.

"Your analysis would have been better if you took a moment to think outside the box. Consider this constructive criticism," Maddox said, his gaze on mine. "I hope you don't mind my little tip."

I bit on my lip, trying so hard to hold back from saying something stupid in front of the class. "*Thank you.*" The words tasted bitter on my tongue.

Pressing my lips firmly together, I retook my seat.

I was hyperaware of Maddox staring at me. He hadn't skipped one English class since he made it his goal to irritate me. Maddox made sure I could feel his presence at *all* times.

He didn't want me to forget – I was the prey; he was the hunter.

As soon as the bell rang, I was the first one out of class. It was hard to admit… but I was running away.

Riley was already waiting for me in the courtyard. "Uh oh. That expression tells me Maddox pulled another one of his asshole moves again."

I threw my hands in the air, holding back a frustrated scream. "He embarrassed me in front of the class."

"What did he do *this* time?"

Riley and I settled down, cross-legged, on the cold grass. I handed her the sandwich my grandma packed for us this morning, Riley's favorite. Turkey, lettuce, cheese and homemade smoked mustard. We bit into our sandwiches while I recounted what happened in class.

"Are you pissed that he was right and made a smarter analysis than you... or, are you pissed that he called you out in front of the class?"

"I–" My mouth snapped shut because Riley...was right. She knew me so well. I'd always been competitive by nature.

I made an aggravated sound at the back of my throat before admitting the truth. "Okay, fine. I'm pissed he had a better analysis, *and* I'm annoyed he called me out like that. And, he called it *constructive criticism*. Maddox can shove it up his ass. He was trying to embarrass me."

"We've established that. You're on his shit list, but you're letting him get to you, babe."

I chewed aggressively around my last bite. "I'm not."

Riley was right, though.

Maddox Coulter, with his pretty smirk, pretty eyes and surfer hair, was having the time of his life messing with me, and I was letting him.

I clenched my fists on my lap. *Not anymore.*

CHAPTER FOUR

Lila

F irst, I heard my mom scream.

Then, there was silence. It happened within a nanosecond.

The world tilted suddenly, my vision blurring, before everything went black. I sunk into a very dark place. For the longest time, I stayed there... awake... fading... heart beating... numb... lost...

The silence slowly faded away, a buzzing noise replaced it, filling my ears. It felt like the only thing inside my head was static.

My throat was dry, scratched raw from the inside, and I couldn't make a sound.

Mommy? Daddy?

I couldn't see anything. Everything was so dark... so empty...

I remembered the sound of crushing glass, mixed with the distinct cracking of bones breaking. I remembered my mom screaming, and my dad... I remembered...

Pain came next.

My bones and fragile organs felt like they were being crumbled and smashed into a tiny, suffocating box. I couldn't breathe. It hurt so much. My torso burned like acid was being poured on it. There was a knife dug, painfully, into my chest... no, not a knife... I didn't know... but it hurt. It felt like a knife or a hammer being pounded into my chest.

I blinked... forcing myself to breathe. I couldn't. My lungs contracted with such force that I was afraid they would fold into themselves. When I coughed, agony strummed through my body, and my cracked lips parted with a silent scream.

Mom... Dad...

I couldn't speak. The buzzing noise wouldn't stop in my ears.

The taste of coppery blood pooled in my mouth; it tasted bitter, and I could feel it soaking my tongue and the inside of my mouth. Blood...?

No...

How...

What...

I remember...

The fight...snow outside... in the car... mom... dad... me...

I remember the screams...

My bones felt like they had been mangled together, and my chest, it was being carved open. I lifted my head up a bit and looked down at my chest to see... blood. Everywhere. So much blood.

I sucked in cramped air and tried to scream, tried to breathe, but my lungs refused to work.

No. No. No. Please. No. Oh God, no.

MOM, I wanted to scream. DADDY.

The pain never ended. The darkness never faded away.

I woke up with a gasp, my mouth open in a silent scream. Drenched in a cold sweat with my heart beating way too fast, I tried to suck in desperate breaths.

Ten. *Inhale.* Nine. *Exhale.* Eight. *Inhale*

I didn't die. I wasn't dead.

Seven. *Exhale.* Six. *Inhale.* Five. *Exhale.*

It was only a dream, I told myself.

Four. *Inhale.* Three. *Breathe.* Two. *Exhale.*

My chest hurt; the pain was almost crippling.

One. *Breathe, damn it.*

Hot tears stung my eyes as I held them back from spilling over my cheeks. I rubbed my chest, trying to alleviate the hammering ache. A whimper escaped past my chapped lips, and I choked back a sob.

Don't cry. Don't you dare cry.

I breathed through my nose, the fear slowly receding back, and I locked a cage around it. The pain and the taste of coppery blood faded away, and my senses came back to me.

Just a dream, I told myself.

Except...

My eyes closed, and I sniffed back my unshed tears. I did as my therapist had trained me to do--count backward from ten and breathe. So, I did, and while doing so, I locked the *memories* away.

Once my racing heart calmed to a soothing beat again, I got off the bed and started my morning routine.

While combing my hair, my eyes fell on the picture frame on my nightstand. A picture of me on my thirteenth birthday. I stood in the middle with my parents on either side of me. We were laughing; our faces smudged with cake icing.

My lips twitched at the memory, a phantom of a smile as I reminisced our time together.

I laid the hairbrush down beside the small frame. My fingers slid over the picture, caressing their faces. "I miss you," I whispered to them. "But I'm okay. I promise you. *I'm okay.*"

They kept smiling back at me.

"Lila!" My grandma's voice broke through the moment. "Breakfast is ready."

"Coming!"

I grabbed my bag and strode out of my room. Sven Wilson, ex-military man and now a retired veteran, my dearest grandpa sat at the breakfast table. With a newspaper in his hand and Grandma Molly making us pancakes, it was a typical morning.

"Good morning," I greeted them with a smile.

"Sit, sit. You're going to be late."

"She's fine. Lila is rarely late for her classes," Grandpa said. He winked before taking a sip of his tea.

I winked back because I knew he had my back. Always.

Grandma handed me a plate and patted me on the cheek. "How's school, sweetie? You've been holed up in your bedroom or the library. We haven't had time to talk."

"It's going good," I replied around a bite of my pancakes. "I like my teachers. Do you guys need help at the store? I can come over during the weekend."

Grandpa waved a hand, shaking his head. "No need. We can handle it."

I held back a smile. He refused to acknowledge that he was getting older, and they did, in fact, need help. Both of them were in their seventies, and they could no longer run the grocery store on their own. But Sven Wilson was stubborn.

"How about we put a hiring sign up? I'll do the interviews and even train them for a few days."

"Maybe that's a good idea," Grandma agreed, a tender smile on her lips.

"Got it. I'll put the sign up this weekend. I'm sure you'll get plenty of students who want to work part-time."

I quickly finished my pancakes and stood up. "Thank you for breakfast." After quickly pecking them both on the cheek, I waved goodbye and ran out of the house.

The cold breeze of October hit me, and I breathed in the morning scent. It poured last night. The smell of grass after the rain teased my nostrils, and it soothed me.

If it were any normal day, I'd say today was going to be good. But my days were no longer *normal*. Not since Maddox decided I was his plaything.

It'd been a week since the Medusa argument, and Maddox was still irritating as always, if not worse.

God give me patience.

I was standing in line in the cafeteria, waiting to get my food, when I saw him. Our eyes met, and Maddox stalked closer, as if he was on a mission. *Shit.*

I quickly put my earphones in and stared hard at my phone. Maddox came to stand behind me, the heat practically rolling off him. I could sense people staring at us, again… waiting for another dramatic scene. I'd quickly become everyone's favorite joke.

Berkshire Academy was a shark tank.

You see, in Berkshire, only the strong survive. The weaker are preyed on, chewed up, and spit out like garbage.

Maddox was on the top – the pack leader. He was *the* King, and he wore his crown with a cocky grin. He was untouchable to his rivals, and he was every girl's favorite dick to ride.

And I wanted nothing to do with him.

His body brushed against mine as he slid closer to me. Maddox nudged me with his elbow.

I ignored him. "Hey, Garcia."

I scrolled through my playlist, refusing to acknowledge him. "Damn, are you ignoring me?"

When I didn't reply, Maddox let out a mock gasp. "You wound me."

I rolled my eyes for the umpteenth time but continued to ignore him. I didn't expect him to be so bold, but when he reached forward to pull my earphones out, I released a low frustrated growl.

My body swiveled around, and I faced him. The first thing I noticed was that he was wearing his full Berkshire uniform today. The navy blazer molded to his chest and shoulders like it was tailored made, especially for him, and the beige slacks didn't hide how strong his thighs were. Instead of putting his hair into another messy man bun, he left it loose today. The tight, blond curls ended up a good inch above his shoulders.

"Do you know that when people have headphones in... it means they don't want anyone to speak to them? That's the universal sign for Stay-The-Fuck-Away-From-Me-And-Don't-Speak-To-Me," I snapped, loud enough for the people around us to hear. *Ugh.*

If looks could kill, he'd be seven feet under right now. Irritation bubbled inside of me at the fact that I had been checking him out.

Yeah, he was hot. So what? Maddox was a fine specimen to look at. Too bad, he had an aggravating personality.

Maddox leaned closer, a little smirk playing on his lips. His hot breath feathered over the skin of my exposed neck, and when he whispered in my ear, his voice was low and deep. "I'm not everyone though. I'm special."

He pulled back, his blue eyes glinting with mischief. "And I know you want me to talk to you. We didn't see each other yesterday, and I wasn't in class today. Miss me, Sweet Cheeks?"

Ha! I had two very peaceful days, and I wasn't complaining.

Crossing my arms over my chest, I let out a laugh with absolutely no trace of humor. "Cocky much?"

"I love the sound of that word coming from your lips." His gaze shifted to my lips for a second, watching them with rapt attention before he met my eyes again.

I felt the blood rush between my ears and I attempted to hold back my growl.

"Say it again," he calmly demanded, which pissed me off even more. "Slowly this time."

I took a deep breath before letting it out. I was trying so hard not to punch this dude. "Listen, Coulter. You need to back off, or I'm going to do something really bad."

"Like what?" He was testing me, pushing and pushing – waiting for what I'd do, or what I was capable of.

"I don't know. Maybe punch your dick so hard it'll retreat back into your asshole. Have you ever heard of personal space?"

My body was tight as a bowstring. He was too close to me, so close I caught the scent of his cologne and aftershave. He smelled clean and...

I didn't like the way my body suddenly decided to appreciate the way he looked or what he smelled like. "Take a step back. Now," I growled.

Maddox took a step *forward*, crowding into me and forcing me against the wall. His blue eyes darkened and all signs of mischief were suddenly gone. "I don't listen well to demands. I think you know that already. I always do the opposite. Did you, by any chance, want me closer?"

I brought my hands up and pushed against his chest, but he wouldn't budge.

"You're so full of yourself."

"You could be full of *me*. Time, date and address. You choose, Sweet Cheeks," he rasped in my ear, his lips whispering over my skin.

What... the... hell?

A voice interrupted us before I could explode. "Next."

The lady at the end of the food line called again. "Next!"

Maddox pulled away, and I could finally breathe again. I hadn't even realized I was holding my breath or that my heartbeats had been strangely irregular.

I shouldn't be feeling this way. I wasn't weak.

No, in a tank full of sharks – I would *not* be preyed on.

Straightening my spine, I pushed past him without a second glance.

Fuck you, Coulter.

And game on.

CHAPTER FIVE

Lila

"Do you want to go to the haunted house this year?"

I couldn't remember the last time I'd been to a haunted house. I hated them as a kid, but my dad would always hold my hand through them. With him, I was safe, and nothing about the haunted houses scared me.

Every Halloween, Berkshire Academy builds its own haunted house on the school grounds. It was a tradition that started a whole decade ago, and to this day, we still honored it.

I took a bite of my pizza, chewing while I contemplated Riley's question. "I guess we could check it out."

She clapped her hands, her face lighting up with excitement. "I heard it's scarier than last year. They're going all out this time. It'd be fun! How about some girl time? We go to the haunted house then a sleepover at my place? Movie and pizza?"

Riley continued to chatter with enthusiasm while I tried to ignore all the eyes on me. It was difficult when they made it so obvious. The cafeteria had become a nightmare now. I could have tucked my tail between my legs and made a run for it; I could have hidden – but I was never one to accept defeat.

Since Maddox had made me his prey, I'd been the center of attention. A year ago, when I enrolled at Berkshire, I got used to all the judgmental eyes.

Lila Garcia, the 'poor' girl. I didn't have Louis Vuitton shoes or Chanel bags or the latest iPhone. I didn't prance around with a kilo of makeup on my face nor was I a cheerleader who constantly rubbed herself against the jocks. I wasn't a *follower*.

I'd always been the outsider, but after a few months of critical eyes on me and their constant judgment, they had forgotten about me. I blended into the crowd and soon became invisible. It made life easier.

Until Maddox.

Now, the girls looked at me with contempt, like I was the dirt under their feet. They gawked at me with envy because I had Maddox's attention while the boys stared at me with obvious interest.

None have made a move though.

Riley said I was Maddox's trophy. Nobody would dare to approach me. The moment he laid eyes on me, I became untouchable to the rest of Berkshire Academy.

Ha, lucky me.

Riley snapped her fingers at my face, causing me to flinch. She smiled sweetly. "Ignore them, Lila."

I hummed in response before taking another bite of my cold pizza.

"So, haunted house and then sleepover?" Riley asked again.

"Okay, I like that idea. I'm not a big fan of haunted houses though."

"I'll hold your hand. It'll be romantic! Me and you, walking through the dark. I'll protect you from the bad guys." She cooed, like a romance hero – way too dramatic.

"Funny. Very funny. If I didn't know better, I'd say you were into pussies."

She paused, looking thoughtful for a moment. "I kissed a girl once. A few years ago. It was a dare, and I liked it. She had really soft lips, and she said I was a good kisser. Wanna find out?"

When she leaned across the table, puckering her lips up, I let out a small laugh. "Um no. Stay away from me, Riley."

"I'm disappointed," she said with a cute pout.

Riley's gaze landed behind my shoulder again, before she blushed and quickly looked away. "Okay, that's it. What's going on?"

"What?" She feigned innocence, batting her long lashes at me.

I half-looked over my shoulder before facing her again. "*Him*. You keep looking at him and blushing. What's up?"

"Nothing." She was too quick with the denial. I called bullshit.

"Riley, who is he?"

I saw the moment she gave in. Her eyes softened, and she chewed on her bottom lip. "That's Grayson."

"And?" I kicked her under the table, demanding more answers.

"I heard some whispers in the hallway. They weren't really nice. He was bullied a bit last week. Jasper and his friends were being assholes, but Grayson just ignored them and walked away. Apparently, he was living on the streets for a while before he was recently adopted by a famous lawyer and his wife. They can't have kids. We don't know much about him yet, but he's in two of my classes."

I looked over my shoulder again, finally taking a good look at Grayson who was sitting at the far end of the cafeteria in a corner by himself. "I didn't know you were into nerds."

Grayson wore a black pair of glasses perched on his nose, and he was reading a book. I could see the appeal and definitely understood why he caught Riley's eye.

"He's a nerd, but did you see him? He's hot with a capital H O T."

54

But he's kinda moody. He doesn't really talk to anyone. Typical loner. But he's smart and we bumped into each other last week. Remember the bruises on my knees? Yeah, Grayson took me to the infirmary after I fell down, and he noticed my knees bleeding."

Aha… I remembered that incident. I had found Riley in the infirmary; she was alone, but now that I remembered – she had been blushing heavily and was a stuttering mess.

"Well, at least he's not an asshole."

Riley let out a dreamy sigh. "He's sweet. Except he barely spared me a glance. I said *hi* to him a few times, and he just…ignored me. Apparently, he doesn't like when people talk to him."

"I didn't think the nerdy ones were your type…"

The last boy Riley dated was a jock and an asshole. After Jasper, it made sense why she'd swear off all the guys like him.

"Fine, I'll confess my secret. I like nerds. There's just something attractive about them."

I couldn't deny that Grayson was indeed appealing to the eye.

"Hot and moody nerds, you mean."

Riley popped a piece of mint gum into her mouth. She looked over my shoulder again, where her new crush was sitting. "Exactly," she chirped.

I quirked up an eyebrow at her. "*Grayson*, specifically."

"Yeah. Too bad he won't even look at me." The pout was evident in her voice.

"Is that why you wore extra makeup today, curled your hair, and rolled your skirt higher?"

I already knew the answer, but I still wanted to hear it from her.

A nervous laugh bubbled out of her, and she twirled a lock of hair around her finger. "You noticed that?"

My sweet friend. Gripping her hand over the table, I gave her a small, comforting squeeze. "Just be yourself, Riley. If he likes you, you'll know."

She let out a sigh, her eyes moving to Grayson one last time before she focused on me. "So, what's up with you and Maddox?"

I crooked my finger at her, and Riley leaned closer, as if we were about to share a secret. It kind of was – *a secret.*

"He wants a fight? I'm going to give him a fight."

Riley's face lit up, and a huge smile spread across her lips. "We're going to be bad?"

Well, if she put it that way… then yeah, we were about to be very bad.

"Oh, we're going to play *his* games, but with *my* rules."

She slapped the table loud enough to rattle our trays and smirked. "I'm in!"

My lips twitched, and I held back my own smile. Maddox was about to be bested at his own little, shitty game.

"Can you see him?" I asked, leaning closer to Riley. It was two hours after school, and we were hiding in the hallway, which also overlooked the huge football field. Where, very conveniently, the boys were practicing. They had a very important game in a week, and I heard the coach was being extra hard on all their asses.

"I can't believe we're hiding with binoculars, Lila. But yeah, I can see him. He's playing just fine. Did you put a lot of the powder in his pants?"

"No, just a little, but enough to make him lose his mind."

An unladylike snort came from Riley. "You're so petty."

I let out a mock gasp, but the urge to defend myself was strong. "He started it."

"Aha! Okay, he just stopped in the middle of the game."

"Yeah?"

Riley looked into her binoculars, her shoulders shaking with mirth. "Oh, he looks confused. The coach is walking over to him. Lila!" she whispered-yelled, before bursting into laughter. "He's scratching at his inner thighs now. Oh my God, he looks like a monkey. The boys are hollering. Oh, oh, shit. He's walking back this way. Ohhh, he looks pissed!"

Good.

"How pissed?" I demanded, feeling mighty proud of myself. Maddox was made of rock. He was untouchable, and if little ole me, Lila Garcia, could get him *this* pissed off – then I won.

"He's reaaally mad. He's still scratching himself. You should see the look on his face!"

Riley handed me the binoculars, and I looked through them. True to her words, Maddox was marching across the field like a mad bull. His face was filled with rage, his nostrils flaring like a wild beast. He was seething, and I could bet, he figured out what happened. Maybe not *who* was behind the prank, but at least *what* was done to him. It should have scared me, the brutal look on his face, but I couldn't help but chortle with laughter at the way he couldn't stop scratching at his muscled thighs and crotch.

As if he could sense me, his stormy eyes connected with mine through the binoculars, although I was sure there was no way he could see me. Riley and I were hidden perfectly.

But just in case, I lowered myself to the ground. "Hey, are you sure... it's safe? I mean, I wanted to prank him, but what we did isn't too extreme, right?"

Riley waved away my concerns. "Nah. He'll be fine. The itching powder doesn't leave any lasting side effects. It's harmless. I kinda feel bad for Maddox Junior though."

My jaw clenched as I remembered the cafeteria scene where he had cornered me. "He deserves it after the comment he made in the cafeteria. He propositioned me for sex, like I'm some kind of paid who–"

Riley slapped a hand over my mouth before I could finish my

sentence. "Shh, he's coming in."

We both ducked around the corner, the same time Maddox stormed into the building and right into the locker room.

"I feel like a spy," Riley announced in my ear, giggling softly.

Basically, we were *spying* on him.

Riley and I snuck closer to the locker room. The door was partially opened, and we peeked inside. It was empty, since everyone else was on the field – except Maddox. From where we stood, we could hear the shower running.

"He must be itching really bad right now."

I shushed Riley when she couldn't hold in her laughter any longer.

"Can you see him?"

I stood on my tip-toes, trying to get a look inside. "Nope."

A few minutes later, the shower turned off and then I did see him.

"Oh," Riley whispered behind me.

Yeah, oh.

Maddox was bare chested, with a towel wrapped loosely around his hips. His body was still wet and glistening as if he didn't care to dry himself the moment he stepped out of the shower. He roughly rubbed another towel through his long curly hair, before running it over the rest of his body.

I hated him; I truly did, but there was no denying it; something about his physique was making my lady brain go mushy and all my lady parts tingle. I inhaled deeply as I took in the sight in front of me.

Maddox furiously wiped the ringlets of water from his muscled chest until his skin was glowing pink. I tried to look away – it was the decent thing to do, but I failed miserably. My curious eyes found his torso, and I bit my lip, mentally slapping myself but I. Could. Not. Help. It.

It was like studying an expertly, carved statue in a museum. Beautifully chiseled chest, strong arms and well-defined masculine thighs. Auguste Rodin would have begged to sculpt a man like Maddox Coulter since he was damn near close to rugged perfection.

"Even his nipples are sexy," Riley whispered.

My heart slammed in my chest, and I bumped back into her. I had completely forgotten she was there with me, and she was also getting an eyeful of Maddox.

I watched as he wrenched his locker open and rummaged through it. The effects of the itching powder were still not gone since he was still scratching at his crotch.

I could tell the moment he read the note I left him. His back went rigid, and the muscles of his shoulders clenched tensely. Maddox turned sideways, giving me a perfect view of him as he scrunched my little note in his fist.

How does your crotch feel? – Lila

First rule of enacting a well, plotted out revenge plan: always leave a note behind, so your nemesis knows it's you. Play dirty but don't be a coward.

He muttered something under his breath and shook his head, before he did something unexpected. I knew he'd be furious, and he was, but then his lips twitched. Maddox rubbed his thumb over his full, smirking lips.

"Uh oh," Riley muttered from behind me. "I'm not sure I like the look on his face."

"Ladies, what are you doing here?" Another voice joined us, loud enough to have my heart leap in my throat, and I choked back a gasp.

Riley and I jumped away from the locker room, and we swiveled around to see a teacher giving us *the* look. Oh shit, busted.

"It's late. Why are you two still on school grounds?" She demanded with her hands on her hips.

"Um, we forgot something," I stammered, looking back toward Maddox while contemplating my escape.

Maddox's head turned toward me at the same time, and through the partially opened door, for only a nanosecond, our gazes collided.

His deep, ocean blue eyes flared in surprise, and I could swear his stare burned through me, causing a warm flush to spread through my body. Then... the moment was gone.

Riley grabbed my hand, already pulling me away. "Sorry! We're leaving."

We sprinted out of the school, and once we passed through the Berkshire's main gate, Riley and I came to a halt.

"Shit. That was close," Riley panted with her hands on her knees.

"So worth it though."

She straightened her back, one perfect eyebrow raised. "Are you sure? Maddox is not the type who is going to let you off the hook. Revenge is a dish best served cold. He's going to get you back, probably not tomorrow or the day after, but he will – trust me, and I don't think it's going to be pretty."

"He shouldn't have messed with me. I'm prepared for anything he's going to throw my way," I responded, fighting back a smile of my own.

I remembered the look in Maddox's eyes when our gaze briefly met in the locker room. I didn't admit it out loud, but I wanted to see what Maddox could do and how far he was going to push me. It was too tempting to mess with him, to retaliate after seeing Maddox's reaction – he started this game, and now, I was all in.

CHAPTER SIX

Maddox

The girl on my lap grinded against me. Her tits were practically spilling out of her tight red dress, and she shoved them in my face. I gripped her ass in one hand and smoked a blunt with the other. Miss-Fake-Tits let out a moan, which sounded straight out of a porn video.

Although I've seen better acted porn. She was inexperienced and quite an amateur. Trying too hard, with too little self-respect.

Easy pussy, easy fuck. I didn't have to hunt for them; they landed right on my lap.

"Maddox," she purred in my ear. My jaw twitched as I caught a whiff of her strong perfume and the stench of alcohol was strong on her breath. She was drunk and humping me like a bitch in heat.

Any other day, I'd be all up in her pussy... tonight, my dick was not in the mood.

Or I guessed, I was not in the mood for *her*.

On the opposite couch, Colton had his tongue shoved down a girl's throat. Brayden and Cole were in a heated conversation about this week's football match. We won, big time. Leighton High School wasn't even worth our time. Knox, our best linebacker, was missing, but he was probably in a room lost in pussy.

And I was fucking bored.

Drunk and bored.

The party we crashed was lame, and I needed some kind of action, something to get my blood pumping – something dangerous. I was itching for a fight and a good lay. Too bad the girl on my lap had absolutely no effect on my dick.

Her lips parted, and I felt her tongue on my neck. She sucked on my throat, biting teasingly. "Let's get out of here. Go somewhere quieter."

"If you wanna fuck, we do it here."

She pulled away, her green eyes hooded and confused. "*Here?*"

I lifted an eyebrow, amused. The only reason she was sitting on my lap and humping me was because she needed to sleep with a Berkshire football star, so she could go around and rub it in the other girls' faces. I was her ticket to being Miss Popular at Leighton Public High School -- Berkshire's rival.

"Too shy for a little audience?"

She looked around, stammering, "No-o."

I squeezed her ass, not even bothering to be gentle about it. That was a warning. "I don't do sweet girls."

Nah, sweet girls didn't do shit for my libido.

Feisty girls, though, yeah… they made my dick hard.

Full of sass with brown eyes, black hair, curvy hips and a pretty Latina ass that would make any man drop to his knees, begging for a taste.

Goddamn fucking trouble she was, but she was exactly what I wanted.

Lila Garcia.

Too bad she didn't want me anywhere near her.

I took a hit off the blunt one last time and exhaled a puff of smoke, not bothering to move my head away. I knew I was being an asshole, but hey... chicks like her wanted jerks like me – so who the fuck cared?

Dropping the now useless blunt onto the ashtray, I leveled her with a look. She scrunched her nose, but her eyes flared with determination. What she didn't realize – I ate girls like her for dinner before spitting them out two hours later, no guilt with one very satisfied dick.

I curled a hand around the back of her neck, bringing her head closer. "You want a taste of me? We do it *my* way."

She looked around again, her cheeks flushed, and she was already a little bit out of breath. "Do you even know my name?"

"Do you know mine?" I threw back, although the answer was obvious. Of course, she knew who I was. Miss-Fake-Tits was only here to use me like I was about to use her. Fair game.

"Who doesn't? You're Maddox Coulter. And for your information, my name is Madison."

She thought she was special. Newsflash – she wasn't the type of girl I'd wake up the next morning with. I arched an eyebrow with a *tsk*. "Here's the thing, I don't need to know your name to fuck you."

Miss-Fake-tits, er... *Madison*, wrapped her arms around my shoulders. Her hips moved in a circular motion, quite tempting as she practically grinded against me through our clothes. Any passerby would have thought we were fucking.

She let out a fake giggle. "Didn't your mommy or daddy teach you some manners?"

She was teasing; it was only a joke.

But the silent rage inside me bubbled over, threatening to burst through, without any care of the consequences. Fuck her. And fuck mommy and daddy dearest, too. Manners? No, they didn't teach me any – just like they didn't give a shit if I lived or died, either.

I crashed the party because I wanted to *forget*.

63

But Madison, aka *Bitch,* right here, just pissed me off even more.

She reminded me of why I was *here*, made me think of my parents when I was so hell bent on forgetting their existence.

Daddy dearest caught me smoking today, lounging on the couch and watching TV. He walked in with his business associate. Oh, he knew I smoked, except he never cared. But Brad Coulter didn't want me to set a bad example in front of his business partners; his image had always been more important than my health.

"You don't smoke in my house," he hissed in my face, taking a threatening step toward me. There was a time when my father was taller and bigger than me. He used to be intimidating, and his words were law in our house. But that time was long gone.

Now, I was bigger... taller... meaner.

He didn't scare me.

Now, he just pissed me off more often than not.

"I've been smoking since I was thirteen. Never knew we had a rule. You didn't seem to care before, father."

His lips curled up in disgust, and I felt it. I fucking felt it – his anger, his disappointment, his revulsion. My hands clenched into fists, and I exhaled through my nose. At a young age, I had quickly learned how to mask my emotions until I became a solid wall of nothingness. You'd cut me open, and you'd find something hollow inside.

"I constantly question if you really are my son."

When I was seven years old, my heart had frozen in my chest. But his words, to this day, could still burn me like acid in my veins. My father held an arrow in his hand, the tip of it aflame, and it was aimed right at my chest – my goddamn heart was his target.

"Nah. I'm definitely your son. You're an asshole, I'm an asshole. It runs in our blood."

His blue eyes – the same as mine, darkened and his face was vicious.

"Brad." My mother's soft voice interrupted us. "They're waiting. Let's

go. Maddox, go back to your room. This deal is important to your father."
I heard her unspoken words. Please, for Christ's sake, don't ruin it.
He took a step back, his jaw hard and twitching. Without sparing me
another glance, he walked away. I saw the look in my mother's eyes, her
parted lips, and I waited for her to say something. But there was nothing
left to say, so she walked away, too.

And so, I'd been dismissed. I saw my parents after three weeks, and
without even a greeting, I had been brushed off and forgotten. Yet again.

Just like ten years ago...

When I had needed them the most. I was left behind, locked away in
the dark... forgotten.

"Maddox," she purred in my ear again. I blinked, the past going out of focus, and I crashed landed in the present.

I had called Colton after the 'fight' with my father. He didn't have to ask me questions, he *knew* what I needed. So, here we were. Crashing Leighton's party, knowing full well we were about to piss off a whole bunch of people.

Yeah, that was exactly what I needed.

A good fight, a good fuck.

Marley – wait, no – Madison rubbed her hands over my chest and shoulders. "You're so big and strong. So hard, in all the right places."

She was so eager to please me, so eager to be *just* another girl on my list.

My fingers tangled in her hair, twisting the thick blonde strands around my fist. My knuckles dug into her scalp, and she winced, before quickly hiding it with a fake-ass smile. Without care, I pushed her on the ground. She collapsed to her knees with a low whine, her wide eyes blinking up at me, unfocused, confused, and with way too many expectations.

Her pink lips parted, *waiting,* and I figured why-the-fuck-not. With one hand, I unbuckled my jeans. "Let's put your deepthroating skills to good use, shall we?"

Her face lit up, and she scooted closer between my thighs. Maybe she wouldn't be such a bad lay after all. At least she was willing to suck dick. Some bitches thought they were too pretty and fancy to be on their knees.

A loud snarl came from outside, making all of us pause. There was more shouting, and through my hazy mind, I realized Colton was no longer in the same room. Brayden and Cole looked at each other, too, confused.

"Isn't he from Berkshire?" The whispers started to get louder.

Brayden and Cole shot off the couch at the same time as me. Miss-Fake-Tits shrieked as she fell back hard on her ass. "What the hell?"

No fucks were given.

I buckled up my jeans before marching outside, Brayden and Cole following closely behind. *Ah shit.*

Colton was standing in the middle of the front lawn, smiling like a goddamn maniac, while he was surrounded by a bunch of Leighton boys.

"Your girl wanted her pussy eaten," he announced, loud enough for all of us gathered to hear. "You weren't doing a good enough job, man."

The girl in question, who was the same girl on his lap a few minutes before, sputtered a half-ass excuse. Her face was bright red, and she hid behind her friends.

I noticed Samuel, Leighton's Quarterback, charging forward. Ah, so he was the boyfriend. This was also *his* party, and *we* weren't invited.

Yeah, we were trouble with a capital T.

Colton was able to block the first punch, which only served to piss off Samuel more. He was livid as he tried to bring Colton to the ground, quite unsuccessfully.

It was a fair fight…until it wasn't.

The Leighton boys came forward, surrounding Colton until he was trapped.

"Fuck no," Brayden growled.

My jaw locked, and the fire inside me burnt like lava, liquid hot and fiery. We cut through the mass of people, the itching need to fight putting all of us on an adrenaline rush.

Without giving it much thought, I yanked one of the boys away, and he fell backward. Weak and useless.

Samuel spun around, his face red and a mask of fury. My fingers curled into a fist, and before he could blink, my fist made contact with his face. Not so pretty face anymore, huh?

He roared but swiveled back around quickly, blocking my next hit. The alcohol was fucking with my senses now, and he caught me in the ribs. The pain coursing through my body fueled me to fight harder and meaner.

He lunged at me, swinging but missing. I could hear the others fighting, the brawl getting louder and messier.

This wasn't just a fight. It was retaliation. It was a fight based on ego -- who had the bigger balls, who was stronger.

I drove my shoulder into Samuel's chest, slamming him into the ground. He tackled me back, but I was able to land solid punches into his gut. We were both walking out of here with at least one cracked rib.

My father's disappointment – *punch.*

My mother's lack of care – *punch.*

My fucked up childhood – *punch, punch, punch.*

The suffocating darkness, a constant reminder – *punch.*

My knuckles were bleeding and raw, my left eye was swollen shut, but I. Couldn't. Fucking. Stop.

Brushed-off and forgotten.

Enraged and lost.

Through my hazy brain, I heard Colton shouting. My head snapped toward him, seeing him rush toward me. My eyes widened for a nanosecond before the bottle cracked against my temple.

My body slumped forward as the ringing of my ears amplified, my chest caving in as I tried to *breathe*. My heartbeat slowed and the metallic taste of blood filled my mouth.

My vision blurred, and I didn't see the punch coming.

I only *felt* it.

My jaw cracked, and I fell back, my head hitting the ground.

Breathe.

Breathe.

Fucking breathe.

The world slowed.

I blinked. Once. Twice.

Silence replaced the ringing in my ears as the world went black.

CHAPTER SEVEN

Lila

"**Y**ou're late, Mr. Coulter."

My head snapped up at Mrs. Levi's voice and Maddox's name. Everyone seemed to have the same train of thought since we all looked up at the same time as Maddox walked into the classroom. Contrary to his usual swagger and smirk, he was brooding and quiet.

Except that wasn't what caught my attention.

No, it was the fact that his beautiful face was messed up.

His left eye appeared swollen and that side of his face was heavily bruised. He had a band-aid on his eyebrow, and there was a cut on the corner of his full lips. It looked painful, and even I winced at the sight of him like *this*. Instead of a man bun, his curly hair was left loose, and I had a feeling he was hiding behind them.

People talked; Berkshire's hallways were never without rumors. There was always something going on. A new break-up, a new student, a bully, someone caught cheating. There was always some kind of drama.

Yesterday, when Maddox didn't show up at school, we heard there was a fight between Leighton and Berkshire boys. They said Maddox landed in the hospital with a slight concussion.

I had brushed off the rumors and thought it was a peaceful day – finally.

But now, seeing Maddox like *this*...

He didn't spare me a glance, taking his seat at the back of the classroom. I waited for the warmth that would always accompany his burning stare, but I felt... *nothing*.

Glancing over my shoulder, I took a peek. Maddox stared down at his notebook, a frozen statue in time. He didn't stare back, didn't tease, and unlike the last few weeks, the playful Maddox disappeared. In his place was a bitter, sulking boy.

I turned away and looked at my own paper. Why did I care? I shouldn't be bothered by his change of attitude. He was having a shitty day, so what? Everyone had bad days. Hell, *I* knew the exact meaning of shitty days.

When the bell rang, I didn't move from the chair. I couldn't bring myself to, even though I should have gotten up and walked away. *Like always.*

Instead, I found myself waiting.

Maddox walked past me, without a word or a fleeting look. He didn't bump into me, didn't pull my hair, didn't throw me one of his annoying smirks. *Nothing.*

I blinked, confused at my own mixed feelings.

I didn't care; I shouldn't care.

Any other decent person would have ignored Maddox and moved on – probably be thankful for another peaceful day.

Me?

I found myself following him.

Oh, how the tables have turned.

Maybe it was the fact that I was ready for him today. The last few weeks, Maddox had been a constant pain in my ass, and as much as I hated to admit it, I'd grown used to him being a jerk. The verbal sparring and the pranks became a part of my daily routine, and somehow, I found myself *disappointed* that Maddox wasn't in the same mood.

"You're dumb," I muttered to myself as I followed behind Maddox, only a few steps away. "Stupid, stupid, stupid."

Turn back. Walk away. Now.

You see, there are two sides to Lila. The indifferent side of her and the intrigued Lila – I was currently the latter.

Something about Maddox was different today, and it intrigued me. I had always liked puzzles, and Maddox Coulter was a difficult one to solve.

Maddox stopped by his locker, and he carelessly stuffed his books in there. His irritation was apparent, and he wasn't even trying to mask it. No wonder everyone was keeping their distance from him. The students stared, but quickly scrambled away, when he directed his scowls at them.

I should have kept my distance, too. Ignored him and walked away.

But apparently, I liked to play with fire and to push my boundaries. Maddox and I were playing tug-of-war. It was an everyday battle between us.

Stopping a mere foot from him, I leaned my shoulder against the locker next to Maddox. "Is it shark week?" I remarked with a grin.

He didn't spare me a glance, but his lips had thinned into a hard line, his jaw tensed. Maddox's blue eyes darkened, but he otherwise ignored me. The scowl on his face was intimidating, but it only made me want to push his buttons even more. "Did your period attack you today?"

He blew out a breath before slamming his locker shut. His knuckles were red and bruised. The wounds on Maddox only made him appear more brutal... and slightly *broken*.

Maybe that was why he piqued my interest.

My grandma always said I was fixer. Since I was a kid, I always picked up the stray cats and the injured birds. Our house was a tiny zoo for all my little friends.

Too bad Maddox Coulter was not a friend.

He was my nemesis, and I didn't want to fix him, I reminded myself.

"What do you want?" he asked, his voice low and hard. A shiver ran down my spine, and I stood up straighter, hiding the obvious effect he had on me and my body.

"Just wondering if you need a tampon. Or, do you already have one stuffed up your ass? Is that why you're so grumpy?"

"For fuck's sake," Maddox grumbled.

"Ah. Definitely shark week." I waited for him to snap, but he only gritted his teeth together, so hard I wondered how his jaw didn't crack under the pressure. "It's okay, you'll eventually get used to all the messy hormones. If you need any advice on how to deal with it, I can make a PowerPoint for you."

"Not in the mood for your pranks, Garcia."

"You love my pranks."

My stomach dipped when his chest rumbled with a low growl. "Get out of my way."

He tried to walk past me, but I was having none of that. Could be my curiosity or my stubbornness, but I wasn't ready for him to leave.

I sidestepped into his path. Maddox squared his wide shoulders, standing taller, and his eyes narrowed on me. "*Move.*" There was a warning in his voice, but I chose to ignore it.

"Are you okay?" I asked before I could stop myself.

I told myself I wasn't worried nor did I care, but still… the question popped out before I thought it over.

Maddox leaned down toward me, bringing our faces closer and crowding into me. I fidgeted with the straps of my school bag, holding myself in place and refusing to step back. He didn't intimidate me.

"If I didn't know better, I'd say you *care*, Garcia." My breath caught in my throat when our eyes made contact. He held me there, in the moment, before he flashed me a sardonic smile. "What is it? Finally decided to sit on my dick? I might make an exception for you. I'll tell you all about my day if you let me in your pus–"

"You know, two minutes ago, I actually cared. But never mind, I take it back now. You're still a jerk, Coulter."

Maddox pulled back, straightening to his full height again. "Always have been, always will be. Remember that, Sweet Cheeks. Ain't no pussy gonna tame me and definitely not yours."

Good. Lord.

The urge to smack him was strong, and the urge to slap myself for being stupid enough to care was *also* strong.

I came to a very important conclusion: I preferred Maddox silent. Why did I even try to get him to talk? The moment he opened his mouth, I realized why I *despised* him. He was an asshole, through and through.

I shuffled through my bag and took out two very important items, shoving them in his hands. His dark eyebrows pulled together in confusion.

"Tampons and chocolate," I explained with a fake smile. "You're welcome. Have a good day, Maddox."

I pushed past him, and just before I walked away, his lips *twitched*.

Did I just get Maddox Coulter to smile?

"Can you stop following me?" I paused and then turned on my heels quickly. Maddox caught himself in time, coming to a halt, so he wouldn't bump into me.

After our 'conversation' right before lunch, the rest of the day took a sudden turn. Maddox decided to follow me around; he was like a lost puppy – Riley's words, although I only found him to be irritating, so maybe more like an *annoying* puppy.

I wished we could go back to 'silent, brooding' Maddox. That version of him was ten times better than *this.*

I looked up at his bruised face, making sure to harden my heart at the sight of him battered and bruised. "Stop. Following. Me."

He shrugged, nonchalantly, and then stuffed his hands into the pockets of his beige slacks. "Can't do that. I'm having fun looking at your ass. By the way, do you mind if I warm my hands up?"

Exasperated, I let out a tiny growl from under my breath before I could stop myself. He was smiling now. As if pissing me off was his favorite pastime.

"That's sexual harassment, Coulter."

"You looking at my dick print is sexual harassment, too, Garcia."

My eyes widened at his words, and I felt the air being sucked out of me. "Wha-at? No…no I wasn't," I sputtered. My gaze fleeted to his crotch before I could stop myself. Shit. Biting on my lip, I blinked and looked away – anywhere but at *him.*

Maddox let out a throaty chuckle, and my eyes snapped back to his. He gave me his signature smirk, his dimple popping, creating a sexy indent into his left cheek. "You were, Sweet Cheeks. You were probably calculating how thick and how long I am, too."

My jaw snapped together, and I hissed through gritted teeth, "Shut. Up."

"Want me to tell you?" He quirked up a mocking eyebrow. "Or, you want to check for yourself? It's a little cold today, maybe you can warm my dick up with your little hands."

He acted as if he was reaching for my hands, but I slapped him away. In a blink, his arm snaked out, and he gripped my wrist, pulling me closer until our bodies were *almost* touching. My neck craned up, so I could stare into his face – he was too tall compared to my own tiny height. The top of my head barely came to his shoulders.

"You are disgusting," I hissed, feeling my cheeks warming up under his dark, teasing eyes.

His breath feathered over my cheek; his lips way too close to my ear. "I am proudly *filthy*, Sweet Cheeks, and so are you. For having these dirty, dirty thoughts."

I suddenly felt hot. Sweat beaded on my neck and between my breasts. My chest heaved with a shallow breath as my insides shuddered at the mere proximity of him.

His lips grazed my earlobe, and my body tensed. I tried to twist my arm out of his grip, but it was pointless. My other hand landed on his hard chest, and I shoved him back. "Fuck off."

He let go of my hand and took a step back, his bruised lips quirking up on the side. "See you tomorrow, Garcia."

I flipped him the finger and started walking away. *Asshole.*

CHAPTER EIGHT

Lila

I felt him before I saw him.

His enticing scent engulfed me as he pushed against my back, barely touching, but still way too close.

"What do you want, Coulter? Was today not enough for you?" I asked with a heavy sigh.

It was not a good day, not after the stupid prank Maddox pulled on me. My wet hair was currently soaking the back of my Berkshire's blouse, the soft material sticking to my skin. I was irritated and absolutely exhausted. One more class left and then it was the weekend. Two blissful days without Maddox.

"Looks like you were able to wash your hair." He chortled at his own lame joke. "Sorry about the feathers, but it was payback. Don't be such a grumpy ass, Garcia. You can be a sweet ass, though. I'll eat it."

I swiveled around and leveled the douchebag with a glare. "You think gluing feathers in my hair is funny?"

I wanted to throttle him and his stupid, smirking face.

"Don't exaggerate. I didn't use glue. I used flour, water and feathers. Simple and harmless. Anyway, you looked cute with a nesting head."

Mr. Asshole here glued, oh wait, my bad – *pasted* feathers into my cute beanie with flour and water. So, naturally, when I put on my beanie, all the sticky feathers transferred to my hair. No, I didn't look at my beanie before putting it on. Who does that, anyway?

My fists clenched and unclenched as I sucked in a deep breath and held back a snarl. Maddox rubbed his jaw, and against my own accord, I took notice that his face was healing up nicely. His bruises were barely noticeable, and his left eye was no longer swollen, black and purple.

He was back to his sexy, irritating self. *God give me patience.*

Maddox closed my locker, leaning against it like he owned the thing. I gave him a blank look, waiting for this to be over. The hallways were empty, except for the two of us.

"The pink hair prank? That was actually a good one, I'll give you that. The feathers were payback for the pink hair you gave me."

Ah, the pink hair. A few days ago, after Maddox left a butt-plug in my locker, *a gift*, he had written in his note – I decided to retaliate. The need for revenge was strong, and it was easy. I had sneaked into the locker room while Riley kept guard outside. I found his personal locker and switched his shampoo with temporary pink hair dye.

"Itching powder though? Lame as fuck, Garcia."

"It was a reminder."

He arched an eyebrow, waiting for me to explain.

"That's what happens when you lay around with whores. You end up with an itchy dick. Also, a reminder that I'm not someone you can mess around with. *Remember* that next time you proposition me for sex like a paid whore."

"That was a nice thought, except… I don't need to pay someone for sex. My name comes with a label, baby. Maddox-Coulter-Will-Fuck-You-

77

So-Hard-You-Will-See-Jesus."

"Where did you find that definition? Dickpedia?"

"If you open dickpedia to the word *orgasmic*, you'll find my name there."

I rolled my eyes while mentally facepalming myself. Why did I even bother to have a conversation with him? It was completely useless. The only thing that came out of his mouth was sex, sex and more sex. Or something completely dumb.

"You know what your problem is?"

"What?" I raked my fingers through my wet hair, frustrated.

"You want me," he said, as calmly as if he was announcing the weather. *Oh, it's sunny. Oh, you want to fuck me.* This man was mentally unstable, period.

"Excuse me?" I placed my hands on my hips, astonished he could even come to *this* conclusion.

"You want me, but you don't want to admit it. You're fighting the chemistry." Maddox lazily eyed me up and down. There was no embarrassment, no awkwardness from him. He was practically undressing me with his eyes, and he was being so casual about it. When he spoke again, his voice lowered to a deeper tone. "Does fighting with me make you wet? We could fight in bed, let's not waste time here."

"If your brain was as big as your ego, maybe you'd be more appealing."

Maddox grinned harder and then let out a deep chuckle. "I'm not sure about my ego or how big it is, but I can assure you, I got something big here." He cupped his crotch and raised a mocking eyebrow.

Annoyed, I pushed away from the wall. He was so goddamn rude, immature and vulgar. "You think every girl wants you. You really think you're every woman's wet dream, don't you?"

"I know I am."

Maddox moved closer, forcing me to take a step back. He stalked me, coming closer and closer until I was forced to press my back against the wall. I shivered, not because of him, I told myself. Because my hair was wet and cold and now that I was plastered against the wall, it only caused my wet blouse to stick onto my back like a second skin.

He leaned forward, bending his head to be level with me. His lips caressed my ear, and it tickled. I went to pull away, but he was quicker. His arms came up, and he caged me against the wall, his palms on either side of my head. He barely touched me, but his body was so close, his heat pressing into me, caressing me and causing a warm flush to spread throughout my body.

My thighs quaked, and my lower stomach tensed with his close proximity. "And you know what? One day I'm going to be your wet dream, too. Picture this: You'll be alone in bed at night, unable to sleep. My face flashes in front of your eyes and your stomach clenches. Your thighs are spread open and your pussy feels warm but strangely, empty. There's an aching need in the pit of your stomach. You won't be able to stop yourself. Your hands find their way into your panties, and you feel how wet you are with your fingers. You bite on your lip to keep from moaning. You touch yourself slowly, a little confused. A little frustrated. You'll think: Why can't I stop thinking about him? You're going to hate it, but you'll still love it. And you know what you're going to do?"

My skin was on fire, my body burned, and I couldn't *breathe*. My stomach dipped and twisted as the air felt like it was being sucked out of my body.

My heart stuttered when I felt his body pressing into me, finally *touching* me.

"You'll finger your pussy while imagining it's me on top of you, pressing against you, and it's *my* cock fucking you. Not your little fingers," Maddox breathed into my ear, whispering the dirty fantasy as if he was making dirty love to me.

Horrified, I could only blink, trying to remind myself to breathe. He shouldn't be able to affect me this way, he shouldn't be able to control my thoughts like *this*.

I was not weak, no... Maddox... couldn't...

He pulled away slightly to look into my face. His eyes were so blue, I almost drowned in them. "It won't happen today. Or tomorrow. Or next week. But one day, for sure. And no, I'm not being cocky. Cocky is for boys who don't know what they're doing. Me? I know exactly what I'm doing. I know for a fact it will happen. Fight it if you can."

He pushed away from me, and the cold washed over me as if I had been carelessly dunked into the ocean.

I silently gasped for breath as Maddox walked backward, away from me. The look on his face was something I've never seen before.

"I dare you, Lila."

I padded barefoot into my room, fresh from my shower and still wrapped in nothing but my fluffy towel. My phone pinged with a message, and I walked over to the nightstand to see it was from Riley.

What time are you leaving?

I typed out a quick message back. *I'll catch the bus in 20 minutes.*

The three little dots appeared on my screen, indicating she was typing.

If you want, I can pick you up, and we can go together.

My thumb paused over my phone as I read her sentence. My ears rang with the distant sound of glass shattering and bones crushing. The taste of metallic blood filled every corner of my mouth, and I almost choked on it. Except, there was no blood. I was choking on my own saliva, and the air surrounding me turned heavy, cold...suffocating.

My fingers trembled as I typed back my message to Riley. *I can't. You know I can't. I'm sorry. I'll take the bus.*

She knew the reason, and I also knew she was only trying to help, but there was no need. I was beyond helping when it came to...

I shook my head, clearing out the blurry flashes in front of my eyes and refusing to think of the night my whole life changed.

Grabbing my blow dryer, I leveled it over my head and made sure to work through every tangled strand of hair with my comb. Once my hair was dry and shiny, I made a French styled twin braid on top of my head with twin ponytails. It was cute and made my face look rounder and more symmetrical.

My reflection through the floor length mirror stared back at me. My hand traveled to my chest over my towel, where it was slowly coming undone. The top of my breasts came into view, and my eyes caught the scars. The long, jagged white lines snaked straight down from the middle of my petite breasts.

I let my towel slip through my fingers, the full scar now visible through the mirror. The skin around it was a bit pinker than the rest. It was healed up properly, but I didn't think it would ever completely fade away. Sometimes it ached, like a ghostly echo of the real agony I went through.

Pain washed over me like a raging storm, and my knees threatened to buckle under me. My eyes burned as tears hung on my lower lashes, and I furiously blinked them away, refusing to cry. My heart wailed, but I refused to shed any tears.

I slowly brought my hand up and lightly brushed it down the scar, tracing the pink-white lines. The tips of my fingers barely touched my skin, and I clenched my hand into a fist, holding back my tremors.

They said I stopped breathing on the operating table – I died for a moment before they brought me back.

I wondered... if maybe. . . it would have been easier if I really was dead.

But then I remembered... I was alive for them – my parents.

I averted my gaze from the mirror. It has been four years since I got the scars, but I still couldn't look at them for longer than two minutes.

They were a beautiful reminder that I was alive... but also an ugly reminder of that night and all that I lost.

Grabbing my ripped jeans and a matching sweater, I quickly got dressed, so I wouldn't miss my bus. My grandparents were still at their grocery store, so before locking the door behind me, I made sure to turn on the alarm.

The moment I stepped out, I was thankful the sweater was my first option when the cold air hit me. It was mid-October; the sun was already at the horizon, and the Haunted House opened in less than an hour.

The bus ride was short, and Riley was waiting for me outside the main gate of Berkshire. This year, they used the gymnasium and the outer field as the haunted house. Apparently, it was a big project, and I could see that. Everything looked expensive and... creepy.

Creepy and scary things were not my forte. Hell, I didn't even watch horror movies because they would give me nightmares for months.

Shit.

"I'm not sure I like this haunted house idea, Riley."

She pulled at my arm, dragging me across the field and toward the fake mausoleum. "Don't be a scaredy cat. Let's go. I already paid for our tickets, and it'll be fun!"

I dug my feet into the grass right before we could pass through the creepy, wooden door. "Wait, Ri–"

With one harsh tug, she pulled me forward before I could contemplate my decision. *Okay, that's it. I'm going to die.*

The moment we stepped inside, we were swallowed by darkness, and the screams of previous victims who have entered this dark place. "And if I die?"

"You're exaggerating," Riley muttered under her breath.

She wrapped her arm around me and guided us through the darkness. "I can't even see anything!"

"That's the point, Lila! It's called a haunted house for a reason, smartass."

She was laughing now, but there was nothing funny about this situation. A loud growling sound came from behind us, and I jumped at least two feet high. Someone was close, way too close to us. I could feel them stalking us in the darkness, their hot breaths on our neck.

"They're behind us," I whispered, my heart taking a dive into the pit of my stomach. The temperature was cold, but I had stress sweats. The air was thick and almost suffocating, or maybe that was just me. My hands were clammy, and I clenched onto Riley's arm.

She let out a shaky breath. "I can feel them, too. Just keep walking."

We walked further into the labyrinth looking path. Metal chains clanged close to us, as if someone had been tied to them and they were restlessly pulling at the chains. None of it was real, I reminded myself. They were live humans with costumes and wickedly good make-up.

I peeked to my left and wished I hadn't.

One very vile zombie man, his face bloodied and disfigured with his eyes pure white, walked out of the shadow, a mere inch away from me. His mouth was opened, and he snarled right into my face.

My lips parted with an ear-splitting scream. Riley jumped, and she let out a shriek, too. Grabbing my hand in hers, we made a run for it.

At every corner, there was a different horror waiting for us.

A bloody clown. Mass zombies. Ax murderers. A creepy nun with a white face and black, rotted teeth. They were snarling and quite terrifying. Another loud shriek came from Riley and I when they reached out to touch us.

They weren't supposed to get this close, right?

Wrong.

Riley forgot to mention this Haunted House was supposed to give us the real experience. As in, the actors were going to be touching us and getting really close.

"Holy shit balls!" Riley screamed as a seven feet man with a bloody chainsaw came forward. I pulled her arm and guided us to the other corner. We moved from room to room, stumbling through tiny dark hallways as dozens of creepy arms reached out to touch us.

"Are you scared?" I whispered again. The exit was near, I could see the fluorescent light ahead.

Riley didn't respond, but I noticed the change in her. Oh yeah, she was freaked out, too.

My heart was pounding like crazy with my whole body trembling. My knees were weak, and I wondered how I was still standing.

We finally walked through the exit and stepped outside through the backdoor. Riley giggled, although I could tell it was forced. She was definitely scared while we were in there. "See, that wasn't so bad. It was freaky but fun."

The heavy pressure on my chest was still there, but I finally took a deep breath.

Fun, ha. No.

"You look spooked," she teased, bumping her elbow into my hip.

"Shut up." I returned the favor, laying a soft punch on her arm.

We could hear other people screaming from the inside. Poor souls. If I had a choice, I wasn't going back in there. Once was enough.

"Are you happy now?" I demanded with a smile, turning to face Riley. My heart was still racing a mile an hour, adrenaline and fear still coursing through my veins.

My smile froze and died when I caught sight of what – who was standing behind her. Riley's gaze went over my shoulder, and her eyes widened, her lips parting as if to let out a scream.

Chills ran down my spine, my heart leaping in my chest.

Someone was standing behind me, just like the creepy mask man was standing behind Riley, too. His arms reached out for her, and my heart thudded so hard in my chest, it *hurt*.

Bile burned my throat, and I tried to warn Riley. Except, none of that happened.

One second I had my feet planted on the grass and then I felt a pair of hands on my hips, before I was airborne.

He lifted me up, hoisting me over his shoulder. I hung upside down, and I still couldn't find my voice. My breath stuck in my throat, and my whole body went limp in fear. Riley shrieked and from my position over his shoulder, as he strode away, I found the mask man holding and dragging Riley backward.

No. No. Wait!

The man carrying me marched through the field, taking it toward the back of the Mausoleum.

Oh My God. No one was coming to save her, no one could hear us scream. We were alone and…

My whole body was cold and numb… I couldn't feel anything, except fear.

I could be molested or… raped.

He was going to kill me.

This was not part of the Haunted House.

This was not an actor.

My pulse thundered in my throat and my vision blurred with black dots as I stayed limp, upside down over his shoulder.

From the distance, I heard Riley scream again, the sound filled with so much terror.

Alarmed, my body started to prickle with awareness, and I began to struggle against my captor. "Let me go. Let. Me. Go."

He laughed, like a mad man. The laugh sounded right out of a horror movie.

"If… if you think you're going to rape me… think… again. Let me go, asshole."

The hiccups between each word made my threat sound less… threatening. Humiliated and panicked, my eyes burned with unshed tears.

The lump in my throat made it harder to speak.

My captor kept marching, my head and arms swinging back and forth as I laid heavily over his shoulder.

"Someone… is going… to come and find us."

He laughed again, his hands clenching over my ass, his fingers digging in my flesh. That did it. I let out a shriek and started to struggle harder. My fists thumped on his back, but he barely even flinched.

Realizing my advantage in this position, I drew my knee back before slamming it forward between his thighs. I missed my target, but he hissed.

His hand came down on my ass, hard. He tsked, taunting me.

I was so close to bursting into tears, dread and horror filling every cell in my body. I continued to wrestle with him.

If I was going to die, I'd die fighting.

When my knee slammed forward again – missing its target once more – he finally relinquished his hold on me. My captor dumped me on the grass, without a care, like a sack of useless potatoes.

He had taken me away from the mausoleum and the haunted house and deposited me behind the school – where no one could see us, no one could come to my rescue.

I inched back, still on my ass. My whole body shook with tremors, and I finally faced *him*.

My chin wobbled at the sight of him, a deep sated fear instilled inside of me. I was going to die tonight. This man was going to hurt me. *That's it.*

I survived on the operating table only to be left to die in the field behind Berkshire Academy.

His face was covered with a black purge mask, with glowing red LED lights. He had a dark hoodie on, with its hood over his head, and black ripped jeans.

The sight of him was right out of my nightmare.

He moved forward, and I put my hands out, as if to ward him away.

"Don't come near me. Don't touch me."

Please.

The pit of my stomach quaked, and I really thought I was going to piss myself in fear.

Purge mask man stalked me as I kept inching back. The cool wet grass soaked through my jeans, but I didn't care.

He was having fun, feeding on my fear and silently taunting me.

He stopped a foot away and squatted down in front of me. His arm reached out as if to touch me, and I shrank away. "Touch me and I'll break your arm. I'll do it."

He pulled his hand back, tsking again. He shook his head, as if he was disappointed in my threats. Slowly, he brought his hand to his face and pulled the purge mask off.

Uneasiness tickled down my spine, my body filled with apprehension.

The mask came off and dark blue eyes met mine.

Full smirking lips and a face I knew very well.

"Maddox," I breathed.

"Boo," he rumbled.

All the horror and confusion slipped away, replaced with anger. My jaw snapped together, and I clenched my teeth.

"Are you freaking serious?"

The previous chill running down my spine disappeared as my blood boiled.

"Why are you so set on terrorizing me?" I snarled. Jesus Christ, he almost gave me a heart attack. Fury rolled off in heated waves. Seething, I curled my legs from underneath me, sitting up. I still couldn't stand up, since my legs were still shaky and weak.

He grinned, almost boyishly, except I saw the mischief in his eyes. I was dancing on the edge of danger with this boy. Against my better judgement, my gaze traveled the length of his body as he stayed squatting down in front of my kneeling form. He was hard and sculptured everywhere, in all the right places. *Definitely not a boy. Man. Fuck. Whatever-he-is.*

"It's fun," he finally said, snapping me out of my thoughts and forcing my eyes away from his body. I looked into his icy blue eyes instead.

I was stunned into silence for a second. "It's fun?" I sputtered. "It's fun to scare the shit out of people? Was that your friend who took Riley away, too? This is not funny!"

Maddox shrugged like it was no big deal. I could feel myself glaring at him, my eyes turning into slits as I regarded my nemesis with utter distaste. If I could breathe fire, I would have fumes coming out of my nose.

My jaw clenched at the way he kept grinning. It made me angrier. It unsettled me. "What are you? A psychopath? Because that's the only explanation. No sane person thinks it's fun to scare someone else to the point they thought they were going to die!"

I fought the urge to punch him and claw his beautiful eyes out. What was it about him that make me lose all my control?

Oh right. Maddox Coulter was an asshole.

He cocked his head to the side, one side of his lip turning up slightly. Maddox then released a deep chuckle, his wide chest vibrating with a decadent sound. "That's new," he whispered, his voice raspy. It made the tiny hair on my bare arms stand up.

"What?"

He was still smirking. *Fuck you*, I mentally slapped him. "I have been called many names before. Been swore at so many times, I lost count about three years ago. But being called a psychopath? That's a first."

I gaped at him. Was this guy joking or seriously just insane?

Maddox brought his head closer to me, his body leaning into mine. He brought warmth with him, and I didn't like that. He wasn't supposed to be warm. He wasn't supposed to smell nice. He wasn't supposed...

"I like it."

His lips were only an inch away from mine. His face so close I could feel his minty breath feathering over my skin. I stayed still, completely still. If I moved, our lips would touch.

My fists clenched, and I squeezed them over my thighs. "What?" I breathed.

"I like it. You calling me a psychopath. It's new. It's different." He was still too close. He was still grinning like a fucking loon. He was still so warm...he still smelled so good...

My body seemed to overheat with his presence. My heart thudded in my chest. "You are crazy," I whispered.

His eyes glinted with something mischievous and roguish. "Wanna see just how crazy I am, Sweet Cheeks?"

CHAPTER NINE

Lila

There always comes a time in your life when your tenacity is tested, and when that happens, you have two choices: you either run away with your tail tucked between your legs, or you stand up for yourself.

Maddox has been playing me, pushing and pushing until I reached the end of my rope and snapped. He wanted to remind me he had the power to make me lose control.

He craved the hunt, to be the hunter – the predator, to be at the top of the food chain, doling out punishments as he deemed necessary.

Being an asshole was his way of living, I guessed he didn't know how to be anything else.

He knew exactly how to make his victims feel small to the extent that all you can do is cower away.

My blood pumped hot. Shaking away the terror and fury coursing through my veins, I stood up. Maddox pulled away and came up to his feet, too, standing to his full height. The crooked grin plastered on his face infuriated me, but I channeled all my frustration.

"What do you want from me, Maddox?"

He raised one perfect eyebrow, without saying a word, shoving his hands in the pockets of his jeans and rocking back on his feet, quite nonchalantly.

"You're the most frustrating person I've ever come across."

"Why, thank you. I take that as a compliment." He was still smirking.

My mother always told me to avoid trouble and look away. The least attention you give to bullies, the more disinterested they'll become.

Maybe she was right.

Still staring at Maddox, I took a step back. "Have a good night, Coulter."

I pivoted on my heels to march away, but his taunting voice stopped me. "Giving up so easily, Sweet Cheeks? I must have been wrong about you."

My fists clenched at my side, and I came to a halt. I *really* should have listened to my mother's warning.

But I never, ever turned down a challenge. Maybe that was my mistake...

Show time.

I swiveled around and stalked forward until I stopped in front of him. Maddox's gaze drifted to my mouth, where I was chewing on my lip – not in nervousness, but to put Maddox exactly where I wanted him.

My hand landed on his firm chest. His eyes widened slightly since this was the first time I've touched him willingly. A roguish smile played on his lips, and I *pitied* him.

He thought he won me over. *Too bad, Maddox. Don't play games with a girl who can play them better.*

He should have heeded my warning the first time.

I rubbed my hand over his chest, sliding it down toward his stomach.

The black hoodie did nothing to hide all the hardness of him. His muscles tensed under my slow, exploring touch, and his eyes glinted with something devilish.

Down and down I went, until my fingers halted on his hips, right over his belt. I hooked a finger into the belt loop and pulled him closer to me, our bodies colliding together softly. Maddox let out a small chuckle, playing along.

Standing on my toes, I brought our faces closer, bringing my lips mere inches from his squared jaw, and I leaned in, so I could whisper in his ear. "I know what you want from me."

"Oh, do you?"

"You've made it abundantly clear. I can give you what you want. One unforgettable night."

"See? That wasn't so hard. Don't know why you've been playing so hard to get." His hands landed on my hips before they curled around my back, squeezing my ass.

"You want a taste of this ass? You can have it. Fuck me sideways, fuck me front and back, put me on my knees, get between my thighs. Put me on your dick, and I'll ride you until the sun comes up. I'm on the pill. If you're safe, we can ditch the condoms, and you'll feel every inch of me. Have you ever fucked a girl bareback? I can be your first. I'll even show you my deepthroating skills. You want filthy? I can make your *filthiest* fantasies come true, Maddox. You can have it all, baby."

My teeth grazed his earlobe before I bit down softly. His throat bobbed with a low groan.

"In your dreams," I breathed in his ear.

I released him and pushed away from his body. His eyebrows curled together in confusion before realization dawned in his eyes. He reached for me, but I sidestepped him, tsking. It was *my* turn to taunt him, and by the look on his face, he hadn't expected it.

Oh no, Maddox Coulter underestimated me.

I winked, and my lips curled into a satisfied smirk. "See you tomorrow, Coulter."

I walked backward, enjoying the look of complete shock on his face. My gaze slid over him, from the top of his messy blond hair down to his brown leather boots.

"Oh. You might want to take a cold shower to help with *that*," I said, pointing toward his semi hard-on, which was indecently poking through his jeans.

Whoops.

Maddox

I couldn't remember the last time a girl had knocked me on my ass. Probably never because it was impossible. *I* played the games, and *they* were my catch.

How did the tables turn?

Lila marched away, shaking her plump ass as if to tempt me further, with her long black hair teasing the curve of her hips. She gave me one last haughty look over her shoulder before she disappeared around the building, and I was left dumbstruck in the middle of the field with a goddamn hard-on.

I should have known – she was fierce. I underestimated her, but honestly, I didn't expect her to give me goddamn blue balls.

With pink lips and a sultry voice, she was a siren with a filthy mouth and I. Was. A. Goner.

There was just something about Lila Garcia that I wanted to explore. I thought she was an interesting plaything at first. *Now?* I rubbed my thumb over my jaw, still staring at where she had disappeared. Her scent still lingered around me. It was some sweet perfume, nothing too heavy or cheap like the other bitches I had hanging around me. It was soft and sweet, and my tongue slid out over my lips as if I could taste her.

I was spellbound, my palms twitched and my dick – yeah, that bastard was more than interested.

I wanted to see how far I could push before she exploded into tiny little pieces at my feet.

Sure, Lila was feisty and oh, so fucking sassy, but for how long? How long would it take to break her and mold her into a pretty little thing like I'd done with all the others?

She was fucking trouble.

Guess what?

I wasn't the type to shy away from trouble.

Come at me, Sweet Cheeks.

CHAPTER TEN

Lila

I walked into my grandparents' grocery store early Sunday morning. We weren't opened yet, but they had been here for an hour, getting everything ready for a busy day. I usually came in to help them during the rush hour, but otherwise, they had part-timers helping them daily.

I walked further inside toward the back storage. "Gran?"

"In here, sweetie," she called out.

Smiling, I stepped into the storage room. "Do you need my hel–"

My smile slid from my face as I came to halt at the door, facing the one person I never wanted to see here.

What the hell?

"You," I said, my voice filled with accusation.

Maddox grinned, still holding one huge box in his arms. "Good morning, Lila."

My mouth fell open, dumbstruck. *No way.* "What are you doing here?"

Grandma patted his arm as if she had known him for the longest time. I wasn't sure I liked the way she was smiling up at him. "I hired him yesterday. He came looking for a part-time job, and since we're hiring, he got the job. He said he's from Berkshire. You won't be bored at work anymore since you two are friends."

"Friends?" My jaw went slack, and I couldn't formulate a better sentence. *Friends? What? How? Who? What? When?*

"Yes. I told Mrs. Wilson how close we are. I didn't know this store was owned by your grandparents. What a surprise," Maddox explained, with a shit-eating grin.

Bullshit. The look on his face told me the truth. Maddox knew exactly what he was doing, and he was here on purpose. His mission was to make my life miserable, in every way. I wanted to knock the smile off his face. So, he was stalking me now. Great.

"Yes, what a surprise," I muttered, plastering a fake pleased look on my face. Gran appeared too happy for me to break the news to her.

This is my enemy, and he's an asshole. Don't fall for his easy smile and charming looks. This was what I wanted to say, but I bit my tongue and held back any snarky remarks. I'd deal with Maddox on my own.

"I just need help to organize the inventory. Sven will be here soon," Gran announced, patting me on the back as she walked out of the storage room, leaving Maddox and I alone.

Once she was out of hearing range, I stalked forward. My whole body strummed with anger. I wouldn't say I was a violent person, but I was feeling quite violent at the moment. "What the hell are you doing here?"

He turned his back to me, lifting another box over his shoulder. He carried it into the walk-in freezer and deposited it on the self. Maddox walked out and went for another box, but I sidestepped into his path.

Leaning back against the wall, he crossed his ankles and his arms over his chest. Today, he was wearing a black shirt and black jeans, ripped around his knees, with brown leather boots like he wore the night at the

Haunted House. It was strange seeing him in anything other than the Berkshire uniform.

He looked... *normal*. Instead of the Berkshire star quarterback I despised.

"I asked you a question. What are you doing here?"

Maddox cocked his head to the side, giving me an amused look. "Working, Garcia. Simple as that."

Impatiently, I tapped my foot on the ground, not falling for his stupid games. To work? Yeah, right.

"You don't need to work. Don't your parents give you an allowance? Your credit card is probably unlimited."

For a brief second, I noticed the way his eyes darkened as if he was disappointed in *me*. But it was gone too quickly, leaving me wondering if what I saw was real or just my imagination. He tsked, shaking his head.

"See, that's your problem. You assume too many things."

I wasn't assuming anything. He wasn't just rich; Maddox was filthy rich. He didn't need a part-time job, especially not at my grandparents' grocery store. He didn't *ever* need to work.

In fact, he didn't even need to be here, in *this* neighborhood, where didn't belong.

But no, he had to be here. The only two days I had without Maddox being a jerk every minute – my only two peaceful days, he had to come and ruin.

"How did you get my grandma to agree to this?"

"That was really simple. I smiled."

A frustrated sound came from my throat, and I rubbed a hand over my face. "Maddox," I grumbled under my breath.

He pushed away from the wall and walked past me to lift another brown box. His shirt stretched over his shoulders as he placed it on the top shelf and diligently arranged all the boxes in expiration date order. "She thinks I'm charming and sweet. Trust me, this is the first time someone has called me *sweet*. Shocking, right?"

I didn't think that was the correct description for Maddox. He was anything but sweet.

"You need to leave. Now."

He shook his head, his messy hair slowly coming undone from his man bun. "Can't. I like it here, and I like your Gran. Your grandfather, though, he's tough. No worries, I'll figure something out."

I grabbed the box he was holding and slammed it back on the ground. The storage room was starting to feel hot or maybe my blood was just boiling.

"Damn, Sweet Cheeks. It's too early for you to be this angry. Are you always this grumpy?" Maddox mocked with a rough laugh.

Yes, since you came into my life.

I stepped closer, lifting my chin up to meet his eyes. "Listen, Maddox," I said, stabbing a finger into his chest. "This is not a joke. You have a problem with me, then it's only me. I don't know what you want but don't bring my grandparents into this fight between us."

Maddox leaned forward, getting into my face. The laughter was gone, and his face was a blank canvas, devoid of any emotions. The change in him was so sudden, confusion clouded my mind. "Why do you always think the worst of me?"

I could've been fooled, but I knew better.

It was my turn to laugh; as fake as it was, I really was amused by his question. "Probably because you've only ever shown me the worst of you. If there was any good in you, I would have seen it already. Too bad you're only focus is on being a douchebag."

Maddox opened his mouth, probably to rebuke me, but I was already turning away, ignoring anything else he had to say. I lifted the box next to my feet and started organizing the messy shelves. Inventory days were always crazy and busy.

Maddox and I worked quietly. He didn't try to speak to me again, and

I wasn't interested in holding a conversation either. The silence was tense and heavy, like an impending thunderstorm looming over our heads, dark and cloudy. An hour later, the storage room was somewhat organized, and all the boxes, old and new, had been put away on their designated shelves.

Lifting one last box, my arms trembled under the weight, but I still pushed it above my head, reaching for the rack. Except, the box was too heavy, the shelf was too high, and I was too short to reach it, even with me balancing on my toes.

Damn it.

I cursed under my breath when the box started to wobble in my hands and a surprised shriek came from me when I could feel it tilting back over my head. The box was going to fall, and I didn't have the strength to keep hold of it.

But before it could slip through my fingers, another pair of hands grabbed the box.

"I got it." His whisper crept along my neck. "You can let go."

I did, and he pushed the box onto the shelf with ease. Maddox was too close, and I didn't like it. Maddox obviously didn't understand the meaning of personal space. His mere presence annoyed me and having him this close had me on edge. I wasn't sure why, but everything about Maddox just made me feel… *irritated.*

I was thankful he saved the box, though, so I uttered a quick *thank you* as my arms fell down to my sides.

His breath was hot on my skin as he pressed closer, barely touching me. I slid away from under his arms before turning to face him. His gaze moved up and down my body, and the burning intensity of his eyes urged me to cross my arms over my chest.

"You're tiny," he grunted.

I hissed under my breath. He insulted my boobs the first time we met and now he had to make me feel *small.* "I'm not. I'm five foot two."

He let out a scoff. "And I'm six foot three. A whole head taller than you. You're literally bite-sized."

"You're just a giant, not average."

His crooked smile should have warned me of what was coming. "You're right. I'm far from *average*, Sweet Cheeks."

Yep, I walked right into that one.

"Wanna see for yourself?" he asked with no shame.

"Keep your dick in your pants and keep your hands to yourself," I warned. Stalking past him, I took the broom and started sweeping the storage room. I expected him to leave now that we were done putting away all the inventory but that wasn't the case.

He leaned against the wall opposite to me, making himself comfortable. Maddox took a small box of cigarettes from his pocket.

My voice was sharp when I spoke, "You're not allowed to smoke in here."

Maddox made a derisive sound in the back of his throat as he flipped the tiny box over his fingers and around in his hand. "I won't disrespect your grandparents like that. I'm just checking how many I have left."

I could almost hear his unsaid words. *Stop assuming the worst of me, Lila.*

Ignoring the silent jab, I continued with my sweeping. Even with me not looking at him, I could feel his stare burning into the back of my head. He was staring *hard*.

Maddox stalked me with his eyes, and I didn't like how he could make me feel... small.

"So, are we not going to talk about the elephant in the room?

"What elephant?" I grumbled, distracted.

"The hard-on you gave me two days ago."

Oh. I had been trying to forget all about that night, but he had to bring it up. Of course, since I left him dumbfounded. Not a lot of people has the chance to push back on Maddox. I gave him a taste of his own medicine, and he obviously didn't like it.

I stopped sweeping and held the broom up, leaning my arm on it. "Oh that. Did the cold shower help?"

"It didn't. I had to use my hand." If I didn't know better, I'd say there was a note of petulance in his voice.

"I didn't need to know that."

He shrugged, quite nonchalantly. "You asked, I answered. Can I borrow your hand next time though?"

Oh, for fuck's sake. "That's going to be a hell no, Coulter."

His lips twitched, and I *almost* rolled my eyes. "You're boring, Garcia," he taunted once again.

"I'd rather be boring than be your next hookup."

Anything was better than being his next meal. To put it simply, Maddox was a lion – it was quite easy to see the resemblance. When given meat, lions pounce without a second thought. They devour their meal, messy and savagely. Once they're done, they spit out the bones, and with a belly full, they walked away.

That was Maddox.

He devoured anyone in his path, without care of the consequences, and he'd spit out the bones once he had his fun. Guys like Maddox would play with you, tear you apart, layer by layer, piece by piece and then lay you down – fragmented and empty -- because they took everything from you.

Maddox pushed away from the wall and took a step toward me. "You hate me that much?"

He actually looked curious, as if he wanted to pick apart my brain to see inside, to delve into my thoughts. He wanted to see beyond my wall. Too bad, he was the wrong person to break through it.

"It's not about hate. I'm simply not excited about your existence."

It wasn't about hate. That was too black and white. *No.*

Boys like Maddox have already stolen enough from me...

My heart thudded in my chest, and I looked away. Boys like him...

they *ruined* me.

Placing the broom back in its corner, I walked toward the door without sparing him a glance. "You should ask Gran what else she wants you to do. I'm going to take a ten-minute break."

Maddox blocked my way out. "Let me change your mind. Spend one afternoon with me."

His words speared me with shock, making me stumble back a step. *What?*

Why would he...

Maddox truly didn't understand the word 'boundaries.' How did we go from enemies to him asking me to spend an afternoon with him?

Well played, Coulter.

He looked at me expectantly, as if he really wanted me to consider his offer.

I scoffed back a laugh that bubbled in my chest and threatened to escape through my throat. Was I a joke to him? Wait... I knew that answer.

"And what? You'll have me putty in your hands?" I asked with a quirked eyebrow.

He grinned, losing the expectant look on his face. He was back to being a jerk. "In my arms and on my dick, yeah."

I leaned forward, pushing my body against his. He never hid the fact that he appreciated the way I looked. My body tempted him; I was aware of that. *So, two can play this game.* "Is this your way of asking me out on a date?" I whispered, my voice sultry but dripping with sarcasm. If he was smart enough, he'd catch that.

Maddox stared down at him, his lips crooked on the side. "I don't date. Ever. My favorite pastime is having girls on their back or on their knees for me."

"You. Are. Disgusting," I growled.

He shrugged.

Pushing away from him, I tilted my chin up, both to look at him and in defiance. He wasn't winning me over. "Tell me something, do your fangirls know how you think of them?"

"Most of them know and don't care. They're using me the same way I'm using them. Sex, fun and popularity. Three things they want and three things I can give them. They're happy with the arrangement. Those who aren't, I show them the door. Simple."

"So, girls get hot and bothered *because* you're a jerk."

"That's the appeal, Sweet Cheeks."

I opened my mouth but then snapped it shut when I couldn't find the appropriate words. I was speechless.

"Lila!" Grandpa's voice broke through our silent battle, and I flinched away. "Can you come and help me with this?"

"Coming!" I called out.

I tried to push pass Maddox, but he didn't budge. On the contrary, he moved forward, forcing me to take a step back and away from the door.

"So, what do you say?" he grumbled.

A frustrated sound spilled from my throat. "What?"

He kept moving forward, and I walked back a step, two… and three. "One afternoon. Give me an hour of your time, and I'll change your mind."

"Not interested, Coulter. You're not even worthy of one hour of my time," I bit out, glaring up at him through my lashes.

He slid closer against me, and I stumbled back into the wall. Shit. "So, you're saying, if I kiss you right now, *really* kiss you… the way you should be kissed and then I slide my hands into your panties, I won't find you wet for me?"

Cocky much? I bristled at his words, and my fists clenched at my sides. He brought his face closer to me, staring into my eyes as his hands landed on either side of my head.

"Lila!" Grandpa called out again, louder this time. He sounded closer than before. If I didn't leave right now, he was going to come and find me in the storage, room and he was going to see Maddox and I… *Oh God.*

"Kiss me and I'll make it so you don't have the ability to kiss another girl ever again," I warned.

"Challenge accepted."

Maddox leaned down as if to kiss me, his lips a mere inch from mine. I turned my head to the side, and I could feel his minty breath feathering against my cheek.

"Move," I growled.

"Lila," he breathed, closer to my ear. His voice sounded deeper, edgier… like he really imagined kissing me.

I kept my head turned, refusing to give him access to my mouth. My eyes landed on his forearm as he kept me caged against the wall. I could feel the bulge between his legs pressing against my hips, and I bristled with anger and displeasure instead of being turned on.

I didn't know why, but I expected something better from him. When he asked to spend one afternoon with me, looking adamant… for a brief moment, I almost believed he was serious about changing my mind.

The muscles in his forearm, where he had rolled up his sleeves, tightened, and I struck out, without thinking much about it. I bared my teeth and clamped down on his arm, biting.

Maddox let out a hiss of surprise, and I lifted my gaze to his. He had pulled away, only slightly to stare down at me. I grabbed his outstretched arm and bit down harder when he didn't make a move to pull away. He froze for a second but then stayed still. I continued to put pressure, where my teeth were clamped down on his flesh.

He didn't even flinch. *No,* he did the opposite.

Slowly, his lips quirked up into a tiny smile. His eyes glimmered with amusement, and he cocked his head to the side, waiting… and the bastard appeared not to be bothered by my action.

With an angry huff, I released his arm and pushed away from him. Mr.

Pain-In-My-Ass looked down at the bite mark and then grinned a slow, lazy grin. "I always knew you liked it rough... but I would have never guessed you were into biting."

Holding back a frustrated growl, I pushed him hard enough to have him stumble back a step. I shoved my middle finger into his stupid, smirking face before stomping away.

His amused chuckles followed me, even as I left him behind in the storage room.

Don't kill him. That's murder. Do. Not. Kill. Him.

CHAPTER ELEVEN

Lila

L ater that day, Riley and I were lying in my bed, going through her Advanced Calculus homework. Riley had planned to major in business and after go to law school, that was her parents' expectations, which wouldn't be difficult for her since she loved Law and Politics.

Her weakness, though, was math. Absolutely everything that had to do with math. It was sucky for her since if she had to major in business, she had to pass her calculus courses with flying colors.

Enter me: Her best friend, her tutor and a genius in math. Lucky her.

"I don't understand shit," she whined, flopping on her back. Riley closed her eyes and threw an arm over her face, hiding from me.

I gave her a gentle nudge with my toes. "Let's try the question one more time."

"That's the third time. I'm a hopeless case. There's no way I'm getting into Harvard if I flunk Calculus."

She was exaggerating. Riley was in no way flunking Calculus. She was currently in the mid-eighties, since she had been busting her ass night and day to practice all her equations and solving extra math problems. Riley Jenson was dedicated to a fault.

"Practice makes perfect, right?" I cajoled, gently. "One more time, babe."

She lowered her arm a bit and peeked at me. "Then we can watch *Riverdale*?"

"One episode," I reluctantly agreed.

"Binge watch the whole season?" Riley gave me puppy eyes, the ones she had mastered, which almost won me over.

I pinched her shin. "Now you're pushing it, Missy."

She hissed, pulling her feet away, and her bottom lip jutted out in a pout.

"Let's go back to the question."

Riley nodded and sat up, focusing back on her notebook. I explained the steps to her again, she nodded along and gave it one more try.

Twenty minutes later, she let out a shout of victory. "I did it!"

Yes, she did. Just like I knew she would.

The happiness on her face was infectious, and I found myself laughing with her as she did half a twerk on my bed.

We spent the next two hours working on our homework. Once we were done and had put all our stuff away, I went down to get us snacks while Riley loaded *Riverdale* on Netflix. She wanted to binge watch while I was settling for only two episodes. It was going to be a battle for sure.

Halfway through the first episode, Riley started to get edgier. She was sneaking glances at me, and I noticed the way she was practically poking a hole through her blouse.

I knew Riley long enough to know this was a sign of nervousness, and it had nothing to do with *Riverdale*. I waited for her to speak instead of pushing for information. If something was wrong, she'd tell me on her own without me having to force it out of her. It was a silent understanding between us. Riley has never pushed me about my past. I told her bits and pieces, and she accepted them without demanding more. I did the same with her. She only gave me what she wanted; we established this understanding early in our friendship.

Her silence didn't last for more than fifteen minutes. "I have to confess something."

I paused the episode and faced her. We were both sitting cross legged on the bed. "What is it?"

Riley swallowed hard and chewed on her lip, her brows pulled together in nervousness. Her body was strung tight with tension, and I didn't like the dreadful look on her face.

She licked her lips, took a deep breath and started. "On Friday, after Maddox pulled you away and Colton grabbed me…"

The night of the haunted house? Confused, I nodded and waited for her to continue. "Yeah?"

"He pulled me behind the dumpster…" Riley trailed off, her eyes wide and glassy.

"Yeah. You told me. They are both assholes. If I could, I'd report them–"

Riley shook her head and cut me off, sharply. "*No*, listen. I didn't tell you everything that happened."

And then she… blushed. She averted her gaze for a second, and she went back to poking holes in her shirt.

"Riley…?" I slowly questioned.

She let out a loud, frustrated sigh. Her cheeks were tinted pink, but there was a guilty look in her eyes. "I messed up. I don't know how it happened but it just… happened. One minute, I was screaming at him and I even punched him; he was laughing like a stupid, madman and then he pulled me close and… it just *happened*. I didn't think. I wasn't thinking."

She was babbling, talking too fast, but I caught the gist of it. For her sake, I carefully concealed my shock. But... oh my fucking SHIT!

"Riley, did you... I mean, you two...?"

"No! We didn't have sex," she sputtered and blushed even harder. "We made out. Oh God, I can't believe I'm saying this. But he pulled me into him and just slammed his lips on mine. I think it was the adrenaline. I was so scared, and then I was excited and like, my heart was beating so fast, I felt dizzy and then I just kissed him back."

Don't freak out, Lila. Don't freak out.

"What happened?" I calmly asked, even though I was anything but calm.

"Colton pulled us down, so I could sit on his lap. And we just... um, kissed."

"And?"

Riley buried her face in her hands, letting out a choked scream. "I'm horrible. Jasper was right. I'm a whore."

"What? Riley!" I scooted closer to her and pulled her hands away from her face, so she would have no choice but to look at me. "Don't say that!"

"We kissed. I don't know when it happened, but he unbuttoned my jeans and put his hand inside and... he *touched* me, and it felt good, Lila. I know this sounds stupid, but it felt really good. It was crazy and everything was happening so fast."

She broke off, looking at me like I could save her from whatever she was going through in her head. My poor Riley. I was shocked, speechless, so I could only pat her arm.

"Ifhame," she muttered too fast for me to catch.

"You what?"

"I came! He was just touching me and... I orgasmed on his lap while we were sitting beside a disgusting, smelly dumpster."

My jaw went slack, and I stared at her. Riley let out a cry, looking so conflicted and heartbroken. "I don't even like him! God, I like Grayson, and I let Colton touch me like that. I'm horrible. Just like Jasper said."

I snapped out of my shock at her words and grabbed her shoulders, shaking her. "Riley, you are not. Stop that."

Her chin wobbled, and she bit harshly on her lip. She was so red now, her cheeks, her ears and her neck were all flushed. "Colton is the first guy... I mean after Jasper. I haven't been with anyone else. I haven't even kissed anyone since Jasper. I couldn't bear it, and then with Colton, it just happened."

"Oh honey. Come here." I hugged her close, and she hiccupped back a sob. Now that she had finally confessed what was eating her on the inside, her mixed emotions had bubbled over, and there was no stopping them.

"He probably thinks I'm stupid and a slut."

"Hush." I soothed a hand down her back, comforting Riley in the only way I knew how. I sucked at comforting people, but I hoped my presence was enough for her.

"He's going to spread rumors like Jasper did. I'm so scared to go to school tomorrow. What if I walk in and everyone stares at me like... before... when Jasper... the whispers, the snickers, the laughs behind my back."

I pressed a firm hand on her back. "Not all boys are like Jasper, sweetie."

"I know..."

"It's okay."

She lifted her face and pulled out of my arms. "He hugged me."

"Colton?" That was... shocking.

"Yeah. After, my... um, orgasm. I think I was in shock. And I teared up. I wasn't crying, but I mean, there were tears. He noticed and broke the kiss. Then, he just hugged me. We didn't speak. That's when you found us. I heard you calling out my name, and we broke apart."

Oh wow.

"He apologized," Riley confessed gently. "Before I left, he whispered he was sorry."

I didn't know what to say. Colton and Maddox were cut from the same cloth. Both were playboys, and both were assholes. It was almost impossible to imagine Colton doing something as sweet as to hug and apologize to Riley.

"Not all boys are Jasper," I said again.

She nodded, her eyes glassy with unshed tears. Riley was always so cheerful, so full of life. The conflicted look on her face tore my heart apart. "Does that make me a bad person? I don't like him. I want Grayson."

"No, it doesn't make you a bad person. Like you said, it was the adrenaline and in the spur of the moment. It happens, and no one has the right to judge you. If Colton hugged you and apologized, then I don't think he's going to spread rumors about you. I guess, he's not like that."

As I said the words, I came to a shocking realization.

Maddox and his buddies were one big package of douchebaggery. They were jerks, they constantly played with girls' hearts and all they cared about was sex, sex and more sex. But I'd never seen them spreading any stupid rumors about other students. Sure, they were irritating – but they had never done anything to ruin someone's reputation. Not like Jasper had done to Riley.

I guess… that was one good thing about Maddox and his friends.

Monday morning, Riley's fear was put to rest when we walked through the gates of Berkshire, and everything was normal, like any other day. It appeared that Colton hadn't spread any rumors, and I could tell Riley was finally able to breathe better. She was back to her smiling self in two seconds flat.

We went to our respective classes, and the day continued without any more drama.

Except... with Maddox being a constant presence in my life, I only had three hours of peace and quiet until it was time for lunch.

The hallways were empty as I walked out of Mrs. Callaway's office, my Chemistry teacher. Our meeting ran longer than expected, and everyone was already in the cafeteria, since it was halfway through lunch now.

I made my way to my locker to deposit my textbooks, only to stop dead when I noticed who was standing there. Maddox leaned against *my* locker, looking like he owned it. He was everywhere I went, everywhere I wanted to go – he was *there*. A constant thorn in my ass.

I was starting to believe there was no escaping Maddox Coulter once he checkmated you. And that was exactly what he did to me. He put me on his radar, and then *checkmate*, I became his unwilling prize. No matter how much I fought and pushed back, he was there, pulling me just as hard and pushing back harder. It was a never-ending cycle, and it was starting to get tiring.

Letting out a sigh, I walked forward. As I grew closer, I noticed he had a toothpick between his lips, his dirty blond locks were rumpled and let down, instead of the man bun, and his Berkshire coat was missing. His white shirt was untucked and his tie hung loosely around his neck.

He looked like an imperfect canvas, flawed and wild. But like every piece of art, you couldn't take your eyes off him.

It was my first time seeing him like *this*. His godly appearance had been replaced with something imperfect and... humane.

"What do you want?" I asked, stopping next to him.

He chewed on his toothpick, thoughtfully. "You hurt me," he said, simply, as if he was announcing the weather.

"When? How? Oh right, probably in your nightmare." I punched in the code to my locker, opened it, and slammed my textbooks inside.

He finally stared down at me, his lips crooked and his eyes lit with mischief. "So, you agree, you're a pain in my ass?"

Me, a pain in *his* ass? This was the joke of the century.

"I'm not roses, Maddox. If you're going to make my life difficult, I'm going to be the thorn that pricks you. Don't expect me to be all smiles, hearts and googly eyes. I'm not that girl."

He kept the toothpick in the corner of his mouth as he spoke. "I know you're not."

When I didn't answer, he slowly rolled the sleeves of his white shirt up to his elbow. The same arm I bit yesterday. He shoved his arm into my face and a huge, red bite mark stared back at me.

My eyes widened at the angry looking mark. I grabbed his forearm for a closer inspection. That couldn't be from when... I bit him, right?

"You hurt me," he said again.

I... did.

"Look at it. It hurts so bad; my arm has been aching the whole time."

My gaze flew up to his, and I would have thought he was serious if I didn't notice the twinkle in his eyes.

"I don't remember biting you that hard, and it was yesterday morning. It's been a whole twenty-four hours. It's impossible that the bite mark would still look like this, except if..."

I let my words trail off, and I squinted at him, now suspicious.

"You think I bit myself? Damn, Garcia, you really are cruel. Why would I cause such pain to myself when I have you to do it?"

He shoved his arm in my face again. "Now kiss it better," Maddox demanded, "or, I'll tell the principal you bit me."

Sweet Jesus, he really was impossible.

"Go ahead," I hissed under my breath. "I'll tell him how you've been harassing me!"

Maddox had the audacity to look innocent. He let out a mock gasp before his bottom lip jutted out in a small pout. "Me? You're the one who got physical with me, Sweet Cheeks. Every. Single. Time. If I didn't know better, I would say you're trying to get me to touch you."

My stomach dipped, and my frustration bubbled to the point where I thought I'd do something worse than bite him. *That's it.* I couldn't deal with him anymore.

I threw my hands up in defeat. It took everything in me to accept it, but I was done. "You know what? Truce. We're even with each other. Let's stop here."

Maddox looked at me for a second longer. His gaze seared into mine, burning through my walls and forcing itself to peek into my soul. I clamped up and met his gaze with a hard look.

He lifted a shoulder, a lazy shrug. "Fine. Truce. But you need to kiss my boo boo better first."

Is he really serious?

So, this was his game? He really wanted my lips on him, somehow. Jerk. But fine, I'd play. "Fine. I'll kiss your *boo boo* better before you go running back to your mommy crying."

I brought his arm closer and slowly bent my head down to the bite mark. It did look ugly and painful. For the briefest moment, I felt bad and guilt gnawed at me before I pushed it away.

Before my lips could touch him, Maddox crowded into my space. I sucked in a harsh breath when his arm curled around my waist and he pulled me into him. Our bodies collided together softly and time came to a halt. *Tick...tock...*

His heat seeped through his clothes and mine, and I could feel the flush on my skin. My heart skittered, and I could feel the beat of his own heart against my chest.

Something pulsed between us, electrifying and powerful... a brief moment in time... something that lasted for only a nanosecond.

His other hand came up and his fingers slipped behind my head, curling around my nape.

My brain screamed at me, angry and confused.

His breath feathered over my mouth; I blinked, and his lips crashed against mine.

I gasped into his hungry lips. My hands landed on his chest, and I *tried* to push him back, but he clutched the back of my neck as he deepened the kiss. With his arm still locked firmly around my waist, he swiveled us around, and my back slammed into the locker. My heart dipped into my stomach when he pushed against me, and he lifted me up, only allowing my toes to touch the ground.

I didn't know if I should kiss him back... push him away...

My mind went blank as he licked the seams of my lips. His chest rumbled with a small groan when his teeth grazed my bottom lip before he bit down. I hissed into his mouth, even though I was trembling in his arms. The gentle bite stung, and I could feel the blood rushing through my ears. Slowly, he pulled his mouth away. The taste of him, mint and tobacco were heavy on my swollen lips.

"Now we're even. Truce, baby," he whispered in my ear, his voice deeper and darker.

My breath caught in my throat as he untangled himself from my body, and I slumped against the locker. I couldn't... *breathe.*

Shock and rage coursed through me, a sea of mixed emotions, too deep while the tides were too violent, I was drowning into the bottomless ocean.

Maddox gazed down at me, and he lazily swiped his tongue over his red, swollen lips as if to taste the remnant of our kiss. "You taste sweeter than I thought."

His lips twitched, and with a ghost of a smile, he strutted backward and away from me. I let out a choked gasp... finally able to breathe.

I inhaled sharply, sucking in desperate breaths as he winked at me, and then rounded the corner out of my sight. My hand slowly crept up to my chest, and I left it there, over my rapidly beating heart.

His lips had tasted like... sin.

And I hated myself for reacting the way I did to his kiss.

CHAPTER TWELVE

Lila

I walked through the door of my grandparents' home and stumbled onto the couch. Gran leaned against the kitchen's doorway, having heard the door open. She watched me closely. "What's with that face, sweetie?"

"Nothing," I grumbled, rubbing a hand over my face.

"That sigh tells me it's definitely something." She took a seat on the opposite couch, waiting for my answer. I knew she wasn't going to rest until I told her what was actually bothering me. "Is someone bothering you?"

Someone? Yes, your precious helper aka Maddox, my enemy.

I groaned in defeat. "There's someone…"

She gave me a knowing look. "A boy."

"Yes, a boy."

"What boy?" Grandpa came down the stairs, and he settled beside me with a hard scowl on his face. He was a tad overprotective.

The last boyfriend I had was two years ago. We dated for about four months before I lost my virginity in the back of his dad's pickup truck in the dark. The next time we made out, he noticed my scar and the look of disgust on his face still burned through my memory. Leo broke up with me the next day. When Pops found out, without any of the nasty sex details, he lost his shit. Since then, he had been wary of any boys who came around.

"It's someone from school," I finally admitted, leaving Maddox's name out, since they both thought highly of him and it'd break my Gran's heart if she ever found who the real Maddox was. Granted, yes, he was the perfect helper on Sunday, and he really did work hard, so I couldn't really ruin his image just because he was an asshole to me in school. Right?

"Is he being rude to you? Do I need to file a complaint to the Headmaster? Molly, where is my rifle?" He stood up, his back straight and his jaw hard as granite. My sweet grandpa, even in his old age, he was fierce.

I grabbed his arm and pulled him back on the couch again. "No, no. He's just... a bit annoying."

"A bully?" Grandpa inquired. His intense stare burned holes through the side of my face. This was his *if-you-lie-to-me-I-will-find-out* look.

"Not exactly. I won't let him bully me. You could say I've been a pain in his ass, too. I dyed his hair pink."

Gran snickered. "Did you know that's how our love story started?"

"You dyed Pops' hair pink?" I gasped, my jaw going to slack.

"Not exactly. It was during summer camp. Your grandpa was a sweetheart, but his friends were vexing. You see, I didn't mean to dye his hair. It was meant for his other friend who stuck gum in my hair."

"She had to cut off her beautiful locks." The forlorn look on his face as he stared at Gran, as if he was remembering that day very clearly, made my romantic heart sing.

"Yes. But Sven went into the shower first and… he came out with white hair."

"Jack Frost," Pops mumbled under his breath.

"A handsome Jack Frost." Gran lifted her chin, a twinkle in her pretty brown eyes. "That's how our love story started. We hated each other until he kissed me at the end of summer. We parted ways, but he followed me. He said he was going to marry me, and he'd win me over. He did."

I was already shaking my head before she could finish her sentence. Love story? Maddox and I? Ha. I refrained from letting out a mocking laugh. "Oh no. There's no love story between us. He's my…."

My what? My nemesis who kissed me? Confused, I couldn't find the right word to describe him. The definition of our relationship was… complicated. He was a jerk, but he wasn't exactly a bully, since I fought back just as hard. Sure, he was my enemy, but he also kissed me, and my treacherous heart had done something weird in my chest. We were both passionate about our ongoing war, but it wasn't *hate*.

Pops patted me on the knee, always on my side, always so encouraging. "If he's making your life hard, make him miserable. Don't be shy. Make him bend the knee," he said fiercely.

I swallowed past the knot in my throat, refusing to admit that Maddox and I had anything more than war between us. It was a battlefield between us. Turning to Pops, I gave him a tender smile. "You've been watching *Game of Thrones* again?"

"It's… *interesting*." He gave his wife the side-eye, his lips twitching with a half-smile. There was something in his look, and when Gran's flushed under his appraising gaze, my own eyes widened, and I fought a gag. Oh shit, I didn't want to know.

"Right. I need to shower, then I'll help with dinner." I got up to kiss Gran on the cheek and Pops on his balding head. They both chuckled as I walked away.

The next morning, I walked down the halls of Berkshire. It was a whole hour before the bell rang, to indicate the start of the school day. There were barely any students roaming the school halls. Berkshire was participating in a science experiment, and if we won Regionals, we would be representing our state. Today was our first meeting. I, of course, joined. Science was my drug, plain and simple.

I was marching down the halls when something caught my eyes, making me come to a halt. Not something: *someone*. Through the window, I caught sight of Maddox sitting outside on a bench.

I didn't even think he'd be up this early since they didn't have football practice today. Why was Maddox here?

He stared at the empty field; his elbows perched on his thighs as he smoked his cancer stick.

It was starting to grow cold in Manhattan, and we now needed a sweater or thicker jacket before stepping out. Maddox was only wearing his Berkshire uniform, as if the cold wasn't bothering him, as if he had grown immune or numb to it.

But that wasn't what made me stop and stare. No, he was *alone*.

He was never alone; he was always either surrounded by his fangirls or his friends, or he was annoying me.

I placed a hand over the window as I studied him from afar. There was no reason for my heart to ache, but it did. Something clenched in my chest, like a fist holding my heart tight. Sitting on the bench, in the cold, with a cigarette between his lips, he looked like a sad, lonely god.

Maddox stood up, his longish hair falling across his face, hiding himself from my view. He took one last inhale before dropping the cigarette on the ground and stepping over it.

His hands curled around the back of his neck, and he looked up at the sky. His blond locks fell away from his face as a gust of wind breezed past him.

Eyes closed, he turned toward me and...

The agonized look on his face made me suck in a harsh breath.

His pain was stark and on display for all to see, but there was no one looking at Maddox except *me*.

He looked like a beautiful canvas being torn apart as sorrow bleed through him.

For the first time since I've met Maddox, I felt something other than annoyance. I really shouldn't have cared. I convinced myself I didn't, that I only felt bad for him because I had a habit of tending to strays.

But Maddox wasn't a stray or a wounded animal.

He wasn't mine to soothe.

But still...

"Why do you always think the worst of me?"

For the first time, I decided to not be a judgmental bitch and wondered what his story was.

"See, that's your problem. You assume too many things."

I did assume a lot of things, but that was only because Maddox had only ever showed me one side of him – the asshole side.

This side of him? The pained, broken one – it spoke to the inner part of me, to my little caged heart. Because I remembered staring into the mirror, my own reflection staring back at me, with the same expression on Maddox's face.

Broken.

Lost.

Lonely.

Scared.

His eyes opened, and my lips parted with a silent gasp as our gazes met. He couldn't see me... right?

But oh, he did.

He watched me, silently, as I'd done to him.

Something unspoken crossed between us, something… personal.

He lifted his chin in silent acknowledgement before he walked away, fading out of my sight.

The heavy weight on my chest didn't lift away. My heart cracked for a boy who probably would forget about me soon enough.

My fists clenched. I shouldn't care.

I didn't care.

CHAPTER THIRTEEN

Lila

"I didn't know you were a stalker, Sweet Cheeks." His whisper crept along my neck, causing me to shiver. I didn't hear him approach me. I had been too lost in my thoughts; I hadn't even felt him coming closer.

It was after school; the bell had just rung, and all the students were filing out.

I swung my bag over my shoulder, closed the locker and turned to face him. "I wasn't stalking, Poodle."

"Poo-what-the-fuck-dle?" He asked, confused.

I didn't even know why I said that. Maybe because he caught me off guard, or it was the fact he insisted on calling me *Sweet Cheeks,* and I needed to retaliate. Or maybe it was because I needed to feel in control again after what I saw this morning. I barricaded my heart, feeling the coldness seeping through me.

But one thing was true.

Maddox was definitely a Poodle.

One eyebrow popped up, and I stared at him, watching as realization dawned on him. His hand came up, and he touched his curly hair.

"Poodle? Seriously, Garcia?"

"Poodle," I said again.

His nostrils flared in brief annoyance before he turned the table on me. "So, stalking is your new hobby?"

Clutching my bag tighter to me, I repeated, "I wasn't stalking."

"I caught you red-handed," Maddox said, his voice gruff.

"What's your problem, Coulter?"

What I really meant to ask was... what... *who* hurt you?

He cocked his head, scanning me. "You."

"Huh?"

"You're my problem, Sweet Cheeks."

Maddox stepped closer. "That kiss..."

"Won't happen again," I finished for him. "That was your only taste of me, Coulter. First and last. Memorize it and sear that kiss in your brain because it's the only one you'll get."

"Harsh," he mumbled. "I like you when you're a spitfire, like a little annoyed dragon."

I lifted my chin, squinting at him. "I'd like you better if you were nicer."

"Nice?" He let out a booming laugh that had other students turning around and focusing on us. "If you're looking for Prince Charming, you kissed the wrong frog."

Maddox Coulter was neither Prince Charming nor the... villain.

He was something else, and I didn't know where exactly to place him.

"I didn't kiss you. *You* kissed *me*."

"Same shit." He combed his fingers through his hair, pushing the stubborn locks away from his eyes.

"We're going in circles, Coulter." I pushed past him, making sure we didn't touch. "Have a good day."

His hand snaked out, and he grabbed my wrist, pulling me back into his chest. His heart thudded against my back, and I stayed still. The crowded hallway faded away as his voice lowered to a mere whisper, speaking only for me to hear. "Next time, make sure you don't stare at me with such a heartbreaking expression. Anyone would have thought you cared, except I'm no fool."

He was referring to his morning, when he had caught me watching him through the window.

Oh God.

His deep voice rolled down my spine. "Don't fall for me, Lila. I'll break you."

Conceited much? Why would he think I'd fall for him out of all the other options I had? Maddox was the last person I wanted in my heart.

"Falling in love with you is the last thing I want. Rest assured, even if you were the last man on earth, I would neither fuck you nor love you; you're too ugly for me."

"Me or my heart?"

"Both," I breathed. *Lies.*

He let go of my wrist, and I could feel the burn on my skin, where his touch had just been. His breath feathered next to my ear. "Good."

I took a step away from him. He followed, to my irritation. "One last thing. If I can't kiss your lips, can I kiss your pussy instead?"

My... what?

Anger coiled inside me, and I swiveled around, glaring. "Didn't your parents teach you any manners?" I spat out through clenched teeth.

Maddox instantly lost the teasing look, and his face hardened to granite. The change in him was so quick and confusing; it felt like I had been dropped into the rabbit hole.

"No. They didn't. They never cared enough to teach me anything," he simply said, his eyes empty.

My mouth opened, although I didn't know how to respond. My brain stuttered for a moment in shock as my heart dropped to the pit of my stomach. Maddox didn't wait, he walked past me, and I lost him to the crowd before I could call out to him... to *apologize*? For what?

I didn't know. Shit.

Shock and confusion coursed through me, and for the first time, I realized that I truly didn't *know* Maddox.

What's your story, Maddox Coulter? Who are you?

"Table eight," Kelly said, handing me a tray of warm food. I nodded, bursting out of the kitchen and going straight to the table she told me.

The soles of my feet were burning and the high heels were not helping. The restaurant I worked at was nice, the ambiance was pretty and welcoming, and because we were the only *Grill and Bar* restaurant for miles, this place could get hectic. I wasn't allowed to work at the bar, though, since I was still underage. I was hired two months ago, and I only served tables. The tips were good enough to keep me here, even though the job was tiring, and some nights, I could feel the exhaustion in my bones.

I swore under my breath when another customer tried to catch my attention, waving his arm with irritation.

It was a busy night, much busier than the last few days, and we were short two servers. Both of them had called in sick last minute.

"Coming," I called to him.

I served table eight their dinner, a tight smile on my face. "Let me know if you need anything else. Enjoy," I said, chipperly. It was fake, I was feeling anything but chipper.

I went back to the man who was waving, fishing out my small notepad from the pocket of my apron. As I got closer to his table, I noticed that he had already ordered and ate his food. The plates were empty in front of him. Ah, so he needed the bill then.

I handed table five his bill and went along to the next table. The rush came and went. Hours later, I was dead on my feet and wishing I was in my bed. Kelly, my co-worker, who was also busting her ass, gave me an exhausting look as she passed me. "Table eleven. Can you grab it for me? I need the bathroom."

I nodded. "I got it."

I straightened my apron, took a last bite of my sandwich, wiped the corners of my mouth and made my way to the awaiting table.

I saw that he had already been served. "Hi, would you like anything else?"

My smile froze on my face, and I choked back a gasp. *Are you kidding me?*

Mr. Stalker aka Mr. Pain-in-my-ass aka Maddox grinned at me, an almost boyish look on his face with decadent mischief in his gaze. The second thing I noticed was that his poodle hair was gone. Holy shit, he cut it? Maddox's long, shaggy dirty blond hair had been cut short. No more man buns, no more surfer swagger. Did he cut it because I called him Poodle? I didn't think he was *that* offended, but I figured it bruised his ego.

"Yes. You," Maddox said.

I recovered from my shock, picked up my jaw from the floor and snapped my mouth shut. "Excuse me?" I asked stiffly, still reeling from disbelief.

He pushed his chair back, extended his legs in front of him and crossed his arms over his wide chest. "You asked if I wanted anything else, I gave you my answer. *You.*" His teeth grazed his lower lips and he eyed me up and down in my waitressing outfit. "I've been wondering if your pussy tastes like cherry, too."

Oh, for Pete's sake.

"Maddox," I hissed.

"Lila." My name rolled off his tongue, like he was tasting it.

"What are you doing? This is my workplace."

He quirked up an eyebrow. "I'm here for the food. I approve, by the way. Five stars for the food, five stars for your service."

"You're stalking me," I deadpanned.

"I am," he admitted, calmly and without any shame.

This was getting out of hand. It was unacceptable, but I couldn't even say anything back. Not while I was still working. My boss was somewhat of a bitch, and I couldn't risk pissing her off, so I bit my tongue and *smiled*.

"I'll give you the bill. We close in thirty minutes," I said, as politely as I could, the corners of my eyes twitching with the effort to keep from snapping at Maddox.

Turning on my heels, I walked away before he could say anything else. I prayed he'd be gone by the time my shift ended.

When the clock struck eleven thirty, I hurriedly fumbled with the strings of my apron. I went into the bathroom and quickly changed out of my waitressing uniform, jumping into my jeans and yanking my beige sweater over my head. Done and done. I had fifteen minutes to catch my bus, and it was the last bus for tonight.

As I walked out of the restaurant, I prayed... and hoped...

But *nope.*

There he was, standing against the lamp post next to the bus stop.

Deep breaths, Lila, I told myself.

My lips tightened into a firm line as I walked to the bus stop, stopping next to Maddox but refusing to acknowledge him. He was starting to become unbearable. Why did I even *feel* something for him before?

The smell of cigarette was strong in the air, and I rolled my eyes. "Smoking is bad."

"Yeah, yeah. I know. Cancer and shit." From the corner of my eyes, I saw him take another long drag before exhaling a puff of smoke through his nose.

My lips curled in revulsion. "I don't care if you die, but you're probably going to give me cancer along the way if you keep smoking around me like this."

It was a horrible thing to say, I knew. But for someone to care so little about their own life and health, it made me pity the poor fool. He really didn't know what it meant to precariously hang between life and death. He didn't know how scary and lonely the door behind death was. I saw it, and it still haunted me to this day.

Maddox let out another puff of smoke before he looked down at me. "Why do you hate me so much?"

A mocking laugh spilled past my freezing lips. It was colder than I anticipated, and I wasn't dressed properly for the weather, stupid me. "Wow. Are you *that* full of yourself you can't figure out why I despise you so much? I thought you were smarter than that."

"Well, I want to hear it from you. I don't like to speculate."

Oh really? I didn't think he was ready for this, but I humored him anyway.

Fighting another shiver from the cold, I hugged my waist and turned slightly toward Maddox. The ripped jeans were a bad idea since my legs were numb now. But I refused to show any sign of being frozen to death, least of all in front of *him*. "First. You still haven't apologized for bumping into me in the coffee shop."

He let out a mocked gasp, filled with disbelief. "What? You're still pissed about that day? It's been two months!"

I locked my jaw, silently bristling. "I don't care how long it's been. I appreciate it when people take responsibility for their mistakes and apologize when they're wrong."

"I'm sorry."

My jaw went slack, and my eyes snapped to his. Wait...did...Maddox

Coulter just apologize to me? Was something wrong with my ears? Maybe I was dreaming. Yup, that must have been it. "What did you just say?"

He threw the rest of his cigarette on the ground, squashing it with his leather boot. He kept his eyes on me, his face devoid of any mischief. He looked... serious. What a confusing man. I couldn't tell which side of him was real anymore. "I said I was sorry," he rumbled, the expression on his face genuine.

I narrowed my eyes on him. "Apologies don't count when they're not sincere."

"You confuse me, woman. First, you want me to apologize. Then when I do, you tell me not to. Pick one, Garcia."

"When someone says he's sorry, he should mean it. Apologies need to be sincere or else it's useless and, frankly, a waste of time. Mean it or don't say it at all. I don't accept half-assed apologies."

Maddox brought a hand up, holding it over his chest. "Jesus. You're harsh, Sweet Cheeks."

"Second, you've been annoying me non-stop, always following me around, and you find every reason to irritate me! Whether it's in class, at lunch or outside of school. You do know that personal space exists, right?"

He looked thoughtful for a second, and I thought he really was considering my words. But then he opened his mouth, and I wanted to smack him. "Girls love it when I'm in their personal space," he admitted as if it was the most obvious thing.

"Full of yourself and absolutely cocky. The list is growing at an accelerating rate."

"So, you hate me because I give you attention?" Maddox took a pack of gum out of his pocket, popped one in his mouth before offering me one.

Against my better judgement, I took it. He was offering; I needed something to keep me distracted. "I *despise* you because I don't want the attention you give me."

"Anything else?" The corner of his lips tilted up, a small grin on his face. There was nothing taunting about it. In fact, he looked *pleased.*

"You keep calling me *Sweet Cheeks* even though I have told you a thousand times to stop. And you keep using vulgar language. You're rude and immature and inconsiderate to other people," I whisper-yelled.

"But you call me *Poodle*." Was that all he got from my rant?

"I call you *Poodle* because you call me *Sweet Cheeks*. I believe everything is fair in love and war."

He stood closer, bending his head, so he could whisper in my ear. "And what do we have between us? Love? Or war?"

"War," I said through gritted teeth.

"I approve," he said too quickly, popping his gum. "Anything else?"

"Yes," I practically screamed now, "You. Kissed. Me."

"Ah. So, you hate me because I stole your first kiss?"

Was that what he thought? That little shit.

A sigh escaped me, and I rubbed a hand over my face, trying to chase away the cold. "That wasn't my first kiss, Maddox. And I despise you because you did it without my permission. That... was unacceptable."

He rubbed his cheek with his thumb and shook his head, still grinning. "Goddamn it. You've got a lot of rules."

My lips curled. "And I guess, you're one who hates rules?"

Maddox flashed me a wicked smile. "I break 'em, Lila. I love to break rules."

"It makes you feel extra manly?" I taunted.

"No. It makes me feel alive." His confession made me still, and I stared up at him, watching his expression for any lies, but all I saw was sincerity.

For a moment, Maddox's pained face flashed through my brain: outside in the cold, sitting on that bench, looking so lost. I didn't want to admit it before, but there was *something* about Maddox that really intrigued me.

I couldn't forget that look on his face, it was tattooed in my memories. Maddox Coulter was more than Berkshire's star quarterback. He was a complicated puzzle, and I wanted to tear him apart, layer by layer, so I could study him, delve into his soul and learn all his secrets.

A gust of wind breezed past us, and I quickly patted my hair down. This time, I couldn't hold back the involuntarily shudder that racked through me. Maddox took notice, and he frowned, his eyebrows pinching together. "Why don't you have a proper jacket on?"

I hugged myself, rubbing my hands up and down my arms. "I didn't think it was going to be this cold. I thought the sweater would be enough."

Before I could finish my sentence, and before I knew what was happening, he shrugged off his jacket and pushed it toward me.

I eyed the jacket, suspiciously. "What are you doing?"

Maddox circled my wrist with his finger and dragged me closer. He placed the jacket over my shoulders and gave me a pointed look, his face hard, until I succumbed and placed my arms through the sleeves. "Keeping you warm. I'm a man, Lila. I know you don't like me and think I'm an absolute asshole."

His lips twitched when I scoffed. "Fine, I'm an asshole sometimes."

I gave him *the* look. *Are you serious?*

"Okay, all the time. But I still know how to treat a lady right."

Treat a lady right? What a joke.

But still… my heart warmed. His scent was still heavy on the jacket, and I chewed on my lip when I noticed how good the smell of him was.

Maddox buttoned up the jacket for me and tugged the collar higher and closer, so my neck was covered. "There. Cozy enough?"

My lips parted, but I didn't know how to answer, so I only gave him a tiny nod.

He pulled back and looked me up and down, a frown appearing on his face. "Jesus Christ. You're so tiny."

I rolled my eyes. "Thanks."

I expected another joke coming from his lips. Instead, he looked tense and his brows were curled with a frown. "Are you sure it's safe for you to be out here like this, so late?"

Huffing in response, I rolled my eyes again. As if he cared. "I don't need a knight in shining armor. I can take care of myself."

His blue eyes were so bright and vivid under the moonlight. It was tempting to get lost in them. But when he opened his mouth, he squashed down all the effects he had on me. "I'm not going to be your Knight because I know you aren't a damsel in distress. You're more like the dragon in the fairy tale."

My lips curled and against my better judgement, I found myself smirking. "If I could fry you right now, I would."

It was easy to get lost in the easygoing expression on his face What were we arguing about before? Shit, I got sidetracked.

His devious grin was back, but there was something… pleasing about it. He was mocking me like before, being a bully, but this was a war with no venom. "I bet I'd taste good as an omelet."

"Do you always have a reply to everything?" I asked, not expecting a particular reply since I already knew the answer.

Now, he was smirking like the devil. As if he had won this round. "Were you born this sassy or do I bring the sass outta you?"

I blinked, my brain stuttering at his question.

I was petty, yes. I never backed down without a fight, yes. But this newfound sass…

Swallowing past the heavy ball in my throat, my gaze skittered away from him. Maddox tended to make me feel on edge, like I was about to jump off the cliff. He irritated me, non-stop. But as bad as it sounded when I admitted it, I had grown used to him being a jerk. The ongoing battle between us was exhausting, but it had been something I started looking forward to. Our pranks and verbal sparring had become something I had grown used to.

The realization had me taking a step back.

I had always been competitive, but I had never found a proper opponent.

Not until Maddox.

His gaze shifted behind me, and his smile slid off his face. "Your bus is here," he said, breaking through my muddling thoughts.

The bus came to stop in front of us, and I started forward, leaving him behind. My hands were shaking as I tried to take off his jacket. He held my hands in place, over the buttons. "Keep it. You can give it back later," he said, his voice gruff and thick.

"Have a good night," I breathed, stepping into the bus.

"Oh, Lila?"

I peeked at him over my shoulder. He had his hands shoved into the pockets of his pants, a few stubborn strands of hair falling over his eyes. "You don't hate me," he stated firmly before cracking a smile. "Sweet dreams, Lila. I might visit you there."

My lips twitched, and I turned away before he could see it. If you google Maddox's name, Cocky will be his definition. Maybe that should be his middle name. Maddox 'Cocky' Coulter.

I swiped my card and took a seat at the back of the bus. As it drove past where we had been, I saw Maddox still standing there, staring at the bus as I left him behind.

He was right.

We were at war, two very fierce opponents.

But…

I didn't hate him.

Realization dawned on me that I didn't loathe Maddox as much as I thought I did. Things just turned out to be a bit more complicated because it would have been easier if I hated him.

CHAPTER
FOURTEEN

Maddox

Hate is a strong word.

It's a bitter but sweet fucking poison. It's like cocaine, and once you've had a taste, it's damn addictive. It becomes something more. It infiltrates your system, running through your veins, until you can't see anything other than red rage.

Hate kept me going.

Rage kept me alive. It became the oxygen I breathed.

See, I didn't hate my parents.

I *loathed* them.

I wasn't angry at them. No, it was something more. The rage festered over the years. I tended to it, watered it and watched it grow into something nasty and ugly.

Years ago, I found out it was easy to hate but so damn difficult to love.

But no matter how deep my hatred ran for them; I still looked into their eyes and hoped to see something *more*. Love for the child they brought into this messed up world and forgot to look after. *Me.*

My mother and I stood opposite of each other in the hallway of our home. She had a cashmere shawl wrapped around her shoulders and the moonlight shone through the window, casting a glow on her face. I was the carbon copy of my father, but I had my mother's eyes. I waited for her to acknowledge me, I waited for her to smile and say a few words. I waited to see if she'd ask me if I ate today or if she wondered how school was. Something simple, something small… but something other than silence.

It had been two weeks since we saw each other. We lived in the same goddamn house, but my parents were never here.

She clenched her shawl tighter to her body and walked toward me. It was way past midnight; I had come home late, yet again, after partying with Colton and the boys. I smelled of alcohol, weed and the scent of cigarette was heavy in the air, clinging to my clothes.

Her eyes met mine for a half second before she averted her gaze. Her lips parted as if she wanted to speak, and my heart thudded so hard in my chest as I *waited.*

The look on her face told me she didn't *hate* me, maybe she even cared… but when she closed her mouth and walked past me, I realized… she didn't care enough.

My heart plummeted to my feet, bloody and weeping, as mommy dearest walked over it and walked away from me.

I marched to my bedroom and slammed the door close, knowing full well my parents wouldn't hear. I was on the opposite side of the house, the distance between us too big.

The bottle of liquor, sitting patiently on my nightstand, called to me. I wasn't an addict, but I *needed* it. Tonight, at least.

Grabbing the bottle, I sank into my couch and watched the shadow dancing over my walls in my dark room. I took a long swig of the bottle, feeling the sweet burn in my throat.

Rage… Hate… I *breathed* it in.

My head swam, the air was thick and hot.

To everyone, I was Maddox Coulter – the golden boy, star quarterback and Berkshire's king.

To my parents, I was a disappointment.

To myself? I was just the boy trapped in the closet.

Hate was cold fire; there was no warmth from it.

My eyes fluttered close. Before I became lost in the space between sleep and consciousness, a mouthy girl with pretty brown eyes and black hair came to haunt me.

I slowly smiled.

Fuck, she was something else.

Lila

The next day, I walked through the halls of Berkshire as if I was on display. If I didn't know better, I would have thought I forgot to wear clothes this morning, but no, I was definitely dressed. Their eyes burned into the back of my head, and the whispers followed me. They made no attempt to hide their curiosity; some of them – Maddox's fangirls -- even looked at me with open distaste.

Shit. Now what?

Riley popped next to me out of nowhere and gripped my arm. "You owe me an explanation," she hissed in my ear.

Confused, I looked down at her. "Why? What did I do?"

"The rumor," she started, but then trailed off as her gaze skirted over my head. Riley scowled hard, and I turned around to see Maddox and Colton walking through the entrance.

I stayed rooted on the spot as he sauntered toward me. My brain told me to run. The look on his face was anything but *nice*. Mischief glimmered in his blue eyes, and a smirk twisted his full lips. Uh-oh.

The hallway became quiet, as if awaiting a long, overdue dramatic scene. I could feel everyone holding their breaths, anxious and curious as they stared back and forth between Maddox and me.

I tried to backpedal out of his way, but he ate up the distance between us with three long steps, stopping right in front of me. "Coulter," I said in greeting, eyeing him with suspicion.

Maddox dipped his head to my level, breathing against my lips. My heart stuttered, and I froze on the spot. His lips skated over my cheek in a chaste kiss, and he lingered there for a second too long. "Good morning, Lila," he said, his breath warm against my skin.

I felt the stares on us, the silent gasps coming from the others at Maddox's public display of affection, even though it was anything but affectionate. He was teasing me, making me the center of attention because he knew how much I despised it. This wasn't good.

I pulled back, glaring up at him through my lashes. Without a word, I stalked past him, but his voice followed me as he called out across the hallway. "Don't forget to give me back my jacket, *baby*."

Double shit!

I snuck a quick look to my left to see people staring at me with open-mouthed expressions. Holding back a growl, I didn't spare Maddox a glance as I stomped away with Riley at my heels.

When we rounded the corner to a fairly empty corridor, she grabbed my arm and pulled me to a stop. "You kissed him!" she whisper-yelled, her face a mask of astonishment.

A groan escaped me. "Is this why everyone's staring at me like I've grown two heads?"

"Someone saw you two kissing at your locker two days ago, and you know how quickly rumors spread," she admitted.

The rumors in Berkshire spread like a wildfire, untamed and unstoppable. The people were hungry sharks in the tank full of blood.

They probably thought Maddox and I were dating now due to the kiss and then the jacket comment made by Maddox.

"Well, here's one important fact. I didn't kiss him. He kissed me."

"He kissed you?"

I threw my hands in the air. "Yes," I growled. "Why is this such a big deal?"

Riley's eyebrows popped up, giving me a look that said the obvious. "You kissed Maddox Coulter after declaring war on him. Yeah, babe. It's a pretty big deal."

"Whatever. It won't happen again."

She followed me, hooking her arm with mine. "Is he good, like the rumors say? I heard some girls say he can tongue-fuck your mouth like he'd tongue-fuck your pus–"

"Riley!"

She let out a smothered giggle, and I instantly knew she was teasing me on purpose. Such a brat. "Sorry, but you should see how you're blushing right now."

Ignoring the warm heat against my cheeks, I leveled Riley with a glare, and she pouted, but, thankfully, chose to remain silent.

I left Riley at her Calculus class before making my way to English. When I walked inside, Maddox was already there, sitting in his usual spot. He had his legs thrown over his desk, his ankles crossed. Two girls surrounded him, and they were giggling at something he must have said, except he didn't look interested in the conversation; in fact, he looked like he needed to be saved from them. Why couldn't they see that?

A little self-respect would go a long way. He didn't want them; it was as clear as the sunrise in the morning and the moon in the night sky. The thing about Berkshire was that everyone wanted to be on top of the food chain. The only way to get there? Date a popular jock, it was as simple as that.

Maddox was the biggest fish in the tank, the best catch, and every girl wanted to get her hooks in him.

His gaze slid to me and the corner of his lips quirked up into a small smile. Maddox gave me his signature smirk, followed by a wink that had dozens of girls melting at his feet.

I lifted my chin in silent acknowledgment before taking my seat.

Soon enough, class started. Mrs. Levi began her Shakespearean lesson for this semester; we were studying *Hamlet*. She wanted to start the lesson with a *Hamlet* movie, the popular one with Robin Williams.

"It's the best adaption," Mrs. Levi explained. "But the projector isn't working. So, I'm going to need someone to get the TV from the storage room. Lila, do you mind?"

She looked at me expectantly, and I nodded.

"Any volunteer to help?"

I held back a groan. *No, no, no...*

"I'll go with her," Maddox said smoothly.

Mrs. Levi clapped her hands together. "Oh, great."

I marched out of the classroom, making my way to the storage room at the end of the hall. Maddox caught up with me easily. "You don't look happy, Garcia."

"Oh look, you're back to your annoying self," I countered.

From my peripheral vision, I saw him give me a lazy shrug. "You shouldn't be surprised."

Actually, I wasn't.

"Did my jacket keep you company last night?" He said the words like he was whispering a dirty secret.

Of course. Everything had to be dirty with Maddox. He probably thought I sniffed his jacket while I masturbated. Fun fact: *I didn't.*

I huffed. "I have it in my locker. I'll give it back to you after school."

"Are you asking me to meet you after school? A date?" A shocked gasp spilled from his lips, but it was fake. I could easily sense the mocking smile in his words.

"No," I growled. "Come to my locker. I'll return your jacket to you, and we both can go on our merry ways, *separately*."

He didn't have a chance to refute me since we were already standing at the storage room.

A note glared back at us, and I rubbed a hand over my face. "Great," I muttered under my breath. "The light isn't working."

I snuck a glance at Maddox, and he looked a bit... apprehensive. Hmm. "Can you keep the door open for me while I get the TV?" I asked.

Maddox shrugged.

The door was heavy as we pushed it open, and I walked inside. It was dark, but the lights from the hallway illuminated the inside enough for me to spot where all the TVs were kept against the back corner of the room. Aha, there it was.

Each TV was sitting on its own small four wheeled shelf, and all I had to do was roll one out. Easy peasy. *Not.*

When I tried to pull, it didn't budge, not even an inch. Goddamn it.

I took a peek behind the TV and saw that there was no way I could roll it out of this storage room. All the cords were tangled up together.

"Maddox, can you help me with the cord? It's stuck, and it's dark in here. I can barely see anything."

"Just pull it," he rumbled, impatiently.

"If I could, I would," I hissed. "It's stuck. Help me."

He was silent for a moment before uttering, "Ask nicely."

"Are you fucking serious?"

"Say please.

"Please," I said through clench teeth.

He tsked. "Say the full sentence."

I straightened, bringing my hands to my hips, as I rolled my eyes. "Maddox, can you help me with the cord, please?"

"Good girl," he praised.

He pushed the door wide open, holding it against the wall, and stared at it for a second, waiting. "It's not going to close. Hurry," I called out.

When Maddox was sure the door wasn't going to close and lock us into the storage room, he sauntered inside. He looked behind him once, staring at the open door for a second longer, before coming to stand beside me.

"Move aside," he demanded.

I rolled my eyes, again, but still did as I was told. Maddox reached behind the shelf, trying to find the cord. "Damn it, what is this?"

"Exactly. It's all tangled up with the others." There were four TVs in all, and they were pushed together into a tiny corner. We hadn't used them in the longest time, since we got the new projector screens, so they had been sitting here, collecting dust.

He let out a frustrated groan before starting to untangle the cords, which would take a lot of patience to do. The space between the rack and the wall was too tight, and I could see he was having trouble. "Here, let me get my flashlight. That might help," I suggested.

I fished out my phone from my pocket, but before I could turn it on, a loud banging sound echoed through the room. We both flinched, and Maddox lifted his head in surprise, hitting the top shelf in the process. He let out a string of curses.

Before I knew what was happening, we were surrounded by complete and utter darkness.

Shit, the door closed.

And… double shit, we were locked inside; the note had said that the handle was broken.

"No…no… No!" Maddox bellowed, rushing for the door through the dark. Huh? Was he scared of the dark? Who would have known Maddox Coulter, with his cocky smirk and eyes that could melt you on the spot, was scared of a little darkness?

I successfully turned the flashlight on, already thinking of teasing him like he would have done to me. My gaze slid to Maddox just in time to see him bumping against a shelf in his hasty attempt to reach for the door. The metal rack crashed to the floor with a loud, booming sound, and Maddox fell to his knees before he scrambled up again. He slipped over the broken shards and fallen liquid, crawling toward his escape.

No, wait. *No...* he wasn't just scared of the dark. This was something more.

A heavy weight settled on my chest, my throat closed and my breath stuck in my throat. Shocked, I stayed rooted on the spot as Maddox came completely undone.

Cool, collected and flirty Maddox was replaced by a stranger. He blindly reached for the door, grabbing the broken handle and pulling himself to his feet. Maddox hit the heavy door with his palm. "No, no! Please! No, no, no. *Please,*" he repeated under his breath. "Don't do this, please Let me out of here! Don't leave me here. Don't do this. No, no, please! *Don't.*"

He repeatedly hit the door, his open palm connecting with the surface with such hard slaps that it should have hurt him. "Help me, help. Please, don't leave me here."

Maddox scratched at the door, as if he was trying to rip it free from its hinges. He was trying to break through. His fingers clenched into tights fist as he started banging on the door, violently. His screams echoed through my ears, and my heart thudded hard against my ribcage, I felt his *pain.* His agony was a reminder of my own silent suffering.

"I can't... I can't breathe. I *can't,*" he whimpered, his voice cracking.

Thump – thump – thump.

"This is what death feels like, and you're going to die alone," a voice whispered in my ears.

My lips parted with a silent cry as I fought to breathe, but I couldn't. I really couldn't.

My breath came out in sharp, hallow panting, and my vision grew darker and blurred. I squeezed my eyes shut and pressed down on my

eyelids. A kaleidoscopic of stars fluttered behind my closed eyes. Help me,
help. Please, help me.

I thought maybe I was having a heart attack; yet, there was no
physical pain. But my whole body vibrated, my skin crawled like I was
picking apart my flesh and trying to jump out of my skin.

"This is what death feels like."

I can't breathe.

Help me.

"Help me," Maddox screamed.

My thoughts fluttered away, and my heart kicked in my chest, pushing
me forward. I snapped out of my frozen state and rushed to his side, my
own hands trembling. "Maddox," I said softly, trying to break through his
madness. "Maddox, please."

He banged on the door harder, and I noticed his knuckles had been
split open from his attempts to break free from the storage room. Oh God,
he was hurting himself. "Maddox!" I said louder, grabbing his arms and
trying to pull him away from the door. He resisted and shook me off him.

"Maddox, no! Please. Don't do that. You're hurting yourself. Just…"
I scrambled, trying to figure out what to do, what to say, so I could break
through to him, reach Maddox in the place where he was lost. I had to pull
him out.

"I need to get out. I need to get out. Get me out of here!" His fist
pounded continuously on the door, a sob racking through his body. His
voice was hoarse as he screamed brokenly. "Get me away from here. Get
me out of here. I need to get out… I can't breathe! I need to get out."

He went to punch the door again, but I grabbed his fist, holding his
hand in my own. It was a risk. I knew he was so lost in his head that he
could have hurt me. Unintentionally. But it was important for him not to
hurt *himself.*

It was becoming clearer that he was suffering from a panic attack. I
knew exactly what it looked it, what it *felt* like.

"Please," he whimpered. "Get me out of here. Please. Please. Please. *Please.*"

I held back a choked sob as he started pleading, each word spilling out of his mouth like a goddamn arrow straight to my heart. I bled *for* him.

He started mumbling something I couldn't hear, his breathing ragged and loud as he struggled to breathe.

When he realized he couldn't break free, Maddox crouched down, his head dropping to his hands as he fisted his hair, pulling at the strands. The mumbling under his breath grew louder as he shook his head back and forth. "Please, please. I need to get out. Help...Help me...Please."

My chest grew tight at the sight of him like this.

My knees weakened. When I couldn't hold myself upright any longer, I knelt down beside his trembling form. My hand landed on his chest to feel his heart pounding, hard and erratic, as if it was beating right out of his chest. His shirt was drenched with sweat, sticking to his body like a second skin.

I knew what it felt like to suffer like this. Chest caving in, all the air being sucked out from your lungs, a fist clenching your heart so tight, blood rushing through your ears, your lungs can't seem to work properly and then it happens... *suffocation.* The need to crawl out of your skin, as if your body is not your own anymore, chasing an escape you couldn't even see through the fog.

The tremors kicked in and Maddox started shaking. It started with his hands before his whole body quaked as he struggled to do a simple thing as inhale and exhale.

I had to get him to breathe first, it was the only way to ground him into the present, to bring him back from wherever he was lost inside his head.

Maddox held his head in his hands, his body rocking back and forth. "No, no, no. Please. Please," he begged.

"Maddox," I spoke softly. "Maddox, I'm right here. It's okay."

A tortured sound came from his throat, and my eyes burned with unshed tears. This was… hard. So fucking hard.

This wasn't Maddox.

This was a boy, frightened and lost.

I gripped his hand and pulled it away from his face, holding it with both of mine "I'm right here, Maddox."

His eyes were squeezed shut; his eyebrows pinched and his face… it was a mask of raw pain. He was tormented by something, his past… maybe, I didn't know, but whatever it was, Maddox was still hurting. I could almost taste his suffering in the heavy air surrounding us.

Squeezing his left hand, I spoke firmly. "Look at me, Maddox. I'm right here. Look at me, okay? Please."

When he kept his eyes closed, I changed tactics. "Breathe with me, baby. Can you do that? Can you breathe with me? I'll count. Maddox, you can do it. I know you can."

He sucked in a ragged breath, his chest rattling with the effort. "There you go. Slowly. Breathe with me. I'm right here. I'm not leaving you. It's going to be okay."

I squeezed his hand again, counting to three out loud. "Inhale," I instructed.

He did. He slowly sucked in a breath.

I counted from four to six now. "Exhale."

Maddox let out a harsh breath.

Squeeze. Inhale. Squeeze. Exhale.

One. Two. Three. Inhale. Four. Five. Six. Exhale.

When his breathing slowly became less ragged, I whispered, "I'm proud of you. That's good. Do it again, Maddox. Breathe with me. Stay with me."

His eyes opened, and I realized whatever I said had gotten through to him, so I repeated it again. "I'm proud of you. Stay with me."

I inhaled, showing him how to do it, and Maddox breathed in a shaky breath. Somewhere in his tortured blue eyes, I saw him trying to hold onto his own sanity. I stared into his dark and bottomless eyes, seeing something I had never seen before. Fear and misery consumed every part of him.

I saw myself in him, and we bled together, our pain seeping through us, similar to how tears would leak from our eyes. Maddox looked at me as if he was staring at something he was about to lose.

"I'm not going anywhere," I soothed gently, rubbing my fingers over the back of his knuckles.

He was still shaking, but he wasn't struggling to breathe anymore.

I remembered my mother singing to me when I was a child, a sweet lullaby as she'd put me to sleep. When I'd suffer from my own panic attacks, my therapist told me to play the lullaby on YouTube. It had helped calm me down. I knew everyone rides out their panic attacks differently, but maybe... maybe I could...

Right now, Maddox looked like a child who needed someone to hold him.

So, I did.

I knelt between his thighs, so I was close to him, and held his hands in my own. I continued to rub my fingertips over his bruised knuckles, letting him feel my touch.

My lips parted, my heart *ached* and I sung him my favorite lullaby.

"Lullaby and good night, In the sky stars are bright, May the moons silvery beams, Bring you sweet dreams, Close your eyes now and rest, May these hours be blessed, Till the sky's bright with dawn, When you wake with a yawn."

I saw brief recognition in his gaze. His eyes turned glassy, and he had a faraway look, like he wasn't seeing *me*, because Maddox was somewhere else.

"Lullaby and good night, You are mother's delight, I'll protect you from harm, And you'll wake in my arms, Sleepyhead, close your eyes, For I'm right beside you, Guardian angels are near, So sleep without fear," I

sung gently.

His lips quivered, and panic welled up inside me. I messed up; I shouldn't have sung to him. He was just starting to calm down and now…

Maddox curled his arm around my waist, and he pulled me against him, his head dropping to my shoulders. The world stilled except for our pounding hearts, beating together like a broken violin, shrieking with violent, pained sounds. A silent sob racked through his body, and I felt wetness on my neck where Maddox had his face hidden.

He was *crying*.

In silence.

He suffered in silence.

His tears carried the weight of his pain.

My emotions became jagged as my chest ripped open, a knife digging itself into my little, fragile heart. It was so hard to swallow past the heavy lump in my throat. Emotional pain bore invisible scars; yet, these scars could be traced by the gentlest touch, I knew that.

Breaking apart was hard. It stung with every breath taken.

Recovering from it was the hardest.

Sometimes, the pieces can't be put back together because they're mismatched, missing or completely shattered, making it an impossible feat.

Tears slid down my cheeks, and I choked back a cry. My own voice cracked as I continued to sing the rest of the lullaby.

He pulled me tighter into his body, and I wrapped my arms around his shoulders, holding him to me. I remembered how it was, coming out of my panic attacks, the adrenaline rushing away as I came back to the present. Everything would hurt, and I'd always feel so lost.

This was Maddox right now.

So, I held him.

Because he needed to be held, even if he didn't say the words.

He needed me.

Maddox trembled in my arms, his whole body shaking with his silent cries and tremors. As the lullaby came to an end, I pressed my lips against his cheek. "You're going to be okay, Maddox. I got you."

Thump – thump – thump.

There was a hollow ache in the pit of my stomach.

I embraced him.

He didn't let go.

His breathing smoothed out, and his pounding heart slowed.

"I got you," I soothed, running my fingers through his soft hair.

His arms clenched around me, and he nuzzled his nose into my neck.

Hold me tighter, he said without any words.

I got you.

CHAPTER FIFTEEN

Lila

Maddox and I were still wrapped in each other's arms when the door of the storage closet opened, and the janitor peered inside with a look of horror on his face.

"What are you two doing in here?" He held the door open, and the light from the hallway bathed the inside of the dark room.

Maddox's grip on me tightened at the new voice, and he kept his face buried in my neck. His silent tears soaked through my blouse as I smoothed a hand down his back. "I'm right here," I whispered in his ear before looking up at the janitor, who was limping inside. He had a bad leg, the rumors said it was from a military accident. He had been working for Berkshire for fifteen years now, and he was loved by everyone. Sweet Mister Johnson.

"We got locked in by accident," I explained, motioning toward the TV with one hand. "We had to get the TV, but the door closed on us."

Mr. Johnson looked down at Maddox and I, where we were still kneeling. I was practically sitting on his lap, and his arms around me were tight. Maddox was a sinking ship; he was drowning in the wreckage of a wounded heart, and I was the anchor holding him together.

I got you.

My heart couldn't bear to let go, even though I knew I had to.

Eventually.

"Is he okay?" Mr. Johnson looked mildly curious, but mostly worried. I nodded. "Could you grab the TV for us, please? The cords are all tangled up together."

"Of course. Let me get it. Which class are you guys in?"

"Mrs. Levi."

"I'll bring it. Get back to class." He waved, shooing us away.

"Thank you, Mr. Johnson."

My nails grazed Maddox's scalp in a soothing manner as I ran my fingers through his hair. "Maddox?" At the sound of his name, he pulled away from me and stood up. I could tell he was still shaky, his body swaying before he found his footing again, and he refused to look at me. Still holding onto his hand, we walked out of the storage closet. His breathing has evened out now, and his face had hardened, his eyes lifeless.

Maddox was shutting down… shutting *me* out.

"We can grab a bottle of water from the vending machine," I suggested, gently.

When I tried to squeeze his hand, he ripped it away from me. Like I was some kind of disease and he didn't want to be infected. "Madd—"

"Stay away from me," he said, and it sent chills down my spine. His voice was like a thunderclap, furious and strained.

"Maddox," I started, but he cut me off.

"Don't." That was a warning, and I should've listened; I really should have because for the first time, I saw a different Maddox.

A boy filled with rage, but blue eyes that held a broken song.

When I tried to grab his hand again, to stop him from walking away and shutting me out, he swiveled around without warning, and I almost fell into him My lips parted with a silent gasp when he grabbed my arm in an unyielding grip and slammed me against the wall. Maddox towered over me, his jaw clenching and his eyes darkening. He looked like a raging warrior, riding into battle with the promise of death in his gaze.

His head lowered, and his breath caressed over my lips. "Tell *anyone* about this and I. Will. Ruin. You. Lila," he warned, his tone thick with threat.

"I would never..." I breathed as my body went cold.

He bared his teeth with a low growl, silencing me. "It's been harmless fun between us, but, trust me, breathe a word about this to anyone else, I will make sure you're never able to walk through the halls of Berkshire again without wanting to cower and hide away in fear."

"Maddox, listen. I–"

My heart stuttered, and I forgot what I was about to say when his hand slid up my arm, and he wrapped it around my neck. His fingers tightened around the base of my throat, but it wasn't a punishing grip. It didn't hurt, but it was a silent promise, a warning, a deadly threat.

"I will ruin you. You'll beg for mercy, and I will show you none, Lila." His voice was a sharp sword carelessly slicing through me.

Maddox pushed away from me as Mr. Johnson walked out of the storage room.

"Everything okay here?" he asked, his gaze going back and forth between Maddox and I.

Maddox swore under his breath, loud enough for me to hear before he stomped away.

In the opposite direction of the class.

He was... leaving?

My voice caught in my throat as I watched him walk out of the building, the double doors closing behind him with a loud bang. I flinched as he disappeared out of my view.

Clearing my throat, I gave Mr. Johnson a tentative smile. "He just needs… a minute by himself."

"He's an angry young man," he commented. "Reminds me of myself after I was discharged from the military."

"He just…"

Mr. Johnson waved me away. "No need to explain. Here's the TV."

I swallowed past the burning lump in my throat, mumbled a quick *thank you,* before grabbing the TV stand and rolling it toward the classroom.

I expected him to come back later, but he didn't.

There was no glimpse of Maddox for the rest of the day. I walked through the halls of Berkshire, looking for him, but he was… gone, and I felt his absence like a sharp sword slicing through me.

Maddox's mixed emotions might have been justified in the moment, but not toward *me.*

I hadn't done anything to deserve being on the receiving end of his anger. Especially not after the time we had spent in that dark storage room.

My gran always told me I was a curious little thing, but this wasn't just about curiosity. This was the *need* to know the real Maddox, the one he hid behind a cool façade and a bad boy mask.

Because the Maddox in that closet, the one I held in my arms… he was a lost boy, and he reminded me of myself after I had woken up from my coma.

Maddox

The scent of a heavy cheap perfume touched my nostrils, and I almost gagged at how strong the smell was.

My head hurt.

My body ached.

What the–?

My eyes split open, and I stared at the ceiling of… *not* my room.

Ah fuck. Why couldn't I remember anything? There was an empty hole in my memories, and all I remembered was…

The pounding headache had me wincing as I rolled over to my side as my stomach twisted with nausea. The bed shifted with another weight and a low moan came from the person beside me.

I let my head drop to my pillow and closed my eyes as the memories came flooding back.

The storage. A reminder of my fucked-up past, carelessly thrown into a living nightmare. *Lila.* Fucking hell, Lila. She was with me. She held me.

She goddamn held me in her arms and rocked me like I was a child.

Lila… sang to me.

A lullaby.

The same one my mother used to sing to me. She had a habit of coming into my room to put me to sleep. She'd sing to me and kiss me on the forehead before turning off the lights and closing the door behind her.

Good night, Sweetheart. Sweet dreams.

Good night, Mommy.

That was all…before.

Before things changed, and I became a stranger to my own parents.

And Lila…

Shit! I remembered walking away from her, threatening her.

A pained groan escaped me when I realized what a shithead I was. Lila was the one good thing in that moment, and I ruined it with my anger and ego.

No, I had been…*scared.*

"Hmm," someone mumbled next to my ear. My eyes closed as I

remembered the party.

I had been drunk and needed to fuck the anger out of my system. It led me to this… grabbing a bitch at Brayden's party. The hotel. Alcohol and sex, then I passed out.

"Hey babe." Her hand smoothed down my naked chest, and my skin crawled at the touch. None of the girls I slept with were allowed to stay after a sex marathon. I hated the after-sex-talk, and I loathed sleeping beside them. It gave them unnecessary expectations that I wanted *more* than just sex.

I grabbed her hand and pushed it away. The mattress shifted again and another weight beside me rolled over, throwing a leg over my hips.

Wait… another?

I guess I didn't grab a bitch, I picked two.

"Get out," I growled.

The one to my left let out a sleepy snort. "Excuse me? It's four in the morning."

"Yeah, get the fuck out." I threw an arm over my face, waiting for them to do as they were told.

"You're an asshole. We're not leaving." This one was from the woman to my right. I could imagine the haughty look on her face without even having to look at her.

I sat up in bed without sparing the two of them a glance. I pushed Miss-Right-Bitch out of the way and climbed out of the huge, king-sized bed. She let out a nasty snarl, and from the corner of my eye, I saw her grabbing the bedsheet and trying to cover up her naked self.

Miss-Left-Bitch was silent but still sitting in *my* bed.

"I paid for this room. So, either you leave, or I call security to have you thrown out. I'm saving you some grace and keeping your dignity intact by only kicking you out and not having you thrown out. Now, Get. The. Fuck. Out," I warned while putting on my boxers.

I turned around, giving both of them a pointed look. "I'm going to take a piss. You have two minutes to leave this room before I have you thrown out. You wanted a taste of Coulter? You got it. Now, shall we go on our merry ways? In case you're wondering, no... I'm not putting a ring on your finger."

Blondie's eyes turned into slits as she glared at me. "Are you always like this?"

The bedsheet was still scandalously wrapped around her curvy body. It was tempting, I had to say. But my dick didn't rouse at the sight, so that would be a no for me.

"I don't even remember your name."

She let out a gasp, her hand flying to her tits in shock. Way overdramatic. This wasn't some goddamn soap opera.

The pounding headache was making it difficult to focus, so I blinked several times, trying to clear my blurry vision. How much did I drink? I couldn't remember shit.

"Two minutes," I snapped, before walking away. The bathroom door closed behind me, putting the lock in place, in case either of them had the stupid idea to join me. I didn't usually say no to shower sex, but I wasn't in a mood for another sex session. My head was killing me, my body was sore and so was my dick.

After taking a piss, I walked out of the bathroom to see that Blondie had left, but her 'friend' was still here. Black hair, exotic sun-kissed skin and brown eyes, she looked like she had just walked out from a magazine.

And those chocolate brown eyes reminded me too much of Lila.

"My name is Tammy," she introduced, breathlessly, with a thick British accent. "I mean, you didn't ask for our names last night."

That was because I didn't need to know her name to fuck her. Nameless and faceless. There were countless women before her; she was just another lay. I was probably just another man on her list, too.

She only had her skimpy panties and bra on, her big tits practically spilling out. Any man would take their time with her body, but I wasn't

156

that man.

Tammy sauntered over to me, stopping an inch away. Her tits brushed against my chest, and she smoothed her palm over my abs, sliding down toward my dick. She cupped me in her warm hand, rubbing me through my boxers. "C'mon, babe. Don't be like this. I thought you said we could go all night. We barely just started. Now that Jenna is gone, it's just us."

My patience was thin, and I snapped, roughly grabbing her arm and pulling her toward the door. On our way, I grabbed her black dress off the couch and dumped both outside the door.

Her face was a mask of fury, her lips parted, probably to curse me, but I slammed the door before she could go on a rage-filled rant. What a typical scene.

Yeah, I was being an asshole.

But fuck, I didn't have the strength to deal with girls like her right now.

I sank into the bed with my head still throbbing.

Sleep took over within a minute, but it was no beauty sleep.

"Run and hide. I'll count to twenty before coming to find you," Nala said to me with a giggle. We were playing hide and seek. It was my favorite game to play with Nala because I was smart, and she could never find me.

Mommy said I was the smartest.

That was why I always won our games.

Nala started counting, and I ran to the basement. She wouldn't find me there. I had to find the perfect hiding place. Our house was huge, and there were corners to hide, but Nala knew almost all of them by now. We had been friends for a few weeks, and she discovered all my hiding spots. So, I had to find a new one.

The closet!

I closed the door behind me and snuck under the shelf. Perfect spot.

I was going to win again. Mommy showed me this spot when we were playing last time.

I waited and waited…and waited for Nala to find me.

It must have been a long time because my knees were starting to hurt from staying in the same position for too long.

I crawled from under my hiding spot and went to the door.

My heart froze when the door didn't budge.

I pulled harder.

It didn't open.

"Mommy," I called out, but then I realized…

My parents weren't home. Daddy said he had a business meeting, and they would be home late. They were always busy, always leaving the house in the morning before I woke up and coming home later, after I'd gone to bed. That was why Nala was here to keep me company. She was Mrs. Kavanaugh's daughter, our maid.

I pulled at the door even harder.

It wouldn't open.

No, no, no.

"Nala! Nala, I'm here. In the basement. Nala, come find me!"

I slapped the door, punched and kicked and screamed. My throat started to feel dry, and tears slid down my cheeks. I didn't like crying. I had to be strong, like daddy. He never cried.

But I couldn't… stop… the…tears…

"Daddy," I yelled, feeling myself go cold.

Scared… I was so scared and cold. Why was I so cold? My teeth rattled, and I shivered, feeling more tears slide down my cheeks. My face was wet as I cried more.

I didn't like this.

Why couldn't I open the door?

Why? Why?

I pulled and pulled, but the door was too heavy for me, and it wouldn't open.

"*Mommy, please! Mommy! Daddy!*" *I screamed.*

Why couldn't anyone hear me?

Maybe... maybe... they'd eventually realize I was missing, and they'd come find me later. Mommy knew of this hiding spot; she'd know where to find me.

I sank to the ground, bringing my knees to my chest.

Mommy and Daddy would find me, I knew they would.

"*When they come home, they'll search for me,*" *I murmured.*

I had to be strong. Strong like Ironman. I had to be strong like Daddy.

I didn't know when I had fallen asleep or for how long, but when I opened my eyes again, it was dark.

So dark, I couldn't see anything.

The lights, what happened to them?

Oh no.

I couldn't see...

I couldn't breathe...

"*Mommy!*" *I scrambled up, searching for an escape.*

I punched the door, but my hands were too small, and they started hurting.

But I didn't stop.

I punched and screamed louder. "*Mommy! I'm here. Daddy!*"

It was so dark. I didn't like it; I didn't like the darkness. I never did. It scared me, that was why mommy always left my night light on.

"*Help! Help me! I'm in the closet... help... me...*"

I couldn't breathe...

I couldn't breathe....

"*I can't... help.... I can't... breathe... mommy...*"

My heart was beating too fast.

I couldn't see anything.

It was dark, so so dark.

My body shuddered, and I stumbled on the floor, next to the door, still scratching and punching.

"Can't... breathe... daddy... please... please... come find... me! Please..."

I cried.

I didn't want to; I had to be strong, but I couldn't stop.

I cried harder.

"I'm... scared..."

My hand went numb until I couldn't feel it anymore. "Don't... leave me here... mommy. Help," I whispered when I could no longer scream.

Everything hurt.

My head. My throat. My hand. My body.

Everything.

And it was so dark. There was a monster in the dark, like in the movies. I could feel it watching me, and my skin crawled.

The monster kept watching me; I couldn't see it, but it was there.

I still couldn't breathe.

"Help..."

*Mommy and Daddy had promised they'd always find me wherever I hid. They said they could **feel** me because I was their baby, and they'd always know where I was.*

They... lied.

They didn't find me.

"Don't... leave... me alone," I begged, but I could barely hear the words.

"Please."

My body swayed sideways, and I fell to the ground, my head touching the cold tiles of the closet. I curled into a small ball, trying to chase the cold away.

Come find me, mommy.

Don't leave me, daddy.

"Please... I'll be... a good boy. I... will... never ask... for another toy... or chocolate. I will...never cry again... I promise. I promise... I will... be good, a good boy... promise, mommy. Please, daddy... please..."

They lied.

They didn't find me.

"Help me."

They left me with the monster in the dark.

"Please."

They forgot me.

"Mommy... daddy..."

I jerked awake, gasping and breathless. My body was so cold; I was numb and shaking like a leaf during a storm. The bedsheet was soaked with my sweat, and I swallowed past the heavy lump in my throat.

It was just a nightmare.

Lies.

How could it be *just* a nightmare if it followed me when I was awake?

My heart pounded in my chest, and there was a dull pain.

The world spun, and I wanted to vomit as my stomach churned with nausea. The pain in my head flashed hard and heavy.

Breathe. Fucking breathe. Goddamn it.

Slamming my fist into the mattress, I let out a snarl. Hate. Anger. Self-loathing. Pain, so much fucking pain clashed together, and my head swam with all the emotions. Fuck this, FUCK!

I rolled over and grabbed the bottle on the nightstand.

I convinced myself I wasn't an alcoholic, but tonight... I had to drink, had to forget.

Taking a long sip, I felt the alcohol burn down my throat, and I winced, my brows furrowed tight with pain. My temples twitched, and it felt like I was sticking hot needles into my eyes as I continued to drink from the bottle.

My stomach heaved as I remembered how I called out for my parents, but they never came... and then I remembered crying on Lila's shoulders, like I had done before in that closet when I was seven years old.

Lila saw me at my weakest, and I hated her for holding me like that, as if she cared.

She didn't.

No one did.

My heart thumped harder, almost angrily, and it pumped acid through my veins, except I was...drowning.

It was then I realized that you didn't need water to drown.

Just like there hadn't been any real monster in that closet when I was seven years old, but the monsters had been in my head, and to this day, I couldn't escape them.

My body swayed, heavy and lethargic, as I took one last gulp before throwing the empty bottle on the floor. I fell back on the bed, sinking into oblivion.

Sweet fucking silence.

CHAPTER SIXTEEN

Lila

Gran pushed a box in my hand. "Storage, please."

She patted my cheek affectionately before rushing away to help the customer waiting for her. Gran was always on her toes. That was exactly why I told them to hire more people to help in the store. Old people were stubborn to the bone.

My gaze slid over to the windows as I walked out of the storage. When I caught sight of who I was looking for, my heart skittered a beat.

Black hoodie, ripped designer jeans and leather boots.

Maddox looked almost too good to be true. If I didn't know better, I'd say he was some kind of fallen angel. But he was anything but.

Maddox stood outside, his hood over his head as he smoked his cigarette in the cold. He had his hands shoved in his pockets, and his head bent low, staring at the ground.

Something had shifted between us since *that* day.

A week had gone by. Maddox was still his usual asshole self, but sometimes, I got the feeling he was purposely avoiding me.

The only time I saw real mirth in his eyes was when I hid a pink, glittery dildo in his locker. It was during lunch, the hallways crowded and bustling with students, when Maddox opened his locker. Mr. Big Ben aka Mr. Dildo slapped him square in the face while everyone around him gasped and promptly started laughing.

I had winked and sashayed away, satisfaction coursing through my veins, after seeing the look on his face. I made him grin, a real smile since that day we had been locked in the storage room.

The dildo prank was two days ago.

Yesterday, he retaliated with fake cockroaches in my bag and my sweater. I remembered throwing my bag on the ground, screaming bloody murder, while the students burst out laughing like it was the best joke of the century.

It was humiliating to say the least. I wanted to be mad. I had every right to be, but the moment I had spotted Maddox laughing, all my anger faded away.

Poof, just like that.

"He doesn't look very cheerful, does he?" Gran came to stand beside me, watching Maddox through the window. "He came in early today to help with inventory, and he hasn't eaten anything yet."

"He didn't have lunch?"

It was almost three in the afternoon.

A customer called for Gran, and she patted me on the arm before walking away.

Before I could think through my actions, call my instinct to help, I had grabbed a wrapped sandwich from the fridge and was walking out of the store.

Maddox looked up as I approached. He took one last inhale of his cigarette before throwing it on the ground and crushing it under his feet. He blew out a cloud of smoke before licking his lips, eyeing me up and down. "What's up, Garcia?"

Silently, I pushed the sandwich toward him.

He quirked up an eyebrow. "Is this a peace offering?"

"Gran said you didn't eat," I said as an explanation. I was just being... *nice.* There was nothing to it.

Maddox grabbed the sandwich from my hand, our fingertips touching briefly, before I quickly pulled away. "Careful there, Lila. You're starting to look like you care."

My eyes snapped to his, and I glared. "I'm being a decent human being. Give me back the goddamn sandwich if you're going to be an asshole."

Maddox was already ripping through the wrapping before I could finish my sentence. He took a huge bite, chewing hungrily. "Sorry, Sweet Cheeks. You can't give a hungry man food and take it away. Just like you can't put a pussy on display in front of a horny man and expect him not to devour you."

I blew out a breath. He was absolutely impossible. "Does everything have to be sexual for you?"

Maddox took another bite of the sandwich. "We were born to be sexual beings. Why not embrace it?"

I leaned against the window, watching the cars drive by, as Maddox devoured his sandwich in big bites. He was obviously hungry. Once he had polished the last bite, I broached the forbidden topic.

"That day... in the storage room," I started.

I didn't have to look at Maddox to feel the change in him. When he spoke, his voice said it all. "Speak of this again, and I will mess you up so fucking bad–"

"Why are you so full of anger?" I cut him off before he could finish his threat. "I'm not your enemy."

He let out a humorless laugh. "That's a pretty ironic thing to say considering our *relationship,* if you'd even call it that."

"It is ironic, isn't it?" I finally turned to look at him. He had a shoulder against the window, facing me. His eyes were bright blue in the sunlight, glimmering and hiding something darker.

Who was the man behind this mask?

"But I'm not going to hurt you. That was never my goal. I've only been trying to get even with you."

Maddox and I had been playing a game of cat and mouse. It was infuriating but harmless.

He cocked his head to the side. "So, you're saying, you won't hurt me unless I hurt you first?" he questioned with a rough, gravelly voice.

"Yeah, it's only fair. If you hurt me, I'll make you regret it."

"You're the first girl who hasn't fallen at my feet and begged me to fuck them."

"What does that make me?"

He grinned, wolfishly. "My prey."

I let out a laugh, instead of being offended like I would have been two months ago. "You have a one-track mind, Coulter."

"You're running circles around my head, Garcia."

Was that a... confession?

I backpedaled away from him. "Gran will expect us back to work in two minutes."

Swiveling around, I went to walk away but then stopped. There was a sinking feeling in my stomach, a gut-wrenching feeling that I was about to do something so stupid. But I couldn't stop myself. I had always been a girl who planned ahead, never doing something so... reckless. After life punched me in the face and left me scars, I vowed I would never be foolish.

Always in control.

Always cautious.

But apparently Maddox's reckless habits had been rubbing off on me.

I marched back to Maddox, standing a mere foot away. So close I could feel his warmth.

"You know what? I think me and you can be really good friends," I announced, the words spilling out before I could stop myself.

Yeah. Stupid, right?

His eyes widened a fraction before he scoffed. "How does me wanting to get in your panties equal to us being good friends?" He eyed my hand, the one stretched out between us. "And are you really waiting for a handshake?"

Goddamn it, what was I thinking?

Heat burnt my cheeks in embarrassment. "I'm trying to be civil here," I said through clenched teeth. "I just think... if we're so good at being enemies, imagine us being on the same side?"

It was true. I was tired of fighting with Maddox, day after day, over and over again. It was time to call truce, to end this war and to start over.

There was an unreadable gleam in his eyes when he spoke. "You'll bring Berkshire to its knees, Sweet Cheeks."

I'm going to bring you to your knees. I kept that tidbit to myself.

Maddox looked thoughtful for a second. He rubbed a thumb across his square jaw before giving me a simple nod. "Fine."

Wait...really? I blinked, waiting for him to laugh and call me pathetic. He didn't.

Maddox stared at me expectantly.

Holy shit.

I swallowed past the nervous lump in my throat, and this time, I showed him my pinky. "We solemnly swear to not share any animosity between us anymore and we'll play nice."

If Maddox thought I was being stupid, he didn't show it on his face. "I solemnly swear not to be an asshole, but I'll still think of sixty-nine ways of how I can dick you down every time you look at me or shake your ass my way."

"Maddox!" I hissed, heat blooming in my cheeks at his crude words. I was no saint, but damn it, he knew how to make a girl blush.

He let out a throaty chuckle, the sound coming deep from his chest.

Maddox wrapped his pinky around mine, squeezing it the slightest bit.

My lungs burnt, and I realized I'd forgotten to breathe.

This is it, I reminded myself.

The end of something; the beginning of something else.

I didn't know how serious Maddox was or if he'd keep his words... I didn't know if he knew the meaning of *friends*, I didn't know what tomorrow would bring us, if he'd be back to his usual asshole self, but I knew one thing – I no longer wanted to be on the opposite side of Maddox.

"Friends?" I breathed.

"Friends," he agreed.

Maddox

I watched Lila walk away, back into her grandparents' store. I scratched my three-day old stubble over my jaw, thoughtful.

The door closed behind her, hiding the perfect view of her ass from my feasting gaze. I had to remind myself to look away because, fuck me, Lila could bring any man to his knees with an ass like that.

Our eyes locked through the glass window, and she was *smiling*. A genuine fucking smile.

Lila waved at me to come inside, and my feet followed. If I was a puppy, my tail would be wagging back and forth.

Ah, for fuck's sake.

Friends?

Friends.

I paused at the door, blinking as I came to a sudden realization.

The moment Lila aimed for my dick in that coffee shop, I was fascinated. Girls were usually on their knees for me, worshipping my dick like it was the best meal of their lives. I never had a girl who wanted to cause Maddox-Junior pain instead of pleasure, until Lila.

When she had smirked over her shoulder before walking away, I was instantly intrigued. Who was this girl?

I made it my mission to find more about her, to study her... and to break her. She was my pet project, and I had wanted to bring her to her knees. Someone feisty as her? It would be sweet when she'd finally *beg* me.

Two months later...

Lila Garcia just fucking friend-zoned me.

Well, shit.

A laugh bubbled from my chest. Little Miss Perfectionist was ballsy, I had to admire that. I never had a girlfriend before. If someone had a pair of tits, Maddox Junior had a one-track mind. Sex. Plain and simple.

Lila had three things that made me weak: tits, pussy and ass big enough for my greedy hands.

I scoffed at the thought. This was going to be interesting. I wondered how long she'd last. The games have changed; the tables have turned, and I was going to play her game now.

Who was going to break first?

The player or the prey?

Well, this was going to be fun.

CHAPTE
SEVENTEEN

Lila

A firm hand landed on my ass, squeezing the soft flesh like its personal stress ball. The warmth of his body radiated against my back and the familiar, spicy scent of his cologne filled my nose.

"Take your hands off my ass. We're friends, Coulter."

When he didn't let go, I elbowed him, and he let out a small *ouf*. Maddox came to my side as we walked to our English class. "Wait, I thought you meant friends with benefits. Because that's the only type of *friends* I do."

I rolled my eyes. Day three of us being friends, and Maddox was still an asshole. A somewhat bearable jerk, but still a jerk. Apparently, he couldn't grasp the concept of *just friends* and was still trying to cop a feel.

Well, I couldn't really fault him since he caught me eyeing his dick print again yesterday. He didn't say a word, but his stupid smirk was enough.

"No. I meant normal friends. As in, you respect my boundaries, and I respect yours. Stop. Getting. So. Touchy."

"So, you mean, I can't slam you against the wall and fuck you?"

Sweet Jesus, help me, or I was going to murder this dude.

Exasperated, I gave him a look that said it all. "That's the opposite of friends, Maddox."

"Well, that's disappointing. You've seen how good I am on the field, but I was looking forward to showing you how good I am at thrusting."

There was a flash of mischief in his eyes, and my lips twitched.

He was being annoying on purpose, the dumbass. Sure, we were still stumbling over this new friendship thing, but it wasn't so bad. At least, I didn't find any more cockroaches in my sweater today and no pink dildo for Maddox.

As expected, when we walked into Mrs. Levi's class, all eyes were on us. The attention had me on edge, but with Maddox constantly at my side, I was starting to get used to it.

People always stared, after all, Maddox was the center of attention. He loved it, practically feeding off it. His chest puffed out like a proud peacock, eyes gleaming, and his signature smirk plastered on his full lips. Girls fawned, and guys burnt with jealousy.

Now that I was on Maddox's side, more like he kept me next to him all the time, we turned heads wherever we went. People assumed we were sleeping together, and I was his latest conquest. Some said I was his girlfriend.

No one believed we were just…friends.

Even Riley was suspicious at first, but she finally understood the nature of our relationship when Maddox stole my apple, and in revenge, I sprayed ketchup on his crotch. Childish and stupid, right?

But there was just something about Maddox that made me feel… carefree.

I ditched the front row and followed Maddox to the back of the classroom, where he always sat. Settling next to Maddox, which put me in the middle of him and his friend, I gave Colton a nod in greeting.

He smiled and fist pumped Maddox. "The whole school is talking."

My lips flattened in a straight line. "They need to stop gossiping."

"That's their job. To gossip," Maddox said with a lazy smile. "What's so bad about being my girlfriend, Garcia?"

"Because I'm *not*."

"You sure?" Colton shot back.

There was one thing I learned during these three days.

Colton and Cole were twins, but they were nothing alike. Cole was more reserved, the quiet type. He didn't always hang around with us, and he was less of an asshole and more of a gentleman. In fact, you'd think Colton and Maddox were twins because... they were both pompous jerks. Attitude and personality, both were fuckboys and infuriating.

Now that Maddox and I were *friends*, that meant his friends were mine. Poor Riley got dragged into this mess, too.

Riley was ready to deck Colton any time now, and I wanted to raise my white flag in defeat, but refrained from doing so. My mama didn't raise a quitter.

"If you two are going to gang up on me, I'm going back to the front row." I went to stand up, grabbing my bag with me.

Colton raised his hands up in mock defeat, and Maddox grinned. "Keep your ass seated on that chair, Garcia. I'll drag you back if I have to."

I plopped back on the chair. "I'm not your pet, Coulter."

He leaned closer, his lips next to my ear, so he could whisper while Mrs. Levi started her lesson. "You're kinda cute when you're pissed off."

"Shut. Up."

He sat back in his chair, looking quite satisfied with himself, like he had just tamed a dragon. As if. I ignored him and focused on the lesson instead. Sure, he was distracting, but I wasn't going to let him affect my perfect GPA.

Hours ticked by, slowly… so goddamn slow…until the final bell rang. It was a long day of being scrutinized and glared at, and the whispers followed everywhere I went. It didn't matter if Maddox and I were enemies or friends; I was an outsider, always had been and always would be.

Some were curious, some were just plain mean about it.

I heard she's poor. She's probably just fucking him for money. Desperate whore.

She's not even that pretty.

Do you think she's sleeping with Maddox's dad, too? I wouldn't be surprised if she has a sugar daddy.

Oh my God, that's so funny! Both father and son. Her hole is probably so stretched out.

She might be fucking her way through the whole football team.

They didn't understand why Maddox was so fascinated by me, their words, or why me and not them. Honestly, neither did I. Maddox was somewhat a mystery even to me. Why did he put me on his radar?

Riley let out a huff, her face red with anger. "What is *wrong* with them?"

"Just…ignore it," I said, breathing out a tired sigh. "They'll eventually grow bored and choose another victim."

"It's not fair."

No, it wasn't, but I was learning to accept my fate.

Riley, bless her heart, looked ready to attack someone, but I pulled her back.

"You have dance practice, right? Don't be late." I nudged her toward the door.

She let out a sigh and gave me a sad look. "You can't them walk all over you, Lila. I did that. I let them bully me to their satisfaction and they took everything from me. My friends, my popularity, my pride… until I had nothing left. They are like vultures. They won't stop until they break you apart. You need to show them who's boss because *you are*."

After all, I had nothing to be scared of. Maddox was on my side now. His friend. His only friend who was a girl. I had more power than any of the girls he slept with. He was king, and as much as I hated it, that made me the unofficial queen. Berkshire Academy was my kingdom.

But no one wanted a cold queen. The last thing I wanted to do was have them despise me any more than they already did.

Once Riley left, I walked into the bathroom since my bladder was close to exploding. The bus wasn't going to be here for another fifteen minutes, so I had enough time.

I was washing my hands when it happened.

When they rounded up on me.

In the mirror, I caught sight of four girls. I recognized two of them. Bethany, probably the most popular girl in Berkshire, and her best friend, Suraiya. The other two girls were familiar, but I didn't know them well enough to know their names.

They circled around me, and I shut off the tap, shaking away the droplets of water from my hands.

"Can I help you?" I asked, suspicious of their sudden appearance.

"She can speak," Bethany mocked, with a fake innocence.

"If you've got nothing to say, I'm leaving." I walked past her, and she grabbed my arm, digging her long nails into my skin. I didn't flinch, but it stung like a bitch.

"Not so fast, *Garcia*." She said my name like it was a stain.

"What do you want?" I wasn't scared, but I didn't like how there was one of me and four of them. They crowded around me, trying to be intimidating.

Bethany smiled, though it looked every bit as fake and malicious as she was. "I just wanted to give you a little…warning."

I laughed. "Maddox? Right, of course. Go ahead, give me your warning."

I tried to appear unfazed, but I knew what was coming. They were here for a reason. The fact that I wasn't cowering or begging for them to spare me angered them.

"Let's just say, I'm trying to save you some face. Maddox will grow tired of you, soon enough, and he'll drop you like yesterday's trash. You're going to be hurt because that's what he does. He breaks girls like you for a hobby."

I returned her fake smile with one of my own. "Oh, like he grew tired of you and threw you out like yesterday's trash?"

The corners of her eyes twitched, and her smile slipped off her lips.

I wasn't done yet. If she wanted to be a bitch, I was going to show her how to play the game right.

I shook her hand off me, tsking under my breath. "I remember that day. Gossip tends to travel fast."

Last year when I was still the new girl, Maddox and Bethany slept together. The next day, she publicly claimed she was his girlfriend, but he turned her down in front of everyone by saying: *You were a good lay but not good enough to earn the title of my girlfriend.*

It was harsh, and things turned ugly that day.

But Bethany was rich and spoiled as well as the cheerleading captain. She was Miss Popular and gossip like that didn't affect her. Sure, her pride was wounded, but she bounced back quickly and kept the title of queen bee.

She growled and lashed forward, backhanding me in the face. I didn't see it coming, and it *hurt*. The metallic taste of blood filled my mouth when I tried to lick my aching, bruised lips. Her friend kneed me in the back of my legs, and I fell to my knees.

"You're easily disposable, Lila. I claimed Maddox a long time ago, and all the girls of Berkshire know he's my property. That's the same as playing with fire."

Maddox... her property?

My stomach cramped, and I busted out laughing. This was probably the most hilarious shit I've heard in this decade.

They looked at me like I was a maniac. Maybe I was.

I was about to get my ass beaten, and here I was laughing at my assailants.

Bethany hissed, her face growing red. Poor little, insecure Bethany.

She pressed her thumb against my bleeding lip, and I forced myself not to flinch. She smirked and pressed harder. It hurt so much that unshed tears burnt the back of my eyes. "You're as pathetic as I thought. Dirt poor, not beautiful enough, so easily forgotten and so easily replaceable that you had to grab onto the richest and most popular guy."

Her voice told me everything I needed to know.

I was poor and beneath them. Maybe I wasn't as pretty or as rich as Bethany and the rest of Berkshire, but... Bethany, she felt *threatened* by me.

"I don't slut shame, but I can smell a bitch from a mile away," I said lazily. "You smell of jealousy. Very stanky. Go take a shower, sweetie."

Bethany gave me a disdainful sneer, her face twisting, and I saw all the ugliness she hid beneath the sweet girl mask that everyone loved and bowed down to.

She was Berkshire's official Queen, a pretty face with a nasty soul and a hideous heart. Her minions still had their hands on me, holding me in place and keeping me from attacking them. They had successfully trapped me; my arms twisted painfully behind my back and their knees were pressed into my shoulder blades, keeping me close to the ground.

Bethany crossed her arms over her huge tits, smirking down at me. "How would your grandparents feel if they lost their grocery store? Their only income and source of survival? They've had the store for fifteen years now, right? I guess, it's time to close down."

So, she did her research on me.

Bethany brought her face closer to me, and I saw the evil glint in her eyes. "Tsk, how sad would it be to watch them beg my daddy? I can ruin you and your little family. All I have to do is snap my fingers, and I'll watch you burn to the ground."

Rage bubbled over. She thought I was weak. She and her minions thought I was helpless.

Bethany gripped my jaw, her long nails digging into my sensitive flesh. "Where's Maddox now? Your hero is not here to save you."

I let out a small laugh.

Maddox, my hero?

She was mistaken.

I was my own hero.

I didn't need him to protect me or my family. I was my own protector in this story. Like Maddox once said, I didn't need a prince charming or a knight in shining armor.

Bethany's first mistake was standing too close to me. She had underestimated me. Once again.

My head reared back before I brought it forward, slamming my forehead into her nose. Hard.

She screamed, her wails piercing, as she pushed away from me. I twisted my arms away, kicked back at my attackers before standing up on my feet again.

I wasted no time and grabbed Bethany by the throat before she could escape and slammed her against the bathroom's wall.

"Don't. Fuck. With. Me," I hissed. Blood gushed from her nose; it wasn't broken, but I knew it was probably painful.

She glared at me, but too bad she was no longer in control. Her friends tried to grab my arms, to pull me away from their queen bee, but I held her tighter. Her throat was small and delicate in my hand.

"Don't fuck with me," I repeated. "You won't like the consequences. You might not like to get your hands dirty, but I don't mind. After all, I'm a poor, dirty rat, right? You don't threaten my grandparents. You don't threaten me. Because trust me, I will destroy you. I have my ways, Bethany Fallon. That's your first and only warning."

I pushed away from her, and she gasped for breath, wheezing. "You... bitch."

Suraiya tried to grab me, but I sidestepped out of her way. "You'll end up with a broken nose, too," I warned.

She smartly took a step back, and I *smiled*. Yeah, maybe I did look like a maniac in the moment, but Riley had been right. I couldn't let them walk all over me.

Bethany's minions surrounded her as she moaned and cried about her nose. I gave them a final glance and walked out of the bathroom.

I wasn't Miss Popular; I wasn't rich or the cheerleading captain... but the lack of these titles didn't make me weak because I was no doormat.

The next time they threatened the people I loved, I'd show them my teeth and claws.

CHAPTER
EIGHTEEN

Lila

I stumbled out of school, my legs feeling a bit shaky. My knees were bruised from where they had slammed me on the bathroom floor. My lips throbbed, and I could feel a headache coming. That was one hell of a slap, kudos to Bethany.

As I walked through the main gates, the bus drove past me, and I stood there, dumbfounded. Damn it, I missed my bus. Fists clenched, I held in the urge to cry because now was not the time for it.

It was cold. I was moody and in pain.

But I. Would. Not. Cry.

"Lila!"

My steps faltered at the sound of Maddox's voice. Huh.

"Lila, what the fuck?" he called out. I looked over my shoulder to see him running toward me. His mouth was curled in a dark scowl as he approached me.

My dark hair fell as a curtain around my face, and I looked down at my feet. I didn't want him to see the bruises, didn't want his pity or his stupid, mocking laugh.

But Maddox, being Maddox...

He crowded into my space, his front pressing against my back. His arm curled around my waist, and he pulled me into his body.

"How did this happen?" he asked, his voice low and serious.

"What do you want?"

"The back of your skirt is ripped. Doesn't look like an accident. Who did this?"

What?

I pushed away from Maddox and reached behind me to realize that he was right. There was a large tear in my Berkshire skirt, big enough for my panties to be visible and everyone could see it. No wonder I felt the cold breeze on my ass.

Anger flared up inside me, and I let out a shuddering breath.

I didn't want to cry because I was hurt or humiliated. They were tears of outrage, and I swiped at my cheeks, refusing to let Maddox see them.

"*Lila,*" Maddox said slowly. The sound of my name came from his lips so softly, as if he cared. It was stupid, but my heart still did a silly jump.

He grasped my shoulders and turned me around to face him. I kept my face lowered, but he was having none of that. His fingers grazed my cheeks, and he brushed my hair away from my face.

When he let out a string of curses, I knew he saw the bruises. His hand clenched my arm, and he dragged me to the bench. I tried to pull out of his grip, but he held tight.

He sat me down and knelt in front of me, looking like a dark, angry warrior. He was...pissed?

"Who did this?" he asked, his voice hard and strained.

"Your girlfriend," I shot back. I wretched my hand from his grasp and crossed my arms over my chest. "She isn't too happy about our friendship status."

His eyes turned into slits, and he gave me a hard look. "Bethany," Maddox hissed under his breath. "She's going to regret this."

I scoffed at that. "I don't need a protector. I can take care of myself."

His lips twitched. Even though his expression was hard and serious, the humor was back in his blue eyes. "No, you're right. You're the dragon."

Ha. Very funny.

I rolled my eyes and looked around us. Most of the students had gone home already, and I was probably two or three of the few who took a bus, since everyone had a car or a driver to pick them up. Perks of being rich, I guessed.

"What are you doing here?"

Maddox dragged his fingers through his hair, still short since his last haircut. I couldn't decide if I liked the long hair better, but I missed his poodle hair.

"Coach needed to speak to me. I was about to leave when I saw you walking out of the building and noticed the tear in your skirt. Nice panties, by the way. It reminds me of your cherry lips."

Mental facepalm incoming: 3…2…1.

Maddox brought his hand up, his thumb brushing over my sore lips. "Are you going to tell me what happened?"

I gave him a sheepish grin. "I can tell you about the part where I broke her nose and choked her."

"Atta girl," he praised out loud. "I was almost worried you were going to tell me you didn't fight back."

He grabbed my water bottle from my bag, and I watched as he wet his handkerchief. Against my nature, I stayed silent and *watched* him. His eyebrows furled in concentration, his lips in a firm, straight line, and his eyes darkened as he studied my bruises.

Maddox pressed the wet handkerchief over my lips, rubbing gently to clean the dried blood. I flinched but stayed still for him. He then swiped it over my cheek, which was almost on fire. Bethany's ring must have caught my skin. I let out a sigh when I realized it would be a nasty green or purple shade tomorrow.

"I don't like how you got hurt because of me," he finally admitted. Maddox touched my cheek, his thumb hovering over my wound. His touch was gentle and soothing.

"Feeling guilty, Poodle?"

His eyes snapped to mine, glaring. "It's not funny."

"What's not funny, *Poodle*?"

"Lila," he warned.

"Yes, Poodle."

"You're hurt!"

I pressed my finger over my cheek and winced, then gave him a nod in confirmation. "Yup, I can feel that."

He fumed, silently. His jaw clenched, and I swore I heard his teeth grinding together. Finally, I let the poor guy out of his misery. "I don't blame you. Bethany was a bitch. I dealt with it, and it's over now. Little scratches can't hurt me because they don't leave permanent scars."

Maddox stood up and offered me a hand. I grabbed it, and he pulled me up to my feet. "Fine. Let me drive you home."

The world came to a halt at his words, and my knees weakened.

I suddenly forgot how to breathe as my eyes watered. Sweat trickled down my forehead and between my breasts. I choked on my saliva as the gut-wrenching feeling in my stomach had me wanting to throw up.

The long, jagged scar between my breasts throbbed with a ghostly ache, a reminder. It wasn't painful anymore, but my body and my mind remembered the pain.

"No," I choked out.

Maddox gripped me by the elbow. "For fuck's sake, Lila. Just let me–"

"No!"

He didn't understand; he didn't fucking understand.

I stumbled back and away from him, desperately trying to count backward.

Ten... nine...eight...

"Lila."

His voice sounded so far away, as if I was submerged under water, and he was yelling at me from the sky.

Seven...six... five...four...three...two...one.

I opened my eyes and took a shuddering deep breath. Maddox was staring at me with an unreadable expression, and it angered me, not knowing what he was thinking.

Was it pity? Or was he judging me? Did he even notice I just had an anxiety attack?

"I'll take the bus... thank you for the...offer though," I spoke, trying to hide the tremors in my voice.

He took a long moment but finally gave me a slow nod. Maddox silently peeled his blazer off his body. I didn't expect it, but he stepped closer to me, his body flush against mine. He was a whole head taller, so he towered over me. He wrapped his arms around my waist, and I stilled, my lips parting in shock. When I looked down, I saw him tying a knot with the sleeves of his blazer around my hips. It laid heavily against the back of my ass and legs.

He was... covering up my ripped skirt.

"I got you," he breathed in my ear, before pulling away.

I opened my mouth to say thank you, but I couldn't find the words. Maddox looked over my shoulder and gave me a small smile. "The bus is here."

I nodded, still stupidly silent. *Say something, damnit. Anything.*

His hands were shoved in his pockets as he watched me climb into the bus. I settled in the back, like always. Maddox was still watching me.

I pressed my palm against the window, and he grinned, boyish and sexy.

Thank you, I mouthed as the bus drove away.

The next morning, as I stepped out of the house, Maddox and his car were there waiting. He rolled down his window and beckoned me over.

"What are you doing?" I asked. "Stalker much, Coulter?"

He handed me a brown paper bag. "Good morning to you, too, Sweet Cheeks. You look better today. No bruises, I see."

My bruises, which I had successfully been able to hide from my grandparents, were covered with makeup. I shrugged and took whatever Maddox was offering me. "Makeup did the trick."

I peeked inside the bag. Mint. Chocolate. Muffin. Oh my God!

"You–"

"You're welcome," he said.

I let out a laugh. "Seriously, what are you doing?"

"I thought you said we were friends."

I eyed him suspiciously. "We are."

"So, I'm getting you breakfast. You and Riley tend to share lunch, right?"

I couldn't decide if this was sweet or dorky, neither of which suited Maddox Coulter. I gave his SUV a once over. "I'm not getting in your car if you're trying to bribe me with my favorite muffin. For all I know, you could be a kidnapper or an axe murderer."

Maddox winked. "I'd make a sexy axe murderer, admit it."

I rolled my eyes, for the umpteenth time, and took a bite of my mint chocolate muffin. "My bus is here," I muttered around a mouthful. I bent down, so we were eye-level and gave him a smirk of my own. "You can follow me to school. Like you followed me home yesterday. You need to improve your stalking skills, Coulter."

The look on his face was comical. Busted, Poodle.

I winked and sashayed away.

We rode to Berkshire separately, although it didn't quite feel like it. The muffin he gave me kept me company. I tried to devour it slowly, but mint chocolate was my one and only weakness.

Maddox was waiting for me at the gate when I stepped off the bus. He hoisted his bag on one shoulder and gripped my hand. Surprised, I looked down at our interlocked fingers as he pulled me into the building. Wh-what?

"What are you doing?" I asked with caution.

"Holding your hand."

His hand was warm and strong. I wasn't sure how to feel about it, but I didn't pull away. "Why?"

His eyes briefly met mine before he went back to staring everyone else down. "Because I need the world to know they can't mess with what's mine."

It was on the tip of my tongue to rebut him. I didn't need a savior, didn't need to cower behind Maddox's back because I could handle all the haters on my own. Yesterday, I let my claws out and I was no longer worried about using them.

But when I saw the look on his face, hard and serious–I swallowed the words.

Something in his eyes told me he wasn't going to budge on this matter.

I didn't know *why* I kept silent and let him hold my hand. It bugged me why I did it, but then I pushed the feeling down.

We marched through the halls, and the students stepped out of our way, like the ocean parting in half for us to walk through.

I bit my tongue, held my chin high and kept my hand in Maddox's. His grip was firm, but comforting. I expected the whispers to follow us but was met with…*nothing*.

By lunch time, I couldn't bite my tongue any longer. The day went on just like this morning. The other students avoided eye-contact, no one glared or sneered at me and no one dared to approach me. Even Riley found it odd.

When Maddox reached for my fries, I slapped his hand away and leveled him with a look. "Did you do something? Did you threaten people? They're acting weird."

Riley gave me a grunt of agreement.

Maddox took a bite of his sandwich, simultaneously throwing an arm around the back my chair, before glancing around the cafeteria to give his *kingdom* a once over. "I think you were threatening enough for both of us."

"Huh?"

"Bethany's nose isn't broken, but you did a number on her. Gossip travels fast."

"They're scared of me?"

"They're scared of *us*," he amended.

I picked at my fries, no longer hungry. "Am I going to get in trouble... for hurting Bethany?"

Colton pushed back against his chair, rocking on the two back legs. "No, you won't. We took care of that already."

My eyes snapped to Maddox, frowning. "So, you *did* threaten someone."

The side of his lips quirked up. "I have my ways."

I should've been mad; I should've told him to mind his own business. I really should have.

But then I had a brief moment of realization – he was *protecting* me. Even though I told him numerous times that I didn't want him to. It was a very different Maddox, from the one who was jerk to me and it was shocking to the say the least. I was curious how far he'd go... to be my friend.

The moment Maddox and I did that pinky swear outside of my Gran's grocery store, it became obvious that my business was his and his was mine. It was an unspoken understanding between us.

We both shared a smile.

And that was it.

The beginning of something Maddox and I weren't ready for.

That day, we somehow sealed our friendship.

Friends?

Yeah, friends.

CHAPTER NINETEEN

Maddox

Three weeks later

Lila slammed her thick textbook closed and growled low in her throat. If she thought she was being intimidating, she was highly mistaken. That was a kitten growl, cute and harmless.

"You're distracting me. Stop!" she said through clenched teeth, keeping her voice low since we were both huddled in a corner of the library.

"What am I doing?" I feigned innocence because, seriously, my favorite pastime was annoying her.

She was studying for our upcoming calculus test while I was watching… porn. Okay, fine. Not exactly porn. But Tumblr was *nasty,* and I was making a habit of showing Lila all the videos I came across. Miss Garcia didn't find that amusing, but it was hilarious to me, so she was growling and hissing. Like I said, a kitten.

I didn't know if I had a semi-boner because of the videos I was watching or because Lila was sitting across me. Probably a bit of both.

"Do you realize you're the most frustrating person I've ever met in my life?" she finally snapped. I bit my tongue to keep from laughing.

I'd give her credit, though, for lasting three weeks as my *friend*.

I thought she would break, but no, Lila was fierce, something I greatly admired about her.

She plugged her earphones in and went back to her textbook. Her notebook was filled with equations as she did the practice questions over and over again. Over the past few weeks, I've learned a few things about Lila:

1) She was a perfectionist.

2) She wanted to get into Harvard and was still waiting on her confirmation letter to come through. Every day, she grew more anxious, although she tried hard to hide it.

    Since I got a football scholarship, I already had an early acceptance to Harvard.

3) She loved her grandparents dearly.

4) She was way too competitive.

Two minutes later, Lila gave up. She snatched her earphones out and glared at me. I tried to wipe the grin off my face, but damn it, it was hard when she was being so... *cute*.

"I know you're getting into Harvard with a football scholarship but don't your marks need to be just as good, or you could lose your scholarship?"

I swiped out of Tumblr as she ranted. My textbook and notebook laid in front me, untouched. "Yeah."

"Then, why are you not taking any of your classes seriously?"

Ah, so she was on my case. I refrained from rolling my eyes and shrugged instead. "I don't care."

"So, you're okay with not playing football after high school and losing your scholarship?"

That made me pause.

I didn't care about school or Harvard… but football was my kryptonite. Similar to how Lila was my favorite drug of choice, sweet and so fucking addictive.

I was MC – Maddox Coulter, Berkshire's reckless quarterback and Casanova.

But there was just something about Lila that kept me…grounded. It wasn't exactly a bad thing but it wasn't a good thing either. I didn't like how she could get under my skin, and I didn't like how she could read me so easily. It made me feel… weak, like that time in the closet. She saw everything I didn't want anyone to see. And even now, she could see through me.

"It doesn't matter. I'm getting into Harvard either way."

"Because your parents are going to buy your way into Harvard. Gotcha."

My head snapped up at the tone of her voice. She sounded… *disappointed*. In me.

My parents were on the Board of Directors for Harvard. It didn't matter if my marks weren't good, I wasn't going to lose my scholarship. They'd make sure of it. After all, that was all they ever did for me. Pay my way through Berkshire, throw a cheque at me, give me a fancy car for my birthday although they were never actually present on the day… it was all ever materialistic to them. Harvard was no different. Maybe paying for me to get in Harvard would actually remind them they did in fact have a son.

"You're getting into Harvard because of your parents." She paused, giving me a look as she studied me. "How about for once in your life, you don't depend on your parents' money and reputation. Why don't you do it for *you*? On your own. Through your own hard work and failures… and success on your own merits."

190

Her eyes bore into mine, looking…searching into my soul.

My jaw clenched and the muscles in my cheeks twitched. "Thanks for the pep talk, Garcia. Do I need to slow clap?"

"Still an unapologetic asshole," she whispered. Lila looked thoughtful for a second before she leaned closer, her face a mere inch away from mine. *"I dare you…"*

Bewildered, I let out a laugh. "What?"

Lila didn't laugh. In fact, I'd never seen her more serious. The look on her face made me capitulate, and my laughter turned into a coughing fit as she waited, patiently.

When I cleared my throat, she nudged her chin high and gave me another one of her I'm-serious-right-now looks. "I dare you to get into Harvard on your own, to keep your scholarship without your parents' help."

I blinked.

Then blinked again.

She was kidding, right?

"Chop chop. Gotta work your ass off, Coulter." Lila paused and gave me a mock gasp. "Oh wait… don't tell me, are you chickening out? Gonna lose this dare? Tsk, so disappointing. Here I thought *the* Maddox Coulter will never turn down a dare."

She was goading me, waiting for a reaction.

Fuck it.

She got me.

Lila got the reaction she wanted.

I gripped the back of her neck and brought her face closer to mine. She had to lean forward, half of her body bending over the table. Her lips parted with a silent gasp, and her eyes darkened. "I accept this dare."

Her lips twitched, and she smirked. Yeah, I was definitely rubbing off on her. Miss Perfectionist was now a she-devil.

"Good luck because you're about to get your ass kicked. First level of

191

this dare, you have to pass this calculus test."

"Easy fucking peasy."

"Really?" She raised an eyebrow, not at all convinced.

"I'm a genius, Sweet Cheeks."

Little did she know…

She cocked her head to the side, her hair falling over one shoulder. Lila looked every bit the wet dream she was – sexy, smart as hell, bold and passionate.

And my friend.

My dick was regretting this and begging for mercy.

Goddamn it.

She gave me a sugary smile. "Game on."

Four hours later, Lila closed her textbook. She leaned her head back against the chair and stretched, a small groan escaping her lips. I didn't know how she did it, but Lila barely came up for air in those four hours. Her eyes barely came off her textbook.

I closed my own notebook and studied my little friend. "Ready to go home?"

"Yeah, I'm exhausted." She piled her things in her shoulder bag and stood up.

"Will you let me give you a ride this time?" I asked, even though I already knew the answer.

Lila paused. "No."

I didn't push because the day she lost her shit on me was still a vivid memory in my mind. She panicked when I asked her to get in the car; I saw it in her eyes, on her face and the way her body trembled.

My fists clenched at my sides. The question was on the tip of my tongue as her lips pursed.

"The bus will be here in ten minutes. You can leave now if you want."
I stood up next to her, and we walked out of the library. "I'll wait."
Because...

Just... *because.*

We waited at the bus stop. Lila shivered, and I could hear her teeth
rattling from the cold.

"Lila," I started.

"Hmm?"

My lips parted; I went to ask the question that has been burning inside
me for the longest time, but I couldn't form the sentence. Lila lifted her
head up and stared, waiting.

"You refuse to get in a car... is it because of your accident?"

Lila gave me a wide-eye grimace, and I instantly regretted probing.
The crestfallen look on her face, as if she had been sucker-punched and
viciously thrown into a lake where she couldn't swim back up for oxygen
– *that* almost gutted me.

Her eyes were tortured, and they reminded me of myself when I
looked in the mirror.

"Your parents..."

"They died in that car accident," she whispered. Each word felt like
they had been torn from her throat, raw and painful. "I was... I was the
only one... the only survivor. They... died...they didn't... pull through."

I cupped her cheek. "Is that why you can't get in a car?"

She nodded, one slow nod. Lila silently spilled her secrets, so trusting
of me, and my heart thudded in my chest.

From the corner of my eye, I saw the bus approaching. She must have
noticed it too because her eyes darted that way, and she quietly sniffled.

Lila looked like she was swallowing a bitter lump of tears. My fingers
brushed against her cold cheeks, and she gazed at me with burning eyes,
her chest heaving.

One single tear trailed down her cheek, and I caught it before swiping it away.

I'm sorry, I wanted to say.

She gave me the tiniest smile, so strong yet so delicate. *It's okay.* *Thank you,* her eyes told me.

Lila took a step back, and my hand fell away from her face. I wanted to keep her pinned to me, wanted to hug her… but when she nudged her chin high and regarded me with red eyes, shining with fierce intensity, I let her go.

She didn't need me to swoop in to be her hero or her protector.

Long after the bus had disappeared from my view and she was gone, I stayed at the bus stop, with an overwhelming set of emotions swimming inside of me.

What started out as a game for me was not a game anymore.

Lila was truly and honestly my…friend.

The last thing I wanted to do was hurt her. In fact, I didn't like the thought of her hurting at all. I didn't know when or how it happened. But too soon, Lila became someone important to me.

Maybe it was when she hugged me in that dark closet and sang me a lullaby.

Or when she had offered me that tuna sandwich.

Or maybe it was when I wrapped my pinky around hers and did that silly pinky swear.

But somehow, Lila Garcia became more than just my prey.

She was someone I wanted to protect.

From the world.

From *me*.

CHAPTER TWENTY

Lila

Two months later

I stayed by my locker after the last bell rang, keeping a close eye on Riley and Grayson. She approached him, blushing and stuttering as she asked him about yesterday's homework. It was an excuse to talk to him. They chatted for less than five minutes before Riley gave Grayson a warm smile and bounced away.

It was so quick; anyone would have missed it. But I was looking and I caught Grayson watching her leave, his stare intense and his lips twisting with amused smile. Grayson rarely ever smiled.

From the corner of my eyes, I noticed someone else watching the encounter. Colton had his hands shoved in the pockets of his beige slacks as he leaned against his locker. His jaw clenched, and I swore the corners of his eyes twitch. No, that must have been my imagination.

But something was up with him, and it piqued my curiosity.

I snuck a glance at my phone, half expecting a text to pop up, but…
nothing. Damn it, I was starting to worry now.

"Colton," I called out as he walked past me.

He paused and jerked his chin up at me in greeting. "Sup, Lila?"

"Did you see Maddox today? He's not replying to my texts or
answering my calls," I asked cautiously.

An unreadable expression passed over Colton's face, and he scratched
his chin before looking down at his own phone as if waiting for it to light
up with a text, too. "No. He's not replying to mine either."

That was weird. Maddox never went radio silent on us, well… *me*
before today. In fact, he was always the first to pester me in the early
morning and until late at night with his horrible and silly jokes.

Maddox: What's black, red, black, red, black, red?

Me: Idk. Let me sleep.

Maddox: A zebra with a sunburn.

He always found a random joke to tell me at night; that was our
goodnight. At first, I didn't know if it was weird, annoying or… sweet.
But after a few weeks, I'd grown used to it and had come to expect it
every night after I climbed into bed.

Maddox: What's green and sits crying in the corner?

Me: Bye.

Maddox: The Incredible Sulk. C'mon, admit it. This one is funny.

Me: Ha. Ha. Ha. G'night.

Maddox's face faded into the background as I focused my attention on
Colton again. "Is something…wrong? What about the surprise party we're
throwing him later today?"

Two months after our truce and the beginning of our friendship,
Maddox had successfully passed the semester with good enough marks to
keep his scholarship at Harvard.

I knew Maddox would never back down from a dare because he was
no loser. But Maddox Coulter forgot to mention he was a genius. Not

Einstein genius, but we all thought he was never paying attention to his classes. Apparently, he *was,* and he wasn't braindead like I believed. In fact, Maddox was probably smarter than me, and this was something I begrudgingly admitted. His brain was working overtime to catch up on his classes, and he did it. Quite successfully.

One semester down.

One more to go.

After our exam marks came in, we decided to throw Maddox a little surprise party. Just his close friends, nothing too big. That was supposed to be tonight.

Except Maddox was nowhere to be found.

"Sometimes…"

I looked at Colton, waiting for him to continue. "What?"

"He likes to disappear for a day or two," Colton slowly admitted.

"So, something *is* wrong?"

He must have seen the alarm on my face because he was already shaking his head. "Not exactly. It's just… some days, Maddox gets low. He doesn't like to be around people when he's feeling like that."

I grabbed my shoulder bag and slammed my locker close. "Do you know where he is right now? Where he goes when he's like this?"

Colton gripped my shoulder, his face intense as he pinned me with a harsh stare. "Listen, Lila. It's best you leave him alone when he's like this."

"He's my friend," I claimed out loud.

Colton let out a humorless laugh. "He's my best friend. So what?"

"I know him." I wrenched away from his grasp and glared.

"I know him better than you," he said simply. "I've known him since we were kids."

But he hasn't seen Maddox like I had… trapped in that broom closet, screaming to be let out… crying and begging for someone to save him.

Colton didn't see that Maddox. I had. I held him and sung to him.

I gnawed at my lower lips, Colton's warnings ringing in my ears, but my need to run to Maddox and to make sure he was okay was strong.

"Don't do it, Lila. Leave him alone. He'll come back when he's ready."

I hefted my bag over my shoulder and stepped away from him. "Here's something you need to know about me, Colton. I don't listen well to warnings."

"You can't fix him," he said to my back.

No, I couldn't.

But that was the thing... I didn't want to fix him.

I wanted to hold his hand.

Nothing more; nothing less.

So, I did the opposite of what Colton told me. I took a bus to Maddox's house, er... mansion. That would be my first stop, and I hoped he was there. If not, then I was about to go on a wild goose chase. If he didn't want to see me, I'd leave – but after making sure he was *alive*.

The Maddox I knew didn't disappear and go radio silent on his friends.

No, the Maddox I befriended was an annoying, pestering jerk. Like the time he gave me roses.

Maddox was walking toward me with... flowers? What the hell?

I leaned against my locker and gave him a look, a look that said – what are you up to now?

He halted in front of me with a smirk I wanted to smother with a pillow. I raised an eyebrow and nodded to the flowers in his hands. "What are those?"

"Roses," he said, looking mighty proud of himself.

"For you." I rolled my eyes.

"They're dead, Maddox."

He gave me a petulant look, like a child who had their favorite toy taken away. "Yeah, dead like my heart because you won't let my dick anywhere near you because you friend zoned me. So here you go. Roses for you, Garcia."

"You need to see a shrink. I don't think you're mentally stable," I announced, already walking away from him.

He fell into step beside me. "You won't accept my roses? I'm hurt."

My lips twitched. Okay, it was really hard to stay serious when Maddox was in one of his pranking moods.

"You're so fucking silly. I don't know if I should laugh or... be concerned."

"Anything to see that smile on your face," he said with a grin.

And it was then I noticed, I was smiling. It had been a frustrating day, one of those days where nothing seemed to go my way. I was feeling moody and a tad bitchy, but here I was...

Instead of being annoyed with Maddox like I would have been before our truce, I was smiling. Damn it, this wasn't good. He couldn't have me smiling so easily.

"Are you flirting with me, Coulter?" I still couldn't wipe the grin off my face.

"Are you falling for it, Garcia?" He shot back, his eyes dancing with mischief.

"No," I deadpanned.

"Good. The harder you play to get, the more fun this game is."

"I'm not playing hard to get. We're friends," I stretched out the last word, putting more emphasis on it. Because obviously, Maddox didn't understand the meaning of 'just friends.'

Maddox let out a small chuckle. "Oh, I know. Besties forever. I'll do your nails and you'll do my hair type of shit." He paused, glancing down at me with a wicked smirk that should have warned me of what was about to come out of his mouth. "That won't stop me from trying to slide into your ass though."

I missed a step and stumbled forward before quickly regaining my footing. Sputtering, I glared at him. "My... ass...?"

Why did my voice come out like a squeak? Damn you, Maddox. You and your filthy mouth and dirty thoughts.

Maddox put himself in front of my path, so he was walking backward, facing me. "I'm an ass man, baby. You got enough to fill my two hands. And my hands are big enough to handle you."

Hmm. Oh really? He was almost too easy because I just found the MC's weakness.

"My ass makes you weak?"

He nodded. "Weak to the fucking knees."

I paused, lifted my chin up and regarded him with a regal look. If I made him weak in the knees, then...

"Great. Get to your knees and beg for it then. You might change my mind if you ask nicely."

He blinked, looking bewildered. "Wait, really?"

"Try and we'll see."

I forced myself not to laugh at the hopeful expression on his face. Poor baby. Maddox quickly got on one knee, in a proposal stance and presented me with the bouquet of dead roses. He gave me his most sincere look and asked, "Can I please fuck your ass?"

He said the words as if he was asking me to marry him, and this was some grand proposal. Don't laugh, Lila. Don't. You. Dare. Laugh.

I brought a hand up, tapping my index finger against my jaw in a thoughtful manner. His eyebrows furrowed, and he started to look suspicious.

I let my own smirk show. "Hmm. Not nice enough for me. Sorry, try again next time."

"What?" He let out a mock gasp, but I caught the grin on his face before I stepped around him.

Giving him a final glance over my shoulder, I winked.

"What a man would do for a piece of ass," he grumbled loud enough *for me to hear.*

I marched away, and maaaybeee, I put an extra sway in my hips –
giving him a good look of the ass he wanted so much but couldn't have.
What could I say in my defense? It was fun teasing a man like Maddox.

I smiled as the memory faded away, and the bus came to a stop at
Maddox's place. I had been here a few times, even got to know his butler,
Mr. Hokinson. I didn't know people in this day and age had butlers, but
apparently, people as rich as the Coulters did, in fact, have butlers.

I waved at the guard and walked through the gate. Mr. Hokinson
was already at the door, as I expected. He must have been alerted by the
gatekeeper the moment I stepped foot onto the property.

"Good afternoon, Miss Garcia," he said politely with a slight southern
drawl and a little bow. Cute, old Mr. Hokinson.

"Is Maddox home?" I asked, sounding hopeful even to my own ears.

He gave me a tentative nod, as if this was a secret. "He is, Miss
Garcia. But he hasn't left his room since this morning. He didn't come
down for breakfast or lunch, so we know to leave him alone."

My fists clenched at my sides. "And his parents?"

Mr. Hokinson swallowed, averting his gaze from mine, but didn't
answer. Ever so loyal, what a joke.

"I wish to see him."

He sidestepped into my path when I tried to walk around him. "I'm
sorry, but I can't allow you."

I raised an eyebrow and gave him a polite smile, even though I was
feeling anything but. "Please tell me, Mr. Hokinson. Did Maddox tell you
to keep me outside? Has anyone specifically said I'm not allowed into this
house? Because from what I remember… Maddox said I can come and go
any time I want. I have free rein, don't I? Even you're aware of that."

The old man blinked and pursed his lips in silence. "Are you going
against his words? I'm not sure he's going to like that."

"He–"

"I just want to know if he's okay, and I'll leave," I interrupted before he could give me another excuse. Before Mr. Hokinson could stop me, I walked around him and into the house.

I took the stairs two at a time to his room. His door wasn't locked, but I still knocked. Once, twice... four times, but there was no reply.

With caution, I opened the door and peeked inside. Nothing. Empty. Bare. No Maddox.

I walked inside to find the heavy drapes still down, blocking any sunlight from entering the dark room. There was something gloomy about the atmosphere. His bathroom's door was open, though, and I could hear the water running.

There he was...

My brain stuttered for a moment and a shocked gasp escaped me. The sight of him had me stumbling and rushing into the bathroom. "Maddox!"

No. No. Please, no.

I fell to my knees beside the overfilled tub. He sat inside, fully clothed with an empty bottle of...

God, no.

Maddox stunk of alcohol and cigarettes. I almost gagged at how heavy the smell was. His eyes were closed, his head barely staying above water. My heart fell to the pit of my stomach, cramped and twisting with nausea at the distraught look on his beautiful face. There were shadows under his eyes, as if he didn't sleep the night before.

I cupped his cheek. "Hey, Maddox." I gave him a gentle shake.

His bloodshot eyes fluttered open, and I could see the naked pain in his eyes. Maddox, strong and carefree Maddox, looked... beaten. Not physically. There were no injuries marking his body, but he looked wounded in spirit.

"Oh, baby. What happened?" He didn't respond, not that I was expecting a reply.

"Go away," he grumbled under his breath. God, he was pissed drunk.

How many drinks did he have?

"And leave you in the tub like this?" I asked gently. "I can't leave you now, Maddox."

Maddox closed his eyes, his shoulders slumping further into the water. "Don't... need a... lecture."

There was a strain in his voice – a voice that used to be full of warmth – now so cold and... empty.

"We need to get you to bed. You can sleep this off, but you need a bed. Not a tub full of ice water."

Maddox was stubborn, but so was I.

He gritted his teeth, a storm flashing across his face. "Fuck... off. *Leave.*"

"No."

He let out an empty laugh. "Then how about... you shut the fuck up... and sit on my face instead? Be a nice... give me good... pussy and cheer me... up, why don't you?"

That was drunk Maddox speaking, I reminded myself. He was barricading himself against me, trying to be hurtful and mean – to push me away.

I blew out a frustrated breath and reached under his armpits, pulling him up. He sat forward, and the water sluiced onto the sides. I turned off the running tap with one hand while supporting Maddox's limp body against the crook of my arm. "I'm going to ignore what you just said. But still, you need to get out of this tub before you catch pneumonia," I mumbled. "Don't be a jerk."

His clothes were soaked through, and I couldn't get him in bed in this state. Shit.

His eyes closed, and his head slumped over my shoulders, with his nose buried in my neck. A shiver racked through my body because Maddox was practically freezing as I dragged him out of the tub.

"I'm sorry," I said in a low voice. "But I'm going to have to get you out of these clothes."

Maddox was going to catch a cold if I left him like this. He mumbled something under his breath as a response. He settled on the edge of the tub as I peeled his wet shirt over his head. It wasn't my first-time seeing Maddox shirtless, but I still found myself pausing to stare.

Maddox was ripped, sculptured and...

No, stop! Don't look.

I averted my gaze and worked efficiently, trying my hardest not to stare longer than I needed at his naked body. He slurred more profanities at me, but I chose to ignore all of them. Once he was clad in his grey sweatpants and a shirt I found lying on the floor in his room, I dragged Maddox out of the bathroom.

My knees almost buckled under his weight. "Jesus, you're heavy."

He snorted in response as his body shuddered violently.

I *hated* this.

I was angry, so goddamn furious, that nobody thought to check on him. His parents or Mr. Hokinson. Anyone, damn it! What if I hadn't found him when I did? He could have accidentally drowned himself or... worse.

I was livid and fuck...

My heart *ached.*

How could Maddox be so careless? Didn't he understand how precious life was... and how easily it could slip out of our grasp? In a blink of an eye... everything – *gone.*

Tears burnt the back of my eyes, and I sniffled. "Why, Maddox? God, why?"

"Stop being a bitch... come and sit on my dick if... you won't stop yapping..." he slurred.

"I'm going to throw you on your ass if you throw one more insult at me, Maddox," I warned him. He stumbled and jerked out of my grasp, swearing under his breath.

"You're all bark and no fucking bite, Garcia," Maddox snarled, his eyes opened into slits.

He was angry – about something. I didn't know what, but if I could take a lucky guess, it had to do with his parents.

I understood that. But he didn't have to be an asshole.

When he stumbled again, his legs giving out under him, I grabbed his arm and hauled him to bed. Once he settled on the mattress, he swatted my hand away. It didn't hurt, but it still stung.

With my hands on my hips, I squinted down at him. "Don't do this, Maddox. I'm going to walk away."

The warning gained me a reaction, a small one. He opened his bloodshot eyes and stared at me, his expression a mask of unfiltered pain. "Then go. That's what they always do anyway. Walk away."

Goddamn it, did he have to hurt my heart like this?

I rubbed a hand over the ache in my chest, attempting to relieve the dull pain there.

"There is no reason for you to be mean to me when I'm only trying to help," I said softly, running my fingers through his wet hair. "Don't push me away."

Maddox let out a mocking laugh and closed his eyes. So be it.

I got off the bed and was only able to take a step away before he grabbed my hand. Firm and strong, even in his state. "Don't go. Don't leave...me," he croaked. The cracks in his voice made me pause. "I'm scared... scared of being alone."

I settled back on the bed again, all fight leaving me in one breath.

Maddox wasn't complicated in ways everyone liked to believe. Once I got to know him, I really saw him, the real *him,* and realized that he only hid behind a mask.

"You can't do this, Maddox. You can't be an asshole and then ask me to stay with that look on your face." Like a kicked puppy, a lost boy, a broken man. My sweet Maddox, with a heart of gold.

"Don't wanna lose you," he mumbled. Maddox grasped my hand in his, albeit clumsily, because he was still really drunk. Our fingers interlaced together, and his hold tightened.

I gave his hand a squeeze in comfort and in warning. "I don't do toxic relationships."

His eyes cracked open, and he gave me a small smile. There was something melancholy about it. He had the appearance of a desperate man, starving and reaching blindly toward *something,* but it always escaped out of his grasp before he could grab hold. Maddox was breaking my heart, and there was nothing I could do to end this suffering.

"We're not in a relationship."

I knew that but I still asked. Maybe I was a glutton for pain. "Then, what are we?"

His gaze fixated on me again, eyes so blue they looked like the midwinter sky – beautiful yet dreary. "You're... more," he whispered the confession. "Don't leave, *Lila.*"

He said my name like a prayer, as if he was whispering all his hopes to heaven.

With that said, he closed his eyes again, and this time, he was no longer conscious. I looked down at our hands, and I swallowed back my tears. "What are you doing to me, Maddox?"

Before I could think twice about my actions, I climbed under the comforter and joined him. His body was still cold, but slowly regaining its warmth. Under the strong smell of alcohol and tobacco, his scent still lingered. Warm, rich and earthy...

I didn't know when it happened or why I didn't realize it until now, but Maddox's familiar scent brought me comfort.

I curled into his side; our fingers still intertwined. He needed me; he needed his friend. "I'm not leaving. Pinky swear."

Maddox was bad.

There was a boy once, a boy just like him, who ruined me and left me scarred.

Maddox was everything I stayed away from; he was everything I didn't need in my life.

I told myself... never again. I'd never let myself be weak around men like Maddox.

But no matter how much I tried to walk away, to put distance between us, to somehow end this *friendship*... he wouldn't let go.

He was bad. He smoked, he was too hasty about life, he liked to break the law, he broke girls like me – he left a trail of shattered hearts behind him, and he didn't care about anything. I thought... maybe it was because no one taught him how to care for another human being.

I saw a few glimpses of the Maddox he tried to hide from everyone, the Maddox who just wanted his parents' approval – *that* Maddox was starving for attention.

There were a hundred reasons why he was bad for me.

But all those reasons became insignificant when I realized he didn't want to hurt me. At first, I was skeptical. I was waiting for Maddox to do what he was best at – break hearts.

But he didn't.

Weeks went by.

Two months passed.

I realized Maddox Coulter was a little bit ruined, a little bit messy, a little bit broken -- a beautiful disaster.

Like *me*.

All those reasons were no longer important, because every morning, he'd wait outside my grandparents' home, he'd hand me a muffin and follow my bus to school. Every afternoon, he'd sit with me and *study* – something he hasn't done in years. He hated studying, he hated opening a textbook, but he did it anyway. Because of a dare, because of me – he did it for me.

It was silly, it was something so little, yet...

I couldn't let go of my friend.

He was annoying but hilarious. He was the world's biggest asshole – a douchebag by definition. In fact, he'd take that trophy home. Asshole of the decade.

He angered me, made me want to scream in frustration, he drove me utterly crazy, but as much as he had me sighing in exasperation and rolling my eyes... he made me smile.

Maddox was out of his mind: too careless, too reckless, too foolish.

But he was the chaos to the perfect world I had built around me – a world where I kept my heart carefully guarded.

Miss Perfectionist, he liked to say.

Hmph. Maddox made my world a little bit less... perfect.

CHAPTER TWENTY-ONE

Lila

A s I came awake again, for the fifth time this night, I realized it
wasn't night anymore. The heavy curtains were still drawn, but
I could see the sunlight through the slits.

My hands landed on a wall of muscle, warm and strong. I could feel
his heart beating under my palm. My gaze slid up his chest, neck, squared
jaw and finally, his eyes.

I realized two things.

One – I spent the night with Maddox, and I slept for over twelve
hours, and he had slept even more.

Two – Maddox was awake, and he was staring down at me with an
unreadable expression.

"Hi?" I mumbled.

Shit, shit. Shit!

I meant to leave in the middle of the night, after making sure Maddox
was alright.

But I must have passed out and now…

This wasn't my first time sleeping next to a man. Well, my ex-boyfriend and I shared a bed a few times. But he was a boy. A lanky, inexperienced boy. Maddox was not a *boy*.

I wasn't shy or inexperienced, per say.

But I wasn't sure I liked the way Maddox was staring at me. The expression on his face made my stomach flip and clench. A shiver racked through my body; except, I wasn't cold. In fact, I was very, *very* warm. Maddox was a human heater.

His eyes were dark and intense, no longer dull or bloodshot.

"Stop looking at me like that," I grumbled, pushing away from his body. The sight of his dirty blond, disheveled hair, eyes glinting with something unspoken, full lips slightly parted, wide and strong shoulders – there was a masculine aura around him. He made me feel small and… feminine.

"What are you doing here?" he finally spoke.

I sat up, chewing on my bottom lip. "You don't remember…"

Maddox rubbed a hand over his face and rolled over onto his back. "I do. But, I mean, in my bed. Not that I mind, but I just didn't expect it when I woke up. Nice surprise there, Sweet Cheeks."

Ah, so he was back to the normal Maddox.

"I fell asleep," I admitted. I didn't know how to make this not awkward. "But I should probably leave now."

I got off the bed, but the sound of my name from his rough, sleepy voice made me pause. "Lila."

"Yes?"

I glanced back at him. Maddox was on his side, facing me and propped up on one elbow, \casual and at ease. There were so many differences between the two Maddoxs I had seen in the last twenty hours.

"Thank you," he said. There was something akin to *affection* in his voice. My chest tightened with an unfamiliar emotion. My mouth opened, but I never got a chance to tell him it was okay.

A knock sounded on the door, and Mr. Hokinson's voice came through. "Your parents are asking you to come down for breakfast."

There was a flash of annoyance and twisted fury on Maddox's face. "You can tell them to fuck off, thanks."

"Good morning to you, too," Mr. Hokinson said before his steps faded away.

"Maddox–" I started.

"No, Lila," he growled.

He climbed off the bed and went into the bathroom, slamming the door behind him. I flinched at that and stood where I was, waiting for him to calm down.

Ten minutes later, he was standing in front of me again. Arms crossed, he leveled me with a warning. "Stay out of this."

"What happened yesterday?" I shot back.

He surprised me by answering. "Bad day."

I took a step forward, reaching out to him. "Maddox…"

In a moment of renewed anger, his chest vibrated with another threatening growl. His jaw clenched, and I wondered how it didn't crack under the pressure. "I called my father to tell him about my final marks."

Oh no. No, I didn't like where this was going.

"He hung up on me because he was too busy. When he came home, I mustered up the courage and told him. You know what he said?"

I shook my head. *I'm sorry.*

His lips curled up into a snarl as he mimicked his father's voice. "Who did you bribe for those marks, Maddox?"

Hot, nasty fury coursed through my body. *For* Maddox. He continued, spitting out the words like they burnt him from the inside.

"He doesn't believe in me. Father dearest probably thinks I fucked my way through my teachers to pass my exams. So, you see? Lila, it doesn't matter. If I get into Harvard on my own or if I passed my semester. None of this fucking matter!"

My heartbeat pounded in my chest. "Yes, it does."

"No," he hissed.

I stalked over to where he was standing and cupped his cheeks. "Look at me! It does matter, Maddox."

He tried to jerk away from me, but I didn't let go. "I don't care what your dad says, but you worked your ass off for this. I saw it with my own eyes. You should be proud of yourself. And if you can't believe it, then let me tell you. I am so proud of you. Got it?"

His lips thinned into a straight line, his eyes going distant. "Lila–"

"I'm proud of you," I whispered, rubbing my thumb over his clenching jaw, the muscle relaxing under my touch.

His eyes squeezed close. "Fuuuuck," he muttered under his breath.

I let out a small laugh, hoping it would rub off on Maddox. "Well, Poodle. That's one way to put it."

His eyes snapped opened, clear as the sky, and he grasped my hand, pulling me toward the door.

"Where are we going?" I asked.

There was a renewed urgency in his voice when he spoke. "Breakfast. Let's go."

Well shit...

"Um, can I brush my teeth first?"

Fifteen minutes later, we were sitting at the table with his parents. It was my first time meeting them, and his father barely gave me a once over before going back to his tablet. His mother sent me a tentative smile before avoiding eye contact. She munched on her toast while an awkward silence fell upon us.

"We didn't know you had *someone* over, Maddox."

His father's voice was deep and uninviting. There was a harsh coldness to it. Mr. Coulter gave me an unappreciative glance, and I frowned. Did he...?

Holy shit, he thought I was Maddox's fuck buddy or last night's conquest.

And he probably though Maddox brought me to the table just for the sake of causing a ruckus. Well, that explained one thing. Maddox got his assholish ways from his father.

I cleared my throat. "My apologies, we haven't met before. I'm Maddox's friend."

"Friend?" His father gave me a dismissive flick of his hand.

"Brad," his wife warned in a low voice. The tension in the air was palpable, so thick someone could choke on it. My throat went dry, and I tried to swallow several times.

"What's your name?" Mrs. Coulter seemed to be more... approachable. The lack of judgement in her eyes had me relaxing, a tad bit.

"Lila. Lila Garcia."

She gave me a half-smile. "You can call me Savannah. How did you and my son meet?"

I took a small bite of my toast. I had been hungry before, although I was not anymore. My stomach twisted with knots, and I knew I couldn't have more than a few bites. "Maddox and I met in Berkshire Academy."

His father's head snapped up, and he speared me with a look. "Berkshire, you said? I don't recognize your last name. Who are your parents?"

He thought I was one of them... the wealthy and the corrupted. After all, Berkshire Academy was a tank full of those.

I took a slow sip of my water, trying to soothe my parched throat. "I live with my grandparents."

I jerked my chin high and returned his look with one of my own. I wasn't ashamed of who I was.

"Lawyers?"

Was this a goddamn interrogation?

I shook my head, pursing my lips in displeasure. "No, they own a grocery store."

"That's nice," Mrs. Coulter jumped in before her husband could utter another hateful word. He was staring at me as if I was a pest. As I stared at Brad, I could see the resemblance. Maddox was a carbon copy of his father. The same hair, same eyes, same angry look on their faces.

"So, have you gotten any college acceptances yet?" Savannah tried to break through the tension, looking back and forth between Maddox and me.

I nodded, chewing on the bite I just took before answering. "Yes, to Princeton, but I am hoping for Harvard."

Maddox's father let out a huff. "Harvard? It's not easy to get in."

My shoulders straightened, and I gave him a tight smile, trying to look polite. If Brad saw the irritated look on my face, he ignored it. "Oh, I know, but I've been working for this for years now," I told him. He didn't scare me, not with his judgmental stares or his cold smile.

Maddox finally spoke. "Lila is one of the top five students at Berkshire."

There was a hint of pride in his voice, and my cheeks heated. I quickly took another bite of my toast before swallowing it down with the tea I had in front of me.

Brad tsked, looking only slightly impressed. He regarded me with a curious look as if he was finally seeing me in a different light. He gave me a sharp nod before his gaze focused on Maddox. "Well, that's good to hear. Maybe you can teach my wayward son how to be responsible."

I wasn't touching Maddox, but I *felt* it as if it was my own – his muscles tightening, his body rigid as a bow – he was ready to sprint away or lunge at his father's throat. There was fire in his eyes and ice in his veins. My hand slid over to him, and I placed my hand on his thigh, holding him down, even though I was no match to his strength. His muscles rippled beneath my touch, and his own hand landed on mine. His breath expelled in a jerky rush.

I got you.

I leveled Brad with a cold stare of my own. This was a battlefield. Maddox and I on one side, his parents on the other. Our words didn't cause any physical wounds, but our looks and the words spoken were sharper than any knife.

I'd go to war for Maddox.

And *this* was war.

"Maddox is working really hard," I started, my eyes flickering from his father to his mother. "He passed this semester with high marks."

Brad looked incredulous. "Oh, did he?"

I held onto my temper and gave them a smile. "Yes. You should be proud of him since he did it all on his own."

Savannah perked up. She was obviously trying to break the ice, but this situation was already too frosty. "That's good to hear! Maddox, why didn't you tell us?"

He tensed, his fork clanking against the plate. "I did."

Her smile dissolved. "Oh."

I realized one thing in that moment. Savannah wasn't ignoring Maddox's existence, although it appeared like that on the outside. But now that I really *looked* at her, I realized she was scared of her son. Maddox intimidated her, and knowing him, he made himself less approachable around his parents.

Maybe I was wrong. Savannah was *trying*, but it was too little… too late.

"We're done here," Maddox announced. He stood up, roughly pushing his chair back and dragging me with him.

"Maddox," Brad called out after his son, his voice threatening and so… cold. "You will show respect."

Maddox wasn't listening. We were already marching away. He didn't stop, even after we were the through the gates of his house. We walked for an hour, side by side. There was an unspoken understanding between us as we walked in silence until we reached Berkshire.

Today was Saturday, so the building was closed. I snuck a glance up at Maddox. He was breathing hard, his lips curled back, and his eyes dark.

He held so much anger inside him, so much disappointment. I could *feel* it, deep in my bones. Maddox felt betrayed, hurt and deceived. He held more pain than he showed to the world.

I gave his hand a squeeze. "You have to train your mind to be stronger than your emotions or else you'll lose yourself every time," I said softly.

His eyes locked with me, and the intensity of his gaze caused my stomach to flip. "Why are you here?" There was a sudden harshness in his voice that had me flinching.

My lips parted, confused. "What?"

"Here," he gritted out. "With me. Why? Why didn't you walk away?"

"Because you're my friend," I simply replied. *Because I care.*

Maddox released a shuddering breath as if he needed that confirmation. So young and so angry. If only I could make him smile again.

A sudden spark of an idea had me silently gasping. Of course, I could make him smile. I knew exactly how.

I let go of his hand and pointed at the building next to Berkshire Academy, opened every day, even the weekends. The library.

"I dare you," I started.

"For fuck's sake."

"I dare you to go in there, no clothes except your boxers."

He paused, watching me with his mouth agape. "Are you serious?"

"Dead serious." I crossed my arms over my chest.

"Naked?"

I nodded, fighting back a smile. "Only your boxers."

Oh, this was going to be a sight to see.

"They'll call the police," Maddox said, still looking at me as if I had lost my mind.

"That's the point, Poodle."

He blinked, still looking surprised. "Holy shit, I corrupted you," he gasped.

My lips quirked up. "Do you dare, Coulter?"

Maddox smirked, a playful and sinful as fuck smirk. "I accept this dare."

He quickly pulled his clothes off his body and handed them to me. He was partially... naked. His Calvin Klein boxers hung low around his hips, the crevice of his ass visible and my throat was suddenly parched. Fully clothed Maddox was... sexy.

Partially naked Maddox was... *gulp*

We were just friends, but damn it, I was a hormonal teenager who wasn't scared to appreciate a fine specimen like Maddox Coulter.

"Stop looking at my ass, Garcia."

"Stop prancing around me naked, Coulter."

He sneaked a glance over his shoulder. "I've a feeling this was your way of getting me naked. Are you feeling tempted, Sweet Cheeks?"

"Tempted to kick your ass to Mars, yes."

He grinned. "Liar."

Fine, I was a liar.

"Damn, it's cold!" His teeth were chattering as he rubbed his hands up and down his arms.

I stuck my tongue out and waved toward the library. "Off you go."

He jogged toward the entrance. "Do a little twerk," I yelled after him.

His warm laughter was heard through the cold breeze. I stalked after him and waited at the entrance, watching Maddox's spectacle through the large glass windows. He pranced around the library, completely at ease and with a cocky smirk. He was completely comfortable in his skin. The people stared, speechless and in shock. A girl had her phone out, probably filming him. Some laughed, others looked outraged.

Maddox paused in front of the old librarian, who was blushing and sputtering, bent down and did a half twerk against the granny before running off.

I couldn't hold my laughter in anymore. My stomach cramped, and I wheezed as he sprinted out of the library, the librarians and security guard at his heels.

"Run!" he hollered at me, his smile wide and infectious.

I took off, and we ran.

We didn't stop until we lost them. Hiding behind the dumpster, I tried to catch my breath.

"You're crazy," he gasped through his laughter.

I elbowed him, grinning. "We make a good team, don't we?"

He smiled.

A real and sincere smile.

My chest tightened, and my stomach did a crazy flip, like little butterflies dancing around in there.

Maddox might seem like he had the world at his feet. He was Berkshire's king, and he ruled with a cocky grin, though no one saw the pain behind that playful smile. To the world, he had everything everybody else wanted: money, status, friends, a scholarship and two beautiful, successful parents. He was untouchable.

But he was still human.

Maddox Coulter wasn't invincible. He had multiple cracks and scars in his soul.

He was a simple, seventeen-year-old boy, who only wanted his parents' approval, with a little messy childhood and now, he starved for attention.

I made him smile.

I did it. And I'd continue to do so.

One dare at a time, I'd chase his smiles – because I realize Maddox needed someone who cared enough about his happiness and his anger. And I did.

CHAPTER TWENTY-TWO

Lila

The crowd cheered so loudly that I wondered if my eardrums were ever going to be the same. Excitement bubbled in my chest, and I felt giddy as the players strode out of the tunnel, leading to the football field. Maddox liked to have me accompany him to his practices but this was my first actual game. I knew absolutely nothing about football but I had to be here for Maddox. This was important to him, hence it was important to me.

"MC! MC! Go Berkshire!" the girls screamed from behind me.

Holy shit, this was huge and it was exhilarating.

The cheerleaders were doing their own thing as the game started. All eyes were on the Berkshire players. I held my breath, and I couldn't tear my eyes off the field. Riley grasped my hand in hers, and she was screaming at the top of her lungs.

Maddox probably just scored a point because the crowd went wild, batshit crazy wild. I knew it was him because of the swagger as he trotted around the field, soaking up all the attention. He banged his fist against his chest, and our cheerleaders cheered even louder. I was too far away to see his face, but I could imagine the cocky grin. Yeah, this was definitely MC – Maddox Coulter, all macho and arrogant.

Tonight was the last football game of the season. Due to the snow in January, the game got pushed back a few weeks. It was still cold, but our Berkshire boys were crushing the other team. I didn't understand much about football or any sports for that matter, but when Riley and our people cheered, I did too.

I tried to keep an eye on Maddox, but everything was happening too fast, so I had no idea what was going on.

The audience hollered once more, "MC! MC! MC!"

They were calling out to Maddox. He was the star football player, after all.

There was one last touchdown before the field and crowd erupted. We… won?

Holy shit, we won! Not that I was surprised or anything, but WE WON!

I was never much of a sports fan; I didn't much care about football, but this was Maddox's passion – his whole fucking life. He was happy, which made *me* happy.

Riley jumped, and I danced in my spot, laughing. "We won!" she shrieked.

My heart thumped so loudly that I could hear the beats in my ears. What a night.

Maddox paused at the edge of the field, and I was standing in the front row, courtesy of being the quarterback's friend. He took off his helmet, smirking. His breathing was ragged, but the expression on his face was one of pleasure and bliss.

Maddox wiggled his eyebrows at me as the girls surrounded him. A cheerleader rubbed herself against him, grabbed his face and landed a big kiss on his lips.

Okaaayy then.

More girls joined the group, all of them trying to cop a feel of Maddox. I sincerely worried for his ego. This couldn't be healthy for a seventeen-year-old boy. So much arrogance and cockiness.

He spared me a glance, challenging me with his gaze. I remembered the words he spoke to me before the game.

Riley stood beside me, completely oblivious of what was about to happen. Maddox waited, giving me an infuriating look, as if he expected me to lose this stupid dare.

Sincerely, fuck you, Maddox Coulter.

As another girl wrapped her arms around him, I lunged into action.

Do you dare?

Ha. Ha. Ha.

Riley let out a shocked gasp as I grabbed the back of her neck and pulled her forward. My mouth landed on hers, and her eyes flared in surprise. I pressed my lips harder against hers before pulling away.

She wiped her mouth, sputtering and glaring. "What the *hell*, Lila?"

Shrugging, I gave her a sheepish look. "Maddox dared me, sorry."

"If I win the game, I dare you to kiss Riley," he said, amusement flashing in his eyes. This was probably some woman on woman fantasy for him.

"You can't be serious!"

His lips quirked up. "Do you dare?"

I turned to face Maddox again, and he was chuckling. I flashed him the middle finger, and he laughed even harder. Maddox pulled away from all the girls as they tried to grab him, vying for his attention, but he shook his head.

He said something to them and pointed at me. Everyone turned to stare at the same time.

Suspicious, I squinted at him as he made his way to me.

"What did you say to them?" I asked with my hands on my hips. My eyes narrowed on him.

He smirked. "Told them my girlfriend was getting jealous."

Huh? Wait… what?

I was in too much shock from his words that I didn't see it coming until I was flung upside down and over his shoulder.

"Maddox!" I screeched.

He swatted my ass. "Be nice. These girls are driving me crazy, and you're my escape plan."

"Let me down. Now!" I banged my fists into his back, feeling his muscles clench under my attack.

"How about you be docile for five minutes?" He rumbled with a chuckle.

Docile? Excuse me, DOCILE?

I hit him with my fist again, although I was pretty sure he didn't feel anything. "What am I? Your pet?" I snapped.

Maddox hummed, thoughtfully. What a douchebag.

"You're such a wild chihuahua," he said.

"Careful, or you'll end up with a nasty bite, Coulter."

His shoulders shook with silent laughter. "Bite me then, Garcia."

I rolled my eyes as he stalked away from the crowd with me over his shoulder, caveman style.

Once we reached the boys' locker room, he let me down, and I blew my hair out of my face. "Why are we here?"

"I need a shower and then we'll be on our way to the bonfire. Berkshire is celebrating tonight. I need my favorite person there."

I crossed my arms over my chest as he sauntered toward his locker. "You do realize if you keep grabbing me and throwing me over your shoulder like this, they will never believe that we're just friends."

We were already getting weird looks. No one believed we were just friends. Maybe that was partially our fault.

Maddox and I spent way too much time together. He'd hold my hands, kiss my cheek or throw an arm over my shoulders while we walked down the halls. He stole bites of my lunch, and we continued to play silly pranks on each other. At first, I hated the public displays of affection, but they grew on me, just like the rest of Maddox's quirks. He still made inappropriate jokes, but he never tried to do anything… more.

Maddox gave me a nonchalant half shrug. He removed his shoulder pads and stripped off his jersey before throwing it my way. "A souvenir, Sweet Cheeks."

"You really don't care?" I asked.

He didn't bother to hide his amusement at my question. "Lila, people's opinions don't matter to me. You shouldn't care either. They live to gossip while we're living our lives to the fullest. So, who cares if they think we're friends or we're fucking?"

Okay, true. Point taken.

Two hours later, we were celebrating with the rest of the Berkshire students around bonfire. There was a lot of us here but the open field was big enough so it didn't seem crowded. Bottles and cans of beer littered around us. A few guys were already a tad drunk, and they were laughing about something, pushing each other around.

Maddox walked over with a beer in his hand and a paper plate in the other. "Got you some Hawaiian Teriyaki Chicken skewers."

I smiled, taking the plate from him. "Thanks." I looked around, seeing all the smiles. "They sure love celebrating."

He took a long pull of his beer before wiping the corner of his mouth. His legs were lazily spread apart, and he was wearing black ripped jeans, expensive leather boots and a hat that probably cost more than my bra. Maddox looked like he owned the world – a god amongst us mere mortals.

He licked his lips, grinning. "This is nothing. The real celebration is at

Colton's house next weekend."

My brows furrowed at that. "I don't want to know."

I munched on my grilled skewers while slowly nursing my own beer.

A moment later, Maddox tsked. "I'm bored. Let's cause a little trouble."

He stood up and went to the middle of the field. He spread his arms out, smirking. "Let's play a game," he announced.

The others hollered in agreement.

Oh, no.

His gaze found mine, mischief flashing in his eyes. I glared, trying to look severe, but my own lips twitched with a smile.

Here comes trouble.

CHAPTER TWENTY-THREE

Maddox

I glanced down at my phone for probably the hundredth time, waiting for a text back. She wasn't replying. I left school early today when Lila missed the first two classes. Now, I sat in my car in front of her grandparents' home like a goddamn stalker. Worry gnawed at me because it was so unlike Lila to ghost me, and she never missed her classes.

I did the same shit a few weeks ago. Bailed on her and ghosted everyone who tried to reach out to me. I didn't expect her to turn the tables on me, and I didn't like it, not one bit. Now, I understood how she felt when I wasn't answering her phone calls and she found me in that tub, freezing and pissed drunk.

Was she hurt?

Did something happen?

Why. The. Fuck. Won't. She. Reply. To. My. Texts?

Goddamn it!

I slammed my fists against the steering wheel, slightly unhinged at the mere thought of Lila being hurt.

I went to their grocery store today and found out that her grandma was home. Sure, I could have spoken with Sven, her Pops, but I'd rather not. He liked me enough, but he didn't seem to trust any boys around his little Lila, even ones who were her friends and didn't want to get in her pants.

Okay, that was a lie.

I still wanted to get in her panties.

Maybe he could read me better than I thought. Was I that obvious?

Oh, she was my friend, but I still wanted to fuck your granddaughter. Up and down, sideways, on our knees, every possible position.

Well, yeah. No wonder he didn't like, *like* me.

I rang the doorbell, and Lila's grandma opened the door, a pensive look on her face. She looked tired and weary. At the sight of me, she smiled a little. "Maddox, what are you doing here?"

"Hi," I said, peering behind her shoulder, expecting Lila to pop up. "Is Lila home? I tried to contact her, but she isn't answering, so I grew worried."

She was silent for a moment, her eyes turning glassy. "You don't know?" She spoke the words so softly that I almost missed them.

My heart skittered a beat, and I started sweating. The blood rushed through my ears and my heart hammered in my ears. "Is… something wrong? Did something happen to her?"

She shook her head. "You don't know what today is?" she questioned, but then answered her own question before I could say a word. "She didn't tell you. I'm not surprised. My Lila always suffers alone."

Suffers… alone?

Fuck, no. She would never. Not alone.

Lila had *me*.

True, she didn't need a hero to save the day, but the more I got to know her, the closer we grew – I wanted, no – I *needed* to protect her. Maybe it was to return the favor since she took care of me when I was at my weakest or simply because I…cared. I'd ever confess that out loud to her. She'd sock me in the face because Lila Garcia hated to be pitied.

Except, I didn't pity her.

I just wanted to… protect her.

"What are you saying? Is she hurt?"

Her grandma gave me a heartbroken smile. "She's been hurting for a long time."

That… hurt. Right there, in my fucking chest.

Mrs. Wilson leaned against the doorframe, looking more haggard than her age. "Did you know that Lila never cries? Never, except one day of the year. On that day, she cries alone; she hides her tears from everyone. That's the only day she lets herself feel pain."

My heart nearly spilled out, and I rubbed my chest, trying to alleviate the ache. It didn't stop the pain. It infiltrated my veins and my blood, for *her*.

Her shoulders shook and slumped, as if she had finally been released from a heavy burden she carried. "My Lila is strong with a fragile heart," she whispered.

"Where is she right now? Where can I find her?" Even I could hear the urgency in my voice, the desperation.

And I was not a desperate guy.

But Lila made me feel many things I'd never felt before. Not for any other girl.

"Lila left this morning. She's at Sunset Park. You'll find her sitting on a bench."

I nodded my thanks and took a step back, clenching my car keys in my hand. Sunset Park, I'd find my Lila there.

"Maddox?"

I paused and glanced over my shoulder. "Yes?"

"Are you Lila's friend?"

Confused, I blinked, and my brows furrowed. Grandma was well aware we were friends; we had been for months. But she stared at me, expectantly, as if her question held more meaning behind those simple words.

And I realized they did.

That question was powerful because it made me *think* about how important Lila was to me, how close we were and how much she meant to me. One simple question, and it put our whole relationship in perspective.

Yes, I respected the hell out of Lila. She was smart, funny, wild and… caring.

Yes, I still wanted a taste of her. Wanted it since I first laid eyes on her. But she meant more.

We had each other – she got me and I got her.

Suddenly, the idea of us being more than friends became taboo. Because if we were ever more than friends, we risked losing what we had now. A silent understanding. A friendship based on honesty and loyalty. Lila saw behind all my bullshit and didn't let it deter her. She pushed and pushed until I cracked open in front of her. Lila and I were alike in so many ways, yet still… different. Maybe that was why we suited each other so well as friends. We balanced each other.

She was the calm in my reckless life.

I was the chaos in her peaceful one.

"Lila's my best friend," I finally confessed, with a curl of my lips.

Grandma looked thoughtful for a moment before she gave me a melancholy smile. "Take care of our girl. She refuses to let any of us lend her a shoulder. Maybe you'll be different."

Thirty minutes later, I was sitting in my car at Sunset Park. My gaze found Lila the moment I parked and turned off the engine. Like her Gran said, I found her sitting on a bench, alone. Sweet Lila was cuddled up in her winter coat, trying to stay warm against the cold. I couldn't see her face from where I was, but I didn't like what I was seeing.

She was hunched over the bench, her legs up on the seat with her arms wrapped around her knees. Lila looked... lost.

I stayed in my car for a few more minutes, giving her some time by herself. I knew *why* she was here. Sunset Cemetery Park.

Her parents were here.

Did you know that Lila never cries? Never, except one day of the year. On that day, she cries alone; she hides her tears from everyone. That's the only day she lets herself feel pain.

And I knew what that day was, what today was, and why it was so important for Lila.

Sweet Lila – the fiery dragon with a fragile heart.

I stepped out of the car when I couldn't stay away any longer. The cold wind blew hard, and Lila hugged herself tighter. There was a magnetic pull between us, and I walked toward her without even realizing my feet were taking me to her side.

She didn't move when I settled at her side on the bench, didn't look up, didn't even acknowledge my presence. Silently, I grasped her hand and pulled it away from her knees. She clutched my hand, and I squeezed hers in return, a silent vow.

I'm not letting go, Lila.

She didn't speak, and I didn't dare break the silence. Lila quietly sniffled and dashed away her tears with her other hand, but she couldn't keep her cries in. She cried her little heart out, a desolate sob coming from a person drained of all her hopes and dreams.

As if realizing now that she was holding onto my hand, she tried to wrench it away from me. I held fast, squeezing her hand in comfort. "Go...away," Lila murmured.

I stayed silent, refusing to utter a word, but also refusing to leave.

Minutes probably turned into hours as I sat with her. She cried until I thought there would be no tears left, but she still cried. She didn't speak again and neither did I. Lila needed to grieve in silence, but I'd be there with her. I was staying, and I'd fight any motherfucker who'd try to make me leave.

Each sob that racked through her body wrecked my stupid heart even more. A whimper escaped her, a tortured sound, and she gripped my hand harder, her nails digging into my skin. Her other hand came up, and she clutched her chest, a broken sob slipping past her lips. Her whole body was shaking, whether it was from the cold or the force of her tears, I didn't know.

The sound of her struggling to breathe through her crying decimated me.

"*It... hurts,*" she whimpered. "It... hurts... so much, Maddox."

Her breathing was ragged, gasping, and her body slumped forward as if all the strength had left her body. She shouldn't be able affect me so strongly, but wild emotions swirled inside me as I breathed in her pain and suffering.

Watching the Lila I knew, the strong and confident Lila, break apart like this...

There was a phantom ache in my chest, like an invisible knife digging and twisting viciously into my flesh – the pain becoming unbearable.

I grabbed her before she could slide off the bench, her body weak in her grief. Our knees dug into the damp mud, but I didn't care as I pulled her into my arms. She was half sitting on my lap, her face buried in my neck as her tears soaked through my shirt and against my skin.

"Why doesn't it... stop? Why? Why? *Why!?*" She wailed. Her tiny fist clenched around my shirt. "It hurts... even more. Every time... every year. The... pain... just never goes... away."

I didn't know what to say, didn't know what to fucking do, so I just held her. I was never good with words of condolences, never had anyone to comfort until Lila.

For fuck's sake, the moment a girl started shedding a few tears, I'd be running the other way as far as I could go. Girls and tears were the one thing I didn't do, nope... never.

Until Lila.

Life had broken her.

Just as it had broken me.

Maybe it was why we found each other.

Call it fate, kismet... or maybe it was God's doing...

Lila was meant to hold my broken pieces together; just as I was meant to hold the shattered pieces of hers.

No, she didn't fix me, and I didn't fix her. We just... held each other; it was that simple.

"I got you," I said softly against her temple.

She trembled in my embrace. "They didn't deserve... to die. They didn't!"

I murmured soothing words to her as she wailed her agony. "Why did they... die... and why... me... why am I... *here*? I want... to go... to my mom and my... dad. I don't... want to be here. I don't!"

I'm sorry, so so sorry, baby girl.

The pain flowing from Lila was as palpable as the frigid wind around us. Such agony and such a lonely, broken soul.

More time went by, and eventually, her sobbing turned into hiccups and quiet sniffles. Lila was still on my lap, face still tucked into the crook of my neck and her fingers still clutching my shirt as if her life depended on it.

I brushed her hair out of her face, my thumb rubbing over the trail of her tears. "I got you."

She hugged me tighter.

"Can I meet your parents?" I asked.

Lila gave me the tiniest nod. She stumbled out of my lap and stood up on shaky legs. I did, too, trying to ignore the tingles prickling through my legs after sitting in the same position for too long. She took my hand in hers, and we walked toward her parents' headstones.

"Hey, mom," Lila said, her voice cracking. "I've got someone for you to meet."

Catalina Garcia.

The sun shines brighter because she was here.

Beloved mother, wife and daughter.

She pointed at the tombstone beside her mother. "And that's my dad. Dad meet Maddox, Maddox meet Dad." A small, wobbly smile appeared on her lips. "And no, daddy. He's not my boyfriend."

Zachary Wilson.

A gentle man and a gentleman.

Loving father and loving husband.

What a beautiful memory you left behind.

My throat clogged with emotions, so I nodded in greeting. "It's good to finally meet you, Mr. and Mrs. Wilson."

Lila knelt down in front of the headstones. She brought her legs to her chest and wrapped her arms around her knees again. I realized, now, that she was trying to physically shield herself from the pain. I joined her as I tried to understand what I was feeling. There was a heavy weight on my chest, and it almost made it harder to breathe. Lila was eerily quiet for the longest time before she finally spoke.

"You scare me," she whispered.

"Why?" *You scare me, too.*

"Because I trust you. Because I want to tell you what I've never told anyone before."

Same, Lila. Fucking same.

"Do you know what hurts the most?" Lila said, sniffling. "The regret."

I waited for her to continue to tell *her* story.

Lila

"I think I'll always carry that regret in my heart because the last thing I said to my parents was that I hated them. I remember whispering it in the back of the car, but I don't know if they heard it or not. Because right after I had said those words, I heard my father scream, and my mother cry out. Then... the car... I was in the air... and the next thing I knew, everything hurt. So much pain."

A single tear escaped and slid down my cheek. I dashed it away, almost angrily, because right now, anger tasted bitter on my tongue while the pain laid heavy on my heart.

"I was only thirteen, well... almost fourteen. So young, so foolish, such a stupid, stupid brat. They wouldn't let me attend a birthday party that all my friends were attending. Mom said they didn't know the girl whose house I was going to, so they didn't feel comfortable with me going. Dad didn't think it was safe because it was too far from our neighborhood, and they didn't know the parents. I wanted to go. I wanted to have fun with all my other friends. But they refused, and I was so, so angry. We were in the car, and we were arguing. Then I said... *I hate you.*"

The memories were vivid in my head, as if it were just yesterday. I could almost hear my parents' voices, and if I closed my eyes, I could see them.

I looked away and blinked away the burning sensation in my eyes, but the tears didn't stop. "I didn't mean it. I *didn't.* I just said it because I was angry, but I didn't mean it, Maddox. I... didn't. Those were the last words I said to my parents. That is my deepest regret," I broke off, letting out a pained whimper. I choked on my shame. "It... hurts because I will never get to tell my parents how much I love them. I will never feel my mother's arms or my dad's warm hugs again. My mom will never sing me happy birthday in her silly voice, and my dad will never tickle me because he loved to hear me laugh. He said my laughs sounded like a chipmunk."

I ducked my head, hiding behind the curtain of my hair. "Sometimes,

I forget what it is to feel okay, to feel normal because I'm filled with… so many unspoken emotions."

Maddox was silent, and I wondered what he was thinking about. Did he pity me? Could he feel my shame? I didn't want to be pitied, though… for the first time since my parents died, I just wanted to be held.

I'd been pushing the people who cared about me away: my grandparents and Riley. They tried, but I always shut them down because I hated being pitied, I hated the sympathetic look on their faces. When Gran suggested therapy, I refused to see any shrink. Talking about my feelings to a stranger? Letting them see me at my weakest? No way.

Realization dawned on me, and I choked back a sob. By pushing them away, I was causing myself more pain. I needed someone to talk to.

I needed to be held.

I needed to cry and have someone tell me it was going to be okay.

Sniffling back a cry, I dabbed my tears away. Maddox was here, and it was ironic because of how much I despised him when we first met.

"Do you know why I hated you so much before?"

He let out a dry laugh, without any humor. "Because I was an asshole?"

If only he knew the truth…

Maybe it was time.

I took a deep breath and let it out. "No, I despised you, hated the mere idea of you, because you reminded me of my parents' murderer."

His head snapped up, and I could almost hear his heart beat rattling through his chest.

Thump.

Thump.

Thump.

There was a moment of silence, his lips parting as if to speak, but he couldn't say a word. His eyes bore into me, searching, and I saw matching pain in his. My words hung heavily between us, and we both bled from the invisible gunshot, a festering open wound.

I swallowed past the heavy lump in my throat, my whole body shaking with tremors. "We wouldn't have gotten into an accident if we hadn't been hit by a drunk driver that night."

Four years had gone by, and I was still haunted by the memory.

"He was seventeen and very drunk, way above the limit, especially for someone underage. The road was slightly icy, so he lost control of his vehicle. Our cars were travelling the opposite direction, and he hit us from the front. I still remember the bright headlights flashing in front of me as his car crashed into ours."

"He—"

"He should have been jailed for a long time. He should have been punished, right? Maddox, right?"

He nodded, his eyes red. *Don't give me such a tortured look, Maddox. My heart is already breaking.*

"He didn't," I said, hugging myself tighter. "He didn't even spend a night in a cell; he wasn't punished, and he walked away from the accident, unscathed. Do you know why?"

"Why?" Maddox whispered, but he already knew the answer.

"He was the rich and spoiled son of a wealthy and influential attorney who had the whole world at his feet. His dad swept the accident under the rug and was able to get his son out of trouble. I was in a coma for a few weeks, and when I woke up... I found out the case was closed and had been filed away. We were told the chauffeur took the blame and had been pardoned by the law; except, he wasn't the one driving that night... *that* boy was. I know because I did my research after I woke up. My grandparents helped, and we tried to open the case again."

"Lila," Maddox breathed. His head fell into his hands. "Goddamn it."

"I was in the hospital, still recovering from my injuries, when the dad walked through the door. The look on his face, God, I can still see it so clearly. There was no remorse, Maddox. *Nothing.* He didn't care that I just lost my parents because of his son. He didn't care that I was practically crippled in a hospital bed, in pain, in so much fucking pain. He took out a check…"

"No," Maddox let out a curse. "Fuck, no. Lila, *no*." He banged his fists against the wet, muddy grass.

I laughed and laughed, dry and empty and cold. "Yes. He offered me one million dollars to stay silent. He said he'd give me more if I'd just shut up and leave his family alone."

Then I cried.

And cried… and cried.

"We… lost…the… case," I hiccupped back a sob, but I was only choking on my own saliva. "Money and power and too many connections, he had everything, and we stood no chance against him."

"He paid off the judge?" Maddox growled, his words laced with anger.

"I assumed he did or he didn't have to. They were buddies."

I tried to breathe, tried to stay alive, forced myself to survive. *Inhale, exhale.*

I wanted to scream until I pass out and forget all of this happened. Maybe when I'd wake up, I'd find myself in a world where my parents were still alive, and we were living happily ever after.

"When you're rich, you can pay for someone's silence, buy life and death, play god and win. That's what he did. I'm a mere mortal… I lost."

"I'm sorry."

I am too.

"I hated you because you were a reminder of the boy who ruined me and stole my life from me," I croaked, my ability to speak fading. I rubbed my chest, over my scars. "So rich, so spoiled. Such a brat with so much arrogance."

Maddox made a sound at the back of his throat; it sounded almost like a silent cry before he spoke. "I'm sorry," he said again.

With all my strength gone from my body, I couldn't sit up anymore.

My body swayed, and I fell onto my back and closed my eyes. I was drained of everything, all the pain, all the suffering… my past and all the memories.

I felt… empty.

And numb.

I didn't have to open my eyes to *feel* him. Maddox settled on the cold grass and laid down beside me. I felt his warm breath against my neck. He was really close.

I breathed in the fresh air, and there was a comfortable silence between us. It lasted for a long time, and I soaked it in, the warmth from his presence. Until Maddox broke the silence.

"Tell me about your parents. How did they meet?" he asked gently.

So, I did.

I told him about an unlikely love story.

"My mom was the only Hispanic in their neighborhood, and all the other kids would pick on her. My dad was apparently one of her bullies until she grabbed him one day and slammed her lips against his then pulled back, looked him straight in the eye and told him, 'If you can't shut up, I'll shut you up.' He said he fell in love with her right then and there. My father always told me to be with the person who makes your heart beat a thousand miles an hour," I told Maddox.

We stared at my parents' headstones, and I wondered if they could feel me since I was so close to them? Were they watching over me?

There was a dull ache in my chest, but I didn't feel like crying anymore. Maybe I'd finally spent all my tears; because even though it *hurt*, the urge to cry was gone.

Until next year, until I allowed myself to break down again. I hated being vulnerable. The last time I was; I had been in a hospital and I couldn't give my parents' the justice they deserved.

I didn't know why I let Maddox see me like this, why I allowed him to see my weakness… but all I knew was the moment he sat on that bench next to me and held my hand, I didn't want him to let go.

I didn't even cry at parents' funeral until everyone was gone, and I was alone. Except the moment Maddox touched my hand – the dam broke, the cage around my heart shattered, and I hadn't been able to stop crying.

We sat there for a long time. The sun was starting to go down, the sky turning a bright orange. I guess this place was called Sunset Park for a reason; it had the best sunset view.

"Do you believe in love?" Maddox asked, roughly.

What a strange question in a moment like this.

"Yes. But I've long decided that it's not for me. Not anymore."

"Why not?"

"Because I don't want to lose anyone else." I've suffered enough loss for a lifetime, and I survived it, but I didn't want to test my luck.

How much pain can a person bear before they break down completely?

I was stronger than the magic of love.

I wrapped my arms around my knees and brought my legs closer to my chest. I laid my head over my knees and turned to look at Maddox. He was staring at my parents' headstones, looking thoughtful.

"Do you believe in love?" I asked him back. My cheeks felt tight from the cold and my dried tears. My face was probably blotchy and red, but I couldn't find myself to care in the moment.

This was Maddox, my best friend.

He blinked, as if he wasn't expecting the question. "I don't know."

Curious, I pushed for more. "What do you mean?"

"I used to think love was fake. It didn't exist. Love is too complicated and shit. No one belonged to me before. I was never close enough to love someone or to even understand the meaning of it."

Wild emotions clogged my throat, and my heart flipped like a caged bird, beating its wings, looking for an escape.

"And what do you think now?" I whispered the question.

Maddox faced me, his blue eyes staring into mine, looking right through my cold exterior, pushing right through my walls and knocking at my caged heart.

When he spoke again, his voice was deep and rough. His words were a silent confession.

"Now, I have someone to lose, and I know it will break me. I know what it means to fear losing the person who means the most to you. That person has the power to destroy me."

Silence fell upon us, and I couldn't find the words to convey what I was feeling. I turned my head away from his probing gaze and went back to staring at the headstones.

Seconds turned into long minutes, but we sat there in comfortable silence.

"Maddox?"

"Yeah?"

I took a deep breath and made my first promise to Maddox. "You won't lose me. Ever."

He was quiet for a moment, and I thought I messed up, until his hand came into the line of my vision, and he showed me his pinky.

"Promise?" he asked softly.

I hooked my finger around his. Maddox was warm and familiar. He felt solid and safe. I wanted to cling to him and never, ever let go. "Promise."

He flexed his pinky around me and then he smiled.

For the first time today, I smiled, too.

Pinky swear, me and you... forever.

CHAPTER
TWENTY-FOUR

Lila

"**S**o, is it like…a date?" I asked. "A real date?"

I couldn't see Riley's face through the phone, but her giddiness was apparent as she let out a small squeal. "Well, yeah. I mean… he called, and he asked if we could grab dinner, and he told me to dress warm since it tends to get a bit colder at night," she breathed, each word laced with excitement. "And Lila, his voice… over the phone… I think I almost orgasmed. Holy shit."

I fell back on my bed, a wide grin spreading over my lips. "Honestly, I didn't think Grayson was going to do it," I said. "I mean, ask you out."

He was so reserved, so quiet and didn't mingle with the rest of the Berkshire students.

In fact, he was a loner.

Riley didn't give up though.

She giggled, and I heard some rustling in the background. "It's been three months. It's about time he breaks down and ask me out. I can't decide what to wear. Jeans or a dress? He said to put on something warm, but maybe a dress is fitting? Something cute or something sexy?" She paused, thoughtfully. "I don't want to come across as easy or trying to fuck on our first date. But I also want to feel pretty and sexy."

After Jasper, Riley had sworn off any Berkshire boys. She said they were all the same, and the pain of what Jasper did was still too fresh, even though it had been over a year since their breakup. It was the first time I'd seen her *this* excited; I just hoped Grayson didn't end up breaking her heart.

Although, I liked to believe that he was into her as much as she liked him. He was always subtle about his feelings but I had seen him sneaking glances at Riley and trying to hide his smile. There was a look in his eyes when he watched her – something akin to adoration.

The same look I had seen in Colton's eyes, too.

I wasn't sure if I should've talked to Riley about Colton, but she was happy with Grayson and that was all I wanted. He was a good guy, and Riley liked him. The end.

She made her decision. Colton would just have to accept it.

"Remember the black dress you wore last Christmas? The mini one, V cut? You looked cute but smoking hot," I offered.

Riley made a sound of agreement. "Oh, that one! My boobs look nice in that dress. I can wear those new high heels boots I got!"

"Atta girl. There you go. What time is he picking you up at?" I looked at the clock and saw that it was almost six pm.

"Umm… an hour. Shit, I gotta get ready. Talk later?"

Her happiness was contagious. "Yeah, babe. Text me when you get home. I want to hear all about it."

Riley let out a small giggle before she mumbled. "He better kiss me, or I'm going to be reaaally disappointed."

Oh yeah, he better.

Because I wanted to know all about that kiss.

We said our goodbyes and hung up.

Riley was happy…

The ringing of my phone jostled me out of my thoughts, and I stared down at the screen. Maddox. His name flashing on my phone screen reminded me that I was supposed to be angry.

I answered the phone, and Maddox cut me off before I could say anything. "Come outside. Now," he demanded. The low rumble of his voice had my stomach fluttering before I remembered to hang onto the anger.

Ugh, asshole.

"What do you want?" I shot back, rather rudely. What he did was… unforgiveable.

"Lila." There was a warning in his voice.

"Maddox," I hissed.

"I'm outside. Come out. *Now.*"

"Maybe if you say please." The sarcasm dripped from my mouth easily. *Watch out, I got my sassy pants on today.*

There was a frustrated growl before I heard him sigh. "Please."

Huh. That was shocking.

My lips flattened in a straight line. "No."

"Are you still pissed because I ate your muffin?"

"You stole my muffin!" And it was the last one.

"I thought you didn't want it. You left it on the table."

I growled in response. He was silent for a second before he laughed. The jerk actually *laughed.* "Are you on your period?"

"Fuck you." I ended the call with a growl.

Yes, I was on my period.

Yes, I was cranky. Because this asshole, aka my best friend, ate my mint chocolate muffin.

A second later, my pinged with a message. ***Come out, please. I'm sorry about the muffin.***

I typed a quick text back. *Why?*

My screen flashed with another message. *Just trust me.*

I rolled my eyes and bounced off the bed. Maddox wasn't going to give up. For all I knew, if I didn't come out of the house, he was going to come in and get me.

I stepped out of the house to find Maddox leaning against his car, arms crossed. At the sight of me, he licked his lips and winked. My breath caught in my throat because he was so sinfully handsome. Then I remembered he was my best friend... and I was supposed to be mad, right?

I crossed my arms over my chest and glared. "What do you want?"

Maddox crooked his index finger at me, beckoning me to come closer. I did.

"Come closer. I'm not going to bite, Garcia."

"You're annoying me, Coulter," I snapped.

He tsked before he looped his arm around my waist and pulled me closer. I stumbled against him, and our bodies clashed together.

A cocky grin spread over his lips. "I can't decide if I like you feisty or I like you quiet."

I huffed and blew my hair out of my face, before squinting up at him. He sobered, the mischievous glint in his eyes gone. My heart dropped to my stomach, and my palms started sweating.

"Lila, do you trust me?"

My eyes flared in surprise. "Why are you asking?"

"Answer the question." His gaze didn't waver from mine, absorbing me and holding me captive.

I shook my head and tried to move away from him. "What's going on?"

I didn't like the look on his face. Something was up, and I wasn't going to like it.

"I want to try something with you," he slowly explained.

"Jump off an airplane? Scuba diving? Bungee Jumping? Rafting? Something stupid and thrill seeking?"

Maddox loved the adrenaline rush, loved any outdoor activity that would have my heart spilling out through my mouth. We went mountain biking a few weeks ago. Well, *he* did, and I watched from the sideline, convincing myself not to pass out.

It was too dangerous, too reckless… everything that Maddox needed in his life. The thrill and the rush through his veins. He *lived* for it.

Maddox shook his head, the expression on his face still too serious. "No, this isn't about me. This is for you. But I want us to do it together."

"Maddox, spit it out." Nerves gnawed at my gut as I waited for him to speak.

Still holding me in his arms, Maddox turned us around, so I was facing his car, with my back against his front. I was trapped between him and the car.

My breath expelled through my lips with a harsh exhale, and my knees quivered. His hands landed on my hips, and his breath feathered next to my ear. He reached around me and pulled the passenger door open, his intention clear.

No. No. No.

I was already struggling against him before he could say a word. "Maddox–"

"Do you trust me?" He said in my ear.

"No, I don't." My throat convulsed, and every muscle in my body turned to ice. There was a roaring in my ears, and my heart pounded so hard it felt like it was about to beat right out of my chest. "I… can't," I wheezed. "Don't make me do this."

"Lila, do you trust me?" The baritone of his voice reverberated through my bones, commanding and strong – grounding me and forcing me to face reality. My hands shook, and I started sweating, even though the spring air was cold against my skin.

I swallowed. "No."

"Don't lie, Lila." His hands tightened on my hips.

My lungs burned, and I couldn't *breathe*.

The panic began with a cluster of sparks in my abdomen. My skin itched, feeling too tight around my flesh. My own body was causing me to suffocate. Chest heaving, breath coming out in gasps and tears threatening to fall, I crumbled to the ground. Maddox came with me, not letting go. My heart jumped in terror, in fear, and each breath I pulled into my body became painful.

Why? Why was he doing this to me? Why, Maddox?

There was a hurricane of emotions coursing inside me, threatening to burst through. I couldn't stop shaking, my mind playing continuous tricks on me.

"Breathe," Maddox said, his voice breaking through the chaos in my head.

"I... can't."

Breathe! Damn it, I told myself.

I clutched my chest and gasped. Ten... nine... eight...

The world around me slowed and became a blur, my blood turned to ice and my body felt... *numb*. There was a vicious pounding in the back of my head and the veins in my neck throbbed.

"I believe in you," he whispered.

Seven... six... five... four...

"Breathe, baby."

Three... two... one.

For the longest time, we stayed just like this.

My head lolled backward onto his shoulders. "Is this fun to you? Seeing me like this...?"

His lips brushed my temple, softly. "No. But I'm about to help you conquer your fear. You only live once, Lila."

"I... can't do it today," I confessed.

Maddox shook his head. "Not today, not tomorrow... but maybe next week. We're going to keep trying."

My chin wobbled, and I nodded my head.

I did try. For five days, I tried. Maddox successfully got me closer to his car. Every day, he opened the passenger door, and I'd crumble to the ground, shaking and gasping.

Day by day, I tackled my past and pushed past my fear until my body threatened to give out.

On day six, I could barely step out of my grandparents' house. My legs were shaking so badly that Maddox had to help me walk down the gravelly path to his car.

Again, my knees weakened, and I slumped forward.

A sob escaped past my lips as the crushing anxiety made its way into my body once again.

"I'm... sorry," I choked.

Maddox waited for my panic attack to recede, his presence commanding and his hand steady on my back. He dominated my panicking, soothing me with a gentle touch.

I lifted my head from his shoulder, and his intense, beautiful eyes locked with mine. Panic coursed through me, making my eyes wild and my face white as a ghost, but he didn't stare at me like I was some pathetic loser.

Maddox waited patiently. Because he believed in me.

I chewed on my lip as I tried to calm my breathing. The muscles in my body spasmed, but I fought to stay conscious.

"Put me in the car, Maddox." I tried to sound firm, but my voice only came out as weak as the cries of a newborn kitten.

He pressed his lips together, searching my eyes. Maybe he saw the resolve in them because he nodded. We got to our feet, and I struggled to stand upright. This time, when Maddox opened the passenger door, I climbed into the car on unsteady legs. I slumped into the seat, my heart banging viciously against my ribs.

He placed the seatbelt around me as I held onto my seat, knuckles white, fingers aching with how tight I was holding on.

He pressed his thumb over my full lips, putting them away from my teeth. "Trust me," Maddox rasped.

Trust him? I did, wholly and truly, with all my heart.

That was the scariest part.

"We're doing this."

He grinned. "No, *you* are doing this."

Maddox closed the door, and I watched him move around the car to the driver's seat. He climbed in, and I took a deep breath. His hands were on the steering wheel, waiting.

"Do it, Maddox." *I trust you.*

"Before we do this, I need to tell you something," he paused. I cocked my head, waiting. "Those yoga pants you're wearing should be illegal, Garcia."

My lips parted, and a sudden laughter bubbled up from my chest.

"Maddox!" I was still laughing when he turned the ignition, and, without me realizing, the car started rolling forward.

My smile slipped off my face, and I *gasped.*

"Oh God." My breath stuttered.

That night… the memories…

Everything hit me at once, and I was drowning, sinking… dying.

I can't breathe.

Maddox grasped my hand. "I got you." His deep voice was soft but powerful, with a rich silky tone. "Lila."

My eyes closed, and I breathed through my nose.

Ten… nine… eight… seven… six… five… four… three… two… one.

I was dying.

"You're not dying," a voice said to me.

His voice.

Maddox.

"I am." *Mom… dad… I love you. I love you so much. Can you hear me? I'm sorry.*

A warm hand folded around mine. "I'm right here. You're not dying."

So warm, so strong, so familiar.

Cold wind brushed against my sweaty, overheating skin.

"Open your eyes, Lila." *No.*

"Trust me," he said.

Anguish twisted my stomach. I pressed a hand over my chest, trying to rub the ache away. My eyes fluttered open as I wheezed through each breath.

My window had been rolled down, hence the breeze brushing up against my hair. And…

Oh my God.

"Beautiful, isn't it?" Maddox spoke.

I couldn't blink, couldn't take my eyes off the pink and orange sky. The sunset. We were apparently driving over a hill, and I recognized that it wasn't too far from my house. I never knew the sunset could be so beautiful up here, like this…

I couldn't stop the tears burning my eyes and threatening to spill. They slid down my cheeks, and I choked back a cry.

"Maddox," I breathed, my hands shaking in both fear and… something else, I didn't know. Maybe in relief?

"Look out and feel the wind, Lila. I got you. You're safe."

I brought my head closer to the window and felt the breeze against my face. More tears spilled down my cheeks. My stomach churned with an anxious feeling. Panic and fear thrummed through my veins.

But…

I was in a car.

Maddox was driving.

I was… alive.

My lips wobbled with a smile. "Hey, Maddox?"

"If you're about to confess your undying love to me, I'm going to tell you to stop right there, Sweet Cheeks," he rumbled.

"Still an asshole, I see."

Maddox chuckled, and my stomach fluttered. *Thank you.*

"Friends?" I asked, showing him my pinky. It was something so silly to do, but it was *us.*

He grinned and hooked his finger around mine. "Friends."

Maddox drove for hours, until the sunset disappeared and the stars came out in the dark sky. He eventually stopped the car over a hill and cranked up the radio, which was ironically playing Lauv's *There's No Way.* He reached behind him to the backseat and handed me a small brown paper bag.

I peeked inside and smiled. A mint chocolate muffin. I took a bite, my eyes going to Maddox to find that he was already looking at me.

I didn't have to confess my undying love to Maddox. What we had; it was an unspoken understanding with unsaid words and a feeling we couldn't explain. Love was too simple of a word to describe it because love was black and white. Love or don't love – there was not really an in-between.

What we had... it was a kaleidoscope of colors.

CHAPTER
TWENTY-FIVE

Maddox

"I don't like him," I growled, folding my arms over my chest. I stayed rooted in front of the door, as if I could somehow stop her from leaving.

Lila rolled her eyes, bent over and touched her toes. She stretched, and I had to look away because, goddamn it, her ass looked good in those jeans.

I was pissed at my own reaction and this whole situation. And I didn't exactly know *why*.

"It's not up to you," she said in a sing-song voice. Somedays, I wished she was intimidated by me. It'd make this whole friendship thing easier, but nope. Lila Garcia was feisty, and she constantly butted heads with me. "You're not going on that date with him. I am."

Yeah, that was exactly my problem.

She was going on a date.

With someone. Grayson's friend. A date that Riley set up. Now that she had a boyfriend, she was under the assumption that Lila needed a man in her life, too.

Well, too fucking bad, she already had a man. *Me.*

"I don't trust him," I said again.

Lila faced me, hands on her hips. She was wearing makeup, which she rarely did. Ripped jeans, ankle boots and a black tank top that should be illegal. Sure, Lila didn't have big boobs, but her tits looked juicy in that tank top. Juicy, sinful, forbidden... and–

She even painted her nails. She looked... beautiful. For *him.*

"You never even met him," she argued. My jaw clenched, and I was about to pop a vein.

"He could be a fucking murderer for all we know!" He could hurt her...

And he wasn't *me.*

Lila's eyes turned to slits, and she nudged her chin high, giving me that haughty look of hers. She really mastered that look that says – You're not the boss of me and I can do whatever I want.

"I've met him twice, and he's a gentleman, Maddox. Stop it."

"I don't like it. I don't like him," I said for the hundredth time tonight. "What if he touches you, and you don't want him to?"

Touch... her. He could touch her and fucking kiss her...

She rubbed her forehead, her eyes looking bleak. Lila was already tired of my bullshit. "Maddox, stop it. You're not going to ruin this date for me."

"He could... hurt you."

A smile ghosted her lips. "Daren can't and won't hurt me."

Daren? Even his name sounded dumb. I imagined Lila moaning out that name, and the urge to pummel his face, someone I had never met before, was strong.

"Can you give me a guarantee that he won't hurt you?" I shot back in my defense. "I won't complain and let you go on this stupid date if you can give me a hundred percent guarantee."

I was playing dirty because I knew she couldn't.

I didn't know why I was reacting this way when Lila told me she was going on this date. There was an uneasy feeling in my stomach and a heavy weight on my chest.

"You're acting like a jealous boyfriend, Maddox," she warned, her lips twisted in displeasure. Her words were laced with a warning.

Jealous... boyfriend?

Jealous... me? Ha.

"I'm acting like a caring *friend*," I amended.

She snorted, quite unladylike. I loved that about Lila. She wasn't fake around me, and she wasn't vying for my attention. Lila didn't mold herself to fit my standards. She stayed true to herself and gave whoever dared to douse her fire the middle finger.

Lila fixed up her winged eyeliner and glanced at me through the floor length mirror. "No, you're being a child. A petulant, bratty child. You went on a date last week, and I didn't stop you. Does that make me any less caring?"

"I didn't go on a *date*," I mumbled, fighting back a grimace. She didn't need to know the details.

Her eyes hardened. "No, you're right. You don't date. You fucked her."

I rubbed my forehead and sighed. This was getting us nowhere, and I was only growing more agitated as the seconds ticked by. Dickass-ren or whatever his name was, was about to pop up any minute now, and Lila would be on her way... to her date...

Jealous?

No, that wasn't it.

Lila and my relationship was clear – there were no hidden feelings and no secrets. We cared for each other, deeply, but that was it. The mere thought of us being anything *more* was a forbidden idea, and my stomach churned.

I'd rather have Lila like this, than risk losing her later because our feelings were fucked up. There was no going back if we crossed that line.

"He'll hurt you," I said one last time, hoping it'd change her mind.

It was just the idea of her being with another guy, as close as she was with me, that didn't sit well with me. I wasn't jealous.

I was just a bit territorial of my best friend.

Lila stared at me for a moment, the expression on her face unreadable. Her gaze was unflinching, and her small fists clenched at her side. She looked like she was having an inner debate with herself.

She swallowed, her throat bobbing with the small action. Then she did something I least expected and sure as hell wasn't ready for it. Not at all.

My eyes widened as Lila dragged her tank top over her head, letting it slide through her fingers. She stood in front of me in her jeans, boots and bra. Lila wasn't shy, never was. In fact, she could be as crass as me if she wanted to, and most days, she was. She had always been bold and confident.

The determined look on her face should have warned me, but I was too focused on her... chest.

I inhaled, and my dick twitched, straining against my jeans. Shit. "What the fuck?"

"What do you see?" she asked calmly.

I see... tits. Titties I could fuck. "What are you doing?" I groaned. "Lila?"

She took several steps forward until we were standing toe-to-toe. Lila was my little midget, so tiny that the top of her head barely came to my shoulders. She had to nudge her head back to stare up at me because I basically towered over her.

Her gaze was somber as she waited. "Maddox, look at me."

My fists clenched and unclenched. I kept my eyes on hers, refusing to let my gaze wander... down. I'd probably bust a nut if I did. "I am."

"No, you're not. Look. At. Me. Look closer," she persisted in that same soft voice.

I did… and I finally saw what she wanted me to see.

"Do you see now?" she breathed.

My heart stuttered, and I lost my breath as my stomach tightened. My eyes fell to her chest, where her breasts were clad in a lacy, black bra.

And I saw…

Pink and white jagged lines… scars…on her beautiful pale skin. Right at the center of her chest and between the two heavy mounds.

"No," I choked. Jesus Christ, sweet Lila.

Before I could stop myself, my hand came up as if to touch her. When I realized what I was about to do, I stopped an inch away from her skin.

Lila took my hand in hers and placed it on her chest, right in the middle, where her scars laid. She let out a shuddering breath the moment I touched her. Her heart thudded hard against my palm.

"Is this–?" I couldn't finish my sentence.

Lila nodded. "From the accident."

My shaking fingers brushed over her scars, feeling the slight bumpiness on her skin, whereas the rest of her was soft and smooth. "It's ugly," she whispered, trying to hide a grimace, but her face said it all.

"You're beautiful," I confessed, my voice strained.

And she truly was.

Lila had been through hell and back. That was the most beautiful part of her; she was a woman who wore her pain like a diamond choker around her neck. Strong, unyielding… a survivor. Lila Garcia straightened her own crooked crown because she didn't need anyone else to do it for her.

Lila let me in, not because she *needed* me.

It was because she wanted me – as a friend, a companion and a partner.

She gave me a bittersweet smile. "Daren can't hurt me because I'm already hurt. He can't break my heart because it's already broken. Do you understand now?"

I nodded. Lila exhaled in relief.

I stepped closer, our bodies pressing against each other. Mine – fully clothed. Lila's – in a state of half dressed. Her skin was warm underneath my touch. She peeked at me through her thick lashes with a look in her eyes that should have told me *something*... but I couldn't understand what she was trying to convey.

She breathed.

I breathed.

The world came to a stop, and the colors faded away, leaving us in a state of black and white.

Lila shivered, a silent tremor running through her body. It wasn't from the cold because her room was hot, and I was sweating. Her gaze fell to my lips before they wavered, and she looked back at my eyes again.

My head descended toward hers, and my lips brushed against her forehead, a simple kiss. Lila sucked in a harsh breath, and her eyes closed.

I'd never given a girl a forehead kiss before. That shit was cheesy, but it came natural with her. It wasn't like I could kiss her... lips. Lips that looked so soft, so kissable. She'd sock me in the face if I ever tried.

So, we settled with a forehead kiss. That was safe and friend-like.

"Lila?"

"Hmm?"

"You're a beautiful dragon," I said.

Her shoulders shook, and a small laugh escaped past her lips. "Dragon, eh?"

"Dragon," I agreed. "Daren should be worried because you'll probably eat him for dinner if he accidentally steps on your tail."

I closed my eyes and breathed in her scent – she smelled of peaches from the shampoo and body lotion she used.

Lila slowly pulled away, and I let her go. She grabbed her tank top, and once she was dressed again, she checked her phone. "He said he's on his way to the restaurant."

"Can I chaperone?" I asked, only half joking. Actually, I was serious.

Lila wasn't amused. "No, Maddox," she said. There was a note of exasperation in her voice.

She walked past me and out the door; I watched her go with a sinking feeling in my stomach.

I considered following her to the restaurant and keeping an eye on them, just in case, Dickass-ren tried to do any shit to my girl-*friend*. But Lila would never forgive me, and I'd rather stay on her good side. She could be brutal, and she had sharp claws.

I never thought of myself as a possessive person… but apparently, I was.

Of our friendship.

Well, fuck.

CHAPTE
TWENTY-SIX

Lila

I watched as Pops let out a robust laugh at something Maddox said. Grandpa said something else of his own that had Maddox shaking his head and grinning. Sure, Maddox worked for my grandparents, but only Gran had welcomed him with open arms. Pops was a little apprehensive; he always had been with any boys hanging around me.

He said he didn't trust them, and he was right.

But Maddox and I had been friends for months now, and Pops slowly started to warm up to him. In fact, if I wasn't mistaken, they were on the same team now.

Project: Don't let Lila date and protect her at all costs.

It only took two weeks for me to realize my best friend had been right about Daren. Dickass-ren, as Maddox liked to call him, was indeed an asshole who was only interested in sleeping with me.

Grandpa was a hard man to win over, but I wasn't surprised Maddox did. He was… genuine, and even Pops could see that. I was just glad that the two men in my life were finally getting along, well enough for them to share a beer and watch a football game together while discussing sports.

Oh, you know. A usual Sunday night.

Maddox had spent the day with us. Gran even dragged him to church, and he went without complaint. I never pegged Maddox as a religious person and neither was I, but I humored Gran every Sunday and let her drag me to church. Sure, I did believe in God, but if He really loved me, my parents would have still been alive. So yeah, God and I didn't share an amicable relationship.

We had brunch together, then went over to the grocery store for inventory day. After we closed for the night, Pops invited Maddox over for dinner and football. If I had to guess, Pops was a tad lonely, missing a buddy to talk with and he was making a truce with Maddox.

"I think they're best friends now."

My eyebrows rose, turning to Gran as she helped me put the dishes away. "They are?"

"Your Pops doesn't laugh like that with just anyone." She smiled, glancing back at them. "Trust me, I've known him for too long time and been married to him for decades."

Well, yeah, it was Maddox after all. He could easily win anyone over. That was my best friend, ladies and gentlemen.

The men hollered from the living room, and I was guessing it was probably a touch down for their team. I grinned, watching the two most important men in my life finally bonding. Maybe if my dad was here too…

My chest ached, and I rubbed the spot, trying to alleviate the pain. Somedays, the skin around my scars would itch and the scar itself would *hurt*, like I was pouring kerosene on already burning skin. The doctor said it was all in my head. The pain wasn't physical anymore, but my brain and body were used to it, and sometimes, they liked to remind me of the pain.

I thought of the day I showed Maddox my scars. It was weeks ago, although it felt just like yesterday, the memory still fresh in my head and my skin still burning from his touch.

Maddox had brushed his fingers over the marks left on my body, touching my past, lingering over the jagged and ugly lines, tracing the dents of my soul and the rough edges of my heart.

He didn't run away, not like Leo did after taking my virginity. I didn't see the look of disgust or revulsion on his face. Maddox didn't flinch.

He stayed and called me a *dragon* – that was Maddox's way of telling me what I needed to know.

And when his head had descended toward mine, I thought he was going to ruin everything by kissing me that night. For a brief moment, maybe I had wanted him to, but then I felt an immense rush of relief when he didn't.

My phone pinged with a message, snapping me out of my thoughts. It was from Riley.

Quick question. Does this make me look slutty?

She had a tight black dress on – one that molded to every curve of her body. Her boobs were practically slipping out, and she had on red lipstick. Her blond curls bounced off her shoulders, in a Marilyn Monroe style, since she cut them last week. Riley was pouting in the picture.

Slutty and cute. I texted back. **He's gonna be shooketh.**

If he doesn't fuck me tonight, I'm going to taser him.

I choked back on my laughter and disguised it with a fake cough before Gran could ask me what I was laughing about. Poor Riley was dickprived, or in Riley's words, she was suffering from dick deprivation. Grayson was being a thorough gentleman and courting Riley, his words, because she didn't deserve anything less.

I agreed, but apparently, he was withholding sex because he thought Riley wasn't ready yet after the fiasco with Jasper. They were doing everything else, except sex – well, a home run. Riley did say they were on third base. She spared me the explicit details except she mentioned how good Grayson was with his tongue, and she saw Jesus. Lucky her.

They had been dating for a while now, and Riley... well, she was deeply and irrevocably in love with Grayson. I didn't doubt Grayson's feelings for her because it was apparent in the way his eyes followed her every move, the way his gaze searched for her in a crowded place and how he always had a possessive arm around her hips. Sure, he was *gentle* – but it was obvious he was trying to tone down his territorial instincts. Anyone could see that.

Especially after all the testosterone went flying across the room last weekend at Colton's party. That was... intense, to say the least. They both wanted Riley. Riley already made her choice, but Colton was having trouble accepting that.

You should just tie him to your bed and sit on him. Problem solved.

I was only half joking when I sent the text, but then... apparently, Riley didn't get the joke. *Holy shit. That is the best idea.*

I quickly typed back a message. *Wait! I wasn't serious.*

My phone pinged with a message a minute later. *I am. Thanks, babe (;*

Oh God. Grayson had no idea what he was about to walk into.

"Is that Riley?" Grandma asked. "Tell her I'm sad she didn't come over for brunch today."

I nodded, fighting back a giggle. Sorry, Gran. Riley was a tad busy right now. Busy convincing her boyfriend she was ready to be dicked down.

As I put the last plate away, my eyes found Maddox. He was intensely focused on the football game, a pleased smile on his lips. The indent in his left cheek, a small dimple, winked at me as he let out a laugh at something Pops said.

He looked... at home with *my* family. Like he belonged here, with us, not in the cold and sterile Coulter Manor, alone with his dark thoughts.

"Lila," Gran said softly. I looked back at her, and her eyes were glassy as she watched Pops and Maddox, too. "He does a good job of hiding it, but that boy needs a family; he needs love. He's far too young to hold such pain in his eyes."

She patted me on the arm and walked away to join them in the living room, leaving me alone with my thoughts.

He had *me.*

Some days, I wondered if *just friends* would ever be enough for us. We friend-zoned each other; well, basically, *I* friend-zoned *him,* but he eventually went along with it, which means I've tried to date other guys and he still fucked around with some girls, but they never lasted for more than four days. The last one only made it three days; he kicked her to the curb because she called me a bitch for accidentally cockblocking them.

It only made me roll my eyes, but I had never seen Maddox drop a girl so fast. He was pissed, although that was an understatement.

That night when I showed him my scars, we had a moment. Maddox and I had looked at each other a little too long to be *just friends.* That eye contact was more intimate than any words or touches would ever be. There was something unspoken between us, and in that moment, I almost thought he was going to… kiss me. It was both mixed signals and my own overthinking.

He didn't kiss me.

I had been both relieved and… disappointed.

Although now that I thought about it, it was better this way. Just friends. He was safe and familiar. Being anything *more* would ruin what we had, and I wasn't ready for that.

Our eyes met as I walked into the living room and joined him on the couch. Folding my legs under me, I leaned against his side and sipped my tea. Maddox casually looped his arm behind my shoulders, probably doing it without realizing. His fingers drummed against my biceps as he continued watching the game.

As the football game came to an end, Gran and Pops retired upstairs for the rest of the night. Maddox searched Netflix, and we settled on watching *Anabelle*. Maddox loved horror movies; I hated them.

"I'll keep you safe." He grinned with a mischievous glint in his eyes.

I popped a tiny pretzel in my mouth from the bowl of party mix chips.

"Actually, I think you're going to use this to your advantage to scare me, aren't you?"

Maddox gave me a half-shrug, but he pressed his lips together to avoid smiling. Jerk.

Halfway through the movie, I realized Maddox was handing me the pretzels and ringolos because those were my favorites while he ate the other chips.

Yeah, it was the little things. I needed my partner in crime. I didn't need a lover in Maddox. Friends were better than a boyfriend, right? Too much drama came with a relationship. Whatever Maddox and I had, it was safe from any unnecessary drama.

My eyes fluttered close as I fought to stay awake. Before I lost consciousness, I felt his lips brushing against my forehead.

"Sweet dreams, Lila."

Just friends, I reminded myself.

CHAPTER
TWENTY-SEVEN

Lila

I stood on the stage, the light in my eyes blinding me for a moment, before I blinked away the blurriness. My gaze found Maddox in the crowd. He was dressed in his graduation cap and gown, a lazy smirk on his lips. He winked, which helped with my nerves.

We were graduating today.

We fucking did it, as Maddox would say.

I shook hands with the Headmaster as he handed me my diploma. My hands trembled, and I smiled as pictures were taken. I walked down the stage, my stomach twisting and feeling beyond exhilarated. I was excited but I also hated having everyone's attention on me.

This was my dream – everything I had worked my ass off for in the last few years.

I remembered the day I received a white envelope – an envelope that held the fate of my future in it.

"I don't know… I mean… what if… it could be a… rejection letter,"

I stuttered, my heart galloping a mile an hour. "Do… they send out… rejection letters?"

"You're freaking out, Lila. Calm down," Maddox said in his smooth voice.

"Calm down?" I screeched. "This," I waved the envelope at his face, "is everything I ever wanted, and what if it's not what I think it is?"

He raised his hands up in mock surrender, and I plopped back on my bed. My whole body was shaking. "I can't open it, Maddox."

"Lila," he started.

"No, I can't." My stomach twisted with nausea. "I think I'm going to be sick."

"Lila, I don't think they send out rejection letters." Maddox rubbed a hand over his face, and I could tell he was fighting back a smile. What an asshole. He was laughing as I freaked out. I was a little miffed.

"How about I open it?" he suggested.

I popped up and bounced off the bed like a jack-in-the-box. "Yes! You do it!"

Shoving the envelope in his hand, I paced the length of my room. Sweat beaded my forehead, and I swiped it away.

Maddox tore open the envelope, and my stomach churned harder. Oh God, I really was about to throw up.

My eyes closed, and I reminded myself to breathe.

The sound of him opening the envelope filled the room. My heart thudded, and I inhaled… exhaled…

"Open your eyes," he said, his voice sounding closer to me. He was standing right in front of me because I felt the heat coming off him. The closeness of him helped… calm me.

I squeezed my eyes close.

"Eyes on me, Lila," Maddox demanded more forcefully, his voice deep and thick. "Now."

Helpless against his command, my eyes snapped open, and I tearfully *stared up at him.*

He was... smiling.

My knees weakened, and I grasped his arm to stay upright.

"Congratulations, Lila Garcia."

The breath I'd been holding shuddered out of me. Maddox waved the letter at me. "You're about to go to Harvard."

A loud squeal left me, taking Maddox by surprise. I launched myself into his arms, unable to contain my excitement. He hefted me up, and I wrapped my legs around his waist, laughing. "I got in!"

His arms came around me, one hand on my back and one hand planted firmly on my ass as I clung to him.

"You did it," he murmured in my hair, with such pride in his voice that my heart nearly burst out of my chest.

I breathed in his musky scent before pulling my face away from his neck. Our faces were mere inches away from each other. His prominent Adam's apple bobbed in his throat as he swallowed. Maddox nudged my nose with his, and his minty breath feathered over my lips.

"You did it," he said again.

"Thank you. For opening that letter, for not leaving my side, for holding me, for forcing me to face my fears... and for being my friend."

Maddox hugged me back. "You're welcome."

I untangled my legs from his waist, and he settled me back on my feet. "You need to tell your grandparents."

I licked my dry lips and nodded.

Harvard, here I come.

I had gotten my acceptance letter two months ago, a little later than usual, but when I found the envelope in our postal box, my heart had dropped and the first thing I did was call Maddox. I didn't understand *why* I did it, but I knew I needed him with me.

He was at my house in less than ten minutes, out of breath and smiling.

Maddox never left my side as I freaked out, and he didn't leave when I told my grandparents the news either. It meant a lot to me, that he stuck by my side. I never expected us to go from enemies to friends...to best friends.

The rest of the graduation ceremony was a blur. Soon enough, we were outside under the blue sky with the sun shining on us.

Grayson had Riley in his arms, and they were laughing and kissing. Each student found themselves surrounded by their family. My gaze lingered over the crowd, looking for Maddox's parents.

Please be here, please be here. Don't hurt him anymore.

They were nowhere to be found.

I seethed, anger simmering through my veins and gut. How dared they? They should have been proud to have a son like Maddox.

Yes, he was a troublemaker – a total misfit.

But damn it, he was sweet, and his heart was pure. He worked his ass off to graduate with honors. Time and time again, he proved himself to the world that he wasn't just a rich and spoiled kid.

My fists clenched at my sides, and I growled. They didn't deserve to share this day with Maddox.

There was a tap on my shoulder, and I swiveled around, coming face-to-face with Maddox. He stood tall, his shoulders squared, and I had to admit, he did look hot in Berkshire's navy-blue graduation gown with his cap on top of his head.

His lips curved in an easy smile, and I searched his eyes, looking for the disappointment I expected to see. But there was none.

It was then I realized that he no longer expected anything from his parents. They were strangers to him, not a *family*. Because they had never been here for Maddox for the most important days of his life – his football games, his birthdays, his graduation.

"What's up with that kitten growl, Sweet Cheeks? Did someone step on your tail?" he teased.

I swatted his arm. "Watch it, Coulter."

"You don't scare me, Garcia."

"I'll bite you."

"Bite me then," he dared.

I snapped my teeth at him, and he threw his head back, chortling. My anger at his parents melted away at Maddox's laughter. I refused to bring up the topic of his parents not attending the graduation ceremony. He was happy, right here and right now, and that was all that mattered.

I crossed my arms over my chest, pouting.

His laughter died, but he was still smiling. Maddox shoved his hand in his pocket, and he fished out a teal Tiffany box. What...?

My lips parted in surprise as he snapped open the small box. No way!

Shock coursed through my body. "Maddox," I breathed, shaking my head. My cap slid down, and I fixed it on top of my head again, still staring at the box he was holding.

It was a necklace, exquisite but simple, with only a sterling silver charm.

"A dreamcatcher," I whispered, my fingers brushing over the intricated webbed floral centerpiece and the delicate feathers attached to the round center.

"Now, we've got matching dreamcatchers."

I let out a laugh at that. The memory from a few months ago flashed in my mind.

"What is this?" Maddox asked, giving the object in my hand a weird look. He appeared unimpressed.

"A dreamcatcher, silly." I gave it to him, and he looked even more confused.

"Why are you giving me a dreamcatcher?"

I realized Maddox sometimes had bad dreams.

We fell asleep together last night, on his couch, while we were studying, and he had woken up from a nightmare. He didn't speak of it, but the bleak look in his eyes broke my heart. He couldn't go back to sleep and ended up going to the gym that was open twenty-four-seven.

Maybe it was fate or just pure coincidence, but as I was scrolling through Instagram, I found an ad for dreamcatchers.

Sure, it was a silly thing to give to him, but I remembered the dreamcatcher my mom used to hang on my headboard when I was a kid. She said it'd keep all my bad dreams and monsters away.

I didn't really think much of it when I ordered it. True, Maddox and I were too old to believe in this, and he was obviously too macho for something so childish, but maybe...

Damn it.

I didn't even know why I got this dreamcatcher, and now, I was doubting myself. The first gift I ever gave Maddox was a dreamcatcher. Oh, what a story to tell the world and our friends.

His eyebrows rose. "You seriously expect me to hang this on my bed?"

It wasn't the response I was hoping for. My shoulders slumped, and I chewed on my lips, the feeling of bitter disappointment gnawing at my stomach. I thought maybe he'd be a bit more... appreciative?

I rose to my feet and squinted down at him, hands on my hips. Fuck him. "Look, if you don't want it, you can throw it away. It was cheap anyway, so I don't care."

Maddox didn't say a word. He just went back to looking at the dreamcatcher as if it was the weirdest thing he had ever seen.

I had thought he threw it away, like I told him to.

Except the next day, when I walked into his room... there it was.

The silly dreamcatcher I gave him, hanging onto his headboard. It looked so out of place in his bedroom, but Maddox kept it, close to him, right next to him while he slept.

We never spoke of it again, but every time I'd walk into his bedroom, that was the first thing my eyes would notice, and it'd always be there.

And months later, Maddox still had it. It was my first gift to him.

The dreamcatcher he didn't want but never threw away.

I flipped my curled hair over my shoulders and stared up at Maddox. "Can you put it on me?"

He took the silver necklace out of the Tiffany box, and my throat went dry as his hands slipped around the back of my neck. He stood close, crowding into my space, but I couldn't complain. His body heat caused me to flush, and his fingers were warm against my skin – a teasing touch, so featherlight that I barely felt it.

Maddox placed the necklace around my neck and the dreamcatcher charm laid on the base of my throat where it belonged.

"Beautiful," he rasped, his breath caressing the tip of my earlobe. It made me warm and breathless, though we had been this close so many times: we hugged, we slept in the same bed, and Maddox would give me piggyback rides. We were always touching, one way or another, but some days... it felt more than just a friendly touch. Like today.

My eyes fluttered shut as his thumb brushed against the pulsing vein in my neck. His touch lingered there, feeling my heartbeat through my throat.

"The necklace or me?" I asked, my eyes still closed. Why... did I just ask that?

"You," he said. "Always you." His voice was soft and hot, leaving me feeling things I couldn't explain, couldn't put into words.

I leaned into him, my palms landing on his chest. The hard thump of his heart had my eyes snapping open. Maddox's gaze flickered to my lips. His hands fell to my curve of my shoulders, sliding down my arms, and his fingers curled around my hips.

A single heartbeat passed between us.

I pulled back, breaking the moment between us. Maddox blinked before releasing a shuddering breath. My skin still burnt from where he had touched me, and I hated how cold I suddenly felt from pulling away from him.

Maddox took a step back, too, pulling us farther from each other. He ran his fingers through his hair, which he kept short since the first time I called him Poodle. He thought it'd make me stop calling him that stupid pet name if his hair was no longer long and curly like before.

Ha, he *thought wrong*.

Once a poodle, forever a poodle.

"Pictures!" Gran said. She waved Riley over, who came forward with Grayson.

"Closer everyone," Pops demanded as he held a camera in his hand.

Colton and the boys – Brayden, Cole and Knox – all whom were Maddox's teammates and close friends, surrounded us. Riley stood beside me, with Grayson on her side, while I stood next to Maddox. We formed a semi-circle and Gran was smiling from ear to ear.

"Say cheers!"

"Cheers," we called out and the camera's shutter clicked.

Picture perfect.

The moment our circle broke apart, we were surrounded by the other Berkshire students. I lost Maddox in the crowd, all the girls vying for his attention one last time. They were probably hoping he'd take one of them home for a graduation fuck fest. Colton and the boys had their own little harem around them, too.

I found Grayson and Riley, holding hands as they stood under a tree, watching from a distance. Grayson looked slightly relieved that Colton's attention was no longer on his girlfriend.

Riley was convinced that Colton didn't have any feelings for her. She was either in denial or she truly was blind to the tension between Grayson and Colton, which was extremely palpable.

Gran came to my side, pulling my focus away from the lovebirds as she hugged me, surprising me by her strength. "So proud of you, Lila. Your parents would be, too."

I blinked back the tears at her words. "Is it weird that I felt like they were with me during the ceremony? Like they were right there, watching me?"

"No, sweetheart. It's not weird because I know they're watching over you." Pops rubbed my back. "You've grown into such a beautiful and smart young lady."

"I'm going to miss you two when I go to Harvard," I confessed, choking back my tears. My heart was heavy in my chest as I realized I only had a few weeks left with my grandparents before I moved away to a whole different state.

Gran cupped my cheeks, smiling. "You have Maddox and Riley with you."

In the end, Riley, Maddox, Colton and I were going to Harvard. Cole got accepted to Yale and that was where he was going. The other boys were leaving for Princeton or Dartmouth.

I sniffled, nodding. "Yeah, but they aren't you."

Even Pops looked crestfallen – I was his little girl – the one he raised and his only grandchild. Pops was rarely emotional but times like this reminded me just how much he loved me and Gran. He placed a chaste kiss on my forehead. "You're going to be okay," he said with strong conviction.

Hours later, I found myself in Maddox's car. We no longer had our cap and gown on, but instead, Maddox was wearing a white buttoned up shirt, black slacks and a black tie. He was… in other words, sinfully sexy, but I wasn't about to tell him that. He rolled up his sleeves to his elbows and flexed his forearms, his hands on the steering wheel.

"Where to, Sweet Cheeks?" he asked, flashing me a half smile. There was light in his blue eyes, and it glimmered with teasing mischief. "The world is ours. Let's cause some trouble."

My lips curved upward. "You've got a bad reputation, Coulter. Stop trying to corrupt me. I'm a good girl."

Maddox didn't give a damn about his bad reputation. In fact, he loved being a bad influence. Such a rebel and a troublemaker.

"Good girls do bad things sometimes," he drawled. "It's me and you, Garcia."

"Me and you?" I breathed.

Maddox and I against the whole world. Partners in crime and best friends.

"Me and you," he agreed, starting up the car. "So, where to?"

I raised an eyebrow, smiling because there was only one answer to that question. "I have a dare, but it's dangerous."

I loved the way his eyes lit up to the word *dangerous*. Such a rulebreaker.

"Do you dare?" I asked.

Maddox grinned, a devious grin, and I had my answer.

Who would have known it end this way? From that day in the coffee stop, to us being enemies… and then calling truce, being friends… and to *this* moment? Maddox and I had come a long way *together*. Fate really had a way of playing with us.

I used to despise him.

And now he was the most important person in my life.

CHAPTER TWENTY-EIGHT

Lila

Three years later

I tapped my foot against the asphalt, waiting for Maddox to show up. I shot Riley a text, letting her know I was going to be late for dinner. She was cooking tonight, her infamous ravioli dish. We were celebrating since she finished her thesis last night. We were currently halfway through our second semester in our third year at Harvard.

While I had gotten accepted into Harvard for Chemistry, Riley was studying Sociology. She was planning to pursue a post-graduate degree in Criminal Law.

Colton was majoring in Statistics while Maddox was studying Business, although he wanted to pursue a football career. Him getting a business degree at Harvard was just to appease his parents, although he did say he enjoyed it. At the end of the day, football was where his heart belonged and he was really good at it.

I still couldn't believe it had been three and half years since that day in the coffee shop – the day I spilled my ice coffee on Maddox and the rest was history. I tried to think of a moment when I hated him, but although we had been enemies for a short period time, I never truly *hated* him. Sure, I had despised his arrogance and douchebaggery attitude, but it wasn't hatred.

Maybe that was the reason why it was so easy for us to go from enemies to friends to best friends.

Such a strange twist of fate – from that day to now, almost four years later.

There was a tap on my ass and I rolled my eyes, knowing full well who it was.

"You got to stop touching my ass, Coulter," I warned.

He chuckled and walked around me, coming into view with his glorious self.

A lot had changed in three years. Maddox, for instance, had grown *bigger*. He was already brawny in high school from playing football and working out, but now, he had packed on extra muscles. His shoulders were half a size bigger than before and now twice the size of my own. His biceps bulged, his arms full of veins and muscles. He filled out the black shirt he was wearing, the fabric stretching tight over his wide chest. He had a six-pack before and now he had eight. His abs were hard and cut. My fingers itched with the memory of touching them. I had seen him shirtless countless times and had seen his progress from seventeen-year-old Maddox to twenty-year-old him.

Me? I was still the same. Same height, same weight – still a midget compared to Maddox, and he took great pleasure in reminding me of that fact every time he manhandled me and put me where he wanted.

His blue eyes glimmered in the sunlight. He eyed me up and down, his gaze lingering longer on my bare legs. I wore denim shorts that were frayed at the end and a black long-sleeved shirt with a brown leather jacket over it and ankle boots. It was March, and the weather was slightly hotter than normal. To our surprise, spring came early this year.

"My eyes are up here, Maddox," I teased.

He glowered, and I fought back a smile. I stuffed my hand in my bag and pulled out his phone charger. "Here you go. Thank you for letting me use it."

I handed him the charger and waved for him to go. "I'll see you tonight. You're going to be late for your next lecture. Go!"

"I'm always coming to your rescue." He tsked with a slight grin. Maddox gave me a finger salute as he started to backtrack. "Always at your service!"

"I don't need a knight," I said, loudly enough for him to hear a few feet away.

"I know you don't. You're not the damsel in distress who I need to save."

My heart warmed, and my lips twisted in a smile. "You're right. I guess I am more like the dragon, eh?"

"A cute and sexy dragon," he called out.

Maddox jogged across the open field toward his building. Since our programs differed greatly, his classrooms were on the opposite side of the campus while mine were on this side.

He faded away in the distance, and I strode away to our apartment building, which was only about a ten-minute walk through the campus.

I took the elevator up to our apartment, which was on the third floor. I found Colton at the door with a girl in his arms. They were kissing, and by the look of it, they were about to fuck in the corridor.

I cleared my throat, and he peeled himself away from the chick, his eyes hooded. "Sup, Lila?"

My eyes narrowed on the girl beside him. Her mocha skin glistened with a sheen of sweat, and she flushed. It appeared like they had clearly already fucked on the way here.

"Are you coming over for dinner or...?" I asked.

He gave me a half shrug, his gaze moving to the apartment next to him. "She didn't invite me."

I grimaced and smiled sheepishly at him. Things were tense between Colton and Riley – well, tense was an understatement at this point in their 'relationship' or whatever they had.

To put it simply, they... *hated* each other.

But that story was for another time.

I opened the door to my apartment, the one I shared with Riley, which also happened to be next to Maddox and Colton's; we were neighbors.

"Baaabee, is that you?" Riley called out.

Colton's jaw clenched at her voice, and he grabbed the chick, pulling her into his apartment. The door closed with a bang behind him.

"It's me," I said, walking inside.

Her back was to me as she stood in front of the stove, humming a song under her breath. She had sweatpants and a shirt on, her blonde hair up in a messy bun. Riley spared me a look over her shoulder. "Did you get the garlic sticks I asked for?"

I lifted my arm up, showing her the grocery bag I was holding. "Gotcha. It smells good in here."

She brought the spatula to her lips and blew on it. "Wanna taste?" she asked, cheekily.

I nodded, and she offered me the spoon. The richness of the sauce hit every one of my taste buds, and I moaned. "Yummy!"

We set up the plates, and she placed a bottle of wine on the table. "Is it just us? Is Maddox coming?" Riley asked as she took her seat at our small dining table, opposite of me.

I shook my head, piling some ravioli on my plate. "No, he missed his lecture this morning, so he's attending a later class today. Isn't it too early for wine? It's not even six yet."

Her lips curled up. "Lila, it's always time for wine, and we're celebrating today."

Riley loved to drink – wine and margaritas in particular. She had been obsessing over red wine lately. It was her favorite and now my favorite as well. We were besties for a reason, right?

Riley swallowed a bite of her dinner and then gave me an inquiring look. "How's it going with Landon?"

My heart stuttered. Landon, my boyfriend of five weeks.

"Good," I said, moving a piece of my ravioli around in my plate.

Riley sighed, carefully placing her spoon on her plate, before leveling me with a look. "Lila, don't give me that shit."

I chewed on a piece of ravioli before swallowing it down with red wine. I drank half of my glass before slamming it back on the table. "He's not replying to my text."

Riley let out a curse. "Did you call him?"

"I'm not that desperate," I snapped.

"Lila," she sighed. I refused to look at her because I didn't want to see the sympathy on her face.

Landon pursued me for three months before I finally gave in. He was a good guy: smart, sweet and nice. At first, I refused to give in since I thought I was his rebound. Landon had broken off with his long-term girlfriend four months before he turned his attention to me. But he courted me, flowers and all, and he was different than the other guys.

Maddox was hellbent on keeping us apart because he believed Landon was no good.

But then again, that was his excuse for every guy I dated over the years.

Granted, none of them really lasted for long – four months maximum.

Sex wasn't some sacred thing to me. I wasn't a virgin; I had a few hook-ups here and there, but I never had a one-night stand. I needed the intimacy before and after sex, and one-night stands didn't give me any of that. I've had a few boyfriends over the years, but Landon was the one I felt… comfortable with, enough for me to give in and have sex so soon into our relationship.

That was three days ago. And he was acting weird since then.

Leo was the first guy to turn away with disgust when he saw my scars. Since then, I either had sex while half-dressed or when we were in the dark–dark enough they couldn't see the jagged, pink lines between my breasts – just so I could spare them the disgust or shock they'd feel if they saw it. I didn't need or want their sympathy either.

My scars never bothered me, and I wasn't really embarrassed of it.

But maybe I was lying to myself.

Landon… he saw my scars. He didn't really flinch away, but I noticed the way he kept his gaze averted during sex. He didn't look at my boobs and kept his eyes on my taunt stomach or the spot between my legs instead.

I'd be flattered… if I thought he was focusing on my pussy, but I knew he was just trying to avoid looking at the marks on my chest.

He didn't act weird afterward, so I believed everything was okay.

Until yesterday.

Landon wasn't replying to my texts, which was unusual. He had always been very attentive… until now.

"Damn it," I growled and poured more wine in my glass. "Maybe he's just busy."

"Too busy to send you a single text?" Riley stabbed her ravioli with too much aggression. She was a tad bit overprotective of me. Maddox was probably rubbing off on her. "It'd take him two seconds," she added.

I cleared my throat and took a slow sip of my wine. Drinking too much and too fast would have me tipsy in less than an hour. "It doesn't matter."

She made a face at me. "He's an asshole."

I shrugged and continued with my dinner, shoving a spoonful into my mouth.

"You don't care… if he breaks up with you?" she asked slowly.

"I'm not in love with him if that's what you're asking," I said around a mouthful.

It was true, I didn't love Landon. He was nice, and I *liked* him.

But that was it.

"Maddox–"

I cut her off. "He doesn't know and you won't tell him." I leveled Riley with a hard look, and she leaned back against her chair, looking only a bit intimidated. "If he finds out Landon is ghosting me or if he thinks I'm hurt over this, which I'm *not* honestly, he's going to kill Landon."

Riley cocked her head to the side, thoughtfully. "Didn't you… um, spend the night over at Maddox's last night?"

"We fell asleep while binge watching *Friends*," I amended. I woke up in *his* bed in the morning; he carried me to bed after I had fallen sleep, and I had been all cozy against *his* pillows and *his* blankets while Maddox slept on the couch.

"Do you think maybe the issue is Maddox? Not that I'm saying he is, but you know how all your exes were sensitive about him. Maybe Landon is too?"

She raised a good point.

Maddox *loathed* every guy I dated.

Consequently, they hated him, too. And none of them were too happy of my relationship with Maddox. They didn't like that we were *that* close. They didn't approve of Maddox having access to my apartment. He could come and go freely and vice versa. They didn't like that I attended all of Maddox's football games and some of his practices.

It was a lot to juggle, and granted, yes, it made sense why they didn't approve of Maddox's relationship with me.

But none of them came close to what or *who* Maddox was to me.

I wasn't going to fix what I had with Maddox to suit these guys.

Maybe that was the issue in all my past relationships, but I wasn't willing to change anything between Maddox and I.

My stomach twisted at the thought of losing Maddox. The mere idea of being without him made me sick.

We were best friends; no one and nothing was going to change that.

Not Landon... and none of those girls Maddox messed around with.

"Lila!" Maddox called out from the bathroom.

I settled back into the couch and stuffed a handful of sweet caramelized popcorn into my mouth.

"What?" I responded, before taking a sip of my energy drink. I was a bit tipsy from all the red wine I had tonight with Riley. She was passed out in our apartment, and I had come over to our neighbors' place to bring him dinner.

Colton and his new conquest had disappeared when Maddox came home.

Maddox walked out of the bathroom with only a towel wrapped low around his waist, bare chest and his v-line teasing me. You see, I've seen Maddox half naked many times over the years. But each time, my mouth watered at the sight of his wide, muscled chest and washboard abs and that nipple piercing. He had gotten it one night when he was out partying with his football team. They had been pissed drunk and they went into a tattoo and piercing shop. The rest was history.

I never considered a nipple piercing sexy, but on Maddox? *Puuurfect.* Yes, I just purred.

I was his best friend, but I wasn't blind, and I had a pussy, which meant that I appreciated the male species. A lot. Including my best friend.

Was I drooling? I wiped the corner of my mouth just in case.

Maddox huffed and gave me a look that bordered between comical and exasperation. "Did you get in my phone and change your name to *My Main Chick?*"

Oh.

I had been a bit drunk when I did THAT a few nights ago. And then I had been too lazy to change it back.

I shrugged, trying to act nonchalant. "Well, yeah. Because I am your main chick. All the other girls are just your side chicks."

Maddox opened his mouth and then shut it, falling silent. He blinked and then just shook his head.

I gave him a cheesy smile. Maybe I was more than just tipsy.

"It's okay, though. You can fuck around with them. At the end of the day, you come back home to me. And I know I'm better," I muttered around another mouthful of popcorn, sending him my best smile.

He growled and the sensitive area between my legs clenched. Shit, this was bad.

Abort mission, abort mission.

Maddox ran his fingers though his wet hair, exhaling sharply. "For fuck's sake, woman! My only side chicks are your other personalities. And there are like twenty-five of them."

I paused midchew. Ouuh-kaay.

He showed me his hand, ticking off each list with his fingers. "Grumpy Lila. Lazy Lila. Pouty Lila. Funny Lila. Lila when she's sleep-deprived. Sugar high Lila, like right now. On her period Lila. Normal Lila."

My mouth opened then closed. My lips parted again, trying to say something. When I found nothing to say, quite speechless, I stuffed another fist of popcorn in my mouth and chewed in mock aggression.

"Do you want me to go on?" He paused, giving me a blank look as if daring me to argue with his claims.

I had no legit argument, and I had lost this round.

"Whatever," I mumbled. "Go shower. You stink."

"You're impossible." Maddox shook his head with a slight curl of his lips. He walked back into the bathroom.

"You love me," I yelled loud enough for him to hear even with the door separating us.

"YOU ARE A PAIN IN MY ASS."

"You still love me, though," I whispered, once I heard the shower turn on, with the silliest grin on my face. I knew he did because if he didn't... we wouldn't have lasted this long as a friend.

CHAPTER
TWENTY-NINE

Maddox

As I walked out of my class, my phone pinged with a message. It was from Bianca. ***R u coming over tonight?***

Did I want to? No. I'd rather be home with Lila, watching some stupid Korean series with her, which most of the time were cliché and too cheesy for my taste. Riley was obsessed with anything Korean: K-POP and K-Dramas. She made Lila watch one of the shows *once* and then...*BAM*, Lila was now a K-Drama obsessed, too. We were currently watching some period/historical drama called *Scarlet Heart Ryeo*.

I had to admit, though, that shit was good.

So, did I want to go over at Bianca's tonight? No, I didn't. Bianca was too...clingy. I didn't even go on any dates with her. We fucked a few times, and she declared herself my girlfriend.

I didn't correct her. She was now going around the campus, telling everyone she was Maddox Coulter's *girlfriend* – flaunting our relationship status in everyone's face. Including Lila's.

Lila would just roll her eyes and subtly put her hand in my back pocket, which would make me *smirk* because, damn it, Lila sure knew how to push all these girls' buttons. They were jealous of Lila and my best friend? She firmly believed none of these girls were ever good enough for me.

So, Bianca, my girlfriend?

Ha.

More like recent fuck buddy – but okay, I'd humor her. For a while.

I typed out a one-word response. *Yes.*

After all, it was Friday. Lila and Landon were supposed to have date night.

My jaw clenched at the thought, and my teeth gnashed together. Why couldn't Lila see he wasn't the man for her? There was something off about him, and apparently, I was the only one who could see that. I didn't like him, period. Why? I didn't know.

I just didn't want him anywhere near my Lila.

"Yo, Maddox!" Turning around toward the voice, I saw Jaxon jogging over. He was Harvard's linebacker, one tough motherfucker. He was a beast on the field.

His dark skin glistened with a sheen of sweat, and he flexed his neck left and right. "Can I crash over at your place tonight… and the rest of the week?" His brown eyes pleaded with me.

"Let me guess, Rory kicked you out? Again."

Jaxon grimaced. "She's pissed because she found a lipstick mark on the collar of my shirt. Told her I didn't mess around with any bitches," he sighed, rubbing a hand over his tired face. "It was before the game when I was hugged by one of the cheerleaders, but Rory doesn't believe me. I'm no cheater, man. But she's driving me fucking crazy."

Jaxon was faithful to his girlfriend of five years. They were high school sweethearts and shit, but Rory was one fucked-up bitch who had major trust issues. I wasn't about to tell Jaxon that, though, because he'd pummel my face into the ground.

"Yeah, you can crash at my place," I said. *Oh, the drama.*

He slapped me on the back and nodded. "Thanks, man. I owe you one."

"You owe a lot. Pretty sure you live at my place more than yours."

He grinned. "I'd say you were goddamn lucky you didn't have to deal with a psycho girlfriend, but I can't complain. She's the best thing in my life."

I didn't need a girlfriend.

Lila Garcia was already the best thing in my life.

As Jaxon jogged away, my ringtone blasted through the pocket of my black slacks. I held back a growl of annoyance and checked the screen. I picked up the phone after seeing it was Riley calling. "What?"

"Lila has been locked in her room for the last two hours; she won't come out, and I think she's crying. That asshole. Landon, it's him. You need to come because Lila isn't opening the door for me," she rattled out in one breath. "Maddox! Are you listening?"

I was already sprinting toward our apartment. "I'm coming," I growled.

Red, hot anger coursed through my veins, and I swallowed it down, but it grew in my belly. I felt it pounding through my blood, vicious and brutal.

If Landon had caused my Lila any pain... if he hurt her...

I took the stairs two at a time, stumbling in my haste, but I couldn't find myself to care. The door to her apartment was opened, so I hustled inside. Riley was pacing the length of their living room, worry etched over her face. Colton was leaning against the wall, also looking a bit pensive. That was the only time I had seen the two of them in the same room without being at each other's throat.

"Maddox," Riley said, looking relieved at the sight of me.

I walked past her and stood in front of Lila's bedroom. The door was locked, like Riley said.

"Lila?" I called out, pressing my ear to the door. There was a sound of her sniffling.

She was… crying?

No.

FUCK, NO.

My gut churned as my fist pounded on her door. "Lila, open the door."

There was no response from her. "Open the fucking door or I'm going to break it down. Trust me, I will."

"Go away," she called out weakly.

My heart stuttered. "Lila," I said, trying to keep my voice gentle. "Baby, open the door. *Please.*"

"Just… go away, Maddox."

My eyes pinched close, and I rested my forehead against her door. "Don't do this to me. Don't shut me out. Don't hide from *me*. I'm not going to walk away, and you damn well know it. Let me in, Lila."

Whatever Landon had done to my girl, he was about to regret it for the rest of his shitty life.

"If you don't open the door, I'm going to think the worst, and I'm going to hunt down Landon… and I might end up in prison tonight."

I didn't give a fuck if I was about to spend the rest of my life in jail because I was still going to hunt down Landon either way, even if she did open the door.

He made her cry – *that* was a death penalty.

"You're not killing anyone," she mumbled through the door.

"Open the door then," I pushed.

There was some shuffling around and then she unlocked and opened the door. Lila came into view, but she kept her head casted down, her black hair covering half of her face.

I placed my finger under her chin and nudged her head up. Her eyes were red, but there was no sign of tears. "I'm not crying," she said, begrudgingly. "I don't cry."

That was right.

Lila never cried, except for one day of the year. She hated being vulnerable and the only time she ever allowed herself to be, was on the date her parents died.

Her cheeks were flushed, and her eyes were red, a clear sign that she wanted to cry, but she was holding her tears in.

Lila pressed her palm over her forehead and squeezed her eyes close. "I'm just... God, he made a fool out of me."

"What did he do?" I asked through clench teeth.

"I was his rebound," Lila said, her voice small. She swiped at her cheeks even though there was no evidence of any tears. "And he has been cheating on me... with his ex. I guess they're back together now, but he was a coward and didn't tell me. I don't understand. Why did he... why did he sleep with me... if he was already back with *her*? I mean, he basically cheated on both of us."

Riley let out a curse under her breath from behind me.

Colton hissed. "He's dead meat."

Anger simmered in my gut. The more she spoke of her situation, the angrier I became.

It consumed me, and my skin itched with the need for revenge, to *hurt* him, like he hurt Lila.

My Lila.

My fingers curled into fists as the fury slid through me like acid, burning inside the pit of my stomach.

Riley pushed past me and enveloped Lila into a hug. She whispered something to her, and Lila nodded. They talked quietly to each other. "I'm more angry than hurt. Embarrassed, too, because I let him touch me... we had sex... because I *trusted* him."

Lila's head came up, her gaze finding mine instantly. "Maddox–" she said, but her eyes flared, probably from seeing the look on my face.

"Maddox, no."

Lila came forward, her arms out as if to grab me, but I sidestepped her reach.

She called out after me as I stalked out of the apartment. "Maddox!"

I wasn't listening; I was too far gone to stop now.

I charged down the stairs, faster than I knew I could and climbed into my car. The passenger's door slammed shut, and I looked up. Colton settled in the seat.

"You're not stopping me," I snarled.

"No, I'm coming *with* you." He cracked his knuckles, his lips splitting into a deadly grin. "He fucked with one of ours."

After breaking every known traffic law, we were at Landon's apartment two minutes later.

"You stay out of it," I warned Colton. My Lila, my fight.

"I'll let you beat the shit out of him, but I'm just here to keep you from killing him."

Colton rang the doorbell. I heard a high-pitched giggle through the door – a woman – and anger boiled deep in my veins. It churned with the hunger for destruction.

I wasn't thinking clearly, I fucking couldn't.

All I could *see* was Lila's sad eyes and blotchy cheeks as she tried to keep her tears inside.

The door opened, and there was Landon.

His eyes widened in shock, and I pushed forward. He stumbled back inside his apartment, gaping like a fish out of water.

"What the fuck?" he sputtered. "You can't just push your way inside like that."

"We can't?" Colton taunted.

"What's going on?" the woman asked. She was partially naked, the look on her face telling me she had just been fucked, multiple times.

Landon pointed toward the door. "Get the hell out of my apartment.

Now."

I took a step forward, a promise of violence. He saw through me, and his eyes darkened. He shoved at my shoulders, wanting to assert his dominance in this fight, and I *snapped*.

Lunging forward, I grabbed him by the throat. He retaliated quickly, landing a punch in my gut. I quickly threw my weight on him, sending both of us crashing into his glass table in living room.

"Oh my God!" A shrill voice screamed.

I felt his nose crunch under the force of my punch. It was so loud, it vibrated through my ears.

Grabbing his hair, I pummeled his face over and over again. "You," *punch,* "don't," *punch,* "fucking get," *punch,* "away," *punch,* "so easily," *punch,* "after hurting," *punch,* "Lila."

He broke Lila's trust and embarrassed her by cheating on her. *Motherfucker.*

Landon struggled against me, and he knocked me in the jaw, hard enough that I stumbled back. The sound of fists against flesh was all I could hear. Blood leaked from my nose, and I punched him in the ribs again and again.

"Stop! Help! Someone help!" The stupid voice was screaming once again.

I drew my fist back and ploughed it into his stomach. He coughed and sputtered blood. Stars burst in my vision when he got me in the head, but I shook it off.

There was blood on my knuckles but I. Could. Not. Stop.

"Maddox! Maddox, no."

Lila. Her voice broke through the red haze, and I blinked, seeing Landon's bloodied face.

Hands grabbed my back and arms, trying to pull me away from Landon. My eyes connected with Lila's brown ones, and she looked completely... distraught.

For Landon? For this fucking asshole?

Lila whimpered. "You're hurt. Oh God, Maddox. Oh no."

Me?

"Ah fuck," Colton roared. "She called the police. Shit!"

Lila's face crumpled, and she pushed her face into my neck. "No, no, no."

I stumbled away from Landon, and his bitch came forward, falling to her knees beside him.

"Maddox," Lila said softly.

"I got you." I wrapped my arm around her, lifting her so her feet were dangling an inch from the ground.

She let out a choked sob. "No, you don't. They're going to take you away. Landon is probably going to press charges. *Why?*"

Why?

Fucking why?

Because I can't bear the thought of you hurting. Because watching you hold back your tears for an asshole like Landon has me losing my mind. BECAUSE HE FUCKING HURT YOU.

I never got a chance to say any of that to her. Glancing up over her shoulder, I saw the cops walking inside the apartment. They looked around, studying the mess.

"That's him, Officer," the woman cried, pointing at me.

Lila was shaking her head, holding onto me tighter. I had Landon's blood on my hands; I broke into his house... there was no getting out of this. And I wasn't the least bit sorry for turning Landon into my punching bag.

"Colton will take you home, Lila," I rasped in her ear.

She gave me a stubborn shake of her head. "I'm coming with you."

"No," I deadpanned, with my hand gripping her chin. I made her look at me. "Colton will walk you home, and I'll see you in the morning."

"But–"

"No, Lila."

Her face hardened. "You don't tell me what to do."

"I am, right now. Do as you're told." She glared. Lila was stubborn, and I knew she'd sit with me in jail if I didn't get her home. There was no goddamn way I was letting her spend the night in a cell, even if it was with me. "*Please.*"

I placed her back on her feet, and her chin wobbled. She turned to face the cops. "It's only a misunderstanding, officers. It's my fault."

"Misunderstanding or not, you're under arrest." One of the officers was staring directly at me. I nodded, compliant. There was no point arguing with them.

Colton had to drag Lila away from me as I was handcuffed, my hands behind my back.

"Please," Lila pleaded. "Can I just… hug him?"

The officer who handcuffed me beckoned her over. She slid closer to me, pressed her nose against my throat. "I'm sorry. This is my fault."

Lila sniffled, and my heart twisted. My lips brushed against her forehead, and she hugged me tighter. "I'm sorry."

"I got you," I said again.

Her teary eyes were the last thing I saw as they pulled me away from her. Lila brought her hand up and she touched her dreamcatcher necklace at her throat, as though it soothed her.

It gutted me, because she was crying for *me.*

CHAPTER THIRTY

Lila

I couldn't sleep, there was no way I could when Maddox was in jail, and here I was, in my nice and cozy bed.

He was locked away in a cell because of *me*. My gut twisted with guilt, and I stared at the ceiling through the darkness. Colton had to drag me home with Riley right on our heels.

After convincing me to get in bed while he handled the matter, Colton left.

Why didn't he stop Maddox from getting into a fight?

Why wasn't I fast enough to stop him?

Why... why... *why?*

I always knew that as much as Maddox was laid-back and easy-going most of the time, he was also short-tempered and easily triggered.

The guilt became harder to bear because if I only had put on my big girl pants and didn't cause a scene, Maddox wouldn't have run off to beat the shit out of Landon.

But I had been *hurt* and embarrassed.

Not that I cared much about Landon. I wasn't heartbroken, but I felt...
used.

Used and discarded after he had his fun with me.

If Landon didn't want to be with me, he could have easily walked
away. I wasn't clingy; I had no expectations. But he cheated on me, after I
let him inside my body.

That hurt me.

And I had been furious.

I wasn't 'crying' because he broke my heart. They were angry tears, at
him... and myself, because I trusted the wrong guy.

I felt foolish, but I didn't think Maddox would react the way he did.
Everything happened so fast, and before I could have grabbed him, he was
already out of the door.

Then I walked in on him beating the shit out of Landon, not that I
cared if my ex was hurt or not. But Maddox was wounded too and that
guilt became much harder to bear.

When the cops came, it took everything in me not to beg them to take
me with them. Goddamn it, I'd sit in a dirty cell with Maddox if it meant
he wasn't alone behind those bars and I was with him.

Landon was pressing charges. His precious girlfriend attacked me
after the cops left and her sharp nails have left a nasty mark on my arm. I
returned the favor by punching her boobs before Colton pulled me off her
and dragged me out of the apartment as I cursed them through their next
lives.

My door creaked open, snapping me out of my thoughts, and I
squeezed my eyes shut. There was a relieved sigh, and I peered at the door
from behind my comforter.

"She's asleep," Riley said softly to the person behind her. Probably
Colton.

I was right, because a second later, his hushed voice came through.

"Good. It's been a long night for all of us."

The door closed, and I sank back into my soft mattress. My body was still tense, and I couldn't find a comfortable position.

It was a long time before I fell into a restless sleep.

Hours later, I jolted away when my bed dipped under a heavy weight. Someone settled behind me and a strong arm slid around my hips, pulling me back into *his* body. Hard and familiar... warm and solid... strong and safe.

Maddox.

He curled his body around mine, and my ass was nestled indecently against his groin. He didn't shift away like I expected him to. He kept me there, my back against his front, so close not even a string could fit between us. We'd laid in bed many times, but this was... *different.*

More intimate, less 'friendly,' and there was an unspoken tension between us. I licked my lips and cleared my dry throat, feeling the way my stomach dipped and fluttered as he touched me.

Maddox pushed his other arm under my neck and tucked the back of my head against his shoulder. I released the breath I was holding and inhaled his familiar scent, also catching a whiff of alcohol. Did he drink before coming home?

"Landon dropped the charges?" I asked in the dark.

I felt him shake his head. His arm tightened around mine, as if making sure I couldn't escape or maybe he was scared I would.

Little did he know...

"Then?" I pushed for more.

"My father handled it," he confessed, his voice a raspy croak.

Ah, so his father bailed him out. Shit. He found out. *Bad. Bad. Bad.* Colton and I thought to keep this incident lowkey and hoped Brad Coulter wouldn't find out his son was in jail.

I guess Maddox's father had eyes and ears *everywhere.*

"Was he pissed?"

"He didn't message me, didn't call me either. Didn't even talk to me. He handled everything behind my back and without talking to me. I only knew he did it after I was released, and Colton came to pick me up."

Oh. So, his father hadn't even bothered to speak to him, to ask what happened, why it happened or how his son was even doing.

I snuggled deeper into his embrace and slid my hand into his, the one on my hip. I squeezed his fingers. "I'm sorry."

He expelled a long breath. "I'm not. He deserved every punch I threw at him. I think I broke his nose. Nobody makes my Lila cry. No one. I won't fucking allow it." He slurred his words a bit. Yeah, he was definitely a little drunk.

My eyes filled with tears. I didn't peg myself to be an emotional person, but Maddox made me *feel* so many things at once.

Sorrow... fear... anguish... hopelessness...

My heart thudded in my chest

"Maddox?"

"Um, yeah?"

"I love you," I whispered.

His arm flexed around my hips. "I know." His hold tightened around me in the slightest bit. His lips feathered over my forehead in a whisper of a kiss, before he placed his cheek on top of my head again. "I love you, too."

It wasn't the first time we had said those words to each other but my heart danced in my chest. Without lifting my head, I brought my hand up, showing him my pinky.

"Friends?"

Maddox hooked his pinky around mine, and I could feel his smile without even having to look at him.

"Friends," he said.

My eyes closed, and I fell asleep to the sound of his heartbeat.

In the morning, I woke up to an empty bed. For a brief moment, I wondered if it was all a dream, and Maddox hadn't come home. But when I breathed in, I caught the familiar, musky scent that he left behind. My body still tingled from where he had touched me.

After quickly freshening up, I walked out of the bedroom to find Maddox sitting at the kitchen table, staring out the window. The morning sunshine shone through the glass, and Maddox looked beautiful sitting there. He was shirtless, with only his grey sweatpants on. It was the perfect sight...but my chest tightened at the look on his face.

My wounded warrior.

He had a black eye, and his lips were cut and swollen. His ribs were turning into an ugly shade of purple and green.

"Want some coffee?" I asked, hoping to get him to talk and lighten up his mood. Last night was hell for all of us. I needed to make sure he was okay.

But his next words were not what I expected.

"Am I a disappointment?"

I flinched. "What!? Maddox, what are you–"

My next words caught in my throat when I saw the expression on his face. Utterly defeated, a look that could only be described as *heartbroken*. Like a beaten puppy, whimpering silently as it suffered.

My heart caved inside my chest at that look, and I walked over to him, kneeling between his legs. He spread his thighs wider, encasing me against his body.

"Why is it that whatever I do is never enough?" he said, his words choked.

"Maddox," I whispered.

I saw the phone in his hand and finally put two and two together. Grabbing the phone from him, he didn't stop me, I searched through his messages. The most recent message, two hours ago, was from his father.

You keep disappointing me over and over again. I can't believe I

almost thought you had finally been redeemed from your messy ways. This is the last time I will bail you out from things you fuck up.

Oh Maddox. My poor, sweet Maddox.

"I'm sorry," I breathed, looking down. This was all my fault. Why did I ever let Landon in my life?

I grabbed his hands, holding onto him, letting him know he wasn't alone. It was then I noticed his knuckles were bruised, and there was some dried blood left on it.

Shit. That was from last night. He didn't clean himself up.

I got up and quickly and went to get to first aid kit to clean his wounds. His knuckles were slightly swollen, but thankfully, not broken. I attentively cleaned his bloodied knuckles, wincing as I brushed the antiseptic wipes over the broken skin. Maddox showed no outward emotion. He was silent until I finished with his left hand and grabbed his right hand to do the same task.

I kept my movements slow and careful as I cleaned his wounds and wrapped a bandage around his hands. He probably didn't need them, but the bandages would keep them clean, so there would be no infection.

His eyes raked over my face before his gaze slid away – looking bleak and distant, lost.

"I got into Harvard. I worked for it. I worked so goddamn hard that I was able to keep my full scholarship for three years. I'm on top in my football career. Why is it not enough? Everything I do... it's *never* enough. I always, somehow...end up lacking somewhere. Always somehow disappointing him. It's never enough, Lila."

"No. No. *No!*" I rushed to say. "Baby, no. Maddox, everything you do is enough. It's more than enough. You. Are. Enough. Please don't say that. I'm sorry about last night. I'm sorry your father is an asshole. I'm sorry he never told you he's proud of you. But *I* am. I'm so proud of you, Maddox Coulter. Everything you've done, everything you do... it's enough," I said in urgency.

He leaned his head back and closed his eyes as if soaking in my words. He entwined our fingers together and clutched onto me. I squeezed his hands back. *I'm here, Maddox. I'm here, and I'm not leaving. Me and you, forever.*

I wanted to ask him what he needed right now. From me. If I could lessen his guilt, his suffering in any way, I would do it. Without a second thought.

As if he could read my mind, his eyes opened, and he leveled me with those beautiful blue orbs. I saw everything I needed to know.

"Can you..." he paused and swallowed. "...hug me? Please?"

He whispered those words so brokenly, like he was scared I'd refuse me, like a child begging for affection. To have someone *just* hold him.

I nodded, mutely, because my throat was closed up as I choked back a cry and forced my tears away. I couldn't let him see me cry.

I stood up, and he pulled me into his lap. Maddox buried his face in my neck. "I got you," I said, softly in his ear.

His grip tightened on me.

Maddox got hurt because of *me*; he got into a fight for *my* honor. The realization was overwhelming because I had underestimated his protective instincts for me and how much he actually cared.

I felt him breathing against my throat, and under my palm, his heart slowly started to beat at a calmer pace. His lips brushed against the pulsing vein in my throat and maybe he hadn't meant to do it or he didn't want me to feel it, but I did. My body was hyperaware of his touch.

"I got you," I said again, as a reminder. My fingers combed through his hair, and slowly, he started to relax in my arms. The tension left him, and my aching heart soothed itself at the fact that Maddox was going to be okay. He was strong enough to be okay.

Once he lifted his head up, I smiled at him. "Okay now?"

His lips curled up in a half smile, and he nodded. "I guess I just needed a hug from my Lila. I swear you're my goddamn therapy. Why waste money on a shrink if there's a Lila in your life?"

I let out a laugh and smacked his arm. "Oh, shut up."

He was grinning now, his eyes lighter, his expression calm.

"So, how about I make you pasta?" It was his favorite thing to eat whenever he was feeling low.

"Woman, you know I'd never say no to your pasta."

"Okay, sit tight then."

Pasta for breakfast. Hmph. Who cared? If that shit made my Maddox smile then we'd have fucking pasta for breakfast. Every. Damn. Day.

CHAPTER THIRTY-ONE

Lila

*S**end me a picture. Wanna see your sexy face.*

I opened the text from Riley and then stared around the loud club. We were sitting at a corner booth with pretty bad lightning.

Still, I humored Riley and brought my phone up, deciding to please her with one picture. She wasn't able to join us for a night out since she had an essay due tomorrow morning. Riley pouted as I left our apartment with Maddox, Colton, Jaxon and Rory. She made me promise to send her photos of us being pissed drunk, so she could live vicariously through us.

I ruffled up my hair a little, then pursed my lips in a sexy pout. Just when I was about to click the perfect photo, I was suddenly jostled. Something wet touched my cheek, and I reared back in shock. Maddox's head fell into the crook of my neck, and he inhaled deeply before pulling away, giving me panty-melting smile.

"Eww, did you just lick me? What is wrong with you, Maddox?" I growled, slapping his chest and shoving him away. But he was a wall of muscles so moving him was an impossible task.

He gave me a mock pout. Yeah, he was a little drunk already. "I thought we were supposed to lick the ones we love. I licked you, so you're mine."

I blew out an exasperated breath before hissing. "Are you a dog?"

Maddox paused, as if he really was thinking about my question. And then he shrugged. "Doggy style is my favorite position to fuck. And I'm also your Poodle."

Before I could have stopped him, he leaned forward and licked my cheek once again, leaving a wet trail behind.

His mouth moved to my neck, licking me there, too. Against my own accord, my thighs trembled, and my core clenched as his lips brushed over my throat. "Maddox!" I whisper-yelled. "Stop licking me!"

He leaned back, and his lips quirked up dangerously. "Why? It gets you wet?"

"No," I barked, suddenly feeling the urge to smack him. "Because your *girlfriend* just walked in, and she's coming our way. Oh, she doesn't look very happy."

Maddox looked toward the entrance before sinking more into his seat, as if trying to hide from the raging chick coming his way. "Ah. Shit," he whispered.

Bianca wasn't exactly his 'girlfriend' anymore. They broke up when Maddox didn't show up the night he was supposed to go over to her house. The night he got into a fight with Landon and ended up in jail.

The next morning, Bianca threw a huge tantrum and even called me a 'homewrecker' and 'bitch' for trying to steal her man. Maddox dropped her so fast I thought she'd suffer a whiplash.

Her man? Yeah, right.

Maddox was never hers in the first place.

A week after their breakup, she still didn't grasp the idea and has now turned into a stalker. Bianca stopped at our table, hands on her hips, and glowered at Maddox. "I need to talk to you."

He lifted a shoulder in a shrug. "I'm busy, as you can see."

"Now," she snapped.

My eyes widened at her tone, and Maddox tensed. "You don't get to come here and make demands. I'm not your boy toy, Bianca."

She tapped her foot, impatiently. "You owe me a better explanation for breaking up with me, Maddox."

Maddox rubbed his eyes and slurred a bit as he spoke, "I don't owe you shit. And we were never together in the first place. We *fucked*, that's it."

The distaste was clear on her face as she gave me a nasty look. "It's because of her, isn't it? You're choosing her?" Bianca said in a shrill voice, pointing an accusing finger at me.

Here we go again.

Another 'girlfriend,' same drama.

Maddox growled low in his throat, the sound so threatening even I winced. "Listen—"

My phone rang, breaking through the tension, and Maddox stopped mid-sentence. I gave him a sheepish look and slid out of the booth, phone to my ear.

I walked away from Maddox and Bianca as they continued arguing with each other.

"Hey, Bea?" I answered the call.

"Lila, shit. We're in trouble," she gasped.

"What? What is it? What happened?" I strode out of the club since it was too loud to hear anything Bea was saying over the phone.

Bea was a professional dancer, and my chorographer of the dance club at Harvard. Two years ago, I joined the club as a hobby and soon realized that I enjoyed dancing. It was therapeutic.

I wasn't the best dancer, but I also wasn't too bad. In between my studying and waitressing part-time, I needed something to do to relax and just unwind. Dancing seemed to do that for me.

"Owen is hurt. He broke his leg from a biking accident. He. Can't. Dance," Bea said, out of breath. I could feel her freaking out through the phone.

"Owen is hurt?" I asked, because I couldn't believe what I just heard. "How bad is it?"

"He's okay. He's home, and he just called me. Owen isn't in a lot of pain, but it's bad enough he won't be able to dance for the next three months. *Oh God.*"

Oh shit.

That didn't sound good.

A month ago, our club partnered up with a non-profit organization that put on charity events for people with disabilities. This year, the fundraising event was for blind people.

Our small group of dancers were supposed to present a show for the attendees at the event who would be contributing to the charity.

Owen was my dance partner.

Shit!

"There's no backing out now. This is top-notch, Lila. The organization, the event – *everything* – has to be perfect. We're representing Harvard. We no longer have a dancing partner for you anymore, and *you* open the show!"

My throat went dry, and I tried not to panic, but Bea freaking out like this was causing *me* to freak out. "Bea, you need to calm down. We can figure it out."

"The event is in a week!" She screeched loud enough I had to pull my phone away from my ear.

She was right though. We couldn't mess this up. Every dance number at the event was a couple's dance; the organization specifically asked for a partner dance since they thought it would be more attractive to the attendees.

I took in a deep breath, trying to calm my rising panic. I was used to perfection – my grades and my work. I was obsessed with it, although I wasn't always like that.

My therapist said it was my way of dealing with the death of my parents – chasing perfection and wanting to always be in control.

Right now, everything was happening the opposite of what I wanted.

"So, we need to find me a new dance partner?" I questioned Bea.

"Even if we do, who's going to learn the dance in less than seven days?" She took a shuddering breath and let it out. "It's not possible."

"Nothing is ever impossible," I said.

"Your optimism is admiring but not suitable for the situation since we are thoroughly fucked!"

"I'll find a dance partner," I announced with conviction. There was no giving up after we'd come this far. The event was happening. Owen was hurt, but we had to find a way to make it work.

And I knew exactly who was going to help me.

Even if I was about to hear him grumble about it for the rest of our lives.

"Lila–"

"I know someone."

"Who?" she asked suspiciously.

My corner of my lips curled up. "Maddox."

I had struck Bea into silence, only her breathing could be heard over the phone.

"You're serious?" she whispered, as if we were sharing a secret.

"Yup."

"Holy shit. You mean, *The* Maddox, right?"

"Yup." I grinned harder.

"Holy shit," she said again.

We said our goodbyes, and I walked back inside the club. Maddox was going to hate it, but I knew he'd never say *no* to me.

Back at our booth, I saw that Bianca was nowhere to be seen, and Maddox was nursing a beer. "Where'd she go?"

"I handled her," he said, not giving me any more details. "What's up?" Maddox seemed to have sobered up a bit.

"I need to talk to you about something."

His eyes narrowed on me. "Is it bad?"

I half-shrugged. "Not exactly. Do you want to go home?"

Maddox stood up without saying a word, and I guessed I had my answer.

Maddox

"No," I calmly stated. "Not happening."

"But Maddox," she dragged out my name, pleading with her eyes. When I shook my head firmly, she stomped her foot.

She peeked at me through her lashes. "This is really important to me."

Then Lila got a look on her face, a look that should have warned me of what was coming.

"Lila–"

"I dare you."

Jesus Christ, this woman!

"Take that back," I warned, my voice low.

Lila smirked. "No." She crossed her arms over her pert tits, pulling my attention to her chest.

I was a goddamn weak man.

Weak to my fucking knees for Lila Garcia because she was the one temptation I couldn't have.

She was wearing a crop top that should've been illegal. Her dreamcatcher necklace hung around her neck; Lila never took it off after I put it on her three years ago. Her stomach was taunt, and her belly button looked cute, and as fucked up as it was, a brief image of me licking her belly button and her giggling flashed through my mind. My mouth watered at the thought.

I shook my head and cursed myself. No, I *couldn't*.

This was... not happening.

Never, fucking ever.

Even though it grew harder every year to remind myself that we could only ever be friends and nothing more.

Every time she smiled at me, it became harder not to kiss her.

Though, I had refused to admit that even to myself. I refused to even entertain the idea of touching Lila in a manner other than 'friendly.'

But I was little drunk, and I couldn't get the image out of my head. She was standing in front of me with a crop top and shorts that hugged her curvaceous ass like a second skin, her pink lips glistening and her black hair falling over her shoulders.

Lila looked like a Rated-R Snow White. I wanted to slide between her thighs and make us both forget that we were best friends.

No. FUUUCCCK. NO!

That was drunk me thinking of that shit. Sober Maddox would never think of fucking his best friend, I told myself.

"Maddox, are you listening to me?" Her voice broke through my burning thoughts.

I swallowed and forced myself to look away.

"Yeah," I said, my voice deeper, hoping she didn't notice the way I strategically adjusted the pillow over my lap.

"Do you dare?" she asked cheekily.

I sighed, running my fingers through my short hair and pulling on the strands. "This isn't going to be fun, Lila."

She was asking me to be her dance partner. I wasn't much of a dancer, but I wouldn't say I completely sucked. This was important to her; I was well aware of that fact.

It was the fact that I was going to be too *close* to Lila for a whole week, especially since it had started to become harder for me to control my urges – my dick – around her. *That* bothered me. After the incident with Landon… there had been an unmistakable tension between Lila and I.

We both refused to acknowledge it, going on with our lives, but it was there, and it was becoming harder to ignore.

I didn't know why… I was feeling *this* way.

And I didn't understand what it was.

Angry at myself, I held back a growl, and my eyes snapped to Lila's. She was waiting for an answer, oblivious to my inner turmoil.

Lila Garcia was my best friend, and the last thing I wanted to do was lose her because I couldn't keep my dick in my pants.

I'm drunk, this is why, I convinced myself.

She tapped her foot impatiently. Any other girl doing that would have annoyed me, but *Lila* tapping her foot was cute as fuck.

"C'mon, Coulter. Are you about to lose to me?" She tsked. "It's a simple dare."

Simple?

Little did she know…

She grew cocky when I didn't reply, her competitive nature shining through. Lila knew I'd never turn down a dare, and she knew exactly how to get her way.

"Fine, I accept the dare," I said, my teeth grinding together. "You're going to regret this, Garcia."

Lila pressed her lips together to keep from smiling, but she lost the fight. A beautiful smile spread across her lips, and she laughed a bit, the little happy sound shooting straight to my heart.

My fingers curled and uncurled at my sides.

What is wrong with me?

CHAPTER THIRTY-TWO

Maddox

My body was on fire.

I fought back a shiver, and my pulse throbbed in my throat.

His hands traveled up my arms, slowly… taking his time, as if he was memorizing every inch of my exposed skin. His touch was so soft, so featherlight, but it felt as though he was writing a word, painting a picture or playing a song on my skin. My breath caught, and my heart raced, tripping over itself because it could longer beat in a normal rhythm.

Our eyes connected through the floor length mirror. The intensity of his gaze made my stomach do a crazy flip, and my thighs trembled.

Maddox was wearing a black sleeveless shirt, the muscles in his arms on display, and they clenched and tightened with every move he made. His whole body was a work of art. I wore a tank top and shorts, comfortable enough for dancing.

His blue eyes smoldered with *something* I couldn't read – dark and intense.

Friends, I told myself.

We were best friends.

But friends didn't look at each other the way we did.

The past five days had been sweet torture.

Sweet because I spent every waking hour with Maddox.

Torture because I spent every waking hour with Maddox.

Dancing… touching… breathing so close to each other's lips… but reminding myself to pull away.

I refused to acknowledge what I was feeling. It was *forbidden*.

Or maybe I didn't really comprehend my own wayward emotions.

Why does my body react the way it does when Maddox is close?

Why does my heart hurt… when he's hurt?

Why does my stomach flutter when he's touching me?

We were friends, weren't we?

Being anything more than friends could risk what we had for the last three years and whatever we had was *beautiful* the way it was.

"Lila?"

His voice, a deep timbre that traveled down through my body and all the way to my toes, snapped me back into the present.

"You just stepped on my toes," he mumbled, his breath against the tip of my earlobe.

I quickly apologized and went back into the position I was supposed to be in.

Our eyes locked, and I moved my hips against his. He followed my movement, and his grip tightened on my waist, his fingers almost digging into my flesh, and it didn't seem like he noticed.

Our height difference had the curve of my ass right at his groin, and my eyes fluttered close, my cheeks flushing in embarrassment and… something else.

Maddox made a sound at the back of his throat, and I looked at him through the mirror. His face hardened, and his eyes grew darker, his pupils dilating.

He grasped my hips and spun me around, taking me by surprise. He pulled me closer, our bodies clashing together. His hand skimmed over my bare thighs, right where the shorts ended, and he slowly lifted my left leg up, hooking my thigh around his hip. Fire licked its way through my veins, and I burned hotter.

Maddox dipped me low, and his warmth seeped through my clothes all the way through to my bones.

"You look a little red, Garcia," he rasped. "Am I too hot for you?"

He pulled me back up, and my heart thudded in my chest. I turned around and rolled my eyes, trying to look indifferent to his stupid remarks and his close proximity.

Maddox chuckled low, his chest vibrating with the sound, and I felt the vibration against my back. "You're rolling your eyes at me, I know. I can see your reflection in the mirror, Lila."

My eyes narrowed on him, and I swiveled around again, swatting his chest. "Concentrate on the dance, Maddox."

His arm snaked around my waist, and he pulled me hard into his body. I stumbled into his chest. "I have you," he muttered softly, and his arm tightened around my waist.

Maddox fished out the white blindfold from his pocket, and he covered my eyes, stealing away my ability to see. I was supposed to be blindfolded for half of this dance, making it trickier. It was all about trusting your dance partner.

It forced me to feel every one of his moves, his steps, our matching rhythm, our shuddering breaths and the heat coming off him. My body was even more hyperaware of Maddox's closeness to me.

His warmth left me for a brief moment and our song, the song we were supposed to be dancing to, filled the tiny dance studio.

"Time of my Life."

There was no way Maddox and I could compete with the original dance and actors from the movie *Dirty Dancing*; they were legends, but it was my favorite movie and song and it was perfect for *this* dance.

Blindfolded, I waited for Maddox to return to me.

I could feel him somewhere around the room, *watching* me. The heat of his gaze had my stomach clenching.

The longer he took, the more nervous I became. Tick, tick, tick.

His body brushed against my back, and I sucked in a breath. I squeezed my eyes shut behind my blindfold and reminded myself to breathe. His hand drifted down, his fingers whispering over my body. My ribs, my stomach, my hips. Maddox touched me like I was a made of glass, fragile to his exploration.

Maddox pulled me into him, and he started to move. I followed his steps through our mixed tango and contemporary dance.

He gripped my hips and twirled me left and right before I fell back into his arms. My heart raced faster, and his breathing was ragged. I imagined his hard face and eyes that were so blue I drown in them. Beautiful.

Mine.

Oh, I wished.

I embraced the music and swayed with the flow, matching Maddox's rhythm and letting him lead me through blindly. I was at his mercy.

After spinning me around and with my heart in my throat, Maddox pulled me back into his body. With one hand on my waist, he grabbed my thigh and slowly brought my leg up to his hip. I hooked my ankle around his thigh, right under his ass. I was breathing hard now, and I wished I could see his face.

His breath brushed my nose. "Is this right? That's the correct move?" Maddox asked, his voice deep and gruff.

I nodded, mutely. Then, he slowly dipped me low. I released myself into his arms and let him move me. With me bent backward, his body molded over mine. He pressed his face against the crook of my neck. It was just part of the dance, I told myself.

Maddox inhaled.

I exhaled.

He brought me back up, and my leg fell from around his hip. He spun me around to the right and then one quick twirl to the left before Maddox brought me closer to him again. Our movements were synchronized.

I lifted my arms up, and his hands slid down my waist, just below my ribs. I swayed and moved my hips to the music. His fingers tightened on my waist before he lifted me up. My feet left the floor, and I wrapped my legs around his hips before he bent me backward again.

When we were finally standing straight up, I hugged him close, burying my face in his neck. I felt slightly dizzy, my heart beating too fast. But so was his.

Body against body. Chest to chest. I felt his heart beating to the same maddening rhythm as mine. Maddox twirled both of us around once.

My stomach tightened as I slid down his body, and my feet touched the ground once again. His fingers grazed my flushed cheek, and I wondered if he could feel how hot I was. Maddox removed the blindfold as he was told to do during our dance practices.

I blinked, and our eyes locked together.

His face shone with sweat, and my hair was sticking to my sweaty forehead and cheeks. His eyes narrowed on me, hungry and searching. Blazing with *something* – I didn't understand, I couldn't explain.

The expression on his face… I wished I knew what it was.

Maddox took a step back… then another and another, walking backward from me. The song was coming to an end; this was our final move.

Once there was enough distance between us, he crooked his finger at me, beckoning for me to come to him.

I did.

I walked, and then I took off running, one final lift, the same climatic lift as the one in the movie.

Once I was close enough to Maddox, I jumped. His hands gripped my hips, and he lifted me up and over his head. Strong and firm, he kept me steady.

Oh God.

Every muscle in my body tightened. I released a shaky breath as I slowly slid down the length of his body, feeling every hard inch of him. My palms pressed over his chest, sliding down his ribs and abs.

"I got you," he rumbled.

Do you?

Once I was touching the ground again, I curled my arms behind his neck, and our foreheads pressed together. His lips brushed against the tip of my nose, and my eyes fluttered close.

I can't breathe.

I swayed, dizzied by the mere proximity of Maddox. My heart hammered in my chest. He exhaled, and his minty breath was on my lips.

Don't kiss me.

Kiss me.

No, don't ruin this.

A loud clap against the silence of the room had me flinching away. My eyes flew open, and Maddox's darkened as he pulled away.

I swiveled around and faced Bea. When did she get here?

"Lila!" she squealed, clapping her hands. "That was amazing... explosive! Oh my god!"

Bea walked further into the room, looking quite pleased. If there was any tension in the air, she ignored it.

She fanned herself. "The chemistry... Sweet Jesus, have mercy on us. Just wow! No one would believe you two are just friends. That was... yeah, wow." Bea pointed at Maddox and I. "This is exactly what I was looking for. You need chemistry with your dance partners. You need the

314

audience to *feel* your dance even though they aren't dancing."

Her smile widened. "Oh, I'm so excited. Thank you, Maddox. For doing this on such short notice."

"Lila asked," he grumbled, running his fingers through his hair. "I couldn't say no."

Bea turned to me. "Are you guys hungry? We can grab lunch."

Maddox took a step back, pulling further away from me. He grabbed his duffel bag, his jaw clenching and his body tensing. "No. You go ahead. I'm leaving."

"Maddox–"

But he was already stalking away without glancing back at me.

Without a goodbye.

My heart dropped to the pit of my stomach.

The moment between us was gone, the spell broken.

It was better that way, before either of us made a mistake we'd both regret for the rest of our lives.

Friends?

Friends.

CHAPTER THIRTY-THREE

Lila

I walked in on Riley and Colton. They both looked furious, glaring and spitting venom at each other. He had her caged against the wall, and their heads snapped toward me as I walked inside the apartment. Colton pulled away from Riley as though she burned him, and Riley was glaring daggers at his back.

Without a word, Colton left and slammed the door behind him. Welp, this wasn't looking too good.

The animosity between Colton and Riley was getting out of control.

I cleared my throat, and Riley sniffled. Her face crumpled, and she choked back a cry. "I hate *him*."

"Colton or Grayson?" I asked, already knowing the answer.

"Both," she hissed, fury burning in her eyes. She stomped into the kitchen and filled herself a glass of water.

"What happened?"

"Grayson called," she deadpanned.

Oh. Shit.

She made a sound at the back of her throat. It sounded like a whimper. "Why did he call? After so long... *why*?"

I placed my shoulder bag on the counter and sat on the stool. "What did he say?"

Riley huffed, her lips twisting with a sneer. "Nothing."

My eyebrows rose, and I waited. "He called, I picked up. He didn't say a word. I could hear him breathing over the phone, but he's such a damn coward. I hung up."

Poor Riley.

Three years ago, I thought Grayson was the best choice for her.

Two months after graduation, he broke her heart.

Grayson wasn't going to attend any universities. Riley wanted to do a long-distance relationship. Hell, she even thought of quitting Harvard and moving back, just so they wouldn't have to break up. She was ready to put her heart on the line for him.

But Grayson was adamant and said it wouldn't work out. He wasn't willing to do long distance, but Riley knew it was a bullshit excuse. Something had been up with him, something he had been hiding from all of us. We figured it had something to do with his adoptive parents and his past, but he wouldn't say a word.

She wasn't ready to give up on him though. After going back and forth, making things difficult on Riley, he left. Grayson broke up with her right before the start of our first year at Harvard.

Grayson was back in Manhattan, and Riley was *here*.

She was still very much in love with him, and I knew, if Grayson showed up now, she'd give him another chance.

Enter Colton – who thought after Riley's break-up, he'd have a chance with her.

Oh boy, did he try. He cared for her, any one could see that clearly. If there was someone who could heal Riley's heart after Grayson broke it...

it was Colton.

But Riley refused to give into his advances. Tension brewed between them, growing much volatile every day.

"I miss him," she confessed, her voice barely a whisper. "If only he had given us a chance."

I grasped her hand in mine and squeezed. "I'm sorry, Ry."

She swiped away a tear, almost angrily. "Do you think maybe… Grayson has a good reason for staying away?"

Something bothered me about that day.

The frantic and desperate look in Grayson's eyes as he pushed Riley further away from him. And the words he roared.

"I'm protecting you, damn it!"

Protecting Riley? From what? From who?

She let out a humorless laugh; her eyes glistening with unshed tears. "He's had three years, Lila. Three years I've been waiting for him, three years for him to realize we could have been so good together, but he gave up on *us*."

I hugged her, and she fell into my arms, crying softly. She had been holding it in for so long. My heart ached for her.

For all three of them.

Once her cries turned into tiny hiccups, Riley pulled away and rubbed a hand over her face, as though getting rid of any evidence she had been crying over Grayson.

She half-smiled, the corners of her lips twisting slightly. "How was the event? Where's Maddox?"

I left the stool and went to the fridge, taking out last night's leftovers. "The event was great. It was pretty… exhilarating, and they loved the dance. The fundraising part of it was a huge success, too," I told her. "It was fun."

And it truly was. The whole night was pretty epic until…

Riley appeared curious when she asked, "Maddox didn't come home with you?"

No, he *ran*.

The moment our dance ended, Maddox left. He didn't even stay for dinner, and with him gone, just like that, without so much as a word, I could barely eat. My food stayed untouched in front of me, and for the rest of the night, I *smiled* while my heart was breaking – hidden from everyone's eyes. I suffered while they enjoyed the rest of their night.

How could he? Why did he leave?

Why didn't he say goodbye?

Why?

A subdued anger burned in my stomach, threatening to break through. I couldn't understand why Maddox was acting the way he was – why he was running away from me, pulling further and further away from me.

Anger and… fear.

Because it felt like we were hanging on by a thin thread, and it was about to snap, catapulting us into two different world and away from each other.

Maddox and I… if we weren't careful, we were about to *break*, to shatter, and there would be no turning back once that happened.

Me and you, he had promised.

I hoped he was keen on keeping his promises.

My chest tightened. *Don't break me, Maddox.*

"Lila?" Riley's soft voice broke through my stormy thoughts.

"He left. I don't where he went," I admitted out loud, the words tasting bitter on my tongue.

Riley stared at me, her eyes searching. "You don't see it, do you?" she said gently.

"See what?" I shoved a piece of roasted chicken in my mouth.

Her lips twisted. "Nothing. When you see it, you'll know what I mean."

"What–"

Riley shook her head and stood up. "I've had a long day. I'm off to bed. Are you going to sleep soon?"

I nodded. "Probably."

Riley paused at the door of her room and glanced back over her shoulder. "Stop hiding and stop ignoring it. You know what you feel. You're just refusing to acknowledge it."

Without waiting for a reaction, she closed her door. I stood there, mutely. What was I supposed to do with her cryptic words?

It felt like there was a hole in my chest, and I was bleeding out. There was no way to stop the flow of blood. I *bled,* the knife digging into my heart carelessly.

Drip. Drip. Drip.

The dam broke, my blood flowed, and I lost those pieces of me I had carefully glued together.

Tears of frustration blurred my eyes.

I was so…*confused.*

Between wanting Maddox and not wanting to lose him.

For years, I'd swallowed down my confusing feelings and kept them locked away in a forbidden place, refusing to acknowledge them. My throat itched as I forced back a cry, and my lungs seemed to collapse.

You know what you feel.

No! I didn't!

I couldn't.

Never.

Stop hiding and stop ignoring it.

I… couldn't.

I chewed on my lip until it bled, and my knees buckled from the realization – what I felt for Maddox, it was so much *more* and I was damn afraid to acknowledge it.

Why was this so hard?

Maybe I was stupid.

Maybe I had completely lost my mind. It was the only explanation to why I was in Maddox's apartment, waiting for him to get home. It was almost midnight, and the last time I had seen him was...

When he had left the event right after our dance.

Maddox still hadn't come home yet.

I wrung my hands in nervousness, the feeling of anxiety pooling in my stomach. God, what was I doing?

Why was I even... here? At his place, waiting for him.

Stupid, stupid Lila.

What was I going to do when he came back? Hug him? Kiss him?

Nothing.

I'd stare at him, and he'd look into my eyes, that would be it. Because we were... friends.

Such a brutal lie it was. Friends...

The closer we became, the more I noticed smaller things about Maddox. What he loved, what he enjoyed, what pissed him off or annoyed him, his quirks and his ticks, and with every new thing I learned about him over the last three years, it became harder to pull away.

To ignore whatever was brewing between us; yet, we refused to acknowledge it.

He slept with other girls.

I dated other men.

We were best friends.

It was simple to the world, to *him*, but I was battling a war on my own.

My head fell into my hands and a choked sound escaped me. *What am I doing?*

The clock ticked with every second that went by, and when I finally couldn't take it anymore, I snapped to my feet. No, I shouldn't have been here.

This was a... mistake.

I was confused and…scared…and feeling *too* much.

The last thing I needed was to be this close to Maddox if he came home. I had to leave. Shaking my head in desolation, I strode for the door.

I never reached it because the door swung open and Maddox entered his apartment, stumbling inside drunkenly. Sweet Mother Mary, he was out… drinking?

He halted at the sight of me, and his lips curled. "Lila." He breathed my name like a whispered prayer to the heavens above.

Was he praying for absolution or destruction? Because whispering my name like *that* could only destroy us.

He slammed the door closed behind him and stalked forward.

"You're drunk," I accused, taking a small step back.

He hummed, smiling. He stood in front of me, our chests barely touching, and my gaze met his. "You're so beautiful," he blurted out.

God, he was completely out of his mind. Maddox wasn't just drunk; he was *really* drunk.

He bent his head and stuck his nose against the crook of my neck, inhaling sharply. Was he…sniffing me?

"*Beautiful*," he breathed, before his body slumped forward into mine.

"Maddox!" He was so heavy, my knees almost buckled under his weight. "Maddox?"

Did he just… pass out?

I took his shoulders in my hands and tried to shake him awake. He groaned, but otherwise, didn't move. Shit.

With the rest of my strength, I dragged his heavy body into his room. Maddox barely made any effort, because he was practically dead to the world. How much drink did he have? And why?

God, I was so tired from asking that question – *why?*

I pushed him on the bed, hating that he drank so much in one night. Before I could pull away, his arm curled around my waist, and he tugged me forward, and I fell on top of him.

His throat bobbed as he groaned. I shifted over his body, trying to break free, but for someone as drunk as Maddox, he was still too strong for me. His arm was a band of steel around my hips, keeping me locked against him. He wasn't letting go.

I shifted away but then sucked in a harsh breath when I felt...

My throat went dry. This wasn't happening.

His cock strained through his jeans, the bulge pressing indecently into my stomach.

"Lila." My name on his lips sounded like poetry. So right, so perfect... so filthy.

I pressed my hands over his pecs and pushed. "Maddox, let go."

He did the opposite.

Maddox rolled us over until I was underneath him, trapped against his body. My legs fell open, and I gasped as he settled between my spread thighs. His eyes split open, hazy and filled with... *hunger.*

His gaze fell to my lips, and he lingered there, his eyelids hooded.

"Maddox," I whispered.

"Say it... again. My... name."

I was utterly helpless in his arms. "Maddox." His name echoed from my lips.

"Again," he demanded.

"Maddox."

He released a shuddering breath before bending his head, pressing his face into my throat. He nuzzled me, his lips caressing my skin. I trembled, goosebumps breaking over my flesh.

He ran his lips down my collarbone, his teeth grazing the sensitive skin there, and I let out an involuntarily shudder. "Don't," I warned, but it was a weak attempt.

Maddox hummed low in his throat, his chest vibrating with the sound. He lowered his body over mine, forcing me into the mattress. He wrapped around me like a cocoon.

We were chest to chest, hips to hips, his hardness against my heated core – so fucking close. There was not even an inch of breath between us.

The area between my legs throbbed, and I clenched, seeking for something but feeling... *empty.*

Maddox was still nuzzling my throat, kissing me as if it wasn't atypical, as if we weren't best friends, as if everything around us would crumble as we remained intimately wrapped in each other's arms.

"Fuck," he grunted against my skin, and his hips jerked, pressing against the most sensitive part of me. My lips parted, shocked, and a silent gasp escaped me.

My hands fumbled toward his shoulders, and my nails dug into his back.

This was so wrong.

Stop.

Don't stop.

Maddox swiveled his hips before grinding against my pussy. We were both fully clothed, and my best friend was humping me like a horny teenager.

And I didn't want to stop him.

How long had I forbid myself from imagining *this*? Too long.

He was drunk; it wasn't his fault. I was fully aware, and it would be my guilt to bear.

We should have stopped.

No, don't stop.

Maddox grinded his erection against me. He was so hard; I could feel him through the layers of our clothes. My core grew hot and wet. Molten desire spread through my veins, and my stomach dipped to my toes.

His breath hitched, and I let out a moan when his hips jerked again, the zipper of his jeans pressing hard against my sensitive core through my shorts. The friction left my body wanting more, and I became needy. My pussy clenched as the need to be filled became strong.

Maddox thrust into me, again and again, the motion too similar to fucking.

My thighs trembled, and my heart seized.

He kissed his way down my throat, biting and sucking softly at my skin. His palm caressed the curve of my breasts, feeling the heavy mounds in his hands. His grunts and his groans were music to my ears, even as I tried to remind myself how wrong this was.

It's wrong. I released his shoulders and pushed a hand between us. *This is wrong.* My fingers traced my wet slit through my shorts.

Maddox rubbed against me again, and it was a delicious sensation that had my eyes fluttering closed.

I shoved a hand into my shorts and tugged my panties aside. My eyes blurred with tears as a whimper echoed from my lips. It felt so good, even though it was so wrong.

"Fuck, goddamn it," he cursed, the muscles in his neck corded, and his face tensed.

His thrusts grew jerkier and faster. He was chasing his orgasm, climbing toward something forbidden between us.

My thumb slid over my swollen clit, and my hips jerked up. I was so hot, and my fingers glided over my wetness. My knuckles brushed against my pussy lips, feeling the way my core contracted. I was so turned on; I'd never been this wet before. I gathered my wetness with two fingers and rubbed my pulsing clit. Pleasure spiked through me and my back bowed.

The feel of Maddox's lips against my throat and his hands kneading my breasts had my eyes rolling back into my head. His thumb skimmed over my hardened nipple through my top, and I shuddered. My body easily responded to his touch, and I realized I had been craving *this* for the longest time.

"Lila," he groaned out hoarsely. "Fuck, Lila. My Lila."

Maddox humped me, thrusting, and I rocked my hips against his in unison, finding a rhythm between us. I imagined he really was *fucking* me.

No clothes, no barrier between us, and our bare bodies pressed together in the most intimate way two human beings could be together.

The image of us fucking was so decadently sinful and filthy. My calves tightened, and my whole body clenched as I climbed up and up toward my release.

I rubbed myself faster before sliding my thumb over my clit and pinching it. My vision blurred, and my whole spasmed as I choked back a gasp before biting on my lip. Wetness pooled between my thighs, coating my fingers and panties with my shameful release. Wet and sticky, I continued to rub myself in leisure strokes, feeling the little twitches of my pussy after my orgasm.

Maddox thrust *hard,* and I gasped before a moan spilled past my lips. He tensed above me, and his hips stilled, his head thrown back with a low, deep grunt. Warmth spread through his jeans, and I could feel it through my shorts. He just came.

Maddox's eyes pierced me for a second and then he slumped over my body.

The moment was gone, and I was instantly filled with shame and immense guilt. My stomach twisted, bile coating every inch of my mouth.

What have I done?

There was absolutely no excuse. Maddox had been drunk, and I took advantage of the situation for my own pleasure. He probably wasn't going to remember this tomorrow morning…

But what if… he did?

My heart thudded in my chest, and I swallowed back a sob. I removed my hand from my panties, the stickiness on my fingers a harsh reminder of our actions. I stretched my arm out and kept the hand I pleasured myself with far away from us.

Maddox buried his face in my shoulder. His body went slack, and I felt him soft snores against my skin. The heaviness of him sank into me like a warm blanket, and for a brief moment, I imagined how it'd be to fall asleep in his arms every night and to wake up next to him, just like this. As much as the fantasy was sweet, it would only have a bitter ending.

My fingers slid through his hair, my nails grazing the back of his neck softly, just the way he liked it. My lips parted, wanting to whisper my secret, but I felt choked. The heart is a traitor, and, in that moment, I could feel all my defenses crumbling to the ground.

Maddox grumbled something under his breath, and it sounded like my name. His arm tightened around my hip, and my arms curled around his shoulders as a lone tear slid down my cheeks. I didn't want to let go... but I had to.

"If I love you, I give you the power to destroy me. I'm not strong enough for that. I can't be just another girl to you, Maddox. I need to be more; I deserve more, and I don't think you can give that. I can't risk *us* and what we are. We're beautiful... just like this. Friends."

I prayed Maddox woke up in the morning with no memory of what we had just done.

I'd take this secret to my grave, and I would bear this guilt on my own.

CHAPTER
THIRTY-FOUR

Maddox

A week later

My fingers drummed over my thighs as I waited for Lila to come down the stairs. I left her an hour ago to get dressed, and if we didn't leave in five minutes, we were going to be late to the gala.

I was in a tuxedo, which was appropriate for the evening gala we were attending. It was an auctioning event and dinner, my parents being the guests of honor. My dad called me last night and *demanded* me to be present. I told him to fuck off and hung up with absolutely no intention to attend the gala. I didn't give a shit if this was important to him or that it was appropriate for me to be there to show my face and support to my parents.

It was Lila who convinced me.

The gala was being held in California, and she wanted to visit the beach. Lila said it was a great opportunity for a small vacation after such a long semester, and I couldn't say *no* to her. I could never refuse her of anything.

So, we took a plane here. We'd go to the gala tonight, and tomorrow, I was going to teach her how to surf.

The sound of heels clicking against the hardwood brought my attention to the stairs. Lila came into view, and my breath caught in my throat.

Breathtaking.

She descended the stairs carefully, a silky black off-the-shoulder dress clinging to her slender curves and fluttering around her feet, which were adorned with glittering silver heels. It was plain and simple, yet elegant with a thigh high split. Her creamy thigh was visible through the gap as she walked toward me, a silver clutch in her hand.

Her hair was piled up on her head, in a bun, with a few curly strands of black hair fanning her cheeks. Her dreamcatcher necklace hung between the valley of her breasts, and she wore a smile that made my knees weak.

She did a slow spin. "So, how do I look?"

Her pouty red lips had my dick straining against my black slacks and I stifled a groan.

"Pretty," I rumbled.

Lila pursed her lips, pouting. "Just pretty?"

I took a step toward her, unable to stop myself. "Gorgeous. Beautiful. Exquisite. Stunning. Lovely. Angelic. Breathtaking. Ravishing. Elegant. Bewitching. Alluring. Heavenly. The angels would bow to you because they can't compete. So. Fucking. Exquisite."

Her lips parted, a hitch in her breathing, and she blinked at me through her long, thick lashes that should have been unnatural but everything about Lila was natural. "You said exquisite twice," she breathed.

My fingers skimmed over her bare arms. Her skin broke into

goosebumps and a small shiver racked through her small frame. "Because you're twice as exquisite," I confessed, in a raspy croak.

My body burned with a sensation I knew too well, and my pants grew tight around my groin as my dick became harder in her mere presence. I didn't even have to touch her, and I was already leaking cum at the tip.

It was lust, I told myself.

But I lusted after other women before, and whatever I felt for Lila didn't come close to *lust*.

And I hated myself for feeling this way.

Just like I hated myself on that morning, a week ago. I woke up to be an empty bed, but I still felt Lila's presence next to me. It was a dream; though, it had seemed so real, so vivid.

And my boxers had been sticky with my release. I couldn't remember the last time I had a wet dream and spilled cum in the middle of the night like a horny teenager, but Lila... *fuck*, she invaded even my dreams with her sweet voice and sinful touches.

I dreamed of fucking her... my best friend. The same friend I made countless pinky swears with.

Friends?

Friends.

I destroyed the innocence of our relationship – the sweetness of our friendship. I made it into something... dirty, and it was no longer pure and no longer untouched by my forbidden desires. It was my guilt to bear for the rest of our lives.

Little did she know...

Sweet Lila, I fucked up.

Her lips curled. "Such a sweet tongue. I'm almost jealous of all the girls you've said those things to."

My heart squeezed at her words. "Your jealousy is not needed because I've never called another woman those words."

No one had ever measured up to Lila since she came into my life. No other woman had ever been... beautiful or *exquisite*.

Her eyes widened before she quickly tried to mask her surprise. "Liar."

I cupped her elbow, steering her away from the stairs. "I don't lie."

Lila mumbled something incorrigible under her breath before she rolled her eyes. We walked out of the beach house, which was owned by me – well, my parents. We had a caretaker who cleaned up and kept the house safe while we weren't here. My parents and I used to spend a lot of time here when I was younger, a child.

Before everything changed and I became a stranger in my own goddamn house and to my own parents.

A limousine was waiting for us outside. Lila let out a breathy laugh. "Seriously, a limo?"

I shrugged, halfheartedly. "The host for the gala tonight arranged it. Apparently, he sent a limo to all his guests."

Her eyes crinkled to the sides as her smile broadened. "Damn. I don't what it means to be *that* rich. Pardon me for being a lowly peasant."

We climbed into the limo, and the driver peeled out of the parking space, taking off through the neighborhood I was familiar with. The drive to the gala was short, and we were only about fifteen minutes late due to traffic.

We walked into the ballroom, and all eyes fell on us. Lila's fingers tightened around my elbow, gripping me hard, as though her life depended on it. *I got you.*

I met my father's gaze with a hard one, and he jerked his chin at me in greeting. My mother smiled, though it was tight. Probably fake, too, but I didn't know any longer since I long stopped caring if it was real or fake.

The moment we descended the stairs, I was surrounded. I was Brad Coulter's son –prestigious, important and held in high honor.

The night ended before it started. My bow tie suddenly felt like it was restricting my air flow, and my skin itched. This was exactly why I didn't want to attend this gala because all they were talking about was when I'd take over my dad's company – asking about the future. He built an empire, and I was the only heir.

I was approached by businessmen left and right. They laughed, and we shared a drink, appearing as courteous as I could be.

I *loathed* it.

Lila stayed by my side until she was pulled away by the wives. I kept my gaze on her, watching her every move. She didn't know these people, and I knew this was beyond her comfort zone.

But she was here for *me*.

My date for tonight, my friend and my ally.

A slow song came up, and the couples spilled onto the dance floor. This was my chance. I nodded at the gentlemen and made my brisk escape, stalking toward Lila. Her head snapped up as if we were connected by an invisible thread, and she could *feel* me coming for her.

Her brown eyes brightened, and a small smile twisted her lips with relief.

"Maddox." My name spilled from her lips, and my chest squeezed.

"Sorry, ladies. Can I steal my date away for a dance?" I asked, offering Lila my hand. She giggled and took my hand, and I whisked her away.

"My savior," she whispered as we joined the other couples on the dance floor.

"I thought you didn't need a savior or protector."

Her eyes narrowed on me, and she pinched my bicep. I swallowed back my laugh. "Forget I said that. I take it back," she grumbled.

Beautiful Lila, sweet Lila.

My hands landed on her hips and hers curled around the back of my neck. The second her soft skin touched mine, I realized what a mistake it was.

We were *too* close, after I'd been trying to put distance between us.

Her body pressed against mine, and my fingers teased the top curve of her ass before I gripped her hips again. She swayed to the music, and we slowly started dancing.

This was a bad decision, and my dick was pissed at me.

Her cheeks were flushed, and I wanted to ask her what she was thinking about.

Was it as forbidden as my own thoughts?

Did her desires match mine?

I shook my head, trying to clear my mind.

"What's wrong?" Lila asked, her voice delicate. She tilted her head to the side, her eyes sparking with curiosity.

My eyes swept over the ballroom, and my gaze landed on my father's. He was watching us dance, an unreadable expression on his hard face.

Anger burned like acid in my veins at the fact that we were in the same room. I didn't want him anywhere near my Lila.

I bent my head, my nose brushing over the tip of her ear as I whispered, "Let's get out of here."

CHAPTER THIRTY-FIVE

Lila

His voice was gruff when he spoke, "Let's get out of here."
Maddox dragged me out of the ballroom, and I tried to keep up in my heels. I knew he was going to hate tonight. As much as he was cocky and arrogant and he loved the attention from the chicks, he loathed being surrounded by people like his father – talking business and mingling with them.

The subject of him taking over his father's empire one day as the only heir was something we never discussed. He refused to talk about it, and I knew he had no intention of taking over.

Instead of waiting for the valet, he took me around the building to the parking lot. "There's our ride," he said under the moonlight of the California sky.

I halted in my step, forcing Maddox to pause, too, as I took in what was in front of me. Maddox chuckled, and he let go of my hand, striding over to his motorbike. His bike?!

I gaped as Maddox climbed onto the beast of a bike – one that was similar to the one back home -- and offered me a helmet. He looked sinful in a tuxedo, with disheveled hair, straddling a bike. I licked my lips, hating the feeling of my heart racing at the sight of him being so devilishly handsome.

I had never seen a man so overtly masculine, so confident in his own skin and with such a dominant aura. The sensitive area between my legs pulsed with need.

"You coming, Sweet Cheeks? Or do I need to steal you away?"

I blinked, still shocked. "*How...*where did you find this bike? We came in a limo."

A crooked smile graced his perfect lips. "I was already planning an early escape." He winked.

I strode over and took the heavy helmet he offered. Maddox helped me buckle the chin strap, his fingers lingering longer at my jaw.

I swallowed and let out a nervous laugh. "Why does it feel like we're doing something very, very bad? Like we're some naughty kids... when in actuality, we have done much worse than running away from a stupid charity gala?"

"Because if my father finds out we ran, he's gonna skin me alive," he said with a slight twist of his lips.

My eyes narrowed on him. "Ha. Funny. Very funny."

I looked down at my long dress and figured this could be a problem. We weren't really clothed for a bike ride. But thank God for the thigh high split. It allowed me to bunch my dress up and tie a knot at my thighs; this way, the fabric wouldn't get trapped in the monster wheels.

"Where are we going?" I asked, curiously.

His gaze fell to my bare legs, and I could swear he swallowed, his eyes darkening in the slightest bit.

"Some place not *here*," he announced smoothly, the deep baritone of his voice vibrating through my bones, all the way down to my toes. My body temperature spiked, burning with unspoken and forbidden need.

He offered me his tuxedo jacket, and I took it, pulling my arms through the sleeves and wrapping myself in his smell – his cologne and his familiar manly scent.

"Well, let's go. Steal me away, Coulter." I pulled down the visor of my helmet, obscuring my face from his gaze, a perfect hideaway for my flushed cheeks.

I straddled the bike behind him and wrapped my arms around his middle. It wasn't the first time he took me on a bike ride. We had plenty of those during our times together.

We rode for a long time, the breeze in my hair and Maddox's warm body against my front. It was… comforting.

This… this was exactly why I didn't want to risk losing him.

This was why I kept my secret and locked away the night we spent together, the heated moment between us. Maddox didn't remember our time together, and it was better this way. Even though I was the only one left haunted by the memories of us, me fingering myself as he humped me through our clothes.

Every time I stared at him, I remembered the look on his face as he orgasmed. My body tingled at the memory of his lips on my throat and his palms kneading my breasts.

It became harder for me to keep my untamed desires in check.

Maddox eventually came to a stop and the sound of crashing waves filled my ears. "We're at the beach?"

He helped me off the bike, before straightening up to his full height. Maddox unbuckled the chin strap and pulled the helmet off. Once the weight was gone, I almost groaned in relief.

His thumb stroked my collarbone in a delicate manner before he caught himself and pulled away. "I brought you to my favorite spot. Let's go."

He grasped my hand in his and pulled me forward. My heels sank into the sand, and I stumbled forward, a surprised giggle spilling from my lips. Yeah, that wasn't going to work. I kicked off my heels, my bare feet sinking into the soft sand. It felt so nice.

We walked closer to the waves, hand in hand. I could see the reflection of the full moon in the ocean, and the sound of the waves were melodious to my ears. We came here last year, with the rest of our friend group, on our summer vacation. It was good to be here again, but this time – just the two of us.

I didn't want to admit it… but it was intimate.

Maddox and I settled on the sand, watching the waves crash against the shore. We fell into a comfortable silence, and I watched him from the corner of my eye. His face was hard and pensive, with shadows under his eyes. Maddox was okay without his parents in his life, but every time they made their presence known… I've seen Maddox retreat within himself – a place filled with anger and hate. He battled his inner wars on his own and in silence.

My heart ached because I wanted to hold him.

I wanted to soothe him, save him and to love him in ways he has never been loved before and in ways only I can love him.

If only he'd let me.

If only he was mine.

If only...

"Are you cold?" His voice echoed through my ears, and I shook away the muddling thoughts.

"No, not cold." I went back to staring at the ocean. The urge to dip into the water was strong. "I want to take a swim."

"We can, tomorrow."

"Or…" I left the sentence hanging.

Maddox read my mind, and his eyes narrowed on me. "Lila," he warned.

"Troublemaker. I learned from the best." I blinked at him in fake

337

innocence. "I dare you to go skinny dipping. Right now."

He gave me a blank stare, before releasing a sigh. "What am I going to do with you?"

"Well, I don't think this is that big of a deal. You dared me to wear a potato sack to the club last week! Do you have any idea how embarrassing that was?"

The tension in his shoulders unraveled. Maddox half-shrugged. "Can't be as embarrassing as you making me wear a fake pregnant belly. I was waddling around campus all fucking day, Lila."

I pressed my lips together to keep from laughing. Oh, that was a sight to see. I'd never seen Maddox so offended in his life, and Colton still wouldn't let him live down that fateful day.

Over the years, Maddox and I have done countless dares. Some of them wild and crazy. Some just plain… stupid and embarrassing.

Maddox taught me how to enjoy life, how to let go of fear and the need for control and to just… *live*.

I wasn't just surviving any longer or simply going through the motions of life after the death of my parents.

I was… living and breathing life.

"So, do you dare?"

Maddox stood up and slowly unbuttoned his white shirt. He tugged at his bow tie, and it fell on the sand beside me. He peeled off his shirt, and my mouth went dry.

His stomach clenched, his abs rippled, and my stomach pooled with heat. My eyes traveled up the length of his torso up to his chest. His strong pecs and his nipples…

My pussy tightened. The silver nipple piercing shone under the moonlight.

I had to remind myself to breathe. My gaze slid up to his face. Chiseled jaw. Full lips. Nose that was slightly crooked, but it was only noticeable if someone paid close attention and his eyes blazed a deep blue

– as deep as the ocean--eyes that could see inside my soul.

"I'll get in the water on one condition. You have to do it."

"Is that a dare?"

"No, I'm not wasting a dare on that."

"You think I'll get in just because you asked?"

He smirked. "Yes."

"So cocky." I rolled my eyes and crossed my arms over my chest.

Maddox toed off his black, shiny dress shoes and kicked off his slacks. He left his boxers on and strode toward the waves. "Don't be a chicken, Garcia," he called out over his shoulder.

Oh no, he *didn't*.

I held back a growl and came to my feet, glaring at his muscled back. I should have thought more about it... skinny dipping with Maddox was a bad idea, but I didn't think.

I made silly decisions around Maddox.

I shrugged off my dress and my bra. Covering up my breasts with one arm, I left my lace panties on and jogged toward the water.

Maddox was already waist deep, wading through the cool water, before I jumped on his back. "Boo," I said in his ear.

It was too late to realize my mistake.

My bare tits pressed against his back. Skin to skin. My eyes widened, and my breath stuttered.

Maddox tensed, inhaling sharply, as my puckered nipples rubbed against his shoulder blades. I squeezed my eyes shut, silently berating myself.

"Troublemaker," he grumbled without any heat. Maddox reached behind him and grabbed my thighs, keeping a hold of me. I loved swimming, but it was night, and I couldn't see a thing. The water was too dark, and the ocean wasn't a place to trust. There could be *anything* in this water.

I clung to Maddox, already regretting my dare.

Maddox chuckled, his back vibrating with the sound. My nipples hardened into two aching tips, and we both ignored it. I told myself my nipples were only reacting to the cold ocean, not because of Maddox.

"Don't be a chicken." He was keeping this from being awkward.

"Asshole," I hissed, swatting his bicep.

Slowly, I untangled myself from his back and waded through the water, away from him. I kept afloat on my back, looking at the dark sky.

How did this happen...?

How did Maddox and I go from being enemies to friends... to best friends... to *this*?

Something slimy touched my feet, and I jumped, snapping out of my thoughts with a terrified squeal. Maddox swam over to me, and he pulled me into his arms. "What's wrong?" he asked urgently, his hands sliding down my bare body, searching for any injuries.

Whatever it was slid over my foot again, and I shuddered. "Something just touched me!"

I wrapped my legs around his waist, peering into the water, as if I could see something, but it was too dark.

Maddox stroke my back. "It might just be a fish, Lila."

"Um, I want to get out. Now."

My thighs tightened around his waist, and it was then I realized...

Maddox's eyes darkened as if he just came to the same realization. My core was seated right above his hard length, the thin layers of our underwear the only barrier between us. Chest to chest, hips to hips, skin to skin.

My lungs squeezed, and I forgot how to breathe. My hands curled around his shoulders.

Time halted, and the world came to a stop.

The look on his face was something I'd never seen before, and I wished I knew what he was thinking. His jaw ticked, the muscles twitching. His pupils were dilated and dark, his blue eyes stormy with unreadable emotions. We looked at each other a little too long to be *just* friends.

"Lila," he rasped. His head descended toward mine, his breath feathering over my lips.

I saw it in his eyes; Maddox was going to kiss me.

No, don't.

Yes, please.

His lips parted, captivating me. He pressed me closer to him.

My heart stuttered, and my stomach twisted, butterflies raging inside. I could feel his hardness between my thighs. Maddox, of course, wasn't unaffected. He was a guy, after all. His dick jerked, pressing against my pussy through the layers. I was hot, my core molten lava, and aching.

He just had to slide my panties to the side and thrust into me.

He could...

I was open to him; my thighs were spread around his hips.

As though unable to stop himself, he rocked against me, slightly thrusting up against my pussy.

A small whimper echoed through my lips, and my eyes fluttered close.

It was then he snapped.

Maddox roughly pulled away, the water rippling around us harshly. He slipped out of my embrace, forcing my legs to fall away from his waist. "It's cold. We should get out," he said, his rich voice hoarse. It sounded like he was swallowing the words and having difficulty speaking.

My chest cracked open and a searing pain racked through my body as Maddox swam away from me without another word.

Feeling more alone than ever, I ducked my head under the water and came back up for air, hoping the coldness would ease the heat of my body and clear my mind.

It didn't work.

Slowly, I got out of the water. Maddox was sitting on the sand, still half naked, with his back to me. My throat seized with emotions I couldn't explain, and I settled on the sand with him. Back to back, facing opposite directions. I watched the waves, letting it soothe my bleeding heart.

After a while, our breathing had evened out, our bodies no longer wet from our skinny dipping. Maddox cleared his throat. I turned my head to the side, keeping our backs pressed together. His hand came into view.

He was showing me his pinky.

God, Maddox.

Unshed tears blurred my vision.

"Friends?" he asked in a low voice.

I hooked my pinky around his. "Friends."

We both lied to ourselves, but it was better that way. It had to be.

Maddox

A low groan escaped me before I could stop myself. Grabbing my pillow, I stuffed it over my face as my hand strayed toward my cock. This was so wrong; I shouldn't want her. Not like this. Never like this.

So. Fucking. Wrong.

Last night, our bodies pressed together in the water under the night sky – I almost lost control. I almost fucked her, right there.

And for a brief moment, I thought Lila was going to let me.

We were both edging toward something dangerous, and I didn't know how to stop.

Because all I could think about were her lips – the way they part when she says my name; her eyes – the way they darken when she stares up at me. Her smooth neck – the way I wanted to bite her soft flesh and leave my marks there. Her hands... the way I wondered how they'd feel around my cock. Her goddamn tits, small and perky, perfect for my hands. She was made for me.

Fuuuuck.

I palmed my cock, squeezing at the base before pumping my length in my fist.

She was in the room adjacent to mine. The walls were so thin, she could probably hear me jerking off. But I couldn't stop. I tried, goddamn it. I tried.

I was hard, aching and... I wanted her. More than I had ever wanted anything in my life.

I shuddered as I imagined thrusting two fingers into her sweet cunt. She would clench around me, moaning, and I'd pull out, teasing her until she was writhing with need, before pushing the same two fingers inside her mouth and demanding she taste herself.

Such dirty, filthy thoughts.

Ragged, guttural groans spilled from me, and I muffled them with my pillow. I pumped my cock with my fist, angry for feeling this way but filled with so much need that I couldn't force myself to stop. The muscles of my thighs tensed, my dick heavy and swollen in my palm as I got closer to my release.

So. Fucking. Wrong.

So. Fucking. Right.

Thick ropes of cum sprayed my stomach and coated my palm as I came, spurt after thick spurt, and I kept fisting my cock, pumping it, until my body twitched and a ragged, breathless groan came from my lips.

"Lila."

CHAPTER
THIRTY-SIX

Lila

The unmistakable pressure between us was becoming harder to ignore. A month after our time in California, which was tense and awkward, the situation between Maddox and I was still same. Maddox had become rigid, and the distance grew between us.

I wished there was a way to fix this, but it was clear there was no going back, no matter how much either of us wanted to.

I was sitting on my couch, staring at the TV, although I wasn't really watching the screen, when Maddox walked inside my apartment. He wore a blank expression and had a piece of paper in his hand. The last time we saw each other was two days ago, after our last exams. This semester was officially over.

"We're going to Paris," he announced. "Me and you."

Me and you. I almost laughed, a cold-humorless laugh. It used to be cute when we'd say that, but now, it *hurt.*

Me and you. But for how long, Maddox? We were already at the breaking apart.

"Paris, why?" I croaked, before clearing my throat. I didn't want him to read the emotions on my face.

"It's my birthday in four days. Daddy dearest gave me tickets to Paris as a present. Well, he mailed them to me."

This meant his parents, obviously, weren't planning to spend Maddox's birthday with him. In all the years we'd known each other, I'd never seen his parents celebrate his birthday. No hugs, no love, no affection. It made me angry, so furious with the way they always treated Maddox.

He deserved better.

He wasn't as complicated as everyone thought. Maddox Coulter was just a misunderstood boy who needed and deserved someone to fight for him – to show him that he was worth it.

And I was going to be that person. Even if I couldn't do it as his lover, I was going to do it as his best friend, at least.

Because, truly, he was worth all the love – all the love he never had but deserved.

"I've never been to Paris," I finally confessed.

Maddox finally cracked a sincere smile. "I know, and you're going to love it."

City of love. And two best friends who didn't have the courage to acknowledge whatever this was between them.

What were the odds? Fate really did like to play cruel jokes on us.

I dragged my nails over my thighs. "When do we leave?"

"Tomorrow night. That's enough time for you to pack, right?" Maddox asked, walking further into my apartment, but still keeping a distance between us.

I nodded and then patted the couch. "Join me. I'm watching *Friends*. It's the pivot scene."

Maddox looked indecisive, a troubled tension hanging between us.

Please say yes.

Please don't leave me. Again.

He swallowed, his Adam's apple bobbing with the movement, and his eyes flickered to me and then the TV. Relief coursed through my veins when he took a step toward me and settled on the couch beside me, not saying a word.

A moment passed between us, I smiled – almost a timid smile, and we turned to face the TV at the same time.

A few minutes later, the brutal tension dissolved, and our shoulders shook with silent laughter at the scene we were watching. Our knees were touching, the briefest touch, but my skin tingled. My pulse raced like a freight train, and my heart palpitated; he was laughing, and I was laughing, and the world had never felt so right in that mere second.

I wanted to cherish this moment, so afterward, years later, when Maddox and I had been torn apart by our unspoken feelings, I'd remember what it felt like to be this close to him.

Later that night, sleep didn't come easy. I tossed and turned, thinking about Maddox and our upcoming trip to Paris. Was this going to be a mistake? Maybe. Probably.

But I couldn't say no, and I wanted to spend this time with him.

Just the two of us.

The ache between my legs was back again, my body tensing with frustration.

Ever since that night – the night Maddox was drunk, my body had been on fire, burning, skin tight with need and aching.

And no matter how much I masturbated, I still felt so *empty* after, never fully satisfied.

My clit swelled and throbbed. Reaching over, I grabbed my second pillow and pressed it between my legs. My eyes squeezed shut as I rocked my hips, back and forth, against the pillow, trying to alleviate the pulsing ache in my pussy. I underestimated how much I wanted Maddox.

My need intensified, and I throbbed harder. Pushing a hand between my thighs, I shoved my panties aside, and my fingers grazed my folds, pushing my wet lips apart and then moving higher to my swollen clit. I rubbed and pressed against the bundle of nerves there, while grinding my pussy faster against the pillow, rubbing my exposed, sensitive flesh against the soft fabric. The friction almost had me losing my mind, but it still wasn't…enough.

My hand matched the rhythm of my hips. My index finger probed my entrance, and when my pussy clenched, seeking to be filled, I slowly thrust my finger inside. Oh God, oh God!

My breath hitched, and I grew hotter, my sticky wetness dripping between my legs – a reminder of how wrong this was, but I still moaned out Maddox's name.

I pinched my clit, rocking my hips faster. I imagined it was Maddox between my legs. I imagined it was his cock pushing against my entrance, not my small fingers.

I imagined him pulsing inside me, filling me… thrusting inside… grunting out my name.

My body tightened, and my hips jerked against the pillow as I rode out my mini orgasm; my panties were drenched and my fingers wet and coated with my release. A low whine spilled from my lips, "Maddox."

I rubbed my finger over my wet folds, imagining it was his lips on my pussy, before I pulled my hand out of my panties. My legs were slack against the pillow; my inner thighs still sticky with my release.

I didn't have the energy to get up and change. My eyes fluttered close, and I fell into a restless sleep.

Maddox invaded my dreams. I felt his kisses… saw his handsome face… felt his touch sliding down my body.

Hot tears slid down my cheeks, because it was only a dream, only my fantasy.

CHAPTER
THIRTY-SEVEN

Maddox

I was angry. At myself, at Lila, at everyone… everything and at fate. I'd lost my way with Lila, and I didn't know how to pull her out from under my skin.

We landed in Paris, and my stomach twisted with fury and unwarranted possessiveness as men stared at Lila. Their gaze followed her, lingering over her ass. I told myself I wasn't jealous – just protective of her. These assholes wouldn't know how to handle a woman like Lila.

By the time we reached our hotel, frustration gnawed at my gut, and I was just so damn angry, I couldn't think straight.

Nothing made sense – not my reaction to Lila or the stormy emotions I couldn't understand why I was feeling.

Friends didn't think about fucking each other.

But that was exactly what I wanted to do. I wanted to hear her moan my name, I wanted her to whimper as my dick stretched her tight cunt, I wanted… *needed*… Lila.

This wasn't just lust. I craved her lips and the sound of her voice. She made me feel unhinged, my emotions too wild to control. I loathed how easily Lila could break through my barrier – she could rip me apart and put me back together, again and again – I was her more than willing victim.

I wanted to possess her. And I *couldn't.*

Lila was sunshine mixed with a little hurricane, and I was getting swept away. I was going to put a stop to it.

It had to come to an end and soon, before we both did something we'd regret for the rest of our lives. I was willing to peel Lila off from under my skin, even if it left me bleeding and mortally wounded.

My eyes flickered to Lila, watching her smile at the receptionist. Sunkissed skin, soft lips, pinkened cheeks and brown eyes that captured me since that day at the coffee shop, almost four years ago.

"Bonjour," a voice broke through my thoughts. "How are you doing today?"

A man appeared at Lila's side, suited and standing tall. His gaze landed on her tits first before they lifted to her face.

Lila nodded in greeting, and they shook hands. He introduced himself as the owner of the hotel, the corners of his eyes crinkling as he smiled at Lila. It was written all over his face.

He wanted her.

My blood boiled, and I swallowed down a growl.

His hand brushed against Lila's arm. "Please, if you need any help today, you can come and find me. A lady like you shouldn't have to go through any trouble alone."

Lila let out a small laugh. "Oh, I'm not alone." She stepped closer to me and place a hand on my arm, smiling. "Maddox is with me."

Mr. Owner, I didn't catch his name nor did I care, eyed me up and down. "A friend, I see?" he asked, with a thick English accent.

He was checking to see if I was his rival. If he only knew…

Lila, oblivious to what was happening, replied, "Yes, a friend. We're so excited to be visiting Paris together."

The moment Lila admitted we were *friends*, his eyes lit up with triumph.

I instantly hated him.

He was practically undressing Lila and fucking her with his eyes, and she had no idea. Or she was playing coy…

My chest tightened. Was she interested in him…? Lila was smiling, her body relaxed, and she *giggled* at something he had said.

By the time we got to our rooms, I was seeing crimson red. I'd never been so angry in my entire life.

"He said they have a fancy bar. Maybe we should go tonight after we've rested?" Lila asked, rubbing her tired eyes. "I need sleep right now."

She stifled a yawn and peeked up at me through her lashes. I nodded, mutely, and walked into my room, closing the door behind me.

My skin prickled with the need to hit something. I ripped my shirt off and quickly undressed, getting in the shower. I turned the water to cold, letting it seep through my bones. My body numbed, but my mind was still a storm of mixed emotions. It was that feeling when I didn't know what the fuck I was feeling.

I quickly soaped up my body, my hand drifting to my dick. I stroked myself once, and my eyes squeezed shut. An image of Lila drifted behind my eyelids.

Perky tits, pink nipples, cute as fuck belly button, taunt stomach, curvy hips, and an ass I wanted to sink my dick in.

My cock jerked as I put more pressure on it, fisting the length from base to tip. My hand glided over my dick easily through the cascading water. Pre-cum covered the tip, and my balls grew tight between my legs.

Sometimes, as messed up as this was, I wondered if I could just fuck her and get rid of this itch. But Lila wasn't someone I could fuck out of my system. It was years of built-up tension and sexual need between us. One simple fuck, one hot night… would never be enough.

Because the moment I had one taste of her… I'd need more…I would never be satisfied.

My stomach caved, and my thighs tightened as the pressure built, and it finally released. My knees weakened, and I pressed my forehead against the tiles, thick ropes of cum spilling over my hand instantly washed away by the water. I fisted my dick until every last drop was spent and then I cursed. So. Fucking. Weak.

This had to end, now… tonight…

CHAPTER THIRTY-EIGHT

Lila

His presence was a warm heat behind me as we walked into the bar. He was close; really, *really* close. I could *feel* him. I could *smell* him. He was so close, yet so far out of reach. A dangerous temptation dangling right in front of me.

I wanted to turn around and wrap my arms around him, bask in his warmth. We'd hugged and cuddled plenty of times before, but since the Charity Gala, everything had been different.

He had been different.

Somehow, there was a wall between us now. I couldn't break it or walk around it. It was exhausting and scary – watching the change in him, seeing him so…cold and withdrawn from me. Sometimes, it felt like he was battling something inside his head. I waited silently for him to come to me, to speak of his worries, so I could find a way to soothe him. Like always.

Except…it started to feel as if *I* was the problem. As if he was hiding

from *me*.

A week in Paris. This was supposed to be fun and exciting. An adventure for us, but it was day one and it was already going to waste.

I chewed on my bottom lip as we walked further inside the dim room. It wasn't overly crowded, but everyone here looked fancy. After all, this was one of the most famous hotels of Paris; wealthy and posh people came here often. "I didn't think the hotel would have its own bar. Fancy. I like it."

"It's nice," he replied. There was a roughness in his voice, except his tone was robotic. No emotions whatsoever.

I paused in my steps, expecting him to bump into me. He didn't. Instead, I felt his arm slide around my waist as he curled it around me. Our bodies collided together softly, and I sucked in a quiet breath. His rock-hard chest was to my back, pressing against me, and I could feel every intake of breath he took. His touch was a sweet, sweet torture.

Fuck you, for making me feel this way, for tempting me and leaving me hanging and...for making me fall in love with you...

"This way." His lips lingered near my ear as he whispered the words. He steered me toward the bar stools.

We sat side by side. From the corner of my eye, I watched him as he ordered our drinks. His voice was smooth, and it slid over my skin like silk. Soft and gentle.

Lost in my thoughts, I didn't notice the man standing next to me until his hand touched my shoulder. I swiveled to the left, my eyes catching the intruder. Yes, intruder. He was interrupting my time with *him*.

Maddox Coulter – the balm to my soul but also the stinging pain in my chest. He was a sweet heaven but also the of my existence.

"Remember me?" the man in the suit asked with a tiny grin.

Yup, I did. He was the owner of the hotel. We met him when we checked in yesterday.

"I saw you across the bar, and I knew instantly, you had to be the pretty girl I met last night." His English was perfect, but it was laced with a husky French accent. I had to admit, it was kind of sexy. Mr. Frenchman stood between our stools, separating Maddox and me. He blocked my view of Maddox and I. Did. Not. Like. That.

"Thank you for helping us yesterday," I replied sweetly, masking my irritation.

His emerald eyes glimmered, and his grin widened. Mr. Frenchman was your typical tall, dark, and handsome eye candy. And he wore an expensive suit that molded to his body quite nicely. "It was all my pleasure."

I nodded, a little lost at what else I could say. I wasn't shy or uncomfortable around men. But this one was a little too close for my liking, and since I had zero interest in him, even though he could definitely be my type, given the fact that *someone else* had all my attention, I didn't want to continue this conversation.

"Lucien Mikael." He presented me with his hand. I remembered he told us his name last night, but I didn't tell him mine.

I took his palm in mine, shaking it. "You can call me, Lila. It's nice to make your acquaintance."

Instead of shaking my hand, he turned it over and brought my hand to his lips. He kissed the back of it, his lips lingering there for a second too long. His eyes met mine over our entwined hands. "My pleasure, *ma belle.*"

Oh dear. Yup. Mr. Frenchman was flirting.

I glanced around Lucien and saw that Maddox was lounging back in his stool, his long legs stretched out in front of him, a drink in his hand, and he was staring directly at me. His face was expressionless.

Lucien turned to the bartender and said something to him in French. I didn't understand the words, but I quickly figured out what he said when he turned back to me.

"It's on me. A treat for a lovely lady."

I was already shaking my head. "Oh. You didn't have to–"

His hand tightened around mine. "Please, allow me."

"Thank you."

Lucien opened his mouth to say something else, but he was interrupted by the ringing of his phone. "Excuse me, *chérie*."

As he moved away, I caught sight of Maddox again. Our eyes met, and I stopped breathing. His gaze was dark, and his jaw was clenched so tightly that I wondered if it'd crack under the pressure. I could see the ticks in his sharp jaw as he gritted his teeth. His face – I didn't know how to describe it. Anger made his eyes appear darker, almost deadly. A shadow loomed over his face, his expression almost threatening. There was a predatory feel in his glare as he watched me closely.

He constantly pushed me away, putting more and more distance between us. Why was he so angry now? I couldn't tell. I. Couldn't. Think. Especially when he stared at me like *this*.

Maddox was maddening. He pulled and pushed; he loved and hated. I always thought I understood him better than anyone else. But right now, he confused the hell out of me.

"Lila." My eyes snapped away from Maddox, and I looked at Lucien. He was apparently done with his phone call, and his attention was back on me. Before I could pull away, he gripped my hand in his once more. "If you need anything while you are in Paris, please call me. I could take you sightseeing. I know many beautiful places."

He let go of my hand, and I turned my palm over to see his business card. Smooth trick, Mr. Frenchman. "Umm, thank you."

Lucien leaned down and quickly placed a chaste kiss on both my cheeks before pulling away. "Au revoir, *chérie*."

I didn't watch him leave. All my attention was on the man sitting beside me. He took a large gulp of his drink.

"He likes you," he said, once Lucien was out of hearing range.

"Jealous?" I shot back immediately.

A smirk crawled onto his face, and he chuckled, his wide chest rumbling with it. "He wants you, Lila."

My stomach clenched, goosebumps breaking out over my skin. My breath left me in a whoosh. His words were spoken dangerously low, although the harshness in his voice could not be mistaken.

"How would you know?" I retorted, angry and confused. He played with my feelings, turning my emotions into a little game of his. Maddox had me in knots, twisting me around like a little plaything.

He grunted, shaking his head, and then he let out a laugh. As if he was sharing an inside joke with himself. "I'm a man, like him. I know what he was thinking about when he looked at you like that."

"Maybe he wasn't thinking about sex. Maybe he's a gentleman. Unlike you." I was playing with fire, I knew that. I was testing him, testing *us*.

"*I dare you*," he whispered so softly, I almost missed it. Maddox looked down at his glass, his fingers clenched around it. Even in the dim lights, I could see the way his knuckles were starting to turn white.

He was giving me a dare *now*?

He didn't finish his sentence, and I wondered if he was contemplating his dare. Maddox's jaw flexed from obvious frustration. For a brief moment, I thought maybe he wasn't angry at *me*. Maybe, he was angry at *himself*. He was fighting *himself*. Could it be that the problem wasn't me?

He drank the rest of his drip in one gulp and then slammed his glass on the counter, before swiveling around in his stool to face me. Maddox stood up and walked a step closer to me, until my knees were touching his strong thighs. He leaned forward, caging me in between the counter and his body. Our gaze locked, and he licked his lips. He had me captivated for a moment until he mercilessly broke the spell.

"I dare you to sleep with him."

I reared back in shock. *Wh-at?* No, I must have misheard him. That couldn't be…

"What?" I whispered, my throat dry and my tongue suddenly heavy in my mouth.

Maddox's eyes bore into mine, staring into my soul. When he spoke again, his deep accented voice danced over my skin dangerously. "I dare you to fuck him, Lila."

A tremble started in my core and then moved through my body like a storm. Not just a quiet storm. A tsunami of emotions hit me all at once, reckless in its assault. I submerged under the dark waves, suffocating, and then I was being split open so viciously, it sent tiny cracks of my heart and fissures of my soul in all directions. I clamped my teeth together to stop myself from saying something – anything that would make it worse.

We had done too many dares to simply count on our fingers. Countless silly dares over the years, but we had never dared each other to sleep with other people. Granted, I had asked him to kiss a girl once; they made out, but it was years ago. But our dares had never crossed that line.

Sex... that was never on the table. We never explicitly talked about it, but it was almost an unspoken rule.

Why would he even ask me to do such a thing?!

"What's with that look, Lila?" he taunted.

My eyes closed. I refused to look at him, to look into his beautiful eyes and see nothing but pitch-black darkness. He wasn't looking at me like he used to. The light in his eyes was gone.

It scared me.

It hurt me.

It was destroying the rest of what was left of me.

"Look. At. Me."

I didn't want to. I didn't want him to see the hurt in my eyes.

"Open your eyes, Lila," he said in his rich baritone voice.

I did as I was commanded. He crowded into my personal space, forcing me to inhale his scent and feel the warmth of his body. "Are you serious? Or are you already drunk?" I asked quietly. It was hard to breathe with him this close.

"I never take back a dare."

And I never lose. He knew that. We were both very competitive, and to this day, neither of us had backed down from a dare.

Maddox's hand came up, and he cupped my jaw. His fingers kissed my skin softly. He smiled, but it didn't match the look in his eyes. "What's wrong? You don't want to do it?"

"I don't play to lose." *Asshole.*

Maddox leaned closer, his face barely an inch away from mine. Our noses were almost touching. My heart fluttered when he tipped my head back. *Take back your dare. Take back your dare, Maddox. Don't make me do this.*

He curled his index finger around the lock of hair that had fallen out from my bun. His minty breath, mixed with the smell of alcohol, feathered over my lips. I wanted to beg him with my eyes. Maddox tugged on my hair slightly before tucking it behind my ear. He moved, and my eyes fluttered close once again...*waiting*... a desperate breath locked in my throat as my chest caved and my stomach clenched.

He pressed his cheek against mine, and his lips lingered over my ear. "Don't disappoint me, *chérie.*"

My body shuddered, and I breathed out a shaky breath. He tore my heart open and left me bleeding. He pulled away and stared down at me.

Maddox was mocking me. Taunting me.

He never stopped being a jerk. He just hid it behind a sexy smile and a nonchalant expression.

I thought he had left his asshole ways behind. But no, I was wrong. So fucking wrong about him. About *us.*

Friends. We were friends.

I thought maybe... he wanted *more.* More of me. More of us, of what we were or could be. I was so goddamn wrong.

Maddox Coulter was still an asshole behind a pretty mask.

And I was the stupid girl who fell in love with her best friend.

CHAPTER
THIRTY-NINE

Lila

I waited, my heart thudding in my chest. His warmth behind me had my stomach twisting in anxiety. His shirt brushed against my bare shoulders. Maddox crowded behind me, and my gaze moved to Lucien.

He looked miffed as Maddox came between us. Lucien and I had spent the whole day together. He took me sightseeing while Maddox stalked us from a distance. Lucien didn't know, but I saw him, following us everywhere we went.

Lucien planned to take me out for dinner later at the Eiffel tower. He said it was romantic and beautiful up there. I knew from the look in his eyes that he was expecting something tonight.

A one-night stand?

And Maddox dared me... so it was happening. Tonight.

I tried to pull away from my best friend, but then the fireworks went off in the dark Paris sky, and it stole my attention. People cheered on the rooftop of the hotel where we were standing.

Someone had just gotten married; they were celebrating. The City of Love, indeed.

Because of the noise of the fireworks as well as the music and laughter that surrounded us, Maddox thought his secret was safe; he thought it was loud enough that I couldn't hear the words he whispered in my ear. But I *did.*

"If there's a God, He doesn't want me to be happy. Maybe it's my fault because I pushed you into the arms of another man. But He won't let me have you even though I begged him to let me love you freely. I can't remember the last time I asked Him for something. I guess... I'm not meant to have what I want. My parents. A family. You. You. You," Maddox whispered in my ear, his voice a low rasp.

Another set of fireworks went off, loud and booming into the sky.

His lips caressed my neck, warm and soft against my skin. "All of *you.*"

He sounded so broken, so tortured.

If only...

Maddox and I...

We were more than friends but less than lovers. That was our relationship; there was no real definition. We were somewhere in the middle, tangling over the edge of something that could forever break us.

I turned around and his face held an expression of a wounded beast: a bleeding warrior, a broken boy.

"Lila," he started, his voice a gruff baritone, but Lucien came forward. He wrapped an arm around my waist, pulling me into him.

Maddox's eyes clouded, and he stepped back, without finishing the sentence and whatever else he was about to say. Lucien's lips caressed my temple, and Maddox stalked away, disappearing into the crowd.

Maybe that was all we were or could ever be: an incomplete sentence and a story without an ending.

But his secret confession changed everything.

Maddox *wanted* me.

God, how stupid could we be?

"So, we shall meet in an hour?" Lucian said, breaking through my thoughts. "Is that enough time for you to dress?"

I nodded, mutely, and sent him a tentative smile before striding away.

I walked inside my room, grabbed a few things, and then stalked over to the adjacent room. His door wasn't locked, and I walked inside to find Maddox sitting in a sofa chair, staring out the window – into the dark night.

He was still in his black slacks, his tie hanging loosely around his neck, his rumpled white shirt unbuttoned and his sleeves rolled up to his elbows. His legs were stretched out in front of him. He had a cigarette between his lips and a drink in his hand.

Maddox looked… rugged. Angry. Intense.

He owned the room, his mere presence sending out a dominating mood. His gaze fell on me, and Maddox tensed. His whole body tightened at the sight of me. His face hardened, his expression dark and brooding.

I wished the situation was different, but there was no other way. I couldn't unlove Maddox, and I didn't want to. We weren't something, but we weren't nothing either.

I sucked in a breath and hung on to my courage, while sashaying inside. I dropped the two dresses on the bed, and my lips curled.

My legs trembled, but I locked my knees together. "I need your help."

He simply grunted in response, his face flashing with uncontrolled frustration. I wondered if the thought of another man touching or making love to me was killing him and the fact that it was *him* who sent me into the arms of another man.

My stomach cramped, and I inhaled. Exhaled.

The room was growing hotter, and a sheen of sweat slid down between my breasts. I slowly pulled the robe off my shoulders and let it pool at my feet, standing in front of Maddox in my lace panties and bra.

His eyes widened before they narrowed on my bare skin.

I'd been half-naked in front of Maddox plenty of time before. This time, it was... different.

I grabbed the first dress and stepped into it, shaking my hips a bit, so I could pull the tight fabric over the curve of my ass.

Once the dress was in place, I turned to face the mirror, giving Maddox my back.

A single beat passed.

One breath.

Thud.

I caught his eyes through the reflection. "Is this sexy enough to tempt him into fucking me before we can even get to his bed?" I crooned.

I was playing with fire.

And I was about to get burned.

His gaze traveled down the length of my body. It was a red fitted, sleeveless dress, and the bodice cupped my breasts like a second skin with my tits practically spilling out. The dress was indecently short, and it was the best way to say – *fuck me.*

Maddox's fingers clenched the glass in his hand so hard, I thought he'd break it.

I smirked. *Am I breaking through your walls, Maddox?*

His eyes grew darker, a vicious glint in his gaze. I smiled sweetly, trying to appear unfazed by his reaction, even though my heart was beating so fast it threatened to burst through my chest, and my knees were so weak, I wondered how I was still standing.

I licked my lips and blinked my eyes innocently. We were still watching each other through the mirror. "Can you zip me up?" I croaked. "I can't reach the zipper."

Another heartbeat.

A low exhale.

Thud.

Maddox stood up, tall and tensed, and the harsh look on his face had me whimpering silently. He stalked forward, eyeing me like a predator. I was the prey, the willing captive.

Maddox pressed against my back, crowding into my space and pushing me closer into the mirror until the tip of my breasts were brushing against the coldness of it.

A silent gasp spilled from my lips, and his fingers skimmed over my bare back.

He inhaled and exhaled a shuddering breath.

If I died tonight, it'd be a sweet death.

We continued to watch each other through the mirror, our reflection staring back at us.

Not blinking.

Not breathing.

Maddox then slowly zipped me up, before his hands dropped to my hips, and he held me tight. Oh God, my heart catapulted in my chest.

"If he hurts you, I'm going to kill him," he growled low in my ear. His words were thick with threat.

My teeth grazed my lips, and I bit down, waiting for him to stop me from leaving, to take back his foolish dare. His grip tightened on my hips.

Stop me. Take back your dare.

Thud, my heart hammered in my chest. Goddamn it, Maddox!

Beyond frustrated and angered by his lack of words, my control snapped, and I swiveled around. Maddox didn't see it coming, and he stumbled back as I pushed him into the wall next to the mirror. He let out a grunt, and his eyes darkened in warning.

Dizzied by our close proximity, I swallowed past the lump in my throat. I cupped his jaw and pressed my body against his.

He didn't pull away, didn't breathe, didn't say a word. A line had been crossed, and we both knew it.

My mouth was so dry, I could barely speak the words: "It's my turn, isn't it?"

Standing on my toes, I brought our heads closer, my lips lingering over his. "I dare you."

Maddox tilted his head, and his fingers dug into my hips. "I dare you to kiss me," I breathed.

My heart stuttered as I said the words. Point of no return, this was it.

His eyes widened; his breath hitched.

One heartbeat. Thud.

Two heartbeats. Thud. Thud.

Then, Maddox *pounced.*

I cried out as his lips captured mine. Brutal. Harsh. Unforgiving.

Maddox Coulter devoured my lips like it was his last meal, and I fell into his arms, powerless.

I gasped into the kiss, which opened my mouth for him. His tongue slid inside, tasting me. He licked and kissed and bit on my lips. Savage and cruel.

Anger rolled off him in waves as we became cocooned with our lust and need for each other. He took his frustration out against my lips, and I returned his punishing kiss with a violent one of my own.

He hadn't been the only one struggling with this need… and hunger for each other.

I suffered, too.

My pulse throbbed, and my stomach fluttered. My whole body tingled as he spun us around, slamming my back into the wall. Maddox fisted my hair, his knuckles digging into my scalp. He growled a guttural groan and kissed me harder.

This was everything I ever wanted. Dizzy. Hazy. Full of desire and untamed hunger, I moaned into his kiss.

Maddox shoved my dress up, not so gently, and pushed my panties aside. "Is this what you want?" he grunted.

I moaned.

Yes.

Yes.

Yes.

He growled deeper. "You want to be fucked against the wall like this?"

Yes.

God, Maddox!

I cried out when his thumb brushed against my clit roughly, sending tiny sparks through my body. He tsked darkly. "I didn't know you were such a dirty, filthy girl, *Lila*."

I was already so wet between my legs, his fingers glided easily over my folds. Maddox groaned as he felt my pussy clench against his seeking fingers.

"Fuck," he swore, pressing his lips against mine. He bit down, his teeth digging into my sensitive flesh. I clung to his shoulders, writhing in his arms.

Maddox pinched my clit, and I cried out, my body growing tight as a bowstring. He callously dipped a finger inside my pussy, and I clamped down.

"Lila," he said hoarsely.

He pumped his finger, once, twice. "Maddox, *please!*"

"Lila," Maddox whispered wretchedly. He pulled out, and I gasped when he thrust back inside with two fingers. He didn't give me time to adjust to his long, thick digits; he slid in and out in a punishing pace, dragging out desperate moans from me.

I was so close... so... so freaking close.

He pulled his fingers out.

"Maddox!" I gasped.

He shushed me, his lips capturing mine again. Maddox shifted slightly, and then I felt him – his hard length rubbing against my wet folds. He hooked my thigh around his waist, spreading me for him. My panties were still shoved to the side as his tip probed my entrance. His hips jerked forward, and Maddox groaned as he spread my pussy-lips with his cock, his tip seeking out my swollen clit.

He circled his hips, coating his length with my wetness. "How badly do you want me to fuck you?" There was a possessive glint in his dark gaze.

"If you don't fuck me now... I'm going to go crazy." My clit throbbed, and my heart was in my throat.

Every dream... every day I had been left wanting for Maddox...

This was finally happening. After years of refusing to acknowledge this tension between us, I had Maddox in my arms.

Our eyes met. Silent and breathless. Heart pounding.

Maddox shoved inside in one punishing thrust, stealing my breath from my lungs.

I cried out, and my body tightened. He stretched me; my inner walls spasmed around his cock as he seated himself inside my pussy, buried to the hilt.

His mouth brushed against my neck before it found its way to my lips again. I could feel his hardness pulsing inside me. A curse fell from his lips as he pulled out almost all the way, before plunging in again.

I looked down between our entwined bodies, watching his cock disappear inside me. Thrust, after thrust. The sound of us fucking filled the room, echoing around the walls.

His grunts, my moans.

His groans, my whimpers.

My name was a whispered prayer on his lips.

His name spilled from mine as I cried out.

He ground the hilt of his palm against my clit, and my eyes rolled back into my head as my body spasmed. I spiraled down as my orgasm hit. It was the most intense release I've ever had.

One brutal thrust later, Maddox held himself inside me, as deep as he could go. I felt his release, spurt after thick spurt, as he filled me.

My leg fell from his hip as I gasped for breath.

Maddox pressed his forehead against mine, and I saw instant regret in his eyes. Oh no, no. Please no.

"Lila," he rumbled.

"No." I pushed his chest, and he stumbled back. "Don't you dare," I warned.

His face twisted with a brutal look, but I pushed him again, until he was forced to take several steps back.

One final push, and he stumbled onto the bed, his back flat on the mattress. The look of surprise on his face made me smirk. I couldn't let him overthink this, not right now. Not tonight. Maybe tomorrow. But tonight was ours.

The only way to keep Maddox from pulling away was to… use my body against him.

I quickly got rid of my panties before leaning over his wide frame. "My turn," I croaked.

Maddox tensed as I pushed his black slacks to his knees. His hard cock jutted proudly toward his stomach. Long and thick, glistening with his cum and my wetness. My heart drummed wildly as I brought my head closer to his length.

My lips closed around him without warning, and his hips jerked up as he shouted, "Lila!"

I took as much of him as I could down my throat, and I hummed, loving the feel and the musky taste of him in my mouth. "Fuuucck, Lila."

He fisted my hair, and I peered up at him. His head was thrown back in pleasure, and need pulsed between my legs. He thrusted into my mouth, silently demanding for more. His breathing was shallow as I sucked him and it was the biggest turn on to see him this affected by my touch. I licked the tip, following the thick veins coursing the length of him, before I deep-throated him again.

Maddox hissed and groaned. His thighs clenched, his stomach tensing as I repeated the process. Sucking and licking.

"Lila… stop… Ah shit!"

Maddox was close, and I pulled away. I straddled his hips, both of us still fully clothed. His hardness rested against my wet slit.

His blue eyes locked on mine. "Don't fall for me," he rasped darkly.

Too late, baby.

My lips curled with a smirk, hiding my true feelings. "I just sucked your dick. Who said anything about falling in love? I just want you to fuck me. Do you dare?"

Maddox glowered dangerously, and I moved my hips, slowly gliding down his length as I took him inside my body once again. His hands came to my waist, and he gripped me tightly.

His hips bucked against mine, impatiently. There was a warning in his gaze, so I started moving, bouncing up and down his cock.

He felt so good, inside me… against me.

I never wanted it to end.

Maddox sat up, and his hand wrapped around my neck. My eyes widened, and his fingers curled around my throat. His grip tightened, not bruising, but the pressure was there, and I gasped. Even though *I* was fucking *him*, he still stayed in control.

I moved up and down his length, finding my stride.

Until Maddox grew impatient.

He growled and flipped us over. Hands fumbling, teeth grazing each other, lips fighting for dominance, we tore at each other's clothes until we were skin to skin, bared and vulnerable to each other's desperate touch and hungry eyes.

Maddox flipped me over on my knees, and he spread my thighs apart. Without warning, he plunged inside – one smooth, merciless thrust inside my body as he forced his cock through my tight channel.

His lips grazed the back of my neck, one sweet gentle kiss, even though he fucked me raw and deep, ruthlessly and filled with so much passion. My eyes blurred with unshed tears.

Maddox Coulter was fucking me.

My best friend was making love to me.

My heart cracked and withered.

I was powerless as he continued to ram himself into me, animalistic grunts spilling from his throat.

"Maddox!" I cried out his name, over and over again.

I didn't know where he ended and I began.

"Lila," he groaned in my ear, his breathing ragged. *"My Lila."*

Tears spilled down my cheeks, and my eyes closed.

Please don't let this night end.

Breathless, heart pounding, pulse throbbing, we found our release, moaning each other's name. We were utterly intoxicated by each other. I collapsed into the mattress, and Maddox slumped over me like a blanket. I teetered over the edge of consciousness, my body achy and sore, and my lips curled into a sleepy yet satisfied smile.

"Maddox," I breathed his name.

His arm tightened around mine. "Lila."

My eyes closed, and I slipped away… far, far away.

CHAPTER FOURTY

Lila

I woke up, my body deliciously sore. It was a good ache, and my lips twitched.

And then I remembered, the night before flashing in front of my eyes like black and white polaroid photos. Snap, snap, snap. Click, click, click.

My head turned, and my eyes landed on a sleeping Maddox next to me, both of us completely naked. We fucked multiple times during the night, unable to quench our desire for one another. We passed out, woke up, and then fumbled for each other in the dark, over and over again.

I sat up, my heart hammering in my chest.

Last night had been filthy… beautiful… and everything I ever wanted and didn't know I *needed*.

But we crossed a line, and there was no going back. My stomach churned with nausea, and I suddenly felt sick.

Last night, even though I had been tipsy and Maddox had been drinking, both of us were fully aware of what we were doing. Now that it was the morning after and my mind was clear from the frustration and *need* that had been coursing through my body, I didn't know what to do with myself.

What happens now?

What if Maddox...?

What if he didn't want this to last, what if this was a one-time thing for him?

I didn't even know what I wanted as my mind filled with confusion. My heart was heavy with mixed emotions. My body ached from last night, but my heart *hurt*.

Tears burned the back of my eyes, and I cupped my face, feeling stupid. For a moment last night, Maddox was mine, and I was his.

But that was it.

Just one night.

Maddox wasn't the type to commit, and I needed more from him than just a one-night stand. There was no point in risking our hearts when the thin thread between us had already snapped.

We couldn't undo what was done.

I had to walk away; I had to leave, though I would cherish last night for the rest of my life.

I eased off the bed and quickly wrapped my robe around me, before walking toward the door. I turned the handle but never got a chance to walk out. The door was suddenly slammed shut, and I was torn away from it. The world spun, and my back slammed against the wall.

Maddox loomed over me, his eyes dark, his dirty blond hair disheveled, and he was still... naked. I peered up at him through my lashes, my heart racing. His lips curled, and he looked enraged.

At me?

Because I was leaving?

Because of last night?

"Where do you think you're going?" he asked, his voice dripping with something akin to… possessiveness? His jaw tightened, and my stomach flipped. "Back to Lucien, so you can fuck him, too? Was last night not enough?" Maddox snarled.

I slammed my hands into his chest, pushing him back. But he was much stronger than me, and he crowded into my space with a low growl. Maddox kicked my legs apart and pushed his knee between my thighs, holding me captive.

His palm slid up my throat, and I felt the strength in his touch. I swallowed, my throat bobbing in his palm, and his hold tightened on my neck. The slightest pressure and my clit pulsed. His hand moved up, cupping my jaw.

His eyes were two dark pools, unhinged. "Is your sweet cunt that greedy, *Lila*?"

Holy Shit. Again. What. The. Fuck?

"Let go of me! What is wrong with you?!" I spat, raising my hand to slap him. He clasped my wrist and jerked my hand down, pressing my palm over his chest.

My breath caught in my throat. His heart was pounding intensely. Thud, thud, thud.

There was a moment, between our heated glance and our volatile kiss, where time stopped and then…

His lips slammed over mine, and he took my breath away. He didn't just kiss me. Maddox possessed me, shoving his tongue in my mouth and licking every inch of me.

Punishing. Hard. Unforgiving.

My nails dug into the skin over his heart. He hissed against my lips, and to my utter surprise, his kiss gentled. Maddox pulled away, only slightly. His breath lingered over my lips, before Maddox pressed his mouth against mine again.

Sweet. Tender. Soft.

"I dare you to kiss me." We were already kissing, but I knew what he meant. He wanted me to kiss him like he kissed me; he wanted me to kiss him like we kissed last night… and he wanted me to repeat the words I threw at him.

"I dare you to stay." His lips touched mine again. *Kiss.*

My heart stuttered.

"I dare you to give us a chance." *Kiss.*

I forgot how to breathe.

"I dare you, Lila."

Then his lips found mine again, and he sealed his dare with a long searing kiss, kissing all the pain and doubt away.

EPILOGUE

Lila

Four months later

Maddox sat on the bed, his head in his hands, a choked sound coming from him.

"You're the best unplanned thing that has ever happened to me, Maddox. And I can't lose you. But you're doing everything to push... me away from you," I whispered, my voice breaking at the end. "You've been telling lies. Since when have you started lying to me, Maddox?"

After all we had been through... he tainted everything that we were with his lies.

His head snapped up, and his eyes flared with torment. He was decadently handsome, a little bit broken and a mistake from the beginning.

"I'm sorry," he choked out.

"Is that all you have to say?"

There were tears in his eyes. "I'm sorry."

If it hurts you so much, what kind of love is this?

I knew Maddox would break my heart, but a part of me hoped he wouldn't.

My heart wept, and a lone tear slid down my cheek. "They said you were trouble. I didn't listen. I took a chance on you. And now I regret it."

"Don't leave me." His hoarse voice cracked. "*Please.*"

I took a step back. Maddox looked wounded, and my soul bled to see *him* hurt.

"Lila," he breathed my name. "Please."

I slowly shook my head. "Maddox." It pained me to say his name. "You broke your promises."

My feet took me another step back.

"No," he pleaded. "Lila, *no.*"

I turned and walked away, leaving my broken heart at his feet.

I DARE YOU

YOU

TRUTH AND DARE DUET BOOK 2

PROLOGUE

Maddox

I knew I'd eventually mess up. I knew I'd end up destroying the one good thing in my entire life. *Lila.*

Because that was the only thing I was capable of.

Destroying lives.

Ruining her.

Wrecking us.

I tried to protect her, since the day I made that stupid goddamn pinky swear for the first time. Ruthless in my endeavor to make sure she was always happy, always taken care of, by eliminating anything that would cause her pain...but I forgot to protect her from *myself.*

My lungs seized in my chest, and my throat closed. A choked sound came from me as I held my head in my hands, feeling the burn in the back of my eyes.

"You're the best unplanned thing that has ever happened to me, Maddox. And I can't lose you. But you're doing everything to push...

me away from you," she whispered, her sweet voice breaking at the end. "You've been telling lies and keeping secrets from me. Since when have you started lying to me, Maddox?"

My head snapped up at her words. I didn't have an answer. I fucking wished I did.

Lies, no matter how big or small, was the quickest way to ruin something beautiful – *us*.

Lies and secrets…

Everything I'd ever done, every decision I made was to protect Lila.

But no band-aids would ever be enough to stop the open, festering wounds I've left behind.

"I'm sorry," I choked.

The torment on her face decimated me. "Is that all you have to say?"

My vision blurred – *goddamn it*– I had to remind myself not to lose my shit. *"I'm sorry."*

A lone tear slid down her cheek. "They said you were trouble. I didn't listen. I took a chance on you. And now I regret it."

"Don't leave me." My hoarse voice cracked.

Lila took a step back. My wounded heart lurched, and bile crawled up the back of my throat, bitter and acidic.

"Lila," I breathed her name. *"Please."*

She slowly shook her head, another silent tear leaving a wet trail on her cheek. "Maddox." She looked pained, and her lips wobbled. "You broke your promises."

And now she was breaking *hers*.

Her feet took her another step back.

"No," I pleaded. "Lila, *no*."

My voice caught in my throat as she turned and walked away, taking my bleeding heart in the palm of her hand and leaving me… empty.

I sunk to my knees, unable to stop myself, choking on the heavy taste of bitterness on my tongue. This couldn't be the end… it *couldn't*.

The door closed, even as I called out her name. Pathetically. Because for her... I was a fucking *weak* man.

Love made me weak.

Love destroyed lives.

Love ruined us.

She left.

My Lila left, as the pain piercing through my chest, became almost unbearable.

All my truths, all my lies collided together – my future with Lila now cracked open, bleeding and sending the broken fissures all over, as I knelt in the wreckage of it all.

Once again...alone.

Once again... lost.

She lied too.

She broke her promises, too.

You won't lose me, ever.

Pinky promise?

Pinky promise.

CHAPTER ONE

Maddox

Four months earlier

I couldn't remember the exact moment I realized what I felt for Lila was more than friendship.

Maybe it was the first time when Lila wrapped her little pinky around mine outside of her grandparents' grocery store.

Or maybe it was the time I woke up from a nightmare and found her sleeping beside me, the night she took care of me, pulling me out of the freezing tub, and didn't leave my drunk ass behind – the same night I realized what it felt like *not* to be alone.

It could have been any time from the first moment I laid eyes on her, any moment we've had in between, until our last moment together – when I saw her with Lucien and I knew I was about to lose her forever.

I never could quite understand my own feelings. Lila wasn't a monochrome in my black and white world, she was a kaleidoscope of colors. She had made my life less dull.

I didn't know if I could call it love then.

Or if it was love now...

What is love?

When I was seventeen years old, Lila sashayed into my life with all the fierceness of a dragon, sassy and stubborn. Like an R-Rated Snow White, with an ass that should have been illegal and a mouth that tempted me to shove my dick down her throat.

At twenty years old, I realized that when we first met, Lila and I were two teenagers who were too young to understand what love was until we'd fallen too deeply into it.

"Just friends" was an easy way out, rather than accepting our growing feelings for each other.

It was around three in the morning when Lila fell asleep in my arms, breathless, sore and exhausted. She curled into me, pressing her soft, naked body against mine.

I watched her sleep, her pouty lips, her soft sighs and quiet snores.

Everyone has an addiction, mine just happened to be Lila Garcia.

My best friend

The same best friend I fucked last night.

There was no going back now; the line had been crossed, and now that I've had a taste of her, there was no way I was letting her go.

Lila was my favorite type of drug, and she was so goddamn addictive.

Her smell, her smiles, her laughter.

The way she moved, the way her face lit up whenever she talked about something that made her happy.

I breathed her.

Lila was so deep under my skin, digging deeper under my flesh, mixed with my blood, and pumping through my veins.

There was nothing calm and easy about what I felt for her.

My feelings for Lila were maddening. Like a storm that opens up the sky, violent and raging... *all-consuming.*

I couldn't let her go, not after tonight.

I'd never forget the sound of her moans, her little whimpers as she begged me to fuck her harder, the sight of her pink sex, glistening with need – for *me*. I'd never forget how she felt in my arms, naked and without restraint.

No, I couldn't let her go.

Not now. Not today, not tomorrow. Not *ever.*

Wrapping my arm around her hips, I pulled Lila closer. Her scent was all around me, on my skin, on my hair... on my lips...

I could still *taste* her on my tongue.

If I knew Lila, as well as I'd like to think I did, then...

Come tomorrow morning, she'd wake up and try to escape. We might have been a bit drunk last night, but we both knew damn well what we were doing and the consequences of it. She was going to overthink this and try to put more distance between us.

Too bad.

Too. Fucking. Bad.

She was mine now.

I woke up to Lila leaving the bed. I peeked up at her through hooded eyes, half-asleep, watching her as she silently freaked out.

I waited – hoping she'd climb back in bed.

I was no longer drunk and could think with a clearer mind. And so could she.

Face me, Lila. Face what we've done and don't. fucking. leave. me.

She stumbled toward our discarded clothes and pulled on her robe. Lila sniffled, casting me a quick glance, but she didn't notice that I was awake... watching her walk away from me.

I waited for her to change her mind, waited for her to *stay*.

Make me your first choice.

When she reached the door, I sprang off the bed, my fists clenching.

Hell no.

Enraged and disappointed at her choice, I stalked forward and slammed the door shut. My heart thumped in my chest. Lila gasped when I gripped her arm and shoved her away from the door, caging her between the wall and my naked body.

She was a goddamn coward.

Lila pushed at my chest; her eyes wide.

"Where do you think you're going?" I asked, my voice harsher than I intended. My jaw tightened as I snarled through gritted teeth. "Back to Lucien, so you can fuck him, too? Was last night not enough?"

I knew I wasn't being fair, but I hadn't expected that, although it was there... the intense need to claim her.

She slammed her tiny fists into my chest, trying to push me back but unsuccessful in her poor attempts. I crowded into her space with a low growl, kicking her legs apart, pushing my knee between her thighs, holding *my* Lila captive.

Maybe it was the adrenaline pumping through my veins, but I was so damn angry. At her. At myself.

For wanting her to stay.

I... couldn't... think... straight.

When Lila tried to push me away again, my palm slid up her neck. Her eyes widened as she stopped struggling, her lips parting with a silent gasp, and my hold tightened around her throat.

She came to *me* last night. She wanted me as much I needed her.

My gaze lowered to her pouty lips, begging to be kissed. My hand moved up, cupping her jaw. Slightly unhinged, with a fierce need to push her past her carefully set boundaries, I stepped over the line. "Is your sweet cunt that greedy, *Lila*?"

Yeah, I was an asshole.

But she was a coward for running away.

"Let go of me! What is wrong with you?!" she spat, raising her hand as if to slap me.

Finally, the reaction I was waiting for.

Before she could hit me, I clasped her wrist and jerked her hand down, pressing her palm over my chest. *Feel me.*

She hiccupped a soft breath, and I swore I could hear her heart pounding, just as hard as mine. Thud, thud, thud.

There was a moment, where time stopped, the world coming to a halt, before I slammed my lips over hers.

Feel me.

The moment our lips met, the world fell into a spinning silence.

Before we crash-landed. Gasping, kissing… fighting a silent war. She pushed me away and then pulled me harder against her.

Lila groaned into our kiss and opened her mouth for me. I wanted to *possess* her – her heart, her body… her mind. I must have completely lost it.

There was nothing sweet or gentle about this kiss.

I punished her with my teeth and my tongue, still mad that she even considered leaving me behind.

Walking… away… from… me.

My fingers gripped her nape, and she let me brutalize her mouth, whimpering but not pulling away. My teeth grazed her lower lip, feeling it swell, and the metallic taste of blood filled my mouth. I must have cut her… or *she* bit me hard enough to draw blood. I didn't know. I didn't know where I started and she begun.

Her nails dug into the skin over my heart, and I hissed against her bruised lips. I pulled away, only slightly. Lila's chest heaved with every labored breath she took. Her lips were swollen and red, ravished. Beautiful. Mine.

My breath lingered over her lips, before I pressed my mouth against hers again.

Feel me.

Everything about this kiss was... sweet and tender.

I kissed her as if it was our first kiss – how I should have kissed her the first time – when we were seventeen years old. When we had been too young and too stupid.

Lila melted in my embrace, her arms curling around my shoulders.

"I dare you to kiss me," I rasped between our kisses, throwing her own words back at her. She dared me last night, it was my turn now.

"I dare you to stay." My lips touched hers again. *Feel me.*

My heart thudded in my chest. Lila trembled in my arms, but it wasn't from the cold. She dug her fingers harder into the curve of my shoulders.

"I dare you to give us a chance," I said, looking into her dark, muddled eyes. *"I dare you, Lila."*

When I claimed her lips again, I didn't let go.

I knew Lila was going to fight me on this, but I had to find a way to convince her to stay.

I wanted her to need me, the same way I needed her.

The perks of being Lila's best friend for almost four years...

I knew how to break through her walls, tear apart the carefully put together pieces of her heart.

And break her, I would – so I could put her back together and make her fall for me.

There was no other option.

CHAPTER TWO

Lila

We were going to break each other.

I couldn't find myself to regret last night because it was every bit as beautiful and wild as I had dreamed it to be. But I was already feeling regret for what was about to come. Heartbreak – that was the only ending.

I wanted him.

Maddox wanted me.

It *should* had been easy.

But…

What about after?

This – Paris – was our safe cocoon, but what about *after*…when we'd go back to the real world?

A groan escaped me, and my head fell into my hands, feeling helpless and so… confused. Maddox was simply maddening and so goddamn stubborn.

"Breakfast doesn't suit you?"

My head snapped up, and my gaze found his. My mouth went dry as I gaped at him.

Maddox leaned against the door that led to the balcony, where I was currently sitting. He crossed his ankles, and his lips twitched with a grin. He was barefoot and freshly showered, his hair still wet and droplets of water lingered over his bare chest and thick arms, as if he hadn't bothered to dry himself.

His jeans hung loosely around his hips, halfway zipped, unbuttoned and unbuckled. My eyes lingered over his wide chest far longer than I intended, his nipple piercing catching my attention. The silver barbell was enticing as I remembered the feel of it on my tongue last night, my teeth grazing his nipple and the tip of my tongue flickering over his piercing.

I flushed at the reminder. My gaze lowered to his hard-cut abs and the perfect trail of hair, a shade lighter than the hair on his head, leading from his navel to his...

Oh shit, he wasn't wearing any underwear.

My head snapped up, but it was too late. Maddox had caught me checking him out, and he was now giving me a dirty smirk. There was a mischievous glint in his blue eyes as he walked into the sunlight and onto the balcony of our – *his* – hotel room. One of the finest hotels in Paris, our master suite had its own balcony, with a little breakfast area – an outdoor sofa and coffee table. It gave us the perfect view of the Eiffel tower. One could easily eat a French baguette, while admiring France's famous landmark.

Maddox stopped next to the coffee table and nodded toward the tray. "You haven't eaten yet. Not hungry?"

As if I could eat in this situation.

He perched himself on the coffee table, sitting directly in front of me and practically crowding into my personal space. Maddox reached for a chocolate croissant and brought it to my mouth, silently waiting, silently demanding. My lips parted, and I took a small bite.

He nodded in approval. "Good girl."

I chewed, the taste of rich chocolate on my tongue. Sweet and oh, so good. This was probably the best croissant I ever had. No surprises there; it was a Parisian specialty.

"I thought you'd build an appetite after last night's..." Maddox trailed off and took a bite of the croissant. "... vigorous *fucking*," he finished, still chewing.

I almost choked on my saliva as my face heated up. "Maddox!"

"Okay, my bad. I meant, vigorous *love-making*. Is that better?"

Once again, we were back to him taunting me. "No," I hissed.

He shrugged. "It is what it is. We fucked last night. Get over it, Lila. It's not as dramatic as you're making it out to be."

"Everything is just so easy for you, isn't it, Maddox?" I said, sitting up straight. "Sleep with a girl tonight, find a new conquest tomorrow. This is what you do, isn't it? Fuck and move on to the next available girl."

His eyes darkened, and he leaned forward, bringing his face closer to mine. His breath fanned over my lips. "Who said I was moving on...? You're still here. I haven't kicked you out yet."

My heart thudded hard against my rib cage, but I still glowered. "Do you have to be such an asshole? We," I angrily motioned between us, "are best friends. What happened last night can't happen again. It was a moment of weakness...for both of us."

Maddox seemed unfazed at my outburst, as he brought the rest of the croissant to my mouth. I pressed my lips together, refusing to give him the satisfaction of feeding me and effectively shutting me up.

His lips twitched in amusement. "Open your mouth, Lila. Or I will force feed it to you. Don't tempt me."

I gritted my teeth, the urge to punch him strong. Yes, I was stubborn, but he was acting like his usual asshole self, right now, and I didn't like it one bit.

Warm breeze hit my bare chest, and I gasped, looking down. Maddox had pulled my white robe apart, untying the belt from around my waist without me even realizing.

Sneaky bastard. Why was I even surprised?

His hand snaked upward and inside my robe, before I could even *think*. Mischief flashed in his blue eyes as he cupped my breast, lazily brushing his thumb over my hard nipple. Heat flushed through me as my stomach fluttered and my heart raced.

"Eat," he demanded, rolling my painfully tight nipple between his thumb and forefinger.

Maddox waited, his attitude aggravating, and his grin – so freaking annoying.

I opened my mouth and took a big bite, shoving the rest of the croissant in my mouth and biting on the same fingers that were feeding me. He hissed and pulled his hand away from my lips… and teeth.

I raised an eyebrow, cocking my head to the side. *Two can play this game, Maddox.*

He pinched my nipple, hard. A squeak left my lips, and he smirked.

"We can't be friends after I fucked you like I did last night," Maddox said, ever so crudely. I tensed, my lungs clenching at his words.

Don't do this, Maddox. Don't…please.

"If you think we can go back to being *just friends,* then Lila, you're more delusional than I thought."

I opened my mouth to snap at him, but he was already pushing me back against the seat. "Maddox, what–"

He loomed over me, our chests touching, and his hands landed on either side of my head. Maddox caged me against his body. "Give us one week," he rumbled. His face was the most serious I had ever seen, his expression hard and sure. "Our time in Paris, seven days."

One week…

With Maddox? Not as his friend, but as his lover?

A fling? An affair…?

My eyes widened, and I was already shaking my head. My heart wouldn't survive a one-week affair. Maddox would wreck me, and I'd leave my bleeding heart in Paris.

His thumb brushed against my throat, over my throbbing vein. *"Lila,"* Maddox breathed my name.

My breath hitched as my robe slid open. He knelt in front of me, his big shoulders settling between my spread thighs, pushing them farther apart. I breathed in, but my throat closed, as I ended up silently gasping instead. I was completely naked under my robe, and he took it as his advantage.

He lifted his head, his gaze hot and dark. "Your cunt looks thoroughly used from last night, Lila," Maddox said, unadulterated satisfaction gleaming in his eyes. My fingers curled around the cushion, and I dug my nails in, feeling a rush of heat coursing through me. My skin grew tight and warmth spread through my lower region, my sex growing damp. Damn him and his filthy mouth.

My eyes turned into slits as I glared down at his imposing self. I wasn't going to fall for it; I wouldn't let him sway me with sex.

Maddox's hand slowly slid up the outside of my calves, up my thighs… and…

I squirmed, my voice gone and the fight leaving me. He was meticulously slow, dragging out the suspense and forcing me to *feel* him.

Inch by inch, his hand slid upward, his touch scorching my flesh as he continued toward my center.

His slightly calloused palm felt rough against my sensitive skin, but his touch was… so light, he was barely touching me. Teasing and tempting.

Driving… me… crazy.

My heart thudded so hard I thought it would spill out of my chest. His fingers brushed against my folds, a soft touch, but I quivered in response.

"You're red and swollen," he rasped, his voice thick and hard. His fingers spread me open, still ever so gentle. Maddox tsked, the side of his lips quirking up in approval. "... and wet."

"What... are you doing?" I questioned, slightly breathless.

His chest rumbled with a low growl. "Having my breakfast. You can't deny a starving man, Baby, and last night, I built up quite the appetite."

Goosebumps peppered my flesh, and my core tightened as Maddox lowered his head between my thighs. Maddox wasn't the first man to go down on me, but he was the first one to take his sweet time. To stare at my body like he was about devour me, and it still wouldn't be enough for him.

I *ached.*

I didn't know I could feel this way, this intense... fierce need inside of me. Desire pooled in the pit of my stomach, and my arousal leaked out of me. The moment his mouth was on me, my body tightened, and I felt a rush of wetness between my thighs. Holy shit!

Maddox took his time, lapping at my sex leisurely. He dragged his tongue over my wet folds, before circling around my clit. "Maddox," I choked, my thighs shaking. A whimper left my lips before I could stop myself, and my hands went to the top of his head in frantic need. My fingers gripped his hair, pulling him closer and silently demanding more.

Fire licked through my veins, and my eyes fluttered close. Maddox was *killing* me.

It would be a sweet, torturous death.

His touch was both tormenting and heavenly.

"Maddox," I breathed.

His tongue slid over my folds, and his teeth grazed my swollen clit. My back arched off the sofa, and my thighs tightened around his head. He sucked and lapped, licking every inch of me, until my whimpers rang like desperate pleas.

I wasn't prepared for it, when he shoved a finger inside of me, but I clenched around the hard intrusion. Seeking for more… needing more… It hurt so good.

"Oh God!" I cried out, as he thrust his finger in and out, his tongue simultaneously working my pussy like his favorite meal. I guessed… I was.

"Ma – *Maddox*… Please…"

My stomach tightened, my thighs quivered, and the muscles of my calves were cramping, as I grew closer to my release. I climbed higher on the cliff, writhing and crying out, but Maddox didn't let me fall.

I throbbed, an intense beat that match my thudding heart.

I bit down on my lip, shaking, choking on my moans and on the precipice of orgasm. He dragged my pleasure out.

I just needed…

Just… oh…

The same moment he thrust two fingers inside of me, his teeth grazed my clit, a small bite that left a sharp sting behind. I bucked against his mouth and fingers, my lips parting with a cry.

I had not finished orgasming, before he was starting all over again.

"No…" I gasped, still sensitive and shaking with my orgasm. "Wait."

Maddox growled between my thighs – a warning – and went back to lapping up my wetness, sucking and licking. This time, there was nothing slow and sweet about it.

The first orgasm was for *me*. This one was for *him*.

His tongue ravaged me.

His fingers didn't stop their torturous ministrations, thrusting and twisting inside of me. There was nothing gentle as he fingered me.

Maddox was a mad man on a mission.

Molten desire, strong and lustful, coursed through my veins at the sounds coming from his throat as he tasted me, like a starved man, who would never *ever* get enough of me. His deep, primal groans were as sinful as the sound of my wet pussy – oh *fuck*!

My hips jerked, and his fingers bit into my thighs, leaving their marks there. His bruising grip was almost painful, but my muddled brain didn't seem to care one bit.

Stop.

My hips moved with his fingers, jerking and grinding against his face. I heard him groan my name against my tender sex as pleasure spiked through me, and my back bowed.

No, don't stop.

"Maddox... Maddox!"

My second orgasm threw me over the edge, and a loud moan spilled past my lips. My eyes rolled back into my head, as he gave my hypersensitive pussy one last lick.

What–?

Dazed, I blinked my eyes open, my body still shaking from the aftermath of my release. I couldn't...breathe.

Maddox lifted his head from between my thighs and regarded me, his blue eyes dark and raw. "You can have this all the time. Me, between your legs, worshipping your pussy. Say yes."

I finally came down from my high, and I shook my head, trying to clear my mind. "You're bribing me with sex? Maddox! This isn't about sex..."

His eyes hardened. "This is *more*. I know it, but you're not giving us a chance, Lila."

"What are you so scared of?" he asked, kissing the inside of my thigh, before giving me a playful nip.

Losing you...

Uncertainty flashed through me, but I was already losing this argument.

"One week..." I whispered. The look in his eyes, such raw emotions, almost like he was pleading to me, weakened my resolve.

"One week," Maddox affirmed. "For now. I might change your mind

397

later."

I dug my nails in the back of his neck, not hard enough to hurt but in warning. "You can't seduce me."

His lips quirked up. "Can't I? Haven't I?"

Maddox left a trail of soft kisses across my navel, giving my belly button a playful lick, before he nipped my flesh teasingly. He didn't look like he was about to leave his spot between my thighs any time soon.

My fingers raked through his dirty blond hair. "If I remember correctly, I did the seducing last night.

Our gaze collided. His chest rumbled and I throbbed at the deep sound. "And I'm weak to my goddamn knees for you, Lila."

My heart lurched but all of this was too good to be true. This couldn't be happening, not with Maddox... not after years of friendship... not after years of playing it safe. Now, everything was complicated.

"You probably fucked someone else last week, and you're here, now, telling me you want me? Don't, Maddox." The words spilled out before I could stop myself, and my voice cracked. I bit my lip, hating that I'd shown him a sign of weakness.

Maddox was a predator; he'd pounce on my vulnerability.

Except he did the complete opposite...

"I haven't." His eyes bore into mine, smoldering with an intensity I couldn't put in words. "I haven't slept with anyone for... weeks."

I blinked, my chest caving in. "You've been celibate for months?"

"My dick doesn't seem to like the idea of another girl."

I shook my head, tensing, and tried to close my legs, but Maddox was still between my thighs, forcing them apart. "You *think* you want me... especially after last night. I won't lie, it was amazing. Whatever happened last night—"

I broke off with a choked gasp. *Smack.*

My body jolted, and a hot flash of pain seared through my pussy, before it quickly disappeared, replaced by a dull throbbing pleasure that lingered. Did Maddox just spank my...?

Oh God! I sputtered and glared, but he was already speaking, his voice almost furious. His tone held a dangerous warning and my mouth snapped close.

"*That,*" he growled. "was the best fucking night of my life. So, don't tell me what I think and don't tell me how I feel."

Maddox grasped my wrist and placed my hand over his chest, his skin warm and smooth under my touch. His heart was *pounding*. Thud, thud, thud.

The hard glint in his eyes had softened by a fraction, but the intensity of his gaze was just as fierce. His words rippled across my flesh, and my heart stuttered, before caving inside my chest. "Don't tell me how I feel. You have no idea, Lila."

This was so... difficult.

A pained sound escaped me, but I quickly smothered it. Falling into Maddox's trap would be dangerous for my heart. I'd end up being just another conquest.

Maddox wasn't the type of man to settle down. I didn't think he'd ever be. He was too wild, too reckless, too... *wounded.*

I had always known Maddox would never be the type of man to do a long-term relationship.

This wasn't going to be an easy week or a simple affair. I was already tittering over the edge of a very dangerous cliff; I was already at risk of losing my heart and having it broken by Maddox.

But I had already lost this fight.

He moved up my body, and my legs instinctively wrapped around his hips. His lips skimmed over my throat, before he claimed my lips into a long kiss.

Maddox Coulter – my best friend, now my lover – was maddeningly irresistible.

He knew exactly how to twist my hearts into knots, and he turned me into putty in his hands.

One week.

A seven-day affair.

Seven days to fall deeper in love with Maddox Coulter.

Seven days to have my heart… broken by him.

CHAPTER THREE

Maddox

The hotel's bar was packed tonight. There were a bunch of men who attempted to look expensive and proper with their high-end suits and a drink in hand, as they surveyed the dim-lit bar. Supposed 'Gentlemen' but they were leering at the women, and it was clear as day, there was nothing *proper* about their thoughts.

There was another crowd of people who were too drunk to give a shit.

And lastly, we had the opportunists, the women and men who were here to catch the attention of someone who was probably as wealthy as the President of the United States – for a night of luxury and passion. Or, well… more than one night.

This was Paris' finest hotel, and daddy dearest probably paid a shit-ton for mine and Lila's stay here. My birthday present.

He threw money at me, in my face, even though, all I ever wanted was for him to acknowledge my existence with a simple "Happy Birthday."

I guessed he was too busy for that.

Yeah, fuck you, *Dad*.

Conversations swirled in a dirty cloud of smoke and the stench of cigarettes. My nose tingled at the strong smell of perfume surrounding me, and I downed my drink in one gulp. The alcohol burned my throat, but damn it, it was almost soothing.

"If you keep drinking like that, you'll be drunk soon enough. And here I thought, you were taking me out on a *date*."

Lila's sweet voice whispered next to my ear, her breath fanning over the back of my neck. My lips quirked up as her fingers slowly trailed up my forearms and biceps, feeling every indent and curve of my muscles. Yeah, my girl loved exploring my muscles.

Years of vigorously spending my time in the gym, throwing all my aggression into working out and into the punching bags, had served me well.

I saw the way girls – younger *and* older – looked at me at the gym. Sure, my ego didn't need any more boosting; my dick was big enough for that.

But Lila was the only woman I wanted to look at me with hunger in her dark-brown eyes.

I swiveled around in my stool, and my arm snaked around her waist, pulling her to stand between my legs. Lila pouted, her red lips shimmering in the dim light of the bar. "The bathroom line was too long, and our room is too far away."

"Your hair looks fine," I said, once again. Tucking a stray strand behind her ear, my finger lingered below it, brushing against the column of her throat. "You look beautiful."

"Beautiful, huh?" There was a teasing look in her eyes, as she nudged her chin up, almost haughtily.

She was wearing a black sequin mini-skirt, with a small slit in the hem. The skirt wrapped around her ass like a second skin, and I almost growled at the sight. The black lace crop top hung on her curves, bringing my attention to her tits. This outfit should have been illegal.

"Sexy," I rasped, bringing our faces closer. "Ravishing. I'd throw you on the bar and fuck you into tomorrow," my voice lowered, whispering our dirty secrets into her ears, "until you beg me to stop because your cunt is too sore."

Lila flushed, and her breath stuttered.

"But then again, I don't want any other man to see your bare body or hear your desperate whimpers or... to see you come."

That was for my eyes only.

Mine.

For a week.

Until I could convince her to stay... for longer.

Lila was stubborn, too goddamn stubborn for her own good. I had to play this game right, or I risked losing her forever.

Four years ago, I played a vicious game – to break Lila.

Today, I started a dangerous one – to win her over.

"You have a one-track mind, Coulter."

"Yeah. *You*, Garcia."

She rolled her eyes, before brushing her lips against mine, a teasing touch. "I... have a feeling you've said this line to a lot more girls than me. Is this your strategy?"

If she only fucking knew...

Lila had no idea that I was doing everything the exact opposite I had ever done. I never chased after a woman, never had to win *anyone* over, never had to be romantic and never had to seduce.

I smirked, and girls fell all over me. My last name and my dick were seductive enough.

Until her.

My best friend: the pain in my ass and my favorite hellion.

"I dare you..." she murmured against my lips.

"Now?" My fingers clenched around her hips. It was her turn to give a dare. I used mine this morning, when I asked – *dared* her to stay.

"Quite ironic, isn't it? This is the same place you dared me to sleep with Lucien two nights ago."

I didn't want to remember that. The mere idea of Lila sleeping with that Frenchman had rage coursing through my veins. How? *How* did I think it would be okay for me to give Lila that stupid dare? How did I think it'd help me get over her?

Instead, I hated myself.

It made me want to fuck her, claim her even more.

The need to ruin her for any other man had been all-consuming.

Yeah, that dare didn't work out as well as I expected.

But it gave me something else instead. It gave me *Lila*, all of her: all of what I didn't have before but now I did.

"Go ahead, give me your dare." *Minx.*

Lila pulled away enough to stare into my eyes. Her gaze drifted to my lips, before she speared me with an unreadable look. "Remember the girl who tried to hit on you when we walked into the bar?"

Suspicious with where she was going with this, I refrained from answering. Lila was sweet like an angel and as devious as a she-devil. I didn't trust the glint in her chocolate eyes.

She nodded to my left, and I quickly glanced in that direction. Miss Blondie was staring at me with rapt attention. When she noticed me looking, her ruby lips spread into a full smile.

"Lila," I started.

She cut me off. "I dare you to dance with her."

My hold tightened on her. Lila was playing with fire. "Why?"

She lifted a shoulder, half-shrugging. "Because. We don't get to ask the reason behind a dare, Coulter."

What was going on in that pretty head of hers? Her expression didn't give anything away, but I didn't dare trust the nonchalant look on her face. Her body was tight as a bow string, and her hands were fisted at her sides.

Yeah, she didn't want me to dance with Blondie.

But then why... give me the dare?

I stared at her for a second longer, waiting for a reaction, but she didn't give any. Fine, a dare was a dare. Neither of us played to lose. Lila's fingers twitched against my chest, as if she wanted to grab me and not let go. But, instead, she stepped from between my thighs and stood beside my stool, ordering herself a drink. Goddamn stubborn, she was.

I lounged back into my stool, gliding my tongue over my lips. My head cocked to the side, I crooked my finger at Blondie, indicating for her to come over to me. Her smile widened, and she scurried over, quick to please. She spared Lila a quick dirty look, before taking her spot between my legs.

"Hello, Handsome," she said in a thick accent I couldn't place. Blondie wore a tight red dress that molded to every thick curve of hers. Her face glimmered under the light, and she smelled of lilac and maybe... chamomile, but her scent wasn't more tempting than Lila.

Lila's was... intoxicating. I'd get drunk on her scent.

Addictive.

Crazy.

Mine.

"Parlez-vous Français?" I asked Blondie. *Do you speak French?*

Lila tensed beside me. Hmm, interesting.

"Un peu," she responded with a giggle. "How do you speak French? You're American. I can tell by the accent."

All thanks to mommy and daddy dearest. They made sure I was fluent in at least three languages from an early age. English, French and German. Brad, my father, said it was good for when I was older, when it'd be time for me to take over his empire. I have been trained, like a good fucking dog, since I was a kid.

"Comment est-ce que tu t'appelles, Blondie?" *What's your name?*

From the corner of my eye, I saw Lila clenching her glass. Her knuckles turned white, and her lips were pursed in a hard line. She stared straight ahead of her, ignoring me and the woman in my arms.

"Serena. Et vous?"

"Maddox," I introduced myself, bringing her hand up to my lips and kissing the back of it.

"Oh." She blushed, biting her lip. "It's a pleasure to make your acquaintance, Maddox." My name rolled off her tongue like she was tasting it, *fucking* it.

"Tout le plaisir est pour moi, *chérie*." *My pleasure, sweetheart.*

Serena let out a small breathy laugh. "Charming, I see."

I curled a finger around her blonde locks, tugging her toward me. Her tits pressed against my chest. She wasn't wearing any bra, and I could feel her puckered nipples through our thin layers of clothing. "Do you... want to dance?"

Lila slammed her empty glass on the bar, and Serena flinched. My lips twitched, smirking. Oh yeah, my girl was incensed.

"Another drink. Strong," she practically snarled at the bartender.

Grinning, I let my hand wander to Serena's hips. My fingers tightened around her curves, thick and lush in the palms of my hands, and she gasped, her lips parting. A tempting sight, but it did nothing to my dick.

Sure, she was attractive.

A few months ago, I would have been all up in her pussy, probably banging her against the bathroom stalls. But not tonight.

I wasn't the least bit interested in Blondie, but if Lila wanted to play...

She needed to learn the rules, and then she had to play it better than *me*. She could turn this into a little game of hers, and I'd show her how it's really played.

When our eyes met, something sparked in hers, before she blinked it away. If I didn't know better, I'd say she was a little psychotic. Ah, life was never boring, when you had Lila Garcia in your life.

"This is a good song," Serena breathed in my ear. "Shall we?"

She grasped my hand in hers and dragged us to the middle of the room. We snaked through the warm and sweaty bodies, finding an empty spot on the dance floor.

Serena was biting on her lip, giving me the fuck-me-now look. Her hands landed on my chest, and she caressed me through my shirt. Her thumb brushed over my nipple, and I grasped her wrists, pulling her arms around my neck. This was safe. Blondie pouted but, otherwise, went with the flow.

My eyes found Lila, and she was glowering. *Hmm. I see you, Garcia.*

As if she could read my mind, her face went hard, devoid of any emotions.

Nicely played.

Gripping Serena's hips, I pulled her closer to me, and we moved to the rhythm of the song. The bodies around us were practically dry humping each other on the dance floor. The bar was dark enough that nobody seemed to care.

Keeping my eyes on Lila, I pressed a knee between Blondie's thighs, and she was practically grinding against me. I jerked her hard into my body, and she took that as an invitation. Her arms unfurled around my neck, and her hands inched down to my abs.

We were close enough to where Lila was standing that I saw her expression go from emotionless to sour and *pained.*

I was just about to drop Blondie, enough of the stupid games both Lila and I were playing, when my gaze zeroed on...

Goddamn it!

What was *he* doing here?

Lucien stepped closer to Lila, her attention snapping to him. He grinned down at her and said something in her ear, causing her to smile. I nearly knocked both Serena and I over at the sight of my Lila smiling up at him. He got her another drink, and I watched as his hands trailed up her bare arms, with her still *smiling*.

Lucien nodded toward the dance floor, and Lila's gaze met mine, briefly, before she put her hand in his. Heat prickled the back of my neck, and I grew tense.

Lila wrapped her arms around Lucien's neck, and his hands were on her lower back, too low... his fingers were teasing the top curve of her ass.

An ass that belonged to me.

I could tell Lila was in tune to me and my attention on her, but she was purposely avoiding looking my way. Serena said something to me, but I wasn't listening. The bastard was holding Lila too close, and I swore she fucking fluttered her lashes at him. Where the hell had her reserve gone?

When Lucien leaned down, as if to kiss her... I was done.

Snapping forward, I let Serena go. She squeaked, protesting, but I was already stalking toward Lucien who was still holding my girl way too close.

Bitter jealousy raged through my veins as I cut through their intimate dance, separating them. "Sorry. You might want to find a new dance partner, Lucien. This one is taken."

Lila gasped as I gripped her wrist and started pulling her away. "What are you doing?" she hissed.

"We're leaving," I deadpanned, my heart hammering in my chest.

"You're causing a scene!"

Me? Causing a scene... when *she* started this stupid game of hers? For what? *WHY?*

I dragged her to the empty corridor, away from everyone and their prying eyes, pushing her back into the wall. I pressed against her body, caging her in.

"What is wrong with you? Maddox," she whisper-yelled. "Maddox!"

Her tiny fists thumped against my chest, her face red and her eyes darkening in anger.

408

"What were you doing, Lila?" I asked, deceptively quiet.

Her lips curled in a smile, although there was nothing warm about it. "Dancing. Like you were. Do you have a problem with that?"

She loved pushing my buttons.

"Careful," I warned.

Her eyes flared at the challenge. "Or what?"

My thumb rubbed over the vein in her throat, feeling it throb under my touch. "You won't like what I do to you, Baby."

"You don't scare me, Coulter."

"I know," I said. "But I should."

"You won't hurt me."

"But I will hurt *him*."

Her smile dropped. "Maddox–"

I leaned forward, bringing our faces closer. She caught her lip between her teeth, her eyes flashing with uncertainty now. "Scared for lover boy, your Frenchman?" I taunted.

Her hands landed on my chest, as if to pacify me. "It was just a dance, Maddox. You can't fight him because I danced with him!"

With a humorless smirk, I trailed my finger down the column of her throat and along the length of her collarbone. Her breathing pattern changed, a sharp inhale… a shuddering exhale.

"Why did you dare me to dance with her?" I asked softly, but the threat in my voice couldn't be mistaken.

"Because…" Lila whispered.

"Because," I echoed.

She licked her lips, her eyes flickering with something fierce. Lila pushed against my chest. "You seemed to be enjoying yourself, so why do you care? *Blondie* was very much into it and oh, of course… your *French* was very charming, indeed."

Ah, ah. Silly… jealous, Lila.

She grimaced once she realized her slip, and her red pouty lips pressed into a firm line.

"You like my French?"

"It's mediocre," she shot back. "Lucien has a better accent."

I bit back a laugh. Lila really was testing my patience. Funny, I didn't know if she was doing it on purpose or if she even realized she was walking on a risky path.

Bringing my face closer to hers, my lips ghosted along her ear, and I nipped her earlobe. "Let's not play childish games, Lila. You and I both know it only has one ending."

"And what is that?" she breathed.

"You'll find yourself on your back with me, between yours legs."

I kept my hand around her throat, lingering over her pulse, while still keeping a firm hold of her. My other hand traveled south, snaking into her mini-skirt.

Lila's eyes widened, and she gasped, the sound barely audible. "Maddox…"

My fingers teased her slit through her panties. She looked frantically around us, as her fingers wrapped around my wrist, trying to stop me. "What… people… *Maddox*, someone could see!"

I traced the wet folds through the thin fabric, feeling her softness on the tips of my fingers. Her face flushed, and her lips parted, her breathing turning ragged.

"Are you feeling… hot?" I felt compelled to taunt her. My dick hardened and throbbed. My jeans were suddenly feeling very tight, and I hissed as her thigh brushed against my crotch.

Satisfaction coursed through me when I felt her wetness through her panties. "You don't want anyone to see… but you seem to like the idea of being caught with my hand under your skirt."

"No," Lila stammered.

I nipped her earlobe again, and she responded with a sharp hiss. "Liar," I breathed.

Slowly, I tugged her panties aside, feeling her bare pussy against my finger. My thumb circled around her clit, and she whimpered, her hand tightening around my wrist. In warning? Or, in desire… wanting *more*?

Her chest heaved, as she inhaled a ragged breath. Her hips bucked forward against my touch, seeking my fingers. Wanton need flashed through her dark eyes, as I rubbed her folds, using my two fingers to spread her lips apart.

Lila was all seven of the deadly sins, and I'd gladly be a sinner for her, for the rest of our lives.

There was no concealing what we were doing. Anyone who walked down this corridor would see us… my hand shoved deep inside her mini-skirt, her face flushed, lips parted with quiet whimpers, as she grinded against my hand.

Shoving a single digit inside her tight core, feeling her inner walls clench around it, I slowly fingered her. Lila tensed against me, as I curled my finger inside her, hitting her sensitive spot. Her reaction was instant. A choked moan escaped her lips, before she slapped a hand over her mouth, muffling the indecent sound.

My lips whispered over her, a gentle touch. She opened for me, and I kissed her. I fucking *kissed* her like I was a starved man, like she was the oxygen I needed to survive.

Lila gasped against our kiss when I pinched and tugged on her clit, feeling the little nub throb between my fingers.

"Such a beautiful liar," I rasped against her lips. "Tell me, Lila. Why did you do it?"

Dazed, she seemed to have a hard time focusing on my words. I thrust my finger back inside her cunt, dragging another moan from her. "I… Maddox… do what?"

"Why did you give me that dare?" I hissed, my voice so gruff, even I barely recognized it.

Another whimper from her as I pulled out from her tight heat. "I…

411

wanted to see… Oh God, Maddox, *please*."

I teased her opening, feeling her clench – seeking out my fingers. "Tell me."

"Wanted to see how I'd feel…" she choked out, her eyes glassy with pleasure.

I rewarded her with two fingers inside her. "Go on."

Her heart pounded against my chest, feeling the vibration like it was my own heartbeat.

"If… I'd get jealous seeing you with another… woman. I wanted to see…"

"And?" I demanded, the word sounding harsh even to my own ears.

"I don't like it," she admitted, through her panting.

"Don't like seeing me with another woman?"

I asked the question at the same time I thrust my fingers inside, curling them in a way I knew would drive her wild. She pulsed around me, her wetness dripping and the sound of me fingering her was almost scandalous.

"Yes!" Lila hissed. "I hate it."

"Don't like me speaking French to another woman?"

Her eyes rolled back, as the heel of my palm pressed against her tender sex. "Maddox…"

"Answer me."

She glowered, a vicious glint in her gaze. "You never spoke French to me," she spat, before letting out a low moan. Her eyes widened, her face flushing even redder in embarrassment, and she bit on her lip, hard.

"Je veux te baiser."

Lila inhaled sharply at my French, her nails digging into my wrist. They'd leave her marks behind, that I was sure. It stung, the pain making my cock harder. She was probably drawing blood right now. I'd gladly bleed for her.

"What?" she whispered.

Lila's legs quaked, and her whole body trembled, on the precipice of her orgasm. She slapped her hand over her mouth again, muffling her desperate moans, as they kept spilling from her lips. My head lowered to her chest, my lips hovering over her tit.

"I want to fuck you. Right here, right now," I said, my voice throaty and husky. Goddamn it, I was about to spill in my jeans. My dick throbbed, practically weeping for a slice of heaven... and hell.

Her nipples poked through her crop top. The outline of the tight, hardened tip was tempting. My teeth grazed over the tiny nub through the thin layer before I nipped her, a sharp bite, as I rolled and tugged her clit between my thumb and forefinger.

"You *can't*," she cried out, as I dragged her release from her.

Lila threw her head back, her eyes closed. Her orgasm hit her, at the same time, my gaze found Lucien.

Perfect timing.

His face paled, a mask of shock and anger. His lips curled as he took a threatening step toward us. I cocked an eyebrow at him.

Lila came down from her high, and she gasped in alarm at the sight of Lucien standing there, watching us.

Frantically, she tried to push away from me. *Not so fast, little dragon.*

Gently pulling my fingers from Lila's skirt, I brought my hand up to my lips. "Oh God..." Lila whispered in horror, as if she knew what I was about to do.

Little does Lila know...

She ignited a possessive need inside of me. Something fierce, something dangerous, something... wild.

Her juices and her sweet, musky scent coated my fingers, as I licked them clean, keeping my eyes on Lucien.

He paused, his chest expanding and his face darkening dangerously. Lila's skirt was still bunched up to her hips, her thighs spread open for me, her panties obscenely tugged to the side. Her pussy was visible

413

enough to Lucien, red and swollen from my fucking.

Fuck, I was going mad.

I wanted to smear my cum all over her pussy and have Lucien take a look, showing him what was mine and what he couldn't have.

Lila tugged her skirt back in place, quickly patting down her hair. Her eyes lowered to the ground in embarrassment. Her legs shook, still weak from her orgasm, and she stumbled forward, before I wrapped an arm around her waist, anchoring her to my body.

I licked my lips, tasting the remnant of her pussy juices. "My apologies, Lucien. My girl and I got a little carried away. We'll be finishing what we started in our room. If you'll excuse us."

Lila avoided looking at Lucien as we walked past him, but the moment we were out of his vicinity, she turned on me.

Her fist thumped against my chest, the action catching me so off guard that I ended up stumbling back a step. Shocked, my lips quirked up. Feisty, just like I liked it.

"You... are an asshole!"

Lila stalked away, her red heels clicking over the marble floor. She took the elevator, and still grinning, I took the stairs to the fourth floor. She was already in our master suite when I got there, pacing the length of it.

Her wild eyes met mine the second I walked through the door.

"That was completely unnecessary! What is wrong with you? You knew he was standing there, didn't you? Huh, for how long?" Gone was soft and pliant Lila in my arms as she orgasmed. In her place was my favorite hellion. In that moment, I realized... Lila wasn't fragile like a flower. She was fragile like a ticking bomb, and I just poked her.

"Maddox! I'm speaking to you. You can't treat me... treat me like a paid whore. I'm not someone you just throw against the wall—"

"...and fuck?"

Lila sputtered, her cheeks flushing red.

I tugged my shirt over my head and let it drop to the floor, stalking forward. "Let us get one thing clear. As long as you're mine, I will take you wherever I want and however I want."

She stabbed me in the chest with her finger. Lila was a midget, but damn, she had a temper and the attitude of a fiery dragon. "You will treat me with respect, Maddox."

I arched an eyebrow at her. "I will treat you with respect, yes. A perfect gentleman. I'll open the doors for you, I'll bring you your favorite mint-chocolate chip muffin, and I'll even hold your hand. I might even give you some dead roses. See? Perfect gentleman."

I bent down, my face hovering over hers. Her breath seized in her throat at my next words. "But I'll also bend you over and fuck you however I want, because I love seeing you trying to deny how wet I make you. I'll treat you like a princess, but I'll fuck you like an animal and like the dirty pervert I am, because you *like* it."

Her eyes narrowed with rage, but she kept her face deceptively calm. Taking a deep breath, she took a seat on the couch, crossing her lithe legs. I followed her, standing close, so she had to nudge her chin high to stare up at me through her thick lashes. What a perfect position. This put her mouth right over my crotch.

Lila's eyes lingered over my torso for a second longer, before her gaze collided with mine once again. "Do you speak with all the girls like this? Do your conquests appreciate this... this crassness?"

"What do you think?" I asked, low and quiet.

"I think you're absolutely despicable."

"Oh yeah, I've been called that a few times."

"Oh, when? After leaving a massive line of sobbing, heartbroken girls?"

I clucked my tongue at her, as she goaded me. My hand cupped her face, and I rubbed my thumb over her parted, wet lips, smudging her lipstick. "You know me so well."

"This is why you never had a girlfriend! You obviously don't know how to tone down your asshole-ness!" She hissed, exasperated.

"Keep talking, Garcia. It's tempting me to throw you over my knee to show you exactly why they call me despicable."

Lila blinked, her face paling in shock. "Did you just threaten to spank me…?"

"I *promised* to spank you *and* fuck you. Go ahead, keep being a mouthy little thing." My hoarse voice seemed to drive her even more wild.

"Is this something you do with your other…fuck buddies, too?" she sneered.

Ah, so little Miss Lila was, in fact, *territorial*.

Jealousy didn't only run through my veins, but it was very apparent in hers. I knew it, and I was goading her, waiting for her reaction.

When I only smirked, she was miffed.

"Asshole."

My lips twitched. "Brat."

Lila let out a shocked gasp, and I stifled a laugh. We've been best friends for four years; I knew exactly how to push all her buttons.

"Did you just call me a brat?" *Yes, I did.* Especially after that stunt she pulled at the bar. Daring me to dance with Blondie when she damn well knew she was the only woman I wanted in my arms.

"Would you rather I call you a bitch?"

Outraged, she jumped to her feet and leveled me with a glare that would have had anyone quaking in fear. Me? Angry Lila just made my dick hard.

I could think of sixty-nine ways to fuck the anger out of her system, until she was a pretty mess under me.

"Why are we doing this?" she growled, fire burning in her dark eyes. Goddamn it, she was a tempting goddess. So tempting. So beautiful. Mine.

And I wanted to put her over my knees and tan her ass red for being so goddamn stubborn.

Her fists clenched at her sides. "You're one very annoying person, Coulter. Why am I still here?" she muttered the last sentence to herself, but it was loud enough for me to hear.

I grinned. "Because you like how my dick feels inside of you."

A heartbeat passed before she exploded. She threw the cushion at my head and narrowly missed.

I tsked, darkly. "You shouldn't have done that."

Stalking forward, I hunted her down, as she tried to escape me. But she was too slow, and a predator never loses sight of his prey.

I caught her easily and threw her on the bed. Lila bounced on the mattress with a shocked gasp, and I *pounced*.

She made a sound at the back of her throat, something akin to irritation, but it lacked fire. And she didn't push me away.

In fact, her fingers curled around my shoulders, as I pushed her thighs apart and lowered my head between them. Her skirt was bunched around her waist, and I snapped the strings of her panties, throwing the lace G-string over my shoulder.

"What are you doing?" Lila breathed.

Her wide, brown eyes were hazy and laced with wanton need.

"Speaking French between your legs," I rumbled, my chest vibrating with the low growl. "Your pussy and I are about to get reacquainted on a... more personal level."

CHAPTER FOUR

Lila

I woke up in Maddox's arm, my body sore and my brain… fuzzy. Warmth spread through my body, all the way to my toes, and against my will, there was a stupid smile plastered on my face.

Warm and safe.

Happy and…

Loved?

No. My heart dropped to the pit of my stomach, a sudden hard dive that had me snapping out of my daydream. It wasn't love. It couldn't be. At least not from Maddox.

"Good morning." I had been so lost in my own thoughts, overthinking once again. But his voice, a deep timbre, brought me back to him.

The same low rasp as he spoke his final words to me last night, before falling asleep… after some vigorous… *fucking.*

Or… love-making, I guessed. I couldn't quite decide what it was we did last night. Maddox had been rough, taking me long and hard… then he had been gentle, taking his sweet time. Touching me with utmost care, like I was something fragile – breakable. He *confused* me.

"Best birthday ever," Maddox had rasped in my ear, before his breathing evened out. It was his answer to me wishing him *happy birthday* as the clock struck midnight, while he was buried deep inside me.

His twenty-first birthday.

Our fourth birthday together. Except, we celebrated this one quite a bit differently than the first three.

I turned over onto to my side to face him. His eyes were still closed, but there was a flicker of a smile on his lips.

Folding my arms over his wide chest, I rested my chin on my hands. "Good morning," I whispered, before placing a chaste kiss on the corner of his mouth. I didn't know why I did it, but it was instinct. Almost like a habit I had picked up in the last twenty-four hours. I couldn't keep my hands or lips off him. "And Happy Birthday."

"When I open my eyes, I better find you naked."

It was impossible not to smile at his teasing. Maddox just seemed so… *happy.* "Open your eyes and find out yourself."

He hummed in response, and I felt his hand inching up my thigh, a soft caress. He cupped my bare ass and gave it a firm squeeze. Maddox popped an eye open, his lips lazily quirking up to the side with a smirk. "Soft and naked, I approve," he said, his sleepy voice gruff to my ears.

"You're insatiable," I teased.

His fingers trailed up my hips, and his arm circled around my waist, before he flipped us over. Maddox hovered over me, grinning. "That's four years of sexual frustration, Lila. Trust me, I'm not nearly done with you. In fact, I'm just getting started."

I hiked my legs around his hips, pulling him closer. His morning hard-on pressed against my core, and I could feel the stickiness where his cum had dried on me from last night.

"Seven days of carnal desires, huh? I was expecting some romance, but I guess I'll take what I can get." I only meant it as a joke, but gone was the teasing look on Maddox's face.

His expression turned serious, like he was really considering my words. Damn it, stupid me and my loose tongue. If this was a seven-day affair, I couldn't let this get any more serious than it already was.

His blue eyes flashed with something... I just couldn't place the emotion, before it was gone. His hand came up, and he cupped my face, his thumb ghosting over my cheek. "I've never had to woo a woman before. But I'm going to try. For you. I'm not much of a romantic guy, but I'll try. For *you*."

I let out a small laugh, but inside of me? I was a complete mess. Stomach fluttering, chest cramping, heart tightening... Holy shit. Did Maddox Coulter just say he was going to *woo* me?

Girlish delight filled me, but I quickly shoved it away. "Sheesh. I was only joking, no need to get all serious, Coulter."

His thumb feathered over my lips, a tender touch.

Stop. You're making this harder.

"I *am* serious. I'll give you romance, flowers and all, with a side of dick to go with it."

A snort escaped me, quite unladylike, and I smacked his chest. "I knew it! You can't do romantic to save your life."

Maddox's eyes darkened. "Was that a challenge?"

I chewed on my lip to keep from giggling. Me – *giggling*. Shit, the Maddox's charm was getting to me. "Maaaybe."

A deep rumble came from his chest. "Try me," he growled, before his lips crushed against mine, in one long, deep... searing kiss.

He *claimed* my lips.

He *stole* my breath.

One... simple... kiss.

Maddox *captured* my heart.

I expected him to want more, but he ended the kiss, pulling away slightly. "Get up. I'm about to give you my birthday present."

Dazed, I blinked at him. "Huh? That's not how it's supposed to work. It's your birthday, and I give you a present. Not the other way around."

Maddox grinned. "We're going on a date," he said more softly.

"A date?" I repeated.

He rolled off me, and I watched, as he ran his fingers through his blond hair. "Woo you," he mouthed.

Holy shit, Maddox was serious.

A date... I was going on a date with my best friend.

Wait... my lover?

Boyfriend?

Nervousness zinged through my veins, and my stomach twisted. This wasn't going to end well. No, all of this had just gotten way more complicated.

My breath halted when Maddox curled a finger around a lock of my hair and tugged, pulling my attention back to him. "You're overthinking, Lila. I can practically hear your thoughts."

"Maddox–"

"No," he cut me off. "If I have to throw you over my shoulder and carry you around on our date, I will. Don't tempt me, Sweet Cheeks."

Maddox didn't make empty promises.

In fact, he always carried out his threats, one way or another.

I got off the bed and quickly grabbed for his shirt, pulling it over my head. "A casual date? How am I supposed to dress? Where are we going?"

He turned over onto his side and propped up on one elbow. The muscles of his bicep bulged, and the blanket slid down to his hips, barely covering his crotch. His bare torso and v-line were on display. That simple move shouldn't have looked this sexy, but Maddox made it downright sinful.

His ocean blue eyes flickered to my bare thighs, before he looked up.

"You look good in my shirt," he said, his voice laced with something akin to… affection? Adoration? Something *more*…

"And you ask way too many questions, woman."

"But–"

Maddox shook his head. "Get in the shower, Lila. Or we'll never leave this hotel room."

Huffing back a response, I stomped to the bathroom. I locked the door, just in case he got any ideas. I needed some time alone to think, to prepare myself and my… heart for what Maddox had planned. Because, regardless of what I said or did… or how hard I tried to push Maddox away and to keep my heart in a cage, he made me weak.

I found my disheveled reflection in the mirror and groaned. The end result of a sex marathon.

Rubbing a hand over my face, I leaned against the sink. Everything was happening too fast. Two days ago… the mere idea of sleeping with Maddox was forbidden, almost taboo.

Now, I was so tightly entangled with him, there was no way out.

I didn't even know how to step back, how to go back to how we were before. My throat tightened with a choked sound.

Before Maddox, I didn't know how to fill in the missing piece. I didn't even know I was missing a piece of my puzzle until he sauntered into my life, with a dirty smirk. I didn't know I was incomplete until he made me whole.

Before Maddox… I didn't really *know* me.

I covered my chest with my hand, and my scars tingled as a reminder. After the death of my parents, I went on with the motion of life. I woke up, went to school, reminded myself to breathe, smiled because I was expected to, slept while praying the nightmares stayed away. And repeat.

I breathed.

I lived.

But I wasn't… alive.

Not until him.

My fingers grasped my necklace, feeling the weight of it, chasing the same soothing feeling it always brought me. The pendant, our dreamcatcher, felt heavier than it was before.

How could I risk losing him – losing *us*?

A soft knock snapped me out of my thoughts, and I swiveled around, glowering at the door. "What?"

"I can hear you overthinking, Lila."

"Shut up," I muttered to the door.

The door chuckled, well, *Maddox* chuckled. "Don't make me come inside. You know damn well a locked door will not keep me away if I want to get in. Better remember that next time."

"Is the word 'privacy' not in your vocabulary?" I shot back.

Maddox was silent for a short second before he replied, "No. Now, hurry. Our date awaits, milady."

"I'm not a lady *or* a princess." And yes, I was smiling because, damn him, I was falling for it again. His charm. His stupid attempts to woo me.

Even with a door separating us, I could imagine Maddox standing outside the door, smiling. "No, you're not, little dragon."

Little dragon.

My cheeks heated up. Damn it, was I… blushing?

Oh no, I was in big trouble.

Thirty minutes later, I walked out of the bathroom to find our master suite empty. Maddox was nowhere to be seen, but he did leave me a present. On the bed, there was a white dress.

With a single… dead rose.

A dead rose? What the hell?

And then I remembered *why*.

Maddox and his stupid pranks. The last time he offered me roses – dead roses – he was on his knees, making a grand proposal to my ass.

This was his messed-up way of being romantic, but still staying true to *us*.

Next to the dress, there was a blue Post-It Note. A handwritten note, with Maddox's not so elegant penmanship.

You look beautiful in white. Wear the dress.

Ah, this was Maddox. He didn't even bother to *ask* me to wear the dress or say 'please.' He *ordered* me to wear it.

And where the hell did he even get this dress? It was pretty and elegant. A simple white, spaghetti strap silk dress.

I grabbed the dress and walked over to the mirror, before slipping it over my head. It came down to my calves, a few inches above my ankles. The dress was backless, with crisscross straps to a tie a knot.

"I'm beginning to think I made the wrong choice."

I gasped at the voice and swiveled around to face the intruder. "Maddox! You scared me!"

He stood at the entrance of the room and closed the door behind him. My gaze traveled the length of his body, slowly taking him in. Yes, I was taking my time to appreciate the view.

There was nothing wrong with eyeing your best friend, right? The same best friend I slept with last night...

Instead of his usual attire of jeans and a shirt, he was wearing black pants, a white buttoned-up shirt and a black tie. His sleeves were rolled up to his elbows, his thick forearms coiled with muscles. My stomach fluttered at the sight of him...all casual elegance and so sinfully looking.

Maddox sauntered over to me, his eyes dark and intense. "Now that you're in the dress, I don't want to leave the room," he said hoarsely.

"Why?" My voice dropped to a whisper. "Do you like it?"

He stood in front of me, a mere inch away. So close, I could feel the warmth of him. He smelled clean...his aftershave and favorite cologne mixed with his manly scent. I'd recognize his scent anywhere, even in a crowded room.

Maddox took another step, until our bodies were flushed against each other. His breath skated over my cheeks. I could smell the mint on his breath, and I'd bet he had gum hidden somewhere in his mouth. "I like it *too* much."

I swallowed, my mouth was suddenly dry, and my tongue didn't seem to work. "Um... can... you help me?"

There was a single heartbeat, a short second, a throbbing moment, before his hand came around my hips. Maddox turned me around, so I was facing the mirror. With my back against his front, we stared at each other.

There was a look in his eyes, the intensity of his blue gaze unnerved me. Eye contact was a dangerous, dangerous thing. It spoke a thousand unsaid words; words we were too scared to speak.

His fingers skimmed over my bare back, and I fought back a shiver. My toes curled around the soft carpet, and my eyes fluttered shut as his head lowered to my neck. His lips whispered over my skin, and his teeth grazed my shoulders sharply, before laving his tongue over the bite.

I felt him inhale, breathing *me* in.

I exhaled a shuddering breath in response.

My heart catapulted in my chest when his lips ghosted behind my ear, a tender kiss. I didn't want him to stop touching me. There was magic in his touch, I was dizzy and drunk on Maddox.

His fingers worked the thin straps, and he tied a single knot, before his hands landed on my hips again. "Black is your color, but white makes you look like an angel who has descended on earth. Although, instead of bringing peace, you're wreaking havoc on my heart."

Thud. Thud. Thud.

My heart was falling... breaking... a loud shatter that echoed in my ears. I wasn't going to survive the next five days with Maddox.

His grip tightened on my hips. "Leave your hair down."

I licked my lips and eyed him through the mirror. "You're really demanding today." Like always.

Maddox half-shrugged before he flashed me a dimpled smirk. "You like it."

"Say please."

"What?"

"First step of wooing me: stop being such an arrogant asshole. Say please."

His thumb brushed against my hips, moving back and forth. It was a teasing touch through the thin fabric of my dress.

"Please." My womb tingled at the low rasp, his voice thicker than usual.

Holy. Shit!

Maddox Coulter just said *please*.

"Shall we, little dragon?"

I nodded, simply speechless. He really was serious about wooing me. Maddox didn't have a single romantic bone in him, but he was *trying*.

I wasn't strong enough to escape his attempts.

I just knew...

By the end of our Paris affair, I was going to lose my heart to Maddox – the heartbreaker.

Hours later, my feet were sore from walking around the streets of Paris, and my stomach rumbled with hunger. I was just thankful Maddox had suggested I put on my flats, instead of heels, when we left the hotel this morning.

Now, the day was slowly coming to an end.

And what a beautiful day it had been.

A date, a... real... date with Maddox Coulter.

We spent the morning at the Modern Art Museum. True, it was boring for Maddox, but he did it for me. He knew how much I loved museums and viewing collections of art over hundreds of years. Paris was rich with culture, and I'd never grow tired of exploring the heart of France.

For lunch, we settled for a small picnic at Champs De Mars, a 60-acre garden that used to grow vegetables and grapevines in the sixteenth century until it was repurposed for military training by Napoleon's nearby academy. Today, we could just enjoy the view of the garden while having lunch.

We later explored the Trocadero gardens and had our dessert there, from ice cream vendors. Maddox had his favorite mango flavor, and I chose chocolate mint.

Everything had been so… perfect. As childish as it sounded, I didn't want the day to ever end.

It would have been the same scene if we had explored Paris as friends. A normal outing between two best friends. We would have gone to the same places, ate the same food…

But this was… *different.*

Maddox held my hand. In fact, he barely let me go. He secretly whispered dirty words in my ear, while we explored the museum. We shared kisses while we ate our ice cream, our lips quivering and numb.

He was completely in tune with me, always reaching out for me, watching me closely, *touching* me.

His romantic side was finally showing, and I got to be the first woman to see it.

It was special, I told myself.

But it was also a short affair, I reminded myself.

"So, where to now?"

Maddox grabbed my hand, tugging me to him. He folded his arm around my shoulder, anchoring me to his side. He lowered his head, so he could whisper in my ear, "Your last surprise."

"It's really not fair. It's your birthday, and you won't let me do something for you," I mumbled, even though my heart was doing somersaults in my chest.

Maddox placed a quick kiss on the corner of my lips. "You already are."

"Hmm."

"You're spending the day with me. That's enough."

"A date," I said cheekily.

"A date," he affirmed, with a warm, dimpled smile. It transformed his face. Maddox looked happy, and he suddenly appeared younger than before, more his age. All casual, carefree and young.

He was always busy with school and football, always worrying, always tense. It was a burden he carried as he tried to make his father happy, even though if you asked him – he'd lie and say he didn't give a single fuck what his father thought of him.

He was a good liar, like that, hiding his pain behind the mask he wore, showing the world he was *the* Maddox Coulter: cocky, arrogant, rich–Berkshire's star quarterback and now Harvard's.

To the world, he had everything. Parents. Money. A scholarship. His football career. Girls at his disposal.

He was a king, and he wore his crown, filled with thorns, with an unmatched arrogance and a dirty smirk to go with it.

But deep inside, all Maddox ever wanted was acceptance and love. So he worked endlessly for it… and always ended *disappointed.*

But right now? The usual tensed line on his forehead was smoothed out, his blue eyes practically alive, and his smile was…real.

Oh damn it. *There goes my heart again.*

Once we were back at the hotel, we waited for the elevator. "So, what's the surprise?" I asked again, growing a tad impatient. He was dragging the suspense out far too long now.

"It's waiting for us on the rooftop." Maddox winked, as he took a step back, as if to walk away.

Confused, I grabbed his hand and tugged him to me. "Are you telling me you're about to climb up the stairs to the rooftop?"

He eyed the elevator, and I could practically feel him sweating at the mere thought of entering the tight enclosure. "Maddox, you can't climb fifteen flights of stairs. That's crazy! We don't have to go to the rooftop. Let's go back to our room."

"No," he snapped, before shaking his head. "Sorry. It's just... I had them prepare this especially for us."

"Maddox–"

He gritted his teeth, his jaw growing hard, so much so that I wondered if it'd crack under the pressure. "Take the elevator, Lila. And I'll be there in a few minutes. The stairs are not a big problem."

"But–"

"Lila, *no*."

"You're serious?"

His expression turned stern. "Yes. Don't argue with me on this, little dragon. You won't win this one."

The elevator pinged, and the doors slid open. Maddox was already backpedaling from me. "To the rooftop, Lila. I'll see you there."

I got into the elevator and watched him leave, as the door slid closed once again. I punched in the button for the last floor, which would take me to the rooftop. I didn't even know we were allowed up there.

The hotel was fifteen floors, and it took me a few minutes to get where I needed to be. When I got to the top, there was a hotel employee at the door. He smiled kindly, before he let me out, sliding the glass doors open for me. I stepped onto the rooftop, which, in fact, was a wide-span terrace.

Holy shit.

I slowly took a few steps forward, taking everything in. The terrace had been transformed into a romantic arrangement. The set-up was right out of a movie or a romance novel. Oh yeah, I was definitely being wooed. Rose petals and scented candles on the ground, creating a pathway for me. There was a table set for two, but it was the view that had me in complete awe.

Oh my God!

I must have stood there, in complete shock for a whole minute.

"Surprise," he exhaled in my ear.

I didn't even flinch or gasp. I felt him before he spoke. Maddox's hands curled around my hips, as I leaned against the metal railings of the rooftop. His breathing was coming out harsher, his chest heaving against my back, and I could feel his heart thudding. He climbed up fifteen flights of stairs for *this*... for us.

He pressed his warm lips on my bare shoulder, a soft kiss. "Sunset, the Eiffel Tower and dinner."

My breath hitched. "What did you do?" I whispered, still in shock.

"Wooing you," he easily responded. "I promised you romance."

So he did.

And Maddox delivered.

Flowers... romance... sunset... Paris...

What else could I ask for?

Falling in love with my best friend was never meant to happen, but being romanced *by* my best friend? I guessed, there was no going back after this.

The city of love lived up to its name. Not even Maddox and I could fight it.

We had been told this hotel had the best view of the city and right here...on the rooftop? The view was absolutely magical as the sun began to set behind the Eiffel Tower, and we could see the whole French Capital.

As the sky turned yellow and orange, the sun lowering itself over the horizon, I could only stare and marvel in its beauty.

"Shall we? Dinner awaits."

Maddox gripped my hand in his, and he tugged me to the table. He pushed my chair in and took a seat across from me. Dinner was served by the same waiter I met at the door.

"Real roses, huh?" I nodded toward the vase on the table. That was a great addition, if not a total surprise. I'd expected dead roses again.

His lips curled up, a teasing smile. "I thought I'd change it up a bit."

I looked around the terrace, admiring the view. "How did you plan this?"

"I have my ways." I couldn't imagine Maddox going to the concierge and asking them to prepare this. It didn't really suit him and his cocky ways, but I guessed...

He really did surprise me today.

Maddox poured us both a glass of wine. I took a slow sip, nodding in satisfaction, when the red wine hit all my taste buds.

"Since you wouldn't let me get you a birthday present, we'll have to go tomorrow," I started, cutting up my steak into tiny pieces.

Maddox shoved his fork into his mouth, his eyebrows furrowed. "What do you mean?" he asked around a mouthful.

"I thought we could get a tattoo."

His eyes lit up instantly, and I continued, "Last year, you wanted to get matching tattoos, but I wasn't ready. I thought this year... we could. Your birthday present."

Matching tattoos... something that was *us*.

"Lila," he said my name in a low growl.

"Yes?" My stomach did another flip, and I *loathed* how much Maddox could affect me.

That was a lie. I didn't hate the feeling. In fact, I was starting to love it. Too much.

"If you weren't eating and across the table from me, I'd have turned you over and fucked you into next week."

My hand flew to my mouth, as I coughed back the steak that was now stuck in my throat. I clumsily reached for my glass and took a huge gulp. He grinned, before taking a sip of his own wine.

I didn't realize he'd be *that* happy about the matching tattoos.

"You have to stop doing that," I mumbled, after my coughing fit.

"What? Making you blush? It looks cute on you, Sweet Cheeks," he said, ever so arrogantly.

Damn it, damn him.

The rest of the dinner went by, with Maddox dropping casual dirty remarks and me rolling my eyes. He was absolutely impossible.

But I had four years to get used to all his antics.

Once the table was cleared and while we waited for dessert, I pushed my chair out and walked over to the railing. The sky was dark now, and the Eiffel Tower was lit up for the night.

It was... breathtaking.

From the corner of my eye, I noticed Maddox rising from his seat and striding toward me with purpose. He exuded confidence and arrogance, the way he prowled over to me. His body moved behind me, his wide chest pressing into my back. I could feel the strength of his body against mine.

A shudder rippled through me, as his finger skimmed over my bare back, gently tugging at the lace knot there, but not hard enough to have it come undone. His teasing touch lingered, my skin rising with goosebumps.

His hand slid up, oh so slowly. He brushed my hair aside, and his lips feathered against my nape. My heart *thudded*.

I suddenly felt really, really warm. All over. Inside, outside... my fingertips... my core.

Oh God. His touch was sweet, sweet torture. A slice of heaven, with a touch of hell.

Maddox kissed his way to the curve of my shoulders. "I knew I had no right to touch you, to want you, to crave you like air, but I did. I knew it was wrong, but I didn't want to stop. So, I took. And now, I'm *obsessed*."

A shiver ran down my spine, and I almost whimpered in need. My body shuddered as his words hit me like a violent tide, sweeping me away. His chest rumbled with a low guttural sound. "I'm a mad fucking man for you, Lila Garcia."

My sex clenched in response. "It's not fair," I whispered. "I can't push you away if you keep saying things like this, whispering these words… You're making this so much harder, Maddox."

His teeth nipped the side of my neck. His hand curled around my throat, and he turned my head to the side, his lips brushing against mine.

Kiss me.

That was the only thought I had before his mouth was on mine. He didn't pause, didn't wait for me to think, didn't wait for me to catch my breath…

Soft but demanding.

Gentle but passionate.

Sweet but all-consuming.

Fire licked through my veins, and my body went soft in his arms. For a short second, my world felt off balance, before it finally felt… *right*. Every part of me came alive, as the drums crashed and banged in my chest. My soul cried in triumph, as I finally allowed myself to… *feel*.

Maybe this was the moment I fell for him. Recklessly. Irrevocably. Wholly.

Maybe this was the moment I realized I never wanted to let go.

We kissed, like two drowning lovers lost at sea, our lips seeking each other amidst the crashing waves. Lips. Tongue. Teeth. We kissed like it was the end, and our lips would never meet again. The rhythm of our hearts matched our crazed desperation. Maddox tasted of all things holy and sinful in this world; he tasted like every forbidden thought I had at night coming true.

He tasted like red wine, and I was a little heady, a little drunk on him.

Our lips parted from each other, as we caught our breath, chests heaving.

"Bend over. Pull your dress up," Maddox rasped in my ear.

I swallowed, my heart racing, and my stomach clenching with anticipation. His fingers unwrapped around my throat, but I could still feel their searing touch on my flesh, as if he had *marked* me. His hands lowered to my waist, and his fingers gripped my hips. Maddox brushed his nose along the length of my nape.

I exhaled a shuddering breath. "People are going to see."

The buildings were so close to each other, anyone could see us if they were looking out of their windows. And what if… the waiter walked in on us?

His chest rumbled with a growly sound. "Let them. I want the world to see me owning this sweet pussy. Bend over, Lila. Now. Show me how wet you are for me, and I'll give you what you need."

My eyes widened at the command in his voice, and my body bent to his will, before I could really process what was happening.

"I'm waiting." His voice had hardened, a slight gruff in his tone. "Your dress, Lila," Maddox reminded me, when I stayed bent over the railing.

My trembling hands clenched the fabric of my silk dress, and I slowly slid it up. I couldn't see his face, but his eyes were practically burning holes into my back.

Warm. Intense. Hard.

I pulled my dress up over my ass, and it bunched around my hips, as I stayed bent over. The thong I wore barely covered my flesh. My ass cheeks were on display, my bare legs shaking, as I tried to keep myself still for him.

This was highly inappropriate.

But maybe it was *why*… the fact that it was *inappropriate*…had me wanting more. I grew damp between my thighs, my wetness coating my underwear. My body was tight with anticipation.

"Maddox," I breathed, waiting for him to say something… to touch me.

But he stayed eerily quiet. I could hear his breathing, could feel him behind me, but he didn't make a move to touch me.

His legs brushed against mine, and I let an involuntary shudder. The fabric of his pants seemed to feel rougher against my skin, even though I knew that wasn't the case. I just felt more… in tune with Maddox. My body was hyperaware of every touch, every breath… every movement.

When he *finally* touched me…I almost moaned in relief.

The tips of his fingers brushed across my back, and his hands slid down to my ass. He cupped it almost possessively, before moving closer. His body molded over me, bringing his chest firmly against my back. Maddox kicked my legs open, forcing them further apart.

The slight coldness of the railing seeped through my dress, as I kept my chest pressed against it. My nipples pebbled, and my lips parted, a silent gasp escaping.

He rubbed his palms over my ass, caressing the soft globes. His voice lowered to a throaty timbre. "What am I going to do with you."

I licked my lips. "Was that a question?"

"No, a statement." Two fingers slid inside my thong and between the crease of my ass, rubbing the soft spot there. Right…there. Holy shit! I clenched and bit on my lip, *hard*. "I'm going to do a lot of things to you, Lila."

I gasped with mock indignation. "You won't…"

Smack.

It was a light tap compared to the spanking he had given me during our sex marathon. After manhandling me the night before, this was almost gentle. This one was just enough to sting before feeling more pleasurable.

He popped his hand over my ass again, and I bit my lips, holding in the moan that threatened to escape. My hips lifted on their own accord, as he rubbed the spot immediately, making me feel hot and aroused.

Smack. Smack.

He spanked me harder. Two quick swats that slowly burned my flesh, and this time, I couldn't help but moan out loud. The heat between my legs intensified, and I *throbbed*.

It was painful: sweet torture.

Oh, sweet heavens!

"Maddox." My voice came out soft and breathy. I could only imagine how it looked if someone caught us. Me, bent over with my dress around my hips, Maddox spanking me, as my wetness dripped down the inside of my thighs. The image was so... dirty... so... lewd, I couldn't help but feel even hotter.

I arched into his body, as he peppered my ass, alternating between light and hard swats. He caressed my arched bottom, teasing both of us.

I felt him kneel behind me, his face leveled with my ass now. He slid my thong down my legs, and the soft fabric gathered around my ankles. I tried to close my legs, suddenly feeling overwhelmed by all of *this*.

"Show me your pussy, Baby."

The pressure in my chest built up. My thighs clenched together at his words, but his hand landed on my ass so hard that I flinched, crying out, and my legs instantly fell open. "Show me, Lila. Show me how much you want me."

Maddox nudged my legs open wider with his knees. His palms rubbed the globes of my ass, as my hand sneaked between my legs. A slight moan whispered across my lips, as I touched myself. I bent forward more, pressing my upper body against the railing and arching my hips up. Maddox's fingers dug into my flesh, and he pulled my ass cheeks apart, just as I spread myself open, showing him my entrance.

He swore under his breath, and I closed my eyes, feeling my body flush under his intense, penetrating gaze. "You are so fucking beautiful, Lila."

Of course, he'd say that. I was at his mercy, wide open for him to do as he pleased.

Maddox let out a low grunt. I felt his breath on my ass cheeks, before he gently bit down. I let out a small screech, my whole body clenching tightly, as he speared my heated core with two fingers at the same time. I bucked against him, crying out and feeling myself grow more damp.

I *pulsed*, throbbing with an intensity I couldn't really describe.

Maddox continued to thrust his fingers in and out of me, and I shamelessly started to move with him, grinding against him.

"Maddox...Maddox!" His name was a gasping prayer on my lips. My legs started to shake, my knees growing weak, as he relentlessly continued to tease me. "Oh...Please! Please. *Please*."

He slowly pulled away. The feeling of emptiness made me cry out, and I blindly reached for him. "I got you," he muttered in my ear.

Don't stop now.

I wanted everything he was giving me and more. "Don't move."

His body warmth left me for a mere second. I heard the sound of his belt unbuckling, his zipper being pulled down... and then he was on me again.

Crowding into my space, pressing against me, filling my senses with his touch... his scent... his... *everything*.

His hard length jerked between us, and the tip of his cock pressed against my core. He guided his length toward my center, slowly rubbing the head around my clit.

My fingers dug harder into the metal railing, as Maddox thrust inside slowly...so slowly, punishing both of us. I felt him, inches by inches, until he was deep inside of me. Jesus Christ! Over the last two days, I've had Maddox inside of me multiple times, in multiple positions, but every time felt like the first.

His breathing was ragged, his chest heaving with each breath. My eyes widened, as he rolled his hips slightly, making me *feel* him. All of him. There was no space between us. And I couldn't *breathe*.

I was stretched fully, but the discomfort was barely there. He slowly pulled out and pushed back in a second later, with the same slow and torturous movement.

My gaze found the lit-up Eiffel Tower in the night, as Maddox took me from behind.

Oh God, this was his *surprise*.

Romance and dick on the side, he promised.

Yeah, he delivered.

Maddox grunted my name, the sound so primal, my womb clenched in response. His slow pace picked up, his thrusting became jerkier. Harder. Deeper. His fingers wrapped around my hair, curling his fist around it, until his knuckles dug into my scalp.

"Look to your left, eyes up," Maddox growled, his voice hoarse, ragged.

I did.

My lips parted with a silent gasp as Maddox thrust back inside of me, his cock hitting me so deep, my toes nearly left the ground. "Do you see him?"

I whimpered in response.

Someone – from the silhouette, I'd guess it was a man – was watching us from the building beside us. All the buildings were so close together, and the man was only a floor higher than us, so there was no denying it – he could see *everything*.

A strangled sound escaped me. I would have thought maybe he didn't see us. After all, it was dark outside, or maybe he had been preoccupied. Except, from the silhouette, it was obvious, as the man pulled his dick out from his pants and started jerking off.

While...watching... us.

"Lila," Maddox growled my name. He pulled out, almost completely. His hard length pressed against my folds, and I clenched, feeling empty. "Bad, bad girl. Are you giving him a good show?"

With one hard thrust, he rammed back inside, and my lips parted with a silent scream. *Maddox!*

Maddox didn't pause. We both made a strangled sound, a groan... a whimper.

This was quick, hot and *filthy.*

My gaze didn't sway from the man. Maddox slammed into me again, as I watched the complete stranger make himself come at the sight of us fucking.

My moans grew louder; Maddox's grunts sounded harsher in my ears. "Lila. Lila. Fuck, *Lila.*"

The tension in my core tightened, my womb shuddered, and my pussy convulsed around Maddox's hard length. I tried to swallow my scream, but when he pounded inside me, hitting that sweet, sensitive spot... I let go.

My eyes closed, as I came so hard my knees weakened, and my legs almost gave out. He found his release too, his body clenching as he spasmed against me.

"So. Fucking. Beautiful," Maddox groaned.

The stranger found his release, as well, before he tucked his dick back inside his pants, gave us a tiny wave and walked away from his window.

Jesus, God! Holy shit!

Maddox curled his arm around my waist, keeping me upright, as I wobbled against the railing of the rooftop.

What... did... we... just do?

I blinked away the fuzziness, but my brain didn't seem to work. My heart was rocking so hard against my rib cage, I thought it'd leave a nasty bruise. My body felt like a limp mess... I was just so...

I couldn't think. Couldn't breathe. Couldn't...

Maddox slowly pulled out of me, and I flinched at the sudden empty feeling. His lips pressed against my shoulder before he spun me around and pulled me into his arms. His suit was in disarray while my dress was rumpled. My hair was probably a mess too, adding to my disheveled appearance.

"Pretty romantic, don't you think?" Maddox rasped in my ear, as his cum dripped down my thighs.

"That's a whole new meaning to romance, Coulter," I said breathlessly.

Maddox chuckled, before claiming my lips in a long kiss. "I aim to please, Garcia."

Oh yeah, I was very *pleased.*

Maddox Coulter could do dirty romance very well.

CHAPTER FIVE

Maddox

O ur time in Paris had come to an end.

One week. A seven-day affair.

And now I just had to convince Lila to stay with me…
forever.

But forever was a long time. Forever was just a daydream, a pretty
fantasy, I thought.

I guessed, I just had to convince her that we were good together.
Really fucking good. Good enough for us to work out as a couple and
last for a very long time. As cheesy as it sounded (cheesy didn't suit my
character, but for Lila, I'd be my own version of cheesy romantic), I could
see my future with Lila.

I didn't do love, or I didn't *think* I did. But she was everything I ever
wanted, and it scared the living shit out of me. She was a slice of heaven,
with hellish fires.

By the end of tonight, Lila Garcia was going to be my girlfriend.

It didn't matter if I had to tie her to the bed and dick her down good enough to convince her. If she wanted romance, I was prepared to give her that, too. That and everything else she wanted. Lila wasn't going to friendzone us any longer.

I could already feel her barrier coming up, shutting me out. I knew she was worried; I was too. As we walked out of the airport, Lila kept a careful distance between us. A distance that wasn't there during our stay in Paris. Of course, it wasn't there, I was all up in her pussy in the last seven days.

And We. Weren't. Going. Back. To. Being. *Just friends.*

Fuck that. My dick agreed.

"I'm glad to be back home," she said, hefting her travel bag over her shoulder. "I'm worried about Riley."

"She'll be fine," I soothed, reaching for her hand. It was out of habit, almost like an instinct, that was now instilled in me. To touch her, to hold her, to kiss her.

Lila shied away from my touch, and I held back a growl. Goddamn it! Her lips were pressed in a firm line, as she avoided looking at me. I grabbed her suitcase and rolled it toward my black Bentley. "I had Colton drop off the car for us."

"You didn't have to do that," she said, placing her bag into the backseat. "We could have taken an uber home."

"I knew you wouldn't like that." I shoved our suitcases into the trunk, before walking around to the driver's side. Lila settled in the passenger's seat.

She might have gotten over her fear of cars. She was okay with driving around with me, but she wasn't comfortable getting in a car with just anyone. Not yet, at least.

I was probably an asshole for thinking this… but I liked that she'd only get in a car with me. That I was her protector. She trusted *me*. Only I had seen the sides of Lila, she never wanted others to see.

I'd seen Lila strong and powerful.

I'd witnessed her fragile and vulnerable.

Lila nudged me with her elbow, her lips quirked up to the side. "That was very thoughtful of you, thank you."

Really, Lila? We were back to sharing pleasantries and being... *friendly?*

The more reserved she appeared, the more I wanted to tease her, probe her temper and evoke her passion.

The more distance she put between us, the more I wanted to devour her.

Leaning in, I cupped her face and stole a kiss. Her lips parted against mine, and I shoved my tongue in her mouth, tasting her. I sucked and nibbled on her bottom lip, until she let out a small whimper that sounded so needy. The sound traveled all the way to my dick.

Well, shit. Not now, big guy.

I pulled away from the kiss and licked my lips, tasting the remnants of her cherry lip gloss and the mint gum she had in her mouth... which... I now had between my teeth. She didn't even notice I stole her gum. Her brown eyes were glassy, her cheeks tinted with pink blush, and Lila fluttered her lashes at me. Yeah, I got her good.

"Why did you do that?" she breathed, bringing her fingers to her plump well-kissed lips.

Because you're mine.

I clunked my tongue at her and started the car. "I was just checking if you'll turn into a princess. But alas, you're still a frog – wait, no. Still a scaly, terrifying dragon, I see."

Lila swatted my arm, a small breathy laugh escaped past her tempting lips. "As if you're a prince. Ha!"

"You're no princess, and I'm no prince charming."

She rolled her eyes. "What are you then?"

"Your king, Baby."

Lila's throat bobbed in response. She turned to face her window without a smart comeback, like I expected. She ducked behind her hair, shielding her face from me. Hiding away, shutting me out...

Run, Lila. Run, little dragon. The faster she ran away from me, the harder I was going to chase her.

The drive to our place was rather quiet, and I gave her that. I allowed her the silence, gave her one last chance to overthink *this,* before I'd swoop in and turn her world upside down.

Fifteen minutes later, we pulled into the parking lot. Lila hurriedly got out of the car, before I could say a word. Was she thinking of making a beeline to her apartment without even acknowledging me?

What – the – fuck?

Lila and I were just stepping out of the car, when Colton rolled into the lot in his yellow Ferrari. Last month, he had the latest Jaguar Sport – in green. He liked his cars, like his women: flashy, bold and extravagant. Arrogant little shit, no wonder we were best friends.

We watched, as he jogged around to the passenger's side, opened the door and out stepped... Riley?

Double – what – the – fu–

She wobbled out in her cast and grimaced as Colton wrapped an arm around her shoulders, helping her hop over to us. She waved, a little smile on her face. "Lila!"

Lila dropped her bag at my feet and raced over to Riley, before enveloping her friend into a tight hug. Colton *reluctantly* released his cargo into Lila's arms and took a step back.

I walked over to the little group and bumped fists with Colton. Riley and he barely tolerated each other, and I was damn curious how he convinced her to let him help. I glanced down at the grocery bags he was holding. I could see there were vegetables, chocolates and... tampons. Yeah, that grocery bag definitely did *not* belong to Colton. He appeared to be Riley's personal chauffeur and... helper?

"How's the leg?" I nodded toward Riley's blue cast.

Her lip jutted out, a sad pout. "It's fine now."

Lila made a strangled sound at the back of her throat, sounding both pissed... and cute with the look of outrage on her face. "I can't believe you waited a whole day before you called and told me about your accident! You broke your leg, what the hell!"

"Fractured," Colton amended. "Not broken. She's lucky I was next door and heard her cry out."

"You shouldn't have climbed up that ladder when you were home alone. It was never stable." Lila's forehead creased with worry as she fretted over her friend. "You could have been hurt worse!"

"She could have just called me, and I would have fixed the broken cabinet," Colton mumbled under his breath.

Riley hissed, her eyes flashing with annoyance. "I had it all handled if it wasn't for the cat jumping into my ladder. Rory asked me to cat-sit for her while she and Jaxon were away this weekend." She faced her nemesis, glaring. "I didn't... and *don't* need your help, Colton."

"Funny. I'm the one who drove you to the hospital in the middle of the night."

Her shoulder straightened, and her lips curled up in distaste. "Because *you* insisted."

"You were in pain."

"Who cares? I was fine on my own and could have called 9-1-1!"

"I care," Colton growled.

Riley opened her mouth to snap back at him, but then paused at Colton's confession. She blinked, opened her mouth again, before finally shutting up. No smartass comeback? Huh, interesting.

"Whatever," she mumbled under her breath. "How was your trip, Lila?"

Lila's gaze found mine, as she turned red. She blinked away and sputtered out a half-ass response to her friend. "Oh, fine. It was fine.

445

Everything was nice and fine."

"She said *fine* three times," Colton muttered to me, soft enough the girls didn't catch it.

Riley never shut up, and she asked way too many questions all the time. Surprisingly, today, she seemed more thoughtful. I didn't miss the way she kept glancing between Lila and I, almost suspiciously.

"Was Paris like everything you imagined?" Colton pushed, a cocky grin plastered on his face. The shithead caught on easily. Of course, he did.

Lila let out a choked laugh. "Oh, yeah. Everything was…"

"Fine," I finished for her.

Her head snapped toward mine, and her dark eyes burned darker. "I was going to say, everything was *magical*."

"Was the sex *magical*, too?" I *grinned*.

Lila gasped, absolutely outraged.

Riley stumbled back and almost fell flat on her ass, if it wasn't for Colton grabbing her.

Colton let out a holler, before disguising it with a coughing fit. His shoulders shook with his silent laughter.

"WHAT?" Riley screeched.

"Maddox," Lila hissed. Her hands fisted by her sides, and I was pretty sure she was contemplating decking me. Gotcha, little dragon. There was nowhere for her to run now.

I grinned harder. "My dick is magic, Babe. Don't be embarrassed to admit it."

I ignored my girl, who was glaring daggers at me, and turned to our friends with an announcement. "She's my girlfriend, and she's moving in with me."

Riley blinked.

Colton smirked.

When Lila started to protest, I leaned down and claimed her lips, not giving a shit that we had an audience or that she was going to murder me in our sleep. I *kissed* her, fuck the consequences. "Shut up."

She pulled away from the kiss, opened her mouth to tell me off, but then snapped it shut again. She chose to glower instead.

"Lila?" Riley questioned softly.

My girl was already taking a step back, like she was about to bolt. Not. Fucking. Happening. I lunged forward and drove my shoulders into her hips, lifting her off the ground, slinging her over my shoulder. One hand gripped her ass firmly, while I hooked my other arm behind her knees and pinned them against my chest.

Lila let out a shout and started struggling, but there was no use; I had my precious cargo over my shoulder.

Neither Riley nor Colton tried to stop me, as I marched to our building. I took the stairs to the third floor, careful not to jar her too much. My heart thudded hard in my chest, and I knew I was playing with fire.

But then again, I had a habit of loving dangerous things. They called me heartbreaker, thrill-seeker and danger-devil.

And Lila?

She was danger with a big, red sign. Damn it all to hell, I *craved* her.

Lila let out a string of curses and peppered my back with her tiny fists. Once she came to the realization there was no point in struggling, she let out a soft cry and went limp over my shoulder. That was better. I lived for her fiery attitude, but, sometimes, I preferred her docile.

I walked down the corridor. When we passed hers and Riley's apartment, Lila snarled. "*My* apartment is next door."

I walked through my apartment and shut the door behind us. "This is *our* apartment now."

I smacked her ass once – because, why not, she was mine now – and she gasped, before I placed her back on her feet. Grinning, I raised an eyebrow.

She gaped at me, her mouth hanging open. "No," she sputtered.

"Get undressed."

"Excuse me?" She crossed her arms over her chest. "No. This is kidnapping, Maddox."

I stood in front of the door, blocking her way out of my apartment. "Undress. *Now*. Or I will do it for you."

"Maddox," Lila warned, taking a tentative step back. Her eyebrows furrowed, and she paused, giving me a suspicious look. "Why?"

She was finally catching on, smart girl. I took a step forward; she took one back. "Because you can't run away when you're naked. Simple logic, Sweet Cheeks."

"Maddox," she started, before lowering her head, ducking behind her goddamn hair again. She shook her head slowly and muttered to herself, so softly, I almost missed it. "This can't happen."

Lila sounded so heartbroken, so lost…and I didn't like that. Didn't like the way she hid from me, didn't like the way she seemed to give up on *us*, before she even tried to make it work.

Anger and desperation rolled off me as I stalked forward. "What are you so scared of?"

"*You*," Lila breathed, when I paused in front of her, a mere inch away. So close I could smell her lavender shampoo, so close I could feel her warmth, so close I could *taste* her fear. My heart slammed against my rib cage.

"You're scared of me?" I trailed a finger up her arm, and she gave me a small shiver in return. "I'll never hurt you, don't you know that?"

Lila licked her lips, still keeping her eyes downcast. "Not physically."

Taking her chin between my fingers, I lifted her head up. She closed her eyes and drew in a shaky breath. "Look at me," I said to her, my voice hoarse even to my own ears. "Look at me, please."

My grip on her chin tightened, and she fluttered her eyes open, gazing right into mine. Misery etched her expression for a split second, before she blinked it away.

I had gotten a glimpse of something so good, and I didn't want to lose it, lose her. I broke my rules for Lila Garcia, and this wasn't our ending. We were not an incomplete story or a half-written page. We were the whole goddamn book, and I needed her to see that.

I cupped her jaw, as I watched her say a million unsaid words to me with her sad eyes. "I've put my whole fucking heart in your hands, Lila."

Her throat bobbed, and her pretty brown eyes turned glassy. Her next words, her littlest whisper, was my undoing. "You terrify me."

My sweet Lila. *If only you knew what you do to me.*

"The feeling is mutual." A soft confession, a gentle promise.

I released her and quickly pulled my shirt over my head and threw it on the floor. Lila licked her lips, and her attention went to my bare torso, before her head snapped up again. I could see her trying to fight me, having an internal battle with herself.

She wanted me.

But she was scared of having me.

"We were perfect just the way we were before, Maddox. I don't want to lose that."

I let out a chuckle at her weak attempt. "Yeah, Babe. It's a little too late. We stopped being *just friends* the moment you let me all up in your pussy without a condom."

Lila shot me a fierce glare, and I grinned harder. She was so easy to tease. I gripped her shirt and started pulling, but she smacked my hand away. "Maddox!"

I paused, watching her resolve grow weaker under my gaze. I wasn't going to forcibly undress her. A heavy feeling wrapped around my chest, as I realized she could end this, push me back and walk away.

Thud. Thud. Thud. "Do you want to walk away?" I asked, as my voice hardened. "If that is really what you want, I'll let you go."

Uncertainty swirled in her eyes, and my palms grew clammy.

Thud. Thud. Thud.

My fingers clenched the fabric of her shirt, waiting. My head lowered, and I leaned my forehead against hers. "Walk away, Lila. Now," I breathed against her lips. Not touching, not kissing... I *waited*. I was giving her a choice, a way out. Now... or never.

My heart lodged in my throat, as I waited for her to make up her mind. *Thud. Thud. Thud.*

She finally sighed softly, her lips parting, and she leaned into me, curling her arms around my neck. "*Maddox.*"

My name was a whispered prayer on her cherry lips. I loved the way my name sounded, the way it rolled off her tongue, like she was tasting sweet candy.

Goddamn it, my chest tightened, and I let out a ragged exhale. "Whatever we had before, it wasn't enough. You know it; I know it. We're perfect now."

I pulled her shirt over her head, and she let me. The rest of our clothes quickly followed until we were both naked. Leaving our discarded clothes on the floor of the living room, Lila's arms went around my neck again, and I hoisted her up. She wrapped her legs around my hips, and I walked us to my room. Her lips found mine, as we tumbled together onto the bed, and I slid between her thighs, hovering over her.

A flash of uncertainty flitted in her eyes again, before she blinked it away. I didn't want her to regret this, regret not walking away. I rubbed my thumb across her jaw, and the touch seemed to make her feel at ease. "I'll always be your best friend, Lila."

The worry slowly melted away from her face, and there was a small coy smile on her lips, a smile that went all the way down to my dick. "But you're also my boyfriend now?"

My heart skipped a fucking beat.

Boyfriend. A relationship...

I had never done a relationship, nothing as official as *this*. My dick was happy enough with all the chicks who eagerly landed on it for a fun time.

But Lila wasn't just a chick looking for a fun time.

She wanted a relationship, romance… boyfriend and girlfriend.

And fuck me, I wanted that, too.

I gave her my signature smirk, guaranteed to melt anyone on the spot. "It could be worse."

"What could be worse than this?" She rolled her eyes, but I could see the worry receding from her gaze. She turned soft under me, her hands sliding over my back, dragging her nails over my skin, like the tempting minx she was.

"I could be your husband."

She smacked my shoulder with her tiny fist. "Maddox!"

I clasped her wrist and jerked her hand down, pressing her palm over my chest. My heart thudded at her touch, and her eyes softened. *Feel me.*

"I live for the adrenaline rush, Lila," I said, keeping my voice low. "I love any adventure that gets my blood pumping, my heart racing… I love anything dangerous, anything wild, anything beautiful enough that makes me want to capture it. *You* are my favorite adventure, Lila Garcia."

She hiccupped back a gasp, before catching her bottom lip between her teeth. Her fingers splayed over my chest, caressing me with her sweet, torturous touch. "You're my favorite adventure too, Maddox."

Her other hand curled behind my neck, and her fingers glided through my hair, pulling at the curled strands. My lips brushed against hers, feeling her soft moan. "I want to wake up every morning at 6 AM, while the world's still sleeping. I'll look beside me, and you're there. I want to fall asleep knowing that you'll be the first sight I see when I wake up. I want every ordinary day with you. I want your bad days; I want your tears and your laughter. Give it all to me, Lila. Be my girlfriend."

She returned my kiss with a fierce one of her own, before she pulled away, just enough to whisper the words, "What if we go back to hating each other?"

I grinned down at her. "Then, we'll just hate fuck. Problem solved."

Her brows furrowed, and she tensed beneath me. "I can't hate you. My heart won't allow me. Even if you break me one day, I won't be able to hate you. That terrifies me, Maddox."

"Lila," I murmured, feathering my lips across her cheek. "Lila... Baby, can you stop overthinking for one minute? Just for a minute. Tell me what you *want*."

Her forehead creased with a tensed line. I kissed down her throat, and she gave me an involuntarily shudder. Her throat bobbed, as she swallowed hard, then my kiss whispered over the throbbing veins on the side of her neck, feeling her heartbeat against my lips. "Stop overthinking."

My head lowered to her chest; her bare tits were a very tempting sight. The white and pink jagged lines between the two heavy mounds called to me. I lightly touched her scars with my mouth, kissing her past away with silent promises.

I knew Lila was scared of feeling too much, scared of losing the people who mattered to her. She kept her heart locked in a silver cage behind her chest, like an Ice Queen.

Too late, though, I had already broken through her barriers. I just needed her to accept it now.

Lila whimpered the moment my lips touched her scars, her nails digging into my shoulders, and I groaned at the sharp sting. "Don't," she said, letting out a soft cry. "It's ugly. Stop, Maddox."

My sweet, sweet Lila. Fierce and fragile. She wasn't weak; she was *never* weak. But she was vulnerable.

I let my kiss linger over her scars, feeling the jagged, bumpy lines under my lips. "You're so beautiful. You don't even know what you do to me, Lila."

Her nipples hardened at my rough voice, and her skin flushed. I cupped her breast in my palm and brought my mouth to its puckered nipple. Lila let out a soft mewl, as my lips wrapped around the little bud.

"You are so perfect," I breathed against her flesh. Goosebumps flashed across her skin, and she trembled in my arms.

My teeth grazed her nipple, and I bit down gently. Lila rewarded me with a gasp and then a fevered moan. I knew I had her exactly where I wanted her. She was trying hard to concentrate on her thoughts, but when I started sucking on her tits, she arched her back. Her hands came to my head, almost frantic in her need, and she pulled at my hair, crying out my name.

"What do you want?" I asked, my voice thick with desire.

When she didn't give me a verbal response, I switched to her other breast and gave it the same attention. At my sharp bite, her nipple swelled in my mouth, and her back bowed off the bed.

"*You*," Lila breathed.

I smiled, before sucking on the pink swollen bud, chasing the sting away. I was finally in her head.

"What do you want, Lila?" I asked again.

"Maddox," she whimpered, "hurry, please."

"Answer me."

Her legs hiked up, and her ankles hooked below my ass. There was an urgency in her voice now when she spoke. "You."

My head lowered further, licking and nipping her taut stomach. I swirled my tongue around her cute belly button. She clutched the back of my head, a small impatient sound echoing from the back of her throat. "What do you want?"

"YOU!" Lila screamed, almost brokenly. "Oh God. You. Maddox, you. Goddamn it, I want *you*!"

I smiled, feeling the urge to beat my chest like a caveman. Lila Garcia was officially mine.

Raising my head, I regarded her with a look of triumph. "I dare you to be my girlfriend, little dragon."

Her eyes grew darker than before and flashed, like molten lava – mixed with lust, fear and annoyance. "Yes," she hissed.

I lowered my head between the apex of her thighs and buried my face in her heavenly scent. She was wet, hot and ready. I licked her slit and circled her throbbing clit.

"Just fuck me already," Lila growled, her hips grinding into my face, hard. Her pussy was practically smothering me, and I loved every bit of it.

"Gladly."

Mine.

CHAPTER SIX

Lila

The moment Maddox fell asleep beside me, I sneaked out. No, I wasn't running away. But I needed to breathe, without him stealing away all my breath, to think, without having him distract me with his touch, his mouth… his very impressive, very *distracting* cock.

I knew he didn't play fair. He never did, but Mr. Coulter was such a dirty player. Using sex to turn me soft and have me sidetracked. Every. Single. Time.

I wasn't exactly complaining… but I needed some time away from Maddox.

And I needed my friend. She'd be able to help me process these past seven days.

I found Riley on the couch when I walked into our apartment. Her head snapped up at the sound, and she gave me a curious look. "Is Maddox's dick finally sore enough you guys couldn't go on anymore, or did you happen to run away?"

She knew me too well. I plopped down on the couch beside her and stole some popcorn from her bowl. Her casted leg was propped up on the coffee table and YOU, on Netflix, was playing on the TV. Riley was mildly obsessed with Joe Goldberg.

"Isn't this your third time watching season one?"

"It's my fourth now," she mumbled around a mouthful on popcorn. "You were gone for a week, and I had nothing interesting to do. Joe entertained me."

"I'd think Colton was entertaining enough." I spared her a sideway glance, watching her reaction.

Her face hardened, and she munched angrily on her popcorn. "He's an asshole."

"An asshole who helped you," I reminded her.

Colton wasn't exactly the bad guy, but he was too much of a shithead. Riley barely tolerated him, and he was making it worse on himself by spouting bullshit half the time. Why couldn't he just say something *nice* for once…?

I shook my head. He was friends with Maddox, after all. Those two were absolutely impossible to deal with.

I'm going to woo you. Romance with a side of dick.

Okay, maybe Maddox wasn't too bad. He sure did romance pretty well… and he, of course, was efficient with his err, male appendage.

I pinched myself in my leg, shaking myself away from my daydream. This was exactly why I had to get away from Maddox. I couldn't stop thinking about how good he felt between my thighs, on top of me, and how perfect his lips felt against mine.

"Who cares about Colton," Riley paused, before turning on her side to face me. "I need to know what happened in Paris."

Of course, I had been waiting for that question. The suspense was probably killing her, as it would have if I were in her place.

I cleared my throat, dragging my nails across my thighs. The expectant look on her face was making me nervous. "Paris was… something else."

"You know damn well I'm not speaking about the city. What happened between you and Maddox?"

"He… well, *we* succumbed to the tension between us. It kinda just happened, without us really even realizing it. But it was too late then."

I let out a soft sigh and closed my eyes, leaning my head back against the couch. "I wanted him; he wanted me. We're both adults, who I guess, couldn't keep their hands off each other."

Riley was silent for a minute, soaking in my words. She shifted beside me, and I popped one eye open, as she drew closer to my side. "And now?"

Now?

My heart slammed against my rib cage and… forget butterflies, I had the whole damn zoo fluttering around in my stomach. "I guess, we're dating?"

Her eyes narrowed on me. "Was that a question or a statement?"

I swallowed, feeling the lump in the base of my throat. *I dare you to be my girlfriend, little dragon.*

"I'm his girlfriend," I finally confessed out loud.

Holy shit! I. Was. Maddox. Coulter's. Girlfriend.

The realization finally hit me, like an arrow straight through my heart. My head swam, the room became blurry and the world tilted, catching me off balance.

"Lila? Lila!" Riley grabbed my elbow, and I realized she was shaking me. "You look like you're about to pass out."

"Maddox is my boyfriend," I choked.

"Oh. It looks like it finally hit you," she deadpanned, with a trace of humor.

"I lost," I mumbled.

"Huh?"

457

"Remember when I first bumped into him at Berkshire? I told you I wouldn't fall for his charms. So, I basically lost." My head fell into my hands, and I sucked in a shaky breath.

Four years later... I had fallen hard for *the* Maddox Coulter. Star quarterback, reckless bad boy, infamous playboy. Who was once my nemesis but now my best friend.

Riley fell back against the couch, howling with laughter. Tears spilled down her cheeks, as she choked back on her maniacal laughter when I glowered. "Oh, shut up!"

"I'm sorry," she wheezed. "But this is actually hilarious. I remember how stubborn you were. You were so determined not to fall for him. Remember those days? Ah, the good ole days."

I shoved my middle finger in her face, and she laughed even harder. Rolling my eyes, I elbowed her in the ribs.

She gasped and then grinned. Mischief flashed in her wide grey eyes. "How's the sex? Please tell me his dick game is as good as it has been hyped up to be."

I flushed, feeling the heat go up my neck and on my face. "Better than the hype," I admitted hoarsely, my lips twisted in a rueful smile.

The sex was... mind-blowing.

But it was the intimacy that had my heart clenching and stomach fluttering like a silly teenage girl with a new crush.

It wasn't just physical with Maddox; it wasn't just sex – no – it was more. Maddox took his time to learn how I liked to be touched and to know my sensitive spots.

I was naked, vulnerable, and opened to him, body, scars and all, but he made me feel like I was the most beautiful, the most desired woman on the whole damn planet. The intimacy between us transcended the physical... it was all about the *feel*.

That made the sex mind-blowing.

That and his... very thick, very long, very girthy... *distracting* cock.

My sex clenched, at the reminder, and I squeezed my thighs together, feeling the pulsing need in the pit of my stomach.

"Well, at least you're getting some," Riley said, reaching for her popcorn again. She placed the bowl on her lap and shoved a fistful in her mouth. "My vagina is as dry as the Sahara Desert."

"Maybe Colton can help with that." I shot her a shit-eating grin, knowing full well it would grate on her nerves.

Riley was visibly outraged by my suggestion "Colton is going to keep that thing between his legs to himself." Her nostrils flared, and she grunted in irritation. "If he brings his north pole anywhere near my south pole, he might have to say goodbye to his babymaker."

"North pole?"

"Yeah, because it points up," she explained, as if I was dumb.

I waggled my eyebrows at her. "I'd love to read a smutty scene of yours."

Riley cleared her throat, straightened her shoulders and started in her best narrating voice, "As his north pole came close to my south pole, my center pooled with warm, creamy liquid. Our copulation was sweaty and hard. My rhythmic wails could be heard across the city as the wet friction of our sex grew louder. His bulbous rod jumped inside my sacred tunnel, as he found his release."

I hollered. "Ew, no, stop!"

Riley winked, before bursting into laughter. "I think I cringed so hard my face is twitching."

I nodded in agreement. That was absolutely awful. "Never mind. I don't want to read your smutty scenes."

She patted my knee, before turning back to the TV. "So, what are you going to do?"

"With Maddox?" I asked, although I already knew what she was asking. "I want to give us a chance. Maybe he's right; maybe we could be good together."

"Two souls don't find each other by simple accident," Riley murmured. "You two were meant to cross paths, Lila. As enemies, as friends… as lovers."

"Since when are you a champion for Maddox?"

Her grey eyes snapped to mine, but they were smiling. "He makes you happy. I think that gives him plenty of bonus points."

Maddox did make me happy. I curled my feet under me and settled back on the couch. "Thank you, I needed this talk."

Riley offered me a handful of popcorn. "My pleasure, babe."

She started episode nine of YOU, and we settled in, finishing up season one and starting season two right after.

Five hours later, although time had seemed to fly by, there was an insistent knocking on our door. Riley turned down the volume, and I walked over the door. I barely had it open before someone rammed into me.

Maddox–

My thought came to screeching halt at the raw expression on his face. Something akin to crazed desperation and…*fear*. His emotions wrapped around my chest and squeezed, until I couldn't breathe.

His frantic gaze landed on mine, and they darkened almost dangerously. "You," he accused, sounding out of breath. "You left."

I swallowed the lump in my throat. "I came to see Riley."

He prowled forward, his jaw hard and his expression tight. Maddox only had his boxer shorts on. He hadn't even bothered to wear his clothes in his attempt to hunt me down.

"I wasn't running away," I whispered, pressing my palms over his chest.

His heart was racing, too fast, too hard, too wild. Oh, baby. I stood on my tiptoes, and my lips brushed against his, in my attempt to calm him down. "Take me back… home."

Maddox let out a ragged breath, as if he could finally breathe again.

His arm curled around my waist like a band of steel, and he practically dragged me back to his apartment next door.

His mouth moved with mine, and *I* kissed *him*. Taking control of the kiss, I nipped on his lips and then slid my tongue inside his mouth. He hoisted me up in his arms and closed his door, before slamming my back against it. He wasn't careful, he wasn't gentle, and, in this moment, I couldn't find myself to care.

Maddox groaned into my kiss, and I could feel his thickness against my stomach. Could feel how *hard*...warm, how... heavy he was.

"I didn't have a good dream," he grunted like the words pained him.

My heart dropped, and my arms tightened around him.

"Woke up to an empty bed. It made it worse." His confession surprised me.

Maddox had never let himself be vulnerable around me, not willingly. Sure, I had seen his bad sides, his *worst* sides. I had seen him at his breaking point, but he hid his pain with a perfected mask and would never admit to something like this. His tightly put together defenses were down.

Right now, Maddox Coulter was the rawest and truest version of himself.

Open to me and vulnerable in my arms.

My lungs squeezed, as I shuddered back a cry. "I'm never leaving you, Baby." The endearment spilled from my lips before I could overthink it, but it felt... *right.*

"Lila." There was so much pain contained in that single word, my name on his lips, whispered like he was a dying sailor at sea, seeking asylum from his impending demise.

"Pinky promise?" A little piece of my heart chipped off.

My Maddox: *mine.*

He always wanted to be my protector... and I wanted to return the favor.

Lips on lips, forehead against forehead, hearts thudding together, bodies entangled – I whispered, "Pinky promise."

Four years ago, I met a cocky and selfish asshole. He was everything I despised and everything I thought I didn't need in my peaceful life.

Today, I held the same man... a different version of him, in my arms.

And I kissed him.

Then, we made love.

Raw, passionate, crazy love...

It was everything I didn't know I needed until now.

CHAPTER SEVEN

Lila

Two months later

Watching Maddox's football games never got any less exhilarating. Every time I watched him walk through the tunnel that led to the football field with the rest of his team, heard the crowd go crazy as Maddox strutted about with his typical swagger and arrogant smirk – my chest tightened, and I could feel myself shaking with excitement.

He loved the crowd, as much as he loved playing football and being on the field. Maddox enjoyed the attention of his fans. The energy, the spectators screaming his name, as he threw a perfect spiral for a touchdown.

It was the first home game of the season, and our players were putting on one hell of a show. Harvard hadn't lost to Brown University in three years. If they won this game, which would have been Maddox's fourth win… It would be a record-breaking, and I wanted to be *that* girlfriend who praised her man for their success.

Maddox has played for the team since his freshman year, and this would be his fourth and final season.

Yeah, it was silly.

But I was so damn proud of him. Maddox Coulter was an exceptional player. Okay, yeah… I was definitely bragging – but that was my right and my duty as his girlfriend, wasn't it?

Maddox said their coach was riding their asses about making sure to win this home game.

It was my job to motivate him…

Withhold sex until he wins this game.

It turned Maddox into a grumpy bear the last two days. *I'm a growing boy, Babe. Need pussy, three times a day, like people need food.*

It was hard to withhold sex, since Maddox could be *really* convincing – both him and his dick.

But if Harvard won, then he was in for a real treat.

I smiled as the crowd went insane, once again. Excitement bubbled inside my chest, as I joined in the cheers. Another touchdown by my man.

I had heard that the Brown's defense was weak, and the score on the scoreboard at the half – 21-7—proved that fact to be true.

I couldn't help but laugh as Colton scored a touchdown and strutted around the field like the arrogant asshole he was. He paused a few yards away from where Riley and I were sitting in the front row. I watched him and Riley make eye contact, only briefly… but it was monumental.

Colton grabbed his crotch, winked and smirked, before he swaggered away.

Riley *blushed.*

What. The. Hell?

"Is there something you need to tell me?" I grumbled under my breath. The tension between those two was thick and intense, but I'd like to think that Riley's accident had driven her and Colton to being civil with each other. Civil enough that we could all have dinner without them being at each other's throat.

They weren't exactly *friends*. Not yet.

But Riley was beginning to tolerate him a bit more.

It was… something, at least.

She choked back a nervous laugh. "Nope. Nothing yet. Except I saw Colton's penis yesterday."

"You WHAT?" I grabbed her elbow, forcing her to look at me.

She hissed at my outburst, but her cheeks flushed even brighter. "It was an accident. I walked in on him… You forgot to tell me he was showering at your place."

My place – mine and Maddox's.

After coming back from Paris, Maddox was adamant that I moved in with him. It was hard saying *no* to him, so I didn't see a point not to acquiesce to his demand. We had known each other for four years and were already practically living together. All I had to do was move my clothes over to his place, next door, and that was it.

Nothing much changed.

Except that now I went to sleep in his arms and woke up with his head between my legs.

Which always made for a *good morning*, indeed.

Riley didn't complain much about the move, since I was only next door.

Colton had to move out, since he believed Maddox and I needed privacy… which was true. Apparently, Maddox had a thing for kitchen sex – while I was prepping his meals.

Riley didn't have a housemate anymore, but she said she didn't need one. Not that she had trouble paying for the apartment on her own. Riley came from a family as rich as Colton's and Maddox's. Sure, she hated using her family's money, but she had a trust fund with multiple zeros.

Riley was a bit of a recluse, like me.

Sure, we had a lot of girls approaching us, but we quickly realized they didn't want to be *our* friends; their end game had been getting to either Maddox or Colton.

"Colton's new place is getting renovated. He's only staying with us for three days," I explained. Colton had moved into one of his parents' townhouses.

He apparently liked his new place better. It was much bigger than our apartment and had a backyard pool, so he was back to hosting his lame parties again. *Pussy and alcohol* – he'd said. *Best. Fucking. Combination.*

My attention flickered to Riley. "So, what happened after that?"

She grimaced. "Something I regret."

Oh shit. OH. SHIT!

"Did you and–"

"No," she practically screeched. "We kissed, that's it. And then I left. Well, *I* kissed *him*. You should have seen the look on his face."

"Was he still naked? When you two kissed?"

She nodded and then chewed on her lip, looking a bit nervous. "It was a moment of weakness. I saw a nice dick, and my vagina was like: *Hello there, Mister. How are you doing today?*"

I coughed back a laugh, as she elbowed me in the stomach, her lower lip jutted out in a pout. "Stop laughing at me. At least you're getting some action."

I grinned, my attention going back to the game. Twenty minutes later, the crowd roared, and I could no longer suppress my own cheer, as I jumped down from the bleachers and ran toward Maddox. He was coming right for me, jogging across the field, with a wicked grin plastered on his face.

The scoreboard read 42-7. Half of those points were from Maddox's touchdowns.

The cheerleaders surrounded him and his teammates, like always. But his attention was all on me. I paused a few feet away, but Maddox didn't make me wait for too long. He pulled away from his harem and sauntered over to me. My gaze darted to the crowd; everyone was watching as MC – their favorite quarterback – made his way to me.

He wiped his forehead with his thumb, and he arched an eyebrow at me, looking way too cocky for his own good. My belly pooled with warmth, and his scrutinizing gaze had me feeling all kinds of hot.

I laughed, as he picked me up, twirled me around once, before he smashed his lips down against mine. I smiled into the kiss, my heart feeling like it would burst at any moment. Maddox shoved his tongue in my mouth, stealing my breath away, as he kissed me *long* and *hard*.

This was our first public display of affection. Sure, we went out on dates, shared a few kisses here and there, but no one had been paying any attention to us. We were a normal couple, on normal dates, doing normal dating things.

Unlike right now…

Everyone's attention was on Maddox Coulter.

They were *all* watching, and I could feel their burning stares on my back, both judging and curious.

My heart hammered in my chest, as Maddox cupped my ass cheeks and hoisted me up, giving me no choice but to wrap my legs around his hips, my ankles hooking right above his ass.

This was a public declaration. A silent confession by Maddox. I was his girl, and he was *mine*.

Sorry, ladies. Maddox Coulter was officially off the market.

My chest heaved, and I was breathless when he pulled away from the kiss, just long enough to grin down at me – a very happy grin – before he claimed my lips once again.

Maddox walked off the field, with our lips still locked in a passionate kiss, one that was driving me utterly insane. Hungry lust gnawed at my stomach, and my thighs clenched around his hips, my clit practically pulsing with need.

"You might end up with a bruised pussy tonight," Maddox muttered. "That's two days of sexual tension."

I nipped his earlobe before my mouth latched on his throat, biting and then soothing the sting with my tongue. "I'll hold you to that."

Maddox groaned when I traced my tongue over his Adam's apple. I knew that was a sensitive spot of his. I let out a small, breathy giggle, and his fingers dug into my ass cheeks. "Minx."

We didn't make it back to our apartment.

Actually, we barely made it back to the car.

I was just glad it was dark enough that no one saw me riding Maddox in the backseat.

Maddox groaned against my lips as he bucked upward, thrusting inside me one last time, before he stilled. His body shuddered as he found his release, and my sex clenched around him. My stomach tightened, as I felt thick ropes of cum filling me.

It was a good thing I never missed my pills.

He buried his head into my chest, as we struggled to catch our breaths. My mind was complete mush, and my body was still shaking from my orgasm.

His hands moved down to my thighs, and he caressed me with the softest of touches. "Give me five minutes, and I'll be ready to go again," he grunted, as he circled my inner thigh with his thumb. He pressed his hand between us, where we were still locked together.

His index finger skated over my clit, and I whimpered. I was still so sensitive after our first round.

"Maddox?" I breathed.

"Hmm?"

"Maybe... we should go home first."

His face was still buried between my breasts, and I felt him inhale. His hard length twitched inside me. "I'm happy right here. Tucked away inside your pussy. Ain't moving, Babe."

"Are we going to spend the night here?" I questioned with a small laugh.

"No," he said, raising his hips to give me a half-thrust. Just enough to remind me that he was still inside me, semi-hard. "But I'm way too comfortable right now to move. Fuck, Lila. You're tight and so soft."

My hand curled around his neck, and I pressed my face into the curve of his shoulder. He smelled sweaty, musky with the fresh smell of grass. His favorite cologne lingered around his manly scent. I licked my lips and tasted the remnants of his minty kisses.

My stomach did stupid, silly somersaults, and my heart squeezed.

God, I still couldn't believe it, still couldn't wrap my head around the simple fact: Maddox was *mine*.

I no longer felt any uncertainty about it, but fuck it, my feelings for him still scared me shitless. I wondered if he felt the same way.

But then I felt silly.

Of course, he felt the same. I often caught him looking at me, his blue eyes smiling and warm with affection.

Sure, we never said those three little words to each other, but I liked to believe it wasn't needed. Not yet, at least.

While I didn't doubt Maddox's feelings for me, we were still so new. I wanted our first time saying those three words to each other, and it was probably the romantic in me speaking, but I wanted it to be *special*.

Maddox tucked stray hair behind my ear, and his lips caressed my temple. "You're so goddamn beautiful, Lila," he said in his deep, raspy voice.

My chest fluttered, and my eyes closed, as I shoved my face into his chest and inhaled. I was addicted to him and his scent. It was like I wanted to breathe him in, all the time. Who knew you could get addicted to someone's smell? That was so weird, but damn my hormones.

It scared me. Being so addicted to him.

God, it scared me *shitless*.

And this was why…

"Maddox?"

He hummed. "What?"

"Can you promise me something?"

"Babe, I'm dick deep inside your soft pussy. You can ask me anything right now, and I'd say 'yes,' before you can finish your sentence."

I gave him an internal eyeroll. Of course, I should have known he'd spout some shit like that. Maddox had a one-track mind.

I breathed in a ragged breath, preparing myself for what I was about to say. There was a sudden, hard lump lodged in my throat.

His fingers smoothed down my back, as if he could sense my worry. "What is it, Lila?"

I loved the way he said my name.

I loved the way he touched me.

I loved the way…

I loved…

Keeping my eyes closed and my face buried in his chest, I spoke, "If you ever get tired of this… *tell me*."

Maddox's hand paused on my back. "*This?*"

"Us," I whispered.

He was silent for far too long. My lungs squeezed, until I suddenly couldn't breathe. "Why are you so quiet?"

"I'm thinking…"

Did I just mess this up? "What are you thinking about?"

Maddox's head lowered, and his hot breath feathered across my cheek, sending another round of shivers down my spine. "I'm thinking… that maybe I didn't fuck you hard enough, just now, if you're doubting this… *us…*"

Oh, God.

His hand came up, and he gripped my jaw, lifting my head up. His teeth scraped along the column of my throat. I squeezed my eyes closed. "What do you want, Lila?"

That question again...

"You," I gasped.

His hand inched down to the base of my throat. My breath hitched when he wrapped his fingers around my dreamcatcher. The necklace I never took off. *Our* dreamcatcher.

"Ask me what I want." There was a hard command in his voice, thick and deep.

I swallowed, my tongue feeling heavy in my mouth, and I could barely push the words out. "What do you want?"

"*You*," Maddox murmured.

His thick length hardened inside me, twitching, and he gave me a slow thrust. "Look at me," he grunted. My eyes snapped open. Darkness casted a shadow on his face and oh my, the *look* in his eyes.

It was downright territorial and predatory. "Ask me again."

"What do you want, Maddox?"

"You," he said. "Never, ever doubt my feelings for you again, little dragon. Next time, I'll whip your ass."

I gasped, and my ass clenched at the threat. "You wouldn't dare."

"Try me," he challenged, with a dark look.

"I don't doubt you, Maddox. But I need you to promise me something."

Maddox waited patiently for me to continue. Damn him, for being so sweet... so understanding... so patient with my overthinking self.

"You'll never lie to me. You'll never keep secrets from me." I brought my hand up and showed him my pinky. "Promise?"

Maddox's face darkened, flashing with an unreadable expression, but it was gone too quickly for me to consider it. He wrapped his pinky around mine. "Promise."

I leaned forward and pressed my lips against his. His chest rumbled with a deep sound in response.

Maddox was the person my dad told me about. "Always choose the person who makes your heart beat a thousand miles an hour," he had said to me. I remembered telling Maddox that I didn't want to ever fall in love.

Because I wasn't strong enough to lose yet another person in my life.

That was four years ago.

And now…

Daddy, I found him. Wherever you are, if you're watching over me… I found my person like you found mom.

CHAPTER EIGHT

Lila

I took the pumpkin pie out of the oven, fresh and hot, as Gran set the table. The pie, with its walnut crust, was Maddox's favorite, and I always made sure it was for dessert, as often as I could.

You'd think Gran was feeding an army with all the food, but there were only four of us. She placed her famous pulled pork, made in her newly acquire instant pot, in the middle of the table, as Pops and Maddox joined us. My chest filled with warmth at the sight of the two of them together.

The two most important men in my life. I was just glad they got along so well.

Maddox met my gaze, and the pit of my stomach fluttered. It was some cosmic reaction I couldn't explain because we didn't need words; we just looked at each other and smiled.

This was my favorite time of the year. Only because I got to go back home to visit my grandparents since it was Gran's birthday. It also happened to be Maddox's favorite too because of two things: food, and, even though he'd never admit it, he loved the feeling of being part of our little family.

Maddox took a seat beside me, and a smile hovered over my lips, when he grasped my hand under the table. After Pops said grace, and before we could dig into our food, Maddox cleared his throat. "Lila and I have something to say."

My head snapped up, and I dropped my fork onto my plate with a loud clank. The room went utterly silent as my grandparents watched us with wide, curious expressions.

This wasn't part of the plan! We had agreed to tell my grandparents *after*, just so we could spend this night in peace. I squeezed Maddox's hand in warning, but it was too late.

Pops placed his elbows on the table and leaned forward, giving both of us his undivided attention. He was giving us his famous military look; hard, unflinching, and frighteningly serious. "Go on."

My knees bounced, and I was suddenly glad Maddox had waited until we were sitting down. My gaze flickered around the room, looking for my grandpa's hunting rifle that was on the wall next to the fireplace. Maybe I should have hid it when I got back home. *Oh God!*

Gran looked around nervously, as if sensing the growing tension around us.

"Maybe we should eat first," I stuttered. "We have all the time to talk after dinner, right?"

Pops barely spared me a glance. His hard gaze was fixated on the man beside me – my boyfriend. My soon-to-be-dead boyfriend.

My hands grew clammy, as coldness seeped through my bones. My stomach started cramping, and it was almost worse than period pains.

Maybe if Maddox and I made a run for it–

"Lila and I are dating, Sir."

Nope. Never mind, we don't have time to run for it.

"Oh. Is that true, Lila?" Pops asked, still staring Maddox down. *Could the ground open up and swallow me, please?*

I felt faint and ended up nodding silently, a small, shy nod. Gran came to my rescue. "That's wonderful news. You two complement each other very well." She cleared her throat, when Pops didn't back her up. "How long have you two been dating for?"

"About three months," Maddox confirmed, his voice steady. How was he not shitting his pants with my grandpa staring daggers into him?

"Lila?" Pops finally leveled me with a look, the same one he'd give me when I was little, and I did something bad, as he waited for me to confess.

But I wasn't a little girl anymore.

Although I still respected my grandpa, I was a grown woman who was happy with her boyfriend. I straightened my spine and swallowed past the lump in my throat.

He raised me to be confident and strong, whatever the situation was. Sure, my legs still felt weak, like mush, and my lungs were squeezing so tightly I wondered if I was really breathing, but I returned my grandpa's look with an unflinching one of my own.

"What Maddox said is true. We've been dating for about three months," I said. "Pops, I'm really, very...*happy*."

His demeanor changed the moment the word spilled from my lips. He settled back in his chair, and the corner of his lips twitched. Pops gave Maddox and I both a look, one I couldn't exactly read, before he glanced at Gran. "Took them long enough, don't you think?"

"*Shit*," Maddox muttered under his breath, and he squeezed my hand so hard I thought he was going to break my bones. I grimaced, and it was then I realized he was just as nervous and scared as me.

Gran smiled. "I honestly thought you two were dating for a very long time. We were just waiting for you to tell us."

My breath expelled from my chest in a loud whoosh, and I went slack against my chair. The tension around the table eased up, and the air became less suffocating. "Wait, so you guys… *knew*?"

Pops shrugged. "It was a guess before. You confirmed it now."

"So, you're okay with this?" I questioned slowly.

"Are you asking for our blessing?" Pops cocked an eyebrow at me, but he was… *smiling*. "You have it. As long as you're happy." I sat there, slack-mouthed. Holy shit, my grandpa, who was a very hard man to impress, was smiling at the fact that I was dating Maddox Coulter. Yeah, I must have fallen into another universe.

He turned to Maddox, his dark eyes hardening. "I don't have to warn you because you already know what will happen if you ever hurt my little girl. You might be young, healthy and probably stronger, but I can still whoop your ass, Son."

Maddox laced our fingers together and gave me a gentle squeeze. He returned my grandpa's stare with one of his own: confident and self-assured, so Maddox. If it wasn't for how sweaty and clammy his hand was, with a slight twitching in his fingers, I wouldn't have been able to tell if he was nervous or not.

"Sir, Lila's happiness means as much to me as it does to you. I know you know that. You raised her and took care of her when she needed you the most. Now, it's my turn," he said.

My chest fluttered, and my womb tingled with fuzzy warmth, as the same feeling spread throughout my whole body. I made a sound in the back of my throat, both happy and in warning. "Um, excuse me. I can take care of myself, thank you very much."

Pops let out a small laugh, and my chest expanded with emotions I couldn't place. "Good luck, Son. This one is very feisty, just like her grandma."

Gran blushed, and Maddox chuckled. "Don't worry. I can handle her."

The worry I felt before melted away, as we turned to our food. The rest of the dinner was just like any other Thanksgiving. If I had thought announcing our relationship would change anything, I was mistaken. This was *my* family.

Three hours later, Maddox and I found ourselves in my room. He was supposed to be sleeping on the couch, but we sneaked him upstairs, after my grandparents went to bed.

"I'm so full, I feel like I'm going to burst." I patted my stomach, feeling my food baby. I probably gained five pounds from tonight's dinner. And there was Maddox, still looking fresh and sinfully handsome, like he had just walked out of a Vogue magazine.

I settled on my bed, bouncing on the mattress, as I watched him pull off his shirt in one swift move. He dropped the shirt on the floor and stood there for a second, letting me enjoy the very distracting view.

I took my time to admire him, to truly look at him. His abs clenched as he sauntered over to me. His nipple piercings got my attention next, and I licked my lips, remembering how the silver rods felt on my tongue. My gaze moved up to his wide shoulders that were twice the size of mine and then his face. Sharp jawline that you could probably cut your finger with, full lips, a strong nose with a slight crook – he told me he broke it when he was thirteen years old. Hooded blue eyes, thick eyebrows, with a scar on the left one – he was injured two years ago during a football game.

When he grinned, his dimple popped in his right cheek, a deep indent. His smile was wolfish, looking hungry, as he stood in front of me.

He bent forward, placing his arms on either side of my thighs on the mattress. "Admiring the view, Babe?"

His hot breath caressed my cheek. I *had* been admiring the view, but I also came to a conclusion.

Maddox wasn't beautiful by definition. Sure, he was hot and sexy...but he was an imperfect canvas, riddled with invisible scars and flaws no one else could see, except *me*.

That made him imperfectly beautiful.

My hand came up, and I traced a finger around his left pectoral. Maddox tensed as my touch brushed across his nipples. I knew all of his sensitive spots. He loved his throat – especially his prominent Adam's apple, to be kissed and sucked on. It got him rock hard when I'd scrape my teeth over his nipples.

"Careful, Garcia," he groaned. "I might be too hot for you to touch, you might end up with a nasty burn."

I rolled my eyes. "That was extremely cheesy, Coulter. It's almost nauseating."

Maddox pushed me onto my back and crawled over me. "What? You prefer my asshole side to my cheesy, romantic side?"

I liked all of his sides. The asshole Maddox; the furious and ugly side of him; the pretty cocky side; and especially, his romantic side. But I wasn't about to tell him that.

Maddox rolled over and took me with him. I settled against his side, burying my head in the crook of his neck. His thumb circled over the flesh of my hips, where my shirt had ridden up and around the waistband of my jeans. We cuddled for what felt like hours and hours. I listened to his breathing and watched his chest rise and fall with every breath.

"Are you ready for your driving test tomorrow?" Maddox finally broke the silence.

My chest squeezed, and it felt like the flesh around my scars had tightened. There was a dull, uncomfortable ache around them – the pain, a ghostly echo. I rubbed a hand over my chest, but my skin was on fire.

I took in a shuddering breath and closed my eyes. "I'm ready."

"Are you sure about this, Lila?" Maddox asked softly. I knew he was worried, but he was also the same person who stood by me as I struggled to get into the driver's seat for the last six months.

He was relentlessly patient with me, as I suffered panic attack after panic attack. It took me a month to finally get myself in the driver's seat and then another three months for Maddox to teach me how to drive.

I told myself I could do it. as long as he was beside me.

I wanted to conquer my fears, wanted to leave my past behind. Truly and fully move on…

My scars throbbed harder, and I squeezed my eyes shut.

His hands smoothed up and down my back, ever so supportive and gentle. "Yeah, I'm ready. I'm going to pass this test."

"I don't doubt that for a second, little dragon."

Little dragon…

Only Maddox could handle my fire... my scars... my pain... He was the mirror to my soul.

My lips twitched with a smile, and the fire burning in my chest slowly dissipated.

Maddox

I never understood why they invited me for dinner when it was going to be like this. Icy cold silence… and they didn't even acknowledge their son was sitting right there.

Father Dearest sat at the head of the table, while Mommy Dearest and I sat across from each other. She could barely meet my eyes, her focus on her plate, as she very primly cut her steak into little bites.

Brad, my father, didn't even breathe in my direction. The only sound echoing around the frigid walls of the dining room was our cutlery against our fancy as fuck plates.

My throat closed, and it felt…*suffocating*.

The difference between my Thanksgiving dinner with Lila's family and tonight with my own was vast.

I didn't know why I still fucking tried. I hated this place. Loathed the idea of our 'perfect family' to the outside world, while it was anything but. I long gave up on the idea of us being even slightly happy.

My parents' marriage was probably anything but happy, too. I wouldn't be surprised if I found out they weren't even sleeping in the same room.

With a mansion as big as this one, the distance between us grew even bigger. When I used to live here, I was an outsider and a burden.

Now that I had left for Harvard, I was still an outsider. To my parents, I barely existed… except, I was their heir and their legacy to the Coulter's name and empire. That was probably the only reason why Brad hadn't disowned me yet.

Yeah, fuck them.

I shoveled my food in my mouth, barely chewing. Swallowing it down with water, I finished my plate, before they were even halfway through theirs.

I pushed my chair out and stood up without a word. My mother's head snapped up, and her eyes flared in surprise. "You're leaving?" she stuttered, looking warily between my father and I.

Oh, for fuck's sake, where was her goddamn backbone?

"Maddox," she started, but then trailed off. She was looking at me like a sad, lost puppy.

My jaw hardened, and I clenched my teeth. "What?"

"Why don't you stay for a little while longer? Your father and I–"

I cut in. "Don't waste your breath, *Mother*."

She opened her mouth, but was cut off, when my father started coughing. Her eyes widened, and there was a flash of fear in them, as she jumped to her feet and rushed to his side. He brought his pristine, white handkerchief to his mouth and continued coughing, his chest rattling with the harsh sounds.

"Brad," Savannah breathed quietly, looking slightly pained.

My fists clenched at my sides, and I fought the urge to run, to walk out of these iron gates and never come back. This place smelled nothing like comfort or joy – it was a death trap.

His coughing fit ceased, and he straightened his back. "Maddox, I want to speak with you. Come to my office," he said, in his usual hard voice. There was no familiarity or warmth in his words, like a father should speak to his son. He spoke to me like I was one of the people on his goddamn payroll.

He stood up and walked away, without waiting for me to follow. I was already taking a step back, refusing to follow his goddamn orders.

"*Please*," Mommy dearest mouthed.

My feet paused, and I cracked my neck, squeezing my lips together. The muscles in my chest tightened, and against my own accord, my legs took me toward my father's office.

I walked inside to find him sitting behind his desk. He nodded toward the whiskey bottle on the tray. "Have a drink?"

I let out a small, humorless laugh. Yeah, if I had to survive this *talk* with my father, I definitely needed a drink. I poured a glass full and downed it quickly, feeling the burn in my throat, and my eyes watered.

"I spoke with your coach last week," he started.

"Keeping tabs on me?" I snorted in amusement.

His eyes hardened. "He said you were one of his best players. That's good to know."

Praise... from Brad Coulter? Hmm. I wasn't about to fall in that trap. I could barely remember the last time my father said something remotely nice to me. I had been... maybe five or six years old? That was almost two decades ago.

He cocked his head to the side. "I heard you're dating Lila," he deadpanned. "You didn't tell us."

I placed the empty glass on his desk, and my fists clenched. There was a reason why I never brought Lila here. I wanted to keep her far away from the toxicity that was my parents. They didn't deserve to breathe the same air as her. "Is this why we're here? To talk about my dating life?

C'mon, Father. That's beneath you."

My father was silent for a moment. I didn't want to play his game, I really didn't.

I grasped the bottle of whiskey in my hand and took a step back, raising the bottle up in mock salute. "Nice talk, Brad."

His nostrils flared at the blatant disrespect, but I was already walking away, without waiting for his response. My heart hammered in my chest, my skin crawling and itching with the need to get away from him, from this suffocating place.

His next words halted me, my feet coming to a sudden stop.

"Don't hurt her."

My back snapped straight, and I swiveled around to face him, a low snarl on my lips. "I would *never*," I hissed. "I'm not you."

He stood up, calmly, and it grated my nerves. I hated the pacifying look on his face, like he actually FUCKING CARED.

"No, Maddox. You're not me," my father agreed, almost like he was relieved about that idea. "But you also don't realize you're on the path of self-destruction. You'll end up hurting Lila in the end, Son. And do you know who will hurt the most? *You.*"

Fury burned through my veins like acid. My blood roared furiously in my ears; it was almost deafening. The sick feeling in my stomach was back, and I fought the urge to throw up. In the moment, I didn't even realize he called me *son*. I was too angry, filled with so much loathing at the person who was supposed to be my dad.

Lila was the one good thing in my life.

And he wanted me to give her up.

If, for one second, I thought my father cared… that brief notion was gone, before it even fully came to be.

"Thanks for the pep talk, *Dad*. I'll keep that in mind," I sneered, before stalking away.

My mother was outside the door, and I walked into her, practically slamming into her small frame. Her eyes blurred, and she reached for me, but I side-stepped her.

"Maddox," she called out.

I didn't stop, didn't pause, until I was out of the iron gates.

I was done listening.

Done trying to be the son they wanted.

I. Was. Fucking. Done.

CHAPTER NINE

Lila

Maddox had been... quiet. Which was unusual. His cocky, arrogant attitude had been replaced with a brooding, silent Maddox. He looked like he was lost in his thoughts, and it had been three days since we returned to school from our visit to my grandparents'. We were back to our regular schedule and classes, but the Maddox, who returned with me, was not the same who left for the long weekend a week ago.

"I've never seen you stare at a business textbook so hard," I said, placing my elbows on the table and leaning forward. We were sitting in a quiet corner in the library, and it was one of our late-night studying sessions. But I'd bet he wasn't even focusing on the text he was supposed to be reading. His eyes barely moved across the paragraphs, and he was still on the same page for the last thirty minutes.

I could be overthinking again, but...

Something wasn't right. Something was up with him.

I had been watching him carefully for the past three days, waiting to catch a glimpse of my Maddox behind the silent mask he now wore. He touched me, kissed and fucked me… but something was different.

Our love making was rough and quick. There wasn't much to complain about, since he still made me feel good, but I missed his tender touch, his sweet kisses, his soft words.

I missed him making love to me.

I missed *my* Maddox.

Dread washed through me as I started overthinking the situation. My head told me he was tired of me. Maddox wasn't the relationship type, and maybe, he realized this was a mistake. My heart argued with that fact, refusing to believe Maddox would be so careless with my feelings.

Maddox blinked at me, then scowled. "Sorry, I don't understand shit," he muttered, shoving his textbook away and slamming his laptop closed.

That was definitely *not* Maddox. He wasn't a genius, but he was a smart student and on top of his classes. He worked relentlessly to keep both his football scholarship and his grades up where they needed to be.

"I'd help, but I'm more of a chemistry person," I teased, nodding toward my own textbook, which was filled with highlighted paragraphs and pages. My yellow highlighter laid next to my laptop.

My heart withered when Maddox barely cracked a smile. His muscular neck corded with tension, and he looked a little… *lost*. Maybe angry. Something was terribly wrong, and I didn't know what to do. "What is it?" I asked slowly.

His shoulders went rigid, and his jaw hardened. I could practically hear his grinding molars. His blue eyes, deep as an ocean that I could easily drown in, and I… *did*, were fixated on mine.

"Is there something you need to tell me?" The knot in my chest began to build, growing tighter and tighter around my lungs.

Talk to me, Baby.

Maddox shook his head. "There's nothing to tell. I'm just so fucking

485

exhausted and stressed about the upcoming midterms."

Lies. He was lying...

And when he lied... he didn't meet my eyes.

"Maddox–"

"Maddox?" I turned to face the voice who cut me off.

Bianca.

What the hell was she doing here? The last time I saw her was at the club six months ago, where she threw a bitch tantrum after Maddox 'broke-up' with her. Not that they were ever dating, but she was slightly delusional.

Out of all his conquests, Maddox liked Bianca the most. Or I thought so...

She was the one who lasted the longest, and the only one who got away telling the whole university they were dating, and he never put a stop to it. Until he threw her to the curb after the bitch fit.

I looked for any bitchy signs, but her face was smooth, and she *actually* looked shocked at the sight of us. So, this wasn't a planned encounter.

This library on campus was open twenty-four hours, but, late as it was now, there was barely anyone here, except for a few students scattered around each study corner.

I waited for Bianca's sneers and drama, but she gave us none of that.

It was then I noticed, she looked completely different than her usual appearance. Bianca always looked like she had just walked out of *Vogue* magazine or she belonged on a billboard.

She had bare-minimum makeup on her face, her curly blonde hair, which was always perfectly styled, was in a messy bun, and she was wearing... a baggy sweater and yoga pants. Bianca looked pale, and it was a weird combination, since she always looked her best.

Her eyes bounced between Maddox and I, before she plastered a fake-ass smile on her face. "Long time no see." She was definitely *not* speaking to me. "You look... good. Um, did you get my text?"

Her text? She was texting him...? Bitter jealousy clawed its way to my throat, and my chest burned with it. Was this why he was so distracted the last few days? Like he had something else on his mind and barely... speaking to me.

I knew Maddox had a lot of fuck buddies; although none of them were his girlfriends, they still *had* him. Whether it was briefly or not.

I had decided to look past it... but I wasn't okay with them hanging around him or *texting* him. Maddox had told me he blocked most of them.

Bianca eyed my man, and I didn't like how she was acting like I wasn't even there.

I convinced myself I wasn't a jealous person.

But I felt... bitter and angry. The mere thought of Bianca texting Maddox, even though she knew he was taken and after they ended on such a bad term, had me wanting to claw her eyes out. The little dragon as Maddox liked to say, red and fierce, that lived inside my chest, rattled against my rib cage and wanted to be let out.

I was really trying to not let any negative thoughts get to me, but it was hard, as the little dragon grew bigger and bigger inside me, but she, thankfully, held her fire.

The only relief I got was that Maddox barely spared her a glance. He looked down at his textbook again, thumbing through the pages. "I got your text, and I didn't find a reason to reply. As you can see, Lila and I are busy right now."

Bianca's expression fell, and she finally glanced at me. "I think," she started, suddenly looking nervous, "I should apologize for how I acted last time."

I blinked, slack-mouthed. Was she on drugs? Or high? Bianca was *apologizing,* and she actually looked remorseful.

I cleared my throat. "You should. You were awful and extremely rude."

She gasped, as if she wasn't expecting me to agree. I gave her an internal eyeroll. If she was expecting me to sugarcoat things for her… Yeah, right. Not. Going. To. Happen.

Her face flushed, and she chewed on her lower lip. Where was the high and mighty Bianca? This one was nothing like her.

"You're right," she admitted. *"I'm sorry."*

Maddox grunted in response, and I sat there, speechless. Bianca fidgeted with her hands, as she waited for me to give her some kind of reaction. I sat forward in my chair and leveled her with a hard look. "I don't do well with name-calling, and if I remember correctly, you called me a *bitch,* for no reason whatsoever," I told her bluntly.

Her face turned red, and she opened her mouth as if to speak, but I cut her off. "The last girl who called me a bitch, I broke her nose."

That was in high school, back when I had to defend myself against wealthy, filthy rich princesses who thought everyone had to bow down to them. Ha, right.

Bianca's throat bobbed with a hard swallow. Once I was sure she got my message, my lips widened with a smile. "Apology accepted. Have a good day," I dismissed her.

Maddox raised his head, gave her a final stare – his eyes darkened, and his face flashed with an unreadable expression. Like he wanted to say something, but he was too angry to. He was so confusing!

As soon as she stepped away from our little corner, my nerves eased up, but I was still strung tight with… strong, vivid emotions. *Jealousy.*

God, I loathed that word.

It made me feel insecure.

And… small.

Like, I wasn't good enough or… I didn't *think* I was good enough.

I hated, *hated* feeling like that. Especially after the way Maddox had been acting lately.

"She texted you?" I blurted out, but then winced. My annoyance had been so evident in my tone that I flushed. I was acting unreasonable, I told myself.

"She did, a few times. I didn't reply," Maddox responded.

A few times? But why... why now? He and Bianca were long over, and she had moved on to the next available man.

My chest squeezed. "Oh."

Maddox made a sound at the back of his throat, a deep rumble coming from his chest. My head snapped up, as he pushed his chair backward and leaned back. His eyes explored me lazily, and his lips twitched with a cocky grin. His whole demeanor changed. Gone was brooding Maddox.

I was about to get a whiplash with all his mood changes.

"You're jealous," he deadpanned.

"Excuse... me?" I sputtered.

He grinned harder. "You were practically spitting fire."

Even though that might have been true, I was outraged he brought it up like this. Especially after acting so shitty the last few days. "I wasn't... *jealous*. I just don't like the fact that your ex is texting you."

"She's not my ex."

"Right, she was just a fuck buddy." As if that made it any better.

"So, that was you pissing all over your territory?" Maddox smiled crookedly, and my cheeks heated up.

God, did he have to be so blunt...?

"Don't be an asshole," I hissed.

"You look cute when you're pissed, Garcia." My teeth rattled at his teasing tone, but I chose to ignore the bait. Looking back down at my textbook, I thumbed through the pages.

From the corner of my eye, I saw Maddox moving. He dragged his chair closer and next to me. Great, *now* he wanted to talk.

First, he acted so strangely the last couple of days, making me question everything. Then, here he was... teasing and being cocky like nothing else mattered. Maddox Coulter was complicated, and I accepted

489

that fact a long time ago.

I belatedly noticed that the subject had changed. He still hadn't told me what was wrong… I didn't know if he was going to admit to anything, before Bianca interrupted us. And now the moment was gone… and Maddox was in the mood to play.

I wanted to fall for it… his teasing, his charms, his dorky side. But I couldn't stop the nagging feeling in my chest. The prick of unease and creeping worry burrowed itself under my skin.

I asked him not to keep secrets, but I knew he was hiding something. I just knew.

Maddox settled beside me, and my body twitched at how close he was. His scent and warmth wrapped around me, like a safe cocoon.

His leg pressed against mine, and my back straightened when his hand landed on my thigh. His hot breath skated on my neck, as he leaned close, putting his mouth right next to my ear. "Why are you so mad, little dragon?"

"Why are you lying to me?" I retorted.

Maddox tensed for a brief second, before his fingers started to inch upward, toward the apex of my thighs. "Why do you think I'm lying?"

"Something is wrong, I can tell." My eyes dared him to deny it, to lie to my face again.

Maddox didn't reply. He leaned in, and his lips skimmed over the column of my throat, his intention clear. His hand cupped my sex through my jeans. A breathy hiss escaped past my clenched teeth. "We're… in the library. Someone could see, Maddox!"

"Being in a public place never stopped you before," he grunted against my skin. His teeth scraped across my flesh, and I let out an involuntary shudder. "Spread your legs for me, Lila."

I really shouldn't; I really, *really* shouldn't have.

But I did. Because I needed him, because I wanted to feel like he was *mine*.

"That's a good girl," he praised. His lips and teeth dragged along my neck, suckling and biting on the soft, tender flesh. I let out a little whimper, as he unbuttoned my jeans and shoved his hand inside. I shivered almost violently, as my gaze swept around the quiet library.

His fingers teased my wet slit through my panties, before he nudged the thin fabric aside.

"Why are you doing this?" I breathed.

"You tell me."

"Because you love to torture me."

His tongue licked a tantalizing trail of desire up my neck and another shiver rolled down my spine. My toes curled in my shoes.

"No," Maddox said, his voice taking a deeper undertone. "Because you look so fucking cute when you're jealous, and I just want to eat you up and watch you come."

He shoved a finger inside me, and I *gasped*.

My back arched, and my eyes squeezed shut at the sudden penetration. I was wet and ready, as the single digit slid in and out of me. My sex tightened around the intrusion, as he slowly pushed a second finger into me. "And that's exactly what you're going to do for me. You're going to sit here, with your legs spread, and you're going to let me finger you because you *want* it. Because you *like* being my naughty, naughty girl."

In frantic need, I reached out for him, and my fingers dug into his thigh. He hissed and then chuckled. "Can you hear how wet you are?" he teased in my ear. "Feel how wet you are…"

Jesus Christ!

"You love being fucked in public, like the dirty little minx you are." Maddox taunting did nothing but heighten my arousal, causing a warm fuzziness in my stomach and a pool of desire gathering between my thighs. "Your pussy is practically begging for my cock. Feel how tight it is around my fingers, how hard it's clenching and seeking for something harder and bigger."

Soaked… needy… gasping… wanting…

His thumb circled around my clit, and he rubbed me, as I ground my core against his hand. I wanted to be reminded that I belonged to him, that he was mine.

Wanton need filled me, as I rode his fingers, shamelessly, in a public library where anyone could have caught us. Maddox made me lose control and all sense of decency. He made me want filthy things; he made me crave him in the most dangerous way. My core tightened, and I locked eyes with him.

My heart thudded.

Maddox's expression was hard with lust, his blue eyes flashing with molten desire. He looked at me like I was the most beautiful thing ever, and when his gaze lowered between my legs, I let out a small whimper.

His fingers curled inside me, hitting the sweet, sensitive spot that had my eyes rolling back in my head. Maddox let out a grunt, before his lips attacked mine. "Lila," he rasped into the kiss. "You." *Kiss.* "Drive." *Kiss.* "Me." *Kiss.* "Fucking." *Kiss.* "Crazy."

The feeling was mutual.

The buildup to my orgasm was quick, and I almost groaned in disappointment, because I had wanted it to last. I wanted him to keep his hand between my legs, and his lips on mine.

A loud groan escaped past my full lips when he ground the heel of his palm against my clit. A storm brewed inside of me, hot and intense. My fingers wrapped around his wrist of the same hand he was using on me. My nails dug into his flesh so hard, I was sure I drew blood.

"Oh God, Maddox!" His mouth slammed against mine, swallowing my moans, before anyone could hear them. I almost bit his tongue, as I shuddered and writhed against the fullness of his fingers inside me. He strummed and played with every nerve in my body like he owned them.

"Come for me," Maddox said, his voice low. A hot wave of pleasure zinged through me, before crashing like a rough, violent tide.

His thrusts were brutal, relentless, as he brought me to the brink of orgasm.

I fell. *Hard.* I landed. *Harder.* I cried out and wept into his kiss, as I found my release, my whole body spasming. The intensity of my climax blinded me for mere seconds, before the world fell into balance again.

I came down from my high, my vision blurring and my heart hammering into my rib cage. My body was still twitching from the aftermath of my orgasm. Maddox groaned and pulled away from the kiss. My lips felt tender and swollen.

He pulled out of me and stroked my folds gently, before he brought his hand up to my mouth. His eyes were dark and daring; he waited. My lips parted and wrapped around his wet, glistening fingers. The taste of my own arousal took me by surprise; my clit swelled and pulsed. This was so... *dirty*, but I licked his fingers clean.

"Good girl," he praised in a low rasp. I hummed in response, as Maddox cupped the back of my head and *kissed* me. I forgot where he started and I began or whose air I was breathing. His or mine. My heart missed its beats.

This kiss was pure... raw... so intense, it bled through us, sinking under our flesh and into our bones. If *this* ever came to an end, I'd never forget the feel of his lips on mine. Strong, full, needy. *Mine.*

Mine.

Mine.

Maddox sucked out all the oxygen from my lungs, until I was gasping and breathless.

His kiss slowed, and my heart beat faster, thudding like a raging violin, screeching and loud. "I'm yours, Lila. Every part of me is yours," he whispered.

I wanted to believe him... and I did. Maybe that was foolish of me...

I had a weakness for Maddox. "Do you promise to tell me if something is wrong?" I asked softly, my voice barely audible. He had my fragile heart in the palm of his hand, and he could crush it, so easily, with a simple squeeze.

"Lila." My name was a gentle whisper on his lips. "I'll never hurt you, not willingly, not intentionally."

When his mouth claimed mine again, I felt him breathe something on my lips. But I didn't catch it, and I was too lost in his kiss to care.

I believed him.

Maddox would never hurt me.

Not intentionally.

He was my best friend, after all.

And that was the exact reason why he had the power to destroy me.

CHAPTER TEN

Maddox

L ila Garcia was a minx, through and through.

A dirty, fucking minx who loved to torture me. Payback, she said. Payback for teasing her in the library, payback for daring her to come in public…

My little dragon was quite the vixen.

Lila loved every minute of it, was practically soaking through her panties at the mere thought of my fingers inside her.

And now she was playing hard to get.

I remembered the smirk on her face when she dared me three days ago. *You can't touch me. Not until I tell you to. I dare you.*

Lila had me chasing after her, practically begging for my cock to be relieved, but she wouldn't relent. She had me in a perpetual state of blue balls for three days.

She found every way to get me hard and aching for her. I'd been jacking off three times a day, just so I could handle all the goddamn teasing.

Doing her morning stretches, in her tight yoga pants that stretched over her ass like a second skin, she'd deliberately bend over, touch her toes and wiggle her juicy ass when I'd walked past her. Yeah, that *almost* made me snap.

Or the time she decided to clean the whole apartment only wearing a shirt and panties that barely covered her pink pussy and ass. Oh, and no bra. Her nipples had been poking through the thin layer of her shirt all damn day. I almost busted a nut in my sweatpants.

Lila was well-skilled in the art of torture, and fuck me, I lived for every bit of it.

Loved her teasing smirk... and her gentle smile.

Loved her clawing at my back like a tigress when I fucked her... loved her soft lips on my chest and her sweet caress.

Loved her intelligent brain... loved her dangerous mind.

Her strong will, her unbroken determination. Like two weeks ago...

Lila Garcia was absolutely terrified of cars and driving. But my girl? My fucking girl got her own license. It was a way of getting over her fear, she said.

She did it. I remembered rather fondly. With a confident smile, a fierce attitude and a slight sway of her hips as she had walked over to me and announced she passed her driving test.

Lila was my good days. and the reason my cold heart wasn't so cold anymore. She was my better half, the perfect combination of angel and she-devil. A mess of gorgeous chaos and beautiful brown eyes, black hair and red lips.

Maybe God – if there really was one, created her just for me. My soulmate. My missing piece...

Oh damn, she was turning me into a cheesy romantic and trashy poet.

But fuck me, I was so goddamn weak at the knees for her.

For her... I'd risk it all.

I walked into our apartment and found all the lights off. "Lila?" I called out.

Taking off my shoes at the door, I left my shoulder bag there and walked farther into the apartment. Our bedroom door was slightly ajar, and the lights were on. I pushed the door open and practically stumbled at the sight in front of me.

I blinked, slack-mouthed, and then choked on my groan.

Lila, the minx, was spread eagle, on our bed, with a fucking wand vibrator between her legs. Her back arched off the bed, and she let out a soft moan. At the sound of my answering growl, her eyes fluttered open, and she gave me a hooded look. Her face was a mask of pleasure, on the brick of orgasm.

I stalked forward, my cock already rock hard. The musky scent of her pussy juices was heavy in the room, and I twitched in my jeans. Goddamn it, this woman was going to be the death of me.

Death by pussy. Yeah, it'd be a sweet death, that's for sure.

"What are you doing, Lila?" I asked, my voice gritty and rough to my own ears.

She smiled at me, coyly. "Coming."

I stopped by the edge of the bed, and my eyes lowered between her thighs. I almost growled at the sight of her red, swollen cunt. She kept the wand on her clit, moving it in a small circular motion. Her juices ran down and coated the bedsheet under her. "How many times have you come already?"

Her teeth caught her bottom lip, and she bit down, holding back another needy whimper. "Once… and… Oh, God, I'm about to… *again*."

Her legs were shaking, as she raised her hips, grinding against the wand like she would do to my cock. "Oh, oh… Maddox, Oh God… *Maddox*!"

My control snapped.

With a low snarl, I frantically stripped off my shirt and jeans and crawled on top of Lila. "This ends right fucking now."

Her brown eyes were laced with unadulterated lust, and she grinned wickedly. "You can't touch me," she said. "The dare."

"Fuck the dare," I hissed, slapping her hand away from her greedy cunt. I threw the wand on the floor and spread her thighs around my hips, hooking her ankles behind my ass.

Lila didn't fight me. She just... grinned.

Rubbing my hard length against her folds, my dick was coated with her sweet arousal, and my gaze lowered to the apex of her thighs. I watched as her swollen lips parted, and her opening was practically weeping with need.

She was so fucking primed and ready.

I clutched her waist, squeezing. That was the only warning she got, before I entered her, thrusting inside in one swift move, burying myself to the hilt.

Lila *gasped.* "Fuck."

Fuck, indeed.

My body tensed, the muscles of my back clenching, as I tried not to come from the first thrust. The tight sheath of her pussy was going to kill me. She was so goddamn soft and wet, I easily slid in and out.

"You. Drive. Me. Insane," I snarled, punctuating every word with a hard thrust.

Lila cried out, her eyes fluttering shut. "Open your eyes."

"Maddox."

"Open your eyes, Lila. Look at me." The threat was heavy and thick in my voice.

Her eyes snapped open, and they were glassy with lust. My cock swelled, as I pounded inside her. She curled her arms around my neck and hung on for dear life, whimpering every time I pulled out and moaning with every deep thrust.

Her nails raked my back, clawing at my flesh. I bled for her. Fucking happily.

Our lips found each other, mad with passion. Crazed and desperate.

Her thighs squeezed my hips, and my fingers dug into her waist, so hard, I knew they'd leave my marks. Good. She needed to be reminded who the fuck she belonged to.

And who owned her goddamn orgasms.

My heart thudded in my chest, galloping like a horse in a race.

Lila breathed my name, moaning it over and over again. My balls tightened, and she had a death grip on me, as she twitched and spasmed under me.

She threw her head back, finding her release with a low moan. Lila never looked more beautiful than she did right now.

I came inside her, our eyes locked together. My cum dripped out of her pussy, running down between her quivering thighs and coating the bedsheet with our mixed essence.

Lila buried her face into the crook of my neck, and her teeth scraped the spot behind my ear. "I won," she breathed, with a small breathtaking laugh.

God, I loved her.

I fucking loved her.

"I don't want you to move," Lila confessed in my ear.

I didn't want to move either. My semi-hard dick was quite happy where it was. I rolled us over, and we laid on our sides, keeping us locked together. She pulsed around me, her sex still twitching with the aftermath of her release.

Lila looked at me with sleepy brown eyes and a tender smile. Her black hair was stuck to her sweaty forehead, and she blinked up at me tiredly. Lila still looked so beautiful. *Mine.*

"You kill me," I whispered, my lips brushing the tip of her nose.

"You kill me, too." My chest tightened at her breathy confession.

Our foreheads touched, and my gaze lowered to where her tits were pressed against my chest. Her scars looked red and angry against her glistening, sweaty skin. I traced a single finger over the jagged, harsh lines. She flinched but didn't stop me. Her scars called to me, and I felt the *need* to touch them. Feel them. I ran my fingers over her past, tracing the dents and rough edges of her soul.

Her heart *thudded* against my touch, and I *felt* it. Felt the echoing pain that still lingered in her heart.

"Does it hurt?" I asked, although I already knew the answer.

"Not anymore," Lila replied softly. "Sometimes, it feels like it hurts, not that it really does... but my therapist said that it's all in my head. It's kind of like a ghost pain. My body remembers it, even though my injuries are no longer painful."

Her fingers clasped around my wrist, but she didn't pull my hand away. Actually, she laid my palm over her chest, feeling her stuttering heartbeat. Her skin felt like velvet against my callous fingers, but I kept my touch tender.

"Do you know what hurts the most, Maddox?" She spoke quietly, her voice barely audible.

"Tell me," I rasped. *Tell me everything, Lila. Tell me every bit of your pain and let me carry it for you.*

She let out a small humorless laugh. The pain in her voice was so heavy, my chest tightened in response. "It's the fact that I will never be able to find justice. For myself. For my parents. I've long accepted that fact, but it still pains me."

My head lowered to her breasts, and my lips skimmed over the harsh, white and pink lines. "I'm sorry I wasn't there when you needed me."

Lila dragged her nails through my scalp. "Don't be silly."

"No, I should have found you sooner." I kissed down the length of her scars, brushing over every inch of raised and marked flesh. "If I knew you were out there, I would have come looking for you."

Lila let out a small cry and pulled my head up. Her lips found mine, and I tasted her salty tears through our kiss. *Don't cry, little dragon. Don't cry.*

Her tears were my undoing.

Her pain decimated me.

My heart withered, as she cried softly against my lips. She kissed me like I was the oxygen she needed to live, like I was the very air she breathed.

Our kiss, filled with torment and desperation, burned through my soul and branded me from the inside.

Hours later, I stayed awake, watching Lila sleep. My thumb caressed her bare hips, feeling her soft skin. I couldn't stop touching her, couldn't bring myself to pull away and disconnect our bodies.

My lips feathered across her cheek. "I know you don't need a knight," I said, listening to her slow, even breathing as she slept. "But I want to be your knight. There's a need inside me. A fierce need to protect you. To keep you safe. An intense need that seems to push me to be a better man. It's my driving force. You are not the damsel in distress, but I still want to be your knight, Lila."

I wanted to protect her… but by protecting her…

My Lila knew me too well. She could tell something was wrong, but I *couldn't* tell her.

Not now, not yet. Maybe not ever.

Some truths were better left unsaid; some lies were better told to protect, and some secrets were better meant to stay secrets.

I needed more time with her, to love her longer, *before everything would fall apart…*

Because if she ever found out the truth, Lila was going to hate me.

CHAPTER ELEVEN

Lila

There was a sudden rapping on the door. I glanced up from my textbook, surprised at the interruption. Maddox was in class, and Riley had a test. I got off the couch and walked to the door, peeping through the tiny hole.

Savannah. Oh shit! Maddox's mom. What was *she* doing here? My heart felt like it was practically going to burst through my chest, as I patted my untamed hair down and opened the door. I was in no way presentable to accept guests, but I also couldn't keep his mom waiting at the door.

Savannah gave me a timid smile, and, as usual, she was dressed prim and proper, in an expensive suit and heels. Her hair was pulled back in a tight ponytail, and she kept her makeup minimal. She looked absolutely gorgeous and ready to walk a runaway.

While I looked like a stressed-out college kid who hadn't showered and was wearing the same clothes for two days. I winced, expecting her judgmental stare, but she didn't give me one.

"Um, hi?" I said, pressing my shaky hands against my thighs. When I realized she was still at the door, and I hadn't invited her in yet, my eyes widened, and I flushed in embarrassment. Stepping away from the door, I motioned her inside. "Come in."

I closed the door behind her and noticed her looking around the apartment. "Maddox is not here right now."

Her blue eyes twinkled, the same eyes as Maddox. Maddox was a carbon copy of his father, but he got his eyes from his mother. "I'm here to see you," she said.

My breathing halted, and I felt a sense of panic well up inside me. "Me?" What could she ever want with me?

"Can I sit?" Savannah asked, giving me a small smile.

"Um, yeah. Sure." I motioned toward the couch. "Do you want something to drink?"

"Water is fine." I came back with a glass of water, and she mumbled a quick thank you, when I handed in to her. Savannah appeared a bit nervous, fidgeting with her dress, as she took a seat.

"We heard you moved in with Maddox," she started.

Ah, so his parents were keeping tabs on him. "Yes, about three months ago."

She looked around the apartment with a timid smile. "You have a nice place."

"Thank you." I couldn't tell if she was judging my décor or appreciating it. Everything felt so awkward, us sitting... trying to have a normal conversation, when we barely spoke more than a sentence to each other in the four years since I'd known Maddox.

"It's very... homey," she expressed.

"Is that a bad thing?" I blurted out, without thinking it through. Maddox loved it, our little apartment together. Sure, our taste was quite different, but he gave me free rein over the décor. I left a touch of Maddox

– the curtains were black; our bedroom was all black… but I added a bit of Lila to it, too. Flower pots, paintings and pictures – he didn't have any frames on his walls before, but now, he did. Photos of us, Colton and his friends. He called it… *home*. Ours.

Savannah was shaking her head. "No, not at all. I'm sure Maddox likes it."

Her gaze landed on the huge Christmas tree we'd gone out and chosen together. She glanced down at the gifts under the tree that were slowly accumulating. It was only mid-October, but I was Christmas ready. I was a holiday person and wasn't ashamed of it.

"Maddox didn't like all the Christmas stuff," I confessed. "Because he doesn't really care for the holiday since you and Brad were never big on Christmas. But since this is my favorite time of the year, I know I went a bit overboard, but he lets me do whatever I want. He's starting to like the Christmassy stuff. He says he finally has a home."

Okay, maybe I was taking a dig at her. I was pissed with the way his parents treated him. True, maybe I *was* trying to make Savannah feel shitty about being a shitty mother.

She swallowed and ducked behind her hair. I saw a flash of shame in her eyes, before she looked down at her knees. "I'm glad. You make him happy."

My heart swelled in my chest. "I do," I agreed.

She cleared her throat, and I watched as she pulled out an envelope from her purse. It looked like an invitation. "Brad's birthday is in two days. He thought it'd be the perfect time to throw an early winter gala. We're also holding a charity event."

Oh. I took the envelope from her. "Maddox didn't tell me."

He barely spoke about his parents. In fact, he *never* mentioned them anymore. "That's because he refused to attend the gala. I called him a few days and…"

His mother broke off, sounding dejected. If she called him… that meant Maddox ignored her calls and never got back to her. There was an enormous divide between Maddox and his parents, so much pain and hatred. They had failed him, over and over again. And Maddox? He was stubborn, and he hid his real feelings behind a carefully put together mask. There was a wedge, so deep between them, that I didn't know if they'd ever be able to cross it.

"Brad wants him there," Savannah said quietly. "It's his 50th birthday, and he wants his family present. And that also includes you."

"Does he?"

She blinked, looking shocked at my blatant response. "Excuse me?"

"Does he really want Maddox there?" I questioned, feeling the anger rise inside my chest, coursing through my veins. "Or does he only want us to show up, so we look like the picture-perfect family... since Brad is running for Senator."

I resented them for hurting Maddox the way they did... and if I had to keep him away from them, so they'd never hurt him again, I would.

Her eyes widened, and she was already shaking her head. "No, no. That's not true. Yes, Brad is running for Senator, but he truly does want you and Maddox to attend the gala. For his birthday. Nothing more."

Savannah actually looked sincere... and my lungs clenched. She was giving me a pleading look. I didn't understand it or her motives.

"Why didn't he ask Maddox himself?" My voice was barely restrained.

She gave me a pained smile, looking so different from the Savannah Coulter I knew. "You know him better than us. Do you think he'd let his father get even a word out?"

No, she was right. Maddox barely spoke with his father, and whenever they did, they were fighting about something. I didn't think Maddox and Brad ever had a real conversation.

Savannah reached forward and clasped my hand, squeezing. Her eyes silently pleaded with me. "Please. Maddox needs to be there. It's very important for Brad. And me. Please bring him to the gala. It might be our last…"

What?

My back straightened. "Sorry?"

Her throat bobbed, as she swallowed hard. "I mean, Maddox never attends any dinners or parties that we invite him to. Maybe you can convince him to come to this one. *Please*."

I mulled her words over, chewing on my lip. She was asking me to do a hard task, and I worried I was about to cross over an invisible boundary between Maddox and I. "Maddox is stubborn. What makes you think I can convince him?"

Her eyebrows quirked up; a small smile painted on her pale face. "Because you're Lila."

Because you're Lila.

Because I was Maddox's Lila, she meant.

With my heart in my throat and sweaty palms, I waited for Maddox to come home. Things were good enough between us, after the time in the library. But I knew something was still wrong with the way his eyes would cloud over. Some days, he was quieter than usual.

But it wasn't the peaceful quiet, the type that soothed you.

It was the type of silence that waged war inside him. I could tell he was battling something fiercely, and he wasn't letting me stand next to him, to fight *with* him.

I told myself that maybe he really was worried about his exams.

But then I realized… Maddox was *distracted*. He was drinking more, smoking more cigarettes than usual. That was my first clue that something was terribly wrong. Most days, he walked around like he was carrying the weight of the world on his shoulders. I couldn't wrap my finger around it, but I didn't push. I waited for him to come to me, waited for him to confess his secrets – whatever they were.

The new Maddox worried and scared me.

I inhaled a ragged breath, as the door opened and Maddox walked in, looking like a beautiful, avenging god.

Smoothing a hand down my olive tulle gown, I got to my feet and waited for him to notice me.

He did, slack-mouthed. His eyes widened and then they turned into dark slits. "Where are you going?" he questioned, carefully, pointing at my dress.

Savannah sent the gown this morning when I told her I wouldn't be able to get one of my own in such short notice. I tucked a stray strand of hair behind my ear and gave him a tight smile. "Your mom invited us to the gala."

He *knew*... and he didn't need me to elaborate. Maddox threw his backpack on the couch and angrily pulled off his jacket. "You're not going." His voice brooked no argument.

My throat bobbed with a hard swallow, even though I had been expecting this response. "Why? Your mom personally came over to invite us yesterday, and she was sweet about it," I said, trying to pacify him.

His head snapped up, and he glared. God, that look was threatening. "You didn't tell me she came."

"I didn't have a chance. You were so busy, and we barely saw each other," I argued. With both our exams clashing together on the same days, we barely even saw each other in the last twenty-four hours.

I grasped his arm. "Maddox, please. Just this once. We have to go. In the last four years, your mom never–"

He cut me off with a low snarl. "I don't care what she said. *You*. Are. Not. Going."

You... *Me*? Wait, what?

My brows pulled together in a frown. "I don't understand."

"We're not going to the gala, Lila. Take off that damn dress."

I stood my ground. "I want to go."

His left eye was twitching, as he scowled. I had seen him give others this look, but it was never directed at me, until now. "Why?"

"Because your father wants you there and because your mother actually looked sincere when she asked me." My fingers curled around his bicep, and I squeezed. "I know they've hurt you, but just this once... maybe..."

I told myself that I wasn't going to push him. If Maddox refused to go now, after my attempt to convince him, I'd leave it be. I'd remove the dress, text Savannah and tell her we weren't coming. Then, I'd get in bed with Maddox.

Just because Savannah pleaded with me nicely, I wasn't going to force Maddox.

But then...

Maddox wrenched his arm away. and I stumbled back, almost falling on my ass. He raked his fingers through his hair and glowered at me. "It's not about me. I don't care about the gala! I'll go, for fuck's sake. But I don't want you there."

Something happened.

Something snapped in my chest.

"What?" I breathed. "Maddox, what are you talking about? Why can't I go?

His head lowered and fixed me with an intense, crazed look. "Because I don't want you anywhere near them! You don't belong there."

I flinched, and my heart dropped to my feet, laying there... cold. "Right. Because I'm not filthy rich."

His back snapped straight, and his whole body tensed. His face hardened, and his jaw twitched, as a flash of regret pooled in his blue eyes. "Lila," he groaned, as if he was in pain. "That's not what I meant, and you know it."

No, I didn't know what he meant. He was so goddamn confusing. Every day I had to deal with his mood swings: his hot and cold attitude.

I was sick and tired of him, keeping me in the dark and treating me any differently than before, when I had been just his friend – his best friend.

Now that we were *more*, everything had changed.

Maddox had changed.

And I didn't know how to deal with it.

It *hurt*, watching him slowly pull away from me.

"Guess what, Maddox?" I stabbed a finger into his chest. "I don't care if I don't belong in your world. You are mine, and if I have to weather a storm for you, I will. Even if I go there and all I get are dirty looks, as these people stand there and judge me, I'll deal with it. Because you are mine, and I will stand by your side. For you."

Maddox stood there, like a goddamn statue. Fists clenching, jaw twitching, eyes dark and pained. Harsh realization dawned on me, and I suddenly felt sick. The voices in his head and the demons he carried on his shoulders were winning. They were stealing my Maddox from me.

What is wrong with you? I wanted to scream but held back.

I grabbed my purse and stalked past him. "Your mom told us not to be late. We better get going."

I walked out, without waiting for his response. My heart hammered in my chest, as I counted the minutes.

One... Two... Three... Four....

Fifteen...

Fifteen minutes later, Maddox climbed into the car, dressed in the black tuxedo suit I had laid out for him. We didn't say a word to each other. Not for the length of the thirty-minute car ride.

Coldness seeped through me and acid ran through my veins, as the tension between us grew so thick, I could barely breathe.

As the car came to a stop, my stomach turned, nausea building in my throat. We got out, still not speaking to each other. An apology was on the tip of my tongue, for pushing him harder than I should have, but I never got a chance.

The moment we walked through the double, wooden doors of the venue... all eyes were on us. That was the thing about the Coulters. They were always the center of attention.

Maddox grasped my hand and brought it to his elbow. When he finally spoke, his voice was soft. "Don't leave my side, please."

What was he so worried about? Yes, this was out of my comfort zone, but it wasn't my first time attending one of these fancy parties. In fact, we attended a charity gala just about six months ago.

The same one that led us to skinny dipping in the ocean...

Maddox tensed as his father walked over to us. "You came," he simply said, with a nod of acknowledgment in my direction. If I wasn't mistaken, I saw a silent *thank you* in his eyes.

Tonight, Brad Coulter looked... different. Wary... tired, like he was carrying a heavy burden on his shoulders.

Too soon, we were surrounded by business partners and acquaintances. They were all interested in Maddox and what his plans were, meaning when he was joining the family business. We were approached left and right... and I was jostled and soon forgotten.

I slipped from Maddox's arms, and Savannah was by my side immediately. I breathed a sigh of relief at the familiar face. She grasped my arm and pulled me to a quiet corner, handing me a glass of wine. "I was just like you when I was around your age. We rarely fit in places like this. I remember the first time I attended a gala; it was quite overwhelming." She patted my hand. "Don't worry, it'll be fine."

Huh? She didn't fit in? What the hell?

"I don't understand," I said, taking a slow sip of the white wine.

Savannah fixated on me. "Neither me nor Brad were born into a rich family," she started, and I blinked, my jaw slackened. "Brad didn't live with a silver spoon in his mouth, like you'd think. In fact, when he was a teenager, he lived several months on the street. He was *that* poor. Everything you see today, everything he has – his empire, his legacy, he built it with his bare hands. He didn't happen to inherit his wealth."

That was news. What the hell? I almost had whiplash from this new discovery.

My eyes found Maddox, and I saw the grimace on his face, as people hounded him. He said something, and they laughed, oblivious to his discomfort. "I didn't know that. Maddox…"

"Neither does Maddox," she confirmed. "He doesn't know a lot of things."

I was so… confused.

Savannah was acting unlike herself, talkative and sharing information I never thought she would. Brad acknowledged me for the first time today.

They were acting almost like they… *cared.*

Did they come to the sudden realization of just what kind of shit parents they were?

Savannah must have noticed the look on my face, because she gave me a tight smile. "I know how it looks. But, Lila, his father loves him."

Ha, that was the joke of the century. She could have almost fooled me if I, myself, hadn't seen the way Brad treated Maddox. He was neither a caring nor a loving father.

"Well, he has a shitty way of showing it." I speared her with a look that said I wasn't falling for her bullshit. "So do you. You're his mother. You should have done a better job."

"I know," she nodded solemnly, "but it's too late now, isn't it?"

"It's never too late."

"For Maddox, it is. I just wished–"

"What?" I asked, my heart tripping over itself, when she fell silent.

"I wished I could go back and change the past. But then…"

"Then?"

She smiled and patted my hand. "He probably wouldn't have met you then."

That was a strange way of putting it and an easy way out for her. I was about to tell her what exactly I thought of such a shitty excuse, when another voice joined us.

"Savannah," a sing-song voice called out. "There you are, Dear."

A woman joined us in the corner, looking just as prim and proper as Maddox's mother. Another elite wife.

She barely spared me a glance and completely ignored my existence. I internally rolled my eyes, but I was starting to get used to it. I didn't have a rich family last name attached to my first name, so I didn't matter in their world.

Fine by me. I didn't want to be friends with these stuck-up, trophy wives anyway.

When I tried to slither away unnoticed, Savannah grasped my elbow and pulled me back. Damn it, why was she being so attentive tonight?

"Lila, meet Anna Carmichael. A close friend of mine."

Carmichael.

Anna smiled a fake, plastic smile, but I didn't even notice… didn't breathe…

Carmichael.

"Oh, there are your boys," Savannah said. She waved them over, and my entire world suddenly became blurred.

My heart *stopped* and then it crashed against my rib cage.

Everything happened in slow motion. There was a flimsy barrier over my eyes, and I was watching everything through muddled lenses.

Two men joined us, standing in front of me.

Savannah was talking, but her voice faded away, like I was underwater, and she was screaming from above me.

My flesh crawled, and the urge to scratch and tear my skin off my bones was strong, so very strong.

"This is Anna's younger son, Rion. He's the same age as you and Maddox." She was pointing between the two of them, but I wasn't really paying attention.

Breathe,

Breathe.

Breathe, Lila. Breathe.

"And this is Christian Carmichael, the older brother. They are Maddox's childhood friends. The three of them were thick as thieves, back in the day."

Thud. Thud. Thud.

My chest ached. My scars… burned like someone was pouring gasoline over my torn, opened flesh.

I couldn't see anything. Everything was so dark… so empty…

I remembered the sound of crushing glass, mixed with the distinct crack of bones breaking. I remembered my mom screaming, and my dad… I remembered…

Pain came next.

My bones and fragile organs felt like they were being smashed and crumbled into a tiny, suffocating box. I couldn't breathe. It hurt so much. My torso hurt and burned, the pain almost unbelievable. There was a knife dug, painfully, into my chest… no, not a knife… I didn't know what… but it hurt. It felt like a knife or a hammer being pounded into my chest.

I blinked… forcing myself to breathe. I couldn't. My lungs contracted with such force that I was afraid they would fold into themselves. When I coughed, agony strummed through my body, and my cracked lips parted with a silent scream.

Mom… Dad…

I couldn't speak. The buzzing noise in my ears wouldn't stop.

The taste of coppery blood pooled in my mouth; it tasted bitter, and I could feel it soaking my tongue and the inside of my mouth. Blood…?

No…

How...

What...

I remember...

The fight...snow outside... in the car... mom... dad... me...

I remember the screams...

My bones felt like they had been mangled together, and my chest, it was being carved open. I lifted my head up a bit and looked down at my chest to see... blood. Everywhere. So much blood.

I sucked in cramped air and tried to scream, tried to breathe, but my lungs refused to work.

No. No. No. Please. No. Oh God, no.

MOM, I wanted to scream. DADDY.

The pain never ended. The darkness never faded away.

My world tilted, swaying back and forth, and then crashed.

Christian Carmichael.

Carmichael.

Carmichael.

My gaze found his, and I saw no recognition in his eyes, as he stared at me with avid interest. He didn't recognize me. Of course, he didn't.

I was a nobody. Just like... eight years ago.

Christian Carmichael...Maddox's childhood friend.

My past... my present... my life crumbled around me.

My heart bled at my feet... at Christian's feet.

Thud. Thud. Thud.

Sourness rose in my throat, and I almost choked on it. Acid clogged my veins, and my body started shaking. Someone was saying my name.

I can't breathe.

I... can't... breathe.

The air felt, so thick, I couldn't inhale. The lump in my throat grew bigger and bigger, until it became too hard to swallow. I suffocated in plain sight.

Nobody noticed.

Nobody cared.

Christian Carmichael was still staring at me, and bile rose in my throat, tasting bitter on my tongue.

Did he *see* me?

Could he see who I was? Or did he… forget?

He did…

He forgot…

He didn't know… didn't remember…

Thud. Thud. Thud.

He forgot…

A shuddering breath escaped me, and my body felt too warm and then too cold. I swayed on my feet, and my head pounded, a searing pain in the back of my skull. My eyes twitched, and I took a slow step back.

"Lila."

It was *him*. He said my name. Maddox said my name.

I looked away from Christian, and my gaze found Maddox. The horror in his eyes told me everything I needed to know.

The world spun and spun, and I fell off my axis.

Breathe.

Breathe.

FUCKING BREATHE!

I gasped. Maddox took a step forward, reaching out for me. "Lila," he said my name again, begging me, pleading *for* me. He looked pained, his expression raw and panicked.

For the first time, I felt nothing for him. For his pain.

I felt… nothing.

It was too late.

My heart had withered and died.

Thud. Thud. Thud.

I still couldn't breathe.

When Maddox touched my arm, my skin itched like thousands of tiny ants were crawling from underneath my flesh. I wrenched it away from his burning touch. My scars ached harder, not a ghostly echo, like I used to experience. No, the pain was so brutal, my body almost succumbed to it.

I ran.

From Maddox, from Christian Carmichael... from everyone... from *myself.*

I ran until my lungs gave out, and I stumbled out into the cold air.

I ran until my legs stopped working, and I slid to the ground, my knees digging into the muddy grass.

Breathe...

Breathe...

Breathe...

No... I didn't want to breathe...

I wanted to go to my parents.

I didn't want to breathe...

I wanted my mommy to hold me; I wanted my daddy to kiss my forehead and tell me everything was going to be okay.

"Lila."

He whispered my name.

"Lila."

His voice cracked.

"Lila."

He came closer, and my body tensed at his close proximity. Standing on my weak legs, I buried my shaky hands in my gown and turned to face him.

Maddox.

My love.

My protector.

My mistake.

"Your childhood friend is my parents' murderer," I said, my voice dead and empty.

Maddox stared at me, his blue eyes sparked with guilt and hopelessness. His shoulders dropped, and he looked like he was about to fall to his knees.

He reached out for me, but I stepped back. *"Lila."*

If it was Christian who killed my parents that night, then it was Maddox who smashed my heart to dust.

"You lied to me."

CHAPTER TWELVE

Maddox

They say lies always find a way to catch up to you. Lies never stay hidden for too long. Secrets are never truly buried.

Lies and secrets can protect…but they also can destroy…

My secrets obliterated us. My secrets burnt my love for Lila to the ground.

It wrecked us.

I was the only one to blame, and Lila was my victim.

I'd cut off my fucking arms and legs if I could just go back from this very moment and change the ending of this chapter.

But the black ink on the pages were permanent. I could rip off the pages, burn them to ashes, but then… that would change our story, *missing* pages… an *incomplete*… and *ruined* story.

The look of raw pain on Lila's face decimated me.

I tried to reach for her. There was a fierce need inside of me to comfort her, to take her pain away, even though I was the reason for it. My mouth went dry, and a heavy lump settled inside my throat, when Lila stumbled back, out of my reach.

Away from me.

Like she couldn't bear my touch.

As if I disgusted her.

The reaction sliced through me with the power of a sword. Too bad I wasn't wearing any armor. The sharp blade connected with flesh, and I fucking bled.

Lila faced the other direction, without saying a word, and started walking away. I followed after her, a careful distance behind. "Lila, where are you going? It's so late."

She didn't answer.

She kept walking, walking… walking away from me. Far and out of my reach.

I quickened my steps and *followed*. I finally noticed the direction she took and realized she was *walking* back home. Shit!

"Let me drive you home, please. It's too late for us to be walking home, and we're too far away." She didn't speak. Didn't berate me. Didn't acknowledge me.

In fact, I thought she was barely even breathing.

Lost in her own world, in her head… drifting away from reality. My fingers circled around her bicep, and I tugged her back toward me. Lila wrenched away with a hiss. "Don't."

One single word. Said with so much venom and torment.

My heart hammered, a vicious beat in my rib cage. My chest echoed with a familiar ache.

"Please," I croaked, *pleaded*. I didn't recognize my own voice or its tone. I sounded so goddamn weak. Weak for Lila Garcia. "Let me drive you home. I know I'm the last person you want to see or hear right now. I *understand*, but it's complete madness to walk all the way back home, right now, at this hour," I tried to reason with her. "I won't touch you. I won't even say a word. Fucking hell, you don't even need to look at me or say anything to me. Just, let me drive you home."

"It's madness that you thought you could get away with this. It's madness that you swept my life right out from under my feet and watched it crumble like you had the right to destroy me," she whispered.

I squeezed my eyes shut, feeling the burn in the back of eyelids. My head pounded, a distant ache, as Lila resumed her walking. Her tulle, feathered dress was heavy, and she was practically dragging her feet behind her. She stumbled a few times. I reached for her, but she righted herself, before I could help. She continued walking. Stumbled again, then straightened her back and resumed the same insane pace.

It was maddening, watching her crumble before my very own eyes. Knowing full well who she fell victim to. Not Christian Carmichael and his family. *But me.*

Without even realizing it...

I became her enemy.

And she was my unwilling casualty.

My fingers curled in my hair, and I tugged, until my scalp burned. The pain kept me grounded. I *had* to stay grounded, for Lila.

It took us almost two hours to get home. By the time we reached our apartment, Lila could barely walk. She held onto the walls for support, as she waited for the elevator, in complete silence.

I peeked down at her face, behind the curtains of black hair. I didn't know what I expected. Maybe tears? Anger? Pain? Brows pinched, lips thinned, a hard expression?

But I hadn't expected *this.*

Her face was completely blank, devoid of any emotion. Lila was the image of an empty canvas. She showed no outward reaction or emotion to my presence or her reality.

I watched her get into the elevator, almost like she was on autopilot. Moving around without really knowing what she was doing.

So, this was what it felt like to die?

To crash and burn.

To wither away.

Because I *felt* it. Right in my bones, down to the marrow of me. I...
died as the elevator closed and she was... gone.

I took the stairs two at a time and cursed my claustrophobia, my
inability to stay in closed places. I couldn't even take the goddamn
elevator with Lila.

When I reached our apartment, I found it...empty.

My heart dropped to my feet, and I went cold. My stomach seized up,
and bile rose in my throat. Frantically, I knocked on the next door. She
had to be in there. *She has to be.*

Riley opened the door, her face pale, her brows creased with worry.
"Oh, Maddox. You're here! Something is wrong with Lila."

I pushed past her, not even waiting for her to finish her sentence. Lila
had to give me a chance to explain, even though I didn't deserve it. Didn't
deserve her forgiveness, but I'd beg for it for the rest of my miserable life.

If only she'd give me a chance to explain. If only...

Lila was standing in the middle of the living room, looking so sad...
so lost...

She picked at the feathers in her olive tulle dress.

I had never gotten a chance to tell her just how beautiful she looked
tonight. *Exquisite. Gorgeous. Beautiful. Stunning. Lovely. Angelic.
Breathtaking. Ravishing. Elegant. Bewitching. Alluring. Heavenly. So.
Fucking. Exquisite.*

I wanted to tell her all of it, wrap my arms around her small frame
and kiss her red lips. I never got a chance to kiss her before our world
collapsed and shattered into fragmented pieces.

"How long have you known?" Her voice cut through the air and
sucked all the oxygen out of my lungs. I knew the question was coming,
but still hadn't been ready for it.

"Lila."

She raised her hand, cutting me off. "I asked a question, Maddox. I want an answer, not your excuses. How. Long. Have. You. Known?"

I couldn't meet her eyes any longer, couldn't look at her anymore. My head lowered, my eyes shuttered close, and I struggled to breathe, as my lungs squeezed.

Lila let out a warlike cry, and my head snapped up, just in time to catch her, as she flew at me. She gripped my collar and hissed in my face. "Answer me, goddamn it!" she screamed. "Stop standing there like a fool, like an emotionless statue. When did you find out about Christian? How long have you been lying to me? HOW LONG HAVE YOU BEEN LYING TO MY FACE?"

Her carefully layered walls came down, and I watched as she snapped, right in front of me. Her eyes blazed with fire and hurt.

My secrets had caught up with me, and I was drowning in the aftermath.

"Eight... months..." I croaked.

"Eight months," she repeated carefully. "Eight months."

My hand came up but stopped a hairsbreadth from her cheek. "I didn't lie."

Lila let out a humorless laugh. A dead, empty laugh. She laughed until her laughter turned into a loud sob.

"A lie by omission is still a lie, you fucking bastard." Her gaze shone with unshed tears, but she didn't let them spill.

My little dragon. She was breaking on the inside, but she refused to cry. "All this time...you knew," Lila said. "*He* is your *friend*. Your childhood friend," she gritted through her teeth. "*Your* friend is a killer. *Your* friend was drunk that night. *Your* friend got away with murder. *Your* friend scarred me for the rest of my miserable, fucking life. *Your* friend should be in jail. *Your* friend KILLED my parents, and he got away with it! YOUR friend played god, tried to pay for my silence. He held my whole future in the palm of his dirty, filthy, rich hands, and he destroyed me. YOUR friend."

My stomach churned, and I felt sick. Bitter nausea built in my throat, and I worried I was going to throw up.

Lila slammed her fist into my chest. It didn't hurt. I almost wished it did. "Say something, Maddox!"

"I'm sorry."

"Oh, that's rich." She laughed, almost manically. "That's fucking rich. Go ahead, lie to my face, and then say you're sorry? Sorry for what, Maddox? Are you sorry for keeping this secret? Or are you sorry you got caught? Are you sorry because your friend murdered my parents that night? Or are you sorry that *you* destroyed *me* and trampled all over my heart."

She stabbed a finger into my chest, punctuating every word with a sharp stab. Again and again. Right over my beating heart. "What exactly are you sorry for, Maddox Coulter? For being a shitty boyfriend or for hiding the secrets of your dear childhood friend, Christian?"

If only you knew...

But the truth wasn't always easy or simple. The truth held hidden layers, like an onion. The more you peeled it, the harder it made you cry. The deeper you peeled it, the closer you got to its core. The truth. The reality of it.

Acidic. Sour. Bitter. Pungent.

But the layers... the fucking layers were there to make our life harder. And so, my truth was just like that.

My hand came up again, before I could stop myself. My fingertips skimmed over her jaw. Lila flinched but didn't pull away. She allowed me this *one* touch. "I broke your trust, and I hurt you. I'm sorry for that," I rasped gravelly.

"Aren't you sorry for breaking your promises?" she whispered.

My heart stuttered. "I didn't..."

She smiled without humor, she smiled with cruelty. A smile of disgust.

I shook my head. "I promised to protect you. And I thought I was doing that."

She finally pulled away, and my hand fell to my side. Instantly, I missed the feel of her skin under my fingers. "Lila… just, listen to me. *Please*."

She stepped back, her dark eyes growing darker. Furious. Pained. "Keep your sorry excuses to yourself. I don't want to hear it. I've heard and seen enough."

"No," I growled. Fear tightened around my lungs. If I let her walk away now, I was going to lose her. Forever. "You need to hear the rest. You don't know anything!"

I reached for her, desperate for a chance to explain. I didn't see it coming, although I should have expected it. The moment I clasped her wrist, tugging her back to me, Lila turned around with a vengeful cry.

She slapped me, right in the face.

I stumbled back, and she twisted out of my hold. There was so much… anger… so much *hate* in her dark eyes. "Don't touch me," Lila warned, her voice cracking over the words. She leaned closer, jerking her head back, so she could stare right into my eyes.

Her next words killed me.

Killed any hope I had for us.

"When you touch me, my skin crawls," she practically spat, with so much venom in her sweet voice. "When you touch me, my scars burn. When you touch me, I want to throw up."

"No. Stop," I croaked. I pleaded… begged. "Lila, *no*."

Her eyes were dull again. My Lila was… gone. "Don't you dare touch me, Maddox."

All the air had been sucked out of my lungs, and I was… suffocated.

"Get out." She pointed at the door. "Get. Out. You're no longer welcome here." My chest squeezed, like a heavy metal chain was being wrapped around my already tortured, bleeding heart.

If it hurt for me…

I wondered how much it hurt for her…

"I'm going to leave, and I'm going to wait for you. Tomorrow, you have to listen to me. Please, Lila. You have to let me explain *why*."

"I don't want to see your face," Lila sneered. "Tonight or tomorrow." She was never so vicious, but in this moment, her words were laced with enough acid to burn even the thickest layer. Me? I was just a mere mortal. My heart disintegrated.

"You should leave." Riley walked up behind me. I had forgotten she was even there, listening to us. "Do as she says, Maddox," she lamented.

Lila's face hardened, and she stalked away, into the room that *used* to belong to her. Her place was with me. *Not anymore…*

"What's going on?" I let my head fall back against my shoulders, staring at the ceiling as another voice joined us.

I heard his steps, as Colton approached me. "I was at the gala. I saw Lila and you leave…"

Of course, he was. We ran in the same circles. Of course, he saw. Everyone watched it unfold, but no one knew *why*.

"What's going on?" he asked again, looking between Riley and I, waiting for one of us to answer.

"Ask Maddox." Riley sighed. "Lila is hurt and angry right now. You two better leave."

My chest hurt, and I rubbed the ache with my fist.

"Maddox?"

"I need to get out of here," I murmured, looking at her closed door. My presence was unwelcomed. And I knew I'd cause my Lila more pain, if I stayed.

"Okay," Colton said. "Where?"

I dragged my legs behind me and walked away. With each step that took me farther away from Lila, coldness seeped through my bones, and my body grew numb.

"The gym." It was that or I'd drink myself into oblivion. Maybe I'd do both. Take all my fuckedupness out on a punching bag and then drink until I forgot tonight ever happened.

Colton didn't ask any questions. He drove us to the gym, and everything was just a goddamn blurred mess to me. I couldn't think straight, couldn't even *breathe.*

The punching bag became my salvation.

The pain coursing through my body, as I pushed myself over, became my only solace. It felt good. I *needed* it. Needed the pain, so I could feel something.

Lila's face flashed through my mind, the image searing into my brain. The tormented look on her face. I could almost taste the saltiness of her tears on my tongue.

She hated me.

I hated myself. What a fucking pair, we were.

Two hours later, all my muscles were dead and numb. I could barely feel my arms or my legs. I sank to the ground, my body too weak to keep me upright any longer.

"Better now?" Colton asked, joining me on the ground. He laid on his back beside me with a groan.

"No," I said.

He sighed. "Look, I don't wanna talk about your feelings. We can leave that pussy talk for some shrink, but you don't look good, man."

My eyes closed, and I breathed through my nose. Silence filled the gym for a long time before I finally spoke. "I fucked up."

He hmphed "Yeah, that's obvious."

"She hates me." I could barely get the words past my clogged throat.

"Nah. Lila can't hate you."

"Christian was driving the car that night... the night of Lila's accident, the night her parents..."

Colton paused, mulling over my words. "Christian Carmichael?"

I nodded.

He swore under his breath. "Shit. You *knew*?"

"I found out a couple of months ago, when I was digging into Lila's accident. It always bothered me, and I wanted to know, wanted to bring her justice. I found out it was Christian," I explained.

"Before you two started dating?" he questioned.

"Way before," I confessed quietly.

Colton swore again. "Lila found out? Oh shit, the gala! Christian!" Colton finally put two and two together.

My chest tightened with a vice grip. "He was there. Lila came face to face with the person who killed her parents, Colton. Do you realize what this means? I did everything to protect her from the truth," I croaked, my voice barely audible.

"Shit, Maddox. I don't know what to say."

"Lila hates me." Saying the word out loud caused me to almost double over in pain. I hadn't expected it to hurt this much, but it did. Everything fucking hurt.

"She doesn't."

"You weren't there. You didn't see the look in her eyes." The look of pain and disgust. Betrayal and broken trust.

"I should have fought harder, should have stopped her from going to the gala, but she was so goddamn stubborn. I thought I'd be by her side all night, keeping her safe, and away from Christian. I thought we'd be able to leave before anything... I thought..."

I rubbed a hand over my face, so exhausted, so mentally... done. I just wanted to wrap myself around Lila and forget about this chapter. I wanted to turn the pages over and begin anew. "I thought a lot of things, but I still messed up."

And the worst part of it? Lila didn't even know half of it.

All my secrets...

If she knew the rest of it…

No. The mere thought of it made me sick.

I wasn't strong enough to love… and then *lose* her. Not like this.

Lila was a maze with no escape. Once I had entered the labyrinth that was her, I lost sight of the exit and never bothered to look for it again. I didn't want to leave the maze. I didn't want to escape her.

I wanted to stay and bleed at her feet. Because I found what I needed there.

My salvation.

CHAPTER THIRTEEN

Lila

It is said that pain comes in waves. Whether it's emotional or physical. The first wave hits you unexpectedly. It's usually the most dangerous, the harshest wave.

The second wave, you're ready for it, but it still hurts.

By the third wave, you've grown accustomed to it. The pain starts to take shape, to build up inside of you. Under your skin, inside your flesh, buried in your bones, deep in the marrow of you.

And slowly, your body grows numb.

Your mind goes numb.

You live with the pain; it becomes part of you.

The wave came and went. The pain stayed, with an angry stubbornness. The wound festered, oozing puss. The agony grew.

I drowned. I floated. I sunk to the bottom.

My mom always told me to honor the anger, to give pain the space it needed to breathe, to never run away from my emotions… to live and breathe it. *This is how you learn to let go*, she'd tell me.

But I didn't know *how* to let go of the fury coursing inside of me, of the pain that chased me every waking hour and into my nightmares.

A dull throb spread across and around my scars, and I rubbed my chest, trying to alleviate the heavy pressure.

"Lila, you have to eat something." Riley pushed the plate of pasta in front of me. "Just a few bites."

The smell of the pasta had bile rising in my throat, and I choked on the sourness. My stomach churned with nausea. Maddox loved pasta. Actually, he loved the pasta *I* made, and I'd always make it for him, whenever he was feeling down.

I pushed the plate away and stood up. "I'm not hungry."

"You barely ate anything in the last few days! You've already lost weight, babe. Just a few bites, at least," she tried to reason with me. "You're going to make yourself sick."

Riley didn't understand; she couldn't. I didn't want to eat, drink... or sleep.

I just wanted to fade away, to cease to exist.

The gala was four days ago. My world fell apart four days ago, and I still haven't accepted that fact. How? Why? *WHY*? I wanted to scream at him.

But I refused to see him, to look into his beautiful face and let him hold me. To feed me his sorry excuses. I knew I'd let him win. I knew I was weak for Maddox.

He'd tell me he was sorry... and I was going to forgive him. He had that kind of power over me, and he proved to be my downfall.

Maddox Coulter was my damnation.

He was a mistake I shouldn't have made four years ago. I should have never asked him to make that first pinky promise. It was the beginning of the end, as far as I was concerned. *That* was my mistake. That stupid pinky promise.

Friends?

Friends.

My phone rang, for the fifth time, in the last ten minutes. I glanced at it, even though I already knew who it was going to be. He had been calling me every day.

But today, he seemed especially persistent.

Maddox's name flashed on the screen, as the call went to voicemail. With an angry wail that sounded like a broken record to my own ears, I tossed the phone at the wall. It bounced and slammed onto the floor, the screen cracking and going black.

The call ended.

The wave came again. It crashed into me, and even though my body had long grown numb to me, it still... *hurt.* I still drowned, gasping for air, gasping to stay alive.

Riley let out a soft sigh. "You have to talk to him. Just once, Lila. Not for his sake. But for your own. You're hurting, and you need closure."

"I don't want anything from him," I spat. "There's no better closure than not seeing his face or hearing his voice."

Riley walked to where my broken phone laid. She picked it up and handed it to me. "How is *this* closure?" she asked softly.

My fingers brushed over the fractured screen, and my skin caught on one of the cracks. A tiny prick: a sharp sting, like a paper cut. Blood gathered around the littlest cut. *Bleeding.*

I fisted my hand, hiding the wound. Oh, how ironic.

Riley grasped my wrist and slowly uncurled my fingers. Her gentle touch skimmed over the cut. "*This* is not closure, Lila."

My heart stuttered, and I blinked back the tears. "I can't hate him. I tried, and I *can't.* But I also don't want to forgive him. I *can't* forgive him."

Maddox's betrayal cut deep, so deep... there was no way for me to reach it and wrap a bandage on it. I couldn't stop the bleeding, couldn't stop the wound festering into something nastier, something more agonizing.

How does a wound heal when it can't be bandaged or stitched?

The answer was... *it can't.*

I flinched, as the silence suddenly filled with Riley's ringtone. She padded away to it and then grimaced. "It's Maddox."

I turned and walked away. Back into my room. My sanctuary.

Curling into my bed and sinking into my soft mattress, I tucked my blankets around me. A safe cocoon. Not safer than Maddox's arm... but at least, my bed wasn't the reason for my suffering.

My eyes closed, and I had to remind myself to breathe.

The sound of crushing glass filled my ears. The echo so loud, it was deafening. My world tilted, swayed and turned over. My head slammed into something, and I remembered feeling like it would explode.

The distinct sound of cracking bones came next.

Then my screams. My parents'.

Pain came next.

Darkness soon followed.

The buzzing sound in my ears didn't stop, and my lips parted to speak, but I couldn't. My voice was gone. I tried to scream, but I couldn't.

The taste of coppery blood pooled in my mouth; it tasted bitter, and I could feel it soaking my tongue and the inside of my mouth. Blood...

I remembered...

The blood. So much blood. I remembered the feeling of death.

I remembered passing out and waking up again, in the same position, with the same agony coursing through my body.

I sucked in cramped air and tried to scream, tried to breathe, but my lungs refused to work.

"Lila? Lila!" Someone was calling out my name and shaking me awake.

My eyes popped open, and I let out a gasp, feeling the oxygen burn my lungs, as I took in a deep breath. The nightmares faded away, but the echoes of my screams still lingered.

Riley came into my line of vision, and she looked worried, her brow creased with tension, and her lips were pressed into a thin line.

"What is it?" I sat up, keeping my blankets around my shoulders.

"It's Maddox."

I frowned and hissed, grinding my molars. My jaw tightened. "I don't care."

Riley shook her head. "The stairs are blocked. Out of service. Maintenance is working on them right now."

My heart dropped. *No, please. Oh God, no.*

"Maddox needs to take the elevator," Riley said softly.

I remembered the time when Maddox and I were locked in the closet, back when we went to Berkshire Academy.

That was the first time I witnessed his mask fall apart. The first time I saw that Maddox had many layers, many cracks in his soul. He was a king with a crooked crown.

I shouldn't have cared... I really shouldn't have...

But I was out of bed before I thought it through. I ran out of my apartment before I could stop myself. My brain argued with me, telling me that he didn't deserve my help.

My heart screamed and called out to Maddox. I belatedly realized the repercussions of my actions... what it meant for me to run to him when he was in such a vulnerable state. I realized the fallout could be worse than the original pain I went through, when I realized Maddox's betrayal.

If I went to him now... if I let myself *feel* for him now...

But it was too late. I was already in the elevator before I could overthink.

He needed me.

He *needed* me.

He needed *me.*

It happened in slow motion. I took the elevator down to the lobby and found him there. Pacing the length of it. His body was tensed and locked tight. His fingers tugging on his hair, like a mad man. He let out a small sound in the back of his throat, an angry growl, as he began to hit the side of his skull. "Fuck, fuck… FUCK!"

He crumbled before me.

"Maddox," I said his name, before I realized what I was doing.

His head snapped up, and he stared at me, blue eyes so raw, so deep… deep as the ocean that I could easily drown in them and I… *did*. Drowned and sunk to the bottom.

His face contorted in pain. I wasn't wearing any life jacket when he caught me in his powerful, violent tides and pulled me below the surface, dragging me into the deep end.

"Lila," Maddox said hoarsely. He looked at me, as if I was his saving grace, his lifeline.

His chest rattled with ragged breaths, and I could see the panic setting in. "The elevator," he croaked.

The look he gave me, it *eviscerated* my heart. Destroyed my already broken heart, further fracturing it into little pieces that could not be glued together again.

I walked to him, stepping a hairsbreadth away from his shaking form. "The…elevator… I can't… *Lila*." His deep, broken timbre vibrated through my bones and slid down my spine. I trembled, feeling his pain as if it were my own.

"Do you trust me?" I asked, grasping his hand in mine.

Maddox laced our fingers together, holding on tightly. So tight I almost lost the feeling in my hand.

Moving onto my tiptoes, I brought our faces closer. "Do you trust me?"

Maddox gave me a heartbroken nod. His eyes flashed with darkness and fear.

He trusted me.

Like I had trusted him.

The only difference between us was that I didn't, and would never, betray his trust.

I thought Maddox and I were alike. He'd never hurt me, just like I'd never hurt him. Not willingly. Not intentionally.

It turned out... I was wrong.

Wrong about Maddox. Wrong about us.

"Hold my hand," I told him. He did, grasping my hand like he was afraid I'd let go. *"Trust me."*

It took me a few seconds to register what was happening, to realize what I was about to do. But it was too late. I didn't pause to think.

He needs me.

My lips met his, as I pushed the button on the elevator. It pinged open, and I tugged Maddox toward me, curling my arms around his neck, as I dragged us backward into the elevator.

The moment my lips met his, Maddox went rigid. His wide shoulders stiffened, and his neck corded with tension. He groaned into the kiss – a groan of pain, fear... shock... and so much anguish.

"Lila," Maddox whispered against my lips, his voice gritty with emotions.

"Kiss me." I pulled his attention back to me, when he started to understand *what* was happening and *where* he was. In the elevator. A choked gasp echoed on his full lips, and he started pulling away from me, his eyes wide with terror.

"Kiss me," I breathed. My lips parted, and I traced the seams of his lips with the tip of my tongue.

His breath quickened, and I felt his inner struggle, the pain I knew that plagued his mind. His worst nightmare. The moment he opened for me, I shoved my tongue in his mouth. Maddox grunted against my lips, and his hands went to my ass.

He hoisted me up, and I wrapped my legs around his hips, hooking my ankles behind him. His fingers dug into my ass, and he slammed my back into the elevator wall.

It's okay, I got you. Feel me.

Our kiss was a battle cry, a crazed desperation, so thick I almost cried out as his lips brutalized mine. I inhaled him; yet, he stole the air from my lungs.

He took my soul in the palm of his hand, and I gave him my life.

The kiss consumed us. We lost all sense of time and place.

Maddox pushed both hands into my hair and wrapped his fingers around the long strands. He jerked my head back, kissing me harder.

Kiss. He was greedy. *Kiss.* I was angry. *Kiss.* He was desperate. *Kiss.* I had been ravenous. *Kiss.* Brutal. *Kiss.* Frantic.

I hate you, I exhaled into the kiss.

Maddox groaned, and he clutched the back of my neck, his fingers flexing, as he gripped me hard. *I don't hate you,* I breathed into his lips.

Feel me, he said.

My heart beat savagely against my rib cage. The elevator pinged, and the doors slid open, as we reached our floor. Maddox dropped his forehead to mine, and our lips parted. His chest heaved, and he inhaled a ragged breath. My nails dragged across the nape of his neck. "It's okay. We're here."

He took a slow step out of the elevator with me still wrapped around him. Maddox turned his back to the wall, as the doors slid closed once again. His knees weakened, and he slid to the ground. I was practically straddling him, as we sat in the empty hallway of the third floor.

His demons had been silenced.

Mine were still wide awake.

"Lila," he rasped. "Fuck, baby."

I wrenched away from him and stood on shaky legs. *"Don't.* I was only helping."

My lips tingled, and my skin turned cold, already missing his touch. My lungs squeezed and burned, as I silently gasped for air.

"Why?" Maddox kept his gaze on me. "Why did you help?"

"Because I had to," I said through clenched teeth, "because even though I can't stand to look at you, it was the right thing to do."

Maddox got to his feet, his jaw hardening. *"Why?"*

My fists clenched at my sides. "I pitied you. That's why."

His face clouded over, and I knew I hit the mark. Maddox Coulter hated to be pitied.

"Your sympathy is misplaced," he snarled, taking a threatening step toward me. "Do you why I did it? Why I kept that fucking secret? Because. I. Wanted. To. Protect. You. Because I didn't want you to relive your past."

He continued advancing toward me, forcing me to step back. "I wasn't protecting Christian like you seem to think. In fact, I want nothing more than to throw him behind bars and watch him rot in fucking hell. He. Is. Nothing. To. Me. Except the person who hurt you." He thumped his fist over his chest. *"My* Lila. He hurt you, and I want to hurt him."

My hands shook, and my core trembled. The lump in my throat grew bigger and bigger, forcing me to choke on it.

Maddox grasped my elbow and tugged me to him. I fell against his chest, and he lowered his head, practically snarling into my face. "You are my everything, and the last thing I wanted to do was betray you. But I had to, Lila. I had to, so I could protect you."

I slammed my fist into his chest and pushed away from him. *Stop*, I silently begged. *Just… stop.*

He didn't stop. "Remember what you said to me the first time we visited your parents?" he asked, but didn't wait for me to answer. "You told me that you hated me before, because I was a reminder of the boy who ruined you and stole your life from you."

Yes, I did say that.

I did hate him because the 'Maddox Coulter,' I met four years ago, reminded me too much of Christian.

"Tell me, Lila," he growled, his voice strained. His gaze flitted back and forth, searching my face. "How could I tell you the truth? How fucking could I? The person who killed your parents was the same boy I grew up with. You would have looked at me the same way you're looking at me *now*."

It was a sick twist of truth and our reality. Everything he was saying made sense. But I couldn't accept it. I needed a reason to blame him, to hate him.

"Stop," I said, my voice shaking. Tremors ran down my body, and I felt so... cold.

Maddox manhandled me. He grasped my jaw and forced me look at him, into his manic eyes. "Why did you help me, Lila?"

Shut up. Please.

His fingers dug into my cheeks. It wasn't painful, but it wasn't gentle either. "Why?" He breathed; his lips so close to mine.

BECAUSE I LOVE YOU.

My heart stuttered. I felt dizzied...as realization dawned on me.

I stumbled back, away from him. My gut twisted, a fiery inferno from deep within me.

His arms fell to his sides, and he squeezed his eyes shut against my rejection. His lips parted, and he whispered my name... but I was already running away. From him.

From my truth.

From our reality.

From... everything.

I ran into my apartment and slammed the door closed behind me, sinking to the hardwood floor. A loud, choked sob spilled past my lips.

I felt Maddox, on the other side. He didn't knock... but I *felt* him. Standing there, right outside the door. Slapping my hand over my mouth, I muffled the broken sounds that were spilling from my throat.

Kismet was a demented bitch.

Funny how, four years ago, I loathed Maddox...and would have hated him, if I found out about his connection with Christian.

And now that I knew the truth... I still loved him with every fiber of my being.

I loved him hard.

I loved him without restraint.

I loved him, as much as I hated Christian.

Maddox Coulter.

My best friend.

My lover.

My protector.

My downfall.

CHAPTER FOURTEEN

Lila

I spent two days agonizing over Maddox and our fallout.

Two days and two nights…

It was a battle with my brain and my heart. Anxiety got the best of me. My emotions were in turmoil, and I didn't know what to do… what to think… what to believe in anymore. I told myself it was okay to be hurt, to feel betrayed. Then, I told myself I was being unreasonable.

It wasn't Maddox driving the car that night. It wasn't Maddox who killed my parents. So, why was I punishing *him*? Punishing us?

Two days and two nights…

My overthinking had always been my biggest flaw.

Once I had calmed down, I started to see things clearly. It became easier to reason with myself. If there was someone who deserved the full lash of my hatred and my fury… it was the Carmichaels. *Not* Maddox.

His betrayal had cut deep, but now that I had the time to think about it, I *understood* why he did it. It was still a harsh truth to grasp, to swallow and to accept.

In my head, Maddox took the shape of Christian. I needed someone to be angry at, I needed someone to feel the brunt of my fury, and I directed it all toward Maddox.

I had needed someone to blame for the way my life had seemed to crumble under my feet.

Maddox was there... and I blamed him.

Now that I had the time to *really* think about it, I realized that the gala was a blurred mess in my brain. I had gone into shock, and I was surviving on it. I hadn't given myself time to grieve, to come to terms with seeing Christian again, coming face-to-face with my parents' killer.

I had been reliving my past, too overwhelmed to really process what was happening. My therapist used to say that emotional shock is a shutdown mechanism that is supposed to buy a person time to process their trauma.

Hurting Maddox... pushing Maddox further from me was my way of dealing with it. I had been vulnerable... powerless, and it was my weak attempt at shutting down and protecting myself.

I wanted to believe that Maddox would never intentionally hurt me. I wanted to believe *in* him. After everything we had been through, his feelings for me were honest. I knew that with as much surety that I knew my own love for him.

After coming to terms with my own anger and my sense of feeling betrayed, I finally decided to meet up with Maddox. It was time for us to talk.

I wasn't ready to put all of this behind us. The trust between us was fragile, a thin thread that could easily snap.

But I was willing to try.

Because I wanted Maddox. Needed him. Because our pasts should no longer have any control over our present... or *our* future.

I wanted to give us another chance. Forgiveness was the first step. I was willing to forgive him for keeping that secret. My mom never taught me to give up so easily, and Maddox was worth it.

He was worth the pain.

He was worth my love.

I walked out of class with a renewed determination. My gaze flickered to my, now, fixed phone, but there was no new messages or incoming calls. I texted Maddox an hour ago and had asked him to meet me at his place.

His class ended before mine. But there was no response from him, except radio silence.

It's okay, I told myself. *I can wait.*

I walked down the path that led me off campus and toward the school residence. I counted the steps in my head, feeling my hands tremble in nervousness.

I told Maddox I would never give up on him, and I was willing to keep that vow. For him. For *us*.

Tugging my jacket closer to my body, I shielded myself from the cold. My gaze found the couples around me. Some were walking hand in hand. I caught one couple kissing. There was another one hugging by the bus stop, laughing... *happy*...

It was a cruel reminder of what I threw away... what I had lost. My pace quickened, as I tried to get away from all the loving couples.

I almost reached my apartment building... when something else caught my attention. A flash of familiar dirty blond hair. My feet slowed, and then came to a halt. I turned toward the coffee shop to my left.

Numbness took over, and my body froze on the spot.

When life hits you in the face, it hits you hard enough to give you goddamn whiplash.

My breath caught in my throat. Maddox occupied a table near the window. He wasn't... alone. Bianca sat across from him. I blinked, as I tried to make sense of what I was seeing. My eyes lowered to her midriff.

The sight of it was glaring back at me.

No, God. Please no. Please don't be so cruel to me. No, please. No. No. NO.

The last time I had seen Bianca, she was wearing a baggy sweater. Today, she had a simple black camisole on. It molded around her curves and... her very round, very pregnant belly.

I started shaking, my whole body growing cold... and colder.

I felt the sting of tears in my nose, as I blinked, wishing this was all an illusion. But no matter how many times I blinked, the reality glared back at me.

His truth.

His secrets.

His lies.

Maddox and Bianca looked to be arguing. Her expression was heartbroken, as Maddox shook his head. She cupped her pregnant belly, and she was full on crying now. Bianca tried to reach for him, but he pulled away, like the mere idea of her touch would burn him.

I watched, as he pulled something from the pocket of his jacket. The world slowed down, and the colors faded away. I watched the scene in front of me, like a black and white movie with no sound.

I was still in the same spot when Maddox got up to leave.

He turned... his eyes locked with mine... Bianca gasped...

Maddox paled, and he rushed forward.

I took a step back...

And I ran. For the third time in a week, I ran from Maddox.

I pressed a hand over my face, as Maddox walked through the door, barging inside of his bedroom. I didn't even realize I had found my way in here.

I missed this room. Missed sleeping in this bed, wrapped in his embrace. Missed his scent that lingered on our pillows and the mattress.

Maddox was out of breath, as he rushed toward me. I looked up into his wide, terrified eyes. "Lila, let me explain," he said. This had become his signature phrase. Why did he keep messing up so much that I had to give him a chance to explain. Every. Single. Time?

I swallowed back the cry that threatened to spill from my throat. "The last few weeks, I had been so worried," I confessed, my voice thick with emotion. "So scared. You were drifting away from me. Something was wrong, I could tell. I gave you a chance to tell me, but you didn't. I asked you, but you evaded my questions. The distance between us grew, as I watched helplessly. It was only a matter of days, before everything fell apart."

I got off the bed, away from the musky, masculine scent that kept assaulting my senses. I now realized the reason Maddox had been acting so different, why he had been so aloof.

"Is it yours?" I still asked, even though I already knew the answer. "Is this why she was texting you?"

Maddox gave me a single nod.

"How far along is she?"

Bianca didn't look to be in her third trimester. Her pregnant belly was round and firm but petite. "Almost six months."

Six... months.

My hand came up, and I rubbed my forehead, trying to chase away the pounding headache. My chin wobbled, and my lips trembled. I felt the sting of fresh tears in the back of my eyes. If I did my math correctly...

She and Maddox slept together about five weeks before Paris.

He said he had been celibate for... *months.* Five weeks was definitely *not* months. It was barely even one.

"You said you didn't sleep with anyone for a long time. I didn't know five weeks is considered a long time," I said, almost mocking him. "It must have been torture for you to be *celibate* for *five* weeks."

Maddox shook his head. "I don't remember much of that night. I didn't even know I slept with her, Lila. I hadn't been with anyone for months, but that night... It was the party... the spring reunion party for the football team."

The one I didn't attend with Maddox because I had been sick and on my period.

He rubbed a hand over his face, tiredly, looking more haggard than ever. "God, I was drunk. So fucking drunk, the whole night is a blur."

I swallowed and tried to push the ball of emotion down my throat. "How are you sure you slept with her?"

Guilt flashed in his blue eyes, and he grimaced. "I didn't think about it before, because I didn't remember much of that night. But when Bianca approached me and told me about it... I saw a flash of us together. I remembered going into the room with her," Maddox croaked, the rest of his words barely audible. "When I told you I hadn't slept with anyone in months, I wasn't lying. I *didn't* lie because, honest to God, I didn't remember that night."

I didn't know what to believe in anymore.

An hour ago, I had been ready to forgive Maddox about Christian.

I had been willing to look past the fact that he kept such a secret from me. Had been willing to move on... and forgive... to accept... to love again.

And now?

We were back to square one.

"I don't understand." I shook my head, bringing my trembling fingers to my temple, rubbing the throbbing ache. "Why didn't she tell you before? Why wait so long?"

His throat bobbed, as he swallowed. "She didn't know... if she wanted to keep the baby."

"And you? What are you going to do?" I asked quietly.

His head snapped up; fear was an apparent mask on his face. I had my answer, without him even having to say the words. My heart crash landed at my feet.

Maddox tried to reach for me, but I pushed away. "You lied to me about her. The moment you found out she was pregnant with your baby, why didn't you tell me?"

"I didn't know how," he breathed. "I didn't want to lose you."

"It was simple. You just had to tell me the truth, that's all I've ever asked from you."

His legs gave out, and he sat on the bed, his head in his hands, a choked sound coming from him.

"You're the best unplanned thing that has ever happened to me, Maddox. And I can't lose you. But you're doing everything to push... me away from you," I whispered, my voice breaking at the end. "You've been telling lies, keeping secrets. Since when have you started lying to me, Maddox?"

I already had the answer to that question. Months... and months of secrets.

After everything we had been through... he tainted everything that we were with his lies.

"You said you didn't want to lose me. But you already have," I whispered, my voice faltering, as I spoke the hardest words in my life.

His head snapped up, and his eyes flared with torment. He was decadently handsome, a little bit broken and a mistake from the beginning.

"I'm sorry," he choked out.

"Is that all you have to say?"

There was tears in his eyes. "I'm sorry."

If it hurts you so much, what kind of love is this?

I knew Maddox would break my heart, but a part of me hoped he wouldn't.

My heart wept, and a lone tear slid down my cheek. "They said you were trouble. I didn't listen. I took a chance on you. And now I regret it."

"Don't leave me." His hoarse voice cracked. "*Please*."

I took a step back. Maddox looked wounded, and my soul bled to see *him* hurt.

I had to leave. For me. For him.

"Lila," he breathed my name. "Please."

I slowly shook my head. "Maddox." It pained me to say his name. "You broke your promises."

My feet took me another step back.

"No," he pleaded. "Lila, *no*."

I turned and walked away, leaving my broken heart at his feet.

Pausing at the door, I gave him a final glance over my shoulder. "You're going to be a father, Maddox," I whispered, my voice thick with unshed tears. "Congratulations."

He shook his head in denial. "You already broke us, but for once in your life... do the *right* thing, Maddox. Bianca needs you. And that baby deserves a father."

Like I needed him.

But she needed him... more.

Maddox

I fucked up.

I knew I'd eventually mess up. I knew I'd end up destroying the one good thing in my entire life. *Lila.*

Because that was the only thing I was capable of.

Destroying lives.

Ruining her.

Wrecking us.

I tried to protect her, since the day I made that stupid goddamn pinky swear. I made sure she was always happy, always taken care of, by eliminating anything that would cause her pain...but I forgot to protect her from *myself*.

My lungs seized in my chest, and my throat closed. A choked sound came from my throat, as I held my head in my hands, feeling the burn in the back of my eyes.

"You're the best unplanned thing that has ever happened to me, Maddox. Ever. And I can't lose you. But you're doing everything to push... me away from you," she whispered, her sweet voice breaking at the end. "You've been telling lies, keeping secrets from me. Since when have you started lying to me, Maddox?"

My head snapped up at her words, but I didn't have an answer. I fucking wished I did.

Lies, no matter how big or small, were the quickest way to ruin something beautiful – *us*.

Lies and secrets...

Everything I'd ever done, every decision I ever made, was to protect Lila.

But no band-aids would ever be enough to stop the open, festering wounds I'd left behind.

"I'm sorry," I choked.

The torment on her face decimated me. "Is that all you have to say?"

My vision blurred – *fuck* – I had to remind myself not to lose my shit. My emotions were in turmoil, and I fought to keep myself sane. *"I'm sorry."*

A lone tear slid down her cheek. "They said you were trouble. I didn't listen. I took a chance on you. And now I regret it."

"Don't leave me." My hoarse voice cracked. *"Please."*

Lila took a step back. My wounded heart lurched, and bile crawled up

548

the back of my throat, bitter and acidic, at the thought of losing her.

"Lila," I breathed her name. "Please."

She slowly shook her head, another silent tear, leaving a wet trail on her cheek. "Maddox." She looked pained, and her lips wobbled. "You broke your promises."

And now she was breaking *hers*.

Her feet took her another step back.

"No," I pleaded. "Lila, *no*."

My voice caught in my throat, as she turned and walked away, taking my bleeding heart in the palm of her hand and leaving me... lifeless.

I sank to my knees, unable to stop myself, choking on the heavy taste of bitterness on my tongue. This couldn't be the end... it *couldn't*.

The door closed, even as I called out her name. Pathetically. Because for her... I was a fucking *weak* man.

For her.

For only her. *My* Lila.

Love makes you weak.

Love destroys lives.

Love ruined us.

She left. The one thing she promised not to do... She vowed to never leave me, to never leave my side... but there she was. Walking away.

My Lila left, as the pain piercing through my chest became more than unbearable.

All my truths, all my lies collided together – my future with Lila was now cracked open, shattered and bleeding, as I knelt in the wreckage of it all.

Once again...alone.

Once again... lost.

She lied, too.

She broke her promises, too.

You won't lose me, ever.

Pinky promise?

Pinky promise.

All the promises we made to each other, in the end… none of it mattered.

In the end, we lost our way, and our happy ending faded away.

CHAPTER FIFTEEN

Lila

Not all right decisions feel like they are *right*. Sometimes, they gut you from within and tear you apart. Right decisions should be easy to make, but they rarely are.

I had a choice, and I wanted to believe I made the right one.

The good choice, the right decision.

Walking away from Maddox was the hardest thing I had ever done in my life, but I had to...

Not for me. But for *him*.

Maddox was my boyfriend, but first and foremost... he was my best friend. I knew him better than he knew himself. I could see inside him, so clearly, and Maddox, my God, he was so lost in that moment, and I needed him to see things clearly.

I waited for the wave of regret that had been crashing through me, since I walked away from him. It came and went, similar to the wave of pain. Always there, always constant. But still, I told myself I made the right decision.

For the last three weeks, Maddox tried calling. He knocked on our door multiple times a day. He talked to Riley, tried to convince her to let him inside... to let him talk to me. But Riley was loyal to a fault. She didn't know why I had to walk away, but she knew how much it hurt me.

I never ran away from my problems, but I had to run away from Maddox. He was my one weakness, and I knew the moment I took a look at his broken stare, his wounded blue eyes – I'd fall back into his arms. It would turn into a vicious, never-ending cycle.

"Hey, Lila!" I flinched away from my thoughts and turned toward the sound of my name.

My co-worker snapped her fingers in my face and gave me a questioning look. "Stop day-dreaming. No time for that."

I wiped my wet hands on my apron. "I'll serve the next table." I went to take the tray from her hand, but she held it out of my way.

Amanda fished for something from the front pocket of her apron. She placed a blue post-it note, folded in half, in my open palm. "He told me to give you this."

My heart thudded. "He?"

Amanda shrugged and walked away. I unfolded the note, and my heart cracked, my chest burning with misery.

You didn't even give me a chance to kiss you goodbye.

I looked up and caught Maddox's eyes through the window of the restaurant. His tortured eyes held mine for a single second, a throbbing moment, a painful heartbeat, before he blinked and walked away. Maddox disappeared in the crowd, with only his note, as a reminder that he had been here.

We were strangers, once again.

This was more than a note about our last goodbye. He was letting me know he had given up. Maddox wasn't going to fight for us anymore. It almost killed me where I stood, for a second, my heart ceased to beat.

I should have been happy about this – it was what I wanted, after all. I had been avoiding him for over three weeks, waiting for the moment, when he would stop calling and stop trying to see me.

But it still… *hurt.*

Goddamn it.

Giving Maddox Coulter my heart had been a mistake. But this time… I had been the one to walk away from him.

"I forgot, when are your exams?" Riley settled beside me on the couch, wrapping an arm around my shoulders. I sunk into her embrace and curled my feet under me.

"I have two back to back in two days, and another, the day after next."

We were now exactly twenty days from Christmas. My life fell apart at a shitty time. Exams period were upon us, and life got even crazier. I could barely study, barely focus on my revisions for my exams. My mind was a mess, and my heart just wasn't in it. I constantly worried about Maddox. He was never next door. From what I heard, he was staying with Colton at his townhouse. The apartment that we made into our home – it was now empty. Forgotten. Abandoned.

"How are you feeling?" Riley asked cautiously.

"I feel like shit," I said, shocking myself with my honesty. "How's Maddox?"

Her brows creased. "I don't understand you. He hurt you, you left him. There's so much bitterness and heartache there. Yet, you still ask me about him every day. Keeping tabs on him. I don't understand you, Babe."

Fresh tears stung the back of my eyes, but I blinked them away. "I still love him."

"Then why did you leave?"

"Because sometimes love isn't enough."

She squeezed my shoulders, and I knew what was coming. "He didn't cheat on you. Yes, he lied. He should have told you about Bianca the moment he found out, but is it really that bad? This whole situation is just a big ball of mess, but maybe... I don't know. I just think that Maddox would never intentionally hurt you. I think he was just trying to protect you, in his own messed up way."

"You won't understand." Because she hadn't looked into Maddox's eyes and didn't see his struggles... his truth...

"Help me understand." She scrunched her nose, as she tried so hard to break down my walls. Riley was a good friend, my only friend. My little bundle of light.

"I can't," I whispered.

She let out a soft sigh, and her head dropped back against the couch. "Maddox still hasn't returned. He's staying with Colton, and he hasn't attended any classes since..."

My eyes shuttered close, and I breathed through the stinging in my nose. "He's going to be okay. Maddox is strong and capable of taking care of himself."

"I hope you're right," Riley whispered.

She didn't believe me.

And... as much as I wanted my words to be true, I didn't believe myself either.

My phone vibrated between my legs, and I peeked at the screen, looking at an unfamiliar number. I ignored the call and closed my eyes.

"Someone's calling again," Riley said, next to me.

"I don't recognize the number."

Five consecutive calls later, I started to grow uneasy. Anxiety tugged at the muscles in my chest, and a heavy weight settled there. At the sixth call, from the same number, I finally picked up.

"Hello?"

"Oh, Lila. Finally." A familiar voice came through, and I frowned.

"Savannah?" Why was Maddox's mother calling me?

Maddox. Oh God. Maddox!

I bounced off the couch, my heart feeling constricted, as if something heavy had wrapped itself around the fragile organ, squeezing the life out of me. "Is he okay? What happened? What's wrong? Is it Maddox?"

"What? No – I mean, I've been trying to reach him for the last five days, but he won't pick up my calls anymore."

Okay, that wasn't alarming. Maddox never picked up his mother's calls or his father's, for that matter. He rarely wanted to listen to what they had to say.

"I don't understand. You sound worried," I said, still frowning.

"The last time I spoke to him, he hung up on me," she whispered, and then, I heard sniffling.

I rubbed my forehead, feeling another headache quickly approaching. "Savannah, what are you trying to say? If you're calling me this many time, then it must be important. Is this about another gala or dinner party? I'm not coming, and neither is Maddox. Save it. Don't even bother asking."

Savannah was silent for a second, before she burst into tears and choked out her words, half mumbling and half not making any sense. "No. Not…another… gala. This… Brad… Maddox… won't pick up my… call. His… father…"

I paced the floor, feeling so confused, so lost. Savannah Coulter was crying to me on the phone. For the four years that I have known her, she's never lost her cool, maintaining her calm, plastic façade.

She was…*crying*. CRYING! The world was officially ending, this was proof enough. "What about Brad?"

"He's in the hospital." She hiccupped back a sob.

My feet came to a halt, and I paused, my breathing stuttering. *"What?"*

"He's sick, Lila. Very sick," Savannah whispered, barely audible.

"Maddox needs to be here… but he won't pick up my calls."

Oh God. No! "Did you tell him?"

"I did, but he didn't say anything and then hung up on me. This was five days ago. Brad is… He wants to see his son."

His son – the same one he didn't give a shit about before. But now that he was bedridden in a hospital bed, he needed to see his… *son*.

"I don't know, Savannah. I haven't seen Maddox in weeks. We broke up."

"Please," she begged, her voice cracking. "Please. He needs to be here. You don't understand. Brad… I don't know how long he has. Please, Lila."

I glanced at Riley, and she gave me a questioning look. "I'm sorry, Savannah. I'll see what I can do, but I can't guarantee he'll listen to me. If you want Maddox there and I can't bring him to you, you'll need to find another way."

Savannah inhaled a shaky breath. "Okay. Thank you, Lila."

We hung up, and I fell on the couch beside Riley. "What's up? What did Savannah want?"

"Brad is… sick."

Her mouth rounded with a shocked 'o'. "She wants you to convince Maddox to go see his dad?"

"Bingo."

"How sick is he?"

I shrugged. "I don't know. It sounded serious, because she was crying."

Riley nodded slowly. "I was on Colton's Instagram two hours ago. They apparently have a party going on at his house, right now. I saw Maddox in one of the videos in his story."

"Another party?" During Exams? What the hell?

"Last I heard, it was Maddox who decided to throw the party. Again. Which, by the way, the last one ended with a fight."

This reminded me of four years ago. Back in high school, when Maddox didn't give a shit about anything or... anyone. He was all about partying, drugs and alcohol... and letting his fists do the talking.

He was spiraling. Once again. Oh God.

My head fell into my hands, and I took a deep breath. Maybe it was my fault... An overwhelming sense of guilt filled my chest, and I almost choked on the taste of bitterness on my tongue.

"Do you want to wait until tomorrow?" Riley questioned, rubbing my back.

"No. I have to do this tonight. Maddox might be stubborn, but I am more stubborn than he could ever be."

CHAPTER SIXTEEN

Lila

R iley and I parked three houses away and stared at Colton's corner townhouse. After a few minutes of silence, we walked up to his porch and blinked. "Holy shit," Riley breathed.

The party was loud and crowded. I cringed, as a couple stumbled out, practically mauling each other. He pushed her against the house, and they were practically humping over their clothes, too drunk to care that they had an audience.

It was in that moment when I realized how bad this situation was. I shouldn't have come here tonight. If I found Maddox's in the arms of another woman...

Oh my God.

I almost doubled over, because the pain of that was unbearable. This was the wrong decision. I should have waited until tomorrow morning, when everything would have been calmed.

But what if...

What if he still had a woman by his side in the morning...?

What would I have done then?

Shit. SHIT! I couldn't even bring myself to think of it. I stalked forward, climbing up the stairs, into Colton's fancy townhouse and weaving my way through the sweaty bodies.

I spotted him instantly. Through a crowd, many feet away. It was like my eyes knew where to look, my heart knew where he was, an invisible string tugging my body toward him.

Maddox.

He sat on a couch; his long legs spread out in front of him. He wore black jeans and a black shirt, with holes in it. It looked like he hadn't bothered to shave for many weeks, and his hair was just as messy. Maddox looked completely out of it. High and drunk.

The two girls, one on each side of him, giggled. They were practically salivating for his attention, but his stares were empty, glazed over. Maddox tipped his head back and took a long pull from his joint, inhaling that shit and breathing out a thin layer of smoke. I took a step closer, my body moving on its own accord.

The blonde girl on his right stuck her face into his neck and her hand moved to his crotch. My heart was about to fall right out of my chest, when his fingers circled around her wrist, stopping her movement. He placed her hand on his thigh, a safe distance away from his dick.

My hand went to my throat, and I clenched our dreamcatcher. I exhaled the breath I didn't know I had been holding.

He lifted his head, looking in my direction.

Our gaze met.

I halted.

He paused.

Time just fucking stopped.

My body twitched under his gaze.

He stared.

I breathed.

The dreamcatcher dug into my palm, as my hold tightened around it.

Maddox's lips curled, and there was nothing warm about it.

Maddox slowly got off the couch and stalked toward me. His eyes were angry, crazed. He still had a bottle in his hand, and he was half drunk. I could tell by the way he stumbled toward me. I never got a word out, as he grasped me by the elbow, and started pulling me up the stairs. His fingers were digging roughly into my skin, but I didn't care in the moment.

Maddox pulled me into a room and slammed me against the wall, as he kicked the door closed. His body pinned me to the wall. "Mad–"

His lips slammed against mine, before I could breathe out his name.

The world shut off.

Time stopped ticking.

Everything just halted, and I was stuck in this moment, on a loop.

The colors faded away.

I stopped thinking... only *feeling.* This. Him. His lips.

His lips feasted on me, like he had been craving for my taste all along. It was all-consuming, and with a desperation so crazed, it lingered on my skin, and I could taste it on my lips, on my tongue. He took possession of my mouth, like he owned it. Like he owned me.

And goddamn it. He did. In this very moment, he *owned* me.

My skin hummed under his touch. His arm circled around my hips, and he pulled me up, my toes leaving the ground, as he kept me between the wall and his body. My hands landed on his shoulders, and his muscles clenched under my fingers. His body jolted, at my touch, and he bit me. Bit me hard enough that I tasted the metallic taste of my blood on my tongue.

This was no sweet reunion.

It was a battle cry. So much anger, so much hatred, so much... passion.

I bit him back, feeling his lip swell under my teeth. Maddox groaned, low and deep, and his body shuddered. Almost violently. I didn't know where he started, and I ended. Our blood mixed on our tongues, but we didn't stop kissing. Didn't stop battling for dominance. Didn't stop... touching each other.

This kiss.

This moment.

This... *feeling*. Torment. Love. Fury. Passion. Resentment. Longing. Pain. So much fucking pain.

The kiss slowed, and I wondered if Maddox could feel how much I didn't want this moment to end.

"You taste like mine... and lies. You're a fucking liar, Lila," he rasped against my lips.

Furious, I tore away from him and slammed my fists into his chest. He was hurting, I told myself. He didn't mean it; I whispered in my head.

But the anger was overwhelming and the final thin thread of my sanity snapped. I stabbed my finger into his chest, hard enough that he drunkenly stumbled back. "Me? ME? I'm a liar?" I screamed into his face. "You lived with me for months and lied to MY FACE, EVERY SINGLE DAY! You started our relationship with a lie. You. Kept. Secrets. From. Me."

His eyes darkened, and his face turned red with rage, as he bellowed back, "I never lied to you!"

I paused, my heart hammered in my rib cage, so hard, I thought it'd burst out of my chest. "You still think you're right? You still think whatever you did... was the right decision?"

"I never lied to you."

I shook my head, laughing, but there was no humor in it. My laugh sounded as dead as my heart felt. "You did. You broke me, Maddox. You broke me... more than Christian and his dad ever did. You had the power to do so, and you used it."

"I never lied to you," he said again, in that same lifeless tone. Like he was trying so hard to convince himself.

"What was it then, if not a lie?"

Maddox lunged forward and pushed me back. His chest slammed against mine, and he pinned me against the wall again. "I was protecting you. It wasn't a lie. Yes, I kept secrets... but I didn't lie, Lila. I didn't. All I ever wanted to do was protect you. Keep you safe. Keep you happy," he croaked. "I vowed, damn it. I VOWED IT. I loved you and that was not a lie," Maddox snarled in my face, his eyes deranged, and oh God, I never wanted to see that wounded expression on his face, ever again.

He... loved... me.

I remembered thinking about the moment we'd confess our love to each other.

I thought it would be romantic... I dreamed it would be magical. Little did I know... Our love turned out to be a war zone.

His hands slammed against the wall on either side of my head, so close, I flinched. "But you're a liar, Lila. You promised me you wouldn't leave me, but you did. I needed you... and you weren't there. I fucking needed you, and the only person I ever FUCKING LOVED WAS NOT THERE FOR ME! So, tell me, Lila. Who's the liar?"

"You," I whispered. *I'm sorry,* I cried.

His chest heaved.

My heart stuttered.

Maddox stepped back. My knees weakened.

"You kill me, Lila."

I squeezed my eyes closed and choked back a sob. I killed him...

No, I had been trying to save him... to protect him... to make the right decision.

Maddox grabbed the bottle again and downed the rest of it, barely a grimace on his face. *I killed him...*

Maddox Coulter was a god amongst mortals. He was enraged, a bitter and wounded god. And I wondered if I made a mistake by falling in love with a man like him.

I watched, as he finished the bottle and started rummaging through the mini fridge, taking out another one. God, he was going to drink himself to oblivion. He was going to drink himself to a slow... death.

I swallowed back a cry and rubbed a hand over my face. My tongue felt heavy in my mouth, but I licked my dry lips and tried again. "I didn't come here to fight, Maddox."

"You came here to fuck," he deadpanned, with no emotions whatsoever.

"No," I breathed through the pain. "I found out... about your father. That he's... sick."

"Oh, you *pity* me?" Maddox threw my words back at me. "How sweet. Lila Garcia needed to make herself look like a little angel, coming to my rescue."

I flinched but pressed forward. "I broke up with you, but I'm still your best friend. We used to have each other's back, and I came here... because I thought I could offer you my friendship."

He didn't respond. Barely even acknowledged my words, except for a small twitch in his granite jaw. My hands trembled, so badly, that I had to press them against my thighs, trying to stop the shaking. "Have you... talked to your... father?"

Silence.

"You mom called me."

Utter broken... silence.

"Please, I'm trying. I want to be here for you, right now. I might have broken up with you, walked away... But I'm not giving up on you or bailing on our friendship. If you need me, I'll be here. *I'm trying.*"

Finally, he gave me a response.

Maddox's face darkened. He stepped closer, crowding into my space and pushing me back against the wall.

"Maddox–" I started, but he cut me off with a low snarl, his chest vibrating with the cruel sound.

My chest cracked, wide-open, and the fissures of my broken heart scattered on the ground at our feet.

His eyes blazed with rage and... raw pain. "I'm self-destructing every time I look at you, every time my eyes seek you out when we're in the same room. You make destruction and melancholy taste like sweet, sweet fucking poison."

His hands came up, landing on either side of my head. His minty breath whispered across my lips, a tempting touch, but our lips didn't meet. His mouth curled on the side, a sardonic smile.

"It hurts because you're not mine. It hurts because we could have been good together, but you decided to give up on us."

No. No. No.

His voice was rough and stiff, as he spoke, his words slicing through the air and through me like a sharp sword. He left me bleeding on the spot, and his eyes told me he didn't care. "So spare me the speech and get the fuck out."

My heart lurched and bled, the organ so fragile, it couldn't bear the assault of his words. His dark gaze went to my throat, and we both stopped breathing for a mere second.

There was an unreadable expression on his face. A flash of pain echoed in his eyes, before it was gone. I whimpered, as he curled a finger around my necklace.

Our dreamcatcher.

Snap.

My eyes widened, and I choked back a gasp. A single tear slid down my cheek, as he snapped the necklace away from my neck, holding it up between us.

"I'll be taking this back," Maddox said, his voice raw and sharp, laced with enough heartbreak that my knees weakened, and I slid to the ground.

He... took... my necklace. Snatched it right from my neck...and...

My lungs seized, and a wounded sob tore through my throat.

Holding our dreamcatcher in the palm of his hand, he walked away.

CHAPTER SEVENTEEN

Maddox

Hate is a strong word. But I hated my father. I loathed my mother. And Lila? I *hated* her as much as I *loved* her.

It ate at me, that all-consuming feeling. Like little bugs eating at my flesh, cutting me open, as my blood poured out. No fucking mercy.

I wondered if I'd ever stop feeling numb. The alcohol helped, most of the time. But when I was sober again, I just felt shittier. So I'd drink again. And again. Until I was drunk, day and night. Numb to everything, everyone, every fucked-up emotion brewing inside of me.

Except, the taste of betrayal lingered. Heavy and bitter.

Lila fucked with my head, and I let her in, gave her the power to do *this* to me. Turned me into the 17-year-old Maddox, who was bitter and enraged. She promised she'd be there when I needed her. But she wasn't. And that – *that* betrayal cut me worse than my father's disappointment or my mother's lack of care.

A pounding headache woke me up, and I glanced around the bare room. The clock said it was past one in the afternoon. Shit, I slept the whole morning away. My head hurt; my body ached. I needed a drink, again. To forget. To go back to being numb.

There was a commotion outside, before the bedroom door slammed open. I groaned, pulling a pillow over my head. "Get the fuck out, Colton."

"No."

My muscles tensed, and my heart skipped.

That stubborn voice.

That beautiful, stubborn voice.

Goddamn it. What was *she* doing here?

The memories of last night came back to me, flashing behind my closed lids, like black and white polaroid photos. Lila was here last night.

The kiss.

The fucking kiss that I could still taste on my lips.

Her dreamcatcher.

The pounding in my temples grew worse.

"Get up," she said, in her sweet, sing-song voice. A voice that haunted me in my dreams and in my reality.

I kept the pillow over my face, refusing to look at her. She was my one weakness, and I couldn't afford to look at her and... *feel.* "And you can fuck right off, Garcia."

There was a small growl, a kitten growl. "Don't test me, Coulter."

Oh, so we were back to being Garcia and Coulter.

Lila was silent for a minute. I heard her footsteps moving away, and I breathed out. She was leaving? Giving up already? My ears perked up, when I heard the water running from the bathroom. What...?

Seconds later, her footsteps approached my bed again. I didn't have time to react, before I was hit with the unexpected.

Freezing cold water. I gasped, threw the pillow off my face, only to have more water dumped over my head.

"Holy fucking shit!" I sat up on the wet mattress and wiped the cold water off my chest and face. "What is wrong with you? Jesus Christ, you're such a fucking bitch."

Lila dropped the pitcher on the floor, her eyes blazing with fury. "Listen to me, Coulter. Call me a bitch again, and I will make you eat that word."

"Bitch," I hissed under my breath.

Her eyes narrowed on me and then she smiled. A sweet smile that should have warned me of what was coming, but I fell for it. Fell for that beautiful smile that owned me.

I didn't see it coming. And when I did, it was too late.

Lila marched to the closet, rummaged inside, looking for something. Thirty seconds later, she came back out with a... baseball bat.

Woah. Woah, hold-the-fuck-up.

Her eyes glistened with something unrecognizable. There was anger and frustration there. And more. Lila stalked to my window, raised the bat and...

BAM!

My heart jumped to my throat. I scrambled off the bed, gaping at my window. Lila lifted the bat again and brought it against the window in one hard swing, shattering whatever was left of it, after her first hit.

"I'm nobody's bitch. Good luck sleeping without a window, Coulter."

I gaped at Lila. Her Latina side was obviously showing. I looked at the shattered window and then back at her grinning face – although there was nothing warm about her smile. "You're a psycho."

But was I surprised? No, I wasn't. Lila Garcia might be midget-sized, but she was a dragon. A little, red dragon who was capable of doing the most damage.

She dropped the bat and stared, waiting. My eyes ran over her figure, taking in the tempting sight of her. Today, she wore faded blue jeans, ripped across her knees, a black long-sleeve shirt tucked inside her waistband and black combat boots. Her hair was in a messy braid and her throat...

It was bare.

No necklace. No dreamcatcher.

"Put your dick away, Maddox."

"*You* are in *my* room," I retorted, but still grabbed my boxers off the floor. "And if I remember correctly, you like my dick. A few weeks ago, you were choking on it."

Lila narrowed her eyes on my face; she avoided looking below my waist, as I pulled my boxers on. "Do you have to be so crass?"

My lips curled. "That's my charm, Garcia."

I sauntered over to the nightstand and grabbed the joint I had left there. The necklace on the surface caught my attention. Lila's gaze, as if she could read my mind, followed mine. Her hand came up to her bare throat, as if to grab her dreamcatcher, but it wasn't there.

I lit the end of the joint, rolling it in my fingers, before taking a long drag. I held it in, for as long as I could, before I slowly breathed the smoke back out.

I held it out to Lila. "Don't be shy. It's not like we haven't shared one before, *Sweet Cheeks*."

She crossed her arms, her lips thinning into a tight line. "What are you doing, Maddox? Just look at yourself."

I took another drag, running my fingers through my hair. "Oh, I do. I look in the mirror and I see the effect of Lila Garcia."

Her cheeks reddened, and she stalked toward me, until we stood a mere breath away. Her chest brushed against mine. "I don't *want* to be here," she hissed in my face. "But I am, because I care–"

I scoffed, exhaling a cloud of smoke into her face. She blinked, her nose wrinkling. "Believe what you want, Maddox, but our friendship didn't end with our relationship."

"You want to act like an asshole, go right ahead." Lila poked me in the chest, pushing me back a step. "But I'm here because I know you need your best friend, right now. Not a girlfriend."

"I needed you before. I don't need you now," I barked in her face.

Her neck flushed pink, and Lila looked at me with such heartbreaking eyes... Fuck.

Her fingers circled my wrist, and she brought my hand up. Her thumb brushed over my swollen, bruised knuckles. "You promised that you wouldn't ever stop being my friend, and I vowed that no matter what, we wouldn't let our fuckedupness get in the way of our friendship. I'm not here as your ex. I'm here as your friend. So, either you shower, get dressed and eat breakfast like a normal person, or I will drag you. Got it?"

Lila let my hand go, and she stalked away, only pausing at the door. She cocked her head to the side, looking at me over her shoulders. "And trust me, I can, and I will. You might be a hundred pounds heavier than me, but, remember, *you* trained me in how to use my weight against someone heavier than me."

Goddamn it.

An hour later, I found myself shoveling breakfast in my mouth. Colton tapped his fingers over the countertop, looking everywhere but my face. "Why did you let her in?" I said, around a mouthful.

Colton cleared his throat. "I didn't. I tried to close the door, but she kicked it open."

I dropped the fork on my plate. He was kidding, he had to be. "You're telling me, that you couldn't stop a hundred-pound woman from entering your home?"

"She threatened my dick, man." His voice lowered to a whisper. "She's legit a psychopath. No wonder you two suited each other so well."

Fuck that. I shoved another forkful in my mouth.

"Your mom called me again," Colton said, slowly.

"Same shit?"

"Your father is sick, Maddox."

"Yeah. So? This is probably another trick of his to get me more involved in his business. Not that I have any plans to take over."

"I don't think–"

I kept my face blank. "If he dies, thank fuck. Good riddance." My chest tightened, even as I said those words. Real, fucking pain sliced through me, and I clenched my jaw.

Colton winced at my choice of words. "You know Lila is not going to give up, until you go see your father in the hospital."

I knew that and to stop her from bothering me again, I was going to play along. Go to the hospital, visit my father, listen to what they had to say and walk away.

"Where is she?"

Colton nodded toward the door. "Outside."

"Let's get this over with."

CHAPTER
EIGHTEEN

Maddox

I parked outside of the hospital but didn't get out of the car. "Now, what?" I drawled, drumming my thumbs over the steering wheel.

"I can't force you to talk to your parents, Maddox. I already did what I set out to do."

"And what is that?"

Her lips twitched. "Get you out of bed. Take a shower. Have breakfast. Stop drinking for a few hours. Mission accomplished."

"You're such a bi–"

"Finish that sentence, I dare you," she grinned, almost mockingly.

"Biscuit."

Lila rolled her eyes. God, she was messing with my head. With us like this, I could almost forget the last month. It reminded me so much of the old times.

I could almost forget that I was… going to be a father… and that Lila had walked out on me when I needed her the most. But I didn't forget.

And the reminder sliced through me with a rusty blade that cut open my already painful wound.

I got out of the car and slammed the door. Lila followed me inside the hospital. I was instantly hit with the smell of sickness and death. I went to the help desk, and they redirected me to where Brad Coulter was staying. A private room in the upper floor. Lila and I took the stairs, and when we walked into the corridor, my mother was there.

Leaning against the wall, waiting. "Maddox," she breathed, in what seemed like relief.

"I'm here. Now what?" I said in a bored voice.

My mother flinched and then sniffled. "Your father wants to speak to you."

Lila touched my back, and her touch seared me through my shirt. Even as her hand fell away, I could still *feel* her on my skin. "I'll wait here."

I stuffed my fists in the pocket of my jeans and stalked forward, into the private hospital room. My feet paused at the door, and I came to a halt at the sight that greeted me. My whole body froze, and my heart jumped to my throat. Shit. Goddamn it.

I didn't know what I expected when I walked into the hospital. Hell, I didn't know what to think when my mother called me, weeping over the phone, as she told me my father was in the hospital and sick.

I didn't think.

I didn't react.

Not until now.

I didn't know what I expected, but this wasn't it.

My father, looking thin and frail, in a hospital bed that made him appear even smaller. Multiple machines beeping and attached to him. The Brad Coulter I knew was strong and confident, with arrogance that matched my own. He was always well-dressed, always spoke like he owned the room and everyone in it, always stood tall.

This was not Brad Coulter.

I didn't know what to do, what to say... so, I stood frozen at the door and stared at the man, who was my father. A stranger. My lungs clenched, a reaction I hadn't expect.

I didn't care, I told myself.

But the brief ache in my chest told me that I was still capable of feeling emotions for my shit dad.

My mother grasped my hand, shocking me even more, as she pulled me farther into the room. She let go, once we were standing next to the bed, and sat down on the chair. Taking my father's hand in hers, she squeezed, and his eyes opened.

Dark circles, tired and hollow. There was barely life in those eyes that used to hold so much power. He blinked at her and then smiled, as much as he could. It was a small twitch of his lips.

My mother returned the smile, a wobbly one of her own. "He's here," she whispered. "He came to see you. I told you, he would come. Didn't I?"

Who the fuck were these people? Because they weren't my parents, for fuck's sake.

When did this happen... how did *this* happen?

He looked at me, and his dry, cracked lips parted, as if to speak, but there were no words. His throat moved, but my father, for once, was silent.

My mother swallowed, making a choked sound at the back of her throat. "He tires easily and can't really speak much." She grabbed the pitcher of water and poured a glass full, before helping her husband drink it.

I rubbed a hand over my face and squeezed my eyes shut. This wasn't... real. It was a fucking nightmare; it had to be.

"How sick are you?" I asked, through gritted teeth.

"Cancer," my mother replied, so quietly, I almost missed it.

"Cancer?" I parroted. "When? You were healthy the last time I saw you."

"He wasn't, but he didn't want anyone to see it."

"When?" I barked.

"We found out about four months ago," she said, looking away from me.

Four months. Four goddamn months and they were telling me *now*.

"You didn't think I deserved to know before?" My mother winced, and she had the audacity to look ashamed.

I speared Brad Coulter with a look. "Why now? Why tell me now?"

"Because…" he started, only to end up coughing. My mother jumped and helped lift his head from the pillow. He coughed and coughed, the dry sound rattling from his chest and echoing through my ears. At the sight of blood dribbling past his lips, my hands started to shake.

My fists clenched, and I *had* to look away. This man wasn't my father.

After a moment, the coughing fit ceased, and I started to pace the hospital room. "Finish your sentence," I demanded. Cold, yes. But I didn't know how else to react, how else to speak to them.

"Because… I want… to fix… this… I want a… chance."

"So you don't die with the guilt that you were a shitty father?"

"Maddox!" My mother hissed. I swiveled around and matched her glare with one of my own.

"What? The truth is not something you want to hear?"

"I deserve that," my father admitted tiredly.

Fuck. This. "I'm out of here."

Before I reached the door, my mother's voice stopped me. "I want to tell you a story."

"I'm not here for some fairy-tale retelling, *Mom*," I seethed.

"Nothing about this story is a fairy tale, Maddox."

If you asked me why I didn't leave, why I stayed by the door and listened to her, I wouldn't have an answer to that question.

I simply didn't know.

Maybe it was something in her voice. The pain, the sorrow, the guilt. Maybe because it all sounded so real to my ears. I *felt* things I shouldn't have.

Turning around to face them, I leaned against the door and crossed my arms over my chest. "Speak." One word. It was all she needed.

She gripped my father's hand, her eyes glassy. "When I met your father, he didn't have any food to eat."

Wh – what the fuck?

She kept talking, before I could say anything, as if she was scared, she'd lose whatever courage she had to speak. "I remember that day very clearly. We were neighbors, and he came knocking at my door. He asked my parents if he could have a plate of food, or even a loaf of bread, to feed his younger brother."

Younger brother? My father has a brother? I have an uncle? How the hell did I not know this? My mind spun, and I blinked several times.

"You see, we came from a shitty neighborhood. From the slums. You could easily describe it as a slum part of New York City. We barely even had electricity or warm water, because we couldn't pay for it. We'd eat canned food that we could get from the community church or the food banks. That night, my family barely even had food to feed ourselves. My mother turned Brad away. After my parents went to sleep, I sneaked out of my room and went over to his house. I brought him two slices of bread. He broke down and cried. He was fourteen, I was eleven. He quickly fed his brother and only took two bites himself. I learned that they hadn't had any food for two whole days."

My mother paused, as I sunk to the floor, my legs suddenly feeling weak. I wanted to call her a liar, but I could hear the truth in her words, the rawness in her voice. This was real. My parents were poor... and I never knew. They never told me anything about their pasts or their childhoods. We never... *talked*.

I sat on my ass and stared at my parents, finally realizing that they were truly strangers to me.

My mother made a choking sound. "For four years, I'd sneak food to him. We were both poor, but I had parents who were still trying to get food on our table. Brad didn't. His mother was a drug addict and alcoholic. The little money Brad saved up from working part-time at the church, his mother would steal for drugs. When he was eighteen, he left home with his little brother."

"We were homeless," my father broke in, with a whisper, his voice cracking. "For months, we lived on the streets, under a bridge with other homeless people. We were...starving. I was ...desperate. I stole a man's wallet... and I was...caught. Was thrown in jail for a night. It rained that night. My brother...was... alone under the bridge. He walked in the rain for hours, looking for me."

He took a deep breath and paused with a cough. I was glad I was sitting down when my mother continued. "Your father's brother... your uncle... he caught pneumonia."

"He didn't... make it," I whispered, already knowing where this was going. If I had an uncle and my father never spoke of him, then it only meant one thing.

She nodded. "I used to sneak away from home to go meet your father. You see, we had a dream. We wanted a future together. We worked the cheapest job we could get. I waitressed. Brad worked at a mechanic shop. At twenty, he finally finished his high school diploma. Then came university. We could barely afford it." My mother paused, sniffling. "Those days were the hardest, but it paid off."

Her head fell into her hands, and she cried. "Savannah..." I heard him whisper.

My father picked up, in his weak voice. "We were finally able to buy an apartment, the cheapest one we could... afford, but it was ours. Life... got... better. We were no longer homeless or starving. I got a job, one that paid the rent and put enough food on the table. We lived paycheck to paycheck, but everything was…okay. Life… was good. When your mother found out she was pregnant with you…"

"That was the happiest day of our lives, Maddox," my mother whimpered. "The *happiest*. Truly, the happiest. The best day."

I wanted to call her a liar. All my life, they made me feel unwanted. I had been a mistake… yet, here they were, telling me that I was loved, before I was even born.

Bullshit.

But I stayed silent and listened. Because it was all I could do. I was stuck in this moment, their voices echoing in my ears, their past flashing in front of my eyes. I was… numb and then I was… feeling too much.

"For six years, we had everything we wanted. Sure, we weren't rich. We still struggled. But whatever we had, it was enough. Then, life… it… knocked us down... again."

"What?" My voice deepened, a ball of emotions settling itself at the base of my throat. "What happened?"

"You were five when I was diagnosed with colon cancer," my father said.

I covered my mouth, then rubbed a palm over my face. Fuck. No. This isn't… this couldn't be real.

"I'm out of here," I growled, pushing to my feet.

"*Please*," she whispered, so brokenly, I… just… couldn't. Walk. Away.

"Colon cancer is one of the easiest diseases to detect, and since we discovered it, at the earliest stage, it was curable," my father offered. "But that was a reality check for us, son."

He coughed in his fist once and then rubbed his chest, as if it pained him. The expression of his face was one of sorrow. And shame. "It was then I realized that if something were to ever happen to me… I would leave a wife and son, without any savings. A mortgage, student loans and nothing else. Your mother, she never finished high school. She worked to put me in university. She worked, so I could have a degree, and if I had died... your mother and you would have been left with nothing."

"When we left the slums behind... we promised to never go back to it," my mother cut in. "Never go back to being that poor."

Brad Coulter closed his eyes with a heavy sigh. "I became obsessed, Maddox. So... fucking... obsessed."

"Brad kept saying he wanted what was best for us. And so, he worked. He never stopped working. Never stopped to even take a deep breath. And he climbed up the ladder," she took a shuddering breath, "he went from an office clerk, to a lawyer, to a senior associate, to a business partner, then a law partner, a business owner... he kept climbing that ladder, like an obsessed man."

I shivered, feeling too hot and then too cold. My skin burned, my head ached, my chest... goddamn it, it was being carved open. That shit didn't just hurt. It fucking killed me.

My *father*... he opened his eyes, and there were tears in them. Real fucking tears. Tears I never saw before. "Years passed, I didn't notice. Years passed, I went from a man who lived from paycheck to paycheck, to a man who could have anything he wanted with a snap of his fingers. I had everything, but it was too late when I realized that, in chasing financial security, in becoming obsessed with being wealthy, I forgot... about you. Even though, *you* were the reason I had done everything I did."

"Am I supposed to pity you?" I finally growled, cutting into their little story. "Am I supposed to feel bad?"

They both flinched at my cruel words. Yeah, good. Fuck this. Fuck them.

"While Father Dearest was chasing after wealth, what were you were doing, *Mom*?" I spat out, turning toward Savannah Coulter. "Chasing after your husband?"

She had the audacity to look ashamed. "I feared losing him. After his experience with cancer... it was the one thing that *haunted* me. I couldn't... I didn't know how to cope."

"Does that excuse make you sleep better at night?"

"No." She shook her head. "It doesn't."

"Do you regret it?" I hissed, anger churning in the pit of my stomach. "If you could go back and change things, would you do it?"

My mother's tears-strained cheeks flushed even more, and she looked away, but not before I caught the flash of pain and guilt on her face. "If I could... I would have changed how things were. I was a good wife, but I couldn't be a good mother."

So, *now,* she cared. But too little, too late.

I got to my feet and straightened up. "Are you done?"

Silence. They both looked as if they had aged ten years since I had last seen them. Tired. Frail. *Weak.*

Their story explained their pasts, but it wasn't enough. I still didn't understand a lot of things. None of it made sense in my head, and the hospital room swayed back and forth in front of me.

"It's too late," I said out loud, the words were more for me than for them.

It was too late... Eighteen years too late.

There was no fixing *this.*

CHAPTER NINETEEN

Maddox

I walked out, closing the door behind me. My gaze immediately went to Lila. She was slumped in a chair, her head in her hands. She must have heard me approaching, because her head snapped up, and she straightened.

"Are you okay?" she whispered; her eyes wide. Frightened. Worried.

"He's… sick. Cancer." The moment I said those words, my knees weakened, and I sunk into the chair beside her. It suddenly felt… *real*.

This wasn't a nightmare.

This was real.

My father *had* cancer… *has* cancer. Shit. Shit. SHIT! I felt a tick in my eyelid, my vein pulsed in my throat, throbbing. I felt… sick. The bitter taste of bile made its way to my mouth. God, I was going to throw up.

"Maddox."

Her voice.

My name.

Her sweet, sweet voice.

"Breathe through your nose, Baby," she whispered, running her hand over my arm.

I squeezed my eyes shut, and I did as I was told. Breathed through my nose, like Lila taught me. Like her therapist had taught her.

Once my lungs stopped feeling like they were getting crushed under a pile of rocks, I opened my eyes and stared into Lila's brown ones. Lila Garcia was the anchor; I was the whole goddamn ocean.

"You're thinking about it, aren't you?" she questioned softly.

"Thinking about what?"

"What it would be like if your father is dead? You're wondering why you care and why your chest aches." She nodded at where I was rubbing my chest – doing so, unconsciously, until she pointed it out. Lila knew me too well. She knew me better than I knew myself. To her, I was an open book. I let my hand drop to my thigh.

"Do you know what I regret the most about my accident?"

I didn't respond. She took my hand in hers and slid her fingers between mine, squeezing. "I never got a chance to tell my parents how much I loved them. Our last moment was us fighting... and me calling them bad parents. That's what hurts the most, Maddox. If I could go back in time, I'd shout how much I love them. If I could go back in time, I'd beg to just spend one more *second* with them. Just to see their faces, to see their smiles and hear their voices."

"It's not your fault. The accident," I murmured, looking down at our entwined hands. Her smaller, paler one, in my much bigger and rougher hand. We were perfect together. Had been perfect together... until we weren't anymore.

"I know. But I still feel guilt over our argument and our last moments together."

I frowned and looked up at her face. "My relationship with my parents is not the same as yours, Lila. It's a different situation."

"I know, Maddox. But trust me, when I tell you… you hate your father so much, but deep inside, you just want to be loved by him. Ten years from now, you're going to wonder… What if? What if I gave my parents a chance? What if… I had spent those last moments with him? What if, Maddox? Those last moments won't erase twenty or so years of a bad relationship, but it could be a beginning of something better. Who knows? Who the fuck knows… but what if?"

She rubbed her thumb over my knuckles. I was transfixed by the movement, the gentle glide of her fingertips. "I constantly live in regret and guilt, Maddox. I know what it feels like. That burden on your shoulders, the pain – nothing physical, but sometimes that ache in your heart is the worst. I don't want that for you. One of us living through it is enough. You deserve better than that," she said, wrenching my chest open and squeezing my bloody heart with her bare hands.

Lila reached up and touched the side of my face, cupping my cheek. "You are worthy of love, Maddox Coulter. And you deserve everything you want."

I want you.

All I ever wanted was her. She was everything I needed.

Yet…

A throat cleared behind me, and I snapped away from Lila, as if someone had pulled my strings and I were a puppet. I looked at the intruder and found a tall man, with greyed hair, wearing a white coat. A doctor. Must be my father's, because he was looking at me with a familiarity that I didn't respond to.

"Maddox Coulter?" he asked, with a raised eyebrow.

I rose to my feet. "Yes. You are?"

"Dr. Fitzpatrick. Devin Fitzpatrick. A very old friend of your father's and his doctor."

"Is he dying?" I asked, before I could swallow the words. My voice cracked, showing the first sign of emotion, since I walked into the hospital.

Devin Fitzpatrick gave me a look of pity, and I fucking hated it. He nodded his head slowly. "Your father has a history of polyps and Chron's disease. Colon cancer is the second most deadly cancer. And this time, we weren't able to detect it at an early stage, like before. The cancer tissues have spread. The small tumors have made their way all over his intestines, and the cancer cells keep developing and growing at a rate that's nearly impossible for us to keep track, hence it's spreading faster. Your father has fought a long battle. He doesn't have long, Maddox. I'd suggest you spend his last moments with him."

I felt Lila coming closer behind me, her heat burning into me. She placed a hand on my lower back, a simple touch, as if to remind me she was *here*. "How long?"

"Two months, max. He refused any form of medical help. Your father wants his final days to be in peace." His voice lowered; his expression pained. "Without all the constant pain, chemo, drugs and surgeries. He went through it once. He knows how bad it can get."

"So, you're saying… he's just awaiting his death. Without even putting up a fight or trying to survive?"

"It's inevitable," he said gently, as if to soothe a wounded animal. "At this point, even if we go through chemo, it will only extend his lifespan by a few months. At most, barely even a year. But he'll suffer even worse."

I shook my head. "*The* Brad Coulter never gives up."

He smiled a bitter smile. "All men have a breaking point. We're not as invincible as we like to believe."

Devin clasped my shoulder, as if to comfort me. "I'm sorry."

He walked away, and I was left with his words and empty condolences.

My fingers slid through my hair, and I pulled at the strands, feeling the burn in my scalp. The world became blurred, and the hospital spun.

FUCK.

Lila

I splashed cold water on my face and... *breathed.*

My reflection in the mirror reminded me of a wilted flower. Weary. Frightened. Lost. I hated hospitals. Loathed it with every fiber of my being. It reminded me too much of the past. And I was stuck in a loop. Having to relive my past and forcing myself to stay focused on Maddox.

I closed my eyes and thought of what the doctor said. Brad Coulter was dying, and there was nothing we could do.

It didn't matter how much Maddox hated his father... I saw it in his eyes. He cared. He was worried. He... *felt.*

It was a strange way of connecting all the dots. Who would have thought that the big and mighty Brad Coulter would one day fall so hard? He had been a god amongst us mortals, and now, he was... dying. That was some reality check.

I shut off the tap and leaned against the sink, rubbing a hand over my wet face. The door slammed behind me, and I jumped, swiveling around to see Maddox stalking inside. He closed it behind me. "You're in the girl's bath–"

My mouth snapped closed, when I saw the expression on his face. His furious eyes. Hurt. Scared. Need. Vulnerable. Hunger. So much raw pain.

"Maddox," I breathed, feeling my heart swell in my chest.

At the sound of his name, he rushed forward and slammed into me. My hips knocked against the sink, and I cried out, only to have his mouth capture mine.

He kissed me brutally. So needy. So greedy.

A cruel, deep kiss. Frantic and agonizing. "I need you," he fed the words into my mouth, forcing his tongue inside.

He was so ruthless in his act, I forgot to breathe for a second. Maddox cupped my face with one hand, squeezing my cheeks. I gasped into his mouth, and his tongue swept along mine, forcing me to accept his sweet, vicious kiss.

I wrapped my arms around his head, my fingers delving into his curly, blond hair. His kiss never stopped, as he lifted me up, setting me on the surface of the sink. He roughly pushed my legs apart and forced himself in between, where he belonged.

I deepened the kiss, just as crazed as Maddox. He intoxicated me. I lost all thoughts of time and place.

Fire burned under my flesh. My stomach tightened.

Maddox groaned into my lips, and his hips jerked against mine. He swore and broke the kiss, his fist curling around my hair, to tug my head back, before he attacked my throat. He bit into my skin and suckled the pain away.

He hurt me.

He soothed me.

His palm cupped my breast, squeezing the heavy weight. There was a riot of emotions, brewing inside of me. So loud, so insane, so reckless.

I cried out, as his teeth sank deeper into my throat. It hurt. He kissed the pain away, whispering against my skin. "Lila. Lila. Lila. *Lila.*"

Oh God, it hurt so good.

My nails dug hard into his scalp, and he grunted, a rough sound that had my core pooling with warmth.

The distant sound of the knob turning pulled me out of this insanity. My eyes snapped open, and I saw the bathroom door opening. I gasped, pushing Maddox away and gulping for air.

He stumbled back, his eyes wide and glassy. So blue... deep like the ocean. Burning with so much need. A lust so fiery, it *scared* me.

I jumped off the counter and brought a shaky hand to my lips. Two elderly women joined us in the bathroom, and Maddox pushed past them, walking away without a word, without another glance.

My skin tingled with the aftermath of our kisses, even as coldness seeped through my pores. The two women gave me a knowing look, but I quickly averted my gaze and left the bathroom.

Maddox was pacing the corridor. He didn't meet my eyes, when I settled in the chair, wringing my hands in my lap.

That... would have destroyed me.

That kiss, if it had gone any further, would have killed me.

I wasn't strong enough to stop Maddox, because I was just as greedy for him, as he was for me. Such passion was too dangerous to be tested, to be played with.

There was no way we could dangle such temptation in front of ourselves and not snap. Neither of us was strong enough to resist it. In a single heartbeat, we'd be devouring each other.

Hours later, I still hadn't moved from the chair. Maddox and I hadn't spoken a word to each other. Though, we were, both, hyperaware of each other's attention and closeness.

Savannah walked out of the room, looking completely exhausted. "Should I order dinner? You two must be hungry."

I swallowed past the lump in my throat. It hurt. God, it hurt so much. Shaking, I stood up and avoided looking at Maddox. "I should leave. It's late..."

Savannah gave me a small smile and mouthed, *thank you.*

She walked back inside, but left the door open, this time. For Maddox. A silent invitation.

The back of my eyes burned. It was time for me to leave. I took a step away, my heart dropping to my feet, as I did.

Maddox's hand snaked out, and he clasped my wrist. Our eyes met. There was a heartbreaking silence between us, as if he could tell what I was thinking. He begged me with his eyes. I pleaded to him, silently.

Such foolish love it was.

"Stay," he breathed.

"I can't," I whispered.

This second lasted longer. It lasted a lifetime. This second was the beginning, the middle and the end of our love. It was the first sentence, the paragraph, the page of our incomplete story.

The blue in his eyes darkened, and I memorized every speck in them. Eyes that I could drown in, and I guess... I did. Blue eyes that were the first thing I noticed when I bumped into him in that coffee shop, almost five years ago. It was his... eyes. Always.

A second.

Maddox let go.

I walked away.

CHAPTER TWENTY

Lila

Riley put her textbook away, when I walked inside our apartment, and gave me an expectant look. It must have been the expression on my face or the tear-stained marks on my cheeks, but Riley, wordlessly, opened her arms for me.

I slumped into her embrace and choked back a sob that threatened to escape. "God, it's so hard. Walking away from him hurts, and every time I do it, it chips off another piece of my heart."

She rubbed my arms, soothingly. "Why did you walk away, this time?"

"I thought we could be just friends again." My voice leaked my pain, and I shuddered, holding back another cry. "I even gave myself a little pep talk. I said I won't fall for his charms, won't succumb to his touches. But the moment he kissed me, I forgot all of it and kissed him back."

I wiped away the tears and lifted my head up, staring at Riley's face. Her brows were pinched, and she gave me a sympathetic look. "We almost had sex in the hospital's bathroom, Riley. If those two women didn't walk in on us, he would have fucked me right against that sink, while his father laid dying a few feet away."

"Well, shit."

"Exactly," I grumbled, so pitifully. "Maddox and I can't be friends anymore. Not when we can't keep our hands off each other. Especially not when he *needs* me *physically*. See, Maddox doesn't do well with emotional support. That's not how his brain works. He feels through touches and sex. Angry sex. Hate sex. Revenge sex. That's how he deals with his emotions. I...can't...do... it."

"He needs you right now, Lila."

"I know. But I can't be his friend in the morning and then his therapy sex at night. That's toxic, Riley. And we *can't* go back to having a relationship..."

Riley was quick to pick apart my words. "Why not?"

"I have my reasons." Painful reasons. But I was doing it for Maddox. I didn't walk away to protect myself. I walked away *for* Maddox. "Maddox needs a wake-up call, even amidst all the shitty things that are happening, I can't be there for him all the time. We can't be so co-dependent on each other. That's not a healthy relationship. There are some things that we have to deal with on... our own."

"And you think this is the right moment to test this? Lila, his father is dying!"

I settled down next to Riley, removing myself from her hug. "You think I'm being a bitch and inconsiderate."

She gave me a sharp nod. "Yes."

There was a pang, an ache in my chest. "Sheesh, thanks for the honesty."

"I'll call you out when I think you deserve it. But I think there's something else in your head that you're not telling me." Riley's eyes hardened and her lips thinned. "What happened that day, when you found out Bianca was pregnant?"

"I left Maddox," I croaked.

"What happened before you left him?"

I saw the look in his eyes...

"I'm tired. This was a long day, and I need some sleep."

Riley let out a deep, exhausted breath and threw her arms in the air – *I give up.*

She was letting it go for now, but I knew I couldn't run away from this conversation for long.

One week later

The doorbell pinged behind me, as I was cleaning the last table. I threw a look over my shoulder, calling out to the late customer. "We are closed!"

The sign clearly said we were closed, why did people still walk in? I never understood that. At least twice a week, we'd get customers, past closing, who would guilt us into serving them.

"Hi, Lila."

My back shot up straight at the sound of *her* voice. I squeezed my eyes shut and took a deep breath. Bianca was the last person I wanted to see after the shit week I had.

It's hard to watch your soulmate walk away. But it's even harder to walk away from them.

I never thought leaving Maddox would be easy, but I definitely didn't think I'd suffer *this* much. Our relationship had never been all sweetness. It was pretty roses with sharp, ugly thorns.

Yeah – that was the side effect of falling in love with my best friend.

The last week was pure agony. Maddox was always on my mind. I worried tirelessly for him. Every day, about twenty times, I'd almost give in. The urge to run back to him was strong.

Sometimes, I'd call him late at night, when I knew he was sleeping and wouldn't pick up his phone. I'd hide my caller ID and let the call go to voicemail. Just so I could hear his deep, baritone voice.

I did it once. I did twice.

And then it became a habit.

I couldn't sleep without hearing his voice.

This obsessive need for Maddox grew every day. How could I say goodbye to him when my heart was still so desperately trying to hold on to him?

I faced Bianca, and the moment my eyes fell on her, I felt a sharp pang in my chest. Damn, that hurt. Her belly was swollen and bigger than the last time I had seen her. I could even see the swell over her baggy sweater. She cupped her pregnant belly, and I fought back a flinch.

This was the reminder I didn't want. Maddox was going to be a... dad. But not the father of *my* kids. The heat rose to my face, and my heart catapulted in my chest. The first wave that hit me was anger. Then envy. Resentment. Finally, it was longing. A surge of emotions brewed inside of me, threatening to spill over. For the first time, since I found out Bianca was pregnant with Maddox's child, I felt an overwhelming sense of... jealousy.

I crossed my arms over my chest. As if to barricade my heart against her presence and her words. The last thing I wanted to do tonight was talk to my ex's baby mama.

"I didn't expect you to seek me out on your own," I said, a bitter smile on my face. It seemed I couldn't control my emotions lately.

"I'm sorry," she spilled out, looking quite flustered.

I cocked an eyebrow. "Are you scared of me, Bianca?"

She swallowed and looked around the empty restaurant, nervously. It was only the two of us in the dining area. The other two employees were in the back, cleaning up for the night. "No. Yes. Maybe. You're a... little intimidating. Sometimes. Especially right now."

"Just say what you have to say. I don't have time to play games. And please, don't give me that *I'm innocent* bullshit look. Save that for someone who'll fall for it."

Bianca started rubbing her swollen stomach, as if to soothe the baby. I had to remind myself that she was pregnant, and I had to rein in my psychotic side.

"I didn't want to come between you and Maddox. That wasn't my intention," she murmured, biting on her lips.

But she did. Except, I couldn't fault her, really.

I rolled my eyes, looking indifferent. But every cell inside me was raging, hurting, breaking. "Why didn't you tell Maddox when you found out you were pregnant? Why wait until you were six months along?"

"I was... worried and scared. I didn't know..."

"But you had to tell him the moment our relationship became public," I seethed.

"No," she stuttered. What a fucking liar. "I talked to Maddox. I told him you guys didn't have to break up. We can make it work..."

I raised my hand, halting her words. "I don't need you to speak to Maddox for me. Maddox and I have been friends, way longer than you've known him. I know him better than anyone else, and he knows me better than he knows himself. If we want to figure this out, we will. We don't need you to play mediator."

Bianca nodded, looking teary eyed.

"Anything else?"

Her gaze flitted past my head, and she avoided looking at my face. She chewed on her lip, before whispering, "Maddox and his parents are going back to Manhattan. Brad wants to be in the comfort of his own home."

What...?

Oh my God.

I stumbled back against the table, my knees growing weak. He was leaving. Maddox was leaving, and I didn't know...

My lips parted with a silent cry, and my fists clenched.

Bianca put the last nail in the coffin when she confessed her next secret. "He asked me to come with him. He said... he wanted to be there for the rest of my pregnancy and when I give birth."

"What about... his exams?"

"He dropped out for the rest of the academic year."

My emotions throttled me, and barb wires twisted around my lungs. I couldn't... breathe. Oh God. This was hell. Pure, absolute hell.

How... how did it come to this?

Oh, right. I left him.

And now *he* was leaving, going far away, and out of my reach. My lungs caved in, my stomach dropped... and the butterflies? They just died. The emptiness left a hollow ache inside of me. The silence that came with the aftermath; it was louder than any sound.

I swallowed back a cry and turned away from Bianca.

"I'm sorry," she whispered. I heard her feet shuffling away. The door opened, the bell pinged again, cold air washed inside the empty restaurant, and then she was gone. As if she was never here.

As if she hadn't just trampled over my already broken, bleeding heart.

This had been my doing; yet, it still fucking *hurt*.

It hadn't been an easy decision, but this was what I wanted for Maddox.

For him to grow up, for him to accept responsibility...

For this unborn baby to have a decent father.

I walked away for Maddox...

And, as much as it pained me, I didn't regret it.

CHAPTER
TWENTY-ONE

Maddox

Two weeks later

I fed him another small spoonful. He accepted it weakly, chewing as
if it took all his strength to do such a small act. He lost all his hair in
three weeks. Lost all his weight, until he was skin and bones. Ghastly
pale and wrinkled. His cheeks were drawn in, and his eyes had lost their
vibrant colors – a hollow look in them.

Brad Coulter was frail, almost too weak, to even sit up straight and
have his own meal. In three weeks, his health deteriorated, until he needed
a wheelchair to move around, and one of us to feed him, help him in and
out of bed. Taking his bath, alone, became out of the question, when he
passed out in the tub a week ago.

Frail. Sick. Dying.

My mother refused to bring a nurse home. She was adamant about
taking care of her husband herself, but she grew weary, as the days

passed, so I was forced to jump in and help.

If you asked me why I dropped out of this academic year and moved in with my parents, awaiting my father's death – I didn't have an answer.

I didn't want anything to do with my father or my mother – but here I was.

Taking care of them, as a dutiful son. That was what Lila wanted, after all. She told me I'd regret it later, if I didn't spend these last days with my father. Maybe she was right, I didn't know.

I didn't know shit.

All I knew was that the thought of my father dying left a heavy, hollow ache in my chest. I didn't like it one bit, but it was what drove me *here*.

Back into the very mansion that I spent my childhood in, lonely, scared... unloved.

My father coughed, and I quickly dabbed the corner of his mouth. He accepted another spoonful, before he shook his head, indicating that he had enough. I placed the half full bowl on the table. He was eating less and less every day.

My mother stood up with a weary sigh. She rubbed her forehead, and I noticed the dark circles under her eyes. "Do you mind helping your father to bed? There are a few documents I have to read."

"Yeah," I said.

Brad gave me a small, tired smile. "You don't have to do this."

"You're right, I don't." Except, Lila was going to look at me with disappointment in her eyes, if I didn't.

And maybe I was doing it for... *myself.*

"C'mon, old man. Time for your beauty sleep." I pushed his wheelchair into the guest bedroom downstairs. I helped him out of his wheelchair and into the bed, tucking the comforter around his shoulders.

"Maddox," he said, his voice small and breathy. "I know I never said it before, but I am... I am... proud of you, Son."

I froze, and my stomach twisted, shock coursing through my veins. My fists started to shake, and the thick vein in my neck pulsed. My heartbeat echoed in my ears, almost too loud.

I shook my head once. "Too late," I said, smiling acidly.

Brad nodded, as if he knew that would be my response. He knew he fucked up. "Your high school graduation… your mother and I were there."

"No," I hissed. "You weren't."

His smile was forlorn. "We were. We saw you with Lila and her family and your friends."

Fuck that. He was messing with my head now.

"Why didn't approach me?"

"And ruin your special day?"

He had a point. I just didn't understand him… *why?*

"You were so stubborn, Maddox. Still are. We lost so many years. You were eighteen, and I didn't know to approach my son. How to talk to you, how to be a father again. I didn't know… *how.* My relationship with you was beyond repair, and I didn't know where to start."

I seethed, even when my lungs clenched and refused to let me breathe. "And so you took the easy way out, instead of trying?"

"My way of trying was to make sure you never give up… I know I was hard on you. Too hard. But I was pushing you, because I worried, you'd either drop out of school or you'd ruin your life. One way or another."

He sighed, and his chest rattled. Breathing – a simple act, something that is second nature to humans – he struggled with it. "Remember the last time you walked out of my office. I had warned you not to hurt Lila… because you'd hurt yourself. I said you were on the path of self-destruction because I *knew.* I knew about the Carmichaels. I knew you were keeping it secret, and I… warned… you."

My back shot up straight, and I glared down at my father. "How did you know?"

His lips crooked on the side, a grin that reminded me of my own.
A signature Coulter's smirk. "You were digging into her past, and you
weren't as careful as you thought you were. Maddox, you forget, I have
eyes and ears everywhere. Of course, I knew."

Goddamn it.

His eyes closed, and he sighed again. "I'm sorry I never said I was
proud of you." His voice grew weaker, until he was whispering those
words.

"Too late," I said. But this time, there was less anger, less heat.

There had been too much toxicity between us. Too much hatred, too
much frustration and a whole lot of negativity. Our misunderstandings
grew every year, and it pulled us apart, further and further away from each
other.

It took my father to be on his deathbed for us to try and fix *this*,
whatever was left of this father and son relationship. And trust me, there
wasn't much left.

After making sure he was tucked in comfortably, I turned off the
lights. "Good night."

He mumbled something incorrigible in return.

Numb and mentally exhausted, I stumbled into my bedroom. Turning
my neck left and right, I tried to release the tension there. My skin
prickled with something fierce, too many emotions, rattling inside of me.

I tugged my shirt over my head and discarded the rest of my clothes
on my bathroom's floor, before stepping into the shower.

I stood under the spray for a long minute, and with my forehead
against the shower wall, I squeezed my eyes shut. What the hell was I
really doing? Here, in this sterile place, that reminded me of nothing but
how ugly my relationship with my parents was.

They have been trying, slowly opening up to me. We've had all meals
together, had a movie night every night – *fuck* – my mother even baked

my favorite carrot cake. The last time I had my mother's carrot cake was on my seventh birthday.

Shit. Fixing our relationship wasn't an easy task, when we had a time limit. If only Lila was here...

No. No. Fuck, NO!

My hand landed beside my head, and I slapped the wall. She was the last person I wanted to think about, right now, but damn it, she was everywhere. In my head, in my every thought, in my dreams.

I tried burning that stupid dreamcatcher, but it felt like I had torn out a piece of my heart. My left hand was still sore from the burn it took, when I saved that damn necklace from the fire.

The mere thought of her drove me crazy, an insane desperation for her. I quickly soaped up my body, angrily rubbing my skin, until it itched and burned. Now that Lila had made her way back into my head, I couldn't stop thinking of her.

Her voice.

Her brown eyes.

Her sweet fucking smile. Her mischievous smirk.

Her slim throat. Her scars...

Her juicy ass. Damn it. And now, I was hard.

My hand drifted down to my dick. I gripped the base and squeezed my length, before stroking myself once, twice, and then my dick jerked, as I added more pressure. My hand glided around my dick, easily, and I hissed, as the pressure grew, my hardness growing thicker in my palm. I fisted my cock tightly.

I was assaulted with every image of Lila. Her sexy grin, as she laid on the bed and legs spread open for me. I imagined Lila on all fours, ass in the air. That was the thing about imagination. You could turn it into anything you wanted.

In my head, I cupped her ass and squeezed. Slid my thumb between those two pale, juicy globes and caressed her tight, little hole. My balls grew tight and heavier between my legs. I pumped my throbbing dick harder, as I conjured up the filthiest scene in my head.

She fights me.

Because she knows I want it.

She moans, louder. Her hips jerking, as I pinch her clit between my thumb and forefinger. She whimpers, as I drag her wetness between her ass cheeks, coating that hole with her own juices, using it as lubrication. She already came once, squirted all over my arms and chest, before she started crying and begging for my cock.

"Such a filthy girl," I growl in her ear. "Tell me, Baby. Where do you want my fat cock? Do you want to swallow my cum? Or do you want it in your cunt... or maybe you want it dripping out of your little, tight asshole."

"Please!" Lila cries out louder. Her body starts shaking, as she pushes her ass back against me. "Take me. I'm yours."

"Fuck yeah. You're mine. Always have been. Always will be."

Her asshole clenches, as I spread her cheeks apart, spitting for lubrication. Her breathing becomes harsh, and she pushes her face into the mattress, muffling her moans.

Slowly, I push forward, forcing my thick, hard length inside. Lila cries out. "Maddox! Oh God!"

She pulses around me, clenching tighter. "It hurts. But oh, oh... please, don't stop."

"Good. Because I'm not stopping, until you're so fucking sore, you can't walk tomorrow," I growl. My hard length throbs and aches with the need to fuck her hard and deep, but I remind myself to go gently... slowly...

I thrust forward with gritted teeth and mold my body against hers. I wrap around her, my cock seated fully inside her asshole. She's stretched to capacity, bearing my thick length inside her. She's so fucking tight, I can't breathe. We're both shaking, sweating... and I'm so fucking destroyed.

Lila Garcia is everything I ever wanted, and she's mine. Every inch of her.

The fantasy broke apart, as I spurted cum all over my palm, but it quickly washed away. I came with a hiss, and I kept fisting and squeezing my cock, until every last drop was spent.

God, Lila was going to be the death of me. She killed me then and... *she still kills me now.*

I quickly washed off and walked out, drying myself and wrapping a towel around my waist. I must have passed out, without realizing, because my phone ringing roused me. The digital clock read 11:30PM. Blindly, I reached for my phone.

Bianca. Why was she calling me, instead of knocking on my door? We were literally two rooms apart. Panic flashed through me, and I grew cold. I sat up straight and answered the call. "What is it?"

"The baby is craving mint-chocolate chip ice cream."

Oh.

Her midnight cravings. "Ice cream?"

She hummed. "Mint-chocolate chip, specifically."

Mint-chocolate chip...

Lila's favorite...

I rubbed a hand over my face. "Dairy Queen is probably still open. I'll see if they have that flavor."

"Thank you." I could hear the smile in her voice. I sure as hell didn't know pregnant chicks were this much work. I hadn't been prepared for it. The cravings, mood swings, the extra emotional drama.

"Okay," I said.

She was silent for a second, and I was about to hang up, when she softly called out, "Hey, Maddox."

"Yeah?"

"Thank you," she whispered, like we were sharing a secret.

I growled and hung up.

CHAPTER
TWENTY-TWO

Lila

"It's strange to celebrate Christmas without Maddox," Gran said. She handed me a cup of hot chocolate, and I reluctantly took it. The moment she started speaking of Maddox, I wanted to run upstairs and hide. They didn't know that we had broken up… yet.

They knew about Maddox's father. And so, I let them believe that Maddox was with his parents… hence why he hasn't visited us… and I haven't gone to him. *Yet.*

I only came back to my grandparents' yesterday. Tonight was Christmas Eve. Maddox used to always spend the night with my family. He'd sleep on the couch (sometimes he'd sneak into my room) and we'd wake up, early in the morning, to open our presents. We'd have breakfast together.

Spending Christmas *without* him was another reminder of how quickly our relationship went from one hundred to zero.

This would have been our first Christmas as a couple. I grinded my teeth, feeling so hopeless… so helpless…

I remained silent, giving the TV all my attention. The movie ended. My grandparents said their goodnights and went upstairs to their room. The digital clock read 8PM, but they had a habit of going to bed early. Old age, they'd argue.

My eyes landed on the bowl of mixed party chips and loneliness clawed at me. Maddox would always separate my favorite kind from the rest and feed them to me. *It's the little things…*

That was what I missed the most.

The little things.

A knock on the door snapped me out of my thoughts. When another knock came, I got up to answer the door. I didn't know what I expecting, but it was definitely not *him*.

Agape, I sputtered, "Grayson?"

He looked different. Older, wiser… and a tad more handsome. He now had a beard, was still wearing glasses, and appeared to have gained more muscles. "Hey, can I come in?"

"Um, yeah, sure!" My voice came out squeaky. I haven't seen him in years. After he broke up with Riley, we lost all contact.

Grayson came inside but stayed by the door. It was then I noticed the file he was holding. "I've tried calling Maddox, but he isn't picking up. This is important and couldn't be delayed."

"What is?"

He squinted at me. "You don't know?"

"Know what?"

"Well, shit," he muttered under his breath. "This is awkward. I thought he told you already."

"I haven't talked to Maddox in weeks."

His eyes rounded big, and he stared at me, agape. "You're shitting me, right?"

I put my hands on my hips, glaring up at him. "Do I look like I'm joking?" I hissed.

Grayson raised his hands up, in mock defense. I rolled my eyes and waited for him to continue. He shifted on his feet, suddenly looking less serious and more nervous.

"What is it?"

"I don't know exactly where to start…"

"Start at the beginning?" I prompted.

Grayson swallowed and nodded. "You might want to sit down."

He followed me into the dining room, and we settled at the table. Courteously, I offered him a glass of water. I watched, as he rubbed his chin, looking everywhere but at me. He took a slow sip of water, and I waited patiently, as he licked his lips and finally made eye contact with me. "About eight months ago, Maddox approached Simon."

Simon Manchester. Grayson's adopted father, who also happened to be a well-respected judge. What would he see Simon for?

"Maddox has been digging into your accident. He's been trying to reopen your case."

My heart skipped, and my breath caught in my throat. My stomach dropped, and the world… ceased to exist.

The colors faded away.

Black and white… and then, I was violently thrown into the darkness.

"Lila? Lila! Hey, Lila!"

Grayson snapped his fingers in front of my face. I choked on my breath, and goosebumps peppered my flesh, as I stared at him, too stunned to move or to speak.

"Shit," Grayson swore. "I shouldn't have been the one to tell you this."

"Why?" I croaked.

"What do you mean *why*?"

I blinked at Grayson. No, this wasn't possible. "Why would he try to reopen my…case… Christian is his childhood friend."

"That's a question you should be asking him, not me. Because, I don't have an answer for you. I can tell you what I know, though." He patted my hand, a comforting gesture. "The Carmichaels are rich and protected by the law, in a way. They have way too much money and way too much power in their hands. Christian's father is a well-known, albeit, corrupt lawyer. He knows how to go around the law and how to get it in his and his son's favor. That's what he did before. The judge that handled your case? That was his best friend. These people, they run in the same circle, Lila. There was no way you would have won your case."

"I know," I whispered. "But then, what's the point in trying to reopen the case? We'd just lose. Again. Maddox wasted his time."

Grayson shook his head, giving me a smile full of secrets. "What do you think he has been doing the last eight months?"

I opened my mouth, but found myself wordless. I didn't know what to do with this news. Maddox hadn't told me anything about this.

When I found out about Christian... he never said anything about reopening my case.

He never said anything about fighting for... *me*.

"Maddox spent two months, trying to convince my father to work with him on this case. Then, he spent another three weeks, trying to find the best and most trustworthy lawyer. After all that? We needed proof. We needed a reason to reopen the case. Rolland Carmichael covered his tracks very well. It was almost impossible to gather the proof we needed. It took us months... and months of carefully extracting all the information. And now, we have a solid case."

Grayson nudged the file in front of me. "This is everything. The driver who took the blame? He's ready to speak in court. The cops that were on scene... Christian's friends who saw him drunk that night and getting into the driver's seat. Oh, and the security camera. You can do a lot when you have lots of money at your disposal. Maddox threw some cash at some people... and the job was done."

I didn't dare touch the file, too scared it'd burn me alive.

The world spun and grew blurry, dots scurrying across my vision. "Maddox didn't tell me…"

"I spoke with him last week. I told him I'd have everything by today, but he isn't picking up my calls."

"Last week? You mean, he was still working on this with you? All this time?" I felt faint and cold… so, so cold.

Grayson looked confused. "Yeah? Why is that surprising?"

"We broke up almost two months ago," I confessed, breathlessly. My ears were ringing, and my lungs squeezed.

His mouth rounded with an 'o,' and he nodded, slowly. "I don't know your reasons for breaking up, but Maddox has been very adamant about bringing you the justice you deserve."

And *that*…

That statement… decimated me.

Killed me. Ripped me apart.

Maddox wanted to bring me justice, to give me the closure I needed. All along, he was on *my* side.

All this time, he had been trying to protect *me*.

Oh God, how foolish I was. How stupid I had been. How careless I was with his heart.

My gaze landed on the brown file, and I swallowed back a cry. "Thank you, Grayson."

He cleared his throat. "You're welcome. I'll see myself out."

I closed my eyes and brought my head down to the table, resting my forehead on the surface. Grayson got up to leave, but my voice stopped him. "Riley is back in town for Christmas."

He coughed and thumped his chest. "I didn't need to know that."

Without lifting my head up, I waved him away. "Well, now you know. Do what you want with it," I said.

Long after Grayson had left, I found myself in bed, with my phone in my hand. I debated calling Maddox. It wasn't late at night, and I knew he'd still be awake, right now. If I called him, it wouldn't go to voicemail, like it always did.

If I called him... he might pick up.

And maybe that was why I wanted to do it.

I wanted to hear his voice – not a recording. I wanted to speak with him, ask him *why*. Why he didn't tell me? *Why* he kept it a secret – another secret? *Why* he let me believe the worst... and *why* he kept working on the case, even after we broke up?

I had so many questions and absolutely no answers.

The pain burned deep into my core. Maddox was secretly taking care of me... when I left him behind, especially when he needed me the most. Now all my reasons for doing so, appeared moot.

My lungs denied me breath, and tears burned the back of my eyelids.

Maddox and I were foolishly in love...

And now? *Look at us.*

My thumb pressed the call button, before I could overthink it. I brought the phone to my ear, and, after two rings, Maddox answered the call.

"Hello?"

His voice. Lord, have sweet mercy on me. That gruff, deep baritone, husky voice. I missed it so much. I didn't know how much I had needed to hear his voice until now.

I tried to clear my throat, because I suddenly forgot how to speak.

"Hello?" he said again, curt and irritated. My lips twitched. He was always so impatient, just as I remembered. Some things never change.

My heart thundered. My lips parted to speak.

"*Oh my God!*" There was a happy giggle and then, *"The baby kicked again. He's literally playing football in there. Maddox! Here, feel it."*

My chest caved.

My pulse beat heavy in my throat.

My fingers twitched around my phone, tightening as I was assaulted with a wave of anguish.

Maddox sucked in a deep breath, and I imagined his big hand on Bianca's swollen belly. "Damn," he muttered. I imagined the look of awe on their faces, as they felt their baby kicking.

Tormented, I squeezed my eyes shut. "Merry Christmas," I whispered brokenly, before hanging up.

Rolling over in bed, I pushed my face in my pillow and *finally...* for the first time, since we broke up...

I let the tears fall.

I screamed.

I cried.

I raged.

And I cried some more.

I sobbed, until I didn't have any more tears.

I love you.

I love you.

I love you.

CHAPTER TWENTY-THREE

Maddox

We spent Christmas morning opening presents, most of which were for the baby. Ironically, it was the first Christmas I celebrated with my family, in over eighteen years… and it would be my last.

"Oh! Look at this cute onesie." Bianca cooed and dug into more presents. Her mom had sent her two dozen parcels for Christmas. I pressed my thumbs into the back of my neck and massaged the tensed muscles there. I was bored out of my mind.

My mother sipped her tea slowly, eyeing Bianca with distrust. That look, *again.* To say my mother didn't like Bianca, one bit, was an understatement. In fact, she didn't hide it. She openly scorned Bianca, gave her the dirty looks, was quick to shut her down, if Bianca ever said anything concerning our family.

My mother barely tolerated her presence and did everything to show Bianca that she was an outsider and wasn't welcomed in our home. I kinda felt bad. *Well, not really.*

I never thought Savannah Coulter had the capacity to... hate. She had always been so mellow. But Bianca, apparently, brought out that side of her. The *don't-fuck-with-me-and-I-think-you're-pure-bullshit* side.

"So, have you spoken to Lila?" my mother asked, trying to sound innocent. Bianca flinched, and Mother Dearest hid her smile behind her teacup. *Here we go again.*

"No, I haven't," I grunted. "We broke up. The end. Stop asking about Lila."

Last night, I fell asleep with Lila on my thoughts.

I woke up in the middle of the night, jerked off *again* with her on my mind.

In the morning, I woke up with the memory of her taste on my lips.

Bianca cleared her throat, trying to divert the conversation, but my mother ignored her.

"She didn't even give you a call on Christmas?"

"No."

"What about–"

"No," I barked.

She gave me that fake lip quivering shit she did, every time she asked about Lila, and I'd been forced to shut her up. Who was this woman? Definitely not my mother! "I was just asking... You always get so tense whenever I mention her."

She quirked up a mocking eyebrow at me and took another sip of her tea. "It looks like the thought of her still makes you restless. She's always on your mind, it seems."

I rubbed a hand over my face, tired of this same shit every day. "Mom, stop!"

Her teacup paused halfway to her lips, and her jaw dropped. Her hand started to shake. She opened her mouth to speak, but closed it again, looking like a gaping fish out of water. Her eyes turned glassy, and it was then I realized…

"You called me, Mom," she murmured, her voice breaking.

My stomach twisted, and I felt… something in my chest. A tightening sensation.

I did. I called her mom, without mocking her. For the first time since…

I swallowed past the ball of emotions stuck in my throat. "Yeah, I did," I said, before adding, "Mom."

Savannah Coulter gave me the prettiest, most real smile I had ever seen on her face.

And I finally understood what Lila had been trying to tell me.

She was right. Like always.

Lila

I stood in front of the Coulter's mansion. Security let me in through the gates, but now, I debated if this was a good idea. Randomly dropping in…

Before, I'd do it all the time.

Now? Well, things had changed.

New Year's had come and gone, a few days ago. I haven't spoken to Maddox in over six weeks. I shouldn't be here, but I wanted my necklace back. I'd fight Maddox, if I had to… but I wasn't leaving, without my dreamcatcher. Two months was more than enough time for him to calm down. That necklace was mine, and he had no right to rip it away from my throat.

I let him off before… because I knew he was angry… hurting.

But not anymore.

Before I could lose, whatever courage I had mustered up to come here,

I rang the doorbell. The butler, Mr. Hokinson, opened the door, and his eyes widened at the sight of me. "Miss Garcia," he sputtered, "it's been a long time."

I nodded, smiling softly at the older man. He had to be in his late fifties or early sixties. "Is Maddox home?"

"Everyone is home," he said, gesturing for me to come inside. I could guess he wasn't aware that Maddox and I had broken up. The butler led me through the house, stopping at the dining room.

My heart galloped at the sight in front of me, before withering.

Maddox was there. He still looked the same...

I wasn't sure what I had expected. For him to be mourning our lost relationship? To be heartbroken? Maybe I thought he'd be missing me... enough that he'd be suffering...

Like I had been. Sleepless nights, loneliness that clawed at me, every waking hour, hollow dreams. Hell, even my orgasms felt empty.

But Maddox looked just as handsome as always. He was clean shaven, and if I wasn't mistaken, his muscles looked even bulkier. I guessed he was working out more, with all the free time he had now. His hair was longer, though, and curled by his ears.

Poodle.

Maddox wasn't alone, though. Bianca stood next to him. She smiled and said something to him, too soft for me to hear. He didn't smile back – he looked anything but interested, at whatever she was saying. That shouldn't have made me feel better, but it did. I didn't want him to smile at her... Oh God, I sounded petty and jealous.

Maddox turned, and his eyes fell on me. His gaze narrowed, and I loved that I could still steal his attention, even without a word. Just a single look, and I got him.

He got me, too.

Bianca followed his line of sight, and she gasped, almost dramatically.

"Garcia," he greeted coldly.

613

"Coulter," I returned, with the same tone. Bianca looked back and forth between us, before quickly taking a step back. "Um, I'll leave you to it. I'm going to take a nap." She scurried away, leaving Maddox and I alone.

We were both quiet for a long moment. Arm crossed over our chests, a silent staring battle, neither of us ready to lose. The silence prolonged, until I couldn't take it anymore. My lips parted, and the first thing out of my mouth was, "I want my dreamcatcher back."

Maddox smiled acidly, his eyes gleaming, with a cruelty I had never seen before. "I threw it away."

My heart thundered. "No," I thundered. "How dare you? It was mine!"

His face darkened, and he came forward, pushing into my personal space. His fingers wrapped around my bicep, and he pulled me closer. I stumbled into him, our chests brushing lightly, and goosebumps peppered across my skin with that simple touch. His head dipped low, his breath feathered across my jaw, before he whispered in my ear, "And *you* were mine."

I still am, goddamn it!

I wrenched my arm away. "How could you?" I hissed darkly. "That necklace…"

"Oh, Lila!" Savannah's voice pulled us apart. "I didn't know you were here! What a lovely surprise."

I took a deep breath, trying to calm the brewing anger inside me. I faced Savannah and gave her a genuine smile. It wasn't exactly her fault her son was acting like an asshole right now. "I wanted to see how Brad was doing. I worried about his health. I'm sorry if I'm intruding. I'll come back another time."

She was already shaking her head. "Oh. No, no. You're always welcome. It's been weird. Having Maddox here, but not you. You've been missed. Now that you're here, stay for dinner."

Maddox made a displeased sound under his breath, and I grinned harder. "Oh, I would *love* to. Thank you, Savannah."

He glared.

I winked.

He couldn't kick me out now.

Dinner was awkward, and that was an understatement. Bianca appeared to be intimidated by my presence. She avoided my eyes and rarely spoke. Maddox's face was cold and stony, and he stayed stubbornly quiet. Savannah and Brad tried to break the tension with a bit of small talk, here and there, but those conversations ended just as dry.

Once our plates were cleared, desserts were served. I only had one spoon of the double-layered custard and chocolate mousse when Maddox, pushed his chair away, the wooden legs screeching and he stood up. His face remained impassive, and his gaze locked with mine. Blue that burned with a ferocity that left me breathless. The muscles ticked in his jaw, and his eyes flared with *something…*

Wordlessly, he turned around and stalked away. I watched him, until he disappeared upstairs. I slowly licked my spoon, appreciating my first… and last bite of the chocolate mousse. "Excuse me, please," I said, getting up and pushing away from the table, too. "Please tell your chef, this was the best custard I've ever had."

With a small smile, I followed after Maddox. Because I knew that was what he wanted.

I found him in his old bedroom. The door was ajar, a silent invitation. I walked inside, and there he was, standing in the middle of the dimly lit room. His back was to me, and he stood so still. Not even a slight twitch. Barely breathing. If I didn't know better, I'd think he was a statue.

I closed the door behind me and took a step forward, farther into his room. More into his space. He knew I was here. Could feel me. I knew, because his hands clenched into fists.

Sharing one space with Maddox was overwhelming. My body was

hyperaware of his presence, his closeness. His scent. The room smelled like him. A heavy musky scent and his cologne. I missed his smell. It used to comfort me on cold nights and make me sigh on warm ones.

"Maddox," I breathed.

In response, he swiveled around. His face was dark and cold. *But his eyes...*

"Do you hate me?" There was a manic look in his eyes, a kind of desperation I had never seen before. Stormy. Angry. Crazed. *Anguished.*

I shook my head, my lips quivering. "I hate you... because I *can't* hate *you.*"

His chest rattled with a sharp breath. "Get out, Garcia."

"Why?"

"Because *I hate you.*" His lips spoke the cruel words, his gleaming blue eyes screamed something else.

"Lies," I whispered. "Lying has become common in our relationship now, hasn't it?"

He took a step forward, as if he couldn't stop himself, from wanting to be closer to me. Maddox paused, and his chest rumbled with a growl. "There is no relationship. There is no us, anymore."

"You're a terrible liar, Coulter." I called him out on his bullshit and smiled, because I knew I was right.

"Get. Out. *Lila.*"

I nudged my chin up, stubbornly. "Make me."

Maddox stalked forward; his face twisted with fury. He grasped my arm and dragged me out of his room, pushing me out of the door. His grip tightened on me, and his head lowered, our eyes leveled. "You are what killed me slowly... without any mercy, Lila. You used to be my cure. Now, you're the plague. And I'm dying. *You kill me, Lila.* Your deceitful eyes. Your wicked smile. Your treacherous voice. So get out and spare me this sweet, torturous death."

One look.

One second.

One breath.

Our heart broke in unison.

He slammed the door in my face and that was it. He left me with his cruel words, wrenching my heart out of my chest, and carelessly throwing it at my feet.

CHAPTER TWENTY-FOUR

Lila

One week later

I picked up the call, without looking at the caller ID, practically stabbing the green button. I already knew who it was. I had been waiting for her call for hours, sitting gingerly on my bed and trying not to break down from overthinking *everything*.

Riley's breathy voice came through. "You were right," she screeched. "Jesus Christ, you were so right!"

Shock rippled through my whole body, and I forgot how to breathe. Chaotic feelings gripped the center of my chest. "You got it?"

"Yeah. I'm gonna email it to you, right now." There was some rustling sound in the background, before Riley came back on the call. "Done."

I opened my email on my laptop, and there it was. Everything I needed. All the proof.

"You did it." Holy shit. "Is there anything you can't do, Babe?"

She giggled. "Well, I have lots of contacts."

"You're a genius."

Riley let out a happy squeal, and a laugh bubbled from my chest. "Wait, are you still dropping out this semester?"

There was only one semester left. My last one. Four more months and I'd be done. Have a Harvard degree in my hand, proof that I had accomplished what I had set out to do.

Four years ago, Harvard was my dream.

Now?

Maddox was the destination I longed for. "He needs me here," I said.

A week ago, Maddox practically threw me out of his life. Granted, yes, I walked away first. But now? Well, I had come to my senses.

I was done with all the lies. And the secrets. I was tired of hiding and walking away from the man I promised to never give up on. It was time to put an end to it.

Maddox had been silently fighting for me… and I had been doing the same. Except, we were too stubborn to admit it. Too prideful.

All this time, he had been protecting me.

And I thought I was protecting him.

But we both fucked up…

"Riley, you always ask me why I left Maddox. The reason why I was so adamant about staying away from him…"

She sighed. "Yes?"

"I saw it in his eyes that day," I confessed quietly, my grip on the phone growing tighter. "*That* look. Maddox never thought about having children. I knew he always thought he'd be a bad father. He was going to walk away from Bianca and the baby. I found out he was going to pay Bianca off. He didn't want anything to do with the pregnancy or the baby. He didn't think he could be a father, and I needed him to realize that he was capable of being one. On his own. Without being dependent on me to show him the way, to teach him how to do it."

Maddox Coulter had so much love to give, and I didn't want to be selfish to take all that love for myself.

"You know what made me walk away? I didn't want Maddox to choose me over the baby. I was always his number one. His only choice. No matter what, I will always be his only one. I saw it in his eyes, Riley. So, I made the choice for him. I *dared* him to be the dad, his father couldn't be."

I knew Maddox better than he knew himself. He was scared of losing me, scared of having Bianca come between us. He panicked... and so, he was going to take the easy way out.

I didn't want to be the reason this child didn't have a father.

The more I pushed him away, the closer it got him to Bianca.

Riley was silent for a long minute. She let out a sharp breath, her tongue making a clucking sound. "I don't know what to say, Lila. You have a messy way of thinking over things."

I let out a humorless laugh. "I fucked up, I know. I thought I was doing the right thing. *For* Maddox."

"You know what your problem is, the both of you?" Riley questioned, although she didn't wait for an answer.

"Maddox will do anything to protect you. He will fight for you, even if it means losing himself in the process. And you will do the same. The two of you are so in love, so stubborn, that you'd risk your own happiness, for each other. I saw how it killed you to walk away from Maddox, yet, you did it... because you thought it was the right thing to do. And Maddox? All this time, he was caring for you in his own messy ways. All the lies, all the secrets... it was all because..."

"Because he loved me and he wanted to spare me any more pain."

"Yup."

I pressed the print button and watched, as the documents Riley had sent me, printed out. "So foolishly in love, doing foolish things, and protecting each other like a fool."

"What a pair!"

I grabbed the freshly printed papers in my hand. It was time to put an end to *all* of this, and these papers were everything I needed to do it.

"What are you going to do now?" Riley muttered. I could sense the smile on her face, even though I couldn't see it.

What am I going to do now? Well, that was simple.

With certainty and a firm determination, I closed my laptop and grinned. "Fight for my man."

I found myself in front of Maddox's house again. Unlike last time, I wasn't nervous or second guessing my decision. I stood on the stairs outside the main door and called him – this time, I didn't bother hiding my caller ID.

His phone rang twice, before he picked up. "What do you want?"

"Always so cheery, I see," I taunted.

"Lila," he warned.

"I need to talk to you. Come outside." I killed the call, without waiting for his response. I didn't want to give him a chance to say no.

But I guess, I forgot how stubborn Maddox could be.

I waited ten minutes in the cold.

Thirty minutes later, I sat on the stairs… waiting. Tugging my jacket closer to my neck, I wrapped my shawl over my mouth and nose.

I called him again. He didn't pick up. I paced the driveaway, up and down, left and right.

Forty-five minutes had gone by and still no Maddox. After the fourteenth call, he finally picked up, only to bark out a single word. *"Leave."*

I stared blankly at my phone, when he hung up. Well… okay, then. Time for plan B (because I already knew Maddox was going to make this difficult).

I got the blankets and snacks from my car and parked my ass on his porch. I used a blanket as a cushion, since the stairs were rock hard and rough. An hour later, all my snacks were gone. The sun had disappeared behind heavy clouds, and I could hear the thunder from far away.

I unlocked my phone and sent Maddox one last message. *It's going to rain... I'm still outside. I'm not going to leave until we talk.*

Tucking my phone away, I cuddled up under the blankets. It was getting colder now, even with my heavy winter coat, boots and gloves. *I'm waiting. Come to me, Maddox.*

The wind picked up, and my teeth started chattering. Thunder rolled through the sky. The sky was completely clouded over, growing darker. The drizzle started next.

I *grinned.*

One. Two. Three. Four. Five. Six. Sev–

"For fuck's sake, Garcia!"

I didn't even get to ten. I peeked over my shoulder, with a stupid grin on my face. "Couldn't bear the thought of me sitting here, cold and in the rain?"

Maddox stalked outside and slammed the door closed behind him. "What. Do. You. Want?"

"Tell me... the... truth," I said, through chattering teeth.

He stopped beside me; his shoes next to my thighs. Maddox glowered down at me and crossed his arms over his wide chest. I could see his muscles bulging through the sweater, and I suddenly forgot what I came here for.

"What truth?" he snapped.

"Grayson told me..."

His expression was thunderous. "Yeah. *So?*" he seethed. "What do you want to know?"

"Why didn't you tell me?" I asked quietly.

"You never gave me a chance to."

"You could have yelled it in my face," I shot back, leaving the comfort of the blankets and standing up.

Maddox and I were toe to toe. His jaw clenched, and his shoulders tightened. A strong wind blew over us, and I shivered, feeling the winter coldness seeping through the layers of clothes I had on.

"Why didn't you tell me?" I asked again. "*Why* did you let me believe the worst?"

His blue eyes flared, but his lips clammed shut. He stood stubbornly quiet. I stabbed a gloved finger into his chest. "Tell me! I want to know!"

"*Because*," Maddox barked. His arm snaked out sharply, and he gripped my bicep, shaking me. His head dipped low, his cold breath fanning over my frozen lips. "Because I'd rather you believe the worst in *me* than give you hope, only to have it snatched away from you!"

He released me abruptly, and I stumbled back. Maddox made a wounded sound in the back of his throat, as he ran his hand over his head, his fingers tugging on his hair. "I didn't know if I'd be able to gather all the proof I needed. I didn't know if we could reopen and win this case! I didn't fucking know, and I needed to be prepared. I didn't want to see that hope in your eyes, only for it to wither away, if we couldn't... if we couldn't... fuck, Lila! WHAT DO YOU WANT FROM ME?"

"I want you," I barely breathed through my cold, freezing lips. "Just you."

"Stop," he croaked.

"Thank you," I whispered. "For finally telling me the truth. That's what I wanted to hear."

His lips curled with a sneer. "Leave now."

"Not until you see this." I grabbed the papers I had brought with me, pushing them toward him.

Maddox snatched the papers from my hand and glowered at the documents. "What is this?"

"Bianca... she's lying."

His brows furrowed. For a long time, I had a nagging feeling in my chest about Bianca and her pregnancy. At first, I told myself I was distrustful of her because I had been jealous.

But then the feeling grew, until I couldn't deny it any longer.

So, Riley and I did some digging. Hospital records, phone calls... text messages...

Maddox stiffened. "Bianca gave birth last night."

Oh, well...

"The baby would have been premature, right?" I slowly questioned, watching for his reaction.

"He wasn't." It was a boy. This baby would have been Maddox's son...

Maddox confirmed what I already knew. It wasn't surprising, since Bianca was officially a week overdue. She was farther along than what she had told us.

"You're not the father," I said.

Maddox handed me back the papers. His face was impassive, for a mere second, before he pulled out a pack of cigarettes from his pocket. He put one between his lips, without lighting up the end. Maddox leaned against the wall, rubbing his thumb across his jaw.

I watched him... finally noticing his lack of reaction to the news.

"You knew," I accused, my voice hardening.

He let out a dry, humorless laugh. "Bingo, Sweet Cheeks."

My eyes fell on the papers in my hands, before finally meeting his again. "I don't understand."

"*Lila*," he said my name like a taunt, "I found out a week after you walked out on me. I'm not stupid. I did my own digging, because I didn't trust Bianca. If you had chosen to stay... you would have known."

"All this time... you *knew*?!"

He nodded, the smile on his face pure acid.

"Then why did you bring Bianca here? What was all of this?"

Maddox kept the cigarette between his teeth, chuckling. "Bianca needed a place to hide, while she was pregnant. Oh, by the way... the father of her baby is her boyfriend. The son of her father's driver. She fell in love... but Daddy Dearest refused to accept the relationship. He was the guy on the wrong side of town, and there was no way, the big and mighty Jonathan, was going to accept him, as the father of his grandchild. He threatened to disown Bianca, so she lied. She said the baby was mine. She needed time. To give birth, to wait until she was twenty-one, so she could have full access to her trust fund."

Holy shit.

I blinked at Maddox, too shocked to formulate any other words. "She told you all of this?"

"Yes."

"When?"

Maddox spit the cigarette out. "Before I found out my father was dying."

"Why didn't you tell me?" I didn't know if I was just angry or too overwhelmed to feel anything else.

"I was going to tell you... but then," Maddox broke off, shaking his head. He shoved his hands into his pockets.

The muscles in his jaw tightened. The barrier fell away from his eyes, and Maddox showed me what he was hiding. The pain. The chaos in his heart. *Everything.*

"You didn't leave me once, Lila. You walked away from me three times."

I opened my mouth to argue, but then I saw the mask of fury on his face, and I wisely shut up and let him continue. "Once, when you found out about Christian. You never gave me a chance to explain. You needed me, but you pushed me away. You robbed me of the chance to be your knight. To take care of you, while you were hurting. The second time you walked away, you wrenched my heart out of my chest and took it with you. And the third time?"

He paused, giving me a pained smile. "The third time was the worst. My father was dying, and I needed you. But you walked away, without a second glance."

I finally understood... *why*.

My heart dipped to my empty stomach, where there used to be butterflies, leaving my chest hollow... and *aching*.

My scars itched, a phantom echo of the real pain. My scars burned fiercely, a reminder that Maddox used to soothe the hurt away... but not anymore.

I clenched my chest over my winter coat, the tears burning my eyes. "You were angry at me. For leaving. *This* was you punishing me. This prolonged separation was my punishment for leaving you."

"For breaking your promises," he rasped darkly.

The sky opened up, and the rain came down on us, drenching us. Maddox barely flinched, as the storm raged on us.

I was so cold, frozen down to my bones... but I couldn't find myself to care. I drowned in his blue eyes and prayed he'd save me.

"I'm still falling for you, Maddox," I whispered. Falling. Drowning. The rain washed my tears away.

"Liar," he growled, his brows furrowing. His expression was stormy. Pained. Thunderous.

My lips twitched with a bittersweet smile. "What else do you want me to do? I tried. Maddox. I'm trying..."

For you. For us.

My hand went to my neck, to grab onto my necklace, like I always did. My anchor. My fingers brushed against my bare throat, and my breath hitched at the bitter reminder.

No dreamcatcher.

His eyes darkened, almost furiously. His jaw tightened, and I could hear his molars grinding. "Nothing," he said. "Just like you did nothing when I begged you to stay. The gates are behind you, Lila. You can leave now. You're not needed anymore."

CHAPTER
TWENTY-FIVE

Lila

I said I'd fight for Maddox, but I couldn't fight for him, if I were bedridden with pneumonia. So, against my own accord, and because I knew I wouldn't win a fight in the rain, I drove home, after Maddox slammed the door in my face. Again.

I spent thirty minutes in the tub, as I tried to warm up my body. Then, I spent another two hours in front of the fireplace, and after four cups of hot cocoa, I was finally warm again.

My gran mumbled under her breath, as she packed blankets around me, but she didn't ask any questions. Maybe it was the look in my eyes, but I truly didn't have the energy to give her an explanation tonight.

Hours later and late at night... I was finally in bed, thinking of my next step. Was I pissed that Maddox played me? Yes. I was rightfully angry, frustrated and... *hurt*. The Maddox I knew would never purposefully be so... vindictive.

But then I realized, it was because of *me*.

I made him snap. I turned him into this furious, ugly beast.

Walking away from him... breaking my promises... turning my back on him when he *needed* me the most, I *tainted* our friendship.

I just wanted us to go back to the old Maddox and Lila. Team MALA – invincible and untouchable. Without all the misunderstandings, hurt and miscommunications.

My mission to go back to being Team MALA would start tomorrow. How long could Maddox stay angry at me? Another week? Another month...?

We'll see...

Because I was fighting *for* him, this time.

I was just drifting off to sleep, when I heard it. The scratching sound outside my window. A thump. A louder sound. More scratching.

Was someone trying to break in? Shit! I frantically looked around my room, searching for some kind of weapon. Where the hell was my baseball bat?

A knock on my window made me pause.

I clenched the bedsheet closer to my body and eyed the window.

More scratches. Another knock, louder this time. More desperation in it.

And then...

His voice.

"Lila."

Oh my God!

"Lila," he called out louder.

I scrambled off the bed and rushed to my window, practically ripping away the curtains in my haste. There he was. Maddox.

Looking utterly handsome and breathtaking under the moonlight.

He balanced himself on the roof and gripped the edge of the window, staring at me with a look I have never seen before.

Maddox was here. Outside my window. Demanding for me to open up and let him in… hours after kicking me out of his house. Oh, the irony. Why were we such a mess together?

Wordlessly, I cracked the window open, and sidestepped, to let him in. Maddox stumbled inside and then straightened to his full height.

I forgot how small he made my room feel, whenever he was in here. His presence was imposing, like a storm crashing through. Maddox towered over me, and I looked down at my bare arms. My skin was full of goosebumps.

His gaze slid over me, taking everything in. I was wearing a tank top and my sleeping shorts. This was the most skin he was seeing, since our breakup.

"What are you doing here?" I finally asked.

He cocked his head to the side. "I'm asking myself the same question."

When a cold air gushed through, I closed the window and leaned against the sill. He inspected my room, his attention falling on a photo of us on my nightstand. Our graduation picture. The day he gave me our dreamcatcher. We were both silent for a very long time, the tension in the room growing thicker.

I wasn't cold anymore. My skin flushed under his rapt attention, and I couldn't look away from his face. Thick eyebrows. Blue eyes. A strong nose. Full lips. Squared jaw and what appeared to be three-days' worth of stubble. His handsome, rugged face.

Our eyes met again.

My heart thudded.

And then I felt it… the *butterflies* in my stomach. The butterflies I thought I had lost before. They were never gone. Just silent. Waiting for me to finally snap out of it. Waiting for *him*…

He slid closer, taking one step toward me. I gripped the windowsill, so I wouldn't do something stupid, like reach out to him, begging him to kiss me.

He leaned forward, his chest brushing lightly against mine. My nipples pebbled through my tank top, and my breasts felt tighter and heavier.

"Lila."

I shuddered, as my name rolled off his tongue, like he was tasting molasses. He didn't speak out my name with a taunt. No, it was a plea. My name on his tongue was a whisper, a sacred prayer.

His hands came up, and I waited, with bated breath, before he cupped my face in his much bigger palms. His thumb brushed across my jaw.

"Tell me a lie," Maddox rasped, caging me in with his eyes. There was nowhere to run.

"I hate you."

His eyes darkened with pain, before his lips slammed into mine, stealing my words and my breath away.

My arms curled around his head. Our lips clashed together, fighting, breaking apart and meeting again, like a wild, angry wave across the shore. The kiss deepened, turning desperate. Furious. There was nothing sweet about this kiss, but it was maddening.

The heat between us scorched our skin, as I clung to him, kissing him back, with just as much frustration and frenzy.

The kiss lasted long, until we lost our breath. The world spun and swayed under my feet, but I didn't care. I didn't want my lips to separate from his. I didn't want this to end.

This kiss.

His mad, mad kiss.

This touch.

His mad, mad touch.

These lips.

His mad, mad lips.

I knew Maddox Coulter was my destination, and *this* reaffirmed it. This feeling in my chest that no longer felt hollow.

Our pent-up anger, weeks of frustration, and months of

misunderstandings bled through this kiss. "I'm so angry with you," he growled, into my lips.

My fingers curled into his hair, and I tugged it, hard, bringing out a hiss from him. "Good. Be angry."

That was all the affirmation he needed.

He shoved his tongue into my mouth, tasting every inch of me, forcing me to submit to his assault. Maddox attacked my mouth, and this kiss was purely animalistic.

Hurt me.

Heal me.

Hurt me.

Save me.

Maddox wrapped an arm around my waist, and he dragged us back. We tumbled onto my bed, and he crawled over my body. Without breaking the kiss, he ripped off my tank top. I bit his lip, tasting his blood, and a snarl tore from his mouth, pouring down my throat.

He cupped my breast, squeezing and making me gasp into his bleeding lips. His fingers twisted and tugged my nipples, hurting me with his torturous touch. The pleasure came with the pain. I cried out; I kissed him harder.

Clothes disappeared, naked skin met each other, our bodies clashed together. We were fighting; we were kissing. This was utter madness, and everything I had craved. Maddox finally forced his mouth away from mine, and we both gasped, breathless.

He shocked me by straddling my chest. Lust masked his face, while his eyes matched the storm raging between us. His cock sprung forward, thick and long. He gripped his hard length and rubbed the tip across my lips. Pre-cum covered the engorged head, and I licked my lips, tasting his slick essence.

Maddox groaned. He fisted his cock, and I parted my lips. His eyes flared darker, and he forced his length into the wet heat of my mouth and down my throat. I gagged, tears burning the back of my eyes. My nose tingled, as I tried to breathe and take *all* of him.

This position was different. I was completely vulnerable to Maddox, and it seemed to feed that thunderous beast in him.

I couldn't breathe.

He couldn't breathe.

Maddox grunted, as the tip of his cock hit the back of my throat. I closed my lips around his length. He throbbed inside my mouth. I clenched my thighs tighter, feeling the insistent pulse between them. My cheeks hollowed, as I sucked him.

He shuddered, the veins in his neck bulged, and I felt incredibly... powerful. Even though *he* was dominating *me*.

His hot shaft jerked in my mouth, as I used my tongue on his thick, hard length.

There was need in his eyes.

A frantic look on his face.

His hand curled around my neck, and his fingers brushed along my throat, feeling his hard cock, as I deepthroated him. I gagged when he pushed deeper and then gasped when he pulled out, without warning. He fisted his hardness, and with a grunt, he released all over my neck, my mouth and my chest.

I licked my lips, tasting him.

He swore. *"Fuck."*

I grinned, lost in this euphoria. Drunk and addicted to him. Long ago, I plummeted head first into love and lust with Maddox. Tonight was proof of how much I craved him.

"I made you dirty," he growled, his voice rusty and gruff.

This was everything depraved. This was carnage. This was our mad, mad love. Ugly and beautiful. Desperate and passionate.

I reached out, curled my arms around his shoulders, and pulled him down to my lips. I kissed him with a violence of my own. I spread my thighs, and Maddox settled between them. I could feel *him*, rubbing his tip over my wet folds. My hips raised, chasing more of his teasing touch.

When I pulled away a little, our lips still lingered against each other. His minty breath mingled with mine, and I found myself smiling at the familiarity. My lips feathered over his jaw, before I licked a small path down his neck. His weakness, I knew that.

Maddox released a hiss, and his body tightened at the same time I licked his prominent Adam's apple. His throat moved, as he swallowed hard. "*Lila...*"

I reached between us and wrapped my fingers around his dick, pushing him inside of me. Where I wanted him. Where I needed him. My heated core clenched, and I whimpered, as he slowly filled me.

His nose flared.

His jaw twitched.

His body shuddered.

I moaned.

He grunted.

I whimpered.

He growled.

I dug my fingers into his chest, right over his pounding heart. "Maddox—"

His hips jerked against mine, and I didn't finish my sentence. My mind went blank, and a desperate moan slipped from me.

Maddox bit down on my lip, leaving a painful sting behind, as his hand circled around my throat. He thrust hard inside, stretching me with every thick inch of him. "Take it like a good girl," he said, in a low and guttural voice. I clenched around him in response.

"Fuck," he grunted in my ear. "Just like that, Baby. Squeeze me good and let me fuck you like I need to. Like you want me to. Your pussy is goddamn therapeutic, Lila."

My eyes fluttered shut, as he pulled out and thrust back in, just as hard. There was nothing gentle or sweet about this. Maddox was using me, desperately chasing his release through my body, ridding himself of that pent-up anger inside of him... through *me*.

Maddox Coulter was my hell and my haven.

He killed me.

I killed him.

We were the cure and the plague.

The poison and the antidote.

Maddox's hands slid behind me, cupping my ass, as he raised my hips into the air. He found his stride, and, in this position, his shaft hit every sweet spot inside me. My eyes rolled in the back of my head. My nails dug deeper into his chest, permanently marking myself into his flesh.

His lips smashed into mine, when I came with a cry. Maddox muffled any sounds I made, and he groaned into my mouth, as he found his own release.

He collapsed onto me, and I wrapped my arms around his shoulders. Our breaths came out harsh, and we fought to regain our equilibrium. His heart thundered against mine, and I wanted to weep. For all the days we had lost. Because we had been so stupid.

"Maddox."

"Shh, Lila."

"Don't leave," I whispered, still trying to catch my breath. *"Please."*

His hips flexed, and I felt his semi-hardness inside me. "I'm not. Not yet."

Maddox buried his head into my neck, and I felt his lips on my throat. A brief kiss. A whisper of his lips. He rubbed his nose against my throat, with such tenderness, it brought tears to my eyes.

I love you.

My eyes fluttered close. Our breathing evened out, but our bodies stayed connected. I must have drifted off to sleep, because the next time I was blinking my eyes open, I felt a warm cloth rubbing my skin.

I smiled, stupid and sleepy, at Maddox. He was cleaning off the mess he left on me. I curled on my side, as he tugged the blankets around me. His thumb brushed across my jaw, and his face was devoid of all the anger I had experienced before.

He looked at me like my Maddox used to. The same tender expression on his face. That soft look in his blue eyes. For me. Always for me.

His gaze lingered on my throat, and unconsciously, I brought my hand to it. My fingers slid over something cool...

My eyes widened, and I gasped, sitting up.

Our dreamcatcher.

My heart thudded. I clenched the necklace in my hand and choked back a sob. Maddox forced my fingers opened, and he slid his thumb over the dreamcatcher.

"Don't lose it. Don't break it. Because if I ever take it again, there won't be another second chance. I'll burn it. I'll burn *us*."

Maddox wasn't talking about the dreamcatcher. He was talking about... himself.

I gripped his wrist, when he tried to step back. "Don't leave."

He shook his head slowly. "Go to sleep, Lila. I don't want your Pops to catch me here in the morning. Since I just dicked down his granddaughter, hard, while he peacefully slept down the hall."

Oh. Yeah. Shit. We just did... that.

A small giggle escaped past my lips.

He cocked his head to the side. "Damn. My dick must be *that* good. I just made you giggle."

I watched, as he climbed out of my window, and closed it behind him. Falling back into bed, I closed my eyes and finally... breathed.

We hadn't solved all our issues yet. There were many things that were still very much problematic, and we still needed to talk.

But, for the first time in months, I fell asleep with a smile and hope, flaring my chest.

CHAPTER
TWENTY-SIX

Maddox

Two months later

If five months ago, someone had asked me if this would be my life, I probably would have laughed in their faces. I didn't exactly know where life would take me when I dropped out of Harvard, almost four months ago. Lila and I broke up, and I came back to Manhattan with my parents and low expectations.

And now?

Well… my relationship with my parents was not perfect, but we were cordial and respectful. We, somehow, found a middle ground. All the years of misunderstandings and miscommunication, all the hurt… it somehow blended together, and we realized that the only way to break through that cycle was to address it.

So, once a week, we did family therapy.

My parents and I spent our time, fixing that broken thread between us.

My mother became my *mom*.

My father? Well… he was still dying.

And Lila?

My little dragon. Fierce and beautiful. Brave and passionate.

Lila didn't give up this time. Oh no, she fought me, teeth and claws, until I had no choice but to let her into my life again. She fought *for* me. She had been right. Again.

We turned something beautiful into something ugly, without even realizing *we* were the reason for all the hurt. Not her past or mine. Not Christian or Bianca. It was all… *us*.

Our stubbornness. Our pride. Our need to protect each other in our own messy ways. There was an angry beast inside of me, ugly and vindictive. I was feeding it, unconsciously. And Lila? She had a fucked-up way of rationalizing things.

I regretted all of what I'd done. Ripping that dreamcatcher away? That was our breaking point. Hurting her deliberately over Bianca? That was where I fucked up.

I was going to tell her the truth in the hospital… but when she left *again*, walked away, without a second glance… something snapped in me. The echo was loud, the sound harsh in my own ears, as she ripped my heart from my chest and took it with her.

I hurt her.

I hurt *me*.

Giving her back our dreamcatcher was the beginning of fixing whatever we had broken between us. That night, I came to her with all my frustration, all the chaotic feelings inside of me. Lila embraced them… she held me, while I took from her. Again and again.

When she fell asleep with me still inside her, I stayed awake for hours. Just looking at her sleeping face. So beautiful. So trusting.

I hated what I had done to her…

So that night, I wrapped my pinky around hers and made another promise.

A solemn vow.

I pinky promise that....

"Hey, Baby." She wrapped her arm around my waist, and her lips pressed against my shoulder blades.

"Garcia."

She bit me through my shirt. "Coulter."

"Chihuahua."

"Poodle."

Lila walked around and faced me. There was a tender smile on her face. The black circles under her eyes were gone. She looked healthier again... happier. Whole. Slaying like my favorite dragon. My only, little dragon.

God, how I fucked up.

"Your father wants to go down to the lake."

I scowled at that. "It's a bit cold today. I told him we'd go for a walk down by the lake tomorrow."

Lila scooped my hands in hers and squeezed. "Yeah. But he wants to go *today*."

There it was. *That* look I had been waiting for, but wasn't ready for. I scrubbed a hand over my face. "Do you think...?"

Lila slowly shook her head. "I don't know. I woke up in your arms today, and I didn't want to think about *it*. But then I saw him in that wheelchair, skin and bones, grimacing every time he swallowed and barely able to form a sentence..."

I swore under my breath. Wild emotions clogged my throat. "I'm not ready, Lila."

"I know. But I'll be here, Maddox. I'll be right here." She showed me her pinky and gave me a wobbly smile.

I wrapped my pinky around hers. "Promise," she whispered.

"Maddox." My father's sickly voice broke us apart. I turned around and saw my mom wheeling him toward us. He was dressed comfortably to go out. Spring was upon us, early this year, but it was still quite windy and a bit chilly out.

I cleared my throat. "Ready?"

He nodded, and I took the handles of his wheelchair and pushed him outside. The lake was on our property, only a seven-minute walk away. Lila and my mom followed behind us, from a safe distance away.

After a short walk, we reached the bench that overlooked the lake. I settled his wheelchair beside the bench and took a seat.

"Did you want to talk to me?" I knew there was something... I could tell by his tensed silence. And the fact that my mom and Lila stayed a few feet away and didn't join us. That meant, whatever my father had to say to me, it was between the two of us.

"Always so perceptive," he chuckled, only to end up in a coughing fit. I patiently patted his back and gave him a minute to gather himself again. My eyes fell on the blood in the corner of his mouth, and I quickly swiped it away with his handkerchief.

His hand shook, as he gave the back of mine a gentle pat. I stared down at our hands. His, wrinkled, bony and frail. Mine, big, strong and healthy. The sight of our hands touching made me realize how far our relationship had come.

Time didn't erase the past.

But it did heal some of the hurt.

He took a shaky breath. "My biggest mistake was letting you think I wasn't proud of you, Maddox."

I flinched, not expecting this conversation. My hand dropped from his, clenching into a fist.

He didn't pause. "Despite everything, you became the man I always wanted you to become. You are capable of many great things, Son. You're not unworthy."

Ah fuck.

I opened my mouth to stop him, but he spoke over me in his sickly, trembling voice. "You are worth so much, and I was a shitty father, for never telling you that."

My father clumsily grasped for my hand again, and he tugged me forward. I left the bench and squatted down in front of him, where he wanted me. We were eye level now. His weak hands squeezed mine.

I closed my eyes, feeling the burn behind my lids. "I just wish we had more time together," he said.

Spending the last four months with my father made me realize that I wanted that too. I wanted all the lost time, and I wanted more. I wanted tomorrow, next week, next month and next year.

"I'm sorry," he breathed, his voice cracking.

I bowed my head over our hands. We stayed like this for a long minute. The more time I spent like this, the harder it became for me to… *breathe.*

The ache in my chest intensified. "I'm sorry," he said again, as if last time wasn't enough.

"Dad," I murmured, the wind carrying my voice.

His chest rattled with a choked sound. *"I'm sorry."*

"I'm sorry, too," I said tightly, "Dad."

We stayed like this for a long time. Maybe thirty minutes. Maybe an hour. Maybe more.

Mom and Lila eventually joined us. I finally lifted my head up, to see my mom standing behind my dad, her hands on his shoulders. Lila came to stand beside me. After a silent second, she reached for me, that invisible thread tugging her closer. Lila placed her hand on my shoulder.

My chest expanded, as I finally took a real breath, without my lungs feeling like they were being crushed under a weight.

My father gave me a weak smile. He nudged his chin toward Lila and gave me a nod of approval. I chuckled, feeling the tension dissipating from my neck.

This was the beginning of the end.

CHAPTER
TWENTY-SEVEN

Lila

Brad Coulter passed away a day later, surrounded by his small family. I held Maddox's and Savannah's hand, as he took his last breath, in his own bed.

The funeral took place the next day, a cloudy and windy day. The place was crowded. Brad Coulter, after all, was a respected and loved man to the world. The service was all a blur to me, and the ceremony wrapped up quickly. Many people approached Maddox, sharing their condolences.

He stood stoic beside me, his fingers wrapped around mine. He never let go, and I didn't either.

Savannah stepped up to the podium. She cleared her throat, grabbed the mic and addressed the crowd. They had been waiting for her eulogy.

She stared at the crowd for a long moment, shifting from foot to foot. Maddox's hand tightened around mine.

Savannah swiped away her tears and took a shuddering breath. When she finally started speaking, her voice was choked with tears. "I don't even know what I'm supposed to say. I just lost my husband, and I'm expected to say a few words about love, family… death… when my wounds are still very much fresh. The Brad Coulter everyone knew, he is… *was* vastly different from the Brad I knew. You see, he came from nothing. Twenty-eight years ago, we barely even had a dollar to spare. Brad was a self-made man, and till the very end, he never lost sight of what was important to him."

Savannah eyed Maddox, and they shared a silent conversation.

"I fell in love with Brad when I was eleven. He was my first love, my first kiss… I remember the first time I saw him. It wasn't anything romantic. Actually, if you heard the real story behind our first meeting, you'd think I was lying. I remember…"

She broke off, choking on her cries.

"Brad and I got married at a court house. We exchanged the cheapest rings. Rings that we had bought from the gas/convenience store. It was the simplest wedding, but it was the best day of my life, second to the day I gave birth to our son. Brad taught me to be strong, to always chase what I want in life. He loved unconditionally. He wasn't always good at showing it, but he *loved*. Hard. He'd whisper his accomplishments to me, and he'd whisper his regrets."

Her eyes clung to Maddox, desperate for him to listen, to *hear* her unsaid words. "His last words to me were that he wished he had more time with *us*."

Maddox sucked in a sharp breath, and he held my hand in a death grip. "He wasn't a perfect human, or the perfect husband or the perfect father, but as long as he was alive, he *tried*. And that was all that mattered. If there's one thing my life with Brad taught me was that love…"

Her eyes searched ours, and she held onto us in the moment, holding us still with her gaze. "Love is messy… love is ugly. Love is roses and thorns. Love is… unconditional. You don't give up on love. You fight and fight… and fight for it, because it is worth every tear, every ache… every smile, every laugh."

She smiled through her tears. "This isn't the movies. Or a romance book. It's real, and it's going to hurt. You see, love will become boring, after you've been together for years. Every relationship will hit that phase, where the 'spark' is gone for a brief moment in time. And that's where most love stories perish, or where few love stories flourish. It's exactly, in that moment, where you're supposed to fight harder. Love isn't just a feeling. It's a commitment. You don't quit when it's no longer fun. You don't turn your back on it when it gets ugly. No, love is everything messy and everything beautiful. You *fight*. You *love*. You *live*. And that's exactly what Brad showed me," Savannah finished, her attention never leaving Maddox and I.

She wasn't speaking to the crowd.

Savannah was speaking to *us*.

I brought our clasped hands to my mouth and placed the gentlest kiss on the back of Maddox's knuckles. *I love you,* I mouthed.

He probably didn't feel it, but I wasn't going to confess my love to him at his father's funeral. For now, I was going to let him grieve.

Hours later, Maddox and I were finally alone. I stood beside him, as he knelt down next to his father's grave, placing a single white rose on it. "Goodbye... *Dad.*"

Maddox's voice cracked. This was *his* moment. When his father took his last breath, Maddox didn't even flinch. He didn't cry. He showed absolutely no emotion. He got up and called the people who were supposed to handle the funeral.

Maddox closed his eyes and bowed his head.

Thunder bellowed loud, and the sky opened up, pouring down on us.

I *felt* it, more than heard his roar. A pained cry left his chest, and I watched, as the man I loved, crumbled, as the storm raged around us.

I let him have this moment.

I let him... *feel.*

His pain bled into me, and I closed my eyes. The tears fell anyway, only to be washed away by the thundering rain.

Maddox didn't move from his father's fresh grave for a long time. When he finally stood up again, he stumbled, and I reached for him.

He wrapped around me, and I held him. He buried his face in my neck, and he shuddered in my arms. We were both drenched, both shivering, but I didn't care.

I didn't how we made it back home, but we did. Everything was a blur, the world swaying, back and forth, in front of my vision.

I helped Maddox out of his wet clothes and joined him in bed, both of us desperately chasing for warmth under the blankets.

His cold lips found mine, and I let him take this kiss. Soft. Tender. Sweet.

It wasn't desperate or crazed. Maddox kissed me like he wanted to taste me forever. My lips fused with his, and my arms curled around the back of his head, as he rolled over, pinning me under him.

Maddox settled between my thighs.

Kiss. *I love you.*

Kiss. *I'm never going to leave you.*

Kiss. *I promise.*

Kiss. *Pinky swear.*

Kiss. *Forever, baby.*

I wordlessly whispered all my promises to him, through our kisses.

Maddox tenderly traced my scars, before he cupped my breast and caressed my nipple. I gasped into his mouth and pushed my knees up, wrapping my thighs around his hips, so that we were aligned, right where I wanted him. Our lips parted, our eyes met – his pupils dark and dilated – and Maddox slowly filled me.

It was exquisitely slow and painfully passionate.

I *ached* at the tenderness in his eyes. I *hurt* at the adoration on his face.

He was bare and transparent. Maddox tore me into tatters and shreds, before putting me back together.

His fingers curled around mine, before he pinned my hands on either side of my head. He started thrusting in and out. His thick length stretched me, and my moans spilled from my lips, as he filled me with slow, deep strokes, our gasp and moans filling the room.

My body flushed, and fire spread through my veins. Maddox twitched and jerked, as he grew closer to his release. My muscles tensed, until I was tight as a bowstring, hanging on the precipice of my orgasm.

His forehead touched mine, and my eyes fluttered close, as we found our release. He filled me to the brim, as my muscles slowly eased, and I grew lax in his embrace.

Maddox rolled us over, so I was laying on his chest, but our bodies stayed connected. I loved the feel of him inside of me.

His head thudded against my ear, and I smiled, feeling at peace. This was... home. Maddox kept me anchored to him with a firm arm around my hips. We fit perfectly together; the top of my head under his chin and my smaller body over his much larger one.

My fingers feathered across his chest. "I'm sorry I wasn't there when you needed me."

Maddox hummed under his breath, his hand drawing circles along my back. "You were."

Brows furrowing, I peeked up at him. "Huh?"

His lips quirked with a smile. "You were always with me."

Maddox brushed his finger over our dreamcatcher across my neck. "I had this in my pocket all the time, so you were always with me, Lila. Whenever it all felt too much, I'd reach inside my pocket and feel the necklace. Even though I had been so angry with you, this dreamcatcher still brough me... peace."

"I never left you," I whispered.

"No," he agreed. "You never did. You were always right fucking here."

My lips brushed across his chest, over his beating heart. "I love you."

This was my first time saying it out loud. But Maddox already knew that... without me having to say those words.

He chuckled. "I know."

I tweaked his nipple. "Say it back."

"I love you, my beautiful, absolutely insane, little dragon."

Oh, these butterflies.

"My Lila," he rasped in my ear.

Always his.

Forever his.

CHAPTER TWENTY-EIGHT

Lila

One year later

"We did it!" I ran to Maddox. I jumped in his arms, wrapping my legs around his waist. We laughed, as he dipped me and planted a loud, wet kiss on my lips.

"You're messing up my lipstick!"

"Fuck it," he growled, kissing me deeper.

While all our friends graduated a year before us, Maddox and I were now – *finally* – graduates.

"Sweet Jesus! You guys need to stop with all this PDA," Riley hollered.

"At least let them today," Grayson said.

"I've seen Maddox and Lila do worse," Colton laughed, referring to the time he walked in on us fucking two weeks ago.

I rolled my eyes and wiggled, letting Maddox know I wanted to be let down. He reluctantly let go, and I settled on my feet again. Our friends and family were all here, and I just couldn't be any happier…

Savannah had been taking our pictures non-stop. Pops and Gran had shed a few tears.

A year ago, our lives changed. For the better, I'd like to add. Maddox and I worked on strengthening our relationship, while Savannah and her son grew even closer.

Bianca was officially out of our lives, when she cashed out her trust fund, packed up her newborn baby and boyfriend turned fiancé, and left her father's ironclad hold. She left the state, and we never heard from her again.

Except, every now and then, I took a peek at her social media. She was thriving and… happy.

And Christian Carmichael?

Half a year ago, we re-opened the case. With all the proof Maddox and Grayson had been able to gather, the trial was quick. This time, we had the law and the judge on our side.

Christian was found guilty of felony – driving under the influence which resulted in the death of the victims of the accident – and was sentenced to six years in prison.

After almost eight years, my parents finally got the justice they deserved. *I* finally found peace.

I always joked that I didn't need a knight. But Maddox? Even though I wasn't looking for one, he turned out to be mine.

My Maddox.

My best friend.

My first love.

My last love.

My knight.

Maddox and I officially moved back into our apartment six months ago. Life went back to normal, as we attended our last semester at

Harvard.

And here we were…

Graduating. At last!

We took a few more pictures, until Maddox was done. Surrounded by our family and friends, Maddox cupped my face and smashed his lips down on mine. Tongue and all, as his mom clicked a last picture of us.

He pulled away, long enough to grin devilishly at me, before he bent down and shoved his shoulders into my stomach. I gasped and then giggled, as he threw me over his shoulder and marched away.

"Maddox! What are you doing?"

He gave my ass a love tap. "Stealing you away. You promised me a graduation fuck."

Oh God. Maddox and his insatiable needs.

"Anyway, you have a wedding to plan."

Wait… what.

Hold up.

WHAT?

I struggled, thumping his back with my chest. "Put me down. Now! Coulter!"

Maddox chuckled and brought me down to my feet. I stabbed a finger into his chest, glowering. He just… smirked. Ugh, typical Maddox. "What was that?"

"A wedding," he said.

"Maddox Coulter!"

He grasped my left hand in his and brought it to his lips, placing a tender kiss on the back of my knuckles. And that was when I saw it.

"Oh," I breathed.

"Oh," he mouthed.

"Holy shit."

Maddox Coulter, aka my best friend, aka my boyfriend, *grinned.* "I dare you to be my wife, Lila."

I couldn't even formulate an answer. My eyes went back to my left hand. When did he slip a ring onto my finger?

"When I kissed you," he said, without me having to ask the question out loud.

"You didn't ask!"

"I just did."

"Oh my God! Maddox!"

He winked. *"I dare you."*

The ring was a simple, princess-cut diamond. Nothing too heavy, nothing too fancy. Just... *perfect.*

"Say yes, little dragon," Maddox rasped.

I stuck my tongue out at him. "You didn't ask, so I can't say yes."

"You want me on my knees for you, Babe?"

I raised an eyebrow, waiting. Maddox chuckled and slowly lowered himself to one knee. He spread out his arms. "Lila Garcia... I dare you to be my wife. I dare you to spend the rest of your life with me. I dare you to make me the happiest man by saying yes."

I was laughing... and crying, at his proposal – Maddox style.

"Yes," I screeched. "You silly, silly man."

"You love me," he said.

"I do," I murmured, falling to my knees in front of him.

The world ceased to exist, as we fell into each other, kissing and gasping into each other's mouths.

My heart kept missing beats.

My stomach twisted and tugged as those butterflies went wild.

My lips were swollen and burning from his kisses.

Forever, baby. Forever.

"So, where do you want to go first?" I settled next to him on the hood of his car and opened the map on my lap.

Maddox and I decided to take a trip around the world, before we both settled down for a busy life.

Now that we were done with school, I had to start applying for jobs. Last month, Maddox had 'officially' taken over his father's position. Brad Coulter left a huge legacy behind, and Maddox was responsible for continuing it.

But first… we needed a little vacation.

"I'm thinking Bali, you?" I asked, swiping through my phone to look at the bookmark, where I had saved all the places I wanted to visit.

"Nah, little dragon. I'm not taking your ass anywhere with me until you're Mrs. Coulter."

I rolled my eyes. He just *proposed* yesterday. "You wanna wife me up? Now?" I joked.

His blue eyes lit with mischief, and he licked his lips slowly. "Now."

"Hmm. Let me think about this. I want a wedding dress. I want to walk down the aisle. I want a first dance." I glanced down at my watch, giving it a thoughtful look. "So, if you can manage to make all of that happen in less than twelve hours, I'll marry you today. Before the clock strikes midnight. And if you can make it happen, I'll let you take my ass on our wedding night, as a reward."

"Done," he said way too quickly.

"What?" I screeched. Maddox jumped off the hood of his car and sauntered backward, giving me a wicked grin.

"Never underestimate a man who wants anal on his wedding night."

"Oh my God! Come back here, Maddox! I was joking!"

He tsked. "Nah. The moment you started talking about your ass, I wasn't joking anymore."

I gaped at him, not moving. "Get in the car, little dragon. By the end of today, you're going to be my wife… and yes, I'm fucking your ass. Done deal."

A laugh bubbled from my chest. I jumped off the hood, grabbed the now useless map and got in the car with him.

Life was never boring with Maddox Coulter.

CHAPTER
TWENTY-NINE

Maddox

I made it happen.

Six hours later, we had the Coulter's backyard decorated, fit for a small wedding.

Lila had her dress. And the aisle she wanted. Our families and friends were here. Everything was just as she had dreamed this day to be.

I swore my mother was going to beat me when I told her she had less than five hours to prepare for my wedding. Savannah Coulter glared, huffed, puffed… and then whipped out her magic wand (her cellphone), cast some spells (made some arrangements with the people she knew) and made it happen. Magic.

Colton slapped me on the back. He was my best man, of course. "Nervous?"

I shook my head. Not one bit.

The piano began to play. I sucked in a deep breath and tugged at my tie. Riley walked down the aisle first, in a purple dress. She was Lila's maid of honor. She winked at me and sent a sheepish smile at Colton.

But then I forgot how to breathe when Lila appeared at the end of the aisle, holding onto her grandfather's arm. Her sleeveless wedding dress molded her every curve. Silk and pretty. Simple and elegant. I knew the dress was backless, because she teased me with it fifteen minutes before our wedding.

Yes, I sneaked into her room, while she was waiting. And the things we did… well, there was nothing holy about it.

Our eyes met.

Time stilled.

A second lasted longer.

She walked down the aisle, and we shared a secret smile.

My heart thudded against my rib cage, when her pops put her hand in mine. "Cherish her," he muttered, tears in his eyes.

"I will," I vowed.

I gripped her hand in mine, and Lila gifted me with a smile that completely stole my breath away.

The minister began the ceremony, but all I could focus on was…

Her brown eyes.

Her full, smiling lips.

Our dreamcatcher, settled perfectly in the middle of her chest.

And the fact that, right now, hidden under her dress, my cum had probably drenched her panties and was leaking down her thighs.

Lila winked, as if she could read my mind.

And I was thrown back six years ago.

This was the girl I bumped into at the coffee shop of Berkshire's Academy.

She spilled her cold latte on me and then mouthed off to me. Fierce and sassy.

The beginning.

And the end.

EPILOGUE

Lila

Seven years later

I woke up with a cramp in my lower back. Rolling over onto my side, I tried to find a comfortable position, but it was almost impossible. My arm stretched out, seeking Maddox's warmth, only to find it missing. Oh, so he was awake then.

I closed my eyes, wishing I'd fall back asleep quickly. *Ten more minutes,* I silently begged, Just ten more minutes. But a loud crash had me completely awake. Well, shit. It looked like no more sleep for me.

With a groan, I got off the bed. After brushing my teeth and relieving myself, I went downstairs to hunt for my husband.

I found him in our kitchen.

He wasn't alone.

And my kitchen? Well, it was an absolute mess.

He faced me, as I walked into the kitchen, *grinning*. "Good morning,

Mrs. Coulter."

Something small and rowdy crashed into my legs. "Good morning, Mommy!"

Our son. The exact replica of his father. I ran my fingers through his curly, blond hair. He perked up and grinned with his signature Coulter grin. Four years ago, Logan Coulter made me a mother. He was everything that his father was. Stubborn. Bold. Strong And that Coulter attitude? Oh, yeah.

The moment the nurse put him in my arms, he opened his eyes, blinking at me with blues that were so familiar, I knew he was going to be a problem. And I was right.

Logan was Maddox 2.0.

"Hi, Mommy," another sweet voice joined the first.

I looked up toward the table, where my other baby was sitting on the kitchen counter. He smiled at me; his face covered in flour. He was my sweet boy. The much calmer version of Logan. Quiet and perceptive, unlike his older brother. Brad stuffed his tiny fist into his mouth and licked whatever was on his hand. Chocolate, probably. Brad Coulter had a sweet tooth, and, ironically, like his namesake, his grandfather had had one, too.

"Mo-mmy." With my heart full, I turned toward Maddox, who had our hiccupping baby on his hips.

Levi Coulter, Brad's twin. The prankster. Out of the three boys, Levi definitely had more me in him than his father. He liked reading, loved Disney and was the bubbly one out of all three boys. Although he loved to tease, he was quick to be serious. Oh, and he was obsessed with mint-chocolate chip muffins.

"Good morning, babies. Are you making mommy pancakes?"

God, they were all a mess. Flour. Chocolate. Whip cream.

Brad nodded, shoving more chocolate in his mouth. Oh sweet Jesus. Sugar rush, I could see it coming. I shot Maddox a glare, before scooping up Brad and putting him in his booster seat, away from the mess and the chocolate.

"Pancakes," Levi agreed.

"Uhuh. How come you decided to make me pancakes today?"

Logan gave me a dead serious look. "Because we love you, Mommy!"

Oh dear.

Oh no.

Oh shit.

My nose tingled, and the back of my eyes burned.

"Yeah, love you," Levi and Brad agreed, at the same time.

Maddox smirked. "Love you, little dragon," he mouthed.

And so... Lila Coulter promptly burst into tears.

"Oh no."

"We made Mommy cry. Again."

"Daddy, Mommy is crying!"

Maddox safely tucked Levi into his booster seat and reached for me.
He wrapped me in his embrace, and I hiccupped back another cry. "Why
are you crying?"

"Because... I'm just... so happy. Shut up, okay!"

This was my family. My crazy, sweet family.

Maddox laughed, before his hands lowered to my stomach. He cupped
my heavy, swollen belly, and his lips feathered over my forehead with a
chaste kiss. "I know. Now, let's go eat. The boys worked hard to make
you edible pancakes."

I gave him a quick peck on the lips, before kissing all three of my
boys. They loved mommy kisses, and I wanted to give them as much as I
could, before they grew tired of it.

My boys. The exact replicas of their father.

Funny how, more than a decade ago, in the halls of Berkshire
Academy...

"Remember how you once told me there was only *one* of you?" I
asked Maddox.

His eyebrows shot up, and he gave me his panty-melting smirk.

"Now look at me! I'm stuck with four Coulter boys!"

As soon as I said the words, my stomach tightened, and the baby kicked. I palmed my pregnant belly, and my eyes widened in realization...

"Maddox," I whispered. "If this is another boy, I'm going to lose my mind."

He chuckled, but I was utterly serious.

"No... I can't... I need a girl, Maddox!"

He was laughing, and I was *this* close to crying again. He must have felt it coming, because he quickly cupped my face and smashed his lips on mine, giving me one long, searing kiss, until I stopped freaking out.

"It's okay, if it's not a girl. We can keep trying, until we get a girl for you."

He smirked.

I glared. "Are you trying to make me give birth to a whole football team."

"I want at least seven," Maddox replied innocently.

"And I'm going to kill you."

He just winked, not at all scared by my threat.

"Mommy, hurry. We hungry."

With a laugh, we sat around the table and ate our too soft, too sweet pancakes. Maddox had his big palm over my pregnant belly, and the baby was hyperactive, as if he – or she – knew his – or her – daddy was there.

I loved my babies, truly.

But I was also about done with being pregnant.

Logan was four.

Brad and Levi were two.

And I was seven months pregnant.

I literally had been pregnant for four years.

As much as I loved being a stay-at-home mom, the last few years, I really wanted to go back to work. I enjoyed being a Chemist. After this baby, I was ready to go back to the world of science and research. My four years absence wasn't really an issue, since my manager's boss's boss was my husband. (Yes, he bought the research laboratory I worked at)

Maddox wanted more kids, and I wasn't opposed to the idea. But I needed a break in between.

I ate my pancake and watched, as Maddox fed Levi a few bites, wiped Brad's messy face and flicked some whip cream at Logan's head. They laughed and Logan flicked a spoonful of whip cream back at his father. It smacked Maddox right in the middle of the chest.

He was the perfect dad I always knew he'd be.

Three years ago, Maddox sold half of the Coulter empire. He didn't want it... never wanted to be what his father was. Never wanted *that* life. I had never seen such a relieved look on his mom's face when he told her. She was expecting it, and she supported Maddox in his decision.

And so, he lessened his burden and made sure he had people doing his work for him. He only ever went to the office, when he really needed to. Which was, like, once a week.

As a part-time hobby, he coached our local high school's football team.

And the rest of his time? He spent it with *us*. Maddox was a family man, through and through. He was a hands-on dad. When I was pregnant with Logan, he vowed that he wouldn't miss a day in our kids' lives.

And he didn't.

He was here for our babies' first laughs, first crawls, first words, first steps.

First everything.

"I love you," I whispered.

Those eyes.

This smile.

That face.

My little finger curled around his, over my big belly. "Pinky promise?

661

One last time?"

His pinky tightened around mine. "There's no *one last* time. We're forever, Baby."

MADDOX
& LILA

CHRISTMAS NOVELLA

CHAPTER ONE

Lila

The loud, piercing cries of a baby woke me up. Next to me, Maddox startled awake and then groaned. I grabbed my phone from the nightstand, checking the time, and saw that it was just after four in the morning. We only slept for an hour – *barely*.

The wailing continued, sounding both angry and impatient.

Iris Catalina Coulter came into this world with a loud, fierce cry and she hasn't stopped telling the world how displeased she was with being born.

My stomach cramped at the thought of going into the nursery to try and calm her down. I thought the boys were a handful as babies, but compared to her, they were laid-back and even-tempered. Iris has been a little beast since we came home from the hospital. She barely slept. She was grumpy and wanted to be held *all* the time. She cried twenty-four-seven. At first, we were worried something was wrong, but after countless phone calls and visits to her pediatrician, we were told Iris was perfectly healthy, meaning she was just a grumpy baby.

But it was more than that.

I knew it. I could feel it.

I was her mother, after all.

"I'll get her," I said, already getting out the bed.

"No," Maddox said. He rubbed a hand over his face and then sat up. "It's okay, I got her. She'll be easier to handle if I go."

I barely hid my flinch but he didn't notice, or maybe he didn't want to address *that* right now.

I watched as my husband walked to the adjacent room, the nursery all our five babies had stayed in. He left the door open and I saw him bending over the white crib and lifting Iris into his arms. Maddox held her against his chest and cooed quietly in her ears.

She instantly stopped crying. The only sound that could be heard were little hiccups as she settled into her daddy's arms and fell asleep once again. Just like that. Three minutes flat. Magic.

My chest burned and I rubbed the ache, feeling both *guilty* and *jealous*. But it was silly, I told myself. Who could be jealous of their husband for being the perfect father to their kids?

"Mommy," a little voice called out. My gaze snapped toward the door to find Brad standing there. He had his favorite stuffie under his arms and his eyes were red. I was instantly on alert and off the bed. "Baby, what's wrong?"

He wrapped his little arms around my neck as I lifted him up in my arms and settled him on my hips. He was a big boy, but he still loved his mommy's cuddles. "I had a nightmare," he whispered in my neck.

"Did Logan tell you scary stories again before bed?"

Brad nodded without a word. "Him and Levi."

Logan and Levi were always ganging up on Brad. While the two brothers loved anything horror, Brad was the complete opposite. So, they found every opportunity to tease him. I kissed my sweet boy on the head.

"It's okay. Let's read your Spider-man comic."

Fifteen minutes later, Brad was asleep again. I took a peek at the second bed in the room. Levi, Brad's twin, barely twitched when we came into the room and while I read Brad his comic. I closed their door behind me and went back to my own bedroom to find Maddox still in the nursery.

He was still holding Iris, rocking her back and forth. My chest squeezed at the sight of them together. *Warmth.* There was just something about a big, muscled man holding a tiny baby against his bare chest. When he noticed me at the entrance of the nursery, he gave me a tired smile.

Maddox placed Iris back into her crib and we both held our breath. When she didn't instantly start wailing, he made his way to me. Maddox cupped my face and placed a tender kiss on my forehead. "Let's go to bed. You look wrecked, babe."

We both got in bed without another word. The moment his head hit the pillow, Maddox was sound asleep and snoring.

But I didn't sleep.

I stared up at the ceiling until the sun rose, the boys woke up and Iris started crying again.

Maddox was gone early this morning. He was busy with the new Taekwondo facility him and Colton had opened a year before. It started off as a shared hobby between the two friends but three months ago, it had become so popular that they now had over three hundred students and counting.

I knew Maddox enjoyed the time with his students.

I knew he loved knowing that he was helping these kids find something they liked doing. He taught them with patience and understanding.

But I *missed* my husband.

Maybe I was spoiled. Since we married, Maddox dedicated all his time to me and our kids. In fact, I was the one with the full-time job while he was more of a stay-at-home dad. After selling half of the businesses his father owned, he only went to his office once a week while he volunteered at our local school as a football coach during his free time.

We had enough money to last three generations. I didn't have to work either, but I loved what I did at the Pharmaceutical company. I enjoyed my time in the lab.

I missed my husband.

I missed working.

I missed... being *me*.

"Mommy, can I have one more pancake?" Levi tugged on my sleeve.

"Me too!" Logan practically screamed. He was always the most hyper. Levi was following in his older brother's footstep. Brad was the quietest, with Noah, the youngest of the boys, being the most calm.

"Logan," I hissed. "Your sister is sleeping."

His eyes widened and he mouthed a quick *'sorry'* but it was too late.

The boys groaned as Iris began howling. My breakfast churned in my stomach and I could taste the acidic bile on my tongue.

Oh God, there was no way I was going to get her to calm down without Maddox being here.

Iris screamed louder when I grabbed her wiggling little body from her bassinet. I popped her pacifier in her mouth, but that barely helped.

I had just fed her a bottle and changed her diaper. All her needs were taken care of. She was absolutely *fine*.

Except...

I rocked her back and forth as the boys watched me struggle to calm their baby sister. I cooed and sang to Iris. I did everything that Maddox would do, but nothing seemed to please her.

Iris cried... and cried until she fell into a fitful sleep.

"Momma, crying," Noah said quietly. My cheeks were wet with tears and I hadn't even realized I was crying.

"I'm fine," I barely choked out, trying to convince my boys.

But it was a lie and even they could sense that.

Iris made a hiccup sound and her forehead furrowed as if she was uncomfortable in my arms. I placed her back into her bassinet and prayed she wouldn't wake up again.

Quickly wiping away my tears, I fed the boys more pancakes and cleaned the kitchen while they finished their breakfast. Afterward, they quietly sat on the couch and watched TV without any argument or screaming matches.

Maybe they sensed that I was at my wit's end. Because they were never *this* calm.

My legs shook as I sat down next to the bassinet. After being a little grump, Iris was now sleeping peacefully. Black curly hair. A tiny button nose and a pouty mouth. The cutest little thing ever. Even at six weeks old, she was the smallest of my babies. Everyone said she looked so much like me, and I wanted to believe that.

The back of my eyes burned and the lump in my throat swelled larger with emotions.

After Noah, I thought I was done with kids. Being surrounded with four boys and their father, that was enough testosterone for me. I was outnumbered and deep inside, I always wanted a girl.

When Noah turned two, I told Maddox I wanted to try for another baby. Of course, I barely even got the words out before he was on me and trying his luck to impregnate me.

As Maddox would joke endlessly about his super sperm, it turned out that I got pregnant that same night.

But it wasn't meant to be.

Thinking about it still made me want to vomit.

Maddox held me in his arms as I lost our baby in our shower. We grieved together and three months later, I told Maddox I was ready again. He was reluctant but eventually gave in.

I grew desperate while I still mourned.

It took us seven months to get pregnant. Everything seemed to have fallen into place once again. At fourteen weeks, we found out we were having a girl.

I still remembered the look in Maddox's eyes. The awe and unmistakable adoration. The kiss he had placed onto my lips, like he had been desperate to taste me and to breathe his love down my throat.

At our eighteen weeks' ultrasound, we found no heartbeat.

After two miscarriages, Iris Catalina Coulter was my rainbow baby.

I had so much love to give her, buried inside of me. I wanted to hold her and tell her stories of how her father and I met and our stupid dares. I wanted to tell my little girl how long I waited for her arrival.

Except…

My daughter *hated* me.

CHAPTER TWO

Lila

After the boys had settled down for a nap – all thanks to our two Golden Retrievers, Simba and Nala, keeping them active and tiring them out – I also put Iris down for a nap. That was after thirty minutes of wailing while I bathed and dressed her.

Once the house was quiet, I practically crawled into the bathroom. My head hurt, my body ached and I was just so… *tired.*

I looked at myself in the mirror and saw that I looked exactly how I felt.

Maddox hadn't changed a bit since we got married. Fit and handsome as ever. He barely even aged. But me?

God, I was an absolute mess.

I cringed at the woman staring back at me in the reflection. The dark circles. The vomit in my hair. When was the last time I showered? Two days ago? Maybe three?

I hastily ripped Maddox's shirt off but then ended up choking back a cry when I saw my naked body. I had barely even looked at myself in the mirror since Iris was born.

It was a rough pregnancy and it took a toll on my body.

My flat stomach was gone since the twins but now more stretch marks covered the loose, flabby skin and as much as I loved that this belly carried my five precious babies, I hated the sight of it. The surgical scar I got from my last pregnancy glared back at me.

My boobs leaked and I realized that I only had about fifteen minutes before Iris needed another round of milk.

Fuck.

My knees weakened and I crouched down, letting out another muffled sob.

"Lila," Maddox called through the door. "You okay in there?"

When did he come home? I was glad he came back early, but I didn't want him to see me like this. The last thing I wanted to do was break down in front of Maddox. He didn't need to see me so... *weak.* A terrible ache spread across my chest.

"Yeah," I said, trying to sound strong, but my voice only came out as a whimper.

Maddox was silent for a mere second before he knocked again, this time more urgently. "Lila, I'll give you ten seconds to open this door before I break it down."

I angrily swiped the tears away and yelled back, "I'm fine. Just give me a minute."

"No," my husband growled. "You're not, Little Dragon. Let me in."

Goddamn it. Maddox and his intuition. He always knew when I needed him, always by my side even without me asking for his help.

"Don't you dare break–"

My sentence was cut off when the door slammed open and there was Maddox. Face hard and eyes soft as he strode toward me. "For fuck's sake," I hissed.

"You never, *ever* lock me out, Lila," he said, his voice deep and angry. Maddox crouched down beside me and I tried to swat his hands away, but he was already cradling me in his arms and lifting my body off the cold tiles.

He settled me on the vanity, next to the sink, and caged me with his arms. I pushed against his chest. "Is there no privacy? I just needed some time alone, Maddox."

His eyes glinted with something dark. "No privacy. Not when you're like this."

"Like *what*?" I asked defensively.

"You're stuck in your head again, Lila. I'm not leaving my wife alone when she needs me."

"What I need is to be alone."

"What you need is to cry it out while I hold you."

"I–"

"She doesn't hate you, Little Dragon," Maddox said gently.

I choked on my own saliva, fighting back tears. "She does!"

He cupped my cheeks, bringing our faces closer. His lips whispered over mine. "How can she hate you? How can she possibly hate you when you gave her life? When you have so much love to give her? Iris is six weeks old. She doesn't know anything about hate."

Maddox kissed me and I let out a sob. "But… she does… hate me. She cries every time I touch her… Iris never cries when you hold her. She won't even let me breastfeed her!"

"You're an amazing mother, Lila."

"I don't feel like it."

"Look at me, Little Dragon," Maddox said with urgency. Our gazes locked together, mine filled with tears and his – blue eyes like the deep ocean, brimming with adoration.

"When Logan was born, I didn't know how to be a father. You taught me how to love, you taught me how be a father because I had no fucking idea where to start. I want to say we both gave our best, but Lila, we wouldn't be the family we are now without you holding us together. You're the glue and I couldn't have asked for a better mother for my kids. These boys and Iris will never have someone who loves them as much as you do."

I curled into Maddox's arms, pushing my face into his neck as I let out a loud sob. It was the first time I allowed myself to cry like this since Iris came into the world, with one powerful set of lungs.

"What do I do?" I hiccupped.

Maddox stroked my back, running his fingers through my messy hair. "You do what you always do, Lila. You love us and let me handle the rest."

"But–"

"And stop hiding from me. You want to cry? Fine, cry. But do it while I hold you. You want to rage? Go ahead. Scream at me. But don't hide from me because I want every piece of you. The good, the bad, the beautiful and the ugly."

He caressed the curve of my hips before his hands went under me, cupping my ass. Maddox lifted me in his arms and I wrapped my legs around his waist. "I smell like puke."

"Yeah, so?"

I wiggled a bit until the juncture of my thighs was perfectly settled onto his hardness. "Then, why are you hard?"

"My wife is naked. Her gorgeous tits were just in my face and she currently has her legs around my hips, of course I'm hard."

"I haven't showered in three days."

He chuckled. "I still want to fuck you."

When was the last time we had a private moment together? Actually, when was the last time we had sex? Way before Iris was born, since I was put on bed rest for the last six weeks of my pregnancy.

So, the last time we had sex was approximately three months ago.

That was the longest we had gone without doing anything dirty.

Maddox carried us the shower, while I was still wrapped in his embrace. We stood under the showerheads, letting the water rain down on us as the steam clouded the glass doors. I slid down Maddox's body but he kept me close while he got rid of his now wet clothes. I admired his naked body, his strong thighs, wide shoulders and chest, abs that were still as droolworthy as the day I met him.

Maddox was sinfully gorgeous and he was all mine.

He lathered my hair with my shampoo, running his fingers through the wet, tangly strands.

His thumbs gently dug into my scalp, massaging it. "That feels good. By the way, you broke the door. *Again*."

"I'll fix it."

I rolled my eyes. "How about you stop breaking it?"

"Stop locking me out," he shot back.

I rubbed my hands across his wide chest and down his abs, feeling his muscles tighten under my touch. I nibbled on my lower lip as my fingers travelled south, stroking his pelvis, just above his thick length that was standing up for attention.

"Don't tease me if you're not ready for the consequences," Maddox threatened.

I quirked an eyebrow at him. "Who said I wasn't ready for the consequences?"

"You want my cock?" His eyes darkened with need.

I wrapped my hand around his length, but he was so thick my fingers barely even touched. "Depends. Are you offering?"

He pushed us against the wall of the shower, away from the cascading water. Maddox gave me a slow thrust when I fisted him. He was fully aroused now. His chest rumbled with a low groan. "Depends where you want it."

To be *wanted* by this beautiful man was something exhilarating. But to be *needed* by Maddox Coulter was… more than I could describe in words.

"My fist?" I teased.

"Not good enough," Maddox grunted as I squeezed him and rubbed my thumb over the slit.

I let him go and brought my thumb to my mouth, spreading his pre-cum over my lips before licking them. "My mouth then? Apparently, I'm good at sucking dick."

"Get on your knees," he ordered, his voice now rough and husky. I missed it – the need and urgency in his voice when he lusted for me. My core clenched in response and I slowly lowered myself to my knees. Maddox spread his legs, wide enough for me to reach for his thick, bobbing length. The tip was swollen and red.

He fisted my hair and pulled my face closer to his cock. "Suck, Lila. Don't make me tell you again."

I licked the shaft to the tip, teasing him. "Lila," he warned.

I looked up at him, watching his face grow hard with hunger and longing. I saw what I needed to see. Maddox missed me as much as I missed him. Our eyes locked together as I opened my mouth, accepting him. He didn't waste any time, thrusting into my mouth as I closed my lips around his thickness. The *scent* of him… the *feel* of him… the *taste* of him…

He barely even touched the back of my throat when I heard a scream, followed by the wail of Iris.

I almost choked on Maddox's dick as our bedroom door slammed open and then…

Maddox pulled out with a curse and we both scrambled away from each other.

"Fuck," he hissed. "Fuuuck."

"I got it." I was already out of the shower, grabbing a towel off the rack.

"Mommy! Levi won't give me back my Spider-man toy," Brad cried.

"Liar!" Levi bellowed. "I didn't take it. Logan did!"

"No, I didn't!"

"I saw you take it," Noah added, calmly. "Levi took it."

Iris continued to scream at the top of her lungs.

Maddox and I gave each other a look filled with longing. "You can finish up here." I nodded toward his still very much hardened dick. Maddox glared down at it, hands on his hips.

"Goddamn it," he cursed.

I gave my husband's nakedness one final appreciative look before walking out of the bathroom to handle our rowdy boys.

Riley took a slow sip of her smoothie. "When was the last time you had dick?"

Aurora choked on her own drink, sputtering and coughing. "Could... you have said that any louder." She took a peek around the restaurant but everyone was minding their own business.

Not that Riley cared if anyone heard us.

For the longest time, it was only Riley and me. Until Aurora joined our little girl group about ten years ago. Even though she was Colton's little sister, she was his complete opposite.

"Anal," Charlotte– Riley's stepsister – said, all nonchalantly while Aurora flushed.

"You're all bitches. I hate you."

While Aurora was shy and innocent, Riley and Charlotte were brash and sarcastic. I missed these girls. Riley came over a lot but I missed going out, even if it was just for an hour to have lunch with my friends. The last time I did this, I was heavily pregnant with Iris and that was before I was put on bed rest.

"Please, you're no virgin and we all know that the shy ones are always the dirtiest. Tell us your secrets," Riley wiggled her eyebrows.

Aurora's eyes swung to me, looking for an escape. "When was the last time you had dick?" she whispered.

Charlotte and Riley let out a giggle.

"No, but seriously," Riley started. "Have you and Maddox had any time alone together since you gave birth to Iris? I keep telling you to drop the kids over at my place. I'll babysit!"

"I can help too," Aurora said, taking a bite of her chicken sandwich.

I chewed on my fries, shrugging, but deep inside, the feeling of helplessness clawed at my chest. "I can't remember the last time Maddox and I went on a date."

"You need some time with your husband, alone… to recuperate." Riley's eyes met mine. She understood me best. "You look like you're at the end of your rope and barely hanging on, babe."

"I can't imagine handling twins, let alone five kids. You're Superwoman, Lila. But even Superwoman needs some time off," Charlotte added.

I didn't know how to respond, because I didn't know *how* to take a break. The last thing on my mind was vacation or going on a date with Maddox when my daughter couldn't even stand me holding her.

I took a bite of my burger, stuffing my face with food instead of answering, or worse, breaking down in front of the girls. Riley squinted at me, giving me a knowing look, but she wisely turned the conversation away from me.

"How's your boyfriend?"

Charlotte rolled her eyes. "We're not on speaking terms right now."

"You guys were not on speaking terms last week either," Aurora noted.

"That's because asshole number two came between us."

"I don't understand how you agreed on this arrangement," Riley said, although there was no judgment in her tone. Just mild curiosity. "How can you share your man with another one? I can't imagine doing that."

"That's because Brody shares me too."

Aurora's eyes widened and even I perked up with interest. "Say what now?"

"Um, yeah. It kinda just happened, but it's complicated."

"A three way?" innocent Aurora gasped. "Was it just once or…?"

Charlotte's eyes darted between the three of us, looking only slightly uncomfortable before she blurted out, "I like Lucas too."

"Oh shit," Riley muttered.

I only blinked. Why was I not surprised? She had been complaining about Lucas for a very long time, but there was just something in her eyes every time she said his name or he came up in our conversations.

"So, I'm a little stuck between asshole number one and asshole number two," Charlotte explained.

My lips curled up, grinning. "Why choose when you can have both?"

"Exactly." Charlotte winked. Riley nodded in agreement while Aurora appeared scandalized.

The conversation drifted from Charlotte to Riley and then Aurora, who was shy and innocent, but secretly obsessed with her father's best friend. Oh, the drama.

Lunch was quickly devoured and we were on our desserts when my phone vibrated with a call. Maddox's name flashed on my screen and I was instantly on alert. Maybe it was mom intuition or maybe it was because at this point, with five kids, I was always ready for something bad to happen.

"Lila," Maddox's voice came through, sounding breathless and a little… *worried.* "Don't freak out."

I gripped the phone tighter. "I'm already freaking out, Maddox. Spit it out."

"So…" he let out a small, forced laugh. "I'm at the hospital with the kids."

I must have heard him wrong because that didn't make any sense or maybe I just refused to believe what I just heard.

My blood ran cold and I was frozen in my seat.

"Say that again," I breathed.

"Please don't freak out," Maddox pleaded.

My heart galloped in my chest and it felt like my lungs were closing in. I couldn't breathe. "Maddox, just tell me what the hell is going on?"

There was another familiar voice in the background and then Maddox let out a tired sigh. "The boys were playing and there was a little incident where Noah got hurt. He needs stitches on his forehead but it's nothing to worry about. It's a small cut, nothing too serious."

I was already grabbing for my bag and sprinting out of the restaurant before he even finished his sentence. I barely noticed the girls following after me. "I'm coming," I wheezed in a rush.

"He's okay. Noah is dealing with this better than I thought," Maddox said slowly, trying to placate me. "He's not crying, just a little shocked, but everyone is okay, I promise you."

I swallowed back the tears. My child was hurt and here I was having lunch and laughing with my friends. I should have been with them. My whole body shook and I felt *sick*. The food sitting in my stomach churned and I fought the urge to throw up.

"I'm on my way," I said, my voice thick with unshed tears. "I'll be there in ten minutes."

I hung up and got in the car. Riley climbed in next to me. "Colton texted me, I'll come with you. Charlotte and Aurora will follow."

Fifteen minutes later, I found Colton in the hospital's waiting room. He was with Logan, Brad and Levi. My boys looked pale and in shock. The moment they saw me, they rushed to my side. Brad, my sweet boy, had tears in his eyes.

"It was my fault but I didn't mean to push him so hard," Logan admitted guilty. He looked like he about to cry too.

"It was no one's fault. It was purely an accident," Colton jumped in. He grasped Logan by the shoulders. "Not your fault, buddy. You guys were just playing."

Colton nodded toward the end of the corridor. "He's in room four."

I left the boys with Colton and rushed to room four. The first thing I saw when I entered the much smaller room was Maddox with a sleeping Iris strapped to his chest. When he moved to the side, my gaze finally landed on Noah.

My poor injured boy had the biggest smile on his face as he sucked on a lollipop. He had a bandage around his head.

"This must be mommy," the doctor said as a greeting. "Noah is a big boy. He barely even flinched when I stitched him, right?"

My legs were shaking so hard I could barely stand up straight. Blood roared between my ears and adrenaline coursed through my veins. My skin prickled with anxiety and the room grew blurry, the voices distant.

Noah eyed the doctor, giving her his best puppy eyes and the charming smile that he got from his father. "Can I have another candy?"

Maddox chuckled. "He's using *that* look."

The doctor handed Noah another lollipop. "You're going to break hearts, aren't you?"

My knees weakened and I lowered myself onto the chair next to the door. The doctor patted me on the shoulder. "He's fine. I'll leave you three alone for a moment."

Shame and guilt gnawed at me, digging its deadly claws under my skin. The whispers were back again. Echoing in my ears. Taunting me. Telling me how horrible a mother I was.

Maddox grasped Noah under his arms and pulled him off the hospital bed. Still grinning, he waddled his way to me and wrapped his little arms around my waist. "Mkay, mommy. I'm okay," he said in his sweet voice.

And that was the moment I burst into tears, choking on my cries as I held my boy.

I was spiralling without anything keeping me grounded.

I felt so out of control.

So *helpless*.

CHAPTER THREE

Maddox

A week later

I walked into the house to five screaming kids. I grimaced, already knowing what would greet me. This was a daily routine. The boys were already hard enough to handle, but Iris was even worse. I toed off my winter boots and shook off the snow from my hair and my heavy coat.

I walked further into the house to find the boys running around with the dogs and Lila sitting on the couch, with Iris in her arms, screaming bloody murder. The house was a mess but I didn't care. None of it mattered, except the look on Lila's face.

The tears streaming down her cheeks.

The fragility of her posture and the look of complete *defeat* in her pretty brown eyes.

She didn't even notice I was home. In fact, she wasn't *here*. My Lila was lost.

Without saying a word, I grabbed Logan by the back of his shirt as he sprinted past me. "Get your brothers and take them to the TV room. I want complete silence while I put Iris to sleep. Understood?"

Logan must have noticed the severity in my voice because he nodded without any complaint. He was the oldest at eight years old. He was trouble – *Maddox 2.0* – but mature for his age. After the boys left and the house quieted down, except for Iris's cries, I walked up to my wife and daughter.

Lila finally noticed me. She looked up and there it was… the silent *pleading* in her eyes. The hopelessness and misery.

"I got her," I said, taking Iris from her.

Our daughter instantly stopped crying, burying her tiny face into my chest as if searching for my warmth. My Lila flinched and I saw the moment her heart broke.

Fuck. There she went, breaking *my* heart.

"I'll be back," I told her before taking Iris away.

After quickly giving her a bath and swaddling her up for the night, I fed her a bottle of warm milk before putting her in her into the crib. I prayed she wouldn't wake up, not until after I had taken care of my wife.

My kids needed me.

But my wife needed me more right now.

I caressed her chubby cheeks. "Your mommy loves you so much. You're our little rainbow… I don't know what's wrong but I'll fix this. I promise. I'll fix this so your mommy doesn't hurt anymore."

After turning on the baby monitor, I went on the hunt for the boys. They were still in the TV room, where I had left them. One by one, they all got ready for bed.

Once the house was completely quiet and all the kids were asleep, I sought out my wife. I found her exactly where I knew she'd be.

Fixing the boxes under our huge Christmas tree.

It was already that time of year. Two weeks until Christmas.

It would have been an exciting time if Lila and I were not so exhausted. Lila more than me. She was having a harder time than usual with Iris, I knew that. But she was stubborn.

Lila hated asking for help.

And worse, she hid from me. Her real feelings, what she was struggling with and all the messy things in her head. She tried to act tough and strong, as if she had everything under control.

But I knew my Little Dragon was *losing* control.

My wife was a warrior and she fixed her own crown without needing me to, but some days she was a broken mess. And I was there, to hold her. To keep her grounded while she fought whatever battle she was fighting in her head.

But it wasn't just a battle anymore.

It was a whole goddamn war in her head right now. And my Lila? She was a bloody soldier who was slowly losing her grip on reality.

I let her pile up the presents again; I had lost count how many times she re-organized the presents under the tree. Lila did that every time she was lost in her head, kind of like something she did unknowingly.

"Lila," I called out gently.

She jumped in response, but otherwise chose to ignore me. But I've had enough. Striding over to her crouched form, I lifted her up in my arms. She went willingly, her body going slack in my embrace.

Lila buried her face into my neck and let out a loud sob. "I don't know what to do! What am I doing wrong?"

"You're not doing anything wrong." I stroked her back as her body trembled with every wretched sob that escaped her throat. She was hurting and my heart was bleeding at her feet.

"Then why does it feel like I am?"

I didn't know how to explain this to her. I didn't have the response she needed to hear.

I settled on the couch and turned Lila around in my arms so that she was straddling me. Her face was blotchy, her brown eyes glassy with tears. Her lips were red and swollen and I knew she must had been chewing on them for a long time.

I grasped her jaw between my fingers, holding her still so she could look into my eyes. "Tell me what you need, Little Dragon. Tell me what you *really* need. Don't lie to me. Don't hide from me."

I watched as Lila struggled to find her words. She was so consumed by being the perfect wife and mother, she forgot all about *her* needs. She forgot to put herself first.

Her face crumpled. "I miss... you."

My lips met hers with a tender kiss. "I know."

"I miss me," she breathed into our kiss. "I miss... *us*."

"Me too, Little Dragon."

Lila whispered her secrets against my lips. Even though I had known them all without her having to tell me, I let her rant. I let her spill whatever she was holding inside her for the last six weeks.

She told me how hopeless she felt.

Lila explained how confused she was...

I don't feel worthy.

I thought I was the perfect mother to our kids, but now I don't feel like it.

Say whatever you want but Iris hates me.

I can't sleep at night.

I can't eat.

I feel sick.

My heart hurts.

Some days... I don't want to wake up. I can't stand to hear Iris cry anymore. It hurts.

I don't know what to do.

I don't know how to be the mother Iris needs.

What if the boys start to hate me too?

I'm worried the boys will feel left out or unwanted because I'm so focused on Iris.

I feel ugly and fat. My body is not the same anymore. I can't stand to look at myself in the mirror.

I want to go out with the girls. I want to go shopping, wear makeup, get my hair done… I want to go on a date with you, but then every time I think about it, I'm filled with so much guilt and shame, yet I have no idea why.

Then I get angry at myself. Why am I so upset about such trivial things?

I should be stronger. I should be better. But why am I so weak?

You won't understand. No one will understand. Even I don't understand what I'm feeling.

Some times, I'm angry at you. I'm jealous of you. How is that normal? How can I be jealous of my own husband because he's the perfect father to our kids?

We're drifting further apart. I can feel it. Don't lie to me. There is a distance between us that wasn't there before and I know it's all my fault.

The clock just ticks and ticks, the days fly by, time never stops but everything just feels so repetitive. Sometimes it feels like I'm stuck in a loop, in a separate alternate reality.

And that was how Lila fell asleep. In my arms, her sobs turning into little wounded whispers. The more she spoke of her feelings, the more I finally understood what I needed to do.

Her fingers clutched at my shirt even in her sleep.

"I got you, Little Dragon."

CHAPTER FOUR

Lila

For the first time in years, I woke up to peace. And by peace, I meant… absolute *silence.*

Which was definitely not something normal and it would be worrisome to any mother. I practically bolted off the bed and ran down the stairs, almost tripping on my own feet. "Maddox!" I called out, panic rising in my chest.

I came to a halt at the kitchen's entrance to find my husband setting up the table with two plates and… flowers?

What the fuck?

I looked around and found no one else. "Where are the kids?"

"Gone," he deadpanned.

I blinked. "What do you mean gone?"

His lips twitched and he gave me that sexy smirk that I fell hard for. "I dropped them off at my mom's. Where they will be staying for the next 6 days."

"I don't understand," I said slowly, eyeing him suspiciously.

"We need some time alone," he explained, coming to stand in front of me. He grasped my jaw and planted a wet kiss on my lips, before going lower, nibbling at the sensitive spot on my throat. Maddox knew exactly where I liked to be kissed; he knew all the spots to drive me crazy.

"For a week?" I breathed and then gasped when his hand came up to my tender breast. He palmed me roughly, kneading the flesh before pinching my sensitive nipple. Milk leaked but he didn't seem to care while he plucked and played with my nipple until I was sore and *aching.*

Holy shit. Why did that feel so good? Had I gone that long without sex that I was horny enough to orgasm with only nipple play?

Just when I was about to throw Maddox on the floor and climb him like a tree, he pulled away with a wicked grin. "Time for lunch, Sweet Cheeks."

Wait, what?

I stared at him in a daze. My husband was a fucking tease. I glowered until his words finally registered to my slow, mommy brain.

"Lunch?" My eyes darted to the clock and I saw that it was past one in the afternoon.

My jaw when slack. "How did I sleep for that long? How did I sleep through the kids waking up and you getting them ready?"

"Magic," Maddox winked. "Don't worry about it. I took care of everything."

I was still a little lost, so I only stared at him. Trying to comprehend how I went from an emotional break down yesterday to sleeping through the night and the morning and waking up to no kids.

"Maddox–"

He cut me off. "Stop overthinking, Lila. Not today." His voice hardened, his tone telling me that there was no place for argument. "Just let me take care of you, okay?"

"Okay," I mumbled. "I need to wash my face."

The corner of his lips curled up. "Good girl. Now, hurry up. I've got to tell you our plans."

I looked him up and down. Maddox stood with his hands on his hips, cocking his head to the side. It was then I realized that he was bare chest and wearing his grey sweatpants, hanging loose around his hips. I could see the outline of his bulge. "Why are you dressed like a hoe?" I pouted.

Maddox chuckled. "Why are you over-dressed?"

"Good point," I said, finally smiling. "I'll be back."

Giving my husband a final appreciative glance, I left him in the kitchen and went up to our en-suite bathroom. After brushing my teeth and washing my face, I took an impromptu decision to take a quick shower. The kids were not home; no one was screaming for attention and Iris wasn't crying for milk – so I had all the time to take some mommy alone time.

Sure, Maddox was waiting.

But he could wait an extra ten minutes while I showered in peace.

Twenty-minutes later, I felt much better and refreshed as I joined Maddox in the kitchen once again. He had the table set for two people, with fresh roses in the vase.

How long had it been since Maddox and I had been alone, truly alone in the house? Just the two of us?

Holy shit, it had been a very long time, way before Iris came into our lives. I had been so busy with work, handling the boys and then my rough pregnancy with Iris.

Our lives had become a routine. There was no… *us* anymore. Our married life had become stagnant and the spark was gone. Sure, we still enjoyed sex. Of course, we were still very much in love. In fact, our love for each other only flourished over the years as I watched him go from young and wild Maddox to a responsible father and a mature man.

But when was the last time I flirted with my husband? When was the last time we went on a date without worrying about the kids? I couldn't even remember.

Maddox was right. We needed some time alone.

"So, what did you get for lunch?" I asked.

Maddox quirked up an eyebrow at me. "I didn't get anything. I cooked."

I blinked at my husband – who was, by the way, a *horrible* cook.

"Excuse me?"

"I tried my mother's chicken casserole recipe."

"Are you trying to poison m–" He shoved a piece of chicken in my mouth before I could finish the sentence.

"Oh." I muttered around the piece of chicken.

Juicy. Tangy. Delicious.

My eyes widened. "Um, liar. You didn't make this."

Maddox swatted me on the ass and I jumped, letting out a small laugh. "Don't be a brat. Sit down and let's eat."

"Bossy much." Nonetheless, I sat down at my usual spot.

He towered over me and I had to crane my neck up. Mischief danced in his blue eyes. "You like it when I'm bossy."

I rolled my eyes but he wasn't ready to let this drop. Maddox bent forward, bringing his face closer to mine and he caged me back against my chair. "You like it when I tell you what to do. Don't lie, Sweet Cheeks. You like when I boss you around in the bedroom. You love it when I tell you what to do with your pussy, how to touch it, how to make yourself come while I watch… you love it when I hold your hair and force my cock down your throat and tell you to suck it like a good girl."

I sputtered. "Maddox–"

He grinned, before straightening to his full height as if he didn't just whisper filthy words in my ears and got me all hot and bothered… and achy. He really was taking advantage of being kids-free today.

It was the way his lips twitched that told me Maddox was in a teasing mood today. He joined me at the table and we had lunch, while he told me how him and Colton were thinking of expanding the Taekwondo facility area. They now had more kids than space.

What started out as purely a hobby and they hadn't expected more than fifty students had now turned out to be a somewhat a full-time job for both of them. I saw the pride and delight on his face as he spoke of his students.

After lunch, Maddox grabbed us the mint-chocolate cake I had been saving for myself from the fridge. The first bite into the cake and I moaned. Holy shit, if I thought dick was good… this cake was orgasmic.

"Don't make that face, Lila," Maddox warned.

"What?" I peeked at him with one eye open. "The mint-chocolate cake is *sooo* good. Better than di–"

"I dare you to finish that sentence." He dropped his fork on his plate with a clank, eyeing me with hardened blue eyes. "You won't like the consequences."

I squeezed my lips together, fighting back a laugh.

Maddox glowered. "My dick can make you moan louder. It's a fact."

"Maybe I need a reminder, huh?"

The words barely left my mouth when he was on me. Maddox lifted me off the chair and sat me on the edge of the table, simultaneously pushing our plates away with one hand.

His warmth surrounded me, cocooning me and it was so fucking perfect I wanted to cry. My legs parted and Maddox settled between them, looking quite at home there. His *happy* place.

He slid his black shirt up to my hips, his gaze smoldering. While I was at home, I was always more comfortable in his over-sized shirts. His eyes went to the juncture of my thighs, glancing at my red, satin panties before locking his gaze with mine once again.

There was just something in the way he looked at me. As if I was still the most beautiful woman he had ever laid eyes on. Like I was the only thing he could see. His fingers stroke up my inner thighs before his thumb pressed over my core. Maddox rubbed me there over the fabric, causing me to squirm in his arms.

"Stop teasing, Maddox."

He tsked. "We have all the time, Sweet Cheeks."

His touch was soft, almost feather like. Teasing and playful; making me *whimper*.

I was a woman who was very confident in her sexuality, always had been – and I was not ashamed to confess that I terribly missed sex and my husband's dick. Our bedroom life was never far from explosive and exciting…and utterly filthy. Well, that was *before*.

And now I wanted it back.

I wanted all the nasty thing my husband would do to my body.

As if Maddox could tell I was going crazy, he tilted my hips up and quickly got rid of my panties, carelessly throwing it somewhere on the floor.

He slowly lowered himself to his knees, so that he was eye-level with my mound. For some reason, I felt more naked than I had ever been before. I was never a self-conscious person, but a lot had changed about my body since I had become a mother. It was finally hitting me after Iris's birth.

Maddox brought his face closer to where I was aching and so fucking sensitive. His breath feathered across my bare pussy and I clenched, hot liquid pooling in my belly and I could feel my wetness coating my lower lips. Desire burned through my veins and my hands dug into his scalp, tugging at his dirty blond hair.

He pressed a kiss on the inside of my thigh, before biting gently into the soft flesh. I hissed and then moaned when his fingers parted my folds, his thumb grazing my hardened nub.

I shamelessly tugged his head harder and more into me, pressing his nose into my pussy now. I felt him inhale, a long deep breath and I shivered, my body shaking with silent tremors.

A whimper left me when he traced my wet lips with his knowing fingers. He knew all the spot to touch me that drove me insane and had me squirming and begging in his arms.

I let out the loudest moan when he finally replaced his fingers with his skillful tongue. The pulse between my legs was almost unbearable at this point. He'd always do that. Tease me, leave me on edge, make me ache and burn for him.

"Time for dessert and baby, you smell so fucking delicious. I'm about to feast because I've been wanting to eat his pussy for so fucking long." Maddox spread me open, throwing my legs over his wide shoulders. "And I've waited long enough."

I practically growled with impatience. "You're wasting your time. Just shut up and get to work!"

Maddox flicked my clit and gave me a love tap. It stung because I was so primed and ready, my flesh soaked and hypersensitive. "Bratty girls need to be taught a lesson, don't they?"

"Maaaaybeee," I choked out, moaning when he *finally* wrapped his lips around my clit and sucked.

"Oh fuck!" I twitched and cried out, my hips bucking up as I ground my pussy into his face. But he was having none of that. Maddox gripped my hips hard, holding me in place. He continued to suck and lick, taking what he wants. Drinking me up like he was starving for water and air.

"Maddox," I whimpered. "Oh shit… fuck, right there, oh my God! Maddox!"

I let my head drop back and my eyes squeezed shut when it got too much, too fast. The first thrust of his tongue inside of me had me calling out his name and I *almost* orgasmed. I jerked in arms, moaning and begging for mercy… for *more*.

Maddox Coulter was really good with his dick. But fuck, he knew how to use his tongue to drive me utterly insane.

Soon, I was rocking against his mouth, chasing my own release because I was *that* horny and *that* desperate. Maddox suckled on my clit, before tracing my pussy with his tongue. I pulsated, my body strung tight like a bow.

When he bit on my little nub, not enough to cause me pain, but enough to sting and probably make me sore later – I gasped and then screamed. My eyes snapped open as my orgasm shot through me like fire burning through my veins.

I sagged onto the table and melted into his arms. Maddox kissed and nuzzled my thighs. He kissed me sweetly on my pussy. "Just because," he muttered, before pulling away. He gathered me into his arms and pulled me onto his lap.

"Holy shit," I breathed.

His lips brushed along the length of my jaw and I felt his chuckle vibrating through my bones. "So, even my tongue can make you moan louder than the goddamn mint-chocolate cake."

When our lips finally met, he groaned and I thanked God for putting this man in my path so many years ago. We bumped into each other, *literally* and it was the most perfect coincidence in my life.

The kiss was deep, desperate and needy and I could taste the remnant of my juices from his lips and tongue. Wrapping my arms around his neck, I held onto him. Maddox pulled away from the kiss and buried his face in my neck.

"Fuck, I missed you."

"Yeah…" I whispered.

"The plan is to take you away from here," Maddox explained. "We're going somewhere else, where it's just the two of us."

The haze was gone and the pleasure of being in Maddox's arms disappeared. My heart dropped to my stomach. "But the kids–"

"We need a vacation, Little Dragon and I'm not taking no for an answer."

"Iris needs me. She's barely two months old," I argued. "The boys need me. I can't just leave them alone for some days. That's not okay, Maddox!"

"What's not okay? For a mother to take a break?" Maddox growled. Our eyes locked and the intensity in his gaze almost made me look away but I held his stare. "It's just four days. Do you not deserve a vacation? You've been going non-stop for a long time. You're crumbling, Lila and you'll do these kids no good when you're like this. You're at the end of your rope and they need you at your best."

"So, you think I'm not a good mother to our kids?" I cried, pushing at his shoulders so he'd release me but Maddox held me fast. "Let me go!"

"I didn't say that," he snapped.

"That's what you just said!"

"No." Maddox grasped my jaw and held me still. There was a stubborn glint in his blue eyes that I hadn't seen in a very long time. "What I said was that you're slowly losing yourself and I can't let that happen. These kids need you more than they need me. You are the perfect mother to our babies, Lila and I will repeat that for a thousand times and more if I have to, until I take my last fucking breath. But I can't let you hurt yourself like this. You don't see it but I can. Everyone can. You need to let go and *breathe*. For one goddamn day at least!"

"But–"

I snapped my mouth shut because I didn't know what else to say, how to argue with Maddox because really, I had nothing to argue about. I had not valid responses and they would have lacked truth in them.

Because as much as I hated to admit it, Maddox was *right*.

My eyes tingled and my throat closed, the lump in there growing bigger.

Maddox cupped my cheeks, his big hands practically covering my whole face. "Please, let me do this. Let me take care of you the only way I know how. The kids will be fine for a few days. They absolutely love their grandma and mom will take care of them. She'll spoil them rotten. Riley and Aurora also volunteered to babysit. And you know how much the kids adore their aunts. You've got a whole village behind you. You're not alone, Little Dragon. It's okay to ask for help. It's okay to take a break."

It finally hit me.

When the realization struck, I was left weightless and beyond fragile.

All this time, I had been surrounded by my loved ones. Iris was my rainbow baby, my precious bundle of joy. I had everything I ever wanted. A loving husband, kids I would die for, family and friends I adored... yet the feeling of loneliness had been overwhelming.

I was angry because I worried I wasn't doing the right thing.

I was terrified because I felt out of control.

I was lost because my life had taken a completely different route from my perfect and careful planning.

"I'm sorry," I wheezed, my whole body shaking. The shame crawled under my flesh and the guilt was heavy on my chest.

Maddox stroke my back and his lips met mine, over and over again with the most tender kisses. "Don't be sorry because you did nothing wrong. It's okay to break down, it's okay when life gets messy and don't pretend that you're okay. I got you, Little Dragon."

He kissed me, inhaling my cries down his throat.

I let go and Maddox wrapped me in his arms.

He took me at my worst, a broken mess of imperfections.

CHAPTER FIVE

Maddox

It was hard to convince Lila to let me take her on a mini-vacation. But it was harder to watch her kiss the kids goodbye before I stole my wife away.

I was excited to have Lila alone for the next five days. But most importantly, we needed to have a *talk*.

Two hours later, I finally dragged Lila away from the kids. She complained, she cried and worst of all, I knew she was filled with mommy guilt at leaving her babies. But I couldn't have any of that.

The whole reason of taking Lila away was so that she could focus on herself. So that we could be *us* again. She was riddled with so much overwhelming emotions and after being stuck in her head for so long… Lila needed to heal.

The kids would be fine without us for a few days, I wasn't worrying.

Right now, my wife needed me.

The moment our private plane was in the air, I had her seatbelt off and straddling me. I flicked her nose and she pouted. "That pout will get you in trouble one day."

Lila squirmed on my lap and I hardened in my pants. Yeah, the fucker was excited too. My dick had only known my hand for the last three months and had been pussy deprived.

"Where are we going?" she finally questioned.

"Switzerland."

Excitement danced in her eyes and oh, how I fucking missed that look. "To our favorite place?"

I nodded and her smile widened. "Holy shit!"

"It's going to be a long flight," I said.

"I'm already bored." Her voice was soft, but there was something in it. Something teasing and playful. Her lips quirked up.

"How shall we pass time?" I played along, my hands going to the curve of her ass and I kneaded the soft globes.

Lila leaned forward, so she could whisper in my ear. "I might have an idea." She took my earlobe between her teeth, giving me the smallest nip. *Fuck.*

Her mouth went lower and she suckled on my throat, before her lips brushed against my Adam's apple and she licked me. She knew that drove me crazy. "Goddamn it, Lila."

"You're hard," she teased against my skin, slowly moving her hips over my lap, rocking back and forth. "Let me take care of that. There won't be any interruption today."

Before I could say anything in response – not that I was going to stop her, anyway – Lila had already left my arms and she lowered herself to her knees in front of me.

"You're being cheeky today." I fisted her hair and dragged her head closer to my crotch. "What if the flight attendants walk in on us?"

She smirked. "Let's see if I can make you come before she walks in."

"Do you really dare?" I was already unbuckling my jeans. Lila drew the zipper down and took my dick out, her little hands wrapping around my length.

"I dare," she breathed, her eyes filled with mischief.

A growl escaped my throat when she wrapped her lips around my cock without wasting any time. Lila was a mad woman on a mission. I pushed deeper into her mouth, until the tip of me hit the back of her throat. Lila made a small gagging sound, before she started sucking. Like a goddamn pro.

Her cheeks hollowed every time she suckled me. Her eyes grew glassy with tears as she deep-throat me and if I hadn't already been so madly in love with this woman, this would have been the moment I'd fallen for her.

Her tongue traced the thick vein along the underside of my length, before she circled the tip with her tongue, tracing the slit and licking my pre-cum. "Lila," I warned. My voice had grown deeper and even I could hear the roughness in them.

When I couldn't have it anymore with her endless teasing, I wrapped her hair twice around my fist, until my knuckles were digging into her scalp and shoved my cock deep into her wet mouth.

"Don't be a brat," I grunted.

She moaned around my length and I felt the vibration all the way to my balls. My thighs clenched and my abs tightened as I grew closer to my orgasm. Lila's hands were on my thighs and her nails dug through the fabric of my jeans, pricking my flesh with their sharpness. The tinge of pain mixed with the way she sucked me as she doubled her effort to make me come – *fuck* –

My hips bucked up and I groaned, shooting my release down her throat. She swallowed fast but my cum still spilled past her lips, dripping down her chin. Lila was still choking my dick when–

"Mr. and Mrs. Coulter, would you like something to dri– *Oh my!* Oh, I'm so sorry!"

The flight attendant gasped and the horror on her face would have been peak comedy if my wife wasn't still sucking me like her life depended on it. I watched as the flight attendant rushed away, letting the curtains fall back down to give us privacy. Lila gave me one, last lazy lick before she pulled away. Her cheeks were flush and I noticed the hint of embarrassment in her gaze, but she was grinning. "I won."

My thumb brushed against the corner of her mouth. Lila wrapped her lips around my finger, sucking the remnant of my seed that I had gathered. She was a beautiful fucking mess. Swollen lips, ruined lipstick, my cum on her chin, flushed cheeks and messy hair.

"No, you didn't. She walked in on us," I said.

Her teeth grazed my thumb before she pulled away. "I said I will make you come *before* she walks in. And I did."

I pushed my dick back into my jeans while Lila climbed back onto my lap. Such a devious minx, but I wasn't fooled. "Why did you do that?"

She blinked at me innocently. "Do what?"

"You crazy woman." I chuckled when she slowly grinned, not once looking guilty. "Let me guess, she was looking at me for longer than five seconds."

"She looked at your ass longer than ten seconds. I counted."

When she pouted, I lost it. Throwing my head back, I let out a laugh. "Fuck. You're insane."

Lila nudged her chin up, giving me her best haughty look. "As if you wouldn't have done the same if it was a man eyeing my ass. The last time a man showed even a slight interest in me, you finger-fucked me in the hallway for him to see. Practically defiled me in front of a stranger and all you said was *whoops*."

My laughter died down as I remembered asshole Lucien.

Lila smirked. "That's a scary expression, Coulter."

"You're threading on a dangerous line, Mrs. Coulter," I threatened, my fingers digging into her hips in warning. "You might just end up with a sore pussy before we even land in Switzerland."

"I dare you," she breathed.

Challenged accepted.

When we landed in Switzerland, Lila was both yawning and walking side to side. She had a constant glower on her face and when I reached for her ass, she swatted my hand away, emitting a kitten growl in response.

"Too sore to walk straight, Sweet Cheeks?"

She snatched her suitcase from my hand. "You know what, shut up."

"Don't worry," I drawled. "The hot tub might soothe your pussy, before I have you sore all over again."

Without a word, she strutted away to where a car was already waiting for us. I pressed my lips together, holding back my laugh.

Lila crossed her arms over my chest but I could see the twitch in her lips. My girl wasn't ready to accept that I won this dare, without any foul play. I dicked her down good enough that she was probably going to be sore until tomorrow or the day after.

Plus, that was three months of sexual frustration. And I wasn't even close to being done with my wife.

The moment we got to our hotel; Lila jumped into the shower. I didn't join her, specifically because I knew my dick would want inside her the moment she was naked, but she needed a break after hours of vigorous fucking.

Thirty minutes later, my wife came out with wet hair and a black silk robe. Lila smiled, a breathtaking smile and fuck, even after eleven years of marriage, she still had my heart in the palms of her little hands.

The way her pretty brown eyes always got me; the way her smiles always had my heart beating in my chest like a teenage boy on his first date.

Lila Coulter was so goddamn beautiful and she was mine. How the fuck did I get so lucky?

"Go shower," she ordered, all sassily. And because I was completely pussy whipped, I did as I was told.

By the time I was done and got out of the shower, I found Lila sprawled on the bed and passed out. She was snoring lightly and I grinned.

I knew she had been sleep-deprived for months. It was nice to see her relaxed enough that she fell asleep so quickly – or maybe I had just exhausted her *that* much.

I joined my wife in bed and wrapped her in my arms while she snuggled up against me, even in her sleep.

There was nothing else I wanted.

CHAPTER SIX

Lila

I slept through the morning and when I woke up, Maddox wasn't in
bed. But he had left me a note and a... *dead* rose. I couldn't help
but smile because it was a tradition. A little weird and abnormal if
someone were to ask, but dead roses were our thing.

Join me in the hot tub. Wear the white bikini – the note said.

White was his favorite color on me, I knew that. But it was the bikini
part that had me pausing. I chewed on my lips, suddenly feeling *odd*.

My cramps were back and my stomach hollowed. For a long minute,
I fidgeted with my hands and the bedsheet, before I finally drew the
courage to get out of bed and get ready. I washed my face, brushed my
teeth and combed my hair five times, until I was satisfied.

I opened the suitcase Maddox had packed for me – he didn't even let
me see what was in it. And right on top, I found the white bikini. It was
a halter top with adjustable neck tie that could be worn in different ways
and the bottom was practically a thong.

I didn't let myself overthink this, even when all I wanted to do was throw that gorgeous bikini away. After putting on the bikini, I glanced at the mirror.

I was never shy about my body and I was no prude.

But...

My palms grew clammy and the room swayed. I had been naked in front of Maddox numerous times since I gave birth to Iris. Why was I so anxious about a freaking bikini? This was nothing, yet...

I felt more self-conscious than when I was naked.

A bikini was meant to make me feel *sexy*, except I felt anything but.

Fuck this!

I took a deep breath, looked away from my reflection and strode past the glass doors, where Maddox was waiting for me.

We had our own outdoor thermal pool, which was just basically a huge hot tub. Our room overlooked the blue skies and snowy peaks of the mountains.

Maddox had his back to me as he enjoyed the view so I cleared my throat, bringing his attention to me. The moment his eyes were on me, he slowly grinned.

"Fuck," he swore.

I shifted my weight from one foot to the other as I dug my nails into my thighs. My anxiety was shooting up to the skies and my blood slowly ran cold.

Maddox eyed me up and down, almost like he was *appreciating* the sight of me. Taking the time to drink me in.

What was there to appreciate though?

My stomach knotted up. I could feel the soft panic building in my veins, like poison.

Maddox must have noticed my stiff posture, before he put out his arm, palm up, inviting me in. "Come here, you gorgeous woman."

My body moved on its own, listening to Maddox's demand before I could even *think*.

I got into the pool, the water bubbling and warm, my whole body went soft the moment I was shoulders deep. Maddox grasped me by the waist and I instinctively wrapped my legs around his hips. He pushed my back against the edge.

"What's with that look, Little Dragon?" he questioned softly.

"Nothing." But I was too quick to answer, which only made him more aware of how uncomfortable I was.

Maddox kissed the corner of my lips. "Tell me."

His kisses were tender but insistent. His lips whispered over my cheeks, my jaw... my throat and the collarbone before dipping lower. "Tell me," he urged again.

"I'm just... I feel so... *not* sexy..." I practically choked on the words.

Speaking of my insecurities out loud felt like I had a knife dug in my chest, the blade twisting deeper into my flesh. "How can you still want me?"

Maddox growled, almost angrily. He pulled back, his eyes hard and his jaw clenched tight. I could see the muscles ticking in his left cheek. He wrapped one arm around my waist and lifted me out of the water, sitting my ass on the edge.

His gaze traveled from the top of my head, my eyes, my lips... my throat, down to my chest and stomach, my hips, the juncture between my thighs and then my legs. The scars between my breasts tingled, like they always did whenever I was under scrutiny.

There was just something in those blatant blue eyes that made me trembled. He stared at me, so leisurely, slow and deliberate. Maddox took his time and goosebumps peppered my skin and my nipples tightened.

"Lila," he rasped.

My heart thudded.

His head lowered toward my stomach and his lips brushed against my stretch marks. He traced every single indent and imperfection with his tongue before placing the most tender kiss on my c-section scar. "You're so fucking beautiful; I don't just want you – I *crave* you."

I've never felt more naked and more desired than this moment, right here, with Maddox's gaze on my body like he had never seen something more beautiful than me.

He stared at me like I was his newfound obsession, a yet we had been married for many years and after giving birth to five babies, my body wasn't the same as ten years ago.

"I want you, as recklessly as I wanted you since I first laid eyes on you in that coffee shop. Needing you is just as normal as breathing," Maddox said in that rough, gravelly voice of his.

I lowered myself into the water once again, wrapping my arms and legs around him. "Make love to me," I whispered, tears sliding down my cheeks. "Make love to me, Maddox. Right now, Right here."

And he did.

Maddox pushed my bikini bottom to the side and slid right in, pushing his thick length into me. I cried out, burying my face into his neck. I was still sore from yesterday and still very much hypersensitive, but I *needed* this.

I needed to feel close to him, with nothing else separating us.

His strokes were painfully slow but I didn't rush him. Maddox took his sweet time, giving me gentle, shallow thrust. He palmed my ass, squeezing and pinching the soft cheeks.

His groans vibrated through my body.

He swallowed my whimpers down his throat. I was wrapped around him, safe in his embrace while he worked my body, pushing me until I was on the precipice of my orgasm. Maddox was everywhere, inside me, in my veins, in my heart, stuck in my soul.

His lips wrapped around my nipple over my bikini. He suckled and bit on the hardened tips until I was writhing in his arms.

"Easy, Little Dragon. Sweet and slow."

"I love you," I whispered.

"I love you too," he grunted.

Maddox made love to me tenderly, like I was someone to be treasured. Like I was fragile and he was scared I would slide through his fingers.

And when we found our release, it was just as beautiful as it was explosive.

He held me afterward, while I cried.

We didn't speak a word, because there was no need to. We understood each other, through our silence and our touch.

Four days later, our time in Switzerland was coming to an end. We had spent five blissful days together, practically honeymooning again. We were lazy in bed, went on romantic dates that overlooked gorgeous views of the snowy mountains, had crazy amounts of sex… and we finally had a chance to speak.

It was a relief to finally open up about all my troubles, the insecurities and my helplessness about the situation. Maddox had slowly coaxed me out of my shell. It was hard at first, but Maddox – he knew me better than I did myself.

And that was exactly how this conversation came up. We were wrapped in each other arms, after another lazy afternoon of making love. We were talking about Iris and how worried I was…

"I've been reading a lot, surfing the internet and reading countless of articles," Maddox said, slowly. "I'm no expert, but do you think you're going through postpartum depression?"

There it was. The conversation I was trying my hardest my avoid. But I knew it was coming, because as always, to Maddox, I was an open book.

I swallowed down the heavy emotions in my throat and gave one small, sharp nob. "I think so too," I breathed, my voice shaky and filled with uncertainty. "I didn't want to believe it at first, but over the last few days, I had come to the same conclusion too."

His fingers gently brushed against my arm and he caressed me. Maddox placed a tender kiss on my temple. "You had a rough pregnancy, Lila... and after two miscarriages. That's a lot of stress, tension and emotions to deal with. You never gave yourself a chance to mourn properly because you were *scared* but you need time to heal."

I was finally realizing that. A lot had happened over the last two years since we decided to try for another baby. The miscarriages had hit me the hardest. There were a lot of confusion and numbness, but I never gave myself a chance to go through those emotions. Instead, I had tucked those feelings away and tried for another baby... until Iris came to be.

But the complication that came with my pregnancy had hit me so unexpectedly. Once again, I had shoved everything in the dark corner of my heart without letting myself truly *feel*.

I ran my fingers across Maddox's abs, feeling the need to touch him. He kept me grounded. "But why does Iris behave this way with me? I know she doesn't hate me. She's just a baby, but... I'm worried, Maddox."

"Iris didn't bond with you right away after she was born. You were in the hospital for more than a week after you had those complications with your surgery. The first week of a baby's life is very important to bond with the mother but you and Iris never got that chance. She got used to me," he muttered, thoughtfully.

What Maddox said was making sense. I had thought of that too, but I still *hated* it.

"Babies can feel when a person is stressed and feeling negative. They react accordingly to it," he explained. "They can sense when you're tensed or frustrated. I'm not saying it's your fault she cries when you hold her. She's a grumpy baby, over all. I'm not a professional, but I guess she can *feel* you."

"You're making a lot of sense, and I don't like it," I grumbled.

I could feel his smile against my forehead. "Infants are mysterious in many ways, Lila. We've learned that with five kids. Don't be so hard on yourself, Miss Perfectionist."

"Maybe... I need to talk to a therapist?" I laid my head on his chest, listening to his soothing rhythm of his heartbeats. "I just want... I want to be the best version of myself for our kids, Maddox. You're right. I need time to heal and I struggle with my feelings. This mini-vacation helped, but I know the moment we go home, I'll fall back into my bad habits. It'll be a routine; I don't know how to pause and I'll eventually succumb to the stress again."

"Whatever you want, Little Dragon. If you want to speak with someone, we'll do that."

My phone rang and we both startled. Maddox chuckled and leaning over me to grab my phone. "It's mom. Probably the kids again."

It was an incoming video chat and I accepted the request. Noah's perfect face was the first thing I saw. His ice cream covered face.

"Hi mommy," he said with the biggest smile, as if we didn't just speak an hour ago.

"Hi, baby," I said. My heart was practically bursting with love. The other boys joined, coming in front of the camera.

"Grandma said we could eat ice cream twice today," Logan whisper-yelled. Savannah, Maddox's mother, laughed. She was holding Iris in her arms. My precious babies all in one frame.

"Oh yeah, and Grandma got me a new stuffie," Brad added.

He already told me that three times since yesterday but I only nodded, as if this was the biggest new ever. "Oh my God! Really? I can't wait to see it!"

"When are you coming, mommy?" Levi asked.

I smiled. "Tomorrow. Did you miss me and daddy?"

"Yes," they all practically screamed.

And that was it. Logan went back to watch the TV. Brad and Noah were arguing about more stuffies. Levi was asking Savannah if he could hold Iris.

That was how short their attention span was.

Smiling, I waved at mother-in-law and cut the call. "God, I miss these little monsters."

"Ready to go home tomorrow?"

"Honestly?" Our eyes locked. "Yeah, I am."

Maddox grinned.

And I just fell more in love with my husband.

CHAPTER SEVEN

Maddox

Christmas Day

Exactly a week after we came back from Switzerland, it was Christmas Eve. And it couldn't have been any more louder than this. I stepped through the door and I was hit with the smell of cookies and a lot of other delicious food – and easy laughter, with Christmas carols in the background.

It looked like Christmas exploded in my house, with all the decorations and the overly fancy tree with way too many ornaments. My house bustled with people and the kids were running around, *everywhere*.

I found Riley, Aurora and Charlotte in the kitchen with my mom. But Lila was missing. "Where's my wife?" I asked, putting down the plastic bags on the kitchen counter.

"You got it?" Riley demanded, shifting freshly baked cookies onto plates.

"Yes, I got the icing you asked for. You were so fucking specific but I got it. Jesus, how does he deal with your crazy ass?"

Riley rolled her eyes, showing me her shiny diamond ring. "He married me. So, he *has* to deal with my crazy ass."

Charlotte clucked her tongue at me. "As if you don't deal with Lila's *insane* ass. You're more pussy whipped than Colton and Grayson combined."

"Language," my mom scolded.

"Sorry!"

"It was time for Iris's next bottle. Lila went to feed her," Aurora explained, softly.

I nodded. "See? You're my favorite. Have fun, ladies. I need to find my wife."

"Pussy whipped," Charlotte mouthed.

I waited until my mother's back was turned before practically shoving my middle finger in Charlotte's face. She crackled like a maniac and I strode away.

I went upstairs and walked down the hall to the master bedroom but when I didn't hear Iris crying, I slowly creeped into the nursery, without making a sound.

There, I found my wife and daughter.

And it was a sight to behold.

Lila was holding a cooing Iris to her chest, rocking her back and forth. She was singing the lullaby she sang to me once... and to our boys when they were babies. She didn't notice my presence and I stood there, arms braced against the door, watching my wife hold our daughter.

Iris wasn't screaming bloody murder while Lila held her. In fact, this was the first time our daughter was smiling and cooing at her mother.

My chest squeezed with an indescribable pressure. I watched as Iris fell asleep in her mother's arm, snuggled tight against her chest. Lila finally turned toward me and I saw the silent tears streaming down her cheeks.

I love you, I mouthed.

She smiled through the tears before gently placing Iris in her crib. I opened my arms for her and Lila walked straight into her, melting into my embrace. She choked back a sob. "She didn't cry."

"I know."

"She was smiling up at me," Lila whispered in awe.

I kissed her hair. "I saw."

"Iris fell asleep in my arms."

"She loves you, Little Dragon. Never doubt that." I'd say it a thousand time if I had to, until Lila believed me.

"Maddox?"

"Hmm?"

"Thank you for believing in me."

Always, my Lila.

We joined the others downstairs just as Grayson was walking through the door. He greeted everyone and then went straight to Riley, placing a quick kiss on her forehead. I wasn't surprised that she was the first person he went to. She smiled up at him and he whispered something to her, looking quite intimate with each other. Her eyes widened and then she threw her head back and laughed.

Lila let go of my hand to help my mom with the presents under the Christmas tree.

I sat down next to Lila's grandpa, keeping the old man company. He was watching an old re-run of a football match and soon enough, we were both engrossed in it until Colton interrupted.

"Yoh," he said, handing each of us a beer. "When are we finalizing the extension plans for the building?"

I shrugged, taking a sip of my drink. "After New Years."

Colton nodded. "Works for me." I didn't miss the way his eyes kept going to Riley and Grayson. There was no bitterness or jealousy in his gaze, just... *protectiveness.*

A few minutes later, he joined us on the couch. "They kicked you out of the kitchen?"

Grayson grabbed a beer from the table, stretching out his long legs in front of him. "I didn't even try to argue."

"There's no arguing with these women," Colton agreed.

Truer words had never been spoken. Cheers to that.

Food was served quickly after that and after we wrangled the kids to the table, it was a pretty perfect dinner.

Every time I found myself looking at my wife, her eyes were already on me. She'd smile and then bite on her lips, as if we were sharing some secrets.

Fuck, I loved this woman. Madly.

Once the table was cleared out, the boys and I went to the living room, leaving the girls to gossip among themselves but it was soon after, when Riley came forward to announce something.

"So, I have some news. I can't keep it in any longer," she started slowly. All attention was on her. Riley grinned and her hand went to her stomach, cupping her belly tenderly. "I'm pregnant!"

All the girls squealed, running over to Riley to congratulate her. Aurora rubbed Riley's belly, almost longingly. Lila was crying and Charlotte hugged Riley – well, practically strangling her. "Oh my God, I'm going to be an aunt. Again!"

"Congratulation is in order," I said to the father of the baby, raising my beer in a toast.

Colton smiled, looking so at ease while he kept his gaze on Riley. While there was unmistakeable delight in Grayson's eyes.

The kids went back to running around, all the adrenaline about the opening their presents soon enough, pumping through their veins.

Christmas Eve was always chaos for us. But it was nothing short of perfect.

None of us were blood related, but damn it, this was *family.*

Lila

After desserts, Maddox and Colton disappeared. And I knew exactly why.

"Boys! Who's ready for Santa?" I called out. A chorus of *'me'* were shouted and they all waited, eyes big with anticipation.

"Can we open our presents now?" Noah asked, practically dancing on his toes.

"Well, you have to wait for Santa to give them to you," I explained.

"But they are already under the trees," Logan complained. "Can't we just take them?"

With my hands on my hips, I shook my head. "Nope. Gotta wait for Santa. I want all four of you to sit down, quietly while we wait for San–"

I barely even finished my sentence when the entrance door slammed open and two huge figured walked in, bringing in a cold wind and snow as they did.

Santa Claus and his Elf.

"Ho – ho – ho."

I had to press my lips together, holding back a laugh at how ridiculous both Maddox and Colton looked. It was a tradition since Logan was born, but it never got less hysterical to see them in their costumes.

Savannah took pictures while the Elf handed everyone their presents. Santa had the boys on his lap, one by one as they whispered their secrets in his ears and he granted them their wishes.

Was it possible to fall even more in love? Because I did. Every time I saw Maddox with our kids and how easily he handled them... I probably fell deeper in love, but I didn't think that was even possible anymore.

Once the presents were distributed and the kids were practically ripping through the wrapping, I went into the kitchen to grab another plate of cookies. The boys were going to be demanding for more cookies soon enough.

"Did I get to tell you how fucking beautiful you look in this red dress?"

I shivered as his deep voice rolled down my spine and goosebumps peppered across my bare arms. He crowded into my back, his warmth surrounding me.

"No, you didn't tell me yet," I said, with all the sassiness I could muster. Maddox grabbed my ass, squeezing. My breath hitched.

"Delectable," he rasped in my ear.

I turned around in his arms, so that I was facing him. He had gotten rid of the fake white beard but he was still in his Santa costume.

"You're being inappropriate, Mr. Santa," I said even as I reached out, grabbing his bulge through his red pants.

He groaned. "You're on the naughty list, Mrs. Coulter."

"Oh really? What are you going to do about that?" I taunted. "Are you going to punish me, *Santa Claus*?"

I chewed on my lips, hiding my grin. His eyes glinted with something dark and mischievous. "You're about to find out what happens to bad girls like you," he threatened. "Tonight."

I caressed his dick through his layers of clothing, feeling him grow thick and hard. "I can't wait," I breathed.

"Lila, the boys want cookies." Savannah walked in the kitchen and Maddox coughed, practically choking on his saliva. I still had his dick in my hand, but his body was big enough to hide me and what I was up to.

"Sure, I'll bring the plate over!" I said, in an overly cheerful voice.

Maddox pulled away from me. "You're dangerous, woman," he

growled.

"And I happened to hear that you *love* danger." I winked, before sashaying away.

Maddox swore under his breath and I grinned.

Walking back into the living room, where everyone was present, I watched as my family talked and laughed between themselves. My babies were well loved and I had everything I could ask for.

Savannah came to me, with a sweet smile. We swapped between the plates and Iris, and suddenly, I found myself holding my daughter while Savannah walked away with the cookies.

My body froze and I held my breath, expecting Iris to burst out crying.

My heart thundered in my chest and I swore, my lungs caved inside my rib-cage, I could *barely* breathe.

Please don't cry, please don't cry, I begged.

Her eyes, blue like her father's, blinked up at me. Her lips pursed into the cutest pout and then she did the most unexpected thing.

Her tiny fingers wrapped around my dreamcatcher necklace and my daughter smiled, cooing.

In that very moment, my world tilted on its own axis, the room swayed and I felt both dizzy in relief and breathless with happy.

"You know, this necklace is special to your daddy and me. It was his very first gift to me," I whispered to my daughter.

I felt Maddox's presence before I saw him. His arm came around my shoulders and we both looked down at Iris. "This is our dreamcatcher, little one," he said.

My heart was so full, I could burst.

He pressed his lips against my temple, giving me a chaste kiss. "Do you believe in Christmas magic, Little Dragon?"

I looked down at my precious bundle of joy as she shoved a fistful of my hair into her mouth. She giggled.

"Maybe I do. A little bit."

"Merry Christmas, Mrs. Coulter," Maddox whispered in my ear.

CHAPTER EIGHT

Lila

Three years later

I walked into my house and it was surprisingly quiet. I wasn't going to complain though, since today had been a long day at work and I was completely wrecked.

I dropped my bag and coat at the door, toed off my heels and walked barefoot into my living room. Maddox was sprawled on the couch, legs stretched out in front of him. Bare chest and grey sweatpants. Oh, yum.

"You're dressed like a hoe again."

"And you're severely over-dressed, Mrs. Coulter," he drawled.

I looked around but found no kids. "Where are the monsters?"

"At my mom's."

I paused, quirking up an eyebrow at my husband. "So, you're saying we got the house to ourselves for tonight?"

Maddox rubbed a hand down his abs, his lower lip tugged between his teeth as he gave me one long appreciative look. "That's exactly what I'm saying."

Oh damn. I slowly grinned, before settling into my husband's embrace. He took my lips in a long, leisured kiss until we were both breathless.

I tucked my face into my throat, inhaling his spicy scent. "God, I'm exhausted."

After my maternity leave for Iris, I went back to work. I missed the kids terribly but I also loved my job. It wasn't exactly easy at first, but I had learned how to cope with it. Being a working mother – while not being riddled with so much shame and guilt.

It took me a year of talking with a therapist for me to finally... *heal*, as Maddox would put it. Opening up about my insecurities and fear to a stranger wasn't easy, but it had been exactly what I needed.

When things got too hard, Maddox was there for me. But it was also nice to have a therapist who would put everything in perspective for me. She was patient and understanding. And in her, I found both a confidant and a friend.

A lot of time, I was still stuck in my head, in the dark corner where I'd pile everything up until I burst. But over the years, I had gotten better at talking about my feelings and asking for help when I needed it.

Maddox was my comfort.

He was home and exactly what I needed when I felt the urge to let go. I knew he'd be there to catch me and he always did. Every. Single. Time.

"What's that sound?" I asked. It was very soft before, barely noticeable when I walked into the house but now the noise had grown insistent.

Maddox looked guilty and he pulled away, coming to stand in front of me.

I crossed my arms over my chest, slowly growing suspicious. He took a step back, hands up as a mock surrender. "Okay, listen. Don't freak out."

My eyes widened. "What did you do now?"

"Wait—"

"Maddox, answer the question!"

His eyes darted left and right as if someone would pop up to save his ass. Maddox gave me a sheepish look. "I got Iris the baby goat she wanted. Early Christmas present."

"You did what?" I gasped.

Iris was an animal lover. My little girl had a pure soul, but that meant my house turning into a zoo. She brought home all the injured animals. Birds, lost cats and dogs, squirrels...

Two months ago, she asked her daddy to get her two white rabbits. And what did her daddy do? He got her two pet rabbits, of course.

"You got her a baby goat?" I repeated slowly. Oh my God! Maybe today was the day I ended up in prison. On the possible charges of murdering my husband.

"She pouted and I couldn't say no. You know I'm weak for her pouts," he tried to defend himself as if that explained why he bought a freaking goat.

I took a deep breath, to calm myself down. But yeah, that wasn't happening. When he opened his mouth to justify himself again, I was done.

"MADDOX COULTER, GET OUT OF MY HOUSE!"

"Yes, ma'am. Of course, ma'am," he said quickly.

Maddox backpedaled, hands still up in defense. When he was a good distance away from me, he finally chuckled.

"I'm not even sorry, Little Dragon. But I love you."

And then he was gone. Practically running away from me and the *goat* he brought home.

Who thought marrying this insane man was a good idea?

Oh right, me.

Fuck.

724

Did you enjoy this duet? Come and join my reader's group:

Lylah's Lovelies Therapy Group on Facebook!

ACKNOWLEDGEMENT

Vivvi, how do I ever thank you? You're my rock and a piece of my heart. Thank you for loving my characters, my babies, just as much as I do, if not more. You're the moon of my life.

My wonderful editor Rebecca – your patience is admirable. Thank you for not hating me. You worked with me on such a tight schedule. It's insane, but you legit made this book possible. I thought you kicked me to the curb, but you didn't. For that – I am forever grateful. Thank you for holding my hand. You were my emotional support system.

My parents, thank you for your never-ending support and love.

To my girl, Cat…seriously, what would I do without you? Suse, you've been there, supporting my craziness, and I love you even more. You made my book pretty – thank YOU!

Brianna Hale, you're my girl. Thank you for listening to me rant and thank you always supporting me!

Sarah Grim Sentz – I'm so glad I trusted you with these promo graphics.

Special thanks to my STREET TEAM! I'm so amazed by how dedicated you guys are.

Huge thanks to CANDI KANE PR – you're a gem, and I'm so glad I trusted you with my book baby, because you did magic!

To the bloggers and to everyone who took the time to promote this book, you are awesome! My big thanks to you. To my beautiful readers, a huge thank you to every single one of you. My lovelies. Your never-ending support and love has taken us on this path. Thank you for standing with me through all my craziness.

ABOUT THE AUTHOR

Lylah James uses all her spare time to write. If she is not studying, sleeping, writing or working—she can be found with her nose buried in a good romance book, preferably with a hot alpha male. Writing is her passion. The voices in her head won't stop, and she believes they deserve to be heard and read. Lylah James writes about drool worthy and total alpha males and strong and sweet heroines. She makes her readers cry— sob their eyes out, swoon, curse, rage, and fall in love. Mostly known as the Queen of Cliffhangers and the #evilauthorwithablacksoul, she likes to break her readers' hearts and then mend them.

Connect with me!

BOOKS BY LYLAH JAMES

Tainted Hearts Series

The Mafia and His Angel: Part One
The Mafia and His Angel: Part Two
The Mafia and His Angel: Part Three
Blood and Roses
The Mafia and His Obsession: Part One
The Mafia and His Obsession: Part Two

Truth and Dare Duet

DO YOU DARE? (Book one)
I DARE YOU (Book two, the conclusion)

Standalones

A VOW OF HATE (Pre-Order Now!)

Printed in Great Britain
by Amazon

86036126R00416